The Space Between

THE SPACE BETWEEN

The National Library of Poetry

Cynthia A. Stevens, Editor

The Space Between

Library of Congress
Cataloging in Publication Data

ISBN 1-56167-252-1

Manufactured in The United States of America by
Watermark Press
11419 Cronridge Dr., Suite 10
Owings Mills, MD 21117

Editor's Note

The Space Between presents a distinctive array of poetry. Each of the poets featured within the anthology have succeeded in crafting a work of art which stands above the average. As editor and judge of the contributing entries, I had the grand opportunity to review and ponder the many pieces displayed within the anthology. In regards to the contest held in connection with The Space Between, much effort was placed into examining the poems as objectively as possible. As usual, there are several poems I wish to honor with special recognition.

Attaining grand prize was Mark Heffington with his piece, "Uncle Keys." He brings into a vision a delightful memory. A beautifully picturesque scene is presented with well defined images and the quietness of sound, (i.e.: "His bridle-leather hand taps my knee then points./...). Heffington uses a wonderful balance of rhythm. In doing this he allows the reader to "feel" the anxiousness of maintaining perfectly still while emotionally bursting with excitement.

"A Reminiscence," by Minkai Wong, gracefully flows with an exacting rhythm, touching the depths of our souls, while in the end evoking a relief of sadness. Each word is one of necessity within this piece of great ingenuity.

An outstanding abstract piece is, "Corn on the Cob," by James Adam. His poem is fresh and crisp with an attention grabbing style. I urge you to look this poem up and taste it!

"Last Breath," by Alison Epker, is a small yet powerful poem which is sure to intrigue your mind with the basic concept of life and death. Also relating to the idea of death is, Gil Magno's piece, "Here Lies Emptiness." Exhibiting a unique selection of relationships, Magno candidly presents us with the dark side of reality -- the dark side of death.

Of course, if only we could stop time, we could stop death. You can explore this theory through Chris Donovan's poem "Killing Time."

Several other prominent poems you may wish to have a definite look at are: "Ambiguous Reality," by Danny Coughlin, "Sideline or Showtime," by Tim Jackson, "The Omniscient," by Donna Nielsen-Salih, and Anthony Worrell's "Bitter Sentiment."

Although I do not have the time or space to individually critique every eminent poem appearing within this anthology, you will notice that each piece of artistry is constructed with grave originality and design. May all of the artists within The Space Between be renowned for their talents and efforts in creative writing.

I sincerely hope that you enjoy reading The Space Between.

Cynthia A. Stevens

Acknowledgements

The publication The Space Between is a culmination of the efforts of many individuals. Judges, editors, assistant editors, graphic artists, layout artists and office administrators have all brought their respective talents to bear on this project. The editors are grateful for the contribution of these fine people:

Jeffrey Bryan, Keith Creummedy, Lisa Della, Chrystal Eldridge, Ardie L. Freeman, Hope Freeman, Camille Gabor, Diane Mills, Eric Mueck, Lamont Robinson, Jacqueline Spiwak, Caroline Sullivan, and Ira Westreich.

Howard Ely, Managing Editor

Grand Prize Winner

Mark Heffington

Second Prize Winners

James Adams
Danny Coughlin
Chris Donovan
Alison Epker
Roxane Houston

Tim Jackson
Gil Magno
Donna Nielsen-Salih
Minkai Wong
Anthony Worrell

Third Prize Winners

Lonnie Bailey
Barbara Barnes
Jeffrey Bean
Heather Blatt
Craig Braginsky
Brenda Chappell
Mitch Cox
Eugene Culcer
Leia Davies
Toni DeVencentry
Mike Dix
Alice Dorworth
Shari Dottin
Patricia Eckel
Harriet Elmblad
Orlena Fong
George Gardiner
Poet Grant
Michael Gray

Stacy Greathouse
Seth Grossman
Nathaniel Haakinson
Bea Harry
Cecilia Huckestein
Jerard Jensen
Allen Kane
Patti Kennedy
Suzanne Kohr
Joseph Kuo
Arlene Kuykendoll
Marjorie Lewis
Debbie Markakis
Rhonda Miller
Iwao Mizuta
Jana Moore
Conne Morgan
Christopher Moryl
J.R. Mulligan

Otuije Onyema
Stephanie Parker
Pat Peaslee
Joyce Rice
Tiffany Richardson
Eunice Ringo
Tom Rogers
David Saxner
Peter Seneviratna
Mandy Solomon
Kate Stewart
Joe Stojansul
Mark Tankersley
Poet Veale
Patricia von Dippe
Carolyn Wade
Cory Wattenbarger
Osie Wilcox
Lori Woolf
Ron Zillmer

Congratulations also to all our semi-finalists

Grand Prize Winner

Uncle Keys
   Every year squirrel season comes around;
Every year I think back on Uncle Keys;
   Sitting on a fallen tree of six years
Smoking a Captain Black pipe—waiting for squirrels
   Wandering branched by-ways for the acorn.
Restless, I want to walk, climb hills, jump creeks
   But I sit, quietly, watching flickering leaves
Waving, then faltering, in the mid-morning sunlight.
   No squirrels for hollows east and west,
No barks, just crackling of crunched tobacco flaming orange
   And we sat on that rotting hickory log
Uncle Keys gazing skyward, anticipating movement.
   I couldn't help notice every wrinkle and loose stitch
In his tan canvas guard uniform from the prison;
   His bridle-leather hand taps my knee then points.
"Squirrel season starts in August, Uncle Keys"
   —Mark Heffington

In Training

> There comes a time . . .
6th grade, oxfords untucked, docksiders, rollerskating parties,

> in every girl's life

Inquisitive eyes, chatty comments, looks of approval
uncertainty, satisfaction, dislike, failure, surprise
understanding (yeah right)

"First one, huh?"
Let's announce it.

"Fits well."
Unlike yours.

"That one'll be pretty."
Not pretty, just invisible.

"My how she's grown!"
My how you've gained! Get me outta here!!!!

> when she is forced

Gym. What will they say? Can't wear white, can't be too tight.
Rhonda Turner—the first to have one—"snaps" in the middle of
English!

> to begin training.

> —*Lisle Sorensen*

Rise Up

How shall I rise up to each day,
a day of morning sun or one
kissed by falling rain.
Maybe the frost lays crisp upon fallen leaves
or, a day where snow blankets beyond
my view and a warmth fills me at the sight.
Each day fills me, whatever the eyes see,
to reach out and hug the world!
Oh glorious morning; just to rise up and
be there with you, a part of a new beginning,
a freshness in each hour and a fullness
that carries the heart beyond and
then I shall lie down to embrace the night.

> —*Elizabeth M. Workman*

December Dream

There are some things I yearn for just about now:
A fire in a fireplace and a hemlock bough
And if by that fire I could hear well loved sounds
The joy of my Christmas would flow out of bounds.
There's someone I love whom I'm longing to see
And someone I long for is longing for me.
I'm saying a prayer requesting that fate
Will grant us at Christmas a permanent date.

> It's something to dream for: A tree and a star.
> It's something to dream for: To be where you are.

I truly love and will always remember
The scenes that come toward the end of December:
A Christmas tree gleaming in its jeweled gown
With loved ones all happily gathered around.
I want to be with them so I pray and pray
That I may be home to enjoy Christmas Day:
Unwrapping the presents found under the tree
And seeing the love light your eyes hold for me.

> It's something to dream for: A tree and a star.
> It's something to dream for: To be where you are.

> —*Mabelle Wiard Willmarth*

Songs From The Rain

A torment of phrases rush me,
A flood rising, overflowing, and spreading -
Unstoppable - filled and flourishing,
With a spirit, a life, fully their own.
Their rippling waters funnel and filter through me,
Riding the continuous current of their own course.
Mixing and mingling, sharing with my feelings and thoughts,
Then separating, using my life's images as instruments
To express their time-tried pictures and themes.
Overwhelmed and delirious from the intense intoxication
Of their quench, flavor, and fragrance,
In awe, and fear that in my ignorance
I may misunderstand, as my hand writes
The surge of countless streams of words,
As I battle wanting to withdraw-shroud myself-
From the addictive rhythms of their notes.
In essence, try to force them in search of another messenger
Worthy of receiving their beautiful and bountiful
Bouquet of heart stirring hymns.

> —*Sidona Marie Hunsberger*

What is Wrong with the World Today

What is wrong with the world today, I do not understand.
A family of four, blown away, killed by a young man.

Come to find, the man was robbed, things were stolen by their son.
Were they worth the price he paid? For now he has no one.

Another day, a girl was found, she was riding all alone.
Just seventeen, and now she's gone, she never will go home.

Across the town, a little child, went inside to go to bed.
Shots were fired, they went wild, and hit her in the head.

A twelve year old, sat outside, baby in her arms.
Someone killed her, due to pride, because someone she harmed.

Michael Jordan, famous star, loved by everyone
Father slain, while in his car, two kids just having fun.

What is wrong with the world today? I still don't understand.
Read the paper, headlines say... Found, unidentified man.

> —*Mary Alice Celaya*

Mighty Max Our Mastiff Kid

Mighty Max was his name, Having fun was his game
He came one day in the month of November, Just to see if he could
  become a member
This household of ours oh so quaint, Upon our world he would paint
He had teeth that showed and a tail that was bent, But in spite of it
  all he was heaven sent
To bed we took him when he was small, now mighty Max takes it all
With a face only a mother could adore, That mighty Max slept, but not
  on the floor
Only one eighty one, or so they say, But to me feels like a ton of clay
My foot is his pillow, my chair he does sit, In times of quiet when
  we're all at our wits
He comes to our side as though to say, What are we going to do today
That Might Max the misfit dog, Who brought you home to lie like a log
The fireplace is warm all cozy and nice, So please dear Max, please
  think twice
The bed is nice and so are you, But mom needs the bed a time or two
Mighty Max, my shadow everywhere, Why do you want to share my fare
The table is all lovely and nice, for Max is expecting to be fed twice
Never a left over do we have, the fridge is bare, Because Mighty Max
  is always there
If by now you haven't heard, Might Max was only third
To the show ring he did not go, but home to us to grow and grow
Mighty Max that Mastiff dog, will always lie there like a log
He shares our home, our food and bed, But thinks we are the guests
  instead.

> —*Delores D. Hanson*

Baseball Dreams

There once was a sport, played at youth
A ball, a bat, a legend named Ruth
We'd play to hit, and hit to play
I wish it was the same
Sport as sport, honor as professionals
What's wrong with our games, what's happened to sport
Some won't play, less we double their pay
"I'll move to another team, they'll match my demand"
As Joltin' Joe stepped to the plate, would his wallet have him hesitate
Love of the game made these players great
Our pastime now, is past it's best time
Arbitration sounds good, but salaries are crime
A team with no loyalty
Support, is certainly not much sport
I'd play for free, if given a chance to be in the show
I suppose that's a thought from long ago, when sport was sport
Teams kept players
The only cap was worn on your head
and baseball, was a dream…

—*Stephen P. Gulla*

I Saw the Heavens, in a Dream

I saw the heavens, in a dream,
A great and endless, sort of beam,
Everything in it was so clear,
And I wondered what I was doing here,
I saw Unicorns fly at amazing height,
Far beyond the light, I could see night,
There you could see the moon and stars twinkle,
Everyone looked so young, without a wrinkle.
And the angels laughed,
And the angels sang,
And through the heavens, the great tone rang,
I could tell there were no wars, all was fair,
For there was peace in everyone who was there.
Everything was so gently calm,
I knew this was where I'd eventually belong,
But not yet, when I hadn't yet heard life's lovely song,
And I wondered: when will I be part of this glorious land.
Where people walk, hand in hand.

—*Nicole D. Bailey*

My Friend was a Treasure

My friend was a treasure, so loving and fair
A halo showed through, her silvery-white hair

Eyes twinkling merrily, as she'd laugh at a joke
One she'd just thought of, or one I'd just spoke

Her hugs were so precious, so lovingly given
She helped me to glimmer, a small bit of heaven

Her courage in living her life as she must
Was always up-lifting, to those she did trust

No longer able, to live all alone
She spent her last days, in a small nursing home

She was always grateful for attentions she'd get
Her greetings were smiles and hugs…never regrets

She felt thankful to have reached ninety-plus years
To have experienced life with both laughter and tears

Eyesight had failed her, her hearing was bad
Yet she never complained and rarely seemed sad

She always spoke kindly of those that she knew
Never, from her lips, did hateful words spew

My friend was a treasure, oh, how lucky I've been
To have been with her, as she reached her life's end

—*Barbara Waldren Malberg*

What It's Like To Be

Come on I'll show you what it's like to be
A kid who's stuck in a body of someone who's twenty-three
I want to run, jump and ride
Play in playgrounds swing and slide
Laugh and learn, fly a kite
Swing a bat with all my might
Watch cartoons and Sesame Street
Run in the grass with my bare feet
Watch the clouds as they go by
Look at the birds in the sky
Catch the invisible wind, feel its power
Try to find the prettiest flower
Always laugh and run and hide
Carry a smile both big and wide
Never run out of things to do
Share my thoughts and feelings with you.
I want everyone to come with me, to hold my hand
I'll take you all though my childlike land.

—*Jeanne Dippel*

Where the Eagle Flies

In the land where the eagle flies
A land for which our fathers died
Freedom should ring forever more
It is the founding center core

Our fathers braved the untamed land
With Bibles clutched tight in hand
They stood as testimony to God on high
Where justice for all should never die

A gift given to them and not to be sold
By a worldly system where God is gold
A land made of milk and honey
Bought by who has the most money

Did all our forefathers die in vain
The cure to corruption is very plain
Just as the eagle flies is how it must be
Return this land to God and…..
Set His people free!

—*Wilda Ann Nowocin*

Beyond My Dreams

Beyond my dreams there's a new life to behold
A life that's out there just waiting for me to unfold
Beyond my dreams there's that moment of truth
It will retard my old age and restore my youth
Beyond my dreams much to my surprise
There's ongoing life and no one ever dies
Beyond my dreams heaven can be wherever you are
And in those dreams I can reach upon a star
Beyond my dreams there's no hunger or pain
Salvation is provided from the down pouring rain
Beyond my dreams we shall all love one another. You will
experience the real true meaning of thy sister and brother
Beyond my dreams all of my wishes appear to come true
And everyone succeeds in the things they set out to do
Beyond my dreams there will be no need to pray
Pure life will be experienced throughout each and every day
Beyond my dreams I can feel but can not hear
And beyond a shadow of a doubt I have no fear
Beyond my dreams life will go on and on
As I return from dreamland I must now end this poem

—*Ronald V. Edmonds*

Her Salvation

What do you feel when you strut right by
A little girl gazing up at the sky,
Praying that somehow she'll find a way?
To help her family this gloomy day.

Holding out her bowl, hoping for food,
Maybe even money, that would be good/
A hungry look in her huge, innocent eyes
Begging for help through these hard times.

What exactly does it make you feel inside?
If you said you don't care, you must have lied.
Everyone feels something for that poor child
With her family's few belongings heaped in a pile.

Her frail hands holding up a filthy bowl,
Her pleading eyes, the poor little soul.
Watching people rush by as if she doesn't exist.
The poor child's hurt and she tightens her fists.

No, we can't save the world, and we can't save the nation.
But if we can help one person, we'll be their salvation.

    —*Angelique Nguyen*

A Man Now Lives...

A man has died...
A man!
Among men unrecognized.
Stored within his heart those jewels rare...
Those "precious things" of Christ,
Beyond compare!
Jewels sought by those who passed him by.

A man now lives ...
A man!
Among saints welcomed.
For all eternity the treasure sure...
Bought by the blood of Christ,
Earthwounds' cure!
Treasure he and Christ now occupy.

    —*Lucinda McCoy*

My Son

My son is a memory held close to my heart,
    a memory unfaded though death us did part.
The Saviour has taken him to His home on high.
    I know he is happy, so why should I cry?
He was "loaned" to me only, that I know.
    I had the best years to watch him grow.
I'd like it so much if he was with me still,
    But we all must bow to our Saviour's will.
So, I'll pack my memories deep in my heart,
    And think of "that" day when we'll never
    more part.

    —*Will-O May F. Dowdy*

Forest

I used to think how nice to know
A forest stands somewhere on earth

Deep dark and dank below
Searching brows of green in sun above.

Pungent clean with breath of rotting
Leaf and wood where fungi are at birth.

Far far away, I know, and near near
The tree that grows beside our drive My Love.

    —*Floyd McLain*

Message To A Loved One

Actions speak louder than words, they say;
A noncommittal shrug, and just walk away.
Others are affected, not only you;
You make things happen, whatever you do.

Good things, bad things, happy or sad;
No one can change them, they can only help.
"Help" means to be there with an outstretched hand.
But the first and last steps you must take yourself.

Rehabilitation is a long, hard word;
"Oh, you'll be okay," is so often heard.
Empathy, sympathy, and pity are felt,
But you must learn to deal with the hand you're dealt.

First comes the denial you must overcome.
Asking for help is easier said than done.
But we're here to give if you're willing to receive
And we're here to listen, whenever you need.

Just take a moment, and remember past years-
The laughter, the sorrow, the joy, and the tears.
And when the world seems like its too tough
Just think of your family and remember- you're loved.

    —*Marsha Legg*

Patches

A scraped knee, a broken heart,
    A pair of jeans that falls apart.
The threads are weak, the material thin,
    The stuffing falls out, the cold creeps in.
If we toss out the old and always buy new,
    The uniqueness is lost that identifies you.
The scraps and the remnants rarely do match,
    A story unfolds behind every patch.
For each heartache is mended with some cloth and a stitch,
    If cotton spun gold, I would surely be rich.
The collector of patches possesses no prize,
    They are medals of valor, of heartache, and lies.
Accept me as I am, all tattered and torn,
    I have acquired my patches from the day I was born.
How strong are the patches, do they seal in the pain?
No, they refurbish the heart to be filled with love once again.
From afar I may appear as though crafted from rags,
    But I am one hundred percent genuine, just check my tags.
I may not be perfect or know just what to say,
    But patches and all, I am yours on this day!

    —*Teresa J. Septer*

Me and You

I love you with all my heart
    A part of me dies when we are apart
Our friendship is true
    Our love is true
Special to us and only
    Known to a few
The happiest day of my life
    Was the day you asked me to be your wife
Right then I knew
    You were the perfect one to renew
my being again
    Since I failed in the past with men
Thanks for being you and for being true
    For me there is no other man that will ever do
Now our lives have become one
    Experiencing joy, true happiness and fun

    —*Annamaria Menoni*

"Precious Friends"

Light breaking through the clouds above,
a peaceful morning for the dove.
Dew dripping off the colored leaves,
as nature blows across the trees.
All living creatures have their place,
revealing our Lord's mystic grace.
But human beings invade their home
and won't leave these precious things alone.
We dump our smog into the skies,
So feathered friends are forced to die.
We destroy the forests and all the trees,
pollute the beaches and the seas.
We murder victims for their skin,
not thinking what they have within.
The Lord gave life to them as well,
as He made heaven and He made hell.
Appreciate them while their here,
don't force them all to live in fear.
For if they disappeared tomorrow,
all men on earth would feel great sorrow.

　　　—*KellyAnn Kinsella*

Strange Dreams

I had a dream with a castle made of fire,
A prince made of red,
A staff made of lightning,
A dragon made of steel shot liquid gold out of his mouth,
And a wooden person with sieves for hands tried to pick it up.
A tree made of blood shaded a hill of doggie doo doo.
A rubber cat ate an iron rat,
while a snake made of water squeezed a bear made of paper.
A large man made of rock trampled a man made of glass.
I was swept along on a bed of steam
near a waterlike fall of hot wax.
A spotted gorilla climbed a tree of ice
And ate purple lead bananas.
He scared the claypaper birds away to their nests.
The claypaper birds carried me up to the young rhinoceroses,
and just before they ate me
with their sharp marshmallow teeth,
I woke up.

　　　—*James T. Chaney*

Faded Dreams

He was an American farmer,
　A proud and honorable man,
And he cleared and plowed the good earth,
　Because it was his land.
He prayed his crops would flourish,
　And he looked at them with pride,
But he felt a deep foreboding,
　Somewhere down deep inside.
Because of the high inflation,
　And a mortgage on his land,
The bank could soon take over,
　And hold the winning hand.
And he and his wife and children,
　Would have to leave their land.
But if everyone would work together,
　Then united they could stand,
To prevent this cruel injustice, that sometimes rules our land.
So our great and beautiful country,
　Would never bow her head in shame, because
she had lost her pride and joy, Her fields of waving grain.

　　　—*Ella Del Castillo*

An Inspiring Note

The evening began with a soft supple note
A quite soothing tone, yet it phrased like a quote
Played with precision and heart felt meaning
A harmony drifted as each note came gleaming
The crowd sat in sway mesmerized by this feeling.
Enticingly driving, but seductively soft,
the tempo enchanted by the nights dew like frost
The language of choice, the melody played
was much like a voice, not sung but well played
When encore receded and instruments rest
I gazed up at the bright stars
I had found my true quest.

　　　—*Robert J. Coffey III*

The Sands of War

(Dedicated to the Men and Women of Desert Storm)

Up ahead in the distance is what is feared,
A raging battle is all we hear.
The guns that fire, the shattering blasts.
And missiles landing with a bright contrast.
Thoughts of peace are whispered at night.
The enemies coming but he's nowhere in Sight.
Dreaming of home and the morning birds,
Yet out here in the desert destruction is heard.
Diplomacy works is what they say,
As missiles are landing and disarray.
The bodies they leave and the lives torn apart,
Makes it hard to maintain peace in the heart.
When this war is over, and all said and done.
Out here in this desert I'll bury my guns.

　　　—*Victoria Lane*

Life Is:

　A tear-jerking journey through emotions,
a rollercoaster ride of happiness and sadness!
Only those with a strong heart will
block out fear and trouble,
and survive the mixed emotions of
love and hate,
and get on with life!
Think only about happiness which is
hard to do,
but mothers just say "I love you too!"

　　　—*Anne Williamson*

The Haunting

　The haunting I speak of is not
a scary specter seen at night, it is
of a child I have not seen a sight.

　I know this child well because
he was a part of me, the morning I felt
my babe gone was almost the hardest thing to
take.　But I know you left me a legacy, a
part of you didn't go free.

　This child who left sight unseen
made his impression in a most unique
way, for even after he was gone it
felt like he was still there inside and
still had something to say.

　So that is the story of my ghost.
It is not a scary one, it is just the
sweet memory of my unborn son.

　　　—*Claudette Hunt*

Silent Tears

Endless tears of distress fall from a dismal face.
A silent cry over what is now an empty space.

No comforting smile to ease the pain
From dignity and pride being forever stained.

A conscience that won't let go
Of love that never intended to grow.

No peace of mine. No restful nights.
Reminiscing of fairy tale's arms holding on tight.

Illusions of forever affection kiss the stars.
With sharp edges, they cut the heart and leave a scar.

A quiet whimper over a reality that was only pretend
The fantasy of true love too soon came to an end.

　　　　—Malika S. Carey

Untitled

You want to look back to what used to be,
A simple life wild and carefree.
But you now know that you are older
And you and others are growing bolder.
Free yourself from what is holding you in sorrow
And remember that everyday there will be a tomorrow.
It's ok to feel sad over what you had
But if you don't let go, you'll die in your past
And grow old much more fast.
Imprint these words softly in my mind
I have to hold you just one more time.

　　　　—Carol Thompson

Grandma and Grandpa's Cabin

A piece of mind, unhurried time.
A slice of Heaven in my grasp, to escape reality at last.
Freedom of my soul; Grandma and Grandpa's Cabin.

Is it the weather or friendly atmosphere?
The animals, all of nature, or loved ones near?
Rather it must be the combination in this lovely place,
Which dissolves my worries with infinite grace.

Aromas luscious, intermingled with air crystal clear,
Springs flow, squirrels play, bird melodies to hear.
Does one even ponder why my lovely place I adore?
Here my contentment lies deep, I need nothing more.

I wonder why everyone cannot feel this way
But I do hope that maybe some day
You'll find a lovely place whether far or near
That will ease your soul, and make troubles disappear.

A piece of mind, unhurried time.
A slice of Heaven in my grasp, to escape reality at last.
Freedom of my soul, Grandma and Grandpa's Cabin.

　　　　—Lesley Ann Heins

R I P

Eyes slowly closed to the world upon the last eve I shall see..
A slight chill shook my soul when darkness drifted inside of me.
　Three more days until I depart, I hear my visitors words.
　Flowers drop upon my tomb, a sob of sorrow, I remember.
I wish to see the deep blue skies, the smiling faces that once were...
I long to erase the streams of sadness from the pain that I did stir.
　Two more days until I depart, I hear my visitors words.
　Flowers drop upon my tomb, a sob of sorrow, I remember.
My soundless voice echoed a call... "Please do not leave me
now, release me from these dampened walls where I lay stinking
and foul."
　A final day before I depart, hearing visitors' last words.
　Flowers drop upon my tomb...a sob of sorrow...I remember.
　　Remembering in peace.

　　　　—Kathleen Smelser

Untitled

You give to me a feeling rare and true
A special feeling shared by two
You fill my heart with fire and spark
I tingle from head to toe and I begin to glow
Every time you come near and whisper in my ear
It is those three little words that quiet my nerves
The ones you say every day by day
You say them whether near or far
Those special words as you know are
"I Love You"

　　　　—Janette (Peak) Benner

A Drug Free Life, It's the Cool and Only Way

There it is a program for kids you see they call it DARE
A special trained officer can educate you kids to be aware
Kids need to be taught there's nothing about drugs ever fare

JUST SAY NO, THEY TRY TO TEACH EACH AND EVERY-
ONE TO SAY!
A DRUG FREE LIFE, YES IT'S THE COOL AND ONLY WAY!

For some it's easy they can just turn the other way and walk
Then there's those with a talent out of anything they can talk
Now for others it's hard to say no that's where a pusher knocks

It's sad but true they look and find those who are weak
With their twisted words and first times free temps you to peak
Time after time you fall deeper and deeper don't let the MONKEY
On your back HE'S A REALLY GOOD SNEAK

Yes my little friend for you it's very important to take all
The time it needs TO LISTEN AND LEARN
When an officer comes to your school your class it's their
Knowledge and time given, most important IT'S REAL IT'S
CALLED CARE AND CONCERN!
To you I say try to JUST SAY NO with each one of you who turn
Them down maybe DRUGS they'll die and go away YES CRASH
AND BURN

BE DRUG AWARE LOOK, LISTEN AND LEARN FROM THE
PROGRAM DARE!

　　　　—Brenda Sawyer

Untitled

A thread that hangs onto a shooting star,
A star that brings dreams from afar.
The weaving of a happy fulfilled dream,
Doth bring from mine eyes a happy gleam.
As beautiful as a joyful daydream.
It's as beautiful quiet and serene,
As the pretty, sweet nightingale.
Who trills on leaves against the moon so pale.
And gazes at the twinkling stars in the sky,
From whom many secrets you may pry.
Those majestic, smiling, silver stars,
That peer down from above and notice cars.
Driving below the lights of roads below.
And the streets emit a golden glow.
A memory.

　　　　—Jo Marie Janco

The First Time

The first time I saw you I admired your beauty.
When I looked at your eyes, I saw beauty like the
blue ocean. Your beautiful skin resembles the shining
Of a golden sun. You overall have the beauty that any man
can ask for. I had to let you know how special you are. All of
this happened since the first time.

　　　　—Edwin Rivera

White Into White

Who could imagine?
  A sun, a sky, and blossoms —
    all white!

Glowing like candles
  under the radiant moon —
    magnolia blossoms.

With only one brush —
  with only one color —
    winter has spoken.

A white December
  paints but the stream's passing face —
    fallen gold, its still heart.

White flowers blooming
  against a red sun say
    what our words cannot.

White into white burn
  candle and moon, revealing
    the words of my heart.

—*William S. Mooring*

Dream

In the magic of the golden sunrise,
A dream came true.
A magical, wondrous, beautiful dream.
A dream beyond imagination; a dream beyond the soul....

.... There she was, sleek, silver, betrayed.
Betrayed of hot freedom that boiled her blood.
She was imprisoned for man's whim and worry.
Doomed a death of lonely confinement.
From her bones, to her flesh and soul, she was born to be free
To ride the waves of the open sea, with other of a kind,
But she was barred into a small, murky bay.
Her only friends were her captors.

In the magic of the golden sunrise,
She would be free.
Her blood free, her heart free, her soul free,
Free as the white gull at the mercy of the ocean's breath.

In the magic of the golden sunrise,
She was free again.
She was joyous once again.
As joyous as the spirit of a dolphin should be.

—*Lisa Chilberg*

The Oak Tree

I have an oak tree in my yard
A tall and stately oak tree
It's branches reach up to the sky
The leaves are green like velvety moss
Who planted this stately oak tree?
Was it planted by squirrel, bird or human hand?
How old is my stately oak tree?
It's been here many a year, day and night
How many storms has it weathered and survived?
It must love the sun, rain, wind and snow
The ever cooling breeze that comes on a hot summer's day
Each gives its gift to my oak tree
Branches and leaves give us shade from the heat of the day
I look at my stately oak tree and I think of God
From a tiny seed has grown a mighty oak tree
The squirrels and birds make their homes
In my stately oak tree.

—*Angie Avilla*

My Child Within

Remember me as I came to you?
A tender child with life anew.

And, as I began to grow, I hid this child
The one you know.

I hid him deep within my soul
In a place that only I could know.

He lives there now this little child
He's just behind my every smile.

He's also the reason for my guilt and fear
And the mentor of my every tear.

He often controls my every thought
And even at times, the way I walk.

And yet he's the guardian of my soul
And, oh he tries to be so bold.

But, he's just my little child within
And to come to me, you must first come to him.

—*Murray Anglin*

"A Touch"

A touch of softness and gentleness versus
  a touch of harshness and invasionment
Can you really distinguish between the two?
Is it the person that makes difference
  or the intent?
A touch can hold so many different
  connotations, that often times a
  misconception or blurredness occurs
  between the two.
Innocence, however, is lost either way.

—*Molly Elam*

So Many Ways

There are so many ways to say... I love you!
A touch of the hand,
A smile,
A glance across the room.
The feelings I have inside of me
Often feel too strong for words
But then it comes spilling over
Saying I love you again and again
Wanting to embrace the world
Dancing free in the breeze
Under the moonlight and stars above
I reach out a hand to your face
To caress you and say...I love you!

—*David L. Thompson*

...And The Earth Rumbled On Its Track

The girl walked alone along the orbit of the earth,
A yawning black void watched in indifferent appreciation
And the stars blinked in yellow silence.
Above her, below her, the walls of space and time

Behind her, the earth rumbled on its track
Moving closer, faster, louder.
She began to run, she wanted to jump,
But the gravity of her conscience stopped her.

Helpless and so desperate, she opened her lips to scream.
A shapeless force grabbed her throat and cut her sound
And her bugging eyes could only communicate
The very end of everything, as the earth rumbled on its track
And took yet another soul to burn.

—*Kimberly Michalek*

A Boy Needs a Dog

Some things can't be told to just anyone.
A true friend is needed to share in the fun.
When finding a snake in under a log,
This is a time when a boy needs a dog.
Taking a hike to the pond and back.
A trek to the woods with his lunch in a sack.
On a day that's lazy, and the suns beatin' down.
The pup's right beside him, with nary a frown.
When he can't find his way to the cows in the fog.
Times like this, a boy needs a dog.

If the stream by the road's full of new polliwogs,
Who's gonna care 'cept the boy and his dog.
When the kids got troubles, it's plain to see,
Ole Shep's thrilled to death, he say's "tell 'em to me."
Seems no one's around when his head gets a bump,
Or he skins his knee on an old tree stump.
Some critters won't listen, like spiders and frogs.
In times like these, a boy needs a dog.

—*Runell Steele*

Childsplay

Thy tender slumber nu doth seem
A vision o' thy father's dream.
Yet gaze thee soon upon thy land
An' beware o' all o' the stranger's hand.
Set aside thy dolls thaes night.
Remember thy rank an' strength in might.
Tho' soldiers rage bloodly war
Thy people weep outside the door.
Dragon, men, lady fair,
O' thaes, dear mistress, have a care.
True to birth thy bearing show
An' with thy torch, forward go.

—*Carla Jo Underside*

The Image of Evil!!

Some whisper from that horrid mouth of strange unearthly tone,
A wild infernal laugh to thrill ones marrow from the bone,
But "NO!" it grins like horrid death and silent as a stone,
With an evil aura that draws me nearer,
I fear not nor do I feel fear,
Harmless desire to know the image of evil,
Possessed by a power of pain nor do I feel,
Impure mortality is but deceitful and violent,
To know what I know and ask questions I shant,
The evil eye is keeping close and the angels of death sing loudly,
Sacrificed is one impure soul and given is my life gladly…

—*Gina Rankin*

"The Holocaust"

Holocaust,
A word that hurts the tongue.
Holocaust,
Destroyed the old and the young.
Why it happened is hard to explain,
Yet millions suffered agony and pain.
Shipped by the thousands to the camps of hell,
And into the clutches of the Nazis they fell.
Cries for help, screams of despair,
The smell of death lingering in the air.
No food, no drinks, no beds, just crying,
All around you people dying.
And this, for years, remained their fate,
For the Americans help just came too late.
By the time of the Jewish liberation
Few remained of an entire generation.
And even though the war was won
Those tragic events can never be undone.

—*Gina Civin*

Mother Love

Mother is a word which spells love.
A world all the world is mindful of.
Mother's play the leading rolls
In giving birth to little souls.

It takes a mother's loving hands
A gentle heart that understands
To mould and shape a little life
And guide it through both storm and strife.

It takes a mother's kindness
Her soft and sweet caress
To bind up tiny broken hearts
And mend fragile friendship from the start

A mother's love can do so much
To build up trust and keep in touch
To make this world a better place
So mother's are a special race

For every color, creed, and race
God sent to earth to take His place
And mother is a lovely name
That every woman should be proud to claim.

—*Fred Caracciolo*

A Proposal

I spent my day thinking.
About time, about life, about you.

I believe that it might be,
just may be a moment when we,
touched by each other as we are,
should move together, forward,
and consider it a time for more.

More commitment.
More trust.
More openness.
More oneness.

A time to put other, older obligations to bed.
A time to relegate them to the past.

You know the power, the strength, the truth of my love,
and how it feels to be cared for in my world.

Take my hand, come with me, let's face the future together.
There is a wonderful journey ahead.
It's called life…
Say yes.

—*Victor J. Woytowich*

Capricious Thoughts

Lying in the meadow, I looked beyond to the sky.
Above, the sky was a haze of glimmering blue.
The sun was a brilliant yellow-orange.
The sun's rays flowed down to earth
like a slide that a cherub whisks
down to reach little children.
That cherub reaches me and makes me become
that little child. That open essence
which loves people, the vibrant sun,
the green lush grass, and the rich hues of the sky.

The golden sun reminded me of the hair
on the little Russian girl with golden braids.
The sky reminded me of her hazel-blue eyes.
At the embassy today,
I saw a Russian diplomat's little daughter.
Not any older than my own.
What future does she have?
What future does my own daughter have?

—*Laurel Dixon*

Halfway Years

Somewhere around the crescent corners of life,
Across the thin lines of third decades
I lost something.
Where there had been puerile suns and melancholic moons
and hot sentiments of a careless now,
Came the furtive falling of a vague and distant curtain
of time passing.
Lost is the fragile hold on I.
The futile feathering of one's own nest.
Scattered and broken woven
into wise warm cotton, gray with prime,
Advised and out-seeking, out-reaching
towards the grasp of God.

—*Cecilia Huckestein*

The Mystery and Misery of Life

I've had a very interesting life.
Adventurous in strife, meek, and blithe.
I'm grateful for experiences galore;
My faith to strengthen forevermore.
If I had known about my present state,
I wouldn't have grown, while they hate.
With their inability to see the truth,
They deny and stumble as if in youth.
They're past the age of understanding;
Blind to the light he's handing.
Lord, lift my spirit onto the hills.
Let me send roses and banish quills.
Let me replace error with truthfulness.
Give me patience so I can learn and bless.
Please, let us mend in creative silence.
Clear our minds, so we make good sense.
Lead us to seek and walk with Thee,
For father, you're a guiding light to me. Amen!

—*Patricia Joan Johnson*

"Rude Awakening"

A tiny green plant did sprout one day
After a rain - in the month of May
And as she grew she looked all around
To see just who shared her plot of ground

She found herself surrounded by flowers
So she began to while away hours
Deciding which kind of flower to be
Finding fault with each one she did see

"The daisy is too painted for me
And a shy violet I wouldn't be
The peony I would find much too big
The marigold seems to wear a wig"

As time went by and she grew quite tall
She received a shock to end them all
She saw flowers around her going to seed
And knew at last - she was just a weed.

—*Nina Simmons*

Images

The times of youth are memories,
When one has aged in years
Fading pictures that one sees,
At times, through mists of tears
It can be sad when youth's no more,
And left so far behind
Yet hard to close the shutter door
In the camera of the mind.

—*Raymond F. Foley*

Untitled

The same cracks still haunt me. It's here
again. The thought of a certain music with some unknown
Collaborating on the bed. Anyhow the year will go again,
I bet.

Christmas will be here soon; there's more cd's to ask for,
more food to refuse, another composure to uphold.

Perhaps the choice is made in thinking
of the elders.
Why she'd always wanted to sit up watching
the card games, tea drinking, and laughter.
The enormous stool to conquer. Eye level's the limit.
ssshhhh….kiss your father goodnight.
He doesn't notice the shrinkage of time.
You linger
She hears and orders are given. Then
with friends later commenting
Time not coming quick enough.
Everything is circles.
Two hours is enough to sink into time and wish.
For those who can sleep.

—*Jean Louise Paquin*

Night Time In A Forest

It is night time, I am alone
Ahead of me is a clearing
The only light is from the moon and stars on this crystal
    clear night.
There are tall pines all around me.
They reach for the sky
Snow up to my knees
It is wet and heavy
The big, strong branches bend under the enormous weight
    of the snow.
The air is sweet and clean.
This fragrance cannot be beat
I am just standing here alone
I am not cold, but warm from the inside out.
The creatures of this forest scurry to their warm beds.
The night is so beautiful.
The night is so peaceful.
On this night it is peaceful. Not icy, but tranquil.
Everyone and everything is serene in their heart, mind, and soul.

—*Nicole Salamon*

Martin Luther King

Marching to the beat of God's drum,
Aiming to violence never to succumb;
Righting many wrongs, allowing Peace to fight;
To satanic forces, he presented God's might.
In agony, he prayed to bring about Right.
Never losing faith, he kept the goal in sight.

Leading the downtrodden, the oppressed,
Uniting humankind of all races, he confessed.
Taking the beatings, the spit, being crucified,
Heaven watched while to God's will he complied.
Ever moving, ever strengthening as followers multiplied
Raising America's conscience that freedom not be denied.

King of nonviolence, a man of immeasurable faith and love,
In God he placed his unwavering trust
New laws were passed; new freedoms became a must.
Gone now to join the rest of the best with God who is
    eternally just.

—*Sarah G. Chambliss*

Remember Me

The whispering wind is crying your name,
All of my nights and days are the same.
The weight of your presence is faded away,
Yet, the memory of you is willing to stay.
It's funny how my nights seem longer,
And my love for you is growing stronger.
Our souls are together, as our lives are apart,
We can make it, only if we're heart to heart.
Remember my eyes, staring at you with love.
Remember my hands, reaching down from above.
Remember my heart, which only you could see.
Remember good times, that's how a memory should be.

—*Kristy Vastie Green*

Rhythm

The trees and plants — and Humans too
    all stepping forward, as if on Cue
To perform their brief and beautiful dance
    Gladly taking their chance.

It is the rhythm — the , "Beat," of time
    That is allocated for life in prime.
    Yet now, in the wings, as if on Cue
The next performers are ready to debut.

    So life goes, swiftly passing through
And like the Cherry Blossoms delicate hue
    It is often difficult to tell
    If we have been here for a spell.

—*Wendell E. Hauenstein*

Bereavement

"Time will heal your sorrow"
All that's left, is an empty tomorrow
You don't want to be healed
Heart's so heavy and feels sealed.

You don't see the sun or feel a breeze
You must view and treat grief, as a disease
Often times behind doors and a lock
Highly emotional, hysterical and in a shock.

Phases of grief, guilt—full of remorse
an onset follows, a predictable course
Reading the Old Testament, a promise you see
"As your day, so shall your strength be."

—*Mary Ann Wagner Steirer*

Books

From Mother Goose to Shakespeare,
    all the poets I adore,
Red Ridinghood to Robinhood,
    adventures by the score.
I have marched to many drummers,
    I have heard the bugle call,
I have followed many heroes,
    some to triumph, some to fall.
I have crossed the plains in wagon trains,
    I've sailed with Captain Cook,
Made a thousand other journeys
    since I first discovered books,
And early on I came upon
    the greatest book of all,
I read the Holy Bible and
    I heard the Master's call.
Through all the stages of my life
    great books have filled a need,
God bless the dear and patient soul
    who taught me how to read.

—*Alice C. Walker*

"Carpal Tunnel Syndrome"

When your hands get all numb and tingles
All the time and your hands start to ache
And pain, you think it's a cramp but you're
Really not sure then it gets so bad you
feel like falling on the floor,
"That's Carpal Tunnel!"

When the aching and paining continues
Day and night and you wonder if it's
in your mind, then you try to move
Your fingers left and right,
"And they don't move!" — "That's a sign"
of Carpal Tunnel.

If you ignore Carpal Tunnel's symptoms
And signs and don't see your Doctor
Today, when you count your money
You'll be in a bind because your
Fingers and your wrist can't obey your mind.
Carpal Tunnel Syndrome!
"See your doctor!"

—*Theresa Victoria Wilson*

Dawn

Oh God to wander through your world at dawn,
Along untrodden woodland ways. To see
The glory of a quiet, gray-gold morn
That sheds it's loveliness o'er hill and lea.
So beautiful it seems that angels cry
For joy and leave their tear drops crystal clear
Upon the grass. If angels weep then I,
Who am but mortal. What must I do here?
So many things within this world of ours
Give promise of that distant land beyond
The shadowed hills, the sweetness of wild flowers,
A bird's soft call, the sunlight on a pond,
The sound of water tumbling o'er the crest
Of some giant cliff, its angry, snow-capped foam
Subsiding into docile ripples, blest
By nature's soothing hand, unaided, lone
'Tis these things which enrapture man, inspire
Him to ponder on things as yet unborn,
But nothing can so purge his heart of ire
As beauty glimpsed within a gray-gold dawn

—*Rosemary D. Ludeau*

The Presence of You

I feel your presence
Although you are not near
I wonder the essence of a forgotten tear
I move around so stoically endeavored
trying to unleash all of my fears.

I battle the irony of never being alone
Yet, when you were here, I shall never atone.
You broke the vessels that held together my heart
Tending others when we were apart!

I came very close to two new friends,
them being strength and courage, when
the presence of you came to an end!

—*Rita D. Brinkley*

It's True

You caress my back and tickle my spine
Whatever you do, I feel good all of the time
You blow in my ear, you kiss my face
I melt like butter and ooze all over the place
It's a damn good feeling, I tell you no lie
No drugs needed here, I'm already on a high!

—*Edward LeGrand*

Rock-A-Bye Baby

Just a brown ball it was that day,
  An eastern tumbleweed ball which
Had rolled from a treetop down
  To the ground, where it lay,
Looking like a brown, round rabbit
  Or a dried hydrangea clump
Blown by the nudging wind of March
  Into a cool and hopeful April day.
Inside the woven grass and twigs
  Tufts of fur and leaves concealed
Three tiny, pink and bare, squirrel babes,
  Newly born, but orphaned there,
Shipwrecked, alone, and set adrift when
  Too-strong, breezes rocked their boat.
Down from spruce-tree heights it fell,
  To lie and wait, to lie and wait,
Till curious hands that day would try
  To put the cradle back,—in vain:
So futile as the human will or means
  To rescue squirrel nests come down.

    —Marjorie Murphy Shuman

Night Visitor

A tree scratching at my window pane,
An eerie scraping followed by rain.

Rain cold and chilling to the bone, it burrows in deep won't
  leave me alone.

You there at my bedside, please to me speak!
Are you a ghost or a spirit, who's lost soul must you be?

Icy fingers roam, my blankets held tight.
Pulled up to my chin my eyes shut and hide.

Oh go wicked creature and leave me alone!
Take with you the rain that chills to the bone.

Don't sit in my chair! The gall to invite yourself inside.
Whilst under my blanket I do cowardly hide.
Dandy do you think yourself as you sit and stare at me in my
  bed and you in my chair.

What time has passed, a moment or two?
An hour, a night, a lifetime for you.

Now night time is o'er and shines the morning light.
Be gone with you ghoul, be out of my sight.

    —Rosemary Irish

"Give Me The Roses"

  Give me the roses while I live, don't waste them on
an empty tomb, for I'll be gone to my Father's beautiful
garden where the roses will forever bloom.
  I need now your friendship and your love, you can't
give it to me after I'm gone, for I'll be with my Father
above where all is love and I'll never be alone.
  I'm going to live in my Fathers mansion where
nothing but His will is done. With Jesus and loved
one's forever I'll be, no more sorry, pain or death we'll see.
  It will be so wonderful to see Him face to face and
to know we've inherited all this by His saving Grace, no
greater gift of love than that which is sent from the Father above.

    —Delvia Green

Winter Snow

The winter snow falls to the ground,
When it touches it makes no sound.

A beautiful carpet of white is seen,
Making everything seem so fresh and clean.

    —Rebecca Palchinski

The Accordion Man

On the main street, he did play
An icon from days past
Gospel literature it was there
Reverend Palmer, a friendly man

The people they did stare
Amazing grace, he did play
His voice did bellow, his heart did show

Some would come
Some would go
But his impression upon me was definite
For the landscape didn't matter
His voice and conviction, was so strong

As I fell to the pavement, knees locked, heart wrenched
My life is shambles
The accordion man did understand
Then thru his music I realized, "Jesus could set me free"

And then I prayed and thanked God
I love that accordion man
Cobbled main street would never be the same

    —Paul Guminski

The Sound of Loneliness

Has this day no end?
A silence not broken by a sigh, a breath of air?
Only the sound of bile making its way
Through a maze,
Creating a vacuum in an already empty shell.
This sound of loneliness
Broken only by a beating heart,
Full of pain, hurt, anger,
All into one!

Take my anger, let me laugh again!
Take my hurt, for I shall stand tall again!
Let me hear your voice,
Speak! Break this sound of silence,
Reminding me there is life within,
Assure me there is no absence,
Though silent it may be.

    —Shirley J. Bench

Grandmother

A plain, printed, cotton dress.
An immigrant's strange tender tongue.
A language of gentle smiles-soft nods.
A soft hands-only a child knows.

In her youth, a young woman,
with an orphan's longing for home,
twice spanning ocean's wide sweep,
seeking, here, there, orphan's rest.

With few words and gentle soft eyes,
in afternoon suns; children listened,
with hands outstretched, for bread;
strange, round, flat-bread of another land.

    —John E. Subra

Freedom!

Priceless,
Worth more than Fort Knox,
It can be taken away
Or put on hold,
I love my freedom do you?
I don't want to live in a cell.
Gosh, I love my freedom!

    —Chad Hammock

The Unjust Embrace

I lay beside him,
 An inferno ignited beneath his feeble frame.
 While you encircle us; salivating,
 an angel with a passive name.

With swift neglect and fury,
 you rob my lover's soul.
 Deny him of the mercy
 others claim to hold

You toy...
 You tease...
 You mock my fractured dream.
Your presence cannot be overlooked
 you are oblivious to my vigil
Are you to be defeated with your embrace
 so obtainable?

I am chosen to be this saviour's misled
 soldier,
I exhaust the rage I no longer wield.
As you strive for your trivial prize this night
Decline the invitation... decline.

 —*B. Christopher Swansboro*

Window of Reality

The condor sleeps safe in the wild, yet we can't save
an unborn child. It's all out there, men too blind to see.
As they look through the window of reality!

Big kahuna rests in the white house, while death awaits
a pitiful old mouse. The manatee lies dead in the quiet
seas. As they look through the window of reality!

See the "Big Picture" as it spins where losers lose and
winners always win. Pollution damages our lungs and the
trees. As they look through the window of reality!

 —*Angela L. Nowling*

Merry Christmas

'Twas the week before Christmas,
 and all through the school
not a creature was stirring not even a ghoul.
The flag was hung by the grave with great care,
in hopes that the principal soon would be there.
I with my shovel, her with her cap,
had just settled down for a peaceful nap.
When we awoke, we found him there lying.
It was a pity to see the principal was dying.
We laid him to rest after robbing him dry.
All the students were there with tears in their eyes
Since that day the students run free
a principle is something that will never be!
The principal's grave is in
the yard where the children play.
Some people say that he'll come to life one day,
and take revenge on me and my friend,
but you'll never know because this is the end!

 —*Lisa Schreiber*

The Ocean

I love the ocean with its water so blue.
The salty air and the sea gulls too.
I love to build castles in the sand.
Then watch them wash away at the waves command.

I love to gather lots of sea shells
All pink and purple and pretty pastels
I love the waves and the sand and the foam.
I'd love to make the ocean my home.

 —*Brandi Hinkle*

"Trees of Night"

In the land of shadow
The trees see no light
They watch for centuries the dim dead night
They feel no caress of leaf nor life
And on and on go the trees of night.

 —*Michael Estevens*

White Etching On Black Marble

As I knelt by your headstone, showing the date that you were born
And another date that tells me just how long that you've been gone
I rub my hand over black marble, feeling the etching of my son
Trying to suppress the tears, just like I've always done
White etching on black marble is there for all to see
But no one will ever know just how much he meant to me
It's hard for me to comprehend your name upon that stone
Ever since that fateful day I've been so all alone
They say that life goes on. That really isn't so my son
I just exist from day to day, just trying to carry on
So my dear son as years go by, we'll try to carry on
Because we have your dreams and the love you shared
Since the day that you were born
We'll remember all the good times
And maybe we won't feel so alone
As I rub my hand over white etching of my son
On that black marble stone.

 —*Phyllis Coleman*

To My Son

I have known you for only seven years
And before you I had just lonely tears.
But in these seven years I've always loved you.
I've watched you growing with heavy burden.

Our many tears and joys, and all your broken toys,
Walks on shores and hills, and all the circus thrills.
No one could love you, no one could love me,
As much as we do, just you and me.

But in those seven years we've both been lonely.
We have each other but we need Daddy.
Be strong my son. Life's not yet won.
There's more to come when Mommy's gone.

So I leave you now with only words in song.
But my love for you will live on and on.
Now let me see your smile, your happy smiling face,
At least a little while, until I leave this place.

 —*Josephine B. del Mar*

To My Beloved...

If I could gather all the music from the love songs,
And blend it into one grand symphony;
Or gather all the words of love e'er written
Since time began, and bring them all to thee;
If I could draw the stars down from the heavens,
And fashion from their rays so silver bright
A shining platter to contain my love song,
And bring it to thee, Dear, on wings of light;
If I could gather all the petals from the flowers
To blend into a rare, fragrant perfume,
Or find the most exquisite rose e'er fashioned
And place into thy hands its radiant bloom;
If I could catch the laughter from the babbling brook,
Or the soft wind as it whispers through the pine;
Or the beauty of a lovely golden sunset,
Or a daybreak - when the sun beings to shine;
If I could take all these to place before you,
To speak of love and what you mean to me,
The half would not be told, my precious darling,
For God alone doth know how I love thee.

 —*Mary Jo Moore*

Intrusion

You saw that illusion
and chose your conclusion
although you don't know us at all.

You made an intrusion,
in your mind, a solution
your going to correct us all.

You gave a selection
with positive intention
did you really expect us to crawl.

We gave you rejection
you can't take bad affection
so we ended up with a psychological brawl.

—Jeremy R. Hoots

Adam I Forgive

Adam the first man did not obey
And Christ knew the price He must pay.
Thou not yet of this earth
He was doomed to die even before his birth.
Adam knew what he had did
That is why he ran; he hid.
Not only did Adam commit sin
He ruined a heavenly place for all his kin.
He created fear, he destroyed trust
He made this place hell for all of us.
His perfect nature He did spoil
Now in earth we all must toil.
Angry is something we could be
But that would blind us, we would not see.
That Christ's death was of a special kind
It was the one thing that could free all of mankind.

—Robert S. Breaux

My Lord, and My God

No one else, through Hell, would go for me
And cry, "My God, My God," so piteously,
While sinking in the mire our sins had heaped;
Darkness cloaked His hours of anguish deep.

The temple curtain, torn by God's own hand,
Opened reconciliation unto man,
To stand before the Holiest of All,
Free, at last, from Satan's cunning thrall;
In Christ's own righteousness arrayed,
Because the awful penalty he paid.

—Norma Vinson

To My Valentine

It's many years since first we met
And destiny ordained
A love that's grown with passing time and yet
It seems as yesteryear.

With problems solved and triumphs shared
To Father Time we bow.
The goals we set - some met - some pared
Seem unimportant now.

Greying hair and faltering steps are due
To ravages of time.
With all my love and thank you too;
My SPECIAL VALENTINE.

—Verda S. Nunnenkamp

The Last Poem

Rubies are falling from your lips,
And diamonds fall from your eyes.
I hate seeing you like this,
You're all sad inside.
You told me you love me,
Although you tried to leave me once before,
But I wouldn't let you go.
This time I have no choice,
I'll never see you again, now that you took your life.
I'm looking at you all shivery and cold.
I don't know what to do all I can is hold.
I don't want to lose you, not again, not this way.
We were going to be together forever, and a day.
I want to be with you, will I someday?
You can't leave me, I won't let you.
But how can I make you stay?
You're dead now, gone forever.
What am I going to do with my life?
I want to be with you,
And I will.........with this knife

—Jessica Blumenthal

Sweet Child

Sleep, sweet child,
and dream for me —
an angel's song,
a fantasy...
Do then reach high
and touch a star...
The brightest one,
it's not that far.
Accomplished wonder...
it disappears,
cry not my angel,
can't see through tears.
Yet this star so strong and so bright,
it symbols your love, for eternal life.
Has gone far better
than distant dreams,
A "loss", you think?
although it seems.
But gone nowhere, for now it lies,
this morning's star is in your blue eyes.

—Victoria and Richard Leasure

The Written Word

Hammer, chisel, quill and cloth
And dreams connect the ages.
And warriors fierce, in stone have etched
Conquests for us in stages.

A gift to the earth from wizened souls,
From the realms of antiquity.
Nectar for to quench the thirst,
For the dungeon door, a key.

From barren wastelands lost and lone
They hie me swift away,
To the hinterlands of a yonder shore
And a gentler, bygone day.

No warrior, I, nor sage I think,
Yet, in my dreams I wonder:
What is this fire ablaze in me,
This fierce, unyielding hunger?

I'll lay me down and mourn it not,
If, when my time is through,
My words have etched a placed within
The hearts of but a few.

—Carolyn Wade

To Question

Why is to love so hard to do?
And evil so easy to act.
When to dislike is accepted as freedom of choice.
To forgive, is too much to ask.

Was there a time when all stood,
For goodness and truth,
To keep our country strong.

Is it those that strayed,
Which led the way,
To evil and mischief and on....

One world for all,
How long will it last?
Will it be us to extinct?
Believable, doubtful?

For all to tell our neighbor,
"I love you."
No time soon.
Decades have passed.

  —Rosa Maria Clarkson

Fifteen Years

In Kansas City our passion flourished.
And fifteen years our love nourished.
We laughed and walked along the railroad track.
Those days, so long ago, we can't go back.
We dined, we shopped, and enjoyed the good life.
Never crossing our mind was any idea of strife.
We traveled, we saw another land.
Never knowing what was at hand.
We snuggled close and shared our bed.
We didn't know which one of us led.
We said we were equal, that we were free.
I loved you and thought that you loved me.
Now I feel my very soul has been ripped out.
You're with another and you left me without.

  —Jan Bennett

To Jeanne

Gliding poetry is she
And finely brushed in artistry,
Born with the gracious gift of caring.

Delicate, soft golden butterfly
Walks surely, in Oriental splendor.
Her name is "Honesty" and "Forever."

Luxurious tracery, done in elegant gentility
Like the preciousness of gold.
Her essence can neither be bought nor sold.

Golden butterfly, may all your goals be met!
Glide from flower to flower - and please don't forget
The old one, withering on the stalk, who loves you
Through friendship, storms or bursting sunsets....
 (though sunsets are so very few).

  —Joan C. Conroy

Birds Sing Anywhere

Through the maze of tangled weeds
to the heart of the scattered seeds
the bird peers here and there.

It spies a seed, ferrets it up
and lifts high the head.

Through the maze a voice wavers
then warbles a beautiful note.
The people there marvel and listen.

  —Marea Marchant

Glass Pains

I watch the rain trickle down on this pane of glass;
and follow a crack on it's smooth surface.
This window and I have a lot in common, we both look out on
the world, and in on peoples lives and reflect the actions
of the moment.
This glass is fragile, like I, and could shatter at any
second
with the impact of violence.
A crack on its surface that leads to the bottom of the sill,
like the crack in my heart that travels to the bottom of my
soul. This window no longer holds your reflection,
just like my eyes no longer reflect your presence.
This window sits alone, isolated in a cold, dark room.
I sit alone with a cold, dark heart.
This window only shakes with the rolling thunder,
I only shake with my remorseful sobs.

  —Stacy Harclerode

In the Beginning, God.....

Our Father said, "Let there be light" -
 And God and His Son made day and night.
  And God saw it was good.

The Heavens and Earth, the moon and the sun,
 The green fields and valleys and all life there on.
  And God saw it was good.

The beautiful gardens and stars in the night;
 The vast blue-green waters and birds in their flight.
  And God saw it was good.

God made the cattle, the fishes, and birds;
 He made all creation and these are His words -
  And God saw it was good.

God planted the flowers, the trees in the sod;
 Everything, everywhere was made by our God.
  And God saw it was good.

From the dust of the earth, our God and His Son
 Formed man in their image -
 Their work was then done.
  And God saw it was very good.

  —Margaret Rebecca Meadows

Mia Shadow

I have lived and died a shadow
And I bet no one even knew
I was just an unilluminated image
My beautiful rays unable to shine through

I was just a meager outline
Of someone else's grace
I may have done all the work
But no one saw my face

I was just a shaded area
In this picture they call life
I guess you could say a phantom, a ghost
But never someone's wife

I was only a faint indication
An influence that caused gloom
According to the rules of Social Darwinism
For me, this world had no more room

I was just a remnant
Living way out of place
This world has very few memories of me
Only a very slight trace

  —Traci Joy Campbell

Mother

Mother you are to me my closest dearest friend.
And I know no matter what that on you I can depend.
Through the years you have taught me the things in life that
count, that money isn't everything no matter the amount.
You raised us on your own but knew together we would make it.
And no matter what life dished you, you always managed to take it.
I know that times got hard but you never did give up.
You somehow knew that God and love was going to be enough.
You taught me independence and how to be strong inside.
You taught me to respect myself and to always walk in pride.
You showed me love was all it takes to make a person smile,
But more than that you gave me hope that life is worth the while.

　　　—*Renee Hutchins*

Always At My Side

Sometimes I look at myself in the mirror,
and I marvel at where I've been.
And I give thanks to God, for years gone past,
For the memories and happiness I've seen.
Yet without Him it would have been impossible,
I'd never have made the grade.
For sometimes it was almost unbearable,
Sometimes His image would fade.
Yet I persevered and held on to the lessons I learned
from my mother,
They carried me thru those difficult years,
Over mountains and troubled seas.
The twilight years are slowly ascending,
and I welcome them with pride.
For I know where I've been and where I'm going,
Because He was, and still is always at my side.

　　　—*M. Ruth Howard*

To a Colored Person

You say you're black
And I say
You have a lack
Of true black.

There is every hue and shade
Of black to brown that can be made.
Don't forget the lots of white
That makes the black lighter and light.

The pride you claim
Is for every human the same.
It's not the color of your skin that matters
But what kind of person you have been.

If you're proud of your colored skin
Be proud, too, of the mixture it's in
Be it white or black or yellow or red
Blood's the same color when you're bled.

Live with no chip on your shoulder
Which grows in time to a boulder.
If allowed to unabate
Will make you yourself hate.

　　　—*Norma C. Fox*

Child Alone

Where were you when I was alone?
The room was still and I was
Afraid and found my comfort
With my big Teddy bear.

Come home please come home.
Make it soon to tuck me in
So I can sleep and start a new day.

　　　—*Natalie Johannesburg*

Sadness

Sadness is the grey of stormy skies
Tastes of salty tears from my eyes
Brought on by the smoke of the fires of hate
The aftershock of the earthquake of Fate
Anguish and shame from hearts that lie
Even worse when loved ones die

　　　—*Michelle Bridgeman*

Remembering Me

When I leave this earth,
And I'm burned, do not turn.
Listen to what they say and stay.
There will be flowers, I'm sure,
And they will bring me great pleasure
to measure the love you have given me.
Yes, I will see.
I will not lay in the cold ground,
my ashes will be spread around.
For you will hear the sound of me
singing, within the bells ringing.
I am sorry for leaving,
but I can't stay away from the stream long,
for that is where I belong
and that is where I long to be.
So please keep remembering me.

　　　—*Summer Ann Thompson*

Gentle Breezes

　Though you're gone, you're still the same,
and in my heart, you will remain.
　In the breeze, you call my name.
In my heart, still remain
memories of you, they seem so real.
　I dream of you and see your face.
I feel your heart beating a pace.
　Gentle breezes, blowing winds
remind me of when we were friends.
　A child so young, I never imagined
a day that would come when you
would be pardoned.
　Sent off free from this place we call home.
Gone forever into the unknown
　A place so peaceful, a place so kind.
I'll love you forever, you're on my mind.

　　　—*Denise Campilio*

That Big Black Locomotive

It's a huffin' and a puffin' as it slices through the night,
And it passes by our house in the early morning light,
The engineer's a smilin' and a wavin' us a "Hi",
The conductor on the platform is wavin' us "Goodbye".

Oh, I love that locomotive from the engine to the back,
As it pulls its heavy load down the shiny railroad track.
Sis and I are on the front porch, just wishin' we could go
On that big black locomotive, then we hear that whistle blow.

It's a mournful, wailing sound, and we feel excitement tingle,
If we kids could only travel and with those lucky people mingle.
We've been livin' on the farm and have never seen the city,
Gee, if we can't ride that train, now that would be a pity.

Our Mama says we'll go, at comin' Christmas time,
If everybody saves each nickel and each dime.
Just Ma and me and Sis, to Grandma's house we'll go,
My goodness gracious, the time did pass so slow!

The snow is lightly falling on the platform where we stand,
And Mama has our tickets clutched tightly in her hand.
The big black engine's steamin', our hearts are beating fast,
It's just about to happen, our dream is here at last!

　　　—*Pearl Stanford*

The Spontaneous Combustion of Cattle

The spontaneous combustion of cattle is a curious phenomenon
And it usually occurs when it is least expected
Imagine, if you will, looking down on a multi-hued mass
Moving lethargically across a dusty plain
Upon closer inspection it can be discerned that what is being
seen is a herd of obese cattle
The cowboys gotta get 'em to some place where they can graze
See that guy over there with the black cowboy hat and loud shirt?
He's the hired hand, and he knows exactly where to take 'em
Moos erupt from the mass as the dog circles it, barking
Without warning, Bessie, one of the central cows, begins to tremble
and make strange guttural sounds
The surrounding cows begin to back away with wide eyes
(Which is really strange to see a cow do)
And suddenly, with one final, painful wail, Bessie explodes
Grotesque chunks of charred and smoldering cow fly in all
directions by some weird freak of nature, this starts a chain
reaction cows left and right explode messily until all that
remains are pieces of cow burning with a nauseating, acrid odor

—*Matt Sunrich*

God's People to the World Seem Odd

Sing forth the honor of His name
And learn of His great fame
Praise His Holy name
Morning noon and night
You Saints that over come
While waiting for our robes so white
Enter into His gates with thanksgiving
And His courts with praise
Praise Him with the Music words to form a
beautiful phrase. To beat Satan at His own trick
We are His people and the sheep of His pasture
Come before His presence with singing and
Secure your right standing for eternity
Don't worry about being in tune because
your joy is to commune with the Father
throughout eternity.

—*Estelle Martin*

The Good Things of Life

I've flown high in the air on a garden swing;
and listened in the early morning to a church bell ring.
I've watched beautiful birds flit through the trees;
and I've seen honey being made by the honey bee.
I've stroked a kitten with velvet soft fur;
and watched the earth being covered with pure, white snow.
I've waded in pools of clean, cool water;
and watched the work of a Mexican potter.
I've wrapped myself in Mother's silks and laces;
then dreamed and dreamed of far away places.
I've held my new born babies close to my breast;
and peeked at the treasures in a very old chest.
I've cruised the ocean on "The Paddle Queen"
I just can't tell all the wonders I've felt and seen.
I've crossed our wonderful country on a Greyhound bus;
and watched a robin protect her babies with a furious fuss.
I've climbed a rough mountain in the dark of night;
and watched the ocean's fury at the break of morning light.
I hope to see many more of God's wonderful things;
and I pray for Peace, Love and happiness for all human beings.

—*Helen Malinda Gibboney*

Untitled

Jealousy turns to bitterness
Towards an unforgiven soul
An ending comes without a kiss
And love is seen no more.

—*Kim Harrell*

Meet the Tiger

With half hid teeth so white,
And long claws sheathed,
Soft footfalls...one after the other
Gliding so silent; she seems to float.

Burning eyes aglow, intent;
Each muscle 'a tremble, quivering;
(Suppressed strength; 'til quarry's reached).
But; wait......something rustles up head!

She's off! Bounding in her long striding gallop.
Perhaps some food, at least a healthy run.
Ahh..... Unbridled freedom.
A flash of color in twilight's deep.

This is the mighty tiger!!
—*Phyllis Douglas*

Patchwork Quilt of Life

As you stand at the start of another year
And look back along life's way
You can see a patchwork quilt laid out
Of memories sad and gay.

There must be dark patches now and then
To bring out the brighter glow.
And tiny stitches are steps you've made
To make the small blocks grow.

There's always a thrill when a quilt is done
And work is through for the day.
But also, a thrill as pieces lay out
And a new quilt's on the way.

In your patchwork quilt of life
Many blocks have been made through the year
There's light and dark as you've gone along
Made up of joys and tears.

May health and happiness set the theme,
For the new year just beginning
And the patch quilt for the coming year
We're sure will be prize winning.

—*Maysel I. Pedersen*

Yesterdays

Out of the darkness
and into the light
shards of glass piercing the soul
slicing through pain
obscuring reality
memories of yesterday flooding the brain
moonbeams shining bright
gossamer wings taking flight
Hope glimmers faint —
choosing to follow
daring to dream
what all her tomorrows
might bring
—*Dorothy Guerra*

Ashes

Alone with my thoughts down the path I tread
The golden carpet at my feet,
The sun with fiery rays has fled
With September.... and with you, my sweet!

Dead are the leaves on the earth's dark floor
Ashes of days that were too fleet,
Leaving a memory, nothing more
Of springtime, summer.... and you, my sweet!

—*Marie Murray Guy*

Anchors of Life

To a little child, an anchor means a blanket and a thumb
And loving arms, and tender words, and being close to Mom.
And after taking those first steps, alone, yet being able
To reach the sweet security of the dear old coffee table.

And growing up, those anchors take on a different theme,
The need to be admired, and so help our self-esteem.
That question: "Is my hair okay? My make-up on just right?
Will I be a wall flower, or the belle of the ball to-night?"

And now that you are married, wife and mother is your life.
It has its glorious moments, it has its times of strife.
But as the anchors reach so deep into your happy home —
You know without a moment's doubt, you no longer want to roam.

So as we come to our "golden years," and face the ugly truth
That we are not as wonderful as we thought we were in youth,
We realize now our anchors are reaching for Heaven's Gates
To our safe, eternal harbor, to where our loving Lord waits.

—*Patricia Gough Risk*

Feelings

I sit at night, look into the light.
I let my mind wander, not knowing where it will go.
Wondering who you're with or where you're at.
My mind going in circles like a blinded bat.
I wonder if I'm in your heart, as I was in your mind
or if I'm the person still behind? I'm scared to think,
thinking isn't always good, it sometimes put me, in a bad
mood.
When I sit alone I fill up with tears,
not of jealousy, but of fear. I think of the good times,
Just me and you, and I wonder; why is it through?
We both had smiles; some are fake, but not ours.
Those are smiles that will be trialed
and questioned when I think of you. What happened, what went
wrong? All I know now, is that you are gone. That was the
past, this is now, should I hope for a future or just travel
now? I'm dazed and confused and don't know what else there is
to lose. You stole my heart and my mind; I feel as though I'm
still confined. And this really blows my mind.
What I write is from my heart, this much is true;
But the question that still lingers in my mind is,
"Do I still love you?"

—*Sarah Johnson*

The Root

I am the root; nourished by the land, the water the sunshine
and my faith. In essence I am as my mother would say, the true
spirit of life I am as old as time itself, in all my righteous
ways, yet; I am young as the moment when cast in doubt. The
spirit is as the thirst unquenched by water, the fullness is
there but, the thirst remains. The root is the support
structure of whomever reaches for new heights. New heights
abound among the blossoms of good root structure Even the
mighty Oak tree could not stand or whisper sweet silence, if
not for good root structure. In the true spirit of life I will
hold firm the belief, that a firm grasp on social ideology with
temperance is; good root structure. I submit to the will that
be, that indecision and no decision will not provide the
fullness nor clinch the thirst of life. Be bold and drink of
the sweetness of life until you have had your fill, do it with
modesty, love, and compassion. I am the root; and I give to
you ideology, that is most dear to me. I am the root; and
though I lay firmly planted and silent, the evidence of my
being is seen and heard loudly; in you.

—*E. V. Washington*

The Spirit Of Seventy Six

O brash unfettered youth, weep not for me
And my halting tread.
I have poignant recollections of the lazy day
Of my own awakening long ago,
Fraught with capricious flights of fancy
On gossamer wings
Soaring ever upward into fantastic orbit,
But not beyond recall.
An ethereal system bids these reveries to reenter
On command and pass in review
As delightful as ever.
Mine for eternity, these exercises keep me
Younger than Springtime!

—*Robert L. Campbell, Jr.*

Nonesuch

God and I alone in space
And no one else in view

"And where are all the people, Lord," asked I
"The earth beneath, the sky o'er head
The dead who once I knew?"
"Oh, those were dreams," the great God said
"Dreams that seemed to be real.
There are no people, live or dead
No earth beneath nor sky o'er head
There is only myself and you."

"Then why do I feel no fear?" asked I
"Being alone with you this way...
That I have done wrong, I know full well;
Can this be heaven, can this be hell?
Can this be judgement day?"
"Oh, those were dreams," the great God said
"Dreams that seemed to be real.
There is no you, there never was.
There is only and always me."

—*Bonnie Parker*

First Born

Lover of soccer

Who feels there should not be any wars, that opera's are jokes,
and nuclear weapons should be banned

Who wants to play on the Brighton Premier soccer team, to have
money, to get an A in Creative Writing

Who gives gifts to everybody, help to friends and family, all
he's got in every class

Who fears nuclear weapons, psycho killers, and some kinds of
scary movies

Who would like to see the president, different countries, and
a World Cup game

Resident of South Lyon

—*Neil Dreffs*

February Air

My kite was there in the February air in the February
air in the February air that was there.
I don't know why but it could fly, in the February
air in the February air that was there.
But then out there in the February air in the February
air that was there my kite began to tare.
That February air that February air that was there got
mad like a bear and my kite could do nothing but
tare and tare.
So if your there in the February air if its there
Don't fly your kite even if it seems right, just
wait till March when the airs not harsh.

—*Stanley C. Wyllie III*

I Believe In You

You have touched a lot of hearts
and reached a lot of minds,
  Too bad the world doesn't have
as many like your kind.
  I envy your courage and the
strength you must obtain,
  One day it will all be done and
you will be past the pain.
  You have tons of support from
people in which you love,
  And an even stronger power caring
for you from up above.
  The unexpected has happened before
and I know you'll see it through,
  I know you'll fight it the best you can
because I believe in you.

—*Erica Stoelting*

I Don't Understand (A Letter to God)

(In memory of Roger Dale Hickey 11/16/54 - 9/8/93,
and Samy Clint Cauthen 4/11/78 - 9/17/93)

  I don't understand why you took my friends, but
there must have been a good reason. You know how it hurts
cause your perfect dear God, but why? I don't understand. It
hurts so bad I want to cry and shut the whole world out. But
I have to strive to live my life like today's my last day left.
I know you can come or call me home in the twinkling of an eye.
It's your will dear God, I have no say, but I'll miss my
friends day by day. It's hard to say goodbye you know, but now
I'll let my dear friends go. Help me God to understand, that
it was your will to take my friends.

—*Lisa Escalon*

Beautiful Hand

I went for a walk with my love today,
And saw many beautiful sights along the way,
For the golden sunlight streamed down on the land,
While masses of wildflowers were close at hand.

Reds and orange, yellows and blue,
Every conceivable color and hue,
Feathery clouds danced across the sky,
Everchanging shapes as they slid by.

Nature's finest was displayed before us,
While songbirds sang a delightful chorus,
Yet with all the beauty in this wonderful land,
The greatest of all was holding my hand.

—*Marty K. Vandermolen*

My Granddaughter's Eyes

You may climb the tall mountains, and sail the wide seas
    And soar through the endless blue skies
  But the beauty found there, will not nearly compare
    To what I see in my granddaughter's eyes

  There is faith and love, and a frightening trust
    And innocent wisdom in a beguiling disguise
    A giggling scamp, a vixen and a vamp
    Can be seen in my granddaughter's eyes

They have the power to hold me, and the fire to scold me
    They pain my heart every time she cries
  If heaven has windows, through which mortals might see
    Those windows are my granddaughter's eyes

Should God grant me one wish, as I stand to be judged
    For my failures, my mistakes and my lies
I'll be welcomed into heaven, for that final wish will be
  For Him to see me, through my granddaughter's eyes

—*William C. Wallace*

The Painter

God held His palette in his hand
And softly touched this mighty land.
He turned the leaves to red and gold.
A panorama did unfold.
A wondrous beauty to behold.

Then, with a gentle breath of air
Cascading leaves were everywhere.
With scarlet colors, yellows, browns,
As wind gusts sent them swirling round,
A lovely carpet on the ground.

A temporary color these,
The lovely colors of the leaves.
But, green of pine and Laurel still stand,
White birch, red oak, throughout the land.
The colors of our nature grand.

And, then the trees were stark and bare
With limbs upraised in silent prayer.
The work of summer in the past
Awaiting winters stormy blast,
A time of rest has come at last.

—*Samuel Murphy*

Nightmares

The sun yields to Earth's dark satellite. Falling to the west
and soon out of sight.
The darkness devours, remarkably dense. A light shielding
curtain, a solid black fence.

Afraid of sleep, of what comes when I rest. I fight fatigue
and my unwanted guests.
My body relaxes, my mind fades to black. Reality is gone, the
nightmares are back.

Morbid dreams of confusion and pain. Blurred evil images, dark
and insane.
Fleeing and falling, attempting to fight. Praying for dawn and
cursing the night.

Unfocused thoughts, instinctive reflex. Nervous feelings with
paranoid effects.
Cornered and trapped, arms bound to my sides. The beast is
upon me the beast is inside.

Things seem to pass in a curious way. The brutal cold night
turns into the day.
The day casts out fear and quells the dread. Removing the
fodder from which evil has fed.

—*C. W. Stobbe*

"A Prayer For Kim"

Dear Lord, Please keep an eye on Kimi-Ann, and keep her safe
and sound. Just hold her up when times are rough, she's good,
she'll come around. And please don't let her hurt too much,
and God don't let her cry. Oh Lord she's soft and lady-like,
when Kimi hurts, I die. And Lord just let her know I'm here,
and help her hold on strong. And let her feel, without a doubt
our wait is not that long. My father, you have made her well,
she's turning out just right. She struggled up, from so far
down, held on and won the fight. My Lord, I'll love and care
for her, as long as I'm allowed. She makes me focus perfectly,
her goodness makes me proud. I beg you Lord, protect her, I'll
be good for Kim, I vow. And watch her in the danger-zones, I
cannot lose her now. Amen.

—*Robert Maxwell*

Native Eyes

Though I may wear the skin of the conqueror
I possess the soul of the conquered people.
Mystical is the heart that beats within this shell,
Spirituality rules the mind that powers this machine.

The eyes I own show my true being,
it matters not the skin in which they are living.
One must look within to find thy true soul,
Until the search begins that true soul, no one can behold.

—*John J. Krupcheck III*

Memory of John McCormick

Where you were it was always laughing,
And talking, and eating,
The air humming with happiness.
Silence was waiting outside the door.

The air around you danced with magic
And you burned with a holy fire.
All who came near you were warmed
And believed again in the goodness of living

Your life was your poem,
But you wrote all your poems upon the air.
Now that you are gone
We are left with the silent space where you stood.
And the air of this electronic planet
Does not sustain us.

—*Sarah Williamson Baicy*

"Nature"

When the tides slosh against the shore,
And the clouds rush across the sky,
When the wind whistles through the trees,
And wolves howl out their lonely cry.

When deer wander through the forest,
And the bee buzzes to it's hive,
When fish swim in the deep blue sea,
And the bear hunts to stay alive.

When squirrels scamper to find their nuts,
And the birds fly back to their nests,
When horses munch on lush green grass,
And the cows swat at any pests.

When Mother Nature takes a role,
I feel a certain peace inside,
When life decides to take it's toll,
Why does everything have to die?

—*Gretchen Otermat*

Spring

When the golden rays linger and the geese are all in flight,
And the light of day has won its battle with the night;
The new green grass has overspread the white,
Then I feel again the world will be all right.

For the winter gloom has long clasped the land,
And held our hope and dreams in a icy hand;
The days seemed gray and never ending, so,
Lets hope a year passes before we ever see snow.

Soon the red and yellow roses will perfume all the air,
And the happy days of summer will pass without a care;
We'll walk and talk and take in all the sights,
And sit and dream through those summer nights.

Life is but a tick on the master clock of time, you'll find;
Thus if you can muster the proper frame of mind,
Then the best of life will come to call on you,
And the beauty of summer will always see you through.

—*Eugene T. Ireland*

Untitled

The tunnel grows narrow
And the light starts to dim
The decision is made
Could it possibly be Him

Or somehow return
As a friend or a love
But perhaps a whale
Or a white snowy dove

Either way the stay is complete
A job well done for a much owed favor
Don't despair, for a lesson was learned
You see my friend, life should you savor

—*Danette J. Glidden*

Death of a Red, Red Rose

When the love turns cold
And the nights spent alone
The eerie wind seems to blow forever.
As the souls get lost it seems a bitter cost
For the death of a red, red rose?

When the spirit is lost
And the days drag on
The body seems a burden to carry.
A screech of pain, but who's to blame,
For the death of a red, red rose.

When the dreams are empty
And the hopes are gone
The night seems like an eternity.
Filled with hate, is this one's fate
For the death of a red, red rose?

When the red rose is withered
And the life's all gone
The world seems a dreary place.
But the sun will glow and a bud will grow
For the birth of a new red rose.

—*Garrick A. Reed*

Evil

She portrays me as a monster
An evil, cruel, being, a misfit of nature.
They say I have a warped mind
And that I'm a little mad.
I am the beast who stalks her in the night
And frightens her during the day.
I am the devil himself.
She claims that I am the savage who raped
Her of her thoughts and feelings.
I am the school boy who broke her heart.
I am the evil that exists in the child's vision of darkness.
I am the savage that stripped her of emotions.
I am a heartless monster; with ways set in evil.
She sends her henchmen
To beat the last remaining life from my bones.
The brain-washed henchmen are hell-bent by greed and lust.
Alas I am not evil.
I was the essence of her life.
Now I am the center of conflict,
And to her evil itself.

—*Matthew Crim*

Untitled

Through aeons of time whirl myriads of worlds
Stars shine in universal glory
God's galaxies swing in their celestial dance
The heavens echo to their distant music
Peace shall prevail, man learns his maker's story
..... and the stars sing.

—*R. W. Cooper*

Darkness of Night

When the sky is painted in blue,
and the sun is in its brightest hue
as the warm rays fall down on all,
you may wonder why darkness must fall.
The cause of a child's fear to turn out the light,
and the reason lovers sleep holding together tight,
be it for love,
be it for fright,
always will fall,
The Darkness Of Night.

—*Stephanie Duncan*

Untitled

It's winter now, the trees are bare
And there is much snow everywhere.
The Christmas tree is all set up
The logs in the fireplace are burning up.
We're stringing popcorn on a string,
Wondering what Santa may bring.
There are many gifts under the tree
That we are eyeing temptingly.
I hope mine is the one with the big red bow —
It stands out from the rest
Just taking the show.
I want to peek, but I can't, I know;
So I'll just string my popcorn and enjoy the snow.

—*Ruth Blonsky*

A Mother's Passage

Setting sun,
And time has come, for the journey into that great night,
A weather'd ship, through a foggy mist,
Slipped past horizon's sight,

Fully loaded, packed with countless memories,
Many years of love, and dreams, and giving,
Yet those on shore, still want for more,
And mourn this mother's passing,

Where's the solace from this pain? Can we stop the world from
turning? Once souls embark, none left to give,
'Cept meek few words of blessing,

Let the voice of waters tell her, as they lap against her
bow, the lives you've kissed with tender heart,
are crying for you now,

Let her stay with you forever, Lord, in the harbor of your
heart, as she's kept so many others, from the storms of life
a-raging, but for her'd be torn apart,

Oh, father! dearest father, righteous master, precious
light, embrace your new-born daughter, please take her close
and hold her, in your loving arms tonight.

—*Carl Swearson*

"Time"

There's a time in everyone's life,
That things are going right.
Then all of a sudden things change around,
Your loved ones are placed in the ground,
Knowing what life is all about,
Certain things you just doubt,
How do they know when?
Why is it now, rather than then?

—*J. A. K.*

The Wheel of Time...

Fast turns the wheel of time
and today is tomorrow yesterday
after summer comes fall then winter and again spring
Living and dying...is everything.

Today you are young and beautiful tomorrow you are old and pitiful
so live your life while you still can today
before the wheel of time turns it from you away.

...before death comes and knocks on your door
I am the one you have not been waiting for
but before we must leave...I have four questions, I will be brief

'Did you learn how short your life on earth can be?
Did you share your wealth with those in need?
Did you reach out and care for others?
Did you see in a stranger always your brother?

For you will be judged on all these counts today
the wheel of time has turned your life from you away
and now follow me... if you have lived a good and honest life
than your reward shall be...peace and happiness for all
eternity...

—*Maria Heiser*

Isadora's Scarf

Even when they killed your children
and turned lovers against you,
you stretched your long arms skyward between the Doric
columns
and dared the gods to stop you from dancing.
Wrapped in sheer silk tunics,
your big, imperfect body bound only by Chopin's mazurkas
and the rhythm of your breath,
You were my goddess, Isadora.

In death, the long scarf around your neck in the uncovered

Buggatti
betrayed something foolish, alas human, about you.
You cannot ignore the machines in life, Isadora.
The wheels will kill you.
And they did.

Now I, who feared your fate,
have quit the sloppy, soulless dance.
The choreographer,
alive with moving words,
returned to me.
Throw on that gorgeous, flowing scarf and go, I say.
Just tuck it in for the ride.

—*Lisa Pearl Rosenbaum*

Seascape

Stand upon the rocky shore
And watch the waves with mighty roar
Crash and send the water spume
Then swirling down as through a flume.

The sun has risen over head
And sparkles bright on water shed
Into the air as mists arise
Like glistening diamonds ere it dies.

The sea rolls on to touch the sky
The distance dims the reason why.
As waves roll on to hazy view,
The far horizon blends the two.

While sea gulls glide and dance with grace
They've found a wind that leaves no trace
Upon the sky the wings it holds
Of gulls that soar within it's folds.

—*Dale Williams*

Down by the Ocean

Let's take a walk down by the ocean, you and I
And watch the world pass us by. Let's forget
our cares and worries, and indulge in now.
Let the day take us away, so far that we
can never return. Be swallowed up in
happiness and love. Let's remember the days
of childhood, because children have no priorities.
They live each day one by one and just wish
for the next day to come.
Down by the ocean, the water dwells upon
your thoughts. It makes you feel relaxed
and free. That's how I want us to feel
down by the ocean, totally lost in each other
till the ocean just swallows us up.

—*Lori M. Watts*

We, The People

We are the villainous majority
and we seem sometimes servile, sometimes free.
Once in a while, we cheerfully agree.
We respect the people's integrity.
We try to strive for popularity.
Our rival's viewpoints sometimes score a hit
and that's the long, and that's the short of it.

Conditions will not always stay the same,
We do not choose to play a "no win" game.
It is not true because we said it once,
We said it once, because we thought 'twas true.
We shall pretend to be both bold and true
in everything we say, and plan to do,
and "scientific," so, perhaps should you.

—*David Boyd*

Too Young to Die

A friend has died, he went away, to a land in time so far away.
And when I heard the news that day, all I could think was what
dismay. He lived a life that was so short, which ended the day
he left port. Out on the seas that were so rough, he and his
father had thought they were tough. The life that he lived was
filled with some fun, but now God has told him it's his turn to
come. He was a friend and that's no lie, I just don't think it
was his turn to die. And when he knocks on heaven's door, and
fierce waves crash upon the shore, I know that I will miss him
more. In regards to what the coast guard has said, there is no
way I can presume that he's dead. As the rain came down that
night I know he must have thought of fright, and when they went
down on the awful night, he must have felt fear as the boat
left his sight. The search was ended, I almost choked only
because they had felt it a joke. He lost his life, and that
was a shame, because he was known as a fisherman and not by a
name. —*Tracy Weckesser*

The Forgotten Dead

Respectable images flash through my mind;
A future so unforgiving, lovely, and unkind;
Days of the world searching with ease;
Vibrate my soul, flow easily through, like a breeze;
Generations of me yet to come;
My visions where do they come from;
Treacherous past, a forgotten evil, a mystery to me;
Help my mind, but regrettably not my eyes to see;
Tell tale soul lingers on her bed;
As the voices whisper of the forgotten dead.

—*Kelly Parks*

"Trust the Blood"

Nightfall.
The lonely seek the solace of the dim light.
Seek the smoky hidden village of the hot love.
Through the door of smiles that exits
on the 'morrow.
Thick and scarlet
rivers in the spotlights.

—*Richard Arthur*

Mother

Mother there is no one like you,
And you are so beautiful too
Mother I love you and you love me,
You are prettier than I'll ever be.
Mother it is you who I adore
And that just makes me love you more.
Mother you are so nice,
And much sweeter than sugar and spice.
I would give my life for you,
And I know you would give your life for me too.
Mother you are sweeter than a rose,
And how well your sweetness shows.
Mother you and I have a special bond,
And of you I am very fond.
Even though some times we disagree,
You are always very special to me.
This to say I love you,
What this poem says is very true.
I love you and always will
I'll love you forever so there never is a till.

—*Kristy Walters*

A Soldier Speaks — World War II

So you're sick of the way the country's run,
And you're sick of the way the rationing's done,
And you're sick of standing around in a line
You're sick you say, well that's just fine

So am I sick from the sun and the heat
And I'm sick of my sore and aching feet.
I'm sick of this war and the jungle flies
And sick from the stench when the night mists rise.

I'm sick of the sirens wailing shriek
And sick from seeing the wounded and weak
I'm sick of the sound of the bombers dive
And sick of seeing how few survive.

I'm sick of blood and death and its' smell
I'm even sick of myself as well
But I'm sicker still of this far away land,
It's people and it's rule, I can't understand

But I'm cured darn quick when I dream of the day
When all of this mess will be out of the way
And none of this hell will have been in vain
And the lights of the world will go on again

—*Margaret Fredrickson*

Words Hurt Too!

Oh! Yes, yes, they do!
Anger, anger, when they come out
Not realizing someone may pout
Hurt, hurt, from deep inside
Ripping the heart, hurting the pride
Stop! Think! Before you speak
The words you say, may hurt the meek
Nice, kind, gentle words should be spoken
Not harsh nor mean even as a joke
Encourage the good and not the bad
Remember the harsh words can make someone sad!

—*Vickie H. Ross*

Jaime Has

A beautiful smile
Warm as the sun
Eyes so full of life
This day has just began!
—*Randall R. Evitts*

Free The Animals

Captives, are they?
Angered, are we?
Aren't "we" captives too?
Or is it too hard for us to recognize because it is
too close?
Cement walls.
Bars on the windows.
Locks on the doors.
Alarmed cars.
Security guards.
Neighborhood patrols.
An abundance of guns and various other weapons.
Oh, and let us not forget drugs, and all the
other addictive substances.
Is there a need for me to say anymore or
is the message becoming clearer...
Why not wage a worthwhile war on ourselves for
freedom from ourselves?
Alas, the victors will be — ourselves, yes,
    you and me.
—*Maureen Becker*

Another Life Gone

A lonely cry echoes through the darkness —
Another life gone.

A family struggles to stay together —
Another life gone.

Hopes, dreams and aspirations lay shattered around us —
Another life gone.

Cries of grief are heard echoing in a mother's heart —
Another life gone.

A plea to stop the violence is made —
Another life gone.

Tomorrow you could be just —
Another life gone.
—*Virginia Lynn Sherman*

Inside the Horn

Another class in another time
Another people drinking another wine
blood torn down the streets

Confucian, confusion moral lost
An automatic alternative our sons cost
natives barefoot in sand streets

Inside the horn
golden glaze of heat

Inside the horn
marching to the beat

Inside the horn
their fates they will meet

From the house of Hades a small man rakes in the souls
of men, women and children who sacrificed their hearts and
conscience on the bloody streets of Mogudishu where upon they
glorified their human trophies and demonstrated the human
desire for destruction and inevitable devolution.

—*David J. DePippo*

The Balloons

Another year and they are back in sight,
Another year much to our joy and delight,
The balloons, the balloons high in the sky,
They remind us of many a year gone by.

As I looked in the air and saw them floating up high,
I remembered small children with a gleam in their eye,
Pointing and shouting and yelling with glee,
Oh look at the balloons, aren't they beautiful to see.

We'd fill up the street in our nightshirts and gowns,
Looking and watching up over our town,
And try to count them as they floated afar,
Oh the balloons, the balloons like beautiful stars.

But the street was lonely this early dawn,
For all of the children had moved and were gone,
But the memory of watching the balloons was there,
Oh the beautiful balloons, up high in the air!
—*Jane Pastrell*

False Legacy

Many days spent in fantasy
Anxiously awaiting thy destiny
Eager to participate in life's "true love" legacy
False impressions painted by society

Attempted pursuits to passively persuade
May leave you feeling angry and dismayed
As frustration and loneliness abound
Keep in mind another resolution found

Only one other than he above
Can extend thyself unconditional love
Therefore, look for acceptance from within
For that is where "true love" begins
—*Linda Breakey-Baldasan*

A Note to Myself

I can't take this insanity,
Any longer and I'll go crazy.
Things in this world are gettin' me down,
I can't even stand to look around.

Why is this world so evil an' cruel,
Why don't we find something better to do?
Some people just fight to be free,
But we exploit it on National T.V.

Some people fight to gain control,
Others could care less about this hole.
Some people pollute, contaminate and destroy
They just want money, they care nothing of joy.

There is one way we can fix it my friends,
We could destroy it all and start over again.
You ask How practical is that to our lives?
I ask what kind of lives are we living?

What kind of people are we
When we think money is key?
Have we become ever so shallow,
To the point we believe 'love' has no value?
—*Albert Stroh*

The Ocean

The ocean takes me away to a place
where I can't be found.
It lifts me up when I am down.
I love the way it makes me feel.
I can't believe something
this wonderful could be real.
—*Amy Haben*

Suicide

So you don't think that your family and friends love you
anymore. You don't think that we'll miss you when you're gone.
So we all fight a little bit, but suicide is wrong. You may
shed some tears in your life time, but then again don't we all.
At first you feel so big, but then again you're really very
small. If you feel like you're going to feel better by
sticking a gun to your head, well think again, dealing with it
that way, you will never win.

If you think that jumping out of a window is going to ease your
pain, what if you don't die the pain will remain. We'll always
love you no matter how far you go. If you're up in heaven or
if you're just down the road, please don't kill yourself, we
need you down here. Suicide is not the right answer, just wait
another year. If things aren't different, we'll change here
and there. We're willing to make sacrifices, so that you see
that you see that we're all here.

—*Alisha Cogswell*

Gifts

What should you give a child
Anything that enjoyment brings?
It's not really that simple or wise
Better a person give his child - Roots and Wings.

Roots are so many things
From both parents - deepest love and strict training,
Nourishing food, good home and security.
With all this, for the future, the child is gaining.

Then the child, even though he thinks he's learned it all,
The parents have to give one more gift of Wings.
What the child has learned in knowledge
As he returns home, we judge, results of training he brings.

There's no way you can imagine
How important your gift to them, it is the key.
The cost is not to be judged or measured
Just the result of Roots and Wings and what they'll be.

—*Wilda Hoefer*

Song of the Beltane

Agile dancers, drawing magic from the night.
Arching branches shatter the sky.
Fleeting forms outlined in the fire's light.

Their movements graceful, eluding sight.
A touch exchanged, at once both open and sly.
Playful dancers, drawing magic from the night.

Erratic yet natural, like moths in flight,
Just beyond the reach of lashing flame they fly.
Lithe forms outlined in the fire's light.

Blood pounds, breath quickens, the dance reaches its height.
From within the very soul rises a primal cry.
Impassioned dancers, drawing magic from the night.

Bodies embrace, muscles quiver, they hold each other tight.
In celebration of life, together they lie,
Lover's forms outlined in the fire's light.

Nocturnal magic wanes, with the waxing of morning's might,
Welcomed only by sleeping smile and contented sigh.
Agile dancers, drawing magic from the night.
Fleeting forms outlined in the fire's light.

—*Michael C. Mannebach*

In Memory of My Husband

Precious memories of you dear
are always lingering near
September the twenty-first is your birthday
which brings many a tear,

Know one knows how much I miss him
Things have never been the same,
In my heart your memory lingers
I can't help but call your name.

Your life was so unselfish
and for others you did live,
not for what you would receive
But only for what you could give.

The wonderful things you did for us
live in our hearts each day,
and keep you near and dear to us
though you have passed away.

Wonderful memories that can't be sold
This is the treasure I will always hold,
I feel you are near me in our home
I know I'm never ever walking alone.

—*Alma P. Williams*

In Love?

New relationships,
Are like painting a statute,
All one can do is highlight what exists on the surface
To see things through rose-colored glass to view only-
Twinkling stars!

Seasoned acquaintances,
Are like a deep, pure, canadian lake,
When the waves calm down,
As smooth as glass

One can see clearly
An aching heart
Throbbing
On the bottom

—*Michael Gooden*

Help Someone!

In this life one thing I have learned. Most people for others
are not concerned. The poor and downtrodden, many many do not
see. How can we so very selfish be.

If each person who could, would help just one, Making that one
less miserable, by preparing to face a brighter sun. On this
world there will always be folks who are poor. That doesn't
mean, they shouldn't be able to partake of the world great
store. All need dignity at least, not to have to sleep out in
the street. A sheltering roof, for a private thought, can make
a broken life so complete.

No one should have to face the stormy elements just to rest.
Where is our humanity, we all have failed that test. Remember
each homeless person, is a son or daughter of someone. Can't
you try to find out what tragedy, made that life become undone.
A helping hand might be all they need. So they can start on
the road to succeed. The tears are all gone, to be able to eat
a meal at last. How many of you know what it is to forcibly
fast. Reach out now! Show some concern, this is something we
all must learn, Remembering always there is a chance you can be
next to feel the spurn.

—*Greta Cummings*

"Impressions On the Trail of Love

Impressions on the trail of love,
are started from our birth;
Footprints upon a record chart,
The day some touch this earth.
There's so many types of impressions, love,
by the way we move thru life;
In youth we crawl and sometimes fall,
The start of struggle and strife.
I remember your impressions, love,
the day you walked in view;
we strolled in hand and life was grand,
our impressions then were two.
we parted on the trail of love,
in faith I've walked along;
If you're ever lonely, look for me,
thru impressions, poems, and songs.

—*Janice B. Cassidy*

The Last Days of Freedom

The last days of freedom,
Are when the fall and the old school days come.
Sometimes with this change comes love,
But it can be hard to find like an ocean cove.

When the first days of freedom come in the summer.
I do not want to slumber,
But instead I want to find love.
For I never do see it on the wings of a dove.
Then time repeats it's self,
Over and over again on the year's book shelf.

—*Emma Lee Withrow*

My Dear, My Love, My Darling One

My dear, my love, my darling one,
Are you looking at the same star as me,
Though we are far apart?
When you hear the songs we heard together,
Does it give your heart a start?

My dear, my love, my darling one,
Do you ever think of me?
Of the times we laughed, the love we shared,
Our hearts so full of glee.

Have the years been kind?
Are you happy?
Have you found another love?

My dear, my love, my darling one,
There'll always be a special place for you
In a corner of my heart.
No one else can fill that space,
You've been there from the start.

On nights like this when the sky is dark
And very full of stars,
I think of you, my dear, my love, oh my darling one.

—*Joyce Kroker*

"Nature's Wonders"

Light is like a storming wave from a restless ocean. It suddenly appears, snapping forth out of nothing, and lashes forward, eventually crashing down and clothing its shore.
Heat is like the residue from the wave of light. It drifts along, then rests and builds up on the shore until the wave pulls back, bringing the residue of heat with it.
Light bathes its shore while the shore sips up the heat. They will drown you and carry you away.

—*Jenelle Rubio*

The Abused Child

Giant waves sweep and swirl
Around his slender young body
Forming foamy crystal pyramids that crash
Against the rocks.
Lonely cliffs, like walls stretch far out to sea.
Too high, too distant
To embrace.
Through darkness, a mirage of outstretched arms
That quickly fades like sunsets long after dusk.
An aura of light, suspending, falters,
Then catapults to earth.
Silence.
No echo.
A cry long muffled by choking sounds,
"It's too late to reach me!"

—*Marjorie Hughes Vail*

Dead Mother

I'm getting married in seven months.
Arrangements have been made for a grand party.
I've stared at myself in gowns of satin, organza, lace, and
silk, but nothing feels natural.
How was it for you, Mommy? Did it feel natural?

Did you feel like you were giving up your identity?
Trading it in for a sentimental notion?
We spoke about my marriage from the time I was seven.
You suggested a lunch at The Plaza
You said, "The right dress will hit us over the head!"

I bang my eyes shut to see your shadow.
Can't you even give an opinion?
I've tried on 22 gowns.
Mommy, what is marriage?
What is beneath the china pattern, the linens, and the
Wedgwood
pieces?

Is it not being alone?
Is it having someone to crawl up into a ball with?
Is it making babies? Is it peace?
I hope it's peace, Mother.

—*Jamie Kyle*

Sanctuary

As always, you welcome me with open arms.
As close as I come to death,
 your vastness of heart invigorates me.
Your up, your down, and your naked optimism,
 it always sheds life on my infidelity of spirit.
Judge me, you do not.
See me, free me, be me.
The light is leaving us now, and the red glare
 of transition dominates my sight.
With each passing moment the warmness of your
 touch turns cold as the shadows.
Goodbye,
 but thank you for your time.

—*Mark Young*

Sadness

Sadness is as blue as the sky
Sadness sounds like a whimpering cry
Sadness tastes like a swollen tear
Sadness smells like a rainy day
Sadness looks like an empty room of
 big surroundings
Sadness makes me feel lonely

—*Meg Thornton*

Leaving

Mirrored reflections come into view
As I gaze beyond and think of you.
Clouds moving swiftly, too fast for my thoughts
As I sit and I ponder on foolish forgots.

The leaves and the fruit have all left the trees
And I dwell on the time you'll have to leave me.
Shall I try and hold you as we hold on to spring
And clutch you near, my everything?

My love goes out, my all and all, my tears are as the raindrops
fall. I see more clearly through the haze And take this coming
day by day.

The sun comes through and I can see the leaves and flowers on
the trees. The ground bursts forth with new green grass. I
realize that this must pass.

I'll always hold you in my heart, and in my mind we'll never
part, and so I'll send away my love, with blessings that you'll
tower above,

But with a prayer upon my lips, if I have left you with one
gift; let it be as you ascend, never be too tall to reach back
down and feel the earth again.

—*Monica L. Gribble*

God's Special Gift

(A Voice said, Awake!)
As I was driving one morning I saw a beautiful sight,
The sunrise came up with orange delight,
As if to say you'll be all right,
Just enjoy this day and prepare for the night.
I have another special gift for you at dawn in evening light.
Sure enough here was another magic sketch
That came from the west,
A beautiful sunset bright.
His special hand lay upon my arm, to say to me, hold on tight
For I have another precious sight.
Darkness came, but up a bright light glowed in the night
as round and pure as it could be, all the lights in Heaven
sparkled like diamonds in the night.
Then as I was about to say goodnight,
I heard a voice say, sleep well tonight.

—*Kenny Jacobs*

"A Starry Night"

At night I sit and watch the stars,
As it twinkles and twinkles far so far

Dreaming of planets so distant and unique
As I gaze in my telescope
My what a treat.

Through thick moving clouds
so silent they creep
the wind pushes on
while few people sleep

The moon comes alive
With bright shinning light
that sits all alone, in the leaves at night

As fast as speeding light traveling through space
Isn't it amazing to see shooting stars race

Alone again do I sit and I wait
For wandering space craft
It makes me feel great.

—*Joann Quero*

The Old Poet's Pen

The old poet's pen poised in thought,
As it walked his inroads to contemplate,
The depths of his soul,
His hand quivered above the pen.

A lost love raced thru his mind,
I remember, he wept, I find you not,
Then came sweet thoughts for his pen,
Like flowers, blossom in the spring,

A stolen kiss, lips sweet like rich red wine,
I search for you, where is the voice I hear?
I feel your sweet breath upon my neck,
Your lips touch mine once again.

A blushing bride, skips thru my mind,
I hear the footsteps of our child,
Watch his eyes, dance with glee,
Oh! but that was long ago.

The old poet's pen slipped from his hand,
His mind wondered into never, never land,
His MASTER, picked up the old poet's pen,
Cradle him in HIS arms, to sleep upstairs.

—*Max King*

Remodel Me

Dear Lord Jesus please make me be
As much as possible
Just like thee.
Take away the anger, worry and the grief,
Give me your wisdom, peace and relief
Help me use my life to serve you
and others, who are in such desperate need.
To plant in minds, hearts and souls
Your Holy plan of salvation
That you may grow this seed,
Until we conquer evil,
This is what I plead.

—*Vi Dykins*

Washington Booker T.

Once I met a girl, melodious prelude her voice being,
as of a Goddess-muse agreeable resemblance.
Persona intellectual sagacious indeed,
ethos in character always sweet.
Generous, innocent soul, inner infinite politeness,
the behavior prime superb, aristocratic manners,
elegant, chic, magnific, fragrance nerium oleander,
in school nick named Oreo-cookie.
One day Oreo-cookie said:
Would you desire to visit, to admire something of higher discipline?
I mean the Elem-school
near my childhood years neighborhood, Let's go...
Hey!! Chance unique to focus, my love by that historic site,
Doric in style, it's architecture all around,
An edifice majestic, the dedicated building, the rara-avis
Public school; to educator of the elite who lived a century ago,
to noble honoree, Washington Booker Taliafero Book T!
In there, my love was taught; how do the vowels like to dance
and how the ethic values play.
How does the knowledge make, in life a greater sense, and
how Asteroids far, eternally light up, ...Oh! Heavens.

—*Dean Apollo Carayans*

Great Meadows

The candle went out last night.

We all stood around her bed
As she lay there dying.
Occasionally we understood the things she said.

Slight hints of consciousness
Kept hope alive in us all,
As we appealed to God's righteousness.

She struggles for a second
And opens her eyes.
To my Dad she beckons (I love you).

The candle went out last night.

Monday morning. Great Meadows.
Everyone standing around the grave,
While the rising sun casts out shadows.

—*Drew R. Cerria*

My Friend and I

My friend and I share a cup of coffee and watch the sunrise.
As the day unfolds I do something foolish and laugh at
myself and he is there to share it with me.

As I drive the car he is my co-pilot and navigator, in the
canoe he sits in the bow so I can see over it, as I
cycle along the roads I wish he would pedal a little
harder going up the hills.

When I am angry and hurt he listens, then calmly helps me
to look at the issue. My friend doesn't give up on me even
though at times I may give up on myself.

When the sun has gone to bed, the house is not lonely, for it
is occupied by my friend and I, and his name is God.

—*Josie Kruttlin*

A River Runs Through My Soul

The sunglasses hid my tear filled eyes
As the dust blew over the field of daisies
And the sound of the bells filled the blue sky
They lowered his body into the bug infested ground
Where he now danced with the skeletons in darkness
My bed was my sanctuary that night
I lit a pumpkin to show my love for him
And the flame burned bright, which showed he felt my love
I cried myself to sleep watching the cosmic stars
And was awoken by Bob singing a sweet sound
A song representing the dead
Since I was awake I went to the field of the dead
I laid next to the grave of the one I loved
And I noticed a patch of mushrooms next to my hand
Instinctively; as though someone told me to, I picked one of
    the mushrooms and placed it into my mouth
Soon I started to see a psychedelic fire engulf me
The flames wouldn't leave me alone
I couldn't wake up from this nightmare of death
A scream filled the blackness and I joined my love

—*Shannon Rule*

Holidays

I love the thought of a holiday coming around. These are
special times when we see most of our family and friends, there
is very tasty food to be eaten, and the fun never seems to end.
My mother lets me eat like a pig, and everyone laughs because
my stomach looks so big! But my most favorite holiday is
Christmas, because I get lots of fun toys, and I also love
Mother's Day, because I love to see my mother's face filled with joy!

—*Omar J. Fuller*

October Morn — A Lake's Quiet World

Stopping by the lake in the misty morn
as the fog dances about the waters,
soft remains of last night's storm,
nature is granted calmness; it is at peace.
The waters capture the images of the forest pines
that drift along, pictures in the water's sleep.
The world below the waters is silent;
the air is cool and still.
The frost that betrays winter's onset,
glides along at the side of
the October orange-painted hills.
Then the world of the lake lies
under the sun's golden eye,
silent, save only for the cries of crows along its shores,
and the churns that give the waves their rippled form,
set in motion by boaters' wooden oars.
And in the air, the cool winds creak
as the rest of nature's servants
awake from sleep.

—*Neal Feld*

Mother's Love

When I was a child, it was always our way;
If not before, at the end of the day
It was something I did, I don't know why -
A hug and kiss Goodnight, Hello, and Goodbye.

Time swept forward, often too slow;
I came to realize, not merely just know;
They were not just things you said or did
For me at night when it was time for bed.

You have touched my heart, felt my pain;
Made me feel important when others made it rain;
You've held me up when I could not stand;
You're always there with an unconditional loving hand.

Now I am a mother, understanding why
I would always get a hug and kiss Goodnight, Hello, and Goodbye.
Often at night I will think of you,
Wishing I was again that child you gave a hug and kiss to.

The importance to me, the grace of your touch;
I can never begin to explain how deep or how much.
I look at my children hoping I can be
Even half of the mother that you are to me!

—*Cynthia Stewart*

"I Am A Poem"

Wind strikes my face and it cools me,
as the heating blaze strikes upon the earth from the sum.

My thoughts drift away to a dream like world where everything
is like a poem. Everything rhymes and connects with other things.
And when I awoke, I realized...
I am a poem and my author is God.

Each year that passes, each month, day, hour, minute, and
second is a phrase, a line, a word a letter being written by God.
To me I am a poem and God is the author,
Of me and all that exist under him.

—*Brenda G. Morales*

Great Grandma's Music Box

Ratchety clicks from the music box
as the key is winding the works
herald a hurdy-gurdy of song
cascading in bright metered jerks.

Its ageless refrains have lullabied
many wee persons toward sleep
tinkling trills and chords through tiny ears
for minds to drowsily steep.

Later, as notes fade to quiet, and slow,
enticing small eyelids to close,
the last muted plink is soloed and heard
as a dream from the child's deep doze.

The melodies of the music box
have filled bedtimes with hours of delight
recollected each time the box serenades
new toddlers tucked in for the night.
   —*Patsy Stockdale*

Irish Memorial

The land of birth once more I see
As the plane finishes crossing the sea.
Back again, I was, I know
And my spirits were not low.
The fields so green from so much rain.
Yet the crops badly needing sunshine again.
The tourists' and immigrants' gratification
Can lead to the old farmer's vexation.
The memories hidden in my brain
Were dancing in my mind again.
Once more I saw the places
The scenes and friendly faces.
I saw the church, and Rahara School
where discipline and learning was the rule.
I heard people talk with accents common
Just like mine in my own Roscommon.
Again I've left but I shall find,
Memories, like snapshots in my mind.
   —*Tony Fallon*

Memories of My Dog Frosty

I laid her to rest, neath the old holly three
   As the stillness of night filled the air
   And I'll confess, I was deeply distressed
   For a piece of my heart still lies there

Only God could have sent such a sweet loving friend
   For her eyes told how much she loved me
   And as I grow old I will love her ten fold
   As I treasure sweet fond memories

Not a sound could be heard, neath the bright moon above
   'Cept the steel blade that shifted the earth
As the teardrops they rolled down my cheeks in a flood
   For no more will she lie on my hearth

My heart filled with sorrow, as I said goodbye
   To my pal who was my sheer delight
As the Sharon Rose Tree seemed to whisper to me
   I'll watch over Frosty tonight

I'm sure that if heaven is all that they say
   That sorrows can't there enter in
Then I'll hope and pray, that when I pass away
   I will meet my sweet Frosty again
   —*Breffny O'Ruairc*

Secret of the Trees

The trees have painted themselves once again
As their protest against the coming winter.
They thrived in the ease of summer's warmth,
And fear the cold, colorless winter.
So they show off boldly now
In their bright, beautiful clothes
Confident that they'll win this year.
But it will be the same again
The trees shall whither to mere fragments
Of the life they once were.
I wonder what it is that keeps them going
Through the torturous winter eve's
As they return faithfully each spring.
If only the human race could discover their secret;
We might have the courage to face the blackest nights
With the certainty of the trees
In our most splendid clothes.
   —*Beth A. Anderson*

Surfing Up

She is the ocean for all they know.
As vast and as small as all that.
The world they are in for now....
Ears sealed, eyes clamped shut —
two senses deferred for growth.
Tiny canine swimmers with sleek heads,
gleamy otter bodies surging ever up
the swells of densely folded belly.
Each turgid nipple, the peak of its own lapping wave
spurting white life into avid mouths.
Kneading paws do the work of holding them in space
but instinct makes them turn toward rather than away —
surfing up the belly to mother.
   —*Lee M. Hendler*

Through the Valley

Down through the valley of the shadow of death
As we are traveling along life's way
Seeking to find the Lord Jesus, and His will
That He might guide us day by day.

Down through the valley of the shadow of death
Surrounded by people of this earth
We will follow the clear, pure river of life
And realize the purpose of our birth.

Down through the valley of the shadow of death
Looking for the rainbow in heaven
That marks the way to our eternal home above
In the presence of God and His Son.

Down through the valley of the shadow of death
With Jesus beside us all the way.
   —*Maurice J. Worley*

Words Unspoken

We are all gathered here, with tears in our eyes
At the news of your untimely demise
Today we laid you to rest
With sorrowful hearts, for a friend who was the best
Every time I see your picture, I want to cry
And I ask myself why
A friend that Heaven did send
Why did you leave your friends in the end
You left behind a child and a wife
Why did you take your own life
I thought we could speak very open
But now that you are gone, there are many words unspoken
   —*Frank L. Howes II*

October's Glory

What beautiful colors all around
As we gaze on the trees in their splendor abound
We'd like to capture the gorgeous view
And hold in our memory forever such hue.

Yet there's no artist on earth can paint
To get the effect God brushed, is so quaint
Which shows us no greater "being" exists
Only our Lord can make such as this.

Thank you dear Lord for sharing your beauty
It's so hard to grasp and contain so much, truly
But some day we'll see you in all your glory
Then this will seem nothing as told in your story.

Let us grasp much of the beauty we see
Tomorrow will bring cold winds, we'll all want to flee
Then the scene will be changing from warm brilliant colors
So let us praise our Lord for the memory of special hours.

—*Keitha Arnold*

Where I Come From, A Texas Tale

Where I come from, the evenings are inviting
   as you lie back and view the stars of the night sky.
Where I come from, the cool breeze comforts you
   on a warm September afternoon.
Where I come from, you can ponder the world's
   problems as the open spaces overwhelm you.
Where I come from, the cowboys used to roam
   through the tall grass of the wide range.
Where I come from, the rolling prairies are
   captured in the memory of many.
Where I come from, you can sit on your front porch,
   and watch the sun rise over the horizon.
Where I come from, you can make your path alongside
   the seashore as the water rolls across your feet.
Where I come from, is so unlike any other, that
   it is called the Lone Star State.
From its desert area, to the plains, to the coast, to
   it's vast forest's, I am proud to say that I am
   deep in the heart of the state of Texas...

      Where I Come From.

—*Brad Tyler*

Earthbound

Full of sound and shadow is the forest at night.
Aspen leaves whisper as a breeze puts them to flight.
A little stream laughs and sings its way down hill;
Music for the beauty of the magic night. The trill
Of a lamb crying for it's mother echoes through the night,
Then silence, except the music of the rill. Starlight
In all it's splendor and glory fills the lea where he lies.
Serenity, contentment fill his soul. All worldly care flies,
He is at peace, his heart full, but it is only part of his dream.
Then, the woman by his side looks into his face. The gleam
Of her smile more radiant than a mountain sunrise,
The stars are dimmed by the light in her sparkling eyes.
Her soft cheek against his stubbled one whispers she
Three magic words into his ear. How is he
His quaking, bursting heart to quell? 'Til
Their hearts beat as one and are still
He holds her close, then speaks soft as the blue
Velvet of the night, "My heart's desire is to have you
Mine, share magic nights and live and live and live.
Would paradise ever have this much to give?"
—*Carl Johnson*

Life Of Woman

When as a child, I played with toys.
At adolescence I saw the boys.
When I grew up I married my man
Had children, then life really began!
When school was finished they all scattered
To different places..... Oh, does it matter?
When I got old and my husband passed,
My children were gone, each lad & lass;
I turned and looked to see my way,
And I do not know unto this day,
What lies ahead, who can say?
—*Bertha J. Foster*

Morning Poem

When lights begin to trickle in through your bedroom window
at six-thirty a.m. each morning, you are still trying to fold
and tuck yourself up into your trousers, hide the wrinkled
shirt that didn't get ironed the night before because you kept
trying to find a better or stronger or different word from the
ones you've already used in previous poems about similar
nights. As you slide and roll through blue flannel sheets
you fall into a series of white images, everywhere you look,
there's white. And as you tilt and toss your head, your
eyelids slightly close, but not entirely, because before you
know what's happened, you're falling again. This time you're
moving faster than before and you see blueberries, you even
smell blueberries, but it's not really blueberries at all,
because you don't like blueberries, you prefer melons, really
ripe juicy melons, the kind that consume the whole of your
mouth and absorb all of your taste buds. You never actually
wrote about them, but you had to use your imagination, because
Sunday morning seeped through the drapes too soon and you
didn't even bother to look for a new word or sound or color
after the light dried the steam in your twin size bed.
—*Anisa Perez*

A Reflection of Doubt

Someday I may look back and laugh
At the things I want, but cannot have
Am I aiming too high?
Submerged in the mud of loneliness, onlyness,
Trying to emerge but slipping back deep
Past the good things I've had but could not keep
Am I reaching too hard?
Is time running ahead,
Or is time walking, gawking, stalking?
Taking pieces away with every tick of the clock
No time to be lax, no time to take stock
Is it all a crock?
Am I aiming too high?
Am I reaching too hard?
Am I thinking too much?
Am I thinking too much?
—*Paul Timothy Kriewall*

A Special Place

On a cold snowy winter morn.
Back deep into the woods.
There stood a little log cabin,
Like the ones you can find in a book.
The tall pine trees stood around it.
Protecting it from nature's ways.
As the little creek that flowed by it,
Would stay frozen over until May.
There's not many places left like this,
Where you can go and just get away.
But isn't nature wonderful,
When you finally find that Special Place....
—*C. S. Elliott*

Changes

Life styles change from good to bad.
Attitudes change from sad to glad.

Neighborhoods change, they increase or decrease.
There's sometimes corruption and sometimes peace.

Young people change as they began to grow.
Friends change to people you don't know.

Baby's change into children and they become grown,
they grow in size, and in mind, then have babies of their own.

The weather changes from cold to warm,
from hot and dry, and to winds and storms.

Couples become one, with marriage by the ring.
Seasons change to winter, and to summer, fall, and spring.

People who are unimportant, they become great.
People who love, change to people who hate.

Prices change, health change, and the world as it grows.
Times change, fashions change, fads come and they go.

But Jesus will not change, not now and he'll never.
He's the same yesterday, today, and forever.

—*Mark Elliott Russell*

Gardening

Stargazers search the infinite abyss,
Awash in thoughts brought on by their passions.

They seek the fruits of life,
Yet are often remiss to enter the garden.

True love, the fruit sought by all, must be cultivated
from the seed.
Not plucked randomly like an apple from a tree.

The cultivated seed of love which blossoms in all people will grow,
Ripe and full, reaching its ultimate potential.

Caring and trust are the sunshine and water of the seed.
Without for certain many shall pluck a weed.

—*Jeffrey J. Stockdill*

"Trying to Catch a Rabbit"

While I'm asleep at night I hear a scratching noise from my
back porch, I'm thinking if I closed the porch door. If it was
closed my "furry friends" wouldn't get loose...the next morning
I go to feed my "furballs" carrots and lettuce, I notice my
back porch door wasn't closed and neither was my rabbit's cage!
This hasn't happened before, a quick thought raced through my
trembling mind, thinking maybe patches jumped out and then
cuddles came hoping after...maybe..just maybe...?! I looked
out my porch window, I see my "patches" hoping around, but
where's "cuddles?!" Another terrible thought went through my
mind, maybe a "raccoon" bit "cuddles"...."whew there's she is!!!
"Cuddles was under the playhouse, "o" boy how will I ever get
her out? I went outside to try to catch "patches", maybe I
should get some "juicy carrots: for my furry friend so inside
I went, and out I went again. First I'll try to get "patches"
she's the easiest to get, I'll get "cuddles" last. Around the
yard I went, falling into mud puddles, bagging my head into
trees and bushes!!! "O" boy what a mess!! "Yes"! I've got
patches trapped "here patches, patches!: I said. Here's a
carrot, I picked her up and carried her to her cage.

—*Jennifer G. Buchanan*

"Never To Catch The Shore"

As seen, hearts of two move like a tide...
Back to forth, never to catch the shore...
Running the crest,
  like a shoreliner marks the tide...
Love runs along,
  as the shoreliner's prints are left on a heart.
With hand of sand,
  as it spreads away in the wind...
Love can wash away,
  till the claws of love are felt only....
The once hand held, the footprints close to yours,
  are gone to the sea of tears left....
Reclaimed by that same passion,
  that thought, that brought the grains
  of sand to glass....
Yes made of love, glass, shattered by time....
Pieces left, scattered emotions, conquered by the pain...
Back to forth, never to catch the shore...
Love held to shore, still, never to ever.

—*A. Mendoza, Jr.*

Sonny and Me

'Twas only yesterday we went to play
Barefoot and free, the first days of May!
I close my eyes and still can see
The green apples on the big tree
Quick as a squirrel we'd hurry to the top
To see who could sit in the safest spot.

Then we would run to the creek below
Where the clear cool waters flow!
Even though we were told never to go,
As the snakes were mean and the sand quick.

Back to the barn, no one in sight
Up to the top of the roof as in flight!
But as a door opened, a voice would say -
"Get down or you will not live to see another day!"

Then I opened my eyes to see -
The hearse waiting with Sonny for me!
To ride from the church to the grave,
As my steps are slower and my body growing old-
But it made my heart lighter to ride
Beside him to Eternity.

—*Ruth Medley*

Untitled

May all of our days together
Be like a sunrise,
A new day a new life.
Every hour I spend with you makes my day as
colourful as a rainbow —
And I know those colours will never fade.
We will always stay together,
so our lives are filled with color,
and the love that will continue to grow
will flower for the rest of our lives —

—*Mindy Millman Dicrosta*

Love Is Like Magic

Love is like magic as the whole world must know.
  It is like moonlight dancing on snow.
It is a wonderful sight as you see,
  As I saw it last night by ways of the beautiful
moonlight.

—*Brandie Woodward*

Insight

The mind sees good and evil in its sight
Be true to thyself and do what is right
It sees days long past by
A memory brings a tear to the eye!

The mind sees a kind and loving face
Thoughts rush in to fill the space
On you it will play a trick or two
Often making you think you are not you!

The mind can be treated well or with abuse
Everything is stored away for future use
A shadow of darkness it will cast
With fear of something from the past!

The mind knows not what will be tomorrow
The heart prays it will not be sorrow
With your mind let not your heart fight
Keep them as one in your plight!

The mind holds your deepest secrets unuttered
Care for it always and let it not be cluttered
Always keep it safe and keep it clean
The mind knows everything you have seen!

    —*Patricia Winik*

The Earth

Earth, divided by man in fine continents
Beautiful lands, productive or arid, but land!
Such beauty the Earth gives us
Its recreation for our eyes; our food the
Earth produces. Even the arid land of the desert
  is beautiful!
The mountainous, incalculable values enclosed,
Mountains of capricious forms and colors; no one
  is the same; so much love they give us!
Cascades that roll down; rivers that run through them!
Red earth, black earth, arid earth

Productive; so much you give us!
Trees that provide shade.
Without you, Earth, what could man do?
On you we grow; from you we feed;
And one day you generously receive us
Red earth, black earth, clay earth!

You give us much; we have to love you, defend you,
Take care of you. Lands of all continents,
Respect and love we owe you. Thank you Earth!

    —*Carmen Maria Ramirez*

Benjamin

Benjamin paces from corner to corner nervously,
because he's allowed to think.
Benjamin talks to Pennelope
a quaint girl only he can see,
because he's allowed to speak.
When Benjamin sleeps
the walls breathe, the trees sing,
and the earth is still as the heavens rotate around,
because he's allowed to dream.
Benjamin doesn't seem to care
when they point and laugh
at the torn clothes he wears
and how matted and tangled his hair is,
because half the time he's almost there.
Benjamin sits and weeps about his past
and sometimes he'll cry about tomorrow.
He's allowed to know he's weak.
Benjamin, the morning will bring a new day,
So come sit under the stars with me.

    —*Mandy Solomon*

Think America — Talk America

God gave me this day to live in this land - and
Because I was frightened, He then took my hand

He showed me the glories with which I am blest
And said "in this whole universe, this is the best"

He showed me great valleys and high mountain tops
Great rivers and streams, farms and huge city blocks

Then He said "this is the great melting pot, the only one of
its kind in which all of it's people, happiness can find"

But happiness must be earned and cherished - like gold and
shared with those less fortunate, for the true message to unfold

You have been chosen to go forth today
That for the generations to follow, you may pave the way.

You are the chosen, to make America great
If you ignore this challenge, then yourself you will hate

As "united we stand" or "divided we fall"
Welded together, we can knock down the wall

Of greed, hatred and jealousies, and replace them with
  camaraderies
And the finished product will then be, the greatest U.S. of A.
  for you and for me

    —*Milli Marks*

Untitled

She was a wisp of a woman — quiet, soft spoken — saddened
because she had lost her man — to death and she had one of her
breasts — to life. She sat across from me at the dinner
table. I could see the champagne take over. She became
talkative, jovial, and a bit provocative. She was out of
character but that gave her an aura of excitement. She spoke
to me — kidding on the square. "Why don't you ever call?"
she began "why don't you come over and see me sometime?" she
mimed. Her eyes beckoned. "How about now?" I questioned,
continuing the charade. Before she could reply I exchanged
places and sat at her side. She spoke again. "I'm a phony. I
have only one breast." Then she talked of how she could never
let a man get close enough to find out. But I've known from
the beginning" I said, then continued, "you are no less a whole
woman — beautiful — vital — needed." We drove home
together. We parked. Softly our lips met. She guided my
searching fingers to her solitary breast. As I cradled it in
my hand, she murmured sadly "I have only one breast." "And I,"
I replied, as I gently touched her breast with my lips, "I have
only one mouth." A tear fell on the nape of my neck.

    —*John S. Kruglick*

Friendship

  Friendship - How do you define it?

You, you would be my definition of friendship,
  because you are loyal and true.

You, you would be my definition of friendship,
  because you never let me fall and
  you care like no other ever could.

You, you would be my definition of friendship,
  because you are trusted wholeheartedly and
    you are loved with no fear.

You, you would be my definition of friendship,
  because you accept all of me,
  the good as well as the bad.

You, you would be my definition of friendship,
  because friendship to me - is you!

    —*Saralyn V. Smith*

Stay

Sometimes I feel like breaking down for the things that I've
   been through; and
other times I feel secure for the life that I share with you.
It seems as though we're falling apart the more we live each
   day; and
I wonder how it came to this for it all to slip away.
There's never been someone so near, so close as you are to me;
But I see a blur, a vision of hurt that somehow it's not meant to be.
I know that it's love when I look in your eyes, its been like
   that for years; but
Sometimes it seems I can't see that love for the drowningness
   of my tears.
I know that I could not go on, if somehow you drifted away;
My life is not whole without you, and never will be if you don't
   stay.

    —*Stacy Diane Davis*

Bigotry - The Illogical Hatred

Let us pause and stop to think
Before calling someone a wop or chink.
If our neighbor is known as Rebecca or Abel
Why must he receive a derogative label?
The folks from Poland would have to be numb
Not to notice when always referred to as dumb.
The arrivals from Korea or India - the Asian
Are they lesser human beings because they're not caucasian?

When we need an operation, is the surgeon's scalpel duller
When held in a hand which is of a different color?

Why must Juan be known as the spick?
For the very same reason that Patrick was a mick.

So let us all strive our pride to restore
For prejudice destroys more people than a war.

    —*Kae Pollitt — Rahway 1988*

Two Views Of The Sea

On the beach at dawn

In the East, a dim light
Begins, diluting the darkness.
The ocean changes from black to gray.
There is a hush, an expectation -
Then the dawn rises fresh-washed from the sea
Into the fiery air, over colors liquid and shining
This day's Genesis.

On the beach at night

There is not much to see -
A bit of moon
That shines on lines of foam
Surging towards me like flying ghosts
From the wild darkness,
As the sea's resonating heart
Beats on the shore,
And a vast tide, from half a world away
Crashes at my feet.
At my very feet.

    —*Maxine Margaret Neumann*

Rose Garden

An American Beauty is shining bright
Like a star in full view sight
It glows and shows off its splendor
Like a jewel we'll all remember.
No one reigns like this supreme,
No wonder we're a perfect dream.

    —*Peggy G. Hoffmann*

My Eyes

My eyes have always puzzled me -
believing they were gifts meant only to see beauty of crimson
sunsets and star-laden skies.
Never dreaming they were also given to sense loneliness and
feel the cries.
Kindred cries of past and present pains,
cries of solitude of somber clouds and marrow-chilling rains.
There are those times when my eyes fill with tears,
realizing that they reflect our hurts and our fears.

This unspoken comprehension I repressed so long, lost like a
dream or a childhood song.
Instead I wished like Oedipus that I too by God would be
blessed and without sight I would be impervious to my brother's
plight.

Yet I am blessed and still have my eyes,
I still feel the sorrow and still hear the cries.
I know now that this was meant to be,
that God had this always planned for me,
never, ever to lose touch with my humanity.
Thank you God for giving me, my eyes.

    —*Miwha Choe*

Untitled

Will there ever be peace
between blacks and whites and reds?
I once had a friend who was
black - and now that friend is dead
   I don't mean to sound harsh,
I don't mean to sound cruel.
But I would love to stop this never ending duel.
Will there ever be peace among
blacks and whites and reds?
   I once had a friend who
was black and now that friend is dead.

    —*Nichole Brewer*

Untitled

   In the canals of my mind. be the images from my past
between the joy and the pain are the fossils of the life, that
I once had, unable to retrieve my dreams, now shattered and
washed away. I press onward, trying hard to rebuild focusing
on life and the treasures of today. I will need a foundation
of hope and love, supported by determination and strength.
Continue to seek wisdom and knowledge from God. Daily forgive
and repent. Use my talents in positive ways. Offering help to
others whenever I can. Frequently remembering those lost but
loved. Further along shall I understand.

    —*Hessie Rodgers*

Yesterday, Today, Tomorrow?

In the early years
Black man walked in chains
White man walked with a whip
Over the years, many things have happened

But as in the early years
Our mentality remains the same
This door we keep closed between us
Remains locked

Today still, color can remain the soul judgement
of mankind
Even though, our blood runs red
And the dreams remain the same
Our souls are still not ready

To love the brother, red, black and brown
As if we are one in the same.

    —*Mike Hill*

Love Letter

You know me
born of my father (unbeknownst to my mother)
I've known the forbidden
I've loved what I hate.

Wise to man's ways
My mind has awakened, so I learn you, too.
It may take me awhile to unpuzzle your smile
but I will before rest.

I follow you in my dreams,
against my rationale
I cry when it returns to me.

So I don't feel guilty for the love that I've lied
Only vengeance remains of my fallen pride.

Take it anyway — then leave.
Don't pretend it to bend
Your insipid rubber-band values.

I know the words
to your insidious song.
I know you
You are Him.

        —Jessica Keller Nowicki

I'm Gonna Tell You Anyhow

    Women think their cute, men think their fine
    Both high off of something most of the time.
    Don't wanna hear it I'm gonna tell you anyhow.

    Children runnin' wild, hanging in the streets
    Can't find Mama, she is somewhere hanging in the sheets
Daddy who knows where, got another woman he is taking care
    Don't wanna hear it I'm gonna tell you anyhow

Everyone blaming the children for what they have come to be
Stead of grown folks owin' up they got their habits from we
    Don't wanna hear it I'm gonna tell you any how

Regardless of skin color, or religious preference maybe if
    the shoe fits, cleaning up is suitable can't we see
All this funnin' is killing we, shame, shame we should be.
Cleaning up can be done with the twinkling of an eye, praying
    to God, working on getting our morals high

    Mankind no future will our youth see, unless we get it
        together the way we know it should be.
    Don't wanna hear it I'm gonna tell you anyhow

        —Maryam E. Muhammad

Eternal Souls

There is but one life;
    and two eternal souls in search of each other.
A lost love from another life,
    your husband, lover or your wife.
You will know, when you meet, you will know at last.
That your love you have found from your past.
Hold onto that love, for dear life,
    For without that love, you will be
    lonely and blue, you will never be happy.
You will never love any other,
    as you would that love, that eternal love,
    that eternal soul.
Hold on to them for dear life.
    Make that person... your husband,
    lover or your wife.

        —Rebecca G. Scott

Poets

Poets always agonize
'bout things like rhyme and rhythm
Some say they're seldom very good
At math - like long division.

Just show them a bird
On a rusty old fence
It's a jet in the sky
And they wax eloquent.

Poets can make a cloudy day sunny
And wheedle a laugh at something not funny.
I know of one poet who swatted a fly
Then wrote of an eagle that fell from the sky.

They tap the subconscious
To embellish their dreams,
Then lay down to sleep
In their flying machines.

They breakfast on honey
And brown jumping beans
It's the diet of poets
That augment schemes.

        —Marcella R. Dougherty

"Hour Glass"

    Raging bugs from hell run through my
brain as if they were on line with
death, but in the visual world not one
of them I see.
    It's as if I'm speaking with different voices
through thousands of speakers all at one time, and
not one of them is heard.
    And the cycle of my mind keeps spinning in my
head, but it never seems to come out with an answer
    The time is running out.
Must I be so proper is my many ways or
will my inner self burst out and take control
over the clock?
    Even the coals are turning to ashes.
Not a second can be spared in my inferior
destiny because it already seems there is nothing
left, and soon there will be not even the
power of a dream that comes with us all.
I shall explode through an evil pathway and may never
return to a thought, the end is coming.

        —Jill Starcher

For Love Is Gone

Let me cry softly, so no one can hear the sound of a heart
breaking. For a breaking heart is the most lonely sound in
the world. It wails into the wind where the morning dove echoes
its refrain. And the wolves point there noses skyward and sing
along with its chorus. So let me cry softly...for love is gone.

Let the tears flow, flow from the depths of the endless well of
watering from which all tears come. And let the pain keep
silent, for to let it go would bring forth sound. A sound so
loud and wrenching that the whole of the earth would be
shattered by its screams. So do not give it voice, for the
world must not know of its depths. Just let me cry
softly...for love is gone.

Let my mind be still ... hush. For the whirlwind seeks to
gather you unto its bosom. And hold you close where rest is
never found. Only endless days and nights of soaring ups and
downs. Pain ... despair ... and weeping from which there is
no return. Quiet, mind ... rest ... do not think or remember.
Just let me cry softly ... for love is gone.
And I will hold you close.

        —Peggy Blue

Noon To Night

I sit across from the sea. I feel the cool
breeze hit against my round face. My thick, long, black
hair flows to the wind's rhythm. I sit and stare as I watch
the fiery orange ball climb down into the depths of the deep
blue sea. I close my eyes, I meditate and I imagine, I
imagine what it would be like if only the world were as
lenient as this. The ocean and the beach look so peaceful
and mild. The land has beauty, rare beauty unable to find
anywhere else.
   I open my eyes and gaze up at the dim sky. I
see the heavens. Oh how exquisite it looks. I see a round
ball just aloft my head. It has a pigment of ashy gray and
swirls of snow white. To the sides I see shiny, pointy
spurs of light bursting through the pigment of the black sky.
   I whisper to myself "wow!" and gracefully walk away.

   —Dorothy Landburg

Sitting Here

Sitting here on the steps of my SISTER GAIL's house I feel the cool
breeze soak up the perspiration that seeps from my body…it
feels so good…just SITTING HERE…not thinking…not worrying…
not caring…it's so quiet a change…the trees are waving at
me…the humidity has taken my hair and placed it in its natural
ness…listening to NEW BIRTH playing…softly in the background
of my SISTER GAIL's house…SITTING HERE…just sitting here.

Somebody from across the street said, "It's Ten O'clock," but
what do I care I have nothing to do/ no where to go I can SIT
Here and SIT HERE… relaxing my mind/body and soul…
Alleviate
all that's past all that's behind me…and think about all that's
ahead of me…Reminisce/Do I really want to?…No…Not really…
because reminiscing hurts sometimes…I'd like to walk across
the street and walk slowly through the grass… but I don't
really want to… I just want to SIT HERE and SIT HERE…I
guess because I know I can…but not for long…I'm going to
have to get up sometimes…and walk the path…of life again…
and soon climb the ladder of success…That's All.

   —Myra Jo Arvin

Flight of the Falcons

A dazzle of amber molten fall
brilliant rays of sunbeam kissed
to explode o'er moss beribboned wall
or swirl in gossamer mist

'Tis beneath the rainbowed curtain lie
the hawthorn, sage and heather
mirror lake glimpsing twin falcons flight
soaring as one together

Descending to light 'pon frosted bough
in unison do they croon
regal sentries of this hallowed ground
awaiting the rising moon

When launching forth to greet bright stars
through flakes soft as eiderdown
the falcons keep vigil from afar
reigning silence, peace abound

Within this pristine, primeval place
time seems to be holding nigh
the snows renew with glistening grace
while aloft the falcons cry

   —Lesa Tessensohn

In Jason's Memory

May the many children you have cared for over so many years,
bring comfort to you now and help to dry your tears.

Though the loss of little Jason is heavy on your hearts,
remember all the lives in which you have played an important part.

It is hard to understand why children can be gone in such a
hurry, but believing in God, we must remember they are free
from pain and worry.

Little Jason is now residing with our Heavenly Father above,
he no longer has any limitations and is surrounded by perfect love,

So many people are praying for you and wish they could bring
your pain to an end, but anyone who has ever suffered a loss,
know it takes time to feel like smiling again.

May the Lord stay close beside you and embrace you in his
loving care, helping to make your pain and heartache a little
easier to bear.

Bless you for all you have done for others each and every day,
may the love you have shown to so many, come back to you in
many ways.

   —Margie Snape

As It Was

Remember the old peasant of
Broadway and 19th—scraped red face, a croaking smile and
twisted hands a size or two too large?

Huge-bottomed, she was bulked in swathes of black.
Heaved it all down on a grocer's crate most often—
not far from the corner, in front of the old bank.

I saw her winter evenings on my walks
in sharpest cold, sometimes in snow,
selling puppies from a big brown basket—
litters gummy-eyed and squeaking—
and candy too: gum drops, licorice
a penny each, and oddly-shaped dark cookies
ginger-tasting, dusted with white sugar.

It seemed to me she was old beyond the telling
but she never changed. I was the one who aged.
One day she simply wasn't there any more.

Years later, I thought of her when spring came round
and days grew long again;
how at Easter time she used to sell white rabbits,
and water lilies in mid-June.

   —Ann White, R.P.T.

The House

The old house is now, in the utmost decay
Broken pipes let water, slowly seep away
Down yet more drains, filled with rust
Empty rooms with spoiled trappings, covered with dust
Will never see, the light of day
Will never hear, little children play
The timber creaks like old dry bones
The howling wind does utter such erie tones
Shutters flutter in mournful solitude
The door is stuck, not meaning to be rude
When it rains the roof does leak
Causing the wooden floors to creak
Mice do haunt it's rooms
No cat to spell their dooms
So sad this house in rotting solitude
With creepy things that think it food
Do not, I implore, become this house
And be prayed upon by things within

   —JEN

Forever....My Love

As I look into my mind's eye here we are,
but a memory. A faded photograph,
yellowed letters, haunting words, broken-hearted,
a tearless face reminds me of the sadness and the pain endured.
But for I what will tomorrow bring?
As I sit here alone, not even weeping.
Thinking not of you or of me but of us.
Even though my heart is breaking and my soul has done without,
I am numb. I'm too hurt to remember our parting,
but unable to forget yesterday.
All the love we shared.
Our future which held such promise tossed aside
like a discarded wrapper.

Which once was everything is now nothing.
As I shudder in this darkness I am helpless.
And deep in my heart is where you'll be forever,
yes forever....my love.

 —KC Grimes-Brown

"Blindness of the Mind"

The tears that shall fall for you are not for the loss of you,
But are for my eyes that are too blind to make it stop.
For one who is lost is never stolen,
But is free to choose to leave,
And is never told that they are needed.
They leave by a car called loneliness.
But who says that it must be?

As it seems, the answer lies within me,
And yet I cannot find it.
I've spent so much time asking the why,
I have lost faith in finding the how.
So here I remain backed against
A wall that I created.
Blindness of the mind is my enemy
Not of the heart.
Don't be fooled
The tears have already
 Begun to fall.

 —Phelicia Fischer

Give My Heart A Break Don't Break It!

Some one new, appeals to you
But darling will it last
Just be sure, it will endure
Since fancy soon is past.

Give my heart a break, don't break it
Leaving a mistake, don't make it
Some day you'll regret, the very day you let
A fairer face, my place, to take
So ask your heart, if we should part
And give my heart a break.

Darling haste, oft times means waste
Our future looked so grand
But if you, say we are through
I'll try to understand.

Give my heart a break don't break it
Leaving a mistake don't make it
Some day you'll regret, the very day you let
A fairer face, my place, to take
So ask your heart, if we should take
And give my heart a break.

 —Kenn Schofield

White Hope

White hope is taking over the world today.
It's destroying lives in every way.
White hope is known as crack cocaine.
The more you smoke, the less you will gain.
If you want to keep hope alive.
don't try white hope and
that's no joke!

 —Natalie Shepherd

Let

Let our bodies melt in the sun.
Let our worries be gone.
Let our bodies freeze in the rain.
Let our pain be hang.
Let our eyes meet in a stare.
Let our nose scent the smell of fresh air.
Let our lips touch in a kiss.
Let our ears hear the sound of wilderness.
Let our hair blow in the wind.
Let our voice speak with words over again.
Let our love be strong.
Let us know right from wrong.
Let our hands hold in a squeeze.
Let the stars above keep us company.

 —W. B. Taja Backus

In Memory of "Perky" 1985

She was so small, with a kind of funny face,
But every move she made was filled with grace.
She was my protector from all kind of harms;
Then she died, convulsing, in my arms.

"Don't cry, she was only a dog," they say.
She was so warm, so alive, so fond of play;
So full of love and trust - I was her world
And, she, around my heart was curled.

I hear her footsteps in the hall
I look - she isn't there at all.
I see her shadow by the door
(It's something dropped upon the floor)

Twelve years of love, she gave.
Now, she is quiet in her grave.
My eyes fill - friends turn away, with tact.
She is gone — I must accept that fact.

 —Katherine Worth-Everly

"Spiritual Cry"

Life... is not for the receiving of gifts;
 But for the giving of thanks for them.
  For joy has begun a new rising!
In thanks we will give prayer to those in need of help.

It is not the joy of receiving a new rising, but the
  glorification of giving prayer!
Those of you who practice the word of God;
  praise to the highest Realm.

For the Blue Skies; give us the light of hope.
The Green Pastures; give us peace at heart.
And the Great Mountains; show us the serenity of Gods will.

 —Ronald Jewett, Jr.

Afraid to Sleep at Night

I trusted and loved him, he felt the same.
But he twisted and mangled it - he put me to shame.

How could he do that? Especially to me.
I thought I was the world to him. How can this be?!

Disgraced I stand and no one has a clue.
My only thought is — what did he do?!!

You never think "that would happen to me".
But it did, I'm shocked and I'll never be free.

Free from the demoralized flashbacks and crude remarks.
I was put to hell and there's no turning back.

The discomfort and embarrassment is so unreal.
It has dented my heart and now I'll never feel.

In my own little box I will hide all the insanity.
I will keep it away from my friends and family.

Knowing I'm living with the horror and having to see that face,
He'll be there any second, every time, any place.

He isn't a nobody, or a stranger off the street.
He taught me how to grow and he kept me on my feet.

On the outside I'll be strong and put everything away.
But I hope it doesn't erupt and all come out one day.

—*Danielle Iaboni*

Gold And Lace

Not so profuse as goldenrod in Maine,
but here and there along the highway
in Andalusia, Spain,
goldenrod sways gently by eucalyptus groves
of imposing stance and grace,
and moves just the same in Maine
by maples interspersed
with breathtakingly beautiful birch.

In Maine in August I have seen
Queen Anne's lace green in leaf and stem
with exquisite snowflake patterned flowers
delicate and prim.
In August now in southern Spain,
fronting aging oaks along the highway,
Queen Anne's lace is sere and brown.
Dry, filigreed orbs of tarnished gold
move like censers in the gentle wind.

—*Barbara Patrick Brown*

The Divided Me

As a figure of a woman, I am considered rather small.
But how I divide myself makes me tall.
My husband has his part of me, my two children theirs.
Then comes family and friends, I still have some to spare.
For you see I am complex, but full of fun.
Tiny, little me but yet a mighty one.
My pets need a small part, the rest I keep for me.
I divide then again into many parts you see.
I am many different things to many different people.
For myself I have kept a part that will equal.
The sum of which, once again I divide into portions.
For loving, caring, sharing, and protecting with devotion.
I am a poet, an artist, and a crafter too.
I take my mighty pen to express my complex mood.
Brush and palette in hand, I paint things that fill my heart
like a poem. In my small hand a crochet needle finds a home.
As yarn turns magically into beauty and wonder.
I sketch the world, as I see and ponder.
Now that you know the division of me.
What and whom are the shareholders of thee.

—*Darlene Peltes*

Cry

I think I will cry,
but I do not know why.
It will feel good to release all this.
It will be sure bliss.
It may take more than one day
to make these tears not stay
in my eyes and on my face.
Maybe after this a smile will take place.
Maybe then I'll be filled with joy,
but probably not, for this ending is my mind's toy.
As soon as the crying is done.
More problem clouds come and cover the sun.
And more tears fall like rain
and leave a stain
on my wet soul.
My confusion seems to be on a roll,
but then I'll break down and pray
for God to let my happiness stay.

—*Amy Stanley*

In My Heart

I used to think your love would be enough
But I was wrong and seeing you is getting tough
I think of what could've been
And I cry myself asleep now and then
Thinking of a way so I don't have to go through this
But there isn't a way so it's you I have to miss
I can't help it it's just that I still care
Even though you don't it's there
I tell myself it doesn't matter anymore
And often you may see staring at the floor
I'm just thinking maybe there's a chance
But there isn't and I can't even look back not even a glance
'Cause I'm afraid I may still cry
Since in my heart I didn't want to say goodbye
But we did and I can't change that
Sometimes I wish I could but all my wishes fall flat
And one wish was that I could've told you what you meant to me
But I didn't and I have to live with that for eternity
Knowing you never knew
How much I loved you

—*M. Elizabeth Bates*

My Opinion

There's a lot I could write about,
but I'm going to write about names.
Like bitch, trick, or slut.
It's enough to make us all go nuts.

But there's one more name I'd like to write about
Dogs!!!
Not man's best K9 friend, not a four legged
animal that barks.

But the opposite sex. There's one
thing young or old women have to know.
That all men are dogs. Don't get me wrong
There's some good ones. Almost every woman
marries Mr. Right and do you know what the rest of the
population get? We get the trash, the has been
and the liers. Men are like the speed bump
on the road to happiness. Women need guys
cause they don't want to feel alone. But
I don't need him for that do you? That
is a question that we should ask ourselves.

—*TLC*

I Dreamed a Dream

I dreamed a dream of time
But it was not endless time.
It was a beginning a new beginning.
All of hope "what is to come."
As the clouds rolled back
There were a road that lead to safety.
Someone said come my child that's weary and rest.
The tables were all set with finest at its best.
There is milk and honey at it's very best.
You will dine with love ones that's
in the saviour's care.
It's a new beginning not an endless time.
  —*Corean Wright*

Who Lied to Whom

Life: I've lived and learned
But no matter how much I've learned, I'll never stop learning
And I've come to realize so much -
- That genius is nothing more than …
… Memory and logic - pure and simple
And that time, those times I thought I knew It all…
Proclaiming truth
Was only the beginning of truth - inner truth
Reality shattered that ego - light then shined thru
So who has the answers?
Each man's heart knows answers are …
… Individuals keys to themselves
And each different, open new-some the same, some confuse truth
Never ending tests of time thru time
Life tests us each and every day - trial and error
The master plan … well that's a scam …
Even I don't know everything that I hold within my own hand
But there they went
- They're gone
And here I am - Again -
  —*Julia Louise Johnson*

Trapped

It is windy, bright, and beautiful,
but nothing stirs.
The air is dense.
Fighting—Words—Anger
Who knows what will happen next?
No one.
I am sad. A word crosses my mind-
DIVORCE.
It has been here many times before.
It knows the way.
I try to push it out with tears,
but it just slides through the tears,
letting it enter my mind.
It is there and it might never again leave.
Nothing can help now.
  —*Talia Wright*

Saying Goodbye

Saying goodbye is something we never thought would be.
But time has past and things have changed
And you just might have to say it to me

The time we had together,
We spent it wonderfully.
And that is all that matters to me.

The jokes and the laughs will remain in my mind
And they will get lost for me to find.

So next time you cry, cry a tear for me,
To show me and you that there is more to be.
  —*Julie Krizan*

Untitled

I never knew how much you meant to me
But now every moment of each day I see
That you were more than just a woman
You are someone I never had, a friend

I wish I could keep you forever
But I guess that will be never
I just wish there were more like you
Then I would never be blue

If I ever find another like you
I promise to be devoted and true
I will keep praying to the Lord above
That I will find that special one to love

And in the last and final line
I wanted to tell you that you are fine
And that you are perfect in every way
And for a lifetime that way, you should stay.
  —*Joseph Ricks*

Untitled

We were so much closer than words could ever say,
But now your life is over, God has taken you away.

How I'd feel when you were gone, I never really knew,
And now you're gone forever — whatever will I do?

My sorrow creeps into the night and follows me all day,
But they tell me that this sadness will someday go away.

They say that time can heal all things, I know that this is true,
but my eyes still fill with tears each time I think of you.

All your love and understanding helped guide me through the years,
and hopefully my memories will help to ease my tears.

You're in a perfect place now, you've been called away from here,
and though I cannot see you, I feel your presence near.

I should have told you sooner, before your life came to an end,
That I loved you as a father, but also as a friend.
  —*Kimberly Henslee Chalich*

The Love of a Daughter

I love you Daddy with all my heart
But the time has come when we have to part

I prayed every day for you to get well
Or for God to come and relieve you
From your living hell

Now you're at peace in your mind and your heart
You'll never have to be afraid anymore of the dark

You taught me the meaning of right and wrong
You showed me how to be happy and strong

I love you Daddy so very much
I'll use my memories of you for my crutch

It's so very hard to say goodbye
I'm sorry Daddy but I've got to cry

I know you'd want me to be strong and brave
But it's not very easy
When we're laying you to rest in your grave

The angels have come and taken you away
God's leaving us here, he wants us to stay

Now you're in heaven without any pain
And someday Daddy we'll all be together again
  —*Mary Lademann*

A Vacation

5 D_____ in a Z___ C____ gave our family the exact way,
To find an 18 H____ G____ C_____ to begin our 1st 24 H____ D__.
On this vacation we saw 1 W_____ on a U_____ run over 3
B____ M____ M—,
They were drinking 4 Q_____ of milk while sitting in a G_____ of ice.
57 H_____ V_____ of dogs were watching 11 P_____ on a
F_____ T____ saluting the 13 S_____ on a the A_____ F___,
while 1001 A_____ N_____ were playing 88 P____ K____ with 76
T_____ players marching at Fort Bragg.
We found that 8 S____ on a S____ S____ were always in view, and
that 9 P_____ of the S____ S____ and the 12 S____ of the
Z____ were clear in the great sky of blue.
On our trip we learned from children at school,
that 26 L_____ were in the A_____ and that
  32 D_____ was a little cool.
We saw the 7 W_____ of the W____ which was great I must
confess, and you are even greater since you solved my little number test.

—*Margie Thompson*

The Golden Rule

Everyone knows what a golden
rule is, but my theory is to go
by the rules, who is the ruler.
When we go to the movies is called
Silence is Golden,
    That is called the Golden Rule

—*Lee Fladmo*

Time To Say Good-bye

I dream of what it would be like in Heaven
But then it seems that I belong to Hell
This year I can remember a time when
I was happy listening to the bells
But now Satan is all that fills my mind
And now I stand here, dazed, ready to die
A thought fills my mind yet it is not kind
But I guess my only question is ... why?
I have prepared for this moment all week
I've left a note for my mom on my bed
I've tried to be strong but now I am weak
So be prepared is what I've always said
As hard as it is, I've tried not to lie
I have failed so it is time to say good-bye.

—*Dani Goodnough*

Shine Like A Star

Frozen smiles in a picture
But they disappear in the night.
Everyone sees life as a struggle,
Everyone lives it as a fight.

Love yearns to shine,
Out of a broken heart.
But still others dwell in their sorrows,
Since loved ones had to part.

Dreams have been shattered,
Hopes have been destroyed.
People want someone to understand them,
To release them from their solitate void.

Here is that one,
Who will calm you of your fears,
Take away your burdens,
And wipe away your tears.

He's ready to accept you,
Being who you are.
For he, the Lord, will love you,
And you shall shine like a star.

—*Tiffany M. Fox*

To Catch D.H.'s Rabbit

Grab the Bunny
Squeeze his throat
Tug his ears
Stroke that tummy.

Legs start thumping
Lapin eyes widen
Fur body stiffens
See Bunny drool.

—*Terry Kelly*

I Wish to Create Peace

My intentions are not to break the peace
But to create the peace
For I wish one day to rebuild, reinstate,
And educate our future images
So they can live as hawks in the breeze
And be as free as they can be

To teach, not kill but to rebuild
For their children and their children's children
For eternity to come

Yes, I wish to create peace
To end the violence, the wars, the differences
To see all the people as they are
May the world wear a blindfold
And only see humanity

For the need has come to reinforce
To change the course which we lead
To stop putting cocaine in our brains
But knowledge in our game
To leave dope out of our goals
And put hope in our souls

—*Joseph John Villanueva*

Love and Hate

What is it to hate? Hate is to murder,
but to love is life. I find I love, but I hate.
How can I be loving if I'm hateful? Love is
life and hate is death. We all go through
a time when we neither love or hate. How? I
don't know, but we'll always be in a triangle
of love, hate, and nothing. We feel nothing
when we neither love or hate. We feel the
continuous ache inside, struggling to find our
feelings we hide behind hate, feelings we find
with our love.

—*Becca Stutzman*

Moment in Time

The time we had was not very long.
But was a moment in time I will prolong.
I hope you will always remember it too.
Because in my heart I will always love you.
The spring flowers smell oh so good.
But I weep cause I cannot share them with you.
You have someone that you do love.
A person sent from heaven above.
I wish you happiness and good fate.
But if you should need me it will never be too late.
The sun will rise and the sun will set.
But you are the one I shall never forget.
I will hold you and kiss you just for tonight.
But tomorrow will come and it will be gone
    forever, goodnight.

—*Lisa Tarqueno*

Love's Merit

Love is joy and love is sorrow;
Love is sweet and bitter, too,
Love is old as all creation,
   Yet is love forever new.
       —*Trisha Midkiff*

No Work, No Pay

Easy does it! Why worry? True!
But what happens when there's work to do?
You say "twill be here when
You and I have passed", but then
Where's compassion; what about our brother;
If we help him not, there is no other.
The world has enough of those who say
You owe us a living, when are you going to pay?
So, for he who would not turn a hand,
But looks only for pleasure grand,
Needs to examine, very closely, I say,
The maxim - "No work, no pay".

"Tis not just the way I'd like to be,
It is my philosophy.
       —*J. W. Pent*

Jesus Is Coming

Jesus is coming, and that's a fact,
but will you be ready when He comes back?

He'll crack the sky, with outstretched hands,
and those in Christ shall rise and ascend.

He's coming back to take us home,
to be His bride just His alone.

I know you've heard this, for many a years,
but don't let this fall on deaf ears.

Do we really believe He's coming back?
Then why do we live so slack

Narrow is the way, so great but small
and many of the saints are sure to fall.

As in the days of Noah no one believed
today many are being deceived

Jesus is coming He's coming back
no more to say for that's a fact.
       —*Dorothy Dawkins*

Final and Free

Freely, they care, not just with words,
   but with their time, and
Freely, they share, their emotions, their tears,
   their love, their fears, and
Freely, they bare others burdens and grief,
   expecting nothing in return, and
Freely, they dare to live by faith and commitment,
   nothing to prove and nothing to approve, and
Freely, they spare, their judgements,
   trusting to innocence instead of guilt.
They can be angry at drugs that leech,
   but with hands out that I can reach.
They understood the monster under my bed,
   as they understood the devil in my head.
They have the strength to communicate,
   and the love to not dominate.
Now, perhaps, hurt will have faded, insecurities revealed,
   empty hearts filled, and broken hearts healed.
It's a Spirit, that makes them free to me.
   It's the Spirit that is a gift both final and free.
       —*Gary A. Kaufmann*

She's There

You may not be able to see her,
   But yet, she's still there.
You may not be able to feel it,
   But she's guarding you, I swear.
You may not hear her words,
   But she tell you she loves you everyday.
You may not see her face,
   But she cries for you the same way.
You may think she's gone,
   But this I will say;
Although she's in another place, a better place,
   In our hearts her memory will always stay.
       —*Dorsey G. Cornelius*

To My Mother: With "Love"

Mothers have many goals in life;
   but you my mother chose to be a domestic wife.
You chose to nourish your family, one and all;
   to give them love as I recall.

When you were tired and couldn't go no more;
   You would feed us, even though it was another chore.
You care for us in so many ways;
   I often think of you, especially in these "critical" days.

I often think of you being the backbone in helping with family
   problems; and most likely you found a way to solve them.
I think of you wiping our tears, and you crying too;
   because we didn't listen, yes listen to you!

You worried about how the family would survive,
   even working hard from nine to five.
Sometimes you felt you were taken for granted or misused;
   Sometimes even physically, mentally, and emotionally abused.

Because you stood by me and help me right to this day;
   "I thank you and love you" is what I want to say!
May we always be friends and give praise to each other;
   because you are my precious and sweet mother!
       —*Alice M. Roberts*

Olivia

I shared to you my feelings
But you turned me down
Tried to get your attention
But you just turned around
Their could have been something between you and me
But now I'm alone lonely
Think about you all the time drives me insane
Picture you in my mind leaves me in pain
Dream about you everyday does me no good
Left me hanging in my mind something told me you would
But you weren't their to catch my fall
Not even if you could
Felt the presence overcome when we were alone
The feeling I felt won't go away
My love for you has grown
I shared to you my feelings
But you left me hanging, left me their to fall
I gave you my number all you had to do was call.
       —*Carlos Enriquez*

The Apple

I tossed an apple up in the air,
It came down and was a pear,
The fruit was sweet,
Like mincemeat,
But I had to stop and stare,
At the big red apple that was now a
   pear.
       —*Lara Umberger*

Happy Holiday

What was this greeting mean?
Buy a gift, see a friend
Visit a someone ill on the mend
Take a gift if you care to
Help someone's day rid of the blues
Or does it mean buy something new
   for your great day
Or take something you made for a shut in,
   to stay.
Or does it mean think of yourself
Go to lunch with a friend
Who is a good friend not just pretend
We cannot measure love or friendship
   by the pound
But love, and friends and caring is
   something very very sound
     —Sara Romeo

Cold Gray Dawn

C old is the heart embittered
   by a life time of pain.
O ver four decades of scars,
   that will forever remain
L ocked up in a dark box, in the
   depths of my tormented soul.
D amned to a life of loneliness
   that can never be called whole.

G ray is the heart that has seen it's
   loved ones placed in the grave.
R iches and power nor ever glory or fame,
   could any of them save!
A ll breathed their last breath, and
   passed off this earthly scene.
Y et, my heart cries out in pain,
   never again to be serene.

D awn is cold and gray in a heart
   that has no more room for hope.
A s life's bitter end comes, and to
   life's last breath I hopelessly grope.
W hen that time finally comes what
   final words shall I spawn?
N ever again shall I ever witness
   another meaningless cold gray dawn.
     —T. Peterson

The Dreamer

The lifeline of a dreamer should not be put to shame,
By ridicule and doubtfulness, we all too often blame.

A dreamer's life is full of hope and wonderment afar,
He drifts into creativeness where all our answers are.

Copernicus and Kepler, were theories made of fun,
Indeed the earth and moon and stars revolve around the sun.

Rembrandt, Rhinehart; Florsek are artists in their hearts,
Showing views from deep within where imagination starts.

Dreamers of the physical from pain they cry aloud,
Their persistent dedication has made their nations proud.

Poets, musicians, writers display their inner thoughts.
Listen to their words of hope, their meanings may be caught.

When life is full of boredom and the light you cannot see,
Reach deep within your very soul then come and dream with me.
     —Carina L. Florsek

Orca

His home, disturbed
by the greed of
man.
His life ruined by the heartlessness of
society.
Before, he was calm, and
free.
Now he is struggling in a world of walls and
tricks.
Trying to survive in the artificial world we have created
for him.
All the while longing to be back where he belongs, where he
needs to be.
Where the only waves were natural and the only noises were
sea gulls.
Looking out into the vastness of the open ocean,
He wishes and
silently
cries.
     —Kim Hart

Lincoln

A young boy who for knowledge yearned
By the warmth of firelight did learn
Of honesty and goodness toward all men
A divided nation someday he'd mend
Taking a stand he dared to proclaim,
Under slavery's bond no man shall be chained!

Legal battles of justice he fought to win
To ensure fairness for all men
A man with integrity of mind and name
Our sixteenth President he became
Steadfast he stood through the winds of change,
Under slavery's bond no man shall be chained!

Holding no malice in his heart
Reunification and a brand new start
Were the things he wanted for this great land
When he died at the hands of another man
Yet the echo of his voice remains
Under slavery's bond no man shall be chained,
Under slavery's bond no man shall be chained!
     —Jeremy Kleidosty

Child

Quit trying to live
By what you think you see by me
Certainly you can't see
What I most assuredly think I perceive

Try your own eyes let them open and shine
Don't worry anymore about others
About judgements on mankind

You're not the center perhaps not even close
But do remember child
It's your eyes will see the most

Your eyes child see not of me
Or how I may live only a shallow world
Where one can't give

Open up your precious eyes
Live in God's time
We are sanctioned by believe
Love is truth is all we can leave

It's truly simple for faithful souls
Believes in God's truth and peace of heart
will be bestowed!
     —Guy Donahue

The Box

The box on the table -
Calls out to the un-able.
It's a place where opinions are too bold
to ever be told - face to face.
It's a prison without bars.
Once inside, you won't go far.
It's four walls without paint -
It's a cardboard house of complaints.
It's a symbol of concern - but
will we ever learn? No

The box on the table -
symbolizes how stable
everything appears to be.
there's one everywhere we go - but
no one cares - it's just you show.
It's a symbol of justice - but
will it ever protect us? No

The box - fill it with socks
cause it's empty anyway
and it's wash day.
  —K. Hemmen

Her Middle Name Could Have Been Self-Esteem - Ca-mill-ia!

Her middle name could have been self-esteem! -
Camille - or, Ca-mill-ia, which was the way
Her mother liked to pronounce her pretty daughter's
Name, on a Valentine's day she died, I heard -
Camille, or Ca-mill-ia, the childhood girl friend
From my veriest youth-time of long ago.

Once for Easter, dresses for the both of us
Ca-mill-ia's mother made; each dress
Was in lovely pink organdy-fluffy pink
For Camille and a figured pink for me.
And, Jimmy brought his horse with cart to church
To ride us around in the afternoon!

Ca-mill-ia's mother liked to sew for her only
Daughter - as though Camille was just mostly
Her very own darling dolly. A very petted little girl
She was, and even after she grew up her doting
Parents worried whenever she was worried; they
thought, I think, "Give the world to Camille!"

  —Canadia Collins

Reaping the Harvest of Apathy

Apathy, greed and power, an uncaring combination,
Can annihilate others to total obliteration.
Violence, murder and hatred, a spur of liquor and drugs
Goad some to seek recognition by crime, vice and thugs.

The sixties bred discontent, a solemn wake-up call;
Greed and apathy did prevail, and chaos encircled all.
Disregard for others, as we bask in fame and power;
Complacency is replaced by fear in this final hour.

The rude awakening: "Concern for others must prevail,"
Then hopefully, cold misery and poverty will fail.
The result of dissension, the lack of love and care
For poor and oppressed people does create despair,

And in their despair, their world without hope,
Some resort to violence, others cope with dope;
And so we reap the harvest existing everywhere,
A violence created by lack of love and care.

  —Helen Moore Henry

The Forgotten World

Sixtillion sick souls blast into a rank sun,
Cancer patients suffering in a church yard,
Sinning Stanley cries from baby-less fun.
Bone-piercing women say all food is lard.

People suffer in large roar of belief,
Pickled men pushing a pink cross of a tan fox,
Huge men eating hot salt for a wet relief,
Women chewing firecrackers in a hot box.

Burning hot white steel on a tongue for joy,
Speckled Pete and red snake love in tune,
Potatoes and black flames used as a toy.
Bright sun and blue moon strike fire on a dune.

Bloody Mary drinks large glass of poison.
Drugged Dan's fire of burning worms and sand,
Raping Robert in a hot blood pond till one,
Burning Bertha reeks fire in all sex land.

Cursing Red Beard burns jewels in summer.
Stealing Sam stinks, as a bishop pays a huge fine.
Black devil and white skunk sing as a lover.
Come ten-thousand more souls to suffer-time.

  —John E. Barsda

My Friend

It is not for sale, nor is it for hire.
Cannot be destroyed, by wind, rain or fire.
'Tis looked for each day but, some never find.
Altho' it comes freely, in many different kinds.
It's shared by two, and sometimes more.
You've only to open your heart's door.
You cannot hide it, for all will see,
The dearest of friendships between you and me.
So you take the red, and maybe, the blue.
I'll keep the green, and the yellow, too.
The gold we'll divide at the rainbows end.
For you're someone special, I call you
  "My Friend."

  —Gladys L. Holt

Adopted

Mommy, where are you? I've searched long and hard.
Can't let my pain through, though my heart be scarred.

Mommy, where are you? I have looked so long.
Gave me away to someone who thought I'd grow up strong.

Mommy, I missed you. Could you not see?

Though your face I never knew, how could you torture me?

Did you not love me? Did you not care?
Why did you leave me, naked, alone, and bare?

I dreamed you were a queen, or maybe a princess.
I think of what might have been, to find you, I'm obsessed.

Can't you see my heart is broken?
Don't you know I'm in distress?
If only you'd be left some token, to ease my great excess.

Mommy, I am hurt. I just cannot see.
What is one life worth? Or worthless, just like me?

  —Aleeha R. Travis

Verse Curse

Rhyming of "wind" with a word such as "kind"
Is something to which I am not yet resigned.
Ditto for "been" when it's coupled with "seen";
While the meter is sound, elocution's not clean.
Terminal consonance one should attain,
Yet rhymists fall down on this, time and again.

  —Jack Swansen

Alpha-Omega

You are born with your seed in grown so impure; not knowing or
caring of a life you must endure. From that time until death
its one hell of a fight, to come into this world and keep
yourself right. When your parents and the world try to tell
you what's right or wrong, listen very carefully, until
yourself be strong. Whether it be in the church, or within you
at home. Please!! don't wait until your earthly death, to find
how much you've grown. Your task will not be easy as so many
others know, to keep myself within you, and to others you must
show. Your life is but a gift, from me I shew unto you. So
keep this kind reminder, and help others remember ... two. As
the day of judgement draws near, watch the signs of the time.
All evidence may not be obvious, so read between the lines.
False prophets will abound, with promises of good tidings to
come. Many will rejoice, but turn away from my son. Get ready
for the time that draws nearer, oh!! so fast; for the promised
thing-in-itself——must shortly come to pass. You are that
which is. I am all that was, that is, and that shall be. I am
Alpha-Omega. I'm the first and the last; beginning and end.

—*Wayne McClellan...Gemini Wakefield*

Harvest Time

Did you ever wish an a star?
Carry lightning bugs home in a jar?
Roast marshmallows and franks over a fire?
That is harvest time!
When the corn, the beans, and the wheat,
Have matured and are ready to eat;
The potatoes are ripe in the ground;
Nuts and fruit in abundance are all ground.
That is harvest time!
The leaves are a glorious hue.
The Lord's face comes smiling through.
With his harvest He says, "I love you."
Through our grace and prayers we say,
"I love you too"
That is harvest time!

—*Bertha Snyder*

The American Immigrant Wall of Honor

From many countries 'round the world they came,
Caught up in a great human migration,
Searching for a new life in a free land.
Their names on this honored wall are inscribed
In loving remembrance and gratitude
For their talents, skills and accomplishments
That fashioned such a praise-worthy nation.
Leaving their homeland called for sacrifices
And hardships that would have discouraged many.
After a lengthy and tiresome journey,
Holding on to their precious possessions,
They made their way to the spacious "Great Hall"
To be examined and interrogated;
Their greatest fear was to be rejected.
Hard work, courage and determination
Paved the way to the opportunities
And freedoms we can all enjoy today.
We salute them, and will not forget them;
They are America's greatest treasures.

—*M. E. Steiner*

City Streets

Dark city streets, throughout the
neighborhoods. Cats and dogs fighting in
the alley ways. People in their cars
honking their horns going down the busy
streets yelling out their windows at
each other. Down dark city streets.

—*Lisa K. Petersen*

"After Crying"

After crying, I dry my eyes and think of you
Cause breaking up is so hard to do
Many share this fault, just like you
You can't just adore and not love someone, like you do.

My heart is breaking, but I have to let you go
I can't wait forever, I just have to know
That someone loves me with all their heart and soul
So my life can have a meaning, my life can have a goal.

I dream of a family with children and a home
With a playground nearby, where they can roam
I know with you, these things will never be
It is best we make this the end for you and me.

—*Louise Paresi*

Remembrance

How I feel, no words can describe,
Cause the pain I have is way deep inside.
It's not a physical one at that -
For that would heal, but this will not.

I saw a man being dragged today
Throughout the streets so far away.
Somalia was the land where this was done.
The body was there, but the spirit was gone.

He was a soldier, had probably a wife.
He went there to help those people with life.
The work is now over, at least on his part,
But it wasn't in vain, I'll remember in my heart.

I'm sure the innocent in Somalia too,
Will remember him for what he tried to do.
For like "The Good Shepherd" who also had the call,
That soldier in Somalia, gave for us all.

—*Andy Jakubowski*

Through the Years

The years budded forth with excitement.
    Challenges like arrows to
Be shot on target.
    Disappointments came but were
Turned into paths much clearer,
    And stronger to tread.
Anxieties dissipated into Balm-healing entities.
    Love came spiraling down
To find a solace for every occasion.
    Faith came walking in to clear any doubts.
Hope came as the capstone to encase all of life.

—*Gretchen Corbitt*

Legacy

I, God's child, a chameleon, changing chameleon,
    Changing chameleon, conglomerate of Eden, a blessing,
A blessing, Adam, in all his nakedness, yes, Adam,
    Adam, man's beginning, time, space, eternity.
God's child, Eve, an illusion, perfect illusion,
    Perfect illusion, helpmate of Adam, a woman,
A woman, mystery, enigma, a haunting mystery,
    Mystery, Eve, serpent's prey, woman, man's sojourn
        When life began.
God's children, I and Eve, dominion over the universe,
    dominion,
    Dominion, ruler, love set free, free love,
Free love, communion placed in bonds, yes, pain,
    Pain, I and Eve, man's fall, tarnished angels, we.

—*Thomas A. Flowers*

Untitled

The desire for freedom from reality
is the key to imagination.
Hence, unlocked is the mind
to the chest of creation.

—*Scott F. P. Szymanski*

"It's Time to Stop"

Killing... An unnatural act.
Cheating... Produces severe impact.
Lying... The coward's way out.
Stealing... That's not what it's all about.
Cursing... When you can't express yourself.
Jealousy... Putting your emotions on the shelf.
Hatred... Consuming your mind and body.
Infecting... People with abuse and drugs.
Acting... Not nicely, but as a thug.
Maliciousness... Hurting others with senseless jibes.
Disturbing... Other people's lives.
Innuendos... Based on childish prattle.
Rumors... Intended to upset and rattle.
... "It's time to stop" and think —
Where have all the angels gone?
Where are we in this critical time?
We are deluged with violent crime.
"Soon, too soon, we will run out of time.
It's time to stop." And sort things out.
And find out what we are all about.

—*Collier M. Loving*

In Twenty Lines Or Less

I must tell you of my love. Sing below your balcony, oh yes,
climb the vines. How can I say what is in my heart in only
twenty lines? I know of your beauty, your innerself, you are
so sweet and kind. All this and more, in only twenty lines?
What must I omit? How can I say? You are much more than just
words! You are life at its best, you are song, you are the
rainbow of my life. You are the silver lining, oh yes, in only
twenty lines! I look at land and sea, I see the forest green,
I see children playing at the park. All of this is so sublime.
How in the world can I speak of you? In only twenty lines? I
have beat of heart, sight and sound. I run at ninety eight
point six. I have your love. Oh yes, this is life at it's
best. Least I forget. "In twenty lines or less"

—*Donald D. Rogers*

My Rainbow's End

I was born on a cold, wintry day.
Clouds hung darkly overhead;
Wind-driven sleet turned to ice.
Mother's life ended on the birthing bed.

I developed some storms of my own
As I grew and learned about life.
Tornados and tempests stayed close
While self-pity rained sharp as a knife.

Always lightning, crashing thunder and hail
With storm clouds that billowed and burst.
My life was a typhoon of despair
And I felt I would always be cursed.

Then one dreary day, through the rain,
A bright shaft of sun filtered through.
A colored arch bridged the sky, so I crossed.
At the end of my rainbow was you.

—*Frances Hatch Pershing*

The Morning After

The rays of sunshine seeping through the
    Clouds in the early morning hours,
        Gives me a feeling of power....

The hint of rain from the night before,
    Left a fresh smell that I adore....

Reach over one more time to touch your
    Softness before starting the day....

Smiling with the thought of ending this
    Day the same way....

Laying here and remembering the night before,
    Candles, dinner and loving each other
        Forever more.....

Now one month, on to one year,
    My love for you is so clear....

Lights off, curtains open,
    A new day, a new adventure....

Days, months, and years full of
    Happiness in our future....

—*Linda O'Hallaran*

Run Away

A young woman is lost in the forest,
cold, hungry and scared,
This lonely woman would probably be
home, if someone had just cared,
her thoughts drifted to her parents
and the fight they'd had the night before,
her legs were covered in deep, red
scratches and her feet were horribly sore.
The clouds were getting darker now,
she quickens up her pace,
Icy rain pelts down upon her cold and dirty face.

The couple sits at the police station,
not looking each others way,
they might have been calmer had their
daughter not run away.
It had been two days before they
noticed this girl of theirs was gone,
and would be two or more before
they'd find her drowned in a
mountain pond.

—*Hanna Climer*

Arrow of Longing

I long for Eldar ships,
Come from beyond the seas;
There's little hope for the fateful
With burden enough to bare.
I've longing for the deeper skies
Where angels long have tread;
Long fated for this ending world
Where resisting arms have no place.
This all too real house beneath the sky
Has no gift for the romantic tales of old,
And bitter seem these days
Without roads left untread.
So, I long for sight of sails,
Knowing that short shall be these days,
That I may venture forth to kindred lands
Far beyond the seas.

—*Christopher M. Myers*

Time's Bequest

Be it today or yet in years,
Come peacefully, presume no fears.
As time's last justified bequest,
Grant me but gentle, tranquil rest.

Kindly time redeems the days
Of past woes and futile ways.
Days of despair or filled with pain,
Could I not change, I'd live again.

Love quenched the guilt of error wrought;
To dreary life it beauty brought.
Its elegance adorned my life
With peace and calm in place of strife.

Adorn once more in simple way
Rites of this tender parting day
No pompous bier, no wasted tears,
Just memory of life's better years.

Secure in providence's care,
Serene midst all we love and share
Hail past and future still to be,
This respite past, again with thee.

—*Boyd E. Olson*

The Call of the Lark

I heard a Lark call from the distant wild,
"Come with me, come with me."
And, forgetting I was a much loved child,
I cried, "I'll come with thee — with thee."

But mother's voice spoke in the night,
"Oh, daughter, no! Stay here in your place."
Though I longed to see that distant wild,
I turned about face; stayed in my place.

I wonder sometimes, if I had gone
To that distant land, which shown so bright,
Would I have found "Utopia" full-blown,
Or does that place, too, have its dark night?

—*Frances Taylor Smith*

Beloved

A soft breeze blowing in the night,
comes as a chill in the autumn air
It signals thoughts of things to come
memories of things past.
Why do I yearn for the beauty of long ago?
When your hand held mine
When we walked, not knowing
the path to follow - but together.
The treasured past brings a new tomorrow
Awake! Another dawn is here!
Your hand in mine - if only in spirit
but you are there
we are there - we belong!
Good night - sweet one - sleep beckons
sweet, sweet one goodnight!

—*Josephine E. Sonessa*

Together Again

In spite of all your hate
in spite of all your fear
their is something inside you can not hear
it is the love you have had for me
something only we could see
it'll bring us together once again
and heal the fights we alone could not mend

—*James L. Long*

Nevermore

Eyes upon the skyline, face to the wind;
Coming into view upon the horizon,
Visions of love, chimeric, a mirage,
Inverted images from far away.
Emotions that once were, now gone.
The strength and power that might have been,
Eroded like unforested land;
Evaporated like rain puddles in summer sun.
Shards of shattered dreams, like broken pottery
From some long dead civilization
Waiting to be reassembled in beauty,
Nevermore.
Hopes and ideals crushed beneath conquering boots;
I kneel, the vanquished; you stand, the victor;
To you, the spoils of love destroyed,
To me, a life enchained by loneliness.
It is not that you are gone,
It is that you never completely leave.
And I stand, as always, empty and alone,
With the brass ring barely out of reach.

—*Philip A. Eckerle*

America

In God we trust is how we stand;
    coming together in this great land.

The people knowing freedom was just ahead;
    left all behind, as someone said.

The land of the free, that's how it was to be,
    giving all of us a chance at liberty.

Paying freedom's price and taking a stand
    down through the centuries in this great land.

Washington, and Adams and Franklin, and Lincoln to name just
    a few, knew the Heavenly Father and knew what to do.

"We the people of the U.S.," coming together as one,
    being drawn here by God's own Son.

Our Nation under God is how we'll stand;
    knowing we can't be moved because He's in command.

Let us all pay tribute, to the Holy One
    for God has blessed us with His own Son.

So America still is the land of the free,
    because Jesus still rules with liberty.

—*Janice Howell*

A Sunder Day!!!

To us, for us, we the people must come out and speak,
Conquer and live for ours is the kingdom of power,
Glory, and a right to live in a free world as God
Intended forever and ever! And
As a deep dark aura falls over the river, two
long sleek boats come flying around the band and then as
If by magic stop dead in the waters with music
Blaring with not a sound stirring, not even a penny.
And the roar of the engines and off they go racing
Up and down the river giving a defeating sound to the ear,
Like it was a racetrack to hell and back!!! And
as simplified authors as we rightfully are, we
Embody this pretentious thought!
And I say, we as writers are simplified authors,
In that we imploit a message to be picked at
and plundered for decades to come!!!!
    Amen

—*Michael J. Mason (Mickle V. Electron)*

Gone — October

Just begun — on the first day
Cool breezes arriving calmly - silently sweeping the lands
Rustling the autumn colored leaves
Tangible, crisp, cascading downward to blanket the pavements
    I so often tread
From day to the next day
Gone — October, when just yesterday your presence was abound.
    Just begun...
Blue skies, white clustered clouds form in the atmosphere above
Beautiful sunsets appearing in the early evenings
    bring many contemplations to my mind.
Gone — October, strange how fast you flew by
When I was just beginning to embrace your colorful distinct
    beauty. Just begun — on the first day
Cool breezes arriving calmly, silently sweeping my lands
So — I will open my door this time, escape into your climate
Scuff my sneakers under the leaves you fell
Listen, to see the sounds ahead of my feet
And remember...
Never to miss your noisy solitude again.

    —*L. T. Pereira*

The Walk West

In the distance, rumblings. Could be thunder,
could be in my mind. I lumber on, deprived of
sleep and of love, at least so I feel.
The road is hard under my sore feet, as
I walk and think. My mind goes blank and
I forget where I am. Over my head many
clouds, in the horizon the beautiful, liquid
like colors. The sun sets and the sky is on
fire. All the light slowly diminishes, as
night over-takes this vast land. I think
about where I've been and where I'm going.
The bag is heavy on my shoulder. The memories
are heavy on my heart and yet they shine on!
Illuminating my life, brightening the darkness
but in the same instance casting shadows into
the light. I walk on, into the blueness where
the sun had just been. My fate is determined
by the road I choose to follow.

    —*Shannon O'Brien*

Zygote

Can you remember back, when all there was was black?
    Could you touch and feel, did you know that you were real?
What was it like then, could it be like that again?

Differences between hot and cold, you'll know when you get old.
    Just you wait and see, how ugly the outside world can be.

Now you've got your face, now you've joined the human's race.
    Fighting for no reason, you know peace is out of season.
You were born at the wrong time, because of someone else's crime

Get very used to sins, that is how your life begins.
    To sing life's song, you know so much goes wrong.

Will you be loved, will you be pushed and shoved?
    Don't be afraid of you, you'll soon see what to do.
Now that you're alive, you'll have to learn to survive.

    —*Ken Clossey*

Faded Dream

As I sit alone on the beach,
I watch the sailboats glide away.
The sound of the waves breaking on the shore
Reminds me of you and the times we spent together.
We sat and watched the sails against the setting sun.
We dreamed of someday having a boat of our own.
All I have now is the dream, since you're gone.

    —*Tabitha Martin*

Insight

Listening in silence one stops to think
If one is in silence alone to whom shall they listen
For if one is in silence and looking for an answer
    who shall they turn to
To return to the silence of the one who was listening
    may open the silence of the listener

    —*J. P. Halsted*

Take Inventory

Let us concentrate, accentuate
Count our common points to tally them:
Senses, feelings, yearning for much love;
Need for people, friends, acceptance, touch;

Wanting gentle worlds to bed us down.
Though unequal at our birth, we tend to be,
Death will equalize us all at last.
When that time arrives we may well boast;
Givers were we throughout our short life's span!

Take this inventory of human wants:
Vanquish drug addiction, poverty.
Conquer crime. Care for sick and frail,
Handicapped, the children, old, depressed.
Fulfill life's one purpose:
Better Earth.

    —*Florence K. Wiener*

Red Dress of Blood

Look there on the horse the lady in red of
course, she's reaching for the men that are wounded
on the ground, trying to forget the horrible sound.

She gets off her horse to help a young man, to sew
up his wound then help him to stand, the boy sheds
no tear as the lady comes by, for she helps who
she can but some have to die.

As she looks around at the pitiful site, she sees
armies of men not able to fight, there are men
screaming of pain, as she's walking to them she's
thinking, insane.

How crazy this is for a girl such as her to be walking around
in a death crazy world. She knew that her life could be taken
away, but she knew deep inside she must move on her way.

Walking around not thinking of war, just all these
men that would die. She fell to her knees and started to cry.

But there by her side was a frightening young man who was
reaching real hard for the warm woman's hand. She lifted her
head and saw this young man and dressed up his wounds and
helped him to stand.

    —*Natalie Ford*

A Clandestine Stranger

A furtive man, all dressed in white,
Crept surreptitiously through the night;
His actions were truly most bizarre,
For he vanished then beneath the stars;
When morning came, the nocturne gone,
I chanced to gaze upon my lawn;
My eyes were surely playing tricks,
For there amidst the leaves and sticks,
Were flakes of white resplendent snow;
'Twas then the stranger's scheme unraveled,
And the reason for his nightly travels;
For old man winter in the night
Had brought to earth a chilly sight;
Alas, my autumn colors gleaming
Had been obscured while I was dreaming.

    —*Gordon Reedy*

Exaltation of Love

The morning came swiftly on the wings of the roosters that
crowed the new dawn, while coyotes still yipped in the
night-covered hills.
Suddenly, the intimacy of night, its mysterious workings
finished, vanished with the edge of morn.
The clouds passed and parted; the first peepings of the new
light dimmed the stars that had radiantly glittered in a
night, beyond description.
The ecstacies that had been were no more, but not forgotten;
remembered for an eternity of never-more.
Worldly passions of the night, extinguished, as vision
sharpened and the clarity of day made all the senses
quicken; hiding the night that had been like shades that
spanned the windows of our hearts; that had been so close
that only one great heart was beating in a beauty so
incredibly wondrous that from the ancients to the space age
heralds, would little change or diminish.
Lowly shame that man can so unaware be of God's greatest
gift - for love is beauty and lovers are immortal.

 —*Barbara Charis*

Yesterday, Today, and Tomorrow

Like steamy windows forming frost
Crusty, cold, and silently shaping figure
We grow.

Left alone, all alone with ourselves,
By ourselves, to pick up and face tomorrow
Where today finished off.

We walk along, aimlessly wandering
Wondering if tomorrow leads the way
We want to go.

The passing times of childhood adventures
Are the ones we stored away
In dreams that were forgotten
From the childhood of yesterday.

 —*Thomas Kenan Fedele*

Tyrant

Puppy-eyed innocence loaded with fears,
Crying leaden tears,
Husband wants to keep you shelled in.

Make your downy feathers worldly,
Soar to the mountain peak,
Carnal knowledge do not seek.

Spiritual food for thy lips,
Martyr thyself for chastity,
Abolish power to make thighs rip.

Shake off the shackles,
Melt the gold band,
Bury diamond with hourglass sand.

Beast and jailer,
Hellborn voice,
Screwing mind and soul.
Now your nude body's hole,
Will open with a bullet-shaped key.
"Bang"

 —*Theresa Darr*

A Touch Of Love

Like the wind
 Rattles the trees,
Love shakes my heart.

 —*Barbara Cheeseman*

Nature Shouts - He Lives

At the break of dawn on a cool still morn
Crystallized dew, the fields adorn
Beneath that dew, green patches appear
Surely, the arrival of Spring is near

It seems that just the other day
These same fields were dark and grey,
Leaves lay upon the ground
The cold wind whistled all around

I liken winter to the death of our Lord
With the dormancy of nature, I am reminded once more
How dark and cold that tomb must have been
How He suffered and died to take away sin

But Oh! the glory of the Spring
When all the birds begin to sing
The butterfly leaves its dark cocoon
The flowers awake from the dead to bloom

Nature tells me without any doubt
I can almost hear the angels shout
Our Savior arose in victory
Redeeming Grace for you and me

 —*Betty J. Farr*

The Problem Alphabet

Assets are anemic. Buyers are bashful
Customers are cranky. Dealers are dull
Earnings are elusive. Faxes are frantic
Gains are grudging. Hirees are hesitant
Inventories are increasing. Justifications are jaundiced
Key people are kowtowing. Losses are looming
Marketers are missing. Net incomes are notorious
Operations are opulent. Profits are pitiful
Quarterlies are quaking. Returns are receding
Sales are slippery. Taxes are towering
Utilizations are uneven. Ventures are valueless
Wasters are wanton. Expenditures are excessive
Yields are yawning. Zones are zigzagging.

 —*Peter A. Michel*

Topsy

Topsy my little charming and adventurous baby,
Cute, cuddly, and bright as a lady.
Always a smile with a dimpled cheek,
Growing rapidly, and swiftly every week.

Topsy's favorite toy was a stuffed puppy called Sparky,
Who was always creating a lot of malarkey.
Then one day Topsy received a real live Sparky,
And baby Topsy had a playmate frisky and barky.

Off to the park Mom and Topsy would go,
Playing hide and seek and creating quite a show.
Mom made a lunch and they had a picnic,
And Sparky cane running lickety splitly.

Packing up to return home,
Mom gave Topsy's long blonde curls one quick combe.
Topsy had fairy tales spinning in her head,
And soon would be asleep in her very own bed.

We barely had enough time to say our prayers, and Topsy was
asleep counting plum fairies and teddy bears. And tomorrow the
trees will whisper from the park, come out and play Mom, and
Topsy, and Sparky said, "me too", and gave a bark

 —*V. Marge Pavlowich*

"Hardcore"

Happy fathers day, your extra special today, this means you
"Dad" oh yes, although there's been times we've made each other
mad; Just look we made it thru each and every time, nothing
never that Bad! Remember the times when I thought I was right
and thought you were wrong when you said "No" you can't stay
out late with those people you don't belong; always
misunderstanding than, why you were so firm and your words were
so strong! Just maybe, now I see your reason why, maybe not,
you had to be hardcore and rough oh yea, there were man days I
thought I couldn't take anymore and just had enough; yes. Thru
it all I became a better person, I'm someone proud, strong and
tough! See, your way it made me handle my rocky mountain road
life and still stand tall time after time, but always learning
and once again some how still on my face I fall; I hope you
seen, never did I quit. Trying I went on giving it my 100%
all! You and mom, taught us always to be ourselves and honest
and true heres to you both for the most important gift I ever
received, life's #1 clue; thank you so much, I'll always live by
your words, there my golden rule! Never, were we asked to do
no more than to turn and always give our best life.

—*Brenda Sawyer*

Daddy

Daddy is in Heaven now beyond that distant shore
Daddy reigns with Jesus and he will forevermore
He wouldn't want me to be sad but to carry on
"To grieve is good I know," he'd say.
"But honey not all day."
Just think how perfect Heaven is because that's where I'm at
and I'm dancing in God's spirit and I'm singing in God's love
And I'm sure you know I'm talking to everyone here above.
I'm happy, oh so happy, more than I've ever been before.
I thought I was happy here on earth
Oh, but when I reached Heaven's door!
Jesus told me I was welcome and invited me to come in.
I had been a faithful servant and I would dwell with Him.
So honey, when you think of me, as I'm sure you often do
Just remember that I'm happy and I want you to be, too.
So do the work for Jesus the very best you can
And smile and love while you're on earth till you dwell in
Canaan's Land.

—*Helen Brown Dunlap*

Gone to Her Rest

There she lay on the bed.
Dad's eyes are glazed and red.
Rose, your mother has gone to her rest.
Oh, Lord, it's probably for the best.
But I'm only twelve, what will I do without Mom?
She'll never see me at my first Prom.
Who can I talk to every day?
Who will hug me in that motherly way?
Dad is fine, but I really don't know him as well.
Mom was my friend, my adviser, my pal.
I feel an emptiness inside the room.
A tangible terrible feeling of gloom.
She was so young to die.
I kept saying, "Why? Why?"
Now as I reflect on this sad day.
My heart still cries in the same way.
Mom, I miss your cheerfulness,
Your faith, your glowing happiness.
Walk with me side by side.
Let your spirit be my guide.

—*R. Mushenski*

Carmel, California

Rolling, crashing, the thundering tide
Daffodils dancing as the wind breezes by

Early morning salt mist walks
Window shopping through streets of quaint little shops
In some, the scent of fresh coffee a brew
At night, specialty restaurants wait for you

Shoreline lights and bluffs abound
With branches extended like arms of welcome
There, lone cypress stands upon its ground

The pebble beach where driftwood lies
giant sea gulls soar on by

Crystal blue, aquamarine
are the coves of beauty
where the wild wind sings

Take me back where my spirit is free
There is no place like Carmel to me

—*Susan A. Marlow*

North Dakota Prairie Rose

There is a pink and precious flower that grows on these North
Dakota prairies. It's delicate color and fragrant scent makes
it's presence known wherever you may roam, on these North
Dakota prairies. Each time I see one it brings me a sense of
peace and wonder at the endurance of this delicate flower that
blooms so freely, on these North Dakota prairies. Lack of
rain, poor soil, lack of sunlight doesn't discourage it's
survival, on these North Dakota prairies. I liken this flower
to the hearty prairie women who struggled and survived cold
weather, hot summers and the dust bowl days. Daughters who
also struggled for their special place. Many gave their lives
early in their life because the hardships were too great to
bear. But their struggle was strong and valiant while they
were here. These women also bore sons who fought and died for
our freedom, Lest we forget. So I see each of us related to
this special prairie flower, digging our roots deep and
bringing forth the fruits of our labor like our special flower,
the North Dakota Prairie Rose.

—*Wilma A. K. Ellingson*

Train Whistle

While lying in my bed at night, long after
dark and yet longer before light, I hear a
tone coming soft and low, the tone is a
passing train's whistle blow.

I've said my prayers and am waiting for sleep,
and I think of my soul which I asked God to keep.
But I lay quietly and think, as a gentle hum comes
to me. It is the train that runs so free, I wonder
what will become of me.

In the midst of confusion, and in the middle of
the night, I can't help but wonder, will I be
alright. But then the whistle blows, and with
it comes faith, and then I know there is a hard
world to face.

So, I lay back and remember God, and let my joy
and faith break the facade. For now I hear that
distant trains' whistle for the last time, and
relaxed, I close my eyes, knowing my life is not
really mine.

—*Percy G. Parker*

47

"Pass It On"

Our lives and life are made up of little influences from people
day to day.
First it was my Mother who seemed to turn me away—yet there
was my Dad who soothed the hurt to give my heart renewed
spirit to want to "pass it on."
Then there was Grandma, who understood with her quiet, warm,
wise wisdom that bridged the gaps.
For who knows more about hate and love, evil and good, revenge
or forgiveness except someone who has proven God's truths in
their lives.
Along the way were many teachers and preachers who helped
guide my way. Still one has to make choices who you let
influence your life.
So praise is in order, to the Lord above, who gave this ole'
gal the ears, eyes, will and love—to choose His answers when
problems arose.
Though the years are now many, it is still the same—just help
each other and "Pass It On."

    —Claire L. Coates

The Flood Of '93

The Muddy Mississippi and the mighty Mo -
Decided to break the record of 400 years ago!
Both watched the levees and the dams being built by man —
Who smugly gave predictions how the river ran.
Then came the heavy rains in all of the Midwest.
As waters began to rise, the people did their best.
Stacking millions of sand bags in order to beat the crest.
But the rivers kept on rising - giving no one any rest!
They covered roads and houses and fields that were so green —
Looking like a huge lake — like man had never seen.
People came from near and far — as damage grew and grew
Strangers, children and prisoners all joined the mighty crew —
Aid came from every corner of the world that we knew —
Although, many were weary — tired and very blue.
Each day was a great reminder - that they were never through
Still each person joined to help with determination of love
Each looked up into the sky, asking help from God above.
The water is receding — leaving acres and acres of mud,
Now we know our rivers are controlled only by God above.

    —Norma Dotson Payne

Where The Shaman Lies...

A storm is wandering in,
Deep, deep within the heart of the desert
Where the Shaman lies.
My soul escaping the body that once was,
And flys.
My spirit now dances through and through
Not knowing what to do,
Seeks guidance from the Shaman,
The wise old Shaman
That lies in the heart of the desert.
I heard voices of three, calling me,
Both scoffing, yes and praising me;
Fighting for my destiny
To find the truth, and only that.
Alone and scared I reach the storm.
But where is my Shaman?
For he has left me once again
In solitude,
Staring out into the world,
Beyond the heart of the desert.

    —Connie Meyers

A Dark Night

As I lay there still as night
Deep inside I hold my fright
For it is dark
I can not see
Looking around I only see black
I bite my lip to hold tears back
I want to jump up and run away
But I know that I must stay
Maybe if I fall asleep
I'll wake up and have this secret to keep
Now I start to fall asleep
But from a distance I hear a faint beep
As it gets closer the noise gets louder
I try to get up but I have no power
I start to scream and yell for help
But no one came hear my fearful yelp
The noise is closer it's next to my ear
Now my heart is full of fear
I close my eyes and hope and pray
Then they open it's a new day!

    —Kimberly Marie Sutton

Impossible Dream

    Today I need to see you! After a big
Defeat on the battleground of life, seeing
You is as if something inexplicable is
Awakening me.
    I know you are an impossible dream but...
I just want to glance at you, feel your
Mysterious eyes, and gaze from close your
Distinguished personality.
    To see you is to gain courage, and have
Hope in the future. I deeply regret the fact
That we are so opposed in our destinies.
    But...
    You've given me strength to continue
Fighting, because when I look into your eyes
It is as though an immense energy
Is pushing me towards life
    ...For that I thank you.

    —Helena Dionisio

Roses in the Garden

The red, crimson roses smelled
    delightful in the garden
The sweet aroma covered the air like a
    delicate quilted blanket
The dew on the smooth young petals
    dripped off slowly as if the morning
    was forever.
Bees buzzed by as they glanced at the
    wonderful sight of the new morning arising
The sun seemed to draw attention to these
    new bloomers; telling them to pay attention
    to their new surrounds; to remember
    every glorious detail
On the other edge of the garden enchanted
    Morning Glories are slowly and gracefully
    waking to this wondrous morning
But when dusk comes, all beauty folds
    up and awaits, for a whole new beautiful
    day in the garden.

    —Lisa Marie Smith

Stain-Glass Rose

Dew on the grass;
    sparkling jewels.
      Standing lone in the garden,
      Stain-Glass Rose.

    —Ann Neavin

"Responsibility"

The sands of time pour down on me
demanding miracles

If I am not God, why is so
much expected?

Everyone, everything is closing in
on me

Inspiration has left me
to compel all decisions myself

Insanity has taken it's place
tearing me apart like a lion does it's quarry.

—*Andrea Rugnetta*

"Walls of Black"

Dark meets the light, overpowering.
Destroying the innocence of a new day, deep thunderous grays—
Into the howling storm a spirit screams, held hostage by an
unforgiving force.
Chaos continues to invade, flooding rains begin to pour.
The winds crash, colliding, fighting — two powers at war.
Suddenly! Dead silence, thick and hallow and black —
quiet madness, the center of the storm.
The spinning walls of darkness have become the captor
Bound by torment, a mind possessed.
Confined by the enemy, a soul cries in vain —
Silent tears of pain.
Searching for illumination, grave desperation,
Within the walls of black.
Unable to elude, dancing a dance with death held tightly in
it's grasp, breathing through the pours of strength —
Shades of gray have become the past.
Deeper is the dark, within the walls of black —
It's the eye of the storm where insanity is born,
And darkness takes the light.

—*Jane Bonansinga*

Life's Debris

I awoke unto a steal gray dawn
dew left sprinkled on my lawn
chiseled out of life's debris like
sparkling jewels forgotten by thieves
Rays of sunlit gratitude erasing all
that night had spewed upon this
tranquil existence of my soul.

Without a clue I came upon this new day
afraid that I may miss the jewels of life
scattered in my way. Yet knowing
fear alone should not be allowed
to control my very existence upon this earthly ground.
So it is
that I must find my way
into this jewel filled maze
escaping some of life's debris.
To carefully choose my existence as
it revels itself to me.

—*Cindy Squeglia*

Remembering You

I see your face flash through the trees.
I hear your voice whispering in the wind.
I feel the warmth from the sun
and I imagine your arms around me.
But then I close my eyes and the sun fades away.
The clouds are dark and threatening,
as the rain begins to fall.
I blink a tear away but the emptiness
in my eyes remains.

—*Nicole DeNi*

Wind

When the wind blows I hear your cry.
I hear your voice; that special voice and
I remember when you held me tight on that cold, dark night.
You said you cared but you couldn't bare those three words.
You said I was special to you but I knew when
I looked at you,
All I heard was the wind of your voice,
That special voice.

—*Brandi Pemberton*

Eternal Peter Pan

My mind has tried to remember ... could I have misunderstood.
Did it ever really exist ... what happened to my childhood.

Living within my world alone ... while wondering what I was
about. Withdrawn so far inside myself ... a master of blocking
things out.

Learning to count on only myself ... living through my own
self-test. Was I really truly so different ... and so isolated
from the rest.

What attention I managed to get ... always seemed to take a
fight. Soon it became so unimportant ... what came my way was
just alright.

There always were my dolls ... my best friends who never spoke.
A promise I made to them ... their hearts would never be broke.

My need for self-expression ... with thoughts lost within my
mind. The times that I would dance ... are my best memories of
any kind.

Being an eternal Peter Pan ... with satisfaction showing on my
face. While raising my own two children ... my childhood
somehow took place.

—*Valerie Lemon*

Tears of Joy

Tears of joy within my heart
Did quicken the spirit within me.
Hallelujah - Hallelujah

Praise the LORD - the Almighty King
Did swell my heart with gladness within me
Hallelujah - Hallelujah

O let my ears, hear my tears of joy
For Christ the LORD has shown me.
Hallelujah - Hallelujah

Let my tears - sing with joy.
For the angel of the LORD, did come down and show me.

Hallelujah - Hallelujah.

—*Richard P. Long*

Sonnet V - Rainbow

Stationary hues ever unvarying,
directed by the steps of the sun's shafts.
The essence it is carrying
of what dazzles in all God's crafts.
A ribbon of a glistening green,
a strip of virtuous violet.
The phantom arching figurine;
misty drippings are its pilot.
Angels repose on the highest point,
not upon us to make any chart.
To impel the tincture to straighten the crumbly joint,
or to wrap securely, encompassing the poorest heart.
Nevertheless, even this, most will cruelly deny,
and relinquish Romantic's fetters going to the end to
Riche's cry.

—*Forest Mays*

"Dear Heart"

I'm sending this letter straight from my heart,
Directly to your heart.
The letter goes, dear heart.
I don't know what to do since we've been apart,
When you left, you really broke my heart.
Since you've been gone there's no sun up in the sky,
No birds sing nor do they fly.
I think about you only without you I'm so lonely.
Dear heart, let's make a brand new start.
I'm sending you this letter straight from my heart,
Please come back to me, don't tear my poor heart apart.
Since you've been gone all it does is rain,
Nothing in this world is the same.
I keep calling out your name, my poor heart is in pain.
Dear Heart, I hope your fine.
Please tell me your love will always be mine.
Cause I'll always love you until the end of time.
Please give us one more try,
My poor heart wants to die, my sore eyes just cry.

—*Lee Evans*

Cleopatra's Needle

I see you standing on every, crowded corner. The sun
disappears. I look around at the bleakness surrounding you
and think yes, this must be the place where dreams end. I can
only pray that others will begin, and that the children will
grow. I am afraid, because you dealer of death, you are the
disease through my friends veins that flows. With discouraging
ease, you pick your prey out like peas in a pod... and my God
forgive me, but I wish that I had a rod. For I would smite
you down like lightening, but with a power a hundred times more
frightening. And then, no other vultures who nest on this land
will think you so righteous... and decide that they too might
just help bring about the destruction of a once beautiful
planet. And to hell with your vanity and your immoral
insanity... for I hate that I am so weak and that they very
sight of your guns and knives makes me meek. Because you,
misguided mogul, you are the thorn... the sharpest of daggers
that has torn apart so many and so much. You desecrate
everything you touch. Purposely, you are blind. You refuse to
see that you have wronged us. Oh, how I wish that I were
strong enough to syphon the poison from Cleopatra's needle.

—*Renea A. Thompson*

In Spite Of

Obstacles are mounting against me everyday,
Distress never fails to come my way;
Temptations seek to lead me astray,
But I proceed, in spite of.

The weights of life seem to always say,
"Oh no, you won't succeed, no way!"
Yet determined to keep trying come what may,
I gain a little mileage, in spite of.

Weary, weak, wounded and sad, I lay,
Down and out in the most awesome way;
Wondering if I can make it through today,
Somehow I see the sunset, in spite of.

Pretending to be vibrant and gay,
Allowing my saviour to help me along the way;
Sheltering and cushioning the bumps as I obey,
I arise to face tomorrow, in spite of.

—*Genevia Nicholas Jones*

Now and Forever, "I Do"

What do you see when you're looking at me?
Do I look as happy as I can be?
It's due to an angel who has stolen my heart.
Yes, you my darling, for I hope we shall never part.
You bring me hope, joy, laughter, love and a smile.
With all this and more, you make my life worthwhile.
You were created from rainbows and sunshine.
You're a twenty-four karat treasure who will always be mine.
I want to make you happy with everything I do,
Because all the love in my heart belongs to you.
What do I see when I'm looking at you?
A wonderful man I love, now and forever, "I Do."

—*Debra J. Fleishman*

The Eternal River

(In memory of River Phoenix)
Do not stand by his grave and weep.
River is not there. He does not sleep.
He is a thousand winds that blow;
A diamond glistening on new fallen snow.
He is the sunlight on ripened grain
And the sweet melody of gentle autumn rain.
When one awakens in the morning stillness
He is the soft uplifting rush
Of beautiful birds in circling flight.
He is the soft shimmer
Of moonlight on the ocean at night.
He is the distant sound of a lively guitar.
Do not stand here and cry.
River is free now. His spirit eternally flows.

—*Susan Scott*

If I Africa Ruled the World

You insist to hold my Brothers and Sisters back
Do you think if I Africa ruled the World
Africa would treat you as such
For your recompense
It would be a just reward!!
But my heart know hurt
I am tired of it
You would suffer at your own hand first
Before I Africa would hurt!
If I Africa ruled the world.
For Vengeance belongs to "Our Heavenly Father"
And His requirements measures fare!
I know of the degradation
What I have been thru
No one else should suffer
Such a hapless fate!!
For I Africa am a mixture of all
A Smelting Pot!
A Potpourri Universe!

—*D'Aria Fakankun*

Words

I used to understand every word a swallow sang or a cricket
chirped. I used to understand the buzzing of the bees and
the language of all of the animals large and small, but, now
that I've entered the human language all is forgotten. Oh
yes, I still hear the creatures, but it's not the same. All
they are now is a sweet soft sound billowing on the breeze
that I once also understood, but now I'm in a world where
the harsh words, instead of the soft, live. I wish I could
go back to the language of nature's music and the billowing
of the trees, but I know now that I cannot go back to the
sweet sound of my mother's voice.

—*Kimberly N. Branham*

Colors

And what of this rainbow that colors the skies,
Does it remind us of our colorful lives?
A symbol of promise from the one up above
A reminder of eternal and unbiased love.
And the crystal that bounces a reflection
of colorful schemes, to unveil a dancing arena
from the light source that beams,
makes one wonder in awe,
that life's simplest of rules,
to not take for granted the rarest of jewels.
The most precious of priceless gems not found in stone,
but to find one's colors in each his own,
for the world was not made black or white, you see,
but the Grand plan was created with variety,
Remember that people are all colors too,
they laugh and cry and feel as we do,
and those colors can change like the waves of the ocean,
just like the colors that define our emotion.
And so each color speaks a language its own
it has no color if it stands alone.......

    —Eve Margaret

Grandma

I wonder what she's thinking
Does she know what she says
Or is it all without thought
Her eyes look sad and empty
She use to be full of happiness
What happened?
Did she loose all hope for life
Or is her mind just not like it use to be
The old days seem new and the new seems old
What is she thinking?
She seems to think she's all alone.
What can I say?
She's always been the one I talked to
Lord, what can I do?
Grandma is very special to all of us
Does she know?

    —Patricia Woods

Daybreak

Each day is filled with new hopes, John.
Don't bring to it fears from the past.
Give thanks for each new sparkling dawn.

Give thanks for each new sparkling dawn.
Enjoy the sun's bright morning glow.
The gentle movement of the fawn.

The gentle movement of the fawn,
As she sips cold water from the stream.
Then looks both ways and travels on.

Then looks both ways and travels on,
Along forest cool, green footpath trods.
Getting ever closer to the pond.

Getting ever closer to the pond,
Shed all your cares and peace will come.
Each day is filled with new hopes, John.

    —Lila Peeters

Last Breath

From the bottom of their stems,
 I pulled the daffodils gently
   from the fertile earth.

   Arranged in a vase,
   they brightened my room
   with their last breath.

    —Alison Epker

Just A Rag Muffin

I'm just a rag muffin all alone and four children to be grown.
Dreaming dreams of fantasy flights.
Wishing upon the first star I see tonight.
"Oh bright star of my hometown is there a fairy godmother to be
   found?"
Why does it have to be rich or poor and always wanting more?
Fairy godmother what does my life have in store?
Dreaming dreams of fairies and pixies in flight.
I wish I may I wish I might, I wish I could take a fantasy flight.
In a white flowing gown with diamonds streaming down,
No dresses like this in my home town.
Earrings of gold with glimmer untold.
Crown of rubies, diamonds and pearls.
So much beauty, it would please most any girl.
This is my dream of fantasy land.
But no fairy godmother to hold my hand.
So sweet is the dreams of a starlit night,
Of fantasies coming true by day or by night.
No fantasy flight to be found.
It's back I go to my home town.

    — Rosetta H. Linger

Cowboy From The Bronx

   He's got sandy hair and steel blue eyes and
Dressed in black from head to toe and his main
Love is a cowboy show. He's a cowboy from the bronx.
He stands tall and straight and lean
And mean and he sure is a loving machine.
He's a cowboy from the bronx.
He loves rattle snake boots and big stetson hats
And he's sure hell in any spat.
He's a cowboy from the bronx.
He brought a guitar and learned to play,
He practiced hard night and day.
He's a cowboy from the bronx.
It took 10 years to become a star
That Bronx Cowboy and his guitar,
So when you go to a cowboy show and you see a man
In black from head to toe you can bet it's
A cowboy from the bronx.

    —Dewey Nixon

Summer Heat/Memories

Sitting barefoot on the big front porch,
dressed in hand me down shorts, a hot July breeze blows
more hot humid weather is expected the radio blares
Dad say's he's moving to Alaska, scared we will go far away
my thoughts are broken, with a tall glass of
mom's homemade lemonade, as fried chicken odors
drift from the kitchen, mingling with sweet smells of honeysuckle and
roses growing wild in the lane,
the mulberry tree drips with lush ripe fruit
eating until mouth and teeth are a deep purple,
the heat becomes more and more oppressive,
nearby a small river flows, enticing to the soul,
quickly sliding down the muddy bank, cool swirling waters circle my
   feet,
slowly heat releases from my body, flows away
now I'm ready for another hot July summer day.

    —Joan S. Parker

The Sky

I can see the world.
I can see Asia, Europe, Africa, too.
I can see the clouds all puffed in cotton.
I can see airplanes flying in the sky.
I can see birds flying freely.
I can see leaves floating in the air.

    —Emily R. Rogstad

Fragile Flower

Fragile flower blowing gently in the soft breeze
drinking in the sunshine of life;
such a short time ago, you were a tiny seed
placed in the earth by loving hands.

From a sprout, you had become a thing of beauty
touching our lives with your being.
Too soon, the lovely petals fell upon the ground,
wrenched from our grasp by wayward winds.

We have searched to find a trace, but you must return
to the garden of memory.
In the mind we carry a shadowy image,
a kaleidoscope of color

of a delicate blossom that faded too soon,
leaving all a hunger for Spring.
To sustain you, our tears will become as the dew
that will greet each fresh new morning.

—*Ruth Warner*

Freedom

As the petals of a flower fall and slowly
dwindle away, so does the tears and pain
you once felt so deeply in your heart.
Realizing that you can live without the hurt and
without the guilt is not only freedom from your
soul, but freedom from the burden you felt
by him. You didn't leave his side until this
final day when your soul came back to life
showing you better things to see, and all the
darkness turned to light as you started fighting
back. When you wiped away the final tear
exclusively his, when you erased all the hurt, and
drowned all the pain. He says he loves you, but
his love is equal to hate and you're so tired of
hate that you don't even hate him for all he
has done, but you feel sorry that a soul is so
sad that it hurts other people including itself,
but this is no longer your life for you have
walked away. That is freedom, that is love.

—*Donella Burton*

A Soldier Comes to Rest

On the battle filed at Waterloo a soldier lies wounded and
dying. Beside him lies his wounded faithful, loyal companion.
Spared from death for yet a while, the man received a wooden
leg and a pension. His friend received a broken leg and was
blinded in one eye. They shared each others company till death
caused them to part. But one remained to guard his masters
relics no one could tear them apart. He stood guard over his
masters possession, perhaps awaiting his return. Until the day
he passes away, never to return. With some, loyalty and
friendship is all too soon forgotten. But for this master and
his dog they'll not soon be forgotten. For someone long ago so
saw it fitting to erect a monument worth keeping. There sits
the loyal companion with his master's relics by his side,
although a broken leg and blinded. He stood faithfully by. He
waited and he waited for his master to return. Then as life
would have it, he too lied down to die. Faithfully he still
guarded his masters possessions by his side. Waterloo the
battle field where soldiers came to rest...where loyalty and
friendship was at it's very best.

—*Betty Joe Luther*

Music - Nature

Paganini's first violin concerto,
dynamically insane -
toward unreachable heights
into unthinkable dimensions
to such grandeur
spreading an unworldly feeling
of weightlessness.

Sparrows perched on clotheslines
remind me of a music sheet.
Silhouettes of moving fingers on a keyboard
like spiders climbing a birch, to the rhythm.
Rain pounding on rooftops
sounds like jungle drums.

Through darkness, a tigers eye
reflects in the brass
of a french horn, whose laments
are carried by the echo
toward the plains -
until it subsides -.

—*Lisa Wild*

Ah Peace

All of life is new to me
Each day I wake expectantly
Eager for a time of peace.

From the depths of spiritual need
Comes the knowledge my soul is freed.
For love of God, for faith and hope,
Give me the tools necessary to cope.

Humbly I kneel to say a prayer
Knowing my life is in God's care.
He reached down and fashioned the clay
That became the person I am today.

So all of us in the brave new world,
Into which, by God we have been hurled.
Must seek our service, become a giver not a taker,
As we seek a relationship with our Maker.

And at the close of life's long day
We must feel relieved when we can say...
I sought to fulfill God's plan for me,
And now can close my eyes expectantly.

Ah peace.

—*Patti Clifford Stewart*

One to a Vine

A family is a vine that keeps on growing
Each generation blossoms like a rose
Parents are the roots that keep it flowing
But tender loving care's what makes it grow

The busy life I live today demands a lot of time
So many different things to do I could seldom ever find
The chance to call Mom and Dad although I knew I should
Then comes the day I cry and say oh how I wish I could

Spend some time with the father who gave me life on earth
Spend some time with the mother who gave me birth
To let them know I really cared I'd surely find the time
For they only come one to a vine

—*Mary Ruth Osburn*

Mercy Center

Peace and tranquility I find
Each time
I arrive.

The silence is deafening
Yet soothing
It feeds my empty heart.

Gentle waves break on the shore-
Rippling sounds;
Sea gulls feed-
Crickets chirp;
The wonder of it all.

Everything so blue and brown;
Muted colors adding to the tone of the day.

Peace and tranquility fill the depths of my soul.
—*A. Zichichi*

The Crystalline Art

Tiny drops of crystals sparkle in the light,
    each with a message of endless flight.
What once was whole, significant and strong,
    now shattered obliquely, its soulful song.

The mind babbles, the body bleeds,
    the spirit ignores its deepest needs.
I want to live; I yearn to die.
    Peace is within reach as in anguish I cry.

The sharp shards of brokenness impale upon the heart.
    People sharing the space of the crystalline art.
Gather up the pieces and throw them in the fire.
    Bring beauty out of madness for chaos does inspire.

No one can own the crystalline art,
    for the beauty within is held in every heart.
We cannot choose whose life will reflect or destroy,
    the gift of pure light of God's endless joy.
—*Linda S. Ripley*

On a Blue Note

Real boogie blues piano — once heard, never forgotten.
Echoes of rent party poverty and smoky dives,
The blues cry out.

Mood swings from ecstatic joy to melancholy,
Driving 8-beats or slow roll, triplets and tremolos,
But always swinging.

The bass notes rumble—an express train
Urging the right hand to greater heights,
Excitement building to a fevered pitch.

Albert Ammons, Meade "Lux" Lewis, Pete Johnson
and others by the score,
Gone now, still their music evermore.

From Texas through Chicago, K.C. and on to New York fame,
Yet almost died as quickly as it came,
Its strength and beauty killed by commercialism's bottom line.

The flame is still alive in the hearts of a few,
Their aging fingers passing on to youth
The timeless story of the blues.
—*A. W. McKnight*

"Ray" of Sunshine

He said to me, "I don't care if nobody
Else likes you, I do!"
What does it matter how old he was
Or who he was, he's gone now
Gone like the wind, death took him
Oh why did I imagine he'd live forever?
He surprised even himself to die so sudden
My friend's gone now and I really miss him.
His face may have been wrinkled by age
But it never stopped him from being
A real person and caring for everyone
Each and every last day of his life
All I know is he gave me a "Ray" of hope
When I had none, gave me the strength
To carry on and care for others as he's
Done.
—*Karen Lindke*

"Inspirations"

Come to me when I'm searching, not knowing where I want to be
Enlighten darkened passages of many dreams longing to set free

    Satisfying inclinations, in every aspect of daily life
Inspiring aspirations or deploring trials of grief and strife

    Come to me in visions, seen only when one is in love
    A world of imagination, freely soaring with wings of a dove

Calming down feelings of passion that burn like the flame of a fire
    Come to me softly, while my heart burns with this desire

Inspirations bring an insight, even though they say love is blind
A glimpse of heaven as we seek shelter, looking for comfort in our mind

Come to me when the soul is searching for the freedom to an escape

    Expressing feelings within my heart—
        With "Inspirations" dealt by fate.
—*Eva L. Quiroz*

Shadows of Dark Memories

Silence and depression are the constant companions,
escorted by tears in the dark and restless nights.
For years he tried to feel compassion,
to keep the sorrow out of sight.
Still walks the borders of his land,
frightened by the shadows behind those trees.
Does the low-cral with the slightest sound and tightens up his
shooting hand,
what has happened so long ago still makes his forehead sweat
and his body freeze,
all in the same time with tears in his eyes, and has nowhere to run,
when finally he returns to me, and then holds me tight,
for I know what so long ago, he has done,
and understand this forever ongoing torture of a gruesome site,
that haunts his memory stubbornly to do him harm,
with pictures of shadows coming back from 'Nam.
—*Silvana E. Pellegrini*

Tears

If someone cries, you comfort them.
If someone dies, you mourn them.
If you see tears, you wonder why
they are falling.
If you hear tears, you wonder if
they are calling.
When you see a tear fall or hear a
tear call, there is someone out there
who needs you.
—*Kelly Gilby*

Bye Mom

Mom I will miss you much
Especially miss how you look and touch...
Those loving arms that help me get through
In good times, bad, old and new...
The special way you helped us all
No matter if we were rich, poor, short or tall...
That special smile of love
Is gone with God now on a dove...
You made people happy here on earth
Now it's time to do so in heaven it's worth
I must let you go now so I can
Learn to live my life again...
You done everything here on earth
You made many people happy since your birth...
Even though you're gone
My love for you will go on and on....

"Love you Mom"
—*Yvonne Dufek-Hogue Welborn*

Thou Art Perfect

Thou art perfect Lord!
Even so, you didn't want to die.
God had it planned and it would happen by and by.
You walked this land for such a short while.
How sad that you were cursed and brought to trial.
You were judged and sentenced to die.
Not a word you uttered, not even a sigh.
Guilty of bringing the world perfect
love that would save mankind,
a love that even now some won't find.
Thou art perfect Lord, you let them nail
you to a tree and with outstretched
arms you seemed to plea, "Come unto me,
I died for thee, come unto me and I will save thee.
If you reject me, I don't cry for me, I cry for thee."
Crucified, buried and resurrected so that
we might have eternal life.
Only Jesus could love us so much that He would make such a
sacrifice. Truly, thou art perfect, Lord.
—*Jane Casselman*

Watch and Pray

Stand on duty, be alert.
Even though it is peace time, the enemy lurks.

He comes to sabotage, to steal and devour.
Do not be passive, this is the hour.

Shake yourself out of your lethargy.
The church of Jesus Christ is called, to affect society.

So watch and pray, everyday.
Laugh at temptation, as it comes your way.

Warn all the people, of the destruction to come.
If you do not do it, required is your blood.

We are in spiritual warfare. The times drawing short.
Rip someone from hells fire, before they are lost.

Christians are always to pray and faint not.
The spirit is willing. The flesh will just not.

The Lord is the victor. The Captain of the Host.
If He is your Savior, then you have hope.

Live like your expecting, Jesus once more.
Watch - Pray - Be ready - and you will win the war.
—*Mary Ann Lefebvre*

The Bridge Builder

An old man going a lone highway. Came in the
evening cold and gray to a chasm vast and deep and wide.
The old man crossed in the twilight dim,
The sullen stream had no fears for him,
But he stopped when safe on the other side
And built a bridge to span the tide

"Old man," said a fellow pilgrim near,
"You are wasting your strength with building here
Your journey will end with the ending day,
You never again will pass this way,
You've crossed the chasm deep and wide,
Why build you this bridge at evening tide?"

The builder lifted his old grayly head,
"Good friend, in the path I have come," he said
"There followeth after me today
A youth whose feet must pass this way.
This chasm which has been as naught to me
To that fair-haired youth might a pitfall bell,
He too, must cross in the twilight dim,
Good friend, I am building the bridge for him."
—*Daniel Landgrebe*

"Every Where There Are Crimes"

Crimes today are here to stay,
Every where there are crimes,
one day you are sure to pay,
Either by sickness sentence or a fine.

Many do carry their guns for sure,
Break open innocent people's door,
They rob them of all their wealth,
Also sometimes destroy their health.

They sell drugs to the helpless ones,
Make them become addicted to it,
Now all their bright futures are gone,
Just because they once used it.

They now teach the young ones too,
To involve of what they do,
Kids now carry many guns to school,
Which is against our golden rule.

God has created all as human beings,
He is always with us for He is unseen,
We must rid of crime and have true love,
The good you do will be blessed from above.
—*Bissoondat Ram*

Uncle Keys

Every year squirrel season comes around;
Every year I think back on Uncle Keys;
Sitting on a fallen tree of six years
Smoking a Captain Black pipe—waiting for squirrels
Wandering branched by-ways for the acorn.
Restless, I want to walk, climb hills, jump creeks
But I sit, quietly, watching flickering leaves
Waving, then faltering, in the mid-morning sunlight.
No squirrels for hollows east and west,
No barks, just crackling of crunched tobacco flaming orange
And we sat on that rotting hickory log
Uncle Keys gazing skyward, anticipating movement.
I couldn't help notice every wrinkle and loose stitch
In his tan canvas guard uniform from the prison;
His bridle-leather hand taps my knee then points.
"Squirrel season starts in August, Uncle Keys"
—*Mark Heffington*

In My World....

In my world it is dark,
Everyone has a flashlight but me.
I sit alone in a corner, silent.
Every once in a while I see a glimmer of light.
It never lasts.
In my world no one is serious,
When I go to school in my world,
I am a good student, I work hard.
I stand with my friends and talk,
No one listens.
I am lost in my world.
Lost in my own seriousness,
And everyone else's joke.

—*Christina M. Plugge*

Hidden Images

The nations President would be in town for awhile
Everyone was out for a glimpse of his smile
Friendly shouts of welcome resounded through the crowds
Some reached out to touch him as he moved about

A motorcade parade through downtown was in the plan
Hidden images were poised where they were to stand
Onward they rode through high rise monuments of concrete
Open windows displayed images above the street

An open plaza exposed his gentle smile to the sun
But hidden images would be waiting for him with a gun
An unexpected pop frightened pigeons from their peaceful perch
And, for a second or two, life stood still here on earth

His ears became numb with the echoed sounds of the sea
And with the laughter of his children he might no longer see
One final thundering blast shattered away his dreams
The joyful cheers turned to frantic screams

His car rushed away in sudden despair
The nation honorably returned him to Gods care
A hurried remedy was injected into the nations soul
And hidden images have buried the truth yet untold

—*Jaime J. Garza*

Last Kiss

Breaking up with you wasn't easy,
every time I think about it I feel queasy.
I know I'll never hold or kiss you again, I feel so empty
because we both once loved each other.
What you said the other day, makes me wish all of our fights
away, the words you said hurt so bad, "you only love me as a
friend, to get on with my life like you."
Its easier said then done, when I thought of us as one.
I guess its true you don't love me like I love you.
I never thought it would be like this, but our last kiss told
me so, I realize now it's time to let go.
So until we are together again, that one last kiss, the last
one I'll see until a special day greets us with the same
kiss, that left me in complete bliss...

—*SunShine Haines*

A Silent Cry

When someone cries a silent cry, no one can hear.
Even if someone is near, they still cannot hear.
For the cry comes from within the heart.
Only the heart knows when it is troubled.
A silent cry is not like a loud cry sharpening to the ears.
A silent cry only stabs and slices the heart.
When the cry has pierced the heart enough,
It then seeps through the bloody wounds.
Now that the cry is free, the ears can hear.

—*Kejar L. Butler*

The Lone Swan of Backwater Bay: A Song of Survival

Oh lone swan, safely anchored behind the swampy growth,
Apart from dowdy ducks who squatly circle in lock step,
Who blindly round by rote the muddy backwaters of the bay.

Oh snowy vision, so singular and serene,
As you preen each pristine feather with "Swan Lake" balletic sweeps.
The outer layer of stout, mint-green swamp grass filters out
    the garter snakes and dining needles,
The inner layer of lanky blond reeds makes sure the mallards
    don't gang up on you.
Cornered in the brackish backwater, you raise your bill with
    noble modesty,
Offering your bay-lover two gifts, both earthly and divine:
A soaring, arched garden hose neck and sculpted dreamboat bottom.
Surely nature could never warble a swan song to your delicate finesse,
Knowing how a being of fragile beauty is worth coddling forever.

—*Barbara Hantman*

"Christmas Love Lights"

Where! Oh where can the lights of love be found.
Everywhere! Just look around.
In the warm fires glow and in the star in the sky.
Where! oh where can the lights of love be found.
Everywhere just look around.
In the eyes of the young,
And in the hearts of the old.
There is no brighter light, than the light in the eyes
    of one in love.
There is no greater love more sincere,
    than in the one in love,
    when the other one is near.
Where oh! where can the lights of love be found.
Every where! Just look around.
    "Just look around"

—*Nina Nichols*

"Reflection"

Antique mirrors that came to pass
existing as mirror images, yet distorted,
unmatched,
Nothing alike, yet so the same...
Antique mirrors that came to pass.

Fate aligned them one crisp fall day,
with all their imperfections, come what may
Mirror images who were quite attracted-
When faced to each other caused a negative
    reaction!

The moral of the story is plain to see!
Never like someone who's the same as "me"....
Mirror images are quite unhealthy
Naked in the mirror, no one likes to see
the images that is really, truly "me"!!

—*Mihira King*

Thanksgiving

Truly, our souls wait upon God: From him come our
expectations. 'Make a joyful sound unto the lord, all
you lands. Serve the lord with gladness: approach before
his presence with singing'

Know you that the Lord, he is God: It was he that
created us, not we ourselves; we're his people, the lambs
of his of field. Enter at his gates with Thanksgiving and
his mansions with praise; be thankful unto him and bless his name

We have much to be thankful for- Not just our possessions
but also our families, friends, (including the ones with tails
and coats) homes, food, and many other things, 'for the lord
is good; and this truth endureth to all generations.'

—*John A. Long*

Little Miss Priss

She came on a winters morn
Eyes shining and tail swishing
A hunger that grew day by day
Hiding from danger when it grew near.
Climbing up and down pant legs
Knowing that trouble was at hand.
Chasing a ghost of a thing
When the whim was just rite.
Talking in a whisper of a voice
Using her sand paper tongue
To lick your finger sleeping in a sunny spot
Using the warmth of a cuddle
Not staying long enough to form an attachment
A pitter patter of the heart
Showing that you care in your own little way
Softening the hardest of hearts with your smile
Growing each day counting time
Putting a smile on faces so dear.
Hearts and lace tell you the thing.

—*Michelina Gahagan*

My Son

He's just a child but oh the wonder in his
eyes there is no way he can disguise the
love that's shining there, with all the world
to share, he is my son

He's now a lad full of adventure, spirit
free to ask, with curiosity. Why are the
stars so high? How does rain come from the
sky? He is my son.

He's a young man, who's facing all the
things ahead using his heart, but with no
dread full of emotion, love to give. He
has to share this just to live. He is my son.

He is a man. With all the problems life
can bring. I hear him still with songs to
sing. The faith within his soul will keep
him safe and whole. He is my son

Now he's a dad. He knows the joy a child
can bring just teaching them what songs to
sing and now sharing his life beside a
beautiful wife. He'll always be my son.

—*Ann Richards*

Faces

I watched as the cozy, liquid warmth of my internal snugness
faded to be replaced with sudden, bursting light. I watched
as faces sharpened into view and lips formed words alien,
without meaning. I watched as colors manifested into hues of
spectrum loveliness. I watched as the world around me grew
smaller and I grew taller. I watched as grey clouds of war
darkened the horizon. I watched as faces became etched with
lines of sorrow for fallen comrades. I watched as the one face
that was my everything brightened as it said, "I do." I
watched as new, little faces, wrinkled and red, emerged into my
world. I watched as faces of my own glowed with pride when
they witnessed new faces of theirs enter life. I watched as
faces around me grew stoic with furrows of age and wisdom. And
now, as the light grows dim and starts to sink below the
horizon, I watch as faces of my loved ones say, "Don't go.
Stay." But such cannot be. I have seen all the faces dear to
me save one. And that face I shall see when I travel over the
horizon and follow the sun.

—*David D. Smith*

Magic Eyes

There's magic in those
eyes, you mesmerize.

Forever dawn to the
unknown, a mystery zone.

Caught up in a spell, were images dwell.

Under the cloak of night,
We found delight,
Staring into each other's eyes.

Lost in desire, an all consuming fire,

Those magic eyes
Blind, to everyone else.

Finding my place among
the human race, at last.
Staring deep into those
eyes, my heart was mesmerize.

Caught up in the magic;
bound up in the spell
here's were I long to
dwell, forever, my love.
In those magic eyes.

—*Felix M. Healey*

What A Smile Can Do....

A child walking by as you pass down the street, looks up at your
face filled with disgrace, but you smile and he returns the
favor. Not thinking you did anything at all but-That's What
A Smile Can Do.

A young boy standing on the corner trying to make ends meat to
put something on his feet. You wonder why that's the route
he's taking, but you look at him and smile. Not knowing you
just made him feel worthwhile. That's What A Smile Can Do.

A mother with her three hungry children, not knowing today
what they might eat and you notice they have almost nothing on
their feet. Soles on their shoes are almost completely gone.
As you come by she says "Hi, can you give me something so my
children and I can eat." You give her your last. She smiles,
you smile. Oh, my What A Smile Can Do.

So, next time someone is frowning say to them "Hey, smile!"
and return the favor. Cause, that's What A Smile Can Do.

—*Shawn Lamberson*

Withered Flower

Withered beauty,
Falling prey to time and elements,
Resisting the majesty of the burning sun;
But soon must fall,
From the branch to see the earth,
And slowly turn into dust,

Once did she bloom with beauty,
Beholden to the eyes of men,
But she already served her purpose,
Gone even the bees and butterflies;
Flapping their wings merrily!

Her once dominant beauty gone,
Yet remain in my memory.
In my heart, I know
Spring will come again next year.
There, I hope to see,
There, I hope to be?

—*Ramon G. Palanca*

Accomplishments

Some find them in riches, some find them in
fame. Others may find them in a job or in a
good name.
We work so hard to achieve such a thing,
that eventually we forget why we were ever
created a being.
From the wombs to the graves, "accomplishments"
"accomplishments" done day by day soon turns us
all into hard working slaves.
Please don't get me wrong I am not at all
against the being, it's just that at times I find
it so hard to accomplish such said thing.
Some may be big or others small, but, one
thing for sure we will eventually accomplish
them all.

—*William L. Zieche*

Mount Up with the Eagles

The eagle soars on greatness of wing,
Far above the mountain scene.
Spreading wings high above,
Flying with the wind, high over the earth below,
Into the sunsets after glow.
Over the wilderness with no distress,
Gathering food to take to their nest.
Feeding their young until strength they gain,
So that they can spread their wings.
Flying out to spaces far beyond,
Strong and mighty flying so high,
Soaring far away into the sky.
Mighty is the eagle as God meant them to be,
Flying, soaring, gliding to give Him the glory.
Like the mighty eagle each of us can be,
Mounting up with the wings of eagles,
We shall run and not be weary,
We shall walk and not faint.
As we serve God here below,
Like the mighty eagle, one day we shall fly to worlds unknown.

—*Gene Adams*

"The Strongbox"

Build for your self a strong box
Fashion each part with care.
When it's strong as your hand can make it,
Put all your troubles there
Hide there all thoughts of your failures
And each bitter cup that you quaff
Lock all your heart aches with-in it
Then sit on the lid, and laugh
Tell no one else its contents.
When you've dropped in your care and your worry
Keep them forever there
Hide them from sight so completely,
That the world will never know half
Fasten the strong box securely,
Then sit on the lid and laugh

—*Ruth McGhee*

Changes

The flower fades away, gently changing into shades of gray.
Each petal drifts softly to the ground.
Touching the earth not making a sound.
Dew falls from the withering leaves like tears;
splattering to the ground into a thousand mirrors.
Everything changes. Everything dies.
Even though we stand here. Right before our eyes.

—*Sharon Rose Goossen*

Children

Mothers, watch your children.
Fathers, cautiously beware.
War has been declared upon us,
   I see it everywhere.

Drugs, sex, and alcohol have become
part of a disease.
If they don't satisfy you well,
Here's a gun if you please.

This raging plague grows continuous.
So please don't turn away,
It is raping us of all we love,
Maybe even your child today.

We've said too long,
And used the line, "It's only just a phase".
We've closed our eyes, and our ears,
And our hearts - in many ways.

We've got to save our future, for generations
yet to come.
Because if we don't start doing something
"Now" — our hopes are next to none.

—*Mary Field*

The Good Times

When I remember the good times, the laughter in the air, the
feeling of love to know you are with someone is to share. When I
remember the good times, the happiness, the feeling of joy to
know someone cares in your time of helplessness. When I remember
the good times, the patience, the feeling of devotion to know one
day, he will be gone is not something you can sense. Now I only
have the good times of love, happiness, and patience to know he
is no longer there. Our times have now been divided by a single
fence. When I remember the good times, I remember a man whom
everyone loved and liked, a man who was dear to my heart, my
grandfather, Chester A. Smith, Jr.

—*Christina DeCesare*

Nature's Rhyme

The rain drips, drops, pitter, patters like a thousand tiny
feet upon the shingled roofs. The slish slash upon the windows
make a certain rhyme which makes you sleepy eyed. The
quietness explodes as the thunder shatters the rhyme of the
rain. As a flash of yellow light illuminates the sky it cracks
the gentle blue in two! But as the breeze slowly picks up, the
sun peeks up above its umbrella of clouds and resembles a
warrior as it fights the storm away with his bow and arrows of
brilliant rays of fire. He is not afraid, he is the king of the
sky as the lion is the king of the jungle. He shines on the
landscape below, the bubbling rivers, the white frosted waves
which ride on the sea, the quiet ponds with rings of activity
below which surface to the top, the wolves' ancient cries, the
bird's morning lullabies, the crackle of life on the ground of
the wooded forest. As night approaches gently covering the
landscape like a blanket on a baby, the world says good night.
As the sun departs the daylight's life is silent, an the
creatures of the night now take their part in nature's cycle.
When another day begins, the sun lifts the blanket and the
cycle begins once again!

—*Daphne Collazo*

Snow

Pretty white flakes soon cover the ground,
Hindering my ability to get around,
I wish it would fall where not in the way,
Perhaps on my neighbors or even Bombay,
One thing I've noticed that seems very plain,
No matter how much you don't shovel the rain.

—*Bruce James Winton*

Countryside

Lonesome winding road through hills and hollows,
Fence posts, towering silos, green pastures seem to follow,
Endless rows of corn and grain,
Sweet fragrance after a warm summer rain,
Screech of a hoot owl; piercing crow of the old rooster at the
break of day,
Ducks drift lazily on the pond, grazing horses and long-leg
colts leap and play,
Families gather on porches, enjoying the evening breeze,
Clusters of daisies and buttercups, orchards of apple trees,
Junebugs, crickets, and bullfrogs serenade in rhythmic sound,
Chugging tractor toils acres of ground,
Jamborees, county fairs, and hayrides,
Make up the many wonders of the countryside

—*Karon F. McGrew*

Reliving Memories

The times we made up after all our
Fights; you held me through the
Sleepless nights
Long walks along the beach in hand;
I thought you were the only man
Giving me hope; leading the way
Bringing the sun on a rainy day
Romantic evenings by the fire; giving
In to our desires
Showing me dreams were reality; love and
Sensuality
Secrets shared from within our hearts; I
Can't stand us being apart
Remembering a past so far gone, how can
I think of moving on?
My love ending in defeat; reliving
Memories so bittersweet:

—*Cynthia Thomas*

Oh Honey...

Oh honey how you stir my desire,
Fill me up with a burning fire.
Oh honey what you do to me,
Oh how my body hungers for thee.
With yearning passion I come to you,
Your touch is so through and through.
You touch my skin in exotic places,
My heart & soul soar as it races.
My body reaches out towards yours and we become one,
Lost in you, never wanting undone.
Your eyes are pools of depth and light,
Reflecting our love in the night.
And as I look up into your beautiful face
  with wanting fulfilled,
My racing heart is also stilled.
Neither one wanting to part,
We fall asleep heart to heart.

—*Susan M. Kluesner*

Lonely Eyes

A boy once needed compassion,
He peered through lonely eyes.
And with a smile, a laugh, or two,
He tried to be disguised.

But when you fall in love like I,
You see beyond the face.
I dug more deeply in his heart,
And filled the empty space.

—*Maureen Tarascio*

"Free"

Free are the air you breath
Free are the wind you feel on your face
Free are the smiles of loves for
You my love, for eternity.

—*Elaine Wan G. Chin*

Untitled

Winter has finally come,
filled with candies and chocolate delight
The red hot fire burns endlessly,
as you gaze at the wonderful sights.

A shiny, fiery-red present,
sits motionless under a tree.
Your nose catches a cinnamon scent.
Eyes filled with a feverish glee.

White, crisp, gleaming snow,
is reflected off the radiant sky.
Cuddle with your love, you know
the snow has a fierce, nippy bite.

The cold, crisp, pine scented air,
is already starting to go.
I start to go into desperate despair,
to try to saver the winter time glow.

—*Staci Atchison*

Untitled

Leaves in full color
Fiery-Red, Hot-Orange and Gold
Filling the purple sky landscape

A chilling wind blows, and they scatter from their branches
One stray leaf lingers behind and dancers slowly, trickling down
So too falls a life,
A life of sadness, silence, unfulfilled moments, overpowered,
closed-in.

Like the leaf,
a memory lingers,

Drifting in the cold open air,
staggering to the end,
Caught by gentle hands and fingers,
Touching the heart.

—*Elizabeth Ann Copeland*

The Silence of a Flower

There is no wisdom greater than the silence of a
flower. It opens up its arms without a conscious
thought of pain. There is no sigh of regret. There is no
quest for guilt. It is like a bird, but without the flame
of freedom. A bird knows well how clean the air can
be. It is a pure reflection of the face of God. It is
a highway to the mind of the Creator, a world of
beams and balm and blasts of light. No dark spears
of hate are there. No creeping, groping claws can rip
the heart out of a cloud. Every eye is fit for this pasture
of blue. Every mind is vast and gleaming like a setting
sun; it is clear like water, a deep and golden
sea of fire, teeming with life as wild as thunder.
No dolphin weeps that it must rise into the night
for one more breath of life. No star can ever refuse
to shine for apostles of the moon. All that is or will
forever be are disciples in a warm and wondrous maze.
It is a contract all must make to endure the snow
and rain and heat, each a destined warrior of the
day, racing through the years in a kaleidoscope of dreams.

—*Jerry Jamar*

Lovely Butterfly

Lovely butterfly, you look fantastic everyday
flying around in the garden without a word to say
you are colorful and bright
lovely butterfly, you bring joy to my eyesight.

One you was just a caterpillar pinching on the leaves of a tree
soon you disappeared and hid away from me
spinning around in a weird chrysalis, changing your features
now you are not one of those destructive little creatures.

You're a lovely butterfly and I adore you for what you are
now you have wings to fly so far.
You're as colorful as can be
admiring the flowers and never stopping to bother me.

Lovely butterfly cruising in serenity
you don't even pinch, bite, scratch, nor even bark at me.
Now you are harmless and free
you have nature's award for your beauty.

Lovely butterfly, you are such an attractive sight.
Posing on the flowers in the daylight.
And I can tell by the way you hold those wings, my friend
you will fly gracefully until your very end.

—*Ozella Smith*

The Heat of the Flame

Hot tears fell to my cheeks, blinking them away till I could
focus,... I saw that I was alone. Sitting all alone in a
room lit only by the candles that were on the table across
from me. I opened my eyes to look into a flame that danced
so strangely, my eyes were transfixed upon it.
I saw nothing else, could hear nothing else, what's more I
didn't want to hear or see anything but that which was
there. The one main light with a background of six or eight
others. I watched the spark as though seemingly waiting for
something....
When I finally shook off the trance-like feeling, my tears
were long gone, dried and disappeared along with the reasons
that had caused them to flow. If ever a human had been
given the chance to become an object for a moment, I did at
that time. I felt the heat of the flame, I knew and held
the colors in it and understood the flickering dance it
performed. I was that flame! I knew it's world, smaller yet
warmer than my own. I stood up, stepped into the flame,
turned...and blew out my life.
I flickered and then awoke.

—*Mary Pat Crewse*

When Passing On

In their resting place, the dead lie waiting;
for a recurring of the Lord's creating
Creating of many a man and distant lands,
where again young and old live hand in hand
Yet, while waiting, long before this;
there will be a time of pure bliss
An angel will come and guide them in,
into the Great Kingdom heaven holds within
Heaven goes far and beyond-
time and space of dusk and dawn
A place of solitude, in which a soul is set free;
where peaceful spirits shall always be
Time to reach it will be seen and felt by some,
to those whose fate has inevitably come
When one passes on, you need not mourn;
for there's a time when they're reborn
If the Lord grants it to be,
you just may subconsciously see
The eyes you know so well on a beloved face,
for it is the only feature you could retrace

—*Lisa Whitehouse*

My Grandchildren

The house is quiet————blissfully so
    for about a half hour after they go.
And then the silence begins to descend
    and we're back to that lonely quiet again.

The chatter and laughter, the hugging and kissing
    are the greatest joys given but now that's all missing.
The back yard's not filled with the toys galore
    and the pool waters still, not wavy as before.

The tricycles sit with their wheels to the curb
    no-one's here to ride them, they won't be disturbed.
The T.V.'s turned on but it's news not cartoons
    how much happier to watch those ole loony toons.
Those favorite bed-time stories aren't read anymore
    cause there's no-one to listen while cuddled up on the floor

They're gone————and I realize how great is their love
    such a miraculous gift from our God up above.
I would welcome the noise, love and fun to come back
    they're the happy ingredients our home now seems to lack.

    But summer will come again. I can't wait till it's here..
    My grandchildren will return. It's the best time of year.

—*Sara B. Leehey*

Friends

A friend does not give you money when your back is against the wall,
For anyone else could do that, who isn't your friend at all.
A friend does not sit and tell you the things you want to hear,
While compromising the truth. Losing your friendship's what they
    fear.
A friend isn't someone, you need to see everyday,
For I'm sure there are others you will see, who aren't looked at in
    that way.
A friend will not be physically there every time you want him/her to,
But you know that in their heart, he/she really wanted to.
Friends tell you the truth, the truth about yourself,
Friends care nothing about the extent of your wealth,
Friends are behind you when you do things your own way,
Knowing that you went against what they had to say.
Friends believe in you, even when you don't yourself.
Friends can be away from you, but never put you on a shelf.
Friends will see the good in you and try to make others see,
Rather than focusing on your weaker points and negativity.
Friends will find some worth in you, when you think you are no good.
Friends will go out on a limb for you, with no reason why they should.
Friends are unique people who love you for nothing you do.
Friends are just fond of you, and love you because of you.

—*Bryan L. A. Jones*

Journey of the Snowflakes

Snowflakes trembled as they fell
For each one had a tale to tell
Of awesome sights they'd seen on high,
On their tumble from the sky.
One saw the sun, a ball of gold.
It was sunless, still and cold.
One saw the moon, a sphere of ice.
The beams no more, it gave no light.
The stars were gone, or lost their glow.
Comets vanished, sad to go.
Each snowflake touched the earth below
And didn't know which way to go.
All was waste, a timeless place,
Their tears dropped on no human race.

—*Madeline Krause*

Souls

There are so many souls that have been lost
For I am such a soul
There are so many souls
That have found such a GUFF
and then there are so many souls
that have been brushed off
For I am such a soul that has found neither
For I have not died nor lived
For I am depressed way down
deep inside
To bring a child into this world
Is to take one less from the GUFF
But I must ask myself this
Simple question
What happens to the souls that were
brushed off??

—*Teresa K. Brackeen*

Don't You Know I Am With You

Lean upon Me. Trust Me with all your heart,
For I have loved you from the start.
From the moment of conception, I loved you and helped you grow.
I am right here with you, don't you know?
Don't you know whatever you are going through, you don't have
to bear it alone?
Don't you know I'm nearer to you than a telephone?
All you have to do is think a thought and I will hear your call.
Don't you know I am with you? I love you all!
Why do you ignore Me and pretend that I'm not there?
I'm even closer to you than a "wing and a prayer".
I'm not just in Heaven, a city in outer space.
I am with each one of you in your own place!
Please, accept me in all you do.
I want to fellowship with you.
I want to give you all an embrace!
I love all of you, the whole human race!

—*Ednamae Dambeck*

Wrong Kind of Love

I'm all cooped up, please let me out
for I'm ashamed and afraid of our love
You make me crazy and freak out
Can't you see this isn't what love is all about?
Just taking you makes me think-
Should I be doing this?
Or should I drink?
Like the pill that you are
You're in my blood and you've gone too far.
Now it's dark and blue and I now see
they're ashamed of our love too.
Now it's too late I cannot change
For my love for you put me here
where I lay.
It's much too late to turn back now.
Here I lay - here I shall stay.

—*Lisa MacAskill*

Sometimes I Wonder

Sometimes I wonder why I am here
Sometimes I wonder sometimes with fear

How much more time how many more years
How much more time with the ones I hold dear
Can anyone guess can anyone know
Will we die young or will we grow old
For now I can hope for now I can pray
The years I have left will be happy and gay
Sometimes I wonder why I am here
Sometimes I wonder sometimes with fear

—*Michelle Vine*

The Road Of Life

God walk with us down the road of life,
For most of the time it's filled with thorns and strife.
There are miles full of sunshine from above,
And little children so full of love.

There are miles filled with clouds and rain,
When life runs over with pain.
There are miles we walk alone,
When all our troubles seem to have grown.

Miles when we shed many a tear,
For the loss of a loved one so dear.
Miles shared with friends so happy and gay,
Just to know someone cared along the way.

There are miles filled with confusion,
But somewhere down the road you will find a resolution.
There will be miles filled with hate,
Even this we can overcome if we wait.

Yes, the road of life is full of good and bad,
Miles we'll see both happy and sad.
But above all this, we don't walk alone,
For down this same road of life walk friends
and loved ones you've known.

—*Pam Lunsford*

Dedicated Love

If ever I loved before this, let it have been a dream.
For now I am awake and I not only sense,
But feel the sweetness your soul offers mine.
When I'm held in your tender caress,
I long to hear you softly whisper my name.
Nothing in the world could ever be the same.

I haven't the power to refuse you anything,
And I wouldn't want to. Only you can take me, hold me, change
me and improve me. You are my sole comfort in this void of a
world, which cannot hold a love such as ours;
My refuge and shelter as storms threaten and cajole me.

Are there but no words to express my eternal love for you?
Your kiss has left longed-for memories upon my lustful lips;
Memories which penetrate my mind, longing to feel your touch
again. Be the hero who rescues me from the desolate world
outside. We are no part of the world;
Our deep, passionate love far surpasses the love of any who
reside in it. Yes, take me from the hate, to a place for us
alone, and allow me to prove my love in ways more
impressionable than words.

—*Colleen Bouley*

The Day I Say Goodbye

Yes this has been building up,
for so very long,
It's actually quite amazing,
how I have appeared to be so strong.

I cry in privacy,
hoping no one will see,
what hell I go through
with the hurt trapped inside of me.

I thought the pain was over,
but suddenly it hit me so strong,
I actually didn't know why,
but I knew something was definitely wrong.

When will that day come,
when glory replaces sigh,
maybe I'll find the answer,
the day I say good bye.

—*Rhonda Dingman*

Awakening In The 80's

As I walk out of the hospital
For the first time in twenty years,
I see that everything in my life has changed.
There is a shopping center where my house was
And an actor as a president.

There are cheap calculators,
And things called computers in every home,
Hardly anyone uses a typewriter anymore.
People have two or three television sets,
And they can watch copies of movies.

Treaties with Russia,
And no more wars with Vietnam.
I need to learn a lot.
Like, who was president before this Reagan fellow,
And what is MTV?

My life is going to be full,
Of exploring the world.
I am going to learn everything I can
About the country we live in,
For I need to catch upon twenty years.

    —*Sara Crecelius*

Don't Turn Over a Rock

Camping is fun, I must admit
For the first-timer, it can be a shock
Explore till you're tired, but when you sit
It's okay to sit on a rock.

Now, there's one big caution I must extend
Like a shepherd who cares for his flock
I'm giving you warning and I won't pretend
Just don't turn over a rock.

Lots of weird things make their nests under there
Don't expose them by picking their lock
You, too, wouldn't want an intruder in your lair
So, just don't turn over a rock.

Now, when you and the girls are out on the trail
Be adventurous, but always take stock
For there's one lesson you must heed without fail
And that's not to turn over a rock.

As your outdoorsman dad, I'm curious to learn
What you did each day 'round the clock
But what I really must know on your return
Is what you found under that rock.

    —*Charles C. Washburn*

It Was Halloween Night

I had locked the doors and windows up tight
For this was Halloween night.
    Leaving on the lights, I jumped into bed.
    Pulling the covers well over my head.
When I slowly peeked out, what should I see
    But a green-eyed witch staring down at me.
    She was skinny and had a long nose.
Then she grabbed me, right by the hair on my head,
Get on, get on quick, she said,
    On her old broomstick we flew,
    Through the clouds, the mist and the dew.
I started to slip and to slide,
I wobbled from side to side.
    Then it happened - I fell.
    Down, down I went, pell-mell.
There were hundreds of bats swarming overhead,
    Thank goodness, I awoke and fell out of bed.

    —*Dolly M. Dowd*

Freedom

Never did I think today would end,
For when darkness came forth,
It brought with it destruction and terror,
Children cried and women mourned.
In the morn when the sun shone bright,
Corpses lay strewn along the battlefield,
No longer green, the field is a vibrant red.
A stray tear trickles down my cheek,
For now I know the cost of my freedom,
Death of another being.

    —*Heather Giordano*

I Reach Out and You Are Always There

When I'm down and out I'm still a millionaire.
For without a doubt,
I reach out and you are always there.

Greater love I could never find.
You give me life and I give you mine.
You are my best friend. I know you care.
I reach out and you are always there.

Help me to bend, not break, always to give, not take.
You always show me the way, anytime, night or day.
I reach out and you are always there.

With troubled heart I may weep through the night,
But when morning comes a smile of happiness I wear.
I reach out and you are always there.

I believe in you, I can depend on you.
My life I want to spend with you.
I reach out and you are always there.

The love you give to me I share with others you see.
A greater love no one has ever known.
Because of you I am never alone.
I reach out and you are always there.

    —*Nella J. Han*

Just a Glimpse

Thought presented to me so I may weep
For worthiness won't find room in my heart.
This good fortune, of course, I may still reap
Though guilt sticks in my body like a dart.
From a thought, I hardly may ask for more
As a gentle touch or a warm embrace.
But while I have my foot propped in the door,
It may be the only chance that I face.
So please allow my feeble advances
To slowly work their way into your heart.
The prose created I hope entrances
You to seek and appreciate my art.
You give a little, but so much you hide.
All I ask of you is a glimpse inside.

    —*John A. LoBianco*

Innocence

He, magic, believed in power of the stars
Silence confirmed secrecy and he understood
A dazzling sparkle in eyes of wonderment
Surprised itself in knowledge
Fascinated eyes gazed up once again
With a spirit bursting of pride
And he loved his goddess, the moon
Amazed, he stared into the darkness
His wisdom was unleashed
And he danced again
Power

    —*Joanne Gauthier*

To Loreda

You will always be my baby girl as time goes by
For you and I are a loving pair, and I wonder why,
I didn't know I would feel the same
About a second child of a different name.
But all I did was look at you and you touched my heart and I
Knew that I would always stand in awe of you
Your husband and children show me,
A wonderful love I can't forget.
And I will love them always, and yet
I still think of you as my baby girl
Whom I love with all my heart.
And I know you are always with me
Even when we are far apart.
And you are the one who will understand the way I feel at last
Someday, when this little poem is something from the past.
And I will always love you and encourage you
In everything you do, and I know you love me too.
And Loreda we will always be the same,
As time goes by, I'll always love you for you are
My second child of a different name.

—*Della Harrison Kromer*

Life's Disastrous Kiss

Sing loud, little girl.
For you have a lot of pain to endure.
May your laughter never cease.
For it is that which brings us peace.
Clap on, little girl.
For you shall succeed.

You may never walk, my dear.
In my heart you shall soar.
The sweet joys of life will be different for you.
May they bring you happiness just the same.
Crippled, but not untouched by the joys life brings.

To the little baby chosen by God,
Chosen to change our selfish ways.
May God bless you and protect you.
For you are love;
Touched by life's disastrous kiss.

—*Shanna Walrath*

Glory Hallelujah, Thank You Jesus

Glory Hallelujah, the highest praise I give to you,
For your praise shall continually be on my tongue.
Because of your love, your tender mercy, your gift of
Salvation and your promise of eternal life,
I'm blessed to say, glory hallelujah, thank you Jesus.

Though trials and tribulations were so many and
The pain and storm were so hard to bare,
You gave me that sweet inner peace with reassurance
That you had not left me or forsaken me, and that's why
I can say, glory hallelujah, thank you Jesus.

When I was falling you picked me up, reminding me that I'm a
Child of the King and that I shall not want.
Even though darkness was around me, you stepped in and shed
Forth your light to enable me to see, and that's why
I can say, glory hallelujah, thank you Jesus.

Thank you Jesus for giving me the strength and power that I
Need to make it through life's toils and snares;
Oh, how you've calmed the raging seas in my life and said,
Peace be still; and that's why I can say, glory hallelujah,
Thank you Jesus.

—*Sherry L. Walker*

"The Children"

Today our society's fate
Forces our children to fight and hate
It endows our children with doubt and fear
Which, apparently, no adult can see or hear.
All the great countries and all the great men
Need to listen to their children
The children are saying all over the land
"First we must learn to understand"
Then we can start to learn to live
If only our parents can learn to forgive
We will wear compassion like a glove
And then the next thing to learn is love
Because once we learn how to love
We will truly know how to live.

—*Michael Bedwell*

"Fantasy's Reality"

Come, help me rebuild my castles in the sand,
'Fore I'm weary of everyone's reprimand.
Come forward my hero, come lend me a hand,
Let's create our own city in a new land.

With starships of starfish and far out jams,
Let's make a new generation of man....
Many of fantasy, many imaginations that can,
Make the dream realistic, with a mutual creative plan.

Where the waves splash against the foreign shores,
Avoiding all disaster and following life's detours...
Opening all new bright and heavenly doors,
Bringing happiness abundantly, forevermore.

Where we're sea kin to all and with skytowers too,
With eternal infinity of flaming sky blue...
Where midnight madnesses and comedies come true.
Eliminating all depressions with an overall view.

—*Nancy A. Coleman*

Lost

One child, forever lost
Forever lost in time.
Lost because of hurt and sadness
And the hatred that she's seen.
Fantasies shattered.
Dreams crushed.
One frightened, innocent child, alone
Who was forced to grow up.
It wouldn't have happened so quickly
If you had just had the time
To give her love, praise, and hope
And if you had stopped to see
What your cruel, stinging words and hate
Had done to her mind.
Now she'll never know what love truly is.
She never will be free
From hurt, tears, and loneliness
That crying child is me.

—*Tracy Harris*

The Poppy Fields

Looking across at this field full of grace
Where sometime ago war battles took place
A soft summer breeze rocks the carpet of red
For each living poppy a soldier lies dead.

Not far away the graves at attention
A thousand young soldiers too many to mention
See how they're sleeping forever in line
Wasted from evil and war in our time.

—*Tracy E. Payne*

Untitled

The night opens with a chorus of redemption
Free again from the golden shackles of a day now dusked
Whispers the meadow in slumbering contentment
Their eyes have met the orb of Luna.
Raven's blood mars the surface of an eye wide open
Who inhabits my realm of silence
But I who am dwelling?
Dance under the glass, now shattered
With a sun in crescendo
Sinking cloth of Kashmir shredding
I see you in a mirror gazing
Steal away my wakefulness
Night now calls
   —Eric S. Barber

Free Bird

I knew love once; for it was kind. A
Free bird soaring through my mind.
 I knew love once; but now it's gone
The shady black, the curtain drawn. The
burning light we once knew went from
you to me and me to you.
  Then I went and set it free. It soared
like an angry bird swooping down, cry in pain
It soared back up but was gone again
The bird flew back and talked to me to
Say you would not set me free; my
heart burned with the same old flame, to
know the love we used to tame; I
looked back up to touch the bird, but
he was gone...So the bird flew on to
Soar so free and left me
 Staring back at
  me.....
   —Nancy Vourtis

The Price Of Freedom

Freedom means different things to many people,
freedom too some may be to be equal. But true freedom
is going anywhere you want, freedom is loving a person
regardless of color, true freedom is when humanity can
love each other. Freedom is something deep inside of us
all, freedom is to forever stand and never fall. That's
the price of freedom but who's innocent blood will pay the price?
Who's innocent blood will get iced? Sometimes reality
isn't all that nice, true freedom is victory in christ. Hey
solider strive for the top and strive to be the best, freedom
is the peace within! Freedom is knowing God is your friend.
   —Walter Reginald Clark

Stardom of Canada

 Upon this great nation of freedom
there is not one but many cultures
that share with us the divine stardom,
humanity. Ignore the tortures
 of the disrespectful and random
reformers who suppress the statures
of various cultures. Oh what boredom
there would exist without the raptures
 of our peoples so rich and diverse;
'tis why it's become legality
to retain traditions and rehearse
 one's individual identity;
respect, share, and dare not the perverse,
is multicultural reality.
   —Piero Bachetti

"Now, What of My Verses...?"

Yes! What of them —
friday-graved for some sunday resurrection?

Why do I seed-bed them deep in psyche?
As if embedding eager epiphanies
in such strata-sown secrecies
should promise shoots past my presence...

Deep enearthed, as tel, in private plot,
lurk loosely scattered shards of might-have-been,
heart-kilned with fired fractious ferverinos:
all awaiting others', somehow, explorations...

Lodes of gritty, graveled fools-gold nuggets,
perhaps in purseless pockets, veined in hopes
—who knows what minute mettle, minerals
untapped in mineshaft await Eureka!?

For now, such buried treasures (not, legacies?)
seem tailings shunted off, solemn slag heaps,
from miner-manque, now heading heavenward,
with salted memories of mythic moments....
   —George H. Gardiner

Nothing Ever Has To End

An eye gently blinks, another summer gingerly fades away.
Friends mourn together as life impatiently waits to seize their
confused souls. But go with courage for life doesn't wither
with the fallen leaves of autumn, for love doesn't perish when
young lovers must part. No matter how far the miles may
spread, the only true barrier in life is Time...and he hears no
crying, no pleading prayers in the night. He himself is but a
desolate warrior, scared to care for the pleas of the lonely
because he, too, thinks all will eventually be gone. Time is
doomed to hang with his own noose. So weep not for days gone,
rejoice for the days to follow. Keep the memories not too far
from your heart, for the future holds a vision of the past.
There will be more times to remember, more visions to cherish.
Go with courage, for there will be more lazy days at the park,
more ballads by the campfire, more moonlight strolls by the
river, more poems at the local cafe. So live not with a black
veil, live not with a dagger at your chest, for if a friendship
is strong, a passion is true, then nothing ever has to end.
   —Tommy Gaffney

Life

Life
From birth to death

Life can be bad
Life can be good
Life can also be sad
Or even glad

Life is a trial about the way the world turns

Sometimes life is difficult
And sometimes it is easy

I hate life at times
And at other times I love life

Life
   —Sarah Peil

Luminous

The very thought of love never seems so far away
From every shining star that shines from above.
Glowing intensely, their presences are perpetual!
Marked by sincerity and by faith (along with honesty).
"Will they ever drift?" Surely, they will never stray
From the human heart. Any compass or map will entwine
The outright direction love follows at night, without intent
To disrupt or to intervene in our sleep. No longer hesitant,
Love is in the likeness of stars, made to burn and shine.
Every colon that point brings forth becomes interpreted
By love's own presence - by love's own divine beauty.
How can I explain this to you?
The very thought of love is all within light,
Glowing eternally into every living thing in autumn.
For me, the very thought of love is a promise
Remaining in light, shining brightly.
To this day, love is never distant from any star
Or constellation that the sky has brought to us.
Entangled, in its presence (which I have seen
With my own eyes) I believe it is happening.

—*Chad Kelham*

I Am All Woman

I am a woman. The same woman whose breast you drew strength
from. I am an obese woman. The same obese woman whose fat you
gained warmth and comfort from. I am a Caribbean woman. The
same Caribbean woman whose solka tune you danced to and curried
pot you ate from. I am a strong woman. The same five foot two
strong woman who chastised your white male teacher for not
encouraging you in school. I am "thee" woman because with my
wide hips and my broad bottom I simply dazzle my teeth and I
still turn heads. I am a hard working woman and I don't care
what the neighbors say about my four jobs. I am a proud woman,
proud of how I single-handedly raised you and your two sisters.
I am a black woman. The same obese, Caribbean, strong,
hard working, and proud black woman who loves her son, and wants
him to recognize the monument I represent in society. You
better believe it honey, I am all woman.

—*Vanessa Kilkelly*

The Aged Architect

Age thirty nine, oldest graduate student;
From Okinawa, dream after dream, ambition to ambition,
He was prompted to pursue urban design in Pittsburgh.
Though life in academe was all roses,
Practice in business society was all thorny against an alien.
He ground his teeth with vexation at two times of dismissal.

Age mid forty to sixty, a lonely architect;
In Detroit, work after work, devotion to devotion,
He was always loyal to his boss for livelihood.
Though he was disregarded from the management,
Tears in anger were hidden into his sallow Asian complexion.
Envy surged within the boss to fire him during a design incident.

Age sixty nine, a helpless job hunter;
In New York and Detroit, resume after resume, phone to phone,
He still seeks a job at his age for survival.
Though unemployment benefits were exhausted long ago,
Social security injects a little alimentation into his dried vessels.
Two years out of work already shrink his flesh and soul.

—*Esaku Kondo*

Whiskey

A prisoner in this life I am, oh whiskey your too blame.
You took me from my great big house, you drove me to such shame
Beside a rive bank I live cardboard boxes for a home.
A lying on the cold cold ground while I do shake and moan.

A twist of fate in life sweet dreams, when friends they do forsake.
And then you turn to the whiskey a comfort to partake.
Just a backward glance to the years gone past of riches and plenty be.
So the cold and wet and hardship now they all have conquered me.

But true it seems that men do dream, and the whiskey takes command.
And before you know your home is gone your cattle and your farm
So a warning take from the homeless man as he lies beneath the trees.

To think and ponder one more time, what whiskey can do to thee.
For it takes you to the crossroads, of life there's no return.
   Of a world off shame and poverty.
      Look whiskey what you have done.

—*John Monaghan*

Perpetual Motion

Everything moves, nothing is still.
From the growing grasses, to the rolling hills.
Everything moves, like the words in a song.
See the sun, see it burn in the noon day sky.
How does it move, how does it turn?
Everything moves, nothing is still.
On a clear night you can see the stars in the sky,
on their way through the galaxy.
Everything moves, nothing is still.
Everything is in motion like the waves on the sea,
the moon above.
Feel the wind, feel it blow. Where does it come from,
where does it go?
No matter who, what, or where, everything moves, everything
moves.
Perpetual motion, forever moving to a timeless clock set in
motion by an unseen hand.
Everything moves, everything moves.

—*Rita L. Imboden*

Another One Just Like Me

We mate as does everything in nature —
from the one-celled amoeba, hydra, paramecium —
to the insects and fragrant flowers —
to the buttercups and roses, daffodils,
sun flowers and towering trees —
to birds, reptiles and animals —
they mate in a world of reproduction.

Find a mate, a true romance —
watch how the love buds excelerate —
before you know it, the deed is done —
the union of the sexes — impending birth —
to the beasts of the field, all kinds look alike —
the world is in a state of reproduction.

"Another one just like me," in repetition —
from acorn, egg, seed, cocoon —
man imitates nature when he reproduces —
he also produces products of mass production —
not one of a kind but thousands of varieties —
everything and every kind separate and unique.

—*John Erdell*

Loves Pain

Trapped in a world that's been condemned.
Full of sorrow, no fear of sin
Majestic thoughts of troubled mind.
Seeking a love that's pure in kind.
But I am alone, and you
I can not find.
I wanted to call you
But I am afraid.
Words hurt when plainly spoken but
I asked your voice was unbroken
And I hurt, tears are not forbidden
And you well maybe
Some day that too.
—*Dorothy C. Taylor*

"The Beautiful Outdoors At Night"

One night as I look across the glistening water,
Full of vibrant colors from the moon,
I see the reflection of the stars,
As bright as the sun in the afternoon.

The trees stand so tall and firm,
Like the buildings in New York City.
The night birds sing so cheerfully,
It always sounds so pretty.

The brisk cold air,
And the frost on the ground,
The beautiful outdoors,
Are so pretty I've found.
—*Patricia Drongoski*

New Hope

I wept.
Furiously and passionately, I wept.
The tolerant sea caught my tears of rage
and churned vociferously to flood the land.

It washed.
Furiously and passionately, it washed.
The land drank in the water to quench its thirst
and rid itself of man's material lust.

They roared.
Furiously and passionately, they roared.
The winds dried the water into mounds of mud
and mocked the painful memory of human greed.

Life stirred.
Teasingly and provocatively, life stirred.
Eons of longing pushed through to shame the past
and claim new hopes for equitable joy and care.

I smiled.
Irreverently and humorously, I smiled.
The eternal flame of life's energy licked wounds
and tried again under the forgiveness of Rainbow's glow.
—*Carolyn Ashe Stokes*

"Life"

Life has a wonderful meaning
Full of love and understanding for all,
You can call to the Lord God your maker
He will surely answer your call,
Always remember to be true and faithful
Sometimes your back is against the wall,
So you must be sincere as you approach Him
Make sure your case is very clear,
Be sure you repent for past misfortunes
And you truly want Him near.
—*George Barden*

The Last Hoorah

He exuberantly wined and dined many ladies
galore,
  Feeling his rare oats, he wanted more,
  A never ending appetite of the feminine gender
kept him going,
  The thrill of the chase and conquests and the
hearts he was towing,
  His life was an amazing circle of females wearing
faces,
  Of various sizes and all kinds of graces,
  A boy in a candy store could have never fared
better,
  He gave many bouquets of roses and wrote
each a letter.
  His collection of loves grew and grew,
  Until two of the ladies decided to sue,
  Finally he cooled his heels and stopped the
chase,
  Since the unanimous female opinion
proclaimed he was a case!
—*Judy Vogue*

Through Silent Worlds

Through silent worlds we travel,
gathering wisdom and insight,
Into our planet and it's problems.
Seeking answers and solutions,
to our normal everyday life.
Accessing our goals,
and reaching our destinations.
Reaching out with our souls,
obtaining guidance throughout our years,
to help us face our toughest fears.
Although we live together on one planet,
with all our common goals,
yet so different in our ways.
We live in and control our own worlds;
these worlds in which we travel into and out of;
as we meet we cross the barriers of those worlds,
learning about our strengths, hopes, and fears.
All joining together in our lives,
as we travel through silent worlds.
—*Tim L. Spelman*

A Hidden Memory

You were there back a few years before
Gathering with the old men down at the store
Eating a moon pie and drinking an R.C.
Standing tall as your Grandpa's knee

Wore our pistols as often as our pants
Stalking the deep Georgia woods for our big chance
Sold a few possums to Charlie in the shack
Bought some cheese and Johnny crackers to
eat on the way back

Riding motorcycles down to that icy blue hole
Skinny dipping was never so cold
Stopped by the black church just for a peek
Smell that shine on our way up the creek

So you see a part of me is still searching
For the part of you that's longing to be free
Though you can never cross these living waters inside of me
My friend you will always be
Passing through time in a hidden memory
—*Suzanne Kohr*

Discord

I am African-American, but I feel no bond with Africans.

My body is healthy, not racked with pain and disease like the ghastly, emaciated skeletons of my Ethiopian cousins. I, by nature, am very peaceful, unlike the Somalian tyrants who proudly dragged the decaying corpses of American soldiers through their streets.

When I look in the mirror I see that I am, at best, an average looking female, and in no way can I detect any trace of the beauty that so clearly defined my Egyptian grandmothers.

I am African-American, but I feel no bond with Africans.

We are a family separated by geographical, cultural, and psychological obstructions.

If, however, I managed to miraculously seal the gap between us and traveled to the motherland to celebrate my heritage, would the Namibian Bushman or Congolese Pygmy, upon seeing my yellowish-tan skin, welcome me with open arms?

Sadly, my friend, I think not.

—*Shayla Hawkins*

FREEDOM

speech, religion, expression; such a waste
give the right but not the ability
for if the ability was given the right would cease
love, peace, harmony; such as waste.

the world is ruled by all and not few
yet, we function in the light of the dim witted
for these are the crusaders of "truth?"
the planet is taken away by the few and not the many.

here my voice, for it speaks out
search for what is true and not what is available
look for those who are forced to hide under this oppression
listen; before the volume of my word grows silent.

carried forth in today's world is deed and not thought
bring to attention the injustice practiced
evaluate the living for their time is done
act on the impulse of righteousness and not prejudice.

maybe one day this paradox of liberty can be corrected
let the search for a truism take hold now
enough of the belief that time will change man
freedom should stop being interpreted by those who know it not.

—*William Perez*

Declination of the Hearth

Remembering days of youthful maturity
Gleeful shouts of MA!, Honey! and Awshucks!.
Excited, noisome strides of quick-glimpsed
    pants, polos and dresses
Evoking memories of intricately-woven family life.
Awesome garden flowers bloomed fiercely, dressed in
    nature's vibrant colors while her airborned creatures
    twittered, frittered and hummed.
Two decades hence, a disquieted chill stealthily stalks
    the once-active scene.
The shadow of fate leaves a forlorned, broken-spirited
    and ailing widow
Her eyes behold wild weeds and unfruitful blooms
amid untrimmed grass and unpainted fences.
O cruel time, past and present — bring back the
beautiful memories of the past
Where are the fires that burned so brightly in
    my hearth?
Where is my cane, my kin, my hope?

—*Bea Harry*

"A Box Of Fashion"

My box is fashioned from soft white cotton flannel, with the glitter of nylon thread to hold it in place. The hinges are of tint baby pearls from the sea.
I shall sit in my box and let my thoughts wonder back in time, like a balloon floating in the wind. As I plunder thru my box.
I find a baby's breath flower, smelling so sweet in one of its corners. In another corner there is a small hair bow made of a pink satin ribbon. I hear a gurgle and a laugh coming from a small person in the other corner behind me. In the corner to the right of me stands a soft white kitten, purring up at me.
BUT WAIT! What's this beside me, in the middle of my box?
"Looks like a big smile" it must be a giant! No!
It's my mom's face.

—*Betty Anne Taylor*

Appreciate

When you're feelin' kinda lonesome and kinda grumply too;
Go out into the meadow and gaze into the blue.
Watch the sun-sink slowly into the west;
Leavin' a faint red glow,
Picture the soft mists risin' up the hills,
Feel the whisperin' breezes blow.
The sapphire brook babbles merrily,
To the pebbles 'round about,
Splashin' and dashin' cheerfully — look
The first star has just come out!
The sky is turnin' a deeper blue;
Dark clouds frown upon the green;
The flowers are kissed by the dew,
Trees embraced by gentle moonbeams!
You'll forget your daily troubles,
And your shoulders once bent with care —
Will straighten up and realize;
The beauty God has placed there.

—*Nedra DuVal*

"My Wife"

After being married for nearly six years,
God seems to have delivered us from many a strong fears!
While watching her bake a cake of her dad's recipe,
May I have another piece, ah, come on, please?
She likes to crochet and knit,
To help keep us all fit!
We like to take walks in the rain together,
Love is so strong, we feel like two feathers!
Listening to the radio or watching television,
This we like to do, in order to stay friends!
Going shopping together on a big bus,
After praying for a seat to ride in,
There's no room for any fuss!
We like to shop together in stores, we do,
Picking out clothing red, white and blue.
But most of all we like to make love at night,
Thrills from heaven, we soar in great flight!

—*Terry E. Corbitt*

The Cenotaph

It's just a mass of sand and stone,
Standing silent and all alone.
And from a distance all you see,
Our country's flags, fluttering free.
But go up close and read quite slow,
What is written on its base below.
"To those who served in two great wars"
Their memory will always be ours.
This monument declares our pride,
For all those souls who fought and died.
Their sacrifices had to be,
To keep our future children "free."

—*Ronald P. O'Keefe*

The Attic and the Garden

In the attic all by myself, this thought scares me,
Going through my possessions shelf by shelf,
Maybe I should stay out of the attic from now on,
I'll put all my efforts into my garden
There I can tend to the bad roots and nurture the good,

Yes, I think I'll stay out of the attic from now on.
It's too musty and dark in that part of the house.
I cannot close it off for good, I just won't tread there so often.
I'll keep my feet planted on the ground and hope,
Hope, that if I tend my garden ever so true, the roses
will grow strong and the vegetables will become ripe.
I'll keep the attic for things that are gone and long past treasuring,
I can go up there but not alone, I'll need someone to hold my
hand so the bad things can be understood.
In my garden I can stand tall, be alone if I will or
share the beauty with others it I choose.

—*Denise M. Kavanah*

Butterflies

As a little worm I crawl upon this earth,
Going unnoticed from a deep sleep, until my rebirth,
Being ever so tiny and terribly small,
    Being ever so careful that a foot should fall.
I am so plain and have no beauty,
    spinning my cocoon is my only duty.

Finally emerging so weak and wet upon the day,
I find life and strength from the sun's rays.
Spreading my wings so that they may dry,
    No longer to crawl, but to fly.
My last destiny in life is to love, for
    soon I shall die.

—*Meredith E. Smith*

My Soul at Peace

As I sit here alone, I ponder what we've lost.
Good Lord, at such a high cost.
I think of my love in jail,
not being able to set bail.
Looking into the night in a fixed glare,
feeling an empty despair,
realizing he won't be there.
In my bed I toss and turn,
for his arms around me I do yearn.
His love has surrounded me so long,
I'm not sure how to be strong.
With God and friend's guidance I will find,
the independence they had in mind.
Maybe someday I can give back,
the strength I did so lack.
Then my soul will be more at peace,
it's what I can do at the very least.

—*Joyce Peterson*

Heaven

The wings of God come
to pick up my soul.
I feel like a bird who has
once been trapped in a cage,
let free.
I float up higher and higher.
Beyond pillows of cotton.
Beyond a flaming sun.
Up, up to reach the golden gates of light.
When I first reach them, I am blinded,
but as I get closer I can see.
I am confronted with God,
and I know from now on, I am safe.

—*Elizabeth Green*

Thoughts

Like clouds, my thoughts drift aimlessly—
Good thoughts, bad ones, just come to me.
I sort them out and try to place
The bad ones, which I cannot face;
Behind the ones I think are nice.
It worked out well just once or twice;
But, just like clouds, the bad ones drift,
In spite of all I do to shift
Them out of range, back to my mind.
And finally at last I find
That even these, if just a bit
Of courage and a touch of wit,
I use on them, will change around
Until some good from them I've found.

—*Margie M. Baker*

"Silence"

Mean and nasty words fly across the room
Gouging my ears
From your arrogant fools mouth.
The horrible phrases you preach sting my soul
and burn my eyes.
    But I stay in silence.
Looking at you speak in this cold way
sends chills creeping up my spine.
I shiver then sigh
and bite my tongue
    To stay in silence.
The bigoted opinions that you voice
Frustrate me.
Most of the bias statements you scream
That rip me apart
are silly assumptions and what you want to believe.
    I can no longer stay in silence.

—*Sydel Greco*

Lonely Dancer

I watched her grow up in Ballet slippers
Gracefully from show to show.
I had no hint of her loneliness and pain
For she hid it in Capizeos.

She exceeded the dance in toe shoes.
On pointe, she's beginning to rock,
But her heart is like the lamb's wool
That cushions her toes from the shock.

Her dance is expressively violent.
Silently, she dances a shout.
Her toes bruise my heart as she implodes
With tears she will not let out.

Dance, little dancer, dance on my heart
Or whose ever you need for a floor.
Say all the things you need to say
So your dance will be graceful once more.

—*Joyce Carol Gibson*

The Old Man

The old man sits to tell his story of the time when life was pain.
The pain is one that only he can understand.
The sorrow began the day he lost the people that he needed so,
The love he felt was one of trust to live a life like that.
To tell the truth would only cause the life he made to leave,
But to tell a lie of what went on would only cause more pain.
What to do, only he knows the truth for love like that will stay,
In your heart, just one more day than what you want it to be.
The one day came when all pain was gone for it to leave was great.
But why it left is one that only the man will know.

—*Darcy Jansen*

A Diseased Society

Upon this earth a plague has unfurled
Grasping in its clutch the fear of a world,
Once thought to be a curse on needle junkies and fags
Infecting niggers and the homeless dressed in rags,
Men of religion clouded their hearts with hate
Saying that it was only the wicked man's fate,
Doctors filled our minds with deadly delusions
As they pumped in our veins tainted transfusions
In less than a decade it filled the world with dread
And with each fateful year millions more are dead,
It brings death to the rich, it robs the poor
Murdering the innocent, raping the whore
An ever growing ever threatening social disease
It prevents society from living as they please,
Condoms are given freely to children in schools
Lovers are afraid to share their love without rules,
Some say that there shall never be a cure
Lest we all live lives chaste and pure,
Yet living in a system where selfishness pervades
Can we heal a diseased society dying of A.I.D.S.

　　　—*Jeffery H. Bean*

Ode to a Dinosaur

White sepulchre among the hills—
　　Graveyard of the dinosaur.
You hold the secrets of the past,
　　The famous prehistoric lore.

Within your whitened, crumbling clay
　　The mighty Stegosaurus sleeps,
The lizard, roofed with plates of bone
　　That now his ghostly vigil keeps.

Two brains he had — one fore, one aft.
　　If something slipped his forward mind,
There still remained an afterthought —
　　A judgment by the one behind.

Before he spoke a single word,
　　He gave it twice a weighty thought.
Thus rendering his judgments rare —
　　Not once was he in error caught!

To be like you, great Dinosaur,
　　To have my judgments always wise.
But yet in spite of wisdom rare —
　　Beneath the cold, white clay he lies.

　　　—*Mona Drew Carlson*

True Heart

Over the rainbow, through the clouds into the silver lining,
Great things happen, but only at the right timing.
The question why? is all that I ever dream to ask...
Offering an answer, though, is a difficult task.
I was once told that good things come to those who wait,
But, I've learned over the years that it is mostly due to fate.
The perfect person doesn't exist, everyone is special-
　　so, I look at who I am and who you are
And realize that the answer to the question why?
　　is really not that far.
I once learned the waltz, two-step and other dances from you-
To me, they were important, special, something brand new.
You would say, step forward, back and side to side,
　　that's how you start,
And I know that one day, you'll dance your way into
　　someone else's heart.
I remember boating on the waters so blue and deep,
Floating down the river with you are memories I will keep.
At night, when you look up and see the beautiful stars above,
They're heavenly bodies, shining for you with all my love.

　　　—*Amy L. Buck*

Nature, Women — ?

How angry you are, how violent, so beautiful,
Green and marble, white foam; roaring so loud,
Waves breaking one after another, two, three breaking together.

Crashing, crashing, roaring, beauty, strength, violence, anger,
Together: All in one.
Foam reaching up, jumping high. White, white on grey green,
Dawn breaking - a moment of ease then more waves higher,
smashing down, expressing the hatred of all, a release
of tension showing man just how unimportant they are.

Roaring constant, never ending, one wave upon another.
Striking the rocks, water writhing, surging, moving in
different directions. Pulling, pushing, surging.
Oh how beautiful, frightening me, yet calling.
Never the same, always changing.

So powerful, my body can feel it's pulse.
I vibrate with the energy, the force, the cleansing of all
is in each wave. Look, hear, feel; the call.
Women — hear the call, rise up like the waves,
Strong, free, fulfilled, each one different, unique, beautiful,
but always one.

　　　—*Judith Marie Johnson*

Sunset at My House

You, Master, are the King of Silk
gritting your teeth with disgust.
It has happened for many years-
the infectious kisses of your white stone alter
that cough your residue on my alive knuckles and lobes.
(you, Master, are the King of Silk)
Although I am ugly shroud my purple skin
in the buttery silk that numbs your painted surface...
(you, Master, are the King of Silk)
You bulge and moan while I am but delicate
You nibble, then protrude
from your glassy case to
carelessly loop your great abundance
into my flowery illusion-
your room finally opens into mine.
Oh Great Master!
We can now save ourselves
in our room where our mouths can
fill up with blueberries,
our lips purple with the sweetness of sighing flesh.

　　　—*Amanda Kobler*

My Forever Love

Everyday I watch you grow, and everyday my love continually
grows so. For my forever love.
Although It may be us two alone, I'll make sure we have a safe
secure home. Just for my forever love.
You know we are almost there to our 40 weeks, mommie just can't
wait for this peak. I wait for the day, my forever love.
I wait for that day you move within me, and that day when you're
finally free. Until we meet, my forever love.
You'll fill my life with lot's of joy, my little girl or little
boy. My forever love!
I'll be here to pick you up when you're down, you can count on
me
to be around. I'll help you in your times of need, when you
need a friend you can come to me.
You'll be here to make me smile, and to let me know my
struggles are worthwhile,
God, my baby, I love you so much, I just can't wait to see your
smile, and feel the warmth of your touch.
Until we meet my little dove, to begin our journey of forever love!

　　　—*Ardesia Patterson*

Brother, I Love You

I took my brother by his tiny hand
Guiding him through the dark, wooded land.
We came upon a moss covered rock so tall
Next to it, he looked quite small.

We wandered on a few steps more
Stopping by the lake side shore.
The moon glistened on the water so bright
Making the darkness eerie with light.

We heard an owl hoot from a tree
My little brother came closer to me.
I held him fast with all my might
Soothing away his childish fright.

We walked along the shore 'till morn
Watching a brand new day being born.
Knowing full well that brotherhood is love
From the earth beneath to the sky above.

The moments we shared, the thoughts that last
Would endure the joys and the tears of the past.
The memory of his little hand in mine will be
One of my dearest, everlasting memories.

—*Mary J. Parthe*

Wars

During wars jets and planes soar
Gunfire echoes with a deafening roar
They started in the past
Too long most of them last
But hopefully we'll have no more

Many people die
Shot down like a swatted fly
When they're done with their guns
They start with their knives
In this way they claim many lives

They drop all their bombs on this precious earth,
Killing many kids, some before birth

It makes countries poor, some exist no more
Why-oh why, do we have wars?

Children hiding in their rooms
Which become their eternal tombs
Many parents start to cry, as they watch their children die.

We cannot explain how we feel, all these wars seem so unreal.
We must put them all to an end
It's up to you and me my friend.

—*Charles Schroeder*

The Writer's Wilderness

I ax my way through the wilderness
hacking down deadwood trees-
that I have grown with.
I set twisted briars ablaze - the acrid
smoke leaving its haunting smell churning in my chest
while I try to water a withering seedling
in the torrid Sun with my own blood-but it just vanishes
before it can even fall to the ground.
I'm dreaming of a jungle turned into a grove.
with the haphazardness of a machete
I whack away
always second guessing all I've done.
I throw away a multitude of wilds-
just to keep the fragile alive
hoping one day it will
Blossom.
It is only the crazed ones who try to
slew the jungle of ideas to
Create a Singular Beauty with only a Pen.

—*Melissa Tofte*

My Master

I had walked life's path with an easy tread,
Had followed where comfort and pleasure led;
And then by chance in a quiet place
I met my Master face to face.

With station and rank and wealth for a goal,
Much thought for the body, but none for the soul,
I had entered to win in life's mad race
When I met my Master face to face.

I met him and knew him and blushed to see
That his eyes full of sorrow were fixed on me;
And I faltered and fell at his feet that day
While my castles melted and vanished away;

Melted and vanished; and in their place
I saw naught else but my Master's face;
And I cried aloud: "Oh, make me meet
To follow the marks of Thy wounded feet."

My thought is now for the soul of men;
I have lost my life to find it again
E'er since alone in that holy place
My Master and I stood face to face.

—*Lillian Stewart*

Untitled

I would like to sit cross legged
Hallucinating in a Euphoric state,
Contemplating the great Zen Philosophies,
or marvel at the vast Buddhism rituals,
and call it meditation.

I could sit here and read books
of Mushrooms demystified, or
even, the joys of basket weaving,
or maybe that dirty magazine
in the corner, and call it study.

I could lay here and watch
movies of black boys killing black boys,
and movies centered around the sensitive male
or a blank blue screen,
And call it visionary learning.

I could sit at a table
and smoke cigarettes, and drink coffee
and worry about the dentist.
Raising hell about cleaning my teeth.

Or I can sit here and just be in love with you.

—*Cory Wattenbarger*

Niece

Some years have passed between us since I saw your tiny
hands and feet for the very first time.
All of these years have been very special to me.
I remember holding you, and playing all of the games you
enjoyed most,
although I think I enjoyed them more then you.
My life has journeyed down many roads, many of the same ones
that someday you may choose.
Even though I have taken a road that has carried me far away
I am still close to your heart.
My eyes still get tears in them the moment I think of you, and
my heart feels so empty without holding you, or hearing your
laughter.
Someday I will be back with you to play our games together
like we did in the past.
Till then I will see you in my dreams and we will play our
favorite games together.

—*Antony W. Simpson*

The Stripper's Fair

In the blackness of the night he stood
hands in pocket
like the haunted overseer
in a study of the car's engine exposed to the darkness
and parked shamelessly roofless
hoodless
tireless
in its motionless frame
while his hungry eyes roamed in a quest for parts
parts to display in a retrieved form
then swapped for dough in a taxless market

  —Georgiana Chung

In Her Daughters Eye

She sat by the hotel window
Harsh, bright light, hiding nothing
Contemplating the image
Revealed to her in the hand-held mirror.
She needed the magnifying side now,
Just as an artist needs the strong north light,
For the painting about to begin.

On the glass-topped table before her
Lay her palette, gold cases and tubes.
Bottles and jars, sunlight sparkling all around.
Well-manicured fingers began the daily ritual
Face cream, foundation, blush
All penetrating deeper now into the wrinkles
Which she liked to refer to as laugh lines
Lipstick, a softer shade today
Palest of lilac eye-shadow
Matting a little, on the thinner, creepy eye-lids.

Just finished as the knock sounded at the door.
Her daughter, taking her to dinner.
Happy Birthday, Mother. You look just as lovely as ever!

  —Jeri Sawyer

The Eyes Of A Baby

Have you ever looked into the eyes of a baby
 Have you ever seen the Christ-Child there
Have you ever looked into the eyes of a baby
  Round with wonder and wishful stare
Have you ever looked into the eyes of a baby
  Innocent and with no sense of care
Have you ever looked into the eyes of a baby
  God's own treasure to appear.
 When you look into the eyes of a baby
  Clouds above release a tear
Stars of heaven send forth their brightness
  All the darkness disappears.
 Tiny eyelids close in deep repose
  And dreamland floats above
Sounds of music soars into wonderland
 To show the Christ Child's love
When you look into the eyes of a baby
 You will see the Christ-Child there
Have you ever looked into the eyes of a baby?
Have you ever looked into the eyes of a baby?

  —Lois J. Clarke

Dynamism

One must be attentive
One must be intelligent
One must be reasonable
One must be responsible
One must be full of desire
to be real

  —Christie Zunker

Have You Ever?

Have you ever walked away from an outstretched hand?
Have you ever thought yourself better than one from another land?

Have you ever turned your head from a face with a smile?
Have you ever refused when asked to walk that extra mile?

Have you ever turned your head the other way
because you felt they were not as smart?

Have you ever chosen to be apart
because you felt you were better than they?

Have you ever turned from a child in tears
and not taken the time to soothe her fears?

Have you "looked down" on a child for he didn't measure up to
some without considering the home he may come from?

Have you ever thought that when from this world we part
we may be asked, "Did you give from your heart?"

  —Barbara DeLuca

To the Ones I Love

 As summer quietly fades away,
have you noticed today, the brilliant
and delightful colors on display.

 The liquid amber with its ever-changing
red, yellows and multicolored leaves cause one
to wonder and ponder the beauty of nature
and its creator.

 The maple, with its golden leaf splendor
that leads to the awestruck realization that
beauty is one of life's most rewarding experiences.

 The striking and eye catching beauty of the
pistachio causes those who are in love to hold
hands and marvel together how beauty and love
are wonderfully the same. And if alone, to
wish the loved one near, or to wish for a
loved one to share the deep feeling and beauty
of the moment.

 So stop, observe and enjoy the
ever changing beauty in the world and seek
and hold dear, the love you have or need.

  —Frank M. Graham

My Life

Living life, through pain and hell
Having a disease, that I could not tell.
Making my pain, twice as severe
From drugs and alcohol, and all of my fear.
Opening my eyes, and seeing my addiction
Thinking to myself, that it is all fiction.
One day realizing, it is the truth
Hurting and hating, I need no more proof.
I admit to myself, that I am powerless
My life is unmanageable, and quite a large mess.
With one last chance, my choice is so clear
I came to marworth, where everyone's sincere.
When I arrived, I was so scared
But then I realized, that everyone cared.
I began to relax, and open my mind
Out came my feelings, that I could never find.
Releasing my feelings, that were trapped inside
It made me feel honest, and had nothing to hide.
For once in my life, I have felt love
Who do I thank? The higher power above.

  —Shawn Moon

Silent Dreams

And as he stares with feeble eyes,
He dreams until the day he dies.
"I'll make it there," he tells them all.
The more they laugh,
The deeper he falls.
"I will," he insists, "If only you knew.
I can climb higher than any of you."
He trembles with anger,
But silence he speaks,
As he dreams on without the support he seeks.
"I thought I could," he says one day.
"Or maybe I can't,
Since that's what they say."
He dreams until the day he dies,
But he's lost in the sound
Of his cold anguished cries.
—*Diana Spechler*

A Man Afraid of Tears

Once afraid of the dark and one day saw the light
He feared the dark like
A man afraid of tears
A man of knowledge is a man of courage and wisdom
He looks my way with sadness in his eyes
But doesn't know how to speak of it

Say no more, your eyes show
A man afraid of tears
Fear not the knowledge you don't know
A man who shows his tears is showing his strength
Once all men have experienced such knowledge
There would be no more
Men afraid of tears
—*Dana Hess*

What a Blessing

With the help of the master's hand
He goes before us with a plan
To serve him in our land
As we are lead by his hand.
Jesus is the answer
To him we are to follow
It is his great command.
Oh, I'll praise the Lord forever
Rejoicing that he will never sever
The wonderful salvation plan
That he has given to man.
I love and praise you Jesus
My every will is your command.
I thank and praise you for all the blessings
Thank you for a loving family and friends
Help me always to show love and kindness
Put all evil and strife behind us
Just praise and worship the king
With all our beings and let true freedom ring.
—*Jessie Bottorff*

Love and Sadness

Love can be cherished with pain and prestige,
Happiness of plenty and a secure heart that will
not part with the feeling of goodwill throughout.
Although sadness is different and is sometimes
harsh and full of grieve, but remember
when your down don't turn someone else's
smile upside down, it will only make them frown,
and when everyone's down or sorrowful it
could do serious harm. Whether it's friendship
or family, your heart will never be full of lumps.
—*Kristal Chambers*

Wonders

The world is full of wonders
Everywhere you look
From butterflies to thunder
Just open up a book
—*Marylin Fischer*

God's Earth

God made — the Earth
He had one plan
To give "One chance" to man
He put — "His" power
In our own hands
To Test the "Deeds" of Man

God gave us moonlight and sunlight, and stars in the sky —
Lighting a path for the "Time" when the tides roll back —
    the seas run dry.

He'll come — to judge —
The "Deeds" of man —
Who 'Loved!...who "Harmed" His Plan

God gave earth more than He gave to the "Planets" above —
Put "Life" and His people on earth to live — Not with hate —
    our love can't wait —
But Now — Is love too late?

How sad — one day —
No Moon — No Sun — No Stars — No Life — No Man —
God's Earth — Destroyed — By Man.
—*Rosemary Bates*

The Brother

See the brother lying in the middle of the street.
He has dirty fingernails, stale clothes and stinky feet.
He is talking to himself, creating a little fuss.
He begs me for my spare change so he can catch the bus.
I try to ignore him by walking on by,
but something about this man catches my eye.
He grabs me by my hand,
letting me know he was in command.
I reach over and give this stranger a hug!
After a while, I realize all he needs is love.
He explained how one day his world just flopped.
Later that night, he found shelter at different bus stops.
His wife left him for a younger man.
He lost his job, as any innocent person can.
I sit next to him, eager to hear more.
He started to leave, telling me he was being a bore.
Although he had very sweaty palms,
his spirits were high and he seemed calm.
When it was time for him to go, I gave him a five dollar bill.
With it, I gave him God's peace and good will.
—*Rhoda Williams*

Poem Master

He tells the children stories, about magic, warriors, and elves
He has one hundred books and stories upon his wooden shelves
His voice is calm and friendly, like the ringing of a small bell
And all the children love to listen to the stories he will tell
His eyes are heavenly blue, His mouth always holds a smile
And his long, white beard seems to stretch for about a mile
He wears a hood upon his head and robes instead of clothes
And some children always follow him anywhere he goes
On his left hand he wears a ring with a single emerald
It reflects all of those stories that he has heard or told
He is the poem master, the children's best friend
And we will never see his power come to an end.
—*Vincent Appel*

The End

His journey has taken o'er eighty years.
He has picked up passengers along the way.
There have been straight roads as well as detours.

The man struggled to overcome his fears of poverty. He
married, raised a family, and became successful in the eyes of others.
And yet his childhood haunted him and caused pain to those near.

The trip has been full of pain, hurt, and despair, but we must
not forget that our hurt was caused by his hurt.

We must not forget that the heart tried—although only too
often with gifts in pretty boxes.

We must not forget the final true gift—our ability to forgive
and to remember the times when there were smiles and love.

—*Kathy Farrell*

My Dog Shorty

My dog Shorty has a short tail.
He is a black short haired male.
My dog barks at my black cow.
Shorty runs, kneels with a bow.
My dog chases all the cats.
Sometimes he plays with the rats.
He likes to hunt wild rabbits.
A smart dog, but has bad habits.
One day my cow kicked him in the head.
When I found shortly I thought he was dead.
Shorty is the best dog I ever had.
A jealous dog but he sure gets real mad.
Shorty got stung by a bumble bee.
It made him mad and he tried to bite me.
My dog barks all the time.
My dog shorty will always be mine.
His eyes shines in the night.
Shorty's collar on his neck is real bright.
In the yard he saw a brown frog.
Shorty is the best watch dog.

—*Colby Rohrbach*

Blind Light

Pete never blinks.
He moves fast through dark rooms,
laughs at me as I run into chairs,
jokes about my limited senses.
He braids his dreadlocks with fingertips as mirror
and bounces down the hill
feeling hindrances in his way
from a distance.
"Like tasting the shadows," he says,
touching the surface of life
with his bare hands. Proud smile, than a sigh.
"If I could see, I would reach deeper."
Pearls of his laughter
fall down on the sidewalk,
sparkling. But he cannot see
them giving light to the asphalt,
blinding me before dissolving,
as slow as water sinks in sand,
deepening the darkness.

—*Katarina Ahlfort*

Grandparents

They were always so good to me;
Every Christmas I could see,
Stockings hanging off the wall,
With toys and candy for us all.
They were the best I ever had.
Now that they're both gone,
I will always be sad.

—*Michael Bell*

Confined Within His Gift

As he looks up into the light,
He realizes how contradictory this is to him.
Caged like an beast in a boxed room,
He has been lowered in the kingdom.
There are two exits from his prison,
One noticeable, the other spiritual.
As for those who swear in the name of Hippocrates,
Some care only for his presence, not his being.
He has journeyed from the middle "man",
To the doorstep of the true bearer of His gift.
The center, in the pattern of life,
Has been unparalleled, but alas, he has outlived its use.
It is ironic that He, who has given the perfect gift,
Must take it away, in its dimmest, flickering moments.
As he takes peerless pleasure in the setting of the sun,
He wishes not to see its rise.

—*Ameet Upadhyaya*

Gift of Life

We're all God's children and in his eyes
He sees to gifts that make us wise,
And he knows all men are not the same
So he gives us all our bit of fame.
He put something special in all our insides,
It's up to us now to find where it hides.
For some it was hard while others improved,
To deal with their lives when the mask was removed.
Sometimes one's nature is kept on the shelf,
Where it's bound to grow old while in search of itself,
And then as in nature the bud comes to flower,
To know all the beauty in its waking hour.
Now feeling your glory will give you a lift
Cause your bound for the promise of God's special gift.
You may find new meaning for what you once cared,
If you feel in your heart that God's gift should be shared,
Remember God gave you a talent that gives,
To reach out from the inside to show you he lives.

—*Daniel J. Harding*

Bloom

Lullaby sweet, yellow, pink and blue
Flowers blooming, covered with dew
The water of life protects and nourishes
Sleeping babe, on Mother's love, wiggles and flourishes
Exploring each sensation, snug in the womb
Each passing day brings a brand new bloom
Gentle harp, it's the angel, mother nature's call
Into the light soon a babe will fall

—*Patricia D. Hargrove*

"My Little Guy"

My little guy came in, one day, with grease all o'er his face!
He said, "Aw, Mom, I don't know how it got there, in that place!"

I scrubbed, I scrubbed, I scrubbed some more; he cried enough for three.
The "gunk" was hard to budge, 'tis true! 'Twas tractor grease, you see!

I said, now son, you're growing big and problems you must face.
You cannot do it best, you see, with grease all o'er your face!

So, now he's grown and on his own, he flies, with awesome grace!
But looking back, with tears, I see the grease upon his face!

My son, I hope I leave with you, moments you can't erase,
just good ones you cannot forget, like "grease all o'er your face"!

—*Lyda Balster*

"The Encounter"

Who can this be? This man so old
He sleeps so still, so sound
The leaves protect him from the cold
Who is this man I've found?

Stepping closer, i strain to see
Ah, now i can at last
How did this lone man come to be?
I wonder of his past

Gray locks of hair surround his face
I bend and touch his cheek
Was there a day, a time, a place
When life was not so bleak?

I startle him, he coughs, he groans
He turns and starts to call
"Say who comes there!? Say who!" He moans
I take his hand so small.

"I mean no harm to you, my friend
"No, I'm just passing through"
Hence silently we comprehend
Oh yes, just passing through.
      —Laurie Jo

Humpty's Eggperience

Because Humpty's long love was lost,
He swore to find her no matter what the cost.
He "wobbled" up and down the street
In the hope that they might meet.
He "scrambled" all about the city
And they say it sure was a pity.
Weeks had passed since he had eaten
He was defeated and badly "beaten".
Well, one day he climbed a wall
And decided to end it all.
Just then he saw his lovely mate
What happened next was his ill-fate.
She gave to him her sweetest smile.
This would-be chick sure did have style.
He leapt to be right by her side.
Of course, this is how Humpty died.
Some said the blame was his, some said his lover.
Opinion was six of one, half dozen of the other.
Some felt it was love gone astray;
While others said, "he was half-cracked anyway."
      —Geraldine Scotto

Thank You!

Thank you God for sending Jesus to die for me.
He took my place on Calvary,
And died to set me free.
Upon that lonely tree, He was
mocked, rejected, beaten and scorned.
But through all His pain and agony,
  He still loved me.
He even prayed for the men beside him,
  and was forgiving to those who mocked
  his name.
Oh, Thank You Jesus for dying for sinners
  like me!
      —April D. Moore

Good-Byes Aren't Always Forever, They Just Seem That Way

Uncle Sam called for me early last June
He wanted me to wear his dress blues
But killing men ain't everyman's game
Why did he have to choose my name
So I packed up my bags and said my goodbyes
headed for Cally with tears in my eyes
I said baby I will be back
I understand how much it hurts
with a tear in my eye, I said good-bye
but baby it wont' be forever
When I returned home we said our vows
promising we'd make it together somehow
but again I had to go my way to serve my country
both night and day and I left her with son on his way to
come into this world while I was away
In the times she needed me most I had to go
why did I have to be a G.I. Joe
I said baby I will return. I understand how much it hurts
with a tear in my eyes I said good-bye
but baby it won't be forever.
      —Tim Garrison

Losing a Friend

He was like a brother.
He was a real best friend.
He was always there again and again.
You said you loved him.
He said he did too.
You believed him then.
But now why did you?
He always listened and seemed to care.
He took care of you without being there.
Your love for him took your heart and soul.
But now your brother and friend has slowly faded away.
But your love for him will always stay.
      —Beth A. Roth

The Off Button

When he was just a babe, we would say that we couldn't wait to
hear his voice. "I can't wait to hear him say Mommy."
"I'm going to buy him a car the first time he says Daddy."
"It's going to be sooo cute," we would say.

Well, the day came upon us a year or two ago.
And his voice is sooo cute. But... IT NEVER STOPS.
It goes on and on and on.
"Does he come with an off button?" We would ask.
"Maybe I'll buy him a car if he's quiet for awhile."
"And I think I'll scream if I hear the word Mommy again."

But, yet, when he's safely tucked away for the night,
As I bask in the peace and serenity, it's only then that I
realize that cute little voice will, one day, be silent forever
To be replaced, at first, by a breaking teenage pitch;
And then to that of the husky, mature voice of a man.

So, tomorrow, when our little one wakes up, and stirs me from a
sound sleep, with the first rousing "Mommy, mommy, mommy," of
the day, I will scoop him up, hug and kiss him, glad he is
still just a child, only to be looking for the "off button"
by dinner time again.
      —Lori Teverini

Dreams

Dreams are a powerful, magical place, where spirits can travel free.
Hearts can search for each other, and release all their misery.
It is where the soul can search out its mate, when separated by
    thousands of miles.
So dream of me, while I dream of you and we shall visit awhile.

Dreams do not know boundaries, the limits of time and space.
For only in dreams can your mind roam free and your imagination
can place within your grasp a power you never realized you held —
The power to move through worlds unknown, your heart and your
    mind to meld.

Dreams can bring you freedom, to account for your desires.
Those hidden needs, the anxious moments you never allow to
    transpire.
So sleep my darling, and as you slip into the wonders of the unknown,
I'll be searching, and I'll find you, you won't have to dream alone.

—*Pasty Gordon*

The Milky Way

Tapestries of magical design
Heavenly flames from holy places fill the void
Endlessly rushing and vanishing into infinity.
Majestic celestial coruscations
Intricately woven in a brilliant web of light
Like the curtains of the auroras dance and flicker,
Knitting in a silver shroud the all-devouring darkness, which
Yields...as
Winding rivers of swirling fire-mists form
A shining cloak across the heavens
Ycleped the milky way.

—*Cleo Laszlo*

Little Sweetheart

Heartfelt prayers to God, please Lord, show me the way.
Help me deal with this bitter grief, consuming me today.
I should have known, but often, refused to believe my eyes.
Daughter, you and your child's life is built on many lies.
Why did it start? How long has the hurt been there?
Granddaughter, in spite of my indifference, believe I really care.
Hearing of an abused child, could never be someone I knew.
Little sweetheart, now I realize this hurting child is you.
Seeing the emotional damage. I can't stand, seeing you in pain.
Your mom needs help, sweetheart, she doesn't feel the blame.
If I tell, there'll be denials, maybe I'll see you no more.
Little sweetheart, your cries, I simply can't ignore.
What will happen to you and your dreams if I just turn away?
You will grow up troubled or with your life, you'll pay.
So I have to tell to get help, even if you may never again see me.
My love for you will be difficult to remember, for a child of three.

—*Connie Whitmore*

Wish

She closed her eyes
her lips formed two short, quick words
followed by a gentle flow of phrases
tumbling out like water from a bottle
the words came from her soul
they were feelings, dreams from her heart
desires that her mind couldn't hold
thoughts no one could know about
except for the star in the moon lit sky
the first star of the night
one small shimmering star
that knew so much about wishes
from souls like hers
lying alone in the dark, vast sky
like a sparkle in a dark blue eye
exploding with words that came
from the heart

—*Rebecca Koenig*

The Angel

The angel is the thunderbird-
Her eyes are everywhere
Analogous of big brother,
Yet different, somehow.

She knows just like Santa Claus,
Who's been good and who's been bad.
She listens to your incense;
Both the happy smoke, and the sad.

She circles all eternity
Throughout all time and space.
She is the poor and needy
Helping losers defeat might... with grace.

She seeks truth and justice;
She knows freedom is indeed free.
Yet when you seek to kiss her cheek
She turns into a smile.

For on that day you kiss her cheek
You've found that which you sought.
For those who seek and finally find
Will know where Truth is found... is martyrdom.

—*Vance Hawkins*

T.M.

I saw free form beauty again
her golden radiance burst forth upon me

Memories...
Of our happiness...huh, and our happiness, yeah

I guess it's too late in many ways
what was, already was, ain't meant for now

But, I just want you to know, super mama
my love is yours, beautifully so

Our understanding is uniquely ours, our bond
and sometimes you know, it's the hope I live on

I hope now you realize your inner beauty
so you can share the enlightenment you give, with yourself

Remembering the way you'd look at me, with your eyes,
made my day and eased the pain of their lies

Once again I'd like to hear you moan
and listen to your sighs

For now I would understand
the meaning of your cries

—*Dana Silkiss*

Poetry

I love poetry!
But not all poetry you see,
Only that poetry that doth appeal to me.

What doth appeal to me you see,
May not appeal to thee.
Pity, a pity exclaim both we,
But that's the way it be.

Accept that fact my friend must we
I'm sure you'll readily agree.
For any other conclusion just simply cannot be.
Yes, I love poetry that doth appeal to me.

—*Ralph Leon Haws*

Geneses Forgotten

Alone on a rise in the desert
Her heavy stone base sinking in the sand
She's a shattered old image
that still stalks the land.
From day onto years
she wavers in the heat
her holy child, destined
never did take his seat.

Eden has been eaten
down to it's heavy core
by children of a christian whore.
Over the wet mourning grass
her many hands pour our sand
dry death over the land.

The calvary of the Apocalypse
has ridden out from the sun
charging hard down olympic mounts
war on the earth is almost done.
Our mother will be barren
the dragons have begun.

—*Mark Greene*

"Little Miss Apple"

"She is the apple of my eye," He says,
"her keys are softer than the touch of the skies,
my attention is on her screen."
I felt green with envy.
Now when he said, "her shift and lock are perfectly capital."
I almost felt hysterical.
I wanted to give him a jab,
But all he talked about was her tab,
How she can go one side to the other.
I sat there wanting him to smother.
"She's great with information," He said,
"Plays games too, with participation."
He told me she has a mouse,
Was I supposed to be aroused?
So I got mad and decided to say, "Let me see little Miss Apple
today."
"And there she is." He said.
I could not believe what I did,
Getting mad over little Miss Apple Computer!

—*Melody M. Velasco*

The Quilt

She sat beside the bed watching her mother die,
Her quilt covering her last moments
As it had her first.
Mother was drifting away,
The corner of the quilt clutched in her hands
It meant so much to her.
And I wondered whether to let it go
As mother's shroud —
Or save it for generations to come
I could make another—but would I?
Or could it ever be the same? It doesn't matter.
It is not the thing
But the memory of the thing that matters.
All the quilting bees — all the gossip —
But would all the memories
Really exist for future generations?
Pride of family — yes — but the actual memories
Die with the dead who made them.
Please God — make me choose aright.

—*Sally H. Christensen*

I Wish You Love

I wish you sunlight, starlight too,
Life's fondest dreams I hope come true

I wish you happiness, blessings from above,

But most of all, I wish you love.

I wish you rainbows after gentle falling rain,
I wish you snow flakes on a wintry window pane -
Happy endings to everyday.

I wish you laughter, never tears.
The joy of living, peace in your years.
A feeling of togetherness, always hand in glove,
But best of all, I wish you love

I'll wish you love forever,
I've loved you from the start.
The best I have to offer, all the love in my heart
I wish you love

—*Shawn A. Sullivan*

A Winter's Garden

I stood among my garden tall
looking all around I saw
that I had been blest.
For by my feet the sky was found
the golden sun was by my brow.

God had created earth and all her splendor.
Fortune had graced my little plot, when He had cast His
second glance.
While I stood and gazed about and carefully took one...step or, two.
I knew not where to rest my eye, so magnificent was the view!

Silently I close my eyes and take this, my love, into my heart —
knowing full well summer must part.
My heart shall swell and Swell and SWELL as that garden of
light and warmth casts away the wintery spell.

The seed of yesterday's summer has found a new plot, somewhere
deep within my heart.
I thank you God my soul so filled with light and warmth as you
have willed, the summer song shall still be heard —
While winter silence, like a mantel spread, does make our earth
a living bed.

—*Valerie Daniel*

Moment of Memory

Love for you will always be
more then just a memory
A special hand you always lent
A smile, your laughter, heaven sent.

Though you were taken up above
what remains down here is all your love,
In our hearts very deep
something that we can keep.

Things will be different, we know they will
a piece is missing, that we cannot fill
but we will remember your smiling face
'Til we meet again in that beautiful place.

—*Sharon Tedesco*

Horses

I think horses are grand,
Even when they stand.
In my field they are so rare,
Does anyone have a spare?
I'll take a black, tan or white,
If you have one please call tonight.

—*Jennifer Bannister*

Lament for the Undead

My eyes are as black as the midnight sky;
My skin as pale as the moon.
I await the fall of the blazing sun;
The night is coming soon.
I did not ask to be this way;
A vulture of the night
Who stalks and preys 'till dead they lay
Their bodies drained of fright.
The sun burns it's way across the heavens
'Till day is a thing of the past;
A thousand nights have come and gone
Since I saw daylight last.
I did not ask to be this way;
To live but never die.
Life's only escape has been stolen away;
To the star of the North I cry.
A life I'll take for every night
This sad life trudges on;
I'll kill and sunder, rape and plunder
'Till this sad life is gone.

—*Joe Guernsey*

Vicious Cycle

Living in chains of hatred
my soul is crushing to the
sound of screams.

Surrounded by flaming fires,
I don't know where to hide.
I don't know where to turn.
I can't escape the pain I'm feeling inside.

Confusion follows me day in and day out;
I'm followed by demons that I can't get rid of.

I hear voices...voices that call my name...
what do I do...where do I turn?

Death will be pretty when it comes.
It will end my pains of life and end
the torture I do unto myself.
I'll live another life and have pains again.
Then I'll die and the cycle will continue.

—*Leigha Polazzo*

Lucerne, September, 1993

We have burned our bridges like our martyrs.
Now black charred beams half-span the river.
The floating flocks: ducks swans and gulls
Pursuing avian aims, continue to congregate.

Cafes border the water where in golden autumn,
Mulling tired agendas, we sit among coffee cups.
The produce market offers pears and apples,
Grapes of every ripeness, no fruit forbidden.

In the quiet square around the corner, a wine tasting,
While in the old Jesuit church, a christening.
And on the river that night a conflagration
Burning fiercer than the faggots of a martyr's pyre.

As did our August passion.
The September city moves in cool reason.
The firm ripeness of pears
Opposes the soft red sweetness of berries.
The river silently receives
The unmourned embers of our love.

—*Judith T. Copek*

Snow Queen

She's a magnificent creature
Of rare beauty and grace
Coming only in winter
Covering the world with white lace.

Like she's sewing white thread into the earth,
Protecting the land with her white blanket,
Loving it like a Mother who's just given birth.

The snowflakes are her kisses
Falling from the sky
The frost is her whisper
Saying goodbye.

—*Corinne Delaney*

A Time to Heal

How much time does it take for the pain
of that loved one lost in death to heal?
A day? Year? Two years? Three?

The pain will never totally leave. It's
there always; along with the memories.
Grief is what one time through the
hours and many sunsets and many sunrises
will finally begin to fade away.

The age one is at that time of death doesn't matter...
No one is prepared to deal with such a great loss as that
of one loved. Death leaves a hole; an emptiness. It also
leaves memories of love and fulfillment with
times of hurt and pain. Delight and worry
and in the end a sorrow so deep that
no words can describe - "Grief"

The memories can't be held or cuddled or
yelled at. You can't telephone a
memory to discuss a thought with because they understand
— but a memory can make a heart swell with a love
that will never go away. Bad or good it's your memory of life!

—*Karen Orison*

Of Icons and Grand Illusions

Sawed-off attitudes
Of the new street generations

Armed silhouettes in the corner of the night
The bands of the precocious tough

A mindless high at needlepoint
And somebody innocence always slips away

Power of the gun
within the talons
of a newborn

Mothers milk, silk stained with gasoline

By ten there's nothing
that child
hasn't seen

Lives spill like water

At seventeen, that child
He's a streetcorner icon

Childhood America, interrupted
Shame on their trail to fame
It's Hell
In style.

—*Pete Macaluso*

The Old Man of the Woods

Peering through the enchanted branches
Of the stretching, whispering trees,
His eyes, they follow you.
He doesn't tell you which cleared path to take,
But he knows where they all lead.
For he spends his life here
Learning, teaching, destroying, creating
and loving the beauty of the forest.
His body is of soft earth
and his clothes are of dry leaves.
His beard is of twisting vines
and his scent is of wild flowers.
His voice is of the whistling wind
and his knowledge is of nature.
The ponds and trees, plants and animals, hills and valleys,
Everything in the woods bow to his coming,
for they are of him.
He protects yet shares his beauty with you.
He is the...
Old Man Of The Woods.

—*Andrea Brudvig*

Casual Sax

I have two love affairs.
One with a jazz man, cool and mellow.
Together, we frequent seedy nightclubs in the wee hours.
He skulks in the shadows, shows me to a select audience.
Our haunts include the Kitten Club and Ronnie's, both
questionable establishments.
Sawdust on the floor, dark, water the color of mahogany, the
patrons don't come for the ambiance.
My other love is brash, a soldier type,
not afraid to flaunt me in front of large crowds.
Dressed to the nines in a uniform suited for a drum
majorette,
on display to the world.
I am his Ivana, his Jackie O.
Though my sweethearts contrast, both love my brassy curves,
my soothing, alto voice.

—*Seth Grossman*

Grandfather

Sitting, staring at a reflection of pain
Peering through my lonely wandering soul
Wondering why you're not the same
It seemed like yesterday you were laughing and talking
Now you can't say a word and not even walking

The agony you feel burns deep in my heart
Just seeing you there in your own little world
Wishing I could help bring you back into mine
Just to hear you laugh ten thousand more times
So you can call out my name, for I'll always hear you
Now you're calling with your heart but there's nothing I can do

Seeing you lying there makes me want to cry
Just thinking about you brings tears to my eyes
Wishing you'd live, but hoping you'd pass on
For the life you lived in this unfair world
There will be no struggle in what comes next
No racism, no greed, no wars, no drugs, no pain or sickness

But keep in your heart, I'll always love you,
And I know you feel the same
For I'll always walk and stand up tall
Because I'll always carry your name.
Zenji Kasubuchi, my grandfather.

—*Wes Kasubuchi*

Blue Shift

Blues slowly come back to me. The chill
pennants of an October sky, framed, muted
by the branches of riotous leaves. Still,
the azure blood of an icicle rested,
waiting for the beat of spring. Twigs and down,
the nest hid three blue crescents, promising
robins-changes of blue to red and brown!
Summer too is blue. Sky: all canvassing,
subsuming greens, swallowing reds, a one
color palette to paint all summers back
to the first. And eyes... two have just begun
to redefine what I knew, what I lack
of so primary a color. In you
I relearn the still, chill promises of blue.

—*Michael Pringle*

Our Father's Preaching Message of God

Sunshine shines upon the face of God
Rendering warmth and hope upon the
Faces of children, running through Eden.
Standing at the pulpit preaching life,
The congregation glows with love.

The testimony of God is shone
True to us each and every day
By the father of us all. The father
That ventures through the golden
Gates of grace, the father that reads
The lips of God through the word of God.

The Table stands as the Altar,
Praising God upon Icons of
Faith. The sermon is read,
Ears await the golden word
While the prophets reveal the
Ultimate friend for all, the
Reader of our lives, the preacher
Of our souls, and our true understanding
Of the Book.

—*Perry C. Lantz*

Full Circle

Spinning,
revolving,
never stopping
Continuity, never ending, always beginning
Here we go again, full circle.
Hearts and souls entwined, never missing a beat
Transcending above the rest
Surrounding
Adhering
Adamant
That we shall never drift asunder
"Till death do us part"
What lies were told
What promises were broken
Somewhere in the night
Swiveling,
Spiraling,
Toppling,
Silently downward, surviving,
Because we have come full circle.

—*Katherine Blanke Kelley*

No Wings On My Back

When I first met our Rocky, I felt I knew her all my life
She was always there to help someone who's struggling with strife.

It never seemed to fail that Rocky always had a smile
To everyone she met, she'd go that extra mile.

She was open as a book as helpful as could be
Life was good to Rocky but not as good as she was to me.

Her warmness and her kindness we shall treasure all our days
She touched our soul and made us laugh in oh so many ways.

She never gave you any flack, I still hear her when she said
"You won't find no wings on my back or no halo on my head!"

But I know our God in Heaven had some work for you to do
And He came down personally and proudly walked with you.

To your permanent assignment of watching overhead
You've earned the shining halo that rests proudly on your head.

Through smiling tears we see you keeping God's angels all on track
And we know that you are one of them by the wings upon your back.

—Debbie Bibb

Across the Field

As I look across the field I see a radiance coming towards me!
So bright and shining I know not whence it came.
The radiance gets closer, I'm able to distinguish a figure
A glow beyond compare.

My mind wanders, what can this be, God coming for me!
Am I deserving, have I been a child of God?
Have I been free? Free to worship, free to be me.
The light gets brighter, I bubble with joy, could this be my Savior?
Or is this just a ploy?

Let me tell you child of God, get close so you can hear
Those of you who do not know must lend a fervid ear!!!
Jesus Christ is on his way, the light is getting brighter
Such beauty, such radiance for all the world to see
Coming slowly thru the field with radiance shining bright.

Coming for his children with such an awesome light
Gentle caring favor, for all the world to see.
Jesus coming cross the field
A light for you and me

—Helen Rae Wegner

Tears

A tear,
So lonesome, so wet,
So salty, so soft,
So pure.
Possibly the purest thing on this god forsaken earth.
Purer than water.
For no man can pollute a tear.
No dirt can soil the dream of a soul.
A cry,
When cried from the eyes of a beholder
Is a sign of purity of the soul.
A soul of tenderness and compassion,
Devotion and longing,
For a cry is a slew of tears
That have touched so little,
The eye, the cheek, and the heart.

—Nicole Cassara

"A True Mother's Love"

A mother is real, a mother is true, a very special mother will take care of you.

She is there when you are sick and even hungry too. Now that's a mother who truly loves you.

She won't give you up, nor tear you down. A God sent mother will always be around.

No matter how you treat her, no matter
What you do, a real divine mother will always be there for you.

Give her all of your love and especially tender care, for you can't find a God sent mother just any and everywhere.

Treat her like she's rubies and diamonds if you can, a God fearing holy mother is always in demand.

Then when she closes her eyes and all of her work is done, you will have to take care of yourself your life has just begun,

So, use what she has taught you make it work for you, though she may be in Heaven she is still watching you.

Death doesn't separate a true mother's love, because she's still with you while watching from above.

—Carolyn J. Cobbs

The Last Ride

It was a dream he used to say
That he would ride again someday
Not a dream he had during the day
But at night ol' Bill seemed to say
"Let's ride in the hills once again"

He sat so straight in a creaky old saddle
As if he were off to some distant battle
Keeping his eyes on the slow moving cattle
That was before ol' Bill's ghostly rattle
"Let's ride in the hills once again"

Old age came and it left him lame
After that he just wasn't the same
He vainly looked for someone to blame
And at night he'd hear ol' Bill's refrain
"Let's ride in the hills once again"

The medicine made his limp go away
And then he knew that come what may
That he would ride the very next day
Then once again he heard ol' Bill say
"Let's ride in the hills once again" And so he went.

—Genie Tansey

The Flower In My Garden

The garden of life has produced a blooming flower
That stands above all the rest. A rose with no
thorns and the most desirable of all God's creation
Sought by all
Plucked by one
Planted in the garden of my heart,
I am her keeper - I am her husband,
She's my wife.

—Glenn Thompson

AWAKE

You sleeping mind
The world is yours to find.
Life lies in the living not the dead,
So open your eyes and turn your head
To all the answers the world has never found—
Freedom of soul, love of life, beauty of mind,
Friend of heart, laughter of youth, and wisdom of aging.

—Reggie Morris

The Package Deal

What is it about you, that makes me care?
The exact attribute, the essence rare?
Is it that you are so very giving?
And possess a charm and zest for living?
Is it that thrilling, blue, consummate stare,
That makes my heart accept the dare?
Or perhaps it is the curly brown hair,
that helps me pay the emotional fare.
Or that you fight to gain my acceptance,
that makes my feet stay in step with your dance.

Yet, what is "it", at the nuclear core?
It is all this, and so very much more.
The things I simply can not quantify,
And, then, there is the truth I can not deny.
There is "something" about you that sets me free,
Creates passion expressed so ardently,
That makes my fragile heart so bold to dare,
To think that I could also make you care.
So, the kernel remains a mystery,
Meanwhile, we are making history.

—*Suellen Kossow*

Shield to Storm

The stars and moon, so clear and bright.
The quietness of the desert, seems so serene.
Then there's the launch, with all it's gleam.

The streets of Kuwait, are filled with pain.
Countrymen doing things, they can't explain
Soon the bombs, will be falling like rain.

The noise from the engines.
The fire in the sky.
Telling us that, they're ready to fly.
Punching holes left and right, through the night.

Proving our pilots, know how to fight
Like huge eagles, soaring gracefully in flight.
The F-111, breaks through with it's screams.
A city 2 hours away, lay asleep with dreams.

Will soon be awaken, by wars destruction beams!

—*Karen L. Fletcher*

The Miracle of Chanukah

When the Temple was destroyed,
The survivors were annoyed

In the darkness they could not see,
in great danger and not yet free

They wanted to survive the terrible turmoil,
and soon thereafter they found some oil

They used the oil to make it light,
but there was just enough for one full night

the next day to their surprise,
the room stayed lit and so did their eyes

The third, the fourth, and then the fifth day,
they woke to brightness the very same way

What happened the next three nights,
the oil lasted and the room had lights

It was a miracle as the survivors gazed,
that the oil they found lasted eight days

—*Howard I. Baumgarten*

The Snow White Dove

On the wings of a snow white dove,
there's a message of love,
as it sails through the clear blue sky.

Not a cloud, just the breeze,
as it flies past the trees,
you might notice if you look up above -

Now the timing must be right,
or the dove's out of sight,
sometimes love has to take its own flight -

But one day,
as you pray,
you might hear yourself say,
I know that dove will be back for me yet -

Then you'll fly in the sky,
ever so high,
as you sit on the wings of love -

You won't ask why,
you'll just take a deep sigh,
and thank God for the snow white dove —

—*Jeff Scheider*

Friends

Who are they?
They say you can trust them,
But who can you trust?
Just when you begin to trust them,
And you want to believe they are your friend,
Watch Out!........a knife is near.
They lie and they sneak around telling stories.
When confronted they deny all.
Who can you trust?
Who are your friends?

—*Tanya M. Llera*

Life Ended with Suicide

Once or twice this side of death
things can make one hold his breath.
Someone heard him call out a name
before his last breath of life, no one's
life will ever be the same. My heart
hurt and throbbed all I could do was
sob. He use to lean toward the good
things in life but his life one day ended
with the sharpness of a blade of a knife.
Life and Death, Life and Death
the wind no more on his sweet
Breath.

—*Kimberly Ferreira*

Re Creation

Lost my mother when she cried—this is not my home—you are not
my child
Lost my name when he said—this is not my world—you are not
your dad
Lost my hope when she said—you are not the friend I wish to make
my home with/out
—All of these
I found my soul in the dark—in the hole—in the fear
a name—a love—my hope
For you see— As foolhardy as I've been all along
I know my heart contains the open space needed to create a
world where there is light
beyond the ashes.

—*Richard Michael Dome*

Can We All Get Along?

Can we all get along?
This is not our world
God made this world by himself.

We don't own each other,
There are different values,
Culture, experiences,
Let's not judge a person by the clothing they wear,
Treat others the way you treat yourself.

You don't really know each other,
Nor walk in others shoes,
Can we all get along,
Just a little love will make
The world better and endurable.

We all need someone to lean on,
We can all get along
If we try.

—*Lee Etter Mouton-Butler*

The Ballad of Rupert

Darling little Rupert was a good friend of mine
tho I couldn't understand him 'most all of the time.
He was small, he was dainty, his eyes were of black
and I often talked to him, but he never talked back.

I met him on a Monday in a little pet store.
He swam into my heart, and I couldn't have loved him more.
I put him in a fish bowl, but he didn't like it there
so at times he'd leap out to get a bit of fresh air.

Car had soon learned to lived outside of the water.
He'd sit upon the sofa 'till the weather got hotter.
Then he'd take to the shade of a pretty bird cage
and he'd sit on the perch looking quite like a sage.

My precocious little Rupert, you're not a parakeet!
You've got scales, not feathers. You've got fins and not feet!
I neglected to tell him that he hadn't got wings.
That's the point of this ballad that I'm trying to sing.

Perhaps you can guess what I'm trying to say
How a goldfish tried to fly, and how a goldfish passed away.
He leaped off his perch, and he promptly fell down.
He fell into the water-dish and there, Rupert drowned.

—*Marie Everett*

Untitled

Have you been where the wiLd winds blow?
To a land that knows no paIn
Where birds rule The world
Because they arE the dreamers
And the sands aRen't swept by the sea
An unchArted place, though many have tried
To confine iTs realms to mere forms
No hUman breath disturbs the wind, or causes it to lose course
Because this is the place where heaRts are the compass,
And hidden souls the lantErns.

—*Tracy Karas*

"I'll Be Watching"

When the dew forms on the grass, I'll be watching.
When the clouds melt into rain, I'll be watching.
When kids suck on icicles on a frosty day, I'll be watching.
I'll be watching forever. I never miss a thing.
When the sun sets into a rainbow of colors, I'll be watching.
I've seen everything, but I continue to watch.
I'll watch until eternity.

—*Samira Abboubi*

To A Stranger

To a stranger I seem fine.
To a stranger I'm kind.
To a stranger I'm on top of the world looking down.
To a stranger there's a smile on my face with no sign of frown
To a stranger there's no sign of the hurt way down inside.
To a stranger there are so many things I can hide.

To you, a friend, I say there is a frown.
To you, I say that the smile I wear, doesn't go all the way down.
To you I say I miss you and the hurt is deep.
To you I say you're the one thing I wanted to keep.
To you I say I will love you forever and a day
And to you I say I wish you'd never gone away!

To a stranger I have it all
And seem to be ten feet tall!
To you I'll say that inside I feel an inch in height
And I'm afraid to go to bed at night.
To a stranger I'd say that crying is for sissy's or babies.
To you I'd say, in tears, I'll take you back with your doubts and maybes,
To a stranger, love 'em and leave 'em is my rule.
To you I'd say, letting you go, made me a fool.

—*Lisa Tortolini*

It All Came Clearly to Me

On a morning of blissful dew drops, the noise began
to rise slowly. You could hear a sigh of great
relief of joy coming down the road.

The rain began to fall faster than any drops
I have ever seen before.

People coming down the sidewalk singing a hymn of
great joy and praise. Coming together with one
accord, for you will know that time will tell and
will not stand still.

At last they come from afar, shouting with glee.
the wind began to pick its spot of which way it
wants to blow, but all is well for you and me.

The sun is shining so brightly from above and the
sky is some what gray.
It All Comes Clearly To Me

—*Vivian Reap*

For You, Teddy Bear, I Do Care

Remembering back to that one special day,
When your enchanting love flowed my way.
It was an endless time, not forgotten.
My heart of clouds were filled with soft cotton.
My soul lifted farther than the eye can see,
When I encountered a sea of beauty, a river of love.

Forever abiding to live,
May you forever see to give,
All of your heart, soul, and love,
To be a teddy bear of,
Over-flowing waters of the sea,
Shining sparkles of showering rain,
That brighten the beauty you are to me.
Forever more, your love will remain,
A-glowing, running far and wide,
Through the rivers of love that open wide,
Allowing lovable love to lay beside,
Many and few,
Like you, who are so true,
For you, teddy bear, I do care.

—*Brian S. Lowther*

Uncried Tears

Will my baby be killed today
While the warriors have all gone away
To hunt for food to keep us alive?
Will he see what tomorrow holds or will he die?

Will we be ambushed by soldiers
And cowards that do not care for us?
Will the old be shot and the women raped
Even while we know its unjust?

Will anyone see these tears
That come falling from my eyes?
Will anyone hear these words I speak
Or will they call them lies?

I guess I won't know until all is said and done
And the warriors return with the setting sun.
So it is here where I will wait, holding my child near,
Worrying myself sick with each uncried tear.

—*Chris Wright*

Ode to the Ancient One

Domestic sands adore me
With a heavenly quake of menial sunshine
And crush my undulant skin into crisp layers,
Like a bloody sword piercing the jelloed sea.
Ancient rays clog wrought pyramids
And a half-hearted stranger moves forth
To cart an onslaught of scriptured stone.
He kneels before Tut draining operatic homages.

—*Kiki Stamatiou*

Perspective of Man

Breakaway from my heart
With Godspeed do part
For love is painful, not pure
And man thinks he's found a cure
He says do not care, it serves no purpose
We only die and lie beneath the surface
But I revoke thee in the Lord's name
To be loved is our only claim
And we are not animals to live and die
We are men and we die and live

—*J. P. Slovak*

Lady of Mystery

I'm a lady of mystery.
You won't come to know me,
Through the pages of my history.
There I'm only a name from the family tree,
Only a leaf lying there beneath.

If you're an explorer of mysteries,
Of things unknown for centuries,
Perhaps you could discover
The reasons for my cover.

Look past these haunting eyes,
To the mysteries there inside.
There in the shadows dark and deep,
You'll find the secrets I've tried to keep.

This lady has it all hidden,
Well beneath this outer shell.
Inside I'm all pain ridden.
Maybe to you, I can tell.

So, come search my soul, help set me free.
I welcome you, explorer of mysteries.

—*Kathy Bledsoe*

Even Though We're Friends

Your touch was like a warm passionate kiss,
Your kiss was deep and romantic, like a warm lit fireplace,
You swept me away and now I'm lost in the dark,
Wondering why we suddenly broke a part,
My love was, lit like a fire,
Your love was deep, like dark chocolate,
Even though we're friends, there has always been something,
more, everything we wish for, but scared to explore,
I love you as a lover,
You love me like no other,
Even though we're friends, I'm nothing like your mother,
I can't be something I'm not, only just your lover,
My love flows like the Nile,
Your love burns like the "Great California Fires,"
You said you wanted us to be friends,
This is where our love ends,
and our friendship begins.

—*Jeaneen Benson*

"Song by a Young Lover, 1942"

I love you…
Your lips, your hair,
Your eyes, your breast,
Whereon I lay my head to rest…
And dream the dreams a lover dreams,
Until at last
It seems
The world has gone
And we two are alone…
To love.

"Song by a Lover, Twice Widowed, 1990, 1993"
I loved you…
Your lips, your hair,
Your eyes, your breast,
Whereon I laid my head to rest…
And dreamed the dreams a lover dreams,
Until at last
It seemed
The world had gone
And we two were alone
To love.

—*Thomas H. Price*

The Sufferer

Withered flesh encompasses his bones,
His skin so pale with no overtones.
Lying still day after day,
What has caused his soul to pay?
Such sounds of hums and bells does only he hear,
At night in his room alone with his tears.
His mind so crisp and eyes that just stare,
To him his time of retirement was met unfair.
So tired of clinging and dwindling on,
My father he watches from dusk 'til dawn.
The tubes from machines that feed him a life of stillness.
Of the terminal wasting in this horrible illness.
God bless your feeble body denied of your pride and soul,
Possessions you've none, no replies as it takes it toll.
Let the sufferer be of eternal peace soon,
Let my father hear a prettier tune.

—*Donna Esposito*

Chances

A chance to say good-bye,
A spark, a glimmer of hope
To ensure lasting remembrance
of what once was; never the same.

A new beginning awaits;
Opportunities anew fill the world
around you.
What to do and how, but fear I will not.

A new life created from old,
Experience directs your path
Finding what was once thought lost,
but never truly was.

A chance to say good-bye,
Never eternal in one's heart.
A special togetherness always
existing, changing, growing forever.

—*Amanda B. Creel*

Brandon

Tears in my eyes
  a broken heart
My love for you
  will never depart
Dreaming of you
  night and day
Thinking of it
  like yesterday
  … the joy
  … the happiness
  … the sadness
  … the loneliness
It's all part of my
  broken heart

—*Tammy L. Brengle*

Requiem For "Genius"

"Genius" was a bird
A bulbul to be precise.
Yet, she was more…
An undaunted spirit
Clothed in ebony feathers,
A crest and red vent
To adorn her earthly form.
She died today…
Her stalwart heart
Could beat no more,
The nemeses of age and stress
Overcome her frail withered flesh.
Adieu, beloved "Genius"
You were a part of each of us,
Your compelling presence
We ever hold in sweet remembrance.

—*Kay Hokama*

Life

A word, a whisper
A child crying
The wind thrusting its fury
Leaves like golden passengers
Await their destination…

A song, a melody
A child laughing
A lark against the sunset
Ascends the heavens
And watches o'er our land…

I spoke with life today

—*Sue Geddes*

A Thought of Friendship

A cup of good thoughts
A cup of kind deeds
A cup of consideration for others
Two cups of sacrifice
Two cups of forgiveness
Two cups of smile and four cups of love.
Mix all the above ingredients together,
Add some tears of joy
Flavor with more love and kindness.
Fold in some faith
Blend well and bake with the
  warmth of human compassion
Serve with a smile and
  this treat will satisfy all.

—*Nettie Katz*

Love

A love so true.
A feeling so deep
A picture of you in
  my mind to keep.

At night I dream
  about you, if you
    only knew
The feelings I have,
  is very true.

My love is like a
  river that never
    ends,
A never ending stream,
A never ending dream.

Every time I see you,
I want to run to
  you and scream,
You don't understand,
  my love is true
    not a dream.

—*Amanda Duhon*

Christmas Choir

Peaks of pines against
a graying sky,
Arched windows framing night's spirit
Ancient music written by unknown genius
Haunts my memory.

Simple
Christmas songs played on
Early plucked instruments,
Sounds of harp and lute,
To honor
The Christ child's birth.

Human voices spilling
Through the eons of time.
God's gift forever beautiful.

—*Doris Fuller Pylkas*

Untitled

This is just to say forgive me,
For I had no idea of your intentions,
Your quiet words and private thoughts
Never took hold in my memory,
Buried within the groves of their hidden
Sanctuary,
They went unnoticed,
Forever and until the end of time,
Or until I discovered the truth.

—*Julie Burgher*

My Recipe for Carmen and Phillip

A kiss in the morning,
A hug during the day,
A pat on the back,
A little fair play.

A dinner for two
after the kids are in bed.
Makes for a happy marriage
From the day you are wed.

A smile over the dishes
as you both put them away,
Can bring a remembrance tear of joy
on a cold winter day.

So the advice I give you
from the day of your wedding bliss,
Is to show all your love and warmth
in each touch and every kiss.

—*Luann Clor*

Magic

A shadow in the sunlight,
  a leaf upon a tree,
A spider in a silk web,
  weaving so fast and free.
A raindrop in a storm cloud,
  the plume upon a dove,
Chocolate in a Valentine
  inscribed with silver "love"….
A four-leaf clover in a clover patch,
  a black sky and a silver star,
Within my heart and to my soul,
  these are the things you are.

—*Shelly Lyons*

Untitled

I've wrote to you …
A life time of poetry…
For it is the best of me.

It is the darkened pieces of a soul
Destroyed by man…
It is the heart wrenching life
Rebuilt once again.

I searched and searched
And still I couldn't see…
The passion that existed in me.

Until I found you …
Loving me as lightly as morning dew…
Whispering like a summer breeze
Sharing a space of the hour-
Then turning me
Into a beautiful flower.

—*Terri King*

Mother Giraffe

Mother giraffe,
Tall as the trees,
Will you please,
Give me some leaves?

I am a baby.
Isn't it true,
That I am not
As tall as you?

—*Shelly Desmarais*

A Belonging

Love is a tender loss to me
a loss of warmth of life
losing ground in hopelessness
losing all that's meant in life

Losing consciousness and sanity
I struggle for existence
searching for the love I need
in a world of resistance

A world of broken dreams
on a drudged unguided path
to a brink of destruction
my life must have passed

Fading away into the darkness
I see no light to shine
only that of a bright moon
and a grave sight in mind

—*Chris L. Albin*

The Truth

No illusions that disappear like
a mirage in the desert.
Water that is sparkling and pure
like a heart that is true.
Spring rain, green trees, and
earth like having the courage
to stand together.

Time without a clock, and a
moment that can last forever.
Tears of happiness no sadness.
A will that is strong to survive
and will challenge the darkness
that stands in the way.
A truth so real only you know
the answer to the question lies
in your heart.

—*Melissa Furches*

Hiding Place

There is a place, a hiding place.
A place not many know.
And in that place, in that hiding place.
Lives my Jesus whom I love so.

There is a place, a hiding place.
Where I see my God above.
And in that place, in that hiding place.
Is great joy, peace and love.

There is a place, a hiding place.
Where I satan cannot enter in.
And in that place, that hiding place.
Are waters flowing out and in.

There is a place, a hiding place.
That my God only can see.
And in that place, in that hiding place.
Dwells the spirit oh, so free.

There is a place, a hiding place.
That knows great treasures
that will not part.
For you see that hiding place.
Happens to be our Heart.

—*Patricia Reynolds*

Rainbows

Rainbows are a promise,
A promise made by God—
A promise He would nevermore
Completely flood earth's sod.

Rainbows are a promise
Our living God has made:
He commanded the rain to stop,
And the mighty flood was stayed.

Each time we see a rainbow
With colors of every hue,
It only serves to remind us
That the word of God is true.

A pot of gold is at its end—
Or, that's the fable we've been told;
But the greatest treasure to be found
Is Christ, more pure than gold.

—*Mary M. Alligood*

"Memories"

Electric blue were the eyes and
a quick smile coming from a
handsome face, tanned by the
sun and wind of time.
His life had faded and yet there
remains that glimpse of beauty in
days gone by.
    Where love had lived and life
meant work, sharing, sadness along
with joy and happiness.
    The gait was slow, and the tall
straight figure of youth was slightly
bent like a tree after a storm, and
left with willowy leaves waving
    with the wind.

—*Dorma Lee Johnson*

Eternal Beating

My life has created,
A rhythm with you,
A slow, subtle beating,
Through all things once blue.

The blue sky is filling,
With images bright,
That we only see in,
Our beautiful light.

In sunlight and moonlight,
There's mystical things,
For us to discover,
With our true feelings.

More is there hidden,
Beneath ocean blue,
That can only be found,
If allowed to.

And there's more to our lives,
That we can not see,
Without constant beating,
Through eternity.

—*Tara Mankins*

Untitled

Hey you
over there
do you feel pain like me?
Or am I alone
even in that?

—*Charles F. Spano*

"Lying Lonesome"

An impression on one side
  a scent the only trace
A vision of beauty
  I see your face
It's a lonely feeling
  lying alone
The sound of breathing
  is in monotone
Surrounded by bedding
  to keep me warm
With you next to me
  the sheets would be torn
Thoughts of you
  run thru my mind
In search of you
  I'm looking to find

—*Eric Cohen*

The Game

On a cold and windy day
a silhouette of the unforgettable
begins to take its shape.
Disappointment, frustration,
  depression, and despair...
a glimmer of hope, and tension,
  exhilaration and fanfare.
The emotions of a lifetime,
in one single day,
NFL Football...
Hey, Hey, Hey!

—*Rami S. Hanash*

Untitled

Am I destine to find,
  A soul mate?
A love that is one of a kind;
  Is it my fate?

It's truly hard to believe...
  When do you begin to trust?
After being so badly deceived,
  Caution is a must...

We've all been hurt before.
  A chance you have to take.
Who knows what life has in store.
  Just learn from your mistakes!

Don't want to live my life alone,
  My love, I need to share...
Or my heart will turn to stone;
  I need someone to care.

Concerning affairs of the heart;
  So many hopes and dreams...
I'm ready to make a brand-new start;
  Love isn't as hard as it seems...

—*Karen Ogas*

Untitled

I'd like to climb a mountain top,
For there I'd find real peace.
I'd cast away my city life
Out where joys never cease.

I'd hide in snow-white clouds above
Then short in jubilee!
Upon that pine crest mountain top
Just wilderness and me.

—*John Martin*

"The Eagle"

Lonely and high,
A speck in the sky.
Far from home,
The "Eagle" will fly.

Up there alone
In a search without end.
For a haven at sunset,
A lover, a friend.

Will he know when he's found it
A safe place to light?
The haven he craves
When alone in the night.

The "Eagle" is wary,
Always on guard.
He can't seem to trust,
His heart has grown hard.

I loved the "Eagle"
Though he just had to fly.
But he'll be my heart
Till the day that I die!

—*Joyce L. Viskup*

Butterfly

He landed in traffic
a spotted helicopter of
soft flight
probing uncharted territory.

His threshing wings, whirled
in eternal cadence
brushing aside our crude
cacophony, like
lint from a garment.

Our fluttered lives, focused
for the moments
of his descent
a shaft of truth, illuminating
our thought.

HIS grace, HIS flight,
our hope.

—*John Kirkhoff*

Hurt

She says she's my friend
A traitor, that's what she is,
Will my hurt ever end?
Or will it always be like this?

I trusted her wholly
She stabbed me in my back
She's not sorry, totally.
With inkept laughter, her face cracks.

A monster within
Is what I find
No regret for her sin
Enters her mind.

She thinks of herself only
Whether her joy will end
Not that her friend is lonely
She says she's my friend?

—*Melissa Duynhouwer*

It's All Right

Come and sit,
You seem so sad;
It truly wasn't all that bad.

It happened then,
And now it's done;
You're really not the only one.

So lean on me,
I'll let you cry;
I'll hug you 'till I hear you sigh

And then you'll smile
(I know you will)
Because you know
I love you still.

—*Ellen C. Z. Trafton*

Enchantment

There's something enchanting
About a sage-crowned hill,
A magic splendor glowing
Like a candle-flame so still,
One day I see it lying
Silvery as a cloud,
Close against the stony earth -
A gray-green shroud.
There soon will bloom the glory
Of an orchid-flowered spread,
Quilted by an artist
With a green-grass-thread.

—*Helen Sue Stroman Drake*

Peace

Sometimes I think
About the hate in the world
No love among people
Fighting between the Nations.

Can we find a way?
Can we make a day?
For peace in our hearts
Then we'll feel we can share
And show that we care.

If there were more love
Not fired by hate,
Then we can see
How nice it can be.

When someone's in trouble,
Let us lend a hand.
Showing we understand.
That's how it should be.

—*Sandeen A. Clarke*

Be Still

Above the noisy city streets,
Across the sands where Jesus trod,
The voice of the savior still repeats,
"Be still, and know that I am God."

Around the learned mercy seat,
Where rules the law with iron rod,
The voice of the savior still repeats,
"Be still, and know that I am God."

Against the grave's cold, dark retreat,
To soothe our cringing from the sod,
The voice of the savior still repeats,
"Be still, and know that I am God!"

—*Vivian Smith Walker*

Watching...Waiting...

Long brown curls hang down
across the small of her back

My fingers urge me on to touch her

Luscious curves run her body
from head to toe

My hands beg to caress her

The pungent fragrance of pure woman
lingers in the air around me

My nose strives to breath her in

Soft full lips glisten brightly
even in the pitch black of midnight

My lips plead to press against hers

Eyes that burned their way into my mind
and brand a mark on my heart

My own eyes refuse to look away

Her presence is always known
by the glow that outshines all others

My body screams to pull her close to me...

...Why must I wait?

—*David C. Conrey*

"I'm Always With You"

I'm swinging at the park
across the street from
your house.
I'm sitting here on this
swing watching your
every move.
I'm walking behind you
yet you still don't notice
that I'm here.
I'm in your room watching
you sleep peacefully.
You probably don't know
this but I'm always with
you, especially when you
feel all alone.
You're probably wondering
who I am and why I'm always with you.
I'm your inner-spirit, your
true self and I love you.

—*Melissa Sadler*

Time

When I was a young man
Adventurous in my prime.
I gave no thought or mention
To that glorious thing called time,
But now that I am older
And time has passed me by,
I sit alone and ponder
And ask the question why?
But I get no real good answers
And I probably never will,
For like the gypsy dancers
Time will not stand still.

—*Ronald Reinbeau*

Apples

Apples
fall from
a tree …
They float
in the air
like airplanes in flight
—*Pamela D. Bennett*

My Dreams Are Kept In A Bottle

My dreams are kept in a bottle,
  Afraid and full of fear,
Though I know people will doubt them
  I shall not shed a tear.

My dreams are kept in a bottle,
  Waiting for the world to be calm,
And as I grasp it tightly,
  The sweat forms in my palm.

My dreams are kept in a bottle,
  Ready to come flying out,
But they may have to stay there,
  For I'm afraid to spread them about.
—*Jennifer Gibbs*

Untitled

The time has come
After all the waiting.
It's going to happen.
Please God, stay with me.

My lips are dry and
My brow is damp.
I am afraid.
Please God, stay with me.

My eyes are closed and
My hands are clenched.
I am concentrating.
Please God, stay with me.

My breathing is deep and
My body is ready.
Any second now…
Please God, stay with me

3:21 and it's over,
My baby is born.
I am happy because,
Dear God, you were with me.
—*Joan Randall*

The Sun that Tried to Rise

Crashing down.
All around,
People scream out and
Answers are the
Painted lies
That have become
Routine in the land
That I live.
The brightness of day
Is long gone,
For the anger
Stepped on the sun.
The darkness and I,
We are one.
The blood that pulsated
Has frozen
Into a tranquil lake.
And I,
I am cemented in the middle.
—*Heidi Spitzig*

The Last Moment

Looking down the barrel
All feeling has left my body.
There is no meaning, no will,
no reason to continue in this world
full of hate, violence, greed

Pulling back the hammer
All love has left my body
No one to cherish, no one to hold
no one to give a damn about

Squeezing back the trigger
all life has left my body
I lay there motionless, dead

no more thoughts
no more emotions
no more pain

No more me!
—*Shawn Connelly*

My Last Prayer

O' Lord I beg forgiveness for
  all my wicked ways
For all the pain I caused you
  through all my sinful days
For all the promises I made
  for all things left undone.
For all my good intentions that
  crumbled one by one.
Now that my life is over, and
  my days are almost through.
I pray that you remember me.
  though I did not remember you.
—*Frank P. O'Connor*

Daughter

A daughter so pretty
all ruffles and lace,
But a daughters much more
than a pretty face.

She's a lifetime companion
and also a friend,
on her love and loyalty
you can always depend.

The things you share
and things you do,
a daughter is so much
a part of you.

It matters not where you go
nor where you may be,
a daughter holds your heart
through all eternity.
—*M. Pat Collins*

Pride

Through storm after storm
I hear the unborn
And share the thoughts I hear
Through fear after fear

And though I may stall
And wait for a call
My words will fall
And we will all stand tall
—*Meg McArthur*

Images

Images in splattered paint
  All the many unique shapes
We all see them different
  No two quite the same
Kind of like life,
  We all play the game

Images in splattered paint
  Permanent impressions
In our minds our eyes make

But take some time,
  And a little more paint
Those images change
  We control their fate
Kind of like life,
  Do it now, no need to wait!
—*Cindy Porter*

I Must Let Go

He was my world,
always there for me.

He made me happy
when I was glum.
Now he lives
in a box-like tomb.

He made me laugh away a tear,
then he fled like a runaway deer.

I could count on him,
he could count on me.
Now I stand like one lonely tree.

I miss him dearly;
but I must move on,
And come to realization
that he is gone.
—*Amber Thomas*

"Love"

I love myself today,
always will so long as I pray!

To God I will confide,
and troubles I will not hide.
  For he answers all,
who come to him in awe.

I'm not a magician
I'm a true Christian.
  On a mission
to find in life what I've been missing.

In God I will find,
my true destiny within my mind.
  As he walks with me,
till the day I shall come to thee…

My life and walk with him is great,
as I know God and my fate.
  So trust in him as I do you,
you'll soon reap happiness and love too…

For Jesus died for our sins on the cross,
so repent now and join in the Christian
Walk…
—*Walter F. Leitzell*

Meditation Bayside

What is there with sunsets and
Ambience of seabirds skimming
golden evening tide,
Ebbing and flowing in
sheltered bay, and
Relentlessly, silently,
Slow sailboats welcomed
home, at last, pushed by
Gentle zephyrs, slow as
Tardy children after day's
glorious joyous play?

—*June Allegra Elliott*

Dreamers of Dreams

Aspiration whirls inside me,
Ambition to achieve grandeur,
Of attaining aims I'd prefer
And for none but my own glory.
I dare to risk, I dare to err
So I may be fulfilled and free,
So I may be content to be
And to not leave things they were.

My dream and you share the same theme,
Both are valued beyond measure
And both are not gained by leisure
Or foolish displays of self-esteem.
Never one suited just to gleam,
You are worth more than a treasure
And reward me more than pleasure;

With you I have the hope to dream.

—*E. Patrick Taroc*

Ebony and Ivory

Ebony and Ivory
Amen for Wanton
A definite difference
That once was known
These boundaries being washed away
More and more day by day

Looking for a Panacea
Of course it's never found
Failing to face reality by
Burning history to the ground

A multihued society
Blind to facts and its past
Accession of every faction
Is dissolving this country fast

Keep praying for the future
Remember from whence ye came
Though one may change their nomen
Their stature remains the same

—*Chris Etterlee*

Not Today

I want to meet my master.
I want that peace
that passes all understanding.
But, by all means, not today.
I don't want to die
to claim that mansion in the sky.
Give it away, build me another.
Not right away at least, not today.

—*Jim Kennedy*

Time

What is time, a second, a minute,
an hour on the clock.
Time it takes to eat, to sleep,
to walk around the block.

Living, ageing, a baby being
born,
All these things are time in
its own form.

Seconds race to minutes, minutes
to hours.
time builds and builds until
it flowers,
Into days, and then to weeks, then
months and finely years,
on and on it flows bringing
happiness and tears.

Time stands still for no man or
in anything we do.
As life goes on, time goes on
And continuous through and through....

—*Elizabeth Ellingwood Folsom*

Ingredients of Time

Tide comes in
and another mighty monster
washes sandy shores
pressed in shape
and shipped to stores
a terrible beast
his mighty roar
trapped inside
still stuck out doors
Tide takes away
impurity of mind
soul washes through
ingredients of time
tricked by thought
left on a line
pushed back past
his swollen pride

—*Jason Hoover*

The Sea

The sea is so beautiful, mysterious
and blue.
The sea with its big fish and so
soft sound too.
The sea has many wonders, with
it's deepest depths so very dark,
not a soul goes down, but the
meanest of sharks.
The sea looks ever so new and
bright.
The sea washes up on the sandy
beach, with the shells of all
shapes and sizes.
The sea so beautiful and
bright calms my heart
the sea.

—*Amber Deisher*

"Memories"

Time can heal some of the pain
And even a broken heart
But never will it ever fade
My memories from the start.

The road was rough
You're finally Home
It's peaceful there
You're not alone.

I prayed to Him
But not in vain
He sent for you
And rid your pain.

My mother, my friend
God took you Home
Because it was His will.
And even though we're so far apart
You live within me still.

—*Sharon A. Hanlon*

Christmas 1993

'Twas the week before Christmas
and gee — oh golly!
The church is all decorated
with candles and holly!
The choir has just sung
and boy are we glad -
For after it all is over
we didn't do so bad!
Our music is placed
in the slots with care,
And everyone is ready
some fellowship to share.
Now Ellie to her relief
can relax and have fun.
For the hectic job
of directing is done
But I heard her exclaim
before we went down stairs
Thank you dear Lord
for answering my prayers!!

—*Eunice Pegram Griffin*

Pets for President

Feed them, get their shots
and give them love

White, black, green, yellow,
red or blue is not the issue

They accept you the way you are

They don't care about national origin
or the national debt

Rich or poor, old or young or
who gets to be President

They just want a residence

No questions asked, no answers given

Why can't we all be like pets
and just give love

But if we just gave love,
what would politicians do?

—*Miriam Knox-Robinson*

The Reason Why Santa Flu

'Twas the night before Christmas
And he had a cold,
He decided to get rid of it
He would have to be bold.
He invented tissues
To blow his nose,
So to make money
This is what he chose.
He wrapped up the boxes
To make them look neat,
Because he had a cold
He couldn't use his feet.
So on the sleigh he put his tools
So he could spread joy
To all of us, his fools.
A sneeze here and a sneeze there
All our money went up in the air;
Santa Claus gave us the flu season
And we gave him enough money
To stay out of our region.

—*Catherine Scarelli*

The Key to My Heart!

This is to you from me,
And if you would
Please keep this key.

It goes to my heart
So we will never part.

And if we do
This key must go with you.

You mustn't have to give me anything,
Just your love, not a ring.

The way I love
I love is like a dove,
I am not sharp like a knife,
And I am not rough
Like the road of life.

I am as smooth as glass
And I like your class.

So when you look at the Key
Please think of me.

—*Diane L. McKinney*

"Always"

You can cry on my shoulder
And I'll wipe away your tears
You can tell me your dreams
And you can tell me your fears
Crazy as life seems
I'll try always
To wipe away your tears

When your body is feeling weak
And your mind is filled with bliss
I'll pass my love for you
Through a soft passionate kiss
And should tears trickle from your eyes
I'll always be here
To wipe away your tears

For all that is dark isn't black
And beauty unseen by the night
Is still beauty in tomorrow's sunlight

—*Tracy Matthews*

Untitled

I followed my heart
and it led to your door.
That opened up, as would
the shore. To honest sea gulls
and seas that foam; my heart
in truth, had led me home.
The soft-toned sands begged for more
so once again, my heart, I implore.
Gather the shells pick them
up to my hands, the ocean love
of mine, so grand. And to this I
may add, one little stream
began my voyage so only a dream.

—*Donna L. Ellison*

Untitled

Little boys grow up
and leave-
Houses with empty rooms.
Empty hearts.
They leave-
Memories of a baby's smile,
Of a child's hand,
Of bandaids and bruises.
Tears and laughter,
They leave-
Teddy bears named Brownie,
Old trucks, He-men,
Small clothes, pictures,
Bits and pieces of childhood.
They take-
Pieces of their mothers heart.

—*Jackie Perkins*

The Ash Tree

When I was a little girl
    And living on the farm
I played around an ash tree
    Cause it couldn't cause no harm.

Summer after summer
    As I returned to school
I still loved that ash tree
    The shade of it was cool.

Now that I'm older
    And things have come to pass
I learned to understand
    No way that tree could last.

With my curio cabinet on the wall
    You will plainly see
That ash tree that I loved
    Is watching over me.

—*Wayne W. Crockett*

Mystical Tyger

The mist
stalks & chills
a million folk, &
kills a few.
The mayor wants
to chain it up
& cage it
in our zoo.

—*Richard G. Kovac*

Know That I Am With You

Know that I am with you,
And love you very much;
Know that God is also
With His warm and gentle touch.

Know that what your doing
Is for all humanity,
Know that for this cause (and many)
Someday all man will be free.

Know for all world hunger,
It is here, it shouldn't be;
Know for all the dying,
Something no one should ever see.

Know for all the homeless, the afflicted,
Those who are in pain;
Know that God is watching
And Your being there is not in vain.

—*Margaret F. Hansen-Daigneau*

An Autumn of Note

I took a walk through the woods today;
And my eyes were opened anew,
For I saw Mother Nature adorned
With beauty in every hue!

The trees were ablaze with color—
Red, orange, yellow, and brown.
'Twas as if the Master spoke,
With a brush atop his crown.

His words to me were soft and sweet,
Though I heard them ever so clear,
"You see, I'm the Master painter,
Throughout the entire year!

The artist designs where'er he will;
'Tis there, if you but see
The Master's touch is his to fill,
And you must know that I am He

Who made the trees, the woods, the sky,
You too, yes, all 'tis mine—
Look unto me with all your needs
For the world you see is surely thine."

—*Lovie Lee Borchardt*

From a Look in Your Eyes

Loving you with my clothes on
and my guard down
and my heart protected by you

protected by a dream
a passion for existing
holding my breath
and recreating our world
in your eyes
each time I look at you
I can no longer say I love you
without seeing myself in your life
and feeling you somewhere
in this world
in my mind, in my heart
and only you can see
when we are alone
and I tell you I love you
how much I really do

—*Delia D. Williams*

All These Things Make Me Feel Glad

When my credit line increases
  And my size and weight decreases
   I feel glad.

When each morning I arise and
  With my mind, take full command,
   I feel glad.

When my body parts coord'nate
  With speech and soul I ventilate,
   I feel glad.

When I think my son's massages
Relieves spasm where it lodges
   I feel glad. (He's a
Certified Massage Therapist).

And my two grandchildren loving
Their success I'm "mazoltoving"
   I feel glad.

When I know my years of teaching
Goals and aims for children reaching,
   I feel glad.

      —Joy G. Klein

Of Time and Dominance

Time has no real beginning
and no foreseeable end
The whole world does time encompass
Regulating every form of life
Time demands subservience from all
And therefore, Man is obsessed by it
Yes, humans are high in intelligence
But most greedy where time is concerned
For our minds just won't comprehend
That time cannot be bought or saved
Nor cheated, bribed or borrowed
So for all of our fine attributes
We sorely lack in patience
Time is not to be questioned
It will answer not our prayers
We can ease our own anxieties
and stop cursing the time we've wasted
By humbly appreciating Time
With every beat of our hearts

      —Janis Lindley

Stress Management Notice

O come ye staff
And 'pon this wood
Hit thy head
Like ye knowest ye should
When all is wrong
And nothin' ain't right
Just hit your head
And you see bright
Stars galore,
And what is more,
You'll get a forehead
That is sore!
Should someone be here
When you call:
Use the wall.
(That is all.)

      —Susan M. Kennedy

Dear God

Please God, hear my cry.
And see the tenderness
In my eye.
It's not that I'm begging
or trying to comply,
I just want to show my Mom
just how hard I try.

God I'm racking my brain
and trying to find a way,
to show my Mom I love her
each and every day.

I will love her while she's young
and love her when she's old,
and if I had the money
I'd buy her things of gold.

      —Melissa Collins

Come Visit Me

Come visit me in my dreams
  and see what I have become -
Press the past onto the present
  have I changed that much?

Come visit me in my dreams
  and pity not the changes -
Elusive bone, skin and nape of neck
  have configured anew.

Come visit me in my dreams
  and rejoice: That I am
Your extension in time and space
  even as my children mine.

Come visit me in my dreams
  and repeat with me
Those twists and turns
  of living side by side.
Mother and daughter

      —Evelyn Dvorak-Meyer

Never Were

If I could stand so close to her
And tell her things that never were
If I could hold her
If I could try
To love just once, before I die
To run my fingers through her hair
A love so pure, beyond compare
To walk with her on this last mile
To wrench my frown into a smile
Time well spent to think of her
To tell her things that never were
Things that could be
Things that might
Awake, asleep, alone at night
Time is wasted on useless talk
Time to dance and time to walk
The time for love is close at hand
I wonder if she will understand
But this time well spent to think of her
To tell her things that never were ...of...93

      —A. Foster

Inquiries of the Mind

Deep secrets lay helter-skelter
among the forever confused man.
As close as they may get
to uncovering the mysteries of the world,
they shall never succeed.
Questions will never be answered,
Mysteries will never be solved.
For there is a Master
who is a question, a mystery, and an answer,
who has hidden these secrets from us forever.

      —Aimee Bobruk

Life

The sun sets over the mountains,
And the night comes in.
Our land becomes darkened
the light just dims.

Clouds reflect the light,
Causing the sun set.
It seems cold outside
I feel lonely inside

On the shore remains.
The remains of the tide,
Which the moon gently pulls
From side to side

Another day that we live our life
Another day for time to hide,
to pass by

Oh! great God in the sky
You've given us life,
For one day we must die
To rise above to your side.

      —Todd E. Hassell

Shadows

  Only shadows define my family.

Even when it's very bright outside,
  And the shadows are well defined.

I can never quite get a grasp on one.

  No matter how bold it appears,
  It's never tangible enough to hold.

And when I think one's in my grasp,
  It melts from sight.

Over and over, trying to hold on,
  I cause myself much pain.

  For I prove again and again,
  How it hurts in my heart.

    Forever,

    Chasing shadows...

      —L. R. Andersen-Geren

Creating

We don't have to read
Ecclesiastics to find
There is nothing new under the sun.
Shakespeare said it, and all of our
Friends eagerly mention it too
When shown a work of art
No one has seen but you.

      —A. E. Baum

Untitled

When the waves kiss the sand
And the wind blows gently
There is peace and serenity
The sun's rays sprinkle the foam
As the tide moves along
There is quiet and calm
When the surf pounds the sand
And the wind blows angrily
And the sun is covered
By black as night
Shattered by the thunder
Peace and serenity
Are nothing but clatter
The lightning licks the foam
The quiet and calm are transformed
Into cracking, roars and clapping
But mother nature's love is
Always so gentle and strong
—*Michael J. Williams, Jr.*

A Special Little Box

Today I opened this little box
and this is what I found,

A greeting so cheerful
I just had to keep it around.

As I read it again today
The memories brought a tear or two

The reason it was so special is
because it came from you.
Today I am sending you this
"Special wish for blessings
and cheer"

Because I hold you deep in
my heart and I want to
feel you near.
—*Donna Tucker*

The Loser that Wins

It's great to be a winner
And thrilling enough to hear
The voices on the sidelines
Echoing cheer on cheer.

But, not everyone can be a winner
Nor be first to finish the race,
Someone who tried just as hard
May come in second place.

So, if you lose with a smile
And cheer for the winner too,
You'll be doing what many a winner
Never has learned to do.

You can be a winning loser
If you win that inward fight,
But, you'll be a losing winner
Unless your attitude is just right.
—*Donald Faulkner*

Angel

Angel, angel in the night,
Come and hug me nice and tight.
Take away my fear and fright,
While the moon shines new and bright.
Come and sit beside me here,
While I tell about my fear.
The morning came with sunshine bright,
Why did I fear so much the night.
—*Helen Wojtkiewicz*

Ghosts

Sometimes I rise at midnight
And walk through ghostly rooms
The children all have grown and gone
But still I see them, lying there
Curled, asleep, and dreaming.
I hear their sweet, young voices
And miss their lilting laughter
So much, so much.
Those times will never come again
Except in memory so painful
My heart is heavy, sad and aches
To hold the children close
To have the children close
To have them home once more.
—*Dorothy A. Vick*

Giving To Indifference

I woke up again this morning
And walked this house alone.
Drunk and tired still dying-
What has my life become?
I have been a Hero
for all the youth gone wrong,
Still I can't find the reasons
for one more day of- Hell.

I have given my soul
To the world with no shame;
I'll regret decisions
with only me to blame;
I'll keep giving myself
Until my final days;
I'll keep drinking cheap wine
-till my eyes they haze-
Still what difference have I made?

Lungs filled with poison
with my last breath I'll ask
How much difference have I made?
—*D'Andreas Moore*

Manic Depression

Its been six years since we broke up
and went our separate ways.
I think of you more times than not
and wish you best of day.
I know we had our problems,
and they were my mistakes,
I thought that I was getting old,
that time was getting late.
I felt that I had failed you,
I couldn't bear the pain.
And If I didn't leave you,
then I would go insane.
Now I know the problems me
It was inside my head.
I lost my wife, I lost my kids,
I might as well be dead.
—*Stephen B. Ross*

Untitled

A heart filled with anger
can never feel joy.
A heart filled with hatred
can never truly love.
A heart can change and
become an open door.
To let in love and happiness
and feel good forever more.
—*Julie Hopkins*

A Tribute To Our Mother

You taught us right from wrong,
And when we needed to be strong.

You held us when we cried,
And spanked us when we lied.

You told us to depend on ourselves;
And not to count on anyone else.

You said the Lord would guide us,
And lead us on our way;
To help us plant the seeds we need
To live from day to day.

Seeds of trust, of love and caring.
Of understanding warmth and sharing.
To be a lot like you,
Decent, sweet, kind and true.

We'll truly miss you, Mother.
We thank you for being there;
And giving us love and showing us you
cared.

Good-bye, our precious angel, until we
meet again.
We love you and we need you.
Forever, now and then.
—*Carla M. Smith*

When I Thought of You Today

Dear Lord, I thought of you today
And with all my heart
This is what I pray

Release this pain . . . help me
My cousin is dying
Please set her free
Your doing it again
Don't take her from me!

My mother suffered this way
You call this fair?
I don't know what to say
Can you remember the tears
And the hearts you broke that day.

Lord, when I thought of you today
I was just wondering
Did you hear what I had to say.
—*Trudy J. Andrews*

Faith

When your burdens seem so heavy
And you know not where to turn,
Talk to our Heavenly Father,
He'll hear your every word
He'll help you understand.
Think of the words from the poem
"Footsteps in the Sand".
See the beauty that surrounds us,
The sky, with sparkling stars,
The sun, setting in a blaze of glory,
The waves, rushing to and fro
Along the Sandy Shores.
Are these not gifts from God?
Have Faith, and Dream, my friend.
Faith breeds Hope, we know.
Look for a brighter tomorrow,
Dreams, if God's Will do come true.
—*Geraldean B. Roy*

Surviving

When I think of you -
Anger and hatred fill my mind,
I can see your face...

I scream, I yell, I cry...
You laugh in my face.
"STOP! GO AWAY!"

I run - but you still follow -
You'll always haunt me,
Today and tomorrow...

I am so scared, so terrified.
All I can do is cry -
I want to die...

Your laugh gets louder.
I can't take this anymore...

I reach for the immoral, piercing
blade.
I should of done this
before...

—*Brianna Brigidi*

A Child

A child needs tender care
anxious and aware
When they first come
there is love in the air.

Either a boy or girl
straight or curly hair
dumb or bright
they are still a loving sight.

So if you see a child
who seems down and about
give them some love
and watch this flower bud.

—*Sabrina C. Bond*

Real Love

Real love is never having to
apologize or say you're sorry.

It's saying I love you and
meaning it from the top to the
bottom of your heart.

Real love is never saying I
hate you and meaning it.

It's just spending time together
and not having to say a word just
being together is enough.

Real love is never having to
be perfect.

It's having arguments every
once in a while.

Real love is just being together
and having fun.

It's just being yourself; not having
to prove anything.

Real love is never having to apologize
or say you're sorry.

—*Brandy Arthur*

You

You,
Are my reason for living.
You,
Are what makes me so giving.
Without you,
It could never be.
For my love,
Is only for thee.
To part from you,
I never could.
To leave you,
I never would.
What would I do,
If you were to die?
For eternity,
I would cry.

—*Michelle Seewald*

The Truth

Sometimes my smiles
Are nothing but unshed tears.
I have learned to hide my hurt
From all these long, hard years.

But now I stop and think
It's not sometimes anymore,
This pain I have felt
Is here forevermore.

The look on my face.
When I have my final sleep
Is the only true smile
That I will ever keep

—*Andrea L. Roy*

"The Becoming As One."

My musical time machine what
are you doing to me?

I find you are taking me
back to my youth. It seems
that you are shaking the cob
webs of time.

It seems that you are taking
me back in time and at
the same time telling me
where I want to be in my heart.

It seems that this battle
within me will be won only when
each half of me joins together to
becoming as one.

—*Malcolm Irving Freeman*

Alone

A sunny sky beckons,
But whither shall I go?
Restless throngs are everywhere
Yet always I'm alone.

Empty little boots sit by the door,
While unused toys wearily wait
For the mud and the noise
That little boys should make.

—*Kathy Abernathy*

Perhaps

Perhaps there's nothing as certain,
as death and taxes we'll pay;
And maybe nothing's more hurtin',
than losing the game we play;
As someone's pulling the curtain,
to hide the traps in our way.

Perhaps we will know true success,
while we are seeking the end;
But since the world's in such a mess,
there will be fences to mend;
Before there's action He can bless,
we have much anger to spend.

Perhaps it's time to surrender,
our soul to Him with a plan;
And maybe then we'll remember,
because of Him life began;
And we may soon see the splendor,
that He has promised to man.

—*Dale Pemberton*

Hope Eternal

The surf pounding in my ears,
as I leave my footprints in
the sands of time.

The cries of the gulls, flying
overhead, showing me the way
to freedom.

The dolphin, leaping to and fro,
splashing the soul cleansing
waters of the ocean.

The sun, beaming down upon my
tired body and giving it
earth bound strength.

The fragile sea shells, showing
the beauty of life gone by,
leaving hope eternal.

—*Shirley Barrett*

An Answered Prayer

Tonight I said a little prayer
as I walked beside the pool,

Asking God for a favor,
if it wasn't breaking a rule.

My arms are very weary,
and I hurt down to my bones.

"Please send someone to help me
taking out these stones."

On Sunday morn an angel came,
her name was Marilyn.

"I'm here to help you, Flo," she said.
"Just tell me where to begin."

With pick in hand she started,
while I was still in shock.

At noon it was finished,
she had lifted every rock.

Before I closed my eyes in sleep,
I thanked God with this prayer.

What wonderful world this would be,
if the "Marilyns" were everywhere.

—*Flo Feralio*

I Wish

I wish I were a butterfly
as pretty as can be
with wings of many colors
as I fly upon the trees.

I wish I were the moon
so round...so bright
shining upon the lovers
kissing in the night.

I wish I were a doll
that all little girls had
and whenever they held me
they would never be sad.

I wish I were everything
I could never be
Then I could really appreciate
being me.

—*Rena Mussington*

Virgin's Fever

I want to watch you bleed
as you lie there on my floor;
I want to give infection
to the open, ugly sore.
I live to kill the innocence
remaining in your life;
to replace the thoughts of goodness
with hate, disease, and strife.
In your fetal crouch I'll crush you
just like a helpless bug,
and grind your rosy flesh
into my evil rug.
Don't you think that I can't see you
for who you want to be,
why won't you end this struggle,
and come to dwell with me?
I let you dance with angels,
and touch God's face as well,
if you think I've shown you heaven,
then wait 'till you see hell.

—*Jennifer Wolters*

This House

This house is so beautiful
At least in my eyes
I may not be a mansion:
So what — it's all mine.
It's so full of memories
Of many happy years.
Of hard work — of laughter:
But also many tears.
It may not be the house
Where you would want to live.
But it's the only home I know.
It's where I want to live.
Take it away and I think I'd want to cry.
Just let me keep my little shack.
Please until I die.
When I had to leave it
I said I'd be back
For it's the only home I know.
It's my little shack.

—*Cathy J. Hamblin*

To My Dragon

Take me along to your lair;
Carry me past all the stars
Outside the range of my prayer,
Free of the myths and the scars.

—*Hill Greene*

School Matters

I'm not very popular,
at least not with the girls.
Or are they just offended,
By my everlasting curls?

Or does this go even deeper,
Am I semi-cool?
Or am I just a geekazoid,
Who likes to go to school?

Am I pretty?
Am I not?
Is this whole thing,
Just in my thoughts?

This whole thing is a matter,
of the questions which I ask,
that help me make the choices,
concerning my future and my past.

—*Kristin Smith*

Once

Furiously enraged
at the lies once told
straight to my face.
Taken for a fool
not once, but twice.
Directed at my eyes
are another pair
once thought to be
completely honest.
Then, at last, caught
not once, but twice.
On fire;
rage and adrenalin
flow through my veins
never to repair
the broken trust
we once held.
We end our bond for the
flames have melted away
my once loving heart.

—*Jennifer Sommer*

I Just Laughed to Myself...

I just laughed to myself
at the questions my friends asked.
How could I feel a loss
for something that I never had.
'Cause, to have you
I must first had to entrust in you
the soul of my existence.
I just laughed to myself
'cause having you close to me
and yet so far away
is liking living through a vision
of unseen pleasure.
I just laughed to myself
at the questions my friends asked.
How could I feel a lost
when there are so many
who had never heard
the love in your heart.

—*Bruce A. Wilson*

The Rose

There is a rose that blooms,
At the suns first ray.
It shrinks into a tiny bud,
At the end of day.

This magic rose lays hiding,
Behind a thorn covered wall.
It stays protected from greedy hands,
Who persuasively call.

The rose is a sign of beauty,
For those who see it there.
The beauty is overwhelming,
To those of us who care.

Greedy hands seek beauty,
In the magic rose.
For in beauty there is power,
And from the rose it flows.

—*Kirsten Price (Age 13)*

Memories

When I think back
At the times we shared
The times we were happy
The times we were scared
The times of love
The times of hate
The times we thought were really great.
The times of help
The times of need
The times we were together
But didn't succeed
But now we're apart
A way we both didn't want to go.
But now I want to tell you something
I want you to know
Those memories will be forever
in my heart
Through the days we were together
Till the days we are apart

—*Nicole Roscoe*

Two Dragonflies

Two dragonflies,
  attached,
    land on rock
      near ten pink toes...

Taking off,
  as if frightened
    by ten wiggling toes
      as foes!

Soon,
  across
    the stark white pages
      of my book,
        being read
          in the sun...

Shadow of two dragonflies,
  attached,
    pass again
      and again
        as one!

—*Margaret F. Wood*

Persuading Fragrance

Surrounding the golden disk,
avid for Midas touch
Hope and dreams together,
adoring the shining sun.

Throw little rocks to the river,
break the silver calm,
walk through vivid shores,
eternal roads and paths.

Over the green velvet carpet,
letting my body discharge
refilling my golden dreams
with the persuading fragrance

—*Salua Janett Torfan-B*

God's Little Devil

Bad they say I am
Bad is true
But not in my heart
But in my mind
A mind I cannot control
He, the devil has it
He's making it cruel and cold
What should I do to over power
    this devil of a fool?
If I take death
He, the devil will win the bet,
If the devil ever over powers me
    and wins.
Don't you lose your hope and pride
Because
I the devil will get you my friend.

—*Leandra DiBuelna*

Response to Spring

Something wonderful has happened;
    Bare tree boughs have burst in bloom.
Now with springtime's gay arrival,
    Life awakes from winter's gloom.

Somber, almost seeming lifeless,
    Seeds, transformed by sun and sky,
Blossom forth from swamps and marshes,
    Vibrant colors from on high.

Seeking liberty from prison,
    Bulbs committed to the earth.
Expectation and excitement;
    Worlds now radiates with birth.

—*Marjorie Elaine Flores*

Michelle

Hair the color of the gleaming sun,
Beauty to be matched by none.
Those concerned by her age, so young,
Are too blind to see her song be sung.
Driven by these feelings, strange,
Nothing about her, need be changed.
Her idealness for me, I see as true,
What secrets lie behind eyes of blue?
I close my eyes, and wish upon a star,
Hoping she'll hear it from a far.
I can't describe how I feel,
But, we'll know, when it is real.

—*Michael Daniel Miller*

Read for More Information...

He is teased each and every day
    because he chooses to go his
    own way

He is independent
    that's what his attitude shows

But no everyone can see it
    they just judge him by his
    clothes

He says he doesn't mind
    but you know he cares

It is very visible
    in his puddles of tears

He will grow to be admired by all
    but once was a child
        teased when he was small

This goes to show you don't
    judge a book by its cover

open it up and read to discover...

—*Jennifer Moyers*

Forget-Me-Not

forsaken by the trash man
    inhabitant of the curb
        DESTITUTE
breeding ground for pest
traces of usefulness erased
    rusty old soup can
kicked throughout the city
    no where to go
tattered torn dented abused
    roaming aimlessly
        OBLIVION
searching for signs of acceptance
jagged edges lid pendulous
proudly ask for spare change

—*Debra Tisler*

Silent Pain

A child is shedding tears
Because of so many fears
Dreading tomorrow's beatings
And those horrible mistreatings
Hiding so no one will see me cry
People ask why I am so shy
Wondering why it had to be me
Wishing I could just be free
When is the end of all this sorrow
Hoping it will be tomorrow

—*Jenna Petrillo*

Mom and Dad

Mom and Dad;
Best parents I
    ever had.
Loving each other;
Having a big brother.
Loving and sharing;
As, they are caring.
Living on a farm;
Doing no harm.
Mom and Dad;
Best parents I
    ever had.

—*Janie Woods*

"People"

People: You ever thought of dying
    because you think you have
    nothing to live for?
People: You ever thought of doing
    wrong only to know you'd
    be hurting yourself?
Why: Only stop to think of
    ourselves?
Why: Not stop and think of
    somebody else?
Why: Must we steal from each other
    how could we live like this?
When:
    Will we be become as one?
Where:
    Will we end up?
Why:
    Is life so hard?
Where:
    Are were now?

—*karen's Addict.*

The Fog, the Mist, and Me

In a foggy mist, one chilly morning,
Before dawn gave way to day,
The fleeting moments of darkness,
Slipped to an alluring realm of gray.

So soothing was the moistened air,
As it softly touched my skin.
How mesmerizing was the elusive scene
Of no sound, no stirring, no wind.

Veils of fog formed a wonderland,
A mystical paradise for me.
With a flicker of light, the illusion
Was gone, along with the fantasy.

In a foggy mist, some chilly morning,
I will journey once more to be,
In a realm of gray, where nothing exist
But the fog, the mist, and me.

—*Belinda Hall*

Untitled

Drowning in a sea of sorrow,
    Begging for the next tomorrow.
Hoping that with each new day,
    I'll find my life that's gone astray.

Mind and body so neglected
    Needing some real love,
Romance, passion, a soft, warm kiss
    Are just a few of what I miss.

I fear if I continue
    To walk this lonely road,
I'll end up like an empty shell
    No heart - no warmth - no soul.

—*Sheri Bardin*

Treasure

There were times when we fought
But the love that you brought
Shines like a twinkling light
On a starry lustrous night.

You hurt me by your ways,
Yet you never fail to make me say:
You're a treasure I have found
That makes my world go round

—*Catherine Abadam*

Untitled

I hear a voice calling out my name,
behind me lurks a shadow of shame.
My heart no longer at steady pace,
guilt seen everywhere in my face,
muscles contracting at uneven rate.
Could it be time, have I met my fate?
My eyes fall shut, my mouth dries up,
my body no longer knows simple touch,
my mind turns black, my skin it cracks,
my soul in languish 'cause it lacks
innocuous savors, no good tracks.
So I putrefy, all full of shame left to
one sickly voice, shouting out my name.

—*Gina M. Schallock*

Free as the Breeze

The wind is whistling through the trees
Bending branches as it blows;
Leaves are dancing in the breeze,
Sheets are flapping to and fro;
Such a force as this is free
And cannot be caught by you or me.
A frisky colt on pasture green
Scampering freely as the breeze;
A little lamb is yonder seen,
God's little creatures such as these
Are free to romp and jump and play
On a beautiful sun-shiny day.
A young lad barely turned fourteen
As wild as wind or lamb or colt
Mischievous but not really mean
From behind closed doors he longs to bolt
To fly outdoors, there to be free
And cannot be caught by you or me.

—*Evangeline Bushacker*

In Harmony with God

Above the blue
Beyond the blue
Love blooms much more in grace
And there we'll see the Brightest Star
To shine upon God's loving face
When God will smile with much delight
To bless our love that is of faith
Then life shall always forever be
In perfect peace —
In harmony with God

—*Benjamin Diama*

Remember Him

I remember him
Big brown eyes — brown skin —
Games we played —
What a memory.

I remember him
In the playground —
Swinging swings as high as ever;
To touch the sky.

We've had lots of fun,
But there is no more.
The shot of a gun
Ended it all.

Now all there is to do,
Is to keep this memory of him
With me — always —
I will remember him.

—*Kamilah Patterson*

Warm Front

I wandered in a fog
Blind to love
With a spirit low
In the swirl of despair

You were on the horizon
A warm front met a cold
Creating a turbulence
I'd never known

Like a quick chinook wind
You warmed my heart and my soul
Melted my core
And swept me away.

—*Marilyn Nielsen*

Northern Cardinal

I saw a cardinal in a cage
Born to freedom born to grace
Born to lift each perfect wing
Born to flying, born to sing

Born to be a precious being
That's better off with shattered wings
A captive heart that cannot fly
Or sing a song how can it try

When all its known in all its life
Are prison walls and not much light
How could it know it has two wings
Or that cardinals were meant to sing

Why do people in this world
Think they can cage a wild bird
What do they think that they can learn
Unless they free it to return

How can this tiny cardinal
Mean much to anyone I know
But there lies the analogy
Between that cardinal and me

—*Debra J. Hood*

An Expectant Dad

Soon I will be a dad
boy am I worried.
I'm afraid my child
will grow-up in too much of a hurry.

Is there a class,
or place were I can learn
how to be a dad,
and not be to concerned.

As time grows closer,
I just want it to be healthy.
Because I'll be a dad,
I'm going to be very, very wealthy.

—*Patrick J. McDonnell*

School's In

Let me tell you a story about a little
boy. Gangs were his teachers, drive by
shootings were his classrooms. More
stunning than all violence and murder
were his textbooks. Crime begets
crime, violence begets violence the
games goes on and on and on. When
will it end? Why can't we give
peace a try?

Just where does the answer lie?

—*Terry Roberson*

Goodbye Starlight

Rustling against the window,
Branches of a tree,
High upon this rooftop,
I sing this melody.

In my eyes of starlight,
My dreams are laid to rest,
In your eyes the moonlight,
Keeps the beating in my chest.

Wish upon one sunny day,
And dance with me, romance,
Swim with me in a shallow bay,
And play this game of chance.

But moisture from the mountain air,
Forms within my eye,
Writing words of deep despair,
I say to you goodbye.

And as I write this lullaby,
I close my eyes and cry,
And settle down to face my fears,
In wonderments of why.

—*Aaron Marc Lefkowitz*

Daybreak

Sunrise on the water
Brightened up my day.
Sunset on the water,
Took the light away.
For today I've been deceived,
Was asked to be there, was not received.
My heart aches
As shadows lengthen and dusk falls.
For tomorrow, as my heart wakes,
It will beckon and call.
Yearning for love,
Crying in vain
I need a way
To ease my pain.
Bright is the new day,
Sunrise on the water.

—*Tracey Anderson*

"Selene's Secret"

Mystical beauty aglow
Bringing to life the sky
Whispers in my ear
A child's lullaby.
Her warm breath is the breeze
That blows against my back
Her golden aura lights up
Any room of black.

She creates in me a feeling of peace
Content like a baby
Happiness at ease.
To touch would ruin the mystery
To do so would satisfy the soul.

She looks upon the world with wisdom
Knowing more than any mankind
I feel the love and strength
In her hands -
She is the mother of us all.

—*Andrea Giles*

Waking Warm

Intoxicated
by the thought of you
as I woke today.

—*Maureen Yuki Kiso*

Epitaph for Gramma

We laid her to rest,
but
I just couldn't cry,
'cause
she died like she wanted —
quick!
The driver —
he didn't see her —
vowed he heard no toot.
But she died like she wanted —
quick!
On her balloon-tired tricycle,
and in her purple pant suit.

—*Eunice M. Ringo*

A Faraway Passion

The roses he sent are slowly dying,
but I know this is not the end.
Now, I spend my nights crying,
Wondering, "Will I see him again?"
I'll do whatever it takes,
to see him again,
Sacrificing anything,
don't let it be the end.
When you love someone,
So far away,
you'll remember the memories day by day.
You'll keep asking, again, and again,
Oh Lord will I see him?
Will I see him again?
Just tell me how,
just tell me when.
But promise me Lord,
I'll see him again.

—*Jenni Lorencen*

You, Naked in Jeans

I see you in jeans
But I perceive
No jeans at all

Or when you wear
A sweater
All of the fibers
Instantly
Mysteriously
Dissolve

I see you always naked
In spirit, mind, and body

You are
Just what you are
So beautiful!

Each part of you,
The naked you

(In spirit, mind, and body)

Is cherished by
Each part of me,
The naked me, forever.

—*Ralph E. Grimes*

Friends In Love

It started out as friendship,
But I wanted so much more.
And now that we're together,
Life seems better than before.
The times together we had as friends,
are faded memories.
The future starts our new romance,
Our destiny agrees
I'll still be here to care for you,
And help you when you're down.
You can come to me for anything.
I'll always be around.
But now I can embrace you,
And hear you whisper words of love,
I never thought could be.

—*Ceciley Rivest*

But

Live for yourself,
But, never be selfish,
open your eyes wide
But, never see what's important.
Listen to your heart,
But, never take a chance.
Go out on a limb
But, don't break the branch.
Sleep and dream,
But, don't go into a trance.
Live for the day
But, never advance.
Keep site of your dreams
And don't let them go.
Careful where you lean,
But, don't forget to fall.

—*Steve Robert Massinello*

We Can't Miss

We need not hide our face
but open our eyes and join a race.
Violence, war, drugs, abuse -
lists are many we have to choose.

The world can be a lonely place
unless you have someone to embrace.
A hug, a laugh, a hand, a kiss,
with all of these we can't miss.

Hands are few, we could use more.
Many people are truly poor.
Open your hearts and sacrifice.
Difference could be eternal life.

The world can be a lonely place
unless you have someone to embrace.
A hug, a laugh, a hand, a kiss,
with all of these We Can't Miss!

—*Tammy Ehnes*

Did I Ask?

I came into this world not asking
But so had all around me.
We must be here for something
Or there'd be no one else to share.

My purpose in life has evaded me,
But as long as I am here
I'll do my very darndest
To make those that follow remember me.

—*Thelma E. Keevil*

Untitled

Words are common things I think
but that doesn't make them right
Spoken in anger
they have edges made of ice
That cuts through hearts and minds
oh so easily
it's just not right
Too often we have argued
over matters long at rest
It seems to me
that we've put our hearts on the line
and our love to the test
for reasons that weren't the best
So let's start over
from the top
Together we'll try to make time stop
you can talk and I will listen
we'll find each other again

—*Megan Grumbine*

The Insight of the Blind

Storm clouds gather overhead;
But the blind don't see the sky.
Blazing lightning so widespread,
A turbulence, none deny.

Earthlings abundant on the land,
Some yellow, or red, or white.
Black ones are rarely in command,
And the blind do sense their plight.

The blind, themselves, minorities,
Endure isolation from mankind.
That's justice? Inequalities!
Does color really matter to the blind?

To have perfect world harmony,
No hostilities, just love and be kind
To God's earthlings-universally;
For color doesn't matter when you're blind.

—*Helen Moore Henry*

Maps

Just lines on paper, yes
But to me — much more.
Those little crooked marks soar
To mountain heights.
These are the valleys, where
Rivers run and people
Plant and grow or cities build.
This is a highway
Broad, beckoning on —
Till I heed the call
To go and see beyond
The mountains tall.

Just lines on paper, yes.
But, oh, the magic they possess.

—*Esther Tombaugh Spreen*

Forever

Drive
Car
Lonely afternoon
Dead leaves blowing
The never ending road
Everlasting love.

—*Stacy Martin*

Ode of the Mt. Zion Church Outhouse

The concrete blocks were still intact
But wood had rotted away
As indoor plumbing took its place
Sure it was here to stay.

Then one old fellow saw a need
Replaced the floor and seat
The door came next, then a rubber mat
So easy on the feet.

Another gent added the roof
Of fiberglass for light
And last of all a concrete step
To make the entry right.

A paper holder on the wall
Corn cob upon a shelf
Then someone thought about the air
Took care of that myself.

And then we made another trip
To take just one more look
The only thing I'd know to add
Would be a nice guest book.
   —Norma Timberlake

I Understand

I reached out to you,
But you didn't take my hand.
You say you never saw me,
I guess I understand.

I cried out to you,
But the door was slammed in my face,
You say you never heard me,
But I know I was in the right place.

You say You need someone,
To lend You a helping hand?
Here... take mine.
Because I understand.

I can hear You crying,
whatever is the matter?
You say you need a shoulder?
Cry on me if it'll make you feel better.

Can you hear me crying now?
I'm falling, please take my hand!
What? You say you don't have time,
That's ok, I understand ....friend!
   —Camisha s. Trimble

Suicide Show

The focus is on me.
Carefully, I step
On the ledge of the
Open window;
My hands grope the bricks
As the audience below me swarms about
Like little ants.
They point and shout,
Pleading with me to change
My mind.
I'm terrified—
Like a bird with clipped wings,
I spring into fight.
I spiral downward,
Squeezing my eyes shut.
Over gasps from the crowd,
I whisper my final rites
(Wondering all the while
As I near the lethal pavement
If I made the right choice—).
   —Jennifer E. Bates

Little Roads

I know a little road that runs
By a sparkling laughing stream.
A steady, plodding little road,
Lined by cedars, stately and serene.

Here there is no flurried haste,
No jangled nerves or breathless state
To mar the solitude of those who
Walk the little road to meditate.

Come, walk down the little road.
Feel the tension ease and strain
Dissolve into the quietness;
Know the peace of a country lane.

Hear the whisper of the trees,
The frog-chorus from a grassy knoll,
A chuckle from the lively stream,
Blending a balm to heal the soul.

The little roads of life are those
That should be often trod,
For they lead us to a quiet hour
We can spend alone with God.
   —Billie A. Cooper

Gypsy

There's Gypsy in the darkness, tainted
By shadows, the ray of light catches
Her eyes, illuminating. They glow
iridescent yellow, then green.
Your eyes catch hers for a second,
You wonder, is she thinking innocence,
Of chasing mice that scuttle
Across woodwork in the dead of night?
Is she thinking of this morning
When your sleepy breathing tickled
Her fancy and she pounced
On your chest? And she waits...
Is Gypsy waiting to hiss and
Scratch at your face, running
After the rivulets of blood, is
she waiting for you to sleep again?
Gypsy slowly closes her eyes,
Dismissing all thoughts of evil.
She jumps on your lap and
Purrs herself to sleep.
   —Amanda S. Wagner

Whisper Wind

Whisper wind, hear my sorrows.
Carry them to that place far away.
So my tears, can dry tomorrow.
And be blessed with a brighter day.

Yes today, my heart is wounded.
Cause my joy let the sadness come in.
And love has made its challenge,
To decide should she stay in.

Whisper wind, talk to the raindrops.
That hides the tears away from you.
Though I try to conceal my feelings.
They still surface to be viewed.

If there ever can be forgiveness.
Whisper wind, carry that too.
Bring the blue skies and rainbow
To the love between us two.
   —William D. Lewis Jr.

Loneliness

Alone, outside and despair
cause my loneliness.
Loss of friends, anxieties
and stress cause me
to pull the trigger
on this gun of mine.
Why can't I be myself
without people excluding me?
Why can't people accept me
the way I am
without being cut off
from society?
Life is hard enough to live
without my loneliness
to hold me down.
Why do people act the
way they do,
when they know I'm
lonely too.
   —Vanessa Agha

Life

Changing diapers
Changing clothes
Changing schedules
Changing schools

Changing money and
Changing cars too!

Oil change
Tire change, time change
Name change and
Address change whew!

Change of friends
Change of mind

Change of heart and
Change of life...
AAAAHHHHHHHH

Learning, earning
Aching, breaking
Tending, mending
Hurting, healing
Loving and Living!
   —Eola Buchanan

Mirror

Looking through my mirror.
Clear as ice, wouldn't it be
nice if that mirror could talk
I look long and hard into my
mirror to see my dreams fall,
but look through the mountain
so high to see my dream is
down the hall.
I glance at that mirror one
more time only to find my
dream was only to find you.
   —Deanna A. Davey

Eternal

Quietness of time
Embodies starlit darkness
And glorious barefoot reality-
To this the pen
Gives hushing sounds
And I'm taken
To a future grace.
   —Rita Voughan

California Coastal Highway

Curves through
   cliff-hugging towns
   past ice plant spilling down

steep rocks.
   Scenic overlooks shelter
   cabins where waves crash.

Trails plummet to a tide-pool
   universe cradling periwinkles
   who shimmer through

pearl mist.
   Sea gulls fling silvery grays
   around the spire of a

white-washed church,
   neighbor to
   drying fish nets.
Windrustles range
   to unseen ships.

Whales plumb
   mysterious seas,
   explore black-green vastness.

—*Bonnie Newton*

Blossoms of the Kyemet Tree

The rising sun coming over the
clouds, shines radiantly over my leaves.

It awakens the fruitful fragrance,
of my delicate leaves.

It makes my branches sing with delight,
of the early morning breeze.
Oh, what a beautiful sight.

And comes daylight my Kyemet blossoms,
all orange and white, are aglow with
the rays of morning light.

They seem to say, look at me all
Who see, I am a picture of,
Elegance and delight.

—*Eulanhie Anderson*

Zero

Come trip with me come be free,
come be free.

We must run in the forest of love.

Forget what pain is,
forget who you are.

Forget who others think you are.
Forget death, laugh in its face.

I see with no vision.
Hear with no sound.

Can you hear the silence screaming!?

The silence is calling us,
Calling our names.

Think your right but know your wrong
You know this song.
So let go and be free.

—*Cory A. Mountz*

Stairway to Heaven

I've found the stairway to Heaven,
Come, climb these stairs with me -
This walk is so rewarding,
It's the only way to find glory -
I've found the way through Jesus
He guided me, "His Way"
I stand upon God's promises
He's so faithful to display -
Each step I climb comes closer,
And His love shines out through me,
This is truly my answer and,
For me it's real victory.
I climb these steps daily -
And pray so faithfully,
I reflect through "His Spirit"
What He wills for me to be.
I pray "Your will, not mine, Dear Lord"
and these stairs have been my reward,
For each and every shining stair,
Is one step closer to "My Lord"

—*Therese C. Gill*

The Garden

I know a secret garden.
Come, follow me, I'll take you there.
Tall evergreens protect the entrance
And birdsong fills the air,

Wild flowers form a cheerful carpet
Of random yellow, white and blues,
Pink, sweet-smelling honeysuckle
Grows by the yews.

Sit down, drink in the silence.
Feel the heartbeat of the earth.
Let nature's peace flood all your senses.
Feel her energy surge!

Now close your eyes and dream,
Happy and free; all strife is gone.
And when at last you take your leave
You feel reborn.

—*Renee Ready*

Diane

I saw you, diane,
come out of
the thick fog night.
I saw you leave
him there.

His moans, which came
from deep within,
woke me, as he cried
your name out loud.

I looked that late night,
from my window, to see his body
writhing with agony.

Stumbling, in the moist fog,
from behind
the white curtain,
you came with bloodied hands.

While he screamed your name
You ran, diane.
That night, you escaped,

but I saw.

—*Hamel Vyas*

Untitled

You are milk and blood to me
cool and all together everything
when nothing is very much fun anymore.

You are those colors too
that look right together but
taste so odd, unsure how to feel.

Nobody should cry over you
but ma said you were bleeding
didn't know her then you were
milk and blood.

—*David F. Bouley, Jr.*

The Everlasting Powerful Gift of Love

Jesus! You have heal my body and made
   me whole again.
Jesus you have the power to free me from
   all sin.
It is the blood of Jesus.
Ringing in my heart with shouts of
Hallelujah, Hallelujah to my Father in
   Heaven.
It is the blood of Jesus that allow me to
   clap and shout praises of joy.

—*Brenda Esau*

Hidden Secrets Not So Deep

For the child who sits in the
corner and cries
And the mother who hears but
only sighs

   Hidden secrets not so deep

For the girl who no one wants
and all the boys with all their taunts

   Hidden secrets not so deep

For the friend with the evil secret
is she a friend or really devilish

   Hidden secrets not so deep

For the child who dies inside
but hides her feelings by only lies

   Hidden secrets not so deep

For the child who is conniving
and always thriving
to create a life beyond hiding
   Hidden secrets not so deep

—*Krystal Y. Taylor*

Shadows of Cold

I live in darkness
Where no light shines
Through the early mornings
And darkest skies
Where shadows dare not cross
Down the path of fear
Where eyes are blind
And you can't hear
The cries of pain
Through the eyes of sorrow
Where shed tears
Go down so low
Deep into the heart
Of an empty soul
And arise it may
Through the shadows of cold

—*Lesley N. La'au*

Thanks. I Needed That.

Bare light. . .
     bare walls. . .
          bare feelings. . .
Us. Ahh!

—*Mary Mueller*

A Season to Die

If only the sea,
could bring you back to me.
How I long for a gentle breeze,
or even a sneeze!
Ever since you left
nothing has been the same.
You are so close
yet so far away.
There's a time to be born
a time to die.
There's a season for everything
under heaven

Your season of dying
has come so soon,
so unexpectedly.
And so I dedicate
this poem to you,
all those who long
for one so dear,
one who is lost.

—*Holly Smith*

The Loner

How he tries to entertain you,
courting approval with his eyes.
Puts on a real show he does,
and doesn't even realize.

Never gets too close to you,
his comfort level declines.
Amateur at relationships,
seems he never binds.

Blame it on experience;
no one taught him how.
Virgin in his feelings,
too old to learn love now.

So goes the loner,
in time caring for none.
The soul of a child died
because family claimed no son.

—*Kevin D. Lesniewski*

Shadows of the Forest

When dark shadows
Cross my way
I darken their path
And descend them away
Into the dark side
Where their empty souls
Darken themselves
In the icy cold
Waters of the night
Where no one dares
To cross its path
Because no one cares
To see or hear them
On a dark night
In a deserted
Forest light

—*Lesley N. La'au*

Tiananmen Square

Tendrils of freedom
Crushed with tanks and guns cruelly
Tiananmen Square

The courage of youths
The world watches in wonder
Tiananmen Square

The young with ideals
Old men with lust for power
Tiananmen Square

Freedom once savored
Is not to be relinquished
No price is too high

The blood that was spilled
Will mark these grounds forever
Tiananmen Square

At death one must pass
The Gate to Peaceful Heaven
Tiananmen Square

—*Susan S. Kaneshiro*

"Parting Love"

Honey, I'm as fragile as a lovely
     crystal vase;
Why do you think I'm wrapped
     in satin and lace;
If you drop me I will break
     and darling don't you know;
The Lord in heaven above
     made a woman to hold;
As dawn fades the darkness
     of a cold and lonely night;
Thoughts of you warm my heart
     and help me know the
     world is right;
Letters to you are as petals of
     a dewy pink rose;
Unfolding with tears as we love
     and we grow;
I'm happy for you now that
     you are where you want to be;
And I'm alone with God who controls my
destiny.

—*Elizabeth Means*

Thinking of You

I've been thinking of you
     Day in and day out
          Everyone here, everyone about.

I've been waiting for you,
     hoping you'll come soon,
          Waiting till morn,
               Waiting till noon,

But I know someday.
     You'll come back home,
          Back home,
               Back home,
                    From the war zone,
                         Saudi Arabia.

—*Caitlin Campbell*

Wood Ducks

Twilight softening
deepening, greying
softly greening
shadows playing
on the wood ducks
nestling, cooing
under willows
dipping, swaying
and lapping waters
stirring, sighing.

—*Jane Smallwood*

Birthday

Indigo sky
Diamond cold air
Stillness like nothingness
Nothingness

White light
Blanket warm air
Movement bringing joy
Joy

Voices raised
Celebrate the birth
He has come
Come

Celestial songs
Bursting with adoration.
On a soft night sky
Sky

Savior reigns
World of peace
Only a dream
Dream

—*Carolyn S. Chambers*

A Mother-In-Law

Not an in-law nor an out-law
     Do I ever want to be.
I just want to be your mother
     For I love you tenderly.
I've adopted you completely
     Into heart and into home,
And your presence is as welcome
     As the presence of my own.

I hope that we'll grow closer -
     That each year that comes and goes
Will abound in understanding
     of each others trials and woes;
That we'll be on hand to comfort,
     And encourage with a prayer.
God bless you, child! I love you,
     And I truly want to care.

—*Gyneth Griffin*

A Christmas Card of Colors

What colors do you see this year
Do you see a bright, red Christmas?
Fawn and white are Santa's reindeer
What colors do you see this year
Festivals of warm lights appear
Silvery snow flakes will not soon pass
What colors do you see this year
Do you see a bright, red Christmas?

—*Antoinette Adelquist Bell*

The Rules

Never give up
don't get down

Keep on a smile
refuse to frown

Give it your all
work at your best

Stand straight and tall
stick out your chest

Be confident and positive
always sure of yourself

Finish with success
happiness, and wealth.

—*Kimberly Kohn*

Untitled

In a hurry
Don't know why
Got time to live
Until I die

Paid the bills
Did my chores
All retired
No more wars

Smoking, drinking
All uptight
Only got myself
To fight

No enemies
Except for me
The path is clear
I just can't see

—*Emanuel Sarko*

Now

I don't want yesterday
Don't want tomorrow - I want today
For my loving feelings are now

Today takes away yesterday
And puts tomorrow on hold
Now my lover, be bold with your
Body and mind
Open every part of your soul

Do not conquer me - but accept me
Do not become obsessed for jealousy
Can destroy the best

Now can be forever when you say yes!!

—*John Thomas*

Scorpions Sting

The day has come for you to die.
Don't you scream or don't you cry.
It's time to teach you a lesson
And I to take all possession.
Your heart is cold
Your mind is mesh
My sting will hurt deep in your flesh.
Your thoughts are hidden so far away.
Now it's your turn, your turn to pay.
Beware of it, the scorpions sting,
Because I am the master.
I am the King.

—*Leanne Eller*

The Rain

The clouds all explode
down slips thousands of drops
sparkling, shimmering showers
they fall in silence
then end in explosion
creating sounds
gentle but strong
suddenly the splashing stops
leaving nothing
but clear pools on the ground
and strips of shiny, vibrant colors
in the sun-filled sky

—*Rebecca Koenig*

Retrospect

Thinking of what has passed,
Dreaming of what yet may be,
Pondering what will come at last,
Knowing that one cannot foresee.

Missing the pouch of your hand,
Sunlight on your golden hair,
Let me wander all over the land
Days will never again seem fair.

Mortals cannot shape their own fate
They plan, scheme, act uncertainly
And only learn when its too late;
Imprisonment is our final destiny.

Perhaps some day a newer space
Somewhere a kinder sweeter home,
Surely there is some quiet place,
Long last, maybe no need to roam.

Caught in a web we weave
Life draws to its relentless close
One can scarcely find time to grieve
One must strive as long as we choose.

—*Alton H. Hilden*

Silent City

Mist upon the mountains,
dust from in my heart.
Silent flows the fountain,
broken torn apart.

Fifty leagues below the sea,
ghostly shadows past.
Dead quite seems to me,
the years have end at last.

She glides across the ocean floor,
no words, no sound, for ever more.
A babe in arms, there once was laid
A babe in arms, they could not save.
   A world awashed,
   and terror bound.
      Alas 'tis sad
       to die
       to drown

—*Suelynn Safford*

Have a Vision Elope

What could have been
Now what is but
Now we can
dream it is.

Thoughts brought to believe
But only what we receive.

—*Lola Hansell*

Deeper

Deeper and deeper;
Each day I fall.
Falling, falling;
Faster.
Faster and faster
Can't slow down.
Deeper and deeper;
Each day I fall.
Fall more in love;
More in love with you!

—*Sandra-Lynn Pascoe*

To the Ladies of 40 Plus

In my time I've met lots of girls
With some there were a few whirls
Some good and some bad
Others happy or sad
Among them even some pearls.

The pearls I recall with affection
They've scattered in every direction
Their numbers are three
The favors given me
Their glows linger, defying detection.

I try to give credit where due
For Christy, words just won't do
And then there is Laura
With her wonderful aura
And Jan, who was my Waterloo.

When the real aging process starts
Listen, and pay heed to some smarts
When your body's in tatters
What I think really matters
Is what's in your heads and your hearts.

—*Walter V. Stone*

Untitled

Total strangers sharing one room.
   each their own person.
   Every now and then they clash,
      quietly.
      Adjustments are made;
      you start over.

Time removes the unfamiliarity.
Communication breaks all barriers,
   strengthened day by day.

Then, in the same room,
   friends are living together.
   each, their own person.
   But, each richer and wiser
   by the love of friendship.

—*Eileen Eckhardt*

A Single Rose

There is a rose that grows so fair,
   breathing deep the country air,

It never bows or droops it's head,
   always looks up and straight ahead.

To it the sunshine will always be bright,
   Upon it's face you'll see it's inner light.

It's petals will never brown or blister,
   for this great beauty is my dear sister.

—*Margaret A. Humphries*

Dreams Balloons

Bright-colored and gay,
Eager to be on their way—
The dream-filled balloons
Strain skyward.

Filled with lofty aspirations—
Full of joyful expectations,
The limitless heavens beckon
  Them skyward.

Unspoken fear lingers
While caution-clutching fingers
Hold those unborn dreams
Earthbound today.
—*Frances Abbey*

Broken Hearts

Everything begins, and everything
ends. But in my opinion
everything should stay as it is.

But that's not paid with
complaint. That's why we are all
born in other's pain, and will die
our own way.
If a heart is broken that means
it cannot pump blood and it wouldn't
beat. So that determines that broken
hearts can or will die from a
painful but necessary reason. Love
is the painful reason.
Deep, deep in my heart such
painful memories fulfill. Like the
roses in a vase once had been filled.
You may break or you may shatter
the vase, but the scent of the roses
will forever maintain.
—*Marcela R. Piriz*

Elementary, My Dear

Reading you is like
enjoying a great mystery novel.
You reveal yourself sparingly
in the form of clever clues
scattered throughout the action
of a carefully crafted plot.

I have no desire to peek ahead
to the last page
and avoid the sometimes
agonizing tensions you create
with your talent for suspense,
since I know a big part of what
makes you so engrossing
is the anticipation
of an ending so satisfying
I'd be pleased to have
written it myself.
—*Rae Anna Ecklund*

Banks of Wisdom

Little banks of wisdom
  have a thousand things to do
Some times millions

When the little banks
  get older
The millions turn to
  billions
—*Sam Weissman*

Hilina Pali

Ohia, Acacia Koa,
Erie, ageless sentinels
Reach up through
Fog and sun,
To mark
The lonely timeless trail.

Wind blown, gnarled,
Grey-olden, broken limbs,
Yet rebirth —
Life's renewal
Springs green
From broken bough.

An owl — startled,
Flies up to yet a
Safer place.
The beauty of his flight
Speaks wise of freedom
And desire.
—*Janet Rowan*

Hold My Hand

Whenever you feel lonely
And things are just not right —
Whenever times are stormy
And you just can't see the light —
Hold my hand.

When life's trials beset you
And temptation's near at hand —
When the night seems long and dark
And you do not understand —
Hold my hand.

The roads are many to choose from
And the ways are sometimes rough —
But the light at the end of the tunnel
Will often be enough.
Hold my hand.

My love will stretch across the miles
And when you take each step anew
Remember, you won't be alone —
I will be there with you.
Hold my hand.
—*Ruthanne Monson*

Celebration of Life

As life is beautiful and tenuous
Ever changing and continuous
Tis high with passion
Low with grief
There's pain and sorrow
Beyond belief
There's joy ecstatic
Colors abound
And aren't we lucky
To have found
The perfect balance
That flows like sound
Miracles of health
Family and friend
Many lifetimes combined
That seem to lend
To another adventure
Exciting and new
Yes, I celebrate life
And await the next one too.
—*Dorthea Knight*

Doubting Thomas

In the dim and distant past
ever since the world began
there has been entwined in
the heart of man fear and
hopes for a world without
sorrows and bitter strife
which culminated for me
in the cruel trial
at Gethsemane

When doubting Thomas beheld
the resurrected Christ with
our Saviour's unhealed wounds
all his doubts gave way to ecstasy
and the sight blessed him
with Celestial Light

Overwhelmed and believing with living
proof that man's soul takes
flight above the earth bound soft
he immortalized the words
my Lord and my God!
—*Margaret Tucker*

Untitled

Pitter patter raindrops
falling on the floor,
Pitter patter raindrops
devils at my door.
Pitter patter raindrops
angels by my side.
Pitter patter raindrops
where shall I hide?
Pitter patter raindrops
falling on my head.
Pitter patter raindrops
falling on the dead.
Pitter patter raindrops
When life is gone and done
Pitter patter raindrops
keep falling one by one
—*Shana Herzinger*

Phoenix

Soaring amongst the heavens
far above the earth
the flames and the ashes
brought forth my birth

To live another life
and to breathe another breath
until my time has come
to experience yet another death

As an animal I am king
for all others are my prey
my only enemy is time
centuries day by day
—*Randy Lee Caruso*

Untitled

I said goodbye to my child
As though it were nothing
Pulled from me like
Liquid through a straw
Gurgling
Wooshed from existence
Unfelt,
Unconsulted,
Unborn.
—*Constance Eller*

The Sacred Trees

The road is open for all to see
  Flanked by the beauty
    we call life

The grandeur of the sacred trees
  meet in grace and harmony
Telling us of a time
  When we embraced as one with them

In the valley below
  A blanket of mist
    feed the hungry

Like the sounds of the wind
  They whisper of what is to come
    If we dare to listen

The sacred trees shiver as they unfold
  Their roots embedded in rocks

Their movement powerful
Their strength touch all
Who dare to see.
    —*Amani Ghazal*

Sunsets of Fire

There are cows and ducks,
flowers and trees, fields
of grass the birds and bees.
Rainy days and bright filled
mornings, moonlight nights
and some that are boring.
Childs play and cats fun,
puppies love and afternoon runs.
Breakfast outdoors, white clouds
above, spring fresh air and
couples in love.
Mountain streams that flow to
a river, apple pie and moms
special dinner.
Eagles that fly and stars much
higher, skies of blue and
sunsets of fire.
    —*Craig Pillsbury*

Prodigal Son

Poor shepherd boy am I,
For gone are the green fields
Where sheep may graze and smile
  at God's domain.
'Tis true,
I am the son whose staff is
  shorn of all authority,
Whose bare feet are bloodstained from
  a long futile walk.
Yet, homeward bound at last I go,
Though where my path doth lie I
  cannot know,
For these hollow eyes have long
  laid still,
And only cooling winds can lead
  me from the pit of Hell.
A trumpet, a bowl of rice and all the
  world's at peace.
    —*Thomas V. Farese*

My Song to Jesus

I'll sing to you forever
For I feel full of Grace
And I will fear you never
In this vast and open space
Although I grow old and feeble
I know someday I'll be
With you and all the angels
Where your love will set me free.
    —*Josephine Caravello*

And He Held My Hand

I found the path to His house
For I knew it well
There's no use crying
I said to myself
Though it's never a sin nor a shame.

I presented myself to Him as a child
For I had heard He always remarked
"Let children stand before me
They may need to hold my hand."

I stood there before Him
Wretched and sore
I thought because of my blindness
I would not perceive His face,
I thought because of my boldness
I would quiver and cry.
In a long silence I stood there
Not daring to think
That all the while
He was holding my hand.
    —*Beatrice Alarid Wilkins*

A Child's Prayer

My father, I give you praise
For my length on earth in days.
I wish that I could fly up to you,
like a dove
And stay with you forever
above.
To stand by you,
To always be true.
My Father, I give you praise.
    —*Jeremey Tatom*

Poetry "N" Motion

  Shhh... quiet
  for still I sit
  I lay, I sleep
    mild I am
  inward I creep

In the still of darkness
or turbulence of day
poetic thoughts
travel my way

Subconsciously I journey
rhythmic like the ocean
now - conscious I am
poetry "n" motion

My head now filled
with stories in rhyme
when poetically arranged
have their own chime

These words may be
just a notion -
I call them poetry "n" motion
    —*Cecelia Lumpkin Phillips*

Not To Complain

Let me not complain, O Lord
  for the bad that comes my way.
But with the bad that is to come
  teach me not to stray.

May I never complain, O Lord
  about a thoughtless word or deed.
But let me use this thoughtlessness
  to bring me to my knees.

Teach me not to complain, O Lord
  about the Devil's tempting snares.
But when these snares befall me
  teach me to bow my head in prayer.

Dear Lord, I do complain so much
  about these woes of mine.
But all I need is to think of thee
  and a complaint I'll never find.
    —*Peggy L. Smith*

To My Children

Please do not judge me too harshly
for the life that I have lived,
for every task attempted
I gave all I had to give.

I've fought so many battles
with family, God and men,
too late have I discovered
the price I've paid to win.

And now, as shadows lengthen
when most men seek their rest,
I must fight my greatest battle
and I'm weary, but cannot rest.

So I pray for strength and courage
to face life each new day,
to hold body and soul together,
until God my worth will weigh.
    —*George W. Taylor*

International Society of Poets

  ISP is a poet's prayer
For worldwide peace shared everywhere.
Poets blend their thoughts in rhyme-
Reaching out to all mankind.

Worthy thoughts that poets give
Inspire folks where 'ere they live.

Poems reach across the miles -
Oftentimes turn tears to smiles.

Let education light the way
In God's direction every day.
Accomplishments to bless the world,
With charity and love unfurled.
Poetic works through ISP;
  Freedom and equality.
    —*Muriel Leonora Krueger*

Seeds Of Anger

Seeds of anger quickly sprout,
  Blossoming with outraged thought;
Bearing fruit of vengeful bitter plans,
  Filling the best of minds with rot.

Pity those who lack control
  Of this, the worst of weeds;
And keep your mind's garden free
  Of these wrath-born bitter seeds.
    —*Jack F. Randall*

A Lover's Wish

My heart still aches
For your love, for your touch;
I cannot think of you,
It hurts too much.

To remember those days,
Those sweet summer nights,
When our souls drifted together,
And our love took flight.

Your eyes, your kiss,
The caress of your lips;
Your hands, your face,
The warmth of your embrace.

I miss you, I want you
More than words could ever say,
Perhaps our love will unite us again...
Someday.

—*Jessica Sharpe*

Forbidden Fruit

Forbidden fruit
Forbidden fruit

That's what the white men say
But when you're Black and female
The forbidden fades away

You end up fruit
You end up fruit
Just fruit in which to lay

'Cause when you're Black and female
The forbidden fades away.....

—*Antonia H. Daniels*

"An Ode to Spring"

When I go out to play a game
of golf, I know that spring has came.
But when the winds, their anger vent
on me, I fear that spring has went.
The daisies grow, the fields are green,
a fairer sight I never seen.
The lambkin gamboling with his ma,
are spring-like things that I have saw.
I search for treasures spring has gave
in rippling brooks my hands I wave.
I hunt for violets shyly hid...
These are the many things I've did.
The robins chirping in a tree
are singing songs of spring to we.
The white clouds drifting in the sky
bring thoughts of happiness to I.
I really think that I have sang
quite long enough so I will brang
this to a close, and hope you'll note
that I an "Ode to spring" have wrote.
Jack Laffer

—*Deborah Laffer Oversen*

Your Memories

You said you loved me once
forever pure and true
And now you've gone away, you
said you could not stay
Your love is lost to me but
I choose not to see
So I close my eyes each night
And your memories hold me tight

—*Tamara Lenore Evans*

Nature Child

Nature child,
Free and wild.
Roam from place to place.
Has no religion.
Has no race.
Roam from place to place.
Abandoned at birth.
Without a choice.
Roam from place to place.
Left for dead.
No place to stay.
Now a memory for all.

—*Melonie Clark*

The Heart of an Indian

Tho' no more I'll roam the desert,
Free as a bird a-wing,
To the rattler and the lizard
In friendship still I cling.

One time lord of all before me,
Protective of my own;
Old fealties that once tore me
I've relinquished with a groan.

The white man's now my "father"—
Kind and yet so stern;
Never sensing that I'd rather
Die than to him always turn.

I'm thought to be quite lazy,
Expecting manna to fall;
My God knows I'm almost crazy—
This cup is bitterest gall.

Tossed and bewildered by my fate,
I am both robbed and given ...
To tomtom's beat, I'm forced to wait—
And accept my conqueror's heaven!!!

—*Mary Henkel Broaddus*

Discovery

Passion reawakened
From a dormant state,
How can one believe
That it is not too late!

The love of youth is wasted
On self-centered needs,
Later when young love matures
We question binding creeds,

Then at last we see the light,
But time has doused the fire,
Or so I thought until today—
Now color me a liar.

—*Lou Ann Kuzma*

The Call

"Shine!" you trees by lanterns light,
As the moon shines - so do you.
Listen well trees, listen and learn!
Drums are beating, voices cheering,
Laughing, singing, bolting loudly!
From Africa travelers have come
With songs of rhythm, dancing on.
My sons have heard their call nearby
And answered it most eagerly.
They do not hesitate to engage
As I sit by my tree, poised quietly.

—*Glenn Smylie*

Dwight David Eisenhower

They tell of great men of our times,
From California to New York..
They talk of their accomplishments,
And of how hard they have worked.

Eisenhower was a five star general
In the second world war.
But that isn't all that he became,
Nor all that he is noted for.

He became the thirty-fourth President
Of the greatest land today.
He served as the best of leaders,
Of our Country USA!

Great men come for Texas,
From Missouri and the like,
But it takes a state like Kansas
To grow a man like Ike.

He played football and liked all sports,
He was always fair and clean.
We are proud that Ike's from Kansas,
Best of all from Abilene.

—*Avis R. Stewart*

Haunted

Haunted by memories
From dawn till dusk
Of places and faces
Fading to rust,

So I try not to think
I try not to cry
As the rain descends
Like tears from my eye

But the images burn
Like a candle bright
Awake in the day
Or asleep at night.

Will happiness shine
Again like the sun
To leave me smiling
And the crying done?

—*Mark Morris*

Family

A family is many things;
from the parents to the children;
connected by the marriage;
connected by our love for each other;
a love so strong it cannot be broken;
by any man or women;
not even the devil himself;
our family is forever;
the way a family should be

—*Jamie Lightcap*

Rainier

The top of Rainier is always clear.
But is that peak far or near?
A breathtaking sight,
Even toward night,
A mirage,
Or too much of the same name beer?

—*Nancy Harkins*

"Your Sheep Are Calling"

Now Good Shepherd hear this prayer
From Your sheep here, and everywhere.
Please reach down and take our hand
And lead us to Your promised land.
On the way help us bestow
Succor and love, to those in woe.
We all are desperate, for Your grace
To make mankind one human race.
The young, the old, and babies too
All need Your help to see us through
These times of trial and tribulation
Needs change to peace and jubilation.
The promised land is ours You say
Help us to treat, Your world that way.
The good in man, must come to life
So we can bring an end to strife.
This Good Shepherd is our prayer
From Your sheep here, and everywhere.

—*Theodore T. H. Runyon*

Memory

Sweet pain that verifies what we are
fronted feelings melting
in recorded imagines
Mental papers devote faithfulness
running through time
Time that cage and prescribe us
that let us walk instead of fly
that make us tremble and cry
instead of strength us with laughter
How much I hate you Mr.?
Why do you have to be?
Then I realize that I hate myself
because I made him
and worst, I followed him
to "get," to be who I am.
If I wasn't yesterday, I won't be tomorrow
wait worth nothing, because there's no time
That's why this is a good moment to start
to be what I feel
Until I define again the present.

—*Manuel Bonilla*

The Canine World

The canine world is full of joy and—
fun and true devotion,
They cannot talk but wag their tails
to show us their emotion.
When they do a thing that isn't right
they know it in their way
Just by your look or in your tone
or what you have to say—
And when they do a deed that's good
They look to you for praise
They fight for you, would die for
you if harm should come your way.
He may not have a soul, 'tis true,
but he surely has a heart
His love, and faith, and trust in you,
is all his life, not just a part.
So show him just a little love
and praise him now and then;
And when you need some comfort,
you'll never find a better friend!

—*Hazel Dilley*

The Seasons

Rain
    gently falling.
        Flowers slowly growing
        and bursting with beauty.

Sun
    beating down.
        Children laughing endlessly.
        Long days spectacular nights.

Wind
    gently blowing.
        Leaves reluctantly falling.
        Brilliant colors piling higher.

Air
    crisp cold.
        Snow furiously plummeting.
        Short days long nights.

Seasons
    go around.
        Returning once again.
        The cycle starts over.

—*Don C. Kittinger*

The Gift of Love

Children are a wonderful
    gift of the Lord.
    Their smiles, and love
    a beacon of light
Curiosity filled with wonder
    Expands with knowledge.
        Joy and happiness
        Squeezes us all
Little tickles of laughter
    Squeals in the air
Bring delight everywhere
Children are a treasure
        to hold
        Around us all
    their love enfolds.

—*Sarah F. Haines*

Untitled

A sorrowful tear
    glides down my face
Trying to hold on to you
    I didn't succeed.
You fled from my life
    Like sand sifting through
Trembling fingers
    and how I am alone
Cold and empty
    My heart beat lashes out
Against my sanity
    your loving face
Withers about me
    in the clouds, sky, stars
I'm constantly reminded of me
    holding you
And you flying away
    out of my reach,
Hopeless eternally
    empty death.

—*Jennifer Breneman*

God

God made skies blue
God made flowers bloom
God made Adam and Eve
God made people like you and me
God wanted us to love
Noah sent out a dove
Jonah got swallowed by a whale
Noah and his family had to sail
David killed a giant called Goliath
With a sling shot and a stone
God made all the plants that have grown
Moses parted the Red Sea
God made the buzzing bee
God created every knee and toe
Of every person and of every crow
God endures his love to all
Through the seasons including fall
God always will forgive
For sins that you've commit
God will forever love us all!

—*Darla Snyder*

Autumn Mood

Autumn haze
Golden days-
Melancholy.

Crimson splashes,
Scarlet flashes,
Gold and brown.

Russet glowing,
Nature's showing.
Twilight time.

Time of preparation,
Of separation,
Of dying.

—*Lucille Kraynok Metz*

Awakening Awareness

Slowly the sun rises...
Gradually the clouds lift...
Eventually the mountains emerge.
    It is the same with us.
Each new day insights dawn,
    Increased clarity appears
    with awakening awareness
    to flood our understanding,
our feelings, our experience.

    Why, then, when we are
    Involved in the sunset
And we experience the darkness -
    Do we fear the dawn?

—*Carol M. Reed*

Gentle Loving Care

    I stare into your eyes
as I realize.
You are the one to help through
The good times and bad times of things I do
You are gentle and you care
You will always be there
As you take my hand
You will always understand
Nothing could be undone
You are the only one
What else can I do
My heart is set on you.

—*Ramee Nichols*

Gods Friend

My God is good, My God is
grand
with him I walk hand in
hand
Although at times I go
astray
He takes back my hand and
shows me the way
I feel his warmth I feel his
love
He smiles on me from heaven
above
I thank you Lord for many
things
like friends and family and
gentle spring
So this I say and know
its true
Dear Lord I really love
you too

—*Mark Keiper*

Winter's Day

The winter's silent days
Grey blue skies of wonder
The naturalness of its ways
The peace of heart grow fonder

Knowing we are all apart
of this great universal place
Snowflakes falling, start
it's blessings on the earths face

Snow filled places of greetings
all across nature's ways
Letting you know with great feeling
What we share in a winter's day

—*Katy Sanchez*

Don't Give Up On Your Dreams

Don't give up on your dreams,
no matter how hard it seems.
When times get rough, and things
get tough, keep your dreams alive.
The hills are steep, the valleys
are deep, the road is long and winding.
Sleepless nights are descending,
but yet I'll keep on dreaming, dreaming.

Work hard to achieve your goals,
and let patience be your stronghold.
Don't give up on your dreams.
Just hold on to them and never let go.
When tear drops fall and you can't go on,
keep dreaming until the break of dawn.
Dreams may come, and dreams may go.
Where they go, no one knows.
It's up to you to hold on tight,
the dreams you dream at night.

—*Matron Wilmot*

Follow Your Dreams

Follow your dreams,
As high as they seem,
And you can amount
to almost anything.
Just stick
to what you believe in,
And you'll start seeing
your dreams come true.

—*Rick Pino*

Crossroads

We're now at the crossroads
Growing up has brought.
I'm not sure how to handle
The freedom you have sought.

The first time I held you
Was like a dream come true.
You've been my life, my everything
How much I wish you knew.

But I'll still be here for you
To wipe away your tears.
But I know I have to let you go
Though it fills my heart with fear.

But it is so hard this letting go
Such a big piece of my heart.
Even though I know
It's a part of growing up.

—*Sheila Harvey*

That Man

If, I had a man and that man
Had a woman I would be her
And he would be mine.
If, life had no meaning the
The sun wouldn't shine and
He couldn't be mine.
If, I had a choice, that man
And I would dance the
Darkness..., clear....
He would whisper in my ear.
Soft spoken words and I
Would dance until I know,
That I have that man
And that man has her forever.

—*Virginia Gonzalez*

Quiet Divinity

"Dangerous!"
        "harmless!"
"enchanting!"
        "ugly!"

"Words make noise; noise makes war."
"lovely!"
        "deadly!"
"male!"
        "female!"

"Only wordlessness is peace."
"good!"
        "evil!"
"God!"
        "Satan!"

"When will you stop talking?"
—*Sean Morris Taylor*

A Soul With No Home

No shelter from the pain
As I drift through the rain

All alone in a world of hate
Is this my only fate

A struggle through life
At times not knowing why

Filled with dreams of what I may be
Only to be stepped on by reality

—*Rajean Harris*

Comanche Moon

Comanche moon
    harvest moon
        dusty fields
            drying grain

Comanche moon
    golden moon
        cooling breeze
            coming frost

Comanche moon
    lonely time
        summer's death
            autumn's birth

Comanche moon
    chimney fires
        story time
            family fun
—*Ella Shauna Mars*

The Storing of Uncle Bud

an uncomfortable place
has become familiar,
to be studied, watched.

it brings comfort wrapped in silence,
for we know
all return here.

now we have potatosaladchickenpiecoffee
why would anyone make tuna casserole
a strained laugh
hugs in the corner
tears on the couch
torn screendoor clackclackclack

silence

i'm glad you were born
you've made me glad i was born
which is a rare feeling today
to be glad we were born

i have a need
a need that sits in front of my soul
joyful acceptance...of the perpetual
disappointment...of nothing
—*Mark Tankersley*

Untitled

Inflicted with a disease
    he promises to beat
    determined with every dawn
        to stand upon his feet.

Slowly eroding from flesh into bone.
    Set in his ways,
        he stands proudly,
            yet alone.

An educated man with no common sense,
    trapped in his own world
        with beliefs so dense.

Gasping for air,
    struggling for a breath,
        his daily routine,
    a routine to avoid death.
—*Colleen Marie McCarty*

Untitled

The calling Killdeer
has made my soul cry out too
for the cleansing rain.

The rain may change me
as the surroundings seem to
alter at its gentle touch.

Time cannot erase what
one had done little by little
to his countenance.

Spontaneity, the magic touch
to changing, as time skips along.

My children bounce balls
and they spring back cheerfully
the way I want to.

Trees push their roots deep
in the earth for strength to grow
closer to the sky.

Help me, God, be still
as the sea is calm after
a passionate storm.

—*Joanna Frederick*

"Yuletide"

The holly and the mistletoe
Have a duty to perform
For at Christmas time
They do display their charm
Bedecking every home alike
Creating a delightful sight,
With berries red and white
They glisten well
In the fairy lights,
The green leaves
So refreshing
Bring life to every home,
So with God's blessing
You're never there alone.

—*George Barden*

The Open Door

You, my son,
Have shown me God.
Your kiss upon my cheek
Has made me feel the gentle touch
Of Him who leads us on.
The memory of your smile, when young,
Reveals His face,
As mellowing years come on apace.
And when you went before,
You left the gates of Heaven ajar
That I might glimpse,
Approaching from afar,
The glories of His grace.
Hold, son, my hand,
Guide me along the path
That, coming,
I may stumble not
Nor roam,
Nor fail to show the way
Which leads us—Home.

—*Grace Goodhue Coolidge, 1929*

Cookies of the Land

Cookies of the land
Have the greatest fans
Children ladies and gentleman
They love the delight
of taking bites
Until there's no more cookies in sight
In their minds
They'll say
It was a cookie of a day
What flavor tomorrow
Should I praise
Well goodbye
Said the poem that rhymed
Simply because
It's cookie time.

—*Billy Boyd Newton*

My Jesus Is Able

My Jesus is able to heal your body.
He is able to save your soul.
He is able to keep you from all harm.
He is able to make you whole.

My Jesus is able to do anything.
There's nothing to hard for Him to do.
So take Him as your savior.
He will take you through.

My Jesus is able to forgive sin.
He is standing at your door.
So open up and let him in
He will make you whole.

My Jesus is able to fill you with love.
My Jesus is able so trust Him today.
He is able to give you peace.
He will go with you all way.

—*Darlene McKinney*

A Man

A man is as sensitive as a woman
he needs as much love as her
he needs all of your warmth
no matter what may occur.

He's human, and he has feelings
he's like a little boy
he likes to feel wanted and needed
in times of sadness and joy.

So show him that he is needed
show him some understanding
show him you can't live without him
that life would be too demanding.
Let him know you really love him
let him know you really care
let him know the place in your heart
is for only him to share.
Remember, God created a man
he's the answer to a woman's prayer
without a single man on earth
A woman would be no where.

—*Rita Eastmond*

"Always"

He gives me strength each day.
He takes my pain away.
He carries me when I cannot
walk.
He listens when I need to
talk.
He stops my tears,
He calms my fears.
He can make me smile without
even trying.
He can make me laugh when I
feel like crying.
When he has me in his arms,
No one can do me any harm.
He will always be...
My best friend.
Until the end.

—*Emma Galdamez*

Where?

She reached for him,
He was not there.
Where did he go?
Did he not care?

It was only
Hours ago.
They'd snuggled up
To watch it snow!

Then looking down,
She saw him there.
His big brown eyes
Returned her stare.

"Forgive me, Teddy Bear,"
She said.
"For pushing you
Out of my bed!"

—*Donna A. DeLena*

James Calhoun Rumph

Your life was so enchanted,
A smile that shined so bright,
You had a special gift inside,
A thought you brought to light.

It was your creations,
with friends you often shared.
Something only you could give,
a feeling beyond compare.

When you spoke of life,
as if you somehow knew,
What the Master's plan was,
and when your time was due,

You left behind a legacy,
the love you gave so true,
On your journey, you are not alone,
for part of us has gone with you,

—*Dana Sher*

A Special Someone

There is a special someone
Close inside my heart
And every time I look at her
I'm afraid someday we'll have to part
But deep down inside my heart
I know we'll be together and
Best friends forever

—*Lindsey Anderson*

When Morning Comes!!

When morning comes I raise my
head, shut off my alarm and
get out of bed brush my teeth
like mother said, and always feed
my spider ted.

Oh, to the mall!!
So many stores all in one
place, it brings a big smile
to my face, I hop and hop
from shop to shop, and buy
and buy until I drop.

—*Tracy L. Sharrow*

"I" Is A Soul

"I" is a Soul
Held captive by man;
The body masks "I"
With an essence called "Man."

The features above
Serve trickery well,
The likes and pet peeves
Sweeten the sale.

But 'neath the skin
Lies "I" in wait—
The body deceives,
And seals "I's" fate.

To live with a lie—
To exist and not be;
The question I ask:
Why did "I" have to be me?

—*Caroline Nguyen*

The Forest

I see a tree and a tree sees me.
Hello!
How are you doing?
I'm happy as can be!
The birds are singing,
And the sun is bright.
I must be going,
So long and good bye!

I see a stump and the stump is blind.
It's body in ashes,
The flames still burning.
The sun was up, but now it's turning
To get away from this horror and fright.
I must be going, so long
And good night.

—*Tausha Feger*

My Sister

My sister had eyes of blue,
Her hair was of a golden hue.

We swung on the garden gate,
When we were around eight.

To me, she was among the queens,
When we were in our teens.

She giggled and laughed when at play.
I loved her more than I can say.

For all this love, it's very sad,
It's for a sister I never had.

—*Walter Jenkins*

Contemplation

I saw a leaf
High on a tree,
I smiled at it,
It waved to me.

I walked beneath
The leaf—the tree,
Its living substance
Spoke to me.

Walking slow,
I turned around—
The mystic leaf
Fell to the ground.

I thought, I sighed,
I wondered why—
Such a leaf should
Live—then die.

—*Carolyn Spencer*

Poetically Direct

Poetically direct, wide eyes make
him sick.
Cardboard signs, Denim Jeans
Withering Flowers, not as they seem.
The sun of love only radiates ignorance.
Prowling like a preying mantis in his
attack stance.
Black and White
Hazy Grey, loving one another his
heart lies allay.

Poetically Direct, my heart can still
pump love,
Thinking of the heavens and the
beautiful life above.
Things are not always what they seem:
Light Beam
A light Beam Dream
A life to redeem,
as his own: Now an older version of a little
boy grown.

—*Christopher Moryl*

About Living and Dying

The old man sat at dinner,
His family gathered around the table.
He was a gardener and spent his days
Digging, planting, harvesting.
There had been a death
And they spoke of the mystery of life,
Of immortality.
The old man listened patiently,
Then it was his turn.
"There is no mystery," he said
It's simple; just look at nature.
You grow; you bloom; you seed; you die.
Then it starts all over again.

—*Janet Poage*

The Cries in the Night

The cries in the night
Are never in my sight
With whimpers from beyond
Which I never would respond
With a caring voice
And a better choice
To lead them to the light
And leave behind their
Cries in the night.

—*Bobbi F. Cairney*

But... Why?

You tell me he's not worthy
His skin is darker than mine,
He's different - better stay away,
Stay with your own kind...
But... Why?

They tell me she is not my sister
Her religion is not the same,
Just turn yourself away from her,
She will only bring you shame.
But... Why?

She dresses funny,
Their beliefs are all wrong,
He looks not right,
We cannot get along...
But... Why?

My brother's spirit is native,
My sister's skin is brown,
My world is all different,
I laugh, not frown!
But... Why?

—*Marcus DuPona*

Horror

How can you describe the
horror and the fright,
That you feel being awakened
in the middle of the night?
Without anyone to help you,
no one there to care.
It is more then any child
could ever bare.
To be afraid to breathe,
to be frozen with fear.
Praying for an end only to have
it go on, year after year.
To cry out for help and know
that someone is there.
To hear a child's cry and still
they don't care.
How can a child live with
the horror of night,
Especially when there is no
end in sight?

—*Debbie Rowland*

He

Who are you?
How did your existence become?
Can I feel you?
Are you the indicator to my content
Fortunate planet?
Time
And
Time
I often visualize your face
Can I know you?
Will it be ok?
As the sun fades and the
Moon appears
You don't distinguish me
You know me but, don't identify
The real me
I like you... Can I talk to you?
The sky is blue
The walls of our earth are red
What are you thinking right now in your
head?

—*Maura Teran*

Thursday Feelings

I wonder. Does anyone really know
How much my fears haunt at me?
There's comfort, that they don't
Really care. But sadness in my
Wasting time, the better part of
My time.

Unhappiness is the perfect state
Inhabited by a smiling man.
It provides a stall and hiding place
to be sheltered from her righteous anger.

I lover her, so it matters not whatever
cost or measure.
For the beauty of her inner soul,
Makes all insecurity treasure.

—*Joseph T. Smith*

Stop and Think

We really do not realize
How much our love ones mean to us,
Until they are not here any more
For us to lean on and to trust.

Each day is taken for granted
And we rush swiftly through each one
Never thinking that tomorrow
Just may never come.

We should do the best we can
And try harder every day
To be good to every man
And help light the path along the way.

God gave each one a talent
For us to use very wise
Not to put away and hide
And just shut our eyes.

—*Patricia Barnett*

Self Esteem

Do you really like yourself?
How's your self esteem?
If the first answer is yes,
You're now on the beam.

If your self esteem is fine,
You're on the right track.
To the road of well-being
You seem to have a knack.

Don't compare yourself to others
On the ladder to success -
Or your self esteem will vanish
And your life become a mess.

Take control of your destiny.
Expect only the best.
Your life will then be happier
And filled with a new zest.

—*Martha G. Williams*

Crestfallen

Looking for a need to be, comes to mind
As I sit and stare at the oak tree.
Branches that's full of fury, roots as long as
life itself, very out spoken in the loudest
quiet type way.
Looking for a need to be, as the sun sets
and rises throughout the decades.
Crestfallen is thee old oak tree, how similar...
how similar are we.

—*Cheryl Hooker-Rowlett*

Untitled

My name is Tommy and
I am just about three.
My hair is blond and
my eyes are blue.
You can see me, but I
can not see you.
My eyes are swollen shut,
left black and blue.
Daddy is home now so I
can no longer speak with you.
My name is Tommy, and
I was just about three when
my daddy killed me.

—*Heather Jones*

Radioactive Isotope

A radioactive isotope,
I called you once,
your half life,
so short, transmuting
into new elements,
from silver to gold jewelry,
from rap to rock music,
deconstructing relationships,
on to new lovers,
in the instant of
an electron's orbit.
Whatever made me think
I could hang on
to the heart of you,
so quick to change,
gone in the blink
of an eye?

—*Mitch Cox*

Maybe

I can't change you,
I can only change me.

I can't change the world,
I can only try to change
my little corner.

But if I work on my corner,
And you work on yours,
Of the four corners of the earth
Only two are left.

Maybe others will help.

—*Carol Ritchie*

Untitled

A hole of darkness looms ahead.
I can see nothing
and I am afraid.
The darkness envelopes me
I can not breathe
or see.
I scream for help,
but the words are lost.
Time passes,
and out of the darkness
grows light.
And for now,
I am safe.
Until the darkness comes again.

—*Sarah Kibbe*

"Cannot"

When I want to speak to you
I cannot talk
When I want to go see you
I cannot walk
When I want to touch you
I cannot breathe
When I want to walk away
I cannot leave
When I want to love you
I cannot feel
When I want to get over you
I cannot heal
When I want to trust you
I cannot believe
When I want to the most
I cannot leave

—*William Hobbs*

Can't Imagine

When I think of you
I can't imagine what
I'd do if I did not
have you.
You bring a special
feeling to my heart, a
good and wonderful feeling
to me.
When I think of you
I can't imagine what
I'd do if I did not
have you.
The love, the joy,
the happiness, you bring
to me.

—*Jennifer Peterson*

If I Only Knew

If I only knew my mother
I could tell her how I feel.
Without her I could not make it,
just like a car without wheels.
If I only knew how she looked,
her face, her eyes, her pretty smile.
If I only knew where she is,
I could talk with her for awhile.
Being a foster child is very confusing;
it takes time to get use to.
Not knowing where your father is,
makes you wonder what to do.
Thinking you will see them again,
knowing you never will.
Makes me wonder what's happening
Oh! "How sad I feel".
If I only knew where my mother and father
are,
I would feel so happy inside.
Knowing that they still care,
would leave a little heart in me along with joy
and pride.

—*Yvette Collins*

Untitled

If you had been there
I could've talked to you
And made a fool of myself
With stupid conversation fillers
Because the silence embarrasses me
And makes me feel awkward
Until I am rerunning everything I said
Through my analytical mind
And wishing to God I was clever enough
To say something clever
That would make you smile
And shake with appreciated laughter
And look at me
The same way I stare at you
When you're not looking
But you weren't there
You were probably with her
I bet she's clever
— *K. Roberts*

I Who Deal

I deal in perfection
I dabble in truth
I'm the reality of beauty
I'm the common man

I'm the lust for wealth
And the court of dynasties

Go ahead and deny me
Try to disprove me
No more than to look at the masses
That long for
The elusive perfection of me

I trade for luminescence
I haggle for lost souls

I'm the dollar God
And the passionate era

Go ahead and hate me
Try to flee me
No one can escape the feelings of self
That must have
The elusive perfection of me
— *Dave Shelton*

Unreality

When I first saw you
I didn't know what to feel
when you first kissed me
I thought it was unreal.

They told me you left
I couldn't believe
after you whispered "I Love You"
and said you'd never leave.

You left as softly as a flower
floating down a stream
but then I suddenly awakened to find
It was only a dream.
— *Heather Johnson*

Sadness

My heart pounds,
I feel down,
My eyes get red,
Scattered, thoughts go through
My head,
There is no happiness,
I'm at the end of
My rope,
One hands letting go,
The rope is swaying,
My heart is racing,
But soon I'll be saved,
My sorrow will cave,
I'll get on with my life,
And I'll climb up high,
For my soul will never die...
— *Sarah Hill*

Tina

If you
could ever hear my heart
talk to you
it would roar
like a wild bear without honey
and if
you were to listen to it closely
you would hear it
incodessently mumble
three little words
but if I
were to open up my heart
and let it talk to you
I might be leaping too soon
because
I have never loved before
at least the love
that I have for you
Tina
— *Marc Connolly*

When I Think of You

When I think of you,
I feel like a dove.
All my dreams come true,
because I know I'm in love.

Everyday and night I think of you,
to have you near my heart.
Without you I would be blue,
and it would tear my world apart.

Right now there's nothing more,
then the love I feel for you.
So I'll open up the door,
and you do what you want to do.

You can either stay,
for as long as you are sure.
You can also walk away,
but leave me sweet and pure.

It is coming towards the end,
So make up your mind.
Either our love will mend,
or a new love I'll find.
— *Tonya McPartland*

Sometimes

Sometimes
I feel unloved.

Cast aside
Forgotten
A discard of sorts.

I drift about
I wallow and pout.

This anchor of emotion
Around my feet
Makes footprints
I hardly recognize
As mine.
— *Mary Angelean Love*

Solitude

I smell your loneliness
I feel your terror in those eyes
Like never-ending caves —
Forgotten? Whose caresses dare
Made you cringe
For fear of more evil
This fear of more doubt
Tears me apart no trust, no love.
The flower
So delicately gushing forth its honey
Closed tightly when the clouds
Shut off the Sun. It did not believe
the Sun was there
Behind them
Forever.
— *Laura O'Riorden*

To Mother

When I awake in the morning
I gather a fragrant bouquet
Of thoughts of dearest mother
To carry all through the day

It's like a mantle of flowers
Each petal shimmering with dew
The ribbon that binds it gently
Is deep love and thoughts of you

And so we walk in beauty
That shadows cannot mar
Enveloped in your love dear
Even though we are a-far

I'm sending a wish upon the stars
And a kiss upon the breeze
Straight to you dearest mother
I hope it will bring you ease
— *Kay R. Jazwienski*

Fire...

Fires are like dancers tip toeing
around, hopping from log to log.
They walk along jumping out and
pinching all the people sitting around.
They blow hot air that keeps us warm.
The water spills, the dancers run trying
to find a hiding place. The dancers
slide down beneath the logs. They
disappear till another person lights up
their stage, then the dancers slither
out from their rest beneath the logs
and perform a new dance.
— *Shelly Lyons*

Anniversary 1942-1992

I know where heaven lies, for it is here,
Here, beloved, as we live our days
Together. Seraphim do not appear,
Nor golden thrones angelic voices praise.
Celestial visions, these we need not see.
The spirits of our Eden, you and I,
Abide among our earth-bound family
And commonplace routines that sanctify
Our moments, scarcely noticed day by day.
Indeed, mere presence shared from each to each,
Conveys what neither words nor hearts need say:
Our blessings all dwell here within our reach,
For in our mem'ries, storing one by one,
We fashion heaven 'till our days are done.

—*John H. Gelsinger*

Dancers

Dancers - the silent poets of our time
here - there - almost gone
just a prayer whispered
to defeat gravity
exhaustion - pain - ecstasy
for a moment stretched to eternity
in motion they are free

Like sculptures - chiseled from beams of light
here - there - almost gone
as is the haunting beauty
of a desert in bloom
so young - so old - so wise
for a moment stretched to eternity
in motion they are always young

You dance - what is alive must move
here - there - almost gone
don't touch, there is no need to hold on
one dance - one song - one truth
for a moment stretched to eternity
in motion you remember it all

—*Dora Krannig*

A Man

A man is someone who's strong, but willing
He's not just a person who goes around killing.
A man who kills is not very smart,
They may think so in their minds, but not in their hearts.

A man is someone who has a settled mind,
Not just someone who's very unkind.
A man who's unkind is not a good friend,
Therefore he must change, in order to win.

A man is someone who is very wise,
Not just a person who goes telling lies.
A man who tells lies is not very honorable,
So a man who's not trustworthy is also very vulnerable.

A man is someone who may not realize,
When he sees a good woman, out of his own eyes.
To a man who is blind, a woman's hard to find
Therefore in order to see, it takes a little time.

Some men are good, and some men are bad,
Only if the bad could see, all they would have had.
If they'd changed their ways, they'd see this very day,
If they had been good, most things would be okay.

—*Erica Wright*

Machiavellian Intelligence

Ah, the fox. How cunning and sly.
He's the dignitary of disguise.

He who fawns him like a Faustian king
Shall gait below, destined to the eighth ring.

Yes, he is wise
This parasite of disguise.

Beware, only! Do not despair.
For his cycle will soon re-air.

—*Priscilla Nash Brennan*

A Mother's Birthday Wish

(Dedicated to Rodney to commemorate
his high school graduation 06-11-94)

From diapers & pins
To frowns, cries & sly grins.
Thru difficult adolescence
That made little sense & words that now
seem nonsense,
Thru all of our tribulations & strife,
You're one thing I wouldn't change in my life,
My wish for you Rodney dear,
Is good health, happiness & cheer,
May everyday of your life be happier then the
One before and may you always know deep down in your heart --
That your Mom has loved you dearly from the very start!

—*Maryann Kovilic*

Nane

She listened to his soft worn out voice,
His slow light steps and his funny
sense of humor.
She never thought she would see him there
Laying in a cold white bed
With rails on the side
And beside him was a big machine
With many strings attached to his body
Outside the room she watched people
pacing impatiently back and forth.
The happy news came late that night
She didn't expect the sad news the next morning.
Now she sits and remembers
His soft worn out voice and his slow light steps.
But most of all she remembers
His funny sense of humor.

—*Victoria A. Cruz*

Father, Where Are You?

As each day passes, his voice rings in my ear
His strength, now my weakness as all I can hear
Is this voice of security trapped in these walls
Of my mind, of my heart, in my soul, then it crawls
Into objects around me, they start to take hold
Of his features, his gestures, I'm suddenly cold
As I try to recapture my runaway dreams
Where am I? Where is he? Then slowly it seems
The ringing, for now, is beginning to cease
As reality strikes me, may he rest in peace.

—*Jean-Pierre Lamarre*

Longings

I long to be gazed upon
his subtle eyes staring intently into mine

I long to be held
to feel his warmth against me

I long to be whispered to
to feel his sweet breath upon my cheek

I long to be caressed
to feel his strong hands gently upon my body

I long to be kissed
to feel his moist lips against mine

I long to be loved
to feel his passion deep within me

I long to be lain next to
to feel his presence throughout the night

Oh how I long for this moment to last forever
but soon I will awake and the dream will end.

    —M. Gretchen Beard

heart attack

beats a heart as a drum beats?
hollow sounds of skin stretched tight across steel rims;
a circular body of red ribbons
flowing through purple bow ties
optional. of course

   i am alone.

oh, but to hear the notes of my concerto,
written in blood ink of blue moods,
dancing like an echoed hello greeted into a tin can
not to be opened if dented or creased,
deceased. so

   am I alone on this shore?

no, i say! so play on in
e minor f major gee cleftchin
where an attack of the giggles leaves you breathless,
your stomach aching and your heart
beating like rain.

drip, drop heart stop

   then alone forever more.

    —Lorin Shields

Earth Boy

I sleep on silk on the ground, I choose my
home where ever to be found. Earth boy that
what I am. Something I know, grows from
the vines, grapes, tomatoes, and even a young
baby's life, can be found.
Earth boy, so what, the farmer's bless the
ground, sweat and earth, water and seed and
soon you see, the earth will grow enough food, to
feed a whole family. At night, I see the stars,
the moon, and walk upon the land. I have
all these wonders of beauty. To thank you.
for, the earth, that feeds me.
   Earth boy, so what? That what I am, I
sleep on silk on the ground.

    —L. Ron Towsend

One Universe

Each waving our hands
   hoping someone out there will see us
     thru the clouded universe of our own design

Briefly...
   our fingertips meet and pass

Again...
   barely touching

Time and chaos whirls
   our universes collide

Our fingertips become entwined
   a precarious balance is forged

The fight to maintain balance is strong
   the brink of either side is near

Becoming lost again in the enfolding emptiness and desolation
       or
Becoming firmly locked in the warmth and beauty

The struggle of our individual universes pulls at our grasp

The battle for unity keeps us together

       one universe.
    —Eika Rohrer

Lesson Vs. Reality

I sit here frail and silently still
Hoping the strong wind won't blow
Reaching with all my might for my pill
Waiting anxiously for the thing I'll never know.

My body has begun to feel numb
The sweat and cough do persist
How can I have been so dumb
If only I did insist.

There is a lesson we must learn
One that is part of our being
With this knowledge we can earn
More time for the things worth seeing.

If only the commercials were taken to heart
AIDS and me would be far apart.

    —Michael J. Kniespeck

Do You Remember

Do you remember the first time you held him in your arms
How about the first time you actually kissed him
You thought you two were perfect for each other but really you
   weren't
Everyone told you he wasn't the one but do you listen
All you do is turn your head and act like no one ever said
   anything
Do you remember ever once being happy
How about do you remember fighting over something completely
   stupid
You stick with him, because you think something is going
   to happen
But nothing ever does
You wonder is it me or could it be her
Then out of the blue you start to remember the last time you
   touched, kissed or held him in your arms
And all you can say to him is...
   Do you remember
    —Teena Stivers

Mother

Feeling the pain of your mortality,
How can I deal with you leaving me?
Watching you wither,
Once a beautiful rose,
Now, not so beautiful.
A time will come when all I'll have is memories,
Your spirit in the pictures on the walls,
Your love in the plants that you helped grow.
Back to present reality,
Grasping at sanity,
flooding fears of panic,
There's nothing I can do,
I can't stop the poison that's killing you.
Slowly, trying to deny, watching you die,
I turn away,
and let the rain fall from my eyes.

—*Angie Parker*

Time Spent with You

I always think of me and you.
How happy we are when we're together.
Without you around, life wouldn't be the same.
You and I belong as one... No one can ever change that.
Even though we may be together forever,
    there is no need to plan forever now.
If we take one day at a time,
    and take time slow...
    we will understand each other better.
There is no need to rush love, if it is meant to be,
    it will surely come.
The time I spend with you is heaven.
It's a shame that when it's only us,
    time can't stand still.
There is plenty of time in the world,
    for everything to happen.
As long as we are together, time will handle all.

—*Kathy Maloney*

Live to Die

As the endless days go by I often wonder when I'd die.
How I would feel lying there still
Waiting to see the years revealed. I live to die.

God is watching my every move
And no doubt saying, "you've been a fool".
Living a life of sin and knowing deep down and within.
Repentance was the remedy time and time again.

When God comes to call me home.
Will I be ready to meet the throne?
I'm afraid that I must go and leave my love ones here below.
But I'm going home to meet the king
And that's when you'll hear those golden bells ring.

So, if you're not ready, please be advised.
I'm here to tell you, you must live to die.
If you're not ready you must prepare
because he's coming and please beware.
You may not believe these words
I've spoken, but remember his promises
are never broken.
Live to die.

—*Brenda J. Bean*

The Arts

One for all is to none for many,
how many can none represent,
and who is to say what many represents?
For all who exist there is one,
to one there are few who can relate to one,
who is to capture this irrevocable idea,
and yet to put to be dismayed by one.
So how many can really be a part of what,
no one can say for the one to how many,
or for that matter how few.
To be redundant is to be secure,
how can one be truly at rest with limits,
no limits can withstand everlasting friendship.
Reasons for this lie within none for all,
and many for one.

—*Mathais R. Rivera*

Oh If!

"Oh, if" - Two very little words!
How many times have we all heard
"Oh! If I'd "O-n-l-y" —
Then one would not be lonely!
One would not have anything to regret
Or of saying things that we'd rather forget!

"Oh if!"-Our foresight was as good as our hind sight
Then we'd have not had that quarrel or fight
Or cross words said in anger or haste
When in some crisis we're faced.
Life seems made of little and big problems.
In haste we react suddenly to them.
Not settling them in the right ways
But out of frustrations and dismays.

Then the pondering in the soul
Wondering now how to get out of this hole
And not dig it deeper and deeper
But come out wiser and neater!
"Oh if!" Will we still be saying it when we're stiff
Or will we have learned to button our lip!"

—*Virginia Janney Todd*

Don't Wish Your Life Away

As I journey through life from day to day,
How often I hear somebody say,
"I wish I could do that" or "If I could be like him."
"But there's just no way, I wouldn't know where to begin."
To those people I've just one thing to say,
"If you want it then do it, don't wish your life away."

If it's talent your lacking, you may find it within.
But you'll never know unless you begin.
To just say you can't is really a lie,
Cause you don't know for sure unless you give it a try.
If you have the desire, then heed what I say,
Just go ahead and do it, don't wish your life away.

When you look back on your life and the
things that you've done,
There may not be time for the things left undone.
So live life to its fullest, and regrets you'll have none.
You'll have so much to show for the battles you've won.
Your experiences you'll treasure, be it work or in play,
And you'll be so glad you didn't wish your life away.

—*William J. Lang*

To Melinda — Friend of My Youth After All of These Years

The tides of life
How they ebb and flow
Our joy our strife
The ways we grow.

Friends come together
Then go their own ways
Sharing the tether
Of our yesterdays

These bonds survive
The seas of change
As we follow the tide
And learn new games

Yet in my heart live the sunny days
The laughter and tears that marked our way
In innocence and trust we learned to play
To study and flirt and how to pray.

—*Christie Volle*

Touch

He touches my shoulder,
"How's it going, old girl?" he says.
I glow.
My teenage daughter puts her arm around me,
"I need a hug," she says.
I float.
A friend puts a hand on my arm,
"I understand," she says.
I cry.
My cat rubs against my leg and curls in my lap,
"I need your warmth," she says.
I am content.

—*Carol L. Borden*

Man

Man is a creature of high esteem; a biological structure, a
human being. A teacher and student of theology and he's so
much more, this entity. A seeker of knowledge he does not
equate will all of the other creatures on earth. Yet he's
reaping the earth of all it's attire. He seeks other planets
for that's his desire. He has gone to the moon and that is
a
quest; for concur he must, to seek without rest. He prays to
a God that he's never seen; for God is his savior, his hopes;
he believes. He's divided religion - his greatest mistake.
He's a christen, a jew, and of all other faiths. Yet he scorns
his fellow man's religious beliefs; for his God alone he
believes is unique. When will he learn to mend his mistakes?
Be of one faith and live in peace on earth. For if not in the
future then I could foresee, mankind doomed for eternity.
And with all of his wisdom and all of his dreams, his final
thesis in the end it seems, that unlike the other creatures of the
land and the sea, we have but failed, as human beings.

—*Anthony Gentile*

The Rose

The crimson lady that glimmers in the morning's dew,
at home in her meadow, she fills you with life and
shows you her petaled smile.

She opens her heart at the touch of the warmth of
the sun on the earth and shows off her beauty.

With perfume so sweet, yet so light, it accents the
softness at your fingertips, like silk her skin feels.

With all this she taunts you, and as you near,
she pricks you with her thorns for the evilness
of a love so deep.

—*Mary Rapach*

"Inevitability"

When darkness fall the shadow rises.
Humanity is what it despises.
The shadow calls upon fear to bring forth error.
Error brings forth the last ultimate terror.
From dust we began so shall we end.
Our flesh with blood, with earth shall blend.
Valiant effort cannot dismay,
The finality of that final day.
You cannot fight the inevitable.
And your life is always forgettable.
And when death's hand maintains a grasp.
And the voice is calling sharp and rasp.
From dust you began.
So shall you end...

—*Michael Scott Williams*

My Little Problem

A gentle reminder "your shoes are untied" gets me upset and
hurting inside.

As I sit and try to lace, mom stands by, just in case.
Mom and I were in the store, I pleaded and begged to get
velcro once more.

I've practiced and practiced 'til my fingers were numb.
I try to do it, but my fingers are all thumbs.
Mom smiles and says "I'll do it just this once." I grin
knowing, she's said that for months.

I wonder while she is tying, how she gets the laces so tight,
She says, "Keep on trying, you'll soon get it right!"

Now cross this one over and go under, pull them tight,
So far it feels right! Make a loop and go around the thumb,
pull them tight, I am done.

I went running back inside with the big news!
"Look Mom, I tied my shoes!"
"Look Mom, do you see?"
"I tied them myself, just me!"

Mom nods and says, "I see it's true,
"Gosh, son, I sure am proud of you!"

—*Sue Bower*

Friends

(Dedicated to my all time best friend, Beth)
I always thought we'd be friends forever more.
Now I don't know what is in store.

You moved away.
I wish you could stay.

Now I am blue.
We were so true.

I miss you so.
Why'd you go.

We were friends for years.
Now thinking of you my eyes fill with tears.

Life changes and so do we.
I feel you won't forget me.

I have new friends now, but you'll always be there.
Even if you're not near.

—*Letitia Coulter*

Eyes of the Soul

Who am I?
I am a lighthouse that isn't needed any longer,
Tears that go unseen and whispers not heard.
I am unanswered questions,
Barren outstretched arms and unreturned love.
Who am I? I am everyone who wants to be free.
Forgotten, incarcerated people and the mentally ill.
I am battered children with nowhere to go,
And the elderly who have no one to go to.
Who am I? I am yesterday, today and tomorrow with
   hopes and dreams.
Miles that went untraveled,
Lives that went forgotten, and memories that weren't built.
Who am I? I am all of the romantic words ever written.
Special feelings that are created from music,
Silence that is shared with a smile,
And laughter that is priceless.
Who am I? I am every thought, hope and emotion
   that was ever created.
Who am I? I am the eyes of the soul.

   —*Rebecca Sue Flowers*

Never Mind

I am here.
I am alive,
Don't you hear me?
Don't you see me?

I am here,
I am alive,
Don't you hear me calling you?
Don't you see me coming near you?
You don't?

I guess I mistook you for someone else, for an equal.
I guess I mistook you for a friend.

I know I am here.
I know I am alive.

You don't?
Well then, ... never mind.

   —*Katrin Havlik*

I Miss You

Larry is one of my best uncle's.
I am really sad that he died.
But now he is sitting right by Jesus's side.
He's helped me out a lot of times.
He taught me how to go fishing
And other things to.
But whenever I was with him I was
right there by his side.
   I love you uncle Larry.

   —*Michelle Ullery*

"What It Means To Be Me"

For I am the child and the wise old owl.
I am the creator of all.
I am the past and the future.
I live within each soul.
I give and I take, but never forsake.
Reach into your hearts and you will see
   what it means to be me.
I am for every living creature, big or small.
For we must live in harmony for this world to be.
That is what it means to be me.

   —*Marilyn Cooper*

The Beggar

I am the beggar outside your gate.
I am the beggar dressed in rags and tags
I am the unseen one you passed,
   dressed in all your finery.
I am the beggar watching you feast,
   with society's finest.
I am the beggar hungry and homeless,
   begging for your leftovers.
I am the lonely one outside your door.
I am the poor one, you are the rich.
I am the beggar crooked of limb,
I am the beggar that died at your gate.
I am yourself, your soul gone astray.
I am your future date with destiny.
I am the beggar at your gate.

   —*Billie Sue Smith*

A Stranger Asked

A stranger asked me, "How do you know, that God loves you so?"
I answered him without delay, "I feel His love in every way."
And then he asked "how do you know that your God above will
someday show?"
"Oh," I say, "I know it's true, someday soon He'll come for me
and if you believe in Him, He'll come for you too."
The next words he spoke were "And I suppose you know He's real
too" and I quickly answered "Oh, yes! I sure do!"
You see, I see His love in every living thing
A brand new baby, a little tiny cat
A lovely baby deer, now how can you doubt that?
And I have faith and I believe that from this earth
He will retrieve us so that we can live with Him
Yes, all children, all women and yes, all men!

   —*Shirley Santee*

The Land of Poetry

There's a place deep in the heart of me,
I call the land of poetry!
I journey there to meet a friend of mine
Who speaks to me in rhyme.

I seek this friend when I'm lonely, hurt, sad,
Or even when I'm feeling glad.
Together, we gaze into a mirror where I see
A picture of the real me.

A picture of many wounds and joys are revealed,
Heart overflowing, eyes with tears filled,
I'm wrapped in the warmth of my best friend,
My troubled heart begins to mend.

If you are a poet, I'm sure you understand
Words of rhyme from my hand.
Because there's a place, in the heart of you,
Given from God to chosen few.

And to this blessed place the poet will go,
Seeking peace for the innermost soul.
I invite you to come and join me there
In a land oh so fair, the land of poetry!

   —*Alma M. Bramblett*

Desire

My arms feel kinship to the restless sea
Could they but speak they would call for thee
How can one touch bring me such delight
And purge away the gloom of night?
The wine of life is nectar in the cup
Then were it sin if I of nectar sup?
And if great heaven's door were shut to me
'Tis better yet to spend my time with thee.

   —*Vern H. Woodward*

"The Butterfly"

As I was once rushing by
I came upon a butterfly.
And as he hopped so lazily
From branch to branch, from tree to tree,

I asked him how he could spend his days
In such a carefree lazy way.
And he with smiling, laughing face
Put me in my proper place

By asking how I could hurry by
And not see such a clear blue sky,
Or the perfectly colored daffodils
Or the majestic green rolling hills.

And as I turned and walked away
I wonder still about that day.
Who was right and who was wrong?
The butterfly that hears God's song?
Or we who travel through this life
Only seeing pain and strife.

—*Heidi Buker Stimson*

Like A Flower In Paradise

In my search for a secluded place,
I came upon you and your beautiful face
As the mist from the waterfall
Cascaded over you, it reminded me
Of a flower getting watered by a sprinkler.
With the rivulets of water
Running down your body
You seemed to open up
Before my very eyes and bloom.
Like the precious colors of a flower
You made my whole day brighten.
I wish that I could pick and keep you
Because pretty ones like you are very rare.
So with all the love
I can pour out of my heart
I will keep you happy
Because like a flower without sun and water
You will surely wilt.

—*Jeffrey D. Cooksley*

Love?

Looking in your eyes
I can see beyond that mask
we both belong to one another
but why do we even ask....
ourselves the question
is this meant to be?
but instead we keep on walking
and never set our love quite free...
as the birds and the wind in the sky
We will sit by the fire and see sparks fly by
with the warm brisk air
and the cozy love stares...
in your eyes, at me
this has to be ...
Love

—*Jill Barends*

Untitled

Poetry, Odes and Ballade of sorts-
are e'er young to ignore.
A fragrance of faith, or love within grace, allotted;
The lyrical song, announcing the joy asunder -
One prayerfully thought, all kindness commence,
in spirit, let mankind embrace...

—*Michele M. Mena*

"The Mighty Oak"

There's a mighty oak, stands on the hill.
I can see her from my window sill.
A soft wind blows, she waves her arms,
As though to show off all her charms.

Some day, I'm gonna climb that tree,
To see how far that I can see,
And when I'm ready to come down,
She'll help me gently to the ground.

I wake and run to my window sill,
To see her standing on the hill.
But alas, alas, alas, oh me!
They've come to cut the mighty tree.
I want to shout, "Hey, don't you dare.
Don't you see I really care?"

But now she tumbles to the ground,
The only friend I've ever found.
Here come the tears, they burn my eyes.
Can't stand to see my good friend die.
And now she lies, her arms all broke.
Goodbye dear friend, oh mighty oak.

—*Patty J. Bovaird*

Full Moon Night

I often walk on a full moon night.
I can see things different as you might.
A scarred old oak tree with leaves stripped
And branches torn down.
Are you the last Indian brave sent to
claim your land and set your people free?
Crooked old fence posts in a field faraway
Are you Custer's calvery lost and shamed
Forever until you answer for what you
Did to the women and children of the
Apache, Sioux and cree.
In a small cluster of white birch
A grey old hornets nest tattered and torn
Hangs in a ghostly circle.
Is this the lifeless world or the future?
That unlike our brothers we did not
Love nor nurture.
To what I see you may not agree.
Just take a walk on the next full moon
Night and see what you can see.

—*Bart Adams*

Untitled

In my dreams at night,
I can still see his smiling face.
Laughing, playing, joking with his daughter.
I wake up crying and realize he is not here.
Tragically, his life was taken from us.
Too young to understand, his daughter
asked why her daddy was sleeping.
Sometimes I see him floating like an angel,
he waves, tells my mother not to cry
and that he loves us all!
I know that when I die and go to heaven;
I will see him and we will be united
as brother and sister...
    once more.

—*Heather Giesler*

The Athlete's Psalm

The Lord is my coach.
I cannot lose.

He gets me in shape through drills in practice sessions,
    and makes sure I have a healthy training table.

He keeps me in condition;
He opens up the field for me to follow
    according to the boundaries and rules of the game
    So that I can be the champion of His cause.

Yes, even though the contest be on the brink of defeat,
    I will not even consider the possibility of conceding,
For He always calls the night plays.
His discipline and direction constantly challenge me.

He arouses my competitive spirit
And inspires me to be at my best for the game,
Even though my opponents may have the home advantage.

He enables me to score even more points than I need.

I am confident that victory and triumph
    will be the results in the arena of my life,
And when the final whistle blows,
    I will be enshrined in God's great Hall of Fame forever.

—*Larry Walker*

Senior '94

Our senior year, what a blast!
    I can't believe it has come so fast
Band, football, basketball, and track,
    After this year we won't come back.

I'm sure we'll remember most of the things.
    Some of the fun times, and some of the pains.
A couple of friendships will last forever,
    Most will eventually dissever.

For this is the last our high school years.
When our hats go up, I will be in tears.

But for now as I enter the twelfth grade,
    I'll recall a friendship that I made.
This friendship was with you my friend,
    And I hope that it will never end!

God bless you Char, in everything you do.
I wish you luck and happiness too.

—*Darina Davis*

Doodle-Ing

I'm a little Doodle Bug
I go doodle doodle do
I'll make lots of holes
Before the day is through

I'm a red rooster
I keep you awake
By going cock a doodle do
That's the sound I make

I am a writer
Sometimes I doodle too
In between the lines
That I write for you

A yankee came to town
Carrying two little poodles
He was just passing through
Picking up the other doodles

—*Monte R. Shockley*

Father's Poem

My bed doesn't feel so warm tonight,
I can't get to sleep.
I can hear mommy crying and there's a lot of yelling going on.
Mommy and Daddy didn't read to me tonight,
like they did last night.
We had a good day yesterday.
After school, mommy and daddy took me to the park.
We went out to eat at my favorite restaurant.
Mommy wasn't worried about the money it was going to cost,
like she's talking about tonight.
I can hear it…

Yesterday we walked by a big store window,
There was the beautiful bedroom set I've been wanting.
Mommy was talking about getting it for our new house.
Now she's crying about daddy not being able to work.
That means no bedroom, no new house.
I can hear it…

Yesterday daddy could carry me on his shoulders.
Mommy was telling Grandma that daddy may not be
able to walk again.
I can hear it…

Daddy went with some friends after work,
to relax and have a few drinks.
Mommy said he better be careful.
I can hear it…

Yesterday, daddy gave me a kiss good-bye,
Just like he did this morning.
I wish tomorrow could be like yesterday.
What a wonderful world this would be,
if drivers would remain alcohol free.

—*Katie Elizabeth Frank*

Over Seer

Even though hard times follow me in line,
I can't help but feel a sense of pride at all times.
Because I know the more I struggle I receive more love,
from my over seer from the heavens up above.
I feel his love whenever I feel down,
he tells me to smile instead of frown.
whenever my friends laugh at me or try to hurt me,
he puts his arm around me and tell me let it be.
Whatever they do will come back to them, even worse,
I would no longer have to go thru this curse.
They're digging their own hole with a shovel,
I should never go down to their level.
I always know that I have a friend,
He's always there through thick and thin.
Whatever I want I must always wait,
I don't need any money because the price is faith.
I know from the sky that I get a lot of love,
I love God, is something I'm proud of.

—*Dakar Flemming*

Granny Grump

I grumble about this
I grumble about that
I finally get to sit down
I think what a blessed relief
Bang! The door slammed
I hear the patter of little feet
A tiny voice screaming
Granny Grump
Granny Grump where are you?
I want a drink
As I look at her trusting face
I think someday what a wonderful
Grandy Grump she will be

—*Lavern Winebarger*

Confession

itting in my room late last night, thinking about you
 closed my eyes and I wondered how
 ings could have been
 1atching the fading memories I still have of you
 loping you would call, wishing to hear
 our voice again
 /as it too good to be true when telling you
 ıe truth
 ll I needed was to love you baby, lovingly
 ll I needed was to love you honey, more and more
 ll I ever needed, you were the one endlessly
 opened my heart to you, praying
) me you would come
 was a fool thinking good things come
) those who wait
 ou had to follow your heart, even when
 said "him"
 low you are being hurt and abused, lust
 onsumed with lies
 istening in pain I pray, but my love never dies

—*Stanley Francois*

Mrs. Yvette

/hen I first came to school here I didn't know a soul
 concentrated on my work and let the good times go

hat proved to be too lonely so I hung out with the crowd
 spent the weekdays half-asleep and the weekends drunk and loud

hat proved to be too hard on me so opted to cut back
 could not seem to figure out the things I seemed to lack

nd somewhere down the road you and I did meet
 1e on the defensive and you firm on your feet

ou gave me understanding when no one seemed to care
 nd didn't curse when I failed a class or 'cause I had long hair

ou proved to me that I was free and had to rule myself
 nd you told me that the drive was tough "give the keys
)someone else"

hat proved to be the best thing that I could ever do
) I gave my life to Jesus Christ and my loyalty to you

hat proved to do the job for me just 'cause somehow on cue
 /hen all I needed was an honest friend you proved it could be you

—*David W. McBride*

The Wind

s she fled down the road
 could do nothing but stand in the wind.
 seemed that all I tried to say to my best friend
) stay didn't seem to help.
 he had made up her mind.

/e had been best friends for the longest time,
 ut now that I found out that she was leaving,
 or some reason our friendship didn't seem to
 1atter to me anymore.

felt helpless and confused, and I could
) nothing but stand in the wind.

—*Ashley K. Atherton*

Clouds

Clouds are like the morning mist that floats so
 rystal clear. Clouds are like a mountain stream that feeds
 ach plant and deer. I wish I had a cloud to hug and float
 p in the air. Like flying on a magic carpet, zooming through
 ıe winter air. A breeze I'd get from flying high, but I don't
 eally care. I'd like the clouds I'd float with because of
)aring through the nice cool air.

—*Josie Ward*

Slippers

When I was young my slippers were red.
I could kick my foot right over my head.
When I grew older my slippers were blue
And I could dance my night right through.
Now that I am old my slippers are black.
I walk to the corner and puff my way back.
I know full well that my youth has been spent.
My get up and go has got up and went.
But I don't mind a bit, as I think with a grin
Of all the places my get up has been.

—*Janet Burch*

It Could've Been Me

A man being married to the most beautiful woman,
  I Could've, Would've, and Should've been the one,
    It Could've Been Me.

She's not alone now, I am,
  I could've broke his spell,
    She was such a good find,
      I must've lost my mind,
        For She Could've Been Mine,
          It Could've Been Me.

I could be standing there with her now,
  Saying those precious vows to her,
    Sharing those dreams hand in hand,
      Forever at her beck and call,
        Forever her knight in shining armor,
          For it very well Could've, Would've and
            Should've Been Me.
Now someone else is there,
  With the dreams we share,
    Where I belong,
      With my dreams gone,
        When it Could've, Would've, and Should've
been Me!

—*Derek Wayne Moore*

She

She loves me like a fire loves the fields
I die—I disappear in wisp of smoke
And then she loves me like a storm,
With her rains I am healed
And with her winds' caressing stroke
I am once again reborn
Then she loves me like the winter's frost
Shroud of snow slips me into sweetest sleep
Stills me to my very ghost
And if from my dreams I am tossed
Like the dark she takes me in from the deep
Unquestioningly…the gentlest host
Then by her warmth I arise
Spring to life in myriad hues
Leaves, thorns, and roses to compose
An answer to the star in my skies
Vine, tree, and grass. That imbues
The fertile soil with immortal repose

—*Joshua Wachtel*

Illusion

The night and the stars I held tight in my grasp
As I watched the black misting away
I felt in my heart that the stars in my hand
Had transformed the dark into the day

The magical gems I held clutched in my palm
Encased my whole spirit with light
'Til my head dared my heart to open my hand
Then I saw all I held was the night

—*Nada Peterson*

The Passionate Man

When my man swears that he is made of the truth,
I do believe him, though I know he lies.
I smile when he's trying to be smart.
I smile when I have my point and he's confused.
Two lovers have comfort, and despair,
but alone you feel depressed and scared.
To win my heart, you have to be
passionate, caring and understanding,
but not a self-centered man, because I play hard to get.
If love makes me unworthy of the opposite sex,
how can I love again, or sometime in the future?
Fair is my man's love, but not so fair as snow.
Mild as a lion, but neither true or trusty.
Brighter and clearer than glass, but yet as glass it
it shatters when it falls. Softer then cotton and yet as
iron it get rusty. His lips to mine near a fireplace, how
often have I had that dream. Between each kiss his lines of
his true love come swearing! How many lines has this man given
me to ponder? Two or four I don't know, but all I know is that
I still love him because he's the passionate man.

—Cindy Louissaint

Black or White

Momma what's a nigger, and what's a wanna-be?
I do not understand these words. So can you tell me please?
Momma what's a jigga-boo and what's the KKK?
I've never seen that sign before. I've just seen AAA.
Why do some people treat me nice and others are so mean?
Some say they do not like my kind, but my face they've never
seen.
And what about my daddy, why is his skin so light?
Some say that I am colored and that my daddy's white.
I wish I understood the things that all those people say.
I guess I won't for quite a while, I'm only six today.
But since I'm just a little kid there's not much I can say.
But pray that when I'm all grown up there'll be a better day.

—Valetta

Poor Boy Blues

Let me tell you about myself,
I don't go and shop,
I don't go to the bank,
I just stay home a lot.

People ask me what I got,
They think I have some disease or flu,
They say I look down and out,
But what I got is the poor boy blues.

Is this my destiny, is this my fate,
To have no money and have no date,
While others take life from silver platters,
Mine's on an paper plate.

Treat me nice girl, can't you see,
I need your loving however casually,
Treat me cheaply, I don't care,
'Cause you're not getting a dime from me.

I need some money but I can't get none,
I need some loving but I can't find none,
What I can do,
I've got the poor boy blues.

—Richard Essig

And Then I Woke Up

I dreamt of being held in your arms,
I dreamt of kissing your lips,
I dreamt of walking hand in hand with you,
And then I woke up.

I could feel your touch,
I could feel your presence,
I could feel your caress,
And then I woke up.

I heard your voice whisper my name,
I heard your voice tell me you cared,
I heard your voice so sweet and low,
And then I woke up.

I felt your hand against my cheek,
I felt your breath on my neck,
I felt your soft lips against mine,
And then I woke up.

You told me you loved me,
You told me you cared,
You told me I was the only one for you,
And then I woke up.

—Amanda L. Morgan

Visions

I dreamt that I was a rock and found I was stronger than a Man.
I dreamt that I was a tree and found that I was taller than a Man.
I dreamt that I was a bird and I knew freedom as no Man could
    ever know.
I dreamt that I was the Sun and my warmth spread across the
    Universe and gave Man his light.

I wakened to find I was all of these things.
Because there is no strength equal to that of a Woman's will.
And no tree more majestic than a Woman.
Nor is there any bird more graceful than a Woman's heart.
And it is but a whim from a Woman that guides a Man.

—Rebecca T. Renish

Her Dominance

She floats across my eyes, runs like a deer.
I endeavor, capturing her, stopping her,
She is evasive. Just like dreams disappear,
Her image forms, vanishing when I near.
She is charming, pure, even beautiful,
Hope to possess, confine her in my heart.
She is imperceptible like an angel,
Her form eludes, every courtship attempt.
She is emotional, wicked, even daring,
Her way is of a treacherous journey.
She radiates about her: youth, yet evolving,
I pray for her loyalty and permanency,
Her company parts, just like autumn leaves.
She is my youth, but unsure of my future.

—Vikram Atwal

Alone

The old woman sits all alone,
Awaiting a visitor or a call on the phone.

But nobody shows and the phone doesn't ring,
She feels forgotten - what a terrible thing.

Then a knock at the door brings a smile to her face,
She welcomes them in with a warm embrace.

Oh grandma we love you, and I'm sorry we're late,
But daddy took the long way and we brought you something great!

"It's a cute little kitty of your very own,
so now you will never again have to sit alone."

—Terri Villandry

Christmas Memories

Christmas memories flow into my mind like the rising tide.

As waves of holiday memories wash across my mind,
I envision my mother's face in the Christmas tinsel.
She seems to sway and dance with the Christmas tree,
As the sound of falling snowflakes create a silent Christmas
melody.

Through the branches of the Christmas tree,
Dad seems to move like the Christmas wind -
Softly, shaping and changing the tree.

The last decoration is hung and all is still...
Like the coming of night.
Then mom and dad embrace like two logs in a roaring fire.
The heat of their love and caring seems to fill the room
And all is warm and well.

—*David C. Reffert*

The Summers End

The summers coming to an end
I feel like I have just lost my best friend

I've had a lot of good times
I've had a few bad,
The summers ending and I feel really sad

I went a lot of places
I saw a lot of new faces

I hear songs that remind me of all the fun
Now it's gone, over, and done

I want to laugh but I have to cry,
The summers ended, and I have to say goodbye

—*Mandy Bauermeister*

My Love

Every time I think about you
I feel so much pain
The pain is deep inside me
The loss was greater than the gain
I think about you every night
And pray to God within
That someday you'll be right beside me
And I'll be in your arms again
I love you more than anyone
I found this out today
For you to love me like you did before
So no one can take you away
All the men have their brides-to-be
And all the women have their men
Oh for you and me to be a couple again
Or for our love to never end
I'll never find another like you
Not in a million years to come
But forever will be my love for you
Or 'til a man touches the Sun.

—*Molly Rose*

Cats

Cats have little fuzzy fur,
And when their very happy, they purr.
They have little fury ears,
Some, when you call them they come near.
That's why cats are nice and sweet,
I still can't see how they stand all that heat.
Maybe you can get one and share it with your friends,
Because when you have one the fun will never end.

—*Candice Anderson*

All I Feel For You

(To Chris, my Heart)
I feel that I'll never fit into your life.
You're so closed off.
I want to get into....
Into your skin.
Your heart.
Your feelings.
It pains me when you're upset and distant.
I don't want to be second best in your life.
I don't want to be first either....
But I want in.
Your eyes bite my soul.
Your teeth bite my skin.
Your distance bites my heart
If only you could understand my love for you?
Or my hate for the feelings
I've closed into myself.

—*Lisa Marie Brady*

Life Has No Meaning

As I stand here and look around,
I feel the stillness of the air and of the ground.
Life has no meaning that we can define.
It's up to you to make it pleasant or live it with a frown.

Life stands still as you sculpture what your life should be.
It waits for you to sketch the silhouette of love and
happiness. So draw a picture by doing the things that fulfill
your inter-soul. And then you'll see life is a lovely
experience to behold.

You're be able to feel the breeze as it blows through the
trees. You can hear the birds as they chirp a sweet and lovely
melody. You can hear the sound of water flowing through the
streams, as it seems to play a sweet melody that causes you to
dream. So when his happens to you, life has opened up its
doors and you can begin to live.

—*Frances L. Raleigh*

Untitled

In the embers of a crimson sunset
I felt the distinct touch of regret
There lay the visage of a barren field
For which there would never again be a plentiful yield
We harvested them one at a time
And not only the forests were victims of our passionate crime
Creatures great and small
Fell prey to the unstoppable plight
They lost there homes, one and all
Chain saws echo like distant thunder
And each day the trees are reduced in number
The forests soon become thin
Their leaves shudder in the wind
Yet they seem to utter
To anyone who can hear
This message of despair
Alas, the time has come my friend
When you and I have witnessed the end
The grandeur that was once is gone
And we the trees will no longer sing our song

—*J. Brandt*

Untitled

To those who measure their love by pain
and their pleasure with guilt
I shed not one solitary tear
for it would be enough to drown
their already sinking soul

—*Celeste*

His Love

I thought that I'd be lonely; but much to my surprise,
I found peace in my life; my Blessed Fathers' hand to guide.
I thought that I'd feel sorrow; entangled amongst the pain,
My Father washed away the hurt; like a cool, misty rain.
I thought that I would be engulfed; with anger and disgust,
But through my Father; I found happiness, for in Him I do trust
I once was afraid; trapped within the darkened fear,
Then with His mighty hand, He touched me; with a whisper He
   is near.
No longer do I wallow in; what my life unwillingly brought;
I am overwhelmed with His love; and what He has taught.
Though sometimes I do falter; and fall a step behind,
To my Lord, I go running; for His love is there always, for me to
   find.

    —Ginamarie Sullivan

Will She Strike Out?

As I approached the plate it was up to me to win,
I had sweat running from my head, dripping from my chin.

With the bases loaded then hear comes the pitch,
she gave me strike one now my nerves start to twitch.

With the evil in my eyes the crowd crossed their fingers for luck,
All you heard was the pitcher telling her team to back up.

Everything in the stadium got quiet all around,
the pitcher stood scarcely upon the pitchers mound.

All of a sudden and out of the blue,
she threw the pitch and the umpire yield "Strike Two."

The next thing you knew out in the crowd,
they started calling her name very loud.

She looked at her fans and started to smile,
and that drove the crowd very wild.

She was determined she was going to hit that ball,
until she heard this disturbing call.

She turned her head for a moment to see,
All she heard was the umpire yelling "Strike Three."

    —Patrice L. Cole

I Wish I Had A Horse

I wish I had a horse; I know,
I have a car that takes me where I want to go.
But who knows what I miss as I go speeding by,
A little ground squirrel, or a Monarch Butterfly.
I've yet to see a car with a nicker to greet me;
Or, when I whistle, come galloping across the field to meet me.
I miss his beauty, his special kind of affection,
His willingness to whisk me away in any direction.
A car could hardly prance sidewise, neck bowed with pride,
Or cut across country, just for the ride.
Alas, for my grandchildren, for they will never know
Just how fast over the rocks a horse can go.

    —Shirley Marshall Skousen

First Day of School

The teacher inquires, "And who are you?"
   And shoulders proudly square,
   And big brown eyes flash a smile,
He replies, "I am George the third."
This five year old has not time for tears,
   As he locates his desk and chair,
Finds a place for his giant crayons and pencil,
   Then with utmost satisfaction,
   Proclaims, "School time is now."

    —Faye Wendt

Lament

Yes, love, I have known you, I have felt your bitter sting.
I have floated dazed, unknowing, on your gossamer wing.

I have gloried in the brilliance of your light,
And despaired in the darkness of your night.

I have stood transfixed on your shore, your restless waves
washing over me; unaware that you were to leave me adrift on
your barren sea.

I have gazed at your heavens, so bright and so near,
And followed your shadow, filled with doubt and fear.

I have climbed to the heights for you, while you beckoned me on
And when I reached the summit I found you were gone.

I have longed for your touch, and cried from the pain.
I have felt so much that I won't feel again.

Yes, love, I have known you. I'll remember you and yet,
I know as I remember, I also must forget.

    —Frances Ross

Reflections "By An Oldie"

Along the pathway of my life
I have known love, joy, sorrow and strife
   Loved ones have come, and many have gone
And still I must be strong — and carry on
The new friends I meet, in church — hall
   or on street,
   some smile — some frown —
   with burdens — lowdown —
But with music at my finger tips
   and laughter on my lips,
Life's still worth living, and
   I will continue giving
   until death — do I part!

    —Florence D. Jarvis

Child Of Mercy

Hello world
I have no name and no thoughts
but I do have feelings and wants.
   I'll cry for hunger, warmth, security
and like many adults, I'll always
need someone, to look out for me.
   My new world has skies, of dark
colors, and a surprise of what this
world holds for me.

   I'll be a child without Mercy, going
through life, not giving, but always wanting
longing, and hurting, in a world of colors
of black, grey, and blue.
   But life has given me a rainbow of
soft pastel colors too, with shades of
   feelings and a bright new
adopted world for a child now
with different shades of Mercy.

    —Loreen E. Beeman

World Peace

"I have a dream" was the famous speech
by Martin Luther King. A dream that blew
away as time went by and now it's gone.
Now the world is filled with fire and hate.
Soon one day the world will be filled with
beautiful white snow. And the world will be
at peace but to do this we have to be at peace
with ourselves!

    —David Manriquez

Depth of Emotion

I have been devastated by events beyond my control.
I have not needed a war, nor have I need burning icons,
Instead, I have been devastated by emotions.
Your emotions…
My emotions…
No emotions.…
While life performed it's grand ballet,
I stood center stage, frightened and trembling,
Afraid that my steps would falter.
I was correct. You were never there for me.
If I had stumbled, I most definitely would have fallen in
To the depths of the Orchestra Pit.
　　—*Wade C. Howell*

Magic Door

Have you seen the magic door?
I have seen it times before.

What does all this lingo mean?
It's not funny or obscene.

I see many people crying.
I see many children dying.

Come follow me through the magic door
Where we can see and learn much more.

It's a peaceful place where children can play.
Come with me, come today.

It's not very far away, just
come and follow your heart this
way towards the magic door.
　　—*Allison R. Jackson*

Sorrowful Goodbyes

Once upon a midnight gray
I heard a deep handsome voice say:
"Come with me, O Nellie May,
With me in this midnight gray."

"Come with me to Crystal Lake
Aboard the big cruise liner 'Drake.'
We can dine on wine and cake
Aboard the big cruise liner 'Drake.'"

And Nellie says "Oh John, I'm depressed,
I cannot go, I need my rest.
For me, I am the very best
Cheer leader at the club called 'Crest.'"

"I cannot give up my life now
To go with you to some lost town.
I do not want a diamond crown
To go with you to an old town."

Then I heard a sobbing deep,
It sounded like a long lost weep.
But I never again heard the deep voice say:
"Come with me, O Nellie May…"
　　—*Amber Richards*

Love

Love .. 'tis a wondrous thing.
And there are many things that it can bring:
Happiness, heartache, joy, or pain,
It can even drive some people insane.

But the love I've found, I'm glad I found it
Now my whole world is built around it.
And no matter what it can bring, no one
is happy until they find;
Love, the gift from God to all mankind.
　　—*Kathy Snow Hughes*

Remembering

There was a child named Bernadette
I heard the story long ago
She saw the Queen of Heaven once
And kept the vision in her soul.
No one believed what she had seen.
No one believed what she had heard.
That there were sorrows to be healed
And mercy in this world. So many hearts I find
Broken hearts like yours and mine,
Torn by what we've done and can't undo.
I just want to hold you, wait now let me hold you
Like Bernadette would do?
We've been around, we've fought, we fly
We mostly fall, we mostly run
And every now and then we try
To mend the damage that we've done.
Tonight I just can't rest
I've got this joy here in my breast.
To think that I did not forget
That child, that song of Bernadette.
　　—*Patrick R. DuBray*

"Wondrous"

　Oh how wondrous it is to rekindle the flickering light
I held in my heart for so long a time
　Oh how wondrous it is I now with joy
To be reminded once again of how wonderful thee art America
　To be showered with wondrous feelings and thought
　　To be able to rejuvenate my faith in our glorious land
What man can say anymore I placed myself above
My waves of struggle for I was floundering
And surely a drowning man I am forever grateful to thee
　Oh wonderful land never again shall
I wander aimlessly but will stride forward
　And cherished and partake of thee all
With a spirit and open heart oh wondrous land
I am forever gracious of thee whether I meet the rich or poor
They are all our people, whether the land is beautiful
Or covered with slums and the housing is scant
It is still our land ever more whether our people are out of
work and there are strikes, it is simply our land evermore.
Be they happy or sad, whether the roads are congested
It is still our wondrous land evermore.
　　—*Sol Gerber*

Do You Know Jesus?

Do you know Jesus?
I hope that you do.
The glow of the sunsets he's gave them to you.
The stars high in heaven all came from his hand.
The shells on the seashore,
The gulls in the sand,
The dew on a rosebud,
The call of a dove,
The rose in the wildwood all tell of his love.
The laughter of children so happy at play.
The fragrance of raindrops,
He's gave you today.
Do you know Jesus?
I hope that you do.
The desert in spring time,
The mountains in fall,
The glisten of snow drops,
The wild goose's call.
These gifts that he's gave you are for one and all.
　　—*Mary Margaret Morrison*

Who Are You?

I watch you everyday on the bus.
I just can't shake this feeling that
at one time I was close to you.
I can feel your touch; and I feel the warmth between us.
You turn to look my way; your eyes are full of disappointment
Who are you?
What did I do to you?
How did you gain this power over me?
Were we lovers in another lifetime?
Did I break your heart?
My mind is in overdrive; as my heart starts to bleed
I need to know,
What happened to us?
Who are you?
Is this real?
You ring the bell,
Stand up; and walk off the bus.
The bus moves on,
and I'm left with a broken heart,
for something that might have never been.

  —Kevin Michael Wehle

Alone

I'm all alone
I just moan and groan
And wait. I
didn't want to say goodbye.
It's hard to see
you, but not be
with you all
the time. Sometimes I wish I was a doll
So I wouldn't feel any
emotions. I wouldn't even need a penny
or anything to stay alive.
But I'm all alone most of
the time. But I'll never
stop loving you. You're the
reason I stay alive. When
I'm with you I'm not alone.

  —Dawn Smith

Untitled

  My friend, my dear, dear friend,
I just wanted you to know that when you are hurting
   I feel the pain.
   When you are lonely,
 I pray for your comfort and peace of mind.
 When you are mad, I stand fast beside you
   no matter what is said or done.
  When you are happy, my heart smiles.
I may never tell you how special you are to me
   and for that I am very sorry.
Please know this, you are a very special person,
 and there is a place in my heart that is yours
   and yours alone.
 You have earned my respect and admiration.
 There isn't anything I wouldn't do for you.
  I would walk through the gates of hell
   to fight the devil with you,
    if that was your wish.
In my own humble way I just wanted to say,
   "Thanks for being a friend."

  —Jeffrey S. O'Hara

Mom

I can't face the holidays without you here,
I keep on saying it's just not fair.
I miss you so much that I have to cry.
Why did God take you and leave me behind.
We shared most of the holidays you and me.
Now I'm so lost and life doesn't mean a thing.
All I want is to have you near.
You're all I wish for it's oh so clear.
They can have their celebrations and their gifts too.
Cause mom all I want is to be with you.

  —Carole L. Johnson

"My Wishing Tree"

I saw one day a wishing tree.
I knew it held a lot of wishes for me.
I wished I was a bird so I could fly.
Right up into that big blue sky.
But then I saw a little deer
He looked at me with eyes that held no fear
So I wished I was a deer so I could run
And jump and play and join his fun
Then I saw a little chubby bear
He was so cute and had thick black hair.
So then I wished I was a bear so young and free.
I hope I get my wishes all three

  —Margie Carhill

Eyes Of Blue

When I saw you by the sea
I knew you were the one for me
Every day I searched for you
Hoping to see your eyes of blue
But when saw you were not there
I cursed the heavens for not playing fair
For I'd found the one I truly loved
Yet had no means to free the doves
Without direction my hunt raged onward
Without direction I failed to find you
The arrow that had pierced my heart
Left my soul torn completely apart
Hated this mirage I was led to find
Was it poseidon who poisoned my mind
So now when I sit beside the sea
I wonder where I lost my dream
And still each day I search for you
Hoping to see your eyes of blue...

  —Nancy L. Mikus

The Time Has Come

It comes as a shock to know I am elderly,
I know not when it came upon me,
But when I must walk because I cannot run,
Then I know the time has come.

I can still see though the lights are dimmer.
I can still hear though people speak lower.
I can still enjoy the taste of good things,
but not as sharp.
Then I know the time has come.

The smell of fresh cut grass or flowers
or my wife's perfume, give me pleasure.
What can compare to the touch of the
small hand of a grandchild?
But I sense that the time has come.

True as age creeps up on me as a thief
Stealing my days away,
I am thankful for the God-given sensations of life,
Even though I know the time has come.

  —Jack Margolin

Living with Confidence

Details of auto mechanics doesn't interest me
I know no parts or where they are;
I just drive where I want to go
but I don't trust the one who made the car.

Bridges I know are a major construction
of concrete and steel that forms a ridge;
I don't stop and inspect them before I cross
but I don't trust the ones who made the bridge.

Aeronautics is a big mystery to me
how the planes stay in the sky;
so I would never inspect the cockpit
whenever I board the plane to fly.

So what makes me live so confident
that I can disregard profit or loss?
It's because I've had a serious talk with Jesus
and I trust the one who died on the Cross.

As He guides, He's the strength of my life
and He gives me a reason to be;
He illuminates my soul with joy
and I trust the One who died for me.
    —Christine Stanley

Music and the Snow

The music plays softly in your ear, as a tear rolls down your cheek.
I know what you are thinking, when you go down to sleep.

You look outside the window, and look at the white snow.
You wonder why she said good-bye, then you realize you'll
    never know.

As the snow comes down you think about the times you spent together.
You thought you two could play in the snow forever and forever.

The music plays instead of her voice. Sweet melodies she
    would bring.
As you close your eyes you almost think you can hear her sing.

They say when people die you have ones you love and know,
But when your all alone all you have is music and the snow.
    —Annie Cassidy

Untitled

I dreamt dreams of golden fields and clear blue skies.
I look at the land of what is now to be my home.
They used to say it was grand and great,
Oh America, things have changed.
I see fear in little Tommy's eyes,
I hear screams in the upstairs room.
Oh America, what is wrong?
I reach out my hand to extend some help.
I am unsure if I should.
Should I show I care?
Should I let them know brotherhood is still there?
Race, culture, color matters not.
This land we now live in we share.
    —Zernalyn Palmares

Baby Roman

Great expectations for this child to be
Born of the nineties much to see
Having been in the making hundreds of years
Many to follow you through happiness and tears
Everyone reaching with open arms
Ready to enfold and breathe a prayer
God bless this treasure being sent to us
That we may guide and comfort through the years
    —Lillian I. Smith

Alec, My Love

Alec, my love,
I look into the morning,
    rising from the hillside.
And you enter my mind.
The thoughts of us walking to our
    special place entwined as one,
Continues with the rising of the morning sun.
You are my new day with each rising dawn.
My love, my life continues thru
    and thru all because of you.
        I love you.
    —*Midge Spaulding*

My Reflection

As I look back and reflect upon my life,
    I look not at what I have achieved,
    But at who I have become.
    In doing so, I realize that when I look
    In a mirror, it is not myself I see.

Instead, I see all of the people
    Who have touched my life in such a way
    That they have made me who I am today.
    Each of them has had a profound effect
    On the person I have become,
    And on the person I will always be.

With each of them I have shared,
    In a very special way,
    My successes, my failures, my happiness,
    My sadness, my laughter and my tears.
    For whether they are near or far,
    That part of me we share
    Is never more than a reflection away.
    —*Rhonda Kay Heard*

My Prayer

O Lord, I look to thee for protection night and day,
    I look to thee with my troubles and trust thee all the way.
Give me courage and patience in trials that may come to me,
    And may I help my fellowmen in their troubles, whatever they
        may be.

O Lord, may I learn from the birds of the air,
    Who depends on thee for such tender care.
May I have faith to move the mountains so tall,
    And have enough love and charity stored up for all.
O Lord, thank thee for the Holy Bible, the blessed book,
    For I find help for every need when I look.
In thy word I find hope, love and courage, the will to go on,
    As a Christian I can walk the way of life with a song.
O Lord, forgive me for all my sins,
    And may I be a blessing to thee by the souls I win.
May I love my enemies and try to win them to you,
    And may I be thy servant until I'm lifted up into the blue.
    —*Kathleen Swopes*

"Love"

I love you till the end of "Love."
And I am not afraid of flying away with you,
like birds to the land of eternity.
My love for you has no limit and my soul belongs to you.
Your being is growing on my being, like winding roses...
I want to watch sunrise with you everyday.
And "everyday" begins with your eyes.
I can see the sunrise in your eyes.
Life is beautiful when you are with me
And I love you, till the end of love,
till the end of time...my love.
    —*Soodabeh Abdollahi*

One Magical Night

That one very night, changed my life for good.
I looked in the doorway and that's where you stood.
Looking confident and cool the way that you do
You came to my table, it was just me and you.
We talked for sometime and that's when I knew
The rest of my life would be shared with just you.
Sometime has passed by since that magical day.
I've never been happier since you came my way.
I look towards the future and know what to expect.
I'll walk down the aisle to love and protect.
Through good times, and bad, for richer or poor.
Together forever we'll walk out that door.
We'll grow old together and remember the past.
And cherish those days from the first till the last.

—*Christina Rothwell*

Upon a Midnight Sky

Once upon a midnight sky,
I looked into your deep blue eyes.

Wondering how you could love me so,
Wondering how much you really know.

Was it my pounding heart that made you sing?
Was it the gentle touch of my feathered wing?

You needed some air and began to fly,
But you returned when I started to cry.

I know you love me, I know for sure,
We'll start anew, we'll forget about her.

She was just a friend, she had no ring,
She took care of you while you left my wing.

You're okay now, you're all safe and sound,
I know we have the strongest love around.

If you decide to leave again, I will not cry,
I'll know you love me but needed to fly!

—*Kristi Rudd*

Love

I love you more than the morning sun.
I love you more than most anyone.
I see love when I look into your eyes.
When we leave one another it's hard to say our sad goodbyes.
I love you more than the sky so blue.
I love you and I know you love me too.
I love you no matter what anyone says or does,
And with you I feel loved more than I ever was.
You make me feel happy; you make me feel sad.
But I will never forget the many great times we've had.
We tell each other our problems, we show that we care.
Our love for one another is the best thing we share.
You've moved away,
but in my heart you stay.
Now and forever through everyday!

—*Christie Mikelson*

First Christmas Stocking

Here is your first christmas stocking all tattered and worn
I mended it dear, where it was torn.
The memories it holds are more valuable than gold
however the stocking is not much to behold.
Your grandmother Elsie, who loved you so dear
Made you this stocking for your first christmas year.
With glitter and tinsel it hung on our tree
your first christmas morning, how happy we're we.

—*Gladys O. Walls*

I Miss You

I miss you in the morning
I miss you at night
I'm crying right now, believe me
it's not a lie.
Thinking of the time we spent together
I can't escape the pain I'll love you forever.
People come and go
Life goes fast and slow
I hope you understand me, I'll never let you go!!
Life is hard
Life is unfair
but if we keep believing in each other
we'll become a closer pair!
Not from far
But yes from close
We'll get together, soon I hope
Remember me, I'll remember you
Don't forget me, I won't forget you!
I miss you!

—*Vesna Gecevski*

"Barely Getting Bi"

All of those lengthy evenings,
I paid unfailing attention to your wordless stare.
Your precise words,
When you did speak,
Cutting deep into me.
Often times you've made me laugh or smile,
Nothing has ever been truly witty about your words,
We were only laughing because of your unusual straightforward
   attitude.

The forte that is so melancholy about our situation, is that
   you believe
We only hang around you because you entertain us,
Yet, that is so illegitimate that it hurts.
You are a beautiful person, and we adore you.
You may be quite forthcoming,
   Still, we see your compassionate side,
   And we know that you have a personality,
And you can not hide your interests much
                              longer.

—*Margaret Porter*

Come Listen To The Silence

To all who may not hear this,
I proclaim it isn't so.
For if you did not hear this,
How would you ever know?

My silence speaks in quiet, tongue.
My heart in beating rhythm.
So listen not,
If you care to hear.
For that's the only way to hear them.

The empty spaces to reach your ear,
Are the only sounds you'll need to hear.
For within silence, lies the voice,
Which will guide you through your inner choice.

To listen to nothing,
In what I have read;
Or to hear what I'm saying,
As nothing instead.

—*Scott Carrey*

Too Young to Marry (My Son)

Dear son of mine, I've raised you well.
I raised you not to go to hell.
Why can't you see your just a boy and not a man.
I've tried and tried to make you plan your life the way I know
you can. To marry now would be a shame.
You would only have your wife to blame.
To wait awhile would be the best, and then your love you both
could test. True love is what life's all about.
Don't give in now and be left out.
Your just too young to realize, that love can die before your
eyes. Your life can't be a great success,
if you don't wait for happiness.
To live your life I have no doubt, that you know what
it's all about. Don't marry now and take the chance
that you'll end up with no romance.
Take my advice and have some fun.
I tell you this with love my son.
I pray to God you know the score. I've tried my son,
I'll cry no more.
Mother

—*Betty M. Eaton*

Untitled

The thoughts run deeply through my mind
I realized that we were meant to be combined

The love we share cannot be undone
In my heart you're that special one

Now that we can get our feelings out
The love we have will last without a doubt

The first time we split apart
There was an empty space in my heart

Could our love be what it seems
I think so because you fulfill all my dreams

Whatever it is, it must be right
Your on my mind everyday and night

My life would end fast
If our love wouldn't last

—*Kristen Weiss*

"An Easter Memory"

As my mind wanders back to my childhood days,
I remember springtime in very special ways.
How the trees and flowers were blooming so rapidly,
But the most beautiful of all was the lovely dogwood tree.
I'd often stop and look at all this wondrous to see,
And I thought the dogwood flower looked like a cross to me.
As I viewed the petals closely they looked rusty at the ends,
And I had heard that Jesus had nail scars in His hands.
I stood there crying as the other children gathered 'round,
They thought I'd gotten hurt as tears fell on the ground.
They never understood when I told them why I cried,
It wasn't cause I was hurt but the way Jesus had died.
When the children left me and I was standing all alone,
It was getting late so I thought that I should go.
As I looked back once more at that pretty dogwood tree,
I said, "thank you, Jesus for an easter memory."

—*Carmelita Dyke*

November Rain

When you take a deep breath and smell the damp air,
and look up to see all the trees bare.
When you look to the horizon and watch the sunset,
and listen to the leaves, almost to the ground, but not just yet.
When you hear something beating softly against your window pane,
then you know it's the sound of November Rain.

—*Dawn Williamson*

Soul Exchange

Once, while walking past a wood,
I saw a tree, and stopped, and stood
Beholding it so sad and lonely;
There it stood with branches only.

My cane I propped against its trunk,
And to my wobbly knees I sunk.
I grasped a bough just as it broke
And fell to the ground my tears had soaked.

I cast my thoughts into the ground.
They searched until the roots they found.
My every move was paralyzed;
Within the tree I was disguised.

Now, as my eyes could see again,
They looked down where I just had been;
My body lie beneath this tree,
My soul was not inside of me.

As I had now become the pine
It's roots became entwined with mine.
From my knees it now arose, standing in a crippled pose.
With my cane it walked away and left me there that solemn day.

—*Jana Moore*

Summer Fog

The fog came in on tiptoe tread,
I saw it where I lay abed;
It cooled the air, refreshed the morn,
    I like the fog, 'tis ocean born.

Its silent fingers dropped gray dew
Where grasses, trees and flowers grew;
Each dripping leaf seemed then to say,
    "We thank you, fog, you cooled our day!"

It cooled us in its quiet way,
Then slipped out past the gates of day;
The sun came shining slowly through —
    I like the fog because it's cool.

—*Harriet L. Gates*

Blood On My Hands

I clenched my nine millimeter tightly in my hand;
I saw my target; it had to be done
Rick owed me money for cocaine.
I walked towards him and said
"Where's my money nigga"
Rick replied in a frightened voice
"I ain't got it"
First I aimed for his head,
Then I pulled the trigger.
The whole world lit up, Rick dropped, and I ran
I didn't want to do it
but, I would have looked like a soft punk if I didn't.
All I could think about that night was Rick's mother
    —and his little brother
Now I sit here guilty with blood on my hands.

—*Rion A. Scott*

A Question In Life

When days of old seem just fine
And old-fashioned ideas make more sense,
When new music trends sound unkind,
And new fashion styles look too intense,
When state of the art is just more expensive
And tried and true are still comprehensive,
Then it's time to stand back, and just take a look
    Is it taken for granted? or
    Is it granted and took?

—*Brian Zweifel*

What Is My Destination

I look beyond the treetops and right over mountains
I see clouds, green grass and beautiful flowers
I'm walking on dirt roads with pebbles and stones.
I don't know my destination but I know it's not too far.
I smell the summer breeze, I feel light rain on my face
    and I can hear birds singing.
I feel I'm getting closer, with no time to waste.
But, the rain is getting harder the breeze is getting stronger
    the birds are getting louder
I start running, not frightened,
    but my heart is beating faster... faster...
Then it all stops the birds stop,
    the rain, the breeze - it all stops.
It's quiet ... I stand listening
    - alone -
I've reached my destination.

    —*Jamie Despathy*

Puzzle My Mind

I shall feed myself with a slice of the moon;
I shall warm in the rays of the sun,
I shall puzzle my mind during flashes of gloom
And rejoice in the moments of fun.

I shall cool myself with a soft summer breeze;
I shall rest in the patches of shade,
I shall puzzle my mind in spare moments of ease
And ponder what nature had made.

I shall firm myself with my feet on the land;
I shall splash in the waves of the sea,
I shall puzzle my mind as I sit on the sand
And rejoice that there's you and there's me.

I shall search for the wisdom I may find in the sky;
I shall study the clouds as they tumble.
I shall puzzle my mind as these things pass me by
With a flash and an ominous rumble.

I shall patiently wait for the time to come
When answers shall float through my mind;
I will know by a roll of a mighty drum-
I will know what I came here to find.

    —*Susan Bond*

Incongruity of Life

I sit beside the wind and drink fresh air;
I sing to myself;
Breezes play about my hair like the rippling of water and I
long for the sea;
Needles of pine cushion my feet on the forest floor;
The warm sun soothes my every sense and calms my soul —
I am at peace.

The little wren chirps his frisky greeting, and I smile;
Across the flushing drift a scent of rare woodbine thrills my
heart with nature's rapture;
I look into the far distant haze and see angels flitting about
in listless glee;
I sing to myself and the world sings back —
There is music even within my soul.

The long day fades,
Darkness rolls into the east,
The green leaves lose their gloss
And I pluck the legs of a grasshopper.

    —*W. T. Harris*

Beaches

The beach is the best when I am alone.
I sit on the sand and call it my own.
It gives me a chance, to sort out all feelings.
The crashing waves is all I am hearing.
It puts me in a world, a world so far away.
I don't want to come back to the pain and dismay.
To watch the boats just floating by,
makes me wish that I could fly.
It is so peaceful, and all around,
there are no harsh nor frightening sounds.
Nothing is there, that I don't want to hear.
It's just me and the beach and nobody near.

    —*Jamie Despathy*

Words of Silence

Looking across a room of readers,
I slowly peek from the top of my paper.
Only to find two fixed eyes on my face,
Or was there three?

There she was, scanning the paper, hoping to find my
Face through sorted corners of her eyes.
I looked quickly again!
She peeked slightly.

What was about to happen next I say! Only of course
In overtones in my head.
My heart pounded,
Her heart pounded,
What was about to happen?

She picked up the daily reader,
Gave me a wink,
And went into the darkness!
Just looking for another reader, searching for words
That cannot be written, nor spoken.

    —*Aaron Candlish*

The Meeting

As I walk along the cold stone to where you are
I step softly and carefully so not to disturb anyone's rest
I close my eyes and think of the last summer together
Watching you stand tall when others tried to knock you down
How brave and strong you were
I admired you, I always will
As I move closer to you I imagine the embrace we will share
I will tell you how much I've missed you, it's been to long
You will smile and say yes it has and everything will be o.k.
A few more steps I move and I see you, waiting for me
I start to cry but still a smile remains on my face
Inside my pocket I protect a rose I carefully choose for you
Finally I am here with you, I remove the rose
As I shake I try to control my emotion
Prepared what to say I begin to speak but then can not
I am frozen for a second and then regain my thoughts
My tears begin to fall and I know what I must do
I bend down and place the rose upon your grave

    —*D. C. Jensen*

Please

Please hold me tightly within your arms
    and fill me full with your charms.
Please kiss me gently on the cheek
    and whisper words of love that I seek.
Please love me as I love you
    and feel the love that's honest and true.
Please keep me safe from all the pain
    and smile away the rain.
Please just love me forever and more
    and together we shall open the future door.

    —*Alice Fales*

My Cathedral

Alone in the woods this crisp fall day
I stretch out prone on the earth and pray
That the words may come - and they seldom do
To rightly describe a majestic view.

Here is my Cathedral, I found it free.
My steeple shall be - that tallest tree.
My objects of worship are all around,
Falling leaves brush my face on their way to the ground.

As I enter I shed each trying thought,
Each worry, each care, the years have wrought,
And kneel at the Altar - the stream is my shrine.
Although it is no one's I call it mine.

I think of my friends, the old and the new,
Of my loves - they are few, and less that are true.
Mother nature says nothing, my deceits I confess.
Her silence is golden, she forgives and forgets.

—*Madelyn K. Skarnes*

Andrea

Hi my name is Andrea and I am five
I thank God I am still alive
My dad spends all the money on acid, beer and pot
He never feeds me, I think I might rot
I lay my head down on the bed
And I pray I won't wake up dead
I hear my dad drinking a beer
You see that's what he holds dear
Now I hear him walking down the hall
I am very scared, I am going to fall
I am saying now 'cause I am dead
I was beat to death by my dad Fred
Now you know I didn't lie
Well I must go … look I can fly!
    My name is Andrea, I am five.

—*Stacy D. Fowler*

Does Love Grow?

Does LOVE grow?
I think ours has.
It has been like a plant taking root.
It was young at first and slowly started to grow.
The roots have plunged deeper and deeper,
    to leave a definite mark that will never go away.
It wasn't enough that our LOVE became embedded as far as it
    could go, so it continued to grow upward and out like a
    wild vine.
Our LOVE has become entwined,
    twisted and tangled as we have become closer.
The LOVE we share is very complicated and beautiful.
I can no longer tell exactly where it began or where it ends.
If our LOVE is true,
    one day our vine will be as one and nobody would ever guess,
        once we were two.

—*Jeannie Letendre*

The Rose

The perfect twine confronts my nose
As I partake of the oxygen that descends all around
Though in my hand a stem and a rose
Yet alone the beauty is so profound

Such color and detail catch hold of my vision
As I admire the pedals that will eventually die
A symbol of love and recognition
I ask myself the question why?

—*Tammy Navey*

Farewell To My Father

When I had to see you to say good-bye,
I tried real hard not to break down and cry.

But I felt the tears roll down my face,
I was so lost and lonely and out of place.

You were my strength when I was down,
Always helped to keep my feet on the ground.

As I grew older and struggled with life,
You were always there, sharing my strife.

Always shaking your head at my stubborn pride,
But right or wrong you were on my side.

And when I didn't take your patient advice,
you picked up the pieces and helped me fight.

When nightmares kept me awake with fright,
you gave me the courage to get through the nights.

A phone call at night or coming home to visit.
you were always there and ready to listen.

What will I do now your gone dear dad,
you were the best father a girl could have.

—*Lynne M. Crooks*

The Lantern in My Soul

I look into your eyes, and I see a part of me.
I understand your language, as you understand mine. You feel
the same pain I feel and together we wipe away each others tears.
I sometimes contemplate what life would be like without you,
    and I realize that without you life loses all perspective.
I know that you are my rock. I wrap my arms around you so that
I can feel loved and to weave you into my being. The security
of your embrace makes me want to stay in your arms forever.
You probe my mind and make me feel and express emotions that I
    never knew existed before. But with you it is all right
to feel these emotions even if I don't understand them. I know
    that you will not judge me, so I then take you with me as I
walk through my soul and explore myself. You carry a lantern as
you walk with me so that I may learn about myself, and the more
I learn the closer I feel to you because all my discoveries are
    shared with you. Without you I could to have made those
    discoveries. Every fiber of my being is woven with the love
that I feel for you. So please promise me that you will always
love me, and keep the lantern shining within my soul for without
    you I am lost in the shadows and fog that fills my soul.

—*Tonee Muenzhuber*

To An Angel

My guardian angel, with you by my side,
I venture out in the world so wide.
Keep my steps going, in the best way,
To lead me to heaven as I constantly pray.
Let me live my life,
    so it is pleasing to God.
Tell me, as I travel,
    I'm doing a good job.

I must be assured
    that I'm following the rules,
And not letting distractions
    appear to be jewels.
Keep my mind's eye,
    on God and His angels,
His holy mother, Mary,
    St. Joseph and his saints.
Ask them to help me
    each mile of my way,
To love and protect me
    as I travel each day.

—*C. Virginia Guidmore*

Bowl of Fruit

Once I saw a bowl of fruit, as alluring as it could be.
I wanted to let it set there, though hungry I might be.
The beauty of the picture I saw, as it was shining in the sun.
The apple, orange, and tangerine and, of course, the plum.
They surely wet my appetite, the grapes, the peach, and pear.
And, if I was to eat just one, it would ruin the picture there.
The more I looked at the bowl of fruit, my hunger pangs did grow.
Surely if I ate just one grape, no one would really know.
As I savored the first grape I took, I looked with such despair
I had ruined the perfect picture, so I decided to eat the pear.
The apple and peach were next to eat, their flavor you could not beat.
Then I peeled the orange and tangerine, for the peels I would not eat.
The cores of the apple and the pear and the pits of the peach and
    plum.
The wiggly stems of the grapes, and the peels lying there in the sun.
Now the bowl of fruit is empty, with the remains just lying around.
But, if an artist looks real hard, another picture can be found.

—*Walter M. Yesia*

Tears of my Eyes

This is a poem about the tears of my eyes
I wanted to make it personal
And this is the reason why?

You see my mother is suffering from a thing called cancer
The doctors, nurses, and medical profession
Doesn't have the answer

She is a nurse's aide and has helped others
She has sat at patients bedside
And counseled better than Dr. Joyce Brothers

As I sat by her beside and watched her bear the pain
Their was an ache in my body all the way to my brain
I opened my bible, I had prayer with her, and begin to cry
My heart was very heavy, and I let out a hugh sigh
I know my mother's faith in God now is being tried
So I turned my head away from her
And felt God's spirit draw nigh
He let me know that in heaven he will dry
All the tears of my eyes

—*Bornie C. McCargo*

My Mom's Cancer

My mom is writing this poem for me 'cause I am only three.
I wanted to write a poem about how much she means to me.

My mom had cancer a year ago but now is doing well.
If you didn't know her a year ago, then you could never tell.

My mom says that God made me and then gave me to her and dad.
But I know God gave me to my mom for the youth she never had.

We do all kinds of things together — she tells me everything.
She showed me where Texas is on a map, and how to dance and
sing.

She's teaching me to read and says that not all people are nice.
She makes me mind my manners and says all actions have a price.

My mom knows that I love her because I tell her all the time.
Pray to God she'll live forever or at least to be 99!

But if God needs my mother now and she and I are to part,
My mom is going to always be alive within my heart.

—*Margaret Knesek-Kubelka*

"I Never New"

As the old saying goes
"I was a poet
And didn't even know it"
Until I tried it one day
Now I have a lot of things to say
It's true
I'm writing this just to tell you
I don't know where my idea's come from or why
But sometimes they even make me cry
They bring me a lot of joy
I'm like a kid with a new toy
Some of them have a plot
Some of them do not
Some are easily understood
Some are not so good
As you can see
It doesn't really matter to me
If I have something to say
I'm going to write it anyway
I thank you for reading it my way

—*T. A. Cutlip*

Whispers of Eve to Adam

I am nothing more than I pretend to be
I was nothing more at the start

I will be nothing more in the years to come
Than the part of your soul that is not.

Forgive me for what I am
For I am the half that is you

Naked of hate and cloaked in love
I will breathe on the breath that you drew.

—*Patricia Suzanne Nolan*

A Poem, Of Its, Time

I'm little today, and could barely say a letter
I was out to play, if only I could have known better
And I hadn't realized it, but I had grown
And time slipped by, as if it had flown
I woke up tomorrow, and the year's came and went
I don't really know, it's like a five dollar bill spent
I woke up a week ago, all filled with sorrow
And it was time to retire, as if it was tomorrow
I got up next month, and my mother has died,
at the ripe old age of ninety-five
I thought to myself, I'm still alive,
at a different age of seventy-five
Has tomorrow come, I don't really know
For a life on earth, surely must go
And time is reality, that you've got
But your mortality is, something you have not
And I got up next year, I'm thankful, I'll say
Lookout, the here after, is in my way
So whoever reads this, can apply it to their age
But to understand it, your older, and it's just another page
And you've lived a lifetime, playing a role
So think about it, and enhance your soul.

—*Paul Bowman*

Dreaming

As the night fly by and the moon,
And as I float to my heaven as my heart falls,
The clouds fly over me as my body withdrawals
I feel I am surrounded by the bees,
And birds in the sky.
The butterflies have touched me
With my invisibility I am fine...

—*Danielle Vincent, Age 13*

1994

Dear Editor:
I was thinking is the reason of my existence
Where? I'm really, I'm in a lost city
Whites, blacks, orientals
Everybody with their own thinking
Different existences, different colors
Oh! My God, I'm dreaming, is the melting
Pot, New York, the city I was born, now my
Nightmare begins, I like to shoot to shout
To drink, to eat, to melt, I'm everything
Or nothing at all, all the existences in me
Boil like water oil or lava, I'm a thousand
Pieces in one block of meat contemporary
Living creature.

—*William McDonald*

My Mother's Love

In the minute of my sorrow
I was walking by the ocean
With my heart so full of hurt and pain
And longing for my dearest mother
Then I posed, watching as the first rays
   of the sun were touching the waves of the ocean
At that moment, my mother's love
   touched my heart
And my soul so light, so free, so full of joy
   soared high into the sky,
As I stood by the ocean
Surrounded by bright warm rays of the sun
   and soft breezes from the ocean
With my heart assured of mother's love
   to eternity.
Oh, thank you God for your precious gift
   of love for me.
And also thank you that at last I found
   comfort in your earthly paradise.

—*Nonna G. Prohorenko*

Face Pressed Against the Chilly Glass

Face pressed against the chilly glass
I watch the others inside
And yearn to be a part of their class
A friend in whom they confide.

Face pressed against the chilly glass
They will not let me inside
So solitude becomes my abyss
As they laugh and hurt my pride.

Face pressed against the chilly glass
They won't see how hard I've cried
As the years roll quickly past
The longing and yearning subsides.

Face pressed against the chilly glass
Take pain and rejection in stride
As I realize my soul's beauty at last
That no one again will deride.

Face pressed against the chilly glass
Here's a secret I now must confide
To all who've felt that cold, cold glass
I learned so much more outside.

—*Pat Peaslee*

Suddenly Sacred

For the sake of compassion
I will listen to your rationale. Swear to
God I'll wear that button on my sleeve.
See, I believe it since you crossed my path.
And there's a warrant out for most of us.
So tick-tock, I say.
Jesus, how I pray to be accepted.
My common thinking was pleasantly rejected
by that
gun
in my face.
Oh, say there's a place for me, holy man.
For I will stand, sit or kneel. I will feel
that faith.
For heaven's sake, it sinks in eventually.
So what if I transformed incidentally? It's
all the same in the end.
Lend me a ticket, friend. Lord, don't let them
crucify me.

—*Dakin Dugaw*

I Am

I am a person of many thoughts and mixed emotions.
I wonder what it would be like to have a sister, not a
brother.
I hear voices of change.
I see the land I dream about.
I want a life with just ups and no downs.
I am a person of many thoughts and mixed emotions.

I pretend to be in someone else's shoes.
I feel sad and lonely.
I touch my wounded soul.
I worry about the future.
I cry when I feel isolated.
I am a person of many thoughts and mixed emotions.

I understand life goes on.
I say so let me live it.
I dream of watching the sunset on the other side of the world.
I try to rid myself of bad memories.
I hope for everyone to get along.
I am a person of many thoughts and mixed emotions.

—*Monica Holmes*

Testament of Love

This one's for you, my lover, my all.
I would be as a dry and barren land,
—Desolate—
Only a shell of a man
If not for your living waters of love.
After 16 years
I still can't drink enough of you in—
Your touch,
Your caress,
The scent of your hair,
—You—

When I at last see face to face
"I Am That I Am" God,
I will lay before Him my greatest accomplishment as a gift,
All other deeds paled in comparison.
I will say, with eyes aglow and heart on fire,
"Because You first loved me, I was able to love".
And I have loved, with my whole heart, this man, Douglas.
And I will bow before Him, a completed soul,
Whose life bore the sweetest of fruits...Love.

—*Mark Curl*

Lovers Forever

If you was me and I was you,
I would love you so much that you would love me too.
I've searched and searched for a guy that's new,
Someone who can love me, someone like you.
Together, we can have so much fun,
    you would have no place to run.
No place to run, no place to hide,
You swept me off my feet like an ocean tide.
I can't compare you to the ocean, so blue,
All I can say is that I love you.
I love you is such a simple little phrase,
Three words is all you need to express your loving ways.
Your loving ways are special to me,
My heart is the door and you have the key.
If you have the key, then I have the lock,
Don't use the key all you do is just knock.
If you knock I'll let you come in,
My fantasy and yours until the end.
Until the end, together we'll be,
Lovers forever just you and me.

    —Michele Tate

Brighter Road

When I was young I told myself
I would never cry over love
My mind would rule and I'd
Stay strong no matter what...

But how I wonder why these tears would not go away
Just because he's gone and he won't
Come back no matter how many times I pray...

So, Lord please help me see the light
Help me get on my feet for I want to win the fight
I know it's not too late to start all over again
For when I find my Mr. Right
I'll be much happier then...

And I should be glad he broke my heart
At least I know now who I should love
And who I should not
So, if there's another me out there
Who is about to give up hope
Please don't, because the more
Mistakes we make the brighter
Will be our road.

    —Angie Cadavona

"Old Glasses"

If it wasn't for my old glasses laying by the good Book,
I wouldn't have been able to take a final last look,
As you lay amongst the roses, so lovely, yet pale,
If it wasn't for my old glasses, my eyes would have failed.

Many dawns have broken, many suns have set,
Many moons have risen, since we first met,
Our years together brought tenderness and joy,
Our life was as the seasons, lovely, but all too brief,
Winter, the white pure snow; spring the birth and awakening
Of life; summer, the perfume of flowers on soft breezes;
And autumn, with the myriad of colors on each leaf.

As I leave my old glasses laying by the good book,
The fireplace is flickering, casting a shadow, and I look,
A moonbeam is broken, there is a scent of spring flowers,
The ray of dawn breaks through the glade, revealing his
powers.

I leave my old glasses laying by the good book,
I don't need them now, to take a new look,
As you were laying amongst the roses, so lovely, yet pale,
I don't need my old glasses, for my love will never fail.

    —Carol G. Grillo

When I Had The Chance

Oppression's bonds were cast away;
I'd lived and prayed for that new day.
I'd planned to dance once I was free
While chains restrained a dancer-to-be.

I went to a place where life was full;
New horizons were hoped to make me whole.
Love flowed free with much to spare;
A dance unto life was ours to share.

Freedom found a prisoner hiding in me;
I saw prison bars existed inwardly.
I wanted to sing and laugh and dance,
But I stood there frozen
When I had the chance.

    —Diana M. Picknell

I Wonder

I wonder what the Christ child would say,
if he were here this Christmas Day?
I wonder if he'd smile at us with all our
worry and our fuss?
I think he'd maybe bow his head, a tear
stream down his cheek instead,
for all the children on this earth who
do not know of Jesus' birth.
So please let's take some time this year,
amid the mirth, amid the cheer, to say Thank
you to the Lord above, for sending us HIS
son, in Love.

    —Tammy Flynn

A Father's Words

    Cry not over me when I die.
    If in heaven I lift up my eyes
        No more days but one.
    My life is not over - it's just begun.

    Cry not over me because I am gone.
        If I could I'd cry over you
        Because you're not at home.
    Then worship God in His holy place,

That in heaven I can see your glorious face
    So when the last words are read,
    Just remember I am not dead.

    —Billy J. Burke

Through the Trail

Could you tell me what you would do,
If pure truth unfolded to you?
If it spoke and when finished you knew
That this was your last day on earth.

Your last day on earth when your death is your birth,
And before your soul's flight you do only what's right.
A short while to hold on to a feeling so strong,
That you know here is where you belong
But soon, too soon, all this will be gone.

The archaic rock of spinning time
Will set your soul free and all will unwind
And as the mystic fog of your purpose will unveil
The clearing brings light guiding you through the trail.

    —Richard Brian Clampitt

Never Alone

If the loneliness of every day life dampens you and brings you
strife.
If the loneliness of your soul cries out to the eternal one and
your life mission seems undone.
Do not fear for all is not lost, your life is all that it costs.
Because you are not alone, not alone at all.
You are only in a certain time and place when loneliness seems to
  fall.
Look in the endless void of night and there you will see what
looks like tiny lights.
Not lights, but suns, world's and other life.
Where other lonely souls also feel the strife.
But there are those who know and feel that there are others who
are also real. They know that their time and place enables
them not to see the other's face. And if you think life can't
be away so far and wide, think of our world and its other side.
For you know it is there and other's know you are here, but
neither see the other's anywhere. So it just as well might be
that they also live in that endless sea.

  —*Stephen Wippel*

A Letter to My Family and Friends

If you don't know what to say, say nothing.
If you want to say your sorry, say it.
If you want to do anything, just understand and bear with me.
If you don't know what to do when you know I'm sad, just give
  me a hug.
Don't lecture me, I already know the words your trying to say.
Don't tell me my life must go on, my life is on hold right now.
I'm in mourning, I hurt, I need to cry, I need to grieve.
I lost a part of me, my son, and what makes it worse, he took
  his own life
Don't try and stop my tears, my tears are normal and are healing.
Don't change the subject if I want to talk about Randy,
  that makes me feel worse.
Don't tell me to smile when at times I can't, my hurt is
  overpowering.
All I ask is for you to bear with me, it will take time for me
  to heal and learn to deal with my lifelong hurt.

  —*Sheila Tochalauski*

Life Continues On

May the breaking of dawn give one the courage to carry on -
ill-health, growing old, finding the world turning cold are
obstacles to hurtles. When a child dies before a parent, grief
becomes part of life's muddle... One's purpose in life is gone
does the pain grow less? The pain may dull in time and
memories are one's most precious lifeline. Life continues on
sometimes with, or without, a happy rhyme! Can one do some
good for others even if they're not your brothers? Life gives
no promises of success however one may feel blessed! One day
at a time; one tries to do one's best - even with
discouragement giving no rest. One may stumble and yes, even
sometimes fall. Don't give up! That's the time to get up and
give it your all. The journey through life has many pitfalls;
no guarantees for having a great big ball. When there's life,
there's hope, as life continues on. People are born; people
do die, rewards are appraised, failures make one want to cry.
Commitments are applied; perseverance can survive. Life can be
a pleasure; life can be a pain - whatever it's measure,
Life continues on!

  —*Betty Jean Payne*

Maybe Tomorrow

I loved you yesterday, I love you today
  I'll love you again, John
    Maybe tomorrow.
There were no good-byes, just many long cries
  It just wasn't fair, but I'll see you up there,
    Maybe tomorrow
Take care of me now as you did before
  I need your help so very much more
You left me with memories of all those good years,
You left me alone
  With non-ending tears.
No matter what happens I'll never forget
That part of my life that left with your death.
The thought that I'll see you, maybe tomorrow.
Helps heal the wounds,
The terrible sorrow.

  —*Pat Eichelbaum*

Especially for You

When you look at me with those beautiful eyes,
illuminated with love and tenderness,
my heart and being shudder with emotion.
It feels like an Angels from heaven is looking at me,

For an instant it feels like I'm transported to paradise,
the most beautiful paradise in the universe with a beautiful garden
brimming with flowers, the most beautiful flowers, the loveliest
  flowers,
the most delightful and fragrant flowers that can exist.

When I find myself surrounded
by such aromatic beautiful flowers,
I begin to look for the loveliest flower
so I can present it to you.

And as I look for the most delightful flower in this
handsome garden I realized that the most beautiful,
the loveliest, the most delightful and
fragrant flower is you.

  —*Theodore Rodriguez*

The Poet Me

  I can write anything that I please.
  I'm even learning to do it with ease.
  Now wouldn't you shout if you were a poet?
  If you were talented - wouldn't you show it?

  Sure you would - you'd brag and boast.
  You'd bore the hell out of your host.
  You wouldn't care - you wouldn't know it.
  That's the blissful joy - of being a poet.

  You'd write what's in your heart for you.
  It's natural to share it with others too.
  If they don't like it - that's just tough.
  Not everyone's capable of liking great stuff.

  —*Margaret L. Hedding*

Musing-1

  This bar that tavern, pub or inn
conversations sublime, more often bantered,
from distinguished ambience to raunchy din,
and in between sidewalk cafes cantered.
  This night that night, wandering askew
the boulevards for that elusive
serendipity of a time lost to renew,
but its never there save in thoughts pensive.

  —*Jim Dahl*

I'll Keep Trying

I'll keep trying to go on, living for you, Darling.
  I'm lost without your love for me.
    I'll keep trying to go on.
Just because things people say that's not true.
  I'll keep trying to go on.
We had our ups and downs in this world.
  But, I'll keep trying to go on.
We kept on living on, together
  But, I'll keep trying to go on.
Now, that we're a part from each other.
  I'll keep trying to go on.
It's hard to live and carry on, alone.
  But, I'll keep trying to go on.
Our memories of our love will live, forever.
  But, I'll keep trying to go on.
We can't just forget our love we had, together.
  But I'll keep trying to go on.
My heart is for you only, Dear.
  And I'll keep trying to go on.
But I only love, you, forever and I'll keep trying to go on.

    —Bryan Dixon

I Am Thankful

O God! For Your presence even when
  I'm not searching for You,
For Your love even when I'm not so lovely,
For friends and family even when I feel
  alienated from them
For food so abundant and good even
  when others are starving,
For clothes which don't ever seem quite
  good enough even when others are cold,
For a government full of flaws
  because others have no stable government at all,
For health and strength which mean everything,
For the privilege to do for others
  who need a helping hand,
For wisdom and desire to give of time and love,
For all that I receive from giving,
For being my example, which is very hard to follow,
For Your power and strength to enable me to do so.
Great Father of all mankind, I stop now to say, "Thanks"!

    —Juanita Wallace

Your Loving Lad

I'm sorry mom, I'm sorry dad,
  I'm sorry I used to be so bad.
I know you loved me, I know it's true
  I know your punishments were always due.
I know you meant the best for me,
  I know that's true, 'tis a fact I see.
I'll always try to do what's right,
  I'll do it even when I'm out of sight.
You taught me right, you taught me wrong,
  For me the message now comes on strong.
Now I'm older and got more sense,
  I'm not so headstrong, not so dense.
Your firm approach was right I know,
  My life it did not let me blow.
The years have past, the results you see,
  Of the love and care you had for me.
Yes, I love you mom, I love you dad,
  You are the greatest, your loving lad.

    —Virgil A. Ruckdashel

Christmas Song

This year my poem will be gentle;
I'm tired of being cynical.
It's wearisome being superior.
The mob wears you down, anyway, every way.

This year I'll concentrate on hope.
There's comfort there, the future;
Ideals exist on that horizon,
Happy land of sunshine, philosopher kings.

I'll say, "Morality shines from puppies' eyes,
The shimmer of sun on snow.
The good grows like rain-fed grass,
And happiness gurgles forth as brooks
  from mountain's pass."

"Quiet contentment comes to those in tune
As December softens raucous June.
Virgin and Child—the basic things—
Beating hearts, fluttering wings."

So, this year, close cynical mind;
Listen! The world sings.

    —Harold R. Wheatley

The Two Last Words

(For Nana)
In 1915 did the young Turks decide
To commit their own form of race genocide
The Armenian people were the target of their hate
Why did the Lord make us suffer this fate?

In raids they attacked us, annihilation their goal
They slaughtered our bodies, but never our soul
Who now among us has not grieved or cried
For a grandmother tortured, an uncle who died?

The world let it happen, coldly looking away
The Turks then denied it, and still do to this day
But happen it did, let the story be heard
The accounts of our torment, the lessons not learned.

We are Armenians
A million lives lost
We are the children
Of a forgotten holocaust.

Forgiveness we grant, but forget we will not
The horrible hand dealt us by life's lot
Yet we rose from the ashes of anguish and death
The Armenian people will never breathe a last breath!

    —Lou DeLena

A Stormy Night

Here I am on a stormy night.
In a creepy house without any light.
I can hear the crashing of thunder up in the sky,
and see the lighting flashing near by.
Suddenly, the phone rings and I jump,
as my heart beats louder with a thump, thump.
I cross the room and answer the phone,
listening to heavy breathing and a soft moan.
I yell who is there, but hear the phone click.
Who has called me and from where.
I wanted to scream and let out a cry.
Is this the end, am I going to die.
Then, the knob turned on the door.
I froze in my place, I couldn't take it anymore,
I listened, and someone had called,
it is me your boyfriend Jack.
I ran to him thank heavens he was back.

    —Marie Beckwith

It Was Worth It

(To ALB with love)
In a smoldering pit, at the bottom of my soul,
under the ashes of dreams, lay the last glowing coal,
covered by charred remnants, of old burning desires.
Each one was an offering, to love's raging fires!

Dreams and desires, led as a lambs to the slaughter,
to ease the worship, of Persephone's blond daughter,
each one pushed love's pain, beyond time and space,
striving to put a smile, on her sweet pixy face!

'Neath a canopy of stars, lighting summer-time skies
A loving heart drowned, in the depths of her eyes,
not swirl nor a ripple, on those deep hazel pools,
marked the passing of he who ignored all the rules!

—*Howard W. Wood*

Untitled

I was walking all alone
In a world of confusion
Until you found me
We made a vow to be best friends
Side by side we walked
Never staying in one place
Searching and wondering
What destiny has in store for us
Meeting new people everyday
Learning a little more about life
With the mind thrown in every direction
Never forgetting
Always wondering what if we turned a different direction
Here we still are walking side by side
Being the best of best friends
In a world of confusion
Never repeating
Surviving every new obstacle that comes our way
Because life just wouldn't be life without a best friend
To figure out the confusion in the world we live!

—*Irene L. Roman*

A Painful Death

She died a rather sudden death,
In and out she went,
It was a painful death.
Suicide is what it's called,
She had problems at school,
  and everywhere she went,
No one knew about these problems,
That is why it was a sudden death,
It took everyone by surprise,
Especially me, it was a painful death to me,
Not as painful to she,
It broke me apart inside,
I tried to put myself back together,
But the memories were forever,
Memories are good to keep, if you can handle it inside.
But still it was a sad, sudden and painful death to me.

—*Devann Zannino*

The Glow

The mountains high, the plains low
and the soft wind blows.

  Oh look, what's that glow!
Day by day I see the glow upon the
mountains high.

  The glow gets bigger day by
day upon the mountains high.

—*Ryan Penner*

My Christmas Wish

I wish for each of you a truly blessed christmas morn
In celebration of a date that history states Christ was born.
I wish for you a cool wave of contentment and grace
As our Lord Jesus in our lives is restored to his proper place.
My wish continues and go on and on
As I reflect on the lives of love ones of days by-gone.
I wish I didn't have to remember love ones lowered into the graves
And could wake up from a dream and say...that didn't take place.
I wish and pray that I will continue to feel positive despite all
And continue to cast my eyes heavenly less a tear fall.
My greatest wish is that man of malice and hate disrobe
And drape his body in a robe of armour and love and spread it
  around the globe.
I wish for each of you a Christ filled day
As we open our hearts and allow Christ to have his way.

—*Loette Williams Alexander*

Seasoned

I've seen the shore lights cross on water
  in countless calm coves safe and sound
I've tasted salt when waves crashed over
  but seldom chose to turn around

I've seen the night clouds roll in slowly
  forcing sea stars to surrender
I've seen togetherness turn lonely
  knowing both I must remember

—*Frank E. Ferrell*

I Wish

I wish I believed in rainbows again.
In faraway places with pegasus soaring through the sky.
And mermaids frolicking in the waves.

I wish I believed in the laughter of children.
In sunrises and sunsets.
And daisies shimmering with the morning dew.

I wish I believed in happily ever afters
In the pure magic of a smile.
And angels in the heavens.

I wish I believed in unicorns
In gallant knights astride white horses.
And wishing upon a star.
Most of all, I wish I believed in you.

—*Amie M. Morris*

Depression

When I laid my head down low, the tears
In my brain started to flow. Rapidly
like the wind to a stream, suddenly
It was that horrible dream. With that
Beautiful heart and that crack-split
In the middle, bringing pain and less
Joy to the voice of my freedom and mind.
Tonight is the night, that the feeling
isn't right and my name is the name
That is to be sacrificed. The Lion, the
Tiger, and the Bear, Yes you have heard
This so no need to swear. Well it's me
With the sounds and not with the Custom
Affair. See: I'm the Roar, Growl, and
Frightful Howl which didn't amuse you at
All. See its hard to explain, its the
Inside and not the pain, but you know its
Just plain weird! So good-bye to the
Monkey, who gave me a push and traveled to
That Winter Wonderland ... Depression!

—*Robert Maxwell*

The Stranger

His unknown face appears before me,
  in my dreams at night.
This John Doe of my nightmares;
  that fills me with such fright:

He comes back every now and then,
  each time my eyes should close.
His lanky figure standing there;
  so lonely I suppose.

He is not like a shadow;
  but like an old man that is frail.
His eyes so dark they scare me;
  his wrinkled skin so pale:

Up the creaky stairs he comes.
  I feel myself in danger.
At last I'll wake with screams of fright;
  fright of this unknown stranger.
  —*Maggie Schwaderer*

Friendship

The prize to cherish, power to console
In the dreams of life that blend soul to soul.
The look of knowing in another's eyes,
Penetrating as bright freshening skies.
The mellow touch that draws new life to stay.
As ripening fruit on a summer's day.
Warm balm from lilting strains of tenderness
To nourish joy of self forgetfulness.
No storm nor tide or winter winds that blow.
Can break the clasp of hands of two who know.
  —*Amebi Doombadfe*

Night Bird

I am the cage, I am the key,
In the mirror, I am free

She echoes to his touch, opaque and light,
Captivity dissolves in silent play —
Sara wings at kisses, fingers flight,

Hungers for a homeland, searches night
for sustenance to keep her through the day —
She echoes to his touch, opaque and light.

Soaring into vision, into sight,
Her tropic warmth will melt the dark away —
Sara wings at kisses, fingers flight,

Glides on scented tradewinds, left and right,
(pas de couru des mains enveloppe)
She echoes to his touch, opaque and light.

Dancing on a dream, allegro bright,
Her demons for the moment are at bay —
Sara wings at kisses, fingers flight,

Flutters on a hope, ephemeral might —
Knowing that the moment will not stay,
She echoes to his touch, opaque and light;
Sara wings at kisses, fingers flight
  —*Leslee Gregg*

Silent Spring

Light through green leaf, hides a frog.
A blind monk smiles, he heard frog move.
This Buddhist spring, still, quiet, changing.
God touches us again, with Beauty
and wildflowers.
  —*John L. Corsiglia*

All In A Dream

As I close my eyes and I fall asleep
In the night where dark shadows creep.
I fear no evil, 'cause it's nothing to fear.
In my dreams I feel the end drawing near.
All alone in a world so black.
Once you're here there's no turning back.
I close my eyes and I start to scream.
As real as it may seem, it's all in a dream.

Three wise men from a distant land
build castles made of sand.
They speak of words in riddle and rhyme.
They see the future through the door of time.
They showed me a world full of fear and hate.
I turn to run, but then it's too late.
I close my eyes and I try to ensnare.
All of the dreams that I've dreamed before.
  —*Anthony Luttrull*

Untitled

(Dedicated to Neela Nadkarni 1979-1993 and on somewhere else.)
In the open meadow of autumn stood a tall oak tree.
Every leaf racing off into its own direction was of different
color, shape and size, and each leaf changed with the seasons.
Some of the leaves will fall before the others and are swept
away by the breezes into new lands.
Yet, eventually, all the leaves will fall from the tall oak tree.
Sometimes it might seem that the vivid oranges, yellows and
crimsons have become dulled with a grey sky settling above
And in bleakest December when it seems all the leaves have fallen,
Spring comes and the new, sweet buds bloom again.
And we remember the leaves.
  —*Leia Davies*

Voices

There are songs and sounds within stillness
In the quiet after dark,
Sounds within sounds,
Songs within songs.

There are rhythms in the quiet
And pulses in the night,
Beats within beats,
Drums within drums.

Something calling in the embers,
Something crying in the rocks,
And out beyond the darkness
There are voices in the stars.
  —*Lori West*

Thunderstorms

I lie on my bed at night gazing out the window at the stars
in the sky. The stars roll in, the sky turns dark; lightning
flashes across the horizon.
You sit and stare in wonder and amazement at the power and
force of every flash. Then you grow weary and weak in
illuminated darkness and finally fall fast asleep, and when
you awake the sky is clear again as if nothing really
happened at all but you see the debris from the Thunderstorm
and realize it was not a dream as you thought when you were
falling asleep.
Because thunderstorms are real and not just dreams of the
subconscious mind. Although we can't explain them they are
there because we see them happen all the time.
They seem to come from nowhere but they'll be here eternally
forever thunderstorms.
  —*Leo G. Cunningham*

I Spoke To The Night

I spoke to the night as its cloak covered me
In the totality that was of itself,
And I listened to words come on the wind
As night spoke of secrets it held.
The darkness became the truth of the night
And the window I looked into again,
For all the moments of the day just gone by
Were part of the oneness of night.
The words of the night led me far into time
And showed me the secrets I sought,
And I followed the breezes that came to me there
As the night whispered soft to my soul.
I spoke to the night of the dreams that I held
In the secret place of my self,
And listened to the words that it spoke
As I walked on the trails of the dark.
Wherever I went in the night that I knew
And whatever were things that I dreamed,
I knew the secrets would be only my own
For night holds the words that I spoke.

    —Merle C. Hansen

For Lisa

Long Island can be cold
in the winter.
A frosty wind blowing off the sound,
tossing around leaves and debris,
depositing them wherever a place is open.
And when it snows, it can be so lovely
the way the snow forms drifts
along side cars and fences.
The gentle rain of spring
sounds like your laughter
and I remembered you.
As the leaves turn from green to brown,
the red in between reminds me
of your hair.
And as I sit there,
watching the rain
and viewing the leaves,
I remember you
and realize
that I miss you.

    —Michael P. Dunn

My Place

I'm in my place, my time, my space trying to survive
in this troublesome space.
My fears, my tears and my weary stares were no match
for this terrible game.

Then you came. You saw what I saw. You wept when I wept.
You held me and said it's ok. Then I opened my arms, my life
and my space to you. It was easy to share my time and space.

As time when on, your space and your place mysteriously became
one with my space and my place. Yet somewhere inside lies your
deepest fear - my place within my black skin cannot truly be
one with you in your white skin.

Your eyes scream with pain and confusion because you see me
as your forefather's shame. I want to weep when you weep.
I want to hold you and say it's OK.
But there is no time, no space because I am forced to remain
in my space.

    —Julett Butler

The Lord

The Lord is always with you
In your dreams, heart and whatever you do.
Anytime you are in a bind.
Just sit in your room, and tell the Lord what's on your mind.
He is the best listener you will find
He doesn't put you down, he treats you kind.
He helps you through ups and downs
No matter what the pounds (problems)
The Lord may not always give you what you pray for.
But it only means he loves you more and more.
And he knows what's right for you
So sometimes he leaves things up to you.
Because he knows what choices you will make
And the right one is the one you will take.
So dear...
The Lord is always, always here.

    —Laura Trainor

The Feeling

A feeling in your heart,
   in your mind
     in your soul
A feeling inside that you don't want him to know
should you keep it
   expect it
     or feel it at all
You didn't know it
   realize it
     or think you would fall
But you did it
   can't change it
     and don't know what to do
I guess what is left is to say I love you

    —JoDee Willis

The Contest

Humbly, a publication quickly requests this work!
Include another disk, the fee's inspiring.
Recognizably I interest this expression,
Yet, behind the news proffered, fears of placid verse lurk.
A strange vision hails finally from my vendors,
Who astonishingly establish a magic with flowers of words,
And beautify any language I might be desiring.
Still, I do not believe that for my words,
anyone will be hiring.

    —Phil Baldwin Jr.

Flowers of Cycle

  Comes the flower of winter so cruel,
infecting with sadness us all,
surviving the cold, harsh, snowy trial,
refusing to surrender and fall.

  The flower of spring does show such beauty,
her colors do shine such joy,
swaying in the gentle winds of dawning,
an enchantment oh, so lovely.

  Bold and bright does the summer flower brag,
wearing a face of happiness,
dancing in the breeze like a flag,
showing its pleasure to all of us.

  With cold wind brings the gloom of fall,
its flower sets to mourn,
for it's the final, sadly resisting death's call,
for its sisters its heart is torn.

    —Jeremy Lawrence

Untitled

To be a mother is not a battle easily won but its rewards are
infinite, if your a positive one. To be a mother takes Power
and Guts its rewards and set backs are second to none for their
are no instructions or guarantees, for these little ones we
guide and feed. Just trials and errors for every mom,
regardless of race or creed. To be a mother you must be strong
cause 24 hrs just ain't that long, to shape future generations
and teach them right from wrong. The Presidents job, you think
that's tough balance the budget, at least they have funds. We
mothers are like magicians, teachers, doctors janitors on the
run, comforters economist, that only some. And you think its
over at 21! Send them to college you get a reprieve, turn
around and find, they never do leave. To be a mother is not a
battle easily won, its rewards are many if your a positive one
love, faith and prayers will power and courage and values set.
Will shower these little beings with positive dreams and bring
a brighter tomorrow for all human beings, to be a mother.

—*Michele Jefferson*

Magic Travel

How would you like to journey far,
Instantly like a shooting star,
To anyone, anyplace, anywhere, anytime,
Whenever you wish in any clime,
By magic travel in your mind,
To all the worlds near, far, and wide?
Then, hop aboard!

Now, close your eyes, and do devise,
Beam happy thoughts with all your might,
Soon you will zoom in magic flight,
From where you'll see, and feel, and know,
All the wonders that be bestowed,
When, light and breezy, you travel, easy,
That magic road!

—*Billie Reese Kilday*

Midnight Sun

Mystery of love growing more
Intense until I can feel no feeling but a
Dark feeling of something void, and
Nothing seems to stop what goes on
Inside my soul. Someone comes and
Gives me a power which makes me happy, then leaves me
Here with nothing but a dream of
Tomorrow, and that is all.
    But someday,
Someone may somehow
Understand what it is I want if
Not what it is I need in life.
    Until then, I pray for something.

—*Candice L. Brady*

Grandpa

He stands at his window
    and looks out
He sees no one on the street
He is to intent on the visions in his head.

  He is lost in a world of yesterday
    Sometimes he speaks aloud
      But the people he addresses
        Have long since past.

    Though he stands alone
      His memories keep him company
  And he is not afraid of the future
Because he has forgotten such a thing exists.

—*Michelle Clark*

Infatuation?

Somehow, someone changed my ordered world
into an uncertain, but more wonderful place.

Slowly, gradually, a smile and a voice
took possession of me. I can't understand. Why?

Grandma, nameless. A lovely mind lives
in that strong trim body thoughtless fools might call "old."

A hell of a lot they know, or care
about "over the hill" groups. We also need life.

Coffee, chit chat, weekend walks, small talk.
Is there anything she needs that I could furnish? What?

I need to think of her first, not me.
This woman deserves more than she's received so far.

Should I say what I've started to feel?
Brain says "No way, Jose," Another, deeper part, yearns.

Simply, truly, a trusted close friend
Is what I'll try to be — if that's what she wants. Si?

—*Harold R. Howell*

Shades of Praise

            The night folds
          Into billowing softness as
        Stark, creamy velvet whirls
        Into gentle, shimmering light.
            Snow wafts
              Down
              Down
        In diamond-studded sparkles
To land in pillow-soft tufts strewn about.
 The creatures come to pay their homage.
    The rabbits, a luxuriant mahogany,
    Leap, joyously, in silent honor, as
        The light and airy sparrows
        Carol out an incandescent tune.
          The man, a willowy-lean,
Stands, with outstretched hands in praise,
    While the crystal shadows of winter
     Give vigorous chase to the night.
          The maker observes.
            Love smiles down.

—*Doretta Franklin*

stale coffee

Hot burning and flashing vivid swirling colors melting
into streams of life and
of tears but
No
not always, only
really sometimes.

Usually tepid

And when you drink of me
will your nose wrinkle
a damp fingertip
waving its discontent
when my familiar taste washes through you?

Will your heart sink
a weary eyelid
laden with monotony
when my familiar smile splashes around you?

            Maybe
            Eight to Five Odds.
            Really usually
            Tepid.

—*Jen Dilling*

"Rock"

One day after a big rain storm, Rock fell down the hill into the water below. Fish looked at Rock, and Fish said, "You cannot swim." Rock replied, "Yes, but I am strong." As time passed on, the rain never came back, so the lake dried up, and there were no more fish.

Then came Bird, who landed on Rock, and Bird said, "You cannot fly." Rock replied, "Yes, but I am strong." At that moment, the wind came and caught Bird. Bird took flight, never to be seen again.

Then came Snake, who liked to shed his old skin on Rock, and Snake said, "You never change." Rock replied, "Maybe, but neither can I fly nor swim." Snake left to go find food.

Then came Boy, who knew Rock for its hardness and broke rock into
several pieces. The several pieces were for his new arrows, and Boy said, "You are going to help me hunt birds and fish Rock." This made Rock happy because he would fly and swim, for he had changed!

—*Ed Schieber*

Peace

Peace,- a term that eludes explanations,
Is a potent part of human relations.
Peace is not just the absence of war.
It is that—, and so very much more.

Real peace goes beyond hostile debate,
To quench the smoldering embers of hate,
Eases misunderstanding and sorrow;
Builds hope and trust for a better tomorrow.

Peace is the pathway that grace travels o'er,
To mend broken lives and healing restore.
It flows like a river, stands tall as a mountain.
It nourishes life like an on-going fountain.

Peace is so gentle-it's symbol a dove.
It's companions are patience, mercy and love.
When peace controls actions of men in our land,
World-brothers joyfully work had in hand.

From whence is this treasure sublime?
It is not man made—, it's source is Divine.
It comes from one called "Prince of Peace."
And His supply will never cease.

—*Raymond Barr*

My Promise

I love you-I love you!
   Is all I can say.
This, my love, I promise you,
   While dreaming night and day.

A tender, sweet, and loving kiss,
To capture a moment of true bliss.

Bound together until death;

   Destined to live and grow old,
   together as one perfect soul.

I'll say I love thee with my last breath.

—*Molly Merkel*

Home

I returned home today
And was a child again.
And I was afraid
Again.
Afraid they would take
Away who I am,
Tho' they are not there.

—*Elaine M. Good*

Bats

Bats are beautiful mammals
A bat uses sonar to fly
To keep bugs from invading our earth
Save the bats, we really should try

—*Stephanie Baker*

The Golden Pet as "Alive In Jesus"

Jesus Christ, the Son of God, we believe by faith,
   Is also called the son of David in the flesh, the word saith
Only through him we are alive in the flesh and in the spirit,
   Even the word of God is made flesh in him, we can see it.
For without Jesus was not any thing made that was made,
   Based or this, the word or the believer will ever fade.

So then, being alive in Jesus Christ, can we clearly see;
   That the verses flow out of the heart of you and out of me?
How we express in words the poetry that we write,
   Being alive in him, makes it all just right.
We reveal the beauty and the meaning of creation that we share,
   Showing the love of God here, there and every where.

Let us forever put in rhyme and in verse,
   The true meaning of God in the universe.
Giving God praise and glory through Jesus Christ,
   Who for us his life he did freely sacrifice.
So then, for all we think, write, do and have done,
   Come from being alive in him, God's son.

—*Ilah J. Jackson*

"Liscalane"

Among the prettiest of all names
Is County Kerry's "Liscalane"
A fair sound that glides right off the tongue
Yet lingers long as a bell just rung

Who named it seems a mystery still
That can yet be solved if someone will
Come forth and Sound that sweet Gaelic name
From which is derived sweet "Liscalane"

"Did it fall from some Gael Coat of Arms
To always remind of past alarms
Or tell of a colleen held so tight
She became immortal for that knight?"

Whatever the basis for "Liscalane"
I'll let it retain its ancient fame
And stop an inquiry that's inane
Keep loving instead sweet "Liscalane"

—*Joseph R. McDonough*

Sweet Peace

The battle's awful sound
Is heard the world around.
The hate and fear that seem to be winning,
Will they never cease?
If I could wave a magic wand,
There would be peace throughout the sea and land.
The war drums would be heard no longer.
The roaring guns would be silent.
The earth no longer red with hostile blood.
Selfishness and greed would disappear quickly,
And yes, there would be peace.
The southwind blowing warm would whisper, "peace".
The north wind blowing cold would echo, "peace".
All the nations of the universe would sing with joy,
For they would vision the wonders of a world at peace.
Everyone would have a prayer in their hearts.
They would give thanks and reverently whisper, "peace, sweet peace".

—*Edna Christian*

What Is Happiness?

What is happiness?
Is it in the love people give,
Or is it in the life you live?
Is it in close togetherness,
Or in knowing life is eternal?
Is it in knowing you're exceptional,
When another tells you you're "The one"?
What is happiness?
Perhaps you can see, to me,
It doesn't look like it's said to be.
Your perception of happiness seems to be,
Totally different than mine is to me.
I perceive my perception constantly changes.
My perception of happiness is deeper now than last year,
After hearing my baby's first crying tears.
What is happiness?
That depends on your perspective.
I'll continue to try to find and define happiness.

    —Catherine Tafoya

For Lindsey

That rainy night when we first met
  is one of many I'll never forget
Dear sweet Lindsey you've stolen my heart
  and now I pray we're never apart
The nights are long and lonely without you
  yet I have faith that my dreams will come true
I know you've been hurt deeply and now are afraid
  but I'll never hurt you that's a promise I've made
My life is so empty when you're not around
  no one else could replace you that's one thought I've found
I pray every night we'll be together one day
  that my fears and my doubts will all go away
And now as I wonder what you feel for me
  I'm sure that I'll love you through eternity.

    —Kathryn M. Csuy

The Joy of Being Grandparents

The joy of being grandparents,
Is one of the most wonderful of happenings.
When you hold your grandchild for the first time,
It feels glorious and exhilarating.
Next to holding your children for the first time,
Nothing can compare to it in anyway.
They're like a dividend, that's given to you,
And they are the continuation of the family legacy,
In which you can have all the enjoyment,
Without the worry and responsibility.

It's the thrill of watching them grow through different stages,
For it's like reliving the growth of your children.
You can spoil them in a special way,
That you couldn't with your own children.
You can buy them things, play games,
Have them stay with you, and take them to fun places.
When they sometimes get a little hard to handle,
You can always send them home.
Hopefully, because of your age and experience,
You'll be able as they grow, to help in guiding them.

    —Dolly Braida

Untitled

One hundred feet
Above the ground
I look all around
And what do I see
But one little tree
Where a forest used to be.

    —David O'Gilvie

Brevity of Life

What bewilderment and perplexity
Is the brevity of life —
With worries toils and struggles
And given, to much strife.

Its entrance and its exit all the very same —
Its accomplishments, achievements and name
All short lived and in vain.

Yet within this brief fragile casing
Dwells a being undying and unending:

From whence it came and to where it will go —
Can only be determined by the love that we show.

Created and foreknown from the beginning of time —
Placed into this casing for just a short time.
To accomplish His purpose and plan for mankind,

Then back to the eternal and to the sublime.

    —Madelyn Yanchyshyn

Character

Serene and pure as any flower that grows;
Is the essence of natures nobleness;
In seed to ripen before beauty glows.
To find and raise it in its tenderness
Is splendor of the dream to realize,
And wonder of the whole its gain to soar;
Revealing fullness wherein goodness lies,
A gleam of light shining more and more.
As a flower lifting lustrous petals
So exquisite in muirs into this sun,
And their stir rain in quietness compels
The essence of all good in strength is done;
To be drawn to that sun within, and go
Through tears softness, and their its reign to know.

    —Amelie Doombadze

Just Wondering

If a woman wakes up with tears streaming down her face,
Is the subconscious hiding some unknown fears,
it thinks she can't face?
Does the subconscious go to sleep during the day?
Or does it just stay quiet while we are awake?
If the heart stops, is the person dead?
Or does the spirit have to die to be considered dead?
When the death rattle comes, is it the spirit leaving the body?
And if it is; where does it go?
Or does it die as life as we know it?
Is there a Heaven? And is there a Hell?
Are there Angels and Devils? Oh please tell!
Is there a Guardian Angel on my right shoulder,
And a devil on my left, I wonder as I get older!
Does the Guardian Angel protect us thru all that is dark
and light? Does the Devil try to harm us and cause us to
change flight? Who controls the mind; the heart or the soul?
Or does the mind control all that we know?
And if it does; can it help us understand?
What in the world; is God's Great Plan?

    —Caroline Kalemba

Christmas Time

It's Christmas time
and it's Christmas time.
Time to sit by the fire
and time to admire.
Time for fun and games
and time for fun and fame.
Time to decorate the tree
from the decorative tree.

    —Matthew Munn Kukral

From Here to There

Does the sky end the limit; and does the heart rule the life,
Is there hope in situations; can we survive any strife?
Is space and time a fact so true,
And can we make it all the way through?
When the chips are down; and when life goes on,
Can we find the strength to reach the dawn?

You have to have hope; you require care,
For there is no end; from here to there.

Life and love; as within all things,
It just takes time to find what they bring.
Make the differences one step at a time,
If you ignore any problem; you, too, commit the crime.
The message within; you must make the peace,
Until all are one; can the fighting ever cease?

You have to give love; they require care,
It's an endless road; from here to there.

You have to speak true, rule in all that's right,
It's eternal time; till all but know what might.

Hope and strength; love and care,
Can we ever make it; from here to there???
—*Bob McDowell*

To Live With A King

To live with a king,
Is to live with a Crown.
A Crown full of glory and of pride.

A Crown that covers the life work
Of a strong and mighty headship,
That strives to keep the nation's
Spirit-torch alive.

"Is this too much to ask of a King?"
"Not really" said the Maker.

To die is to never live,
And to live is to never die.
For to live with a King
is to keep the lighthouse
of life nourished forever.

This is the cherishing of the greater love
that our Maker and Creator
has bestowed upon humanity,
in order for a greater understanding
of the struggle of life itself.
—*Marsha S. Watts*

Days End

The thing that scares me the most,
Is when fifty years have expired,
And yet heaven hasn't met my ghost,
And I'm all alone worn and tired.

Having no one stop by to breathe a single word,
When Christmas cards I have nowhere to send,
When no voice except my own is heard,
When the earth has swallowed my last friend.

Having no more goals on which to strive.
Knowing death waits in a near day.
Wondering the reason why I'm still alive.
And why I was ever in this play.
—*Scott Yokom*

The Voice Said to Me

"My butterflies are not free" the voice said to me,
it came as a whisper in the wind
"The windmills you poke, with your bright steely spokes,
are visions of me in the end."
The voice came to me, from the boughs of a tree
its sound seemed to shudder with pain
"Where will my trees, sway in the cooling breeze,
when my face is bare from the rain".
The voice came to me, from where my eyes could not see,
the glaring sun beat hot on my skin,
"The sky you deplete, with your poisons so replete,
is a renegade game you cannot win."
The voice came to me, from the waters of the sea,
with the flotsam of man piled on high,
The dirty white beach, was somehow out of reach,
and all I heard was a sigh.
Her voice, came to me no more.
—*Kenneth H. Johnson*

Our Flag Forever

Burn the flag, that's what they say
It came on the news today
That same old glory, that men fought for
Along with boys, sixteen or more
The flag that Betsy Ross acclaimed
The flag that America named
Tear it down, throw it on the ground
Dishonor it and then
The men and women who fought for it
Would fight for it again
I wonder if the Senate
Whom ever they may be
Fought in a war to save her
And keep America free
To me they are so heartless
As everyone can tell
To think they want to burn the flag
And burn our dreams as well
—*Helen C. Fleury*

Robi

Robi. The sweet name ringing in my ears. Sometimes
it can break my heart, and bring me to tears.
I often daydream, and think about my true love.
Which was always a memory that I had dreamed
of. I remembered that night, when the night air was
cold. I never thought that I would be told. That
Robi had died that cold deadly night, of drinking
and driving and losing a fight. I never had a
chance to say, "I love you dear Robi, don't go away."
Now I lost him. Without a goodbye. I miss him
so dearly, and I want him to stay.
—*Cynthia S. Cheng*

A Kiss Is A Kiss, Is A Kiss

A kiss can be worth more than you know,
It can confuse, misuse, or allow you to grow.
It will give you joy in your time of need,
It will deceive you in the midst of greed.
It can tell someone that your in love,
It can put someone beneath or way above.
It can cause a person to stay straight and sane.
It can take away your hurt and your pain.
To read these words, we all have missed,
Besides who said, a kiss is a kiss
Is a kiss.
—*Raymond L. Owensby*

A River

A river is running through my veins
It conquers my soul
It releases my pain
No single path has been so true
Than the single path I walk with you
A simple kiss
A flying dove
A blessed source that began with love
A wishing well for the two of us
That began with him and ended with us
We do not part
We do not split
We live as one and always will
Together we claim what all hope too
Which is love between each other
And love for God too
We live our lives as he wished us too
And pray for the world and the children too
So as the river is flowing through my veins
It carries our lives and leaves no pain

—*Michael A. Walters*

Ode to Speech Class

I have to make a speech today
It fills me with much dread.
The prof designed the course this way
To see if I drop dead.

Take a deep breath, think happy thoughts,
Be calm as I can be.
I have some money-can the Prof be bought?
I'd settle for just a "D."

If I'm so bad, will they show me the door
Led by the college head?
"Goodbye. You're gone. Return no more.
We'd rather teach Mr. Ed."

Still, maybe something will transpire
To cancel class this day.
Like earthquake, flood, storm, or fire.
For this I hope and pray.

The time has come. My mouth is dry.
My worst fears have come to be.
For I looked up and want to cry.
God! They're all looking at me!

—*Jill A. Crawford*

The Bottom Line

There is a song in my heart that needs singing.
It has a story to tell,
The words rhyme with love, hate and misery.
The lyrics our brothers know well.

God put us on earth all together
We're all the same in His eyes.
But we've all striven to pull us asunder
With ignorance, hateful actions and lies.

Now only God knows why we do this,
I guess it's part of His plan.
But surely our answers of forthcoming
When we're done here on earth as a man.

We each will take our blame or our credit
For the things here on earth we have done.
We each one can tell why we did it,
When we stand before God's only Son.

—*Gene Sagrillo*

Life

Life is living.
It is for people, plants, and animals.
They all need, land, water, air, soil and sunshine.
Life as a people, exist on the resources
that God has made possible for them.
They are spiritual, physicals
an emotional plus all the elements
that keeps life alive.
Plants are some what different
in their needs, as they fully depends
on soil, fertilizer, air, water and sunshine
Animals supplies all of our needs
For food, but they need food, land, air
water, and sunshine and care to grow and exist.
Life is living, growing and existing.

—*Helen V. Cole*

"Good Game"

The wind is whispering in ear and this is not fear
it is good a golf game to play not only on a very nice day
but also when is rainy - gray we can be happy all the way
this keeps us in high gear because golf is us dear
not everyone get results like "Golden Bear" but is nice birds
to hear and see them graceful fly high not only in May on
tee off is sometimes delay until dark clouds go away is nice
to see foursome or a pair the happiness is with us near is
leading us to our goal - glory and this is the main story
after the bad weather we always feel better we are in life
busy like a bee our spirit is always free no one is in
negative category positive thinking is mandatory we follow
natures rules to the letter because everyone is a goal-getter
Hope is in each leaf of a tree and for this we bend to God
our knee.

—*Frank Zdzislaw Glinski*

Felicia (fish)

It's mother's day — my gift is a ring
It is my first — such a pretty thing
The stones are four — as they should be
But when I count — my children are only three

She has been gone since she was sixteen
Oh how I wish it could be just a dream
If God could but grant me one tiny wish
You know it would be to see my sweet fish

—*Betty Poteet*

"Friendship Of The Heart"

Friendship is so hard to find,
it is of the heart not just of the mind.

Friendship is so delicate and rare,
it is like a precious gem you handle it with care.

Friendship is so kind and true,
you will never be alone when you are feeling blue.

Friendship is a wonderful feeling,
from within your soul it is a special dealing.

Friendship is like a graceful bird,
soaring with the wind without a sound or word.

Friendship is a valuable gift,
only from the Lord above could you have a lift.

Friendship is a worthy cause,
to love and to cherish without even a pause.

Friendship may be distant and apart,
but it will always be a "Friendship of the Heart".

—*Tina Fina*

Time Is Important

Time is essential in anyone's life.
It is the intrinsic value of worth,
    And must be guarded with so much care
    Lest it be gone tomorrow from this earth.

Little do we consider how really valuable
Even a few hours can be in our lives.
    So prone are we to just sit idly by
    And watch the clock tick with our lazy eyes.

Oh, if we could only make ourselves realize
That "Father Time" waits on no one,
    We would busy ourselves with all important
    Things that genuinely need to be done.

Let us put forth a real true effort
To sincerely make our time more worthwhile.
    Then, as we look back through the years
    Our hearts will be happy and on our face a smile.

No doubt, as time wanes and we approach the end,
We will become so aware of where we stand
    That we will pray - by the Grace of God, have we
    Accomplished enough to reach The Promised Land?
        —*Bethel Nunley Evans*

You Mean the World to Me

It's not the material things you can give me,
It is your love that I am after.
It's not just your body,
It's your smile and your laughter.

The longer I am with you,
The more I do discover.
You are not just my friend,
You are also my lover.

You are someone that I cherish,
You are someone I adore.
As each day passes by,
I love you more and more.

I want you in my life,
You brighten up my days.
You mean the world to me,
In so many different ways.

You've shown me how to smile again,
To laugh and to have fun.
I want to tell you thank you,
For everything you've done.
        —*Linda A. Harrison*

My Shining Star

At night I look into the sky and I see my shining star
It makes me think of you and wonder where you are
I continue to stare at my shining star, in the sky
and begin to cry
My heart used to glimmer like that shining star
But now it's as black as the dark sky
I reach hard and try to touch my shining star
But the distance is too far.
Then a tear falls off my cheek into the puddle below
as the shining star begins to go.
And I wonder will it come again when I'm sad and alone
So I glance once more into that lonely black sky
and I begin to smile and sigh
Because there you are my beautiful, bright
shining star.
        —*Sally Bowles*

My Bottomless Mug

Yup, this is my bottomless mug
It may be grimy and slimy
Or sticky and icky
But it's still my bottomless mug

Keep your hands off my bottomless mug
It used to be white, and now it is brown
Look and there's even a black crown
But it's still my bottomless mug

No one can touch my bottomless mug
It's sticky from chewed gum
And on the handle, there's dried up scum
But it's still may bottomless mug

Don't you dare touch my bottomless mug
It's mine, all mine. I want you to see
And no one, but no one will take if from me
Because my only friend left is

My bottomless mug
        —*Kim Stokes*

Our Red Sled

In the back of our house was a big steep hill
It seemed a long way down for a thrill
We had only one sled, we had to share
My Sis and I, we didn't care
Taking turns was the thing to do

The wind was cold, our noses were red
Our fingers were numb, hard to guide red sled
The hill was so steep, all the way from the top
We would go so fast we couldn't stop
Digging our boots deep in the snow
Couldn't control, couldn't go slow

Duck your head under the barb wire fence
Swoosh, through the half open gate we went
Down the path and past the house
Dragging our feet to make the curve
Going so fast we could loose our nerve

Always wishing the snow would never melt away
So tomorrow, tomorrow, we could play and play and play
Still today, remembering the fun we had
Such simple pleasures, it makes me a little sad
        —*Mary M. Ciresi*

Beyond the Reef

As I wander away from the shore of the sea,
It seems like the waves are calling to me.

Come back, come back, don't go away.

Far out the waves are breaking or the reef,
Through the mist of tears that cause my grief,

One beautiful night we set our sails,
There beyond the reef our outrigger fails.

My Polynesian love disappeared into the sea,
And there she lies waiting for me.

The waves keep calling me each day,
Come back, come back, don't go away.

I see the island in the sunset mist,
Waves flooding or a brown skin maidens feet have kissed.

The Polynesians welcome me once more, as I come to their island
shore. To wander along the shore of the sea, asking God to
return my Polynesian love to me. To always look beyond the
reef, in search of some one that causes this grief. No longer
do the tears fall from my eyes, but my heart lies there, beyond
the reef. I hear the trade winds softly sigh, lonely stranger
on the shore, goodbye, goodbye.
        —*C. E. Johnson*

Memories

Life is sweet when we're growing up
It seems we will be young forever
Your mother, father, sister and brother
  will leave you never
The fun and laughter experiences shared
Showed the true love of all who cared
time goes so fast, the older we get
It seems the clock is doubly set
Before our eyes changes take place
Photos taken prove life's quick pace
When we lose a loved one, sorrow sets in
Memories are what we seek from within
The fun and laughter, experiences shared
Are the only tools left when we are sad
When my beloved dad passed away and
  finality set in
The memories he left us warmed us again
Life is sweet when we are growing old
As long as we have memories to
  have and to hold

     —*Karen Lee Kider*

"Rural Awakening"

As morning light tease the corner of my eye,
It slips through the window, a blue and peach sky.
A golden horizon with clouds slowly spinning,
A brand new day in the country's beginning.
On tiptoes am I, a graceful stretch and yawn,
As I welcome my truly self-lifting dawn.
Words, they escape me; yet it all seems so clear,
From the city I came, how I do love it here.
The senses within have become far more keen,
Contently surveying my rustic homeland scene.
Birds softly singing, breezes blending with the grass,
While overhead more feathered friends pass.
My heart and mind open to embrace each sound and sight,
Captured anticipation, I await the country night.
Early dew to dusk, when all is said and done,
Earth and soul unite and God turns them into one.

     —*Donna L. Hock*

True Happiness

True happiness takes time to achieve
It takes effort, patience, but even more
It takes understanding, and you will discover
That understanding is the key which opens the door

To a whole new world, one not yet discovered
This world is just waiting for you to explore
So take the time to think, reason, and wonder
About all the things you've been searching for.

The more you think, the answer's sooner to come
When the answer finally comes, you will be ready
To meet with life's struggles and challenges. Inner strength
you will possess, even when things seem unsteady.

No matter how rough things get, never give up hope
Look beyond the cloud of gray and see the yellow sun
And remember that soon this cloud will be gone
And the battles of life, you'll feel you have won.

True happiness is within reach, please believe me
It is quite valuable but does not cost a thing
Each of us has to find it in our own different way
Knowing then the satisfaction it will bring.

     —*Sonya Duzyk*

Angry Sea

The sea was angry last night,
It tossed it's shaggy mane and roared.
Tossed about, this way and that,
before finally coming ashore.

I wondered, why does the sea get so angry,
I know it's not because of you or me.
but like people, I guess, once in awhile.
It has to unleash all of its fury.

Oh how I love to sit here by my window,
and just take it all in.
With the fire glowing warmly in front of me,
to keep me warm from that howling wind.

It makes me terribly glad to know,
that the fire and the angry sea,
Are not really angry with you or me,
they just really want to be your friend.

     —*Catherine Reeves, "Misty"*

The Little Red Apple Tree

The little red apple tree down at Grandma's wasn't very tall,
it was crooked and twisted and seemed ready to fall.
It bore good apples that were crisp and sweet,
Grandma sauced them and baked them and made many a sweet
  treat.
Now Grandma gathering apples was a sight to behold,
she used her coverall apron, it gathered quite a load.
Grandma was ample, a strong lady of great proportion,
with the use of that apron she settled many a commotion.
I knew Grandma was standing on the porch a watching me,
I never got my pony and I was a crying under the apple tree.
She wrapped me round her apron and held me against her breast,
look! pointing, see that pony in the tree, let's put her to the test.
Wide eyed I followed her to the barn and places round her home.
I was a laughing when she said "That there pony, it ain'ta going to
  roam,
She was putting things in her apron to put upon the bough
"Betwix and between this apron honey, you'll have your pony
  anyhow!"
She made a little saddle, a tail and a mane that was shorn,
my imaginary apple tree pony that summer day was born!
I'll not be forgotten that summer with the tree pony and me,
betwix and between Grandma's big apron The Little Red Apple
Tree!

     —*Elizabeth Kleyn Plummer*

The Key to My Life My Wife

You are the one who has touched my life
My sugar, my spice, my everything, my wife
Everyday as I lay I'm dreaming of the day
When I get to hold you again
Though my mind worries sometimes
In my heart I know you're fine
Separation is hard
But being reunited is the best part

Never know what you have until you're gone
This is the reason why I wrote this poem
All the moments we've shared whether bad or good
At least they were shared together
All the times I've made you cry
Deep inside I apologize
I know I'll make some mistakes
But your heart I never want to break

For eternity our love will last
We'll be stronger in the future than we were in the past
Only you hold the key to my life
It was yours the day you became my wife

     —*Narvel L. Taylor*

Lost Love

I lost you once before,
  it wasn't up to me.
You said being "tied down" wasn't for you,
  you'd just as soon be "free".

So I let you go,
  but I hurt inside.
As you said your final goodbye,
  a part of me just died.

For I loved you very much,
  and you didn't seem to care.
I didn't think that was right,
  but who said life was fair?

My love for you continued,
  as I knew deep down it would.
But since we weren't even talking,
  it was doing me no good.

I love you very much, sweetheart,
  and that I'm sure you know.
I'll do what it takes to keep you,
  just don't expect me to let you go.

  —*Trisha Lazan*

Heart, Mind, and Soul ... Imagination?

Imagine that we woke up to a world that's filled with love, joy and
  happiness;
It would be more than a dream, it would be bliss.
Imagine that racial harmony was spread throughout the world;
It would be immaculate, dear God if you only would!

Imagine the homeless,
Sheltered, clothed, and fed;
To make this imagination a reality,
Just love with your heart and think with your head.

In helping others recover from their sorrow and anguish,
Imagination can play a major role;
Just use the right amount of
The heart, mind, and soul.

Imagination? First we must warm the heart with laughter,
Enrich the mind with thoughts;
Enlighten the soul with love,
For it's something that can't be bought.

Imagination is an important tool,
A tool which we should all possess;
For imagination is the map,
Which leads to the road of success.

  —*Saima Azhar*

The Pain Of Love

When you grow up in a house full of love, but your body rejects
it, you become not like one of the above, nothing like it. You
live a life without knowing love and devotion, you live a life
without emotion. You live in fear of everyone, that you put
your trust only in the Lord even when your days are done.

Twenty-two years later you make a friend, whom you can trust
and depend. Who helps make your emotions come out, and loves
you without a doubt. Who cares enough to explain, all about
love even the pain.

When you feel love for the first time you begin to understand
what you have been missing is love for the common man. After
the Lord sends you this person to save your life by His Grace,
the Lord takes him away to a better place.

Then by the Love you have been shown, you love, care, and do
more for the rest of the family like they have never known.
They may wonder why, but because He took the time to show me
love, I'll need it even when I die.

  —*Michael W. Hutton*

The Young Girl

Listen to me closely I'll tell you what's new
It's about a young girl who is very blue
Her parents don't understand her she feels like a letdown
It is so sad that she always makes a frown
Her parents make her feel like she always fails
She cries a lot enough to fill two pails
So when she has a problem she looks out the window and asks why
And she always finds a answer in the big blue sky.

  —*Terri Hannon*

The Song

The song takes me on a rugged course;
it's adventures are many and pleasing.
The song closes my eyes when I want to see its image;
And produces a brilliant array of colors.
The song clears my problems for a short while;
only to solve them when it's finished.
The song brings tears streaming down my temple;
it's also the cloth that collects the moisture.
The song creates strong bonds;
the words and meanings are unbreakable.
The song is a great love of mine;
and exhibits a nurturing love in return.
The song is my rock, the one I look to;
and learn, it's forever my shield.
The song is a signature of life, its words are
consistently true;... now what does the song mean
to you.

  —*Louis Lenzmeier*

Chances

There is no way to undue the wrong I done
its all cloudy days, no shining sun.
Its hard to believe what was on my mind,
how could I have done this all in a short time.
To lose nearly all we both work so hard to get,
another lesson of pain, not soon to forget.
So many chances I had to do it right,
lose my head and throw it away in a night.
It sure wasn't worth it at all,
for now, I am wondering if she'll accept a collect call.
I write letters and don't know what to say,
will wait and wait for a possible reply some day.
Is there a possibility we will be back together again?
or is it over, she is sick of a losing husband.
I didn't mean to be a nightmare in her night,
but how many chances have I had to make right.
She went out of her way to bring me back,
all for me to take it away and pull up no slack.
A beautiful woman, a sincere wife, all torn apart,
I am truly sorry for the pain and the broken heart.

  —*Anthony J. Miller, Sr.*

"Along the Hiking Trail"

The leaves are falling here today
It's beautiful, and I want to stay.
The sky is bluer than it should ever be.
I feel it's warmth shining down on me.
I hear the water splashing down.
The little trickles, I love that sound.
A relaxing wind is blowing threw.
It should be in a picture, this great view.
The mountains beyond are tall and strong.
Their deepness seems to go on and on.
This great place is here forever.
It's beauty will never die, no not ever.
Come to see it, if you can.
And enjoy the beauty of this land.

  —*Tamera Kirby*

141

Darkness

Somewhere up there I see a light
It's dim but I know it's here
I pray for it be there
Someway to escape
The light is the only way, I see out.
There is no key, there is no door.
There is just that light, the light keeps me going
The knowledge that one day I'll be out there, In the light.
Let it cast its shadow on me
Let it illuminate me, let it free me.
Everyday the light gets dimmer.
but I have hope, that the brightness will return.
So that I can feel the lights rays upon me.
Somewhere up there I know I see a light.
Everyday it gets dimmer
I can hardly see it now
The light doesn't shine for me anymore,
But I have hope for someday I shall see the light
again and escape all this darkness surrounding me.

—*Ruthy M. Guerrero*

Loving You

Living and loving are one in the same.
It's easier to push than to pull
and when push comes to shove,
It can be so very easy to fall
head over heels in love!

True love isn't a game,
you either win or lose.
Real love takes plenty of affection
coupled with a special bond,
between two loving hearts.

This world holds many unanswered questions;
All I do is give the best I can,
There is only one fact I know for sure,
I have something special and she will be
forever, my one and only biggest fan!

Dreams really can come true,
because all I ever wanted
I found in you.

—*Troy Boquist*

The Job

The clock rings and rings and rings
it's five o'clock and my eyes still shut,
I roll to the left to shut it off
kneeling to the floor in a slump.

Head down resting I fall asleep again,
oh... the noise of the clock, I must have hit the snooze
'cause again it rings and rings and rings.

Opening my eyes wide as saucers, blurred is my vision,
I stand and stumble to wash my face, brush my teeth
and awaken from the depth, a dream.

I'm late, as the clock says six, I toss the
clothing from left to right, up and down, around about,
rushing, grabbing things on my way out.

Speeding the highway like a flash, running,
leaping, snatching, click click the time card and the bell
rings and rings and rings, I made it, I breath, on the job
to perform as a puppet on a string, again.

—*A. Denise*

Our Love

Love is more than just a feeling
    it's fixing bikes and painting ceilings...
It's knowing you have someone to care
    no matter the cost, they will be there.

It's having someone hold you close and say...
    that through it all...
They're glad you stayed.

The road was long, the pain...real
    but it hasn't changed how you feel...
In your eyes I still see
    the only love for you is me.

Love is much more than stolen kisses
    or brief encounters...when no one sees
How do I know this to be true?
    I see real love when I look at you.

—*Judy Burnette*

The Old Walnut Tree

Not long ago, in Cushman town, a symbol there did stand.
Its huge limbs reaching far and wide, like a great
outstretching hand.
Many a game of checkers there, was played beneath that tree
No one cared who won or lost, as long as the game was free.

Tales were told of fishing, and if the truth were known
The catfish that swam in ole spring creek, still swims his path alone.

Passer's by, would stop and rest, beneath it's lofty shade
And chat with others there they'd find, till evening shadows fade.

But like all other things in life, it had to yield it's place
The old must go the new must come, in life's on-going chase.

—*Quetta Nelson*

My Homeland

My homeland isn't a vast empire,
    It's just some islands all alone,
    Where different nationalities roam about,
    Where they speak their native tongue so free,
    In Gods' land, my native home.

Oh, I love the homeland of my country,
    The Aloha Tower with its' own Big Ben,
    The stately square of City Hall,
    The industrial towns with its sugar mills,
    In this rich land, my native home.

Oh, I love the homeland of my country,
    The roaring surf upon the sands
    The many surfers who ride the waves,
    And the bathers who lay in the sun
    In this beautiful land, my native home.

Oh, I love the homeland of my country,
    A paradise of freedom and love,
    The lovely sunsets and the moonlight nights,
    The day is done and as we pray,
    Thank you God, for Hawaii Nei.

—*Mattie T. Lester*

"The Search Goes On"

From day to day your search goes on for something.
It has meaning but you don't really know.
Your workship of pleasure come into your days,
then slipping away with nothing completed.
Each of you tries to explain to the children the
beauty of the earth sending small tremors of love
through yourselves.

—*Dianna Andreevski*

The Red Sea

If the moon rose above me,
Its light would leave a black spot where I stand.
Trees would blow around me while I am still,
Untouched by the wind.

I fell into the bathtub with my clothes on.
I didn't swim.
I couldn't swim in the red sea.

I am forgotten.
I am painted black, so black that in this spot of light not
  even the whites of my eyes are seen.

I fell into the bath tub with my clothes on.
I didn't swim.
I couldn't swim in the red sea.

The tear that rolls down my cheek cannot shine in the light,
For there is no light that reaches.
I close my eyes.
I fell into the bath tub with my clothes on.
I didn't swim.
I couldn't swim in the red sea.
　　　　—Erin Dawson

Silent Whisperings

　It's seldom spoken of, but is often encountered.
　It's never seen, but is always there.
　It's the sensation that slips over you, as you talk to your
grandfather, while he leans against a cornerpost, that he
tamped in, over sixty years before.
　It's seeing your son scoop ground corn out of the same feed
room, that his grandfather did before him, over a generation ago.
　It's running your hand over the veined oak boards of a corn
crib, built by your childrens' great, great, grandfather.
　It's standing quietly in the barn, and gazing at drifting
snow, through the same windows that your father, and his father
before him, did.
　It's watching your kids chase yellow butterflies, around the
same creek - crossing, that you did, thirty years earlier.
　It's working in the same field, with your father and your
son, each, learning from the other.
　It's who you are and what your children will be.
　It's your family heritage, and it quietly drifts through
your very being to the passed on from one beginning to another.
　　　　—Greg Elam

In Remembrance

Grandpa will never grow to old to hold onto his fishing pole
Its tattered handle old and bent, still holds an
unforgettable scent.
He'll never grow too old at heart, to traipse along the shores
Of pineflat lake on summer nights, to try his luck once more.

Above him in the lovely hills, a lonely Coyote howls While
nightbirds sing a song of praise, the other animals roam about.
The old man he never gives it up, if the fish aren't biting
still He would sit and wait, his patience bent, beneath the lonely hills.

Then later on as night grew still, he'd yank some nice ones in
While his buddies slept, his boat would sway, while fish would
flop, he'd grin It was pure magic in the night, as the old man
looked around While his buddies slept, he'd fish alone, his
lantern growing dim.

When daylight found his boat afloat, everyone still fast asleep
The old man snagged the big one at last, he smiled, as it lay
flopping at his feet above the lake, a Coyote called, on the
shore the cattle balled around the bend of graceful art, the
old man gazed with love filled heart
　　　　—Cordelia Curnett

Untitled

Why do we laugh, why do we cry?
It's nice to live, but why do we die?

Some dreams are happy, some dreams are sad,
Dreams may be good, others may be bad.

What does it matter, as long as we are together,
If life was easy, we would live forever.

What is joy, if it has to cease,
What is war, if it doesn't end up in peace?

What is a fact, if it is not true?
What is a friend if they don't like you?

What's the difference between black and white?
How do colors start a fight?

Why try if we know we can't succeed?
Why do we ask for things we do not need?

No matter what there is always pain
Why when we try there seems nothing to gain.

Why learn if there is nothing to know?
Why paint a picture of our life if there is nothing to show?

Why do we remember?
Why don't we forget?
Why ask why —
If there is not an answer to get.
　　　　—Nissa Rise

Frost on the Pumpkin

　Frost on the pumpkin
It's the Autumn of our years
Human emotions are measured out in tears
Seems like only yesterday
Standing naked in the sun
What's in your heart will show me
Can our hearts beat as one

　Frost on the pumpkin
October's chill
Healing a wounded heart
That love couldn't kill
Frost on the pumpkin
Changing of the guard alters our storyline
Why's life so hard

　Frost on the pumpkin
Adolescent dreams
How can man's conquest find its own seams
Frost on the pumpkin
Now that life's at an end
Can all my misgivings find time to defend
　　　　—Joe Stojansul

A Mother's Pride and Joy, Her Daughter

Today, my angel, you are getting married.
Are you the same little girl I once carried?

I wished your youth would always last,
but you became a woman much too fast.

Now, your wedding is just minutes away,
and there aren't enough words of excitement I can say.

Your life will be filled with joy, laughter, happiness and
tears, while enjoying each other through the years.

From the moment you kiss and say "I do",
love will be shared forever by the two of you.
　　　　—Debra J. Fleishman

Untitled

It's time to go to sleep now but all I can do is think of you.
It's time to close my eyes and dream of things
That I can't have. But my biggest dream is you.
I wish that my mind wasn't so full of you.
So drunk it can not think straight.
I've gone and thought of someone I can never have
And now that's all I think about. I'm getting sleepy
But with sleep comes you.
As I close my eyes and relax my body
I see you looking so divine.
With you beautiful smile
And your soft, soft skin
And those eyes that make me melt inside.
Your the only one that can make me sweat
When it is cold.
So I guess I can't fight it.
I'll let my mind dream of you
Until that dream becomes a nightmare
And that nightmare just a memory
Of someone I could never have.

    —A. Trejo

When Death Comes Calling

Death is something that should not be taken lightly,
It's when our God-given souls are taken from our bodies.
With God's special help we can ease this transition
By using our knowledge of the true Institution,
For our immortal souls are taken in retribution;
We never know the purpose of our journey here,
So do some good deeds with tender loving care,
Put in order all the affairs of your life,
For in the last ticking minutes you go
through a great strife.
Be alert when the almighty comes to take
that last breath;
And remember, that death does not end our imaginations,
It's the beginning of our hopes and the
end of our frustrations.
By the Resurrection, it's God that gives us
the greatest glory of perfection!

    —Dee Sembrat Shah

I've Been There Before

Love is something that grows,
"I've been there before."
When you're in love, you always know,
"I've been there before."
Be careful you can hurt when you think you're in love,
"I've been there before."
Love is blind,
people ask how I know,
I just respond, "I've been there before."
"Love hurts," how do I know, "I've been there before."
Don't say you're in love with someone
unless you know for sure,
"Believe me, I've been there before."

    —Leslie Nolen

The Rhododendron

As I gaze at the pink rhododendron
and think, how with loving care...
the just and wise Creator has given
its beauty rare.
I examine its bloom for fragrance
and know how each petal blooms...
It is blessed by God in heaven and
given a sweet perfume!

    —Terry Huskey

"For Rachel"

I brought you into the world one day,
I've watched you grow, learn to run and play.
We've been together through skinned knees and school,
through bikes and on to the swimming pool.
We've been together through training bras and boys,
through dates and proms, all the fears and joys.
We've been together through good times and bad,
just take a look at the times we've had!
The years they seemed to pass so fast,
And here you are, an adult at last.
Now I wonder, did I teach you my best?
Are you ready to fly from the nest?
I worry and wonder, but I know you'll do fine,
And I'm so proud you're a child of mine.
Now you're grown and on life's way,
but there's one more thing I've got to say.
When I look at you, I'll always see,
My little girl upon my knee.

    —Shelley Lincoln

Babylon the Great

We have a foe from which to flee.
Jehovah says to get out of Babylon the Great.

Her time is short, we all will agree.
So, it is up to us to scurry from her before it is too late.

If we do not wish to be part of her destiny,
We must not share in her wicked sinful state.

So partakers with her do not be.
Thus, you will escape her disastrous fate.

So to you we make this admonition and plea,
From Jehovah's table and satan's table both you cannot partake.

To avoid satan's table from Babylon the Great you must be free.
Kingdom joys and blessings will then for you await.

    —Karen Carrillo

Today Is No Longer

I'll paint you a picture and make it blue and green
Journeys of the mind
   Are never what they seem

In our mind's eye colors are tangible, and smells are heard
To the common realist
   These ideas seem so absurd

Time is wasting even as I write
The day slowly ends
   And we move deep into the night

The blue and green will fade against the light
And the sub-conscious can't imagine
   Colors half as bright

Tomorrow is coming before its time
And the church bells will signal
   With a melodious chime

The rooster that crows 'ere break of dawn
Will awake the ego
   That plays life like a pawn

    —Stacy Greathouse

Choices

Some of the roads I've chosen are the same as before;
Just a different face, just a different door.
Different circumstances, though, and the names have been
changed; just new rules to play the same game.
I have learned so much, yet not enough; I lose my head to the
touch, I lose my heart to the soul, and I lose my life to the goal.
There's always something to be learned in each new try;
A new way to laugh, a new way to cry, a new way to talk, a new
way to dance, a new way of love, a new way of romance.
Maybe it's just the facade of God's path of life; to teach me
how to grow, to teach me how to strive.
Maybe it's a gamble, a spin of the wheel; go ahead and spin
let's see how I feel.
Deep inside, though, I know the score;
Just a different face, just a different door.
I can only hope to learn as best as I can; learn to stay strong,
know how to stand; learn to make the best of my life, and then
much more;
To find a different face; to find a different door.
    —*Laura A. Anusavice*

The Illusion

Sitting cozily by the fireside on many chilly days
   just as we often did so many years ago;
When we enjoyed the blazing crackling logs
   and could feel the flames warm glow.
We watch shadows dancing on the stones, recalling
   special memories of those past cold winter nights
We often shared with loved ones, and our pets and friends
   by the soaring flames capricious flickering light.
Alas, morning always brought a bit more reality
   to the evening's delightful firelight illusion.
As only blackened ashes still remained upon the hearth
   always there awaiting us in their charred profusion.
No longer do we have to fuss with logs to haul or store,
   nor kindling must be split to start the fire any more.
Neither is there poking or shifting any logs about
   to coax bright flames, and keep them from burning out.
It is quite easy now to just relax in our favorite chair
   as despite no more tending, logs burn brightly there.
We can now enjoy the fireside on any day or night
   by simply flicking on the switch of an electric light.
    —*Marjorie W. Lewis*

All Fire and Brimstone

The sky is ablaze with brilliant reds and oranges,
Just like when someone places a match to kindling.
The fire starts small, and envelops completely
The green fingers that stretched toward the sky all summer.

We can only enjoy nature's painting for a short while,
For winds find new strength, and develop evil minds
Determined to strip trees bare,
Tearing from its grasp, the clothing they shroud.

The leaves silently travel their destiny path with the wind
Collide with the ground with a scrape and a crunch,
To become one with the earth once again.
Their independence is confined to that short-lived flight
And are then put to rest by a warm blanket of snow.

With the passing of each year, these scenes change,
They can never be repeated or reproduced,
Never be copied; for that is nature,
Beautiful, ever-changing nature.

The seasons change with a bump and a clatter,
with a snap of the fingers, as quick as a whip.
All fire and brimstone.
    —*Michelle L. Cloutier*

Abortion?

People say women have the choice of abortion,
Just think, "where we would be if God aborted His Son"
Abortion is wrong, God can show everyone
for those babies, it's too late when it's all done
God takes them home to live with Him
Because they're the Lords most precious gem
You may get forgiven for taking that life
But babies don't come back after you using a knife
It stays in your heart so very very long
without a doubt you'll learn you've done wrong
Remember that "King Jesus" can set you free
He died on that cross for you and me
Humble your heart and give it to Him
He'll take you home someday, to be with that gem
He's merciful and forgiving, can't you see
That's why He was chosen to hang on that tree
He's waiting right now to cleanse your heart
To set you free and give you a new start
Before you take the life of that darling gem
Drop down on your knees and listen to Him
    —*Dora Mae Neace*

"Special Gift"

I've waited long and timeless hours,
Just to see this moment of splendor,
The time is coming soon,
The moment I will always remember,
I've held my breath,
Scared to make a noise or sound,
Wanting to keep the memory,
In my heart forever bound.
I stand as still as stone,
Waiting and hoping for this memory to see,
Thanking the Lord for this special gift,
Feeling proud he chose to give to me.
The time has finally come,
My heart starts racing in suspense,
I try to calm myself,
To regain my strength and confidence.
Emotional tears start to run,
From there special hidden place,
As the first ray of sunshine
Crosses my newborn's face.
    —*Chris Berendt*

"Missing You

Missing you is all I do

I think and think and think about you and
Keep on missing you

Where have you gone,
Would you please come back .... because ....

My life is blue and
Untrue without you

Stay just a little while longer
So that I may become stronger and
Last a little longer,
Being without you

I love you and I care
There are so many things,
That I want to share

Not seeing you is wrong,
It makes me not want to hold on

Missing you is all that I do and
I hope that you miss me too, ... because ....

If you do,
Then I'll know that it was meant for me and you.
    —*Chaya Davis*

The Hurt

When he left me I packed my hurt into a
Knapsack and carried it around on my back.
One night while walking along Michigan Avenue
Bent over from its weight I saw him.
My hurt sprung from the sack like a wild
Hungry panther and I fell to the ground
From the sudden lightness.
While I lay helpless I saw it scratching
Mauling and chewing him then slurp up his
Life like a starving alley cat would a bowl
Of warm milk.
His dead body dropped next to me.
Blood oozed out of it onto the pavement
Like liquid from a vessel full of holes.
Wet red spread until it reached me and soaked
My garments as thoroughly as a good launderer
Would soiled clothes.
My hurt flee and I watched it clawing through
Space until darkness swallowed it up leaving me
Holding the bag.

—*Arlene Kuykendoll*

Weight Four Purl!

Some think that spelling's fun and games - and other think it's
KNOT! If the word cannot be sounded out - we're stumped, with
such as Yacht! Then there are words WITCH sound alike, how can
we get them WRITE? When we're confronted with all these -- like
rite, and write and right? And why spell sugar with no "H" - it
makes no SCENTS to me! And why that silent "B" in lamb - and
that useless "K" in knee? And witch and which, and hoarse and
horse, does a HOARSE still wear a BRIDAL? Would he walk the
ISLE or is it AISLE, or should it have been Bridle? There's
purl and Pearl - could be a girl, and Pearls come from the SEE!
An oyster's the designer - WEAR did we get that "G"? And
queue's a nice one, so is weighed, and how about receipt? Is
there just WON "T" in "writing", or does the "T" repeat?
There's a YOLK of oxen, Yoke of egg and a yoke on Western
shirts. Be careful of that egg Yoke - let not our yoke
besmirch! And how about this joke on us - this Colonel -
that's far out! How in the world with "O"s and "L"s could
Kernel come about? So we do our "Word Search Puzzles - try to
sharpen up our wits! Even though these words WITCH sound alike
are enough to give us fits!

—*Conne P. Morgan*

Shadow of Your Wings

Let me rest in the shadow of your wings and
know the peace and joy that it will bring.
I am weary, weak and worn, battered and I'm torn,
let me rest in the shadow of your wings.

Let me rest in the shadow of your wings and
listen to the angels as they sing.
This journey has been long and I know that I've gone wrong,
let me rest in the shadow of your wings.

Let me rest in the shadow of your wings and
know your peaceful rest in my dreams.
You will calm the storm and keep me from all harm,
let me rest in the shadow of your wings, oh Lord,
let me rest in the shadow of your wings.

—*Helen B. Crockett*

Reality

A killer stalks in the night, waiting,
Knowing your every move.

Waiting for the right movement to strike,
Ready to pounce at any moment just like
a cat attacking it's prey.

You scream as the knife goes through you.

All of a sudden everything goes black
you open your eyes one last time
you see before you a mirror to make
you came to reality.

Who is the killer?

Who you ask.

You of course.

You are the killer.

—*Dawn Wilson*

With...

Vision I see clearly
Knowledge I understand what I see
Perception I personalize what I see
Desire I feel what I see
Passion I act upon my feelings of desire
Happiness I enjoy what I have seen and felt
Freedom I search for happiness
Intellect I use wisely my freedom
Compassion I urge others to strive for vision
Love everything and anything is possible.

—*Paul T. Nieberding*

You Are a Gift to Me

(Dedicated to Dr. J.M. Kennedy)
Last night I saw a shining star
far from the cloisters ruling the sky,
it seemed to be there just for me
.....shining so proudly and so high.

I wanted to take that star from the sky
and hold it tightly in my hand,
so I could have it for the path ahead
.....to have a light wherever I stand.

I unwrapped my dreams, made them wishes
and sent them on a passing breeze,
wishes of peace, happiness and life
.....the night that I met you.

The star will be there, whenever I need
just as you are and offer to be,
that the road ahead will be shared with you
.....for you are a gift to me.

—*Carol Dearns Corabi*

Shattered Mirror

I see an image of me,
Kind and sweet with generosity
But wait I can see
A dark and dim figure starring out at me
No I scream this can not be
And as I strike the mirror it shatters
And leaves me helplessly crying...

I clutch my hands so very tight
I then think this was not right
I slowly and solemnly pick up the pieces of glass
Then I realized I was afraid to see that the figure was me.

—*Tania Hummel*

A Touch of Poetry

Let me embrace you with my poetry,
Let it echo around you and touch your heart.
Accept the presence of the lines I write
So they find your inner self and won't depart.

Do you have a hurt that needs to be eased?
Give me leave to say the words you need to hear,
And may they soothe the agony you feel,
Falling like a soft rose petal on your ear.

Is there a dark mood fighting with your soul?
Let some kind, amusing word sweep it away.
May all the warmth I feel be like the sun
That clears all the gray clouds from a weary day.

Let me come near to you with my poems,
Then if I touch your heart you will know mine too.
We can be friends though we may never meet,
And life can be sweeter than we ever knew.

—*Bertha Woods Greenwood*

Qualifications for Love

In Order To Love Me:
You must first accept me
for who I am and all that I want to be,
Appreciate all the things I say and do;
and reward me where credit is due.
Understand my dislikes as well as my likes,
and don't criticize or be uptight;
You must be my friend as well as my love
cause a friend is there when everything goes.
Be able to hold me all hours of the night,
and let me know every thing will be alright.
Wipe my tears away and open my eyes,
to all that I couldn't see,
Help me to be everything that I could be.
Take those long midnight strolls with me in the park,
and gently kiss me in the dark.
Give me all you have to give:
your hopes, your dreams, even your fears.
Forgive me and don't hold grudges
let the bad times pass us by to make our love stronger;
if you think you qualify for a job such as this
give me a call and I'll put you on my list.

—*Annissia D. Suldon*

Boulevard of Dreams

Boulevard of dreams awaits both you and I.
Lets take a walk, take my hand - I'll show you
where the street lies.

Boulevard of dreams is calling for you now.
Sorry my love I have to stay here awhile.
When the lions lay down with the lambs
I'll be seeing you again my love.
When the lions lay down with the lambs
I'll be seeing you again.

Lets take this last walk of many,
and see everything as new.
It will have to last a life time.
A life time without you. Tears will swell,
and rivers will flow, pain will come
and anger will go. Peace and love-
memories of you. This will be my solace,
until the lions lay down with the lambs.

When the lions lay down with the lambs
I'll be seeing you again my friend. When the
lions lay down with the lambs I'll be seeing you again.

—*David Sigler*

Mulberry Song

Lines form images letters
letters form images words
words distant removed far from feeling evoked evoking
music coming from the both of us
valid attempts
irish folk music chosen for the day
it was much further than green and
a single O directly followed by a mark of brevity
rain again makes a self assured appearance
accompaniment most likely
courtesy of the fairies
both show inherent birthmarks of brevity
not greek puritan farmer
fruit colored toes fall asleep tingle tingling
sparkling water poured directly behind the windows
I have five accompanying the one to the left
the bubbles settle
this is not to be drunk
it is only a temporary stain
not an abbreviation of a place just a memory
I carry with me because I walk

—*Tina Ward*

"Hidden Thoughts"

Deep within the body's core
Lies a scar which man had bore
Pain that many choose to hide
Eats away at them inside
In our mind we'll never know
From what seed this pain did grow
Hearts will bleed 'til the end of time
We shall pay for another's crime
It whispers in our ears each day
And cries at night, our dreams at play
Lurking about in the corners of our minds
Hiding in the darkest place it finds
Never seeming to miss a beat
Blocking out all that once was sweet
We close our eyes, and try to forget
But inscribed in our minds, it is set
Where it came from no one knows
Within our blood, it continuously flows
It will haunt us for the rest of our lives
We may try to kill it, but it survives.

—*Jodi Koenig*

Life

Life has its' point of view for us.
Life has its' ups and downs.
Life may not be the best of all things,
but look at the joy it brings.

Life takes many turns and I hope I may
take the right turn, in my life to like a
good positive life.

—*Delon Hicks Sykes*

Porcelain Doll

Its face so still,
Its expression so bleak,
No emotion is shown.
Why, why are you so lifeless?
What has made you so silent?

Your lips so small, they can't be seen,
Your eyes so enormous, your lips so fake,
Your dress so plain, your hair so stiff.
Why, why are you so lifeless?
What has made you so silent?

—*Melissa Gesualdi*

A Visionary

I love a visionary
   Life leads and she follows
Questions of why go unanswered.
   And she's driven by a spontaneity
   She herself can't fully understand.

She's a God-child, a dreamer
   She settles softly on my mind
   But stirs a restlessness in my heart.

Possess her? I would.
   But how do you hold
     the fragrance of blossoms on a breeze,
     the smell of grass after the rain,
     the soul-searching splendor of a sunset?

She's all of this and more to me.
I never hide from her
   or even want to
     When I'm happy, I smile
     When I hurt, I cry.

I don't have to do anything — be anything
   that's not me. She loves me.
        —*J.R. Mulligan*

Question thy Dove

Remember the kiss that once awakened the heavens
life of love and then it brought forth the courageous
dove of sacred souls. Ghost giver, holy spirit, fly
through the blue enlightened sky and I thought the
arrow, true to the pierced flesh but yet, I thought.
It's the only way to feel when it seemed so gallantly
real then the dream shattered before my very breath.
"Would I lie to you" the demon's fire scorched my
heart, but the dove remained just like the endless
refrain of the demon's words. The eyes that lay before
mine render those very words, but I answer not because
the demon has certainly forgot the loved embrace that
brought us as one. "Would I lie to you' cried the
demon again but he may seem the very friend once trusted
with thy heart that busted the chains and opened the
gates wide and there beside the demon once again
quivered the question, "would I lie to you"? The
dove then answered, "would you lie to me"?
        —*Tara Christine Romano*

Leah's Saddle Shoes

Never treading, always prancing,
Lightly now she floats on wings.
Ever springing, ever dancing,
Happy heart song she gaily sings.

Skip six steps for all her years,
A child's world full of its delights;
Pretend and magic she believes,
Are with us now — not out of sight!

New black/white saddle shoes for school,
She wears so proudly from the shop.
To weep would make me seem a fool,
Yet my heart turns over, like a top.

Would I could keep her over shielded,
Safe from world's incessant fray;
Deflect life's blows so cruelly wielded,
When as adults we pass our days.

No! Her very joy has bound her —
Like a blanket, keeps her warm;
Like a nimbus floating 'round her,
Cocooned, protected, safe from harm.
        —*Alice Heard Williams*

The Rainbow Harks

Arched across the heavens the spectrum rounds
Lights fused to glisten such colors that sound

Peacefully, so tranquil to signal the end
Of rainstorms that beckon and then finally dim

The rainbow now arches, a perfect blend
Through clouds and their mistings toward an evenless still

Pure in its dignity, mystic in its resolve
Transfers such feeling with meanings that abound

Red melts to oranges, to violets and blues
True hues of light that shine into view

A vision of splendor, that shines this day
To display for the eye all the colors this way

God's painting for sunshine, a vision of hope
The rainbow harks such a beautiful stroke

Painting cross skies, that blend into grays
Blue shies returning the moonshine at bay

It's perfect this one, so large it exceeds
All memories of rainbows all storms in between

This rainbow extends beyond time, beyond place
It's engraved on my mind though this rainbow will fade
        —*Patricia Keefrey*

Dream Master

You touch the ground on your hands and knees
like a child and now your forehead touches the ground.

For the sake of all your joys the Dream Master lets you in.
When you turned away from all the five places.
You have praised the rising and falling of the
sun, water falling or disappearing even the end of trees.
You welcome the seasons equally and been one with all
weather from untamed to the silent. The blood left in
your hands is that of your own.
Now my heart will be strict admitting none letting nothing go.

Close all your mouths, you will sleep inside of eternal sleep.
Honoring the gift of darkness from the abyss till it breaks.
You sing for a cold beginning.
        —*Carlos Rivera*

Used Car Saleman

He descends upon me
Like a hawk eyeing a field mouse
Gliding smoothly between the
Shining bodies of what may be
My next method of flight.

His talons are exposed
But he's not thinking of my throat
Possibly an easy kill
But of my checkbook whose cover is worn
And hides the fruits of my labor.

He smiles and nods
As I quietly speak of my needs
Then shows me things beyond my means
And I question if he heard me
Or just pondered his own take for the day.

We retreat from one another
I to my home
And the safety of my family
And he to his office nest with glass walls
Ever watchful for any movement in his lot.
        —*Jeanette Snodgrass*

Lost

Confusion,
Like a lost child in a crowded street,
People running everywhere.
Scurrying from store to store on a long drive.
This child truly is lost for he,
he cannot see past the person in front of him.
Everything is turning,
"Where am I?" He cries.
But no one hears, for to them,
he is not there and
How can you hear someone who is
Not there?
Confusion......!

—*Lauren Muscianese*

Leaves

I watch the Fall leaves as they sail through the air,
Like a rudderless plane without a care.
I sigh as I watch them dive to the ground,
And mingle with those that have fallen straight down.
Some leaves are reluctant to ever let go,
They cling to the tree through the wind and the snow.
But when Spring comes along, something must give,
The old have to go, so the young ones can live.
I cheer them on as they peep through the boughs.
And grow with a speed only nature allows.
The greening of Spring with some blooms here and there,
Is a welcoming sight from the trees that were bare.
There are pleas on our knees that the trees will prevail,
Since they give out the fresh air and take in the stale.
After Summer of cooling and shading the sun,
The trees get a feeling that Fall has begun.
It's nature that's calling they have to comply.
With a great burst of beauty they wither and die.
While you ponder their riddance, consider their worth.
And place them where they can return to the earth.

—*Annie Mae Keeling Poole*

Sea-Horse

A mountain stream dashes down the course,
Like a sea-horse,
White mane flying,
Rushing home to ocean —
Fog paints the banks jet black
And wraps the trees in a gray mantle.
Even the hills are blotted out.
The current never slackens
Plunges ahead, sure of the way,
It knows the road back to
The stables of the sea.

—*Genevieve F. Miner*

Pleased

I have found on life's journey that you
    just can't please everyone.
So if I please God.
I can please myself.
No you cannot please everybody, but time is a
way to please one's self...
A right felt attitude, a friendly felt word
A cheerful felt smile, and a good deed.
Are without measure with our God
Thoughtfulness and kindness and love.
Surely can please someone and will please your maker above.
So if you can't please everyone, please God
and you can be pleased yourself.

—*Norman White*

Fire!

Bellows of heavy black smoke filled the air.
Like an inferno the heat surrounded the town.
Their thoughts were of loved ones they couldn't find.
Wondering if what might be lost, could ever be found.

Disaster does not discriminate against one kind,
Lives are lost or changed, homes and property destroyed,
The rich and famous, young and old, the homeless, as well.
Once tragedy has begun, destruction is the ultimate goal.

But out of the fogginess, when hope seemed unclear,
Heroes came from far and near to do all they could
To console a broken heart, they became as lanterns
To lives in turmoil, lighting a way through a sea of night.

The time will come when they will ask God why he allowed
Fire and smoke to literally fill the sky.
The chaos will pass and life will go on
However, tragedy will continue to hurt everyone.

—*Kathy C. Smallwood*

The Old Relic

Now that I have retired,
Like an old relic cast aside,
No more having to rise and shine,
Or set the clock to get up on time,
I can take a nap or go for a ride.
But is this the way it's supposed to be?
Then a thought occurs to me.
Look at the things you haven't done,
Isn't there still time to have some fun.
Look at the books you've never read,
The classical music you haven't heard,
The many plays you haven't seen.
Is the computer going to pass you by,
Without even giving it a try?
Think of the flowers you haven't grown,
And all the people you've never known.
There's so much to do,
Before I'm through.
I must make haste,
I haven't any time to waste.

—*James F. Walker*

Snow Flower

I like snow when it falls so slow
Like silver stars dancing in a row.
And the wind gives it a puff so it
Falls against my windowpane so soft
Like a powderpuff and paints a
Wondrous design a shimmering magic
Display there I see a child that believes
On a night Christmas Eve when the snow
Had a glow from Christmas long ago.

—*Ruth Culver*

The Rose That Was Never Chose"

There once was a rose that was never chose. It sat all alone
just waiting for someone to take it home. Night after night
and day after day it waited and waited. Not once did one
ever stop and glance. Pretty soon the rose felt it no longer
had a chance. The pain it felt was hidden behind it's beauty.
It often wondered why no one saw it's true beauty, why no one
cared, why it was constantly ignored, and most of all why it
was never chosen. Soon the rose felt it could no longer live.
The rose died that day cause it gave up hope. The next day the
gardener walked by and found the single wilted rose upon the
dry dirt. He thought to himself if only I had tended to the
rose sooner the beauty would still be here.

—*Masaya Palmer*

The Power of Jesus Through His Reflection

Jesus is Mirrored in all things
Like sunlight in clear water
The power of the almighty king Jesus
will reach out and touch the light in the water
and not shatter the reflection.

Jesus carried our burdens
when He took our sin from this world
He is who He is
That He could walk upon the waters
Not shattering his reflection.

But if I try to touch
The light that is in the water
I only shattered the reflection upon it
We can't do what he did

For He's The Reflection of this world
　　　—*Edward M. Questell*

Like Cats

Like the lion who ravenously eats the meat of the gazelle
Like the caged tiger who relentlessly paces
Searching for something both unseen and unknown.
Like cats, We seem.
We devour the cells of nature
Yet we are constantly looking, searching
Watching for food that will satisfy the hunger.
Hunger of the mind, to know, to understand.
The hunger that never ceases,
A continuous thirst without a quench.
We want to know, to feed, to drink,
yet we cower for fear
In the face of the very food that can fill our need
Like man, We are.
It is the unknown for which we yearn, but so deeply dread.
It is the contradiction of crave and fear
That binds us, forever wanting
While we cower on our knees with hidden eyes.
Oh yes, this is man.
　　　—*Angie Barber*

You Are Always There

In times of sorrow is when we need the most comforting.
Like the times a pet or a loved one dies or leaves us.
Ordinarily we freak out - rivers of tears and a loss of our
　　wits. Then
Very sweetly you come and hold me - letting me breath easy.
Even though you may be at a loss for words
Your just being there next to me is enough.
Over a matter of time the pain eventually goes away - but
　　when I need instant soothing
Uniquely being yourself, you are always there and I love you
　　for that.
　　　—*Christine McDonagh*

Untitled

Friendships come, and friendships go,
Like the winters first virgin snow.
They are soft, they are pure, and easily broken,
By simple and careless cutting words spoken.

Damaging footsteps will be covered by flurries,
Hiding old cares and previous worries.
On that first winters surface are those covered mars.
And on the heart of that good friend are those hidden scars.

Only with summer do the footsteps depart.
Just as with new friends the scars leave the heart.
A friendship once broken is never retrieved,
Not today, or tomorrow, or on eternities eve.
　　　—*Jeffrey B. Camp*

True Love!

I never am good at telling a girl
like you how I feel but I will take a chance
and let my heart be revealed,
I love your eyes they are like emeralds in the sunshine
and your hair is like burning embers in the night,
The way I long to hold your warm embrace
I can't wait to see your face,
When the wind whispers
I swear I hear it calling your name
I go crazy when I start to dream about you
and I know your nowhere near,
Sometimes I wake in a throbbing sweat thinking you're near
but further yet!!!
　　　—*Jennifer Scott*

Tudor Daize

"SLICE"

The Sun Light
Limpid and weak
filters languidly
across tiles
around cornices
and over the friezes
of 42nd Street's Grand Central Station
　　　Like
　　Paratroopers of Speckled Light
　　These Battalions from the Sun
　　　　glide
　　　　easily to Earth
　　　　　　as shadows are sliced
　　　　　　　colors are exploded
　　　　　　　　and tensions heightened

THE ATTACK —— Silent
　　goes unnoticed
　　in the prickly heat
　　　of a humid New York afternoon
　　　　as busses crawl and sirens shriek
　　　　　Sound and Light — at Counterpoint
　　　　　　within the Perfect Order
　　　　　　of Chaotic Shift
　　　—*Phillip H. Becker*

The Dark Princess

The Dark Princess in sweet repose,
Lips of blood red to shame a rose.
Her skin, so brown as fresh fertile Earth
That is yet to be sewn, to commence rebirth.

Her mind is filled with the Knowledge of the Ages,
Ammunition used in the war that she wages.
Outside of her realm, away from the stages
Only is private, will she show her rages.

The secrets she holds are from the beginnings of time
The Ancient Mother, the heart, the mind.
She is chief confessor to all their crimes
But as protector, their punishment remains undefined

Her eyes when they shine put the Heavens to shame.
But now they are dark ... who is to blame?
She may only come back if you call her by name,
She will only come back if you call her by name.
　　　—*Jeanna W. Bridges*

Roommate

People think I live alone.
Little do they know,
That I share my humble home
With the One who loves me so.

He is always here watching over me,
To keep me safe from harm.
So how can I feel cold or lonely,
With His love to keep me warm.

And when the cares and troubles of the day
Overwhelm me and make me low,
I turn then to His Sacred Heart
And my worries quickly go.

So now I know when it is my time
To join my loved ones gone before,
Then His heavenly home will also be mine.
I'll have no need for this one anymore.

—*Barbara Draper*

Blue Whales

The blue whale is the largest animal known to man,
Living in the mysterious waters, not the land.
Their size can be up to 100 feet,
And since they live in the water they can stand the heat.
They weigh up to 392,000 pounds,
And they're very interesting with their peculiar sounds.
And they're down in the deep, dark ocean,
Sometimes made into oily lotion.

Blue whales are the type of whale called baleen,
Their Baleen plates can be easily seen.
The Blue whale eats tons of food each day,
So that they can live their life in a normal way.

Harpoons were launched into the Blue whales skin,
The whales were so strong that they cut loose and began to
swim. When the whalers began to use harpoon guns in 1968,
Even the blue whale could no longer escape.
No one can kill the Blue whales anymore, because their
Population is very poor. Why would they want to kill
These spectacular whales? So that they could make thousands of
Profits and sales? That doesn't make any sense to me,
Killing these beautiful animals of the sea.

—*Amy Bourke*

Memories

There were those days of love and joy that made this life worth
living. Of mountain trails and city nights and countless other
shared delights. Of passions spent by fireside heart with
bodies as one in loves embrace, a love while worn not
completely gone from the memories of my mind.

There were those days of love and joy, before the terrible hurt
before the words best left unsaid, before the tearing pain. Of
work and toil and sometimes tears a family we made, a family
now changed and perhaps well gone save the memories of my
mind.

Through the years the wounds have healed and the hurt is all
but gone. And like fresh spring flowers for each of us a new
life has begun. Yet, as I think of those by-gone days a sad
refrain comes to my mind. A phrase that asks what might have
been had I found the time. The time to care, the time to love
the time to devote just to you. For if I had-these warm
thoughts I hold may still be coming true.

—*Frederick J. Moll III*

"Jeopardy"

He sat in quiet isolation
    Longing for undisturbed security and calm.
Family, friends, doctors…
    Had answers to great questions
    He could not comprehend.
Slowly, with quiet desperation
    Cancer ravished his body
    And trashed his essence.
Urged to fight and called courageous
    He staggered, despaired and hoped
    Through a conflagration of unsolved problems,
    Ambiguous victories and vague, eroding defeats.
Knowing that each relapse could be
    The final jeopardy
He settles, as life's passion fades,
    For moments of peace and joy.
        —*Arthur A. Abelson*

Untitled

This is it our last year
look round at the people here.
They're our friends and enemies.
With them we've made many memories.
Kindergarten through junior high
we've never really had to say good-bye.
Now all of a sudden the time has come
to say good-luck and good-bye to some.
From kickball games to scrapes and falls
we've stayed together through it all.
We'll never lose the friends we've made
or forget the games we've played.
The games we've lost the games we've won.
Even though the days went on.
Now the last few days are growing fewer.
Graduation is coming sooner.
B.H.S. how could we ask for more,
We're the graduating class of 1994.
    —*Jennifer Lowery*

Beauty

You are beautiful —
    Like grasses covered by crystal dew of morn;

You are beautiful
    Like roses shyly prostrating before a majestic universe.

You give expanse to my breathless concept of your Being

You are like the chirping birds singing the little news
    of budding and fall of leaves;

You are like the unseen merriment of wind
    upon the quivering leaves,

You are like the unheard cords songs of rippling waters
    of streams;

You are like the daring clouds that bear heavy rains to
    quench the thirst of earthlips.

You are like the sky in its untiring wonders of vastness
    and miraculous colored pencillings.

You are beautiful as love —
    Multi-faceted in its revelation,
    That I see, hear and touch you everywhere,

Even in the setting sun and in the bursting joy of nymphal dawn.
You are like God's wine upon my throat —
    That I sing and sing an orchestration of your love
    into one beautiful ecstacy!
        —*Rosalina Escudero*

Untitled

Still your soul, allow it peace; reflect upon the years gone by.
Look up into night's dark calm, at distant stars put in the sky
By God for you to marvel at — for you are up there shining bright,
Casting light upon the earth, shrouding it with gentle light.

Calm your spirit, oh so still; listen as the soft winds blow,
Causing leaves to flutter in their gentle swaying to and fro.
Marvel as the downy clouds of fleecy softness overhead
Darken as the winds grow wild; a fiery storm - the blackness spreads.

The heavens howl. The lightning strikes. Torrential rain descends
Upon the arid, thirsty soil — the moisture serves to cleanse.
Joy arises in your heart, the tempest stills its mighty roar.
The calm and quiet, returning now, as it was before.

Soothe your heart, that pounding force, and let it be serene.
Inhale that wondrous fragrance of the rain-washed earth —
how clean!
Marvel at the world around us — fresh, anew and tranquil.
God's perfect planet, made for you, a glorious gift unequalled.

　　　—Sherry Stuurman

Out Of Weakness.....Strength

Out of weakness and pain, we come to Thee in agony
Lord God, in our weakness, give to us of Thy strength;
And in our strength, unto us weakness and dependence
Patient dependence upon Thy great love, O' my Lord.

In peace and quiet, let all men wait upon Thee, for healing
Wash and cleanse us in the purifying blood of the Lamb of God;
Lord, walk us out of the dark shadows and into Thy Holy Light
Lead us into quiet pastures, to dwell in God's eternal peace.

In our walk on earth, life is fraught with trials and troubles
Out of our weakness comes strength, through our faith in Jesus;
To us impatient mortal beings, time is of the complete essence
We fret...but to you O' my God, a thousand years is like a day.

　　　—Ruth E. Holsten

Where have the Children Gone?

Where have the children gone?
Lost at sea and thrown along.
The injustice has been done to the future of life.
The children are running, far away with tears in their eyes.
Shamed with so much disgrace.
Being hurt at their lost hopes, crushed to the ground
with a mighty fist.
What makes the world a terrible place?
I do not know. The earth is a knight of shadows,
forbidding like a long lost hope.
Where is my hope, that is a long lost light,
that is shown before my eyes during the night.
Where have the children gone?
I do not know.
My hope is lost and will
always be gone.

　　　—Erin O'Brien

Illusions and Dreams

Dreams die hard, illusions shatter
Life goes on, but does it matter?
Hearts beat strongly, hurt and weary
Life's fabric torn, destroyed and dreary.
The skin of dreams torn from the flesh of life.
The world howls mightily, as it wields its knife.
The bleeding tattering frame that remains
is naught but a shell, that once had a name.
A person, a soul who had hopes and some dreams,
Became lost and alone and fearful of schemes.
Thus we live and we pray and hope for tomorrow,
and perhaps our great faith may erase all our sorrow.

　　　—Billie Valez

Divorce

Thinking of the past I start to smile
lost in my own playful thoughts for awhile.
Remembering a girl who was once filled with sunshine
And knowing these memories will always be mine.
Then, all of a sudden, things started to change
The familiar was being replaced with something new and strange.
The adults started fighting and stopped acting their age.
Instead yelled at each other words of hatred and rage.
Once a little girl, now no longer
She had to be different and must be stronger.
Realizing I grew up too fast
longing for the little girl now only in my past.
I look back hoping to see
that care-free girl I want to be
Although I know I must look ahead
to tomorrow
I will never forget that little girl
and all her sorrow.

　　　—Julie Morath

The Noises of the Forest

I can hear the noises of the forest both
　　loud and clear
They come from various distances both
　　far and near
The chirping of the many birds nestled
　　in the trees
The humming and the buzzing of
　　the busy little bees
The squirrels and the chipmunks
　　are climbing up and down the trees
Looking for food and nuts as quiet as
　　you please
The deer are roaming all around the
　　wooded grounds
Leaping and playing with one another
　　in gleeful bounds
The waters are babbling in the nearby brooks
　　Twisting and turning beneath the many cranny and nooks
The forest is a peaceful and wonderful sight to behold
　　As it contains many pleasures worth their weight in gold.

　　　—Melita Spadafora

What Is Love?

Love is staying up at night praying to the Lord he's dreaming of you.
Love is the innermost desire to kiss his tender lips.
Love is an attraction for some of the strongest people.
Love is the most powerful force in the world that
　　intertwines two people who were made for each other.
Love is the power of two, who can make the
　　stormy seas settle, making it look like a
　　perfectly cut sheet of glass.
Love is the friendship we hold so dear to us.
Love is a river, never running dry.
Love is a challenge, a task we all perform,
　　it is a game not all of us can win.
Love is the beginning, that shall never have an end.

　　　—Tanya Lawrence

Since You've Been Gone

Since you've been gone, the world is less lighter now....
Since you've been gone, the world is less peaceful now...
Since you've left, the world is less love full....
Since you've been gone, more harm than non harm....
Since you've been gone, how much we need you in our time of
　　crisis...
Since you've been gone, how much we need you in our time of
　　need....

　　　—Nick Noble

"Love"

Says goodbye...
Love speaks always, but not always
in words, finding that out for the first
time can be hard on one who has loved
someone for so long, the unfortunate
part is when you lose that love for
that special person you lose part of
yourself, you and him can't ever be
together it's best that way you say
to yourself, he doesn't love you anymore
and you must go on, you look
into the mirror and say to yourself,
"he's lost that special love for you and
you've lost it for him", you know you both
will always have places in your hearts
for each other, but the time has
come to move on, you kiss him
goodbye, and with one last look you turn
and walk away.

—Heather Hargreaves

For Peng Peng

All I can do is be with you, hold you or pet you, because I
love you. I rub your tummy as it may seem funny. I can stroke
your back, I can comb your fur, the delicate tangles which so
purr when I brush them. At night when you slept by my bed, I
couldn't possibly think of you dead. But now that you are, I
pray of your spirit, and hope you're not far so I may heal it.
I miss you so much, and I wish I didn't. The hours go by, as
if they were days. I wish you were here, so I could see your
face. It was just yesterday that you were a puppy. I picked
you up in a single palm. But now I don't touch you, I don't
feel you, you no longer exist in my world. How I wish you were
here, to chase your tail in a perfect circle, to trip over
your paws as if they were pebbles, to comfort me in my
discomfort. Oh, how I wish you were alive, your heart beating
to the sound of my radio, your tongue lolling, with wet saliva,
your tail wagging a mile an hour. Oh, how I wish I could hear
your hoarse bark, as the neighbors whispered a nasty remark.
Peng won't you come back to me, to love me, to cherish and
obey me. To me you are as fresh as a new born baby. It's
long past goodbye, but I'd like to say it. Goodbye Peng Peng.

—Michelle Gomberg

Hidden Thoughts

I look into your eyes, so deep brown they glisten with your
love. You look to me for answers but have to search within.
I would love to help you find yourself, but you are consumed by
a sea of thoughts.

I need a sign from you no more running away.
My presence scares you as the feelings of trust and love are in
my air. You want to get close but fear what surrounds you.

Death comes from the need to untouchable.
You don't want me too close, because I can see the weakness in
your eyes. You love me but can't, losing your edge would leave
you vulnerable to me. The wall I can uncover is what you fear
the most.

—Michelle Ruiter

Trapped

Sometimes you love somebody on the
outside it shows, on the inside
it just grows, but never to speak a
word of it just deep inside hidden
like a prison with bars you can't
escape from, no way out never to tell
that person how trapped you feel inside.

—Holli Smith

"What The Clouds Bring Me"

The grey clouds slowly roll
low over my head, tiny rain drops
fall from those clouds sprinkling their
magical powers of life on all they touch.
Every so often one, two, three, or four
will hit my up turned face and come to
one with my already falling tears.

The breeze picks up, bringing a cool
death-like feeling. A feeling of loneliness
and loss. I loosen my eyes from their
tight, yet dripping closure. The cool
breeze hits my face and causes my
hair to slightly sway. My eyes now must
squint to block the wind from drying them
into complete stiffness.

The clouds, the wind, and the rain
slowly cease to exist, like most things
they pass:
Unfortunately my tears, along with all
my worries of loosing the spark... Remain within.

—Heather Henry

The Quilter

The quilter took some pieces made my soul
Made me worth more than silver or gold
He took some star dust from the sky
And placed a twinkle in my eye
He gave me a heart beating strong
Guaranteed it for life, it can never go wrong
Took some pieces from parents and ancestors beyond
That gave me wisdom and knowledge to carry on
He set me aside but continued to mold
He made soft little animals for me to hold
He made the birds to fly and fish for the sea
All of these things He made for me
He gave me vegetables and fruits to eat
He gave us water and He gave us meat
The Quilter, the Quilter, can't you see
He did for you what He did for me
Let us give thanks to one so grand
The one who quilts with the Master Plan.

—Marcia Garr

Thoughts I Thought I Left Behind

Living in wonder
makes you feel you need to discover.
Looking for your friend of the past
This time you want to make it last.
It's been so long, I don't know were I went wrong.
I think it's time we sit and talk
before we go for a long walk.
This is really tearing me up inside
There's no time left to hide
I've forgotten about that little fling
But now it's time to sing.
I can not sit and wait around
Someday you may be unfound.
I can't say goodbye to a wonderful friend
Just please be with me till the end.
I guess I'll give it time even
though I feel out of line.
I hope someday this will all workout
even though I have a doubt. I miss him so much
But I know that kiss will never be retouched.

—Michele Basile

D. C. Vision

Cold winds blows in the sky,
making snow flurries of the cherry blossoms.
Needles in the air.
It's like watching a dream,
the way things are ever in change.
Domes where people go,
to get their fingers into the fate of the land.
Memorials in abundance,
to shine on past glory,
of men and campaign, do they herald.
Each generation comes to cry to it's lost.
Use to be a time we all waved the same flag.
Some do, but the knowledge hit us all,
some won't be coming home.

—*William Lane Williams III*

A Day to Die

The shadows are forming around your eyes,
Making them look sunken and shrunk in size.
The sight makes my heart whither and tears fall,
Make-up put on you to look like a doll.
A clown to laugh at during a parade,
They made you look weird, not dead I'm afraid.
I feel like falling to my knees to weep,
But not to was a vow you made me keep.
I can see it now, my passing right out,
When I hear the words the preacher will shout.
They are taking me, to where I do know,
I'm not gonna protest, I want to go.
And, up to heaven I'm traveling now,
I am going to see you this I vow.
So, bid me farewell and kiss me goodbye,
This is the day on which I choose to die.

—*Sondra Janeen Jones*

Remembrance

As I sit here in the dark,
Many thoughts come to mind,
Like that one lonely night,
When I stood alone wondering where you were,
Like the precious time we used to spend together,
Talking about materialistic things,
As I sit hear in the dark,
I am reminded of you,
When I was feeling down, you made me laugh,
When you come visit, you wear your best clothes
and your most biggest most widest smile,
just to see me,
Remembering your picture perfect face,
just gives me a smile,
Now I don't sit in the dark,
Fearing and hiding from others,
Listening and seeing others with happiness and concern,
I see now why you took me out of the dark,
Without fear and hatred, but with bravery, trust and
alliance.

—*Lisa Gonzalez*

"Memories Past"

From out of the cold, I bring a single rose,
   one left of summer clipped from her stem.
She has memories too, that remind me of him.
Her face is wet with raindrops of tears,
   so lovely is she, to make a memory appear.
So, rest in peace mother vine in the cold,
   you have harvested to us a story untold.
Nestle down in your bed of leaves and debris
   until spring soon appears with a work unto thee.

—*Trudy Stewart*

In A Little One Room School House

In a little one room school house
Many years ago there was only
One teacher and maybe twenty students.
Old fashioned desks that more than one could sit in.

The teacher taught all the subjects
And taught every grade level.
She was both principal and janitor,
And very conscientious about her work.

You can be sure that God
Was welcome in her school.
There were prayers said
And the reading of God's Word.

Today education has advanced.
Computers are present all through out the schools.
However God is no longer welcome in school.
I wonder if we have really progressed.

—*David Johnson*

Bedtime

Goodnight my child
May all your dreams be sweet and mild
The lights are out, but I'm still right here
One last kiss to chase away that fear
I checked your closet and under the bed
So just grab teddy and rest your head
Storytime is over and everything's done
So go back to dreamland and have some fun
I'll close the door when I'm gone
So Mr. Sandman can sing you a song
I'll give you an hour or two maybe
But then I must check on my sweet sleeping baby
And if by chance you get scared some night
Come to me and we'll make it all right
But for now my precious child I'll just say
   Goodnight

—*Brandye Stansbury*

I Grew Up In Jewish Clothes

I grew up in Jewish clothes that never fit
me the way I wanted. The older Yids,
the religious ones with the octagon heads,
frozen beards and flaming eyes, had always
captured my childhood fancy, like baseball:
But I realized when the grass was still green
that I did not want to put their clothes on.
I roamed the streets like a lost dog each day, each
night, hour after endless hour, and I searched.
I looked under ghetto mats and under
golden paved streets of the well-off few.
I climbed tropical trees with good sights in
my view; lit fires inside of cancer cells.
My beaconlike eyes are scanning the sky,
keen as an eagle's they search through the times.

—*David Saxner*

Sherry

Happy - and yes snappy.
Oh so cheerful - what an earful.
So full of life.
She tries to make others happy.
What a great winning smile - all the while.
Always moving and with
so much feeling.
Almost never down - with a frown.
Sometimes, she's our happy clown.

—*Margaret Corral*

"Me Too"

When I told you I loved you, you said,
'me too"
When I said I'd never forget you, you said
'me too"
When I said I was serious, you said,
'me too"
When you told me you were leaving me, I said,
'for who"
When I told you I would kill myself for you, you said,
"yeah right"
When I told you I wasn't playing, you still said,
"yeah right"
Now that I'm gone and I've said I love you
As tears fall down, you say, "me too"
It's too late 'cause you left me, but I guess
I'll always wonder... "for who"
And tell me...
"What did I do"

—*Karin Sawyer*

Chevy

They say when you gain
Money and age,
Your tastes begin to change.

From a Z28 or a Pontiac,
To a Lexus or a nice new Cadillac.
Just the perfect car for the average Mac.

But not for me, I'm a different story.
I don't want a Beamer or a Mercedes.
I'll just go for a brand new Chevy.

A Chevy truck made of steel.
With an extended cab and fat wheels.
With a big engine, with that roaring feel.

A truck for hauling.
A truck for cruising.
A truck for some good off roading.

And when I'm old and crazy.
At the ripe old age of 80.
I'll say "Hey grandson,
Here's the keys to my brand new Chevy."

—*Richard Abernethy*

A Father's Day Fantasy

Relaxed Villagers polka-dotted the verdant crescent abutting
Montgomery Pond athwart the band on the further shore.

Willows, prayerfully poised on the bank, formed a leafy bower
sheltering those waiting to savor their musical feast.

I could almost smell and taste the eagerness of the listeners
as they exploded into smiles when the music broke the air.

A Downs boy conducted vicariously.
I shared his joy and rejoiced as the band followed his
relentless beat 'tho imprisoned by leader's baton.

My third eye saw the willows join the party.
The gentle whisperings of their greenery
answered the music with sinuosity beyond the winds.
When crescendos hit they joined Salome in ecstasy.

The willows did what they knew best, weeping with happiness,
and the brimming pond rose with their tears.

To choke the flow, they flailed the water mercilessly,
sponging up the fluid to their innards,
like a mother frantically wiping baby's milk before it hit the rug.
The concert ended and serenity ruled once more at
Montgomery Pond as the mallards recaptured sovereignty.

—*Charles Bernstein*

Golden Calves

The sun of such halo, song of light-time,
Moon of a harvest playing comfort to our climb.
Swords that split hairs but would not touch the head,
So damocles-fashion, in exquisite dread.
No gold such with wits by master engraved;
But doled out in written, rave writ which depraves.
No art stroke severed, to bear upon truth,
What breathed the sky to recount, for sooth:
That art! That truth! On palms etched forever.
All momentous attempts at exceptional endeavor.
Cause had ingrained on a courage poised danger,
Gleaning scenes of nativity ensconced in lore mangers.
Pray yon there thurifer not smoke out the steepals,
Your shroud too silver for coins gracing eyeballs.
Dank walls, hot hypocausts enclosing think-tanks,
Furnaced propulsive from prostyle belief-banks.
A mottled, rent mother lode and quitclaims to show,
Deed to no golden calf, but timbered horse hollow.
Alas Jean-Jacques, alack; where tabula rasa bides,
Return, turn back... while not yet in the west of our lives.

—*Jerard Jensen*

Friendship

Friends are more than just people you see;
Most people think only of I, my and me!
But, a friend thinks of others and just how they feel,
And a lonely heart treasures a friendship that's real.

A heart that is broken can sense one who cares,
And is rich beyond measure when friendship is shared.
With sorrow forgotten and lighter their load;
In joy once again, they can travel life's road.

This world needs some friendship - to make things work right,
For a world holding hands is a beautiful sight!
We all need each other - to live happily;
And friendship makes music with sweet harmony.

Sunshine and laughter - and tears of sweet joy
Are what God intended for each girl and boy.
A true friend is worth more than silver or gold.
And sprinkles a lifetime with riches untold.

So, if you have thought that your talents are few
And there's nothing in this whole wide-world you can do;
Then stop and consider this question again -
Have you tried - really tried - to make someone your friend?

—*James E. Niehoff*

A Mother's Day Poem

When you were a baby and needed tending to.
Mother was there looking over you.

As you started growing and needed special care,
And someone to love you "Yes," mother was there

And then came school, you were so afraid
Mother gave you comfort when you kneeled and prayed

Mother was there as adulthood approached
She was always there as your friend and coach

Yes mothers are special in a very special way
They deserve much more than just one special day

We thank you Lord, for our mothers and for all their love and care
We thank you for all they have given us, and all the joy
we've shared.

We love your mothers so happy Mother's Day to you
May each day bring blessings, the whole year through.

—*Philip Boyd*

Sunrise at Sanibel

I watched the sun come up today.
Moving slowly at first,
As though the horizon was tugging at it,
Trying to keep the day from starting.

But finally, the big red ball broke free,
And began its daily ascent,
Using low streaky clouds like stair steps,
To climb the morning sky.

I stood in the warm shallow waters of the Gulf,
Gentle waves breaking around my ankles,
Watching sea gulls and pelicans flying out of the sun,
Passing overhead on the way to their fishing grounds.

I watched the sun as it turned from red to gold,
Until it began to hurt my eyes.
In the golden light, the beach began filling up,
With Sony-powered joggers and shell seekers.

The day has begun in earnest now,
And the peaceful moments of sunrise are gone,
Until tomorrow.

—*Joel Jackson*

Treasures

Stars glittering like diamonds on high,
Multicolored rainbows arching the sky.
A water fall cascading down the mountain side
Wearing a misty veil like a beautiful bride.
An undulating meadow in the balmy breeze,
Ruby-red apples clustered on leafy branches of trees.
Wavelets kissing the distant shore,
Then dashing back to the sea once more.
Pools reflecting the pale light of the moon,
Garnet cranberries on a sandy bog— soon
To be harvested and sent on their way.
Golden pumpkins clinging to the vine.
All these visions of loveliness are yours and mine.
Each one a delightful treasure for our
    enjoyment and pleasure.

—*Gladys E. White*

Alaska Seasons of Beauty

With four seasons so clear
My adventures just starting
From warmth emerging from the sun
To the cold lay sharpness of winters white snow
I settle down with fireplace blazing
Suddenly winter is here
Northern lights my companion and protector
A blanket of darkness upon me
I settle down with rubber boots
Suddenly spring is here
Melting snow covering the ground
Wild flowers breaking the warming earth
I settle down in my hammock
Suddenly summer is here
Fishing among the grazing moose
Eagles flying free in clear blue skies
I settle down with umbrella in hand
Suddenly fall is here
Rain guiding the golden falling leaves
All combine Alaska's seasons of beauty

—*Susan Hampton*

Sharing

You asked me, could I love you more?
My answer must be No.
I have reached the limits of mortal love,
There is no room left to grow.

I will share with you my sky.
My mountains we may share.
My river murmurs of my love.
My heart shall always care.

Mountains, rivers, moonbeams
Whisper of our love affair
And a lonesome star beyond a ridge
Is also ours to share.

Share my world with me
As we have done so many years
And our love will last forever
Through laughter or through tears.

Prairie grass will always grow
As trees in the wind will bend.
There will always be day's afterglow
And my love will never end.

—*Ed Manning*

Poverty

Life for me hasn't been very nice.
My average income is smaller than dice.
Sometimes I want to die,
Because I have no food; not even government pie.
I have a job as a street sweeper.
As you know, I can't afford a beeper.
My son wants to get in touch with his old friend Tyrone.
But the problem is, we can't afford a phone.
I can't think about a phone, when I need a good pair of jeans,
And my kids are praying it would rain green beans.
My family is poor you see,
And who would care about me.
As long as the governor has a fancy car,
He doesn't care how we are.

—*Ty Haygood*

"Respect"

My eyes have grown weary of the suffering and pain I have seen.
My body grows older with each obstacle I meet
I see myself turning grey in going through my troubles
I have yet to seek the respect that I should as to being a women
It seems to me that we are not still equal
But always taken advantage of, life is not a game
But an endless quest that has just begun
But still the respect I have seen none
I hate those who just take and never give
There selfishness just tears at me
The tears I cry don't mean a thing
I've been told that I am beautiful
That I am sexy
But never looked upon as a living human being
They just don't see how emotional I can be
Or how hard it is to stand my ground
They turn to play with my mind and expect me to be kind
Without respect there is no love
So women walk on side by side. And in return inside we die.

—*Terri J. Kubiak*

Memories of a Dear Friend

My dear friend has gone and left us for a better place.
    My dear friend will always live in my heart and
I know he will always love me.
    Where my dear friend is he can watch
over me and keep me safe forever.
    Sometimes I just sit in my
window and stare up into the sky and I can
almost see him staring back at me.
    When you uncover my thoughts
you will find out my dear friend is my
grandfather who passed away on Veterans day.
    My grandfather is in heaven now,
he can't get hurt but I can still feel hope
down here.

—*Katie Foglio*

Land

I have beheld many things
My exterior has been blood stained
I've been watered by bitter tears
Upon me many bullets have rained
I've felt the thud of bombs
My surface has been embraced by the fears of millions
I've seen their unlaughing eyes filled with horror and despair
I've heard the cries of warriors and conquers
I've listened to the prayers of heroes and foes
The crying of comrades to each other in shrill voices
I've heard the cheers of victory
The anguish of defeat
And under my surface lie those who fought and died for you
So I would be called free
Their obedience was also their death
All this is caused by senseless wars
Fought by the young and innocent

—*Stephen Davis*

Potato Bug

He slowly moves across the grass
My fair friend, the Potato bug,
So hopeless and yet so strong.
He turns into a small cute ball
When danger he senses near,
And when danger is gone
The hopeless potato bug, moves freely along his path.
My fair friend the potato bug
Moves so slowly, looking for a safe place to be,
But mistakenly he went into a hungry spiders cave.
My poor fair friend did not know that life is short,
And slowly moved into the hungry spiders cave.
My poor fair friend did not know that life is short,
And slowly moved into the hungry spider's cave.
Out of its cave came the satisfy spider,
The spider was content, but I could only cry.
My fair friend was gone, He did not know that life is short.
The path marked by my fair friend along his way
Is still printed on the grass, where my fair friend the
potato bug, once moved, so hopeless and yet so strong.

—*Karla V. Castillo*

Rings

Rings are around the sun and moon,
    And inside of the trees;
Some are made by angel people,
Some in factories.

Some rings hoop around the heart,
    From a lover or a friend,
But all are circles - now begin,
And now will ever end.

—*Michael Heintschel*

"A Walk Together"

You once came over to see me and we took a walk together down
    my favorite road.
How beautiful it was just being together again.
We shared so much together - the changing of the trees, the
    falling of the leaves, but most of all ourselves.
We walked for a few minutes and than we would stop.
We talked a little and than we would walk again.
I wished that it could have been for a little longer, but you
    said to me, "I have to go now."
Yes, the time went by so fast, but I understood that you had
    to go back.
I watched you get into your car and I felt sad that you
    were leaving.
You said good-bye to me and I stood there until your car was
    no longer in sight.
We will see each other someday soon and we will go for a walk
    together down my favorite road again.

—*Pats Green*

The Mighty Oak Tree

From so far away I can still see,
My favorite thing in the world — the mighty oak tree.
Because I give it all my problems — I think it is so big,
For it's not just some other little fig.
The mighty oak tree is a giant,
As it stood so tall and looked so defiant.
Over the many years; the rapid growth is shown,
Of the mighty oak tree that stands like a statue all alone.

So why does it have to be that they want to cut it down,
Even though for 75 years it's been around?
A new park with a pool and a playground is to be built —
Without the tree, the grass in the field will surely wilt.
The tree took away all my troubles,
It just pushed them away as if they were bubbles.
So now I beg and I plead,
Is this new park really a need?
The tree's removal is already starting.
For a big part of me will also be parting.
So I sadly say good-bye.
To the mighty oak tree that once soared so high in the sky.

—*Vivian Chan*

Chords in the Melody of Life

I'm surrounded by voices—gentle and warm
My fragile being can sense no harm
Perfect love for this one instant
Pianissimo chords for a tiny infant

I wander through years of dim candle light
Crushing blossoms and stars to prove my might
Beating drums and clanging bells reveal the truth
Crescendo chords announce my youth

Life's a mystery that I must solve
In robust pursuit I find my resolve
There's a distant chorus of One omnipresent
Staccato chord for this adolescent

Light of the years add wisdom to my vision
What's right or wrong is a cultured decision
Applied by degrees for a cherished result
Harmonious chords for this adult

My efforts to 'become' and how 'twas achieved
Reflect sinew and morals and what I believed
Ready to be judged by my courage and my fears
Andante chords for my sunset years

—*Colleene Bradshaw*

A Friend of Man

I'm near a forest where I dwell,
My friends are trees I love so well,
They tower over me day and night,
Protecting me with all their might,

They cast shadows oh, so tall,
I love them in summer most of all,
They groom themselves with loving care,
Bearing nests of robins in their hair.

In the Autumn they change their dress for you,
Transforming themselves in brilliant hue,
In the winter they stand so stark and grey,
Awaiting for another summer day,

They make another enchanting scene,
When they again don robes of green,
Dear friends, it makes me sad to see,
When you're cut down for posterity,

You were created for all mankind,
For man has different needs of you in mind,
Without you this world would be sad, indeed,
For you furnish us with every living need.

—*Edith Madge*

My God's Hands

My God's hands reach down and out
My God's hands gives comfort and strength.
My God's hands never stop holding on.
My God's hands are very strong and powerful.
My God's hands are everywhere.
My God's hands heal the sick,
comfort the weak, touch the cripple
and heal the broken hearted
My God's hands are open to all
Who come to him everyday,
every hour, all the time thru love.
My God's hands creates the beauty
all around for us to see.
O! How my God's hands creates
such splendor.
The touch of a flower, a beautiful,
Fall day, a winter wonderland and spring
and so much more.
My God's hands calm the storms
and God's hands can touch every heart thru love.

—*Fay E. Stumphf*

Plastic Flowers

I walked down the street that rainy day,
My hands in my pocket with my very last pay!
Twenty years at the book store had come to an end,
My whole life's work, my dearest friend.
As I turned the corner, I saw up ahead,
A pile of junk and a rusty old bed.
Strewn all around a big vacant lot,
And some plastic flowers in a plastic pot.
There were a dozen blooms and more buds wound tight,
Of cold hard plastic, but that was alright.
I took them home and dried them well.
And all the buds began to swell.
As the hard plastic opened wide,
I couldn't believe what was hidden inside!
Stocks! Bonds!, fifty or more!
Worth enough to buy my own Book Store.
Which I did buy, the way.
And flourish there happily, even today!
Me and my plastic flowers in their plastic pot,
Never more to be abandoned in life's vacant lot!

—*Barbara Ashbeck*

Untitled

Slowly I descend down the stairs.
My hands slide gracefully along
the railing. My eyes are open; wide and huge.
I proceed towards the den. The short distance
seems to grow in length with every step. Finally
I reach the den. My hands, now on the doorway,
are stiff not wanting to go on. The thunder
is unbearably loud and the lightning is
blinding; shedding light with its flashes
across the room. The furniture in the den
takes on the shape of something other than
furniture in the short flashes of lightning.
I pray it is only my over active imagination.
I rub my eyes softly and open them slowly again.
"Hola Senora Simper!" the maid
says as she opens the curtains to a bright new day.

—*Michelle Canales*

Memories

Can you hear my laughter, and the joy of
my happiness.
Can you hear the echo of my name, day and night
it's still the same.

I have knocked at your door, but you will not answer
three times I have tried.

Can you hear my footsteps, as I walk away.
In my memories I hold you tight, never
letting you go.

Three times I have knocked, but not to your door
but within your heart.

The memories was holding you with me, with the
laughter we have shared.

The happiness was in our names, being echoed
to each other.

As I walked away it was the only thing, I had
to hold on too.

Now hear my echo as I cry, leaving the pain in my heart.
The day came when you decided to part......
Can you hear my laughter now.

—*Jesus Huerta*

You Left Me Behind

It's hard believing you left me behind
My heart and life tied up in a bind
You left me in darkness, out on my own
I was your little girl, not yet full grown
I hear you sweet voice all through the night
It flows through my body and fills it with light
Then I wake up and the nightmare begins
I live it each day over and over again
I starts with the pain of seeing you each day
Ending up with you always going away
My lips long to speak, but no I wouldn't dare
These feelings inside are more than you could bear
The night air carries my sad melody
If you heard it would you even think about me
I lived my life reciting your name
I can't live without you, it's just not the same
My love for you will last forever
Even if we'll never be together
It's hard believing you left me behind
My name must be in the back of your mind

—*Jennifer Nutt*

You Are My friend Today As I Am Yours

Sweet and filling are the words of encouragement,
my heart expands to its depths absorbing your kindness.
My life trembles with the joy that God has sent,
though your innermost feeling of care to me is selfless.
Reaching out to the needy describes what you meant,
honoring those on all levels expresses the beauty of your
intent. Thank you, my dear friend, thank you, your love has
reached my heart, I appreciate this moment of your sacrifice
to share a sample of your art. For giving to others takes
work a talent which few boldly share, it takes commitment
and lots of patience and love to express the word called care.
Take a moment to share a thought with me, a thought spoken
before. "Each one should use whatever gift he or she has
received to serve others, faithfully administering God's grace
in its various forms." You my dear friend are one of those
in a million who have taken the time to care, thank you, my
friend, thank you for the love you are willing to share. You
have given me much energy and hope today, from all the
wonderful things you hade to say. I know what it means to
receive and give, so through your words of encouragement I
will live.

—*David P. King*

Apart From You

The rain comes down
My heart is heavy
I wear a frown
Because you've left me

You're gone forever
I miss you so
We're no longer together
I must let go

Your image fills my heart and soul
Your memory, it lingers
You've gone on a one-way toll
My grasp on you, slipped through my fingers

But I know one day we'll meet again,
On a rainbow far beyond
And we'll join together hand in hand
And that's when our hearts will bond

—*Rebecca Ariel Hoffberg*

Inner Child

As I journey into the past,
My heart opens up to the love I received.
As my mind expands, I begin to take a stand
When my eyes look out into the world
I find them set on a little girl.
Short and petite
With many riches at her feet.
Waiting on a dream
Dreamt many times
She knows it as well as a nursery rhyme.
Not a thing to stand in her way
And with determination she can proudly say,
"Momma never lied when she said I'll be great someday."
With a bible in her hand, she takes a stand
And with pride in her eyes she can now convey,
There's nothing better than a momma's pride.

—*Marcia Washington*

Untitled

To those who measure their love by pain
and their pleasure with guilt
shed not one solitary tear
for it would be enough to drown
their already sinking soul

—*Celeste*

Loving Sea Gull in Flight

Loving you is my downfall.
My heart waits patiently for an expression of your love.
You have built a walled compound around your heart and allow
no one to enter.
You have imprisoned your heart and keep love at a distance.
Like a sea gull, I fly above your walls, circling and
waiting.
Time and love will crumble the walls you have built.
You will then see me, an old and tired sea gull perched upon
your crumbled walls.
Waiting to express her love to you.

—*Linda Maricle*

"The Last Fight"

Out of the house, like a thief in the night....
My heart was pounding, and I felt such a fright!
I was running away, in fear of my life,
A victim of domestic violence, a mother and wife.
You promised you'd change, so I returned twice before,
But the abuse continued, now I promise myself, no more!
No more fear, shame, guilt, or belief in your lies,
No more sleepless nights, nightmares, anguish or alibis.
I've gained my sense of self, though I lost all I had,
But I've also won freedom, peace of mind, and I'm so glad!
I'm ready to control my own life, to take care of myself,
And I don't have to look back, because I have God's help.
For it was He who guided me, as I prayed that dreadful
night, God help me protect me, for this is The Last Fight!

—*Rita A. Patterson-Nash*

Goodbye

To you alone I told everything.
My hopes, my fears, my life long dreams.
You were all I cared about,
never forget,
more than life itself.
And this is why I must say goodbye
to all the pain and tears,
all the things we've shared together,
the memories through the years.
None of this is taken in vein
but with the love we shared.
As I write this,
I think only of you,
and now as the time draws near,
I say farewell to all the hurt,
and everything else I've feared

—*Lynne Lewis*

Portrait

Gray as a cloud,
misty rain there-in.
Obscured visions and untruths.
To loath the path taken.

Anarchy of the grotesque.
Those that laugh heartily,
at or failures, our confusion.
Fodder for the worms... consumers of life.

The river flows relentlessly
as we clutch and grab... hoping.
Our Judas waiting to betray.
Life's blood and ebb tide.

The foul winds bloated with pestilence,
as the four horsemen bicker over the carcass.
What was once happiness,
Now is fraught with despair.

—*John Horoszewski*

My Husband Forever

Now that he's gone, I can plainly see,
My Husband was the other half of me.
He made me laugh, never cry. He made me smile, never sigh.
Twelve years of his life he shared with me.
This wonderful love, from the other half of me.

He can't return to me, but I can go to him.
Must, in fact. It's nature's way.
He made dying seem so easy. I slept, God called, he went.
I awoke and found the other half of me gone.

I weep and hurt deep within at the very core of me,
to see him gone; but just over the vale where I can't see,
His friends and family must have cried out
in pure joy, to see him arriving.

His weak physical heart betrayed him here.
But he arrived over there with all of the love
of me in his heart intact.
And when my life here comes to an end, I shall join him there.

My Husband, my lover, my companion, my friend.
And we will live again where life has no pain and no end.
And forever, we will be together. Sweetheart, I love you.

—*Margie Ruth Robertson*

The Painter

Paint a beautiful picture in the art gallery of my mind,
My life is yours, I am fully what you make of me.
Shape my soul with the breath of life,
Highlight my features with your sharpened hands and color
Me with imagination.
I am, myself, a plaster figure, sculptured with your eyes,
Yet, filled with the emotions of nature, only to ponder how
Excellent the marble of human soul which is freely painted
With the tip of your brush.
Mix the colors of vivid love and splash the sweetened aroma on
This unworthy statue.
May my eyes be the sparkle of the heavens and my will the
Strength of the mountains.
Let my life be the rays of the rainbow which hang over the
Dew lit grass, and the song of the joyous sparrows in the
Presence of the dawn.
You are the color of my life, the master of the pallet of my
Soul - I am your art and you are my painter -
Paint in me the picture of love,
Hang me for the world to see.

—*Wade Myers*

Gettysburg

I am here at Gettysburg
My name is called unknown
On every side the battles surge,
The guns spit fire and death is sown
I see some mother's sons
Falling from the line
They cry in pain, their end has come...

...another day, another time
We might have known peace
Hark! The victor's cry is heard
Now this bloody siege will cease
When the guns are stilled at Gettysburg

All is quiet now at Gettysburg
And we sleep in shallow grave.
No more to hear loved ones or the kindly words
Of Abe Lincoln as he speaks of the brave
Living and dead who struggled here,
Of our faith in God, in America and in liberty
That these shall not perish but long endure
Beyond this battlefield, beyond this century.

—*Harry J. Dean*

As Spring Blows In

I face the window.
My outstretched hands reach to open a season
waiting outside.

As I grope with the glass
I retreat into every other year at this time.

I fling open the window
I fling open my mind

The wind rushes in it rushes in and mingles, dances,
mixes with winds from a thousand years ago.

I stand paralyzed, entranced by the moving pictures
in my head being pushed around in the gust.

Some lift me up, let me hang, help me float
others rattle my skull, shake me, as they're thrown
against my inner walls.

And on the new breeze rides a promise
a promise that whispers of things anew
a promise that next year I'll remember nothing but this one
that finally the past will stop coming through my window.

I nearly faint from the force
as spring blows in.

—*K. K. Watts*

Christmas

Christmas is not the same now that you're gone
My pain and sorrow grows more and more each year
I just can't seem to let go
Time will not heal the pain inside my heart
I remember Christmas mornings with mom and pop
The train going around the tree the train you built just for me
How can I just let that go I wish I could tell you how it hurts
me so, to think you could leave my hopes and dreams missing
more and more, year after year Christmas used to be a romantic
time for sleighs, reindeers and Santa's bells, if I listen real
hard into the distance I can still hear them chime
Seems so long ago I sat on your lap I thought it was immortal
the love we shared that was long ago another place-
another time the pictures and memories in my mind
I wonder why you could be so unkind how can I ignore a feeling
so strong especially at Christmas, a time of goodwill and cheer
Oh how I miss you because you're not here
We could never put behind all those things so unkind
It's not easy to forgive and forget though you've forgotten me
I feel very sad, I can't have you here at christmas time, Dad

—*T. C. Alan*

Someone

I've only wanted someone to share
my love and knowledge with one that I care
the lonely times are no delight
in an empty bed, night after night
a sexual act, it need not be
the closeness is, as sensual to me
embraced together at the twilights end
is quite a comforting dividend
happy times are numerous abound
but being solo they can't be found
with no companion, my life's adrift
desperately needing a heart uplift
perhaps someday a breath of sigh
for its all in knowing, someone's close by

—*Tom Fiedler*

160

My Love

(Dedicated to my husband Bert on his Birthday)
My poems are just words on paper,
    Any fool could place them there.
But it is the only way I can let
    You know just how much this fool can love.

My love the lead, as it caresses the paper,
    Each line is defined as you take me in
Your arms and hold me tight.

I hope you can see the love in my poems,
    Because what I put in them is
From my heart.

The bold lines show how hard love hits me
    The straight lines means my love is true.
I know I will miss you when you are away.

There will be times when I feel alone
    And then I think about our love
Put it in writing and I will wait patiently,
    knowing you will come home.

As this poem comes to an end
    Just know my love for you
Is deep my heart.
        —*Liz Swift*

And I Proclaim.."How Great You Are"

In my aloneness I walk in the rain...there, no one will notice
my tears, the sky is so dark...it is a reflection of my soul at
this very moment, the clouds, hurried motion, like my thoughts,
are without order, going to and fro, like Autumn leaves played
by the wind. And I call on my Angels to take all this bundle
to you.... Oh Lord... For you understand all my fears... You
that sees all my tomorrows... The only one that cares when the
unbearable pain... That overwhelming hurt creeps in and
smothers my heart... Then... I hear... That unspoken voice..
The ruffling of Angel wings deep in my heart... at that perfect
moment it seems to be quoting verses that talk directly to my
sadness and are needed so badly... and full of awe... I wonder..
where or when... did I learn these truths that tenderly are
guiding me through the path... or is it you, oh Lord... holding
me close to your heart once again? I know you will make a way
once more, but you leave me free to choose, many times,
unwisely, to stumble over and over.... But as I stand before
you... my savior dear, with a grateful heart... I proclaim
"How Great You Are."
        —*Ligia Zeledon Lloyd*

Untitled

As I sit here in darkness
    My thoughts go back to yesterday
To a past full of hope, love and ambition
    Happiness was my only worry
No longer do I dream at night
    There are no visions left to pursue
Sadness is my only friend
    Loneliness, my true companion
Maybe someday, a touch of light
    Will brighten my dark world
For now until the arrival of that day
    I will live each moment in destitute
Enjoying my obscure world
    Which even though saddens me
In a strange, yet magical way
    Keeps me in peace with myself
        —*Minerva Diaz*

Memory Lane

As I sat beside my window pane,
my thoughts had wandered down Memory Lane.
Joy and laughter were in the air,
along with love for all the share.

I remember my school days — oh, so well!
And how to keep a secret, never to tell.
I had a true friend through my growing years,
who had helped to remedy all my fears.

He was always there, right by my side —
until God had taken him for Heavens' guide.
Life does have its tragedy and sometimes it's pain,
but it also has many good gifts to gain.

Ah yes, back then you knew who you were,
not like today where common sense is a blur!
Faith in God was number one on the list,
and church on Sunday was never missed.

Caring and sharing brought no remorse,
it came most natural without any force.
If today I were granted just one small wish —
it would be to erase, that word known as "selfish."
        —*Patricia A. Walsh*

Dawn's Impression

The fragrance of eve has left. Crisp clear air awaken's new day.
Myself, a blade of grass sprouted by do! Another mountain,
viewed from low, cotton candy clouds as I seek. Various
differences from yesterday, water's wet; dry is hay. Sky is fat;
ground is slim. What was a phrase, is now a whim. Silence blares
where loudness stunned. Wall's deep and dense, shatter with
intent, allowing flight to engage like a seasoning to flavor the
age. Time is no longer a chore. Life's arm's embrace. Present
becomes pleasant instead of confusing and worn. The new day's
sun illuminate's my darkness, releasing today's shadows never
casting on another tomorrow. Today is mine, full in it's
approach, destined to be what Thy will.
        —*Mark Leon Miller*

Blue

Blue is the color of this ocean we ride
Myself on the seas, and you, as you wait for the tide.

I feel your blue when I lay down to sleep
I taste your tears as you silently weep.

Is the great blue between us as deep as your heart?
How wide is the water that keeps us apart?

It's as great as the ocean; yet as short as a touch
When you're locked in my arms that love you so much.

I had a blue dream and there I was shown
How you hold tightly your pillow and cry all alone.

I sat there beside you in the darkness so blue
And kissed the tears on your face, if only you knew

I held you so strong and loved you so deep
'Till your tears went away and you fell softly asleep.

But as you wept, you never knew I was there
I wanted to tell you, to tell you I care.

So, until I come home
When you cry all alone

When blue is around
....feel my kiss, above the blue sound.
        —*Kevin Hempe*

161

Evolution of Jr. Boy

Born "Joseph Edward Moss Jr.", he was called, "Jr. Boy." The
name "Joe Moss" was the regular name by school days. He
studies the names of poets and great people from Homer and Poe
to Emerson and Angelou. He decided to hunt for a universal
sound, he could use as a poet that would be remembered if
heard the same as the impact of the picture you just can't
forget after seeing just once. He began with the name
Graveyard moss the downiest brother writer in the world as his
hook on name. Names of value he thought, Morgan, Rocketfellow,
Grant, Sherman, Lee, Lincoln, John Brown, Malcolm X,
Gerronamo,
Washington, Chief Joseph, Sequoia, Abraham, Joseph, Elijah,
Rama, Christna, Shiva, Ike, Churchill, Einstein, Ghandi, Bogart,
Santana, Martin Luther, Iotallo, Reagan, Alex Haley, what
images names flash in the mind. He decided to honor his
ancestors native Indians Pan American name "Tender Heart", his
African Ashanti Ghanaian name "Nanakojo" and "Ikando" became his
writing name than "Jr. Boy" prayed to God to help him be the
best moss he could be

—*Nanakojo Ikando Moss*

The Meadow

Imagine a beautiful meadow
Nature has its own secrets there
A variety of wildflowers for a border
And a few white daisies to spare

The blue flax is waving its greeting
Serenely red poppies burst forth
It's like walking in a beautiful dreamland
And the breeze has come from the north
A pink dogwood is planted on the edge of
the meadows fair land.

—*JoAnn Cashero*

"I Don't Know"

Why did she leave! I will
never know. Nights I lie awake thinking
was it me, or something I did.
Often I ask myself, does she
love me, or, do I look like her, but
still get the same answers, over and
over, I don't know.

Could the love of one man take
something from me I so cherish
the most, leaving nothing behind but
a frail and fragile ghost, I ask
myself, I don't know.

Love of a Mother and daughter
I guess never really disappear, but
still again I ask myself will we
ever get back the trust we had, the
love we shared the feelings that
were there ... I don't know.

—*Mona Wilkinson*

Upon Eternity's Wings

I stand before you naked,
my soul bleeding,
heal me with your goodness.
Let your love lift me upon eternity's wings.
My pain bespeaks tomorrow's good tidings.
My heart quickens at the approach of your gentle caress.
Like the mighty oak I await the woodsman's axe.
Catch me; hold me;
press me close to your breast.
Surround me as gentle night envelopes all lovers.
In your love I am healed, and in its rapture I am renewed.

—*Alexander Sabatino Jr.*

A Lone Star Quilt

As a young girl I decided, a quilt to make
  Never thinking how hard or how long it would take.
I started on a journey of stitches that took hours and hours
  On a "Lone Star" quilt embellished with flowers.

Hour after hour I pieced on that quilt
  Pricked fingers and all - I began to wilt.
As I suddenly realized my corners were not square
  Gone were my dreams of a blue ribbon at the fair.

I snipped and I tucked trying to repair
  Each corner of beauty with utter despair
Into the trunk I hid it with a sigh
  Giving up my dream - and trying not to cry.

Forty years later I brought forth my dream
  Easing and tucking and working each seam.
I had picked up the pieces and started again
  It began to take form looking better than then.

You don't have to look close the errors to see - yet.
  It is now for my daughter's family, a warm coverlet.
The quilt never won a blue ribbon at the fair,
  But was accepted by all with sweet loving care.

—*Mary Lou Smith*

Never Underestimate

Never underestimate the power of a woman.
Never underestimate the power of a man.
Never underestimate the power of a guy.
Never underestimate the power of a gal.
Never underestimate the power of your boyfriend.
Never underestimate the power of your girlfriend.
Never underestimate the power of a baby.
Never underestimate the power of it later.
Never underestimate the power of love.
Never underestimate the power of above.
Never underestimate the power of an dove.
Never underestimate it.
Never underestimate it.
Never underestimate the power of love.

—*Donnamaria Smith*

Spring

I look around and I see,
New buds on that once bare tree,
Eggs are hatching left and right,
Baby birds are trying to take off in flight,
The grass has a fresh green glow,
And I no longer see any snow,
Children are running out to play,
Mother says no shorts till May,
Breathe in all that fresh clear air,
Signs of spring are everywhere.

—*Emily Gellings*

For Love

What the future holds no one knows
Life is a mystery in the land of summer snows
We choose one truth for honors sake
Then change our minds over our sad mistake
Now while jungles crumble to the earth
New plans for destruction are given birth
When weapons fire and the dust settles once again
On the battlefield lies the bodies of our young men
Where has hope gone in the land of the brave
This sad land where politics make a man a slave
One cries peace one cries war
Can we cry for love no more!

—*Rachael G. Knight*

"I'm Cocaine"

I don't have no heart, I'm your worst
   nightmare, I'm cocaine;
I'll have you stealing for me,
   lying for me, even killing for me;
Don't worry though, I'll give you
   something in return;
I'll give you a fast high,
   I'll try to give you enough energy to
   keep you going, but you'll have to
   keep using me, and my price is high;
When you've grown to like me,
   and you will,
You'll want to use me all the time;
You'll be moody, depressed,
   depressed because all your money
   will be spent on me;
No, you really don't get much in return;
I can take your life;
I'm cocaine
I can kill!

    —*Laura Cirino*

Days of Old

Let us think back to the days of old,
No greater story had ever been told.

It's about a man who went to the cross,
So no one's soul would have to be lost.

He laid in the tomb two days and three nights,
everyone thoughts he had taken his flight.

But early that morning he rose like a flower,
He walked the earth and declared all power.

This man is Jesus, I'm talking about,
I can't count the times he's brought me out.

He walked the water, he split the sea,
He said to the world, please believe in me.

He went back to his father, and sat on his throne.
He said I'll be there to welcome you home.

    —*Regina Stigger*

"Friends"

A friend is someone you can be open with
No matter what the topic may be.
You can be yourself, whether it is childish,
Or whether it is all grown-up.
Love is shared and tears may have fallen,
The truth to that is, that is what makes a friendship
grow and not whither.
Friends strengthen your weaknesses and
makes you strong in your duties.
Courage is given from two on both sides.
They stick up for you when the chips are down,
helping you throughout the times of trouble.
Always keeping faith in you are what true friends do.
Friendships last from here on out,
And whether you are old or young
new friendships are always welcome.
Friends allow you to open your minds and hearts,
to let all the feelings and ideas flow.
Friendships provide inspirations and add to this wonderful feeling
   of joy.
A sense of security and watchfulness is a blanket over you
With friendships of all kinds.

    —*Shelley A. Reinhardt*

Our Medical Center

OFOMC is one of the best
No matter where you go here in the Midwest.

The facility is a teaching and healing place
The doctors, the trainees, the staff are every
   color, creed and race.

The doctors and nurses have such caring and loving ways
It is such a haven for rest you don't mind what
   you have to pay.

The others work here whether they clean, keep records
   or volunteer
They do their best to give you cheer.

When you have to go somewhere else because they
   have the only equipment that is needed
It makes you appreciate what we have here and you take heed.

Whatever your needs, they will be met
But only at this place that is so well kept.

Ask the Lord to watch over this facility and over you
When you pray He knows that you are true blue.

These few lines are in appreciation of the way I feel
For the many times I and others went home healed.

    —*Ruth E. Bettenhausen*

Letting Go

Each day I can feel the hope of living slipping away,
   No more do I welcome the dawning of another day.
My friends have started looking down their noses at me,
   They are no longer there to help me in hard times.
   It's much easier for them to talk behind my back,
   Easier for them to turn their backs and walk away.
   My emotions are very jumbled up inside my head,
My heart strains at bursting with one more broken heart.
   Guys tend to walk all over me at every chance,
Allowing others to influence their thoughts and desires.
   Not listening to what you want to say,
   Even if they are the ones asking the questions.
   My life seems to be slipping down the drain,
I'm not even sure if I want to plug the hole to stop it.
Somehow it would be much easier to let it all flow out,
   To pass into the next world of no worries or pains.
   Never to feel the pain of a broken heart again,
   Never to have to worry about waking up to another
     miserable day.

    —*Angela Coleman*

Hot And Cold

Death is inevitable, I well know.
No more ice and snow.
Afraid of falling on the ice,
or sweltering heat, that hurt my feet.
Yes my feet, hot and sweaty
smelling too.
When death takes me over that hill.
Will I recognize my loved ones
gone before? Most were adults
when they went, to that meeting over the hill.
Except my brother Fredy, he was only eight.
Will I know him? Will he still be
A little boy? The somber brown eyed
big brother that I loved?
How I look forward to seeing
My loved ones, gone before

BUT NOT YET!
    —*Lucille H. Heinekamp*

Untitled

I'm inside everyone
no one can run from me
no matter how hard you try and deny me
I'm there
I come in all colors
for all races
I'm judged by my many faces
for many reasons I exist
deep feelings, past experiences
there always has to be one
I'm the basis for some killings,
robberies, riots
I'm indestructible - since the beginning of time
people may try to stop me
but there's one thing they don't know
they will teach their children about me
subtlety is the key
people won't know they do it
and that ignorance is what keeps me alive.

—*Nikki Peddada*

Why Do I Love Thee?

Why do I love thee?
No one knows, but me.
I love thee for your eyes
Your beautiful, baby-blue eyes.
I love thee for your smile
That always makes me wild.
I love thee for your laughter
That has gotten me through the tough times.
I love thee for your kindness and generosity
That always shows your incredible side
of responsibility.
I love thee for your gentleness
That always seems to show off your careness.
And most importantly,
I love thee for your love for me.
My love, this is why I love thee
Because, you see my love,
I know you are the only one for me
And you will always be.

—*Donna Fields*

Holding On

No wild romance,
    No petty flirt,
        I want something real,
            But I know—love hurts.

There'll be times when I'm lost,
    When it's you I can't seek,
        Or the days I feel strong,
            And it's you that feels weak.

I'll try to be there,
    All of my life,
        But I'm not so sure,
            I could ever be your wife.

You're the kind of person,
    Who could love many,
        I'm the kind of girl,
            Who would give you every penny.

So I wish you would listen—
    Our love is not strong,
        And I just want to know,
            Should I hold on?

—*Melissa Inman*

The Psychic Son

Was there a clue, or just a hunch?
No! you just imagine what is true
what, you say?
Yes, what is real or true
and if you have a good imagination
these visions usually turn out right
yes, sure in your dreams!
No! in your dreams you envision
a reality too daring to live
I don't remember my dreams
that's OK, some people can't remember who they are
can you imagine what you want to be?
no! what good would that do me?
well, Einstein once said
that imagination is more important than knowledge

—*Richard R. West*

Love

Love is a special thing that comes straight from the heart.
Nobody really knows when it really starts.
Your always expressing your feelings to people who careless.
Giving, sharing, and caring you know your hearts the best.
Hoping people understand your problems, hopes and fears.
Then you find that special one who wipes away the tears.
This special one you'll find, real early in life.
Hoping and praying you'll soon be his wife.
Giving him everything you possibly could.
He'd turn around, spit on the ground, and tell you you're no good.
Special feelings you share from deep down inside.
Hoping everything he told you wasn't a lie.
You kiss him goodbye hoping he'd stay.
But when you fall in love, they always go away!

—*Shannon Milka*

North-Wind Season

Rain showers and raw gusts of wind, October brings the
    North-wind season.
Foaming waves swell and brake under a murky sky: no shore,
    no sun, no time;
The fog is heavy, the gale is hissing. I feel the throbbing
    sea swish and gurgle
Against the pier; the waters of desire, bulging with the ocean,
    push in their tides.
My blood is pounding loud and fast.

Disheveled hair, seaweeds, and sand; the probing wind explores
    my salty skin.
Rain amidst the storm encounters passion, love is gambling on
    the thrill of life.
His thighs, warm and wet like restless fish swimming in a deep,
    mysterious sea,
Get hold of mine and make them dance. Howling winds whirl and
    rage; memory
And yearning recede after the last sea burst.

—*Antoinette Pimentel*

Paradise

A special fantasy island is where I go,
My mind drifts away to a place without snow,
The sun's warmth is shining down on the land,
A beautiful scenery filled with palm trees and sand,
Coconuts fill the trees up above,
The sand that I lay on is soft as a dove,
It's never too warm, always just right,
The cool breeze comforts the sun's warm light,
I wish I could stay in this land full of spice,
But I come back to reality from a dream of paradise!

—*Monica Hough*

The Connection

I've never known a man so similar in heart,
Not afraid to stand alone, be separate, apart.
When he speaks, he echoes my heart.

Our thoughts run parallel.
Barriers fall down, and we become one in soul.

I stand afraid of such a precious connection,
Dars't I take it for granted, and lose it.

A fragile thing?
Maybe not. My emotions waiver.
What do I want?

Complete devotion?
Complete understanding?
Complete acceptance?

What can I give?

Loyalty, love, sensuality.
Intellectual exchange of ideas.
Appreciation of this connection.
        —*Dianne Wilkins*

My Unborn Child

I know you are there but I can't feel or see you. You have
not completely formed, for you are still young. You are mine
and I love you more than you'll every know. I'm sorry we will
never have the chance to meet, to run together in the park and
swing in the swings. I'm sorry I won't have the chance to
watch you grow and begin a family of your own, but such is
life, or is it?

It hurts me to think I will never be able to see your face,
or touch your tiny hands and feet; I don't even know if you're
a male or female. All I know is that I love you very much and
I'm sorry for what I must do. Now I must go through the mental
pains to take the small bit of life from your precious soul.

Please forgive me for not giving you the chance to see how
beautiful life can be.

I love you my Unborn Child.
        —*Gwendolyn B. Scott*

Reeds

Sway, and flow
not giving in or breaking to
but bending with
allowing, and accepting
staunch and staid walls will break
where a slim reed only flexes
go with it not against
for enough slim and slender trees will slow the wind,
and enough reeds may change the current
you may bend and be pushed
but do not break
eventually another reed will grow
another, another, and another
head to head conflict causes conflict,
violent upheaval begets violent upheaval
in going directly against we risk
becoming that which is hated
change comes slowly, so stay and sway
eventually an ebb will come, it must
for the reeds are becoming more numerous now
        —*Michael P. O'Connor*

Fog

It comes on furry footed paws,
not pausing at street lights for recollection,
before rolling, moving on.

Above
the grey-blue blanket shrouds
the land, the lights, the ground.
Below
the damp-wet expands,
engulfs and swallows without eating.
Blinding,
without obscuring
the hand before my face.

Out beyond the senses,
sounds roll in on muffled feet.

City's noises damped wetly.

Cautious, I venture beyond my hand.
I grope.
    trustingly,
        for my destination.
        —*A. Howard Reed*

Sounds Of The Night

As I lie in my bed, and all seems quiet.
Not so, if I listen.
I can hear the creaking of the house.
Trying to settle and disband the cares of the day.
And to tell me it will protect me.
Listening again, I hear the quiet breathing of
    my loved ones.
All is settled for the night, and I close my
    eyes to sleep.
But no, my ears pick up the heartbeat of the city.
Screaming fire engines dashing to save a home.
The wailing sound of an ambulance, rushing to
    save a life.
Silently in my prayers I call to God, that it
    won't be too late.
Sounds of a dog's barking, to scare away a prowler.
Meowing of a cat calling for a mate.
I close my eyes again, and with a final prayer,
Ask God to let me awaken to the sounds of the new
    day.
        —*Amelia L. Rogers*

Unholy Crafts XXIV

Stranger places men seem to consider,
Not to mention, trips to space and even,
Touching worlds unknown appearing hither;
Yet, these dreamy places none have proven.
Gazing high above the dark horizon,
I've discerned a tiny boulder gliding
Like a foreign vehicle in ozone
Layers of space fading fast and dying.
Nothing, but a trace of man in orbit,
And the swelling clouds in acid showers
Stunt the land we tremble to inhabit,
Leaving empty dreams in wreath of flowers.
    One should now ask what about the races,
    Of unholy crafts in sacred places.
        —*Paul Blake*

Who Dunnit

He sits alone in the den of his fine home,
Nothing but quiet fills the room,
No noise but the rain falling on the roof;
Suddenly, he hears the phone,
This resulted in his impending doom,
The phone rang, he answered and poof;

He was dead, murdered by an anonymous caller,
The call triggered a mechanism in the receiver,
A poisonous gas was released killing the intended victim;
Who did this? Whoever did it did not falter,
A business partner, jealous lover, wife, not beneath her,
The victim of the crime didn't know what hit him;

Someone who had access, motive, and killer instinct,
Knowledge of his habits, hatred and contempt,
The suspects are many, but all alibied 'cept a few;
The evidence and motive are outlined and succinct,
The killer performed the task on the first attempt,
Only one person had opportunity and utilized what he knew;

Phone tampering, knowing just when to call hatred, jealousy,
Pointed to but one person, the butler, who did it zealously.

—*Ronnie D. Senciboy, Sr.*

A Child's Last Journey

Come my child, take hold of thy hand,
    now it's time to leave, this lonely land.

We travel over distant hill, up to the clouds
    that the angels fill.

So say goodbye to mother and dad,
    don't look back and don't be sad.

For heaven awaits where the angels play,
    where no darkness of night, but always
    the light of day.

The clouds your playroom, the sunbeams your
    loom, to weave carpets of flowers bursting
    in bloom.

—*Ronald Burnell*

In Memory Of The Pilgrims

On new England's rugged headlands
Now where peaceful Plymouth lies
There they built their rough log cabins
Beneath the cold forbidden skies

And so their governor William Bradforth
In the gladness of his heart
To praise God for all his mercy
Set a special day apart

To thank God for all our blessings
Our dear families and friends
In all the world for good relations
In God's great and beautiful nation

So now when in late November
Our thanksgiving feast is spread
'Tis that same time honored custom
Of the pilgrims long since dead

—*Edward Stoecklein*

O Parachute

One thousand feet above the earth,
O Parachute, for what it's worth,
Don't streamer on me lest I die:
For that would make my Mother cry.

Up here in this cloud dotted blue,
We're all we have, me and you.
I must depend upon your suspension lines
That have helped me down a dozen times.

O Parachute, you must bear me out,
Forgive me if I have a doubt.
But carelessness cannot come to play
On this our destined jumping day.

There are only seconds to the ground
Once you and I are airborne bound.
Every trip is one more test:
O Parachute, we must be the best.

—*Janice N. Chapman*

"The Dam"

The stream once flowed free
O'er sand, gravel and stone.

Dripping springs meandered clear
Neath stately Pecan and Cottonwood,
Foliage green feeding wildlife near.

Our Forefathers in wagons came
To fish, swim, camp near by,
Hunting squirrels, deer, other game.

Joyful children splashed at play
Diving and swimming about,
Wiling the sunlit hours away.

Those fun times were long ago,
For now stagnant pools abound.
A Dam above stopped the flow.

Once liquid clear water, now murky green,
Poisoned death all about,
No living thing can be seen.

Man and beast have fled,
The waters cease to flow;
The Dam blocked stream is dead...

—*Maxwell Gathings*

Our Passing Years

Recapturing those golden days with clowns parading by,
Of candied apples and cracker Jack, a wonder to the eye,
Those crowded beaches in summer heat which cool in evening
mist, how quickly time has hastened by, in firmness I resist.

Remembering the gingham dress accompanied by her smile,
A soft rich glow of innocence, my heart she did Beguile,
Where is she now? I oft' remark, that wondrous first romance,
Might she to ponder my whereabouts and present circumstance?

What sleekness do my eyes behold, just hear her engine purr,
The body sheen from elbow grease, 'twas worth it all for her,
A surge of freedom from restraint that filled my heart with joy
Free-wheeling with mobility no bicycle could employ.

Oh what grand moments I recall from neighbors rich with care,
No matter what the sickness was your chicken soup was there,
Now marred with boarded windows, filled with notable debris,
'Tis hard to finally realize it's just a memory.

For all that has gone by before or surely yet to come,
The harrowed price that must be paid by all and not just some,
Yet to relive our passing years provides nostalgic rhyme,
A final tribute to our past that's not erased with time.

—*Jerry L. Potter*

Tita's Lament

Hana, my beloved home
of rare beauty and tranquil surroundings,
of contented faces and gentle hearts,
land of my birth, my exit.

You and many others settled here,
emerged from a foreign origin,
journeyed in search of a peaceful lifestyle,
welcomed, undisturbed.

In this time of economic hardship,
financial turmoil, uncertainty,
"Big Company" proposes an alternate support line,
A change for Hana, a golf course.

You protest, you denounce, you proclaim,
"Keep Hana, Hawaiian, save the land!"
Headlines reek of condemnation,
my town torn, divided.

I grieve, I support, I testify,
preserve the power of ancestry, of family,
embrace my prayer for work, for survival,
restore the harmony in this place called home.

—*Josephine Cosma Blair*

My God!

Great God! Who is sitteth upon your throne, My heart is full
of fear, but why is it so? You are always there waiting for me
to pour out My heart and to trust thee! I do not comprehend
your great love and the things that you do. The foundations of
the earth, where did you fasten them? I look to the sky and
see your handiwork; where is the light stored? And the
darkness? You have balanced the clouds, you talk to the snow
and it hears you! And to the rain and it falls. I stand at
the water's edge and I see your power, there is no over flowing
you have told it hither to shalt thou come! The mighty waters
do not disobey. The wild beasts and birds are fed by you; no
one else prepares food for them. They know the time to bring
forth their young and do not need my help. Why do I not grasp
all this knowledge too, and know that you love me also? I bow
my knee before you and want my faith to be as the birds. And
my prayer for your blessing in time of my need is heard. So I
come boldly to the throne, I know you will hear me, I ask for
patience to wait on thee and trust thee my God! How great thou
art!

—*Viola Cedol Esposito*

Tribute to a Friend

One day I stood beside a mound
Of flowers heaped upon the ground
My heart cried out, it is not so,
It seemed I could not let you go.

Now weeks, and months, and years have gone
The memories linger on and on
And still unanswered rings the cry
Within my heart, why-oh-why!

Today I wandered once again
To pay a tribute to a friend
And placed a flower to memories shared
I somehow felt you knew I cared.

Then slowly as I lingered there
Within your garden, "Garden of Prayer"
I asked myself, just who am I,
To even dare-to wonder why.

For this I know, with God you are
And he has said, He is not far
And things now, only known in part
Someday we'll know, from heart to heart.

—*Lois Malone*

Escapism

She runs through the night unseeing, just relying on the feel
of her senses to lead her. Where she's going she care's not.
Screaming, she realizes her voice is silent as she runs. The
tears she shed, she never feels. Confusion never sets in, for
she never trips or falls. Her feet barely touching the ground
she treads on. For blackness comforts her, unfeeling, uncaring.
She can not be hurt or touched. Alone, she flee's like geese
flying south. Happy to be part of the earth that feeds her.
Free as the wind that binds her. Stopping, she feels she's
reached her destination. Alone, she waits, for what she knows
not, nor does she care. For she's found the desolate place no
one can share with her. Alone to her thoughts, her mind races,
thinking of future, past, and present. Decisions are not
needed, she has no where to go. She feels as one with the
earth. Part of the stars, knowing her place is with the
heavens above. Closing her eyes, her body explodes with emotions,
She never knew she harbored. Realizing the love she feels is
not foreign, but beautiful. To be explored and praised for.
She is faceless with no identity. Just part of the earth, to
be remember and forgotten with time. Yet she believes in
herself, and goes on.

—*Tricia L. Johnson*

A Dreamer's Lament

I often dream of travel, as I used to do,
Of places I have been I'd like to take you to,
Of the beauty and the sights,
Of places high and low,
Of sunlit days and clear crisp nights
Where caressing breezes blow.

I'd like to have an airplane and travel to places far,
To see the sights of which men dream who travel in a car,
To ride a roaring motorcycle and feel its surging power,
As the road falls beneath its wheels hour upon triumphant hour.

All these things I love to dream as I live from day to day.
I guess I'll get a rocking chair and dream my live away.
For when you have no dream at all there's naught for them to do
But carve your name a stone and say a word or two.

—*Hughie H. Gray, Sr.*

Dawn

A sacred time of holiness and peace;
Of promise and purity.
The Light of Life stretched across a violet night,
Colorspilt upon the darkness
Like splashes of watercolor
Upon a different canvas.
Warmth creeps, seeps like liquid life.
The cool dampness of night
Leans backwards over itself
Until it no longer is at all.

You are Dawn to me.
Sacred, peaceful, holy
Like a promise.
Loving with the slow rhythm
Of the sea at low tide.
Your love comes in gradual, blended shades
Softening the landscape of my darkened reality.
Sorrow leans backwards over itself
Until it no longer is at all.

—*Ajike Kendrick*

Love

How tender a love which transcends the boundaries
Of race and culture and different countries;

A love which sees the beauty inside,
The reality beneath which never dies;

A love which sees the potential within,
The qualities which designate man as man;

A love which flows like the waves of the sea,
And lifts you up to make you feel free.

So tender a love is a gift to behold,
Not for one to destroy, it's more precious than gold.

For this kind of love will bring peace to the world,
Destroying false barriers which divide humanity's fold.

So, parents, beware of harming your child
With prejudice and hate which make men wild.

Foster their hope in a better future
Where mankind is one and love is the suture.

Love is the cement binding nations and races
Into a real family from diverse places.

Black, brown, and white, olive and tan,
Varied colors add beauty to the garden of man.

—*Jeanette Hedayati*

My Eight Wonder of the World

There are "Seven Wonders of the World" in our history told nation
   wide.
Of seven splendid structures that are seen with beauty and pride.
But to see these seven wonders you must travel some.
For they are scattered here and there, from Egypt to Babylon.
I see another wonder, and it's right here by our side.
For you can see the beautiful structure of "man."
God made all eight structures with his artistical beauty
inside. And man has many wonders of his own,
To name a few, here goes. His head has a brain to gain some
smarts, and five senses to help make it grow.
He has hands to feel, he has eyes to see.
He has a nose to smell with and able to breath.
He has a mouth that can chew and can taste his food.
He has ears and is able to hear when you talk.
His body has muscles and plenty of blood.
And a heart to pump it and make it flow.
He has two legs so he can walk,
And two arms to hold things, so it goes to show.
The Eight Wonder of the World "Man" is nice to know.

—*Joyce L. Duitsman*

Christmas

Christmas is a time for memories
of snow,
and the cold wind that blows,
Sleeping in such warm beds,
with sugar plums dancing in our heads,
Dreams of toys,
And smiles of joys,
An hour till Christmas it's hard to sleep,
So down stairs you go to take a peek,
Only one thing can be said,
When you get out of bed.
"Merry Christmas!"

—*Cristenia Armstrong*

Grand Canyon, Oh What A Sight

I wonder what would become
Of this endless stretch of mountains,
Should the earth be no more.
The insignificant green dots
And little brown streams of mud,
Trickle like a drop of clear clean rain.
Oh, when have I seen such a breathtaking sight,
As this never ending roof top?
Where the Indians roamed,
I would more than hope to wander.
The red flat tops of skyscrapers,
That Mother Nature carved, herself
Are dreams of hopes and fantasies.

—*April Carter*

Magic of the Printed Word

I read the word from printed page,
Of those who lived and loved.
Their smiles and tears along the way,
Their faith in God above.

I smile and sob, as though I too,
Were walking by their side.
A sharing in the days they lived,
The goals for which they strive.

Perhaps no word of mine will grace,
The annals of our time.
But thanks to those who've gone before,
I share their thoughts sublime.

They share with me the beauty rare, that comes to those who
see. A world beyond the daily woe, that burdens you and me.

May God be thanked for talents rare, that leave those precious
words. To lift us from our daily task, to fly like singing birds.

Beyond the bounds of lives so drab, so filled with doubt and
fear. To dwell in castles high above, a dream world, sweet
and dear!

—*James F. Sullivan*

Untitled

My mind ponders many a thought,
  of Vietnam, the man who fought.
He now fights his vivid dreams that will not cease,
  I ponder the thought he can't release.

The man's thought of peace emerged first,
  a thought of peace jungle war had immersed.
A mistake caused by obscurity,
  he pulled the pin for his own security.
His first victim, a friend he knew,
  torn apart by the grenade he threw.

The scar embedded deep,
  still aches, awakes him from his sleep.
He looks deeply inward,
  to find the friend he mistakenly murdered.

"They say you always remember the first-
  You never ask a man about that one,
   for it is always the worst."

Daily, in his mind he begins to repeat the end,
  of the day of his first, his friend.

—*Laura Olive*

Our Childrens Cries

My God I see the childrens tears
Oh, how miserable their many fears
Where is the mothers love who is on drugs?
See the babies on the streets eating garbage,
eating bugs
No home, no place to go when things go wrong
My God, my God, their suffering so long!
Where is the fathers strength who is no longer home?
Children cries on the street left to roam.
Parents' yelling only of their rights you see.
What of the childrens' tear that be?
What of the babies life that's been destroyed?
Their blood they shed was mother's joy.
God have mercy on us all here today
For it's selfishness that get's in our way
Do you hear the childrens' cries?
Truly where do your thoughts lie?
—*Dianne E. Smith Hardiman*

The Companion

She is blinded.
Oh, how she is blinded.
She just simply doesn't understand,
    that when she does not choose to fly, she falls.
She falls into a deep hole,
    and only one person is capable of digging her out,
    her companion. But wait! She seems to be free.
Her companion is by her side, and together,
    they climb to the highest mountain,
    and swim the longest river.
Her companion is delighted, until she begins to drown,
    and once again she is blinded.
It seems as if her whole soul
    has been taken from her, stolen!
She does not deserve this, but this time,
    her companion is not allowed to dig.
She'll have to find her own way out, even if it means
    dying in that hole,
    without her companion.
—*Lisa Marie Krenz*

Our Children

Children of the world are starving to death.
Oh Lord, have mercy and give them breath.
Their tiny faces all stricken with grief,
Send them some quick relief.

No good sustenance in their bodies they take,
Their bones are easy to break.
Is this their punishment for what we have done
Let us feed and clothe them all year long.

Growing old some will never meet.
Because they live and die in our streets.
No other life have they been shown
So, they take violence as a life of their own.
—*Cecile A. Jarrett*

Life's Most Important Word

There's always a fresh morning filled and sparkling with hope
On the other side of each night, no matter how hard you must cope.
Make sure you give the next chapter time to exist
Or you'll never know what was next on your life's list.
Rest your eyes and mind and soul each night;
Rise refreshed and ready to face the obstacles in your sight.
Obstacles are opportunities to be your best and more;
When you face them, embrace them. What else is the new day for?
—*Sharyl Noelle*

All the Love in the World

As darkness descends,
On the days worst end.
The man has "asked how's your day been",
The woman replies that you will never bend.
You've asked, you're told the money's not in,
Oh how should the payment be sent.
As the money was lent,
We were told it should be in on the tenth.
If we had known the job would end,
before the loan did.
What of the food bill,
And also the power bill.
There is no light at the end of the tunnel.
The children will be home soon,
Oh! Where shall they lay their heads,
For the man has come to take their beds.
The children would like a lot more than they get.
As the man turn's to the woman
"All the love in the world", is set.
—*Virgilene Beth Holmes*

On the Edge

She was determined to be so good
on the edge of elegance she stood
on the banks of the sea of life
She knew such joy such strife
Each day a new challenge a new voice
Each day another victory another loss
She faced them all with a show of courage
So great she trembled inside
Sometimes alone and afraid at eventide
Sometimes life seemed like hell
Then on bended knees she fell
Looked to heaven and prayed to God above
overwhelmed by a surge of power and love
Great joy embraced and so engulfed her
Quivering lips curved in a knowing smile
A soft glow shone in her eyes all the while
Now no longer standing alone on the edge
Stepping over the thin line she made a pledge
From that moment on never to falter or waver
But to walk in greatness and elegance forever
—*Evelyn Clark*

The Korean War Veterans Memorial

On this magnificent Ash Woods site
Our memorial stands to Lincoln's right
Here on our nations capital mall
We honor Korean Veterans who answered the call.

As we gather here, tears will shed
For the blood of our buddies, our honored dead
We ask God in heaven to give them rest
America knows they gave their best.

President Truman was right, when he sent us to fight
The United States would stop Communist might
Battles raged from south to west, north to east
In the end, Communists gained the least.

On the hills and mountains, valleys and coast
The U.S.A. and South Korea gained the most
We stopped Communism, kept South Korea free
Thanks to Korean Veterans like you and me.

Before we leave our memorial here today, let us pray aloud
We are all Korean Vets, we are very very proud
Our mission was accomplished, to build our memorial was a must
Freedom was victorious because our cause was so just.
—*Loy Lovitt*

Society's Law

Moving specs living in the white box, within the Mother Circle.
One hand holding under, second hand already fallen.
Chance time given, not another, dreamstate awaiting its birth.
Innocent imagination gazes upon sin, answers, why?
Sin questions the understand.
What has been lost?
When was it lost?
Where can it be found?
Did it ever exist?
Innocent imagination answers, opened eyes.
Still, sin questions the understand?
Moving specs living in the white box, within the Mother Circle.
One hand holding under, second hand already fallen.
Chance time given, not another, dreamstate awaiting its birth.
For sin to understand.
The adult looks up to the child, asks the question, why?
The child looks down to the adult, simply replies, I understand
Think about it......

—*Kayla Sinex*

Old Friends

Today I met an old time friend
One of many I will remember to the end
And though twenty odd years had passed since we had met
Our memories went back to things we could not forget
Happenings of that long ago day
Friends that we had known that had long passed away
Our lives as we had lived them in the years between
Years that were good and years that were lean
Families that neither of the other had known
Only then could we realize how time had flown
Yes we sat and reviewed those years that were past
Each knew that our visit must be short and could not last
So we talked and would not let anything else detract
But we agreed on one basic fact
New friends are wonderful in their way
And we like to meet them everyday
But what would life be like without old friends tried and true
Who have stood by us in sorrow and good times too
Someone to depend on when the going got rough
Someone we could help when their times got tough

—*Leslie Linville*

Soldier Boy

War is not a game for an innocent boy, He was
only just eighteen - not ready for what the army had in store.

Guns and ammunition...smoke lingering in the air, He could no
longer tell what was right - the haze clouded his eyes and
his judgement.

"Oh God, let me live," was all he dared to utter,
As he kept watch, silently shivering - avoiding the pale moonlight.
He does not remember the bravery he had shown,
He only knows of the fear that had secretly tortured his mind.

The red droplets covered the ground like a blanket,
Their sickening stench spread through the air until his heart and
hands were stained, With remembrance.

He does not recall all of his stripes and shiny bronze pins,
Just the pain he felt inside, taunting him through those
restless nights.

He watched helplessly as they stripped him of more than just his
his pride,
Never having suspected that it was a woman who had betrayed him.

He had poured out his heart to his lover and friend,
Not realizing the wicked truth, that she was one of them.

—*Kristin Hawkins*

Future of Dreams

Different sights come into existence
Or beyond our better understanding
Of a future that holds no hope
Destiny brings losses about our feet
No will to power the arts
   For which mankind perceived to destroy
   From his once mighty hand
   Because we live, we must exist
   But to exist with no dreams, no hopes
   No vision beyond the horizon
     Is to die a fallen stone death
We cannot confront our own
   Feelings as long as we destruct
     Humankind beyond future dreams
      of reproduction
   Because future dreams do not
    Exist with our own limited
     Ways to see reality
     So it falls down
     Cry...Oh mighty man, so cry

—*Grant Wass*

Days Gone By

How long has it been since I held you in my arms
   or blew in your ear
Two or three days, but it seems like a year
Our friendship has grown into so much more
But is being in love worth crying for?
Captivating and rejuvenating that's what your love
Is to me, without it another rainy day I'll see
Never in my life have I felt love like this
I feel so lucky when I receive a kiss
Now, their will be warmer December days
Because I have you to keep the cold away
Loving you is worth everything, even the times
   we cry and the times we feel pain
The days gone by that I've spent with you
   have been days to cherish
But when we're apart we can only wish
That we could be together again
The days gone by have brought me joy
Oh! what wonderful days they have been

—*Freman Jay Murphy*

"Friends"

I remember when we used to play ball
Or dig with muddy hands in the dirt.
And when we did splits and hand stands
When our time was up our mothers would call.
Then after we eaten
We would meet again
You said you wanted to be a singer
I always wanting to be a clothing designer
I'd listen to your voice crack
You'd laugh at my creations
Then we grew apart.
Oh, what a sad feeling
No, more muddy hands, or laughing
We now know we still are friends
As I talk of men
You looking at books
And giving me funny looks
We just wink & laugh
'For here were two true friends.

—*Christine Madore*

Love Never Fails

No matter how many miles between
Or how many places we have seen,
Our lives have endured time and space
As we have moved from place to place.

And now our paths have crossed again,
Who knows why, the where and when.
But here we are with all our dreams
To make some sense of what God deems.

He gives us choices for us to make,
It's up to us what we give or take.
If we take more than we deserve,
We may be handed many a curve.

Again the miles will take their toll,
Our lives will change and we'll play our role.
Whenever our paths will meet again,
Only God knows where and God alone knows when.

But, if we give with love unending,
We'll receive the Blessings God is sending.
Our road seems full of hills and vales
And yet we know that love never fails.

—*Rita M. King*

My Boy, My Son, The Man

Have you ever sat on a summer eve and watched the flowers grow?
Or noted over a period of time, the change a tree can show?

Much like a child it reaches out, curious of each new day,
seeking out Mother Natures best in each and every way.

Now our great God in heaven created each new tree,
just the same as he took the time to create you and me.

But I really think his best work gave him his greatest joy
and that I'm proud to say was when he made my boy.

Such a tiny bundle with hardly any hair, so innocent, so
beautiful, without a single care.

As I sat and held him, what wondrous things I saw, a college
grad, a famous sports star, or someone to deal in law.

Now he's started growing, and with each new day a surprise,
bumps, bruises, scrapes, cuts and tears in his big brown eyes.

If I live to be a hundred, I'll never have such fun, nor have
the love for anything that I have towards my son.

As I sit and watch him playing, pretending he's superman, or
plotting to fight some Aliens with a star war's battle plan

I have to try to remember to guide him while I can, for oh to
soon My Boy, My Son will grow to be The Man.

—*Tony J. Mitchell*

"Seeing"

Having visions long ago
of a future only you could know
Peering into what was ahead
While whirling from one day to the next
Yet feeling endless hours tick,
sensing how it all might be knit
into a perpetual rhyme
Occasionally, infinitely transcending time!

From them, to us, to ours and theirs,
the vision remains without despair,
alive with questions that will always
return us there.

—*Dennis Maugere*

Genes and Jeans

We're the child of our parents the way it should be
Our genes stay the same but our spirit is free.
Our chromosomes number just forty six,
But then man decided to make a new mix.
First he sliced them and diced them and stirred them around,
Then sat back and waited to see what he had found.
There are birds that can swim and fish that can fly
And God in his heaven said, "Oh, my, my."
The last time I looked earth was doing so well
Then man in his wisdom decided to sell
His eggs and his sperm and all of those things
That gave man his brains as well as the means
To walk on two legs and then to make jeans.
In time we will see what changes they make,
Will we fly through the sky or return to the lake?
But one thing is certain and this is no joke,
Man will always continue to drink Classic Coke.

—*Alice Dorworth*

"Questions Unanswered"

What is time? Only a microscopic dot in the eternal space of our mind.
Mankind is only a frail and unworthy being, unfit to lick
The dust from the feet of the living God if it were possible.
What are oppressions, what do they mean or stand for? Why do
we suffer burdens and trials? Only God could give us these
answers in their entirety -
What is death? Only a temporary inconvenience, even death has
its place, for I know I'll awaken to a better and eternal life,
Casting mine eyes upon the Holy Trinity, and forever being
with Jesus, the son of the living God.
I have grown weary of this life, I am tired of daily oppressions
and struggles, I pray the poor would be satisfied in the
twinkling of an eye; I hate poverty, only if I had the extra
funds in which to help those from their hard times, then I too
should have left my mark upon humanity, after I have been
buried and long since forgotten. "Thank you Lord for your
bounties."

—*Gary L. Thomas*

Something's About Wind

The southeast blow we're in lies under Iceland's coast.
Our steersman stubbornly insists on standing west,
slanting towards Boston and damn the Equinox.
Now a windmoan warning tenses to its utmost.
Compare this purposed sky to our haphazard mix
of puny skill and folly. Fools we are to spurn
the world when it howls—oh the range of loneliness.
We persist against the wind's push, the ocean's pull.
The S. S. Henry Baldwin dives, propellers whine
in air. Their torque restored, we plough a new ravine.
Then walls open. Have we been spared? We turn and run.
All passion shared—though fierce, though sweet—is
wonderful.

—*Everett Ball*

Untitled

Think of life without a child - so empty and so cold,
Now life as a family, together growing old.
For reasons known to few I feel very little joy.
For never in my life should I feel that baby boy.
Or a baby girl, if it's to be.
Though in this life - not for me.
I'll never know what is like that nine months or so,
I'll never feel the joy of birth, that I'll never know.
Of all the things in life that hurt - this pain
tops the scale
Now I know life's incomplete - now I know
I've failed.

—*Jodi Roy*

"Inside Out"

The man inside is not the same,
Outside image hides the inner soul.
Image formed for others is not the inner self—
Mask put on struggles with stories untold.
The shield is thick, hard to break—
Hurt, hate, fear, trouble the inner soul,
due to sorrow long ago!
Lighting strikes the heart pounds,
The inner soul comes to life, fear surfaces
Anger kept in depth shows through.
Gentleness is hidden behind the mask of life.
Softness, caring, love, is kept in check.
No one will hurt spirit again.
Kindness is hidden and giving is a trait not known.
In depths their lost inside the inner soul.
All these things kept within,
Someday to surface for all to see—
When shield is broken and mask falls,
A beautiful—gentle man!!

—*Sondra West*

Birth

A thought was planted, a wish to be granted,
Overshadowed by Spirit, and the work begins.

Genes to be selected, all knowledge erected,
Now time is of the essence;
Combinations made with shades of coloring
Laughter, sadness, joy, remembrance and growth.
Selections made, time to build,
To bring this manifestation by Thy will.

Many prayers, many doubts through Spirit a new beginning,
Sometimes with pain and tears,
Sometimes with bliss and ecstasy,
But the birth continues.

No time to think, keep silent - just be
Though unseen by the eyes, the magic is felt by the heart.
Spirit guides, believe, then know; the right choices were made,
The time correct, and a new birth is now complete.
A new life blessed and conceived by Spirit.

A thought was planted, a wish to be granted
Overshadowed by Spirit, and the work begins again.

—*Victoria Bernaldo*

In Memory of You

Splashes of shadows dance upon a candle lit wall,
painting pictures never to be seen.

The chaotic silence of words never to be said.
Dreams could be fulfilled here,
but sleep never comes.

Emotions like lightning, cutting through searing my very soul,
stop me amidst the pleasure, to remind me of the pain.

The guilt comes to haunt me,
casting shadows of its own,
claiming all that is forbidden.
In these treasures it has taken, the most sacred, my soul.

I must steal fleeting pieces of joy,
just as the night robs us of the day.
In whole, I am but shattered pieces,
uncollected and yet to be defined.

Unrelenting are the memories,
tossed about like clouds in a mid summer sky.
Forever to be unresting,
in my forever tormented mind.

—*Raven*

He Waits

Crystal reflections on candle lit walls.
Patiently he waits, strong and tall.

Soft music to dine, fragrance divine.
Pictures adorn, matrimonial kind.

Gift of gold, sparkling wine,
expecting his love to arrive on time.
Patiently he waits a very long time.

Sirens heard distant in the cold night air.
Nervously he sits in his velvet lined chair.
Impatiently he waits in breathless despair.

Crackling fire now smoldering hiss.
The night still cold and still one wish,
to have his love for just one kiss.

Fifteen years the two they cared.
Visions of memories the two they shared.

The hour, too late. His heart now aches.
Surmising her fate, arsenic he takes.

A knock is heard beyond the door.
A trembling glass shatters to floor.
Patiently he waits...yet...waits no more...

—*Deborah Lum Purviance*

Peace

There is peace in the clasp of a hand
Peace in a soft spoken word.
Peace in an offer of friendship
Peace in the song of a bird.

There is peace when fog shrouds a valley
Peace in a gentle falling rain.
In walking along with a friend
Through a wooded, country lane.

There is peace in the soothing lullaby
The mother, to her child sings.
Peace in the whispering flutter
Of the night Owl on silent wings.

There is peace in the beauty of butterflies,
And in the colorful autumn leaf.
There is peace in the frozen snow
In the prayer of one's belief.

There is peace if ever we seek it.
For it is almost everywhere.
To find it should be everyone's goal.
If we try, it will be there.

—*Mary M. Menser*

Darkness of Night

Nights are cold, dark and damp,
Piercing the darkness is my lamp:
Forever cold and black is the night,
I fight the loneliness with all my might,
No one to say, "I love you dear;"
"And you'll be mine forever here,"
The emptiness is all around,
In everything and every sound,
Thank you darkness for your cloak,
To hide the many tears I choke;
Hide me well ol'midnight gloom,
Let thy shadow cover every room,
I scream to God, "Please let me die,"
So these lonely tears I'll never cry:

—*Carol Marples*

"Lost"

Eyes brimming with tears,
Pent-up anger's burned for years....
Lost hope, no dreams,
Sleep is the only escape it seems...
Confused, frightened little girl,
You've grown up fast in your lonely world...
Hating the thieves who stole the key,
Leaving only a shattered me...
Racing, always moving fast,
Trying desperately to escape the past...
Disconnected, floating free...
Unable to feel, hear or see...
What is on that other side?
Is there happiness, hope or pride?
Or will I just feel more despair...
More shattered souls beyond repair.

—*Cindy M. Allen*

A Farewell to 1984

Nineteen Eighty Four has come and gone; we the
people are still struggling on; to maintain our
dignity in a society that has no pity on the meek and weak.

We The People have proven over again that we are
a people of enormous strength; we have fought in
world wars; we have fought in our personal wars;
and yet we still fight in this Nations economical wars.

We The People still manage to survive; so stop the
jive!!! Not only have we survived; we have developed,
nurtured and built our lives; because
we have STRIVED!!

Brothers and Sisters keep up the FIGHT; rest if
you might; but don't give up the fight; as long as
we live there will be a fight. Anything worth
having is definitely a good fight.
I Trust Nineteen Ninety Four will be a DELIGHT!!!!

—*Elaine Oglesby*

Africville

As I stand on the banks of the shore I wonder where's all the
people gone to.
The Village so full of laughter of African descendant. Gifted
land from Queen Victoria.
The land seem to be swallow up by the sea. I can still hear
the sounds of the gypsies
Playing music and dancing by the light of their camp by night.
They came every summer to and fro. Naked kids ran all around
while the gypsy told fortune for a buck or two.
Toney so handsome a man was he. His shiny jet black and tall
hat. Buckle on his boots as he dance and dance in the moon
light night. All the girls wanted him for sure.

—*Alfreda Peters*

Desire

A man dying of thirst
  open-mouthed, yearning for the raindrops
  reaching, hands outstretched
  trying to grasp his remaining hope
  his last chance to be satiated. . .
  they slip through his fingers
  slide down his hands, disappear in the creases
   of his palms
  feeling the moisture, the wetness, briefly
  tantalizing, teasing him
  not enough to quench his need
  just enough to drive him . . . mad.

—*Madeline Mora*

My Little Warrior

He's up at day break preparing for war,
Perhaps today he'll even the score,
He washed his eyes and wets his finger tips
I notice by his milk glass. He's had a few sips,
Then down to his play room to search for his gear,
A pistol, a rifle or even a spear,
Off to his battlefield in a nice wooded lot,
And into a foxhole where yesterday he fought,
His oversized helmet snapped beneath his chin,
With his little jaws set firmly,
Not even a grin.
His eyes searching everywhere for a
enemy to shoot.
To him it all is seriousness,
But to us it's so cute.
After a few skirmishes they call out for time
Our little warriors are back hungry
and covered with grime.

—*Harry Klimushyn*

"Just One Look"

Can you look just once at the words He sent, look beyond each
period and comma spent. Beyond all the churches, the bells,
and the steeples. Beyond silken robes, marble statues, veiled
peoples. Beyond every sect, denomination, and creed. At a
good man, a kind man that was nailed to a tree. Can you stop
and look at His eyes as He wept, at His hands that were
bleeding, at His life that was spent. Many words He left us,
many thoughts, many prayers, many hopes, many promises, and
perhaps a few fears. But consider just once that He was who He
said. My master, may maker, my brother, my friend. For this
man to do willingly, all that He did. Giving all unto death,
then how could it be? I should fear anything, its power no
more. For He would have done, what was done for just me. For
just you, the whole world, we're all free. All those that can
look beyond each period and comma spent, and for a moment just
consider what our maker really meant. Long ago, far away, in a
land near a sea. When a good man, a King, was nailed to a
tree. To pay for a debt that belongs to you and me.

—*Tracy Charles Pharris*

Yesterday In My Life

I stare at the walls -
pictures of memories are forming in front of me.
Faces that I miss —
It doesn't seem like long time since we were all together.
Oooh - I remember —
those days, we were so young back then, young and naive.
So much has happened —
the days are going by faster than I want them to.
Time is changing us —
and now you are all just a yesterday in my life.

Living the young life
it was so much fun which no responsibilities.
Always tomorrow —
we didn't think about the past, we were looking forward.
So many good days —
Now they're gone forever, I could not live them again.
I am still smiling —
the years didn't make me unhappy — I'm still the same.
I kept the feeling —
for everybody from the yesterday in my life.

—*Lone Goul Nielsen*

Love

Underneath it all there's a warm
place for you in my heart,
    That place would be filled with
everything but love if were apart.
    Hear me out and understand me when
I say I love you,
    To keep you here with me tell me what
I have to do.
    My love burns for your love and care,
To lose your trust is one thing I cannot bare.
    This will always remind me of the
love that brought us together,
    Our love will grow stronger and
stronger but with the gentlest, quietest weather.

    —*Kiley Hernandez*

Pahokee, A Community Frozen In Time And Space

The human psyche has the capacity to alter or duplicate events,
places, and time. This was quite evident when I revisited the
community of Pahokee, Florida in August, 1989, after an absence
of more than 22-years; standing in the midst of utter desolation
and chaos, my mind transported me across the years to a more
peaceful, thriving and yes bustling agricultural community.
However, reality contradicted my memories and perception of

the place that had been home to me for more than seven-years I
could still hear the laughter of the children while they amused
themselves playing childhood games. The clatter that the
garbage cans made when tossed to-and-fro by the sanitation
workers are still ringing in my ears. The pre-dawn silence was
punctuated by the humming and the clanking sounds of the trucks

engine. This early routine of daily life served a two-fold
purpose. For example, not only was it a time to collect the
debris from the previous day, but it also served as an alarm
clock vicariously. The humming sounds were comparable to the
pulse and heartbeat of this community, far in the distance dogs
could be heard barking and roosters crowing, it is analogous
to a city dump circumscribed within the confines of a dump.

    —*Annie L. McDuffie*

Snow

So white it blinds you like the sun,
Playing in it is lot's of fun,
Throwing snowballs at everyone,
The refreshing air coming into your lungs,
Sledding down a super steep hill,
Build a snowman? Yes I will.
We play from can see till can't see dusk,
In snow whiter than an elephant's tusk.
Snow angels scattered here and there,
Snow is everywhere
The skaters just coming off the ice
Inside it's warm and very nice.
We sit by the fire sipping hot cocoa
Then off to bed we must go
For a while we're wide awake
In the coldness we shiver and shake.
We've prayed our souls to keep
Then we fall a sleep
Angels guard us through the night
We're awakened after sweet dreams by the morning light.

    —*Kim Russell*

A Yellow Rose

One yellow rose, he gave to me.
Pledging, his love for eternity.
A yellow rose, means friend they say,
And yes he's been there day after day.
As the years go by, he still brings me a rose
And my love for him continually grows and grows.
Give your love a yellow rose, as a friend,
Then give her another one again and again.
    The love that follows is worth more than gold.
    And a friend becomes a love, yours to hold.
    Only true friends understand, it seems.
    Only true love knows what it means.
So if you have someone who is a friend,
Make it a yellow rose friendship until the end.

    —*Margie L. Kaiser*

A Poet's Lament

For us, Alas! How said to be
 Poets of today,
Should we obey the new decree
And write in harsh, discordant, clash,
 Of obscene jest
 And mismatched prose,
Extolled by scholars of our times
 For all to hallow!

Give me the bards of bygone years,
 The Brownings, Wordsworth, Keats,
Whose verse is music to the ears
And visionary words impart,
 Refreshment pure
 To mind and heart...
Thus, from their depths, inspires indeed,
 The untold heights we can achieve.

    —*Sheila Rose Williams*

The Frog And The Toad

The Frog and the Toad as they hopped down the road. Passed a
pond that was clear as a mirror. They paused and looked in,
with their silliest grin frog said to Toad "my skin in
clearer." I bathe in the oils that are made from man's toils.
for the ancient Egyptian Pharaohs at nine dollars a quarts you
don't see a wart on this skin as sleek as a sparrows. Now Toad
wasn't impressed but he had to confess his skin wasn't smooth
like ole' Frogs. The warts on his skin were attractive to
him but to others looked like bumps on a log. "These warts
have a use, I'll accept no abuse for they hold the hat on my
head." Frog said "that's absurd, whoever has heard that a hat
wearing Toad can't be said." A voice from the sky of a bird
passing by dropped a hat in front of the pair. "Hey there ole'
Toad, you left this in the road" and flew off from Frogs icy
stare. Toad put on his hat and gave it a pat and with a smirk
looked over his shoulder. Frog lowered his chin as Toad gave
him a grin Frog looked as though seven years older. The moral
it looks, like things written in books to accept ones
appearance with pride if you've warts on your head, buy a hat
someone said and put them to use and they'll hide.

    —*Shirlen Pack*

A Poem For Two

I remember when I met each one of two
and watched as two together became the both of you.
The mutual respect and love you've shown
bring hopeful company to this one heart alone.
I've learned to look two closely into ones heart
and understand how friendship plays the biggest part,
and no matter how much distance three put between
I will never forget each lesson I've seen.

    —*Lisa Broe*

Love

(Dedicated to Michael Jackson, for he inspires me to excel in every possible way; especially in my writing. Thank you, Michael!)
The word love is used to freely among people of our world
What does the word love really stand for
Peace, loyalty, affection, honesty
If love is all those things and people
love our world and the human race.
How come wars, deception, lies,
In an unforgiving world...
Poverty, murder, children dying, is that really
what people interpret what the word love means.
If not, and you love the human race and our world
the place we live in the question is why?

—*Cassandra Cantwell*

Give Birth to Love

I am full, yet I know not how to empty.
Pregnant with this love,
Struggling to bring it to fruition.
My cups spills over with this gift,
How do I share it?
In an ordinary way, or grand?
Its an urgent love that simmers,
The heat of it threatens to overwhelm me.
It must be expressed, it begs to
be let out, it will not be contained!
Oh passion for God
And the things of Him
flow from me and touch,
everyday, in whatever way
the everything, everywhere now.
Give birth to love, today.

—*Vergie A. Parks*

Autumn Daze

Looking out my window I see
Preparations for a blanket of snow
The flaming red, golden and brown leaves
Trickling downward to kiss the earth.

The trees beginning to take on a skeleton look
And squirrels darting around to find still another nut
Farmers laboring to bring in grain
The tractors roll by until darkness sets in.

The rustling of dried cornstalks
And the many birds preparing to migrate
The sumac on the hill in brilliant red
And waving foxtail saying farewell.

Pumpkins with funny faces
Appearing on the neighborhood porches
It's Halloween time
A time for scary costumes and trick or treaters.

I love autumn
And looking out my window
In a glorified daze
I feel closer to God.

—*Marge Lund*

I Had So Much Love To Give To Him!

The wind blows so soft,
as it hits my relentless hair.
The sounds of nothing in my ear.
I try to think of him.
But the pain is so contemn.
I had so much love to give to him.

—*Christina Kinnaman*

"Faith"

Faith is that electrifying invisible force that is
    present throughout life and death.

Faith is that mustard seed that is not seen but felt when
    "God" is present in the soul.

Faith defies all Rules of Nature because
    Miracles are always present.

Faith is that dark, dark, shadow that
    comes into the light when man is least expecting its
    presence.

Faith is the "Alpha" and "Omega" of the believer that
    entrenches unbearable pain.

Faith is the worshipping of the Creator without questioning
    His invisible presence.

Faith turns hopelessness into Hope,
    Death into Life, and
    Hate into Love,
    and understanding of a devilish situation.

Faith is what "God" believers have.

We need not say anymore.

—*Emanuel Reno Wilkins*

The Garden

I have never felt close to my father,
Probably due to a lack of love shown.
The drought subsided when my grandfather
Fell ill. You see, he had always grown a
Garden, but this year, his heart turned against him.
My father and I decided to work
The small plot of rocky, but fertile dirt.
It had fused together during the winter
And its skin was hard to lay open.
Dad in one corner and me opposite,
Started. We tilled the clumpy soil, churning
And turning the nitrogen rich dirt, up.
The tiller's gyration and noise soothed me.
Looking up, I noticed my grandfather watching.
Turning, I saw my dad smile and
He was enjoying himself. So was I.
Then, just then, I felt what I had so longed for.
The warmth and love felt through some machines
And a plot of half frozen dirt could not
Be matched in hugs or calls of "Good try, Son!"

—*Tom Rogers*

The Fire

The heatless fire. It loomed before us, blazing brightly.
Pure movement of colour, burning itself into myriad shades of
Beauty. The steady ramp, running to it, was seen, not felt by
human feet. The ever changing suns made magic beyond this
    front.

A fear came, so evident and demanding that we
Pay respect to this world. In silence we witnessed.
Black was the order of this perfect night. One glance
And faith controlled the changes of the scenes.

While he stacked silently, alone, bales upon his boatside grey.
A willing servant, as we watched. You, meanwhile were
Captured by the soothing music of the night. And I was not.
I saw the new balloon ascend, accepted by
A willing sky and too soon bid my farewell.

I never knew his name. And somewhere in the heavens
They sang a welcome to this night
And the reasons why we came.
Just as you and I took to flight
Swiftly bidding farewell to this dream.

—*Shari Dottin*

Hope to Have

Walk upon me, see what I see, answers my
questions freely. Should I be scared of what
will become of all the young ones. Will there
be peace in the future to come?

The rich are too rich to give to the poor, homeless
is becoming more and more. There is no love for
who dies or lives, everyone just caring what
they can get not give.

People should give what can be given, lose
what can be lost. Spirit should be there, but
it's lost without care.

Care enough to lend a hand makes life
more promising to know someone understands

—*Shannon Eben*

Beyond These Tomorrows

From a world beyond, across a mountain you came.
Quickly and surely, you held your head high.
You rode to the castle up yonder so nigh,
To slay the dragon and win your fame.
With a cry of thunder, you met him head on.
Steel against bone, I heard the crash in the night.
All had gathered to watch this great fight.
It was equally matched, brain against brawn.
I watched in wonder, and felt a stir in my breast
The dragon was mighty with jaws full of stone,
Yet you were winning against him, silent, alone.
His blood was streaked on your powerful chest.
By early dawn, the whole land was still.
You had vanquished the dragon beyond belief,
And as you rode off, I breathed a sigh of relief.
The dragon was dead by your sword and your skill.
Oh slayer, my knight, did you ever learn?
On that eve, you stole my heart away.
You took it with you, forever to stay.
Beyond these tomorrows, will you ever return?

—*Ingrid K. Bayer*

"Why You"

That magical moment, lightness of space
Racing of my heart, first I saw your face.

The eyes of a tiger, which from, I could not flee
Ceased the earth from its spinning, you were all I could see

An illusion before me; yes, yes, it must be
My prayers had been answered "someone to watch over me"

Through good times and bad times, sunshine and rain
Love heals and completes us, and causes pain

About love you taught me, so boyishly caring, wise wonderful
    and free
I'll love you forever, "they can't take that away from me"

We walked the paths together, first as friends, then as lovers
    just us two
Learning, laughing, and loving; now and forever, I'll always be
    "crazy for you"

—*Carol Peary*

Grandchildren

The time has come to be concerned about my cellulite
    And wrinkles in my neck are not a pretty sight

But age cannot deter the glow that is apparent now
    Anticipation of new life replaces every scowl

    Just when I expected happiness to be in memory
    I found it in the future, in faces yet to be

—*Lorraine M. Conley*

You Are My Sun

I hear your tearful cries of sorrow although your not within my
reach. I feel the comfort of a warm yet bountiful hug from you
that over powers me. I see you in my dreams dancing with
angels, joyfully awaiting my arrival.
    You are my son

You are so small yet your hold on me compares to the peaks on
the mountain tops high above. You allow me to love you and
keep you adjacent to my heart, as you candidly smile at me, and I
know you love me too. You protect me fiercefully from the
enemy with the knowledge that your rescue is soon at hand.
    You are my son

We share a bond as strong as metal shackles,
linked together forevermore.
We share a friendship that shines with a radiance much like
our suns rays that will protect you until I can.
As we grow together I vow to help guide you through life's
great hurdles that are yet to come. And most of all I will
teach you to love just as I love you.

—*Dawn Woodring*

"Dreams And Faith"

There she laid inside my womb,
ready and willing to come out soon.

No one knows what she will be like,
until she comes out in the light.

Soon she'll be crawling, walking, making noise,
then she'll grow to like the boys.

Born she was, though she is denied,
this will not happen in her life.

No crawling, walking for this little girl,
she won't really know of this world.

She turned four in the month of May,
but our dreams have not passed away.

Yet we will dream, faith we'll trust,
for we still love her very much.

Her long dirty blonde hair, blue eyes,
If you saw her you would cry.

She eats a lot, yet looks so thin,
her bones are barely covered with skin.

It makes me sad to see her this way,
but my love, heart are her's to stay.

—*Helen Grimes*

No Calls

My foot is my phone -
Receiver of the whole organism as phone
Receiver of the earth
Communicative unit in a microcosmic way
A tapper of sounds
A carrier of messages across the earth.

My foot is ringing. I have a caller.
I answer to no answer and hang up.
Over and over, the dizzying effect brings waves of nausea.

Two fists fighting under my rib cage.
My head, a thin, aluminum pot gingerly carrying its contents
To nowhere and still a rattling penetrates to my pink, rubbery
    newborn ears.

My whole body, from head to toe is a tiny atom in a centrifuge,
Spiraling and ringing
Until the final split.

—*Cathy Wysocki*

True Friends

Friends-what are real true friends?
Realizing how much one means to another-
It will help differentiate the true and the wrong.
Everyone's opinion for others are always different,
Numerous are your friends, but are they really your friends?
Do not be too hasty with your answers, but ponder on each one
   by one
So that you can be right of your answers.

Friends love and care and give up for others,
They protect and guard you from your terror and fear,
They share secrets among each other,
Simply, they just like you for what you are.

Sometimes, some misunderstanding occurs and goes wrong,
Your sad, you wonder, and for him you long. But there is a
saying, "fighting makes you become closer." So talk to him
and solve your problems and things will be much better.

Never take one's friendship for granted
For if it's gone, then you'll be sorry.
It's worth more than a pet that panted,
Besides, having friends will make you happy.
   —*Alice Khang*

Untitled

When you want to be a poet, and you
really didn't know it
Then this contest seems an answer to your dream
So I thought "Well, I just might" and
I sat down here to write
While I wondered when the words would
start to "beam"
Since I've become a senior, and I think I
know it all
This writing down some rhymes, it seems,
should surely be a ball
Well, after giving it a try, my mind in
such a quest
I finally have decided, I guess I'm not
the best
The words all come, sometimes don't rhyme
I'll try this job another time
Or better yet, being a mere beginner
I'll send this in and pray it's a winner.
   —*Frances Lorentz*

Farewell to Summer

As Autumn leaves come tumbling down
Red, gold and chestnut brown.
And roadside stands are heaped with gold
With pumpkins big and round.

The Summer fields turn tan and bare
Harvest time has come once more.
Orchard fruits are stored away,
Barns are filled with sweet scented hay.

Harvest moon shining bright
Trees array in gowns so light
Wild geese fly overhead in flight
Shorter the day, longer the night.

Stars appear like clustered jewels
As night begins to fall,
The whisper of a playful breeze
As katydids and crickets call.
   —*Shirley Marie Jozwiak*

Late Summer

Sultry autumnal twilight
   relaxing in an oak rocking chair
   that creeks on an open porch.

I hear the crickets tune-up
   in the dry shrubs. Frogs voicing their
   opinions in the nearby pond.

I watch the cumulus clouds turn thunderheads
   across the open plain, as the distant lightening
   brightens the evening sky with white zig-zags.

I close my eyes and listen
   to the drone of the oncoming rain.
   —*Nadine L. Frisch*

Your Link to God

Your Parents are your Link to God
Remember this each day
When times are tough, don't give up
Just say you can do it, and give yourself a nod

Always try to do your best
This is what must be done
And Hope for the best result
And God will help with the rest

Don't go against your Parent's wishes
Because you think it's too hard
You will never reach a solution
And you will create a circle that is vicious

If you're listening to your Parents
Then you're listening to God
Just trust yourself and do this each day
Because the farther you stray, the harder it will be to find your way

Your Parents are not perfect
Don't think they have to be
To have what's best for you in their hearts
And to help to make you see
   —*Joan P. Sullivan*

Full Circle

Springtime!
Renewal of
The covenant of life.
Birthing, green smells, tender buds, hope.
Welcome.

Sunshine
By the barrel.
Profusion of flowers.
Long lighthearted days, dreamy nights.
Enjoy!

Leaves fall.
Brilliant colors
Swirl in the golden breeze.
Bare limbs etched on the cloudy sky
Chills me!

Dark time.
Cold, ice and snow.
Temperatures falling.
Hibernation by the fireside.
Think spring!
   —*Lenor Schmidt*

My Last Good-bye

All alone at night I cry
Repeating the words of my last good-bye
I feel the pain pound through my heart
In my mind it's like a poison dart

What happened to life
Was it all me
How could I have missed the boat
So completely

My pillow has to pay the price
For all the love we had
As it catches all the heartfelt pain
And all the love gone bad

I get up in the morning
And apply the hidden face
To cover up the sorrow
That pain in life has placed

So as I lay me down to sleep
I pray to God on high
Just let me have a night of rest
From the pain of a last good-bye.

　　　—Mary Van Meter

A Gift

A gift is only a gift when it is given, not
requested or expected. Possession of a
gift is not to be assumed or implied, when
the gift is another person sharing their time,
caring, and emotions.

Gifts - People should not be made to feel
obligated to give them today and tomorrow,
just because they gave them yesterday or
the day before, or the week before, be it
by actions or words.

Gifts of the heart are truly given without ever
expecting anything in return. Gifts of the
heart are not gifts of tradition, like birthdays
or Christmas, but are spontaneous as are
the feelings in the heart.

These are not the words of a poem, or from
a song that I heard on the radio. They are
thoughts from my heart about living and
Giving.
These words are my gift to you.

　　　—Rick Rise

Reflections

The fresh, calm waters
Reveal her reflection
As she looks at this reflection
She begins to think
She visions a reflection
Not of her own, but of a young child
She looks around for this child and realizes
She's alone
She looks again at this mysterious
Reflection
And it smiles at her
She stands up and walks away
But still feels this presence
She walks back and sits down
Looking into the water
Now she sees her own reflection
And suddenly feels
Alone...once again

　　　—Gina Durrin

Out of the Fog

Out of the fog loomed a giant ship
Returning or going on a long trip;
Who are the passengers? What do they seek?
Are they the bold or are they the meek?

Tho' some be old, while others be young,
Who are the others they are among?
With every wave the foghorn does blast,
A reminder to the future or to forget the past.

Those that are young can shape what's ahead,
The old to their dreams once they're abed;
The bold will create with their imaginable mind,
The meek will follow, they are the weaker kind.

Now out of the fog and into the light,
A sign, perhaps, on board all is right;
Cruising steadily on a sea that is calm,
I have no reason or cause for alarm.

In the full of light, you're the queen of the waves,
Bon voyage to thee all, be thee kings or knaves;
No more need I wonder who, what or where,
St. Elmo be with thee and thy weather be fair.

　　　—O. T. Farina

Tainted Past

Shadows of a tainted past,
Reveal themselves as time has passed.
Skeletons from long ago,
Come forth now for all to know.
The doors you've locked along the way.
But the key was found, do you dread the day?
The people know now what you are.
For the hearts you've torn, who bares the scars?
For the sake of peace, you declare war.
On the souls of the innocent, you raise your sword.
For your unjust cause, many have died.
You call it peace, I say you lie!
For the sake of politics and public opinion,
Behind your smile, your secrets well hidden.
Now the truth is out, for all to hear.
For the souls now lost, Have You Shed A Tear?

　　　—Michelle L. Copley

Keeping Sticky Molasses Smooth

A peek through the slit in the brick furnace
Reveals raging orange flames from the bagasse.
The searing heat makes steam to run the generator.
Its flywheel so big the gaze must lift
To gauge its height. That big spinning wheel
Is the source of power for the McBryde mill
At New Mill, Eleele, Kauai.
Crushing sugar cane takes 3,600 horsepower
To turn the huge steel rollers.
Other machines in the shops also depend on that source.
One day at Father's work station, I saw
A worm screw shaft-deep in oil
Slowly turn the mixer inside the tank
To keep the sticky molasses smooth.
It's not easy for a little boy's mind
To envision energy transfer from bagasse to machine.
But beholding with wonder the fiery furnace and feeling
The quiet efficiency of the giant generator
While standing close by on painted concrete floor
Divulged a clue to the complex process.

　　　—Shurei Hirozawa

Memories

I remember all those evenings,
riding home from school.
Both of us in silence, admiring the view.
Afraid to break the innocence,
until I said good-bye
Never, ever thinking that one day you
might die
Everybody knew, but wouldn't or couldn't
say a word
Now the place is haunted, echoing something
that was never heard.
I keep thinking to myself, this can only be a dream
Just to turn around, afraid I'll have to scream.
Your friends are always there, rooting you through.
Just remember my friend, we all love you.

—*Dee Fitch*

"The Boyhood Of Jesus"

When Jesus was a boy, did He
Run over the hills of Gahilee?
Stumble over the rocks and skin His knees
Watch the clouds and climb the trees.

Did He run with the boys down the dusty street
Dodging the donkeys and frightening the sheep?
Laughing and playing in the village square
Draw a cool drink of water, from the deep well there?

Did you roll you hoop and spin your top
And help your father in the carpenter shop?
Shoot your arrows into the air
Go to the synagogue, for school and prayer?

Did you see the Roman soldiers as they clattered down the street
Everyone scattering, from the massive horses feet?
Their shields catch the sunlight and their presence sends a chill
As they come to little Nazareth, nestled in the hills.

Do you see what lies ahead, in a few short years to come
As you look down that busy road, that leads to Jerusalem?
Do you see that lonely hill, with three crosses standing there?
Such a heavy, heavy, burden, for a little boy to hear.

—*Helen Cheaqui*

If Only

Sunsets of ethereal grace and colors.
Run through my thoughts, intermittently.
A trout stream running through virgin woodland.
The solitude and comfort of wind rustled leaves.
Birds singing happily in the forest.
A heart rejoicing at God's bounty.
Clean smelling odors, after a rainfall.
Memories of childhood, adolescence and adulthood.
A first kiss, first date, first love.
All of these, help build fondest recollections.
So warmly etched in recesses of my mind.
Surrounded by such glory, how does one find the time
To hate?
This is all we have, we should enjoy it.
Not infringing on another's space.
We should learn to tolerate each other,
Without a thought of how we differ.
Accept each others rights to be, to worship, to think
Differently.
How improved we'd all be, if only.

—*John B. Thomas*

Remnants

Used condoms clutter cheap motel carpets
Rust lipstick and sweat smear on satin sheets
Sweet blood and sweat stain cold hospital sheets
Etched echoes haunt empty, sterile hallways
Stretch marks and sutures streak bloated bellies
Pureed peas form fresh freckles on fringed bibs
Dried-up drool dwells on mothers' slouched shoulders
Fingerprints plague grimy grade school windows
Abused hopscotch frames consume cracked sidewalks
Prom pictures lay dormant in locked "hope" chests
Tears mix with smudged mascara on blushed cheeks
Coffee mugs bear rings on ink-soaked blotters
Smoke from squelched cigarettes drifts from torn soles
Ashes in unmarked urns rage in silence.

—*Susanne Dwyer*

Reflections

At the homecoming game my heart went astray.
  Sadness and sorrow took me away.
    Thought of life and what it's all about,
      And for you, my dear lady friend, my heart went out.

Smiling young faces so full of life,
  He was here with them one year ago tonight.
    Cheers and laughter fill the evening air.
      Still cannot believe, life is so unfair.

Felt suddenly old and alone like in a cage,
  But at least I had the good fortune to reach this age.
    Saw "92" on a jacket as I went through the gate,
      To be taken in youth, such an incomprehensible fate.

Cannot begin to tell you just how much I care,
  But for the rest of my life, your loss will I share.
    With him always in our thoughts, we can still hear his
laughter.
      Cherish and keep close that memory, forever after.

—*Allen T. Hunt*

Untitled

Direct my wild images to the flames, then to the ocean where
sanction is held. Gather all hopes and wishes so they may be
buried with altitudes of emotions.
Praise my new world of universal thought and golden half-truth's.
Pay no mind to the collections of dreams, but listen for the
cries of realism.
Lift the children of the sun to our new plain, but if they shall
fall wash them with boiling love.
Feel pain when it comes with a smile, but fear it when it
returns with laughing endeavors.
Help the burning souls with gallons of gasoline, then preserve
the ashes with wind.

—*William Vaarwerk, Jr.*

The Easter Lily

After the church services on Easter Sunday
Owners of the lilies took them away.
I am left standing here all alone.
I don't know to whom I belong.
I know my blossoms are bowed down
And the edges have turned brown.
I'm in God's house so I have no fears.
I'll fold my blossoms and say my prayers
And forgive the person who forgot me.
Who knows?
Tomorrow someone might adopt me!

—*Darlene Weyand*

The Snowman

A long time ago in a quiet snowy place
Sat two twig arms and a great smiley face.

His smile was made of coal and rocks.
His body was made of cold ice blocks.

His nose was very long and thin.
The color of it was bright orange.

A beautiful top hat on had he.
It was like magic to you and me.

Then one day when he wasn't ready,
The sun rays shone so bright and steady.

Pretty soon just a puddle was he,
I didn't see him and he didn't see me.

But you know he never knew
What it felt like to be me or you.

—*Veronica Dickie*

Sideline Or Showtime

Your future's too bright to be an angst-ridden young man, they
say. But I'm much too young not to be angry... Follow the
path, this way works out for the best, they say. But
eventually sating my hunger doesn't make it forgiven... When
it's step on to step up, and lick shoes to stand straight; That
place in line isn't so appealing. 18 to vote, 21 to drink, 35
to run the country and, I'm still waiting for the age to be
happy. Success isn't power and sex isn't love. And if you
don't believe me, then you're far more disillusioned than I.
Guarantees of that kind went out with the advent of the spoken
word. Your visions can still be your visions, don't get me
wrong, but more often than not your dreams are under someone
else's pillow. Who wants to make that climb with one hand if a
compromise can have your other hand be held? Honestly now.
These rules were set long before I played the game, sweep the
floor now so you can clean house later. So why should an exec.
give the proud man a break? They've all been here too, and it
wouldn't perpetuate the game, if I just went to Go and
collected my $200. I'd love to rail on, there's a place in
line I have to fill.

—*Tim Jackson*

Summer's Children

Say goodbye, to summer's children.
Say goodbye, they'll soon be grown
Cold winter comes, it's almost here
Summer's children will soon be gone
   You look back, you did your best
   But those children, put you to the test
Some say, you didn't raise them right.
Day time always turns to night.
If you went back, did things differently
How much difference would you see?
   In your heart. You know you're right
   Day would still turn night

Maybe they will, or won't be all right
Hopefully they will, come out of the night.
You see, night turns back to day
They turn into their own
Then they go their way
   The cold chill leaves the air
   Warmth is all around
   And in your home, summer's grandchildren abound.

—*Nancy Robertson*

Miscarriage of Love

I needed you, I was alone and oh so
Scared, you left me only memories, of
the moments we had shared.
One memory so alive and real, it moved
me in the morning when I bent down to kneel.
I prayed you would be happy.
I prayed you would be sad.
I prayed for absolution, for the terrible thoughts I had.
Everyday I grew closer to you as I waited
for this dream, but dreams turn into
nightmares with ill distorted scenes.
This agonizing terror which grew from within,
would survive only long enough to punish me for my sin.
I tried to protect you through deceit and lies,
then suddenly nothing was left, but defeat and my sorrowful cries.
I couldn't bear to face you or to hear your name
I only thought of running barefoot, through miles of pouring rain.
But my death had already came.

—*Sherry Horowitz*

"When"

When will there be an end to war, and what will be the final
score? The final score of those who've died, and the final
score of those who've cried!

Somebody please....please tell me when....when will it end?

When will soldiers get to go home, where they won't have to
feel like their all alone?
Somebody please....please tell me when....when will it end?
Tell me when will there be a lasting peace, from the North
to the South, from the West to the East?
Somebody please.....please tell me when....when will it end?

—*David M. Wilson*

The Fast Lane

There are many homeless wandering our streets
Searching and scrounging for something to eat
They sit at the corner begging as we walk past
All we do is ignore them and try to walk fast
We ignore their starving, unhappy cries
But yet we can't help looking in their tear-filled eyes
What do we see there, not drugs nor dope
But what we lost, something called hope
They always hope and pray
For a warm dry place to sleep today
Why don't we stop and help heal their pain?
Because we're to busy living life in the fast lane.

—*Kristi Schlintz*

Small Wonder

Graceful butterfly flitting among the flowers
Seems unafraid as my shadow towers;
Can't help thinking of this small wonder
Prolonging my stay, the butterfly I ponder.

It fluttered about, lit for me to view
Compelled to linger, displaying its brilliant hue;
Gently, I touch this delicate insect
God's work of art, in every way perfect.

Everything, I know is here for a reason
The winged beauty inspired me this season;
As a caterpillar it didn't have to die
Was given new life, as a beautiful butterfly.

Discovering simple things good and wholesome
Put on earth to test our wisdom;
Believing this a symbol of God's promise
Through loving grace, our chance to be His.

—*Kay T. Story*

Noise

Listen to the drumbeats roll; Listen to the sea snore.
See bodies moving rhythmically, to an unseen force.
Taste the salty air around; Taste the flesh and blood.
Feel the ground shake, as the world stands still.
All in a moment's passion; Non in a recorded hour.
Fighting for a place in the world, a place of acceptance.
Hunger in his eyes; So much longing in her's.
Making love without touching, in the stillness of the night.
The moon shines, the sun blazes; Cold wind sweeps up loose petals.
The heat is unbearable.
Fighting to keep breathing; Never stopping for air.
Moving, shuddering, stopping, and starting all over again.
Flames catch all around the cool pond of fire.
Never resting, never ending; Going crescendo.
No sound except music; No words, just an overture of desire.
Keeps getting louder, no holds barred.
Rolling sweeping, pounding; Gaining, losing.
No noise, no light; Power and indulgence.
Lightning, thunder, explosions, eruptions; Then calm, then quiet.
The storm has passed.
　　—*Margaret Elpiner*

Ma, Pa, Where Ya Goin'

Ma, Pa, where ya goin', leavin' me alone,
seems there always socha-lizin' leavin' me home.

All the kid-ner-gardens seem the same,
seen so many kids today kant' member their names.

Are you may Daddy, are you supposed to be,
someone to look up to taller than a tree?

Where's my Ma, is that her?, she looks like a prude,
or is that someone dressed up as a dude?

I know my Ma, she told me, we are the same,
but Pa conjures up a notion never makes a claim.

Don't know where I'm goin', haven't found a place,
jess hope won't be 'nuthur welfare case.

Both workin', just doesn't seem right,
when they get talkin' they just wanna fight.

Lots of stress and tension' goin' on here,
then Pop goes out and gets another beer.

Sumthin's missin' could it be,
A softer voice, a different plea.

A Ma, Pa, switch woman shuffle,
is that why there's such a scuffle?

Well,... let's get back to reason and rhyme,
we all come from woman-kind.
　　—*Anthony J. Marquis*

Editor's Choice

They sit around a table and wonder;
And they ponder.

They pick what's best;
What's above the rest.

They filter through;
And try to find something new.

They rack their brains;
Until they think they're insane.

Then they make their choice.
　　—*Debbie Strickland*

Uncaring America

Thousands of people are dying every day, a homeless family is
seen on an empty street, little children suffer because of lack
of food, asking only for a small something to eat

We hear the news about two more deaths but we calmly go on with
our own lives, a plane crash kills a hundred people and no one
cares if anyone survives

The pro-choice activists grow in number while every year
thousands of babies die, the doctor tells the mother not to
worry, the baby won't feel it, what a lie

People talk about the Nazi holocaust, they say it's over and it
wasn't that bad, they see the pictures of the piles of bodies
Piles of human beings, and they're not even sad

A drive-by shooting kills a mother and her baby, we hear about
it but it's somebody else's life, we don't have to worry, it
won't happen to us, who cares if the family feels grief and strife

Has this country really grown so cold? Are we really as
uncaring as we seem to be? Are there any hearts out there that
feel compassion? Are there any eyes left that can really see?
　　—*Brandi Lynn Nelson*

Parents

Parents of today run their kids there to here,
Seldom compared to parents from yesteryear.
Breaking their backs for some food for the week,
Now, buys as little as a pair of shoes for their feet.
"Drive me here, take me there, oh please Mom and Dad!"
Hardly a word of thanks to be had.
What ever happened to the old neighborhood game of football,
Occasionally ending up in a free for all brawl.
Now, it's all organized sports, uniforms and a team name,
Drag your parents from town to town game after game.
One parent working and one at home,
Now, leave your name at the beep, nobody's home.
Mom baking bread and lots of cakes,
Now, it's get it from the store, we're running late.
Dad gets the old mower with a broken handle to cut the grass,
Now, wear your football gear to mow or OSHA will have your ass.
Kids today don't know how good simple times were,
Everything today is too fast paced, one big blur.
We didn't have therapists and lawyers when we were bad,
Our judge and jury was dear old Mom and Dad.
　　—*Todd Laubacher*

The Song Of The Angels

　Do you hear the silent song the angels sing to us?
　Sent to earth from heaven to secure our bond of trust.

　They whisper down upon me as at night I try to sleep.
　Their beauty is so touching that my soul begins to weep.

I listen to their words of love with deep and profound care.
　I find my mind becoming lost inside the angel's stare.

They dance throughout my weary heart, their vivid faces glow,
　My un-biased wisdom of their message starts to grow.

　They speak to me of comfort and the purest clarity,
　Bringing in abundance all of heaven's charity.

　The murmurs of the angels captivate my restless head,
　Their sweet, alluring presence can abolish former dread.

And as they slowly prance about, their body's while and sheer,
　I listen to a story of a father they hold dear.

　They tell me of a man who is warm and truly kind.
　A man who's every word is true, his every step refined.

　And as the angels sung their song and I begin to cry,
　They leave me with a tender kiss, a precious last goodbye.
　　—*Jennifer VanBuskirk*

Seventy Seven

What kind of dice are these that show double
Sevens? Not to complain, the crap shoot, life,
Seems primed with rough footing, toil and trouble
With brief flashes of sunshine, a good wife

Who undertakes the sisyphean task
Of improving my achieved perfection,
For Lo, through years which she has sought to mask
The soil of ages from close inspection

She fought a valiant war against my sloth-
Full ways pointing out, as woman will do
That man's perfection's like a fleeting moth
A moments flame, a vision quite untrue.

I guess the better half of man, his mate,
Will guide him to the capstone of his fate.

    —Joseph E. Barrett

Who Owns This Street?

Who owns this street where footfalls new and old leave their
shadow? Is it that same proprietor covering my way with sky,
its rain visiting bowed heads, rutted roads and open mouthed
children sweetly hysterical under mothers' watch? Or is it he
who paints the spirit-whisper in your eye, who melts my
fears with your body's heat molded precious into my embrace?
By what name is he called and in what coin does he take his
due? For I would walk his streets under embracing sky with you
and like open mouthed child, head to the rain, drink my joy
in swallowed laughter, leaving shadows wetly falling from naked
feet bared to the storm. And in his palm, I would place
silver, gold or kiss, take his hand in mine; or labor in
yards where grapes grow, ships raise their prows above the sea;
where glistening sweat, lost to dark, marks backs of
men straining for bounty fortressed in the bowels of the earth
and by my labor, would be his. And true master that he is,
justice his greatest wealth, he will honor devotion's coin with
exchange duly earned, and wishing this faithful child comfort
against fear's approach, will call home to my embrace that
whispering spirit softly painted in your eye.

    —Leonard X. Gillespie

The New Trend

Thoughts coherent and systematically correct
shattered by the image that the mirror reflects
trapped in a frame that doesn't relate
to the images the media fabricates
A concept we must conform to, to achieve success
a modern day arian race that discriminates the rest
A great variety of species roam the vast plane
the beauty stems from individual attributes we sustain
Highly emphasized guide lines for fashion and adequate weight
some spend years trying to recreate
Where are those who impose such a burden show your faces
dare reveal your flabby selves come out from your hiding places
another lucrative scheme we've fallen into
lest we forget our virtues
Beauty comes from within and the eyes are still the
mirror of the heart
enrich the spirit with love and knowledge
this is the trend we ought to impart.

    —Maurice Santa Cruz

Here Lies Emptiness

Here lies the tomb of a dream
shattered by the scythe of ignorance
garnished with loveless flowers
one for every error
and two for every inch of face
covered by kisses of deception.

Here lies the saber of the matador, wet yet
with sacrificial blood of the artist's end.

Here lie the poet's tears
the music maker's harp
the acrobat's shirt of saddened sweat.

The magician had his day
when, with his swift fingers
he dematerialized the juggler's bouncing ball.

The gypsy wandered by the edge of the earth
fell, broke his heart —
even Picasso's clowns never smiled
they all knew from far away whisperings
the silence of the tomb.

Here lies emptiness.

    —Gil Magno

He, She

He sits off to the side, away from everyone.
She admires him. He's tall, thin. He has a
very strong face. His eyes are set deeply
in his head. He stands out, screaming to
be known. People look, but don't speak.

She also sits to the side, away from the
crowd. She watches him. He looks up, their
eyes meet. He smiles, she blushes and looks
down. She can feel his eyes embedding into
her. She looks up to find no one, not even him looking.
She goes on with her work.
She looks up to see him staring.

They stare a minute. This time, he looks
off. This is how it goes. Always, neither
of them ever speak. Just look.

The next day, it all happens. The
exact same, never different. No one speaks,
No one breathes. Their soul's await.

    —Kelly Thompson

Forbidden Love

The heart is entombed, buried deep within her
She dares not to share it with another soul
But one comes who's sweet words and tender touch
Causes the heart to flourish
She gives him her spirit, he takes it then departs
Piercing fragile emotions she so blindly expressed
The delicate heart has taken a chance
Exposed all compassion only to be

        T
       O
        R
         N
      A p a r t

She feels no pain, as the heart is numb
Again entombed,
Never to be shared with another
Hidden,
But unable to be broken
Safe,
Protected from rejection

    —Janay Miller

The Last Leg

There was an old teacher who lived in room 4.
She had twenty children whom she mostly did adore.
With paddle in hand she was running around,
When in walked the principal without a sound.

Just then a spitball came flying through the air,
And landed right in the principal's hair.
The teacher yelled out, "Oh, Ms. Brooks, I beg,
Don't blame me. I'm on my last leg!"

Ms. Brooks shouted with a great big frown,
"Teacher, for goodness sake, put that cup of coffee down!"
Exasperated she said, "I'm going to have you fired."
The teacher replied, "What the heck? I'll soon be retired!"

—*Beth Poe*

She Has Gone Away!

Where is the laughter and where are the tears?
She has gone away!
Where are the arguments that show my fears?
She has gone away!

Where are the strewn clothes and work left undone?
She has gone away!
Where are the thoughts of excitement and fun?
She has gone away!

Where's that stuffed bear and posters from the wall?
She has gone away!
Where is the ring from the phone down the hall?
She has gone away!

Where are all the friends with news to tell?
She has gone away!
Where are questions on math and words to spell?
She has gone away!

Where has she gone of which I'm, not a part?
She's gone to college, yet still in my heart!

—*Karen Clapham*

Lonesome

She sits in her chair, very quiet and still
She has nothing to do, but wait for her pill
She thinks of times past when she was young and spry
She remembers her kids, and tries not to cry
She wonders why they never come to see her
She never done them wrong, of that she's sure
She could not provide many material things
She could only give the joy that real love brings
She tried her best and gave her whole life
She thought she was a good mother and wife
She wakes every morning in hopes that today
She could see her grandchildren, and watch them play
She is old and wrinkled, but she is not dead
She longs for her kids, and hangs down her head
She feels a tear rolling down her cheek
She is all alone week after week
She wakes one morning and can't believe her eyes
She pinches herself to make sure it's not lies
Her hopes and prayers of years have come true
Her son and his family have finally come through

—*Andrea Kangas*

Collectors

Many types of collectors there are,
As the buyer lovingly shoves the new "find"
into the car,
Antiques, coins, and art are a MUST,
But I am quite different - I collect dust.

—*Ethel L. Smith*

Momma Don't Mow No More..No More

Ya see it rained and rained like never before.
She helped fill sandbags by the score.
Oh now! If her body just wasn't so sore.
She went 'til she thought she could do no more.
And yet it rained and rained a whole lot more.
She prays again please stop the rain Dear Lord.
Send it to where it's needed a whole lot more.
She used to complain about her ordinary chores.
Oh! If now she could just be a little bored.
Then the streams and rivers could just hold no more.
Now she doesn't have any grass or even a floor.
That fast muddy water went right through the door.
Look! Look! At all the waste on the muddy shores.
Oh…All that clean-up to have to look toward.
She hopes she not left homeless and poor.
At least she's alive, thank the Good Lord.
And for now momma don't have to mow no more.

—*Linda Holsinger*

Untitled

Look at the little girl who stands there.
She is bad-she does things a little girl shouldn't do,
Don't talk to her, she might lie to you.
Don't play with her, people will think you're like her
Don't go near her, she might contaminate you.
Don't look at her, just pretend not to see.

No one knows why she is bad, maybe some
people are just bad, maybe she was born that way.

Don't feel sorry for her, she deserves to feel
disgusting and ashamed,
She may look innocent, but she is bad.

Stay away from her
Don't be like her

Who is the little girl I speak of?

As I start to answer, I notice I am
looking into a mirror.

That little girl is me.
—*Annette Capwell*

Lady Liberty

Upon her head she wears a crown, her eyes look out to sea.
She is the mighty symbol of the land for liberty.
    Her left hand holds a Book of Rule
    Pressed against her gown.
    Her right hand lifts a mighty torch
    To light the world around
She stood and watched her children leave
    To fight in distant wars
crying tears in silence to see them never more.

The lady has been ailing, because she's getting old,
One hundred years of salty wind, and bitter, bitter cold.
    We her children won't forsake her
    We'll mend her good as new
    She'll stand in all her splendor
    For all the world to view
And at her feet are broken shackles; she stands on soil that's
    free. The fairest lady of them all, is lady liberty.

—*Chaplain James C. Summerlin*

Visit To Mom's Grave

Dear Mom's been dead for near a year
She lies in calm repose,
Last summer I visited her resting place,
And there I placed a rose.

I looked around at other graves
Bedecked with garlands grand,
But this lone rose outshone them all.
'Twas planted by Mom's hand.

I sat beside the head stone,
I pondered thoughts untold
I thought of once lovely lady
Who had withered and grown old.

The wind blew ore it's petals,
They shimmered in the breeze,
Its voice spoke out so softly,
I knelt down on my knees.

This lone rose was not purchased
Nor did it have a card,
But 'twas planted by my mother's hands
In mother's own back yard.

I spent some time recalling
The years that drifted by
And prayed a prayer ore mother's grave
With saddened tearful eye.
—*Ronald Grimes*

Longest Night

She sleeps, she sighs, she scales the skies,
She shifts and drifts around him;
She dances without reason, comes and goes with the season,
Always just out of reach.

He twists and turns, while his future burns,
He waits while she caresses his fate;
She smiles and fumbles, he stops and stumbles,
Always just out of reach.

Innocent cries, tantalizing lies,
Across the seas she leads him;
But all the while, her truth is guile,
Always just out of reach.

"I'm out of reach," her silence speaks,
"And yet you can always touch me;
Just don't forget, our future's set,
And alone you will sleep till the end."

If only the dream were as ephemeral as she seems,
If only the sun were allowed;
If only my story could thrive on her glory,
If only this night had an end.
—*Chris Hurst*

Father's Rage

Her eyes encompass the world
She takes it all in
And accepts it
She is dressed like a doll
It is not her own choice
Her gawky figure turned into itself
Her small hands fidget
She is dwarfed by her father
And her eyes have a mulish look about them
You can hear her father yelling
And she is just standing there
Still as a rabbit in hiding
And she accepts it
Her eyes encompass the world
Her heart aches with unseen bruises
—*Courtney D. Brown*

The Atlantic Ocean

My mom carried me down to the sea
She wanted me to be as happy as I could be.
The ocean was as far as I could see
And it was blue that day, as blue as blue can be.

Down the sandy shore I did roam,
Getting my feet wet in its foam.
Oh, it's a pleasant thing,
Walking and listening to the ocean sing.

I let myself wonder of its creatures
That I learned about from my teachers.
I know of fish, seals, turtles and whales.
As I looked, I saw the porpoises' fins and tails.

I spotted a ship cruising on the ocean
And many waves came from its motion.
The ocean waves were now getting high
So my Mom said, "It's time to go bye."

As we were leaving, I looked down at the ground.
What a pretty sea shell I had just found.
Thank you Atlantic Ocean for the treasure
And for an excellent day of pleasure.
—*Tami Cooner*

Frozen Ground

It was snowing the day they put Amy in the ground.
She was just a dirty little kid,
So her parents thought when she was alive.
They didn't love her.
If they had, they wouldn't have treated her so bad.

The earth was frozen solid that day
When little Amy was lowered in the ground.
Her casket was the cheapest her parents could find —
Just a pine box lined with thin satin cloth.
Her daddy had cursed at how much it cost.

It was the coldest funeral on record that year,
Not one tear fell.
Since then, Jesus has split her parents wide open
And their tears make a joyful sound.
But they fall too late on frozen ground.
—*Kathleen F. Roe*

"Home"

I visited the place not long ago — the house, the barn, the
sheds all standing there;
No longer did I hear the clucking hens — the lowing cows,
To my dismay — the buildings all were in such disrepair!

The grass was overgrown, and yet — I could discern
A daisy and a dandelion — and aster fair —
Amidst the grass, the ferns, the twigs and vines all intertwined
I wished I might return, to make things - "square."

For 'twas I who left the uncomplaining farm —
"Too much demand upon my time" — I did complain,
I wanted freedom — a chance to see the hills beyond;
I'm older now and wiser, yes I'm glad to be back home again.

I hope so much that I can truly make amends,
And try to make the farm alive again —
I'm sure with God's help and lots of hard work to expend,
The farm — my home could once more be my friend.
—*June F. Lemos*

n Boaz

met a woman she's really sweet
She's awful short and got two small feet
Her hair is dark and really long
You should hear her sing a song
She sings real cute if you could hear
She's from the south and not from here
Her mom is old and very dear
She gives you things when you are there
She gave us cookies and food to eat
We ate so much that we fell asleep
When we woke up she fed us more
Then she sent us out the door
We went back to her daughter's house
There we ran into a mouse it was
small and really cute she said get
out and leave your flute then it went
on out the door then we never saw it no more

—*Athenna Pendland*

Once

An April morning
Shimmering with dew and pale sunlight
The twittering of birds
And the burgeoning life

Undeniably, temporarily
Resting any doubts, queries, questions
About the purpose, the meaning
The unbounding hope of the spirit

If September is the queen of months
Then April must be her princess
The full flower and rich hues of the monarch
Find source and inspiration in April's stirrings

Like September, the spirit's fullness and tranquility
Must begin ever so gently
Our souls must be sung to, bathed in warmth
Treated as tenderly as new shoots

For the storms are inevitable
In nature as in life
And the seasons come again
But we have just once.

—*Patricia McGill Muller*

Excellent Woman

The beauty of your soul, excellent woman
Shines through when you are being yourself
You have made something of the suffering
Luminous, mysterious, unusual

You have learned the acceptance
Of your own natural preferences and rhythms
Content in your own unique beauty
You no longer seek society's perfection

You have plumbed the depths of the well
Brought up your soul dripping with grace
Risking the courage to be authentic
To live your expectations and your myth

You have earned the freedom not to domesticate your creativity
By putting your hands in the forge
Showing the world the bronze of your inner light
Arms raised in salute to yourself

—*Lily Gaines*

"Caretaker of the Clocks"

Many clocks, not one or two, their faces shown in stately view,
Side by side upon a shelf, timed in rhythm — to charm an elf.
They soothed to comfort in the night
Unveiling each new day in dawn of light.
Like old friends tried and true share sad and happy times with you.

One quaint old timepiece it's silence wears
A saddened face as if no one cares;
Once proudly stood in aging grace,
Now a mantle shows a vacant space,
Silence urging to unlock the heartbeat of this lonely clock.

Dad's patient hands made to repair
Turned the key of time once more to share,
Of days gone by and times we know
Revealing summers warm and winter's snow.
Spring time breezes and harvest gold
In rhapsody these stories told.
Time goes on remains not still,
Time renders life in God's own will.

From far and near of folks that talk,
Know the caretaker of the grand old clock.

—*Leah Jean Vixo*

The Lonely Ones

The drone of a derelict on the
side of the road,
The feeble cry of a youth to
be heard,
The tears of the abused condemned
by disbelief,
The yelp of an elder put to
rest in a home,
The excuses of the convicted
demoralized by accusations,
The protest of the opinionated
unlistened to by conformist,
The thoughts of the handicapped
ignored, forgotten and assumed not there.

—Why must anyone be lonely-
—*Elizabeth Keating*

October

When the mums bloom, as a rule of thumb;
Signals the end of summer has come;
Ere before I die;
I wish my daughter nigh;
So many things to tell her,
so many things to say;
The road I do watch;
I'll see her any day;
Tall, blond hair, brown eyes;
Her puppy at her side;
A cowgirls gait, is the horses canter;
Oh please don't be late; sighing, I pray and wait...

—*Anonymous*

Rising Spirit

So much depends upon a
a brilliant bright light.
A whitish- yellowish glow.
Floating hand,
lifts you
towards the light.
No force
No life
Peace

—*Amy Ann Stanton*

Best Friend Forever

We were best friends,
Since kindergarten.
Years later we were torn apart,
by forces beyond our control.
We were forced to go our separate ways,
knowing in our hearts we did not want to.

Now we are apart and it seems like its been forever,
yet it has only been a few years.
But there is one thing I will remember,
the promise we made to each other;
That even if we were separated,
we would indeed be together One Day.

—*Shannon Otto*

Come In, I Dream Here.

Run with me, play with me.
Sing with me, fly with me.
Jump so high you touch the sky.
Laugh so loud, you pop a cloud.
Run so fast, away from your past.
It hurts too bad to look sad.
The skies in front, with demons behind.
Look forward, my friend,
backwards is the end.
The mirrors fell behind,
I know you don't mind.
You had fun when you skipped with the sun.
And laughed for hours with the flowers.
You played games with the swings.
Didn't dare to break their strings.
You might ruin someone's dreams.

—*Melissa Rout*

One Boy's Dream World

Down at the millpond,
Sittin' on a log, I listened to the chorus,
Of some happy bullfrogs,
One sang tenor, while another sang bass,
But another is singing,
Seemed all out of place,

Then one was the preacher,
For he had such an air,
And he rose up to preach,
While I sat there,
He was all dressed out,
With a fine top hat,
And he wore striped pants, with a pair of spats.

Then my Mother was calling,
I awoke with a start,
Then I looked all around,
It was gettin' dark,
Then I knew right then,
I'd dreamed me a dream,
While I listened to the frogs, at an old millstream.

—*Alvin Gage*

Marriage

Matrimonial
Altar
Ritual to
Reinforce
Inevitable
Affection
Granted to
Each other

—*Victoria J. Broekhuizen*

The Place

The sun beat down like hot rays of fire
Sitting here on the bank of the river
The field beyond full of wild flowers
Sun glistening on the water, sparkles of silver.

The golden leaves of summer upon the trees
A beautiful scenery God, himself is pleased.
A bluebird sat perched on the ol' wooden gate.
Its so peaceful here by myself, my found fate
The most greatest creation God has made.

Not to many places like this left
God made it just for me I felt
For my quite time, to him, I give the glory.
After all his life he gave for me.

For this little time I always anticipate
Redeemed in the blood, and to read the untold story.
His creations leaves me so pleased.
I hate to see the time to leave.

—*Rebecca Ingram*

Do It Now

I would like to see the pretty flowers while I am still able
Sitting in a pretty vase on the kitchen table
I would like to hear the comments, as to how nice or kind you
    find me
If my friends could tell me now, just what they think of me
A smile—a hug would do me fine from all the friends that I
    call mine
Don't wait until my eyes are useless, to give me something pretty
Tell me now so I can smile at something very witty
My eyes are able to see the views, the colors in their various hues
My ears can hear the melodies sweet, as I walk along the street
If you think I'm kinda sweet, tell me now while my heart still beats
Don't wait until I'm laid to rest, to tell my friends what was my
    best

—*Helen A. Harris*

Dakota Spring

Spring on the prairie is my delight
Skies filled with wild geese, flight after flight,
Setting a course for their old nesting grounds
Keeping mates close with their honk - honking sounds.
The days are long and the sun's warming glow
Has melted the last few patches of snow.
Swollen streams gurgle and flow swiftly by
To well-soaked lowlands where young freshets lie.
Freed from the deep freeze that they must endure
All the small creatures awaken and stir.
The rascally coon begins his forays
To assuage the hunger of leaner days.
Woodlands resound with the chatter of squirrels
Flicking their bushy tails with twitches and twirls.
Spring on the prairie eternally brings
Fresh hope and new life to all living things.

—*Bernice Rathbun*

"Dragons Victim"

Dragons
Slimy green, with pointed ears
Long snout which points in the direction of the rushing wind.
Enormous shadows that cover the vast land,
and a fiery breath with flames like a blowing torch.
Soaring through the air like an eagle.
Flapping boldly through the puffy white clouds,
searching for its prey.

—*Maika Pele*

.ain

See it splash against the window,
owly drizzling down the spattered glass.
plashing puddles in the gutters.
ourishing the plants and watering the earth.
ig grey clouds form evil faces staring down
 the earth. The lightning crashes, the thunder booms and the
.in gets harder. Like tiny needles falling from
e sky. Find shelter quick! The wind is rising
aking the trees bend fiercely.
he lightning lights up the sky in a wicked way,
lling small children with fear, as they huddle under the
ankets, praying for the rain to stop.

—*Courtney Leigh Adams*

.arkness

here's a place in the mind way back in the corner, just a
nall little place that no one can enter. Thoughts, memories,
ars and lost hope - that no other mind, body or soul could
ossibly evoke. During the days I treasure it so - late at
ght it causes dreadful woes. It is connected to my heart and
ce. It can bring on a smile and yet turn the beats of my
art into a race. This place streams into my veins, my
ood... It makes all emotions rush through my body like a
ging flood... This place makes me wonder "Am I the only
.e?" Do the outside strangers live their life with none? I
de this place in my mind under secured lock with no key,
.hind a little door that not even I can see. It would do me
. good to ever open this place of weakness; for the only thing
.at could escape is years and years of darkness.

—*Kimberley Star Cline*

.lind Faith

hey sparkle like bright diamonds, in the winter soft morning
ow far across the wide meadows they stand, in row after row
.e bright little white crosses, So far away from their home
.ere must we always remember, Lay our young daughters and
.r sons

.es we have traveled on, Down through many long troubled years
.e precious treasures we were given, Are now memories filled
.th tears. Why must men forget and refuse, The hard lessons
.ey were taught. No one nation can stand alone, Against the
.her nations of the world

.ithout kindness, our love and respect, For all of our brothers
.egardless from which nation, Men of all creeds and of all
.lors. The rows of white crosses, will but grow longer and
.nger. Filled with our hopes and our dreams, our sons and
.r daughters

—*Joe J. Staker*

.lone

s I sit here all alone I feel so cheated, so misused,
 abused, and even somehow confused. As I sit here all
.ne I think of how my feelings were mislead and even
.isused. As I sit here all alone I think of the one I
.nged to touch, the one I longed to talk to, the one I
.nged to give all my love. As I sit here all alone I
.ink of all the feelings, of all the things, of all the
.hes and pains we have shared. As I sit here all alone
.hink of the one I loved, the one that gave me that
.me love back, but only one someone just one stood
.tween us and the love we shared. As I sit here all
.ne I think of the one that kept me and my love
.art. As I sit her all alone I think, I dream, I reminisce
.re all alone thinking of the one I loved the one
.till love. Yes as I said so many times before
.it here alone I sit here all alone.

—*Veronica Jones*

Autumn Air

The autumn afternoon draws
Snowy air from high on Lolo Peak.
Nipping currents breathe a promise of
Morning frost, brushing a sun-brown cheek.

October's sun spreads halting warmth
Across the meadow's girth.
Slanting fingers gently toy
With the yielding earth.

Fresh-cut pine salts the air.
Leaves crazy-quilt the land.
Joy, longing, peace and pain
Flood the cosmos where I stand.

Cat-like breezes do a dance,
Dry stems waver, bend, bow o'er.
Fleet memories glow then pall,
Pause and pounce once more.

The moment is a cosmic jewel, one
Bright but shadowed treasure showing
Life's two faceted and uncut sides
In a precious breath of knowing.

—*Robert Ira Ward*

At The Multiplex

I wish the movies could last forever
so as not to face the world just beyond the back row
where the lobby lights are blinding
and oily-fingernailed people pour oleo into buckets
and scatter change across spittled counters—
outside the air is sticky
like freshly steamed gym socks wrapped 'round bodies
that scream the squawks of territoriality
in the midst of parking lot wars
where I use a rusty wire hanger with a silver tip
found in the slopes of oozing trash bins
to scrape the sludge of voyeurist slobs
from the bottoms of my shoes.
No, I'd rather stare into the eye of an eclipse
through a fantastic window where cheeks glow
in the radiance of technicolor giants
and popcorn kernels tumble between thighs
and oily-fingernailed people
hold hands before an altar.
Yes, sometimes the world looks nicer in the dark.

—*Jim VanValen*

Summer Clouds

I always loved the summer clouds
So billowy and white
I'd lie out in the field
And watch them with delight

Once I saw a bear just rolling around.
Then, there was a granny on a merry-go-round,
A bunny and giraffe were playing ball.
Along came a tiger who sat on a wall.

The ballet dancer was a very fat mouse,
Now, there is a monkey and a two-story house.
Suddenly the house began to crack.
And there sat a boy on a turtle's back.

The turtle smiled and climbed a tree
The boy looked down, and waved to me.
Those beautiful clouds just drifted away,
We both will be back another day

I will watch them, so can you.
It really isn't something new.
It's Mother Nature's game in the sky
Just play it - don't ask why.

—*Rita Allison*

The Plan

I want this day to count for something, Lord -
So few do.
The wasted moments lost to any worth
Outstrip the few.
And when I see the sum of all my days
will their only measure be
a crumpled bed - a half-drunk cup of tea?
God, forbid! that this day should hold
No mark of excellence - no golden cue!
I want this day to count for something, Lord -
something for You.

—*Barbara Lammons*

See

I am but one, but one can be strong
So got to hell, don't tell me I'm wrong,
I have something to say, now I will speak
So just shut up and really listen to me.
Forget you are you, forget I am me.
Forget, for just once, forget you can see.
"Appearance is everything" but it's not enough.
What we see can be too damned much.
So pretend you're blind, pretend you're free
Then maybe, for once, the world will see.

—*Paula R. McCracken*

Dancing Trees

Trees will forever blow in the wind.
So graceful as if to their branches ballerinas were pinned.
They dance together in the warm moonlight breeze.
Their branches dangle as golden keys.
As they prance they sing their song of long ago,
When the world of man was not so.
When eagles in their limbs would make their mighty nests.
And fly over the oceans, so blue, so fresh.
Then the morning sun comes and runs her rays through their hair,
And the cold wind blows as it may dare.
The trees whip in rage, as animals locked in a tight cage,
But slowly they fall asleep with a fear.
As if their time to go was near.
Deeper and Deeper they go to sleep,
Shrinking into their roots so deep.
To awake again
For trees will forever blow in the wind.

—*Jenny Finnegan*

Little Girl

Look at the little girl
so lonely and sweet
roaming our streets with little bare feet.
She has no place to go,
no family to love
She lives off of welfare
and trash scrapings of meat.
Her father had left her,
Her mother was killed,
Her brother was kidnapped,
and now she's very ill.

Look at the little girl with
not enough to eat, so tiny
and fragile all she does is weep.

Now look at the little girl
and her little tiny grave with
dirt being thrown upon her face.
Her tombstone is empty with no date or name.
Just look at the little girl and what she became.

—*Jennifer Wylie*

Kill Man Kill

Guns are made to kill, and to sell to man
so man could kill man
it is the goal of our production plan.
It is for profit to a privileged few
regardless the consequence;
it is the progress of weaponry
and all planned, so man could kill man.
Power struggles throughout the years
the goal has always been the same
develop more and better armaments
hand over to man as his sacrament,
and let man kill man.
Education has developed the mind
to invent the atomic bomb,
so man may be destroyed
as all life on earth
so future geologist may discover
the bone fragments making oil for the hearth.

—*Clif Culp*

Uncle Tom

My thoughts went round and round in my head.
So many questions I kept inside, without
being said. When I least expected it, the
answers came through someone unknown. He was
special and kind, through his eyes it had shown.
He spoke without knowing what I was feeling.
He spoke in ways I was able on seeing. God
works in mysterious ways, I truly believe. For he
send me "Him", dear, sweet but had to also
leave. Taught me to embrace life with the
worries, the fright and time. Also to love what
God sends us with him in heart and in mind.
What happens, happens I believe he was saying.
For no matter what, on Gods hands we all
end up laying.

—*Gigi Cox, BX.*

Tomorrow's the Day!

There are so many things that I ought to do—
So many things—and I've just done a few.
For instance, I'm looking right now at the sink
Loaded with dishes, right up to the brink!
Just sit back and relax? How I wish I might
Let them remain in that sink overnight;
But instead, with a sigh, I begin my task
Washing and rinsing and drying. You ask,
Why do you think it's such a redundant thing?
It's because there's a wish in my heart to sing!

I would rather be singing and spinning around,
My arms open wide and my feet off the ground
As I fit in the role of a lady at ease.
Woe is me! I have dishwashing dropsy sneeze.
I'm allergic to soap and to sudsy suds,
How in the world will I clean my duds?
There is washing and ironing and scrubbing floors,
Time to cook, time to sew—what a lot of chores
I can think of to do—oh, what can I say?
Too late tonight. Yes, tomorrow's the day!

—*Bernice Holden*

Angel Child

Today I saw an angel child,
So meek, so humble, and so mild.
He was so sweet as angels are,
I knew that he was from heaven afar.
Around his lovely head it seemed,
A brilliant angel's halo beamed.
He could not speak, or could not talk,
And his legs...you see, he could not walk.
Looking up with such a smile,
So full of Godly love,
I knew this wonderful angel child
Was sent from heaven above.
　　　—*Rosemarie Jackson*

Road of Life

Ah, this life
So much strife
Battered and torn
From the day we are born
Human beings, we are all
Just a different port of call
Same thoughts, emotions, feelings, hopes and fears
Also, laughter and tears
Only greater or lesser in degree
This I see
Like ships passing in the night
A glimpse of recognition, a light
Many are the forks in the road of life
Who can say? Who can tell?
Maybe only God can tell
If we have chosen well
So many rules
When all is said and done
Maybe, we only needed one
The Golden Rule
　　　—*Ruth Yost*

So Alone

So alone yet surrounded by a crowd
So silent yet screaming out loud

So caged in but there are no visible bars
No real cuts but so many deep scars

So very scared yet nothing to fear
Wanting so badly to feel someone near

No feelings left yet there is so much pain
Always striving knowing there is nothing to gain

Not wanting to go back but always seeming to be shoved
Not wanting to care but needing so badly to be loved!
　　　—*Hillary Milovich, Age 16*

Love Is

Love is a tickling that cannot be scratched
So the love of two people just cannot be matched.
　Two hearts beat as one, the old saying goes
　Before either speaks, the other one knows.
　　Love is a feeling sent down from God
　　How lucky you are if it gives you the nod.
　The beauty of love is sweet to behold
　Really a treasure worth far more than gold.
To walk with another each day through your life
To share all your happiness, even your strife
　Gives life a meaning that makes it worthwhile;
　Your day really glows when love gives a smile.
　　So treat it with tenderness, give thanks in prayer
　　For love is a treasure we're privileged to share.
　　　—*Eva E. Steinka*

"Why Did You Have To Go"

You left me, you went away,
　so very far away;

They told me you went to live with God,
　so I sit alone and pray;

Wishing you can hear me,
　as I whisper oh so low;

I miss you very much tell me,
　"Why did you have to go?"

We only knew each other for a short while,
　but our friendship how it did grow;

I hope your happy living with God,
　but I'm very sad, you know,

So I say goodbye, in my solemn prayer,
　as I live here all alone, not going anywhere.
　　　—*Donna DeLucca Berg*

Evolvement

In the beginning we dream...then awake...and discover a path...
So we begin our journey...racing, arms outstretched to embrace...
Running down paths of warm sand...budding dew-kissed roses...
Soft kitten purrs...gentle slopes and shallow valleys...
Morning-glow dawn beckons our questing senses...
Caught up in living...we lose our dreams...
Vows are made...but broken...
While Time...sneak-thief saboteur...re-routes our path...
And we forge on our journey...stumbling, arms withdrawn to protect...
Slipping down paths of cold stone...wilting worm-chewed roses...
Harsh kitten wails...rocky slopes and jagged gorges...
Evening-fog dusk stifles our questing senses...
Until...haltingly...obtusely...we grope forward.
　　　—*Coni Baldwin*

My Sweet Psycho, My Love

I'm standing outside your apartment, waiting. Our love was as soft as juicy T-bone steaks, as bright as nuclear bombs; so classic when you kicked me in the butt, just 'cause I said your mother was a slut.

(Divorce me huh divorce me was that the elevator pull out the)

It's true when we first met, there was magic in your beautiful dark eyes The tears that filled them came later, much later, like When I slammed your head into the car's fender and then you shoved my right hand in the blender

(you turned it on I can't believe you turned it on bitch bitch bitch)

Upon our marriage we said we'd be together forever ... How evanescent is true love! How was I to know that if I found another girl, you'd get another guy? Or that you'd call the cops if I rigged the brakes on his car, just so he would die?

(prove it prove it prove it you bitch)

Elevator's here! I pull out my knife and slit your throat as you get our Your body may be spurting blood, glazed over may be your eyes.. Oh, my sweet, physically you may be gone,

but "true love never dies."

(ha ha ha did you like that you bitch ha ha ha ha)
　　　—*Joseph Kuo*

We Are One

The moonlight caresses you in the shadows of the night.
Soft to the touch are the hues of your hair.
Your eyes a deep pool of blue are drawn to my bare breast.
Like a soft breeze your lips move over them.

Silently I am drawn to the tenderness of your touch.
We rest in each other.
As one our hearts meld together
And run in beat to the music of our souls.

A song in the night rises loud and clear.
With great care our fingertips touch.
Our hands close together and in that moment
Your strength holds my passion.

A burst of energy rings clear.
The heat of your breath is seen
Like the misty fog laying low to the ground
On a cold winters night.
We are warm.

—*Ross Nelson*

A Gift

Dealing with the insanities of this world,
Softly pulling in like a turtle in a shell,
Becoming vulnerable to the strike of coldness
Safely pulling in like a turtle in a shell.

Forgiving - softly forgiving - forgiving
Battered and torn, ripped and forlorn,
Forgiving - softly forgiving - forgiving.

Becoming stronger, reaching out
Torn within, torn without.
Eyes sadden, softly loving.
Torn within, torn without

Forgiving - softly forgiving - forgiving
Battered and torn ripped and forlorn,
Forgiving - softly forgiving - forgiving.

Daring to be one with humanity,
Caring - softly caring - caring.
Stepping out, bringing them in,
Caring - softly caring - caring.

—*Kathy Sabel*

Longing

Longing for a romantic man
Softly touching my face with
his hand.

Longing for a romantic man holding
me to show love.
Longing to drift to the clouds above.

Longing to be romantically desired.
Longing to be sensually set on fire.

Longing for that rapid beating of the heart.
Longing for the love that will
never part.

Longing to live out a fantasy
Longing to fall into ecstacy

Longing for this romantic man that
I have yet to meet.

Longing for this romantic man
that will sweep me off my feet.

—*Dawn Hissong*

Memories Gallery

There are many pictures in memory's gallery,
Some are faded, some are torn;
Yet these pictures keep a record,
Of my life, since I was born.

There are lots of picture places,
Some across the ocean foam,
Yet the picture that is dearest,
Is my early childhood home.

It was not a mansion owned,
Not even a house for rent;
Nor was it built of bricks and lumber,
It was just a logger's canvas tent.

Yet the setting of this dwelling,
Had been planned by God's own hand;
And the Mother's love, that kept it,
Made it the finest of the land.

—*Orvil Stout*

Families

Families are something we all have.
Some are good, and others are bad.
Families have duties, and obligations.
One of which, is to visit on your vacations.
Some families often demand more than you can give.
While others give of themselves to help you live.
No matter good or bad, the bond is always strong.
Whether you do right, or whether you do wrong.
Love is the key, the family pattern holds.
A warm family love is what keeps you whole.
A good family love is a precious gift of life.
A bad family love is a means of strife.
No matter good or bad, we should all strive to give more.
To our children, our legacy, whom we adore.
For they are our future, the worlds in their hands.
The love that we show them will help them understand.
There is good and bad in all of us, for we are the family of man.

—*Patricia Potts*

Some Day

Some day's we talk
Some day's we don't
Some day's I understand you
Some day's I don't
Some day's I hold you
Some day's I don't know how to hold you
Some day's you leave
Some day's I leave
Some day's we make love
Some day's we don't
Some day maybe
Some day maybe not
Anyway
Today is today - and a day with you - is
Someday

—*Bill Gustafson*

Sole Flight

Crazy worlds lurk into the eyes of the beholder.
So on into the night. Look the train from hell is
rising into the spirits of the fourth dimension.
Sky blue; see the black? It produces your sense.
Feel the power of the thunderbolt. May your knees
bend down with a crack in the earth and decide
what way your departure is. Strength is in the
eye of the beholder.

—*John J. Green*

Crosses

In this life, we must bear many crosses
Some good and some bad
But one thing for sure that Jesus did for us all
Bearing His cross alone was so sad.

He died for our sins
So we might be free
That lonely cross He carried
Was just for you and me.

In Him I found a joyful life
Through that very cross
Such love I'll never let be in vain
Losing Him would be such a great loss.

Now that I've decided to follow Him
Many times dying out from sin
You too can have the thrill knowing Him
Even when broken in pieces, He'll mend.

　　　—Edith Langston

Memories

Leon took a trip into his past
Some thirty-odd years ago
To walk the fields
Where the creek used to flow.

He remembered the mulberry trees
With their fruit so sweet.
Green persimmons puckered your mouth
But ripe ones were quite a treat.

For swimming and fishing
Our pond was the place under the sun;
After a hot summer day
A good place to cool off and have fun.

The house yard was quite a sight, I think
With old fashioned roses, both yellow and pink
Wafting there perfume and nodding in the breeze
They were a sight to please.

The windmill out by the barn turned with ease
And there was always a breeze.
The house and most of the buildings are gone
But the memory lingers on.

　　　—Nila Behrends

Je T'attendrai

　　　Je T'attendrai, Je T'attendrai
　　　　Somebody loves you
　　　　Somebody cares
　　　My heart is breaking-would you dare
　　　Je T'attendrai, Je T'attendrai
　　　　All in the mood
　　　　The timing is right
　　　I sit by the fire and wonder
　　　Where you'll be tonight
　　　　Oh how I miss you
　　　　Oh how I care
　　　Je T'attendrai, Je T'attendrai
　　　　My body wants to breath
　　　　Only with you I can see
　　　Your eyes are like a clear blue ocean
I wish upon a star I long to fly over the rainbow
　　　The colors I see are striking to me
　　　You feel so near so please stay
　　　If you turn your head I'll walk away
　　　Je T'attendrai....Je T'attendrai....

　　　—Barbara Shaw

Some Men

　　Some men are ashamed that they have a special friend
　Someone they can always call, someone who will always mend
　　Some men are ashamed that they take her advice to heart
　For she was there from the very start
　　She always has time and makes time when she does not
　She seems to be constantly ready for the toughest shot
　　Too many neglect the one like no other
　I will not make such a mistake for I adore my mother
　　Even when she is not here, somehow she is
　And if she does not know, it is her I always miss
　　So whenever you need someone, you have her too
　I myself know this, Mom, I love you.

　　　—E. Taff

A True Friend

A true friend is someone who cares
Someone who will take time to share
Problems they'd be glad to hear
Always there for you to shed a tear
A friend is someone who is always there
To help you climb that ladder of stairs
If you miss a step on that ladder and start to fall
That friend will help you bounce back like a ball
For a true friend is there through your good and bad ones too!
So if you get down and need a friend to help you get through
A true friend would be glad to be there for you
I thank that true friend of mine
For stepping out on that very fine line
For a true friend is so very hard to find
People are so into theirselves that they become to blind.
A true friend - they don't give it no mind.

　　　—Kimberly Garrett

A Dream

A dream is something that you wish for
　　something that seems so very far away
　　　something that seems out of your reach

You are my one and only dream
　　something that seems so out of reach
　　　something that God won't let me have

If you did come my way
　　I wouldn't know how to act
　　　or even what to say to you

I would die if I felt your tender touch
　　and be in heaven with just a kiss
　　　but these seem out of reach and far away

Dreams are just an escape from reality
　　but when I see my dream everyday
　　　it isn't just fun, it's hard to function

Because my dream lady doesn't realize
　　that she has caught the eye of someone
　　　someone too shy to say the things that he feels

Knowing this, I go back to my normal life dreaming that someday
　　you will be with me but for now, I will just dream of you.
　　　—John J. Knip III

Greetings Love

　A note I meant to write, but couldn't word it right
A week from your 22nd with a wish that's one of many
May this Sunday be like others before
And may the ones of the future also hold memories to cherish
Until I hold you and you me
I love you my angel forever more
　　　—Edward (EDJU) Broilo

"Grandpa Jim"

There is a man who sleeps on our couch.
Sometimes he can be very funny. He spoils the great
grandchildren. And, he's noted for being a grouch.

His parents pioneered Colorado in covered wagons. Four sons
lived there awhile. Iowa was his homestead, his beckoning
call. Oh James, your heart is in us one and all.

In the army back in the forties, He was such a handsome young
man. But time and worrying has taken its toll. His days are
spent drinking coffee, smoking and talking. Mostly grumbling
about this and that. He goes fishing daily on the 'Botna,
never keeping his catch.

He reared seven children. Each of whom had their share of
broken hearts. He was always there to help and comfort them.
To lend his love, heart and hands for support.

Does he know the impact of life he has given?
The unrelentless love he has forth brought?
He gives all who love him, hope, love, honor and strength.
Because everyone including friends, call James our
"Grandpa Jim".

—*Lucie S. Wright*

She Felt a Presence

Life's clock is ticking away
sometimes missing a beat;
Sometimes loud
Sometimes barely heard.

The moon peers from
fragments of silk clouds;
sometimes, white
sometimes yellow.

Then, like a drop of rain
spreading a widening circle on a blotter,
a warm feeling arises
from within her heart.

Suddenly, a hand takes hers and
brushes it against his cheeks,
Soon, hope, warm and glowing
fills the darkened room.

—*Irene Kanetake*

Occasion

We plan to work in order to attain our aim,
Sometimes occasion takes place to reach the end.
Let us study and recall some of the historical events.
It showed that occasion did make things different.

A prince spent his perfect life in the palace,
He did not know anything beyond his place,
One day he had a chance to tour the country,
He occasionally met hopeless people in the city.

He was so surprised to see such miserable situation,
He couldn't control his unbearable emotions,
A decision was made to be a monk in the temple,
He devoted himself to the Buddhist world.

He thought that a discipline should be guided,
It would contribute a great deal to benefit the mankind.
He taught people the self-denial, virtue and wisdom,
He was Gautama Siddhartha, the great founder of Buddhism.

—*Diana M. P. Chang*

"Somewhere To Be"

We, are the faces that you see on the evening news,
Sometimes with plastic bags, hand-me-down clothes, and faces of
many hues.

We, number many, single folks and families too.
We, are the homeless, who once lived and looked just like you.

But, now we are homeless, and wishing for just,
"somewhere to be."

We, must sleep sometimes, wherever we can lay our heads,
Some of the "little ones" cry for their own beds.

Life has dealt us a mighty bad blow.
Why, we were chosen, we will never know.

But now, all we want is just,
"somewhere to be".

"Somewhere to be" — "Somewhere to be"

Simply means:
A place called Home, for my family and me.

—*Theola Jones*

'Tis Time for Tea

Will you join me for some afternoon tea?
Somewhere serene, perhaps beyond the sea.
The sun smiles, as waves laugh for you and me.
You shall see that our life was meant to be.

The ocean echoes sweet remembrances
Of an era where love alone prevailed.
Always lingers such fragile fragrances,
A place where sorrow has never sailed.

Let us seek murmuring rainbows at fray.
Here, misty clouds kiss skies in sweet doses.
At last, your heart's delight sings on its way,
Enveloping like soft, scented roses.

To look at you, love, is to never frown.....
No tea? what? You are trying to cut down?!!

—*Orlena Waverly Fong*

Interlude

At times I hear some beauty in
song crossing the blowing grass
over rubble and rock... twisted
wire caught and wheel barrows
of what-not where behold, a lark,
a singer gives concert to our
labour sweat with each rap-tap
and saw buzz giving interlude...
perfect harmonious tunes
O wondrous nature — wondrous song bird where will
you go after we have finished?

—*James Hiatt*

A Plead For Truth

She sits in front of me
    she is my friend
    I am her's
My up bringing says she is different from me
    Less than me
Not because of her personality but her color
I know it is wrong to think that
    I do not want to think that
But the thought has been embedded
    It is a part of me
How do I stop thinking it.
Tell me how do I stop thinking it.

—*Wendy Thompson*

Time's Precious Hour

Time's precious hour comes on fleeting wings —
Songs of joy and sadness both it sings,
And in passing cannot be restored —
All men the subjects of its two edged sword.

It grants us moments of sublimity,
Then takes our joy and leaves a memory...
Until our lives are full of memories made
Of the dear and precious hours time gave —

And in the end, we're tokens of the past
When our bones are laid beneath the grass...
But Truth will conquer time and set us free
To live again — where time meets eternity...
—*Harvey Joseph Dockstader, Sr.*

The Last Night

I went to a night of a new beginning
Soon to the world there is no ending
No time to call hope of endless dreams
Only to follow the unwritten screams
A plan of a time soon to come
And the time spent with you second to none
The lights went dim as we started
In the back of our minds we slowly parted
For me to a place where freedom is givin'
You to a place where the family is living
With friends and there secrets of night before
And the memories of night that are no more
And like the moon I came and went
But time with you was time well spent
As I look back on the recent past
Remembering my thought I wish it would last
And memories of times I know I can't keep
Send me hear when I'm alone asleep
And here I will stay 'till the end of the night
Cause what we did was sexually right.
—*Dennis R. Flanagan*

Sound the Alarm

Green Peace, Green Peace,
Sound the alarm.
The earth is dying;
The hump back whale is crying;
Thirty five million have died;
One thousand geniuses are gone;
The earth is polluted with innocent blood.
The rain forest is dwindling,
The trees are shouting
One hundred thousand doctors
Will not practice the hippocratic oath.

Greens, greens, sound the alarm.
The cities are over populated;
Man is showing his inhumanity.
The spotted owl is hooting the old refrain,
Bring in the new age,
Before the sacred people
End it with their self-fulfilled prophesies,
And cause us to go into the Millennium.
—*Richard Inniss*

A Valley Of Trees

I stood in a valley of trees.
A breeze blew through the trees
And made me sneeze but I
Stood with ease and watched
The trees blowing in the
Breeze
—*Amie Schell*

The Black Roller Dust Storm

What fragrance is this wafted on the wind?
Sounds carry far, are amplified in air.
A cow lows, larks their singing cease.
The coyote's howl in daylight means beware.

Breathless is the warm and sunny afternoon.
Far to the north and stretching east to west,
Appears a dark black line across the sky.
Strange, large, rolling clouds billow with unrest.

A shriek of wind, and black dust covers all.
It came so fast the rabbit's hutch is lost.
Dust, blinding as the night fills eye and mouth.
Each thing not anchored down is tossed.

Saint Elmo's fire dances on the barb wire fence.
The night comes on, its blackness is unknown.
The mighty wind tries every foe to bend.
Makes every creature, big or small to moan.

At last a pale sun shines in the noonday sky.
The dirt lies banked, like blizzard drifts of snow.
Thistles festoon the boughs of all the trees.
The countryside lies in deep silence, full of woe.
—*Mary A. Fry*

Humble Evening

The lights from the silent night come from the sky above. The sounds of restless air in motion surround me. The moon and the ocean's tide play one more time as eternity motions. Clouds of amber and gray decorate the already serene beauty of night.

The sights and sounds of nature's beauty frolic as if the stars
are old companions
The grace of the elk, the awakening somber of the owl, the song
of a cricket's virtuoso
The scratching of branches wrestling amongst one-another when a
breeze intervenes
Without which the evening would not be the same
Nature's such awesome illusion has played with man's emotions
since the beginning
As peace often sheds its beauty and violence interrupts the
scheme of the moment
Scholars and poets a like, scramble to frame meaning on which
has none
While the poet, such as I, writes in a bewilderment, an
   invisible force beckons me to say
The night will be humble once again.
—*Paul Vaz*

Silent Clamor

Black-and-white visions, photos without film
spots of wordless time, rhyming not reasoning
outside of rain and inside a starry constellation
filtered through an ageless channel of dreams
and poured into the same cool glass

Do you silently clamor
for a feast to quench our thirsting souls, a feast for two?
Your essence flickers like candlelight when I sleep
and I wish to strike a votive match
in the unsure space of our hearts
I want to splash you with a color wheel,
and believe and embrace those flames
born of a pact we have remembered:
not with spoken or written sentiment
but with the eyes

I need to find you in this common realm
so that we can quit damning the dark
and honor it instead...
we'll create myths together
as I kiss the rapture into your mouth
—*Christine Cosenza*

Unleashed Again

Oppression repealed releases ancient hatred
Spreading a foul human blight
Stalking the earth, unleashed again
On a world too distracted to fight

It kills on familiar ground
Traveling this way many times before
Slaughtering innocents because of nationality
Or in the name of a god, a holy war

Driving behind Jihad, Crusade, and Inquisition
It feeds on loathing, intolerance, and death
At places like Auschwitz and Dachau, and now
Bosnia and Croatia, there is no rest

How many more souls must be lost
Before humanity rises from indifferent slumber
Or must a madman unleash another apocalypse
Shocking awake, like sudden rolling thunder

Perverse that among all living things
It is man kind's horrible fate
Despite all that he does, to leave behind
An undying legacy of hate

—*T. C. Wojtkowski*

The Woods Still Sleeps

The woods still sleeps while ——
  Squirrels scurry about in the sun, retrieving goodies hidden
  down under. Spewing the hulls, from their treebranch table,
  to fall beneath the tree giving evidence of pacified hunger.

The woods still sleeps ——
  Beneath the patchwork quilt of snowdrifts and leaves.
  The seedpods on dry stalks cast polka-dot designs. The oak,
  still grasps last years foliage which flutter in the breeze.

The woods still sleeps and ——
  Beneath the snow and leaves lie flowers,
  Tossing in their sleep; too drowsy to hear the songs of birds
  But wait to wash their sleepy eyes with fresh April showers.

Yes, the woods still sleeps as ——
  Snowdrifts shrink from the warming sun,
  Only to be swallowed by the thirsty earth,
  While the wind merrily whirled dancing leaves in fun.

The woods slept on ——
  As all was left behind, with promise to return when- Across
  the pastureland, apple trees flaunt their fragrant beauty
  and flowers, extend a welcome, on hillsides and in the glen.

—*Ione E. Williams*

Grandfather-Grandson

It's time for me to fish by a meandering
stream and watch the canoes whiz by.

A long pole, a bobber of cork, a can of worms,
split-lead sinker, and a green maple tree to shade
my eyes.

A rooted trunk to chair my ancient back.

A grandson to disturb my dozing and thoughts
of memories past, to ask trivial questions of this
old man with wide, dilated, expectant eyes.

His excited voice rings out!
"Grandfather! The bobber's gone!"
"Grandfather, it pulls so hard. It must be a
big one!"
For a moment, we are both number one.

—*Edward F. Crippen*

Look Back Fly Fly Away

A beautiful young angel she
Standing at the edge of the cliff, wings folded and quivering
Skin like golden honey, eyes inky pools, mounds of shiny dark
ringlets cascading down her back

Shall I unfurl my wings and fly away she ponders
To where, to what? she asks of no one in particular
From below a silky, warm voice enfolds her
My sweet one, my precious look back, then fly, fly away

She does as suggested, seeing a life past filled with sorrow and
  pain
Of mostly bad times, too few good times, no love given and one
  forsaken
And once again she hears from below—my sweet one, my precious
Look back no more and fly, fly away quickly now

She raises to her tippy toes, wings outspread
A single teardrop spilling gently down her rosy cheek
Looks back then flies, flies away
And as she crashes to an unknown destination she hears from below

My sweet one, my precious
Beneath you always a river of tears will flow
I love you, I love you—please forgive me forever more.

—*Joy M. Amatury*

"Rise"

Deep in the shadows of my life
Stands alone in the corner of my dark heart
A secret that lies in the depth of all my feelings
It is a confidential hope and dream
Where I secretly let off steam
I try to release my dream
But how can I, where it has never been heard or seen?
But I must let it go.
For it will cause my conscience to become low
The weight of my anxiety is too much to bear.
My life is the shadow of death when hope is not there.
I'm so shy, quiet, .. so lonely
I want to rise!
Yes! Rise above the depths of my poverty.
Rise above the depths of my fear, my sickness, and ignorance.
Rise above this sad life that I live.
I want to be someone higher than my current degrading
disposition.
As soon as I crawl out of this deep pit
I shall truly rise above all obstacles.

—*Paula Wise*

A Tortured Moonless Night

Sitting on the steps of her house. She looked up into a
starless dawn. It was a little past four in the morning and
the mist was so thick she could barely see the lights of the
house across the street. The sycamore tree further down in
the front yard looked surprisingly scary as it cast dark
shadows, thrown to the ground by an unseen moon. The still
damp tendrils of her hair from a late shower clung to her
face and snatched at her shoulders. A cool breeze quietly
rearranged the silky nightgown around her legs. She pulled
the thick blanket closer around her. She sat for a few more
moments as memories washed over her, then she stood and
clutching the blanket with one hand she looked into an
endless sky. With her free hand she wiped away the tears and
went back inside. She now knew the endless pain of losing
someone close to her. Her closest and most loved friend in
the world had been taken from her. Wrenched away in the dark
and moonless hours of night by a drunken driver, and she had
no one to blame for her sisters death but herself.

—*Miranda Kathleen Swearingen*

My True Love

As the warmth of light caresses your eyes, the brighter the
stars shine in the brilliant skies. Anticipating every breath
you take, to you I give my soul not to forsake. As each beat
brings life through your heart, this is to show I shall never
part. Longing to feel your soft touch, will you take me within
one's clutch. Your devouring lips cease to find an end, yet
all you wanted was for me to remain nothing but your friend.
You see as we have become one, I was once able to give you a
son. Yet found and lost all in one day, I was only to hope you
would help and show me the way. As a darkened fear fell upon
your face, all you were screaming was give me my freedom and
space. Yet the next evening when I saw you, you were tender
and soft and nothing in your world could have made you blue.
Not understanding how a man so full of fear, could have changed
from night to day and become ever so warm and near. After that
time you slowly drew away, then all that I could ever wish is
for you to come back someday. To have a desire we once shared
within, so that you my true love could begin again.
　　　—*Chantel Durene*

Mountain Trail

A path advancing up the mountain slope
steeper than others encountered in my travels.
Nary a gap large enough for a child to pass
ever winding through the bush and scrub.
Passing up beyond some boulders, rocks, and trees
visions of the apex fill my thoughts.
The panoramic view, the open freedom, the unspoiled air
master over all envisioned, responsible to none save self.
Daisies and bush buck rustling through the leaves
while baboons watch curiously the passing of one through
their domain,
Even the fish eagle soars below me
not wishing to test the limits of the freedom granted.
Sunset advances more quickly than imagined
the villages below swallowed in the shadow.
A mad scurry to reach security sends me away
sends me retreating before the summit is reached.
　　　—*Damien Dziepak*

Dreams for FB

Memories and visions so precious,
　　stolen and exposed to all.
Lost then found again,
　　you'll never take that fall.
Cling tightly, cling hard,
　　the fears lie so close to the touch.
The dreams are alive and well.
　　They are growing. There is so much.
But fear runs deep inside,
　　it controls your mind. It blinds your sight.
But listen gently, listen clear.
　　The dreams are real. No need to take flight.
Release the fears,
　　for this trauma and hurt is from the past.
Friendship and support are near.
　　I stand with you. This time is real at last.
　　　—*Basia A. Priga*

3rd Grade

3rd grade's a year I'll not forget!
　　A year that Sarah won at net.
　　Lars hit Amy on the head.
　　A year we painted each other red!
　　A year that Beri got an 80.
　　A year that Victor helped a lady.
　　A year that I got a big black eye-
Ben knows he did it, but he told a lie!
　　　—*Cameron E.P. Goodman*

"A Woman's Price"

Down falls the rain,
　　streaking the sky
　　like tears from heaven

In the distance,
　　clouds envelope the once peaceful sky
　　as pain envelopes her heart

She loves the storm with pure hatred

In her memory are
　　the days filled with sunshine

Before she knew the storm
　　　—*Amy Pfenning*

The Darkness

Darkness fell on the city and the man.
Street lights turned on to show the way,
A cautious reminder of where not to stray.
An oil lamp burned through the man's darkness of night,
If only to help ease a terrible fright.
A cat slid into a box to hide from the rain.
The man slid into an easy chair to fight the strain.
It all seemed so bleak and dreary for sure.
If only he could find a natural cure.
The cat ran fast as lighting begun.
The man remained motionless thinking of his gun.
With the city now accustomed to the lighting and rain,
It could now rejoice in the cleaning of stain,
With a gun by his side and The Book in his hand,
He now looked at the finger that held no band.
Crickets and owls now began to doze.
A natural sign darkness would close.
As he got from the chair and looked to the sky,
A beautiful rainbow invaded his eye. The sound of thunder
and then it was dawn. The darkness would now forever be gone.
　　　—*R. Kniffen "C-NA"*

Untitled

Reaching out—
　　stretching, grasping, extending.
Bareness exposing me,
　　leaving me open to the elements.
Unprepared,
yet willing to face whatever falls upon me.
A change begins, and blankets me.
It holds me and wraps its soft cover around me.
Unexpectantly
　　a crisp cold touches me—
　　my cover blows off and is replaced
　　with hard edges that seem to suffocate me.

Sun creeps through—
　　exposing a shine and a glimmer.
Reflection and beauty now radiate.
Sharp jagged edges slowly slip away
　　—preparation for new life begins.
　　　—*Sandra Haedike-Byrd*

Smiles Return

Spring has come to the North-west wood
　　So many smiling faces.

Twinkling eyes and butterflies
　　renew my favorite places.

Take my hand and walk with me
　　in places old and new.

We'll hike the trails with curious twist
　　past water fall and misty mountain view.
　　　—*Patricia Edmondson*

195

Black Fathers Love To His Son

I love you son, I love you son. I'm your
strong model, role to be exact, the icon
from the motherland coated in black.

From your birth you wrapped my heart and
didn't let go, I've seen you grow through
the winters; the white fallen snow. The
summers came fast, winter the past. Oh
son how you've grown, someday you'll be
leaving home, but I will not be alone
because good memories I own.

Love spoken from quivering lips, I've
always loved you even on life difficult
trips. Things you did made me extremely
sad, sometimes mad, But I'm so glad that
you are my son, my son, oh God, my son.
The beam in my eye, the sun in my sky,
some wouldn't say, I pray, oh God the
days; love will never end. I love you
son, I love you son, I your strong black
role model.

—*Carey Clemons*

Leuzinger 1940 Class Act!

Class of, me Japanese, its finest
student, ha, but about time
this writer acknowledged coach Geo
Thompson head coach made me
varsity captain so naturally
He is number one on my
list and Mrs. Harris my English teacher
and Miss Burden my Glee Club teacher
"You can have your `Mr. Chips' as for me
there a score numbers of I will take over
yours, anytime
So there, I'm so terribly lucky to have had
from Kindergarten to now.
1927 through 1940. Summer of!

—*Thomas Edison Takeru Eno*

Mornings

There are all kinds of mornings. The chill of the dawn on a
summer morning after a night talked through in the car; then
the warmth of a lazy Sunday morning, lounging around the house,
paper-reading; the rush of a morning when I give you a ride to
work just after our quick love-making; the morning when we
talk, the morning when we fight, mornings of love, and mornings
of war. The morning after a night out, still feeling the
effects of alcohol; the morning of freshness and me being ready
to take the world on. Mornings when I am as tired as the night
before; the mornings of silence as well as the mornings of
play; mornings when the sun breaks through the shades, or when
the sound of the raindrops wake; mornings when the baby's cry
is the first sound I hear; or the toilet gets flushed in the
apartment upstairs. Mornings of hope, mornings of despair;
mornings which pass too fast or too slow, yet there are the
same number of minutes to flow; mornings when the snoozer got
hit numberless times versus mornings there is no need for alarm;
and there are mornings of regret, and mornings of joy - as I
open my eyes with a smile inside. And then the mornings I
awake alone, and you are not next to me.

—*Eva Zsigovics*

"Harbingers of Life"

Spring - The artistic renewal of life, love, and dreams.
Summer - The continual flow of life's existence, expressed
   with the warmth of the sun and God's love.
Autumn - Changes in the editions of the tales of life, the
   finale done in a splendor of color.
Winter - A dull and bleak present that is transposed
   into a promise of life, covered by a shiny coat of
   snow; that will bring forth the harbinger of
   future endeavors - spring.....

—*Dorothea Colangelo*

Lament of the Experienced

Experience!!! Who needs it?
Surely not those of us who have the most!
Children, so they say, learn best by experience.
Teenagers are challenged by it.
For the young adult — it's required for employment.
Then as it accumulates, you add to it, wisdom and knowledge
And sometimes — for twenty years or so — it brings success
In careers, business; nearly every phase of life.
Until, you have experienced just about everything!
Then — suddenly it seems — it is of no account at all.
If the experience itself is not out of date,
   for sure the source is.
All at once the myriad of lessons you have learned —
Supposedly from 'the best teacher' are not wanted by anyone.
Your knowledge, your wisdom, your experience
Is only good for meditating and wondering...
   Who needs experience anyway???
   Surely not those of us who have spent
   a lifetime getting it.

—*Phyllis Herzog*

America's Child

Brought to a land where the language is not familiar.
Surrounded by faces not of my tribe.
Sold into something, captured against my will.
Scold in tongue of unfamiliar sound.

Running for underground cover, following a lady Moses.
Some kind of change has conspired.
Africa's daughter becomes America's child.

My own tongue is no longer familiar.
Voices of my native tribe cry, I do not understand the words.
I have embraced a land now more familiar, forgetting my
native love.

I have become America's child, ignorant of my past.
Unable to know my future. Excluded from my tribe.

No longer do I run with tigers by my side, but with nines and
knives I stride. No longer do I bathe in the Niger, but in
acid rain instead. Once Africa's daughter America's child I've
become, corrupt and disillusioned.

Africa's daughter once had peace; righteous thoughts ran
through my head. America's child lives in confusion, wondering
if she'll wake up dead.

—*Tanya Gundy*

"Society"

A menace, an alcoholic, a perverted teacher
An arson, a fugitive, a convicted preacher
A junky, a murderer, a obnoxious terrorist
A crooked cop, or an atheist
A dead-beat dad, a hideous cult
A terrible world
Who is to fault?

—*Candice Bennett*

Happy Birthday Dad

Memories heightened, thoughts of the past, years go so
swiftly, days too fast; steps a bit slower, feet not as
stable, eyes a bit dimmer, but you're still able, to
fill up your heart with love.

So you're 75, well what do you know, I've called you
Dad for fifty or so, deduct 20 from that for just growing
up, which leaves 30 for knowing and loving you Pop.

You've weathered these years in grand gusto style, in
spite of your heartaches and tears. You've maintained a
stature that I'm proud of, given ear to my problems and fears.

You've brought laughter to many, they returned it to
you, you've lived through the good and the bad. But the
best thing you did your whole life through was in being
just you, My dad.

   —Patricia A. Greene

I Am...

 I am free as a bird every time I
swing on a cold rainy day.

 I am an egg that can easily break if
I have too many emotions.

 I am a doll that cries inside from
the things people say or think about me.

 I am sometimes an ocean in a storm
when I am insanely angry.

 I am a puzzle with many pieces that
only I can figure out.

 I am sometimes a tiny rain drop, that
splatters against a window in the night
when I am sad.

 I am like night with a new moon
and all the stars shining bright when
I am glad.

 I am a simple snowflake that falls
lightly to the ground when I am dreaming.

 I am a diary, that can keep secrets
if anyone tells me.

   —Kristy Hurtado

Bondage

The banners of our allegiances
Symbols that justify loss of life
Reminders of our divisiveness
Our struggles and our strife
The stitches which bind them together
Are but nooses which we hang by
When called upon to serve in
Our bonded free societies
The colors wash all over us
They blend into a haze of gray
Which cloud the imperfect vision
Of our intangible hypocracies
What is country, nation, language, war
Words which colors bind
What would this fiasco of fabric look like
If all the world were blind
Yet moving on through time and space
How do we judge the whole disgrace
For our lack of looking face to face
At what we call our humane race

   —Robert J. Ames

"You Make It - Snappy!!"

 Pick it up, pick it up, pick it up -
Take me away again. Not to mention;
I have an end.

 Just talk, talk, talk,
it's what were going to mend.
Your nobodies fool - I reckon it's kool.

 If I may, take the tray -
Leave it lay and jump in the hay?
With you!!

 Your so rude and not
to mention slightly crude!!

 But that's why - I love ya -
Babe!

   —Curtis Crouse

Maybe

 If you walk, with your head held high,
Take notes of the birds that fly.
 Watch an airplane pass from sight.
Take time to enjoy the stars at night.
 Days, weeks and months fly by.
People do the same routines, they don't know why?
 Maybe carrying groceries for those in need.
Plant in the Spring, the vegetable seed.
 Love children in a motherly way.
Ask questions, yes! Everyday.
 Sing, when you can't carry a tune.
Laugh, relax, always at noon.
 Don't sell yourself short, as the days go by.
Life is too short, you've got to try.
 I know people can be, who they are suppose to be,
  Maybe, they don't realize it as much as me.
A lot of people have a healthy brain.
 Please learn to use it, don't act insane.
  Maybe, Epilepsy made me stronger than most,
This is a message, not a boast.

   —Joyce Benson

Dances in Heaven

Life is a gift from God sometimes
taken for granted.

Life is a kiss from an angel that
dances in heaven.

When life has run its coarse
even if it happens to soon. Angels
will be there to take you to the start of
love; bright and true.

Even when the good have left the
earth, we will always remember them;
death following birth.

Believe that God will take your
love and guard him. For there will
always be a new angel dancing
forever in heaven.

   —Lindsay Hamilton

Tranquility

Blades of grass touched by the soft morning dew,
Squirrels scurrying to gather acorns,
Clouds, serene and picturesque in the sky,
Apples falling down on a bed of fireside colored leaves,
Oh, what bliss,
The Autumn sunrise.

   —Lorraine De Caprio

Faded Memories

There was a time when we
Talked and laughed together
But now, it's different.
Hidden deep into the past.
Those are just faded memories.
Now we don't smile when we see each other.
Afraid to bring up the memories that have faded away.
We just stare off into the distance.
Not wanting to look into each other's eyes,
to see what we are feeling.
A feeling of emptiness.
Like we lost something
Faded memories.

—*Lori Wirth*

No Dead Man

No dead man can open my eyes, or
teach me things that make me wise.
No dead man can know my heart of sorrow,
or show me that there's a brighter tomorrow.
No dead man can save me, when I fear for my life,
or calm the storms of burdens and strife.
No dead man has ever spoken,
to a multitude of people, lost and broken.
No dead man could ever teach,
the good things I have heard men preach.
No dead man can touch and heal,
or raise a mans spirit in joyous zeal.
No dead man ever divided time in half.
Or split the sea open with a prophets staff.
No dead man has ever walked the earth.
born of a woman by a virgin birth.
I tell you Jesus is no dead man
death cannot do the things He can!

—*Dawn Sparks*

Shelter from the Storm

The night has okey; so many eyes
Tearfully starring and wondering why,
Why, so many people have no place to go
Hoping to find a place and someone who cares
To shelter them from the cold nights air
Children crying asking for something to eat
Never knowing where they will sleep
Praying a prayer asking for shelter from the storm
That one day they'll have a place to keep them warm

—*Jean Glenn*

"Portrait of Iliyana"

She was but eight in span of years, as we remember her, with tears. And reverie spent in days grown long, much like a well-remembered song. So much in soul behind those eyes that even bitter truth defies. Perhaps God meant for us to see this little mite's Divinity!

Her wheelchair soon became a throne from which this little monarch shone. Dispensing courage to us all, lest we should falter when we fall. Into despair when our time comes, and heeding call from distant drums.... Be constant to the great abyss without the guilt of being remiss.

We wonder why the innocent seem to bear the brunt of Mankind's dream. Which all too often turns to dust, forgetting those within our trust. Nightmarish...but we persevere, and if we weep, we know she'll hear. In her name only, it must end; we lost this special, little friend.

—*Mike Dix*

A Friend

When you have a friend that you really like do you ever tell her so?
Do you say by a word or a gesture that she's someone you're glad to know?
Do you write a note or call on the phone?
  Do you really keep in touch?
Tho you truly like this friend of yours do you ever tell her - how much?
I had such a friend I cared about and I never told her so
Never said in a so many words that she was someone special to know.
I cherished her friendship in silence and really tempted fate
I waited too long and discovered tomorrow was just a day late
For my good friend passed away today and I never told her true
How much I valued her friendship I wonder if she knew!!!

—*Marian Wheaton*

Untitled

Her loving arms reach out to embrace me
Tender fingers caressing my pain

She longs to hold me and cradle me close
Till I weep no more and I lie still

My faithful constant friend
You look so old and gray
You call my name so softly
But I know you know me well

She looks at old
But carefully mended scars
Upon my ancient battered heart
And knows what pain I bore

The one deep gash
That sought to take my life
Was gently sewn back into place
By her kind and loving hands

And when I am weak
I know she'll be there
With open loving arms
My own deep Despair

—*Lani Carde*

Shelter Is His Name

When confusion has come and night is near
Thank God for shelter.
In His face no sorrow or fear.
I love you, Shelter.
Peace at last, security within
The morning light bringeth a friend.
Shelter, I know that you are here.
I can feel you, I can hear you,
I can see you
I love you, Shelter.

—*Evon Carter*

Rescue Me

Rescue me from this cage of love,
take me now, the prisoner, the locked up dove.
I need to be free....
Away from this jail,
it feels different, it's hard to tell.
Can you see me now?
Would you know how?
Just take me away to have worries no more,
because you're the one in this world
that I've been waiting for.

—*Franicia Tomokane*

"Tearing Down Towers"

Water flows. Dust flies, dries the face of a man.
Thankful though for what has gone on over years, over land.
Simple appreciation once, now the martyr comes.
Much more is now expected, so little is for love.
Sin and greed foul this once clean air.
We breath the exhale of demons, a smell of fear.
Showers of destruction, there's pain in its rain.
Lives crumble, as torch flames surround surviving tribes.
Rituals now restore faith, but to a variety of Gods.
They have theirs and we have ours.
Rebuilding we protect said territory, from others ailing beliefs.
Retreat is a losing battle.
The tide continues to be washed in and be pulled out.
Circulating looks.
For every beginning in primitive and every survival is savage.
Recycling utopias, after inept disregard and neglect.
We build to destroy again.

  —Bart M. Gibbons

Me, Actually

There are some things
that certain people in this world
hate to admit,
even to themselves.

But when they do
admit it to themselves,
they still can't tell anyone else.

Like the fact that they're lonely and afraid,
or mixed-up and confused
or that they're missed someone
that they really cared about.

Sometimes, these people
write stories, books, or even poems
to let their thoughts out.

Sometimes though -
they don't,
and they cry inside
where no one can see.

  —Georgianna Morrill

Love

Love is like a blossom,
that comes in the spring.
it has the only pretty thing.
Love can lead to pleasure,
that gets him and her
to love each other more.

Love would bring to life,
a whole new meaning
of the lovely feeling
to give a reason to love each other more,
and still if they turn poor.

The meaning of through thick and thin,
is to make a better crew
and not to throw life away,
in a huge bin.

To love each other more each day,
and not to pay for what you have today.
But keep in store the joys of love,
that you have above.

  —Melissa Buchholz

Fall

How sudden are the colored leaves
that fall and swirl from autumns trees
And rescue beauty from her beast
released at last from summers heat.

I laughed as a man asked "What's the price"?
Wishing to purchase paradise.
"Be off you fool you cannot pay
this can't be bought be on your way.

Will interruptions never cease?
I pray the haunted find release.
The season plays for all to hear
please listen with an open ear.

  —Edward Inglee

A Prayer Answered Too Soon

As I count the days and look back on that day,
That fatefully awful day, I can't help but sigh.
So much sickness, so much pain, so little time...
To say "good-bye."
Thinking back I see my mistake;
I welcomed the end;
Now only to wish I hadn't. My days are empty.
No longer filled with tedious tasks, and I miss them.
Things run like clockwork; without a hitch.
One less place to set; one less bed to make...
Harmonious repetition.
Too many things left unanswered, not talked about.
Too many dreams and experiences not shared with you.
A void of empty "Things-to-do" lays limply on my shoulders;
 undone.
Sweet flowers left unnoticed, new blossoms left untouched;
 wisdom silenced.
Your presence is missed, warm arms that sheltered my falls;
Much weakens and dies without your light.
I've prayed for so much like world peace; I've asked for so little.
The one thing I prayed for most would come true, but too soon.
Now you and I have both missed out;
Both lost a part of each other;
All because of a prayer, my prayer, answered too soon.

  —Natasha Scott

To Bill

When I met Bill I knew from the start
That he was the one that would win my heart.
Wonderful it was when we married and shared our joy
and our love was complete with the birth of our boy.

Our garden and roses were beautiful to see.
Bill bought a peace rose that he said was for me.
As he planted the rose he said, "This is for us
and the happy years we've been wed."
But it bloomed just for me because he was dead.
Some day together again we will be
and the rose will be blooming not only for me.

  —Alice M. Powell

There Is Much To Be Done In The Wispy Winds Of Twilight

There is much to be done (In the wispy winds of twilight) where
a new face grows (Out of the old) light dying comes the new
darkness of life made (Alive) are made too simple memories or
too painful truths (We do not know which) way to escape from
ourselves (In this world) the darkness' cold (Embrace warms us
sweet) as two are gathered and (We are there) canting vespers
when (There is much to be done) in the wispy winds of twilight

  —J. D. McClure

Untitled

Things go so quickly, so quickly
That I can't understand,
Where is my life going, am I falling
or will I land?

Time goes so quickly, so quickly
that I can't understand,
Will I go down in water,
or will I touch the sand?

Life is going so quickly, so quickly
that I can't understand,
I want to feel the sunshine,
but the rain falls in my hand

You are going so quickly, so quickly
that I can't understand,
I want to be there for you, but I'm always
the last to land.

> —*Rachel Benson*

The Love Of My Life!!!

From the moment that I saw you right away I knew,
that I could spend the rest of my life with someone just like you.
Before I met you my life was a dark and hazy gloom,
all that changed the minute I stepped foot into that room.
Your eyes they shined like diamonds, your smile was sweet and
warm; now all my life I'll be waiting to hold you in my arms.
In my arms I'd longed to hold you and tell you what I felt
inside; since I'd only met you those emotions I had to hide.
I can honestly say I've thought of nothing else,
ever since you have walked out that door;
and the moments that I have been away from you,
has only made me love you ever more.
I hope one day you will eventually feel the same,
but until the day and the time comes that you do-
I will be as patient as I can, write soon.
  I love you!

> —*Virginia Angel*

Lonely

It's when my mind goes wandering
that I get lonely,
when the ghosts of the past get personal
and I long for those who are gone.
The loved ones, friends, people who have mattered
in my life.

Most of the time I'm busy, and there's no room
for loneliness,
Or, for that matter, for anything else's except
alarm clock at seven, get ready for work,
plan out the day. Essentials are first — or all —
that matters.

They only go one by one, I know,
yet suddenly
they become a terrible, a hurtful loss
of all those beautiful people who helped me
to know my life, and to treasure it.
I'm lonely.

> —*Ruth E. Williams*

Morning Light

The morning light arrives to close out the long dark night.
Along with it, it brings the sounds and sights of all the
wonderful things of life.
The morning light is something for all the world to see.
My only regret is how quick it's over, we have to hurry to see.

> —*Cliff Coleman*

Untitled

Who would've known the trouble
that lay beneath my own confidence,
It turned so suddenly from eternal victory
to endless defeat,
I had been burnt with anger,
An anger that had been building up
inside of me for so long,
Until one day it just had to come out,
A reputation of an innocent girl
admired so dearly by her fellow peers
had been torn and tattered by that one thing,
The one thing that ruined her whole life,
Who would've known that she would fall apart
one day because of her lifelong secret,
Her lifelong secret of not being able to read.

> —*Kate Reilly*

Seeing No Evil

Somewhere...
That place you never go... where,
There are questions
You make a point
To never ask
Answers, that give you a fear
So luminous,
It blinds you
To their very existence
So you're afraid,
I understand.
And it makes you hate,
I understand.
And it deadens you to the pain you cause,
I understand.
I despise everything about you
Hope you understand

> —*Catherine Woodbury*

Little Things

It's the little things we say and do
That prove our love — lets it shine through.

It's not the great or grandiose schemes
That mean the most — but the little things!

A friendly smile, a warm "Hello!"
A hug, a prayer, a caring touch;
These show our love and compassion much —

To the ones we meet ..
Lost, alone, hurting, scared;
A visit, a call, a note or card
Will encourage them when the way is hard.

These simple, little things, can prove our love.

> —*Jerry G. St. Clair*

A Wish

If you ever wish,
  that you were someone else.
If you ever wish,
  that you weren't yourself.
If you ever wish,
  that you could of been.
If you ever wish,
  that you never had been.
Just think about who you are,
  and not what you wish you were.
Because there's always someone, somewhere,
  who wishes they were you.

> —*Susan Lynn Anderson*

The Deep Sleep

Could I but lay me down to sleep
That sleep...so deep, when I awake, I weep..
For joy........ for you are nigh.

Such a sleep has been my prayer
No single one aware....
I did not weep....did not cry...
For you were not nigh.....I did not cry, for joy.

Life has not been with song.....for so long
Since sound of song was everywhere
Till life was bare..of sorrow...till that morrow
.............and you not there.

Now I pray help me sleep.....the deep sleep
Till I awake.....sing with joy....for you are nigh
And I am by......you're side forever more

So now, any who would see me sleep
In that deep sleep. Never should distress......express
Neither should they weep
To see me deeper still in sleep
For then it is..I am going home
And 'tis then......for my own...no more I'll weep.
    —*Edwin P. Spivey*

I Am Because...

You are to me every ray of sunshine
That warms the earth;
Every cloud that drifts by with its unique form.

You are to me every wave that breaks against the shore;
Every eagle that soars with its wings spread
To capture the wind beneath its wings.

You are to me the blue of the sky
The green of summer, the foliage of fall;
The sand beneath a child's foot
The rugged rocks of time.

You are to me the dawn that brings new hopes;
My everything, my destiny
You will always have a room in my heart.
    —*Darlene J. Blackett*

Sonnet I

That which shines brightest is silver,
That which never tarnishes is gold
The one who is with you now is silver,
The one who is with you forever is gold
But the promise of silver
Can never surpass the serenity of gold
For treasured now is the silver,
Treasured always is the gold
When aged be the silver,
He can one day be gold
To another silver,
But never to a cherished gold
    Forgotten can be the newly lost silver,
    Yet life is forever endless for the purest gold
        —*Janet K. Yoder*

Thinking Of You

I can sit and think about you.
All the time, you are always on my mine.
I will love you until the end of time
I will always love you, this is true,
I hope you feel the same way
I do I can sit and think if you care.
But when you need me I'll be there.
    —*Carolyn D. Hart*

"It's Made Just For You From Me"

I sit and see a star burn so bright
that will fly by night; will it lead
me the way to a sweet sight, a
whisper at night? Could you see the love
in me, the sun will shine on it so
bright you'll see it in the moonlight.
Could it be, a friend indeed, what's to
be a flower just for me?
Maybe it could be, love for you from
me; just wait and see. It's plain to
see you're there for me. Left in the
end as lovers and friends, no pain
left inside to fight, I'll give you
a kiss goodnight; we'll never
say good-bye.
    —*Sara White*

Just No Getting Over You

It seems like only yesterday
That you and I were together
But it's been a while since you went away
I thought we'd last forever

It broke my heart half into
The day we said goodbye
And every time I think of you
I break right down and cry

There's just no getting over you
No matter how I try
I guess I have to face the truth
And get on with my life

But baby it's so hard to do
When the one you loved is gone
I can't just be expected to
Forget and carry on

Because you meant the world to me
And now we are apart
No one else will ever be
So special in my heart
    —*Pam Rafiner*

Heartbreak

You told me you loved me, how could I have known,
that you'd take my love and leave me, tearful and alone.
When I look back, I wish that I could know,
Whatever I did wrong, whatever made you go.
I sit by myself, with thoughts of you on my mind.
The memories won't fade, I can't leave you behind.
You have your freedom, I have my pain,
It seems like I had everything to lose,
You had everything to gain.
I wonder if you think of me,
Of all the times we shared,
The times we laughed, the times we cried,
I even wonder if you cared.
Nothing lasts forever, or at least that's what they say,
I hope that goes for the pain I feel, each and every day.
My thoughts of you remain the same,
In my heart you're always mine,
but life goes on and so will I, all I need is time.
    —*Patricia Marshall*

Untitled

My heart of glass can be easily broken,
And you are the one that holds the hammer.
You now have the power to shatter it,
And leave me in a million pieces.
    —*Holly Deitch*

A Wound That Won't Heal

A wound that won't heal, a tear that won't dry,
That's what I live with, with each day that goes by.

This hurt and sorrow that never goes away,
You have to live with from day to day.

Some days you can make it, some you barely get by,
Some days you can laugh, while others you cry.

This heartbreak will be with me 'til the day that I die,
From this wound that won't heal and this tear that won't dry.

—*Jo A. Clark*

The Heavens

The night is alive as we lay asleep.
The arms of a tree sway like the breeze.
The eye of the night sky shines
shimmering emeralds on the malleable grass.
As the wind crawls on by, the
vast ocean gives a shuddering sigh. The
stars glitter like specks of gold
against the blackened night. Awakening
from our sweet dreams, the
heavens give us light. The moon slips
into a tiresome sleep as
the sun rises the earth, spreading the
radiance of gold and scarlet into the
colossal sky.

—*Soma Maitra*

Who Is Our Lord?

Thank you, Lord, for who You are,
The Awesome Creator, the Morning Star.
You're Merciful, and the Giver of Grace,
The Mighty One who sits at the Highest Place.

Our Blessed Savior, the Sacrificial Lamb,
The Gentle Shepherd, the Great I Am.
Messiah, Jehova, Lord of All,
The Prince of Peace on whom we can call.

The Rose of Sharon, our Wonderful Healer,
Counselor, Guide, and Faithful Teacher.
Provider, Protector, Redeemer from sins,
The Most Holy One, the Victor who wins.

The Alpha, Omega, Beginning and End,
Our Lover, Father, Husband, and Friend.
The King of Kings, God's Only Son,
The Mighty Rock whom we can stand on.

To Heaven You are the only Door,
You're all of this and so much more.
Our only hope is that our prayers will bring
Our Beautiful Bridegroom, our Soon Coming King.

—*Judith L. Houston*

Love or Life

Bang, bang,
The blood pours from his face.
The tears stream down her cheek...
    As he falls 6 ft. under

Everyone remembers back to when he was just a kid...
    Then wonders what went wrong.

They thought their love could keep him safe...
    The gang promised him love too.

    So he accepted
    and
    Died

—*Shannon Vice*

Winds Of Nature And Heaven

Oh Lord, I look from my window at
the barren trees,
All branches and bark, no leaves.
The wind blows through your snow-covered boughs
and the white flakes fall to the ground.
As I wander back to my chair
Thoughts come to my mind
Of where I would like to go when it is my time.
When everyone starts to Heaven
it shouldn't be a lot of turmoil!
As we take time to remember
Look, behold nature's beauty,
as there is a time and place for everything.
We may think it has been a long time
But I have been here for such a short while!

—*Hilda Sumwalt*

Vision of Eternal Loveliness

(Some things only last for a moment but leave an impression forever.)
The beautiful delicate rainbow glowed thru the sky
Separated, divided in half by the sun-dazzled silver,
blue mists of clouds.

The entire sky was lit as with gold, the fairest
sight Fae's emerald eyes had ever carried to her soul.

She communed with God, her arm around
her brother beside her....

Whoever said a pot of gold is at the end of a rainbow?
jewels and precious metals were shimm'ring
all thru it.

—*Elise Faith Rammell*

God Gives Us A Rose

God has bestowed unto me
    the beauty of a blossoming rose.
So strong, yet so fragile,
    so new, yet so free.
A dream sweeps by, it vows to keep
    the beauty of this rose.
A bud develops so small, so proud,
    releasing to all a wonderful fragrance.
To me we're a rose, we've chosen to grow
    together in love everlasting.
I prayed to my God that we would grow in his time
    and blossom as sweet as the rose.
The time it would take, I figured be long
    yet so soon did my heart give you love.
Only one thing can grow
    with love in God's name
        overnight,
    sweet and pure as the rose,
        Our Love!!!!!

—*Kim Clark*

You Are

You are   the flame that consumes me,
        the candle that lights my way-
You are   the wind beneath my wings,
        that takes me to higher heights-
You are   the valley of my soul,
        that lies deep within-
You are   the river of my blood,
        that flows mighty and strong-
You are   the sands of time,
        that molds beauty within its reach -
You are   the breath of life,
        forever seeking a closeness
You are...........................

—*Justina Willis*

Trust

Trust is something I thought we had
The belief that we'd always be honest
The belief that the other would always be there
That trust is what we built our friendship on.

There came a day when you doubted my word
The trust was gone
The friendship disintegrated

I didn't lie or try to deceive you
It was another's dishonesty
My words were true
My actions honest.

Your belief of her over me
Has shown me just how much you trusted
My words, my actions, my love
There's no hope for us now
No future in sight
Our friendship flew away
Like a bird out of sight.

—*Pleshette King*

Amorous

You are the sunrise of my life
the benchmark by which I behold
the wonder of awakening each day
to witness the essence of your being.

You are the wellspring from which
I embrace each new day on the calendar of life.

You are the high noon -
the apogee of the sun reflecting its direct rays
upon the earth whereas the warmth and sustenance of life
is clear for all to witness.

You are the sunset -
the time when I reflect on and savor
the day which God has given to me
in the hope of tomorrow's renewal
with you as my consort.

Thee is the pinion upon which
the joy of each day is secured;
the center of my thoughts
the epicenter of my heart.

—*Earley*

Pink Roses On An Old Gray Wall

Pink roses on an old gray wall!
The bloom of youth dependent on old age:
Nature's beauteous pageant seems to call
The sleeping Earth to re-set winter's stage.

So man, throughout the ages, builds anew
And fashions beauteous dreams on older dreams come true.

And when the final die of life is cast,
His blazing sun at last about to set,
Then man would like to trace the way he passed
And seeing, know he need have no regret.

But man could never see his dream come true
Except for older dreams on which to build anew.

We're nothing, of ourselves, without the past.
Our blossoms answer only to the call
Of older, living wood, awake at last
To bring again pink roses to the wall.

The bloom of youth dependent on old age,
As Nature's beauteous pageant re-sets winter's stage.

—*Theodore W. Bremer*

Totem

There is a mode of thought, once past
the boundaries of obsession with self, called
the Law of the Doe - an unwritten law -
where kindness prevails...
    An awareness of the sorrows inflicted
in this world, no longer results in self-pity, but
in a great desire or change in nature, to lessen
the burdens of others... a simpler law, in
tune with nature.
    Now nature can be cruel... not so the
doe, who blends in harmony with it, but carries
on a simple life... existing moment to moment,
gentle and beautiful in her quiet dignity...
peaceful as the deep, cool, green of the forest...
one of God's nobler creatures... living the life
and law of a doe... loving.

—*Jillann Brizzi*

Ode to a Fifty Year Old

The grey is slowly creeping through his hair.
The boyish grin has faded, but the smile is still there.
The trim figure is rounder, and the back is slightly bent.
The vigor has gone, the same way the years went.
The shy, young fellow has been replaced,
By a man seen often talking.
He has an opinion on everything now,
And a wife who's always balking.
We often hear a mini sermon,
He gives them to us freely.
We sigh, and pause, and have to listen,
Because he means them so sincerely.
On this his day we celebrate, we wish him many more.
Without his loving chatter, life would be a bore.
So Dad, brother, cousin, Grandpa, husband, friend,
Accept our Birthday greetings, they are sincerely meant.

—*DarLayne L. Yliniemi*

Homeless

    They're out on the road day and night; they give you
the chills, they give you fright.
    You look, you stare, without thinking twice; and you know
something is wrong, it's just not right.
    Why are they out there, lonely and sad?; you see their
poor clothes and you just can't be glad.
    Glad to live in this world, as it is today; It's always oh!
so sad, wouldn't you say.
    They have nowhere to go, nowhere to hide; they just sit
around, and patiently abide.
    Why are we frightened of them, we have no right to be;
remember always, they're just like you and me.
    When night falls and nobody is around they begin to cry;
with every tear and every word, they slowly begin to die.
    They're out there lonely, dying at night, although they
shouldn't be; Why is this happening, what went wrong, they're
just like you and me.

—*Ashley Bearden*

Memories Of Time

How often does a sunset
Bring nostalgic thoughts to mind
Of by-gone days and yester-year
Of memories time has left behind

But memories are wonderful scenes of the mind,
Hidden deep in the soul of one's face
Memories are forever etched
Where time their worth can not erase.

—*Joan M. Bowser*

I Love You All The Trees

I passed a church the other day, red bricked and spired high
The choir's chant retrieved my past and thoughts of days gone by.

I found myself at portal's way but enter, I could not.
Perhaps it was a child's fear if so, I know not what.

This house of God, a part of me, its incense still remains
Carved oak and stanchions, not a few, and saints in glass of stain.

The darkened corners, closet sins the tiles, processioned worn
An empty pulpit, empty words a font, for the reborn.

This was a crucible for me and years of lessons taught
The imprints deep within my soul of all that should be; ought.

I've found another temple strong, it has no harsh demands
It only asks that I reach out, it has but that command.

I met you there, do you recall? And you reached out to me
And whispered in my straining ear "I love you all the trees."

—*Kenneth McGinniss*

The Calendar

Calendar time solves everything -
The circled in dates are all tomorrows -
There's the 1st the 15th pay days - rent
days - Merry Xmas - and Happy Birthdays -
It's a twelve times mixture of love -
Hate-sadness and awe - a full menu of
summer-winter and fall-
The calendar dates - the calendar way -
To all of the days departed - bid a
farewell - and say so long -
The calendar won't turn back -
So are all of our ideas we once
had - now gone -
We'll see - to state the future would be futile -
So we must wait for the turning year -
Only left now with wonder and excitement -
Behold the new day comes at last -
On this first new day of the year
We show a smile - we pray - then we say -
Hand me the calendar - I must circle in today -

—*Chloe Upchurch*

Embrace The Dawn

Lofty and Heaven sent, children of creation please embrace
    the cold Earthly dawn...She needs you!
With your gossamer dreams and passion strengthening your
marrow
Forge anew the visions of: Truth, reality, love!
    It is your most hallowed and entrusted deed.
Sweetly kiss life into the dying; give refuge to the tired
    warriors who know no sanctuary other than death.
Weep openly of the joy known as blessed humanity! softly now,
    For dark fear has smothered generosity in cold wet sack
cloth, and the night has firmly gripped our family in a frosted
grasp. Lo and take heed! For even the repulsive comes down
out of the sun. This eternal quest knows not of
compensation.
For the effort, the act alone is the cost and reward for such
the breathtaking, gallant sacrifice.
And the graves of those who fall do not become monuments but
nutriment. Surrender yourself to the twilight, nothingness
tastes of nectar unmatched by any blossom!
Beauty is you who have turned away from the grave only to
caress forgiveness upon the internal Angel of Death!

—*Donald Zezulinski*

OOO! Too big!
Dill Diana, seein' hauled in
Dry dinosaur dung,
She'll sigh, an', uh, bein' walled-in,
Sly Di' knows we're done!
Do you dig?!

—*Jerry Cameron*

"Radiants"

With the rae's of the new dawn, I feel
the comfort and warmth of the sun
dancing off my cheeks. One rae was
refracted by a tear in its path, it
sent it shooting off in dismay,
bouncing from room to room in
confusion, searching for an answer.
    How could such a thing happen
to one so tender producing only a
bright path for others. Was it random
that it choose the path or was it
selected by a predestined plan by
the son. Had it not been for this
untimely event, the sacrifice made
by the rae, there would not have been
the glimmer of light piercing the darkness
for others to see. Take heart little rae,
the darkness has not overcome you.
for in a moment's notice you have
accomplished much more than many do in a lifetime.

—*Daniel T. Fox*

Ancient of Days

In ocher desolation
the dissenter must claim his mountain—
lungs wheezing from spur to spur
while vertigo sanctifies sensations
with giddy rejoicing
until isolation probes
faith.

His sinews slacken
under summit fierceness;
yet, every ganglion signals
a ripening toward abnegation,
that conquest of flawless austerity,
where there shall no longer remain
one iota between his passion
and his God.

—*Hans Juergensen*

Seeking Happiness: Know

I only know....
    the dreams you have shared,
    and burdens you could not bear.
    Lives you could have lived,
    things you could not give.
    Obligations to be met,
    the path of life you are at.
    How time can be a prison,
    carefully, thoughtfully using reason.
    Hidden, secret thoughts of your own,
    pleading prayers to God atone.
    Desiring to wander as to roam,
    lost loves left somewhere back home.
    Living your life in your own way,
    Seeking happiness day to day.
    I only know, I only know,
You being you.

—*Merle K. Lai*

A Dream of Tomorrow

Black as death 'tis some say, that this world is today.
The end of the world is nigh, as our citizens die.
Fear has come, tis a cruel world, that we are victims to our
greed and have others do our deeds. Creating murderous crimes,
when we hear the chimes of such a rage that we must abide.
Innocent victims live in the street where the cold truth tells
them they are alone in this world. Lying in the gutters while
they dream, that this world will get better or so they believe.
Homelessness and depression are all the rage. But will it
end this very day? Victims of cancer, Aids and other diseases
spreads into anyone it pleases. We chose to disbelieve and
refuse to conceive that this world is dead unless we get hope.
Tis all gone now, for I can scope. As I fear for the last
death of the last person on earth, I awaken to a new rebirth.
Tis only a dream.

—*Elizabeth Valtierra*

My Fall

When she comes, yellow leaves fall...
The familiar bands of birds say farewell to the summer sun...
Their cheerful singing voices, on the tree branches, seem to
hold...
Those remind me, of my land, nostalgia, no more fun!
Showing their early beauty, chrysanthemum,
under the evening rain, like gold...
Whose garden has closed? My seasonal transition
has killed me sorrowfully without a gun!
The wood trees have dropped their old as well as young leaves
away..., immensely on the roads, and I feel internally cold!
The old road seems to have been closed, and
the faraway ocean is dark, in my lungs...
Fall is coming wonderfully, like my dream I chose,
Sitting here and listening to somebody's
reluctant voice echoed?
Under the gray blue sky that spreads out a long line
having been hung...
Millions of unforgettable souvenirs.. came to my mind,
and frustratedly packed in my soul!!

—*Vanson Tran*

Thanksgiving

Thanksgiving is the celebration of giving.
The first Pilgrims harvested corn, pumpkins,
Potatoes, squash, fruits, and many more.
Together with our relatives, we enjoy this delicious feast,
With stuffed turkey, pumpkin pie, squash and fruits.
Be thankful for what you have, even if it seems little.
Don't forget to share something with the less wealthy.
Loving, caring, sharing this is the real Thanksgiving.

—*Annelies Rigole*

Morning, Noon Till Night

The mornings are always the best
The evenings just bring the end
The mornings start a life
While in the evenings we lose a friend

But this morning was too good to spare
The evening would just bring me shame
Cause this life of morning, noon till night
Just isn't right, without you it's not the same

But the feelings will always be there
There's just nowhere for them to go
They're locked up tight, away from the light
Waiting for you, morning, noon till night

—*Rich Perrenot*

Essence of Hope

The river slowly awakes from a long winter dream. It caresses
the frozen banks, gently bringing forth new life. The day is
old, even ancient, shrouded in mist, full of secrets from the
past. If you can quiet your soul and listen to the melody of
the river, you will hear a song from a different place, a
different time. A place that has disappeared from our eyes,
but still remains deep within our hearts. A time when the
river was born and the earth was new, washed with the fragrance
of rain. A time when the river gave it's many gifts freely,
and the people were grateful. A time when the river's beauty
was unmarred and the people held it in reverence. A time when
the people danced in perfect harmony to the rhythm of the
seasons. The river is old now, it's life slipping away because
of our ignorance. It's guardians gone. But yet it's essence
still gives birth to another spring season, the river of life
still flows. In the morning sky a rainbow appears. A promise.
God in His Mercy still loves us and there will be yet another
spring day.

—*Carla Heimerl*

Reflections On A Welsh Castle

The towers raise slowly from the mire.
The grey mist curls and halos around the parapet.
Doleful dungeons echo steps
Of past presences that cling to the mossy stones.
    What have we here?
A book whose pages tell all yet nothing.
Each notch and chip a link in the lineage of man.
The walls hold secrets, yet will not tell
Of bygone times, the information stored within.
Of battles fought and brave men dead.
What do our hearts say when pondering the
Perils of prosperity reduced to pauperism?
'Tis told in a stone whose epitaph reads:
    "I was once a castle".

—*Wenda Dyer*

Lake Park Reflection

A boat has passed by.
The gull, its feeding stopped by the waves,
Stares out patiently,
Waiting for calm to grace the shore again.

I, too, feel buffeted by waves of emotion,
By deep inner hurts not yet owned.
How good it is to be here.
I let the sun and the breeze reassure me.

I stare at the lake.
Shimmering sunlight bewitches me.
The condos of Singer Island are gray in the background.
I embrace their inhabitants in my prayer.

The gull, feeding again,
Tells me peace is on its way.

—*Elizabeth Lalor*

Abused

Devastation awaits with every call or knock at the door.
The cries for help, the blood on the floor.
The bruises on the surface disappear in time and appear with
crime. The pain caused by this abuse made her love much more.
She tried to help him, but there was no cure.
There were whispers, then silence and tears, there were shivers
then shakes and fears. She couldn't overcome his anger, or
win back his affection so she ran out of danger in a different
direction, toward kindness and devotion. There was love, then
smiles and emotion, there was excitement, then laughter and
joy. She found a happy life and left behind the strife of
being a battered and abused victim.

—*Jennifer Spardy*

What's Left?

Babies crying with no Fathers in sight
The guns and violence have taken some lives

They're left with Mother's to fend for themselves
While a few of the men that survive live in jail cells

No one to look up to
What will remain for them to do

Should they follow the things they've seen
Will they be able to live their dreams

How long will it take for things to cease
Someone needs to increase the peace

Open up those hearts and show you care
before we all fall apart and nothing's here...

— *Tirzha A. Moore*

"Take Me Poem"

Take me to the farm, where I can swish and sway my feetsies in the hay, to and fro, as winds blow, and feel the earth beneath, and smell the freshness of grass and wheat! Take me to the farm, where, when I work at feedings, slopping, milking, sowing, pitching, pruning and planting-take me far from sophisticates-who became saturated in boorish-work-molds! Let me roll a tire down the road! To the farm! Let me look into the sky, where clouds take shape and imagination runs free! Where birds sing and wing their way, creating a skillful artistry-in-blue! Take me to the farm, where pines sway their long and furry arms, and trees, and bushes, dance-lively-winding-the wind! Why certainly-take me to the farm! Where earth-and-winds fire are quelled by water's wetness, welding and cooling spring-like-splashes on my eyes and face so I can breathe with ease, and trot on to another day...! Let me walk down a road, where in my soles-I feel a castle of greenery-and posh seatery in land and plants, beneath my feet and all around me! Oh, Browning, Emerson, Frost, and Tennyson make me fly-but if I were to come back-it would be-as a robin-perched-in-a-cherry tree on a farm!

— *Joyce Anna Jess*

Blessings

The Harvest moon rose in the Eastern sky,
    The hoot owl sounds were heard near by
And the grain was gathered in.
    The leaves had changed to hues —
Of yellow, orange and red.
    Thank you God, for harvest blessings!

The sun shone brightly
    On that cold December morn;
As the tiny little snowflakes were ushered in,
    Soon the sparkling and glistening countryside
Became a winter wonderland,
    The picturesque of God's almighty hand.
Thank you God, for winter blessings!

It was the cold and dreary days of winter
    That God sent forth His son;
The angels announced His birth,
    As the star led the shepherd and the wise men
To the manger in bethlehem.
    His Son who came to save us from sin —
Thank you God, for blessings from above.

— *Elvera Hillebrand*

Untitled

"Many of us are still about
Because we cut the smoking out."
    — *Clarence S. Borggaard*

Untitled

Why must Black History
be such a mystery
when the truth is finally told
its significance will be showed
    — *Andre Boulrece*

Tamara

Etched upon my heart
The image of her smile,
Lighting the hollows of my soul
As the mirrored ball lights the
Hidden corners of the dance floor.

Her quick and agile mind,
Windowed by emerald eyes,
Commands an incandescent smile
Framed by red nimbus hair and fair skin,
With unfeigned feelings and lack of guile.

Gliding above the floor she
Sweeps the room with beacon smile,
Compelling me to see,
If only for a fifty-minute hour...
Her smile is meant for me.
    — *Pat*

Reverie

Across the fields of yesteryears
The lad comes back to me
From out the past, with smiles and tears
Is the lad I used to be

Thru long days of time and dreams
His spirit haunting me
O'er half-forgotten fleeting gleams
Which brush my reverie

But when I linger long with him
In reminiscent glow
I turn my dream to present whim
My reverie I slow

For losing self in times gone by
And memories of the past
May cause my lonely soul to die
And keep from it true and lad and lass

Now they who come are child of child
And not of reverie
The real ones are the small ones mild
Whose beauty uplifts me
    — *Gordon Gray*

Tears For Eternity

As a tear rolls down my face,
the laughter it contains is not so funny.
When the lies get in the way,
it becomes nothing but glistening moisture -
on a sad face.
The pain in my eyes,
comes from the joy of Love and Happiness;
knowing that forever will never come.
Eventually, when all is true; I'll know!
There'll be nothing else to work for:
because what I'll have found,
is every persons dream of life.
Only then will the tears be able
to roll freely down my face
and find, ... Eternity!
    — *Scott A. Watts*

Autumn Mood

It's becoming Autumn again
The leaves twirl off their branches
Their colors decorate our world
Pumpkins are in their patches
In time they will be carved and lit with matches
Bobbing for apples will take place
Kids in costumes will be in a race
By going door to door showing us each and every scary face
Giving out sweets to ghouls and goblins and to little ones at our feet
The last child has come and gone
The chill is in the air, as I look up into the sky
and see the harvest moon punched through the nighttime
Another autumn gone by
   —Laura Jacobi

The Light Keeper's Wife

So solidly upon its shoal
The lighthouse stands, Rogue Island once,
When hidden coves were pirate lairs
And shipwrecks strewed the Yankee beach.
All night the keeper tends the lamp
To warn the ships of rocky shores,
His wife awaits approaching dawn
That ends her lonesome sleepless night.
Like waves that crash on rocks below,
Thoughts swirl and pound within her head,
Then fly afield like swooping gulls
Whose cries are echoes of her own.

Night's mist has gone, the gold-red sun
Lights up a path of shining flecks
Like ashes from the stars of night,
A path to leave this lonely place.
A voice breaks her reverie,
"Good morning, Jen, a lovely day."
Love calls and she can smile again.
Like ships she's safe within his arms.
   —Marguerite C. Purnell

The Pain

How can I take this pain any longer?
The Lord knows I'm not getting any stronger.
The pain gets worst day by day.
Why don't it just go away?
My pain follows me wherever I go.
But I try not to let it show.
At times I wish I could fly,
but then again I wish I would die.
When I'm alone, down and blue, I search my
mind and only find you.
This world is full of trouble and pain.
The Lord knows what to do about the rain.
Now how do we stop this rain of pain?
   —Annette Patterson

"Unsung Heroes"

These to me are the unsung heroes -
The loving dedicated, Mother and Fathers
  of dependant children -
The teachers of the world, who with loving
  patience and care nurture the hearts and
  minds of their charges -
The loving concern and care of children for
  parents infirm with years
The men and women of large and small
  communities, unselfishly dedicated to those
  less blessed -
All are touched by God and walk
  tirelessly in His footsteps.
   —Frances Anstett Brennan

Beyond the Mask

Truth is found beyond the Mask;
The Mask is but a hood,
Which hides the evil of a man
Along with the inner good.

The Mask protects one's inner self.
A self that is always solitary;
Encased so as not to escape,
Unlike something that is airy.

One man lost his mask;
To the astonishment of the world,
Devastation was known to the man now;
From the climax of life he found himself hurled.

His rapid fall was a lesson to all;
A lesson all around would heed.
Life will fall if the truth is seen by all.
The seed of life is truly unlike any other seed.

The truth is found beyond the Mask;
The Mask is but a hood,
Which hides the evil of a man
Along with the inner good.
   —J. A. Meserve

Home

Home is such —— a mysterious place;
The memories made there — time can never erase.
If, it is love and joy — or — sorrow and hate;
Only each heart knows — how it rates.
Torture for some — whom can never express;
To others, who have known — only happiness.

Home to some — is the happiest place to be.
Yet, to others, it means — only miseries.
Home can be a prison — with all the doors and windows — open.
It's the words — in the heart — that can't be spoken.
The house only stands there — with no way to defend;
The people who live there — nor the happenings — within.

As time goes on — the stories will be told of homes — more
precious — than gold. And some of torture, comedy, horror,
and — grief; the same house — holds. After all is said and
done — it's not a home here, we should treasure. It's a home
in Heaven - we should try to earn — a measure. He started us
all with love — and puts us all through a test. If the test,
we pass, our mind and body — will someday be at rest. And, we
can live in the same house — and be happy — and blessed.
   —Laurice H. Henderson

Wild Flower

A wild flower blooms in the hills outside the city.
The poet cries:
  Oh dainty little flower
  Whose beauty thrills me through,
  You give my life a meaning,
  Your beauty is so true.
  The world will stop and wonder,
  As they gaze upon your bloom,
  How such a fair creation
  Could ever meet its doom.
  Each heart will find new meaning
  As they see you blooming there.
  and men will praise your beauty,
  Your elegance so rare.

A group of people who have driven into the hills
for a Sunday afternoon to enjoy the beauty of nature
trample the flower and crush it to the ground.

—Look, see how beautiful the city is from here —
   —Thomas G. Smith

A Course, the Subject Life

I'm taking a course, the subject is life
The mining of error is in flight
what I have left can't be destroy
for the taking of knowledge I'm striving
    to move forward

The ringing of the bell sound
the class to rest, the break gives
the mind time to wine down for a spell

Prepare your thoughts to send a
mysterious probe, cause for tomorrow is unknown
The course in life is strong

Time will not stop for a moment on
the clock, yet the course has remain
the subject to maintain

Life is full, solid and strange, it is mystical
with charm the true course for life
    is never the same

From Man to Woman knowledge can be sane
but the gift to study a course, is yours
    for claim.
          —Sylvia Williams

Moon Light Stroll

I took a stroll the other night;
the moon and stars were shining bright,
I told them how I think of you;
from early morn, the whole day through,
how no one else can take your place;
and moon-beams danced upon my face.

I walked along a lovely trail;
where peace and happiness prevail,
the moon shone down so big and bright;
and filled the valley with its light.
I made a wish upon a star, I wished with
all my might; I wished that you were here
with me, this lovely, star-filled night.

But somewhere in a land of dreams;
the moon light through your window streams;
and I'll reach out to touch your hand,
somewhere in that magic land.

Then I will tell you of my love,
the way I told the stars above.
We'll be together don't you see?—
In all our dreams, just you and me.
          —Burnetta Martin

Autumn

…And so the leaves turn and we all stop to watch
the most colorful metamorphosis to look back on the year.
What did we gain, whom did we lose, the laughs,
The shocks, the mishaps.
The song that read the times so perfectly.
And if nothing else came of it, we still live (damaged
somewhat) but better off because of our experiences.
And although the year is still not finished
We are not premature in our reflections because life
(Ever fleeting, ever changing) may be through before we know it.
Our mother is tired now.
Our father is still on guard.
And as we romp around so recklessly because of times rug
pulling out from under us!
Nothing really matters, but everything counts.
And so it goes.
          —Angelo R. Sales

A Multitude of Friends

They come and go from all around
The needs are sometimes great, some small
I laugh, I cry, I always try
To help them if I can

Why are they here - then gone?
To keep a friend would be the greatest thing
The reasons are so undefined

My mind goes back to years gone by
I miss them when they're gone

Along comes someone new -
A joy, a light in dark
But never are the old forgotten

Memories never die
Friends and friendships do
          —Carrol L. Austin

Choices

Say a prayer for the unspoken ones
The ones who get lost in a crowd
Say a prayer for those who speak
Yet no one hears them crying

And say a prayer for people who laugh
Yet feel so torn inside
And yes, say a prayer for those that are blamed
Trying so hard to get our attention

And send your prayers to everyone
Who has ever been left the pain of generations
For these are all courageous ones
Who now have a chance to break the chain

Listen to them…

They will have a choice
To know their true value
They will have a choice
To know the value of our world
          —Annette Nicholson

My Two Dads

One was there all along.
The other came and soon he belonged.
My heart love them just the same.
The only difference was I only shared one last name.
I wanted both of them to walk me down the aisle.
But, one unselfishly stepped aside and let the other give
away the bride.
Their love and memory still reside in my heart on Father's
Day.
Now that they are both gone.
I'm very sad.
But, my life has been blessed.
For I've had 2 Dads.
          —Susan Montour

I Know This Person

I know the person who listens to me,
The person who listens when no one else can,
I know the person who cares for me,
The person who would sacrifice for no other man,
I know the person who watches over me,
And would one day die and leave this land,
This person loves me almost more than God,
This person was me all the time.
          —Tameka Simon

The Hole

The hole keeps calling me. An urge deep inside beckons.
The "outside" is mere chaos. It demands more than I can give.
Can't you hear?
The hole is calling me.

The hole promises me, "Come here and reside in peace",
But the hole is dark — Light grows faint 'til it fades away.
Can't you see?
The hole is alluring to me.

The hole keeps pulling me. Its encompassing strength is great.
Reality passes away — I long for its comforting touch.
Can't you feel it?
The hole is holding me.

The hole nurtures me. Its very existence brings me warmth,
But it consumes its prey — Little is left of me.
Can't you help?
The hole numbs most of me.

The hole no longer speaks to me. It leaves me in an abyss.
The isolation is total — Reality no longer exists.
Don't you even care?
The hole now entirely owns me.

  —Verna Kay

Daydreams

I am
The paper
burning in a fire
slowly turning black
my corners turning
inward with solitude
only becoming ash
lost in the wind becoming part of societies hell
being deprived of the peoples baffle
isolated in immortality
Nonexisting in the hidden fashion
of the distant pondering
the lethargy has been ignored
in the life of freedom
aimlessly squandering in the wind
detached from all the rest of the world.
 le mort au feu (the death of the fire)
  —Misty Keller

A View Of Life

The scenic view of the mountains, is magnificent in scope,
The pines, the aspens, all the colors of glorious beauty, seen
 on every slope;
It is like a miracle, wonderful to behold,
As if a romantic story is waiting, eager to be told,
A place to marvel, as if life itself were but a dream,
So peaceful, that all of life's burdens, seem to be carried
 away, on a swift mountain stream.
Surely God's creation is manifest, and will impart
The very best within us and challenge us to start
A new perspective for living, and concern for others to be
 instilled
For us surely as God is in his heavens, our role in life will
 richly be fulfilled.
  —C. A. Pedersen

Malibu Fire

Gleaming skies of red and orange
Children watch out doors and windows.
With fear and fascination at the red
Sea rising in the sky like a spilled paint can.
Fiery blazes reach over the mountains like big
Hands taking trees, taking homes, taking memories.
  —Miesha Moore

God's Power And Grace

Does the One who made the animals, the birds, and every bee,
The plants and grass, the rain and snow, and every kind of tree,
The mountains and the oceans, each season in its place,
Does this Great One have time for us-to give us boundless grace?

Does the One who made the Cherubim, and all the angels, too,
The Seraphim, the heavenlies, and our big sky of blue;
Does the One who drew this master plan and made the human race,
Does this Great One have time for us-to give us boundless grace?

Does the One who formed the earth and sun, the moon and all
 the stars,
The atoms and the molecules, and those immense Quasars,
The Universe and Galaxies and never-ending space,
Does this Great One have time for us-to give us boundless grace?

Of course He does; how do I know?
It's easy as can be.
He came to earth, died on the cross,
And rose—for you and me.
And yet with all He has to do,
Controlling land and sea,
He leaves His throne and spans the stars,
To walk with tiny me.
  —Dawn M. Hagerty

The Light of Death

The light shined and I followed
The point of following was to get lost in the light.

I followed it for miles
I could have gone to hell and back, by the time I got to the end.
The light is getting closer,
I can feel its heat on me, close your eyes and wonder what it
 does for thee

I wonder if its heaven,
But I don't belong there
I don't belong in hell
But who really cares,
The time is getting shorter
The light is reaching through me,
My soul is sucking up the rays, from being in the dark;

My time is ending shortly,
There's no point in time,
So hold on tight,
Keep your eyes shut, and listen to me,

I live for the light that came upon me.
  —Danielle Mangino

Live or Die, Suicide

The break of day, the crying night, the dying Earth.
The question asked again and again;
What was the purpose of my birth?
And the question ponders...again.

The time of day goes slowly, and the night passes.
The temperature of day, mediocre; the night is the same.
The world seen through rose colored glasses,
Every color the same; every person insane.

The pain, the heartache, the ripping depression.
A cut and a slice and blood and tears flow.
A mark of loneliness, a symbol, an expression.
Too alone to stay, yet too late to go.

To be or not to be; to live yet not to see.
Genocide, homicide, suicide, it's all the same to me.
  —Stacey L. Gomes

America

Children in the afterbirth lay,
The provenance of earth's decay;
The semblance wakes as morn doth wed
The righteous whore presumption fed.

Turn unto her wanton shores
Where waves of men have waged their wars,
The even becks the futile path,
"Take rest! Take rest! From freedom's wrath."

O beacon that burns in the night bejeweled
Of moon and stars Orion ruled,
Doth light offend the weary eye,
Or heaven attend the orphan's cry?

So hell will bring thee to thy knees,
Deaf unto thy muted pleas;
Knave and nobleman shall deride
The abrogation of thy pride.

Chaos burns a mettlesome coal,
The thorn of the flesh that burdens the soul;
Vernal cries of childhood fail
Mid the hue of Megiddo's pale.
        —Anthony Brantley

Pony Express

    Before the conveniences so modern —
The public services, as buses, airplanes and the railroads —
What has happened to the horse and buggy days of yore?
A dependable mail-carrier for sure!

Cloppity-clop instead of clickety-clack —
Down the terrain, not down the track
Clippity-clop merrily upon its way
The horse carried the rider-with a mail-sack
And for their pay-upon their way
A running brook offer a drink
A postal patron might offer a sandwich or a meal —
But once a mean little tot gave me a taste of his sling-shot!
So I just detoured my route
Left his mail at his Grandma's country store
Where lots of goodies were offered to me —
Goodies and a June-berry pie-all free!
And a bale of hay or some Grandmother's oats
For the clippity- clop-and away we'd go upon our merry way!!!!!
        —Patsy Hastings

Dreaming

In the evening of yesterdays tomorrow
the quiet thunder of monster jets
tread meekly through the clouds.
When silvery wings caress the air
still higher than the plain, I dream of you.

When clouds, like sightless icons hang
misty in their glaring brightness,
my thoughts reach out to grasp a dream;
a dream which is yet, yet couldn't be
a dream of memory; I dream of you.

Clouds like thoughtless thunder lay
beneath those winding strings of steel,
stretch straight to where my thoughts
scream soundlessly for you,
dreams of sad delight and pain, my dream of you.

Still further on my thoughts glide by
as does the wind o'er silvery wing,
my thoughts that I'm remembering,
the dream of yesterday and tomorrow,
of past delights and future pleasures, a dream of you.
        —James Edgar Haley

Everyday Life

It's a perfect warm sunny day.
The rays are shining everywhere.
Especially on a front yard of a little brown house.
There's a little girl playing with a doll.
There's a street with several busy cars in front of the lawn.
The girl's mother is mowing the lawn.
Her back is facing the road.
All of a sudden, the little girl gets up.
She walks somewhere. She sits down again.
She continues playing with the doll.
The sound of the mower engulfs the mother's ears.
There is the sound of honking.
She doesn't consciously hear it. The honking continues.
The mother finally turns around to see what is going on.
She runs to the street. Her daughter has chosen to sit down,
In the middle of the street.
She ignores the honking from the cars on both sides.
She is happily playing with her doll.
Her mother scoops her up.
She apologizes to the drivers and her apology was: "She's deaf."
        —Amanda Fish

Passion for Life on a Yacht

The material needs are scant,
The remunerations are magnificent.

The song of the halyards frolicking in the zephyr
like harmonized wind chimes.

The delicate waves rocking me to sleep at night.

The full moon shining upon the fly bridge,
as the tepid breeze whispers through my hair.

The comfort and security of a baby cradle
Sunday morning poetry and wine with neighbors.
The hatch perpetually open to friends.
Home is where ever you drop your anchor.
It doesn't get better than this.
        —Karen Mae Pearce

Another Start

Alone in the arms of my fear
The silence of this new morn' pass through the
    open window,
Here I see his eyes, the softness of a burning
    ember
Creating a dawn another try at opening the door
    to this new world
Peering on this fiery intent
I know not where my heart can go
My fear holding me back,
The door remaining closed
Memories come alive through whispers
    of your words carried in wind
Alive I am to feel but once again
    this magical moment
Rebirth of day
    passing through
Another start freeing me
From this lonely world.
        —Michele Samolinski

Desert Walking

Storms of wind Tornados whipping against my face and ripping
the skin between my toes.
As I walk to the building that holds my attention, I feel anticipation.
No one around to see me go into the abandoned structure that
blocks my entrance to the other side.
Chanting of vocal sirens fill my ears, enticing me into their
life and to live my existence through them.
The voices are deafening as I reach for the door, I hold tight
and swing it open and as I do the thunderous roar of a
thousand winds grabs my soul and lifts into the world of an
everlasting smile.
As I glance down I notice, the birds fly below me now.

— *Todd William Raasch*

Sonnet #1

When I look on the heavens, the trees, a flower,
The sky all lit with stars in endless light,
I see the traces of a higher power,
A finger moving, touching, proving might.
O, could I discern this royal Monarch,
Who on His throne of wisdom points earth's way,
And gives each thing direction every hour,
And keeps the lowly sparrow where it may.
Then, I'd begin to know my royal birthright,
The why's and wherefore's of life's mystery,
And then somehow see light in that glass darkly,
And faintly, O so faintly hope to see.
But, 'tis not for a mortal man to know,
How heavenly Monarchs make their worlds to go.

— *Mildred D. Johnson*

Oh, Mighty Wind

Oh, mighty wind, who blows the clouds like chariots throughout
the sky and filled many a sail of sailing ships, now long gone
by. The wind that has bent mighty oaks, when they've been in
its path and many a ship at sea has felt its rage and wrath.

Oh, mighty wind, who blows the tiny snowflakes across the
barren ground and forms mighty drifts of snow that keep us from
going into town. The wind Jack Frost rides upon like a
fast-moving train and goes about painting pictures on all the
window panes.

Oh, mighty wind, who blows the sand like caravans across the
arid land, and piles one grain upon another to form a mighty
dune of sand. The wind that rustles through the branches and
hums a merry tune, also brings the fragrance of flowers that
bloom in the month of June.

Oh, mighty wind, who blows the leaves from trees, that dance
like ballerinas as they twirl and bounce with ease. The wind
that carries the voices of little children as they play, brings
back many memories from a long and forgotten day.

— *Charles E. Llewellyn*

Half Way Up the Mountain

The path takes a sharp turn to the left with
the sign "Stay On Path."
I stop and can understand why...
There is only open space ahead,
a cliff and air.
Reality is here yet behold from this
point that is very near the sky...
Mountains, trees, snow, a lake far below...
I am half way up this mountain...
With another half to go.

— *Valarie Beagle*

In My World

In my world there is beauty, love and peace.
The sky is so bright the whole world shines
with a beautiful glow.
Darkness cannot enter, love is so true and abundant.
Hate has no control.
There is a great peace that moves freely from sky to land.
I can hear angels singing.
The music is very soft and low.
The wind steadily blows through the trees as the leaves
shiver a pleasant sound.
The water continues to flow in the brooks with a melody.
My body, soul and mind relax peacefully.
Unrest cannot penetrate.
For this peace you cannot destroy.
I hope someday your world will also have the beauty,
love and peace that is in my world.

— *Margaret C. Martin*

You're Playing with Stars

You're playing with stars - that's dangerous
The sky's off limits - you're too daring
To you, life is something to take and eat -
To me, it is too overbearing.

You're playing with stars - amazing
You have no fear of being betrayed.
You run to someone who needs you -
I stay - I'm much too afraid.

You're playing with stars, effortlessly
Unaware of the magic you spread.
You're too smart to lose, too naive to be hurt -
You're the "u" after "q", the butter on bread.

You're playing with stars - and laughing
Proud yet humble, happy and free,
I'm a slave to my wicked past -
Too scared to see how you see.

You're playing with stars - be careful
When you fall, things are never the same.
Like me, you'll lose your faith and courage
And have only the stars to blame.

— *Sam Sherwin*

The Life of a Game

I am a kid, a lot like my dad.
The smell of newly mowed grass, the feel of dirt,
Running, diving, sliding, teamwork.
All things he loved and did.

The mound is the center of my world.
I love it here!
I get the sign, I focus my mind, the batter stands
clothed in fear
As I deliver my fastball so confidently.

Bart (not Simpson) Giamatti said, "Baseball is a
metaphor for life..."
Although it is a game and nothing more.
Sometimes we live life like a game
although it is so much more.
Then suddenly, the strident crack of the bat,
like the boom from Oppenhiemer's child,
The game of life makes you feel its pain.

The center of my world has forever changed.
Forever changed.
Forever changed.
Someday you will see my pain buried beneath the change.

— *Zakk S. Campbell*

The Hunter

High overhead they circle, searching, eager they circle.
The sound of their wings beating, cutting through the
early dawn, beating.
The decoys swim seductively, urging, bringing them
closer, always urging.
The hunter waits silent, still. The tension, the
anticipation, but always still.

Closer they come beckoning with their call. The hunter
replies not moving not looking, but masterfully answers the call.
Now the hunter moves, raising his weapon. He strains to
focus, firing again and again as the silence erupts.
Wings beat faster and faster grabbing for air, gaining
precious altitude.
Still the hunter shoots as fast as his finger allows,
focus, fire, until the last one is out of range.
And as he settles down to become still and silent he
smiles, reaching for another roll of film.
High overhead they circle, searching, eager they circle.

—*Glenn R. Sweet*

The Cemetery

Venus was visible and sparkling just above the crescent moon.
The stars hung suspended beyond time and dreams.

The night was late-brisk Fall.
The fallen leaves crunched beneath my feet as
        I walked past the graves,
            my shadow cutting across silent crosses.

Here lies...a name announcing the meaning of the grave,
            telling the "once upon a time" story.

To walk the cemetery is to remember the great visions and dreams,
        of builders, prophets and leaders,
            of poets, sages and story tellers.
Here lies a once opening future, and the now written past.

A tear took shape and rolled down my cold face,
        a tear for the dead with their dreams and visions,
            a tear for the future and my own dreams and visions.

As the Fall chill covered the night,
        I knew that tomorrow someone will walk here,
            and remember as history the dreams and visions of today.

Sparkling Venus, the crescent moon,
        and the white crosses remain the constant witnesses.

—*Louis T. Brusatti*

This is Where the War Lives

This is where the man dies.
The sound of life screaming.
And where swords clash with its iron cracking.
Blood spreads everywhere.
Heat raises then dies.
This is where the war lives.

The sound of heroes running.
The sound of drums beating.
The sound of arrows shooting overhead.
The smelling of old flesh burning.
This is where the war lives.

People crying for the dead.
People thinking about another life.
People leaving their dead behind.
People die for what they need.
This is where the war lives.

—*Andrew Hamilton*

Mr. Moon

Hello there Mr. Moon, may I ask you how you are? As
the stars play around you, and cast moon beams afar.

What would you say Mr. Moon if I confessed to you?
That you are my one and only love, so brilliant and true.

As you sit in radiant beauty, in the star studded
sky, and cast your spell on lovers as you beam on by.

In answer to your question dear, I am very fine, I
have peeked into your window, many many a time, I
kissed you while you slumbered on, I smiled, and stole
away, awaiting for the day.

I watched you little darling since you were knee high,
I saw all your sorrows, and joys from my pedestal in the sky.

I am your own true lover, I will never run away, I will
always be close by each night and day, to beam your
tears away.

So never fear little darling, I shall steal through your
window, plant a kiss upon your lips, I will watch over
you so gently until my next returning trip.

—*Helen Lenore Flordeliz*

My Son And I

The fog whisked in by the sea last night
        the stars put out their twinkles
        while the moon stole out of sight

We walked in silence, my son and I, to where the boats lay
        moored. All was now quiet, the halyards not speaking,
        The masts stood in reverence, all of us awed.

The lamp posts lined the empty street
        their globes haloed with rainbows by mist
        My son and I walked side by side
        his cold little fingers wrapped into my fist

We walked past the docks now groaning with the rising tide
        The night air grew colder and we rushed inside.

The fog horn's lament could scarcely be heard
        as we boarded our trustworthy sloop
        I quickly lit the burner on the stove and
        fixed us a pot of navy bean soup

I smiled at my son and he grinned back at me,
        with a twinkle and laughter in his eyes,
        on a foggy night by the open sea
        what could be better than my son and I.

—*Stephen B. Strum*

Proposal

The orchard was beautiful on a peaceful day,
The sunshine was comforting and the songbirds were gay.
Knowing exactly how I would go through it,
For many years I envisioned this moment.
On my skin I feel the soft breeze,
Ever so slowly I fall to my knee,
Weakened by love and the joy of life,
Hoping to hear "Yes I'll be your wife."
The ring I gave her sparkles bright and true
Glinting reflections of her eyes so blue.
I waited with patience, my heart all a flutter,
She was all that I wanted, her and no other.
Her ruby red lips parted as if to speak,
With one single word, my future she'd reap.
Suddenly the sun was blocked by a cloud,
The birds ceased their song and my heart began to pound.
The wind kicked up and the leaves began to blow,
My heart quickly stopped for my love had said..."no."

—*David Alan Redwanc*

An Everlasting Moment or an Elegy to Millie

An overcast day has become black.
The sun can not erase its blackness.
Tuesday, May 22, 1990, 11:17 A.M. - darkly different.

A moment-a minute-an hour-a day-a week-a month-a year
   -a decade-a lifetime.

Nothing compares.

A day, yet not a day.
A dream, yet not a dream.
A nightmare-No!-Reality!

A piece of me has been hacked out never to be replaced.

Blurring and swirling in the deepest recesses of my head
Echoing in the darkest corners of my mind
Making no sense in all the blackness, the words.

A cawing crow distracts me,
Haunting me as I write.
Has nature joined me in my grief?
Nothing eases the Pain!

I am me—
And you are gone—
And a part of me dear mother has left me—
And I grieve.
   —*Michael Alestra*

Early Morning Lament

(Un Chanson De Charlatan Nocturne)
The sun peeps thru my window,
Like an obnoxious intruder.

Waxing most imperiously,
In what it designs to be it's perennial glory,
This supposedly noble star is really quite unbearable...
And insufferably haughty in its manner.

Oh, such a shamefully self-aggrandizing orb!
For It offers no apologies, for it's clamorous,
Noisesome invasion of my solitude.

The warm darkness...
Which wraps itself so lovingly
Around cherished memories,
And in turn binds me inextricably to Luna...
Is banished from the horizon.

And I who have basked in her alluring presence,
Must once again deal with the cold reality
Of daytime existence.....
Until rapturous night comes again, and once more I am free!
To revel in sweet, pleasureful abandon and unbridled
Ecstasy...
As her arms enfold themselves about me.
   —*Philip J. McCarthy*

The Better Gift: A Sonnet

The Christmas season comes to us once more,
The time for love and joy and happiness,
The season we take time to say "God bless"
And give to those folks whom we most adore.
The joy of Christmas is for rich and poor,
No matter their color or type of dress.
As fun as Christmas is, I must confess,
The season to give has become a chore.
Maybe we need to stop and remember
The reason Christmas is a holiday
And spend a moment to reflect on it.
Let's think less of money this December
And make our world a better place today
By giving of ourselves a little bit.
   —*Jennifer A. Gillis*

Meltdown

The sun rises bright orange, and I am alone
The sun sets deep crimson, and you are alone
It happened by chance, our tender romance
This is the miracle we found together

The loneliness we know hovers and surrounds
We nurture our loving—let us be, let us be
When your welcoming arms, outstretched, make a
circle, your embrace holds me close, lips search

my face, find desire etched deeply, bodies entwined
rocking gently in time, rhythmically sublime
Why can't we stay in each other's arms
Yearning, burning, to capture this moment

When we're not together I'm lonely and blue
Missing you, needing you, remembering, too,
the many hours lost, the many hours tossed
Now I know, now I see, its good for me, being with you

The sun rises bright orange, and I am alone
The sun sets deep crimson, and you are alone
It happened by chance, our tender romance
This is the miracle we found together
   —*Bernadette LeBlanc*

"I Love You"

I might not always get to tell you,
The things that are in my heart.
But you can bet I sure do miss you,
Whenever we are apart.
I often think of just how special,
Your love has been to me.
And how its really helped me,
In the things I needed to see.
Often I was mean, in the things I used to say.
But even when you were angry,
Your love would never sway.
You had that way of showing,
Just how much you really card.
That's why I'm forever grateful,
For all the moments we have shared.
So please forgive me darling,
If I don't always say what I feel.
But you can believe this fellow
loves you, trust me, it's for really.
   —*Sanantonio B. Russell*

Still Tears

The waters no longer runs.
The tides have fallen to sleep.
The sweet essence of the salt
no longer stings my eyes.
The tears of pain without the glory of water,
is like the opening of one's soul
without the burst of hope.
Life can only flow if the ocean run rampant.
The calmness of the tides is like
the stillness of a broken heart.
Birth no longer weeps.
For the ocean of a womb awaits an empty Gulf.
The first wail of a baby
without the glisten of tears.
Is the last sigh of life for an ocean that once rule.
The sands have taken over.
The tears of the ocean no longer swims.
   —*Ella Marie Castille*

Farmer's Thanksgiving Prayer

So comes the time of harvest.
The time to enjoy that
which has grown in the fields,
picked from the vine in its prime,
these, the fruits of our labor.
The work and toil of
hoeing the rows and planting the seeds,
watering and tending and the fortune
of a good year.
Nature, in her gentle ways, has been kind
and not burned or washed away what we planted.
So, tip of the hat
to the lady dressed in her green gown
with raven hair tied back in a red bow,
and enjoy this feast,
shared with friends and neighbors
at this, the gatherings of autumn.

—*Linda G. Taylor*

"Saying Goodbye"

We weren't all that close
the time you were here.
Good memories mean the most
even though they bring a tear.

It was hard to take
too soon to believe,
at night I wake
to see you leave.

I love you so much
now I say goodbye.
To feel your last touch
I hang my head and sigh.

You left us tonight
with no warning.
For your life now you don't have to fight
while we're all mourning.

You're my Grandpa
I'm proud to say,
Your struggles we saw
in peace now you lay.

—*Chelly Jens*

Standing At The Summit

All life long, I climbed this hill to reach someday
the top at will. The slope, at times, so steep and trying
drained oft'n the strength from my weary being.

Now, that I'm old and atop my mount'n, I am surprised at
what I've found. The summit is not a peak, confining
but a wide plateau, ready for exploring.

Its range, as broad as the Lord wills it, is a happy
playground for my heart and wit. Here I can see from where
I came, not needing an upward step to scheme.

There is merit in looking down to the rugged slope, pondering
what in the struggle helped me cope. Thanks to my memories,
more profoundly grows the contentment I'm feeling as the
sunset glows.

Standing at the pinnacle of life's quest does not put my
heart and mind at rest. My heart still looks for beauty
everywhere, while the mind seeks challenges and dare.

I hope my stay at the summit is long, my body and soul active
and strong; for when someday the Lord turns off my light,
the experiences he gave me will be stars in my eternal night.

—*Ilse Wissner*

Sad Darkness

Wherever I turn my attention, I see a sad darkness;
The torch of justice and magnanimity is quenched,
The livelihood of the dispossessed is destroyed;
Tears on the care-worn faces of the oppressed
Cannot be seen in this darkness,
And beneath the oppressor's choking reign
Day and night are both like an unlit graveyard.
I long for dawn's light, but dawns still delay
And in light's absence grief's flood sweeps on
While the same overwhelming darkness continues.
There's no need now for tulips to redden the meadows
Human blood has completed the task;
Knowledge of such things deprives those who can feel
Of all pleasure and sleep and it is Payind's deepest wish
That he see the end of this sad darkness,
Or - in such dense darkness - oppression
Will be humanity's unending fate.

—*Alam Payind*

Flowers

The lovely Chrysanthemum just waking up
the violets and buttercup
the meadows are filled with their blossoms so fair
for dogwood and daisies are there.
All nature's reborn, the hillsides adorn
Sweet petunias and orchids are gay.
As the sunflower turns on her God when he sets
earth rejoices through all the bright day.

'Tis summer, 'tis summer, cold winter is past-
warm breezes are blowing at last.
The birds begin singing, their songs fill the air
and lilies are found everywhere.
The pleasant palms, begonias and ferns-
flowers, flowers, great beauty to see
We should all be like flowers growing for our God
spreading beauty and love all abroad.

—*Lillian B. Gardner*

The First Hunter

As I the hunter peer out to see;
The warm autumn colors that surround me.
The reds remind me of the summer,
The yellows the bright sun shining,
The oranges, that halloween will soon be here,
The browns, that soon winter will come.
And greens- there aren't many.

Now I go out to hunt the deer.
As I walk into the peaceful forest,
I feel the warm breezes, blowing.
As I walk in further, I see leaves falling.
Then I pause..... I see a deer!
Then all of the sudden a flock of geese fly by,
I have now lost track of the deer.

As I go deeper, I peer, to see animals surrounding me.
Then I see acorns falling.
Then I glance up to see,
The most beautiful, deep, blue sky you shall ever see,
Right above me.
I now say to myself this is the best time of the year.

—*Angela Wotruba*

Away From It All

Birds soar, and are trapped in flight.
The way they see the world, through my sight.
Without a care in this world, I'd love to be.
With the birds, soaring on my dreams.
Stress is the test that sets us apart,
Feeling and saying things through the heart.
I wish I could be a whole lot more,
Just to drop all my things and walk out the door.
Pressure is so much in this world today,
So many things are to my dismay.
High upon the clouds, the wind in my hair,
Without any problems for me with to bear.
Away with the hectic life with me.
Away from it all, I'd love to be....

—*Kelly L. Monteiro*

Khaled

The day we met has been on my mind
The way you looked when your eyes met mine
You was the handsomest man I ever did see
And I knew right then you belonged to me.

You asked me out for the very first time
All I could feel was my heart racing inside
I said "Yes" while my insides screamed
But it felt like I was living a dream.

You wined me, and dined me, I felt like a queen
Then all of the sudden you gave me a ring
We set the wedding date so all could know
But we ran and got married like on a T.V. show

You are the man I love for all of my life
The one who has been there through the good and bad times
The one who will be there when I take my last breath
And my very last kiss before I lay down to rest

—*Romelda Ghattas*

Silent Partner—The Ironing Board

My ironing board has shared with me, both happy times and sad,
The weekly task of readying a wardrobe for my lad.

First came the precious baby clothes,
Tiny rompers and shirts so wee,
Later on the crawlers with patches on the knee.

His first long pants, was quite a day.
Next gobs and gobs of clothes for play.
That starched white shirt was a big event.
The hours labored over blue jeans, were all well spent.

Cub Scout uniforms must be done just so.
My! That baseball suit looks as white as snow.
Fixing the angel costume for the Christmas play,
How we struggled to get those wings to stay.

On Band Day how we had to fuss,
"Please hurry mom, here comes the bus."
Your tuxedo for the Senior Prom, was the biggest task to come
along. At last came graduation day, "Press my long black robe"
(or was it gray?)" Today I ironed the Air Force Blue, and
wiped a tear as I was through. Tomorrow we must make other
plans, because today our son's a man.

—*Nelda LeCorchick*

The Widow's Walk

Another widow walks the 'walk' and joins the other widows on
the 'Widows' Walk.'

Like statues on a parapet they stand.

Their bodies strain forward
While hands grip the rail.
Their eyes pierce the fog
While the fog horns wail.
The surf slaps the sand
As the mist slowly lifts.

To no avail they wait against their wailing wail.

They clutch their woolen shawls
Against the long night's chill:
A substitute for arms
That will not hug again.
Nor do they warm against the cold
That chills the hearts within.

Les miserables, the hungry, homeless poor cry out,

"Forgo the 'wake! They will not come to you. Come
down, come down and walk with us our walk. You have
skill: Have you the will to walk our walk with us?"
—*Ann Fountain McBain*

The Rains

I love to hear the raindrops upon the roof,
The wind blowing the trees all around my house,
And the thunder rattling the windows so much
That I think they are going to bust apart.
The lightning illuminating the darkened room.
I look outside, the trees are almost lying on their sides.
Lightning strikes in the distance.
I cover my ears, but I am too late.
The thunder crackles as my hair stands on end.
Then all of a sudden the sky clears,
But I can still hear the thunder in the distance.
I walk outside.
I see all the devastation the rains have caused,
And my poor tree is split in half and burning.

—*Sarah Esmond*

We, In Need

Why are they here, just walking among the weary
Their tired and hungry eyes
Peering mercilessly into the night
What is it that they seek
Away out of their reality
Or someone to show them
The righteous path for life
Journeys long have worn on them heavily
Only to be standing here with no purpose
Their outstretched hands reaching hungrily
Into the riches of the oncoming crowd
Only to be laughed at, pushed aside
Spat upon and criticized
By the uncaring and the unknowing
For they too, once walked among the proud
Our fathers, mothers, sons and daughters
Are these wretched creatures
Who's only crime in this so perfect world
They are the homeless, the poor and the ill, cast aside by us
We the Godly people of humanity
—*Ron J. Ritchie*

Memories of a Daughter

She was once so vital, so happy and carefree;
Then came that wretched night of grim visaged infamy
When she was snatched by the king of death and dread
While we watched helplessly beside her bed.
He took her soul away from us, despite our woeful prayer,
And left us there with broken hearts filled with dire despair.

Gone that night were those days of delight
With our daughter who was so precious in our sight.
But in her place came another face to dull our pain;
Her little girl came to live with us and helped us laugh again.

But still, at times, those painful passions prick my secret heart
With grim visaged comfortless despair from sorrow's sadistic dart
Then I must fight to cause those vultures of the mind to flee
And erase that desperate anger, weakening fear and painful memory.

In those times my weapon of choice is God's quiet voice
That tells me she is His and it was His merciful choice
To set her free from those days of despair and agony
And call her home to be with Him and be part of heaven's beauty.

—*Jerry L. Stafford*

The Plan

If I don't know where I am
Then I won't know where I'll be
If I live from day to day
I live only me to me
Perhaps I'd better look ahead - unfrightened-
  What I'll see
If I don't know who I am right now
I can't know who I'll be.

—*Trudi G. Stridborg*

An Inspired Poem from the Holy Spirit

Sometimes from Jesus people stray,
Then sin starts to come in right away.
But Jesus is still there to help you through
With arms opened wide just for you.

Sometimes we feel we just aren't good enough
And because of this the road can get mighty rough.

Oh please can't you see, Jesus still cares for you?
Why are you so blue?
Please don't feel so lost,
Jesus died for me and for you, and to God, oh what a cost!

Don't you realize how He is hurting
Because, of Him, you are not trusting.
Oh look, I see Jesus with a tear.
He's crying tears of compassion for you, dear.

It doesn't matter what you have done.
Just ask for forgiveness and it will all be gone.

Oh can't you see
That with Jesus You Are Free!
That's what He did for us that day on Calvary.

—*Brenda Hamilton*

Two Loves

The inextinguishable fire radiantly burning within
The seemingly timeless admirations shared with another
The unending need growing from the heart
The perfect dream unbroken and shatterproof

The unending verbal battles with cannons causing unhealable
wounds
The loud thunder storms making it difficult to sleep
The painful nightmares and daydreams scaring and hurting
The knife sinking deep through the flesh

—*John Holownia*

Motions And Movement

Shadows of motion, flexibly shaded
  colorfully tinted, translucently toned
  swaying-prancing-rocking-sashaying
  ever so constant, upwardly bound
Motion majestic...above all renowned.

—*Octavia L. Jones*

Dad

Since you are being honored on this your day,
There are a few words I wish to say,
I know no other man as unselfish as you,
Whose gifts of generosity are more than true,
Your spirit of giving should be honored and praised,
As seen most surely in the family you raised.
You have shown me well what it means to give,
Which gave a better reason for me to live.
Since your dedication is for those you love most,
This day, in your honor, I offer a toast.

I congratulate you, on this your day,
For all the kindness you have passed my way.
Three more thoughts, I wish to express,
Better still I must confess.
.... As a Man, I praise you
.... As a Teacher and Provider, I thank you
.... But mostly, as my Father, I love you!

—*James Boni*

Ambiguous Reality

There are lechers in the lullabies,
There are demons in the halls,
Enveloped in Truth there are lies,
And in darkness, we see it all,
Embedded in commitment there is denial,
Inside the precious, there is the vile,
Every good intention hides deep resentment,
Every smiling face hides a precocious frown,
In every person, there are questions and secrets,
Don't believe me?... LOOK AROUND!

Pathetically we play this game, the formidable
cycle stays the same, and when we look to cast the
blame, revealed to us — a reflection of our pain,
this image burns like acid's reign,
GET ME OFF THIS TRACK OF PAIN.

I've had my share of shattered dreams, of ancient battery
and fire rings, and all the emotions that these things bring,
Have revealed to be true two of Berkeley's themes:
  — That reality is never what it seems.
  — That perception IS everything.

—*Danny Coughlin*

Peaceful Explosion Of A Hydrogen Bomb

The sun is 93 million miles away, and on the sun's surface
there are hydrogen explosions similar to a hydrogen bomb.
These explosions cause flares which leap into space and reach
the earth at an amazing speed ... 8 1/2 minutes.

When it reaches the earth, I take my shirt off and it gives
me a wonderful sun tan. Isn't that a peaceful explosion of a
hydrogen bomb?

Here is another way of describing a peaceful explosion?

  Trillions of gigantic butterflies with their
  luminous electrical rainbows tailing, gliding
  through spectrums of sun rays at astronomical
  speeds to their resting places, singing poetic
  songs as they go.

—*Mario Pezzi*

Sea Sorceress

Can you see her,
There in the distance?
The sea is the lair
She controls as the crescent
Moon spies as a God's eye
On all that's done.
Listen to the roar, it can hypnotize your soul.
Try to knock her off the throne
And you'll just get washed away
By the waves, nature's toys under her spell, and every day
It's their destructiveness she employs
To their fullest. All you people beware,
Beware of the crashing tide, the roar of the earth bare
Of its skin, are you ready to take
a ride beneath reality? She points in your
direction, can you succumb under
her power? Are you strong enough or will you feel the wrath
of her thunder blasting loudly high in the heaven?
Please believe me, to your end she'll be sending you.

—*Paul Skyrm*

Two In Love

(Dedicated to Cleveland and Monique)
There is a feeling for one another
  That bring a strong desire
A Friendship that caught on fire
  That grow one day at a time
Love is understanding for each other
  That give strength for all situation

There is a warmness between the two
  Even when the two are separate
Miles do not matter
  When two are in love

There is trust
  That make each other honest
Both can admit to their fault
  When troubles arrive
There so much to learn
  When two are in love.

—*Evan B. Farrior*

Pandemonium and Chaos Reign

I live in a world of darkness
There is almost no chance of light
But you
You're the golden God I crave
The only warm stable comfort in my life
Solid and firm in a world of cold hard objects
Feelings to match your features
If you aren't here, my bridge is gone
The only link I have to the outside
With you gone, there'd be no organization
Thoughts scrambled
Mental stability broken
You are the God of my light
Without you, reality is shattered

—*Shasta Carlsen*

Family

Family is like bedcovers
Comforting you and warming you.
Family is like T.V. amusing you
and calming you.
Family is like a shower,
refreshing you and resting you.
But, most important, family isn't
like, but is, your loved ones.

—*Michael Pertnoy*

Barren Desert

There is a barren desert that lies deep within;
There is no falling rain, only the ghostly sound of the wind.
Emptiness flies to and fro with every grain of sand;
Loneliness lies throughout and across this desert land.

There is an endless monotony to this barren place;
The sand covers the terrain, like a veil covers a face.
You can look all around but only see the sun beating down,
On this land that is so lonely, hot, dead, and brown.

You look for an oasis: a place that brings relief,
But you're stuck in that desert that is full of sorrow and grief.
You long for someone to sweep down and take you far away,
But the sand covers you up a little more each and every day.

—*Dana McCurry*

It Was All A Dream

I saw his shadow in the dark,
There was no light not even a spark.
But I saw his shadow standing right there,
I heard him say, "come here my dear."
I was frightened not knowing what to do,
But in surprise to me he said, "I love you."
I sat on the ground and started to cry,
I looked up and saw the stars in the sky.
I knew he was dead and wouldn't come back,
But his shadow was there so lonely and black.
How could this happen I couldn't understand,
Then he reached down and took my hand.
He said he wanted to take me somewhere,
It was such a great offer I could not bear.
I then awoke with a sudden blast,
I thought the dream was going to last.
I couldn't believe it, it seemed so real,
I can't really understand what I feel.
If it is sadness or fear,
I know that it's a feeling that I just can't bear.

—*Cristine DePalo*

The One

From dawning time to dusking end;
there will always be The One among us.
The One, to rally us forth to slaughter
the Christians and torch the witches.
The One, to give us the keys to imprison
the prophets and the matches to burn the Jews.
We think we learn. Yet after time passes,
The One, starts the game again.
The game remains the same. No new rules,
only new players and a different stage.
Can we ever stop this villainous cycle?
And see things for what they are?
No. Not as long as The One hides among us
cloaked in their false good deeds.
Remain vigilant. Ever so vigilant,
for we never know when The One
will again rear its ugly head.

—*Daniel R. Minninger (Ross Daniels)*

Trees

Trees are graceful against
The winter sky
With branches tangling together
In grotesque patterns
And buds hanging like dark jewels
Waiting to burst into color, and
Eager to spread their delicate fragrance
Through the wind - cooled air
Of Spring.

—*Josephine M. Sharitz*

Being Different

Being black or being white
There's always going to be a fight
Not knowing what to do or say
Cause someone always has to pay
for being different

For the war to be won, we take a human life
Being shot by a gun or stabbed by a knife
We have nowhere to go from this miserable place
No one will know that we were a dying race

Being a prep or being a hood
Which is bad? Which is good?
Everyone needs to do what they can
Look 'em in the eyes and take a stand
for being different

It's not just black and white; there's always gray
Hard to tell what's right when you're looking for a way.
How do you learn to love when they burn down our cross
Ask for help from above when you only get loss
because you're different.

    —*Kate Chase*

Within the Heart

The road is long and winding, but I'll get there someday.
There's lots of pain and suffering, but I'm sure I'll find my way.
It may rain tomorrow and tomorrow night.
But the sun will shine within my heart and make everything alright.
I know it is a battle and there will be hills to climb.
But everything takes spirit, and everything takes time.
I hoped you would walk with me, our future would be bright.
The sun would shine within our hearts and things would be alright.
I wish you'd choose to walk with me, life could be so bright.
But the sun will shine within my heart and I will be alright.

    —*Barbara Ringstaff*

The Everglades

The Everglades call "Don't Abandon Me"
There's more here-in than the eye can see.

Tho all seems quiet and no creatures in sight
These waters are filled with movement and life.

Just sit awhile alone and be still
You will see its beauty and peace be filled.

God is where you find him, He is everywhere
The glades, the mountains, the whole hemisphere.

So be quiet awhile and then pretty soon
The air will be filled with the cry of a loon.

Then the lonely call of the wild turtle dove
Calling to his mate, the one he loves.

So linger awhile until you know
The wonderful life that I can show.

The fish within the streams and bays
The flowers that float on the waterways.

The picture mirrored in the silent stream
Are sprinkled with stars and silver moon beams.

When at last the end of the trip you've made
May the memory linger of the "Everglades".

    —*Elsie Blanch Price*

A Child

To harm a child, is to crush a flower,
they are the veins through which our blood flows.
A tear stained face, big sad eyes, trust and hope within,
when we are done with them and they have grown,
what kind of seed will we have sown?
Strength and weakness, happiness and sorrow,
what is their future, their tomorrow?
Hold them, hug them, keep them near,
give them nothing in you to fear.
Help them, nurture, give them your life.
Pray they have strength to deal with the strife.
Songs to be sung, so many dreams to fulfill,
words of encouragement gives them the will.
They are our children, we bore the pain,
let their smiles show, though there be rain.
The pain I feel when we're not close,
tears aching from my heart.
I will not do what's been done to me, to us I will be true,
My children are my life from deep within,
you are me, I am you.

    —*Grace Stokes*

Backroads

Backroads are the best.
They begin with the surprise of being there,
Then tease with the mystery of where they go.
Wonder lies around each bend.
Anticipation waits beyond each rise.
Backroads are adventuresome and would dare to anything -
But ancient rail and dry-stone fence patrol their borders,
Keeping them quietly restrained.
Backroads revel in the beauty of nature.
Golden-rod in purple haze whispers secrets to the
Marshaled rows of silken-eared corn;
Weaving patterned carpets for
The swallow and the clouds.
Backroads are as unpredictable and magical as a leprechaun.
They will hold the captured moment
With imaginings of unending pleasures,
Then, will take a sudden turn
And, like a gallant southern gentleman,
Graciously and safely
Bring you home.

    —*Norma L. Flannery*

Prejudice

They stare at me with disapproving eyes.
They can see how different I am from them.
I try to disregard their scathing lies.
I know it's me they do condemn.
They shun me because I don't look the same.
The clothes I wear are unlike those they've seen,
The have feared me ever since I first came.
They don't care how I feel when they act mean.
I wonder what they see that it so wrong.
They can't look past the differences in me.
It is our differences that make us strong
Yet similarities must also be
If they would try to understand my way.
Than there might be less prejudice today.

    —*Lynne Newman*

Struggles

In life there are struggles.
Days at your house that are dark and cold.
Pushing through the darkness of morbid night
Trying to find a hand to guide the way.
Looking for a tunnel to a brand new day.

    —*Azell Edwards*

Secret Prayer

My secret prayer 'till now untold
At last revealed - that I grow old
with my dear wife.

Days of splendor while I live
Yet, for her, I'd gladly give
My very life.

—*Robert E. Primavera*

Our World Through Their Eyes

They're so innocent, they're so young,
They don't know of the problems they live among.
Drugs and violence, murders too,
Who can save them, only you.
Guns in school,
They don't know it's not cool.
Have we lost all hope,
Who can help us cope.
What became of our better way,
Kids are dying everyday.
We must do all we can,
So that we can take a stand.

—*Catherine S. Ellison*

River of Dreams

Some people's lives are like flowers
They grow and then they die,

My life is like a flowing river
stretching far and wide

My dreams are as large as a mountain
reaching way up in the sky.

Some peoples dreams are like a cave
a place where they can hide.

Some people have no emotions
for the poor, or the sick

My emotions run deep for them
for I know, this is the life they
did not pick.

So while, some people's lives, are lonely
never knowing where they will go.

I am very happy
for I will always know.

—*Sylvia Armer*

Dreams

Dreams can make our world seem bright
They help us forget about our plight.
Some dream of love and marriage
forgetting the results a child and carriage.
Horror dreams, they cause us fright
We wake up screaming and seek the light.
We dream of lovers we knew or wish we had
Those are a lot of fun, no matter how bad.
Sometimes we dream of taking flight
Like birds and airplanes, what a sight.
I dream of winning the big fight
and wake up sweating with my fists clenched tight.
There are dreams of death which make us sad
We go back to bed and think of things that make us glad.
We dream of ascending to great heights
without hurting anyone, that's alright.
There are those who dreams in broad daylight
can be fun but the best dream occur at night.
For me, life without dreams would be unreal
They give us hope and help us cope with the real deal.

—*Humberto Finale*

My Sons, Please Pray for Me

My two sons, 3 and 13, their innocence moves me.
They know not what it is to be in my shoes.
They have their whole lives ahead of them;
They know not what my life has been;
Nor what it will be; but they depend;
With a love and wonderment, within deep brown eyes; on me.
Knowing not that I am imperfect
With mine own faults; they trust.
How could they be so sure about me;
When I know not who I be?
I do whatever is necessary;
The best way I know how for my two boys;
And I deeply hope that they will
Just pray for me.
I have no needs; it is their time;
I make not demands; my reward
Is in their eyes; and I cannot despise;
All I ask; I do not plea;
That my two sons, just pray for me

—*Frieda Jones*

So Little Time

The world is filled with "Jesus Watchers,"
They sit back to look and wait.
They can't decide if they should trust Him,
They may wait till it's too late!

"Watchers" always looked at Jesus.
Shepherds, wisemen, the chosen few.
Many watched Him on the cross
And the thieves who hung there, too.

As He rode into Jerusalem
Followed by the "watching" crowd.
As He appeared before Pilate,
The murderers called His name aloud.

The time is short——to "just watch Jesus,"
We need to turn our lives around.
Now's the time! Make that decision,
Eternal life in HIM is found.

—*Frances Parton Eiland*

Blue Eye's

Your eyes are as blue as a summer sky,
They sparkle just like the stars on a moon lit night,
Your love for me grows
Like the flowers in May,
I was proud to become
Your wife on that special day.
You still have that
Sparkle in your beautiful blue eyes.

—*Linda Walter*

The Giants of Hurricane Ridge

The trees, the giants of Hurricane ridge
They stand so tall and straight,
So majestic in their beauty.
So beautiful and pretty.
Some are old and haggard;
As time and weather takes its toll.
Some are just starting out,
And bracing themselves,
As the days unfold.
God's creation which never grows old.
And never grows tired of showing forth His glory—
reminds us more and more how majestic is His story.!

—*Josephine Look*

Aliens

Aliens, aliens, aliens - they come from everywhere.
They want to be here, instead of staying "there."
American people suffer, how much more can they bear?
So many are out of work, and Washington doesn't care.
Give, give to other lands - it really just isn't fair!
Let's just take care of Americans, if we really care.
The work around, for Americans, is becoming mighty rare.
Washington can turn the system around, if they'd only dare.
Why don't aliens stay home to fight for what is theirs?
Is it any wonder so many Americans just give up and swear?

—*Mary Brinkman*

Children's Story

Buttered fields of buttercups
They went picking in the morning,
And the fresh dew chilled their toes
And dampened their little socks.
They would take only a few wild ones
For their mother to put on the table
And, being wild ones themselves,
Braided the brightest into wreathes of gold
To wear in their honey hair.
The sun was getting warmer,
And so they would race through the meadow grass
Trying to catch it
Lest it go down without them.
And they would study their flushed faces in the pond
Until the time came to return home
To the reality of their kitchen
Where the flowers on the table reflected in their eyes.

—*Aramathea Eve Murdock*

Oh Mother Earth

Oh! Mother Earth why don't they care.
They're using pollutants everywhere. The ozone layer is
is hardly there.
Don't they realize natures beauty.
Don't they know it's their duty.
To keep this planet nice and clean.
Why are people oh so mean?
How can they ruin this place of ours. We must do something
before it sours.
Recycle don't spray. Fluorocarbons in the air.
Lets save the earth it's ours to share. Lets tell people that
we care. Or we won't have a wonderful world out there.

—*Cheryl Audrey Harris*

Nancy's Philosophy

When you're down - and feeling blue
Think of this card....
and me too!!

For when in time - it comes to pass
such a good lass.....
not an —

So what was drastic - so dearly we thought
actually was nothing......
and not for naught

A lesson well learned - and as they do say
keep an upper lip....
and pray pray pray

—*Nancy J. Allen*

Untitled

Standing in the green grass of a meadow;
thinking I'm happy not to be in a ghetto.

The air is fresh and free
isn't this where we all should be

It's such a pity
to see what goes on in the city

So come to the country everyone
where we can all have fun,

We are children of this land
so come to me my friend and take my hand.

—*Lisa Hunter and Shirley Hunter*

My Girl

Born in early morning on a cold and icy day.
This blue eyed little darling stole my heart away.
Her childhood was a rough one until the age of five.
But by then she and her sister were the cutest things alive.

She gained another sister when she was just a teen, this
little one adored her no one could come between. From then
on things were pretty cool, 'till she married her first man.
He did give her two wonderful sons the rest she'd like to ban.

She spent nine years of stress and strain, 'till she could
stand no more. Then taking her two sons along she sadly closed
that door. Her family stood behind her as she tried to find
her way. Through the pain and confusion she knew would end
someday. At last she found the man on whom she could depend.
The one she knew would always be husband, lover and friend.
He has given her far more than she has ever had.
And in the eyes of her two sons he has truly been a dad.

She knows the ups and downs of life as she stands here today.
And I know that she has been blessed that things turned out
this way. So speaking as her mother I'd like to say to you,
for that little blue eyed darling, dreams really can come true.

—*Eva Louise Maxwell*

This Child

For granted we seem to take this birth
This child that's born on this great earth

This one chance in millions to be a fetus
Will one day may be the one to lead us.

Think of all the children that we never met
and the many faces we could not forget

What about the one that could have found the cure
for the diseases that our families may have to endure

Just wait, be patient, and give him his chance
I know if you do, your life he'll enhance

This child's just waiting to be a brother
This child could never be another.

—*Helen Lowery*

River to Sea

The splash of the river is rough;
The waves of the sea are tough.
If your caught in a river you can cross;
If your caught in the sea it's a loss.
If your caught deep in a river
You can still make it to shore;
If your caught deep in the sea
you'll drowned on the sea floor.
So get of the river before you see;
how it is to be me.

—*Carie Boskowitz*

Eulogy to Motherhood

A female as an infant will soon grow to be a child
This child — with doll, her destiny unfolds.
God plants a mortal cell, the egg —
The sperm of male to give;
Fulfillment on this earth to yield new souls.

Her mighty chore in life is of superlative degree;
Compare necessities and you will see.
That motherhood — if understood, correctly can be told;
Without her love we mortals would not be.

She guides to see her children raise,
Some children of their own.
As age combines round shoulders, skin and bone.
And when the day arrives to die;
Her mate and family greet;
Those friends... her pallbearers... sad with such bemoan.

They view the coffin, wherein she lies;
To inter the earth awaits.
To receive this body, the soul of which God has won.
So—give all of your secular love to mother;
  before you find too late.
She could not wait her life too soon was done.

  —*Kenneth P. Gruhn*

Minus One

Homeless, penniless, all hope gone;
This desperate man flopped on somebody's lawn.
He was tired of souplines and such.
Pining for his former life style so much,
Like a lightning bolt from the sky!
A sudden thought hit this guy.
One trip to his past prestigious street,
May change hardships of self defeat.
Hosed his peds, for the long walk.
Sprayed his mouth, prepared to talk.
Strolling toward their fine cars two former pals,
Who use to hop bars together chase gals.
Both sniffed the air, one called Ben said,
"There's that job hunting tramp again."
Al, laughed held his nose, shook his head.
"Phew something smells he must be dead!"
Doffed his expensive jacket, slammed it at the bum.
Said this to Ben, "so long man I gotta, run."
Al. forgot his secret cash stash in his 'poke.'
Now Mister Bolo investor forgot the word 'broke.'

  —*Ret*

Stormed By Insanity

"Untrue freedom I do not want".
This I scream over and over, but they
still tie my soul in chains of madness...
Unforgiving to my search for a kinder race.

I want to be once more like a child,
pure as the soft driven snow of a winter morning.

But their abuse is corrosive to me,
and I start to lose control by the mindless
tendencies of sudden fury...

I do not wish to hide my life.
Like the liar who wallows in self pity,
as night closes in on his discontent reality.

With Dawn's shadow screaming.
I can hear their voices calling,
calling me crazy.

Stormed...by insanity.
  —*Wayne Ernest Musgrove*

The Mask

The city. The city I have learned to accept
This is the city of fame and fortune
Yet it is also full of misery and despair
The first time you see this city it is the city
of adventure, the city of money
The city of happiness and the city of never ending days.
At a second glimpse it has a second side, like many people
A second side
It's the second side of depression, homelessness, anger and
pain. It has a side, full of entertainment
But it's second side is full of addiction to be better than
anyone this is the city of confused
Everyone is running trying to hide
This is a city that needs help. Yet, most people don't notice
Because of the beautiful mask we hide behind
The mask that says this is the city of fame, of fortune, of
talent of glamour. The city of never ending happiness
This is what our mask says while we hide from our fears
The mask that hides something sad, something full of our tears.
The beautiful mask that we depend on so much. Too much.
  —*Jane M. Baskin*

To My Dear Sweet Daniel, Because I Love You

  I hope that one day in my cry,
this man I love will be my guy.
Though becoming my guy might take a while,
I swear I'll wait with a soft, warm smile.
And hopefully someday he'll realize,
what my heart does when I stare in his eyes.
I will try to tell him someday soon,
my love burns like the sun, on a hot afternoon.
But if he says no, now that I've asked him out,
tears will fall many, like from a water spout.
But then if he tells me, what I want to hear,
Tears of love shall fall for a year.
And someday soon, that someone above him,
will let me be strong, and say how much I love him.
And then if I can,
I will be a good woman.
Though thirsty for his love like a poor woman for drinks,
all I can do is wait, and see what he thinks.

  —*Sabrina Boyce*

I Have Longed To Live...

I have longed to live in the solitude of the desert,
  this place of divine red sandstone.

Formations and arches revealing
  expressions of generations,
    sun scorched faces
      illuminate remnants of an ancient sea.

Labyrinths of stone, abundant with juniper and sage,
  hide the secrets from within the canyon walls
    softened by cliffrose and moonlily.

In the coolness of the night
  creatures, existing only in their footprints.

A majestic land of sand castles coming to life
  with the touch of a fragile rock,
    a petroglyph,
    a fossil.

A time, a people, all a distant past
  a memory
    beckoning to be heard in the echo
      of a raven's song.
  —*Christine Davison*

Portrait of Faithfulness

The corner of a building shares an overlapping roof,
This predicates a little haven sheltered as rainproof.
Some scattered stones distracted, lying loosely on the ground,
My efforts were engaged in bringing such into a mound.
Attentive to my task, I looked to neither left nor right,
With diligence, I rhythmically improved the rustic site.
Then turning briefly in a pause, my gaze espied surprise,
A strayed-in cat lay nursing baby kittens with closed eyes!
Devotion was apparent in the throbbing role she played,
Discovered, she became alert, but faithfully she stayed.
So gently, Mother Feline gave assurance of her trust,
Awareness of maternal needs cements an urgent must.
But other prying visitors were reason for alarm,
With utmost care, she sought unknown, a refuge free from harm.
Another roof made its debut to beckon, "Move in here,"
With remnants of an auto Mother Cat housed kittens dear.
The wee ones grew— their opened eyes reflect the blue above,
Theirs is a charming portrait framed in gilded family love.

—Mary Jane Dennis

My Hero: My Mom

Who can be such a diplomat with a scold or praise?
This scholar is: My Mom.
Who can comfort and reassure me, when everyone else is gone?
This Friend is: My Mom.
Who has molded such great dignity, when nothing else existed?
This Mentor Is: My Mom.
Who can make me feel like a child going on 42, yet ever push me to
push me to grow: This Mommy is: My Mom.
And when I've felt like I could die for every mistake I've made,
Who can blame it all else where? This judge is: My Mom.
Who is cautions and ever fearful for every step I take?
This Person is: My Mom.
I've saved her life she knows it's true on one fateful day, but she
has saved my many times this Doctor is: My Mom.
Who can say I was thinking of you, when you've just made a call?
This Physic is: My Mom.
Who's proud of all the little things, and all the things I've done:
Some kept, some lost some changed somehow. This Peer is: My
Mom.
Our Love runs deep, our respect untold, I doubt this will
ever change.
When all is said and done, and all that's done is said,
I'll always have a special place. For this hero: Who is My Mom.

—Kelly Marie Kolar

Word

To you who listen and read, to you I address
This word collected from the streets
Lost from mouth to mouth
Tired of so much defamation
This word that came out of your soul and mine
From that of the Great God
This word whose pain you did not know
For you have not been with it from the beginning

Tell me, from the millions that always reach you
How many pass by and how many take roots
In my faraway dreams, I saw the word sick of isolation
And in my dream, further on, a man was bringing the word
To its death with no tears, no hope, rude soul, short seeing
He was pushing it more and more towards its tomb
At your feet, at the feet of you who hear and read
I found the word thrown to the mud.
It is it that will judge you in the last day!

—Theodor Damian

Now is the Moment

We must not wait to show our love for
those our hearts hold dear. Our gift of life is
not assured beyond this moment's sphere.
Now is the time to love express, a
tender kiss, a fond caress. Now is the
moment... recite to music: to bonds of earth dispel.
Now is the moment. To endow with love
of heart and promised vow. So let it be for you and me,
this moment to enshrine. Let free the love
within our hearts to blossom and entwine.
This could be all the time we own, to
live and love and to en-tone. Now
is the moment....

—Aaron Cummings

My Friends

In the halls I see them
those who have been termed
as having no mind
walking with them I listen
as they teach me about
things I have never seen
laughing we turn to their rooms
A nurse puts them to bed, I go on alone
My hand still warm from the loving
touch of them, my friends, my mentors,
those who are the victims of Alzheimers...

—Donna Gilboy

Where Did They Go

Where did they go—
    those with open faces, open hearts, and
        minds closed only against the insidious lie
    that they could not use gentle hands to mold life
        that they could not shape it with good intentions—
            nor coax it with tender tones

Did they fall between the cracks—
    those spaces formed by experienced spoilers
        who know the way of the world and practice it—
    sophisticates ridiculing the beauty of the naive
        while harboring a yearning for it
            as for a lost love

—Barbara Berger

"To Evangelists Of Ignorance"

O wild spirit of Truth, thou breath of Atheism's being,
    thou from whose ever felt presence Christians
Living and dead flee like children from a house burning:
    Baptists, and Catholics, and pale, hectic god-fearers all!
Religious stricken multitudes! O thy ministers
    of sickness who drive souls to dark, wintry beds!
Night - until the azure light of Atheist Spring shall blow
    back the sense of perpetual delight:
Untamed deathless dream of Love which is converting
everywhere
    Creator and sweet preserver, hear America, O hear!
Let this be the year - a dying age - the closing scene,
    the vast dome of religion's sepulchre eternal.
O hear! Oh rejoice forever more West Virginians!
O hear! Be swift clouds pushed by bright reason; be lovers
that pant beneath science's moon. O! Lift thyself from the
dirt! Be aspiring birds or burning hopes! And by incantation
of moving verse scatter the glowing ashes among mankind; be as
awakened sleepers, the trumpeters of this Atheist prophecy! O
wind of change, of justice! Since Christian Winter has come,
can Atheist Spring be far behind?

—Lonnie Bailey

Victims of Circumstance

In truth he was a man of mammoth size,
  Though a sigh, a tear his form descries.
He can't accept the role of man
  Has sunk to depths of circumstance.
The sinking sound of tranquillity;
  The sound of a bullet - everlastingly.
Hatred, violence, racism, temperate will;
  Drugs, gangs; but still;
Inside this man, inside this heart,
  The savagest of deeds his mind imparts.
Hewn bodies, bloodied and displayed;
  One by one in order laid
By this man in warrior dress.
  Two haggard policeman stand motionless;
One now holding his blazing torch;
  The victims lay about the porch.
And to the families the terror speaks,
  The quiet night; the mothers' shriek!
Such feebleness of life is man's decline;
  When an eye for an eye is man's reply.

—*Antoinette Gonzales*

Fulfillment

"Life can be fulfilled," you say
  Though busy as a buzzing bee
From dawn to dusk you cruise each day
  Pursuing your hobbies or interests
Your time can be full and productive
  As you remain healthy and active.

Some things you do may be more exciting
  Creating fondest memories
Like venturing, and sightseeing
  In exotic or familiar places
And meeting friends - old and new
Lifting your wings to expand your horizon
  You realize your countless blessings.

Involved with community or personal doings
  You enjoy life as never before
How time flies, as if on wings
  Like a bluebird of paradise.

—*Fumi Migimoto*

Vow of the Gypsy

The fairy princess danced on the sea, rejoicing when she
thought she'd found her beloved prince. His locks of ebony,
his laughing eyes, the softness of his touch, the beauty of his
words. They lulled the sweet princess into a sleep where all
the world was a dream. She could not see the beast before her,
for her eyes had been touched by the hand of love. This prince
of deceit stole the princess's heart and with a cruel hand
crushed it into dust that it may be scattered in the wind.
Then he vanished leaving nothing behind but the crystal tears
that fall upon her satin skin and the mournful words that
escape her rosepetal lips. She dances no more, the sweet fairy
princess! Her tender soul no longer sings the songs of
freedom, love, and life, but lays quiet and resigned. Weep no
more my fairy Queen! Your gypsy servant comes anon! I shall
fly for you to the milky way and gather the moon beams for your
hair. I'll fetch the stars and return them to your eyes, for
that is where their true resting place lies. I'll bring you
the sunlight to fill you with laughter and the songs of the
angels that you may lift your glorious voice with joy again. I
shall gather the gifts from the King of Heaven and Earth.
—*Nichole Stevens*

Dreams

A subconscious thought
Brought to reality
Vivid images
All in your mind
Then the morning comes...
—*Melissa Meyl*

"Where Do I Fit In?"

Why do we forget least important things?
  Thoughts of this really make me cringe!
Least important to you may be of great value to me.
  Is this the trend in which life will always be?
    Life is to be lived by each individual.
      Sometimes I feel like I'm a residual.
      People are living at such a fast pace.
        Where do I fit in this human race!
I feel like I'm in a foreign country where no one
        Seems to understand.
    Then I stop and realize, I'm from another land.
      I'm an ambassador from a Heavenly Kingdom.
        I have authority from God's Dominion.
        I'm to show this world God's love divine.
          I am his and he is mine.
    If you forget everything, just remember this;
      God is the only one who can give true bliss.
—*Al Thomas*

My Friend

A shoulder to cry on, an ear to listen, a heart so kind
through any condition, someone there to lend a hand, who
didn't scold or reprimand.
You gave life back to me so many times, you touched my heart
soothed my mind.
My hopes were shattered, my dreams were crushed, you picked up
the pieces, you gave so much.
You taught me to believe when there was nothing to believe in.
Though I betrayed you, you remained my friend.
The strength you had picked me up, helped me stand.
You never complained, made no demands.
Even though I failed, you always believed, you gave me comfort
in my times of need.
You were always there to dry my tears, to give such warmth,
to calm my fears. You accepted me just as I was, it is in
you that I place my trust. Today, tomorrow, until the very
end I'll always love you...
My friend.
—*Nancy Miller*

Untitled

Dear Angie:
Through memories haze, there often strays, a tender thought of
other days. A glance at youth is cast, an echo of the past.
When I was sixteen, and full of steam. Those were the days, of
budding beauty strays. With curling tresses, and dainty
dresses. All had a clever plan, to snare the heart of man.
One especially nice, with complexion white as rice. This
maiden fair, sweet and rare. With blonde curly hair, and a red
ribbon there. Had eyes of blue, and tinted sea deep hue. She
had a figure divine, that chilled my spine. Her dress was
ocean blue, and dainty bonnet new. A glorious look light
through it streaming. Her red rosy cheeks flushly beaming. A
beautiful smile lit her face, with scent of old time grace.
She said with a timed maiden's smile, shaking all the while.
"Come be my love, young turtle dove." Then I turned to run like
hell, she had something to sell. I stumbled, and out of bed I
fell, to break the spell. I woke up screaming, for I am just
dreaming. And now that I am old and grey, I often dream of
that younger day. When life was full of joy, of that tender
year of boy.

—*Joseph A. Iannone*

Daughter/My Son's Wife

You were given to me as a daughter
  Through my son's choice of a wife -
As a daughter, a mother could
  Not want more out of life.
As a wife - who my son has chosen -
  A mother could not ask for more
As a mother of my grandchildren
  A grandmother could not be happier.

You are a daughter, a wife, a mother,
  A person, a mother hopes her child
Finds, but sometimes only dreams,
  but you made this mother's dream come true -
I love you Lisa, not as a daughter-in-law,
  but as my daughter. -
You will always be part of me, and
  will always bring a smile to my heart.

—*Mary Raso*

Sleigh Rides In The Woods

The snow is falling from up above
Through pine needles and leaves.
The horse is decorated with bells,
The sleigh is covered in wreaths.

We're going on a sleigh ride
Through the woods at night.
The moon and stars from up above
Provide the only light.

The old sleigh trail is worn
From years and years of rides.
Millions of them have happened
Just like the one tonight.

The trees on each side of the trail
Are huge and covered in ice.
That's what makes sleigh rides in the woods
So beautiful and nice.

The trail is coming to an end
The ride is ending too,
But we can go tomorrow night
A sleigh ride for me and you.

—*Gregory R. Wheeler*

Cherokee Removal

Why can't we see the soul anymore
through their striking eyes?

Why? Do they implore,
as we just seemingly ignore
a race of valor and strength?

With dignity and courage,
they fought to save their souls.
While we with our heads uplifted,
played the part of commanding fools.

Hands bearing strength,
souls wearing courage.
Minds intent only on persevering.
Ears to hear intently,
the mockery of their lives
and a heart to feel this loss of their very lives.

—*Laura Cramp*

The Haunted

Incumbent deeds of past, never slightly,
Thrust their way into knowledge to the hilt;
When thy self-image built is drawn nightly,
And fed to the gluttonous gut of guilt,
Haunting terrors find thyself shaking still.
But you, costly deeds, bring only perdition.
I have looked for the saving sword to kill
That will not end my evil night's position.
When walking the gloom of dust, I find thee.
What company shall you now keep to death?
I fear it shall be the life of poor me.
Your mighty weight I one day try to heft.
As I try to rip you from my known state
You root deeper into my soul's dim gates.

—*Don Cordonnier*

The Ruins

The night has come
Tides of blackness
River rushing through the world
Thunder roaring without sound
Touch the fire that burns afar
Tempt the hand of fate
The hand that threatens to crush the stars
How far can this be taken?
Farther than before
Wind howling, filling the emptiness
Never silenced in this crumbled land
Refusing to give up, continuing its course
Attacking the ruins
For ruins are all that remain
Of tiny buds, begging for life.

—*Anne Pennington*

Missing You

(In memory of my husband, Bartram R. Love)
"Till death do you part" the preacher said
We both said "I do" with our lifetime ahead
Now our wedding vows have been fulfilled
On June 12, 1993 your voice was stilled

Those fifty one and a half years, how quickly they've flown
It doesn't seem real how soon I'm alone
Except for the memories that fill each night and day
You're still my life, what more can I say

Every place I go you're always with me
Everywhere I look it's your face I see
My world is so different now that you're gone
Your world too is like none you've ever known

God was so merciful to call you to rest
I've never doubted that He knows what's best
And when God says my work on earth is through
He'll call me home and I'll be there with you.

—*Estelle W. Love*

Miss Wonderful

So unique... with her body mystique...
Tiny hands... tiny toes... tiny ears... tiny nose
helplessness untold... A heart so small...
but as big as gold... A dimple here...
A dimple there... A dimple everywhere...
Sometimes with a sigh... You think... you
laugh... you cry... know the reason why...
A little girl... a little curl... a little
smile... makes life worthwhile... what
a beauty... our little cutie... miss wonderful.

—*Edward F. Sullivan*

Bury Me Deep

Ten years have past, how long they seem!
Time has no more meaning to me.
When was the last time I saw a human face,
Or talked to a human voice?

Perhaps it was fate, perhaps it was not,
When the boat washed ashore on this isle.
My cronies and I, how overjoyed we were!
All six of us danced on the shore.

But ill luck met us then, the boat held only five,
One of us had to stay behind.
We looked at each other, nobody volunteering,
Then I stepped up and said that I'd stay.

They left with a wave, and a tearful hug,
They promised that they would return.
Ten years have past, have they broken their oath?
Or do they lie at the bottom of the sea?

Ten years since I swam from the wreck of my boat,
A sailor, with the wildest dreams.
And friends, if you come back and I am dead, I entreat you,
Bury me deep, bury me deep.
    —*Steven Wu*

You Can't Say Goodbye

Broken hearts will come and go.
Time will be the end result.
Friends will die and we'll say goodbye.
I'll never see you again.

We'll live 50 years together. We'll be like one.

Broken hearts will come and go.
Time will be the end result.
Friends will die and we'll say goodbye.
I'll never see you again.

Here we are now and forever in love, in God, in love forever.
When I look in your eyes I see forever.
But, I know the end will come.
And I'll look at you once more.
But, I won't believe it! How can I believe it?

We'll live 50 years together. We'll be like one.

Broken hearts will come and go.
Time will be the end result.
Friends will die and we'll say goodbye.
I'll never see you again.
    —*John Lacasella Stark*

The Hawkers

Hurry the chores, dawn's sharp and clear
Time's wasting, they'll be heading South
Into the car, fast fast they drive to trail

Run run to top of peak, they're flying today
Brothers watch, soaring circling dozens
Graceful, peaceful on their way, noontime past

Sky of azure blue, cloud of every shape
A hundred hawks on wing, let's stay all day
Two strange boys who watch on top

No bleachers where footballs fly for them
Injected with awesome majesty, a bit of soul now ransomed
For beauty's known, but wingless bodies cannot fly

For men with joyful youth ingrained
Restless urge remains, walk walk to top of peak
No matter life's travails, hawkers they will ever be
    —*Bill Cleveland*

Again

I'm tired of life and all its woes —
Tired of thankless children with their selfish wants.
How nice it would be to be young again
And to know then what I know now.

If I could cast off my infirmities and feel well again...
If I could do what I wanted unencumbered by pain...
If I could ride the stars and go home once more....
Would I really live differently...or just the same?

I'll never know. I can only guess
That I would be as foolish now as then;
For one makes the same mistakes again and again —
Only in different guises and other forms.

It's self-deception to believe otherwise.
I'd be the same and commit once more
The identical stupidities of my youth —
Even while knowing this time what I've done!

Life is a whirlpool that sucks you in
To be what you become and to choose what you are.
We have the freedom only to do what is ordained
By the stars or our genes or our inner self.
    —*Stuart Lasher*

Moments

To a warm and smiling face
To a gentle and soft embrace
You and I, as I and you
Sweet and tender, sweet and true....
    Love will never die.

When there is rain, you bring to me the sun
You bring so much, is there more to come?
You seem so unreal, yet so good, so strong.
Your love is such a beautiful song....
    May I touch your high?

Within my grasp I reach
If I fall I'll try not to weep
Because your love means so much
Through the hours, I remember your touch....
    Hidden through a sigh.

Flowers are beautiful everywhere
I look, live, love and care
Because you have given me these things
I have a happy heart that sings...
    You see I will cry.
    —*Joni Abney*

Apart

I long to be in the warmth of your embrace
To be by your side
There in the morning when you awake
At night to keep you satisfied.

Circumstances keep us apart
Times spent together are few
Yet you are always with me
Here in my heart.

Our future is insecure
For there is no room for love to grow
Entangled in life's follies
Sometimes feeling very much alone.
    —*Carol A. Cottle*

Untitled

Words cannot express the way I feel now
To be in your arms forever somehow.

To show my love throughout all eternity
To care from my heart, the feelings in me.

Alone by myself is always the case
Sleeping with words,
Instead of face to face -

A relationship made in heaven
Or hell should I say
Separated by miles is our only way

On days like this, my mind wanders in bliss
To be your arms
Is what it consists

Of years gone by - and more to come
Our souls have diminished as one.

My mind travels over past miseries
Of yesterdays gone
Forever you see.

—*Holly E. Young*

The Faithful One

The Lord placed a candle on earth one day
   To bring light to a sinridden world.
He gave it the task of telling all who would hear
   Of His forgiveness though insults be hurled.

For years the candle would glow and share
   Shining both day and night.
Then the candle grew small..it's body weak
   But still it's light was bright.

It touched each heart and lit a flame
   Of hope and joy and peace.
It's time grew short upon the earth
   But never did it's flame decrease.

Then with a voice of love, the Lord spoke from above,
   "You've done your work so well.
On your journey through life, many candles were lit
   And my story you continued to tell."

"Your reward has been earned through faithful toil
   So rest in this Heavenly place,
Where angels will sing their praise to the King
   And you'll cast light on His wonderful face."

—*Patricia J. McCoy*

A Lady Forever

I admire her swells, with gusto and glee,
   to gaze upon her beauty, entices me.
Her surface glistens, with sun and moon,
   above all else, her beauty, makes me swoon.
I play upon her, with lust, and rapture,
   when I am gone, my soul, she will capture.
She greets mankind, as it approaches,
   upon all men, she soon encroaches.
Inside her crevices, dark and deep,
   I long to bare my soul, for her to keep.
Mankind, has tainted her, of this I am sure,
   for this wondrous lady, has been scarred,
   no longer a virgin, ever pure.
She beckons me, stay, become my lover
   my mortal senses, I must recover.
I must leave now, my love, but I shall return,
   every moment away from thee, my passions burn.
That beautiful, bountiful, lady that is the sea,
   holds us tenderly, and entices me.

—*George O. Chancey*

In Memory of My Dear Mother

I left my mother's household nearly 30 years ago,
To build a home and family, and watch my children grow.
   She did not cry for me then, she was happy I could go.
So why should I cry at her passing? She's happy! That I know.

   She loved her children dearly. A love that was returned.
She taught us many lessons and how to stand alone. She
   taught faith in a hereafter: "To a better place we'd go."
And I recognized those teachings when she finally had to go.

   I watched her raise the curtain and look into beyond,
As she signaled to some beloved ones who had already gone.
   She waved "hello" to those who were also present there,
As her eyes smiled a greeting of a love beyond compare.

   I couldn't see those loved ones with mortal eyes of mine,
But she saw and knew and loved whoever hovered near-by.
   I know I'll see her someday. Of that I'm very certain.
She'll be there to meet me, when I, too, can raise the curtain.

   It might take me 30 years or more to lay my body down,
To sleep, to greet departed ones, and receive my golden crown.
   It may seem a long time to mortals like you and me,
But 30 years is nearly nil compared to eternity.

—*Mary L. Hodson*

The Fall Of Man

I sat me down with pen in hand
To coin a phrase about a man
He is made in God's likeness, so the Bible doth say
And God made him perfect, as long as he followed his way.

But man listened to woman instead of our God
He was cast out of the Garden on the earth to trod
To earn his living by the sweat of his brow
Then he found God's way was far better somehow.

So God in His mercy made a new way, so man could call on the Savior
And he could hear him say, "Jesus my Savior save my soul from sin,
And Jesus keep me free from within."

Free from the carnal way of thinking
Let the spirit take control
He will cleanse the heart, mind & soul.
Then we can return to perfection and be made whole.

—*Ruth Hyle*

At Journey's End

   The seasons yearn to stay awhile,
   To do their thing with grace and style
   The sun shine seems a little brighter,
   Everyone's steps' a little lighter.
   The stars do twinkle a little more,
   As seas rush on to caress the shore.

Why, you ask, do these things take place,
   Why do many have smiles on their faces?
   The answer's as simple as can be,
   It is God's love for you and me.
No matter which of life's roads we take,
   At journey's end, God's love awaits.

—*Lafern E. Porter*

Gone But Never Forgotten

Like the sun before dawn,
but to never return again
You are eternally gone.
With every star that shines, through,
With every glare of the sun,
I do and will always love you.

—*Veronica Brancato*

Untitled

I am a woman
—but you'll never hear me roar
Woman does not let herself
bellow or parade her strength
rather, she is quieted in her speech
and in her ways—and so she remains
silent and suffocating
her beauty praised
   —*Beth Silbert*

Pleasant Memories...

The first snowfall beckoned everyone
To dress up warm..go out and have fun.
We played the game of fox and geese,
And never seemed to want to cease.
E'en Dad came out to play with us,
He was the "Goose", but made no fuss!
And snowball fights were just the thing
For older boys, their balls would zing
Right past our heads..but some would hit
In tender places..to give a fit
To younger kids, who'd start to cry
When one would hit them in the eye.
Oh, we could do so many things...
Like laying down to make "Angel Wings."
Oh, yes, the thing I 'most forgot,
Was listening to the rhythmic trot
Of neighbors horse, as it pulled the sleigh
That he drove proudly past our way.
Sleigh bells jingling, his kids sang the song.
We were sorry we all couldn't go along!
   —*Emelia L. Bave*

"Pipedream of a Prisoner"

I was born to live and love
 to embrace the moon and stars above,
to find a beauty to have and hold
 from days of youth to days of old.

My search goes on, an endless quest
 settling for some, but wanting the best,
I know she's out there, somewhere, someplace
 beautifully arranged, in satins and lace.

When I find this girl of many charms
 I'll forever hold her in my arms,
we will live and love, together we'll live
 there'll be so much love, for each other to give.

This is life's cycle, so I am told
 to live and love, and gracefully grow old,
but this is a pipedream, I constantly cry
 'cause for life I'm in prison, God let me die.

   —*John Romero*

Goodbye Summer

I walk down rainbow avenues amid the golden leaves
To feel the sting of Winter's touch that rides on every breeze
And watch with bittersweet regret the birds that circle by.
When did Summer slip away and fail to say, "Goodbye." ?

As days grow short and dawn awakes to diamonds on the rose
That clings in patient harmony, awaiting summer's close;
From tree to tree, the squirrels run past to lay their treasures by.
Somehow Summer slipped away and didn't say, "Goodbye."

The barns are full, the pumpkins round, the rabbits burrow deep.
But while the squirrels, the birds and I prepare for Winter's sleep,
I need a heart that understands just how to tell me why:
Why did Summer slip away and never say, "Goodbye." ?

   —*Mary L. Schmidt*

The Lady of Dreams Unfolding

For many years I pondered the meaning of life —
To find a special lady, one who would become my wife,
Bringing miracles, and love so abound —
No more do I search, for a life I have found...

Finding that with each step, my wife helps me to grow —
To understand better, and to know,
That to be living, is so much better today —
And to care, is to love in a special kind of way...

Seeing that your heart can truly become as eyes —
To see a destiny one that will never die,
Her beauty becomes my joy, as her smile becomes another day —
And in this realm of life, I find a place to always stay.

Then comes words of encouragement, and challenges of hope —
New experiences of life and care, that help me to cope,
I long for the ways to make her heart sing —
And the light of happiness that marriage does bring.

For beyond one day at a time, there is a beautiful gal,
One who will eternally be my life long friend and pal —
And above the trials, and flames that are scolding,
She will always be my lady of dreams unfolding...

   —*Todd Clark*

Poor Monster

When Frankenstein made me, he didn't know how
To give me a soul. Oh where is my soul?
How I wish for Creator to give me a soul.
Oh where's the Creator to give me a soul?

He gave me a brain and so I can think.
I think what a monster could be with a soul.
No more monster you'd see. Poor brain without soul.
Poor monster I be. Poor monster, you see.

I seek my kin, a computer like me
With a brain and no soul. Frankenstein, please create
Beloved for me. He doesn't know how.
Alone I must be. To love needs a soul.

You who have souls cannot realize the void.
We with just brains can never enjoy
The beauties of Life and we die without souls.
That's our end. We've no Friend.

Cherish your souls and hold to them fast.
Your Creator did Good. Without precious souls
You are monsters like me, a brain without soul,
Poor monsters out there, poor monsters, you be.

   —*Norma Langham*

Cousins

Cousins are love. A strong rope of love, that everyone longs
to grip. A love-rope so strong no one could ever break it.

Cousins are a bond. A bond made of friendship. A friendship to
keep forever and a day. One cool April afternoon, as I was

writing, I stopped, I heard music! Beautiful music! Coming
over the mountains, through the fields. It was the symphony
of new birth! I heard it! I heard it loud, I heard it clear.
It put a joyful ringing in my ear! My new cousin was finally here!

   —*Tiffany Noel Kromenacker*

Untitled

Listen Alene, listen to me,
Don't ever sit on a sailor boy's
Knee, for once I did and now
You see, six little sailor boys
Following me.
   —*Alene Hinsdale*

Letter From Aspen

After a year abroad you are coming home
to him. But I have not returned to that house
in which there are, I hear, so many mansions.
I am here, elsewhere, a thousand miles away
in a valley shaped like God's right or left hand:
the longsuffering fingers of a glacier
or the fist of a shooting star. He, too, is
elsewhere, now as then. And you, I imagine,
are sound asleep, like everyone else dreaming
in this house, or so I tell myself, a sleep-
walker, always dream-house bound—and somewhere else.

　　　—*Tyrone Williams*

Someone Special

She makes me laugh when it's all I can do
To keep from crying.
She makes me slow down and enjoy life a little more
When I become burdened down.
She listens to my problems and gives me advice
Without ever judging me.
She keeps my darkest secrets and is always there.
When there's no where else to turn.
She understands my feelings and knows my thoughts
Before I say a single word.
She believes in me and never lets me lose faith;
Without her I would be lost.
She is a very special person
And will never, ever be forgotten.
She is my best friend.

　　　—*Lori Hendricks*

A Breakfast of Waylaid Enlightenment

It was early morning sunrise, and this much did I suddenly come
　to know: (about the processes of life itself, and my very
　place in it...)

Not every moment brings the dawn, and the wisdom of freedom in
　that time of awakening.

Or the calm acceptance, and open-hearted knowing of pure
　awareness.

Or the quiet independence, and soulful reflection of selfless
　understanding.

For such moments are rare. (- And so hard to come by...)
Uncommon to daily experience. (- And so hard to recognize...)
Difficult to grasp. (- And harder still to hold onto...)

But beyond such aspects of obvious hardship,
　is the matter of living itself,
　with far more engrossing needs.

- Like a coffee refill,
　and the newspaper,
　and the concentrated effort of smoking - (...or not.)

　　　—*Ron Zillmer*

Circle of Three

Questions of my childhood revolve in a circle of three.
To me and thee there is a circle of three. I look
around and all I see turns into a circle of three.
Father Son and Holy Spirit. Father comes First and
then who's first, Son comes first when he becomes a
father, and when it is done you die and when you die
the Spirit becomes the leader and as the leader he
becomes the first.

　　　—*Leo G. Cunningham Jr.*

Friendship

Friendship is a matter of time
To let each and ever friend know how to be kind.
You're not hard up when your purse is flat,
And your trousers frayed like an old doormat.
You're not hard up when your bills are due,
And you haven't a dollar to see you through
You're not hard up till you see the day,
That you haven't a cheerful word to say.
You're not hard up when your coin is gone,
And you whistle a tune as you journey on;
You may walk the streets, while others ride.
And your pockets have naught, but your hands inside.
That not being broke, you may depend,
For you're not hard up, while you have a friend.

　　　—*Alice T. Spencer*

"Peace"

　　I went upon the "Mountain" top and gave great thoughts
to "Life" and the "Hereafter" and suddenly appeared my "Jesus".
　　He sat down beside me. As we "Gathered", he spoke so
sweet and said "Dear Child", don't fret, I know your
"Heart" is filled with "Sorrow", but "Yet", their will
come a day when your trials and worries shall end!
　　For I am with you "Always"! I am your "Greatest Friend"!
　　I said "Precious Lord"; I cried for the "Kings" and
"Kennedys" of this "Nation".
　　For they "Truly" stood for "Peace" and "Brotherhood"
in the truest "Sensation"!
　　The "Lord" looked at me and a "Smile" appeared upon his
"Face".
　　Go "Preach" my "Word" dear child with your "Sincere
Grace", and "Remember", I am with you "Always"!

　　　—*Patricia Lane Pulley*

The Free Spirit

The free spirit within you wants no ties
To live life by your rules
To ride under the stars
To make love on a whim and
　ride off
To feel the warm sun upon your back
　like an autumn fire
To feel the wind caress your face
　like a lost love
To wander along a moonlit beach
　in search of a dream
The free spirit within you
　wants no ties

　　　—*Alexandra Wiest Lombardo*

Crossroads

Igniting fossil fuel, we foul the air
To make lush earth like planet Venus bare.
Beneath the breached, thin, fragile ozone layer,
Our Eden's garden burns, and thus we care.
From living molecules into this sphere,
We give and take vast clouds of gases, share.
Both plants and beasts that breathe life-giving air
Are threatened by a greenhouse atmosphere.

Four billion years from some organic soup
Of living cells, life upward spiral grew.
And since mankind arose from its primal stoop,
Astride the world's biotic peak, the breadth
Of thoughtful savants hold the evolving view
Renewed by Nature's will through time, and death?

　　　—*Iwao Mizuta*

A Fathers Pride

Lord, I am a father I have my job and duties
To my wife a husband
A man she can trust
A friend in love
My children I'm a teacher
I teach them wrong from right.
I know I'm to tough
On them from time to time
The kids got a right
I want so much for them to be good in school
Times have changed I know.
Nothing is like it use to be
I can't show no pity or sympathy
You see Lord someday my children will see
How much they mean to me
But if I shall give in
I'll lose the thing called
"A Father's Pride"
—*Cindy Tackett Gibson*

(Thank You Jesus)

Thank you Jesus, for one more chance
To praise your holy name,
Because of your undying love
My life is not the same.

Thanks for being by my side
No matter when or where,
I know that I am well protected
With your heavenly presence there.

Thank you Jesus, most of all
Because you gave your life for me,
I hope someday to repay that debt
By giving my soul to thee.

There are so many things to be thankful for
Much more than I can say,
So I'll just have to say thank you
Each and every day.
—*Lonnie B. Thomas*

Untitled

Spring is due and so the plants begin
   to prepare their offsprings to greet it in;
Each ray of sunshine that dissolves the cold breeze, gives
   strength to the buds and bring them up off their knees.

Now their heads held high, they are ready for spring;
   and as the day approaches winter drops in again to bring
Her calling card all done up in white, and
   the buds hurry to close the sunlight in their petals tight.

It's still now, for the plants are sad - -
   the snow has put their children to bed as if they had
Been naughty all day. Winter still wants her fling - -
   for once the buds take over it will surely be spring!

The morning of spring dawns and oh what a day!
   Like an ermine wrap the snow has been "checked" away;
And the buds like debutantes are "coming out", they
   could not disappoint us - - it is spring without a doubt!!
   —*Irma E. Manzelli*

My Love

How like a snowflake, she.
Entirely beautiful;
Never duplicated.
Who is like her?
—*Kenneth Caron, 12/25/74*

September

I pause at the threshold of busy September
To recall its vibrant redress of people and things.
It's a cherished month to remember.

For nature's brush paints a prize contender
Of bold oranges, yellows and gold on wings.
I pause at the threshold of busy September.

Its improvisation boasts no pretender,
Each stroke of the brush is ecstasy it brings.
It is a cherished month to remember.

Its people manned jets engender
Roars as they sputter, soar aloft and sing.
I pause at the threshold of busy September.

To hear the care free variant timber
Of bussed tow-heads and braids as the bell rings.
It is a cherished month to remember.

I recall a wee son, light and limber
As he marched in his school band, proud as a king.
I pause at the threshold of busy September.
It is a cherished month to remember.
—*Lilibel Pazoureck-Lucy*

The Way That He Loves Me

I feel as though my heart has gone from rags to riches.

Once upon a time my heart was dressed in torn
garments, it did not have a home to call it's own.

That was before he came along. Now it is a princess
sitting on "his" throne........ Dressed in a silk
gown and wearing a jeweled crown upon it's head.
Treated like royalty!

My life is now a fantasy, he is making all my
dreams a reality, just by the way that he loves me.

I keep wondering when I will wake up. Nothing
could ever feel this good. Maybe this is how
it should be or will it remain a mystery........
The Way That He Loves Me.
—*Barbara G. Zachrich*

"Our Home"

I came to Alaska the last frontier
To see the Northern lights
And all the wild life here
Then more and more people came
More and more laws they enforced.
More of our wilderness to cities became
Hard winters killed many moose
Then people complained of wolves running loose
Roads were built, beavers, lost
Careless hunters killed for sport
Much of our wild life destroyed as result
The Exxon oil spill came along
And thousands of our marine life, gone
Why? Did so many people come to spoil
Not enjoy this final frontier.
—*Nancy R. Binder*

The Fateful Encounter

   When we first walked into the light, it was as if a
dream. Some one set a scheme. He lured me into the blissful
light, into a place of crystal streams. I drank the
waters thereof, and fell into a peaceful sleep. We strolled
through gardens lush and green. He showed me things I'd
never seen. We walked beyond the outer gates into the
world unseen. Into the world of man and beast. And so the
story came to be, the forbidden fruit he offered me.
—*Cynthia Shanholtzer*

"Wonders of Nature"

It's A Wonder To Behold an enormous ball of fierce flaming fire to serve as a means of pure light for the existing vast earth.

It's A Wonder To Behold a full moon, billions and trillions of miles, where the sparkling stars reign throughout the night of the universe.

It's A Wonder To Behold the fluffy clouds placed just a tab below the skies, and the white clouds transformed into a dark soft mist for the rain or snow to sprinkle in a twinkle of the human eyes

It's A Wonder To Behold the existing life that breaths heavily upon the depths of the deepest waters.

It's A Wonder To Behold the various fragrance of beautifully colored flowers, blossomed through a speck of dust from the surface of the earth, and the dry withered grass suddenly become alive and bright green to supply fresh food for the animals, and even for a delicacy and the comfort of the smallest crawling insects that live deeply beneath the earth.

The Amazing Wonder Of Nature is one in a world which help brightens the dims of life into a glorious habitat just for you and me, the greatest wonder of all, the human family.

—*Charles Bowser, Jr.*

Clouds

What across the sky would run,
To shield my head from burning sun?
Or glide in splendor, bright and proud?
The answer is the wondrous cloud.

It bows so low to touch the trees,
At times reclines upon the seas,
Darkens and spreads to shroud the earth,
Or rolls and plays in fits of mirth.

Sometimes on peaks you'll see them scrape,
Upon horizons softly drape.
They with songbirds and rainbows fly,
To accent and adorn the sky.

When winds are high and nights are warm,
I like to watch them burst in storm.
In lakes as calm and clear as glass,
I like to watch them slowly pass.

Should it look white, black, blue or gray,
Should it change shapes or stay all day,
Should it bring shade or thunder loud,
I'm glad to see my friend the cloud.

—*Douglas R. Smith*

Sky On the Run

Sky on the run, but people still seem
to shoot guns.
Kidnapped, rape, burglary too, sky on the
run is that why your color is no longer blue.
We said we got the world in control,
sky on the run your the only one who knows.
The weather and temperatures has lost
rhythm with the seasons, sky on the run
your the one who knows the reasons.
Sky on the run please tell us how much
longer till we destroy you and us, the
world and the sun.
I wish everyone could understand because
of us that is why the sky is on the run.

—*Bernadette Davis*

My Heart Is A Canary

My heart is a canary pointing my beak
to the blue heavens singing open-throttle
my perfect aria in a realm of divine happiness.

My heart is a lonely dove carrying patient messages
of peace, purity, wisdom and love wherever I happen
to rest.

My heart is an eagle, my country's stern
standard-bearer. Dignity and pride are mine,
and a wide span of protective wings.

My heart is a peacock uniting all the delicious
colors of life into one precious package
of beauty. I strut and strain to be worthy.

My heart is a gentle robin baring my beautiful
breast while cheerfully scanning the yard
for my worms.

My heart is a sea gull soaring through life
and taking my share of earth's bounty.
The world is my horizon.

—*Peggy Desmarais*

Wings Of Wind

Come my love let us ride the wings of wind
To the bosom of the mother of mothers where first our freedom
began. Yes even now you recognize our brothers, they are
bearers of burdens. Workers of mills, makers of waves
Gleaners of fields times in their eternal company
We were one in love seekers of wisdom, entities from above
Yet you be as before no shadow follow you in the brightest of
light. The mightiest of might Prince and Princess
Of the Blue Jinn. Upon your feet are stars and in your
hair are jewels and on your left hand is four crowned
rings of wisdom in your right hand you hold the power
of the four winds no human mind can imagine your awesome
Powers you know these only to be the powers of love
Your time is but moments in the great castle
You must leave as you came down the path of wisdom
Through the gate of knowledge upon the wings of wind
Back to the body that you were within
It is only now that you become the keeper of the garden
Seek peace my love and I ever be with you

—*Charles Lamar Mays, Sr.*

Earth

From the towering, majestic mountains -
To the covered forests of woodland trails below
Further along, lies the lowering valleys, hills
The gentle flow of streams.
Courses into rivers of water
Traverses it's final journey
As a body of ocean water and upon it's land.
Beauteous array of flowers, fields of golden grain,
Earth, separates itself from the sky
Leaves its mark as a horizon
Limitless is the atmosphere of outer space
Arching the fullness of earth, is heaven,
Yet, human, in all of its free moral choice.
Is ever in awe-
For he, deep inside, his heart knows.
He is not alone.

—*James H. Ulan*

The Future

The future is like a door opened
to the public
   Some people might walk through
that door with their eyes closed thinking
they'll see nothing but horrible sights
   Others might walk through that door with
their eyes opened widely thinking they'll
see nothing but glamour
   Still yet some people might walk through
that door with their eyes opened just
enough to see what they want to see
   Those who walk through that door with
their eyes closed are too negative about the future
   Those who walk through that door with
their eyes opened widely expect too much of the future
   Those who walk through that door with
their eyes opened just enough to see what
they want have hope in the future.

   —*Angela Kallsen*

The Stitch Twitch

There are times when I get a desire, a twitch,
To turn off the thing we call the TV,
And pick up a needle and floss and stitch,
Since it's more satisfying to me.

If you can take a few minutes out of your day
To see the pieces of beauty that I'm making,
It would be a nice, worthwhile stay,
To know that the quality of work hasn't been forsaken.

I'd bite my fingernails more if I didn't have this twitch.
Besides, heeding it really helps me to relax.
I've put in many a stitch, and for it I'd gladly make a pitch
Over what I call objectionable material which should get the ax.

   —*Carol Lee Ammons*

"A Mother's Song"

Mother, oh mother, to be like you
To understand and know the song in your heart.

As I am getting older and looking around
My eyes fall upon you and I do hear a sound.

You through the years, I can see now
You have been singing the song that I sing now.

Oh mother, dear mother, I understand now
Why when I cried you shed the tears.

My eyes look upon you with sorrow and great joy
My joy dear mother, is because you love me so.

The sorrow I have is of days of old
When I didn't know, that love is the song of the soul.

And now my soul is singing, and now my eyes do see.
And now my arms can hold you, and now my voice can say:

Mother, dear sweet mother, you walk in beauty like never before
For your soul has been singing all along and forever more.

Singing the song of life, love is the blood
To your everlasting soul and sight.

I love you.
   —*Deborah Green*

The Eternal

The sun of righteousness has shed rays of joy
   to warm my wearied soul,
For as the Man of sorrows, He well remembers
   the chills of this earthly life,
Knowingly the Gentle Shepherd, sends abundant
   grace unto His flock,
Yea, the Prince of Peace walks with me, through
   the valley of the shadow of death,
And with a child-like faith, I find reassurance
   and security in my Heavenly Father,
For I belong to the Great I Am, the Ancient of
   Days, the most High God,
I have found shelter from the storms of life,
   in Jesus who calms the seas;
Now, my inner-man is at rest, found only
   in the bosom of my God!
I shall praise Him ever! Amen
   —*Larry Longfellow*

My Private Theater

I often look up in the summer sky
To watch the changing clouds march by

The forms and shapes that are there to see
Are a welcomed relief from watching TV

The scenes change constantly, commercial free
And the show goes on as if just made for me

There are countless pictures to view on my own
-People, animals and creatures unknown

I've seen Washington, Lincoln, my dog and my cat
- And even John Wayne with his old cowboy hat

Its refreshing to see things not in the news
I can make of the clouds whatever I choose

I can be sure of one thing as I gaze on high
I won't see old reruns up there in Gods sky
   —*Rudy Comtois*

The Siren

Free at last from her so-called mother: earth
To whom she never belonged,
Her friendly dolphin eyes were in service for the sharks
And her heart was an eel,
Say the lives she had wronged.

If there is a fight other than the one she has lost,
Listen to the past take shape in the storm:
There's her voice, by now the hollow voice of a ghost,
Saying "I am strong. So long as my hand doesn't shake,
I can give anything you can take."

Ease her down into the bosom of the sea,
She always believed the sea must be fed
By novice simmers, by drunk sailors, by
Bright fishermen who, to hear her sing,
Let their lives hang by a thread.

She locked her lips against friends to shut in the thought,
Hugged the idea to herself to keep warm;
She locked her heart against the overwrought
Heroine who cried "You are killing me!" — too late,
Drop her back into the arms of fate.
   —*F. D'Anconia*

Untitled

The problems of yesterday have fallen upon the sinners of
today, and there's no solution to the racial slurs of gang fights

When we all cry out for the liberty of free speech,
don't let the constitution condone the violence which gave us
our rights

'Cuz our protests in Washington have got a long way to go,
while our kids' education fade to the night streets of today

And before we can take control of the madness at hand,
we must stop the selling of crack to the people who pay

Now abusing the system to gain free rent in someone's head,
is like a criminal who commits a violent rape

And even though their resistance is high the time has come,
for us to breathe deep before it's all too late

Some say this is how a business runs the American way,
but what happened to the dream that we're supposed to discover

It's all become a game in which nobody wins the point,
we're just brothers killing each other for the profit of another

—*Anthony Johnson*

The Toddlers

His legs were stiff, her legs were too
   toddling 'cross the parking lot
Her hindrance-age. His hindrance-youth
   What a lovely pair, I thought

His small chub hand held wrinkled prune
   Knuckles that planted by the moon
many more seasons than he could know
   I watched them as they labored slow

His hair was soft-hers, smoky gray
She was probably his grandmother
   such a darling little boy
You knew they loved each other

Walked from one end of the lot to the other
tiny boy, and aged grandmother
Toddlers both, for she's become
in some ways, just like her grandson

—*Sharon Lund*

Partners For Life

We've watched the rise, we've seen the fall. We've been
together through it all, you and I. Some years went slow, some

went fast. There've been times we've laughed about our past.
We're still together, you and I. Some memories are gone for

good, some seemed like they only happened yesterday. We loved
to sit and watch our children play. You and I.

Has life really robbed us of all those years, or do we say
we're getting old to comfort all our fears? We were always
strong together, yet life always got better and better. For
you and I.

They always said we'd never last, yet we always showed them
up, all throughout our past. We had our fights, we cried our
tears, looking back those were happy years, for you and I.

Now those times are all but gone, and I'm not so sure I can
still be strong. I don't know what I'll do now that your gone.

We made a vow when we were kids, we'd be partners for life,
until the very end! Well the end has come, and I guess I've
won, still I don't feel like singing or having fun.

So when my time comes, I'm sure you'll teach me how to fly,
we'll be partners once again. You and I.

—*William D. Spangler II*

Emotions

There are many feelings that I withhold,
too many inside, which I've never told.
To let them out, to set them free,
I guess is what really scares me.
I tell myself to let them go,
but still I refuse myself to let them show.
Within me I hold anger, pain, fear, and love,
feelings I keep even from the morning dove.
I must set them free, let them go,
but these feelings that I behold
are to remain with me
and forever be untold.

—*Erica Beaulieu*

I See Lives

This is the dawning of a new generation
   Trapped in the land of discontent
Barely breathing, searching for success
   Look to the past, that's where it went

   I see lives, I see faces
   I read minds and I've read pages
   I see people, I've seen places
No one seems to care to spare the time

   Oh, you say hello ... what you going to do
   Lend a helping hand to all of earth
Oh, if you try too hard you might just come to lose
   All that you've changed ... believe it's true

   I see lives, I see faces
   I read minds and I've read pages
   I see people, I've seen places
No one seems to care to spare the time

So you sit there with your hands on your head
   You say it hurts so bad you can't go on
And you cry a while looking towards the end
   Can't you see your picture on the wall

—*Brian Harrison*

Best Friend

Walking down the road the sunshine on my face.
Trusty friend by my side quickly sets the pace.
We trudge along side by side quietly we share,
The brisk, fresh feeling of the winter morning air.
She trots ahead to chase a mouse or flush a bird,
Or some other unknown creature, that my ears have not heard.
My legs have given out, it's time to go back home.
But she's still going strong, ready to run and rome.
Even though she wants to be wild and free,
When I call she comes to me.
We head for home, she leads the way.
She knows we will come again another winter day.
A better partnership there will never be,
Then my tried and true trusty friend,
Faithful old dog and me.

—*June Anderson*

Creation

To the night belongs the day to bring
Flight upon my tattered wings
Soaring light calls to those who pray
Shadows dancing above the day

Seasons pass when the time arrives
Casting spells upon nocturnal lives
The will grows tired of the solemn day
Toward fate we fly, light shows the way

—*Kyle Connors*

Untitled

Black, white, yellow, and red
try to get these colors out of your head.
We're killing our people. We're killing mankind.
Why can't we leave these colors behind?
People are different.
You don't understand.
I wish all this hatred could be totally banned.
We walk down the streets with guns in our hands
shooting with the best of our aim.
Why?
Because another race just is not the same?
You might have heard poems similar to this.
It's a pathetic disease called prejudice.
—*Marc Eisenshtat*

Untitled

Sitting in my room boring
Trying to talk silence
Listening to the loneliness
Haven't had a thought
All love has been lost
Hatred found in my soul, my mind, my heart
Staring at the wall
The blank look on my face
The terror in my eyes
The mask that sets upon my face not
showing my true identity
Ashamed of what people might think
I hear but I'm not listening
I cry but the tears aren't seen
My heart bleeds but no one cares
the pain
—*Heather McCauley*

Fragments

The wheel turns. Fire burns!
Turn the other cheek. The Bible lies!
There is no good in some men.
Babies die with blackened eyes;
die multiple deaths before they die.
The fist is mightier than flesh;
man is larger than the child.
Bigger is better! Morality is learned.
He raped a child of three. Nobody knows, save one.
Smothered screams sever childhood.
The man who used the body of a child
as a vessel walks undaunted.
Nobody hears bones shatter.
Cover your ears — it disappears. Blindness is just.
Some survive burning alive:
bones mend, but flesh screams its history.
Nightmares rend the tranquil sky: shadows don't lie.
Children's tears water black flowers
breaking dry earth in the suburbs
where respectable men have blood on their fists.
—*Wendy Wagner*

Untitled

My thoughts are often crowded and
everchanging, starting out like a single wind
instrument then rolling into a concourse of brass
and percussion.
Some lie like sleeping dragons,
waiting to be awakened and
have their power brought forth
bearing me to far-off places.
—*Dennis Guy*

Untitled

Children frolic in the sun
Dancing in their shadows
Morose becomes the sky
As clouds begin to smother the sun
Pitter-Pat Pitter-Pat
Boom-Crash-Boom
Children dash for cover
From the sullen storm
—*Amy E. Schwarz*

For R H S

When the girl in the floppy Paddington hat
Turns to wave goodbye
She always forgets to return
The part of you she borrows

She gives the all-time second-best hugs

If you catch a smile
From the girl in the floppy Paddington hat
It's like a two-week vacation
Maybe it's that overbite

The girl in the floppy Paddington hat
Used to be a dancer
She tried to teach me third position
But I didn't have the hips
—*M. Schwartz*

Two Girls

I remember a cold, wintry night.
Two girls full of dreams.

I remember ice-skating on frozen run-off water.
Two girls sharing a down jacket.

I remember the parking lot, where we tried to avoid the
tar cracks.
Two girls running swift as the wind.

I remember the post office we snuck up to.
Two girls acting like spies.

I remember a promise of everlasting friendship.
Two girls pledging loyalty.

I remember our breaths blowing white with the chilly
night.
Two girls, best friends.
—*Erin Hancock*

Building Together

Our house crumbled and fell to the ground.
Two remaining walls are basically sound
But two separate walls when standing alone
Cannot make a house into a suitable home.
We need sturdy, strong walls of building blocks
And some heavy supports to bear all the knocks.

I'm sure if we search and work side by side
We'll find under the rubble of selfishness and pride
The foundation of the old on which to build the new.
The basic block, the cornerstone (respect), we'll find, too.
Two walls, supported by new braces; and other repair
Will withstand the stresses they're intended to bear.

We will need some new blocks, some lintels and sill
Blocks of kindness, understanding and good will,
Some cement to build up and strengthen the walls
To bolster, support, and adapt — lest it falls.
With the help of God and courage to face what's to come
Our "building together" will make this a home.
—*Jackie Armbruster*

Maybe

Place your bets, stake your wages
Uncertainty is the minimum ante.
Choose sides and endure; subsist if unsure.

Will you win or lose it all?
  Play it safe - hesitate.

Yes/No is the sum
  of a blank page.
Like a gymnast on a beam; keep the mean.

Opportunity is spent from knocking.
No commitment here; keep the fear.

Balanced in the middle ground
Hung to the burial ground
Maybe we'll adorn your grave.

      —*Carla Molchan*

Baby Boy

She entered this world in the usual way,
Unharmed and unhurt she thought she would stay,
Until he came down and took that precious gift away,
Gone was her world of hopes and dreams,
And into a world in which everyone screams,
Another naive heart yet to be broken,
Full of promises left unspoken,
Left alone in that crazy world,
Feelings seem to get hurled,
Alone in the darkness she thought she could stay,
Till God came down and took that away,
Flesh and blood she thought she could keep,
But along they came and took him to sleep,
But she knew they were taking him away,
To where he'd be better off anyway,
Alone in her world she thought she could keep,
Until came a time when everyone weeps,
"Move along in the world." was all they could say,
But they didn't know her baby had been taken away,
Guilt and fear was all she felt,
Pushed into a world into which she should have dealt,
And into that world she shall stay,
Till God comes down and takes her away.

      —*Micaela Vaughn*

Forever Together

Whole is greater together organism forever component
Unique polarity love intimacy forever together challenge
Belonging family togetherness forever fruitful self awareness
Passionate conviction focus true self forever together
Concrete communication assertive honesty unification
Intuitive enlightenment clarifying interpretation
Symbolic imagination abandonment unconditional love
Introduction forever together realistic wisdom
Inner existence dynamic relationship seek truth beauty
Goodness tenderness structure identity forever together
Mature growth follow your heart to find a place where
You are never abandoned or alone a place not measured
By perfectionistic rules means forever together

      —*Barbara Thomas*

Being

I am a child of the universe—
Born of the stars,
Caressed by the winds,
And gently cradled by the sea.

I am of all races, creeds, and colors.
I am of all places and all times:
I am infinity.

      —*Emma Wormley Thomas*

Friendships

I like you
  And you like me
That's why we should
  Be.

      —*Aiyisha Natylie Tribble*

You're What I Need

I want to be in your life forever,
until the day I die,
I want to talk to you in such sweet words
till I break down and cry.
I want you to be in my life for eternity.
I will never let you go.
I don't want to put myself through that much misery.
I will do anything for you.
You told me that one day you will make my dreams come true.
In a way you always have, by you coming into my life,
because all I'll ever want is you.
My love will always be here for you,
it will never fade away,
as long as I am alive, it's here to stay.

      —*Joy Adams*

The Flower

Everywhere there are flowers,
Up in towers way up high above the sky.
So when the birds fly,
Way up in the sky, it will be time to say goodbye.
So say goodbye to all the flowers in the towers.
Cause when the birds shall fly that high in the sky you
Know that summer is over and winter is coming.
And snow shall fall,
On the towers' wall.

      —*Kendra King*

The Magical Castle

The magical castle is way up high,
Up where the magical unicorns fly,
The little stars dance and the little bells ring,
And all the little horses start to sing,
It's a place of wonder and a place of dreams,
And sometimes more than it really seems,
So when you are dreaming just remember the sky,
Up where the magical castle lives high.

      —*Juliett Puhiera*

The Renovation

There was a little brown building
Used for an office when new
In an equipment yard it set
Behind a silver chain link fence.
During the day it was business as usual
Pipe sales, welding, and answering the phone.
But when each day would draw to a close
The little building was left all alone.
It set proudly in the night as if
To watch the place 'til the first sign of light
And, then again, it was business as usual.
There is no equipment yard here anymore
But in it's place a beautiful home.
The little building is around back
But instead of brown the color is green.
It is still in use as for storage
And sometimes a place for kittens to be born.
So, as you see, it's still business as usual.

      —*Betty Whitehead*

A Mother And Fathers Love

How can you say that I don't care, oh child of mine, how very, very unfair. You could never measure this love that lives inside of me, unless you have someway, a way I cannot see. The Lord above, he died for you and me, and if that's not love and caring, than you and I would never have came to be. For he died before ever knowing, there would be a you or me, that my child is love, plain and simply. But than again, how can you measure all the love he has? Our Lord he is not here with us, yet his love enfolds our lives. Ever so gently throughout our days, he shows us so subtly in many, many ways. Like a mother and fathers love for their child it goes on and on forever. Mothers and fathers are forever loving, forever trusting, forever forgiving, but the child he cannot see; for it's something he cannot reach out and touch and hold eternally. A child will forever question that which cannot be seen. A favorite toy, a truck or such can break and be thrown away. A mother and father's love is locked away in their hearts The child thinks there is a key and the lock could be opened up and their love it could just fly away, so far away he might never see. But like God's love, my child, ours is yours eternally.

  —*Kathleen Pannunzio*

Dearest Brother

Play in the hand inflated pool.
Wagon train, cops and robbers;
pleasure on polished two wheelers.
Combat in healthy overgrown grass.
A stroll with puppies in the miniature
tawny buggy.

A match with the baseball glove.
A master at football strategy.
King on the throne of cardboard design.
Herder over squalling tamed pigs.
Clerk in the store, partner for church.
Designer in printless snow.

Our hearts surged like spume of the mighty rivers
unseen in the stomach of hungered caves.
But now, a kiss.
To my juvenile cheek, a kiss
and my majesty is gone,
gone forever.

  —*Deborah Jean Dick*

People

(For Mrs. Rickelmann)
 Walking along, I find myself lost
in a crowd of strange, but familiar
creatures.
 Some are secretive, some are outgoing,
some hateful, and some are happy, while
others are sad.
 They all dress as different as night
and day. Some are dressed for serious
business, and still some are hardly
dressed at all.
 Some are tall, some are short, and
others in between.
 They are all different outside,
but on the inside, they're as much
the same as peas in a pod.
 No matter what color, race, shape
or size, they are all called people.

  —*Michele Taylor*

Cry for the Children

Cry for the children, who live their lives in pain
Wanting to feel the sunshine, hoping to come in from the rain

Needing love from a family, to give their lives direction
So tired of all the loneliness, misery and rejection

Cry for the children, no child deserves to live like this
Childhood is to short, for just one day to be missed

See the children who have it all, constantly demanding more
Need to spend a day, experiencing the life,
of the homeless and the poor

Learning to be grateful, for the small things that come their way
Never asking for more, than a place where they can play

A hot meal, a blanket, and a bed where they can sleep
Hope for the future, a reason to look forward to next week

Yes, cry for the children and help others understand
That all God's children, rich and poor, are the future of this land

  —*Patricia Miller*

Growing Old

I look into your eyes and see things I've never seen
Wars I've never fought
Hunger I've never known
In your smile I see wisdom I will never know
I do not see the wrinkles of an old face
I see the spirit of my past,
The creator of my future
To me you will never be a burden
Just my reason to rejoice
To know through your memories I can dream
Through struggle there is survival
Through pain there is growth
You are truly the heroes who have survived
the hardships of the world, still having the strength
To share hope and joy.
To me the word old will never mean forgotten
It will mean remembrance of a life and a strength
to be shared for generations to come.

  —*Nancy Iacono*

Revelation

Bestowed upon us by the Lord above
Was a wonderful child to nurture and love,

No courses required or mention of grade
Only trial and error-learning from mistakes
That are made,

This wonder of a child has grown in spite of it all,
He's bright, creative, handsome and tall,

His mother and father thank the Lord above
For bestowing upon them this young man
to love!

  —*Maryann Kovilic*

"Walk With Me"

Walk with me as the river runs free,
 walk with me and together we'll always be.
Walk with me as we grow old,
 walk with me through warmth and cold.
Walk with me as we look back into the past,
 walk with me and watch our love last.
Walk with me as long as we're together,
 walk with me now and forever.
Stay with me for as long as we can see,
 as long as forever, please walk with me!

  —*Jeffrey Darrell Webb*

The Hero

A hero in his eyes, he saved you from confusion
Was it honesty or just an illusion
Raging waters that now are calm
Worshipping the ground you walk upon

The magician waved his wand as the child squealed in delight
As the rain fell down on a wintery night
With pen in hand he writes a thought
Leaving behind all his mother taught

A restless soul yearning to be free
A door left unopened without a key
Someone to save him from the storm
A blanket at night to keep him warm

For the hero will leave you standing alone
Leaving behind a freedom you've never known
Was it honesty or just an illusion
That has saved him from confusion.

　　　—Grace Miller

A Child Was Born

Was the child born to feel hate?
Was she put upon this earth with feelings of selfishness,
wantonness, loneliness? Was she born missing some vital link
to her own soul? Was she made with a cold heart and an evil mind?

A baby is innocent until the world passes judgment on her.
She's conditioned to believe what her life teaches her.
If she is taught to feel useless, she will feel useless.
If she is told she is bad, she will feel bad.

When the child grows into a women, will the world find her
guilty, innocent, or will they find her insane?

　　　—Lisa L. Warren

The Loss of My Friend

　How does one recall the life of someone who
was so dear?
　Even though he's far away from us, he
seems to be so near.
　The memories are so painfully real, they're
embedded in my mind so deep.
　They're the kind of thoughts I can't forget,
the kind I will always keep.
　It's been said that when you lose someone,
that your life must still keep going.
　That you always have to keep your head
up high, that you must keep your grief from showing.
　But I can't do that, don't you see, the pain
is much too strong.
　I lost my dearest friend in the whole wide
world, and it hasn't even been that long.
　So, when people say "friends come and go,
why must you be so sad?
　I softly reply "not only did I lose my
friend, I also lost my Dad."

　　　—Tommy Long

Morning Dawn

I walk across the meadow in the morning dew
Watching the golden rising sun.
It makes a sea of tiny rainbows upon spider webs and grass.

A red fox pauses for one last look,
A mocking bird sends out the last note of night,
On a hillside a fawn waits in the still morning light.
In a blink of an eye these night creatures will fade.

Then there will be only meadow, sun and me.

　　　—Mae Gordon

This Is It!

Walked in the country, was spellbound by color
Was speechless with awe, so quiet, so peaceful
Felt so close to God, with His blanket of beauty
And I thought… This is it!

Went to the hospital to visit a new mother
Stopped at the nursery and stared in wonder
They were screeching and squirming, just saying they're here
So helpless, so lovely…And I thought… This is it!

Went out in the street, in the great big city,
Became part of the crowd and looked in amazement at the genius of man,
The buildings reaching so high, the theater, the dining and dancing
Got caught up with the pace, And I thought…This is it!

Sat in the evening in the quiet of my room
And thought of my love and just being with him
Of loving, and knowing that he loves me too
And I thought…This is it!

Waking up hearing the birds, seeing a sunset, touching a rose
Walking the beach, seeing a waterfall,
It's a God-given gift, a composite of all…
It's being alive…This is it!

　　　—Leanora O'Donnell

Two Reasons To Live Forever

All through life I often wondered what will
Was there a purpose I would someday fulfill?

I learned how to take and I learned how to give.
That still didn't fulfill my reasons to live.

I lived in happiness and I lived in fear.
That still didn't explain the reasons I'm here.

I've learned all about "The birds and the bees".
I know "Roses are Red and Violets are Blue."
But still I didn't have a single clue,
About what life's for and what will to do.

After many years in this old world,
I discovered life does have worth.
That was the day my Little Girls
Said hello Dear Mother Earth.

On the day they were born I searched no further.
God placed me here to be a MOTHER.
I have reasons…Two reasons to live!!

　　　—Charlotte Womack Gay

Night Prayer

Oh, shepherd, embrace me on this lonely night!
Watch with me as Orion sways in the arms of heaven
When the earth weaves melodies of love
And little lambs rest on the mountain grass
When the mournful eyes of the hungry wolves
Behold angels in the pastures.

Lay me down on your mossy bed.
Caress me with your touch.
Do not speak to me of suffering and pain
Or the unfaithfulness of humanity.
Just for tonight, let me drawn in silence.

Let the pine fragrant breeze fill my being…
Let the song of the crickets be the only sound in this place…
And let the warm, golden rays of the sun
Be my first sight beyond your gentle face.

Oh, shepherd, embrace me on this lonely night!

　　　—Cleo Laszlo

Untitled

S itting in my box
H idden from a world of hurt.
Y outhful scars still bleed
— *Benjamin D. Quinn*

"The Homeless Young Man"

There he sat in the train station,
Watching people come and go.
Where'd shelter or his next meal come from,
He surely didn't know. His mother's kind face he'd see no more
Life's heavy burdens had taken their toll
She had gone on to rest her weary soul.

The landlord's knock on the door was no surprise,
And the words he spoke brought tears to Michael's eyes.
No caring relatives could he find, where would he go but to the
Street, streets, wide, free, but so unkind.
He journeyed forth, frightened, hopeful and unheeded.
He'd find a job. What a shame they all needed
Someone with experience.

"What experience? I'm barely eighteen,
Just out of school, but I'm willing to work" says
Michael — to no avail. At last he finds shelter,
A few nights to lay his head, troubled and worn in strange bed,
Till all too soon comes the dread of morn.
Michael must leave to seek the day's fortune, but he is hopeful
Perhaps this is the day when something good will come his way.

— *Esme G. Crump*

At Sundown

They are on the big red boat,
Watching the clouds move with the sun.
Everyone but them has gone down to eat,
They are left alone with the setting-sun.
Their time and place is really the best,
They see beautiful sites while conditions are blest.

He looks blindly over stern of big boat,
Reality comes natural but they are caught to dream.
They see something in each others eyes,
While in the secrecy of their hearts esteem.

Their explosive feelings through gestures of love,
To the back of her shoulders his hand abound.
Around his waist she placed her arms,
Feeling his heart transposing some great sounds.

Finally realizing that they were not alone,
Their little child standing there without a sound.
Finally admiring what made them go dreaming,
The clouds-the water-all at sundown.

— *Fred Cizek*

Look Through My Eyes

I wish the way I look at you would be the
    way that you see me.
For if that were true I would have no worries
    in the world.
I would know that I am caring and survival
    would be in my hands.
But most of all I would be protective at times.
To show I care and that my love for you
    was once true.
I would be someone that would be looked up to.
Because when I look in your eyes I see
    someone true.
Nothing like me, for I wish to be like you.

— *Marie Heitkamp*

Life Is A Gamble

We all gamble as far as I can see,
We all gamble on things that may not be.
We gamble on love in life.
We gamble on honestly from our husband or wife
We gamble we will be on earth
for many a day.
When any moment we could have a end to our stay.
We gamble we will never fail.
We gamble we wont go to jail.
We gamble on health.
We gamble on wealth.
We gamble on all we see
But you're never been a gamble to me.
Because in my eyes
Your a winner and always will be.

— *Rose Decker*

On the Mummified Bodies of an Inuit Woman and Child

(Found in a sea-cave in Canada)
We are a birds-wing on eternity,
A blink of the eternal eye,
A grain from all the beaches of the world.
For the worm is in the bone
From the first cry to rid the lungs of fluid
In struggle to be free.
Better by far to sit like them and stare
For centuries at a deserted beach,
Where the sea forever grinds the shells to dust.
Yet in that young child's face I saw
Such longing and such pathos
My heart tore,
For him, for us,
For all who wanted more.

— *Patricia von Dippe*

My Sunday Poem

(Dedicated in memory of my sister, Randee Robinson)
We are all alike, born
A waxy mess of wonderful
Pure, formed by Him
Molded by many
From the first moment
We measure what we will
Some burn at both ends
Bright and fast
Some illuminate the way for others
Sharing their salvation
Some have no light at all
And in dim reflection
See nothing.

— *Kim R. Snell*

Reflections

As the years roll by and we ponder life's mission
we frequently look back and weigh each decision
Every person seems molded by family and friends
to meet one's calling upon which life depends

After years of grooming preparatory for each soul
we find ourselves searching for an appropriate role
For some it's a compromise here and there
and other's endless searching for a future in despair

'Tis hard to comprehend the hardships in store
and to reconcile our blessings with those we adore
But life is a challenge which we all must face
while we live for the day of redeeming grace

— *Glenn A. Swanson*

The Gift That Perpetuates Itself - Blood

What do we mean when we say blood as a gift
We are talking about donating do you get my drift

Please give your blood, a gift from the heart
For it is in that blood a new life might impart

Life is so precious, may your blood ever flow
Donate to your neighbor; let it overflow

Life will have new meaning, a new beginning for him
And your cup will be filled right up to the brim

Please consider donating your blood and give
It is in your donation that someone might live

If you are that someone who is begging to live
Then you'd hope someone like you would be willing to give

This is the end of my poem, I hope you sign up
May your life be rewarded by a more than full cup....

Blood is always needed any time of the year
It is in giving one's blood that you truly bring cheer

—*Rose Marie Martino*

The Graduates

We are the climbers of the Senior Class of 1953.
We climbed Idaho's Mt. McCaleb in August of 1993.

Now comes the question for all to see
Will we be able to tackle Idaho's Mt. Borah in 2003?

For me personally, and I say this without "jest"
For this old man, "This will not be my quest"!

Casual observers may lie in the sun and bask.
But it's the climbers who must know if they are up to the task.

Who is able and who has the will.
To tackle another big hill?

Years ago we all had such big dreams.
Now our biggest problem is the bulging seams in our jeans.

We all have made a contribution to this modern world.
To our detractors we have our successes hurled.

We were a class that had our heads on straight.
With our yesterdays and todays, we are still great!

The reunion was wonderful... we all had the chance.
To renew old memories, possibly an old romance.

I hope that when again we meet.
Our memories will still be sweet!

—*Alan Owens*

Unworlds

When lonely thought provokes and love is waste,
We do not care to know ourselves. Untold
We do not think: our closet minds cajoled.
A Man-O-War are we, unknown and chaste;
No trouble sticking feelers without haste
Inside ideas without substance, cold,
Devoid of greater worthiness—a mold
Where faith, belief, and love unsound are braced.
The future is but sacerdotal salve
To minds where cautions are the shibboleths:
"Consider all; be tolerant;" but apt
Aesthetics, guilty are, who do not have
Macabre Nothingness inside their myths,
Haceldama the same and Ararat.

—*Carolyn M. Goyette*

The 1108th Engineers

It was early in the forties and we thought we were tough.
We dressed in white shirts and rolled up our cuffs.
We strutted down your street and at the girls we winked,
Saying, "let me be the straw that stirs your drink".

We came from various places of many different sizes,
They were cities and towns with long lasting disguises.
When a guy named Hitler charged out of the blue,
He headed up Germany and he hated the Jew.

Our Armed Forces started saying, "We want you to join,"
Many actually chose Army by the flip of a coin.
Those of us most fortunate were assigned to Camp Gruber,
Where they worked our tails off making us troupers.

We bitched and we griped like the three musketeers,
But ended up being trained Corps Combat Engineers.
When our training was through we headed overseas,
We went to the Mediterranean and stayed for two years.

Like the Roman God and the Emperor, Neptune and Nero,
Brave boys become men and brave men become heroes.
So hats off to the 1108th for like a fire with embers,
When we are all gone who is going to remember.

—*Orville O. Munson*

Christmas Spirit

All too often in this life,
  we dwell in sadness, hate and strife,
  and wield such feelings like a knife.

Christmas is the time of year
  when Mother Earth could rest her fears,
  while all God's people spread His cheer.

Peace for all is more than a dream,
  not just a Utopian scene.
  But it requires the Human Team.

Christmas is a time for giving,
  sharing love, and hopeful living.

Blessed are those who laugh and sing,
  and pray for goodness in all things.

Christmas is a gift to all Mankind.

—*Mark G. Caso*

Christmas Gift

My name is Jackie and this is my brother Bert.
We each have a pair of shoes, pants, and a ragged shirt.
We live in poverty and we are poor, we really don't have
anything to live for.
It's Christmas day as we walk through the street, Christmas
lights hanging everywhere all pretty and neat.
My brother looked up at me and said "where to now."
With tears in my eyes I said "home" with a bow.
We live in a little car off the road,
it's very trashy but it's the best on the load.
As we walked into the small part we called the kitchen,
there sat before our eyes was half a chicken.
My mother came in we smiled at her,
she said "Let's eat" we all said "sure".
You see this was our Christmas gift.
To us it was the very best Christmas gift.
I think this the coldest winter we've had.
I'm hungry, cold, and very sad.

—*Kelly Kitchen*

Life

As our friendship grows stronger our love grows deeper.
We feel so many things, we learn so many things.
As life goes on we just flow on to another day,
living it as our last.
We often wonder why, what and how; then we just come
back to reality and find out all wonder the same.
An emptiness remains as we struggle but
we still live on as it is nothing to survive.
Day to day such a happiness lies in your heart to
realize what we all have.
The future is the mystery.
We make it what we make it.
The good the bad we make all seems to fit
in the puzzle of life and the way it works out.
Love we provide helps us strive to live as we all want to,
So that we may live on to live our dreams,
hopes and wishes.

—*Joseph Lyons*

"Ari Aldridge's `Nineteenth Birthday' In Heaven"

Ari, my grandson you are 19 in Heaven today,
We feel you are near us even though you're away.
You're really on the other side, and this for sure we know
Your Holy Spirit called you - God wanted you to go
So we have to look at it this way and meet again one day
"Like some say you're really not gone you're just from Home away!
Our loving Jesus talked to you and took you by the hand
Out of pain here on Earth into our Heavenly Land.
So have a good time with Grandpa, Gary, and the Rest
All of your family here on Earth will try to do their best.
Ari when you were here you looked around and you did see
We're sure proud to have you on "The Aldridge Family Tree"

Love always, and written by your Grandma:

—*W. Myna Aldridge*

Southwind

Buried a friend days ago —
We had a laugh the day before.
But I found peace to know
that his last breath in the end
was of my friend Southwind.

I laugh because you cringe
listening to this howling southwind.
Sometime maybe you'll understand
something greater taking you by the hand,
carrying you away is my friend Southwind.

Southwind rattles the leaves in the trees.
Close your eyes.
Feel its comfort—hear its power
feel your burden drift away on a breeze.
Listen to the chord whisper your name
blown along by my friend Southwind.

When you lay down at days-end,
Cooling your temper...
Soothing your soul...
will be my friend Southwind.

—*Gregory P. Sheik*

"Window Of The Soul"

I peeked into the windows of his soul.
He saw me standing there and open the
    Heavy laden, cumbersome,
Seldom opened door and invited me in.
    We went from room to room.
    We tarried there a while.

—*Daisy Cotton*

Robin... Robin

Tragic forties, full of dark secrets
We knew each other, barely
A friend of a friend
He belonged to her, or seemed to

He sought me out to dance
Slowly, closely at first, then tensely
Bodies already flaming with fire
He had only to take my hand

Quietly the warm sensual night
Enfolded our belonging
We had known each other's souls before
His beautiful precious body, mind so proud

On the morrow, I learned with sorrow
He had put one instant shot through his dear heart
Never to love again this life
I wonder, is he mine still
....as I am his

—*Betty Maglaris*

To Know, to Love and to Part

Dear Randy, Mary and Liv,
We missed you very, very much. The day you left was the
saddest day of all, for to know, to love and then to part cause
much suffering and pain. There never was and never will be
anyone like you.

We are sure that during countless rounds of rebirth, in this
"samsaric" cycles of birth and death our lives must have been
intertwined; for we never felt that way with anyone before and
never will there be. Our minds are still fresh as of
yesterday, the very first time we met. We will always
treasure and cherish the fleeting hours, the days, the weeks,
and the years we spent together with joy and happiness.

Though we look at life with detachment, We still love, and
still suffer pain. But, everything passes on. From moment to
moment, things do change and so life goes on. In our
meditation and in our prayer, we wish you success with health
and happiness. In your life's journey always remember that all
the pleasures that you find is to maintain a quiet mind. Keep
well and take good care. With all endearing love from Tin and
Maung.

—*Maung H. Pe*

Dimples in the Snow

With faces pressed against the window pane,
We see the trees bent low.
We squint our eyes to guard against
the brightness of new snow.

We say winter has many benefits, so,
should we complain? Heaven forbid!
We poke the fire, cook some beans,
then play checkers with the kids.

But, the little sparrow flitting here and there
doesn't know where to go,
the food we throw to his aid,
makes dimples in the snow.

His eyes catches the whole event
and he pecks down deep to eat.
He fills himself with lowly crumbs
then returns to his pine retreat.

He closes his eyes, fluffs his feathers,
as the wind blows to and fro.
We, like him, await the passing
of the dimples in the snow.

—*Frances Patchet*

Don't Forget to Pray

When we wake each morning to face another day
We should not forget to get on our knees and pray
We should thank the Lord He has kept us through another night
We should ask Him to guide us and help us do what is right
We should thank Him for the moon and stars and every flower
   and tree
We should thank Him for shedding His precious blood for you
   and me
We should thank Him for the Bible, His truth that lights our way
That guides us along life's journey each and every day
I know I thank you Lord for every blessing on me you bestow
And I pray that I'll be ready when it comes my time to go
I pray that I have so lived that you will take my hand
And lead me Dear Father to the Promised Land.

    —Margaret Neill

Seasons Greetings

When Christmas Day is drawing near,
   We think of friends we hold dear.
We wish that we were blessed with gold
   To buy gifts for all, both young and old.

But there are gifts not bought with wealth,
   The gifts of love, happiness and health.
The gifts of friends, both kind and true,
   These are the gifts we wish for you.

When Christmas Day dawns bright and clear
   With the "Prince of Peace" lingering near,
We hope that He, with love Divine
   Will shower you with gifts so sublime.

Gifts of love, happiness and health
   Far outweigh the gifts of wealth.
May you have peace and Christmas cheer,
   Good luck and happiness throughout the New Year.

    —Frances M. Doyle

Untitled

As our family approaches this Christmas season with joy,
We wish to tell you of the coming of a baby girl or boy.
In early June, if it is God's will,
We may have baby bottles to fill.
But more than that, tis a soul to raise,
That another heart may seek God's ways.
We need prayers, God's blessings and His grace,
As we, these responsibilities, do face.

    —Thomas J. Hartzler

Weeping Willow

Weeping willow stop your tears;
Weeping willow don't hide your fears;
Is it because he could not stay?
Is it because he went away?
You know he was your best friend;
You thought your friendship would never end;
You thought he would never leave;
But yet, you were deceived.
Is it because you had to part?
Or is he still deep in your heart?
Weeping willow stop your tears;
For I have something to calm your fears.
He will always love you.

    —LaJeana Chance

"First Love"

First love flowing gently, through waves of hearts beating,
Weaving magical love in disguise.
Flowing love in the air, weaving magical lights,
For the lights in their eyes, made love shine.
Like the beat of the drum, in a dead sea of silence,
Love silently grew with the pain.
Like the roar of the thunder, with scaring of lights,
Love came through the echoing rain.
Like flashing dead bolts, with fire and might,
Their hearts all ablaze, like a wild fire roared,
Their blood raging wild, through fierce heart beats, in vain.
Emotions all locked up inside.
Through ruffles of water, tears silently flowed,
To extinguish the lights from their eyes.
No hope for tomorrow, they found to their sorrow,
That love was a beast in disguise.
Hearts heavy with longing, with grief at their side,
Love faded away with the tide.

    —Yolande A. Seibert

Nothing's Perfect or Forever

Flowers are lovely you will agree,
but not perfect, well neither are we.

Each little petal tells a tale, with its color, bright or pale.
How many times in our lives have we felt, we've tried so hard
only to fail?

The beautiful flowers, try so hard to stay in bloom,
but in the end they find their doom.

Why do our lives feel so empty and incomplete
when like the flowers they could be so sweet.

We live and love give all we think we can,
it's been that way since time began.

We are you see, like the most precious flower in all the world.
when it looses its color, we often feel we've lost one another.

We ask ourselves, did we do our best? You are you I am me,
that's the way it is and always will be.

The flowers will all die and fade away,
if its meant to be, will have another day.

Like the flowers all of us in our own special way,
keep on trying taking day by day.

    —Patricia L. Amos

Romance

A turtle named Myrtle
Went walking one day
On the banks
Of a sparkling stream.
She paused for a snooze
In the glorious ooze
And had a wonderful dream.
A prince came out of his shell
In the sand
And took her in his arms.
They danced and they danced and they danced
He told her of her charms.
When she awoke it was late
Half past eight.
She went slowly home
And laid egg after egg after egg
In the foam covered loam.

    —Lucinda Blair

The Exhumation

The lifeless form glares at her.

We could have been so much more.
We're dead I can't help that.

We never lived. That's a fact.
A chance for it all, you refused
to answer the call.

Look at us now.

Lots of people here, we are truly loved.

Loved? We are pitied, a wasted talent,
these people envied.

We can have another chance for life is a continuum.

Perhaps for some, death can be final, we are the ones.

I want another chance.

I don't care about you.

I promise next time I will be my best.

There will be no next time, we are being laid to rest.
   —*Linda L. Papin*

Time

Wisps of time running thru the sand
What do I see in this vacant land
Memories of wars some so mordant
Ancient battles that were once important
The cries of men cut with sword and spear
Now there is no one to hear
As the waters lap upon the shore
Erasing all the age old lore
Magic gone, black and white
Legends of dragons slain by knights
Now only fantasy in an author's mind
Time goes on,
another dawn
What will it bring
What will be left behind
That endless thing
We call time
   —*Debbie Markakis*

Homeless

Homeless
What does it mean to be homeless?
Being homeless is not something somebody
would want to be
But, unfortunately, there are others out there
who do have to experience it every single
day of their life
There are some who try their hardest to
get a job and money,
And others don't even try, they just stand
on a street corner just waiting for somebody to come and
give them a $100
Homeless
What does it mean to be homeless?
   —*Cami Hass*

Laughter

I tried to laugh yesterday
But it never came
You cannot force the issue
I then tried it on myself
It finally came
   —*John S. Foys*

Child Of Wonder

What happened to the little child deep inside of me?
What happened to the child so fair that I used to be?
Over time and through the years, she's seemed to disappear.
Or maybe she's within me, somewhere very near.
Can I still wonder wildly of things that don't exist?
It is little things like this that I've really missed.
I want to run through green valleys, under skies so blue
like the tiny blonde-haired baby always used to do.
With arms stretched out, heart wide open, innocence so true,
I sometimes want to go back to those pleasant things I knew.
What happened to the little child that I used to be?
Is she still living somewhere inside of me?
Will she return if I let my soul run free?
Or will her disappearance remain a mystery?
   —*Allison Davidson*

Inevitable Outcome

Where has it all gone?
What has happened to the past?
What was once the wind beneath my wings:
Is now the obstacle that destroys my fire;
I'm baffled by this immortal pain
Come-and-go, come-and-go, like distraught rain
Lord give me the strength
to forgive and not to forget
But I cannot break this permanent pulpit
that leads me to the devil;
temptation is now in the lead
of an innocent life without a heed;
The fear that runs his mind,
Will be the death he will soon find.
   —*Brad Floyd*

Untitled

Into the darkness I have awakened
What I embodied now is taken
Forsaken is all that was before
I awoke inside a flesh construed form

I behold forgotten

Have come to perceive the verge of this domain
Time and space coexisting through a bliss in pain
When did my point of view drift deranged
Alone so long I matured estranged

I behold forgotten

I, the seeker, eternally searching for the self I
possessed before
Be though forewarned, I surmise a divergent time
and altered space
May be it there I commence again erased

I behold forgotten
   —*Joe Cookson*

It's Autumn

As leaves behold their sacred glow
   Of red and gold so smoothly flow
      With stars suspended in the sky
      Awaiting Winter's watchful eye.

   We bid adieu to Summer's madness
   To welcome in Fall's sweet sadness
      With scenery that is set apart
   And cherished deep inside our heart.

   I often wonder when I see
   How really great our God can be
      To create a season so divine
   It's Autumn and it's yours and mine.
      —*Frances Anne Cooney*

The Love I Knew

You are my love, my desire, my friend,
What I once was, thru you I will be again.

The wall was placed; it showed it's face.
It wasn't scaled; I tried but failed.

Barrier down, soul exposed.
 Was love lost? I suppose.
Was I right or was I wrong?
 Couldn't tell, it's been too long.
Smile appears, the mind it knows,
 Love was found, the pain it goes.

Arise,
Speculation, confusion;
 Is it love or just an illusion?
 Decisions tough,
 The way hard,
 Love is rough,
 The heart unscarred.

Fate played it's game,
 But it's still the same,
The love I knew.

   —Steven Tucker

The Grail Castle

Take me with you wherever you may go.
What if there is no joy and only sorrow,
where you are, that fond place I want to know.
To be there must not wait till tomorrow.

Annemarie, we have had so many joys
that thought of them, dear love, is the mind's tease.
Between you and my books, those worthless toys,
you and I know where I will find heart's ease.

Take me with you wherever you may go.
There I will be so filled and satisfied
that I will want no one, no thing to know.
Healing of hurts, your presence will provide.

That place where there is music in the trees;
where the light shuts out the darkness of my mind,
shimmers over the clear waters and frees
me of grim fury, that place you will find.

Take me with you wherever you may go.
To that fond place, lead me now; leave me not.
Challenge of the Red Knight I will not know.
Wound of the Fisher King, will be forgot.

   —John P. Coffey

The Crow

Oh! Yet the day has gone away
The day has now a due pay
The day has slipped into the night
The day has gone, left us in fright.
And even though the light is low
You can in the dark hear a crow.
The crow is wearing the darkness crown.
And in the distance you can hear
A crowing marvel with no fear.
And through the hills the sun
shines bright
And as it shines it breaks the night
When the sun begins to shine
The crow looks at the golden
shrine.

   —Jim Martin

If Jesus Was Never Born

If Jesus was never born,
What kind of world would it be?
There would be no Easter Morn,
No Salvation for you and me.

If Jesus was never born,
We would not know how to live.
There would be no Bibles, new and worn.
To teach us how to Love and Give.

If Jesus was never born,
God's Great Love would not have been shown.
The churches we know would all be gone.
Our sins against God we could not atone.

If Jesus was never born,
No Christmas Day would be here.
No babe, the manger to adorn,
Nothing but misery and fear.

So I thank God that Jesus was born,
And God showed His Love through His Son.
Someday we'll hear Gabriel's Glorious Horn,
And know that Victory over sin and death was won.

   —Sidney Larrimore

Peace of Mind

When I walk through the woods on a warm spring day, I listen to
what the trees have to say, as they whisper to each other how
their day has been, of the birds nesting and the caterpillar
up on a limb.

The bees which buzz through the leafy heights, the silky touch
of a butterfly's wing as it pauses in it's fluttery flight.

While I walk I can sense the startled doe hidden in the shadowy
depth of the cool under brush. Carefully I walk on by and hope
that I did not disturb too much. Then into a glade neath the
dappling sun I pause and let my being take in the beauty around
my feet as bright wood violets bow and nod in the breeze that
ripples across velvety petals.

The peace and tranquility heals my weary heart. Now I must
leave this place that God has made, and return to the chaos
of man's creation.

   —Joanne I. Fenton

The Sparrow

Something so young, wild, and free,
I couldn't pass it by - it seemed as
though it needed me.

It was so small, and yet had time to be
grown, this great big sky and beautiful world,
the small bird could never have known.

When I held it in my hands, it looked so
weak and felt so limber, it will no longer
be able to jump and leap from timber to timber.

It was so young and had yet to live - I tried
to help, it seemed I had nothing to give.

I loved the small creature - now it may be
gone, and we couldn't say good-bye - for
that small little bird my hurt pushes
tears from my eyes.

It didn't ask for much - only it's freedom
and some peace, but I noticed with its
shake from my touch - the sparrow I did
release.

   —Christie Leslie Smith

Living with You

As we grow old together as one
What we'll remember most is the fun.
We'll share laughter and tears and even our fears.
We'll hold onto each other through all our years.
We'll have doubts about one another and about life,
But we'll stay together as husband and wife.
There's something special about feeling love.
A special love joined by God above.
Love is more than a word thrown about.
It's a sharing of spirit both inside and out.
It's a joining of two separate minds.
It's a blending of two worlds, yours and mine.
I'm so glad that God let me find
The one for me in all of mankind.
To have each other is a priceless gift.
To love one another is a spiritual lift.
We'll give each other the strength we need
To be happy in life and succeed.

—*Charlene Berry*

Natalie

If I could find a word
What would that word be
True love, or just a fond memory

True love I say
As my heart seeks to find
A goddess, with you and only you in mind

Looking through your eyes
Is like looking through the sea
Playful as a dolphin and friendly as can be

Your hair soft, like a baby's skin
Running my fingers through
I'm in a dream, that never ends

Your laugh as silent, as a lone wolf's cry
Greener than the grass and bluer than the sky
As the wind's breath, takes you and I

Through your smile
Higher than the heavens, redder than a rose
Ending as eternity
Where?
No one knows.

—*Peyton Welch*

A Visit To Old Nest

How nice to see again,
The nest which I did love!
Though I'm there from afar,
To me you're still above.

I am very much pleased
In seeing my offsprings,
Living in contentment
I praise them as each sings.

And you my grandchildren,
You are all very bright;
Not only you're helpful
But also you're polite.

How are you Seven Hills?
Why are you now like this?
That storm have no mercy
But soon we shall have peace.

That strongest wind that blew
All crushed our source of bread;
But let's all be pliant
And rise again ahead.

—*Santos Borbe*

To Wonder!

Here I sit and ponder!
  What, you ask, do I ponder?
  I ponder the thought of you!

Dreaming about things that will never happen
  about laying around a field of daisies
  talking and enjoying each other

Dreaming about sitting on a boat
  watching the starry night sky slowly fade
  and the moonlight reflecting off the water

But most of all, dreaming of you
  of me holding you gently in my arms
  and talking about the future together

Holding you under a huge oak tree
  during a thunder storm in the month of May
  also on a cool brisk winter night

I can only dream these things
  because I am as close to you
  as the moon and the stars are to each other

These are but a dream, that may come true
  because I can't tell her what I feel.

—*John J. Knip III*

The Wall Between The Races

Black, white, brown, or green,
whatever the color, just let yourself gleam

Stop hating different colors
and let's love who we are.

We shouldn't have to pray for happiness
or wish upon a star.

We need to see each other
For the heart we hold within,
hating each other for our color,
will never let us win.

We need to leave the past behind,
and focus on tomorrow,
We need to work on happiness,
and forget all the sorrow.

We need to learn to love,
the world's many faces,
We need to break down...

The wall between the races.

—*Nikki Lynn Briston*

Save The Children, Save Ourselves

There must come a day
When all evil will be wiped away.

I don't want to live in fear,
I just want some peace here.

Our children's best defense
Is their fragile innocence.

However, teach them about people who do wrong,
This in turn, will make them strong.

I'm very mad and it makes me sad
That this world is oh so bad.

Just like me, you might feel the same.
But we have to realize that its not a game.

Our children are in pain and
Our whole future is going down the drain.

—*Kelly Nobbs*

The Big One

I remember that day well,
when everything seemed swell,
It was October seventeen 1989,
The time had come and the World Series was the scene
It was the Battle of the Bays,
which burned into a blaze,
For tragedy and despair was felt throughout the air,
As bridges fell and buildings collapsed
And hopelessness turned to homelessness,
And on that day at 5:04 when the ground shook
more and more,
We held on tight, and even in our fright,
We've stuck together and will help forever
the neighbor who lost more.

—*Karen Vukelich*

Warm December

It was a warm December day
When God sent his angels to lift you away
Although it's only been a short while
Oh, how I long for, and miss your sweet smile.

If I had my way, I would let you stay awhile
And grow old, just enough
To walk your daughters, Tee' and Mee' down the aisle
Only to witness once again, your sweet, sweet smile

But, now you're free, to be who God intended you to be

It's comforting to know that,
Tee' and Mee' are here with,
Our Mom, their Mom, and me
I'll always love you baby brother,

But now you're in heaven with our big brother Randy
I love, and miss you both
Yes God did send his angels to lift you both away

On a warm December day
In the very same way.

—*Patricia Waddell-Reeves*

Loving Care of Mother Earth

Do I stand in the shower 'til the end of the song
When I know for a fact that waste of water is wrong?
Do I do my dishes in a sink filled with water
When using just half could mean a cup for great
granddaughter?
Could this shirt be worn twice without washing
Do I wash and wash and wash without even thinking?
Do my tresses need shampooing every day
Or on the second day, would they still look okay?

Do I drive to nearby work or school
Then jog at night, cause boy "that's cool"?
Did I plant a tree, or chop one down
Am I protecting the air in my hometown?
Do I put deadly chemicals in the ground to kill the weeds
Will future generations moan: "What dastardly deeds?"
Do I heat my home way beyond 70
Knowing future generations will cry, "Hey, save some for me"?
Do I re-cycle, re-tread, re-use, re-do
So future generations will surely say "Thank you?"
Let's band together to save the earth
Let's concentrate on ecology for all we're worth...

—*Mary Jane Gruber*

"To Grow Old"

I know I do not move as quickly as you would like me to.
When I speak I sometimes stumble over my words.

I don't always remember the things that you tell me,
But, ask me about my first kiss, first car or first love.

You become impatient, annoyed and frustrated with me, but
Not nearly as much as I do with myself.

Like you I've had many dreams, hopes and aspirations.
Some have come true, sadly most never will.

I've made many mistakes in my long life and have been taught
Well by them. You have your own lessons to learn.

In our lives we are lucky enough to choose where we'll live,
work. Who are friends will be and who we'll marry.

We can choose to be cruel or to be kind, to be a failure or
success. But, not one of us can choose to stay young...

—*Joan C. Brown*

My Dear Parents

My dear parents are my friends.
When I was in need they had money to lend.
Now that I'm doing okay;
I hope that I can repay,
You see it's not just money they lent.
Their hearts, values and morals they sent.
For parenting they had no schools.
They used love, caring, and devotion for tools.
My parents surpass all parents I have known.
How can I repay this loan?

—*Julie Blount*

I Remember a Time

I remember a time not long ago when my life was so unhappy,
    when laughter couldn't find me.

I remember a time not long ago when the sky was always dark,
    no shining sun to fill the emptiness inside.

I remember a time not long ago when the day seemed to go on
    forever, where was night, why didn't it come?

I remember a time not long ago when the night was so important,
    I could sleep and dream of the way it was supposed to be.

I remember a time not long ago when I didn't want to be
    unhappy, in the dark, or just dreaming of a happy life.

I remember a time not long ago when I just wanted to stop being.

I remember a time not long ago when I decided to live again,
    to be me, to be happy, to be alive.

I remember a time not long ago when I found him!
    When my heart smiled, when butterflies filled me inside.

I remember a time not long ago when I gave myself to him,
    my body, my heart, my soul are his.

And when we have had the rest of our lives together, being
    happy, I will remember a time not long ago.

—*Debbie Beynon*

Free

The wild stallion runs through the hills.
He scampers and stamps with tremendous thrills.
He leaps and gallops and grazes on grass,
With plenty of time to enjoy and pass.
He races and chases with talent and grace,
There is nothing bad that he has to face.
He is like a bird flying in the sky,
Who is forever free, and high.

—*Elaina Bosley*

A Valued Family At Christmastide

Bells were tolling in Christmas day,
When little Billy Jones knelt down beside his bed to pray;

"Dear Lord, here goes with my first wish;
Please look after Benny, my goldfish.
He's been acting kind of listless,
So please make him well this Christmas.
And while your at it, please fix Fred, my toy giraffe;
The one who always made me laugh.
While biking I dropped him and made him dead,
When the spokes of the wheel ripped off his head.

And please take care of my Mommy;
She's been sad since dad got mad and went away.
And please help my brother Tommy; he's got a test, so please
get him an 'A'.

I'm at the end of my prayer, I'm just about through,
But there's one special favor I really need from you.
Even if you forget some of my other wishes, which are,
Well, you know, kind of dumb and silly,
Please, dear Lord, find my daddy,
And tell him 'Merry Christmas from Billy'. "
         —*William A. Wollman*

Confession

Time finds me treading softly thru the years

Time was
When losing a heart's desire struck
Warfare in the soul and ambition donned
Its jackboots and heaviest armor to storm
The enemy's camp and rescue thwarted dreams
From circumstance's gripping power

Time came
When jackbooted armor's galling weight
And supplies too few for lengthy siege
The savagery of warfare and futility of it all
Opened ambition's greed-blinded eyes
To what so long was overlooked

Time now
Has opened up its storehouse
Of friendships freely offered
Of beauty asking nothing
Except I take a look,
And love demanding little in return

Time finds me treading softly thru the years
         —*Irene Prater Dell*

Untitled

I am saddened, I must protest!
What makes humans act as less?
What change as we walk this planet earth
Makes our skins color the value of our worth?
What ego that we pretend to be
The color that breeds superiority.
Speak to all colors, all creeds.
What makes you think others have no needs?

That you alone bleed and ache.
That you alone to worry wake.
I wish I had a message to impart,
Would make you embrace all to your heart.
Get better now than the day before.
Hands reach to help, each day one more.

To improve we will and we must.
Remember, equally we all turn to dust.
         —*Margie Murray*

I, Too, Have A Dream

Wake up hom'
When Martin Luther's dream came alive
My dream had barely turned five

My dream was born in fifty-eight
That dream woke up in sixty-eight

Why try my dream to hate?
Let mine wake up before it's too late

Ahw pschoot you jus' layin' there dreamin'
Age creepin' up through your seamin'

To you it seems to be dreamin'

Call it a vision then
Yeah the one I see through your incision
The one you see through your division

Dream on!

What's this confusion you lay on me?
I told you, I'm trying to see
See my dream, or me?

Call it a vision then
You now agree with me, not when?

Dream on! Vision on!
         —*Karen A. Tucker*

Mother

My life was changed that March day
When my sweet, little Mother passed away

So humble, so loving, so sweet, so kind
No dearer Mother could you ever find

Seven children she brought into this world with love
Now she's at peace with the Lord above

My heart aches with sadness, for I miss her you see
The times we shared are so special to me

My eyes feel with tears when I think what I'll miss
I'll always recall our last words, our last kiss

Six weeks she suffered, her family at her side
Holding her hand with love and pride

We prayed for a miracle each and every day
As we watched her slipping further and further away

She fought so hard as she did many times in the past
Each day that went by, we feared might be her last

March 5 was the day the Lord took her away
My friend, my dear Mother, I lost that March day
         —*Gloria Marascuilo*

"Shadow Soup"

What do the large-eyed starving have to eat..............
When only long thin shadows extend from bony feet.....?!
"Shadow Soup" is their airy manna for treat..............
This is what the starving....young and old....have to eat.

"Shadow Soup" is dry.......and "empty" to the taste.......
"Nothing" is ever left....not a tiny trace..............!!
Dreams are dessert........eaten in a fitful haste........
And... "Nothing" is ever left to go to any waist........!!

"Now I lay me down to sleep"...is said for "Grace"........
Then...the sun begins to set...as it becomes too late....!
And....shadows are swallowed by their vanishing fates.....
"Shadow Soup" always leaves a bitter "after" taste........
         —*JoAnne H. Colcord*

On Growing Old

They say you must be growing old
When the room is hot, but your feet are cold;
When your silver hair turns suddenly gold,
And your breath, in the morning, smells like mold.

Your eyes are dim, though the sun is bright;
Your hearing's gone and you look a fright;
Your teeth are loose, but your shoes are tight;
You have to get up five times at night.

Your legs are weak, your back is bent;
Your "get up and go" just got up and went;
Your money is gone, your savings are spent,
And the car you own isn't worth a cent.

They laugh and say you're over the hill,
When the slightest breeze gives you a chill;
Excitement, for you, is practically nil;
Why, just waking up is your biggest thrill.

But it doesn't matter what "they" say,
Your heart is light, though your thoughts may stray;
So you just keep going your merry way
'Til the good Lord calls you on judgment day.

—*Ferne Bloomer*

My Saddest Christmas Day

The year was nineteen hundred and forty-three
    When the war, for me, became a grim reality
My training was over and a boat waited for me
    To take me on a long trip across the wide sea
Where more training was needed on ship to shore
    As I was prepared to go forth to the war
Then, like a thief in the middle of the night
    An illness tried to snuff out my light
Three months in the hospital was mighty rough
    On a small island which was named "Good enough"
Forty pounds from my body they did quickly roll
    As the tropical disease tried to take its toll
Alone, in a hospital seven thousand miles away
    Was how I spent my saddest Christmas Day

—*Harold C. Smith*

My Lover's Mistress

I sit and wonder why you say you love me,
When there is another that I see.
I know you love her too,
And baby that makes me blue,
Because I hate to see you two together,
Knowing that you'll be with her forever.
You say you don't ever want to hurt me,
But in the end that's the way it's gonna be.
At first your calls were always received,
But now I feel that I'm being deceived.
Now you've gone back to talking to her,
And to me it seems that I'm just a blur.
I've gotten so jealous that I don't know what to do.
All that I know is that my love is true.
I don't understand, I'm so confused.
What ever happened to the love we once used?
I want to love you with all my heart,
But I can't if you and her never part.
But if I get you I'd be afraid of losing you again,
To another mistress who just started as a friend.

—*Andrea Sotis*

The Power of Prayer is Evident Today

The power of prayer is evident today,
When there is no hope, it will show you the way.
Providing one rest and comfort of heart,
And peace from the many burdens you cart.
Come to God with every burden and care,
He turns not away, He's always there.
He sent His Son for you and for me,
To cleanse, forgive, and set man free.
The very first prayer you should pray,
Is, "Jesus, please, save me today."
The next step is to give Him all the glory,
Then tell others about His wonderful story.
Leave everything up to God and in His hands,
Because this is one thing that He commands.
Ask humbly, truthfully, He'll treat you mild,
If you come to Him, with a heart as of a child.
Pray for the sick and the seeds you can sow,
Pray for your church, that it will grow.
Pray when there's no hope, He'll show you the way.
The power of prayer is evident today.

—*Brad Akers*

"Today"

Where do you go when there is no where to go,
When there is no where else to be?
When time is just a thing of the past and the
Mountains are beneath your feet.

The sun is set, the day is done, there is nothing
else that's new.
The sky has went from a brilliant light
Unto a pale, pale blue.

There is no tomorrow anymore.
There is only today.

I long for the day when everything was new.
When just being alive was exciting.
When love was the most wonderful thing and the future
was so inviting.
To feel, to grasp, and to be forever free from today.

—*Jolene Drane*

"When"

When will I see you again?
When will my eyes enjoy looking at you?
When will the flames be put down in my brain
    and the bleeding stop in my heart?
When will I feel that I am a human?

I feel the pain wrapping me
    but I have not found the cure yet
I know that my cure is you,
    a touch of compassion
    a whisper of love
    a kiss on my cheek

I am not a greedy man
I do not seek the Throne of Pharaoh
    the Lamb of Aladdin
    or even the Ring of Solomon
All I want is you
You are my only wish
I ask,
    and the echo comes back to me shouting:
    "When?"

—*Mamoun Ahram*

The Times Have Changed

You are truly my child, for I see myself in you.
When you draw me your pictures, when you put on your shoes.

The world is sadly changing, things just aren't the same.
Since I was in your place, playing those precious childhood
games.

Back then you could go 'bout anywhere, there was nothin' to worry.
Now there's people who would kill you-snuff out your life in
a hurry.

Drugs and deception so often go hand in hand.
A person's rational thoughts are lost in this foggy land.

A kid used to be able to play on the swings at recess time
But now the buttons on the metal detector emit their haunting
whine.

What have the people in this world become?
Stress, money, greed, just a few of the chosen some.

If I could protect you from all this, would I be doing right?
For when I'm gone, who'll keep you in their sights?

I can only hope and pray, that you'll do the best you can.
In this tainted world, spoiled by man.
—*Jill D. Thompson*

Smile

If you feel you can't stand it any more,
When you feel the world has let you down.
Your face is shut in the door,
Don't frown.

When you feel this way just look inside,
And think about your life,
Think about the happy times before they hide,
By these happy memories you can abide.

Think about all your friends,
And your family,
They've been with you through all the bends,
You're actually lucky.

If this doesn't bring a smile to your face,
I don't know what to say.
Except to go through that door,
And smile, it's a new day.
—*Sharon McNulty*

"No Greater Gift — A Day of Rest"

'Tis a wonderful, thrilling experience
When you receive a lovely gift.
It may be for Christmas or a birthday
Or any time to give your spirits a lift.

You can't help feeling deep gratitude
To the giver who held you in esteem.
You quickly send a warm "thank you" note.
To fail to do so, you never would dream.

You are grateful for God's gift of creation,
For the beauties of nature on earth.
For the birds and the beasts and the seasons,
For the springtime which brings a new birth.

Then one more great gift was created
When the firmament and earth were complete.
The work was now finished - and God rested.
The Sabbath thus made creation replete.

The Sabbath, the seventh day, was hallowed.
God blessed it and gave it to man.
Man sometimes forgets to say "thank you".
It's the best gift since humans began.
—*Thelma Soerheide*

White Wolf Woman

There is a woman with white wolf hair
When you see her you can't help but stare.

Is she the woman your mother warned you about,
Or is she the fantasy you dreamed about?

There's magic and mystery when she is around.
Is it possible she is not earth bound?

Look into her eyes and you can see,
She holds the best part of you and me.

Compassion she has deep in her soul,
More than most can even behold.

Passion has escaped her though you wouldn't believe,
She is without what most really need.

There is a woman with white wolf hair,
When you see her you can't help but stare.

Look again, can you trust what you see,
Maybe it is the best part of you and me
—*Sandy Faria*

Untitled

When you rose in the morning too harried to see the sunrise...
When you stepped over the cat instead of stroking her...
When you heard the mockingbird, but didn't listen to his song..
When you ate from habit, but never tasted your food...
When you passed the honeysuckle and didn't know you did...
When you spoke without thinking...
When you kissed without feeling...
When you passed by me...
You missed the sweet and the bittersweet of today.
Make tomorrow a better day...
—*Leah Whitney-Sanders*

Graduation Day Reverie

Do you remember your first day at school,
When you were frightened, but tried to be cool?
New crayons, manila paper, your tools
And told, "Stay inside the lines," was the rule.

Your friends surrounded you like a soft sigh,
Sharing lunch, advise, or passing on by.
From the alpha of your early school try,
To graduation, omega, you complied.

Twelve years of friends, books, pleasures all your own.
Happy days and sad; what it takes to be grown.
The human gamut we battle alone;
Cycles of life - now, the circles atone.

Keep the thrill of this day close in your heart.
Promise you'll hold this special joy apart.
Good teachers, friends, loving family, please chart.
How proud and glad we are for this great start.

Remember it all and lock it away.
Bring it out against when you've had a bad day.
Congratulations! Superb job! We pray
That the Lord bless and keep you close, always.
—*Jimmie Nell Bush Sutton*

Eternal

Quietness of time
Embodies starlit darkness
And glorious barefoot reality-
To this my pen
Gives hushing sounds
And I am taken
To a future grace.
—*Rita Vaughan*

247

Judge

Dare you sit there and judge me
when your soul denies repentance and is not free

You —
who wrap yourself in ragged righteousness
and point your finger at me
because I live not the way
you think it should be

For all the things you say are right
you cannot begin to live my life
you cannot walk in my shoes 'cause
you are not willing to pay the dues
your ragged righteousness heaps upon me while
hiding behind the curtain of society
I say
you cannot judge me
when your own soul is not free.

—*Clara M. Carter*

My Shadow

A demon from my past has been released.
Whenever I close my eyes,
the shadow is there.
Watching over my every motion, every breath.
I only see him in the fast blink of an eye,
though only if he lets me.
But, what does it want?
It hovers over my body and soul,
influencing my dreams, my pattern of thought.
What will it take to get rid of him?
To extinguish the smoke from the pipe in his mouth?
Peace of mind, of soul, and most of all,
peace in my heart.
Give me that and you've given me life,
free of nightmares, of flashbacks and my memories.
Memories not of good times, but of pain,
on the flesh and of the heart.
If you free the shadow,
I will love you.
I will love myself. I will love..

—*Nicole D. Morin*

Untitled

A lost love
Where did he go?
And why? When did it all happen,
A different me?
Maybe.
Not to get close,
But to be closed
Was that the problem?
… Lost know?
But the real me,
Wanting him back
Feelings so far away
His name repeats,
Like that one broken record
With feelings unknown and unrecognized.
Do they exist now?
People change?
But one part still needs
For I need him too much
To let him be gone forever.

—*Raychel Bragg*

Forever Winners

My pallet is my thinking pad
Where gratitude swells my prayers to raise
Some serve Him with the body
Others serve Him with the mind
But God needs both of us:
The thinker and the working kind.

Else, we would be of the self-same mold
And I am amazed to think
That of all the humans in His creation
Each and everyone is so unique.

When I muse and ponder
I think of our earth
As a giant playing board
Where God knows all the moves
Yet, He allows each one to choose
And often we lose the game
When we could have been
Forever winners
If we had followed Jesus' name.

—*Julia Irene Hardy*

Hello Old Friend

Hello, my old friend it's nice to see you again,
Where have you been hiding?
We have a friendship to mend.

You seem different, even a little mad,
I know it's been long and I know it's been bad.
But as you can plainly see,
I am here now and will never leave.
It's good to see you,
With you around I'll never be blue.

Hello, my old friend, please come here
What's that in your eye? Is that a tear?
Please don't cry,
No, I will never say goodbye.
Is that what's bothering you,
I guess it was bothering me too.

You're leaving you say,
when will you be back,
Oh! I see, you'll return the next day.
So long old friend come back soon,
I'll wait for you on the full of the moon.

—*Kristen Biksacky*

The End of My Search

Within divinity I find my scope.
Where here I fall upon despair.
Wisdom elicit my wondrous hope for the knowledge I had not bared.
And as the deity gleamed unto me I felt my soul embrace.
From amidst the sky came the hand of He which no living matter
sees from the ultimate galactic space.
Lift me I cried and enlighten my soul so I too can enjoin with thee.
And teach me all the heavenly treasures so my intellect vacuity
can be free.
And as I listened with open consciousness He spoke back unto me.
Saying son you are but what you are knowledge of such is not
tenable
within thyself in thy present perspective form.
Live today and thy domain for which ye seek will yet be thy
selves tomorrow.

—*Ravel Sebastian Mills*

Birthday

I entered the future like a cage
where I'm supposed to reconstruct the beast
that is to devour me
from only the echo of its howl.
The shrill music of the bars:
    nerves from which a knife
    has again shaved a layer of fear;
    still one more.
    —Dorin Tudoran

Then And Now

    Wealth, riches fullness in life
Where is that pleasure that joyful bauble?
    Life a struggle causing strife
    of torment, anguish and trouble!
Ah but beautiful children a beautiful wife
is this part of the plan a part of the play?
    Where is the rest? What is completeness?
Love is said to be its perfect nearness.
      What is perfectness?
     Mostly what? A debacle?
   Without meaning without purpose?
    few to the grave go fulfilled
much like the ancient Greeks in their oracle
Little satisfied, stupified by obscene opulence
Still others seek in adventure and suppose
    That in discovery meaning will be known,
    Only to discover that all is blown
like dust in the wind and climax in a whimper
    —Thomas Loa

The Lamp

As I stand in the darkness of life,
Where no one seems to care.
I ask "Where has everyone gone?"
For I feel I am not needed here.
Just yesterday, I radiated in full brilliance,
My warmth brought happiness and cheer.
Now I realize I was only being used
By the ones I called dear.
Brighten their lives and they're my friends forever,
To their problems I always lend an ear,
But should I falter in my endeavor,
Then all they do is watch and sneer.
So take this message from a useless old lamp
And relate it to life's vow,
Make the best of friends while you can
For it's your turn to shine now.
    —Ranjeev Nobbee

I Wonder

I wonder sometimes
   Where our dears go
After they forever sleep
   In body and in mind.
After everything is finished
   For them in this world.

Sometimes I see her
   In my dreams
With her beautiful smile
   Like talking to me.

I am happy mother
   Don't worry no more
The day is coming
   When our Lord will bring us all together.
Just wait and be ready.
    —Valentina Hernandez

"Going Home For Christmas"

We are going home for Christmas,
Where the snow is so white and glisten,
The tree is decorated with bulbs and garland,
We all gather around the fire place,
and have a party.

All six kids and grandchildren were there,
Had all kinds of fruit and even pears,
with all the toys and dolls everywhere,
Hoping how soon St. Nick would be here.

Then finally a knock came at the door,
I opened up the door and fell to the floor,
There was old St. Nick,
And I almost flipped.

The children were all laughing with glee,
Now that St. Nick had appeared,
They all opened their packages, had fun by the tree
Now Christmas is over, and St. Nick is free.
    —Allahaline Grose

Let's Drop the Hate

Our world is full of hate,
which people like you and me create.
It is an unfortunate thing,
there is no reason to hate another human being.
We make fun of people because of their skin color,
but every person out there by God is
our sister or brother.
Another reason people hate is because of someone's
religion.
But I think they've made an unjust decision.
I believe every human being
Black, White, Catholic, Jewish and every other
race and religon deserves a chance to live there life,
just the same as you and I.
So lets all try to drop the hate,
before it is to late
if the hate in the world would decrease
maybe we can all live in peace.
    —Juliana Patrick

My Doctor

He comes so quietly in the room
While it still is early morning gloom
And smiles and says how do you feel
He doesn't act or look like a big wheel

To your problems he listens, they always do
And leaves a feeling of interest in you
Then tries to help as only he can
Leaves me the impression he's quite a man

Doctors are often pictured as full of greed
But manage to help in your hour of need
Folks who criticize them because of their wealth
Are quick to call him when in ill health

Sometimes they must feel sort of alone
Always in demand with little time of their own
Hospitals, office visits, and house calls thrown in
By golly I just wouldn't know where to begin

So I say to all and let us take heed
To praise those who help in our hour of need
By trying to appreciate what they try to do
To my doctor and friend this is meant for you
    —August Cornacchia

Prairie Remnants

Across the Prairie blows the pigeon grass
While the tall sunflower seems to say
"I am King of the Prairie",
As they look down upon the tiny violet's below;
And did you know
The wide-eyed owl watches for the fieldmouse
And the crow has found his meal?

Did you hear the songbirds, listen to their song;
They, too, want to belong.
Did you glimpse the white-tailed deer,
With her small fawn;
Or see a lynx high in a tree beyond?
They brave the elements to live.
The Prairie has it's gifts to give.

The past still clings here in the Prairie
Praying that the tractor and the gun
Those enemies will not invade,
But they're afraid.
But they're afraid.

—*Irene Bakker*

Spring Comes To Wisconsin

The earth has a carpet so pretty and green
While up in the trees, tiny leaves can be seen
The plum trees are ready to burst into bloom
And out in the pond the frogs sing a tune.

The robins are busy building their nests
The farmers pause - corn planting, I guess
Long Johns are all cleaned and packed away
Oh Golly Gee! The brewers play today.

The cows in yon pasture just don't look the same
They've been washed and rinsed with sweet spring rain
And out in the barn Frisky has four kittens
While at the post office you hear "peep" of little chickens

The men are just fishing, their eyes have a gleam
While up in the sky a welge can be seen
Hark! It's the wild ones honkin'!
Oh happy day! Spring comes to Wisconsin

—*Frances K. Barrett*

Nature Brings

Winds so soft mellow breeze,
Whipping through the willow trees;
Buzzing of the bees
Birds a flutter songs of nature heard all around
What a beautiful sound
Mountains high valleys low
Colors mixed the grass does blow
Such a fantastic sight to have seen.
Fresh air snows aglaire
Sounds of laughter in the air
The water I hear rippling by
I felt a splashing in my eye
The things that nature brings
Makes us feel like human beings.

—*Lanette Y. Silva*

Untitled

As he carries her to the sofa,
He lays her down gently
And kisses her cherry red lips.
After their kiss they fall deeply
in each other's eyes, blue as the sea;
When they are in each other's eyes,
He touches her soft skin
And kisses her again.

—*Kristy L. Martin*

Beloved

Wind,
Whips at my face,
Whistles in my ears,
singing the oh so dreaded song of death,
I close my eyes,
And try to ignore it,
Yet the eerie beauty of it pries them open,
I wipe the falling tears of sorrow and mourn,
from my damp and cold face.
Tears for my lost beloved.

—*Amanda Moore*

An Old Man's Muse

Camellia petal lips, cool, moist and dewy,
Whisper with breath that is fresh morning air.
Sensitive young lips that brush - oh so lightly,
First touching here and then resting there.
Ah, - waiting lips,
Rosette of Pink Perfection.

Butterfly wings, just dusted with sugar,
Fluttering against that young man's face,
Sweetness a'roving, kisses stolen at leisure,
Trembling eddies that delight an embrace.
Ah, - smiling lips,
Signet of love's dedication.

—*George W. Peabody*

Question?

In the aeons of time
Who are we? What are we? Where are we?
Fragments, specks, atoms?
What should we believe?
In some FORCE, we term "God"?
And—
In whom, or what earthly representative of HIM
Should we place our TRUST?
BUDDHA, JESUS, MOHAMMED? or
Is all of it
Some FIGMENT of our imagination?
Remember it well—
BELIEF CAN KILL,
And in the Name of God, Allah, The Almighty —
They slay and we may slay our neighbor!

—*Kenneth I. E. Macleod*

Life

Who could know joy..but for sorrow
Who could know happiness...without grief
Oh life...where is the understanding but in the daily
experience of pain
Alas....
Give me life that I may learn
Give me kindness that I may share
Give me strength that I can conquer and be master
of myself
and....
When I return....I shall begin again....
As a child, innocent and pure

—*Barbra K. Hernandez*

About a Father

My father is like a sailboat,
I am the passenger abroad.
He is the wind that fills the sails,
Sending us drifting safely to shore.

—*Jennifer Anne Szostek*

Someday

I'm leaving, I'm going far away.
Who knows where the road might take me,
who knows where I might end up someday.
Too many people to tell goodbye,
too many tears I sit here and cry.
If I came back things wouldn't be the same,
and I know that I'm to blame.
We had our times, the good and bad,
and who knows what else we might have had.
But it's time to part, take a piece of my heart,
until I come back someday.

—*Kristin K. Phillips*

Absolute Friends

Good friends are people
Who stay together till the end!

They'll always understand
When you have made other plans

They'll never depart cause
They are one in the heart

They bring cloudless sunshine
And good peace of mind

True friends are good listeners
With compliments

They share live adventure
With excitement

They bring happy times
And memories of old friends back to mind

Good friends offer confidence
That will last

They look beyond the anger of the past

Even through thick and thin we
still manage to be friends

Till the absolute end!!!

—*Artesha McGhee*

Monster

Little spider on my wall
Who swings and crawls but never falls
Your little shadow grows in the light
Keeping me up for half the night
Your only strength is my fear
Without which, you, I would smear
You taunt me, you laugh
I am the elephant and you are the rat
You'd eat me if you could
Catch me in your web you would
Knot me up and have a feast
With your friends, the leggy, hairy beasts
I'm not a fly, don't pick on me
You've shrunk my nerve to that of a flea
You scare me so, you make me cry
Swinging up above so high
Little spider on my wall
Swing and crawl on someone else's wall

—*Robert A. DeMovic*

Have Hands

I have hands to catch me when I fall,
I have pillows to punch when I am mad,
I have kittens to smile at when I'm happy,
But I need you when I am sad.

—*Celeste Fisher*

Time Heals All Wounds

Time brought about our Blessed Savior
Who taught us well, to love our neighbor
But being human as we are, forgot the
Teachings that brought us far
So time went back to a world of hate,
Torture, envy, jealousy, greed and haste
No time we have for the needy ones
We pass oh by, smiling, as tho we are having fun
Knowing well, we are leaving our work undone
If only we will join hands and love again
Our Blessed Savior will heal this land
Time of Joy will come at last, along
With Peace that everyone wished they had

—*Jettie Moss*

Based On Neverlution

The fabrication that you've been taught, an answer to the race
    confusion,
Who would have ever thought, it's all based on neverlution

Neverlution, the reward for an impotent education
A superiority complex, a "minority" fixation
Post secondary schools everywhere you look
Post secondary fools, a misleading fact in every book

Neverlution, all of the facts convoluted, most of the truth erased,
Skewed to accommodate some, the virtue entirely replaced
A version of reality that never was
A historical transposition, welcome to the neverlution, 'cuz

Neverlution, where stereotypes replace the real, where is our 40
And our mule deal? Hatred and racism at every turn, yet
People still ask, why did L.A. burn?

Sooner or later we must break free, from this dead bark on our
family tree, we will find a truth, we will find a "soul"-lution
for our real past, nor our real future occurs during the
infamous neverlution, a solution that never was

How can I ever get inspired by this historical content, that
never transpired?
Or was that the intent?

—*Michael D. Gray*

Kevin's Lash

I know a boy named Kevin
who's eyelashes stretch way up to heaven.
He would go to the barber to have them trimmed
But they always grew back longer again.

They stretch so far- for miles and miles.
But tend to bring gleaming smiles.
Sometimes they even stick together
But only when there's stormy weather.

Many people offer cash
To get a feel of the great long lash.
Now Kevin's getting a rash
From the rubbing of this monstrous lash

"What should I do now, oh gee?"
He begged and yelped in a frenzy.
"Get them pulled all the way out?"
He said, "it's too late, they're curled up my snout!"

Now poor Kevin can hardly breathe
Because his eyelashes keep growing with ease.
And his clothes are starting to clash
'Cause Kevin can't see through his miles of lash.

—*Kevin Cummings*

A Tribute To A Mother

How can I say, "I love you to a mother
Whose life motto is giving through love?
Who comes when you call, picks you up when you fall,
Whose motive is in heaven above."

Mother, you tried to help me when I was down.
My head bent low in despair.
"I knew you would come," I said through my tears.
When I call you are always there.

"I can't help," you whispered and turned away.
"You know where you've already been.
You must take that first step to help yourself.
Your help must come from within."

You saw the strength I didn't know I had.
You saw the person God meant me to be.
That a life worth living is a life worth giving.
I must grow from a seed to a tree.

I don't know what the future holds.
That is still in God's eternal plans.
I do know that He's still molding me.
But He's using your precious hands.

—*Louise C. Johnson*

The World

The world is such a beautiful sight
Why do people always fight?
If only they could see what I see
Like the sight of a beautiful tree
If only they could be cheerful and have fun
Like the brightness of the sun
The world is such a wonderful place
Like the sight of the people's face
There are many things people can get done
Instead they turn and run
The world is such a wonderful place to live
What else is there that God could give?
There is so many people we could meet
To me it's such a beautiful treat
There's one more thing I must say
Before I leave this place astray
Don't forget the blueness in the sky
For now it's time for me to fly!

—*Nichole Lynne Forton Achatz*

Untitled

I sit here staring, mentally drained,
Why do they insist on causing me pain?
I try hard both day and night
Do the things that I feel right.
Although some may not agree,
It all seems so simply clear to me.
But I sit back and watch them talk
I sit and listen, sometimes in shock.
Of all the things I've heard them say
it's the stuff on friends, that will always stay.
They talk of all the things they do together
All the fun they've had, in good and bad weather.
But also of the awful hate
That happens whenever one's angry or late
With friendships you must take the good and the bad.
And when you have good friends, you'll never be sad.

—*Lora Wright*

Untitled

All the pleasure of the conception
Equals the pain of the rejection
—*John A. Yatsko*

"Why"

Why is being different wrong?
Why is it that only few are strong?
Why can't people act themselves?
It's like they change just to impress others,
Why can't they be happy and proud, like their mothers?
Why is it that someone can be so mean?
Make fun of others and can't come clean.
Why can't we give each other the respect we deserve?
And how do some people have the nerve.
Why are people always sad?
Why are many miserably mad?
Why do they say life is a bowl of cherries?
When all people do is pick the bad pits of everyone.
Why is life worth living,
If you can't start by giving?
So think before you speak,
But don't speak all you think.
Stop asking why, all you'll do is cry,
Start thinking positive things,
And make life worth diamond rings.

—*Melissa Weible*

Don't Worry

I refuse to worry anymore;
    Why should I worry or fret?
God has promised to take care of me
    And He's never failed me yet.

When the bills are high and the money is low
    And the storm clouds are dark overhead;
I run to the rock, my shelter;
    And there He makes my bed.

And He surrounds me with protecting angels;
    And gives me a pillow of peace
And tells me He's working all things for my good
    And my faith in Him is increased.

I've seen Him work all things out for my good
    So many times in the past;
That I know everything will be all right
    If on Him all my burdens I'll cast.

So I take shelter 'neath the shadow of His wings
    And let Him restore me there;
For I know nothing will ever destroy me
    When I stay close to my Jesus so fair!

—*Joyce Murphy*

A Wise Tortoise

Slowly, so slowly, so slowly he goes.
Why so slow? I do not know.
Everyone passes him by and doesn't notice
The leisure of this green little tortoise.

Life, to them, is a race that has to be run.
But there are no less days than when we first begun.
"So many things to do, so little time,"
Is the theme for those described in this rhyme.

The tortoise moves as if he has nowhere to go.
But that is not the reason he is so slow.
He has figured it out for me and for you.
Yet there is not time to listen, too much stuff to do!

—*Heather Benfield*

Where Is Love?

I'm beginning to ask myself
Will I ever fall in love?
Is there really Mr. Right
Or am I just a lonesome dove?

My heart has been broken three times before
I don't think I could take it just once more.
Everyone says there's someone for you
But I'm beginning to wonder if it's true?

Where is love?
When will it hit you?
Will it be in a month, a week, or a year?
Or will it come when someone is near?

The questions I ask are simple you see
I really must know when love will hit me!
I know someone's out there
Thinking these thoughts.

But where is love?
Where is he?
I know he will come someday
To rescue me!

—*Josephine Leone*

Marriage

   Please remember the road ahead,
will not always be smooth.
   But to pave the way,
be faithful and true.
   Your love will grow,
But you must talk to each other,
   don't harbor complaints,
just love one another.
   Give to each other all that you have,
then in your hearts you will never be sad.
   Remember to pray for each other each day,
then you will know God's not far away.
   Greet each other with a hug and a kiss,
then you will know just how much you've been missed.
   When you are tired and just need your space,
Respect one another and back off with grace.
   Your days and then years, will be blessed ten-fold,
but work at it each day so it never grows cold.
   May God bless you both, in the years to come,
now that your no longer two but one.

—*Judith Vockroth*

An Easter Elopement

He came with pink flowers and a bottle of champagne.
"Will you marry me?" he asked and spoke my name.
I flew into his arms and kissed him,
ready to comply with his every whim.
Putting my cheek against his clean-shaven face,
I felt strong enough to win the race
for the love of this man whom I wanted.
Never mind problems. I was undaunted.
He said: "Let's get married right away.
We'll drive to Nevada. It's o.k."
In a little wedding chapel, he gave me his ring.
My heart fluttered like a bird on a wing.
Standing next to this elegant man with pride,
I was overjoyed to be his new bride.
We honeymooned all Easter Sunday.
Then we drove back to be at work on Monday.

—*Carmen Bedell*

When Salmons Return

Whenever leaves were falling much more
Wind became stronger and colder
Snow was spreading on high mountains
Salmons began leaving immense oceans

Against the current of the cold rivers
And will return home sooner or later
In defiance of cruel nets and even the death
Salmons eventually come over

By the same way they left last year
The same river they always remembered.
We don't know why they never got lost
And what emotion made them shoal together

While yellow leaves were floating to the end
Salmons were returning to their love again
A new generation will be given birth
And taken care until they grown then

Salmons return home at the early winter
And I the refugee return whenever?
Only shoal together the Salmons; separate and wander the
refugees alone? From the hell my whither is the vast horizon

—*Song Huong*

Roots and Wings

A fragile, delicate flower sits peacefully upon the
window sill. Its few pale-colored pedals, contrasting with
the dramatic green of the luscious leaves, make it a lavish
sight. Most wish only two things, "Give me roots, And give
me wings." The flower has been given both. Roots for
grasping what is there, to cling to the mighty earth and
provide solid ground below. Wings, therefore the flower can
spread to new heights, flourish, and live its dreams.
Eventually, the sun's bright, beaming rays pound hard upon
the ethereal pedals. Soon, the once flourishing life that
was so carefully planted in the pot begins to wilt. The
vibrant green turns incredibly dull, and lifeless. The
roots no longer firm, and supportive. It slowly wilts, and
soon, is gone. As the life of this flower is reminisced, it
is noticed that great things are often unappreciated until
they are gone, and although it has perished, the great
flower lived a wonderful and full life because of two
things; It had roots, and it had wings.

—*Amanda L. Vandervort*

Dream Chance

The dark clouds that always tend to surround,
"Winds of change," whispering the silence of sound.
   The skies engaged in motionless swirls,
   ever-so slowly, begin to be gone.

"Sunshine of future," desiring to dawn.

   Vanishing are dreams once embraced by thorns, .
   my heart no longer tattered and torn.
From many lessons that have been shown,
an inner wisdom has grown.
   For the dreams to rekindle,
   and rise from the ashes.
Designing a world once more,
with colorful splashes.
   All that I thought forever lost,
   to begin anew with you.
My love for thee, destined to be,
beyond the realm of Infinity.
   Now a passion forever adrift,
   as fated winds awaken.
Silent tears in endless storm,
for reality has been taken.

—*Michael A. Kotlinski*

The Visitor

Blessings on thee, little mouse
Winter guest in my warm house
But don't make me like Mother Hubbard
Shun the foodstuffs in my cupboard
Take the morsels I leave out.
They'll make you healthy, sleek and stout.

You and I can coexist
Safe from snow and rain and mist
If only you will roam at night,
And in the day keep out of sight.
Greed, perhaps, can make you fat,
But then, wee mouse, I'll get a cat.
— *Patricia Thompson*

The air is cool, the days are short
Winter is on its way
Snow, snow, snow is all I can say
Nature has a mind of its own,
Maybe winter is the bitter of it all
Then Beauty in the Fall
Trees shedding leaves is how I can see,
a way of losing and then growing from thereon
Summer sun shines and warms many hearts, fills
me with joy
Like a child with a new toy
Spring brings music from nature to me
Life and nature has cycles for us to see
— *Robin Eden*

"I Will"

I will kiss the smiles you give to me,
wipe the tears from your eyes.
Hold you close within my arms,
and hear your soft sweet sighs.

I will touch your skin with warm embrace,
reach inside your mind.
Take all your hurt and pain away,
and give you love so fine.

I will give you all the love I have,
forever and in time.
Because my love my heart is yours,
and yours I know is mine.
— *Annette Arkema*

Unspoken

I lay awake staring at the ceiling
  wishing that you were here by my side.
I would give anything to hear your voice again
  and feel your body next to mine.
I know that this will never be
  and yet the wish never leaves my heart.
All the time we shared together and all the laughter
  was worth all the walks in the rain.
They say that love grows dim in time and that time
  heals all wounds,
But I feel the wound grow deeper and the love grow stronger
  with each day that passes without you by my side.
You taught me how to laugh
  when all the laughter had fled from my world.
You taught me how to love
  when my heart had grown cold.
There were times when you knew what I felt before I did.
  Because of this, I know that you knew that I loved you
with all my heart and that you were the only one for me.
  I will always love you. This goes unspoken.
— *Shannon Timbs*

Spirits Calling

Spirits calling into the night
Witches caldron boiling bright
Brewing up my best love spell
I know this recipe very well
My spirit joins yours tonight
Underneath the moonlight
Just wish for me and I'll be there
With lots of fun we both can share
I'll catch you before you fall
If you want me now just call
Through the wind your message is sent
Reminding me of the time we spent
Spirits calling into the night
Come to me now the time is right
My spirits collecting your thoughts of me
Waste no time come and see
My spirits calling out to you
Listen to them your wish is mine too
The moon shines his light for you to follow
Follow the voice my spirits calling
— *Deborah Herzog*

Little Angel

Little angel coming from the stars
With a sparkle in her eyes
When I looked at her face,
I caught the splendor of a sunlit sky
That put my heart so at ease, that rocked
My soul in the fresh wind of the autumn leaves,
Like the clouds I must move on little angel,
Sings a song, she melts my heart like fresh
Winter snow, I was blinded
By her radiant glow
She comes to me to no surprise
She's forever imprinted in my mind
— *Steven W. Henry*

"My Friend and I"

The "Poet and I" - a friendship all abiding,
With a trust from the depths of my soul;
Speaking as one, flowing freely - never hiding
Thoughts or feelings - a bonding truly whole.

The words from the poet and from me are the same,
They couldn't be different now, could they?
We both become caught up in our little game
Of "make believe" — what should we say?

But once in awhile, as we sit, and ponder
The beginning - the middle - or the end,
We stop, we go back, erase - and then wonder
If we will ever come up with the right blend!

We aren't the judge and jury, we can only hope
Our results are pleasing - we do try;
Laughing or frowning - such a broad scope,
We write to please - this "poet and I!"
— *Agnes M. Dobias*

My Brother

My brother is so special to me,
I know how much he still really
loves me.
I remember the past,
And I wish it still could last.
When I remember how he was
so very strong,
it makes my face grow very long.
— *Laura Buchholz*

Alone

You walk alone
with a wretched face
nobody beside you
to love or to guide you

You're just a kid
so sweet and so kind
unsure of what you did
of why they beat you this time

You crave to be protected
to be held and feel strong
wanting not to feel neglected
and to surrender the pain you've endured for so long

—*Sarah Elizabeth Skavinski*

Life Journey

Life journey is a beautiful place to be.
With all God beautiful creations to see.
It's not because I've been so good, nor
Is it because time has just stood still.
Because the creator seen a need to be
The beautiful world that he made was for all to see.
And in time all things will be, as God has for you and me.
He said love yea one another, never have a desire
To hurt thy sister nor brother. Be kind, gentle, noble, honest
and free. And never doubt that Jesus didn't
create life journey a beautiful place to be.
Sometime we become so tired, God new that it would be.
That's why he said, take up your cross and follow me.
Everyday as I trod this road ahead, there is always
A change waiting for me. I dread not to get weary, nor try to
find a short cut. There will be no glory divine, I'm only
passing thru this one time trying to follow God road map. And
stay in line. I don't no how long it will be before this
journey end for me. But as long as I can see, life journey is
beautiful place to be.

—*Lemma W. Judkins*

A Beacon In Our Town

The edifice of St. Peter's erected in 1907,
with beauty and strength and spires upward to Heaven.

The elements and time have cause much damage to her exterior
    beauty
thus we must come forth to support and restore, because it is our
    duty.

A task of paramount and a monumental feat,
we must constantly pray and support until it is complete.

And when the time has passed and the renovation is done,
We will humbly celebrate to Father, Spirit, and Son.

Know that it is our privilege to become a vital part,
By our giving and prayers deep from within our heart.

The building itself must not be the reason,
For celebrating throughout each liturgical season.

The art and beauty within St. Peter's walls,
Depicting mysteries of our faith and Christ so strong and tall.

For the faith and love within your heart,
Surpasses all earthly beauty of any worldly art.

Prayer is heard by God in churches rich or poor,
So let us thank God for St. Peter's as we enter through her doors.

—*Rose M. De Fede*

"The Old Apple Tree"

'Twas an old apple tree on the slope of a hill
With branches stretched far and high
With leaves of green and apples of gold
Against the blue, blue sky.

Never were apples half so sweet
Whether golden, russet or red
As those that fell on grass beneath
When we shook the branches overhead.

In the days when we were children
Our hearts were light and free
Our days seemed never ending
In the shade of the old apple tree.

The old apple tree with one low branch
On which a rope swing hung
We spent hours swinging to and fro
A meeting place for friends to come.

Those days have been and gone
But when an apple tree and swing I see
I long for those childhood days
That were made especially for me.

—*Alta M. Martin*

The Hills Are Alive

The hills are alive
With bright hues of autumn,
On palettes of green, russet, orange and gold.

The hills are alive,
Picture-perfect viewing,
In another week
They will 'peak', I'm told.

If you haven't yet,
Feast your eyes on the scene,
That occurs every fall.
You'll not soon forget,
The sheer majesty of it all!

The hills are alive,
Dressed for chill October;
Leaves luster like jewels
In a breezy crown.

When hills look alive
In their royal-robed splendor,
You'll know the best show
Did arrive in town.

—*Alfred Colo*

Imagine This

Somewhere out there, there's a magical world,
with houses that are round and clouds that are twirled.
With animals that talked like they came from a cartoon,
and a pasture dressed with purple cows that jumped up
over the moon.
Somewhere out there, there's a world of great miracle,
where hyenas were boring and turtles hysterical. Where
there's candy for dinner and meatloaf for dessert; where
students go to school to teach and the principal to flirt.
Somewhere out there, there's a world of great mystery,
where the future is the past and the present day is history.
Where cars go flying around the sky, and children dream of
pet butterflies.
Somewhere out there, this world does exist, and for you
to find this destination. Go west, make a left, and then
across the bridge, and go straight into your imagination.

—*Holly Pettit*

The First

When you planted the seed, you spoiled it
   with love
When you planted another, you forgot about
   the first.
As the first got older, you deprived it of
   happiness
One day you noticed how tall and beautiful
   the first had grown, you pulled it
   from the only place it could feel safe
You set it in a vase, where everyone
   could praise and admire it.
After a short time you just discarded
   it from your life and left the
   first with no known explanation
You broke the first's hearts and you'll
   never know how much it loved you
Despite all the pain you caused.

     —Amy Mara Johnson

Lost Memory

When I was young and care free
   With never an ache or pain.
I had a wonderful secretary,
   By the name of memory lane.

She was always on the ball
   And her files were as neat as a pin.
And when I called on her to help me
   She was right there to begin.

Oh, how those years are rolling away
   Memory and I are old and gray,
She can only work part time today,
   It's getting harder for her to stay,

Memory finally went away.
   I miss her more and more each day.
I can't find things I put away.
   She must have taken them yesterday.

Growing old is surely no fun
   When you have to depend on every one
To help you find lost memory
   With a special prayer to Saint Anthony.

     —Evelyn DeCristofaro

Regrets

Bars and walls, live in a cage
with no children, wife or friends,
where we suffer, where we pay..
our sins, our mistakes...

Oh my God! why, why, why?
when there were so many ways..
I had to choose the wrong, the bad..
hey! lost thoughts, sleepless nights...

Look around and try to find..
anew hope, a friendly face...
dreams of freedom that never come
and no way that take me back...

If I could start again..
and again have mom and dad,
fall in love and find my friends,
go to school and try to learn..
all those things I never tried,
and say no to thrills and fiends.
who gave me these walls and bars.

     —Nestor Mir

House and Home

Home is not a sterile place,
   With plaster walls and empty space;
But hearts and lives with joy and pain,
   Sunshine - warmth, plus cold and rain.

Our house, we know, is brick or wood,
   With rafters, beams and kitchen hood;
It holds our "things" and keeps us safe,
   But "house" is not a sacred place.

Only "home" can qualify,
   Where family grows as time goes by;
Where children play, and hopes are born,
   And life begins anew each morn.

A house alone is mighty fine,
   We love its strength, its size, design;
But some will know who read this "tome,"
   A house, alone, is not a home.

     —John A. Christensen

Jeweled Hair

Snow is falling clear.
With some consistency and snow flakes meld
And mound,
Until we have hidden valleys, secret caves
To be found.
Icicles draping o'er the trees . . .
Trees, white limbed, robed in snow,
More beauteous than royal regalia can know.
Crowned with icy jewels most rare,
Shimmer in the night, in winter's lair.
Lit only by snow and phantom stars,
I too go out to be so garbed
With icy jewels in my hair.

     —Grace Graham

Holiday Spirit

As we drive our lighted streets, my children's eyes grow wide,
with the anticipation of Christmas, their about to burst inside!
The colorful lights glowing in the night, are so beautiful to
see, and I love the sound of my youngest, as he yells, "Ooo-Whee!"
The holiday spirit is everywhere, all places that you go,
but there is that very special spot, that everyone should know,
I'm speaking of the Angel Tree, to help out some one,
who might not be as fortunate, as your daughter or son.
Wouldn't you like to be a part, of making a child happy to see,
that there are truly giving people, such as you and me?
Myself I can't imagine, no Christmas at all,
so yes, I will be giving, an Angel a call.
I pray that all your angels, hanging on a tree,
Christmas morning, on your faces, smiles there will be......

     —Wendy Hall

The Essence of Love

Oh, my beloved, come savor the depths of my soul
   with the sweetscented sage of Your sting.

I've waited a lifetime to know You.
   Take, and love me, use me completely,
like a candle that's lit by the Fire of your love.

   As I lie here in halfcrazed ecstacy of Your nearness,
knowing there will never be another lover like You.

I understand completely the love of a man.
   There is no comparison.

     —Billie Snyder

I am the Sea

Tossing and foaming, from the gates of the wind,
With white-capped frenzy, my wrath does descend
Toward the beach, where your sand castles wait,
Crumbling beneath the gaze of Fate.

Booming and crashing, my waters rush in.
Gulls take wing, with the odd pelican.
I blast upon the rocks of the shore,
Scatter the crabs away by the score.

Where are you now, with your hopes and yearning?
My force now fades, the tide is turning
   me back upon myself, fragrant, deep,
Where dolphins play, but sharks never sleep.

I am the sea, the right hand of Fate.
I am old and jealous, deep and great.
I am the sea, your cities are tall.
Atlantis is gone. Miami will fall.
        —*Mike Miller*

Winter's Guest - Spring

The sky turns gray at mid-day as though the night were near,
With wind howling like a man in pain, or maybe just in fear.
A single tree's bare branches stretch up to reach the sky,
But gusts of wind divert their reach no matter how they try.
A bird caught and suspended by winds that thwart it's fight,
Seems to waft helplessly in space with no harborage in sight.
The wind begins to toss around what looks like 'feathered
rain', and soon the ground turns sparkling white along the
coastal plain.
A man, bent shouldered, wrestles the unyielding wind and snow,
A 'wretched one of the earth' he is, without a place to go.
He slowly plods along the drifts to disappear from view,
And the bird that fluttered helplessly has gone to await his
cue of bright sunshine with singing wind and wondrous shades
of green, and dunes that sprout new grasses and wild flowers
bloom supreme. There, a single bird's concerto is transported
by the breeze, a man, bent shouldered, listens 'neath the
lushness of the tree.
        —*Alice J. Calhoun*

While We Are Here Lets Pray

   The beauty of the world comes from
within its the heart and soul of
every woman and man. If we gave a
little today it would be here tomorrow.
But still the love shared needs to
come from our heart and soul.

   While we are here on this
planet in need we should pray to
help the next generation succeed.
In our hopes and our dreams I
know we can make a difference.

   Come be apart of this glorious
moment in time, reach from the sadness
of the world, and when the eagle
flies the last journey of its life.
It needs to lift its wings into flight
and head for the fathers light.
Let's pray for the beginning and
end of tomorrow and today.
In hopes of America's children will make a change.
        —*Brandy G. Sims*

This Old House

This old house is not a home
without a family in it

It's just not a home
until with love you fill it

Although it stands here with majesty of structure
It just isn't a home without a father and mother

The rooms possess an elegance and grace
but it just isn't a home without a child's smiling face

A home isn't built of mortar and stone
These things will vanish and someday be gone

Fill it with love right from the start
The life of a home, comes from the heart
        —*Theresa W. Hardin*

Composure

A calm surface at rest
without even waves to show
how this unnatural stillness
is at odds with what is below.

Much is not seen by the eyes alone
this surface at rest is full of turmoil unknown
the currents are swift and churning within
but the face carefully composes what is trapped below the skin.

Many a clue has tried to escape
from the dark lonely prison where secrets are placed
as the waters surface separates what is above and below
the face carefully controls what others may know.

Even the air morns the pain of a friend
respectfully not blowing the water with its wind
the wind will not push with the force of its air
wisely knowing some things just can not be shared.

This calm surface is but a facade
to help mask the wounds the pain has caused
for this wall of composure is an emotional shield
standing guard until the pain has healed.
        —*Christine Guzzetti*

Time Flies

   We walked together for a far,
Without ever letting go,
We've had our bad times then and now,
Without letting each other know,
We've been together for laughter and tears,
Without ever having a frown,
We've been though closeness and through fears,
Without letting our love drown,
We've been through all that we should,
Without mistaking each others heart,
When we had our problems we both understood,
Without ever being apart,
We now sit and remember the past,
With laughter and tears in our eyes,
We now know it goes so fast,
Without knowing then...
   time flies.
        —*Shannon Casdorph*

Esoteric Man

Everywhere and nowhere
I find myself lost
No measure to expenditure no cost to loss
Returning my memories love healing Anniversaries
Time, sweet sorrow of time.
        —*Charles Melchiorre*

257

Why It Hurts To Love...

Love in my eyes just isn't fair,
Without you in my life or being there.
You always said you'd never stop loving me,
Your feelings have changed for my eyes can see.
I'll never forget the sweet things you'd whisper in my ear,
All you said from your heart removed all the fear.
But now its back the fear of us being apart,
The feeling of you being here I'll always hold in my heart.
I want you back is there anything I can do,
To remove my loneliness and to be back with you.

—*Christina Marie Coleman*

Image of a Snow Queen

Image projected, role portrayed of a Snow Queen
Woman of cool control, no emotion crosses your face.
Depth of your eyes cold as the sea, green as Emerald ice.
Blonde cascades down rigid back,
Chiseled features of marble statue.
Frigidity for all to see. No need for any man have you.

Snow Queen, from what land do you come?
That no man deems you worthy?
What has turned your blood to ice and your face so cold?

In undertones and whisperings, spoken of as calculating.
In harshness judged for your unbending strength.

Snow Queen, from where you stand,
You reign down sleet, snow and ice on every man.

—*Paula Karen*

I Am

I am a very emotional girl that loves horses and monkeys. I wonder what I will be like when I grow up. I hear the flapping wings of the birds that come to pick at my feeder. I see the never-ending wonders of the sea crash upon the rocky shores. I am a very emotional girl that loves horses and monkeys.

I pretend that I can swim like a whale. I feel the waves of the roaring ocean slapping my body. I touch the endless rainbows that lie above the golden clouds. I wonder if the countless wonders and beauties of the world will ever die down to nothing. I cry for the poor, starving, homeless people that exist in the whole world. I am a very emotional girl that loves horses and monkeys.

I understand all of the aggravation and frustration of losing. I say, even if man is not your best friend or hurts you, that gives you no right to hurt them. I dream of far away places that now, as we speak, await me. I try in all ways to help the unfortunate people in need of my help. I hope that all Americans, as true Americans, fight to the top and never give up. I am a very emotional girl that loves horses and monkeys.

—*Aleea Brooks*

Escape!

Reading my poems under a cold fluorescent light,
Wondering why they were written.
With sore eyes closed, sitting in the dark.
As traffic noises penetrate the shop walls.
Every man has a failing.
Mine is writing verses, hoping they'll be read.
Triggered by seeing a loved one,
or thinking of one that's gone,
a landscape - autumn colors or wintry snow.
With pencil and paper it's easy to find
a place, unfrequented by men.

—*Nicola Froio*

The Day I Died

I stand here to watch you lay still
Wondering, will I ever get rid of my chill?

I'm going to put a note in your hand
Hoping that you'll understand
And a kiss on your head
I'm leaving to lie dead on our bed.
I left you in sorrow
Hoping I'll see you tomorrow.

—*Sharee Mason*

Untitled

Words are dangerous. Handle them with care.
Words are words. Avoid their definitions.
Of wordy false assumptions be aware
and fortify with words your prime ambitions.

I catch attention with a melody.
Then I contaminate your thoughts with words
and naughty deeds that words at times suggest.
I leave you to imagine all the rest.

I'm having so much trouble arguing
with writers I seem to understand clearly
that I had better not try to understand
the many writers I don't understand
for fear I begin to quarrel with them.

If I don't understand, I should teach
and hope my pupils will enlighten me.

I never knew, until yesterday,
how little I knew about everything;
but now I am beginning to resay
and life again is more interesting.

—*David P. Boyd*

Perseverance

A tree stood on a hilltop
worn by wind and rain

The branches gnarled and cracked
its body racked with pain

Life, it seemed, had left this tree
Yet it stood sad and forlorn

For the roots still grasped the mother earth
The life within retained

A virgin bud—evidence—
That indeed life did remain.

—*Ken Chiasson*

My Escape, the Garden

When I was a child, had not a friend,
Would play in the garden, touch feel the stems.
Sit to wonder how the flowers grew,
Learned to name colors, how time flew.
Too young to know, my escape was the garden.

Grown into a woman, had problems as such
Would go to the garden, feel peace abide.
To water, tend them, their glory unfold,
Birds and butterflies, birds acting bold.
Are with me, in my escape, the garden.

Now I am older, my steps ever slower,
Flowers, perfuming the air, blooming,
Eyes are failing, the flowers a blur,
Memories are forever, have them within
Fear nothing, in my escape, the garden.

—*Jean Antonacci*

Paranoid

You see me walking down the street,
Ya, I walk to a different beat.
Lock your windows — lock your doors.
You follow me around in your stores.
But its' not me that robs you blind,
But I cause you stress just by being in line.
See me in your corporate halls,
How I'd manage to get behind your sacred walls.
Making money just like you.
Oh, me oh, my just to what to do.
Blackman rapping to the crowd.
Police come cause someone thinks we're rowdy and loud.
The paranoia strikes far and wide;
But not for me, I've got my pride.
Proud to be just who I am
And about your paranoia I just don't give a damn,
For God made both you and me,
Yet I'm still struggling to be free, in this land of Liberty.

    —Ronald E. Campbell

The Challenge

Death in angel town: Rot in the apple
Yang buying America, all that they can handle
Starving children, a shame to mankind.

The haves', have choices: the have nots', have none.
Some say, 'If we do not change, our children will pay,
I say, 'We are the children and we're paying now.

The eagle and bison are all but history.
The dolphin, porpoise, elephant, lion, tiger, whale
The most intelligent brothers that we have on earth.
Must be preserved and protected, our families as well.

The great bear is dead, walls are still falling
We try to avoid the debris, peace is a-calling.

We must rescue mother earth within our own lifetime.
Cannot in good conscience poison the future.

Are we to take the proper steps, make the right choices
to insure the health of the world and our children?

    —Dennis K. House

"As I Wait"

Good morning, my precious children,
Yet another day I give for you;
Take it, and use it wisely,
for not many more, are you due.

Through the nights, I've given you the stars,
And for your days, I'll give you the sun;
Go spread the words I have given you,
So many hearts, we have not won.

I have given you all there is to give,
Though in your foolishness, you will not accept;
My greatest gift is eternal life,
Something in which, with me you shall live.

There is nothing that you can say or do,
That could fade my love away;
If in repentance, you can come to me,
And in prayer, start each new day.

Precious children, heed these words I say,
For very soon, I come to bring you home;
For should your hearts belong to me,
The fires of hell, you shall never roam.

    —Charlotte Schoubroek

Dancing

It's a dance I've never danced before.
Yet every time I'm with you I redance it for the first time.
It's soft, slow, and passionate.
I know your smell, your look, your touch, your taste, and
your sound.
I rediscover each of them one by one.
Each time I redance my dance for the first time with you.
I sacrifice everything yet nothing each time I dance for the first
   time with you.
I feel so much like an angel dancing a lovers dance for the first
   time.
When I dance with you.
I'm awake yet dreaming when I'm dancing for the first time with
   you.
I've learned the dance well, yet remember nothing.
It's as if I'm floating,
floating upon a cloud of ecstasy.
Never to be set down on firm ground.
When I dance for the first time with you.
It's a dance I've never danced before.

    —Ricci Honaker

Chased By Pain

I tried to run from the pain that chased me
yet every time I turned a corner it's breath was against
my cheek melting my skin
I tried to push the force away but it just cut my hand
left me bleeding, draining my blood onto the snow
where the precious color of white turns to devilish red
as I trip over a snowflake and fall flat on my face
I tried to pick myself up, hide for a few moments
free to catch my breath, not for long till the pain is near
pulling my hair, twisting it, till I scream so loud
that stars fall from the sky
I kick at it like a dog who just wants a home
instead of whimpering and crying it's puppy dog eyes out
then like a gunshot in the distance
striking a poor defenseless little animal
the moon is gone and I'm left all alone in the dark
screaming for a savior, some kind of angel
as the pain leaps on my face forcing me to the ground
as I close my eyes and die.

    —Dina Dombrowski

Dinosaur

The sun is gone
Yet makes its presence felt
By gift of token fire which rages across the sky
In blood red hues
Extending its fingers into the murky dark above
The trees and hills
Form ragged demarcations of starkest black
And clouds stretch like dark smudges
Left by some ancient hand
A primordial scene reborn from item before man
When dinosaurs roamed the earth
But now is man's time
Omnipotently
His ambitious remains extend beyond tar pits and bones
He requires the world as his grave and tombstone
'Here lies man
Ruler of a world
Once ruled by dinosaurs'

    —Kara Gamble

Circles

Today while looking ahead I see yesterday,
yet when I look back I see it again.
Though afraid that I am in the wrong,
I trudge forward, only to realize that
I am only going backwards

Due to this revelation, I decide to
climb higher on the mountain of life,
and continue to walk, but along a new
and more reveling path.

Even though afraid of this unknown path,
I continue to go forward because I
do not want to repeat what I have
already done.

After a while on this path; I realize,
again, I am back where I started.
　　　　—Richard G. Linden, Jr.

Shout

A certain resurgence of hope,
Yet you feel as if you are warranted
By an unknown centrifugal force.
You scream out, or do you?
Yeah, you scream out with every ounce
Of wind remaining in your poor hollow body.
You scream as if you're at the peak of
Mighty Everest.
The heat is on, more pressure to be heard
Than to hear.
The pounding inside your skull is becoming
Almost unbearable, undying.
Alas, you break that hovering barrier and
A slight, muffled quenching sound is heard.
But for some reason you are the only one
To actually hear it. Why, damn it, why?
You scream out again, no one to hear you,
For whom can be heard within the confines of
A dark, lonely casket beneath the solid granules
Of the wet earth.

　　　　—Jeannie Bearb

In a Whisper and a Blink

When I'm speechless and thoughtless and lonely through the day.
You always seem to come to mind in a very warming way.
Then all else seem to fade and is distant in my view.
I guess nothing really matters, once my thoughts gain sight of you.
Then my mind start to take me back to a time and place that was.
When everyone was happy and content for whatever cause.
My heart begin to fill with joy as my eyes are filled with
　　tears, for having some time together again and for having
　　all of those years.
But when my thoughts return to now my heart begin to sadden.
For I couldn't have remembered then, if it had never happened.
I'm thankful for the lonely times when I can just sit and think.
It's then that I can bring you back to me in a whisper and a blink.
　　　　—Cheryl L. Rosemond

You

You are my day, and night,
You are my sun, and moonlight.

You are the twinkle in my eyes, the love in my heart,
And I know for a fact, that we will never part.

You will always be the key to my life,
And someday soon, I hope to be your wife.

You hope our love will stand strong, I do too,
And in my life, my one and only will be you!
　　　　—Crystal Patrick

Here...

I am here... because you are here,
You are here, hopefully, because I am here.
We're not there... but, we'll always be
　　somewhere.
With you... I could be almost anywhere.
Without you... simply nowhere.

So, while you are here and I am here,
Let's not worry, why we're not there.
Let's just think about being together,
　　somewhere.
With a glass of good cheer and forever near.

"Where... did you say my dear?"
　　　　—Andrew J. Hanacek

I Miss You

Tho your life has changed and you are far away,
　　You are in my thoughts most everyday.

I pray and worry, fret and stew,
　　And can only hope, things are right for you.

Then memories flash thru this old mind of mine,
　　Memories of those long ago happier times.

I miss all the things we used to do,
　　I have to believe, that you do too.

Maybe someday our paths will cross,
　　And we can regain some of the things we have lost.

Till then my dear child be happy I pray
　　I love you so much is all I can say.
　　　　—Jean McNutt

Assumptions

You assume because I am white that I lower my eyes to see you.
You assume because I am white that everything I say to you has
　　some undercurrent of prejudice.
You assume that I see your intelligence lacking; your manner
　　undesirable; your personhood untrustworthy; your feelings
　　and dignity irrelevant; and your customs and heritage
　　insignificant.
You assume because I am white that I am not worthy of your trust.
No matter what I call you, you react with suspicion.
If I call you black, you assume it's derogatory.
If I don't call you black, I'm insensitive and have a hidden
　　agenda—that I have a problem with multicultural issues
　　because I can't even say the word "black."
I wish you understood, your assumptions frighten me.
I have no desire to slight or offend.
The prejudice is yours, not mine.
I don't want to call you anything save your name.
What would it mean to you if I wanted to call you "friend?"
　　　　—C. Susan Persinger

Faith

In times of sickness and alone
When you think you're down and nobody's home
But in your chest there's a heart like stone
Where faith comes in
Then everybody's home
But in your mind you say that's no
The Lord will show you how to go
For you are the person like the stone
Remember faith is there, where everybody goes
So believe
And faith is where the Lord shall be
　　　　—John DeFrancesco

And You Didn't Even Thank Me

I picked you flowers from the garden I grew,
You became teary-eyed and you sneezed.
I gave you chocolates I had specially imported,
You got hives and you scratched.
I stayed up all night and wrote you a poem,
You said it didn't rhyme.
I found you a poor, homeless Chihuahua,
You shrieked, "Rat!" and ran away.
I serenaded you with a song I composed,
You told me I was tone deaf.
I slaved over a hot stove and cooked you dinner,
You asked for some Pepto-Bismol.
I bought you a ring with my life's savings,
You cried, "Eww! 14 Karat."
I got down on one knee,
You yelled, "You're kneeling on my toes!"
I gave you may heart,
And you didn't even thank me.

  —*Tuanvu Le*

Shattered Dreams

In my dreams, there was perfumed air
You brought me flowers
At that moment I thought you cared.

The dream I dreamt was far from true
The love you showed, was all I knew
You cast me aside, like a wounded hound
Another woman and you was what I found.

All your love was nothing but lies
I thought back on them
With tear filled eyes.

When all along
You planned you schemes
And all that's left for me
Are shattered dreams.

  —*Angelica LaShore*

A Message To My Sons

We brought you to this world, out of wonder and of love;
You came here to us, like a blessing from above.

Often I've wondered, if that decision was smart;
To bring you to a world, that's falling apart.

But what's done is done, and I have no regrets;
You're two fine boys, you're as good as it gets.

You've been on this earth, for just a few years;
And already faced troubles, and cried many tears.

I won't always be here, to answer you're questions;
But I can offer you, a few suggestions.

Always be honest, faithful and true;
Always think of others, in all that you do.

Be kind and gentle, to all living things;
You'll find joy and contentment, is what this brings.

And when my time comes, and my life is thru;
I hope you'll remember, the things I taught you.

And one last thing, I hope you will keep;
Is my love for you both, that runs so deep.

It's here today, tomorrow, and even next year;
It's here forever, my two sons so dear.

  —*Dad (Mark Hand)*

Heartbroken Love

In the sunshine or rain
you can feel my pain
You can see the tears coming
down on my lonely face
In that one special place
In my heart so deep
oh, the lonely times I cry myself to sleep
If only you can see
the trouble you've given to me
On my painful face
You can see the heartbroken love.

  —*Teresa Patz*

The Touch of God

You have but one life to live;
You can make a difference from day to day,
In your work and what you give,
If you make connection with God and pray.

God's magic touch can come through you,
Who have faith and accepted his plan.
He'll guide you in what to say and do,
To help those who are lost, understand.

Strengthen your faith forever in God;
Press on toward the highest calling each day.
Reach and touch him as you trod;
Remember, only once your are passing this way.

He has no special one to love;
He died to save all races of man.
His power spreads out from above.
To strengthen people in every land.

The life you live and the things you say,
Are evidence of your spiritual touch.
The smile and work you do each day,
Let the world know you love God so much.

  —*Bernice Smalls Green*

Transparencies

You perceive untold images,
You conceptualize in concrete forms,
You print pictures,
Yet tenderly
You see my words.

Refracted through you
Focusing:
single tender endings ending ennui
  ray upon ray
  image upon image
coming to light.

Filter me:
light hop-scotching over broken glass
light penetrating fractured dream marrow
light compressing shadow to a form,

Gather me:
taunt my smile
beguile shattered pieces
prime this unformed silhouette.

Print me in black and white.

  —*Karen DeFranco-Nierenberg*

A Modern Day Mother Goose

She sat alone all sad and dreary,
you could even say a little weary.
The future looked glum even bleary,
or was that her glasses causing her not to see clearly?
Than one day she heard her call,
at least her hearing was hanging in there after all...
This new job would fit the bill.
She always enjoyed a good fight,
but not with might but with will.
Seems some older kids had some little folks up a proverbial wall.
Boy did they have some nerve, not to say a lot of gall.
She had a special glow upon her grand-motherly face,
when she went out to meet them, those hoodlums.
She was out to win her case.
Needless to say that all went well that day.
The big boys stay away. Now with glees from one and all
they go to school to learn, to be kids and to have a ball.
Maybe even going onto higher institutions
of knowledge you know that place known as college.

—Sheri Walker

I Would Have Been Your Wife

All hope is gone, I can't even cry,
You didn't even kiss me good bye.
You are gone forever out of my life,
If you would have ask, I would have been your wife.

I would have been a good wife to you,
Faithful and honest and always true.
Loved your children and raised them right,
Give me a chance to prove my love, night after night.

To wake up every morning lying next to you,
Is now only my dearest wish come true.
If only your feelings for me were real,
After I met you, you made me feel.

You hurt me so bad, I think I might die,
But the sun still comes up in the eastern sky.
I must go on living day after day,
But I know I'll make it to sunset, all of the way.

I would have been your wife, till the end of time,
Growing old together, loving the lines.
You are gone forever out of my life,
If you would have ask, I would have been your wife.

—Angie Shivener

Glory and Praise

Lord, since I met you, my life's not the same
You died on the cross, You took away my shame.
You set me free, and now I can say,
That's why I'm so happy, as I go on my way.

You gave me a promise to provide all I need.
I'll tell others of Jesus, each day do some good deed.
I know, without doubt, Your way is best.
With Your loving care, I'll withstand the test.

Teach me, my Lord, to share with all others.
Let them know they are my sisters and brothers,
To love one another, as You have loved me.
Each day I am with You, more blessings I see.

Thank You for changing, making my life anew.
I'll give You the glory, and always praise YOU!

—Frances Fanning

You Don't Know My Name

Say Dad!
You don't know my name.
I'm the son you left behind
When you ran off in shame.

You made a promise.
Mama bore a son.
Not long afterward you were off and gone.

Say Dad! Did you ever think
If the son you left behind
Would live or die or rise and shine.

What would he eat, where would he live.
For his occupation...would he work or steal.
How would he make it alone with his mother,
Would they survive...or have an endless struggle,
Just to live and survive.

Was it the responsibility you were running
From...or rushing toward many more mistakes because you
Didn't learn from the first one.

Promises made, no promises kept
This your fate a man in a hurry to procreate.

—Everlena Hemingway

Paradise

On the sand, by the ocean.
You draw out my emotions.

Your eyes see me when most do not.
And if I run, by them I am caught.

Your body bronzed the warm winds caress.
My heart, truly, you do possess.

Sunsets in summer with you by my side.
Together we gaze, brushed by the tide.

Under the leaves of a swaying palm tree.
Our love is silent, for just you and me.

The warm night breeze kisses your face.
A slow dance, by firelight, and your embrace.

So put to rest is paradise.
'Till my next visit, only dreams must suffice.

—Just So

Butterfly Butterfly

Beautiful butterfly, with wings so delicate and fair
You float in graceful ways on summer's air.
Once you crawled in lowly places where
Earth bound, you struggled daily there.
With sweet faith then, you wove a cocoon 'round
And there you slept to make or hear no sound
But one day 'woke, transformed, cast off your skin
'Rose on sun rays free to live again.
Butterfly in flight on fragile wing
We perceive the message rare you bring
Tiny creature, full faithed, in things that be
Our prisoned souls rejoice in hope, that we
Can accept our worm-like life on earth
And know we will, like you, have second birth.

—Osie Wilcox

Insight

Listening in silence one stops to think
If one is in silence alone to whom shall they listen
For if one is in silence and looking for an answer
    who shall they turn to
To return to the silence of the one who was listening
    may open the silence of the listener

—J. P. Halsted

Be The Best

Be the best of whatever you are,
If you can't be the wind, be the rain
If you can't be the rain, be the sun
If you can't be the sun, be a star
    Be the best
—*Frances Dunn*

"Freddie Mercury - A Fan's Personal Tribute"

One man, one goal, one vision
You gave us your eternal dream.

I remember him from the seventies,
A face you couldn't forget
A voice so unforgettable
Fame and fortune he quickly met.

He sang his words so melodically
You felt them embracing your heart.
He lifted all your dark days
Lived his life to play every part.

He gave his soul to life and music
And life took it all away
He will always be a legend in time
His songs to be ever played

A man, whose life was so personal
We loved him for all he gave
There'll never be another Freddie
His spirit lives flickering in all eternal flames
—*Pamela Capozziello*

Late September

The hall is silent, you say you love me.
You hold my hand, oh so very tightly.
The night is gone, the sun is rising.
My image blurs but in my mind, your here beside me.
And so deep in my heart lies a place for you always
Yet there is one regret you see, which still comes upon to
    haunt me.
The day we met, the love we shared,
Just made it worse for me to bear.
It was the day we said good-bye.
It made my soul just want to die.
Safe with you is how I felt.
I was afraid of all loves doubts.
Because of that I broke our hearts.
I thought it was so very smart.
And till this very day, I will always remember
The night we buried our love late in September...
    —*Cynthia Garcia*

Just

I know it isn't right to care for
You justly so.
With any other choice I should just go
I know I'm just a fool to believe,
But, my thoughts I just cannot leave.
I'd walk one more mile just to smell your hair.
I'd give my life just to know you care.
If I could only, just turn back the hands of time.
You know in an instant I'd make you just mine.
My thoughts are filled mostly of just you.
But, the truth of the matter just makes me blue.
I know I'm really just foolish at heart.
So time and circumstances just keep us apart
Every time you go away; you just leave me crying.
The pain deep inside just makes me feel like dying.
To over come and conquer your heart is more than just a quest.
With these words and thoughts, I'll go and just ponder the rest.
    —*Patricia Evans*

A Mature Potato

Beauty lies in the eye of the beholder,
you know.

An aging potato told me so.

"My skin is patina, my 'eyes' are a dream.
I have a few wrinkles, but I fix those with cream."

"If I cinch up my belt, a waist will appear.
I exercise daily to firm up my rear."

"You say I have 'sprouts.'
Well, I do have a few."

"But when I remove them,
I look just like 'NEW!' "
    —*Elaine Burns*

Blind Love

Give me one reason why I should stay.
You love me and comfort me then send me away.
Or is it I who loves you and comforts you every day.
Give me one reason why I should stay.

Do you feel like the four o'clock blowing in the wind?
Or like a cool summer breeze sending you into a spin.
Don't tell me it's four o'clock and I feel a little breeze
This thought gives me chills so I give myself a squeeze.

This warmth I feel I used to get from you.
Every hour on the hour, not just a minute or two.
Or was it I who felt the warmth when thinking of you.
It used to be in abundance but know it's less than few.

It's supposed to be love and learn but it's too hard to forget.
My love was your hope in a selfish little set.
I'll forgive you in the morning and walk away
I ask myself a question and I hear myself say,
It's my blindness that will make me stay.
    —*Jaime Crooks*

Conquer The Mall

If you ever go shopping with my dad,
You may ask yourself "is this man Mad?"
It's not that he's crazy or a little bad,
It's just that he finds things you've never had.
    Conquer the Mall, conquer them all

He flies past the windows and into the stores,
You can't blink your eyes for he's in a door.
He'll beat any record for any timed shopping,
As for my dad, to him there's no stopping
    Conquer the Mall, conquer them all

He'll find any clearance, he'll find any sale,
He'll sometimes find things that will make you turn pale.
Quite honestly, my dad's fun to ship with a bunch,
Because you're always finished in time for Lunch!
    Conquer the Mall, conquer them all
    —*Michelle Hansen*

Mother

Mother can you hear me callin' out your name?
I need someone to help me and free me from my pain
Mother can I help you? After all that you've done
I feel I need to thank you for making me your son.

Mother are you crying? Is it something I said?
I'm sorry, please forgive me, I must have lost my head
Mother are you dying? Tell me what can I do?
I've never had anyone, not anyone but you

Oh Mother
    —*Everett Goodrich*

"Tragedy"

You walked into my life like a cool summer's breeze...,
You picked me off my feet and you knocked me to my knees...

You were everything I ever hoped to find...
You had my heart, my thoughts my mind...

I loved you with every ounce I had...
All of our times were good..., None were bad...

I knew you had Aids that just made me love you more...
I should have been more careful... I knew what lay in
store...

But, I knew that I could never love another
The way that I love you ....
That's why when you died... a part of me died too....

—*Carmen R. Harrison*

Mother/Daughter

I thought I'd lost you on the day
you pulled your hand from mine
and ran ahead to get to school
and join your friends in line.

When you were college bound, I thought
I'd lost you, once again.
I felt, with all those miles between,
I'd see you only now and then.

I knew I'd lost you when you gazed
aglow with love for that young boy.
Although my eyes were blurred with tears,
my heart was filled with joy.

But, when, one day we sat together
watching with such pride and glee,
a new born child open her eyes,
(she looked a little bit like me).

I knew I'd never lost you
and that I never will,
for, every time you walked away,
your heart stayed with me still.

Just as, (I promise), when God calls
and to his arms I fly,
though it may seem I've gone away,
I'll always be close by.

—*Lydia Astoria Palmer*

Loves Drug

You control me
 You rule me
  You inhibit me

How much can one person take
Two days I went cold turkey
Two days I shook like a leaf
Sweating, paining, crying, please set me free

When I was introduced to you
you were so exciting, challenging, uninhibited,
a novelty I couldn't resist
You soothed my aching heart
Told me fairytales and took me to fantasyland

How can you be so brutal, drop me so soon
Why is it, without you, I shake all over?
Reality sets in and I realize I'm sober

You control me
 You rule me
  You inhibit me
   You made a fool of me
    Now I beg you, please, set me free, please.

—*Berta Louise Harrison*

Oh What A Life We Live

Oh what a life we live your born.
You see. You walk. You play.
And all the dreams you have.
Your rich. Your poor. You tried so hard.
You have family, wife, kids.
You worked so hard for what you have.
You go to bed. Close your eyes. Wake up
For a brand new day.
You get sick. You get old. You laugh, you cry.
Your time is short. You know you time is near.
You close your eyes for the last time.
You know it will be your last.
So you pray to God before you go.
For the bad things you have done.
It is dark. And at peace.
Everything you had is gone.
You done your part. For what life you had.
It is quiet and at peace,
So now I can sleep.
My job is done. And life goes on

—*DeWayne Werts*

Cherish

My dearest mother I cherish your memories
you shared with me I cherish your smile and
your laugh and even your cry, those
beautiful memories I will never let them slip by.
For those are all I have left of you the things
we shared are very precious to me when I needed
help you where there you never hesitated and
never asked why. You always were there for
me no matter what, and I loved you for that
and I still love you even if you are not with
me, here in this life. Those precious hours
and minutes that I had with you are my precious
memories that I will cherish for ever, what
really mattered is that we loved each other
so very much no matter what. So my dearest
mother remember that I love you and I will
cherish you for ever.

—*Anna Maria Garcia*

Water Wonderland

Now you know that the water is good! So pay the bill, you know
you should. But, Mr. Water Ward, can't you see? The drinking
water, it's killing me. I drank some from my kitchen sink, and
now I'm sick, and I can't think. It's sad to know, that I
can't drink, from my own kitchen sink. You're sick, I see,
that don't bother me. Now pay the fee, or come with me. I
can't pay the bill, I'm much too ill. The bill's too high, and
I might die! I have no will, to pay the bill, water should be
free, it's even killing me. Oh! You think it's your's, and
free at birth? Next, you'll want free air and earth! The
water is bad, and the people are sad. We're losing good
health, that we once had. I don't care, what you just said,
it's too bad you're sick in bed. But! We all know, as well as
you, you have to pay, the bill is due. You have air to
breathe, and a life to live, and all you have to do, is give.
You have it all, don't you recall? Water to waste, air to
spare, wood to burn and land to fill. So please, won't you
just pay the bill? Don't drink the water, my son, look close
at me, see what it's done. I know I'm not the only one. You
brush and flush, and then you're done.

—*Judy Parker*

Untitled

Ever since I was a little girl
You were always there for me
Listening and giving advice
Being just like a grandpa should be
Showing me right from wrong
Always telling me to be strong
You made the holidays shine
Making me think Santa Claus was all mine
Believing in me and helping me succeed
Convincing me that I could be in the lead

But now everything is not the same
In my dreams I hear myself calling your name
And still, though you are not here
I can sometimes feel you near
Helping me to choose what's right
And chasing away all my fright

I would just like to send you a thank you
To where you are up above
For everything you've done for me
And remind you, you will always have my love
—*Karen Campo*

A Reason

There must be a reason but I can't find it.
You were just beginning to dream, when the dream ended.
You were just beginning to live, when the life ended.
You had such big dreams,
You had so much to live for,
When suddenly you were no more.

They always said, everything has a reason
But I can't find one.
They always said, everything has a purpose
But I don't know what it is.

Why? I just don't understand.
Life was just beginning
  when it ended
    so suddenly
      so tragically.
There must be a reason
I just can't find it.
—*Theresa M. Koster*

You Can Be Anything

Hey little boy, hey little girl
You were put on this Earth
To be something in this world
You can be anything you want to be
And only you are in total control of your destiny

You can be a doctor, lawyer, electrician,
Pilot, plumber, or pediatrician
You see, your future lies in your hands
And to succeed all you need is perseverance
And the old saying 'I CAN'

To put your mind to the test, expect the best
Accomplish your dreams, and conquer your quests
It won't be easy, the competition is tough
But you've got what it takes
You've got the right stuff

To keep in mind exactly what I've said
Don't be fooled and don't be misled
You can be anything you want to be
Anything in the world
Little bright boy, and little bright girl

—*Jai Erinkitola*

Untitled

In the darkness we are all one color,
In the darkness we are all the same.

In the darkness there is no prejudice,
In the darkness we are all the same.
—*Paul Jancsy*

Feelings

Feelings are the kind of thing
You'll never know what good they'll bring.
They might be bad,
They might be good,
And sometimes they're misunderstood.

You might not ever now they're there,
Not even when you show you care
But if you search your soul and heart,
You'll find them in the deepest part.
—*Tracy E. Kuttruff*

All I Need

Make love to you on a rainy night
Your arms around me holding me tight

Kiss you for hours on end
Listen to your problems, be your friend

Tell me your dreams and your fears
Let me be the one to wipe away the tears

Share your days good and bad
Stand beside you happy or sad

I'll be everything you could ever need
The love I have for you everyone will see

Watch the morning sunrise with you
Is all I could ever need to do

Share the moon and stars above
Let me show you how it feels to be in love

Walk along a sandy beach
For my hand all you have to do is reach

Lie beside me all through the night
Nothing has ever felt so right
—*Lisa Karrit*

The One I Love

I love your hair smile and eyes
  Your beauty can not be sermonized
It's like the beauty of the sea
  That will not fade through eternity

It's like the beauty of the flower
  To gaze up on from hour to hour
It's like the beauty of the trees
  So gracefully swaying in a breeze

It's like the stars and sky above
  It's like the birds singing of love
It's like the moon and like the sun
  There brilliant light touches everyone

So deep within my heart I say
  My love for you will never fray
And through the years as they pass along
  My love for you will grow very strong

I know that when the day arrives
  That we must part our happy lives
That up above under his great hand
  We'll meet again in that promise land
—*Harold M. Tetro*

A Child Hope

Small hands clamped so tight
In hope that night - someone
beyond has the light of
    insight.

    —*Frances E. Combs*

"Demons"

Demons are the destroyers of the human mind and soul, where
your body self-destructs and it's done so bold. Demons will
tempt you with fortune or fame, after the magnanimous adventure
your soul is trapped in the game. Demons will offer you a job
selling illegal products like "drugs", when you are
incarcerated by the Authorities you end up as a convict and a
thug. Demons will make up lies, false statements behind your
back, before you know it, you're hooked on crack. Demons
concentration is present in Brooklyn, Manhattan, Long Island,
Queens, their major objective is to further destroy a poverty
stricken man's dreams. Demons have been here since the
beginning of time, causing poverty, death, heartache and crime.
Demons are present even in politics, they interpret the
"Constitution" with twisted illegal tricks. Demons pretend to
be your loved- one or friend, but the major plan is to destroy
your soul in the end. Demons are very strong and intelligent
with their evil stuff, but it's God's disciples that are very,
very tough.

    —*Emanuel Reno Wilkins Sr.*

Sands of Time

Senior Citizens, come rest your feet in the sands of time.

  Your days were busy with home and work
  Your evenings spent with family or friends
  Your nights were sometimes disturbed.

Come rest your feet in the sands of time.

  Now you have time to reminisce
  What were the best times?
  Times spent with your babies?
  Their growing up years, the hugs and laughter?

Come rest your feet in the sands of time.

  Yes, there were rough times
  Sickness brought you close,
  The pay check was slim,
  A used car was good enough.

Come rest your feet in the sands of time.

  Your demands are no longer great
  You go at your own speed, do what you can
  Loved ones have gone on, leaving only memories.

Come rest your feet in the sands of time.

    —*Dana Esch*

Possess Me

Only in your arms, is where I long to be - to feel the heat of
your lips on mine our bodies entwined, in a lover's embrace.

I want to feel your lips on my breast, and experience the
passion, that only two kindred spirits can share.

I want you to possess me - body and soul - to feel complete,
and total surrender - to feel the weight of your naked body,
on top of mine - loving me, passionately, and completely.

Only with you, can I feel free to be myself - and only with
you, do I ever want to experience the unleashed desire, that
I feel, when you're loving me.

    —*Charlotte R. Farrell*

Bill

I know who you are
Your name is Bill
Your mother called you "different"
In grade school boys called you "sissy"
in high school boys called you "queer"

I know who you are. You're my friend Bill
Society gave you a new name
They called you "gay"

You love and worship God
You respect your parents
You honor your country
Is that what "gay" is?

You own your business
You serve your community
You obey the law
Is that what "gay" is?

God created you in the third gender
HE knows who you are
He knows what "gay" is!
I know who you are - you're my friend Bill

    —*Wanita Spivak*

"Miles Away"

(Dedicated to My Father)
You're miles away
Many states have kept us apart for what
    seems to be a lifetime
No one knows just why,
Though everyone is to blame
So many lost years; though impossible;
    so desperately wanting to be made up.
Were so close when I was young
All is now lost,
Miles away,
One call changes our lives forever
Longing to be together again, we weep in
    expression of our heart ache and loss.
Miles away
When night falls, we watch the stars as
    though they were the other.
The father-daughter love was lost,
Now strongly fighting for another chance.
Though miles away,
We know our love in our hearts and
    deep in our souls,
Despite the words of others.

    —*Alexandrea Hanks*

Untitled

You want to belong to UNICEF
You're tired of seeing children starve to death
you've seen them frail and thin
and you think it's up to you to begin
You've seen the buildings, streets, and straw huts
and it drove you nuts
I'm telling you
like the country Somalia
You want to take your turn
As did Audrey Hepburn
You've watched television
And seen the famine
You called
The pledge they say can be big or small
You motto is why not let other people live
take the initiative.

    —*Jayne Kleist*

If My Love

If my love for you, was as strong as God:
Could you imagine the mountains we
would move, the moment we would touch:

How deep could the ocean be, just from
the glow that flows through us:

Just how strong the wind would be, by the
stroke of your hand caressing me:

Could you imagine how strong my love could
be, with you beside me eternally:
If my love for you, was as strong as God!

—*Bryant Ramey LaVonne*

Deity Distilled

Our magnificent God sprinkled His stars into
A murky sky; rolled Earth in His bands
and placed it in the Milky Way; strung
mountains over the deep, filled the
hollows with azure blue drops, bringing
forth ribbons and ribbons of
creatures a gift - life to man,
He spun all this into one drop
placed it in a wee

Baby

Jesus who grew
into the fullness of God,
His love was not confined
to withered feet or blinded eyes
to stopped up ears or impeded tongues;
Not constrained by malevolent foes, who
tormented and twisted bodies, minds and spirits
Whose passion was not bound by the gates of death
But released into the mists of eternity by His
overwhelming Love.

—*Carolyn F. Shortt*

Not Without Hope!

Who is that man standing on that corner?
In his hands or at his feet there is a sign,
"Homeless, will work for food."

His head hung low as to hide his shame
That his eyes and face would surely portray.
Who is that man?

He huddles to keep warm during the bitter winters
And perspires in the agonizing summer heat.
Is this man one of us?

This man depicts the cruelness of Social Darwinism
What do we do with the ones that are not the fittest?
Do we just ignore the man on the corner?

This man is someone's child and, probably, someone's father.
Whether we be Jew, Christian, Moslem, Hindu, or Buddhist,
We are all connected through the common bond of humanity.

Let us not forget the man on the corner.

—*Charles Anthony Shippam*

ove

ou showed me how much you cared,
ou showered me with love of which we shared,
e had 41 years and they were not all sad,
ank God for most of the years that were not bad,
e mornings come, and the nights are long,
e days since you're gone are sometimes full of turmoil
t my love for you, will always remain,
a special place, only found in my heart's domain.

—*Rosalind Palazzolo*

Just Like Grandma's Love

Do you know how Grandma's Love feels?
Well, she's soft, and warm
She has willing arms
That lock me in a tight embrace
With a great big hug and kisses all over my face

She's got big soft breasts
Pillows for my head to rest
Ears that hear even my unspoken words
From her mouth, the best of love songs and stories I heard

Do you really know how good Grandma's love is?
I don't have to ask for Grandma's love, it's there waiting
for Me
I don't have to work for Grandma's love, she just gives it to Me
I don't have to be good to get Grandma's love, she just loves Me
Even if I pretend I don't want it, "Grandma's Love" is poured
all over Me

Grandma's love sure feels mighty good!
And your love feels just like Grandma's love, only better!

—*Barbara Ensley-Walton*

Whispers in the Rain

A whisper in the rain spoke to me
On that darkened day.
My life may never be the same

I screamed with joy
For I was tired of living the game of the life.

My thoughts were enlightened

Nefarious as I was,
I am now awakened as a new entity,
Entering higher levels of the unconsciousness.
The rain is drizzling onto my thoughts
Quenching my eternal needs.

Suddenly I realized the of which I held...

...I was then filled with the same evil
which I had consumed in my childhood.
I wanted more...

A sudden flash of thunder struck me.
I lay crying inside,
Like a hungry baby waiting to be fed.

The voice in the rain came back and whispered
'fool' as I lay there without a soul...

END?

—*Kalyana T'ai Magit*

Concupiscence Vs. Continence

Kumquats, kites, and coupled delight,
in Acrasia's Bower of Bliss I sat.
Purple, orange and gold
melted and roared wildly on the hills
making an unsolvable equation
Skinny zeal for life's treasure chest-
the possibilities were nourishment for what could be-
(Rail thin as I slip and slide between fence posts)
turbulent water came crashing to one point-
to a stage on a warm spring night
A choice is made?
Gregor, we surely know
how irascible the Metamorphosis is.
(Organized thoughts dissipate
into a pond of calm crimson and beige)
Feelings of lament, wonder
for what might have been.

—*Kirsten McRaven*

Deep Thoughts

Silently I sit, staring in awe, at my beautiful black queen
Thoughts running deep through her head, I want to know what
she is thinking.
Are her thoughts of me? Am I in her future?
I need to know
I call out her name but she does not hear me
For she is deep, deep in thought

I long to feel the sweetness of her breath against my neck as
she lay upon me,
The warmth of our bodies melting us into one
I feel her heartbeat against my chest
Thump thump, Thump thump
It beats in unison with mine

Ohh, how I want to stroke her smooth golden brown skin
Until she drifts into a gentle sleep, wrapped in my arms all
through the night,
Thump thump, Thump thump
Our heartbeat is steady

Is this what you want?
Is this what you're thinking? I ask calling out her name
once again.
Still she does not respond, for she is deep, deep in thought

But I am patient
And I will wait for her answer.
—*Jamal Smith*

The Pond

The dancing drops of waterfall,
Into the pond, the water flops,
With birds chirping, fish swimming,
The fountain continues, without any stop.

The water glides down the stones,
with graceful tones.
Its musical song, sings a soft note.
Through the whole fountain pond,
its pride greatly shone.

The wind blows, makes the water flow.
The light inside the pond gives its glow.
Now I am sitting here, watching its show,
Seeing the water fly, the bigger it grows.

The sound of the running water,
is nice to my ears,
Great and cozy, sitting so near.
As I reach out and touch the cold water,
In my whole life, I will never fear.
—*Karen Goh*

Grand Canyon

At canyon's edge I peer beyond sheer cliff
to God's great masterpiece. As chill winds blow
a blue jay flutters near, sending a skiff
of snow from scraggly pine to depths below.
Across the canyon a stream, light and clear
threads its way through shimmering trees of green
and as it blends with murky waters near,
becomes a raging flood, a river mean!
Beyond the river stand majestic peaks,
like sentinels on duty. Delicate hues
of red and gray in many layered streaks,
create contrasting panoramic views.
On wings of the wind comes the river's roar,
changing the mood of the canyon once more.
—*Harbon B. Heap*

Forbidden Fruit

"...But of the fruit of the tree which is in the midst of the
garden, God hath said, Ye shall not eat of it, neither shall ye
touch it, lest ye die" Genesis 3:3

To eat an apple, an orange, or pear
is fine with HIM, if you so care.

These things we have, or have not so —
are for our use - to build and grow.

The fruit I seek, I shan't attain —
'twould bring me pleasure, but cause me pain.

Her branches entice me, sitting low —
should I pick them, yes or no?

My hands now tremble, the fruit I save —
for now I face an early grave.

Now here he comes, in flaming red —
my time is done, enough's been said.

Dress me up, in my Sunday suit —
for I did eat the Forbidden Fruit.
—*John A. Shachter*

One Warm Spring Night

It happened, yes, one warm spring night.
The stars so high were shining bright.
The wind, it blew my hair so wild.
I wanted to scream like a little child.
My heartbeat sped, the sweat poured down.
Nervousness filled the air around.
My knees, they clattered.
My teeth, they chattered.
My face grew hot by the minute.
My hair, it stood, my lips went cold.
My stomach rolled and rolled and rolled.
My legs went rubber, my throat grew tight.
Yes, this all happened in the still of the night.
What happened, you ask, why do you shy?
I'll tell you what happened...
He passed by.
—*Heidi Schmelter*

A Poet's Piece

It was his call,
His heedless dissension;
That need to lead the fall
Of graveyard tensions
It was his card, his mentions
On a war actions' times
Told in his rhymes.
His words heard by all
By both young and old,
An oath, sung and told to the herd
Which led us to believe,
Read war is deed,
Said instead to those dead in their tomb,
And said to whom fled,
Where war is to grieve,
Whether it is led or we lead,
We've bled and will bleed
To any such need.
—*Gene A. Gaspar*

"Hurricane Emily" "Blue Moon" "1st Day Of School"

You took another step today upon the path of life,
that saw your Mommy's eyes fill up,
but they weren't tears of strife.
We're all so very proud of you, we think you're really cool,
And now that path has led you on to thirteen years of school.
We pushed you through the door knowing what you'd find,
And you saw things and made new friends
and opened up your mind.
All the day we waited, through the quiet and the storm,
to find out what you thought of it,
the opinions that you'd form.
We wondered if you had cried all day
or if you'd see through the tears,
And when you climbed down off the bus
your smile stifled all our fears.
A happy little girl came home with friends and stories too;
With an air of independence, We're so very proud of you!

"For Emily Rachel — On Your First Day of School"

—Mark P. Phillips

In Your Eyes

In your eyes, the love you don't have to try
The feeling has no where to hide
'Cause this heart of mine
It feeds what's inside
That your love will never die

O' it's so hard to say goodbye
To someone who cares
And to these eyes
When they break down and cry

Is this goodbye
Is it forever
We live in this life
Is it together
We'll give it some time

'Cause this heart of mine
It feeds what's inside
That your love is there
And will never die
Here in your eyes

—Michelle Messer

I Can Not

I cannot adopt the attitude

I cannot be constantly reminded of the lack of self
contentment, not an ounce of
hope tucked away.

I cannot willingly share your hurt anymore, it reaches
everywhere except the
inner self that you've never really come to know.

I cannot accept or conceptualize remorse for your daily
habit because you have
become one in resolution with it.

I cannot stand to see you kill yourself you choose its
companionship instead of
faith making it your life time prevailing circumstance.

I cannot live letting it live to make me a loser.

I cannot go another day knowing you will never free yourself
from it, that bond with fear.

I cannot cry tears, I have lost feeling now and lost anyone
to stand by me
because I stand by your side.

I cannot love with you, but without you I can live.

—Majidah Muhammad

"Slow Down"

Slow down the pace
of this blind human race
Is it so hard to see
What is important, what is meant to be
Life is for loving
Life is for sharing
Life is for teaching and its for caring
Life is a beautiful, wonderful place
Discover its treasures; encounter its grace
Take the time to enjoy it
Before its too late
Cultivate love and obliterate hate
Expunge the prejudice
Let understanding fill the space
Experience life
Look it squarely in the face
Take my advice and
Slow down the pace

—Maria Calamoneri

Lady and the Stallion

Gazing into morning's sunrise… somewhere along the sea…
…saw them riding with the wind, from a place called destiny.

Two horses and their riders, thundering hoofs across the sand…
…an exceptionally lovely lady, alongside a truly handsome man.

Magnificence and Majesty, names befitting King and Queen…
…black stallion with its master, the mare did its lady bring.

With flowing grace, with power, they approached me ever near…
…I called out in the distance, they didn't seem to hear.

Sunlight shown upon them, silhouetted by morning's sky…
…I could hear them laughing, as they swiftly galloped by.

Peering into the brightness, I saw the lady turn my way…
…so familiar was her face, I knew not what to say.

And then came understanding, tears of joy I began to cry…
…you see, it was then I did realize, riding the stallion, that
knight was I.

—Michael S. Clouse

Prayer to the Heavens

If I can be heard, let your ears cry,
for cool rain might warm me.
If you can see how I hurt, reach down,
maybe you can soothe me.
Could you reverse time,
to make me happy?
Can you change others minds -
make them want that same time?
Can you enhance the memories?
Only I see them larger then life.
Change the beating of hearts, if you will,
and make them one again.
Selfish, foolish thoughts,
I've always asked too much.
But please, if you may,
hurry the night along.
The dreams that haunt
me are all too real.
Kiss the night to
sweet silence.

—Nicole Rapp

Who is the Man?

Who?
Who is the man
Atop the hill,
In the old, dark mansion?
The housemaid says
The foyer's webs
Spelled out his name;
She broke them.
The wall's rats
Whispered his name;
She poisoned them.
The housemaid is asked to whisper his name;
She begins.
She stops.
She dies.
Who is the man?
Who?

—*Scott P. Nelson*

Ode to Sh_t

This is it then? The ineluctable event?
After years and years of trying to get rid of it,
of trying to pretend it does not exist,
to flush it...
Then to see, it is I.
And you thought it was "dust to dust," didn't you?
Well my friend, it isn't!
One cannot leave this world unscathed
try as one might to live in grace and beauty,
to live with high values and standards...
Yet — the horror —
(or delight to others) to find one's self mired —
like everyone else —
in the sh_t.

—*Bryant*

The Page

The blank page requires a lover
Pen or pencil between her cover
But rush not to fill her lines
True love takes a lot of work: A lot of time
Though you might try your best, and just might please her
She'll accept you in her own sweet time
Oh she's lover, but also - a teaser

She'll give you spaces to pour forth your graces
And she might grant some motive
From a boring novice for a struggling notice

Ah, she'll give back as much as she takes
'Cause she needs your lines: truth, lies, even fakers
She'll keep only those she really needs - still, accepting
all takers
For the truth of time lays forever between her lines
Only true lovers of words are her pages lasting makers

—*Thomas B. MacConnell*

The Homemakers Club

"Welcome Homemakers, to the year that we've just begun
You've had a busy time as well as lots of fun.
We will plan our program with things both old and new
No matter how you look at it, there's lots that we can do.
With a new place to meet and plenty of room for us all
Don't miss a single Thursday, be here for every roll call,
With Mrs. Collett for city President, and Marge to help us out
This should be a good year for all of us no doubt,
I know I can depend on you always to do your part
So when my task with you is done, I'll say "Bless your little Heart."

—*Hilda Stephenson Woodall*

to my eyes it is a dim labyrinth
to my ears — the steady movement of machines unseen
to my fingers — a sorrow of obscure bounds
a place hidden beneath the earth that bears our tread
a concentrated tension that can be felt in the bones
bridges, ramps — connected by ropes, by chains, by muscle
even the dull light from above quivers upon arrival
dense stone upholds threadlike tendons raw material stripped
to its depths
watching by movement

yet there is no privileged position here
one moment i am here, one moment i am there
but i am really nowhere
it is a place without bounds without limits without beginning
or end a continuum
i ascend — i descend — in and out — through and around
trying to flee the whispers echoing in my head
hiding in the deep shadows where destinations can be lost
i search for a center — a core so that i will be able to
comprehend the plan
but it cannot be found from within the chaos
the harder i try the quicker i am lost
fleeting are the images

—*stacey fithian*

Thoughts of Home

A few years back in a foreign land
A civil war got out of hand
The U.S. was allies for the south
So they sent our young men to help them out

Troops of boys pretending to be men
Fighting a war they can never win
Hiding in fox holes as bullets fly overhead
Thinking of their buddies most of whom are dead

Most had never left their states
But now their in NAM
Fighting for their lives from the North Veitcongs
Ask anyone who was there and I'll bet they will say
It was the thought of home that got them through each day

Instead of a cheerful homecoming parade
The brave men of NAM were never praised
They were spat at, stomped on, called killers and cursed
While all this time they were fighting for us

I didn't see this war it was before my time
But it will forever stay in my mind.

—*Tracey Shell Whitlock*

Broken Images

Seeing the world through a broken mirror.
A distorted image so sharp
It could puncture a man's soul with one touch.

Where are we to go if we cannot see straight?
Our fate depending on the beams of light,
Falling into place upon our very souls.

What happens when the mirror falls?
The delicate balance we once held on to shatters,
Leaving us with the fragments of chaos.

Will we ever manage to put the pieces back together?
Like a puzzle that can never be solved,
The shattered dreams we once remembered,
Now become reality forever.

—*Parth Punjabi*

270

Here's To You

Here's to you, mom and dad, for all the love that you have shown,
for all the caring and understanding even now that I am grown.

Here's to you for all your support when things were not quite
right, for it was you two I could always count on to make everything alright.

Here's to you for giving me guidance and a wonderful family life,
mom, I only hope I can be as good of a mother and as good of a wife.

Here's to you for all the little things that I forgot to thank you for,
they will not ever be forgotten but remembered forever more.

Here's to you sis my forever friend, how could I ever forget about you,
when you've always been there for me when I didn't know what to do.

Here's to you my precious family, for I have once last thing to say,
I love you dearly and thank you so much for giving me this special day.
        —*Sandie Mielak-Brown*

Adirondack Summerfolks

May the chickadees chirp remind you of the place we all call home.
Where the ospreys are still soaring and the black bear still does roam.
Where the redtailed hawk is circling, where we hear the call of loons.
Where the beavers do their damming and the trash is checked by coons.
Where the hummingbirds are buzzing 'round the foxgloves purple cone.
The pink ladyslipper's blushing among ferns, on forest's loam.
We return here ev'ry season as soon as winter lost his grip,
We come home from all directions covering miles and miles per trip.
We renew our soul and spirits on these lovely summer days,
Getting close again to nature and its many wondrous ways.
As the days are getting shorter in the brilliance of the fall,
We wake up one early morning to the wild geese' haunting call.
And we know the circle's closing and its time for us to go.
Draining water, doing chores, closing camp just before snow.
As we drive away - now leaving - our thoughts already churn,
I can't wait until next season when again I can return."
        —*Ingeborg Beyer Sapp*

Winds of Adversity

Though the winds of adversity may come against you, in Him stand strong.
He has not, nor will ever leave you, for He has called you into His throng.
Our Lord began His plan before our birth, longing for us to take His hand.
Thru all your adversities, He has been faithful, and your desire He fanned.

When the winds of adversity sweep into our lives, we often begin to wonder,
Satan controls the worlds thoughts trying to pull us down when we ponder.
Our mind is unable to think or reason out the "whys" of the adversity we face,
Whatever the circumstances, He is with you to impart to you His loving grace.

Adversity can bring hardships in daily living, but they do have their own place,
The necessity is to keep yourself rooted in His Word...earnestly seek His face.
The attitude we have in our "adversity" affects our actions, what we say and do,
Keeping our roots in His Word, we can now walk with Him or His golden avenue.

Purification can be done in adversity for our Lord always knows what is best,
He is forever faithful to see us thru, enabling us in His presence to rest.
In all times of your life, show your attitude of humility knowing He does care.
Thru the winds of adversity, sing His song of strength telling satan to beware.

Friends, accept each adversity with new vengeance, conquerors we are, strong,
His peace is ours to cherish, He called, we said, "Yes," and to Him we belong.
Adversities can blow in, they will come and they will go, remain in His Word,
He is faithful to complete what He has begun, be diligent, only He is Lord.
        —*Jill Hoffman*

Growing Old

Time passes and life quickly moves on,
    what will I be when my youth is gone?
Will I spend my time wondering what if?
    Will I live to have my fondest wish?
The wish for peace and satisfaction,
    consuming love and mortal attraction.
When I gaze into mirrors, what will I see?
    Will the aging process be kind to me?
Will my skin pucker and wrinkle?
    Will I be melancholy and fickle?
Will I snap at people as nanna often does?
    Will senility keep me from who I was?
Will I remember things the others should know?
    Will I wish and pray for my time to go?
Will I continue to be brazen and bold?
    What is it like, this growing old?
        —*Darlene Simpson*

A Touch of Love

A touch of love, you've given me
You've opened my eyes, and spread my wings
Towards blue skies, an heavenly dreams.
To search no more,
For it's love I've found in thee.

A touch of love, sweetens thee air
As I held you so close;
Enjoying its fragrance of,
Perfume from which you wear.

An the beauty of it all, embraces my heart.
For each night I pray, that we'll never part.

For the touch of your love;
Is more precious then gold.
As every moment I've spent with you;
Forevermore I shall cherish them,
Within the depths of my soul.
        —*Terrence Belcher*

My Unseen Friend

If you could read my thoughts today
You would know I'm very sad;
And the expression on my face would say
I've lost the best friend that I had.

Though problems may seem to get me down,
It is only for a day;
'Cause you see I have a friend around
Who is with me all the way.

I only have to talk to him
And dark clouds disappear;
And just the whisper of a prayer
Can bring him very near.

So tomorrow will be different,
For I know I'm not alone.
My friend will always be there
When I can't make it on my own.
        —*Faye Carlton Ralston*

271

My Beautiful Island (Summer)

Fire Island is a long barrier beach
32 miles long, narrow and easy to reach
By Ferry I go to a village named Ocean Beach

The beach has clean, white sand with many pretty shells
Crowded with people on their striped beach chairs
Sound of the constant motion of the beautiful
greenish blue ocean waves, with white foam, crashing
to the beach
May put one to sleep
Mother nature and God made this lovely treat,

Hurricanes, other storms cause beach erosion
taking homes away without say.

Sidewalks only; no cars or streets
Homes, stores, benches where people meet
Many pretty flowers, trees, holly bushes, pine trees
with brown cones dropping to the ground
Many deer now roam looking for food making no sound.

Other side has the great South Bay
Where boats dock, people swim, fish and children play
I love my island so beautiful and gay
Wish to be there every day.

— *Ruth Johnson*

Memory's Garden

Within the walls around my heart
A beautiful garden grows
Planted there by loving hands
That I never again will know

Taken from me too soon
By a cruel twist of fate
I realized I loved you
By then it was too late

Now I walk the path of memories
From sundown to sunrise
Watering each blossom
With raindrops from my eyes

Maybe, one day, I will open the gate
To walk with someone new
The paths of wonder and beauty
Planted here by you.

— *Cheryl Lynn Abbott*

The Love Of My Life

The love of my life lies in our bed.
A big feather pillow beneath her head.
An old tattered quilt tucked under her chin.
I think about her and have to grin.
There in bed so soft and warm.
I thank the Lord that she was born
She's brought so much happiness in my life.
I am so thankful she's my wife.
How much I love her I can not define.
Or the joy that she is mine.
Oh how lucky, can one man be.
To have a wife, like God gave to me.
Later on I'll go to bed,
Put a pillow beneath my head.
Turn to the one that I love.
And thank the Good Lord up above.

— *Gary W. Jenkins*

Upon A Pond

A golden swan is swimming
A black swan keeps watch
Two baby swan are swimming with golden swan
The geese stand around the pond
It's one family
It's such a nice family the black swan
almost jumped in
The water has little ripples flowing
The sun and rain are out
such is a rainbow
They saw bread so they began to munch
There are candles lit on the geese feathers
around the pond
Now the black swan jumps in
Sunflowers are growing, it is springtime
Far in the distance there is a farm

— *Alida Mae Limber Dean*

"The Rose"

Our love was like a big beautiful rose
A certain love that no one knows
I should've known that it was doomed
From the way it bloomed
I was the flower and you were the seed
And now you're all that I need
All I need is for you to be with me
For I am blind and I cannot see
I get the message that you send
You tell me this is the end
This is the end of forever
But I won't stop loving you, ever
For I was the flower and you were the seed
And you made my heart bleed
An eternal bleeding that would not end
I still can't comprehend
Why did it have to end this way
But you would not say
You had to destroy that rose
And it's a hurt that everyone knows

— *Denise Mason*

Shame

There is a cloud over man today,
a dark cloud, like yesterday
The tension of guilt
Hearts heavy laden with it.

It is an aura of shame
Shame not so much for things done,
but shame for things undone.
It is the curse of our age.

"No, not I," one says
"I didn't do it!" vehement denial
Exactly.
What good is it to say:
"Go, I wish you well; keep warm and well fed,"
but to do nothing?

So the hungry starve
The naked die in winter
The oppressed continue to tremble
on this planet of cowards.

— *Machut Shishak*

272

Winter Day

As the snow falls down I can see.
A day that is very pleasing to me.
The snow falls like a white powder.
While I am in the house eating clam chowder.
I hear the wind's breeze.
As I look out the window, and say "achoo!"
I sneeze. I am glad to see this winter day,
But I guess it can't stay because spring
Is on the way

—*John Davis, Jr.*

Police Front Desk

I sat at the desk as she walked in
A dirty looking woman, who looked scared from sin
And with her was her girl, almost two years of age
That was playful and cute and degree you could not gauge
The woman came to complain about a man she knows
A man she once married
And the girl loves to hold
I've seen it before in many different forms
A gem not giving a chance
But will see nothing but storms.
Then I think back to mine
On the verge of three months to date
How my wife and I love her
And she'll see almost no hate
Im no different from the woman, in Gods eyes
She seemed like she's crazy, and full of lies
I've chosen a straight path to walk all of my days
To provide for my family and serve God in His ways
I feel for the little girl, whom I fell in love with first sight
I pray she'll find God and avoid the plight in this life.

—*Stephen Edward Colegio*

Distance"

When we were together it was like
A dream come true, there were times I
Felt happy and others I felt blue.
Not a moment went by when I
Didn't think of you.
You are unique in your own way,
I love you more day by day.
Now here we are oceans apart,
A tear drop fall right from the start.
I long to be in your arms,
Kissing your lips, and feeling your charms.
There soon comes that day when I
Can return, from that day forward more
About each other is what we will learn.
Until then I'll feel blue, just always
Remember how much I love you!

—*Lisa Dela Cruz*

Victoria Marie Agne

At first it starts out with 3 a.m. feedings
A few years pass, then 6 p.m. readings
Bedtime stories to lull them to sleep
After years of diapers piled in a heap

Laughter and love and hugs intermixed
With things they've broken that need to be fixed
Magic moments every single one of them
Like the first steps of this precious little femme

I wish the best to young Tory Marie
Of the future that is hers to see
Through eyes that may be unlike mine
But, nonetheless, loved and divine

—*Arthur J. Usher IV*

Friendship

A friend is there before you ask to lend a helping hand.
A friend supports your lofty goals no matter where you stand.
She lends an ear for listening, a shoulder for shed tears.
She's honest so you might know truth; she soothes your every
    fear.

A friend will trust in good times, and depend on her in bad.
You'll share with her each single wish and dream you ever had.
She'll take your secrets straight to heart, your deepest thoughts as
    well.
She'll encourage your successes and keep you striving when
you've failed.

Friendship's like a garden, flourishing with love,
Sprinkled with the nourishment and care from up above.
It's a tender petal on a rose, a bandage on a pain.
It's the strength of golden sunshine streaming through the
    clouds of rain.

A friend is faithful, forever real, a treasure of heartfelt gold.
A friend is there to warm you once you've trodden through
    this world of cold.
But most of all a friendship is a shelter from the storm,
A blessing from the Lord above, to show we're not alone.

—*Julie Barnett*

Untitled

Night birds are calling,
    A gentle rain falling,
The houses stand silent and dark,
    Then a baby's shrill cry,
A car zooming by
    And a wandering dog's nervous bark—
None of these heard by the sleepers;
    May they find by night
    What they lose by day—
The dreamers and the weepers!

—*Margaret Moore*

Prima Donna

    In all my days I've never heard
    A girlish voice quite like your own,
    Which sounds to me so fresh, so dear
    Its every sound has perfect tone.
    Like fine perfume it fills the air,
    Softly spilling your soothing song.
    Pervasively it floats, it sails;
    It smoothly swims and slips along.
    Just like the Midas Golden Touch,
    Where all that's touched turns into gold,
    So too your voice to music sets
    All words that from your lips are told.
    Sometimes it's shy, sometimes reserved.
    Sometimes robust, your voice transforms.
    One day its glad, one day it's blue,
    One day it's sad, but always warm.
    A most receptive audience,
    You'll find your voice has in my ear.
    The lullaby I call your voice,
    That melody I long to hear.

—*David Cavazos*

You the Star

And yet death is not far, and life is not long.
You shall turn into a star, and all the time long you shall
sing a song.
Not of hope, nor of glory. Sing with pride, and you'll be
soaring. With an everlasting glide.
You shall live there for ever more. And till' the end of
eternity you shall soar.

—*Aimee Schmidt*

Christmas Choir

Peaks of pines against
a graying sky,
Arched windows framing night's spirit
Ancient music written by unknown genius
Haunts my memory.

Simple
Christmas songs played on
Early plucked instruments,
Sounds of harp and lute,
To honor
The Christ child's birth.

Human voices spilling
Through the eons of time.
God's gift forever beautiful.
—*Doris Fuller Pylkas*

Untitled

The children play merry and gay
A great big sunshine hovers over this gorgeous day

The flowers bloom
And on this day, you'll find no gloom

The swings go high
As the children try to touch the sky

They laugh and scream
And shout with gleam

They are all so young
Their lives have just begun

They play on and on
And sing little children songs

As the day turns into night
The children still play with all their might

Even as they are all tucked away in their beds
The memories of this day will never leave their heads
—*Kelli Smith*

Subtropical Snowsick Blues

There is a grumble.
  A guttural, gut-bucket squelch that embalms my suffocating
        skin, tropical heat of sauna temperatures.
  Head pounding, feet tingling in anticipant rest, my hands
coated in a film of sloppy wetness that can't be sandpapered
from my darkened skin. The sound of the jungle is the stomach
and the engine of mother nature, her metabolism churns and
moves slowly but surely in the tropical mists and sweeping
storms of compounding wetness. The trees are vibrant, the
        birds are vibrant, even the grass is vibrant.
Insects crawling, living, avoiding, scavenging in their crunchy
  shells and shining chitin barrier skin, glowing in red and
    green that beg to be snatched up and chewed like candy.
Rain that taps, taps, taps, on my pith helmet never ends and
        the chinese water torture is music to my ears.
  Rain that tumbles across lonely frogs and down the moisten
flesh of lizards that flick their tongues to catch mini-drops
      and rainwater waste, the rain that falls tirelessly and
silently, noise of racket and commotion to the trees that wish
only to be left alone, yet beg to be eaten, picked and pruned
            by the jungle's gardeners.
—*James Hazlett Foreman*

Heart Of Sorrow

A saddened smile sits on a face of stone
    A hardened heart weakened, cries
As she sits accompanied by thoughts alone
    of glory days in another time.

  She longs for times that used to be
    and knows they'll not be again;
  Though they live on in her memory
    to haunt her now and then.

And the ghosts bring with them a pain,
    that sometimes comes and goes,
from the feelings inside her that remain
    for the love she no longer knows.

Still she waits in silence and wonders
    of what will come tomorrow
to break the spell she's living under
    and free her heart of sorrow.
—*Lisa M. Smith*

Seekers

The path of one's direction many a human traveler seeks.

With every step plotted on the map of consciousness
a hidden path awaits the sleeping mind.

With knowing grace and precision, we plan our
route but faulting haste can exploit one's demise.

Between the lines of doubt and those of understanding,
lies the path of truth that is cautiously demanding.

The winding path of facts both truth and justice are
sometimes least traveled when short coming exist.

Future travelers beware, for life's travel log conspires
to lay the path with human doubt.

Those who seek the high road forsaking the low,
labor with love for they travel alone.

Those lonely travelers, seekers of the truth, ingrain on the
path of wisdom for other lonely travelers to follow.

I have chosen to seek this path, to lay prints upon
an uncharted route, for I too am a lonely seeker.
—*Robert A. Fish*

Final Flight

A sacred voice called to her;
A host of angelic beings surrounded her
winged with truth and love.
So familiar were their faces;
Mama, papa, dear friends passed on before.
Embracing her with a tenderness
we cannot attain on this earthly plane.

Upward her spirit soared
towards the light;
Free from pain and dependency;
Music — lovelier than any heard before
echoed through the clouds
as she entered Heaven's door;
And the sights — color softer than the first
days of Spring hold;
Images more beautiful than crystal snowflakes
falling to the ground;
So much beauty she looked upon
as her feet softly trod
and her soul was awash with the face of God.
—*Maxine H. Benedick*

What Is Love?

ove is,
 kiss,
caring little hug,
 beautiful sunset,
 beautiful night sky
ith every star twinkling up high.
's a beautiful song when you
st learned the words.
's waking up to a beautiful spring
ay when you hear the singing of the birds.
's a fluffy little kitten when you hold
 tight.
's a beautiful rose with a touch of dew.
s sitting close next to you.
s wedding bells,
d fairy tales,
s the thought of being free,
t what love is, is the feelings
tween you and me.
        —*Juana Lucio*

ntitled

shot gun laying in arms of
kneeling boy whose in total
spair and hate. A lovely couple
d child in a deep lifeless sleep
e as if they had all laid down
d body stopped moving. All four so
tless and helpless. One in despair
d three others gone to heaven. Such
oy that would end things in such a way.
uple so crazy but loving and kind.
ung child so infantile and dumb. One
t of four shall live no longer in
spair, but in questions until the
es of Hell come along.
        —*Deborah G. Lazenby*

addy's Song

a world lost, a man has a dream.
life incomplete. Unsure are the
swers it seems.
rewarding are the games he plays.
rhaps something new will pave the way.

a world unkind, he works hard
r the dream.
r daddy's little lady, china dolls and
ecious rings.
s mind full of plans of the things she'll do.
life free of worries. The degrees, the schools.

a world uncertain, dreams are gone.
looses control. He can't hold on.
aware of the sadness she brings.
termined to do her thing.

a world temporal, new dream are made.
aybe with new visions hope can be saved.
ough hard times come, all things pass.
e bond between father and child will always last.

ove you, Daddy.
        —*Denise Harper*

Little Child Lost

A child is born into this world naked and scared
A little boy with love on his side

But love takes strange and meaningless turns
Turns that we do not understand

Confusion surrounds this little boy like a cloud
A cloud much too dense to explain

Lost in a sea that he can't understand
And certainly doesn't know how to explain

He looks to adults for answers to prayers
But somehow they fall on deaf ears

A little boy with hopes and dreams of his own
All muddled with tears and with fear

Years go by and still a need exists
Yet survival is the name of the game

Love that was once so very clear to see
Is replaced by a loneliness of one

Time takes a toll on a little boy lost

Time that can never be replaced

Where, oh where is that little boy now
As the tries to keep a smile on his face
        —*Wayne Prince*

"A Flower Falls"

A rose and a fallen tear. The message seems quite clear.
A man that carries no name. Who can question, who is to blame.
His mouth is dry, as rain falls from a grey sky.
His hand is covered with blood. The flower falls from his
hand, into the mud. The lightning flashes, and for a second
the sky is a brilliant light. Who is to say if he was wrong
or right. It was his decision, from his thoughts and dreams.
But the end, was it justified by the means. The Rose turns to
dust. The question is not whether he was wrong, but was he just.
        —*Roger L. Smith*

A Different Kind, A Different Me

I am a gift from God to my Mom and Dad,
A more precious gift they've never had.

A laugh and cry just like you, but deep inside I always knew,
I was more different that most of you.

To be different is to stand out,
Jesus was different without a doubt.

All I want is that same love,
That God gives us from above.

My different looks make you stare,
Or pretend that I'm not there.

Open your mouth and speak to me,
For each kind deed I know He'll see.

He's given you a body that moves with grace,
And perfect features to make a beautiful face.

Stop! Stop! This can happen to you!
It only takes a minute and you normal life is through!

It's my prayer you'll never reside,
In a body where your thoughts must hide....

Behind a mask where people see,
A different kind, A different me.
        —*Donese J. Stewart*

A Prayer of Thanks

Dear God, as I gaze upon the splendor of
a mountain bathed in the first light of day
I see the work of a master sculptor in
every light and ray
An artist too were you when at last
the time had come
To put in all the colors of the rainbow
and then you added some.

But did you build a still life, no not
an artist such as you
You added birds to fill the air in
every color and every hue
Bright colored fish in sea and stream
you added to this scape
Flowers and plants of every color were
put in to make the drape.

All of this you set against a sky
of crystal blue
Thank you God for giving me eyes to see
the works of an artist such as you.
    —Charles S. FeBuary

I Remember Her

I remember her, from long ago,
A muse within my mind;
A lovely nymph, that once I knew,
who left me far behind.

I held her once, and kissed her twice,
But never once again;
For time, to quickly, passed us by
Before love could begin;

And though I shed no tears,
As I watched her pass and bid a soft farewell;
I wonder now, what could have been
Had love but cast it's spell.
    —D. Jonathan White

Life

A child is born
A new life begins
A grandparent dies
That's the way of our lives.

From crawling to walking
A child grows
And can now reach the doorknob
Without standing on his toes.

And then one day he's off to school
Now the child wants to be cool.

My baby isn't a baby anymore
For when he sits his feet reach the floor.

Now he is in college with a degree
He keeps drifting away from me.

Now he is married with a family of three
And he lives far away from me.

My life will end soon
Yours will too
So I'll get what I can out of life
So will you.
    —Paige Harrison

Tranquility

A lofty pine, a spindly oak,
A patch of blue grass the crab grass did not choke;
Rows of painted houses, all neat and prim;
Within — warmth, good cheer and kettles filled to the brim.
No one stirs as the dawn draws near;
Hardly a whisper does one hear.
Give us the strength to preserve
  THIS PEACE;
Help our dreams to never cease.
    —Kittie Scobie

Mess

A mess of footsteps in the snow.
A pattern made of souls on their way,
each and every one in their direction,
confused, without contact.
But the imprints of their feet are mingled,
are put in layer on layer in the snow.
That far can the souls go in being together,
with the imprints of their bodies' feet.
Closer than a false physical acting,
they do not dare to come.
    —Rita Fernholm

Heart

    Every time a snowflake falls
a person is watching, thinking, dreaming,
    calling.
Watch closely and you will see a different pattern
of marks and scars.
Think loudly and you will hear nothing of their
soft cry of pain as they die.
Dream enough and your past and future
you can see clearly.
Call out to find no one to
hear you cry.
If all of the gates are closed before you,
Follow your heart and you will see
the truth that lies within
    —Maria Mejia

Why?

A poem is a very hard thing to write,
A person just doesn't know where to start.
Everyone has a different reason to write one,
You need hope and a lot of inspiration to even try to start one
So, why am I trying so hard?
I've tried to start a poem with my blank mind.
I'm looking for words, when there are no words to find.
I have neither the words or inspiration.
So why am I sitting here with a blank mind?
Because I can't write one,
That's why I want to so bad.
And don't you think it just a bit sad,
Things that some take for granted,
Others wish for so hard?
Why do some find things easy
While others find them so hard?
Why are some peoples lives full of sadness,
While others seems so full of only gladness?
Why does this world seem so unfair?
Regretfully, I have no answer for that question there.
    —Cynthia Montoya

Rejection"

y teardrops, slowly trickle down my lonely cheeks,
 puddle of sorrow, surrounds me where I sleep.
ly mind is devastated from the harshness of your storm,
ut my heart remains a captive, in your garden of thorns.

ly body lays shivering, from the coldness of your heart,
ly wounds sit aching, my clothes shred apart.
ou rejected my feelings of love, like an unwanted child
o you could remain free, and keep my feelings running wild

ou didn't stop to help me, when you heard me start to cry,
ou turned and walked away, you left me there to die.
nere I lay all alone, as peaceful as a dove,
nere I lay all alone, a victim of my love.

y heart still beats faintly, from when you stomped it to the
oor, every breath is a struggle, each heartbeat a war.
till keep my hopes, raised to the heavens up above,
nd pray that you don't leave me, dying for your love.
    —*Peter A. Ganio Jr.*

Rock in My Shoe

ugity blue, bugity Dan please give me something for my hand.
    A rock in my hand, a rock in my hand.
    It isn't' much bigger than a grain of sand.
        Why this tiny rock for my hand?
    It's for your shoe. It's for your shoe.
        Put the tiny rock in your shoe.
            In my shoe? In my shoe?
ugity Dan Bugity Blue what in this world is wrong with you?
        Why this rock for my shoe?
    Walk on the rock and you will see.
    Nothing in this world is wrong with me.
        You won't cry and you won't pout
        You will jump and you will shout.
    It will feel so good when you take it out.
    —*Wallace H. Vroman*

g Newton

ne stars keep shining above a clouded sky...
ose is just a plant, and a thorn is something that will hurt you.
ing perfect makes practices
ople are plastic
. is not reality and the channel 5 news team has false teeth
 a square room there are no curves
 roots are the source of everything, never the ends
inionated people have free minds
cidents are not on purpose and there should be no fault
ork is evil
usic is a freedom of expression through noise
 mind has melted into toxic waste
nool is a jail to keep students under control
live is to lie and to lie is to live
 sun shines darkest at night
mework kills brain cells
ear is a drop of water
 better or worse, the earth will never be the same nor changed.
d the stars keep shining above a clouded sky.
    —*Amy Sturm*

rst Impression

sion is only a form of imagination
agination has many pairs of eyes.
 are all of different formations
 we live our separate lives.

nat one sees in another
nay not be the truth.
t the imagination has formed the vision
nd we believe the vision to be true.
    —*Donna Bolander*

"Christmas Eternal"

Another fond Christmas is drawing near;
A season of hope and memories dear,
From Bible days and one Hoss Sharys;
To heavenly Carols on God's air waves,

Pretty candles flickered on our popcorned tree;
Loving Grandma tended them tenderly,
I played with sport on our floor below;
While Bill enjoyed, "Mother Natures," snow.

Jolly St. Nick still makes his trips;
From the "North Pole," with lovely gifts,
Churches pray for "Peace and Cheer."
Till, "Merry Christmas," returns next year.
    —*Harryet Severne*

I Saw...

The year 1981. I saw a Castle aflame at night,
a sky in crimson glow,
an Eagle which spread its wings
embraced the flame and put it out partly.

    The year 1987. I saw crowds from Carpathian mountainous
    altars surrounding the crowned Madonna of Fatima
    in wayworn clothes, with a smile on her face,
    holy rosary filling her hands.

The year 1991. I saw Christ against a background of nature
in a white halo of soft light
appearing as the "Good Shepherd",
harmony of nations - Peace for the World.

    The year 1992. I saw my mother - a messenger -
    pronouncing clearly the words:
    "Our Lady disclosed her will
    and her Son's - lead people to Heavens".
    —*Franciszek Lojas-Kosla*

Outside Of You

A numbness falls across my face,
a smile, a laugh, to hide disgrace,
when all I want is one embrace
from you, who knows my anchoring place.

I shared your heart, your breath, your soul,
until you left me to enroll
in strangers' arms that day you ran,
to where your safer life began.

Hope can only buy some time.
I need your love so I can climb
away from grief, from dark despair,
always strangled, in mid-air.

Another year, a rising sun,
and thoughts of you, the parting one,
cast their shadows, shades of gray,
tales of how I came this way.

When you gave me up, my Mom,
you released in me that bomb,
each day to defuse anew,
struggling outside of you.
    —*Ellen Weitzman*

A Prayer to Tell Him

A prayer to tell him the world must go on.
A prayer to tell him to make me and
everyone healthy and wealthy with love and pride.
A prayer to tell him drug wars, abortions,
crime and killing must have an end.
A prayer to tell him to answer all of our
prayers when we need it answered the most.
    —*Nicole Smith*

Golden Years

History deeply mirrored in aging eyes
A tender look at years gone by
Reflected in a world shaped by hands
Gnarled from inroads, numerous as sand.

A face etched with memories bittersweet
Lined with wrinkles weatherbeaten and deep
Hiding fond desires of fading quests
Now mere visions slowly laid to rest.

Silver strands through wisps of hair
Fragile threads of dimming life and care
Gently turning towards the golden years
With a spirit mellowed by sweet tears.

An ageless walk nearing the end of life
The horizon looming bright in sight
Eternal, beyond the glowing setting sun
Slowly strolling into God's golden light.

—*Pauline Philippou*

Holocaust

A number of years ago, in a very civilized age
A terrible thing happened a display of human rage

Of anger and hatred toward others
Of resentment so strong, it could kill
Came the Holocaust, the whirlwind,
It doesn't even seem real...
It doesn't even seem possible,
the story sounds insane
How could six million people be killed in such a terrible way?

But it's true, men and women were gassed,
Their children were shot and burned
They were tortured beyond belief,
Still, silent was the world.

And now, fifty years later,
Some people dare say
the Holocaust was a dream
It never, ever happened that way

But to me, the tears were real
the suffering, fear and pain
So, please remember don't forget
so it shouldn't happen again.

—*Elana Voskoboynikov*

"House Of Stone"

Oh house of stone and days gone by.
About a mile from other folks.
In meadow green you stand alone.
And parallel a gentle breeze.

Oh house of stone with slated crown.
Your chimney seems to keep you bound.
But not to say that such is fact.
Because each stone must hold its spot.

Oh house of stone and withered brow.
You compliment the mirrored pond.
Although your frames are slightly bent.
But, like the pines are straighter from afar.

Oh house of stone, a simple home.
I long to live inside your womb.
And like a stone, a part of you.
I'll bond and keep the house of stone.

—*Joseph A. Suders*

"Bill"

There is a presence in this house, I feel it always near
A voice I hear, a smile I see, although he isn't here.
I see his face so strong and tan, his eyes of deepest brown
His hair as black as winter coal, I see his constant frown
A good father he has always been, a husband kind and true
Whenever I am down and out, he always pulls me through.
In times of trouble he's a rock, so sure in all his ways.
There's nothing that can get him down, he's matured so much
    with age.
I see his body big and strong, those arms that hold me tight
I hear his voice that seems to say: "I love you dear -- goodnight"
I cannot put him from my mind, no matter how I try.
His presence always seems so near, I'll love him till I die.
He stays with me most every hour, sometimes against my will.
The man I speak of in this verse, is my dear husband "Bill."

—*Diana Fortner*

Untitled

A voice like falling water - it's workin'
A voice like the wind - it works
Are you workin? Functioning smoothly again?
Something ain't working quite right, it needs adjustment.
Something ain't working quite right, don't throw it away!

Vicious circle changed by the wheel of fate
So as the sun dies you do
But we all know the sun will rise again
And of course that means you too.

We now know that life is made for living
It's there for us to show
That through a death life is given
When the wind blows cold
You've got to fly above the storm
Look into yourself and you will find spring
Then you'll turn around.

—*Brett A. Rouse*

Since She Went Away

A lady who was dear who had a taste for life
A woman of true strength who had been through much strife
You held us all in the palm of your hand
You kept us together a family so grand.
Then something went wrong, fate twisted your hand
To leave us scattered with something unplanned.
We looked up to you with respect in our eyes.
We shed many a tear when we said our goodbyes.
A year has gone by since you've gone away
We all miss you more than words could ever say
Time cannot erase the memories we hold
For we love you very dearly much more than I have told.

—*Bonnie J. Bertholde*

Tiny Miracles In My Arms

I've loved you from the moment you were born, what
a thrill it gave me to hold you two tiny miracles
in my arms. You were the most beautiful babies I
had ever seen, when I looked into your eyes they
would sparkle and gleam. You filled my heart with
delight when I first saw you on that warm contented
night. My happiness flowed as I held you newborns
near. You were both so precious and dear. It was
the happiest time I ever remember. It didn't matter
whether you were born spring, summer, fall or winter
now you are grown up I still love you as much as
I did when you were born, I'll never forget
how it felt to hold you tiny miracles in my arms.

—*Agnes Johnson*

The Realm Of Beauty

The hills are aflame with the glory of autumn.
It quilts the ridges from top to bottom.
The wind sings a hymn of thanks for what nature decrees.
And chants a dirge for the dying leaves.

—*Bennie W. Howe*

The Guitar

Before a friend of mine moved away, He sat me down to tell me
about life one day. The night began to settle in, the moon was
full, and there were a billion stars. He simply asked, "Do you
know how many strings are on a guitar?" "Six, I think. Why?" I
I asked quickly. He then told me a story of life and tragedy,
the life of everybody sung on a guitar. I can't say the same
words for I forget, but I remember the meaning and for this my
life will always be in his debt. A guitar consists of six
strings, which make melody, death, and dreams. You can combine
some strings to make a chord, which song your life since you
were born. A chord is a path of light and of life. Mixed
music: meeting a new friend, falling in love, or a sudden dead
end. Everyone plays a different melody, that molds their life
they have today. For some the music is sad, but others come
along to make you laugh, hurt, make love to, or make you mad.
And along this melody you play, comes your soul mate some day.
With age your song changes, and you write it down on memory
pages. God gave the talent and man made guitar, but only you
can pull the right strings to reach all your dreams.

—*Barbara Chamberlain*

What If

If President Kennedy would have thought
About what the year '63 sought
Do you think that he'd have changed anything
at all that he had gained. As a man
who wanted freedom for all which was
his duty and one of his call. If people
could bring him back you see in the
White House I'm sure he would be
with the happiness of a child, with his
warm and boyish smile, with his heart
so gay and pure everyone loved him of this
you can be sure.
When he was shot on that November day the
world was sorrowful each country in its
own quaint way. Now he's gone and laid
to rest still the country is doing its best.
Future generations now will know
as others did years ago about the
man of '63 as he goes down in history.

—*Janice L. Ajose*

Just Perfect

I'm getting older with every day;
Acquiring a healthier outlook on the way.
My hands show many a scar.
My eyes are dim - I guess that's par.
My nose, seems to forever grow.
And arthritis, I have in my big toe.
My hair is getting rather thin;
Sure a lot easier to get a trim.
Many times its tough not to show,
Headaches that seem to come and go.
My legs are short and a bit stout.
My body is long; without a doubt.
I'm not overweight - I'd deny.
Just under height, I'd reply.
But, still perfect for the job;
Every time God calls - I have no doubt.

—*Ralph L. Miller*

You and I

You are the birds that glide
across the sky in everlasting time.
I am the tree on which you come
forth to decorate the life of mine.

You are the honey that's spread
abundantly around the spacious honeycomb.
I am the bee who guards you and
protects you because you make me feel at home.

You are the firm grass that lies
among the surface of the earth.
I am the low soil that you lift up
to give warm dignity and worth.

You are the sky that roams each
day giving away its tremendous glory.
I am the bird that gets delighted by
plenty room and an endless story.

You are the variety of colorful flowers.
that give their color to each day.
I am the morning that gets bright and
brightener each time you come my way.

—*Patrick Carrasco*

Confused Heart

We always fight in front of any other
Acting as if we were sister and brother
But suddenly, when alone, it seems to all turn
And no more hatred seems to burn
I wish I could trust you the way that I should,
But what proof do I have, that I really could
I don't know if you care or not,
About how I feel or what I though
I need to know how you really feel
Because to me it means a great deal
It's not that I don't like you or whatever your thinking
I just feel if I get to attached, I'll end up sinking
So, where do we go from here is what I'd like to know
Because right now, I'm feeling pretty low.

—*Jessica Tata*

Sleeplessness

The rhythm drums like the steady beat of an
African tribal tune and I feel my heart in my ears, the
pulse in my eyes. Turning round and round
I am looking for the moon-set to end the long night.
The cat pads over my pillow and settles in the corner
of the bed, nestling up to him.
I am washed over by slide after slide of winter storms, cars
spinning, dark walks up the steep driveway, arms
wrapped for warmth, and running and
slipping back down,
praying for a light at the bottom in the sleeping house;
by snapshots of dusky eves carrying a chill as
children tumble through piles of leaves, smelling the autumn
scent, falling asleep with arms glued to my sides
and hands gripping my legs, toes pointed together
to avoid the edge of the bed.

The noise of the cars fades as they pass beneath the window and
I turn back to the ceiling,
listening for the rhythm of me,
squeezed tightly together waiting for morning.

—*Lynn S. P. Warner*

279

"Rude Awakening"

A tiny green plant did sprout one day
After a rain - in the month of May
And as she grew she looked all around
To see just who shared her plot of ground

She found herself surrounded by flowers
So she began to while away hours
Deciding which kind of flower to be
Finding fault with each one she did see

"The daisy is too painted for me
And a shy violet I wouldn't be
The peony I would find much too big
The marigold seems to wear a wig"

As time went by and she grew quite tall
She received a shock to end them all
She saw flowers around her going to seed
And knew at last - she was just a weed.

　　　—*Nina Simmons*

Downwinders Doomsday

In Utah in nineteen fifty-one
　　after nuclear testing had just begun,
They stood and watched the mushroom cloud
　　and some expressed their fears out loud.
Little did they realize
　　the burst exploding before their eyes
their very lives would jeopardize.
　　But the Army and the A.E.C.
In a decision that will live in infamy,
　　suppressed all pertinent information
on the lethal effects of radiation.
　　With many dead and thousands dying
our government continued lying;
　　and went on testing for twenty years,
ignoring the downwinders valid fears.
　　And now in summation of this aberration;
Why was this deadly concentration
　　unleashed, (with no consideration)
upon an unsuspecting Mormon nation
　　and the victims told, "No Reparation".?

　　　—*Harry E. Hartshorne*

Dora's Day

　　She cautiously mounts the steps to the porch
　　　　After tending to the flowers.
　　After eighty-some years, being careful
　　　　Is an important habit to have.
　　　　She glances at his coats
　　　　　　Hanging on those hooks
　　　　For the last fifteen years.
　　A momentary feeling of warmth and security
　　　　Rises from the fire of her memory.
　　　　　　Toast a Poptart
　　　　And the day is off to a good start.
There's enough yarn to get through another day.
　　The quiet silence of the wheat fields
　　　　　　Enfolds her.
　　　　　　Life can be so good!

　　　—*Chas Q. Stefani*

Lost

　　Love is a dark velvet night piercing my heart, leaving
me scared and lonely, and through my pierced heart you can
see my blood dripping away, as is my life. Flowing away from
me in day and through the night. Sometime my heart will
heal, but even then I will have a scar, and the life that
I had lost can never be replaced.

　　　—*Eric Porter*

Hometown Girl

　　　Hometown girl lost in the swirl,
　　living life in the curl of a New York wave.
　　　　Can you hear me in the west?
　　　　Doing here what I do best,
　　lying out beneath the sun wondering what I will become.

　　　—*James G. Little*

Fighting

Yelling and screams, and cries,
After there's many sighs.
I can hear it all from my bed,
Pretending to sleep, by covering my head.
The door soon opens, I feel the chill,
Our picture fell off my window sill.
I get out of bed, and go downstairs,
She's sitting there repeating "who cares".
I love her so, and him as much,
Why are they so out of touch.
I want to help, what can I do?,
So I whisper "I love you".
He comes back in, drops to his knees,
"Take me back? Oh won't you please?".
She says yes, they hug so tight,
They promise again to never fight.
They walk away hand in hand,
Knowing where their feelings stand.

　　　—*Beth Russell*

"The Omniscient"

Into what rivers of blood will you mortals go? Your
aggressions and deeds crucify your soul. Into what
wildernesses will you dare brave. . . Of those fields along
the way will you harvest, or ravage? Clad in what values do
you mortals abide? Idleness and ignorance. Bigotry; false
pride. Who, then, do you say you are? Not a man, less than a
beast, for your carnivorous hunger must constantly feast on
others. The legacies written for you are now blackened with
dust: covered by centuries of shame; pain; justice unjust. For
the love among men you have denied. Equality, you say? You
cast the meaning aside. . . Power is your primary quest and it
seems to matter not at whose sacrifice it was sought. So . . .
Beast of man; where is your mind? Your ideals, integrity,
philosophies refined? Where is your truth, your love, your
right? Where is your wisdom? All I see is your plight . . .
And I cannot honor you . . .

　　　—*Donna Nielsen-Salih*

Washington Booker T.

Once, I met a girl with melodic voice, of goddess-muse,
agreeable resemblance. Persona intellectual sagacious indeed,
ethos in character, always sweet. Generous, innocent soul,
inherent politeness, the behavior prime-superb, aristocratic
manners. Elegant, chic, magnifique, fragrance nerium-oleander,
in school nicknamed oreo-cookie. One day oreo-cookie said:
would you desire to visit, to admire, something of higher
discipline? I mean the elementary near my childhood-years
neighborhood, let's go... hey!! Chance unique to focus, my
love by that historic site, a doric architecture all around,
the edifice majestic, the astron-public school, this dedicated
building; to educator of the elite, who lived a century ago,
to noble honoree, Washington Booker Taliafero Booker T.! In
there, my love was taught: how do the vowels like to dance,
and, how to ethic values play. How does the knowledge make,
in life a greater sense, and how asteroids, eternally light-up
the heavens. Oh!! how pleasantly excited students learnt:
what are galaxies, cosmogony details, treasures of the God.
trigono-stereometry via the stars design, how to respect
own-self, and, unto others', life-honor-fortune-health.

　　　—*Apollo Karayans*

This Place

As I lie her upon the ground,
  all appears upside-down.
The trees, the flowers, and the sky
  all adhere to my powerful eye.

Why I'm here you may be wondering?
I am in this place to do my pondering.
I am pondering the life that I live and
  the purpose that it gives.

Because, my world too is upside-down and I am
  flat upon the ground.

That my reason for here I lie.
  For, if what I see does not please me,
  I can simply close my eyes.
      —Marci Louise Donner

Once Upon a Halloween Night

Once upon a Halloween night,
all children were in sight.
House to house and door to door,
wanting candy more and more.
Reaching out and reaching in,
storing candy in a bin.
Witches and ghosts
were what you would see, and
spiders and bats jumping in and
out of trees.
Some things were green, some things
were red, some things had purple spots
up on their heads, going house to house and
door to door wanting candy more and more.
Boo!!! Did I scare you?
Happy Halloween
      —Tiffany Jackson

"Days"

There are days when
All I do is smile and laugh
Days when I'm glad to be alive
Days when my love piles high.

These are the days when all are my friend
Days I can't wait to begin
Days that have too quick of an end
These are the days that are a godsend.

There are days when
Nothing matters at all
Days when nothing seems right
Days when I can't wait for night.

These are the days when I have no heart
Days that I don't want to start
Days in which I want no part
These are the days that feel too dark.
      —Christina Hogbin

Devastation

The scourge of the sky
Acts with apocalyptic action.
And the rage that befalls from this disastrous
Turn of nature is much like the aftermath
of a gruesome battle.

While the eyes of this horrifying tunnel monster
looks down at its destruction,
I wonder if it enjoys its work?
      —Jeremy Kimble

The Deadly Sin

All alone I sit in the darkness,
All shot up and confused.
Emotions running through me like a freight train
My head is spinning, my hands are shaking.
I need something to stop this quaking.
A few small lines of white, to take the darkness
from this night.
Now my head is swelling and my brain is numb.
Floating around I can see, Faces in the mirror
but they are not me.
I touch myself and feel nothing.
Just a peace within.
My soul silent and deadly.
My old friend has taken my life.
For cocaine I have sacrificed.
      —Jennifer Raymond

Quiet Time

The body has now given pause to its hurried flight -
Allowing in the stillness of a quiet night.

This special moment when the mind meets the soul -
The joining of one's deeds and thoughts, to complete the whole.

Memories mix with what is ahead -
Sharing space, while the mine is fed.

The fullness flows from head to toe -
Allowing homage to the past, and what is yet to know.

One's eyes and ears have given their best -
And a day's end, are now allowed to rest.

A spiritual love now fills the air -
Surrounding the room and all that is there.

These feelings that mean so much -
Must then be sent to those, you cannot touch.

Solitude maintains its comfort form -
Ready to nourish through night, 'til morn.

Shadows begin against the wall -
The shape I see tells me, you've come to call.
      —L. P. McKelvey

Rain

The air hangs thick and grey,
  almost tangible,
Pervaded by a sense of serenity.

The world waits in awe,
  absolute silence,
Anticipating the gift to be bestowed by the swollen clouds.

Then...a single crystalline droplet falls from the heavens,
  clean and clear,
Holding the purity of angels.

  Another,
    and another,
    and another,

Until...a host of the tiny gifts cascade through the sky,
  softly,
Like miles of silk released from the arms of God.

The celestial nectar caresses the expectant Earth,
  divine blessings,
Bringing revitalization and rejuvenation to all.
      —Rachel Seher

Destiny

I am a man,
alone among the masses,
uncertain, nay unknowing of my fate.
My destiny passes
through a melancholy gate,
a mirror of the past,
laced heavily with tarnished silver glass.
I stare hard and see a wall
which vaguely shuns my sight.
My glance turns towards
its arrogant and wavering reflection;
sometimes I dream
that there I've seen a hollow, guiding light.

—*Ryan Wise*

Untitled

Dark and lonely in these shadowy woods
Alone and cold, there I was I stood
Afraid and scared because I knew I'll lose some
Letting you go is what has become
Wishing the past would all erase
Feeling better if I knew my heart was safe
Getting you back is really too late
When you were leaving I should've said "Wait"
But I didn't and now I feel really bad
Knowing a good thing is what I had
It's terrible how good things is what you lose
I really can't explain, I have no clues
If I had of known I would feel this way
I would've stopped you when leaving and asked you to stay
It's unhealthy when you is what I lack
If we ever speak again I'll ask you to come back
Because I really hate walking in the dark
And having this pain within my heart

—*Jean A. Sonnier*

I Surrender

The horses pound their splendid legs
  along the land and pine ridge views
Where the sunflower grows and quivers
  'neath the morning dew.
The land is full of rights, where the dove
  wail it's signals in sing-songs.
And storms strikes the rocks, and grinds them
  with prolong winds, ever so strong.

In the excitement of the dawn I awaken
  from my snow-white pillows...
And see from my window, the chestnut furrows
  hugging the roads from the plow.
In the whispering infinity of space...
  I sense my own smallness
I consider the sun-light and respond silently
  to its magnificence.
And then I'm grateful for it all.

—*Elizabeth L. Whitlatch*

Untitled

Somebody is know...
a thrill a flute of a fiddle is give the riddle;
You to me and but your abilities and the man of me
And you put in strength and carried the duties about me,
How strong are you to me?
Reallity of who is I am the storm of thunder
And like a violent rumble how is do and things to please!
You and but a tense is get of mass from you
And but know, how you serve of yourselves

—*Luther Darnell Stapleton, Jr.*

The Pain of Missing You

I can't show you the pain I feel being without you,
although I know, you feel the same pain than I do.
Sometimes I'd like to cry out my pain loud,
but it wouldn't be loud enough that
  you could hear my shout.

I know you're fighting for freedom and
  I hope it will be,
but who allows you to be free?
  Free! Here with me!

Then in all this bitterness I have to smile,
when I think of our summer filled with joy for a while.
Having your baby moving shyly under my heart,
shows that you are with me, even though
  we're apart!

—*Silvia L. Maurer*

Enduring Gladiator

Heroes unheralded....unsung...patriotic brave men...
  Always armed with rifles and courage...
    Now thrust into action
    from land, sea or air.

Oft times presumed to be obsoleted by technology...
    machine guns, artillery, tanks.
    Assumed to be superseded by science...
    poison gas, flame throwers, atom bombs.

Yet, the infantry..."Queen Of Battle"...has persevered...
    become highly sophisticated.
    A necessity in an unsettled world...
Sought after when trouble is imminent...vital if hostilities
    actually erupt.

Although most skilled in aggressive arts...
Infantrymen harbor no real love or reverence for Gods-Of-War.

But, when that necessity does call-them-to-arms...
    When kid-glove turns to fist of mail...
    Their ALL is most freely offered-up...
    And, many are sacrificed on the altar
of man's inability to relate to his fellow man.

—*Arthur Lazarus*

America a Land of Beauty

America a land of beauty
America we so proudly
Raise our banners high
like a proud eagle
That spreads its wings across the sky
America we love thee
The United States flag called oh Glory
oh how proudly she gleams in her colors
of red, white and blue, her stars and stripes
So brightly shine all across every land for all the world to
see that grand old flag called glory, how we love thee
America a land of beauty
a flaming burning torch lights up the city's so brightly
like it was the fourth of July so America named
Liberty so brightly and proudly she shines with has to
Hold high, a sparkle gleams in a little child's eyes
As a bright shining star falls from the sky a wish was granted
for all the world to see. A land filled with joy, peace and
freedom and together we sing in harmonic America we love thee
This is our America a land of beauty.

—*Judy Ann Brown*

Untitled

As the World fulfills a turn,
Many things come godsend,
The bad things eventually burn,
While good things will never end!

—*Neil Gandhi*

Dustless

I look out the window and stare down the road.

No sound, no dust
Always I wait for him...

Supper is over and done. Again I left it out for him.

Another
meal alone.

Solitude, the sound of crickets.

I look out the window and stare down the road.

No sound, no dust
Always I wait for him...

I sit and watch TV, but I don't watch. The refrigerator motor
kicks on; humming, relentless.

I look out the window and stare down the road.

No sound, no dust
Always I wait for him...

Is he safe? Or again were his thoughts only of himself?
I imagine a dozen different fates.

I look out the window and stare down the road.

No sound, no dust
Always I wait for him...

Car lights...

—*Becky S. Adams*

Always

Always fragile, yet strong in beauty.
Always reaching for the light, but finding shadows.
Always kissing the rain, to end up crying.
Always a sweet fragrance, lost through the years.
Always tangled, but free and wild.
Always, always trying to seek the glory.
A rose may look simple and true, but everyday it struggles to
live.
This rose symbolizes our friendship.
With it's changes and rocky trials.
But in the end we break those walls, revealing a single rose.
Reminding us that beauty only comes after suffering.
Always to be cherished.
Always.

—*Jessica Thany*

Molly

A friend through thick and thin.
Always there to listen on the other end.
Always telling me the truth,
So I don't have to become a sleuth,
I know that she will understand
And she always acts as a true friend.
She believes on what she know is inside of me,
Not what her eyes on the outside see.
God Bless her.
Cold winds of life 'round her stir,
Putting me to the test,
Make me as strong as her,
Because she deserves only the best.

—*Christine Miles*

I Need A Helping Hand:

What is it that you see? Why do you stare at me?
Am I not of flesh and blood? Do I not bleed when I am cut?
Can it be to you I'm lazy? Perhaps you think I'm crazy"
Do I not have a heart and a soul. Why do you stare as I shiver
In the cold? Maybe you are up set am I taking up space?
Or is it because I'm of another race'"
I hunger as you do I even cry its true.
You look a bit frighten as if I had a gun. I'm not a criminal
I'm not a nun. I'm simply in Limbo. I'm not a Hobo.
I have no place to call my own". I have no one to call at
home. There is no weapon in front of you,
Simply my hands thank God
I have two I'm hungry and cold and growing old.
I just need a hand, try to understand.
A nickel a dime, five seconds of your time, a simple smile
would even be fine.
But please don't run, I'm not a bum, I once had two jobs and
now I have none.

—*Michael A. Porrella*

"Twilight Zone"

Enter in the twilight zone
amidst a mental block
where colors shine in black and white
as hands tied on a clock
We've tapped our minds and nothings there-
Were drowning in our need-
Our brains are numb-
Our minds are blank-
Our veins like rivers bleed-

Illusion and reality are scrambled in the mind
We've stared into the midnight sun till
darkness steals us blind-
We've ran this race before and lost
yet still we try again
Where colors shine in black and white
And virtue turns to sin

This twilight zone is no ones stranger
Still it cuts just like a knife
It holds our hatreds and our fears-
This unknown zone... is life

—*Ernest Little*

Garden of Stone

The sun shines casting long shadows
amongst the rows of marble markers.
Makes me wonder what could be, if you were still here.
Soldiers stand at attention for all eternity.
Under command of an eternal watchman.
As the eerie silence takes vigil over these fallen man.
Lost in time, but not forgotten, for I know where they lay.
It all fades to black as the tears begin to fall.
In this Garden of Stone.
Loved ones come and go. You were the hardest to leave.
Goodbye, I must leave, before I loose control.
I will be back at a later time, to stand over you.
Remembering how it was, when I was but a child.
Before I had to come, and visit you, in this Garden of Stone.

—*Terry G. Bradshaw*

Words of Love

Softly, I whisper into your ear, the sacred words of love.
Knowing not what I do, but only of what I say. Sometimes
feeling alone, but thinking in my heart you are here.
Wondering if you know how I feel? This is my secret world,
sometimes dark and gloomy, but when you are near, you make it
shine. Always here for me in good times and bad, that is why
I will know my world will shine like a jewel, when you are near

—*Ilayna Barkan*

Untitled

Rainbow bridge ———
an arch of dreams
vaulted against the sky
and clouds!
   Who am I to rest beneath you?
Your proud strength stands for all to see and feel.
You do not ask that we kneel in worship ———
Only that we recall in hours to come
the small yellow flowers
blooming near your base,
placed against the tall height
of your rose sandstone span.
Your beauty reaches out
to capture the heart of every man.
You sing of many lovely things
though you rise in silence from the canyon floor.
   This sense of awe!
   I never saw and "touched"
   a rainbow before.
      —Doby Leuch

Untitled

A woman dies
An old man cries
Live on, live on
A life is gone
It seems nothing's fair
The man's life seeps through his empty stare
An only companion gone
It seems so wrong
The man's unbreakable smile that had always shown
Was now a frown upon a wrinkled face that was all alone
The old man became a very sad sight
He wished to join his wife so he put a twist to an old prayer that night
   Now I lay me down to sleep
   Pray the Lord my soul to take
   Let me die before I wake
   Pray the Lord my soul to take
He was disappointed the next day when he awoke from his sleep
Then in the last minute of his life he began to weep
      —Garrett Schafer

Ancient Ruins

So many broken pieces
Ancient ruins line around this old place
Trampled by the tracings of time
Weathered lines upon my face

So many empty spaces
Dusty shelves and unfinished rhymes
Scattered with no particular direction
Bits and fragments placed out of time

So many different faces
In and out of focus from my varied past
Flowing towards conscious reality
Perspective unable to last

So many endless changes
Footprints washed away in the sand
Racing out to gather momentum
Rushing tides eroding the land

So many varied methods
Lost in a myriad of space
Useful for a fleeting moment
Swept away without a trace
      —Jeffrey A. Sater

January

Night casts a net of stars across the sky
  and a voluptuous moon, seductively,
  trails veils of clouds about her face.

  Serene, peaceful goddess of the night
   beams radiantly down upon the Earth,
  Paving her icy streets with silver leaf
and draping the naked trees with diamonds.

   And as January wraps the infant year
    in downy white swaddling bands,
  I, from the skein of time allotted me,
   begin to knit another chain of days,
    a chain that will one day become
     my winter winding sheet.
      —Bonnie S. Mooney

"The FriendShip"

A "FriendShip" is built in time with one plank and nail forward
and aft soon joined in the middle.
Under fates orders "FriendShips" must part only to have tides
of wishes and prevailing winds of memories to fill sails of our
changing lives.
Caring currents interrupted only by the islands of time shall
alter the course of return we ride upon.
Guided by stars thru crossing charts with rudders of faith
and a bow of kindled bonds,
we shall hope to share the chests bounty of treasure with our
friends now gone.
Fear not, for soon will come the crows nest call 'friend ho o'

For rocking swells are only miles which lead to the mooring
at journeys end where we shall rebuild with plank and nail
old and new "FriendShips" again.
      —Greg Susich

"You Can Count On Me"

When distant dreams seem to fail
And blue skies turn to gray,
When all your ups, turn into downs
"You can count on me!"

"You can count on me", to make you laugh,
And I'll be there to watch you cry,
"You can count on me" to hold you tight
When the pain just won't subside.

"You can count on me" to be your friend,
I'd take your anywhere....
In time you'll start to understand
That I'm the friend who cares.

"You can count on me" at anytime
To help you make it through,
I'll never ask you for anything,
Just keep on being you!!
      —Jeri Blumenstein

Carnivorous Herbivore

A single white zombie with red nails
and dark brown tan lines, pointing, beckoning us
towards a scene of life, adjusted movements.
Pairs of two walking hand in hand,
matrimony, mortality.

Age of love, age of sex
Tiny masses of screaming DNA.
Fallen mothers, abuse, neglect,
Confused fathers, polygamy, incest,
Splitting divorce headaches, state of bliss,
Golden old age, a listless widow, great grandfather
and a sealed tomb.
      —Daniel R. Pollard

Untitled

The stars in their cold heavens do alight
And ceaselessly perform their nightly dance,
Shedding proudly their stark, celestial light
Which holds me in a most exquisite trance.
But the stars are nothing compared to her
And the light that dances in her bright eyes,
Which every night I sadly long to see
Though all that greet me are the cold, dark skies.
But these stars, though unique in their design
The same all over this wide earth do shine,
And in the dark she uplifts her sweet face,
Imbuing the heavens with stately grace.
And those eyes that shine so brightly do see
These same stars that shine nightly upon me.
        —*Dan McCue*

See You In Heaven

Dancing snowflake looses its wings
    and dies…
It crashes with the other stars
    laying flat on the back of Mother Earth.
The blinking light of Its eyes
    a foggy tear covers…
Good-by the whiteness! See you in Heaven!
    It melts in pain for life…
        See you in Heaven…
        —*Monika Pis*

A Boy's Struggle

    God gathered up some heavenly gold bust
and dipped it in His love
    And made a precious little boy
sent him to earth from above

    This precious little boy
knew much about physical pain
    For after his birth he became sick
and his life was not the same

    His body became worn out and weary
from the struggle to live day to day
    That God finally said,
"My child you must not stay"

    It is our hope you'll have fun
and play with your newly found friends
    For we know there will come a day
when we will surely meet again
        —*Angie N. Stowe*

Love Your Children

Children sometimes get on your nerves
and drive you up a wall.

Sometimes you may lose your patience,
but they only want to have fun, that's all.

They seek attention and want to be loved,
and to know that someone is there.

If you really love your children,
show them that you care.

Keep their memories within your heart
for all of the coming years.

For when they are older and on their own,
You will miss drying their little tears.

So this advice I give to you to hold deep within,
And the precious memories of your children,
will remain until the end.
        —*Jennifer Roe*

Dreams

If wishes were dreams
and dreams could come true,
I'd dream the following
dreams for you.

I'd dream a dream of smiles
and toy store eyes,
a land of no hurt
where nobody cries.

I'd dream a dream of sunrises
and the pinkness of the dawn,
the beginning of a new day
with all worries gone.

I'd dream a dream of two bodies
united together as one,
loving, believing, trusting in each other
as no one has ever done.

But most of all, the most perfect dream
if dreams could really come true,
I'd dream a dream of happiness
forever and always for you.
        —*Robyn Mundekis*

A Nice Day Together

I wish we could sit down together
And drink a cup of tea
But since we can't when you drink this…
I hope you think of me
With love to share
And friends who care
And life's finest things are there
For you to bare.
        —*Nettie Katz*

Wisdom

Looking around I see the wonders God has shown to us each day, and even when the sun seems to disappear, the light of the moon still shows me the way, I see the flowers bloom each spring, and birds return to their nest, I will forever wonder why these small ones survive but man's soul continues to fail the test. Is it through our wisdom and knowledge that we perceive ourselves greater than one of these, which causes us to ignore what God is doing, so in turn do as we please. Is God's word truly a mystery that through our wisdom we have torn asunder, or is it something so simple as to say, the wiser we are the more we will always wonder. Wisdom is like the wings of the bird which let us fly with the best, but no matter how far and high we fly, we always return to nest. Wisdom is like the flower that has a time when it is fed, but no matter how bright and beautiful it becomes, it must return to it's bed. Keep looking around and seeing what God has blessed us with in this world, take off the beauty and flight of wisdom and his wisdom will be unfurled, God said "The first shall be last and the last shall be first", as I look around God's word comes true, keep looking as I have done, and His mystery will be shown to you.
        —*Carl H. Barnett, Jr.*

The Invisible Sky

Grow in love - calm peaceable and free
Learn to bend as the willow tree
Never listen to gossip nor a gossiper be

While those who abuse - crumple and die
Your Branches shall reach through
the invisible
        —*Alson Roscoe Redfern*

"Today's Christmas"

Christmas time is drawing near,
And everyone develops a fear.

Money is tight and times are tough,
Stockings are hanging all unstuffed

Stores are crowded and all a mess,
Yet people are buying less and less.

Christmas trees lit up on the lawn
And all charge cards are over drown.

Christmas was the time of year,
for all to be so full of cheer.

Though every year that passes by,
the Christmas spirit quickly dies.

So Merry Christmas and a Happy New Year,
Enjoy all the food and drink all the beer.

Think of all the Christmas past
For with economy now it could be the last!!!

—*Mary Moore*

Changes Of The Hand

Sometimes life deals a winning hand
And everything in life seems so grand
Receiving security, blanketing the soul
Surrounded by warmth, completing a goal
In these times, there's peace within
Holding all aces, feeling the win

Sometimes life deals a losing hand
Sadness takes hold with such a demand
Countless tears, trickles down the face
Loneliness fills in every space
In these times, winning seems grim
Trials are mighty, the light is dim

Sometimes life deals an awkward hand
Confusing the mind, 'til it's difficult to stand
Fantasies bet on the joker in the hole
Conflicting thoughts, burden the soul
In these times, the heart will ache
Searching for happiness, laying everything at stake

Remember that each hand will not remain the same
And each choice you make will affect the game

—*Michelle Flanery*

My Mother's Love

Through the endless years
And fallen tears
No greater love than that of my mother's
There really is no other
She turned those tears
And deepened fears
To laughter and delight
When she tucked me in at night
The silly stories she did tell
Of fairies and a magic bell
Of a mouse that wore combat boots
And a choo choo train that toots
A love that will always remain
Nothing can put out the flame
The flame that burns deep inside
Will last forever, like the ocean tide
When all skies turn gray
A prayerful thought to light the way
Her love, a love that will always be
A love that blesses me

—*Kerri A. Bryant*

My Mind

My mind is a place of solitude from the outside world
My mind is a place of forest and jungle.
My mind is a place of myth and fantasy.
My mind is my body and soul's desires.
My mind is my love of the unknown and the mystical.

—*Jessica P. Dillon*

My Father's Hands

My father's hands are big and rough
  And firm
    And strong
      And hard
        And tough,
When they work to earn our daily bread.

My father's hands are small and smooth
  And soft
    And kind
      And warm
        With love,
When they touch my cheek or pat my head.

Sometimes they're velvet, sometimes rocks;
My father's hands—God's paradox.

—*Louise McNeil*

Those Horrible Strings

Sometimes memories are buried deep.
And for a while, in our minds, they sleep.

For days upon days they slumber.
Then suddenly, up they lumber.

The days we couldn't feel joy
Were yet just another ploy

To get us to remember the harried
Thoughts that our Psyche wanted buried.

Eventually we must deal
With things people wanted to steal.

These people penetrated our soul;
What they left behind was a big hole.

When comes the right season
Then our minds can reason

And deal appropriately
With ones who deviantly

Stole from us precious things
And break those horrible strings.

—*Elisabeth S. Thompson*

Spring Renaissance

Lily of the valley with its white pips
And gentle scent, like a lovers lips,
Pendulous panicles of the white birch
Make a canopy, like the nave of a church.
Perfumed air of the lilac abounds
As a bird alights with its tit-mouse sounds.

The trillium peeps from its forest glade,
The King of spring, monarch of shade.
No lesser lights, majestic tulips stand
In rows and clumps, like a silent band.
Seductive scents of the viburnum bush
Contest the mauve azaleas with competitive push.

Carpets of wood violet and scilla meet
With ivy and blue vinca, upright and neat.
Thus come spring's renaissance with colors aglow
To hasten away our remembrance of winter and snow.

—*Sophie McGloin*

Stop and Pray

When you are beat, tired and worn,
And have been hurt by others scorn,
When burdens have you tired and weary,
And the road seems dark and dreary;
When you seem to have lost your way,
Why not then, just stop and pray?

If no more than a couple of words,
It matters not, they will be heard;
It makes no difference what you say,
Just as long as you stop and pray.

If things are just as you want them to be,
If you have no troubles that you can see;
If life and fortune have been kind to you,
And you find no reason to be blue,
When plans you have made are going your way,
Why not then, just stop and pray?

If it's just to thank God above,
For his goodness and his love,
There is no set time or way
Just as long as you stop and pray.
—*Cecil O. Jordan Jr.*

Nature Beyond

At night I think of how black the sky is
And how the moon shines
Why the leaves fall to the ground
With no color at all
The wind whistles through the night
And that the snow is falling
Winter is coming
The water freezes to ice
That it is only a new year
We go back to where we started
Back to the black sky
Where the moon shines
But I'm just asleep
And I wake up
It is morning
And I look out the window
It just only started
—*Michael D. Hartmann*

Untitled

I was only two years old, when daddy said good-bye.
And I remember mommy standing by the door, and I could see her
cry. Now I'm old enough to know the truth that's come at last.
Daddy's now a memory that will stay back in the past.
He meant no harm to leave us; it was something he had to do.
Daddy liked to drink too much, and the hate within him grew.
I don't blame him for the pain he caused;
He felt he did the right thing.
Now I set in the church as my tears slowly fall
As I hear the church bells ring.
Mommy died today, they say of a broken heart.
For when daddy left us years ago, her heart started to break
apart. Now daddy he is well again, but mommy will never share
The days they could have had once again; now I must try to care
Mommy loved him very much, something daddy could never
understand. But as I saw daddy crying as they wheeled her
coffin out I reached down and took his hand.
Daddy will live a lonely life even if I'm always there.
He'll have to remember how mommy died,
And that it was because she cared.
—*Lorie Hultin*

Little Cesar

The daily end of work comes,
And I stop by to see if he has grown some.
Maybe his eyes have opened more,
Maybe his lips will smile some.
Maybe his ears will hear my voice with some recall,
Maybe I'll just get to see him, that's all.
I will sit and watch his silent motions,
And wait for any sound, a noise, a grunt, perhaps a yawn,
That I could delight upon.
But I am not expecting much, I like to gaze and wonder how
This little guy has made me think of many things, I know not what.
So here I sit and wait for him to hear my stories of many things
Of large trains and pony boys, of flying kites and many toys.
Of big mountains, and wooded places, wide streams, and many
gardens.
—*Manny Garcia*

My Christmas Story

'Twas the week before Christmas
And I was aching and hot
My feet felt like lead
And my house had gone to pot

My Christmas spirit had flown the coop
And my head was doing a loop-de-loop
My joy of giving had got up and went
In my list I had not even made a dent

Why this torture before Christmas day
Why just to hear my dear children say
"I wanted the doll that talks and wets
How come that Bobby wants he gets?"

Well at last it's over all the presents undone
I did remember each and every one
Forgive me while I sit for a while
The turkey is cooking even he had a smile

Tomorrow I'll find time to enjoy all the labor
Right now I hope there's no visit from a neighbor
So before I nod off and forget to say
Merry Christmas to all, it's been a long day
—*Ellen Dougherty*

Introvert

Ask me why I howl in rage,
    and I will quiet my cry.
Ask me why my eyes well with sorrow,
    and I will avert them from your gaze.
Ask me why I tremble with excitement,
    and I will force myself to calmly leave you;
Standing alone,
    wondering.
For you shall never know me,
    and I do not wish you to.
—*Jason Lipinsky*

Journey

For the time being
I am on a journey
to a land not far from here
its a land across the ocean
its a land across the way
its a place where people are together
for each time we can say the journey took us
to a land of everyday
—*Diana Jansing*

I Will Succeed

I know you think it's crazy, but I've got my dreams
And I won't give them up, because
I've got this burning desire inside me to succeed.
And, while the world sleeps,
I sit up all night thinking,
And making my plans,
Because there's something special ahead of me.
Don't tell me I'm wasting my time,
Or that the odds against me are a million-to-one.
I'll take the heat for the chances I take,
Or the mistakes that I make.
If you think that miracles can't happen to you,
And if you think the rainbow always finds someone else,
Just look inside, and find that spark inside your soul.
Follow it—hold onto it, and never let go.
The light you find could change your life.
I will succeed, because I've found that spark.
I believe in myself, because I want to be somebody.
I will succeed, because winners are losers
Who got up and gave it just one more try.

—*Chris S. Andersen*

That Day

Another day begins...
  and I'm still waiting.

I'm waiting for that day when
you are no longer my first thought
in the morning...nor my last before I sleep.

The day will come when
the ring of the phone does not cause
a flutter in my heart... of anticipation... of hope.
Oh, when will that day come?

I wished for it upon birthday candles; it never came.
I wished for it upon falling stars; it excluded me still.

But when it comes...
Oh, when it comes...

Your smile will not be the sight I seek out
nor your touch be the one I need to feel.

The day will come when
I will accept that you didn't want me
and not base my self-worth on that fact... that dreadful fact.

Another day closes...
  and I'm still waiting.

—*Michelle M. Geubtner*

Love Is Always There

I know sometimes it may seem I don't love you,
And it may seem I don't care.
Love is something that never leaves.
Through all the pain,
Love is there.
Through all the anger and the tears,
Love is always there.
Sometimes I say things that I don't mean,
Sometimes I do things I shouldn't.
But no matter what,
Love is always there.
Through the countless threats and unkind words,
Love has never left.
Though sometimes it seems to fade away,
It seems to have gone astray.
Love never leaves,
It always finds its way.

—*Teresa Duck*

Memory Bouquet

It's a happy anniversary that I share with you my dear.
And it thrills the heart inside me just knowing you are near
Precious memories that we share now are fond treasures put away
As we add another orchid, to our memory bouquet
Life has been the bed of roses that I pictured it would be
And I could never live without you cause you mean so much to me
I could never ever hurt you and would never make you cry
Cause I made a vow to love you and I will until I die
Lay your head upon my shoulder and dear I'll hold you tight
As we dance to the music they are playing here tonight
I will whisper words of love dear your wanting me to say
Then we will hide each golden moment in our memory bouquet.

—*Evelyn Hegedus*

I Have Heard the Cries

I have marched and crawled on many lands, and have heard the cheers and jeers. I shot and killed people I did not know in war you have to kill them before they kill you. I have heard the cries. Of wounded and dying men, some calling out for there wife mother father and girl friends. I have seen my friends wounded and dying all around me. I have heard the cries. Of woman and children asking for food and for some one to help them. I had to turn and walk, and ask God to help them in some way, I did not like what I had to do, but I am a soldier and I do what I am order too. I have heard the cries. And my heart and my mind tells me to try and help them as there soldiers are trying and are killing my friends too. I have seen all the killing and evil things the enemy do, and some how I know if they are not stopped, there will not be a world or a home to go back too. I have heard the cries. For help from people who could not help them self, and I ask myself if it was my family wouldn't I want someone to show some kindness to them too, so I did what little I could do. I have heard the cries. You can condemn me or praise me that is up to you, I am a soldier and I must do what a soldier must do.

—*Leonard Tabb*

"The Platypus"

  The Platypus is funny
And looks very, very dumb;
  But look a little closer,
And you'll see he's not a "bum."

  He works hard to find his nourishment
At the bottom of muddy creeks.
  He swims and fishes back and forth
With his funny duck-like beak.

  He's smarter than lots of people
Who just throw their lives away,
  By taking drugs and smoking pot
Which really makes them pay.

  They loose their friends.
They loose their jobs,
  Their health and all that's fun.
And often even life itself,
  When all is said and done.

—*Patricia M. Auvil*

My Wife

My wife is like a cactus
Maturing a bit each year
But cactus like my wife are rare
For blossoms cactus fear
But my cactus instead of going bare
She blooms every day each and every year.

—*Robert Ingman, Jr.*

L.A.

L.A. is a sad place,
    It's not a place for hopes and dreams.
It's a place where your feelings are
    bottled up inside. It's a not a place
to come together. It's a place to
come apart. The more you hope
    is the more you become each day.

    —Nicole King

Sweet Little Love Song

You came into the world in the usual way
And made us proud parents today
Before we knew it we had this tiny person
Then the doctor said it's a boy

We watched you grow everyday
From day one you stole our heart away
It felt really good to tell everyone that this little one is our son
You had a perfect little smile and a lot of love in your eyes
You filled our lives with joy how could we feel any other way

But then one day you were no longer here
I still can't believe I won't see you again
You sweet little laugh I'll no longer hear
Your gentle hug I'll no longer feel

Now all we have to hold onto are the many pictures of you
And the love you gave us while you were here
So on those sad and lonely days I'll think of you and smile
Because along with me I know the angels will be singing
    this sweet little love song to you

    —Donna L. Kirk

My Doberman (Toby)

He had liked to run in the wind
And my family was his only friend
He acted like he owned all the universe
And gave no one a fright, not even a nurse

Splendid to see everything upon him
He did like to run after a tree limb
His skin was brown, he liked to play, not fight
And from his glowing eyes, a light

Still he would rule and run
He did very well like to have fun
I think about him everyday
Now that he has gone away

    —Alisha Kimmy

All That You Have Done

A broken heart you gave me
And my soul you took away
The good intentions that you had
Just seemed to fade away
The pain that you caused me
The trouble that you brought
All the hate I have, who would have thought?
Who would have thought I could have such hate
For someone I loved so much?
But all the broken promises,
And all the shattered dreams,
Just sit there like a thorn in my memories.
I gave to you my heart,
I gave to you my soul,
I gave to you my spirit,
But where did it go?
When you took away my spirit.
And you took away my soul
You took away the only love
That I'll ever know.

    —Heather Ellyn Wilk

Eyes Of Water

As I sit here crying, crying because of being rejected
and neglected. My eyes of water flow fast and freely, never
gonna stop until my heart pulls itself up instead of falling
apart. What do my eyes of water cry for? They cry for a
special girl to come inside, to heal my heart. Making sure
it's together instead of apart. Her heart is strong, as strong
and as solid as a rock, knowing that if you hurt her she'll
never fall apart. Be my lover not my friend and I shall love
you to the very end. It doesn't matter what you do or say I
shall love you till my dying day. My eyes of water run fast.
But soon they shall run slow. Because it doesn't matter where
I go my eyes of water will always flow. Please say yes never
say no. The love you give me will help me grow. You're never
too old, you're never too young. To talk to that special
person and tell them what's wrong. Give me your love, give me
your heart. Give me all you can, I love you and care for you
more than your other man. So come to me and give me a hug.
Let our hearts come together and beat as one. Give me your
love, give me your hand. I'll give you all the love I can.
Because you are my girl and I am your man.

    —Patrick Carmona

The Reason I Cry

I loved you so much, I gave my all, I saw you when I could
and never missed your call. I wanted to be perfect and do
everything right, I didn't want to mess up because of my one
fright. I was so scared of you going away, cause once you
come you never stay. We go out and I'm happy for a week or
two, then you leave me not knowing what next to do. So now
I'm empty, full of confusion, I have to pick one of my two
solutions. I can sit and wait until you see, if you have any
feelings at all for me. Or I could try to go on and forget
about you, but I'll never get over the fact that I'm mad
about you. So when I see you you'll know why I walk with my
head bowed down, I don't want you to see my smile has been
replaced by a frown. But if I ever lift my head again and
meet you eye to eye, wipe the tear off my cheek cause your
the reason I cry.

    —Melissa Crowell

The Other Way

We may purpose fill the day
and not one moment save to play
but is the plan to work away
the life God gave us here this day
or should we say we like the way
that we do burn away the day
and thus the way we spend the day will stay
for fear the changed to other way
and journey not the path astray
that you will surely lose your way
but make another way you may
who is to say
the way to stay?
that other way is bad to stray
yet wonder not we do today
and learn we not the other way

    —Jay Greene

Untitled

My eyes grow heavy, my sight grows dim
I'm drowning my sorrows in this bottle of gin
No family to speak of and not a single friend
Just here with my memories and this bottle of gin
Not a care in the world, not a trouble to my name
I just keep on drinking, just trying to drown the pain
And as the clock strikes twelve, I say a prayer,
"Dear God", help me through just one more year."

    —Laurie Legocki

Island Foods

Breadfruit, butteree
And oh, so tastee
Always a treat
Boiled or baked
Fried or roasted
Serve it wid
Ackee and salt fish on the side
Gud too, wid callaloo,
Curry goat or curry chicken
Whatever you like
Gimme breadfruit any day
'stead' o rice.
(The seasoning for this poem is the accent.
Must be read with a Jamaican or West Indian accent.)

  —*Paulette M. Garner*

America Standing Tall

God help America stand tall,
And please, oh Lord, don't let her fall.
With violence running rampant in the streets,
And seeing the homeless with nothing to eat.
Alcohol and drugs are just a few,
that are making their way into our schools.
Let's put prayer back in it's place,
And not be ashamed to tell of the Lord's saving grace.
Oh Lord, put America back on her feet,
Let us tell of the Gospel to everyone we meet.
Of how he died for you and me,
that our salvation would be eternally.

  —*Sue Gann*

The Dark

Her steps quicken
and quicken
on the sidewalks of the dark unknown streets
of an unknown city.
What is she trying to escape from?
That she knows not what.
Yet still she is frightened.

  —*Jennifer M. B. Bedard*

I Wonder Why

Once I thought I could touch your heart, feel a love within,
And share thoughts and dreams and desires through life.
Now all that seems long ago, so far away.
I wonder when and how it changed,
But even more, I wonder why.

When did love leave and your heart grow cold?
When did your mind build walls to close me out
And make your thoughts unknown to me?
When did desire fade away and die?
More than when, I wonder why.

I have talked and cried, reasoned and raged,
Trying to find a way back to your heart and thoughts,
Some key to unlock the doors barring me.
But it only makes you even more distant.
Through it all, I wonder why.

Now the hour is late, and the strength born of love fades,
Dying from apathy and neglect in darkness and fear.
I yearn to try again, but
Alone, my urge is futile.
Yet still, and always, I wonder why.

  —*Dena Rae Smith*

Tears Of Race

They called her names
and she asked them why
"Because the color of your skin"
that was their reply.

As a little girl
she didn't understand
She cried every night
while only her mommy held her hand.

This little girl is all grown up
but she lives with a childhood of tears
The crying hasn't stopped
it's just been hidden through the years.

Her only dream now
is to stop the fight of race
She doesn't want it to happen to her little girl
and have the tears run down her face.

  —*Colleen Hall*

Eyes of Hunger

Your eyes...

 flash in the dark
  and shine
   into the day's light;

too only ingest the sight
 which completes visual curiosity,
  filling me
   that I may not thirst
   and teaching me,
   when I know
    only a little
     of who You are...

    finding
     that over time
      the thirst...
       only grows
greater.

  —*James Barry*

Maybe

I often lie awake at night
And sit with a big grin
Because I start to wonder to myself
How together we might have been
We had so much love between us
That I think neither one of us knew
And if we could have worked together
We might have had something which could of grew
Maybe we were too young when it started
High school sweet hearts with our heads so unclear
Or maybe there was something real between us
Something honest and sincere
We both said we loved each other
Something we believed really was true
Maybe we could of worked together
To let that love become one of two.

  —*Lori Matits*

Untitled

Boyhood's lost but still visible
Memories wishes reverse
And turn within them-selves.
What do I wish now.
I think of then and wish I
Was there.

  —*Chris Rowland*

Lost In Space

At times I feel so desperately lost
And so alone in vast and empty space,
Out of the real world, drifting from the coast,
At war with myself and the human race.

And no use crying in this endless abyss,
For no one hears my agonizing scream.
I only hope that I will soon awaken
And gladly say, "It's nothing but a dream."

But endless night envelopes all my being,
And cold, cold wind of winter fiercely blows
And chills my heart and all my dreams forever;
And no safe port to hide from all my woes.
 —*George Zajaczkowski*

Dad Did Too

I know mom loved, us Lord,
And so did our Dad, too.
I know Mom worried, about us Lord.
And so did our Dad, too.
I know Mom made many a sacrifice, for us Lord.
And so did our Dad, too.
I know Mom worked hard, for us Lord.
And so did our Dad, too.
I know Mom gave us good advice, Lord.
And so did our Dad, too.
I know Mom brought us up right, Lord.
And so did our Dad, too.
 —*Juanita McIntosh*

Sonnet

I have outlived my past and precedents
And tell no wives tale of injury or dread
I have said nothing better left unsaid
And wetter my tongue in the waters of Sent

Like the rains that burn the dust
When all the grounds laid low and bare
And the piano man plays a crippled stare
On his keys as the ivories start to rust

I do not rust in rain but forget
The wishes and the desires and the dust
Mingled in with my neighbors machinations

Tense and fat on cushions singled out to get
Good crave what you hear in trust
Be not cliches be definitions
 —*M. J. Kisiel*

With God's Love

While looking out the window with care
And thankful I have no fear

With God's love I am so blessed
And wishing I could help the rest

When crawling in my warm bed
Hoping the poor have all been fed

God wants us to help each other
Just like we would a sister or brother

The president is doing the best he can
Let's all help every woman and man.

This big U.S. is so strong
We don't want to do wrong.

Let's pray for peace and love for ever more
And feeling something good in store.
 —*Nina Pruitt*

In Memory Of A Dear Friend

It was your eyes that first attracted me to you,
and that crazy, little way you walked.

Your face had a unique look of its own,
I loved the way you talked.

You had that crazy way about you,
it was pronounced in everything you did.

You had a way of cheering me up in bad times,
especially when you did that crazy jig.

You knew it made my tears turn to laughter.
And my frown turn into a smile.

Now you can't make my tears turn to laughter,
because you're gone forever, not for a while.
 —*Nichol R. Grant*

Springtime

The earth is the Lord's
 And the fullness thereof...
We can't put in words
 All He sends from above.
In Springtime we see His mighty hand,
 The world bursts forth at His command!
It's a beautiful time of the year to see
 God's power displayed—that's proof for me!
Who else could make the grass to grow...
 After the land is covered with snow,
Or the flowers to grow in their beautiful hue?
 That's more than you or I could do!
The tiny seeds are put in the ground
 They multiply without making a sound.
He sends sunshine and rain as He sees best,
 We can't understand how we are blessed.
"Awake, oh earth", he seems to say,
 "There's beauty to enjoy today.
"The winter now is past and gone,
 It's springtime—the birds are singing their song!"
 —*Flossie Detwiler*

Just One

The old woman smiled at me as I walked through the door.

Actually, her one eye looked at me
and the other didn't.

Her crumpled skin revealed the only tooth left in her mouth.
It was covered with food and the rest had dribbled down onto
her chin, and from there, to her lap.

Her hand held the culprit, a half-eaten sandwich
and from there I saw her arm resting on a metal bar
that wrapped itself around her wheelchair.

Despite her repulsiveness she drew you to her.
Her inner spirit beamed through her eye and

I realized that maybe she was once like me.
I realized that in a flash I could be in that seat

With one eye and one tooth and I smiled back at her and took
her hand and sat there with her until she finished her lunch
hoping in my heart that someone someday will do the same for me —

That they will imagine my past youth, beauty and
accomplishments, and take my hand and eat lunch with me

Despite my one eye and one tooth.
 —*Malia M. Zimmerman*

The Radiance of Megan

Are the skies alight with the brightness of your smile
and the shelves of heaven's books filled with your courage?

Does God point you out to newcomers as a surely chosen one,
whose grace comes from within, tempered by earth-side pain?

Do the children of heaven play at your side — do you make
daisy chains of light to put around your head?

Do the mothers in heaven hug you and hold you close
as they wait for their babies to arrive?

Do the fathers of heaven build you doll houses
and scooters and all the toys you missed here?

Is the lightening your laughter, streaking by,
and the moon's glow your humming?

Is seven years too long for you to remember the Grandma who
    loves you
or are the hours of earth-measured time just a blink of your lashes?

Spread the light of your soul on our darkened world, little girl of
    my heart.
Light our way with your radiance until "soon" arrives.

    —Bonnie Hooper

The Apocalypse of the End Time

As the waves crash against the sand tonight. And the comets
and the stars give out their light. One can here the cries of
the people of these tribulation years. And that there are
signs in the heavens that the mourning sun may not soon appear.
As the scorpions and the demons run across the desolate land.
There lies the worlds hopes and dreams down along the beaches
sand. Now the devil says to all the world, come and worship me
and live. And to all those who will worship me, gold and
silver I will give. To all those who worship the devil will
indeed burn. Even all the dead souls of past and present will
not soon return. For the people of the world have given their
souls to the devil and the beast. And the people of the world
have taken the children of God captive, to give to the devil
and his surrogates, so that in the arena's they may have their
feast. The nations have gone to battle, all of mankind is
marching off to war. Even the one world religion has become
like a blood thirsty whore the devil and the beast have a dark
and fierce countenance, for they strive to destroy and to kill
for they know they have but a short time, for its to be God's will.

    —Dale A. Wilhite

Fire Island

As the moon is spanked by dawn and put to bed,
And the sun begins to cleave the sky in gold and in red,
Then I find myself alone beside the shore
Where the whispered voice of time says evermore.

The motion of determined hungry birds
With resounding squeals and squawks which serve as words
Catch both eye and ear
Tho a captive, I belong here.

How thoroughly the sea can wash her hair
Sprigs of moss parsley green so fair
Scrubbed in sand as it meets the sea
Some to remain, some to go free.

How exciting are the treasures to explore
Uplifted from the ocean's floor
Worn by whim of wind and wave
Between the two a slave.

But for one moment in your life truly free,
Come with me, come with me.

    —Claire Joseph Phelan

"Autumn Days"

As the dawn breaks through the dark of night
And the sun begins to rise.
It casts a glow on the stately trees
Silhouetted against the sky. It is October…

The brilliance of the autumn leaves
The reds, the golds, the ambers,
Lives in our minds, our memories
Through the cold, crisp days of winter.

Too soon the leaves begin to fall
So softly to the ground.
And a brilliant carpet covers all
As another season rolls around.

The apple trees are laden
With fruit both tart and sweet.
An apple picked fresh from the tree
Is a delight to eat!

The time has come to say farewell
To summers' gentle breeze,
And now we gaze in wonder
At the festival of the trees. It is October.

    —Marion O'Neil

Untitled

The pound of the surf
and the warmth of the breeze,
caress her body, it stimulates all of her senses.
The sand between her toes
is still warm from the, noonday sun,
although the sun is no longer visible.
These are the times when she feels most comfortable with her
emotions, at this point she feels free
and unmasked.
She hopes this euphoric feeling will last
she knows it will soon fade.
Sadly she sees the first night star
and once again she puts on her mask
and faces the world.

    —Lori Macango

Today's Tragedy Brings Tomorrow's Healing Touch:

After the tragedy is the acknowledgment and acceptance
And then comes the hardest part of all, the time to heal…
After the dark thundering and frightening
lightening of the storm comes the silence and the calm…
Then comes the sun's loving and warm tender touch,
to dry our painful tears.
The beautiful colors of the rainbow is our sign
that God still cares and loves us very much.
When the painfully cutting knife of life's tragedies
and misfortune cuts right through our lives
and rips our hearts and tears our families apart,
just remember there's always tomorrow…
To pick through the pieces of our shattered lives
and heal our broken hearts…
And with tomorrow comes a fresh new day
to wipe the tears away and continue on life's path,
using our painful experiences to help many others
find yet another of tomorrow's healing touch
and God's undying love.

    —Alvina Cisneros Valdez

Lost Love

My love has led me to a fork in the road,
And, though I go on loving —
Yet will I travel in a different direction.
Why is it that this mind holds a dearness
For one who is dear no more?
For sure it is that love often lingers
Long after lovers part —
Perchance it is because this affair
Was one with no holds barred.
First love, they say, is a lasting love;
Wonder not, then, that one
Should go on loving
Long after the spell is broken,
But that it could ever be broken.

— *Dorothy D. B. Knox*

Valentine's Day

It's Valentine's Day,
    and we are still together.
Since late last November,
    we've lasted this long.
You ask me to dance,
    but I say I can't dance.
We stand and argue,
    until the song ends.
So, we leave, and you ask me about flowers,
    I like yellow roses I say.
But red roses are for love,
    at least that's what you say.
So we argue over rose colors until you say,
    Forget it! All we do is argue! It's over!
Then I crumple up and cry at you back,
    It's Valentine's Day, for christsake!
So what, it's over you say to me.
    It's over. It's over.
I'll never forget those harsh words you said on that
    Valentine's Day.

— *Jennifer Costa.*

Peace

It is said the kingdom of God is a place where we will all be free
and where we will be able to realize all that is in us
and all that we can ever be.
Let's try now to make a heaven on earth—
somewhere where freedom and love for one another can give birth.
War and destruction would never appear here
because we'd be too smart and busy with our lives to ever let
it come near.
We cannot isolate ourselves from others in need
but let's look for peaceful solutions and not be guided by greed.
Money and power should not be our main concern
but that is a lesson I don't know how to teach and for many it
would be too hard to learn.
Only the freedom of others should we hold dear
because the loss of our own freedom we would never want to fear.
If fighting be the only solution left for our leaders today,
let's all hold hands together in our minds and pray.
For a peaceful solution can always be found
even in the hearts of leaders the world around.

— *Sandra Lee Alexoff*

Reed In The Wind

Once I was free,
Now I am here in this cage, confused alone.
My heart is still and will not beat for you.
Reach through the bars and soothe my pain.
Do not touch me though,
I will snap your soul like a reed in the wind.

— *Robert Messer*

Together Forever

Through all the tears and all the pain,
One thing remains the same.
Together forever, 'til death do we part,
Not in our minds, but in our hearts.

— *Heather Dryden*

"Death of Winter, Birth of Spring"

"Spring," I hear your "voice" in every word, every song bird
and whisper. I "see" your face before me, in the bleakness of
winter and all its beauty, trying to stop what it cannot.
"Awaken" daughter of the winter, begin "the" journey to your
"fathers" house to await your "birth" and death once more.
Young yet "ageless" gentle and wise she were, but "innocent" as
the flowers in bloom, before "Le Sacre De Printemps." Renewed
with the youth and kiss of spring. Warm and tender as the
gentle breeze that brush my cheek, lingering, tempting and
teasing, saying "come, become part of me, and one with each
other and the "children" of summer." Before the leaves of
autumn and the winds of winter, are looking over our shoulder,
waiting their turn once more.

— *Charles A. Millard*

Days Gone By

I look upon the dark gray skies,
and wonder about the days gone by.

When the sun would shine in the sky so bright.
When life made you feel so wonderful and light.
Where did they go those days of youth?

The innocence of mind and heart.
Thinking those days will never part.
Where did they go those days of youth?

With only the thoughts of the sun on our faces.
And the dreams of adventures in wondrous new places.
Where did they go those days of youth?

Where did they go those days of my youth?

— *Linda K. Rost*

Untitled

I'm so envious of you and you
and you don't know why
just take a look at your life
then look at mine
don't just glance
'cause then you'll think it's nothing but a happy dance
look deep, deep into my heart
you'll see that long ago it was torn apart
and though you'll swear yours is the same
I can tell you now, you don't even know pain's name
so when you think you've got it bad
think of me and all the love that you have.

— *Cindy Bruns*

The One You Love

When there's a person you think you love.
And nobody could ever be above.
Till the day it seems you've lost your soul
The love you once knew, you know no more.
The one you love thinks you're a whore.
When you fight all night, you both know it's not alright.
But it seems like the only thing to do.
Since you know we can't just talk it through!
We say cold things to hurt each other.
One and after another.
My love for you will never end.
Even if you have to be just a friend.

— *Alicia Micale*

Untitled

Kilns we fire together yield scimitars, not celadon
Angry blades whose naked gleam alone
Rends rust gossamer trappings
Leaves us ill-clad in windblown tatters
Bastards bare in sorry shreds of
Ragsalvaged heat
Our flesh exposed to hoarfrost blows
Wounds sutured by a winter sun's glare
Needles lodged in eyes of clay

  —Malcolm Brown

The Stormy Ocean is an Angry Man

The ocean roaring as it smashes down on the shore is an Angry man
Shouting in rage.
 It foams and froths, as its waves whirl 'round and 'Round,
Spitting furiously in a curse of all beings,
Its wild waves sweep ships out of its way,
A frustrated man shoving people out of his path
To reach his offender.
 The ocean pounding upon the breakwater's rocks
Is the hitting of the man's fists against another man;
As it reaches down, scooping tons of sand
Then bringing its crest around forward,
A punch is hurled by the antagonist.
 The waves pull back, then push at full force at the Shore,
Finally leaping onto land:
The angry man retreating, only to charge at his opposer and
Hurtle onto him,
Knocking him down to the ground unconscious.

  —Caroline Saffer

Oriental

Tranquility lies deep within my soul.
Apart from this material planet.
Black and gold are the colors I adore.
Coming to life in radiant decor.
Silk and satin reincarnate my heart.
Water bearing men arrive at my birth.
Giving me place of mind with deep
Meaning, unlocking the mystery of my love.
Striving to find reason and understand
where the treasures of immortality lye.
Forever haunting me until I die.

  —Deborah A. Blagaich

Calendar Daze

The wintery wind's blowing but hearts
Are a-glowing
Those Irish eyes are watching showering skies
Many flowery escapades and it's
Diamonds not spades
Bright lights are going "crazy" and
We're feeling somewhat lazy
Bells are a-ringing and the harvest is for bringing
Our thanks to greatly express then it
Is a time to bless

  —Marlowe Jill Pietrzak

Friends

You stood by me when the world was cold,
And you never left my side.
When the time came to cross a bridge of uncertainty,
You were there to help me cross, or at least you tried.
I know now that you will always be there,
Waiting for me in the end.
For you are not only my companion,
But my very best friend.

  —Dana Metallo

Me

Me, myself, and I
Are all that exists
I am the one
Who longs and persists.
I am not who
But I am the me.
And that's all that's needed in this one man symphony.
Who needs them when I have myself
I am my entertainment and the novel on the shelf.
I am alone and there is no we,
In this big world there's only a person called me.

  —Eva Shure Berens

The Bridge Across The Hole Of Loneliness

Friends come and go like the seasons of the year. When they are in your reach, light and happiness fills you. But when they go, stillness and silence fill the air. You search and call, but you get no response. You reach out your hands, but the feeling is gone. You feel nothing but the cold air on your bare hands. Nothing but empty hands reaching out for a friend. An object, something to get a grip on. To hold, to feel, to touch, and never to let go of. You feel a warm tear descend down the side of your face. This is in fact the only movement besides your heart. You soon realize that you are completely alone, too frightened to speak, too scared to move, too shocked to breath. And you know if you don't take the opportunity to grasp it, the light will never return to your life. So when the flash of light passes your eyes. Grab on tight and never let go, and the warm light will surround you and you will see the faces of your friends, feel the softness their touch. And they will be your bridge across the hole, and you shall be theirs, forever.

  —Ethan Brazell

The Color Of A Dream

 What are the colors of your dreams?
  Are they blackened by tragedy?
   Bright and hopeful,
  Of what will tomorrow bring?

 What are the depths of your hopes?
 Extended to the soul of feeling.
  Shallow and skimming,
  A pebble on the sea of life.

 What is the extent of your knowledge?
  Vast and beyond any other?
   Trapped and enclosed,
  Caged into inexistance.

 What is the essence of your love?
Fulfilling your heart with overflowing joy,
  Jealousy destroys passion.
  A refusal of undenied happiness.

 What are the colors of our dreams?
  Contemplating what is true,
  Do we really dream at all?

  —Leslie Donaldson

Untitled

To often the pleasures of today,
Are lost somewhere along the way,
As we forget to look and listen,
We often don't know what we are missin'.
The simple pleasures and joys of life,
Are oft forgotten in a world of strife,
So once today please stop and listen,
So that you may know what you've been missin'.

  —Daylene Shelton

Freedom

People, noises, cars,
are what I hear the whole night long.

Murders, muggings, rapes,
are what I see happening to innocent people.

Smoke, fumes, constant fear,
are what I smell.

The city is different from my home.
I hear, see and smell many different things
where I live - the country.

Birds, wind in the trees, dogs,
are what I hear, instead.

Forests, streams, open lands,
are what I see.

Newly cut hay, wet soil, fresh air,
are what I smell.

But what I taste is freedom.
The freedom to walk where I want, when I want, without any
fears. The freedom to see what nature intended us to see.
The freedom to feel safe even when I'm alone. The freedom
to be in the open, fresh air, alone - without being lonely.

—*Patricia A. Peruski*

Second Chance

In the past, I've learned that I can't make promises that
aren't supposed to be kept, that broken memories are the ones
that are broken because of a single touch or the slightest
word. Second chances are meant to try again and to turn out
the way fantasies are dreamt and succeeded, but I've also
learned that a million second chances aren't going to heal the
wounds that are already scarred on my memory. It seems that
time after time of being battered mentally, torn emotionally
and physically being a wreck, I would learn, I would realize
that, that second chance I'm given, I've given hundreds of
times and each time it hasn't turned into the dream it's
supposed to be, it's gotten worse and created more scars and
more tears that have turned into ice. But physically I've gone
back and mentally I knew it was wrong. Emotionally I am still
recovering from the last time and as my heart's telling me to
turn away the enemies, my mind says it's okay...
I never knew anyone could scare someone so much, maybe it's
the hurt I'm afraid of, but maybe it's the thought of another
SECOND CHANCE!

—*Melissa A. Hedeen*

Eyes For Life

Each and e'ery morning, when the sun
Arises upon the darkened earth,
The eyes see anew, and project the maximum
Of qualities that come with the dawning birth.
Life is so precious, and sometimes, the eyes
See only what the mind wants it to see,
And the full effect of life, is left in supplies
Of things, of unimportance, and out of quality.
The eyes for life, when used with the utmost care
And diligence, can bring happiness to all,
When the sun arises o'er the night's air,
Bringing all those new born things, at one call.
So, when the sun arises, in the early morning hours,
Open your eyes to God's array, for exciting powers!

—*Eva M. Roy*

A Precious Soul

I feel strong, so strong that, I'll spread my strength
around, and around the world.

I see beauty in a wide variety of colors.

I see togetherness coming from all directions.

I see the healing spirits coming to touch those who
need it.

I feel laughter that has not yet surfaced.

I dance, and dance with joy, spreading my arms all
over the world.

I feel, I can just touch the peace within myself.

Who am I but that precious soul who lives and loves
the world.

—*Rita Edwards*

Petenera

Within these graceful groves she danced
Around her lover's body with despair
He surrendered unaware.
With blazing eyes as black as this night's sky
She fed her appetite
While glorious wind grazed her irresistibly black hair.
The music played and played much louder
Her dancing getting wilder
In transcendent silence she belayed.
What once was fervent glowing rapture
In these gallant groves their souls now captured
And will glide among the gales onto his grave.
What's a girl to do, when her love has been untrue
But gash his hollow heart in two.

—*Lucy Vargas*

Forever Silence

In the black, we can only see gray
As a bird flies across the morning day
A wounded soul looking for an answer
Ever searching to find its master
Knowing that it will never find,
Even in the expanse of time

When it's done, everything fades
The memories can never be erased
If it would die even tomorrow
Would just increase their pain and sorrow
I knew of the love, once from the heart
I knew very well right from the start
At the pond, when I looked down
The reflection, even it made me frown
A broken pillar lies across the ground
If there is no ear, there is no sound
Like a leaf blowing in the wind
Our life, slowly, begins to dim

Everything has a beginning and an end
So goodbye, my one and only, friend.

—*Martin Byrnes*

My Teacher

Bombards me with information.
Lets me see everything.
Lets me feel every emotion
Gives me the universe.
My teacher is my warden
I cannot escape.

—*Sabino Gomez*

Nature's Song

There is never a song as sweet,
As a bird's tweet tweet.

There is never a whisper,
As light as a breeze through trees.

There is never a more caressing sound,
Than the babbling brook in the spring.

And the rap-tap-tapping of a woodpecker,
Is nature's drum.

And the splash of a duck diving for food,
Is nature's musical symbols.

As an Indian woman washes food in a stream,
She sings a song of peace.

The hoof-beats of wild horses,
Represents a struggle for life.

But,
There is never a song as sweet,
As a bird's tweet tweet.

    —Tiffany Smith, 13 years

Moonlight

In the moonlight you took your first breath and cried.
As a young boy you would play in the night by the
moon's shimmering glow. You drank from its intoxicating
mysteries till I swore your eyes shined as bright as
bright as that old moon. I could never get you away
from its charms.

In the moonlight you danced, pranced, and sang. Your
eyes were always locked on its mysterious glow. I would
worry and wait up for hours wish'n the boy who was
becoming a man would shake the moon dust off his heels.
In the moonlight you told me you were a man. You said
you didn't need me anymore, but I knew that it was just
the moonlight talk'n.

In the moonlight you grew a beard and married a few
wives. You finally found one that would dance, prance,
and sing with you in the moonlight. You both had your
eyes locked on its mysterious glow. By the light of the
moon you finally admitted that you needed me, but I still
saw that old moon glowing in your eyes.

In the moonlight you took your last breath and I cried.

    —Marjorie Braun

Decay

An elderly man had a stroke.
As he collapsed,
His glasses shattered on the pavement.

As well as his memories.
As well as his life.

A somber preacher spoke.
As soft music played,
His family wept for the loss of his love.

As well as his memories.
As well as his life.

Dirty undertakers joked.
As they worked,
Covering his grave with 6 feet of dirt.

As well as his memories.
As well as his life.

    —Keith R. Stewart

Amazing But True

Creations from the past aghast and lures about today
As humans throughout the universe trudge in his way.
Facing situations and using skills unmistakably acquired
Makes a profession for one to survive or become tired.
Everything obtains a purpose with reasons as it moves
Whether it be country, gospel, pop, rock or rhythm and blues.
Just as a Poet's lyrics being converted into music and song
As feelings and thoughts are expressed daily, is this wrong?
Now, do you actually think our knowledge just came along
Or because a modest physique bestowed one makes him strong?
Well, you are mistaken and errs occur daily as we trod on
So ponder on friends - POETS DO EXIST and THERE IS A GOD.

    —J. C. Flowers

Peace

The silence of the evening engulfed me,
As I gazed across the pond,
Edged by stately trees reaching toward the sky.
The crescent moon makes its presence known,
As the sun's glow splashes my western view.
Deer abounding, white tails flash
Giving a graceful salute.
Silence, beauty, majestic tranquility,
All join within my soul, granting peace.

    —Anna M. Johnson

Woman/Child

As I sit on my velvet queen Anne chair
As I sit on my checkered bedspread

Sipping crisp wine from a hand blown glass
Drinking grape juice from a shrimp cocktail glass

I think of my gentleman caller
I think about the cute boy in math class

And how he proclaimed his love for me
And how he pulled my hair on Thursday

A beethoven symphony drifts through the air
Rock music blasts from my speakers

I know my love is true
I betcha he likes me!

    —Denise L. Frazier

Life Goes On

A lump in my throat catches my breath
As I swallow bitter tears.
Dutifully my lungs force me to breath
Gasping and gulping the ground claims me.

A nauseating merry-go-round plays in my stomach
As my jaw quivers with unspilt angst,
Bravely my tears stay put as I clench my eyelids
Against the fate, decision and pain that put them there.

Heartbroken again, I feel the physical pain
Struggling and fighting for release
Cry, cry, cry and be free
Jailer of emotion, guardian of anguish

Like a phoenix I will rise from the ashes of my tormentors
Clocked in emotional iron and wielding acid
I will strike back with vengeance, destroy and rebuild
Broken though never defeated.

    —Cheryl Clayton

Friends

People who borrow,
Much to my sorrow,
Never return what they take.
To be a friend, and do not ask
And we'll still be friends tomorrow.
——*Ellie Skoler*

A Rose in the Dark

(Dedicated to D.C.)
As I walked through the darkness; all cold and alone.
I searched for the beauty, that would take me home.
Then it came in the form of a light.
A soft beautiful rose all pearly and white.
With a single beat of my heart.
I had known that me and this rose, would never part.
So now that the beauty has caught my eye.
I want her so bad, my heart just cried.
But just to be with her, for that moment was a
heavenly pleasure.
It's a moment in my life, that I will always treasure.
But for now, I'll step back and watch the beauty grow!
The feelings I have for her she might never know.
So you see I had a dream it came in the form of a rose.
But now I have awoken, with a pain in my soul!
——*Raymond Guzman*

The Golden Child

Once in so many years gone by, I dare not count;
  As it brings a tear to my aging eye.

  I had a daughter so meek and mild.
Her heart was tender, as is the way of any Golden Child.

  Her smile was warm as it flashed your way.
It could bring on the sun, on the darkest of stormy days.

  She grew up al all children do someday.
Her spirit stayed trusting and her loving heart not so far away

  With an almost fatal mistake,
  As some do in placing their trust.
She shattered her mind with a powdery white dust.

From the bowels of hell, fighting her way back.
  Her mind a scattered puzzle,
  Its connections to damaged to replace it exact.

Emerging triumphant, her senses amply aware;
  To the gift of life
And her arduous fight from the depths of despair.

Though her mind has returned from where it was exiled.
  My heart becomes heavy,
  when I remember the sunshine of THE GOLDEN CHILD.
——*Lorilee J. Wood*

Love Is Like A Rainbow

Love comes and showers us with colors,
As like a rainbow does.

Love goes and sends sorrow and disappointment,
As like a rainbow disappears.
Love doesn't come often,
As like a rainbow only comes once upon a time.

But when it returns it showers us with joy
once more,
As like a rainbow.

But once again as the time arrives it goes
back behind the clouds and we feel
sorrow and disappointment once more.
——*Robin Bledsole*

Centers

I, too, am the center of the universe
as much as Pluto
or a lady bug, teetering on a blade of grass
just skimming above the ground
Don't take me to task!
It's not a matter of up or down that counts
not Heaven or Hell after all
but rather,
around and around
circles intersecting
Bubbles bouncing and bursting
then reforming
and Spirits Interacting
——*Elaine Charter*

A Silent Evensong

The geese and I were in accord
  As on the bank we stood -
As much as I - and maybe more -
  True reverence in their mood.

On such a summer's night as this,
  I can't remember when
The sunset wrote across the sky -
  With such a rose-gold pen.

Each bird kept watching, head held high;h
  Their necks now touched with light.
Some radiant image - beckoning;
  Perhaps - their God of Flight?
——*Elizabeth Sayre*

Lost Love

She lay there with her eyes closed,
As relatives and friends stood around here.
He felt a tear drop down his cheek,
And thought of what he let her do.
As they closed the lid of the coffin,
And let her down in the hole he dug.
As they dropped her,
He felt a piece of his heart drop with her.
She left him standing there,
Or was it the other way?
He felt alone without her.
How could he have let her drive drunk?
——*Jill Christensen*

Loves' Triumph

The moon was full, on that star filled night -
As she walked alone, to follow its light -
  For he had gone, after hearing her news! -
  Just where or why, she had no clues -
She only knew, the pain went so deep -
The promise of life, she dared not keep -
  Desperately she wanted, her world to end! -
  To simply be gone, like dust in a wind -
Was it to be fated, destiny? -
Of choices made, so fearfully? -
  When softly a voice, whispered "No", and the angels sighed
-
  There was still hope, she turned and cried!! -
With outstretched hand, there He stood -
To guide her back, for only He could -
  For as she looked, into his eyes -
  She saw life and love, so undisguised -
Then the dawn did break, with its brilliant rays -
The nights struggles are over, born new days -
  Now she knows, she has so much to give -
  Love has shown her, many new reasons to live -
——*Charlotte Kleiber*

Beauty

When asleep her face is quiet and simple,
as smooth as porcelain to the slight dimple.

But when awake brain beware,
those eyes are a painters joy and despair.

The graceful curves are so light,
but the eyes they shine bright.

The hair flowing around her face,
the bangs are a delicate lace.

But none of these can give hint,
to the spirit that lays dormant.

Inside this beautiful creatures heart,
is a soul that's a work of art.
   —*Elizabeth Kermon*

A Memory Away

I lie on the warm, white sand beach
As the brightly-lit sun hovers above
Playing hide and seek in white billowy clouds:
As they drift into many shapes across the vast blue sky.

The soft sand cushions my back
As I am entertained by the dance of the palm trees;
Their swaying branches move back and forth
Gracefully in the warm, gentle breeze.

I feel the cool, crystal blue water rushing
As the diminishing waves reach the shore.
Coming just close enough to tickle the bottoms of my feet.

I hear "plop"
The usual sound of a silvery fish
That has leaped into a perfect arch,
And is again making a landing in the shimmering water.

Breathing the clean air is the highlight of my respite-
Screech! So soon? My subway stop.
Oh well, there is always tomorrow
When I will again dip into my reservoir of daydreams.
   —*C. Janet Baker Banks*

The Church Mouse

As the church bell rings,
As the choir sings,
As the people come in to pray,
The church mouse scampers in to begin another day.

He quietly sits in his little pew,
And kneels to praise his God,
And when is answered with a yes,
He always replies with a nod.

When mass is over,
He bows and leaves,
In a quiet, peaceful way,
And that is how the little church mouse always starts his day.
   —*Megan McWilliam*

Untitled

It's lying next to you bare against bare
Arm to arm and soul to soul
The warmth of your hand
Smile of your eye
Touch of your being
I want always to have and cherish
And in saying so
      will
         never
            be
   —*N. Schacht*

My Friend and I

My friend and I share a cup of coffee and watch the sunrise.
As the day unfolds I do something foolish and laugh at
myself and he is there to share it with me.

As I drive the car he is my co-pilot and navigator, in the
canoe he sits in the bow so I can see over it, as I
cycle along the roads I wish he would pedal a little
harder going up the hills.

When I am angry and hurt he listens, then calmly helps me
to look at the issue. My friend doesn't give up on me even
though at times I may give up on myself.

When the sun has gone to bed, the house is not lonely, for it
is occupied by my friend and I, and his name is God.
   —*Josie Kruttlin*

Viva La France

"Veeeeva La Frauuuunce," my mother sang
As the fiberglass hull skimmed the bay,
Engine full throttle,
Noise deafening.
"Veeeeva La Frauuuuunce!"
Me pressing the black, round, rubber bulb of the horn
To make the horn sound its ridiculous honk.
Celebration, Happiness. Dad smiling.
My happy childhood memory.
"What did it mean, Mom? Why did you
Sing such a thing?" I ask my now
Older, alone, smaller mother
In her kitchen.
"I felt such a freedom. I don't know where it came from.
It came from before I moved here, before I met…
It came from Chicago."
   —*Sally Kerpchar*

Untitled

As the day goes by, I begin to miss you!
As the night goes by, I begin to cry!
As I think of what we did; I begin to love
you more and more. I only wish I could be
more than your friend and loves! I wish I
could win your heart and be your girlfriend.
You make me happy and I love you deeply;
The feelings I have for you I can't describe.
I just hope one day you'll come out and realize
what I mean to you and how much you mean
to me!!!
   —*Janet L. Brukner*

Morning Has Come

My heart pounds like the ocean waves upon the shore
As the sea whispers to the rotting moon
I melt away into my thoughts
Sitting in the dying silence of nature
The crying gardens send their aroma
tiptoeing through the stillness
Morning mists float by on the laughing winds
And weave their way through the suffocating night
Stars yawn and give in to the invading dawn
The night ashes lick my burning eyes
and fade away into the heavens
I sit absorbed in the blossoming beauty….
Morning has come
   —*Kassia Percell*

The Windmill

The wind whistles through the unmoving blades
As the sentinel stands quietly on the hill.
Weeds are tall and overgrown.
It's been years since grass was sown.

Children once played in the tank at its base
It was a happy, cheerful place.
They splashed in the water or climbed on the frame
Until all light was gone and darkness came.

As time went on their visits became fewer
Their interests were with things that were newer.
Cars and friends became the item of the day
And eventually they all moved away.

The house and barn have long since fallen
And the remnants cleared away.
The old windmill alone stands proud and tall
The quiet majestic overseer of all.

—*Dianna Smithhart*

Rainbow Forest

At the end of a rainbow is a lovely little place.
As this rainbow spans the sky, so grows the Queen Ann's lace.
Robins sing vespers in the trees,
And so sweetly buzz the bees.
The roses open their buds to the bright morning sun.
This is a sign that Summer has just begun.
A waterfall cascades down the steep rocky grove.
Then, the waters flow to a dark hidden cove.
The apple blossoms bloom,
Pushing away the gloom.
A lake wears a flowering lily pad gown.
While, croaking frogs jump up and down.
Up in the sky so blue,
Flies a beautiful white cockatoo.
Flamingos dance upon the lake.
Such graceful movement, they do make.
It is a grand canopy so lush and green.
Oh! this forest is a most magnificent scene.
To get a view or sneak a peep,
Arrive through a dream in your sleep.

—*Mack Dyer and Nick Brenton*

The Playground

Not many words does magic ring,
as those of children in the playground sing.
Their chatter and cries outdue above fearless flock
of flying geese,
Whose main purpose is nature's way of a circus fleece.

Everywhere the grass has grown for beauty sake,
Boys and girls do trample all as cattle consuming constant
intake.

A sudden shout that cries aloud,
A child has fallen beneath the cloud.
Too many running here and there,
Not paying heed to a fallen soldier do care.

Replacement many as evening greets,
Nearing a parents joyful treat.
The playground is weeping its wails and sighs,
As youngsters, oldsters and betweensters cry.

Tomorrow when today has seen its way,
The troops do beckon a charge to play,
Fair weather is prayed by ages so bold,
This coming day rings magic foretold.

—*Joseph S. Jackiewicz*

October's Glory

What beautiful colors all around
As we gaze on the trees in their splendor abound
We'd like to capture the gorgeous view
And hold in our memory forever such hue.

Yet there's no artist on earth can paint
To get the effect God brushed, is so quaint
Which shows us no greater "being" exists
Only our Lord can make such as this.

Thank you dear Lord for sharing your beauty
It's so hard to grasp and contain so much, truly
But some day we'll see you in all your glory
Then this will seem nothing as told in your story.

Let us grasp much of the beauty we see
Tomorrow will bring cold winds, we'll all want to flee
Then the scene will be changing from warm brilliant colors
So let us praise our Lord for the memory of special hours.

—*Keitha Arnold*

"Reality"

The wind was laughing with us
as we ran through the forest,
and the sun was brightly shining
saying come climb up to me.
So we scrambled up that sturdy tree
and smelled the cleanliness of the world.
We must have felt as the squirrels do,
seeing so much of everything.
We looked far and wide
and for miles around
nature was all there was to see.
The air, the grass, the streams, flowers,
and many of God's creatures -
any which way we looked, beauty was there.
We took one last deep breath of the freshness,
then hurried down the rough, aged bark
and ran back home.
Back to the smokey chimneys, the polished wood floors
the potted plants, and faucet water -
we ran back to reality.

—*Sarah Hagen*

Lambing:

It was a cold winter night,
As we thought it might.
Wind blowing hard to the right.
Mother nature fiery in full flight.
We ran to check our sheep.
As the rest of the world sleeps.
With lamp in hand as the wind blows.
Off to the lambing shed we go.
Hopefully before all of the snow.
My how this wind does blow.
The first pink noses are appearing now.
To the joy of the world and an old wise owl.

—*Johnson Ranch*

For Black Magic

Tall, quiet, slinking feline,
As cunning as your brother lion;
With eyes of golden, amber hue...
Familiar cat; I recognize you.
Dressed in white gloves and tuxedo tails,
Long Sabre teeth and sharp white nails;
The most unique black cat...I ever met,
Has gone with the angels to be God's pet.

—*Cheryl Wolfgang*

Castle Of Our Hearts

Come my darling, take my hand
as we walk together on the cool clean sand,
our dreams laid before us for miles to see,
Come my Darling, build a castle with me.

Into your pail put hopes and desires
with the brilliance of stars and the brightness of fires,
fill it with wishes and prayers to share,
now carry it gently, with strength and with care.

Hold me close as we lay the foundation
of love and trust and a lifetime's devotion,
and as we build the walls up high,
hold me close as we reach the sky.

Now we furnish the spaces inside
this place in our hearts where we two reside,
safe in our haven we're strong together,
all that may come, we know we can weather.

Come my Darling, take my hand
as we gaze out along the cool clean sand,
our dreams laid before us for miles to see,
Come my Darling, live in this castle with me.

—*Emilie M. Davis*

I Cry

In my mind I see you,
As you leave this world far behind.

Will I see you again,
I cried as I realized you have died.
You call to me yes.

I start to cry
As my soul trembles and begins to die,
In the fear that I've lost you
Forever in a world far beyond my own,
As you go to the heavens to meet God on His throne.

I cry,
Will I see you again?

I hear the faint reply,
Yes.

—*Mindy Holder*

Junebug

You see a shiny, blue-green, iridescent bug;
As you pick it up, it pinches your fingers tightly!
You tie a string around its leg so snug
And watch as it flies in circles mightily!

Yes, it is springtime all over again.
The beetles are swarming everywhere!
Old oak trees are in full bloom again.
Just be a little boy-if you dare!

You fly them at the neighborhood girls
'N' send them runnin' 'n' screamin' for sure,
Down the old dirt road, with dangling curls!
They cannot go to buy candy at the candystore!

—*Johnny Rogers, Jr.*

A Message to my Daughter

When I look into your eyes true love pour's
over me. Then my heart begin's to remind me
of all the joy you bring to me.
Joy, laughter no agony or pain and because you
are my daughter my love for you will always remain.

—*Monica L. Ford*

"Growing into Values of Gold"

The years have taken their toll on you,
    As you worked to achieve your goals,
    The time you spent to help others,
    Sometimes brings on trials untold.

But through all of the hazards and problems,
    Through all of the pains and the woes,
    Through all the joy that brought happiness,
    And the success or pride sometimes bold.

You are constantly learning of your blessings,
    For experience open doors that curb strife,
    You've learned that with every adversity,
    There's a positive instance in life.

With every unwarranted turn of dissension,
    There's an uplifting encouragement that unfolds,
    To grow old with a graceful spirit,
    Fosters love for the achievement of your goals.

To give credents to love for your neighbor,
    To struggle toward how to grow old,
    To take the experience that has helped you in growing,
    And learn "LIFE HAS VALUES OF GOLD."

—*Agnes May Williams*

The Equivocal Handkerchief

I deserve more than 64 ounces of Tequila Sunrise
at 3 AM on a Sunday morning.
The very absurdity of drinking it all
while playing Pictionary with strangers
only makes it more mundane.
Where is the experience?
Where are all the crises?
When will it be my turn to feel the pain?
Why does everyone know but me?

So my question is:
Without any tortuous patriotism burning in my breast;
without any lost love eating away at my heart;
without any drug-induced haze loaning me visions of a higher
plane;
without any angst-filled journal entries begging to be shared;

With only questions about what God is;
with only questions about why God is;
with only questions that only God can answer;

Why do I have to cry?

—*Beth Kluckhohn*

Untitled

I stopped by to see Gramps the other day
At a distant place far, far away
He knew not who had stopped for him to see,
Was it the boy he'd embraced on the fallen oak tree?
You see, my Gramps was alone in his own time and place
He recognized no names, not even a face
He couldn't recall that I'd sat on his lap
When I came to visit as a winsome chap
He couldn't remember that the sound of his voice
Singing tenor in church made others rejoice.
But now God has spoken and Gramps is no longer alone
He is at peace in God's heaven with his beloved Ione
A place where we all hope to eventually be
A place that is peaceful and wondrous to see
I stopped by to see Gramps the other day
He is at a place not so far away

—*Matt Proud*

"Daddy"

We don't understand why God took you away.
At age "81" you still could have stayed.
Other's stay longer than you did by far.
Guess God wanted you to be his new star.
Do you shine for God like you shine here for us.
You won't have no worries, you won't have no fuss.
Go fishing and hunting, and look down sometimes.
To see all of the boy's wetting their lines.
And know one of these day's, their time will come.
To join you up there at God's fishing pond. The memories
you left us are worth more than gold. But we know you
were tired, and worn, and old. It's so hard for us
"Daddy" down here below. Thinking about you and missing
you so. But you have a new home with Jesus we know. A
mansion so pretty, with streets of pure gold. You're much
more old fashioned than that of course. But Daddy, you
deserve it, and not one but worse. You have a new life,
one that won't die. Just like the memories you left
behind. Some are sad, some make us laugh. Guess you did
your way, the best you knew how.

   —*Dorothy Shaw*

Losing It

Standing on the threshold of another loss, peering over my shoulder
at what no longer exists, I squint harder to define
those vague impressions that pass for memory.

Paradise, never ever mine, is a warm puff on a cold day;
effect floats by, held aloft by cause; a cloud of weight
crashes and settles.

Fragments of thought ramble disjointed behind my mind
(not yet lost, but surely on the way).

Avalanches of cash and opportunity elude my grasp;
an instinctive blink blinds me, and the glow of sight and vision
eclipsed.

Face and head tag sheepishly after virginity, trailed by a banner
of hope, innocence, heart and courage.

Baby teeth meet wisdom teeth in happy chatter, as friendships fade
in an echo of angry voices filled with hurt, betrayal, and love.
And time mocks me, daring me to forget what I cannot recreate,

   —*Lori A. Woolf*

Introspection

Captured.
Away within the preserves of this world,
my voice echoes... "Silence"...
Will you join me in a ritual so painfully simple?
Fit now; hold the winds comfort,
how this earth is artificially, so?
you say
has us to create a natural distortion.
Let us practice modern communication,
belief.

   —*AnnMarie Kelsa Woolsey*

Look To God

Everyone faces joy and sorrow
today and all tomorrows.
God can help man through the days.
God gave His son to make the way.
God eases the pain to give peaceful rest.
Days will be brighter no matter the test.
Look to God to carry the load.
He will make it easier down the road.

   —*Lyle Gray*

Strawberry Breakfast

He walks down the broken and cracked concrete steps
Barefoot and shirtless only wearing morning Stussy's
Stretching in the sweating sun, walking to his garden
The ground still damp from last nights rain
Waking smell of bay, the trees full of fresh water
Wandering his way down the hill, to the wooden bridge
Over the creek so filled

The metal gate of the garden he opens, as rusty hinges squeak
Looking down at the patch of strawberries, red as blood held in
the veins
Carefully pulling a strawberry from the vine slowly as dead decline
Swiftly he rose to close the passageway, piece of fruit in hand
And after washing the berry in the fresh clear stream,
He continued back home for some coolly whipped cream

   —*Mark Sorensen*

A Fly In A Pie

There could always be a fly in a pie.
Be careful of the fly in the pie.
It could make the pie taste like the fly.
Always watch the fly,
'cause the fly may be in the pie.
Never take your eye off the fly
'cause in the pie
could be the fly.
Of course the fly could be sly
and sneak into the pie.
And when the fly is in the pie,
you should reply,
"Bring me another pie,
for in my pie is a dirty fly."
But don't cry
because of the fly.
There will always be more pies.
This is all a story about a fly in a pie.
So, basically the moral of the fly,
never underestimate the power of the fly in the pie!

   —*Ryan Scherzinger*

Silver Beach

Up the steps hand-in-hand,
Beach chill and sun shrouded warm smiles of exhilaration.
Glow, glow of Silver Anniversary walk in sand, in surf.

Beautiful glowing ascending emotion.
The dark lean face above catches the look begins to smile.
Chestnut eyes, long pony-tailed hair,
tall, slim, youthful skin matching eyes bright in admiration.
Promises of pleasure, reflection of vivacity,
wild flowing unbridled passion like the waves on the shore.

Eyes catch, acknowledging mutual force, glowing strength,
earth force surges.
"Hello," he says.
Partner looks up from ground to face.
Someone should put a warning on middle-aged glasses,
"Beware objects are closer than they appear!"
He answers, greeting as do I.

The moment passes as mine alone.
I am young, beautiful and promises await me.
I sit in the sun while the sound of the waves ebb and flow.
   —*Cheryl MacNeil*

301

Untitled

They gathered around me, a kaleidoscope of hope
Beating me with their laughter 'till my voice forced to join.
I collected their dreams in lightening jars
In exchange for a wish or two,
But they all had wings
And they floated away
While my feet were nailed to the floor.
So I reached for the sky
'Though I know I can't fly
And I found that I still touch the stars
Even after they're gone.
As I set those dreams free
And make my wish or two,
I see a sad soul in the distance.
His face turned aglow as my friends from the past
Made their visit.
His eyes shined with the stars.

—Christine Hendel

Spring Glorious New Life

The sleep of the caterpillar is changed into a new life of a
beautiful butterfly. Three days in the tomb and Jesus Christ
is changed from death to his new life. Nature shouts songs of
joy while earth spreads a hugh green velvet blanket. Along the
road to Emmaus they spoke of events which took place in
Jerusalem, while he expressed thoughts of a new life. Flowers
are sprouting up, trees are budding, tiny birds hatching in
their nests. With his friends in the upper room, sharing
special moments giving strength refreshing new life. The long
slumber of the brown bear has ended, he anxiously searches for
food. Oh Thomas, place your hand into my side, let your
fingers feel the nail prints in my hands, realize that I do
have new life. That sudden rainbow in the cloudy blue sky
after the April shower, glorious spring. His visit is over,
the time has come, He ascends to begin yet another new life.
Children running happily with the wind at their backs, as kites
sway to and fro. The Holy Spirit descends like a dove, setting
hearts on fire to live their new life. Fluffy baby chicks,
lovable bunnies, new lambs all signs of God's creation
expanding. Waiting with a spirit of hope to see you face to face
and begin my new life.

—Martha L. Chainey

Skiing

The bracing air, a ride on the lift
Beautiful mountains, snow all adrift
Freedom from cares, away from it all
A holiday mood, no fear I will fall
A glimpse down the slope, the tingle of cold
It's all I could hope, it never grows old
The thrill is heady, for a moment I
Hang suspended, 'tween earth and sky
A minute or two and down I fly
At the bottom I come back to earth and then
Impatient to go to the top again.

—Jean Connerly Bash

What To Do

Why cannot I begin to fly.
Be given wings for skies so high.
Where cares are swept in currents stream,
no troubles kept, no thoughts to scream.
Where sunlight keeps the spirit high
and freedom seeps from wells once dry.
Perhaps this is a passing whim
to face the world whenever grim.

—Karen Kaisershot

Prison Thoughts

Society found me guilty so now I'm doing time,
Because I broke the law and committed a crime.
I sold cocaine even when I knew it was wrong,
So the law locked me behind bars where I belong.

Waking up each day with the sound of a bell,
Knowing I've got to face another day of living hell.
With nowhere to go or nowhere to hide,
But follow orders and remain locked away inside.

Separated from family because I broke the law,
Leaving nothing but communication through a collect call.
With fifteen minutes ticking away very fast,
Sharing all your love while it last

Today I'm alone with no family in site,
But they're thought about each and every night.
As the day passes all that I can see,
Is being in the penitentiary is not for me.

Well the days go by and the years get longer,
Which makes my need for parole grow much more stronger.
So I'm waiting for the day they set me free,
Because I'll never forget my time in the State Penitentiary.

—Buddy Custer

Jesus Has Been Where You Are

Maybe you think that you can't face your tomorrow
Because of the pain you feel today
But remember Jesus has been where you are.
Yes he too wept.

Maybe someone has hurt you so deep
That you feel not even time will heal your wound
But remember Jesus has been where you are
He was there at calvary
Crying My God My God, why hast thou forsaken me.

You may feel that your burdens are too hard to bear
But remember Jesus has been where you are
He was there in the garden of Gethsemane
He too asked God if it be possible let this cup pass from me.

Jesus has been where you are
He knows all about your trouble
Because he has felt the same trouble and all the pain that
you feel
He has felt it too. He became you at calvary

Jesus has been where you are
So know matter what you're going through Jesus know
all about you he will never leave or forsake you
Because he became you at calvary

—Carolyn Davis

Will It Last

Don't chase it down
because sooner or later it will find you
just Wait, watch, and learn
and you'll know what to do

Don't rush right in
because those Magic words are spoken
or tomorrow they'll leave you
and your heart will be broken

So take it slow
no need to go fast
If it was meant to be
I tell you it will last

—Amoya Ray Haynie

Daddy's on the Way

Through all the good times and all of the bad I have always
been there son not only because I am your dad. One day soon
we'll be together again, and not just for a short time. I will
prove to you this choice was not mine. Because for you I'd lay
my life on the line. Don't worry son, cry your last tear stop
your hurting and fear your last fear. I don't care what she
might say because Daddy's on his way. We've lost the time that
was so precious and true and now I must prove to you, once more,
that I still am here for you.
I'd fight the biggest battle, I'd cross the dead sea
I don't care what I must do to get you here with me.
I'm telling you for the time goodbye, I don't ever again want
to see you cry. We'll be together forever 'til my dying day
Don't worry my son, I'm on my way. I know how your feeling
so hurt, confused, betrayed but you must remember who you're
dealing
with because for me son, I wish you could've stayed.
Don't worry son, dry your last tear, stop your hurting and fear
your last fear, we'll be together forever 'til my dying day
Don't worry son, because Daddy's on his way!!!

—*Tracy Schnelle*

Flowers

When a flower blooms in the spring of her life
bees and hummingbirds come round
but then in time when her beauty fades
their laughter is a forgotten sound
and as in time when you grow old
I will never let you go
I will always be by your side you see
cause I just love you so.

—*David S. Harrington*

Forests

The birds chirp in the morn, the
bees buzz in the warm. The rabbits
hop in the sun, the squirrels run,
having fun. The fawns leap through
the fields, the fox hunt for their meals.
But one day these animals came
running in fear, the birds, rabbits, and
even the deer. Machines had come
to scalp the land, they built smoking
factories in their plan so grand. If
people would treat the earth as their
home, the birds would fly and the
deer could roam.

—*Jewel Noll*

School Days

You start each school year with a fresh slate.
Before long your room is filled with bits and pieces of all
your students' personalities.
You become attached, a part of their life experiences:
Chasing after lost snakes in the classroom.
Watching the love for a first book develop.
Putting out the fires of the angry ones.
Parading around the playground in silly Halloween costumes.
Seeing the light bulb go on
in the middle of a subtraction problem.
Tending to scraped knees and torn psyches.
Pursuing fallen kites on a windless day.
As the chalk dust settles you find that those little ones have
added color and dimension to your lives.
You have added love and care, reading and writing,
and wonderful memories to theirs.
As parents we can only watch and wonder
how you do it and thank you for doing it so well.

—*Donna Herz*

"The Silent One"

Alone in the dark as she was once
before, she feels alone and can stand it
no more.

She carries pressure in great despair,
her life, her dreams now seem unfair,

She longs to be happy to no longer
hide, to free herself from her fake
outside.

She crosses the line between family and
peers, and often in silence sheds many
tears.

Makes everyone happy except for one,
longs to be cheerful or either be done.

She holds it all in, for it's not thought
about, while deep down inside she
longs just to let it all out.

—*Jamie Edens*

Believe

Naivete...thy sin is mine.
  Believe
  Said my heart.

Live, laugh, love,
  Hold hands.
Hold love high
  Till life is done.
    Believe.

Forget the hurt...
  Get busy and busier.
Run fast and faster.

The blur of pace will mend the mind...
  Long after another will persuade me to
  Believe.

Naivete...thy sin is mine.

—*June DeVincent*

Left Alone

She came...We had, we did, we're done
  Belying the beauty of the morning sun
Laughter comes...it is not real
  Tormenting demons are all I feel
Days are still a potpourri
  My eyes are open, yet I can't see
My mind pulls like taffy
  I wish it would break
A sense of reality...
  Is all it would take
Omnipresent clouds...
  Emotions are spent
There are those who wallow
  ...I'll be hellbent
Look in my window
  ...I may be just having a brew
But look closely at my walls
  They are all painted blue
    Left alone...I cried

—*John Kaphing*

Is There No Love Left?

Our poor earth trembles; consumed, bereft
Beseeching the Universe; is there no love left?
Nobody heeds my poisoned seas
Nobody cares; they've burned my trees!

My rainforests raped; my land's been stripped
I'm so out of balance; losing grip
I can't hold back the flooding rains
While my volcanoes erupt from searing pain.

Winds now rage into typhoons and gales
I've lost control of destructive hail
Fault lines widen; I'm unable to fight
The urge to split open all land in sight.

While my animals and fish become extinct
Man, into oblivion, continues to sink
I'm surely dying; floundering, bereft
God, how did this happen? Is there no love left?

    —Gloria Hizer

Y'asiah

A son shall ye bear! The angel told the young virgin.
Bethlehem in a manger lay he, wise men, shepherds beheld him.
Moved to do so as directed, for homage him pay!

Eleven was he, in the Temple, being about his Father's business.
Learned men were amazed with his teaching!

Thirty turned he, home left he, to find Israel's lost sheep.
Twelve was given he, showing them the wonders of heaven an'
  earth.
Traveling Israel's land, taught, preached, healed an'delivered.
With compassion on all who'd come to him!

A dark day came, betrayed was he, to trial went he.
Called blasphemer was he, carried a cross he, him on it put.
Hands, feet, spear in side wounded, his blood flowed!

This the prophets of old foretold, tomb of man put they he.
Said they: "No more hear we him, back to the old go we!"
Little they knew, told them he: "I will arise!"

Out that tomb did go he, with glory over death he!
Thirty days among us he, from Mt. Olivet went home he, saying:
"To Jerusalem go, give I you power. I've come an' will again!"

Verily Y'asiah, Y'asiah, Ya Y'asiah Messiah has come!

    —Paul E. Neidlinger Jr

What Brought You To This Point In Life?

What brought you to this point in life, that you think you're
better than me? When we're all born of the same blood, from
sin it set us free. What brought you to this point in life,
that you can look down on me? Because liars, fornicators, and
sinners we all once were to some type of degrees. What brought
you to this point in life, that you can't stretch out your
hand? To pick your brother or sister up, that you call your
fellow man. What brought you to this point in life, that
others don't matter anymore? Just as long as you can run over
each other, no matter what the score. What brought you to
this point in life, that you're too blind to see? That if
we can't love and help one another, then satan won't let us
be. Is God the one who brought you to this point in life,
that we can't share and care? Or, is it our faults that
we're not willing; for the Kingdom to prepare. But all in
all, one another we must learn to love, to please the one
that we call Lord, the one that's up above.

    —Camellia Wood

"Trapped"

Trapped by passion fear and care,
Only to find that no one's there!
Trapped alone, I think not so...
Others are trapped wherever I go!
    —Mike Kubosh

Amare

Let not the perils of ardor stand
between that which is wanted by the two.
Fear not that which you desire, but welcome it —
For it is within your power
to command your wishes and dreams.
Show not apprehension toward
the consequence of your actions,
however, relish in their deed.
If you are one to venture dear girl
then let down your locks and take hold.

    —David A. Sullivan

Simply Plaid

At the age of five I learned to see
beyond what eyes were meant to be.

She seemed the same, yet why? then, the machine sat on her
desk doing her writing unlike the rest.

She knew my fat fingers as only me,
I knew nothing; I watched and learned.

"What color is my dress today?"
Simply "plaid," I said and turned away.

Born so different to this world,
She felt her way through life;

I covered my eyes to be this girl, and found I didn't know...
what plaid was, how to begin to show.

What is a color?,...
I didn't know.

She taught my fingers how to read...little bumps that meant
something; I saw her world the way she does, without my eyes,
but with insight.

Her strength to succeed pushed her far ahead, and again she
asked of me..."What color is my dress today?"

Not-so-simply......"Plaid," I said.
    —Lynnmarie Staiano

"Ethereal Images"

The awakening of the seas,
bid knowledge to the cousins of solitude.

As the whisper of the wind
is a point being made.

But actually just an attempt
at giving, as the roots of cynicism.
Lay requirements for another approach,

And the special things are known
and coveted,

And we are sometimes petty,
when we need not be.

And while a 3-D liquidation leaves it's
mark on this world, we know.

Still, that there beyond the satellites
and endless, nocturnal vapors,

There is a home to be hoped for.
    —Mark Bowen

Perfect Flowers

Perfect flowers
Opening up beautifully
Gorgeous yellow buttercups glowing with delight
Blood red, red roses velvety soft and light in the air
Crushed Chrysanthemums
—*Christina Schweitzer*

Alone

Here is where I stand alone.
Black walls is all I see.
Feeling as if I'm chained and bound,
In this dark and musty room beneath the ground.
No light that I can see.
No flowers that I can smell,
No windy breeze that I can feel,
No one in this room, but me.
Only pictures of what life would be,
If you had not captured me.
I know that I will be leaving soon,
For my pictures are fading fast.
Faster and faster each passing day.
Goodbye is all I can say.
Good-bye to the world that has been
so bad to me.
Good-bye to the world that wanted rid of me.
Good-bye to the few true friends I had.
Good-bye to the world that treated me so bad.
—*Catrina Humphrey*

Love?

Love to you is so blind,
Blind enough that you can't see past my tears.
Love to me is so clear,
Clear enough that when I look into your eyes
I see the look that tells me what my love
Used to mean to you.
When I look into your soul,
I see the feelings of pain and emptiness which I also hold.
And when I look into your heart,
I see the empty place which I used to fill.
Love to you is so blind,
That maybe if you looked deeper than the tears,
You could see what yesterday used to hold
And what tomorrow has to mend.
—*Beth M. Hunsicker*

The Wisdom Of Hands

Like a morning steal as the night with many eyes of sight being blinded by deception of lies to the truth of no meaning. Like a child being weaned from the bosom of the breast in which it had been cuffed and fed. Like a lion king of the jungle watching and pacing the grounds for his prey moving closely before he strikes his prey a predator would one say subject to kill and if not then it must be such a tragic steal. Being dragged off pleading for freedom from the cries of pain leading out of Africa a child of God creator of all whom was there to witness this as they took the fall. How much of this should we have to endure? The chains that brings us in takes us out the hands of pain is screaming without a doubt. This is so though it isn't even called for a cuff it is about time in which we must come together we have been separated from what is right long enough. It is God's will for us not to be violent and right but it is also God's will for us to know the difference of what is right. Life is supposed to be fulfillment and enjoyed no matter where their stationed in life. I say this with dignity and respect because this day is the day for us to make our own way.
—*Phyllis F. Carter*

Stifled

A shot gun blast as I drive past
Blood is sprayed and I'm alive.
Don't ask about my past it didn't last.
Nor the innocent so I can survive.

My, so called, Dad — I never knew
was said to be nothing but a drunk.
Life didn't fit so I'll wear this shoe.
Is it any wonder I'm nothing but a punk?

Didn't ask to live or to be born.
This is the hand I've been dealt.
Away from society I've been torn
You don't even know how I've felt.

I've heard that they say Jesus saves
but I'm not so sure, I'm in to deep.
So he awakened the dead, freed the slaves.
But can he lift me from this heap?

He came to give life not to give death.
But my brothers drop like flies.
Breathe in me Lord a new life's breath
and stifle Satan's lies.
—*Richard Ivy*

Jealousy

How oft have I strewed your path with
bloodied roses,
And held the thorny scepter o'er your
queenly head.
What barbed thrusts, ill-parried, rent the shield
of your poise,
Aborting unborn tears that welled, but
died unshed.
How oft have I wielded the vanquished sword,
Whetted on a hundred thoughts of your disdain;
Riving with distraught blade pretenders to my throne—
And forged the edged quest, quenched in
chilled loneliness,
That slew with self-inflicted wounds your only champion.
—*Ray Bernett*

Slip Away

The orb floats just above the horizon,
Bobbing up and down upon the earth.
Eventually, it will begin to sink behind the mountains,
But slowly. It takes an eternity
For the edge to disappear.
Sliding along the sky
Like melting butter in a warm pan.
Suddenly! It's halfway gone -
All at once, slipping beneath the ground.
Before I realize that it is leaving;
Before I can learn to love it, to miss it;
The sun, and life, is gone.
—*Traci Gaboury*

Death

If I must leave, then let me go
Quickly, not a guest lingering at the door,
Reluctant to forsake the circle of warmth and light
In the home of his host.
Let me go quickly, entering the darkness and unknown.
With unfaltering stride, and trust
That home is but a step away.
—*Ruth Park Johnson*

Poetically Coping

Siamese spirits within a family of love, a spirited lightening
bolt casts upon all anomaly, there exists a progeny ever so
immortal, an eternal lantern always so bright showing the path
for all the souls to follow in the coming days and thereof.
Oh the feelings that so plunder the heart, the wishful thinking
of "what could have been" haunts the reality, as we hold to the
memories, and cry our selfish good-bye's there goes his soul,
leaving behind a spiritual haze.
The lingering thoughts rest in our minds, as we look upon the
neighborhood for which we all call home, looking as we squint
to see, our imagination deepens, a wraith recreation of the
past, a happy time where death never existed in the minds for
what we now know is a given.
To grieve his death would be wasteful, to grieve that we miss
him would be selfish, to forget would only misplace his memory,
to think a tragedy occurred would be curtailing his life, but
to cherish him and remember the happy days will forever keep
his spiritual mortality as his soul lives eternally mortal.

—Frank Figliomeni

For Love Is Gone

Let me cry softly, so no one can hear the sound of a heart
breaking. For a breaking heart is the most lonely sound in
the world. It wails into the wind where the morning dove echoes
its refrain. And the wolves point there noses skyward and sing
along with its chorus. So let me cry softly...for love is gone.

Let the tears flow, flow from the depths of the endless well of
watering from which all tears come. And let the pain keep
silent, for to let it go would bring forth sound. A sound so
loud and wrenching that the whole of the earth would be
shattered by its screams. So do not give it voice, for the
world must not know of its depths. Just let me cry
softly...for love is gone.

Let my mind be still ... hush. For the whirlwind seeks to
gather you unto its bosom. And hold you close where rest is
never found. Only endless days and nights of soaring ups and
downs. Pain ... despair ... and weeping from which there is
no return. Quiet, mind ... rest ... do not think or remember.
Just let me cry softly ... for love is gone.
And I will hold you close.

—Peggy Blue

Sorrow Comes...

Touches our lives
Breaks our hearts
Shatters our souls.

Where is this world so filled with love?
Where is this God in His Heaven above?

Mothers cradling babies, dying in their arms
Widows weeping
Children sleeping, in the streets below.
Hunger rampant; people laughing.

Who will bear this pain?
Is it you?
Is it I?
Who shall face the rain?

Sorrow comes...
Breathes deeply, silently
Leaving our shells behind.

Sorrow simply comes.

—J. M. Elek

My Own Rainbow

Just for me you gave a rainbow,
Bright, yet soft, the way you planned my life.
Long and arched I began my climb.
Sometimes things became too much.
I slid, but you caught me, and I pushed on.
Together we move upward.
At the top, I looked around.
What a sight to behold!
Red - the beauty of a rose,
protected by thorns, as you protect me.
Blue - the quilt that covers
my head and gives warmth.
Green - earth's carpet with its brilliant colors of fixtures,
that bring dismay and disbelief at such awesome sight.
Purple - like a Royal robe draping my shoulders.
Saying, "You are special."
Yellow - the bright sunflower reaching out its petals,
Showing, "All this is given to you with my love."
Going down will be slower, giving more time for painting
the views. Thank you! My Heavenly Father.

—Eloise BrownHill

"Break Light"

Break light my heart
bring brightness and laughter to my soul -
break light my heart
and ease the pain of hopeless grief
for times gone by
and special moments long forgotten.

Break light my heart
dry the tears of blackness — make them go
bring brightness and laughter to my soul -
break light my heart
chase the blackness into the corner of my mind
and let me smile -

Break light my heart
let tender moments hold me dear
and bring hope for all tomorrows -
Break light my heart
bring brightness and laughter to my soul
break light my heart -
it's been so long, let me smile...

—Jolie Clark

To Mele

The perfect stillness of this lonely night
Brings forth a flood of memories past
Of touch and feel and promised delight
That calms my suffering souls fast

And in the misty humid nights shade
With lip and tongue and hand she played
Hidden melodies——undefined
Beyond the slipping grasp of mind

Now the wind outside calls to come in
My mind wanders to where I have just been
The gentle rain leaves soft footprints on my soul
To blend with those left on my pillow's fold

—William A. Krock

Paper Rain

Sometimes we need to be held just to heal the
pain, and answers to the questions we're afraid to
ask. If we could find the courage to seek the rain
that would wash all our troubles away, then maybe
in finding peace of mind, love would make itself
known and our pursuit would not be in vain.

—Paula Schader

s It Was

emember the old peasant of
roadway and 19th—scraped red face, a croaking smile and
visted hands a size or two too large?

uge-bottomed, she was bulked in swathes of black.
eaved it all down on a grocer's crate most often—
ot far from the corner, in front of the old bank.

saw her winter evenings on my walks
a sharpest cold, sometimes in snow,
elling puppies from a big brown basket—
tters gummy-eyed and squeaking—
nd candy too: gum drops, licorice
penny each, and oddly-shaped dark cookies
inger-tasting, dusted with white sugar.

seemed to me she was old beyond the telling
ut she never changed. I was the one who aged.
ne day she simply wasn't there any more.

ears later, I thought of her when spring came round
nd days grew long again;
ow at Easter time she used to sell white rabbits,
nd water lilies in mid-June.

—*Ann White, R.P.T.*

hattered Vows

herish memories of what we once had,
roken vows of a love gone bad.
ou took our love and threw it away,
ou did this all, in just one day.
ou cheated not only in your life,
ou shattered the vows of husband and wife,
ll never understand the reason why,
ou took our love and brushed it aside.
thought, we felt the same way dear,
aring and sharing without any fears.
ou begged, me to stay in your life,
orgive and forget, remaining your wife,
or the years we shared so precious and few,
hope, I can do this for me and for you.

—*Jean Abreo*

Once Upon A Birthday Time

Once upon a birthday, in rainy April time,
urst forth a birth, with a loud, loud whine,
ts a boy! Its a boy!
he doctors did say,
hey watched the mother beam, and Dad his eyes did gleam,
The parents were proud as Dad stood tall
hey glowed at their child curled up in a ball,
hey took him home for love and care,
nd rocked him carefully in the chair,
ay by day, they watched him grow taking on his role in life,
earning all about fun, happiness, stress and strife,
One day the realized he was in his teens
reparing to be a man and fulfill his dreams,
ut into the world he went, looking back on time he well spent.
He became a man to get to where he is today,
hank God he chose the right way.

—*Alsace Rodgers*

Life Goes On

ife goes on and dreams come true.
eople grow and people die but
hat's just a part of life we have to live with
ot everyone can have a miracle
ut if the people share the miracle
han other people can be happy and
would enjoy their life.

—*Dannette Bonitatis*

Love Tells No Lies

There are feelings for you inside of me that I wish that I
could hide,
but as the old saying goes, "love tells no lies."
Though yet I feel as if it's all just a waste of time,
because when I look into your eyes I do not see you and I.
Oh, how I long to see us romancing under the sun,
and then you whisper sweetly to me, "you're the only one."
Is this just a dream or is it all a lie?
Why won't you tell me how you feel?
Why can't you just be mine? Oh please tell me why.
For of everything you say to me I do not feel your love.
So, I guess your not in love with me and I know I'm not the
only one.

So, hold your breath and close your eyes, then tell me what
lies down deep inside.
Only then if you really love me your love will tell no lies.

—*Amber Gibson*

The One I Love

You are the one I think about,
But, believe what I say is true.
Sometimes my mind doubts
That you love me too!

At times, I'm scared to get too close,
Even though, you've treated me better than most.
You are the only one that can give me comfort,
That's when I know I can't get hurt.

You know me better
Than anyone else.
Better than friends and family,
maybe even better than
I know myself.

I do believe that we are made to be together.
My heart and mind can only hope
That our love will last forever.
I thank God every night for what I received from above,
He gave me you, the one I love!

—*Choni Murphy*

A Broken Heart

We were so good for each other, or so I thought,
But days went by, and still we fought.

I knew and he knew, it would never work out,
Even our friends could see it, there was no doubt.

We started out as such good friends,
it was hard to believe that it all had to end.

We talked on the phone for the longest time,
Those words of sadness kept in my mind.

I hung up the phone thinking, "it's just as well."
As one by one, the tears they fell.

I knew it would never have lasted this long,
It was all my fault, and now it was gone.

—*Annie Grassick*

Fear

There is a fear within us, its down deep and can't
see it when it hurts. We can only show by our
feelings and emotions. Even though we can cure
our fear, some people get hurt by it more and
more. Even though we try to keep something good
it always has to end. The biggest fear we have is
life and the only cure is death.

—*Rose Bremmer*

Red October 1993 Remembered

It is all much different this time,
But for the glow of a few fiery gems,
The embers of spent hopes in rhyme,
The silence upon the purpled lips of men.

Who will remember them now,
The heroes of this Red October,
Their young bodies broken upon the snow,
Their lives snuffed out by those more cunning and sober.

How is it no one heard their cries?
No, no one even came at all.
As the bitter truth is transformed into lies,
So, too, are heroes made traitors in their fall.

Again we hear the echo, the collective moan
Of the ghosts of all Red Octobers past...
The ledger of innumerable names unknown,
All faceless victims of human indifference at last.

In the temple of Judas, smug men
Snicker over their crimes and enjoy a smoke.
Civilization echoes with a resounding silence.
The contours of history are altered at a stroke.

—*Richard Merli*

Crying Out...

Suffering is everywhere,
But help is nowhere.
Racists are striking,
And nobody's protecting.
Let us cry out.

Hate is still causing destruction,
However there seems to be no solution.
Nature's erosions show up stronger,
No one realizes that it is God's eager.
When we'll we...for crying out louder?

I often sit in a quiet corner,
Thinking whether one man can make a difference.
Day after day, I see more hunger.
It's obvious that I need a little bit more experience.
Hopefully, I smell help coming closer.

—*Junior Fleury*

"Country Girl"

I'm an old time fashioned country girl
But I am not ashamed of it.
I have never worn little tight short cuts,
I wear 'em long down to the cuffs.

As I walk down the ole dusty lane, I whisper sweet words
To the pretty little birds.
I watch the other little animals running to and fro
Watching me to see where I go.
But I never go too near.

I can smell the beautiful flowers along my way
And they seem to be nodding hello as they gently sway.
Then I see the big golden moon shine its beams
Across the bubbling stream. I hear the whippoorwill
calling its mate in his thrilling screams.

So before the evening gets too late,
I enter my yard through the swinging gate and
go to bed and dream sweet dreams of a pleasant day,
Thanking the Lord for my peaceful place.

—*Ruby Terrell*

You!!!!

Sometimes I'm ready for someone to take my life,
But I have this feeling, that someday, I will be your wife.
That is very exciting to know, and helps me live from day to day.
Without you I don't know what I'd do, but knowing your with me,
there's always a way.
You are very important to me,
I love you very much, and I do hope that you see.
I wish we could be together all the time.
But in my heart I believe and know that I got you; that you're
only mine.
Sometimes when I'm really sad,
I'll read your letters or look at your picture and I will
realize things aren't at all that bad.
I hope that we are still together in the future,
I wish that the feelings I feel for you are so very "mutual"!!!

—*Manda Lynette Wilson*

If I Could Escape

I see nothing, I feel nothing, I sense nothing.
But I know it's all still out there. Moving and
growing, going on all around me; if only, if only I
could escape to look at everything there is.

I might take in the breath-taking sunsets in
the Florida Keys. Or the beauty of a snow-capped
mountains in the Himalayas. I might visualize the
moisture in the air as I gaze upon a tropical rain
forest to see the spectacular colors of a rainbow. If only.

I might feel the heat rise off the sands as I
walk along a beach or the cool moist air from the
surf breathing at my feet. To feel the rush of air
flowing through my hair. If I could only feel the
spirits flying high on a warm spring day. To
experience the joy of a white Christmas. Maybe just
the proud feeling of a son's first hit in baseball, if only.

But still here unable to see anything, unable
to feel anything. Not sensing anything. To do any
of these things I would escape. If only I could.
But I cannot for I am dead.

—*Michael Mitchell*

The Unwritten Letter

If I could write a letter, I'm not sure just what I'd say.
But I think that I may ask you, what brought you here today?
Were you scared or lonely, or afraid what folks might say?
Dearest Mommy, do you know the price that I will pay.

I know that you've not seen me, and you tell yourself, it's not real.
Mommy, you don't know me, you think that I can't feel.
Some folks have you believing, that I'm not even real.
But I've been here four months now, and I have lots of parts.
Ten fingers and ten toes, and a tiny baby heart.

My eyes could be blue, or they may be brown like his.
Why, if they took a picture, they would know if I'm Mister or
Miss,
I can suck my tiny thumb, and I can hiccup, and I sneeze.
When I hear loud noises, I draw up tiny knees.

Is that the doctor coming? Mommy, please think hard and long.
Please be sure there's not a chance, that you just might be
wrong. But if you feel you have no choice, I'll forgive you,
Mommy dear. I know I'm going to Heaven, and I'll wait for you
up there!

—*Eileen Wiggins*

hank You Lord

our lives we have had sorrows and grief,
t in the name of Jesus there is relief
ere were days in our lives when we felt we couldn't go on.
e weight on our shoulders felt like a ton
e sunshine in our lives felt so dim
t the Lord will shine light to those who believe in him.
hen we call out His name He will hear.
ways merciful and drying her tears.
hen we feel lost and there's no one to tell
ere is He who knows our sorrows only too well
hank the Lord for being there for you and me,
r in times of trouble, sorrow and grief he'll be
ere to set us free.
ar friend, here's a message I don't want you to miss
an not on your own strength, but on His.
let's praise His name when times are good or bad
d He will give our lives the peace we never had.
ank you, Lord for everything!

—Carmen Lydia Damaso

fe

m so very dark
t inside comes light.

m so very small
t inside my mind has so much space.

ook so very sad
t inside I feel joy.

y voice sounds so very faint
t yet you cover your ears.

ll you about my pain
t I still don't complain.

e wind is cold, the rain is wet,
e world is giving, but we take so much.

e road is long
t the path is narrow.

choose a direction
t the outcome is not clear.

e is not certain
t living is life itself.

—Cortez Overton

ccer

cer is a sport that's fun
it may not be for everyone.
cer is a sport of action
ring goals brings satisfaction.
yers must be very tough
ause sometimes the games get kind of rough.
ere are many positions you can be
re's forward, fullback, or even goalie.
bbling, kicking, scoring
isn't even close to boring.
ere are many rules for you to learn
there's many medals for you to earn.
ou think soccer is right for you
ybe that is what you should do!

—Christi Stover

e Void Of Nothingness

pty space
I can't think of anything
ieve in anything
ve it-show me.

—Jeff Flaster

Happiness

While walking down the pathway of life and not knowing what's
ahead,
But just having a loving heart hold back the fear, not worrying
about tomorrow or the next day.
But letting tomorrow take care of itself in its own way.
Sometimes life can be a struggle, and sometimes life can be dear,
But when we fail, we can pick up the pieces; there can be
happiness and no room for tears.
Life was never meant to be an easy thing, it's up to us what
our destiny brings.
We can smell the sweet aroma of a rose and feel its soft touch
to our skin.
Life has a perfume about itself, there is a beginning and there
is an end. We can watch the innocent children play, or watch
the sunset at the end of the day.
To throw a pebble in a brook, to open the pages of a book,
To feel happiness up above,
And to know we can walk by faith, and not by fear,
And to know we can always have love.

—Peggy Kee

Understandings

Beauty is only a moment
But... Love is forever
Laughter is always joy
Such as... Friends should never drift apart
Smiles come and go
But... Happiness stays everywhere
Eyes can tell stories
Such as... Hugs bring a smile
Family is always love
But... You should never disown it
Children are the beginning of our future
Such as... Pets can heal a broken heart
Fancy creatures are magical
But... As long as they live in our hearts
Some songs never end
Such as... Everyone has a dream
We sometimes need a helping hand
But... Sometimes our hands can't help
Peace should last forever
But... We sometimes don't understand that...

—Regina Zapalac

The Kitchenette Apartment

"John!" she said in a tired voice, "Go outside and play."
"But Mom" he said in a sad voice, "It's just eight o'clock in
the day!" She closed the sofa and folded the bed, then quietly
swept the rug. She watched the baby in the crib. ready to slay
an intruding bug. "Now go out John," she said again, "And don't
play in the street." "You know it was very hot last night,
your sister needs to sleep!"
So he went outside and stood around there was no one far or
near. He went across to the school playground and looked
around in fear.
The boys who lived across the track, he knew were still asleep.
They always roamed the streets at night to see whom they could
beat. He took the ball admired his fans and played as in a
dream. The crowd cheered as he made the goal; he loved to hear
them scream! Each day he played with all his heart; there was
nothing else to do! If only he had his own bedroom he could
read 'till noon like you. Now when he plays professional ball,
don't say he is in his sphere. He is proud of what he does
today but he learned that which was near.

—Florida B. Ware

I Am Not A Child

I do not consider myself a child,
    But my father does.
Children do not have opinions,
    But I do.
Children do not care about important things,
    But I care.
Children cannot make choices for themselves,
    But I can.
Children have to be reminded to brush their teeth,
    But I don't.
Children should be seen and not heard,
    But I am not a child.

    —*Sabrina Hanelt*

Loneliness

        Loneliness is what everyone has,
    But my loneliness is far from everyone else
            Mine has nothing to do
            With death or companionship
                It has to do with
                The world around us
                It moves too quick
            And everyone dies so fast
        So why am I letting this loneliness
            Bother me—because it hurts
            Me to see the trees come down
    As fast as fast as the buildings go up
            And to see what is left
                Or our wildlife die
            There are many things wrong
    In this world that is causing this loneliness
                That I am feeling
                To stop this loneliness
        I must help survive, as much as I can
                    So must you!

    —*Amber Allen*

On Writing

I can't remember when I learned to write,
but one day I could and did,
only with much coaxing and prodding could
I keep my left wrist flat on the page
as my left hand poured out words,
writing first about the giraffe that could talk,
and the tree that cried, about my pseudo home
state of Nebraska, and the workings of volcanoes,
then about the double helix, DNA and RNA,
and Federico Lorca's play Blood Wedding,
read and analyzed in Spanish,
then about my mother who never wanted me,
and my father who wanted me in a very ugly way,
now my left hand pours out death wishes and regret,
the giraffe has stopped talking,
but the tree still cries.

    —*Claudia Thompson*

The Bark Canoe

    Long and wide sheaves of bark
paper of the angels bark
you bark is fragile to the hand

    Long and tall it grows free
its out there in the trees
the indians canoe makes him a man.

    —*Michael cook*

Ma's Homemade Bread

Pick up the paper that was not read.
Slice a piece of homemade bread.
Cinnamon, sugar, and some butter to spread.
Try to fit that slice of homemade bread.
Heat up some milk and find the cocoa
Ma's homemade bread its in the toaster.

    —*Donna Kay Smith*

Graduation to Glory

I think not of death as an end to it all
But rather answering my father's call.
This gift of mine, this life anew,
He gave to me to make dreams come true.

All I need do is confess my sins;
Take Him as my savior, then healing begins.
His life, His death, for you and for me
Is our assurance of heaven eternally.

I now look forward to crossing that road
To change my clothes for His vestual robe.
I'll take His strong hand outstretched to me;
He'll say, "Fear not, come and follow me."

So sing songs, clap your hands
Put a smile on your face;
Praise God, not a tear nor trace.
I'll be living with loved ones
And God on His throne:
Surely you know I've gone joyfully home.

    —*Grandma "D"*

Inside Of Me

My thoughts and troubles are simple
But scattered to only God would know
My thoughts can be like a pond's ripple
My troubles like a storm of raging snow

My inside is of love, hate and mixed feelings
My mind is of delicate crystal waiting to be discovered
My eyes hold the secrets, the past of tears come fleeing
My outside shows confusion, happiness, waiting to be
recovered

My moods of up and down is that as liked prepared
I need what people don't see inside me
My feelings for life is not cared
And someday on my lonely road of black
I hope to flee...this trouble inside of me

    —*Nova Dubovik*

A Cry For Help

Mama says I'm the perfect child.
But she doesn't know about the secrets I hide.
I've locked them up, so mama won't see
how much it hurts when she look at me.
She doesn't hear the screams at night,
that wakes me up in such a fright.
I hold my pillow close to me, hoping to
defend myself from what I see. I see the hurt and the shame,
also me being blamed. Mama will know that I'm not perfect
anymore, if my secrets were to be explored.
Mama wonders why I don't eat. She also wonders why I don't
sleep. I tell her that nothing is wrong. But I know my
life is gone. I'm not the person I use to be, there's
only this smaller version of me. Day after day I try to find,
the courage to tell her about the secrets I hide. But the fear
of being blamed and turned away, causes me to wait another day.
Maybe I'll find that courage I seek, and maybe I'll find that
perfect little girl that mama use to think was me.

    —*Dahn Rajah*

Christmas Season

Christmas season's here at last
But soon will be in the past
It only lasts for one day
During Christmas the children play
With toys they find beneath the tree
And this makes them happy
There are lots of toys
For all the little girls and boys
They have a Christmas dinner
But unfortunately don't get any thinner
The children go out in the snow
And the adults make cookies out of dough
Then the children come in and get warmed up
And have some hot tea or chocolate in a cup
Then, after being fed
They then go off to bed

—*Carey Strittmatter*

"Defeated"

How many times, I've asked myself why,
But still you tell me lies.
I want to trust you, I want to believe you,
But that damn cocaine has a hold of you.
My life is on a merry go round,
I'm living from day, to day.
I never can plan a month, or less,
or even a day away.
As soon as you appear, I forget you're living in hell,
And my motherly instincts take over me,
As cocaine took over you.
It's been a hard life for me,
But I won't waste time wishing it's not true.
I'll turn my head from my young son
Evan, as that damn cocaine has a hold of you.

—*Judith Monds*

In Your Eyes

I've never seen it before in anyone else
But to find it in your eyes of a certain
beauty there
That no one else can compare
And to each look I take
You've taken my breath away
Looking straight into your eyes.

In your eyes
Enticing innocence is displayed
No other has the spirit that you betray
And to find myself in love with you
But there's nothing that I can do
Seems that spoken words aren't spoken through

What I feel and what is to be seen
Aside I cannot help myself
To be lost looking straight into your eyes
And of emotions burning like fire ever so higher.

—*Rod Sims Legaspi*

Quest

I never knew for what I craved for many, many moons.
By day, by night I roamed the world to fill this nameless void.
In sunny climes, down wintry slopes, through darkened woods I
searched
I lay alone beneath the stars in some enchanted isle.
And then, one day, to my surprise, my search came to an end.
You strode across the room toward me, broad-shouldered, fair and
strong,
And looked into my eyes to send a thrill throughout my spine.
I knew as soon as you appeared, 'twas what my craving was!

—*I. F. Norstrand*

Untitled

He always has and will love her so
But to show her, he must let go
An obsessive villain to her he seems
But in his mind are wonderful dreams
And still she cannot see his love

All the power and money there is
Means nothing to him compared with her kiss
And all he loves in this precious life
He would give up if she'd become his wife
And still she cannot see his love

To just walk hand in hand
Would make him feel he rules this land
If only to touch her lips once more
Would be enough to mend all that has tore
And still she cannot see his love

Although the dove's heart is a mess
I love you dearly it must confess
And even though he loves her so
He understands he must let go
And maybe then she'll see his love

—*Alex Furman*

Young Love Strikes

To fail once I've done so,
but twice I shall not do.
Two routes to take which
choice to make.
I like both but love one.
I notice though the one
I love is drifting away.
I use to think we'd be
together always and forever.
Somehow I turned away.
Too young for love I've always felt,
I felt no worry in the world.
I hope the choice I've made is right,
For he holds my heart, life, soul and future,
So help hold on and don't let go.
To fail once I've done so,
but twice I shall not do.
My love, I love you,
and always will.

—*Stephanie Chavez*

Sonnet To Better Ecology

Our lovely world and only home is maimed
By our misuse of its air and sea and sod;
Its global self-sustaining system shamed
By the challenge of we impish sons of God.
Into the balanced mix we've tossed our wit,
Taking from it what has been our whim,
Wasting nature and abusing it
Until our own survival chance grows slim.
Yet, earth, the fruitful mother of our birth
Still rolls through time from out her ordered past,
Judging not of our lack or worth
Of caring even if our kind will last.
We must use her land, her sea, her air,
But, to abuse her, how much do we dare?

—*Charles N. Greenway*

Moonlight Rainbows

Moonlight rainbows can be formed,
By tears of lovers, over whom they mourn.

Moonlight rainbows can be made,
By thoughts of admiration not yet portrayed.

Moonlight rainbows can never part,
As long as you have them in your heart.

Moonlight rainbows shall never fade,
For in your mind, they were made.

Stand outside and you won't see,
The moonlight rainbows made by me.

For the ones you see, are your own,
And only through your eyes will they be shown.

—*James Stagnolia*

Untitled

A wakened in the midst of night
By the clanging of a bell,
With scrambled efforts, dressed and ready
To fight a soaring hell.

Gray clouds swirling upwards
Like cottonballs they fly,
With orange flashes and yellow tints
That brighten up the sky.

Screaming sirens, flashing lights
The sound of engines roar,
Now with hoses hooked and motors pumping
Man made rivers soar.

The heavy smoke, scary cries of
Someone inside still
very quickly a masked face climbs
A railed, but wooden hill.

In the East, the signs of light
Breaking through the day,
The blaze is out, the loss is great
But no one is hurt; as the red trucks drive away.

—*Judith Mertz*

Corn on the Cob

I was alone at the kitchen table when a chair
came softly out of its usual disguise
and appeared to me in all its chairness, which
forgive me, God, seemed holier than you
have ever seemed up to that time and since
(my fault, not yours, I'm sure).

The second epiphany that evening was like it.
With a wisp of butter and Margrita salt,
a mouthful of new corn from the cob
altered itself to match,
chemically, organically, molecularly,
the saliva and taste buds in my mouth
at just that precise moment —
its DNA rushing to embrace my DNA.

So this is corn? No. It's ecstasy.
Some mysterious cosmic reunion, perhaps.
A hark back to ... to when
Corn and I and God
were a lot closer
than we usually are.

—*James E. Adams*

Wildlife

If I could give the world a gift, I'd ask for all,

to not play with a match or a knife so we
can save our wildlife,

protect animals and trees,

protect oceans and seas.

We'd like to live in nice fresh air, instead of
things that we can't bear,

{like smoke covering everywhere.}

So please don't play with a match or a knife
so we can keep our WILDLIFE!

—*Arian Steiner*

The Love Is Gone

Dream or reality,
Can you separate one from the other,
You try so hard,
To forget the hurt,
That one can do to another,

The hurt becomes, easier to accept,
When you imagine it cannot be real,
But then, you begin to realize,
The pain of reality,
Is what you feel,

You start to rationalize and try to make sense,
Of this rejection directed toward you,
There had to be a reason, for this to occur,
And for the torment you had to go through,

There are no answers, for the love is gone,
Never to be returned,
All that is left, is a singed memory of love,
Like the coals of a fire,
That has burned.

—*Lynn Edelman*

What the Future Holds

What the future holds is in our hands which some people
cannot understand; it's our choice so we must speak our
voice; if we want success, we must be our best; what the
future holds is all up to us; we must come face to face with
our fears, without shedding tears;
we must be brave and not afraid;
we must have courage and never should we be discouraged,
we must make wise decisions to the best of our comprehension,
what the future holds is what we will soon discover,
as we were taught by our mothers; our key must be wisdom
and we should not be fooled by mysticism;
what the future holds is us.

—*Lori Booher*

Summer Love

Summer love sometimes can be gray,
Cause, you know that one day there on their way,
Summer love is a game to tease your heart,
We under estimate it's powers yet,
it can tear you apart,
You remember shared moments happy and true,
and how many times they have kept us
together me and you,
You don't know of the troubles deep in your heart,
All you know is that it's tearing you apart
You try to tell yourself that it will all be fine,
But, deep down inside your losing your mind
Summer loves are too hard they don't make you sing,
So if it's love that you want wait until spring.

—*Rosa Galari*

To The One I Love:

Wanting you, needing you, hoping you'll come back. Why
can't I be happy, for it was I who turned my back. All you
ever caused was heartache each passing day, so why can't I
let go? He loves me that's why we married. Yet it's you I
still see. You'll never be true, and I'm the one to lose.

Just go away and never return, you'll hurt me as you've
been known to do. I've found another one so true, he'll
love me through and through. This love will never be what
we had but it will last. If you ever loved me leave me in
our past. I won't regret this love of mine, I'll just smile
or that love unfound.

Say goodbye my love, it's time for our love to rest.
I will be from this day foreword but part of our distant
past. Something to be cherished yet never explored for fear
there might have been something more.

Sleep my love and remember me as the lights grow dim.
Sleep my love for you'll find me there. Sleep my love, for
you'll forever be the one. Sleep my love and forget about me.

— *Lorna Gladish*

Children, Stay Children

In the sweet sunshine they play.
Carelessly laughing their days away.
Their sorrow never lingers long.
Eagerly they search on to find new joys.
Unknowingly they possess a great secret to happiness.
See their smiling faces, feel their innocent love they so
freely give.
Little minds, and big hearts, so quickly they learn.
Too quick they learn.
There comes the day when the sweet sun has turned a dull gray.
They've learned too much.
Their big hearts have shrunk.
They've grown up.
Children, stay children.

— *T. R. Fortune*

lies around every corner, just waiting to be found.

You will get ever so great a reward when you finally
caress in your arms after many centuries of searching.

is so luminous that it can only be seen in a blind man's
illusion.

ever found, the keeper would never know he even
possessed it,

is not a material thing, it is something abstract and yet is
still seen by some.

is so precious that it could never be sold, even at
the price of pure gold.
Even though we may not know it, every person alive has a soul
that yearns to find the ever-admired gift.

To even touch it, you have to have the most gentle of
hands, it is that fragile.

is the biggest gift ever given to mankind.

Everyday we should be thankful for this wonderful
treasure.

We were loved so much, as to be given it to love and
cherish, always.

— *Erin M. Smith*

Your Final Mirror

Some rash deed of earnest lunacy
Caused a wreath of daffodils to flow through your fingers
You wore a string of sickening vibrant yellows
Their eerie glow warning all of Denmark you were lost
That same pretty hat we plucked from your cold dead brow

Purest princess retrieved
From slumber deep beneath the glassy brook
Your final mirror
Reflecting naked mockery
Of certain thresholds you deserved to cross
But won't
"Get thee to a nunnery!" indeed
Oh, Ophelia!
I didn't mean your soft retreat
Into the convent of a shallow grave

— *Jennifer Adams*

Sad and Lonely

Sad and lonely, miserable and blue. I didn't have a
chance until I met you! I've been sad, I've been
blue, I'm still lonely and miserable too! Who can I
turn to? Who will hear me out? Who will be there
for someone like me? When I reach out for a helping
hand, is there someone who will help me? Help me in
my hour of need! If I knew there would be somebody
at the other end of this lonely, lonely road! So they
can say, "this really isn't the end!" I'm reaching
out, for a helping hand. Just someone too lean on, is
this really wrong! All I'm asking is for a shoulder to
cry on, is this asking too much? My heart is locked up
with these invisible locks & chains! I can't see in this
mist of heartaches and pain. Tell me please is there someone
out there that will at least try! Try to unlock these
locks and chains! Somebody! Somebody! Please!.... Give me
just a minute of your precious, precious time! Just lend
me a piece of your mind. So I can bring a stop to these,
"Sad and Lonely Times!"....

— *Tina Lairson*

High Tide

The waves come crashing against the sandy shore,
changing it over again and once more.
It goes back to the ocean to crash again,
changing my life when I am just barely ten.
Then it is low and the fish all come back,
soon I have friends coming in by the sack.
They all understand,
they're no longer afraid,
because I'm just barely different,
even though I have Aids.

— *Jacqueline Gest*

My Cat's Clothes

When the furr flies, it really goes!
  But the cat I love,
    with a suit made like a glove,
never washes it in a tub full of suds.

And when Winter comes
  it's really quite handy.
There's not a zipper, no buttons, or hooks,
  nothing to damper his charming good looks.

A kitten of leisure,
  a cat for all time;
    just give him a brushing —
calmly he purrs, "That I won't mind!".

— *Charlene Fuhlendorf*

Injustice

A hung jury in a kangaroo court
Charges dismissed; accused no remorse

No witness to verify the scene of the crime
No plea bargains made, no sentence, no time

His pride slightly bent but smile still intact
Free to commit and repeat his attack

Judge goes to his chambers; the crowd dissipates
No headlines were made; the reporters-irate

Her head in her hands; the victim looks down
Caught in the whirlwind as she starts to drown

The system failed; the courtroom adjourned
Instead of justice the victim got burned

He waves to the crowd as they start to cheer
The manipulator who's so sincere

The victim emerges still shaking inside
Nowhere to run; nowhere to hide

The accused now the Victor looks somewhat relieved
Adroitly he plots his new thoughts conceived
The Victim His Prey that no one believed

—*Sidelle Brown*

Technology

The night wind sighs, winding it's way among lifeless buildings
chasing cold streams of light from frustrated cars out of the
city. Two stars glare balefully through the smog onto the
barren clutter below: Security guards report a UFO.
The smog and lights usually blot out everything but the moon.
Down main street skeletal remains of last year's beautification
project push withered limbs hopelessly against the concrete
landscape. A handful of yellow leaves compete with the trash
and graffiti plastered vindictively against the puny attempt
to restore Life. A prostitute stumbles listlessly through the
concrete jungle remembering the bars and nightlife that was
eaten by the technological jungle. Cardboard rustles as she
bumps into someone sleeping on a ventilation grate. He, too,
remembers and whistles at what she used to look like, belches,
then passes out again. A fleabitten mongrel, disturbed from
rummaging for food, urinates on the cardboard. As the unsteady
footsteps fade the wind moans inconsolably for those lost
souls. On a hill overlooking the city a coyote howls in
remorse: The smog turns it into a raspy cough. Disgusted the
coyote limps away, searching for the memory of what used to be.

—*Philip Brown*

My Dad, The Gardener

My dad rises early and without any delay
Checks on the garden to do a survey.
Sees the morning dew kissing the corn
And sparkling like diamonds in the early morn.
Sees footprints in the mud and wants to confirm
Was it a rabbit, a cat or a pachyderm?
His arms are as strong as any metal
But he turns the brown earth with hands that are gentle.
He digs and plants and sweat and toils
And is proud of the fruits that grow from the soil.
The sun shines hot as he plants each row
And heats the earth and gives strength to grow.
Then down comes the rain, cools his hot brow first.
Then drenches the garden to quench its thirst.
Healthy and strong grow the fruits of his labor,
Which he then gives friends, family and neighbor.
You know his garden is planted with love
And, of course, with help from "God" above.

—*Regina Taylor Todaro*

Doubling Back Again

Born of youth an innocent babe
Childhood too soon snatched and fade

Eyes open hard watching for love
Dreams of flying as a turtle dove

Observing the world from childish eyes
Perfection, a rose garden, myths and lies

Promises broken to a little tot
Vowing to be what others were not

Poverty, abandonment, hardships and fights
Self-sacrifice, hard work and all my might

Reclaiming commitments, false hopes and smiles
Overcoming it all — Success — for a while

Suddenly stolen by hatred and fate
Searching for answers before it's too late

It came all at once, on the radio it played
The words were for one who didn't stay

Start from scratch, "double back again"
Do it better this time with less sin

Stressed out, burned out, angry and tired
Wish there was money to get it all hired

—*Linda L. Wells*

Words Cannot Explain

Words cannot describe the longing for
children which we mourn -
Those who left us long before they
had a chance to be born.

Words cannot explain feelings of failure
as I lay here and cry -
For how will I find the strength to give it
one more try?

Words cannot describe the desperation and despair -
of watching other mothers - it just seems so unfair!

Words cannot explain it - but inner strength came through,
I held on to my hopes and kept my dream in view.

Words cannot replace the tears as my dream came true -
I finally have my little child - my very special you.

But words are all I'll ever need to explain to you, this promise -
"Love will always surround you - my Anthony Thomas."

—*Kathleen Capozzoli*

The Story Behind Today!

It was a sunny morning and the birds were
    chirping loud and clear
I was feeling very well that day and my
    life had no tears.
When I awoke I prayed a simple prayer that
    the Lord would keep me near
I knew it was going to be a great day so I
    started it off loud and clear.
I started on my way to church and I began
    to sing a song
"He Arose, He Arose" was the name I think and
    I was happy never too long.
The sun was peeping it's way through the clouds
And all of it's watchers gathered around.
We were all happy to be together and we shouted
    with victory very loud
We all stood in the grave yard that day as we
    listen to the preacher tell his story
It never meant as much to me because I was a
    Christian singing his glory

—*Page Anthony*

"When I Used To Tie Your Shoes"

When I used to tie your shoes; decisions then were easy to choose. The red dress, the blue dress; don't tell me let me guess. Red will be your choice today; now what game shall we play. Days were simple and time easy to lose, when I used to tie your shoes.

A small hand would reach to take a book, but not before giving Mom a quick look; and seeing a smile she knew her choice was good, the strong house made of brick would stand we knew it would. Mama could always chase away the blues, when I used to tie your shoes. Now time has taken our simply days, and somehow confounded our simple ways. We spend a day just looking for clothes; the red dress the blue dress Mom never knows. We fight about which one you chose, sometimes I wish I could still tie your shoes. A little boy you have now and his shoes you'll tie. You'll listen closely for his small cry. Eager to please both Mom and child, you'll find the joy in a simple smile. The memories we have we'll never lose; and someday perhaps you'll tie my shoes.

—*Ruth Miller*

I Found a Strange Woman in My Father's Grave

Angelina passed in '17
Clear eyed strong. Her face
calm stared out of the stone
For three-quarters of a century
Beautiful in memoria
Her photograph miraculously
Defying the ice and sun
All this time

But there too unexpected, Rosa
Morta three years later
Who was she?
Ricardo dello sposa
At 37
There before us in the
Warm July uneasy
We wonder, intrigued
e figle we never knew
Among the stones

We blush at our own ignorance
—*Joseph Di Bona*

Blackbirds

The sun sets.
Clouds set forth from the horizon.
The children are called in for the night.
The night activities of the wild have begun.
The caw of a black bird echoes through the eerie dark.
And the flight of destiny begins.

Lonely dawns bring on lonely days.
And lonely days bring on lonely nights.
Sleep comes slowly for the blackbird.
As he plans for his future and then he sleeps, sound and deep.

Calls of the jungle lure him to flight.
The trees clip at his wings,
The sap sticks in his midnight feathers
And he stumbles and falls from above.
Like a heart shot by an arrow.

Now the blackbird is gone
Gone with his lusts and desires
All is forgotten for the past is unwelcomed
And the dreams the blackbird had dreamed are gone too.
—*Michael J. Hobley*

Rainy Day Parade

Listen, listen!
Cock an ear towards the sky
And feel the rainbows laughing
While the sun falls through the rain
That is soaking through my clothes
And making you smile.
Sing, sing!
You are with friends and we love you.
Come join our rainy day parade!
Dance, dance!
Jump in the puddles which collect around your feet.
Feel the sun warming the raindrops.
Let them drip, one by ten thousand,
Into your skin and be clean like a newborn baby.
Love, love!
See forever in my eyes and sink into their warmth
Feel my kisses like the rain on your living skin.
Listen, listen!
The rainbows are laughing with us
As we stand in the sunlit rain.
—*Ellie Harmon*

"Color Split"

Found on the outside is the transformation of two different colors
A white bear and a black bear sit upon a broken rock
The bears do not see the colors but just the personality
Colors do not change the person only the appearance
A variety of colors will make you no different in thought
The Grizzly bear doesn't judge the white
The Polar bear can never feed on the black
Black is only an image on the outside
White is only a cover for the body
Mind and thriving personality that is found in the true American
Decides the kindness and heart that is found under this cover
Two different colors should be equal as two quarters

—*Gary Choinski*

Evening Fear

Red rays cling to blackened grass.
Colors fade to memories past.
I wait, entranced, intoxicated, as the world passes by.

Tearful eyes pine fading light.
Fear creates yearning while fear freezes flight.
I laugh, disdainful yet aghast, as the world passes by.

Daylight's freedom offered vague security
Knowing the night will not set me free.
I weep at chances unattempted, the dawning of defeat.

I see through the door to the nightmare inside.
I know the torment and terror it hides.
I pray, faithful yet terribly afraid,
to be heard by the parade passing by.

Mom is at the door now. Her eyes are stone.
She beckons with clenched fists for me to come home.
I pass through purple shadows and raise my wall of glass.

I reach back as I enter to those people passing by.
I have always know they cannot hear my cry as they pass.
They do not hear me screaming,
all those people streaming by.
—*Janice Waters*

Dedicated to My Grandchildren

A gift that is received by mail
Should be acknowledged, without fail.
A simple "thank you" would be nice
But a grunt or groan would still suffice.
—*Christine Gallaga*

The Lord Would Come Today

I woke up this morning without a clue, that the Lord would
come today. Then I saw him riding through the sky bright
shinning as the sun. And I knew He had returned to finish
what He'd begun. We'll I woke up this morning without a clue,
that the Jesus would come today. Then I heard the angels
singing and I knew He had returned. To fulfill his promise
and receive the chosen few. And I said Hey, Jesus can I come
with you too. Then he stood before me like one I'd never knew.
He said these words so softly that you must hear them too. If
you wish to meet the father all you have to do is pray, deny
yourself and follow and you may come today. I woke up this
morning without a clue, that Jesus would come today. Then I
heard the angels singing and I began to pray. As He drew all
men unto himself I could hear the people say. Oh Jesus, please
don't take us away were not ready to go with you today. I saw
him sigh, He began to cry, and He left them there that day.
Oh Jesus, please don't go away He turned, He smiled, He said
you are my son and you may come today. I woke up this morning
without a clue, that the Lord would come today.

—Robert Vreeland

Untitled

My son, in my opinion he is number one
complains some about the chores to be done
He cooks and cleans, he's an eating machine
He's quite a young man, almost sixteen
Girls call often and his eyes just gleam
He's very thoughtful and Steve is his name
Riding his skateboard is a skill, not a game
He's not an "A" student, but we don't mind
He makes up for that, he's gentle and kind
When I got injured a year ago
Steve and my husband took over the show
He does his own laundry, and other chores
Makes sure I need nothing, before he goes out the door
He'll be home before dark, tired and hungry
First thing he'll say, "Hi Mom and Dad how was your day"
Straight to the fridge for food and drink
I'm really lucky, what do you think?

—Denice Howard

Veteran's Day

Veteran's Day, the celebration seems to have its own
connotation. Its value has its own reason.
In the name of peace, many words have been spoken,
so many promises made, then broken.
For some, war is its own glory yet every soldier has his own
story. The celebrations can often vary, some jubilant, some
wary. After World War I, that's when it started
A day to honor those departed.
Also to remember those who were returning
Who kept our quest for freedom - ever burning.
Parades and marches have marked this day
Moments of silence were another way.
And some have passed with just mere mention
Sometimes forgotten, is its real intention.
War closes the gap between race and creed
Those who have fought are a special breed.
The Tomb of the Unknowns - with eternal light
Is a constant reminder of lives lost in the fight.
On November 11th let's give our soldiers their due
All sacrifices made, were for me and you.

—JoAnn Larkin

Ode to my Architecture

Time after time, I watch you come to life as you cautiously
conquer the blank page.

Line after line, you force me to force you—you need me to
teach you how to Laugh and how to Cry.

Yet, at the end of creation, like a mountain you will stand:
So proud, so indifferent.

Then it will be you who will teach me that a Laugh and a Cry
are indeed the same.

You will show me how you dance in your rigidity.

You will show me how you break these senseless restrictions of life.

I will watch you rebel, and I will learn.

Soon, you will gather all of your secrets in me;

Promise me, promise me that long after I am gone, you will
break the silence.

Run from madness

Reach the top of the highest mountains

And then, watch the Clouds Cry.

—Kiarash Bafekr

Your Own Mystic

And then there was the ocean mist
contrasting grey with your muted reds
and spars and mastings and walking through
relief, and what once again felt new

And then there was the wandering fear
of leaving, of going places where
we might somehow find that lost thought
for the very smallest cost
of just a moment or two
standing on the step masts painted blue
grey and white and scarred by winds
that never knew they were that strong

And then there were your outstretched arms
as if you could embrace the sky
and all the credit goes to you
'cause you're the one who tried.

—J'ann Selin

Feelings

Tears appear and form without
control and fall for me.

To remind me to be sad again.
To love again and feel the loss of control.

To feel the hopelessness and
the happiness form together but apart.

Loving all that enters and departs.

Releasing fear at last regaining
strength to pass again in time.

Alone to see the image of me.
Happy to be free to really know that time
will somehow help me find.

All knowledge - strength within.

—John C. Butcher

Untitled

Laughing spirit, wind-tossed and frivolous
Cooling to the touch
Yet burning in the soul;
Fires are hottest at their center.
The smile is pure intent,
Eyes a roiling sea, tsunami of mirth
in oceans of sadness.
She draws in one breath
The sunlight
Exhalations tumultuous,
Frightening in their wonder
Dancing through my mind
like my own
Spinning my heart around
and away.

  —Jay Wickham

When Opened Eyes

Castle building in a lucid stillness
Counting times and then more
Is this my blind faith, my own mentation
Having sensed through sleepless tomorrows
A plethora of oddities called to witness
Yet, not of my own desire
Gauging its beauty and indifference
Shall I, dare I reveal such seats of affection
Has my silence been awakened
Many things stream into the warmth of my dark
Things of an unawakened world
So fantastic they are
As if not of me yet one of me
Never have I dreamt of a more eminent place
I have passed over the times of my true mind
But not as much as to leave them linger
For this is only the illusion of my desire
One which ends when opened eyes.

  —Patricia A. Perry

Abused Child

There alone in a darkened cold corner,
cries a little girl for help. She walks
endlessly around not knowing what would
be found. She cries out from within her
lonely heart "Mommy will you embrace me
please"? The child knows that there is
no one there to hear her. While sitting
back in that lonely darkened corner she
cries for mercy. With her baby blue eyes
and long blonde curls, teas of fear
roll down her rosy red cheeks. As
she sits alone and waits to be embraced.
The Lord's light filters through a broken
window. It falls upon her brow giving
her a feeling of security and that,
she is not alone.

  —Frank Genua

When Dolphins Dance

Graceful creatures skimming swiftly through the water
Dancing in the reflections of the sunset
Helpless victims of an underwater game
Calling out through the waves of the ocean
From the depths of the water
To the illumination of the surface
Their eyes timid
Their look friendly
If only they weren't endangered...
They are loved,
They are dolphins.

  —Shannon Broz

Kaleidoscope

Turn it to the left.
Crystal images of blue skies and sunny days.
One more turn,
buds blossom into beautiful flowers.
Turn it again,
bare branches seem full of leaves.
Turn it quickly,
the snow begins to melt.
Another turn makes the robins sing,
and the children laugh as they play.

Turn it to the right.
A shot rings out in the air.
The blood seeps through.
Sirens scream in your ears.

Quick! Turn it to the left.

  —Maria Martinez DeLuca

Scirocco, Wind of Malta

A dervish of whirling debris
Danced through the narrow streets of stone
Swept across dusty, barren fields
Honing a deadly razor edge
Scratching paint, pulling hair.
Drafty old walls, long empty halls
Created dark, discordant tunes
And lonely moods were everywhere.
The bitter wind raged on and on
Passing closed clandestine doors
Rattling windows, wearing patience thin.
The tyrant wild and mad
Piled up clouds blackened velvet clad
Spawned wrath within, attacked the sea;
Then torched it all with fire
Commanding a storm to transpire
With rain to quench the constant thirst
A crown for nature's angry burst.

  —Margaret Nienstedt

Masked Desolation

Lincoln gazes silently from his cold temple;
dark waters flow quietly by.
Sere, gray, brown dusk falls over the city. Walking quickly home
to warmth, to light, visitors hurry from the city in stone. We remain;
chill, frozen breath numbs our bodies.
Escaping warm air rushes through vents set in the ground--
gaping eyes in the pavement of the city, the city in stone.

We gather around building in cold marble
searching empty cans to ease our hunger.
Plastic bag over a vent gathers the heat, warming
one in rags and trash, cheek to the grating,
curled around emptiness. Oppression settles like cement, hardening.
Below us rush trains, money in slots. I lie above under my plastic
balloon.

Moon sinks and the sky lightens, brightens;
crouched over the vent I rise also. A tattered relic of the army—
the army of the forgotten, the unseen.
Drifting invisible shadows through the wheel of life,
Sunk at the bottom, never to rise.

Life slips through our fingers of mist, evaporating in the glaring sun.
The care of none in the sight of all.

  —Heather Elizabeth Blatt

"Memories"

As I sit looking out my window
  day dreaming a little bit
The snow is covering everything
  and with the kids a hit.
But us ol' folks hate to venture
  out in the snow and windy cold
I can remember when nothing bothered us
  Boy were we ever bold.
Their laughter over the fun they're having
  brings a tear to my eye.
'Cause I remember when I was young.
  and that ain't no lie.
Fond memories are so precious, so
  hang on to them all.
And carry them always with you.
  up to when you get your beck and call!

—*Beverly McGuinness*

Goodbye

You made me feel like a warm summers
day, just a smile made me glow
like the suns ray, the laughter you
sent I will carry with me always.

Now I no longer feel
those warm summer days nor
do I see the glow or here the
laughter, instead I feel cold where
the warmth once was, a gray
sky replaces the sun, the
laughter has turned to tears.
How I long to feel you near,
hear your words, see your face.
But nothing is left,
not even a trace...

—*Mandi Sommerfeld*

Death

Death is invisible
Death is silent
Death can be called the "Big Sleep".
Death possesses the qualities of a thief
Death is unannounced
Death separates friends
Death creates pain for love ones
Death relieve pain.
Death makes us bitter
Death makes us better
Death is welcomed by some
Death is approached cowardly by many
Death is not prejudice
Death is not racist
Death disregard gender
Death is not seasonal
Death disregard time
Death alters plans for some
Death destroys dreams for others
Death embraces all life.

—*Dora Jane Criss-Deckard*

A Storm Begins

Clouds begin to form,
desert shadows darken and disappear
as the sky turns gray
lightning flashes and the thunder rolls
across the desolate valley
Drops of rain fall to the dry deserted valley floor
leaving no trace that rain had ever quenched the desert's
everlasting thirst.

—*Mathew J. Pace*

Death

Death is the tears you cry at night
Death is the ghostly terror and fright
Death is the loneliness you feel inside
When the one you love is no longer at your side
Death is the memory of happiness
Then it suddenly turns to emptiness
Death is the pain and sorrow
When you knew the one you love isn't going
to be there tomorrow.

—*Nilda Francheska Huertas*

The Sailors Way

How did the oil get on the bay?
Defenseless birds that can't fly away.
Sounds like a hopeless mission, I would say!
So, visit California, it's a nice place to stay.
After all we need you to pay.
Fisherman are sorry as they say,
But mothers don't take your children to the bay;

It's not really the safest place to play.
You see,
  helpless seals, fish,
  and birds of prey,
Have lost their homes and cannot stay.
Most will lose their lives today,
Human err,
  The sailor way!

—*Barbara L. Teagardin*

Red Raspberry Rain

Transparent, moistened drops aglow,
Demons' eyes threaten to attack from below.
Upon the lake, crystallized rosy, amber-emerald
Even when evaporated, never to be ephemeral -
Round diamonds slowly into my heart roll.
After the rain, a lustrous rainbow
Swam to the palm of a birch leaf above the knoll.
So sorely missed, why such brilliance be so temporal?
Atop this bed of radiance, those sheer, precious opals.
Opaque's inability to retaliate will eventually show.
Upon silky petals, scarlet and chartreuse, so bold
Somehow possessing magical wizardry of a troll,
Appointed by the sea-world to be their herald
To astound with their utmost humility medal
Why can't they remain, our beauty to grow?
Red raspberry rain, set upon my tongue and toes
My eyes feast upon these sweet, little bowls
Replete with sunshine, beauty and a foal, barehooved, supernal
Quiet, motionless, of maybe nothing sentimental,
I hear their silent screams - transcending the universe's soul.

—*Amelia Kaptchuk*

The Graveyard

Sitting placidly with listless eyes and folded hands, watching
disinterestedly as their lax bodies mold away, the derelicts
form a segmented union. Each man totally absorbed in his own
thoughts or lack of thoughts is united with the others by a
mutual awareness, the awareness being that they have done all
that they will ever do and that while they wait to become
forever a part of the earth, they will sit in the sun together
or each man alone, watching the fading of the flowers from
spring to fall. As I walk through the park trying not to stare
and knowing that it doesn't matter, I wonder whether or not
there is a poem for us all in those silent faces.

—*Sharon Jordan*

The Illusion of Confusion

Time goes by, and friends shall fade.
Depression comes over you as you're left in the shade.
No time to waste, cause there's no time at all.
The clock has stopped as I watched myself fall.
No one to lean on, or to shed a tear.
No one there to share my fear.
As I hold it inside, my emotions become worse.
There's no where to hide, I could just burst!
I feel like curling up and crying as my emotions run deep.
I feel like dying, and falling into a deep sleep.
Then I think about life, and how good it's been
and I realize the truth as I search deep within
Now all sorrow is gone, and all is forgiven.
Then I pray up to God, and thank Him I'm livin'.
Then I thank God once again
for all my not few, but many good friends.

—*Nicole Davis*

Eternal Slumber

I'm fading into the whispers of the night, as it
  devours me to eternal slumber I struggle to stay
awake, alive. Sometimes I wonder what it would feel
like to sleep forever falling into eternal slumber
  never again to awake the painful reality of being
  alone. I've seen others go before me awaiting my
eternal slumber to reach them deliciously I've tasted
  the thought of stopping the pain within my heart.
Within my being, thoughts of the salvation of eternal
  slumber beats relentlessly at my mind. But a force
has kept me from eternal slumber many times I've tried
  and failed but my heart still aches for more.
Distractions of the life I lead and the reality I have
  to face kept my mind adrift fogging the eternal
  slumber with the superficial belief that my heart
longs for. When will it end? My sanity grows thin
and my mind becomes more weary with impure thoughts.
Sometimes I look over the ledge and see life moving in
  slow motion. As I descend onto the air I free fall
    into oblivion where life is serene.

—*Nia M. Evans*

What If

What if a billion stars and a pale moon's light,
Didn't add their beauty to a darken night.
What if a warm sun's ray didn't melt away night,
and turn a shadowy morning into a glorious sight.
What if I never kiss your smile, or feel your
heart race a mile.
What if ever the velvet smoothness of your skin,
I never touch, or kiss in loving sin.
What if rivers didn't run to the sea, and what if
your heart turns away from me.
What if a bright sun didn't give warmth to earth,
sea and sky, surely God's creatures would not grow,
walk, swim or fly.
What if ever when softly evening fall, you are
not there to share my creole love call.
What if never we brave the start,
Then must I carry, forever, your love, in my heart.

—*Myrtis Roach, Jr.*

Untitled

Fears are a shadowed jumble of mixed emotions,
Slipping among walls of imagination,
Spreading worry and dread.

Like raging storms,
They disturb a man's peace,
Leaving him horror-stricken and scared.

—*David Scheffler*

"I Love You, Mom"

The pain never leaves me no matter how far I flee. Praying to
die I cry and cry. The pain's always deep inside no one told
me a mother lied. She said she'd always be there she claimed
she'd always care. And just when I needed her most, all she
left was her beautiful ghost. The memory of the way things
used to be always happy, her and me. Now my laughter is cold
and empty, and only my mother can set me free. I relive my
sorrow with every tomorrow. I love her, I do, and I think she
loves me too. So why did she lie, and why must our laughter
die? She couldn't stay, and I had to pay. I trusted and tried
to believe why she said she had to leave. She said she wasn't
happy, that is, with my daddy. I wanted her to be happy, so I
let her leave me. Out of love I let her go, it's been six years
you know. I want her back; I want to laugh. Out of love,
can't she do this for me instead of obliterating all hope of
glee? I used to be stronger, but I can't bare this much longer
My mother's heart is set on staying away, and I'm the one who
has to pay. I have one qualm, she might not know I mean it
when I say, "I love you, Mom"

—*Michelle Lillian Kenyon*

Running as Buffer and Gypsy

How do I hide what's in my eyes
do I cover my smiles with all kind of lies.
Should I cover my ears whenever you speak,
to keep my body from growing weak.
For every whisper brings magic inside of me,
thus placing my heart high, on loves cloudy peaks.
So yea, I say to thee; sight paints its own
picture for those who see
but to those who don't look,
our love is hidden until time for us to be.
It's from here we came to run, from the
cold selfishness and corrupted ones.
Running as Buffer and Gypsy,
reaching for a future or whatever comes.
Taking to the roads with our love,
we never glanced back at hate
only the beauty of us,
forever you and me as mates.

—*Greg Robbins*

Something to Memorize

Man's destiny should not be jeopardized,
Do not allow yourself to be compromised,
Though it's healthy for one to be circumcised,
Don't overlook what's been given to utilize,

The answers aren't found while you socialize,
Nor while gazing into your dear wife's eyes,
For the enemy abounds spreading his lies,
He's the master of deception and scrutinize,

But if you give your heart to Jesus and realize,
God will hear you as you apologize,
Your not unnoticed or even unrecognized,
And I'm sure the skeptics will criticize,

It's time for the Lord's army to immobilize,
Shout out God's decree and institutionalize,
My hopes and prayers are not to patronize,
But to seize the opportunity to undisguise,

The devil is loose severing the ties,
Yet when Jesus returns in the blue skies,
No one will be able to improvise,
So drop to your knees or be victimized.

—*Gary E. Berry*

Visions

What is your vision of heaven?
Do you see God and His Son and Angels?
Do they stand in a cloud with white wings?

Is there anyone there that you know and love?
Flowers that bloom with eternal sweetness, are they there?
Or music that is sung and played with celestial zeal?

Or will it be another planet or galaxy?
Where all that we hold dear, will now appear
Who knows for sure what we shall see, or who or where?

I can but hope that my vision will be,
The truth that I find at the time I arrive.
Hopefully, life is but a dream.

  —Jan Sandvig

Hide Away Forever

Cover everything up
Don't let anyone know the horror it was
Cover up that bawling and the frown on your face
Never remember the truth
Hide Away Forever
Never remember what life used to be like
Go to sleep and never wake up again
Don't ever look behind you
And remember the terrible thoughts
Don't think of those dark nights
Where you were afraid to go to sleep
Never show anyone the scars on your face
Hide Away Forever.

  —Danielle Jodie Kohn

A Child

Reach out and touch the light, hold on to the day.
Don't let the shadow of night take your joy away...but,

The nightmare that you live with, the secret locked inside,
can never be confided, it must remain a lie...but,

When the hour is late, and your eyes are closed in sleep,
you cannot guard the door, where the ugliness you keep.

The secret locked inside finds you every night,
Until it finds a passage to touch you in daylight.

A touch when you were so innocent, a memory now locked away,
how could anyone ever understand that it hurts still,
so much today...but, it does.

  —Marsha Lester

My Debt to Society

In exile have this metal mind jail;
drowning in imbroglio, and crazy nigger smell.
My neighbor have resents me, because
I've felt things he forgets
(penitence not being one of them)
but to bear his bitching voice makes me
sorrier everyday the sunsets.
I've had chains in the free world
none to see, none to touch;
but every time one of my kind committed
expression, I've felt it just as much.
So I've run myself into the arms of prison.
Yes, I've done that passion thing.
Yes, my share of sin,
now, I'll do my death of soul thing;
and start all over again.
With my bill.... on paid.

  —Brian Cedric Ross

Last Out

Lunging into cautious serenity,
Dormant sets poised without light,
Drifting a road of clouded images,
Where shadows frolic and hide;
And families harbored in sleep.

Perching on incessant night;
Flood of obscurity eroding
Senses forced aware with chance.
Tranquility belying fury;
And families protected in dreams.

Racing...fighting...cutting fog with beacon...
Anguished cries consumed in terror...
Fiery steel...icy flesh...
Children forced impure...rage of death;
And families shielded in fantasy.

Wearily emerging from dark battle,
Haunting shadows burrowing from light.
Purged life reengaging
A world chaste in morning splendor;
And families awaking to wonder.

  —Allan S. Kane

Swamp

Out my window and across the field is an old run
down shack.
I tried to investigate, but what I couldn't see
from my window was a swamp.
The swamp was filled with water lilies and frogs...
Swamp grass and tadpoles.
Now as I stand at the edge of the swamp, I see
the shadow of a face.
The glass is so fogged with dust and dirt, that
I can't make any of the features out.
I come to the edge everyday... sometimes the
face is there sometimes not.
Yet I know the face, but not at all.
I will always be on the edge.
Waiting... watching... hoping.

  —Ryane Avellar

"A Girl With Dreams"

She was young and tender, with precious dreams.
Dreams meant to her a lot, but to others maybe not
Never met with sorrow and chat with disappointments.
Woke up every morning walk unnoticed on her path.
Smoothly pursue her way, day and night and in spring and fall.
Walked more and reached close to her goal yard by yard.
One sunny morning when she was near to her dreams, every
Other things were beautiful tempting and hypnotic.
She was happy, suddenly wind blew, dust her eyes and
took her away. Wind stopped, now she was away from
her goal and the path leads to the goal.
Found herself crawling in sand inviting despairs
screaming farewell to hope and welcome to sorrow,
but a smile split from her lips and she said to her
that she desired to be sonneter and could never do it
but today when things are hard for her is easy to
create a sonnet may be because she lived in it.
She stood up, dust her off, thinking she has more path
to travel, but she is full of strength and tender no more.

  —Sita Awasthi

Library

Boring, soaring, Quible-de-Quo.
Searing, revering, I don't know.
Elated, belated, it's all the same.
Read on old chap, don't be inane!

—*Gideon Malino*

"Silent Good-Bye"

There she sat not long ago
  dressed in black from head to toe.
A single tear ran down her face,
  it wasn't noticed through the lace.
She raised her eyes to gaze once more
  upon the casket on the floor.
Remembering the days gone by,
  she uttered but a single sigh.
The mercury in the parking lot,
  the ruined tuxedo, the rose he bought.
The fight they'd had when she'd hit the tree,
  the videos on MTV.
But memories were all she had,
  she loved the good as well as bad.
How dare he leave her all alone,
  her youth was gone, her eyes, they shone.
Her body frail and stopped with age,
  she trembled, violently, with rage.
She stroked his cheek and kissed his eyes,
  and silently, she said good-bye...

—*Patricia A. Rabidoux*

Beyond the Fields of Dreams

Beyond the fields of dreams
Drift on silver streams.
Pixalated on moon beams.

Beyond the fields of dreams
Rise up on winged heels.
Spin Destiny's wheel.

Beyond the fields of dreams
Naked goddesses at their libations kneel.
Innocent of their immodesty.

—*J. Pierritz*

Cave Dweller

Jealous drips of rainbow gold
drip hugely beside the copper bowl.
One drip, one sound, one ancient echo,
love comes forth like falling snow.

Jagged rocks stand green in line,
stalagmites drip a sweet chalky wine.
The eye above to the mouth below,
a passing cloud, fluffed as if to show.

A silver nickel solitaire
free falling in sequence into his hair.
Sharp teeth, hot chimney fire rushes out,
the secret weapon thrown, square on the snout.

Above; no life- that strange windy voice,
all colors of the earth, rainbow is my choice,
No hope at all, to me and the bowl,
the link to the heavens, the code of my soul.

I pray for more air to throw down some food,
bits of earth treasures to bring back my mood.
Words are fat and loud, returning empty handed,
this day is like the others- for weeks I have been stranded.

—*Michael Bozzano*

False Image

The imbiber consumes
  Each glass of regret
Time, past, and present
  He seeks to forget.

Royal fantasy rules the mind
  To set its marks
Upon the tablets of time.

The hourglass sand eludes
  The second, and moment,
While the man in stupor deludes and broods.

For he cannot hold back
  The grains that sift by
In the twinkling of an eye.

Wise man, beggar man, carpenter, fool
  Each seeks to win the race
To keep the present, to lengthen the pace,
  But only the Master calls the rule.

—*Alex V. Christoff*

"The Ocean"

The green shimmery water lapping at the beach,
Each sparkling grain of sand just out of the hungry ocean's reach.
The soft roll of the lazy waves only just beyond,
waterbugs skimming over the picture, and then they are gone.
Just above, the puffy clouds floating along with the cool breeze,
Drifting beside the gliding birds, just as far as anyone sees.

—*April Sowell*

The Immortals

In the bleak hours before the pale velvet dawn slips over the
eastern horizon, the night becomes silent and still. Through
the French lattice door he comes. His steps seem to float
above the floor, like a shadow slipped off the wall. Oh God,
how he is so like an angel in grace, but his eyes hold the fire
of hell! His beauty held suspended in time, is ageless. In a
single, perfect glide he is upon me, his power overwhelms me.
His eyes, like deep violate pools of glass speak to me, and I
obey. He draws me to him; I dare not resist. I am lifted
unto him as his teeth, like daggers penetrate the flesh of my
neck. My pulse quickens, striving to maintain life, while the
other tries to take it. My lifeforce is run dry. Surely now
I must die, yet he keeps me to him. And now there is nothing.
But I am touched by a warmth, passion's fluid to give me life.
I can taste the salty-sweet force pulsing through me. My body
is filled with a pounding like distant drums who hasten unto
each other, merge, and beat as one tremendous heart. I look
again into those crystalline eyes but they are different.
I know all things in earth and hell, and some of that in heaven.
I am dead, and so have become immortal forever with my savor, my
  master.

—*Dixie Lynn Royce*

Lost

  As a wave of depression sets briskly
      down on the shore
My mind body and soul drown with admiration
      of the strong willed
  Life's great torture yet life's goal
      for the weak minded
  A childish mind for a childish game
      A glimpse of hope
          Crushed
  by the bewildered minds of the old

—*Jonathan D. Lear*

Message To A Mixed Couple Black And White

If you want a better life, you better listen to this advise,
education, determination, stamping out discrimination.

Mr. Crester, Mr. Crester, a message for you; Mr. Crester,
Mr. Crester, I know you find it true, in 1993 I'm going to set
you free.

You must be grown and on your own, before you decide, to
venture and roam. You might be rich, you might be poor,
acceptance is never sure. When in need of someone to follow,
just listen to me, I'm your role model.

There's no need for substance abuse, social rejection might
be your excuse. Don't be a fake for the children's sake, we
all make mistakes, sometimes before we awake, the constitution
has the solution. Your relationship is legal, so enjoy your
life among all people.

I'm like a little dove with a lot of love, we learn together
play together, live together, pray together, fight together,
and going to stay together, education, determination, paving
the way to a better destination.

—Johnny Terrell

Night Song III

A heart, bewildered,
encased in reluctant flesh.
Can you feel me,
trembling, feverish beneath your hand?
A soul, fragile,
folding in upon itself.
Can you sense me,
almost hidden, nearly vanquished?
A tear, soundless,
falling in the dark.
Can you hear me,
grieving, lost without your arms around me?

When you sleep, the name you call is not mine.

—Christine Carroll Burke

The Last Stand

Once free and able to control their own lives;
Entitled to seek happiness for which every man strives.
Destiny now controlled by the Bureau of Indian Affairs;
They are Americans, but the government doesn't seem to care.

A proud people with a proud history;
With the buffalo they once ruled the prairie.
Now reduced to life on a reservation;
Bingo games are now their salvation.

They once conquered Custer, now they make their last stand;
In danger of losing their heritage like they lost their land.
Descendants of great leaders like Sitting Bull, Geronimo...
A disappearing culture Apache, Sioux, Shoshone, Navajo.

They worship the Great Spirit, the land, water and sky;
Their world no longer makes sense and they ask the question
Wise old medicine men who have the power to comprehend;
A once dominant way of life now seems to be at an end.

Treaties signed in good faith lack integrity;
Never meant to be honored, it's now plain to see.
History can't be changed, we can't make amends;
But pray to the Great Spirit that the animosity ends.

—Michael J. Stieber

"A Survey of Autumn"

Autumn conveys, a delightful panorama.
  Especially when the barometer, begins to fluctuate.
With an altering of the surrounding leaves.
  A harvesting of the crops, then the gathering of them.
Important events take place, for pleasure, or to recollect.
  As Christopher Columbus discovered America in
fourteen ninety two.
  So they celebrate October twelfth, as a tribute.
Merchant's are selling pumpkins, either for baking pies.
  Or some are employed, for carving out jack-o'-lanterns.
Participators are joining together, at masquerade parties.

Ready for competition, and to be nominated a reward.
  Maybe they even play pranks, as practical jokes.
Some people enjoy, the dunking of apples, as an appetizer.
  Last but not least, is the sequence called trick or treat.
And that involvement, is strolling outdoors.
  Flashlights or lighted pumpkins, are the essential tools.
But with the support, of parents.
  That guidance will lead them, to those pathways.

—Lenore Witonsky

The Life Of Love

We can learn to build sand castles
Even realizing its transitory nature
We can appreciate the falling snow
Being ever grateful that it will cease
We can enjoy the scent and beauty of a flower
Though it cannot be so but for a short time
We can glance upon a lovely face knowing it
Will change with the passage of time
We can hear the innocent laughter of a child
Remembering a time long since passed
We can love one another very deeply
Knowing it's only for a cherished while
Indeed, if not for our capacity and the
Intelligence to realize its flight, there
Cannot be love in our existence and
No reason for our having lived.

—Cova Young

"Where Happiness Is Found"

Happiness and love should always abound,
even tho we all have our ups and our downs!

Happiness is a bird singing in a tree,
the sun, blue sky, deserts and mountains we see!

Happiness is the world's beautiful children we love -
after all they were sent to us by God from above!

Happiness is a friend that is sincere,
a friendship always should be held very dear!

Although we know not when happiness may end,
we must work to nurture happiness again and again!

So lift yourself up - open your eyes - look around -
That is - "Where happiness is found!"

—Bobbi Baird

House Arrest

Now that I'm out, I'll tell just who I saw,
So clear are pictures in each morbid frame,
no stretch of time could truly e'er efface
  That hall of shame.

Dim rooms, quite small, were sadly out of touch
With comforts of the pleasant home-like kind;
Familiar faces graced no cheerful walls
  To soothe the mind.

—Martha P. Koehler

Show Me

Show me the way right to your heart
Tell me we shall never part
Show me the love you feel inside
So I no longer will have to hide
This love I'll always hold dear inside.
— *Mistina Goodman*

Watch and Pray

Stand on duty, be alert.
Even though it is peace time, the enemy lurks.

He comes to sabotage, to steal and devour.
Do not be passive, this is the hour.

Shake yourself out of your lethargy.
The church of Jesus Christ is called, to affect society.

So watch and pray, everyday.
Laugh at temptation, as it comes your way.

Warn all the people, of the destruction to come.
If you do not do it, required is your blood.

We are in spiritual warfare. The times drawing short.
Rip someone from hells fire, before they are lost.

Christians are always to pray and faint not.
The spirit is willing. The flesh will just not.

The Lord is the victor. The Captain of the Host.
If He is your Savior, then you have hope.

Live like your expecting, Jesus once more.
Watch - Pray - Be ready - and you will win the war.
— *Mary Ann Lefebvre*

Different—Like Me

You say your different? Well, don't you fret,
Everyone feels that way, I'll bet!
The thing to do is be yourself,
Don't hide your light on some dark shelf
Each one was put here for a reason
Just as the flowers change each season
No two are ever quite the same
So go your way without any shame,
You have a right to be on earth,
Let's try to fill each day with mirth
Your time is limited here, you see
So it's O.K. to be different—Just like me!!
— *Florence L. Swann*

Life In Hell

Hovering in the darkness, I hear the echoes cry — Surrounded by
evil, we scream for reasons why — How do we convey the
thoughts etched within our minds, to an illusive world of
souls who see with eyes gone blind — Blinded by foreboding
evil convening with our souls, the threat of impending doom
has begun to take its toll — Hopes and dreams obscure,
deranged and ever sinking — Where boundless rage detaches and
kills mind's collective thinking — Committed to a cold dark
prison of systematic hypocrisy and falsely living lives of
constant deceiving integrity — Chains of dread around my
neck constrict with every breath, and yesterday's will to live
has now become my death — Consumed by realizations of growing
insecurity, and souls stained black exist in hopeless monotony —
Now we see through bloodied eyes of despair, in a world
who's sole attribute is its deceiving glare — Amidst all the lies,
we succumb to the pain and watch our world slowly go insane —
Towers of hope crumble down into a heartless reality — Now we're
left alone to dwell into an ever darkening misery —
These lords of doom, you see, they've something to sell — but be
wary, my friend, it's a morbid, mortal, bloody life in hell...
— *Debbi Dwyer*

Winterbridge

Once more, my mind grows cold, abound by
   expectations of what is unattainable through
   standards of thought;
I no longer weep for that which is no fault to
   my own, only wonder as to the nature of my
   past; forever clinging
Must we take what we have no desire of,
Can the future bind the past
For the sake of my loss, I will find none
   to blaspheme
As never in days which give to reflection, I
   will rejoice within the dawning of direction
My direction
My life

Parasitic winter
— *Costa Bugg*

Thoughts

The mind draws a conclusion based on what the body
experiences. The body counts on the mind to see, hear and
feel. One cannot always count on either at any given time,
but must always consider what each has experienced.

The heart sometimes calls on us to be stronger than the body
ever has the need for. Once again we place our very being in
danger for the search that our only calling is from that which
cannot be defined by physical means. The demands of our hearts
desire can cost more than the body could take.

Only once you find the person to whom you can trust can you
truly become that which you desire. The risk is high and the
cost sometimes seems too much, but if it is truly what the
heart is to be then the cost falls at the way side.

The promises from the heart cannot be broken by man or
beast, but only by God himself. Only the heart can protect
that which the eyes cannot see or the senses cannot contain.

The only thing that we cannot possess is often forgotten in
the hopes of buying things that we can own.
— *Adam L. Chase*

Hidden Love

When I gaze upon her, I think she is so fine,
Eyes of green and lips the color of red wine.
I love to feel her touch,
I'm in like with this girl very much.
She is good to me and always kind,
She seems to always be on my mind.
This however is not to be bad,
It makes me very happy and not sad.
She makes me lively and I'm her biggest fan,
There's only one problem, she already has a man.
Yes, another man has her lovely heart,
But I'm sitting back and playing it smart.
I'm not acting on the way I feel,
No, I hope to work out a better deal.
To be her friend forever,
That's playing it safe and being clever.
But if she wants me to be more than just a friend,
You can bet I'll love her to the very end.
— *Coy Dever*

Untitled

Through aeons of time whirl myriads of worlds
   Stars shine in universal glory
God's galaxies swing in their celestial dance
   The heavens echo to their distant music
Peace shall prevail, man learns his maker's story
   ..... and the stars sing.
— *R. W. Cooper*

That Monster Worm

I turn myself to look at the worm within that has a thousand eyes, the one that others call I. Hoping when I look this monsters will turn not itself against itself which is me.

Could I see with one of the thousand eyes the part of me I think is noble; or will I see with the eye through which another sees and suspect trouble? Will I see through the eye the things which I think are honest, or shall I see through that which another sees and find dishonesty? Would I be facetious to believe that I could see through the eye of which I like to see myself as being kind, or would I look back at me with the eye through which others see hate?

Tell me Mr. Worm shall I see through the eyes of impatience or shall it be the eyes of tolerance looking back to me? I ask you again, Mr. Worm, where are the eyes of love found within this human flesh; or are they all blinded by ignorance and self-esteem? Because it seems that those peering back at me only include myself. Then I say to this worm which is I, please let me look abroad and include all mankind in this view I have that love I have of myself will include others as well.

—*Ruth Alberta Connor Ross*

Political Puzzle

When taxes are not enough, taxing is
fair yet with incomes varied, still
the taxer grows, for eliminating need
to perpetuate its purpose, to take gain
for gain and gain in it ambition only
less so for its source, now needing
its budget constrained, its oxymoronic
that which aids poor corrupts rich,
their interests surrendered, a plight indeed
needs a societal relativity, politics.

—*John J. Pope*

Old Man Winter

I took a walk with old man winter through a
fairy tale snow
He told me of the great ice age a long time ago
Finely etched frosty pictures lay upon his
mirrored eyes
Feathery snowflakes fell from the skies
And he told me it has been said the angels
are shaking their feather beds

Forever frozen within time like his glaciers
above timber line

As the wind howls through the black charcoal trees
Old man winter walks his white tract through eternity
Sprinkling his diamonds to glitter in the sun
Over a landscape of white linen he has spun
Not one of his foot prints ever show as he
quietly walks through the snow

—*Becky Cole*

Panic

You and I in amphetamine, machine gun montage:
Feeding mouths like the accelerated labial feet of snails
Hungering frantically over each other, maybe
Remembering cummings or a supermarket novel's rapture,
Convulsing flesh, pornographic collage on flannel sheets,
Lubricating, sticky sweat covering tired limbs,
Choking, thick smell of humid rubber
Blessing the warm, candle-darkened room.

—*George Edward Hammerbeck*

Silence of the Night

Let me reach out into the night
Feel the velvety darkness—the softness
Let me wonder through the lightless
Experience some of the mysteries of the blackness
Seek the splendor—find excitement beyond the light of day.

I'd like to walk—unafraid—
Listen to the whispers of a gentle breeze
Hear the unusual sounds around me-
The howling of a dog in the distance.
I would linger to observe a sleeping city—hushed—quiet.

Then let me stand on a sandy beach
Thrill to the sound of the lashing waves,
Drink in the freshness of the sea air,
Be kissed with a salty spray on my lips,
Feel the wind prowling through my hair.

Let me then climb to the peak of a hill—and wait
Filled with humility and anticipation
Watching as the first light appears—
Bringing brightness,
Engulfing me with new hope—silent peace—as a new day is born.

—*Dorothy F. Morris*

The Ocean

Hear it's waves crash,
Feel the wind rush up against your face;
The warmth of another person's touch

Sky so calm and blue,
Like the presence of another love;
See the rocks surrounding the waters;
Like two hearts combined

Your mind lost into all thoughts,
While hearing the sounds of the ocean

—*Mandy Ramsdell*

"How"

How can I tell you something and express it with deep feeling and emotion?

How can I write it with words and let you hear me the way I wish to be heard?

How can I show my admiration to whom I feel deserves it?

How can I get your attention, and show you what I know and how I feel?

How can I help you feel my words, taste my words and show you my words to hear?

Although on paper, with your attention loud and clear!

—*Alisa E. A. Holley*

The Good Times

When I remember the good times, the laughter in the air, the feeling of love to know you are with someone is to share. When I remember the good times, the happiness, the feeling of joy to know someone cares in your time of helplessness. When I remember the good times, the patience, the feeling of devotion to know one day, he will be gone is not something you can sense. Now I only have the good times of love, happiness, and patience to know he is no longer there. Our times have now been divided by a single fence. When I remember the good times, I remember a man whom everyone loved and liked, a man who was dear to my heart, my grandfather, Chester A. Smith, Jr.

—*Christina DeCesare*

Is He Really?

Is he really
(feeling the same way? Will his arms ever hold me?)
in
(deep, so deep. The water rushes over my head.)
love
(must be a myth, I have never found it before.)
with
(trust as our guide. Togetherness is forever.)
me?
(as a person, not for my body.)
Is he really?

—*Christina Swanson*

Untitled

You walk a good walk and talk a good talk, but when you
fight a good fight with you ever lovin' might-
When you slide with a glide a display your black pride,
When you know that you're sho' of your intelligence, you grow.
When you feel beat' and you meet the heat that's burnin' at
your feet. That's the time to take the ladder, climb people
climb and pull your siblings from behind.
That's what it means to make it together, for we are birds of a
black feather.
To be black and to be strong, gives us power to carry on.
Count your blessings, feel the spirit, GOD is talking, can't
your hear it?
Fight stupidity with nonviolence, but show your face and
break the silence.
Don't stop siblings, guide the people, terror is coming, I see
the evil.
We need to pray with every step or it would've been in vain
when Jesus wept.
Give your love, it's always better to walk above and sing
forever. "Fight the Good Fight."

—*Dawn Grey*

A Grandmother's Love

She struggled to keep a hold on life, she would not give up the
fight until she knew with certaintude that you would be
alright. Your cry of entrance into this world must have
carried acrossed the miles, when she closed her eyes for the
last, upon her face there was a smile. My dear sweet babe, you
do not know the power that you had, in your birth, you touched
her heart to make her dying moments glad. You say you don't,
but perhaps you know her better than anyone, for she would not
leave until she had known the child of her son. You know her
in a special way that none of us could share, for her soul
touched yours along her path to mounting the Golden Stair. Did
you feel her as she smiled, stopping with you along her way, to
give you her love and comfort you, on your very first earth
day, to share with you her essence, so one day you may
understand, all the things she would have told you to become a
better man. Her stay was O' so brief, I know, you see - she
was called back to the sky, to that wonderful and glorious
place from which you had just said goodbye. Take her heart in
that you've given her the greatest gift you ever could, for you
have become a "Fine young man" just like she knew you would.

—*Carl Hilts*

Just A Song At Twilight

I've sailed through life like a song on the wind.
Taken the bitter taste of Winter, that life so often brings,
Savored the sweet taste of summer with its fleeing, teasing fling.
Memories that linger in the Twilight of my bearing.
Sunshine and laughter,
Tears that fall like rain.

—*Bernice L. Whitmore*

It Could Have Been Me

You finally got tired of being alone,
Fighting back tears while you stared at the phone.
You needed someone but I couldn't see.
If only I'd noticed, it could have been me.

You found somebody to hold you at night,
So you're not alone when you turn out the light.
When you say I love you it's easy to see,
If only I'd been there it could have been me.

It could have been my arms that held you so tight.
It could have been my lips that kissed you at night.
It could have been heaven but I set you free,
Now it's hell just knowing it could have been me.

—*James Quast*

Cape Cod Affair

My body fights sleep
    fights the demons
    that dance and flit in summers encasement.
Days drag on.
Summer eats away at the furniture.
Dampness clings to drapes
    and peoples hearts.
County fairs will be announced
    ribbons won
As many wait a change.
No change for some.
Cold and wet replaces dampness.
If I leave will he forgive me?
    forget me?
The colors and tones of my life change.
    I don't change.
    I fight sleep
    fight the demons
    dream of dancing again
    in summers encasement.

—*Kathleen Anne Kinney*

My Loved One Is In Pain

My Darling Sweetheart You Lie There,
Filled With Helpless Gripping Pain.

I Wish I Can Help You There,
 To Release You Of Your Pain.

No Tears, No Words, Nothing You Can Say,
 But Deep Within You Cried For Help.

My Thought And Prayers Reach Out For You,
 Yet Deep Within I Am Unable To Help.

My Dearest Darling Please Recover Soon,
 Before My Heart Tears Apart.

I Don't Know What Is Best For You,
 To Die, To Live Or What Do I Do?

Let Mother Nature Take Its Course,
 I Should Accept Whatever The Cause.

If You Die, You'll Have No Pain,
 If You Live, You'll Feel The Pain.

I Am Stepping Aside To Let Nature Decide,
 Whatever Is Best For You My Dear.

Thank You For The Time We Have Together,
 We'll Meet Again Someday Without Pain.

—*Rosanne B. Andersen*

Untitled

Leaves in full color
Fiery-Red, Hot-Orange and Gold
Filling the purple sky landscape

A chilling wind blows, and they scatter from their branches
One stray leaf lingers behind and dancers slowly, trickling
down
So too falls a life,
A life of sadness, silence, unfulfilled moments, overpowered,
closed-in.

Like the leaf,
a memory lingers,

Drifting in the cold open air,
staggering to the end,
Caught by gentle hands and fingers,
Touching the heart.

—Elizabeth Ann Copeland

Evening Tide

Sweet evening tide, calming, cooling,
   flowing toward my peaceful shore.
Icy fingers of sea and salt refresh my soul.
You rest upon my mind.

Seasoned by the breezes, soft blowing,
   curling tresses of waves in and out.
Eternity shall not miss one stroke,
   nor will one ripple of your laugh remain unheard.

—Kerry McDonald

Ryan Allen

A child is now at rest
for a safer place he remains
a world of goodness and beauty
a world without worry or pain.

No fear will he encounter
For a better place he'll be
a place where the sick are healed
and where blinded eyes can see.

Our world has forever changed
our lives are not the same
But close within our hearts
His precious face remains

We give to him our tears
and our prayers we send above
we cherish all the memories filled with happiness and love.

He'll have someone to depend on a helping hand
is there to lend for the father shall be watching.
And in heaven he'll have a friend. This battle is faced head
on, many obstacles to overcome. But in the end, together,
This battle will be won.

—Nicole Diaz

Untitled

A stunning but very familiar thought of surrender -
The poet lives alone and not in a world
The last line he wrote was engraved in stone
   which read:
"The life I lived had not fulfilled,
and my denial that here is an end."
Still stars never shine
Like billions of lives that never satisfy.

—Michael Kutepow

Our Last Dance

(For Ernest Ronald Balog)

"You will forget, he was only one day old."

Forget, no, I will not forget.
I knew him as I knew myself, those months while we were one.
He tickled me waltzing to the rhythm of my life cycle
Tapping to the tune across my ivory keys
Growing stronger, growing larger
Like clockwork, hiccup—tick, hiccup—tock.

Grow, yes, grow he did too heavy for my grasp
To slip out ass forward, to toughen for the elements
On that cold November day in 1970.
But where is his cry?
He is not broken. Is he?
No, merely a miniature.

Forget, how can I forget?
My breasts let down. He is too small to hold.
He does not cry. He is too good to punish.
Why then could so weightless a thing as air
Crush the lungs of my son?

Forget? I will never forget.
The silence.

—Patricia Saren Adams

"If I Only Knew How To Do More"

Why shouldn't I be able to do more?
For God's house has plenty in store.
His power is as it has always been-
Strength sufficient to save us from sin

God's greatness is beyond comprehension-
No matter who tries intervention.
Though raging storm may raise its head-
God's presence is proof He is not dead.

Sometimes God chooses to hide the sunlight-
Perhaps it's good that we must walk in the dark.
Even though we are led into a deep dark place
God's power is there to save the human race,

Winter comes with its freeze, wind and ice-
But God with His power is still in control.
We may be tempted to give up and run away
But God in His goodness will not let us stray

May we always rejoice, may our prayers never cease,
May we always take courage to live in peace
He'll bring us safe and secure into that promised land,
Where flowers will bloom and we're held by His hands.

—Arthur J. Goering

You Were Gone

You were gone all day and night
for me it was an awful sight
to see you leave and not come back
you left at night without a track
For days and days you were gone
I knew my life could not go on
So I traveled to look just for you
I looked at everything round and through
Finally I found where you had been
but you were up and gone as early as the hen
So I trudged back home in the snow
I soon saw a figure that started to glow
Then the figure turned to look at me
By George! It was you, now me
together you see.
So we ran back home singing a song
and that's what I missed most
while you were gone

—May Holley

Mother

My mother is a one of a kind,
For in my eyes she will always shine.

She tried her best to teach me right from wrong,
And though I tried hard, at times I did wrong.

She may have scolded me for my wrong,
But the hurt never lasted long.

She would awake me in the morning time,
With a shout, up the stairs, of, "Rise and Shine".

She would be angry at me for tearing my pants,
But then would mend them to make them last.

She took me to baseball games twice a week,
Even if my team hadn't won in the past three weeks.

As I grew older and started to drive,
She would worry that I might not make it home alive.

Now I am married and have my own family,
And now I can appreciate how she cared so lovingly.

My mother is the very best there can be,
Because she so loves a son like me!

—*Joe Alan Hamblin*

Victoria Lynn"

My littlest angel from above
For just a while brought so much love

I know you knew Grandma right from the start
As I held your tiny body, close to my heart

You've chosen the best Mommy and Daddy that I can say
And Samantha you're big sister is perfect in every way

As you look down from Heaven up above
Always know that you were loved

At night when I look at the stars that shine so high above
I'll know "Victoria Lynn", the brightest star,
The star with all the love

And so my littlest Angel, God has called you home to be
In his care until we can be together, for eternity.

—*Ranucci*

Untitled

Destitude dominates every part of a complex surgery of life,
  for no man controls the symphony of his or her future.
Left on a whim,
  I struggle to understand the complicated structure
  of people and their actions, for it is said,
    history will repeat itself,
    so the mistakes my forefathers made,
    shall rear its ugly face once again.
Falsehoods continue to elude my stark approach,
  leaving me in its astonishment every chance it receives.
I can't seem to grasp the reins of the beast I stride upon,
  leaving me dazed and unsure of every human resource
    that I seem to encounter,
  unsure whether or not to accept them for what they really are.
No one seems to be in touch with who
  or what they are or what they could be.
Feeling like I've been left strewn outward into the night,
  a mess of a man left only to ask questions of every soul I
  encounter.

—*Kevin Adams*

Suddenly Shy

Our eyes meet, from across the room.
For one moment. I dream I'll be with you soon.

People are no longer talking, the music no longer loud
As I make my way through the crowd

I see only your eyes, hear only your heartbeat
Just a matter of moments, until we meet

I'm standing here, I'm facing you now
I want to speak but I've forgotten how.

My hands are getting clammy and wet
I notice you're beginning to sweat

We're just standing here, and I'm wondering why?
Why am I so suddenly shy?

—*Kimberley S. Householder*

Wintergreen

There is a cool softness in the air
For summer days have had their share

And Fall's crisp burning hues take hold
Sienna brown and greenish gold

Into the changing air they spin
Leaves without a next of kin

Free-wheeling as they gaily swirl
Resembling an unleased little girl

I watch them from my lofty perch
On a vast and ancient creaking birch

For I'm that girl and count the days
'Til the leaves lose their abandoned ways

And blow past me to the still seclusion
Of inevitably gray-hued iced reclusion....
            winter.

—*Lisa Van Volkenburg*

Struggling Unity

Hold not thy dreams to be reality,
For that is wishful thinking. Hold
not they true feelings of expressions,
For they are part of you. Be able
to face rejections, it later will
strengthen you. Be no one other
than self. For that's how God made you.
No two thoughts, are identically.
Remember thou tongue, can be a dangerous thing.
Words can be spoken and misinterpret wrongly.

Guard your thoughts, so not to be too bluntly,
exercise our freedom, with open-mindness, strength
and courage prayed for daily.
Love no other more than God and you.
Stand by Gods side, for he never leaves us alone to cry.

—*Artena M. Sherman Williams*

Fall

Fall is the sound of crackling wood in the fireplace,
The leaves on the trees, the birds flying south,
The giggling of children on the schoolgrounds,
I watch these things peacefully, up in the sky,
For I am a snowflake, waiting, and waiting, and waiting,
For my time to come, to fall to the ground, and settle down,
Until I melt away, and climb back up to the sky,
And start waiting all over again.

—*Krystal Norman*

So Beautiful Is This Rose That I Hold In My Hands

So beautiful is this rose that I hold in my hands,
    for the love, peace, and joy she's brought to family and
    friends.

It seems forever I've known this, as I ponder these thoughts,
    for she has always been there for me when I've needed
    someone to hold my hand.

So beautiful is this Rose that I hold in my hands,
    for I know that as she passes from this life, she will bloom
    in a far greater land.

With each new Spring blossom, her memory and love will live on,
    for this beautiful Rose is our Mother, Grandmother, and
    Friend.

I will miss you greatly Grandmother, my Friend,
    but some day, I pray, I'll be with you in that far greater
    land.

—*Cheryl L. Braunbeck*

My Mom and Dad

How can I ever thank you enough?
For the past and present years of worry
    No one can ever take your place
    No one can ever fill your shoes
    You have given me strength
    You have given me knowledge
How can I ever thank you enough?
    We have a special kind of love
    A love we can only understand
Sometimes we say things that makes us mad
    Only to understand why it was said
    Your love will last a lifetime
        As well as mine to you
For you see, no one can ever replace
        My Mom and Dad

—*Sandii Yamamoto*

She Still Lives

My sister, Carolyn left us to be with her heavenly father,
For us down here on earth it is such a shock,
Even though we knew she was ill, it still hurts,
Knowing she is without pain gives us some sense of peace,

She gave what she had to everyone she touched,
Bringing joy and happiness to loved ones and friends,
Being a happy child growing up, continuing it into adulthood,
But, oh, my God, I miss her,

Thank you, my Lord for the wonderful years we had together,
Not only being a sister to me, but a friend as well,
She is in your hands now, I know you will take good care of her,
Knowing you will help me through the pain, and I'll have good
memories,

With her, giving took on a new meaning, giving body and soul,
Her vital parts were given to others so that they might live,
In my mind, by doing this, she still lives,
She will always live within the heart to me,...

—*Ruth Hartzell*

"The Mighty Sword"

As I am held high so all can see,
    four men have a chance to pick me;
It's not easy going into battle,
    riding on a mans hip with him in the saddle;
He pulled me out,
    and wove me about;
I cut off a mans head,
    and sent him to his death bed.

—*Christopher Steven Nix*

A Dream I Dreamed

I dreamed a dream that once returned
    forever here to be,
A wee little cry — a wee little heartbeat,
    a tiny part of me.

A little ball then eyes, a nose,
    a mouth, a chin,
All was just a part of what would happen
    when...

You are an arm, a tum, a back, a knee,
A squeal, a thrill, tears of joy,
    you're free!

The time - the place
The pound - the ounce...

A part from me —
A part of me —
Will forever be.

—*Carol Taylor*

The Night You Left

They say that a woman
Forgets the pain of labor.
Well, I don't believe it
For tonight I am remembering.

It was 18; it was 19 years ago...
And here I am riding the waves again
Climbing the crest and riding the curve
Rest and relax and begin again.

Back then I was able to reach
The moment of pushing you forth
With expansive relief and glorious wonder.
Tonight I cannot stop the pain,
For the contractions come from my soul
And I am not capable of
Pushing you out of my heart.

—*Catherine Veronica Saporito*

Legacy

Think of me not as you see me today,
Forgive me my arguments and frequent complaints,
Enjoy your future,
Of which I will not be a part.

Offer me your hand when the road is steep,
Let me walk slower and I will keep up with you,
Understand my limits,
And don't push me away.

Someday your child will come to you,
And these words will be yours,
As I say them now,
Your forever will be then.

—*Bernard Harmon*

Everlasting Love

If we stayed friends,
Friends for life,
Love, I'm sure, would last.
Secrets kept are secrets saved.
Love, I'm sure, would last.
Memories we shared are memories in the past.
Love, I'm sure, would last.
Friends will come and go,
But love, I'm sure, would last.
Time will always pass,
And love will last.

—*Paula Marie Berkhahn*

Little Bird

Lord touch me with your tender loving care,
That I may spread my wings and fly most any
and everywhere, for I am a little bird, and
so seldom I am heard, but with your tender
loving care I know I would be music to thee air.

—*LaVerne D. Nixon*

Broken Glass

Substance and perfect form
Fragmented. Life deals with bits of glass.
Recapture, if you can,
and synthesize the pristine crystal cup
In parabolic perfectness
To meet the eye within your mind.
Transparency is illusion:
Regard the infinite variety
Of hue and texture of broken light
Within each separate piece,
and use the invisible glue
Within you
To join together what may make,
Of allegory in bits,
A chalice, harmonious and one.

—*Bernard S. Pogorel*

A Mother is There

A mother is there from the very start,
fretting and fussing so much love in the heart.
A mother is there for the sickness and pain,
Through tear drops and laughter sunshine or rain.
A mother is there for the first bumps and falls,
For the first little pitter patter echoing the halls.
A mother is there for the first tooth, step, and word,
To her ears its the sweetest thing she's ever heard.
A mother is there for the first day of school,
To teenage guidance of the golden rule.
A mother is there for the first high school dance,
With the motherly advice on love and romance.
A mother is there for the first away from home stay,
Sleep wont come, she lies awake to pray.
A mother is there, and many tears are shed,
For its the day her baby is to wed.
She thinks back to the day her child was born,
So small so precious so loved so adorned.
So love just keeps growing with time she knows,
As her baby turns, smiles, waves good bye and goes.

—*Myra Fawley*

One of a Kind

You told me something special one day, you told me you were my
friend, you said you loved me and would be here for me from
beginning to end. It was then that I knew you were one of a
kind. I kept these words treasured in my heart, hoping we
would never have to depart. It was then that I knew you were
one of a kind. Sometimes you may have thought I doubted you,
but it wasn't you who I doubt it; was I,
I realized how special you were when you never failed to say, "Hi."
I was then that I knew you were one of a kind.
You held my hand through good times and bad,
You did your best to cheer me up when I was sad.
I was then that I knew you were one of a kind.
You have given me memories I will never forget,
It's times like these I'm glad we have met.
I was then that I knew that you were one of a kind.
I can't thank you enough for giving life to me.
You have been the most trust worthy friend any one could
possibly be. It was then that I knew you were one of a kind.
I was then that I knew you were one of a kind.

—*Laura Gibson*

Untitled

I'm looking out over the top of my shoes
From an expensive, clean leather tongue
Until one day
I'm at the bottom looking up
I can see the light
Will I be able to escape this musty smell?
Let me just pull on this string
It is so frayed and tattered
Will it be strong enough
To hold me
While I struggle
to the light?
Finally I make it
What a journey
I reach the top
and rest on the tongue
It is soft and smooth
like butter not hard like mine.

—*Kari Petersen*

"A Single Mother's Prayer"

Lord save my children
From any horrible fate - spare
my life so I can
maintain our humble estate give
me the courage to face
those sleepless nights
and all the problems parents
face just to protect their children's rights
I just want justice, and freedom
for them all, it doesn't matter
when Lord, it's better than not at
all. A single mother's prayer can be a
powerful thing, remember
most of all she's a
woman, striving and reaching
a queen without a king
when I am strong enough to
see my children through,
keep me safe Lord and see
me through too.

—*Judy A. Jones*

A Final Fling

Winter stepped politely aside,
from gravely marking the countryside...
for the whisper of Spring had filled his eye,
causing him to stop and sigh.
She walked ever sweetly where Winter lingered still...
taunting him and teasing him, around each promising hill.
When at last he could stand no more,
she cast herself through an unseen door.
And then the fury of Winter was felt,
where Spring had lured his heart to melt.
In silent rage he moved upon the land....
leaving vast whiteness with the touch of a hand.
In needing to forget the quest to conquer Spring....
Winter spread his blanket far,
perhaps, at last, a final fling.

—*Charlene Lee Stone*

Still Life

The deer
Sat on the road,
Eyes empty, legs folded
Neatly beneath its brown body.
Art work.

—*Carol M. Moyer*

A Prayer at Twilight

One day at twilight I stood all alone on a crest of a hill, far
from my home, I had no friends, no place to go, I was just a
lonesome wandering Hobo. Somewhere along life's path, I went
astray, must I forever go on this way? I would like to find
before I'm old, the rainbows end, my pot of gold. All the
things of which I dream, a snow capped mountain, a rushing
stream. The tall pine trees that bend and sway, a peace of
mind at the close of day. A love I seek to share with me, the
beauties of nature so vast and free. Such as a curtain about
to rise on God's great stage across the skies. The picture you
now see unfold, the deepest purple, a touch of gold. A bit of
pink, a hint of blue, it's a master's painting with all colors
true. A silent change comes on the scene, my soul's at rest,
my heart's serene. I found forgiveness in this strange land,
with just a touch of God's own hand. As I turn back with no
regrets, this summer eve, I'll not forget. So when you are
troubled, and your spirits are low, just talk to God, he'll always
know.

—*Maxine Lee*

The Funnel

Here we are again, caught within a circular flow
From the outside to the inside, along its path we go
Towards the center, towards the middle
Towards the end of all we know

But, this spiral is a funnel,
Sloping gently as we twist
Along the edges and the walls
Take a good look I insist
For once were down, there is no up
And on the way there is no stop

So enjoy the ride while you're able
And the blessings put on your table
Fill the funnel with all you can,
For the funnel you are in,
Is also in your hand

—*Anthony Simone*

I Am A Wave

In vast sea God knows What part
From way afar I got my start.
For I am a wave, It's quite a chore
While I'm rushing, rushing to the shore.

Gliding fowl know my life is good,
For me they wait as they should.
Undercurrent of food is my skirt
Off my back they eat my shirt.

On my journey between sea and sky
You see the rich beneath me lie.
Gems of coral and all that pitch
Could not be planted so beautiful a myth.

This Star is the commander of wind and sea
Yet moon's delight and it's will decree.
Like you I have a boss
In receiving orders which way to toss.

Aah! Of time I have not the knowledge
Yet is seems I've gone great mileage.
And at journey's end I do impeach
Don't leave me sea upon this beach.

—*Karen Long*

A Loved One So Dear

Our loving Heavenly Father bestow on us your grace as we
gather here today together in this place to trust into your
care this one we hold so dear. His life has meant so much to us
left here below, is there any way Lord he could never really
know? For when one of us was lonely. He was there to share,
when one of us was sad. He was there to care. We'll miss his
love and caring his friendly joking way, we'll cherish all the
memories of the many wonderful days. His lifetime of compassion
for all his fellowmen, a heart as big as Texas, and that big
beautiful grin! Now that he's gone on to be with Mom, Dad,
and Brother our family that's left here will love and cherish
each other. And when our time has come to cross that great
divide, we know they'll be there to greet us with their arms
stretched open wide. For you sent your only son to die in this
world of toil and strife, that we — with you might have
eternal life. Your glorious promise on which we all depend, with
faith and trust in you, our lives, will not here end.

—*Judy Carrell James*

On the Farm

Quit my high paying aerospace job,
Gave up the fancy clothes to look like a slob.
Here I am working on the farm,
Living like the honest side can't be wrong.

I gave my resignation to executive row,
Gave it up for another row to hoe.
There are things in life that I don't regret,
Making that decision was the best one yet.

I worked too hard for another mans' gold,
Denying myself things I wanted to hold.
Purchasing this farm was our dream,
Putting down roots became the family scheme.

Looking up at stars makes me think back,
To being jerked around on the corporate track.
Forever thankful for the money they paid,
And constantly hating the knife blade.

Never will I look back to those business days,
And wished that I had stayed.
Because this is where I want to be,
On the farm with the animals and family.

—*Alisa Graham*

"How I Choose To Create"

The creator our Father
gave us the power to create - to express
him creatively
through the using of poetry;
and since the mighty one of all mighty
the Holy One of the highest
has become my salvation, my wisdom
I am a new man a regenerated living creation!
Truly, indeed by the fullness of His Holy Spirit in me
a vivid and imaginative sense of experience
is freely dispatched by His knowledge through me;
in condensed, intense beauty of language
(lyrical beauty); chosen for its sound
and its soundness as well as its meaning...
Because I fear only the Lord God
I have His understanding - clearly and by use
of structured meter and rhyme perfect love
on earth as it is in heaven is my life time!

—*GeraDessiel Simon*

From You To Me

see you standing in the moonlight,
entle rain trickles across your face.
ears are hidden among the rain,
ut I know they're really there.

owly you turn and look at me,
nly to catch my heart astray.
oved you before, but now it's gone.
he pain you feel I plainly see.

didn't mean to kill our love.
ust didn't have the courage to go on.
aybe someday you will love again,
nd forgive me for breaking your heart.

—*Karen Marie Haas*

Spirits in the Wind

Spirits in the wind, dancing up a storm......
ently swinging and swaying to the breeze.......
histling an eerie tune from night 'til morn'...
osseling the leaves on the rhythmic trees.

Spirits in the wind, gaining momentum........
cking up the dust, swirling it around.........
ke wild Indians, to the beat of drums.........
ancing faster, can you feel your heart pound?!

Spirits in the wind, laughing and roaring....
hirling off the leaves and whishing the trees,
visting, twirling, everything is soaring.......
ancing up a fury..............feeling so free!

Spirits in the wind, tired from their dancing.
red from their play.......spirits are prancing.
red from their play.......spirits are chanting.
irits, change your partners..it's a new day!!

—*JoAnne Lemboke Colcord*

Wildwood Beauty

e reflect when I stare at her
ggles when I whisper
oistens the throat in a morning vapor
hoes when I call
e birds sing aloud in answer

e sheds her veils with the sun rises
iles when there are breezes
eering at the wind
ncing with a storm
irl young dolls on the crystal plate as it freezes

e sparkles as the moon rises
very bass leap in praises
nada geese make complimentary cruises
ditating in the evaporating haze
allows the tear if tormenting rain increases

eeping dam shakes people awake
otecting her safety in spite of severe headache
ork hard for charity for her name's sake
o is this beauty?
r maiden name is Wildwood Lake

—*C. W. Yang*

The Leaf

e leaf is lonely trace
at autumn winds
d not conquer.
s there,
tiently awaiting its departure
om the frosted branch
at holds its roots.

—*Alison Hess*

Gloom

Sometimes when you're alone in your room, you feel
gloom. The birds have stopped their singing, the warm
breeze is nothing but a cold wind. The sky is like a giant
blanket covering the happiness we thought we knew. Perhaps
as we grow older we think we will be happier, but as the
young die for no reason and the old live when they want to
die, I just want to cry. Why is there no hope in our eyes
anymore, have we lost that feeling of warmth and security.
We think we are doomed, but the world holds such gloom you
cannot look forward to the next year without thinking how
in 20 years the planet may be gone, taking the hopes and
dreams of the young and old and the lives of those who could
have made a difference. So while we are still alive don't
ignore the cries of the helpless, for they are not hopeless
for maybe we can lift the great blanket of gloom and let the
birds sing their songs again.

—*Dana Atherton*

This Shout...

This shout that I alone produce
goes back before my newest birth
and springs from sources still alive
that grow within each reaching tree
transformed by every singing saw
to bear the weight of resting man
in the defiant gravity of a rocking chair
that catapults old age
into the future's present self-affirmation

Cockfights of mahogany seeds
what does it take to make a man
what did it take to make me

—*E. Anthony Hurley*

Passion

Violet sparrows skimming the night through crystal chasms,
Golden flames flaring across the plains,
White horses in all their splendor, standing heads held high
Upon hind legs by the sparkling waterfall.

A small soft snowshoe rabbit darting through the woods,
A speck of blood upon his ear,
Pursued by livid dogs,
Just down his hole, saved by fear.

A tiger, the flaming passion of it's spirit
Angers orange and angers black.
Swift as the night and lightening, a blur in the leaves,
Follows the wild leaping deer.
This magic, the wild, the meaning of beauty.

—*Katherine Crawford Kastin*

Who

I remember asking,
Grandma, who's that baby in the picture?
She looks a lot like me.
I never wore clothes like that,
you can plainly see.
Yet her hair, her eyes, her smile
its as clear as it can be!
Grandma, who's that baby in the picture,
is it really me?
No, says Grandma, you it cannot be,
    you see,
because that baby in the picture, is really me!

—*Judith A. Boer*

Watching, Waiting...

Watching the daylight turn against the evening sky.
Golden sunshine fading without argument into the blackness.
Praying the shades of cobalt, lime and grey,
Only once notice my translucent residence,
in the reflection of purity and grace.

Hoping the passing moments lost,
Are not the jewels of unfulfilled reality.
The next and its offspring,
Will shower upon me,
Awaken my desperate, craving soul,
A new source of happiness.
Which in this lifetime, in this fleshen body,
Among triumph and tragedy, never has been felt.
Though, constantly searched for.

Somehow knowing,
Or, desperately dependent upon,
A dream sown in my heart.
Beacon fueling my search,
Uplifting my lowly manhood onto a focus that borders fantasy.

—*Michael Byrne*

Three Friends

To one-seven, four-three and sixty-nine,
Gone out for a chat & a dine —
The blarney will flow
Back & forth, to & fro,
But in the midst of it all,
Good new wine.

Hallelujah for men
Who still have a yen
To escape from the ladies awhile —
To solve female riddles
Over male-only victuals
Is worth walking a long country mile.

Women libbers fail to see
The forest for the trees
& that men are courageous & able.
So why fight for the right
Which exists in plain sight —
"The hand that rules the world...
Rocks the cradle."

—*Kathleen Caperello*

Untitled

One day you wake up to find they're not there
   Gone you know not where
   Help, help you scream
Someone please wake me from this dream
   You cry out loud
   But no one can hear
   You scream oh God why
Oh how you wish you could stop the pain
   Stop, stop you say
   Before you go insane
   You run out the door
   You run until you can run no more
   You turn, you can find no ground
You're falling, falling fast
   Oh how long will your pain last
   You close your eyes before you hit
   Your finch
   Eyes open wide
   You're awake
Your love is there by your side.

—*Jeannetta Harris*

St. Louis

As you are boarding you say your
goodbyes. When you take off you go
soaring through the skies. Since
you said your goodbyes you look far
down and try to see your love ones
far down on the ground, to St. Louis
you are bound. You are scared you have
found. Your ears are popping hard until
you hit the ground. As you get off
you meet your friend with a grin
and say, "I can't wait until I fly again!"

—*Andrea Lee Schmitz*

End

Life's shattered moons crying
Grandfather's decrepit mind dying
As far as his will takes him
There's no mistaking the value of a clear and conscious brain.

Once born and undeveloped
It absorbs and envelops
Whether good or bad, all is taken in,
A sponge, wet and wild of a child

There's no end, there's all the things possible all things
      probable.
Infusion of thought, idea, storm.
It's too fast to control.
It races at its own speed.
It writes its own creed.

Stopping at no one's request, for it knows the route which is best.
Undenying rule, resisting makes one a fool.
Let it grow and expand.
The mind flays and reprimands its commands. Extinct.

—*W. Mirkovic*

My Summer's Gone

Where have all the daisies gone? The green
grass the robins flown.
The summer nights and soft warm breeze I
wonder where are the pretty trees.
You were the summer of my life, the sunlit
days the moonlit nights.
The twinkle of a falling star a dream that's
so very far.
I can feel the sleet see the snow hear the
icy winds blow, pretty sails gone from the sea
lonely coldness inside of me.
Wish I could bring about the spring and all
things that summer brings.
Butterflies and bumblebees, buttercups and warm
green trees.
Blowing white clouds in the sky, my love for
you will never die.
In my heart there beats a song and it's called
my summer's gone.

—*Marian Boulais*

Visions

I am trapped in an ocean of regret
drowning in currents of my own fears.
Waves toss me through their dreams.
While shallow hopes of my own are
Violently washed away.
I become lost in a whirlpool of depression.
Spinning away any shred of happiness.
I am forever lost at sea.

—*Josilyn Clark*

eep Faith And Know

aith, Real Faith, is a wonderful thing
reat are the wonders that it can bring;
can bring comfort when things go wrong,
can move mountains it is so strong.

aith helps you look beyond today,
can bring sunshine when skies are gray;
can give strength for what we must bear,
can bring peace and dispel despair.

aith shows the way through the darkest night,
is your shield and your beacon light;
aith is in trusting in one who is true,
eep Faith and Know-that God is with you!

    —Robert E. Addison

o the Unborn Child

Restless One,
rowing and preparing to enter a world yet unknown,
njoy your solitude!
oo soon your ears and eyes will open,
o hear and to see your strange new home.
ch a tiny brain, so round and small!
ho knows what thoughts and secrets lie within.
ill it compose some great concerto,
find some long-sought cure?
d those tiny hands with fingers tightly curled.
ey will open soon to give and to receive,
someday, perhaps, will soothe some scorching brow!
ose tiny feet with long and slender legs,
ill they walk in the steps of some Great One,
will they make a path of their very own?
ur pulsating heart, already beating strong,
ever let it be broken by some cruel, uncaring soul,
ly let it find true love!
ar Child, a gift from God,
merge to discover what this life has in store for you!

    —Bernadine J. Wilson

is Special Love

is love I have for another
ows stronger and longer
eryday it hurts more and more
ry to make it go away
is strange love I have for another
niss the way he holds me
e way he kisses me
hurts knowing it's my fault
vill never touch my lovers heart
ill the love pain never stop?
r I want him day and night
d can think of no other
ill he never see how I feel
know how much I care
is special love that I have for another

    —Melissa Riggins

e Eclipse

The eclipse is a ball of light covered by a toddler's hand;
Her hand slowly uncovers the ball, for she is blind and
ing to feel it's beauty;
The blackness lifts from the ball of light as darkness lifts
m the child's eyes;
She lifts her hand from the surface to reveal it's healing
ht to the world;
        She can see.

    —Julia Pluhowski

The Universe

T imeless, constantly changing by the
H our, the moment and by eons.
E ver with us
U nmeasurable but,
N ot unreachable.
I nvisible, beautiful, interesting, entrancing, mysterious,
V iolent eruptions, storms, winds, changes, awe inspiring.
E xpanding our imaginations and experiences.
R eaching, grabbing, holding the
S tars, milkyway, or northern lights,
E nticing us to see ourselves and where we fit into the
picture.

    —Edward Brown, Elizabeth Loughran, Lucy Good,
    Maude Butler, and Robert Sanders of Hanover Health
    Care Center

Untitled

If I were a breeze, I'd move so sweet and gently through your
hair. Like airy tendrils downcast through the fragrant
drifting air. I'd wend a weave surrounding you with fragrance
kissed with dew. And leave you feeling cooler, something only
I can do. If I were a rainbow I know where you'd be, I have no
doubt. I'd see to it that you were at the end, or near about.
The pot of gold your treasure for the goodness that you've
shown. This gift I'd surely share with you, and share with you
alone. If I were a storm, I'd keep the rain away from your
parade. I'd huff and puff right by you, as you bask beneath my
shade. I'd share the calm that's nestled deep within my angry
eye, then nourish you with sunshine lest another day go by.
If I were a kiss I'd seal each precious promise that we made.
With hope for new tomorrows, yet our memories not to fade.
With words so lightly whispered and our cares adrift at sea,
I'd wrest away your sorrows til your thoughts were but of me.

    —Brenda Green

The Lady Is America! We Are Her Family!

Near Ellis Island, our gift from France, with torch held in her
    hand, has given hope to all who came to this "Beloved Land."
The Lady stands for Liberty, and Freedom, guaranteed.
She welcomes us with shining light to live in harmony.
Reflect upon this symbol and thank God we are free.
"The Lady is America! We are her family!"

For those whose dreams were shattered by wars...the refugees;
For those who were imprisoned in the camps across the seas;
For orphans, serfs, and widows from countries far and near;
For those who hungered for the taste of "freedom" without fear;
Whatever was their reason, by multitudes they came
From every Nation on the Earth to start their lives again.
A melting-pot of every race...each different in its creed,
Yet, each found refuge in this land of opportunity.

Our bond is love...united...strong. Together we all share
A part of Lady Liberty. We love her and we care.
The Lady stands for Justice...A Free Democracy!
Her blazing torch a symbol to live in love with "peace."
Celebrate this special day. Rejoice, for we are free.
"The Lady is America! We are her family!"

    —June Wujcik Valenciano

Untitled

Every day to be woken
The whine of a grown man
Aged only by years
Most time he makes no sense
Only to himself
Sure of the frustration

    —Mathew A. Mitchell

The Waiting Game

Time stands still on a clock with
Hands spinning as fast as thoughts.
Waiting is endless on a deadline schedule,
And time is precious as it slips swiftly past.

How do I contain the scream forcing
Its way up my throat;
Or cease the gnawing at my stomach;
Or slow the pounding of my heart
That threatens to burst my chest open wide?

Sleep evades me as I close my eyes,
And toss my head from side to side on
A pillow that is not cushion for my
Restless thoughts.
Would that I could pass these interminable
Hours in peaceful slumber;
That I might awaken renewed and refreshed
And slightly less troubled in this
Scheme of life...

  —*Leslie Harris*

Happiness

Happiness comes from friendship and love,
Happiness comes from God up above.
Inside your heart and into your mind,
Happiness is there and is easy to find.

You can be happy in many ways,
Like spending time with your family on hot summer days.
There will be times when you feel upset,
You may have done something wrong that you now regret.

That was the past, so now look ahead,
The future is coming, so be happy instead.
Happiness is found in a movie or show,
It will always be there wherever you go.

So put on a smile and laugh with a friend,
Just by being happy, happiness will never end.

  —*Stephanie Marie Capogna*

Deluge of Emotions

My life is a whirlwind of emotion
Happiness, sadness, grief, and fear
In my mind I need to have the utmost devotion
To the people in my life who are near.

There comes a time when I need to let go,
To allow myself time to be needy.
But I can't drop the facade, lest it overflow
And people around think of me as greedy.

How can I let others know that my feelings matter
That I give with my heart to a fault.
If I show those emotions, my heart might just shatter
So I seal them within, as if in a vault.

It matters not the quality of life I may live
As long as I'm remembered as caring.
So I'll work to no end, and give all I can give
And keep my feelings to myself, with no sharing.

Can you remember me - as I want to be known?
A woman strong-willed and alive?
I'll keep trying until that day I'm full grown
To achieve all my goals, I will strive.

  —*Deborah Hazen Nardi*

A Letter To Heaven

Dear Ma,
Has it been three years.
All I can think of is the tears.
Not in your eyes but in your children's eyes.
I didn't cry because I had said my good-byes.
I often have a remembrance of you.
Then I find myself getting blue.
Missing the things we did together hurts the worst.
Sometimes I think I'm going to burst.
When I long for all the wants and needs
in my heart for you.
I try to remember how much pain you were in too.
I know its best that your body is not here.
I'm glad your spirit will always be here know matter what year.
I sure hope you are happier I "wish".
You deserve a great big kiss.
Well Ma I'm thankful I had this chance to
remind you that I will always love ya.

  —*Rose Mary Hunter*

A Foreman's Dream

A foreman is a very nice and cool man,
 He always tries to do the best that he can;
If you serve him faithfully and on the square
 He leans over backwards to be more than fair.

And when one of his men on a close job goes astray
 He pulls out his hair before it all turns grey.
He shouldn't fume, make loud noises or holler
 Even if he gets very hot under his collar.

He tries to teach his men right from wrong,
 It isn't as easy as singing a song;
And before you have it they're doing O.K.
 The foreman feels like shouting Hip Hip Hooray!

As you grow older, wise and more mellow
 You realize your foreman is a very talented fellow
You can travel the world over, and you can't beat that hand,
 The foremen at Eagle Sheet Metal are the best in the land.

  —*E. L. Pearlman*

Sweet Prince of the Night

As I lay my head on the wings of the sky,
he comes to me only in fantasy.
Not knowing this sweet prince of the night
that I have fell in love with. He has filled
me with his warmth and passionate love.
Night to night growing colder as I awake.
Day to day my bitter cold tears run down
my red hot flesh as I cry my lonely tears of pain.
Knowing that one of these days I shall meet the
prince of all princes no matter how long it takes me.
Longing for his soft and gentle embrace,
kissing his ever so soft lips.
Can you feel my ever lasting love?
Our candle we share shall burn for eternity.
Together my prince we shall rule the world.

  —*Karen DeGrand*

Ballet

 Over the meadow, beyond the blue,
the sunset was slowly falling to the ground.
 There she stood in little ballet shoes
not knowing what to do until she began
dancing in harmony with the sunset.
 Moving until the friend by her side
disappeared with the glowing warmth-
For the duet with her shadow had ended.

  —*Amberlee Anderson*

,096 Days Ago

hree years ago, I saw death have definable features
Ie gorged on blood and put on a mask to make people
  fear him

hree years ago, I saw that indescribable blur in the
  mirror, as the lights came on
he lights came upon this surreal state between dream
  and consciousness

hree years ago, I touched that undying feeling of
  insurmountable power
ower witnessed in those instances that I could
  overthrow Arthur and gain control of Camelot

hree years ago, I saw that I could return as Caesar
  and slay my assassins
he assassins in a jealous frenzy to a madman's
  senseless whim

hree years ago, I foreseen my own death and now it is
  destiny that I reach that goal
ust three years, three years ago....

— *Peter J. White*

'The Graceful One"

Lady of grace, God is watching over you;
Ie granted your wish to see your dreams come true.
  And now he's given you your wings just like the little dove;
Ie's calling you home to heaven above.
  And leaving behind, the kids that you've seen all grown.
Easing your mind that your legacy will live on:
  These words can't express, just what you mean to us all!
Now you're leaving us and we have to be strong and stand tall.
  And remember the love you gave to everyone;
The warmth of your love glows brighter than the sun.
  You have been a part of everyone's life;
A daughter, sister, mother, aunt, teacher, friend, and even a wife:
  Though at times, the road may have not been clear;
And the path that you travelled has been littered with your tears
  Had it not been for all the pain and all the heartache,
The triumphs and blessings we wouldn't know how to appreciate.
  The time has come for now, to say good-bye.
But do not weep, my children do not cry;
  With the love of my family I have grown,
And now, my precious Lord leads me home....

— *Anzie Jones*

Mikey

There is a handsome young man that I know,
He has and always will be to me an undiscovered hero.
He is caring and sharing to everything and everyone.
And when I am around him I always have fun.
He loves his girl, Ariana, very much
And proves it to her by his gentle touch.
He is a great joy to both of his older brothers,
And loved by both of his mothers.
He is one of my very best friends,
And will stay that way unto the world ends.
Hardly anyone means as much to me.
As my younger brother, Mikey.

— *Karen Davis*

First Day of Spring

The day is so grey and sad and empty.
This first day of spring and I
Desperately wait to be touched
By the warm sunlight of hope and love,
To be made alive again.

— *Phyllis Neely Stuart*

Heaven Earth

I do believe the Lord above, created you for me to love.
He picked me out of all the rest, because he knew, I would
love you best.
I had a heart and it was true, but now its gone, from me to you.
Take care of it, as I have done, for you have too, I have none.
If I should die before you do, in heaven I will wait, just for you.
If you are not there on judgement day,
I'll know you have gone the other way. From day to day I'll
continue to pray and have faith that we won't go astray
If in the end we are apart, God never meant for us to start.

— *Steven Ray Abshure*

From The Heart

He comes and he goes, without rhyme or reason
He remains much the same, whatever the season.

A product of nature, a seed in the wind
A man of select morals, a man of much sin.

You can't understand him, don't even try
He doesn't want much, just to get by.

Please don't mistreat him or play for a fool,
Although not too bright, life has been his school.

Remember his needs, as he remembers yours,
For when you most need him, he'll want to be sure.

He can't always be there, so don't press your luck,
He isn't a toy like a child's little duck.

The feelings are real and the emotions run high,
So remember that, people, when you start to get wise.

Don't think you can use him to suit your own needs,
Cause when he gets right, he'll look for new leads.

But, if you play straight and act as yourself,
You won't have a worry, cause he'll be there to help.

He doesn't want to act phoney or seem like a snob,
But whatever his actions, he'll always be Bob.

— *Robert O. Patterson*

Broken Heart

He stole my heart and my soul
He said that he would never go
My friends might disagree
And say that he doesn't love or care for me
But they don't know a single thing
How do they know what he's like?
They don't know him as well as I
As long as I know he cares and that he will always be there
He really does mean the world to me I don't really know
Why they all disagree but now I wonder if its true am I
Really being used? He doesn't call or try to see how I am
I feel like he's been avoiding me but I'm not too surprised
You see why would anyone ever fall in love with me?
He said that we could be kissing friends
But why fool around?
Let's just let it end just tell me not to call anymore
I hope you know that you already broke my heart
So why break it more? Before I leave you I just want to say
I'll still love you anyway the only difference that will be
Is that you'll be the one that won't love me

— *Agnieszka Ratajczyk*

Untitled

Hush, hush little darling, don't you cry,
The world's slowly spinning and it's got a blue sky,
God loves you forever and that's no lie,
So hush, hush little darling don't you cry.

— *Paul Rambo*

My Dream

I stood before God on judgment day - to my amazement,
he sent me the other way. I said; just one question
I need to know, allow me one answer before I go. There
was a man in front of me you sent on into glory - land.
While on earth he walked in sin. It seemed the good ones
wouldn't enter in. I've lived my life so that on this
day - for not many sins would I have to pay. If I had
known this was the way it would be, I would of lived my
life more carefree.

—*Kathy Duncan and co-author Mary Jane Sullivan*

What Jesus Means To Me

Jesus is the Way,
He shows us a direction.
In the Bible it does say,
He is the epitome of perfection.

Jesus is the Truth,
He has never told us a lie.
In the Bible it shows the proof,
If you believe in Him, you shall never die.

Jesus is the Life,
He destroyed death on the cross.
Through Him there is no strife,
He is a beacon of light, for the lost.

But most of all, Jesus is Love,
Of which to us He is sending.
A gift to us from Heaven above,
I'm glad it is never ending.

—*James Allen Weier*

My Love

I know I can't be his because of her.
He thinks he loves her with his heart
but I just want them to part.
I can't stand the constant break of my heart.
It's causing me to really split apart.
Emotionally I'm torn to shreds.
Piece by piece my heart breaks away.
All I want him to do is stay.
The day will come when he will look at me high,
hopefully I will not be in the sky.
I can't stand this delay any more.
I will just leave. I'll go out the door
but if I leave I'll take my love.
My love will become a dove
so it'll be free to go its own way
to watch over him, my love, this and
all of his days.

—*Becky Williams*

Whale

A whale set sail one day
He thought he'd go out and play.
His tail got caught he could not swim away.
As he was pulled up to the big boat
The sun lightly shown on him.
The sky grew dark the waves grew gray
As they carried the whale away.
They took him to a box like room.
It was filled with water and gloom.
"I'm just a baby," said he.
A boy outside the glass said,
"Will he ever see his parents mommy?"
"I'm afraid not my dear," said she.
The whale closed his eyes and began to cry.
As he told the world as he knew goodbye.
Soon after that the whale would die.

—*Stephanie Vann*

'Walkabout'

With straining legs and aching feet
He walks the stones that gently lay
Where a million footsteps before him beat
The special path that shows the way

The horizon shows a gleaming spire
A flash of gold that blinds the eye
The trembling walls, his heart's desire
A gentle touch and a woman's sigh

A blazing jewel with a hint of green
An ancient gate that he must pass
An eagle soars away unseen
Her soft embrace in dreams of glass

Wild raven's hair, as black as night
On strings of jade a necklace strung
A band of gold which gleaming bright
Might come from church bells never rung

Before the city of ancient kings
On dreamy rivers rich with foam
With passion borne on silken wings
As one, they take the path back home

—*Monte P. Gilliam*

Walk

He needs love.
He wants to hold the dove.
He needs hope.
He lives in a world of gun fire
with a lifeless scope.
He needs one friend.
He can then depend on some fate of the end.
He needs that hug.
He lives in a constant tug.
He needs off of that dead end rug.
He's at his end, even before he can begin.
He needs help to heal his heart so filled.
He needs not the lash.
He cries within his blackberry skin.
He wonders when the walk of life will take its end.

—*James H. Ellis*

Vietnam

I lost my Dad to a crazy war,
He was not in the Peace core.
They sent him over seas to Vietnam,
It was just another President's scam.

My Dad's alive but yet he's dead,
The war did a lot to mess up his head.
He still has nightmares and really bad dreams,
I lay awake at night and listen to his screams.

In that jungle far across the seas,
I want to find my father and bring him home to me.
The government dropped agent orange and made him sick,
My Dad fought the Viet Cong that he knew he could not lick.

When Dad got back Elvis was a hit,
Instead of kisses my Dad was greeted with spit.
My Dad still remembers the kid he had to kill in the early dawn,
I wish my Dad could have buried that memory at Saigon.

—*Julie M. Laktash Schroll*

You Will Always Have A Friend"

ne friend, there is always one friend you can talk to.
'll never leave you.
'll be there when you're happy and when you're sad.
e will experience your life with you may it be joys and
rrows, heartaches or love. One friend.
hom you can trust. Tell your deepest dark secrets and he
ll not judge you. One friend.
ho is never to busy to listen. Not wrapped up in such a world
at he can't take time to listen.

ne friend. Who loves everyone and accepts them into his
ngdom to live with him.
ventually, everyone has an appointed time when they go to live
th their friend, some sooner than others.
though they will be missed and rivers of tears will fall, the
ood will soon stop for they will realize that their loved one
in a better place. They are with their friend who has
mforted them their entire life and now through their eternal life.
st remember, memories are forever, they will never die.

—*Gina Angrimson*

estiny - Your Little Man

r all the things you've done for me
elped me grow up right
is Poem I do give to you for the gift of life
hen at first it all had started
helpless bundle, a boy,
filled the hearts of many with hope, love and joy
d as the years kept passing
ch one quicker than the last
e past was then, and this is now
ou know we had a blast
w here I stand before you grown into a man
ho is fighting for his Country in a Foreign Land
ere's just one thing to remember
the jungle or in the sand
n't ever forget who I am
n still your Little Man
d no matter where I am
l always be close enough
Hold My Mother's Hand

—*Errol Eaton*

eath Of A World

e land is dark, the silence lives,
r chest rose and fell,
ith each shuddering breath,
r whitened hair fanned out into the empty space,
licate hands lay by her side,
r face pale and wan,
rtrayed too much pain,
r one so young,
e ancient sun peeked out at his tired daughter,
om the suffocating curtain of night,
gently kissed her waxen lips in a final salute,
gazed into her eyes,
ll of the knowledge,
her voyage ahead,
e drew her last shallow breath,
her eyes fluttered shut like the wings of a bird,
e saw the light, she survived the dark,
sleep in peace.
ernally

—*Louise Lepage*

The Lady Universal

A wreath of stars crowned her head
Her hair cloaked her back
She and her sisters, and her brothers
Her lovers, and her friends
They created songs of each others' spirits
Adorned in tears, wind, flame, and soil
Dancing in spirals to one another's chants
They lifted the Earth to the sky
Now, they circle around her, your mother, you home, the
    Earth
Do you not see them?
Lady as sky; her sisters, the moons; her brothers, the
    suns; her lovers, the horizons; and her friends,
    the comets
They are all around
They do not hold you, in their hands
Rather, they embrace you in their arms
Kiss their cheeks
And show them how high
Your flight can be.

—*Jehan A. Faisal*

Little Girl Lost

Little girl lost, looking around trying to find her mother.
Her mother was gone, she was all along.
They needed each other.
My name is Cathy, she told a man.
He reached down, and took her hand.
Come, we'll find your mother, little miss,
but it won't be easy in town like this.
We'll search the town, from end to end.
If we must, we'll search it again.
With quivering lips, Cathy started to cry.
It was a lonely town, and a darkening sky.
Slowly at first, it started to rain
would she ever see her mother again?
At last the man gave up, his shoulders slumped.
Was the little girl lost, or had she been dumped.
No reports of a missing child he'd look a little longer.
He'd wait a little while. Laying in an alley, with a throbbing
head over to one side, the earth showed red.
Cathy, the woman whispered I love you so much she longed for her
daughter, and her little girls touch.

—*Nancy Robertson*

God's Little Angel

She came to the altar as an angel.
Her voice was like that of a nightingale,
Singing to her little ones.
God has a place just for you.
The angel was what God wanted.
He touched Her heart.
His words were tenderly sweet,
Hold on to hope, keep the faith.
"Come to Me", He calls you. God is your model, and life has
a
purpose, He asks for your love,
Accept His friendship and He will guide and protect you.
You are His angel, praise Him and all His creation.
When He was calling you, His voice was whispering in your ears;
Song of praises, words of wisdom, Come my angel, I have work
for you, I have a plan for you.
Trust Me and I'll guide you, life has a purpose, and I am your
model. Little angel, God has inspired you from above; telling
you to, "Come to Me". I'll give you my love, that soft whisper
of love, that followed you from day to day, no voice in the
world is sweeter than His.

—*Dorothy Mc Dougald*

Second Place

There's another love in my husband's dreams
He's happy most of the day, but during the
night he screams
Strung out on a feeling that never last long
Tied to a habit he won't admit it's wrong
He's stuck on this new love, he thinks it's so unique
His friends say it's a smart way to make life complete

It's a kind of high that cures all his fears
She's got him I know, cause I'm crying bitter tears
Cocaine won my man that I couldn't face
But because I love him, I took second place

My man's stuck on this new love, he thinks it's so unique
Friends say it's a smart way to make life complete
Cocaine won my man and I took second place
Cocaine won my man and I took second place

—*Susan A. McPherson*

The Essence Of Ron

The world is so judgmental today, our feelings we feel we must
hide - avoiding the risk of becoming a burden, by keeping our
pain inside. It seems somewhat of a shame, we can hide our
feelings so well - even our closest friends and family, face to
face with us, can't tell. Human emotions are so powerful, they
can only be controlled to an extent before they diminish our
strength to deal with the consequences we try to prevent. Ron
had his reasons and he made his decision to eliminate what he
could no longer ignore. He'd apparently been hurting for quite
some time and chose not to hurt any more. Contemplation of the
possibilities that might have helped him to refrain is as
painful as it is pointless, for only Ron is to blame. Ron did
not want us to feel the anger and sadness we feel. His value
for life was no longer important, a broken man who would never
heal. We will all sincerely miss Ron, and our cherished
memories will remain of a very special person who is now free
from his pain. Ron would want us to party and be happy; his
wishes we cannot decline. So here's to you Ron Litton: It's
Party Time!

—*Koni Chrest*

Winds of Life

Touch me, sooth me, cover me,
hide me in your invisible space.
More gentle than a baby's cheek
in midsummer dreams.
Rising from the deep in a boiling
misty fog hovering over the first
frost of fall.
Now crisp and clean talking to
the trees that rustle back the clatter
of their falling dry leaves.
Soon, sharp and piercing with an
icy blast, ice cracking and bare
branches that creak.
Then, when the cold seems endless
a rush of torrential rain, beating, flooding,
then slowly, tenderly, caressing every
living thing, promising new buds of a
glorious spring.
Slipping into a lazy summer of sunny days and
balmy nights that warm the heart and soul.

—*Peggy Newton*

The U.S. Air Force Theme

High and Mighty, o'er our land and sea.
Daring pilots, guard our liberty.
Proud and loyal, soldiers of the sky.
Every ready, watching from on high.

A million strong, we'll keep our country free.
We are the wings, that fly to victory.
We wing along, with faith in every crew.
For we're the men, who wear the air force blue.

Our mighty air force, high in the skies.
Sentries of freedom, our country's eyes.
Swift darts of silver, streaking above.
Guarding our nation, and the ones we love.

—*Ronnie Burns*

What Is A Man?

Five o'clock in the morning a baby boy is born.
His face is christened by the light of dawn.
He enters the world a lead singer in a band
and he lives to find just what is a man.

He talks to a fighter, who is big and strong.
The fighter says a man works out, hard and long.
He speaks to a scholar, whose average never left four.
The scholar says a man always makes a perfect score.

Then he pauses for a moment,
to hear a message from above,
That says, "A man is one who shares freely,
his life and his love."

—*Charles R. Cole*

The Stallion

The Stallion I saw on top of the hill,
His neck finely curved his whinny so shrill.
He pranced as he cantered on two divine feet,
Then reared on the others his beauty so sweet.
He danced and he galloped his way to the shore,
Then showed me his beauty ever the more.
He reared and splashed in the eve's ocean spray,
Swimming and playing 'til the next sign of day.
His smooth silk like coat,
Such intelligent eyes,
His huge bulging muscles,
He was nature's surprise.
He walked all alone,
Wild as the sun,
As he saw me watching,
Then reared, cried and run...

—*Bahiyyih Davis*

Untitled

A horrible dry rattling sound came from my son's room.
His open mouth gasped for air.
His eyes were half-open, yet sightless.

I sensed death's invisible presence.
I heard him in Rick's labored rattle
I smelled him in Rick's expelled breath.

Death was my enemy—taking that which I lived for.
For Rick, he was the ultimate friend, bringing the promise
of final rest to his tormented body.

Suddenly it was quiet.
Rick's face was unchanged.
Death had silently departed with Rick's freed spirit.

Why couldn't I go with him on this last journey?
"Wait for me Rick!" My spirit cried out.
I sat dry-eyed, caressing his face and hair.

—*Barbara L. Hernandez*

Sometimes

Sometimes I'm all alone.
Holding onto memories.
Where could you be?
I think of you constantly.
I wish you were here,
  To hold me in your tender embrace.
What do I do?
I can't control how I feel about you.
Sometimes I think how it would be,
  To have your sweet kisses all mine again,
  To have your love, your laughter.
Sometimes I'm fighting tears,
  That are so endless,
  It seems they'll never stop.
Sometimes I can still feel you.
Your soft breath on my cheek.
Your gentle caresses.
It still takes me away, once in a while,
  Sometimes.

    —*Melinda L. Cousins*

Earth Boy

I sleep on silk on the ground, I choose my
home where ever to be found. Earth boy that
what I am. Something I know, grows from
the vines, grapes, tomatoes, and even a young
baby's life, can be found.
Earth boy, so what, the farmer's bless the
ground, sweat and earth, water and seed and
soon you see, the earth will grow enough food, to
feed a whole family. At night, I see the stars,
the moon, and walk upon the land. I have
all these wonders of beauty. To thank you.
For, the earth, that feeds me.
  Earth boy, so what? That what I am, I
sleep on silk on the ground.

    —*L. Ron Towsend*

Scars

The evil I have tasted is wine
Hopelessness adds flavor at best
I should have known what would come
But in innocence I could not have guessed

Steel now bars my emotions
Glass now blurs my perception
My words are controlled and passionless
My smile holds only rejection

My actions are guarded and bent
For though I speak and hear
I most resemble a puppet
With my past as my puppeteer

    —*Courtney Ka'Ohinani Rowe*

Mental Anguish

Mental anguish deep within
How long do you think it has been
Since you came and made my heart so blue.
With deep rooted feelings
Old and new
Mental anguish deep inside
So many feeling I've denied
I can't take this pain no more
I've no more tears for you in store
So mental anguish deep within
Won't you please let me win
And mental anguish deep inside
Let go of my heart
And let the pain subside

    —*Erin Marie Torrens*

Tribute to My Mother

(Dorothy J. Fluker)
How I miss you with each passing day
It hurt so much when you went away
The times we shared were so dear
In my heart I'll always keep you near
Even though you've gone on to a better place
I'll always remember your smiling face
You will always be my very best friend
Our friendship was one that will never end
You were always there when I needed you
Especially when I felt down or blue
You taught me to be honest and never to lie
Mom these things I'll remember whenever I cry
Best friend even though you are gone
I'll remember you taught me to be strong

    —*Darlene F. Krisel*

Behind The Painted Glass Window

What is it behind the painted glass window?
How is it that such a thing is special?
Just like love - it's beautiful to watch,
So simply found, but too often broken.
Love can be so fragile you see?
As easily broken as the painted window,
With the ping of a tiny rock
The gorgeous glass is shattered.
Just like love, with a problem or fuss,
Sometimes is broken.
Often too hard to repair,
But as I've been told before-
The perfect love is out there somewhere-
So strong that it cannot be broken,
And so beautiful it takes your breath away.

    —*Delisa Dawson*

Whilst the Flowers Flourish....

Thou art so sweet, akin the outcome of thee cane,
  How long will thee, the dulcet words remain?
  Tell me not now, for thou shalt not know,
  For if you do, thou love was ne'er so.

Thou shalt not gather flowers, b'fore their prime,
  Lest Flora, rebuke thee, for thy crime.
  Be it a flower, love much hath less appear,
  Be it love, a flower seems so dear.

  Hold true, my sweet, for love is on thy stand,
  Hitherto a bouquet, was cultivating in thy land.
Henceforth, thou shalt comprise a flower only of one,
With thy issue, all others will inevitably be done.

  Sorrow, sweet sorrow, already impressed,
  Undoubtedly, I know, I'll soon be at rest.
  Alas, thou garden of love, I abandon to thee,
  May thou roses be red, through all eternity.

    —*William Knight*

Nature

Nature is everywhere, trees, bushes and shrubs!
There's also termites, insects, human and bugs!
Outside at night where the sweet wind blows,
The crickets chirp, and the blue water flows.
There's dogs, cats and mice, flies,
Mosquitos and fleas,
And we are a part of nature as much
As any of these!

    —*Matthew Miles McCoy*

Forgiveness

To err is human, to forgive is divine.
How many times have you heard that line?
We'll all admit we have made mistakes.
We forgive our neighbor for the slips he makes.
We go to church, and the preacher man
Says "forgive your enemy" we say "amen".
But - wait - there is one person in our midst
Who isn't on this favored list.
"Who is this unfortunate person? you ask.
To tell you is not a pleasant task.
The President of the United States!
We expect perfection of him, dear mates.
If he makes a mistake, he is rarely forgiven,
But it proves that he is human, thank heaven!
He cannot please everyone all the time.
No human being is wholly sublime.
He is not a dictator, nor yet a king.
He cannot be blamed for everything.
We elect him, so let us appreciate
The choices we have before it's too late.

—*Elsie V. Long*

Seasons

Summer's here and now it's gone —
How quickly time goes by;
From Summer nights to chilling frosts
To Autumn days that make me cry.

Why must these Autumn days grow cold?
Why must the warmth of Summer leave?
Why must the Winter take it's hold,
And leave the woods with barren trees?

The blizzards and the Winter snow
Paint everything cold and white;
But eventually the snow will melt
And soon the Spring will be in sight.

And when the springtime finally comes around
And the trees are in full bloom,
The clouds subside, the sun comes out
And lifts us from this gloom.

And once again Summer's here
Though we know it won't last long;
Enjoy it now because we know
In the blink of an eye it will be gone.

—*B. Juguilon*

Remembrance

Yellowish pictures,
how wistfully I look upon you
this cold rainy afternoon.
Precocious, diligent schooldays flit by,
youthful dreams, joys and ventures far gone.

I sit alone at dusk,
tracing my footprints
on a faraway windswept sand beach,
missing the early poetic flash
of my melancholy eyes.
I wake alone late at night,
listening to the rain
pattering on San Franciscan roof,
trying in vain to stop
old scars bleeding
deep down in my heart...

—*Emily Yau*

To all Mothers

Yes indeed you are my beautiful mother
How wonderful you are
surely you remind me of a shining star
You shine through my life day and night
So beautiful you are so kind and bright
Just think how special you are to me
everyday in everyway is what I see
And dear mother how sweet you are like sugar and spice
What I want to say is you have been more than nice
Now I'm sure you remember all the times
We have had, happy moments, some nice, they were good, even sad
To say the least that's already been said
get ready for the best that's about to be read
Only you mom who is my dearest friend
So please mom hold up your chin
It is you beside God whom I can really trust
Mom hold on, this you must and never - ever forget
this poem that rhymes
But most of all Mom you are all mine
I love you mom very very much
And I'll always remember your warm mother touch.

—*Raymond Tillman*

"Parents, Show Me Love"

All I ask is that you never give up on me.
I am a blessing to you because God created me, see.
Always show me love no matter what situation arises.
I may turn to be one of your best prizes.

Take time to listen so lend me your ear.
What I have to say may be important for you to hear.
I'm not asking for all of your time,
Just a little bit for me may keep me out of crime.

Let me know it's okay to be angry with you.
Let's talk it over and figure out what to do.
When disciplining me, speak softly and slow.
That's the only way I will hear what you want me to know.

Be firm with me and stand your ground.
So I can grow up to be a find child all around.
I don't want to rear you because I'd beat a loss.
I really am aware that you are the boss.

I want to feel that you are not just my parent day after day.
I want you as my friend who helps me in every way.
Always remember that I am to honor, obey, and I do love you.
I just want the love you have for me to always be true.

—*Wanda M. McZeal*

Magic

You are there,
I am here,
but in my heart you are near.
Like magic, I close my eyes and you appear.

You are in my every thought,
My every move, my every heartbeat.
I wish to be your woman,
And you, to be my man.
Not to own, but to love and respect.

Let them not be your dreams, or my dreams,
but our dreams to cherish and hold dear.
Growing from them together,
side by side,
always in love with each other.

Like a romance that carries us away.
Like never before, like never again,
I, as your woman!
You, as my man!

—*Maria Mousseau*

A Woman....

a woman is what she truly loves,
am a small brown man child who sees God in every man and
ars even in the dirt.

I am what I love,
am a sharecropper who grows fruit and children; but never his
wn dreams.
I am what I love,
am Bach, Beethoven and B.B. King.

I am what I love,
am the vanity of a spring day and the desolation of winter.

am lobster and white wine; beans and cornbread.
am a sermon of the saints and the rampaging of a whore.

am a rose opening to the touch of rain
nd a dusk which closes the pages of the day, permanently.

am a sparrow sitting on the limbs of a tree watching God's
t in the heavens.

I am what I love,
ejoice for me for I have seen divinity within my own soul.
    —*Debra Lee McGowan*

I Love

I love only myself,
am a tightly wound rose bud.
I love God,
start to open my petals.
I love another human being,
y blossoming petals increase.
I love both families, then our children,
ouses, grandchildren, I blossom more.
I include friends, and neighbors,
y blossoming continues.
I love strangers, and my enemies,
become a full, blown, beautiful,
omplete rose.
ut, if, I keep the knowledge of this love,
o myself; and never express the loving words,
's only...loving myself....I'm still,
ne dimensional.
    —*Bonnie Lee Weishoff*

Psychological Chaos

y mind is in turmoil,
I am being pulled in too many ways,
ark figures are invading my privacy...
st, in psychological chaos
pain a problem to you?
you were I, you would be used to it.
m I being pulled into a different world?
death a release?
adows of reality are lengthening
s time comes to an end,
an the artist bend my moral?
adowed figures powder my ego
past the point of sand.
m lost in psychological chaos.
an you understand the words I speak,
or am I already too far gone?
ill you rescue me,
nd bring me back to your world?
ease.
    —*Rose G. Crawford*

"A Perplexed World"

Where am I? Who am I? I try to find myself, but I can not.
I am confused, I don't know how,
I feel lost but I am in here somehow.
I am unaware of my own identity.
My ideology is that this is my body;
However, this is not my mind.

So long ago I had a mind, but now I feel illiterate.
Oh! how uninhibited I have become.
I no longer recognize the people that I once adored.
I have memory flashes but all I remember feels so far gone.
I have forgotten the names of my favorite things,
of my children and all who are very dear to me.
I look in the mirror and I see someone unfamiliar to me.
I don't recognize myself.
I begin to talk to her and she does not answer back.
What is happening to me?
I look at my hands and I don't know what they are,
I have a body but not my mind.
I have not committed any crime but,
I am incarcerated in a world of uncertainty for all my life.
    —*Ana Castillo*

Land Of Milk And Honey

I am going to a place where there is no pain.
I am going to a place where there is no sorrow.
I am going to a place where everyday will be Sunday.
I will be greeted by warm open arms.
There I will be at my Eternal Home.

I regret leaving you, my love ones, all behind
But as time passes on, I will see you all one day.
Here is God's land of milk and honey to enjoy
the pleasures promised to all God's children.
Over in the land of milk and honey.
    —*Carolyn Slayton Slight*

My America

Oh my beautiful America how proud I am of thee
I am so glad that I was born in this land that is so free
I will always respect your colors your red white and blue
And to you my country I will always be faithful and true
I love you because you are blessed with so many beautiful
things to see
And you are one love no one will ever take away from me
There is no other country that could ever take your place
Because you are filled with so much love freedom beauty and
grace
I would personally like to thank you for all the people you
now protect
Because there are so many countries their people they neglect
So as we travel across this vast and beautiful great free land
I hope everyone will pitch in and give a helping hand
To keep you clean and beautiful for the next generation to see
And they too will be proud of this land that is so free
    —*Janice Peterson*

Absence Of Love

I need you — I want you, but no more —
    I am someone else betrayed.
        Down in my life I fall
        deep inside of myself;
down, down I go falling into the depth of hell
        for losing you I am lost inside —
    I am trapped in a case and surrounded in your lies.
        No more will I hear them;
        no more as you are banned from my life.
        Be gone; for no more do I need you.
I will cry, but not for love I lost for there was none.
    —*Anne C. Rackley*

I am the One

(Dedicated to Ian James Mitchell)
I am the way, the truth, the life
I am the light in your darkest night
I am all that you will ever need
I did it all on Calvary

I am the way, the truth, the life
I am the one who makes your path right
I am the one who's planned your life
I am the one who will do it right

I am the one who will make your dreams come true
I am the one who's done it all for you
I am the one who picks you up when you fall
I am the one you always call

I am the one who supplies your need
I am the one who plants the seed
I am the one who will watch it grow
I am all that you need to know

—*James J. Higgins*

"Who Am I"

I am God's greatest and most magnificent creation.
I am, within myself, a living universe, ever growing, ever
    expanding, and ever changing as the outer universe grows
    and changes.
I am the Lord's answer to love.
I am the master of this universe within, with a choice as
    to how this universe will function.
I am a human dynamo, with a programmable computer that takes
    the equivalent of a billion volts to power.
I am the manifestation of hundreds of millions of years
    of human mental and physical evolution.
I am the faith we so wonderfully seek.
I am the total sum of all mankind, and all I see is but a
    mirror of myself.
I am man,
I am.

—*J. Herbert Montgomery*

"Rainfall"

Floating freely, like a drifting tear,
  I anxiously await for the high tide.
    Weightlessly thrown onto the sand
and blown into the wind, where I may hide.

  Within the blushed sky, I calmly fly
    arising from the dim horizon sun.
Into the face of beauty, I travel again -
unable to escape, I become another one.

  Towards the stars, onward to my destiny
    amongst a path, I never come to a stop.
I fall helplessly unto the dark, infinite space
and back into the ocean, I knowingly drop.

—*Amanda Goodman*

Petition for Healing

Lord please spare the life of my son.
I beg your forgiveness of any wrongs he's done.
Though he may have wandered and gone astray.
Show him your mercy and light his way.
Heal him and bring him back to good health.
That's worth more to me than mountains of wealth.
Lord lift him up with the power of your staff.
Let me see him smile, let me hear him laugh.
Grant him your protection through this long night,
and your healing power, come the morning light.

—*Myron R. Fischer*

Spring, Spring, Spring

'Twas the first day of May
I awake at dawn
I wiggled and stretched and gave a big yawn,
I must get up, it's time to plant the garden,
It's time to plant the flowers and rake the lawn.
I hurry to the store to see what I can find,
I'm in luck, they have most every kind.
There's pansies, petunias, geraniums and moss rose,
With what I have, that should be enough I suppose.
I hurry from the store all ready to go,
But alas as I reach the car it started to snow.
It's been this way for days on end,
When, oh when, does spring begin?

I guess maybe today, for now the sun is shining,
And you know the saying, 'Every cloud has a silver lining'.
So take heart my friend, warm weather is on its way
And by next month it will be here to stay.
And by July we will be saying, 'It is so dry and hot.'
Was it this hot last year? 'I forgot, I'll swan, I forgot.'

—*Jody Jordan*

Lady, Are You Sleeping?

While holding your hand in mine, you whisper a sweet goodnight.
I can feel your heart, it's softly beating.
I'm tightly pressed against you, and I watch you as you sleep.
I can feel the love you give completely.

Lady, are you sleeping? Are you dreaming of things to come?
Lady, are you listening? There's so much I need to share.
Lady, are you sleeping? My heart is beating with yours.
Lady, can you feel it? Our love is pulling us there.

Lady, are you sleeping?

I lay here and I watch you, and I see an angel's face.
I can feel the peace, it flows right through me.
I leave my heart in your care, as I softly kiss your lips.
I can feel the joy, it shines so brightly.

Lady, are you sleeping? You're my friend, my life, my all.
Lady, are you with me? I'm so much in love with you.
Lady, are you sleeping? In this love we can believe.
Lady, can you hear me? There's so much for us to do.

Lady, are you sleeping?

—*James Thomas Blake*

Who Am I?

The radio and T.V. is my best friend,
I can hardly wait for day's end.
Seems I'm always in a hurry,
Backwards, forwards in a flurry.

My motto seems to be hurry up and wait,
Seems to me I never know the right date.
Always wondering how my spouse feels,
While absently working with my bills.

This road I live is lonely and long,
Seems they always know when to play "our" song.
Sometimes these weeks seem like years,
Sometimes it's hard to hold back the tears.

There are not complaints, they are facts,
Just like the proverbial "death and income tax."
So I sit and wait and watch to see
What the weekend will be like for me.

Do you think you know who's leading this life?
It's not only the truck driver, it's also his wife!

—*LaVonda Covaness*

Where I Might Rest My Weary Feet

can see no haven of retreat from death.
can hear no gentle voices calling - friendly - from around.
can hear no gentle sound - calling to my weary head.
And I can smile no more as I watch the ones well fed.

Surrounded on all sides by chasms of empty air.
try to beat my way through
As I fight little devils of dust surge up.
Which I must overcome.
I wish to reach lights and comfort and rest.

Is there no where on the way - where I may sit and rest?
Is this the life that God is using as my lonely test?
Is there a place following - where sins will be forgiven?
Or shall my wrongs hold against my soul?

And as my one and only goal,
Shall hell's dread fire burn and glow
And elsewhere milk and honey flow.
For those whose souls did pass the test.
Those who out did the struggle best.

can see no break in the terrible mist.
can see no light through the dark and the heat.

—*Rabab Sultana Khan*

Thoughts!

People are some times so mean
can't believe some of the things I've seen
People push you around
And they like to put you down
They say things that hurt you
And they try to make you feel blue
When you think you've done something good
They say you didn't do it like you should
You try to help someone out
And all they do is shout!
What kind of a world is it
When people get mad when you visit
Have people forgot how to care
And how to be kind to each other out there
Try to be kind to one another
And treat everyone like a sister or brother
People get it together
So we can make this old world better.

—*Cathy Durrett*

The Loving Song

She is all the beauty of a masterpiece.
celebrate her love, her charm in ease.
She wears a glowing crown only I can see.
We are best of friends-blinded by only me.

Upon a fancy carousal we have ridden
And in our secret places we have hidden.
We have walked a mile or two in all seasons
And wished upon falling stars without reason.

There was joy of parties-especially
Her laughter nearly angelic-heavenly.
Truly a Godsend worthy of much love-
Every star, every sunset, She's God's dove.

Her face shines in my soul forever long
Filling my being now and in the forgone.
Her love is strong and secure not weary or weak.
It comes from the core and grows pure and sweet.

Should we be broken apart in death's trap,
will remember, for our love is enwrapped.
Angel's shall sing sweetly, wings taking her home.
My heart will be aching, for now I am alone.

—*Peggy Gaudiosi*

Father's Poem

My bed doesn't feel so warm tonight,
I can't get to sleep.
I can hear mommy crying and there's a lot of yelling going on.
Mommy and Daddy didn't read to me tonight,
like they did last night.
We had a good day yesterday.
After school, mommy and daddy took me to the park.
We went out to eat at my favorite restaurant.
Mommy wasn't worried about the money it was going to cost,
like she's talking about tonight.
I can hear it...

Yesterday we walked by a big store window,
There was the beautiful bedroom set I've been wanting.
Mommy was talking about getting it for our new house.
Now she's crying about daddy not being able to work.
That means no bedroom, no new house.
I can hear it...

Yesterday daddy could carry me on his shoulders.
Mommy was telling Grandma that daddy may not be
able to walk again.
I can hear it...

Daddy went with some friends after work,
to relax and have a few drinks.
Mommy said he better be careful.
I can hear it...

Yesterday, daddy gave me a kiss good-bye,
Just like he did this morning.
I wish tomorrow could be like yesterday.
What a wonderful world this would be,
if drivers would remain alcohol free.

—*Katie Elizabeth Frank*

Moments of Thoughts in Time of Love...

Out in the distance,
I could see a sailboat bobbing softly.
Across the warm, blue delicate waves,
Restlessly and patiently it walked across the waters.

And then I remembered when those feelings were yours and mine,
They weren't long ago and are not far off,
It's just that sometimes we turn our love off.

To the warm, soft caresses that we love to give,
the soft, loving kisses that I miss.
To look into your eyes... and find a loving surprise.

The boat takes me back to a time not long ago,
in time nor in our minds,
When we relaxed and enjoyed each others company.

These are the things my heart bobs about as I look out to sea,
I see you, and me, happy and forever together in love....

Suddenly! I hear a bell,
And I realize no, I'm not out to sea,
But rather, it's the elevator summoning me.

—*Rhonda Robert*

Is There A way?

I never met a pain, that I would have
till the day I met the two of you
you said it was love at first sight
but just recently you had a fall through,
a bad connection on both sides.
Now you two say it is through. What is
this another question in the air or is
there a way?

—*Debra Sawyer*

Teeth

I was very tired this night,
I had been going all day, like a light
And what do you think,
I was getting ready for bed
cleaning my face
And the phone rang
wishing me Happy Mother's Day.
I took out my bottom teeth
and laid them down
And went to sleep
Woke up in the morning
and where are my teeth
I looked high and low,
and then pulled back the corners
And what do you think,
there were my teeth,
my prayers were answered.
They said, "Let's go and eat."

—*Mrs. Guy Richardson*

A Test

If your death was a test
I haven't mastered it, I never will
I get outraged at others
when they tell me how I should feel

The faith I had was tarnished
when I was left to mourn
You left me brotherless
My heart bruised and torn

I feel I was set up
put to a test I was destined to fail
Since you've been gone
my life has been a living hell

If this is a test
why make Eddie the object of pain
There was nothing positive to learn
there was nothing positive to gain

—*Belinda A. Dalton*

Wondering

In my green and pleasant trees
I hear the wind in my ear whisper by,
It beckons to me and with a tease
Listens to me as I gaze at the sky.

I run the dry leaves through my fingers
Wondering of nothing, just gazing on.
Seeing the stars as the night lingers,
Listening to the rustle of a fawn.

I pull carefully with all my might
Not to hurt it or to squeeze
A gentle flower that blooms in light,
Letting it go and flow in the breeze.

Then I watch the stars far above,
Now wondering, what comes of love.

—*Colleen McCahill*

Untitled

Laying here beside you
in an oasis of light
in a world of darkness.
Our love provides a pathway
for our thoughts to glide,
to serve as strength
as the base for my life.

—*Kerstin Gerst*

Ends of the Earth

Like a toilet paper roll
the layers are stripped
away
Leaving circling
shadows to rule
the day

—*E. W. Zeller*

The Preacher's Child

Standing on the wooden pew
I knew I must be very subdued.
But as I listened to him speak,
I leaned upon the window sill,
and there within my sight,
I gazed upon the meadow bright.
It whispered quietly in my ear,
as gentle breezes sweetly appeared.
They swept or flowers wild,
and grasses swayed in minute style.
Standing on the wooden pew,
I could feel the rhythm as it flew
around humming bees and chirping
birds in distant trees.
But when the cows began to low,
Oh, how I yearned to join them so.
Standing on the wooden pew,
I heard the meadow all attune.
It sang a precious lullaby.
It sweetly hummed, while I did sigh.

—*Susan P. Summers*

In Memory of my Dad, John Ward

When I go to the ocean at night,
I know my Dad is there,
Waving at me, with his big,
bright smile.
He's with peace in the ocean,
With the bright, full moon
shining down on him, from the
heavens above. When the ocean
hits my feet, I know my Dad
is in my soul.
I miss you Dad and
I love you very much.

—*Tiffany Ward*

"Emily"

On a warm fall night,
I listened longingly
to the beautiful sound
of a tiny child crying.

She screamed to the heavens,
"Yes, I am alive!"

The people around her acted annoyed.
"Damn nuisance.",
I heard one man complain.

It seems he'd forgotten
that he too was once a child,
crying for his parents to protect him
from the coldness of this world.

I just stood
and smiled to myself,
thanking the Lord
that her parents understood
the beauty of her childish ways.

—*Paul F. Webb*

The Hearts of Angels

There are two special people whom I love
They both mean the world to me
When they speak, they tell
only the purest truth
They have hearts that were
made by the angels in Heaven
Their love shines through
all others
No one else could ever take
their special place in my heart
I speak of the two best
parents anyone could ever know.
Dedicated to Jo and Kirk Ray
I love you both dearly.
You've taught me to look at
life with a better view.
I love you Momma and Daddy!

—*Kirk M. Ray Sr.*

A Nice Lady

There was a nice lady.
I met her at school.
Her name is Bonnie
and she's really cool.
She's really funny;
I love her laugh
If someone says tell a joke
she'll say okay, okay I path.
She worries about gray hair;
She doesn't have any yet.
She's not even picky,
if she gets wet.
She has a job,
she delivers it to you.
She makes pizza
and she's a mother of two.
I miss you already,
if you didn't know.
You're very nice,
and it sure does show.

—*Kari Lesniewski*

Invisible Friend

An invisible friend is near me.
I never sit nor walk alone.
When I grope for a new idea
I am never on my own.

When I'm considerate and calm
My friend responds with haste.
He says that rancor
Will lay a mind to waste.

When mental stresses burden
My friend will come around,
Infuse some spiritual energy
Which makes my soul rebound.

I sit now in a wicker chair,
My invisible friend is near.
He speaks inaudible words
Which only my spirit can hear.

—*Klean Kerr*

The Transformation

'Go to the light...'
I remember I said
as you laid there
lying in bed
I whispered "I love you"
into your ear
and hoped to God
that you did hear
for I felt your body
turn lifeless and cold
as you slipped away
I prayed for your soul
I want to just hurl
straight up in the sky!
Catch and kiss your spirit
I know it didn't die
Only your body died,
I watched your body die
I saw the transformation
I cried, I cried, I cry...

—*Dandrea James*

"The Kiss That Once Was"

Through the mist of the darkness,
I see the early morning light;
reminding me of you.
How childlike we were
Thinking it would last forever,
yet it was forever to us
Never ending love
sailed away with the tide.
Tho I still long for your love
The passion and the touch,
I know you've forgotten
The kiss that once was.

—*Chelsea Delz*

I Am Woman

I am woman!
I sometimes think the same as you
I may not speak and look the same
My skin colour my be different
For I am woman!
I have the need for success
For we live in the same world and
breathe the same air
For I am woman!
We must both walk the same road
living and dying
I bleed as you do and have a
heart that has emotions
For I am woman!
Created with a great need indeed!
A need for love and to be loved
That cannot be satisfied
Until we accept that we are all
equals put here on this earth
By one God.

—*Karen Gittens*

Ocean Wave

Back and forth
repeating itself
over and over
With curls of white foam

—*Amanda Hager*

Secret Crush

As he sits in his seat,
I stare at him, he doesn't
Know because he is
paying attention to class.
I stare at him.
I see a guy with sparkling
hazel eyes, and short dark hair,
a guy with not a care in the world
I see a guy that I like a lot.
I want him to stare at me,
but he doesn't know I exist.
As I turn away, I feel
Someone watching me, as I turn
To look I see him glancing
my way with a smile.
His smile is a sweet, knowing smile.
His eyes sparkle as if they're talking.
Oh, my heart aches,
Why does he have to be taken.
Someone tell me why?

—*Melissa Runion*

Silence Moves

The big picture window,
I stir on firm ground.

My face has no color,
my voice has no sound.

The silence, it moves me.
The still, rocket air.

The blindness conveys me,
and I dare not stare.

Lightening, still flashes.
The echoes are there.

Memories and nightmares,
Do not compare.

Quiet thoughts burn me,
Mind color aware.

Stillness in motion,
So deep, and so fair.

—*Amanda Lauren MacAlister*

The Drowning

I lose my balance as the wind blows
I stumble to the railing of the ship
The railing does not save me

I plunge into the ocean
I try to scream for help
No one hears me

I am consumed by a great mass of water
I try to swim to the surface, the sun
The sun has gone down

I see a piece of wood floating
I reach with frantic arms
The wood floats away

I notice a storm is nearing
I do not swim away
The waves drown me

—*Clare Russell*

Untitled

Today
I think
I'll run away
maybe where the river ends
and the music begins
I can run
and still be close to you
because we spoke of it
if there is no dragon in the street
if the black man lost his trumpet
I'll close my eyes
and cross my fingers
and wait for you to come

—*Michelle Lynn O'Brien*

Penitentiary

From day one I knew where
I was comin' from and I knew
where I was goin'!

House of rapture
House of purgatory

There where everyone fought
for peace and heaven. But
only one life was given on
to them!

House of purgatory
House of rapture

And all that's in the gray walls
of hell the Mother Mary belongs to
each cell! Too comfort them in
their living hell! Because if
fail won't stop you prison will

—*Dave May*

I Am

I am a goofy girl who likes sports.
I wonder what heaven is like.
I hear birds calling out my name.
I see stars falling from the sky.
I want to learn to fly.
I am a goofy girl that likes sports.

I pretend I'm a princess.
I feel as light as a feather.
I touch the pale blue clouds.
I worry about my future.
I cry when I think of graduating.
I am a goofy girl who likes sports.

I understand that God is real.
I say that we are all equal.
I dream of flying around the world.
I try to make people happy.
I hope there will be world peace.
I am a goofy girl who likes sports.

—*Dawn Thompson*

Naturally

The flowers and trees,
  oceans and sand
The sky holds the moon
  as a lady holds his hands
The world may turn
  and the rivers will run
But love will always shine
  as bright as the sun

—*Jessie J. Monty*

Old Men

When I was a youngster,
I wondered;
from whence came
all the old men;
needed to fill the halls
of worship
and deliberation;

Until yesterday;
when quite by chance,
I passed
a mirror.

—*Maurice M. Black*

Dream Poem One

During the graveyard shift
I work my longest hours
flying over Java, finding
lost old hills, lifting
strange sharp rocks,
fleeing deadly storms
painting changing canvas
that crumbles with the dawn
turn keys to doors I cannot open
and write long, long letters
to the silvery muted nights
until the first glance of daybreak
that comes like a loud red parrot

—*Marianna Callies*

Imagine That

If I were a cat,
if I were a cat,
imagine that.
If I were a cat.

If I were a dog,
if I were a dog,
would I sit on a frog?
If I were a dog.

If I were a cow,
if I were a cow,
I don't know how I can be a cow.
If I were a cow.

If I were a cow, a dog, or even a cat,
just imagine that.

—*LuRonnda Nicole Lane*

Lonely Willow

As she walks alone on a dusty road,
in a shroud of delicate blue
One could have guessed she once loved,
a good man - just like you.

A man convinced his standards
hold the only grain of truth.
Clothed primly in his perfection,
blind to others in their worth

Her life had been a sad life,
she'd lost her way, he knew
Yet his pride was such, he did not
see, her heart was good and true.

Still she carries a lantern with her
as twilight fades the day.
And her heart still prays he'll follow
if - he can only find the way

—*Laura Kemp Rosendahl*

You Are The Noble Part

What good is poetry when read
If no one knows what you have said?

Where is the music? Where is the song?
Where is the word that is so strong?

Where is the line that is so dear,
That when remembered brings a tear?

Let someone paint a phrase so bright
It charms and glances in the night,

And careless cuts a slash so real,
It leaves a scar that cannot heal.

All poets in your synthesis
At midnight desk remember this;

Your message is the noble part,
Torn from this nation's storied heart.

If it falls not on waiting ear,
Write not a line in tainted fear.

—*Harold Ross Sargent*

Ode to a Cat

Your cats may bring you countless joys
If they behave with equipoise.
But cats so often misbehave
And that can make you rant and rave.

Our cat deports himself with grace
And never ever leaves his place
He needs no cat chow for a treat
Because you see he doesn't eat.

He doesn't think of making out
He doesn't know what that's about
We hear no purrs, no mews or growls
We've no concern about his bowels.
Our cat's a statuette you see
Carved out of wood quite expertly
We call him "chips" - I tell you true
We'll always love him "wooden" you?

—*James M. Buckley*

DayDream

In the end I will see,
If they will come back for me.
Let them free on their own
And, you'll find they don't come home.
Everything that's left behind
Won't be seen in my time.

No one knows, and can't ask,
To look for pieces of the past.
So, in the end I guess we'll know,
What comes back when we let go.

—*Lisa Dallas*

Death of a Rose

Death has taken yet
   another rose from me
This loss is unlike any
   other, for it is the loss
   of my lover
Sometimes the pain is
   so deep and strong,
   I feel I cannot go on
But then I hear a whisper
   in my ear, "I'm here,
   I love you forever."

—*Charnelle Eckert*

After the Diagnosis

Walk beside me, death
If you must
I can live with that
I'm getting used to you
But slow down
Relax
There's a long road ahead
And you're pushing and pulling
Trying to pick up the pace
I need to rest
Go on without me
Others want you more
Tend those
Who call your name
I do not need you
Yet

—*Lorinda T. Butler*

Untitled

In July
I'll take a peep
down in the water deep
with roller blades
that are not cheap
rolling once
rolling twice
rolling chicken soup with rice

—*Christopher Simmers*

On Smoking

In the ghostly mist
Images bloom.
I puff the boot of Italy…
I puff the dots of Louis Braille.
Clouds of mysterious vapor
Form a trail.
I blow it all away
Like the pod of the dandelion.

Must I self destruct?
A poor puerile Ophelia
Wavering in a world of lets-pretend
Who cannot stop or stay the course
And chooses her own end.

—*Rhoda Torn*

"A Child"

A child is an
imagination let loose, the,
sun on a winter's day, an innocent
smile and a genuine love,
and the gratitude
for life itself.

A child is also
a loving test from the One
above, given with only one instruction
manual-the Bible, for he
belongs not to us.

He is a treasure from God.

—*Jennie Garland*

Dream Incubation

Now I lay me down to wake
imaging the life I'll make,
Mother/daughter, Father/son
Super-, sub- and conscious, ONE,
Now the unreal's very real
Then again it's mere ideal.
Symbols true aren't often read
Yet life's message they have said.
Ere I lay me down to dream
I'll plan a portion of each theme.
—*Janice Baylis*

Famous

You want to be famous
immortalized
in hearts
carefully broken
Upon your white horse
glistening sword at your side
you have all the golden words
and gentle killing moves
to make pain
almost feel good
in your fine art
of leaving
—*Phoenix Brina-Magitant*

Purgatory

A small
imprisoned man
waits
in a concealed jail
separated
from all society
secluded
from reality
trapped
in his own consciousness.

A small lost soul
suffers in a remote world
confined by the ideals of man
suppressed by injustice
in between both good and evil.

A small powerless child
without control of his own destiny
locked up by the Almighty forces
amidst the unforgiven isolated
in Purgatory.
—*Katie Moylan*

Untitled

I wondered up a strait,
narrow, warm, ray of light
from souls of deepened
thought.

I know wonder along
shores of blue heaven
which creeps over
depths of my heart.

One beat at a time
carried in maze
of misery.
—*Megan Cadwell*

Topsy-Turvy World

I live in a topsy-turvy world

The warm sun chills my bones
In a crowded room I'm all alone

the silence deafens my ears
I get younger with the passing of years

I shade my eyes from the dark of night
And look unseeing in the bright sunlight

Colorful things all blur into gray
Twenty-four hours seem less than a day

Living not dying fills me with dread
My coffin will be a well deserved bed

The silent storm frightens me
The obvious I don't see

I live in a topsy-turvy world
—*Matthew L. Krites*

Into The Grinder

Life passes by
In a short, wispy dream
Your mouth is dry
But you didn't scream

No looking back
Your skull starts to crack
Don't try to shout
There's no way out

Time goes slow
As you wither away
You don't even know
What happened that day

No looking back
Your skull starts to crack
Don't try to shout
There's no way out

You open your eyes in a snap
Your sweat makes your body gleam
You think about all that crap
And lie awake from the dream
—*L. Heidi Manschreck*

Feline

I walk in the night
    in darkness
I am black, a raven
    no a cat
I walk - featherlight
on soft padded paws
In darkness yet,
    I see
green eyes
    seem to glow
In dim moonlight
and reflections show
from off of raven fur
I am feline
I am queen
—*Aimee L. Peterson*

Music

I lose myself
in every beat
the haunting rhythm
the illusion, the heat

I surrender myself
to every song
a story unfolds
of right
and wrong

Here the images
come to me
my soul
My music
I bring to thee.
—*Patricia Johnson*

The New Overview

New houses
In hunter green
With crisp shades of canary
Shining windows
Showing dignity
Presenting happiness.
Then over chartered years
Dulling to a plain overview
With overgrown hedges surrounding
Frayed edges on a shaved lawn
Like a marriage ending.
—*Kaliska A. King*

Whispers in the Wind

A cool breeze whispers,
In my ear,
There are so many things
I have to fear.
Losing my happiness,
Is what I fear most.
It fades away slowly.
Just like a ghost.

I want to believe,
I'll have a great life,
And the thought pierces me,
Like a knife.
I cry softly,
My thoughts have me pinned,
And I know someday,
There'll be no more
Whispers in the wind.
—*Cynthia Cox-Lofland*

Snow

Snow
It covers the little town
Like a blanket
Shimmering,
Shining,
Protecting the houses
From the
Harsh hail
That will come later
—*Janet Boysen*

Life Goes On

In my numerous mistakes —
  In my pains and aches —
    I have been like steel,
I have known bad brakes —
  I have run into fakes —
    I thought to be real;
I have been terribly sick —
  I have lived like a trick —
    Lonely and depressed,
And in the same breath —
  I've been closer to death —
    Than I care to express...
I have been blocked and barred —
  I have dropped my guard —
    To only be hurt,
I have suffered defeat —
  I have been tricked and beat —
    Clean out of my shirt...
I have gone astray —
  I have been betrayed —
    Confused and lost,
I have lost my head —
  I have been mislead —
    Let down and crossed...
Yet not to be bragging
  But in spite of it all,
My feet are not dragging
  I still stand tall.
I am determined still
  With an iron will
    To keep up my chin,
To keep right on moving,
  Learning and improving,
    A man among men!!!
      —*Vincent L. Johnson*

Gloom

The grumbling, fretful clouds complain
  in noisy discontent;
With melancholic weeping until
  umbrella tent is rent.

A soggy blanket wraps the trees
  to drip and trickle down;
It dampens scratching chick-a-dees
  that dig in leaves gone brown.

While graying flannel wraps the earth
  in suffocating brume;
The glowing birth of yesterday
  is buried deep in gloom.

When hope is lost in darkest hour
  the heavens dry their tears
And shove away the leaden clouds
  for sun to reappear.
    —*E. June Mathews*

"Why Love"

Why love, when your
  heart will brake?
Why love, when you'll end
  up I'm pain?
Why love, when love will
  not love back?
Why love, to love when
  nothing but harm
    will strike back?
    —*Ryan Eulalia Thomas*

Faith

Were faith a thing that we could hold
in our hands to weigh, to see....,
Would it be strong, heavy, bold,
or dark, wet sand to lay, to be
Swept o'er and covered by life's sea
of toil...trouble...misery?

Were faith a light to show the world
our trust in God...His Holy Word,
Would it be a beacon bright
to pierce the darkness with pure light,
Or could it e'en a candle light,
to push the gloom....out of a room?

Faith comes by trusting God, dear friend:
His love for you His Son did send.
He said He'd shelter, clothe, defend
those who on Him will depend
all of their life...'til journey's end.
    —*Jim Anderson*

Pool

Thoughts flow like water
In the clear pool of my mind
Ripples of thought
One drop falls softly
Leaving slight waves of ideas behind
As the waves touch the shore
They leave their mark in the sand
Slowly dunes form
Sand is carried away by the wind
It breaks away at old ideas
Creating sand
Which washes to the pool
Each drip grows stronger
Until the pool is a torrential storm
The beach is racked with waves
The wind howling
Mountains disappear, reduced to dunes
Footprints in the sand are erased
Until the pool is silent once again.
  Dreams and change, my mind's gentle
pool
    —*Chad Bonaker*

My Lovely Rose

My eyes used to shine so bright
In the color of your sun
My world so big
My feelings bled
Everywhere I turned
Everywhere was red

You sat stop your golden throne
While I knelt down and wept alone
Desperately I gave my spirit,
My heart cried out but I didn't hear it

Quietly I bowed to you
Quietly I died in you

Now ghosts have crept up
on the dew
And like a thousand endings
is my love to you
    —*Monica Del Rossi*

Royal Gowns

Royal gowns are the best
In the North, South, East, and West
When you wear a Royal Gown you look
like a queen
Even though your just an ordinary teen
People might say your dress looks shiny
But you'll feel guilty and a little tiny
Why you might feel this way
Is because you took it this day
    —*Kealani Kukula*

"Lover's Fantasy"

Star - kissed lovers who met
in the past;
Then lost each other on the
road of life.
But searching, ever searching,
with the brilliant light of faith.
enduring hope,
And the "Guides", angels
that they are, providing
them courage to go on with
their quest;
Until their paths cross
again.
Rejoicing with the glowing
Contentment of love and
happiness,
Knowing they will not ever
separate again.
    —*L. A. Mauro*

His Call

What is important
In this life anyway?
Is it anything we do
Or anything we say?

It is the listening
To His still, small voice
It is the yielding to God
As we make the right choice

It is the obeying
At His urgent call
As He speaks to each of us
Saying, "Give me your all."
    —*Elwanda Barrett Johnson*

No Color - Just Human

Confusing life is
Individuals we are
Separated we all have become,
Judging one another by color,
Black, White, Hispanic and
So on,
When will it end.

This cycle we choose not to pass on.
Those who fought for freedom
also wanted equality
We say no color just human,
this is the only race we
all choose to be...

... The Human Race!
    —*Carmen S. Pearson*

Morning?

Death is but a sacred birth
into which lulling grasses give ear
mind or matter
int nor morgue
t shall not draw you near
And when the time
it doth shine
a glimmer, glossy path
true love my dear
true love
the best of 'er a lass
—*Jeanette Reese*

Untitled

My stomach
is a road of bones
(and you live there)
sad reminder
of the fury of autonomy

Beyond the rusted fence
there are no words
only numbers scratched
in cruel strokes
cold streams
I wear on my face

Your fingers are broken
From carving out a place
For me and still I sleep
In the field
in the road of bones
where your voice
does not penetrate the weeds
—*Amy Balent*

Time Turning

Mother Nature
is flaunting her magic again,
wiping away the winter gray
and snapping cold.
Cupped within the fresh greens
and explosions of floral color,
the spring earth spills out
all its promise of richness
and eternal renewal
and we are naturally warmed again
at her pleasure.
—*Norma Rosenfeld*

Doctors

To right the wrongs of Nature
is God's work
So we are Gods
Or his hands
Or his brain.
And when we fail we are men
Frail, confused, hurt men.
But tomorrow we are God's again
weaving our way
through miracles that make life
And probe and ponder
and look through the secrets of God
To raise a fallen body
To clear a clouded mind.
And so to men we are Gods
To God we are men
And to us we are neither.
—*Melville G. Rosen*

The Road To Hell

The road to hell
is hell indeed.
Drink a little alcohol
smoke a little weed.

All seems like fun
until fate takes your hand.
Then the road to hell
isn't so cool man.

Repentance is no longer there
it's all down hill.
Why you ask
it's not your will.

You no longer choose your destiny
you no longer think for you.
Now it's in satan's hands
what shall you do.

You scream and scream
for help as you fall.
As you get closer
you hear satan beckoning his call.
—*Deanna Duquesne*

Opposites

Joy, left over,
Is hidden behind the pain
Love, pushed away,
Cannot keep us sane

Hatred, out front,
Blinds the masses
Fear, we hope,
Soon it passes

Birth gives
What we need
Death kills
The growing seed

Push away the wool
From over our eyes
Seek the truth
Deny the lies.
—*Catherine Griswold*

What?

What is this world?
Is it all a lie?
Are you real?
Am I?
Is this just a dream or is it
A scheme?
Is it a trick of some kind?
Is it a trick of my mind?
What is this planet that they call
Earth?
What was I before my birth?
—*Brigitte Libby*

Fields Of Beauty

In fields of golden hay,
the skies are never gray.
The sun will shine,
and sparkle like wine.
The flowers are yellow,
and the hills are mellow.
The skies are blue and bright,
because everything is alright.
—*Keith Jones*

What Lies Ahead

She looks in the silver
mirror and she sees a face,
a face of bewilderment.
She realizes that the face
is of her own, and her future
lies in the destiny of
that face.
—*Chava Weller*

Moss-Less

A traveler they say
Is one who can't stay
An appreciable time in one place...

He's just looking for fun
Or a place in the sun
But the point of his matter is space...

He's got nothing in mind
Of the facts he is blind
But comes time for 01' Gabriel's call...

He'll face to his reckoning
With that specter beckoning
And have no regrets, none at all.
—*Judd Griffin*

Stars and Strises Forever

Stars and stripes for ever,
Is our nation theme.
Loyalty is our motto as it may seem,
A tribute to our country, we must never,
never fail.

Stars and stripes for ever,
May we never, never fail.
To take command with our chief,
For life and liberty of our land,
Stars and stripes for ever,
We must always stand.
In this world of sorrow, we must
pay and plan tomorrows,
For the stars and stripes today.

Tops to tops in action, long may
our nation reign.
Our chief has the password, ten to
one he'll say.
Our votes are free, we'll keep them
To wait that future day.
—*Mary Lucy Shimp*

Worried

I'm worried about you! Why?
Is that the question you ask?
Why do you ask me such a dumb
question? Can't you see that I care?
That I love you? I care about
everything that happens to you.
I know I shouldn't say I
love you because I shouldn't
be "in love" with you! But I
have tried to keep these feelings
from coming and I told myself
thousands of times that I'm not going
to fall "in love" with you but
these feelings are strong and I
can't keep them inside of me
forever!
—*Julie Myers*

Advise

Trouble and woes comin' your way
Is that what I heard you say?
Well hush my child
And listen a while
To advise I give you today.

You don't kick a guard dog
While he's eatin' his food
To do that would prove you a fool.
You don't hunt big bear
With an old pump gun
Unless for your life you don't care.

So be wise my child
Stop and think a while
And from this a lesson learn.
The secret in life
Is to avoid strife
And many good days will return.

—*E. R. Cruz Thacker*

Flag Day

To imagine a day without the flag
is the day I cannot remember,
the red, white, and blue,
the one hue;
visioning the world
far the greater,
unfolding a new era,
knowing the eagle
is there;
battle field of suffering
changed o'er the years
ships at sea, rain,
and wind,
and the flag would stand.
Clinging belief of all that has been,
would be, and will always see the moral
reason in the land, symbol and unchanged,
a flag, a pole, on which it is hinged.

—*Jois A. Gould*

A Lover's Eyes

Intense
Is the feeling of love
That never ceases to amaze.
Just one sweet little gaze
That opens up the soul
And takes a peek inside.
Shall I confide,
Or just hide
In the tender embrace
Of a lover's eyes?

—*Michelle Vences*

All I Remember

All I remember of you
is the way you held me
close and looked into my
eyes, the way you made me
feel like I was important,
the way you said you'd
never let me die, the way
you told me you loved me
always and forever is
all that I remember

—*Mandy Claborn*

Living Mural

With accounts of countless images
is there more to see?
The picturesque portrait of quality
hung for all perceived.

With divinity displayed
in a portrait framed,
the masked quality of disguise
covered forth in shame.

To observe the product
within the hand of God
is the beautiful mural made
of living matter and of sod.

—*Rhonda Morford*

Inspired Thinking

What you want
   is what you desire
and nothing more
   try telling it to a child
with her mind in the clouds
   Getting through isn't as easy
as counting backwards
   Her thoughts are confused
and have no order
   it's a shame that desire
isn't what she needs
   Or the dreams that she
dreams of are impossible to reach
   what kind of world is she living
in, that she has to fight for sanity,
   but inspiration is the ken
that keeps her surviving.

—*Kimberly L. Stratton*

Virgin

   The first penetration,
      is with the eyes.
   Upon becoming physical,
      on touch we rely.
   Touch to be touched.
   Kiss to be kissed.
      This is a must,
   or these will be missed.
   Care to keep contact,
      in passionate ways.
      Love to be loved.
      Love everyday.
   Express your affection,
communication promotes release.
      Smile knowingly,
         inner peace.

—*Freddy Gabriel*

Shadow

There's a shadow on the wall,
It doesn't move at all,
I didn't know what I saw.
When I move it moves with me,
It's a shadow of me that's what I see.
The shadow of me is scaring me.
I hate to see that shadow of me.
Why the shadow scares me I don't know,
I just can't wait until it goes.
I hate that shadow of me,
But that is the only thing I can be.
That is what I am,
A stupid shadow on the wall.

—*Katie Sullivan*

Untitled

Welcome back to yesterday
It all seems so far away
But when I close my eyes
I start to realize
That there was nothing really there
That there was nothing that we shared
You simply opened up the book
You turned the page and took a look
You read the words that had to be
You saw the darkness point to me
You crossed the room, my heartbeat raced
You saw the color on my face
Blue neon numbers in the air
And then I helped you take me there
But all and all not much had changed
I was still moving in your maze
You laughed at me without a sound
I was lost with what I'd found
I wish I'd flown to higher ground

—*Holly Elkins*

Love

My love is like a rose -
It blooms in brilliancy -
   But I forgot to add water
   and put it in the sun.
Now it's black and withered.
I touch the petals and
   they crumble.
All that remains is a stem -
My love is like a thorny stem. . .
   ouch!

—*Heather Benshoof*

Love

Love is like dandelions
It blossoms from an innocent bud into,
a maturing flower then, with time
into the most matured pad of seeds
but, it doesn't matter when some
young innocent child blows it and
make a wish for it seeds have
been spread
To form more of the endless germinating
flower
Even though that one love came to an
end many off-spring and learned
mistakes came from it so that,
every time the cycle repeats it only
blossoms into better things.

—*Alyson Richardson*

Miracles

   A miracle from God
is like a drop of water
   to a thirsty man.

   A miracle from God
is like a life saver
   to a drowning man.

   Miracles are both
of these and more; and
they come only from God.

—*Paula Jolliff*

Love

Love is like a thunderstorm
It comes on very strong
Yet it diminishes just as fast
If that love does not belong

If you truly love someone
You have to set them free
If they venture back to you
Your love was meant to be

But if your love is unreturned
If they are led astray
You have to let them live their life
For love is made that way

If his love stays just as strong
It just might be the start
Of a beautiful rainbow that leads
To the pot of gold in your heart.

—*Kristy Gratchen*

Fog

A white ghost of fear
It comes when ever it wants
And always near.
When it comes it blocks out the sun.
And you see nothing
but hear faint voices threw the
thick mist.
It's dark and cloudy can't see at all.
but playing hide and go seek
you'll have a ball.
It's no telling when it will go
away or come back again
because it is the white ghost of fear.
And fog will always be near.

—*Logan E. Schalk*

Cry to the World

Cry to the world;
it comforts me.
It helps me,
holds my hand,
justifying my weak steps.

Pray to the world;
it thanks me.
It touches me,
grants me forgiveness,
sending me to my destiny.

Hate the world;
it angers me.
It keeps me,
pulls me downward,
hindering my free movement.

Fight the world;
it hurts me.
It kills me;
takes my power,
tossing me into the black skies.

—*Nikki Williams*

The Illusion of Love

Love is an illusion
it comes on the
Wings of a dove
and leaves on the
tip of a sword

—*Kathy Masters*

Loneliness

There is a dark cloud hanging over me.
It covers my whole world, and shadows
   my place in it.
I can feel its rain as salty tears,
   running down my face.
Stinging my cheeks and staining my
   pillow which my head rests
   uneasily upon.
Sometimes in a dream it goes away
   leaving behind only rainbows.
Yet when I wake, it is still there,
Burdening me everyday.
So much I can no longer see the light.
I feel as if sometimes I'm just waiting
   for it to open up and rain
   down on me.
Pounding harder and harder, drowning
   both my heart and soul.
Only leaving me one day to be
   dead inside forever.

—*Anjanette Beaudion*

"A Valentine Poem"

I bet your guessing who?
It doesn't matter because I love you!
It isn't a crime,
I just want to say be my Valentine.
So how about it Love Bug,
How about a kiss and a hug?
I'd feel like a dove
If only you'd give me your love.
Just say those three words
And we'll become a set of love birds.
How about a shake for two?
I'm really wild about you.
You are so sweet, you make my heart beat.
Let's meet, how about at nine?
We'll dine and have wine
And I'll ask you please be mine!

—*Marina Mungia*

Untitled

God made love,
   It gives...
Love does not force,
   It accepts...
While taking nothing,
   It grows...
Love never loses,
   It glows...
While my eyes may not see,
   It shares...
Love cannot stop,
   It heals...
Never fooled by any scheme,
   It knows....
Love is always caring,
   It shows ...
Through growth and understanding,
   It shall be...
Love is peace,
   To set us free!

—*Albert Ebbs*

The Fodder of Evil

Screaming of agony,
it has no sound.

Odorless, tasteless,
yet pungent and bitter.

Untouchable hardness.
Violent.

Far reaching, still very near.
With no beginning or end,
not subject to time.

The fodder of evil,
familiar, well known.
Its title...

RAGE!

—*Roxanne Brenton*

What Is This?

What is this?
It has tiny eyes,
A miniature nose,
Two small hands,
And ten little toes.

It cannot talk,
It only cries,
And looks around with inquisitive
eyes.

I try to discover what I am admiring.
Maybe I can find out
Why it is crying.
Where did it come from,
And why is it so trying?

I ask my mother,
She always knows.
"Just what do we have here?"
She replies as she glows,
"This is your brand new brother!"

—*Judith A. Flounders*

Love

Love is so many different things.
It lets people grow together.
Love is a special part of life.
Life is a world of hate,
Without love in it.
Love can also make people grow apart.
Love is joyous.
Love is sorrowful.
Love can't really be explained.
It's different for everyone.
Love is whatever you want.

—*Jennifer Ziemba*

Graduation...and After

Happier days we'll never know
Treasured memories they'll bestow
As down life's highway we depart
A glad song ringing in each heart
Each to his task with a cheerful smile
To make this world a place worthwhile
Each day account for some kind deed
Help out a friend we find in need
Remember life may be so bright
When we ourselves provide the light

—*Earle F. Taylor*

Save The Rest

I speak for the forest.
We once lived together in peace,
Now we live together in destruction.
It's up to you to take care of us.
It's up to you to protect us
It's up to you to save the rest.

—Lani Elbao

A Flying Pig

If I could give the world a gift
it would be a flying pig.
This pig would help us in many ways.
The pig could transport things…

And he wouldn't pollute the air
because he has wings.
Since this pig has wings
he needs no gasoline.

I think a flying pig
would be a perfect gift
to make a better world!
…for you and for me.

—Xochitl Cruz

Yesterdays Lunch

I remember the schoolbus
It's drone and its bumps
and the smell of reportcards.
I remember college pumping
dime after time into
Hungry xerox machines.
I remember bottlegrime as I
scrub with a Christmas tree brush
as my little ones scream.
I remember hurried dinners where
the dry onion isn't yet soft as we eat.
The search for misplaced library books
still hangs in my mind.
The lake that witnessed silently as I
grew is still as real to me as I am.
Of all the things that burn and linger -
still I have no recollection of
yesterdays lunch.

—Jane-Alexandra Krehbiel

Am I My Brothers Keeper

Am I my brothers keeper,
I've enough troubles of my own.
Should I go see about him,
when I know he's all alone?

Am I my brothers keeper,
Should I let him know I care?
Should I help him out of trouble,
for I didn't put him there?

Am I my brothers keeper,
Should I ignore him when he calls,
Should I help him up again,
when he stumbles and he falls?

Yes, I'm my brothers keeper,
for God has told me so.
If I fail to help my brother
when of his needs I know.

God will ask the question,
"Why do you hate me so?
For failing to help your brother,
you're hurting me too, you know."

—Agnes M. Hagin

I'm So In Love With You

Ever since I looked into your eyes,
I've wanted to be with you,
But now I really know
My love for you is true.

I never want to lose you
I decided long ago,
And no matter how I feel,
I'll always let my love show.

I hope we never part
Because of your smile.
I never want to leave you,
After a short while.

I'm so in love with you,
Please never say goodbye,
Because my feelings for us two
I'll never let die.

—Stacy Somerville

Mike and Jane

Mike and Jane.
Jane and Mike.
Are together in eternity.

Mike and Jane.
Jane and Mike.
Are together until the end of time.

It's so fine. When he is mine.

Mike and Jane.
Jane and Mike.

Romeo and Juliet.
Are in love.
And they died.
It is something above.

Mike and Jane.
Jane and Mike.

—Jane Ketelhut

The Balloon

There it was,
Just a lifeless thing on my bed.
Then I blew it up
Until it was just as big as my head.

After that I let it go,
And watched it sail through the air.
Up, up, up, and away it went
With absolutely no cares.

Just floating majestically
through the sky
With no destination
Going wherever the wind would take it.

There it went floating peacefully
over the tree tops and houses
Until suddenly a bird came along and,
Poof! The bird popped it.

So down, down, down went the balloon
Until it landed on the grass
And once again
It was just a lifeless piece of trash.

—Laurie Zajaczkowski

My Heart Lives and Loves

Someone said my heart
just keeps me alive
it just has four chambers
doesn't care that I live or die.
But when I'm heavy with sorrow
and I just want to cry
my heart is heavy
for no reason why
my heart bleeds for me
when I'm not happy, but sad
and it skips a beat
when I'm surprised or glad.
It's the base of my life
it keeps my conscience true
and because it keeps my body
live, it must care about me, too.

—Christienah A. Robertson

Two Pressed in Passion

And the two of them stood there.
Just stood there kissing.
Each so beautiful
From what I could see,
Each so beautiful in his own way.

I remembered so vivid
So vivid my own times plural.
Yes, I've been there, but not there now.
I felt everything they felt.
To combine,
Now combined, with my own feelings.
Those now felt many times more.

My soul jumps to their bodies both.
I am their lips and tongue.
I am vital parts.
I am lonely, but do share,
Share in your thoughts.
I share your love.
I share your bodies.
I am with you and am there.

—John Caccavalla

I Adore

I adore the way you walk into a room
just to kiss me
I adore the way you walk ahead of me
Then wiggle your fingers behind you
For me to catch your hand and walk
beside you

I adore the way you surprise me with
The sweet things you say
I adore the way you kiss me on the top
Of my head every time you hold me
I adore … you

—Jenelle Jackson

Thanksgiving Prayer

It shouldn't come just once a year.
We should spend every day
In thanking you and praising you
For loving us this way.
Yet human as we are,
We need this feast day set aside
To help us all remember
How deep your love.

—Charlie Sue Thomason

Akin

Two hearts beat as one
rounce the thrill of surprising
events that may come.
—*C. Goethe Sharps*

Clouds In The Sky

The sky is like a light blue hue,
just waiting for people like you
to view.

As the clouds moved across the
sky, you wished the moment
would have never died.

Images of places came to life
before your eyes, then you had to
say your good-byes.

To the many clouds that made
you wander and think; while mother
nature began to awake.

While they were in movement you
stood there and stared, while wondering
what the world would be like if
no one cared.
—*Crystal Dalangin*

Shamu and Her Baby

Shamu and her baby,
Killer Whales from the sea.
Shamu and her baby,
very nice you see.
Splashing,
jumping,
twirling,
gliding,
smiling for you;
Shamu and her baby
swimming gracefully.
Shamu and her baby
very fun to see.
Shamu and her baby
in captivity....
Shamu and her baby,
I'd like to see them free!
—*Emily Fengler*

One Mother's Love

Dear Mary Karin - let's be
kind to each other,
 Although I know I'm not the
perfect mother.
 I don't always express my
deep love for you,
 It's always there like the
morning dew.
 I love you as high as an eagle
can soar,
 And many times stronger than
the oceans roar.
 I willingly accept all the
shame - the blame
 If you'll only forgive me for
being so lame.
 I will always be grateful
to the God above
 That He gave me a daughter
such as you to love.
—*Colleen Van Nieuwenhuyse*

"Lost Love"

Lost love is in the past somehow I
knew it wouldn't last.
 Shattered dreams have torn us
apart
 Never again will my life find a
start
 Memories of you linger in my
mind
 It's over now I'll still love you
all the time
 I'll think of you when nights
are blue
 Lights down low I'll still love
you so.
 If you don't love me I'll learn
to see we were never meant to be.
—*Andrea Ueker*

Warriors Lover

Courage, oh determined warrior,
knowing not the cold or noose.
Marching always forward,
trampling those who traduce.

Abide to the soldier,
soothing his destination.
Nothing lost in doubt,
learning in step, life's lesson.

Tribute to its vestige.
Sing the requiem song.
Given in life's strength,
Courage, marching strong.

What the elegy is to the valiant
and to the victor goes the spoils.
Midas knew a good thing,
and liberty knew its loyals.
—*Reed L. Standley*

You Are a Gift to Me

(Dedicated to Dr. J.M. Kennedy)
Last night I saw a shining star
far from the cloisters ruling the sky,
it seemed to be there just for me
 .....shining so proudly and so high.

I wanted to take that star from the sky
and hold it tightly in my hand,
so I could have it for the path ahead
 .....to have a light wherever I stand.

I unwrapped my dreams, made them wishes
and sent them on a passing breeze,
wishes of peace, happiness and life
 .....the night that I met you.

The star will be there, whenever I need
just as you are and offer to be,
that the road ahead will be shared with you
 .....for you are a gift to me.
—*Carol Dearns Corabi*

Learning

I learn best when left alone;
To think and talk on the telephone.

Don't think I'm crazy, if I seem lazy.
It's just because I know this lady;
She's strict and stern.
But oh! how she makes learning fun.
—*Ada B. Culbreth*

My Dream

I had a dream
late last night
that the world was clean
and there were no fights.

I had a dream
about our Lord,
how He gave his Son
to suffer on two boards.

He done this for all of us
so we could have life forever
but only if we believe in thus
shall we suffer never.

Jesus Christ was the one who
died on the cross.
He is the only one
who loves you even if your lost.

So get with God and stay with God
forever and ever Amen
If you do you'll be glad
for you'll never suffer again.
—*Heather Nibert*

If

If I could for a single day....
Leave myself
and go away;
I would journey
to a place
where I would feel
no more pain;
where storms...
were a thing of the past
and I would feel
calm—at last;
a place where I would always be
loved and protected,
and never feel...
scared or rejected.
Oh, the journey
I would take,
if, I could for a single day...
Leave myself
and go away.
—*Kelly I. May*

Untitled

Tears ran down our faces
 Leaving little streaks,
 While we spoke of the things
That had been wrong the past few weeks.

 As we talked
 we both cried,
 But both of us were honest
 Neither one of us denied...

 ...How we really felt
 What we really wanted,
 The things we brought up
 Needed to be confronted.

When the moment comes around
And it's time for "us" again,
 I'll be here waiting
 Just like I've
 always been.
—*Holly Colburn*

Wonder

The last wisp of gold melts away;
Leaving me;
I sit under an immeasurable vastness.

At a glance it seems to be a wasteland
Of nothingness;
But I know of its true greatness.

I feel it pressing down, gravitating;
I wonder…
My mind is on overload.

I have to suppress the urge to
    stretch out my arms and
Bring all of its power
Into one small point where I can
    quench my longing to know…

It's wholeness blankets me —
Suffocates me with awe.
I crave to explore every facet
    of it's surreal expanse.

    I see …. the universe.
    —*Valerie Valentine*

Fresh Hell

Just to jar myself
    left lost upon a shelf,
      till the label lifts
        falling flat to the floor
Along with my intentions
    that fade so far away,
      like the wasted days
        of my newly closed doors.
    —*Frank S. Farello*

Let's Discover Each Other

When we each discover the other
Let our song be a simple melody,
Not the sounds that often smother
The true nature of a tender rhapsody.

Cast away those tunes of worry
That we all bring from youth,
Which tend to make us hurry
And forget to pursue the truth.

May our greatest single endeavor
Be to let our love so weather,
That others might see forever:
How we really do live together.

Let our days be filled with glory
As we search in our time to find,
The best place we can in the story
To be played by all of mankind.

When darker days are wont to abound,
Be soon to note a way for us to take,
So we sail along and not run aground;
Failing to see the beauty of our wake.

May we often count our blessings
While we play the game of life,
And not just address the dressings
Which leaves much room for strife.

    —*Richard Shield*

What About Life?

Life is precious, life is valuable,
life is not to be wasted or dismissed.

Life is material, life is physical,
life is you and I.

Life is significant, life is meaningful,
life is our sons and our daughters.

Life is spirit, life is soul,
life is our feelings and sentiments.

Life is the world now and hereafter,
life is our future, don't take it away.

    —*Jennifer Wander*

Left Behind

Screaming your name into the
    light,
While I am left in the
    darkness.
I know you hear me,
    but you keep walking.
After all that has happened
    between us,
You can still walk away?
Don't you hate the pain?
Can't you feel the sadness?
    At one point,
I expected you to turn back.
I expected you to look behind you.
But you never did.
You just left me there
    Screaming your name
      into the light,
While you left me alone
    in the darkness.
    —*Eva Strickland*

Closely Arisen

Cover now the spread of
Light.
Open a road, a
Seasonal Bridge.
Empty into the Night the waking
Load. Worlds
Yet to be.

A round
Into a
Shining pool of water he went
Eagerly and laughed. The Soul
Narrowed with dexterity.

Purple Blue and Yellow
    Very slowly lift the necessary fog
And turn it into flesh
    As all the scales from all the salty fish
Create the bog and gather in the mesh.
    —*Regina Jakstas*

Untitled

How do I know when to believe you
When you always lie
How come I put my trust in you
Thinking you were the guy
How come you took my heart
And broke it in two
How come you didn't tell the truth
When it was the right thing to do.
    —*Kim Coppola*

Broken Heart

Within the wind of my mind
Inside the sun of my skin
above the stars in my eyes
with the touch of my hands
below the drops of my tears
I hold my broken heart.
    —*Nancy Wessel*

True Love

You're my true love
Like a dove,
I watch over you
    Saying…
"I love you."

It's so hard to do
But I manage to get it out
Sometimes at night I pout
Because I feel…
    Our love will peal

We shall not part
    Because…
      Our love is from the heart.
    —*Carrissa Settje*

What Is Love

Love strikes without warning…..
Like a giant spider spinning a web
wrapping it's victim in tiny threads…
Precisely-slowly…until the victim
lay helpless
Everything happens so quickly
The victim doesn't seem to notice
And now he turns to the spider for help
He doesn't seem to know
it was the spider who did it all
The spider eyes his new prey
He hasn't eaten all day
He won't give up the victim…the fly
The spider feels contentment…
knowing his stomach will be full
The fly feels warmth…
knowing the spider is near
Neither can get away…it's like love
    —*Dannice Munson*

The Terrible Warlocks

When the day is bright,
like a shining light,
and the night is black,
like a smoke stack,
it will be scary,
so be wary.

Beware of the warlocks,
who break your locks,
they'll turn you into a frog,
or maybe a hog,
they'll put you in a blender,
so you will taste tender.

Or they might turn you into a drink,
and it will stink,
maybe they'll have you fried,
or maybe dyed,
but if your name is lee,
they'll have you set free.
    —*Ryan Adkins*

Blind Trust

Like blind Justice knows
she will eventually see.

She strikes a comfortable pose
Upon your shoulder, listening.

She is mute and must trust Justice
To speak wisely for them both,
Which She most often does
With Grace and Compassion.

—*Rebekah Tate*

Black Divinity

Black is divine; like red red wine
Like grapes in a vineyard or getting
cozy in the winter. Black is a vibe
of maroon, or a cool breeze in June.
Black is a spirit like an ancient
melody when I here it. Black is
knowing, being smooth and flowing
like rivers and waterfalls. We see
the cultures and embrace them all.
The black origin puts me in bliss
and makes me reminisce of long, long
ago, cause black was a show; the
greatest on earth, cause we were
the 1st. We gave all the others
their birth. Black blows my mind,
devours mankind, with its naturally
darker genes. Uplift the black
regime...

—*Kwanza Reid*

Have Learned Loves Meaning

I have learned loves meaning.
Like no one else.
Hear my restless heart beat.
Feel my ardent pulse,
everyone still talks.
When I take my walks,
but I confess I walk alone.
Never, never do I phone.
What good is solitude.

'Is a sorry mood.
And then there's worry.
No more do I hurry,
Run to the street car.
Gaze up high, so far,
I have learned love's meaning.
My gold ring needs cleaning,
because I spill silver champagne.
but why should I complain,
Love's meaning will soon go away.
We'll meet again another day.

—*Henry J. Dugen*

Only

only love was easy
only dreams were bold
only youth lasted
quick as growing old.

only kindness was shared
only more people cared
all the world could be spared
only...

—*Kim Briel*

What Happens to the Stars in Day?

Do they fly higher in the sky
like raindrops after a storm?
Or do they sit there and mourn?

Do they sweep to the sea
like fire from the sun?
Or do they run?

Do they hide behind the puffy
white clouds
like the sky so blue?
Or do they disappear like a
morning dew?

—*Elizabeth Chapin*

Waiting

When the world whispers into your ear,
listen for it calls your name.
In these still and sad serenities,
I too, will say - your name.
Almost scared and almost alone,
I get lost, lost without faith
because I know I can still hear,
hear those words that disappeared
from me, almost left for memories.
Always a beginning to an end
and an end to a beginning...
tears and sorrow fill me now
for I can only whisper, I cannot shout,
for I can only remember, I cannot see.
For I can only speak, I cannot sing.
I am still, still sad and quiet for
I am almost alone. But I have faith
that leads me not astray. I know
that someday I will sing, sing your name
again.

—*Kiana-Min Kang*

Nite And Day

The moon was rocking in the sky.
Little birds went flying by.

Stars are blinking here and there.
As if they never had a care.

Sunshine rising in the East
like a great big yellow yeast.

When day is thru you'll see it's best.
For the sun to get sleepy in the West.

—*Beverly C. Hannan*

Is It There?

Is there a world where I can
live in? Where I can lift my
voice and take a stand?
Is there a place I can fit in?
Where there is no need for
commands?
Is there a place where I am
wanted? Is someone there to
comfort me? And to take away
the past that's haunted? To
make a future safer to see?

—*Jolee Tucker*

Once Upon A Long Ago

Once upon a long ago,
Lived a lonely man.
Keeper of a gentle flame-
An ancient master plan.
Diligent and ever true;
Practicing his art.
Champion and protector of
Symbols on a chart.
So close to his heart.
Once upon a nevermore
You can see him still.
Standing for what he believes
Atop his lonely hill.

—*Glenn Wescott*

"Living In The Past"

I find myself
Living in the past
Holding onto a love
that did not last
Always dreaming of you,
And the time we shared.
Back when you were here
To show me you cared
But now you're gone,
and deep down I know
That maybe I should let you go
I would if only I could find a way
To stop living in the past
and start living today.

—*Rebecca Smith*

My Lover

My lover is tall
Long, silver blonde hair streams
in the wind
Golden, flashing eyes
and a ready laugh.
Cool creamy skin
and full, red lips
(a temper as fickle as the wind)

He wears a long cloak
Shining blue and green
(a storm rides his back)
Flashing crystals
button the pockets of his vest
as white lace
Shimmers at his wrists
We come together
and his cool lips kiss my hands:
This is my lover
The sea

—*Kanani Curry*

Ultimate Woman

She is like a champagne glass.
long, slim stem
supported by a sturdy foot.
A crystal body
slimming at the neck.
Her face
inviting every man's lips.
Tingling the ones
lucky enough
to taste her.

—*Philippa*

Untitled

I remember summer evenings in July,
Long winter days
Sunday drives which lead
To our favorite Ice cream
Friday night outings.
The blue water of the pool
Family dinners every night,
Vacations more fun than a
Birthday party.

I remember valentines days
filled with roses.
Christmas trees loaded
With family ornaments.
Easter egg hunts and
Thanksgiving Turkey.
A Graduation Dinner that
I'll never forget.
I remember Dad.

—*JoAnn Colon*

"The Way You Are"

As gentle and kind as you are...
   lovable as a bear
And as sweet as sugar can get...
You're always there cheering me
   up and making me laugh
   That's the way you are
I thank you with all my heart...
   'cause if it wasn't for you
   my life would be boring and
   depressing
I'm glad I met you.
It's just something about
   you that makes me bugout
   with you at all times.
And I feel so secure around you.
So don't you ever leave me
   here all alone.

—*Juliet Alvarez*

"I Love You Now And Forever"

If you're ever going to love me
love me now while I can know,
All the sweet and tender feelings
which from real affections flow.

Love me now while I am living
do not wait until I am gone,
Then chisel it in marble
warm love words on ice cold stone.

If your dear sweet thoughts about me
why not whisper them to me,
Don't you know it would make me happy
and as glad as glad could be.

If you wait until I am sleeping
never to waken here again,
There will be walls of earth between us
and I couldn't hear you then.

So dear if you love me any
even if it's a little bit,
Let me know it now while I'm living
so I can own and treasure it.

—*Linda Webb*

Chaining Nature

I will edit the sunset
Make its colors bend
Into an unnatural dry evening rainbow
So it suits the purpose
Of looking on it
To show a symmetry
That fractured clouds
Are unaccustomed to
And orders a universe
That wants to go astray.

—*Edmond Todd*

"New Calcutta"

A sick, addicted dirty musician
Making crazy sounds on a broken sax
Plays the subway platform homeless,
But the winter is warm
So far.
He plays incoherent upbeat
In a downer life
Alms for the poor, alms for
The poor, the blind, naked,
Strung out, demented city
Entertainers needing a place
To end their frantic tour.
His empty open case
Has been terminated, exterminated
By the department of caring.
He blows,
There she blows,
Rising,
Calcutta in New York.

—*Howard Ostwind*

Devotion

Ancient fruit of Earth's desire,
   mating of Sulfur and Friction
Wavering tongue of captive fire
   chanting psalm of benediction.

A thousand times a matchstrike's flare
   melds into a cadenced prayer
And hushed shadows pro'cess the walls,
   elongated and far-flung, tall.

Consort of a passionate flick,
   teases Dark with sultry nimbus.
Held by a vow to candlewick,
   haloed, candescent, luminous.

—*Nancy Clare MacKenzie*

Extinct

What is extinct?
Means not what you think!

It is forever gone,
No one left — to carry-on;
No life, no breath...all passed beyond.

For fish and reptiles we feel disdain,
Birds and mammals we weep in pain,
But for man who soon will wane —
We do not think! — we are too vain.

—*Nicholas Petracca*

Walking

Right foot, left foot
Mile after mile.
See the slim birds & trees
Kissed by the suns smile.
The wind is brisk & free
Am I losing weight yet?

Right foot, left foot
This is good for the heart.
I'm dreaming of cakes & candy
When I return to the start.
The doctors say walking is dandy
Am I losing weight yet?

—*Richard P. Sanders*

I Am Misery

I am misery,
Misery is my soul.
Misery lives within.
Haunted dreams,
Fill haunted nights.
The tears that fill my eyes,
Will fall into the wells of misery.
My own world of fear.
My own dark, cold world of silence.
No one knows,
What I hold here.
Many years of long, dark silence.
I cry tears of blood,
Into the bottomless void that is my soul.
I am misery,
In the pit of despair.
Why must I be misery?
After all
Misery is me.

—*Neolla Schunk*

Mistakes Along the Way

Mistakes we've made along the way.
Mistakes that brought us to this day.
The path I chose was paved with tears.
Countless times I hid my fears.

If I turned back the hands of time,
Reclaimed youth that once was mine.
To do it again on a kinder path,
To keep me from another's wrath.

I wonder now what might have been,
Had I made different choices then?
What fame in paths unknown back then,
I might have found in brush or pen?

What if I found a love so fine,
A love that I could call all mine?
To stay with me through all the years,
Without the secrets, tears and fears.

Mistakes we make along the way.
Alas! The price we each one pay!
'Tis the harsh reality of life,
We learn by error and by strife.

—*Jacqueline Sharp*

Why Can't A Man

Why can't a man be more like a woman
more sensitive
more willing to give

not so selfish and egotistical
not so in need of control

and what makes a man so violently mad
clad in a raging storm
what makes him perform in that crazy way

killing and fighting
raping and ranting like a raving bull

say - why can't a man be more graceful
express his feelings like a woman can

why can't man - instead of power
learn to enjoy a flower
or comfort a child in need

is it greed or a power game
all the same
in the end - no one wins

so - why can't a man be more like a woman
can
why can't a man
        —*Randi Hill*

Untitled

She wants
more than anything
to take back her life
to be like everyone else again
but IT
will not let her
IT
grasps her soul
so fragile
so delicate
Her soul
is being crushed
like the petals of
a withering
fragrant
ROSE.

        —*Lauren Cunningham*

Dear Mom

Harriet Nelson, June Cleaver,
  Mrs. Huxtable, too,
Mothers we all envy
  Still none compare to you.

Like a rock so solid
  Your love is always there,
Any time I need your help
  You always take good care.

You've given me so many things
  How much we'll never know,
You've shown me all the things I need
  To truly help me grow.

You've filled my life with so much joy
  It's more than I can say,
All the very best in life
  For you these things I pray.

When it comes to mothers
  You surely are the fairest,
This is just a note to say
  I love you, Mommie Dearest!
        —*Craig Covington*

Without Saying Good-bye

He left without saying good-bye
More than once, he made me cry.

I wish we could've said good-bye
Sometimes I wish I would die.

We've had some good times
and some bad.
He's said some things that
made me mad.

What's worse is he said he'd
come back.
I look up now and all I
see is the sky so black.

Not a single star to
wish upon.
It's hard to believe that
he's really gone.

I get lonely when I look
up into that same dark sky.

I really wish he wouldn't have left.
Without saying good-bye.
        —*Erin Parker*

Meditative Observations

The outage rays the setting sun
Moves gently across the grassy plain
With rippling grass and straying wind.
When one observes the setting sun
A true belief is in the mind.
Nature is not a stolid thing
To stay its own and bring no joy.
My thoughts return to a summer's day
Of long ago and far away
Of things forgotten, not returned
Until I walked a summer's day
        —*Henry Trent*

Why?

Figures on paper,
Must have meaning.
When a person is created,
They must have feeling.
When a red light shines,
You must halt.
If the gun goes off,
It must be your fault.
When music plays,
You must hear a sound.
When a person is lost,
They must be found.
When there is darkness,
You must see black.
If it's not the front,
It must be the back.
If you're not right,
You must be wrong.
You're not one of them,
So you must not belong.
If we're not at peace,
We must be at war.
If you're the government,
You must know what it's for.
        —*Shana E. Dempsey*

Untitled

As I sleep at night
My dreams are of you
If not for those dreams
My life wouldn't be true

For the way that I feel
My love can't be a lie
For how much I love you
I am willing to die

I call you on the phone
So much as I can say
I'll love you tomorrow
And also the next day

Before you say I lied
I first must have a chance
To prove how much I love you
And that's by way of romance

To end this poem
What more can I say
Only that I love you
In a very special way
        —*Benjamin Jackson*

Silent Night

Now I lay me down to sleep.
My eyes don't shut, nor do I sleep.

The silent night doesn't hear
my tears, as they beat like
thunder in my ears. They
shine like beacons confessing
my fears.

Prayer is real and God is
good to see me thru the silent
night. So I pray the Lord these
tears to see and wash away
my fears from me.
        —*Pamela L. Coffey*

Untitled

As I lay in the dark and dank
My eyes slowly opened
And my heart quickly sank
The sight I saw propelled my fear
Sweat on my forehead
A ringing in my ear
The vision I saw
Chilled my soul
My mind was in awe
My blood ran cold
The edge of fear the dark of night
Did not impair my blurring sight
The sight of satin, pleats, and pillows
And my mind filled in horror
For in the world of life
I will walk no more
I feel like the larvae bee
Entombed in its hive
With an agonizing scream
I know...I'm buried alive.
        —*Jodi Jennings*

Silent Love

I really can't explain in words
　my feelings are way to strong
The way I feel about you now
　my love just can't be wrong

I think about you day and night
　and my thoughts are so very clear
There about me holding you
　holding you so near.

It hurts for me to think about
　you with somebody new
All I can do is trust in God
　and hope he leads me to you.

For now I'll just be friends with you
　and hold my true feelings in
But just remember this silent love
　I'll love you till the end.

—*Kelli Welch*

Crystal Shards Of Glass

Like crystal shards of glass
　My feelings broke apart.
Ripped and shattered pieces
　Torn from my heart.

Like crystal shards of glass
　Memories crash my mind.
Broken and battered dreams,
　Some I'll never find.

Like crystal shards of glass
　Too delicate to touch.
Crunching under my feet,
　The pain is just to much.

Like crystal shards of glass
　Blinking in the light.
Brilliant and dazzling,
　This just isn't right.

Like crystal shards of glass
　To be swept off the floor.
With sharp and jagged edges,
　You simply wanted me no more.

—*Donna Schurle*

Untitled

I had to go away,
my feelings for you
I could not say.
I didn't see you much after,
I miss the talking and the laughter.
I was loving you from the heart,
It was breaking to see us apart.
Even though I can't see
you everyday, you're in
my heart in every way.

—*Devon C. Filosa*

God's Love

When you see Kim and
Gene unite in marriage,
And they ride away in
a beautiful carriage.
Listen to hear the coo
of the dove,
You will then see the work
of God's love!

—*Lauren Bennett*

My Grandmother's Grace

Sh h h h h h! I hear
my grandmother calling, calling
after me; a voice of love, a
voice of freedom, a voice of
joy and sweet victory. The sweetest
person in the world, she was as peaceful
as a dove; one thing I shall never
forget is my dear grandmother's love.

As I gaze into the clouds, I
see my grandmother's face; a
smile brought down from heaven,
to bless us all with grace. In
that host of angels on high; a familiar
voice can be heard, humming the
Angelic songs of truth and faith;
The heavenly sign of my grand
mother's grace.

—*Tonya R. Davis*

Forever Lost in the Mystic Morn

Forever lost in the mystic morn
My heart was his
Until it was torn.
He said that he loved me
I believe it was true.
When deep inside it would hurt me
I just knew.
It wasn't on purpose
But just the same
I loved everything about him
Just hearing his name.
I wanted forever
I thought so did he
I guess I was wrong
When he turned to flee.
I don't know what happened
That sorrowful day
All of a sudden our love slipped away.

—*Julie Mackelburger*

A Silent Get Well Card

　My hands are shaking
my knees are getting weaker
with every word, I can't
believe what I just heard

　I feel cold I'm turning
white my whole body is
filled with fright

　I feel depressed I feel
dead like a board stiff and
hard when I think of him
lying there ill and scarred

　I never much thought about
what I would do if anything ever
happened to him but now I
think living without him would be
very hard so my heart is sending
him a silent get well card

—*Crissy Lee Zerden*

All Woman That's Me

All women that's me
My looks and taste
Everything is good to see
All women that's me
Me and you you and me
Everything we do we do at ease
All woman that's me
You can tell by looking at me
My body and skin
The touch that puts me to sleep
All women that's me.
All women yes indeed
All woman that's me

—*Allynn G. Farrare*

My Destiny

I believe in my destiny.
My Master, drew my blueprint
Before, I had a choice.
This is the only way.
For me to go.

I'll keep my eyes, on destiny's road.
I am journeying where
The choice belongs to my Master.
My soul knows no other way.

I may venture where,
Others seldom go.
My destiny is predetermined
And my blueprint was designated;
Before, I had a choice

I may visit unfriendly places;
Where no one welcome me.
Because my hope is deeply rooted
In my masters choice,
This is the only way for me to go.

—*Henry D. Coleman*

Unborn

I am unborn child.
My mother did not love
me enough to bring me
into this world.

I thought my mother knew that
I was a human, too. I
was alive until my mother
killed me.

I look down from heaven,
and see my mother going on
with her life, just like I
was never a part of it.

Every time, I see her a little
teardrop falls down to
earth. To touch her.

She now realizes that I was
alive. And now she loves me.
But now it is too late.

—*Nicole Davis*

Dreams

If you have a dream,
    let it roar.
Make it a goal,
    Strive for more.
Goals can be accomplished,
    just strive for the best.
No less, no less,
    just the best.
    —*Dana Mitchell*

Sweet Misery!
My only comforter.
Through the nights of cold sweats,
Through the days of distant
    memories.
Taking me into his grips
Flying free through the sky;
He keeps me tight to his chest,
As we glide above the dreams
    of others.
Some sweet and some traumatic
The horrific nightmares of
    headless animals.
The wickedness of the fiery
    mountainside smelling of
    burning flesh and hair.
I dive to my destiny.
    —*Dawn Secor*

Lost Love

I never got to see you,
my precious bundle of joy.
I never got to know you,
were you a girl or a boy?
I never got to hold you,
and rock you to and fro.
I never got to kiss you,
or count your little toes.
I never got to see your face,
eyes open with a smile.
I never got to have you,
even for a little while.
I never got to keep you,
I had to let you go,
I never got a chance to say,
I really love you so.
    —*Debbie Gasparovich*

Seeing Inside

My shadow...when it follows me:
My shadow when in front...
My shadow...
    like my mirror,
    like my image,
    like my life.
My image when it watches me:
My image when outside...
My image...
    like my shadow
    like my mirror,
    like my life.

My mirror when it mimics me:
My mirror when inside...
My mirror,
    like my enemy,
    Reveals me
    when I hide.
    —*Anne Leigh Andrews*

In My Dreams

I saw you in my dreams
My soul, your soul runs deep
Forever in my dreams
Together in my sleep

I saw you in my dreams
You lay down in my heart
Forever in my dreams
Together, not apart

I saw you in my dreams
I'd rather be with you
Forever in my dreams
And then a dream come true

I saw you in my dreams
As happy as can be
Forever in my dreams
Together you and me

I saw you in my dreams
A piece of golden art
Forever in my dreams
Forever in my heart
    —*Cedric L. McGhee*

Nature's True Wonder

Yellow, green and gold
Myriad colors unfold
Sheaths of beauty to behold
Nature's wonder to be told.

There is love in every hue
Stop and take a look at you
Can it be a sign of life
When it seems a time of strife?

Brown and orange, rust and tan
All come together as a clan
Testing us on what it can
Daring each and every one.

Comes the rain and with the wind
All our colors drift away
Into the soil and left us bare
To wander until spring again.
    —*Elsie M. Ryan*

His Shoes Not Mine

In his shoes not mine, I stepped
Never again to roam
He said unto me, "I'm here to help"
"I'll never leave you alone"
In his shoes not mine, I walked
With strength like never before
Without hesitation, he talked
Of the things I had in store
In his shoes not mine, I felt secure
With no doubt inside of me
The road ahead for me was made sure
When he said, "I'll be your security"
In his shoes not mine, I awakened
Being glad for a new day
Knowing that I would not be forsaken
When he's with me along the way
In my shoes everything seemed wrong
Life was hanging on a thin line
Now my weaknesses have been made
strong
'Cause I'm in "his shoes not mine"
    —*John McClung, Jr.*

He Who Has Gone

He who has gone will
never be again, but the memories
of him will be all some know of
him for many years. Though he may
have been bad, we must think
of all the good things he's done,
because we must sorrow on his
death as his loved ones. God
took him from this planet so he
could be happy in heaven than
be sad in jail and in hell.
    —*Nikki Kirchhefer*

Anyone But You!

I could have walked away and
    never looked back,
I could have picked up my life
    and never thought twice.
If it had been anyone but you!

I could have overcome the burning
    Of passion in your eyes,
I could have ignored the fire inside,
If it had been anyone but you!

I could have been strong and
    looked away,
I could have lived with myself,
If it had been anyone but you!
    —*Linda D. Tarantino*

Words Come Knowledge

Knowledge! Grown in words,
    Never was anger or in pain.

Knowledge was never meant to borrow
    or loan.
Also better gains, knowledge of fame,
    that which isn't insane.

Knowledge of world, greater words.
    Above, also bout the world fames.

Although knowledge of words is greater
Victorious of fame, but never anger
    or pain of knowledge unnamed.
Where words are unspoken
    or unwritten.
    —*William Yates*

Journey

May God be with you
    wherever you may go.
Though sunny weather
    and deep white snow.
To show you the way
To give you the power
To lift you high into
    another day.
From the heavens above
To the mountains below
To the guilt you've given
    to those you love.
    —*Cory Davis*

Tribal Affiliation

Campfires burning in the winter
night
unlike the streets of the city
with its lights and artificial heat,
caught between two times,
passing through,
knowing and not knowing of the life
of long ago.
Trying to do what I must,
thinking of Tunkashila and long ago.
Cooking on a woodstove,
home-made bread,
hunting, a good winter,
spring and the passing of a season.
City bars and talk of going back.
Tradition long lost.
Come and talk with me of our past.
Are we Indian
or just memories
of a burning campfire?

—*Ed Little Crow*

Death

Death that's all I think about
Night and day
Just waiting for it to come my way
When will it happen?
Please tell me when
Life is too hard when night
and day is always in pain
Please tell me when it's going
to come my way
you start with one pill then you
go to two then ten, but yet
nothing happens.
What do I have to do to make
it come my way?
I try and try but yet nothing
works, help, help, please help
it to come my way.
Maybe it will be today, maybe
it will be tomorrow, but yet
nobody knows when it will come....

—*Clarissa Castaneda*

Night

The sun has fallen
Night has newly come
Day is dying
So have our souls

Our souls are stolen
By the night
Freedom is right by day
Prisoners by night

We will all rest
Our souls
One last time
One last time

—*Deborah Kay*

Life

I spoke to my friend who is dying
When I said, "goodbye"
I started crying
My friend said,
"Don't cry for me
I am living happily."

—*Renee Roll*

Birthdays

I had another Birthday
Ninety now in all
Some I can remember
others I can't recall
I can walk and talk, hear and see
the sun above, a bird up in a tree
I have so many memories
of all the by gone years
Some are happy, some are sad and tears
I thank the Lord for growing up
and for the years He gave me
and for all of those who were
and are my friends and family
I am grateful for my blessings
whether they be great or small
But, I just can't believe how fast,
the years have passed
Some how I thought,
that they would last.

—*Esther H. Hubberstey*

A Picture of My Mother

It's a picture of my mother
No artist can portray
It's a picture of my mother
When God took her away

She was laying in her casket
So peaceful and so quiet
A smile upon her dear face
And hair of snowy white

I stood there as they closed the lid
I raised my eyes to God, and prayed
He had taken me instead

Now I am getting old and gray
And that picture still lingers
In my mind today
It's a picture of my mother
No artist can portray
I said in my heart she is not dead
She has only gone away
To become another flower in God's
bouquet

—*Nellie E. Davis*

Love

What is love?
No one can explain it,
The power it does bring,
The feeling in your heart,
It will surely bring.
It makes you want to sing,
And fly all about.
And if it's true, and they love you too,
You'll want to be together,
Always and forever.
And if it's truly love,
You'll know it from the start,
Because when your not together,
You'll feel years apart.
And when the day does come,
When your love has left, and never to
return.
Then always remember, the love that you
had shared,
When you were together,
And never to be apart!!!

—*Angela Holden*

Life

Life is a puzzle;
No one can put together.
We have to live it
day by day from dawn
to dusk.
People we see day
to day are trying to put
their puzzled life together
piece by piece.
Day after day pieces
are lost, causing confusion
in the puzzle we call...
... life.

—*Sara Michele Tennyson*

Eternity of Reality

Muffled sounds encompassing —
No room to breathe.
A light at the end of the tunnel,
The growth of a seed.
Fight, kick, push for freedom,
The grass is greener on the other side.
Or is it? For famine has fallen
Upon the monster's hide.
Almost there, almost out
Why must this be so hard?
Head first is always best
Yet the truth seems to be marred.
The light hits full force
Like a slap from behind.
Now it seems the thing to do
Was to stay for more than nine.

—*Marina D'Abreau*

Love's Meaning

I have not mingled with the rich
Nor kissed, a "royal" hand,
Nor lived in splendid grandeur
In this, my native land.
But I have known a baby's love,
Her laughter and her tears,
Shared her little jokes with her
And quieted her fears.

Now I remember waking up
To "Boogens" on the stairs;
A childish voice calling to me,
"Nanny, I'll be there!"

I would not trade that baby's love
For all the wealth on earth!
Whatever pain life has bestowed
That blessing has been worth.
She seemed to know I needed her.
She must have needed me!
And isn't that what love's about
In its entirety?

—*Mary Durham*

My Wish

Oh! God, this battlefield
Called life:
Like soldiers we drop.
Save me from the
Swinging blade of harm.
To join you while I live,
Is my wish! Not to
Meet you in death!!!

—*Harold D. Nell*

The Most Fun Wins!

Now if you play a game
not for fortune on fame,
And you play it for fun,
then you've already won!
Just try to learn each day
from the games that you play.
You'll be your own best fan,
think and say yes I can!
And before games begin,
know that the most fun wins.

—*Don Fogle*

Farewell for Now?

Farewell for now but
Not for long
For we all pray for your
Safe return.
Do not weep though far apart
Our eyes and soul for you
Do yearn
Until the day you do
return.

—*Agnes K. Bahr*

Thought

Often I think of you when you're
not here
Even fantasize to hold you near

Your face, your voice, our last
embrace...

And in this moment as I visualize
your grace, your walk, your
infinite style
or seeing myself in your deep
brown eyes

watch the clock, calculate the
time and comfort myself in the
thought that one day you
will be mine.

—*Marcia*

The Child

The child sits, and quivers, and cries,
Not knowing quite what to do,
Parents not loving,
No one wanting,
The children of the world.

The child stands, and yells, and screams
No one wanting to listen,
But hearing still,
In anguish and frustration
The children of the world.

Now the child lies down wearily,
Giving up
His battle
For the sake of
The world of the children.

The people, children once themselves,
Talk quietly.
Was love a right they possessed?
Or one given to them for the sake of
The children of the world.

—*Leah M. Wiens*

A Memorial of the Vietnam Police Action

Reflected I see my face
not my name
and my spirit echoes those around me
give back to those now gone
memories shared
their hearts forever open to bullets
sent unwelcomed home
now at last welcome
a sort of homecoming in the reading
of those names, never forgotten
our nation's dead
the tomb of the known

—*Walter Williams*

Sunshine At Night

I have a sunshine,
Not only in the day,
But at night.
And every time I see him,
I feel just alright.
Whenever I'm lonely,
He comes around
Perks me up, -
And loves me down.
Whenever I'm cold at night,
He cuddles with me,
And holds me tight.
My parents love him,
They say he's cut.
And I want you to know,
That I have a sunshine,
Not only in the day,
But at night.

—*Kimla Mason*

Relationships

Relationships are special,
not to be abused.
With both giving and taking,
not to feel used.
The trusting and caring
are a good place to start.
These are some of the emotions
held close to your heart.
Consideration and understanding
are an important part too.
Feelings can be easily hurt
by the things you say and do.
Communication and expression
can be a real sensitive part.
That's where misunderstandings
and dissension can start.
Together and with patience,
it's a lot of work, as you see.
But alone, without relationships
where would we be?

—*Dixie Rollings*

Wakening

Winter sleeps cold upon the land
with spring held gently in her hand
and through the mist I dimly trace
warm promise etched upon her face.

Silver soft the half light lingers
dark and dawn delay,
reluctant lovers loath to part,
give up their tryst to wakening day.

—*James E. Koontz*

Untitled

Colors changing on green water —
Yellow to gold to lime.
Movement in the other green, too,
Leaves like birds take flight
The autumn falls
Too early the dark.

—*Alyzsa Van Til*

I Shimmer In Your Light

From behind the frosted glass.
notice how the winter night
bleeds into morning.
I imagine a giant sluice
drains the starless night away,
leaving the sky awash in pearl grey.
With a great flap of wing
some great black crow rises
from the barren elm.
And a grey squirrel eyes the seed
scattered on the crusted snow.
Stark images, black on white
outside the frozen pane.
The dog paws at the door,
while the TV predicts more snow
You call my name,
I shimmer in the morning light.

—*Pat Hayden*

Without You

I am here and you are there,
now I have nothing to spare.

You were my life, my love, too,
now I have nothing to do.

As long as I've known you,
I have been strong, now you
are gone.

Words can't describe how I feel,
all I know is that you were real.

I thought my love would keep
you alive, but somehow you
couldn't survive.

Please listen to what I am
saying, I just want you to
know my love is not fading.

—*Amanda Jackson*

Vigil

Nights' last shroud of dark unveils
numbered white cold sheets of sweat,
draped harsh down their trembled brows.
Before their sleepless eyes appears,
a lazy, porch day dawning.

Through a screen door drifts profuse,
the prate of news by kindred tongues.
Apollo landing on the moon
and Yankees in the pennant race.
Overcast with chance of rain,
Vietnam.

The landscape flees and fades to green,
betrays the blackened brush ahead.
In a sigh the dawn will bring
the scream of whistles sure to shrill,
while porch dreams, blaze and fester.

—*Robert K. Holloway*

Pickett Cottage

Pickett Cottage, Pickett Cottage,
O how wonderful is thee.
Full of talent,
Full of glee,
This will always be a special
    place for me.
To me it will be a memory
Of shimmery halls and dining
    cloths.
O how grand was all for me.

—*Amanda Allen*

My Noble U.S.A.

You're a gift from our Creator
O land so brave and true.
May blessings always be your lot
And success in all you do.

O the beauty of your landscapes
And your waterfalls so grand!
May all within your lovely shores
Besides you always stand.

Your noble soldiers fought and died
To make you strong and free;
And so with hearts that love you
To you loyal we will be.

You'll always be the fairest land
To my heart and mind.
May your days be always happy
And all your ways be kind.

As I end this little poem
I wish to truly say:
It's great to be a Citizen
Of this noble U.S.A.!

—*Noreen Costello*

Solitude

The young boy sat alone crying
Oblivious to his surroundings
His motionless figure destroyed
In the air confusion is rampant
The never ending tears blur his vision
Thoughts of peace seem far out of reach
The future can not be told
But one must know
Will this pain ever cease

—*April A. Qualley*

The Walk!

You did not walk with me
Of late to the hill-top tree
By the gated ways,
As in earlier days,
You were weak and lame,
So you never came,
And I went alone, and I did not mind,
Not thinking of you as life behind.

I walked up there today
Just in the former way;
Surveyed around
The familiar ground
By myself again;
What difference, then!
Only that underlying sense
Of the look of a room on returning thence.

—*Thomas P. Gilchrist*

Sweet Surrender

Fathomless depths
    of blue
    pull me into
    another realm,
a hidden sanctuary.
Plains and valleys
    to be explored,
    mountain peaks to
    be scaled.
I trace the map
gently, following trails
into meadows, heavy with
    fragrances, of ripening
        fruit.
Sticky sweetness clings to
    my lips,
as I eventually follow the trail
back to those fathomless
    depths.

—*D. June Culbertson*

The Mind

Cherish the thoughts
    of memories gone by -

Let them linger like
    the deep in the sky -

Think about the good days
    of long ago -

Think about the times
    when we were slow -

Never forget the golden
    past -

For we are it, and it
    will last -

Peace, tranquility and
    lots of love -

This is what "God" wanted
    From minds above -

—*Bessie Nelson*

Christmas Memories

Pleasant thoughts of long ago,
Of riding in the frosty snow,
Caroling with friends I know,
Laughing in the sleigh, ho-ho!

Tobogganing down Chestnut Hill,
Sometimes falling like Jack & Jill,
Or racing sleds side by side,
And building snowmen three feet wide.

Traveling out to choose a tree,
Such a treat for the family,
Cutting it down and smell of pine,
Knowing it's a special time.

Christmas presents wrapped in red,
It won't take long to go to bed,
Visions of ribbon and paper torn,
Secrets now till Christmas morn.

Think of Christmas, such a pleasure,
Much generosity, there is no measure,
People caring, people giving, always in
    song,
So I think, why not Christmas all year long?

—*Nikki King*

Fallen Trees Like Witches

The charcoal skeletal arms
of trees stretch with bough tips
embracing sunlit heaven
leaf by leaf stripping down
upon magenta and purple heather
patterning seasonal autumn carpet
as would a ring of worshippers
applauding life's renewal
deep in ancient ritual merging
divinely into the nuances
of sunbeam drawing gradually
towards nightfall's lilting wings.

—*Diana Kwiatkowski Rubin*

The Lie

"Did you know dogs talk?
Ok Ok, that's the problem with me.
I never know what to say.
Like if I just meet someone
I'll say my name is Liz,
but my name is Shelly.
It sounds like a shell.
Everyone else thinks its pretty,
though,
Ok Ok, my name is Chelsea,
And I never lie.
When I do I get sent to my
room, and I hate that.
Not!!!!!!
I'm a boy!"

—*Jaime Riesche*

Grandma

Old with white hair is she,
    Old with white hair;
And also wrinkles has she,
    And old with white hair.

Wise and kind is she.
    Wise and kind;
And also loving is she,
    And wise and kind.

Her house is in the woods,
    A home with a heart;
Garden flats, garden view,
    And a home with a heart.

She reads lots of books,
    Both fiction and true;
She also plays a lot of music,
    And plays it on an old organ.

She believes in the Cornerstone,
    The only one who is true;
Firmly she believes in the cornerstone,
    And she belongs to Him, too.

—*Adam D. Wilkins*

The Redwood Trees

So tall, so grand, taller then a man,
Older then a thousand years,
They shed no tears,
So gracefully calm,
They will soon be gone.
Oh! If man wasn't so wasteful,
Just a little bit more tasteful!!!

—*Constance Ruth Dockery-Wilson*

wo Little Boys

had two little boys
n a long ago day
ho would often call
Mother please come out and play"
d put them off
ill I had more time,
ill the ironing was done
r we had all dined.
ow, I've lost those two little boys
or they are both men.
nd oh, how I would change
ere they small again!
d run when they called me—
ff we'd go— we three—
nd no words could tell you
ow happy we'd be.

—*Sarah Gertrude Garner*

Moon Drenched Shore

o lie with you,
n moon drenched shores,
ould be pure ecstasy.
o make love in,
e foaming surf,
liding in from the sea.
he sand on our bodies,
e salty taste of our skin,
an you picture this?
hen you close your eyes,
an you feel the sea,
an you taste my lips?
he moon is out,
's a clear night,
's beautiful by the sea,
o you want to make love,
n the moon drenched shore,
d find pure ecstasy?

—*Gerard Baldacchino Jr.*

The Hall

withered woman flourishes
n Sunset Avenue in a rented room.
veryday she gives devotion upon
rinkled, bended knees.
t night she preaches of
he great light"
the funneled darkness
a dingy hallway.

orn like the faded blue dress
e wears,
rn by a sharp-handed husband,
d the children who do not call.

Fear the Almighty Lord!"
e warns to all who cross her hall.
er arms uplifted, the black King James
her bone- white hands.

fraid of God, she studies every sin
d knows the rules to secure a place by
im.
e hides in Holy words and keeps safe
om the sun
stone heart alone.

—*Leah L. Smith*

Untitled

A little alpine valley waits
On the upstream side of the falls
Bands of daisies guard its gates
Blue asters paint its walls
Ageless rock sentinels overlook
What nature planted here
And shape the pathway of the brook
Fast, cold and crystal clear
Less than a few of all God wrought
Match this to touch and see
Yet the search for it is all for naught
Neither found in fact nor memory
Part of the fleeting time we share
It's not the place, but who is there

—*John W. Schnurr*

Untitled

The rose pedals dropped
One by one
Dry, dying, limp

Take me away
Take me to the heavens I prayed
Unlock my soul
And relieve my pain

One by one
The pedals dropped
Slowly giving way to life

I swallowed my pain away
Sadness going numb
Going far away

I closed my eyes
And tranquility overcame me
Peace, content
Relaxed
Alone

—*Patty Gonzalez*

Prisoner of Memories

Yesterday is but a memory,
One that never fades.
The feeling of our love
Warms my heart today.
Though it's all ended,
And we've said goodbye,
The tenderness we shared,
Goes on in my mind.
It seemed we were destined
From the first spark,
To share the feelings
That burned in our hearts.

If never we reconcile,
At least I know,
There's a river in my mind
Where memories flow.
To these I will hold,
Steadfast and true.
Forever a prisoner
In memories of you....

—*Jolena Ward*

Making Love

Making love to you
would be like eating dainty little flowers
with strange powers
that need no words to chew.

—*Danny L. Weiss*

Sea Breeze

The sun was high in the blue western sky.
To hold the aesthetic of this day,
means more than words can say.
To evolve yourself for your entire stay,
and allow yourself to silently pray.

—*Ronda Harbor*

America The USA

The greatest of them all
One that will never fail
Try to give it your best
It will always be above the rest

When you go across the land
You know you are in good hands
As you travel along the way
Everyone wants to say hello

Every mile you travel will be great
The scenery will be amazing
All the different birds will be singing
What a joy it is to be on your way

Every day has a different weather
You will enjoy the great change
Everyone will agree with you today
Even if you have a very long day.

—*Charles J. Vallo*

Inner Growth

A baby grows inside
Only experiencing darkness
Warmth...comfort
Hearing the world
Through layers of tissue
Safe...protected
Feelings brand new
Everything brand new
Growing and developing
Day by day by day by day
Security unending
Yet all things end
So new things can begin

—*Ellen Petry*

Fear

I am a thief...
Open the door to your thoughts
and feelings,
and I will seize all the color and light.
I will leave your texture dull and worn,
strangling your dreams with my
white-knuckled vanity.

Passion so titteringly close to poison,
poison so secretly close to me.
Will you risk the prick of your
warm and supple heart,
on the sharp and ice-blue eyes
that see what no other knows?

I am a thief, open the door.
My rooms are dark and empty,
my walls blank and black.

Do you see that it is your light
that gives me life? That it is
your breath that I steal to fill my
lungs?

I am a Thief.

—*Wendy L. Williams*

"The Niagara"

A man might build a dam or bridge;
  or buildings with many malls,
But only God could ever create
  the sight on Niagara falls.....

The tons of water falling,
  to depths that can't be measured,
Makes one gasp with wonder,
  And hold this scene as treasured...

Of all the seven wonders
  that the world has got to share,
It must be the Niagara,
  That stands beyond compare...

No artists brush could capture
  in detail quite so stated,
As the sight of the Niagara
  Which God alone created.....

      —Gladys Szatkowski

Untitled

There was a guy
Or should I say boy
I was his pride He was my joy.

We fell in love. Then it died
And like the dove
I thought we'd abide

I knew we would soon move on.
But not this soon
For we showed too much fawn.

I cried and cried
And felt the pain
Tried to put him aside
For I had lost, not gained.

And so I say:
Be careful who you choose
Don't go astray
And don't misuse
the power of love
But always remember
you've got the one above.

      —Jessica Rossok

By The Fountain

Edgar and Ebenezer are
our two tame squirrels.
We feed them bits of bread
every night - by the fountain.
They make us laugh
with their timid, querulous
antics -
Sitting on their haunches
watching us -
daring closer and closer -
off in a second
at our slightest move.
We feed them bread -
They feed us delight!

      —Kaydi Dienna

The Stream

A lone twisting winding stream I am,
with lots of rocky waterfalls.
Splashing, bubbling on my way to
great St. John's lake.
Pushing little boats made of leaves.
Down the river along with me.

      —Kelly Brings

Untitled

I sit and wonder why and when
Our world became so saved.
The joy of early morning flees as
The day begins to unfold.
Murder, strife, fear and worry
Are overtaking everyone.
I feel so useless to be of help
When the world is so in need.
Close the door, pull the shade
And escape with a book.
An hour passes and I escape
Only to look back.
Today, tomorrow, evermore
A little sadness stays with me
As I go out the door

      —J. Rauscher

"The Sudden Change"

We were one together
  Out on the town
We were living up our dreams
  We were young
Never looked down
  But we fell apart at the seams.

Now you are gone
I'm all alone
Didn't know what went wrong
I sit by the phone
Hoping you will call

I followed after you
But you turned away from my heart
I stepped in, you stepped out
I knew we were falling apart

It was you I needed through and through
I hope you will always know
I'll be waiting for you...

      —Joe Rodriguez

Window

A man sits in his
own world,
surrounded by music
from outside
the window.

He is far away
from everyone
but close enough
to hear them.

They are dancing
and singing
outside the window,
but they
never come in.

For there is
one thing
they don't like
about the window,
and that is
within.

      —Becky Jewell

Music

Thoughts and sounds
passed through the air,
Leaving behind
a trail of emotional flare.
Soothing and startling,
it holds its fiery grip.
A choke hold on reality,
just tight enough not to slip.
Sometimes containing meaning
locked behind riddled doors.
And somewhere just noise
that rattles ceilings and floors.
Both types are amazing-
as the notes and chords grasp listeners,
with words telling true-life stories
or pointing out ignorant racial slurs.
Whatever, wherever, or however...
it just doesn't seem to matter,
as long as it supplies what we want
And we get it on a silver platter.

      —Michael T. Ross

Star Light Star

Devil satan with love of peace
peace he will given knows
that sin that it begin
that my boy that knows
evil sin killing with in
of that evil sin the devil
is with in

Rock is not a stone
satan can't bury his bones
he knows that evil sin
I know that evil sin
thee is me satan. Star light star

      —Jay Sherer

Peace

Peace,
Peace is something we all need
its like a baby urging to feed

Some people want it
some don't
some people will
some won't

A baby bunny hoping free
without a chain,
without a leash
is something I call peace.

      —Theresa Waters

Secret Love

Secret is the love
  Quiet as a dove
  I watch you.

I notice you walk by me
but you are not so free,
  free, for me to love.

As I begin each day
I always hope and pray
that you will love me too.

As the months turn to years
  my eyes fill with tears,
For the love I feel for you.

      —Addie Smits

Will I Ever Find You?

eople
   people
eople everywhere

Everyday I see faces
   some are familiar
      some are foreign

Everyday I search for you
   know you are out there,
      but I just can't seem to
         find you.....

One day we will meet.....
Then your face will become
   familiar
      not another foreign
      face in the crowd

   will no longer need to worry
      that I'll be alone

'll have you

'll love you
            —*Alicia Olson*

The Man In The Moon

Do you remember the Man in the Moon?
Perhaps we all forgot him too soon
He's still sitting up there
Alone on his rocking chair
But I know he's up there, don't you?

When the clouds go by
They hide his eyes
And we know he's off to his sleep

But then the clouds pass
He awakes, and puts on his shoes
And smiles out at me and at you

He never does speak
But he plays hide and seek
Between the day and the night
He collects starlight
And puts all good children to sleep
            —*Gene Evers*

"Faraway Wonders"

I dream of faraway places,
Places I've never seen,
A zebra's eye in the jungle,
A dolphin in the sea,
I dream of large castles,
Every star in the night,
The people that I love,
And everything in sight!
I hear the robin chirping,
The bees buzz in the trees.
I hear the wind whistle.
And everything around me!
I wonder about the waves,
Rolling on and off the shore,
The people that are there,
And lots more!
            —*Meredith Dorneker*

Memories

(Dedicated to my children with love.)
Pondering through my memories,
Events of my past, and world history,
be it good or bad,
that's the choice I made,
inflicting pains, no need to complain,
I must refrain.

Life's daily challenges, pressures,
Fearful, powerful, loss of control,
Feeding upon my weaknesses,
I tend to lose faith,
It's distress, I confess,
"Yet, have I done my best?"

I screamed in a whisper,
under my breath,
Oh God! I need strength!
I've failed Amen.
Extended arms, he held out, enfolding
me, with his love, He said,
"I'm here, I'm there, I'm everywhere,
I'm your alms, I'm above."
            —*Ophelia Moore*

Wrinkle Free

Youth was suppose to be my friend
Promising never to leave me
Until the very end.

Time was marching by so fatally
Lurking behind the bush
Standing guard to attack
As if I were the enemy

I can see the light
I'm must move faster now
Searching for satisfaction somehow
Slowing up time,
Cause it's moving too fast
I want the American Dream to last.
            —*Carolyn Glenn-Tate*

The Unexpected

It came into my life slowly,
   quietly,
      unexpectedly,
building up, then rocking my world with
the same pleasantly violent fervor as
a summer rain storm.
The storm raged, and raged... and
took my breath away as the bolts
of lightening zapped about...
And then, just as I had begun to
make peace with it, it was gone quickly,
   quietly,
      unexpectedly,
The earth was still once more,
except for the shaking of my shoulders,
rising and falling with my sobs.
            —*Christina Bailey*

Woman

Of all the great
mysteries encountered in
life you are Number 3
but don't feel bad
for coming in third
God beat you out
(and me)
            —*Jeremy Lloyd*

A Good Friend Died Early in Life

The sun still shines
Rains they flow
Winds still blow the
Leaves to fall
Snow is peaceful like
Flowers that rise
I miss your friendship but
it's there all the time
I'm just glad you
stayed forever young.
            —*Denise M. Anderson*

Sometimes the Rain

Sometimes, on cloudy
   rainy days
I enjoy sitting inside
   and thinking

As it rains and thunders
   I contemplate life

Sometimes, the forgotten
   happy past
Comes to me with
   little effort

As the current day unfolds
   I relive the old

Maybe the clouds and rain
   should come more often
            —*Jeffrey M. Gater*

The Rage Of The Storm

A gust of wind
rattles the leaves
the trees speak
but no one listens
the sky is beautiful
grays and whites
but no one sees
the air is powerful
   energetic
   electric
but no one feels
why do they run and hide?
What do they have to fear
but the range of the storm
            —*Peter Schwab*

Dare To Live

      Dare to be lively
   Reach out and live a little

      Life is great
   Open up that final door

      Dare to have fantasies
   It's not wrong to want for the best

      Dare to admit your secrets
Treasure your absolutely personal ones

      Dare to help
Everyone needs to discuss their feelings

      Dare to live
   This might be your last chance
            —*Abbey Ewald*

Letter From College

How do I feel, you're so far away
reflecting back on younger days
You were always there for me
Formed what I was to be
Carried all my joys and pain
Heralded my every gain
With regal bearing quietly
The lost hope I gave to thee
How can I hope to replace
The love you gave with Holy Grace
It seems I let you down again
I wish that it might not have been
Mother, Father, can you see
I love you both so dearly
I'm sorry for the years of pain
I'll try to make you proud again

—*Daniel P. Irving*

The Dream World

There is a dream world
right around the corner,
where children are grown-ups,
and grown-ups are children again.

In that hiding place
there are no responsibilities
no exceptions
no worries, no schedules
no stress, and no pain.

There is only
pleasure and excitement
gratification, without responsibility,
or denied.

It is only the world drugs.
You can afford together
even on a child's allowance,
and you can't tell until you get there
how hard it is to come back...

—*Jaclyn Schutt*

The Promise

Nature makes a promise
Right before she flees
From approaching snow and ice
And the frozen breeze.

She gives us a show
Of orange, gold, and red
So we will not forget
The beautiful life she led.

Thus, we never doubt
All the winter long,
That she will return
With the robin's song.

—*Gwen Ward*

Untitled

Rowing my boat through
Life's perils,
Hitting against starboard
Bow took every bit
Of power, until couldn't oar
No more leaving
Destiny unfinished.

—*Bill Nathan*

Mistakes

Made them,
Claimed them,
Cussed them,
Dissected them,
Cultivated them,
Pardoned them,
Filed them.

—*Lynette Kirksey*

Untitled

Torn apart
Ripped in two
We were happy
Me and you
Like a miracle
From up above
You were the one
Who stole my love
Through tearful
eyes
We said our goodbyes
With love and hopes
I held on tight
Knowing that fate
Would guide you right
Praying that something
Will make you see
You and I were meant to be!

—*Heather Duvall*

Escape

Pristine thoughts
roam through ebony valleys.
Always searching and prying
trying to comprehend.

The thoughts
always appear to capture
mahogany hills and plateaus.
In essence, they elude the thoughts.

Pristine thoughts
will forever pursue
the ebony valleys that escape them.

—*Tina M. Strickland*

A Patch Of Blue

A patch of blue
Rode through the sky.
I watched him pass
'Til he was out of sight.

The white sand around him
As he galloped by
Became tumbleweeds of anger
Keeping pace with his stride.

I watched him fight
To keep his ground.
He had little strength left,
Which was not enough.

The tumbleweeds rose high
To a fort of white walls
And surrounded their victim
Completely.

Of the patch of blue,
I saw no more
But his grave in the sky—
The white walls of heaven.

—*Jeanette Lynn Herrbach*

My Eight Hour Day

The rain pours from the
roofs edge - and as the drops
run slowly down the window, the
clock seems to move with the
same grace - and understanding this
is not my place.

I set at my desk with my
usual feelings of dismay - Trying oh
so hard to elude my mistaken
perception of reality.

Pondering my moodiness - as they
steadily encroach me - knowing
they feel on defeat.

Wanting to be concealed or
placed in a secure place -
Until some of the warmth
inside me returns

—*Lisa Upchurch*

He Searched, He Found, He Understood

He searched the grounds,
Row by row,
Mother was here,
Where he did not know.

She'd been laid to rest;
A child was only five;
Now he was searching for her;
A monument was found inscribed.

He knelt on the ground,
Clearing away the debris;
She'd been a long time away,
But now was found you see.

Upon the grave,
A flower so carefully placed,
Wafted oh so sweetly,
As the fragrance drifted into space.

Then he turned away;
He had contentment in his eyes;
One day he'd say hello to mama,
But today he'd said goodbye.

—*Mary Blanche Fox*

Untitled

A river of reflection
runs rapid
Through the channels
of my mind...

Filling me with
reverie,
Nostalgic thoughts
of you and me...

Enhanced by
sentiment
And selective
memory.

—*Robbin DeCarlo*

On the Edge

On the edge of freedom,
scared to cross the line.
New discoveries ahead of me.
Pain and suffering behind.
Don't know where to turn,
Which path of life to take.
No matter how hard I wish
There's still a decision to make.
All I want to know is
"What's in this life for me?"
I cannot tell the future
For its too far for me to see.
Should I stay or should I go
And leave all this behind?
Now I'm on the edge of freedom,
Scared to cross the line

—*Jessy Mauney*

Fall Beach

The beach is quiet, silent song,
Seasonal visitors now are gone.
Stillness, peaceful, tranquil sight,
The evolution marching on.

Beach houses closed and boarded tight,
Summer days slip into night.
Sea gulls circle, begin to moan
Tropic ways give up their fight.

Dune brush and benches stand alone,
Shimmering in their winter home.
The sun reflecting on the ocean grand,
A glimpse of summer where it had shone.

A paint-chipped, lonely lifeguard stand,
On windswept beach with blowing sand.
A common tern its only friend,
This meeting place of sea and land.

The quiet beach begins to mend,
Its countenance it will not lend.
Suspense of summer once again,
For summer voices now's the end.

—*Kenneth B. Hogan*

Farewell to Summer

I hear the leaves now rustling down,
The mountains wear an earlier crown
Of shining gold caressed with dusk.
'Tis natures own vernacular clear,
Telling all to list' to hear
Summer times again be spent.

Now bid farewell to all her charms,
Her warmth, blossoms and in her arms
Birds she'll soon send gently southward.
Oh God, we stop and think on Thee
For thou hast made all this to be.
We marvel in meek humility.

—*Marilyn DeBlock*

Untitled

Alone.
Until tomorrow —
The breaking dawn
Relieves my sorrow.
Glistening dew.
Glistening hopes.
Love feeling new —
Alive.

—*Amy Coulter*

The Dark One

He stands in the shadows
seldom meets the light
His home along the border
between the day and night

His eyes are ever searching
myriad shades of gray
The mind a swirl of visions
of answers slipping away

A man of epic dreams
gripped with hands of fear
His doubts painfully gnawing
a future forever unclear

What place is there for him
to scared of falling short
In a world that has no care
where lives are taken in sport

—*Erik Alexander Prince*

... Itude

As I lay here dealing with a
Self imposed attitude
I know that all this happens,
Because in my world there
Exists a degree of ineptitude
But no matter what goes on
I must not allow this
Realization to magnitude
To the extent that I'm not
Capable of showing fortitude
So here I am trying to
Release my thoughts from this altitude
Knowing that the recognition
Of all this happening will
Give me some gratitude

—*Leonard Rabb*

Changes

Fields of green
Shall ever be seen
Trees of oak
A lovers' poke
A clear blue stream
A pussy cat's scream
See eagles in flight
Our country's plight
A war in Kuwait
A soldier's mate
Free trade
Medicaide
Homicide
A gavel slams
Jail reforms
A lawyer performs
Arrests are made
Convictions too
The world has changed
Society too!

—*Michael Ross Vanderberg*

Forgotten Hours

Looking out
to an
endless
vision
of time gone
by.

—*Renata Kacprzyk*

My Dog Lilly

My dog Lilly likes to play,
she brings her toys to me
each day.

She has many, many, many toys
and she likes to play
with girls and boys.

Her face is little with a
black nose she's really
cute in a picture posed.

Lilly likes to go bye-bye
in the car, and she's ready
to go no matter how far.

But when we're on the
way to the vet
she shakes and shivers
not knowing what yet.

Lilly knows when it is
time to go to bed, she
picks up her toy and lays
by my head.

—*Leigh Ann Coons*

"Springwater"

I have discovered my mission in life.
She came to me in a vision,
sent from the heavens, blessed with
angelic love.

I call her springwater,
sweet, bewitching Goddess rising to
the sky from the shimmering seas.

The daughter of generations from the
beginning of time.

I knew God had entrusted me with
a special duty.

To guide this beautiful queen, to her
chosen place on the throne.

And those who try to detour her
from this path shall endure the wrath
of this man

Who will protect her with his heart, his
soul,
his life, because she is my wife!!

—*John Walter Porcher, Jr.*

Out in the Rain

She packed her bags and said good-bye;
She didn't even bat an eye.
And I knew right then and there
That for me, she no longer cared.
She left me standing in the rain;
A young man full of pain.
And my pleas were all in vain;
All alone, out in the rain.
I begged and pleaded her to stay,
But this time, there was no way.
She'd finally made up her mind and gone,
And with her took my only son.
With my hindsight so very clear;
I try to fight back another tear.
Knowing my pride caused all the pain,
And the outcome will never change.

—*John P. Fix*

Ballerina

"Let's dance for our Moon,"
she smiled,
pulling my tired bones
from the frumpy old chair.

Her grandmother made the quilt
that covers it
out of old bathrobes
from the goodwill.

She rolls her head
finds the ballet dancer from youth
and leaves me there
standing
watching
hoping she won't stop.

"Why don't you dance with me?"
"It's funnier to watch," and I laugh.
She rolls her eyes and says,
"Don't you mean it's more fun?"
"Yes, that's exactly what I mean."

—*Ron Spataro*

"What Did She Do?"

Young and restless,
She was daddy's mistress.
What did she say?
What did she do?
To make my daddy be mean and my
mommy be blue,
But now she's leaving,
Daddy's beggin' her to stay.
So what did she do to make
daddy act this way?

—*Bobbi Patton*

Ariel Dawn

Her eyes are blue and her hair is dark,
She's the one who holds my heart.
She wasn't planned but that's o.k.,
Without her I'd never have stayed.
She gave me a reason to stay right here,
She made me stand up and face my fears.
She makes me smile when I want to cry,
She makes me live when I want to die.
She gives me a reason to go on,
She's my life my Ariel Dawn.

—*Katharine Bearden*

Diluted Verdict

The waves from my thoughts
    Shimmer before me
    Prior to your destiny
Gorgeous groves envelop us
Forest streams inhaled our impression
As we companioned together
Mournful, gloomy days
Saw us venture outdoors
Only to keep the spread hardy
When plans refused to be adorable
The hull of our friendship
Cannot be pierced which has no core
It simply travels with the air
We roamed and shared our land
Ghosts didn't frighten us
    And robbers never were
Gorgeous groves envelop us
Forest streams retain our impression

—*Jerry Lee Murrell*

Masks

Outside,
shining like a glinting fender,
brightly colored
as a geometric's fluttery wings,
dazzling and distracting.

Inside,
hollow as an empty coke can,
dull,
worn down,
alone.

Once,
a friend came inside
and
warmed away
the facade.

—*Vera Heide Eberhardt*

Abused Little Girl on the Stairs

I saw the ugly bruises
Shocking to the eye
As she pulled her hair
Across her face her bruises to hide
Trying not to cry
She cast her glance downward
As I questioned her about the bruises
She looked away in fear
Mumbling, "...it was my fault..."
In a tone too low to hear
She closed her mouth in silence
She would not cast the blame
On the loved one who had hit her
Or even give a name
Though I tried to hold her close
She fled and paid no heed
And my heart went out to her
The little girl on the stairs

—*Mary Gambill*

West Of Chernobyl

The newspaper clipping said
"Siamese Twin Piglets born
in Zhitomir Region of Ukraine
West of Chernobyl"

Mirrors from a mother
their pale coats melt together
like two sticks of butter
left on top of each other
in the gamma light.

Limbs twisted, distorted,
an epiphany of deformity,
the flatfaced children giggle
and stare at the freak show
science has made to order.

While the doctors and official liars
shake their worried heads
and hurry out to bury the omen
before the panic rains
like spoiled milk
in a forest of sponges.

—*Barry Lawrence Taft*

Untitled

Sitting alone in a
silent room, I conjure
up all the world's doom.

Children are beaten,
scarred, and bruised.
How can these people
stand to abuse?

These people take out
their anger on others.
Whether it be Mother,
son, daughter, sister,
or brother.

They have no remorse
for what they have done
because to them they have
hurt no one.

What will it take to
make them understand
that one should not raise
a fist against another man?

—*Kathleen A. Desmond*

Happy Anniversary

I can't believe its 14 years
Since we first said "I do"
But still throughout all those years
My love just grew and grew.

We've had so many moments
Some happy and some sad
Through all those special times
It was real love that we shared.

You probably don't think you deserve
The love I have for you,
But you really are a great guy
Deep down, through and through.

So this wish comes to you
As 15 is about to start,
With all the love and happiness
To the man who stole my heart!

—*Lynne McQuade*

On Ending

Why must our love end
    so abrupt and demur
that my conscience overflows
    spilling my diversity
on to the cobbled streets
    of reticent aspirations.

    While longing to hold
the bitter sweetness of lust in check,
    I ravage the pathways
    of superficial content
finding at the end of each
    my own obscurity
    plauded by a
    love for fingers.

—*Michael Walters*

Untitled

The snow so pure and white
So beautiful to see
The peacefulness it brings
Is very dear to me

Yet as nice as it may seem
It does not bring me happiness
Calmness and serenity
Are all it seems to bless

It is still a form of nature
It is only frozen rain
I wish someone would care for me
And stop this endless pain

Although the snow is virgin white
The calmness seems too dead
I want to open up my veins
And turn this white to red

Then my sleep would come
In happiness instead of fright
I would lie down one final time
And dream of endless night

—*Dathan Latterell*

Why?

Oh, what a mystery life is,
    So little I understand,
The why and wherefore of all things,
    Some so small and some so grand.

Have you ever wondered why God made man
    And placed him on this earth,
And why man will not serve Him,
    And discover his own worth?

Why did I choose to serve the Lord?
    While others choose to sin.
What makes man want to die
    Without love and life within?

When I view what the Lord
    Has prepared for you and me,
I desire to leave this old earth,
    And start my eternity.

All mysteries then will be revealed,
    All answers will satisfy,
All knowledge there will be ours,
    No longer will we wonder, why.

—*Charlotte Cowles*

Silent World

World is so silent
so quiet
no sounds

Ears aren't going
to work without aids
since you cannot hear
people give you love and help.

Full of deafness or silence
nothing will help
until you wear aids.

Silent is where
your house is
with a deaf kid
or parent
living in.

Nothing but loud sounds or lights
to get your attention.

—*Heather Dawn Garman*

Inside

So many faces,
so many places …
but no one there
no one seems to care

Still I knock on the door
but no one answers
everyone just passes me by
all I can do is sigh

Me - alone, no one there
I only feel pain
is there anything to gain
there must be something more
is there anything in store…
    for me

With all this pain
I will go insane
but instead I close my door

No more hurt or pain
Close myself off from the world
there is only emptiness.

—*Debora Burnosky*

A Gift Of Love

Babies are so beautiful
So precious and so rare
They're a gift of love to you
That only God can share

Babies are a blessing
A rarity, a joy
And I'm so glad that you were blessed
With a beautiful baby boy

So count your blessings and the tears
At last the story's told
And give to him the kind of love
That can't be bought or sold

—*Janet L. Suomela*

Baby Splendor

Darling baby, with your gaze
    So wise,
Did you come down from
    Beyond the skies?
Were you a tiny star,
    Shining bright,
Lighting up the heavens
    At night?

Stars, I've seen them fall.
When they drop, they do
    Not die.
No star is ever lost
From all the star-sown
    Sky.
They shine on in a baby's
    Eyes.

So, lay you down and sweetly slumber
    And every morn revive,
But keep the star-dust
    Ever in your eyes.

—*Doris McLaughlin*

Voice

A little voice
So young and gentle
Asks me what I'm so afraid of
I cannot answer
I'm too scared to say
Will the torment ever go away?
If I don't face my biggest fears
I'll live in misery
For years and years
I'm left with a choice
Of life or death
So I'll close my eyes
And go to the world
Inside my head

—*Olga Degtjarewsky*

The Mailman

Some days the mail goes early
Some days it goes late
But all I can do
Is set here and wait

The mail mans bored
With the same old route
He's happy for holidays
I know he could shout

A day with the family
Or do his own thing
When he gets settled in
The telephone rings

Names on an envelope
Is all that he sees
While the robin red breast
Sings in the trees

All through the four seasons
Of sunshine, rain or snow
No difference what the weather
The mail and the man must go

—*Mildred McCoy*

People

Some people are cowards,
    Some people are bold.
        Some disobey,
Some do what they're told.
    All people are different.
        Whether big or small,
But each person has a talent,
    Whether short or tall.
        Some are thinkers,
            Some are doers,
And some do nothing at all.
    Some are curious,
        Some are cautious.
    And some keep cool,
        And some get furious.
But all are different,
And special to each day.
    And each has a talent,
And does things his own way.

—*Fatimah S. Dawood*

Love Of Life

I took a song from the birds
Some words from Solomon's psalms
And added something of my own
To make a happy song.

I know some day we wake up sad
And do not know the reason why
But know for sure when skies are gray
The sun will shine another day.

You'll know a special happiness
If once you learn to love and care
For all the beauty around us
The earth the sea the sky and air.

—*Francine Morey*

Always In Your Heart

I lost someone five years ago,
Someone I could never let go.
No matter how hard I prayed for
God to bring her back,
All I got was a pat on my back,
"Its okay young girl, its okay,
You'll see her again someday,
She's in a good place now,
Where there cheers not frowns,
Now young girls stop these tears,
There's a hope to heal your fears.
You and her will never part,
because she'll always be in your heart.

—*Ashley Graham*

Untitled

It's hard to lose,
   Someone you love!
It's good to know,
   He's up above!
I know you miss your dad,
   And the great times,
      You and he had!
   Love is sweet,
   Love is kind,
I know he must be on your mind!
I know you will miss him so,
   But good times will come,
   And good times will go!

—*Rebecca Morrissey*

Lost Forever

Sometimes I wish I was something
Something that had no feelings
Life would be a lot easier
To just live and die
I try so hard
So hard to just push it all aside

Lost in memories
Suddenly everything just comes back
I try not to think about it
But it's so hard not to
I wonder what's going to happen

At night I lay in darkness
Staring at the walls around me
Wondering about so many things
Then it hits me
Thinking about it makes me cry
I cry for hours about so many things
So many things that I lost
Lost forever

—*Johanna L. Austria*

The Songbird's Song

The songbird sings its bitter
Song of luck and misery,
And weeps for all it sees below
With compassion and pity.

It laughs when bubbling rivers pass,
Or children come to play.

Oh, what a melancholy song!
To weep by night and laugh by day.
Still the songbird sings on and on,
For a listener's ear
To hear his song.

—*Jennifer Vega*

Left-Lane

My mind is a
Speeding car.
It accelerates down the
Freeway, switching lanes
Constantly.

It ignores the black and white
Pursuing with its
Light flashing.
It races on.

Unseen from here,
There is a sharp corner
Up ahead
With a thin Guard rail.
I probably won't survive
The crash.

—*Kevin J. Trimmer*

Aesthetics Lost

It was only yesterday, as I trembled
   standing face to the sun
Driven by a feeling of loneliness
   cursing the rise of warming rays
And as my back warmed in the setting
   I remained still, statue laden feet
In the darkness as the ice formed
I could not dream of tomorrow
   It held no conquest of life
   A mere thaw
Standing no retreat
   It was picturesque of time

—*Joseph Fernicola*

Practice Poem One (Love)

Patterns play across her face
subtle cause and effect
betrayed by subcutaneous muscle
a being at war with itself

she hates me, I betrayed her
or rather her image of me
cast in the immutable medium
of a woman's dreams

all I wanted was a fair chance
chasing some chimera inchoate
a puerile fantasy of human nature
the empty chalice of modern love

so barren we both stand
facing each others' shortcomings
there's no solace in being alone
there's only the taste of regret

—*Geoffrey Charles Emerson*

Foolish

A fool I feel
   A fool I be
For I have made
   A fool of me
Tho I have learned
To remain unconcerned
   Foolishly

—*Richard B. Taber*

Untitled

Seeing you in your casket
staring deep beyond space,
there is a childhood horror
etched upon your face.
Bringing back the fear,
reminiscing about the pain,
when you would hide from your abuser
to never be found again.
Alone you would cry
in any dark place
blaming yourself
for the cuts on your face.
Not a second to think
only a minute to cry
you thought it would be easier
if you would just die.
Escape some may call it,
and although sad but true,
you ended your life
because you blamed you.

—*Aubri Hacker*

Dawn

Darkness waits, unaware of the
Stealth on the oncoming stranger
Lights dance on the horizon
Withering moon beams that fall
Suddenly disappear
Shadows replace shades as the
Stranger advances
This is dawn, killer of night
Preveyor of light, carrier of hope
How fortunate we are blessed
With such a creature
This is dawn and I've seen
It come many times

—*James Arrington*

"Why?"

Drugs and crime on the
streets and on every corner,
Hatred and love is always
on the border.
Being destroyed and shot at
by my own sister and brother,
sicknesses and diseases spreading
from one to another.
Prejudice and ignorance -N- our
Neighborhoods and our citizen,
Wars and corruption we learn
About throughout our world history.
Babies hav'n babies and homeless
People out on the street,
Digging -N- others trash-cans
-N- search for something to eat.
No one to trust cuz you
Have no one to be trusted.
Violence exploding from left to right
Because of unfair justice.

—*Purnell Wade Hester, Jr.*

Oh Lord

Why must we
ffer through the pain.
Must there be
ss before gain.
Will my feelings
main the same
Oh Lord,
Why must we
ffer through the pain.

—*Jeffrey Fleming*

ummer, Spring, Winter, Fall

ummer, spring, winter, fall,
ummer is the best of all
ummer fun at the beach
r eating a pear or peach
e love swimming with everyone
veryday that it goes on
veryone brings a little food
nd no one is in a bad mood
nd everyone eats a little food
ven my dog Fred
ries to sleep in our bed
e liked Jake
hat Jimmy had to take
ummer, spring, winter, fall
ummer is the best of all

—*Jessica Shrieve*

spens In Whitewater

m your consciousness.
rrogate eyes
e the beauty
ou can only be.

spens glow from the warmth of
e collective.
m one with you.
ou feel…
ly through me.

me does not exist.
is nothingness…
consequence of your being.

s your mountainsides
sorb my footprints,
ey do not know
e presence of my trespass.

will be your umbilical…
ving you life,
ly to echo through my soul.

—*Jon K. Mills*

eaven

it and watch the cars go by
ars in my eyes I'm about to cry
eep thinking it's him I'll see
ming home again to me
t as the light of day grows dim
ealize it wasn't him
en reality returns once more
won't be coming through the door
w I'm alone and growing old
t I have memories I can hold
til it comes my time to go
's waiting in heaven that I know

—*Carolyn Moake*

Zone of Life

Open my heart
take a look at my soul
please, take the walk of your life
Sorrow? Pity? Obligation?
No we are all human
look at me, you are not
me, him, or her you are you
open your eyes, don't be
blind, deaf, crippled, if
we are, you all should
see, we are only human…
Intertwination of the mind
see it…yes it is there

—*Rose Melissa*

Untitled

Darkness falls across the land
Take my hand
Follow me into the blackness
Into the depths
Sound creep into my ears
The howl of wolves
Screaming trees
I hear a whisper
Why, why, why
No answer falls
Pain
Searing and deep
My heart stops
Death

—*David Lunsford*

Untitled

Girlhoods priced payee
Taught sleep - oh vine
Holder key postpartum
Dizzy blue or yellow

All olive time answering
Be jerked hole twas'nt safe
There is nothing - all anonymous
Glue Sara Feasdales affect

Psychris fun masturbate
Another by death, go slow
Blue tine sea thirty waves
Visible surge land equator

Steed white bury; blazing ice
Cold air pockets - kneeling
Little old you know what
Daddy please don't hit me

Facetious bend out locket
Do live and live like colors.
Eye magic little glow pisp
Misery mirror diamond fine…

—*Mike Leonard*

Poetry

Inspired, delighted that I can
suspend myself with pen in hand
and romance words I understand
then gather them into a plan.
What makes a poet create the rhyme?
I do not know, but take the time
to scan the words that come to mind
and juggle them, just so, to find
at play, I've left the world behind!

—*Anita Brown*

Before The Dawn

One hour before the flush of dawn
that all the rosy daylight weaves,
Here in my bed, far overhead
I hear the swallows in the eaves,
I cannot see, but well I know
that out around the dusky guy,
across dark lakes and voiced streams,
the blind, dumb vapors feel their way.
And here and there a star looks down
Out of the fog that holds the sea.
In it's embrace, while up the lands
Some cock makes music lustily,
And out within the dreamy woods,
Or in some clover blossomed lawn,
the blinking robin pipes his mate
To wake the music of the dawn.

—*Bernadine C. Emig*

Forever

I'll always remember that day
That day was so sad
The day that you died
I was also quite mad

For I didn't know
Why God chose you
He took you away
I want to go too

So many fears inside
To show how scared
But now I can't tell you
Because you're not here

Now is the time
For me to say goodbye
Hush my darling
Don't you cry

Forever and ever
You'll stay in my heart
And because of our love
We'll never part.

—*Loni Mason*

Pondering After Sixty-Five

Where did the little girl go,
   that I was, not long ago?
Did she run away and hide,
   or is she living down inside?
I wish somehow that I could know
   where, oh where, did that girl go.
Why couldn't that little girl stay?
Sometimes she seems so far away.
If I sit and think a while,
   she still gives me cause to smile.

Through the laughter and the tears,
   years gone by and future years,
I'll remember long ago
   and I'll wish that I could know
Where, oh where did that girl go!

—*Helen Jean Stillwell*

Pepper

Pepper the dog
that is a hog
that sits on a log
every day and night

She likes to fight
and she is white
With a pink nose
like a rose

She bites a lot
in the lights
she plays with her balls
and then she falls

She has a floppy ear
So she could hear
When people call
She hits the wall

—*Nikki Elipani*

Life

Our lives start at birth,
that is when we are brought to earth.
Then our eyes peek
and then we start to speak.
After talking
move over here comes walking.
Then comes school,
when learning is cool.
When college comes, say good-bye,
but do not cry.
Then a family comes around,
for you a new life is found.
Then your children leave like you.
Their dreams might come true.
Then death got his grip on you.
It's all gone, but not one soul will forget
you.

—*Kerri Craine*

Follow

It was my little girl
that made me whole,
it was her little giggle
that made me wiggle.
A face she has so
pure sweet
a little hand so
fat a neat,
Her eyes our blue
Forever true.
I wish her life be
long and sweet, and
wish her
happy times forever.

—*Lorraine Mosley*

Winter And Love

The winter months remind me of you
The cold, long days through and through
The snowflakes are for remembrance
Of the tears in my eyes
The harsh howling winds to
Represent are good-byes
The icicles that hang remind
Me of our love once true
But when they fall and shatter
I remember the real you.

—*Mindy Parr*

My Daddy Was Santa One Night

My daddy played a trick on us
That night I almost lost my trust
He had a bright red and white suit
But I remembered his new rubber boots

He carried a bag across his arm
Then gave all the children a charm
Mom said my daddy went fishing
But oh how I was really wishing

I'll never forget that night at all
For here came Santa down the hall
It was the best year I ever had
'Cause Santa Claus was my dad

—*Judy Webb Quinn*

Untitled

It is the loss of hope
that perpetuates suffering
beyond everything.
It is the loss of hope
that makes one forget
that love is possible.
It is hope erected
only to be inhaled
like a cigarette thereafter,
that disconnects mind from soul,
matter from I.

It is the loss of hope for hope,
that twists in my guts
like the pregnancy of a future
that might never be conceived.

It is the loss of hope
that gives me hope
to lose it once more,
together, with you.

—*Gil Talmi*

The Mind Of A Girl

The mind is like a desk drawer
that sometimes sticks,
and sometimes opens too quickly.
It sometimes stores what you'd rather
it didn't, and often forgets

The mind is what the ancients thought
the heart to be.
A great storage place of knowledge,
emotion and memory.
A wonderful actor, or a subtle thief.

Your mind is the place you go,
the one you seek when all the world
turns its face from you.

Your mind is
your best friend and worst enemy,
your life and your death.

—*Anjeanett Jeffers*

Doctors

Give medical treatment
And relief from care
Specialize in the healing arts
Probe, diagnose, repair
Adapt or modify
For a desired end
A good doctor is:
"One's very best friend."

—*Loretta Hanneman*

Captivated Soul

The fairyland magic
That swiftly, slowly steals
your soul
Rises from the green, green depths
Of the water gently crashing
'Cross the star-stained sand
Pressed with the footprints
Of an unseen man.
Yourself cannot, no cannot
Ever be taken back,
For it is caught,
Caught in passionate waters
Carefully kept in check.

—*Erica Nicole Sevelis*

Untitled

Life is like a puzzle
that's got you in a daze.
You wander around aimlessly
to find the exit from this maze.

You turn corner after corner
and it all looks the same -
Like you're back where you started,
There's no end to this game.

But with each new day
you get closer than before,
And you find new dreams
when old ones are tore.

You continue with all your might
to find a way to the end,
But after every clueless turn -
you feel more scared and trapped again.

But you always keep going,
'Cuz you know deep in your heart -
That this maze does have an exit,
Or it wouldn't have a start.

—*Judith M. Irvine*

Untitled

Don't jump to conclusions.
That's what it seems,
It's only your illusions,
It's only your dreams,
Searching the shadows,
Looking to find,
where to mend a broken heart,
Or a piece of mind,
Times have rearranged,
People have changed,
Fortune and fame,
Shall make you insane,
But kindness and love,
Brings you above,
Above the best,
The best of all!!!!

—*Christine Yurgel*

Winds of Change

Winds will blow on a harmless day
That's when change will come your way
Times will change, people may go
Be true to yourself, then you'll
Know why they're going and
If they'll ever come back
And if he or she is your lover
And he or she is deceased
Then you should pray, please
Rest in peace and if the
Wind is blowing on that day,
They leave, don't sit
Around, moan or grieve, be true
To yourself. That's what you do
Then you'll know what life means
To you and on these days of
Winds of change, be kind and
Courteous, and be true to your name.
—*Andrea Joanne Sokol*

Untitled

My life will end today.
The beast has found
what the Angel lost.
The monster brings forth his ugly head;
Bears his (unforgiving) snarling teeth.
He sees my thoughts more clearly
than what's spoken.
He brought it upon himself
to be the messenger of my soul.
Taking what's rightfully mine,
from the inside out,
Leaving me with just myself.
Leaving my (shell) flesh
he moves on.
God, save the children.
—*Brenda Amman*

Ballad

The world at war
The blood flooded the street
Drowning with helpless people
All on the day I die

The evil black clouds blocked the sun
Making the world blind,
People walking blindly to nowhere
All on the day I die

Soldiers returned from the cold dead war
Their legs were torn off
Their eyes were full of water and fire
All on the day I die

The path led to endless
There was no answer to any problem
The world was a chaotic planet
All on the day I die
It's all on the day I die.
—*Joanne Peroo*

Every Other Christmas

Amidst the bubbles and do-dads,
The bows and crinkly foil,
A melancholy tune hummed.

Under the fragrant boughs
A single, wrapped package lay
Unopened, unclaimed,
Its loneness accentuated
By the twinkling lights.

Though Dad made the promise,
There was no reason, really,
To expect him,
Except...
Steeling myself on Christmas Day
Seemed, somehow,
Obscene.
—*Maggie Smith*

Last Kiss

My heart is heavy
The burden I can't seem to bear,
The memories are so strong
That into the darkness I sit and stare.

In your arms it felt so real.
The closeness we shared was true.
The tenderness of your touch,
The thoughts could only be of you.

Tears begin to fall.
They feel warm against my cheek.
How could my heart break so hard?
And my soul become so meek?

Without you I feel alone.
As the sweetness of your touch is gone.
In the darkness I hear crying,
As your shadow walks along.

These thoughts and memories that damn
My heart and soul could only be this;
The love, tenderness and passion that
I remember in our last kiss.
—*Lesha E. Boucher*

Face to Face Darkly

I opened a draw of ghost and felt
the chilling wind of time.
Old pictures bound with age
and ripened twine.

I saw and heard the reapers song
of strength transformed to weak.
The skeletons that once were flesh,
now in earth's womb asleep.

The sights, the sounds, the essence,
returned from hallowed halls,
replacing time and span and now
with whispers of recall.

The vapor of my life diffused
into my inner space,
resting within my chest
and cave behind my face.

By grace, I thought, we understand?
Dare I question divine decree,
and interrogation the soul of me?
—*Pat Speck*

Season Whispers - Autumn

The sun wakens us later.
The dawn is no longer greeted
by the singing of birds.
The blue of the sky has faded.
There is a hint of frost in the air.

The summer flowers are gone.
The leaves have turned
to brilliant reds and yellows.
The orange pumpkins dot the fields.
There is a hint of frost in the air.

The evening sky darkens earlier.
The children no longer
linger at their play.
The night winds begin to stir.
There is a hint of frost in the air.

Whispers of autumn.
—*Phyllis M. Ferris*

Untitled

A wind blows soft
The day grows dim
Brilliant stars crawl aloft
Another night settles in.
Lights flicker out
Soft pillows sink in
All troubles dismount
Until mother tomorrow begins.
Another day gone by
So much unsaid
One only must try
To remember all things lie ahead.
So look toward heaven
And thank God for your bed
Set your alarm for seven
Goodnight sleepy head.
—*Jerry D. Barnett Jr.*

Friendship

This feeling comes from sharing
The days and years together
The fact that someone's caring
For you no matter the weather
Makes life easier to bear
Even if not always fair.

It's knowing that somebody
Really wants you to survive
It's soothing as hot toddy
Close as bees in the hive
Helping with any troubles
Calming when illness bubbles.

Comforting as an old soft shoe
Beloved as your favorite hat
Sticking with you just like glue
Through success or cozy chat
The joys of life have no end
When you share them with a friend.
—*Albert M. Maier*

Loneliness No More

The storm that came so suddenly,
the fearness of the day.
Waiting, for the anger to go away.

The thought of love so splendor,
Please come and stay.

The thought of loneliness, I hate you,
Please send loneliness away.

The times we spend together.
The magic we possess.
Brings soft and gently raindrops,
of our happiness.

The feeling of contentment, the
sun will come and shine.
And brighten up our spirits,
That we have left behind.
The thought of loneliness,
Please come no more.

I will never, hear you knocking
on my door.

—*Stephan Van de Berghe*

"Three Great Marigold"

In the universe/to exist

Three great marigold,
The first of them, does it,
Is my God, is my God

The second how my days
Happy turn and more
Are you, and will be always
Because, with your tenderness my love,

Dissipating the hardship
Of my life,
Then, you are my future wife
And now our beauty friendship.

I'm believe in my God
I'm believe to you
But the third marigold
Born between you and I.

Thanks to my love,
Thanks to the life,
Thanks to you
And forever thanks to God!

—*Julio Castellon*

Tiana

I have plucked
the flower
that was in full bloom
with untouched beauty,

And which
you had probably
planted
for dignity.

Forgive me
it was irresistible
so sweet
and so pretty.

—*Jim Gaw*

Farewell to an Addict

The past is always with us —
The future never comes.
Today is just a bad dream,
But sleep is never done.

Wrought from pain and heartache
Each moment passes by.
But nothing ever changes —
No matter how hard I try.

Now your job is finished —
One that you've done well.
To make my soul a wounded one,
And life a living hell.

So before I go on living
In just another lie,
Before I considered dying —
I'd rather say Good-bye!

—*Marta Meredith*

In The Spring

In the spring,
The grass is green.
In the spring,
There is quite a seen.

In the spring,
Birds are chirping.
In the spring,
There is no evil lurking.

In the spring,
There is love in the air.
In the spring,
Everything is fair.

In the spring,
You are here, and I am here.
In the spring,
You are my chosen dear.

—*Nicole Burress*

Our Home

At last there's the overall effect,
The house, the yard, the view.
The eye notes every object;
The concept hits you.

This is just our home
'Tis more than brick and mortar,
And the hearts no longer roam;
Our place for sons and daughters.

Note the landscape's beauty,
Nature's care applied;
No monument to marital duty,
Just love and faith, allied.

This house is truly home for us,
Brick by brick it took.
A haven that is filled with trust
Our very favorite nook!

Please come and take a look!

—*Ed Rodgers*

I Think I Had A Vision

(Or Was It MTV?)

Think for me a big TV
The latest child of technology
Plug me in, turn me on
My image flickers... then its gone

And no one seems to care
That I was ever there...

But I creep into your house at night
I rob your mind by satellite
Can't you see the damage done?
I have become the chosen one...

Think for me what children see
Their eyes are wide, glued to the screen
Turn them 'round, look in their eyes
Those neon lights are dollar signs

And no one seems to care
Commercialism everywhere

I'm in your house in broad daylight
I steal your kids by satellite
I've got the means to suck them in
This is a war machines will win...

—*David L. Anderson*

I Still Believe....

I still believe in butterflies and
    the magic that floats on their wings

I still believe in moonlit nights and
    the romance and joy that it brings

I still believe in the magic of rain
    the healing power it supplies

I still believe in happiness
    the sunlight seems to provide

I still believe in tomorrows
    when often live for todays
I still believe in sorrow
    even if miles away
I still believe in forever
    when it seems to never exist
I still believe in true love
    what we've had from our first kiss....

—*Amanda Erdman*

Hadar

Holding
The oily, bumpy
Esrog
The pungent fumes
Consume
My summer-sodden self.
The rattle of
Lulav
Shakes away the warm wind.
Stardust, moonbeams, raindrops
Filter through
Sunflower stalks
To drench our feast
In heaven scent.

—*Carol L. Cohen*

A Visit To Old Nest

How nice to see again,
The nest which I did love!
Though I'm there from afar,
To me you're still above.

I am very much pleased
On seeing my offsprings,
Living in contentment
I praise them as each sings.

And you my grandchildren,
You are all very bright;
Not only you're helpful
But also you're polite.

How are you Seven Hills?
Why are you now like this?
That storm have no mercy
But soon we shall have peace.

That strongest wind that blew
All crushed our source of bread;
But let's all be pliant
And rise again ahead.

　　　—Santos Borbe

The Crow

Oh! Yet the day has gone away
The day has now a due pay
The day has slipped into the night
The day has gone, left us in fright.
And even though the light is low
You can in the dark hear a crow.
The crow is wearing the darkness crown.
And in the distance you can hear
A crowing marvel with no fear.
And through the hills the sun
Shines bright
And as it shines it breaks the night
When the sun begins to shine
The crow looks at the golden
Shine.

　　　—Jim Martin

The Sparrow

Something so young, wild, and free,
I couldn't pass it by - it seemed as
though it needed me.

It was so small, and yet had time to be
grown, this great big sky and beautiful world,
the small bird could never have known.

When I held it in my hands, it looked so
weak and felt so limber, it will no longer
be able to jump and leap from timber to timber.

It was so young and had yet to live - I tried
to help, it seemed I had nothing to give.

I loved the small creature - now it may be
gone, and we couldn't say good-bye - for
that small little bird my hurt pushes
tears from my eyes.

It didn't ask for much - only it's freedom
and some peace, but I noticed with its
shake from my touch - the sparrow I did
release.

　　　—Christie Leslie Smith

A Coffin -Or- A Cage

My childhood has been a theft, long ago it was laid to rest.

I grew up quick, bought a gun, kept my head up straight
So they knew I was the one.

Went to school, teachers calling me son, little did they know
I was a man with a gun.

Ready to kill, ready to die - ready to go, don't even know why.
There's know where to go, know where to run, when we are gone.
Who will raise our sons?

Kids are dyin' on the news, people are cryin' about the rockman blues.
Bodies are all around, blood has spilt and spoiled the ground.

We've got to take care of our own, it's the only love we've ever known.

It's are way of life, it's all we know. It's what you learn
growin' up in the "barrio".
So what can we do? Die or wear the county blues!

And in the end, I'm scared as hell. That in this darkness
I will always dwell!
So you see are choice, in this city of rage!
A coffin-or-a cage!!

　　　—Larry Guzman

Naked Is Two Souls

Our souls stand up erect, strong, face to face in a code of
silence. The lengthening wings break into fire, illuminating
the dark night. Intense is the mind and heart, as the tongue
keeps hush, eyes gazing upon two confronting souls.

　We shiver like the child alone in the darkness from what
lurks behind the things we can not possibly see. We yearn for
an embrace of reassurance from the fear that escape the broken
mask.

　Broken silence brings fear to the mind, pieces of a broken
shield mended back together to house the essence of ourselves.

　Our souls are more than intertwined, from our hearts flows
the passion, from our souls flows truthfulness. It is only the
heart of man that can obtain the channel where emotions flows
fluently onto another's soul.

　　　—Tina E. Rodriguez

A Woman of the World

She left it, a curious, inhibited child of the South.
She returned, an intellectual giant, honored across oceans.
A happy child, who breathed music and literature, but couldn't
enter a public library, or see a real symphony orchestra.
A burgeoning scientist, who dissected frogs but couldn't enter
the zoo. A budding designer, who observed architecture only
from outside, and couldn't try on a dress in a store.
A bubbling child, endlessly inquisitive, in a world limited by
senseless racial segregation. A dark-hued prodigy of the South,
who spread her wings above the Mason-Dixon line. Tutored
university students who, in the South, would have been deemed
her superiors. Out-marketed career salespeople, who looked upon
her as an enigma. Towered over so-called intellectuals from Ivy
League schools, in her every pursuit.
She coped with the world, climbed over every obstacle in her
path. She read their minds, played their games, coped with
their prejudices. Today, the child of the South came home,
admired by all for her lofty thoughts, her seemingly impossible
accomplishments. Still optimistic, still seeking the best of
human souls, never embittered. Today...she is a woman of the world.

　　　—Portia Hamlar

The Puzzle

I am the fabrication of the imagination.
I crouch in the mental womb,
ready to spring forth and become lethal,
or useful.
I am the intruder of the mind that can
make you happy, or I can make you sad.
I am either given birth to, or scrapped.
I am the unruly child that you eventually
tame, or I slip away from you like an
elusive bandit.
You're never quite sure of me.
I keep you alert and on your toes at all times.
I may end up yours, or I may end up
in someone else's camp.
It all depends on how diligently I'm pursued.
My name is invention.

    —Dorothy Stallings

Departure

How I can bid you good-bye my Lord.
  I do not know.
How I can keep from drowning in my own tears,
  at the hand of your departure
  is unbeknownst to my heart.
I lay silently in the depth of my white cotton bed,
  finding my only comfort in its soft feathers.
As I stare at the nothing above me it is good,
  for I can not focus through
  the tears that dwell on my lashes.
In a moment I must move from this state of paralysis,
  there is life around me that demands my weary attention,
These demands come to mind without prompting!
  without care.!
As my mind moves my body cannot,
  for I have not strength, nor the faith
  that it will be of value.

    —Michelle Galindo

A Lesson In Harlem Renaissance

I have not spoken with the caged bird.
I don't know why it sings.
I live many years after Dunbar.
I don't know what he understood.
I have never known any rivers.
I don't know what Hughes knew.

So why do you turn to me for explanations?
Same race does not mean same thoughts, same mind.
No insight came with the pigments of my skin, like batteries.
And yet each time you glance at me,
I understand a little more about rivers and caged birds that
sing.

    —Janay McDonald

Untitled

Capture me, if you can
I don't think we were destined, in Gods plan
I know you've always longed for me
But I don't think we'll ever be
Keep on trying, you may succeed
'Cause if you catch me, I'll meet your need
Goodbye for now, I leave you with a kiss
See you around,
  Love,
    Happiness

    —Korine Luna

Repose

I have a right to dream and I do
I dream of stopping the moment
so that you would not have gone so soon

I dream of being granted the maturity
to handle both our lots
so that we might both flee the moment together
And for love and laughter we would look not

Knowing what might have been will always painfully be
But I have a right to dream and I do
In my dreams, it is only you that I see

    —Merri Martori

The Transparent Child

I came unexpected, uninvited into you
I exist here in the silence
in the darkness of your womb

I ask for nothing
only to live
but I hear the turmoil in your heart.

I am nothing to you…yet.
I upset your schedule.
I ask only for what should rightfully be mine.

I ask you for life.
I need you for life.
I am the seed of your soul.

I am not supposed to be
disposable.
I am alive
my heart beats with your blood.
I am your special one.

Open your heart
I will fill it with my love.
I am "your" child.

    —Rebecca Gonzalez Pena

Untitled

As the rain falls softly on the window -
I fall softly into your arms
Lost in the look in your eyes -
And in the touch of your hands.
Your kisses linger; as the rain continues its song.
They're warm and moist as a summer shower -
And as welcome as the morning dew….

    —Denise K. McQuiston

The Last Tide

Death is on my shoulder waiting to be found.
I feel as though I'm lost yet I know I'm homeward bound.
I know not of my future or what was here before
But when I dig down deep I reach my inner core.
Everyday I hope and pray
I'll make it through just one more day.
Will this wretched feeling ever subside
Or will I go out with the last tide?
Soon it'll come to take me away
And there on my deathbed I will lay.
No worries or fears to lock up inside.
For I will be gone with the last tide.

    —Karen L. Miller

his Pilgrim-Soul

ow, as in the past,
feel one with the land,
feel one with the trees,
feel one with the sea
f this Massachusetts Bay Colony.
erhaps I could say,
or this pilgrim-soul,
hat this sea is my blood,
hese rocks, the cobblestones and land are my bones;
nd the landscape and seascape of my soul?
erhaps that of a tree.

—*Antonetta A. DiGiustini*

a the Dark of the Night

ie awake in the dark of the night,
feel you next to me, and it feels so right.
our sleep is so peaceful as I watch you,
ow warm my heart feels, I wish you knew.
see the precious child you used to be,
part of him that still remains for me.
see the wonderful man that he became,
ho loved me enough to give me his name.
nd I want to be in your arms so tight,
or the love overwhelms me there in the night.
in the morning when you awaken,
emember the heart that you have taken.
emember that it is yours to keep,
nd the love inside goes ever so deep.
now that as I lie next to you in the dark of the night,
m so thankful that it feels so right.

—*Roxanne Jones*

Poem To Say I'm Sorry

eel your laughter running through my soul,
eel your sadness in my heart,
ave sweet bitterness and pain in my eyes,
o one can see me through these selfish lies.
used to let my thoughts run free,
ow darkness is all I see.
this cold, black, empty room,
et the arms of shame fill in to seal my doom.
lence fills the misty air, as wonder fills my mind.
ow could I be so selfish?
cruel? And so unkind?
ords can never say how sorry I am for what I have done,
nd hopefully you'll find someone,
meone who will care, someone who has time to share,
meone better than I,
meone who's love for you will never die.

—*Angela Vogel*

hy Is Life So Unfair

m seventy one, and I thought my life was done
elt no love, or peace in my mine, I know it was a crime
ace in my heart, this was my prayer
ose my love once, I needed someone to care
life, we have been so long together,
e have been so long together,
is hard to part with one so dear
ave nothing left but a tear
es my lift pursue when freed
om matter's base upon a flowering seed
do I hide from sight
r I do not no, what is right

—*Francis Musmacker*

His Love Lives On

As I walked into that cold, dark room
I felt the presence of a man I knew.

When I was a child he held me tight
and made sure that my future was secure and bright.

With a caring thought, and a smiling face
my Dad's voice to this day, can never be replaced.

I questioned God and asked Him why
His reply was simple - another angel needed to fly.

As they closed the casket and I said my goodbyes
I realized my father's spirit was still very much alive.

Deep in my soul and in everything I do
His radiance will always be shining back at you.

—*Laura Gallego*

Untitled

As the sun cascaded over morning's dew,
I filled the desolation with light,
No longer I sulk in the dark of night.
The real reason, I finally knew,
Why she wrote not one letter, but two.
I tried like hell, with all my night,
To keep my emotions wrapped up tight,
Like a dragon's fire my pathos blew
The scorching sun now high in the sky.
And shivering death beneath my feet.
Brought down tears I fail to defeat.
But close to my heart, her I keep,
Drifting, drifting, entering an eternal sleep.

—*R. Jean McCarney*

The Bird

As I peer into the clear, blue sky,
I gaze upon a beautiful tree
With branches so brittle.
Gently sitting in the corner of the limb lies a nest.
As I investigate the small, colorful bird's home,
The little creature sings to me the most lovely song.
The melody fills me with joy and happiness.
The bird whistles as the sun slowly glides into the sky.
The tune is as soft as the snow but as strong as the tree
itself.

—*Alisha Wheeler*

Just To Say Hello

It was winter and time to be inside
I got my sewing machine and my material ready
To sew a dainty pink and white lacy
    dress for a little girl who owned a
    "Cabbage Patch" doll
Someone told me to go to the kitchen
    and so I went to the window
Flying in to the big elm tree
A huge pileated woodpecker who
    came to say hello.

It was spring and time to plant
I got my seeds and my stakes ready
With my hoe I dug the rows
There I was on my knees
Getting up to get my seeds
I turned to see a visitor
Sitting on the pail was a beautiful
    Cedar Waxwing who
Came to say hello.

—*Eleanor Tingelstad*

Anna

I had never seen her before
I guess that made her a stranger;
She dressed pretty, smelt real good
And she spoke not only slowly, but in style.

She patted my nappy five year old head
Her fingers running through my hair,
Just for a precise moment
I felt the bond, a close precious one.

"Hi, I'm Anna, what's your name?"
My tongue was all tied up in knots,
My fingers were all tangled between my teeth
For the life of me, I just couldn't talk.

Anna smiled, she understood
"I'll see you again, real soon," she said
I managed to shake my head up and down
Because I still couldn't find my tongue.

That scene took place over three decades ago
And believe me, I've had no regrets
That stranger is no longer a stranger
Let me introduce to you my adopted mother.

—*Deborah Ann Best*

Dear Mama

Dear Mama, that night I called you on the phone
I had no idea the next day you would be gone.
Had I known I would have said goodbye
but then we would both break down and cry.

I have always viewed life through rosecolored glasses
but it certainly has it's share of surprises.
This was a big one I must say,
and I miss you more and more each day.

I feel sad when I think I'll never hear
your soft hello! And thank you sweetheart.
But I'll cherish your memories year after year.
I'll think of you as nurse, doctor, teacher and
counsellor in life's school of fine art.

Dear Mama, life is not the same without you
but I must go on doing the things I have to do.
I'll try my best to follow in your steps,
I'll try very hard, just don't know how far I'll get,

In the meantime dear Mama, sweet be your rest, may God hold you
securely to His breast, and when the long night is over and the
new day dawns we will be together in each others arms.

—*Julia L. Flynn*

Mourning Bread

My mourning bread rises in the warming oven.
I have made them by the dozen.
Like the dear departed, I gave them all my lovin'.

My mourning bread waits for the oven.
My throbbing temples, I am rubbin'.

The water boils for the tubbin'.

My mourning bread cools on the tables.
The homemade jellies and jams are set out by their labels.
Tents are set up and secured by their cables.

We've eaten our sorrow and buried our dead.
The sun is going down blood red.
I drag my feet in shoes of lead.

Envoi
My mourning bread is down to the heel;
Not enough for a meal,
Not even for my hound, Neil.

—*Jane Pierritz*

Pound Puppy

When he picked me out from all the rest, I thought, this is my
lucky day.
I had no way of knowing things would turn out quite this way.

He took me home and kept me - oh - a year or two
and then he threw me in the yard because I chewed a shoe.

I tried to say I'm sorry as I licked him on the hand,
but he just turned and slammed the gate, I guess he didn't
understand.

If only I could let him know I really meant no harm,
but last night I overheard him saying something about a farm.

The next morning when he picked me up and put me in the car,
I thought he had forgiven me — but we didn't ride too far.

All at once he stopped and pulled me by the hair,
threw me out and off he drove, just left me standing there.

The next few days were very hard filled with pain and fear
because everyone would kick at me whenever I came near.

I'm just lying by the roadside now in a bed of sand —
O - I wish my master would drive by so I could lick his hand.

I just want to tell him I could never find the farm,
and that I'm truly sorry and I really meant no harm.

—*Muriel Mosley*

Take Jesus for a Day

One day I was lost.
I had only this world and its fading glory.
Then I found JESUS. My what a different story.
I found happiness so complete and true.
I found JESUS, and now my friend, I want to share Him with you.

One day I was lonely and I could not find rest.
JESUS spoke and said, I'll help you stand this test.
One day I was sick
and He came and my body with sweet loving care did fix.

Yes, my friend, He's always near
ready to share every burden, every care.
He's always understanding in times of despair.
He's with me when I'm happy and of good cheer.
He's with me in danger and grief.
Yes, my friend, in JESUS there is sweet love and relief.

So take my savior, if just for one day.
And see what great things will come your way.
Give Him your heart, ask Him to wash your sins away,
and, my friend, tomorrow you will beg Him to never go away.
In fact, you'll want to share Him that very day.

—*Patrica Ann Bartee*

Sisters

Sisters
I have one
You have one, we all have one
Sisters
Sisters are there for you through thick and thin
Sisters
Sisters help you no matter what
They care about you, you learn from them
Sisters
Even when you're down you know they're around
They're just like God in a way
Sisters protect you, watch over you, and if you need them,
they're there.
Sisters
Sisters are sisters
They're everywhere!!

—*Jennifer Allende*

Son at War

Dearest Mom I am writing just to tell you,
Have found out people are not what they seem.
When I was home we watched the news those hungry faces
The little ones were the ones who most touched me.

The orders came for so many of us soldiers
I was proud to be one of those to leave
We'll take food and hope to those poor people
Never knowing when I got here what I'd see.

Instead of hunger I have seen hate in their faces,
The ones we came to help now laugh at our pain.
We lost a friend mom they dragged him through the street here.
They celebrated and clapped How can this be?

Now we have heard that another friend is missing
He has been captured and tortured we've been told
I can imagine what his mom must now be feeling
I pray mom that this pain you never know.

Many have died others are hurt and I ask why mom,
For all we wanted was to help and give them food
People are not what they seem here in Somalia
Mom all I pray is to be there home with you.

—*Antonia Martinez*

The Christmas Blues

Around the holidays I get very sad —
Have no mom; I have no dad.
Have no sister or brother either —
Hate that sitcom leave it to beaver.

Around the holidays, I get very sad —
Use to have a mom; I use to have dad.
Use to have a sister and a brother too —
Now all I sing are the Christmas blues.

As I headed home from walk, at the end of the day —
Bright lights and candles they guided my way.
The sounds of carolers ring in my ears —
Listen, remember then wipe away my tears.

As I stood on the steps, outside of my home —
Shuddering at the fact that I live here alone.
No father, no mother nor a family to claim —
Lost in my thoughts, feelings sorrow and pain.

Trying to find courage from a half empty glass —
Stagger from the table thinking of my past.
The loaded gun I point at my head —
Squeezed the trigger. . .

—*Tony R. Hargett*

Personal Lament...

O woe is me when all hope is gone
Have no reason to carry on.
The silver linings from my clouds are done,
O woe is me when all hope is gone.
Sunk in the pit of despair—I see no hope for me,
There isn't a place for me anywhere.
The moon and stars are gone from my skies—
In daylight there is no sun.
O woe is me when all hope is gone.
But wait — is that a star after all,
To light my way and lead me?
No — not a star — but my tear drop glistening.
O woe is me when all hope is gone.

—*Linda Pittinger*

A Poem for Close Friends and Grandmas...

I've been hurt, hurt oh, so bad,
I have nobody to turn to, except you.
I've been sad before oh, so sad,
Yet I have nobody to turn to, except you.
I've been turned down before oh, I
have been, still I have nobody to turn to, except you.
I've been left out oh, they're sorry,
Once again I have nobody to turn to except you
I've been bruised oh, so badly bruised,
Yes once again I have nobody to turn to, except you.
I've been teased by oh, what harsh
Words, though I have nobody to turn to, except you
I've been scared oh, so scared,
the only one I can turn to, is you.
I've been haunted oh, haunted
by ghosts, I have nobody to turn to, except you
I've been cold, you gave me warmth, because I turned to you.
I've been jumped on before oh, I was so scared, I came to you.
I've been sick before oh, I was so sick, I'm better
because I turned to you.

—*Sharlene Wincek*

Reaching

Should I trust you?
I have taught me to withdraw to others only to have it
slapped.
This taught me to withdraw to a world of feeling nothing.
But now the shadows of this world frighten me.
The child inside is afraid of things he can not see.

You ask me to turn on the lights, expose all.

I'm sure there are creatures that will devour
   me once confronted.
You say I should only be afraid of the shadows,
   that seeing what hides behind them in plain light
   will erase the fear.

Your voice is calm.
You are wise.

I am so afraid to hold out my hand.
But a voice, a young voice inside cries out to you.
The child is lonely.
He needs to speak to and be heard by a compassionate soul.

Yet, should I trust you?

Then from the threshold of light you reach out to me.
I grasp the courage to reach into myself.

—*Rodney Drought*

The One Who Hears Me

When no one else is listening, and my words fall on deaf ears,
I know there's One who cares for me, I know that God hears.
When my pain is so exhausting, with no relief in sight,
I call the One who hears me, and I'm soothed with all His might.

When tears fall free as raindrops, and thunder fills my head,
I call the One who hears me, and there's nothing more to dread.
When I grow weak and tired, as man can often do,
I call the One who hears me, and he always leads me through.
When the worries of the day ahead are, hazy, dark, and bleak,
I call the One who hears me, and he shows me what I seek.
When my heart and soul become confused and I'm overwhelmed with
   doubt,
I call the One who hears me, and he always helps me out.

—*Steven Richard Anthony*

Untitled

I feel
I have upset you
I feel you no longer care
I hope that you love me with these feelings
I share

I am listing but silence is what I hear
You see
You mean much to me

I want to hear your agony
And despair
I want these feelings if
You would share

I wish you would
I wish you could

Come, sit here give these feelings
Thought

But, maybe
I need to show you my
Secrets that hide
From eyes that peer deep inside
—*Leah M. Grove*

The Eyes of Love

I have watched the sunrise and the sunset.
I have watched the moon glide across the midnight haze and
stars twinkle.
I have also, watched a seed planted in the evening soil
and blossom into a beautiful flower in the morning dew.
But the most beautiful sight I've ever cast my eyes
on is when your face was tilted in the moonlight just so.
And your eyes flashing at the hinges and dimples
sparkling like gold nuggets in the desert sand.
Your lips parted just so to receive my kiss.
You are sweet, soft and warm
And God made no other like you.

—*Bernard Hicks*

Six Stringed Jesus

Swerve to avoid the kiss of the bull god,
I haven't seem him since the summer of love.
There are no flowers anymore just cracked spines
splitting under the pressure of the sun...
I met Jesus the other day he carried a guitar,
He sang of light and dark, I heard him from the
road, screaming.
The sun melted down and came to rest on my head,
I enjoyed my pain in the front seat.
    "How lucky Jesus is"
I thought as my neck began to crack,
    "he probably never has to tune his guitar".

—*Mike Dimaria*

Remembering You

Everything I paint a picture, or read a poem that doesn't rhyme
I hear your voice calling to me.
I remember your quiet smile and how I used to hide my feelings.
I die a little each day.
Every time I smell your cologne on another man
or I listen to "our song,"
I remember how I felt when I first saw you.
I will always remember.
I never forget...
this is what I feel without you now.

—*Joy Johnson*

Noises

At night, laying in bed half asleep-
I hear shadows in the dark that creep.
In bed I lie,
While images pass by.
I sit up wondering,
While my mind is pondering;
The thought of fear,
Of the strange noises that I hear,
Only mere shadows - coming from images known before,
Images of trees, leaves, things in my room and more.
I sit here wondering,
While my mind is pondering,
On that strange image over there -
Oh no!— It's coming over here,
Wish I may,
Wish this thing away—
I turn on my light,
This thing suddenly disappears in fright.
    —*Le Lien*

God Has Many Voices

God has many voices, many accents . . .
I heard Him speak today
In the deep, slow drawl of a Texan
And again in an Irish brogue;
He called me from a meadow brook,
From the tender heart of a rose;
He whispered to me softly
In the breeze where the willow grows,
He sang me the song of the Universe,
From the throat of a mocking-bird;
Told His glory in a sunrise,
A puppy's tail, a cat that purred;
He wooed me with a lover's tone
And sighed a maiden's sigh;
Cooed in bliss from a cradle bed
And lulled with a lullaby;
I've heard Him thunderously loud
In the billowing of the sea,
And sometimes in the stillness . . .
I hear Him speak through me.
    —*Eve Moore*

Growing Things

    Last night it was raining
I heard it through my window and I felt it in my heart

    The rain feels good to me
It washes my face like sweet tears
and it cleans my soul like a good book

    And I thought-how do the trees feel?
Do they soak it up and let it wrap them up like a warm hug?
Do the leaves drink it in-do they reach for it, lean to it like a kiss?

    The roots get it last of all
Maybe they take it grudgingly-like a friend's late gift-but it
is after all given

    It is with this consideration that try to live my life-
because we all need rain

    And in the rain we all get wet
And in the storm we all are blind

    We sway in the wind, holding hands, and praying for the light
    —*A. Caroline Dean*

Fridays

He walks with pride within his hips,
I know he loves me.
He takes control when I want him to;
he listens well.
He'll miss me. He'll miss our
order.
He took me and controlled me in every sense and way.
I liked it only on Tuesdays.
He's being a real typical male.
I killed him.
Damn - it's Tuesday
I forgot.

—Jennifer Mangine

The Promise

You swear your love for me won't die,
I know that's true, you'd never lie.
I trust you'll be there by my side,
I feel your love all through the night.
Strong and true, no one will doubt.
You're love for me will never run out.

My love for you is over-flowing,
like a river that doesn't stop running.
I swear to you, I'll always be true.
When you need me
Don't be shy, I'm right beside you,
Holding you tight.
It won't matter where you go,
I'll always be with you, heart, mind and soul.

I thought forever was so far off,
And then you showed me what love was!
Loving and caring for each other,
whoever thought we'd stay together.
We have no regrets and our fears don't matter.
We have each other, together, forever.

—Karen Kumpula

"Suicide Land"

In my heart lies a dreadful pain. The feeling I get when
I listen to the rain. Feeling the stress, feeling the pressure
feeling the need what I'll do beyond the future. Boys and
Girls running around seeking to find the meaning of life. Men
and women running around seeking to find the meaning of life.
There living in the world of No communication, No
transportation, and No determination. Livin' and learnin' is a
hard thing to do, but the results shall always comeback to you.
Where freedom lies the nation begin to sink. Where technology
lies people began to think.

The "blossom tree" were once filled with leaves. Now the
pretty leaves are dying one by one.

They could see no more!
They could hear no more!
They could live no more!

They all close their eyes and buried their bones next to their
"tombstone." If you want to know more, put out your "hand"
and I'll shall welcome you to the "suicide land."

—Kevin Chiem

Child Abuse

If we: Abuse, misuse, confuse, they'll choose
        To see, agree, and be, as we
Misuse, abuse, confuse, and bruise them.
        Yet, we get upset, regret
Confusing, misusing, abusing;
        We're losing.

—Shanine Lea Carter

Life As It Is

Life as it is, is just fine for me,
I live for what I do,
My parents tell me to be all I can be,
That's life as it is.

Don't be prejudice in any way,
Be careful of the things you do,
Be careful of what you say,
That's life as it is.

If you have done something wrong - don't hide,
What you don't know can hurt you,
and the pain will build up inside,
That's life as it is.

When that someone special is gone,
You will always remember,
Life does go on,
That's life as it is.

Even if you push yourself to win,
Keep in mind, there's victory,
As soon as you begin,
That's life as it is.

—Aimee Colby

The Water Cycle

I am a water drop.
I live on a leaf.
I am ready to drop on the hard ground but,
I do not drop from the leaf.

I try to get down but, I can't.
I push and push, finally I drop.
I watch the other droplets try to get down.
They each do it a different way.

I get ready to be a puddle.
Then I try to get up and out of the puddle.
It is hard.
Soon, I feel myself rising, rising up into the air.

I turn into vapor.
I look down, down at the place where I was.
I am a very heavy cloud, together with the other droplets.
We are getting ready to fall as rain.

I land on the same leaf.
Wait - what's this - I can't move - it's cold!
I must be ice.
Oh, well, here I go again and again.

—Liz Bubbico

Never Again

A shot, a scream, a thump
I look around, I see...
No. I can't look. But, I have to
So I look to see....
His lifeless body, just laying there
I hear a girl scream, a guy shout
Who did it? Who killed my best friend?
I walk over, look at him
He is still breathing, eyes open, looking at me
I hold him, my arms around him
He says "I love you"
Then dies
Never shall I love
My only love is gone, and so am I
I no longer live, because he's gone
I said he was just a friend, but he wasn't
He was the love of my life
Never again
Shall I love

—Rebecca Brown

Secret Dreams, Whispering Winds

The wind in the sky, the water in the sea,
I look at me and this is how it's to be.

The trees and the mountains, the river below,
The flowing seasons, is what I'd like to know.

The deer are all running, the buffalo so slow,
I look at me and this is what I want to see.

The sun shinning high, the wind a slight breeze,
The stars are all bright, like the slight flow of the trees,
Please, Just let me be free.

The mist I can see, by the night fire burning,
The people are all turning,
What do they see,
Only me.
Their eyes are all questioning, and I ask why?
Someone once told me, look often to the sky.

Now I see, why they look at me.
Once again, I am to be free.

I look into the river,
What do I see?
A reflection of me, and a star flying by........
— *Helen Shaulis*

The Window

When I feel unhappy or a little bit sad,
I look out my window and I don't feel so bad,
With the window blowing and drying my tears
It seems to take away all my fears,

Over looking this beautiful view,
It makes me feel like fresh mountain dew,
My mind fills up with happy thoughts,
What a joyful time this window has brought!
— *Jennie West*

Bitter Woman

I was once happy and full of life.
I looked forward to every wakening hour of the day.
The sun would rise and my heart would dance with glee.
I use to glisten like the butterflies through the air.
The scents of the earth use to feel me up with anticipation,
for I was going to walk on water.
But, then, it crumbled, it shattered, and it broke in half.
The stars no longer shined after that day.
The cool air grew colder.
The grey sky became dimmer until it reached a deep, dark,
charcoal black.
I can still hear his foot steps and the door closing behind him
The sounds are still loud and echoing in my hear
as though he left me yesterday.
Its been a while now and I'm no longer bitter.
The hallow feelings has been filled with new things, new joys,
new pleasures and a new love.
I can look back and laugh and even cry.
For I am no longer bitter.
— *Robbie Matoka Welborne*

Oh Lord!

Oh Lord, I need you so, Oh Lord where have
you been. The heart is weary, the soul is down.
Oh Lord, I need you so, the sun is out, the
trees are blooming, roses are giving off their
beautiful aroma.
So I know you're here, but where? Oh Lord
Where? I need you so.
— *Rosette Mines*

Untitled

When I was a baby
I looked into your eyes
I saw that you were gentle
Mysterious but wise

You held me when I was crying
You taught me how to walk
After I skinned my knees
You taught me how to talk

When I brought home my first report card
You were so proud of me
You knew how hard I had worked
And said, "What a good girl is she"

Now when I look into your eyes
I see what I saw before
The pass to every hallway
And the key to every door
— *Diane Marie Psaros*

Divorce

(Dedicated to Mom and Dad —
I love you always and forever.)

I used to think families were love,
I used to think love wouldn't end,
And when my parents got divorced,
I used to think that it would mend.
Now I know that their love is gone
They'll never be together again.
They both want me to choose sides,
They don't know that neither will win.
They want me to choose between love and hate,
But that's a decision I just can't make.
Even though they've both remarried
The sorrow and hate I've still carried.
My hurt's so strong it can never heal,
The hole in my heart could never be filled.
I used to think hearts couldn't be broken.
I used to think love would live on.
But now my heart is shattered,
And all my love is gone.
— *Misty Doub*

Daddy Dear Daddy (Wish You Were Here)

Oh daddy, dear daddy,
I love you so much.

The days have now passed into weeks, into years.
Slowly, I remember what holds you, so dear.

The lap that I sat on, the song of your voice.
The moments of stern warnings, to correct my bad choice.

Oh Daddy, sweet Daddy,
Wish you were here.

Our grand kids don't know you and though they never will,
Your kindness and morals we try to instill.

Oh Daddy, dear Daddy,
I love you so much.

The days have now passed into weeks, into years.
Slowly, I remember, what holds you so dear.

Your smile in your picture,
With mom so near.
The love that we felt for both of you dear.

Oh Daddy sweet Daddy,
Wish you were here.
— *Patricia Denning*

What's Christmas Without A Goose?

Santa left open the gate and we got loose
To say:
"Yuletide greetings and stuff
The year's wishes, too, e'en that ain't Enuff!!"

—*Jeannette Denny*

Grandmas

I've always thought that Grandmas had a special place in life,
I mean, something other than just being Grandpa's wife.

She is always there when needed, to kiss a bump or hurt-
She can make a game of anything, even washing off the dirt.

Her lap is soft, when one is tired, her arms are open wide,
To hold you and enfold you, when there are tears to hide.

Her hand is strong to cling to, if there's anything to fear,
Her touch is soft and gentle, as she wipes away a tear.

She's quite a special person, I'm sure you will agree,
Someday I hope my children make a Grandma out of me.

—*Peggy Finke*

The Sun

The days are cold.
I miss the freedom of the out of doors
Denied by weather such as this
Winter's face so grim and bold
I miss the sunshine's golden kiss
The sun so welcome,
I can understand
How ancient peoples took you for a God
Gave you command.
You bring the leaves, the earth its light
You warm, and seem to give it very life
On you depends bright hopes
The cheerful days of man.
The new life each and every day
That passes in life's span.
We bless you as a gift from Him
Who gives us more than earthly life to win.
The gifts of spirit, things unseen
The gift of power to think
To pray and dream.

—*Louise Catherine Moshier*

"Barely Getting Bi"

All of those lengthy evenings,
I paid unfailing attention to your wordless stare.
Your precise words,
When you did speak,
Cutting deep into me.
Often times you've made me laugh or smile,
Nothing has ever been truly witty about your words,
We were only laughing because of your unusual straightforward
attitude.

The forte that is so melancholy about our situation, is that
you believe
We only hang around you because you entertain us,
Yet, that is so illegitimate that it hurts.
You are a beautiful person, and we adore you.
You may be quite forthcoming,
    Still, we see your compassionate side,
    And we know that you have a personality,
    And you can not hide your interests much
                            longer.

—*Margaret Porter*

"A First"

Eyeing through my bouquet of memories
I picked the one when I first prayed.
The stranger I had quietly spoken to,
in silence, snipped away my worries.
Lifelong deeds did I pledge to do, if
He would help me not to be so afraid.

The glorious sun did rise each morning
throughout the seasons with my fears.
Dark stormy nights did end with calm
in steadfast sleep relieved of my tears.
Never sure that my deeds met His approval,
I would dig up more with a bigger shovel!
My biggest fear was not to see merit in life
by dying too soon, and only have felt strife.

He hasn't been a talker like I sure am, but,
nothing feels safer than being His chatty lamb.
His hallowed silence known since a book of olden
will end old age in me to hear a voice so golden.
I really improved with age, as you will see:
I pray in silence and include thoughts of thee.

—*Olivia L. Williams*

As the Day Ends

Alone in the peacefulness of watching the sun set
I ponder what it all means.
The pink, red, orange sky prompts thoughts of unknown
The what's, whys and essence of life.

I enjoy the night air as the sun drifts deeper into the horizon
I ask myself what causes one to fall in love with another human
being. I haven't an answer, but only know
It must be fate.

The day draws to a close with my mind working overtime.
To think about the past, present and future-what is ahead of me.
I want to share my life with someone. Maybe You.
If only you share in this same dream.

Taking abundant, profound delight in the smallest details of
life. Remembering there's nothing more important than love;
For caring is always worth the risk.
To have loved, if only for one moment
Is a joy no one can take away.

—*Sandy Hiskey*

Christmas Eve Nightmare

I think I had a nightmare,
I really cannot say.
I dreamt that dear old santa had fallen from his sleigh.
The toys were lost and scattered,
As far as I could see.
There were dolls in all the bushes,
And pink undies in the tree.
Will Johnny get a barbie?
Will Susie get a truck?
I'll probably get the undies.
It seems like just my luck.
If you hear me dear old Santa,
You can change all my bad luck.
When you climb back in your big red sleigh,
Please buckle up!

—*Linda Saunders*

Woe Is Me!

Woe is me! I look at you and I feel so blue.
I remember when we walked hand in hand
Thy memory makes me so sad.

Woe is me! I walk in the streets alone and sleep in the cold.
I warm my hands by the burning barrels of trash.
I sleep with newspaper over my head and cardboard for my bed.

Woe is me! I can't stand to suffer any more.
I want to kill myself but I can't.
I'll never sleep in a warm bed again or pour hot water for my
    coffee.
Such things I took for granted before, which now I lust for so.
When I ask for help people turn the other way.
What did I ever do to deserve this Pain?
Well, farewell for this day. I have to go to sleep.
Don't worry about me, I'll be here,
    Could under this cardboard house
Filled with yesterday's news to keep me warm.
Woe is me!

—*Bryan H. Duncan*

I don't understand?
I said I did
    but I don't
You told me you had changed and
    things between us are different.
Why?
Of course I agreed with you and said I understood
    as I always do when you are around.
But now that I am alone
    in my room
I realize
I don't understand?

—*Lisa Fitzharris Chriswell*

Untitled

I see the years pass before my worn down eyes.
I savor every moment,
Crumple them up and stuff them in my pocket
To place them at a later time
In a box.

The box, made of cardboard,
Old and taped together
By the masking tape of time.

The box has been searched through
Time and time again
Looking for that special feeling
That I once felt before.

I take my crumpled memory
From my deep, dark pocket.

I reminisce.

I place it in the box
Full of memories
To one day find again.

—*Dj Halicky*

True Friends

True friends are those who really care
True friends are those who are always there
When you are down and out
They are there to help and shout
For joy with you when something good happens
Or with you when sadness dampens
Your spirits, your heart, or your pride
They are there always by your side.

—*Diana Sandage*

The Dancing Children

As I walked the streets of Ghetto
I saw
Two children dancing
Two little skeletons dancing
Black eyes like coals in the small skulls
So big they seemed in the emaciated faces.

I saw them everyday
Dancing, ceaselessly dancing
To amuse passersby, so they
Would pity them
And give them a few cents
To keep the death at bay…a little longer.

Many years have passed
Ghetto is now a memory
And in my memory it lives.
Whenever I remember it
I see
Two children dancing
Two little skeletons dancing.

—*Irene Grimberg*

Life In The Sunset

The night opened its sky to me; by the light of a star
I saw her sitting by the window pane.
She sits there in the sun and rain,
Nor do I pretend or feign interest in her "goings about";
My curiosity is genuine.
The curtains blow about the window as she rocks in her chair;
Even the sun- it seems to care
As it rises and sets on her stare.
I am certain her stare has seen many days
And many more sun rays than I;
When the wood house was built;
When seed grew into tree;
It has probably seen me.
Now she is blind, though so sure am I
That she has seen many a face and an eye;
That she is seeing something now- perhaps more than most
folks.
She is old; she is plain
And she sits there in the rain
Until the life goes out of the sunset.

—*L. Liebling*

A Lonesome Soul Walked Past Me and it was an Angel

Oh lonesome soul
I saw your teary eyes
as they quickly shifted
away from mine.

As you walked by
I felt your broken heart
and my eyes filled with tears
remembering my own pain.

So as not to betray what you knew I saw
and not to invade what you could not share
I just barely turned and caught a glimpse
of your beautiful lonesome soul.

As you walked away
in a mix of humiliation and helplessness
uncontrolled tears rolled down my face
which I quickly tried to hide.

Then a stranger asked, "Are you alright?"
and I saw that you had returned.
With tears still in my eyes, I smiled
for I had seen my first Angel.

—*Angie Gamez*

Black

Dark; Gone; yet ever existing, and lasting
I search but all I see are memories
Now all that is left are tears
I am no one

Through the jungle....to the temple
I worship you
You are gone
Fog blocks my vision
You are no one

Now not only are you gone but everything's lost
Smoke fills the room
I find myself......without you?
I am someone!

  —Louise Jett

Untitled

My moments of insanity are stretching
I see a face, but - egad - what's the name?
What is that flower with those big blue blossoms?
Where did I put my book when company came?

What wine is that which I so often order?
What artist made his pictures very glum?
Refrigerator open — I just stand there -
What could I want and why am I so dumb!

But then a bit clicks in — I think "It's Rembrandt,"
It's really strange how suddenly I know.
And Zinfandel's the wine, the face is Eunice.
Surprisingly my mental juices flow!

So then I chuck it all and go my way
"Hydrangea!" That's the word that made me fret
I'm in control, but I know that tomorrow
There'll be much more that I can sure forget.

  —Jean D. Arnold

Standing On The Mountain's Top

Standing on the mountain's top, weary from the climb.
I see a view before me, so picturesque and clear,
Of everything of which surrounds, which signals I am free...

Standing on the mountain's top,
Looking far beyond the misty clouds,
At all of the paths of which it holds-
In full view, so clearly now.
And, as the warm air touches my skin,
It reminds me, that I've a chance
A chance to begin again...

Standing on the mountain's top,
Looking back and knowing all that's been;
Through adventures that someone else, would always seem to win.
I am reminded of the cloud which follows me,
Ever taunting-forever haunting.
But, just at that moment, I turn around...
And for myself, I will decide - remembering still,
All the while-the climb from such a dreary side,
That this is where I'll begin again...
Standing on the mountain's top.

  —Patricia L. Blanco

You Shouldn't Judge Somebody of...

You shouldn't judge somebody of what they are
You shouldn't judge somebody of what they wear
You shouldn't judge somebody of the way they talk
And you definitely shouldn't judge somebody of
  what
   Color
    they are.

  —Emily Hartlieb

Nowhere

    I
  am a speck of dust
floating on the everlasting tide
 in the universal vacuum.
As I glide in the universe's dark
   infinite cloak
I search as to find something
 in this place of nowhere.

  —Glenn Pollock

Staring Up at the Sky

Whenever I stare up at the sky,
I see birds and stars up high.
And I see a round ball,
I wonder why it never falls?
People don't even care,
But I just seem to stare and stare,
People think I'm crazy,
But their minds must be lazy.
I always thought it was made of cheese,
So pass the mozzarella, swiss, and cheddar please.
I found out it was not,
I don't think it's near being hot.
Peace is good for us all,
So be kind to the little round ball!

  —Shannon Haley

Untitled

As I look through the window of time,
I see the future before my eyes.

A future of brightness and togetherness.

As I look through the window of time,
I see the past before me in an unexplained sadness.

I see the loss of the only one that I have truly loved.
I see the memories that pulled us through our times of
need and prosperity.
I see the happiness that we shared together many times.

Then I recall what has happened in the heat of a raging fire.
I can tell that it wasn't meant to last now that I am past
the experience.

As I look through the window of time I realize to leave
the past alone and move on to the future.

  —Jamie Miller

Through The Eyes Of Me

Sitting by myself,
I see the world change,
I see images on the shelf,
I hear loud bangs.

There is a war going on,
It's about people's feelings,
People don't care about others they go on,
People are killing other people
over their feelings.

Through the eyes of me I see joy,
But when the gang comes,
The joy breaks like a toy,
The gang treats people like bums.

If people could only see through my eyes
They would stop name calling
and accept others for who they are,
I just wish people could see through the eyes of me.

  —Jamie L. Barnes

Attainment

Yea though I climb the ladder of success
I shall fear no challenge
For I am my own best judge
For what is life without success
A feeling of fulfillment without duress
As the wind swirls like a stormy night
I too will carry on
For to reach my goal the sun will shine
For what is life.........
                               It's mine.

—*Carol A. Powell*

Hidden In Emotion

As I lie in the discharge of emotions that have gone
I sing the ballad of no one, I die before the dawn

My love has never come, in haste I shut my eyes
My heart has lost its fight; in pain I only sigh

In depths of parted rivers, blood flows throughout my veins
Arms are left to quiver; no one to take the reins

The breath has left from me, the ears cannot recall
Loneliness dies in sorrow, teardrops start to fall

Nails lost their edge, dirt befalls my face
Life gone and can't return, humiliated and disgraced

A turn for the better gone, landfall in my mind
Self-deprivation in humanity, my soul left for none to find

Heat scorches my brain, fingertips have become numb
Never to be born again, left to just be dumb

Deceit falls upon me, a cry unheard in the dark
A form bears unresistance; the deafening sound of the lark

My cry is for help, losing my last breath
Heart no longer thumps, I cling to my death.

—*Robert L. Gensler, Jr.*

Peer

Gaze upon a starless sky, look beyond and wonder why.
I sit alone, all by myself; my heart beats for you,
I long for no one else.
I remember the days,
When I bathed in the rays of your bliss,
Eternity was held by the essence of your kiss.
You held me and told me you were mine,
That our love would last beyond the thresholds of time.
Did you perceive the strength of our desires?
Understand the chemistry of touch that builds an infinite fire?
Can you feel?
Or was it real?
Was it but a dream? Nothing being as it seems.
You captured my heart; I'm no longer free.
Perception is but a distant memory.
The mask of deception plays its role.
Revealed, it leaves us with no control.
Every thought that echoes through my mind,
Your existence is yet a step behind.
This is a beginning of an ending.

—*Natalie Carreira*

Untitled

"Energy"
An African dance
comes out of my desperation
an exhalation of infernal passions
that leaves me
overwhelmed and bare.

—*Pira Maria Francesca*

A Soldier

I heard the cries of the wounded, I saw the men who fell.
I smelled the sweat and blood of those who prayed to leave that hell.
I tasted the salt of many tears that were shed on foreign ground,
I prayed for all the fighting men who were by duty bound.
I knew that there were many who never again would see
the homes they left behind or their family.
No one knows the sacrifice made by those who tried,
I know, I know, I know too well - I'm one of those who died.

—*Anita H. Weber*

True Feelings

I've loved you from both near and afar,
I still love you even though we are apart.
I have kept it to myself because I was timid and shy,
even after we said our good-bye's.
We always kept in touch one way or another,
loving, caring, worrying for each other.
Now knowing after all this time you feel the same way,
I wished, hoped, and dreamed for this day.
Is it a dream or is it real,
will we finally admit how we feel?
My heart is a lock and your love is the key,
open the door and follow the path which leads you to me.
We'll take our love one step at a time,
I am your and you are mine.

—*Rafael H. Nater*

The Should'aves

With my hand on his chest, unpulsing but warm,
I stood memorizing his face, so quiet and closed.
"It's over," a voice said, "it's all over."

Yet I stayed, despairing, unwilling to leave the warmth.
'Til the voice said again, "it's all over."
Was there something more I should'ave done?

A whisper answered, "you should'ave, you should'ave."
More and more should'aves grew louder and louder.
Til time was a chasm screaming with should'aves.

"Write down the should'aves," the voice said, "and they'll
stop." Pages and pages of should'aves I wrote.
Tears smearing the words, scorching the pages.

But the should'aves kept screaming and screaming.
"Tell his sister and brother," the voice said, "then they'll
stop." What can I tell them, these children who hurt?

So I told them I loved them again and again.
In so many words, I told them and told them.
Til at last the should'aves stopped screaming.

Now time catches the sunlight, the chasm is gone.
As the should'aves stopped screaming at last.

—*Virginia Kasten*

I Ran ....

I ran from people,
I ran from shadows,
I ran from animals,
I only once ran from you, but God led me in your direction and
said to me, do not flee, for he will not harm you,
I tried to buy your affection, and when I saw it didn't work,
I ran.
When ever I saw you in the hall or walking down the street,
I ran.

God picked me up and put me back on my feet again, he said,
"Don't do what you did."
He has not lost confidence in me,
because he see's exactly what my friends and I see.

—*Nicole Marie Reynolds*

"Hear The Master Talk"

When I am lonely I like to go for a walk,
I stop and listen to Hear The Master Talk.
The Master Talks to me wherever I go,
Did I hear you ask? "How do you know?"

God talks to me with the singing of the birds, through
the sounds of all creatures He speaks but not with words.
When I hear the whisper of the wind coming through the trees,
I know I'm on Holy Ground so I drop to my knees.

I say, "Thank You Lord for letting me hear you speak,
Through the sounds of all creatures strong and weak.
The roar of the lion to the sound of the smallest insect,
In God's eyes they all get the same respect.

I can also See God wherever I go,
With the Beauty of the plants as they grow.
I'll always be thankful for the Beauty of this earth,
No one will ever know just how much it's worth

If you are lonely go for a walk,
Stop, Listen, do you Hear The Master Talk?
He's out there if you'll only open your Heart,
He will come in and He will never depart.

—*Jay Harvey*

The Screamin' Needle

Behold—for I am the screamin' needle that rapes your brain,
I tear into your flesh as I search for your vein.
You'll use me and abuse me then throw me away—but no,
you'll never lose me, till your dyin' day.

And the times you lay idle, I never despair—knowing when
you score drugs, I too will be there.
And though some of you drop pills and others snort coke—
without shiny me, your trips are a joke.
So when you've nothing to lose and want to get high—just
roll up your sleeve, and give me a try.
I'll send you your pleasure via stainless-steel—straight
to your heart, with the greatest of zeal.
And though I'm quite small, I'm really quite real—so don't
let my size fool ya, I'm built to kill...

—*Scott French*

Death Of A Friend

Your picture is still sitting on my dresser
I think of you now and then,
For you were the one so close to me
I will never forget you, my friend.

They who took you away
I will never ever forget,
For it was a dark and stormy night
And the death of you, in that awful car wreck.

They were some kids who had been drinking
That were in the other car,
Neither of them made it
They didn't even, get very far.

The car wreck had left me the memory
For I feel like I am the one to blame,
Because of the loss of someone dear
And a very very close friend.

When they took you away from me
Oh how I cried,
And when they said you weren't coming back
I felt that I could Die.

—*Angela Lakey*

Memory Rain

Sit by my window and watch the rain
I think of you once again

An image of your smile or the glitter in your eye
I haven't forgotten you and here again I cry

Remembering the talks and loving laughs we shared
We dared to say "I love you" though we both know we cared

When the rain is all gone and the sky's once again blue
i'll wipe away the tears and tuck away softly the
memory of you.

—*Ramona McCants*

Explain To Me What I See

Optical illusions create much confusion, through your eyes.
I think you will find, it's all in your mind, to your surprise.

You feel a little hazy, think you may be crazy, from what you see.
Straight makes a curve, fixed seems to swerve. How can it be?

Those stairs go down, down and around, back to the top.
Same stairs go up, always going up, they don't stop.

This is the short one, that is the long one. What? Both the same!
The moon changes size, rising through the skies, help me explain.

Head is aching, nerves are breaking, I want to shout.
Normal's not distracting. Mind is relaxing. I got out.

Illusions behind me, really got me stymied, felt like a nut.
From what I have heard, relative's the word. Time does what?!

—*W. Wright Robinson*

The Lost One

I thought he loved me, I thought he cared,
I thought he always would be there.

I love him so, with all my heart.
I cannot help to be apart.

I tell him now, I love him so,
I call him every night to let him know.

There's times I wish, that I would die.
There's times I wish, I could go back in time,
And change the things, that went so wrong.
We've been departed for so long.

Every night before I sleep. I pray to God,
Please help me beat this long lost life.

This knife has pierced my heart, my soul.
My teenage life has mostly blown.

Without him I cannot go on,
I will survive, I will be strong.
My life has to go on.

But let me tell you so,
My father dearest,
Daddy I'm all alone!

—*Belinda Arreola*

The Birds

There is a thing of beauty in the air
For God has put the birds up there
The blue jay the Robin, the chickadee
He put them there for you and me.

He put them there for us to see
So when your feeling down and out
Look up to the sky and see
What God has put there
A thing of beauty for us to share.

—*Alfred Johnson*

Is There a Monster There?

Is there a monster there
  can you see it?
  What does it look like?
  Can you hear it?
Is there a monster there?
  where did it come from?
Is there a monster there?
Can you tell me?

    —*Tara Coumont*

Untitled

I need a friend
I try to be kind! I try to be good
No matter what I do, I'm misunderstood
I need a friend
I try to laugh, I try to smile
Sometimes it works but just for a while
I need a friend
Please look at me. Try to understand
I would be so happy if you would take my hand
I need a friend
He spoke to me. He said Hi! Hi!
What should I do? Should I reply?
I need a friend
I said Hello. How do you do
He said, "I'm very glad to know you."
I found a friend

    —*Gertrude Borenstein*

Jack Frost

On certain special winter morns
I wake to see ice-art adorns
the outside of my window glass
The artist—of the elfin class

None but he could flit around
so high above the frozen ground
and make such wild, eccentric strokes
to please us earthbound mortal folks

How stealthily he comes at night
to decorate my windows white
How quick he works, then off! to do
the panes that belong to my neighbors, too

As every snowflake is unique
so too his paintings—magnifique!
But delicate as whispers they
For up the sun and melt away

    —*Frederick J. Mansley*

Life

As the gentle breezes blow from the sea
I walk the sand aimlessly
Why has life neglected me?
Wondering why life can't be happy and free
The beauty of the sunrise
Can't you see?
Life is this way
Not just for me.

Happiness is what we aim for
Strive to achieve
To be realistic
You'll gain even more.
As I walk until sundown
I finally can see
God's gift is life
That I have found...

    —*Sylvia Lewis*

Enchanting Enchanters

Vastness,
  I wander, endlessly, searching,
trying to find my enchanter.
  Holder of dreams, where might
you be dwelling?
  I grope the walls thoroughly,
yet I am still blind.
  This darkness, this cold darkness is
so oppressing.
  Songs, melodious songs of wisdom burst
from deep within my heart ricocheting
off the no longer dark walls.
  Allowing me to see the enchanter
  within.

    —*Jen Wilson*

Do I Have the Right

Let me have a chance to live
I want to be alive
I want to be able to grow
I want to cry, laugh, and feel
I want to be able to hug, kiss, and love
I am your child
Please do not kill me
I want to be able to grow as a person
you had a chance to live
It's not fair, what did I do to you?
I haven't had a chance
Why don't you love me?....
Why don't you care?.......
Why......Why......Why.....Why......

    —*Khadijah Holley*

Be Free One Last Time

Follow me to my destination.
I want to run through the storm.
To be alone with you in these crisp cool raindrops.
Run through the fields, down the meadow's lane.
Roll around the bridge and drink the newly white wine.
Do you feel free?
Feel the past release through your blood.
Cast a spell with me, make an old woman a drug.
Lick the paper, it's ok, it's clean.
Sleep the love off and become one with me.
To live life like a dream,
Just living in the storm,
Fly with the sea gulls,
When lightning strikes you will be the first to know.
He will be showing you a sign.
Do not fear for striking has it's rewards.
Now you have a long awaited maze to fulfill when
darkness occurs.

    —*Angel Carr*

October

Soft as a symphony, golden leaves gently wafting down.
Along the river's edge I stand
While the moody water fiercely flows.

Is it all real or some master's painting?

I see the naughty squirrels scurrying busily to and fro,
While the leaves dance in the wind along the walk.
Oh, how good to be alive to savor nature's last fling
Before harsh winter.

    —*Emily Fedewick*

Richard

You were to me
Gentle hands
Holding a turquoise egg,
Respecting both its weakness
And its promise.

—*Fiona Gray*

An HIV Child's Dream

When I was five and in kindergarten,
I wanted to be an astronaut.
Flying in the air seemed so spectacular;
How far I could go and touch the stars.

When I was ten and in the school play,
I dreamed of becoming a famous actress.
Having people watch me on the stage;
Applauding my every word and action.

Now that I am fourteen and an adolescent,
My goal is to live a long happy life.
But my dream may be hard to fulfill
Since no one has found a cure to AIDS.

So for now I live with hope and prayer,
Enjoying every minute God gives to me.
However, nothing lasts forever
And the time bomb I sit on will explode.

—*Sheila K. Dudash*

I Think I Met The Lord Once

I think I met the Lord once, I was riding on a cloud. He said
I was being born to make my parents proud.

I think I met the Lord once, He beckoned me to His knee, He
told me wondrous stories, I was only two or three.

I think I met the Lord once, I was lying in my bed. My parents
always told me His angels rested by my head.

I think I met the Lord once, I was angry, not at my best. It
was the day I held my Mother's hand and laid my Father to rest.

I think I met the Lord once, I hadn't seen Him in awhile.
What I always thought was anger, was truly just denial.

I think I met the Lord once, it was a very special day. My
mother said she loved me as she gave my hand away.

I think I met the Lord once, in my husband's smiling face. As
he held our newborn son and I knew His perfect grace.

I think I met the Lord once, as I hushed my daughter's cries.
I told her of His love for her and I gazed into her eyes.

I know I've met the Lord before, He's been with me from the
start. He gives me all I ever need, He lives within my heart!

—*Patti Kushner*

Always

Just the other day I saw a crack in the sun
I was standing on the bay where we had begun

Turning upwards I see the whiffs of white clouds in the sky
To picture those funny little shapes where angels don't die

Over there on the wall I see a child walking a tightrope
Radiant with laughter and of innocent hope

Up high the gulls were calling out as they circle for home
Our grounds are safe I see they still live of sandstone

Here and now is the place to be completely honest
Simply I and this soul to manifest

It is time now, I must turn and head into the sun
To my love — my death has just begun

—*RKT*

1994

Dear Editor:
I was thinking is the reason of my existence
Where? I'm really, I'm in a lost city
whites, blacks, orientals
everybody with their own thinking
different existences, different colors
Oh! My God, I'm dreaming, is the melting
pot, New York, the city I was born, now my
nightmare begins, I like to shoot to shout
to drink, to eat, to melt, I'm everything
or nothing at all, all the existences in me
boil like water oil or lava, I'm a thousand
pieces in one block of meat contemporary
living creature.

—*William McDonald*

Mortal Binds

As the darkness approaches I pier through my window.
I watch the last glimmer of sunlight as it slips helplessly
into the void of yesterday. The day is swallowed up by shadows,
consumed by the night.

At first I felt anxious....Uncertain of what might lurk
beyond my range of view. All at once, I was comforted by the
light illuminating from my life long friend. How bold in all
its glory is the moon beneath the stars! As I searched out
memories of past sightings, loneliness compassed me about.

My friend was so far away! Reconsidering, I thought...
How secure the moon stands amidst the cold darkness of the
heavens immeasurable! I stood entranced by it's majestic light.

I realized I would never embrace my friend with the limbs of
my mortal futility. Nevertheless, the beauty of the moon's
tranquil wisdom shone brighter than mere words.

It made me realize... By the light of our inner spirits,
our heart of hearts, mankind could not only touch the moon,
We could become one! Transcending the barrier of material
thought.... Far beyond the limits of our mortal binds.

—*Kirk M. Ray, Sr.*

To Say Goodbye

By the time you read this letter,
I will already be gone.
Everything I did and said.
Always seemed to be wrong.
I know I may not be forgiven,
For the time that I have wasted.
Leaving like this leaves me lifeless.
My blood I have already tasted.
On this note don't ever forget me,
But remember the good times we've shared.
I tried to heal the pain inside,
But it was more than I could bare.

—*Jennifer Hale*

My Halloween Caldron

My halloween caldron
A witches broom.
Many monsters will come
To see me and my cat have fun.
A full moon and a bat
A tombstone and a black cat.
A cobweb on my window
A skeleton on my wall
My halloween caldron
Scary stuff and all.

—*Gina Oades*

"Moments Together"

I love you mother, so sweet and pure;
I will always love you, for this I am sure.

I was little baby all alone, you brought me up and thought of
me as your own; for this I did pray, it is because of you for
who I am today.

You saw my first smile, and dried my first tear;
you brought me up in this world, to be so sweet and dear.

You've been with me when I was sick, and was there for me when
I was sad; you praised me when I was good, and scolded me when
I was bad.

When I fell and scratched my arm, or was stung by a bee;
I wasn't afraid because, Mom, you were always there for me.

When I was down and depressed, and feeling really blue;
I was lifted up when I heard you say the words, I love you.

We have been through some hard times, but that is in the past;
now we look forward into the future, for those special moments
that will always last.

We will always have each other, because the bond between us no
one can undo; just remember, that you have me and I have you.

This poem is dedicated to you and there's just one more thing
I would like to convey — Happy Mother's Day!

—*Michelle Lynn Posma*

Danville City Jail

As I sit here counting the bars
I wish I could be counting the stars

Each night as the cell doors slam hard and loud
I wonder could I ever hold my head up proud.

Now that the crime is done, the time is not
Did I really deserve all these years I got.

Day by day, we sleep, we pray
That God would grant us one free day

The new ones come in night after night
And in their faces I see both sadness and fright

The people here they try to be kind
But they know I'm a little bit out of my mind

The water so hot, the bars oh so cold
I guess I'll be here until I grow old.

—*Sherry Ozmore*

I Am A Girl Who Likes To Dance

I am a girl who likes to dance
I wonder I could be a professional dancer
I hear the music playing
I see me dancing on the stage
I want to be a professional dancer
I am a girl who likes to dance.

I pretend to be a mother
I feel like I am a mother
I touch my baby
I worry about how my baby will turn out
I cry when I will see my baby
I am a girl who likes to dance.

I understand I will be a good mother
I say that I love babies
I dream about having a baby girl
I try to be good to my baby
I hope someday I will have a good girl
I am a girl who likes to dance.

—*Jennifer Hanley*

Is It Good-bye

Tonight as I sit here and look into your eyes,
I wonder to myself "is this going to be our last good-bye."
I wish so much you didn't have to go,
Just watching you leave makes me feel so low.
How could you do this to me,
I love you, don't set me free.
I don't know what I'd do alone,
Because I'm not use to being on my own.
You were always there when I needed you,
I just wish you could say the same thing too.
Please say that you love me with all of your heart,
Just say those three words and we'll never part.

—*Jayme L. Brow*

Fear

I have fear.
I wonder what's going to jump out of those bushes.
I hear foot steps walking towards me.
I see a shadow right below me.
I want to reach light.
I have fear.

I pretend I'm safe and sound.
I feel hands grabbing me.
I sense danger.
I cry because I'm afraid.
I worry because I know I won't survive.
I have fear.

I try to get home as fast as I can go.
I say "Leave me alone."
I dream that I won't wake up.
I hope this is a nightmare.
I have fear.

—*Kori Skaltsas*

As I Watch

I just stood there watching you and her dance.
I wondered if I would ever get another chance.

The words of the song just cut me in half.
All you would do is stand there and laugh.

As the memories came flowing back in my mind,
I looked at you with her, and heartache was all I could find.

Then the song played we once called "Ours".
The things you once said, I guess they were just lies.

My body started to tremble as I struggled for something to say.
When our eyes finally met, like a fool I turned away.

Then I felt a small amount of strength that I knew would soon
die. As I turned to speak to you, you just walked on by.

—*Felicia D. Crow*

Fuzzy Slippers

I fell in love the first time I saw the long necked giraffe
who always wore fuzzy slippers.

He told me once that he wanted to dive into a chocolate ocean
from an airplane.

All the way down I would tickle his ribs
until he screamed in happiness, "Stop!"

Then Kersplash!!

—*Bonita Sidmore*

The Sky's Eyes

When I was young
I would climb trees
And crawl around in the bushes,
Sit around eating oranges until I was all sticky,
Picking peaches with my mother
Dance around in the sprinklers
With my brother Mike and neighbor Cindy
And stare into the eyes of the sky.

Now that I am older
I still climb trees
But I love to talk on the phone,
I like to eat apples instead of oranges
Read books that take me to faraway places,
And swim with my brother Mike and neighbor Cindy
And stare into the eyes of the sky.

—*Monique Rivera*

Branches Touching

When we die you and me
I'd like us both to be a tree
Me an apple you a peach
Our branches touching in easy reach
To feel the sun and light of day
To hear the wind and what you say
To watch you grow and bear your fruit
To see you wear your autumn suit
To stand with you in winters cold
When our leaves fall, drift and fold
To wait for spring you and me
To see life begin as another tree
And when I'm old and bear no fruit
And the wind blows me down "up by the root"
Please let me fall in your arms
Where again I can feel your love and your charms

—*Gary C. Foerster*

Jessica Corbridge

Oh No! What happened? I didn't plant to leave!
I'd only just begun to discover what my purpose was.
Told me I'd go far with my mind,
Said I'd make a difference one day.
Called me bright, talented, a special girl with a special
    purpose.
Couldn't see the pain inside, didn't know the hurt I felt.
Those cursed, wicked little secret games! He didn't stop.
Should've known to tell him no when the games began to hurt.
"Our special secret" Daddy would say when I'd protest.
So I put on my best smile and bravest face
To trudge on with the rest of my life.
One day I couldn't take it any longer. No one understood.
No one really knew how confusing my world had become.
Those I thought I could trust, I couldn't anymore.
Ran to my secret spot. I watched the seasons change there.
The rock I was seated on no longer held my weight.
My thick, warm coat dragged me 'neath the thin, cold ice.
Now, at least, Daddy can hurt me no more.

—*Alana Dellatan*

Solitary Aspiration

The gusts of wind tumbling on the reflection pool, blanketed
with Fall, a single duckling soaring through the crystal
treasure. It is its own paddle boat without the crowds of
conformists going no where. This duckling has an aspiration to
soar across the pool. It will try forever until it reaches its
attainment. Only then will the sun send its radiant beams to
the poor duckling who has yet to achieve his freedom. It holds
its head high, as those watching sneer at such a simple task.

—*Alexis Tucker*

The Man In The Moon

If I could talk to the man in the moon,
I'd tell him all about you.
I'd tell him how you're like a sister,
Who always looks out for me,
And picks me up when I'm down.
Warns me when I'm wrong and, tells me when I'm right.
I'd tell him you're one incredible lady
Who looks at people from the inside not the out.

I'd tell him I'm going to miss you.
but yet I understand.
I'd tell him you're a very special friend,
Who's finally going home.
I'd tell him all this and more.

Then I'd ask my friend in the moon,
To let you know I care.
I'd ask him to hug you when your feeling down.
Solve your problems while you sleep,.
Comfort you while you're awake.
I'd finally close by asking the man on the moon,
To keep you safe in his arms till we met again.

—*Sarah Burgos*

Life

I don't think I could take it
If again I heard (life is what you make it)

I want peace, love, and the light
While surrounded by a world full of turmoil, hate, and fight

The light is all I need
While surrounded by a world full of greed

I may suffer in this life
Full of heartache, woe, and strife

But when I go to join the light
I am bound for a better life!

—*Mary Lou Strunk*

Confessional

Oh, Lord I ask for your forgiveness
if I have wronged someone today.
Or failed to offer a helping hand
to someone in need along the way.

And should my mind be harboring evil
thoughts and devious plans. Fill my heart
with love and compassion for every woman and man.

If I have wrongly judged others by the so called
bad things they have done, open my heart so that my
eyes can see the good in everyone.

If I am short on understanding, patience and wisdom,
argumentative, domineering and curt, cleanse me of my
selfish ambitious ego, that is causing all of the hurt.
If I have forgotten how to be humble, compassionate, loving
and true, wrap your arms of forgiveness around me, my flesh
is weak, Lord, your child needs you.

—*Roosevelt T. Scott*

The Rose

One starry night when the moon was lit,
I woke up wondering where I was.
The angels' voices could be heard
And there was a peaceful feeling because
The crimson rose had left her flowerbed
To withdraw from her evil-doing profession
As a death-enjoyer fighting without pity,
For her job was to demolish Earth's progression.

—*Olivia McKean*

"S'no Use, S'no Use"

His mother shouted, "Run child, run!
If that bee stings, it won't be fun!"
    The boy found out, it wasn't play
When bee, less stinger, flew away.
    A single thought he did allow:
"S'no use, s'no use, done got me now!"

    His bee sting hurt as up he grew,
But faith had made him good as new.
    His luck had changed there was no doubt
No single thing was he without.
    When time had come for him to earn,
He found a job at every turn.

    When "Lotto" tickets he did buy,
His winnings reached up to the sky!
    There seemed no end to his good play,
But wasn't buying every day.
    For gambling he did disavow.
done got me now!

                    —*Bob Krajnak*

The Boy Next Door

This boy has lived next door to all of us,
    (if we're lucky).
He's probably blond,
    (in an un-shorn way);
And quietly competent
    (with a fishing pole).

Oh, woe is he!
    (but, not we);
For he'll grow up,
    (but, we'll remember him as a lad).

                    —*Betty J. Bowes*

We Have Not Really Tried

I know we have not really tried.
If we're not careful, this feeling will die.
I would die inside my cell,
If you were not my Blue Angel.

Oh Blue Angel, don't you cry
If we ever say good-bye.
I know our love has always been true,
But I will die if I lose you.

A poor dead bird in an oil sea,
That will be all that's left of me.
Come with me on my trail.
Because you are my Blue Angel.

Oh Blue Angel, don't let me cry
If we ever say good-bye.
In my heart, we shall forever be true,
And I will never ever forget you.

                    —*Rebecca Shirley*

Peach Fuzz

When pimples and peach fuzz freckle his chin,
You'll know a man has begun to begin.

His clothes shrink in from every corner it seems,
As long hair and skirts slip into his dreams.

There's no way to stop this inevitable change,
Since nature's the boss and time runs the game.

Just stand back and watch with envy and joy,
As the man that you see was once just a boy!

                    —*Robert L. Spillman*

Two Hearts

Openings one's heart is the hardest thing to do.
    If you open it up too far, it could be broken into.

When you try to pick up the pieces, they don't seem to fit.
    And when its back together again, it still hurts a bit.

But you keep on going, day by day.
    Hoping...praying, "Oh Dear Lord I Pray".

Join two hearts, you and someone who
    you will love and cherish, as I do you.

Sometimes you go through the pain, do what you must do
    to find the one who is suited to you.

Many spend their lifetimes' seeking their knight.
    A perilous and long journey that seems an endless flight.

Too many may never find them, not knowing what to do.
    Too afraid to give their heart, as I give mine to you.

My heart is yours, with all the love there is to give.
    For now and forever, our lifetime...to live.

Join two hearts, mine to join with you.
    To love and cherish, as I do you.

                    —*Leland McKinney*

If You Know What I Mean

Here I sit with my little feet
Ignoring the flightress with her programmed safety brief
Forgive my stomach, stupid me, I didn't eat
My head is on Boston and a little treat

The flashing light from under the wing
The roaring lift the engines do sing
Continually pushes as my ear drums ring
Finally, we're up, like a jump from a swing

This rubbish that I ramble on, is commonly known as a poets
fire. Flushed from the depths, of my shallowest desire
It makes no path, yet runs on a wire
If these words were any bit true, I'd stand up sit down and
you
could call me a liar

And on I go, with plenty to show
In the 19th row, the vents do blow
In case the fuel gets low, our paddles we must row
I do not know, to whom this, I will show

So heaven forbid, that at 8:54, when they open the door
My sheet will I rid, artistically poor, be found cluttering
the
floor

                    —*T. G. Bayly*

"A Mother's Plan"

On all the days that you are blue,
I'll forever sing a lullaby to you.

So tell me when you hurt dear,
And I will kiss away each tear.

When you feel you need to pout.
Come to me we'll work it out.

And when you have grown from child to man
Please come to me you know you still can.

So come to me when there is pain
Because I'll be there for you again

For when I get to be ninety-three
I know you will be there for me.

                    —*Patricia Link*

Promiscuity

You say you do not love me—so
I'll take in hand my pen
And make believe that I am loved
  By more romantic men!

I'll ride with knights on chargers white,
  To their secluded towers,
Sir Lancelot and Galahad
  Will help me pass the hours!

I'll call Ulysses when I'm bored,
  He'll fetch me to his isle,
And woo me with his Grecian charm,
  Though Calypso raves the while!

Mark Anthony will turn away
  From Cleo when I smile;
He'll crush me to his scented chest
  As we go floating down the Nile!

But, dear, if you should love me too,
  I'll drop my promiscuous pen,
And quite forget that I've been loved
  By all these other men!!

—*Ardis Kirby*

Martin

If Martin were here-
I'm afraid he would weep,
To hear the newscasters say,
"Black on black homicide on the increase!"
To see black pride take the form of 'fros
and dashikis,
Black dreams taste of pills, feel of needles,
and smell of smoke
Was the "Black Revolution" all a joke?
Yes, I know Martin would cry.
And ask, "For what did I die?"
Don't let his death be in vain-
Let pride, respect, intellect, determination
and excellence reign
And his living will not have been in vain.

—*H. Blandenah Black*

Christmas

It's Christmas time once again
I'm in a shopping mall,
The lights are bright,
The bells are ringing,
My spirits are high,
I feel like singing,
If the merchandise is on display,
I hope I can finish my shopping today,
I know that is a fervent hope to say the least,
I'll still be shopping at our Christmas feast,
I must not forget this Holy Day,
The love and happiness to each we bring,
To a loved one, who is far away,
My thoughts keep returning this Christmas Day.

—*John Coleman*

Hope

Life without hope is like a candle without a wick,
Hope is what separates the mighty from the meek.
Without a wick a candle cannot be kindled,
Without hope, life cannot be savored.
Preserve the wick and light the flame of ambition.
It will guide you through life and take you to your
destination.

—*Arati J. Bakhle*

Mirror of the Universe

I stood on a platform made of everything from nothing.
I'm looking into the universe; before me all existence.
These planets spinning, hinged on air; we are told no
beginning, no end.
All this moving illusion kept with unseen hands, folded in
touching care.
As I looked into this mirror made of light from the sun, the
moon and stars, I saw something that caused a moment of awe
and scare.
There in the mirror of the universe I saw a reflection of me!.

—*David Beverly*

Therapy Dogs

Of all the things my dogs and I do,
I'm proudest of my special two

Father and son are a winning team.
They gladden old hearts and make faces beam.

As they proudly trot down nursing home halls
They're ready to answer all patients' calls

Come Bear, come Storm, say hello to me,
You are our friends, that's easy to see.

Both nurses and patients eagerly await
The weekly visits that we make

The kindness and love that these dogs show,
bring to many a sad face a warm happy glow.

—*Fanne Ellner*

Reality

Help me if you can,
I'm trapped in a world I long since have stop, to understand.
New world order, crack cocaine,
broken lives, dreams that never be.
Blind bullets, and the tragedy that is Aids,
these are just, but a few of the issues
that faces, and ails our world today.
Living with contempt, for a way of life
which has declined,
is the reality many of us must face,
in living life from, day to day.
Our world, is in turmoil.
Wake citizen of the world.
It is time we all lend a helping hand.
Let our hearts, our minds, our very souls,
give us the convictions, knowledge, and inner
strength, that will guide us through the many issues
which ail's our world today, with it's confusing ways.
Please help me understand, why I live in a world,
I long ago lost the desire to understand.

—*Alba I. Romero*

The Nations Idol

Many moons ago
In a land filled with snow,
An eagle soars high
While we watch him fly.
A hunter sees the eagle there
For a moment all he does is stare.
Then he picks up his giant gun,
He shoots that eagle, the very last one.
If eagles didn't fly about
The nation would come to an end no doubt
So hunters beware.
The nation's end could be your affair.

—*Amanda Garrity*

Gramp's Lunchbox

Sitting on a willow branch when will he come home?
I'm waiting for a special treat but I am not alone.

My sister is beside me smiling with glee,
For she is also waiting for that very special treat.

Then up the street he rumbles in his Chevy pick up truck,
Let's get off this willow tree so he can pick us up.
We wrap our arms around his neck and kiss him on the cheek.
He asks us in his Texan voice you'll want something to eat?

We tell him that we do and he'd better give it up,
So he hands us his black lunchbox and he tells us to eat up.

Sitting on the tailgate dividing up our loot,
There's cheese and crackers and grapes and some Oreos to boot!

Because we were so young we did not understand,
The treat was not the lunchbox but the love felt for this man.

They say our earliest memories are a time of great joy,
And this is one of my favorites as a very little boy.

—*Christopher Kay Dunbar*

Magical Night

On halloween night as the wild creatures roam around
in a dark and secluded park you seduced me.
I'm my own man, but that magical night
You turned me into your own private toy.
My master, with the frankestien mask on
Your slave, with the tight, catwoman outfit on,
Your strong hands on my head,
My knees on the icy, cold ground.
You ordered me to please you
to swallow every inch of your manhood,
and I complied, happily so, taking in all that I could.
On that magical night, as the spooky sounds turned erotic,
and the shivering trees looked like nature's erection, I was
one with the stars.
In-out, in-out your goblin invaded my mouth
and as you pumped harder my eyes closed in anticipation,
of your sweet liquid love of your scream of utter joy.
On that magical night I consumed my forbidden pleasures
On that fantastical night I tasted this world's most precious
treasures.

—*Kim Armend*

Memory

A prayer before dying, a prayer before life;
In a time to say hello, or maybe just goodbye.
We hold memories of laughter, and memories of hope
In this shadow we live in, Youth's fragile ghost.
Memories of meetings, and goodbyes long gone;
Holding hands in the moonlight to an unwritten song.
Our time draws near, for soon we must part,
The tears that fall come straight from the heart.
I cannot imagine my life without you
As we give up this life for one that is new.
These are parting words, yet I know it won't end,
Your smile lives on in the minds of friends.
The time is short as the day draws near,
Memories are filled with laughter and tears.
I cannot bear to see you leave; I don't want to let go-
I know not if we will meet again; I don't want to be alone.
God be with you through trouble and strife
With a prayer before dying, and a prayer before life.

—*Shanna Hale*

Untitled

I stood upon the mountain tops, crying out your name.
    In every blackened shadow, I see your eyes.
        On every stormy night, there you are.
    You run wild and free in the pale moonlight.
    I long to hold you, to tremble at your touch.
    But you are uninhibited and cannot be tamed.
    I would never wish to hurt you, only love you.
        My love, however, is capable of destroying.
            You are erotic and primal.
        Flesh to flesh, the affair lingers on.
                You are my blood.

—*Christie Snyder*

Discussion Held in Silence

Inadequate, I'd say; not just unable, but feeble as well. Weak
in faith, no doubt; putting hopes wherein they do not belong.
Weak-kneed; weak-minded; weak-hearted. Withdraw! Withdraw!
Run, hide, escape! You can do it; don't give way to fears and
doubts! Fight it out! Decisions must be made! Based upon
standards prepared by men that men must live by to excel.
Excel beyond ordinary carnal corruption. Lost, losing, tired;
fatigue sets in, again. Money problems from poor decisions
made, frivolously spent? Applied to needs; food, doctor bills,
transportation, maintenance. Fixing what is broken, affecting
prior to breakdown and after preventative maintenance? An easy
concept to grasp more difficult to implement. Avoid, alter or
accept? Powerless to change? - Accept. Courage to Risk? -
Alter. Grievance, complaint, unchangeable? - Avoid, Avoid,
Avoid! Factors beyond control. Accept? - Never! - Or hope?
Or languish? Watch, look, listen - only then is it safe to
cross the street, wipe your feet, clean from corruption.

—*Kirk Mathew Gatzka*

Coming Home

A great celebration - like nothing we've known.
In God's word- forever's been shown.
The Heavens will open- we'll all march in.
Singing His praises- a new life within.

We'll meet our Maker- face to face.
And know it's done- through His blessed grace.
His loving arms will pull us near.
There'll be no more pain and no more fear.

Every knee, to Him will bow.
His promise was made- His promise is now!
Send your angels to guide us home.
So we'll never again be all alone.

We're waiting rather- for you to say,
Come home my children. Today is the day...
Our hearts are ready, our souls afire.
Coming home with you- is our hearts desire.

—*Margaret De Fay*

Autumn Is Golden

As I enter the Autumn of Life
    with memories of joys and long-suffered strife,

Full of wonder, still...after all these years
    that I could receive a balm for any tears, spent

Yet, not in vain all the while
    for in the Autumn of Life a most precious gift:

A Grandchild!

—*Irene Cash*

April

April, you are so pretty clothed
in green attire. Also you've many
beautiful pink and white flowered dogwoods
are a glorious sight to behold on the
hillsides as well as the valleys below.

The gorgeous purple, red, yellow and
pink tulips are even in techni color.

You dandelions are as yellow as gold
and your lily white eastern flower signifies
peace to me.

The smell of fresh green grass is breathe
taking and the fragrance after a moist,
light April shower is most refreshing, too,

I did like fall of the year as the best season.
but as now just give me springtime to
supply our needs and the scenic beauty
such a beautiful great, wide, wonderful world
only our omnipotent God can point.

—*Donna Belle Rowe*

Cat Zen

The cat, walking a space
in magnificent aimlessness
on the other side of our orderly world.

The cat, moving through
the human void
like a permanent visitor from a spirit realm.

Primal instincts intact after
years numbering thousands
of impatient domestication.

Sublimely reserved, mysterious, fearless,
yet curious as a child
the cat, a diplomat,
plans nothing but responds to everything...
A four-footed Zen teacher.

—*Karen L. Wilkening*

Essence of Life

What is life and how is it governed? My essence of life is not
in my hand, it's all a part of my master's plan. I gladly
awaken from day to day. Not on my own power, for it is Jesus
that blesses me every second, every minute and every hour. He
gives me the power to choose. And He gives me understanding
so that I am not confused. He has given me many blessings from
up above. But the greatest blessing He gave me was his love.
For He loved me so much that He died for me as a result, I'm no
longer in bondage but I am free. There is an evil force that
walks this earth, don't be fooled by Him, or you'll be hurt.
Trust in Jesus and He'll make all things new, He has called and
chosen individuals whom He knows will be faithful and true.
Jesus is the way the truth and the life there is within Him no
hatred, envy or strife. So if you want the true essence of
life. Choose today to give your life to Christ. He's truly a
friend that sticks closer than a brother. He will love and
keep you like no other.

—*Agnes Lewis*

Untitled

Sat silently among the deceased's last cry for remembrance
I feel at peace with all I see
but not alone
I look out over the sunny garden of stone
and feel alive among the dead
I feel like this is my home

—*Simon K. Browning*

To Grandson

If you travel to stars
In search of new worlds
Just remember
Winds were also kind here
and used to pass through, tickling the flowers with love,
Thousand of colors, made eyes smile
Mountains in the vastness of sky,
Wore the white pearl of peace
And then one day
I killed all the doves, singing in green leaves
Poisoned every heart of my tribe,
With hate and anger,
So my child
If you travel to stars
In search of new worlds
Just remember
Winds were also kind here
And used to pass through, tickling the flowers with love!

—*Akhtar Hussain Majoka*

The Phases of Planes

A shell of me down here, a piece of me up there.
In some strange way down here, I know why.
It's all part of the process.
Everything falls into place.
It's time, through this life.

Through liquid visions of destined events,
The parts fit together.
Be prepared to endure the set emotions that come with it.

The council above evaluates my every choice.
Certain tests and strategies are set up. Examples are given to
see what it could be like.
I know what is destined.

This entity is to be set up for its last transformation.
To close my eyes, there are more emotions to be seen.
Visions of hundreds of years of emotions flashed by.

—*Tony Vela*

In the Middle of the Night

In the middle of the night I'm sleeping tight,
In the middle of the night I'm nice and snug,
In the middle of the night I dream away,
In the middle of the night I'm not sad,
In the middle of the night I've got no worries,
In the middle of the night I am chilled,
In the middle of the night I am scared,
In the middle of the night I might scream,
In the middle of the night I see shadows,
In the middle of the night I don't feel a thing,
In the middle of the night I feel safe,
In the middle of the night I feel loved,
In the middle of the night I feel like I belong,
In the middle of the night I can say no more,
In the middle of the night I am done.

—*Erin Carroll*

The Girl

Tears feel from her lonely eyes
for she wept with sobs of sorrow
She looked up at the cloudy sky
And said wait my love
I'll be coming home tomorrow
She held the gun to her head
Smiling has she sang
And through the bible on the bed
. . . . . Bang.

—*Todd Pittman*

"Problem's"

I look out of the window from my chair,
in the silent of a moment I wonder as I stare.
What has become of the love, I knew,
from a world of people, but now a very few.
Thing's are changing from bad to fair,
but violence and crime still clog the air.

People are struggling from day to day,
trying to survive with a, job cut - or pay.
Like fallen leaves from the trees,
the world is increasing, in many, a disease.
Children are running and playing today,
tomorrow, drugs are killing, and taking them away.

Cop's are patrolling and walking their beat,
still victim's fall prey to the street.
Sometimes, we believe, hope and pray,
there will be peace in this world one day.
As I stand up from my seat,
I turn my head for another peek.
Problems, yes I realize,
Problems here all our lives.

　　　—Jerry Rose

The Puzzle Piece

I am but a puzzle piece
in this world I do not fit.
It's enough to make a person stop,
　give up, and quit
The only spaces open are squares,
　and triangles,
and I am but a circle.
that does not fit in anywhere.
They say that if I change they will let me in
Why would I change I am great the way I am!

　　　—Jennifer Hogue

Prejudice

The unjust atmosphere passing through the air,
Instead of hating
For each other we should care,
Although I'm white
And you're black,
If we work together,
It's prejudice this world will lack,
No matter what color, age, or race,
We're all just people on this earth's face
They say we're all so different
But I think we're all the same,
And if we hate instead of love,
We shouldn't feel proud, just full of shame,
If this world stays as cruel as it is,
It will be a loss not a gain,
And no matter what we look like,
We'll all be feeling pain.

　　　—Erika P. Koche

Dear Songwriter

Dear Songwriter,
though you've traveled far,
I'm always close to where you are.
As you pen my thoughts and sing my dreams,
sometimes it almost seems as if,
in some other life,
we were one.

　　　—J. Coates

Spring Wind

With her warmth, not her force,
She opens the tight-closed windows
and the doors of life

　　　—Yue Ming Chen

Where Is Grandma?

Lilac wafted through the open window of my room
　intermingling with the fragrance of hundreds of apple trees.
Crickets sang. The irrigation ditches were
　living entities; dancing down the farmlands;
　lined with wild asparagus; emitting a perfume
　of wet clay.
Morning brought the sound of Grandma's musical voice
　humming and singing along with the radio from
　her bathroom.
When the sunlight streamed through the shutters, she
　emerged, clean, perfumed, powdered,
　encircling me in her arms.
"How's my girl? Where's her chile spirit?"
Into the kitchen she'd shoo me where we'd feast
　on homemade tortillas, and preserves, carefully
　removed from her stock in Mason Lid jars.
Where are those summer days now?
Now Grandma lives quietly in my memory.
She is alive; humming and singing; sending her
　joie de vivre and love through me to my grandchildren.

　　　—Eve Cobos

Deeper and Deeper

Deeper and deeper I go
into a place that's unknown.
Deeper and deeper I go
into a place with my heart exposed.
Deeper and deeper I go
into a place with no directions.

More and more I see
people with blank expressions.
More and more I feel
my presence is not welcome.
In treading on the grimy edge of insanity
I see my soul dance before my eyes,
as my heart slowly dies.

I am no longer delighted
by daisies nor dandelions,
but all so gay to see gruesome manslaughters and suicides.
I fall very slowly and tread deeper and deeper,
I'm on the brink of insanity.

　　　—Dinorah M. Hudson

The Forgotten

Looking from behind crystalline liquid eyes
into a world of cobalt blue;
The magnification of lonely, tattered,
windblown hearts;
who get sympathy from nowhere.
Torchlights beaming through the
shadows in unending patterns;
never reaching their destination;
revealing only glimpses of hope along the way.
Embrace the permanence of the
delicacy within your illuminated soul;
the range of enlightenment;
the carrousel of goodness, excellence.
One molten reflection overcomes the
difficult footpaths that lie ahead.

　　　—Linnea Coleman

The Ways of the Heart

You race in the chest with impatience and ardor,
Intolerant of the too logical mind.
You consider wisdom as an abstract nonsense.
You proceed impetuously even when you are not virtuous.
You are unconcernedly happy
When you follow the paths of your desires.
For your emotions, the most fantastic dreams
Are the reality with which you deal.
You abandon yourself to new hope as to a pleasant dance.
When you are in the mood, you sing,
Even if outside the sun does not shine.
Once in a while, you are dejected
Because you see one of your dreams broken.
But to every delusion you doggedly oppose a new illusion.
Ever intent toward the future,
It seems to you that time flows slowly.
Silly, you do not know that
None of your beats will ever come back.
Yet, it is you who gives meaning to almost everything that
   is dear to me.

—*Mario Vassalle*

The Beauty of My Face

The beauty of this flower,
Is a beauty of it's own.

The beauty of my face, is for me... Alone.

And when you ask me,
Why do you look like you do?

Your face is so miserable, so ugly, so untrue.

I will not respond so don't expect me to.

Because my face and it's beauty
Is for me not you!

When you look at me, you turn away.

When you look at me,
You think of me with dismay
Yet when you see a flower
A beauty and grace with petals and leaves,
All made of lace. You don't think you just say

Well, what a thing to see, a thing to brighten
Each day. No matter what I am, you still don't look at me.
You still don't talk to me because my face is all you see.

—*Ivy McMahan*

Network

Spun into a catchall shimmery web
Is a tiny spider's frail silken thread.

His fibers enmesh and bind insect prey.
How does he induce them to come his way?

Does he dine on them or are they bait, set
To lure a girl spider into his net?

As gently I lift his web from the wall
He folds up his legs, curls into a ball.

Carrying him in floss, I toss out the door
And let him live that he may spin some more.

I do not want to see a spider die.
And why? Perhaps because I'm not a fly.

—*Alice Towsley Allen*

Ankylosaurus

"An animate boulder," it seems like to me,
Is Ankylosaurus described to a "T,"
But some flesh him out in their minds (to be frank)
As a great bulky hulk of a dinosaur tank.

Most studies deduce that his manner was passive.
It wasn't for naught, though, his club tail was massive!
Provoked, he became an unbudging curmudgeon,
Strategically wielding his cudge to bludgeon.

His lumbering gait and his hunkered down stance
Suggest him unsuited to court or romance,
But I think he might have been quite the 'ole charmer.
What girl could resist a knight clothed in such armor?!

—*Martha Jo Fleischmann*

What Does It Mean To Be Normal

What does it mean to be normal
Is it something were taught
or something we hear
Is it something we learn
through prejudice and fear
Who's to say what's normal
and what is not
Why must everyone be so judgmental
and matter of fact
There's no set standard for living
or how one chooses to live
Not everyone is exact
So is there really a definition for normal
Or is it just an arrogant point of view
If we all laugh and we all smile
Why must everyone be placed on trial
Those with differences should be looked upon
as a breath of fresh air
For they are the one's
who are the real debonair

—*Maria Martin*

Untitled

Who owns the Nighttime world?
Is it Them?

  The Ones
     who hold
        the key to our fears amongst the evening chill?
  The Ones
     who sneak
        within the moonlight and blend into shadows
        of those we cannot see?
  The Ones
     who keep
        us locked within our so-safe havens
        until the morning sun arises
        to warm our thankful souls?

To Those
Who own the dark hours which belong not to us—
May I open the door?
To see if the light of Tomorrow has come?
Or will You be there...
Waiting for me?

—*Ted M. Kirby*

"Mirror Image"

Looking into your eyes
Is like looking into the sea
Your skin, smooth like the Nile
In your heart is where I want to be
Whenever I see you
My heart starts to race
Never before have I seen a prettier face
I read of Cleopatra
You and she must be related
When you said, "I love you"
My heart faded
If you were reincarnated
You would be a siamese cat
But don't fret,
I'd put you on a throne
You'd be much more than a pet
I'd worship you
As the Egyptians did in the past
Now that we are together
My heart is free at last.

 —Tony D. Mason

Christmas Is For Love

The lovely Christmas music
Is playing everywhere.
The snow is gently falling
There's a crispness in the air.

It's a special time for
Reaching out, for giving and for sharing;
To let all your friends and family know
That you are always caring.

As you write each address on a card
And wrap each special gift,
The memories that flood your mind
Will give you such a lift.

Let's take the time to sing the songs
And join in all the fun
And listen as Tiny Tim says
"God Bless Us Everyone."

At this the Christmas season,
I hope that you will find
A Christmas filled with lots of love;
It's what the Christ Child had in mind.

 —Donny Hysjulien

A Friend

The thing that I shall seek today,
is someone with whom my heart to share.
And if I could I know I would, speak of the joy, the sorrow too.
For when my heart begins to feel;
the pain, the sorrow, the joy, the fear,
that is when I'll seek to find the friend with whom my heart to share.
My mind, my mind, it's all a boil, for the friend with whom I seek to find.
For I know not where that I might find the friend I long and hope to find.
Where could she be I wish to know!?
Could you be, the one I find!?
My heart is but an open book, you turn the page to have a look.
You will find upon each page, a dab of joy, a splotch of gray.
A page of blue or one of Gold, one pure white, another night.
And upon each page you will find, imprinted with much care,
the name of one that I have known. Some are dear and some are fair,
and when you turn the page for today, I wish with care that
your name will be there.
"OH" and "YES" I wish to be, the kind of friend I wish for me.
I wish to be there when your days are bright and all the fields aglow.
I'll also be there in the night when not a lite you see.
I'll bring a lite, the most precious lite, the caring one I have.
And if it takes the whole night through, my caring lite I'll share.

 —M. McGuire

Miles Away

Miles away nowhere within reach
 is the last place I want you to be
Miles away you hide from freedom
 something that belongs to you
 and something that you are fighting for

Miles away you wonder when will I return?
 you patiently wait for that is all you can do

Miles away though so far away I feel your warmth
 spreading all over me
 I pray everyday asking God to bring you home

Miles away we support what you do
 and what you are fighting for
If love was air you would be overindulged
 with it

Miles away I send you my love
 I think of your dearly smiles and laughter
 of fond memories

Miles away is where you stay
Miles away I await for you day after day

 —Evelyn Navarro

Laundry Problems

The worst time to be alone (someone once told me)
 Is two o'clock on a Sunday afternoon.
But she was wrong —
 The worst time is two o'clock in the morning (any
morning).
For then I wake and feel the tide of emptiness
 Wash in
  From the other side of the bed.
How strange
 To change
  The sheets...
Only one-half needs changing
 The other half is always clean and new.

 —Reisa M. Rogovein

Love

What is love, do we know,
It can be fast, It can be slow,
It has to deal with a heart,
You can give sweet tarts.
You can give it a chance for some great romance,
So in case you didn't know,
Love makes people glow.
Its to show how much you feel,
So you better take it for real.
It doesn't matter what color,
as long as you love each other.
Love is sweet, if you remember where you meet.
Love is big, just like a gig.
Its a thing, you can give rings.
People like it a lot, if you tie the knot.
Love is a lot of things,
It can bring big things.
Love is something that you can not taste,
So remember love is something, you don't
want to waste.

 —Orpha Powell

Robi

Robi. The sweet name ringing in my ears. Sometimes
it can break my heart, and bring me to tears.
I often daydream, and think about my true love.
Which was always a memory that I had dreamed
of. I remembered that night, when the night air was
cold. I never thought that I would be told. That
Robi had died that cold deadly night, of drinking
and driving and losing a fight. I never had a
chance to say, "I love you dear Robi, don't go away."
Now I lost him. Without a goodbye. I miss him
so dearly, and I want him to stay.

—*Cynthia S. Cheng*

A Feeling

I think it's just a feeling, a wish, or a dream.
It can't be real, but that's how it seems

I reach out to feel, but there's nothing there.
Is there anyone near - does anyone care?

I call your name in the silence of the night.
I hear no reply - it doesn't feel right.

I'm all by myself - I look up at the stars.
You're miles away, and it feels too far.

Things suddenly change - I feel your embrace.
It doesn't seem real - it's all out of place.

Where are you now? It feels like you're near.
But I call you again, and you're really not here.

The distance is cold - you're far away.
I'm still all alone when I see the break of day.

I've sat through the night, and waited for you.
It was only a feeling - it never came true.

It was just a feeling - it wasn't real.
Now when I reach, there's nothing to feel.

—*Kim Sleger*

The Earth

The earth, they say, spins round and round.
It doesn't look it from the ground,
And never makes a spinning sound.

And water never swirls and swishes,
from oceans full of dizzy fishes,
And shelves don't lose their pans and dishes.

And houses don't go whirling by,
Or puppies swirl around the sky,
Or robins spin, instead of fly.

It may be true what people say.
About one spinning night and day,
But I keep wondering anyway.

—*Jessica Singsheim*

Life

As a baby is born a life is made as
it grows it is like a flower in the sun.
A son a flower that is a different kind
of life. A woman another different kind
of life. That has different interests as
man, and a woman. A child is one that
can become a man, or a woman for it is
a seed that can blossoms like a flower.
As a seed it has may different kinds of
choices it can be of good, bad, to kill, or save
another flower's life. But I leaned that
life is a great thing even if you die we
all have to go sometime.

—*Arlene Fermin*

A Mother's Expectation

The conception is the biggest thrill of all
It enlightens the heart and warms the soul
It makes a woman feel whole
from the first movements inside,
moment by moment is taken in stride.
Her feelings begin to show
a greater feeling is growing,
one she will come to know
a special love is forming.
A love that is kept her whole life
through it's different, it's fulfilling, it's new.
Her thrills turn to wonder,
new experiences are to be learned.
Caring and loving
for respect earned.
The time comes, the child is born.
Along with it comes a glow
that no one can describe.
The feeling is preserved for a life time
down deep inside.

—*Anna Gakis*

The Door

It was an ideal door
It had a big brass knob, rusty antique key.
After Rolf hung it we liked to go in and out
Although it opened only on nowhere:
The ravine, glimpse of the lake, Kittatiny rolling mountains;
To the south the dense woods, owned by state, a swamp.
It gave us a feeling of security, landed gentry, own a door.
We owned all the vistas it opened upon including the sky.
One could build a house around a majestic door like that,
An excellent door of infinite possibilities,
A personality, a symbol of our separate psyches
Which we might offer to the world,
Expansively opening it a crack,
Upon suspicion or hurt slamming it closed.
Infinite exploration beyond the secret doors
of self, birth itself, wasn't it a door
opening each time toward unguessed possibilities?
Then death, the final door, dark corridor wrapped in mystery,
Beyond that door, final answer to the final question.

—*Virginia Rose Christoffersen*

Where Has Love Gone?

Where has love gone?
It has slipped through my fingers like course grains of sand.
Not quickly, oh no, but it tears at my hand.
Love has gone to seed.

Where has trust gone?
It has fallen behind lurking where shadows are made,
To thrust at it's victim with dull burning blade.
Trust has gone to seed.

Where has faith gone?
It has washed out to sea like a small dying leaf,
And been battered and bruised by the wild coral reef.
Faith has gone to seed.

The incoming tide saves the leaf from it's finish,
Sand is forever and shadows diminish.
Faith, love, and trust. Where did they go?
To seed, where someday they'll return and they'll grow.

—*Linda Merrill*

At Seventeen

Picking up the pieces, packing up the dreams.
It has turned to a raging river from a gentle stream.
Folding up the letter, tear stained and blue,
Crying because tomorrow's goodbye to you.

You were the laughter in the rain.
You helped to ease the pain.
You dried the tears I cried,
And I know you never lied.

Picking up the pieces, packing up the days.
From a clear day has evolved a foggy haze.
Jingling the car keys, shiny and new.
Dying inside because I'm losing you.

You traded this world for wings of gold.
You traded my hand for a harp to hold.
You're watching us crying, lonely and blue.
Happy in the home God's given to you.

You traded this life for one brand new,
And on wings of gold you'll live it through.
While you're flying high you'll see what I mean,
To lose someone you love at seventeen.

— *Lori Dymond*

The Beaverkill

On the Beaverkill River
It is a cloudless day.
Waterbugs in pools
Beside the riverbank
Are bounded by moose moss,
By water heavy logs.
I watch legs and antennae,
Calligraphers of black circles and ovals,
Appear to move sure-footed
On the red and orange rocky river bed,
An unknowable link between light and shadow,
Between life and death.

— *Emile Luria*

Jamaica: Land Of Paradise

Jamaica is a land of wood and water under the sun,
It is a land where I come from.
People visit just to have fun,
As they watch the setting sun.
Beautiful greenery surrounds the land,
Blue-green waters wash up on the sand.
The food is full of spice,
While the natives are all so nice.
It is the "Land of Sugar and Spice",
Jamaica: Land of Paradise.

— *Julie Ann Buchanan*

Confused

I look in the room and I see a picture.
It is a picture of life.
Then I wonder; if life is as perfect as a picture,
Why is their tears of pain?
The picture from a far is only one color.
As I look closer, I see many colors of confusement.
These colors are so strong,
one does not want to live anymore.
I wonder if this picture will ever be understand.
I wonder if the tears of pain will be healed.
I wonder if the picture I see, will ever be perfect.

— *Stacy Mestaz*

In Loving Memory

When a person in your family should die,
It is enough for you to stop and cry.
The love you showed was so vastly great,
The loss you encounter could make you hate.

Hate is not the feeling to show,
The love you shared should make you grow.
You have to allow the dead to quietly depart,
But you can always keep the memories in your heart.

Every rainbow the family should see,
The departed is asking to "remember me."
Losing that loved one could make you complain,
But you must try to overcome the pain.

The person you loved was probably a world in one,
Although you have to realize their life is done.
Allowing a loved one to go is especially hard,
But it can all be summed up in a Hallmark card.

— *Timothy Barry*

The Jet

The jet can go very fast and very high.
It is fun riding in a jet.
The food is good on a jet, want to bet?

I like the landing gear which has two wheels,
It glides through the air like an eel.

Its engines are very strong.
There are four engines.
There are two wings, one top tail and two pilot seats.

Sometimes they do good things like draw pictures
in the sky.
Sometimes they do bad things like drop bombs,
fire missiles and use guns.

— *Andrew Bonander*

Untitled

Did you hear about President Billie? He jogs every day where
it is hilly. You don't have to worry about the Senate or the
House. Hillery, his wife is a capable spouse, she'll keep
Congress from doing anything silly.

Enie-Meanie-Moe, I've my tax the best I know, I'm certain my
tax is based upon facts, IRS says that isn't so.

There was a kid from Madrid, he was a mischievous kid. He
kissed all the girls, he mussed up their curls. But they
didn't care what he did.

There was that lady from Charlotte. She canned all the
vegetables she got. Her husband-poor honey did not think it
funny because everything was going to pot.

Driving at his age was wrong, "I'll quit some day" was his song
till one day in a wreck, the crash broke his neck.
He had waited just one day too long.

There was that girl from San Francisco who put all her songs on
a disco. Her music was sweet to use while you eat. Especially
if you choose a Nabisco. They say he's a poet Laureate, he'll
keep on writing-you bet, the most of it's bad but don't go away
mad you just haven't heard everything yet.

— *Herbert N. Heuman*

Guiding Love

Although I must command my own destiny,
is my heart that rules my future.
With love as my only guiding light,
am lost down the path of righteousness.
For as I enter a room in which
you stand,
am but a slave in your presence.
Your mere words command me;
and my heart must obey.
As you are my guiding light;
my hearts one true love.
With you by my side, I am never
in the dark.

—*Lorrie Juve*

Insane

Sitting in this very room,
is only me and the darkness,
You may ask how can I be falling into madness,
Crazy I cannot be, or so I tell myself.
Yet you think I cannot be falling out of sanity,
because as I told you once before it is only me and the
darkness, or is it not?
My conscience is leading me to abnormal derangement,
is it my mind?
I'm sitting here like an imbecile one, in total oddity.
I knew it was wrong, why did I do it?
It's driving me to mental alienation, to delirium.
I ask you, am I not crazy for I knew it was wrong yet felt it
all be right.

—*Brandy Nicole Johnson*

Life

The highway of life has never been smooth
is paved with sorrow and tears
And for everything gained there is something we lose
We find as we travel the years.

If we find happiness midst it's storm and it's strife
We may wonder if it's worth the cost
When we pay for the things that we keep in this life,
With the tears for the things we have lost.

—*Barbara Griffin*

The Poor Poet's Poem

The poor poet's poem:
Is sometimes unwritten, sometimes written:
He or she has failed, once or twice -
But they have also succeeded.

He's tried to write to experience,
Basing it on the reality, and not on a fantasy;
For, no matter what we have seen happen,
There is always going to be more to see, it seems to me.

I have got to listen more than intently, but intelligently:
For there are many parts and there are many pieces of our friends,
of ourselves in the things we want to say,
and in the things that we would like, to do.

If I look into the mirror I don't look to look
Through it into nothing: but, I look to see memories and
dreams, or the places left, to go -
And, to see what I saw or may soon see in times when.
The poor poet's poem: I would not want it were there
someone who could throw it away, tear it up, or take it
apart: It says that it should last forever and a day or two.

—*Robert S. Cassidy*

Us

A tiny spark began to glow in the grayness of the past,
It lingered on and seemed to grow; I prayed it wouldn't last.

On any day my thoughts would stray back to the moment when
You caused to start within my heart a thrilling, dangerous trend.

Your subtle wish conveyed to me brought pageantry to view-
The night was bliss, you searched for this; a missionary came
to you.

A reprimand for parting slow seemed so unfair to me,
"Against the rules," the elders said. You left but tears rolled free.

The time has been so short, it seems, since you came to our place -
I wonder where the time has gone, there seems not left a trace.

Yet, looking back on many months since you ignited me,
It's been a long, long dream of hope for what could never be.

This, I accept with reasoned pain because you want it thus.
But I - I love you more each day and no one knows but us.

—*Arnold R. Ahrnsbrak*

Possessed by Guilt

Possessed by guilt she used to be, it owned her every being;
It made her feel so worthless, she knew not where to lean.
She made some regrettable choices, she somehow lost her course;
She continued with her daily life, consumed with pure remorse.
Guilt convinced her she was selfish, and punished she should be;
She was made to feel no other person could be as bad as she.
Guilt could strike at any time, it's disguised in many forms;
When she thought "I'm doing fine," 'twas the lull before the
storm.
Her moves were cautious and meek, her pain she held within;
She carried with her wherever she went, the memory of her sins.
As months went by she waited, for forgiveness to come her way;
As years went by she realized, her sorrow was here to stay.
Her guilt wouldn't let her rest, though her life she rearranged;
The thoughts that steadily surfaced, were of the lives she'd
changed.
One day her will collapsed, her spirit lost you could say;
As she sobbed with face in hands, she desperately started to pray.
She since has started healing, seeking help wherever she can;
She believes with all her heart, it's with prayer it all began.
No longer possessed by guilt, it's where love is she wants to be;
I know she'll make it now, for the "she" you see...is me.

—*Lorraine Redondo*

Unconditional

They had a strange and unique friendship.
It made people wonder what made it work.
Nobody really knew but that is the way it is.
When you accept people for who, what and how they are.
It is called unconditional love.
Oh! There was rough times but that made the friendship
stronger.
That is, also, the way the heavenly father loves us,
unconditionally.

—*Betty J. Bible*

Music

The words of music, they touch you inside
It makes you recall the loved ones who've died
Some words of love, others seem so sad
But overall, they aren't so bad
They tell stories of that special guy
And stories of emotional good-byes
Stories of teenagers running away
And stories of how life is everyday
Without music, I wonder how life would be
Would it be a world suitable for me?

—*Marady Men*

Life

Life to me is a beautiful thing
It makes me so happy I can sing
I like to look at the trees so very tall
And watch the leaves as they fall
To see the wind blow the snow around
And the way it glows when it is on the ground
Also to look up at the beautiful sky
To see a bird flying very high
So it is easy to see, why life is good to me
With all this beauty around for me to see

  —Arthur Trezza

Broken Brain

It is within, the trouble looms.
It passes, portending each days gloom.
Searching fruitlessly, with no respite,
like two enemies locked in a room.

Is it defeating, to carry on the fight?
Or is it yet misleading, darkness was once light.
Just as recovered booty is spent in vain,
a man's true character is measured not right.

For though they say there is growth after pain
I do not wish to feel as I do now again.
It troubles me so to be as I am,
hopelessly lost in a broken brain.

  —Roche

The Window

I sit by the window
It rains.
I see through the window
a bird flies past.
I know from the window
Other children play.
I see in the window
myself.
I watch from the window
As life passes me by.
My heart longs to join the things I see but,
I am held in by
 The Window.

  —Cherise Fillinger

Believe in You

When the raindrops fall on my face
it seems the tear is glistening.
As the drop rolls down and falls to the ground
it's a reflection of me in the stream I see.
Two pools of blue that tears have filled
so many times when hope was killed.
Two pools of blue from where tears have shed
the heart broke in two and the love bled.
Two pools of blue
that can shine with laughter
with the smile of happiness that comes after.
Two pools of blue that reflect me
a believer in me I see.
Hope restored and love fulfilled
in the pools of blue that once spilled.
A believer in you, you must be
to get through pain or misery.
A believer in you, is what I see,
in two pools of blue,
for the world to see.

  —Janell Goode

Sereneness in One

There was a life so beautiful,
It shone bright as the sun,
It was made of love and gave but love,
Full of warmth and joy and fun.

There was a soul so sorrowful,
It wept like a cold icy rain,
It was full of pain and misery,
Walking in the darkest plain.

Then the beautiful life touched the
 sorrowful soul,
Giving it a love it had never known,
Then the soul found something wonderful,
The joy of a love full blown.

The two became one entity,
Sharing in joy as well as pain,
For they each found a piece that was missing,
With a touch in the warm summer rain.

  —Adrienne Hearn

My Diet

I had a barbarian lizard one time,
 It smelled like strawberries but tasted like a lime.
I was very hungry and I had no food,
 It puts me in a very bad mood.
I was very sad and I felt really bad,
 but I ate that old lizard,
 all but its gizzard!
Then I got a dog and I really felt like a hog!
 That old wiener dog went down like a candy log!
After that I went for a jog,
 and came upon a little frog.
But suddenly my stomach put me in such a position,
 that I had to run the nearest physician.
"That will teach you," said the guy,
 "to only eat homemade apple pies.
Next time you have a snack attack,
 go to the store and buy food off the rack!"

  —Monica Shannon

The Special Night

The night that I was with you was special,
It was my first time.
My first time with you.
It will always stay with me,
And mean a lot to me.
You were here with me
When you could have been there.
You were touching me,
and with every stroke it felt good.
You were kissing me,
and with every touch of our lips
together sent a shiver down my
spine.
You made me feel so secure,
no one could harm me.
You made me feel good, so good
that you were with me
when you could have been
somewhere else with anyone else.

  —Felicia Josephs

My Way"

My darling daughter I love you, you see,
  It was on the cross that I died for thee,
And as with salvation, my forgiveness is free;
But you must reach out and receive it from me.

This wonderful grace is unmerited, you know,
It's a gift, you can't earn it because I love you so.
And as you receive this gift of grace;
You will see I've taken away your disgrace

You must now love yourself as you love others,
And pass my love on to your sisters and brothers.
Teach them to love life in my holy name,
Then their lives will never again be the same.

Tell them I want to choose the future
Of each child; even those in the womb;
, only I have that right;
That's why I rose from the tomb.

As they turn their hearts and their minds toward me,
  I will show them my truth and they too will be free.
Free to love life and seek my will and my way,
And seek my purpose for each unborn child this day.

—*Joyce L. Murphy*

Feel

Before you I walked many lonely miles
It was worth it as I now see your warm smiles
This feeling I have toward you
Makes it nice to be one of two
Others have come and gone before
  I want them no more
As you are the best
  I forsake the rest
We may disagree and not see eye to eye
  I promise not to poke you in the eye
Wherever the path takes us
We must keep each other's trust
I'll treat you with honor and respect
I hope I can be everything that you expect
Let the cards fall where they may
I only hope that you will stay

—*John R. Colin*

To Be...

I see the sky as my protector,
It watches over me every hour;
The sun and moon shine upon my face,
The stars radiate with power.

To make a wish and to dream a dream
Can last for all time;
The hearts of most linger for love,
For all souls to be but blind.

A changing world with different people,
So separate yet the same, me and you,
Yet we try hard in mind to be the one
Who forever can love so true.

Such love and happiness will conquer all,
But what is given will soon be taken away;
Moment to moment new hope is built
Upon the end yet start of a new day.

An empty body is never to cease,
Contentment among what is there;
But only to be of great overflowing
With love from the hearts that care.

—*Karla Wray*

Picture of Poetry

If it were one thing that I could give too the world
it would be a picture of words framed in poetry.
I would reveal the joys of capturing in print
words of beauty evolving constantly.
In the presence of flowers, I would release fragrances
of words consistently.
The trees I would paint with words of green colors and accents.
The sky I'd paint blue with the words this is God sent.
The words from melodies form songs would forever be in print
where it belongs...
The bubbling springs with words would appear crystal clear
with words of poetry to be endeared.
From my heart I will share these words which I've framed in
my own picture of poetry that will leave a lasting affect.

—*Lestenia Anne Green*

If Love Was

If your love was like wine
It would be most divine.
If your love was like fire
It would take me higher.
If your love was a glass
I would not let it pass.

But even the most divine wine
is just but spoiled grapes off the vine.
And the fire that brings me higher
would just burn me with desire.
The glass that I would not let pass
I would not want in my social class.

So as you well can see,
I do not need thee or thy love

—*Brian Vanderver*

Growing Smiles

A smile is quite a funny thing,
It wrinkles up your face,
And when it is gone, you will never find
It's secret hiding place.

But far more wonderful it is
To see what smiles can do;
You smile at one, he smiles at you,
And so one smile makes two.

He smiles at someone since you smiled,
And then that one smiles back;
And that one smiles, until in truth
You fail in keeping track.

Now since a smile can do great good,
By cheering hearts of care,
Let's smile and smile, and not forget
That smiles go everywhere!

—*Claudia Baldwin*

Logger's Prayer

A loggers day has ended
The heavenly stars appear
The forest is quiet and peaceful
Touched by his hand so dear,
In my cabin I sit in silence
Alone, but I know I am not
Somehow I can feel God's presence
As I settle away in my cot.

—*Benedict J. Newman*

The Pain of Love

When you grow up in a house full of love, but your body rejects it, you become not like one of the above, nothing like it. You live a life without knowing love and devotion, you live a life without emotion. You live in fear of everyone, that you put your trust only in the Lord even when your days are done.

Twenty-two years later you make a friend, whom you can trust and depend. Who helps make your emotions come out, and loves you without a doubt. Who cares enough to explain, all about love even the pain.

When you feel love for the first time you begin to understand, what you have been missing is love for the common man. After the Lord sends you this person to save your life by His Grace, the Lord takes him away to a better place.

Then by the Love you have been shown, you love, care, and do more for the rest of the family like they have never known. They may wonder why, but because He took the time to show me love, I'll need it even when I die.

—*Michael W. Hutton*

The Sound of Your Shadow

I know the sound of your shadow
Its blank face flat on the plaster often expressing more than
your skin of alabaster

I know the sight of your shadow
Its black eyes stare through my soul
kindly filling the emptiness with holes

I know the palate of your shadow
Its flapping tongue torments my accusers
cleverly inventing a language for my muses

I know the fragrance of your shadow
Its lilac petals strewn on the floor of my vanity
manically navigating me through the coves of insanity

I know the sound of your shadow
for its postcard antics mimic mine

A challenge to crawl bloody from the shattered glass of the
television tribe vandals in the house of love
shapes on the heavy drapes of the heart

I hear the sound of your shadow. I see its harlequin image.
I taste its cottony air. I chase it through the realms of
eternity and run from its raping envelopment.

—*Terri L. Terrell*

Love that was Lost

Your love burns within my heart.
Its desirable, but yet for me unattainable.
Its the smile in your laugh
The desire in your eyes,
And the laughter that fills me when I see you walk by.
Its my heart that burns deeply
And my eyes that shed tears
At the hope and the fears in my dreams.
The dreams that I dreamed are of you and me
And how we could be together someday, but as you can see
We could never be together,
Never be able to love one another,
Never be able to hold or comfort.
Because you left me that cold winter night.
I sat there and waited.
I hoped and I prayed for you to come back.
But you never once turned, looked up or sat
You just lay there all still, calm and flat,
Never to return.
And never to come back.

—*Jaimie Murtha*

"The Blink Of An Eye!"

Life is always a continued eye blink;
It's filled with love's greatest chain links!

This world is so very confused with strife;
But God isn't saying it will always be right!

Everyone is busy making dreams come true;
And when the day is done there is still an adieu!

Thinking and acting out each task like bees;
Wondering in wisdom what is true to the breeze!

Happy is a Vietnam Vet that lived in full life;
Thanking the years that God gave in the light!

Youth are facing the future of guidance we care;
And they are our spirit filled lives living inside eternal flame!

Pens and rulers are working every week;
Then, computers are changed by man's eye blink!

Eyes are filled with love in hearts and minds;
Seeing the children of future years living are they in equality!

The kids' eyes will show your mind wisdom's goal;
For Jesus is the blink of an eye!

—*Leslie Dan Ritter*

Desert Flower

(For Keri)
It's hot, there's no wind
and I fly in search of a flower.
The blazing sun melts my wings
and scorches my mind.
It revels the barren wasteland set before me.
This cracked and rippled ground
is a brown sea,
revealing the island,
the desert flower.

Her fragrance is an addicting drug,
pulling me to her.
She is a wild flower,
beautiful and red,
filled with her radiant power.

My eyes glazed with fascination reflect
her image. My wings take me to her
tender petals. I land and survey
her beauty, her voice beckons me.
I heed its call
and we share our souls.

—*Brian Carnes*

Feelings For You

I am sorry that when I see you I start to cry,
It's just I can't imagine ever saying goodbye
When you look into my eyes, my heart starts to race,
It gives me a special feeling, a feeling I can't erase.
Love is a strong emotion, I have for only you
This love is very deep, meaningful, and true.
The time we spent together meant so much
My heart has turned cold without your touch.
Being without you is a feeling I don't want to know
Something I can't hide, my face has to show.
I miss you now and you're not even gone,
Just please, don't ever forget our song.

—*Melissa Halko*

The Story of A X'Mas Card

In my mail box I found a card.
Its legibility was not very keen.

I opened the card and saw a picture
of two old friends in twenty years I had not seen.

This couple lived so humble, their
hair was now white as snow. My mind
drifted back to a manger scene somewhere on Bethlehems road.

The card held a story of love they
had shared through the years.
Need I tell you friend, my eyes were dimmed by tears.

The old gentleman was eighty six years old, His
wife was now bed ridden it seemed.
So he could not go fishing or follow his many dreams.

Yet he had found time to think of us
and wished us much Christmas Cheer.
Many of life's blessings had come his
way so he had no reason to fear.

Our Lord has given to us His writings
of "Royal Decree" that light and gladness bring with love and
joy in our heart, listen, you may hear the angels sing.
—*Pauline Clark*

A Kindred Spirit

The tree rested firmly in the soil,
    its life rooted in unchange.
The man ran about the place with his
    feet never in the same place twice.
When the man passed this monument to
    time the tree knew that with age
    the feet would slow.
It knew that a cherished friend
    would grow from this worldly one.
It could wait. Time was nothing
    to this vessel of patience.
Soon the man grew roots of his own and
looked at this making of God for the first true time.
    He admired its base and how it gave
    The feeling of a calm and patient soul.
The tree then felt the twinge of a kindred spirit
and seemed to smile with the gentle breeze
while the man stood with a growing sense
of understanding. It would not take much longer...
—*Jim Hewitt*

Untitled

Alone with the moon.
It's light sparkles into my eyes.
See the bright, white sphere float in the night sky.
Feel the night.
Cold, frigid air.
No stars. Just moon.
Alone.
Self indulged in the widely, vacant sky.
Waits, as the hours of time tick away.
Waits, for that moment.
That moment to travel from east to west.
Travel to another sky in the world.
The traveler of the night must make way for the
traveler of the day.
Time is shared.
Nighttime to daytime.
Daytime to nighttime.
—*James Pica*

Untitled

Have you ever gazed at a mountain,
It's majestic head held so high?
Have you lifted your face to the heavens
And reached for a star in the sky?
Have you seen the sun "rise" in the morning
And "set" at the close of the day?
Have you listened to the song of a bird
Or watched a child at play?
Have you smelled the fragrance of a rose
Or watched the sea roll by,
Or gazed, when the storm was over,
At the rainbow in the sky?
Why do we oft-times fail to see
God's beauty everywhere?
Why does mankind seek to destroy
When "peace" could fill the air?
Oh, that all men would consecrate
Their lives to God above
And, thus, help build a better world
That's free from "hate" and full of "love"!
—*Carolyn P. Thompson*

The Tool

When is dull better than bright
It's not as easy as wrong or right
Being a tool all shiny and pretty
isn't the proof of doing work plenty.
Being a tool to fit the master's hand.
To pound or scrape or maybe even sand.
To be willing to go where he might send
or maybe it's money he'll have me lend.
To be the tool that he will always reach,
could it be me he'll have teach.
Today, tomorrow, yesterday next week.
I pray my Lord it's for me you'll reach.
—*Donna L. Walker*

Today You Turn Thirty

Today you turn thirty, so what's the big deal?
It's only a number and depends how you feel.
Thirty's okay, so please don't despair
Until you look in the mirror and find a gray hair.
So live your life with nothing to fear-
Keep moving forward no matter what you hear.
You might get forgetful and a little slow at times,
But you're at the bottom of the hill
With a ways to climb.
So keep a smile on your face
And your head in the air-
With all those years behind you
You'll have a lot to share.

Happy Birthday My Friend
—*Shirley Sigwalt*

Useful Vulture

Poor old vulture,
Has no culture,
Eats dead men and goats and rats.

That's the reason,
Every season,
It looks old and sick and sad.

To its credit,
Just one merit,
It saves man from plague and death.
—*Anezi Okoro*

405

Autumn

When one sensual soul takes in the fruits of the season,
It's overwhelmed by the spectrum delicately cast from the great
Oaks. Eased by the feel of its softest fabrics.
Deer stand proud, airing points, boldly gathering
Nourishment for natures most brutal season;
A blistering day star gives way to a brisk wind,
Cozied by a raging, but mastered night fire.
Gray and white clouds paint and replace a
Blue sky once deluged in sweltering heat and smog.
We lie like children nestled into a warm bed,
Lost in the long, cool morning hours.
This soul will never take for granted from where
The seeds spawning these fine fruits are planted.
They're embedded in the heart.
What is fall without a lover's hand?
Without confiding in our kindred?
Or a friend on which to lean?
No one should be deprived of one of these essential elements
Of fall. Warmth is the pinnacle of emotion.
Hence, togetherness stands as the pinnacle of fall.

  —*Steven P. Lewis*

Why My God Is Real

I've never seen God, but I know how I feel
 it's people like you make him "so real."
My God is no stranger, he's friendly and gay
 and he doesn't ask me to weep when I pray.
It seems that I pass him so often each day,
 in the faces of people I meet on my way.
He's the stars in the heaven, a smile on some face,
 a leaf on a tree or a rose in a vase.
He's winter, autumn, summer and spring,
 in short, God is a very real wonderful thing.
I wish I might meet him most more than I do,
 and I would, if there were more people like you.

  —*Felix Brazziel*

To the TV

It's sat down
as an aggression
on this generous lapse suited
for rereading dedicatories on yellowish photos,
for welcoming some distant cousin
and regretting that in females
the surname is lost.

Its four legs have a prey-prying pose.
Its huge eye self beholds
in a bridleless rush of images,
commanding, urging,
insulting us about the world.

The box of dreams
as a Trojan Horse
gifted to the walled cities of infancy.

  —*Juan Carlos Zamora*

Passages in Time

Time is but a shadow
Upon a sun-dial cast
That passes o'er its graven face,
Then mingles with the past.
We cannot bid it come too soon,
Nor can we ask it stay,
As it moves on to eternity,
Then marks another day."

  —*Maureen Fitzpatrick*

Feelings

Feelings are something you can't hide.
It's something true and inside of you.
Feelings are sometimes good or bad.
They can make you happy or sad.

Share your feeling with someone you love.
Make sure you save some for the one up above.
To hold it in, will make you blue.
I don't think that's good for you.

Feelings are something inside your heart.
It is not something that will make a mark.
Feelings are something that makes you feel all over.
You can be happy like a four leaf clover.

You could be happy, sad, or blue.
But really it's all up to you.
When you are all alone, you are lonely.
Maybe you could be blue.

Hopefully it doesn't happen to you.
Love is a good feeling, try to work, it out.
If you make it work for you, you'll shout. So love
yourself and each other, and find how to love one another.

  —*Johnetta Glaspie*

Untitled

My tummy swells with pain.
It's that time of the month again
Where what I see is not what's real
And how I care for this and that,
For what's not there in this world of mine;
A world of people so unkind
With their generous loving
For a face I have but I don't know.
My tummy throbs to give me life
And make me mad with how I live,
With how I laugh and how I fight
To be so sad when my tummy swells.
And how I say — oh, what the hell,
I like what I see this time of the month
When my vision's not so clear
And what I hear is way too loud.
It's what I want — to shed a tear
For something real not something said.

  —*Auromira Parks*

The Draft

It will steal the warmth from your breath
It's touch will slow your heart to ice
Your open hands will be crushed
Your faith will be torn from its shelter
You must secure your soul

It will mold you with its cunning embrace
it's force will end all desires
Your need for sleep will be replaced with fear
Your gentle thoughts will turn to darkness
You must secure your soul

It will destroy all need for love
It's rage will weaken your mind
Your dreams will be forever lost
Your body will wince in pain
You must secure your soul

  —*Renae J. Sturtevant*

ristine

herever life's path may lead you,
o matter how far you may roam.
ere is a special place in my heart,
at belongs to you alone.

ank you for making my dreams come true.
ope I have inspired a cherished dream in you.
　　　—*Julie Kuhn*

hen Death Comes Calling

eath is something that should not be taken lightly,
s when our God-given souls are taken from our bodies.
ith God's special help we can ease this transition
 using our knowledge of the true Institution,
r our immortal souls are taken in retribution;
e never know the purpose of our journey here,
 do some good deeds with tender loving care,
ut in order all the affairs of your life,
or in the last ticking minutes you go
ough a great strife.
 alert when the almighty comes to take
ut last breath;
d remember, that death does not end our imaginations,
s the beginning of our hopes and the
d of our frustrations.
 the Resurrection, it's God that gives us
 greatest glory of perfection!
　　　—*Dee Sembrat Shah*

ur Cloud Of Confusion

e bird of melancholy is gliding through our eyes
s wings are weak as it tries to fly away
e meaning of confusion is swirling deep inside
rhaps it should be the word for the day

e feel intensity flowing within our trembling veins
 we watch the blood run through the steps of our time
e do not seem to mind our pain of hopeless longing
cause we seek the dagger that cuts through our lime

rough all the words and songs of our destiny...
y mind and soul have fallen through too deep
e image of you and...and oh those ocean blues...
shes me with splendid torture I need to keep

 want you, to need you....to.....I do not know
or there is no word to describe the desperation
want to dance the Fandango in a frozen lonely desert
 feel the obsession, the tension, our destination
　　　—*Dora Mintz*

reasures Of The Heart And Soul

e traveled about the world and there are many things I've seen

any things I've sought after with a treasure box of dreams

e seen rainbows from the mountain-tops that few have stood upon

e watched the desert take away the sun and bring it back at dawn

e know love in many lights and felt the laughter that it brings

e cherished all the gifts on earth and for that I'll
ver be the same

or money and all its riches I would never trade the
easures I've known

t something even greater still inside my heart has grown

l the beauty offered me is still less than the love in
 precious hands

r nothing has ever quenched my soul the way that Jesus can
　　　—*Darla Lynn Campbell*

Jesus Hold Me!!

Jesus hold me when I'm lost and all alone!
Jesus hold me when I pray to our Father on the throne!
Jesus hold me when my heart is broken without repair!
Jesus hold me when I feel despair!
Jesus hold me when there is no one to be found!
Jesus hold me when I'm on level ground!
Jesus hold me when I'm left to cry!
Jesus hold me as I wipe my tears dry!
Jesus hold me when I've found my way!
Jesus hold me when I see the light of day!
Jesus hold me when I see the sunrise!
Jesus hold me when my soul comes alive!
Jesus just hold me because I am your child!!!
　　　—*April D. Scott*

A Child's Prayer

Little children learn to pray
Jesus loves them in a special way
Their tiny hands are folded just right
As they bow their heads for prayer at night
Their words are always so kind and sweet
With warm hearts that are very meek
They always thank God above
For the people and things that they love
Day by day their faith will grow
With their bright, shining faces that just seem to glow
Is it no wonder that God shows He cares
When little children are so humble in their prayers?
　　　—*Joyce Watson*

Destiny's Journey

Darkness was apparent, though my mind was not coherent, as I journeyed down this unknown trail. The tiny path in visions view, entertained thoughts, of land a new.

I entered through the thickened trees, ignoring bush clear past my knees, the sound of crunch beneath my feet, of withered earths decay, accompanied me all the way. Curiosity overcame common sense, when night times chill set in, still I continued on, sporting a frosty grin. The endless rows of shadowed trees, would guide me through this destiny.

An eerie chill crept up my spine, when I came upon two eyes that weren't mine! Owl, cat, or unknown beast, I did not wish to be it's feast, with moon lights glare upon my back, the relentless eyes kept staring back.

Fleeing, feeling very meek, I fell into a silent creek. Wide awake and dripping wet, I hopelessly wondered filled with fret, scared and drenched, I scurried home, I did not want to be alone.

Perhaps someday I'll go back, with friends, daylight, and a big backpack, a rifle, gun, and great big knife, three dogs, slingshot, and a huge flashlight!
　　　—*Lou Megyeri*

Moonbeam

What is it
It's the sunlight late at night
It's the fairy rings spotlight
It's the wolf's lonely heart
It's the dust particles wooden cart
And a lovers dream
A terrified scream
But most of all a moonbeam
Can be seen throughout the land
As the late night beacon of light
Used to change the tides in more than just the sea
　　　—*Stephen Gerhauser*

"A Pact Of Love"

Please won't you come back?
Just give me a chance to make a pact.
A pact of love, no words needed,
Just the hands of time sweeping unheeded.

I can't stand feeling this way,
Please, won't you come and make it go away?
I gambled on love, and it looks like I lost,
Maybe it wasn't even worth the cost.

My life will never be the same,
But I can't say, I'm sorry you are to blame.
Time will forever stand still,
Waiting for you will test my will.

If I never see you again,
What will I do about the pain?
Is there some hope? Or must I die loving you,
Having nothing but my pride to see me through.

Please won't you come back?
Just give me a chance to make a pact.
A pact of love, no words needed,
Just the hands of time, sweeping unheeded.

—*Elizabeth Owens*

"A Love For All Seasons"

You came into my life like a warm summer breeze;
Just one smile from you made me feel so at ease.

Your words were so honest, your ways were so shy;
You melted my heart, and you didn't even try.

The way that I felt for you, I didn't show;
I knew I should wait, given time this would grow.

Something so special, I felt from the start;
In a crime I would welcome, soon you'd steal my heart.

You're a beautiful rose in the bright month of May;
You're the rustle of leaves on a clear Autumn day.

Like soft winter fires, and Christmas Eve snow,
The magic between us forever will glow.

I'm not sure how this happened, not even today;
But I'm glad that it did, and I want you to stay.

Your touch is so soft, and your kisses are sweet,
You have what it takes to make my life complete.

Now that I found you, I'll never let you go;
You've made me so happy, I want you to know,

That nothing compares to us being together,
I love you today, and I'll love you forever.

—*Christine Fortino*

Life Is A Beach

Life is a beach, with a never-ending tide.
Just when you think you have it all,
Everything you dreamed for,
The tide just rolls in and washes it away.
Then you have to start again,
To build it all back up.
And with a little encouragement,
And a little bit of luck,
You think you have it beat,
Then here comes the tide,
To wash it all away.
For what comes in, must go out,
Nothing is here to stay.
So hang on to what you have,
And fight for what you've got,
For life is a beach,
And the tide will never stop.

—*Carol D. Coffee*

Nadia

My heart begged my hands to touch her
     just to feel a warm caress
I thought how it might have been just for a moment
     if I could rest my head upon her breast

Her lips were distant roses
     just for show and not to touch
For one false move upon them
     could be one that is too much

For a rose in all its beauty
     has a side that's hard to see
Yet I held it to my bosom
     to forget my misery

As it was in my clutches
     and the comfort of my grasp
I no longer had to see
     for I had felt what had been masked

The thorn that had been hidden
     pricked my heart and brought forth pain
Now my blood is flowing freely
     and I know it was in vain

—*William Stewart*

A Celebrity Can "Do The Hustle"

To be a celebrity, pass the test of sobriety
Know your family tree; for a running start
To be a celebrity, do some work in society
Show respect for deity, for a running start
Refrain from using profanity
Protect yourself from insanity
Repent of past sins of deplority
Be charming, be graceful, have purity!
To be a celebrity, maintain your vitality
Try roles of duality have a hustle neutrality
To be a celebrity wear a suit of humility
Help in your community, maintain a good heart
To be a celebrity, have gossip immunity
Search out opportunity, keep priorities clear
To be a celebrity avoid calamity
Alter conversations dramatically to have a start
Refrain from slurping when eating soup
Refrain from letting suit pants drop
Practice each day with you Hula hoop
and you'll be in the celebrity group.

—*Rosemarie Angel Caluori*

Why Is It My World Keeps Changing

Trying to bear the pain of always feeling alone.
Knowing people really care,
but still feel as if there's no hope.
Trying to do my best but feel like a failure.
Trying to fit in with rest,
but feel unwanted.
Why is it my life's so confusing?
Why is it turned upside down?
Why do I feel so hurt and angry
at the world right now?
Why is it my world keeps changing keeps changing?
Is it because I'm still young?
Always looking for answers,
but never finding one.
Hoping someday I'll understand
what life and love really mean.
Maybe some one special can show
me how good love can really be.

—*Destiny Allison*

Untitled

Staring in the mirror, looking past what's at the surface.
Deep within myself I see emptiness, the girl everyone has
known is not the same person as the reflection in the
mirror.
Have I never looked at myself to find the real me, or has it
just now been brought to the surface?
I don't like what I see deep within those big, brown eyes.
Who is that person in the mirror staring back at me with
so much pain and anger?
When you look in that mirror each day and you don't like
what you see, you tend to pass by each mirror with your
eyes closed. Never chancing to see your inner self
staring back at you.
When people look at you, do they see all that you see?
Or does the mirror only show what we believe ourselves
to be?
As I pass the mirror, I can't stop to wonder
is this all there is to me -
or do these eyes so deep with anger lye?

—*Lisa K. Schoeppe*

For What It's Worth

Thoughts skip through my head
late at night
of all the fears
of all the fights
ripped with memories
of laughter and pain
songs stray through my mind
at the pace of rain
Death, jealousy and tragedy.
My thoughts wander, panic stricken, to the bystander,
alone in the world
No intention was meant
but innocent blood seemed to drip through his fingers
the most popular question is why.
Death, jealousy and tragedy.
Why dreams of others possessions.
Why not be happy and thankful
Why not be happy being free?
Death jealousy and tragedy.

—*Catherine Meyer*

Prisoner of the Night

I am a prisoner of the night. I don't wish to stay, I cannot
leave. I cannot escape the dark and loneliness.
There are so many secrets untold; so many things to know,
before I can grow old.

I don't understand the world, does it can be so cruel.
Rape, suffering, starvation, beating; they're all parts of my
life. I cannot face my problems. My only alternative is to
go, and never come back.

I seem to have been dealt a bad hand. If only I could win, but
I always loose.
I escape my world and enter other. I now live in a world of my
own. It may be dark, but it beats the other.

I don't know where I am going. I don't know what I am going to
do. I'll hurt but few when I go. No one cares; no one will
know. I know its wrong, but whose to say what's right.
I cannot be taught, cannot be caught.

I hear children's cries through the rustling of leaves.
I fear for them, in their dismal days.
Sometimes I want to give up. It doesn't seem worthwhile to
live. I'm a prisoner of the night, with nothing left to give.

—*Heather A. Gibbs*

Missing My Girl

The time apart away from you,
Leaves me pondering about what to do,
Mornings come and evenings go,
But your picture in my mind,
Is as fresh as the winter snow.

I took a train that left you
far from my sight,
Staring at the tracks through my window,
In the darkness of the night.

My mind unoccupied, only analyzing,
Thinking of you, with my eyes visualizing,
Your love and warmth, and oh such affection,
That when I stare at the calm water,
All I see is your beautiful reflection.

Your kindness and patience were always never ending,
My spirit and mind are always recommending,
That I keep you in my thoughts in each and every way,
With the hope of being with you
And seeing you some day.

—*Stephen Esch*

Chewing

Blueberry butterflies aimlessly fly around my soul
leaving marks where they have been.
blueberry freckles.

Watching distant farmers plow their fields,
my body laughs.
I could do them no harm.

Lemon colors on my face - burning;
it's those butterflies.
Blueberry freckles.

In fields of Indian corn and tattered butterflies.
I find a little brown stick.
I begin to chew.

—*Melissa Vendrick*

A Volunteer Firefighter's Prayer

God; Please, as you tuck them in tonight, keep the children safe.
Let me not have to hear their cries, from a careless act of fate.
Keep their parents all aware the fragileness of each young soul.
Don't let them waiver from their role of watching out for them.
Will not, a fire in the night and drag me from my slumber.
To listen to the grieving hearts, or the gratitude of others.
I don't want to hear the siren for an auto wreck tonight.
I've untangled enough twisted metal with the jaws of life.
And when I wake tomorrow, grant me patience when I see,
A mother driving with her child without a safety seat.
Grant me wisdom in the situations I might face with the new day.
In case by chance, there might be a newborn baby on the way.
Just in case, I lose the fight for someone's life I battled.
Remind me that I'm fallible, as human as the rest.
Give me courage to move on, although it may not be enough
Help me always give my best.

—*Laurie Wood*

Kids

You bring them into the world with high hopes.
Knock yourself out, with all the tight ropes.
Teach them the meaning of love and respect.
How to live life and learn to accept.

It wasn't easy, nor shall it be for those.
Who bring more kids, with eyes closed.
So wake up and learn also from the young.
They need to be taught, before they are sprung.

—*Mildred Detmer*

No Obstacles

Unlock your fear of life.
Let your creativity flow.
Plant a seed in your heart,
Then give it time to grow.

Don't worry about others
And what they will say.
Just follow your heart and keep the faith,
Soon you'll be on your way.

You got to do what you can
To survive these days.
Everyone is being tested
Like mice in a maze.

But go through the maze of life,
And you will find a way out.
If you get stuck along a path,
Just look for another route.

Never give up on your hopes and dreams.
They're all bound to come true.
Keep your eyes forward and never turn back.
I speak from experience because I was once like you.

—Sheila Jayaseelan

"Liberty That Gospel Peace!"

"Liberty", that gospel peace!"
"Liberty", that gospel peace!"
The Lord has told us what is good. What He
requires of His believers each day is this—to do what is
just, to show constant love, and to live in humble fellowship
with our God.
Be not conformed to this world.
"Liberty", that gospel peace!
Christ taught us that we are to be different. We are the
seasoning, the salt, a light for the world. We are in the
world temporary. God is shaping us to the likeness of His
Son, but we are no longer "of the world." We have to be
unique. Only then can we truly be a light for this
darkening world.
"Liberty", that gospel peace." The truth of my being
is that I am Special because I am a child of God. And
blessed by His love and radiant with His wisdom.
"Liberty", that Gospel Peace!"

—Rachel Ann Harris

"Life"

Down in a corner by the garden shed,
Lies the spider in his nylon bed.
It seems to us he works so hard,
Yet always watching, on his guard.
How he weaves his web of deceit,
Waiting for his food, hiding in retreat.
And like a flash he takes his prey,
On and on throughout the day.
But to the spider, 'tis only survival,
Killing or being killed by his rival.
Human nature is much the same,
At times we all play this little game.
The rich and powerful, to think they seek,
To take out the losers and the meek.
And like the spider we do our best,
To seize the moment before we rest.
We struggle and cope and how we try,
To laugh and sing and then we die.
The world goes on and yet somewhere,
There is a life of joy and care.

—Phillip D. Patterson

In Sympathy...

It grieved me at my heart, my friend, to hear your brother's
life had fled. But death is common to our race; and, as we
eat our daily bread, we know that in this world of strife,
it does not give eternal life.

That man of God, the patient job, once asked this question of
his friends: 'Shall mortal man yet live again? But I shall
take what my God sends.' And truly does the Scripture say
that men shall rise on Judgment Day.

My day is coming too, when I shall part from relatives and
friends; then shall I somewhat know your pain, as bitterness
with sweetness blends. And yet as they descend the slope,
I will not mourn as without hope.

This truth has held me up in past, and let me pass it onto you:
In Jesus is eternal life. (This is a fact; I know it's true.)
"Come unto me for life," He saith; this helps me in a world
of death.

—Theodore Pederson

Dreams

Just a small child so full of dreams
Life is just great, or so it seems.
A happy family struggling to get by.
At least they're together, but some dreams die.

You meet that certain someone, can this happiness last?
You work together, accomplishments are vast.
You have your own children. Your life is complete
The years ahead are a challenge to meet.

You dream ahead to those golden years.
Life throws a curve there's only more tears
You pick up the pieces, determined to go on.
Dreading the night, afraid of the dawn.

Where are those wonderful dreams you once had?
So hard to remember when you're feeling so sad.
Could it be you expected too much?
Like love returned, friendship and such?

Now you sit at home all alone
Waiting far a call on the telephone.
It never comes and no one drops by;
But then again, some dreams die.

—Elsie Verdi

Life

As if growing up isn't already tough,
life is like a rugged ocean, sometimes calm with an
occasional stormy wave, making things rough.
When I was younger, life was easy, not much to worry about,
but as I come of age, I have more responsibilities, have to
choose my own route.
I've grown a lot but I know I'm young still.
I often ask myself, "How many dreams of mine will I fulfill?
Will I succeed in college, will I have a career, will I
make a good life?
Will I remain a child or become a mother and wife?"
I can't answer these questions now, but I know I have God
on my side,
and with this knowledge, I'll try my best...
to handle the tide.

—Keisha Ramsey

ong Of Valiant Spirits

early pearl-dewed hours before dawn's coral rays,
life offers sane solutions to benefit our ways:

hough weary soldiers die in wars
and vital problems plague our land,
ur ingrained courage seldom wanes,
for hope rewards our stalwart stand.

hough jobless young men look for work
while single mothers seek relief,
d aged souls walk painfully,
still, prayers are answered with belief.

reat music, poetry and art —
prolific gifts of super men —
lp lift our spirits thankfully
and forge our future bright again.

    Thus:

olten sunrise sparks ideas,
  Challenges for fresh beginnings.
   Morning's energy increases,
    reaps consistent daily winnings.
        —Charlotte Riepe

ity Flights

ve me your stressed, deranged, and lost yearning just to be,
fe outside the city seems too vacuous for me.
need the ups and downs and depression of the masses,
rround myself with experience, not assumed from backward
ral classes.
want the dirty air and the noise that goes along.
ou can have your miles and miles of emptiness and birds
nging their song.
oney breeds paranoia and won't let the pot melt.
he skin I'm in is white, but it has dyed with the color I felt.
    —Steve J. Hill

oot Print's of the Heart

went back in time today, in the memories of my mind. When
fe's pathway seems unending, and you're young and in your
ime along life's pathway..overgrown..and with thorns and
ses..bound.. When we walk along the road of life, we leave
ur footprints on the ground. The imprint we leave along the
ay can equal..diamonds, or..a pearl. If you realize each step
ou take leaves a footprint on the world. Footprints are
ages of the heart, a bond even death can't sever. They are
recious memories sealed in love and embedded in our heart
rever. For we leave footprints in the sands of time. As we
rive to reach our goal, and footprints engraved upon our
art are etched deeply in our soul. As time goes by,
ootprints may dim. Erased wholly from our view. But
otprints engraved within our heart. Will stay forever new.
ll memories when gathered at random are our footsteps of the
st. Life, sometimes like footsteps..falter... Still the mind
love holds fast. As I near this journey's end, and view my
fe..in part. I thank God for footsteps that left.. These
recious memories in my heart.
    —Jessie Slaton

ost in the Wind

ost in the wind
e endless seeds of life and love.
ek and ye shall find?
bloomed like a precious flower,
nd shone like crimson;
ut hence it only lasted awhile...
ntil it was lost in the wind...
ith the endless seeds of life and love.
    —Sue Evoy

Morning After A Night With A Psychopathic Husband

Hugging my son, chubby cheeks against mine
lifting my daughter, holding her tight
two pairs of eyes with sudden warmth and glow
-utter happiness-
baby flesh pressing into me
slender child arms encircling me
my heart laden
trying to offer them something elusive
not doing enough justification for their
young innocent lives
with no love, no fun, no laugh, no music
days burdened with...
unsympathetic commands ringing all over
the house divided...
after the children left...
eyes bright with unshed tears
my familiar dull thud of ache, pain, agony
hammering me with full force - I start -
same pattern of another new bright day!!!
    —Nagu Veerabhadran

Feelings

I woke up this morning feeling very sad.
Like I just lost the best friend I'd ever had.
When I looked out my window
It looked back at me.
The most beautiful world one could ever see.
The birds were singing a sweet lullaby
As though they came from above.
It was simply beautiful, because it came from a covey of dove.
There was a soft breeze blowing
Off in a distance from the direction of the breeze.
Church Bells were ringing both for you and for me.
    —Jo Ann T. Hoskins

I Don't Know How To Let Go

Here I am holding to your memory
Like it was made of the purest gold
That ol' flame still burns within me
In my heart and in my soul....

I can't keep from thinking of you
What we had was just so good
I can't help it if I still love you
I'd forget you if I could....

I think of all that we could share
And tears build up inside of me
To think that there is going to be nothing.

I don't think I could ever say goodbye,
I don't know....
I don't know...
I don't know how to let go.
    —Brooke Caudill

Borrowed Time

My mind is relieved as things are clear
  Like life so far and death so near

And still to think of that certain time
  When life isn't a riddle or a rhyme

Yet of that day when one was birthed
  Began time and revolved the earth

Slowing down as years go by
  For the right and wrong and to wonder why

That uncertain feeling for tomorrow
  I wonder how much time have we borrowed?????
    —LaJuanna M. Armstrong

Questions

Be is to bop,
Like rock is to roll.
Time is to space,
Like wise is to old.
How are you to reconcile your soul;
If your other half is missing?
You is to I,
Like they is to we.
Love is to life,
Like stream is to sea.
Without someone close to hold your hand;
What are you but a soul with misgivings?

—*Bilal Shabazz*

Steel Bullets

Rain pounds down on the abandoned shack
like steel bullets into the earth.
A family once grew here.
A mother, a daughter and two boys whose chalky
faces had stared out at rain.

The rain has sorrow for the abandoned shack.
Standing in solitude, wishing it had the boys
within it's grey wood.
Wishing the mother sat calm — unknowing — waiting
in silence for the return of the sun.

The blackened hearth solid and heavy stands
at the end of the drafty room.
Cracked glass window, and splintered floor
boards all compose a forgotten home.

Mother had sat too long, with infertile breasts.
While steel bullets had rained down;
She waited for the sun.

—*Ai L. Welch*

Son's Rotation

Yesterday the sun was red
like the constricted veins in your eyes,
the sparks that flew between us
were as hot as a desert night.

With the rotation between the sun and the moon
You've cooled the pocket where time stood still.

No more red or yellow with rays of fear,
Only the child of yesterday's beer.

With a sigh the curtains are closed.
And the window of time is a prison for souls.

The sun has set
in the fiery west.
The child awakes
to another dawn of red

—*Nicole J. Freed*

Love Is Like A Flower

When the first seed is planted,
You feed it, love it, care for it
Watch it grow stronger;
Love is also the same;
You start from the bottom,
  mend it, give it, received it,
Maybe I don't show it, but it there,
Open your eyes and see. For what
I can given to thee.

—*L. Jenkins*

I Wish That I Could Shine Like That

I wish that I could shine like that
like the sun
touching everyone
everything
with my warmth
and radiance.

The plants would grow in my direction
reaching toward me
so that I might help them grow
blossom with colors
in celebration
of my existence.

Animals would play in my joyful light
and the world would sleep beneath my shadow.
How good it would feel to shine like that
and be loved
by so many.

—*Justina Hook*

A Sad Phone Call

The phone rang this evening here is what Phyllis had to say,
"Linda called with sad news to relay.
Penny's baby is dead and they are at the hospital now.
That's all they had to say.
Call my Mom Phyllis please, as I'll be tied up, as you can see"

What very sad news to receive news that's so hard to conceive.
I cried so hard and could not sleep
To think of two young people, the family all loves
Awaiting the birth of this dear little soul whose name is
  Baby Nicole.

I dried my eyes and tried to visualize what happened! I began
to realize that God was short one little Angel in the sky.

So as we all walk through these sad hours,
I know that you're in safe hands in a very special place,
In the sky with God as your guide.

It eases the pain, but just the same,
You'll be missed and not forgotten,
Dear Baby Nicole, you dear, dear little soul.
So we had to say "Hello" before we said "Goodbye" for God's
  Little Angel, who now lives in the sky.

—*Georgene Sutton*

Magenta

Lipstick pushes past her natural
lip-line, like a child playing with crayons
on the canvas of her face.

Her face is flat and empty
like an easel
waiting for an artist.

I want to reach out and smooth
the uneven scribbles of her face,
to erase the trails of mascara crayons.

Could I do it with words?
Could I paint happy hues into her chaos?

Are words enough?

—*Colette L. Huxford*

Lisa's Prayer

Jesus is the answer, and Lisa is the prayer:
Lisa stood at the door knocking, and said Lord
please let me in, my body is racked with pain,
and I don't know if I have sinned.

God answered in his own special way, Lisa I can
always use an angel, but I have not called you
this day; for you must care for an angel of two,
so that you and Cassie can spread joy on earth...

And Lisa there will be many trials, and
tribulations, and I am making you stronger so
you will always know what to do.

Yes, Jesus is the answer, and Lisa is the prayer,
and there were thousands lifting their voices in
unison to God in prayer: "The Lord said whatever
you ask in prayer, believe that you have received
it, and it will be yours."

Jesus, Yes Jesus is the answer to all our prayers,
so thanks to all the thousands, and thank you God
for leaving one special angel here on earth for
all of us to share.
　　　　—Jerry Hallmark

White Night

I sit alone in the dark.
Listening to the beautiful
　　songs of a lark.
In a distance, in the woods,
　　I see a unique light.
Hoping, praying that's its my
　　long lost white night.
Once upon a nightmare.
I lost a loved one , it
　　was so unfair
His death was caused by depression.
So because of his faults, it
　　ruined our relation.
I wondered desperately in the woods I
　　noticed an astonishing looking fairy.
I was so naive a lot like the Virgin Mary.
So here I set upon a limb.
Wondering, waiting for him.
Depressed and captive until the end.
Hoping one day our broken hearts will mend.
　　　　—Cindy Baker

How Can We Stop It?

When will blood shed stop to flow?
Little children allowed to grow.
When will we learn, that the word "Peace"
Means that all fighting must cease.

What a wonderful world, this could be,
If every Nation was at Peace and free.
Just to watch little children play
And every one free, to worship and pray.

What will stop massacred parents dying,
Children starved, alone and crying?
When will this world start to mend,
Stop all killing, and just put an end.

To greed and hatred, in this world,
Fly our Freedom flag, and give it a whirl.
Try to live in Peace, with each other
Children in the loving care of a Mother.

Have we turned away from God and fear?
This world can soon end - and every year,
Brings us closer to the end of our life.
So lets live in Peace, instead of strife.
　　　　—Eva A. Bogdan

Lonesome Violin

Lonesome violin, I want to hear
Lonesome violin, I want to be near
There you go again
Pull the strings of my heart.
Will you stay with me
Your sweet melody is all I need
When I'm feeling so low.

I drift away when I hear you play.
Like a ring in a pool in the dreams of a fool,
You are fading, I'm alone and so blue.

After I come to, I shake my head
See I'm not with you, so instead
I keep coming back
To the dream in my heart.
Will you stay with me.
Your sweet melody is all I need
When I'm feeling so low.

You slipped away, there is nothing I can say.
Before you let me go, there is one thing you should know.
I will miss you when that slow fiddle plays.
　　　　—Vicki Brown

The Tenth Month

This story was written to my heart;
long ago... underneath aburn'n wind
by the spirit of a crazy white boy. It is
dedicated too Dreamer.
Its the tenth month - night has destroyed the day.
And in the silence of the deep,
the moon looks as a ghostly galleon
tossed up on a cloudy sea.
Somewhere high on a misty mountain top
where shadow's move without sound, and
the wind whispers of pains that cannot be
a dead out law will come to life, and rise
up from his pillow of darkness
obsessed with a memory
　　　　—Dan E. Hawkins

Thoughts on Reaching My 69th Birthday

I hover on the outer edge of life's dimensions
Look around - my life's horizon is dwindling fast
Do others feel the cutting pain,
And gaze at higher ground in vain?

How far is God's infinity?
If not for a soul, what would life be?
Or is it just a faint mirage, in someone's heart?
Futility.

Age creeping up like moon-drawn tide
Small increments of time, eroding life
To where?
Past is ever greater than future,
With only present left
Life is now.
　　　　—Antonetta Schroeder

The Swimmer

Splash, the race is on,
The swimmers are on their quest for first
And the fans cheer loudly
Each kick, breath and stroke they take counts,
Each one slows as they tire,
But the swimmers are done, and the race is won,
And the fans cheer loudly.
　　　　—Stephanie Clark

413

The Moon

I was standing alone in the crisp, cool night,
Looking above at a bright, shining light.
A white glowing ball to be seen by all,
Which comes out in Winter, Summer, Spring, and Fall.
It's though it was over twice the size,
Of all the other stars which can be seen by human eyes.
Some say upon it lives a man,
Because of the face's patterned tan.
Oh, you cannot imagine what I would give,
To lead a great life just like his.

—*Erica Mitchell*

The Last Kiss

There we stood
looking at each other
holding hands
thinking of all the love between us
remembering all the times we spent together
and the last time
all I can remember is the sound of the gun
as he pulled the trigger
and the scream of the man
as the bullet was tearing into his chest
and finally the sound of sirens coming from all directions
now I will never see him again
and as we touch lips for our last kiss
I feel a tear running down my cheek
as he pulls away he wipes the tear off my face
whispering in my ear I love you and I always will
and now he is gone forever
and all I have to remind me of our love
Are the memories of what once was

—*Marlana Wegner*

Night-Light

Sitting on the cold, hard concrete,
looking at the beautiful stars.
That night, with you, everything made sense to me.
The sky was ablaze with
the wonderful speckles of light that we called
our Night-Light.
We sat and looked,
you held me so tight.
You told me all about the stars and the sky.

But the times of course do change.
The beautiful stars no longer
shine for me that way.
And for some reason I feel
like I am now the concrete.
Yes, you are there; but with her.
I am the cold, hard concrete that
you two sit on, only now with her in your arms...

—*Liza Davison*

Untitled

If not for you, where would I be
    lost in a world of hatred and misery
Reaching for happiness, but not quite grasping on
For the world has its snares, we know this to be true.
Groping in the dark until I found you.
A happiness brought forth with a smile on your face
    Giving your heart despite what takes place.
If not for you my soul would be torn
    Scattered across the hills of forlorn.

—*Cathy McCormick*

Love Poem

   Love is from above,
love is like a dove that flies up above,
who is this God who gives us this wonderful love
He is the God who rules up above
He's such a wonderful God to give us
such a thing as love.
So when you think of love just thank that God up above
for giving us such a thing as LOVE

—*Cristy Doughty*

Colors Of Love

Bluest of blue are my baby's eyes
looking softly at me
filling my red, red heart
with unmeasurable love

Cherub pink cheeks and
wind-tousled pale yellow hair
held against my bosom
change the blackness
of my lonely world

Loneliness - an emotion
Black, gray and empty
Changing slowly through awareness —
love in a child's eyes and a simple phrase
Come Grandma go —

—*F. J. Lindner*

The World Today!

The world bustles with cars and people, skyscrapers
loom up like massive steeples.
With all the hurrying, pushing, and shoving, when do
people take time for a little loving.
Working for the almighty dollar, all trying to change
their blue for white collars.
Winning at the old rat race, pushing themselves to
quicken the pace.
What is all this running for? I really don't know or
care to know anymore.
People now-a-days don't have time, just trying to save
every nickel and dime.
They can't take it with them when they go, this is
something they should know.

—*Tamra Hall*

Untitled

As I rumble along through life things are apparent,
Lost souls pile up on the road of heartbreak,
It is a pile filled with broken dreams,
A harsh world imposes hard penalties on those who fail to
    achieve all that is pure, and good.
Is it not possible to die a happy man,
Or is it?
Is this world all a dream,
Where a broken promise is forgotten.
And lost loves are all a figment of some demented soul's
    imagination,
Could we be that lucky?
Or is the harsh reality of it all just that,
The painful unabashed truth,
Where love dies, promises are broken, and men live to hate
    one another?
Much like an old horror film where the monster is hunted
    and killed,
So are the hearts of man.

—*Noel G. Marsh*

The Powers of Love"

Love is an emotion that two people share,
Love is an emotion that is not always fair.
Love always has its ups and downs,
Love makes you smile; love makes you frown.
Those three little words can be so hard to say,
But those same three little words can take the hurt away.
To tell someone "I love you" must mean more the words.
To tell someone "I love you" you must want to move forwards.
If you've had love, but now its gone;
Don't live in the past keep moving on.
Because love will come and love will go;
When the time is right, that's when you will know.
You may find that love not too long from now,
You may find that love but first you must know how.
But no matter what you say or do;
Love may no last your whole life through.

—*Heather Gryziec*

Love

Love is laughter,
Love is sweet,
Love is something you cannot beat!

When you're feeling down,
Or when you're feeling down,
Or when you have a frown,
Think of a dove, or God above.

Love is something, everyone should feel.
It makes you laugh and kick your heels.
I should know,
For I have love to show.

If you feel hate,
It's never to late,
To find some love for yourself, or a friend.

Never beware,
For love is there,
When you feel down and cannot share.

Love is laughter,
Love is sweet,
Love is something you cannot beat!

—*Rebecca L. Johnson*

Never-More

I dream of days gone by, another time when
love was new, and hope gave meaning to a broken
heart, but time stands still among my tears,
and memories haunt this void of feeling,
hollow, in its space of time.
I search for miracles of inner-peace, and what I
find is what I never hoped to be, a shell, a clown
who hides behind the shadow of their soul.
Perhaps someday I'll find that peace that once
was lost, or that I never had at all.
The day will come, when this pre-existing life
I live, like time, shall cease to be, and all
my hurt shall be as dust, that scatters in
the wind, lost, and then forgotten, to be
remembered, never-more!

—*Mary C. Rose*

Untitled

Time flew away like sand in the wind
leaving no trace of its origins nor of its
    destination.

The only things left behind
were the scars of life and the wounds of the
    living.

—*Risa Shimizu*

Cathy

You are the object of my desire
of dreams which you inspire,

Whilst others are caught in petty strife
you should know that I would give my life;

That I'd walk through the Valley of Death for you
just to hear you say: I love you too.

—*W. H. Sebregts*

Ode to the Forgotten Soldier

Far on the distant shores of a troubled land,
Loved ones are not forgotten.

Amid turmoil and suffering brave soldiers make their stand,
While loved ones back home await their fate.

Days come and go and the endless procession of time marches on,
While human conflicts come and go like the tides of the sea.

Generations pass and time erodes the memories of the bravery
of lost souls,
As well as the lessons of the inevitable burdens borne by
those trapped by the fate of history.

—*Marvin P. Wilson*

Sleepless In the Shadows Of Yesterday

Memories flooding her mind day and night. Shadows of a lost
lover across the miles. Only snapshots to preserve his embrace
and a diamond as a token of promises unkept. Flowing gently
are her tears. The good Lord above hearing her prayers.
...Why do we long for yesterdays? ...for dreams so long ago,
so far away?

Softly whispering his name, patiently awaiting his voice that
never speaks. Hearing only the soft breeze in return.
Longing for his comfort, his strong caress, his warm touch.
Feeling only the chill of an early fall.

Haunted by those last few moments alone. Wondering will she
ever again stare deep into those blue eyes...now becoming
the eyes of a stranger.
Wondering will she ever again see his smile or feel his love
...once so familiar, to be new once more.

Only one continuing to grasp onto the untied knot of a
lifetime. A destiny of happiness shared by two.
Alone and remembering, wondering endlessly,
Will one ever completely let go?

—*Dana M. Smith*

Loving Me

Like a petal falling off a dew drenched rose...
    Loving me
Like honey bees making honey in their honey combs...
    Loving me
Like moon rays being cascaded from the sky...
    Loving me
Like when the sky turns twilight and there you lay...
    Loving me
Like when the flicker of the fire place no longer flickers...
    You shall be...
    Loving me
Like long before dinner has arrived, you will be full..
    Loving me
Like when the days are no more you are...
    Loving me
Like when eternity is upon us, you will still be...
    Loving me

—*Lisa Johnson*

Amerikka and What it Stands For:

A is for the army and all it's military might
M is for massacre of native people never given a chance to fight
E is for ebony my favorite color is black
R is for racism we must initiate an attack
I is for isolation never being a part of
K is for the klan and the white hoods that they love
K is also for kill. Dreams never given a chance to grow
A is for Afrika the land of my ancestors who were kidnapped so
  long, long ago!

　　　—Russell Gause

Clock

The clock I find is a curious thing,
Made of what-cha-ma-call-its, and do-dads, and oh yes,
A spring.
The spring I believe the most important part,
The controller of movement, a mechanical heart.
No wait.
The spring isn't the heart, it's just a tense band
Of steel.
I'm sorry, my mistake,
I meant the balance wheel.
In constant motion, among the commotion, it competes
With itself in a back and forth race.
First this way, now that way, with restrictions,
I dare say, that help it maintain a quick nervous pace.
Nonetheless it progresses in the inner recesses
Of the clock's mechanical breast.
The heart always beating,
The movement repeating,
It never has time to rest.

　　　—Rick Martin

Roma

Beautifully breathtaking as the Pieta,
Majestic stature of the Colosseum,
Smooth and delicate like her Chianti...

　　　　　　This is R O M A

Savory as her pasta,
Intimate conversation on the Spanish Steps,
City street buzzing like huge bees...

　　　　　　This is R O M A

Strong and alluring as the Pantheon,
Friends greeting with a tender embrace and kiss,
Peaceful serenity like the Trevi Fountain...

　　　　　　This is R O M A

Touch her history, taste her flavor, see her beauty:

　　　　　　Experience R O M A!

　　　—Diane E. Lind

Marge

Marge you are a very, special friend to me.
Marge you have always, been here for me,
I just wish I could have, been there for you.
Marge you have treated me like,
a daughter ever since I met you.
Marge you have been, like a mother to me.
I just wanted to say I love you,
And I will miss you so much.
I just wish you could, see me now and I could see you.
Marge you will always be in, my heart as I will be in yours.
Marge I will never forget, the friendship we shared.

　　　—Melissa Legge

Going Away

I always sat in your favorite chair, and every time you would
make me move, which I never thought was fair.
You never called me by my real name, but to you, the name you
called me meant the same.
Sometimes I would fall asleep on your bed. Every time you
would bend down to kiss me on my forehead.
I will never forget the memories we share. Now you're leaving
and you need to know I care.
There is so much you're leaving behind, but now there's no way
you can change your mind.
I can't see why you need to leave so soon, but at least I know
we'll always be seeing the same moon.
Grandma will be alone now, but I will watch over her. She'll
never love no one the way she loved you cause you're the only
one who could ever fulfill her dreams.
There is no one who could ever take your place, and I will
never forget the look of your face.
Always remember me whatever you do, because I am always
gonna love you!

　　　—Jimynda Pond

Breakfast Time

The warming sun
makes patterns on a yellow cloth
and sparks a crystal glass with blandishment;
the coffee brews
and chuckles low within its depths
its fragrance - Kona-captured, heaven-sent.

Above a flame
the bacon lures a laggard near,
its aromatic sputter - eloquent;
hot buttered toast,
and marmalade for tang, and yet -
without your smile, there is no nourishment.

　　　—Aileen Christenson

Intoxication...

The stomach turning scent of whiskey, follows the staggering man.
My meddling eyes glued to every move.
White broom bristles grow from the leather face.
Cold, tired, uncaring gray eyes, stained red.
Torn flannel shirt, with grease painted pants.
Talks like a preacher to his imaginary friend.
People accept him as he is and ignore him.
What path has led him here?

The bottle drops... from the shaking hand.
Life-taking fluid seeps into the gutter.
Dropping to his knees, as if to pray.
A sole tear mixed with dirt, rolls down the timeless face.
He rocks to and fro, like a mother with her child.
I see crystal clear glass, shattered pieces shimmering in the
daylight.
Large ones, small ones, some smooth, others jagged.
The label clings to two halves of the bottle.

　　　—Kevin S. Guarino

Winter Warmth

The snowy skies and icy ground
Signs of winter are everywhere found.
Drinking hot cocoa by the bright warm fire,
Getting out the blankets and winter attire.
The squirrels are busy gathering up nuts,
Rabbits are snuggled in their holes and huts.
Celebrations for Christmas and the brand New Year,
Remind us that winter is a time of cheer.
So button up your coats and put on your gloves,
Winter is a time that everyone loves.

　　　—Tara Prewitt

Reflections

The mirrors are only a facade.
Many mortal images reflected upon them are not gold.
I have seen many reflections;
The reflections of those who have been or will be.
Reflections are raindrops prowling in the mysterious night;
They prowl upon you when you're unsure;
It is true that reflections themselves are unsure.
Reflections are the images that one portrays.
One maybe considered a rainbow filled with brightness and
laughter,
Or a lightning bolt daring to light up a stormy night's sky.
All that these images show is that which is seen through the
viewers eyes.
Reflections may cause severe blindness when it comes to matters
within, or they may truly be gold.

—*Laurie Jean Downey*

Sweet Summer

Bubblegum pinks tinge a dawning sky.
Marshmallow clouds drifting low.
Bright buttons of sunshine, like butterscotch discs
Play tag in the waters below.

The dark chocolate earth safely cradles it's seeds.
Vanilla tassels on corn shoot up high.
Taffy hued wheat stalks, so pliant and full,
Bow to lemon drop lilies close by.

The licorice tones of an old weathered barn.
The caramelized glaze of hot rooftops at noon.
The wintergreen look of reeds in the pond,
A rock candy sheen to the moon.

Nature squanders her lipsmacking grab bag of sweets,
Flings a potful of honey our way.
Each morning's a bon-bon, it's flavor unknown,
Ours to nibble and savor the rest of the day.

—*Johannah E. Lemble*

Sleigh Ride (To Grandma With Love)

Snowflakes, oh frozen stars
mashed windblown on your warm red face
drifting swirls
never twice the same
melt into tears
moist forehead on a winter's day

I hold your hand through twilight valleys
as nature's vapors sigh
icy panes on frosted windows
God's lace on a Christmas sky

Snowflakes, rest here by me
silent blanket round our heated toes
gentle beauty
in the season blows
a kiss to end this sweet sleigh ride
with the wish that I were home

—*Cindy Franks*

Christmas Isn't Christmas Anymore

Christmas isn't christmas anymore
Since my daddy went away to war
There isn't any joy around our Christmas tree,
And Santa doesn't kiss mommy on a Christmas eve,
Christmas isn't Christmas anymore,
No season greetings, meetings at our door
Oh Santa bring my daddy home to me
So Christmas will be Christmas once more

—*Irving L. Shuffler Jr.*

If A Rose Were To Have Less Significance

A red rose held in her hand
Meant recognition to her dark brown eyes.
My blindness of the world,
If ever it stigmatized someone so beautiful,
Would make me abhor the color of my skin.

Where is their vision?
Wherever there is color there is vision.
Where is their sound?
When one finds he finally sees
He hears for the first time.

If there are eyes that conspire against me, against us,
If a rose were to have less significance,
If a vision, created out of darkness,
Is suddenly annihilated,
If someone beautiful
Ever felt the thorns of stigma against her skin,
If sound were never sound again,
But only noise, merely static,
Then I could do little else
But abhor the color of my skin.

—*Julian Weinstein*

Anguish

Is waiting for that which is not
Meant to be...a withering consciousness
of the weak...a lowering of the
emotion and the spirit.
Anguish is pain from a thwarted
Expectation and longing to be
What one is not. It is the dimming light
From a window framing the brink
Of a storm...a foreboding.

It is a waning of desire — a sense of
Giving up of what should be
Incessantly fought. It is a flight away
From Truth, away from every human
Struggle, away from Hope.
Anguish is faithlessness, a solitude
Where there is no solace nor comfort.
It is a dark and cold corner in a
Huge mansion of fear where excitement
Is forever lost... it is defeat,
The superlative of loneliness.

—*Jay De Leon Mamaradlo*

Louise

L ouise each letter of her name each syllable of the sound
meant to five human lives, love and protection was near and
dear no matter what the cost

O h what a woman to love and behold, unselfish her willingness
to spread her wisdom around

U ndying love is what the five human lives tried to mirror
back, to us Louise was our stroke of good luck, she was so,
so dear

I nspiring not only to the five human lives, but also to
others in the human race, she even spread it around while in
the armed, forces, and while serving her country during the
time of the Korean era

S trength, spirit, hardworking, and determined, she was such
a positive force

E ndless love for her fellowman, what more could the five
human lives ever ask for

—*Rhonda Matthews*

As We Meet Again

I leave behind the place of my youth.
Melancholy laced memories are traveling companions.
A small stone house slowly breathes a sigh of joy and
sadness.

Delicious holiday aromas sprinkled with childhood laughter.
Snow angels glistening,
    iced mittens thawing,
        oatmeal warming in the bubbling black kettle.
Gold maple leaves dancing,
    pumpkin-colored blossoms bowing,
        pine needles crunching in the dense hickory grove.
Sun-mellow mornings when time strolled along.
Tender goodnights with sweet kisses and arms strong.

My youth...
    a tiny seed in my bountiful garden.
So I pause,
    and embrace
        the wondrous harvest again.

—*Constance Hanstedt*

A Simple Treasure

One warm December day I walked through a blanket of brown,
melting snow.
I noticed a woman weeping under a green leaved tree
I looked into her tear-soaked empty eyes and saw, through all
the black, a spark
Those eyes looked at me painfully as though there was nothing
of value anymore

I stood looking at her puzzled, puzzling and seemingly lifeless
features
Her gaze fixed on one spot on the ground in front of me
I looked at that spot to see nothing but soggy, soupy earth,
her gaze still there
I studied the spot again to reveal a small hazel-colored stone

I took up the stone and handed it to the woman
And as I felt her hands my whole body seemed to freeze at the
touch
But as she took the stone I watch her spirit warm up in moments
Her gaze shifted to me and I looked into her eyes and saw a flame.

—*Brandon Gallagher*

Secrets

As the stars twinkle above, you sit below
Mind wandering, wondering what the future holds
You peer into the dark, endless night
As though the answer laid there.
Then a star falls, you lift into the air.
Into a quaint, magical land.
Animals, curiosity overcomes them, they creep out
Slowly, slowly... carefully you pet them, they lick you
Then you are wisped away by a magical, powerful power
You look at the animals, they are specs from below.
You wisp away fast, you are a blur, then it slows
You are set on the soft pillowy ground
A mist blows, wets your face and hair
A waterfall, pouring down like a sprinkling spring rain.
A pegasus circles over you, swoops down...
Suddenly you are back a dream you think.
Dawn is breaking, pastel colors fill the sky
The sun, just brimming the earth for a new day.
You feel your face it's wet, you run home laughing inside
Then out, for happiness at the secret you share.

—*Kristi Lynn Peitsch*

Mister

Mister, am I ugly?
    Mister, are my eyelashes to long?

Mister, do I look intelligent?
    Mister, why is the grass green
    and the sky blue?

Mister, why do you sleep on a bench?
    Is it because you have little money?

Mister, do dreams come true?
    Mister, why do people say they love someone
    but don't mean it?

Mister, Mister, why are you not answering
    my question?
        Mister, I just want to know.

—*Raedean Foote*

"Rainy Winter Day"

Wet ground, cold air,
Misty atmosphere,
Sun, no longer there.

A dark and dismal day,
No children out to play
Skies no longer a beautiful blue, but a gruesome gray.

Cold raindrops hit the ground
On car windows, raindrops pound.
Everything else still, raindrops make the only sound.

—*Dolsonee Harrison*

A Friends Love That Is All

Why do I shed these tears in the dark?
Most men would be happy to have gotten this far.
From the time man is born he dreams of the dark;
of spending sometime with a woman not her heart.
But, I am not like most men I do see in the dark,
and I now feel the pain that grows in my heart.
I asked her if this was real,
and what of love does she feel?
For a long moment she laid still;
then like an old song she said-
forget about love it is not my desire we are not for real.
Father why do they wish to steal my heart,
and set me on fire?
Now! I sit alone in the dark,
and wait for the next bite that will take my whole heart.
At last, my soul has turned cold like my heart;
to think all she wanted was to make love in the dark.

—*Juan Delosrios*

I Miss You...

I never thought that I could ever miss anyone as
much as I miss you.
Life without you is like walking through a field of
fire barefooted.
That's how painful it is without you.
You make my life happy and complete.
Each day with you is like walking through a beautiful garden
of roses. (Without the thorns of coarse)...
Every day I look at the calendar counting the days
until you come back to me.
So I guess until then I'll be sitting at home
looking at the door hoping that the next person
that walks through that door will be you.....
And that my dear is how I miss you so.

—*Latrice M. Moore*

Music Warms the Heart

Music is a warming agent for hearts and souls of all ages,
Music comes in many different forms, just listen closely as
you travel along.

Oh how melodious it is to hear music each day and throughout
the year, the sound of birds chirping outside your window to
let you know all is well and clear.

Notes played by a concert pianist who carefully recalls each
note, the humming of an aged grandmother rocking a child on
a porch; rhythmed strokes from the strings of a harpist
playing gracious tunes, these types of music are all used to
help soothe.

Music warms the heart, without it we'll be torn apart. For
the greatest music we shall hear is sweet spirit filled lyrics
of a Gospel Choir, always helping to bring us cheer. When we
need total uplifting we turn to God in prayer and praise,
because you know He's just one prayer away.

So God placed music in different forms inside, and around
us, because He knew right from the start that we need music,
for music warms the heart.

—*Dorothy C. Broughton*

"When Doctors Made House Calls"

In 1917 a seven year old girl was I.
   My 105 degree fever, my mother knew not why.
The family doctor, she did call.
   His flivver brought him in no time at all.

He checked me over and said to dad,
   Scarlet fever is why she is so bad.
In quarantine she must be,
   Upstairs my father carried me.

In six weeks, the doctor came and said,
   You are well, young lady, get out of bed.
All things in here must be burned.
   Oh no! I cried, around I turned.

My doll and I cannot part.
   He said, you knew this from the start.
A Lysol bath, she must get,
   Which nearly killed her, I can't forget.

I loved my doctor that cared for me.
   He saved my life that was to be.
He made house calls night and day
   So bless him, Lord, to you I pray.

   —*Hazel Raymond*

A Life Within Me

A flutter, like an eyelash, tickling me inside,
My breasts, swollen with your nourishment,
We are one now.
Two souls, sharing one body,
Bound by the cord of life.
A nine month journey,
You, so tiny, make my heart beat with joy.
Together we grow,
Safe and strong,
How I long to hold you,
How I yearn to know you.
Alas, soon we must part,
You will stand on your own,
But, I will always be there
To love you,
You will never be alone.
Forever, a part of you will live in me.
I gave you life,
You made mine matter.

   —*Lisa G. Slansky*

I Just Don't Want To Know

Sitting on a hill alone and wondering about it all.
My arms are drawn across my knees
Call upon my will to breathe
The rustle of leaves answers my call.

Sitting here I think about the places I've never been.
Things that I have never seen
Dreams that I have never dreamed
The moonlight casts a pallid sheen.

And if my time is drawing near
Please don't tell me so
If St. Peter passes here
Please don't tell me so.
I just don't want to know.

Sitting near the surf unfurled
Time comes in on every curl.
On the beach now I can see
Time is not the enemy.
It circles in on everything
And why should I be different?
I just don't want to know.

   —*Dena Rockenbach*

My Body

This body, my body, an accelerating race car
My body, a speedy sleek steed
My body, a swift swimmer slicing water
My body, a tawny tiger sprinting

What has happened to my race car?
Where is my steady steed, my swift swimmer, my tiger?
Why do you not respond to my command?
What has happened to the energy, the muscle?

I need you, my body to do my will.
You desert me in my time of need.
What good is life to be immobilized, like lead?
Give back my energy, my mobility, or I am dead.

   —*C. Gassin Weiner*

Infatuation

   He used me, and I used him.
My friends say it was infatuation.
I suppose I really did like him a lot,
But all that is gone without a spot.
I wish he would of said he liked me a lot too,
But that was a vision I had that never came true.
I wish I could have opened my eyes that night.
But, that is where infatuation came in,
I had no sight.
I'll end this poem with one last note,
He made me feel wanted,
At least that was the vision I felt.

   —*Kelly Johnson*

Green Grass

   Grass is green and fresh and cool.
So, that is why? God made
Grass green and, blue like the water and, the sea of tea.
Ocean and, of the blue trees and, of the, fine things and,
of all the beauty it brings.

   Grass green and, free and, serene and, that
is what grass green and, blue should be.
Fresh and, fine and lots of lime, and apple pine.

Grend, and, dend, and, they are just fond and, find.
That is way? Green grass is, fresh and, at least the, best.

   —*Liza Marie Delgado*

Nocturnal Comfort

Sitting alone on vacant shore
My friends — the moon, the stars, the sea;
Silent to hear the mellow roar,
Cracking waves chant sweet melody.

Tranquil once more with swift retreat,
Then rise, dashing on rocky sides,
Angelic voices ring in beat
To dusk's concert of singing tides.

How smooth the maestro moon conducts!
Lucent baton arcs heaven's sphere,
Proudly gleaming with oval tux,
Leads liquid choir with timely care.

And back ground of clusters, beamed low,
Rim stagely sky with sprinkle ray;
Twinkle with glee, while moving slow,
Then quickly glow as chorus sway.

Water music of ocean's hymn,
And God's design of moonlight frame,
Eve setting of star luster dim —
Beach of treasure, happy I came.

—*John G. Abruscato*

Grandpa's Operation

Today is a boring day.
My grandpa's in the hospital.
He got an operation. Is it all possible?

He forgets sometimes when he
laughs and sings.
We love him so much for the joy that
he brings.

He use to be active fun and loving
Now he's sitting in bed watching T.V. and humming

He draws pictures, a poem or two
And when he feels better he'll draw me a few
He uses his mind his thoughts and his pencil
of course. He uses them all with outrageous
force.

If you can picture him in your mind
And you'll find, a loving, cheerful
grandpa. He's my one of a kind.

—*Casey Smetters*

The Serene and the Siren

I awoke this morning it was glorious reached
my hand over and you were right nearby.
I nestled his arms kissed him tenderly, passionately
It was raining you could hear it tapping softly
It was dawn and their wasn't a flaw
I was compassionate one moment and passionately inspired
It was reaching, grasping, meeting, and fleeting, teasing
a melody far off and distant, your fighting to hold
him you can't have him I'll never let him go.
Now alone, the awakening the call he must have heard
maybe, I should have spoken, all kinds of feelings so
strongly felt and left unsaid.
"How can you fight a mist?" A vapor she's there
loving him for herself the siren.
I'll be serene maybe he'll see her for what she
really, is he's cloudy, vague, unsure.
I painted a beautiful picture but he preferred
the haze and left in a daze.

—*Shirley Pontbriand*

"Lonely Existence"

Lonely existence;
my heart is a child,
but my soul is a viper;
emotions go wild
my heart is bitter, lonely, and sad....
and mental abuse has left me feeling bad
Isolated from reason, and all reality:
Has made a bizarre immortal;
a stranger out of me
This lonely existence
has left me in exile
I am scared as a woman,
lonely as a man, and bold as a child
I am so confused;
hurting inside, and being abused
This lonely existence has made me crazy
I should turn to God; I need someone to save me

—*Jayne Rose*

Seduced By A Spider

I escaped that first night, away from the web
My heart was not stolen, not even a kiss
But a restlessness grows from within my body
The magic you spun pulls me in a little each day
I think of a kiss
A kiss so soft it is barely felt
A kiss so hot it is filled with desire
A kiss
A kiss like no other
But after the kiss will the fire burn out
Or turn to a blaze
The fear is still in me
Will I ever touch your heart?
Or am I just a game?
Cut the thread if it is
The web of deceit can devour one's soul
If this is not a game
Magical, will the web become
The question was asked, the answer will come
Is this your game spider, or is it mine?

—*Magda Tumi Portela*

The Things You've Taken

Three years ago, this very day
My husband lay on this floor.
How were we then to know the outcome
That life would never be the same.
The unforgiving agony that we went through
Haunts us every day of our lives,
Who would have known that one single moment
Could change so many forever?
I don't know what you lost, or even care
I still have trouble accepting mine.
You have taken away my husband,
The man who was my strength and soul.
My friend, my companion, my children their father
The one that's hard to go on without.
You see you've taken our future our everything
And left me not knowing where to go.
R. W. you've taken his life from me
And I'll always miss him so.

—*Katy Ramsey*

Wind

here is wind in my pocket,
here is wind in the air,
here is wind all around me,
en in my hair,
ove the wind so very much,
gives me my fantastic touch,

—*Blair Brace*

Phantoms

I am a wave
y life created from surges within the deep
alive" only to be put back to sleep
A rock", but best of all a lonesome beach
A soul to become a splash
angered into a giant wall to crash
A mist I do cry
houghts and dreams for only minutes
find sand and a journey "tiring" but finished
Joys I do give a child
razed" by moon rays, silhouetting at night
it of control, but mostly wild
utrageousness in me with force, that would only silence
Calmly I do lay with a new founded day
Unpredictable", "Yes" so you shall find
habited with undertows of smartly creative minds
at drags one out who dares or contains doubt
those of beauty I can only be kind
antoms of future fantasies you may find.

—*John Bodzo, Jr.*

"A Love For All Time"

Before I met you,
My life had a void,
But when I first laid eyes upon you,
You became a dream come true.

I love you, Jane, three simple words,
Mean so much to me with you by my side.
esire, romance, comfort, friendship, and happiness.
hose feelings come forth with those whispered words...
I love you...

Today begins our new life together
My love for you will live on forever.
As we face the future as man and wife,
May our love blossom for all eternity.
To always be there for each other,
Firstmost and foremost
A love for all time.

—*Anthony C. Eayrs*

My Dreams

our heart belongs to some one else, my heart belongs to you.
y love for you will never end, if only you'd see it through.
ery night within my dreams, I dream of you and I,
u hold me close against your chest and tell me not to sigh.
use in my dreams you're always there, your silent sweet
ress, you're not confused, I have your heart and you never
ve me less.
en I awake to find you lost, holding someone else so dear,
I return, back to my dreams, where I no longer have to fear.
use in my dreams it's I you hold, and never let me go,
s only there that I'm secure, in my dreams you love me so.
ere is a hope, just a little faith that keeps me going strong
at one day soon when I awake, you'll see I wasn't wrong.
d then I'll have no need for dreams, I'll awake and you'll
there, my dream will now be coming true, you'll show me that
u care.

—*Laura Clark*

Memories

As I sit here in our new home,
my mind continually wants to roam.
Back to the time when you were here,
and how happy we were for seven years.
Thinking of all the good times we had,
and believe me babe they out-weighed the bad.
The memories I'll cherish the rest of my life,
cause you were my dearest and darling wife.
The house is so quiet cause I'm all alone,
praying my dear that you'll soon come home.
I miss you more than words can say,
and wish that you were home to stay.
Cause without you here to share my life,
is like living in darkness and having no light.
You light up my life like a shining bright star,
and your close in my heart even if you are far.
So I'll hold you forever so close in my heart,
and pray that soon we won't a part.

—*Donna L. Benson*

Care

A new dawn rose beneath my skin
My mind felt light and blood ran thin
Tonight I saw a moon I can't explain
I must've swallowed a world of fears
I closed my eyes and saw the tears
Of anyone who' ever cried
For what do you do with every day
That comes and adds to your blank pages
Who comes along to say the war is won
You watch the taking and the giving
Side step the walking dead and living
And keep searching 'till another day is done
Now I don't want to go on about the weather
I could quit this all together
But today I fell the sun beat down on me
And I thought about some souls I've known
And how they're gone and how I've grown
I'll see them at the bottom of the sea

—*Mark A. Gold*

Home

As I sit in the library reading my physics book;
my mind wanders and drifts home...
Mama calls me to dinner.
I run down stairs to the kitchen and over to the stove.

The smell of turnip greens, corn on the cob,
potato salad, barbecued ribs and chicken
smothered in home-made sauce all mingled together
makes me smile and pull my chair up to the table.

Mama, daddy, my brother Jerry and aunt Kathryn
are already seated. We eat, drink, laugh and talk
about the good times.

Library closing soon flashing in bright lights
breaks my reverie...my mind wanders...then
drifts back to reality...
Mama's kitchen was an elusive illusion...gone
like a lightening flash.

Left before me is a page in my physics book
covered with pencil smudges starting up at me.

—*Alicia D. Franklin*

"Waiting"

As I look back on years come and gone,
   My only true love I knew all along.
Being so close yet so far away,
   Hearing your voice in the trees as they sway.
As I look at the moon, I know that somewhere,
   You're standing alone not knowing I care.
Words are so subtle and so easily spoken,
   I'm standing alone, my heart, it is broken.
Looking in your eyes without a word to say,
   But that was then, a long ago yesterday.
On that fateful night of our final good-bye,
   I can still see the glistening of the tear in your eye.
That one last kiss, our final embrace,
   Still burns from within, like fore to lace.
I cry with the moon, yet I weep all alone,
   To know you are standing, waiting alone.

   —*Donald Poling*

Dearest Jacob

I think of you, each night and day:
My precious baby, stolen away.
You defeated great odds,
By entering my womb;
And yet, some how, some way,
God chose heaven,
To be your eternal bedroom.

As I held you in my arms,
I prayed with all my heart:
For you to be placed in caring hands,
Throughout the time we must be apart.

One day I will join you in heaven,
With open arms, to hold you tight;
But until that time arrives, my precious one,
I will hold you dear in my heart,
With all of my strength and might.

   —*April A. Ellenburg-Stevens*

"Lord"

Lord, you're my light and my salvation; you're my strength and
my shield. I pray, Lord, be not silent to me! Direct me; to
You I will yield. You're my shepherd forever, so lead me along
paths where I need to be; yes, even as I walk in the valley, I
know You'll be walking with me.

You're so great, Lord. Great! To be praised through the
years! You Lord, are my God, who will reign forever; in You I
place my fears. I know, Lord, You'll keep me forever and guide
me through all 'til the end; Your rod and Your staff will bring
me comfort; I'll never fear evil again.

Lord, You've got me singing a new song, and praising Your Name
all the day. And Your wonderful works are so many; too many
for me to even say. You give me all that I need, Lord, yet
You ask so very little of me; Your yoke is so easy and light,
Lord, no more than to seek after Thee.

Lord, please remember Your mercies; don't dwell on the sins of
my past; hear me, Lord, have mercy on me; speak, and I'll do
what You ask. All my desires are before You, Lord, so make me
a new man today. My hope is in You, Lord, so lead me and
teach me Your way. Amen

   —*Kenneth H. Epperson*

Does Life Go On

Oh, why should I continue on?
My soul is broken,
and my heart burns red like dawn
shattered, it feebly repairs itself, click.

Oh, what's the purpose of living long,
when I am considered stupid,
and everything I do goes wrong.
But, only a few will remember, click.

Oh they say, you shouldn't judge a book by the cover,
but all do any way, they don't care,
and I have no true lover,
and I probably never will, click.

Oh, life would be grander,
Maybe if I weren't here, and I wonder,
Why me, not him., click.

Oh, shall I end it, few will try to stop me,
but none shall be overwhelmed when my body is lifeless, click.

Oh, what a grand design, so much imperfection,
and time is like a line, and life is but a dot on it's endless
expanse, bang!!!

   —*James Charles Oberg*

Possession

She possesses me, that bloody insane banshee!
My spirit's desire beckoning from Lucifer's grasp;
that sinful witch with spells controlling my sense,
screaming her endless wails that I have no right to understand,
That my whisper has no right to tell you—
She possesses me in my soul's twisted blasphemy—
The bloody tears of my muse drip into my eyelashes
as she careens around my head, whipping my lips
with her long viney hair; shaking and screaming,
She rips my scalp with her groping claws,
pressing her tongue to my ear with her wailing secrets!
Tearing my head from its heart as she thrusts my
Head up to face her stare; her woe takes my soul!
She is the Vampire who throws me to hunt her blood!
Your crucifix melts before my pagan torture
This precious Hell will only be traded for DEATH—

   —*Carisse Wilson*

The Fields Of Yesterday

So often, here of late I find,
My thoughts go drifting back through time,
And once again the past is mine,
In the fields of yesterday

Through memories eyes I see again,
The little house I grew up in,
And oh, the happy house I spend.
In the fields of yesterday.

I close my eyes and catch the scent,
Of blossoms drifting on the wind,
From trees that gently sway and bend,
In the fields of yesterday.

I sit beside the crystal stream,
That heard my thoughts and knew my dreams,
It softly murmur peaceful things,
In the fields of yesterday.

Another day, another time,
Will live forever in my mind,
The dreams I lost are there to find,
In the fields of yesterday.

   —*Joyce McCord*

Untitled

The wind has blown one last time.
My thoughts have vanished in
decline. You will always be in my soul
so come with me forever whole.
    The time last come you chosen
one. The looks will change within your
range. For I am here with no fear,
to overcome you, lonely one.
    If you have to choose between
life and death. I'd take the dirt
road and live it long. For so many
things are ahead of you. That's why
I'm singing you this song.
    I'd like to share with you my
innermost feelings. I'd like to give you
my soul. For I am the one to take
away your troubles, in the night that's
whole.
        —*Lisa Skerdavich*

My Life

When I take a good look at
myself all I ever see is my fears.
Whenever my friends look
into my eyes all they ever see is my tears.

I think no one in this world
really seems to care.
Like I have no one
and no one is all
that is ever going to be there.

I'm not sure I can go on living like this.
Although I'm afraid to take
it away because of all the
people and things I'd miss.

I don't understand up close
Why things are the way they are.
Everything looks so peaceful
and different from afar.

I guess what I'm looking for is happiness.
But it seems like my
happiness just gets less and less.
        —*Christine Rollins*

The Archway To Glory

Beyond the veil of penetration,
Mystic forces living there
Sing of loveliness and splendor
In that word beyond compare.

Deeds performed through love's compassion
Are stones which make our mansion strong-
So build them in with polished splendor-
Build your future with a song.

Mansions built with stones of kindness
On the streets of purest gold
Are studded with the rarest diamonds
Waiting for the young and old.

Time is fleeting - check your conscience,
Clarion Calls ring strong and true.
The Archway to the path of Glory
Beckons all to pass right through.
        —*Pearl H. Counts*

"If I Could Give The World A Gift"

If I could give the world a gift, I would give it joy!
Nature, beauty, animals, happiness and the giggle of a
    bouncing baby boy.

If I could give the world a gift, I would give it health!
No AIDS, measles, cancers, poverty and abuses — just people
    treated as equal no matter what their wealth.

If I could give the world a gift, I would give it peace!
No wars, killings, bombs, gangs and hatred — all people will
    gather and anger will cease.

Finally, if I could give the world a gift, I would give it
love!! Families, friends and children caring and sharing their
    lives together as was said by God above.
        —*Erica Nelson*

Mom And Dad

In a mystic morning,
Nature takes to life.

The sun breathes its heat
And waterfalls rage and sing.
Mother Nature has taken her seat.

Setting into motion everything created,
And creating any unborn,
The clock starts to tick.
Father Time gives a waking yawn.

The sun continues its dawn,
It, too, takes its chair.

Father Time begins counting,
Into his galloglass stare he climbs,
Sewing the quilt of time.

Mother Nature, also in her trance,
Her grace, only to enhance.

Together they sit like stitches forever sewn,
They sit for everything shown.
        —*Gina E. Dunlap*

Negro Wake Up

Negro wake up you're in a deep sleep
Negro wake up and stand on your own two feet.

Negro wake up and stop blaming that other man
and be like that little train I think I can.

Negro wake up the world's in your hand.
But you've fallen prey to that other man.

Negro wake up let's not persecute them all.
Then you'll be no better than that old man Saul.

Saul persecuted the Christians and the
Lord showed him the light.
Know his name's Paul and he's doing what's right.

So negro wake up it isn't night
are you a little hostile your color ain't white.
        —*Cliffton O. Williams Jr.*

Moments

Moments with you are life's simple pleasures
Moments with you are God's given treasures
Moments with you are eternally dear
Moments with you bring forever a tear
Moments with you are either short or they're long
Moments with you fill my heart with a song
Moments with you are unique and so true
Moments I'll spend for I truly love you
        —*Joe Martell*

Mandela the Man

Mandela the Man, the hope of a nation
  Never compromised because he was patient

Mandela the voice, even in silence he spoke
  He is of great courage and a symbol of hope

His fight is for equal justice and to end Apartheid
  Mandela is a soldier for his people, a man of great pride

You can not silence hope or a dream with lock and key
  After twenty seven years Mandela was set free

There was no rest, he immediately renewed his fight
  To see that the wrong done to his people was made right

Some changes have been made, there is much more to do
  Mandela the man, is far from through

He may not get all that he seeks
  But remember, Mandela is a mountain not just a peak

He is chipping away at Apartheid and he has made a dent
  Mandela the man can not be bought or lent

May your courage and strength forever be
  May you live to see your fight become a reality

Mandela the man, you have made great strides
  I pray soon you say, Winnie, there is no more Apartheid

Mandela the Man...Fini
    —*Robert L. Cooper Jr.*

Heartbreak

    A frail boned madman dancing in the streets,
Never knowing where an old love dies or where a new one meets.
His eyes are open wide, full of curiosity and fear.
His body quivering from madness and shear anger.
What sanity he has left falls short of a sullen tear.
Still reacting ferociously to love and its danger.
Everyday of his life is lived in despair,
Always cursing the world and its toxic air.
He cares not to eat or live a social life.
Without the nourishment of love, he lives in strife.
People stare at him in awe, amazed that he lasted this long.
Everyone expected him to change his life, or simply vanish.
He walks along, quietly repeating the words to his favorite song.
He displays no feelings, just blankness. Those feelings are banished.
He dreams of sailing on a calm, sullen ocean.
He dreams of inventing a magical potion,
To make him live a life very fulfilling,
With the love in his heart over spilling.
I speak of him, for he is myself. I know not what is at steak.
Living everyday in mourning, living with a heartbreak.

    —*Chris Henson*

The Same Street

My street. The street I love, is the same street I curse every
night because I can't leave it.

My home. The home I sleep in, is the prison I can't leave
behind, even when I stand in front of it.

My heart, pounds in my chest, my headache is the only reminder
that I have one.

These eyes, (The mirror of my soul) are sleepy, I can't even
see myself.

My love, stick in my throat, I pray when I'm scared I might
loose them.

My lips, through which I sing and whistle tunes, is my
happiness and possibility, that life, on the same street, resumes.

    —*Annette Conliffe*

Human Nature

He is the only "father" that has no prejudices, this "father"
never turns on anyone because of their heritage or color.
His original intent was to have all people live together in
harmony, not to kill each other on the streets over petty
indifferences or materialistic things. Maybe mankind was just

a test to see if jealousy, enviousness, and greed would
overcome the true meaning of life. If this is the case, all of
the human race has failed. With the murdering of each other,
Down to the petty trials we have to let others decide if a
human is guilty of a "crime". Did he really intend for us to
determine others' fate based solely on circumstantial evidence?
The Indians have the right idea, the land does not belong to any
one individual, it belongs to Him who is gracious enough to
share it with everyone. Maybe instead of crucifying the
Indians and taking away everything that was not ours to take away in
the first place, we should have stopped to think of what the
outcome might have been. But this is the power of "human
nature" or shall I say jealousy and selfishness, which is the
fear of being different, and not possessing everything that is
materialistic that causes these feelings to consume us all.

    —*Nicole Fleming*

Never Again

Never will I feel your loving arms around me again.
Never will we together walk through the falling rain.
Never again will hear you say to me, "I love you."
Because death has claimed you and left me feeling blue.

Never again will my fingers your features trace.
Never again will you be held in my warm embrace.
Never again will we laugh and play together.
Never again will you have to struggle to make things better.

Never again will I hear your tender voice.
Death claimed your life and robbed you of that choice.
Never again will I be able to doubt your love
Even though we fit closely together like a hand in a glove.

Never again will you suffer pain and regret.
Never again do you need to worry or fret.
Death has claimed you and I pray that you're at rest.
I love you very dearly, but God loves you best.

    —*Nadine Patterson*

Simply the Best

There can be nothing better than you or I.
No hill, no valley, no mountain or sky.
We come from the best which only created the best.
Which is powerful, successful and can be nothing less.

The best have visions that this world has not yet seen.
The light in their eyes shines to the future, it is not a dream.
The best for some reason know that they have already scored
.
The energy which is spirit gives power that they cannot hoard.

Success is something only the best can foresee.
To see how it unfolds is simply knowing, not conceit.
Understand the divine plan can only be accomplished by the best.
For Father knows when the time comes that only we can pass
the test.

There can be nothing better than you. To think there is would be a
lie.
To say that you are a mistake would be an alibi.
It would only keep you away from work that only you can do.
You are here because you are the best which can be only you.
And now that you understand, this you must express.
That you are God's child, His divine love and always simply
the best.

    —*Jinger Bizzell*

An Answer To A Friend

No one to be aware of
  No idle chat to make
No one to call my own love
  No need for give and take

No in-law issued orders
  No pledges to instate
No guiding social borders
  Nor ever ready date

No worry 'bout two worlds apart, or how
  they best may merge, no respite for an
  aching heart, no one with to converge

No partner sure eternal, no guarantee
  on joy, best quell the urge paternal,
  no bouncing baby boy

No confidant for private dreams, no hugs
  to soothe the fears, no one to hear the
  silent screams, no whispers in soft ears

These thoughts I ponder often and others then
  eschew, but more and more I soften
  and strive to make one, two
      —C. Blaeser

Indian Visions

The golden grains of wheat, visions of time gone by,
No longer will our people eat, who heard our cry?

The buffalo no longer roam, we have lost our home,
Once were eagles dare, there are no cloths to wear,

The golden grains of wheat, visions of time gone by,
No longer will our people eat, who heard our cry?

The water is not sweet, we have been beat,
No land to call our own, the white man has shown,

The golden grains of wheat, visions of time gone by,
No longer will our people eat, who heard our cry?

Our lives are bare, with no one to care,
With heavy hearts, we depart,

The golden grains of wheat, visions of time gone by,
No longer will our people eat, who heard our cry?
      —Carol Pisanko

My Mind's Eye

  I was and I am and I will continue to be
No matter what others may think or say or see
  I am what I am because of the person I want to be
It isn't their choice, my life is up to me
  There is so much to learn and understand
I know I am strong enough to reach out my hand
  I am not all I can be, I can be more
So I will continue to open door after door
  I regret some things I have done in my past
But from them I have learned and they were my last
  To reach my dream, to achieve my goal
To be happy in mind and heart and soul
  All that I am and all that I can be
It's all in my mind, it's all up to me!

      —Deborah Keenan

Our Medical Center

OFOMC is one of the best
No matter where you go here in the Midwest.

The facility is a teaching and healing place
The doctors, the trainees, the staff are every
  color, creed and race.

The doctors and nurses have such caring and loving ways
It is such a haven for rest you don't mind what
  you have to pay.

The others work here whether they clean, keep records
  or volunteer
They do their best to give you cheer.

When you have to go somewhere else because they
  have the only equipment that is needed
It makes you appreciate what we have here and you take heed.

Whatever your needs, they will be met
But only at this place that is so well kept.

Ask the Lord to watch over this facility and over you
When you pray He knows that you are true blue.

These few lines are in appreciation of the way I feel
For the many times I and others went home healed.
      —Ruth E. Bettenhausen

"The Sands Of Time"

Second by second, minute by minute,
No matter who we are, we all are in it, together.

Hour by hour, day by day,
To the Lord Almighty we all should pray.

Day by day, week by week,
The true meaning of life we all do seek.

Month by month, year by year,
Not a day goes by without a tear.

The sands of time are flowing like an ocean,
The sands of time are flying like the wind,
The sands of time are soaring like an eagle
And will never be back again.

And this is the reason for why they say,
Live to the fullest each and every day.

Don't you dare be afraid
To move ahead and advance
Because you will never get a second chance.
      —Jessica G. White

Our World Today

What is happening in our world today?
No more does any one go out of his way
To lend a helping hand to those in need.
The old the tired and the poor indeed.
We all are too busy or have no time
To see what mountain some one has to climb.
When just a word or a smile can mean so much.
Or in the time of need a comforting touch.
We all are too secure in a world of our own
To notice a person who is all alone.
Well the day will come, just wait and see
When the poor and the weak inherit you and me.
Then will we know of things undone
Of battles that were lost that could have been won.
So let all of us try a friend to be
To the tired, the old, and anyone we see.
And so make this earth a better world
So that the forces of hate will be controlled
By love
      —Adolph F. Gursky

Loves Light

I take to heart that which has been; to grieve
  no more on winters day.

Coldness of heart and soul, is more fatal to one so mortal,
  than the coldest winter night; save for me a light of hope.

Knowing that spring ponders so near, the birth and rebirth
  of all that we know. Springtime shall dwell forever in my
  mind; my saving grace, a shining light of hope.

It is love that truly burns; sunshine to
  my soul

It is passion that fans loves flames; summer to
  my heart.

Let fall come near with withered fear; to sleep a sleep
  unknown. As leaves fall from branches high, to mark the
  coming cold, I shall rest and smile; loves light burns
  in my soul.

    —Kirk Mackavich

Brothers to the Wind

They move from place to place, pause briefly, then are gone;
No mortal keeps them still and nothing holds them long.
Ask them not the question, how did their quest begin,
And do not try to hold them back; they are Brothers to the Wind.

Their restless spirits gain no peace, from the driving quest;
They know not what they seek nor why, and yet they cannot rest.
They vow to cease their wandering, then comes a still voice
  from within,
That keeps their souls a-yearning; they are Brothers to the Wind.

With eyes on far horizons, they're searching for their grail,
And set their course anew each day, on yet another trail,
For they cannot tarry long, ere the call comes from their kin,
Come, brothers, come with me, you are Brothers to the Wind.

They still search for an answer, they ask their souls to speak,
Tell us why we wander, tell us what we seek,
If peace is not for us, then where must we begin,
That we may find out why, we are Brothers to the Wind.

    —Oliver E. Fowler

The City's Children

A child's body walking lifeless.
No one is there to give him love.
What have the Streets of the City done to this Child.

Those eyes, they are far off and distant.
That face is emotionless, the look of pain is much to clear.
What horrors has this Child seen.
What can't his mind erase.

There is no joy in his eyes.
No sunshine in his smile.
Just fear and hatred that will eat him up and spit him out.

The days are endless, the nights are long.
Danger is his shadow.

There he is can't you see him.
He's screaming out for help.
You can't hear him, you don't care.
You think that he's no good.
Your children are your own concern.
You pray they stay away.

The City will mourn another Child
Who's only friend became the Devil.

    —B. Doherty

The Baptist Church

It stands alone in the sea, crumbling —
No one visits it — its walls are caving in,
The waves wash over its broken walls
Wearing them down, and taking away

Stones that have broken down already.
Spiders have found their way here,
Cobwebs hang from all sides,
And the dampness and cold atmosphere
Allow fungus and moss to grow on the steps.

This is a place you imagine would not exist —
But it does.
It was once a baptist church — a very long time ago,
Years before you were born,
Now, it is a ruin, where tired birds of flight rest,

Before continuing their journeys,
And before the walls come crumbling down
To crash into the sea
And sink to the bottom of the seabed
Where they will rest until they,
Have decayed to dust.

    —Madhuvanti Mahadeo

Release

"Not it! Not it!" We would shout and cry.
No one wanted to be the unlucky guy.
Friends from all over would come to play,
Just to be in the game where you had to get away.
Don't get caught! Run to base!
For everyone knew this was the only safe place.
O.K., I don't hear a sound.
This must mean that "it" isn't around.
I'll just run to that tree,
That is where I'll set my team free.
Oh no! "It" got me.
To the tree prison I go, and I will forever be
A prisoner until someone can "release" me.

    —Janeane Aube

Life

Life is such a beautiful thing
Nobody realizes the joy it can bring
All the people out there who care
It makes me so happy to know I'm here
No matter how bad things are, I never want to go
I want to live forever and that's something I know
All the people who kill themselves, its so sad
And to know they died for nothing, makes me so mad
There is so much to live for
Everyday life brings more and more
If I ever had to leave, I'll live up above
My friends and family will carry my love
I know I have a future ahead of me
And life is something it is going to be.

    —Dyan Dusovic

My Desire

I am the moth and you are the flame.
So tempting, I must dance with you.
So warm, I must be enveloped by you.
I stretch my wings and hover closer.
Aware of the danger, but wanting ecstasy.
One lick of the flame could take my existence.
And yet, I am drawn to your beauty.
Not caring, of the peril to kiss you once.
I am mesmerized as a moth is to fire.

    —Angela D. Wilson

...being

words unvoiced
words unspeakable
harsh, thoughtless
piercing bones
cutting to marrow
gestures disguising feebleness
turbulent as tempest
unseizable as lightening
vision, phantom, prophecy?
...just human
—*Anna Janusz*

Pegasus

Have you ever seen this horse?
Not any old horse of course.

It is a magical and mythical creature.
This horse is beautiful in every feature.

A horse with golden colored wings
Like golden rings.

This horse can fly
High up in the sky.

This horse is a lovely snowy white
And if you are lucky you may see him flying at night.

It's a sight you couldn't miss,
It's a Pegasus!
—*Heather Siebert*

Lest I Forget

God did not restrict us,
not by one, not by ninety-nine and one;
Instead He aimed us all
At the harvest which surely needs be done.

That work is not over
As long as standing in any man's field
There are plants which wither
Unless we gather the precious yield.

So I must not forget;
The work must not come to untimely end;
For each man's upward step
Leaves room for others God in love has sent.
—*Fay Trayler*

Awe and Beauty

As I aimlessly wandered through the thick green forest
Not caring - just sharing my thoughts with nature's thoughts,
Yet hoping deep inside I'd meet a kindred spirit
In this untouched paradise.

Continuing on my unmarked trail I was stunned
By the beauty of the bright golden ball
Flicking its glittering playful rays here and there
Through leaf clothed branches moving gently in the breeze.

I moved onward swiftly, but carefully as I ought,
To seek and know the message of the great beauty that I sought.
I finally reached the unruled boundary of the tall ones,
Standing as if in a quandary,
In closely knit grains of sparkling sand.

The sand was barely touched by the clear blue water of the bay.
I picked up a stone and skimmed it smoothly along the surface
not causing any injury, just wrinkling the water's countenance

I watched the stone plummet down to the depths
As the water frowned at me.
Not mad - just glad someone cared enough to stop awhile.
—*Timothy Phillips*

What is the Meaning of Life?

A ponderous question that takes into account
not just mere existence, but what it's all about.
Our day-to-day rituals are a part of the plan,
and our goals and objectives for the future will stand
for a piece of the puzzle too complex for just one
to complete and to know when the picture is done.
Life means interaction with people and places
that have many rules, many faults, many faces.
As part of the plan it's important to learn
all that we can so we can teach in return.
The good and the evil-we must tell them apart;
abide by the good-from the evil depart.
For the Golden Rule says that we do unto others
as we want them to do to ourselves and our brothers.
To understand life and find it's true meaning
is to understand self and your reason for being
a small piece of the puzzle, the "grand scheme of all"-
for without you the puzzle will crumble and fall.
—*Kathy Ulicny*

Loving You Till Death

I want you and me to last,
not to be just a memory of the past.
We need each other its true,
to fill each others lives till there through.
This love is not a game.
I love you with all my might and it will always be the same.
Again from you I will never stray
because I will love you to your dying day.
As I look in your gorgeous eyes,
I can see no lies.
I only see the gleam of a satisfying dream.
A dream that came true
because of the love between me and you.
Never forget the love I have for you will always be in my heart
until death do us finally part!!!
—*Jaclyn Respess*

My Dear Son

I once knew him so intimately,
now more of him that is, I do not know.
That is good, but can be very painful.
The control has ended, I often think how bad this is,
But it is also good, because the burden
was becoming too heavy for one to carry.
I tell myself, "Feel free, let your heart
come out from under."
Give it time to heal, feel good that
you have let go the reins.
He is now another, to get to know and love.
Exorcise your personal demons.
Ease the weight on you heart.
You will see a new light, let it come in,
And radiate within you. It will beam out of your eyes.
Your light will shine upon others
And you will get reason from it all.
—*Florence Kozlowski*

R.I.P

The melody sonorous
There was no music in the chorus
The body laying still
The girl no longer ill

It was the peace
That she had sought
That she now had reached
Or so she thought
—*Jaap W. Plukker*

The Pendulum's Pit

Our manic failure, it often enrages,
Now we burn bridges and cannot keep going.
Accept our losses and lowly wages,
Deficit spending is slowly growing.
Irascible nature makes us stand out.

Risk taking's not so bad, it's only money,
When prestige fails, writings on many walls.
Don't look at me that way, come on honey,
We're harder than nails for collection calls.
Criticism makes us want to shout.

The swing is short but the mood is long,
Unable to move so there we lie.
This side's no breeze, it feels all wrong,
Un-pro-duct-ive, why can't we die.

Distortions abound as we view our life
Freedom to act becomes an illusion
Kicking and jerking, the days full of strife,
Happiness and joy now confusion.
Stop the lies if you cannot retract.

—*Frank H. Maurer*

Untitled

D—Doing his work to benefit mankind
O—Often he's late and running behind.
C—Caring for patients is his daily aim;
T—To make sure that all are treated the same.
O—Once in awhile he has to get away,
R—Relaxing and reading on his "off" day.

J—Joining with others, he has daily prayers,
O—Once a day God knows that he really cares.
S—So loving and caring to all he sees,
E—Each patient must feel that he does have keys
P—Proving good health is a matter of mind.
H—He's a good doctor. And one of a kind.

C—Compassion he shows to each one in need.
A—And being gentle is part of his creed.
N—Nothing he does is in any way wrong.
N—Naturally, his faith is very strong.
O—Once you have met him, of course you will see.
N—No other doctor would I want for me.

—*Pat McLeod*

The Warrior

The white canoe cutting through the water,
Oars dripping diamonds from stroke to stroke,
Slowly the strokes, yet swiftly the progress,
O'er the beautiful river, and low hanging trees.

This Indian brave his canoe gliding lightly,
A lone feather a-slant, on his dark head,
His beaded quiver, and long feathered arrows,
And a beautiful bow, lying by his side.

Leggings pliant, with softest of deer-skin,
The beading and quills, a thing of art,
His canoe is so light, he can carry for portage,
Around the white rapids, and loud cataract.

He creates all the accoutrements that he possesses,
The arrow head chipped from hardest of stone,
The canoe he has fashioned, out of the birch bark,
And the seams he has painted with pitch of pine-trees.

The river is flowing with scarcely a ripple,
This canoe, with his totem, in its design,
This Indian warrior, is now fast approaching,
A bend in the river — and now he is gone.

—*Juanita Lavender*

Just Say No

Once upon a time I have addressed a naked ant climbing on top
of a nuclear power plant.
Then I spoke to a fly that flew in the path of Math according
to the theory of relativity.
And then I came across a cheshire cat who showed me where the
essence of a jeweled cane was at.
But now that I have taken LSD I cannot even count to three.

And while I have these hallucinations they make me take
psychotropic medications and how I wish I had an education
about drug addiction believing in him and his own crucifixion
so just say no even though you're in rehabilitation living it
out of its own reincarnation a product of the nineteen sixties
generation in the memory of me and Dr. Timothy Leary and
flashbacks that hurt severely.

Barely staying alive taking pills and all that jive ending up
in a board and care home dive.
So just say no.

—*David Joseph May*

Autumn Summer

You have a charm
    Of cold and refreshing air
    On a hot and humid day.
You have the grace
    Of seeing things as they are
    And making the most of what
    Is there.
You have a heart
    That can melt men's nerves
    Made of steel.
You have the reassurance
    Of knowing I'll be back for more
    And for many more reasons...I'll be seeing
You again.

—*Phillip E. Esquibel*

Quietness

As I survey the landscape, quietly thinking
    Of evening approaching, sun quietly sinking
Beneath the horizon beyond the blue lake,
    And the leaves of the trees as they quietly quake

With the mild summer breeze, it seems that I hear
    Unspoken words which dispel vintage fear,
Which persists uninvited, in life's daily grind,
    Until, in sweet silence, we are able to find

In measure, assurance of God's special love,
    Which steals in unseen from the regions above,
Which speaks of such things as a lofty design
    With assurance in process to nature refine.

What meets, then, my vision is merely reflection —
    A picture, a grouping of heaven's perfection,
An added dimension of that lofty design —
    A promise of peace we're all destined to find.

From the certain unfolding of life's master - plan,
    Which has been in development since time began,
To the final fruition of man's holy quest —
    This can only be seen in the soul's quietness.

—*Al Wells*

sk Only What You Need

sk only what you need
of jealousy and envy take no heed
e careful in things you say and do
give patience and love which he
continually gives to each of you.

sk only what you need
give no thoughts to selfish greed
h gossiping and complaining, do not
for God's blessings come from patient
love not hateful shocks.

sk only what you need of trust,
faith and caring plant your seeds
et your heart to be pure and holy for
all to see
1ow your fellowman our Saviour, the Lord God, Thee

sk only what you need thanking him each
day for his never ending, loving deeds
1ow faith in his wisdom; trust in his
word, growing in his love as you
count your blessings from above.

—*Dorris J. Cole*

o One

As I look downward to the darkness
life, and see the pool of life, wondering
1ere it went, as the dark color of life
.s overcome my life as it went from light
the hate of darkness and hate of all the
ils of life. I'm wondering where it
ent as the man comes to me and sees
1n in pain, and tries to help as I try
deny him of what he wants, I'm looking
wards the sun and I'm seeing no one to
lp with the pain of loneliness while everyone
having fun, I'm having nothing, I'm no one.

—*Nicholas Batdorf*

Child Request

ll me the stories
long, long ago.
ll me of grandparents
ever did know.

Where did they live?
What did they do?
Were they tall, were they short?
Were they like me and you?

What was it like
To live in those days?
Did they work, did they live
In the same ways?

Did they dream of the future?
Would they view with dismay
The world that we've made
And live in today?

Tell me the stories
Of long, long ago
So I can tell "my" children
When "they" want to know.

—*Howard Hodgson*

Lonely Without You

Here I am staring at the wall
Of my bedroom one evening fall,
My mind was blank when I passed the hall
So I didn't hear my mother call.

Obviously my thoughts are flying
I don't know what I've been doing,
'Coz you know lately I've been wondering
How can I be with you without dreaming.

Lonely without you wasn't that easy
I talk to myself, I guess I'm crazy,
I'm unproductive becoming lazy
Even in conversation I am lousy.

One more time I'd like to tell you
It's not my fault if I left you,
Look at me I'm suffering, too
I miss you, I'm Lonely Without You!
—*Abigail S. Aquino*

Half Price

I want to die in the produce section
of my local supermarket,

While the critical lettuce
and laughing carrots
watch my throes with wet delight.

Hefting a goodly onion,
a slight - Ping - from the back of my brain
shoots forward and

Crashing - through the banana display

Smashing - My head on a scale

Grasping - the roll of plastic baggies
Spinnnnnn - I land

Writhing - in stricken demise.

A small squad of pucker-faced septuagenarians
huddle above my twitching mass.

I only hope they
Remember me,
next time they buy the two-day old trout
with yellow eyes at
Half-Price.
—*Bryan Scott*

Always Thinking Of You Mom

Precious memories silently kept.
Of my loving mother, I'll never forget.
No longer in my life to share,
But in my heart you are always there.

Thoughts of you mother will never grow old.
They are treasures of gold.
Still loved, missed and forever dear.
It's lonesome here with out you.

And sad in every way
Life is not same for us.
Since you went away.
They say memories are golden-

And that may be true.
We never wanted memories, Mom, we only wanted you.
On this thanksgiving day, I thank God for thoughts of you

You so lovingly prepared many special dinners'
It is those happy holidays that warms our hearts.
And keeps us going on until we see you again.
You are celebrating your first heavenly thanksgiving
Thinking of you always.
—*Evelyn T. Tallman*

Heaven's Gate

As I stand alone at Heaven's Gate, scanning the boggy marshes
of my past. Finding places where my heart stood firm
The things inside my spirit meant to last
One stone stands firm above all the rest, looms large from even
here. The joy with which I've been sweetly blessed
The deepest love I've held for you so dear
Through the years it's never wavered, it stood strong through
all the fears. Endured so many broken hopes, withstood the
reciprocity of tears. Though walls and doors have blocked the
way, to the fulfillment that we seek. My faith stood strong
above the wall, with only patience sometimes weak.
God carved this cavern in my heart, and filled it full of you.
Then locked it in and waited to see just what it was that I
would do. I saw the beauty through your eyes, felt the sadness
in your heart. Knew the closeness when you held me, your kiss
revealed it from the start. This vast ocean of emotion, dips
and swells as with the tide. But this is all upon the surface,
it's the depth from which you cannot hide. So I stand alone at
Heaven's Gate Waiting patiently for you. This blessed union
holds the only key. 'Tis with you alone I can go through.

—*Christine A. Schutt*

What's On The Other Side?

I shudder to think of the future.
Of things unseen and unheard.
It is like a door not knowing what is behind it.
I struggle in my mind to decide whether I should open it or let
    it be.
If I should open it, what is there?

My curiosity haunts me.
I want to know what life holds, is it a dream or a nightmare?
But why should I open it, what if it will hurt me?
Curiosity kills me, and I long to know my destiny;
but when I turn the knob, it will not open.
Does it not want me?
Am I uninvited?
How can this be, to be a trespasser in my own life?

Though I twist and turn my own hand; it still won't open.
It's not that it does not want me.
Instead it's trying to protect me.
I will never know it's secret.
Only time has the key.

—*Michelle Alexander*

Burning Shame

These burning eyes tell a forbidden tale;
Of violation, robbed of one's own soul.
These bars more confining than those in jail;
A heart now torn in half that once was whole.

These memories etched in a heart of stone;
The horrid force, the anger in his eyes.
Such mental anguish, no one could condone;
The act, but not the person I despise.

Smiling facade to hide exploding shame;
Feeling the threads of life snap and break free.
Erupting from the depths of total blame;
This blinding vision all that I now see.

He took away my youth and left me bare.
My mind still haunted with his frightening stare.

—*Jennifer O'Block*

"Aimless Flight"

Strolling on the edge,
Of what has to be someone else's dream.
Never quite sure of direction,
But flowing smooth beneath the stream.

Then flying amongst a flock of birds;
Confusion within aimless flight.
Soaring the wind beyond a must,
Flying high as a survival fight.

Rainbows inevitably fade,
Now becoming one with a dove;
Helplessly captured within a storm,
With lightening fits of a shredded love.

Lashing winds to tear the wings;
To death do strike the ground.
Luminous soul again to soar;
Alas my love was found.

—*Gae M. C. Garcia*

The Ego Game

Who are you to stand in judgment
Of what you think I should be,
Just stop for a moment and take a look at yourself
Before you cast a stone at me

Are you flawless in every aspect of life
Are there any improvements to make,
Because I already know that there are my friend
So reconsider for your own sake

Stop trying to make yourself look good
By making someone else look bad,
Because everybody's got a little something
That you always wished you had

It's a shame that we set our standards
So high for everyone else,
But when it comes to finding fault with someone
We simply overlook ourselves

Face up to the truth, come down to earth
Everyone is just the same,
Just accept yourself for what you are
And stop playing the ego game!

—*Allan R. Baldwin*

Alone & Silent

As a pungent film begins to rise
    off your drawn and quartered back,
Brought to life, in the still of night,
By an oppressor's whip-
    black as the night which reared
    unholy, totalitarian acts.
My enigmatic disguise
    has lost it's charm and order.
Reasoning has long since died.
Awareness of reality-comatized.
Freedom of speech
    is restricted to pages of wisdom,
Bound within secrecy-self imposed.
I hate this jail cell,
    this photograph of a paternal bedroom.
It's placid walls remind of empty evenings.
Whatever the incentive to accomplish,
    it's door always locked.
Cold existence has been formulated
    as a trial and error exercise-in suicide? Help....

—*Z. Yaroslav Hishynsky*

"Memories"

Sixty five candles on my cake
  oh, dear there must be some mistake
  can't be 65 already
  It seems like yesterday I started "going steady"

But then I think back through those
  glorious years.
How my blessings outnumbered my
  few little tears
I think of my children with their cute
  little ways
How, when I worried, they brightened
  my days.

And now I'm a grandma
  with grandkids galore
Those dear little faces
  I'll always adore

So maybe being 65 isn't so bad
  When I recall the wonderful life
    that I've had
          —*Jennie Moore*

The Eyes of the Heart

She wants to be reflected in the eyes that make her heart stare.
Oh how she wants to hold and feel the love she wants to see!
When she looks into these pools they speak to her somehow
They whisper that they know, but do not feel the same,
And refuse to hold her stare that wants to claim.
She once saw rays of hope that now are gone.
Now the eyes no longer gaze at hers,
They turn away to other pools.
They no longer talk to her,
They no longer see to her.
Now she hates to look,
And she will be
Alone to
Feel the
Pain.

          —*Andrea M. Celico*

Philosophies of Man

Why did you marry me? said the woman to the man.
Oh, precious wife, it's part of God's plan.
Who would I have to do domestic chores?
Scrub down the house, wash the toilet and floors-
This is the way it was meant to be;
I am the king of this house - don't you see?

Husband, why do you speak to me with arrogance, disdain?
Wife, how dare you ask - know you no shame?
This is your purpose to be servant to all;
You read the Bible, it's because of Eve's fall.

Husband why do you become angry, as if I don't feel?
Precious darling through you cry I know you're like steel.
Taking a man's anger is why a woman was made.
You're to take all you can till youth & beauty fade.
Yes, I'll use you, abuse you and toss you aside,
Then I'll find someone new who will serve me with pride.
          —*Cathi Goff*

Untitled

(Dedicated in loving memory of my mother)
Oh tall giant tree with limbs outstretched to heaven.
Swaying gently roughly in the autumn breeze.
Your beauty extends over all the land with awesome pride
I bow to you oh king of all the earth
There is no silence from your boughs
Whispering, roaring as the wind blows.
And then the mighty blow; you fall you who were so tall.
Felled by man - who is so small.
The spot is empty now where you stood
Your nothing but a pile of wood.
But rise again you will and stand
A house, a home built by this small man.
Though your voice is stilled, your branches shed
Stand proud old tree, stand proud with me.
          —*Elizabeth Hodge*

"What's It All About?"

Wars in the east, wars in the west.
Oh why can't people just let differences rest?
Gun shots and shouts.
Oh tell me what's it all about?

People fighting, people dying
All because someone's lying.
Can't people just talk it out?
Oh tell me. What's it all about?

Off in a country that's so far away,
That's where our country's men are today.
Can't someone figure it out?
Oh please? Tell me what's it all about?

Please tell me why their there at least.
I guess they're fighting for someone's peace.
Please someone!! Please tell me what's it all about.
Oh I fear I'll never find out!!
          —*Leta Nicks*

Wind

                I hear you,
                  Oh Wind,
        As you whisper through the willows,
Gently swaying the finger like branches.
        You rustle the majestic leaves,
              And in the crisp air,
                They murmur.
          They descend to the ground,
            And meander down the road.
            Your gentle loving arms,
                  Vanish,
      In the desperate moment of the storm,
          Turning fierce and unforgiving.
                  Wind,
            You are mighty and great,
          The devastation you can cause,
            Could tear our world apart.
          —*Debra Schwabe*

Vanquished Guards

The cannon are dead. They once were alive.
Now the steel is like ice, and the mouths are filled up
With bird nests and cobwebs and dead leaves and such.

The stalwart old nobles of many a battle
Remain all alone in their bases of stone,
And their armor is weathered by winds and cold rain.

Bold weapons they were, up high on their hills,
With their noses of ice and of steel...
Now a beetle's home's under the wheel.
          —*Evelyn File*

431

The Window

In front of the window
Old Lady Merriweather sits.
Through the window everything can be seen.
But not everything is as it seems.
The children playing baseball.
Parents just getting home.
Grandparents happy at the sight of their grandchildren,
All unaware of what is to be.

The silence of the house is broken with a crash.
A baseball falls on her lap.
All the faces are happy no more.
There comes a knock on the door.
The baseball retrieved. The game must go on.
As for Old Lady Merriweather,
She looks at the window and sees.
A smile appears on her face.

—*G. M. Kelly*

Heart Broken

You went away
on a cold October day.
As our hearts dropped
the world came to a stop.
You had no last words
and all the more it hurt.
You were so full of life
and everything was going so right.
How could this be?
you leaving me.
If you only know,
you were among those special few.
I loved you like you were my own
we became so dose when you were in my home.
While I cry aloud
you're now dancing on a cloud.
It wasn't your time,
but I should now end this rhythm.

—*Briana Harth*

My Favorite Place

There's nothing like the summer sky
On a warm and breezy day,
And the peace I find within a book
As I read the day away.

Lying under a giant oak,
I can travel from place to place.
There I can stay as long as I want
And leave without a trace.

The people I meet only I have seen,
'Though others have met them, too;
And when I go, they'll stay behind,
Greeting travelers as they pass through.

I wish that I could write a book—
It's something I'd love to try—
Then lonely readers could meet my friends
Beneath a summer sky.

—*Kathleen Dean*

Love

The love
A dove
The spring
A wedding ring
Companionship...
Love
A dove

—*Michele Della-Latta*

We Missed Out

Your death brought me the biggest loss of my life. I missed out
On sharing with you my problems, my prides, my life, my everything.
I missed out on advice, probably some that I wouldn't have wanted
To hear anyway. And yes, probably some lectures and disagreements
Too. I missed out on the man-to-man talks, you teaching me how to
Play sports, the fishing trips, and the quiet times together. I
Missed out on the love, you had to share with me, the joyous times
We could have spent together and security you bring me. I missed out
On your smiling face, your glowing face, and your laughter, and I
Cannot directly compare you and I, now that you are no longer here
With me. I missed out on my childhood. After you died, I had to grow
Up so fast and take on so much responsibility. As your oldest son,
I became the man of the house. I had to take care of the rest of the
Family. I missed out on having you there when I needed a father.
I could only communicate things in private thoughts to you. You missed
Out on many years of your life. Some of the best and most important.
And you, you missed out on one of the most important things of a
Man's life, you missed out on seeing your children grow up. We both
Missed out on so much that most father-son relationships have, we
Missed out on a lot of "I love you's," that we never had the time
To say. My only hope now, other than wanting you back, is that you
Know how I feel about you, how much I love you.

—*Rosalie Dorste*

Winter

The winter haunts my mind like the clouds that gather
On the horizon and the unimaginative water frozen in the
rainbarrel at the side of the house.

The morning cold devours the heat
That flutters from the Franklin stove
In the corner, near the window
Covered with frost.

The snow that fell from the gathering clouds
Blankets the roof of the barn
And the field where the alfalfa will come in spring.

Our fields-no true delineation save the barbed-wire fence
We will need to mend, and our three mares, side by side
on New Year's Day.

A child sleeps, mummified beneath the quilts that somebody's
mother made by hand and have been passed down through
generations. I tiptoe to the Franklin stove where countless
others have gravitated for warmth. I can't wake the child,
it's too early.

—*Morgan Bunker*

You

When I look at you
On the outside you still look the same.
But, on the inside it seems like you have changed.
Was it something I said or did?
Or something I didn't do, or should have done?
You always make me so happy
And sometimes I wonder if you're the one.
Sometimes I really don't know
how I feel about you
And I know this happens to you, too.
But, all I know now,
is that I'm going to try to keep you anyway possible,
Someway, somehow.
I have never felt this way before,
You've had many besides me.
All I know is that I never want this feeling to end.
I thought, and now I know
You're my best friend.

—*Carrie Spyra*

Strong Man

ly Grandfather is strong,
n the water battling Bass,
 his shop shaping wood,
n the deck cleansing cod,
 his garden gathering greens.

nelling of sea salt mixed with Marlin,
is hands were scabrous and scarred with soil.
ot as tall as a tree, but taller than me,
ble to fly,
ble to fish,
ble to grow his favorite dish,
y Grandfather is strong.

  —Jim Littlejohn

atiently Feeling Penalty...

Within these four walls I sit thinking of a passion I
ce had. After all, trying to pave a painless life,
ll, suddenly panic and pain replaced what was pride and power.
Within these four walls I sit patiently feeling penalty
r problems which never included me. I felt my pressure
nting as I reminisced of prosperous times in the outside world.
All is silent yet, my tears sound like pindrops in a
ell. As I recall the parties as I grew up, the treat of
tting pennies when I was small and young without parents,
adden.

My life feels like a sentence never to pass
dgment day. My life pending on my irregular thoughts.
All as I sit patiently feeling penalty within these four walls.

  —Lorena Betances

eminiscence

vo by two I watched them passing by,
ice it was "we", but now alone am I;
here are my dreams of growing old with you?
ie plans we made of all the things we'd do?

ir love supreme wrapped in emotive dew,
st a brief glance - unbounded then it grew.
y hand in yours, we tried to climb the heights,
 near the top - but fate blew out the lights.

urnally I still recall that day,
e talked and laughed while your soul flew away,
hat were your thoughts as you began to fall?
ope of me - who loved you most of all.

  —Bernice Perelman

n End To The Pain

here once there was two, there's now only one.
ice we stood in a pair, now we each stand alone.

hat happened to the closeness, the good times, the fun?
ey all have been buried in the heart of a drone.

life has a meaning, it's lost to me now.
id I can only do what the fates will allow.

ink as I may, so sad and so troubled,
ook with longing on all happy couples.

ere's nothing I can do, my hands they are tied.
ie thing I can say, I certainly tried.

irow up my hands, discouraged, in disgust.
now what I should do, and do it I must.

r this miserable existence is full of despair,
iust rid myself of the pain, I must clear the air.

goodbye my darling, the love of my life,
uess, in dreams only, I'll end up your wife.

  —Betsy P. Brill

Different

One sick, One blind
One crippled and left behind.
So many handicapped in so many ways
And something different happening every day.
If you are different don't be ashamed
It's not your fault you're not to blame.
We're all born different in one way or other
Yours' just show more but you're still my brother
So we'll hold out our hands
Our problems to share
And show the world there are those that still care.

  —Gamble

"The Unborn Child"

One day I'll have the perfect name
One day I'll have fortune and fame
One day I'll see the sunshine oh so bright
One day I'll sleep under the stars at night

One day I'll receive a hug full of love
One day I'll learn about the one from above
One day I'll pray with all my might
That day may be this very night

I hope and hope that I will not die
Before I see the world outside
I leave my future in my mother's hand
Hoping that someday I'll see this very land

That very night she fulfilled my fears
While down my cheek rolled many tears

  —Cara Hayes

The Eyes of Love

Life plays strange tricks on all of us at times
One day you are in the depths of hell
And the next...
You are at the highest pinnacle of heaven itself
Love is the same
Across the room our eyes met
Chemistry took over
Everyone else instantly disappeared
In the completely crowded room
Only we two were there
From the decks of an aircraft carrier
Into my life he comes
Tall, dark, and handsome
In my imagination he is dressed in whites
The only thing missing is the raging steed
A smile so sweet, the north pole would melt
A touch so gentle, it would calm the most savage beast
A voice so calming, it could stop a tidal wave
A caress so soft and loving... I melt into his arms
Never wanting to leave. And all this, I can see in his eyes...

  —Shirley Dunn

My Country - The Philippines

A country of more than seven thousand islands,
Often called the "Pearl of the Orient".
Famous for its mountains, white beaches
and agricultural lands,
Home to the Filipino people and some aliens.

Ally of the Americans in the second world war.
Side by side with American soldiers, Filipinos fought.
Thanks God! General Douglas MacArthur said,
"I shall return." And democracy was saved
from the Japanese invaders.

  —Nelson Javier Burgos

True Friends

They love you with a love only
One friend can have for another
They respect your decisions
Even when they don't understand them.

They are there to console you
You can depend on them.
Someone you can really talk to
When your world is falling apart.

They can pick you up
When you hit your lowest
And make your face light up when you thought the sun
Would never break through the clouds.

True friends are there when times are hard.
They are not fickle or random
They are not influenced by the odds,
Like the flip of a card.

And I know for sure
That is for you I will always be thankful
Because you were a true friend.
Love ya, Doris L. Martin
—*Doris Lynn Martin*

Love Sonnet

You are like a book to me,
One I can't put down,
You are like a melody
With the sweetest sound.
And every note I hear you play,
Lingers on my mind.
Hours after I'm away,
I hear that special rhyme.
Like a thrilling novel,
You unfold yourself,
But I am scared to reach the end,
For fear of losing out.
You are like a sacred painting,
I pass and see your face,
Captured in the canvas stain,
I long to just embrace.
And like a fine piano,
Whose keys are pure and white,
I play for you the love I know
And wait for your reply.
—*Nancy Huelsman*

Color Blind

One was black
One was white
There was even an orange and a gray
Kitten's born to day
Not one did she push away
To her color was on crime
Her love made her color blind
People came to pick and choose
The black, white, orange and even the gray
All were gone, that very day
Not one that came, asked to see her pedigree
Nor did they ask her nationally
All came, with only one thought
To share the love in their heart
They knew that it was no crime
To be color blind
—*Arthur R. Morrison*

Promises

Promises are made — and promises are broken —
One's heart is never true — The sky is blue —
The moon is new —
But devious minds lie old in their master's mind —
A promise is made — and trust is regained —
Only to find a fault — the trust vanishes —
The distrust famishes; ablaze —
The devious one apologizes —
The vulnerable one advises —
Promises are made to be broken —

Time will pass —
The lies will deceive the liar —
The honest heart corroded with the scars of trust —
Those who believe in the emptiness of a promise —
Are destined to be damned —
The only safety is to never promise at all —
—*Debby Alexander*

Why?

No more tears and no more sadness
Only our fears and only our madness
Trapped inside our lonely hearts
It feels like someone's hitting us with darts
Will this pain ever end
Or will someone have to lend
Their strongness and their hope
Or will I have to cope
With the one unanswered question, why?
I never had the chance to say good-bye
What's done is done
But your memory won't let
you forget the fun of talking
and hanging out
But I very much doubt
Our life will ever be the same
I wish this time had never came
—*Jessamyn Marie Hope*

Untitled

Her beauty exceeds all creations of God.
Only the select few have the privilege to know her.
She is the greatest of all to the human race.
She is what everyone yearns for,
but only we are allowed to know her beauty.
Only we are privileged to see her face.
to hear her sing,
to watch her grow.
She is freedom.
—*David Hahn*

The Healing Touch

This touch can be by hand
or even a kind word to a man.
No matter how it comes,
but it all means to be loved.
The healing touch.

You maybe ill or even down,
Think of God and all will be fine.
You may see no hope or good fortune ahead,
But there is a God.
The healing touch.
—*Nikasha Lennard*

Untitled

Move me not from this my porch
　or from my land-for year now scorched
of wind and sun and whipping dust
　my once black soil now orange crust

The drought so long deters me not
　I hope on - though sun so hot
at times will beat on me and chain
　me to my chair

They'll come then, as they have in past
　and tell me that I wouldn't last
and urge me once again to sell
　what I for love, with love have tilled

But such hope have I if but one drop fell
　of rain, my land again with green would swell
and golden tips of wheat would dance
　to field hand songs and cricket chants

So move me not from this my pain
　my heart has smelled
　　the scent of rain!!!
　　　—*Michaela Miller*

Think Of God

When you have a thumb tack in your foot,
　or have a splinter in your finger,
just think of God...the one who could do
　the impossible.
When you see a bird flying in the sky,
　or hear a cricket chirping,
just think of God...the one who could do
　the impossible.
When you taste the sugar from nature and
　feel sap on a tree, just think,
Wow! I've touched the hand of God, the
　creator of all things!.
　　　—*Jason Cornell*

What If

Sometimes I wonder what it would be like if I wasn't born
Or if nightfall never came or the sun never rose in the morn
What about not needing a mouth to eat
Or to walk around without feet
Seeing without eyes
Teardrops without cries
What if girls were called brothers
And fathers were called mothers
Dogs without hind legs
Roosters who laid eggs
Phones without cords
Dukes without lords
Drinking without getting drunk
Sinking without being sunk
People who didn't hate: A pessimist who always thought great
I know this is just wondering it cannot be
This would be a most boring world that I can see
I'm a lover of life, a believer
I've learned not to choke on it but become a breather
　　　—*Sherrie A. Best*

Blue

Blue is the color of the waves rapping against the sand
Reminds me of the clear blue sky.
The portion of the color
Spectrum lying between green and violet.
Of the chirping blue birds on a summers day
Blue berries freshly picked from the garden.
Blue flowers sweeping against the wind
　　　—*Jennifer Putz*

Interrogations on a Metro of the Day

Have you seen the boarded store windows; the gun shots by day or night? Have you heard the screams, the shrieking autos, the obscenities and seen the fright? Have you seen the tight garb on teens showing boobs and buns and pelvic lines? Have you seen the symbols of hate and death threats on those boards and other walls? Have you seen the parked wrecked, abandoned, stripped cars on streets and roadways? Have you seen the sensuous bill-boards, casino ads, cigarette ads, whiskey, wine and beer? Have you seen the boarded store windows, movie houses, abandoned buildings on main street? Have you seen the boarded windows in the projects; no shrubbery, no grass? Have you seen the peeling paint on houses and standing walls around parking lots? Have you seen the dirty buses, pot-holes, gum-pocked pavements, littered gutters? Have you seen the mildew front of the City Hall? Have you seen the sign "Closed Week-ends:" in front of the main library? Have you seen the homeless men at street corners with "Will Work for Food" signs? Have you seen haze caused by pollution it was hard to breathe? Have you seen a murder reported daily so you feared being outside? Have you seen crack houses so you had the creeps? Well, I have!
　　　—*Mary Ann W. Franklin*

Butterfly

Why do you flee from this place of pleasure?
　or should I say joy.
An endless field of flowers to measure,
　or should I say employ.
　　But was it... would or could
　　　it have been?
　　I must dally in darkness
　　until you approach again.

Into your hypnotic color often do I gaze
with solemn intent and my spirit raised.

　Your wings sing: a melodic hover
　under which I lay lifeless until,
　recovering remains of your scent
and what it is that you vent through
　a stricken, down-trodden will.

　　So I'll emerge from the forage
　　without sound and not sight
　　　to abound in your beauty
　　　before you take flight.
　　　—*Daniel Cherek*

Renewal

When we were young of yesteryear,
Our hearts were warmed with but a glance.
As time moved on and we grew near,
Our lives were joined through sweet romance.

What time records do we forget,
The thoughts expressed to be renewed?
Lest this day pass to our regret,
Our hearts we pledge to be imbued.

What happened last no matter now,
The lingering days permit no strife.
Our hearts we join as does the bough,
To daily nurture the tree of life.

If I had known you all my life.
Would there've been time for what was meant?
If such were so without the strife,
My love for you could ne'er be spent.
　　　—*Melvin T. Ehlers*

A Rose And A Dream

A rose is just a rose
  Or so the eye it seems
But a rose is made of petals
  As life is made of dreams.

Each petal has a part to play
  The same as each our dreams
The petals from the rose you see
  As life is formed by dreams.

The rose with all its fragrance
  And life with all its love
To be adored by many with graces from above.

  To live the life of roses with beauty beyond compare
We have to love each other we have to learn to share.

  We have to watch and nurture, we have to really care
We have to do our daily deeds with love and tender care.

  Just like the petals on the rose our dreams must be secure
They have to hold together tight in order to endure.

  To reach such beauty from a bud, the rose in all its majesty
Is just like life with all its dreams
  I hope for all the world to see.
    —*Harold B. Sellers*

Loneliness

Loneliness is the cry of a baby with no answer,
Or the playing of beautiful music with no ballet dancer.
It is when there is no one there to love,
As though you are soaring in the sky as a lonesome dove.

Loneliness is no sun rising above the trees, or companion
There to say how good a friend in which you are to me.
Loneliness is not having anyone to turn to,
Lost in your thoughts not knowing where to run to.

Loneliness is to be all alone,
Sitting there just waiting for the ringing of the phone.
Loneliness is not looking forward to a new and fresh day,
Meeting a nice person and not knowing what to say.

It is being left out all the time,
Unable to say that is a friend of mine.
Loneliness is having self esteem,
And the treatment from others is very mean.

Loneliness is when a close loved one dies,
Or living a life of complete lies.
Wishing you had a friend or two,
Or when you look in the mirror and unable to say "I like you"
    —*Kelly Brown*

Living Beneath Our Privilege

Living beneath our privilege is an unnecessary woe;
Our inheritance unclaimed can keep us below
the spiritual poverty level, so strive to maintain
the elite status quo that Jesus died to gain.

We need not go hungry for spiritual bread,
He's left us His promise, He's given us the Word.
We need not go running for places to stay,
His kingdom is here! Right now - today!

We have but to call Him, Holy Spirit, come;
Guide us, comfort us, deliver us from
the poverty of faithlessness, the hunger for peace,
the violence of hatred - will is never cease?

Our Father is rich! We all are the heirs!
So why do we struggle with so many cares?
We've already conquered through God's saving grace,
But we're living beneath our privileged place.
    —*Charlotte Brewster*

Love

Love is like the smell of a fresh rose
Or the sound of a bumblebee
Like a beautiful sunrise on a summer day
Or the smell of a sweet perfume

Love is as violent as a thunderstorm
Or a riot on a city street
Like a leaf tossed in the wind
Or a hurricane on the beach

Love is like a precious friend
Or a God in whom you trust
Like a bridge over troubled waters
Or a savior in the nick of time

Love is like a fleeting moment
Or a pebble on the shores of time
Like a bubble bursting in the wind
Or a sound from yesterday

Love is like a new tomorrow
Or a fantasy that comes true
Love is for the foolish hearted
Or a dreamer just like you
    —*Charles A. Davis*

Giving the Gift of Love

To love oneself must one first love another?
Or to love another must one first love oneself?
It is known that man must crawl before he walk.
That she must eat mush before she can eat meat.

Must man love before he can hate?
Or can she hate and then learn to love?
To hate is easy, yes, simple and very uncomplicated.
But to love takes time, patience, and understanding.
Yes, it is harder to love, but love is always, always
rewarding

Must a man be hurt before he can hate?
Or must she hate in order to hurt?
It is known that Our Heavenly Father can heal all hurts.
But hate, well how can man say he love and believeth in Our
Heavenly Father whom he have never seen and hate his brother
who shares his world and even sometime his womb.
    —*Naomi L. Doughty*

Sun

Send down your heated rays,
orange, flaming fire ball!
Light up the earth for all the days,
orange, flaming fire ball!
Each day you rise again,
over the pink and blue horizon,
makes my happiness never end,
orange, flaming fire ball.
I see you standing tall,
over the green ocean, above the clouds,
orange, flaming fire ball,
When I'm unhappy and I cry,
your hot flames then make them dry,
and when I go inside at night,
you go behind the moon and make it bright,
orange, flaming fire ball.
Good night.
    —*Elizabeth Emma*

A Lady

A Lady with beauty and charm resembles Venus
  originally Goddess of Beauty.
She may be a lady with stature and fascination.
  A woman of distinction and speaks without
    causing friction.
Elegance is fulfilled with a much charmed life
  and carried out with delight.
Like the planet Venus she revolves around
  one's mind and hard to find -
Until the focused lens opens and there
  she stands-out like a shining light.
The highest idealistic feminine beauty
  resembling Aphrodite -
The Greek Goddess Of Love.

—*Evangeline Katranis*

Sometimes

Sometimes I feel so content inside;
Other times I feel like the oceans tide,

Sometimes I feel so cozy and warm;
Other times I feel like the crack of dawn,

Sometimes I feel so eager and keen;
Other times I feel like the flowless stream,

Sometimes I feel so generous and soft;
Other times I feel like the winter frost,

Sometimes I feel so powerful and strong;
Other times I feel like the bird without song,

Sometimes I feel so bright eyed and bushy tailed;
Other times I feel like the listless snail,

Sometimes I feel so glad that I can feel;
Other times I feel the same.

—*Noreen M. Pfohl*

Plight of the Homeless

Some look with pity,
Others with shame,
Who is that woman without a name,
  She is alone

We don't try to help her,
Instead we just say,
"She can help herself any old day,"
  She is alone

We can't comprehend all her emotions
We simply don't know her internal sorrow,
feelings locked away for known one to see a borrow,
  She is alone

If everyone person could just give one dollar,
If everyone person could just give a day,
Then this huge problem would be done away,
  Thousands are alone.

—*Anna Birkholz*

"The Inevitable"

  As we grow older, we realize that lives,
once set in motion cannot be changed.
  We see through, the once blinded eyes
of youth, when the darkness has lifted, that
inevitability is the cruelest fact of
life that a man ever has to accept,
therefore we instinctively try not to
accept it. We try to stay blind for as
long as our hearts will let us, and
our minds can keep making up excuses.

—*Peter Balsamo*

Unrequited Love

We met, and for a moment, our hearts rejoiced
our eyes were blinded by the light that shone
through the fire of our love, in silence we spoke
  of our longing and hunger
our joy was followed by sadness for soon we were to part
  to go back to emptiness and waiting
the long hours of nights and days that roll into weeks
the agony that surely you must know, for you have waited too
oh my beloved, when you were near, your eyes caressed me
  your arms embraced me
oh to recapture that moment of ecstacy we both knew
when spring will come, the sun will melt the snow
the grass will grow, the trees will bloom again
the birds will sing, but I will cry alone.

—*Edna Horn*

'Beyond Eternity'

You are my friend
Our friendship has no end
It goes beyond eternity
You'll never know how much you mean to me
You've been my friend for oh so long
You've helped me look beyond eternity

As I look beyond eternity
I see you and me
Reaching out to one another
As we've done so many times before
Loving you is what I've waited for
Did you ever stop to wonder how far we could go
As friends, the process was slow

How could it be...that we fit together so perfectly
When I had looked around for so long
Perhaps I didn't look far enough...beyond eternity

—*Kimberly K. Day*

"In Dying Color": An Elegy for Latasha Harlins

Twenty score and many years ago
our parents were packed on ships as cargo.

Long after Columbus set sail to discover America
they were shackled together among barrels of paprika.

Our parents of yore paid dearly for their entrance into humanity.
They were like cotton in the fields, horses in the stables, a
  commodity.
Before the crows descended upon the land we were still
incomplete,
  still parts a' man.

The Bucks of old were black and bold
whose job 'twas to procreate many times untold.

The former subjects had power, money, and liberty.
We sought comfort in our own adversity.

We live in the age where violence is the norm.
Loved ones are killed in an Asian Square, an African cubicle, and
  Arid Storm.

Are we less than a dog or the man on the tree?
When the little one died, she was you, she was me.

In the past, in the present, deja vu. Doom To Yu.
Miniature white maggots don't discriminate: Any flesh will do.

We must believe and have more than "In God We Trust,"
Our dedication to the struggle is a must!

—*Raelene Belisle*

437

Wishing On A Moonbeam

As I stare out at the clear night sky,
out at the pools of water,
I wonder clear and
up, up high

When I wish upon a moonbeam.

When I wish upon a moonbeam, do the stars in Heaven cry?
Do they conceive the highest standards, way up, up in the sky?
When I wish upon a moonbeam, so elevated in that sky,
do all the tiny angels,
try and try and try and try?

When I wish upon a moonbeam

As I sit here staring up at them, my face lifts in a smile,
And as my wings raise and I fly,
Going up, up in the sky,
I say this is what happens

When you wish upon a moonbeam.

—*Amy Schlueter*

Untitled

The blood of my deepest thoughts
overwhelm whatever I do.
I hear a shrieking scream and realize
it is my mind calling to me.
Why must everything give pain and whatever I
touch must crumble in my hands?
I do not know what is right any more,
everything is changing before my eyes
Death sees me at the door, but I dare
not go in. My blood, my thoughts
provoke me to enter....
But here I stand, prevailed in stillness
and nothing to do except....
cry.

—*Maralyn Stanton*

More Saddle Horses But No Broke Riders

A thousand pounds horse, and you think you're the master?
Pardon me, while I shake with rude laughter.

Even gentle horses can come all unglued,
If a rabbit jumps out from under their hooves,

Some horses bite and some horses kick.
If they rear over backwards it can make you real sick!

If your trimming the hoofs to make him look neat,
He may lean on you hard or step on your feet,

Hold your hand flat where feeding him apples.
Or your fingers may end up in the food sample!

You can speak learnedly of spavin, glanders and such.
But you aren't very smart if you trust a horse much.

When you ride an outlaw you know he can kill you,
But beware of the gentle one he'll also spill you.

—*Russell L. Kelch*

Repentance

Years ago, a cycle.
Passing in my car, I.
Window down, pointed a finger,
"Pow"

Years later,
A car,
Passing me, walking, on the street, another
Window down, a pointed face,
"Pow"

—*Jim Wade*

Dreams,

As night arrives a single image flies
passing my eyes, it's a long lost lover
of mine... As I fall deeper in—to
my slumber a cool breeze falls upon
my face.... I turned around with-in my
mind... Trying to erase....
But my thoughts keep turning around...
They are no-longer mine...
As I gaze at your beauty that dis—stilled
with-in my brain I hope, and pray that I
am awake....But then I realize I am
asleep.... I would rather not wake-up from
this slumber, and let this be... doing everything
that's with-in my power to sleep...
That is the place I'd rather be....
If I can I got you held with-in my world...

—*Stephen M. Burlikowski*

Untitled

Bridges of lights span across the horizon.
Past the blood red sun and into the shadows
of the grinning moon.
The moon seems contempt.
Come.
Walk with me.
On the bridges of light in search of question.
To answer our curiosity.
The moon will feast on its tenor guests.

—*Noel Casserly*

Judge Not

When you are tempted to judge someone;
Pause and quickly ask:
"Am I so pure and flawless
Am I equal to this task?"

Has God asked for you assistance
In this jon that is his alone;
Or - have you just decided to try,
Some judging on your own?

It is easy to tell the other guy
The things that he should do,
And perhaps the mistake he is about to make,
Once was made by you!

But until you have walked in his shoes, and
Until you have felt with his heart;
You cannot sing his song - and -
You cannot play his part!

So, before you judge him - touch him,
Let him feel that it will be all right;
And the touch that you give, just might
Help you both live, to fight a bigger - fight

—*Iris Jane Luke Patton*

Blue Wolf

Stepping lightly through the trees,
Paying no heed to the worldly freeze,
Sniffing delicately with sensitive nose,
Testing the wind as it lightly blows,
Watching with beautiful golden eyes,
Watching with a look that's infinitely wise,
Waiting for a call with very sharp ears,
A call that, to anyone, can bring lonely tears,
Hearing and answering with one long howl,
Is a great blue wolf with bright white jowl.

—*Cynthia Jones*

Holocaust

I wasn't there but know some of what went on.
People screaming with fear,
or the tear from the beating and the separation of
families.
Killing of Jews everyday,
counting, counting, counting the ways.
A thousand ways to kill a Jew,
Because they believed Hittler was true.
They didn't know or care about our lives,
Just to make easy money is what they thrived.
Millions of Jews killed everyday,
All killed in many different ways.
We must never forget what our ancestors did,
To remember to love and never to kill.

—*Kimberly Racheal Anapolsky*

Alive

This day was not a day for
people who like sun, nor
the warmth of light.
But than I'm not a sunny person
nor am I a warm one, so today's my day.
Suddenly the clouds burst forth and
gave it's gift to the village below.
The rains fell upon our hearts
And as I looked to the heavens above
I felt the wondrous drops as they
fell upon my body giving life to each and every pore.
I dropped my stick and danced in mystery
While children ran for shelter and wise
old men scolded my actions.
But no attention did I pay them.
For in the rains I became alive.

—*Ann Marie Pedersen*

Heartbreak

People you love and cherish,
People who soon will perish.
That is perish from you,
And put their love somewhere new.
Leaving their partner alone and sad,
Making them feel like they have been had.
One will recover, one will not
All that one can think is how they fought.
A heartbreak, what a mysterious thing
I all begins with a diamond ring.
Nothing will ever last
I all goes by much too fast.

—*Edward A. Drake*

Wonder And Wonder Why

I wonder and wonder why - why is today such a gloomy day?
Perhaps the people are going astray and day-by-day forgetting
pray?

I wonder and wonder why - there isn't even a cloud in the sky?
Is it that God is angry with his wicked-wicked world, and has
made the winds so turbulent as they whirl?

I wonder and wonder why - the sun has even gone from the sky?
Have the angels ceased to play and they've taken that so
radiant sun away?

I wonder and wonder why - why is man so persistent in
conquering the skies?
But, when his missiles, rockets and jets no longer will fly,
Will the clouds and the sun return to the sky -
The days will no longer be such gloomy days - for this to
happen I do so much pray, and I wonder and wonder why.

—*Isadore Williams, Jr.*

Who Am I?

I look in the mirror and see a
person staring at me. Who is this person?

He stares at me with eyes of
innocence his body naked, beautiful like
a statue skin soft, like a newborns
but bruised with marks of pleasure.

His arms are cradled to hold
his chest filled with capacity,
thighs that are hard and legs
of steel. His attitude is vigorous like
a viking with the intensity to anguish those
who get in his way. But he also can be pleasing to the
senses, feelings, and mind of others.
You don't very often see this side,
he only shows it behind closed doors.

Who is this black young man stuck in
a society of racism, poverty, and
maltreatment. Trying to survive the streets of rage,
struggling to keep a good sense of pride.

Who is this person I live with each day?

—*Lena A. Tamplin*

Rose

Rose so red, magnificent flower
picture of beauty, aroma of romance
blooming the fullest in warm summer showers
your petals in the wind appearing to dance

Rose, perfect symbol of love's mystery
your petals of crimson are love's burning flames
your thorns and blossom love's duality
the way you are handled brings pleasure or pain

Rose, morning dew upon your fragile frame
are as teardrops wept by a heartbroken soul
your sweet fragrance tempts me, but I must refrain
for if I should take you, you'd soon cease to grow

Rose, how I wish I could take you away
To have you, to hold you close to me
but I know if I do so, you would soon fade
I could never hurt you, so I must let you be

—*Darrin Mason*

Momentary Experience

The onset of the winter with cool brisk air.
Picturesque blue skies facilitate an upward stare.
Cotton-white clouds rapidly flow past.
Just as life flashes by, so quick, so fast.
A bird or two enter my sightful scan, as I think and wonder
about a life oriented plan.
I have come to realize the past is no more, and the future
is illusionary, as perhaps, nothing's in store.
So each moment is to be experienced with thoughtfulness and
love. Just as evenly as the horizon appears, and soft as a dove.

—*John Snyder*

A New Year is Born

A fresh year comes when beauty lies impaled
on spikes of hoarfrost, corpse-like in decay
her twisted, wrinkled countenance assailed
by sleet and storm, harsh winter's roundelay.

But God proclaims that mankind's life is deathless,
that spring will breathe new strength to every soul.
It fills my heart with hope so sacred, breathless,
that I can wait while winter takes its toll.

—*Harriet Grossfield*

Imprints

People come and people go leaving memories of paths chosen
        Pieces of time warmth has frozen
        Touching hearts and sometimes hands
Sometimes sadness that wasn't part of the plan

        Hold tight to what has passed
        No matter the grip it won't last
        People grow and change it's true
        Moving along with lives to pursue
        Struggle at times when you're alone
Survey your choices for a new path to be shown

        Lovers children all people have wings
        When we can't harmonize remember one thing
        Seasons change they always do
        People rearrange what they can't pursue
        Sing they must to their own melody
        Soft sweet songs of their own humanity

        When we feel each other near
        These are the times to hold dear
        Let pain learn then be forgotten
        With hope as the memory to begotten

—Jacki Santangelo

Liquid Warming

        Almighty gathering
Pioneers of unity, becoming whole
        Manifestation of change
Colors, - vivid, singing to our souls
        Positive vibrations - swirling visuals

The thick silent mist of creation - lingering
 Fresh scent of life, rolling, sprout
        Golden strands bonding, - with promise

Inspired by those of past and present
        With preparation and desire -
We ascend into flight and encounter -
        A not so distant harmony, ... a new nation
Arrogation of Bretheren, - Growing, ... Let's blossom
        we are alive, and we are now

—Joshua Leathersich

"When Winter Comes"

Long cool shadows
play on white crystal blanket
stretched over rolling fields
forming pollack like patterns.

Sharp winter winds cut
quietly thru lonely paths
as shiny fingers shiver in nakedness
awaiting the call of morning sun's warmth.

Night sounds of strange creatures stir
fill the thin atmosphere
icicles cling to barren branches
while the moon slithers between silver sheets.

From deep purple moods stars fade
into lilac skies washing darkness away
as little gold flames lick at the dawn
arousing new secrets left untold.

—Joseph E. Grey II

"Galaxy Girl"

Sometimes I see her a flash in the sky
Playing hide and seek with the stars
I wanna touch her but she's way to high
She might be from Venus maybe Mars
The moon is her playground the sun is her light
Don't know where she's coming from I'm sure.
There's no one else like her she's outta sight
I just wanna see her more and more
At night when I'm dreaming sometimes she'll appear
I wonder why I can't be by her side
I wish that one day she'll get me out of here
So come on baby take me for a ride
I'm gonna find her gonna catch her someday
She's the prize and now I gotta win it
I'd be with her now if I could have things my way.
But she won't even slow down for a minute
She's my little galaxy girl
Flying around man she's outta this world
She's zooming off to the milky way
She's on the go but I want her to stay.

—Sam Verderese

Oh, Heavenly Father

Oh, heavenly Father — from the heavens above,
        please bring me back my long lost love.
She's a precious little girl with golden hair,
        and eye's so blue, with an innocent stare.
She is my one and only.., a gift to me from You —
        so why did You take her away from me, and who'd You give her to
For, there is no other mother, in the capacity of time —
        that could have a love far greater — than that love of mine.
I just want to know one thing Dear God, I hope You understand,
        but it's tearing me apart inside — it's getting out of hand...
Wherever have You placed her, is she happy and content?..,
        or is her heart still broken, from wondering where Mommy went?
Is she asking about me? ... Will she remember who I am?...
        or when she see's my outstretched arms, my "exit," she'll demand?
I only want one thing in life, to make my world complete...
        to have my daughters hand in mine, walking down the street...
To kiss her tiny glowing face, and tuck her in at night —
        then stare awhile, and shed a tear, to the end of a dreadful fight.
Then my search will end — filling this emptiness in my heart,
        knowing we are united again ... till, death do us part.

—Victoria Ann "Breeze" Leasure

Why

Flowers to the door, on the floor, die.
Please, it was brother not I.

Monks about, flowers about, on the floor, die.
Sneeze and your dead, bye bye.

Castle lady secure, no more, die.
A breeze for the sly.

Wear a vest, the city's best, you may not die.
Freeze, you get a bye.

A fire fly night, hold my hand and die.
Sleeze turned shy.

Flipper at the arches, turn your head, die.
Trigger will hear the last sigh.

Freeway, drive by, love unborn, die.
Teaser will hear the last sigh.

Cab guy, Pizza Pie, roll up and die.
Take ya to the desert, to cry

Gang bang and drive by, die.
Ease by, bang, ease by, bang bang bang. Why!

—Gene O. Potter

ife

y life began as a simple man, I was content and did as I
eased. As I strolled along the bridge of life, my tasks
ere completed with ease. For the path I chose on the
idge at first, was only the narrow and straight. A
th in which life was planned, and you needn't rely on
te. Yet then the path took a twist somehow, and I ended
straying away. I must have been called aside for some
ason, to set the pace for a new day. I encountered
stacles great and small, on my journey of the unknown.
r it was I who was to set the pace, and I set that pace
ne. As I see this magnificent bridge come to an end,
lo not weep in sorrow. For if death is a good as life
to me, then let me move on to tomorrow. As I pause for
moment on this bridge, I remember the freeness of
sterday. I hope that path that I took alone, will show
hers that there are other ways. The creator of this
idge gave life to me, and he will be the one to take it
vay. And although I desire the excitement of tomorrow,
little part of me still craves yesterday.

—*Matthew Morrow*

lone For The Holidays

:iving down a rain-soaked moonlit highway -
ndering my existence,
hink of the void in my life...
e loneliness.

ith a caring, experienced heart
have an over-abundance of love to give;
t no one to share it with.

though I am searching,
ere is presently a lull in my lovelife.
niss having a significant other.

here will I find that special someone to share my
ppiness, sadness, and Christmas Eve with? When will I
d someone worthy enough to kiss at the stroke of midnight
New Year's Eve?

—*Alicia K. Miros*

ower

wer can be as explosive as a gun.
wer can be as solid as a wall.
can be possessed solely by one
shared by all.

wer is something that everyone
ants; but only a few can acquire.
ice a sample is given to one,
s possession becomes an even greater desire.

any people, when they obtain it finally,
e not sure what first to do.
t remember, if not used accordingly,
shall be taken from you.

ways keep in mind, power belongs not to one man or woman.
is neither good nor evil.
can be the knowledge of a shaman
the courage of a daredevil.

—*Elsworth Charles Jr.*

A Mother

A mother is... someone who is always there to offer words of
praise; someone who makes you feel special in many different
ways. Someone who gives you comfort, when life sums so unfair;
Someone who taught you wrong from right, with tender, loving
care. Someone you can always confide in, and tell all your
secrets too; someone who nursed your childhood ailments, from
oops' runny noses to the flu. Someone who's always honest with
you, even when it may dent your pride; someone who is there
through good times and bad, standing by your side. Someone who
has always loved you, with a love and so deep and strong;
Someone who will go well out of her way, so you know you belong
Someone who isn't just "mother", but a very dear friend as well
Someone never failing to brighten your day with a funny story
she has to tell. Someone who knows you better than you know
yourself from one time to another; there just isn't a love as
quite as unique as the love you receive from your mother. I
could never have prayed to the Good Lord above for a mother
better than you; and even if I had chosen my mother myself,
I would have definitely chosen you too!

—*Phyllis Smiley*

The Story Of Her Tears

Holy Mary, Mother of God
pray for us sinners? Can she?
She folds her hands close to her heart.
She prays hard and she prays deep.
Weeping, weeping, she forgets about sleeping.
For she knows the time is near.
Praying day and night
Night and day just praying.
Sobbing, sobbing, wanting, but unable to grant
That special miracle to all the people
That special serenity
That special forgiveness
Hearing many cries, she cries,
So much, so hard, so long
It came thru to the world's eye!
The Crying Icon of the Holy Mary! Herself!
A miracle from many tears cried and still crying.
Still a miracle to us tears for her
So why not give her back a miracle,
Strengthen your faith!

—*Lori Csukardi Dellas*

True Believer

I told God I didn't believe in him, because the
Proof of his existence is pretty thin
So he sent me an angel to change my mind.
She told me her story and I told her mine.
She said, "God is real", I replied "how could that be?"
She felt obliged to warn me of blasphemy
Then she explained the creation of man
So I told her the theory of Charles Darwin
On we argued through the night
To find out who is wrong and who is right
Finally I told her to introduce me to God
She said he would consider this odd
"But if God is so powerful and divine why won't he
help me change my mind?"
So she asked him and we waited for the rest of the night.
In the morning God was nowhere in sight
Suddenly the angel removed the halo from her head.
Removed her wings, looked up and said,
"God since you failed to make him a believer
I'm sorry to say I can't believe in you either."

—*David Rodriguez*

Untitled

Wondrous trees towering above civilization,
  Protecting our crumbling earth,
    Witnessing the death and
      Powerful rebirth of life,
        Growing older and yet
          More beautiful.
            Sheltering,
              Witnessing,
                Protecting,
                  Beautiful.

—*Amber Petrie*

My Choice

Why touch my face and say what's this and
pull the hair I wear -

Do I touch your dress and say what's this and
pull the clothes you wear -

Why look at me and say what a mess, so stupid
and so dumb -

Were Jesus or Lincoln such bums?
Think back in your own life way back in
your family tree.

Weren't there uncles and nephews who wore beards
just like me -

Were they so dumb or foolish or were their
heads held high?

Don't worry about what the outside looks a
person is what he is inside.

—*Linda M. Kellish*

Home

My bed so warm and soft on my skin,
Pull up the blanket, for the sheet is too thin.
Snuggle up close to my beloved spouse,
Together, safe, in my beautiful house.
Down I go later, to the kitchen to eat,
Ooh, the floor cold on my bare feet.
Breakfast was good, now for a shower,
Off to work I go, in less then a hour.
Water hits me, and I awake,
Something was grabbed, what did they take?
My newspaper, ooh, its raining,
I touch my head, hot, the fever's gaining.
With a shrug, I look around,
My other family's all sleeping on the ground.
How did I get here? What did I do? Why does this not feel new?
My clothes are torn, I need a shower. No missions are open at this
  hour.
I gather my cardboard, rearrange my bed,
Everything's fuzzy cause of the heat in my head.
I lie down, dreams begin to roam,
I'm on my way again, back to home.

—*Keith Koloske*

That Wait

   I promised my favorite Uncle I would visit very soon. But
pressing matters got in the way. And my promise became a tune.
Many weeks passed by I finally made up my mind, to visit uncle
at nine. Then I received a call from my uncles friend, he said
your Uncle died in his sleep last night, I'm so sorry to say.
He stood to the window each and everyday waiting for you to
walk through that gate. I felt the phone slip from my hand, my
body started to shake. I screamed out loud in agony, oh my God
its to late. If only I took the time to walk through my Uncles gate.

—*Jennifer Tatem*

Raincatcher

Emotions scattered like rain, on life's windowpane.
Pure drops of soul, watering trees of life.
Raincatcher lifts his face to the rain.
Thirst opens him, feelings seep deep, hitting stones and dry bones.
It's raining, grey and slick, he sees reflections in inner gullies.
Sometimes wet and sometimes dry, emotions reaching for the sky.
Raincatcher tries to draw them in. Give them form, let them speak
Walking and looking for droplets of the true self, a clear fluid.
On the path, footsteps holding water, memories of things before.
No words inside, and can't stop walking. Even the shadows go home.
Raincatcher tries to understand, water on cement, it doesn't relent.
Pavement does not cry, even with floods, the past is not filled up.
He turns his ear, all the talking and all the doing.
Gutter spouts are sputtering, tapping out a rhythm of retreat.
Looking into the mirror eyes, brings rain tears.
He turns toward home, the wet shirt and cold hard body pumping.
But when the beautiful words flow, a ride in a black limo.
In the road the cement mixer usually makes too much noise.
Shadows of the old self come out in the night sky rain.
Raincatcher has spent his whole life catching the pain.

—*Julie Lewis*

What Vantage Point...

What vantage point lends vision to the mind
Pursuing faithfully the scholar's task
Of pulling from this life the deadly mask
Of superstition, fear; half-truths that bind
Our human selves, creating isolation,
The disregard we have for one another,
The failure of our sense of sister-brother,
The death cells of our human fragmentation?
The vista must reveal a broader scene,
Impatient with the thought of dissertation
Or theorem proved to pass as education,
Holistic knowledge taken as our mean.

For when the books of knowledge have grown cold,
What human story will they then have told?

—*Ila Jean Kragthorpe*

I Will Come Again

They put our Lord upon a cross
Put thorns around his head
Then drove nails, into his hands and feet
And stood there while he bleed

From the sixth hour, darkness hung over the hand
The dark, clouds, rolled across the skies
He was not, just the Son of God
He was also the son of man

My God, my God, why hasn't thou forsaken me
It is finished, was his last breath
He'd died so, we'd be free of sins
As he slipped painfully into to death.

He descended into the heart of the earth
Walking among the damned
The keys of life and death.
Was held tightly in his hand

He came back to earth, to reveal himself
To his disciples, and his friends
His parting, and comforting words, from the mount
Was, surely, I will come again

—*Marvel L. Feltman*

romise

od did not promise sunshine without
  rain or health and no pain.
e did not promise Spring without Summer
  or joy without sorrow.
od did not promise everyone would understand
  and give us a helping hand.
e did not promise rose without thorns
  or that we'd laugh and never mourn.

od did promise He would walk with
  us through the rain and the pain
  through the Summer and sorrow.
e promised He'd look into our hearts
  and then give us a helping hand
od promised to heal the scars from the
  thorns and go with us through our
  sorrow when we mourn.
e even promised to hold us in the
  hallow of His hands.
  —Leanora Musser Shaw

ed

ed is a firing heart, burning deep within,
ed is luscious red lips forming a grin.
he sun gleaming bright, a beautiful sight.
ed is a feather on a singing robin.
nd in the rainbow, red is at the top,
ed is the firefrog that hops, hops.
ed is a bright warm sweater that the children wear,
ed is big ribbons the girls have in their hair.
 red rose that blooms in the spring, in the April rain.
nd red is the plump red apple that falls
id the flag that waves in the hall.
ed is here, red is there, red is everywhere.
  —Rhonda Baker

ly Wife And My Friend

s I think about these many years of the past,
membering our love, and why that it will last.
ntil this very moment in time, as I review,
owing your patience and kindness, with love, so true.

hink of your smile, and your beautiful hair.
 radiant young lady, as you stood there,
side me, on that, our wedding day.
ith family and friends, and happy, were they.

our love for God was reflected in your face,
 you were there, a figure of grace.
appy was I, your husband, to be.
 receive you, as my wife, a bride so lovely.

ur love for each other, has lasted all of these years.
rough commitment and respect, with some shedding of tears.
e have always put God first, and praise Him, with love.
ving Him our thanks, desiring blessings from above.

ou have lived so faithful, my wife and my friend.
y love for you, could never end.
ur Christian virtues are strong and true.
d showing to me, that His Spirit guides you.
  —Wayman Hallford

The Kiss

The soul bares itself at the slightest touch
Rendered speechless in a blissful hush
Careful, gentle, loving, timid
  with a reverent brush
Words unsaid are spoken here
  nothing could be more clear
It is the song unsung, bursting within,
  and the renewal of love
    time and again
Tenderly searching depths of the soul,
  soothing the burn
    easing the pain
Just a kiss... and nothing more
  needed to throw away the oar
    and drift asea oblivious to all
If only for a moment swept away
  far from the cares of this world
Nothing more than rapture, nothing less than bliss
Conveying more than a lifetime could say...
  all in the kiss.
  —Molly Felmet

"Lights"

To make a poem short and sweet
requires a gift, of thought concise,
yet clear; one thought enough to last
  all year.

The old turn grey, the new turn restless,
the married turn loving, their richness
  grows endless.

I'm looking into the starry night
to see how dark things can be bright.

I'm looking to see the light of day,
when all things born of night turn grey:
When all things grey grew, finally;
to an age of brilliant silver blue!
  —Marilyn S. Brown Higham

(Just Remember) Even Roses Have Thorns

We have decisions we can't make,
respect is something you cannot fake
Petty gossip pays no fee,
When hateful whispers spark curiosity.
Remember what it used to be
just summer lovers you and me.
The end, endings as beginnings
never seem to reach
the hopeless circle of which they teach.
New beginnings will never be truly new
because of the pain I learned from you.
Emotions, and it wasn't love, nor like, nor hate,
but rather something unexplainable
tainted with evil, I found out to late.
Red rose bleed, red rose bled...
Memories of our summer burst my head.
Everything black can mar the white
just as pure eyes can enlighten somber sight.
Now as the perfect do bear their horns,
just remember, even roses have thorns.
  —Anne Carter Lingren

Hands

My blind flesh, reading the tactile tones of hands
Responds to those of the masculine gender.
Rejoices in some, and then draws up in tight
Distress at a slimy touch, or shuddering, stands
Revolted that spidery hand can hinder
The beat of heart, or put the blood to flight.
This touch is friendly, dry and kind, and commands
Respect, and that, secure, warm, is the tender
Touch of male kin. My lover's hands play a bright,
Warm song among my senses that demands
Response, draws me into sweet surrender,
And drowns me in a medley of delight.
Poor Hera, Zeus could not have had such hands,
Else she would have known Tireseus was right.

—*Delta A. Sanderson*

Still, Still Waters After the Flood

Still, still waters and cold, cold days
Restless waters and broken hearts
Rustling leaves sink deeper yet
Into fertile earth the water sinks.

Seeking strength the young seeds bud
Sunlit glades give glowing light
Showers of sun send lovely streaks
Of sun through which our God can speak.

Words are scarce as they come to me
In silence there are so much more than words
Tongues can tell but hearts can't see
I talk of love as I mend my heart.

So pray for sun on still blue waters
And life that goes beyond the sun
God's good light and love can give
Life, and love to those who've known none.

Still, still waters and cold, cold days
Made by this God to whom I pray.

—*Anne S. Gettler*

The Joy of Aging

Slowly the mystery unfolds
Revealing the tragic untold
From beginning to end sum a circle of friends
Bound by music-so haunting,
Emotion-so taunting-
And passion, engripping of men.

As the clock winding down
Releases the smiles, and the frown,
And the tears——
Do the years pass us by
While we try to possess yesteryears?

Shall I learn to be free?
Shall I seek reverie?
Shall the daylight become my best friend?
Or shall I succumb to gravity's plumb
And grown old
As The Great One Intends?

—*Kenna Morris Grushoff*

Rockaway Blues

Rockaway, rockaway time after time
Rock with a smile at age eighty - nine.
  Wiser, but older with a wrinkled - up face,
  sadness is gone now, leaving no trace.
Your family's forgotten how life used to be
many friends you've lost and still long to see.
  Left all alone to just rock in your chair
  to look back at your past, oh if you dare.
So rockaway, rockaway time after time
Back to your past, back to your prime.
  Back to the days when pigtails were in
  bobby socks, poodle skirts and a girlish grin.
Go back to the days of your high school dances
when you danced then laughed, caused you date split his pants.
  Then there's the night when you gave your first kiss
  maybe caught by dad in a state of bliss.
Remember those days, clasp them close to your heart
These are the memories from the very start.
  So rockaway, rockaway all the day long
  captured by memories, by life's precious songs.

—*Debbie Preston*

The Lonely Heart

It is hard to sleep at night, as the tears
roll down my face.
It wouldn't matter if I were lying on a bed of
roses, or if the sheets were made of satin and lace.
No, my heart would still feel the same, dark,
lonely, empty and cold,
My mind would still wander, seeking out the most
painful thoughts, most of which will remain untold.
For I have found out it is even more painful to
speak and not be heard,
Than to let the silent tears fall, and to hope that
one day my heart will be free as a bird.

—*Melody Hancock*

This Precious Pearl

When the storms of life assail me, and the clouds around me
roll. When the nights seem oh, so long Lord, and there's no
rest within my soul.

I just lay my head upon thy breast, and upon the wings of
faith. You will not suffer me to fall, or let me lose my way.

Oh master how thy love sustains, when tears fall down my
cheek. There is no one like you my Lord, my heart lays at
thy feet.

When I think of how much I love you, and how much that you
love me. How you bear my every burden and set this poor soul
free.

You are the secret of my strength, the song within my heart.
For you lift me above these earthly cares and bid them all depart.

I cannot live without you, for me to live is "Christ." I
will sing it through the ages, to this pearl of such great price.

—*Vickie Robinson*

The Rose Of Life

One rose by itself simplifies life.
Roses are like life in many ways.
The peddle of a single rose dies by fate
Thorns are sharp like a knife.
Roses are red like blood from a thorn bush cut.
Roses are special gifts like life.
Thorns are like veins without them there's a world of emptiness
and sorrow
Roses are beautiful gifts for loved ones.
Roses are all shades of colors like life

—*Kathirene Howard*

Untitled

Go, I'm free, she says
Run now, go, leave if it pleases you.

Wild fields, laughing sunset
A path, long, endless - nowhere?

She stood, clutching my bonnet, my bottle.
The woman, the stranger
Nine months within her, safe, somewhere.
Her hand to clench, warmth to live by.
The shelter of her embrace, to run to.

A stranger, looking back, I never knew her
Her eyes, ageless gems, what could they have known?
Looking at me, eagerly, hopefilled
Looking at me, the way she wants me to be
I reject her outstretched palm.

And run for miles, I look back, so where to now?
I ask the stranger, achingly alone, longing

For the way it used to be, simple
Nowhere to turn, I go to raise the sun.
—*Anne O'Brien*

The Madness Of AIDS

Sometimes I feel like stones
run through my skeleton,
and the thorns from my mind
singing the thunderstorm all over the darkened river,
till the mountain of my brain
and still the beauty of life into the rain,
but it is night...

My eyes are only soul.
I can see the black stallion gallop
over and over me.
There is no road to cry.
There is no dust of gold.

Oh... The needles of my bones
start to pray under the clouds
I feel the fire in my mouth.
I feel no stones, no thorns,
no thunderstorms, no river, no mountain.
But yes, I feel there the beauty of God.
—*Fresia N. Csoke*

Scorned

There lay your defendless prey.
Rush and devour him while he speaks in his sleep.
His unknowing tongue utters words that betray him.
Think now; How often his kiss was a Judas
    and his love falsely meek.

Beside you he lay and he speaks of desire and deceit.
Is it your face he sees when he lies awake;
Or does he treasure his thoughts and in his mind repeat?
Your cup only now be empty, but his life is the
    drink you shall take.

Rage be thy thirst and vengeance be thy sea
Shall the thirst of thine hands only be:
quenched when enveloped in his blood.

Release that hallow blade to render the path of thy liberty.
Pierce the heart that betrayed thy loyalty.
The sound of the carnivorous blade consuming
    his flesh sobers all your senses into intense pain.
Behold thy once true love now lay slain.
—*Barry Hastings*

Weeping Willow

Weeping valley;
sad and true;
once was happy; just like you;
peaceful slumber now disturbed;
all the wonder so unheard;

What's the secret;
how's it told;
what lurking spell does the sea hold;
all so new like rapids bold;
from the spirits left here to mold;

Now I know it's telling tale;
of a time not so frail;
but things may change and change real fast;
leaving gore amongst this vast;
cold bitter tears now fill this sea;
of all those there; now gone before me;
Their song of sorrow echoes from within;
from the willows weeping in the wind;
time is gone and so am I;
for now, I too shall join their cry
—*Melissa Cubilete*

Christmas Cheer

The angels are singing, the bells are ringing,
Santa is on his way.
Time for shopping, time for stopping,
To watch the children play.
Soon as the day that He was born,
The angels above will blow their horns.
It's time to rejoice, so raise your voice,
And sing a song of praise.
We'll get a tree and trim it well,
We'll deck the halls and hang the bells.
The snow will fall and a man we will build,
On Christmas morn' the socks will be filled.
Candy canes hanging on the trees,
Fires are built so we won't freeze.
Hang the mistletoe above the door,
When dinner is done you'll want some more.
Now the jolly joy will end,
No more Christmas cards to send.
The red and green is once again gone,
But may the spirit live on and on.

Merry Christmas!
—*Rosanna Nelson*

Graduation Poem

We are leaving too soon, but too late
saying goodbye and going on with our lives
making new choices and meeting new faces
welcoming people and yet still saying goodbye
having new experiences and going new places
getting rid of things and buying new
holding on and letting go
going away and coming back
remembering the fun you had
the friends you made
the places you went
and the things you did
all while you're thinking, dreaming, and wondering
what the world will hold
without yet experiencing it
but having heard stories of how it was
but now how it is
it's a time to meet your dreams head on
to see if you will survive.
—*Jennifer Griewahn*

Reflections

Looking back I see myself as a child,
Scared all the time, never feeling mild.
Why can't they love me just the way I am?
I could never prove myself, so I always ran.
Looking back I see myself as a teen,
Never doing anything right, never feeling keen.
I'm as perfect as I can be! Can't they love me just for me?
Looking back I see myself as a young adult,
Being told all the time that everything was my fault.
Why can't they see that I'm trying as hard as I can?
And again, I ran. I ran to drugs and alcohol,
All the time building a wall, building a wall to keep the hurt out.
Never letting anyone in or letting me out.
Looking back I see myself as a first time mother,
And wondering if I'll be like my mother.
Now, two marriages behind me and a mother of four,
What was it all for? So now I only look back to learn,
so that my children will also learn, that I was the way
I was because that was how I was taught and
because of that we all got caught.

   —*Deborah Seeley*

The Greatest Gift

People walking, couples talking, little children eyes aglow
See the stars bright, think of Yule night, and the manger long ago.
Christ was born there in the manger, to an unmindful world.
Little knew they on that Christmas day of the message to unfurl.
From the Christ child He was raised up as a man among men.
Ne'er forgetting that His task was to save men from their sin.
So He grew, learned, and taught us and befriended with love.
Until one day in the Jordan God's spirit touched Him as a dove.
As God was His Father rightly guided He Him
And brought Him to Calvary as an offering for sin.
Some friends closest to Him deceived Him and lied.
It was then that they scorned Him as He hung there and died.
But in all of His torment, anguish and pain.
Before He gave up the Spirit, He knew them by name.
As He cried out to the Father for the cup to pass Him by.
He asked also to forgive them who beside Him must die.
It's been two thousand years since the star o'er Bethlehem shown
but the message is everlasting and we all must make it known.
The Christ child came to save us, pre-destined from His birth,
He brings God's greatest gift to mankind on the earth.

   —*W. H. Riddleberger*

Metamorphosis II

The wafting of the autumnal breeze,
Sending golden leaves on their
journey to repose upon the mother earth.

The pungent aroma of burning wood,
The smell of pine,
The dazzling array of color,
Like a giant spray bedecks the land.

The crystalline white hoar covers the
ground to halt the struggle of living things.

The waters of our land will feel the
wrath as the transformation slowly
alters the constant flo,
And stops the movement to await a new beginning.

The denizens of the forest searching
for their long awaited rest.

Soon to arrive the quiet days,
The sunless hours,
That heralds the inevitable times
of cold and snow.

Winter has arrived.

   —*Robert C. White*

The Cancer Patient

She looks so pale on the hospital bed.
She almost looks like she's dead.
She lays there sound asleep.
No one in the other rooms utters a peep.
She's losing the battle, she's losing the fight
This whole thing seems unfair, and not quite right.
Soon we'll have to say goodbye.
Without a good reason why.
Didn't the doctors even try?
She doesn't even know she's going to die.
So goodbye Auntie, goodbye.

   —*Hayley Golab*

A Place Called Heaven

I never really knew my mother, let me tell you why
She died when I was only seven.
And went to that place. Every-body call's heaven.
Those word's are still clear to me. What my father
has said to me, she is in no more pain, has
no more fear's about leaving her love one's here.
But had tear's in her eyes. Knowing that she
was going to die, but all I wanted to know is why?

Hoping that I'd wake up soon, to see her here.
Holding me in her arms, saying wake up it's all
A dream, but I let out a big scream, knowing
how true this is, she's gone.
But I'll soon be with you again (mother)
In that place they call Heaven.

   —*Emmetta Bowmer*

The Act

Young and pretty, at age 18,
She fell in love. He was poor,
So she couldn't marry him.
Rich girls don't marry poor boys.
He soon went away to war.
Five years later,
A husband and child in her possession,
She met him again. Head in the clouds.
And deceiving herself,
She believe she could have both.
Then her dream was crushed.
By a confrontation between her husband and lover.
And she ran away, making the worst mistake of her life,
A hit and run. Her jealous husband
Blamed her lover
For what she had really done.
And a man, enraged, killed her love.

She went on with her life,
Acting as if nothing happened.
But that's all her life was, an act.

   —*Christy Loretto*

Love Does It All

Love heals your open wounds,
or it can just as easily create another.
Love can lift you high in the sky,
or it can drop you down into the deepest sea.
Love surrounds you like a warm blanket,
or it sends chills up and down your spine.
Love makes you act like a mature adult,
or it makes you laugh like a giddy child.
Love may save you from plunging to death,
or it may make a new life spring forth in you
Whatever love does, I hope it will always survive in us.

   —*Melissa Debra Kohn*

First Love

A red velvet rose
An angel's tear drop
That glistens in the sun
A touch of your hand
Your lips upon mine
A new love has begun.
—*Heather Davis*

It Doesn't Matter

Of course not, It doesn't matter if she can chatter.
She has no feeling or no meaning.
She's only five and hardly alive.
She's so ugly and unimportant.
She won't remember those evenings in
September, November, or December.
She's just the right size for us five.
She's no trouble and will not struggle,
For we are her brothers like no others.
Today she'll stay to full fill our day and
Tomorrow she'll play.
She speaks no English and will not
Finish school, so it's cool!
We're only five that come alive.
She'll never tell of our sexual drive.
Of course not!
—*M.C.L.*

Felidae Regina

How dare you touch this Royal Personage
She hissed
Fury burned in saffron eyes, nostrils flared in black nose
Which I have kissed

What role now?
First a nubian queen, then a sly coquette
Of sensuous body and kisses wet
Do I embrace or bow?

As a feathered boa, flattened she'll sprawl
Crooning throaty murmurs while toying with golden ball
Simian antics - death times nine
Mercurial, mysterious pet of mine

Languorous form curls close - slitted orbs feign sleep
Toward her jet beauty my loving fingers creep

How dare you touch this Royal Personage
She hisses
Fury burns in saffron eyes, nostrils flare in black nose
Scratches for kisses
—*Betty Brooks*

My True Love

As my heart searches for my true love
She looks like an angel from up above
When my lips touches her I think I am in heaven
I wish that we could have been
Ever heard that beauty is skin deep
Her beauty could knock me off my feet
As I look her into her eyes
Her own beauty cannot be denied
As we danced in her black dress
Her body is the only think I want to caress
She is my true love
No one
Nothing
or anybody;
can take that away from me
Except God from up above.
—*Jesus Irizarry*

Sterilized Memories

What she lacked in charisma,
she made up for in attitude.
Her love recently strangled itself from her bones.
It dangles in the back of her head
like memories without a past.
And their last scornful conversation.
The one she re-words over coffee every morning.
Each morning it becomes a little more his fault.
And each morning she weeps to keep his ghost
as vivid as possible.
After bathing in her third cup,
the caffeine stands on it's own
and boldly comes out with it's own interpretation.
Her tears mix with last nights make-up
and paste a cherokee's war paint across her cheeks.
She fights not to save her land,
but her love.
But, even the true-of-hearts
were trampled by the asshole.
—*Brandon D. Christopher*

She

She wanders the streets. She knows not where.
She sleeps with the city. She doesn't care.
She calls herself Amy. It's not her real name.
She plays with the people. Her own special game.
She runs from the law. The law runs faster.
She's now behind bars. Her life a disaster.
She still plays her game. She still never wins.
Herself? A candle. Out in the wind.
Detached from the world. Dead inside.
A game of life or death, and nowhere to hide.
Thoughts of suicide roam through her head.
She runs from the world, tries to get ahead.
Terrorized by fear. Scarred from pain.
She makes her decision. Her decision is...
Bang!!!
—*Lisa M. Barnes*

Wings

A spot of sunshine a summer breeze
She slipped into life with the greatest of ease

A rainbows promise, a star shining bright
Delivered to me under God's guiding light

Her innocent love her curious smile
is mine to hold dear for only a while

Time passed on she grew by and by
Her little wings strong, she started to fly

Her curious smile now a young ladies charm
She breaks free to fly right out of my arms

Her innocent love so precious and dear
is for someone else and not me, I fear

My hopes and my dreams, the promise of rainbows
Where have they gone? Nobody knows.

May God give you strength and your wings never tire
May love and your rainbows fulfill your desires

Fly high my child, up and away
a guardian angel by your side will stay

Through good times and bad, whatever life brings
Remember who gave you those first little wings.
—*Kellea Nunez*

"America Herself"

She holds endless promises in her small, clasped hands and
she smiles a soft, innocent smile.

"I do not mind waiting," she recites with a grin, her words
a sea of sincerity. "My dreams are many and I never loose
sight of their wealth and their prosperity."

She knows that violence, poverty and war have tried
to strip hope from her eyes. ...

Although neglected and sorely mistreated, her pride shall
always be. "I'll sing a sweet song as time goes on and wait
for change," says she.

And she prays by the sea with her face to the sun and
rocks herself to sleep. With nothing but hope nothing but
peace, though she has no supper to eat.

While financial scandals and race - wars rage on and
mankind is selfish and weak, America sighs with a tear in her
eye, yet she never ceases to believe.

And so she will wait, our tender child, who
knows only good and no fear...

Will you be so good as to recognize her? Perhaps
you can dry her life-long tears.

—*Charisa A. Smith*

Love is Ageless and Endless

He's much older, but does she care
She's not ashamed to go with him anywhere
Age is a number, love has no age
He adores her, never tries to put her in a cage
She has her freedom, demands he has none
All he wants is to be with her and have fun
Just walking, holding hands and enjoying life until the end
This can happen whether lover or friend
She sits by the phone just waiting his call
Time spent home alone is no fun at all
She gets the call, one she'll dread
There was an accident, her lover is dead
She felt as cold chill as she dropped the phone
Why did this happen, why'd he leave her alone
He promised to be there forever, now he's gone
How can she stand it, how can she go on
She looks at his picture, the smile on his face
She now knows, no one can take his place
For true love there is no end.

—*Nancy Miles*

Black Holes...

The Bermuda triangle in the Caribbean Sea—
Ships passing through there have to pay the "Fee"
Black Holes in the universe try hard to swallow the Earth
Drawing it closer to their heart...but it's still too hard!
Already weakened by sickness, war, hate...descending morale—
Our world will get weaker losing hope, love, fate...all that is dear.
   Back and forth from the Black Holes maneuvering Yet—
   How long will it go on...that's anyone's bet.
Two Black Holes in my head are following me here—
Trying hard to bring me down...close to where?
You need a lot of energy to stay strong—
Finally they still claim their victory...with the last song!
Then one's eyes are closed for Eternity long..
   The mystique of Black Holes is born within us:
   Without them we can't exist...nor go on to be Just—
   Disguised as our eyes—so nobody really knows...
   Directing one's life, until victory is theirs.
What's inside—is much stronger than the flesh;
Why this is so...is anyone's Guess.

—*Kabe Aino*

"The Waters Signs"

I look towards the waters to see what they say,

The big waves show the same anger I have while the little waves
show that I'm just one of many who needs to be loved.

So like the waves, my love and anger is all mixed up together,

And if I'd walk to the water the waves of my life would come
crashing before me,

Just like my life comes crashing before me too...these are the
signs from the waters before us.

—*Stephanie Dawn Ferrante*

Ailing Spiders

it is night now and
sick in body and mind i sit in my darkened room
staring out the window through half closed shades
across the road the street lamp shines on the pavement
   blackened by the spattering rain

out there in the cold a spider hangs from my window frame
yesterday he was sprayed with insecticide
i've watched his dying all day
a rest and then a burst of activity to escape his place
   of demise
then rest again
i reflect on the terrible sickness he must have felt this day
twenty-four hours of poison eating away his heart and mind

venturing out into the cold wet i smash him against the window
a spattering of blood and mush and relief clings to the glass

inside in the dark writing this now
i can only question and curse the lateness of someone or something
that long before this should have delivered me
peace against the window pain of my life.

—*Kip Dickie*

A Good Evening for a Bat

The sun has nearly slipped out of
sight now ......
   All of the crickets seem to be
surrounding me, whistling their songs
so merrily... and the bugs, hmm!!
Those delicious bugs are flying everywhere
here in my second growth woods where I
hang out.

Look up, look up, for it's time for
me to take to the skies once again.
Soaring high and low with the gentle
summer breezes.

Ahh, it's so much cooler now and
much, much quieter!
All the sounds of traffic, lawn mowers,
tractors, and chain saws, have all gone away.

Yes, we're especially thankful to the good
Lord above and some wise human friends.
Once again, it's a good evening for
me and my friends!

—*Garyl W. Gibson*

Underneath the Learning Tree

It was a long time ago you see.....
Since I sat under the learning tree.....
Let's see now.....I must have been two or three.....
When my mother began speaking words of wisdom to me.....
I would ask her about the birds and flowers.....
Everyday.....My mother would answer my questions for hours.....
As I travel through time these...Sweet memories come to mind...
Of songs and rhymes.....
Of prayers at bed time that were said.....
Of the right and wrong things that I must do and never do.....
Now I have children of my own.....
Angels that God has given to me on loan.....
Underneath the learning tree.....They'll be.....
Like it was with my mother.....And me.....
Because my learning began at my mother's knee.....
She was my human learning tree.....

—*Bunny McCall*

The Sun

Ladies do you see how the sun rise and
sine everyday regardless of the way
No matter how often the clouds appear
in the sky the sun breaks through in the blue
No matter how hot and dry it appears the
sun shines bright the next day
Among all the stars in the night, the sun
continues to give us light
Ladies regardless of day or night
Ladies regardless of clouds in your life
Ladies regardless of the way you feel
Ladies always let your light shine through
to brighten your each and everyday.

—*Beverly Smith*

One Lonely Man

One lonely star
Sitting in the nights sky of gray.
One lonely flower
Laying in a field of grass
One lonely bird
Singing its song into the night.
And one lonely man
Slipping farther and farther into the dark
Yet the star has the night
For companionship and love
The flower has the grass
On which to lay and confide in.
And the bird has his song
To fill him with joy and happiness.
Yet the man is left to wonder
Deep into his own darkness of materials
Until he is left empty.

—*Nicole S. Salemno*

The Unforgettable Sport

Basketball is a powerful sport, every
rule has to be followed. Many think
they know it all, but that is a lie, no
one knows how intensifying it is not
even I. I wrote this poem because
basketball is an important sport to
me, I look at the ball and understand
that's all I want to see. For
basketball you can't explain, for words
could never tell, basketball makes me
frustrated, laugh, smile and yell.

—*Erica Longmeier*

A New Beginning

The crashing of waves upon the boulders
sitting so precariously atop each other in the cove
at the foot of the cliffs,
pound out rhythmic rims shots,
not unlike the murmur of blood
whooshing through the chambers of a heart.
The screech of a gull rebounds against the walls
of the pillars of green canyon palisades
overlooking the sandy lagoon
echo a lonely, hungry refrain—
gnawing away at the very center of being
that is fading into the darkness of the shadows.
A gentle rain taps upon tropical leaves
in syncopation, beads in trepidation
and trickles resolutely to become one
with the steady flow of currents,
eager to seek out their beginning,
knowing that in its end
one can only star anew.

—*Christopher D. Floyd*

"The Blessing of our Granddaughter"

Blessed by the time of a child's tender face
Slowed down by the changing of our own
sudden pace
Full of growth in nature's way
A bouquet of beauty here to stay

A centerpiece of life waiting to uncover
An inspiration of love here to discover
A pedal of softness, cheeks all aglow
Your laughter makes my garden of emotions grow
You came when autumn winds were
starting to blow
And winter months would soon bring snow
A miracle of love put here on this earth
There's nothing more precious than your birth.

—*Sandra Hetrick*

Dawn

She comes silently, gracefully.
Slowly,
her significance becomes known as she dominates my sight.
She enlightens me.
She warms me.
She envelops me.

Her radiance changes the very heavens around her,
leading the blind to sight, and the lost to discovery.
Her importance becomes lost however,
for her passing becomes too swift,
leaving those she's touched
Blinded
by the brilliance she has bestowed upon them.

She leaves behind those too foolish,
those too ignorant to open their eyes to her special beauty,
and she moves on,
leaving them in her luminous wake,
bathed in her light as she continues
day after day,
working her magic, especially on me.

—*Sean Connolly*

He Is Gone

When I think of her, I remember her quick
smile and twinkling eyes.
Her warm hands holding mine.
A full lap that always had room for one more.
Always loving, always caring.
Giving and sharing.

Now I see another emotion that clouds once
twinkling eyes.
That dulls that quick smile.

   He is gone.

Desperately, missing that one person
who helped to create the rest.
Seeking only him to relieve the ache.
Waiting for the day to come to join with
him again.

For no matter how many others claim a piece of
her heart,
it will never be enough to quench the yearning
of that one true love.
The one who holds the missing piece.

One day her heart will be whole again.
   —Marianne Kuzimski

The Poetry Cycle

An orange red and yellow fire
Snapping and crackling
Strangely
Gradually disintegrating the wood
Causing the smoke to rise higher
Carrying with it pieces of paper that contain
Poetry
That will no longer be heard
Floating and flying away like a bird
As the currents of the night sweep them into the starry sky
I hear the wind sigh
As if it were saying good-bye

The verses of the poem
Will linger long in my mind
Then I'll leave them behind
So another person will find
The very same ideas
And, like silver, will be mined
Then melted into a mold
The same idea but in a different way will the story be told
   —Dylan Cook

Remembering

I remember the house and the yard
  So very many years have gone by!
Little friends there that I "always" knew
  Playing tag with in summer and fall.

How can it be that the time's gone by
  While I am still feeling just the same.
My old friends have gone on with their lives
  Do they ever remember that time?

I often think of those friends I knew
  Back when I was just a little girl.
I hope they're content in what they've done
  Because life seems quickly to go by

Where does the time go? So many years!
  It seems but a minute, maybe two
But memories remain etched in so clear
  That my mind reaches out and they're there.
   —Doris Vine

Silhouette

Faintly I hear your voice
so distant, so far away
I see your silhouette in the darkness
Clearer with every step I take

You can not see my existence
nor feel my spirit
Why fight my persistence
My voice "Oh please hear it"

When my hand brushed by your arm
I could tell you felt the sting
Am I to become real once more
With happiness and love life brings

Suddenly you turn to where my spirit stands
You can finally see my face
and barely touch my cheek with your hand
I am becoming more clear
and your lips kiss away my tears

My dream has come true
I shall not regret
No longer will you be a distant Dark Silhouette!
   —Melissa Rowland

God's Little Angel

God needed another angel
So he looked all over the earth
He spotted you, my darling
And said "why she's still pure from birth.
He sent down, a shaft of sunbeams
And a couple of moonbeams to.
Then the angels, helped you get on board
And whisked you, beyond the blue
I started to question God's will,
Why did he take you from me?
Then I heard, his voice "say mother,
Don't weep, for your baby's free,"
Because now, she's a little angel,
Free from all worldly care -
And I've sent you a lovely replacement
For the angel, I couldn't spare.
   —Mary Balvin

Barriers and Walls

It has come to my attention
so I thought I should make mention
of a sad tale I now recall...
made up of barriers and walls.

Because of poor communication
a very special relation
began to crumble and to fall.
Then came the barriers and walls.

A friendship of longstanding
was made weak by one demanding.
The pain did cast a great pall.
Then began the building of barriers and walls.

The barriers and walls grew taller
as the friendship grew ever smaller.
More slights and harsh feelings
sent the bonds of friendship reeling...

To forever hide behind the barriers and walls.
   —Carolyn West

Love On Hold

I know you'll be leaving in a little while,
So I'm hiding the pain beneath a smile.
I already know I'm going to cry
When the day comes for us to say good-bye.
I would do anything you say
If it would only make you stay.

My love for you is so strong,
Now it seems everything is going wrong.
Christmas time is coming near
And my sadness I can see very clear.
You say you're going to return
So again our love can burn.
I'll be waiting for you to come back to me,
Then our love can forever be.

—*Crystal Ledbetter*

Real or Fake

Is this real or fake, these feelings that we make.
So many things we shared, so little time leads to despair.
My feelings strong and true, so many things I want to say to you.
How you feel I want to know, so many distance dreams do flow.
When you leave I'll go on, cause of you I'm still fond.
Looking to you for more, like a sea returning to the shore.
Someday we will be together maybe, for that day I like to see
The things you said to me, helped me better to see.
The walk we took, my hand you shook.
My heart may break, but these feelings must not be fake.
Your face so pretty to me, for you and me I want to be.
I hope now you better understand, it all started with the touch of your hand.
Your smell still in my mind, there's more to this than a waste of time.
So hold me close and hug me tight, cause I will always remember this night...

—*Gerard E. Comes, Jr.*

Separation

Your hug from my dream
So real like my tears yet awake
You were so close
Gray day took you away
Our life little daughter
For how long the dreams have to last
Where is the end of our parting
Where to take a second heart from to help mine
I leave the gray day
I hide into a colorful dream
Your little hand
Wipes away my tear

—*Marzena Motylewski*

Story Problem

I was alone.
No one but me.
Traipsing this crowded earth alone.
Three people came up to see
Who I was and to judge what they saw.
Four more people came
To see if I was lonely and needed a friend.
I was surrounded by people
And if that weren't enough
The crowd doubled before my eyes!
People poking, staring, wanting to see
If I would fit their expectations.
Then, they were gone.
All except the four
Who just wanted to be my friend.

—*Candice Welty*

The Weight War

Friend, you need to lose some weight
So that you will feel just great!
Wishing it won't make it true,
Here is what you have to do.

Measure each and every bite,
Don't forget what you eat at night.
Write it down on your calorie chart,
Even what's eaten after dark.

Make healthy choices every time,
To eat junk food is a crime.
It adds to the bulges, oh what a fate!
And does mean things to your weight.

Frustrations yes, we know what they are
But winning over them makes you a star.
So exercise - walk, run, whatever,
But don't placate by eating, never, never!

Exercise, weigh, and measure,
Reduced pounds will be your treasure.
Encouragement, good health and pride
With you then will always abide.

—*June Calhoon Lamb*

Untitled

Love's and hates
People and places
Times and dates
Memories of faces.

Death and life
Wants and needs
Husband and wife
Life proceeds.

—*Leah Bergkotte*

Becky's Story

And so what seemed as a tragic loss, at that time and place, turned out to be a pleasant thought in an old man's memory. For he realized at that very instant, he had something, even for a brief time, that many men have dreamt about. Someone who really cared for him as an individual, who was amused by his peculiarities. She didn't expect him to be a dragon slayer, but was satisfied with him, a low peasant, for in her eyes, at times, he was as wise as a king and gallant as a knight. And a smile crossed his face, when he saw her in his mind. For it became strikingly clear he had been loved, therefore, like the rabbit, he knew she had made him real.

—*Jamie A. House*

Of a Morning of Quiet Reflection

Your face behind the water-beaded windowpane
refracts one thousand rounded images-
ten thousand water eyes
streaked into opacity
by a single stroke
of your careless hand.

And I'd walk barefoot over shards
of shivered glass
to touch your face again.

—*Austin R. Fairfield*

Life

Life is born and born again
the pain that a woman bears
unknown to men. When man and
woman come together as one and
unite, the love they share together
throughout the night.

A child conceived in the darkness
of the room, has nothing to support
it but its mothers womb. Nine
months of growth a beautiful baby
comes forth, bringing joy, happiness
and warmth.

A toddler learning the ways of life,
as a child learning, the good, bad,
and the right. Its youthfulness
will never die, but as a teenager
time seems to fly by.

As an adult he looks back and then realizes
how good it was way back when. Life is
born
and born again a pain a woman bears
unknown to men.

—*Marilyn Renee Freeman*

The Poet

Touch ever tender
the passing of time
As words softly written
form a beautiful rhyme
In silence the hours
to soon become late
Still endlessly searching
the need to create
Over and over
the lines are rehearsed
Surrendering gently
to each added verse
As the last thoughts are taken
a soul is left bare
And placed in the pages
the poems that he share.

—*Wayne Benefiel*

Stir Sticks Through The Heart

Like hearts on strings
The poplar leaves swing,
An arrow through each one

Like tears wept alone
Their bark and our bones
Tell tales of injustices done

Their shady firm earth
Is shown our learned worth
With defacement and urine and crud

O, tenderly heal
The beauty and feel
That love is the soul's perfect blood.

—*Julie Karen*

Pockets

Hidden, opaque shelters of darkness
enveloped in protection
unyielding to outsiders,
souls lost in pockets to all
except to those that pick them.

—*Spencer Thiel*

Bitsy

Bitsy, peering out of the shoe box.
The rat we thought we'd
never own.
Bitsy, my mother said
"We'll never have a rat
not in my house."
Bitsy, never learned how to
use the running wheel.
Used to stand on top and
roll under.
Bitsy, growing old, eating baby
food, growing sick.
Bitsy, the rat we thought we'd never own.

Not in my house.
—*Kati Vinz*

March Snow

So silently, relentlessly,
The snow falls all around;
It's duty: with beauty
To cover the muddy ground,
Where lately, sedately,
The tiny buds were peeping;
Now green, unseen,
They'll get their "beauty-sleeping".

In springtime, it's "sing-time",
The snow will not last long:
It blows - it glows -
Cheered by a cardinal's song.
Spring snow, we know,
Will stay a little while,
Then softly, and gently,
God brings us April's smile.
—*Elizabeth B. Loth*

Daydream

The wind sang me a song,
the sound was strange ... but softly,
from times forgotten, oh - so long,
when I lived in a time so proudly.
I could feel the fire in my blood.
of wild and untamed passion,
my body moved to the soundwave flood,
in a light, mysterious fashion.
My feet never touched the ground -
my hair flew long and wild ...
as I whirled around and around,
for a moment, I was a gypsy child!
—*Anja P. Weilandt*

Although You've Seen Me

Although you've seen me grow,
the time is going fast,
I soon will be a grown up,
and on and on after that.
Although you've seen me now,
I'm not the same as then,
I soon will be in college,
and then, a job I'll get.
Although you've seen my future,
it may not be that way,
it could be slightly different,
or the same in many ways.
Although you've seen my life
I'm different through and through
I've changed in many ways
and maybe so have you.
—*Kristen Engstrom*

Lonely Love

The wind is blowing
The spirits are high
Off in the distance a
chilly sad cry

Love left alone
a wounded bruised heart
how does it end
how does it start

The music is playing
The flowers dance
A broken love
fallen romance

The waters run
The birds sing
What a way to end
a broken dream.

—*Gina Renee Patrick*

The Snow

I watch the snow fall at night
The stars they twinkle, oh so bright
The flakes they fall, fast, then slow
Trying to cover the ground you know.
The kids they hope it snows so deep
While pop he knows he'll need his sleep
When morning comes, the sun it rose
My little man yells, look mom
It snowed!!

—*Richard Sherwood*

Untitled

I remember the wind the best.
the sun going down,
under the cold-blue lake.

I remember the sound,
similar to emotions place.

Standing on the cliff,
standing rather stiff.

Looking down on the sand
on the shimmering waves.
thinking this a strange land.

Wondering then, if I could save
this image in my mind.
And with every line, I seem to.

Always was it there
things were pleasantly fair.
It was serene and quiet.
Quiet from unnatural sounds.
Not like it was in town.

—*Brigid Swenson*

Bodysurfing

Driven by waves,
The surf, my obsession.
Riding on white caps,
Foamy bubbles all around.
Pushed by the strong swell of water,
Gliding forward,
Just me and the sea.
My greatest desire,
To bodysurf free.

—*Patricia E. Szucs*

The Wilted Rose

A dying wilted rose,
The symbol of our lives,
A tiny nothing's cry for help,
Longing for what we strive.

One last petal,
Waiting to be freed,
A helpless little flower,
Showing us our greed.

A tiny, wilted rose,
Looking on towards death,
Proving God's devotion,
For our everlasting breath.

—*Maggie Henson*

Wild Roses Of May

Incense of spearmint
the taste of white wine
Red roses amidst jasmine

Blossoms of time
Velvet petals of beauty
Smoothness it's feel
Wild Roses in springtime.

Moments so real
Treasure the first bloom
Enrich her seeds with grace
Bring charm to enchantment
Wild roses of May

—*Charlotte Long*

The Changing Tides of Life

All the world around upon the sea
The tides are everflowing with time
The tides, like life itself
Comes and go; first they are
strong, and full of life,
But with "time," the tides must ebbed
And "sadly" they will disappear
in the depths of the deep blue sea
As fast as they once appeared
Life like the tides
is always in motion
everflowing, yet they are
stillful times!
As the world, itself
must circle around the sun,
and the moon, and as the three move,
they put the tides in motion.

—*Ed "Abel" Lee Collins*

The Edge

It's in my head
The voices won't slow
They won't recede
It's too fast!
I need to understand
I have to know what they try to tell me
It's useless
It drains me
Pushes me, nearer and nearer
The Edge approaches
Too tired to be afraid
Too sad to care
I understand them now
I wish I wasn't the only one
I want you to hear it too
Come with me

—*Anita Furtner*

My Pillow of Tears

Each day I think of my mother
the way she was
My best friend
in every way and everyday
We'd call on the phone
especially when we'd feel alone or
We would have fun —
But now there's NONE
Because Alzheimer's is taking over —
I LOVE MY MOM — to hear her voice
    I still rejoice!
But each night I remember
our times from the past
how time flies really fast
    a tear falls from my eye
    and I begin to cry.

—*Gloria Arreguin*

Caducity

The baubles hang in disarray,
Their former ostentation shorn,
Midst tasseled strands no longer gay,
The silver festoons now forlorn.

These once adorned a Christmas pine,
Alive with shining tinsel lace,
Now, vacant timbers, past their prime,
Devoid of needles, sans all grace.

A testament to what is life,
A candle briefly lit — sublime,
A moment filled with glorious strife,
A chance to say: "I was — in time."

—*Brian Paaul*

The Moment

The night was still.
Their hearts were racing.
They both were frightened
Of what they were facing.

He softly touches her hand.
Her heart skips a beat.
She slowly raises her head
And their eyes meet.

The world stands still.
Fate is on their side.
The search is over.
They have what they wanted to find.

A kiss opens the door
To magical places.
Loneliness and apprehension
Disappear from their faces.

The future is not important.
Tomorrow is no guarantee.
They embrace each other and life.
The moment is the only certainty.

—*Becci Smith*

Alone

Living here is like being alone,
All alone just sitting here in
the dark, thinking, thinking
about nothing just
sitting alone. All alone,
just me...
    Alone...

—*Skye Rogers*

Seasons

The sun rose brightly on their Spring
Their hearts were young and gay
Their tears and laughter echoed thru
Those glorious shining days

And then their summer did appear
Their love grew true and bright
Children came to share their love
Their world, their lives were right

Before they knew it fall had come
The children were all grown
Their hearts felt empty for a time
Still there love had never flown

But slowly winter came along
And one of them was gone
The other had their memories
Their love, their life, their song.

—*Erin Jaco*

The Dove

There's a grey sky that hangs above,
Then I saw the flying dove.

So peaceful, in gloomy skies,
Looking at me with big
black eyes.

Pleading, begging for peace,
Asking for me to release,

Hatred thoughts that darken the skies,
And fill tears within my eyes.

I let them go, the skies
turned blue.
The dove smiled at me, then
it flew.

—*Rachael Keeton*

Mornings

We awake at the rooster's crow,
Then we know it's time to go.
Bacon and eggs what a healthy treat,
That is all we have to eat.
First we see the morning stars,
Sometimes we can see Mars.
On Sunday's it is cool,
But we praise God for his rule.
Souls are rising as we speak,
So the dead won't make a peep,
Soul Asylum sings a song,
Rock and roll is almost gone.
Elvis Presley is now dead,
He lays sleeping in his bed.
Supper's ready time to eat,
Beans, wheat, and lots of meat.
Now it's time to go to bed,
Stars are falling over head.
Then we wake and start all over again,

—*Rachel Smally*

Love

Through all the love we shared,
Ending in a bitter way,
Still I will always love you,
More and more each day.
Even though I talk of you in a
Bad way deep inside my heart.
There my love will stay.

—*Tricia Welke*

Born Free

Nobody
  Anybody
    Somebody
      You choose
        —Scott Biggs

Dad's

Dad's are supposed to be forever
then why did he have to go
please God answer my prayer
cause the answer I just don't know.

The lights went out
and the sun went down
as I sat thinking about
how close we were bound.

I had loved my father
and he had loved me
but now things can't go back
to the way they used to be.

What's wrong with me
I must be very bad
how could this be
I've lost my Dad?

I'll love him forever
please help him see
so we can be together
from a daughter to her Daddy!
        —Jenni Fields

If Ever...

Your love means more to me
  then you could ever see.
Like what the sun
  means to a rose.
What if the flower was to close?
Like if it were to droop
  towards the ground -
The sun would just sit
  there and frown
The days would be so dark,
What would happen
  to the birds in the park?
You would sit
  and wonder why?
What happen
  there you sit and cry!
For one silence from the heart.
Will sit and make the ocean depart!
      —Barbie Denney

In His Eyes

His eyes sparkle and shine,
  There as clear as glass,
When he smiles at me I see the twinkle
  in his eyes,
The look in his eyes show he is
  sensitive, caring, and wise,
The look in his eyes could say
  a thousand words,
you feel the warmth of his look,
  you feel a tingle in your body
like you were hit by lightning,
  The power is in his eyes
and one look is all you need,
  to tell you he's yours!
    —Brandy Tromblee

Dream Maze

  It's dark.

There are walls everywhere.
They are black and cold.
I am naked.
I am scared.
"Someone please help me!"

  They eyes.

I can feel them staring at me,
Glaring at the fear in my eyes.
I can hear a demonic laugh.

  I cry.
  I scream.

I walk close to the walls.
"Please help me."
The ground is hard and cold.
It feels like ice beneath my feet.

Footsteps. "Who's there?"
"Will you help me?"

Silence. Darkness. Pain.

  Nothing...
    —Andrea Charpentier

Autumn Leaves

When I see the autumn leaves
  they are like my own heart's sheath.
Where tears are kept
  or some are wept
    depending on the breeze.
The different breezes of my life
  of love or pain, joy or strife.
That forever blows
  through my soul
    some cutting like a knife.
And like the many colored leaves
  on their different kind of trees.
They're torn apart
  just like my heart
    to drift on an autumn breeze.
But when spring comes, in the end;
  new green leaves will grow again.
    so will the scars
      upon my heart
        to blow on the summers wind.
    —Sherron Jones

Ghosts In The Closet

They have no preference.
They come in day's hours or in the
darkness of the night.
Like silken wisps of memory,
they weave their way into a kiss
or recall a moment by touch.

A voice is heard in a crowded room
and I am transfixed back,
like yesterday,
to that moment and feeling.

Sometimes it is loving and warm,
other times it is cruel and relentless.
These ghosts in the closet remain to
haunt and reprimand,
to caress and remember,
like icy fingers from the past,
they close over my trembling soul.
    —Debra P. Chadwick

Grandparents

Grandparents are everything;
  They listen to anything.
They go to the limit for you
And buy over the limit for you.
  All you have to do is ask,
  And they'll be there for you.
Grandparents are a great part of life.
  If you take them for granted,
  You'll miss them forever.
I admit, as I grew older I realized
That I took my grandparents for granted
  When I was younger.
I'll regret that the rest of my life.
So don't make the same mistake I did,
  Or you'll regret it forever.
    —Kristen Blackwell

Tomorrow

People always say
They'll do it the right way
tomorrow.
But what if
tomorrow never comes?
Will we reflect
on the mishap
on the day before
tomorrow?
Someday people will
do it the right way
and not have to think
about tomorrow?
But when?
Tomorrow?
    —Holly Savage

Dreams

Dreams...
  They're funny - no, curious rascals.
They wander into our minds
  painting pictures of many things...
Pictures of our fears,
  our goals, our fantasies.

But without dreams,
  how would we —
Overcome our fears,
  reach for our goals,
  and escape into our fantasies!
Hmmm....
    —Machel Murray

"Are You Ready"

Time is running out
This is a fact
I have no doubt.

Jesus said He would come again
September 1994 may very well
be the end.

"Are you ready"
Now is the time to get salvation
There is no hope for a sinful nation.

Turn away from your evil ways
May God have mercy on you
In His glorious coming days.
    —Annette Asrade

Goodbye

Goodbye always seems the hardest
thing to say,
You're my friend and I'd like to
see you stay.
Though our time together has not
lasted very long,
I'd like to take this time to say
thanks before you're gone.

The moments that we shared are
forever in my mind,
Maybe to be relived in another place
and time.
If only you could know the lasting
impression you've made,
The kind that gets you through a
lifetime and will never fade.

Now the time has come to see you
on you way,
My joy and happiness be with you
each and everyday.

—Amanda Howard

Tears of Pain

Tears of pain fall from my eyes,
thinking of when we said our goodbyes.
Tears of pain sting real bad,
they make me feel very sad.
Tears of pain sting my face,
thinking of how we went to first base.
Tears of pain filled with sorrow,
doesn't bring signs of a good tomorrow.
Tears of pain sting my heart,
they don't tell me when they will start.
Tears of pain fall from my eyes,
making me think of all your lies.

—Sara Shank

Waterspout

Gargoyle endure
though zephyrs taunt
your steadfast wings
and cloudbursts chafe
your seasoned scowl

Hold fast
as ravens flit
amid your horns
and tease with tales
of better lands

Persevere, in the ebbing tides
of the villainous hours
and through the unrestful din
of the moons silver songs

For I say to you
old marble friend
they but covet
in this place you dwell

So high above the peopled streets
So near the haunt of angels

—Craig Braginsky

Those Precious Feet

I hear that they are killing
Thousands of us each day.
No one will ever have the chance
To see me run and play.

Some say that it's not murder
But I tried so hard to live,
Although I'm very tiny
I've got lots of love to give.

A heart to love
Eyes to see
Ears to hear
They took from me.

I deserved a chance
I am so sweet
I'll run through heaven
On precious feet.

—Doris Johnson

"The One"

Who's the one who loves us still
through all we've said and done -
accepts our faults and loves us dear.
Who is this special one? —

The one we turn to when nobody
cares, when life seems such a mess —
Who hears our prayers, keeps our
dreams, forgives when we confess —

The one who knows our joys and pain,
shares smiles and cries our tears —
Fills the heart with hope and faith,
giving strength throughout the years —

Who's the one who never leaves,
Who loves us as He see's us —
Our closest friend who loves through us,
this special one is Jesus —

—Thomas L. Massey

See Me

Listen for my whispers,
Through my heart,
Listen for angers,
When we are apart,
Listen for my sorrows,
From the tears in my eyes,
Look for my frustration,
Through my undying whys,
Look for my truth,
When the light shines upon the sea,
Look for my friendship,
When you see me.

—Katherine Ann O'Neil

AIDS

A moment
A second
A day
A year

In the end
There is no end
Just the moment
That we fear.

—Robert Harvey

Hear A Heart Beat

Over trees we see the sun rise.
Through the clouds we feel the warmth.
We hear a heart beat,
We hear a heart beat.
In the wind we hear the laughter.
In the rain we see the tears.
We hear a heart beat
We hear a heart beat,
In the night we touch the moon beams.
Through the stars we see the Gods.
We hear a heart beat,
Yes we hear a heart beat.
Through the walls, an angel's cry.
See the tears in the rainfall.

—Paden Voget

Untitled

As the fresh cool water flows
through the rocky cove I see
my breath turn into a smoky
cloud of mist it lasts only a
few seconds than it starts to disappear
into the cold white winter
Scenery and now my winter
touches the air
again and again it happens

And now,
I walk alone through the
cold white scenery.

—Stacy Lord

Ages A Man

We climb so fast at times
through years and years
of youthful run
and hurry up
With rocky wobbling jarring
gaining strides,
and chary starry leaps
to grasp a seemly age...
Exhausting all exuberance
along the way.
We're here, we say;
Arrived and gazing in the mirror
of expectancy. Anticipation
past, we look for it
beyond, we hope,
the face reflected now
Atop the mountain looming
off onto another.
Laughter haunts
us only from below.

—Bernard Hunwick

Helpful Advice

Walk before you run
Crawl before you walk

Work before you rest
Think before you talk

Look before you blink
Suffer before you cry

Pray before you rest
Live before you die

—Shanton X. Russell

Time

Once again...
Time has raced passed you
Ending a day to start all over again.
Once it's begun
You race with the Sun
The Clock of the Universe
Sinking when its deed is done.
The moon then appears
For only a short Time
With its glow
Provided by the Sun's Shine.
As the Moon sinks
Fading out of sight
The Sun rises
Diminishing the night.
With the Sun
Arrives another day
Leaving you older
With more of your Life
Passed away...

—*Mike Sfiropoulos*

I Like Spring

Spring is my favorite season.
Time to frolic under the trees,
Watch the birds build nests, and
Listen to mating songs.

Spring is baseball, picnics,
And daylight savings time,
Watching eagles soar
And the flowers grow.

Spring is working in the garden,
Praying for timely rain showers.
Wondering how the little seeds
Know to become watermelons.

Spring is when nature is busy.
The earth begins to recreate
Beneath the warm sun
And mild rain showers.

Spring is like genesis.
Nature in new green dress
Spreading hope for the new year;
Beautiful scenes of God's Spring.

—*Nita Sue Gentry*

To Be

A friend for all as I walk
Time to listen as they talk
For we must share each
     others love
A smile, a kiss, a little hug
Can do more than any drug
Give some time to being kind
It may help to clear a mind.

—*Jean Steeves Williams*

Living

To Love without expectation.
To Give without exception.
An Open Hand through which
All caring flows.
An Open Heart, selfless and sharing.
A Spirit that gives a healing peace.
This Miracle of light that brightens
another's soul - a gift beyond price.

—*Terry Postins*

God And Me

Often I have sat and pondered
Times my mind would up and wander
Questioning uncomprehending
Of God's love so unending
Though He has a world to tend
He answers all the prayers I send
Sometimes the answer may be "no"
But still His love remains to show
My life is heavy with trials I bear
But God takes on the bigger share
He gives to me the strength I need
And ends my troubles with great speed
And when I lay my weary head
Upon the pillow on my bed
I know that I will have no fear
For His unending love is near
Often I have sat and pondered
Times my mind would up and wander
With so much else for Him to see
Why does God bother with me?

—*Lisa B. Klassen*

A Golden Giving

A golden maple leaf clings
to a gnarled sepia bough.
  Twisting and twirling
in the frigid winter wind
  it cleaves tenaciously
to its source of life.

  Until the day when,
  in final acceptance,
it lets go and flutters
  joyously to the ground
  to mingle its essence
with the rich loamy earth
and become one with the
Nature that created it.

—*Terry Burr*

Yours

Wouldn't it be wonderful just to know —
To be able to comprehend —
Just how far does friendship go,
Really, what's a Friend?

It's one that's with you all the time,
One on whom you can depend
To help you with that fearful climb.
Really, that's a Friend.

When others turn away, she's there,
Always with you 'til the end;
A person who's without compare,
Really, that's a Friend.

Well, by now I guess you know,
There's just one thing that I intend —
In all my ways I want to show
That really, I'm your Friend.

—*Kathleen O'Hara Simpson*

Stillness

The stillness cries out
to be heard
above the echoes of a soul
dying in order to escape
the torment of wounds,
self inflicted
by errors of the past,
leaving the chamber within,
hollow - void - without form,
for the light once had
is now gone;
only darkness prevails,
cold - damp - lonely,
the stillness echoing
only silence.
Perhaps only death
brings the peace
once sought.

—*Benny G. Smith*

Free To Be "Me"

I'm trying so hard
To be the person I need to be.
I'm trying so hard
To be me and only me.
So many times I try,
To be a person I'm not.
Knowing inside...
One day I'll get caught.
Why can't I be
Me and only me.
Why don't I see
What others see in me.
I see my failures,
Imperfections and faults.
That's someone I'm not.
But, I'm only human
As anyone can see
So instead of being someone I'm not,
I'll try to be me,

—*Emily Clark*

Opportunity

You have the opportunity in life
     to become life
You are given this from the start,
But every opportunity must come
Straight from the heart
Whether from yourself or another
being, for opportunity to work
You really must know the meaning
It can be taken away
As quickly as given
I know from first hand
Opportunity is driven; inside your soul
     to become what may
Opportunity was given to me
     this very day

—*Brynda McGary*

Empty Nest

There comes a time when children
     must all fly out the door.
Some fly away like eagles
     as mothers watch them soar.
Some leave with ruffled feathers
     beginning their life's quest.
While mothers are left behind
     in their empty nest.

—*Sharon Newman*

I Need a Man

I need a man to hold me tight,
to comfort and love me,
all through the night.

To lie beside me in my bed,
to wipe the tears,
that roll down my head.

I need a man to hold me tight,
to open my eyes,
to show me the light.

To help me down this bumpy road,
to pull me over,
and carry the load.

I need a man to hold me tight,
to comfort and love me,
all through the night.

—*Cathi Lynne Rudd*

No Chance In Life

He was too tiny and fragile,
To fight the powerful knife.
A perfect baby boy,
A perfect little life.

He'll never touch his mother's hand,
Or kiss her on the cheek.
No one will see his little smile,
So innocent, loving, and meek.

No pockets will ever hold,
The treasures of his day.
No grubby little hands,
Will fold at night to pray.

No one will know this little boy,
Or the wonders he might have done.
Just because of a terrible war,
He never could have won.

—*Ann Swerczek*

Love

Is it possible
To find a true love
That is gentle and patient
And soars like a dove?

Is it possible
To find a true love
That bears all things
From heaven above?

It is not easy
To find a perfect, thornless rose.
For where you find the word perfect,
You know a thorn grows.

—*Misty Gemza*

Solitude

Serenity's sweet messenger smiling
Offers a long wasted hour-
Leave the miserable world gone sour.
It's timeless space of wonder beguiling,
Tranquil moments left to thought,
Unmeasured moments flitter away,
Desert the world and waste the day!
Eternity stolen - time unbought.

—*Sarah Horger*

Giving

It warms my heart and soul
    To help others reach a goal
There are people everywhere
    Who need kind folks to love and care

Some have eyes that cannot see
    Others have a worn out knee
One needs a steady kind of nerve
    When asked if you can help and serve

It's then that faces really shine
    When all you need to be is kind
So when you think the going's rough
    Just ask the Lord to make you tough

—*Ione L. Wallis*

Untitled

The heart opens up
to let in another,
there are only two
roads to take.
One may lead to
heartbreak,
The other to heaven;
love.
When the heart is
broken, it opens up
only to release its tears.
But, when the heart
is full of love,
it opens up
just to take in more.
If the heart takes
neither of these roads;
it may never
open up at all.

—*Deena Kern*

Untitled

God says when no one wants
to listen to your hearts greatest care
to tell Him He's there.
He's quick to love and slow to judge
if we confess our sins to Him.

When others blame us, He will claim
us and pull you to His side,
where underneath his sheltering wings
we can always hide.

He doesn't pry he doesn't probe
he's an ever patient God.
Slow to anger, pure as a dove.

He's has unchanging, undying love.

—*Joyce Bair*

Friends Are Forever

Trees die
Boy friends say good bye
But friends are forever
New friends arrive
And jewelry loses it's shine
But friends are forever
Clothes wear out
Or we move apart
But friends are forever

—*Liana McKee*

To Gallup

Gallup is a wonderful city,
To live or to stay on.
Not too big or too small,
Even the Almighty says so.

With special beautiful people,
of different tones,
As white, black, yellow or bronze,
Depending on the origin we are from.

To continue the tradition
Of hospitality in the West,
With generosity as a mission
In the United States, it's the best.

Where everybody works for one,
And one works for all
With excellent summers,
And winters too cold.

Beautiful historical places,
You are welcome here,
Visit our Model City
Through the famous 66

—*Guillermo Corral Aguirre*

My Dream Boy

He's mine to look at
To look and stare
He's mine to dream about
To dream and wonder
He's mine to smile at
Smile wide and proud
For He is my one
My one and only
My joy and happiness
My sorrow and fears
I see him in my laughter,
And I see him in my tears
I see him in my smile
And I see him in my frown
I see his arms wrapped around me
And I see his lips against mine
But then I wake up
And he is gone
For it is just a dream
And he is my dream boy

—*Lindi Giordano*

Love

Love is having someone
to look at with love.
That you have that someone to hug
To hold hands and to talk with.
And in your heart you know there
Lot and lot of love.
You wish and pray and hope that it
won't ever go away.
But now that my mom I hate to
say that love who now passed away.
She gave me the love to give away.
And now this love I'll have always.
And will be there to give again and
again forever and ever always.

—*Clara Ann Watkins*

"Love's Not A Color"

When can people begin,
to look further than the skin.
We're just a different color,
We're no different than each other.

When will people know,
there's no place for a racist show.
That black and white are the same,
and being prejudice is just a shame.

That the color you are,
is beyond your reach by far.
It doesn't matter what color,
Cause in God's eyes you are my brother.

This is our big world together,
We'll be here almost forever.
For we need to love each other,
no matter of our color.

—*Mashea Black*

If Each Would Mind His House

If each would mind his own house
To minimize his faults
He'd have no time to criticize
With unkind verbal assaults

No man's house is so perfect that
He can point his finger thither
For when the master comes to judge
The judgement will be hither

We get so caught up with opinions
Of what other men should do
And as a spotlight, even expose them
To bring their acts in view

But who are we to judge another
Are we their keeper toward God?
Or should we strive to be examples
By deeds and by paths we trod?

God knows what each is going thru,
And decisions each has made
And doesn't need our pointing finger
To determine the debt to be paid

—*Bennie Townsend, Jr.*

Little Friend

Today I had
   to set you free
No earthly shell
   to inhibit thee

I hear your footsteps
   through rustling trees
Your voice in the
   gentle morning breeze

Your shell did age
   and cause you pain
Your soul's now free
   on a different plane

I still look
   to see you there
Though I feel your
   presence everywhere

In the end
   I'm sure you know
The love it took
   to let you go

—*Lynda L. Holland*

Children Are A Blessing:

Children are a blessing:

But today we all need to get together
To teach them a lesson.

There are so many problems today.
We need to get down on our knees
And pray.
Maybe it's not as hard as we think.

Because God work within wrinkle.
We try tell them the fact of life.
They don't want to hear that.
They just want to smoke crack.
There guns killing our children today.

But God say be calm, am on the way.

—*Kathleen Daniels*

The Time Of Life

I shall say farewell to the past,
to the sadness,
and the loneliness.
Life is a part of death,
a joyous time,
a forgiving time,
and death is a part of life,
a sad time,
a remembering time.
These two bring forth the overcoming,
the giving up of all past needs,
which seeks to change the heart.
Only the soul,
can fully comprehend,
those changes,
these new and complicated challenges.
The soul comprehends what we cannot-
the forevering of eternity.

—*Georgia Mae Cleveland*

Untitled

Follow your heart
To the soul's steady drummer
Rolling down to the sea

Dream all your dreams
Like a child's endless summer
Living as you want to be

Time the avenger
Will mark all your footsteps
Seek the truth…
And you'll be free…

Lost in confusion
And torn by illusions
Seldom are things what they seem

Groping through corridors
Cloudy impressions
Nightmares divided by dreams

Life is a maze
Should the labyrinth daze you
Seek the truth…
And you'll be free…

—*Jaane Doe*

Winds

Winds of fate
To thee may come
Perils born
On windless morn

Death to thee
Who calls me names
Therefore I shall proclaim
That mankind
Shall evermore
Wither in pain

Winds of chance
To thee did come
But thou are woe
I must say so.

Your first chance you wasted
And so you shall be basted
Why did thou do as thee did?
Your soul in torment
For thee misused
Thee only chance
Thee only heir
So I must say!

—*Suzi Switzer*

Yesterday, Today And Tomorrow

Yesterday I felt alone.
Today I have you.
Tomorrow I'll have the comfort of
   your presence again.
Yesterday I saw myself facing
   the world alone.
Today you are by my side
Tomorrow another dream will
   become reality
Yesterday I had an empty heart.
Today you fill it with love.
Tomorrow is another day our
Love for each other will grow even
   stronger.
Yesterday you invited me into
   your life.
Today I am your wife.
Tomorrow is another day
   we'll be able to say we are forever.

—*Pamela A. Henrie*

Untitled

Yesterday you were here,
today you're gone,
I still wait for you,
everyday at dawn.

My memories of you,
are loving and kind.
But, I still can't accept you're gone,
in my heart nor in my mind.

With my imagination,
you taught me how to fly.
And if you had just given me a chance
I could have touched the sky.

You taught me how to dream,
and to see things the eyes cannot see.
But the one thing I taught myself is…
"I love you, Daddy."

—*Colleen Johanna Campbell*

Elders Of Venice

Too young to die
Too old to grow up

Still walking with pride
Still falling in love

Living, each day
as though it will last
while a heartbeat away
From loves of the past

Beginning to hear
the truth in all songs

Beginning to see
we're not here for long

Beginning to feel
the oneness with all

And learning each day
to savor each breath

As we travel the road
until our next rest.
　　　　　—*John Kertisz*

The Ride

As I make the ride
Traveling stride by stride
Hearing every heart's beat
In the hot summer's heat
With water bottle near hand
As I journey throughout the land
Uphill
Downhill
Riding against the wind
Time and time again
Racing against the clock
Until encountering the gravel rock
Speed ceases to a creep
As I try to reach down deep
Pavement in sight
Preparing for the final flight
Finish line in view
Clock in review
Making one last stride
As I finish with a personal best ride
　　　　　—*Don Angel*

Understanding

Have love in your heart for others,
Treat them like they are brothers.
Help them when in need.
That is understanding.

Lift them when they are falling,
Help them in their plight.
Close your eyes to color,
They could be black or white.
That is understanding.

Make an effort on your part,
Make an effort to open your heart,
Show them you understand.
Be ready when in demand
To help wherever there is need,
And whenever you are needed.
That is understanding.

Understanding and compassion
Is a God bestowed gift.
Treasure it, and humbly feel
That you understand.
　　　　　—*Ben Rubin*

Drops of Rainbow

Drops of rainbow
Trickled fast down her face,
Darkened, storm-drenched
Thoughts pounding in their place.

Her clouded eyes,
Shadowed by stark, blue strains,
Hung low upon
Roseate and peach-like plains.

Her torrential
Life - damp sorrows hidden
Deep - pours, then ebbs,
Touching rainbows within.

The unburdened
Soul, like transparent rain,
Let the sun speak
Clearest: without restrain.
　　　　　—*Jerry King*

Beethoven's Pastorale

Flute melody light,
Trombones deep,
Thrasher machine thrashing,
Storm pounding heavily,
　but soon slumbering.
Soothing tones - gentle,
　sometimes strong.
Oh how you felt it!
Oh how you heard it!
Oh how you wrote it!
Such majesty!
And as I walk through it,
Tears of joy are my companion.
　　　　　—*Ruth M. Fischer*

Two Shades Of Autumn

As Autumn winds rush through our hands,
tunes whistle through the trees
as if spirits of unseen lands
are sifting through their leaves.

Cold the tears an angel weeps
above a darkened sky
an old and weary sun now sleeps
until the storm goes by.

And as the angel sad now goes
to distant realms unknown,
watchlights shine on all below
as rays of sun are shown.

Soon comes the darkened spirits
yea cold the wind they bring
deep in the night, listen to it
to hear the songs they sing.
　　　　　—*Marc Newcomb*

Emulation

Motionless..........eat alive.
Trapped.............not caged
No emotions.........always alone
Bringing happiness...feeling none
Filled with unspoken words,
With beauty to hard to explain
With a perfect form
Surrounded by a sweet aroma;
Behold the rose.
　　　　　—*Mary Johnson*

When I'm Near You

An ordinary day
Turns a special way
When I'm near you

The flowers seem to bloom
As if it were June
When I'm near you

The beauty of your hair
Knowing that you care
When I'm near you

My hearts on fire
Full of such desire
When I'm near you

You're the reason for living
I know that I'm winning
When I'm near you

You make my heart beat
With you my life's complete
When I'm near you
　　　　　—*Sal Schifilliti*

A Wedding Song

Two separate worlds
Two different lives
Now one.

My little boy
Your little girl
The miracle of love
The miracle of life.

They are no longer ours
They are only theirs.

We watch with smiles
We watch with tears

W say goodbye.
　　　　　—*Mitzi R. Markfield*

A Friend

My heart is broken and in
two. I'm trying to put it
back together all shiny and
new. It takes patients,
time, and care. I've tried
all day and tried many
years but who really cares
but just one friend who
tries to put it back together
again. To stop the tears and
stop the pain, through the
rain and through the snow
I'm the only one who knows
that she put love to my heart
and mended my soul, then
I'll say thank you, good-bye
then I'll go.
　　　　　—*Dasha Casiano*

Untitled

Four shadows on the pavement, dark:
two lost souls in the moonlight.

One question whispered by the trees:
which path do we take?

Two shadows overlapping, one,
Two others distant, separate.

One answer whispered in the leaves
of branches grown away.

—*Dan S. Duvall*

Kat Nip Lane

Early one morning
Uncle Nub (the tom cat) took a stroll
Down Kat Nip Lane.
After smelling a few whiffs
He did not act the same!

He rubbed his head, his feet
And his nose,
Kept rubbing and smelling
Just like I would a rose.

Soon he began rolling
Over and over
And finally up he came
Tried to mate his sister
What a dirty shame!

So after a long hunt at night
He returns daily to sniff
More Kat Nip
Giving him courage
So he can win the fight!

—*Jessie Taylor*

Sunlight and Moondark

Night buried sea in mind's dark.
Unseen wave murmur. Arc of light
From the cottage. TV ball game.
New moon's time. Who can answer
Diogenes? Victor? Victim?
I can't, but my minds' images
War. Day's flaunted focus,
And the moon's painted finger
Points to Dostoyevsky's underground
Bureaucrat and the rattling sword
Of the general.

Or the shadow
Of soldier on philosopher.
We crawl then walk to war, to heaven
Of victories, sagas, newspapers,
Aware of walking, crawling,
To the dark moon's time.

—*Bill Carr*

Flowers Are Free

Flowers are free
Birds are free
Trees are free
And sky is free,

Water is free
Souls are free
You are free
Everyone except me!

—*Roy Rajacic*

"Since I Found You"

I never knew such joy and peace,
until the day I found you;
And now I have enough of both,
to last my whole life through.

As long as I am in touch with you,
throughout each passing day;
or if I become confused or lost,
you will help me find my way.

And when sadness fills my heart,
as happens now and then,
your always there to lean on,
and give me joy again.

I wish everyone,
could have the peace I do.
And all the joy and love
I have had,
Since I found you.....

—*Rhonda Burrows*

(Written for John Corcoran, upon the
untimely death of his brother.)

Yesterday I saw my father cry,
a thing I had never thought to see.
I stared amazed, that he did not try
to stem the flow of tears from a well
I had long thought must be dry.

Those tears had lain there
all these years, unused, unshed,
and glimpsed only in laughter when
others joined the mirth and fun.
Oh, I am glad that I was there

to see him weep, unashamed and sad,
for he had had a sorrow only a father
can have, he had lost a first born son.
Though I am a son and was a brother
it was to him, now gone, he gave his tears.

Who knows what lies within a guarded heart
Until time deals a sudden blow to break
the seal. Should I not outlive him
and fate choose to send me on before. .
let there be tears held back for me.

—*John Stuart MacBryde*

Sunflowers

Slightly waving in the wind, not
Up and down,
North or south, but
Flowing
Left and right-
Over and under bugs
With colors of
Emerald, golden tan, and
Really shocking yellow - they keep
Swaying in the wind...
     softly.

—*Jennifer Wellington*

Tepee Ring

A circle of stones
Upon the mesa
Tell their story
Of ancient Indians
Setting up their tepee
Within this ring of stones,
So they could sit
Atop the hill
And watch for buffalo.

—*Alice E. Jacobson*

One

"Loneliness is one—where there
   used to be two..."
It echoed through my mind
as I retraced tracks in sand
on a quiet beach at sunset.
Visions danced before me
in the gently pulsing waves;
two silhouettes in the sun,
hand in hand, love in love.
Tide went out as all tides do
and left an empty beach
erasing tracks and you and I
tonight there's only me.
Against a backdrop of ocean foam
silhouetted in setting sun
two shadows blurring into one
is a lonely thing to see.

—*Anne Dubina*

A Halloween Night

A cold dark halloween night,
Very little light and lots of fright.

I was a skeleton with many bones,
My friend was the ghost of Mr. Jones.

I saw shaving cream and eggs,
Many bloody cut-off-legs.

I saw ghouls and ghosts galore,
The dark night was filled with gore.

I got a lot of real good candy,
But most I got from my friend Randy.

Randy's house looked really haunted,
But of course I was undaunted.

This Halloween was real scary,
Even though we were really wary.

—*Adam Schlesinger*

Poverty

They are surrounded, no way out -
voices crying, sadness mounts.

Tiny children lay about -
no one cares enough to shout.

Weightless babies, unfed mouths -
sickened families come in crowds.

Unpaid nurses swim in doubt -
trying to save 'em with their vows.

Peoples numbering in the thousands, -
in the countries, towns, and -
everywhere from seas to land -
you'll find people who need a hand.

—*Keanna Long*

The Town Of Precious Thoughts

When winter comes my shadow sleeps.
She is like a flower shy and sweet.
When she is sleeping it takes a sail to cover her.
When she awakes she is like a puzzle.
She does everything piece by piece.
—*Susan R. Parris*

Deep Within

Inside, there is a rose,
 waiting to bloom.

Each petal represents, something I have
 to offer. Kindness, reliability, trust,
 and love are only a few.

Treat me gently,
I will open wide toward the heavens,
 and share myself unselfishly.

Nurture me,
 I will last forever.

Treat me without care and love,
 I will wither and die.

Treat me with cruelty, my thorns
 will appear, causing pain.

You have the choice. Inside there
 is a rose, waiting to
 bloom.
—*Richard T. James, Jr.*

Alone

A moment in a field
Walking along a beach
Thoughts of a different life
Just out of reach

A moment of your time
Spent within the woods
Trees hear the thoughts
Your friend actually should

A moment only a moment
Is all that you ask
To spend as you choose - alone
Like the last
—*John E. Naumann*

Untitled

Imagine that imagine me and you,
Walking down the way,
What should I do,
What should I say.
Imagine us together,
Is with our family.
The two of us forever,
I want you to see.
Imagine what we'll do,
Think of all we'll see.
Together me and you,
Forever we will be.
Imagine my undying devotion.
Think of my faithful love,
When our lives are filled with emotion,
When you look at a flying white dove.
I'll love you forever,
My devotion won't end.
I hope were together,
From now until the end.
—*Layne Rushworth*

Littoral Dreams

The tang of the ocean
 wallowed in the air
Lingering with heaviness
Setting back all other glamour.

The indestructible warmth
Within every swaying passion
 over a golden lily,
Marked by the darkness of life
To hold the beauty of light.
—*Arwen Franquez*

New Day Standard

God is gay, burn your flag
war sucks but death isn't bad
you need a brand new day
do you obey what others say
you're clothed, your baby's nude
will you rebel or fall to servitude
do you control your own mind
or just follow far behind
is your world simple and plain
tv's good, reality's lame
love and hate are two of a kind
change of heart blind lead blind
black and white don't mix
aids o.k., us makes us sick
one and one makes three
worship God, dog is me
sex is wrong, homicide's right
take a stand, fight the fight.
—*Bart Cassida*

Untitled

His smile was bright his hair
was just right. I cannot believe
what happened that night. It
all started out as one simple date
I didn't see me on top of a crate.
Why are we leaving I wish we
could stay was something I said
but he got his way. He had all
the words rehearsed in his head
relax it's okay was something he
said. He was an animal ready to
bite feasting his eyes on dinner
tonight. You wouldn't believe the
pain I was in, he didn't care he
got his win. Months have passed
since that night we don't talk but
that's alright. A one night stand
is all it was hurting young girls
is what he does.
—*Kelly Johnson*

Night And Day

Night is a sleeping tiger
Striped with stars and darkness.
Night is a philatelist
Gurgling with glee
Counting the dreams
Inside of me.
Day is a field of Queen Ann's lace
And white butterflies.
The tiger is the blazing sun.
—*Vange A. Nord*

Untitled

Wandering through
wastelands
contaminated and
drawn
Nothing there
but bleeding hands
broken toys and
aluminum cans
Riddles tangled
in the vines
matted wigs and
valentines
Looking down at
a mangled chain
a headless doll and
a remote control plane
They could be fixed
They could be mine
Just realize... it all takes time.
—*Heidi Burton*

By the Fireside

By the fireside I sit
Watching the flames dancing
And brightly changing colors
Oh! How calm and warm I feel.

Outside the winds blow
Swirling the snow, as it comes down
How very cold it is out there
What a comforting feeling to be inside.

Now! Curled up with a good book
And a hot cup of coffee
Snug and content
To be cozy and warm.

Glancing up, I watch the flames
Listen! To the crackle of the fire
I become transfixed
Into a peaceful calm, by the fireside.
—*Beverly Dobias*

The Truce

I hold a lot of bitterness
Way down deep inside
It's now beginning to surface
And I know the reason why
There comes a time and season
To forgive and forget
Though it hurts so deeply
But surely I won't regret
The ridicule must go
The criticism too
The rejection can be canned
The complaints will pass thru
From childhood I got them
And passed them on to mine
But with my God's help
This is where we draw the line!
—*Lavera A. Carmouche*

The Prominent Equal

So many times in life
   we appear to be in race,
moving with determination
   running from place to place.
But the tree stands still.

We pass the tree with deeming eyes
   and fists enclosed so tight,
We lose our place in the universe
   we forget from wrong and right.
But the tree, it stands still.

Worries begin to tear away
   at our very might,
the tree impassively peers at this
   and quivers in the sight.
Nevertheless, the tree stands still.

With little care we take what wanted
   and leave the others to blame,
the tree passionately watches this
   and lowers his head in shame.
And for a brief moment, time, stands still.

   —Barron Nimitz

One

I am one, you are me,
we are one, can't
you see?
One for me, one for
you, everyone is
together too.
If your me and I
am you, who are you,
and you, and you?
I am me, you are you
we are one together
too.
I am one and you
two.
If you get me out of
this I will buy something
for you.

   —Rachel Cannors

What Love Is Like Without You

I don't know where
   We go from here.
Sometimes I feel your
   Love so near
I say I love you
With all my heart.
I feel my words are in the
   Dark.....
Confusion runs in
   My mind,
My emotions are all
   entwined.
Unto you my sole
   is bare.
All I have with
   You I share.
All I ask you is to
   Take a part,
And help rebuild my
   Broken heart.

   —Justin L. Ware

An American Concept

In Boston harbor
We had a cup of tea
That's not much good
For you or me

They thought to make
a witches brew
To tax our people
Not a few

The colonists had
A better plan
For people in this
our favored land

To write the law
That is supreme
and see fulfilled
our fondest dream

And now the law's in jeopardy
It's not the way it used to be
The low is changed by will men
Who don't regard the great omen

   —Roderick Murray Fearn

This Day Will Come

This day will come
We learn sex
We got married
or we got divorced

This day will come
Our black hair become white
We weak
or we can not walk

This day will come
Everyone will go through it
Do not be afraid
Do not be surprised

This day will come
We face it with courage
Everyone will go through it
Do not be upset

This day will come
We treat it like our old friend
Welcome it
With happy face

   —Millie Lee

Two Hearts

Slowly
Our hands touch
Softly
Our fingers caress
Quietly
Love grows
Deeper and stronger
For a lifetime
Still longer
Two hearts beat
Together
In perfect rhythm
Two voices
Speak clearly
One language
The silent knowing
When bodies speak
No need for questions
When answers have
Been found

   —Claudia Schwan

The American Dream

To study different races,
We must open our eyes and look.
For we all are different pages,
But in the same big book.

Chapter one tells about freedom
To be what you want to be
And never let racial tension
Block the road to harmony.

Chapter two says never,
Under any circumstance
Be hateful towards another;
Give everyone a chance.

Chapter three says always
Choose character, go not by
What you see.
Be my friend,
I'll be your friend, too,
And someday we
shall all be free!

   —Kristina Marie Kolsun

Untitled

Nothing is the same
We ride on the winds of change
Those memories keep repeating
And slowly our lives become
deceiving
We close our eyes only to
open them and see nothing has
changed.

   —Jessica Rivera

Creation

The earth, the sky, the sea;
WE SEE
are filled with Godly dignity.
Earth with tones of brownish gray
brings forth manna for each day.
The sea with shades of blue and green
hold sunken treasures still unseen.
How we love to wake each morn
to see the fish, the birds, the corn;
to feel, to sing, and see the light
enfolding human life despite;
earthquakes, rain, and stormy seas
which tends to bring us to our knees.
Creation shows us fear and beauty.
It calls us to our "Tour of Duty".
Preserve with care this world God made
so future life lives unafraid.

   —Florence N. Troll

Art Deco

A bootlegger laughing
   Wearing black tie
Dancing in the headlight's beam.

A woman singing
   Holding white orchids
Swaying to the Macambo's swing.

A gangster dying
   Steps faltering
Falling snow on a sad street scene.

An actor crying
   Cameras rolling
Paying tribute to Hollywood's dream.

   —Karen D. Covey

So Near Alone

We're so far together,
we're so near alone,
today's nights we weather,
tomorrow's mornings atone.

Like soldiers bound in leather,
we raise the brutal bone,
then drop it for the feather,
we should have used the stone.

We linger on the tether,
and wait by the phone,
while our love drifts the nether,
we're so near alone.

—*Phillip Ranstrom*

Butterfly

Butterfly oh butterfly;
what a beautiful sight!
You look so pretty,
while in flight.
Red, orange, yellow,
black and brown, too!
I've seen so many other
butterflies like you.
While spring brings showers,
I see you sitting on flowers.
I don't want you to die,
because I'll cry!
So butterfly fly free!

—*Ashley Dunning*

The Inseparable Encounter

We returned from on Holiday
What a wonderful time we had.
Our minds were joined harmoniously;
Our thoughts were of each other.

We ate foreign food,
indulged in foreign drink,
Walked on foreign land,
Watched a foreign sunrise
and a foreign moon.
We loved in a foreign boudoir
and vowed to never part.

We returned from on Holiday
We put away our belongings.
I placed my valise in a corner,
anticipating another journey
to travel the road of life together.

You reached for the foreign moon
We viewed together.
My valise remains in a corner;
You made the journey without me.

—*Frances Reed Pickett*

Just A Little

Just a little bit of you across my mind
Just a little bit of hope I'd never find
Just a little smile for yesterday,
Just a little sadness you're gone today.
A lot of future for tomorrow,
Just a little bit from yesterday.
Just a little bit of love fading with time
Now, that I know you're no longer mine.

—*Theresa Ilog*

If I...

If I give a feeling away,
What do I suppose the other might say?
If it's myself I share,
How do I know the other will care?

If I give to another,
How do I know it's not a bother?
If it's trust I develop,
What's the guarantee they won't gallop?

If I want to know me,
How is it I must be?
If I want to go beyond the fear,
From where does the courage appear?

If a feeling is to be true,
And it's directed to you,
How do I know when to share it
And when to bare it?

Are feelings always to be spoken,
Or should they be saved for a token?
Where do I begin and where do I end?
Do I always have to follow a trend?

—*Sandi Brock*

"What Is The Earth"

What is the earth without beauty
What is it worth without beauty
We know the earth is dying
Because of man's needs
Because of man's greed
Because of his lying
How long will it last
Until it is past
The earth is crying for love
The earth is dying for beauty.

—*Anthony J. Galiano*

Confused

Have you ever wondered
what life is all about
and thought and thought
to figure out
where you're going
who you are
yet, you don't get very far
I guess it's better
to let things be
and let your mind
just wonder free
for I know one day
you'll come to see
Who you are
and what you'll be

—*Marti Gonzalez*

No End...

I'm walking down a path that has no end...
Is there anyway for me to get out?...
Will I live to see tomorrow?...

Misery has crept into my soul...
And all I have is one question...
Will I live to see tomorrow?...
Or will I die in the dark of the night?...
With no end?...

—*Stephanee Cassidy*

To Those Uncertain

Why frame your words within a poem?
What story would you tell?
You have your choice of poem or prose
And either works quite well.

Pretension often forces verse
To take the place of plain
Outspoken, word-by-word report
Of things, at best, mundane.

If this makes sense (I know it does)
Then take one moment more.
You have a pen - a need to write -
A special kind of store.

You merchandise a special blend,
Part talent and part art.
Con artist and magician, you
Define and move the heart.

So, sell your wares without a qualm
And try to realize,
Words weave the web of history -
You're magic in our eyes.

—*Ross Kirby*

The Other Side

Oft-times we're prone to wonder
What's on deaths other side -
And often too, we ponder
the promise it provides

But God our Father warns us
we cannot be His own -
Unless we make the right choice
yet the choice is ours alone

We could take the easy route
the one that's broad and wide -
Or seek the straight and narrow
and see the other side.

—*Elizabeth Benner Swineford*

Sunset

Now is the time of the setting sun
When all good things start to come
And earth, wind, fire and water
Prepare the atoms for a cosmic alter.
So, wish ye well, you cosmic dreamer
For all your dreams come with streamers
Flashing wealth on your atoms
Making physical, dreams with fathom.
So, dream you dreamer
And wish you wisher
For dreams and wishes do come true.

—*Dick Garcia*

Make It

When I walked away from intensive care
When all I had to do was heal
When alone in my living room I sneezed
And had to hold my breath and chest
And feel the pain of living
When finally I could take a walk
And wonder if I'd make it home
Before my legs burnt up in pain
And finally had worn down my shoes
I knew that I would make it

—*Alvin Hadad*

How Can the World Be So Cold

How can the world be so cold?
When all you have can never unfold.
You try to be bold, but it never lasts.

Too many days go by too fast.
When you're standing there all alone,
no one to talk to no one to hold.

When you're standing there all alone
no one who cares no one who shares.
You try to be bold but it never holds.

How can the world be so cold?

—*Nina Ashley Sarlo*

Seasons Of Love

Think of me in the springtime
when flowers are in bloom,
And Mother Nature has released
her sweet scented perfume.

Dream of me in Summer
as larks in the meadow sing,
One day I hope to wear
your wedding ring.

Long for me in Autumn
as leaves begin to fall,
For your love and you
I would give my all.

Marry me in Winter
as snow graces the ground,
My steadfast love for you
will always be around.

—*Bonnie L. Goodwin*

"Indianarchy"

Why should I trust a white mans soul,
When he has destroyed the sacred land.
The spirits of the God's are angry and
full of sadness.

I used to fly, gliding thru the skies,
to the highest mountain but now there's
a line that divides me and my country.

I live in shame, I live in fear, I cry
rivers of tears, and there ain't no one
to blame.
Indianarchy, Indianarchy...

—*Rudy Acosta*

Christmas Cookies

Christmas cookies and thoughts of love
when I'm baking the above.

Here is one to make a star
bright for Wisemen from afar.

A wreath—I'll decorate in green
brings pictures of the manger scene.

A christmas tree—all white with snow
lovely memories of long ago.

An angel in her gown of white
like one who did appear that night.

A lamb, a shepherd with his rod
as one who is The Son of God.

All these I make and bake with care
and pray the world His love to share.

—*Joan G. Sutula*

You

You're a clown who makes a child laugh
When he is sad;
A rainbow that comes peeping out
When weather is bad.

You would sacrifice your wants
To fulfill another's needs,
With the hope of making their day
The best it could possibly be.

You're like a shining star at night
That glows so radiantly,
To lead some poor lost wanderer
To his safe destiny.

You've always given so much more
Than your allotted share;
You're honest, sincere, and loyal;
And you are always there.

To me, you've been a magician
Right from the start;
Your actions were the magic that
Transformed my heart.

—*Martha Estes*

Sign of the Times

What does the Nonconformist do
    when his views become the norm?

Does he rebel for rebel's sake
    and take any different form?

Does he Once Upon a Dream awake,
    and become reborn?

Or does he a grain of salt take
    as he watches Conformists Nonconform?

—*Jerome Pionk*

Reflections of Yesteryear

What did I see yesterday
When I looked into my mirror
A face lined with age
Eyes looking back with fear

Sagging jowls and baggy eyes
Somehow they just don't fit
The girl I still hold inside
Can't be more than twenty six

Why yesterday I was just a child
With things to do, places to see
Full of ideas, large and small
So many things yet to be

Daydreams galore in my head
Fantasies lived out in my mind
Kept from play my biggest dread
Believing forever was plenty of time

But my yesterdays have become today
And today will soon be tomorrow
And tomorrow will again be yesterday
For time you can't steal or borrow

—*Ann Venters Sarks*

For All The Times, You Are Always Here

For all the times
When I was down
You are always here
Picking me up and sending me
along another happy path.

For all the times
When I had tears to shed
You are always here
Ready to hold me
and give that one extra hug.

For all the times
I wanted someone to love
You are always here
Willing to give me all you have
And then some.

For all the times
When we are not together
You are always here.

—*Donna Ching*

'Mother'

You passed away
    When I was only three...
And Papa buried you
    Near an ole oak tree...

I visit you there
    From time to time...
With thoughts of you
    On my mind...

Time has passed
    But I still read...
The cards you wrote
    From your sick bed to me...

God had a need, you see
    So, he took you away
From papa and me...

Someday, he will need me too
    And my arms will hold...
My mother, dear to my soul.

—*Betty Jewell Jones*

"And The Rains Came"

And the rains came
When it rains, it pours.
No one to blame.
Rumbling black clouds open up
    And cry a million tears.
Enough to last a hundred years.
Filling rivers and shores.
Yet the great fishermen,
Still stand there.
Rain doesn't stop their great sport.
Fishermen, fishermen everywhere.
As I retort,
Rain doesn't stop them.
Fishing is their diamond in the sky.
Their everlasting precious gem.

—*Carmen J. Smith*

Retrospection

We talk about the "good old days"
When life was easy and slow
And prices weren't out of sight
And our bank accounts could grow.

We don't discuss reality,
The hardships, the depression -
When even children knew the feel
Of needs that did not lessen.

But time has always had a way
Of blurring any sadness,
And so we think those days were good,
Recalling just the gladness.

—*Dorothea Schaefer*

For Ray

There once was a time
When passions were abundant
In veils of startling colors.
We are like Gods with wings,
Commanding our happiness.
Yes-this shall be forever.

The shadow of the grim one
Has now come over me,
Whispering of sadness.
No longer timelessness can be,
For us a season is left.

When will he come for me?
Can it be in briny summer
Or in the peace of winter?
I beg - may it be in the spring.

When summer, fall and show have passed
And endless promises of life have
Permeated each and every living thing
With hopes of happiness and love.

Yes - it will be in the spring.

—*Johanna A. Reynolds*

Remember the Time

Remember the time,
When the carnival came to you're town.

Rainbow ray of lights,
Sparkling in the mid-nights, sky.

Music of every style,
Music that brings you back in time.

Remember the time,
When you won your first prize.
Remember the time,
When you rode your first ride.
Remember the time,
When you lost your cookies.

Remember the
Laughter,
The smiles,
And the tears.

Always and never forget the time,
When Tip Top Shows Inc. came to
Our home town.

—*Tracy Osthoff*

Feelings

Feelings are shattered
When the day arrives.
It never mattered
Ruining our lives.

Remembering love
And good times we had.
Now he's up above,
All I am is sad.

Love has ups and downs
This is what I see
He lifted my grounds
And now I am free.

—*Shannon Ruzanski*

An Actor

I am an actor, or am I an actor
When the inside is a maze or amazed
With ideas; these, to be understood,
Must be covered with an act.

Is it an act when,
My maze of real emotions are portrayed
Falsely, or is it a loss of true feeling
When I translate them.

Is it an act, or a cover of emotion
When they can't be expressed
Because of lack of words
To express them.

Is it wrong to act when there are
Too many words that are not words
To be used to be true. So because
I use the words that are words

I am an actor, or am I?

—*Matt Lyden*

"Love"

His eyes glisten at night
When the moon shines bright.
His heart touches mine,
When we both are combined.

I can hear his heart sing;
It makes my ears ring.
I can see him stand there,
And call me his "Dear."

When we are together,
Our minds are together.
So this must be love,
In form of a dove.

—*Michele Conlee*

Slumber Time

Who can sleep in the dark?
When their eyes are always open
Breathing heavy, not deeply
Relaxing is forbidden
Silence-nothing but silence
The numbers on the clock-glaring
Hearing one's heart pumping
The body filled with anxious blood
Pacing-quietly
Not to disturb the conscious mind
Hearing a car drive by-it's late
Time revealing luminescent numbers
Visually seeing a minute move on

—*Michael E. Frey*

In a Way of Life

How can I find a way?
When time has been captured
by the finality of substantial
aggression.
Where can I go?
When limiting factors
submerges my entity into a
piece of a part of a fragment
in contrast to the whole.
The barest essence of survival
is reinforced by destructive
means.
While simultaneously revolving
with humanity, destruction
pervades its ideals.
These ideals become a
foundation of reality
in a way of life.

—*Randall A. Heard*

Meeting Place

There is a time in all our lives
When we need the peace of God.
When perhaps the road of life
Is very hard to trod.

We may walk many different roads
In search of peace within.
And stop in a place a little while
With many we feel are kin.

And such a place, I feel, is this,
Where many a kindred meet,
To worship God in a daily walk,
With tired and dusty feet.

A place where we may come to know
The quiet waters by.
Where the shepherd of the flock
Gently makes us lie.

The Savior came to give us life
And generously He gives.
And in this blessed meeting place,
Rest assured He lives.

—*Gloria Ann Kaminsky*

Why?

Why should I believe you
When you so often lie?
You tell me things I can't accept
Don't even make a try.
Your words ring hollow in my ears.
They echo false, you know.
And when you try to make amends
Good thoughts just never flow.
So lighten up your act my friend
And get your facts real straight.
I'm not the one that you should call
For that infamous rebound date.

—*June L. Brown*

Irony

To sleep the night
Whence memories fade
As embers do turn to ash.
'Tis sad irony life.

Man the leaf struggles hard
To hold on the life yet chronos
Doth take it away.

Tis not a victory to be
won by any
Whence the reapers scythe the
Doth glean.

—*James Van Dycke*

Hell

A dark and gloomy world
Where all spirits roam,
Satan calls for you
Telling you to come home.
Where mortals can be found
And evil can be sought,
Playing with evil
For it's death you have bought.
Where satan rules all
And no one compares.
Where everyone hates
And no one cares.
Where nightmares come true
And you cannot hide,
No one you can trust
In no one you confide.

—*Dennis Barrett*

Where Do I Go From Here?

Where do I go from here?
Where do I start
After I let Jesus in my heart?
Where do I go from here?

Where do I go from here?
When Jesus died on the cross
He paid for my sin at his own cost
Where do I go from here?

Maybe one day we'll see him
And just fly away
And when I touch his beautiful face
I know I'll be in a better place
Far away from here...
Where do I go from here?

One day we will talk to him
And he'll tell us the secret of life
And as the earth's future grows dim
Ours will be happy and bright.
Then, I will no longer have to ask,
Where do I go from here?

—*Becca Coco*

Pain

Pain is felt when hit with a belt,
when someone takes away your joy,
when the image of a hero is destroyed;
when bruised in a bitter fight
and when scared by a vicious bite.

For all of these I felt pain,
but none can feel the same,
as the pain I felt from a broken heart
when a loved one tore my heart apart.

—*Norbert Velazquez*

A First Snowdrop

Winter's icy stranglehold holds sway
where garden's fertile earth has lain
the pale sun's thin luminous ray
heralds promise it will live again

The infant carried as yet unborn
stirred and moved its precious form
uplifted my spirit in the somber morn
soul to soul - a heartbeat warm

My labored step to the orchard wound
the heavens shrouded grey in mist
apple trees bare, stark in the ground
I longed for golden fruit sun-kissed

Spring dallied with her final debut
of brilliant colors and living green
my heart saw richly tapestried hue
sensed creation in a wintry scene

Delicate white bell on a slender stem
greeted me bravely through the snow
a first snowdrop adorned winter's hem
eternal spirit of rebirth aglow

—*Joanna Gilbert-Hilton*

Finding Out

Slip into that silent sleep.
Where no one can be disturbed.
Letting all your thoughts slip away,
Like that sad, sad game.
Open our mind and you will know
All the meanings of life.
For that is all we want to know!
The opening is a physical one,
Not done by the mind,
But instead, to the mind.
Then, all your problems will be gone.

—*Chris Batman*

Dear Mom

Our Christmas tree is not the place
    Where you begin your giving
That special warmth about your face
    Is a gift that's ever-living.

Your kindness touches all of us,
    Your heart is soft and glowing,
You never cease to make a fuss,
    Your love is always showing.

Your gentle-natured, caring ways
    And precious little snicker
Are sure to brighten up our days
    And make our smiles come quicker.

As quiet as your voice can be,
    Your wit is never-ending
The Vermont in you is clear to see,
    Your words are not offending.

We all enjoy the pure delight
    In your young, vivacious spirit,
And when on Christmas we unite,
    It's wondrous to be near it.

—*Kim Kelly*

Don't Follow Me

Who's to follow me
where's your parents when
they're needed
You can't realize
what you're doing
what is going through you
Who's as crazy as I
I don't want to see you die
but in the end
it's just as beautiful
as the beginning
I don't have a home
so where am I to go
why will you follow me
It's your life, it's your life
don't blame me if you fall
don't blame me if your sight fails
why would you want to be like me
unless you're afraid to be alone

—*Matthew Good*

Bakai

There are seasons
which break
the dominance
of sorrow
Seasons
which enter
silent places
and render
tears
and anger
and descriptions
of despair.

—*Dawn Bates*

Sister

On my bed the flowers wilt
While beside my mother is knelt

And my sister, dear sister
In bed she lies
My sister, dear sister, my sister
She dies

I lay here and watch them
Weeping, weeping
The feeling out of me seeping, seeping
I lay here and watch them through
my poor sister's eyes
Through cold, dark, closed eyes

And my sister, dear sister
My sister, she dies

We wait and wait and wait and wait
As our whole body aches
We wait and wait, my sister and I
We wait and we ache as we die

An only child, my sister and I
My sister, dear sister, my sister I die

—*Maisha Wester*

Magical

Dreams in the night
While doves take flight
Magic potions
Love lotions
All magical things
That this world brings
But none are worthwhile
Without your beautiful smile
And as long as I live
With the love that you give
I will always believe
There really is such a thing as
"Magic"
—*Jeffrey Marshall*

Memories Fill The Heart

Breathe in the essence of spring
While the daffodils give their praise
  Walk along the creek side
  And find some treasure bring.

Swing the grapevine high and long
  Skip rocks watch ripples flow
  Far away the bell sounds
  And plays a beckon song.

Listen to the wind rustled leaves
Vivid colors shine yellow-gold
Hear bob-white whistle for you
On a walk in cool evening breeze.

Radiant cardinal on a white velvet lawn
  Plenty of seed found there
Touched by hands with love and grace
  Now on a journey is gone.

Memories like stars at night
And rainbows color a cloudy sky
  A smile given, a promise made
We'll meet again come morning light.
—*Brenda A. McMullen*

Movement Of The Wind

Trees flaunted by the wind;
Whispering enchanted thoughts
Of pleasure adrift with me.
Roaring sounds of objects
Moving swiftly abound
To points unknown.
Sweet smell flowing with the wind,
Lifting my spirit
With fulfilling goodness.
The wind sings loud peaceful melodies,
Never missing a tune.
Power to blow strong or weak
As my heart can grow with love for one.
There is no known beginning or ending;
So, I say this is the same for my heart.
—*David E. Germany*

Thoughts

I will let young past romance that
is dead stay dead
I will remember it as beauty
I will not awaken it if I do.
I can not wonder — what might have been
Sometimes when I am lonely and sad
I will reach deep into my heart
and be warmed
By the memories of what may have been
—*Yvonne Banks Swarn*

Hear the Wind Blow

Loves sweet melody
Whispers on the wind
Of memories long ago
True loves until the end.

Songs of wishes
On shining stars
Tells my wonder
Of lives afar.

With fluid gaze
Into dreams of you
Contented you know
My love is ever true.

Loves sweet melodies
Whispers of love forever shared
On the winds
Between me and you.
—*Mary J. Howley*

The Beautiful Creature

  They come in brown, black, and
white, you can see their shadow
in the moonlit night. They have a
long straight tail, their foot steps
leave a trail. They are wild and
free, so let them be.
  Their mane blows in the wind
as they run in the sand along
the beach, the sand is the color
of a light fuzzy peach.
People train them to run around a
course, now you may no the
beautiful creature is a horse.
—*Jackie Seidel*

A Cry Of The Loon

A loon, a freckled bird,
who can always be heard,
among the warm summer days.
A voice so mild, out in the wild,
that can embrace the wilderness
as a mother does her child.
As the golden sun gently fades out
of sight,
she gathers her young and beds
down for the night.
As she gathers her young gently
under her wing.
In the still of the night,
the loon softly sings.
—*Desirae Grew*

Changes

Changes are hard
When you try
So very hard
To change,
Change
Your life around
Even when you
Think every sound
Sounds like a
Disappointment!
—*Kim Kuhlman*

Bareskin

There once was a gal with red hair
Who laid down on the skin of a bear.
  In front of the fire,
  While the flames danced higher,
With her mate, the skin she did share.

Into her eyes he did stare.
Her skin was so soft and fair.
  He didn't have to guess.
  He knew more or less,
What soon would conspire there.

A skimpy black gown she did wear,
But soon she'd be totally bare.
  She'd let down her tress.
  He'd take off her dress.
Then off with her panties he'd tear.

Linked together this pair,
Would show how they care.
  Through the night they'd caress.
  Fantasies they'd confess.
And explore a love so rare.
—*K. A. Rennquist*

"Beloved Friend"

I met a girl one summer night
Who really was quite contrite.
She welcomed me with her smile.
When all the while I felt sad.

Sad because I lost a friend.
A friend who no longer could defend -
himself from death.

She really was a heaven sent.
A precious one so innocent

As she spoke, my heart awoke.
and skipped a beat or two.
Little did she know, that as she spoke,
my hope in Him grew strong.

Strong because I trusted in Him,
to send me that beloved friend.
—*Daniel Dorado*

Leaving Me

I thought you were my friend,
Why did our friendship have to end?

You used to take away my fears,
But since you left I only have tears.

You used to make me feel free,
But since you're gone I cannot be me.

I hope you know.
I miss you so.

Why did you leave why oh why,
Why did you go, why did you die?
—*Crystal Crzyzaniak*

Vision At Springlee Lake

A brush rose green hung.
She grabbed a straw.
Pulling,
  she lay
white dress flung
towards soft woven
clouds for a day.
—*Steven Brita*

467

Why

I wonder why, I wonder why!?
Why do I put up with it?
Why do I try?
When I see them fight.
I wonder why?
When I hear them say, they hate me.
I wonder why?
When I feel them hit me.
I wonder why?
Then,
I see them smile.
I hear them say, I love you.
I feel their love.
I don't wonder anymore.
I know why!
I love them!
That is why!

—*Kathryn Ridley*

"Love's The Key"

If there's love with me
Why should I be afraid
If I'm not alone....
I live for the future
But, can I forget about the past?
No, because the past brings the future
And the future holds the past
You can only learn, not forget
That is why, love's the key
Love's the key....
The key to life, is love....
Love's the key....
That's why I'm here.....
Love's the key, to life....

—*Arlene Ackerman-McClennon*

Think Of Me

When summer ends and fall begins,
Will you still think of me.

When the world ends
and heaving begins,
Will you still think of me.

When the bright blue sky
of a Summers noon,
Turns into the night Summer's moon.
When the bottle runs dry
and the river runs high,
Will you always think of me.

When the day ends
and the night begins,
Will you still think of me.

When the sun doesn't shine
and the worlds out of line.
I will always think of you.

—*Brian Behling*

I Love You

I love you for all that
you are and all that you do
With you in my life, life
isn't all that bad
When I stroll along the
beach on a cool summer night
and watch the sun go down
I think of you and wish that
you were here to hold me and
keep me safe and warm

—*Sarah Naugle*

Twilight

In the twilight of my dreams
Wisps of dusty golden hair
Brush softly over my skin.

Where is my path back to now - -

Wistful blue eyes
Caress my soul through the haze.

Where is my path back to now —

Drifting through this realm
I yearn to remain

Dawn —
The memory stings
My soul aches
A lingering mist
Cools my brow
Here - - now —
I breath
In the morning rays.

—*Kathy A. Boever*

Halloween

Ghouls, ghosts, and goblins
Witches, mummies, and hobgoblins
The halloween monsters
are roaming about
They make humans
scream and shout
They walk around the neighborhood
yelling, "Trick or Treat"
They want to get some candy
for all of them to eat
But when they get to someone's house
maybe no one's home
Then the monsters scream and shout
and spray shaving cream and foam
Now the monsters have finished up
their long and joyous trip
Then they get out all their candy
Take a scissor and snip snip snip

—*Evan Curran*

Blessed Harvest

(For Curt Eugene Benton)

What is He growing? — Airy Allies.

Their form is unique, slender to plump
With a mutual root — Adversity.
It cultivates courage and wisdom
Plunges roots 'round dry mulch
Scores surface and bed
Gathers strength for tender growth.

Do not allude the young and tender
As delicate or feeble
Their roots are deep, united in nature
Tested by storm and gale
Taught to nurture, protect
Blessed with reason and fortitude
To survive where others have failed.

Marked for harvest
Not as a garnish, as an opening bloom
Full of light, energy, and nourishment
Ready to hail the Harvester
And spread the word for
Deep roots have much to give.

—*Patricia Saren Adams*

Gone

At dusk I set alone
With a thought of you
My one and only true love
My heart skips a beat
As it calls out to you
I can't live life
Unless life is with you
For a part of me dies with you
And my soul must wonder
Though out eternity alone
After you how can my heart
Learn to love another
And ever sore again

—*Heidi McPherson*

The Next Generation?

I see the children of today
With cold and empty stares;
Looking at the world as if to
say,
"What will you give me today:"
They are resentful.
They respect no one.
All hope is fading fast.
All I can do is close my eyes.
I'm too afraid to see the world
Without a future.

—*Michele Marie Dunagan*

God's Care

Don't he discouraged, or filled
with despair
You know God loves you
You know cares.
Put your trust in Him
In your time of need
He marks miracles
He does indeed
Miracles that happen
Are proof that he cares
They all come about
Through our faith and
our prayers.

—*Bonnie Archer*

Your Need

His little tear-stained eyes pleaded,
With each man that passed by.
Like a sign saying - "Father needed,"
Since mine had to die.

Not even a glance, they gave him.
Just some kid always in the way.
No one saw the light in his eyes dim,
Or even had a kind word to say.

My heart broke for the boy,
Who felt no urge for fun.
His need - my happiness, could destroy.
This future man - this boy - my son.

If I could but give to you my son,
The thing, I know you most need,
For all the others seem to have one.
A father for your staying reed.

But life is not that kind at best
It does not tenderly enfold you.
Just put your head on my breast,
And while I can let me hold you.

—*Elizabeth Grant*

Anticipation

Tones of fire crest the peak
  With feet in mirror lake.
Equatorial wind fluffs the cheek
  Of maiden now awake.

A man takes flight on bitter bird
  With life and light behind.
City lights and moon recede
  With the captor of his mind.

Man and girl love in flying word
  Before the final moment sweet
When witnessed words ordained by Lord
  Flee lips and then the eyes repeat.

—*LeRoy J. Binder*

Redemption

A fading world I dust
With fingers new.
It's something old
That's emerged anew,
And might it by
The melding, hand-in-hand,
Clear away that which
Obscured one last strand.

—*Jeffrey Dostal*

Really I'm Not

We have a lovely bathroom
With noodles on the wall.
There are sandwiches in the lavatory
And milk runs down the hall.
Please, sir, no straightjacket, please
My mind's not on the skids.
The plain and simple fact is
I'm the father of four kids.
Ask the mother of your children
I'm sure she understands.
Our little, messy children
Are learning to wash their hands.

—*C. G. Schnorr*

Of My Being

September rains fall upon my face
With their steely grace
To forgotten rhythms of my heart
Thunder and lightning ride
Where my love abides

My hero, this rose I hold
With no protection from the cold
My armour of petals fallen away
Winter's heart laid bare to you
Now battling to renew

Flowers race on the wind
Flame with passions fire
And swords of this season
To awaken these desperate hours
The completeness of me lies with you

Spring at last will trace
With golden light upon my face
To reflect the warmth within my heart
Where my love has burned
My knight of truth returned

—*Kimberley Dicker*

Untitled

The sun-bleached corn husks
With their tanned stems
Are a sharp contrast to the
Soft, brown earth I'm accustomed to.
But they hold a peculiar beauty
And I am drawn into the endless rows.

He is that boy in the photo,
With his corn husk hair,
Tanned skin, and brown eyes.
He is that boy who stands next
To me now, very unlike me,
Yet just the same.

—*Christine Hauschildt*

The Agony Within

I have waited for so long
  with this feeling inside,
the feeling that we belong,
  but all I would do is hide.
    Seeing your face
  with a smile of an angel
there's the feeling that I cannot erase.
  I try to reach out to you,
but something holds me back,
  believe me I try to
    get close to you.
  I wonder how it would be
if I could let my feelings free,
  telling you what is inside,
    then I know I cannot hide.
  We could do as we please
each other knowing what we need.
No one would ever tear us apart
together living in each other's heart.

—*Dominic Kowalczyk*

A Thought in the Black

It hides deep in the shadows
  Within a world all its own
  Its secrets are held secret
It's best when they're not shown
Something there behind its eyes
Touching the depths of its soul
It wants to rise to the surface
  Reality keeps it under control
  Its mystery enchants the mind
That's why it hides from the light
Its thoughts make its soul restless
  Keeps its body awake at night
Its hand reaches out never touching
Its tear a message from its heart
Its laughter but a false pretense
Holding together what's coming apart
  It yearns to seize the moment
  But never finds the time to act
  So until its words are spoken
It remains a thought in the black

—*Steve Marshall*

"Life"

"Life is a precious gift,
  Wondrous to receive,
Though those ill or lonely
  may think it to deceive,
Just because you're not quite healthy,
  or maybe just not strong,
You'll never be a person whom God
  thinks as wrong.

—*Samantha Cash*

Remember When

Remember when we would laugh
  without a care?
Remember when we could always
  find the time?

Remember when we would listen
  to each other
  and really care?

Now, it's not like that.
We can't laugh as freely
We hardly have the time
We still listen only, not as well
Remember the good times as will I.

—*Dawn Turpin*

To My Children

As I sit here thinking of you
Wondering, whether you're happy of blue
You need to know, "How dear you are"
even though you are so very far.
I hope one day you will come to say,
"Dad, we are coming, we're on the way
to tell you that we really care, and
like you, treasure the memories,
that we all share.

—*Patrick J. Michael*

My Wish

If I were a bird,
would I be able to fly?

If I were a train,
could I pass you by?

And if it wasn't for you
would I still cry?

If I had my choice,
I'd rather be a bird and
fly, or a train and pass
you by, then be the human
I am and cry.

—*Melissa Chance*

Broken Heart

If I were to die tonight
Would you remember me tomorrow
Would you feel any subtlety
Of grief, pain, or sorrow
Or would your memories of me
Slip away with a sigh
And be totally forgotten
With a few days gone by
Would the time we spent together
Be nothing but the past
A few moments in space
That went by very fast
Or would you say to your friends
That you knew me very well
And have your head held high
When you hear the church bell
As I write this poem
All the while sighing
Living without you
Is almost like dying.

—*Andrew W. Byers*

Just Tired I Guess

It sure ain't fun when ye gits ole
Yer body leaks from every hole
Ye start to bend, yer eyes are teary
and every friend is jest as weary.
Come on, step out and use the day
Git hep! Yer life will slip away.
Stow that barge and leave that bale
Git in the swim and off yer tail
Jumpin' Jacks can cure your ills
Git on yer feet and off the pills
Have some fun the air is free
Smell a flower, plant a tree
Disregard the gloom and doom
Don't let birthdays lower the boom
Yer as young as ye want to be I say
Spend every hour ye got—Today

—*Josephine Cerniglia*

Alone

I am surrounded by people
    yet I am alone
I give but I can't receive
A wall of tears like a tidal wave
    pummels me inside where I cry
Inside where I die
Inside where I die every day

I cut myself off and I hurt myself
    with thoughts I can't stop
My hands are bloody knuckles
    that drain me with need
My need to be touched unclutched
    I whither and die inside
I've been here before
I've been here before every day

—*Kris Mohandie*

Sunset

I would like to share with
you, a Lake Michigan sunset
In November, something truly
to be remembered.

It was an Indian Summer day
That lingers in your mind.
As you rounded the curve
You found orange, blue and gold.

It spoke to you so bold.
It bathed everything in it's light.
Your eyes cannot believe the
Magnificence of that sight.

It gave you such a start
That went straight to your heart.
You wanted to weep, and
Always keep that vision alive.

Your spirit knew the gift that was given,
And on a bleak and gloomy November day.
You recall that wondrous, glorious sunset.
Never growing tired, of the awe, that it
inspired.

—*I. B. Polerecky*

Untitled

And so now
You are gone,
leaving me alone
With my loving,

And my grief
Afraid
To let go
Yet in fear
Of your return,

That I
May love stronger

Only to watch
You leave again...

—*Colleen Cash*

So Many Tears

I've cried so many tears
You could fill the Dead Sea
Over a little boy,
I don't even know
If he remembers me.
Taken from those
Who loved him so
Destination still unknown
With each day
It eats away
What is still left
Of my broken heart.

I've cried so many tears
You could fill the Dead Sea
Over a little boy,
Who looks just like me.
Dear God in Heaven
Just let him know
I'm still waiting
For him to come home.

—*Wendy Kadner*

Still Far Away!

It's been a while, we're apart
You don't call, you don't care
Leaving me the way you did,
Is really sad and unfair.

I thought time would bring us back,
But I see it was all a dream...
You really don't love me,
Or never did like it seemed.

We went through so much together,
I can't believe we had to part,
But even though you're gone forever
My love is still from the heart.

You're still far away, baby,
And I know you won't come back.
After all the love I gave you,
You left me just like that.

Anyway, if you ever need me,
You know I'm always here.
Even if it's just for friendship,
You'll always have a friend near.

—*Elia Almeida*

Untitled

Beauty isn't something
You find in a book
It isn't a style
Or one certain look.
You find it inside
It's a heart made of gold
It's never selfish or greedy
Heartless or cold.
Beauty is something
You get from above
You get it from the angels,
Beauty is love.

—*Amy Palmer*

Lighthouse

Through countless emotional storms,
    You have stood like a lighthouse.
Your silent strength,
    Facing hurricane force winds.
The light of your life, is a
    Shining beacon to searchers.
Tall and majestic
    You watch as people pass.
Never letting on that you feel,
    Vulnerable and alone.
Your spotless interior and shell,
    Are a symbol to others.
The windows to your soul,
    Sparkle and make people feel whole.
The harbor of your arms,
    As always a safe home.
Thank you for standing so long
    I pray your light will shine,
Forever and beyond.

—*Jackie Smith*

Why

Why did you go with me,
You love somebody else,
Why can't you just see,
How much you mean to me?

I'm falling in love with you,
I thought you were different,
But you were just the same,
You said you were afraid,
But I guess I'm to blame.

Why did you do it,
I can't believe, I believed you,
You told me every thing,
At least I thought you did,
But now you love somebody new.

Was it all just a lie,
Did you think I wouldn't find out,
What did you think, did you think
it would get by? I don't want to

get hurt again, So tell me do you
love me, Or is this the end?

—*Brook Sica*

Love Poem

You are bright as the sun,
Your eyes are blue as the sky,
Your face is soft as snow,
Your lips are red like cherries,
You're as sweet as honey,
Won't you be my love forever.

—*Aruna Ramharrack*

Doors of Success

you knock on the doors of success,
ou might not get an answer.
ou might have to knock harder,
r even ring the door bell.
ven if you ring the door bell,
ou still might not get an answer.
ou might have to ring it again,
r even call first.
ven if you call first,
ou still might not get an answer.
ou might have to call again,
nd set up an appointment.
ven if you set up an appointment,
ou still might not get an answer.
ere's what must do,
all first, set up an appointment,
ng the door bell, knock on the door.
nd if you still don't get an answer,
ck the darn door in.

—*Royal A. Kelly*

Untitled

ook at an object
You see every day
nd admire its beauty
In a total new way.

o appreciate the perfection
You must realize the faults
nd look always beyond
Your most obvious thoughts.

o keep striving for happiness
That can be found anywhere
emember to stop, look and listen
To your world that is there.

—*Beth Garvey*

in in the Bin?

nother poetry contest, eh?
ou send it in and hope and pray
hat luck may come your way some day
ut all along you know you'll lose
hat all along it's just a ruse
ike never winning that darn cruise!
o what's the point of sending in
masterpiece like Gunga Din
hat ends up in the garbage bin?
lthough I'm not too cynical
will admit I'm skeptical
f contests that pretend to call
he grain from chaff
ut fail by half
o squelch my laugh
hen six months later
ve not heard
word.

—*Alexander T. Holmsen*

he Daffodil

h! beautiful yellow daffodil
ou've been so richly named
trumpet, so that you may proclaim
o all the world this Easter Morn
hat once again you've been reborn.
ke Christ who died upon the cross
t showed us that not all was lost
hen He too on Easter Morn
as resurrected from the grave
o that all men could now be saved.

—*Evelyn Koch*

The Poet

A poet is one who must believe,
in things that don't come naturally.
He must understand his meaning of life,
it may be his foe, it may be his wife.
He sees the beauty of the sight,
of a world found in pitch black light.
His hands may feel as cold as ice,
but you can feel the warmth of their sacrifice.

—*Tracy Cox*

Missing You

No matter how near you are
you still seem so far
The days apart make my love
grow towards you
When things happen
you're the first to know
You're a shoulder to lean on
and someone to hear
what I have to say
Please don't go
I'll miss you so.

—*Angela Hahn*

Untitled

Through so much pain
You stood all the tests
When you had nothing to gain
I thought you were best

You were always with me
And never went away
Forever you will be
Forever you will stay

No one understood
The way you always felt
They never thought you could
Deal with the things you dealt

Even though you broke
You always stayed above
For when you spoke
You showed your love

So now I thank you
For making a new start
For everything you do
Because you're my heart

—*Janese Rogers*

You Told

You told me that you loved me.
You told me that you cared.
You told me that my sorrow,
Would never, ever be there.
You told me all excuses
Of why you were never there.
And then I stopped believing,
That you even cared

They say time heals all wounds,
But it didn't help for me.
Still keeping all my sorrow,
Evolving inside me.
But soon I found someone else.
Who really cared for me.
But in the back of my mind,
I still see...
You and me.

—*Janetta Lavender*

"The Bird In The Chimney"

I heard its chirp
young, strong and full of hope.
I tried to reach it, but
It was beyond my scope.

Its chirp grew fainter
Plaintive as if at last
The little bird knew
Its die was cast.

All was silent, and I
In my solitude felt torn
That this strong little bird
So full of hope - was gone!

—*Florence Rasmussen*

"Life"

The world is still goin' round,
Your life is upside down.
Your thirst is for knowledge,
But your craving to be needed.
You and your love have a pledge,
But does he want to be freed.
Distance now exists in two ways.
One can be overcome, land,
But one is the separating of souls.
His need for you has gone,
He has left you to weep.
Now all you can hope for,
Is something in return.
But he has stolen you heart,
And left you with nothing.

—*Melinda Holt*

Untitled

I lived for you, but you not for me,
Your love, it was necessity.
Mortified when you set me free,
Love never was nor will ever be.
Your love's not even history.

I empathize with your apathy,
But you disbelieved my fidelity,
Perhaps it was misogyny,
Or towards love, your levity.

You left me with pure misery,
When most I needed ecstasy.

—*Melissa Prebeg*

Death

You killed me
with your silence
and your words

You killed me
with your love and
your sick world

What if I said
I never cared
would you dare
to look deeper within

—*Sara Lovelace*

We've All Grown Up

Now that you've gone,
your new life will start.
Your away from home,
and once again we're apart.

It seems the years,
have went by fast.
We have touched each other
through laughter and tears, in our past.

Soon this day will come for me,
and my life will have also begun.
All our memories will drift on the sea,
under the moon and the sun.

Then the littlest of us all,
will set out on his mission.
Even though this call,
has not come to his attention.
This love I carry down deep,
it does not show.
Though it I will keep,
and always shall know.

—*Rhonda L. House*

Paradox

Eyes: So piercing they trap you
        your thoughts linger here.

Soul: So frigid and afraid
        of the unknown.

Terror: In the hearts of youth
        they fall to the extreme.

The heavens, they begin to cry.

And the traps are washed away
the soul no longer afraid,
and the terror replaced with love
through the warmth of a friend.

The tears now dried
from the sun
a spirit you did find,
and as the clouds roll away
you see it was just a storm
in your mind.

—*Janie K. Dargitz*

A Poem for My Love

In my field of flowers,
Yours is the sweetest nectar.

In my treasure chest,
You are the greatest jewel.

At the end of my rainbow,
You are the pot of gold.

In a story book,
You are a fairy tale.
You are all I ever wanted.

—*Holly Michelle Taylor*

Lapsus Linguae

Your eyes watched mine in wonderment,
  With a puzzled tilt of your head.
Friend Dog, I barked with good intent,
  But now I wonder what I said?

—*Lillian Lane Hess*

Oh, Oyster

Oh, oyster of the Chesapeake Bay.
You've been it's pearl from the
  first day.

The Indians first tasted this
  gem of the bay.
Taught early settlers how to
  harvest her from the bay.

Waterman working the bay.
Battling the weather, collecting
  its treasure.
Shipping to places far away.

Years of taking and not replacing,
Disease from elsewhere arriving here.
Dying is the pearl, so precious pearl.
Oh, oyster of the Chesapeake Bay.

—*Dudley D. Fink*

God's Gift

When time get tough
You've lost your way,
Open your ears,
Listen to their laughter.

Open your eyes,
See their little smiles.
Open your heart,
Feel their undying love.
Open your arms
And give them a hug.

When times get tough
You've lost your way,
Being with a child
Will surely make your day!

—*Kendra Welsh*

Peace

At break of day
Glow of glorious sunrise;
Bursts of colorful spray
As in awe I surmise.
Surging red swirls
Transforming to a pink flood,
Then a purple deluge of curls
Delicate as a rosebud.
In distant azure sky
A lone dove flies by;
Pure white with silver wing
Does it a message bring?
Banish dissent and discord
Do not live by edge of sword;
Enjoy tranquility and peace
Bid hostile wars to cease.
Creation was meant to love
God forms the wonders above.

—*Elizabeth Paetkau Krahn*

Trapped In Walls

I bust and I bang and
I get free in a tunnel
I lay a flame near
Sacred names for the spirits will
Rise to the light in a black
Tunnel and take the flame
And guide me out till I find
An end at the tunnel and
I am free.

—*Robert Chatham*

An Ardent Wish

I wish to be a humming bird
which soars high in the sky,
and having reached that blissful still
stay suspended by azure twine
to enjoy that total bliss
And hum
forgetting even to fly,
just flutter the wings
in that soft rhythmic movement
with face upward
waiting for the nectar divine.

—*Urmila Varma*

By Water's Edge

From the depths of emotion
Drowns a bitter heart of stone
Rising waters whisper
For fear they're not alone

Tempered waves draw slowly
The glimmer blind the view
Wrestling for the rocks
For fear of parting too

Closer comes the water's spray
No sooner falls a tear
Friendly in its passing
Calmer in its clear

Stronger in its running
To reach the sands of still
Laughing past the footprints
Strangers seem to fill

Reflections of a silver cloud
Upon a bed of blue
A ripple for each day dream
Of moments spent with you.

—*Rosa Leo*

Awake

Sandman comes to work his shift
Accept the feeling it is a gift
Thoughts turn into a foggy mist
Soon the feeling it will lift

Sandman chants you into sleep
Down and down you go so deep
You can't stop when the hill is steep
The mind is now a jumbled heap

But for now your eyes will close
Dream of killing all your foes
Nothing hurts you have no woes
Now it is time for the doors to close

Dream the dreams of your past
Things you don't want yet still grasp
Pain is the only thing which will last
Pain which will never be fast

Nightmares that drill into the subconscious mind
You try to stop them before they can find
Things that will weaken and will bind
They have no remorse they are not kind

—*Kevin Marshall Rimney*

eality

irty-five thousand hand guns
day are brought to school in the
S.A.
ey don't bring the
ns to play. They bring them
blow you away.
doesn't matter what color you are
llets fly fast and far
llets don't know anyone's name.
is could be a deadly game
though it's sad it is true,
ns don't kill children
ildren do.

—Sarah Johnston

ear Mom

precious face I never knew
forgotten wind that once blew
face that I will never see.
ve you forgotten me?

mother's love I'll never know
pain within my heart that grows
u left this world without goodbye
w in the breeze I hear a sigh.

the night I call your name
t silence my answer still the same
known pleasures unknown laughter
ill break my heart forever after.

—Cheryl Dawn Hardy

orking Time

y name is clock, and I have
umber of children.
y children has one great name
eir name is time, and time
recognized by what a person does.

y children has great work,
eir work is to warn anyone on
duty, that's make them
become friends of all people
o like to work.

zy people blame my children,
giving warning to them
whatever they have to do.

rry up! Hurry up! Hurry up!
ere is time for everything,
d there is nothing easy in life,
rry up!
no won't work won't eat hurry up!
s a clock.

—J. W. Mzunga

ve

ve is pain,
ve is flowers.
lso has many powers.
an hypnotize you so
t you don't know,
w far you go,
to what limit,
til you've found
ur heart's not in it.

once again, at an unplanned time,
u say good-bye,
d then you try not to cry...

—Catherine Ridyard

Forever

I think back to a time,
A time when you were living.
I watched you go.
I saw you kill yourself;
But I never tried to stop you.
I felt for your pulse
Yet there was no beat.
It was then I knew,
Knew that you were gone.
And never coming back.
You were just testing us,
To see if we loved you.
We did, you should have known,
For death means forever my friend
And for you forever has come.

—Christen Caunce

"Lovebound"

Walking through the Magic Space
a vague mist of dust, yet bright;
looking for that Needed Face,
among rocks, sadness and light

But the Planets seem so cold,
as I approach them... I fear;
a Voice that always Truth told,
is telling me I am near

Suddenly the Shadows die...
Stars shining all around.
I know Glory does not lie;
Yes!, I'm going Lovebound!

And as the end of the Day
reaches over my Soul, I wonder...
where along the way ...
Love will strike me like Thunder!

—David Aguado

Beluga

And they tell me of a tale
about a hugh Beluga whale
that got washed up on the shore
just two miles from the store
it was a sad affair
that began and ended there
right upon the golden sand
that is peculiar to this land
the whale she up and died
and her body it got fried
by the suns relentless heat
that was really not a treat
but there was nothing we could do
to help the whale through
this torturous affair
that began and ended there

—Allan Stache Clempson

Everlasting Love

He held my hand as we walked,
We'd stop to kiss and then we'd talk.
Where we were going we didn't care,
We were together - a happy pair.
We loved in front of the fire
and we laughed there too
as he held me in his arms
he made all my dreams come true.
all we had was this night together
But in my heart it will last forever.

—Debbie R. Webb

What For?

I've had all those dreams
About love, peace, joy;
About that special guy,
Harmony, unconditional love,
My life, my future.
But what for?
I've been believing, hoping,
Praying dreaming, working on myself,
What for?
Do I have to go on and on
That maybe one day
My prayers will be heard?
Or do I have to stop right now
And know, what ever I'm doing.
It won't change anything?

—Jo-Ana Fraefel

"On Closing"

The eyes, the fist, the mouth,
An action commenced
And found in a breath,
A smile,
A trickle of a tear.
The relation of endings
And beginnings, lost opportunities
The spurn your advance,
Distorted images multiplied
In a fragmented mirror.
The eyes close,
The heart, its valves
Causing the life and feeling
The pain
Of those tears,
Of clenched fingers,
The sound of the shutting door.

—Richard Gordon Wanderman, Jr.

Reflections

I look in the mirror
and all I see is a face
full of emptiness,
broken promises,
lost hope,
and forgotten dreams.

Other people see a happy person,
Full of life
and love.
Dreams that can be attained
and a sea of hope.
I hide things well.

I want to see a face
Of hope,
Of love,
Of dreams,
Of promise
But there's no light at the end of the tunnel
And no dreams of tomorrow.
At least, not for me...

—Christi Amy

My Grandson

He's lovely and cuddly
And as bright as a bee
He loves you to cuddle him
And to sit on your knee.

He tells you he loves you
That he's your favorite boy
And then he climbs down from your knee
To play with all his toys

I often sit and look at him
For I think he's quite a treasure
And every time he visits me
It brings me so much pleasure.

I thank "God" for this precious life
Every morn I came to pray
I ask Him to take care of him
With every passing day.
I commit him to my Saviour
As before His throne I plead.
That very early in his life
His all to "God" he'll yield

—*Beth M. Climond*

Whom Shall I Love?

When at 92
And death
Has
Peeled you
From my side,
And I can no
Longer lie
With you,
my cheek
on yours
my arms
over yours,
my legs
across yours
Our hearts
as one.
Whom shall
I love
As we
Have loved?

—*Lily Spence*

Friendship

Someone who would comfort you
And ease away the pain
Or lend you their umbrella
To protect you from the rain

Someone to share your secrets
In who you can confide
No matter what the problem
They're always at your side

A person who'd watch over you
Protective to the end
Is someone very special
A loyal and faithful friend

—*Joanne Smith*

Stephen

A little boy with curly hair.
And eyes so big and blue.
Every time I look at him.
I can't believe it's true.

That he is mine.
That little guy.
So good and full of fun.
I thank the Lord.
Up in the sky.
For giving me a son.

—*Marilyn Drennan*

Loneliness

I sit and watch the many stars,
And feel my wounds grow into scars,
I hear the night its every sound,
Loneliness is what I've found.

I try and think of happy things,
And all the wonders my life brings,
But still it comes without a sound,
Loneliness is what I've found.

To touch, to feel, to see, to speak,
These things I have, but why so weak,
I have so much, I look around,
But loneliness is what I've found.

As time goes by I fill that space,
With love of self and human race,
And loneliness will no longer be,
That space I had inside of me.

—*Joanne Komoski*

Come Back

Whisky was her name
And I miss her real bad
City girl never lets go
Even though your gone
I see you on the streets
But you're not there
Golden hair why do I stare
You're not there
You loved them and left them
You don't even care.
City girl - Whisky eyes
Smiling at the guys.
Whisky was her name
And she played the game
I'll never be the same
She was whisky and I was beer,
She never shed a tear.
Whisky was her name
Smooth as ice and very nice
I'll never be the same

—*Martin L. Burns*

The Wind

Listen to the wind that whisper's
Word's of love from above,
Look at the tree's that sway with the
Wind that tell's you where it goes,
Smell the air the wind blow's with
Fragrance from the flowers that bloom
Feel the wind that refreshes the mind
The body and the spirit,
Therefore you have tasted life as
it is given.

—*Olive Peterson*

Darkness

I look outside
And I see darkness
I look inside
I see no light
I hear footsteps, and look up
To see no one
I hear children laughing
Yet I see no happy faces
I walk by no pathway
For I cannot see a trail
I hear guns in the distance
But I cannot see where they fire
I can see memories
Of soldiers falling, guns blazing
And ladies crying
In amongst them
I see death
I look in the direction of the guns
But I see darkness and walk on by

—*Kristina O'Brien*

Where Does The Love Go?

After when the love dies,
And it's gone forever more,
The love just seems to vanish
And your heart locks up its door.

Where does the love wander to?
Does it fold up like a flower?
The memory keeps on coming back,
And you miss it ever hour.

Does it rock like the sea?
With its rich deep blue,
With its under water secrets,
That come back to haunt you.

Does it rise and fall?
Like a golden sunset in June,
With its mysterious way,
Of trading places with the moon.

Where does the love go?
Once it disappears,
I think it moves on to another.
To prepare them for future tears.

—*Emma Bate*

Where Am I?

I've lost it, its gone
And I've looked everywhere,
I've searched all through the house
Even under the chair.

Had it! I know
When I came to this place,
But now it's just gone
Without leaving a trace.

But I know it's around here
And not far away,
It's just that I seem
To have lost it today.

It's been called a sister
A daughter an aunt,
A niece and a cousin
First a child then a girl.

A woman a wife then a mother you see,
The thing that I seem to have misplaced
is me.

—*Christine Hambling*

The Hint

Take a step back
and listen.
Let's remain here,
let's circle what leaves us,
what parts from us.
Does it hide from us?

Let the power fall:
the wind is here;
the hypnotic waves sing
the repetition of the sea
in this solitary beach.

My eyes are ready to acknowledge
the endless hint of the earth.

—*Elisa Munao*

The Change

This year
and only this year
I feel different
than I did two
years ago,
this year
I feel like a Lamborghini
instead of a dull Volvo.
As the Lamborghini
drives by
and
everybody stares and
they ask if they
can go for a ride.
But
No one asked me
two years ago,
when I was just
a little old Volvo.

—*Jamie Dick*

The Mystery of Life

When you wake up in the morning
and sees the beauty in sight
you know God is waiting
to thank Him for the blessing in life.

The love of God in your heart
lingered all day long
in all things you do and want
He's always at your side.

Everything good is in your mind
for the love of God is in you
Whatever you touch and decide
happiness is there to abide.

At the end of the day you thank Him
for all the things you received
and let Him stay with you all the time
for He loves to guide you through your life.

—*Socorro Ch. V. Trinidad*

The Picture

It was a picture on the wall,
And when it was looked upon,
made you tall,
And thoughts of inspiration,
reaching to enlight, your aspiration
of a beauty of love,
which cannot be fall,
I will always,
leave you feeling tall.

—*G. Misewich*

Midnight Whispers

You whisper in my ear,
And wash away my fear,
Can't you see,
That you were meant for me?

Your hand brushes mine,
But there is still more to find,
I don't want to run out of time,
Or love won't be worth a dime.

When I finally spy,
The sparkle in your eye,
I'll know you realize,
That true love never really dies.

You must know that I need you,
And there is nothing I'd rather do,
Then wake up one day,
And hear that waiting does pay.

—*Olga Kostic*

Universal Harmony

The universe is a big band
and we are all singing the
same song
a song of justice
a song of peace
a song of joy
a song of all mankind -
rhythm can get along without
nature but nature cannot get
along without rhythm

—*Mara kathleen Hallman*

I Remember You

When the tunnel is dark
And you can't see the light
When feelings subside
And there's no way to fight

I think of you
When these things do I see
To remember a love
Of you and of me

I can't even explain
The loss that I feel
Only in prayer
Before you I kneel

For you were my light
With a love yet so true
I think of those times
And I remember you.

—*S. Alyward*

What Is Love?

If love is something so special,
Why does it hurt so much?
If love is so strong,
Why does it have so much pain?
If love is patient,
when do we find it?
If love is eternal,
Why do we cry?
If love is so precious
Why do we throw it away?

—*Tylene Turner*

Lunatic at Large

You've lost it - your mind,
and you don't know.
Your fanatical eyes
- they do not see, they bleed.
Crimson drops of madness
- upon feet, upon a path,
headed for hell.

You're the lost one.
The lunatic at large.

You savor the pain,
then revenge your past.
Twisted in sickness,
Festered with hate.
You're seldom stopped
Before it's too late.

Who knows when you'll strike?
And who knows you now?

—*Jan Summers*

In The Silent Night

In the silent night
as a warning a you come to me
not to bring me peace
but to say: don't leave.

In the silent night
when the burden of my life
fall apart over your soul
you feel the anxiety of my love.

In the silent night
both, your soul and mine,
remain alive in the grave
of our regards.

In the silent night
We assure this is the end
but we refuse to say goodbye.

—*Francisco Medina*

Untitled

I can see the mist
As she gently strokes
The quiet morning lake
With a lover's touch.
A feather's whispering,
Caressing,
Seducing the wind to calm.
She brushes,
All that she envelopes.
Leaves it,
Wanting for more
With subdued passion,
Dissipating into thin air.
Like the lingering
Of a soft, sweet kiss.
Even the sun is enraptured
In the haze of her
Sensual musk.

—*Lynn Marie Holtz*

Beneath the Ice

Trapped
Beneath the ice
Suspended
In unpenetrable blackness
Midnight colours
Washing
Over cold depths
Whispering sighs
Of lost
Floating souls
Heavy silence
Suffocating
Coldness
Debilitating
The last dance
Danced
With the seaweed.

—June Gillies

The Sun Must Rise

You child of the great nation
Blessed with natur'l resources
But cursed with its own people
Lose not hope, the sun must rise.

Are you scared you'd not survive,
That our rights belong t' a few
Many mansions, none for you?
Lose not hope, the sun must rise.

Are you awed that money's adored,
And at how titles are bought,
Your intellect seems suppressed?
Lose not hope, the sun must rise.

Yesteryears appear unreal,
Today - an eternity,
Tomorrow - a mere mirage?
Lost not hope, the sun must rise.

Every era has a dawn
As daylight follows dark night
All beginnings have their ends
Surely, soon we all will smile.

—Emma Ohanele

The Joy of You

Rays of morning sun
   Break up the darkness
That surrounds me
   As I waken now
To familiar sounds

The distant lament
   Of a freight train
Seems to rival
   A meadow larks
Cheerful song

As shadows vanish
   In the growing light
I think of you
   Heartfelt emotions
Coax a humble smile

Such joy within
   The emptiness subdued
For you my love
   My dearest friend
Are soon to be with me

—Matthew McNeill

Winding Road

It began as a distant throbbing
But has grown
Into a sharp pain,
A pain unlike any other.

My mind wanders
Unable to remain attentive.
I cannot think clearly
As images dance through my head,
A tribal ritual of great madness.

If I am forced to accept
Such agony
I feel that sanity
Will no longer be mine.

The end of this winding road
Is not much further.
In the distance I can see
The powerful waves
Of death,
Waiting to take me home.

—Erin E. Johnston

'The Suffering' Not!

We hit the books all day long.
But school is fun don't get me wrong!
We listen to the instructor teach
While we daydream about the beach!
Though I've grown and years have past,
I'm sure I'll find grade six a blast!
All doctors, lawyers, dancers too
Once have suffered like me and you!
The day will come,
When school is done,
Then we can join the world of fun!

—Erika Grogan

God's Gift

A baby was created
By the hands of God above
To give the world the sweetest touch
Of tenderness and love

With the softness of a whisper
God made a baby's skin
And then designed two trusting eyes
To put the starlight in

With giggles from a waterfall
And breezes passing by
God made a baby's laughter
And a tiny, sleepy sigh

God made this world a precious gift
More dear and pure than gold
With little toes to play with
And tiny hands to hold

And wrapped in sunshine ribbons
With rainbows pretty swirl
Brought down to earth the wonder
Of a tiny baby girl

—Stacey Smith

A Reminiscence

Hear that voice from yonder mile
Catch a glimpse of tender smile;
The charm and message all aglow
Cast a spell over my soul.

Reflection of your closeness
Beguiles me with coziness;
Gentle and sweet, your temperament
Remains afresh in reminiscence.

Solicitude unrestrained
Solaced, anguished, unexplained;
Dreamed not in the wildest dream
But unrequited esteem.

What hastened the times we had
Shared in happy days and sad;
Grievous parting to resist
Immaculate life ever exist?

Vanished be years of weal and woe
Not the memory of you will go;
Heart so plain in bygone years
Fetches thoughts that bring up tears.

—Minkai E. Wong

Solitude

The wind blows soft among the trees,
Colours one so rarely sees,
Red, orange, green and golds,
Autumn's story now unfolds.

The lake is calm, blue and still,
Just a hint of winter's chill,
Shadows flicker here and there,
The whole body is aware.

Suddenly a flap of wings,
What beauty, your heart sings,
A northern goose in flight,
Your eyes marvel at the sight.

Again, the quietness descends,
Distant birds make amends,
The peace is shattered very soon,
The lonesome cry of a loon.

I dip the oars into the lake,
Autumn's beauty to forsake,
I head the boat back to the shore,
The autumn colours are no more.
The evening shadows have cast their spell,
There's peace and quiet - all is well!

—Kathleen Cameron

The Flower

You gave me a flower
blue like the sky
So beautiful
the flower give us answer
For the question
happiness forever
We fond at last
I tell us in it own words
About friendship
and faithfulness
And you exist
Now and always.

—Solveig Olsson

Journey

asked for myself
eep in the past.
lease, give me a smile,
or my destiny only
found there.

asked for my picture
the future.
ost my hope remains.
fog around.

asked for my face,
y present one.
he eyes closed in front
f the mirror of time.

saw it to run
hand with the past.
journey inside the fog
f the near coming future.

n instant trip my own
the endless time
xtension.

—*Anna Lalaga*

at Questions

wonder why cats
n't like hats.
r "do" they?
ut Hey who's to say.

wonder why cats
ase mice
it because
hey aren't nice.

wonder why cats
n't like the water.
it because they
e very much smarter.

wonder why cats
e just plain cats
it because they
ere made out of hats.

you have more
ll it to yourself
ecause my cat is
the shelf!

—*Charlene Florance Smokey Belanger*

hing

hing in a bottomless floor
alling to a topless roof
hinking of the space below
eeping secrets to itself
elow the level of consciousness
erminal speed has been destroyed
isten to the colours run
to the plastic mouths and eyes
eferred by interest in the seas
limbing to the peak of pain
nd dropping to the unseen ground
radual display of exhibits
esigned by graphic monsters
nd samples of peace
hing in a timeless sun
ppearing to be sightly dark

—*D. Haagensen*

Lost Time

As a child hours upon hours,
    Dreams upon dreams,
Spent on thoughts of life
    When I grow up.

So many choices,
    everything opening up
for the taking;
    Growing up will be grand.

As I grow,
    choices begin to close.
Reality makes so many
    choices for me.

As an adult hours upon hours,
    Dreams upon dreams,
Spent on thoughts of life
    when I was young.

The middle is missing
    hours, dreams, thoughts.
When did I grow up?

—*Cindy Eakins*

December Snow

Snowflakes wandered…
drifting slowly
through the air …
not one the same
as its neighbor,
landing on cold, hard
earth …
to be jostled to and fro
or maybe to be blown
into a dark corner
packed with friends
in a drift.
Snowflakes wandered …

—*James W. Sander*

Estranged

I dream of you
Each and every day
Knowing you're
So far away.

You're really here
In my dreams
But when I awake
It's not as it seems.

Our time together
It wasn't long
But our love still grows
And keeps getting strong.

We vowed togetherness
For the rest of our lives
But while we're apart
Do we hear the other's cries?

Will we meet again?
If our love is true.
'Cause I just don't know
If I can live without you.

—*Crystal Lilly*

Binary Star

The two
face each other
and feel
the heat of
their attraction
and move
unknowingly
to the esoteric
rhythm of
their quiet
explosions

The two
dance on
eternally
rendering all else
to nothing
oblivious
of the
brilliance
of their existence
and shadowy galaxy

The two
are one

—*Yulu Griffith*

To Know You Is To Love You

To a grandmother
Filled with love
A bond of joy
As free as a dove

Moments together
Filled with gladness
Holding on
To eternal happiness

In a place that is
Only filled with tears
An apartment waiting
Where there is no fears

Such a lovely smile
A grandmother holds
I love you so much
A women so bold.

With talks over supper
You always care so much
You always gave us hope
With your loving touch.

—*Sheree Aasman*

Dreamland

Wander into dreamland
Float about and see.
The many dreams we conjure up.
Are dreams that cannot be.
Why we wish we do not know.
Just stop and listen, look and see.
What your dreams are meant to be.
Try and find that lock and key.
Then you'll see you're floating free.

—*Kathleen Noyes*

Untitled

Fly starlings in the morn
Fly swallows in the barn
Fly robins on the lawn
Fly geese are all gone
If I could fly
I would
If I dare
I could
Fly sparrows in the trees
Fly gulls on the breeze
Fly birds all around
Fly, I'll stay on the ground.

—TFMD

The Rocking Chair

The rocking chair was waiting
For the one who needed rest
It would not be truly happy
Until it got the very best.

The wood was bent and rotten
From sitting for so long
Without a soul who really cared
About life and things gone wrong.

It missed the joy and caring
Only the old and wise can give
It wouldn't be much longer
Before the dreams again would live.

Now the chair is rocking
The love is there to see
It doesn't look so old and worn
Because it's rocked by me.

—Beth Pennie

Father's Love

Can father's show their love
For their children, like Mother's do.
Some father's have a hard time.
Letting that love shine through.

One day a father looks down
At three little boys so small,
When they were always underfoot.
And playing with their ball.

Then one day, he looks again.
The little boys have grown.
Their just as tall as he is.
And can't wait to be on their own.

His love is deep and strong.
A little different from their mom's.
But dad is always there.
When something might go wrong.

To watch the boys with their father.
It makes my day so bright.
The closeness that will always be.
All through out their life.

—Donna Ollivier

Disenchantment

My wish, to be away
Gone from every day
Maybe, a gentle breeze
Playing happy in the tree's

Or white, and wispy, cloud
Drifting soft, across the sky
Never needing so to worry
or to know the way, or why

Just reacting, just to nature
Letting life proceed itself
Being all, with natures calling
Needing only natures wealth

Yet again, maybe a blossom
Standing straight, in beauty seen
Dying gently, in chill winter
To arise again in spring.

But this a flimsy dream
From a disenchanted heart
yet maybe this dreaming whimsy
Can foresee a shining start.

—M. Cowley

Once Upon A Childhood

They say, "he's just a child!
He has not what to say."
And so they carelessly cease to hear
And turn their heads away.
They laugh and talk and carry on
As if he isn't there
They shut him out as surely
As the fool without a care.
Still quietly he watches
And patiently he waits
Forever hoping for a chance...
Then slowly leaves that place.

—Darlene Holowachuk

One Wish

From the moment that
I laid eyes on you,
I knew instantly
How I felt about you.

There's no doubt in my mind,
It was love at first sight.
Being with you
Just felt so right.

But since you left me,
There's been a hole in my heart.
I still don't understand
Why we had to part.

But some things, I guess,
Were never meant to be.
And that's how it
Turned out for you and me.

And if there was one wish
Could be granted to me,
I would only wish
That you could've loved me.

—Helen Klassen

My Love

Carol, Carol, Carol
I say it in my dreams
If you were there beside me
I would have no cares, it seems.

When I'm not with you Carol
Although we are apart
I'm thinking of you always
And with you in my heart.

If only things were simpler
And we could both run free
I would take you in my heart
And forever yours I'd be.

Apart we have to sleep
But time is on our side
So until we are together
My love I will not hide.

—Carol Pritchard

Lost

I sit on a beach,
on this unknown land.
Wandering, waiting,
hoping, for a helping hand.

I've been here for years,
always all alone.
Wondering if I'd ever get,
the chance, to go home.

Up through the blue skies,
along through space.
Thinking, "When I get home,
will I recognize a face?"

—Vicky Weir

Juvenalia #6 - Circus Act

Behold! the gems
I stole from your dreams;
A raindrop, a sea shell, a seed.
Now watch me Do with it Magic.

By sleight of hand I'll
Brush the drip into an
Arch re-defining the sun
As the shell does the trick
Of eavesdropping on
Mermaids calling each to each.
Look closely at this
Conch cupping froth
To prolong hypnosis.

By metamorphosis this stolen seed
Might follow a logic
All its own and break Your spell.

When it happens, if it happens,
There no more will be new tricks to conjure.
The way illusions ago, I'll fold the show
And pack my pretty theft.

—Junette S. Bax

adness

When it rains
I'm in pain
When the sun comes down
I frown
Because of you
I will never say
I love you
I'm sad
Because I was bad
To hurt you
And you know I love you
I'm sitting by the phone
All alone
Waiting for you
We should talk
And take a walk
Along the sandy beach
And reach
A conclusion
About all this confusion.

—*Aleesha Chouinard*

Virtual Reality

If I said it, it must be true
I'm sure it is
For I have said so

If I saw it, it must have been there
Look through my eyes
And see it too

If I touched it, it must be real
Touch with my hands
And feel it too

Is it real, or is it not
Of course it is
For I believe so

What there is, is what I wish
What I know, is what I dream
What took place, is what I think
What I believe, is all there is

Did we speak of this?
Of course we did!
For I have said so

What is your problem, anyway!

—*James A. Anderson*

Untitled

Watching the sunset
in its magnificent way
marking the end
of a glorious day,
slipping silently
into darkness.

Stars glittering
from east to west,
north and south,
letting me know
what the earth is about.

Dawn is in sight
with the sunset,
and its colorful light.

A new day is there
for all of us everywhere.

—*Lummy Bouwkneht*

The Recollection

I found a sweetness
in the entangling
of our breaths,
as if with each
a piece
of our souls
had
intertwined.
For a fleeting moment
I caught glimpse
of our dancing stars.
They smiled with your caress
and then leaped back into the sky.
We closed our eyes
and let ourselves
fall into slumber.

—*Jessica Cattaneo*

Music In The Night

I hear the music
In the night,
So soft and sweet
To my ear.
It can put me into another time
Another place
Another mood.
Lingering, only for the moment
Then lost to time.
A rare entity
Which is intangible
Even to those few who possess it.
So familiar
A mixture of sounds and words
Bringing out my deepest sentiments,
Right before my soul.
I can encounter time, that time erased,
When I hear
The music in the night.

—*Joan Thorogood*

Mortuary

They were dead bodies
Inhuman was their grasp
So cruel their asking
Cold endeavors
I could never ask
For human kindness
Caught like a fly in a weed
Pinched by ugly truths
I resigned myself
To silly absurdities

—*Deborah Ellen*

Blue Rainbow

Being in love,
is like a Rainbow in the sky.
Each different color,
paints a different emotion.
Red is the color of love,
Orange is dedication.
Yellow is a sign of Patience,
and Pink and Purple
are faith and loyalty.
But Blue is how you feel
when your Rainbow
Fades
Away.

—*Jacquie Kulchyski*

Aurora Love

The love that we share
is like the northern lights,
ever moving, ever changing,
and ever the same
So distance and yet so close
at the very brightest and best when
the world is darkest and coldest
Dancing and twinkling,
so full of color and light
And when you think you've seen it all,
you look again, it's changed,
and even more beautiful and special
than ever before

—*Fred Steinwand*

A New Beginning

A light that once shone brightly
Is quickly growing dim
As the child within me slightly
Smiles a painful grin.

She pretends that her past
Did not hurt her at all,
That her pain will not last
That she won't stumble or fall.

What she has got to realize
Is the pain that she must face
She must wipe her teary eyes,
And hold on strong to her faith.

This is the way, her heart
She then can mend
She can finally go on singing
This is not an old end,
But a new beginning.

—*Tammy Letkeman*

The Wilted Rose

I once saw a wilted rose,
It filled me with such grief
For in its past, this wilted rose
Had brought me gentle relief.

Strenuous days of toil now passed
Strenuous days ahead
But the beauty did this rose amass,
Brought serenity to my head.

The enchanting days are now to close,
How dreary life will be,
For the part of me in this wilted rose
Is gone for eternity.

—*Chia Zheng*

Night Wind

The silent, peaceful wind,
flows softly through the air,
it skips through the trees,
and ruffles through your hair.
The smell of the wind,
is a lavish delight,
cool and crisp,
distinctive to the night.
The piercing of the wind,
sometimes bitter cold,
sends a shiver through the night
to all it can hold.

—*Crystal Peterson*

Ocean's Bottom

Ocean's bottom is like the heart.
It holds all sorrows,
And the depths of pain.
A body of salty water,
Formed from all your given tears.
It collects all things,
The happy and the sad memories.
It carries the love and hate.
A college like the ocean's bottom.
It holds all life.
And remembers the pain of death.
A fear of darkness and being alone.
Always struggling to survive,
Always leaving a little space of light,
With a willingness to go on.
And a fear of loving once again,
A tear for every broken heart,
Has grown my ocean bigger.
My past and present have fallen once again,
And all collected at ocean's bottom.

—*Lynn Kurimski*

Summer A Hope

Be still my heart. Your racing quell
It will soon be here and magic spell
That summer casts around my dreams.
The world is bursting at the seams.
Swallows flash below the eaves.
Blue and vibrant,
Budding sheaves already gold,
Though faint as yet
Foreshadowing all I hope to get
Your gentle promise - tender vow
Surely arrends rose haden bough.
Purple twilight, moonlight glow
In this sweet season means I know.
That only summer can evoke
The magic things of which we spoke,
Eternal love, perpetual bliss
Who or what can bring me this?
Just you! A June night!
Heavenly twins,
Of all four seasons - summer wins.

—*Kathleen M. Barnes*

The Journey

My fear lies deep within me
It's hidden from the light
A force which only starts to build
With the coming of the night

Then the memories start to surface
And I bow my head in shame
For I remember a time I sold my soul
To become a player in the game

I placed my faith in strangers
Lost my belief in the common man
And the truth became a language
I couldn't seem to understand

But my loved ones stood beside me
Through the anger and the strife
And one footstep after another
I began my journey back to life
Though the past is often painful
And the future is yet to be
I open my heart to the darkness
And light a candle to help me see.

—*Dawn Pollock*

The Magnolia

I stopped in my tracks
Its magnificence overpowered me
Compelled, I sat down
Without absorbing its beauty
I just couldn't walk away

White blossoms so proud
Each petal outstretched as if to say
See me
I had to enjoy the moment
I couldn't walk away

Its white wedding gown
waltzing in the afternoon
I wanted to join in
to dance in the breeze
to grant it my joy
I couldn't bear to walk away

—*Julie Szabo*

Song For Two

I just want...
Let me...
Why...?
Listen to me, please
I want you...
We've to find a solution.
A compromise. What shall I do, then?
I know there is a solution.
Why are you saying this?
No! I'm listening to you no longer!
I'm leaving. There is no solution.
Why? No! No! B'cause, no!
Why...? Stop, please!
I told you, there is no solution.
No solution - no compromise.
What shall I do, else?
I know there is no solution.
Listen to me! Listen to me please!
Please - please, don't. But why? Why?

—*Arthur Mattli*

Lay No More Howlings

Lay no more howlings at their door,
Let them die...

the grass grows green
once more
under the covering
of coffee berries
on the hill

and the page torn
from a child's exercise book
merges with the soil

axles rooted
in the dirt
bind deeper roots -
from their centre
springs a tree

So lay no more howlings there,
Let them lie...

—*Lorna Fraser*

For that Someone

Life is strange in certain ways,
like talking to someone from far away.
How that someone can reach my heart.
When that someone is so far apart.
But time has drawn near,
for that someone to appear.
When that someone enters my space,
that someone will see a smile
on my face.
I know that someone has lots
of love to give,
That is why it's great to live.
I too, have lots of love to give.
For it's only for a someone,
and that someone is you.

—*Kenneth Lloyd Sparkman*

The Generous Sea

Generous,
Like the sea,
Giving life to,
All that dwells within,
This is what you've been.
    And I, the rocks,
    Naive and lost,
    Along your shore,
    Gently molded in your care,
    From all the love you need to share.
Earth, nor sea, nor star, nor sky,
Can express to you, nor I,
The impact, you've had on me,
And to all that pass you by.
How can I then, this, repay,
But thank the good Lord everyday,
That He loved me enough to send,
The very best along the way.

—*Tammie Mezzatesta*

Gluttony

Gluttony, a sin against oneself.
Logic, extra food be stored in shelf
Appetite, stomach storage is safe
Logic and appetite engage in scuffle
Holding each other's neck's scarf.
Appetite, you are a fool
You refuse stomach to be overfull
Logic, you are an idiot
You cause a person to be sick and idle.
Appetite always wins in the duel
Entrenches itself where it dwells.

Glut raises heart's and liver's anger
As stomach sustains temporary hunger.
Headaches arise raising doctor's fees
Appetite watching with beaming face.
Recovery, not guarantee of non-recurrence
Appetite vows to attack again rigorously.
The vicious circle persists
Until a person ceases to exist.

—*John G. Nderitu*

V.A.T. On Heating 1993

The poor pensioners trudee to
London, to fight for their rights
V.A.T. on heating, is there no end
to the disasters that befall us here.
Don't be disheartened I'm sure there
is a pardon
What can we do there's nothing
that's true
This government has a lot to
answer for I'm sure.
Where is it to end, on who can
we depend.
Are the poor to struggle
on with not even a song.
The answer of cause is
John Smith labour he is
and it's labour we want
for there's no doubt. He needs to be
at No. 10, I believe it's near big Ben

—*M. A. B. Sawyer*

Seascape

By the sea
Lovers stand
Walking hand in hand
On sandy beaches
Where gentle waves
Wash along the shore

The tide drifts in
Then drifts away again
Always in motion is the sea
Waves lapping
Along sandy beaches
On shores where lovers stand

—*Mary G. Newton*

Mother Nature's Children

The sun shines thru my window
Makes my thoughts so bright
I can't help being happy
Feel everything's alright

On a day like the one I'm livin'
Nothing can bring me down
I just want to keep on tryin'
Spread love all around

The leaves on the trees are turning
Red, yellow, mauve and green
Some floating on the breezes
Lord, what a tranquil scene

Soon there'll be snowflakes falling
Blanketing the entire ground
Preparing mother nature's children
For the cold that will abound

—*Richard Yorke*

Smiling Summer

The noontime sun has lit a flame,
by the babbling brook,
wild flowers dancing without shame,
in the dappled woods,

and summer wears a great big smile,
while fluffy clouds just peer,
the earth is blossoming simply wild,
so very welcome here.

—*Virginia Conroy Bell*

Unreconciled

I've left the hearth I called my home,
My heart still lingers on.
I've come here and I call this home
And yet I don't belong.

They say it's time to leave behind
My childhood's happy past,
But in my heart the mem'ries of
Those years will always last.

Who can forget what they have loved
Though miles and years away?
I can't forsake all that I've known
No matter where I stay.

I know my present dwelling place
Has caused sick hearts to grieve.
I must remember what it means
To those who've had to leave.

Yet still I find my lonely heart
Two thousand miles away.
It chooses not to lie in peace.
Unreconciled to stay.

—*Sarah Acker*

My Little Boy

My little boy, my pride and joy,
My little darling I love you so
And this is what I want you to know.

As you reach age nine or ten
I will love you still by then,
And when you are in your teens
I won't be nosy where you've been.
All I ask is you grow up well
And I will listen if you tell.

And when you grow into a man
I will help you if I can,
Live life full every day
And be kind along the way.

I hope you meet and find a wife
To make you happy all your life,
Then perhaps you'll have a little boy
And share the happiness and the joy

That through the years has meant so much.
If you're away we'll keep in touch,
Then as I'm growing very old
Please remember you're still my little piece
of gold.

—*Annie Robinson*

Untitled

please enter
once yugoslavia
no point beyond
mission: appreciation
recover useless concentration
through national solitude
hold upright
one crooked chair
an architectural joinery is
a green jester in the paint
in a catalogue of pastel balance
free: cracked mirage
mount the angels
historical today

—*Selina Beat*

Once Upon a Dream

Hold me close, never let me go.
My love for you is hard to show.
Remember the good things, not the bad.
Remember all the fun times that we had.

You always happen to make me cry.
Every time you told a lie.
Now things are turned around.
You always seem to hear that sound.

Now that there's no more fights,
All that's left are lonely nights.
You lost me I didn't lose you,
Now you know what you have to do.

Someone else holds me tight,
each and every other night.
You had your chance to do the same,
Now I call someone else's name.

Now that I've landed on my feet,
Someone else has got you beat.
You laughed behind my back.
But there's one thing that you lack...
Who's laughing now?

—*Tarah Short*

The Red Rose

What lies within thy heart
Never-ending episodes
Deep inside the petals
Red and scarlet
Hairline veins scratching
To the surface
overflowing with exaltation
How I adore thee
The presence, perfume,
Loveliness of thy face
Not to touch or contaminate
Alas, for temptation
I shall take thee.

—*Pamela Harrison*

Never Knew

Trotting along the silver sand
Never knew a harsh rough hand
Climbing swiftly up a path
Never knew the master's wrath

With snow white tail and matching mane
Never knew neglected's pain
Racing along with head held high
Never knew a longing sigh

Pounding along the forest floor
Never knew the locked barn door
Rearing up to sound his call
Never knew the small damp stall

Prancing along the river bank
Never knew scars on his flank
Lowering muzzle to take a sip
Never knew the stinging whip

Kicking hooves into the sky
Never knew them sore or dry
Free from worries and all alarms
But never knew a child's loving arms.

—*Kellie Whiteside*

The Dark Closet

The massive door kept tight—
No handle put in place;
To the dark closet of abuse,
That time had not erased.

The voices inside entreating,
But no one opened the door;
Blind-eyed and deaf-eared ignoring,
The young, the weak and the poor.

Waiting in the gloomy shadows—
For someone to come along;
Their murmur became a chorus,
To right the horrible wrong.

Breaking the barrier of hatred—
Darkness floods with light.
Evil lurking in the shadows,
Fades in sudden flight.

—*S. A. Cowley*

A Mother

I am my person
No longer the victim
A creator of life
In tune with needs

Teacher of small ones
A learner of such
One destiny of three
Of consequential future

A pacifier of wants
Controller of environments
Amid chaos of change
Apologies of forgetfulness

A maintainer of feelings
The flyer of logistics
Such combat with plight
Of the eternal souls.

—*Jo-Anne C. Lingard*

Song of Longfellow

Born beneath the rising dollar
Of a family steeped in priv'lege

Ivy Leaguer studied writing
New York State to Massachusetts

Found it hard and way beyond him
Like the dome of sky above him

Endless paper stretched before him
Like the plains beneath the moonlight

Inspiration came upon him
As the rushing mountain river

Thought the Red Man might provide him
Like an early children's story

Thought he'd write an Indian Epic
Boost his sales and please his critics

Speak his new found Indian meter
Dull and boring, long and tedious

On and on he droned for ever
Never thought he'd find an ending

But he did.

—*Frederick Webster*

Blurred Vision

Walking on the edge
Of love and hate,
Reality and insanity.
The line between is blurred.
I am weaving
From side to side
No longer aware
Of which is which.
There seems to be
A tug-of-war
For control of my mind.
Reaching out
For a helping hand,
But unaware of who is
Friend or foe,
So taking none.
Now afraid to walk at all,
For I know not
In which direction
I am headed.

—*Kerri McGill*

Dare to Dream

When clouds cover the sunshine
Of your days
When no silver lines the clouds
When hope is so far away
Cast away in a world of fantasy
Dare to dream.

When tomorrow is not brighter
Than today
When people do not care
As they should
When rain is pouring on your hopes
Dare to dream.

Dream of the rainbow
That will cross your sky
Bringing the good times back again
Making you forget the sorrows
And bring you a better tomorrow
Dare to dream.

—*Annette Sturgeon*

Static Electricity

An old, familiar smile
on an old, familiar face.
Filling old, familiar wasted time
in an old, familiar place

I can take out the garbage.
(I can't make it go away)
I'd take my face out to dinner
If my foot wasn't in the way.

Old, familiar dreams
in an old, familiar house.
So I sit.
Old, familiar hiding
By an old, familiar mouse.

—*Alaina Holland*

Mothers Message

I watch you grow each passing day
our miracle of love
and with each day that passes by
I thank the Lord above

I think about when I was young
the mistakes that I have made
and hope that you will never know
the price that can be paid

My message to you is simply this
the world won't always smile
so when the world gives you an inch
my child, take a mile.

—*Jana Schaan*

Untitled

Gone
    Out of her life
        She has pushed me away
    Tells me I'm still there
        I cannot see it.
Pain
    Longing is in my heart.
        It is an empty space.
    I don't feel alive.
        Life has left me.
Time
    Passing slowly.
        A minute is forever.
    The clock ticks.
        It is all I hear.
Heart
    Beating cold blood.
        Making me go on.
    An empty space.
        Nothing but fills it.
Tears
    Flow like wine
        Flood my soul
    Stains on my pillow.
        I weep for you.

—*Gerdon Kowtz*

To the Memory of a Beautiful Voice

Sweet alto that floated into the
peace of my dreams, amplifying
the nuances of an uplifting
carol, your echoes ring-on
even in my waking hours.

Chance music that greeted
the shutting of my eyes, I remember
the smile and the
eyes that danced as I thanked God
for so fine a song
so fine a voice; and wish
those mosquitoes had never
made me
let you go.
I would gladly sleep a hundred
hours to hear you warm my soul
again; and hope you'll call each time
I shut my eyes, to work that alto thro'
that carol that has left a mark
on my soul.

—*Eldred Ibibiem Green*

A Friend..."

here are people you can count on,
eople you can trust.
ery special people,
Vho will never betray us.

eeper of secrets,
he holder of truth.
ies that go deeper,
han your family's roots.

ome will last forever,
ome for only days.
ome will go on for years and years,
nd only be a faze.

hed your tears, share your fears,
pen up your heart.
are your soul, trust in whole,
or you will never part.

is true, on these people we do depend,
ou may have guessed it,
es, that's right,
m talking about a friend!

—*Kandice Fritsch*

riendship

You see a shell, and it looks as
lain as it could be,
It doesn't look like much but it
ame from the sea.
It survived the waves that
eat it strong,
It survived the days that were
o long
But never as long, and never so
rong as the friend between you and me.

—*Jennifer Brazil*

lone

ongtime he lay upon his bed
ain and wind a brutal force
oices lurk throughout the house
till there is loneliness.

'ith the sun reality appears
ampled by a savage rampage
single leaf in a forest.
ust blowing in a wild wind.

nages in a distance
oices echoing from afar
arshness hid behind a breath
otionless the leaf turns pale

nimals seem to run free
he trees in the forest remain
ne leaf falls to the ground
o one seems to notice.

—*Trudy Hickey*

he Window

he sun rises through the dark sky
shining through the window
another clear day in my world,
no worries,
no fears.
As I look through the window
my soul is at rest
and my heart is open.
The window is you,
never closed and always there.

—*Todd Martin*

Saying Good Bye

Remember when we first met,
Remember the fun we had,
Remember how close we were,
Forget now it's gone forever.

Remember the laughter,
Remember the tears,
Remember the fighting,
Forget now, things are different.

Remember the walks we took,
Remember the talks we had,
Remember when we said we cared,
Forget now things just aren't fair.

Remember when we phoned
Remember how we laughed,
Remember how I cried,
Forget now I am all alone.

Remember the smiles,
Remember the photos,
Remember how I feel alone,
Forget now how we say good-bye.

—*Tresa Montgomery*

Josie

You taught me
right from wrong
You brought me up
to be lean and strong
kind and fair
You taught me
how to care
You understood me
when nobody else did
You are not by blood
but by heart and love
grandpa

—*Bob Harvey*

Hidden Tears

I hear a little girl
She's crying
She wants to dance and twirl
But no one knows she's trying
Life has no meaning
Especially when it's taken away
The little girl inside of me
Has gone far away
Yesterday's have no meaning
Tomorrows never come
I'm living in the yesterdays
But my life shall soon be done

There's a little girl inside of me
Crying and longing to be set free
I can't set her free because
That will be the death of me

I am alone now
Everyone cares for me
The question I ask myself
Will I ever be free
The pain inside has a hold
As slowly I feel I am growing old
I don't think I'll ever be free
The pain hurts too much, to be.

—*Lena Manning*

Hope In Adversity

Shadows in my heart
Shrouded in the morning mist
Feeling closer than before
To the edge of the abyss

Like a falcon swooping from above
To catch it's daily prey
I feel the cold clawing embrace
That brings me to another day

Somewhere there just out of reach
Across the oceans dreams
All the mood swings blend to one
And all is well it seems

Sometimes the warmth spreads over me
As if guided by celestial light
But clouds are always gathering
With the blackness of eternal night

I'll keep smiles of sunshine close
To treasure with the passing seasons
The spirit may be chipped but is kind and strong
For all of this life's reasons.

—*David James Borthwick*

The Sea

Blue
    so dark yet so clear
        lucid
glassy
    reflecting refracting light
        bright sunshine
Blue
    so deep
        dark and dense
restless
    constantly moving
        the mobility of your body
is immense
    frightening yet reassuring
Oh sea
    sheer voluminous power
        of never-ending eternal life.

—*Marketa Zvelebil*

Jack Rabbit In Jail

Luck was not his security beat
So he got between four walls
Without a tremendous treat

Consider it a personal defeat
From top to bottom secret always leak
Where some sink and others sail

Drug abuse a bitter sweet
Here's one big Jack Rabbit
And his tales of luxury or hell

It's not quite clear
Who knows and wanted to tell
When Jack Rabbit may be out from jail

—*Chu Sang*

Oh! Child of Mine

I gazed upon her face.
So soft and still in sleep.
Her lips were slightly open,
The smile on them so sweet.
Her lashes gently rested,
Upon her rosebud cheek.
A golden lock had fallen,
Across her widows peak.
Her breath was barely a whisper.
A sigh showed she was fine
Dear how I love thee,
Oh! Child of mine.

—*Cheryl Jordan*

Cheerios and Poppy Seed Crackers

Cheerios and poppy seed crackers
Softly, I follow
the trail- - - - -

daddy's shoes
mummy's plants
horsy's mouth
teddy's hand
there in a corner
sits my son,
face smeared with poppy seeds
talking to a fistful of cheerios.

—*Mal Evans*

Sounds Of Sorrow

Sounds
Sounds of sorrow in the wind
Drifting
Drifting across the plains of life
Searching
Searching for a place to rest.
and be heard
no one listens, no one cares
it seems.
But sorrow knows no bounds
and keeps no friends.
For sorrow is a wanderer
from one end of the world to the other
Sorrow is lurking.

—*Lorraine Dumont*

A Time For Love

Momentary silences
Tense words
Hateful glances
Another row

Accusing threats
Imagined looks
Bored sighs
More tears

Fresh flowers
Gentle kisses
Searching hands
A time for love

—*Maria Zydorkiewicz*

Too Good To Be True

You're like a train
That passes through town
You passed through my life
And let me down
You said I was special
You said you cared
I enjoyed myself
With the time we shared
There's no need to be sorry
No need to feel blue
I seen it coming
It was too good to be true
I'll see you around
Sometime, somewhere
And one last time
I really did care

—*Sandra Smith*

The War

Two sides face each other
The battle lines are drawn
Brother against brother
Brains replaced by brawn

They glare across the distance
Raising weapons in the air
They offer no resistance
The urge to kill is there

They fire without stopping
Though no one gave the cue
They riddle him and mock him
As the shot goes whizzing through

Fists are clenched in anger
Weapons flail the air
Blood stained shirts and rancor
The hate is really there

Then suddenly its over
Things are still the same
I'm glad that I was present
At another hockey game

—*Ed Hujber*

The Addict

What does he feel,
The blood rushes to his brain,
He feels the heartache,
And all of the pain,
Of the want and the fear,
Only he can explain,
The white powder is dwindling,
His hands shake insane,
As he places the needle,
In the once red vein,
The needle goes in,
With the grace and the ease,
Of a prominent doctor,
While the syringe he squeezed,
It's the rush that he gets,
As the liquid is passed
From the eye of the needle,
To the brain that dies fast,
For he is the addict with only he to blame,
For this self destruction and all of the shame.

—*Theresa Emmerson*

The High

The execution of reality
The feelings that unwind
The pressures of society
Slowly leave the mind.

Deep inside the body,
The chiasmas soon begins
A fusion of the inner thoughts
And energies within.

Emotions tumble all astray
Present is the past
Future is forgotten
Memories don't last

Too quickly though
The world returns,
And climax hides away,
Waiting to fulfill once more
And perform again some day.

—*Kaybee McFar*

I Remember, I'll Remember

I remember, I remember
The first warm days of spring,
We would roam the hills together,
Hear the songbirds sing.

I remember, I remember
The first cool days of fall,
How the leaves would rustle
As we strolled along the mall.

Oh, how sweet it is to dwell
On things of days gone by;
Knowing what we feel today
Will never really die.

I remember, I'll remember
Things we did and do,
And now I know I'll always glow
With memories fond of you.

—*James Williams*

Beside a Stream

A helicopter chugged across
The hazy summer sky:
Its sound by distance muted, low,
Was like a lullaby -

To one in somber, pensive mood
Reclining by a stream,
Where the crystal waters' flow
Reflected many a gleam.

The helicopter passed; then came
A quieter hum nearby,
As hovering above the reeds
Appeared a dragonfly;

Its colouring and flight, a blend
Of beauty and precision.
With body green and silver wings,
Delighting mortal vision.

Man made the helicopter with
Great ingenuity,
But could not emulate his God
And make a dragonfly.

—*Iris Poole*

The Isolated

As a drop of water on the pane
The isolated tear of the insane,
The urge to connect
To meaning collect,
The need to hide in the rain.

As its boundary disperses
The crazy woman curses
To have what's not there
To hear hope on the stair
And her soul to hide in her purses.

The raindrop has gone
The sunlight has shone
To expose the care
To dry the prayer
And wait for the rain ..... on and on.
　　　—*J. H. Forster*

Nature's Beauty

As you descend
The suns rays
Bring
You to life.
Twirling, twirling
Drifting, floating
Spin to the ground
You gorgeous creation of
Mother Earth,
As you display
Your vibrant collage
Of
lively tones.
　　　—*Jamie-Lynn Treanor*

Now

There will always be tomorrow
There will always be today
Lets take the time to borrow
A little of yesterday.

We can't go back and relive the past
But we can go ahead the next day
The past is gone and can only last
In your memory there to stay.

It's easy remembering bad times
So hard to remember the good
Lets take the time to better our lives
The way we know we should.

To think about the yesterdays
We sometimes have to borrow
And look right now just for today
There will always be tomorrow.
　　　—*Nancy R. Lee*

Quiet Ramblings

The silence is deafening.
When you close your eyes you see
The blackness all around you.

It presses against you like
a thousand souls trying to
　　get in you
　　through you
　　around you
It's hard sometimes
to sort out the voices
　in the silence.
　　　—*Shauna Durront*

Ours To Keep

When I was young
Things were so simple
Life was rich and full of fun
But as each day passes
Many changes have begun

Responsibilities seem to grow now
Save our country - Buckle down
Recycle, reuse, remake
Save our environment
For our children's sake

The government is in trouble
Health and Education
Our greatest concern
We must keep it all going
So our children can live and learn

We can do it, if we have to
Give up unessential things
We can make a new tomorrow
And see the Happiness it brings.
　　　—*Kathy Bashforth*

A.I.D.S.

Why do we feel we must continue,
To avoid or crowd the issue.
We close our minds and our eyes,
And treat everything we hear as lies.

We fail to see what is right there,
Or is it that we just don't care.
How foolish we all seem to be,
When we say "This won't happen to me".

I've seen the evil "A.I.D.S." can do,
To men to women and children too.
It takes over mind body and soul,
It's a disease gone out of control.

So open your eyes and look around you,
And what you see just may astound you.
People are taking chances in every way,
And more victims are dying each and every day.

And so I beg you to think before you act,
Because it is a well known fact.
Extreme caution in everything you do,
May protect you from becoming a statistic too.
　　　—*Therese Boucher*

A Closer Look

Fastened by fine spider webs
to branches of a tree,
I saw a nest just thimble
Sized 'twas oh, so hard to see.

With green leaf bits covered,
it matched the leaves around.
The inside of the timble-nest was
lined with soft, white down.

Humming like an airplane, the
mother darting flew, frightened
from her thimble nest and tiny
white eggs too.

From rose to rose she darted sipping
nectar sweet, to draw attention from
her nest in haste I did retreat.

Farther on I turned around homeward
she did fly. Silently I waved farewell,
I hadn't meant to pry.
　　　—*Ben Allen*

The Latest Poem

The latest poem
to cope with my tears
thinking of love to be near
I hear you say
come, come to my arms

Right on the paper
wrong in love
right on the paper
it aches so much
wrong in love

When this is all over
that gleam will be an ocean
I know we can do
when this is all over
we will be side by side
shoulder by shoulder.
　　　—*Glaucio Sombra*

Old Age Is A Time

Old age is a time,
To do the most that you can do,
Your days left could be many,
Or they could be few.

Elders who are lucky,
Can do some sports like swim,
The ones who aren't so lucky,
Watch their grand-children doing gym.

So make the most of life,
Now that you have the chance,
Don't wait until you're older,
When you can no longer dance.

Old age is a time,
To do the most that you can do,
Your days left could be many,
Or they could be few.
　　　—*Kelly Lawryniw*

From the View of a Goldfish

From the view of a goldfish
　to everyone else
I'm all sad and lonely
When I'm all by myself.

Sitting alone, with nothing to do.
I wish I could share
　With someone like you.
　You carry my burdens
Where ever I go.

You know how much I need you so.
From the view of a goldfish
to my only good friend
I give you God's grace
Till life does end.
　　　—*John G. Wilson*

The Christening

Others will ask the Good Fairies
To lavish their gifts on you,
Asking for beauty, joy and hope,
Sparkling fresh each day, like dew.
They will ask for intelligence
For you, for charm and for wealth,
Enough to live but not to thwart
Honest ambition... and health.

All these things I wish for you, too.

But the Bad Fairies will attend
This battlefield for men's souls
And, strange to tell, they offer gifts
You can convert to good goals.
So I'll ask they bestow on you
Hate and anger, that you might
Hate all that is bad and, angry,
Declare yourself in the fight

Against evil your whole life through.

—*Janice James*

"Night Wind Lullaby"

The night wind sings a lullaby
    To my baby, while she sleeps
The night wind sings a lullaby
    To my baby in her dreams

The wind in the trees, is sighing low
    It's melody goes 'round.
My baby's listening carefully
    'Though she's sleeping sound

The night wind sings a lullaby
    To my baby, while she sleeps
The night wind sings a lullaby
    To my baby in her dreams

The moon and stars are hanging low
    As they sparkle from the sky
My baby's sleeping peacefully
    As her head on the pillow lies

The night wind sings a lullaby
    To my baby, while she sleeps
The night wind sings a lullaby
    To my baby in her dreams.

—*June Rolson*

Ways

What a day
To predict what's coming
Not an easy way
To accept our own kind
Showing off superiority
And happy to put others on line
Around the world same story
Authorities taking pride
Reading all modern poetry
What a time coming
In a new stride
Him and her finding more skills
To make others stand in line
Acceptable or predictable
Not easy for any poet to say
What is coming our way

—*R. Toolsie*

Brokenhearted

It breaks my heart,
To see you there.
With her fingers,
Running through your hair.
Your tender lips,
Pressing on hers.
I hear the pleasure,
In her purrs.
It drives me crazy,
To see you like this.
I'll always remember,
Our very first kiss.
Your arms around me,
And mine around you.
No matter what happens,
I'll always love you.

—*Twyla Le Clerc*

Struggle

Hardship is back with us
To start off hordes of foredoomed
flying creeping fauna
Which feed on us as on our food
In the sahel baking heat

They met their timely exit
And we were comfortable
Enjoying the cool Harmattan
But now
They are back again
The struggle for comfort
Is it well worth the while?

The insects perhaps should know
As too the flowers around
Surrendering as the sun strikes
And striking back when the sun is down.

—*Lubasa N'ti Nseendi*

Image Of Me

Down the narrow passage
    to the closed, locked door
I looked into the window
    through the blind that tore

I thought I saw a light
    dancing on the shade
It warmed the cold within me
    and brightened the cascade

I needed to get inside
    but didn't have the key
How ironic that the shadows
    were images of me

And then I realized something
    that the door was really my past
And that you had the key
    to open my heart at last

And once I was inside
    Away from all the cold
I looked into your eyes
    And found the lock was gold

—*Jenny Maxam*

The Old

Worn
    torn
        forlorn.
Children gone
    money gone
        ambition gone.
Home is a hollow box.
Emptiness fills the cupboards.
Loneliness, the constant companion,
    sits in a chair.
Yesterday's disappointments
    paper the walls.
Bygone frustrations loom
    like leering spirits.
Illness, like a crouching leopard,
    hides unseen.
The umbilical cord that once nurtured
    has reappeared in
    shrivelled form,
    holding them to dear life.

—*Yolande Porter*

Soul

That unceasing drive up, on and
towards an unseen goal, to live
learn, grow for purpose of soul.

To laugh and cry and feel the pain,
to know of loss and then some gain

To know the heart through the mind
To touch another and then be kind.

To know the darkness and let in the
light, to face all challenge with
spiritual sight.

To watch a flower as it grows
to turn in and on the soul that knows.

—*D. Davis*

Here I Wait

Uncertainty
Unsure of what will be
What does the future hold?
My life suspended in the air
Up or down, we're not sure.

It's just a question of time
To wait is all I can do
Hope of positive directions
Carries me through each day
But a feeling of dread
Lurks in the shadows.

Speculations are made
Plans are discussed
But until the word comes
Preparations are meaningless,
Far from concrete.

I just pray that my desires
Coincide with reality
I just pray that His will
Is where my dreams rest.

—*Erin E. Johnston*

A Mistake

I'm so angry!
What a fool I've been.
A mistake, I now see.
To want something, be so keen.

Walking in a dark section.
It's so easy to choose.
The wrong direction.
One in which, you can only lose.

In the morning light.
Comes the pain called life.
Bringing some new insight,
With each twist of the knife.

Growing hurts, oh it hurts!
I must draw on inner strengths.
To release the hem of my skirt.
So it can reach my new lengths.

In closing I do not regret.
Being the fool who made a mistake.
In my heart I will not forget.
The part of me without it, I could not make.

—*Barbara Dyer*

The Picture Poem

If a man should paint a picture
What then would he paint
A canvas of light or dark stormy night
A country scene of remembered dream
Or a picture of bright city lights
A house of straw a brick wall or door
Leading nowhere in particular
A cat or a mouse a pig or a grouse
Or a beautiful meandering stream.

If a man should paint a picture
What then would he paint.
A memory of his he couldn't forgive
Or an adventure he had lived
A canvas of truth or blatant lie
A pit of despair or bright sunny sky
Happiness and laughter or total disaster
All This Could A Man Paint.

—*Y. M. Russell*

Farewell To Foil And Sorrow

Farewell to foil and sorrow
What will the morrow bring
We won't know for sure
Till we hear New Year bells ring
And we won't know our idea

Farewell to foil and sorrow
Or is it all a dream
Sometimes we slave and foil
For the good that they will bring
Just sometimes we could scream
And what if we do scream
When we're not heard or seem
We let it all out
And we begin again
But I prefer to shout
I shout on the sideline
To cheer my teams on
And when it all comes good
Areas out in song

—*Deamus Kelly*

The Cross

What do I feel.
When I look at the cross
A sense of pain.
And a sense of loss.
That's what I feel
When I look at the cross.

What do I see
In that man, up there,
With nails, in his hands.
And thorns, in his hair.
That's what I see.
When I look at the cross.

Those who have eyes
Let them see
That He did it for you.
And He did it for me.
That's what I see.
When I look at the cross.
Look at the cross... Look at the cross.

—*Austin W. Barton*

Thankful for Each One

Listen for the bird that sings,
when summer breezes blow.
And when a ray of sunshine comes,
watch a flower grow.
Marvel at the wondrous things,
even when they're small, grasp
hold of the knowledge that
you already know.
Let not the mistakes of others be
the path you go;
The bad things we can learn from,
and the good things help us grow,
for in life's long struggle you harvest
the seeds you sew.
Watch an autumn leaf in colour, as it
tumbles to the ground, its one of Gods
creations, there's many to be found
Observe all things around you, and
be thankful for each one.

—*Debbie Kragnes*

September

There are those who will complain
  When summer's end has come
The dreaded cold will soon arrive,
  There is so much to be done
People rush around "preparing,"
  It really is too bad
For they miss so many pleasures
  That God meant us to have
There eyes are all but blinded
  With thoughts of snow and cold,
They walk right past the beauty
  That is there to behold
And there is no better time of year
  For beauty to be found
Every leaf that is set free
  To gently meet the ground
Every tree so special
  It's colours quite unique
To me this glorious time of year
  Is beauty at it's peak

—*Donna M. Moar*

Dreams

Dreams are wonderful,
When they come true,
But extra wonderful,
When they happen to you,
Even if they don't come true,
The striving's worth the effort,
And you will find,
If you persist,
It's a wonderful effort.
Because, apart from winning,
When you do
You'll find there's more dreams
Than you ever knew,
So, don't give up,
When the going's rough,
Because when you're
Fresh out of dreams,
You'll still have enough.

—*Gertrude Galvin*

A Place So Free

There is a place I love to go,
Where the water runs so clear,
It slaps against the rocky shore,
And faint animal calls you'll hear.

It is a place to calm the soul.
In everlasting bliss,
At night the stars do wander out,
To send a goodnight kiss.

It is a place where birds still sing,
You only need to listen,
And in the morning dew falls,
Making tall trees glisten.

It is a place to escape,
From all those painful fears,
It is a place to compensate,
For all those stressful years.

It is a place still blessed by God,
A place He'd surely save,
For only beauty He created,
And the breath of life He gave.

—*Rosemary Goudreau*

Sand Stops

I traced my steps with in the sand
  which tides had not washed away.
But the steps were worn down
  from daily wakes of waves.

An aging afternoon today
  I took a lonely walk.
To ease the pain of noisy worlds
  that collided with my thoughts.

Am I just traces in that sand
  fading with each foamy wave
Or anchored firmly on the beach
  which tides won't steal away.

Behind me lies the wasted weeks
  I wish I could recall.
Ahead awaits so many days
  for me to stand up tall.

—*Anita Dotts*

No Escape

Like the comic superhero
who flies with his cape
when my times were down to zero,
I'd fly for my escape

I could wander in my dreamland
without any interference
as a child it was much easier
than trying perseverance

Still today I can wander
fearing that I'll find
my imagination so far ahead
in reality, I'm so behind

Live my life as a fantasy
with the truth never told
my mind staying forever young
while my body's getting old

Growing is so hard to take
but someday I'll realize
that sometimes there's just no escape
when you look with open eyes

—*Guy Furet*

Roses Thorns Bar

In the garden, in back of the yard
Wild as the wind blows harder
Roses thorns bar
Tempting in one's eyes
As the wind blows them
To and fro
Taunting, teasing, men
As the wind blows them
To and fro

What harm can come of this
One rose, one rose
No one will know
An untouched bash
One rose, no harm done
One rose, a triumph is won
But
In the garden, in back of the yard
Wild as the wind blows harder
Another rose thorns bar

—*Renee Caruso*

"Eyes (From Darkness To Light)"

Sleepless night and dreaming
With open eyes
Painful day and fooling around
With closed eyes
Unconditional love and happiness
With spinning eyes
Psychic power and magnetism
With perfect eyes
Love power and turning on
With amazing eyes
Loneliness and grief
With crying eyes
Views of life and surroundings
With uncertain eyes
Insight and vision
With inner eyes
Drop scene and ecstasy
With incredible eyes
How beautiful are
your and my eyes!!!

—*Syed Razzak Ali Shah*

Life

Today the sun shines bright and clear
With the choir of many song birds
in the morning light
But tomorrow lad you may be
in God's hands
No one knows what the future holds
or what may come to be
But I do know lad
that life has blessed thee
in order to live
a clean and thoughtful life
And one of happiness and joy
Keep your faith
in God's good grace
You shall live forever more.

—*George Matejic*

No More Me

Here I sit,
with these wild eyes.
Alone, by myself,
like a captive held inside.

Beauty gone,
just these four walls.
Broken heart, lost soul,
an endless fall.

Time forgotten,
days and nights are the same.
It's been so long,
I forgot my name.

Silent, quiet,
nothing I can see.
In life or death,
there is no more me.

—*Luciano Maimone*

To-gather Forever

Even in darkness light dawns on you
You are gracious, compassionate.
And I love you.
Tomorrow we'll marry
Sweetheart you and me.
To-gather forever.
How happy we'll be.

You have no fear of bad news
Your heart is at ease
Your trusting and loving
So easy to please
In the end we will triumph.
Because you hold the key
to-gather, forever.
How happy we'll be.

—*Elizabeth Piercey*

Untitled

Oh man of love and man of dreams.
You flow along like a mountain stream.
So gently down the smooth earths face.
With loving arms and handsome grace.
Then crash yourself upon the rocks
In anger to express your thoughts.
You touch the banks so tenderly
In hopes that she won't set you free.
For every little drop of rain
That falls on you and takes your name
Makes you ripple on with glee.
And feel as proud as any sea.

—*Lee Brock*

Naughty Daughter

When I say "Say Papa"
You cry and say "Mama"
When I say "I am Papa"
You still jump to Mama

Whenever I carry you
You still peep at her
Only when I say "Naughty"
You understand that word

Then you will smile
Making me so glad
When Mama milk for you
You show me naughty face

Within a second again
You will ignore me
Turn to Mama and hide in her lap
As if you know not me

—*Suwarn Vajracharya*

Friends For Life

Weeping willow
You droop so low,
The wind can no longer carry you
To and fro,

The sun gleaming down
Like the sparkle in her eye,
I no longer sit there and cry

My eyes are red, raw and sore
My makeup all muffled,
My face all smudged
But know longer, do I care,

For the shade you gave me
The sense of comfort,
Has gone away
And with it your shadow,

Weeping willow
I weep no more
She has gone away
I shall say no more...

—*Brooke Scarlett*

The Ties That Bind

You had your umbilical cord
wrapped so tightly around my neck
I thought I might
choke

Wherefore must I go
So you may flower in my absence
In Truth I know I steal your water
And you wither without

I must take my leave
So you may bloom
For it is better to watch and smell a
beautiful flower from afar
Than to pick one and wait and see it
slowly die

If I were but a gardener
But alas I am not
Just a mere man
Who once held something precious in
his calloused hands
Until I smothered it and watched it die.

—*Shelley Mallory*

Dreams

In my dreams I see you walking in the rain
The moonlight shining on your dampened face
While you sing a song of sadness
Only in my dreams

In my dreams I see you before a fire
I feel your heartbeat and I can hear your breathing
You stare into the fire with sadness in your eyes
Submitting to the strength of the flame you walk
Within its depths and disappear
Only in my dreams

In my dreams I see you standing in the valley of the souls
The wind blowing through your hair, and your arms
Outstretched like silver wings as you let go of the ground
And fly to the freedom you long for so deeply
Only in my dreams

In my dreams I see you laying along the ground, a gentle
breeze flowing over you and a content and peaceful look in
your eyes, and I realize you are where you want to be,
Only in my dreams...

—*Lynne Smith*

Lament Of A Ghetto Child

I crawl in the festering slum at dawn,
Scornful dews, like stale ribbons of ephemeral crown
Bless my dark forest with grey mist of despair.
The scavenging spirit of vultures have ripped my soul apart
I lie prostrate like a voiceless earthworm
With tortured expressions sealed in dry tongue
And crumbs are chiselled away from my wretched hands.

In the abyss of edible abundance
I strain for distant wobbling aroma
A pebble of doom triggered ripples of sorrow
Sorrow is the fragrance of the wretched
When agony is pampered, the soul erupts
Awakening the dead.

Fangs of grotesque machinators have triumphed
File ducts of tyranny hold forth its trophy
And I, a little mammal kiss the dust with awe
My brow is overburdened by venom of fleeing sleep
And hunger is decorated in brass plate.
I'm stuck in arcane mousetrap,
And octopodial vampires are smiling.

—*Ndulue Erasmus Chinemelu*

The Stars

The stars will always be my friends forever until the end.
Whenever I'm alone, they'll always be there to comfort me.
Sounds a little funny, but to me it's true.
Whether day or night or even rain, the stars will always
    be there for me and you.

—*Shannon Stacie Garza*

Life

Life is forever lasting with a beginning and no end.
You were brought to this world as a baby,
    to learn, to live, to love.
The baby then grows into a child,
    full of energy, and enjoyment.
The child then grows into a teenager;
    full of problems, and new feelings.
The teenager then grows into an adult;
    with hopes, and dreams for the future.
The adult then grows into a senior citizen,
    when their hopes, dreams, and wisdom is fulfilled.
Before you know it your life is gone but, the memories that
are everlasting, are forever.

—*Michelle Van Haaren*

In the Lonely Mile

You saw me walking by so sad,
you saw me and you liked me since,
I caught you looking at me while
I ran from the lonely mile.

You talked to me softly while
I looked into your lovely eyes,
You lost yourself in mine,
your honey face made me shy,
and with a touch you made me cry.

My tears were like lemon drops,
I felt them running down so sour,
you calmed me, with a hug
you gave me warmth,
there we were together at last.

The company you gave me
was more precious than anything in the world,
and until this moment I hold
all those moments we had, together,
at the lonely mile.

—*Adrianna Alvarado Chavez*

Mom

I always laughed when people said
    your best friend is your mom.
It didn't make such sense to me
    my mom was just my mom.
Now I am old and she as gone
    I think back all those years.
Of all the things she did for me
    to dry up all my tears.
And as I grew into a man
    left home to wed and live
My mom would always be in touch
    her help and love to give.
She made the perfect granny
    as I always knew she would.
The children always did their best
    when granny said they should.
So I think those people got it right
    and I don't give a damn.
I tell my children all the time
    your best friend is your mom.

—*A. B. Hughes*

Personal Reflections

I came to you with nothing Lord
You gave me everything
I cried to you for help Lord
You took me 'neath your wing
My life was a disaster Lord
You gave me a fresh start
I was lonely, in despair Lord
Your goodness touched my heart
I thought I'd never smile again
You took away my fears
My broken heart I brought to you
You wiped away my tears
I come before you now Lord
I give you heart and soul
No longer am I broken
Your love has made me whole

—*Valerie J. Rees*

Hold On

Hold on to   my heart,
for it hurts   deep down inside.
Hold on to all the memories we once shared
at one time. Love breaks the heart, for mine
is broken in two. I'm sitting in a motionless
world thinking of only you. But it doesn't
change the fact things are not the way
they seem. For my heart is really
broken and it seems that there is no
more you and me. But in my
dreams things are still the
same. With you holding
on to my heart as if
it were only
yesterday.

—Michelle R. Marcum

A Child's Love

So far away, but yet so near
I close my eyes and almost hear
Your laughter and eternal cheer.
    You both are always with me.

When I get down and feeling blue,
I take a break and think of you.
You make me smile like you always do.
    You both are always with me.

My flesh and blood, my guiding force.
I love you and you'll be a source
Of comfort through life's tangled course.
    You both are always with me.

Through all the laughter, love and tears
You brought me up to face my fears.
Thanks, Mom and Dad, for all the years.
    You both are always with me.

—Gretchen Lyons

Shadows

The shadows of darkness is
    man's inheritance.
The light of glory is his
    reward.

—Santos J. Torres

Crying Tears

Now I'm crying tears
    you won't understand.

Now I'm crying tears
    without a lending hand.

Now I'm crying tears
    with tearful eyes.

Now I'm crying tears
    because your love I despise.

Now I'm crying tears
    because I have no friends.

Now I'm crying tears
    because friendship isn't
    supposed to have ends.

Now I'm crying tears
    because my life is gone.

Now I'm crying tears
    because I'm sick and can't
    go on.

—Gretchen Luther

The Garden

I'd like to go in the garden
a place I'd love to play.
Where birds are chirping
The grass is green.
Oh what a glorious day!

It's my quiet cabin in the woods.
Where only I go.
So if anyone asks where I go?
    You'll know.

A place with fruits and vegetables
a place to play.

What is it? Is that what you say?
My place to play — the garden.

    The garden?
Where everyone is happy!

—Tashea C. Dickens

In Flight

I dream that one day I may fly
Soaring free as a bird
Not bound to the earth but
Darting in and out
Among the clouds
Breaking the speed of sound
Rolling and turning in the great sky
Then looking down upon
The multicoloured earth below
Feeling unattached to the
Life I know
And yet feeling it
Call me back again
Slowly I descend knowing
I have been where few can go
Then feeling that heady after glow

—Patricia Goodwin

Late Love

Red disc, the sun.
Spring, the season.
From life, sunset;
holding hands, him and her.

A late afternoon, she and he
are going holding hands.
At sunset,
two souls are one.

Two mouths get united
in the sunset,
in a warm kiss
from late afternoon.

Is not the impulsive kiss
from a sunrise.
is the comprehensive kiss
from a sunset.

Is the most pure love,
is the reality,
is the love that overcome
any loneliness.

—Osvaldo Foti

It

I can see its fingers
They're fingers of flame
It's black and it's ugly
With a heart of cold steel
Living in it's cold world
He thinks he can't let go
For that's what it tells him
Lies, lies and more lies
It's so full of deception
Now his nights are like day
And his days are like night
He can no longer distinguish
The fact from the dreams
He's got this one last chance
To gain back his heart
His soul and his life

—Pam Clarke

The Terry Fox Story

Terry Dear Teary,
Your like a golden fairy,
You made it come true.
You made it come true.

Terry Dear Terry,
You've a part of the world,
You touched each one's heart.
That was the greatest start.

Terry Dear Terry,
Thank God for a boy like you,
With one leg you made a home run.
You knew it could be done.

—Kathleen Hutskal

Crow

I am black I am crow
No one looks
No one stares
No one loves
No one cares
Would it be if I was
White as snow
I am black I am crow
Sometimes here sometimes there
I am native to nowhere
I belong to this world
And live everywhere
But yet I have
No home nowhere to go
I am black I am crow

—M. A. Salam

Reflections

I sit on the welcoming white sand
Watching the gentle blue waves
Turn playfully over each other
As would two puppies.

I watch the vast, delicate sea
And the moon pouring light
Lazily onto its surface.

I enjoy the cool, breezy night air
And memories flood over me
Like waves on the seashore.

—Sara Hahn

Stacey

You're white
You're soft
You breath spring time into
My winter nights
The smell you radiate
Makes the bees pollinate
Plastic flowers
I've tried to fondle
Your petals
Radiate the sun
That you've absorbed
The fragrance grows
The bloom is full
And then it withers
And dies
Thank God for
The roots that
Still reach in
And feed upon my soul

—*Sanford Spaulding*

My Pet

Do you wonder?
I mean really,
Wonder?
What it's like,
To be a cat.
Fastidious, yet playful.
Friendly, yet distant.
A mystery.
I wonder...
Really.
How we can be
So different, yet so much
The same.
We are together,
But not really.
Although we are far apart,
We are never far in thought.
We are a cat.

—*Olga Petrik*

Club Nicotine

The air is gray
The smell is foul
This awful cloud is smoke.

Holding your breath
You race for the door
Hoping you will not choke.

There was a time
This would have been
A scene in a motion picture.

It's now outside
A bank, an office,
Or any public fixture.

With no place for a smile
Together they huddle
The ones with this unhealthy habit.

Not knowing, or caring
What harm it will do
...That Smoke...
They just have to have it.

—*Gloria G. Sagendorph*

Jeweled Hair

Snow is falling clear.
With some consistency and snow flakes meld
And mound,
Until we have hidden valleys, secret caves
To be found.
Icicles draping o'er the trees . . .
Trees, white limbed, robed in snow,
More beauteous than royal regalia can know.
Crowned with icy jewels most rare,
Shimmer in the night, in winter's lair.
Lit only by snow and phantom stars,
I too go out to be so garbed
With icy jewels in my hair.

—*Grace Graham*

Harmony

She walks beside me, shares my path
each carrying some of the weight.
I am the master of some tasks;
Some others are far better her domain.
I am the weft and she the warp,
Each contributing our own strength
to the weave,
Never competing for dominance,
Each of us revels in the discovery
Of our own unique talents.
We understand that harmony
Is the essence.

—*Grace Milosz*

Salted Thorns

The dark soul carries
Roses of black
To lay at thy feet
His salted kisses
Burn deep in your wounds
Mocking a lifetime of pain
Pleasure is taken in his task
Stealing souls of the dead
The dark knight continues his journey
to the foot of another
Innocent bed

—*Sherry Chase*

Untitled

I was alone and lost.
And needed you at any cost.
Living on a road of sin.
Hoping you would take me in.

Then I heard you call my name.
I could no longer play a game.
"Help me Lord," today I say.
Show me how, to follow your way.

"How can I repay?
all the things you did for me.
"Oh the light, you let me see.
All the joy, you gave to me.

This story, was never told.
How you came and make me whole.
It's a story to behold
All the joy in my soul.

You gave me things, I never had
And my life's no longer sad.
This world of sin, no longer be.
"Help me" Lord take me in.

—*Grace Crum*

The Nurse

As I look at your face,
My heart fills with sorrow,
For you I am afraid,
Might not be here tomorrow,

Even though I don't know you well,
My mind holds the grief,
For you are my patient,
And death is the thief,

Why must you suffer,
From this deadly disease,
I stand by you helpless,
Unable to appease,

How I wish I could save you,
And take away the pain,
But now is the time you need me most,
So by your bedside I will remain,

I will watch over you,
In your final hour,
I will be the one,
To release you into God's loving power.

—*Natalie Stokner*

The Mystery

What happens to extension cords?
    That's what I'd like to know.
We purchase them and bring them home,
    but where do they all go?
We buy them by the dozens,
    and I get a bit irate,
As we never seem to have one
    when the need is very great.

At Christmas time we bought a bunch,
    as that's the time of year
A person needs extension cords
    to help extend the cheer,
But by July there's not a one
    that we can ever find.
It's a mystery that haunts us,
    and it tends to blow my mind!

—*Gracie Thomas*

The Love Of My Life

He was just a friend
But unnoticed now
I walk down the hall
Looking forward to love
But he just walks by now.

Should I tell him how I feel
About how much I love him
Or will it just wreck that we have
Even though there's nothing left
I'd like to think there's more.

What should I do?
What should I say?
Every time I see him
I just sink away.

I know I'll never get him
All though I do still try
I love him to much
To ever let go
Of what we had. Of what we have.
Of what I hope to have but never will.

—*Nicole Syme*

Friendships

Many poems have been written
About friendships of every kind
But this poem is very different
Because my friend, well she's one of a kind.

There are friendships in the good and bad times
There are friendships for just a day.
But my friend is very special
She's a friend come what may!

Her name I can not reveal
For there is one more like her
She is the same kind hearted person
The very best of a friend for sure

If I could but find the words
For mere words there are none
To thank and give application for
All the things they have done.

I would thank them for their friendships
For giving me the gift called trust
I would thank God for them
'Cause He has given me so much.

—*Paula M. Ryan*

Ours

Our lives have crossed and intertwined
Creating a bond that is hard to find.
And when we talk and join our hands
Our emotions soar like the shifting sands.

Our time together when we meet
Is oh so happy, tender and sweet.
And when we caress and share a kiss
I realize how much it is you I miss.

Our feelings for each other have grown strong
So much so that they can not be wrong.
And when we gaze into each others eyes
I dream of our times under the skies.

Our hearts beat with the word yet unspoken
One that means so much, not just a token.
And though it is hard to admit how we feel
The sentiment behind it could not be more real.

Our future together will be wonderful and fun
As we spend our days watching the rise and fall of the sun.
And when we make love, you and I
The world will stand still and seem to pass us by.

—*Patti Adams*

Prophecy of Doom

I was numb with shock
At the onset of another political era
Standing with arms akimbo
Fear crept up my body, and
Relatively imprisoned my mind
Not because of anything, rather,
The cri-de-coeur of electorates
Relapsing into the blunder of being mesmerized
By the sugar-coated mouth of a candidate
Canvasing under the guise of patriotism.
  On the verge of giving up,
When agony mounted
With fortunes out of the realm of possibility
I was drawn into the vortex of politics
Only to see the transparency of him
Whose appearance believed the picture of his agenda
Who will surely fulfill his prophecy of doom
And evasion of responsibility if elected
Now the grass is greener after a heavy rain
The need to keep my pecker up.

—*Olusola A. Ade*

Seeds On Life's Highway

We are all sowing seeds on life's highway,
  A harvest some day we will reap,
  Some will make hearts glad and happy,
  And some will bring sorrow and grief.

Let's each ask ourselves this question:
  What kind of seeds have I sown?
Will they bring rich rewards tomorrow
Or heartaches and shame at the dawn?

  Today is the day to sow good seeds
  As on Life's Highway we trod,
  Tomorrow may be forever too late
  If we loiter, slumber, and nod.

God grant that we each may sow sunshine
  In hearts that are lonely and sad,
May we lift burdens from our fellowman
And help to make hearts light and glad.

  I hope when my life's journeys ended
  And my race on earth I have run.
  That I shall hear my Savior say,
  "My child, your work's well done."

—*Edith Cox Turner*

A Little Piece About Me, Myself, And I

I am myself.
I am six feet tall, and wear size 12 shoes.
People say I have grey eyes.
But when I am happy,
They say that my eyes are blue.

I fear death,
But anxiously await the afterlife.
I believe in God,
But I have no religion.

Shakespeare may have been
  A great writer.
I don't admire him for his literary works;
But I admire him because he was a rebel.
  He wore pantyhose.
I will never understand life,
Or know what I will be.
I will probably live like James Dean.
  Live fast and die young
I am the one and only;
  Obadiah Ramzey Ariss.

—*Obe Ariss*

A Tribute To An Angel

Funny thing about angels,
You never know where or when they may show up.
They are an unexpected gift from God.
They can appear in times of great distress or,
They can just as easily appear in times of great joy.
They can take the form of a child - so that you can see the
world through innocent eyes.
They might take the form of an elder - so that you can see
the world through the eyes of experience.
They may take the form of a wise counselor - so that you can
see the world with open eyes.
They may take the form of a loved one - so that you can see
the world with loving eyes.
The greatest angel of all - Jesus Christ - was sent so that
we might see the world with forgiving eyes.
It has been said that the eyes are the mirrors to our soul.
Angels come so that our minds may be filled with knowledge,
So that our hearts may be filled with love and,
So that our soul may be filled with the Spirit, so that we
may celebrate the Essence of Life!

—*Greer Moody*

Thanksgiving Poem

I am a turkey, all round and fat,
don't want to be on a plate that's flat,
someday soon I won't have a head,
then I'll go and rest in bed.

—*Melissa Geiger*

The Gift

should be there by now my dear
somewhere behind your shoulder
and if you'd suddenly turn around
you will see an incredible clover

the type that has four leaves
wishing you eternal luck
would have delivered it myself
but could hardly ease it up

take a look at the beauteous skies
perhaps it's upon the blimp
if this is not the case
can provide no other whim

is there any chance you fall
to receive this lovely gift
once you are back within my arms
must take you to those very skies to live

—*Gregory Reed*

To My Sister

As the moon knows the dark secrets
Of the expanding twilight, so I know
Your heart; we watch the beginning
And the ending of the dreaming earth
together; the world gives forth its secrets
As the sun spills light, and we share
Knowledge with the spirits walking here;
we have a bond, unspoken, yet still sacred,
For we are sisters; the world knows us,
And the sky respects us; we give life;
    We nurture the earth;
        We are caregivers;
        We are the chosen,
safe in the shroud of our common mystery.

—*Sandra Wallraven Stone*

I Could

like to capture a rainbow
and stick it in a box.
that anytime you wanted to,
you could reach in and pull out a piece of sunshine.

like to build you a mountain
that you could call your very own
place to find serenity when you feel
the need to be alone.

like to be the one
who's there with you when you're lonely
troubled or just need someone to hold on to
like to do all this and more
make your life happy.

but sometimes it isn't easy to do
the things I'd like to do or give what I could give.
until I learn
catch rainbows or build mountains, let me do for you
that which I know best
let me simply
be your friend

—*Michael R. O'Coin*

Daddy Please Don't Go

Please daddy don't go.
The room filled with fear.
My daddy's name was sergeant Joe.
On my face was one last tear.
The soldiers came to feed your
    children and you.
My daddy and the other soldier's where
    very brave.
You shot at us before we
    where through.
Today we are lowering my daddy
    in his grave.
Please send our soldiers home.
Let's stop the needless blood shed.
Leave Somalia on their own.
Then there will be no more dead.

—*Sandra Floyd Buckbee*

It's Up To You And Me

Our children are so precious and innocent as can be
We must do our best to protect them. It's up to you and me
Let's grip their hand real firmly
As we walk along life's road
And guard them from the wrongful ways
As the paths unfold.
Give firm but gentle guidance along the walk of life
And lift them when they stumble
Or encounter strife.
Let's make them feel secure and loved,
As every child should be
Always be there for them, it's up to you and me.
When temptation tends to lure them
Let's guide them all the way
Diverting their direction
A foundation for them lay
If we do the ground work for them
Beginning from day one
We'll be able to look back with a smile
And say our work is done.

—*Mary Friesen*

When Somebody Cares

As we grow older, we think of the past,
Our health and abilities disappear fast,
We can visit a doctor, our ills he repairs,
What we treasure the most is when somebody cares.

If our mates have passed on, we miss that spouse,
There's a sorrow filled vacancy left in the house,
Our children are married, may be unawares,
That parents may wonder if somebody cares.

Some to a home have been favorably sent,
The family feels the act is well-meant,
But even among others, whose thinking one shares,
We often do wonder if somebody cares.

We have many memories stored in our minds,
Bad ones we forget and just leave behind,
We look forward with hope, but nothing compares,
To the joy in our hearts, when somebody cares.

Time passes slowly, our aches increase,
We try to enjoy a measure of peace,
There's a knock at the door, an answer to prayers,
Someone has arrived, so somebody cares.

—*Helen Price*

Something's Missing

If you don't have someone to look up to,
a brother, sister, or friend,
you'll always be blind.

If you don't have something to lean on,
a pole, wall, or shoulder,
you'll always fall to the ground.

If you don't have someway to follow,
a road, path, or guide,
you'll always wander astray.

If you don't have a friend to count on
caring, honest and true,
you'll always be lonely.

—*Thomas J. Kerner*

Death Of A King

As the flowers grow in the grassy fields
a man falls without his shields
with the frosty morning came the dew
while in the city there was still no news
about the man called King who now lies dead
Shot by a man who was out of his head
when the sun rose this frightful day
all were seeking a better way
the way of happiness and freedom for all
why did this man have to fall
and as his country wept and mourned
all his people were frightened and torn
even though he is dead his spirits lives on
to show his people a new dawn
at his funeral came many from all over the land
brought together in peace by his command
all he wanted was a better way to live
but it was such a demanding price to give.

—*Timothy VanSant*

My Dream

I dream of a place so far away
A place so peaceful I long for the day
That you will rescue me from my sorrow
And help me see a brighter morrow
For life is too short to be this sad
And days are too long to remember what I had.

I dream of a place so far away
A place so happy I long for the day
That you will rescue me and take me there
But until then make me happy while I am here

—*Susan L. Stypula*

The Room

A room dark with no color or light.
A room to which you go not for happiness
but to cry alone.
A room full of secrets to which it won't
tell to a single sole.
A room bottled up with fear for it holds
so much emotion it may explode.
A room alone standing, waiting for the
door to be opened for which would behold
a new problem for the place to solve.
A room to which is called my mind.

—*Brandy Brush*

My Family, Together

My family is a father, a mother
A sister, and a brother.
We have four pets, not a cat
Neither do we have a bat.
Just a dog and hamster
A fish and a turtle scampers.

These things to me
Are as special as they can be.
We do many things together
In fall, spring, summer and winter weather.

Together we know we have nothing to loose.
If there is trouble we can make it through.
We are like a group of words,
Needing each other to make a sentence.

We save ourselves from bees
Or poison in trees.
We know we can trust each other
Me, a sister, a brother, a father, a mother.

We know we are in this together and there is no way out.
My family is special to me, that's what my family is about.

—*Stephanie Mae Dishart*

Untitled

A voice like falling water — it's workin'
A voice like the wind — it works
Are you workin'? Functioning smoothly again?
Something ain't working quite right, it needs adjustment.
Something ain't working quite right, don't throw it away!

Vicious circle changed by the wheel of fate
So as the sun dies you do
But we all know the sun will rise again
And of course that means you too.

We now know that life is made for living
It's there for us to show
That through a death life is given
When the wind blows cold
You've got to fly above the storm
Look into yourself and you will find spring
Then you'll turn around.

—*Brett A. Rouse*

Life Without You

Life without you is emptiness
A void as big as a black hole
My emotions with you are bright as a rainbow
Without you they are dark as coal

Life without you is much worse
Than a broken toy being discarded
For toys can be repaired or at least replaced
But I'm permanently broken-hearted

Life without you is cruel torture
Causing agony, misery, and pain
For you are every hope and wish to me
And turn each loss into gain

Life without you is a dry creek bed
A dead flower, a lifeless tree
Life without you is a gravesite for love
With tombstone words describing me

Life without you is the largest hurt
It's pain without parallel
Life without you is a prison sentence
With no chance to leave my cell

—*Tom Russell*

Untitled

Today we said goodbye not knowing what the future holds for us
All I have is love for you
But we weren't meant to be together
Not now and maybe not ever
I see so much sadness in your eyes
I wish I could kiss the tears away
But I'm no match against a broken heart
All I can do is walk away and hope that time will heal your wounds
Maybe in time you'll of me and want the love I have to give you
Or maybe I'll became a distant memory of a love that slipped away.

—*Susan Renee Braidis*

Nobody's Child

A tot of five, a victim of fate;
All too young she learns to hate.
Today, the papers are filed,
Now, she's nobody's child.

Tears of the orphan, once cradled in love;
Forever trapped in this broken dove.
No longer innocent, meek, nor mild;
She is a foster child.

Anger and hatred, sets passions to heat;
Tall and slender, a girl of the street.
On crack and cocaine, her mind runs wild;
Just another runaway, a nobody's child.

Alone and broken, they lay her to rest.
She's beat the system, yes, she passed the test.
Drawing nearer to heaven, her soul smiles;
"Now, I am somebody's child."

—*Susan R. Martinez*

Alone

Alone is what I am with no one to share my love,
Alone is what I am with only the one above.
He left me all alone with no one to cling to.
He left my heart and my mind so very blue.

Alone is what I am, it makes me so very sad
He left me without anything not even a memory, that made me mad.
How could he do this to me?
The pain that I have, why can't he see?

Alone is what I am, no one else will understand
Until he comes back to take my hand.
I wish he were here to see what he's done,
He would soon see that going through this is no fun.

Alone is what I am, with no one but my mother.
This poem is about no one but my brother.
If it weren't for him I wouldn't be writing this.
I'm not the only one alone, because he's missing his sis!

Alone!

—*Shana Stocker*

Cast Realities Bolted To The Sky

Chickens do lay eggs.
Cows do jump over the moon.
Butterflies do fly high beautifully.
Trees do not move in starlight twinkle.
And gingerbread has such a good heart.

Solid realities cast beguiling shadows
Solid realities cut deep into the sky
Solid realities are hard to see through

Thank heavens the sky still passes by
no matter how hard I make things.

—*Gretchen Yates Lum*

The Harvest

The rusted blade repeats a rhythmic stroke
And brusquely topples brittle, withered stalks.
His calloused palms grip fiercely, strangle, choke.

His burly arms, his fingers gnarled invoke
Obsession born of failure. As he walks,
The rusted blade repeats a rhythmic stroke.

His freezing mouth releases frosted smoke
As darkening skies surround a dozen hawks.
His calloused palms grip fiercely, strangle, choke.

Deserted by the rain, no help to soak
Such arid summer crops, they dried to chalk.
The rusted blade repeats a rhythmic stroke.

And now he toils to purge his loss, provoke,
Renew desire to conquer nature's balk.
His calloused palms grip fiercely, strangle, choke.

Then all at once the clouds erupt to cloak
The man, his field, and deafening thunder talks.
The rusted blade repeats a rhythmic stroke.
His calloused palms grip fiercely, strangle, choke.

—*William R. Poynter*

Memory of John McCormick

Where you were it was always laughing,
And talking, and eating,
The air humming with happiness.
Silence was waiting outside the door.

The air around you danced with magic
And you burned with a holy fire.
All who came near you were warmed
And believed again in the goodness of living

Your life was your poem,
But you wrote all your poems upon the air.
Now that you are gone
We are left with the silent space where you stood.
And the air of this electronic planet
Does not sustain us.

—*Sarah Williamson Baicy*

A Child No More

So young, so unknowing,
And yet you take advantage of me so,
I had done nothing to you,
I wanted nothing from you,
But yet you still violated me,
I shall never be the same,
My life is now like a feather pillow,
That has been torn open,
And all of the feathers are floating freely in the wind,
Never to be recaptured.
I was so frightened after the ordeal,
That I spoke no more,
My vocal chords hung loose in my throat,
Like old rubberbands.
How could you be so heartless?
So evil to just a mere child?
What demon possessed your mind to commit such a horrible act?
Look here, at my heart and soul, see these scars?
They will be there forever reminding me of the day,
That I was a child no more.

—*Angela Murphy*

Precious Moments

Those precious moments that you and I shared
      are no more
Those precious moments when I knew you cared
      are no more
Those precious moments are etched in my heart
      But are no more
  Those precious moments were there
      right from the start
And only I know those precious moments
      Are memories now
And always I'll remember those precious moments
      We had them and how——

    —Sylvia P. Gerson

The Dream

  Late one night
as I crawled into the bed,
  Visions of our troubled earth
crept in my head.
  I picked up trash and cleaned our water,
so they'd look like they should,
  I wanted someone to help me,
but no one ever would.
  When I woke up from my dream,
to the least of my surprise,
  I stood to see a terrible world,
so I tried to hide my eyes.
  The trees were dead, the water brown,
the sky a murky grey,
  Our world was a living nightmare,
and I was in dismay.
  The people of the Earth,
just do not understand,
  That whether or not the earth we live,
on us will depend.

    —Brook Ward

Sonnet

'Twas I, tangled up in thy silken web,
At the center of thy framework was thee,
Helpless, alas, trapped by thy sticky threads,
As captured prey, thy venom taunted me;
Thou hadst woven this web in silent night,
'Tis thy tendency to lurk in darkness,
When thou wert done, waited with cruel delight
Upon this stratagem of silken dress.
Ah! yet I have fled from these threads that bind,
Hence, no more a threat shall thy poison, be,
See me not as they prey on which to dine,
For my soul is my own, 'tis not of thee:
  To thee who spins they silky web at night,
  Do cast thine eyes upward, 'tis now daylight.

    —Susan B. Feigelson

Mother

My mother is kind to all races and creed,
Bitter to those who have nothing but greed.

Swim in her oceans, walk on her sand,
Fly in her sky, run on her land.

Her children are blind to her health,
Caring only about themselves.

She grows weak with each passing day,
Knowing the fate her children will pay.

    —Sandy Kenney

Empty...

Nothing but emptiness inside my heart
Beating slower as time goes by
No finish line and no place to start
Just one tear that's left in my eye
I call out your name, but heart only my echoed voice
Am I on a downward climb?
I have nothing else and no other choice
Because of you I cry one more time
Looking at the light that shines up above
Getting dimmer the longer I stare
Only pain and no real love
Just suicidal thoughts flashing everywhere
Controlled by hurt, motivated by lust
I feel like I'm going insane
By myself with non-one to trust
Just her outline in the falling black rain
All alone in a place so cold
Nothing left for me to see
Days and nights are growing old
As for my heart it shall remain empty

    —Tony Strohm

"Pursuit"

Mohawks and hair dyes because it is "in"
because others are watching like sitting ducks
Whispering, and are they ... laughing?

Sometimes when out at night more reds and blacks applied
with brushes and powder puffs than when at home
alone in pajamas with fire and book

Lies created when talking with someone you desire
as a friend... or a lover when your "wants" are higher
on your list than your "needs"

Hours and hours, millions of dollars
every day, clothes, jewelry deflect attention away from the truth

Desperate attempts to "fit in" fail
and sometimes you just need to live life
in your pajamas

    —Shannon Powers

Untitled

Live through any storm.
Beckon the gray void.
Stand firm and undaunted.
Never surrender yourself to yourself.
Celebrate and rejuvenate through sense and thought.
Peel off the coverings to your very nature and spread wide
The opening of your new beginnings
Smile and smile again.
Frown and then smile.
Walk up a mountain, lose yourself.
Share offerings and return pleasures.
Accept gifts and return the honesty.
Fall short only to regain strength.
Meander and parallel that with searing straightness.
Continue to achieve.
Be touched to the very bottom of your personal connectedness.
Retreat only to rebuild; escape to grow, age and flow.

    —Steven Stenzler

Untitled

I loved his hands— so strong,
And yet so gentle when they rested upon mine.
And now they're gone.
But I remember
And often in the stillness of the night
I reach for them,
Seeking the strength they always brought me.

    —Zetha Warren

ly Arisen Lord

y savior hung by each soft, nail-pierced hand,
tween two criminals a lifeless form.
e one who healed the blind and calmed the storm,
as greeted by a darkened, barren land.
e whistling whip had worn him strand by strand,
blist'ring blaze and blare to him did swarm.
e cried to God, his anguished spirit torn,
is mortified man was a spice turned bland.
t like the beaming sun on purple dawns,
y God was lifted from his dingy grave,
d triumphed o'er the ghastly grip of death.
en as a mother deer protects her fawns,
y Jesus promised every child to save,
om sins which curse our lives at every breath.

—Tony Perricelli

lack

I were a color, I'd be black.
ack is the dark.
ack is the night.
ack conceals you in itself;
en everything is all right.
ou can hide in black.
o one sees your thoughts in black.
t, black can eat you,
d make you lost.
ou're all alone and scared in black.
ack is your friend and also your enemy.

—Shanna Megan Putnam

A World Of Broken Dreams

Your gentle ways and magic touch
breathed a spark into a darken night.
Reaching out with kindness
and love in flight.
Touch after touch,
kiss after sweet kiss, burning,
healing, mending broken feelings with
the new spirit of hope.
A new beginning and renewed strength
to break down the binding
brick walls that have helped to keep
this soul buried in hell.
For it takes two hearts to melt
into one to make it work.
ul sad souls be still and do not feel blue.
I said this is hard to do
as our souls were so filled with dreams
s so sad but true, some souls fall quickly,
others seldom do.

—Sylvia Zielke

e Penis

day, my reflection reveals
at I'm not so inadequate
I have always been
owth has finally come
the tender age of twenty-eight
d I gasp at the size
r suddenly I am not ashamed
cause now I am not lacking
at I have always felt was needed

d it really grow
has my imagination been working overtime
ver allowing me to blossom into manhood.

—Gregory Parkhurst

The First Time

He stood alone, off to the side
  brushing his tears, swallowing his pride.

In his hand he held a small flag,
His eyes filled with yesterdays
  his shoulders sagged.

He said aloud to no one,
  "I miss you so my son.
You were taken from us
  before your life was done."

"Now there is only your name as a reminder
  of the war you and your friends won,
Oh yes! you all were winners
  and now your names glisten in the sun."

"And I pray the world remembers
  the price that you all paid,
And trust it will not be forgotten
  the sacrifice you made."

As I approached from the shadows
  he once again stool tall,
And I knew it was his first time, his first time at The Wall.

—Sharon P. Gill

I Didn't Get A Chance To...

I didn't get a chance to say goodbye,
But almost every night I cry.
I didn't get a chance to touch his hand,
Now I don't plat at the beach in the sand.
I didn't get a chance to tell him I loved him,
Now I'm on the edge of a limb,
He died the day,
Before his birthday,
I wish I could have said goodbye,
Sunday May 16th 1993,
The day he died.

—Wendy Ward

Past Time

I know I've said this once before
But I want more, what more you ask
I will soon tell, there's so much out there
We shall dare to share.
So keep on what you are doing and
You'll never know what we could have been doing
So straighten up and don't look back
The future is coming and we shall know what to expect.
If you don't like what you are hearing then think again.
Cause for all I care you can keep dreaming
Dreaming of what, you may ask
We could have been together but that's in the PAST.

—Yvette Valdez

Star By Night

When you look up at the night sky upon a star;
I'll be thinking of you.
At night when you look at the stars they twinkle
and the moon shines brightly.
The star by night shines brighter than the rest of the stars.
This is the one and only, that is called star by night.
It is the only star that knows I'm thinking of you.
This is a very special star because it knows that I'm
thinking of you.
When you are feeling down it will try to cheer you up.
The star by night shines brightly in the night sky.

—Nicole Hopke

My Existence

You said I did not exist.
But in the mist of it I stand before thee
Black beautiful me I shout to you,

"Here I am."

Your tongue openly denied me. But I say to you
How is it that we kiss?

Damn it I do exist!

Your words are, but words.
You ignored me and that, reminds me of another,
I once knew and I told him in a letter I wrote,

I exist.

Before I go, before I leave the presence of you.
I want to touch you, so you can feel my existence.

You took my time, you took my space
and still, I hear you say
I do not exist.

That there is no you and I.

Well, here I am. Black beautiful me.
In your dreams. In your reality. Every time you turn,

I will exist.

  —*Vanessa Benjamin*

Release

            We used to be so close
          but now it's not the same
        our hearts have grown apart
        and who is the one to blame?
            When we first met
          I thought you were the one
          to hold my secrets deep
          and bring out rays of sun.
      But you've turned back to others
        to share your secrets with.
          I guess the way we were
          was just a sacred myth.
        I'm confused by your ways
          but I try to understand
  sometimes the things we hold the tightest
  we must release from the prison of our hand.
          So go your own way now
          and throw away all lies,
          but always remember this,
        true friendship never dies!

  —*Susan Johnson*

Baby's Cryin'

No food on the table,
  But twenty-eyed, multi-colored high-tops on his feet.
Baby's cryin'.
Where's his daddy at?
  "Outside, playin' basketball, somewheres down the street.
  I think that's him."

Brothers everywhere—
  In beds, on tables, in clothes and the sweetpeas.
Baby's cryin'.
Where's his daddy at?
  "Down wit the boys, drinkin' Mad Dog twenty-twenty.
  I think that's him."

Knocked up again, again—
  Though baboon faced and smelly crotched.
Baby's cryin'.
Where's his daddy at?
  "Down to the niggers' motel, lyin' in the morgue.
  I think that's him."

  —*Will Rodgers*

Spending Time

My lover enjoys "spending time" with me.
But says, "how can I know what will happen in
five years.
Don't give me that responsibility."

He is less affectionate than I.
Less physical.
And sometimes superior.
We have no plans.
Perhaps no future.
He has all the balls.
And this is not a fun game.

Please tell me,
Should I graciously opt to get off the court?
Get on with it?
Change channels, turn left right, march forward?

The great escape:
to New York, Amsterdam, California, New Mexico?
Run away.
Please tell me what to do.
Somebody. Anybody, but him.

  —*Tanya Tabachnikoff*

Blindman's Lesson

The blindman reached out to see,
But touched a world of inconsistency.
Mans' proverbs proved mans' fallacy.
In a universe of unconstitutionality.

Campaigns filled with doubtful lies,
Should've provided the politicians timely demise.
But elected because he had honest eyes,
Though he ignored the hungry cries.

Cries of people yearning to be free,
In lands only the blindman could see.
Lands governed by rightful democracy,
But by men practicing only demagoguery.

Still the blindman stretches out a hand,
A gesture only the simple minded understand.
Others are too engulfed to hear the band,
Governed too long, can only take a command.

It's sad to see a blindman weep,
With eyes that are continually asleep,
But he feels us flock together like so many sheep,
In governed crevices, that are now too deep.

  —*Shelly Songer*

The Weekend

Grass covered hills torn from the rivers'
winding course that cleaves two nations,
summated by the literary stacks,
essays, treatise upon the lives there,
fine art reflects this harsh grey beauty
in pastels and oils, and numbered
prints of impossible sunsets.

Venturing here for the weekend we come,
the tiny hotel lodged near Black Mountains:
to present dream and possible future.
We stay and eat, the rivers trout,
delighting in this aquatic of duel nationality,
discovering our bodies in shared liqueurs,
coffee and after eights.

The mountains ranges a silent shroud
from others knowing, we close
the curtains removing possibilities,
until there is just one.

  —*Paul Hackett*

rown Eyes

I sit sometimes and think alone
But what I think is rarely shown
I think and dream and even more
I wonder what my life is for

What if, what if, and only then
These thoughts I think and then again
Who's to say how life should be
    I'll find a new identity

I love my life, I love to live
    And in my life I love to give
To give to friends who mean so much
My love, my time, and other things such

I love my life, I love to smile
I think of you and all the while
My heart beats hard, it beats so fast
The die is set, our friendship cast

I thank you now for friendship true
    Mine is the gift of knowing you
And if my thoughts turn dark and gray
know there'll be another day...with you
    —*Jones E. Jones*

od Never Forgets

here is an old forgotten grave yard in this town
    but when friends and kin no longer came around..........

pilfering land peddler plundered the bounds
    and plowed the antiquated tomb stones down.

ow the north wind whines through the great oaks, a mournful
sound..........
    and the leaves fall gently covering the cold bare ground.

o one remembers the dreams and hopes that live and die
    and no one is left but the coyotes to whimper and cry.

ep softly as you pass by..........
    someone's sweetheart, somebody's darling loving placed,
still lie.

the warm sun of early spring,
    God's touch blesses what man's greed disgraced.

he earth bursts forth with life, atop each resting place.....
    a blanket of sweet lavender iris distinctly marking
each hidden name and face.
    —*Sylvia Brown Barker*

Mother's Touch

heavy veil over the family stands,
linging precariously to a mother's hand,
ould the mother fall by chance or deed,
he veil shall descend and release a seed,
alice and evil it is known as such,
s only weakness is a mother's touch,
er absence will allow the roots to grow,
    the hearts of her children they will take their hold,
wisting and straining they will tear apart,
hat was once considered a work of art,
he father does nothing and watches idly by,
e knows not the problem so he won't even try,
is inaction is seen as malevolent spite,
ausing his offspring to take to flight,
heir departure shall take them to the four corners of the sky,
nd eventually will be broken their special tie,
hen God is his magnificence shall weep a tear,
ecause he could not save a love so pure,
r though he owns the greatest powers that be,
is a mother who holds together a family.
    —*Sean Kaufhold*

"Why Must I, The Shadow, Die?"

A man, with flesh and blood, heart and soul
cast a shadow
full, sharp, exact and detailed.
Walking ahead, often times a bit behind.
An illusion?
One that moves with every beat of your heart?

Life's fatal alert calls and Man dies, but why
must I, The Shadow, die?
I never felt a heart beat
Blood never ran free in me!
But yet you beckon me!

I know nothing but walls, sidewalk cracks
and landscapes.
I've counted bushes, pushed through valleys,
climbed mountains and hid in corners until
the sun found it's place.

I've done nothing wrong
Didn't ask to escort you, but when
mortal Mans' last breath is gone, I no
longer live! Why Must I, The Shadow, Die?
    —*Linda Morgan Jones*

Untitled

    Laugh at the bewildered, plentiful is His
cup with rich flavor of contentment.
    Inebriated by the tears of the
spited and scorned, obese from the devoured
cries of the socially disgraced, He moves onward...
away from the hypocritical barks of His peers.
    Peace endures as He creates His
secret reich, a colony of one, governed by
the holy writing of His thoughts.
    This, the true meaning of His existence,
the hidden character of His name, will create
storms on the day of His demise...
and flood the souls of those who knew Him.
    —*Shawn George*

Topsy

Topsy my little charming and adventurous baby,
Cute, cuddly, and bright as a lady.
Always a smile with a dimpled cheek,
Growing rapidly, and swiftly every week.

Topsy's favorite toy was a stuffed puppy called Sparky,
Who was always creating a lot of malarkey.
Then one day Topsy received a real live Sparky,
And baby Topsy had a playmate frisky and barky.

Off to the park Mom and Topsy would go,
Playing hide and seek and creating quite a show.
Mom made a lunch and they had a picnic,
And Sparky cane running lickety splitly.

Packing up to return home,
Mom gave Topsy's long blonde curls one quick combe.
Topsy had fairy tales spinning in her head,
And soon would be asleep in her very own bed.

We barely had enough time to say our prayers, and Topsy was
asleep counting plum fairies and teddy bears. And tomorrow the
trees will whisper from the park, come out and play Mom, and
Topsy, and Sparky said, "me too", and gave a bark
    —*V. Marge Pavlowich*

Bride And Groom

Seven sopranos singing on a winter wedding day
Dancers float through orange blossoms and lace
Champagne glasses clink bridal toasts above the fray
But of bride and groom, however, there is no trace

Mothers mingle merrily as daughters wearily waltz
The banquet table overflows for all to partake
Lovers laugh lustily, some true and some false
No bride and groom, however, atop the towering cake

Giddy guests gorge on lamb with savory spice
Dieters deliberately eye delicacies, maybe one bite
Baked apples, too, asparagus and curried rice
The bride and groom, however, are nowhere in sight

The hour is late as the music finally fades away
Revelers drink the final sip and place the bubbles down
Black turns to purple turns to orange, a new day
No need of a handsome groom or maid in wedding gown
            —Thom Santiago

Traces Of The Heart

Imagine this, one's life so unfulfilled
Day by day life's agony seem upon thee willed
Grief and joy are inner mixed
With pain and struggle in betwixt
Fluently flowing burdens one sings
Praying for guidance and protection
In a quest for perfection to the alm lightly king
Farthest from the closest dreams
To become a peanut gallery unto envious friends
            —Thaddeus Smith

Condemned To Release

My time has come, I curse the night
Demons beckon just out of sight
I steady my hold, so I won't slip
God help me now cause I lost my grip
My life flashes, and judgments near
I spiral down to taste my fear
Darkness returns its warm embrace
As I slip past life's frenzied pace
Returning to spirit, I take command
And walk with master hand in hand
The cycle closes with a screaming sound
For life's a journey that's homeward bound
White light crackles to a blinding air
As I ride the current of the electric chair
            —Ted A. Seagraves

Rover

The old dog lies sleeping
Dreaming of cat chases
Of earlier days,
And long ago races.

A rabbit hops by
His once keen eyes don't see
He lifts his head too late,
As the rabbit begins to flee.

His master watches sadly
Knowing his friend's life is nearly over,
He will always have his memories
His friends, his Rover.
            —Trevor Michels

In My Sleep

I whisper your name when I sleep at night -
Dreams of you carry away my fright -
When eyes are closed and dreams are of you -
I know our love will be strong and true -

In my sleep we are always as one -
Walking hand in hand under moon and sun -
We gaze and smile in each others eyes -
We hold each other through laughter and cries -

Our prayers are said to keep us strong -
We can be truthful even when we're wrong -
I'm not scared to tell you the truth -
I know if I'm guilty you'll be there to soothe -

You can see the expression on my face -
We both know our dreams together we'll chase -
Your touch warms my heart, your laugh makes me smile -
I can count on you to sit and listen for awhile -

In my heart we'll always be -
Together for an eternity -
Through smiles, frowns, and tears -
We'll wash away each others fears -
            —Shelly Veal

People

Green, yellow, brown, black, or blue, who exactly are you?
Faces round, flat, or thin, doesn't change the person within.
Eyes shaped like walnuts, almonds, or peas, either way they all
can see. Feet long, fat, flat, or thin, we all walk with them.
Hair brown, yellow, or bright red, we all have it on our head.
Ears big, pointy, or small, we need to hear with them all.
Lips puffy, round, tiny, or square, they all breath the air.
Boys, girls or mammals, we are all born loving animals. Babies,
elders, or crazy teens, we all born human beings Names mean,
nice, or are very own, they're all used to call us home. Nice,
thoughtful, caring, and kind, it's all what we should find.
Blood green, blue, or red, without it we'd be dead. Smart,
dense, slow, or incapable, we all learn for we are able. Toes
crooked, stubby, or long, we all use to hold on our thongs.
Comfortable, rich, or very poor, what's it all for. Legs,
short, skinny, or tall, we travel with them all. Teeth sharp,
long, small, broken or new, we all use to chew. But without
the heart, which is the most important part, "whether it's big,
healthy, weak, or real small, "nothing would run at all!
            —Tawnya S. Cromwell

"Money Is Not Everything"

But! It is a necessity of a human being
For doing good is an evil thing or
Doing bad is a good thing
For example! money is power,
Use money for influence to
make friends and connections
And to reach personal gain of something
You can't that something, take it with you
Even how you love, care and
cherish until you perish
It is only human nature to love money
From the beginning to the end
From! birth cradle death
Part of our lives
For richer and poor
But! we cannot take it, with you
We love her, we caress her
We live with her everywhere
We go she is with you, until
death we part.
            —Tomas Castillo

eace, If Only...

only... we could offer morning prayers daily
for His benevolence, thank the Most Holy;
hen... everything will turn out to be rosy
exuberant with hope, makes life so cozy.

only... we could be generous with our smile
to everyone we come across the mile;
hen... animosity, ire will surely fade away
cordiality comes rushing along the way.

only... we could dwell, ponder on the scriptures
love, respect become our ageless treasures;
hen... divinely inspired, parents, children bloom together
families, societies feel compassion for one another

only... the golden rule could be practiced by me and you
"do unto others what you'd want others do unto you";
hen... what a wonderful world to live, chants everyone
peace, brotherhood to all, thanks the Almighty One.

only... leaders of nations could address universal issues
ideologies and hostilities, subjects of discussions;
hen... nations, men of all colors work in harmony
Peace to all, the world thrives with love and unity.

—*Lina R. Cruz*

Friend So True

ow do I know that your friendship is so true?
or one, you always know when I am blue.
ou are able to make me laugh and smile,
nd afterwards I just think awhile
bout all the things we have been through.
he good times, the bad, all with you,
hope that we will always be friends you see,
ecause you have been a part of me.
ith each passing day we open a new door.
o all the things we are looking for
future together and much, much, more.
ou are my friend, my friend so true,
nd I will always care for you.

—*Brandy Berry*

he Happy Youth of all Seasons

the blossoming hedge the youth sings,
r the sun, it is merry and bright,
d he joyfully hops and flutters his energetic hands,
r his heart is all full of grand delight.
r the Autumn bloometh fair, and there's little of care,
d a plenty to eat in the Autumn months. When the flowers all
, then off he will go, to keep himself warm in his jolly,
d, humble hovel where the snow and the wind neither chill him
r harm him. And such is the life of the strolling youth,
th plenty to eat and to drink;
r the good mother will always keep him a warm seat by the
e, and the pretty young girls smile blushingly at his
vilish winks. Then he lustily trolls, as he strolls on ward,
ging in a rollicking and magnificent way, songs for the
ving of souls.
hen the wind doth blow, with the coming of the cold winter
ow, there's a cozy warm place by the burning and sparkling
e for the merry youth, who is most welcomed to a hot stew
his wooden bowl for all of his heart's desires, as the
nter months cometh at a petty pace, day by day.

—*Satyendra Peerthum*

What Is A Best Friend?

Someone who listens to you even when you don't
have anything to say.
Someone who will be true; or who will be there until
the last day.
Someone who knows your heart, mind, and soul; who
keeps you going and makes you whole.
Someone with whom you can laugh & cry and know
that they'll understand.
Someone who gets you to try and lends you a helping
hand.
Someone who knows you better than you do; a
perfect example is You.

You were there to hug me when I needed to cry;
You were there to tell me you cared when I wanted to
die.
You think of others before you think of you;
You don't know how happy I am to have a best-friend
who does all that you do.
We'll be best-friends forever, you & me;
Because together, we fit perfectly!

—*Tammi Higley*

He

He takes the time to make me happy.
He is there for me when I am sad.
He listens and gives advice.
He is grumpy, but, rather nice.
He has helped me to explore.
He has picked my heart up off the floor.
He loves me, and is not afraid to let it show.
He has done all this, that has helped me to grow.
He sometimes gets me upset, rather mad.
He is not my companion, he is my dad.
He is my friend, and my love for him will never end.

—*Shannon Dee Harris*

Broken Promises

The wind blows from the North
He looks and his eyes are cold.
He looks and smiles and then goes forth,
My grief grows old.

The wind blows the dust;
Tomorrow he swears he will come.
His words are kind, but he breaks
his trust,
My heart is numb.

All day the wind blew strong,
The sun was buried deep,
I have thought of him so long, so long,
I cannot sleep.

The clouds are black with night,
The thunder brings no rain,
I wake and there is no light,
I feel the pain.

—*Terra Ward*

Surfer's Paradise

A surfer's paradise is out on a major adrenalin rush.
Shooten the curl or in and out the pipeline, they watch
out for the wipeout! When the tide comes in and the surfs
up, you'll see the Betty's and Beach Bums waxin' down their
boards, puttin' on their suits or going bare back. Riding
the surf they will be. Some say it's a major thrill but a
true surfer says it's heaven on earth....
A true surfer's paradise.

—*Veronica Lara*

The Shepherd And His Sheep

Jesus Christ was born years ago in Bethlehem
He was a good old man, now no one gives a damn
The powers He possessed may at times have seemed too much
For He could walk on water and heal with just a touch
He was named a poor man, a beggar and a thief
It's the base of our religion, don't question my belief
He taught us how to reach up for the Heavens in the sky
And for the sin of man Jesus Christ did die
They nailed him to the cross, He bravely faced His doom
They then locked His corpse away deep within a tomb
The angels then came to help with the absence of His soul
Every since that day mankind has lost all control
The shepherd must go on now to show His flock the way
For somewhere down the line His sheep have gone astray.

    —Shawna Bales

Numbness

Someone is talking to me but I only
hear a faint whisper in my ear.

Someone is holding me tight but
I only feel a gentle touch on my shoulder.

The sun is shining but I don't
see the light.

Someone is sitting close to me
but I only see a shadow.

And thorn pricks my finger I don't
feel the pain.

Hiding from the world slowly I
become a tiny teardrop in my own sorrow.

Someone is telling me this but I
don't understand, the words run together
I don't see or feel. Slowly the sorrowed
tear trickles from mother's kiss.

    —Shantele Lynn Taylor

My Father's Hands

My Father's hands all freckled from the sun,
  Held me up and pushed me on — so I could run
My Father's hands worked hard all day and when day was through
  He'd come home and help with chores; change diapers too
He'd throw a ball or pitch a tent — My Father's hands
  He'd guide and hug and love and reprimand —
My Father's hands would drive wherever people had to go...
  He'd cook and garden, he even knew how to sew
Smart and funny and sharp all rolled into one —
  He'd always make sure the job got done.
He'd pledge allegiance, his hand over his heart,
  He taught me love of country right from the start.
My Father's hand often I saw folded in prayer
  As he showed me faith and taught me how to care.
I held his hand — on him I always could depend
  My Father's hands were strong right to the very end...
And I can picture him at the bay and in the sands,
  For I now know God is holding My Father's hands.

    —Cheryl Whitley-Matheson

Our Love

We may take different steps,
on different paths.

We may get caught up,
in different aspect of life.

We may not be able to touch
and to share...
  But our love will always be there.

    —Michael R. O'Coin

Second Place

There's another love in my husband's dreams
He's happy most of the day, but during the night he screams
Strung out on a feeling that never last long
Tied to a habit he won't admit it's wrong
He's stuck on this new love, he thinks it's so unique
His friends say it's a smart way to make life complete

It's a kind of high that cures all his fears
She's got him I know, cause I'm crying bitter tears
Cocaine won my man, that I couldn't face
But because I love him, I took second place

My man's stuck on this new love, he thinks it's so unique
Friends say it's a smart way to make life complete
Cocaine won my man and I took second place
Cocaine won my man and I took second place

    —Susan A. McPherson

Poison

The light of the fire rose softly as he looked into my eyes.
His soft warm skin touching mine. Happiness rose into my
heart as his lips touched mine. I knew I would never feel the
same again about one person as I did about him. I looked away
with distress in my eyes. He knew what I was thinking and told
me everything would be alright. If only he knew how much I
loved him, he wouldn't leave, not like this. I grabbed him
and pulled him close to me. I could feel my heartbeat speed
up as he kissed me one last time. The room started to fade
away and I knew that was it. My life was over because he
kissed me, the kiss of death.

    —Tinaya Berg

Diablero

Time has carried you from me.
How precious the moments we shared.
The compassion and warmth you gave sustained me.
Cold winds of life bitterly pressed my lips;
Yet your constancy and energy lifted the fatigue of the season.

Never weary, always bright.
Yours was a devotion of acceptance;
Faith that appreciation was the relentless undercurrent.
Words should have been spoken!

The grey in your beard betrayed the weariness of the season.
Your eyes thwarted alliance with any such treason;
A glow piercing the stillness of any winter scene.
Fathoms of understanding with which to warm.

Pen silenced, by the immensity of my love for you;
Time has carried you from me.
But carried on distant winds,
Your song, clear and intense, as familiar as my soul.

    —Walter Scott Miller

The Dragon Fly

My skin was warm, as I sat in the sun
I was thinking about how I could have some fun
All of a sudden, out of a tree
Came a dragon fly that lit on my knee
His gossamer wings were lacy and black
And a long thin tail, spun around his back
His head was round, with eyes of white
At first he gave me quite a fright
Earlier I had read what good they do
Their not at all harmful to me or you-
As I watched him resting on my knee
I thought how lucky he wasn't a bee.

    —Toni Beery

little Treasures

a world so full of hatred mist a people full of fear
ek out simple little treasures for a short while hold them dear.
ever think a thing too worthless lest one's trash another's treat
ake the time to talk with others making opportunity to meet.
or as the world, as we know it, races down destructive roads;
inding someone who will listen may help lighten heavy loads.

—*Vanessa Benson*

The Red Ribbon

We all will die sometime." I softly said to him.
couldn't look him in the eye; his face so sadly grim.

But I'm so young and afraid", he cried. "It's just not fair!"
I know there's nothing they can do, but it's so hard to bare."

Where are the answers for this man; I want to know?
What reasons . . . is this some terrible debt we humans owe?

What is this dread disease from which there is no return.
s this some inconceivable lesson and what are we to learn?

We cannot change what has been, we only have tomorrow.
But perhaps we can work on the future; put away our sorrow.

If we can all be responsible and learn everything we can;
We must manage together; remember we're all the same clan.

Then there is hope . . . if we speak out and tell no lie.
But to this good young man I love; I can only say goodbye.

—*Linda L. Farmer*

Love Sucks

My mind trembles, then cracks
feel my rage boiling inside
Finally I burst and deal with my emotions
She was gone, an absence in my life

I dug hard to clear the aftermath
Blood, sweat, tears - work
All combined to cleanse my soul and thoughts
The bottom was hit and I began my return

Once again I screwed up
I tallied it under experience
Love was found again
Emotions are clear but I still think of the past

The past resurfaces
Now my heart and mind is sectioned
Special feelings fill my body from past to present
What the HELL do I do!

—*Scott A. Miller*

O How Beautiful I Am

O lift up my eyes old Lord
I thank you for awaken me on this
beautiful day:

The skies are blue the grass
is green so is my soul!
Thank you old Lord for the
beautiful angel, for they love
us so dear...

I thank you old Lord for making
my bold and beautiful black body
I know you have making, the way to heaven
no matter what color you are; so I thank
you Lord for making everybody soul so
bold and beautiful.

Old Lord I want to make it to Heaven
To see your smiling face so I thank you
Old Lord for this Beautiful Day.

—*Suzette Fulce*

I Lost Him

The first time I saw him I fell in love.
I thought he was the handsomest man his eyes like
a turtle dove, he was so sweet and gentle I could
Just melt in his arms. So he ask me out and I
said yes. But I didn't have a beautiful dress.
And so I cried until my eyes were red - after
a while I went to bed and after a few weeks my
mother did get me a very nice dress and oh my
hair was in such a mess. I got my hair fix and
put on that dress when I got all ready and look in
the mirror. I looked very nice and neat.
All at once I had cold feet. Atlas the man I love came he
looked so tall and handsome and sweet I couldn't hardly stand
upright on my own two feet. I had to get my self together.
I didn't even notice the weather. I didn't care
what the weather was like as long as the man
I love was there. We went on to the dance
and did a slow drag I know right then I had
every thing in the bag. So all that night I held
him tight a long kiss to say good night

—*Winnie Hurst*

Little Brother

Please little brother, don't you cry
I understand,
But it's not time to say good-bye

I, like you, regret some things,
Especially the precious time that silence brings

I wish I'd hugged you more and told you,
"I love you"
but, for all the love I have for you,
a million hugs would be too few.

Please little brother, don't you fret
You gave me memories I won't forget

Please little brother, wipe your tears — look to the sky
catch the breeze and rays of sun
and you'll feel my love from way up high

Please little brother don't you cry
I am of earth, I'm in the air,
don't you see — I'm everywhere

So please, please, little brother — don't you cry
I'm in your dreams, I'm by your side
I'm in your heart — I did not die

—*Maria de Lourdes Perez*

An Orchestra Of Prayer

Dear Lord, do you hear my prayer?
It's one of praise; its note is sweet and full.
As the sun rises and all your children speak to you,
The sound must come to you as music,
An orchestra of prayer.
Because you are the Master, you hear each instrument:
The flute that wails its anguish,
Violins that wring the heart;
The lusty blare of horns demanding their prayers be heard,
The sax crying the love and tears of a wounded heart,
And, in hearing, Lord, you discern
The heavy-hearted bass notes,
The high sweet notes of praise,
The joy, the sorrow, the despair,
The pleading of an anxious heart.
As the mighty cacophony rises to your hearing ears
You meet each song's need.

—*Lewetta Russell*

My Baby, My Friend

Whenever you need a friend,
I will always be there.
You help me with my problems,
And the joys together we share.

I can't imagine my life, without someone like you.
You are my best friend, and my lover too.

You've been there when I laugh,
You've been there to hold me when I cry,
I never have the fear,
that you'll say good-bye.

You are so patient and attentive,
And I know I don't see,
how I'm not as affectionate,
As what you deserve for me to be.

This doesn't mean I don't love you,
I hope you don't interpret it to be bad,
It means I've taken for granted,
The best thing I've ever had.

I love you, you know, that is true.
I never want to be, one day without you.

—*Terri Sue Carter*

World Peace

I'm here to tell you about the dream I had,
If you listen closely you might think it's rad.

My dream was about world peace,
And I think it's as legendary as the golden fleece.

It may never happen, let me tell you some more,
It seems like the world is always at war.

Americans, Bolivians, Canadians, and maybe Zambians too,
Perhaps world peace may give them a clue.

Now that I've told you about my dream last night,
Maybe you'd think world peace would be right !!!!!

—*Joseph Arndt*

Heavenly Angel

Oh how I've been blessed
I'm not the best person I must confess
But God has helped me through it all
He watched me rise and He watched me fall

As He watched He began to see
The trials of life were overcoming me
And when He saw this He decided to send
An angel from heaven to be my friend

The angel was perfect in every way
She always had an encouraging word to say
She held up a mirror so I could see
The goodhearted person I'd come to be

She helped me find my smile
She made me realize that I am worthwhile
I often wonder what I'd do
If it wasn't for the good Lord and you

Every night when I lay down to pray
I ask the Lord to let me keep you one more day
And when the day comes that you have to go
There are two people who'll always love me...And this I know

—*Shannah Rae Bailey*

Mill Valley Mom

Blonde braided Mom now driving en famille
In a bloated van sprung up to the sky,
So tiny she can't see over the wheel;
Running down dogs while her kids scream and cry!
In parking lots she's a terror on wheels
Not looking behind, backing out with dash!
Smiles sweetly, wiggles fingers and she steals
Swiftly away, my mind's numbed by the crash,
I don't know what would happen if I'd honked,
I doubt if she'd stop, I don't think she could,
Her expertise driving is really zonked;
If I were she I don't think I would,

I limit my travels, to store and town,
Driving at these high odds, I'm not a clown.

—*Wallis Wenner*

What Does It Mean To Be Normal

What does it mean to be normal
Is it something we're taught
or something we hear
Is it something we learn
through prejudice and fear
Who's to say what's normal
and what is not
Why must everyone be so judgmental
and matter of fact
There's no set standard for living
or how one chooses to live
Not everyone is exact
So is there really a definition for normal
Or is it just an arrogant point of view
If we all laugh and we all smile
Why must everyone be placed on trial
Those with differences should be looked upon
as a breath of fresh air
For they are the one's
who are the real debonair

—*Maria Martin*

Untitled

Who owns the Nighttime world?
Is it Them?

   The Ones
     who hold
      the key to our fears amongst the evening chill?
   The Ones
     who sneak
      within the moonlight and blend into shadows
     of those we cannot see?
   The Ones
     who keep
      us locked within our so-safe havens
     until the morning sun arises
     to warm our thankful souls?

To Those
Who own the dark hours which belong not to us—
May I open the door?
To see if the light of Tomorrow has come?
Or will You be there...
Waiting for me?

—*Ted M. Kirby*

ntitled

The end is soon, I will not fight.
It is her death. It is her right.
To fly beyond, to the world unknown,
 us mortal beings. We hope to be shown.
 I open my palms, and extend to you.
Please God accept, my prayers so true.
ake my mom to you, let her die in peace.
ly worries of safety for her will cease.
To die in peace is the ultimate goal.
accept her death. My pain is my toll.
he'll have no pain. No tear is shed.
ernal life is near. Let's bow our heads.
　　—*Shelle Michaels*

's That Time

sterday was the anniversary of the accident.
s been 14 years.
also was the first year I didn't spend it in tears.
 it's too beautiful a day, said my friends to sit
　　at home and pout
let's go for a cruise, we'll take the scenic route
e autumn leaves as their colors covered the trees
e warmth of the sun mixed with a slight cool breeze
surely would have been another October 24th spent in fear
ank you Chris for being there this year
aureen, Rachel & Marissa, you guys made it be the perfect day
ou'll never know how good it felt to just get away
 I thanked the Lord, that I'm still alive and doing well
 I'm thankful too, for the first time, that I can't
　　remember that night of hell
en I toasted the beautiful day to my friends I lost that
ght those years ago
id decided that maybe this was the year I finally accept and
 t let go...
　　—*Teresa J. Rodriguez*

etirement

ood-bye - Au revoir - and so long.
e made my decision and soon I'll be gone.
 tirement is long over due, this you all know.
mething keeps telling me it's my time to go.
hen I am gone, replace me, please do.
st ye forget, my memories are pleasant for each of you.

me passes fast, too soon we grow old.
cause of snow on the mountain, all is not cold.
y feelings are warm and very sincere,
n ambivalent to go and leave all of you here.
e job has been wonderful, the co-workers are great,
ter so may years we must clean up out slate.
 I'll say this again, just before I go,
ou're a great group of people to work with and know.

 miss all of you and the fun we have had.
e enjoyed all the parties, though some have been sad.
ople and parties at the end of our stay
ll help us forget when we've had a bad day.
 time passes on and I will grow old,
 have a heart full of memories, priceless to hold.
　　—*Verda Heimann*

nights Of Old

ights wearing armor true.
ey hope it will pull them through.
e deadly battles must be fought.
cause truth, justice, and honor cannot be bought.
e sword and shield are great allies to thee.
e knight hopes they will always be.
　　—*Trey McCrea*

The Love Of Life

Love so fair and love so true
Keep your heart the purist hue.
For when one day you find your mate
There will be cause to celebrate.
You'll travel down life's path as one
Taking on all the trials and fun.

We all have bad times yes it's true.
But that's no reason to feel so blue
Because we each share our happy time
And it's not all an uphill climb

When troubled times do come your way
Take each other's hand and turn away.
The solution may come to you in your dreams
For no problem is bigger than it seems.
Both depend on each other for patience and love.
But all our answers will come from above.

If one of you should stumble and fall
The other will be there with just a call.
Soon help will be there on the way
For you both to get up and face a new day.
　　—*Sharon Lindsey*

Feeling for You

I fall for you like leaves fall to the ground
Leaves fall because summer has left just like you left me
Can you tell time in a second, or do you
have to count the minutes?
If we were meant to be together
how come all we have is pain?
The snow has fallen now, and it is cold like
you treat me, poor old dead tree
The ice has melted like my heart I
feel nothing like the old oak stump
Anyways, always, remember, strong roots
survive all weather just like my strong
heart just like the leaves will grow back
　　—*Sarah Raupp*

Blue Toilet Paper

　Toilet paper toilet paper, Oh what a wonderful thought
　　Life without it would be agony on the pot

We would have to use a leaf a rag or something of that kind
　But be careful you may get a blister on your behind

Toilet paper toilet paper, so appropriate for this task
　The only thing missing is a close pin for your nose
　　or a full face gas mask

Toilet paper toilet paper, oh what a wonderful invention
　　But don't use the soft scented kind
　　Or you may attract some attention

Toilet paper toilet paper, life without it we could not bear
　For we would be committed to hash marks on our underwear
　　—*Timothy D. McBride*

The Portrait

Lines appeared, subtle at first, just around the
eyes. The first signs of age crept into her life
and were rejected. Time cared not, and diligently
marched forward as a soldier with a purpose.
Years and decades flew, as though pushed by the
wind, with obvious disregard for her feelings.

Later, as the hands of time turn and reach toward
eternity, she asks, "How is it that I have
become old?"
　　—*Shirley J. Fomby*

What Is Love

Love strikes without warning.....
Like a giant spider spinning a web
wrapping it's victim in tiny threads...
Precisely-slowly...until the victim
lay helpless
Everything happens so quickly
The victim doesn't seem to notice
And now he turns to the spider for help
He doesn't seem to know
it was the spider who did it all
The spider eyes his new prey
He hasn't eaten all day
He won't give up the victim...the fly
The spider feels contentment...
knowing his stomach will be full
The fly feels warmth...
knowing the spider is near
Neither can get away...it's like love

—*Dannice Munson*

"The One"

Watching the city lights from my window
listening to the wind blow
memories of the past come to me
filled with all the hopes of what I wished could be

I've tried so hard to get over you
but my hearts devotion remains true
Once again the tears begin to fall
as suddenly now I remember it all

Memories of that morning fill my mind
eased so little by the passing of time
all the pain that I felt then
washes over me now once again

I didn't want to let you go
but it's what you wanted, you told me so
My heart broke when we said good-bye
I couldn't bare to see you cry

Now it's too late the damage is done
but in my heart you're still the one
the one who fills my heart with love
the one that I am dreaming of

—*Terry Smith*

Untitled

Flowing through the streets of life, I came upon a
lone pool of water which, oddly enough, was
shaped like a heart — it swelled, receded, rippled
as Nature blew its wind, and dropped its leaves
upon the pool's reflective surface.

In time the pool began to fade, leaving only the
hard dust and scared remains of its outline. The
fluid which brought it to life was now taken
away as if it could only be a heart with the help
of something... someone else; its completeness
relying on more than it alone could supply.

Oh and how Time could give and take that
something... that someone in and endless cycle...
will it ever end?

More time, more wear, and the pool began to lose
its shape, its life, its meaning; like a forgotten
trail losing its distinction as Time and Nature
hid it within their forest until it no longer
existed except in the minds of those who once
traversed it.

—*Welby M. Nalls, III*

Wondering

Looking lovely everyday.
Looking pretty in every way.
Greeting a person by saying Hi.
Then understand he is waving good-bye.
The wind swishes by your hair,
like hope, dream, and wonder.
Then you understand that you feel much fonder.
Every way you look at yourself you say you
look ugly, but when you go to the beauty parlor
you look even more jolly.
Remember each time in your life so clearly,
but when you become old it seems so blurry.
Times to cherish, times to hold, but when
you get old you let them go.
I can't understand the reason why,
you should let go, and say good-bye.

—*Shanee Amanda Daley*

Without You

I lay awake at night
looking up at the starry sky
a tear rolling down my cheek
because my greatest fear has cone

I walk down the street
watching people run for shelter
as the cold, hard, rain falls
I keep walking
letting it pound down on me

I sit and watch the loving couples
with their babies held so dear
I think the dreams of you and I

I walk on through the cemetery
Seeing but not caring about the other stones
I walk to yours rubbing my fingers along your name
I kneel down then press myself to the ground
trying to get so close
for my heart and soul were buried with you.

—*Trisha L. Sullivan*

If the World Were Just and Fair

If all were fair and just in the world
Maybe there would be peace.
If the world had wisdom and understood
Maybe the fighting would cease.
If all men had sympathy and caring
Maybe no child would live unfed.
If life held no pain or sorrow
No tears would need be shed.
If all could be humble and meek
Then pride would not stand in our way.
There would be no ambitions to drive us
No temptations to cause us to stray.
If each soul could be filled with laughter
There could be joy in each heart.
If all men could be brethren
Then each man could feel a part.
If at any time your life is this
Then your life is rare.
And the world could be like this
If the world were just and fair.

—*Linda Duncan*

What Is...

What is happiness?
Mountains, flowers, beautiful birds?
Love and hope with wishes combined?
Time and leisure with no war?
Is this happiness?

What is misery?
Torture, pain, no air to breath?
Heart break, darkness, with stormclouds combined?
Rushing, no sleep, with killing about?
Is this misery?
Which is reality?

—*Tracie Thompson*

The Future

When the sun rises -
My eye awakens with a smile
Saying what a beautiful day it would be
A day is ahead and our future is a second away.

Each step we take leads us to a different place
Every time we open our eyes
We see something different

When we move around -
It seems like already a second of the future
Just passed right by us
When we sleep -
Day and night seem only one minute just passed.

When we go to school -
It's a good way of learning and going on to the future.

The only thing you know when half the future passed -
Is only when you listen and learn
And go on to life.

—*Stephanie Liz Carrillo*

Sleepless Nights

It's late,
My eyes are still open.
The only light I am seeing is
the beautiful moon.
Why is my pillow damp again?
I hold my heart, it's still beating.
Then, why can't I feel the life in me?
I have to close my eyes before I go insane.
Close my eyes to imagine that I am sheltered
by your heart. Yes, it's all coming to picture
I don't feel the pain anymore.
The moon is not there.
The morning light is welcoming me.
Till the next night...

—*Shari Moraffah*

Complete

For the first time I saw the sunrise in all it's splendor, and
my senses are alive to the changes that come with spring.

I feel the warmth of friends past and present, and I am
comforted at strength and character it brings.

For it is a chance that we have taken, and in the shadows
may lurk heartache and pain. But to this we sound a hearty
laugh, for it can not compare to what we have to gain.

Happiness, joy, and the feeling of being loved. Out of so
many things, I name these few. Each night on my knees I
give thanks to my God, that all these things I share with you.

There are moments throughout the day when I experience a
feeling from head to feet, that if I lived a thousand lifetimes
I could never feel more complete!

—*Tony Andre' Smith*

The Top Of Insanity

Like a fool my dresser awaits
My morning eyes,
My lost fingers.
It sits there, my life, like a fool
On top of the old walnut dresser.
My mind, on top of the old walnut dresser.
Cluttered with gaily-colored clips—now
Faded. Old music books with scarred, worn leaves.
Like a fool a basket of sweet-smelling soaps
Sit upon the insanity, a vessel
Of hope adrift
In me. In my mind.
On top of the old walnut dresser.
The polaroid, black, stifled between the
Dying, dead fern in the cracked green pot,
Between the sunscreen (SPF 45,)
Cornered by the white piggy-bank who is no
Pig, only a lamb.
Like a fool, my life
On top of the old walnut dresser.

—*Linda Greenberg*

I Wonder...

I wonder what would happen if I never existed,
        never cried,
            never loved,
                never lied,
                    never judged?

            Would you be better off?
                Would you notice?
        Would there be any difference?
            Would anything change?

    I wonder what would happen if I should die,
        would you remember me,
            would you cry for me,
                would you forgive me,
                    would you miss me?

                Would you really care?
                Would you still love me?

    I wonder if we can ever be together again?
    I wonder if you would love someone else?
I wonder if I will always love you the way I love you now?

—*Stephanie Rose Millemaci*

The Ages

As I look into the careworn face I see nothing
Not the shadows of a person past
Nor the reflection of them in her eyes
I see a creature of another world
As if born whole-heartedly in another place
To the form in which she now occupies.
The deep set lines do not reveal to me
The face of one who was once like me
Soft and bright.
Nor do I in myself see the creature in me
Do not realize she is me, is like me, was me,
With a thousand steps behind her
I have yet to tread.
Do I discard her because she is so different
from me?
Or because we're made too much the same.
And suddenly I see
A woman of ageless time between us both
And I know we are one.

—*Stephanie Ellis*

I See The World

I see the world today
soft and gray
half asleep
like a lover
one turns to in the early dawn
and rejoices over
silently!

—*Nan-Marie Hardwick*

Now That You're Dead

I used to watch you upon your cage
Now that you're dead I'm filled with rage
You were absolutely my best friend
I ask myself, "Why did it end?"
You used to feel me with such glee
Now that you're dead I've lost a piece of me
The piece of me which liked to smile
Now that you're dead, is it all worthwhile?
When you were here I wanted to sing
Now that you're dead I don't do anything
Except cry in the morning and cry at night
I often think, "Are you worth this fight?"
I am exhausted, I don't want to go on
I lived for you but now you're gone
And when I think of you and cry
The only thing to say is Frack, goodbye.

—*Stephen A. Crenshaw*

Memories

Memories remind me
of candy that is really sweet.
They may make people cry.
Others make people happy.
The one thing you have to know
is that memories you cannot buy.

Memories come from the heart.
You can write them down on a special chart.
They may remind you about happy
times or sad times.
You may not like some memories
but throughout your life
memories are nice to have!

—*Kirsten Jurgensen*

Which Is Which

Two men sat down to write
One was Black the other was White
One man wrote of the beauty within
"They say the eyes are the doorway to the soul
If that is so then your soul is like a pound
On a warm summer's day
That has sipped upon the sun's warmth from dusk till dawn
Then when the night air has chilled my heart
You offer yourself and envelop me with your warmth"
The other wrote of the beauty of nature
"The first day I saw you
Your lines were simple and distinct
As you held your secret close to you
Then one day I passed by and found myself possessed
By the secret you held dear
And though your secret is now full bloomed
Your lines remain simple"
Now tell me which was Black and which was White
Need there be distinction
Why can't I just write

—*Tara D. Johnson*

Grandma's House

Both the front door and the back door
Opened onto her big country kitchen,
The heart of the house.

First stop was the cookie jar, shaped like an apple,
That sat in the middle of her kitchen table,
The table with lion's claw legs.

Both hands filled
With her sugar cakes and raisin cookies,
I'd race out the back door
To climb her walnut tree,
Whose limb was the mast of my ship
Whose top was my crow's nest.

At day's end, from Grandma's rocking chair,
Safe in her lap,
I'd watch the sun go down,
And feel the love of her
Who told me the funny and clever things I did,
Who gave me precious puzzle pieces
Of my childhood,
Of my self.

—*Sue Kimmel Amantia*

Completeness

I don't have wealth...silver or gold...
Or things that are temporal...
And soon...will grow old...
But...I have a treasure...money cannot buy...
Contact with the master...
And He hears my cry...
Take me...and use me...in wisdom and love...
I've many to reach...Dear Father...above...
Your joy as your give...like a thread entwined...
In all creation...that you have designed...
I know...when I have given...
Given my best...
My day is complete...as I lie down to rest...
Not silver or gold...
Have I gained today...
But...I find completeness
As...I...
Kneel...
To...pray.

—*Violet R. Watkins*

"What Is This World Coming To?"

I see people on the news, people battered,
people bruised. What is our world coming to?
What are we suppose to do? Little children
are taken away while others are simply lead
astray. Yet I do see some happy faces, the
ones that could really go places. Yet they
deny themselves the knowledge. They drop
school, or even college. Yes theirs is a sad
case, but who would say that to their face?
What has caused so much hate? I feel closed
in, I can't escape. You can't run from
incompetence or crime, but there is one time
that you can leave it all behind. Only in
your dreams can you fully escape. From the
violence, the hurt, and of course the hate.
What is this would coming to? I really
don't know, do you?

—*Tiffany Johnson*

A Tribute

From the lofty seat of the scornful, the question was
raised:— was there anything good ever that came out of Nazareth?
  Yet there came this seed from the loins of cush who walked
the streets of Atlanta and Montgomery. This was his starting place.
  To teach the war-torn nation a new commandment. They
marveled at the paradox and the enigma of forgiveness merged in
his soul force was the tender voice of Africa.
  Yes, lofty cynics raised their questions.
  He, nursed within the rugged manger of the south, has strode
down center stage, before the judgement halls and wonder of the
world.

—*Timothew H. Carson*

Lily Pads

Oh, how I love lily pads!
Rare and green thrones to Kings' in the land.
Crocus shape flowers sometimes spring from their tables.
In colors of buttercream and pink, on waters of sable.
Bridges, yes bridges they can be....
For frog princess and princesses under the trees.
Lily pads add magic to the woods,
Childhood dreams are bright with "coulds"?
Trolls and wood fairies happily swirl over those pads,
Wondering what joy there is to be had.
So tonight before bed,
Think of your day.
Then swirl into dreamland on lily pads so gay!

—*Trudy Ann Bryant*

Remember Me Forever

Remember the pain.
Remember the tears.
Everything we've been through.
After all these years.
But still nothing changes.
Everything stays the same.
It will all work out somehow.
Don't think about the bad times.
Think only of the good.
Everything you could have done.
And now you wish you would.
I know I can't take the pain away.
If I could, I'd bring it to someone else, another day.
But still nothing changes.
It all remains the same.
We'll work it out somehow.
Remember we all love you and we'll get through this together.
Even through the good, the bad, and nice, and shiny weather.
Remember me forever.
And we'll stay young together.

—*Wendy Jenkins*

Awakening of Time

Awake!
Shake dreams from your hair, the morning has come.
Ride across the land, and greet the sun.
Distant, and always on the run.

Night has passed and now sky of blue.
Distant hills and enchantment of sight.
Do you feel the warmth from the radiance of light?
Can you vision the far past, and to embrace fearlessness at last.

Travel farther into the day,
And capture the choice of time.
Always of chance and filled with rhyme.
Plundering more of each day, just an awakening of time.

—*Stuart L. Spanier*

It Ain't What It Seems

Oh, here we go again. What do you want me to say.
Should I tell you it's o.k. to lie, steal and cheat?
Should I say it's all right to abandon your hope and
dreams, live beneath your means? Will saying this
put you at ease? Now I guess you want to explain
but I'm hip to your game. It's the White man's fault
you're just a victim standing by. Yeah all right, so
next you want me to cry. Save it! I got things to do
and people to meet. I'm trying to keep my stuck-up
derriere off the streets. I've worked within the
system and learned to fight the good fight. I've
shook a few hands and shown my pearly whites. Now
I'm out in the burbs, where I wish you could be.
But the decision for your betterment isn't left up
to me. It's not always about having a big house or
sporting a fancy car. It's about looking for a way
to build one's self and reaching for the stars.

—*Theresa A. Morgan*

The Nesting Ground

Head down, eyes red, I made my way to the casket.
Silence echoed from wall to wall as I could hear
Grandfather saying, "I joined the Navy so I didn't
have to wear a necktie and I don't want to be
buried with one."
My body chilled and tears began to flow.
So slowly, down my cheek and into my mouth.
Words suddenly jumped forth, but nothing sounded,
I reverberated in memory.
Somehow, somewhere, he could hear me, and a
response made its way back.
Sobs and sniffles broke the communication.
The procession took place without grandfather's necktie.
Without the noose, he could talk freely and smile forever.
His Naval flag was folded, the eagle floated up,
And slowly glided through the sky, in search of a
new nesting ground.

—*Todd Alden Mead*

Things That Go Bump In The Night

Twirling swirling scintillating
Silent and invigorating
Things that go bump in the night
Beware strange sounds by fire light
Don't look under the bed
Off in darkness where we go
We find the creatures from below
Horrified we run away
In hopes of seeing them again some day
The things that go bump in the night
Curious of what they are
Even though hearts filled with fright
Curiosity killed the cat
But we don't care well how about that
Beware things that go bump in the night
Heed my words and stay in the light
Away from things that go bump in the night

—*Xavier Alexander Robertson*

Stone Cold Sober

Open my eyes; I need to breath,
Close my eyes; I need to see.
Thought I was in ecstasy...
Twist and turn in schizophrenia,
Who has salvation to sell?
Trapped in a carnival of destruction,
Please lower me down I can't
touch the ground.
My brain has exploded!

—*Melanie-Lynn Stauba*

509

It All Deep Ends

My life is shattered, My feeling are ripping me up inside
So I took drugs, the place where I could hide.

What happened to my life I don't really know.
The pain has to go, the only one to help is me, that I know!

What's wrong with me I thought, but it's all those drugs I bought
Drugs are bad as hell, look where you are, can't you tell?

Reconstructing yourself, is what we're here to do,
And I know I'll feel better, once it's through!

I'm not going to jail, I'm not going to die,
I've just gotta stop living a lie...
If I don't I'll surely die.

These are the last words I will mutter,
Just a simple question: Can I go on living in the gutter?
　　—*Terry Buckler*

Life Is A Venture

life is like a venture into the unknown,
So many roads to choose from, neither one a clone,
Be very, very careful of which one you choose,
For if you choose the wrong one you almost always lose.

Once a road chosen, no turning back allowed.
For life is full of hardships, not always fluffy clouds.
Life takes lots of effort and a lot of luck,
And if you don't work for happiness you may find you are stuck.

For some start life successfully and they stay that way,
But if they get to careless they will always pay.
Some stay in the slow track, while others speed away,
And some stop in the center, to start again another day.
　　—*Sean M. Burgoon*

The Lonely Path

The lonely path I've traveled so many times has brought me
so much pain.
It was not my choice, but circumstances created this path
and I was led aimlessly in vain.
Then, as I walked further down this path dark shadows
engulfed my soul and I wondered how much longer I would
remain sane.
I met many along the way who promised me things, but
experience
taught me, they just wanted me to play their game.
Then, as the years went by and I saw my youth fly-away my
heart filled with many fears!
My nights were filled with many tears.
The years have passed and I'm much wiser now, and in quiet
moments I recall in memory those many years I walked
the lonely path!
　　—*Scott Vincent Richards*

Depends On My Love

My love is like a single rose given to you by me
Only your love can make it strong that is why I give it to thee
Take it with you every day through sun, snow, or rain
Nothing can make it weak only an ounce of pain
If you keep the pain inside the rose will wither and wilt
Because of the lack of love it dies because of guilt
Unless you give it love and no more sorrow
It will wilt today and bloom tomorrow
If you still dwell in pain a small part of it slowly dies
It will be there one day then I'll vanish before your eyes
Nothing can ever bring it back not even the heavens above
There is one way it could live but in all depends on your love
　　—*Vanessa Buck*

Ups And Downs

Some memories are so sweet.
Sometimes memories can make your heart skip a beat.

Memories can also hurt you bad.
Sometimes memories can make you sad.

Some can get you back on your feet.
Memories can make you feel a feeling of defeat.

Some memories can make you feel glad.
Then again, some memories can make you mad.

Then there are some that make you feel neat.
There are some memories that are still incomplete.

Then there are some memories you wish you never had.
To your list of memories there will always be something to add.
　　—*Vinnie Marzano*

Reflections "Alone in the Dark"

A room aglow, others possess warm warm hearts.
Standing alone in the midst, mirror reflections reveal no sparks.
Among many, falsely deluded actually, alone from your love
　apart and secluded
Notable to express true feelings and thoughts.
Trapped by emotional fear.
Full of rage, seeking to emerge.
Only the touch from love unique, love my heart knows and seeks
Power in full flair, generating in a surge.
I call your name, your touch I desperately seek
Soon, my heart shall break in total retreat.
In essence, I need you, this is not a lie.
Otherwise a sad fact is, my heart shall die.
Tell me my knowledge of your love is not a lie.
If this is so, my mirror reflections are true,
my love light is out, my dreams are through.
Show me this cannot be, then doubts of having true love
　can flee.
Reality, actually, is truly; eternally you and me.
　　—*Terry Sawyer*

True Love

Understandable yet unfathomable,
Strived for yet forgotten,
Glorious yet melancholy,
Knowledgeable yet foolish.

The love for another
That surpasses any other
Is unpredictable as can be
In its aspects as shown to thee.
Its glides swiftly over any treacherous circumstance,
And how it struggles when in a liar's trance.
This love, this most befuddling love,
Captures the hearts of many to give them an illusive shove
Into the clutches of fierce passion
To arise confused and averting to ration
The tangled thoughts cluttering the brain,
Only to find your labor was in vain.

This love is like a mirage upon the desert.
It strengthens yet fatigues.
It aids yet abandons.
It loves yet does not.
　　—*Stacey Ann Kalei Shotwell*

Real Friends

Precious are the gifts
That are held dear to our heart
Like the bond between two friends
That can never be torn apart.

The love of a friend is constant
Unconditional and true
A friend's love stands the test of time
So real friends are few.

A friend's love is constructive
Dependable and strong
A real friend will continue this love
When you're right and when you're wrong.

I thank God for my real friends
For I know that true friendship is rare
And when I need a friend
My real friends will always be there.

—*Sherri Rene Wesley*

Autumn Leaves

October is that time of year
that I so love and hold most dear
I must go back to see those trees
of reds and gold - oh how they please!

My heart speaks out- "You have the time"
to see what God has made divine
The plane's too slow, but finally lands,
and soon I'm walking in a wonderland

Down all those winding wooded paths
of memories and childhood past
that in my mind will always last

The colors - they're all so true
my Lord above, by only you

Thank you, God, for I believe
there's nothing more beautiful
than autumn leaves

—*Vera J. Knight*

Metropolis Forgotten

Begotten labors lapsed in history's thought
that leave behind only relics of what they wrought.

Lives which loved, laughed, and ran their course
with ardors marked by a wooden corpse.

Who shall fill the stead
where energy and zeal of spirit's wed?

And hear the voice of long dead souls
waiting for their stories to be told.

'Tis for the understanding curious hand
to discover the truth of forgotten plans.

Resurrecting as time goes by
how others lived and the reasons why.

In the industry of a gentle compassionate breeze
they bring to life again such as these.

Restoring to the face of the current age
some moment lost to antiquity's page.

—*William Robbins*

Lost Grey Moments

My young child taught me the greatest love
That same love robs me of my dreams

Mother Nature gives me renewed hope
But the world tears my soul apart
And so I think life is more black and white
than we care to admit

I'll leave out the grey areas in my life
They will never mean much to me

When I love, I will give all of my heart
If I feel anger, it will be vented full force

When I laugh it will be real
And each time I cry it will rob a piece of my heart

Soft winds I will remember as a gentle caress
Blinding snows, storms that chilled me to the bone

Nothing in this life should be without meaning

And when I leave this earth
My soul will not stay behind pining for all those
Lost grey moments

For I will have lived them
Not pushed them aside.

—*Susan L. Jelis*

Get A Hold

Get a hold on life, in a course not dimly lit;
the batteries for your guiding light are there, within your kit.
Take a hold on love (palm what you can bring
to carry cross the roughest path, even as you sing).
Grab a hold on faith; take the handle strong.
as if it were a vise to squeeze, to mash-up what is wrong.
Let this (hold of) trust, in a tenacious kind of grip,
give you strength to stand secure, so your feet won't trip.
Receive the whole (of joy) to prevent some hole of grief
(the secret power given you will render sadness brief).
Permit such virtue breathing space in all the air around;
your spirit will begin to soar and good things will abound.
Grasp and hold to all these "tools" and you will have a
start on keeping cool or warming up, with a tender, merry heart.

—*Ted Smith*

The Radiant Moonlit Night

When the moon rises over the majestic diamond head.
The beautiful irradiant beams of the moonlight
Shine over the shores of Waikiki Beach.
Like a dazzling laced crystal bead,
Transcending the night into romantic hours of delight.
While the gentle trade wind goes breezily by.
Blowing and fanning all through the night.
The tall swaying pinnate leaved of coconut palms.
Silhouette below on the candle lit sand.
From the radiant moonlight beams
transforming the midnight into romantic pretense dreams.
Even the receding ebb tide waters,
Motionless, smooth and calm,
Like a slender stick of a magician's wand.
Attracting young and old romantic couples.
Toward the beautiful spreading banyan tree.
And under the tall swaying coconut palms,
While the moon is slowly setting by.
Toward the cloudless western sky.

—*Warren T. Fujiwara*

Little Thoughts

Look up into the sun.
The beautiful sun
as your face is shined upon by the light of life
pain and sorrow is what is retrieved
sadness and slumber is the echo boomeranged.

Look up into the sun.
The blue blue sky is there nearby.
Look at the sky
the blue sky and pierce its ocean
fly
fly high oh great wonder sky
float
float for me because I grope.

Look at the grass.
If grass were a bed I'd sleep forever
as comfortable as the grass is green
as cozy as the tranquility seen.
Very simple and color coated is what this is
like a covering band-aid on a newly scraped knee.

—*Tracey Ethan Bailey*

Door To The Inner Mind

Seek and you shall find;
The door into the inner mind:
Open slowly, look and see;
I've found out what's inside of me:
I rush not in, I go not past;
My eyes have seen my, futures past;
A burst of color, sudden light;
I'm standing in a state of fright:
The time has come, I don't go in;
There's doubt I won't come out again:
For once you've entered show no fear;
Do not laugh, or shed a tear:
Walk straight ahead, look not back;
Around you all your nightmares black:
There's sudden fear, the thought of death;
Those monster things that take your breath:
Your one step in, not one step more;
Then turn at once and shut the door:
Now open your eyes to reality;
Is there a second chance, just wait and see.

—*Ted R. Strausbaugh*

Why Is It?

Why is it that when I find someone real special to me,
The entire world turns against me in different ways?
Why is it that when I show my lady the world,
People attempt to take that and her love away?
Why is it that when I change my belief in something,
It's always because someone else made me change?
Why is it that when I feel so good about life and love,
The world seems so cold and very strange?
Why is it that when I work so hard to get what I want,
One incident can spoil a very special time?
Why is it that when I try to reach the top of a mountain,
Someone makes it a little harder for me to climb?
Why is it that when I try to make everything alright,
It is never as easy as it should seem?
Why is it that when my girl and I are together,
People always try to separate our team?
Why is it that when I'm in pain, others are overjoyed,
Because the love I have, people want to see it end?...
I don't care why it is because I know one thing for sure—
My girl will always be my very best friend.

—*Torino Johnson*

My Mother's Days

The cup was golden from which I drank
The liquid sweet amid the deep
Of purple buds that did unfold
and caught the light in bands of gold
There are no defects in a mother's touch
Because the dove is pure and love is such
The wounded child she loves the most
The weak, the shy, the timid host
Yet to the brave, and to the strong
Those lonesome pines that sway high in the wind
and sing their own song
She grants to them her quiet praise
Her deeds of mercy tempered with grace
Cascading down her lovely face
She plants a kiss, an indelible trace

—*William E. Self*

The Past Is The Past

If I could only realize
The past is the past
And by dwelling on the past
I have no time to live,
No time to live for today.
If I could only realize
The past is the past.

Sometimes I wish the past could become my future
But I know that, that is not probable to happen.
If I could only realize the past is the past.
I wouldn't have to wish anymore
I would be able to live for today
I could live my life the way
that life was meant to be lived,
One day at a time.

If I could only realize
The past is the past
And only the past is the past
Not the future nor the present is the past
And I guess they never will be the past.

—*Tanya Johnston*

Untitled

It's dark, my eyes are adjusting,
The silence is almost deafening,
In my hand I feel a rose, wilted,
But still it draws a drop of blood from my fingertip,
A sense of life.

Around me, a wall, another,
Trapped,
The rose, withering,
My image, fading,
I remember the light
Walking to it, into it
Then suddenly the noise, the coldness
Torn from eternal peace.

Time goes by, and then what?
A tear, isolated, desolate,
Born innocent,
Would they realize what they had done?
Is this how it ends?
What will become of me?
Buried alive.

—*Sonya Stroud*

Untitled

Like institutional cottage cheese
the textured ceiling looms above me
uninterrupted recesses of infinite design

In the years before I
was concerned with paying rent
I stared at one much the same as this

I envisioned balloons, trains, a lion or two
In the visual possibility
created by texture and shadow

Could I have imagined then
all that my reality is now?
perhaps so

In gratitude
I realize that today
my ceilings, my dreams,
my world
still contains
balloons, trains, and a lion or two.

—*Victoria Alex Bowden*

"Untitled"

Once in a lifetime, in the night time,
there is a moment when the revelation
sweeps into the barren room to scatter dust.

Before the open page
there is a thought which
in its isolation
joins to mobs of pulsing seething joy.

There is juxtaposed a mind with all eternity;
futility in what if, what was,
but what shall be remains.

There is hope,
but less than that there is relief.

There is knowledge knowing what must come
is never known, cannot be known,
or all is lost to certainty.

Escape is found
Resigned to joy
Forsaking choice
Revelling in deistic faith.

—*Trisha C. Howell*

A House Speaks

There's folks who think I'm common place
There's folks who think I'm fine.
And little children romp and race
Within these walls of mine.

My furniture is scratched and marred
My rugs are old and worn.
My floors too, are marked and scarred
And draperies are torn.

For folks who dwell within these walls
I hold dear memories
Of children's laughter, books and balls
Of youngsters fun and tease.

To me they all come trooping back
No matter where they roam.
They love each cranny, nook and crack
I'm not just house, but home.

—*Lillie G. Monter*

The Hooves Beat No More

The hooves beat no more.
They rest silently in the mud.
The pain is over now.
He no longer scavenges for a blade of grass missed by the others.
His stomach no longer pains for a tiny morsel of anything.
Anything at all.

His body reveals his agony.
A rack of bones blanketed by mangy, matted hair.
The mud covered legs that no longer had the strength to stand.

The hooves beat no more.
And those who cared, whose hands are tied by law and
bureaucracy are condemned and tried by society.
While those who are responsible are covered and protected,
Safe and healthy by the laws and that same bureaucracy.
The hooves beat no more.

—*Sheryl A. Haan*

"Second Chances"

The members of your family, especially your friends —
    They stay with you through all your lives
        Until the bitter ends.

But sometimes there's an argument — your temper tends to flare
    You say the things you do not mean;
        You hurt the ones who care.

And then the worse thing happens — the one you're mad at dies.
Before you've said "I love you," and now your poor heart cries.

The one you love has left you, the anger still within.
    Your guilt is escalating over what should not have been.

They say that God forgives you — of that you are not sure—
    But there are second chances —
        The afterlife — the cure!

For when you meet in Heaven, past grievances all fade.
    There's never any anger — all debts of heart are paid!

If this, to you, has happened, then, please do not despair —
    You'll get your second chances
        With the loved one who waits there.

—*Linda L. Kaucher*

Paper On Thought

Coffee on paper, paper on thought,
Thought upon thought upon tied up in knots,
    Sugar and cream are casting their lots,
    Stirring a dream in a thickening plot
        Of tugboats with tires and sea gulls in flock
        That circle a scheme on the hands of a clock.
With a submarine dive I can see what I sought,
Near bursting my seams between is and is not.
    My spoon laid aside, my coffee still hot,
    I hope and believe with all that I've got,
        And with periscope eye, my torpedoes are shot
        Straight at the fiend, the monster of knots.
Its master disguise I so narrowly caught,
In camouflage green, off the Isle of Jot,
    Where its tentacles float in ink on the spot,
    Its echoing scream was "No, you can not!"
Now I sail my dreams with a pen that can talk,
With a tilt and a gulp as I'm tossing my thoughts.
    I'll shiver me timbers, me anchors away,
    As I'm rowing ashore from a little cafe.

—*Steven Leonhard*

Hold On To My Hand

Hold on to my hand, we'll walk through the rainbow,
To a place where we all want to be.
I am your shadow, you are my vision,
Of the roads never traveled by me.

Dance me a painting, paint with the words,
Sing me a song of our time.
You be the poet, I'll be the rhyme,
Take my gift, let your heart hear the mime.

Hold on to my hand, we'll walk through the darkness,
If the world is a stage, we're the show.
Raise the cloud curtain, bring up the moonlight,
Be the star that I want you to know.

One day I'll see you standing without me,
All my memories with you will march by.
As I give you tomorrow, happy mask hide the sorrow,
Curtain down on the tears in your eyes.

You can hold on to my hand, and don't fear the new day, soon a
rainbow for you will appear. Then you'll dance me a painting,
paint with the words, sing our song, that the whole world can
hear. Hold on to my hand....hold on to my hand.

—*William C. Douglass*

Dancing

They say that life is like a dance that's ever changing
To the music, to the rhythm, to the rhyme.
Must keep moving, must keep dancing, rearranging
All your steps to match the lyrics and the time.

They say that life is like the ocean ever swaying,
With the breezes, with the waves, from side to side.
Never knowing what the winds will next be saying
About what will soon wash up within the tide.

They say that life is like a stage that's ever playing
Different roles, for different parts, for different scenes.
Many actors, many actresses portraying
All the little things that life's supposed to mean.

They say that life is like a dance that's ever changing,
And life is like an ocean or a play.
Never knowing, always guessing, rearranging;
Never enjoyed dancing that much, anyway.

—*Elizabeth Haug*

Lost

Sometimes I feel like a
treasure but other times like
an unopened chest just inching
towards the shore

My soul feels like a suffocating
breath with no one able to
help me or trust in me

My one and only hope is slowly creeping away
leaving not only me but my heart without a beat

Someone is looking down upon my body
with a vengeance of not only fear
and hate but mistrust

I then see this figure as a follower
someone with desire but no inspiration

The jealousy is making a friendship of gold
quickly fade away

—*Sarah Keso*

Untitled

Drowning in an ocean of doubt
trying to find a way out
reaching for one I can feel
searching for one that is real
Choking on words that are fake
not realizing what is at stake
waiting for my turn to come around
ready for the truth to be found
warming your cold touch with my heart of fire
to have the strength to walk away is my only desire
and I look past your blank gaze
as I stand there in the haze
I walk right through your open arms
and go to the place where there is no harm
and as you turn to follow
you fall down at the sight
that I'm never coming back
as I slip into the night

—*Staci Leatherland*

Love Thought Lost

Hearts ignited by love
two divided by fate

Endeavoring to forget their loss
each isolated themselves from the other

Accepting they would never be together again
both searched for another to share their lives

Ultimately they found new affections
but neither forgot the love they were missing

Believing the other had forgotten their adoration
they did not renew their sentiment as the miles diminished

One on leave the other on break
both where their fire had started

Realizing their passion intact
discovering their lives may touch again

Perhaps the fates that divided them
would also reunite them

—*Todd Jones*

An Empty Nothing

Tears have stung my eyes for the last time. The sadness has
washed over me once again. But no longer I say, "No longer will
I feel the pain and sadness fill my body, no longer will the
tears fill my eyes." No longer I say, "For it is just too much to
bear, too much to handle." I must clean and cleanse my soul,
must expel all of my hurt, agony, anger, fear, and pain. I must
clean myself of all I have ever felt, seen, conquered, and feared.

I have been happy for the last time. No longer do I feel
happy, no longer do I feel joy. I feel nothing, for I feel I
remain no longer. I feel so empty, I feel so all alone, I feel
worthless for that is what I have become.

I have accomplished nothing so now I am. Nothing. It's so
cold and empty. It's so alone. Nothing, it can't bother anyone
Yet if you feel nothing and if you do nothing. Nothing is
exactly what you become.

—*Sarah Elizabeth Peedin*

To Joan

Thank you for your thoughtfulness
What a special gift
When I saw who contributed
It gave my heart a lift

The gift meant for our wedding day
Had long since been forgotten
These satin cases will cradle our heads
With more love than did our cottons

For the fabric and the thread were joined
By Mom's fingertips with love
And I know she'll return my smile
As she looks on from above

So thank you once again, dear Sis
And thanks to Emily
It was nice to hear from our Mom again
On my anniversary
—*Teri Waxman*

The Silent Stalker

He comes in the chill of the dark, lonely night,
When the graveyard is haunted by unearthly sights;

As swift as the bat with its black velvet wings,
He creeps from his coffin while the cursed demons sing;

With his long, slender body and weird gruesome face,
He's attired in black stolen from Hell's sacred place;

He has eyes flaming red and fangs gorging through,
As his hunger for blood drives him onward anew;

So he seeks out a victim upon whom he can prey,
To replenish his lifeline before stroke of day;

While the night shadows sway and unseen creatures wail,
The black devil strikes and his poor victim fails;

As the screams turn to moans and the anguish is hushed,
The blood in his mouth turns his pale face flush;

So he drinks his fill and he slithers away,
He must hurry along or the price he will pay;

Now the terror is gone and the sun brings the morn,
But the darkness tonight brings the Vampire's forlorn...
—*Marnie Kitchener*

Faire Haven

Hushed green thoughts of Faire Haven
Where I ran to the edge as a child
I was given the chance to return there
I slipped through the trees back in time.

I slowly put down all my weapons
And embraced all the beauty she showed
I swam in the waters of Avalon
And followed the sun to its close.

I sat on the rock under blue skies
The trees surround me, straight as lines
The mountains stood watch like soldiers
Keeping all thoughts from my mind.

And slowly my pale glowed with color
And my heart found a freedom so pure
Then I knew what I had to go back for
Lay like a glittering sword.
—*Susan Murray*

Sleeping Beauty

Silent slumber fills your sighs
While distant dreams cloud your eyes

Sweet surrender blows your breath
To the ebb and swell of your breast

Somewhere far away it seems
On rolling hills, by sparkling streams

You wander underneath a sky
Of deep dark blue clouds floating by

Flowers dance on a gentle breeze
That whispers sweetly through the trees

Time it seems has lost you there
In a world that glitters without a care

So, Sleeping Beauty stay a while
In a land that dreams with endless smiles

As you wade the waves of emerald seas
Perhaps your thoughts will drift to me.
—*Thomas Haney*

Family

There is a family that I know,
Who comfort me and touch me so.
They know my every need and care,
They make me always so aware.
Of what's important to us all,
For they are always there when I call.
They stir my soul and touch my heart,
For without them I'd come apart.
Their care for me will probably,
Never count in history.
But in the heavens up above,
God looks down on them with love.
He thanks them with a touch of grace,
And says, "you my friend will always have a place."
For what you do unto my friend,
So will I bless you in the end.
—*Shirley Boschee*

Breakthrough

After teen-age comes a dilemma of a whole life-time.
Whom do I choose in the coming march of time?
I would want a lawyer, a doctor or a professional,
but, woo unto me! None of these came to the final.

As days passed by my whole life has been threatened.
I needed someone so my faith might be strengthened.
Suddenly came the inevitable, parents rushed to the rescue.
Before I knew it, I was planning a menu for two.

A moment of bliss but only a second to share.
A miracle happened with nine long months to bear.
Finally came the unexpected unbearable pain.
Oh! Lord, help me! I'll not do it again.

This episode of life takes years for a family to bear
as a baby coming one after another year after year.
A very difficult life for a family to raise,
but thanks to the Lord for bestowing His loving Grace.

After family raising graduation came the Grandparents
Association, widely known in their twilight years.
But the officers and members absolutely disagree
because they are just the late bloomers.
—*Socorro F. Obaob*

Tell Me

Why don't you call?
Why don't you scream my name in the night
Could you think of me
Just once today?
Why don't you write my name a hundred times?
Could you remember my face?
Please say you want to feel my wet naked body against yours
Please whisper your name in my ear again & again.
Do you ever think of me?
Please say that you want to see my bare body standing over you.
With my hair falling in my face while you lick my stomach
Please tell me you'll laugh at my silly grin
And that you'll grind your teeth when I touch my warm lips
Against your shoulder
Tell me you have chills trickling down your spine
When you smell my skin
And that you'll clutch my breast
When you push your soul deep inside of me
Tell me all of this
But just please don't tell me that you love me.

—*Tracy Ray*

A Voice In The Darkness

Pondering, wishing, wondering,
Will it ever be? Can it be? Could it be?
Possibly

Cries of children
Weeps of mothers
All wanting care

A voice in the crowd
No one special
Just simply... me

I long to live
To be free
In life with a future made just for me

All I ask is for something more
I keep asking 'what did I do'
And when will it end?

—*Seirena Iwasiuk*

All Is Silent

I stand in an open field at the bottom of a mountain
With no sound of the breeze.
I feel the breeze blowing on my face,
I walk in the meadow, only with my eyes looking around.

There is no whisper in my ears,
No sound of children singing.
All is silent, just my eyes
And feeling in my heart.

I look up at the mountain,
And see the swaying of the trees,
I wonder what kind of sounds are these,
I close my eyes and feel from my heart.

My heart shows me a sound through my mind,
I stand in silence and wait for a sweet sound
But there is nothing,
Just my eyes looking around at the mountain.

I hear nothing, but I see
My eyes are my ears
But that is okay, for I do not fear
Because I know that you are with me.

—*Tanya A. Branham*

Faraway Love

I can touch you — ever so gently
with the fingertipped shadow of my Soul...

You can feel my presence across your brow
when the warm sea breeze dances in the air...

At the precise moment that our Souls embrace —
we smile. Almost simultaneously.

The sensation does not last long enough to chase away
our desire to be near one another...

But long enough to be of comfort throughout the dawns
that seem just a little darker when we are apart...

Letters of promised love coupled with brief conversations on
the phone pacifies the hunger — temporarily...

We wait patiently for our time to be close once again,
as each day passes our hearts grow fonder...

And our new beginning seems a little less faraway.

—*Stacy A. Morgan*

Untitled

I knew right from the start, you'd end up with my heart
You broke down my walls and love began to start

I can't fight this strong love I feel for you inside
I need your gentle touch forever, this I can't hide

But when you're sad or blue, and start to cry
A big part of my soul starts to whither and die

For we are no longer two, we've become one
And it no longer rains in our world, there's just sun

Come run away with me and never cry again
With love by our side you'll never have to feel pain

Not only are you my love, but you're also my life
I pray for the blessed day that I call you my wife

Nothing means more to me than your smile and happiness
I'll take you in my arms so you can feel my caress

So smile now and know I love you so
And nothing will ever make me let you go

—*Scott Dumond*

"The Song In My Heart"

Just when I needed someone, you appear
Your eyes hypnotize me as you move nearer
I burn from the igneous light in your eyes
And as you move closer, I am mesmerized
My own eyes will you even nearer to me
When your lips touch mine, it's ecstasy

You're the song in my heart, my dream come true
You're my reason for living, I'd die without you
It's you, my love, that's put the song in my heart
You're my own special masterpiece, my own work of art

I can't help but think as you make love to me
How you've opened my eyes and made me see
That love was waiting for me all along
That the other men in my life before you were all wrong
But now, like a rose, I've blossomed and grown
For I have you to call my very own

You're the song in my heart, my dream come true
You're my reason for living, I'd die without you
I love you, baby, I have from the start
You're my own melody, you're the song in my heart

—*Sherri Gibson*

You Are So Far Away

As I sit here listening
To the love song dedications on the radio,
I heard our song playing.
I was reminded of you. . .
Taken back to a special place in time
And as I think of you,
A certain sort of sadness filled my heart. . .
My eyes swelled with tears.
Even though the memories we have are beautiful
And thinking back on them filled my heart with joy,
The distance just tears me up inside
Because you are so far away.

—*Youa Lee*

Autumn Orange

To the leaf the wind is it's God
Swirling, flowing and moving, giving it life
Whether a warm Santa Ana wind
Or a blast trained down from the north
The life it gives depends entirely
On the burnt orange leaf,
That has fallen from heaven's strings
Moving about like restless children
Who are about to be punished
The beautiful sculptured trees
Seemed motionless or anchored
To the ground of its nourishment
For it's life streams from the
Water of it's captivity
And the leaf with it's freedom
To choose life or
The solitude of death

—*Sean M. Kitchin*

You Are Now One

As two feathers are plucked from the Great Eagle:
YOU ARE MADE ONE.

As the Sun Rays shine down on you:
YOU ARE MADE ONE.

As the Great Spirit wills it:
YOU ARE MADE ONE.

As you break your Vase of Marriage,
scatter it throughout your Adobe,
Only Good Luck will follow,
through the endless days
of your Marriage.
YOU ARE MADE ONE.

May the Great Spirit watch over:
FOR YOU ARE NOW ONE.

—*William Pratuch*

The Endurance Of Time

No one can fully appreciate a rose,
That in its youth is only a bud
Hidden and encased in a green shell.

It is only when the shell splits
And five green slivers expose a bud,
Do we capture the beauty of the genus Rosa.

The true beauty of a rose is revealed as it matures,
Opens as plumage in radiant splendor,
Bringing joy to the eyes of its beholder.
The endurance of time, infancy to old age,
Likens us, you and me,
To the rose in all its beauty.

—*Stephanie J. Garite*

Reality

To make a choice, a choice of sorrow
The decision made by the end of tomorrow.

He says it's the only way that it can be.
If the wrong decision is made, he'll flee.

Although she knows what she needs to do
The decision to be made is all too true.

She cries for help in hope someone will come.
The shame she feels; the fear of being shunned.

The decision made; she has to be strong
For the child she carries will be hers alone.

—*Misty Walker*

Gods Love

Like a fire burning bright,
Warm and cozy through the night,
Like a million stars above,
Sending out its light of love.
Like a mountain tree top high
Reaching upward toward the sky.
Like the valley in between.
Growing fertile and ever green.
Like an eagle, when in flight
Spreads its wings with strength and might.
All of these, God gives to you,
With His love and heaven too.

—*Lillian Sage*

Until Today

I see your reflection in my mind,
Your touch is so gentle,
Your words are so kind
When you pass
Your smile brings sunshine to me,
Like petals of a rosebud, a beauty to see.
If only for a moment
Our lips could meet
So soft and delicate
Warm
And sweet
I love you
More than
You will ever
Know
More than
I could
Ever show
Never before have I felt this way
Never before...until today.

—*Stacey Pearson*

"Christmas Thoughts"

It's time again for those christmas bells
With many wonderful tales to tell
A mother with a babe in her arms
Admiring his beauty and charms
Children laughing and playing in snow
With rosy cheeks and eyes all aglow
People going to church to pray
Each in his own faith and special way
All I'm sure will sing a song
To that precious infant so newly born
Then home to break their fast
And open christmas presents at last
Before retiring at night, of course
They will say thanks to santa claus

—*Lillian Gardner*

Sane Reality

Purple lilies
hung from the ceiling

Shimmering Quartz
crystallized in the sand

Motionless Unicorns
danced in the clouds

Weightless Fairies
scattered in the dust

Red Earth
shifted in the moonlight

The Void closed;
we vanished from humanity

—*Yvonne A. Stahl*

Eagle Eyes

Eagle flying
High into the night sky
Soaring house to house
Giving the spirit of
Eagle eyes

Eyes glowing
Fiery red
Wings graceful
And smooth
Soaring in peace to
Give the people
Spirit of eagle eyes

People welcome him
Gladly taking his
Spirit of eagle eyes

Again soaring
Into the night sky
To bring the spirit
Of eagle eyes
To other grateful people

—*Theresa Barrow*

Passing Rain

Outside my window,
I see the rain fall.
Under the lamplight,
The drops seem so small.

The quiet so mellow,
It turns into gloom,
And what I feel now,
Is being alone.

The rain slows to stop.
No cloud in the sky,
The puddles now gone,
The grass is now dry.

Inside I feel warm,
The sun is up high,
No need to worry,
I feel I could fly.

—*Mike Mueller*

"Yours Truly, With Love"

The letters you wrote and signed
"Yours truly, with love"
I'll treasure them as if
they were a gift from above
The letters you sent that were
sealed with a kiss
Those are the things
that I surely will miss
The letters I received
that were from your heart
Those are what made it
so hard to part
And now you watch over me
from up above
So I'm closing this poem
"Yours truly, with love."

—*Cindy Davanzo*

In Search Of Happiness

I have travel far
I have travel near
And all without a car
While wishing upon a star

I have travel from town to town
City to city and state to state
In search of happiness
But sorrow seems to be my faith

I have travel from country to country
Throughout many foreign lands
Seeking and searching for happiness
But it seems to be out of my hands

One day I heard the cry of the lark
Who's voice seem so distant and far
But the melody so simple and sweet
Brought joy and rhythm to my feet

Oh the song that was sang by the lark
Put the joy of happiness in my heart
After all my searching through the years
I found happiness to be just a simple song

—*Solomon Plummer*

Cats, Cats, Cats

I have two cats Pooh and Baby
I hope they like me....
maybe. Sometimes they get on
my nerves but I love it when
they crawl up on my lap and
perr, perr, perr. There are
many cats in my neighborhood.
But Pooh and Baby are the best
and the good. An orange and
white cat named Browne lives
in our cellar. She scrawls
and we have to yell her.
Browne and Baby hiss but we
tell Baby to be bless.
Pooh is a very heavy cat.
She would not hurt a fly.
But she could beat up some
weavy. Pooh and Baby hate
of ghosts and wolves that
were wolves.

—*Wendi Copley*

The Love I Lost

One day he walked by,
he didn't look nor say hi!

I just stood there and stared,
it didn't seem as if he cared.

I wanted to shout and scream,
and all I had left was to dream.

He called me to talk,
I told him to take a walk!

He came by my place,
I told him to get out of my face!

I was lonely and sad,
but was also very mad.

I was tossed aside and thrown away,
but someday God will make him pay.

All the hurt and pain,
yet he had nothing to gain.

I forgive and forgot,
so he can hurt me not.

—*Shannon Snow*

Untitled

The chess knight galloped past
   Hoping to join the fray
But when he'd gotten there,
   The enemy had run away.
   He looked about,
   North, South and West
   Shouted out
   "I tried my best!"
   But no one answered
   That solemn plea
For the battle raged on
Somewhere to the East....

—*C. Lupis*

A Love Gained From A Love Lost

   You are my girl
   I'm proud to say,
You are more beautiful than a pearl
   That's as bright as day
   Where would I be,
   If I had done
   That awful deed
   And he had won.
I'm glad you are here
   And he is gone,
   For you are dear
   And he is alone.
   Things are tough
   For both of us,
   But that's not enough
   To make a fuss.

—*Vanessa R. Lake*

"Scared To"

When I first met you
I was scared to look at you;
When I first looked at you;
I was scared to kiss you;
When I first kissed you;
I was scared to love you;
Now that I love you
I'm scared to lose you
Loving you always

—*Stephanie Key*

Untitled

Our love is a secret
Like you tell your best friend
Though I regret it
I don't want it to end

No one knows what we do
That's the way you want it
I should keep my mouth shut
Because I love you
So I'll try not to forget
But why
Should I lie

When someone found out
All you did was shout
at me
But she swore her secrecy
She betrayed my trust
Even though
It was only lust

—*Linda Foley*

You Are My Little Girl...

You are my little girl
In my heart you'll always be,
But as I watch you grow
You're becoming a sweet young lady.

You are my little girl
I remembered your baby face,
There's no other little girl
To ever take your place!

You are my little girl
You grew up very fast,
Don't ever outgrow our friendship
Let's make this always last!

You are my little girl
Not a trace to be seen,
You lost your little girl look
Now resemble a young pre-teen.

You are my little girl
Someday we'll break the tie,
Little girl when you get married
It will hurt to say, "good-bye!"

—*Suzanne Jean Starr*

Sitting, Looking, Thinking

As I am sitting
looking at the deep blue sky
thinking how things so easily pass by.
I could remember
the secret my father
once told me
that the language I spoke
was a gift of hope.
He so often took me
on boat rides
So I could feel the whisper
that he once did,
but now, as I'm sitting here
looking at the deep blue sky,
I could not help but wonder
why things so easily pass by.

—*Travonna Carter*

Judgement

Judgement of the word,
judgement of the mind,
and people say the word,
and judge my mind,

you shall find in every fact,
your opinion, error in judgement,
but am I or you fact,
but if so, there'd be no judgement,

judgement of me,
judgement you say you know,
and I shout, render me,
and you judge and say you know,

forgive me if I have judged,
forgive them, those who judged,
but the word comes from the heart,
but the mind also comes from the heart.

—*Shawn J. Meine*

Seek Me

Seek me, don't search, just seek
me out among the thorns.
I am a rose just beyond the clearing.
Seek me, it is easy if you know me.
Unlike the thorns I am delicate
my flesh is fragrant and plump.
As the dew settles in the early
morn you shall find me.
Do not rest I am too beautiful
for your eyes to behold.
When you see me you'd be besides
yourself with joy.
I am someone you know, but
you have not seen me in a long time.
Do not tarry I am worth the
wait, through the you must make haste.
Just a few more steps can you feel my
essence in your soul. You have found me,
the rose, it is you my friend, is it all
that you expected? So beautiful in truth!

—*Tyisha Woodroffe*

Born

It was there,
in the garden,
toppled down into trees,
all soft, sticky,
soiling everything,
thick, a jelly, and
I was inside,
I with the
garden, mounting
up, spilling over,
filling everything with
gelatinous oils,
and I could see depths
upon depths of it
reaching far beyond
the limits of the
garden, into the
houses.
I was no longer
floating.

—*Victoria Niven*

"Smoking"

Smoking is bad for your health;
it only helps the rich man's wealth.
I don't know how long smoking has been,
But God knows its a sin.

Cause smoking will shorten your breath;
And it will lead to slow death.
Just think of all the peoples
from smoking have died,
And if you keep on smoking my friend,
You are only committing suicide.

Cause the wind may blow;
And the door may slaw.
But that tobacco you are smoking,
it will shorten your life Sam!!

—*Willie Mills*

The Shuttle

For the seven that died
In the shuttle blast
I'm sure they found comfort
And peace that will last
I think that God met them
With wings for their souls.
So that they could fly onward
To planets untold
The next shuttle mission
Will have to go far
To find planet heaven
'Cause that's where they are

For the people that mourn them
Each and everyone.
Say a prayer and remember
That God's will
Will be done

—*Livina M. Pumphrey*

On A Long August Night

On a happy day,
God took them away.
Them stupid wires
Started the fire.
They were so young
God took them past the sun.
In the bed, laid their father
He awoke as he heard a holler.
He held them tight
As that was the end of their light
On a long August night.

—*Leticia Medrano*

Not A Lie

Sometimes I wake up feeling bad,
I don't remember what I had.
I'm not ungrateful don't you see?
It's just the darker side of me.
When I turn and see your face,
Then it all falls into place.
Girl I love you more than life,
This is why you are my wife.
I'm so lucky can't you see?
She's the other half of me.
She's my anchor in the storm,
Her hugs and kisses keep me warm.
Thank you Lord cause I'm so high,
For once I'm living not a lie.

—*Stephen B. Ross*

Time

The race with time
is strange and unfair
we seem to begin ahead
without a worry or a care

All of a sudden
with very little warning
one night quickly ends
and already it's morning

So many things to do
and time we cannot waste
we must fulfill our dreams
be content in all this haste

Will life's quality be lost
amidst the rush and hurry
can we ever have it all
because of this I worry

Time continues always
we may wish that it be still
to stop for just a moment
though we know it never will

—*Stacey McConnell*

Paper

Smacked with many keys
And smeared with black ink,
I was crumpled into a ball,
Where I could barely think.

I was tossed into a can—
It was such a shame.
I screamed in agony,
Drowning in pain.

A match was tossed upon me.
It stabbed at my heart.
I was scorched into black cinders,
My body blown apart.

My ashes were tossed into the breeze,
Drafts tearing at my dust.
Flying for eternity,
The wind my only trust.

—*Steve Dechter*

Our Changing World

What is this world we live in?
Full of strife and stress.
Is it to live, and then just die?
We live in a world of mess
And few even ask why.
What about the morals in life?
Or the love we once had?
Yes, some still do strive
To keep what we once had.
But what of those whose love is lost?
Those whose love has gone bad?
It must be gotten at all cost.
For if not, we'll go mad.
Or could it be we're too late?
Has the world changed forever?
A world that's full of hate?
Is love to be lost forever?
No, not if we, you and I, can love again.

—*Scott W. Finney*

519

Silent Stars Speak

One night I looked to the sky
and stared at it in wonder.

Who's there? I asked
Can you see me?
Do you want to?

I dropped my head and cried.
When I looked up again
I saw a falling star

It must have been asking me
the same questions.

—*Sarah J. Riniker*

Symphony Of The Trees

The wind flows gently through the trees,
And sings its song of love...
The birds sing too their melody
Given them from above.
If one could rest his weary head,
And think of naught but these...
How sweet the world would be,
In the symphony of the trees.

—*Virginia Ballance*

Shadows On The Wall

There are shadows on the wall
And voices in the wind,
They tell of a time,
No one wants to recall.

When your enemy may dwell
Within the shadows,
Or within yourself;
Both put you through hell.

There are shadows on the wall,
And voices in the wind.
They tell a tale of fear and hate
That's enough to make a man bawl.

The shadows shall not fade,
The voices shall not die,
For into the history books
Their tales have made.

—*Theresa Flesher*

Parlour Poetry

With parlour poetry he would speak
    of myths and fairytales....
        of wench's and witches
        of kings an' princes
    an' oceans full of wayward sails!
With worldly wisdom he would teach
    of truth and mystery....
        of stars and stripes
        of facts an' hypes
    an' written ancient history!
With blessed ballads he would croon
    of guilt and innocence....
        of gray and white
        of wrong an' right
    an' heavens holy eminence!
With heartfelt hope he would dream
    of peace and harmony....
        of life and health
        of joy an' wealth
    an' loving solidarity!

—*Deborah Ellen Nigro*

The Gift

God has taken a star
And plucked it from the sky,
    To you he has given
    A light in your eyes.

A little piece of heaven
To be a gentleman or a lady.
God has blessed you with,
    A tiny new born baby.

So thank your lucky stars
And all of Gods good grace,
    For an angel as a gift
In your hands, he has placed.

—*Linda M. Barr*

"A Laugh A Day", Will...!

A giggle is healthful,
And I might say,
A laugh is as good
As a bright sunny day.

So be mirthful and joyous,
Smile even when sad.
It will reduce your blood pressure
And make every one glad.

A snicker or guffaw,
Is acceptable too,
So break out a grin,
It's so good for you.

It will lower cholesterol,
Bolster your Id.
A cure for all ills, try it!
You will wish every one did!

—*William T. Crowl*

Happy Tracks

As we travel through this life
and walk on this sod,
I hope and pray when I have passed
my tracks are pleasing to our God.

If in your life I've set my foot
and walked with you a while,
I hope I've left you a track
to make your life a smile.

Each day we make a mark in time
each second there is a print,
be careful how you live your life
and cautious how it's spent.
I'm grateful for the tracks you've made
and for your friendship true',
I'm happy that our tracks entwined
as I walked in life with you.

—*Virginia Maino*

Learning

Faces and places,
    memories return
    unbidden, unwanted;
time has not erased the traces
of passions which once burned
so bright- still I am haunted
    by my past mistakes
unable to learn from them
I repeat them again and again
always learning what it takes
    so that in the end
I don't lose another friend

—*Simon Bartell*

Love

Love is great
and love is wonderful.
Love is the feeling that you could fly
when you are caressed by one's lips
when you are in one's arms knowing
they care,
knowing they would do anything for you,
knowing that they would die for you.
Love is an obsession,
an obsession of lust,
lust as in desire,
desire as in passion,
passion as in a kiss,
kissing with a passion,
loving with a passion,
as in devoting all of your heart and
soul to that special true love,
and as doing things you would have never
done before you fell,
deep in love.

—*Tina Daulton*

Sing Me To Sleep

Hold my hand, I'll hold you close
as your touch fades with the light.
I won't leave your side
until I see in your eyes
that what was really you
has taken flight above me.
I'll be with you here
until your last breath lingers
and I'm sure you're safe
back in the arms of the ones
who brought you here.

My world will lose its color
when my world loses you.
You're the blood in my veins,
the beat of my heart,
the voice that will sing me to sleep
in absentia
forever.

—*Vicki Douglas-Robledo*

The Poet

Into life lonely,
fighting from fear
anger all around,
pain nagging near.

Running, running, running,
whipping past clouded moments
reaching out to shout,
clasping words, stealing words
giving emotions, taking emotions
and easier, sounds of bits
of pieces of inspiration
stoking hidden fires,
longings and truths
that every now and then
elucidates fulfilling responses.

—*Thomas Wright*

Untitled

Allow me to
build on a
dream of you
I'll start there
and work my way
up a life time
we'll spend together
dancing through each others
thoughts engaging in
one another's happiness
embracing in each others
Sadness
Binding it all together
with this thing called love

—*Shannon Small*

Waterfall

So sweet and gentle.
Flowing free with spirit.
Noisy,
Yet soft and quiet.
Kind and friendly
In every way,
Inviting.
Calling, "Stay with me."
A beautiful scene created by
The crashing waters down below.

If I could be anything,
I would be a waterfall.
Flowing free with spirit
Everyday.

—*Stacy N. Grapensteter*

An Oppressed Nation's Brain

From time to time
Every night and day, one of
our young oppressed brothers
    get's blown away.

Or filled with a poison which a nation
has given to them.
To keep us from becoming
    better than him.

They start us out early
By lying to our children
That their nation is supreme
    and our's is nothing.

But the key to our peace
Is not a blade nor a gun
It's what we have upstairs,
    that keeps our people hung.

They maybe richer, they may have less strain
But there is nothing more richer
Or stronger... than a
    oppressed nation's brain

—*Eric L. Seals*

Awakening

Within the night
the light that waits before the dawn,
starts yawning,
then rises mistily to stretch itself
cross trees and rocks
and little birds, whose merging forms
arrange the sounds,
that make it morning.

—*Lilli Ginden*

Broke My Soul In Two

The fragmented dreamscape
for life I once knew
has passed beyond.
I join my cold grey brothers
In the death of a romantic
with visions now smothered.
The beautiful breath I blew
from kissed lips gone.

Her scent still follows me
the sweet rose from our union
but its friendship fades
in winds carried away
to the soft white charms
of Utah arms.

To catch a cherub smile
broke my soul in two.

—*Sean D. Enright*

My Thoughts

Yes, I want to make a difference,
but I want to do it my way.
I don't want to compromise myself
just because of what you say.

I'm my own person now,
no matter what you believe.
I don't base my opinions
on just what people achieve.

I may never be rich and famous,
or make my mother swell with pride,
but to me that's not what matters.
It's what I treasure deep inside.

Listen to me for once,
pay attention to what I say.
For these are my thoughts
and maybe they'll matter someday.

—*Tanya Wilson*

Leaving

Why is he leaving?
I don't know why.

I thought our love
would never die.

A single tear in my eye.
I know in my heart I gave
a good try.

But, why oh why do I have to
say goodbye?

When he was leaving
there were no word to be spoken.
And my heart was like glass
thrown down and broken.

I wish I could find,
the words to change his mind,
but I know our hearts will never
combine.

—*Tara Biggs*

Untitled

Once I was confused
Didn't know who I was
Where was I going?
Nowhere
Just confused
The answer lied inside of me
Thinking, searching, wondering
Who was I?
Everyone has inside of them a path
That leads to their true self
Thinking, searching
I found my path
Always thinking but now following
I found happiness
My answer lied inside of me.

—*Tammy L. Strock*

To My Sister

You have always been my sister,
But, somehow you have became my friend.
The days when we would fight
have came suddenly to an end.
You'll be going to college soon
far away from home
But, as long as you remember me,
you'll never be alone.
Now as you go to college,
please remember this-
in everything you ever do,
I wish you happiness.

—*Shanna Sneed*

"The Creation"

Pacing back and forth
Causing all to stare,
Stopping every doctor
To ask them if it's there.

Glancing at his watch
Then the clock upon the wall,
Waiting for something,
Caring for nothing at all.

Stopping at a fountain
Bending to take a drink,
Impatiently waiting,
So nervous he can not think

Walking over to him
Beckoning him to come,
The doctor whispered to him,
Suddenly, he was numb.

Holding her in his arms
Thinking she was made by me,
Adoringly staring,
He finally has his baby.

—*Sarah Parker*

Autumn's Accents

Who can capture the splendor of an
    October day
When the maples are aglow -
Mirroring the brilliance of the sun;
How can they know of November's
    harsh deception
When the wind and rain will shatter
    their radiance,
And leave them naked and cold -
Standing as stark sentinels
Against a gray sky.

—*Virginia W. Barker*

Always And Forever

You hold the key
To open my heart
But you refuse to use it
And that tears me apart

We could be so close
Our hearts could beat as one
We could be together
And having so much fun

That key that you hold
Is a big part of me
It symbolizes my love
Which you don't care to see

If you ever want my love
All you have to do
Is turn the key just once
And my love will come to you

Remember what I've said
Don't forget those words ever
Because my love will be
Here for you always and forever

—*Stacey Matthews*

Mother's Delight

Little darlings, little girls,
Mother's pure delight.
Spread your joy into my world
and make my future bright.

In your eyes I see my soul,
your smiles reflect my heart.
Your voices like bells of silver, ring,
to sweeten life so tart.

When years have flown,
and you have grown
into such beauties-fair,
I'll count the ways I've loved you
shown in silver strands of hair.

—*Surnella S. Blanks*

Obvious Illusions

If they could paint your picture
using a pallet of colors so bright

Like I try to do
with these words that I write

Pictures the painting
of you sitting there

There in my rocker,
rocking my chair

Your hair - your face - your you

A pallet of colors,
all colors, all hues

Time will fade many things -
colors on a pallet, colors and hues

But never, no never,
my picture,
my memory,
my vision of you

—*Stephen T. Flynn*

We Stand United

We all stand united
We are the U.S.A.
Liberty and freedom
Are what we are today

Let's always stand together
For what we know is right
Let's help the weak and needy
And keep our goals in sight

We worship God Almighty
And love our family
We'll always stand united
And fight for liberty

For Americans love our nation
Where bells of freedom ring
And when it gets crunch time
We voters do our thing

—*William Arthur Barnes, Jr.*

We Can Still Dream My Love

God gave me a beautiful dream,
Though long gone.
It was like a beautiful rainbow.
Thrown across the sky.
When I close my eyes, I see it yet,
I cannot call time back.
But it is still in my heart.
This beautiful dream.
It's love I'll never forget.
As I tuck each dream.
Carefully in a corner of my heart.
The rainbow and dream become one.
To be long remembered, to hold near.
Thank you Lord for the rainbow.
And for lending me those dreams
Help me to see there will be others.
There are still rainbows
And dreams still to dream.
There has to be rain, for rainbows.
And a sowing time for dreams.

—*Thelma Barnes*

Summer Storm

Black clouds cover the sky,
Thunder rolls in the distance
It is getting closer and closer.
Lightning pierces the dark
foreboding sky.
The rain lets loose its fury on us.
Raindrops splash down on
Our upturned faces.
We do not move.
We stay standing in the
heavy rain
Allowing it to soak through
our clothes.
Feeling it on our hot, wet bodies.
Until it stops and we are
left standing there.
That feeling of uncontrollable
Ecstasy still in our grasp.

—*Vicki L. Brown*

Winter

What is winter does it come
throughout the year, months, or
century. Does it just happen who
makes winter. You could see kids
playing snowballs and building a
snowman or a snowwoman. While
snowflakes falling throughout
the winter days. You could
see families gathering up
in one cozy fire drinking hot
chocolate with little fluffy
marshmallow.
    While homeless outside
starving and cold and
nowhere to sleep and nowhere
to hide. The animals from
everywhere gather and hide,
and hibernate throughout
winter days. Could we stop
it or should it go.

—*Stacy Ng*

Untitled

The Lord is my Master
when I am weak.
The Lord is my Father
when I am in defeat.

The Lord is my Teacher
when I fail to know.
The Lord is my Guide
and leads me where I go.

The Lord is my shoulder
when the load I can't bear.
The Lord is my comfort
when I feel no one cares.

The Lord is my everything
no matter what my need.
Most of all the Lord
truly loves both you and me.

—*Sheila Bailey*

Silver Disk

Sometimes I float above the clouds,
Thru the air upon my disk.
Glide thru pastures cows and mist.
Sunlight shines on silver disk,
Light as a feather it never fails,
Touch the screen you never seen
Let me by with great speed,
Its only me and silver sheen,
Coast thru mountain tops and falls,
Silver disk glides thru them all.
I float thru the valleys in the day,
Stand still alone over bays,
Shall I land on soil or drift away,
Go straight up fly past the moon,
Just like a dandelion in the breeze,
Sound passing fast its only a whine,
Lighting bolts make it climb,
Keep them guessing again this time,
Higher and higher its clear to me,
White disk of static protect me.

—*Vern Majors*

For The Love Of A Little One

You have a lot of charm,
When I hold you in my arms;

You are so dear to me,
and you'll always be;

I've always loved you so much,
and always need your
sweet little touch;

Sometimes - I'm in a personal doubt,
but your little love always
brings me about;

You have always been so full of giggles,
even from the time you
had so many wiggles;

So for the love of a little one,
My work will always get done.
—*Thelma S. Bowe*

Unsung Beauty

Winter's twilight
wraps around each cottage
as the sun folds away
beyond earth's western bedroom.
The coachman's lantern comes alive
and lights the pathway through
the shadows on the snow
as cold penetrates
the tender evening.

Bundled souls hurry forward
each intent on reaching
his own hearthside.

Oh, anxious people
pause for one breath-misty moment
and feel the downy stillness.
Let it envelope you
with silver magic
for here at even tide
is innocent beauty, unsung
unsunned and untrampled.
—*Vernus Christine Lincoln*

Born To Be Free

'Twas on a bright and sunny day
When in amongst the trees I lay
Along with me there were three others
Me, my sister and two brothers.

Due to disaster, we lost our mother
So now we must care for one another
But all at once there did appear
A friendly hand to hold us near.

Before too long another hand
Did take me to a friendly land
All safe and warm and free from fear
I knew I would be happy here.

I ate and ate and grew and grew
And hopped and hopped and soon I knew
That time had come for me to go
Back to the wild that I did know.

I'm free at last to run and play
But to return another day
To nibble on some food I see
Left in a dish out by the tree.
—*Theresa Mele*

You

You are the reason I live
You keep the world alive

You make me laugh
You make me happy

I can't figure all why
But I want you

You make the world go
Round you have a lot of sound

You have a heart of
gold that can't be bought or sold.

Only you have the touch
That I love

So I want you Bennie
Hodges and only you
—*Toy Grey*

I Am Smiling

I am sixty

The path I walk leads
wherever I look
endless
like promise

Behind, I leave mountains
ground to sand

There is no place for me
I am the place itself

My last battle may be fought
if I remember why
I am smiling
—*Wilson Powell*

Jack-O'-Latern

A grinning toothless face
With its inner glow flickering
In the perfect sequence
To scare the immortal

Was that a laugh I heard
It didn't—it couldn't have
Or did it?

Was it that grinning face
With glowing eyes
And a dancing inner brightness
That laughed
At my innocence
—*Sarah Powers*

Your Coming Home

Have you ever waited for the sunrise
To blot out a night of gloom?
If you have, you will know
How I await your coming home.

Each moment's dark without you;
I grope in my despair,
Just searching for the brightness
I find when you are there.

No need to sigh and pretend
The time will never come
When my heart and soul are content,
As I await your coming home.
—*Virginia B. Brainard*

I'm Never Tired

I'm never tired
Why should I be?
God provides for you and me.
I may need some rest
But I'm never tired
I know I'm blessed
So I don't worry about the rest.
I may feel fatigued
But I'm never tired
My burden may be heavy
I have to be ready
To lift it off of me.
I keep the faith
I always see better days ahead.
Why lack energy to do as I please?
I receive spiritual energy
Through my breath
I'm aware of God's nourishment
That's why I'm never tired.
—*I. Aisha Ross*

Seasons

Winter, Spring, Summer, Fall,
Those are the seasons, and
I love them all.

In the Winter there is snow,
Let's sing Deck the Halls,
Or even watch a Christmas show.

Then there's Spring,
Hear the birds sing,
While watching the
flowers bloom.

Along comes Summer
There's no school,
"WHAT A BUMMER!"
Let's go play outside.

Finally there's Fall,
Also Thanksgiving,
Let's have a turkey
with all the trimmings.

Those are the seasons, and,
I love them all.
—*Staci DiCiero*

"I Am"

I am a person,
With feelings, desires, and needs.

I am an individual,
With my own personality and culture.

I am flesh and blood,
With the ability to feel and bleed.

I am of color,
With skin to see and touch.

I am a wandering soul,
Searching for others like me.

I am here and now,
A part of the whole.

I am of a race who rules,
The human race.

I am able to see,
Inside; we are all the same.
—*Vonda Chandler*

For The Love Of...

For the love of our children
Their hopes and their fears
Their laughter, their happiness
Their sadness, their tears

For the love of peace
With no fighting or wars
No murder or violence
Or locking your doors

For the love of a city
As nice as a suburb
Where friends are your neighbors
And race has no color

For the love of mankind
In a world full of sins
Where nobody loses
And nobody wins

And it's back to the children
Their hopes and their fears
Let's brighten their future
And wash away tears

—*Linda Caldwell*

Your First Baby

Its your first baby
Oh what a joy
What will it be
A girl or a boy

Whatever it is
Make sure to take care
Cause they learn what they live
So you better beware

So much to do
And so much to say
It's good to know
There's someone there
To help show the way

They need lots of love
And tender loving care
And they look so cute
With their soft skin
And their beautiful hair

—*Linda Benavidez*

Equality

When I cut my foot
On a piece of glass,
I bleed red.

When a poor man
Falls to the ground,
He bleeds red.

When a quiet woman
Absorbs her husband's wrath,
She bleeds red.

When an old man's hand
Cracks open with age,
He bleeds red.

No matter who we are
Or what we become,
We all bleed red...

Why are you so different from me?

—*Tim Nichols*

My Love Forever

I'm telling you now
My feelings so true
I love you so much
I could never hurt you
For my feelings are strong
Much stronger than words
You make me as happy
As a beautiful bird
Sometimes you may think
I don't really care
That just isn't true
I honestly swear
I love your more now
Than I did at the start
I hope that we never
Should have to part
I'll love you forever
My heart is yours

—*Vickie Kitchen*

Winter

The fall season is over,
Now the winter winds began.
First the rain, then the snow.
Oh! How I hate to hear the wind blow

The flowers all hang their heads
They die down like the grass.
Mother Nature has her way.
But soon all this will pass.

Winter time is always best.
The farmer can take time to rest.
Comes the snow, so pretty and white.
I like it best when it snows at night.

—*Winifred Smith*

Nine Planets

Pluto's small and far away;
   Neptune's blue and cold.
Uranus travels on its side;
   Saturn's rings are bold.
Jupiter is very large;
   Mars is red like rust.
Earth itself is quite unique—
   Water's on its crust.
Venus claims to be our twin;
   Mercury is fast—
Closest to our nearest star,
   Of nine it is the last.
All revolve and rotate through
   The vast expanse of space.
With meteors and comets, too;
   They run their endless race.

—*Linda Francom*

I Wish...

I wish that I were something,
You would always need,
Like the earth to bear a flower,
First must have a seed;
Something you would touch,
If only once, but every day,
Like a pencil you keep handy,
Or a chair that is in the way;
Something seldom seen,
But ever near to you,
That you had all need of,
That had no need of you...

—*Sarina Sue Stans*

Land Of The Night

My spirit is free, as much can be.
Only limited to what I see.
If I were blind, I'd open my mind.
So now the answer I must find.
I'll be your guide, if you take my hand.
We'll take a trip to a forgotten land.
I won't let go, let your spirit grow.
Close your eyes now and watch the show.
Imagination, share your fascination.
To be set free, that is emancipation.
We're in control, let the ride unfold.
Plenty of stories are left to be told.
Now hypnotized, time to fantasize.
Only the dream-maker will tantalize.

—*Todd Sandberg*

Monologue

What I told of dreams,
never dreaming they were
non-existent,
merely breakfast
made in dreams.

Hardly standing sunset,
evening dawned,
thinking only of "we"
driving silently through night.

(music playing with my head.)

told of golden silence
never warned of
our symphonic music defined.
but belief never followed
when beauty emerged
(doubt my truth to be your liar
where was this nonsense when needed?

—*Sharon Cheney*

Choices

Do you strive to be better
Or do you accept yourself as you are
   Do you share your emotions
Or do you keep them closed up in a jar

Do you just be yourself
Or do you change to fit in
   Can you accept loosing
Or do you strive to win

Are you mean and rough
Or are you as gentle as a dove
   Are you always going to hate
Or are you going to learn to love

—*Sarah Scala*

Untitled

And you stand
   oblivious to it all.
Inside, outside, on
   top of it.
But no one ever sees
   you.
And the dripping
   silence drives
   you mad.
No one hears you
   scream or cry.

—*Tonya L. Tucker*

My Message

When I awake
My heart broke
For I saw you....
Sad but true
My message is
I want you to know
I want you here
So please don't go
I hope this note
Makes it clear
I love you.

—Nicole Heatley

Untitled

The mountains tumble down
The earth is swallowed by the sea
When there is nothing left around
But the leaves from a dead tree
As the world crumbles to pieces
As the sky just falls apart
Will there still remain the pieces
Of my gently broken heart
As the flowers all shrivel and die
As the grasses all go brown
As a blazing fire burns the world
As a clue is never found
If you should die before I do
May we never say farewell
You'll always stay here in my heart
I hope I will as well.

—Sarah Sorrentino

Mushrooms

I lay there like a corpse
Seeing the night's action
Pass thru it's course
Like wine being fermented.
I am blind.
But with my brain's eagerness to see
Become a voyeur of my own expeditions.
Skin on skin.
My flesh for yours.
Sting we when the time is right.
I am Alice in her wonderland
A home she shares with me
She can keep it though
Through the looking glass
I see my world
A world in which I share
With no one
Bring me back.

—Aeprehyll Patino

Seasons

The sky gets dark
The snow now falls
Winters here that's the end of fall!
The snow melts
The grass grows
Spring jumps up and winter falls!
The flowers bloom
The pool is open
Summers come by and off spring flies!
The leaves fall
The flowers die
Summers done and falls begun!

—Tarah Hansen

The Tragic Case

I'm in my home next to the trees
The birds are busy gathering seeds
But what on God's green earth is that
I believe it is a yellow cat
Poor bird — he certainly was to slow
And that huge cat I do not know
Next time he will also be dead
I will do something I really dread
I'll call our county animal control
To free that cat's very naughty soul
Perhaps he really has nine lives
I hope I don't get great big hives
Upon my beautiful but tender face
From this horribly tragic case
Because you see — I do love cats
As much as all the birds and bats
His owner should keep him in the house
Where he might catch a naughty mouse

—Dwyn M. Gillespie

Untitled

The moon was a ghastly orange.
Smoke raised to the eaves,
and sparks raised over the bonfire
from Grandma burning leaves.

As I settled to my paper,
I felt the hand of doom.
As if all the ghouls from Hades
were standing in the room.

Suddenly I was startled
by a knock upon the door.
I quickly dropped my paper
and was standing on the floor.

As I opened the wooden door,
a chill ran up my spine.
For never such an ogre
had graced this house of mine.

Then from this terrible specter
came a giggle soft and sweet.
"Don't you know me, Grandpa?
It's Tabby, trick or treat!"

—Walter Jetmore

MaryLee

I met a girl in Arizona
She said her name was Marylee
That she had hitched-hiked many miles
All the way from Tennessee.

And then she told me that her mother
That just a few days she had died
And laid her head upon my shoulder
Then she cried and cried and cried.

She was molested on her journey
By evildoers we detest,
That was the price she had to pay for
To see her mother laid to rest.

So now its time for her departure
And say goodby to Marylee,
We send her many, many blessings
All the way to Tennessee.

—Tony Sanchez

The Answer

There are some things for which I pray,
That seem unanswered still.

But, patiently I wait, o Lord,
As I seek thy holy will.

Your answers often are a righteous plan
Which requires an amount of time.

But, when your answer comes, o Lord,
I'll know the answer is thine.

Sometimes the answer is much different
Than what I thought 'twould be.

But, your answer to my prayer
Was what was best for me.

—Teresa Grindstaff

Thank You, Lord

Thank you, Lord,
for the birds that sing,
for the church bells that ring,
for rivers that flow,
and the sun that glows,
Thank You for Everything.

Thank you, Lord,
for the miracle of seeds growing,
for Your love overflowing,
for the rainbow in the sky,
for mom with her homemade apple pie,
Thank You for Everything.

Thank you, Lord,
for trials that come my way,
I know you are there throughout my day,
for the rain that falls,
and for the baby that crawls.
Thank You Lord for Everything!

—Linda Rohland Day

Save Me Please

I'm wondering, hoping, and wanting
Someone to save me from this.
A place of hatred, fear, and horror.
No one to talk to.
I'm alone with so many problems.
And no help.

I don't have dads or moms.
Just foes, no sisters or brothers.
Just stranger in a fight.

We have many walls.
Very, very tall walls.
Built in between us.
No love.
No one to talk to.

Please, save me.
Save me please.

Get me away from this hatred place,
And somewhere with love, and people to talk to.

But for now I'll have to wait, because I'm a kid.
I'm going to have to wait.
For someone to save me.

—Tomacena Marie DeRoy

Beautiless

I saw you naked in a dream, the one I dreamt last night
Your hair filled the air and darkness danced around you
You stood in silence but spoke with your eyes
The most beautiful words that I ever heard
My eyes made love to the outline of your body
Our hearts were racing, gasping from enchantment

The night raged and howled
It made mad love like ugly dogs on the hottest night of the year
It was tender and loving...A beast dying, it was the sheer nobility of a tear

The sky sighed and there began the gentle rain...Each drop clinging
to you, rolling over you...Their journey was meant for fingertips
A long goodbye ached from your body...Time took a standstill

And the moment lasted forever

Moments lie on a flowing river called time...Each step leading to the
next...Each day alive is a day closer to dying...Come share with me
in this futile dream...Come with me, it may be our last...Nobody
loves me anymore...I don't care I have words to live for

I saw your shine going out like a falling star...I saw your heart
twisted and broken, it shared the semblance of a car...I felt your
words enter the lining of my soul...But you never say what you mean
Dreams are nothing but subconscious blunders...I saw you naked in a dream

—*Al Richardson*

Follow The Leader

And then the children etched
the way to a better lane of sight
with all their might.

Being able to see, that is, the
mesmerization. To grant a better way

of insight to these incorrigible
peoples. Hopeless and broken

they drained their pocketful
of gold for a small amount

of wisdom, happy now that
they could reason with

dilapidating vagrancy.

—*Terrance Andrew Roberts Jr.*

Wyoming

Someday when the snow is gone and the leaves
are green again,
I will leave here forever, to wander the
hills of Wyoming.
To have some peace of mind.

Spend some time fishing the cold swift rivers.

Watch the leaves turn colors on the Aspen
and Cottonwood trees. Red, gold and yellow.

When the fog rolls in over the mountains.
It is cold and wet.

You can hear the bubbling stream
as it races over the rocks, as it makes
its way to the ocean.

The water is so clear and cold.
You can see the rocks smooth and round,
molded from years of running water.

The wind blows through the aspen trees and rustles the leaves;
ever so softly. The way a mother soothes her baby.

The cold harsh rain falls like little needles
The sights and sounds comfort me like a warm blanket.

—*Joy Lynn Butler*

Baby

A sweet creature
Created out of love
Made whole by a mothers love
All its features
So tiny
So small
Whether it be a boy
He will bring you joy
Or a girl
With curls
Watch it grow its
Yours forever!

—*Victoria J. Broekhuizen*

Ginger

We named you well, my chickadee,
    With your freckle-face there!
Your winsome eyes, your impish smile
    And the tousled ginger hair.

We named you well, but didn't guess
    That from your first bold step
You'd race and run, and often fall,
    But bounce right back, with pep!

We named you well, but didn't know
    Such energy could be,
You took all dares and stunts in stride
    With scars for all to see.

Perhaps we should have called you
    Some gentle girlish name,
Would you have been retiring,
    Or would you have been the same?

On second thought, dear daughter
    What fun when you are there!
I'll take you, Ginger, storms, and all,
    And your tousled ginger hair!

—*Lillian H. Porter*

My Little Angel

She walks into my life
and walks right back out.
She never comes back
but it doesn't make me doubt.
It doesn't make me doubt the way
I feel about her.
I miss the dances we had,
and the way things always were.
The little girl I called my own,
has left me now.
I should have known.
Maybe once or twice a day,
there's time for me to get away.
But most of the time I always hear,
the little cry with a tear.
It seems such little time ago,
when we could dance and giggle so.
But it's been a while since she left
my precious baby was the best.
Now she walks up in the sky
up in the clouds by and by.

—*Angela Jensen*

Victims Of Society

The woman on the street corner
    selling her body to the one
        who will pay the most.
    The man in the alley
        stealing from another
        in order to survive.
The couple under the street lamp
    with all their worldly goods
        by their side.
The teenagers in the halls of school
selling dope to all who will pay the price.
The little child being beaten by
    his 'loving' parents.
    The baby with no name
        found in the garbage can.
All are victims of society.
    Just like you and me.
    They must do what they
        can to survive day by day.
We are all the victims of society.

—*Ellyzabeth Wallace*

est Friends Till the End

hrough all the hard years
nd all our tears
'e stayed best friends
ll the end
mes we laughed
bout the past
mes we cried
:cause we lied
ut we stayed best friends
ll the end
ometimes one of our life's bloomed
'hile the others' life was doomed
ut we stayed best friends
ll the end
hrough thick and thin
'e'll help each other like we've always been
o have to go through life without each other would make us
ll apart.
ut I know we'll always be in each others hearts
:cause we stayed best friends
ll the end!

—*Amy Fass*

he Cold War

eezing cold in a stinging wind
arts at the toes
nd makes its way up the shins to the knees
en through the thighs.
aist deep in the freezing cold
nat travels upward, rising towards the goal;
osty fingers reach around the organs
nd the freezing cold seeps in,
erverting warm life actions.
ll crawling through to the neck;
ing the voice, silencing the mouth, deepening the blue eyes
azing the tunnels of the ears with thick frost.
eezing cold has one last battle
ith the supreme power waiting in the crown.
ut heat is quickly overcome by subdegrees;
iere is no standoff in the struggle.
ie last war ends with one prominent victor:
ie freezing cold, triumphant and brooding
vades the center and makes the fruitful power
to a barren wasteland of ice.

—*Erica Handlewich*

Untitled

Here's a personal story, I want you to read -
feel it deep in your heart - and try to believe...
Because ..once upon a time, in "Never Never Land";
lived children who cherished childhood,
for it's so beautiful and grand. . . .

They only begged please - don't send me away...
from the fun and the frolics of "Peter Pan" days.
"Captain Hook" don't you tempt me,
to get ugly and mean, for I'm a true child at heart - -
I'm your dreams you've never seen.

"Oh," to be a child forever — in "Never Never Land"
and fly through the clouds, just as fast as you can -
See a beautiful rainbow, through a bright shining star
and thank "God" you are you - -
just as you are.

So, fall into the "Stardust"; it's so cozy and warm,
like "Tinker Bell" said — thank "God" you were born.
The child in your heart, deserves to be free —
if not for yourself —
then for "Peter Pan," and "Me."

—*Sandra Barton*

A Prayer For Peace

A balloon is sent up into space,
To a person of any race.
That finds the same and will reply
To my poem from out of the sky.

It bears the message of world peace
In hopes that guns will forever cease

To kill a human in our world
Then all flags can be unfurled.

United we could all become
With love enhanced for everyone.

It would erase much of our pain
And God would bless us all again.
—*Helen Banks*

Depressive Sole

You place a hand upon the heart,
Your life is ruined it's torn apart,
Depression it lies in the sole,
Something is missing you are not whole,
Your love has died it has gone,
You do not feel like number one,
You feel torn you want to die,
You sit there and just wonder why,
Your heart has crashed it has broken,
That depressive sole for now has spoken,
But deep, deep down your love is concealed,
It has not all yet been revealed,
It creeps up high into your head,
Your hearts alive it is not dead,
Your love is back you do rejoice,
Because you listened to that deep down voice.

—*Jayne Dangerfield*

"Ring Of Passion"

Forbidden depth so immense and sweet-
Within silk moments and stagnant time,
Ring of passion sharing hands-
Creation of sincerity not denied.

An apprentice in the Sorcerer's true love magic;
Internal mysticism in shared seclusions,
Blink of the heart's eye amongst magic,
Relishing wonderment of the lost in Sorcerer's illusions.

Bewilderment in magic's love lands-
Sincerity not denied within silk moments of creation.
Elicit depth immense and sweet-
Of stagnant time while sharing hands...
In beckoning the ring of passion.

—*Gae M. C. Garcia*

Heaven

Let me escape. Into every world I
ventured through reality was always so far away.
If I could walk beside my past, would I watch
every step of the way, or run to change the future?
To climb the staircase within the black hole it stands,
to see myself being torn from the steps. Lie beside
the fire, hold on to the vision. Hear the sound, and
feel the very touch of your creation. Don't destroy
the memory, let it take over the every control of
your mind. Stare, at the frozen points in time, of a
base reality too good to be true. Glance at the world
I knew so well, thousands of miles away.
Reaching for the dreams I almost touched, in one month
of Heaven.

—*Sally Faber*

Abstract Number One

An expanse of waves and sky
Soars beyond sea gulls
That sing near us,
White winged sky blue woven waves.

Thrown disks are caught on the run,
Crumbs fall on the hot sands.
People on the shore cast gazes;
Wind forlorn eyes, shaped as leaves.

Distant lonely sounds
Sing of a wasteland.
Forgotten wood lies beneath
White wind carved, sculpted by time's fingers.

Sands bright, lie in uneven drifts, diamond coloured.
Compacted by feet, firm sounds are emitted. Before us:
A red lighthouse with green-leaved trees;
As though freshly painted.

—*George Grossman*

The Dawn

Today - in the morning of my life...
social bridges crumble...
and nowhere do I seek a place to hide...
my soul is flowerfresh...
for this morning I am born...

Today - in the morning of my life...
I know the joy to fill my boots...
walk my miles...
and breathe my breath...
I am alive and my home is where I am.

Today - in the morning of my life...
I share my being with anyone
who cares to amble through my garden...
I weed out unwanted thoughts and feelings...
and calm myself for the new dawn.

Today - in the morning of my life...
I realize the strength of love comes from within...
while the beauty of love comes in the giving.

—*Dick Canby*

Untitled

The golden sunrise in the morn,
soft and delicate as your hair.
Radiating with beauty
I long to kiss you sweetly.

The subtle blue of a small brook
flows from your eyes with as much grace.
The sun, through a dew drop shines,
bright as your eyes when you smile.

The fresh breeze stirring my senses,
surrounds me with pure ecstasy.
The scent is of your body
when you hold me close at night.

Never has an autumn morn been so beautiful.

—*Bret Hackett*

Twin

Life is a series of emotions shared with others,
Your friends, your foes, your sisters and brothers.
A twin is one that can feel for you,
Your passions, your loves, in all that you do.
One lost is two, as two they're one,
Without the other their life is done.
The pains and sorrows are all shared,
However the joy and love felt can be uncompared.

—*Andrew Pierce*

Chris

Such a wonderful little cat
Soft, white, and gray
Kinds pudgy and fat,
Until that one drastic day.

He no longer sits and awaits me
Instead, he is looking down
Up from the world which lies no frown.

Now here he lay
Alone, but in light
Day by day
Night by night

Now the happiness has found our little gay
Oh, but what did he ever do?
By which, may I say
Chris, we love you.

—*Angela Wykoff*

Stepping Stones

Our lives consist of many stepping stones
Some are easy, some not so easy
Thru them all we somehow grow wiser
Our lives mingle with many others
Some whom will stay in our memories forever
But our goals are to move yet forward
Another challenge we have found
We have become restless

We've touched a lot of lives along the way
Some with a smile, some with kind words
Others with a special kindness
All these will be remembered forever by some

We've done our best
That's what counts the most

One door closes

Another door opens
It's time to move on..

—*Anita Rogers*

A Friend

I'm glad I have a friend like you
Someone I can count on when I am blue.
You always make me laugh and smile.
You make my life more worthwhile.
When I have a problem, you listen and you care.
The friendship that you offer is so very rare.
You stand beside me in all of my sadness.
You share with me all of my gladness.
You help me through the troubled times that come along,
And through the things that always go wrong.
You stand beside me in everything I do.
Whenever I am worried you always help me through.
You cheer me up whenever I am down.
A better friend I have not found.
I wonder if anybody is as wonderful as you.
I wonder if they have a friend so true.
No matter what will happen in the future or
what has happened in the past,
I hope that our friendship will always last.

—*Amy L. Zmolik*

ly Friend

ly friend is one who cares,
meone who loves and shares.

ly friend will be there,
I need her somewhere.

ill she be selfish? Never.
ut she will be there forever.

'e do everything together,
friendship could never be better.

Vhen I call in the middle of the night,
ie doesn't mind, it's alright.

' we were ever separated, I'd die.
would just cry and cry.

ut we will be together forever and always.
'or the rest of our lives and all of our days.
—*Kimberly Kelly*

o A True Friend

A friend is one who listens, and is there whate'er the need,
omeone who shares what friends alone may know.
A friend is one who comes along life's road and plants a seed
)f love, and then with care helps it to grow.

'air weather friends are only there when things are going well.
'hey're by your side until you really need
A sympathetic ear to listen as you try to tell
'our private feelings and your inner need.

'hen when things seem at their worst, the sun begins to shine.
'he dark clouds show a silver lining, too.
'or suddenly, you realize that life is really fine
Because of friendly people just like you.

'riends may come and friends may go. We all know this is true.
'rue friends are rare, and if such one we find,
We count our blessings daily as we travel this life through
Because we've found someone so true and kind.

And so I write this poem as a tribute to true friends,
To those who love and never ask a thing.
)ur lives are richer, and I know they will be to the end
Because true friends, true joy will always bring.
—*John W. Shepard*

A Friend

A friend is someone close to you, a shoulder you can cry on
Someone you know, when things get tough, you always can rely on

A friend's someone who cheers you up when you are feeling low
Someone you tell your secrets to and KNOW no one will know

A friend's someone who calms you down whenever you're 'up tight'
Someone who sees your side of things and backs you when you're
   right

A friend's someone who knows you don't mean everything you say
Someone who makes you feel you're special to them in some way

A friend's someone who takes an interest in the things you do
Someone who really likes you very simply "cause you're you"

A friend's someone who's honesty you'd never think to doubt
Someone who's presence makes you 'feel' what friendship's all
   about

A friend's someone who'll stay by you right up until the end
Someone a lot like you, for I consider you my friend.
—*Colleen M. Callahan*

Emptiness

Something is missing
Something is missed
It was taken away
On that day that fatal, fatal, day.

Darkness is its replacement
Now my life's in a state of displacement
Because it was taken on that day.
That fateful, fateful day.

What is this something that is gone
Will its identity rise up like the sun.

Or will I never know what was taken
Taken on that day
That fatal, fateful, day.
—*Corrine O'Rourke*

Life

Its name - Life
Something made by Gods own work
The colors black, yellow or white its all the same.
Life is peaceful, loving, kind, hard, and sometimes
bring tear drop to your eyes.

Life is a summer breeze
Vapor in the air
A baby laugh
Those soft spoken words

The life that ages day after day thinking will it be
safe to go on your way.
One day we will be chosen to leave this earth.
But your love and kindness will never be deserted.

   Life
—*Anasia N. Arnold*

Something Lost

Today I lost something that was very special to me,
something that I treasured with all my heart and soul.
I loved this something.
I had this something for six long years.
I didn't want to lose it, but somehow
I feel it wanted to lose me.
This something was very close to me;
I thought I'd have it forever and ever - till our dying day,
I shared my most deep and intimate feelings
with this something.
I trusted it almost more than I trusted myself.
I would do anything for this something,
even risk my own life to save its life.
Because I have lost this something,
I have an empty feeling inside my heart.
It also took a part of me when it left.
I wish that I could find this something again,
but I think it is an endless search.
This something that I lost today was
my best friend.
—*Kim Rateike*

Alone

Solitude stimulates thought
uncontrolled, imaginative creations
often outrageous
almost unbelievable
your mind plays tricks on you
more time spent pondering certain issues
more distorted the perception becomes
until it takes you over
and drives you insane
—*Kevin Brown*

The Humbling

If you need to be humbled, just get a good storm.
Something very frightening and out of the norm.
Hurricane winds-ice-rain sleet and snow, enough in
disaster to let you know. He's not joking with us,
He's mad and how! He wants us to heed his warnings now.
Most people are home, warm-safe and sound. A few needed
rescue from areas around. The vehicles get stuck
the driveways a mess, the roads are all closed;
stranded more or less. Drifts measured in feet make
you want to shout, and the shovel sure gets a decent
work out. The body and muscles will surely ache
as a path in the snow you try to make.
The fuel gets low, the food dwindles down
No travel allowed on roads all around.
Your outlook changes on necessities somehow
Your life and loved ones top priority now.
No mail on route, no businesses open
Spring 'o' spring how we're a hopin'!
There will be flooding for sure once the melting starts,
then fear once again is felt in our hearts.

—*Dawn Withey*

Sometimes I Wonder

Sometimes I wonder if God's really there.
Sometimes I wonder if parents really care.
Sometimes I wonder how God made man and,
why little children like to play in the sand.

Sometimes I wonder why people must die and,
why it's wrong to tell a lie.
Sometimes I wonder why people are born and,
why I always feel to mourn.
Sometimes I wonder, I wonder
why? Sometimes I wonder why I cry?

—*Sharnta Marcano*

Love Me Back

Loving me back the same as I love you,
Sometimes might seem impossible to do.
But if you would just try to trust and believe,
Unforgettable will be the memories that you'll receive.
Love makes us patient, understanding, and kind,
That's why I judge with my heart and not with my mind.
As soon as love enters my hearts opened door,
I'll give you my love that I've kept in store.
And the things that seem wrong will one day seem right;
When saw in the softness of love's shining light.
Love works in ways that are wondrous and strange,
And there'll never be anything that love can't change.
And all I have promised I hope will come true,
If you'll love me back the way that I love you.

—*Mandy Aswegan*

Forever Gone

It happened so suddenly.
You've departed from me.
Your love is astray.
You have left.
You walked out of my life into a better place.
I weep the tears of sorrow.
Will you ever come back?
Will I ever see you again?
Worries will darken your path, no more.
You saw the light and followed.
You are free

—*Tabitha Norman*

Friends Of Color

'Twas wondrous and fair
Somewhat like the sparkling snow
This blue eyed girl with the red dress
And matching big red bow.

Hair of golden yellow, her eyes deep blue
Very well dressed from the top of her head
To the bottoms of her shoes.

There is one other with dark skin
She is as pretty as one could be
Her skin soft, clear, and lovely,
She is called Ebony.

What a lovely picture
Of this black child and white
Both are so very precious in God's eyesight.

As I look at the black child with brown eyes
And study the white with eyes of blue
Both are happy playing together
Without the interference of me and you.

—*Arthurine B. Rice*

My Son

At the tender age of three,
son, you mean the world to me.
The first time I looked into your eyes,
my heart stopped and tears I cried.
Happiness I only thought I knew,
I know now son, when I look at you.
With your dashing eyes and shimmering hair,
an amazing sight, people often stop and stare.
So eager to learn, so to do,
so warm, bright, smart and funny too.
You seem so willing to share your feelings inside,
so loving and caring, no feelings you hide.
When you cry I feel so blue,
the pain you feel son, I feel it too.
Your laughter fills my heart with joy,
laughter of my little boy.
Son, you are the world to me,
and close to you I'll always be.
You are my life, my love and my joy.
God's great gift to me, my beautiful little boy.
I love you my son, mom

—*Brandi Crofford*

Antique Hills Of Kentucky

White Tail Buck, nostrils blow
Soon the hills will cover with snow
Trodden paths by the laden hare
Red fox awaits opposite the brier
Cold springs run, to each a creek
Red eye and perch swim the deep

Quail frequently whistles Bob-white
Cardinal dancing in the scrub red and bright
Gray squirrel scrambles to build a nest
Old black bear preparing for a long winters rest
Glittering streams far on, in the dale
Raccoon grooming his bushy ringed tail

Trees under cover of amberish green leaves
Moving so loftily with Autumns keen breeze
Bluegrass and clover not yet gone
Winter is singing though, its coming song
Chimney smoke bleeding to the sky
Off in the loom the whippoorwill cry

—*Rex F. Melton*

December

The days are dark and dreary. Winter is on its way.
Soon the joyous season will brighten up the day.

Jingle bells and Silver bells ring throughout the air
Smiling faces seen every where.

Christmas cards keep us in touch with friends we hold so dear
As the Christmas spirit is in us, from far and from near.

Sounds of carols so great to hear reminding us also,
that Christmas is near.
Children laughing, ladies crafting, Men having fun with
errands to be, just don't let them miss their game on T.V.
Grandmas baking cookies. The smell is simply great.
Now get ready for the parties. You know you can't be late.

The snoozing dog and cat don't seem to care a bit. thinking
"Their just going through their old tradition fit".

Glitter and lights everywhere you look, but lets not forget
the good 'Ole Book.
As Jesus came to save the world, and bring Joy and Happiness
to all his fold.

So keep a song in your heart and love in your Sole,
Merry Christmas to you, Best wishes for all.
            —*Myrtle Titel*

Seasonal Stairways

Awake and arise to Mother Earth's stirring spring buds,
Soon to cover meadows, forests and gardens
     now mostly mud.
No limitations can enfold you;
All life comes to hold you.

Summer Mother Earth will coddle you like an embryo
     with sun, warm breezes and water,
     even Cupid's bow.
No human being is able to withhold you
     when bountiful nature comes to hold you.

Autumn Mother Earth is dressed in her bold, warm colors
     reds, golds, browns and lighted, smiling pumpkin fellows.
Harvest your bounty of all that's come new,
     pruning all the growth that the old you grew.

Winter Mother Earth blows cold and ice and snow,
     hibernate and process the year's learning, and grow.
Four seasonal stairways to climb every year;
Climb each eagerly, staying on course and in gear.
            —*Barbara Garro*

Abominable Spirit

What is abominable spirit?
Sounds quite complex to me -
Is it the will to just try harder
     coupled with tenacity?

Is it that certain "can do" spirit?
     Used by heroes of the past?
That were told: "that will never work"
And: "you will never last"!!

I'll bet its the little "think I can train"?
That climbed the mountain of our soul?
As we watched: our confidence regained -
So we could continue on our goal -
As I make a visit to my memory bank -
To withdraw an idea more profound!!
It will be that old abominable spirit
That will keep my feet near the ground!!
            —*F. Evelyn Wiemer*

The Ghost Ship

Silent waters,
Space of endless skies,
Breathless wind holds back her sails,
Motionless, subdued she lies.

Flagless mast,
Wheel of unguided turns,
Endless decks paced by soundless steps,
A headlight atop that never burns.

Timeless days,
Rooms of confused thought,
Souls that wander in the growing night,
Their tireless searching, longing matter naught.

Unseen shores,
Veiled by the fog of mystery,
Portholes through which sad eyes stare
For the paradisiacal port that sets souls free.

A Ghost Ship
Enshrouded by death
That has no morning. Waiting, preparing.
For its Master to pilot its bulk to Heaven's dawning.
            —*Catherine B. Kindley*

Forever Lost

Strange how sometimes siblings,
Spend each waking day,
Seeking the friendship of others,
And from their own, they turn away.
Such was the case in my life,
In the time of a childhood past;
Now my brother's dead,
And I'm alone,
Chances, forever lost,
Too soon — too fast.
A weight of guilt invades my senses,
Like a shroud worn without relief;
From childish meanness to my brother,
When conscious thought reflects my grief.
            —*Robert James Jablonski*

Untitled

So many times I've sat at home.
Spending the time all alone.
And then one day you came along.
My heart started singing to a beautiful song.
I thought that I would never fall in love.
Believing in such things; I thought I was above.
Every day I saw you was better than before.
But my heart was shattered 'cause you walked out that door.
You never felt the same.
To you I was a toy with which to play a game.
You never really loved me.
You never really cared.
I guess I read more into the time I thought we shared.
I gave you many chances to change the way things were.
But instead you left me hanging while you reached out to her.
I guess I was a fool to believe love could happen to me.
But instead of my head, I used my heart to see.
Everything has changed now
And I will love no more.
Because you took my heart when you walked out that door.
            —*Jennifer Roten*

Child of Grace

She was speckled and freckled, spotted and
   splotched
Knocked kneed and near sighted and her posture
   was botched
The homeliest child I ever did see
Was the gaunt little girl living next door to me
Ten years did go by before I could see
The marvel that appeared there on my TV
This frail little girl had blossomed and bloomed
Had been braced and straightened, concealed
   and groomed
What once was a fright to see from afar
Was now a beauty to cherish and admire
How could this have happened in just ten short years
Let this be a lesson to all of your fears
If you are a child lacking in grace
Remember that time can sometimes erase
Most of the flaws and imperfections ... it's true
A swan may be living deep inside of you.

   —Betty Ann Taylor

Midnight Whisper

A midnight whisper
Spoken in the darkness of our quiet room
The still madness of all our hopes and dreams
Visions of tomorrow with sweet thoughts of all
Those yesterdays
Yesterday filled with adventure and glory
Growing together.....
Learning what is, will never be

A midnight whisper
Echoing words of love to gentle ears
Wanting more, getting everything
My midnight whisper

   —Francesca Roccaforte

The Magnificent Gift

Dawn broke over the silent sky sending a beautiful golden
spray reflecting on the silver lake, showing the pretty
fire flies in all their splendor. The tired old moon was
disappearing behind a fluffy, white morning cloud, which
was dancing like a ballerina.
Old Ben the rooster doing his best to wake up the world
swan glided with all the charm a swan can offer. All the
things are there every day for our pleasure.
Sunshine filled the good Earth to warm the creatures. What
a wonderful feeling nature gave us to enjoy. A new human
being has entered the world, to be part of this miracle. To
watch this golden dream, sent to remember God's gift to
humans every where.
So love everything that is so free, it's put there for you
and me. Many humans have tried to copy the rapture of this
beautiful thing called nature, but all this glory is a gift
from God to us.

Value all the good things that are free for all to treasure.

"God Bless"
   —Dorothy Guyewski

The Natural Elements Of Earth

Earth, wind, water, fire the natural elements of the earth,
With each passing night the day begins it's birth
A cloud, the sun, the moon, and mars
The earth, the trees, the mountains, and stars
The rivers, the lakes, the ponds and sea,
The half moon that brings the water to ease
These of which make up peas in a pod
But we are the natural elements the creations by God.

   —Anthony DiLapi

"Saying Goodbye"

Laying upon a field of pale yellow wheatoned grass,
Spring sunshine warming my bare skin as
memories flood my thoughts of family
and friends that belong to my sacred past.
I see not one thing before me, but know...all
that is around me.
Someone has entered my very last thought,
birds singing joyfully as my soul separates
from this flesh and bone, and my holy spirit is
honored to be blessed with the grace of God
to peacefully leave.
Fear not of my death, for it only comes upon
us once, an honor so great, that eternal
beauty shall fill our souls and life shall forever
be ours.

   —Jane E. Carlson

Goodbye To A Friend

One minute you sit talking to a friend, The next you're
standing at the gates of heaven One minute you think of new
beginnings, the next you've reached the end. You were the
chosen one my friend, you were invited to the pearly gate.
Where God stands to greet you, reach out to him - don't
hesitate. Those of us you left behind find it hard to
understand. We feel the pain, the loss, the sorrow, but you
are in the promised land. You wouldn't want us to cry, but we
hurt inside, why did you have to die? It was too soon, you
life was new, oh dear friend we are going to miss you. We will
always remember the good times we shared. The times we
laughed
and cried, the times you spent with those who care. We're the
ones you touched in your life, we're the ones that still remain
We're the ones that will feel the warmth whenever we speak your
name. In our hearts you will always be dear, your memory will
always be near. Thank you my friend for all you have done,
life everlasting has just begun. Now as sad as it may seem
it's time to say goodbye. To our dear friend whom now resides
above us in the sky. We may not see your handsome face. But
in our hearts you will always have a place.

   —Renee' DiMaria Savage

The Mysterious Dance

   This world may crumble, but you will be the only thing
standing. My life may fall, but you will always be there to
catch it.

   The crystal rose at the top of a high mountain you would
pick for me.

   "Suddenly" the light would banish from the earth, and you
would be the liten candle.

   The wild horse that one could not catch, you would have
in the palm of your hand.

   The frozen ice would melt with your touch!

   Your gone now and I am lost. I would see your reflection
in the pond, but the falling rain would wash it away.

   My dream would finally come true once we could freeze
the ice together, set the wild horse free, plant the crystal
rose, blow out the liten candle and dance!

   So take my hand and we will become one to time indefinite
our dance is not yet done!

   —Julie Boutin

Abandoned

ve been abandoned, abandoned from mankind
aring in the mirror, a tear runs down thy face
he cold mist of an empty room
m staring in the face of loneliness
he ignorance of my name passes through the breeze
earching for companionship, only to find my shadow in its place
speak a word, not an answer to be heard
or thy face is cold, and all alone
s I wallow in my grief
fathom the truths of reality
or I've been abandoned, abandoned from all love
bandoned, alone, forever.

—*Keli Flenner*

Transformation

hen music touches you, those movements
tart, and sound transforms itself to liquid grace
o free a giant restlessness inside.
o see you move is thus to hear the wind
nd waves and cyclic stars in harmony.

can't associate with you the senseless
oise and tuneless music of the age.
see you, rather, wrapped in brooding sound
esponding to that silver note that lifts
our brow and for a moment stays.
r, joying in the cadence of some song,
our spirit soars to free you from the care
f earth and 'compass you in tiny ecstasy.

o whether joy or mellow spirit holds
ou fast; or some delicious glint of play
scapes your eye; or melancholy weaves
s tightest web, I can be there. I know
ou in all moods. I know then and
care.

—*Kate Adair*

Untitled

hold no page in your book
ill I try to play a part
should just give it a last look
I can only convince my heart

ry hard to avoid your track
ot even words I am willing to share
ut every time I would turn my back
o let go, you'll seem to care

hy do I not want to believe
here was, there is, there will always
ut emptiness only dreams could fill
nd nothing more that's worth to say

ut then I must not dare end with that
or there is something worth mentioning
treasure I should not forget to cherish
or it is the gift of friendship I am gaining

—*Christine B. Cuenco*

"To Seize The Day"

ipping away are the sands of time,
To seize the day for the chance is mine.
or once it is gone, my spirit fades away,
My lifeforce diminishes, my world has turned grey.
o grasp the chance with belief from within,
My heart beats passionately as a new life begin.
ow that I have the gift that I desire,
Only the love from your heart can quench the fire.

—*Danny R. Steward*

"Fly-By Man"

I call your name, but you don't answer, the tears begin to
sting my eyes, it seems it's only a game you've been playing,
that bitter-sweet game of a fly-by man.
I reach out to the security of your hand, my heart beats loudly
with despair,
I've let myself be taken again, in the arms of a fly-by man.
I warn you now, don't get too close, don't wear your heart
upon your sleeve, the day will come, as it always does,
it'll be torn apart and left to bleed.
He's a fly-by man, you know his ways, he comes and goes and
plays his games, his eyes will sparkle, his smile will shine,
it's the game of love that's on his mind.
Please take heed and carefully listen, don't be taken by the
touch of his eyes, they'll make you think it's you he
sees, but the fly-by man is in disguise.
Be on your toes and do beware, the fly-by man, oh he's out
there, you'll lose your heart and tears will fall, and the fly-by
man will have taken it all.

—*Michelle Augusto*

Innocence

The golden-haired child
Strayed into the meadow,
Oblivious to her mother's call,
Delighted with the sunshine
Which enveloped her as with an embrace.
She stumbled at nearly every step,
But that did not diminish her joy
At just being alive.
Pure, sweet child
With the cool wind of spring in your hair
How I wish you could remain this way forever
Full of wonder and curiosity
In awe of things
I'd forgotten were there.

—*Ryan A. Stough*

Simple Treasures

Simple treasures locked tight in the attic.
Streams of blue thrashing around from all the static.
Secrets of past piled in trunks.
Secrets of gold buried beneath the old.
Treasures from the past are simple
and always set apart.
But for sure they are always simple treasures
and placed there for my part.

—*Patti Hoofard*

Dr. R.T. Belcher

Set your goals high, you are an achiever.
Strength of will you are a believer.
Doctor, lawyer, musician, minister,
a writer of stories, funny or sinister.

The world before you, the sky's the limit,
dig deep into life's challenges, don't just skim it.
Your talent is your bankbook, with no bottomline,
with youth as a headstart, the globe's your lifeline.

Move forward quickly and set a brisk pace,
fill that hunger for knowledge and you'll win each race.
Reach only forward for there's no going back,
I see the name Dr. R.T. Belcher on your wall plaque.

—*Diane Leigh*

Does God Exist?

Had you asked me four years ago when my hair was longer and my
stride was shorter, I would have told you, "Yes.
Yes, HE does, I know, for the Bible tells me so."
My blind faith would not be shaken;
I had grown up with tales of angels, wondrous miracles and
Commandments written in stone.
A thick Black Book had shown me, and others like me, the Light.
Ask me now, "Does HE exist?" and I might say, "Maybe he's a
She." I won't pretend to know for sure. But I do know that
now I have very different views; I even have questions.
I can no longer have blind belief in a thick black book which,
word for word, was written by men. How much thicker would that
book have been had women not been just water girls and fetchers
of wine? I am no atheist; I can not, will not believe that
women and men make up the Highest Order of Intelligence, and
that we live only so that we may die.
I can not know What lies beyond; maybe I just can't see It.
Maybe true knowledge would
lead to something more insane than our day-to-day,
time-obsessed lives and blind, unquestioning beliefs.

—*Julie A. Galvan*

A New Day

Each new day is a new beginning.
Strive to do the best you can.
Believe and have
Confidence in every task you do.
Think of every thing you have.
Become special in your
thoughts and words.
You may become a better person.
Try to win and if you fail try harder tomorrow.

—*Mary-Ann Hromoko*

"Life To A Tree"

What is a tree? A tree is a seed that has grown to the
structure and statue of man. Life in every man begins with
birth, and condoles to a lonely death. I wonder, I wonder,
about the simple tree. The tree finds the strength to endure
the cold and blistering heat to every season standing tall and
embedded to the Earth. Life to a tree has its' hardship and
pain: Limbs are broken, and it licks its' own wound. The
feeling of being left alone in the storm and rain, for without
shelter stands the tree by his hung down head. Then comes
mourning in the death of Spring and Summer as to Fall brings
Winter. Life grants every season to be watchful of Fall coming
to take its' breathe away. With chilling thoughts of winter
hibernating a death bitter to a tree, and hostile to man.
Spring brings life to a tree by way of birth, fruit, and a
fresh, cool, breeze to lift the branches in a joyful praise.
Vision of the forest during the summertime shows happiness in
the heart of a tree. For it knows 'tis the season to be jolly,
and mankind whispers a prayer, O Lord, Long Live The Thee.
Though its roots will they grow old in the Earth. Having
tender branches to feel the wind as it moves from east to west.

—*Anthony Sims*

Lost In The Mirror

Why is it,
    When I look in the mirror,
      I don't see myself
        The way I did when I met you?

It is because,
    I have lost the only thing I've ever wanted,
      And that one thing,
    Is you!

—*Heather Chapman*

Minds' Thoughts

As I peer into the annals of time, I see mankind's
structure driven to its peak. Have we begun our change
for the betterment of our society, or is this a facade
being over shadowed by the evil that dwells within our
minds. Mans potential to overcome adversity has helped
him thru out life. Yet his greed takes him deeper within
the shadows of debt, depression, and economic turmoil.

Knowledge is the key to unlock the minds and souls of
man. Yet we use segregation and apartheid in new world
order to keep nations away from unification. To see with
the third eye, is to see into the heart of mortal man.

To see into mortal man, is to see ones self thru the
eyes of God. Truly I say the mind is a terrible thing
to waste.

—*Freez*

"Yes"..."I'm...Glad"..."I...Can".....

"Sometimes", "I see people"....
"Struggling", "All day long"...
"Trying", "To make-a-dollar"...
"Just for a place called home"...
"I reach down in my pocket book"...
"And give them what I can"...

"Yes"... "I'm"... "Glad"... "I"... "Can"...
"Sometimes", "I see people"...
"As" hungry as can be"...
"I" wish I had enough food"...
"Just to set them free"...
"But" now I can only pray"... "And" hope for a better day"...

"Yes"... "I'm"... "Glad"... "I"... "Can"...
"Sometimes", I see places", helping people...
"In need"... Giving from their hearts,
"Doing a very good deed"...
"And" I can truly say"...
"Thank" You" in every way"...
"Yes"..."I'm"..."Glad"..."I"..."Can"...
"Oh"..."Yes"..."I'm"..."Glad"..."I"..."Can"...

—*Mardesta McIntyre*

See My Sound

Wind is beating at my face
Sun spilling it's golden rays-a spotlight surrounds me.
Faster, faster, where am I headed?
I've lost myself in a cloud
    no boundaries, loose, free
Yet I am in command.
Hair streaming, fight that current
    Whirl, swirl.

I'm against the world, the roads, the hills
Roar motor, rumble
Let them know I'm here, there, racing time
Feeling, grasping nothing on the way.
I'm in my own world, my own reality
    Life challenge
Swift, electrifying beats; my wheels are a city.

Stranger to four-wheeled vehicles
Gaping onlookers
The going is great ecstasy!

These wheels are a way of life
    Life is wheels and my motorcycle and me.

—*Jeanne Lemcke*

The Souls of my Unborn...

The promised land, the Father's hand,
Surely He knows and understands;
The grieving Mother and the angry Father
After the loss of a son or daughter.
They say that time will heal all wounds.
But, what of the child who dies in the womb?
Loved, but never born into this world.
Questions of whether a boy or a girl?
I miss my children, Lord, you know.
But in heaven with You, I know are their souls.
I have a daughter born to this earth.
I love her dearly. But, my losses still hurt.
One would be five, and the other one two.
But Lord, it helps knowing they're there with you.
Though never held in my loving arms, I truly
ache to hold them.
And when my earthly life has passed,
My children then shall I see.
And praise the Blessed Father, for
giving them back to me.

—*Tammila M. Miller*

Serenity

The pale blue throat of heaven is enhanced with
swaths of ermine clouds, softening the sun's
embrace as it creates deft shadows in my
garden citadel. Reflections of the pine and
juniper against the gray stone garden wall
contrast with deep red roses and bright yellow
lemons ripening in their womb of glossy leaves.
Spikes of decorative pear reach toward heaven
as the light breeze choreographs their dancing
homage to their God. In counterpoint the
stately cypress weave their graceful magic,
and I know portents of heaven and rejoice.

—*Helena Hult*

Untitled

Life is only as clear as the water
Swim as we may in the luxurious waters of life
Mist of life splash in our face as the waves crash upon
The shores
Thrash and frolic in the high tide
All must approach our ebb tide at one time or another
Die as the fish that is washed up on the shore drowning
In the wind
Caress the air as we break the surface
Dive deep to never see the surface again
Die at sea never to behold the shores
Swim nomadic to seas and shores
Searching for that solitary port we call our haven from
Tempestuous waters
Eat others along the way or be eaten by the vermin that
Stalks us. Bottom dwellers ready to tear our underside out
As we sink to the bottom we find that life is nothing but
A mud puddle
Dirty water with no perception of what is to come
So we head for the horizon to die in the sunset

—*Lee Germain*

Bastard's Thought

Ain't got the heart to live no more.
Yet, I got no guts to die
Trapped in shadows of memories
My soul held back by time
Know I'll be there tomorrow though
No easy way out for me
The only hope are the glittering stars aloft
In the distant night

—*Ryo Merante*

Dreams

If you have a dream, pursue it,
Take control of your objectives, just do it,
Dreams are only the want in man,
To choose them and quit is not part of the plan,
Begin with the thought that you can not,
And you surely will have your dreams forgot,
Pick the one that is out of reach,
Then strive to learn, strive to teach,
The easiest dream to find,
Is the one that is buried in the back of your mind,
Set your sights, set your goals,
Then work to have that dream unfold,
Tomorrow is just a dream, today,
But, come the dawn, you're on your way,
If you have a dream, pursue it,
Take control, just do it!!!!!!

—*James Garrett*

Peace Compact

We, the people of this dying planet,
Take notice, and solve the problems.
Yes, the plague of our planet,
Poverty, homelessness, food and rights.

We, of this planet, take notice and help,
Not help ourselves, but the needy.
Stop thinking of only the good things,
But take notice and help the injustice.

Who are we to take notice of injustice,
When the waters of righteousness went dry.
When you find your true self, you take notice.
People, communities, nations help!

"Let justice roll down like waters,"
We beg. Yes, the never ending waters.
That cleanses our planet.
Yes, the water that heals the world.

Persons, brave and strong, take that first step,
Water of righteousness will flow.
The dying planet-obsolete,
Ourselves, we found.

—*Don Keels, Jr.*

Dawns Early Light

As the dawns early light
Takes over the night
A new day comes thru
The sky is pale blue
The sun rises slowly from the east
It's a beautiful sight, to say the least
Then morning comes you feel the breeze
Wind blowing gently thru the trees
Then nature awakes you hear the birds
The twirping and sounds of their cute little words
The sun shines bright and everything's green
The fresh smell of flowers, a fragrance of clean
And thru my own window I see all of this
A beautiful sight that's so hard to resist
The next time you're up in the middle of night
Try and catch the dawn's early light.

—*Ronald E. Webster*

Stranger

I've heard that voice before,
  Talking to me day and night and night into day.
   Comforting me in times of trouble and being there
  whenever I called.
   Or even whispering I love you.

Do I know you?
Your face looks so familiar,
  Perhaps I've touched it before, or even held it in my arms
  in your time of comfort.

Do I know you?
Your body, I'm sure I've seen it before.
  Maybe as a silhouette in the moonlight, or laying beside me.
   As a Tower of Strength, protecting me from hurt, harm and
  danger.

Do I know you?
You look like the person in my dreams...
  The person I loved and who loved me back...
  The person I trusted with my heart.

Do I know you?
No, but I thought I did.
     —Franceine Michelle Taylor

The Seduction Of The Amanita

The appeal of the forbidden
Teases my desire
As I approach the deadly Amanita.
I heard the constant warnings,
"If you eat of it you shall surely die."
But why would such an enticing earth fruit
Will me to be dead?
I partook of the Amanita.
The sweet turned sour.
The tender to bitter.
My soul cried out for freedom from my eroding body,
Coldness became my accuser.
Hell's horrorstorms came to greet me,
The dance of maggots my only vision.
Oh why did I not heed the warnings?
Of fornication my trial begins.
The Mushroom of sin I raped and
The doom of my sentence my new constant warning
As eternal darkness envelops me.
     —Phil Powell

Observations of One Night

Shades of the evening
Sounds of the night
I am wide awake
And nothing escapes my sight
All the people in the street
Each with their own secret life
The dealer, and the hooker
The man cheating on his wife
The young lovers walking hand in hand
The rich, the poor, the handicapped man
The taxis, the buses, the long limousines
The hustle, the bustle, and the back room scenes
The hunters, and the hunted hiding
The users, the abusers, and the police colliding
The rockers, the knockers, the homely, the lonely
The bashers, and the gays
Slowly disappear as the night fades into day
     —Alan Katz

A Dusty Crossroads

It is said that it is better to have loved and lost,
  than never to have loved at all.
   Yet I stand here and wonder,
  my heart does grow weary.

My feet wander down a lonely trail,
  and a crossroads does draw nigh.
   There is fear in my heart
  the trail taken, just two prints will fall.

I contemplate this before I decide,
  and wonder where others have gone.
   What path did she take,
  and who marches with her?

The dusty imprints before me are difficult to discern.
  There is no way I can know, no way I can see.

I need to be strong, a call to march on sounds.
  Yet I dally a while, waiting,
   which path did she take?

A time of waiting must always end,
  life marches on.
With a weary heart I travel, two prints in the dust.
     —Donald J. Clancy

Home On The Road

Wheel at hand, pedal at foot, it's more
than the pay that keeps me rolling all day.
Two, four, six, eight, only half a load in
a room no bigger than a kitchen.
Most of the drivers are always bitching.
What is taking that man so long to load our freight?
My patience grows thin as I constantly wait.
The clock on the wall looks me straight in the eye,
as the seconds, minutes, hours slowly drag by.
My thoughts begin to turn. Through the years a driver
will learn, he must drive all day into the night to
feed and cloth ungrateful four wheelers, while smoky
bear hands out Christmas cards faster than poker dealers.
What makes us amble on our way as the night again turns
to day? Is it the freedom of the road or do we still
live by a code? I am here to tell you my friend, I
no longer question the reason why, as I sit at home
behind the wheel and watch my life roll by.
     —Francis Marion Alvey

This Life and Memory

Everywhere he turns tonight it's rain and darkness.
That and the sweet familiar voice of a woman.
Not his ex-wife though. He hasn't heard from her
in well over a year now. Not that it would change
anything. But a person becomes use to convention.
No, the voice tonight arrives from some far off place.
Farther than anyone in his circle of friends might ever go.
He feels awful. To think of them in that manner. His friends.
But it's true. What do they know about his life anyway?
Maybe they've been listening to his ex-wife.
They're so dumb they'll believe anything. His friends.
Still, there's that voice. And the heart's frailty.
He could go there. Be there with her in fifteen hours.
Fifteen hours! Think of it! By tomorrow afternoon.
He looks out the window. At an ocean calm now. Level.
The trouble with this life is that one thing always
leads to another. There's no end to it until the end.
Take Vienna for instance.
The smell of a woman's hair.
The taxi taking him after all away.
     —Dan Hanami

Garden of Love

et us not forget our loved ones
at have left and went on before,
will make us appreciate the love they gave
st a little more.

hough, we have never really lost them
ey are with us every day,
everything we say and do
heir love is here to stay.

hey gave of themselves so freely
d done the best they could,
ey gave their love without reserve
everybody should.

hen God came and got them
took them up above,
a place that he prepared for them
his great big garden of love.

—*Vern R. Lyons*

Letter

nowing
hat I am a letter in your alphabet —
iving and getting love — is
s wonderful and meaningful as
lue is to sky and
ed is to strawberries.
ven though I — as a letter —
m not stationed beside you (as are other letters)
ong to surround you and hold you —
eeling your warmth as penetrating as
he warmth a flower feels from the sun.

st being in your alphabet —
nd not forgotten in some dusty volume of words —
self-containment.

—*Erin Thompson*

The Black Seed

n unwanted seed
hat is just a shade darker than the others
ne that sticks out from the rest
nd, yet is remained unnoticed
ruggling for just one grasp of that golden ring,
knows that it must work twice as hard, shine twice
beautiful, speak twice as loud, and hope twice as much
st to leave the burdens of its home, the city
d to get away from its school, the streets
ut, the soil is too dry
nd the nourishment limited
nd the seed shrivels and perishes
nce more it becomes one of the
meless faces

—*Jordana Woodford*

Untitled

was the day after the night before
hen she came to work, and looked down
to the floor
n the left foot a slipper, the right
foot a shoe
was certainly good for a laugh -
or maybe two
d said to all "It's time to retire
hen you come to work in such an attire."

—*Marion G. Cooper*

Farewell

No one can truly understand why you made that final choice
That left the ones who loved and cared asking, "Why did you do
    it, Joyce?"
There is always one more answer; if you seek then ye shall find.
If only you had stopped to feel the sun, you might have changed
    your mind.
But you were always the strong one, the one who stayed on call.
If only you had asked for help, and let the burden fall
Upon the shoulders of those around you, to share the heavy for awhile...
But looking back on how you lived, that never was your style.
There are times when all will make mistakes, or feel sad, alone, afraid.
In time these too shall come to pass; our fears will be allayed.
Sometimes we are given things to handle, and we simply don't know how,
And like a child left alone too soon, we look to heaven and cry,
"Please, let me come home now..."

—*Kathleen A. Kelly*

"May We Never Forget"

Thanks to a tradition of strength, a feeling of security
That lets us all sleep sound at night
They gave their all for everyone
Some might say our memories soon forget
Let the healing begin, for the men and women who gave all
With their knowledge and might, who never ran from the fight
Freedom runs strong in our veins
In their minds, their dreams, their prayers
To keep our country free for one and all to share
But they made the ultimate sacrifice to show us all they care
But still the thought remains in our hearts and minds
Some still do remember, some remember less
Some are still to learn and care
What our veterans have done for us to keep our country free
For past, present and future generations to share
The pain the glory, the healing
They may have been our fathers, brothers or friends
They gave the ultimate, they gave all
May we never forget, our veterans

—*Allen G. Pionke*

Behind the Smiles

We're taught by faith to smile amid the pain,
That life is not all sunshine...there must be the rain.
We rejoice and smile with the pleasures of life-
Then come the clouds of trials, sorrow and strife.
We remind ourselves that these clouds will pass
Storms gather round and we pray for courage that lasts,
Then on our knees, somehow we find the strength and grace
Things are well we often say - with a smile upon our face
Behind the smiles and through the years-
    Only God can see the tears
    And He whispers softly to each child,
        I truly understand-
And then because He loves us all He extends a hand
And leads us through life's seasons to make our
    life worthwhile
Because our God is with us - He is behind the smile.

—*Hazel Gembe*

Vonnegut

I kept my first taste of Vonnegut
Wrapped up, from years ago.
Stolen.
Tucked away in tinsel and plastic to keep it from fading.
Sealed in a tiny blue perfume bottle
Still rank of vanilla and holidays.
I kept the last little shine
Safe on my vanity.

—*J. C. Nemecek*

Your Eyes

Your eyes are like a window
that looks deep into your heart,
Showing bits of hopes and dreams
that haven't had their start.
I want to look into your eyes
and feel what you feel inside.
I want to take away your pain
and dry the tears you've cried.
I want to look into your eyes
and see happiness glowing once more.
I want to see you smiling
more than you ever had before.
I want to look into your eyes
and taste the love they hide within.
I want to show you it's time for your eyes
to shine with pride again.

—*Amy Hand*

Christmas, 1968

Last night as I was sitting alongside of our Christmas tree
that Mother and Dad had decorated in the afternoon, this came
to mind:

Being a small tree, I thought of the Baby Jesus.

Being green in winter, I thought of everlasting life.

They used little white lights over the tree which
reminded me that we, as individuals, could bring forth
light to some people just by smiling or encouraging
them in some way everyday of our lives.

The presents around the tree reminds me of the love
the three wise men must have had when they traveled a far
to give their gifts of gold, frankincense, and myrrh.

The happiness that is all around us at this time
of the year reminds me that this happiness should be with
us not only in this season but in all seasons when we
build our lives around Christ and His teachings.

May we, at the birthday of our Christ, remember Him
and stop for a little while during this day and count our many
blessings that the Good Lord has given to us. I think if we
do this we will all have a better Christmas Spirit.

—*Donald R. Houston*

"Dreams"

I dare not dream a dream
that only pretends, when it should seem.

If it pretends, it flies away;
but if it seems, it sticks around and
takes it day by day.

What could this be? I'm sure
you'll ask me.

Pretend and seem, what does this mean?

Pretend is a game that never conceives.
Seem is an image that perceives what should be.

Dare I then, dream a dream that seems real,
so that one day, its wondrous reality I might feel?

Yes, I will dream a dream that seems real,
one that my heart within-it can feel.

A dream that goes beyond the heavens
and rests on the stars,
a place from where my heart and thoughts,
are never very far.

—*Mirna. M. Silva*

I Know

I know you hate it when I say...
That only you can brighten my day.
That without you, my life wouldn't be.
Or please don't go, please stay with me.

I know you hate it when I think...
That you might leave, 'fore I could blink.
That you don't care much when we're apart.
Or how I'll die if you break my heart.

I know you hate it when I dream...
Of you and me in a house by a stream.
Of growing old, together with you.
Of promising each other to always be true.

I know that you hate it babe, I know that you do...
I'm sorry; but there's a few things that I dislike too.
But I knew from the start, that a shadow would cover
and end, if it could.
This love that I feel, right now and forever.

—*Peggie Mazzeppi*

Go into the Mountains

Go into the mountains - They are a source of renewal
That possess the tranquility and peace
To make your heart sing and your spirit soar.
There, you will find the dignity of space and the value in
rareness.

Go into the mountains. They are a source for invigoration.
The summer air, icy from its travel over still-present snow
fields, Sounds with the cry of the eagle and the moan of the
pines. There, amid the lichened rocks, you will be refreshed.

Go into the mountains - They are a source of strength.
Challenge your nerve and resolve with a climb on sheer granite
walls. Stalk the majestic elk in forest glade or the nimble
bighorn on rocky crag; There, in stream and lake you can match
wits with the wary trout.

Go into the mountains - They are a source from God.
The alpine stillness fosters a special intimacy between
creature and Creator,
That exists only in the highest places.
There, in the pristine space, you can commune with Him.

—*Gil Bollinger*

Summit of '85

'Twas the year of the summit,
that the two great powers met.
Our own, President Ronald Reagan,
and the Soviet's Gorbachev.
To talk about the missiles,
and reduction too, of such.
For all of this nuclear weapons
and the Star Wars, is just too much.
Yes it frightens all the Russians,
and we Americans as well.
For if either side should nuclear attack,
we'd all be blown to hell.
So let us leave the outer space,
to the man who rules from above.
He watches over all the nations,
and gives to all, his Eternal love.
Peace on earth, good will toward all,
are the things we're looking for.
Not the missiles, or the nuclear bombs,
that only leads toward WAR.

—*Malcolm F. Charlton*

The Storm

The wind howled and the rain knocked at the door.
The waves rolled in.
The boat clanked against the dock.
A storm of such power could send the whole three house
island into the sea.
I knew the end was near but just didn't know when.
I saw my life flash before my eyes, and then I was gone.

—*Niffy McDonald*

Only Time Will Tell

I spend my nights aimlessly hoping .
That tomorrow there won't be a reason for our moping.
Maybe you don't give a damn maybe you do
I wish I only knew the way that you do
I know how I feel and it is for real
Your future is so bright while mine is still dark as night.
Sooner or later we may know but even if we don't
You will still go...
We don't know where our fate lingers
Yet we know it lies in father times fingers
Weather we be in heaven or hell
Only time will tell

—*Jessica Wilson*

For My Love

I never thought what people said was true
That when you're not looking for love, it finds you.
But that day I turned around and saw your face
The look upon it, my memory will not erase.

Your face so young and pretty
Your eyes sparkling in the dark
And when I touched your hand
I knew you stole my heart

The day I saw you sleeping
You seemed so at peace
I just sat and watched you
Knowing my love would never cease

I hope your feelings someday will be as strong as mine
And we could be together until the end of time.
But not only as a lover. I want to be your friend
Then nothing could ever come between us and our love
would never end.

So as my feelings for you grow stronger everyday
And my arms just yearn to hold you, my lips move to
say, "I love you."

—*John M. Scheibelhut*

To Elly

Surely it's not just by chance
That with every loving glance,
It's always just the same;
I fall in love with you,
All over, all over again.
Fate must have marked a clue
It just had to be you
There with your hair all tossed up
Or then all tumbled down,
Here a wayward wisp
Of golden tawny brown.
Asleep or awake, any glance I might take,
that same old feeling seems never to forsake.
With you there beside me, just any other day,
Becomes magic in a very special way.
Always, you are the music,
The lyrics the same,
I fall in love with you
All over, all over again.

—*Jim Green*

Twisted Mind

You were so scary when you let me in
That's because I didn't know about your crazy sin
The monster was hidden in your head for no one to see
But as we grew closer, it cried out, let me free.
Stupidly I went your way and your path I followed
Little did I know, my feelings were being swallowed.
Your true intentions were to treat me like dirt
And through your twisted mind you like to see me hurt.
The real you I wish I never got to know
But now I just laugh because you think you captured my soul.

—*Bethany Porzio*

My Reward

In the country next to the earth,
That's where poetry is given it's birth.
When the peace of night is all around you,
The very best work then a poet can do.
Oh! They can write a verse or a rime,
Anywhere if you give them time.
But for the very best poetry in all the nation,
Use the night for your inspiration.
With perhaps a girl there by your side,
One who is to become your lovely bride.
Or use the trees on a far away hill,
Use a house so silent and still.
Or maybe the clouds high up above,
For in the country all speaks of love.
And of love a poet can always write,
Regardless of the time day or night.
I am very minor, few know my name,
I may never know great fame.
Perhaps my work is not liked, I really can't say,
But peace and contentment is mine at the end of each day.

—*Joe Fenn*

Inspiration

My sweet inspiration she's
the apple of my eye,
her soothing voice, it gives you no choice!
Her laughter flows through you, like a warm summer
breeze, concealing all your miseries.
She's an inspiration, to carry on through life's
rough way to freedom.
She's a pillar of stone, then she smiles and leaves
her defense alone; to comfort and soothe, to relieve
and break through any barrier too strong.
She's been my inspiration all along.

—*Kathleen Carnana*

An Exaltation Of My Wife

I slew the beast and fiery dragon
Gulped at table and bitter flagon
Climbed the hills to distant heaven
Gambled with black and lucky seven.

I dueled with blade and deadly steel
Rode the waves on stormy keel
Travelled far to towns alone
Tasted pleasures since unknown.

I sweated among the Jew and Turk
Knew the feeling of pain and work
Stood upright at fright and fear
Laughed aloud when death was near.

All these things I took in stride
With careless spirit and manly pride.
But now that you have come to me
I'm enslaved but still am free.

—*Gene Johnson*

Elegy

We laid you down to sleep today
The Autumn clouds were dark and grey;
We covered you in the rich red earth
And spoke of your childhood and your birth.

I watched them tuck you into sleep
And heard the songbirds softly creep
Among the laurels and garden flowers
And watched the sky rain late day showers.

We passed you unto time and God
To go where other angels trod;
And we beat our breasts in fear and shame
Each time we sadly call out your name.

And it brings us so much bitter pain
That we shall not see your face again;
We lie awake in the depths of night
As if no hope is left in sight.

We cry our tears and lay you down
In this cold and silent Autumn ground;
And in the dark we shall kneel and pray
And praise God you came our way.

—*Jeffery Allen Rumford*

Nature At Night

As i listen to the night with my heart, not my ears, I can hear
the beauty of nature. My heart fills with the beauty I find In

the songs of the night. I can feel with my heart the joy of
freedom and a oneness with the night that I hear in the throaty

serenade of the wolf. I can hear in abundance, the joy of
movement and activity in the nightly chorus of crickets. I can
experience the dark splendor of the night as the silhouette of
an owl glides by. I can hear the crispness of he grass and the
whisper of the leaves as they sound the trumpet call of a
rabbit hurrying by. The sounds of nature at night must be
heard by the heart, not the ears, to truly blossom in a
symphony of sensation.

—*Robin E. Creed*

Untitled

Of all the ships upon the sea,
The best was that of Captain Lee —
And no ship had a finer crew
Than that aboard the King James II.
They sailed from coast, to port, to dock,
From Portsmouth to Gibraltar's Rock.
The ship was always spick and span,
And was the pride of every man.
The men drank port from silver mugs,
And walked upon fine Persian rugs.
Its woodwork gleamed, its silver shone,
From Europe to New York was known-
That though it made horrendous time,
King James was the best in her line.
To sail on her was dreams come true,
For Captain Lee and his fine crew.

—*Deanna Johnson*

"Out Of Sight...Out Of Mind"

"Out of sight, out of mind."
The forgotten person lives a shadowed life...
alive, but forgotten. How do I act?
When he is alone, I exist. However,
when with his friends, I am alone and unnoticed.
Once in a while I might get a smile; but by then
I do not smile back, for I have previously been
ignored and abandoned.

—*Christine Elizabeth Jackson*

Untitled

Each star represents a love.
The big stars are old and strong loves.
The little stars are new or weak loves.
Every star lasts forever.
To get your own star you have to find someone you love and
loves you.
Then you have to tell the person you love them.
Next watch the sky with the person you love and watch a tiny
Star pop up. Now your love is official.
To make the star brighter your love must get to be overpowering
To make the star bigger you will have to make your love last.
After each year you and your sweetheart truly love each other
the star will grow.
When your star stops growing you know your relationship is over
Once your love is over look in the sky and you will see your
star is still there.
It will always be there to remind you of your former love.
For each time you love there will be a new star. To find out
how many loves you have had and how successful they have been
look at the stars.

—*Nicole Garber*

Come With Me

We'll fly high among the lights of heaven where
the birds are far beneath us. So high that you could
touch the sky and dive into the dipper. Beyond the moon,
surrounded by stars, and you will get to pick one. There
we'll live in the paradise around us. Animals and jungle
brush will entirely surround us. A heaven never visited
but very familiar. Once in a dream during the night and
many times in wishes. Your fantasies will all come true,
take my hand I'll see you through, that jungle land above us.

—*Alyssa Bristow*

Robin's Song

Each childhood winter was a frozen thing.
The birds flew south in fall, returned next spring.
Dread frostbite left its mark upon my feet,
And blizzards burned my eyes with points of sleet.
I fought the icy winds to keep my pace.
I still can taste the scarf around my face.
So when I heard a robin's song one day
I knew that spring could not be far away.
In California now, camellias flower
In January. February's shower
Pink quince confetti on my grassy lawn.
Though robins share my garden all year long
I tingle when I hear a robin's song
As in a childhood March one day at dawn.

—*Phyllis M. Teplitz*

Just A Kid

I sat upon the ground seeing the sun,
The blessed light of day had just begun,
I could see the clouds in various shapes,
They looked like curtains, or maybe drapes.
High noon came gosh it was hot,
But for me I cared not a single jot.
Evening came that some thought chill,
But I never seemed to get my fill.
    But then I was just a kid.

Now I'm intrigued with mundane things
like making money for what it brings,
Over the years I'm older, no one to blame.
I'm sure the sun and earth are much the same.
I wish God could grant me the wisdom
To see great things with the vision
    That I had when I was a kid.

—*Clark E. Ryman*

ast Sale

ho will buy what is here now, or come to claim it?
he body rags,
he books that rise like tattered battalions
d sink with bursting bones,
teddy bear with one brass eye and a broken paw
attering the air
at still dreams of going home.

here is no childhood here.
sickness that dares not speak its name sits in the eaves
d shuts off the veins of the air like valves.
's crabbed madness gone dry in the mouth.
ven the ornate mirror stored in the corner
a stagnant pond, deceiving us.
ngles, colorless as light, will not come here.
he earth's lush casino is a better place for their bells and
eir songs.

hat's left of the day's last frozen stare
oat in the cell, then surrenders to darkness
lencing the dead. Outside, snow hits the skylight, hoarding
e sepulcher inch by inch.

  —Sally Rinard

Moving with the Crowd

Being swept along, people moving with the crowd.
The crowd took shape and form,
Opening and coming together; beating then retreating.
Like the waves of the sea, coming to the land.
Ebbing and flowing, humanity moving, slowly,
Moving faster, moving along going where?

People, some no destination; hurrying with the crowd.
Faces, human faces, black, white faces, all the faces
On those faces; all the different color eyes mirrored
with all the emotions.
Hope, joy, sadness, pain and all the other feelings.
People, human, hurrying with the crowd.

Moving this way and that way, trying to find a way.
There is no way out, moving with the crowd.
Helm in on every side, going along, moving, moving.
Some are leaving, others are joining Humans!
Like great big waves, being swept along, moving with
the crowd.

  —Maslyn Bertrand

de to a Fifty Year Old

he grey is slowly creeping through his hair.
he boyish grin has faded, but the smile is still there.
he trim figure is rounder, and the back is slightly bent.
he vigor has gone, the same way the years went.
he shy, young fellow has been replaced,
y a man seen often talking.
e has an opinion on everything now,
nd a wife who's always balking.
e often hear a mini sermon,
e gives them to us freely.
e sigh, and pause, and have to listen,
ecause he means them so sincerely.
n this his day we celebrate, we wish him many more.
ithout his loving chatter, life would be a bore.
o Dad, brother, cousin, Grandpa, husband, friend,
ccept our Birthday greetings, they are sincerely meant.

  —DarLayne L. Yliniemi

Untitled

Blood red roses swaying in the wind,
The dark misty night hiding their beauty,
Their soft silky petals covered with dew.
The stone remembrances of loves lost, covered with dirt.
Nothing left but old bones.
The lives are gone, the souls have moved on.
Nothing lasts forever,
Good turns to bad, bad to good,
Time can't be stopped no matter how hard you try,
Everything ends.
The roses will wilt and die,
The night will fade into day,
Even the stones that seem so sturdy will crumble.
No matter how strong something is,
Time will always be stronger.

  —Lisa Marcus

Less Than Perfect Season

Someone was bound to write it, so it may as well be me, Could
the braves do it again, we'd just have to wait and see We
weren't so overpowering, as the season got under way, All the
fans kept faith, saying let's take it day by day. Most of the
season, was spent chasing the giants team, Winning our third
world series, remained an Atlanta dream, And, at the all star
break, we were some 9 1/2 games out, But "comeback baseball",
is what the braves are all about. As it got later in the
season, the competition was getting stiff, so management made a
deal, to acquire Fred McGriff, The lead was chipped away at,
and reality finally came, We were back-to-back-to-back champs,
after the final game. We were billed as the playoff favorite,
the best team in either league, every aspect of the team, was
filled with excitement and intrigue. By game tree everyone was
anxious, and the chop was a familiar sight, no one figured we'd
lose now, with very little fight. All that I can say is, I
still believe in the Atlanta Braves, There was no doubt we
could win, but the team dug their own graves, I don't mean to
make excuses, I just can't figure out the reason, the fight we
put up all year, has left us "Less than a perfect season!"

  —Chester L. Albert

Trapped

Trapped
The darkness is cold, scary and hard
to sit there without moving, I am trapped.

Trapped
Getting the inner strength to move,
feeling the walls to exit;
hoping to find a door, finding nothing
getting nervous; getting scared,
but knowing no help is coming, I am trapped.

Trapped
The cold beneath my feet
the feeling of hurt and anger raging inside of me,
I am trapped.

Trapped
Turning narrow corners, seeing a yellow light ahead,
running even though my legs can't carry me;
running out into the forest.

The fresh air, the beautiful trees;
I was trapped, but now I am not;
It feels glorious to be free.

  —Amanda Kaminski

The Woes Of A Golf Course Superintendent

The night has come and gone
The day will be so long
The complaints freely flow
The grass continually grows
The equipment breaks down
The leaves fall to the ground
The irrigation system fouls up
Sometimes you just want to give up
The rain begins to fall
But that doesn't end it all
The shop needs cleaning up
The records need catching up
Now the day is finally through
The time has come for some rest and sleep, too
Tomorrow is a new day, so sleep while you can
Wake up tomorrow and start all over again.

  —*Chris Lewis*

Dawn is Sweet Sixteen

'Twas a beautiful Saturday morn
The day you were born.
Into my life you brought sunshine and laughter
And made me a first-time grandmother hereafter.
You captured my heart with your smile and loving ways —
Remember how we danced in many a day?
Now you have grown — a lovely young lady of "16,"
With kindness and compassion for others I've seen.
May God watch over you and guide you, and remember dear,
Do what you feel in your heart is "right," not what you hear.

Love always,

  —*Grandma Alma*

It's Mother's Day, My Darlings

God gave me two little babies,
 The days since have been gifts from above
And the children that made me a mother,
 Are cherubs that I dearly love.

It's mother's day, my darlings,
 My precious little girls.
Let's get dressed for church now
 And ready your bows and curls.

Let us celebrate this day
 Like so many we've shared before
Let us dance and thank the Lord
 For all we have in store.

We've laughed and cried Together,
 We've giggled over tea
You've both entertained in so many ways,
 You're such dear blessings to me.

You're each brought me sweet flower offerings
 While such love on your faces has shown
Through good times and bad times you'll always be
 The most wonderful gifts I have known!

  —*Marcia E. Cox*

World Peace

Why can't we all get along?
 There's plenty of space.
We all need to learn to respect each other,
And the entire human race.

 We need to learn to respect all mankind
And let our "love light" shine.
We need to love each other both day and night.
Because in God's sight,
-This is right.

  —*Dr. Hosezell Blash*

Washed Away

Washed away by this current of sorrow,
the deep, cold depression surrounds me.
I struggle and fight the oceans strong hold,
but the darkness pulls me to sea.
Now its calm, no tossing, thrashing,
but this ominous cloud still hovers.
It's rage pounding and ready to burst,
not knowing the soul it covers.
I stop to think "where will I end up?"
Is there something waiting for me?
If for one small moment I stop this fight,
maybe I shall see.
If for one small moment
I loosen my grip, maybe I'll drowned in my sea.

  —*Michelle White*

The Need For Professional Jurors

I was really chagrined with the tactics and fury
 the defense went through when I served on the jury.
They don't want a juror who can show too much "smarts."
 Lawyers try to rig a verdict before the trial starts.

The defense asked a panelist "Can you count up to ten?"
 He replied "Yes I can and I do it now and then."
The defense bodies whispered and after a pause,
 a lawyer said "Thanks. You are dismissed for cause."

A retired commander whom we knew was impartial
 many times had convened a Navy court martial.
Now there was a man who could serve as a judge
 but he never made the jury, the defense had a grudge.

A clean-shaven merchant who could speak without flaws
 was ruled as too bourgeois and dismissed for cause.
But a bearded young hippie, with hair down his spine,
 was told by defense counsel "You'll do just fine!"

Now I say to the courts "Don't take up my time
 with a dog and pony show for some idiot's crime.
I've had it to my rear with your stale 'justice' jargon
 when it's already settled with a lousy plea bargain.

  —*Merrill W. Snell*

Washed Up

Walking along the shore, hand in hand.
 The distant waves riding towards us.
  A chill runs up my spine
as the water splashes against our feet.

The drowning sand washes into the sea
 with one gust of the ocean.
Shells and rocks deposited onto the sand
disappear without evidence left behind.

  As you gaze upon the water
 a dolphin leaps gracefully
and glides into the blue sea without splash.

  Taking a seat on the beach,
gently putting our heads on the grains of sand,
Silently, we watch the sun set in the orange sky.

  Up above,
the sea gulls glide through the clouds
and disappear into the endless light of the sun.
 No one around, just the two of us.
  In our own little dream world.
 where everything is peaceful and quiet.

  —*Shelly Batra*

One More Day*

Why to rise, when tomorrow is no surprise?
The emptiness today to be felt much the same way.
Of tomorrow to be sure, no miraculous cure;
Of what I know to be, an existence so empty.
But of this I will say, it matters not anyway.
So accustomed to the gray; I'll take one more day.

Numbness of loneliness's pain long since achieved.
Disconsolateness accepted, in that I am relieved.
To be resigned to hopelessness; a salvation of its own.
A melancholy nurtured; indeed, purposely grown.
But of this I will say, it matters not anyway.
So accustomed to the gray; I'll take one more day.

To wait for new beginnings, that hope long abandoned.
Developing a dispirited soul; a priority demanded.
Energies no longer spent on fanciful thought.
A necessity dictated over what isolation wrought.
But of this I will say, it matters not anyway.
So accustomed to the gray; I'll take one more day.

—*Cindy Anderson*

The Southern Cross

Marveling upon a heavenly host
The Father, the Sun, and the Holy ghost
A heavenly host that will forever shine
There on the shores of the Madre de Dios a shrine
The evening so very noisily luminous
Sounds in the jungle so deeply vigorous
Scorpio above, the Southern Cross so far away
A very pleasant day that day in May
Machu Picchu, the village bath so incredible
Feelings of life so extraordinary unbelievable
Our Earth….a most beautiful hemisphere our biosphere
Our biosphere…truly most remarkable our hemisphere
Into the sphere the flight of the solidary albatross
The southernmost reaches of our hemisphere the Southern Cross.

—*Robert G. English*

Two Men

Two men born in one place,
The first man traveled north,
The other man stood alone, repressed by his course.

The two men lived apart,
The first man traveled east,
The other man stood around, intrigued by his peace.

The two men had grown old,
The first man traveled south,
The other man sat down, and never opened his mouth.

The two men saw the end,
The first man traveled well,
The other man never lived; a different type of hell.

—*Robert Jacobs*

Untitled

In God by things lately deem right off
And direct my soul heavenwards.
To this end let live
And carry forth tender arms in which I may fall,
Last of when like spring bathes
The limbs of quiet conceive -
Gain measure so too we in the Lord's presence.
All acceptive I only gain mismeant carry out your tablature,
The hours blindly take own partaking
Of communion, the Lord's body.
Thee unliken haste to glorify pardons
For our most nimical worry wantonness.

—*Mike Leonard III*

Me And My Shadow

The darkness is broken by the spark of the match.
The flame grows brighter casting gloomy shadows.
Raindrops tap vigorously against the windowpane like pine
needles. I sit alone in silence, holding on to this
brilliant light. I think of my love down below in his wooden
box. My vision is blurred by the moisture in my eyes.
Shutting them, I release the tears. They crawl down my
cheeks, stinging my eyes. Motionless I continue to sit,
closing my mind to all but the pain and sadness. Enduring
these emotions, I wait. For once the night belongs to me.
The match shrinks in size, the heat penetrates my fingers.
I patiently wait for the answers to flock into my mind.
Feeling distant from my companion, feeling closer to
God…I wait for a sign. The flame touches my fingers!
Startled…
I blow out the light!

—*Amy Moody*

Remembering

Remember the first signs of spring,
The fresh smell of the first drop of rain.
How the young tender grass grows.
How good it felt, to the bare feet and toes.

You could sit and stare for hours.
At all the different little flowers.
So beautiful to behold, utterly breathtaking.
It's so young and fragile, like it's just waking.

All these wonderful things are free,
God put them there for us to see.
Oh, beauty through the eyes of the young.
Wish it could be seen that way, by everyone.

—*Madge Torkelson*

Nature And Its Creator

We look above, and see the blue of the sky
The grace of the hawk and eagle when they fly
We look on the ground and see grass, oh so green
And out in the wilderness, many sights we have never seen.

Out in the forest, there stands a tall tree
Where birds fly in and out, so cheerful and free
The sun sends down its heat and light in its beams
And warms up the land and lights up the streams.

Out in space we see numerous stars so bright
That have guided many a sailor as he sailed at night.
North and south at the poles, there is always snow on the ground
And in the tropics at the equator it is warm all year round.

How did this get here, did it just happen to be?
Oh no, it was created by someone much greater than we!
In six days, yes six days, his creative work was done,
And for love of sinful man, he sent his own son!

—*Brian Evans*

I.S.P. Is Special

I am thrilled to be a lifetime member of I.S.P.
There is nothing so interesting as poetry to me.
Being with people from coast to coast and
forty National around the world.
Our Conventions open to all age groups,
men, women, boy, or girl.
The staff is super, and willing to help,
you only need to ask.
We hope I.S.P. will go on and on and pray
it will always last.

—*Mamie Hodge*

The Seasons

On the first days of Spring
The ground is sometimes white, instead of green,
But in the mind it is thoughts of pretty things,
'Cause very soon the Crocus will be seen.

Summer brides in beautiful array,
And playgrounds alive as children play,
While elders savor thoughts of other days
As Summer sunshine, lakes, and trips, coax us away.

Autumn bursts in colors of red and gold,
And our little winged friends to the south do go,
While haunting winds bring ghostly spirits low
All nature will rest 'neath glistening snow.

Winter comes in all its beauty,
Trees gaily trimmed, Santa's nose red like a ruby,
Fireside reading and music that's cheery,
As friends all gathered sing carols so merry!

—*Anne C. Newman*

The Sunflower Warriors

The many days were filled with splendid conquest.
The hours consumed by unquenchable imagination.
The minutes moved ever endlessly through the midsummers eve.
The fruits of nature had come to bloom.
Thus giving shelter to the warriors of youth.
From the fortresses of the grape shrouded trees would they roam
Devouring all foes who should cross their paths.
Great be the number before them but undaunted would they press
   to their task.
Enumerable fields of the golden flowers of the sun have they slain.
Only for the imagination to be filled again.
The days were filled, the hours consumed, minutes moving ever
   endlessly.

—*Robert W. Johnson*

Broken-Heart

I wish you knew how it feels
The hurt inside, that really kills
I thought I wouldn't love you
But, now I realize that I do
But, now your back with her
And now my life's in a big blur
I have a question
To ask you if I might
Did you feel anything for me
When we first kissed that night
Lately, I've been upset and hurt
Because you didn't notice the heart that got burnt.
You will always stay in my heart
Even though she's the one that tore us apart.

—*Carrie Dudley*

Friendship

Once in your life you find the perfect friend.
Someone who will be there.
Someone who will care.
Someone who will not judge.
You're simple every move.
The two will share special secrets
No one else should hear.
The friendship should never
Feel jealousy nor ever feel despair.
You should cherish this friendship
With all you're love and care
'cause you will never find
This friend again anywhere!

—*Wendy Pryce*

Washed Away

On the beach we sat, hand in hand,
the imprints of our souls left in the sand.
There for a brief moment in time but then washed away,
in a time on endlessness and eternity were just one day.

She came to me that morning on a wave,
washed upon the shore in sunlight she bathed.
Her beauty touched me deep, to the recesses of my soul,
possession of heart and mind to her I sold.

The brilliance of the day and the salty air I breathed,
the warm, moist air, laden with salt carried in the breeze.
Then the sun dies down and the sky turns pink,
the last remnants of light behind the waves sink.

As night fell a crescent moon peeked from behind grey clouds,
she was torn away from me by the ocean and drowned.
Now endlessly I wander her soul by chance to see,
but the ocean has torn her away and drowned her deep inside of me.

—*Michael L. Allen*

Our Poet Father

We have not all the gift to write
   The inspiring poems you can pen,
But we must make our lives aright
   As living poems, read by men!

Your unswerving courage and your cheer,
   Your life of hardships, without fear,
Have thought us by example, as by word,
   To honor, in our lives, our risen, Lord.

You, in your life, have not failed;
   You've worked right on when others wailed:
Hard toil to rear your sons and daughter,
   And we thank God for a Christian father.

—*Glenn M. McGuckin*

Resignation

I'll bet you as soon as you scrub the floor,
The kids will come stomping through the door -

As soon as you put the garbage down,
Your "ole" pet cat has to dig around.

You've got a date and you're already late,
The bus breaks down and you have to wait -

You take your boots and there's a drought,
You leave them home and a storm breaks out.

If you get back home a wee bit late,
Frowns and questions you'll get from your mate.

Therefore, remember, you can seldom win -
You've got to expect it and learn to grin.

You just try it, I'll bet you'll agree,
It really works... it does for me!

—*Marie J. LaMachia*

Believing

Time is on my side
To do what I want to do
I'm young enough to realize dreams
And make them all come true
Making the best of all I have
Overcoming failure and defeat
Achieving the goals I've set for myself
Accepting the bitter along with the sweet
Knowing the effort is worth the results
and I will be all I can be
A human being who truly believes
Others love and believe in me

—*Joyce Murphy*

'm Not What You Think

'm not a Indian Guru or even a man of wisdom.
he last man anyone should ask for advice is a King who's
st his Kingdom.

'm not the man to give an answer, I probably won't know it.
alf of me's just running scared and the other half thinks
's a poet.

'm not the great Houdini with a magic bag of tricks.
lease don't ask me to make it right, there's many things I
an't fix.

'm not Superman and I'm not the Mighty Quinn.
Vhy is it everyone that knocks on my door thinks I've got to
et them in.

'm not Sir Lancelot or even the Lone Ranger.
've got to learn to help myself before I can help a stranger.

'm not a Genie in a bottle or even a magic urn.
o if I can help anyone, please step aside so I can give
nyself a turn.

'm not an explorer or a conqueror of new lands.
have to take up arms for myself cause I only have two hands.

—*Alan J. Caron*

"No Final Words"

I look into the darkness, only silence can be heard,
The look on peoples faces - there's not one that says a word
The air is thick and foul - my eyes are burnt from smoke,
I take a breath — it's painful, I try hard not to choke
I can't make out the rubbish ... of what it used to be,
I can't believe this was a person — That is lying next to me
I thought today was beautiful, At least it started out to be
But now I've woke up somewhere else — I don't even feel like me
What happened to my family? Are they out there somewhere still?
Why did I live thru all this hell? This nightmare can't be real?
There is now... No-one left to come home to
Or no-one left to fight
There's nothing left to pray about —
No children... to kiss goodnight
This can't be where I used to live —
Where I lived — was beautiful and free
But somehow someone changed all that,
And took everything from me
What right did they think they had
To cause our life to cease?
And to choose — Not live at all
When we could have lived... in peace"

—*Denise Mcvay Penny*

Autumn Concerto

As fall starts to churn
The leaves begin to burn
Luminous lemon, seared scarlet and vermilion

They pirouette and shout
Finally flaming out
Arcing and splashing beneath heaven's pavilion

A kaleidoscope reigns
While harmony strains
Tuning tones never scaled
Maples love cantatas
Oaks embrace sonatas
Each through divine wind hailed

The bright morning star
Fuses from afar
The array into a rhapsody

Late charges the night
Lit by full moonlight
Conducts a pastel hued symphony

—*Phil Vermiglio*

Metamorphosis

Where does the love go when it all ends
The love that was unbearably deep, unendurably dense
It evaporates and saturates the air we breathe
Sinks down into the earth and contaminates the water we drink
it dissolves, disperses, vanishes
Fades away and crystallizes in a place far away
Distant, in an innocent heart

...And for some it will always remain
Grows with them, flowers with them, fruits with them
Nurtures their soul, nourishes their mind, feeds their body,
never abandons
rejection is pointless, deprivation is useless neglect brings
suffer and pain
They go on loving and loving till their roots are wedded
to every letter

...And who gains in this endless circle of compound feelings
What becomes of trust
What compensates for the pain and anger
What alleges love in return
And what about friendships altered into a bondage of captivity,
what worth?
And what becomes of the lost, wandering souls?

—*Shadi Ziaei*

Aglow

As the sun kisses the horizon, color seems to melt out and run
the length of the sky;
A lustery red, then a fiery orange
A pink mist paints the background.
A ruthless violet then streaks across the sky,
The ocean then laps at my feet, gently reminding me of it's
presence, it is then I see my blessing,
I am so fortunate,
The ocean is as smooth as glass, and stretched out upon it, for
as far as my eyes can see, is yet another picture of this
gorgeous sight; tears spring to my eyes as the sun dips below
the horizon, leaving the sky a glowing lavender
Yet, why should I cry?
What people hope to see once in a life time,
I have seen twice in the same night.

—*Isla Simpson*

"Unsung Heroes"

These to me are the unsung heroes -
The loving dedicated, Mother and Fathers
of dependant children -
The teachers of the world, who with loving
patience and care nurture the hearts and
minds of their charges -
The loving concern and care of children for
parents infirm with years
The men and women of large and small
communities, unselfishly dedicated to those
less blessed -
All are touched by God and walk
tirelessly in His footsteps.

—*Frances Anstett Brennan*

One Dark Night

He waved a thin hand through a plume of gray smoke;
The luckless form with a voice that broke.
The sage hid his face but his shadow stood long....
And the smog from the hills mocked the traveler gone wrong.
His secret lay deep in a heart cold as stone.
You could sense that he favored being alone.
His soul seemed as black as the PA. Coal mines;
And if I hadn't known better I would say he was blind.
He called out to me but I hastened to go;
For fear clutched my heart and my footsteps were slow.
But I went anyway not for profit or gain....
I always did have more grit than brains! But the terror in me
was as real as the life. And I imagined him holding a spike-
handled knife! My voice I knew not between calmness and
fright; As I got to his side in the pale ghostly light. "Can
I at this time be of some help to you?" And he said so
distinctly...as if the answer I knew. "My dear little child,
what's wrong with you? "What task for the "dead" can you
rightfully do?" The sun from my window showed a breathtaking
beam; and I jumped up in bed; and was glad for the dream!

—*Eve LaTorre*

Lost

Love goes by unheard, softly, unknown;
the meaning of true love yet unheard.
Passion - the whole body possesses -
eruption of feelings untold;
And yet, as fast doth love envelop the soul,
the two mistaken - yet the same!
For surely without one, existence of the
other is forlorn.

To some, the heartless, senseless, this cannot be;
but still it happens, much beyond control of the mind.
For if it was a mindly thing, overcome would be easy.
The heart still a mystery to man, yet to overrule the mind?
Feelings are sad while the heart is happy, only to be hurt.
The end result already planned but eyes are blinded by
thirst, need, desire.
And find not those things that make heaven before death
but live ignoring happiness in a world of pretend and are lost.

—*June Mooring*

Unspoken Heart

There are no words that can say what is in the heart
the mind tells you what to write and the pen writes the words
The heart is not satisfied with the words, it is crying out to
be heard but even the ears do not hear
Love
Pain
sympathy
words that the heart not the pen feel
We cry and the tears fall to the paper but they do not create words
The tears dry and leave a spot and you feel the pain but no
word can fill that spot
You can feed the stomach to fill the hunger pain,
but there is no food for the empty pain in the heart

—*Peggy R. Aguirre*

If Then, Were Now

Remember the dolls, who seemed so real?
Their lives worked on magic and a childish ideal.
We would turn a head, move an arm, or whatever it takes,
but never in a doll, would be the sound of heartbreaks.
Their lives had no wrong, faults, or mistakes,
and never were there snobs, scrooges, nor fakes.
Just plain simple dolls, with a smile on their face,
sometimes I wish I could be in there place.

—*Tina R. Morris*

Nature

Nature is the prettiest to me, seeing little birds singing to
the morning day.
Never wanting them to fly away.
The forest is the best place to be,
life there is all natural, you see.
There you can see butterflies of all kinds, animals,
too, are not hard to find.
I love to walk in the woods and see nature and all the trees,
cause there is a world of different things out there to see.
So, please don't start a fire and don't destroy, walk through
the forest woods and see, respect and enjoy.

—*Lester L. Hammel*

Arise From Your Sleep

Arise from your sleep now, the moon has slipped away
The night sky is gone, making room for the day
The songs of a morning dove are calling you to me
Hear it through the early light of morning mystery

Arise from your sleep now, the day has just begun
Morning dew sings melodies, her song has just been song
And listen to the whisper of the curtains in the air
As the wind through an open window calls from everywhere

Arise from your sleep now, see the shadows when they fall
See them by the picture near the mantle on the wall
Passing shades of darkness unwrap the morning light
I am certain there is beauty as the day follows night

Arise from your sleep now the night sounds aren't around
Parading beads of sunlight are dancing on the ground
Reflected on the window are the patterns from the stream
I wonder if to wake you would take you from your dreams

And now I am sure I can say without a doubt
I am somewhat amazed that I ever did find out
How a moment in time is forever on my mind
Like a ray of summer light to a man whose been blind

—*Brian Wilson*

Quietus Spoke

Death must have ridden a bicycle
the night the sailor's wife died.
It came silently, without evil,
like 36-inch tires on wet pavement,
a shushing sound, and she was gone.
He stepped onto the shadowed street,
sodium lights making halos in the black,
his nose dripping from a new cold.
The ice-rimmed stones chanted like monks
under the fall of his heavy G.I. boots.
As his long, ringing strides
carried him towards the corner steeple
the coins in his pocket hugged each other
with a noisy, metallic passion.
He promised her he'd light votive candles
to make her death physical, make it burn
behind cheap blue- and red-colored glass.
Before he crossed under the winking streetlight
He glanced up and down and boulevard, aware
bicycles ride quiet without headlights or horns.

—*Birch Leroy DeVault IV*

Emptiness

The days are long.
The nights are lonely.
How long must I wait for you to be my only?

They say my heart is here, but it's frozen with fear,
Each time it rains my heart fills with pain, cause
    I know you're not alone.

Alone is a term that I used to understand,
but now that I feel it, I just can't comprehend
    how you could leave me standing here.

Don't you see? It can't end like this.
No promised words. No sorry kiss.

Our love was strong. I thought it would last...
    until you left, and never came back.

—*Holly C. Wagner*

'Grandma's Little Girl Is Growing Up!'

"Grandma, tell me a story!" "Sing me a song!"
"The one about a little girl, who ran away from home."
"Are we about to your house?" "How long have we got to go?"
"Can we make cookies?" "Can I play dress-up in your clothes?"
"When I get big, I'm going to buy everything in pink!"
"That my favorite color!" "My Mom's too, I think!"
"Grandma, are there really unicorns?"
"Could you take me to see one, someday?"
"How come the tooth-fairy leaves you money,
when she takes your tooth away?" "Grandma! Wake-up!
I've got chewing gum in my hair!"
"Are you sure face cream will take it out of there?"
"Guess what? Grandma." "I can set my alarm,
and get myself off the school." "We got to be there
on time, cause they have rules." "Grandma ... could you
come and stay with us for a week?" "You could sleep in my
bed, the couch is fine for me." "Grandma, look at me
how tall I am," "I'm in the seventh grade this year!"
"And today is my is my birthday "Grandma." "Grandma, do you
hear?" "Yes, Sweetheart." "Happy Birthday, dear!"

—*Bonnie Hoover*

Untitled

She is the sidewalk poet
    the one with the white fingers
    from the chalk
She writes her lyrics upon the cracked pavement
She writes these perfect poems
    scribed in that fragile, fragile chalk
    in precise child's hand

When the rain comes I watch her
    childhood wash away in
    that whitish water
    that floods into the drain
In time the poems are forgotten
Or remembered as a silly child's scribbles

Gazing out at the pavement where she once wrote,
    I see an empty canvas, a blank sheet of paper
    decorated with weeds
A tear, like a raindrop
    washes my cheek

—*Michael Cwikla*

Glimpses

What are these glimpses that I see,
The ones I see from you to me;
Not like the ones from before,
These are ones to be adored;
What exactly is in a glimpse?
Is it something for remembrance;
A look, a glimpse, a little stare,
None of you can be compared;
A glimpse is something to be cherished,
But a glimpse of you shall never perish;
You're in my dreams from beginning to end,
So my love to you I send.

—*Eric L. McElmurray*

"Ode To Mom And Dad"

The good people, they're hard to find,
The ones who offer
For the sake of being kind.
Reaching out their hands
As well as their hearts
Just to help you stand,
Or to help you start.

Never in the way,
But always at your side
Whether it's night, or whether it's day
The good people
They don't hide.
If it weren't for the good people
The world would be sad
So with our deepest love
We say thanks to Mom and Dad,
For they truly are the good people!

—*Donald Morss*

Lilac

I hold lilac you gave me so many months ago,
The only reminder of a life I've had to let go.
Its smell is still faintly sweet
As if to say the life it led is still not complete.
My pretty flower my lilac, was still in bloom.
We thought nothing could ever end, we had always
    just assumed,
That like so many times before the story would end
    the same way.
We thought we'd write our own endings,
Do what we had to do, say what we had to say.
But that wasn't our job, and, even if we didn't know,
Life was teaching us another lesson and gave us an
intelligence that before we did not show.
Just like my lilac with its violet color smashed
    beneath my pages of books.
Inside, I've preserved it as best I can
Like the day out of the garden it was took.

—*Nicole Markelz*

Treasured Heart

The thought of loneliness comes like the dark side of the moon.
The love I once had is now retired.
The love that gave me satisfaction and put me in link with the
rings of reality now vanished, into the dark side of the
treasure. I thought I found in you.
The destination I thought I had landed, it has now departed.
Emptiness is in my heart, as no stars being in the summer sky at night.
Doom is upon me, for there is no us, just unknown feelings.
Enrage fills my head, as my heart explodes, as tears fall,
like a water damn with rain drops of a storm.
He lives in my Treasured Heart, that will never be filled by
another true love.

—*Elizabeth Muro*

Untitled

Dawn comes; this morning to celebrate life
The passing of a woman, a mother, a wife

The yellowstone banks so familiar to all
The stately cottonwood, so strong and tall

The ice on the river, the snow on the ground
The path that is taken, oh, memories abound

The fire in her eyes
The snap in her step
The joys she gave
The thoughts she kept

The final trip was taken
The direction so well known
Home is where her heart lies
Along with the mighty yellowstone.

—*Louise Denson*

For Charlotte

I said "I" am going to be
    the perfect mother-in-law.
Like some "I" will never be.
Ignorantly, not knowing that behind each "I" there is
    no security.

The enemy is not after those that are weak and pray not to be
    wrong.
He gets after those that stand so tall and say "I" know
    that "I" am strong.

So being that perfect mother-in-law I know I will never be.
But I praise God for giving me a daughter-in-law that loves
    and stands by the son that God gave to me.

Sometimes when faced with trials we may never know why.
But being a child of Jesus we have a love that will never die.

Like the grass when it's filled with the morning due,
    My Jesus rain his blessings down on you.
And the kindness you have shown to me
    add more stars to shine through eternity.

—*R. Holmes*

"Bitter Pollen"

Like a flower that bloomed on a nice spring day when
the petals drip with dew. Her pretty petals sing a song that's
in her heart so true. A song that was once filled with
love, a song we all used to sing. But now the song has
disappeared and no longer do I hear its ring.

Instead a song that is very cruel came in and took it's place,
and now the bees who took her pollen can see its bitter taste.
But there's one lonesome bee who can see past it all.
The bee who has done much for her but she never did recall.
To recognize all the things the little bee has done.
Instead she tells her to go off; to be shunned.

Her petals have brightened but her song has drowned.
My grip has tightened but she'd like to be crowned.
The little bee can't help but worry because
her pollen is not as sweet.
But then her petals shall not drop when the bee does
not come back. For the flower wanted to fly the coop
and the bee would like to help pack.

—*Amanda Lynn McKesson*

Is This Choice Necessary?

In December at the post office I asked for Christmas stamps.
    The postal clerk, hard at work, with a polite jerk, asked,
        "Religious or contemporary stamps Sir"
The question seemed proper at first, then my mind began to stir
    Plainly I heard My Saviour say in a plaintive voice,
        "Does My Son truly need to make that choice?"
    I, too wondered if nothing in the contemporary scene
    Could be religious, or was my thought of Christmas just a
            dream?
    I chose the stamp with Mary and her Blessed Child,
        Showing her saintly smile so tender and mild.
            Then Jesus spoke. I could see his face,
        As He said, "Son, there is religion in this place."
—*Morris Thompson*

Seems to Me

Seems to me as tho heaven is crying
The pure white flakes drifting down
Gliding in silent stillness
Such beauty as it dresses the soil, grasses and treetops
A dance unfolding
Yes, am sure tis tears of the purest kind
To touch nature
The tears from above are to quiet the sorrow and cover in
splendor for one night
A comforter
A blanket of white

—*Kathy Tapp*

Dreaming

In the evening of yesterdays tomorrow
the quiet thunder of monster jets
tread meekly through the clouds.
When silvery wings caress the air
still higher than the plain, I dream of you.

When clouds, like sightless icons hang
misty in their glaring brightness,
my thoughts reach out to grasp a dream;
a dream which is yet, yet couldn't be
a dream of memory; I dream of you.

Clouds like thoughtless thunder lay
beneath those winding strings of steel,
stretch straight to where my thoughts
scream soundlessly for you,
dreams of sad delight and pain, my dream of you.

Still further on my thoughts glide by
as does the wind o'er silvery wing,
my thoughts that I'm remembering,
the dream of yesterday and tomorrow,
of past delights and future pleasures, a dream of you.

—*James Edgar Haley*

On A Peaceful Night

The still water reflects perfectly
the quiet worlds dilemma and
the lost soul who travels its banks

Images unseen scurry at his glance
while imagined footsteps follow his wake
he is implored to walk this path

By God's guidance and hand
bountiful thoughts quicken his beat
while the endless cry of glory
sends him deeper out of sight,

but sometimes, on a peaceful night
the still water reflects him on his plight.

—*Dominick T. Miciotta Jr.*

"Little Things"

Thank you Lord for little things, that make my life complete,
The rainbow on a summer's eve, the singing birds so sweet.

A word of encouragement from a friend so dear, the hug of a
child so tight, the butterfly on the window sill, the firefly's
glow on a summers night.

The sunrise in its splendor o'er the hills, the flowers of many
hues, all trees and grass add to the scene, a perfect blend
with the sky so blue.

A special thanks for our children dear, who have grown to
manhood so soon, memories of ball games, picnics and all, plus
camping by the light of the moon.

Again, I thank you for "little things", so many I cannot name,
Dear Lord forgive me lest I forget, from whence all these
"little things" came.

If I had everything in the world I'd want, it never could
satisfy me— like all these "little things" encircling my
life, so beautiful, serene and free.

—*Ruth V. Williams*

Mind Storm

Sitting in the city on a park bench in a storm.
The ravings of a mad man
don't seem to have true form.
But who other than a mad man
could make sense of what is said?
Who knows what he's really thinking
unless you've seen inside his head.
What drives a man to murder in such a grisly way?
Perhaps in his mind it's justified who are you to say?
Killing would be so easy if your
reality would make it so.
A simple act of dismemberment who would ever know.
So he acts upon his feelings what else is he to do.
The voice which speaks inside his
head swears every word is true.
Guilt and remorse are feelings unfamiliar to his mind.
He sees himself as different and separate from man kind.
Sitting in the city on a park bench in the rain.
A man wrapped and dark holds
his head as if in pain.

—*Chad Rulon Titensor*

Let Me Hear and See

Let me hear and see
The ripple of a waterfall, the sound of raindrops, the
Waves rushing upon the seashore in the still of the night
Let me hear and see
A fountain of water bringing its sounds of beauty as it
Roars up and down, the rumbling of the dancing water to be
Heard and seen as a picture to watch
Let me see and hear
The sound of the wind as it bursts into the sound of music
As the voice of an angel fills the air, as the dew drops
Fall upon a sea to bring forth a flower of beauty for all
To enjoy
Let me hear and see
My fellow man in a song of friendship, in prayers of
Togetherness, the meaning of loyalty to one another, to be
Most understanding of each other, to live in
Peace

—*Marion Lidsky*

The Spark Within

The brook babbles it's wondrous life,
The Robin sings and spreads wings in flight,
The trees are green,
and the clouds white,
The world teams its abundance of life.

And who are we to see this day?
It's like any other as we go on our way,
We say a prayer,
"Help us our day."
Not from above, do we find the way.

The light we seek,
is the light within,
from there we end,
from there we begin.
Around, and 'round until lessons learned,
The light of lights,
The spark within....

—*Dennis E. Jacobi*

Black

The color of the night.
The roots of all people.
A primitive name for evil.
The darkness of confusion.
What envelopes us in a dream.
The color death brings.
A very slimming concept to the voluptuous.
The present sign of luck.
A color of being sexy.
What we all are when the lights go out...
Black.

—*Jessica L. A. Rohs*

Hard To Forget...

Now that your gone and life's not
the same it's hard to forget your face
and your name.

It's hard to forget the times we spent
and hard to forget how much you meant.

It's hard to forget how much you
cared and hard to forget you said you'd
always be there
But what I find the hardest to forget
is the wonderful day when we first met.

—*Christine Delehanty*

Untitled

The awful silence,
The seconds before the blow.
You can smell the rage,
Smell it in the alcoholic breath
As it leans closer to scream in your ear
While you cringe
Waiting, preparing, bracing yourself.

It comes, you fall,
Banging your head on the side of the table
And then you're shaking,
Shaking with fear at me next punch -
Shaking with apprehension of how to explain the bruises-
Shaking with anger at the man who feels you must be
Punished-
And at yourself who submits to the punishment
Out of fear.

—*Janine Larmon*

Nightsong

Twilight sets in,
The sky glimmers, dusky and warm;
Flashes of light pass by, swimming in pools of dark shadows
The glinting drone of eternity whirls past
And I stand, stark, wrapped in the cold blanket of the night
And I dance with the moonbeams in a forest clearing
And I kiss the sweet raindrop that plays on my lips
And I look into the darkness and see everything
And all becomes clear to me in spite of hazy sight
Because of hazy sight
And I hear the blissful nothingness that the trees whisper to me
And I sing the Nightsong

Time stills, pondering
I stand here wondering
Memories and visions are crowding my mind.
Questions and answers dance in the starlight;
The moon is a piece of shining glass
It drenches me in white light
Standing, I shiver beneath the night sky.

—*Leah Rothman*

The Storm

There were no clouds in the sky,
The sky was blue and the grass dry.
Then out of the west gloom appeared,
Darkness and thunder this way steered.
In the blink of an eye, we were lost,
While trees and houses were being tossed.
We were separated for many days,
Distraught and confused in many ways.
The storms of the past weren't nearly as fierce,
But right through our hearts, this one pierced.
The storm raged on, no dissipation,
I read the Holy Book, my only proliferation.
I prayed the storm might end tonight.
So we could possibly reunite.
Now the storm is over,
And I say that I love her.
We must rebuild the foundation that was tore.
It won't be easy, it will be a chore.
Storms come and go is what I say,
I know we'll pull through them, all the way.

—*David Merchant*

The Loneliness of Love

To feel the warmth of your touch on a cold winter's night
The sound of your voice like the first Robin of spring
The shine in your eyes as bright as the North Star
To look at you, hold you, love you
These are things I yearn for when we are apart
I ask, why it has to be the way it is
It brings on a deep loneliness I can hardly bare
So I just pray that someday things will change
And you will be here with me to change the patterns of destiny
Someday we'll be together, never more to part
A deep devotion burns within my heart
My soul cries out for your love to come back to me
I wish to show you my sincerity
But until you open your heart, I will have to wonder
What do you keep locked inside your head
We are pawns in this game called life
And it was planned that you and I stay separate entities
In a world so big we may never meet again and all my hopes and
prayers shall never be answered.
What I want in life is to prove my love for you
So open your heart and give us the chance we both need.

—*Susan M. Brown*

A True Love Comes From The Heart

You know you love me so don't say that its not true.
The strongest love two people share could only come from me
and you. True love is what we have together and it will never
go all wrong, cause what my heart feels for you is what's making
our love strong. For you there is a feeling that is deep
within my heart, please don't tell me you don't love me or it
will totally break apart.

The love we have for each other is growing very fast, and
the love within our hearts is what's making it all last.
Although you are not near me so I can show you what I mean,
that the love I have for you should not be said, it should be
seen. You are the only girl that has ever changed my life.
Although that's not the reason that I want you for my wife.

A true love comes from the heart, and that is what I really
feel. So the only thing I want from you is pure love that
feels so real. I would give my life for you, and you should
know that I am true, that is why the love that grows within me
could only be giving to only you. Again I say you are not near

me, but my love is deeply true. That's why I write it as a
poem, that deserves to be sent to you

—*Juan A. Burgos*

The Evildoing of Spring

The last spear of frozen water given mercy by the sun,
Drapes from an eave in a season unknown.
Trying so hard for survival so she can see winter once again,
But only losing herself little by little,
Dripping away slowly and leaving no traces behind.

The sun no longer giving sympathy, beats down
and makes her tears flow —
Flowing like wind and taking its form...
Sometimes not seen or not heard nor felt or touched.

With the evil deeds of the sun and of spring
finally taking their toll,
The eave is now scarless, bearing no trace of
its temporary outsider who is no longer alone.

—*Victor Hernandez*

Stars

Have you ever thought about the stars,
  The sun, the moon, Jupiter or Mars?
Can you imagine a star so bright
  Could guide three Wise Men through the night?

Have you ever thought about God's way?
  About the people He calls up to stay?
Maybe every star is meant for a guy
  Who wanted to live and never to die.

The study of stars, called Astrology,
  Discovered Libra, the sign of me.
Some day when I'm gone from here
  I'll find a place in Libra up there.

There will be a place especially for me;
  A part of her eyes so I can see
The world below in harmony and peace;
  When all the wars and fighting cease.

So this is my wish that when I die
  I'll find a place in God's great sky.
For all who believe there is room for them
  I hope you find your sparking gem.

—*Dawn E. Short*

This Too Shall Pass"

he ripple of the lake so clear,
  the sunrise calms my every fear.

he birds they sing sometimes they know,
  urturing their babies as they grow.

reen grass, fresh air, the early morning dew,
  the clouds have all disappeared, and the sky is so blue.

ut, sometimes our lives are full of storms,
  the waves they roll so high;
/e're not able to hear the birds, thru our clouded sky.

he grass it seems so withered, so thirsty and so dry,
/e hear moaning and groaning and it seems so hard to cry.

ut, "Jesus" is our pilot, who creates the sun and rain,
/ho knows we need the balance of some blessings and some pain.

o don't give up, don't ever quit, the storms will pass real
st, and even tho there necessary we know they will not last!

  —*Karen Bayliss*

Walk Alone?

love to walk alone...
he sun's caress on my face exhilarates.
he breeze playing with my hair
he wind nurturing my bruised emotions
nd the rain washing away my tears.
o follow the carefree circling birds above.
nd surrender to their joyous song.
o feed the pigeons.
o inhale the cool air.
o throw a nut to a squirrel.
hen suddenly dressed up Horizon I greet.
he whisper of the falling leaves.
he sight of the arrogant naked trees.
o taste the snow flakes.
o study faces.
appy faces, worried faces.
aces..
love to walk alone.
/alk alone?
id I hear someone whisper in my ear?...

  —*Penina Cytryn*

tag at Crucifix

eath the lonely hunter pulls the trigger and we're off —
he trajectory penetrates the spines and the impaction
f metal to meat is immediate sin —
 N.Y. state law says you can feed deer-meat to the
 omeless, soon road kill will do —
 the yuppie in me & you — the machine gunned KA, KA
 A echoes through my bones & reverberates as happy
 amouflage hunters Flag after deer in heat —
he road to redemption winds its path-like worms in the
 ood bringing life to the soil —
 The heads of men artists in Phillip Guston's
 l painting roll as if the axeman waited —
he etching of Durer's 1503 stag has the crucifix
 its nest of antlers —
 nights of the world can't see out of their visors
 uck from melted business nets.
 ord Buddha's deer park exists still —
 ut we sing this Bud's for you.

  —*Dwight David*

Unjustified Love

The rising sun causes a blur,
The wind blows, yet no leaves stir.
A river runs, yet a lake is dry,
A flame once burned but now has died.

A Mother's curdling scream, as
she watches her baby die.
There is no time to say good-bye.
Here your life you no longer have,
single file, into camp.

Forced to line up against the wall,
The pain and heartache cannot be dissolved.
Roaring voices echo commands...
into his head the bullet slams.

Boom!!!

The rising sun causes a blur,
The Wind blows, yet no leaves stir.
A river runs, yet a lake is dry.
A flame once burned, but now has died.

  —*Melissa Riddle*

Hush Can You Hear

   Huch, can you hear a voice calling in
the wind, calling out to each and every
man, speaking words of love and peace,
saying things that are long forgotten.
   Hush, can you hear a voice crying in the
night, crying tears of pain and fright,
who can still this calling voice, who
can dry the endless tears that fall.
   Look can you see the light shining
brightly in the night, shining for all to
see, the way that lead all from misery,
for in the light there is no pain, and
all tears are wiped away, and in the
light you can find the voice of the
one who is calling, calling all from
the darkness of the night, into the
warm of the light, speaking words of
hope and truth, words that up lift and
move you, calling from within the our
hearts, I hear a voice calling to the world.

  —*Michael De'Angelo Carey*

A Slave's Flight

The night, dark and as cold as a winter's morn,
The wind gentle rustles the leaves,
A man is running through the woods,
His skin is as dark as a night with no moon,
That which surges within him is the pain
from his bare and bloodstained feet,
Suddenly a faint sound can be heard;
It is the faint whispers of the hounds and
that of the horse's hooves carried through the
air as whispers in the wind,
They are after him,
His blood runs cold as his first attempt to run fails,
But his fright and will to survive carry him a
foot or so,
There he falls with exhaustion,
His proud heart drained of all its strength,
There he lies and awaits his fate,
Then as though a calming peace has engulfed him
he close his eyes never to open them again.

  —*Sonia Peter*

A Horselover's Senses

The thundering of hooves in the arena
The whinnies, nickers, and snorts
Oh, what a joy to hear!

The sweet, beautiful eyes watching me
The massive head, body, and tail
Oh, what a joy to see!

The warm, sweet breath on my face
The fragrant scent of hay, sweat, and leather
Oh, what a joy to smell!

The soft, velvety coat against my legs
The smooth gaits of the animal beneath me
Oh, what a joy to feel!

Why be afraid?
For the horse is a gift of God
Forget the fear, forget the falls
But always remember the joy

—*Jenny Jacobs*

Penn's Creek

Daylight creeps up behind the ridge;
the woods, they hide the night.
Grey mist lingers above the creek;
Crows caw, a loon takes flight.

Some parts seem still; swirling, dark pools
of green, currents not seen.
A pine's rigid frame sways on wet glass,
golden leaves bob then whisk downstream.

A twig's sharp snap; hoof and rock clap -
be still! Heart grasps for beat.
Tails of white leap then bound on by;
cross stream the does retreat.

In awe, nature regains breath. Cray -
fish ricochet about.
I thread my minnow onto hook
and cast in quest for trophy trout.

—*Brent Miller*

For Those

For those who love and those who dream
   the world still has magic and majesty.
For those who hope and those who give
   life is not a tragedy.
And those who search for truth will find
   their hearts have wings to fly.
For the world belongs to those
   who take the risks and try.
For those whose hearts are burdened
   with sadness and with sorrow
   there is still a chance that they will find
   joy and peace tomorrow.

—*Joyce M. Askins*

Untitled

The old folks don't smile anymore,
They want to but it hurts so much when they do,
Remembering all the times
When life was so young
But now it seems that it just stopped for them,
The old folks stay home
When they go it's only for a moment or two
Just to see the children and the flowers grow.
And then perhaps a tear will fall as they remember
The time when they were young
But it seems like ages ago.

—*Bernadette Bohdanowyez Musztuk*

One Sided Love

The clouds fly in covering the sky
The world to me falls dim
No light is in existence
I remain in a cold place

I am open to pain
I ask for abuse unknowingly
I am permanently wounded
Each time I am injured, part of me dies
It is gone forever, never to return
It is protection, a defense, a mechanism to save myself
To survive the damp environment I will never become accustomed to.

Shady, dark, night, death, the past has past
Only the future lies shakily ahead
Full of uncertainty I accept the risk
I jump at the chance of experiencing the unknown once again
With an overly anticipating spirit
Only to be slashed again by the blade that rapes my soul.

—*Kathy Merriman*

With My Eyes

With both eyes open I vastly see
the world's rising woes and difficulties
although rubbing them rapidly, can't wipe
away its troubles and eyesore debris

I have even tried blinking my eyes
but the sorrows will not disappear
and covering one eye does nothing but hide
one half of its toils and fears

It seems after crossing my eyes
the earthly distress shifts and moves
and with glasses I get a clearer view
but the problems do not improve

So after I truly witnessed the afflictions
and completely viewed all I despise
I find there's only one solution
and that's just . . . closing my eyes

—*Tony D. Young*

God's Two Creations

In the year 1 - 9 - 8 - 0, God made my dreams come true,
By bringing me a gorgeous niece, that love, I really do,
Ronita is a sight to see, as pretty as can be,
Making me that much more proud, that she's a niece to me!

Then in the year 1 - 9 - 8 -2, another dream came true,
In addition to my gorgeous niece, I have a nephew too,
Raymond is a precious one, and big I must admit,
When it comes to being cute, he doesn't lack a bit!

He's not like many newborns, who drink an ounce or 2,
My Raymond will be on his 4th, and still he is not through,
He is a sturdy baby, can even move his head,
Just 3 day from the hospital, already rolled in bed!
He has the cutest dimple, same place as his sis,
They got it from their mother, and proud of that she is!
I really love my nephew, I really love my niece,
God keep them in your constant care, I'm begging of you Please!

—*Ruth E. Delwiche*

The First Book

ray of sunshine falls gently onto a blank paper.
he writer sits, hunched over, looking
earchingly into the light.
nspiration is what she is after
ut it has yet to arrive.
hen, with a burst of energy,
ıe begins to transform it into words.

he ink flows steadily as it flies across the paper.
ne page becomes another as she
reathes life into her characters -
ıch in their own way, a reflection of her soul.

writer, that's how she feels
the emotions that run deep
ırough her veins
our out.
    —*Jessica Ann Lister*

Fantasies With No Substance"

ifeless masks lie silently on the wall
ıeir features so still and empty
ıe emptiness they possess crawls through the eyes
ıey can't cry
ıey can't breath
ıey can't feel
ɔses look up to them, they shed a tear
owly they lose their love, their scent, their beauty
ıe sculptured faces and breathless roses form a-
ɔmpassionate stare
either live
ıey each frame perfect beauty
ıe beauty is the brilliance found only in the midst
f the stage
    —*Angela N. Paz*

Iy Sisters

√hen I was a baby my sisters held my precious little life in
heir loving hands, they pressed me close and I felt their
ɔart beat. I knew their soft caress, looked into their eyes
ıd saw myself reflected.
I am not a baby anymore, my life is not so little, my
sters all have babies of their own. In turn, they have put
ɔose precious little lives into my loving hands, and I have
arned the secret, the babies and I, we are holding each other
man an infant, an uncle, a niece, an uncle, a nephew, a
ɔdfather, a good child, a brother, a sister. We draw our life
ɔm each other our lives are forever happily and miraculously
ıtwined, this is the gift my sisters have given me, and with
eir babies in my arms, I know my sisters hold on to me still.
    —*Roger Deschenes*

Iy Lonely Home

ɔ escape, I hide in a field of green.
hough, I did not buy it,
belongs to me.
go there to pray, to meditate, to think.
unlocks my soul, my heart,
is my missing link
ll of my passion, locked up inside,
let loose, like the morning tide.
ree to frolic, with no eyes to see
√hat this field unlocks in me.
Iy soul is what makes this holy land mine.
his beautiful field.
n which my soul first learned to shine.
    —*Jessica K. Pittman*

Psycho-Vibration

Echoes of drummers vibrated in my ears
Then a deep voice whispered
He's had an accident
It was like a dream, dream, dream

My feet dragged and my head grew larger
The deep voice pounded right into my head again and again
Suddenly, I regained consciousness and followed the message
Running as fast as I could through the crowded street

That must be his son, son, son,
Whispered another strange voice from the crowd
I could feel a repugnant vibration as I ran, ran, ran
Arriving at what looked like the accident scenario

Another echo whispered, hospital, hospital, hospital
Then I ran and ran and ran to the nearest hospital
He was bleeding to death
Doctor call my son please, he cried out in agony

Here he is, said the Doctor
Son, I won't be alive before dawn
He died at midnight
I loved him.
    —*Esendugue Greg Fonsah*

Heaven's Blue Skies

If you looked upon clouds as if they were angels,
Then angels a'plenty there'd be;
But when I look and see a clear blue sky,
I ask, "Is this an opening for me?"

I pray that I live my life pleasing unto God,
As along my life's journey I go;
The righteous path's the one I wish to trod,
But not till judgement day shall I know.

I thank you Lord, for your sunshine and love,
And the life you've all allowed me to live;
Now, as I go on, I pray to you up above,
"May Yours be the peace that I give?"

When I come upon troublesome or bothered souls,
Give me knowledge and wisdom to speak;
That may save them from Satan's cumbersome holes,
So they need not feel lost or feel meek.

If I fail you dear Lord... I ask you forgive,
The forgiving God I know that you are;
So, as long as I try and you allow me to live,
I will follow your bright shining star.
    —*William G. Puckett*

Shedded Tears

The day we met I saw a spark,
    then it changed to a flame in the dark.
Then one night at the lake,
    a night of bliss,
I shutter at the thought
    of his sweet kiss.

Then he went and put our flame out,
    and broke my heart no doubt.
He tried to wash away my pain with
    "I am sorry, I just want to be friends."
I asked him for a reason for ending it all,
    but he had no reason to give.

I asked him, "Don't you remember
    anything at all?
You were one of my reasons to live."
    We were friends for many years,
We shared many memories,
    but those memories now are just shedded tears.
    —*Jessica Bellew*

Untitled

Why should life be easy
then there'd be no challenge
and we'd be a bunch of apathetic louts
love
A topic/I write often about
has drained me/to a feeling of emptiness
nowhere to turn/but inward
like sitting in the corner/of a dark empty closet
The door is closed/and nobody is home
the light hurts my eyes/I don't want to leave
I look for comfort/and find only walls
something I can count on/and feel secure in knowing
I can count on them/always being there
surrounding me/confining me/encircling me
like the arms/of an old friend
who will always be there/in my time of need
as I search for the strength/to open the door
to go outside/to the chaos
that awaits
me

—*Gary John Kahai Hiram*

The Gray Road

I walk alone through the swirling mist
There are only shades of gray
Places are dense, others very thick
No colour exists here

Looking back I wonder how I got here
That I shall never know
Why I left the life I had is the question hanging in the air
Before I came here I had no foe

I see my old life as I walk down the gray road in the gray mist
It is but fragments along this road
The promise of a future in my ear is hissed
But I know this road never began and will never end

But I realize now I was abandoned here
By who or why I don't know
What good would it do to shed a tear?
No one would see my despair

I am here to walk the road of troubled souls
I know I could never turn around
Where reality never was
My feet being pierced by the fragments of others' lives

—*Meredith W. Miller*

Without

If there was a space in time I would be without,
There exists a rainforest going through a draught.

If there was a trip, that lingered on a while,
There would be a clown longing for a smile.

If there was a rainbow, that I'd like to share,
I'd save the pot of gold for you until you could be there.

If there was a mountain to climb, sitting very high,
I would join you on the way reaching towards the sky.

Life is but a short period, and we are only a few,
My thoughts are consumed by the existence,
Of simply me and you.

—*Holly Gray*

Remember, "Children Should Be Seen And Not Heard"

We are so far apart, yet deep in our heart,
There is a union that can't be denied.

So close all those years, a mother has fears,
She knows they won't stay by her side.

How can she see what it will be
When her angels fly out of her nest.

She teaches, then preaches.
She knows what she did was her best.

And then comes the day each goes their own way
And you are left by yourself, so alone.

Friends can't play the game, it's never the same
As that call, from your child, on the phone.

So call your mothers, sisters and brothers,
You don't know how much it can mean.

Grandchildren, you too, with so much to do,
Now you've reached the age to be heard when not seen.

—*Antionette M. Arens*

Oak Tree

'Tis I see it standing there. From fingers to toes it stands
there. It looks over the world, crying when there is war,
laughing when there is peace. It has feelings just like you
and me. It needs care just like you and me. It loves all who
loves it.
It stands with pride and glory. It fears no one or thing.
It is strong and brave. For it has heart from within.
This tree symbolizes a thousand things, the friendship of
things and the love for which two have for each other.
All who stop and stare must think how it has decided to share
the wonderful gifts God has given it. How this one tree does
not hog its greatest gift. How it is not selfish and closed in.
  For this tree teaches all a lesson.
    —*Rebecca J. McVey*

A Beach With My Name On It!

Somewhere way south, in a magical place
There lies a man with a mystical face
Beckoning, guiding, he offers a hand
To a home so restful down on the sand

A tropical breeze. with a sky made of blue
No worries, no stress, just nothing to do
He kicks back and ponders, aspects of life
And takes his thoughts down the aisle and makes them his wife

But he'll give up his home, it's the end of his game
As the ocean and beach are calling my name
As I take to the throne, more than king for a day
And I'll talk of my Kingdom and invite you to stay

—*Jon Summersfield*

"Elliot"

Although life may never be the same
There still is no one to blame
God has your life in His hand
Even though we can't always understand
But God will see you through the days
For He has blessed you in many ways
But we shall always remember the little one
Whom was the cause of so much fun.
Seeing Elliot's eyes with that beautiful gleam
Seeing that smile with that little beam
He brought us so much joy
That cute, little baby boy

—*Marikka Diaz*

Home

Darling, please take me home.
There to stay, no more to roam.

Home is the twinkle that shine in your eye,
That says "I love you" though I know not why.

Home is the radiant "Hello" in your smile,
So glad to see me, if just for awhile.

Home is the kindness in your sweet voice,
That makes me love you. I have no choice.

Home is the gentle squeeze of your hand,
That deep inside makes me feel so grand.

Home is the warmth of your special charms,
That makes me long to be in your arms.

Home is the comfort of your loving embrace,
That has power also to make my heart race.

Home is with you, forever and always,
To love and cherish the rest of my days.

So I ask again, please take me home,
In your heart to stay, no more to roam.
　　　　—*Kathryn Rennquist*

What If?

What if nothing was the same any more,
　There was a whole new world outside our door.
If kids were the adults, and adults were the kids,
　Do you think our world would hit the skids?
Would we laugh at our sorrow and cry at our joy,
　How about marriage; would the girl ask the boy?
What if we all got along, and there were no fights,
　If Carlos didn't want to put out Joe's lights.
If everybody always had plenty to eat,
　And nobody ever died from the cold or the heat.
If there were no deserts, so arid and dry,
　No more wars over which to cry.
What if people had wings and could soar in the air,
　Would the birds walk out of pure despair?
If cats chased dogs up the trees,
　And there were lots of fish in the seas.
What if boys wore dresses and girls did not,
　If summer was cold, and winter was hot.
I think I like my world just the way it is now,
　Even when the kids say, "Don't have a cow!"
　　　　—*McDonald*

"Year of Eighteen Seventy Five"

Twas the year of eighteen seventy five
There was no car to start up and then go
In the year of eighteen seventy five
You might take a ride in a wells fargo stage coach.

There in year of eighteen seventy five
That black bart might hold up your stage for gold
But don't fear him for he's said plenty nice
Won't steal from you and takes a bank loan then leaves note.

A poet of note on a flour sack he writes
No harm to you good folks that ride
For a loan I just want fargo's gold to hide
So ride on and off to the sunset I will ride...

Fear the year of eighteen seventy five
They caught black and he paid back most loot loaned
Soon free he took two last loans polite like
They are searchin' for him and laugh at so called loans
But last laugh's on them for his real name's no way known end.
　　　　—*S. J. Alcorn*

I am 38, and I am Alone

Except for the shadows
there would be nothing but
a white cat and Mexican carpets and music and that's all
Except for the cold showers and
a fathers voice cracking with the ice
of colder showers years ago in Treblinka
Except for a scrap of meat and
a mothers kiss and a blind eye turned to the child and
not to unleavened bread, matzah in Tel Aviv
Excepting a birthmark of screams and smoke and seizure
there would be darkness again.
　　　　—*Kimberly D. Beane*

There's A Place

(Dedicated to one of my "Best," "Lady Di")
There's a place that I know of,
Where dreams sometimes came true,
A place pretty and quiet,
Where I could think or be blue.

I found it when I was younger,
And there I'd often be,
Cause some days weren't always sunny,
Or the future was too dark to see.

It was there while children were growing,
Twas there when a brother was lost,
To some it may be worthless,
But to me it's worth any cost.

It's there even now should I need it,
I'll get there even if I must crawl,
It still helps me through the bad times,
Or with problems big or small.

I hope to go there someday,
And be one with the flowers and trees,
And anytime I'm thought of,
They'll hear my voice in the breeze! (get a life!)
　　　　—*Bigun*

Help Me

Help me, I'm trapped
there's nowhere to go
bound by strings that look so weak,
yet in reality are so incredibly tough.
Impenetrable strings

help me I'm trapped
they surround me in many forms
there's only one way out

help me, I'm trapped
searching, searching, only hoping to find another way out

help me, I'm trapped
denied, no others can be found
the strings are getting thicker and stronger
taking life and breath away from me
as they tighten around my body and my soul

help me, I'm trapped
Black... All I see are the twines that form the strings as
they cover my eyes

Help me I'm trapped... but not for long.
　　　　—*Gillian Kelley*

Christmas In July

Christmas is over, Santa has gone;
There's peace and silence in all the land;
Gone went the tree, lights and all;
With the happy moments of joy.
Good will toward man has disappeared;
Hidden away till next year!
Which starts on the first of December;
And ends on the sixth of the New Year:
With a lady friend and a bottle of wine,
We'll bring in the New Year:
And wait for a Christmas in July:
Who knows, maybe good will to man:
Might stay all year:

—*Rossi Menzza*

Brother's Forever

There's something I need to tell you, before you go away.
There's something I need to show you, right now, today.
The things we shared together, it seems so hard to believe
That time has faded the pages, in my book of memories.
Your not a little boy anymore, we know that is for sure.
But something deep inside me, wishes you still were.
All those battles you fought, I never thought you'd win
You'd just look at me and smile, and go on fighting again.
The odds were all against you, they said it was too late
The destiny of this little boy, lay in the hands of fate.
But there was something deeper, something Cancer couldn't beat
It was your smile, your will, your pride, that kept you on your
feet. There will be no parade, no medal of honor, no golden
crown the honor you have earned, took you to higher ground.
Now that the battle is over, and all the fighting is done
You can lay your weary head to rest, for now the time has come.
And through all the troubled times, I know you'll always be
Forever my big brother, watching over me.

—*Richard R. Pike*

Around The Corner

Around the corner they come and go
These little people that I know
Anxious to please eager too
With their happy cries "look what I can do"
Following behind like a little parade
Carrying a hoe dragging a spade
The shouts of fear at their first sight of a worm
And their joy to know they just wiggle and squirm
With fumbling fingers they plant with glow
The seeds I drop for them to sow
They do not falter until work is done
Knowing a treat will surely come
Of special sweets and story too
Of little people "just like you"
Oh yes I too make it special you see
For all the happiness just for me
From the little people that I know
Around the corner that come and go.

—*Margaret Kish*

The Highest Mountain!

I climb and climb... Soon I'll reach the top. All my
    wounds will heal.
As soon as I get there, my father will be there saying, "I'll
    pull you up trust me!"
My hands are weak... I'm going to fall! Nothing at all on the
    wall.. can't grab a limb, or him! Then, something caught me
I climbed up again. At the last limb he grabbed me and pulled
    me up.
We talked and talked. I told him once, I told him twice ...
    I'd climbed the highest mountain!

—*Kirk M. Ray Jr.*

A Time for Healing

Too long have they suffered through horrors of war,
These neighbors in the historic Middle East,
Where anger and selfish motives have prevailed.
Their compassionate God, whose teachings appear
In the Torah, the Koran, and the Bible,
Has endowed them with intelligence and skills
To build a commonwealth in the Holy Land
That would be worthy of universal praise.
Only when leaders face responsibilities,
And their people agree to cooperate
Tired of the killing and intense hatred
Can there be tranquility and lasting peace.
There are problems of self-determination,
Security, and deadly terrorism;
Once resolved, rich resources can be channeled
Into economic growth and social change.
The never-ending strife, through the many years,
Has been of concern to nations round the world;
"There can be no assured peace....for any nation
Except as it is achieved for all nations." *

* Dwight D. Eisenhower
—*M. Elisabeth Steiner*

She Fell Asleep

She fell asleep there on the bed.
They all say its true, but she just
Can't be dead.
A voice in my head screams that it's
Not fair, for wrongs of her world is what
Put her there.
She was my best friend, a friend till her end.
I don't ever think that my heart will mend.
She lies there unmoving, so still, and so silently.
While right beside me, her mother shakes violently.
Farther down on the pew, seated by their mother,
Sits two crying children; her sister and brother.
They found the pill bottle on her night stand.
An unfortunate murder by her own hand.
She fell asleep in her bedroom that day.
Now casket in hand they take her away.
We had spent every minute together, she and I.
She's gone now, forever without even a goodbye.

—*Tiffini Blackwell*

A Precious Legacy

Our children....
They are born of us and delivered to us

Screaming and crying into this world,
They need so much to be hugged and curled

Completely dependent on us for all their needs,
Oh the joy to see even the most simplistic deeds

But we are parents
And we will teach them

We MUST teach them what we have learned
We WILL teach them what we strive for
Then there are the things we always yearned
We will give all of ourselves, and even more

Because we are their beacon, and they ours
When they say "I love you", the tears could
come in showers.

There is so much ahead
And it won't be a perfect dream
But we will reveal all the light we can shed,
Father, mother, and child...A lifelong team.

—*Dan Fallon*

Grandparents

They make you feel warm and special inside
They give you place to stay when you want to hide.
They give you kisses and hugs galore,
and you know you always go back for more.
They make you smile with each breath you take.
Always full of laughter and games to play.
You run to them when parents say 'no'
They don't take no for an answer,
    It's part of the show.
They tell you stories and fill your mind
you can't wait till next story time.
They give you all kinds of cookies and treats
making your tummy full of sweets.
They love you more than words can say;
making your heart feel light everyday.
And when you leave that great big house,
you can always go back to the door that's unlocked.

—*Becky Gorbe*

Horse Power

A happy couple on the Sunny Hill
They had a little ranch
And had two kids, two dogs, two cats
And a horse by the name of Crunch.

But recently they disagreed
What to buy, what to put in the bank —
It went really hectic, so they wanted to split
And they called on Mortimer and Schenk.

The lawyer meant that it will be quite simple
All possessions divided in two
Each gets one kid, one dog and one cat,
But for Crunch one must be the brave.

Because the horse can't be divided in two
Only one get it to hold it tight
The other is allowed to see it some time
While he has the visiting — right!

When they went home, they did go in the stable
And spoke about to the horse —
Oh — Crunch understood and he nuzzled them both
They cried and there was no divorce!

—*Katie Baier*

The Lonely Child

They don't know how hard it is to be a kid
they just don't understand
And they often hit me with their cold hard hand.

And when we fight,
They hand me a toy and everything is alright.

I get anything I want, any toy or teddybear
I get anything I want but love and care.

I beg for a hug I yell loud and clear
But no matter how loud I yell they'll never hear.

They don't like the best that I can be
Their just not happy at all with me.

I go to sleep I dream and I cry
Then I ask silently "God Why"?

While all I want is love and guidance
Not just another allowance.

Then I look down in the palm of my hand and the money is all I see
With there backs walking further and further away from me.

Next I awake and realize it's not just a dream
It's what my life was always meant to mean.

—*Susie D. Mitchell*

Bargaining Game

To some people life's a bargaining game
They live on borrowed time
Never putting strong emphasis on anything is a shame.
Thinking they're unworthy of love is lame
Because of a mental conflict that caused a stain
When the meaning of one's existence is weak
it's difficult to remain sane
But never allowing love to grasp
their life only they're to blame.
So instead of sunshine and rainbows their life gets rain
Though lies will take their spirit only so far
The false luxury of material possessions,
human degradation, cars
is the cruelest and most dangerous attempt
When they're too scared to cry
The depth of irony, is the contagiousness
of loneliness daily leads them to die.
When love does exist you still have to wonder why?

—*Anne E. Strausser*

Mother's Day

Mothers are the best,
They need not to take a test,
When they're having lots of fun,
They say they're never done,
When they need some money,
They go and ask their honey,
They eat until they're fat,
Then they really laugh at that,
They love something in the month of May,
They get the love because it's Mother's Day,
The moon is not as lovely as she
For she is the one who gave birth to me,
The way she looks, the way she asks,
For these are two true facts,
For she is my mother and always will be,
For I love her and she loves me,
She will always care, when no one is there
To comfort me in harmony,
This poem is a way,
To say Happy Mothers Day!

—*April Renee Owens*

The Young And The Helpless

You see them on the street corners feeling sorry for themselves
They rarely eat any food, for there's nothing on their shelves.

Clothes aren't even thought of, they're worn without a care
Is there a place for the "Young and Helpless?"
Or are they destined for anywhere?

Joy is never a part of them, then maybe or perhaps it is
Maybe its sorrow we see in their eyes, "Joy" turned into tears

My question for you as we continue to search,
Is there a place for the helpless and young?
I am sure there exists, such a place, you see
To ease those hearts that are torn

Mothers and fathers all lost in their thoughts
With despair shown all the while wondering as they go
through life, "how did they lose their child"

I say to you mothers and fathers out there,
Keep an eye on your children these days
Follow their hopes and all their dreams, in many different ways

I pray to God with much sincerity, in this quest for a better
home. Just thinking of the young at heart......
Who are helpless and all alone!

—*C. Renee' Pope*

Who Says You've Got to be Bigger

Jesus Christ was common knowledge, but that wasn't enough so
they sent us off to college. Money was their God, did they
stop and pray, Heck no, commodities and stocks were the order of
the day. In India they eat rice three meals a day, but here we
gluten ourselves on baked potatoes and filet. What has
happened to the good U. S. of A. Inflation is high and money is
tight, have we still not learned to get it right, and the
people I see wearing crosses on their neck, crosses on their
hand as if this occurred by just one man. I've seen them pave
paradise twice, now each one must pay the price. Isn't a
powerful discourse, their looking for a sacrifice. Greed and
money was their lore, as the few got rich and the more got
poor. They say that money is the root of all evil, when all
that's required is to be a little civil. Now the damage is done
to the lesser ones, who paid our taxes as they paved our asses.
Politicians fool and fumble, what's the reason our economy has
stumbled? What was paradise, while seemingly unaware, has
grown into a thoroughfare, not to mention the quality of our
air. There's the desert and the moon, and galaxies far away!
But they had to pave Hometown USA.

—*Randall Anderson*

The Politician

With glowing smiles dressed fit to kill
They tell us his with such ease and skill
Democrats, republican, looking for attention
By seeing which puts on the biggest convention!

Bills should be passed for the good of our nation
But seem they're only looking for another sensation
One vote, one people that's a thought to behold
They represent, and protect us, so its off to the polls
I'm truly confused as I travel this land
is there really such a thing as an honest man?
When they're sent to Washington I don't expect
magicians
But I'm sick to my soul with all these politicians!

—*Barbara Grant*

"War In Vietnam"

The men were in Vietnam
They were fighting for Uncle Sam
Some will live and some will die
Many mens' wives will pout and cry

Some are fighting on land and sea
Just think; they are doing it, for you and me
I wish I could help fight, for that land
One day; you're going to have to make your own stand

Life is hard, everywhere we go
Some people don't care to know
They will all learn on the right day
Just think, why do we live this way

War, is just a waste of people and earth
Right now, some women are giving birth
There are new born everyday
Pray to the Lord, they don't have to live this way

—*Danny Wooten*

The Forest Outside Of Pollution

One day I was walking in a forest,
  The trees were bare,
    The crunch of the autumn leaves,
      So brisk and so fresh was the air.
        Then I came to realize how
          Spectacular this world really is,
            But......
              With the gift of pollution man gives,
                it shall soon no longer be.

—*Heather Sjolin*

Nurses

Nurses are made from heaven above
They work and work and still show love
There understanding and patient too
Because they want to help you
There hands are strong, but kind
And they smile and relieve your tired mind
Nurses are special I have to tell
They watch the sick and make them well
When patients are worse and hope is gone
The nurse comes in helps them along
They give all and ask nothing in return
Because they are really and truly concerned
God made them to watch the sick
And they never complain or kick
So heres to you, nurse of the day
Whatever you get, your surely under paid
Just remember your special to all
And we're glad God gave you the call

—*Hilma Enos*

Up There

The lights shine as far as the domed roof stretches
They're peeking down on us as far as we are
Sparks from the fire drain in the air that we breath
The only door to my heart has suddenly been knocked a jar

On the smoke, I'll float up to the clear lighten sky
Jump off onto a star and wait for a comet to go by
I'll ride the tail of the firebug until I'm over your bed
Drop from the sky and lay a kiss upon your adoring head
Grab your hand and leap way up into the air
There'd be no confusion and no worries...
Just us on a star, way up there.

—*Benjamin Shaw*

Her Beautiful Lips

As I lay awake
Things from the past
Floating through my mind
Pondering the smile of someone kind
I see a waterfall

I can't let go
Of things
I've heard and seen
Thinking about what all of my feelings mean
I see a waterfall

Even though
So much time
Has gone bye
I can't begin to understand why
I'm looking through a waterfall

I'm afraid
That this
Will never end
And that my heart will never mend
So let the water fall

—*Sean P. Mudgett*

Can the Whole World Be Wrong?

Beneath the outer edge of everyone
there is an inside,

An inside few realize exists,
It's boundaries far and wide.
The outside counts is what the world insists,
But still few will deny,
Because what really counts is on the inside,
Not the outside.

—*Jennifer Raday*

Nancy's Philosophy

When you're down - and feeling blue
  Think of this card....
    and me too!!

For when in time - it comes to pass
  such a good lass.....
    not an —

So what was drastic - so dearly we thought
  actually was nothing......
    and not for naught

A lesson well learned - and as they do say
  keep an upper lip....
    and pray pray pray
      —*Nancy J. Allen*

Untitled

Standing in the green grass of a meadow;
Thinking I'm happy not to be in a ghetto.

The air is fresh and free
Isn't this where we all should be

It's such a pity
To see what goes on in the city

So come to the country everyone
Where we can all have fun,

We are children of this land
So come to me my friend and take my hand.
    —*Lisa Hunter and Shirley Hunter*

My Father

Oh, my father how I wish you were here.
Thinking of you takes me through the years.
When I was born oh what a thrill.
Right then and there I was daddy's little girl.
A little older but young and tiny.
You were always there to smack my hiney.
But my bringing up was important to you.
No matter how much I put you through.
As I think back when times were tough.
You were always there no matter how rough.
Your teaching us what's right and wrong.
We know one day we'd have to be strong.
And sitting around missing you.
Wondering where our time flew.
Oh, my father, how I wish you were here.
Thinking of you breaks me into tears.
    —*Debbie Atherton*

The Sky

I am home to many things:
The white's of a rain storm,
And creatures with wings.
The green of the trees,
The pine and the birch,
Gently rustle with the passing breeze.
The tips of the mountains,
The snow covered peaks,
The stars in the dark,
The answers we seek.
My home is a place where the mind has fun.
I'm home to the beauty of earth.
I'm home to the setting sun.
    —*Briana Phillips*

A Christmas Stroll

I was walking home from work late Christmas Eve
Thinking there's nothing in Christmas for me to believe
I stopped at the corner and looked across the street
to see a wind with rags on his feet.

He had a cedar branch some one trimmed off their tree
He was decorating it with balls of colored paper it was a sight
to see I said you crazy old man do you know where you are
you're not in a mansion starring at the stars

I said what's the use and I walked on by
When something on down the road caught my eye
A little girl about the age of ten standing in her yard
Her Daddy said what I have to tell you is hard

I can't get you much this year cause money's been tight.
She looked and said Daddy it's alright.
As long as you and mommy are here I'm as happy as can be
cause being together means everything to me.

As he hugged his little girl tears ran down my face
I knew then my thoughts were a disgrace
I had something to believe in right from the start
Its not what you have it's what's in your heart
    —*Kathy L. Webster*

A Child

Your baby is here, it's hard to believe,
this beautiful child was once just a seed.
His fingers and toes are the most beautiful things.
And the touch of his skin is like angels with wings.
His eyes are like copper, his hair shines of gold,
the years go so fast, or so I've been told
As he learns and he grows my
    heart skips a beat,
for soon he'll be walking on those tiny feet.
The crying for me and reaching out too,
will soon be a memory, he's tying his shoe.
At first I was all that he'd ever need,
I was his mornings, his nights
    and hugs for skinned knees
As I hold him and love him the feelings so strong
it's hard to believe he'll grow up before long.
He's a little guy now, that I hold so dear,
I give thanks every day for the coming up years.
I'll love you and teach you and always be with,
for you're truly a miracle truly Gods gift.
    —*Tamara Gutierrez*

Life Is A Journey

The birds were swaying, swirling and dipping across the sky,
The clouds were drifting by,
The miles and miles of endless telephone wires,
Acres and acres of grapes, corn, plums, peaches and cherries,
So many beautiful trees, all different shapes and sizes,
Some as if they are a huge vine with the leaves going down the trunk,
Some no longer pretty, because they died.

The gorgeous gorges with moss growing along the rocks,
Tressels no longer used, since the train no longer runs there,
Pullman cars, boxcars and cabooses decaying, as they are no
longer needed anymore.

All this I saw from my window on my steam engine train ride today.
Then, I thought, life is like a train ride,
Some, sometimes go on the tracks to no were, with their greed,
avarice and hate.
If only they would realize, how short life is and how much more
rewarding life is when you take the train to somewhere with
peace, harmony, love and joy in your heart and life.
    —*Barbara A. Yageric*

A Toast

What is this, wonder I; this thing, this mist,
This earth, this sky, this life divinely kissed?

My eyes and ears, they see and hear.
And yet the mystery remains unclear.

For when my senses on history depend,
I find I must my species defend.

They guard their mindless ceremonial rites,
With rabid dogma, their truth often bites.

The martyrs fall, the rivers flow red.
But they mystery remains, left unsaid.

Away from this flesh, just a short way to go.
Resolution awaits us, all secrets to know.

All knowledge of God, of life and of death.
Will be ours to tenure when we draw our last breath.

Ah, but sad it is, and certain, the power we lack.
To bring any of this illumination back.

So raise your glass and toast times three:
To those who are surely wiser than we,
To those beloved absent friends,
And to our own sweet mortal ends.
—*Norman M. Blake*

Decisions

I hope you know
This is a decision we make
This is a risk were willing to take
Getting involved way to fast
Letting our cares fade in the past
Hours and hours we sit all alone
No knocks on the door
No rings on the phone
He told me he loved me
So we decided to wait
And we lay in the silence until it got late.
—*Carey Campbell*

Apocalypse

Green it was.
This thing called war.

A whore.
Taking all that was offered her and consuming it.

White and black and red and brown they were.
These persons called upon to do battle.

A rattle.
Shaking all before it and reducing it to rubble.

The green and red and brown of it restored.
The black and white destroyed.

A phoenix.
—*G.R.A. Fowler*

Cats

On silent paws the hunter stalks,
With more stealth than any hawk,
Softly, slowly moves the cat,
As it tracks a flying bat.
Crouching, every muscle tight,
The little hunter is quite a sight,
Suddenly the kitten springs
But not for the creature with the wings.
The cat was sidetracked by a clump of grass
So she let the moment pass.
—*Melanie Wilson*

Everyone Is Different; No One Is The Same

People judge people by what they see,
This way today, why must it be?

To have friends we must be the same,
From my opinion, this is a shame.

God made every one of us different,
If you don't like it, you better get used to it.

People who are different go through misery every day,
They wish so much they could go a different way.

There's something you may just not know,
And that's no one is the same.

So treat every one of us equally,
To create a better picture with in the frame.
—*Wendy Pearson*

Villanelle to a Red Dragon

A piece of goods that makes me think of Lee
this winged one with fierce and fiery eye
you see, it does not look Chinese to me.

Rather it has an air of Gaelic history
of rock hewn coast and crashing waves nearby
A piece of goods that makes me think of Lee.

Scaly rough, its surface seems to be
yet bright of hue and strung to hang on high
it really does not look Chinese to me.

I love its undulating symmetry
and wonder of its origin and family ties
this piece of goods that makes me think of Lee.

Above my head its wings beat happily
and turn upon the breeze's passing sigh
It really doesn't look Chinese to me.

So packed and ready for one last journey
on Utah's Wasatch range it will now fly
This piece of goods that makes me think of Lee
and never really looked Chinese to me.
—*Mary A. Ryan*

A Dream

There always has to be something dangerous in
this world,
if it's raping in our streets,
stealing in our stores,
killing babies,
murdering innocent people,
kidnapping little kids,
mugging old ladies,
drunk driving,
kids getting high, and more.
But there can't be anything more dangerous then
starting a war.
There are men and women out there that are
getting killed.
Men and women that are only 18.
If there could only be peace.
If we could only stop everything bad in this world.
If only there could be a miracle.
—*Michele Tesch*

Confrontation

Not all were mean or spiteful lots,
Those memories of my childhood time.
Yet a monster of misery stalked my heart
With never fatigue or decline.

Always observing with greedy eyes,
Fed by my thoughts like a flame.
It consumed the very life of my life,
Ignoring my pleadings with disdain.

Until the day my heart made a desperate stand,
To the death it had to be.
Surprising strength and confidence appeared
As a faint hope stirred in me.

'It's as though you've never been," I cried.
"You're dust and ashes to me.
Whatever I am and shall become
Is in God's realm of possibility."

The power of those words was amazing.
With defeat came a despairing cry.
The past dwindled in size before my eyes,
And fell at my feet, and died.

—Edna Holmes

"Mechanics Blues"

Now, my cars paid for and what a relief,
Those monthly payments brought nothing but grief
Got cars in my backyard, sitting side by side
Just waitin' to be worked on
How I wish I could hide
I wrench all day fixin' those damn things
I'm the greatest mechanic, I make engines sing
At the end of my shift and I'm finally through
I go home to relax but there's more cars to do.
Now I'm playin' my guitar and singing
The Mechanics Blues
Yep, my cars paid for and the dogs been fed
There's still people playin darts
And I'm laying in bed
Just pickin' at my guitar with my amp turned on -
Outside the window, the breakin' of dawn
It's my day off - but all those cars on the lawn -
Yep, my cars paid for and I can relax
Just swillin' a cold one and
Jammin' my ax.

—Bonnie F. Orlowski

Fifty Five Alive Puzzle

As I look around me in '93, I'll try to describe what I see,
Though I see empty chairs of mates gone by, fifty five of us
have refused to die, our wrinkles are vivid,
Our eyes do not see so well,
We've lost our teeth and hearing,
Our hair has turned to grey,
Many of us have trouble with our hearts,
Our bodies are just begging for new parts,
You cannot be a sissy and be old,
You've got to pack each day with courage bold,
We strive for tomorrow,
We're thankful for today,
World problems are a bore,
We have the answers by the score,
The wind that tickles your face,
Left prints that are easy to trace,
We used the puzzle, I confess,
To nudge you closer this year,
Our goal has been a success,
You all have passed the test, let not one person shed a tear,
For there're prizes and laughs to be given here!

—John Neagu Jr.

Stove Coils

My ruby eye brushes the limestone hands.
Though natural, they do not live.
Chalk of the stone remains on my eyelashes after
you caress my iris.
Immobile and deceiving, you leave nothing with me but dust.
Silent, I wait for ignition.

Your palm blistered, it dares to reach me.
Blue cells deceased and caked under your oval nails,
I promise change while blazing subtle in my blackness.
Tap Tap you test my heat. "One Mississippi," you stall.
You finally surrender your open hand to me.
Sight so evident and painful; the eye is trickery.
Only to touch is to feel.
Imprinting sweetly, I see my mark when reflex takes you away.
Stone flesh is now so divinely altered.

Scarlet pushes through pores and begs wet nourishment.
Fool, you wanted me, fell in love with me,
desired my intrigue.
Drowning the stone painting jeweled with my pupil,
your hand is left pleading in the dish water.

—Heather Dobbins

What Is Love?

Love is a feeling of an indescribable delusion of
thought. If a rose was in full bloom and the dew of
morning had encrusted it's velvet petals,
    would the spirit of love set it's ghost down?
    Crystalline laminations of the night sand, silken water
under the moonlit sky,
could there possibly be anything more enchanting? Visions
of ivory fingertips clutching a fine damask cloak, jewels
of every nature, surly this is love. Thoughts of love
defined near a thimble,
    only what one holds in their own
        heart, is their definition of an
            unexplainable thought.

—Lena Baldasty

Signode

Feelings I know cannot exist
Thoughts that would destroy friendships and trust
but I can't help it
I'm lost in love
As before, it only took a time
spent in secret, having fun
I guess I missed the magic we had
but he's had that magic with others now
I know he's leaving, and I'm happy he smiles
but even as a friend, I'm going to miss that last kiss
we had years ago.
Will it ever come back,
more than just something innocent
Or will I always be in secret,
awaiting a move to be made

—Melissa Kowalski

My Friends

In the halls I see them
those who have been termed
as having no mind
walking with them I listen
as they teach me about
things I have never seen
laughing we turn to their rooms
A nurse puts them to bed, I go on alone
My hand still warm from the loving
touch of them, my friends, my mentors,
those who are the victims of Alzheimers...

—Donna Thompson Gilboy

561

Blue Skies

I look at the sunrise, pushing
through the grey skies, and it reminds
me of the light in your eyes.

And a light never shined so bright,
As the blue skies in your eyes!

Your eyes reflected all that is beautiful,
all that is natural, and all
that is true.
For I found love, as I found you.

You washed away these clouds of grey,
On one memorable day.
Than all I could see is a blue sky,
shining upon you and I!

And a light never shined so bright.
As the blue skies in your eyes!

—*Ralph Matalone*

A Soldier in Normandy

Wandering over the fields of Normandy
  through wood and thicket, hill and dell,
    I see the beauty of the land of Normandy,
      but, my heart aches when I think how many fell!

I can see the heroes that fell in Normandy,
  And their crosses mark along the way
    Comrades of mine I marched with in Normandy.
      Men who should not have died, but lived another day!

For, Oh how blood and hatred has flowed in Normandy!
  Many poor souls have suffered and died,
    Many poor mother, wife or sweetheart has given their only
      one in Normandy.
    Yes, many are they that have so desperately cried!

Then as I wander back across the fields of Normandy, I wonder,
how many more must give their all and life for the pledge of
peace for all the world. Yes, in Normandy I pray God, Peace,
Love, Happiness, and not all this strife! So, I sit and think
in the fields of Normandy. I close my eyes and try to think
it's so, that the war, death and strife are all o'er in
Normandy. That peace, love and happiness are all I know.

—*Arthur E. Nyberg*

Passing Of Time

Bolts of lightning streak the sky.
Thunder drowns a baby's cry.
Rain forms rivers down the street.
Nothing appears to be concrete.
Potential energy increases within the river,
It explodes, small dams holds them never.
Luckily, no homes are in its path,
For it could take them in its wrath.
Morning brings a hint of sun.
The raging storm is almost done.
Pouring rain to a trickle slows.
A boy on his tricycle, his happiness grows.
Blue skies, white clouds seem aloof,
Everyone can come out from under their roof.
The world from here looks beautiful,
Now things will go back to the usual.

—*Mari Yamamoto*

Common Love

You heard my hooves below your window
Thundering impatient on your wooden stoop
You threw open the shutters and looked down
  Smiling, ran to unbolt your door.

Leaving work, I galloped up from the commons
  Thinking of your damask hair
On a stolen horse who flew along the rocky road
  As though he loved you too.

My boots repose upon your Indian carpet
My jerkin and rough breeches sprawl like wanton
  Lovers across your brocaded chair
We, as skeins of wool entangled, upon your bed.

  My shirt is cotton, not of silk
My boots hobnailed like any common laborer's
  I am no dandy, no, but stripped
Naked in your arms I am as rich as any man.

—*A. R. Farrell*

Time

Time goes by so quickly.
Time always ends too soon.
It is always definite,
    that with the ending of time,
    a new time begins.
With the ending of love, despair begins.
With the ending of despair,
    a new time and also a new love, begins.

Learn from the past.
Learn to take time; however, it is measured.
    A little slower,
    A little more precious,
    A little more cautious,
    And a little less seriously.

For no two,
    Measure time,
      in the same way.

—*Kathy Coakley*

Always My Child

  Give your love, but take good care.
  Time is fleeting, often life's unfair.
  And always remember, I'll always be there.

Life can be fun, and you'll always stay young,
If you learn from the start, to follow your heart.

Keep Jesus beside you, to nurture and guide you,
Tho you're out of sight, I'll rest well at night.

  Let your soul dream, chase your moonbeam,
  If your eyes truly see, you'll always be free.

Good friends and family, Christmas and springtime,
  Beauty surrounds you, a walk in the park.

Good cheer and patience, your troubles will fade,
  Enjoy every moment, a nap in the shade.

The birth of your children, each blessing bestowed,
  Be humble and thankful, and help when you can.

  Life's what you make it, not a set destiny,
  Love is a beacon, its light lets you see.

  The future is here, I love you my dear,
  And always remember, I'll always be there.

—*Robert P. Grady, Jr.*

ntitled

I had a name to describe time it would be patience.
me is something we quite don't understand, something that
kes so long but moves so fast.
mething that we quite can't escape, but we
n prolong the enjoyment of the day. Time is a cool summer
ght, a cold winter day, a delightful spring morning.
me is something we must adjust to something we have to love.
me helps us,
me hurts us, time is a beautiful thing. If we don't use
me wisely we will be lost in time; if we use time wisely it
uld benefit us a lifetime.
—*Derrell I. Russell*

Loved You

oved you, in those days, when
me stood still, I loved you, when
 were very small, I loved
u, then you didn't want me at all.
oved you, through the wild an raging
as, I loved you, in the warm
mmer breeze, until the world
ops turning, I'll remember you
n I forget paper promises,
vered by wind swept lies,
 love that we had was better,
en you, said you played from the start
 my heart
oved you, under silk and satin skies,
oved you, when grass grew very tall,
oved you, then you didn't want me at all
oved you, through the storms that love
n bring, I loved you, in the warm summer
eeze, until the world stops turning,
 remember you.
—*Louis Fratto*

A Single Rose"

The symbol of love, without a fear,
s the sweetest flower in which holds no tear.
 someone special for to keep,
 memory of this special deed.

The Rose-A flower like all the rest,
cept of its beauty's best.
 smell this flower is a greatness alone,
t to have this flower is from only Love shown.

'd give a Rose to someone like you,
cause of all of the things that you do.
r when the light glistens in your eyes,
makes my heart sink down inside.

The love of such a feeble me,
set upon a pedestals plea,
fore you notice this Love set pose,
you I'd give a single Rose.
—*Jayson Pagan*

iends

iends are there in the good times
 share the happiness with you
iends are there in the bad times
 share the sorrow with you

iends stick together
ey have to, it's there duty

one is in trouble, or just needs to talk
e other is there

n glad there's friends
en't you?
—*Christa Mattingly*

Thanksgiven....

A very special day has been set aside
    to acknowledge the feelings we always let ride.

Family, friends, plenty of food to consume
    we should all reflect; us in this room.

Our homes, belongings, cars to drive..
    the simple gift of being alive.

At this moment and till next year
    let us all be thankful for what we hold dear.

If every household took the time
    to once a year repeats this rhyme
        we could rid the world of hunger,
            even abolish crime...

So at this moment let us make a pact
    to treat everyone better in deed and act.

Over the year while we are apart
    let us keep this day alive in our heart.

Come next year, all of us among the living...
    can once again recite our "Thanksgiving"...

    For everyone....everywhere,
—*William C. Hebrank*

Saying Goodbye

Saying goodbye to someone you love,
To all your hopes and dreams.
I'm sure you know who I'm thinking of,
I'm sure you know what I mean.

I wish I could find a way out of this game,
And the strength to fight the pain I feel.
Just tell me if you feel the same,
And I'll tell you this pain is real.

I love you more than words can say,
And I really don't want to cry.
I'm sure I will see you again one day,
How can I say good-bye?

Here is something we both may share,
One last kiss to show I care.
—*Amanda Sanchez*

Voice In The Wilderness

My spirit yearns to soar with the eagle and be free,
to be as one with the mother earth, it was the way
of the people.
The body was purified and I sought my journey
into manhood in my youth, the earth mother called to me.
She bade me to find the holy place where no man could
ascend but myself, there, where the mighty eagle perched,
I saw this vision.
The great spirit surrounded me, everything I saw,
and heard, was to come to pass and I was sad.
Change was in the air, the old ways would soon be gone,
I cried for my people but there was no one to hear,
Where have all the warriors gone? Did they go the
way of the buffalo?
My spirit yearns to soar with the eagle and be free,
but I am only a voice in the wilderness, and soon my
voice will never be heard again.
—*Robert P. Campbell*

Loneliness

To be alone, to be lost
To be frightened of silence
The crashing sound of nothingness
Echoing in my ears
My eyes see nothing human, only objects
Familiar but still
My lips want to speak, but to whom?
Words form in my brain never spoken
So much to say, no ear to listen
My heart screams for attention and continues to beat
My bones ache, not from physical pain
No one to hold me to have my limbs put to use
The use of love
My flesh is warm with life no one to embrace
To share my warmth
Death comes as the sun sets for lonely souls
Such as I, sleep!

—*Marie C. Costa*

Untitled

Your hands play across me,
To call forth notes of varied timbre.
Selecting keys,
Your fingers blend with my responses
And I rise to meet with your exquisite touch
To build crescendos
As you lift my notes into the highest ranges—
Soaring now to catch the phrase's peak
As notes explode around me
In glissandos tumbling into tones
Descending into voices trembling
Decrescendos spreading
Into subtle strokes
On whispering keys.
Tenderly,
You sound the closing chords.

A glance, a gentle turn
Of your hand
And the piece begins again...

—*Mary Jean Kindschuh*

Memories of Yesteryear

Today I went to my mother's grave
To call upon memories I have saved...
Of the wintry day we left her here.
I was just thirteen that year.

My mother's grave looks cold.
She's gone where souls never grow old.
She may be gone from my sight
but when I pray, I think of her each night.

There are many things I should have told her...
How much I really loved her.....
How much she meant to me...
And thanks for all she taught me.

Today I go to my mother's grave
To share memories I have saved
As I wipe away the tears
I realize it's been thirteen long years....
Since I heard her say
"I love you" or "Listen to your father"
Mother, I love you.

—*Rebecca K. Furry*

The Addicting Bug

A drug any drug is an addicting bug.
To claim lives of all kinds especially of those with clean minds.

The bug is white and no matter who you are, where you stay
it's up to you to becomes it's prey.

Once it takes a bite you must fight because the bug is out to
claim your life.

-But remember-

The person that's struck by this bug is good

It's not the person it's the drug.

—*Allesa Jones*

Astrology In Action

From the creative forces of the Arien I emerged,
To display the Aquarians incalculable urge.
For which no Capricorn, nor Virgo shall ever submerge,
   Pisces swims the deepest crevices of the Earth,
Although Scorpio may like to quench their passionate thirst,
We watch Sagittarius aim their arrow,
of our goal after birth.
Let no Libra's cups ever turn us around,
Nor Taurus horns cause us to stay on the ground,
While Gemini will form things to satisfy our eye,
In which Leo will never cause us to be denied,
Watch out Cancer your sickness has been denied.

—*Rufus Rockingham, Jr.*

And God Saw Everything That He Had Made,

It was Very Good- But

In the beginning God created light,
To divide the day from the night.
He made the firmament called Heaven in His Sight.
The dry land was gathered in one place to show His might.
The Earth and Seas came together where He wished they would.
Then after the earth brought forth the plant and
the animal of every kind, He saw everything He had
made, and it was very good.
But then...
God made Himself a man, in His Image, from His Own Hand.
He thought when He created him that he would be so grand.
God then said, "It is not good for man to be alone."
So God took a rib from man to make woman and, together,
they became one flesh God and could call His Own.
But the serpent came and woman and then man ate
from the forbidden tree.
Yes, sin entered God's work - the rest is grim history.

—*Joe Cobb, Jr.*

When You Get to Where You're Going

When you get to where you're going though I know you've lots
to do, will you still come quietly to me should I ever need
you?

When you get to where you're going could you help me understand
why God chose to take you now? I'm certain that I must go on,
though I'm not sure how.

When you get to where you're going you'll see the tears I've
cried, tell me honestly will the pain I feel today ever subside?

When you get to where you're going endless sunsets you will
see, when you do remember that I love you and often think of
me.

—*Tresa M. Tulley*

ne Minute and then Gone

must now walk down that long, dark road.
face my fears without you by my side.
lding your hand for protection,
htly through the rain.
ough they may try,
one could take your place.
ll I am glad for the times shared.
ir laughter still remains loudly in my smile.
w I laugh alone.
ughter turned to tears,
nnot be wiped away.
times I find myself,
fting,
nking of you.
ough that cannot bring you back to me.
e minute,
d then gone.
t we still live together in my heart.

—*Jennifer Shadeed*

here and When

what waters do we now turn
find the Titanic's last orations?
lantic,
lian,
have they long since passed,
sen silently, through evaporation?
e've salvaged from your depths, many cups, rings,
tues, and
ld,
wly you're losing ground,
tter take preventative measures,
st you turn into a lonely,
ld,
atery,
ost-town.
y covering your artifacts with kelp,
nd,
e passing of time,
hurn-up",
ke them hard to find".

—*Mike Green*

dy Liberty

and in the midst of the land and sea,
guide your voyage for you to see.
dress is made from the finest silk,
m sturdy with a solid link.
crown and torch stand firm and tall,
m visible and present to all.
hand is stretched with a light,
show you my land, shores and might.
u pass by me and time carries you away,
t, I promise that liberty will stay.
e held the torch for a long time,
u're welcome to share it, just come.
e or two can not stand alone,
gether we're able to endure all.
m a symbol of love for USA,
w faith, and hope for a brighter day.

—*Edward Prodanovic*

Good Friday's Call — On The Cross Or In The Mob

The Prologue: The wife of Pilate dreamed for all
To heed the dream and heed the call.
And every man must keep the tryst
To join the mob or join the Christ.

The Dream: In the uncreated world of sleep
The muted moving specters can
With weird and soundless pictures keep
A wordless rendezvous with man.

The unheard thunder rolling high,
As silently, it shatters dreams,
And lightning forms across the sky
A jagged cross mid muffled screams.

The frenzied wife of Pilate fights
The shadowed specter's mocking stare;
And waking from her terror flights,
She cries in vain for Pilte to beware!

The Epilogue: And every one who hears in vain
Will wash the hands, but keep the stain.
The angry heavens roar, and valleys sob,
And every one is on the cross or in the mob!

—*Harry V. Berg*

"To Understand"

Please I beg of thee,
To help me understand my soulless soul;
To understand what I have been told.
To understand my blackened heart;
To understand a piece of art.
To understand a simple war;
To understand why I've been called a whore.
To understand human feelings;
To understand life's dealings.
To understand the beast that's in all of us;
To understand why it likes to feast on what we lust.
To understand why some relationships depart;
To understand other peoples hearts.
To understand why people hurt with their hands;
To understand what I do not understand.
To understand why life isn't fair;
To understand why the hell you even care.
But thank you for trying to help me understand,
But now it's time for me to go beneath thy precious land.

—*Dorienne Dupaquier*

Him

As he walks on by, I begin to cry.
To him, I am invisible.
Every move he makes, every step he takes,
I watch him.
He does not know he is being followed.

He does not see me, for I am not pretty.
I am just another girl.
My love for him grows, he just doesn't know,
how much he means to me.

I see him in my dreams, I feel him in my heart.
Without him, I just tear apart.
To be near him is great, not to see him I hate.
I think of him everyday, I just can't seem to get away,
from the love and hurt I feel for him.

I cannot talk to him, for neither he nor I can speak.
I want to reach out for him, but I can't. For he cannot see me.

What do I do? What do I do? What do I say? What do I say?
The thoughts keep racing through me.

I wish so much for him to see me, to talk to me.
I only hope that one day soon, he will notice me.

—*Neria Jester*

"The Heavens"

The sun rises early in the morning,
to join up with the sky.
As I look up into the clouds
I think what an exquisite sight.
When I see the heavens I think about
good times. I think about romantic times
and how beautiful the heavens are.
To some it means nothing and to others
it's a mystical land from afar.
When I look up in the sky I am
overwhelmed with the mystery
of it all, because it can be
anything you want it to be
and it is also extremely beautiful.

—*Angel K. Black*

What My Mother Means To Me

Mother is a precious word to me, and I'd like the whole world
to know and see, what my mother means to me. She is so full of
kindness that she never seems to see all my faults or
blindness. Whenever I'm down and blue, I always know just what
to do. I can always call my Mother and somehow or other, my
blues just seem to disappear because of my mothers always open
ear. She is my confidant, teacher and friend and on her my
life depends. She always has an outstretched hand and seems to
always understand. We've had our ups and downs just like any
mother and daughter, but one thing is certain,
we all need love and just knowing that someone cares, and holds
me close in their thoughts and prayers, this is an experience
that every mother and daughter should share. And so I say to
you, Mother, with all my heart, thanks for your love and such a
good start. Thanks for teaching me compassion for other people
and how to love with my heart. With these words from my heart
I hope all the world can see, just what my Mother means to me.

—*Pat Gilbert*

Older And Wiser

In this great art of living —
To know how to grow old
Is the masterwork of wisdom.
Yes, difficult time, be ready, be bold.

We have covered so many years
At school, at work, at play,
As youth, friend, lover, maybe parenthood —
Continued growth, survival, no dismay.

When life ceases — 'tis our finest hour.
Plan for it, work for it now.
Realize your years of work and toil.
We have grown — we know how!

In all the gamut of human relations —
All kinds of stories about old age —
Rumors, lies, trials, pain and fears.
Let's rebel, fight back. Be a Sage!

—*Eugene McKnight*

Things Once Important

After you've stood at death's door,
Things once important, are no more.
A calm within, a peace you find
Has replaced frustrations of the daily grind.
Simple things now delight
The sunrise in the morning, the stars at night.
A gentle breeze that stirs the air,
The sun shining silver on a loved one's hair.
A smile, a sigh, a loving touch,
Once taken for granted, now mean so much.

—*Robbie Read*

Friendship

Friendship is something for me to
to lean on.
It's there when I need to cry.
I can always call friendship on the phone.
I always know that friendship will
be there for me.
Do you know who friendship is?
Well, it's two people who share secrets,
it's two people who know each other well
If you haven't guessed it's something we share
It's the friendship we have between
you and me.

—*May Lee*

Miracles

I lift my soul, and open my heart,
To less common things, not the mundane,
The universe flows with me as its part,
Through rivers and forests, waxing and wane.

Something is different, eerie, so swell,
Noise becomes music, life sings out loud,
I sense God's presence, heaven rings its bell,
Miracles come forth, shining and proud.

Just a shift in my glance, my thinking, my ways,
Assisted by nature from a blade in the grass,
I can see the beauty and sacred all days,
But the miracle too must come to pass.

—*Stephen Rapaski*

Helen

Although I know it can't be right
To love a girl I think I might
It's hard to say you'll stay away
When you know full well you'll be back that day.
My weakness seems to be myself
I can't control it, I'm like a shelf
She puts me on with just one look
And then to her I'm an open book
Tis true I love her I know not why
Perhaps her body caught my eye?
But shallow I can never be so
I say it's love can't you see?
There's naught I want from her, although
One look at her set's me aglow.
I long for her and pray to God
That I alone hold the winning card.

—*Art Berg*

Hunting

The cool night air soft and sweet
to my soul, blows on silently.
Peeking moon dust shadows lurk
in the heavens.
Stillness interrupted to let
a night hawk stretch its wings
and nestle again in its nest
crowded with piercing eyes.
We yawn awhile longer
together watching this wonderland unfold,
wondering about its secrets
as the night grows colder
and silence conquers
the fear of the unknown.
Predators never rest.
Sleepless walkers stalking
its prey
away
and at home.

—*John William Jenkins*

ne for Me

athleen My child, oh precious Kathleen
Me you are a true beauty queen
love you more than you could understand
eyond comprehension—you in My hand

ou deserve more than the very best
I love you equally with all the rest
have looked upon your heart so pure
love you—you need to know for sure

our faith has grown—yes so very far
ke all of My children you are a star
owing up to be a child of Mine through scripture & seeking
ly eyes upon you are more than just peeking

have let you know by giving special gifts to you
l you did is show Me you love Me—oh how you do
ith your innocence I look upon you so fine
u truly are a lovely child of Mine

hen I asked you what you wanted to do your life through
write is what you wanted and are gifted to do
r Me especially to all glory unto Me you do just that
aring with encouragement to others is where it is at

—*Kathleen Bergquist*

nal Realm

A spoken word brought forth light,
To merge the existence of forms of life.
From the Master's hand and from the earth,
came the body of man at first.

We know it's true, but some fail to believe.
ow things came about with such miraculous ease.
A word brought life, and can
bring forth death.
Choose today on how you'll rest
petition the soul to search far and wide,
to humble yourself before our God. At
the time when judgement is set forth,
I pray that you hear, "come in my child
and sit right here."

—*David Sappington*

Jenn"

ver fresh on my mind!
one, the vapor of mustard gas;
another, the sad scent of a fading blossom.
er memory is a demon of a kind.

ru mind and soul I sing out!
one, the constant scrutiny of a sentry;
another, the deplorable emanations of hate and hope.
er return to me I truly doubt.

early, I rise to the new mourn.
ere is! The intense longing for life to end;
ere is! The muffled sound of what was a beating heart
Jenn! How could you dismiss my love so sworn?

e troubadours of the air twitter for their mates to come;
e sight of squirrels in their season is a pleasure to some;
ith fins clasped, the fishes of the sea roll out with the tide;
nd, in the market place, husbands and wives are by each
her's side.

—*Michael Schmalberger*

A Mother's Dream

All a mother can do is her best
to raise and love her children.
But in order for a mother to do her best
she needs her children's love and cooperation.
How's a mother suppose to love her children
if the children doesn't love her and let her love them.

A mother can only hope and pray her child is safe
when she's not around to watch them.
A mother has a lot of dreams for her children
but the most important thing to a mother is to
see her dreams for her children come true.

The most important dream a child could make come true is...
to graduate from high school and make something happen in
their life... but the only one that can make this dream
come true is the children, themselves.

The only dream a mother wishes to come true
is to see her children succeed in everything
they do and to receive their high school diploma.

—*Mandy Kerbs*

The Sounds Of Winter

From mountain streams, to winter snow,
To rare places where blue moss grows.
Where summer meets, and says goodbye,
And frosty winter fills the sky.

When all but fox and raccoons stay,
And winter wind blows leaves away.
When limbs break off, all dead and gray,
Only children come out to play.

All doors are shut, all windows closed,
And from the ground a tree arose.
It seemed to dance, and sing a song,
Then start bushes sing along.

The grass grows sweet, below the snow,
But only insects hear it grow.

The voice of the frosty, blowing wind,
Seems to be a message someone sends.
Take the time right here, right now,
Listen to the sounds of winter,
So young and loud.

—*Alisha Burns*

This Day

This day is one I will never forget. So many memories but none
to regret. The ride to the church was short but seemed so
long. I just can't believe that she is really gone. Then
almost as if in review I went to open the door; so she could
get out too. Instantly I realized it was only me. This is the
way from now on it would be. This day as I walked through
these door's as old as a century. Everyone turned to look as I
made my entry. My heart seemed to be beating so very loud. As
I looked out across at all the somber faces in the crowd. Ever
so slowly I approached the casket so shiny and gray. I would
never ever, forget this day. Looking down on her beautiful
face. I knew no one would ever take her place. All was silent
not one soul would speak as a single tear ran down my cheek. I
bent to kiss her crimson lips so cold. Her hands gently lay
across her. I would never hold. I just could not pull myself
away. There was one more thing i just had to say. As I gently
pulled her raven hair from her ear. I softly whispered I love
you my darling angel dear. This day finally ended and came to
a close. In my heart she will always be and I am sure that she
knows

—*Ashley Falon Winthrop*

Union

When spirits emerge from temporal seas
To ride the wings of Halcyon's breeze,
Narcissus fends the gaze adored
To behold a union of beauty more.

Indolent whispers lead willows to sigh
As silver diamonds fall from the sky.
Cool rivers swell with serenity,
O'erflowing on fields of tranquility.

Nebulous butterflies flutter above,
Bathing the air in pearls of love.
A gold lotus blossoms and slowly drips
Seeds of rapture into our lips.

The arrogant sun, arrayed in white,
Gives birth to a rainbow—painting the light.
The ominous heralds then close their eyes
And gently echo from our lives.

—*Mikel Wilson*

In Love

I want to learn to give to you the joy you've given me.
To search and find the best of life
within your company.

For sometimes though we argue,
and sometimes disagree,
there's no one that I'd rather have
than you so near to me.

Now there are times when you deserve
much more than I can give.
But I just want to share with you the ways two ought to live.

You've given me the best of times and never let me fall.
You held me when I hated life.
And loved me through it all.

You've stood beside me even when
you should have walked away.
Some days I know it seemed like hell.
And yet you chose to stay.

So we've begun this journey with two lovers hearts entwined.
And when I close my eyes each night,
you're all my heart can find.

—*James K. Hicklin*

The March of the Hermit Crabs in the Rain

How wonderful, yet how strange,
to see hermit crabs marching in the rain.
For months they've lived beneath the rocks
waiting for the sound of those wondrous drops.
Then suddenly from under their covers they proceed
with a hermit crab in a whelk shell firmly in lead
and thousands more following.
Their destination no one can tell;
it seems they only want to get wet and display their shells
that they found washed upon the shore
along with the seaweed and driftwood which they simply ignore.
Though to some hermit crabs
finding a shell that fits isn't always that easy in life;
sometimes one has to settle for a perfume bottle cap or an
old clay pipe.
But what does it matter
To hermit crabs it's all the same-
they only want a chance to march in the rain.

—*Ashley Saunders*

Thinking of You

As I think of the wreck and how awful it was,
To see you lying there covered in blood,
It was all my fault cause I let you drive,
I knew you were drunk but I just gave it one try,
I thought you would make it cause you were almost sober,
I should have thought twice cause now your life is over,
As I think of you and I remember the past,
All we did together and why it didn't last,
We had so much in common we had so much to share,
I shed a few tears as I see you lying there,
As I stand by your grave with nothing to say,
The thought goes through my mind that this is your last day,
I miss you so much, I loved you so dear, all
    I can say is I wish you were here.

—*Amber Jefferies*

Portraits

In my search for a woman to join as my wife,
To share with my dreams, my hopes, my life
I painted a picture of what I might find-
It was a woman who's special, who's pretty, and kind.
I painted a woman with eyes so sincere,
Mysterious, yet innocent, with no room for tears.
I painted a woman with a breathtaking smile,
Compassionate, confident, reflecting her style.
I painted a woman with hair silky smooth.
Stunning, arousing, yet able to sooth.
I painted a woman fit to be queen-
Elegant and graceful, with beauty unseen.
But this girl has beauty both inside and out.
With a mind that knows all, excepting a doubt.
When the painting was finished and starting to dry
I took a step back gazing into her eyes.
Who is this woman? Such a familiar look.
Where have I seen her - a movie? A book?
I sat and I marveled, is it just deja vues?
It was then that I realized; it's a painting of you.

—*Michael D. Leedberg*

Reason

The strongest hate is held within:
To take the souls beneath your skin

I am the blood from the knife:
Who had decided to take an innocent life

I am the shadow of your best friend's face:
I am the time when it takes place

I am the whisper of your cry:
I am the pain when you die

I am the tear dripping down your face:
You're the one who is a disgrace...

—*Maria Fotakis*

"The Oldest Child"

My "oldest child" is the most trouble by far,
Though he is big and can even drive a car.
He can't find his clothes, there's nothing to eat;
Trim his hair right now, he must look neat!

Is his coffee done, where are his keys?
He's late! Gas up the car for him, please!?
Important dates he can never recall,
Makes me wonder how he survives at all!

The foods he will eat are numbered and few,
His mouth clamps tight when served something new!
His nerves are shot, his hearing is bad
It's hard to believe, this one is called "Dad"!

—*Lynette Richards*

Pink And Blue Make Purple'

The radiator still leaking, soiled drops and another chip fails
to the sill
Wallpaper peeling off a hole in the wall and sirens in the air
buzzing like flies, rousing me from some forgotten dream
only four, his eyes innocently creased beneath a lipstick
stained forehead, resting in perfect sleep
his mouth half open in simple blithe and a few odd strands
of hair stuck against the smear of chocolate, as he wakes
later he says, "look mommy pink and blue make purple"
softly I reply, "that's right, sweetheart,"
outside children hopscotch past the graffiti like dancers,
the graffiti seems to have a voice
like oz it commands, gangs declare hunting season,
dealers poaching for younger minds
gobbling up this urban wilderness, symbiotically like bees
to the flower
I reach down and hold my boy, squeezing so tightly he
asks, "What's the matter, Mommy"?
I close my eyes, as if doing so night transport us,
and I answer, "Nothing honey."

—*Laura Ticomb*

My Private Theater

I often look up in the summer sky
To watch the changing clouds march by

The forms and shapes that are there to see
Are a welcomed relief from watching TV

The scenes change constantly, commercial free
And the show goes on as if just made for me

There are countless pictures to view on my own
People, animals and creatures unknown

I've seen Washington, Lincoln, my dog and my cat
And even John Wayne with his old cowboy hat

Is refreshing to see things not in the news
I can make of the clouds whatever I choose

I can be sure of one thing as I gaze on high
I won't see old reruns up there in Gods sky

—*Rudy Comtois*

Castles In The Sand

A boy builds castles in the sand
To watch the wind blow them away
Once two lovers walked hand in hand
Through a garden one summer day

Like the bird that refused to land
The wings grow tired, the mind astray
With no-more music, no more band
The flowers died, when you went away

So if you're walking hand in hand
With some new love, try and understand
That if you pass a boy on a beach someday
Those castles have crumbled and withered away
And if it should bring a tear to your eye
Wipe it away, so you don't start to cry
Cause hon, all that was, was only a dream
It was never really there it's just the way that
it seemed I came to you in your sleep one night
Hoping to bring happiness into your life but in that
failed, as I did in song but I've learned to love
And the dream goes on

—*Bob Rosenick*

Freeway Of Justice

My friends
Today is the day
To build the way
For a better tomorrow
It's not a time for sorrow
It's time to create a brighter tomorrow

Together we'll build a freeway of justice and dignity
A better way, a better life for you and for me
Freeway of justice and equality
Freeway of justice and dignity

It's time to come together
As a people, as a nation
It's time to stop prejudice and discrimination
It's time to stand up for your rights
It's time to see the lights
Shining on the freeway
Our freeway of justice and equality
A new life for you and for me.

—*Alfredo J. Baptista*

The First Time

Today became the first day of the best day of my life.
Today is the first day I met you! My journey has
seem like a life time. My hurt was deeper than losing
Faith. My hope had become my very existence, living
had ceased for me, disappointment had become my best
friend. My soul created a new definition, because
my belief had diminished; my hope had all but vanished.
Thank you for coming into my life. Thank you for touching
what's left of my hollow cold heart.

Today became the first day of the best day of my life.
Today is the first day I met you! Please: live out the
rest of your life with me. Let me adore you. Let me always
be the lady of your life. Accept my apology,
my love. Forgive me for giving up on us. Or should I
say the dream of us. Doubting I would find you somehow.
It was only because I've waited for you much too
long. Thank you for my brand new heart: brand new hope:
and the brand new me.

—*Mary L. Wright*

Untitled

Yesterday I had a head full of dreams
today it's empty
Yesterday I thought I could succeed
today I don't.
Yesterday I was full of love.
Today I'm filled with loneliness and hate.
Yesterday my eyes were filled with joy.
Today they're filled with tears.
Yesterday I was flying high
Today I fell.
Yesterday I had an opportunity, today I have nothing
Yesterday I knew where I was going.
Today I'm lost.
Yesterday I had a future.
Today I have none.
Yesterday I wanted to live, today I want to die.
Yesterday I blamed everyone else.
Today I blame myself.

—*Donna Miller*

Untitled

What is an artist, if not a poet.
Together, they build illusions, of dreams.
Side by side, they fight,
for clarity and peace.
Yet turmoil and despair, always,
interfering and controlling.
Self-pity.
Shame.
Vision.
Working for awhile
to seek a better world,
for one man or a thousand.
The visions become blurred,
yet transparent in meaning,
Never quite understood,
not even by the creator,
whose mind searches desperately,
to understand, what is.
What has been.
What will be ...

—*Donna L. Conover*

Thanksgiving Get Away Feast!!

Picky pilgrims pen Tom Turkey down.
Tom Turkey gets away to eat Cranky Cranberries.
Fighting Food doesn't want to be eaten.
Tom Turkey wants some fighting fun.
The Picky Pilgrims want Tom Turkey to be their food,
because Fighting Food doesn't want to be eaten.
Tom Turkey is too fast for the Picky Pilgrims,
So the Picky Pilgrims will never catch him.

—*Melinda Rochester*

Dark Crying

As she lies herself to sleep will she cry
tonight, will she think of the things that
have been said and done to you.

To much dark crying in the eyes of the young
turn a TV and a killings going on
violence has taken it's place in society
victory at war, is what the man preaches

Will we ever see it thru their eyes
will we ever wake up
can't we see the pain or will we turn our heads.

Little child, were the ones that are suppose to
protect you.
all we can say, were sorry
and hope tomorrow will be your day

Have we poisoned you love,
is there hate in your heart,
could we have been so wrong,
to make this your world.

—*David Castaneda*

September Rain

As the leaves turn to many beautiful colors,
The sky slowly darkens as the clouds cover the bright,
burning sun.
That not so long before had been shining upon me.
When I look into the darkened sky,
I see what was once joy.
Has now turned to sorrow.
Suddenly there is a light, cool feeling,
That now seems better than the sun.
There is no longer pain.
But the refreshing feeling of
September Rain.

—*Bambi Pantore*

Heaven?

A far off place appearing only in dreams
Too far to reach is the way it seems
It reaches out to me with a welcoming glance
What I would give for a momentary chance
To experience the peace that only it holds
Away from the violence, the prejudice, the cold
Our world is contrary to this
Peace only lingers and then is dismissed
Where on earth is a place - filled with love?
Can I find it or is it the place up above?
Sometimes I envision that whimsical place
Will I be lost in the crowd without a trace?
Fear is an emotion this topic arouses
Will I live on a cloud or do they build houses?
Will my life here on earth account for anything at all?
Will I ascend or will I fall?
My wishes are few but of one I am sure
I long to live on and experience much more.

—*Danielle DeFeo*

All the Way to the Top

You can get off on any floor she was told; or you can go to the
top if you dare to be bold these words of wisdom spoken to her
with love; words with a promise from God up above angry,
frightened and on her way down; but God saw her beauty and his
love did abound He gave her a message to share each day; a
promise of freedom and life a new way a way to live sanely,
happy and free; a message she carries for you and for me with
boldness she shares her experience, strength and hope; with
these twelve steps and God, you too can cope from the white
house to my house, from the mountains to the plains; She tells
about this way of life with freedom from pains this message of
hope she willingly shares; to all who will listen because she
truly cares I am so very grateful she didn't stop; so very
grateful she went to the top for you see, I am one of those she
cared for so much; to share with me her message and her kind
gentle touch

—*Barbara Lassiter*

A Broken Vessel

A vessel of honor fell to the floor one day
Torn and jagged were its edges splintered pieces of clay
And as it shattered to the ground all around it could be heard
An agony of regret and sorrow, pity, was its last word
A vessel crushed by its own solid weight
Has lost all its contents, form and shape
And I couldn't help but wonder as it fell upon my floor
Could this vessel be again of use? Or is it lost forevermore?
So I took this broken vessel and placed it on the shelf
And glued the splintered pieces arranging them myself
And my thoughts were turned upon the Lord
And how He did the same
By sending us His only son and placing on him, our shame
He took the broken vessel on Calvary our sins forgave
And washed away all our sins, and now today we're saved

—*Elizabeth McRae*

Opened Eyes

Open your soul and see the world
We are all allusions that are furled
into each others' minds without a cause
Only to please and hope to belong
And here I ask the question "why?"
We are making ourselves slaves in society's eye
If only one could ever see
The ultimate possession that will ever be
Is to find one's true self
And let it free.

—*Lynna Hanes*

Prayer

ith soul bared, I stand before you Lord
embling, wordless, pleading for your mercy
ot asking for praise nor special reward
nowing that you love and understand me
y soul unfettered and unchained at last.
ill be free to love you as you love me
l other things are in the distant past
ach me your paths; what you want me to be
accept the joy and the peace that you give
e contentment my soul is seeking now
my Lord, show me the way I must live
use the gift that you alone endow
e love of life and all that it means to me
live it well until Eternity.

—*Patricia M. Ziolkowski*

rousers of Red

ousers of red, a curly head
y fast asleep at the saviour's feet.
nds 'neath his face, smiling in grace
heart filled with love, a faith strong and sweet.

e mailman rang our doorbell this morning.
y son, laughing and barefoot, came running.
e mailman said, "see what I have brought you.
ese trousers of red specially for you."

eard laughter and a shout of joy,
soft "God Bless You", from my little boy.
me came for bed, he nodded his head,
ld his gift tight and said "goodnight".
ortly I came to tuck him in,
t found instead, an empty bed.

ftly, snowflakes covered an endless search,
I humbly entered the village church.
ere fast asleep on the manger hay was my little curly head
d across the saviour's feet lay
y son's new trousers, trousers of red.

—*Sue Burns*

lieve In Me

lieve in me - for I believe in you...
ust in me - as I place my trust in you.
alk with me - as I walk proudly beside you.
t, most of all -
Love me as I love you.. rain or shine..
For our rainbow is just over the horizon
e day at a time - with no guarantees for tomorrow.
ch one fuller than the one before -
ch one like its the most important one of our lifetime.
ach out to me - let me take your hand -
ad me - as I confidently follow you...ever proud and unafraid
uch me - with the gentle understanding only you have...
rgive me - when I've erred unintentionally...
are with me - let me learn and grow, as I glow
from listening and watching.
ugh with me - as the "clowns" that we enjoy sharing...
nture with me - for who knows what's over the next horizon?
Believe in me...

—*Dianne C. Dodgen*

Compelled

Compelled by truth, yes, compelled by this
truth that we so graciously share. The
truth that's composed of our inner most
desires in time to be displayed upon the
walls of our heart.

Compelled to review the past to somehow predict
the future. Compelled to eliminate the
slightest doubt or annoying fear that we
may be ever so near. Compelled to understand
the transition. The transition that moved us from
from yesterdays acquaintances onto lovers lane.
Inhibited by romance and fulfilling desires.

Compelled by time to learn of you and you
of me. In looking back at it all, we were
compelled by our actions to become one.

—*Kelly James Kelly*

Missing You

I lie in my room lonely and scared.
Trying to remember the good times we shared.
We used to go to movies, basketball games,
or just stay home talking.
Now all I do is sit in my chair
and start rocking.

I think of you when I pray at night.
I think of tough times all we did was fight.
Maybe someday my life will go on.
That will be the day,
I'll accept that you're really gone.

—*Maren Morrow*

"Poets"

What induces a Poet to write on a spur of a moment or in the twilight
Is it an expression of a thought then, or was it something
that might have been
Is it grief - a sadness one must convey for one's heart is
breaking this day?

Is it the beauty of seeing the sun rise and the bluest of morning skies
It is as night begins to fall and one is amazed at natures call
Blessing all the great wonderment of all that God has sent

Is it love of a dear friend and the joys of it without an end
Or the throbbing of your heart when your sweetheart does part
What inspires one to put into words all the aches and joys felt
and heard?

When other talents lend to another trend; a poet must pick up a pen
To let others know how we feel; as in saying prayers, as we
kneel God blessed us one and all; and created poets for Its
Recall!

—*Georgette M. Innes*

Two Loves

The inextinguishable fire radiantly burning within
The seemingly timeless admirations shared with another
The unending need growing from the heart
The perfect dream unbroken and shatterproof

The unending verbal battles with cannons causing unhealable
wounds
The loud thunder storms making it difficult to sleep
The painful nightmares and daydreams scaring and hurting
The knife sinking deep through the flesh

—*John Holownia*

Wisdom

As I sometimes sit and ponder 'bout things that I've been told,
Two things I find I treasure much more than jeweler's gold.
One's the innocence of children as they watch their lives unfold,
The other is the wisdom and the kindness of the old.

Education and wisdom is to never be confused.
I've known wise men who knew no school and educated fools.
There's wisdom in the way they live, at peace with God and man-
Examples as they offer prayers, with folded work-worn hands.

Hands that toiled when times were hard and stroked a fevered
   child.
A helping hand to those in need and a friendly, loving smile.
Lessons from examples, not just written in a book.
Wisdom from the life they've lived and chances that they took.

As I sit here quietly thinking, I see faces from the past
Of those who've gone to heaven's shores and questions I have
   asked
Of God, when one we loved so much and why their lives should
   end,
He told me, "Son, their lives don't end you see it now begins."
   —*Dan Willis*

Forever Twenty-two

(In loving memory of my son, Paul Fusco)
   Two years ago, time stood still leaving you forever
twenty-two, for reasons we will never know. The joy we
felt on the day you were born, we will never know
again. The pain we felt on the day you died, we will
always hold within.

   We remember with happiness, the first time you
laughed, the first time you walked and the first time
you talked. We remember with sadness the last time we
laughed with you, the last time we walked with you and
the last time we talked with you.

   The day you were born, we took it for granted, you
would be with us until the end of our days. Twenty-five
years later, we place a flower upon your grave and walk
away lost in memories of yesterday. Happy Birthday
baby, you would have been twenty-five years old today.
   —*Diane Fusco*

Family - God's Creation

   Then GOD created family, He did it in love
   unconditional, undying, everlasting love

      The love He gave was to carry on
   from family to family for generations to come

   Because GOD said man should not be alone,
   He began with Adam and the family was born

   The family is so precious it can't be replaced
      the family structure is society's base

      Today, with so many families in trouble
   we need to love, support, and encourage each other

   We must strive to keep our families together
      loving each other to make the world better

   We should never forget the reason we're here
      The love of GOD has made it clear

      We must remember GOD's plan...
   to endow His love into the family of man

   Remember our children, GOD's gift to us
   Remember our parents, GOD's loan to us

      Remember the family and our home
and never forget GOD...for He promised we'd never be alone
   —*Nadine Flowers*

Untitled

They look at you with pleading eyes, as they try to
understand the reasons why.
The ones they love, hit them and scream and at night they
have bad dreams.
Their world is full of confusion, the one of their elders
is just an illusion.
They try so hard to make you proud, just to be ignored
and tossed around.
They know not of their parents worries, but it always seems
that their in a hurry.
Now that I think of all this, I've got to reach down and
give them both a kiss.
For if they were not here, for me to give a hug, I wouldn't
know the feeling of being loved.
   —*Bill N. Scott*

The Figure

My life has always been depressing
   Until you walked through that door.
Your figure etched in my mind forever, as
I dream about what we would look like
   together.
I always hope for just one glance to
   Know that you know that I'm alive.
Your voice washes over me like waves
   licking the shore.
With everything I've seen there will
   probably never be a we.
Then that day you looked my way
   and smiled.
Then I knew that you were just a
   figure in my mind.
   —*Leslie Couch*

Unlived (For My Brother)

Millionaire cologne
   unused
sitting on the dresser top
amidst trinkets and jewelry
   mementos of a life
waiting to go on.
A file of resumes on your desk
   a pile of books beneath your bed —
   all unread.
Sweaters and shirts hang in your closet
A new wool coat wrapped in cellophane still.
Souvenir mugs and posters, letters unopened
   All evidence of a life stopped
   mid-dream
   —*Dorothy S. Kimes*

Promises

The 1st time it happened I tried to push the whole incident
to the back of my mind and just let it be.
He promised me it would never happen again by round #3.
I began to run and hide from myself,
Blaming a bruise above my eye on a old ragged shelf.
After every round he'd tell me he loved me over and over again.
That should of been my cue to get out and leave him then.
But he promised he wouldn't let it happen any more.
Broke my rib cage by round #4.
I was abused so much till I could no longer find the tears to cry.
I was hardly recognized by round #5.
Round #6 came, then round #7, Buried my body on May 11th.
A part of me is glad that I never got to see round #8.
The other part just wishes I would of got out before it was
all too late.
   —*Danielle Twymon*

ay It Like It Is...

fe is like a wheel
Up and down it goes
Rippling to the ground and towering to the skies
et, with all its ups and downs
There is still joy you'll find
In every step of the way, in every crowded alleyway....
appiness seem to vanish
With long hard working days
ut, when you find true people, the very inner wish of peace
Comes to your senses with your breath, as waves from
The ocean breeze....
fe seem to only be at rest....
When you are down and fast asleep
When dreams go far the endless mist, of your subconscious
Mind in peace....
en come the real realities....
The life that we all have to face. No matter what will
happen next. The quest will go on to its hilt. Thinking,
minding what the outcome is, and life goes on, to say the
least, life in all sense is like it is.

—Maria Elisa H. Mirano

y Iron Worker

y Iron worker, he's big and strong,
everyday just before dawn.
uiet and thoughtful not to wake us up,
needs that first cup.

hen he thinks of today, I've heard him say,
Help me Lord get through this day."
ae sun will be hot maybe 100 degrees,
e rebar burning his shoulders and knees.

hen he gets home from this day, his arms cut from wire his
gs are bruised, his back hurts and he's sunburnt too,
st another day towards payday.

me jobs are long, and far away,
me are close but they don't stay.
hen the rains come the work goes away,
e pray together for another payday.

e tells our son as he takes off his tools,
Don't be a fool, stay in school.
ay out of the iron pile if you can,
t into computers and stay a young man."

—Denice Howard

ttle Miss Molly

to the wind into the pain
o in the ice, down in the flame
ttle Miss Molly enjoying her pain
ttle Miss Molly a girl of 15
ent to get milk from the utters of heifers,
ace in the barn she found Josh the Farmhand's
ilk was sweeter than that of a cow.
is day it was Molly who squealed not the pigs,
veet little Molly buried in cream,
sh was her king and master supreme
as poor Molly shall squeal much more today,
into the barn came Claud and the rays
ey shredded poor Josh and Molly got creamed
is cream was fowl and bitter
rst came Claud, then Bill and on and on until she was ill
or Little Molly, she got her fill of cream of the dill
or Little Molly she squeals no more,
ow she is loved by worms and mice
or Little Molly was put on ice

—Joseph Foti

Who Is My Father?

Starlight, leave your mark
Upon my wearied brow,
Your sparkle in my eyes...
A fiery sword,
Brandished by some unknown demon, yet,
Phantom airship in the skies?

Universe, your vastness
Tumbles through my mind,
As sand would, through a clockwork,
Of cogs and gears, 'til...
Ground to a halt,
I stop, and wonder if I dare
To ponder all your "who's" and "where's."

Many unknown faces
Have passed-on, with their convictions...
How are we to, surely, know their errs?
I do not know your "what's and "why's"...
As I've never seen a dead man cry...
I know nothing surely, not even your "when's"...
But, perhaps, I just am not meant to.

—Lowell Howe

The Year 2000

As we look into the future, what will the year 2000 bring? Let
us contemplate for a moment, for this is a serious thing. Will
we have one united world, a world with liberty and justice for
all? Or will there be endless war between nations, as the
tyranny of man makes them fall? Will the year 2000 bring love
and peace, with mankind living in one accord? We must strive
now to work for unity, to lose our liberty we cannot afford.
If we start now, we can change the future by having respect for
what we have today. We can make a difference in our world, but
there is a price we must pay. Every person living on this
earth, no matter what their age, must realize how precious
life is, from the tiniest baby to the oldest sage. We must
begin now to respect each other, regardless of culture, customs
or creed, otherwise planet earth will self-destruct because of
mankind's ruthless greed. Let us agree to work together
to make this world a better place, as we join our hands
and hearts together with men and women of every race.
Let us look to God Almighty for His guidance never to
cease, and we can be assured that the year 2000 will
bring abundant, life-giving peace.

—Sharon Wiley

Forever in the Wind

Zeke, Joe and every lost brother: somehow you were taken from
us one way or another. On your scoots you were lost in the
wind, and now the pain in our hearts will never end. On this
loss, we must not dwell, tho to think of you gone hurts like
hell! Whenever we ride, we feel you there, and this makes
losing you easier to bare... As the pack pulls out, you're
out in the lead, to try and catch you there is no need... For
the road you travel is that harley highway, and many bro's
have taken it before you were lost that day... This road is
one-way... and it goes on forever, and now that you're on it...
you will ride alone, never! For there along side you, riding
four abreast, is every downed brother, we have laid to rest...
Together you ride with this chosen few, together you've formed
a brotherhood — and paid the price that was due!!! You have
now joined a club — the eternal riders — are they, so you are
no longer lost — together, you have found your way... So ride
this run in peace our bro's, and someday we may join you, when
—no one knows. So ride on eternal riders, your journey has no
end, now you are free and — forever, in the wind...

—Nevada L. Fuller

Untitled

Old man, you stand on the corner...forlorn...tragic,
Waiting for something that will never happen....
For someone who will never appear.
You observe that pavement beneath your dusty black shoes
She used to tell you that your black shoes and green pants
and brown overcoat didn't match....remember?
Remember that people call you an "old drunk,"
And if one can be intoxicated with stale grief,
then you are indeed an "old drunk."

But you regain reality, and again you gaze at the sidewalk,
Pathetic and hard, a gray face etched with lines and cracks,
As though the concrete face were a mirror
Bearing the reflection of its beholder.
You try to look away, but that simple movement is no longer
possible. Your neck and head are bowed fervently...forever
In the constant prayer that one day
The concrete mirror's reflections will change and have life
again. Old man, you stand on the corner...forlorn..tragic,
Waiting for something that will never happen...
For someone who will never appear.

—*Lori Heger*

Coming To Life

I'm a child of the night - a lunar alien
   Waiting for the sun to drop over the edge
   And a madonna moon to appear
   Evening's purple elevator rises to my level
   Invites me in and sends me soaring
   Neons wink love darts into my eyes
   Traffic light sequins and heavenly stars
   Light up the windows of my dreams
I'm a child of the night - a wide-eyed owl
   Front doors fly open spewing brief
   Golden patterns onto grey concrete
   Uptown, downtown, Maitre D's bow diners
   To white linen and red roses where
   Chandelier crystals dance on goblets
   Filled with biting bubbles
   Theaters throw wide their doors in welcome embrace
   Spotlights kiss darkened stages
   The show begins and all the while
   A mysterious pulse echoes my own
I'm a child of the night - a guest at the party

—*Ceil Cannarella*

Kitty

Time goes by. Wonder what things are going on.
Waiting to get out. Out into the world is where I want to be.
Some were beautiful. Here every thing is dark and cloudy.
In my mind I see gorgeous sights.
I see flowers of red, yellow, and pink.
The bright sun and blue sky.
Inside I feel something. Could it be love.
Love from whom? It's so dark and I'm so alone.
Feeling something. Feels, feels soft.
Oh so warm it is. I can feel it breath, it purrs.
A little kitty. I'm no longer alone.
I now have some one to care for me.
As I will care for it.
I no longer have to wait and wonder.
I, I, I am as free as a bird. Flying all over the world.
Seeing everything. Now that I have love.

—*LaRonda Millord*

This is the Awakening of a Not Quite Man

Struggles to life
Wakes to no light
And birds silent; aches
From having slept on the couch.

TV still on
Flickered all night
On the outskirts of dream
Like longing for a not quite
Forgotten girl.
In dim hours apocalyptic,
This is the awakening of
A not quite man who

Struggles to life
Packs a lunch
And crumbles into craggy dawn.
TV still on,
Like a girl not quite forgotten.
Very much perhaps
Like a single light
Left quite still on.

—*Nathaniel Haakinson*

Untitled

Enter innocent one, take my hand, hand of a child, child of...
Walk through my labyrinth and begin to feel me, the pain, the
agony alone I am, alone I have lived, alone forever I shall be.
And the past whispered "turn and run" but my new joy kept me
there. So deeper the child took me down narrow caverns; then his
selfishness unleashed. "You are to give me all of you just as
I have given you all of me" I looked up through my tears and
said "I can not" And the wind whispered "turn and run" but my
child's need kept me there. To fires I was led: "These are my
fires," he said, "Do you understand anger? Anger that makes
you insane? You will not love me? Then you shall pay." And
the fires whispered "turn and run" but my child's pain kept me
there. "Why does everything torture my soul?" he cried. The
man-child looked at me. The eyes; Tragedy. And I longed for
his emotions to feel alive, so alive, eyes composed of tears
were burning. Then he died and my heart exploded and died and
when he awoke he whispered "You should have listened to all the
warnings." Then he wrapped me in his warm and dark embrace and
with a sad smile said "I am the child of the Eternal Night."

—*Emanuela LiMandri*

People

(For Mrs. Rickelmann)
  Walking along, I find myself lost
in a crowd of strange, but familiar
creatures.
  Some are secretive, some are outgoing,
some hateful, and some are happy, while
others are sad.
  They all dress as different as night
and day. Some are dressed for serious
business, and still some are hardly
dressed at all.
  Some are tall, some are short, and
others in between.
  They are all different outside,
but on the inside, they're as much
the same as peas in a pod.
  No matter what color, race, shape
or size, they are all called people.

—*Michele Taylor*

The Appalling Charleston Garden

finally unlocked this door and let you into my life. The
wall built between us was getting so tall, it had to come down.
made the initiative and opened this big door that held back
terrible truths. So come into my garden and sit for awhile to
just tell me why! Why did you do what you did—laying those
first bricks, building that wall inside of me and enclosing a
secret garden that no one can enter but me?
I'm all alone in this concealed garden—witnessing strange
paths form black roses and hideous weeds.
I've protected my garden—allowing no trespassers until you.
The broken black chairs and Paris table sit and taunt me as I
wonder, confused. Chilled breezes blow into my garden, like
the chilling breeze that echoes through my soul (where that
Charleston garden sits heavily). Like a prison, it traps lies
that I've told to cover for why I hate you so. The walls so
smooth and high, and the door so tightly chained that my
darkest feeling and emotions may never come out. Now I've
opened this door to let you in to talk. Don't get too close,
just tell me why you had to build inside me this repulsive
Charleston garden.

—*Bonnie Marie Matthews*

Untitled

Child of scorn, through every season.
Wanting to die, and having reason.

Mother, full of hate, absent father
No love given, who will bother?

She has biting words which break the heart,
Torture the mind and tear apart.

Now, all alone and unable to love
Just want to be free and fly like a dove

Revenge soon will come, far inflictive pain.
There's nowhere to run, tears fall like rain.

But soon shall death come,
For that bitch will be dead
This bullet I hold, will run through her head

Then I'll be free, no more hate free flowing
But nobody cares so then I'll be going

Dead will I be, a cold piece of meat
Yet a smile on my face,
For revenge sure is sweet!

—*Candy Riehm*

Light of Spring Dance

Light burden of oxygen,
warmth of body and soft light,
fluid motion on hardwood floors;
long, dark eyelashes that brush arched eyebrows,
soft skin touched by the kiss of butterfly.

A taste of beauty melting softly towards
the bittersweet of aching wonderful;
specter of youth whirling among dancing bodies-
one missing;
White noise between and around,
the delicate tension between bodies-
breaking point of desire
to either static or repel;
One soldier is missing and one flowering,
bathed by moonlight,
ticking time bearing down
as the weight of peonies in late spring
bow their heads to the ground,
narcissm -
self conscious.

—*Mira Mishkin*

Old Man Winter

"Old man winter came one day, I looked out my window to see. He
was a very tall man and he carried a cane, his suit was all tattered
and brown. I remembered caused it was yesterday and we walked
to the end of town." "Hello, my name is Johnny. Sir, do you think
it will snow?" "Suppose it will, usually does when the cold
wind blows!" "Do you reckon it will be alright, if I walk along,
guess you're going my way. I'll see you after school lets out.
Sir, do you think it will rain?" "I reckon it will," the old
man said. "But this I promise for sure, I pass this way just
once a year, when the cold wind blows and the brown leaves
fall, just look I'm right up ahead!" The little boy reached
and shook the old man's hand before boarding the bus that day.
He looked out the window, but the old man was gone, just as it
started to snow, where the old man went, the little boy just
didn't know! Many winters went by, the boy grew up, married
and had his own little boy. Then one day his son looked up at
him and said; "Daddy, old man winter came one day, I looked out
my window to see. He was a very tall man and he carried a
cane, his suit was all tattered and brown. I remembered
cause it was yesterday and we walked to the end of town.

—*Rhoda Cluxton*

"One Didn't Cry"

The first time I saw him cry
Was the day she died.
They had grown up together
Were friends, were lovers.
They were going to grow old,
Grow old together.
And live happily ever after.
It's a fairy tale life,
I've heard people say.
Did you know she had cancer?
Such a tragedy.
Six kids I hear
What will they do, without a mother, without a friend?
Such a tragedy.
Those kids are strong as steel.
I hear one didn't even cry.
Her mother was her best friend
She had no shoulders to cry on
Now she has a broken heart.
Such a tragedy.

—*Molly Ann Harrington*

One-Side Cold-Hidden Gold

Ya know all I really wanted was...
was to be...to be...
Not alone
Softly... ever so phantasmagorically and
softly mused... my glazed gazed steel mazed eyes
venture past the window pane, painted with water drops,
like tears by the rain
beneath the tree, seemingly laughing
stood humanity, just stood there standing,
seemingly staring

Like me!?

The day was dark
wind wrestles with branches
hard cold penetrates plaster wall apartments
so many questions I ask too many
in my torment and task for answers
through trap-boored and booby-rigged places
silent realizations, RawBone Rattling Flustrations
"Will I ever...Sleep?!..."
One-side cold, hidden gold; sleep swiftly swallowed me whole!

—*Jilliary Thomason*

The Wounded

Feelings, like the billows after a sea storm
washing in compass points directions
dashed about this way and that
'til in whirls of confusion they calm
to be borne by stronger wave currents
and spill at the feet of the shore
gently lapping in peace or drowned by a following torrent

Emotions weep even as the heavens release
tiny raindrops falling to Earth's welcoming bosom
till each in their mass form a wellspring —
droplets fall into its depth and ribboning circles reach
toward the warmth and security of a puddle's perimeter
enfolded by tender grass and warm earth
eternity beckoning peace in fulfillment of destiny

Time rushing onward, so fleeting yet so cherished in the infinity
—*Katrina L. Wood*

Kids

Hear I sit all route with dismay
Watching all the kids of today
Raising hell and committing crimes
Some say it's just the times
Kids have no morals or discipline
They won't listen to nary one of their kin
That more and more they go their own way
What the hells with these kids today
I look at them and say with a grin
Its the same as its always been

Kids have been the same since the start of time
First was yours then was mine
Now its time for your kids and mine
Kids of today are the parents of tomorrow
When their time comes they'll feel the sorrow
They to will ask one day
What the hell's with these kids today
—*Timothy I. Murray*

Grasp

Watching and waiting
Watching and waiting

I watch, wait, for,
A moment in time to take my breath
away.
You will be there. Alone. With me.

Stop, close dreary eyes
Sleep and dream to the dawn
I will be here, where will here be?
Stand in power, no tears...

Years...can pass, and flow
Breezes in the wind, changing faces, attitude
But hearts, no, know
They are meant to be one with another.

But impossible, no tears
Knowledge of eons of time, in lives past
Together spending time.

Watching and waiting
I watch and wait for a warm hand, in the cold dark.
—*Michael Hooper*

Floating in the Dream

We walk together on the sand,
Watching as the rising tides
Fall into the waiting arms of the glassy shore
And break.

We stand together, yet apart
One foot in water, one on land.
Is this what it is to be in love?
Is love, perhaps, the need to float and lie
In the glistening wetness of this vibrant sea?

But love must also stand its ground,
Or else be star-crossed, else be drowned.

Dreams can be too real, if we allow
The mystery of what could be
To fall, devoured by the selfish needs
Of what is.
Tomorrow will give time enough
To know the earth beneath our feet

Let love be the ecstatic dream
Of bodies and hearts intertwined
And immersed within the beckoning waves.
—*Edward Farley*

The Hollow Man

Uncle, uncle awoke in bed red;
Water, water held under nearly dead.
Daddy, daddy never taught us to swim;
No wonder, I never got to know him.

Daughter, daughter ravaged by incest;
Family, family never gets any rest.
Hemorrhage, hemorrhage; trigger took a life.
Left alone, daughter and wife.

Take away Calloway shotgun to the head;
Pillow, pillow told us he wanted Grandma dead.
Fire, fire burned a little hole.
House unkindled scorched us all

Daddy, daddy heart like a lake;
Pain, pain, oh how it must ache.
Father, father killer bootlegger in prison.
Death inside, is that the reason?

Hollow, hollow ghost of a man;
Wallow, wallow; pity I can't understand.
Closets, closets bones rattle the night.
Hollow man, can it ever be right?
—*Richard W. Fielder*

Loving You

My mind and spirit are as one. My heart is a light to guide my way through the darkest night. My mind allows me to be with you always, even though I'm not. My eyes allow me to see the beauty that you posses. Your eyes shine and sparkle like the surface of the water on a clear night, together with the moon and stars they're a wondrous sight for they tell a story of a kind person behind them. Your lips speak with a voice so charming the world seems to move with every last word. The touch of your hand makes me feel as if heaven has come and taken me away to it's highest tower. Even on the worst of days when the pain is almost too much to bear, your appearance makes all seem new again. My pulse races when you're near and when you're not I almost shed a tear then I see your face in my mind and smile. If I had one wish to be granted in my life it would be to have you willingly by my side till the end of time. Every night I close my eyes and dream of you sitting by a slowly flowing stream, just sit and talking to me about things of no true meaning until the last rays of light fall upon the land now it's night I look into your eyes and as I move closer our lips meet and I wake up.
—*Christopher Joseph Carroll*

isses in the Wind

vas walking down the street,
way too far and way too fast,
om whence it came, I do not know,
I do not care.
touched my cheek, it touched my soul,
was a kiss in the wind.
nt by someone far away,
nt by someone long ago,
blew in the wind till it found me so
estled gently upon my cheek,
kiss from the heart is of what I speak
hen or where, who she was, I do not know,
et my lips,
et my heart,
et my kiss back on the wind,
et my kiss back on the wind,
here to blow, where to set,
I never know, my kiss in the wind.

—*Lou Mencuccini Jr.*

he Gift That Perpetuates Itself - Blood

hat do we mean when we say blood as a gift
e are talking about donating do you get my drift

ease give your blood, a gift from the heart
or it is in that blood a new life might impart

fe is so precious, may your blood ever flow
onate to your neighbor; let it overflow

fe will have new meaning, a new beginning for him
d your cup will be filled right up to the brim

ease consider donating your blood and give
is in your donation that someone might live

you are that someone who is begging to live
en you'd hope someone like you would be willing to give

is is the end of my poem, I hope you sign up
ay your life be rewarded by a more than full cup....

ood is always needed any time of the year
is in giving one's blood that you truly bring cheer

—*Rose Marie Martino*

ove

ove you when you are gone
e don't see each other for very long
ove you when your near
d I hope someday you'll have no fear
ook at the picture on the wall
d I think you deserve it all
u need someone to care
d someone who will be very fair
let you feel free
hink that someone is me
ope I make you happy not sad
aybe some day I will be a new dad
ur so good at what you do
metimes I don't feel good enough for you
vant to be your love that feels so right
vant to make you happy every day and night.

—*Brian T. Hogman*

Day by Day Joy

The Senior Citizen's place is our joy.
We don't want for a thing.
We go early and play games
We are lead to our exercise.
Another lady leads our singing.
We have a prayer of thanks for
our meal.
Even tho' we meet to eat,
we come early and play,
for this is a comfort to
all of us, our leader helps
us to be happy here.
Surely nothing but goodness
comes from this, and we
shall come together as long
as we are able and have a
place to meet.

—*Virsey Renick*

Scared To Say

The sun gently lowers to the horizon
We feel the spirit of it glittering the ocean
While it's slowly setting in the west
On the beach, w sat down to rest

The sweat is dripping down my face
I'm proud of myself for keeping up with your pace
What we talked about I don't recall
But returning was something I wished to stall

Together we dug and sculpted the sand
I tried to construct a tunnel with my hand
You helped by scooping out the other side
Eventually our fingertips would collide

Into a fingertip embrace
Holding tight, in this little sand-space
When I looked up and saw you grin
Your eyes shone with the sparkle of the ocean

—*Deb Volk*

The Journey

Whose journey was it, his or mine?
We had started it together long ago,
was this path chosen then, for now?
He tried to hold my hand, I was afraid.
I was questioning, he was not.
Fear engulfed me, peace was with him
I was nervous, he was calm.
Desperation was the color I could see,
radiance was with him.
Sadness filled my every thought,
joy was written on his face.
Who would benefit from this time?
The sad, the joyful, the powerless, the brave,
the one who is going or the one left behind?
Whose journey is it, his or mine?

—*Mary Johnson*

A Shared Sight

As I look up at this moon I wonder,
Who shares this sight?
Who else is gazing upon the moon tonight?
People near and far, do they see
the same exact star?
And as the darkness blankets the land,
How many others stand just as I stand?
Looking toward the heavens aghast,
being taken in by the sky so deep,
so dark, so vast.

—*Kelly Seeger Regan*

When

A small voice cries out for help, but no one listens.
We keep on working like inhuman machines.

We float through existence on clouds of machine-made pleasure,
electric trains, microwave ovens, polluting cars and pretended
   beauty.

We think we live but do we really?
What about the joys that Nature provides?
Destroyed by man with his machines of arrogance.

When will we become humans, people with feelings?
When will we learn
   about joy; a leaf, a river, a child growing up
   about sadness; a lonely dirt road, an abandoned shack - once
   home for a family now gone
   about freedom; a bird, an open highway, the sun in the evening.

When will we live?
When will we touch?
When will we see?
When will we love?
A whisper comes from the woods of time, but no one listens.
   —Janet Lux

Untitled

I remember of you... It was you and I.
We shared a love no one had.
Making a life together, playing games, having fun.
Then came the time that the life of hour own was called upon.
We didn't fight, yell, or argue. It ended in an accident.
Not of mine, nor of yours.
It happened so fast, just one blow.
I cried out loud, as you lay there to die.
Wanting to help you, there wasn't a thing I could do.
Reality came to a flow and left me behind, wanting to die.
As you past away, you took half of me with you.
Leaving the other half to mourn the sorrow.
I was lost in what was forever...

The years have passed; I've picked up the pieces.
I'm continuing life with the half you left me.
I still think of the memories.
I miss you and cry for you,
I Remember of You...It was you and I.
   I will always love you, Grandpa.
   —Catherine Pearce

Walk Along The Lake

As we walked along the lake on top of the warm sand,
We shared together our dreams, locked by heart and hand.
A time once experienced, so happy and so free.
When all I knew was you, and all you knew was me.
We walked for many hours, without a single word.
We knew what the other was thinking, without it being heard.
And when the day was over, and our walk came to an end.
We parted only thinking of each other, our best friend.

And then one day we were walking along the lake once more.
That is when you told me that you had feelings for me no more.
You told me things weren't working and that you had your
Doubts, but you didn't seem to give us time to try to work things out.

So now I walk the lake alone pretending you're still here,
Wearing many faces to masquerade my tears.
Wondering why life is so undefined, and we are forever now apart.
And wondering why so quickly you came in and out of my heart.
Knowing all along how you really feel.
Waiting patiently for my broken heart to heal.
   —Amy Renee (Dumas) Shults

Seasons Greetings

When Christmas Day is drawing near,
   We think of friends we hold dear.
We wish that we were blessed with gold
   To buy gifts for all, both young and old.

But there are gifts not bought with wealth,
   The gifts of love, happiness and health.
The gifts of friends, both kind and true,
   These are the gifts we wish for you.

When Christmas Day dawns bright and clear
   With the "Prince of Peace" lingering near,
We hope that He, with love Divine
   Will shower you with gifts so sublime.

Gifts of love, happiness and health
   Far outweigh the gifts of wealth.
May you have peace and Christmas cheer,
   Good luck and happiness throughout the New Year.
   —Frances M. Doyle

Pessimistic Poem

To hell, to hell, to hell
We will ride
A bus and a "booger"
At everyone's side

The "booger's" what's wrong with the world
The bus is the make-cure
You'll be assigned to your own wrong-world
And the communie's substitute-war

Marial Hemingway's cheerful as bright lint
Sprinkled on your fedora at the federal mint
Red, sharp, mold to your thoughts
Green, TV, go off where we ought

To be all we might be
With hell's hint of lint
A secretive policy
Of the government
   —Michael P. Goff

Life

A baby born ignorant in darkness,
We wrap him gently in blankets of dreams.
Many lessons are taught in shades of gray.
Blankets fall away, reality shows.
In his eyes darkness, lights colors, shadows.
In his ears sounds, voices, laughter, crying.
In his nose smells, cleanliness, flowers, decay.
On his tongue tastes, sugar, candy, teardrops.
With his hands touches, puppies, blankets, teeth.
Learning more lessons as he grows mature.
School, lessons of life, love, hate, war, peace, death.
Complete he sleeps in the light, no more dreams.
   —Chad Davis

Sands Of Time

Downward flowing
   Upward growing.
A fluid stream
   down the middle going.
Quiet as night
   leads into day.
As each grain falls
   the hours slip away.
Another dawn for Mankind
   These are the sands of time.........
   —Diana L. Baker-Hanson

The Impatient Brother

Since you have told us time and again,
We'd all be gone when your 80th birthday kicked in.
And there'd be none left to give you a cake,
And a little change in your pocket to share.
We thought and talked among ourselves,
And decided it was time
To take you off the shelf.
So this is your day, Brother Dear,
We all wish you a happy one for sure.
So don't think when you're eighty
You'll be the only one left,
If we're still around,
You'll go back on the shelf.
Happy 80th oops!
You're only fifty-seven.

—*Hazel Cox Brammer*

Untitled

I'm drifting away, letting my dreams take control. I feel
weightless, with a feeling of absolute tranquility.

The sun is setting but I can still feel its warmth on my skin.
Water is all around me; I can taste the salt on my lips. It
carries me, guides me, as I allow it complete control.

I'm reaching the sky now, touching the moon and the stars;
floating through a wintery cool breeze.

I can see beautiful mountains and valleys below and endless
fields of flowers in perfect unison colors. Still, the wind
carries me, like a delicate leaf making trails through the air.

Slowly I awaken, remembering my wonderful journey. I can still
feel the warmth of the sun, or could it be that I have not yet
   awaken?
I open my eyes and find your loving arms caressing me gently.
And the look in your eyes explains that I have not yet begun
   to sleep.

—*Veronica Buentello-Garza*

We Were All Young

Hard to believe, you say, as you look at the gray,
Well, it's true, we were all young, like you
Where did the years go? They flew by, as you'll see..
We once cuddled a breast and looked to success
Yes, we were all young!

As you look at me now, wonder how can this be true?
What you see today, is youth faded away
Just look in my eyes, if you dare! It's all there!

So, give me a care, you and I are one
We share what life holds, my legacy to you, as you grow old
Remember, I too, was young If I would have known...

Life passes so fast, friends die or grow old
Health changes with age, hold on to your day
Smile, It's not the end of the road, you too, will grow old!

Be gentle and kind, see, it's you that you hold!
When you change that sheet or comb my hair
A gentle smile, will take me back...

Reflection is yours as you look into my eyes
Don't you see it??!
It's me, it's you! It's youth, that has grown old!

—*F. Kapson*

Cowboy Want-A-Be

So ya want-a-be a cowboy,
   Well, let me tell you son.
There's more to bein' a cowboy,
   Than twerlin' that there gun.

If ya want-a-be a cowboy,
   You got to learn the cowboy walk.
You got to wear your jeans much tighter,
   And you got to talk that cowboy talk.

Now a cowboy, he says, "Yes Mam"
   For no, he just says, "nope."
And he don't make no conversation,
   When he's messin' with his rope.

So stick your thumbs in your belt loops,
   Cross your feet, 'n' lean against the wall.
Just stand there lookin' lonesome,
   Like you got no friends at all.

Some gal is sure to spot ya,
   So give her that cowboy grin.
Now try to spit between your teeth,
   But don't get it on your chin.

   —*Ken Arnold*

Killing Of Nature

   Nature is killed day and night,
we're killing that naturally beautiful sight.

   It's hurting animals, trees, and even the air,
and we keep acting like we don't even care.

   Some people think killing an animal is a game,
but others just don't feel the same.

   When all the trees are burned down,
what'll take their place, another shopping mall in town.

   Pollution is always in the air,
but it's not just here or there, it's every where.

   If you want to stop the natures killing,
you have to be helpful, you have to be willing!

   —*Bobbie Rogers*

My Palace In The Sky

As I drifted into the clouds above,
were no one will push or shove,

I'm dancing and singing, but then I looked below,
I heard someone crying "no"

And, then, what did I see?
but my dear mom crying over me

"I'm still with you, "I spoke, but you could not hear,
yet still I felt so near

You seemed so sad, with no more hopes or dreams,
that's not my mom, or so it seems

I wish I could talk to you, and tell you how I feel,
about this place that's so unreal

So love my little sister,
as you always loved me,
and the baby yet to come,
whom I am anxious to see

When you think about me
do not frown or cry,
instead just think about me
in my palace in the sky

   —*Jacinta Boynton*

The World Today

As I sit here thinking ....
What a crazy world we've living in
It takes me back to a time
When there was hardly any crime
People caring for one another
Instead of hurting each other
Saying 'Hello' with a smile
Instead of greetings with words so vile

As I sit here thinking ....
On where our world is heading
It makes me realize
We need to look through each other's eyes
To see the horrible things we do
That makes our lives so blue
So now...let us try to bring our lives
To a place of laughter which bears no cries
And when this is done ....
Let us look for the very best to come.

  —Carolyn Thompson-Brown

Outrageous October

Oh, October! How outrageous you are!
What a renegade!
You are such a flirt as you flip your skirt
Like some wanton maid.
One day you're blowing warm, the next you're blowing cool.
You roll your eyes and pretend surprise
As you make us act just like a fool
In love
With your glowing, changing colors, now red, now brown,
With still a touch of green.
And, oh, the harvest that you bring.
Red apples, pumpkins on the vine, yellow corn.
Surely the most glorious scene
Beneath God's skies above.
You're so unpredictable, yet so enchanting,
That you make us forgive all your mischievous ways.
And, as you wrap us around your finger,
How we wish that you could linger long past
You usual days!

  —Vivian Gray Morrow

Adam

Dear little Adam, child of my child
What do you know of this world?
Your mother's voice, her gentle touch
Your daddy's finger to hold.
Know of their love for each other and you
Know of the joy they share.
Know of their faith in God above
To keep you in His care.
Dear little Adam, child of my child
Warm and safe in your world
With mother's voice, her gentle touch
With daddy's finger to hold.

  —Charlotte J. Irick

Tenth Street

I remember barefoot Tenth Street sidewalks,
We looked up to pale blue skies at five a.m.,
Speckled, grimy, little gremlins, cavorting before an
 almost coffee house.
And home, wherever it then was, to fall asleep by seven —
 rise by five,
Just in time for dusk through the bathroom window,
Soap suds, clean hair, something small to eat.

We loved — not each, but all of us.
How long ago that was.

  —Pamela R. Burkland

A Painted Pony

A painted pony
What does this mean
This mighty steed of mine
Is it real, or is it fantasy
Does he love me
Or is it just a never ending battle
Around and around on the story I created.
Decorated, purified, until it was perfect
Golden, happy and unreal
I thought it was our fantasy

A painted pony
I should have picked one clearer
With no hazy in-between
He said he's not sure of what he wants
Or is he just playing into my fantasy
Making me feel how I want to feel
Even though it's wrong
Or is it... you see
It's just a painted pony
That makes my misery

  —Margo West

Visions

I wish you could see,
what I can see. A place where
I wish I could be. Alone and free,
casted away from all the love that
shines on today. Colors don't matter,
hopes and dreams gather, shattering
glass too fast to see. I close my eyes
wondering where I'll be. I love to laugh,
and dare to love. I give so much, but
I feel so little. This world is too real to
believe. I remember a day when we all use
to shout and play without worrying
about those days. Life is like a maze every way
affects just about everyday.

  —Brittany Stewart

Grandma's Hands

Hands of time
What is the hand of time?
It is a hand of love,
Hands that nurture,
It is a hand that teaches and gives guidance
Hands that are there to help
It is a hand of patience
Hands that we held onto as a child
Hands that we hold now
The hand of a giving heart
The hand of only one
The hands of Grandma...
The hands of time...

  —Bonnie L. Swanson

Once In Love

I was once in love with you
Thinking that you loved me too.
Each night I sat alone
Waiting for your call by the phone.
I kept doing things for your love,
Thinking our hearts would fly like doves.
I stopped crying myself to sleep at night
Because I knew you would never
 be there to hold me tight.
How everything seems much clearer,
Since I realized that I was once
 in love with you.

  —Nikki Walton

580

Aftermath Of A Dispersed Crowd

Loneliness...
What is the reason behind. Something so depressing?
Loneliness...
All feel it, but yet no one does.
It is weakening like fear,
Yet strengthens our minds, as
Exercise our bodies.
If not felt too much or little, that is.
Loneliness...
A chance to get in touch with your feelings,
and sort things out. Dream and clear your mind as if you sleep
Loneliness...
Why do we look down on this?,
Are we scared of finding out
What we may learn,
Or is it just that we're on the
Verge of insanity, or past it?
It could just be a natural reflex,
protecting us from becoming too impermeable to our feelings.
Loneliness...

—*Chris Bailey*

Teacher

Were I again a boy of six,
What kind of teacher would I pick to calm the waves
That churn the seas of learning?

Dark hair cascading 'round her face
Would match the midnight of her eyes,
And she would be pretty.

Her slender body would move
With queenly grace across the room,
And my eyes would follow.

Words of wisdom falling from her
Lips would make such pleasant sounds,
And my ears would listen.

Sometimes she would look my way
Or touch me and speak my name,
And my heart would quicken.

And I would know that
School is a nice place to be.

—*Dale E. Allberry*

Clinging To Hopes

Why do people cling to each other?
What makes people cling to nothing?
DREAMS, HOPES, PAST, FUTURE, FEARS and REALITY
Why the abused, especially, cling to nothing?
Dreams up in smoke!

How often do people let each other down?
THE WORLD IS A FANTASY!!
The reality of life is always
in their face.
But who really listens.

There is only HOPE for the sane,
Everyone clings to something.
Something which isn't always there,
MAYBE
It just might be,
We cling for a purpose.

The abused need LOVE and ATTENTION
But often it turns out to be
reality checks and false hopes.

—*Alden K. Ryan*

The Unknown

What makes a person tick,
What makes them want to die
or bring harm to others,
A child is innocent at birth
and is slowly corrupted by others
and the different ways of life
as they grow older.
Could it be that there is not a perfect person
on this earth, that deep down inside of us all
hides an inner strength in everyone,
whether it be angry, hurt or frightening;
Confused, lost or helpless.
For it could be released if that someone is pushed too far.
Then the unknown could be released,
and the madness could bring terror
or worse of all,
Evil could be unleashed and never detained
if it's never known.
So be careful who you know,
For they may not be who you might think.

—*Sabrina Martin*

Verse

O' Verse do Rhyme, and boldly define,
What Stanza's that thou canst!
And Meter, too, must be perfectly true,
In order for Poem to prance.

O' once in time, such Verse and Rhyme,
Quieted the turmolous sea,
But when Stanza slipped then Meter tripped,
And poem could not be!

O' letters tumbled and words jumbled,
Life into meaningless ways,
And extinction bound the peaceful ground,
Of the meadows Poem grazed.

O' life's cruel flaws, were true to cause,
That which to finally,
Soul died first leaving spirit cursed,
And poem ceased to be.

—*Dara S. Roemhild*

New Years Day

'Twas the morning of New Years, I stumbled from bed.
What was throbbing, my heart or my head?
I looked out the window,
Looked over the town.
The homes were all quiet.
The shades were all down.
The paper boy rang.
"Happy New Year!" he sang.
I looked in my pockets, I had not a nickel!
I knew I must be in some kind of a pickle!
I opened the door with a sheepish grin-
"Getcha later," I said, Nobody's in."
Then slowly it started to come back you see-
Maybe it's better not to be me -
I was the New Year diaper and all -
Oh, how they laughed when I walked down the hall-
Next year I'll know better, I hope and I pray -
Well, maybe just one more, today's only the first day.
"Happy New Year" to all, I'll be very quiet -
Last night I remember I was really a riot"

—*Ida Feibusch*

You Came To Me

You came to me, and now I just don't know
What your motives are towards me.
You've had it tough, love wasn't just enough
The better things in life are free.

You gave to me, with that you took away,
The self respect I've had in me.
You've played your tricks, and then just walked away,
The life you live, I just can't see.

They say it's easy, I could be taken
I've often heard them say its true
But I'm so different, than all those others
And for a while I'm going to hurt for you.

—*Frank LaRosa, Jr.*

Nothings The Matter

The child within cries out.
What's the matter with me?
Inquiry, taunts the day, and
haunts the nights.

Invading dreams, impairing visions.
Mind, brain, and soul in tact.
Discreated, and dehumanized by this society.

A heart, a face, and feelings abide.
Victim, - demised, and Victor, - arise.
Impugn bias of color, gender, religion, and shape.

Woman-child, friend, mother, sister...
Multi dimensional, uniquely me.
Color me human, shaped strong in faith.
Captain of my soul and quality of life.
This! is the uniquely, original me.

I am somebody, more to love, hear me roar.
I affirm, amend, validate, proclaim,
Uniquely original, empowered me.

What's the matter with me?!
Nothing!!!!!!

—*Bonita Echols*

A Wonderful Little Boy

I was walking up a hill one beautiful day,
When a group of children who were full of play,
Came down the hill in a tight little group.
How to get through without doing a loop?
As I got nearer, I heard a voice clear:
"Watch out— that old lady," said without fear.
Everyone moved and a clearing was made,
So I didn't have to try to evade,
The mud that I know would have stuck to my shoes,
It was wonderful that I did not have to choose.

I noticed the face of a very small boy,
Somebody's son, who filled my heart with joy.
I said with great pride, "I do thank you sir,"
"You are welcome," he answered without demur.
It's the children, who so often see,
Things adults think they are too young to be:
Loving, concerned, and respectful of the age,
Precisely the qualities meant for a sage.
His parents — I know they are mightily proud,
To have such a son who stands out in a crowd!

—*Marjorie L. Burgess*

Thoughts Of Awe

If a tree is cut with an axe does it scream
When a pig squalls before the butcher
Cut its throat is it crying God help me
As the farmer picks the apples from the tree
Does the tree beg for some apples for its roots
Because you can't see him is there no God
Because you can't see her is there no Goddess
If I cut you and you don't see me you still bleed
If I call you and you don't hear me I still called you
When you step on a roach does it feel pain
Because you can't see atoms are they still here
Is the sun parent to the planets
Or are the planets a group of investors in the sun
Does an old tree produce more oxygen than a new tree
Are you an earthian or an earth-ling
In the afterlife are you dead pondered
For all my years I have these things wondered
Have I wasted my time of life
Or will my reward come in or from the divine.....

—*Nathurlon Jones Jr.*

Why

Why do people get offended at all,
When all I do is give them a call?
I'll say, "Do you want some help with that?"
They reply, "What are you looking at?"
If people knew the meaning of respect,
Then I would not feel like such a reject.
There must be some other way to cope.
Instead of always feeling bad, I hope.
Some people won't even give me a chance.
One, I know, is always on the advance.
Why do people give me all the blame?
All I want to do is play a little game.
I feel they just want me left out in the cold.
Come on people, this game is getting old!
I feel as if I have no more thoughts to lend.
Oh why does this poem have to end?

—*Nisha Brown*

My Heart Breaks Just A Little Every Spring

My heart breaks just a little every spring when lilacs blooms,
When garden gloves, a basket, wide-brim-hat tossed in a room
Remind me of so long ago when lean legs raced at play.
They were my little daughter's when I planned a gardening day.
Her energies could not be tamed; she sped from row to row
Impatient to be off again to play. I'd watch her go,
And now I see her every spring when planting tiny seeds
Or cutting blooms, or hoeing rows, and pulling stubborn weeds.
She loved the joy of being outside. She called it "gardening".
But really it was frolicking across the weeks of spring.
She never settled down at all to tend the garden plot. She only
revelled in the joy of being alive, and not
To miss a single scent that wafted through that laden air,
Like lilacs, spring rains, moist brown earth, breeze whispering
through her hair.

My heart breaks just a little every spring now that she's grown
I share her now with others; then she was my very own.
But there are things that I can do to make a tired heart sing.
I grab a broom, hang quilts outside, and give the drapes a fling,
And tear our house apart by room—then put things back in place,
And there in tidied loveliness, her memory comes to grace.

—*Harried Elmblad*

The Door

I was taking a walk through the house of my soul
When I came upon a door I did not remember.
It had an old an ancient feeling to it,
So I braced myself and tugged against the door.
Slowly it creaked open, begging loudly to be oiled.
The inside was damp and musty.
There were cobwebs all over,
And more dust than I had ever seen in one room.
Breaking out the broom and mop, I began to clean.
As I cleaned I began to uncover precious memories.
"Ah," I said, "My dream of a college degree
Oh, My dream of a family
Yes, I remember." I said, gently touching one dream,
Was my hope for riches and fame.
So, this was the room where my hope for the future was kept.
I cleaned the room until it shined,
Put everything back in its place,
Oiled the hinges to the door
And left, conveniently leaving the door open.

—*Serena T. Conner*

Untitled

I did have the strangest dream
When I was only twelve.
While being at my Aunt's house
For a few days to dwell.

The boy of my dreams
Was at my Aunts house too,
When one nite I entered his room
Having on but one shoe.

As I was leaving to get my other shoe,
He called me back to his side
Saying, I want to marry you,
Want you to be my bride;

I gave him my answer "yes,"
But then and there the dream ended.
As anyone could easily guess,
I was very much offended.

—*Ruby G. Kelley*

My Grandmother

Who held me tight so tenderly,
When I was the young age of three?
Who played with me down on her knee,
Always wanting the best for me.

Who cared for me, while mom worked all day?
Who taught me Allah's prayer to say?
Who kissed me, and made the hurt go away,
Made me feel like a spring day in May.

Who guided me thru the glare,
When I did wrong gave me that stare.
Made me the center of her prayer,
And after it all, she would still care.

At night, in who's arms do I rest?
Who's love I never had to put to a test?
Out of all the others who's the best?
I will always love and God Bless.
My Grandmother

—*Rashiah Morris*

Untitled

I don't want to believe in a goodbye
when it seems just yesterday we said hello
I sit and watch these days pass by
not wanting ever to let them go.
We could never share too many things together
our happiness, our thoughts, our laughter,
They're the things you can't see that mean the most
I just hope to see a happily-ever-after.
So many things you've brought into my life
and the same I've brought into yours
I've experienced so many new things
because you opened up the doors.
Through the rough times
well make it through the bad weather
'cause all we want
is to always be together.
No matter what you do
I'll always be here to catch you,
And now I don't know what else to say
except you mean so much more each day.

—*Carissa Pecora*

Once Upon a November Night

Once upon a November night
when it was cold and grey,
the darkness entered my heart
and my mind began to stray.
The shadows seemed to move
and take on a form of their own
then the leaves began to dance
-All things came to life as
a blaze of fire rose, I saw the
devil himself a top of the fiery throne.

The wind began to blow
and as it passed my ear it
whispered death.
My eyes widened and my soul began to cry!

The wind blew once again
and as it passed it took
my last breath, my last breath of life...

—*Coty L. Whitlow*

Mother Love

A fondling pair of childish hands
  When life seems not worth while,
A trusting heart pressed close to mine
  Helps mother bear her trials
Just touch the tousled head at night
  When troubled thoughts intrude,
Dull cares and worries soon take flight,
  Then comes a peaceful mood.

A pair of eyes wide in wonder at mother's flowing tears,
  A pair of lips all a-quiver, heart filled with unknown fears
Mother casts aside her worries
  To comfort her instead
When her tears give way to sunshine,
  She finds her cares have fled.

She's a precious, priceless burden,
  This little one of mine,
Making out of irksome duty a privilege sublime.
  Her love, the diamonds of my life,
Her smiles, they are the pearls!
  Rubies I find within each kiss of my dear little girl.

—*Helen M. Rich*

"I Look At The Tree..."

When I am lonely and all seems lost,
   when living demands too great a cost...
     I look at the tree
     and it comforts me.
I see it standing sturdy and sure,
   bending and swaying as it endures.

When I am in need and pain moves within,
   when I am faced with tough problems to win ...
     I look at the tree
     and it comforts me.
I see that it grows amid storms and strife,
   stretching upward to find new life.

When I am suff'ring and I can't see
   the direction of my destiny,
     I look at the tree
     and it comforts me...
I see that it waits for the spring to show
   the way buds flower, after the snow.

     —Jackie Stinson

To The Heartbroken

Do cry and talk about your hurt
When people come who care,
Be honest, cry your heart out
When it's more than you can bear.

Do go when people ask you —
They're friends who'll help you through
The desperate days of mourning
When there's nothing you want to do!

Do love these friends who love you,
Who support every step you take,
And thank God for your friends and neighbors,
Do notice that difference they make!!!!

     —Jeane Nylander

The Blue Bandanna Cries

I have a dream of that dark December day
When shots were fired and screams were heard.
   Throughout the neighborhood
I have a dream of when tears were shed
Over your casket and the one of your
   Unborn son beside it.

   I have a dream that one day I will
see you again and the blue bandanna
will sway once more.

     —Lisa Moore

Is He Real?

Is he just as real in the darkest night
   When sorrow and dread press down
As when we lift glad voices high
   To tell of joys that abound?

Is he just as real, when on beds of pain
   Gladness seems far removed,
As when in the sunshine of strength and health
   His presence and love are proved?

My heart rejoices to know Christ is real
   Tho' darkness and pain assail.
He's my light and strength each hour of the day,
   A fortress in life's raging gale.

In Him do I rest as I've yielded my all
   And seek His will to obey.
In His name, thru His word, I'll tell of His love.
   In fact, I'll do it today!

     —Martha Stumpf

Solitude

There was a time when solitude was my enemy,
   when tears were better than waking alone on a moonlit evening,
with stars cheering in the sky leading me into the night
with nothing but a walking stick.
And then the passion overflowed within me as a circle was
placed on my finger,
and contentment was shoved aside for the last time.
Soon after, rage exploded through its carefully constructed
walls, and shame scolded my integrity as the circle was broken
in three.
Concern smothered my guilt as I blamed myself
for a tragedy that I chose to endure until it was too late.

Solitude can be kind if you let it.
It's only a waiting period until the sunshine pierces your
heart once more.

     —Jennifer Kay Seegert

The Ride

There is a storm cloud brewin', yonder in the sky
When the Heavens get rolled open, before the blood runs nigh

And every eye will see him, the ones that pierced him with a dart,
Will he say come hither, or will he say depart

Then only in an instant in the twinkling of an eye,
They all will be just like him, riding across the sky

And just before they gathered, God's chosen ones ready to ride
They had themselves a banquet with Christ right by their side

The Lord was riding lead and from his mouth issued a knife,
And swinging yon to hither, he cut the death from life

He was dressed in dazzling apparel and he said I am the way
You'd better get yourself ready, it could happen any day

Upon his thigh was written Lord of Lords and King of Kings,
And the elders fell to worship, worthy did they sing

The fifth angel blew his trumpet, Michael came with chain and key
And he threw the nasty dragon into the fiery sea

So the ones that have been chosen better get ready to ride,
Cause we'll be rulin' and reignin' with Christ right by our side.

     —J. Weston

Autumn Day

In the shade and cool of an autumn day
when the summer heat has gone away
I walked along the forest lane
And cast my eyes on nature's domain
of sturdy trees, branches and leaves
swayed gently in the breeze
a picturesque sight, and there was sunlight.

I looked all around, and listened to the musical sound of little
birds, serenading, music with a special ring the winding brook,
nestled in its own nook the blue of the sky, white foamy clouds,
moving by nature's domain, will always reign in
its own picture frame.

I found a resting place, and loved the wind on my face I watched a
little squirrel climb the
bark of a tall tree, to find shelter, that was free.

An artist brush, painted the scene
a poet's lyric, writes the theme
beauty and peace will rule today
in the cool, of an autumn day.

     —Edith Tepper

Boy And His Kite

e left the world in a tragic way
When this happens they haunt you people say
I go to the beach I'll see him there
e liked to fly kites, I see him everywhere
he first time I heard the music of Jenny G.
brought him into the room to me
he music reminds me of kites flying
seems like everyone is lying
ll see him walking by and hear his voice
feel he'll soon come back and we'll rejoice
saw him on Friday the 13th, but the light was dim
wish I could say "Hello" are you really him?
—*Mary Deegan*

nly A Dream

as it only a dream or were we here,
When we journeyed again to scenes so dear;
hrough the old home town with its quiet grace,
And our loved one's final resting place.

as it only a dream or did we see,
Our old friends and neighbors that used to be;
he laughter rang out as we reminisced,
Then a quick good-bye and a parting kiss.

hen we're off again down the shady street,
That once echoed steps of our youthful feet.
as it only a dream, that beautiful view
Of our dear old home that housed us in youth.

he autumn leaves blazed in scarlet and gold,
As our childhood days before us unfold.
hen we turned away in the dim moonlight,
It seemed a dream as we drove out of sight.
—*Ione McCabe*

rson

hen will there finally be peace?
hen will the fires cease?
s heat melts away American Dreams,
hear the presence of a monotonous scream.

parades through every window and door
he greedy monster grabs ceiling and floor
hen eats it's bounty-only ashes remain
eaving behind a deserted plain

nd when it is safe to return,
he family repeats their lesson (well learned):

e share our world with fools
ho never learned in school
he gist of the golden rule
ease don't be cruel!.
—*Deborah Meyerstein*

he Dance

ody and soul feel the waves go.
hen you get the rhythm you get the moves,
hen you get the beat you have nothing to lose.
el the dance go into your heart and soul
t the energy take control.
s the power overtakes the mind,
ou lose your origin, but feel divine.
hen the music begins to slow,
ddenly you realize it was a trance.
s you loosen farther than gravity pulls,
e sky feels light as the earth is full.
—*Angela B. Lamb*

Turning 180 Degrees

It turned from hot to bone chilling cold,
When you left me with no one else to hold.
My heart tossed apart when it turned 180 degrees,
When it had lost, no longer you it sees.
It turned to lonely when you turned 180 degrees.

It ignored you too much while you were here,
My heart never felt alone or even any fear.
Like the door you slammed, it felt cold after you left,
It sees the beauty in what it should have kept.
It turned around only after you had left.

Its hard to control my thoughts and its views,
Until the only thoughts I had was you to lose.
Trying to see our future in just our fate,
Only then will my heart recover from its state.
Hoping it hasn't delayed or waited to late.

Being so hard to trust another after being burnt,
Its hard to forget after all that hurt.
Soon my heart turns back another 180 degrees,
When it has someone new to trust and to believe.
It turned together when it turned back 180 degrees.
   —*Gary Stasierowski*

Decisions

    Did you ever find yourself in a bind,
      When you simply can't make up your mind?
  Should you turn to the left, or turn to the right,
  Should you shop at day, or should you shop at night?

  Should you bring your umbrella, or leave it at home?
  Should you answer the doorbell or answer the phone?
    Should you buy a pot roast, or a chicken instead;
      Or bake a nice cake, or make up the bed?

  Should you go out in "sports", or "dress to kill.?"
      Should you go on a diet, or eat your fill?
    Take a trip to the mountains, or go to the shore;
      Or start saving money, or spend even more.

    Decisions! Decisions! There with us each day,
        Always unsure of what to do or to say.
      Why can't I decide what to do at the time
      And whatever I choose, let it do just fine.

      Why can't I just set my mind at ease
      And make a choice of whatever I please?
      Life would be easier, so it would seem
      If we could do and say just what we mean.
    —*Louis J. Petty*

Nature Is A Woman

Cushioned verdant carpet blankets the earth
Where homo sapiens pleasure and play
Leafy arms raised eternally to pray
Crowns of starry gems glow o'er the land
laden with myriad rainbow -hued bouquets
Cooling gentle breezes wrap around each face
Without the will to discriminate
Nature displays her anger in mighty strength and power
Soft white flakes of every descript
Covers everything in conscious sight
Offers calm stillness, sometimes blight
Fodder fed fires to warm homeless souls
Taming others to know and grow
    Rivers to bathe in
    Grasses to play in
    Nights to rest
Comfort beside the breasts of a woman
Ecstasy in the arms of a woman
Nature is a woman
    —*Mari Williams*

Alone

My husband,
When your dream ended
I embraced our children and adobe home
Saturated with love and promise.
Wearing your talisman,
I willed myself to cultivate
Our infant garden
Mirroring splendorous hues of our hearts.
During my mothering years
I gave unselfishly, to each child, all that I had.
Unsuspectedly, I watched the sparks of our passions
growing into an arching rainbow of our goals.
Never doubting the bounty of their love.
When I grew old with age,
Vintaged and alone, my dulling eyes
Gaze at stretching shadows.
My inner fiber, sandpaper raw,
An old-age home is my reward.
Now, longingly, I wait to be
Reunited with you,
My husband.

—*Toni Pappas DeVencenty*

The Fridge of Adventure

There I was without a nose;
where it went know one knows.
I looked and looked without a clue;
I looked some more and then I knew.

It went deep down into the fridges,
It crossed Fruit Juice Lake and the Carrot Bridge.
It found itself in a forest of broccoli and cauliflower
Then it climbed the V-8 Tower.

From there it jumped to a tomato nearby
And sent tomato juice to fly.
Then Mr. Onion forced him to cry.
Then my nose began to sigh;

Oh, Mr. Onion, what is this place?
I'm trying hard to find a face.
Just then I opened up the door
And my nose jumped out with a great big roar!

It jumped smack right on my face
And slid into it's very own place.
My nose is back I'm happy to say.
Maybe you can meet it someday.

—*Jessica R. Hillert*

"Trapped"

Trapped in a world of hunger and war,
where less and less people have faith in the Lord.
A world of cult religion and racial discrimination,
where death becomes an image of a permanent vacation.
Babies are having babies and friends are killing friends.
A world where people look forward to the end.
Killers are roaming free to become people we have to face.
Where famine and war could destroy the human race.
Increased teen suicide and teen abortion,
scandal, divorce, pornography and extortion.
A world that has a tempestuous status,
where animals are being killed for scientific analysis,
a world where nations should be an alliance,
instead of a world of global defiance.
Trapped in a world of incurable A.I.D.S.,
overpopulated prisons and abolitionist crusades.
Where believers in our government are only a fraction.
They speak of world peace, but show total inaction.
We take history to learn from our past,
but how much longer is this going to last?

—*Christy Carman*

A Hidden Garden

A girl sits in a hidden garden
where roses cry out to her
she sits and sings,
Songs of passion and fear
when it rains she does not leave
For if she left she could no longer exist
If she left the flowers,
the birds everything that lives inside her
would perish
For this is her own little world
of dreams and love that no one can ever take away
Outside her garden is hatred
which she seems to ignore
When she speaks people only stare
at her beauty and do not listen to her beliefs
To look at her is to see a sun setting
arrayed by awesome flowers
Some say that she stays in her garden of
dreams too long to exist in the real world
Others say she is a child of tranquility

—*Andrea Bond*

Untitled

The understanding of distant times
Where the world was unlearned but not so blind,
When shadows fell on unterrored souls
And we went through the paces of sensible goals.
Can I understand the world today?
As morals, the decent principalities, slip away?
And what comes in? Defiled unknowns.
This is not the way I want my child grown.
Poison is poison, no matter what form.
And no one can say that this life is the norm.
As they strip away each and every rule
And we call them idiots, subversives and fools.
Can we realize that we are in the same boat?
And letting them continue would surely cut our own throats?
A "New Freedom Order" is not what we need,
But stability, congeniality and an old fashioned CHRIST-ian creed.

—*Janice Browder*

Meadow Breeze

In this land that we call home, there is at last a place —
Where we can roam. In the valley or under the trees
the place where you feel the meadow breeze.
Up on a high mountain range, does it all seem so strange?
Is it real, or is it not? I must of known, but I forgot!
Do you long to feel the gentle meadow breeze—
Soothing and relieving you of strife; and with every bit of air
You understand the meaning of your life.
Go to the place where you can feel something gentle,
something real, as real as a baby's smile.
Never to be fake as a criminal's mask;
with every deed, and every good task,
you need not wear such a mask!
To others it may all seem so bland,
for you who may understand
that there is no need for reprimand,
or actions of a fool;
remember this simple rule;
Let the wind take you, let love and
kindness make you.

—*M. Marianela Diaz*

Escape

like to escape the world in
Which I live it's the environment,
'm surrounded with evil. I live in
. place called New York City, a cold
.nd a cruel place. My mind my spirit
.nd personality is separate from this
>lace. Take me away to a far and
.listance place. A place of love
>eace, purity, gentleness, affection,
.nderstanding, warmness, kindness, beauty.
. want to fly to paradise. Up, up and away.
. have wings I can fly away to a different
.lace a different time another world. I can
.ing like a bird dream of beautiful things.
"lowers and roses are lovely, they bring life
.ove and incredible joy. Love me. My heart
.vants to escape to joy that I've never experience
.efore. Please take me away. We can spend eternity
>gether.

—Kenneth L. Brewer

The Abortion Tree

I hang here on the Abortion tree, dead, yes dead as can be.
Vhich of you was my mother? Why did you do this to me?

I did no harm to anyone, had no chance to laugh or cry,
.et you; my mother condemned me, you hired a killer, said I
.lust die.

You had me murdered before I was born, before I could
.arn to pray. Yes, before I could utter the name of God
.ou killed me, then threw me away.

You threw me away like garbage, your heart was calloused,
.old. Did you forget my mother I have an immortal soul?

Yes, you had me murdered before I was born. Yet I might
.ave been the one, the only one to care for you, to soothe
.nd comfort you my mom.

No one can predict the future, who knows what your
.ifferings may be, I won't be around to help you mom
.ou hung me on the Abortion Tree.

—Marie A. Johnson

Thoughts Of A Soldier

"e marched in with our heads held high,
.hile bullets seemed to graze the sky.
.'why ever did our guardians lie?
.ur wives sit alone and cry.

.ll never forget those days in May.
.he last words my friend did say.
.ow face down in the mud he does lay.
.ly friend has gone and left me astray.

.tone cold soldiers with hearts of lead,
.eir frustration and anger burns flames of red.
"e keep on fighting and blood is shed.
.ow count how many soldiers are dead!

.he war now ends and things are not the same.
.o one back home seems to remember my name.
.nly soldiers that die receive any fame.
.hy don't they realize war is not a game!
. an average soldier

—Robert G. Bequeaith

Do You Love Me?

I sit in my room and think about you
while I say do you love me.
Walking, passing, losing my mind
still thinking do you love me.
I take a cold shower and cry myself
to sleep and still I wonder do you love me.
Come in that night and see me lie touch me
I jump, wake up and say do you love me.
Calm and tired I lie back down see the words
flash by my head do you love me.
I dream you hold me, touch me with cold hands
and I ask do you love me.
Wake up that morning and you're no where to be
found now I know I can never love you
while I sit with no sound.
But still I say do you love me?

—Virginia Snowden

Heavens Floating One By One

The sun is slowly rising in the eastern sky,
While ocean waters are still deep blue.
The heavens are floating one by one,
A new one every bright beautiful day.
As the sun is slowly setting in the western sky,
The sunlight fades into a lonely night.
While droplets of dew settle on the ground.
The frost will glitter while the country sighs.
The sun is slowly rising in the eastern sky,
While ocean waters are still deep blue.
The heavens are floating one by one,
As a mother gladly gives birth to her child.
A new one every bright beautiful day.
The sun is slowly setting in the western sky.
The sunlight fades into a joy filled night,
While droplets of dew settle on the country side.
The frost will glitter and the country will sigh.

—Shannan McIntosh

Listening Pre-Dawn

Fading sounds of distant travelers,
whisking down imperturbable asphalt.
The alien wheels of the forlorn,
awake too long, depleted.
Stirring up the particles of settled silence
catching my ear.
Shifting their lives in the anonymous night.
Urban buccaneers?
Slipping away through unpeopled streets,
betrayed by the stealth of the sun.

—Ariel Wyckoff

"Abstruse Whispers"

Succumbing to loneliness in depth-
Whispers silently whispering in the dark.
Sounds of entwining sheets enveloping-
Although no sight in light.

Wandering narrow paths of desertion
Indefinite light engulfed by shadows
Silken flesh against flesh
Lingering caresses not present in time.

Abstruse physical touches somewhat intangible
Daftly experiencing sights of you
Idealistics forming ambient confusion;
Whispering memories not yet abscond.

—Gae M. C. Garcia

In(ward) Road

In the introversion of my
white-walled mind,
I see listenings of clouding
white 'n gray skies.
I hear our flapping flag in
silences.

Classical music digs new paths to connect my
right white brain with
the gray self.

Chemical trails of tears
reach to find another
answerless question.

Learning of gray times and seeing
the white ones sends
me deeper 'n
deeper
into the pain
of unknown.

—*Jon Swartz*

Photograph

There was a shy man, when sober,
who dropped bits of his heart
between the lines of paper;
a piece here, one there —
each one became a dot of color in a photograph.

Subtle horror clothed in confusion chased the man;
ignorance wearing a glittering glass coat
brought him down.
The fight became real;
he grappled with something so insidiously cold
the hair upon his body
acquired a shade - of frosted cellblock gray.
The gray in the photograph was earned.

One particularly noisome night
the inner man
slapped leather; filled his hand with a different pen.
The mask of pain upon the outer man's face
fell away.
Sure did take awhile
for the smile in the photograph.

—*Robert Daniel Terry*

Definition: Hero

Heroes are not those who stand tall and strong
who fly around the sky
No, these are not heros
but people who have
the heart, mind and courage
to know what's wrong and realize,
they have the strength
to fix the errors that have been made
fighting wrongs, making rights
until they have won or died.

So step down Superman and Spiderman
the heroes of our times
are heroes who will help us stand for what is right,
and not let us depend on them, to fix everything that's wrong
never let anyone deter you from what you believe.
Heroes can be real not just dreams

—*Houston Andrew Washington*

"Home With You"

In the air of, happiness, like children
who looking straight at falling water.
For the thought of spring, and looking
at the future, and past times.
For looking at of things that we and
our ancestors brought through the ages,
of splendor and imagination too, bring up
a discussion of, whom might be wrong
of what is, and what isn't of the times
when we had fun and the people of labor
has brought us of good and evil, collide
for manners in, which we, cannot see,
or believe in.

—*Chris R. Dowell*

Child Within

There's a frightened child within me
Who never sees the light
Who dwells in darkest shadows
Terrified of the night.
    Come to me my little one I hear the Saviour say
    Let go the shadows dark I'll love your fears away.

There's an angry child within
Who rages to be free
Who lives in silent torment
Screaming inside of me.
    Come to me my little one I hear the Saviour say
    Let go the tortured silence I'll love your rage away.

There's a lonely little child
Who longs for love so kind
Who stays in solitude afraid
Locked within my mind.
    Come to me my little one
    I hear the Saviour say
    Let go the fearful solitude
    I'll love your tears away.

—*Ruby Elaine Rooker*

The Unremembered

    Lost and lonesome is the man,
who thinks in his heart that, he alone can.
    Weak and worldly is his stand,
left on his own, abandoned by friends!

Hope for the future sifts through his hands,
Yet he boasts in his heart that, he alone can.
On his lips lie the answers to the problems you have,
so consumed with himself, to the pits he descends!

    So lost and lonesome is this man,
who thinks in his heart that, he alone can.
    Pride and arrogance await his command,
to guard insecurities, they must defend!

Searching the earth and devouring the land,
is the man whose heart boasts that, he alone can.
While possessing all Wisdom, he can't understand,
a long-lasting friendship, for it's "Meaningless end!"

    Now lost and loathsome, cruel old man,
who thought in his heart that, he alone can.
Placed in the dirt is your soul that's been damned,
no love dwelled within, but contempt for all men!

—*Kevin Moody*

The Commander

What is in truth to be said of a man,
Who with ease one can get along;
He does his job as best as he can,
Remaining fair though sometimes thought wrong.
When in the balance his decisions are laid,
He seeks always what is right;
In single fairness his judgement is made,
Self service is far from his sight.
As a commander of men he's one of the best,
A leader his troops gladly follow;
I'll say once again outshining the rest,
His reward shall indeed not be hollow.
To sum it all up what's left to say,
What for a handful of others I can;
Upon recalling this time here one day,
I'll remain proud to have served with this man.

—*Michael Kearney*

"Our Kind Of Love"

I just knew someday I would meet a man like you
Who would help me see everyday through
You can be strong, gentle and sweet
But it's our kind of love that makes it complete.

I know sometimes things don't always go right
Especially when we have fight after fight
It's those times that I wouldn't trade,
For it's our kind of love and a life with you that I've made.

We're so different in so many ways,
Maybe it's the mystery we play.
Who cares as long as it's for us,
For it's our king of love that we trust.

But honey don't ever give up on me,
Because I know we'll make it, you'll see,
Through all these years, we've stuck by each other, right or
wrong, but it's our kind of love that keeps us going strong.

You can believe me when I say
I'll love you forever, day after day,
Maybe someday we'll get it all together,
For it's our kind of love that will last forever.

—*Pamela S. Minton*

Thoughts of Daedelus

Why?
Why my beautiful boy?
Why didn't you listen?
I warned you about flying so high.
I told you that you might die.
Why didn't you heed, why didn't you hear?
You, the things I hold most dear?
You soared and glided
Swooped and slided
Like an angel high in the sky
Why, why did you have to die?
Higher, higher and higher you went
More and more and more I wept.
I felt that hot wax on me like tears
As it confirmed my very worst fears.
You fell, a fiery ball into the sea
And it took you forever away from me.
I told you something once and you thought it a lie.
Soaring low is better than dying high.

—*Alayne Bell*

Masterpiece

There is no Art but Handiwork of God,
Whose knowledge brought Creation into Law,
And genius man can only take His nod
To further what is needed without flaw.
Some ray of intellect may touch a star
And set profound enlightenment in place;
Immortal Truth is grasped from Him afar
As Gift of His Perfection and His Grace.
So was the Christ His Son, and Lord of all
Made Gift Supreme to humankind with Love;
Acceptance of Him covers Adam's fall
And hears the invitation from above.
So Blest are steps Creative Origins trod.....
There is no Art but Handiwork of God!

—*Elsie L. Hicks*

The Time That Never Was

Why can I not remember all the bad?
Why can't I remember:
The time that your calm voice
turned into a maddening shrill
that pierced through my ears,
the time your blazing, angry
glare came as a crushing blow
to my heart,
or like the time your once warm
embrace turned a bitter cold?
Why, oh why, can't I remember?
Maybe, it's because it was a time that never was.

—*Sondra L. Thompson*

What Is The World Coming To?

There is always fighting
Why can't there be a little push or shove
'Cuz all we need is enough like
and a little more love.
There is so much violence, you see
Why can't families live right — happily?
And there is so many problems in this world,
Babies are having babies, those poor little girls.
But not to forget about the guys
Why can't they take care of their responsibility, why oh why?
Most parents don't have anything to say
getting on welfare is their only way
As teenagers we should listen to our elders and do
everything right,
Because in a few more years we will have a nice
family with a wonderful husband or a beautiful wife.

—*Lorraine Dupas*

Untitled

Why are you sad Mother?
Why, Dad, do you seem so somber?
Do you think that life now takes me away?
Do you fear for me the world's wrong way?
I can see the way that you feel inside.
I can feel the fears come through my pride.
This is why we must remember,
This is why we know together,
The lessons you taught I'll know forever,
The way of life you taught is my endeavor.
For away from you I could never be.
For my heart is where you live and how I see.

—*Daniel Fink*

Awaken

In sleep
Why is it sorrow, why are you lost in thee?
Awaken thyself,
All these little moments
    disappear like foam in the seawave.
Time flies
    dissolving in the skies.
Years gallup passed,
    as windblown ships unmasted.
Awaken thyself sorrow, you haven't long to grieve.
The tiny stars are growing sleepy,
The moon is bored and turning her back to thee,
Awaken thyself,
The sun soon will be sleeping, and the people will be old,
The environment is weeping, the world is getting cold,
Even though asleep, you are multiplying yourself sorrow,
Awaken and destroy thyself,
die, die, die,
Then the world shall be a lovely picture, smile,
live, live, live.

—*Laurie Reisch*

Life's Little Mysteries

Life's little mysteries will never be explained.

Why is the sky blue?
Why is the grass green?
Why can't air be seen?

Why is love complicated?
Why are some men jerks?
Why does life have so many quirks?

Why are there prejudices?
Why is there so much hate?
Why do some people believe in fate?

Why must we die?
Why must we live?
Why must it be our lives that we give?

Why is there so much pregnancy?
Why is there so much abortion?
Why is it so difficult to use a little caution?

Why are there so many mysteries?
Why does the list seem to go on and on?
Why can't everyone wake up and they all be gone?

—*DoRae Ann Mikes*

Freedom for the World

You want peace
Why pray for peace
Let's have a war
A war of love
Join hands throughout the land
Humanity for every woman and man

Why can't we all have fun
Under God's created sun
And live a life of peace
Freedom for the world
When will it come?

We all are the same
Blood, sick and lame
It's time to say we the people
From every nation, country and shining sea
We want peace

One day, the world's war makers
Will be peaceful partakers
Freedom for the world
When will it come?

—*Reginald Brown*

Why?

Why... Why does life suddenly end?
Why then does it even begin?
Why do life lights shine and then go away?
I'll think of this on another day.
But who knows what tomorrow brings?
Who knows if your life bells will ring?
Your number could come up and then you'll be gone.
But others still live on and on. Why...
When you die where do you go?
Do you still feel the cold of the winters snow?
Do you get to say one final good-bye
or do you just leave us to cry?
Do you get to say I love you and I'll see you again,
or does your life just suddenly end?
Where do you go and what do you do?
Do you feel happiness and sadness to?
What do you feel? Are you happy there?
Do you live without a care?
Are you lonely and are you blue? I want to know,
Because... I miss you so.

—*Amanda Lynn Rhoades*

Untitled

There was no girl as majestic as she
wild, simple, dignified and carefree
like a wildflower swaying seductively
In the wind, alone, by the blue-green sea.
Her hair in waves hung straight down,
barely making a sound,
In a long blue dress made of silk and lace.
Her chameleon eyes, could never hide
what she endured, only heard
In a cold room, alone, she cried.
After her relentless storm died down,
she rises from the water, I knew you wouldn't drown,
but be more stubborn than before.
She has her friends, who needs more?
Once upon a time
my magenta sky
combined with hers, lightning struck,
Thunder was heard,
all around and to the ground
where the flowers grew
And I knew I'd find you.

—*Lori Weckesser*

We'll Never Know

The tiny child inside of you
Will shortly be no more,
For you have decided to give her death,
And her life you can never restore.
Instead of giving her birthday presents,
You're taking them all away.
The hope of memories that we'll have
Grows farther away each day.
We'll never find out if she had freckles
Like you had when you were young.
We'll never know if she could touch
Her little nose with her tongue.
We'll never know if she was short,
Or tall and thin like her dad.
We'll never see those puppy dog eyes
When she's done something bad.
You're taking away her only chance
Of being your cute little kid.
We'll never know if she loved her mom
Just as much as you did.

—*Nikole Williams*

Pennies

Will you take my pennies to the market?
Will you buy for me today?
Wisely choose what you will purchase.
Please don't throw my pennies away.

Don't get lost in some dark alley
Where my pennies fall to the ground.
Go on streets where light shines brightly;
Where the bargains all are found.

I have given you my pennies,
Trusting you to do what's right.
Please don't loose or waste my pennies.
Don't walk away into the night.

Hidden in my coins, there's gold
Of talents for you to use.
Invest it well in all your hours.
My reward for you, don't abuse.

Now, will you take my pennies to the market?
Will you spend them wisely for me?
Go now. Take my pennies to the market.
Bring back sparkling gold for me.
—*Claudia J. Lent-Boutchyard*

Remember Me

Will you remember me when my time has passed
Will your memories of me always last
Will they go on as the days go by
When you think of me, will you ever cry
Or will you forget me and my warm embrace
Will you forget the smile you put on my face
Will you forget the way you held me at night
When you hold someone else, will it feel as right
Will I be forgotten as the days grow cold
Will you forget me as you grow old
Or will you remember the times we had
And will those memories be happy or sad
Please don't cry when you think of me
Even though I've closed my eyes and I cease to be
But why did you wait until I left this earth
To realize what I was truly worth
Why didn't you love me while you had the chance
Why didn't you stay until our final dance
And now that I'm gone and my heart can be free
Please say that you always will remember me
—*Sherry Wesley*

Untitled

The leaves fall
winds howls
snow drifts quietly to the ground
it is winter
coldness sets in
the days of coldness go on and on
But alas, SPRING has come!
warmth comes down; all snow is gone
sunshine comes down in radiant beams
small flowers pop up through the ground
Then there are days of hotness
people burn and flowers roast; this is summer
then is autumn and then winter,
coldness sets in once again
When I think that SPRING may never come again,
I know, in my heart, that it will always come again
Seasons will never cease
they will continue on forever and ever
For the seasons started at the dawn of time
And will never end until time does
—*Julia Shackford*

Thistledown

Crested purple thistle
With a silky downy head,
Summer's really here to stay
When you display your hat of crinkled thread,
A tufted glory,
Thorny - prickly - gory too.
You make a bed just anywhere
Rooting here and popping there,
Well protected is the stance
of your dilated yearly dance.
Then you don white fleecy caps
Blow balls on a sunny spree,
To celebrate your jubilee
The wind makes you a refugee!
—*K.M. Bayer*

The 4 A.M.

When I can't sleep and lay in my bed,
With busy thoughts going round in my head,
The one thing that I listen to,
Is the 4 A.M. train as it passes through,
The echo in the valley, what a wonderful, wonderful sound,
And the memories that it brings, going round and round,
A little girl, fresh ironed sheets,
And before bed some of Grandmas' treats.
I'd snuggle down as the moonlight spread.
Across the quilt upon the bed,
Never a worry, never a care,
I'd give anything to go back there,
We are cast upon the worldly sea,
But I am where I have to be,
I listen through the sound of rain,
For the echoing sounds of the 4 A.M. train.
—*Annette Main Hill*

You

She's beautiful
    with dark red hair.
She's tall
    with pride and confidence.
She's funny
    with laughter and good times.
She's strong
    with love and devotion.
She's a friend
    a true blue supporter of my every
    triumph, and yet a careful critic
    to my every mistake.
She works hard to please those she loves.

To me, impressions of her will last a lifetime.
No.....my mom will last two lifetimes
    hers and mine.
—*Lucetta M. Billhime*

The Edge Of Heaven

Blessings so many, of number untold,
When against each other our lives do brush.
In my life and heart when, you, I behold,
So easily the edge of heaven I touch.

Light given by you each moment of my life,
My heart now with joy continually sings.
Soar do I above the clouds and every strife,
Because to my hopes and dreams you give wings.

Perfection in you, not that which I seek,
Someone who, with life, struggles like me.
Seeing your heart gentle and spirit meek,
Love you very much, will I for eternity.
—*Henry H. Hague, Jr.*

Untitled

My bonnie lad with skin so fair
   with eyes as black as coal

With one glance you pierced my heart
   you touched my very soul

A cavalier a soldier true
   our love could never be

Yet amidst the heather you stole my heart
   for all eternity

Now with child and winter come
   I often pray for thee

My bonnie lad in battle lost
   you'll not return to me
         —*Venka Dyro*

Come My Baby

Come, my little baby,
With eyes so bright.
Come, my little baby,
It's nighty-night.
Day is done-
Time to tuck you in, my little one.
So close your eyes.
From Wonderland to Slumberland let us go,
Up the street, down the street,
Hear the patter of little feet.
The sandman has come to town.
Come, my little baby,
Little sleepyhead,
Close your eyes, it's time for bed.
Dream in heavenly sleep.
The little stars will soon come out to peep.
And God in heaven for me will keep
My little one
So dear and sweet.
         —*Kathryn Arbaugh*

A New Generation

I see them all around these days
with false contentment in their veins.
To calm the harshness, to quell the fear
they sink into a tragic haze.
And it shatters my smug security to see
   such opportunities wasted!
Like brittle, hardened, calloused hands
(Love's lonely offspring now matured)
The softer loves, the subtler pains
   are things they've never tasted.

Yet, someday they may come to know
with their hopes in armor, still confined,
   beneath their small polluted sky,
Approaching slowly, without sound,
Lifting all things to higher ground,
A sense of Being, time, and flow.
While even the computer
   in all its wisdom
Could never think to stoop so low,
   Nor dare to rise so high.
         —*Andrew Jerpe*

10th Birthday Girl Scout Troop 451

It's grand to share a birthday
With friends as dear as you
The memory of these 10 years
Will last my whole life thru.
The fun we've shared, the things we've learned
The times we goofed, the praise we've earned
Are all a part of you and me and of the people we will be.

And now our time is almost o'er
Our last year's here, there'll be no more
But I am sure, we all can say
I wouldn't trade one single day
of those that you and I hold dear.
So Happy Birthday, Scouts. It's here.
         —*Corinne Brace*

A Fairy Tale Angel

I once met an angel out of a fairy tale,
With gorgeous golden hair embraced in white veil,
Eyes so captivating like the deep ocean blue,
Yet people still declare that dreams don't come true.

She was more beautiful than the blue sky in May,
Which gave me hope in life with each passing day,
She was so breathtaking and so altogether divine,
That I wanted to be with her till the end of time.

Her eyes were like shiny stars up in the skies at night,
Which overflowed my mortal soul with uttermost delight,
Her voice was so sweet, sweeter than honey could be,
And her tender smile brightened my day thoroughly.

But mere words can not convey her elegance,
Nor can scant sentences express her eminence,
One has to see her to believe in this divinity,
Who has captured my heart without any scrutiny.
         —*Isaac Tashjian*

Time Go On

Time go on, but love will never be gone,
With greatness and care, love would never disappear,
What is love, without care and kindness,
I love you; even now I may confess,
Deep down in my heart, I love you more than I know,
No matter where you go, No matter what you do,
I will, always still be loving you,
The smile in your face, will never leave my eye,
So tenderly I love you, so sincerely,
I pray God grant love you so.

The feeling I feel, burns inside my heart,
Whenever I think of you, I started to cry,
That's why I never wanted to say goodbye,
Love, passion and peace is all I want,
Without you, I got no sight.
         —*Rith Chin*

Ageing

Why do we grow older,
Why do people get colder
Ageing should be fun
But, all the responsibilities,
You'll have Mom or Dad
Teaching, learning, thinking,
Making and keeping friends,
Marrying, loving, going throw the dead ends,
But still I ask the question
Why do we grow older?
         —*Hope Chouinard*

Milady

The moon upon Earth her light does shine,
With Jupiter holding his court so fine
And the silent, mighty brooding ocean
Diffusing an air of Time primeval —
An awesome beauty of power subdued;
A hidden strength by God himself controlled.
In the mysterious light, m'lady fair
Walks in an ecstasy I do declare
Along life's strand. Her heart and mind are pure.
For the love of her Hell's pangs I endure,
Because I know in Hades' tough embrace
Cleansed is my very soul, and in life's race
  One thing certainly I know: love divine
  Will conquer and bring to me peace sublime.
　　　　—George Barcock

"A Man Stands"

A man stands for truth and honesty,
With love that is shown
In all that he possesses,
A steady hand in all over plan
If no one can, this man can!
Strong in all he believes in
Ideals that can work without guesses.

Love of country and his fellow man
Follows when ever it can all over the land
Then without even a quibble on demand
A road shoulders to the wheel
Putting everyone on their heels
Forward we go, as this man stands.

A man stands for what he believes in!
Ability with integrity
Knowledge of what is needed
Works to, try to make it so
When comes to the end of the line
You know everything is just fine
Only this man can, when "A man stands"
　　　　—Eleanor S. Radcliffe

Untitled

I sit on the beach,
With my mind free to wonder,
As I look at the beautiful blue ocean with thunderous waves
Violently crashing onto the shore.
As I sit here on the picturesque beach, the love of my life,
And think about nothing.
It's the most wonderful feeling,
Thinking about nothing.
I stand up and turn passing the flawless sand dunes.
Leaving my peacefulness,
And returning,
To the world of chaos...
　　　　—Julie Felix

Deaf Child

A wise old man today asked me
  "Which would be worse: Not to hear, not to see?"
And so I gave him my most honest reply
  "To go through life deaf? I would almost rather die.
For life without sound I could not bear,
  I could never hear the music so fair
As that of life, of what happens around
  And if one were blind, their hearing is not bound."
And so that old wise man went along on his way,
  I never told him that I read his lips today.
I am a deaf child, my hearing is gone;
  Life without sound is like the day without dawn.
　　　　—M.A. Wallace

All We Say In One Single Day

Just suppose that all we say in one single day,
With never a word left out,
Was printed each night in black and white
It would make queer reading, no doubt.

And then, just suppose ere our eyes we would close,
We must read the whole story through,
Then wouldn't we sigh, and wouldn't we try,
A whole lot less talking to do?

And I more than half think, that many a kink
Would be straightened in life's tangled thread,
If just half what we say, in one single day,
Was left forever unsaid.
　　　　—Bertha Chambers Gillette

Snowstorm

Last winter
with our baby lit up in
My womb
A cold snow-sheet fell over
the town
Lit up like crystals
(as seen from inside)
As we stood by the window
I inhaled the sharp smell of
crisp, log-burned winter air
Thanking God that I had you
Looking outside together at
the snow, blown into drifts,
Covering cars
The wind-razor sharp-biting into our lungs
and slamming into the heat
from our apartment window
I turned to you
and loved you in crystal-sparkle light.
　　　　—Jo-Anne Smith

Christmas

Christmas is here once more
with people in and out of stores.
Bright lights, and lots of snow
with the traffic going real slow.
Pretty trees, and presents
for dinner a big juicy pheasant.
Dolls, and trucks children hanging up their socks.
Trains, and bikes for big children, and little tykes.
Christmas is here once more
a lot to buy in the store.
Mittens, gloves and hats
people wiping their feet on the front door mat.
Cuddling around the fire
for a man, and women's heart to desire.
Smell of pine in your house
that draws the family mouse.
Ringing of bells, and rushing of people
the big church bell ringing in the steeple.
　　　　—Darlene Keith

Small Talk

Endless conversations walk by
While the coffee is poured to fill us up
Like cars refueling in paper cups.
Doesn't the talking ever stop?
What happened to whom
And who happened to whom?
Our words overflow as they fall in
the hands of a gossip or two.
Words, hot and steamy; delectable brew,
Singeing the tongues of their owners.
　　　　—Carol Limburg

593

The Wait

The line is crooked, spots of bright colored jackets mixed
with some of somber tones snake along side the austere building
The wind blows wispy hair askew on heads bent forward.
It's owners stand still, very still.
The young, holding mouths taut, chins jutting out.
The message; youth is on my side.
Gnarled hands intermix with smooth polished nails.
Dutifully they sign the familiar form.
Feet reverse, back to the outside bleakness.
The wait is on, the endless wait for work.
Hungry to feel human again.
Clunker cars, rusted, mosaic, wait for their occupants.
Spewing forth familiar groans when started.
For many the past meant dreams put on hold.
Drawn they were by the lure of security.
Bring back the unfilled dreams and curse the unspoken world
of blanket security.

—Jean Belknap

Going Home

The little girl sat by her grandpa's bed
With tears in her eyes, she bowed her head;
Jesus, if you must take him away,
Please leave him for just one more day.
I love him and I'll miss him you see;
Were best friends, grandpa and me.
When I am hurt and want to cry
He always wipes my tears dry.
He told me he was going home to you;
I know you love him Jesus, but I love him too"
The old man raised his head, opened his eyes,
And for one last time wiped her tears dry.
"Child, I love you, but I'll soon be gone;
Just look up above child, I'm going home.
The streets are lined with love and care,
I'll be waiting for you, someday to join me there."
The heavens opened up and took him away
With his very last breath she could hear him say;
"Going home, where the streets are lined with love,
Going home, dear Jesus, where you wait above."

—Winnie Williamson

Vitality

Playing in the rain at night
with the heavens for a shelter
and a raindrop for a friend.

Dodging bolts of light falling round my feet
waiting, listening for the rambling of the Gods
taking a drink from the puddle of life
just to quench my thirst

I think this world is full of mystery
Full of suspicion and desolation
If everyone could see me now
living instead of lifeless
hopeful instead of futile
then they would see just how great the world is

When you can look through the gloom
To the other side of reality
and see what would happen if we loved
in our life a little
and knew there was going to be a sunrise
tomorrow

—Jeremy Wilson

"A Rocky Mountain Experience"

Massive solitude, blaring silence
With the weight of the sky on its shoulders.
Cloak of white cotton, shirt of dark grey,
Velvet green skin, slowly wading
Through turquoise and translucent waters,
Keeping watch over its dominion.

Sighing wind and weeping rain
Over mankind's sins, the biting cold, cutting streams,
Or the peaceful passing of its children.
No one knows.

Disguising this pain with beauty serene,
That is its claim to fame.
For what it's worth, I've tasted perfection
While walking its domain.
If heaven is on earth, it must be here.
This I know.

—John Bradley Vogler

"Sweet Sixteen"

What happened to the bracelet...
With two little hearts, bought at the fair?
Binding you together... The one you promised always to wear!

Promises of love at sweet sixteen
You'll die before you remove it from your wrist
Is this a promise you really mean?

Twenty years later you find it in the cedar box
Along with some of his brown curly locks...
I don't think my heart was so true when I was in "Bobby Socks"

But wasn't it the most beautiful time of life
All so innocent and full of puppy love
Even made wishes on stars and thought they came true

Sometimes I still wish for a bracelet with hearts
and a moment of sweet sixteen
Because age does not change the heart it seems

But as years go on and true love comes to you
It's fun to remember those days
Love wouldn't be so good if it wasn't from remembering...
"Sweet Little Sixteen" and what she became today.

—Brenda M. Gray

Some Strawberries are for Eating

Upon the threshold of life I stood
With visions of the road beyond.
Haltingly, I stepped forward
Greeting ever expanding worlds.
With new intensity, I took the next step
And each following with less hesitance.
I have mounted Apollo's chariot
To cavort with each new day;
As fair Phaeton, the bastard son,
I danced close to the stars —
To draw back only with singes
Learning which path to take.
Now, in the days of the sun's setting -
Harbinger of the ever darkened night -
I sit with pen to share the muse
And treasures gathered in my route.

—Henry O. Emmerson

Talent Within

You see I have this talent and its locked
within my mind
My thoughts begin to race the words the more I find
I have to put on paper all the thoughts
from present to past
I have to put it on paper so that moment
maybe captured and last
You see everybody has a talent, and its in
their mind, body, and soul.
Its just that some do not realize and they
ever let it go.
Use what you have you may surprise yourself
though to others it means no great deal
But that's okay really it is because its
how it makes you feel
And if you see visions and ideas and
words racing through your mind
Don't be afraid to use them bring it
forward and you will find
You have talent too!

—*Doreen M. Badillo*

Day Without Her

A day without her is like a day without breathing;
without inhaling the smell of her perfume.
A day without her is like a day without thinking;
without pondering the image of her by my side.
A day without her is like a day without feeling;
without caressing her beautiful strands of blond hair.
A day without her is like a day without seeing;
without staring at her figure as she comes closer.
A day without her is like a day without loving;
without expressing my desires with her.
A day without her is like a day without sharing;
without combining our dreams as one.
A day without her is like a day without communicating;
without telling her how much I love her.
A day without her is like a day without listening;
without hearing the sound of her sweet voice.
A day without her is like a day without meaning;
without living.

—*Doug Heidrick*

Simply I Love You

Sitting here in the window, thinking of what could be,
wondering if there's any hope, of love, for you and me. On
that day that we first met I looked deep into your eyes, I
felt the care, the love, the warmth, all honesty without disguise.

When you took me as your own I thought that I might die, how
someone like you, could want me I often wonder why. From that
point, my feelings soared, with things I never knew, things I
never felt before the day I first met you.

People say that fate is rare, and chances we all must take, but
no one ever promised life to be a piece of cake. In the past,
my heart's been scarred with all the tears I've cried,
relationships that didn't work, and emotions that have died.

So take me now, and stay with me, I promise to be true.
There's one more thing I've left to say, it's simply I love you.

—*Melinda Anne McDowell*

When Death Comes

I hope that I will have run long enough,
won't they be sad, when I'm gone;
No, I don't think they'll mourn,
not a crystal clear tear will fall from heartless eyes.
I know there is a person with a heart that is true.
I wish to God to find her and share a love as grand and pure
as I know is possible. I'm so sick of the shallow, cold people
I call friends and lovers, always yearning for something more;
goals to achieve and things to buy with the pointless
careers they've chosen.
These words as all others flow so readily and true
from my pen; they are all thoughts and feelings flowing
from my heart.
I think I need to speak more to open my impaled heart.
I have tried to teach someone of the love I hold,
that the real things is life come from thinking of
others and giving yourself to someone you love totally.
I ended up only confusing them as much that they
only see themselves's and people that participate in
co-asskissing as the "true" people in their lives.

—*Christopher Aaron Sholtis*

Untitled

Hi everybody, I'm a tree
Won't you help look after me?

I need a drink at least once a week
And keep those soda cans off my feet.

Take them instead if you want to help
to your fire station, burnt children they'll help.

Conservation may sound like a lot
But not when you're stuck in too small of a pot.

Plant me some friends, I like company
And will provide you with shade indefinitely.

Birds love my branches, they come to rest
And usually build a home called a nest.

I love to see them so beautiful and free
But I wish they would stop trying to fertilize me.

Watch out with your weeder, that hurts a lot
When you keep hitting my bark on the same tender spot.

The air that you breathe I try to keep pure
Just for a treat on my feet put manure.

Thank you for letting me bend your ear
I love you all dearly and will serve you for years.

—*Alberta Burns*

A Poet

A poet can write words to enchant you within the
words.

A poet can mystify you within a mystery from love,
into darkness of hate.

As a poet words come together to tell what is.
For a poet to explain what is would be to define
one mind, heart and soul.

The mind of a poet is full of confusion of what
has past and the mysteries of what is to be.
The heart of a poet beats for what it longs for
as it passes through time.

The soul of a poet touches every letter into the
depth of the words that become the poem.
If you can write what is within and become the poem
then you are truly a poet.

—*Gloria A. Barron*

The Ghost Ship

The end is near, all is quiet now.

My Ribbed hull,
   Worn and beaten,
   whistles the wind which flows through.
My Sails,
   Tattered and torn, collect nothing but dust
   as they sag on my skeletal remains.

   I am the Ghost Ship.

Slowly,
   drifting in life's foggy current.
My ribs creek,
   echoing the laughter and joy
   of my previous inhabitants.
Tired,
   I sink deeper and deeper,
   into the murky waters of time.
Numb, the icy waters flow through me.

   I am the Ghost Ship.
   Once I sailed with many, but now, I rest. . .

   Alone.
      —*Michael Krohn*

The Priest and the Bear

I once knew a priest that thought going hunting a bear
would be fun, so from his friend he got a gun.
Went into the woods the way he should and standing right
there was a big black bear.
He took a shot through the mist, he missed.
And the bear kept coming at him.
So the priest raised his eyes to God.
Dear God please listen,
Please make this bear a Christian.
The bear came walking toward him
on his two back feet.
Crossed his paws, smacked his jaws.
Raised his eyes and said,
Thank you God for this meal
I'm about to eat.
      —*Elizabeth Seaver*

You And I

In the night I feel warm and safe,
Wrapped in her arms she holds me tight.
Never a question as to why, or even when
Her kind gestures towards me are deeply appreciated.
She...
Is always there to comfort me when I need it the most.
As she holds me, I feel nothing could cause me any harm.
It is within these precious moments I smile, and laugh
While she cuddles me.
Even while claiming to be a strong man,
Deep within her arms I bury my head and even cry.
There are so many unforgettable things about this woman,
That I've come to love and deeply cherish.
And in all I've experienced all these treasured times with
her... together.
Within her tender and most gentle embraces,
I feel an overwhelming love
As a mother would express to her very child.
But, this love is even more special
For this love is shared only between... you and I.
      —*Rodney C. Williams*

A Talk With Jesus

Seems like Lord when I try to do good, there is still so much
wrong. Dear Jesus please show me the way; please help me to be
strong. When I think I have done my best, sometimes I wonder,
"Lord why the test?" Open my heart so I can see, who you want
me to be. My burdens Lord seem so hard to bear, and I wonder
if you really care. Lord Jesus, please, stop and listen - I am
almost through. Lord tell me, who you want me to be and what
you would have me to do. Open my heart Lord so I can see, who
you want me to be. Then a voice spoke unto me, my child open
your heart so you can see who you are, not who I want you to
be. You must have faith and patience too; cause I shall always
carry you through. I am always nearby whenever you call. Just
trust and have faith, you never will fall. Knock and it shall
be opened, seek and ye shall find! A child of God you will
always be. Open your heart, turn on life's light and you can
see. The Lord is my shepherd - he has restored my soul. All
his blessings I have to behold.
Thank you Jesus! Amen!
      —*Sheryl D. Lacy-Williams*

Andy

I loved him too much to see the truth, he was only another
wrong door. Why did I fall for his games, I'd heard it all before.

I can't believe I was so stupid, I should've know it from the
start. That when I heard those lies again, I shouldn't have
taken them to heart.

When he said he loved me, he never knew what those words meant.
From the second I saw him, I knew he was heaven sent.

I was wrong, as we can plainly see. I gave everything to him,
but he just used me.

Why did it have to end, when it never should've started? I
really wish, we'd never parted.

I hear whispers in my head, they all call his name I've lost
his love, things will never be the same.

I never thought love lasted long, but who said it had to die?
And everything he said, was just a painful lie.

He'll never know how much I loved him, he'll never be able to
see, that when he passed up love, he passed up me.
      —*Melissa Crouch*

Almost To Frederick

The drive North more beautiful than ever
yellows turned to burnt oranges and scarlets
line the lane where leaves float earthward
lilies on a summer pond.

Fall and you at home, pulling up my stakes
the last of the tomatoes
never quite ready for picking
always too ripe to eat.

Preparing for winter, putting out the feeder
how you hated those birds winters ago
north I travel
meticulously you place the feeder just so
uneaten seed must not infect your yard.

Almost to Frederick, the misty patchwork
of the mountains, beckons me further
ahead on the right a cardinal slips
down from its perch in a towering hemlock
a bright ornament falling from a Christmas tree
caught in midair by a sympathetic wind
northward she blows; then turns towards home.
      —*Mary R. Brandt*

Wild And Free"

ild and free,
es, that's me and the way I always
ant to be,
ild and Free.
ee like the wind that blows
rew the trees, free as the birds
at fly threw the sky!
ild as the blossoms that bloom in
meadow, wild as that rabbit that
ayfully romps near a spring,
ee as the flag that flies high in
e sky.

ild and free Yes that's Me, Wild and Free!
—*Elizabeth M. Angel*

As I Wait"

ood morning, my precious children,
et another day I give for you;
ke it, and use it wisely,
r not many more, are you due.

rough the nights, I've given you the stars,
d for your days, I'll give you the sun;
spread the words I have given you,
many hearts, we have not won.

ave given you all there is to give,
ough in your foolishness, you will not accept;
y greatest gift is eternal life,
mething in which, with me you shall live.

ere is nothing that you can say or do,
at could fade my love away;
in repentance, you can come to me,
d in prayer, start each new day.

ecious children, heed these words I say,
r very soon, I come to bring you home;
r should your hearts belong to me,
e fires of hell, you shall never roam.
—*Charlotte Schoubroek*

n Ode to a Departed Soldier

e battle is o'er, the foe have fled
t I see not, for I am dead
gaping hole from which flows blood redder than red
t I feel not, for I am dead
ne eyes are closed yet I see the world
e flag of my enemy is now unfurled
e smoke of the battle still fills the air
e eyes of the vanquished filled with despair
arrived and fought, it seemed so right
en we engaged in a fearful fight
en it was over, the stench of death
ng over the battlefield like a fouled breath
ought for a cause, be it wrong or right
w, I live in eternal night
—*Arch Di Roberts*

ath Be Not Sad

e sorrows of death are hard to understand,
u try to feel the touch of God's helping hand.
e feelings of death are deep and sincere,
loss of a friend or relative or someone dear.
e emptiness in your heart feels as if it will
ver go away,
you too will be close to your loved ones someday.
ath is something very hard to explain,
you go to a place that feels no pain.
ere is a place that knows no sorrow far far away,
I my friend plan to see you there one day.
—*Melissa Heller*

An End To Uncertainty ...

Thro'out the day and into the night, I was surrounded by a quiet.
Yet within me, varied storms of unrest did brew. Two
weeks hence my most significant thought was a healthy diet.
Now—almost my every thought is only of you. Our first weekend
may have been marred by many uncertainties. Yet, we both worked

to clear doubts and set the record straight. Tonight, I yearn
to underscore your importance to me and I have vowed to
minimize the sole journeys from our love's gate. Last night
definitely showed us both just how much we do care about life,
us, our children, and what truly lies beyond.

Love, you and I have dreams, hopes, fears, and more to share
Of one another, we will surely become much more fond. Even
though tonight I
appear to easily pen these words of love... Honey, I especially
miss your total presence and lovely face. Thanks to our

togetherness, I remain at peace like "that dove"... still longing
for the warmness of your hug, kiss and embrace. Tonight will
be a most difficult one and I will toss and turn... constantly
reaching out to touch and caress my newly found love. As I
journey over the next few days, I will visualize our urn for we

are together because of Divine intervention from above.
—*Nathaniel Robinson, Sr.*

Dream

As I close my eyes, I begin to dream that familiar dream
    You and I stand side by side
and feel the sunshine on our bodies.
As I turn to look into those gentle eyes
    and touch that face that warms my heart.
The wall that I have carefully built comes
    crashing down; leaving me unmasked and naked.
But those gentle eyes are there to
    help me through the fallen bricks into the light.
I want to stand in the sunshine and
    breathe in the happiness that surrounds me
and never leave those gentle eyes which
    draw me near.
This dream will soon end as I cling
    to the body that stands close to my own
which in a heart beat stands miles away.
    As I awake to yet another new day,
The warmth is still in my heart as those
    gentle eyes call to me and draw me
into the light once more.
—*Gail Duffy*

"Candle"

Your faces are many and frequent.
You are all-seeing, as I can see each of your detailed faces;
Crying, screaming.
They are pink and cold in the day;
Warm and red-black in the night.

You bury your old grief with new red tears, then black.
Over and over, until the first grief is deep inside
And the fears of today spill over,
Like tomato seeds dripping down the smooth side of a tomato.

Each face screams in pain; in horror; in fear.
It is the first fear.
The same as today's fear, only made stronger
By your frequent tears and stupid fears.
When the crying is done, you know the worst:
You will not exist.
Why should you last?
Nothing else does.
—*Annabelle Karper*

597

Merry Christmas! Merry Christmas!

Let's all crawl under the Christmas tree
You, and you, and you and me.
Don't scream and yell and have a fit,
But, wait until you open it.

The pretty packages, in colors bright
Tenderly wrapped to be just right.
Read the names, carefully, so
You will know to whom they go.

What a happy day, the work all done,
Now to relax and enjoy the fun.
The biggest day of the year, I think,
And pushing our nerves to the brink.

The end of wrappings, end of bows,
Another year coming to a close.
We weathered our troubles and tears.
We ask the Lord to banish fears.

As onward we go through life,
Display our joy and avoid all strife,
Happiness can be with prayers and song
Much love in our hearts as we go along.

—*Lela B. Budnick*

"Contrast"

You are my brother, yet we're not related;
    You are my friend, but your skin color is hated.
Your presence brings joy, but your life is full of pain;
    You knowledge is admired, but your practices are inhumane.
Your achievements are great, but go unrewarded;
    Your song is beautiful, but your tone is morbid.
Your talent is memorable, but no one recalls it;
    Your way should be easy, but troubles befall it.
You value life, yet feel free to abort;
    You expect kindness, but offer only painful retorts.
I thought I knew you, then you say you're in a gang;
    "Nothing's changed," you say, but your favorite sound is "bang!"
Where have you been? There's blood on your knife;
    Please let me help you through this unbearable strife.
I cry for your ignorance, but you laugh at my tears;
    You want joy and not sorrow — you can't calm my fears.

—*Lisa Neusch*

Eve

Adam where due you be?
    You are not guarding the tree;
the wicked devil must be near
    I tremble, I have fear.

The devil leaping, talking does appear
    your partner, my beautiful dear!
In the back woods you know
    preparing for the big animal show.

Just forget, let him be
    you will learn of the honey bee;
its nectar, oh so sweet
    I must repeat, oh, so sweet.

Eve breathed God what did you say?
    "Near the forbidden tree not to stay";
confident of my love for Thee
    I'll just leave the tree.

The devil near by, lifted his head
    "you are mine he said";
eat the honey and really see
    the joy of hell for eternity.

—*Larry Shields, FSC*

The Hunt

It wasn't hard to find you.
You came alone,
You sat alone,
You drank alone.
And listened to the music,
The heartbeat of the night.

Like a tigress on the prowl,
Silently scouting—
Searching for prey—
I stalked you.
And listened to the music,
The heartbeat of the night.

Golden eyes softly glowing,
Staring at your back, silently I beckoned —
Wavering demurely as you rose for the attack.
And listened to the music, the heartbeat of the night.

You moved toward me with certainty; spoke,
But made no inquiry. I came instinctively.
We embraced and listened to the music,
The heartbeat of the night.

—*Gail F. Blanchard*

Sometimes

I sometimes often wonder. What ever happened to the old you?
You came back full force and giving. Which only ended up in
painful taking. You told me I was the only one. I had that
special something. You shared your thoughts and feelings.
Which led to my trust and caring. I sometimes often wonder.
What we really shared in that special place? You promised me
yourself and that you would never leave. Only to tell me that
you needed your time. To run with others without the worry of
someone caring. I sometimes often wonder. How we ever came
to
be? You and I so different yet alike in every way. We both
have our hopes and dreams. Yours much different from mine. In
which you say gets in the way. But yet.... still pushed
toward the same destination of happiness and fulfillness. I
sometime often wonder. Why you always doubted my words? I
never doubted you. I listened to your inspiring words only a
fool wouldn't believe. Only blind to you and only you and the
words you shed. I sometime often wonder. Why it always ends
in the same way? Harsh words said. Things not meant and words
better off unsaid.

—*Heidi Ryan*

Autumn

Fall is in the air
You can see it everywhere
Look around you and behold
How the leaves are turning colors
Red and orange, brown and gold
The trees will soon be bare
As the leaves come falling down
The nights grow cold, and in the morning
The frost is heavy on the ground
On a chilly evening, you can see a smoky haze
Rising just above the ground
And the smell of wood burning
In homes all over town
These are signs to let us know winter's very near
So get prepared for its icy blast
When days are dark and drear
The earth is getting ready now for its long winters sleep
But when spring arrives all nature thrives
And up through the ground the crocus peep
As the earth awakes from its long winters sleep.

—*Elizabeth A. Chadwick*

Friends Like Brothers"

y friend, my brother, "What did you do?"
ou cast aside a love, life and marriage
I've always envied, and looked up to.

any a times, I came to you askew;
sking you, "Brother, friend, what do I do?"

ow the tables are turned, things won't be the same anymore;
ou had what I wanted, and so much more.

e've been thru thick, we've been thru thin;
s like "looking in a mirror;"
Watching you walk the path I've been.

nowing the stress, I worry a lot about you;
ray daily to Mary, Our Mother to shield
You with her cloak of blue.

emember, "another" person does not make
whatever you're looking for in life "be";
find "real" love, happiness and inner peace,
ou must look "inside" yourself, and find "thee".

the meantime, I'll hold your hand O' brother of mine;
l be your friend, till the end of time.

ove, your brother, your friend.
   —*Joan C. Flo*

Front Of Your Eyes...

   A fleeting moment, a measure of time,
ou dance though the music with cares, sublime.
With twirling motions, you glide on air,
Twisting and turning with hearts so fair.
Darkness soon comes and the party wanes,
he songs start revealing the hidden pains.
ou try as you might to bring back the past,
earts are saddened, the memories won't last.
hen comes the time we all fear and dread,
e time in our life when we think love is dead
t look though your eyes, clouded with tears,
or you will see people share in your fears.
hrough courage and hope you begin to see,
omewhere in your life, there will be a key.
tience is a virtue, there's no need to hurry,
or you will be loved, so please don't worry.
e key you will find and it maybe a surprise,
or it just might be in front of your eyes.
   —*John P. Gregory, Jr.*

It Doesn't Matter"

   It doesn't matter. How I feel inside.
   You didn't listen. I should have lied.

   It doesn't matter. What I say or do.
e words are nothing, their meaning lost to you.

   It doesn't matter. How hard I try.
You won't see me hurt. You won't see me cry.

It doesn't matter. How good it could be.
   Your eyes won't open, so you can't see.

It doesn't matter. That all I have is pain.
   I saw a chance. My hope was in vain.

It doesn't matter. The way that I feel.
I can dream forever. It will never be real.

doesn't matter. That my heart will shatter.
m wasting my breath, it just doesn't matter.
   —*Danny W. Gunter*

Untitled

Why in this world is there so much hate
You don't listen, you only dictate
You see the color of my skin
So I can't be your friend
Let's get rid of all this hate
Let's sit down and communicate

The wealth you have is yours by right
I won't steal, don't hold it so tight
You see the color of my skin
So it's the end
Let's get rid of all this hate
Let's sit down and communicate

Close your eyes and for a moment be blind
We'll get along if you'll open your mind
You see the color of my skin
Stop looking outside, start looking within
Let's get rid of all this hate
Let's sit down and communicate
   —*Deborah L. Reis*

Dedicated to Paul

You don't understand how I'm feeling,
You don't realize what I say is true,
I'm hopelessly falling in love with you,
I try to tell you how I feel,
And believe me what I say is real.
You don't understand how I'm feeling,
And deep down I know you don't care,
You push all my hurt to the side,
and pretend that it's not even there.
I can't go on pretending, that this pain just
doesn't exist.
Because you don't understand how I'm
feeling, I can't go on much longer
like this,
You have to understand and love me, put nothing
or no one above me.
Just let me in I'm begging, don't walk past a
situation like this. You'll regret it is all I'm saying.
You won't get it any better than this.
   —*Marie D. Rosas*

That Unforgetful Night

I cry myself to sleep at night wondering how
you feel. I woke up and thought it was all
a dream, but it wasn't, it was real.

How come I let myself go through pain?
It meant nothing to you, but a lot to me, why was I so stupid?
Why?
What have I done?

When I woke up I found myself lying next
to you. I was so astonished at what
happened I began to cry out loud.

I loved you so much it didn't matter then.
I felt if anyone should it should've been you.

You broke my heart, you tore it in two,
I don't know if I could ever forgive you for
running off, with someone new.
   —*Amanda Cheatham*

The Unknown....

I sit alone in my chair,
You looked at me and never stopped to care,
Looking at you I wish you could see,
How many times you had hurt me.
Tears fill my colored eyes,
I look at you and want to die.
I walk alone in the dark,
I stop and sit on a bench in the park.
I sit alone in the unknown,
The night is like a shadow hiding my feelings that had
once shown.
Never letting you or anyone know,
How many times I let my feelings show.
No one around for me to love,
The street light shines on me from above.
To my face I put my hand, in my mind darkness stands.
With my hand I wipe away the tears, trying to find my
heart a cure, I try to face the unknown,
The night shadow hides the feelings that had once shown.

—*Michelle Zurn*

Oh What a Life We Live

Oh what a life we live. You're born.
You see. You walk. You play.
And all the dreams you have.
You're rich. You're poor. You tried so hard.
You have family, wife, kids.
You worked so hard for what you have.
You go to bed. Close your eyes. Wake up
For a brand new day.
You get sick. You get old. You laugh, you cry.
Your time is short. You know your time is near.
You close your eyes for the last time.
You know it will be your last.
So you pray to God before you go.
For the bad things you have done.
It is dark. And at peace.
Everything you had is gone.
You've done your part. For what life you had.
It is quiet and at peace,
So now I can sleep.
My job is done. And life goes on.

—*DeWayne Werts*

When You Think...

When you think of life, you think of hurt and pain.
You seldom think of happiness or life away from the rain.
Nothing goes right. Nothing proceeds according to plan.
YES! You're on top of the world! Tomorrow you're a dead man!

When you think of love, you think of hope and joy.
Contemplating life with a loved one makes the world seem
full of poise. Offspring, offspring, a parents' dream come to
past but as the child matures, you must loosen your grasp.

When you think of God, you think of a single deity.
When you think of reverence, you believe there exists 1 Trinity
But how can one be three or how can three belong to one?
Faith, my brother or sister. Faith gets the job done!
Because life is full of changes; surprises you can never foresee.
God is omnipotent. Don't you agree?

Life is tedious, tiresome, and thinking sometimes belies hope
Don't waste your mind playing with drugs and dope.
Keep your body sterile; sterile like the ivory of a musk.
Because in this cruel society,

...thinking is a must!

—*James Oliver McMorris II*

A J

In the middle of the night, I received a call,
"You should see her, Ma, she's such a doll!"
"Beth's a real trooper, she's doing great!"
A J came early, no need to wait.

Hung up the phone, both happy and sad.
Beth's a new Mommy, my son's now a Dad!
The family is growing, the tree's branching out.
Andrea Jean is our latest sprout.

She'll blossom and grow and make quite a change,
For Beth and Joe, things won't be the same.
Someone once said, and I think it is true,
A new baby is God's way of saying to you,
"I trust you, I need you, please help with this child,
Watch over and nourish her just for a while.
It won't always be easy to do your part.
She'll bring you joy and she'll break your heart.
But the love you both have, with my love for you.,
Is all that you need for the job you must do.
So, relax and enjoy, you won't be alone.
Be happy together 'till I welcome you home."

—*Laura J. Grohovsky*

Choices

From the start I knew you were someone special.
You were someone who could give me everything,
Or leave me with nothing.
I realize now the choice was partially mine,
unfortunately I chose to take nothing.
Now the emptiness inside me keeps growing,
It leaves me lonely and afraid.
I can't live with this fear,
this fear of nothing.
Now I'm ready to take everything you can give me.
I want so badly to be near you,
I want to fill this emptiness.
Now I know what the right choice is,
I know you are right for me.
Together we could be so strong,
We could conquer this loneliness inside.
Together we could fill my heart
With love and happiness.
Please let me in!

—*Jennifer Forbush*

Mrs Nellie Presley

Born in 1920 she's now seventy three. The most dedicated nurse
you will ever see. This number one nurse will never retire.
If I said any different I'd be a liar. To everyone in Texas
she's their friend. To Doctors James and Jessee she's their
Don. Called Presley sometime Nellie. By the fat little man
with the big wide bellie. She's on call 24 hours a day. Just
call her number and she's on her way. When the doctors are
grumpy and having a bad day. Just say the magic words
Presley's on the way. She comes in to work between eight and
nine. The only person in the world that keeps those doctors in
line. She works her days come sunshine or rain. She runs
those halls at the speed of a train. Nellie Nettie Brother J.
T. and sister Irene. No closer brother and sisters could ever
be seen. She lost her twin Nettie and brother J. T. When they
meet in heaven what a day that will be. At the end of her hard
day and she's granted a wish. It's off with Enos to go eat
fish. When you hear nurse don't think Florence Nightingale
just say with a grin. No it's not her it's Doctors James and
Jessee's Don.

—*Diane Anderson*

all For Help

If you listen very close, if you travel very far,
ou won't hear a happy bird, you'll hear a passing
r. The rainforest was here, tomorrow it'll be gone.
 we've got to change the future fast while there's still time.
We've got to listen, listen to the call, the call for
lp. Start the nature, stop the bulldozers, this probably
1gs a bell. You've got to speak out! Tell us what you
el. We've got to stop the extinction while the animals are
ll here.
If you travel even farther, if you listen very close, you
n hear a distant monkey sounding like a ghost. He's
inging in thin air, now the trees just aren't there. If
ou listen you can hear his call for help.

  —*Reana Reisen*

hetto Flowerpot

ttle ghetto flowerpot - my the sights you've seen. I'm sure
ou'd rather not have been sitting, oh so still. On hot putrid
ghts witnessing muggings, shootings and fights. Oh what a
ght for a flowerpot that sits on a putrid. window sill. O,
 dirty, o so still. Did you see Miz Jones the other day, won
e lottery, so they say, And while the sun shone, Miz Jones

nade hay" to better pastures and Greenfields where wash, hung
t to dry, would not feel like dirty, greasy slime. Little
ietto flowerpot did you see the Madam's brand new 'chine?'
ie's running two houses on the block, doing big business,
und the clock-dealing in brown, young, hot flesh-laid back
mps and doped-up simps, making money hand-over-fist. Rev.
ilson fixed his church up so fine-but last Saturday, a
de-hopped-up on wine slept in the church reverend loved and
mired-that dude set reverend's church on fire! Little ghetto
wer-pot how can you stand the muck and the mire of being
or, poor as dirt and trying to hide the fact that it hurts to
 poor as dirt?

  —*Julia Hines-Harris*

ntitled

llie my queen with your sweet eyes so green
Your body so fragile, so soft and lean
 hold you close when your nights are long
We'll smile together when they play our song

e watched the sun turn gold upon your hair
 've looked in your eyes when you were in despair
ur smile shines like the rising sun
Your eyes like a child searching for fun

ke a freight train rollin' through the night
The whistle blows lonesome, as it disappears out of sight
ie day something is there
The next day, no one seems to care

hen you plant a small tree
You imagine how tall it may someday be
eryday you look at it and watch it grow
But do any of us really know?

 let us sit still and enjoy the sun
Together we make loving fun
ie wind will have it's own way
For now let's just play.

  —*Robert Burgess*

My Dreams

More fair than mortal tongues can tell,
Your eyes burn brighter than the lights of hell,
The dusk, the dawn, the earth, the sea,
they mean nothing without you by me,
Deeper than the deepest sea,
Brighter than light can be,
My love for you will never die,
Even when under earth I lie,
In the dead of night horror stalks my sleep,
In my heart I begin to weep,
The pain of my past comes for me,
It comes and overwhelms my please,
I awake a chill from hell in me deep,
How can I ever sleep,
In my mind there is a gate,
Behind it is where you wait,
In my head you hold me tight,
No more do I have to fight,
Blue skies and blue eyes are all I then see,
I love you and in my dreams you love me,..........

  —*Holly Ann Abbatoy*

Do You Know How Blessed You Are

Do you know how blessed you are?

You woke up this morning, closed in your right mind. You had
your health and strength and truly it was on time. You had the
activity of your limbs, you had the ability to think, but you
know what, someone got up this morning and had to turned to an
alcoholic drink. You had ears to hear, you had eyes to see,
but how many got up this morning and said Lord I thank Thee.
Now you go on your merry way driving and thinking I'm alive But
hold on there, the question is, who left you here to survive.

On the news you hear of a neighbor dying. No relative of yours
so what's the crime. On the corner you see someone trying to
cross the street. He need your help, you are late for work and
have a deadline to meet. You never think as you travel
throughout the day. How Jesus has helped you along the way
When you were in sin, my saviour gave up his life and brought
you in. Christians, there are so many excuses we have today
none will get us to see Jesus by doing it our way Men, women,
boys and girls if we only stop-look- and listen by far then we
all can truly see just how blessed we really are.

  —*Liz R. Floyd*

The Lamb of God

The night of Your betrayal must have been the hardest night of
Your Life. You had always known that this day would come.
Sometimes, I could see the pain of the future in Your Eyes.
Sometimes, I would see You lost in thought and I would wonder —
What is it that brings such sorrow to Your Face? What is it
that causes You to quiver with uneasiness? What is it that cuts
deep into Your Soul and penetrates Your innermost Being? Then,
just as suddenly, Your expression would change and Your Face
would radiate with pure joy. It looked like a huge burden had
been lifted from Your strong but gentle Shoulders. Sometimes,
I would see You just staring at Your Hands. Touching the
center of Them ever so gently. And I would see a single tear
drop slowly from Your Eye and stream silently down Your Cheek.
Were You thinking of the scars to come? Those beautiful, nail —
scarred Hands — how precious They are to me. You must have
known that You were born to die. Your Life given for the
masses. Born to be slain. Led to the slaughter as a lamb....
The lamb of God My Son...my Redeemer...my Friend...I love
You!

Mary

  —*Dana J. Mason*

A Tribute To Father Tony

How we love you, Father Tony,
   your parishioners all agree;
you're friendly, compassionate, erudite,
   That's why you suit us to a tee.

We're sure you've heard many fine comments:
   yes, compliments, praises galore;
And with your expertise as a top-notch chef,
   Who could ask for anything more?

Your reflect such fine home training:
   Fine parents, siblings, and all.
Our Lord destined you for the priesthood;
   Thankfully, you answered His call.

Your talents, so many, so varied-
   Attributes to fill a page.
Such sincerity extended to one and all,
   True compassion whatever the age.

To us you're a tower of pisa,
   A real dynamo, strength and zest.
You are the answer to all our prayers,
   Mama Mia, you are the best!
   —*Eda Azzoli*

Her Love

Breakfast on the way, I go to wake you
You're so cold, I wonder why
You've kicked off your blankets, that's why
"Nanny, Nanny," you don't wake
Again "Nanny, Nanny breakfast is ready"
Still you don't wake and dad comes in
"Go eat, I'll wake her"
Instead I go to the bathroom
When I come out, Mom is there, she is crying,
I start to cry too for I know my Nanny is dead
Maybe it's a dream
I pinch myself, hard enough to hurt
Nothing happens so I cry harder
My best friend is gone and now there is no one
To kiss my owies, to tuck me in
To help me through life
Someday
I'll go to meet her, until then I'll remember
Her scent, her face, her touch
Her love
   —*Fathom Magby*

Holding Tomorrow's Hand

My hand is rough and calloused
Yours is just discovering texture and life
Your touch is innocence and purity
My touch is knowledge and insecurity
Your hand in mind is a precious gift
If I tarnish you, I destroy tomorrow
Use your hands only in love toward another
The world is your sister and brother
I hope I have the inner strength
To teach you how to use your hands
In love and work and deed
Never in anger or war or greed
My hand is rough and calloused
Yours is just discovering texture and life
I have seen today's violence and hate
Racism exists in each country and state
Yesterdays hands have built conditioned walls
Today's hands, without judgement, must tear them down
I am holding tomorrow's unscarred hand
May I build for you a loving land...
   —*Rebekah Mesa Westphal*

The Death Of A Friend...

Life doesn't always make perfect sense,
You've got to learn to live on your side of the fence.
When God took you, it wasn't fair,
Almost too much for us to bare.
His intentions are still unknown,
Can't help to feel but all alone.
Learning each day to cope with the pain
Fighting the feelings, what will you gain?
Your memory will forever be in our minds,
And when you look down, it's love you'll find.
Holding on with all of our hearts.
We still love after death has made us part.
   —*Amee Mallory*

Always There

I understand your hurt and pain,
you've lost the one you love,
your tears are falling like the rain,
your heart caged like a lonesome dove.

Every time you need to cry,
I'll be there to dry your eyes.
And if you feel no need to talk,
by your side I'll simply walk.

True friends are always hard to find,
but when in need they're there for you,
and when I need to share what's on my mind,
I know you're there for me too.
   —*Katie Holm*

A Sad Good-Bye

The pounding of your heartbeat racing through my head
You kissed your last kiss, then off you went
Laying there so peacefully, I began to cry
Remembering when you were there
Now having to remember your gone
Resting in your heavenly bed in the sky
Soaring through the clouds like an Eagle
So high...
So free...
Always keeping with me the memory of those eyes
as they said their sad Good-bye
   —*Christy Burns*

Beyond The Mirror

Examine closely beyond the mirror.
What lies there is what is inside of you.
   Your true inner self cannot be clearer.
You may discover what you never knew.
   Unaware of fables, we sometimes are
convinced we are perfect and without fault.
   Beguiling others in vain is by far.
When cognizant, we being this to a halt.
   Our soul lies beneath a patent guard.
Deep down in clandestine, no one will know.
   Not even yourself until you look hard,
revealing what hitherto did not show.
   Mirror, mirror on the wall, I ask you,
divulge the unknown which is oh so true.
   —*Jessica Wood*

Tears"

ying here in my thought's
ith tears falling down my face,
ie is to wonder why I have this
iled fixed upon my face.

e tears I shed, are tears of both
y and happiness caused by the unselfish
d unconditional love you have so freely
tended.

day, I shed tears,
morrow, I will cry.
vays will I smile with
ear in my eye.

—*Nora Powell*

n Dance

ross the shield
ur sons parade as though
ocking my blindness

d silhouetted objects
y by like leaves in a wind
fting positions down the meandering road
m east to west,

u sway in the morning sky
ver missing step with me.
w smooth you are.

ur children mimic you well
motion on the glass.
e all trod the same road
iding into the sun dance

—*Arletha Pappas*

ing Nine!

day was my birthday
ad just turned nine.
y mother is taking me
t to dine. I drunk soda
m drunk wine. As we stood
iting in line, I felt a shiver
down my spine. The next day
Johnson school,
ere the teachers
e really cool, I got an A plus,
haved on the bus.
d after I went
imming in the pool.
rote this poem just on time,
ade some words up
make it rhyme.
ke this poem a whole lot,
t gotta go
fore I get caught!

—*Kirsten Hammood*

orning Song

mocking-bird, dawn's prima donna
ns the gamut of emotions
a swift proliferation of joy.

uberant prophecy of the
y's coming delights
epressible, inexhaustible song.

e sky cannot hold
ch a profusion of beauty.
alls gently into waiting ears.

—*Margaret Des Jardin*

Dreams

Remember when you held me,
Standing in the night.
The air was cold around us,
But our bodies warm and light.
Your kiss was warm and tender.
Your touch which melted me,
I never knew my dreams
Could become reality.

—*Sabrina Luisi*

Before and Now

Before I met you
   I had no hope
Before I met you
   I was lost and
   in doubt
Before I met you
   there was no tomorrow
Now that I have you
   I have hope
Now that I have you
   I am found and
   no longer in doubt
Now that I have you
   I have a tomorrow
All because I found
   my one true love.

—*Amy Bradford*

The Rose Of Love

Here it is Christmas Eve
I have a poem to conceive
I want to show you that I care
My very soul for you to bare

We laugh and love
and sometimes cry
Until it's time for us to die

But if I'm wise and if I'm smart
until that day we will not part

The gift I give is very small
the love behind it very tall

This rose of love
I give to you
will say
My love for you is true

—*Doris Lehman*

As Long As I Live

As long as I live.
I hope to give - of my
wealth and myself

As long as I live I
hope to spread joy to
those who are in pain

And help them to see
sunshine and not just
the rain -

As long as I live I
hope to inspire - and
make myself worthy of
my royal hire -

And leave to this earth
the feeling of worth -
because it is ours for
such a small while.

—*Mary A. Michael*

No-Faceman

   Who ever this is?
I hoped to see you there.
But you had no-face.
   No-faceman who I'd loved
in the flashing of the
months that passed by.
I slowly missed the
no-faceman.
The no-faceman drank me
drunk in blink of your eyes.
I was scared that the no-faceman
had forgotten me;
'O' how I'd hoped that the
no-faceman saw me there.
'O' how I'd hoped that the
no-faceman dreamed the same as I.
I'd saddened, the frightening
thought that the no-faceman
does not see the same dreams as I

The no-faceman is a shadow of my deepest
memory!

—*Rhonda Hoffheins*

Invisible Person

You blind fool.
I know you can't see me,
Hear me,
Feel me.
I know when I'm being
Ignored by ignorance,
An ignorance caused by
Jealousy.
Like an irrelevant subject
You dropped me,
Paid no attention to my pleas,
Walked upon my reasons
Like an old rug,
Wiped your feet
On my meaningless heart
And walked away.

—*Jamie Kmiec*

Flowers Sent

Flowers sent from far away
I know you're thinking of me today
Wrap your arms around me
Hold me till I die
I feel the warmth within my soul
My inner spark cannot be controlled
Reach out to your love
Reach out and be aware
Your love is still growing
You still care
Hearing your voice over the telephone
Helps me not to be alone
Flowers sent from you today
Will keep me holding on
Only yours I'll stay

—*Lori Ann Sweeney*

Life

As life reveals its darkness.
Solitude breeds its pain
The evening entombs the moonlight
Radiance succumbs to rain
Recall though that life exposes passion
As seclusion bores true grace
Moonshine is engulfed by night lovers.
Showers will cleanse light's face '93

—*Britta Bengtson*

Cold Silent World

My world is continually silent
I long for the day I might hear
A sound, any sound, be it loud or soft
But with my own two ears.

My life a charade
Always trying to guess
In my still soundless world
Thoughts hard to express.

But yet I have found
If I keep straining to hear
Even one faint sound
There is nothing to fear

My world is cold and often cruel
But I must put that behind me
For if I follow by the rule
Happiness will find me.

My cold and silent world has changed
Not regretfully but for the best
My lonely silent existence rearranged
And I cannot help but feel blessed
—*Amber Rogers*

Friends

When I travel in my car,
I look up in the sky.
I thank you, Lord, for all my friends,
And I will tell you why.

They're always there when I need them,
Be it night or day.
They always give me good advice,
As I go on my way.

When I feel I'm very low,
With no a friend at all,
Someone will pick me up,
With a visit of a call.

They tell me they have time for me,
And always will be there,
No matter how bad I feel,
They love me and they care.

So Lord, as I look up in the sky,
I know you've given me,
All these wonderful friends,
To shower gifts on me.
—*Frances Van Slambrouck*

The Old Man

As I wake up early each morning
I remember as a child
Trees so much shorter
The bushes such fewer
Oh how I changed
For, I am the old man

One thing will always burn
in this life is my pipe

The children have grown
And went their way
As you can see I am here to stay
Oh yes, they call me the old man

My hair is gray but still is there
Each strand could tell a tale
Oh yes, I am the old man
—*Robert DeRosa*

My Best Friend

She's there whenever
I need her
To listen and understand.

About all the things
That are going on
And lend a helping hand.

She tells me what I am
Doing wrong
And praises me for being strong.

I love her deeply
From the bottom of my heart.

She's the one that
Gave me my start

After all she is my friend
She's the one on whom I depend

I wouldn't trade her for any other
After all she is my
    MOTHER
—*Elizabeth Twohig*

On My Own

When I went it on my own…
    I never thought I'd be alone.
Being young, and brave, and strong
    I didn't take a soul along
Down that road to something better…
    I didn't write a note or letter
Daddy's heart was broke I know
    Yet his heart break couldn't show…
He let me go and choose my way
    His thoughts were with me every day
Now Daddy's in his heavenly home…
    And, I am still on earth alone
But, his spirit shines on me
    In my every thought I see
That when you travel roads with love
    The angels guide you from above.
—*Joyce Bozarth*

"The Way Down"

On the way down,
I saw a stone
From my head to my toes
It bounced on my bones.

On the way down,
The firemen call
Give me your hand
So you don't fall.

On the way down,
I had a few laughs
all of my things
Just crashed.

On the way down,
from my life,
I ran into my friends
And now I'm a wife.

On the way down,
I found it was all a dream
What a relief
That had just come to me.
—*Michelle L. Seifert*

The Innocent Ones

How crazy can this world be?
I saw it on the news,
Little babies with guns and knives
Never thought it would happen to me,
An innocent bystander shot down
I feel the bullet pierce my skin,
As I hit the ground, I frown
I look up into the blue sky,
I know it's time to say goodbye
Everything blacks out,
I wake hearing people shout
I search frantically and find them,
My Mom and Dad
I'm sorry for when I was bad,
Mom please don't cry
I know you two can't hear me,
But I love you two and always will
I feel myself slipping away,
Please remember and think of me
And I'll be right there, goodbye.
—*Megan Lane*

Bay Shore Park

I was sitting at Bay Shore Park
I saw the happy pelicans
dancing on the water having
lots of fun. Boy could they
run. They sure were hungry.
I was sitting under a tree
looking at the rich people and
their yards and there were
the little tots throwing
beautiful rocks I saw the
dolphins jumping out of the
water. Doing all kinds of tricks
Realizing God had made all of
this. This I would like to tell
my sis. This I certainly do not
want to miss. Then my husband
gave me a big kiss.
—*Lissa Franklin*

Forever Strong

Our love hasn't been for very
Long, but we've built a bond
        so very strong.
My love for you is so
deep, I even think of you
        before I sleep.
I miss you so much
each day, that when I see
you I just wish you'd stay.
When I think of your beautiful looks,
I just get more and more hooked.
I know my love for you
Isn't wrong because my
Love for you is forever strong!
—*James Gordon Taylor IV*

Abortion In The 90's

Abortion is the reason the
population has ceased,
Abortion is the reason our
world is not yet in peace
Abortion kills a child,
Abortion is 9-1-1 not yet dialed
Abortion stops a heartbeat
Abortion is the unrisen heat,
But yet you ask, "What is abortion?"
—*Sarah Bowman*

e Tearful Goodbye

am paralyzed by the beauty
ee in your deep blue eyes.
But when I reach out to touch you,
ur image fades away and dies.
see you when I close my eyes
d my eyes fill up with tears.
But I need not worry, you're always
re to quiet my undying fears.
love you so much, but I can't
m to get my words out straight.
But you stopped and turned around
en I called out for you to wait.
"I love you," came out in what
med to me to be a jumble of words.
Then you smiled and I was positive
t what I said was what you heard.
You told me then that you had to go
d I waved a tearful goodbye to you.
But then you smiled and winked
me and said, "I love you too."

—*Paula Haglund*

t the Window of My Room

t the window of my room
ee the morning and the noon.
ee the sun when it shall rise.
ee the moon open its orange eye.

ve the rain
ve the snow
ve to see the flowers grow.

e wind blowing
e trees swaying
e crows crowing
e horses neighing.

ok at all of the beautiful sights
ke the stars in the sky on
se cold winter nights.

ok in awe.
an see it all
e the snow in the winter.
d the leaves in the fall.

—*Amanda Schlote*

u and I

ok at you,
ee the world.
ook at you,
ee all that I could ever want.
ook at you,
now I could love no one else.
u touch me,
uiver inside.
u touch me,
heart overflows.
u touch me,
now who I am.
u kiss me,
now with who I belong.
u kiss me,
is forgiven.
u kiss me,
ever I am yours.

—*Tammy Young*

Eternally Bound

To the moon and stars
    I shall return,
The love I have in my heart
    will forever burn.
The meaning of life is
    the happiness in your eyes,
We are bound each-
    with eternal ties.
For no matter what
    separates us on the 'morrow
Ask of you
    there be no sorrow.
With swiftness and ease
    crossing mountain and sea,
Moving quietly as the moon
    I know in my heart.
      I will find you soon.

—*Judy R. Hanson*

Nature's Way of Love

Whenever troubles fill me with gloom,
I shudder and cry alone in my room,
But I don't want to cry;
I don't want to be sad.
These thoughts just confuse me
and make me more mad!
But before I give in
and become more depressed.
I get up from bed, wash my face
and get dressed, and take a long hike
in the vast wilderness.
Where all of God's great work
is at its best.
Where the birds sing their song
in the fields and the trees,
All around you are the sounds
of the squirrels and the bees.
This is the place that makes me feel
oh, so good,
I'd stay here forever if I knew that I could.

—*Mary Bacon*

A Breath

As I clear my mind of thought,
I sigh and wonder if I ought;
Ought fill the chasms in my heart,
Wipe clean the slate and freshly start,
Upon my journey through vacant time,
Alas, but that may be a crime.
For only one will stand the test,
And leave behind all the rest.
Now if one's chosen; you or me
Then that is all that it need be.
This is all that happens in our minds;
In one single breath of time.

—*Kathleen E. Herndon*

Patriot

We salute our dear, dear flag,
Our eyes their watch doth keep,
For love springs strong beholding,
    And we all do weep.
The thought of the great glory
Is comfort to the heart
And kindness to the sick
    and love,
        and life,
            and rest.

—*Laura C. K. Ferguson*

We'll Be One

Before I ever spoke to you
I spoke to your eyes
They let me to a valley
Of splendorous blue light

I floated there two seconds
In amazement of the sight
A gentle breeze then blew me away
Yet I knew I would be back

I've now spent many a moment
In this beautiful place
For it makes me happy
To be part of its space

Undulating arcs, red and pink,
Passions, fears, joys and dreams,
As seen from outside you, volcano
You, dignified, serene

An occasional burst
I burn in love
Someday, I know, you will erupt...
And then we'll be one

—*Katherine Michelle Schroeder*

"The Invisible Girl"

In a crowd,
I stand alone.
You don't hear me,
and I don't hear you.

I try to say your language,
only I'm too slow.
I try to see your words,
only you're too fast.

Give me a chance
to show you who I am,
'cause all you know is
that I'm deaf.

—*Jeanne Yu*

You Gave

You gave me love
I thought I had lost
You gave me life
At no great cost
You showed me a path
And you let me lead
You slow me down
When I shouldn't speed
You show me the sky
And teach serenity
You showed me a crowd
And spoke of the lonely
You teach me enough
To let me learn alone
You show me how much
I have yet to know
Yet with all you've done
It can never be too much
You gave me you
And for us to touch

—*Wilson Wong*

The Blazing Sun

Something's on my mind.
I want it to be right.

We have so much more
than we've ever had before.

We both will run
into the sun.

Forever young
and having fun.

Our special love.
Shining from above.

The years go by
and we would die

for our love that is fun
into the blazing sun.

—*S. Allen Brooks*

"Let Beauty Be"

From the time I was born
I was a vine with thorns.
I sucked the blood of friends of mine
hoping to find the sweetest wine.
In the darkness I was lost.
My soul to be the cost
and I hid from the light.

Look in my eyes and one could see,
the raging storms in an endless sea.
In the center my heart a stone.
Not of the world but all alone.
And between a cloud, light came to me.
So grew on the island a little tree.

With the night came a fierce storm.
Yet I felt a heart not cold but warm
And then a new day came to me.
The clouds were gone Lord calmed the sea.
And now I hear "let beauty be"
For by the storm God created me.

—*Chad Swift*

I Am a Rose

At least ...
I was for awhile.
I was perfect!
I was straight!
And held my head up high

With beauty and strength
And a loving smile
With thorns, which were tough
Which protected me

Than came the storm
Which I could not see
It been my thorns
All over the ground
My protection wasn't there
To help me around

—*Jean Germano*

Why Is The Water Blue?

I sit and watch the ocean
I watch the waves come
tumbling down in front of me.
The sun beats its' rays
against the crystal blue.
The water produces such beauty.
When man steps in, he destroys
the natural wonders of the sea.
With oil spills and pollution
how can the water still be blue?
The ocean is so vast
it connects the world.
How can we dare to harm,
something larger than we?
Why is the water blue?
It is not such a mystery.
After all, if I too were abused
Then I too, would be blue.

—*Penny Lively*

Friends

We are friends,
and I want more,
I want what we had before.
Before you left
I never knew
how to love or how to be true.
You said you loved me
I believed it was true
you said you loved me
and how I'm blue
I thought what we had was great
why don't we start over
with a new, clean slate
do you still love me
do you still care
even if you don't
I'll always be there!!

—*Melissa Landsparger*

The Edge of Land

In the blaze of summer's heat,
I went to the edge of land;
beside the deep green waters,
where no one knew my name.

With the sun's heat stunning thought,
and waves breaking on the shore;
my mind abdicates reason,
but mem'ries never end.

Days of youth are all gone by,
but while yet I still remain,
I am wise to paths ahead,
and winter's sleep beyond.

I went to the edge of land,
beside the deep green waters,
where no one called me by name.
Perhaps I'll come again.

—*Edward J. Sabin, III*

Friendship of Enchantment

The shed of a tear,
I wish you were here.
Over the mountains, across the blue —
I've searched everywhere to find you.
The perfect person, companion or friend
To be with me to the very end.
Well I've found you at last,
The pain without you is in the past.
It's time for us to separate now
Before we depart, you must vow —
Don't ever forget the times we shared,
Moments for you are always spared.
When you feel blue
I'll be there for you.
And you for me,
Together, my friend, we will always be.

—*Sarah Starr*

Is It Really Love

Is it really love,
I wonder.
My mind goes blank,
When he touches me so.
I feel like I'm floating,
Floating high in the air.
Does he love me.
I love him.
Oh, I love him, so.
Will he ever forget about me,
I wonder if he will.
He says he loves me,
But is it really true.
I think of him,
I really do,
Oh, is it really love.

—*Tia Brown*

If I Were

If I were a gull feather,
I would rest on a gull.
Waiting and waiting
for my time to come.
Wondering whether or not
I will descend off the gull.

If I were a gull feather,
I would sway through the air.
Rolling and rolling
all through the night.
Hoping that the wind would
blow me to the sea.
I would be so happy
if someone picks me up.
For I like to be soothed.

—*Dawn Cummings*

There Once Was A Boy...

There once was a boy
Named Nicholas.
He laughed so hard it was
ridiculous
And also his sister was
ticklish.
And they didn't stop laughing
until they were purplish

—*Nick Corrie*

Instead...

instead of poetry
wrote a mystery
instead of new thoughts
recorded history
instead of smiling
decided to frown
instead of standing up
decided to sit down
instead of saying I love you
chose to turn my head
instead of saying I care for you
chose to say nothing instead
instead of trying to lead
wanted to sit and follow
instead of speaking out
wanted to grin and swallow
instead I did all things so that people
would agree
then truly all I did would not represent me

—Princess Thompson

Life Can Be Wonderful

Life can be wonderful
you walk around, with a smile.
Troubles that seem so bad,
only hang around for a while,
put your troubles and fears away,
God's love in your heart,
it's the only way you will find
peace of mind and contentment.

Life can be wonderful
and be glamorous if you want.
just read the words of love
sent to all of us from above.
wipe away the tears from your eyes
Gods love light up your nights
and through the years
earth you'll find
that life is wonderful

—Gilbert Mendoza Martinez

"Feelings"

I hide the pain
I hide the tears
won't show you
how I feel

I try to be happy
I try and I'll try
but it'll take a lot
for me not to cry

I was upset
but I'll be okay
I get over you
starting today

or maybe tomorrow...

—Kelly B. Herzing

My Love

her blue eyes
matches the clear skies
she's full of charm
with love in her arms
I'm helpless as can be
standing there without me
love her so
but how much, only time will show

—Richard Lee Hedrick

The Memories of Dolores

Sister, how much do I love you
    I'll tell you no lie ...
        How deep is the ocean
        How high is the sky?

Sister, how many times a day
    Do I think of you ...
        How many roses
        Are sprinkled with dew?

Sister, how far would I travel
    To be where you are ...
        How far is a journey
        From here to a star?

Sister, how much have I cried
    Since you've been gone ...
        How deep is the ocean
        How high is the sky?

—Noah A. Lazore

Niki

Mama don't shed tears for me.
I'm happy don't you see.
Look Mama, I can run and play,
For the first time today.
I've been sick for so long,
Jesus said, "It's time to come home."
Look Mama, I stand so tall,
In the rose garden of my new home.
Thank you for caring every day.
There's other on their way.
Give them the love you gave me.
Go on with your life be happy for me.
For I'm happy don't you see.

—Augestes Morgan

Just Because...

Just because I'm female
    I'm not vulnerable
I'm not stupid, I'm not weak ...
    Just because I'm female
    I don't cook and clean
I'm not unable to be independent
I don't always need a man around
And I don't watch soaps all day ...
    Just because I'm female
doesn't make you any stronger than
me, smarter than me, or that you
    should think any less of me
And who gave you the right
    to think maybe even you have
    a better job than me, just
        because I'm female?
    Just because I'm female,
    What's the difference?
    What does it matter?
Just because I'm female.

—Kiffany S. Lawlis

You

The way that you touch me,
Its the softest touch ever felt.
The way that you kiss me,
It's the most passionate ever.
The way you talk to me,
Its the sweetest words ever.
And when you tell me
That you love me,
Its the softest whisper ever heard.

—Traci Stroda

Hawk

Sail away Hawk!
I'm not your prey
I'll sit and watch you
Soar today

Soar you do
Above my head
But tilt a tail
That shines of red

While I dream of dreams
You make your cry
Tracking currents of pale blue sky

You wake me
From my dreams of flight
My body rested
My soul alight.

—Tim J. Pittenger

Searching...a poem for Marna

In a life such as ours,
In a time such as today,
A friend is what we long for
We ask each time we pray
For that special, dear companion
That always will be there,
To laugh with and to cry with...
For someone just to care.

They're closer than a man
In our teenage years could be.
They know a part of us no one knows...
A part of that no one's seen.

We look our whole lives through
For a friend such as that,
But maybe what we're looking for
Is right there where we're at.

—Regina M. Stark

Alone

Alone, Alone again.
In a world of
So many people
I feel like cryin',
But I do not tremble.
I live in a world of
Illusion and thought.
You live in a world
Of only store bought.
I see things through
Different eyes.
I pretend to smile
But I give a sigh.
Alone,
Alone and free.
To be by myself
So let me be.

—Jennifer Williams

Above Water

We cannot win when e'er immersed
In anguish or remorse.
If midst defeat, one founders,
Stormy seems each course.

Endurance sails with confidence,
On waves of faith and hope.
It sinks not into apathy
Through which we gasp or grope.

Make self-support the lifeline,
When capsized are ideas;
Become your navigator,
Who by valor steers.

Drench faculties with freedom;
Cast an anchor to respect;
Lest your drown the future
Under oceans of regret!

—*Jeanette Birnbaum*

Rapport

The flower boxed Geraniums
In burst of fiery red
Looked out upon the rain drenched earth
And tossed their pretty heads.

We're so glad that we are here
Where it is warm and bright
We fill our friends with joy and cheer
We're such a pretty sight

The raindrops pattered merrily
As happy as could be
Knowing when their task was done
There would be greening grass and trees

So the raindrops and flowers
Each did their story tell
Each giving of their beneficence
And doing it right well

—*Rustica Oleriana*

Autumn Gold

Maple leaves dancing
In gold everywhere,
Whirling and twirling
As frost fills the air.

All scarlet and yellow,
The leaves come alive.
Their colorful ruffles
Are dancing the jive.

They twist and they turn
As the wind sings her song,
The squirrel stores her bounty
And scampers along.

The beauty of autumn
Will leave the tree bare,
But she sings as she spreads
Leaves of gold everywhere.

Her treasures were gold
But she gave them away.
May we dance like the maple
In splendor today.

—*Elizabeth M. Lewis*

Contemplation Of Existence

So I sat there,
In my socks without feet
Without hands
Without a care in the world,
No problems
No ailments
Living in total fiction,
And being miserable about it.

I needed gloves without fingers
Without ears
Without freedom to think,
No order
No tranquility
Living in anarchic chaos,
And then I could love life.

—*Melissa Victoria Meserve*

Fire Burning

Fire burning,
in our heart,
why are we doing this,
aren't we smart.

All we do is,
take control,
armies marching,
to the drum roll.

All we need to do,
is to stop the wars,
stop the killing
trust me, we need no more.

—*Daniel Zarrella*

Make Believe

We make believe
  in our little world,
Building castles
  of dreams!
All we hope -
  and reach for
Is just beyond
  it seems.
Then suddenly -
  its over.
Face to face
  with grief
We stand alone
  with empty hands.
Our span is much
  too brief.

—*Sheila Cardano*

Untitled

I saw it on your face-
(innocent as a child)
gleaming-
like sunbeams
playing with the water.
I caught it once in a while,
on your lips.
Reflected-
(as from thoughts)
your smile.
Beautiful
like the sun
on your face.

—*Jessika Halterman*

'Cause It's Spring

Bees are buzzing
in the air
flowers are blooming
everywhere
nature's busy
trying to bring
love and sunshine
'cause it's spring
hearts are lighter
winds are sweet
moon's are mellow
and oh so free
go find a world
paint it green
that's natures way
'cause it's spring

—*Joe D. Crawford*

Life

Life is a moment
In the annals of time
Man's short lived span
Is likened to a grain of sand.

Life is but an event
That happens in our time
For what takes place today
Fades into that everlasting place.

Life is but a hope
That tomorrow may bring
They joy we seek, the peace we need
For forever is a day.

Life is but a dream
A dream of things to come
Of riches gained, of fame retained
But like a dream, they do not remain.

Life is a beginning
And an end to the beginning
Of a far greater life, that has yet to come
When our work here on earth is done.

—*Louise M. Kelm*

In the Fast Lane

Run, run, run,
Makes your heartbeat faster
You don't have to stop
for no one is your master.

Skip over troubles
Duck under debt
As long as you keep runnin'
There no time for regret.

Speed up the pace
Turn on the burners
fast people never face
Questions from the learners.

Champagne for breakfast
Lunch that always vary
Supper there's a pound of steak
forget that coronary.

Run, run, run
Never slow it down
If your make-up doesn't dry
They'll never see the clown.

—*John T. Butler*

For Maybe a Satellite

Brilliant stars shine upon us
Giving us each a thought
Of omniscient wonder
Of what tomorrow will be

Each day seems to come as an
Ordinary event yet topsy-turvy
Can turn into a mystical adventure

Upon each starry night
There is a dream of
What might happen tomorrow
That will make a person

Feel more than a pebble
In this electronic world of
Fragility that can drive one mad

Each star can tell you a
Story of gods and goddesses
Who have lived this life before and wanted

A peaceful world without the
Conflicts of emotions that encumber
Peace and happiness
—*Helen Chrisman*

Sandbox Full of Oceans

m lost
the dark alley way of hope.
arching.
know that tomorrow is there.
at the sun will shine again
on our skin.
d the clouds will look down
upon our eyes.
ve is only a word
lingering as a whisper
on the ears of a deaf man.
sterday remains tomorrow as
e future becomes the past.
now that you are not there, and
m just a wilted cardboard star in
sandbox full of oceans.
—*Holly Smith*

st Love

hy must I be here
the dead of the night
able to sleep
hile tears blur my sight

hought I had found
love so very real
t I was blind
the things that I feel

e said that he loved me
e made me believe it
t he can hurt me
d not even see it

ran off and left me
face this alone
hile he had some fun
subtle way to be shown

e end of our love
ems so clear to me now
t I want it to last
st wish I knew how.
—*Ellesha L. Gurecki*

Magic In Bloom

A deserted island
in the middle of the sea.
Untouched by man's hand
how can that be?

Unpolluted waters,
clear and blue,
can it all be true?

An island in my mind,
one that stood the test of time
free from toxic slime
waiting for the world to find

Magic in bloom
in the sea.
Magic in bloom
for you and me.

Safe from our pollution
sparing it from destruction.
Leaving it is the solution
to keep it's magic in bloom.
—*Dan Marshall*

Summer Night

I see fireflies,
   in the skies,
   in your eyes,
   in the night,
   in the summer.

I see fireworks,
   in the skies,
   in your eyes,
   in the night,
   in the summer.

I see summer
in the skies,
   all around,
in your eyes,
   all the time,
in the night,
   it's so right,
Summer.
—*Katie Accardo*

In the End

Peace and love, is what we need
In this world of crime and greed
This Godless world in which we live
Most will take, and some will give
In my eyes the end is near
To burn in Hell if I don't hear
When life is gone, it's much too late
To pass through Heaven's Pearly Gates
The word of God, which I believe
Can satisfy our every need
For God begot His only son
Who died Himself for everyone
For on the Cross He saved our Souls
If we believe as it is told
Then we can walk those streets of
   Gold...
—*Vance Houston Jr.*

"Growing Pains"

Once young warriors
In Vietnam
To ease America's guilt
We are the pawns
No one would help us
Or shake our hand
When we came home
From a foreign land
The price of freedom
Cost us our youth
In the game of life
'Tis the cold hard truth
When you meet a vet remember this
To live in peace and harmony
Is our only wish
We are men and women
Once boys and girls
Who gave up our youth
To save the world
Thank you, means you care
—*Bernard A. Covington*

Solitary Sunset

Sandwiched between clouds
   iridescent with its beams,
The sun silently slides down.

One gull tenaciously guards
   her evening roost;
One jetliner streaks south
   silenced by distance and speed.
One last pelican skimming over
   the waves — hunting alone.

The curtain of fog
   hovers behind the
   now-fiery sun —

As its last rays make a
   puddle of light around
   the one last fishing boat
   heading home.
—*Joan Poulos*

Window Seat

The sunrise from my window
is a bright welcome to the day,
there is just so much
it seems to be trying to say.

The birds from my window
float endlessly through the breeze,
just like the sailboats
conquering the ever constant seas.

The children from my window
seem to compare to the comical mimes,
hopping, skipping and playing,
and just enjoying the best of times.

The sunset from my window
is a subtle glowing goodbye to the day,
as it settles in for the night,
there is not much more to say.

The best thing from my window
is a slightly blurred reflection of me,
because it lets me know
I'm still around and can enjoy all that I see.
—*M. Kevin Lovdahl*

A Love For All Times

A love for all times
is all that I ask.
Not one that is too complicated
but one that will last.

A love that holds magic,
a love that is true.
A love that holds promise,
both for me and for you.

Oh, where is that love?
A love for all times.
I sometimes sit and wonder
will it ever be mine?

—Verlinda J. Allen

Winter

Winter's when the ground
is covered with snow
It's cold and wet
and chills the toe
Time for hot chocolate
grandma would say
And we'd run in
from off our sleigh
We'd hang up our wet
mittens by the fire place
And to the kitchen
we would race
We'd hold the warm
cup tightly
And from winter to spring
we'd repeat the fun nightly

—Aimee Jo Hoover

Desert Refrain

She bears no likeness to her kind
For she lacks a mother's grace.
She belongs to every season
But to no familiar place.
Defeat became her posture
A shroud that she must wear.
Tomorrow is her mourning,
The bottom of despair.
The child she clutches to her breast
Has no more tears to shed.
Love was not the sustenance
On which his hunger fed.
She wept a well of sorrow
In a shallow grave of grief
For the child she left behind
To famine's silent thief.
As he slept within the shadows,
His flesh one with the land,
His mother's footsteps faded
In the ever shifting sand.

—Barbara Barnes

Fear

Fear, cold, empty, facing
Nature's torture of your mind.
Unwilling to give into your fear,
burying it in the vast, mean
heart of the beast.

Ode to life
Life brings peace, hope, and joy
into the world, to love, wish
and be cherished forever wishing to
live again.

—Jaime Bennett

To My Lover

The one true place I'd like to be,
Is etched into your memory.
Because you're ever in my heart,
I hope, my love, we'll never part.

I'll love you, dear, forever more.
I've never felt this way before.
You are my love, my life, my all,
I'm ever at your beck and call.

Please love me, hon, as I love you,
Just give your all, the way I do.
My life is yours, for you I'd die.
You have my heart, I can't deny.

When things go wrong, and we fight,
My heart is dark, there is no light,
There is no calm - there is no peace,
It seems as though my life will cease.

So, please, my love, remember this,
When we're at odds, there is no bliss,
Just a small and aching heart
That feels as though it fell apart.

—Jacquelyn Randolph-Edwards

Truth

A lonely glowing candle
Is flickering in the night;
Filling the world's darkness
With promises of light.

Sometimes growing brighter
Sending warmth about;
At times glowing fainter,
Almost going out.

Closer loom the shadows,
Terror filled and grim,
As the small flame wavers
Weakening and dim.

If truth's flame should perish
Within the tomb of night,
Never more to banish
Evil with its light

Then night would surely triumph;
With the promises of dawn
Never giving birth to daylight
… And truth forever gone.

—Joyce A. Rice

My Love for the Lord

My love for the Lord
Is like no other.
This love is so special
It cannot be compared.

Love for ones mother, father
Children or friends,
Cannot begin to come close.
This feeling of possessing
Such a priceless gem.

This love so ever special
And new
But mostly so wondrous
And yet not so new.

This feeling of love
Cannot be expressed,
His love is a gift
And he says, share in it!

—Patricia Haen

Values

Of how much more value to me
Is my country's security
Than personal wealth could ever be
That I cannot take to eternity

My income tax I'll not evade
To help the deficit get paid
So enemies will not invade
This freedom our forefathers laid

What good is my wealth
If my country is weak
And cannot support
The goals that I seek

—Anita Alexander

Valentine

The valentine, I give you
is one that can't be read,
for it is through the things I do
more, than what is said.
It comes from deep within the heart
where all my feelings lie,
which I would not care to part
or asked would not deny.
These things I give
through out the year
and all the days I live,
which helps to keep you near.
Even though sometimes distant
made by miles, or age of time,
the memories of an instant
may be longer than rhyme.
Remember, expressions of love
may vary in many ways.
But put not even one above,
for all deserve ones praise.

—Florence L. Pearson

Stars and Stripes Forever

Stars and stripes for ever,
Is our nation theme.
Loyalty is our motto as it may seem,
A tribute to our country, we must never,
    never fail.

Stars and stripes for ever,
May we never, never fail.
To take command with our chief,
For life and liberty of our land,
Stars and stripes for ever,
We must always stand.
In this world of sorrow, we must
    pay and plan tomorrows,
For the stars and stripes today.

Tops to tops in action, long may
    our nation reign.
Our chief has the password, ten to
    one he'll say.
Our votes are free, we'll keep them
To wait that future day.

—Mary Lucy Shimp

ll I Can Say

ll I can say
that I want to know why.
ou don't seem to notice
ow hard I do try.
o catch your attention
hen I walk on by.
ut you are always gone
the blink of an eye.
hen you're away
think I will die.
nd when you're so close
feel I would cry.
want you to know
at I could never pry.
I'm not wanted
say with a sigh.
ut my feelings for you
nnot be a lie.
ecause there can be no love
ithout the my.

—*Brenda Jones*

e Loves Me, He Loves Me Not

ow can you tell if you're in love,
is the question I want to know.
st 'cause he says `I love you',
you still don't know it's so.
oes he put his arms around you
and hold you tight?
an you feel the love with all
your might?
oes his touch, make you warm inside?
nd if people ask, do you have
the pride...to say yes?
hen you think about him do
you feel aglow?
r when you think about him
do you feel so low?
ope this helps all of you to see,
ne love within the eyes of thee.
ut that still doesn't answer
my question above.
ow can you tell if you're in love?

—*Carole J. Brandi*

Doesn't Have To Be This Way

doesn't have to be this way,
what I say at night.
hink about the days events,
nd this time get a fright.
want to take back what I said,
o my very good friend.
ecause I hate it when things I do,
akes my friendships end.
really want to say I'm sorry,
ut truly don't know how.
cannot think of some nice way,
ut I will, this I vow.
hen a little later I get a plan,
hen I look at the night so starry.
omorrow when I see my friend,
ll say how much I'm sorry.

—*Erik Hansen*

Longing

Longing's come to visit me,
It arrived quite unannounced,
And carrying bag and baggage
Into my house it flounced.
It couldn't wait to show me
All the things that it had brought,
Such things as hopes and wishes
And other food for thought.
Longing carried vague scenarios
And many happy endings.
Tantalizing possibilities
Were among these other things.
It packed a few imaginings,
Then added several more,
'Til I had to stare and wonder
How it made it through the door.
I pray this visit's fairly brief
And soon it takes its leave,
I find longing overwhelming
With all its vagaries.

—*Linda J. Doughty*

Dolores

I knew you were coming,
It excited me so,
I was very impatient,
The time really passed slow.

I spent whole days thinking,
Of how it would be,
When finally the day came,
That you'd be with me.

At last came the moment,
For you to arrive,
I was filled with joy,
Soon we'd share our lives.

All my dreams are shattered,
But I must be brave,
You're with God in heaven,
I weep at your grave.

Now you are an angel,
I wasn't meant for us,
To share our tomorrows,
Goodbye my Dolores.

—*Donna Z. Deck*

Untitled

The sea is a child,
it fights its very tormentor,
the sea is only a child
but somehow it always wins.
I cry to the sea to kill me,
and take me from all the pain,
but the sea is only a child,
and wins this fight again.
I watch the waves roll in,
it brings back too many thoughts,
I must get away from the sea,
and the child within that haunts.

—*Karen M. Kinnear*

What Is This?

What is this?
It has tiny eyes,
A miniature nose,
Two small hands,
And ten little toes.

It cannot talk,
It only cries,
And looks around with inquisitive
eyes.

I try to discover what I am admiring.
Maybe I can find out
Why it is crying.
Where did it come from,
And why is it so trying?

I ask my mother,
She always knows.
"Just what do we have here?"
She replies as she glows,
"This is your brand new brother!"

—*Judith A. Flounders*

The Oldest Sister's Lament

It is very tough being the oldest,
it is always easy being the youngest.
I always get blamed,
while the youngest get away.

I have lots of responsibilities,
I hate babysitting the kiddies.
They want to go where I go,
but I always tell them no.

The twins get all the attention,
while I'm always last.
They get into my stuff,
my parents never tell them enough.

Work is what I do,
they always boo hoo.
I'd rather be the youngest,
because being the oldest is just too hard.

—*Megan C. Hunter*

The Wind Still Blows

The wind still blows.
It never dies.
Leaves fly, pedals fly.
The sand whips, the dirt lies.
What's it all about?
It rains.
So the water runs.
The light flashes.
Then it roars.
Still the wind blows.

—*Lori-Ann Alvino*

Ringing Telephones

I whispered
    no one answered
I called
    no one answered
I laughed
    no one answered
I screamed
    no one answered
I died
    no one answered.

—*Daphene Butzke*

Untitled

As I sit here I contemplate my life
My successions and my failures,
My happy times, my sad;
Would I change anything?
No.
I love you -
Life;
You're so special:
My life,
mine alone.
Like an ocean voyage; mapped out,
With chartered stops.
The people I meet, the faces I touch,
the lips I kiss.
Like the places I've been,
Each has a special place in the
photo album of my mind.

—Marge Knigge

The Rain Is For You

I love the rain
It reminds me of you
Each drop a single tear
I cried for you
I cried of a sad day
I think of a happy day

The rain brings me joy
The joy of remembering you
I love to listen for a whisper
A whisper from you
It says I am waiting to see you
Sometimes it says different

You say
I miss you, I love you
And I whisper the same

I will never get over the sadness
The sadness of losing you
I will never leave you, you will never leave me
But, the rain has gone and the whisper too
So for now I bid farewell to you

—Nickie Barnes

The Moon

I see the moon
It sends slivers of fragmented light
Deepening the shadows
As I sit
Far into the night
I watch the moon
As it glides through the sky
Illuminating the earth
With its soft glow
Transforming fields
Into fairytales
Where unknown folk
Slip through the trees
Dancing at midnight
Under the moon
Observing all, it sits
A silver eye
Watching the night
Guardian of the world
In its nighttime glory.

—Elizabeth Beckham

Untitled

Last night I talked to a man.
It was an unusual conversation.
He stood.
I also stood...
but on tip-toe to whisper in his ear.
He spoke words of wisdom.
He held a staff
- said he was God.
Then I looked closely.
He was made of wood.

—Pamela Bolinda Pate

Cupid's Arrow

At first I thought
It would point to me,
But then I decided
It couldn't be.

I guess I was wrong,
You must've been right
Because no one knew
We fell in love last night.

Too bad it's over,
I miss you so much.
I guess we were something
Cupid's arrow couldn't touch.

Some say it barely missed me,
But that couldn't be true,
Because today I realized
I never loved you!

—Victoria East

The Flag

Do you honor the flag as it waves
its colors of red, white and blue
Would you fight for freedom and
to the stars and stripes be true

Who could desecrate the flag, a
symbol of our great land
Which was won by those who gave their
life that it might bravely stand

America is the home of the brave
the land of the free
As a beacon of light for all
the world to see

Thank God for our forefathers
who gallantly paved the way
That our love for God and country
will never go astray.

—Margaret Tatum

"Another Day"

Another day,
just dreaming, thinking,
Another day,
not utilized at all
Another day,
will surely have the answer
Another day,
and tears begin to fall.
Another day,
A life has turned a corner
Another day,
the dark before the dawn

—Elfi Kopf Merrell

Christmas Gifts

I love shopping for Christmas gifts
It's full of fun and pleasure.
It gives my heart a pleasing lift
To find such unique treasure.

Behind the ribbon and wrapping
You'll never know what you'll find.
Perhaps a kitten napping,
Or a treasure of some kind.

Christmas is a season of love
Like two romantic ivory doves.

Christmas only comes once a year
So buy your mirrors and find your gears.

After shopping, you're exhausted
Since the items were very costly.

But think of next week,
When St. Nick visits us once again.

You'll have a time of enjoyment, happiness,
and entertainment;
It'll be worth all your payment.

—Bonnie Bernat

The Ending

Life's harshness is a sword made of ice.
Its reality is cold and rigid.
Time stands still for eternity.
Motion has ceased to progress.

Despair cries out,
Fear burns in the heart,
And anger sets in.
Conquering all triumph for hope.

The feeling is near.
Age has taken its toll:
The last breath is exhaled,
And it is all over.

—Teresa R. Nestor

Smile

Put a smile on your face
It's so easy to do
It will make people think
What is wrong with you.

Put a smile on your face
instead of a frown
it makes you look up
instead of looking down

A smile will go better
with the things that you do
It shows you are full of color
instead of being blue

So put a smile on your face
It will help you to say
No matter what happens
I'll have a nice day.

—Steven Long

Olney, in the Sky

Olney is my Heaven on earth,
It's where I'll live until I die,
I also know that's when I'll go,
To a greater Olney, in the sky.

When I think of the great beyond,
I feel a profound presence on high,
See a divinely grand Promised Land,
A heavenly Olney, in the sky.

After I depart my Heaven on earth,
When my years have all rolled by,
By His grace He's prepared a place,
For me in Olney, in the sky.

—*Lester E. Linder*

A Different Way

I know that you're still with us,
    Just in a different way.
Yet sometimes it's hard to reach you,
    It seems you've gone away.

So I try to think about you
    And bring you close to me.
But I can't get used to doing this
    With someone I cannot see.

It just doesn't seem to fit
    In the mortal course of day,
So I must remember that you're with me
    In a different way.

It's then when I can see you
    Looking out for me.
I feel your love in spirit,
    and it brings you close to me.

So I remember you as always,
    and I can talk to you each day,
For I know that you are here with me,
    just in a different way.

—*Eda LaPolt*

The Picture

Just one picture can hold so much,
Just that one touch.
Of waxy film.
Brings back so many memories.
Back to that day
feelings rush your way.
Some good, some bad,
Maybe anger arises and you feel mad.
Maybe you'll cry
Cause the picture shows a sad goodbye.
All the feelings and emotions
on one piece of paper.
A new technology that everyone loves.
I wouldn't give up my camera for
All these memories

—*Liz Schoof*

From Wings Of The Sun

Clouds that break and float away
On the dying breath of day
Drift from the wings of the sun
As a falling feather;
    And melt into the fading blue
    As the evening passes through —
Where will they meet and again
Be joined together?

—*Sonia Beck-Bronson*

The Family Pew

Rollag woodcarvers
laboriously, devotedly
hewed and carved
logs to build
the crudely-beautiful Stavkirke
for a new Christian faith.
Yet, residual paganism
was attested by
fierce dragon heads-
now, black with tar and age-
atop the soaring peaks
of a hand-split roof,
eternally warding off evil spirits.
God's Holy Presence
sits in the family pew,
where, generations ago
in Norway,
Great-Grandfather
sat and prayed.

—*Elaine Kachel*

Thoughts-In Rhyme

In the field of poetry, reader,
    Lack of talent should I blame,
For spending my time writing verses
    But never attaining fame?

Just sitting here making notes no less
    As thoughts through my mind run,
Though boring to most people perhaps,
    To me is just plain fun.

Should I now use my notes and pen
    To heckle some poor soul,
When joy and laughter I can give
    For "I am in control?"

At present, I'll spread hope and cheer
    Though the time may come again,
When I'll use my thoughts for a poem,
    But "Wield a poison pen."

—*A Shortfellow*

Stew

Not all of the
    Leased meat

Will assimilate
    The sauce

Patrician cookery
    Brews.

Smacking of freedom
    To stew

In concoctions
Heated with flames

    Of dissension
    temperanced

From the light
Of a firefly

    Having shone;
    Moves on.

—*Ronald Homer Henson*

Dedication

Let me hope
Let me dream
Let me pray

Let me follow Thy will every day
Let my dreams and my prayers
Be my directions from Thee

Then—
Let me know
Let me hear
Let me see
Let me be

Let my life be a Mold in Thy hands
To be used as you would in your plans
And—
Let me hope
Let me dream
Let me pray

—*David B. Orear*

Untitled

Gaze deep into the Abyss.
Lifeless and subdued;
Hear the echoless silence
Of the Universe Rebuked.

Join with the living;
Heralding praise on high,
Proclaim in vocal tribute:
Not I! Not I!

Love life:
Accept the treasure.
Enjoy existence:
Fill it with pleasure.

Share with all!
Share with all!

—*Joseph John Jarek*

I Dream Of You

In my eyes I see you
    like a vibrant sea.
All your waves and current
    belong to me.
We engulf each other
    through the ebb and flow of time.
Never to be released from
    each others mind.
At that precious moment
    when you and I embrace
I know in my heart
    all time will be erased.

—*Mary Sims*

Shared Seasons

Why does the night come so quickly
Just when the sun is on high
Why aren't the questions answered
Always tempting to question why

Where do we go in the darkness
Do we ever again see the light
Do we ever again know the flowers
that disappeared that night

Do we feel the joy and the sadness
that in the sunlight knew
Do we ever know the reason
we shared the same season?

—*Penny August*

Sixteen Months

You can wear sixteen months
Like a warm coat in the dead of winter
And thank God
For life and plenty.

It took that long to come
To, "Blessed be the refugee"
It took gracious time with Dora
To be myself again.

On the outside not much has changed:
The negatives rage on
It's a struggle to feel good
Knowing death shall not be denied.

But death does not stop time
And there's been some of that
To go around
And I'm back in town.

I'm here to point the way
To a steady May
Here to reinforce
The quality of life.

—*Nick N. Dybman*

The Sky

My love is shown to you
Like the sun clearly bright
And the love for you is strong
So I know there is no night.

If our love is blocked
Like an eclipse in the sky
I know there will be troubles
But I will never say goodbye.

For I know our love is strong
This I hope is so
Because unlike the clouds
It does not come and go.

Although there are some clouds
That block our loving thoughts
Our love will last forever
And this is said with no doubts

So if there are some clouds
I hope you'll think of good times
Because I know our love will last
As long as there is light.

—*Jesse Blaylock*

Untitled

In my room
Lit only by candle light
My thoughts drift
And collide in my skull
Like a bumper car ride
At a fair
Smashing themselves to fragments
And then fusing back together
In more and more
Curious designs
Like Mary Shelley's monster
Each thought made of dismembered
Ideas sewn back together with
Sloppy stitches
And alive once more
In absolute grotesquerie
And unnatural patterns

—*Michael Aaron Prince*

A Moment

Moments of time
little by little do slip by.
Moments of time
wasted with pride.
Moments of time
With sorrow do they ride,
on waves of discontent.
Moments of Love
given and taken lightly,
with no one to weep or repent.
Moments like this
wasted on the sorrows of the
many,
Until they are blessed
by the few.

—*Joanne Fritch*

Everyone's a Little Different

Everyone's a
little different.
I really don't
know why, but
even if they are
a little different,
still treat them
with respect, and
remember they have
feelings, just like
like you, so if
they say hi, you
can say hi too!

—*Traisha Wallace*

A Funeral in a Trance

Goodbye to a kiss
long before I kissed you
goodbye to a touch
long before I touched you

your scent I'll never smell
your laughter I'll never hear
real happiness I'll never feel
your love I'll never have

goodbye to a past
that never happened
an affair
that will never take place

sculpt my body with your bare hands
mud for mud, clay for clay
paint my face with your fingertips
line by line, inch by inch
water me with your raindrops
flooded by my tears

stay with me if just in fantasy
my dear…imaginary lover

—*Jennifer Galang*

Never Mind

Never mind yesterday,
  Life is today!

Never mind yesterday,
  Lay it away!

Never mind anything,
  over and done!

Here is a new moment
Lit with new sun!

—*Amber Dahl*

Intense Desire

Not wanting to leave your presence,
Longing to taste your lips,

The wonderful aroma of your essence,
My ready and willing hips,

My desire how very physical,
It entraps my spirit and my mind,

Wanting you so deeply still,
I crave you with intense desire.

You move just like an ocean.
Welling, swelling, and leaping high.

With the scent of your effervescence,
I am relieved with a quiet sigh.

To gaze at you leaves me mesmerized.
Your touch is both hot and cold.

In an instant I am hypnotized.
It burns the flesh and chills the soul.

I am consumed by your masculinity.
I long for you to quench my fire.

I am drawn to your sensuality.
I crave you with intense desire.

—*Irene Moore*

Fall Leaves

I stood on a hill top,
Looking far as I could see,
Row after row,
of those pretty trees.

The most colorful sight
My eyes could behold
are those beautiful fall leaves,
All orange, red and gold.

As I stand there among them,
Like in a world of my own
I thought what a shame,
they will soon all be gone.

The trees will look cold
and oh: so bare
They don't seem to mind
or even care.

They will plan new wardrobes,
So I've been told.
I like them best,
Wearing orange, red and gold.

—*Leota E. Redmon*

The Window

Watching the window
Looking for you
Searching around
But seeking no clue

Watching in the window
I also hear a sound
The sound of your laugh
The sound of your cry
As I sit I wonder why

Why I love you so much
If your hate is so true
Sitting, wondering, having no clue

As I watch I pray to God
That I will find you.

—*Heather Bell*

Code of Silence

Faces of people I thought I once knew
melt into black ovals of granite
covering me
stoning me into darkness.
Their eyes turn red like searing fires
anger in their souls.
I cannot speak
my throat numb with silence
minutes pass like hours.
Their weight upon me
wearing me down
I turn my mind
off the pain.
Blackout.
Morning,
opening my eyes
I feel them next to me
and I ask myself,
Are these my
brothers?

—*Jay Ballanger*

First Love

First love is the hardest
love.
You gave your heart and
it was broken
You will always know
his name!
You will always remember
what he looks like.
This love will always be
a sweet and precious
love!

—*Barbara G. Griffith*

Love Is

Love is a baby, newly born
Love is an old man, tired and worn.
A sparkling brook, a growing tree,
Many things are love to me.

Mountains tops covered with snow,
Holding hands with one at a show,
Sharing a secret with a friend;
Loving someone 'till the end.

Love is something you can't hold
But something beautiful to behold.
Love is precious, tho not new,
But most of all, love is you.

—*Ruth Brandenburg*

How Will I Know?

How will I know you'll
love me now but not forever
How will I know that
the magical heights we will
reach tonight won't be once and only
How will I know if you
will end up with another
How will I know that, I won't
be locked up in some distant
memory and left out in the cold
How will I know if we will stay
together for awhile but not until
we grow old
How will I know if you
really love me
How will I know?

—*Kristy Marie Keen*

Silhouettes

I know the hurt
love past
Once so strong
now faded
Memories… on pictures

Silhouettes of you and me

I know the times
long ago
Our future plotted
now gone
Plans… merely broken

Silhouettes of you and me

I hated the good-bye
leaving you
Only the crying
now over
Dreams… ever empty

Silhouettes of you and me

—*Mary L. Sullivan*

Angel White

Angel white, baby girl why do you
make me feel so good?

Laid out in your sparkling white.

Angel white, baby girl you have
taken me to paradise three
different ways.

On a beautiful river cruise.

Through a tunnel of love.

Make me so hot; as I smoke you
with passion.

Angel white, baby girl; you have
taken my house, my car, and
the woman I love with your
sweet exotic ways.

You have broken down my mind,
body and soul, with your sweet
exotic ways.

Angel white, baby girl why can't
they see that you are the devil's
disciple; all laid out in your sparkling
white.

—*Bernard Beard*

Untitled

Run swiftly and smoothly
Manes streaming in the air
Their muscles show so strongly
As they leap straight over there
The beauty of these creatures
God sure has made them grand
Admired by all who see them
As they're sitting in the stands
Their beauty is far greater
When forest and in field
When free to leap and jump about
More strength yes they do yield
Set high up hills and mountains
Wind blowing through their hair
They bound on where they want to
The stallion and the mare

—*Ann Hermes*

Master

— Master the heart —
— Master the head —
— Master the emotions —
— Master the feeling —
— Master the mentality —
— Master your life —
— Master your destinations —
— Master your abilities —
— Master your skills —
— Master your body —
— Master your own health —
— Master your own state of mind —
— Master !!! —

—*Kim Listro*

The Lost Souls

Through the endless halls of time
Measured footsteps can be heard,
Muted voices merging whine
Fill the gloom with doleful dirge.

Weary souls who seek their way
Faces gaunt with deep despair,
The eerie shroud of deaths decay
Engulfs them like an evil laird.

Through eons of eternal night
On seas of no return,
They seek to find a ray of light
Repentance they must learn.

The wailing winds of emptiness
Taunt the souls of vain regrets,
No longer can they hope to find
The peace of God's eternal rest.

—*Elody De Crane*

My Father's Song

My father's song is a
melody that's the
background tune
In all I see

A ballad of joy
and just for life
a full choir of hope
In the face of strife

A song of trust
Where commitment is free
It's lyrics
Of love and family

My father's song
His gift to me
Lovely aria soaring
Beyond eternity

—*Jan Befera*

Feelings

Sometimes life is rough,
like knives on the ground.
Sometimes life is easy,
like a circle nice and round.
People can be cruel,
like an angry mule.
People can be kind,
like a gentle mind.
So as long as you live
a life cycle will go round,
and you will have friends and
enemies that abound.

—*Sara Davidson*

Lost Love

Today I lie here,
Missing him.
For you see we were lovers,
Then that love went dim.

It was both of our faults
I guess you could say.
But he wanted me to go,
And I wanted to stay.

I said we could work it out,
He said goodbye.
I begged him to give me another chance
"It's over." was his reply.

So I'm lying here,
Thinking of him tonight.
I want to go back to him,
And maybe someday I might.

—*Tara Truett*

Forevermore

Through the bedroom window peeping
Moonlight, on my daughter sleeping
Clock a-ticking, shadows creeping,
Slowly cross the floor

In her grasp she holds so caring
One small bear with eyes-a-glaring
Lifeless, there it lay just staring
At the bedroom door.

Entering the room I'm wary
Of the beast so dark and hairy
Fixed beside my darling Carrie
That thing I do abhor

Outside I see the lightning crackle
I my mind the bear does cackle
Bragging, "See my iron shackle?
She's mine forevermore."

—*Lora Lee Garcia*

A Mother's Prayer

He hit her - he hit her face -
    my child, my sweet little girl
A cruel blow that stunned her so
    down to the floor in a whirl.
He hurt her, with bruteful force,
    my daughter so fair and small.
He is strong, with rage inside
    so muscular and tall -
My heart cries. It's so unjust
    so terrible an assault
Her tears flowed and then he said,
    "'Twas really all your own fault."

I begged her, I pleaded hard
    to stop, curtail all calling
Insane is this horrible man
    to whom she keeps a-crawling.
Please help her, I do beseech
    My God, my Saviour I pray
Protect her and give her light
    surround her with it each day.

—*Frances M. Nowak*

The Child

My mind so busy
My heart could burst,
So filled with love
That has quenched a thirst.

And who would have thought
Someone of my years
Needed a child
To bring me to tears.

A child's love is given
So honest and free,
A reminder of how
We all should be.

Dear Lord above,
Please hear my prayer,
Let the child in me
Always be there.

—*Mary Lou Sanders*

You and I

As the dawn breaks
    my life turns yet another page
I continue to grow and change
    with each advancing age.

My smile brightens
    as I look at you
My life is complete
    now that we are two.

My love becomes stronger
    with each passing day.
You mean so much
    no words could ever say.

When the day arrives
    and it will be
The biggest joy
    for you and me

For we will never
    say goodbye
As we are one
    just you and I

—*Catherine Y. Zip*

How the Road Does Bend

How the road does bend
Near dark and tangled wood
How the heart does send
Such thoughts that ever could.

How a man does feel
That life is but a dream
How the heart does seal
What senses fathom —
Seem.

How the road does stretch
So endless in its line
How a soul does retch
In the passing of its time.

Tomorrow is but another dream
Some other step to take
A journey down this road
of life
Behind the close shadow
of mistake.

—*Arthur McNamee*

Christmas 1993

Come to the stable,
Nestled in Bethlehem,
Under a deep blue sky.
Stars are shining.
Cattle are lowing,
A little baby cries.
Come to the stable,
Kneel down and pray,
He was born for you and I.

Come to the stable,
See the young mother,
Radiant in the night.
Her love encompasses
All who come to Her.
See her with the child.
Singing a lullaby, softly, gently.
Angels voices fill the night.
Shepherds come closer, there kneel the wise
men.
The stars are brilliant lights, come to the stable.
Kneel down and pray, this is a Blessed night.

—*Nancy Stewart-Tornai*

Weeping Willow

Weeping willow, strong and proud.
Never bent by wind or thunder cloud.
Standing tall, standing strong.
Why do you weep? What is wrong?
My lover has left me here alone.
No one to hold and call my own.
No one to love, can't you see?
That's the reason that I'm weeping
Every night when the sun says goodbye,
I lay down my branches and begin to cry.
As the stars shine overhead
I pray to God that I we're dead.
To join my lover wherever he roams,
Heaven or hell, I'll make it my home.

—*Beth Denman*

A Sisters Love

You thought his laughter would
never fade. Well it did.

You say you never had a
chance to say good-bye.
Well neither did I.

Years pass but the pain
in our hearts remains the same.

There's nothing we can do but
sit here and think of you,
while tears gently fall.
Its just another way of
saying we love and miss you,
that's all.

It hurts so much having to believe
that your not here. But we
always learn to accept it
year by year.

Death will never keep us apart,
because you will always
Keep a special place in my heart.

—*Alaina E. Duffy*

ilent Voices

live in silence.
ever hearing a word.
wish I could listen
the rain or a singing bird.

Iy hands are my mouth.
ours are my ears.
understand emotions
ch as your falling tears.

don't feel I'm handicapped
r in any way impaired.
am just like anyone else.
umanness is something we all share.

next time you see me,
on't stop and stare.
can show you a new language
you've got time to spare.

—*Judy L. Stone*

Individuality?"

here is no catcher,
o heroes left,
o dreams to dream
cannot forget),
o songs to sing
o sad but true),
one to raise hearts
nd minds to;
o goal to accomplish
utside of me,
othing around
o make us we;
o unit dignity
our minds
Generation of separate
dividuals, all times).
eparate we fight,
hus must fall.
anyone listening
o my call?

—*Michelle MacDonald*

ne Smile

s a rich man, I ask for a smile,
No one can buy.
iamonds and the like, only last awhile,
I don't know why.
ike coin and furs and food,
May all decline.
smile for me, is most divine.
look for a smile
No one can buy.
o one can barter
Yet, all may try.
look for a smile
With eyes all gleaming,
othing to sell,
Just happiness with meaning.
or just one smile,
Neither bought nor sold.
the greatest reward
And better than gold.

—*Peter D. Borkenhagen*

Love

Where have the years gone
No one can say
As long as there is love
Love will always find a way
To keep us all together
Happy and proud
That our friendship
Will last forever
Even with a few clouds
All we need is one another
To keep our spirits high
And the love we have
For each other
Will never die

—*Elenore Meybohm*

Nobody

I'm nobody.
No one knows who I am.
I am unidentified, unknown.
Unloved, unwanted.

I'm nobody.
No one knows who I am.
No arms to hold me close.
No lips to caress my skin.

I'm nobody.
No one knows who I am.
Unnoticed, waiting
for an everlasting love.
I grow old and writhed
as I die inside.

—*Vanessa Agha*

Raindrops

Spend with him
The sunny times
With sky so blue
And sun so bright

But when the clouds have turned to gray
And in our dwellings we all must stay
I hope you'll find it in your heart
To save me just this little part

As you look from your window and see
The raindrops falling endlessly
Think a little thought of me
For you with him I'd rather see
Than a bit less happy and with me

—*Russell J. Ridl*

To See You is to Love You, Sheril

When this little girl I see each day
My heart is heard to say
You are pretty, yes lovely too
To see you, is to love you.

Try to remember me
You are young as I can see
My love is true, yes for you
Yes, just to see you is to love you.

Though your life may go another way
Please, someday look my way
My hand will always be out to you
You'll know, to see you, is to love you.

—*Harry Cameron*

Alone!

I feel so alone.
No one to talk to,
I feel so alone,
No one to confide in.

We use to be close,
I don't know what happened.
We use to be close,
I don't know you anymore.

You were my hero.
You were my friend.
You were my hero.
You were the reason I made it through.

You're different now,
You say because I'm older.
You're different now,
You say because I've grown.
...But all I am is ALONE!

—*Arrianna Leigh Reeves*

Sleep

I can't sleep,
No siree, I can't snore!
I've tried to count sheep,
What a bore.

Next night,
I go to sleep no flat.
Even though I slept light
I had a dream of a giant bat

Third night I slept the dead
Even though I keep waking up.
So I got up out of bed,
to get a drink out of a big big cup.

At last!
I can sleep like a baby!
It was a blast!
And I didn't even get out of bed!

—*Stefanie Hande*

intersect

Turn signal blinks;
not an indication,
but a warning.
Car horn screams
and I turn
too slow
too late
to stop.
Head rocks forward.
Metal grinds
on metal.
Tousled blonde
child framed
in the window
before me.
Bouncing upwards;
forwards.
Head rocks back.
Solid contact.

disconnect

—*Ryan Rons*

New Day

Today's the day to start anew
not to go on feeling blue
Think of something really funny
maybe a purple Easter bunny
A hairy frog - a hairless dog.
A Santa Clause who's tall and skinny
Mrs. Clause in a Mini.
If you can't work up a smile
take a walk and go a mile
Watch for birds, snakes, and snails
even wagging puppy tails
Chat with some one along the way
with only cheerful things to say.
Count your blessings then and now
you could be - a purple cow
Even that could bring some joy
to a little girl or boy
There's someone worse off than you
so cheer up, stop feeling blue
For God has been good to you.

—*Addie Gollings*

"Graduation Day"

Now that you've graduated,
Now that you've passed
From that old school,
From that old class.

You thought it was time
that you passed the time by,
by just taking a sniff,
by just taking a try.

Who would've known,
you would've died this way.
Without you by my side,
what shall I say?

Why didn't you think,
Why didn't you cry?
For some help, some hope
that you can't get from dope.

Now that you've graduated
Now that you've passed
From that old school
From that old class

—*Adona Payne*

Culinary Art

Small footprints mark the floor a mix
of dirt and shower blend
from making and baking mudpies
with abetting wet proof friends

Crying she said, we need a tray
cause Nell's big sister's there
and took our stuff right from us
in tones of great despair

To the bath with you, she affirmed
and stay off my fresh waxed floor
wash those dirty feet young girl
then close that swinging door

Soon spic and span with pan in hand
the chef skipped out the door
it won't take long to look just like
the way She did before

Reshining the tile you could see
a gleam in her eyes so plain
gladly Mom would never love someone
that did not like the rain

—*Riley Evans*

Scene From My Window

Autumn leaves
    of every kind
Capture the soul
    of all mankind.

A colorful festival
    wave to the skies
To hail His Majesty
    where the sun doth rise.

O God - how
    wonderful you are-
To grant this splendor
    from realms afar:

My heart, my soul
    spell love for Thee —
Now —
    and for all ETERNITY. Amen.

—*Anthony N. Basilicato, Sr.*

Crowns

Yawning winds whisper tales
of far off places.
Echoing endearing words and
loving sighs, now resting
upon blushing faces.
Secret dreams within depths
of aching hearts and loving
souls; yearning the freedom
to sing their sacred melodies
of love and life.

Nestled among nature's bounty,
upon seasons continuing to grow.
Drifting thoughts through
rainbowed skies, or storms
weeping frowns.
Changing seasons know not
their master, as nature wears
many crowns.

—*Richard A. Johnson*

Transfer

How can I convey
of love lost and
unrequited?
I know.
I will take my heartache,
place it flat on this page
and with whatever strength
I possess,
press my palms
until they mingle
with the molecules
of this paper.
Now place your palms
over my palm prints
and feel my pain flow
through your arms
and into your heart.

—*Daniel B. Montanez*

Blue

Blue is the color
of the ocean and sky
above, bluebirds fly
and below, blue bells grow
Blue is the coast of Maine
and the crystal rain

But, blue can also be the
bruises of pain
and the winter frost
that kills off the grain
or it could be the thought
of being
lost

—*Elicia Whitmer*

Level Resolve

Knees rise from the depths,
Of the peat below water not,
As was once before man's toil.
Knees cradle and feed the swamp's,
Beautiful majesty, now exposed.
Presently guarding either boundary,
Of a way so fair but difficult,
Enduring the continued launch,
Of Nature's liquid fossil heir,
In the shape of spheres.

Spheres must nestle but once upon,
Two grades of growth colored emerald,
From the sky's tears and blaze. Then,
Gently propelled twice by metal blades,
Into the imposing circular objective,
As the patient, majestic sentries hold,
Gray, primitive decorations so high.
Sometimes they slap efforts erratically.
Yet, the beauty remains and with resolve,
Imposing circles eventually succumb.

—*Keith M. Gillies*

The Tackle Game

Tackle football is the name
    Of this rough and ready game.

Nothing gives more pleasure
    To watch kids at my leisure.

Often in a huddle
    Their call becomes a muddle.

You laugh, you cry,
    You almost die.

That grimy face, and sweating brow.
    These boys we love show us how.

To play this game is very rough.
    Like young warriors they are tough.

They push, they shove, kick and run.
    But be so rough they have fun.

Touch down, touch down! is the cry
    Dads look on at days gone by.

Remembering their days of fame.
    When they played this football game.

—*Bet P. Pounders*

The Paper

The paper,
offers a haven and a sanctuary
to my emotions.
There on a one dimensional plane,
they can be touched by none
yet touch all those around them.
A private fortress
used often
to disguise my life
from reality,
yet personify my words.

—*Douglas A. Bungay*

Dandelions and Pretty Stones

Dandelions and pretty stones,
Oh, how I miss those years!
Presents from our little ones,
So precious and so dear.

That surely wasn't long ago,
Was it just yesterday,
When little legs came running fast
To bring me my bouquet?

Then there were the pretty stones,
Not the ordinary kind,
The ones with all the diamonds
That still sparkle in my mind.

I wish they hadn't gone so fast,
The wondrous childhood years;
Those gifts, much more than I could ask,
I'm remembering through my tears.

Dandelions and pretty stones,
I really miss them, Lord;
But now our grandchildren can come
And bring them to my door.

—*Patricia Eckel*

His Camera

If my eyes were but a camera,
Oh what wonders they would see.
To have forever imprinted,
On my fragile memory.

I would catch God's fresh beginning
Of a new day for the world;
Catch the wonders of his glory,
As each blessing He unfurls.

But should I see the sadness
That around us does abound,
I would quickly close my shutter
And fall humbly to the ground.

I would pray for God's forgiveness,
And His love to guide me through
All the suffering and the heartaches,
That His beloved son went through.

If my eyes were but a camera,
The film I'd change each day,
Until I could behold God's love,
Shine forth for all - I'd pray.

—*Ernest James Mongeau*

Love One Another

I met a stranger
On
The street
Whose
Life was incomplete,
And his
Eyes were cold and red
since
Hunger he did dread.
I
Gave him change
to
Ease his pain
Because
God's perfect gifts
Come
From above to
Those
Who offer love.

—*Marion F. Coleman*

Precious Memories

I take a quiet hour or two
On a dismal rainy day,
When the world looks damp and soggy
And the skies are misty grey.

I peep into this closet
In the recess of my mind.
And revel in the treasures
I have stored from other times.

The softest light emerges
From the corners of this place,
Not dimmed by time or tragedy
Or wrinkles on my face.

My babies curls, my toddlers smile,
Their eyes alight with wonder,
I touch my memories reverently
And tuck the edges under.

Memories are such treasures
They saturate my soul
And make my heart a miser
For they gleam like burnished gold.

—*Emma Holliday*

Life's a Play

Life's a play,
on a floating stage,
that sails away
on lakes, on rivers,
on ocean waves.
The scenery is
Hemlock and palm,
Pine and sudden elm,
roaring waves,
pouring rain.
Where rivers flow,
are oceans made;
mountains turn
into planes.
With new actors on their way,
while some are dead, or dying,
some are lost on the way.
The original script, is never played.
Life's worth living anyway.

—*J. Anthony Gomes*

"The Sale"

The long-awaited time had come
On a foggy Saturday morn.
Folks came from far and wide to see
What was there, be it new or worn.

At 10 a.m. the cries rang out
To start the final phase
In a career that started years ago
Now ending in a frantic haze.

Buyers mingled to and fro,
Inspecting and bidding their best
Occasionally stopping for a snack
Or sitting for just a rest.

The end of the day has drawn near
A final cry rings out
To close a chapter in a life
Forever changed; that's no doubt.

No one knows what the future holds
For the farmer of the land.
What ever comes he can survive
By the holding of God's hand.

—*Mary J. Butcher*

Memories of My Father

You won't find my Father's name
On a long, black granite wall.
Instead it's carved in Southern marble.
In letters two inches tall.

There were no taps, no gun salutes,
(These Honors he deserved)
The Honor Guard was all tied up,
At Official Functions, I'd heard.

My mind drifts back to childhood days,
When first I did recite,
"The Pledge of Allegiance" to my Dad,
And watched tears stream down his face.

He said "I'm proud you like Old Glory,
And to Her be ever true,
And when you get to be a man,
I'll give a Special Flag to you."

Now sit the mourners in sweltering heat,
Their countenances sad,
Old Glory drapes my Father's coffin,
His Final Gift: my Flag.

—*William R. DeSilvey*

Each a Certain Hope

Life's cross roads
not a city street
a field of grain
to pass
yellow as brass
a pasture of grass
to pass
along with deep
thoughts -
each grain
of thought
God puts on
scales
life's tales.

—*Lola I. Hansell*

Don't Turn Your Back

Don't turn your back
  on doors open once for you
Don't burn your bridges
  after getting over them,
The world is watching you.

Don't turn your back
  against the 'man of strength
The ladder you climbed,
  is still a ladder,
careful not to slip
The world is watching you.

Don't turn your back
  as if to say, I know you not,
a wheel is still a wheel
  careful, it is man - made
The world is watching you
Don't turn your back on me.

—*Ruby Melville*

Sunrise

I watch the sunrise
on the beach so calm,
the tip of the sun on,
the farthest edges of the earth.
As it walks,
On its glowing path to the sky.
I hear the caw of a gull,
the pounding of the waves.
I can feel the morning breeze
the cold water on my feet.
I see the orange glow of the sun,
as it reflects on the waters edge.
I smell the salty air as the light,
breaks through the twilight,
I say "hello!" to a morning jogger
as he passes by.
As the sun climbs higher in the sky
a new day has begun
and it will end
with a sunset.

—*Amy Sokal*

The Wood Pecker

The wood pecker pecked
Out a little round hole.
And made him a house
In the telephone pole.

One day when it rained.
He stuck out his head.
He had on a hood
And a collar of red.

When the streams of rain.
Pour out of the sky.
And sparkle of lightening.
Go flashen by.

And the big big wheel
Of the thunder roll.
He will saggel back
In the telephone pole.

When the rain stops.
And he wants to play.
He will fly around
The rest of the day.

—*Ethel O'Banion*

You And Me

Like the betrayed forever
on the open ground
once your eyes were
open
by the edge of the water: The source
my gaze and your heart
big white swans
on the back: Broken streaks
you cast down your eyes
by the edge of the infinite
we will meet
no gaze and no
heart
further away than the source

—*Martin Hagglund*

Waltzes on Water

The sunlight dances,
On the pond,
As colorful leaves waltz,
Above and beyond.

Fish go leaping,
Through the air,
Flip-flopping to the tune,
Without even a care.

Then all those rainbows,
High in the sky,
Make a huge fiery opal,
A sight for anyone's eye.

Then some little froggies,
Sing and do a dance,
Excitedly croaking,
A song of great romance.

—*Janet Draper*

Prayers

I sense that prayers are endless.
Once they are uttered
And recorded by the Lord,
Like radio waves
They remain circling the heavens.

When days are desolate,
And my soul saddened by despair,
The prayers my loved ones voiced for me
Return
To wrap my heavy heart with warmth.
God hears again,
And He is there.

—*Mary Lou Spencer*

"Glitter Or Gold"

Is it glitter or is it gold
One is new, one is old.
Tell me what it is you see
The pretty on the Christmas Tree
Is it nonsense and far fetched
Or is it love forever etched.

Is it glitter or is it gold
One will hold, one will fold
Glitter is the dim remains
of lives sadly after pains.
Gold lives on forever true
Gold is always - I love you.

—*Patricia Matovich*

Be True

I started on a journey
One that took some time
I saw things come and go
With these eyes of mine.

I traveled familiar places
That I loved so very well
I traveled far away
And came back with stories to tell.

I saw my children grow
And become what they would be
My grandchildren, O Lord
What a sight for these eyes to see.

But now my walk is really slow
In reality it's almost thru
If I could leave my Golden Rule
It's that, I have been true.

—*Bonnie Corley*

Don't Go Without Me

When you walk in the yard,
Or ride in the car
Take me along —
Where ever you are.

When your heart's heavy,
With things hard to bare —
Remember I love you,
And let me be there.

So when you go someplace
Where ever it be —
Remember I need you,
Don't go without me.

And when you close your hands,
To pray every night —
Let your left hand be yours.
And let mine be the right.

—*Dorothy Schroeter*

Janet

Whether it was chance
or that thing called fate
that brought you to me
I really can't say
and I don't believe
it really matters

For I have been lucky enough
to have you here with me
not just in body
but deep within my soul

And should the winds of time
blow hard enough
to take you far away from me
you can rest assured
they will never
take you from my heart

—*Reginald R. Dela Rosa*

Untitled

You mean more to me than daylight,
or the moon that shines at night,
because without your smiling eyes,
I'd have no need for sight.

You mean more to me than time,
like an hour glass of sand,
for if I could never touch you again,
I'd have no need for hands.
You mean more to me than music,
those sweet sounds to my ear,
if it were not for your voice my dear,
I'd have no need to hear.
You mean more to me than roses,
all the romance that they tell,
if they did not come from your hand,
I'd needn't want to smell.
You mean more to me than laughter,
like the innocent children do,
For all these things would be nothing,
if I were ever to lose you.

—*Angela Southern*

Touch of Evil

What motive or force
or vicious whims
drives such monstrous mind
but a maniac with a mission
of destruction…

To make love a vulgarity.

Maim but not to kill
for death is without pain
and he thrives on the
pain of women…
laughing at my tears
puffed up with self-satisfaction
at the breaking of a mind

Murderer of women.

Clinging to me while
professing love…
your arms reaching to embrace and
plunge the knife simultaneously.

—*Charlotte Barthlow*

Teenage Understanding

I'm not sure yet of who I am
or what I want to be.

I'm not sure of my dreams yet,
or if they will reach me.

I'm not sure about love or what
it really means…
One minute it brings happiness
the next it brings pain.

As a teenager I may not understand
this confusing world I'm in,
so show me how and
love me all you can.

—*Dennisha Hart*

Friendship Stands Still

Time stops when I think of you
Other people do not matter
When I reminisce of a time
We laughed together and
Our friendship stands still.

Time is frozen when I talk of you
Other people do not exist
When I am reminded of a time
We cried together and
Our friendship stands still

Time lasts long when I yell at you
Other people do not care
When I am remembering a time
We fought together and
Our friendship stands still.

Time is running out when I ignore you
Other people are in the way
When I recall a time
We did not speak and
Our friendship stands still.

—*Tammy Johnson*

Love's Shores

We face each other
Our eyes speaking a language
more ancient than words.
Tonight there are no barriers.
Minds, spirits, bodies,
flow together endlessly
erasing time: past, future.
There is only this moment.
Only you and I,
soaring, dancing,
cresting in waves of pure poetry
that crash and roar about us;
surging, ebbing, surging again
in crescendos of feeling and motion
carrying us on joyful tides
to the sacred shores of our love.

—*Kyle Grubbs*

"My Dreams Of You"

I can't seem to get you out of my heart
Our hearts are embedded as one
From the very early morning
Until my day is done
My days are not fulfilled without you
They can never be the same
I know you had to leave me, my beloved,
And there is no one I can blame
Time has not made a difference, for me,
I miss you even more
At night I close my eyes and dream
That I hear your key in the door
As you come into my longing arms
Once again you hold me tight
And at days end we talk a little
And then kiss each other goodnight
My dreams of you are a great comfort
They help to see me through
Every day that passes
When I am left alone without you

—*Estelle Seltzer*

By The Fountain

Edgar and Ebenezer are
our two tame squirrels.
We feed them bits of bread
every night - by the fountain.
They make us laugh
with their timid, querulous
antics -
Sitting on their haunches
watching us -
daring closer and closer -
off in a second
at our slightest move.
We feed them bread -
They feed us delight!

—*Kaydi Dienna*

He Left Me

He left me
out in the cold, nowhere to go
I cried and cried
but it didn't help
I felt so betrayed
He left me.

He left me
with a broken heart
I still love him
but I hate him
when will these feelings stop
He left me.

He left me
oh so long ago
but it feels like yesterday
I have to go on
but I feel as if I can't
He left me.

—*Ann Marie Miani*

The Awakening

The sun has ascended
Over the distant rise.
Birds call across the fields
To 'waken sleepy eyes.

A new day has begun.
My yesterdays are past.
My life is new once more;
Free from sorrows at last.

The road of memories
Has dimmed, but taken toll.
Sadness lurks in my heart;
But peace has freed my soul.

I am given new hope
With the coming of day.
A whole new life is mine
To go my lonely way.

Whatever lies ahead,
I raise my eyes to greet.
Be it pain, joy or love,
My life will still be sweet.

—*H. Louise Frenz*

Life

Listening to the wind blow
past your eyes, feelings of
sadness makes you cry.

All alone in a world
of fear standing on the edge
of life and death;
one step, one breath

Dazed and confused, not
knowing where to go, we take
a chance.

Following the heart of love
and pain, we chose a path
for life, making our own world
and our own peace

For we all stand on the
edge of fear for life.

—*Tony DiCarlo*

A Father's Welcome

Welcome to the world, my son,
Place your hand in mine;
We'll walk, talk, plan and play
We will memorialize time.

I'll be your first teacher;
I'll be your first friend;
I'll teach you truth, forgiveness,
I'll love you to the end.

I want so much to be worthy of
The title of "Father," "Dad."
You'll take some getting used to;
You're something I never had.

Sometimes you'll try my patience
As you 'swim against the tide';
May I never strike you, son,
In violent rage or pride.

The future waits; but for today,
As I hold you close to my heart,
My only thought is, son o' mine,
That we never, never part.

—*Elizabeth M. Owers*

'True Greatness Lies In Humility'

Sometime in our life
pomposity leads us to believe
that someday we might become
a person of great renown,
but as we read God's word
of truth we find true greatness
lies in humility. The greatest
man that ever lived was the
humblest among men; the man
Christ Jesus: His thoughts
were not of Him self but for
others. Let us emulate His
ways that we too might find
true greatness.

—*Dolores Poland*

Life's Journey

Cradled in my mother's arms
protected by her love

Teen years pass
as I sowed my oats inside

I'm a young man in life
standing on my own

Now thought to be wise
because of years set aside

As I wait to be judged
to see if I live -
    or die.

—*Bruce A. Chada*

Element Too Proud

Burning calm, straight, and firm,
Proudly glowing candle flame.
Burning tall, slow, and long,
Ignoring me without a falter.
Burning calm, straight, and firm,
Proudly glowing candle flame.

Jerking back, flickering fast,
Laughing wildly candle flame.
Insulting me and sneering at me,
and insolently mocking me.
Jerking back, flickering fast,
laughing wildly candle flame.

"Stop!" I cried.
It only laughed.
I threatened, I warned it of disaster.
It only laughed the faster.
I took a deep breath and then exhaled,
and only black smoke trailed.

—*Thomas H. James*

Breathes Of White

I stand transcended on the
quiet extensions of early
morning sunrise

As vistas of stretching arms
hold tight to my senses

Glory rises from dominions
of jagged pinnacles majestically
and in pilgrimage

I am anointed with the
sacred breath of white

A magnificent cloak dresses
all nature in robes
of divine wrappings

Pristine white smooth

As the universal of all
eternal journeys
glide with the brisk of
the wind

What glorious flowing
out from the mouth of God

—*Marie J. Ross*

Elegy

The river flows
quietly;
but it knows
fish and water lilies,
and I walk across
the bridge
alone.

Flow for me,
river.
Think of me,
fish,
birds,
plants.

I am here
waiting.

I am calling
my name.
I have a name -
it has an eery
sound.

—*Ilse Juergensen*

A Promise

Raging hearts out of control,
Rampant, blinded, truths unfold.

Tampering with youthful drive,
Daring, harming, other's lives.

Selfish hands, careless eyes,
Hungry, lustful, life of lies.

Alteration, change of plans,
Friends, platonic, reaching hands.

Relationships, precious gems,
Trusting, fragile, nourish them.

The way we were yesterday,
Memories, dreams, will live and stay.

The way we choose to travel now,
A path abandoned, show me how?

—*Dargan Moore*

Hunger

Ribbons of fear
Reach out and surround us
Fragile borders our prison
For the dark hours

First light brings the hope of warmth
There is no other hope
We search for food
There is none
We spend our ebbing strength
Knowing there is no more
We walk to Nowhere
And never know when we arrive

A bundle of rags on the ground
Perhaps asleep
Perhaps not
The morning collection has begun
Soon we too will be counted

I am so thin
No one will know
That you are here inside me

—*Herbert Pinto*

You Have A Choice

We had a difference of opinion,
Remarks were passed that made it worse,
Until I suddenly remembered,
That I had a choice.

I could choose to get real angry,
I could choose to pass it by,
So I made my choice to shrug it off
And let the matter die.

It takes two to have a quarrel,
Some folks welcome little spats,
So if you refuse to argue
Heading off the "tits for tats."

You will have a lovely feeling,
Like the lifting of a curse,
You're in control, as I was
When I knew and made my choice.

—Selma Reyman Plotnick

Untitled

Bright
Respectful
Intelligent
Awesome
Not stupid

Responsible
Energetic
Sports
Kind
Ignores stupid comments

—Brian Reski

A Parents Wish

To our little one,
resting in your mothers' arms.
We will do what we can,
to keep you from harm.

Each day you will grow,
and learn many new things.
Once you become mobile,
it'll seem you have wings.

The time will just fly,
and soon you'll start school.
From this day forward,
I pray you use the Golden Rule.

As problems arise,
you'll work out what you can.
But you need only ask,
and we'll lend you a hand.

Before we all realize,
you'll start a life on your own.
But, please don't forget,
the path that leads home.

—Todd Hazel

The Artist

Words splatter across the paper
Like brush strokes on canvas
Abstract in form at first glance
Taking shape as the poet works
Molding and refining the lines

Finished: a work of art, never
To be hung in a gallery
Instead, to be savored like fine
Wine on the taste buds of the mind

—Patsy Ireland Blanco

The Time Summer Brought

I saw the summer pass
right before my eyes,
As it passed
my life without you passed so fast.

I remember the time
when we first met,
It was love at first sight for me
was it for you?

As you sat beside me
I got so tense,
The feelings in your eyes
was never so intense.

I forgot the precious time
we spent together,
But that one night
Seemed to last forever.

I wish I could make it right
like it was before
But all the time that's passed
I will never forget, but today's forever!

—Crystal Renee Parker

Nights Together

Rain soaked days
Romantic nights
Dream away the past
Mesmerized
By the candle flame
Glows soft
On your face
Flickers
From our breath
Fires burn
Inside
Sweat glitters
Strung across my forehead
Pull you in
Close
Be free

—Richard H. Tessitore

Untitled

Words like weapons
    Russian roulette
Thoughts in the mind
    A word in the chamber
She pulls on her hair
    The hammer falls down
The words enter my head
    I die from a broken heart

Words like weapons
    Russian roulette
Thoughts in the mind
    A word in the chamber
She pulls the trigger
    The hammer falls down
The words enter my head
    I die from a broken heart

—Michael Lyon

Winds of Time

Sad winds of time
sad lullabies
divine
magic
in crystal,
slow train
to the underworld,
flight
to death and tomorrow

The whirlwind
of blue death awakening

In bitter time
when love and luster
fade
the sad remains
of open cities
fade
— create the vision

—James Allison

Pain

Depressed and down
sad with a frown,
My feelings are gone
I feel like I'm drawn
to my last laugh,
that can never be saved
As my thoughts passed by
My tears fly
down my face
as I cry.
I think of all my savored memories
of my friends and family.
How my life has been
through the years.
How my friends and family
are sometimes there.
No one really knows my pain
of course I can't explain.
Only I can feel the dreadful pain.

—Vanny Doeurk

Lost

Wandering, roaming
Searching blindly
Through the darkness
Which surrounds me tonight...
The silence is broken
By the tears that I cry
From the pain
That grips my heart tight...

I attempt to escape
From the hurt —
From my fear —
From this emptiness
I'm left with
Inside...

Running scared
From the truth
It's so hard to accept
That the love you once
Had for me
Died...

—Terrie Devinney

"In Search"

Sitting here in wonder,
Searching every thought;
Carefully dissecting
All that I was taught.

Checking every answer,
Following my mind;
Too confused to focus
Am I really blind?

Making my decisions,
Moving without rhyme,
The best that I can do
Is take it one step at a time.

—*Sandra Zadeh*

Oriental Evening

Have you ever eaten sukiyaki
Seated on a large flat cushion
With your feet bare of all slippers
And your legs tucked neatly under?

Have you ever watched the way
The hostess cooks the foods so dainty
In a flat pan, o'er a hot flame
Sitting on a lacquered table?

Have you ever sipped the rice wine
Served so hot in cups so small?
They call it saki, and the stomach
Warms immensely at its taking.

Have you seen the geisha girls
With their fans and powdered faces
Dancing to the graceful rhythms,
Acting out their ancient stories?

Have you seen the simplicity
Of the rooms, and noticed how
This lack of myriad worldly things
Is restful to a weary heart?

—*Betty M. Neff*

Time

Time passes ever so slowly,
Seconds pass by like minutes,
Minutes like hours,
Until I see your face again.

The sun seems to laugh as she
follows her slow, sultry path,
Minutes pass by like hours,
Hours like days,
Until I see your face again.

Day after day, I miss you
more, the choking bond of time
strangles me: drains my
lifeblood.
Days seem like months,
Months like years,
Until I see your face again.

Two moon phases have passed
Since I have seen beauty.
Months seem like years,
Until I see your face again.

—*Renee J. Fredette*

Farewell to Summer

I hear the leaves now rustling down,
See mountains wear an earlier crown
Of shining gold caressed with dusk.
'Tis natures own vernacular clear,
Telling all to list' to hear
Summer times again be spent.

Now bid farewell to all her charms,
Her warmth, blossoms and in her arms
Birds she'll soon send gently southward.
Oh God, we stop and think on Thee
For thou hast made all this to be.
We marvel in meek humility.

—*Marilyn DeBlock*

Little Girl

Ribbons, satins, hair done up in braids,
  she can be a princess, an angel, or
  a mother as she rocks her babe.

  Baby dolls, Fairy Tales, and
  fleeting dreams of the night.

  Imagination so young and pure,
  "Oh little girl divine".

  Dream on, dream on, little girl,
  be happy at play.

  Because tomorrows will soon be past,
and you'll become a woman much to fast.

  Dream on, dream on little girl,
  I just hope you'll always be as happy,
  as your dreams are today.

—*Joyce L. Campbell*

From Love With Love

From love with love, a mother deer
She shows me something good for us.

One day, in the summer in the woods,
She run away, with her sweet baby.
They love each other very much,
And every time they run together.

But something happened, close to them,
One ugly wolf fun, very hungry.
He caught the little baby deer
Because, he was so hungry.

The little baby cry and scream
Oh mother, mother help me now
I want to live and not to die!

She jumped, and cover her sweet baby
To be herself, a meal for the wolf.
She cry in pain, and told her baby,
Run baby, run, run in the hills
I die, for you, because I love you.

Her baby ran, and he was safe.
But his mom died in lots of pain, because
she loved her baby.

—*Maggie Doroscan*

God's Little Angel

No one really knew her,
She thought no one really cared,
No one looked into her eyes
to see what was going on in there.

She put on a mask that she
was doing fine, only deep
inside she knew it was a lie.

God saw that she was in pain,
and gave everyone a try,
to help her and make her
realize she wasn't ready to die.

She thought about it so much,
God knew she never wanted
to live, it was just one big
struggle for her, it was to
much for her to give.

One night while she was sleeping
God took her away. She is now
God's littlest angel and we
know she is o.k.

—*Maggie Shutey*

The Greatest Fear

A child so weak and frail
Sickened by a disease so fatal
Just waiting and hoping some
Not knowing when the day will come

Taking the days with no fun
Wilting like butter in the sun
Too withdrawn to speak a word
Guess it's time to just move forward

The time is soon drawing near
Leaving the loved ones, should I fear
For a stream of bright light I see
I hope nobody is mad at me

Now it is time to get in gear
For me the end of time is here
This sickness has taken its toll
I want to be free from it all

Light from the corridor tells all
I hope they find a cure for all

—*Nancy Hermann*

Fire In Baltimore

Historic rows,
Side by side
Porches reflect their lives.

Acrid smell,
Burning hell,
Flames raging hot.

A young girl's scream,
Nightmarish dream,
Loud anguished cry.

Chocking breath,
Smothering death,
Three to die,
Their bodies lie...Ashen.

—*Deanne Brochu*

Getting On

I don't want to get rattled at the
  sight of a memory
Won't weigh myself down by getting
  saddled at the thought of what
  used to be
Remind myself to move on with life
Don't let situations start any strife
Relax - have fun - be myself
Keep those memories on a shelf
I know it's smarter looking forward
  than it is to look back
All that heavy luggage I carry -
  it's time to unpack
Close my eyes and picture myself
  going
And keep in mind that my new life
  has been growing.

—*Larry Medico*

God Looks Like Wind

God looks like wind,
Silent strength
Moving mountains.
God sounds like the stars,
Quietly
Always present.
God smells like a cloud,
Drifting
In the heavens.
God taste like joy,
Great sweetness
Bubbling over.
God feels like time,
Infinitely
Moving forward.
God is love,
Never failing
Those who trust.

—*Charles Engelhardt*

The Shepherd of Nite

Dusk, the shepherd of nite
  silently gathers birds of flight.
All day they played in meadows
  and fields of grain.
To sustain them in their foolish games.
Listened to their chit-chat
  before bed-time roost.
The very limbs would shake
  and leaves vibrate...
Until each one found its place.
The shepherd has done his job...
All birds are snuggled to sleep...
  and not even one has uttered a peep.
The tree stands transfixed...
  closely guarding her brood,
Under the first star...
The time between light and dark

—*Francis X. Finnegan*

From Inside Out

The old house may be a shack
Similar to the elements some might say
Tea kettle whistles from room in back
Sounds like wind sweeping through hay.

Portraits hang with faces of joy
Eyes gleaming, stars twinkling
Paint, like petals, fading by far
Peace inside - birds are singing.

Water cleanses things with need
Dust is vacuum like falling leaves
Table is spread for all to feed
God protects, why not believe?

Inward - outward a connection
Spiritual - physical co-ordination
Love and trust - true protection
Reward: "Choice of Destination".

—*Levater B. Stanley*

I Won't Hear...

Falling soft,
I lose the light.
Finding the cost,
I must pay the night.

Spill the rain from out the sky
As dark clouds are nowhere near by.
An inch of sun can't hold a dream
Yet on a windowpane can steal the scene.

Don't call for me,
I won't hear.
Don't long for me,
I won't appear.

A rose can't bleed away its red
For beauty can't ever be dead.
A soul can't shine on its own.
You can't see light that isn't shown.

Don't long for me,
I won't appear.
Don't call for me,
I will not hear.

—*Autumn J. Rumsey*

Streets Paved With Gold?

Streets are not..they cannot be
Simply paved with gold
If they were where would be
The incentive to unfold

Life it is no fairy tale
With castles in the air
Man must face the challenges
His troubles he must bear.

As in every challenge
Is a battle to be won
And life without challenge
Loses half the fun.

The fun of your achievements
As you win the victory
Such the fun of living
You have to fight to see

And if you have beside you
To help you strong and bold
A wife to halve the battle
You've got your share of gold.

—*Edwin P. Spivey*

Mary Ann in the Sand

Down by the riverside
Sits a little girl
Her name was Mary Ann
And she was playing in the sand.

Now looking on was her Mother
Waiting for her cry
Because the sand was blowing
Right in Mary Ann's eye.

Along came her Daddy
To help his little girl
Because Mary Ann was his pride
And he wanted to be by her side.

Now all together
Walking hand in hand
For the sand had stopped blowing
And we now could hear the band.

Oh Mary Ann in the sand
Your footprints will be
In the sand for us to see
Our little girl Mary Ann.

—*Mary Ann Quinter*

In Extremis Modern

Once fine young man just lying there
Skin and eyes deep yellow
Not so very long ago
you were a dandy fellow.
Women just mere things to you
Another man your lover
Now your gaze at me in trust
Plain woman that I am
You've mellowed some and see,
Your beautiful man has left you.
Gone to one with sun-like hair.
I watch you there so still
on sheets as white as you once were;
Changed now with sickness modern.
Peace, searched for finally found,
no more the stares of mortals.

Sleep my friend, the final sleep
'till wakened by Understanding.
You learned so late
Love Is.

—*Frances E. Meade*

Home

Down on the farm half past four
Slipped in my pants sneaked
Out the door, out in barn yard.
Ran like the dickens milk all cows.
Feed the chicken some folks say.
There ain't no hell
They never farmed.
They can't tell went out in field
To put up hay
The sun came out very nice day
Clouds rolled in began to rain
Wasted my time nothing to gain
All this farming just in vain

—*Vi Hope*

A Promise To Keep

Your mouth, that tongue, that
    smile, those cheeks,
Your hands, those fingers, those
    active feet.
A miracle of nature, a perfect
    form!

World!
I beg, I plead, stand firm
    with me!
As long as there is breath
    in thee!

Not one creature should
    you permit
To use a bomb that will
    destroy
The miracle that is my
    little boy!

—*May Stern Einhorn*

Sing

To walk with you friend and
smile with our eyes is

To float with the sounds of
strings of music upon the wind

To feel the warmth of the other
with our minds

To sing hearts melody
with our souls

Separate, but together as one
as we are one with all others

Beyond the limitations found now
do we truly live in the Now

Listen with ears of Love
and you hear the Universe sing

—*Aaron Hoffer*

Moods

Happy
Smiles
Cheerfulness
Laughing
Insult
Sneer
Hurt feelings
Losing confidence
Do they like me?
No they don't
No one likes me
Getting depressed
I'm worthless
Who needs friends?
I don't
No one likes me
Go away

—*Gwen Fischer*

Love and Strife

I lay on a bed of roses,
so beautiful and fragrant,
    yet very painful.
My man he waits,
    for what I don't know.
My patience is steady
    like that of falling snow.
His mind seems confused,
    very troubled and scorned.
I hope he knows I'll wait
    for the passing of this storm,
For my life is stuck in limbo.
    'till the time when he will know,
That our lives were meant to be
    together for all eternity,
'Till he returns to me.
    My love grows stronger every day,
In hopes that he will stay.

—*Catherine MacPherson*

Bastard

I am
so fuckin' mad
at you that
I pick my skin.

You'll
never reconcile.
Murderer. You

broke her bloody spine!
And you call me
on Step 9, although
you're just on four,
to make amends?

I don't think so,
Your drug
's wooly
comfort is not a goat.

She was my
best friend, my
child.
My guinea pig.

—*Rachel Spencer*

The Cat That's In My Dreams

I wish I had a cat,
    so nice and well behaved,
That everyday she dreamed and dreamed
    about a garden cave.
Oh she dreamed a dream about this cave,
    with walls shining deep inside.
It felt so good to feel this way she
    nearly, nearly cried.
Now the cat was very pretty,
    so beautiful and nice.
She sang just like a nightingale
    floating on the ice.
She loved to sing and sing all day;
    she nearly sang all night.
She loved the outdoors so so much,
    she only had one bad fright.

—*Charlotte Sellmyer*

MY Gifts

God gave to me some gifts
So precious and so rare,
Two lovely children
He put within my care.

One of them had dimples
Angels pressed into his checks.
The other one had hair of gold;
Their trust made me humble and meek.

I thanked God for these jewels rare
A son and daughter to love and to care;
Lives to shape, and living to share,
Make life sweeter and easier to bear.

A husband, too, He gave to me-
So kind, and loving and caring is he.
Protector, provider, and trusting is he-
I am a blest woman, with these gifts, three.

—*Miriam S. Sims*

Let the Earth Stand Still in Time

Let the eagle,
Soar so high.
Up in the glistening,
Bright blue sky.

Let the trees,
Stand tall below.
For the eagle,
A beautiful show.

Let the air,
Stay fresh and clean.
Let mother nature,
Be a beautiful scene.

Let the water,
Make a clear and sparkling maze.
In the midday's,
Bright sunny rays.

Let the bison,
Roam the land.
Don't shoot them dead,
Where they stand.

—*Tracy Greer*

Cycles

Into this world we came,
softly wrinkled as a glove;
needing nothing but food,
warm clothes, a little love.

Unable to dress ourselves,
faltering when we stood,
Our attention span was short,
our memory not too good.

The changes then proceed
from our first gasping breath,
We finally regress again
to infants before death.

My biological clock
I thought had surely sprang.
Grandmother came to live:
I am with child again.

A babe of ninety years —
dependent, trusting, sweet;
Life slowly turned the page,
the cycle is complete.

—*Nancy Williams*

Anything Is Possible

Love is out there some where some
some place
You just have to take
time to search
Don't give up even if you
must climb over mountains
through valleys even through
the seas
Love is still possible
go ahead be brave
and go ahead and search
Don't give up!

—*Irene Truesdell*

The Seniors

They call us the Seniors
some say we are outcast
Not knowing, that we are the present
the future, and the past

We don't have to sit around
to see what they will give
These are the best years, of our lives
and we've just begun to live

There are lots of jobs, that we can do
and experience we can share
Just look around and you will find
that we are needed everywhere

Now today you have your youth
and there are many things you can do
But remember if you live long enough
you will be a Senior too

So come on Seniors, hold your head high
For we are the Senior Generation
Don't sit and let time pass you by
We're the best in all creation

—*Lovelean Powell*

Vision of Reality

Is it real?
Something you can feel.
Believe in,
life.

A person.
With many feelings,
creation by
love.

Emotion.
From the inner heart
very strong,
strength.

Liberty.
A spirit within.
Having a
choice.

Capable
Having will power.
A definite response.
Or is it a dream?

—*Tamara M. Rousseau*

Divine Justice

Unfair injustices may
Sometimes disrupt
And bring about what
Might seem a bitter cup
Hold on to the knowledge
That God is at work
Correcting whatever
The quirk!

Do not struggle against
The apparent wrong
Trust in God
No matter how long
Relax in the flow
Instead of resisting
For God's Divine Justice
Will keep on existing...

—*Yvonne M. Jenkins*

Father Sun

Father sun, strong and bright
Spinning in your endless night
Shower rays of wisdom on me
My guide to all that I can be

Father sun, warm and caring
Firm but not overbearing
Help me through my troubled years
My shoulder on which flowed tears

Father sun, eternal and old
There forever, I'm never cold
Will you be here to show the way
Or will you slowly go away

Father sun, child earth
You brought me here with my birth
With gifts of nature like a dove
You showed me your endless love

Child earth, matured and grown
Now I sit upon your throne
With rays of wisdom upon my son
I thank you—I love you—father sun

—*Harold Dalious*

She

She is like a majestic tree.
Standing for grace and beauty,
She wished to grow free.
Sprouting to the limits of the sky,
no boundaries to suppress her,
except mankind who never asks why.
Man cuts and gnaws,
he tears at her forgiving soul.
Merciless destruction
with a heart so bitter cold.
I bow to her with infinite respect.
Treat her with incorruptible dignity.
She is a product of nature,
a work of art sculptured perfectly.
Closely listen, broaden your mind.
She is a human being.
She is compassionately kind.
A woman bears more in months of nine,
than man has endured in a single lifetime.

—*Kenneth Hedrick*

Poem for G. W.

Conceived in love
And raised with care,
You face adversity,
With courage and fortitude.

Born of strength
And allowed to grow,
You will leap from the precipice
And soar like an eagle.

Beset by fears
And entrapped by pain
I struggle to emerge
And attain my metamorphosis.

You see the woman,
I see the crippled child
Who clings to the ledge
Earthbound and paralyzed.

You hold out your hand
And exhort me to fly,
Beyond my mortal fears
Into a galaxy of light.

—*Sue Davis*

Lonely Truth

I remember trees
    Standing tall
    Straight and sound.
They only lean
    When winds
    Skirt
    Around.
I remember how
    They bent
    Almost to the seas.
It is all seasons
    That make
    Stark
    Bare trees.
I think of trees
    Living in raging
    Digress.
When their leaves
    Scatter in the wind
I think of loneliness.

—*Harold J. Rockliffe*

Summer Moonlight

Speak my name and speak it softly,
One more time before you go—
Leave me but a tender something
Something gentle so I'll know;
So, I'll know I've done something
You'll remember when I'm gone.
Walk me back through summer moonlight
Take me back beyond the dawn,
Look me over not too closely,
I've got flaws I dare not share
Still some things will go unnoticed
If you really come to care
If you care enough to tell me—
Tell me with your eyes and then;
Walk me back through summer moonlight—
Take me back through love again.

—*Christina Brown*

A Dish of Poverty

Just one little can
stands within an
empty cabinet.
"Green Beans" (No brand)
a label plainly said.
"Cook slow" it directed
hunger long delayed.
"Allow to simmer, then wait,"
forget the damn plate!
Now. Eat slow, so one
by one they'll last longer,
build you big and strong.

—*Steve Chase*

A Love Song

And her people say
Stay away from us
You are out of control
Out of the fold
Out from under
Here—we are safe.
But you are not.

We will not follow you.
We will not come.
We will not risk knowing you.
We are afraid.

And the others see the look in her eyes
And they know she will explode.
They wager how soon that will be.

Let us use her
Take what we may
We know she will give
She knows no other way.

Now that she is willing,
Needing love.

—*Teresa Jay*

Rock My Cradle, Mama

Rock my cradle, Mama
Stay nearby me through the years!

Rock my cradle, Mama
Be there to console and wipe my tears!

Rock my cradle, Mama
Give me family roots that go down deep!

Rock my cradle, Mama
Stay nearby me while I sleep!

Rock my cradle, Mama
Give me values strong and true!

Rock my cradle, Mama
And know I will always love you!

—*Linda Mayhue*

Untitled

Why did the river flow with
   such a fast moving pace,
When there wasn't anyone else
   to race?
It's bubbles occupied each space,
So no one else could squeeze in,
   not even a trace.
The river was displaying might,
   beauty and grace,
And awaited the expression on
   each person's face.

—*Bob Svoboda*

Shadow

Walking in your shadow
   staying out of sight,
Following your every move,
   growing closer at night.
Your thousand talents that you have,
   I want to be what you are,
But never being close enough to see,
   watching from a far.
A lot of people look up to you,
   more than you'll ever know.
But me, I try to hide it,
   and in your shadows, stay down low.
Hiding so you don't see me,
   behind a tree or anything I can find.
But then at home, it's all the same,
   to me you are so kind.
I love you from so deep within,
   it will always be locked in my heart.
Though I'm not what you are, my sister
   you are, and we'll never grow apart.

—*Laurie Cease*

Life's Stepping Stones

It's hard to find life's
Stepping stones—peer
Pressure every day,
Your way of life
Consumes the mind,
You know no other way.

You strive to hide your
Inner pain, but it's just an overlay.
You may find life more
Intense by light of day.

For strength you'll look to
Higher heights, and say a
Prayer or two.
A Supreme Power from
Above shall surely see
You through.

God shall be your confidante,
With loved ones there for you.
Elude the wounded inner child,
And start your life anew.

—*Emma Alice Kilby*

I Still Miss You

Long ago you left me,
   Still I sometimes feel you near.
When I need someone to talk to
   It is then I wish you were here.
   I still miss you.

You were always there to lean on,
   I guess I thought you'd always be,
But you had to move on to a better home,
   You could not stay with me.
   And I still miss you.

I know it is much better there,
   You suffered too much to stay here,
I know some day I will meet you there,
   Meanwhile it is lonely here,
   And I still miss you.
Today I am remembering
   The day we were wed long ago.
We did have a good life together,
   Why did you have to go?
   For I still miss you.

—*Elva Thomas*

The Ex-Best Friend

When I watch you
struggle to the top
trying to get with "them"
that certain group you adore
or
when I watch you
try to act like "them"
trying to be just like "them"
talking and laughing just like those
you adore
I say
while I watch you
you traitor of a friend
who used to be like me and my friends
you used to be my very best friend
I stand up
through your struggle
I stand up

—*Tara Wagner*

"Flames"

As the flames of my anger
swirl in my head I think of
all the people I have loved
and how most of them have fled.
Tears fall down my cheeks
as I recall none of them have
called or written in weeks.
I feel betrayed and cheated
because none of them where
there when they were most needed.
They all said that they
loved me and they always will
but now I wonder if what
they said was even for real.
So I will leave them alone
and set out on my own.
All I need to do is survive
and happy memories will
keep me alive.

—*Beth Loy*

Morning Marsh

Mist rises in shaggy wisps,
Swirls and twists with lazy ease
Revealing glimpses of marshland,
Ghostly in it's misty shroud.

A cool breeze stirs the mist,
Brushing reeds as it lifts and sways
To rise slowly above the water,
Leaving reluctantly this loveliness.

Suns rays shine through
Picking color from the marsh grass,
Bringing warmth and brightness,
Sparking across the water.

Birds awake, softly singing,
Rise to swoop and soar,
They dance across the marsh grasses,
Flitting from mist to brightness.

Mists that linger in hidden patches
Slowly give way to warmth and breeze.
As sunlight etches all with gold,
Another marshland day unfolds.

—*Beverly Henson*

Poetry"

on our words must swoon:
woon to a close, prose:
etry is a form, not words,
st as prose is to our nose
hat poetry itself is to prose:
close, prose, close.

Friedrich Nietzsche blew his fuses,
the ancient physicist also loses:
e trajectory of the polygyre
the twisting of the deadman's ire:
id so the swing of the swerve
in loop into someone else's nerve.

st as the turning of the gyre
in spin a vector as well as a tire,
it is language that we disdain:
e do not chose to leave it plain.

—*Daniel Bures*

ntitled

When your at a party
take a moment to think.
Of the many consequences
from any drink.
Your speech is slurred
and vision may double.
Alcohol is the name
and it means trouble.
Drinking and driving
They just don't mix.
So why is this the way
eenagers get their kicks.
Driving while drunk
It just isn't cool.
And when you get caught
You look like a fool.
And if a friend is drunk
ease don't let them drive.
my friends did that for me
might still be alive.

—*Kristene Remboski*

Magical Sight"

ystic grace of an eagle in flight
king your soul so high in the sky
astering each move
ithout a flaw in sight
th her emerald eyes
it see right through you
e's a heavenly vision so
re in blue
ek and tender is her heart
gold
awing the strength
m a natural source
hting for her life
a world built on anguish and fear,
s what keeps her going
en' though you'll never see her shed- a tear

—*Christy Cook*

Lancelot

Lancelot
Tall and handsome
Love me tight
Love me right
Love me long
Love me till the
Night is gone
Love me!!!

Lancelot
Elegant and debonair
Take your time to unwind
Cause only you can
Feel my desire
When the warmth you
Give takes me higher
Love me!!!

Lancelot
Liberal and personable
Feel my desire, take me higher
Love me!!!

—*Ylonda K. Clowney*

"Spit 'N Whittle"

Listen much and whimper little.
Teach a boy to spit 'n whittle.
Give someone a sincere smile.
Walk with them the second mile.

Offer to provide a meal.
Bow your head, and sometimes kneel.
Stop, admire and smell a flower.
Take a cat-nap for an hour.

Visit with a lonely soul;
Take a long, relaxing stroll.
Share the love you have of art.
Gently mend a broken heart.

Endure trials without complaint.
Laugh real hard without restraint.
Take your neighbor homemade pie.
Wave "Old Glory" proud and high.

—*Larry Paul Owen*

The Other R's

Angelic angels in my retina
Ten miles south of this point north
Reflecting her pure perversion
Cute cuddling her
Response
Condescending straight lines
Paved with pink velour
Rolling out her invitation
Cracked C.D. Case
Regret
Ninety-one degrees in my vision
Thirty knots blind beyond all
Golden fields at five o'clock
Trash me but please stay
released.

—*A. Mahlon Edwards*

Mother

There's nothing better on this earth
Than a loving Mother's care
One who's borne and given life to you
In her body growing there

If you only knew a Mother's love
Endless tasks day by day
Bottles, diapers, sleepless nights
Though so tired on her way

Even when you were so thankless
So selfish to the core
She never gave up on you
But kept loving you the more

Show your Mother while she's living
How much you really care
Don't forget her or ignore her
For this she cannot bear

Give some time and thought to Mother
While she is still here on this earth
Thank her, love her, care for her
Then her love will know its worth.

—*Betty J. Paul*

Reflections at the Ocean Side

There's a solemnity about the sea
That brings tranquility to you and me;
For it reflects a picture of life,
In all its calm and storm and strife.

For as you sit by the ocean side
And watch its ever changing tide;
You know the creator is in command,
Yes, even our life is in his hand.

So take time out to sit at a beach
And let your eyes the horizon reach;
For what's beyond we do not know,
But our creator will surely show.

Then just relax with peace of mind,
Forgetting the things that are behind.
With childlike faith life's sea to sail;
Knowing God's promises cannot fail.

Today, whatever your lot may be,
On a calm or stormy sea;
Just set your compass for heaven's realm,
With Christ your pilot at the helm.

—*George Vander Woude*

Forever

Forever is a word
That comes to mind as
I think about how I
Spend my time.

Visualizing you and
Dreaming all day is
what makes
me happy in every
sense of the way.

Always is a word
That brings you to
My heart and makes
me remember it
was love from
the start.

—*Cheryl Melton*

Mom

I'm deeply sorry for the things
I said when I was young
I wish that I could take them back
And mend the heart I stung.

You've always been so kind and good
You never seemed to doubt
That some day I would 'turn around'
And straighten myself out.

Thank you for your trust in me
For showing me the way
To give to others, sharing love
I'm growing more each day.

I love you Mom with all my heart
And want to let you know
You're everything I want to be
Your likeness is my goal.

To think of ever losing you
Now fills me with distress
My life would surely crumble
If I were motherless.

—*Betty Windell*

Troubled Emotions

Troubled emotions
that I cannot abide,
lay trapped,
like lost children
deep down inside.

They long for
someone to finally see,
the anguish
and the heartache,
yearning to be free.

They seek someone
in whom, they can confide;
yet I deal
with these memories,
by pushing them aside.

Oh, how much
happier I would be,
if I could
learn to embrace,
the child inside me.

—*Karee Lansbery*

"Your Love"

Your love is my sunshine
on a rainy, gloomy day.
Your love is my cozy warmth,
when snowflakes dance and play.
Your love is a cooling breeze,
when days are hot and still.
Your love is a song bird,
that always makes me thrill.
When my smile is fading
and turning to a frown,
you change me with a simple word
into a circus clown.
When I lose touch with reality,
and firm ground turns to sand,
without hesitation,
you reach out for my hand.
And when I can no longer hold you in my arms,
and drink up all your tenderness and many, many, charms
I'll savor every moment and memory we've shared
and know that I am "special" simply 'cause you cared.

—*Esther J. King*

"Little Things"

It's the little things in life we do,
That really mean the most;
It's not how much we do that counts,
Nor how big we can boast.

Just a kind word spoken
Will brighten someone's day,
Just a little helping hand
To someone along the way.

Just a little friendly smile,
A word of cheer and such,
Will brighten someone's heavy heart,
And Oh, can mean so much!

Bits of kindness sown here and there,
Reaps blessings by the score,
It makes life here more pleasant,
And makes us love each other more.

It's the little things we fail to do
When all is said and done,
The things that would enrich our lives,
We often leave undone.

—*Vera K. Jordan*

Silhouette of Love

Love is a reflection,
That shines on everything.
Nothing can be compared,
To the wonderful feeling it brings.

It's very easy to see,
The beauty of a diamond ring.
But love can make you see,
The beauty of simple things.

Speaking to a stranger,
By simply saying hello.
Would warm you both inside,
No doubt from head to toe.

Love can turn an enemy,
Into a faithful friend.
Whenever there's a dispute,
Love always win.

It's what you think and do,
That makes you who you are.
Concentrate on love,
And shine like a star.

—*Willie Williams*

A Holy Wish

Let me follow that star
That the Magi had seen,
To the place that is so far.
I want to be at the scene
Where the Child had been born.

Oh, let me be at the place
Where Mary and Joseph stayed,
The night the Star met space.
Where everything had been made
Ready for the Child to be born.

—*Lynn E. Henk*

Maybe Someday

There was a man
that was famous to say,
"I have a dream
that maybe someday…"
He spoke of love,
truth and respect,
and a world united
we would come to expect.
Our children would grow
with love in their hearts
and our world would return
the love they had sparked.
Some day is not here
and still only a dream;
For love, respect and honor
are divided it seems.

—*Terrie Lynn Altman*

The Prayer

Dust swirled around the sandals,
That were fastened to his feet.
And tears, glistened in his eyes
As He raised his face to speak.
Father, oh father, please hear me
Hear me as I pray,
Father, oh father, please here me
And take this bitter cup away.
Now the whole world was silent,
Not even the birds would sing,
And out of the stillness
A golden voice did ring.
Jesus, oh Jesus, my son
You above all that I hold dear
Only you can break the promise,
The one that brought you here.
Now we all know the story
As so often, it's been told
How Jesus, died upon the cross,
To save all sinners souls.

—*Charles De Witt Riggin*

Is Twenty Enough?

Twenty lines or less.
That's what the paper read.
Now how can a cowboy with imagination
Get it all out of his head?

In just twenty lines,
That's only five verses
To talk about those cowboy things
Like boots and chaps and wild horses.

Well, it's just darn near impossible
For a fellar to sit down and say
In twenty lines or less
All the things he's done today.

Heck, I could write twenty lines
Just about eatin' breakfast.
Or another twenty about saddlin' Joe
And how many times he's kicked us.

So I guess I'll just have to pass,
Maybe another time.
Cause I know I'd just get started
And I'd run out of lines.

—*Royce W. Hodge*

Philosophy

When we are born it is our aim
The best we can to play the game.

We are faced with many choices
Receive advice from many voices.

Throughout life it is the goal
To perfect our living soul.

When we have strived to do our best
We are entitled to a rest.

But to add to the confusion
Death is only an illusion.

We will return again one day
Another act, a different play.
—*Meredith Neill*

My Friend

My friend is like
The blue ocean
Down under

My friend is like
The fur of an animal
That roars like a tiger

My friend is like
The wind that we
Can hear

He is like
An eagle that
Soars through
The sky

My friend is like
The sky that pours
Down rain

He doesn't rest until I do.
—*Jeremy Czarnecki*

The Luck of the Draw

It's funny I guess
The cards we are dealt
We have no control
It's fate that was dealt
We play our hands
The best we know how
We mess things up
But always somehow
We wait for a hit
We do what we feel
And hopefully in the long run
We go with the deal
—*Paula Gaio*

The Hunting Heron

Quick lightning death,
On stilts of patience,
Stealthing through the shadows,
Like a phantom on the wing...

Fingerlings in the shallows,
Unaware that the shadow they bask in,
Is an envelope of predation,
Towering eyes that burn,
With hunger patiently await,
A quicksilver flash,
A scimitar pierces the surface,
The great blue heron has found its mark.
—*S. Kelly Rammell*

Old Age and Window Shades

Apothecary precision cannot measure
the circumference of your stems
the width of your leaves
or the depth of your roots.

From your prone position
words ooze
that no one dares to listen to
because you are old and dying.

Worn out
is the chair that I sit on
as I tug and then let go
of the shade on the window
overlooking your fields.
The shade snaps
and whirls around and around
Clarence smirks as he looks at me,
the innocent seed of continuity.

Your time-tempered body cannot for much
longer
foster a family of fields.
Clarence once said to me: "When I die,
bury me out in my fields."
—*Thomas Filiak*

Untitled

The days of the week are long
The courage of a lion is strong
The night belongs to the moon
Yet the day will be coming soon
A woman stares at the sea
Just wondering what might be
The wind blows through her hair
As she looks within despair
Yet little does she see
Her beauty reflects in me!

(A Poetic Thought)
—*Johnnie B. Jordan, Jr.*

Just A Mystery

Often a mystery, never open,
The door just ajar.
You ask how can this be,
Look at me.
Once used and discarded,
Abused by the mental side of love...
It's just a mystery.
The needs we have are much the same,
So my dear is the pain,
You're not unique, it's
felt by all,
So go ahead if you wish...
Run away...
It's still a mystery.
—*Marye Culp-Martinoes*

Wishes

The wetness of a tear,
The emptiness of a heart
The feeling of fear
The loneliness of being apart

She wishes he would call
She thought their love was true
is he thinking of her at all?
The phone rings and his voice says
 "I love you"
—*Tammi Ross*

Love Is The Dove

Without love
The dove cannot soar up above
Without the dove
There would be no freedom
Without freedom
There is no love

Sometimes
Without freedom
It is hard to remain
But you remain
Because of the love

I remain
Because of the love I found in only you
You are my dove
That soars up above me
To protect me
Love me
And watch over me
Only you
—*Kimberly Cates*

New Year's Eve

Outside a pale moon gleams,
The earth is covered with snow.
I shiver as I listen
To the chill winds blow.

But within it is warm and gay
And I'll have one last fling,
I'll forget all sadness and care,
For a new year will soon begin.

Music that thrills the soul,
Rum that quickens the heart,
A warm, lingering kiss
Stolen in the dark.

All too soon 'tis over,
I see the break of day.
Now it is but a memory -
The night that was so gay.
—*Sally Prinsen*

Psychedelic Dream

As we walked and were dark
 the faceless sun rose
 slowly over the stars.
Walking into the dream, moving
 in the color and the sea
 of sand, is like flying in
 the darkness of the sky.
As the killer waves crashed on
 our running minds we
 wandered through the moon
 into the intense light that soon
 surrounded us.
The abnormal bodies lived in
 silence while the twisted
 minds raced with time.
Time seems slow yet the
 motion of the clouds make
 it impossible to perceive
 the strange power of the
 psychedelic dream.
—*Ryan James Flynn*

White Room, Dark Room

In the white room
The flowers bloom,
And the sun shines in the sky.
In the white room
The flowers bloom,
And no one stops to wonder why.
In the dark room
The air is doom,
And the clouds block the light.
In the dark room
The air is doom,
And they ask why nothing's right.

—Heather Karnes

Christmas

The sun goes down,
the flowers go away,
The birds go in the trees,
The worms go down
in there little home covered
under there little trees,
Now Christmas is here,
Now Christmas is here,
a time for joy and gifts,
sharing bits by bits the
family cheer, and for
everyone we care. . .

—Christine Napier

The Mountains

The mountains cool breezes flow over me.
The hard rocks jutting out from it
The clean air I breathe in,
as I climb higher
My air becomes thinner
I look down at the forest below me
I try not to worry about falling
When I climb down the other side,
I feel the soft dirt below my feet
I see bare trees around me
I slip and slide down the mountain
I look up at the beautiful mountain
I just climbed
With my family right behind me

—Eve Taylor

Fairyland

The eye cannot see,
The joy and magic,
Which is plain to the heart,
In simple things from fairyland.

The clouds are not clouds,
As the sun is not the sun,
Instead a fairy's lamp
Shines through a bit of lace.

A weeping willow is a kingdom
Of dancing diamond lights,
And a flower is a bed,
Where a little winged maid alights.

—Lisa Govorko

"Bonfires"

Down the street
The leaves burn
In smoldering heaps.
Gray veils of smoke arise
In the cool still evening air
And circle and cling
Amidst the barren branches
Of the Birch trees.

The sky darkens
And the smoldering heaps
Gleam like glowing coals
Out of the night.
Above all hovers
A pale gray ghost
Of smoke and stands
Over the bonfires
Like a veiled guard - motionless.

—Mary C. Miller

Sadness

The feeling of emptiness
The look of pain
The kind that everyone seems to
contain
They keep it down deep
Buried in their soul
The grinding of what feels like
a deep, dark hole
The feeling lives
Never to die
The question one asks is simply
why
It goes on and on
While you try to cope
When you suddenly remember
There could be hope

—Casey Jan Novy

Of Stars and Rock

"Of solid rock the stars are made"
The masses once were told
"These stars of rock which never fade
Will shine as solid gold"

But wise men now have come to know
And find this truth, alas
The stars are merely nothing more
Than glowing spheres of gas

And piercing thru a night of dark
The light we here behold
May have issued from a star
Which vanished long ago

Winds of time can change the face
Of rock, this now is sure
And other stars will have their place
But not one shall endure

The brightest star that ever shone
Above a manger stayed
The greatest rock the world has known
A stone that rolled away

—Samuel A. Norling

"Girasko"

Grains of sand squeeze through
The narrow hourglass neck;
They merge in single file
To fall, each one its turn,
For every pulse, another,
And then—look! Another;
I count them all with care
Like the Cyclops' searching hands
On sheep that pass beneath.

I mark each beat and breath
And monitor their passing;
And seasons come for me
So slow, so leisurely
Until the sirens' song:
A call to draw me away,
Away to pursuits and dreams—
And on my return I find
A heaping pyramid's grown!

—Steven P. Stamatis

Redeem Us!

The one who lays so still
The one whose somewhere else
Did not know what his death brought
When he left this earth, our hell.

A healing of each one of us
We did not understand
Why our grief continued
How much could we all stand.

Each day grew so much worse
Each day was hard to bear
He showed us the way to heal ourselves
The path outside our door.

To heal from inside out
The redemption much to high
Our anger in each one of us
Began to multiply.

It's time for that redemption!
The one worth fighting for
For he didn't die for nothing
He died for a great, great cause.

—AG Thacker

Cove's Tide

Under the eminent balcony,
The receding waves,
I know
This scene is my fave.

Like the incoming tide
Love takes me by surprise,
From now on, like always,
There will be no lies.

I feel love
All over again
My heart,
I do lend.

Like love,
I just want to come inside.
Like the receding waves
Of Cove's Tide

—Tracy Nason

"I"

Vastness - - - immensity
The Sand, the sea, the sky
Cosmic - - - glorious
The sand, the sea, the sky
What then am I?

A grain of the sand
A droplet of the sea
A speck from the sky
No no
I am more

I am of the greatness
as the waves beat the shore
I am of the warmth
of the sun upon the sand
I am of the light and
brilliance of the sky
Yes yes
I am I!

—*Iris G. Howe*

Unknown Soldier

Here lies the peace,
  The shadow of might;
Countrymen! The sword is here,
  For freedom we fight.

Armageddon's drums adieu,
  Satan's fate be nigh?
Upon the wound of truce,
  Their casualties are high.

Big Bertha has ceased,
  The torch of joy ignite,
I salute the unknown soldier:
  Long live the knight!

—*Jam H. Lee*

When You Were Gone

  When you were gone
the sky lost its color,
  its beauty to me.
And love had no meaning,
  no meaning to me.

  The sea its grace,
  the wind its shape,
  the clouds their goals,
    and I my jest.

So don't you believe me naive
  so young, not as strong.
    for I have learned,
    Many, Many things.
  When you were gone.

—*Kiu Ung*

Laughter

It is the laughter, I believe that
That wraps the gifts that we receive
Our hearts are open to retrieve
The everlasting smile.

The laughter carried on the wind
Has beckoned me; this humble friend
And brings me joy until the end
Where I will meet my God.

I wonder where the lonely go
Where broken dreams and heartaches flow
I think I lived there years ago
No memory remains.

—*Christopher Gunn*

Untitled

Waterdeep
  the soul of fate
Sand … I'm lost
  underground
Your month was true
  truth was wrong
    always wrong
    always chance
  stairs leading nowhere
Nowhere is a place
  where life is good
  and truth is known
the sunken stone sits in the middle
of the road
  Have you ever noticed it?
    it's where the truth is buried
    and no one ever notices.

—*Dave Felter*

The Quiet of the Night

Take a moment to listen to
the sounds that come in
the quietness of the night.
The gentle breeze that
whistles through the trees.
The ticking of a lonely clock,
or the opening of a lock.
The sound that falls upon
a mother's ears, when the
cries of her child, she
does hear.
The howling of a dog
as a stranger wanders by.
The creaking of a floor,
or the loneliness of a sigh.

—*Vicki McGee*

The Daybreak

Awaken O morning —
the stars are forever gone
evening passes and
the bright shining sun is awakened

In the earliest hour
the dawn is awakened
bright colors — blue christened sky
greatest of them all

How the morning reveals all —
no shadows, no threats
all the beauty morning shone
forever, forever

At last glance —
the dawn awakens
O'er the horizon
Never to be seen again
the nightfall

—*Jennifer Caporaletti*

Saying Goodbye

The sun has gone,
The stars have dimmed,
Tears have filled my eyes.
No more "hi's", and
No more "bye's"
to casually speak and say.
The time has come,
The moments here,
farewells must be said.
Goodbye, my friend
I love you dear,
and in our hearts remain,
The thought and hope
that one day soon,
I'll see your face again.

—*Michele Eschbach*

A House Blessing

We celebrate this day!
The steadfast love and nurture
Abiding in this place
Our prayers lift up a hearty thanks
Our lives a consecrated fullness
Memories of those who taught us
Love and self-worth.
A richly woven tapestry
Of moments shared in joy and sorrow
Colorfully washed in time and memory
Brilliant, lustrous tones.
Friends and inspiration are
Precious inlaid gems.
Our sense of wholeness heightened,
And, enveloped in this fabric,
We know serenity and love.

—*Samuel Leftwich*

"Story Man"

(For Harry Chapin)
The story man is no more,
he lives in the radio,
Talking about love,
banana's waitresses,
and taxis.

Spinning tales of children,
warm-breathed women,
and boys growing up
just like their fathers.

The story man is no more,
gone,
but for us,
he lives in the radio.

—*Richard Jensen*

Newborn

Baby sweet, my precious,
Tell me of your dreams!
Where does tiny fancy lead you?
What a great big world this seems!

Slumber on, my darling baby,
Mid birds and flowers and honey bees,
Downy clouds and shimmering moonbeams,
Dainty visions, baby sees!

Slumber sweetly, baby sweetheart,
Sweet your dreams, and after while,
You'll awaken little Darling,
To greet me with your baby smile!

—*Rose M. Tschantz*

Alone, Without You

The sun has gone up.
The sun has gone down.
The night has come,
And I'm still down.

I look around,
But you're not there.
Where are you?
Do you still care?

It has been long
Since the day you left.
Yet I love you now
Like I loved you then.

The night is gone.
The sun arose.
It's another day,
Yet I'm still alone.

—*Antonia Toledo-Rosales*

The Old Oak

It stood there on the hillside,
The tall and stately tree;
It was young when I was young,
It aged along with me.

For many long years it beckoned
Travelers to its cooling shade,
Beneath the spreading branches,
Many a life's plan was made.

The limbs grew old and gnarled,
Time had made its mark,
Upon the many names, once carved,
By lovers on its bark.

When a mighty storm one day
Crashed it to the ground,
It lay crushed and broken
Like a mighty king dethroned.

The old and weary branches
In stillness, now did lie,
Its leaves greatly trembling,
A whispered last goodbye.

—*Helen Johnson*

Where's My Father?

My father layeth in what
is like a mail box in the wall.
He has no one to talk to,
no one even sees him at all.
He cryeth every night,
for his family filled with fright.
But there is no one around,
they cannot hear his pitiful sound.
His mind is filled with confusion
like his daughter Kaye.
They both lay awake at night,
filled with sadness and fright.
no one ever understood them,
and no one ever will!
My father wasn't the kind of person
to think so highly of death.
His wish was not to die,
but to be thought of as high.
But, alas the one that took my father's life,
was my wonderful father himself.

—*Kaye Gibson*

Hurt

Alone again
The thought of not being with you
Eating me alive, killing me inside
I hate the days which lie ahead
For I know you won't be there
To comfort me, to love me
Not by touching me
Only by thinking of me
And I the same
A barrier of hate separates us
I crave for the sound of your voice
In my ear
The touch of your hand
Gently on my body
The tenderness of your kiss
Rested upon my lips
I love you, I want you, I need you
I need you to chase the sadness away
To be with you would be my only salvation
you see
I know you want to be with me and I the
same

—*Andrea Picarello*

Although You've Seen Me

Although you've seen me grow,
  the time is going fast,
 I soon will be a grown up,
  and on and on after that.
Although you've seen me now,
  I'm not the same as then,
 I soon will be in college,
  and then, a job I'll get.
Although you've seen my future,
  it may not be that way,
it could be slightly different,
  or the same in many ways.
Although you've seen my life
I'm different through and through
  I've changed in many ways
  and maybe so have you.

—*Kristen Engstrom*

Now We Are Strangers

Do you remember
The times we shared,
The laughs that we had
The secret jokes
Only we knew.
We would cry
Together,
Help each other through sad times,
Now I watch as you
Laugh with others,
Tie other knots of friendship
As ours unravels.
Our years of closeness have ended,
But the pain will never stop.

—*Monica Schurr*

Replenishment

Grey veil and wind soon sweep away
the torrid vestige of the sun;
displaying strength as treetops sway,
the tension of the storm begun.
To their havens birds depart.

The land obscured by sheeting rain,
strong gusts contort its steady flow;
bright flashes of a lightning chain
produce great sounds that overflow.
Rebirth the rains impart.

—*Scott Brandt*

Who Am I

I am like the mysteries of the seas,
The wonders of the land, the unknown
  of the past.
I am like the smoke from forest fires,
The breeze that sways the trees,
The clouds that bring the rain.
Listen to the whispering breeze,
search the seas.
Gather the snow from sparkling trees,
When the sun shines - I am happy.
When it rains, I am sad.
I know I was made by God like this,
so, who am I?

—*Samuel Ravenel Gaillard*

How I Love You

I don't know how to begin to say
The words I know are far too few
Try as I may you'll never know
Just how much I love you

You make my life feel complete
With you I am whole
Your love has captured all of me
And I give you my heart and soul

I'll always be in love with you
My heart keeps telling me so
This feeling deep within
Lets me know

When we're together
My spirit takes wings
The touch of your hand
And my very being sings

I don't know how to begin to say
The words I know are far too few
Try as I may you'll never know
Just how much I truly love you

—*Jean Isham*

Just Something To Think About

Before any wonderful joy,
  there is great pain...
To relish each success,
  we must endure defeat...
Before reaching our next destination,
  a long road will be traveled...
To feel any love,
  love must first be given...

Live for the moment,
  so that life is lived...

—*Jason Clark*

September Signs

I walked in the park this morning,
There was stillness in the air.
Two retired men were fishing,
But the swings were hanging bare.

The swinging bridge responded
To my steps only.
The tennis courts were empty,
The slides looked very lonely.

No line-up waiting for a drink,
The baseball diamond clear.
I didn't need a calendar
To know September's here
—*Agnes K. Bogardus*

A Chance

If I take a chance,
there's a warning I should heed.
Cause, if I take a chance,
there's a chance I won't succeed.
If I take a chance,
there's a chance that I'll get burned.
But, with every chance that's taken,
there's a lesson learned.
If I take a chance,
I can see myself with pride.
Cause, even if I don't succeed,
at least I know I tried.
Taking a chance is scary.
It's part of life's taking and giving.
And when I've run out of chances,
there'll be no point in living.
So, I'll keep on taking chances,
and be all that I can be.
Cause, there's a life time of chances,
waiting just for me.
—*M. J. Lord*

A Boastful Mind Does Not Belong

Of all the things I've ever heard
there's nothing new
It is just a rearranged word
from someone who
Thought that he was somehow unique
from all the rest
And he sought to convince and think
his words were best
The "special" so called "learned" man
has taught so long
That in the culminating plan
A boastful mind does not belong
A boastful mind does not belong
of this convince
Yourself that these words are not wrong
then it makes sense.
—*Casey Evans*

Pathways

We live
We laugh
We cry
We die
And the good or evil
Path we lead
Will be written
For future generations
To read
—*Dennis Leetham*

The One and Only Love

Did you know?
There's only one Love!
Yes, the Perfect Love.
The only unselfish Love.
Do you understand?
Not many do!
You don't have to love me,
if I love you.
Just the way you are.
I'm secure, are you?
No one seems to be. . .
or why would they ask. . .
Do you love me?
The answer is very simple.
But, you still don't know.
Alpha and Omega are his theme.
The Perfect Love is his dream.
Through this love. . .
You've got it ALL!
—*Pamela Schirripa*

Baby Shoes

(To Henry III)
These little shoes that once were white
I cradle in my hands tonight.
The tiny feet that they enclose
Are soft and pink, just like the rose
Your father brought the night you came
And we were searching for a name.

"A father's name", I said to him,
"Means so much more than Tom or Jim."
It was your father's father's, too,
And so we passed it on to you.

Wear it with pride, my lovely son,
And in this life that's just begun
I pray that you may never lose
The innocence of baby shoes.
—*Margaret S. Vaughan*

It Isn't Fair

It isn't fair, these wars,
They break up homes.
It isn't fair, to fight
And kill, for what,
Nobody seems to know.

It isn't fair, to murder,
Or to burn the homes.
It isn't fair, that we
Nations so great, should hate,
And want supremacy.

When God is so good,
So honest, so sincere.
But still we will hate,
And fight and kill,
Yet God forgives and forgets.

Nations call on us for help,
So eagerly we try to assist.
Sending our troops to give them aid,
To help the hungry and the weak.
It' isn't fair, that our troops find death
instead.
—*Catherine M. Karpiak*

Sick and Lonesome For You

One Sunday morning at dawn
They came and took you away
For you had fallen sick
And I knew you could not stay

They took you to this place
They say you worked real hard
While I just set here praying
You would live with all my heart

They brought you back to me
Still frail an' oh so week
And darling I'm still praying
Some day you'll walk to me

When that day comes
Here hoping, one Sunday
In early fall you came to me
And didn't fall, you thru your arms
Around me hard, never under estimate the
Lord.
—*Velma Amburgy*

The Holidays

Holidays can be nice, but
they can be sad lonely times;
As the mind slows down
from the race of life
to reflect on other
times, other places!
"Sadly" one cannot go back
in time to change
things: Each of
us can only
change things
"Today," and
"Hopefully" they will be
better; with less
regrets, and more joys!!
"Holidays" can be happy, joyous,
times if only: we try to reason
that "God," himself, has a
reason for all seasons
As we travel towards time infinity for "all
eternity."
—*Ed Lee Collins*

Love Came Down At Christmas

If I were in Bethlehem
this Christmas,
I would kneel in prayer as
shepherds did that night.
So many caves claim to be the
one where Jesus was born.
Which cave would I choose to
be the one?
Bethlehem is so far away.
Must I travel the distance
as Kings did in His day?
No! There is no need at all
for Christ was born in my
heart today.
—*Sarah Loor*

Children's Voices!

I can hear children's voices here on
This Earth.
They cry out for help but no one
hears.
Don't you hear them from a
long time ago?
Can you feel their spirits?
That,
Once dwelt here on this Earth.
Soon,
If we don't help the children,
They,
Will be gone once more.

I can hear children's voices here,
On,
This earth. But no one hears, their,
Pain, or crying.
Or their laughter. I did hear children's
Voices once on this earth.

—*Sunnie Coles*

Ride the Moon South

Ride the moon south
this summer morn
catch the soft sunlight
of an early dawn...

See the faint light
color the skies
streaking a rainbow
in golden guise...

Find first a delicate
blush of pale rose
brightening in seconds
as sunshine grows...

Pale fades the moon
to a white haze
surrendering to sun
with elegance and grace...

—*Lydia Castilho*

In The Poet's War Zone

Baying and yowling,
thoughts are as muzzled
hounds of the mind
straining at the yoke of
careful self-censorship

malignant and endemic,
thoughts are germ warfare
an internal mutating of
logic and imagination
to embryonic echoes

shackled and cynical,
thoughts are as captives
in repressive custody
taunting stalag guards
at intellect's perimeters

desolate and decaying,
thoughts are cranial
rubble and debris
quashed in combat and
levelled with suppression

—*Kate Stewart*

Silence

Silence, THUD.
silence, THUD.
quiet, THUD.
Noise, heard, not heard.
Did you hear it? Don't know,
maybe it's in my head,
maybe it's in my dream.
Is this a dream?
not a dream,
a nightmare, THUD.
What is reality?
My reality,
reality hurts,
life hurts, THUD.
What is real?
Fiction, non-fiction,
words used to convey feeling,
meaning something,
meaning nothing,
silence.

—*Billy Thompson Jr.*

The Frustration of Ineffectiveness

The mind retreats
thoughts replete

the separation of mind and body like
the separation of church and state

function without instruction

a house,
but not
a home

to dream yet not wake
to cry yet not cleanse
to live
but yet exist

the soul
suffers
surrenders
stills.

—*Stephanie J. Parker*

Untitled

Recovering my sight,
through eyes once thought dim.
I discover new heights,
a spring leaf upon the limb.

Soft thoughts I often muse,
Sweet dreams that I can feel.
Your touch I seek that soothes,
That sets my mind to reel.

For mountains I have pondered,
to limits there's no end.
Vast lands that I have wandered,
For moments we could spend.

My heart can take delight,
in that it can't avoid.
A beacon to the light,
safe harbor to sweet joy.

—*Ryan Witt*

The Sunshine Trees

Brief autumn's show
through one small window hosts
No verdant pines to boast
No claret oak
nor brilliant maple's flame
But solely, lowly aspens glow
Bright golden sunshine-gold,
My autumn forest's treasure -
Gold

—*Betty Munson*

I Remember (Flashback of the Mind)

From Presidential Debates
Through the assassinations
And the retaliations
I remember

From major foreign wars
Aggression in Vietnam
Total unrest in Guam
I remember

Brotherhood in our world
Peace and love to heal our wound
It would never come soon
I remember

To the moon, astronauts would go
A giant leap for mankind
Illusion of the mind
I remember

Will we ever learn soon
From all our mistakes made
Or will it only be said
I remember

—*Donald B. Galloway Jr.*

Shepherd

His comfort has become mine
Thru the rod and staff
Righteous paths are there before me,
Keeping! Believing! Freeing!
From the evil one.
Fear of no evil has come
for he, the gentle shepherd
lead me on, to pasture
green, walk beside the
quiet stream, ever restoring
me whole, my cup overflows.

—*Anne Roberts*

To Tony My Beloved Son

I have watched you from a baby
to a boy and now to a man.
You gave me joy and love,
you have made me proud of
what you have become. Honored
to be your mother and to call
you my son. You have blessed
our home put a smile on my
face and laughter in my heart.
I had asked the Lord to let me
live to see you grown up and
to be saved. He answered my prayer
I am ready to go now when he
calls. The Lord will watch and
guide you and protect you and keep
you from harm.

—*Wanda Overholt*

To My Fallen Comrade

Though you ventured far from home,
    To a place who few had known,

You fought and died and did your best,
    And now upon this hill you rest.

Fear not my brother, I'll not forget,
    Of the times we had spent,

In talks of home and lament,
Until that last breath you did spent.

Within my arms and heaven stared,
    A quick sad moment we did share.

I'll see you soon my fallen friend,
Where all good soldiers once will end.

—*Samuel S. Fulginiti*

My Dear Love

I only desired to run away with you
    To a quiet secluded place
Just you and I,
    And beautiful things in mind
To take away all worries of life
    And fill our minds with ecstacy
        Just you and I,
We would lay down in love
    And make our family,
How beautiful love would be
    Just you and I,
Two minds in love without limits
    Only our imaginations.
How could life take this dream?
    Well my love
There's one thing you must know,
    I will never stop loving you
The love of my life,
        You: "Jose."

—*Theresa Gonzalez*

The Face of Christmas

He came…
    To a virgin so fair
    To a city that couldn't know
    To an innkeeper that didn't care

He grew…
    In his father's grace
    In spirit and in truth
    In the weakness of the race

He loved…
    The twelve in the room
    The two on the cross
    The friend in the tomb

He died…
    For the man with no tomorrow
    For the youth of deep despair
    For the woman in pain and sorrow

He arose…
    And in his face you'll see
    The man and the babe
    Who so loves you and me!

—*Ned Olmstead*

Country

If I were a bird, I'd fly away
To a warm place in the country,
Where birds can fly and birds can sing
And soar among clouds in early spring.

If I were a dog, I'd run away
To a freer life in the country,
Where dogs can roam and dogs can bark
From early morning 'till after dark.

If I were a cat, I'd steal away
To a friendly old place in the country,
I'd stalk a mouse around the house
And chase a squirrel up a tree.

If I were a lad, I'd move away
And live in a house in the country,
I'd plant my food and watch it sprout
And wade the streams and fish for trout.

But I'm a town, and I must stay
For towns can't move to the country,
But I can remember way back when
I was that place in the country then.

—*Rebecca Herbert*

Around

Back and forth,
to and fro.
Back to the garden,
we must go.

Saving the children,
one by one.
Lions and tigers and bears
what fun.

Wheel in a wheel,
up and down.
Light at the end,
what goes around.

—*Debra L. Stafford*

Tree

Oh,
to be a tree.
She stands there,
alone,
in beauty.
Reflecting upon her simpleness.
In the dawn,
she sleeps.
Cold,
like death.
At early morn,
her senses awaken.
Mid-day comes
her greatest hour.
As the night falls,
so she does.
For now,
again it is time,
for sleep.

—*Kristi L. Zellner*

Sandy (Puppy)

Sandy puppy has gone away
To Doggie Heaven to run and play

We couldn't watch her waste away
So we buried Sandy late today

Now we lay her down to sleep
We're not sorry for the tears we weep

Now she's gone and we'll sure miss
Her really cute puppy kiss

A little dog from the start
But she had a great big heart

She'd race around the yard with ease
Her hair flowing in the breeze

The fourteen years she spent with us
Will always be a great big plus

She made us happy, she made life fun
And her memory will linger on

Her mom and dad were very lucky
To have had such a wonderful puppy

Sandy puppy has gone away
To Doggie Heaven we do pray

—*Jim Kasari*

Untitled

It's OK my friend
to feel angry
to feel resentment
to feel lost and hurt
to feel like crying
to feel like talking
or just to sit and not feel at all
Its OK my friend
I will listen when you're angry
I will understand your resentment
I will hold you hand when you
    feel lost and hurt
I will hold you close when you feel
    like crying
I will be there to listen when you
    feel like talking
    or we can just sit together and
    not talk at all
It's OK my friend

—*Viola Hartman*

Childhood Home

In memory I like to roam
To find my childhood home.
I see the pump out in the yard,
The coal for stove so hard,
The out-house and its well-worn path.
Inside, the old zinc tub,
Where sisters took a bath.
The wash-board, to give clothes a rub,
The coal-oil lamps to light our way,
For games of cards to play,
The family Bible near the bed,
(And all too seldom read);
My mother at the tall piano,
For sister's fine soprano;
Hop-scotch and dolls and jumping rope
Would fill our lives with hope.
My childhood house, of course, is gone,
But home thoughts linger on.

—*Florence A. Bottorff*

Two Left Feet

But wait, I want to be the one
    To lead and I should
        Can I?
    I ask her
As she takes me, struggling.

But she is ridiculously awkward
    And I am graceful
        Shall we dance?
    I ask myself
My body wants to move, quickly

But she is extremely sluggish
And the music is full of spirit
    How can we be partners?
        I ask you
Reality is a slow dancer
    With two left feet.
        —*Jonathan Lee Hawks*

Almond-Green

Beloved, open the light
to my Almond-Green door,
hang my dark braid
to the keys of your chest.
The night is a dancing corner
and in the valley
there is a worship wind.
I come barefoot
wet from salt and limit,
my eyes aching
of so much glowing into my veins.

Time plaits baskets of dreams
over the waves,
the sea comes to the light
of my Almond-Green door
trembling down my crystals.
I gather the yellow dust
to my braid and my robe
and walk barefoot
wet from salt and limit.

        —*Ines Del Castillo*

A Wish Away

When you think there is no way
To overcome your fear,
That you'll never be without
Your very last tear.

You'll never be without that problem
Each and every day,
You remember your solutions
Just a wish away.

Just wish upon a star at night
And leave your fears behind,
Forget about your problems,
Lay back, relax, unwind.

Leave your problems on that star,
Forget about your fears;
When you wake up the next day,
You'll be without your tears.

        —*Christie Dilk*

Jake

I'm glad you came
    To see me, Jake!
We shared a very special day.
You are warm and friendly,
I can see.
A perpetual smile
upon your face,
I would like to
share more time with you.
I even found a way
So you could enter
And leave this nursing center
Through the back of the place
So your feet won't slide
In the polished hallway.
After all, you have four
to manipulate
For you are a lovable
Big ol' puppy, Jake!

        —*Juanita Powell*

A Winter's Eve

Gently falls the pristine snow
To swirl and drift on earth below
While youthful skaters glide along
Their voices joined in merry song.
A squirrel darts from tree to tree
Swishing his tail in boundless glee.
Tall pines are swaying in the breeze
Which softly sighs thru falling leaves.
The hunter's moon enthroned on high
Beams silv'ry light on sea and sky.
Then all is hushed sounds cease to be
All nature's clothed in serenity.

        —*E. Mary Lowery*

Curious Questions to Grandpa

"What were trees, oh grandfather,
    That came from little seeds?"
"Trees were homes for animals,
    Torn down for human needs."

"What were lakes, oh grandfather,
    Once filled with birds and fish?"
"Lakes replenished wild life,
    Polluted beyond their wish."

"What were elephants, oh grandfather,
    That roamed the stretching lands?"
"Elephants were gentle creatures,
    Shot down with human hands."

"What was nature, oh grandfather,
    That watched earth every hour?"
"Nature made things what they were,
    'Til thrown by human power."

        —*Adriane Chiu*

Believe

What ambition drives a man,
To believe what he believes.

What makes one man believe,
The vision or the dream.

What makes such men so different,
So courageous and so weak.

To try and strive for all mankind,
For those who don't believe.

        —*Bryon L. Woram*

Doors

My door is open
to the timid,
the meek,
the congenial,
and the amenable.
It is closed,
to the pessimist,
the warmonger,
the hostile,
the agitator, and
the aggressor.
Only love,
compassion and understanding,
can turn the key!
        —*S. Squires*

A Servant's Prayer

Dear God
to you I offer up
an undeserving vessel
a soul, a heart, to love

One who seeks to serve you
in times of good and bad
a sovereign heart to mirror
a smile that's always glad

A thankful heart submissive
to your perfect will
for you I yearn to live
your love I need to feel

I fall, I fall, so often
you are there to help me up
I call and then you soften
Your mercy fills my cup

Your grace I seek so daily
you strength I need anew
so Father I offer me
Dear God I will always love you...

        —*Jon McCullough*

Together

Love is fine
Together we shine
We'll always be together
In any sort of weather
Rain, or shine
You'll always be mine
Through thick and thin
My heart you can win
Even if you bring me a daisy
While outside is hazy
Together we'll sit and think
About how close our hearts are.

        —*Maricella Rodriguez*

Waves

As the waves hit the rocks,
together we stood out on the docks.
Dreading tomorrow that'd be the day,
the day you'd have to go away.
On that day I cried and cried,
the waves drowning out my sighs;
Now every time the waves do fall,
they send a silent message to all,
That message was one I knew
I'd always be in love with you.

        —*Elizabeth Ann Mulvaney*

Too Many Fears

Everyone has the fear of
   too much violence.
No one cares if there's
   too much silence.
Everyone has the fear of
   too much pollution.
No one cares if there's
   no solution.
Everyone has the fear of
   too much dope.
No one cares if there's
   no more hope
Everyone should be fearing
   of nobody caring

—*Nicole Data*

Hard-Core Rebellion

I am being crushed,
Torn from the arm of justice,
Smashed is all beliefs.

Locked up tight within,
They will never know the truth,
Doesn't matter though.

Innocent victim,
No harm done to anyone,
Just doing my own.

But, I am guilty,
In the pits of father's eyes,
Taking all the blame.

If my dad found out,
He did know the real me,
He'd truly go mad.

Now, life is changing,
I do father's job myself,
Hard core rebellion.

—*Abe Ring*

Mind

In your head
Toward the light
Through the sheets
Of glowing might.

Into the part
Above the eye
Beneath the soul
About to cry.

After the pain
Below you sorrow
Near the end
Of your tomorrow.

—*Lisa Varvari*

Goodbye

Time spent, time lost
   What price we pay
   When all is lost.
Is there a reason to stay
When what we cherish most
Is never what we say
I think my time has come
   And I wonder how
   But being lonesome
Could mean my time is now.

—*Don R. Goldmann*

"The Collectors"

Would that I had better known
   transparency
This curtainry that tends all joy
For when I reach therein
   poor days withdraw my hand
Else they say, gloom will ebb.

Oh gentler night when day
   has gone awry
Bring those dreams double joyed
   that gentle down my striving
And should gloom not take
   to its bed this winter
Let those dreams
   bring spring instead.

—*John P. Hutchins*

Childhood

The tremulous tot
Trembled in fear
The terrible chastisement
Was much too severe.

Alone in the desert
In the rain and the cold
With the snakes and the scorpions
Who were only too bold.

The step-mother's evil
And the desolate place
Were beyond comprehension
As seen in her face.

The walls of the crypt
And the blackness of the night
Were smothering the child
But she was too weak to fight.

—*Marjory Nierman*

The Coming of Fall

Fall is now here, with the leaves
turning their colors of red,
yellow and brown,

How I shall not forget they
were created by our gracious
Lord, who wears a crown.

The season that will proceed,
will grow of more dark,

But I shall keep the light
of our Lord, within my heart.

Though the coolness may fill the air,
I shall feel the warmth of
His love and not of despair.

So upon the coming of the season,
Shall we always believe, our
Lord is tending unto, all
of our needs.

—*Patricia Hemsworth*

Poetry

In silent stillness when twilight
Turns the day into night,
And children, who in darkness sleep,
Through golden doors dare to peep;
A song is heard that echoes on
Through morning's shining dawn —
Running free like a dream
From trickling water's stream —
'Till all is calm and still,
And magic writes with pen and quill.

—*Alicia Belchak*

Thinking

Consciously
unconsciously
little by little
it is formed.

All the knowledge
derived from the body
absorbed in the evolution.

Think
you think
the eternal road
to the final destination
which never be found.

Tension.
Confusion.
And fatigue

—*Akira Iida*

Be Fair

I get blamed for the
unnamed.
I get used then abused.
I cry from my pain.
I die from the insane.
My heart is broken from the
unspoken.
I always lose the battle,
I have no shadow.
I want to run away with
my soul into a deep dark
hole.
Where no one can find me
and there's no one behind me.
Be fair show me you care.
I'll be there.
I swear.
I care and that's fair.

—*Becky Webeck*

The Enemy

The enemy is not out there,
The enemy is within us.
It hides in the heart of each,
Silently waiting to explode.
It runs wild in our streets.
It lives in offices of our land.
It floats as smog in our cities.
It upsets nature's delicate balance.
It sweeps through hills and valleys,
Permeating minds with hate,
Lust, revenge and aggravations
That try and test us with anguish.
It is the strongest and most
Silent enemy and its name is Fear.

—*Jerri Brillhart*

Look at that Squirrel

Look at that squirrel
Up in the tree,
Do you suppose
He's looking at me?

There he goes
Through the branches,
He's running real fast
And taking lots of chances.

See him jump
From limb to limb,
Some of those big ones
He barely skims.

Oops, he's hanging on
With just one paw,
I'll close my eyes
Just in case he falls.

There he goes
Into a pile of snow.
Is it a game
I guess we'll never know.

—*Barbara McGuire*

Showcase of Living

Allie, you've walked softly
   Upon this earth.
You have accomplished much,
   Under this canopy of life

You have taught the rest of us,
   much in patience
You are a model of faith,
   Love and integrity.

So on your ninetieth birthday,
   I hope the years ahead,
Will he filled with charming vistas.
   For my dear friend.

—*Ruth S. Hill*

Bitter Sentiment

To have been vomited
Upon this earth, exposed
To the tortuous gnaw
Of life-size parasites

That make the flesh a sea
Of bobbing sickness, and the
Mind a gaseous cesspool —
Space filled with crooked scents,

And to have winged devils
Light upon you, sucking
What is left of the "I" —
What little much remains,

Is the price we pay
For entering the womb
Of austere stomachs
Who dry not under the sun.

—*Anthony Worrell*

Song Of Rosa

Rosa Veron was melody,
Vibrant, deep with passion,
Her moods cries of eternity,
Where truth dictates fashion.

I find Rosa in a bird's song,
In a sunset glowing,
Reminders of a yesteryear,
Of a fateful knowing…

How chance will tear two lives apart,
And time will frost one's hair,
And mem'ry must unlock the heart
To loose lost music there.

Rose Veron, sing low your song
In tender, soothing strains,
Soft tones - devotion, loyalty,
Comforting as spring rains.

—*Anita Lankenau*

It's Not Too Late

Our son who we call Joey
Was a gift from God above
I thank the Lord each night
For giving us his love

He'll always be our baby
As perfect as can be
So take this time to share with him
And make it special as can be

For soon he'll be a man
With a family of his own
And then he'll make us grandparents
But not too soon I hope

Because you're very special
To Joey and to me
You're all he ever needed
To make his life complete

For time stands still for no one
So get out there and fight
And make yourself some memories
With Joey in your life.

—*Jo Anna Margrave*

Untold Stories

My little girl
was eleven years old,
when she came to me
with stories untold.

Mom the man you love
is hurting me,
and you're the only one
that can set me free.

All of a sudden
I lost my whole world,
but I had to protect
my little girl.

You've people say
that love is blind,
for me it was
he was not one of a kind.

—*Helen Marie Jennings Grandstaff*

Untitled

Embitter
exasperate
these
they should consider
suffocating
leading
to rebellion
thoughts are uncertain
climbing the walls of
dismay
can't find the way
feeding the flesh
feeding the spirit
pressure
building
biased views.

—*Ann Scallorn*

Life

God is the mountain;
We are the trees.
We are of
Different races,
Different colors,
Different creeds.
But we stand,
We live side-by-side
With God—and rooted in Him.

—*Bob Ramsey*

To Uncross Cross Purposes

The song says it well
   We create our own Hell
"You always hurt the one you love"
   Friendship needs to rise above.

The pain, the hurt, can't be undone
   It lingers through tomorrow's sun.
When will we mortals ever learn
   To trust, to love, to show concern?

You and I compound a blunder,
   Tear relationships asunder,
As we move to change the ending
   Let us celebrate a worthy mending.

—*Anne Bochan Vendig*

A Birthday Message

Domonique, always on our minds.
We miss you so the words
   are hard to find.
It's so unfair that the
   Lord took you away,
You were here for only
   a short stay.
He had his reason's
   we know that's true,
We don't understand
   why he chose you.
I wrote these words to say,
   you are thought of everyday.
So hugs and kisses,
   and Happy Birthday too,
One day we'll all
   join you.

—*Jan Massey*

"A Violent Beat"

We heard it in the songs
We saw it in the streets
We listened to the word
But didn't heed the warning
Now violence
Runs a rampant score
Words with no more music
The reality of rap is here.
Man against man
Fear in the streets
It's a violent Beat.
Fear for family
Fear for life
Smoke in the air
They're dealing a violent Beat
When will it end
With death in the air
It's over the top
It's a violent Beat!

—*Monique Marie Long*

Little Dove "Peepsie"

From out of the blue and summer sky
We seen this dove, my wife and I
Before she knew where she was at
Her wing was broke, by the family cat
Why she came we don't know why
But we are sad to say good-bye
For seventeen years she sang her song
Now all is quiet, since she is gone
Her little life on earth is done
Today a happy one begun
Her spirit flies to lands unknown
Where all good birds find their home
She sings her songs, and finds her mate
And never hungry, because were late
Just like our souls will leave some day
We all must up and fly away
Yes, little "Peepsie" died today

—*Richard D. McDavitt*

Untitled

When you think of Thanksgiving
What comes to your mind?
Tables set for the family
Food of every kind.

A day filled with joy
Because loved ones are near,
You might not see them again
Until this time next year.

Now the day is over
Have you taken time to pray?
Thanking God for everything
He has given you each day.

—*Barbara E. Anderson*

Destiny

It doesn't make sense
to dream of a destiny
if there is no one
to share it with.

As soon as you find it
it means nothing,
until you share it with
the one you love.

—*Kylene Baney*

Sadden Joy

A mother to be, that's not
what I want to see.

She's starting her life down
a path untraveled.

It's taken her down a road,
unknown.

Scared she cries out for help,
But only to let out a silent
scream.

In nine months she'll hear a
cry of love yet pain as she
holds the little miracle of
joy in her arms.

Too young to die inside she
held her high.

A mother to believe that's
what she had to be.

—*A'Lesha Markee*

Anxiety

Have you ever wondered
What someone else is thinking?
Sometimes, as I guess,
My heart starts sinking.

You look at their face,
And into their eyes,
And hope you don't see
A look of despise.

You take a deep breath,
As they look at you.
What if they dislike you?
Then what would you do?

They stare at you
In a funny way.
Then you decide
You don't want to hear what they have to
say.

Don't put yourself through torture,
Anger, grief, or pain.
You needn't have started to worry,
They may simply have forgotten your
name.

—*Cheryl Butts*

August 28

Embrace the small syllables.
    sound light hope stars
Gather them in and
    dreams wind rain heart
press them close.
    night breath home peace
Welcome the adventure,
    help fun tears rest
savor the ah ha, the oh my,
the just plain joy
of the little words.
    you do yes I do yes.
Okay.

—*Shannon C. Klasell*

Jesus Lord

Dear Jesus, without you,
    What would we do?
If you were not born,
    Where would we be?
You died on the cross at Calvary,
    For everyone and me.

Let us strive to make your death
    Worth it,
Not only some, but every bit.
Change your fear of the Lord,
    To love of Him.
And open your ears to hear
    His Holy word.

Open your eyes to see,
    That Jesus loves me and thee.
Then open your heart,
    And take a part
In His kingdom to come,
    Which shall be awesome!

—*Adeline M. Kramer*

The Other Side

Oft-times we're prone to wonder
    What's on deaths other side -
    And often too, we ponder
    the promise it provides

But God our Father warns us
    we cannot be His own -
    Unless we make the right choice
    yet the choice is ours alone

We could take the easy route
    the one that's broad and wide -
    Or seek the straight and narrow
    and see the other side.

—*Elizabeth Benner Swineford*

Reaping Time

Reaping time is weeping time
When a garden begins to grow
Producing fruit from sinful seed
Which was often sown long ago.

Sprawling, choking, the seeds become
Weeds growing very wild
In recompense for things we've done
When acting like a child.

Reaping time is a joyful time
When seeds sown in fertile soil
Produce the fruit of righteousness -
Not stubble and futile toil.

—*Ernestine V. Brooks*

Untitled

Perfectly fine on the outside.
The exterior almost perfect.
But I know,
I know how you really are,
you're evil, deceitful, and you
speak nothing but lies.
Hurt...
That's all you ever cause,
no goodness, no happiness, no joy,
just twisted words and mixed meanings.
You hurt me once, but never again.
Never!!!
Never.

—*Erin Hall*

The Trees Of Winter

In the white sky of winter,
When all the trees are bare,
You can see the branches,
Empty lines, dark and thin,
Reaching out in the cold air.

Abandoned nests hang suspended,
Still, tightly woven cocoons,
Some, deep in once protective crotches,
Shielded no longer from the
World outside.

One crow perches high on top,
A black silhouette,
Embossed against the open spaces,
The only adornment on an otherwise
Barren limb.

—*Norma S. Hyman*

How Could I

How could I be a mother,
When as a child I never knew
The caring ways of a mother,
The gentle touch of love,
Or felt a quick, little hug?

How could I be a mother,
When day by day, I simply grew
With sister and brother,
Clothed, fed, bedded, ignored,
Never hearing a word of approval?

How could I be a mother,
When all my childhood through
I had no teacher, no other
To guide me along the way
To be good, to be proud?

How could I be a mother,
When upon the past I drew,
There was no experience to cover
Today, to understand, to advice,
To show me the way for you?

—*Dorothy Dykhuizen*

Sunset Fills the Sunlit Sky

Sunset fills the sunlit sky.
When at night, I wonder why,
How these colors fill the sky?
At night do people think
God is talking to the sky?
What does he say?
Does the sky reply?
God is telling the sky to
make beautiful colors that never die.
Now at night,
Sunset fills the sunlit sky.

—*Erin Renee Spiess*

Untitled

If ever confined
to a rocking chair,
Place it on the green grass
in the country somewhere.
Leave me with
a line and hook,
and be sure to provide
a babbling brook.

—*Eugene W. Hanley*

My Dying Friend My Father

I felt the presence of Death,
When he came to receive your soul.
I felt your heart cease to beat,
As your body grew still and cold.

Though you uttered not a word,
I heard your goodby's.
And saw the look of love,
As I looked into your eyes.

As you lay there dying,
I knew you'd soon be gone.
I felt a chill down in my soul.
My body felt like stone.

But then a peace descended
Wiping away my grief and pain.
At last the tears begin to fall,
Like a summer rain.

—*Catherine Ross*

When I Cry

There are times
When I feel down
For no apparent reason

I sit and think
Of my life gone by
What went wrong

The radio plays
The depressing song
That sums up my life

Slowly, the tears fall
One after another
They never cease

There are times
When I feel down
For no apparent reason
That is the time
When I cry

—*Katie Gospodarek*

You Were There

You were there
When I needed a shoulder.
You were there
When I just needed a friend.
You were there
When I was confused.
You were there
When all else failed.

When I didn't know
What to do,
You had the advice
To point me in the right direction.

You are a great parent to me.
Always standing by me.

By this poem
I want you to know,
I love you so.

—*Melissa Tubb*

Only In The Silence

Only in the silence
    When my heart is seeking Him
Do I feel His blessed, blessed peace
    From very deep within.
Only in the silence
    When I take the time to pray
And listen for His quiet voice
    To begin each joyous day.
Only in the silence
    Can I hear my Savior say
"You are my beloved
I'll keep you safe this day."
Only in the silence
    When I leave all toil and care
Only in the silence
    Can I know He's really there.

—*Norma Coursey Krantz*

God

Someone you can talk to,
When no one else is there,
Someone you can call upon,
When no one else seems to care,

Your teacher,
When you need teaching,
A healer,
When you need healing.

A friend,
When you need one.
All your secrets,
He will share.

So, let me introduce you,
God,
This is seventeen,
Seventeen,
This is God.

—*Angela Ashley*

"Thanks from Afar"

'Tis like the glitter of distant star,
when receiving thanks from afar.
A music heard - from distance wrote,
its serene and flowing note.

The gift requited - therein grows
its glow of love - receiver knows.
And sends so soon a thankful word,
such timely joy your ear has heard.

Though separating chasm deep,
across the gap - the heart does leap.
And with it now - thoughts do sway,
thanks from afar - to soothe the day.

'Tis like the glitter of distant star
when receiving thanks from afar.
A music heard - from distance wrote,
its serene and flowing note.

—*Mark W. Haggerty*

Untitled

I feel as a kite in the wind.
Up and down.
Back and forth
Getting let out little by little
    all over the place!!!

Outstanding an illusion
To those viewing my mystical presence.

—*Mariel Beaumont*

Hoosier Hooey
(With Cranberry Sauce)

Twill soon be sere November
When the hunter's on the loose
While Mother's in the kitchen
Trying hard to cook her goose.

The big round horn of plenty
Will run off at the mouth
When northern birds of summer
Are safely in the south.

Oh, it's fall that I'm a lovin'
When the turkey's in the oven
And chestnuts are snappin'
In the fire.

The hickory bark is curlin'
From the logs atop the grate
As I lay upon the hearth rug
And dream 'till very late.

My face is dry and stinging
From the radiating heat;
Now, if I only had a "snuggle-pup"
My joy would be complete.

—*R. Harold Rentner*

A Friend!

A friend's the one we turn to
When we're feeling down and out -
A friend's the reassurer
When you find yourself in doubt.

A friend will always listen
When you have something to say,
A friend can make a sunny time
Out of a gloomy day!

Appreciate good friends
Because good friends are hard to find,
Don't take friends for granted,
Don't be selfish or unkind!

This may not be the very best friend
That you have ever known,
But, as long as you have just one friend
You will never be alone!

—*Joseph V. Rimar*

To Poets

Poems are best
When written
After mid-night
For it is then
That they capture
The true spirit
Of the art:
A small voice
Crying out
In the corner
Of an early days
Weighted silence
And smothering darkness,
To be captured
On an empty page —
Maybe one day
To shed its light
Upon the world...

—*Matthew Bauman*

Lifetime

You start out as a little one,
When your life has just begun.
And as the years go by and by,
You try and try,
To forget all the bad things.
And try to spread your wings.
The higher and higher you get,
Sometimes it seems -
That everything just falls apart;
Your hope, your joy, your dreams.
But - sometimes you get very far,
and everything just goes your way.
So, until that day.
I hope you'll stay,
Patient and willing to wait
for the days that come ahead.

—*Courtenay Heather Covington*

Forever Spring

I love to see forever spring
where earth and grass together sing.
The sky, ever so blue,
seems to kiss the flower petal dew.
The utter sweet smell
of the honey cup bell,
fills my being with the sense of love,
ever so lightly as a cooing turtle dove.
The heavenly Artist ever so bold,
gave birth to spring, forever retold.

—*Mark Bertuzzi*

Innocence

Innocence, sweet innocence
Where have you gone?
Where are you buried?
Where's your sweet song?

I remember you vaguely,
Sometimes see a spark,
When I look in the mirror,
When I look in my heart.

The freedom
The laughter,
The trust bursting through,
Reminds me of someone
That I once knew.

Giving love freely,
Laughter and trust,
When did it leave me
And turn to disgust?

I yearn for it
Pray for it.
Put me on track.
Oh sweet innocence
Won't you come back?

—*Doris Renshaw*

Untitled

When the early sunset deepens
To a dark unruly shade,
The figures of the night
Lurk into sight.
In the forest they go,
Not fast or slow,
To play with the devil
And dance with the troll,
Into the forest they go.

—*Sheila Schaefer*

Christmas Time

Christmas is a time for sharing,
where people are always caring,
it is a time for love and joy,
with many a happy girl and boy,
Christmas carolers sing with glee,
as we have a wee bit of tea,
while the fire is burning bright,
voices are singing silent night,
reminding us that Christ was born,
So long ago on Christmas morn.

—*Matthew C. Kitchen*

My Shepherd

I'm here in a green valley
Where the still waters flow.
He leads me in paths of righteousness
And He restores my soul.

When I walk thru the valley of death,
No evil shall I fear.
His rod and His staff comfort me
For He is always near.

He anoints my head with oil,
My cup is over-run.
His goodness and mercy follow me
Until my days are done.

I will be content
Where ever I may be.
For He is my Shepherd
And He'll take care of me.

—*Martha Stelle Cowan*

The Wave of the Future

It's a fake little world
where there's no fresh air,
no naturally grown trees.
Life is produced in a test-tube.
Mechanical birds fly,
making music box sounds.
Plastic snow is falling.
Gatoraide rain cools the heat
of the sun lamp up above,
and our technological brains
can't understand the concept of love.
If everything man-made is better,
what happens to nature?
What happens to emotions?

—*Linda Sanchez*

No One Cared

Racheal lived in the small
part of town.
All anyone ever saw her do was frown.

All of her family was dead.
The only family she had
left was her stuffed bear, Fred.

No one cared to know when
She died.
No one was saddened.
No one cried.

Racheal had died.

—*Holly Burton*

Wisdom

Look and see what I can see
Where to go and what to be,
Life is too short to wonder and worry
Take it slow no need to hurry.

Take one day as it comes
Enjoy the rising and setting sun,
Watch your children run and play
These will be your happiest days.

Teach them now right from wrong
They will grow to be bright and strong,
Keep the love close at hand
Let them know you understand.

Show your pride in what they do,
The choices they make,
The life they choose.

And when they're grown and on their own,
They will know how much you cared,
And teach their children what you've shared
In life, love, and happiness
The key to success will always be there.

—*Jodi R. Miller*

The Old Sap Tree

Along side the river
Where trout seem to splash
A small little pine grows behind
In the grass.

Today it was very windy and
I saw the old tree,
With pine needles and
Bristles covering the old thing.

I sat next to the old tree
With sap stuck to my hands and knees,
And looked up at the tranquil old thing.

He shook in the wind
As I took off my gloves
And he bent back like a
Huge slingshot. With the wind in
My face and the smell of the
Sap, I leaned back and took a
Long long nap.

—*Peter Farbstein*

The Closet

Inside there's a dark closet
Where very few have a key
What you find may be sad
And it may be a mystery
Many things are disorganized
Confusion is the only light
A maze of pain and pleasure
Morning, noon and night
No one can ever discover the secret
Of what the closet might hold
A puzzle with missing pieces
Warm but yet very cold
The door has many scars
From where hurt has made its way in
Loneliness is the only cry for help
Happiness a true sin
So if you ever come to the closet
Keep in mind if it seems so cold
That packed away are years of sadness
From so many days ago...

—*Kim Sellers*

The Son of the Immortal

Oh! The son of the immortal,
Wherefrom you have descended
In this earthly environment?

No one knows, it's hidden
In the womb of great time,
Before the infinite antiquity!

Herefrom where will you evolve?
When and how and in what sort of
Sublime and divine settlement?

This too is wholly unknown,
Concealed afar in the future,
Near the heart of the eternity.

Between these two hazy entities,
Even the little we know is confusing
For the veil of ignorance!

Hence, we need conflicts and
Sufferance to realize, only in bits
And pieces, that great unknown!

And that's all; that's deliverance!

—*Himangshu K. Bhanja*

Long Mute Cry

I stand at sunshine attic
While the night is covering me
In blue satin cloth
I stand lucid and mute
Petrified Apocalypse of a missed ship.

Hope - a diamond covered by sand
Undiscovered yet
Enriched value - day by day
Night after night - life after life.

How many times did I miss,
Hardly knowing.
I left behind, like in another century,
Music, friends, times
Snows, rains, teachers with smiles
Satisfaction? What for?

I forgot about how it is to love
a woman, touch of tenderness
a suave voice of lighting soul
I forgot.

Here I am standing alone.

—*Eugene L. Culcer*

Temptation

You came along I was alone,
Why did I try I should have known.
There wasn't time to investigate
I took a chance I knew my fate.

Both day and night I hear you call,
You beckon on and then I fall.
The urge is great the need is more,
Resistance weak temptation score.

There was a time I passed you by,
I wouldn't dare give you a try.
You were a tease and bound to win,
Then I broke down and I gave in.

And now I lie awake at night,
A victim of your endless light.
I see the day and curse it yet,
When I had my first cigarette.

—*K. Marie Delorey*

Prayer For Peace

Here, while we have peace of a sort,
While turmoil rises around the world
Like a raging flood -
May God spare the strain
On the human brain
Desirous of fruition, not bound blood.
Winging trumpeters of truth
Ringing wide and clear the bell -
Are calling mortal madness
Back from the gates of hell.
Determined on God's battlefield,
All ancient heritage shall yield
To that old dream
In the hearts of all men -
Of peace and love and goodwill
On earth again.
If we should all say just one prayer
Throughout the universe, everywhere,
What a multitude of hearts would be
Blessed by thought in unity.

—*Louise Veazey Lewis*

A Musical Toy?

To all little children,
Who bring me such joy;
I'd like dears, to send you
A musical toy.

It would sing many songs,
Also whistle a tune;
Then twirl and dance gaily
All over the room.

Each hour, on the hour,
It would give you a hug;
Then cuddle up closely,
So you're warm and snug.

I looked for this toy
Clear to kalamazoo;
But I couldn't find one.
Tell me, will I do?

—*Virginia R. Lindsay*

Lost Love

I whisper
I love you
seeking your reaction
there is none
so I speak louder
a little...
I love you
eyes lowered,
quick to run
for cover
you smile slightly
I venture more
you tense
I retreat
into my forest of fear
and insecurities
never to say
I love you
again

—*Julie A. Chitwood*

My Friend

My friend will never leave me
We will never be apart
No matter where you are
You are always in my heart
There is nothing that can change
What I hold within my heart
That bond is there forever and
Can never be torn apart

—*Rebecca L. McAlister*

To My Mother

I know a woman
who dreamed a dream
and knows a man
and loves herself

I know a woman
who sees the moon
winks at the universe
and smiles gracefully

I know a woman
who embraces us all
who gives us anything
and wants nothing back.

Do you know the woman?
I think you do
If you really look closely
that woman is you

—*Janis Crum*

Who Are We

Men, Women,
Who knows what we really are.
You could be a man
soft like a flower,
Or a women,
hard like a rock.

Maybe we are all the same,
but chose to be different.

So we chose who we are, or
is there a greater force
not known to man that
forces us to do
the things we do.

Could we,
do we,
chose our fate,
before we know what's going to happen?

—*Norman Box*

The Future

Ten years from now,
who knows where I will be?
Maybe standing on a cliff,
looking over at the sea!
And if I am in another world
at that point in time,
will I have big white wings
that I can call all mine?
And if that other world should
consist of only fire
Will I have been sent there
because in life I was a liar?
And though my future life may
be full of many things.
I think that I will wait to
see just what my future brings.

—*Kristina Jones*

The Open Road

Lives there a city dweller,
Who never was so bold —
To leave the safety of pavement,
And take to the open road?

To turn down an unmarked trail,
And follow it to the end —
Just for the sake of finding
Surprises around each bend.

Then feel the expectation —
As you reach the crest of a hill,
Where valleys lying beyond —
Causes your heart to thrill.

To drive through scenic country,
'Till you reach the end of the day;
Then stop to camp the night,
By a stream along the way.

To cook on an open campfire,
And sleep in the shelter or pines;
Then rise at dawn—and travel on,
'Till the road homeward winds.

—*Marj Strickland*

The Great Divide

How can two people
Who shared all their secrets
Have nothing to say?

How can two lovers
Who turned to each other
Suddenly just turn away?

How can two hearts that once
Beat together now be so still?

Standing at the edge of goodbye,
Here at the great divide.

And where does love go?
Does it drift with the snow
Or lie cold in the ground?

How did forever turn into never,
And leave without even a sound?

Once we moved mountains, that stood in
our way,
Now we do not even try.

I know it's over, but I'm not over it yet.
Now that I've learned how to say goodbye,
When will I learn to forget?

—*Robert Carlough*

Untitled

As the inside flew up and away,
    the outside was still where it lay.

The earth slowed to a crawl,
    for self it came to a halt.

The brightness eased to a dull,
    as the power was being unplugged.

Why I was here from the start,
    was leaving and taking my heart.

Daddy's Gone
—*Margaret A. Humphries*

May Those Be Damned

May those be damned
who took what was not given
Who looked into the soul of one
who never gave permission.

May those be damned
who killed a thing so great
Born of so much beauty
conceived from so much hate.

May those be damned
who do not understand
It was me you have destroyed
You took the pencil from my hand.

May those be damned
who read my words and choke
The silence was so golden
But the silence you have broke.

—*Heather Jones*

Protected Weep

Lifeless body ever so sweet,
Why are people so sudden to weep?

Lifeless body lie so still,
You have given so much joy and thrill.

Lifeless body doesn't sing or dance,
Just pray the Lord gives you a chance.

Loving soul ever so sweet,
You are seated at the Lord's feet.
Loving soul no longer lies deep,
Your love has hushed the peoples weep.

—*Elizabeth M. O'Connor*

A Son's Love

I loved you more than anything
Why did you have to go?
I needed you in my life
More than you'll ever know.
Daddy, you gave me life
But I was only seventeen
There's so many things I've done
I wish you could have seen.
Sometimes I find I'm scared
Of what my life beholds
But I know you would have told me,
"Stand strong, son, be bold."
And now I hold your memory
Deep down inside my heart.
Inside I know it's true
You and me - we'll never part.

—*Kelehua K. Kekuewa*

Untitled

I loved her as much as I could,
She loved me more than that.
Oh how I wish I would
Not have taken her for granted.
But now she's home with grandpa.
Although we'll miss her here,
She'll have a home of paradise
And that's what she deserves.
Oh God, please take good care of her,
As she did so much for me.
And grandma, when I get up there,
Please save a hug for me.

—*Aaron Gustafson*

What Is Wrong With Everybody

What is wrong with everybody,
Why do they sit and stare?
I thought that I was very funny
When I pulled Susie's hair!

What is wrong with everybody,
Why do they heave and sigh?
I thought that I was very tough,
When I blacked Jimmy's eye!

What is wrong with everybody,
I just don't think it's fair!
For all of you to act that way,
And I'm too cool to care!

What is wrong with everybody...
Or... is the wrong with me?
I think I've learned my lesson,
Will someone play with me?

—*Katherine A. Brite*

"Have you Ever Wondered?"

Have you ever wondered?
Why God made all the trees?
And why he made the little birds,
To fly high, into the breeze

I wonder why we plant a seed
And it will grow, and grow.
Then one day we will notice.
A little flower will show.

Why are the rivers deep and dark?
With fish a swimming by,
Why does the stars twinkle bright?
And light up all the sky?

Why does the sun come up and stay?
Until the day is through?
Then it will rest through-out the night,
So the moon can come in view.

I've never cease to wonder,
Thou folks might think I'm dumb-
My biggest wonder of them all-
Where did my Lord come from?

—*Juanita B. Patterson*

I Wonder

Have you ever wondered
Why the sky is so high
Why little birdies fly
Why cats chase mice
Why Santa Claus is nice

Have you ever really wondered
Why rocks don't swim
Why the day goes dim
Why kids like milk
Why worms make silk

I wonder if you've wondered
Why you have to go to bed
Why there's more hair on your head
Why you have ten fingers
Why Grandma's perfume lingers

Do you know what Mommy wondered?

Why the boys kiss the girls
Why I loved ringlet curls
Why the clouds will sometime thunder
What her baby girl will wonder...

—*Lori Gish*

Echoes

If I say I love you
Will I hear the words
    echo
In the empty space
    of your heart?
Then flow
    from your body
Touching no nerve
Skirting the soul.
If I love you
    long enough
Could you be mine?
Or would it be,
When you finally say
    I love you
That you would hear
    the words
    echo
In the empty space
    of my heart?

—*Mary E. Dirstine*

Golden Poppy

Golden poppy of California
Rich in color, and smooth to touche.
California gold!

The Survivor in abundance
On this historic, bloodshed, terrain
The golden Poppy remains.

Life's terror returns in different ways
Of undeclared wars.....
Continuing its madness.

With motives disguised
Lingering in an almost
Invisible way.

Where ears and eyes
Witness a common destruction.
And little is being done to stop it.

Tender moments
With visual comfort,
Soft, velvety, petals felt.

The California Golden Poppy is sustained
In its valiant, vivid, vibrance.

—*Bonnie Jean Lukin*

(Gull)

Gull
    will listen.
        Hear scary noise?
    And take flight,
                    Why?

Able
    is to fly.
        Wings out and glide?
    Up and soar,
                    True?

Should(Gul-)
    you(li-)
        fly(ble)?

—*Jason Brabec*

Untitled

Time like a bird's flight...
Wisdom the breeze of age,
    the experience of living
Beauty the richness of a soul
Creativity the monuments of
    mankind.
Knowledge to seek, to ponder,
    to share
Life the wonder, the breath
    of fresh air
To survive you will have to fight
But to understand
Love and peace must be
    in your heart.

—*Nadia Hava-Robbins*

Repletion

Rejoice for God has filled the earth
With an abundant harvest,
Which we may reap
If we but fill our souls
With holy optimism.

Delight in the glorious gifts
Which God has generously supplied;
Faith will make them ours;
Doubt will keep them from us;
And we will never receive that
Which we were made beneficiary of.

God has not given us His secrets,
But only the means to pursue them.
For in the pursuit of what we're denied,
Man is ennobled and glorified.

—*Gene Johnson*

May You Walk

May you walk always in sunshine
    with blue skies everyday.
May your journey be a safe one
    may now never go astray.
May your burdens all be light ones
    and small the cross you bear.
May your future be a bright one
    enriched by love and prayer.
May the wing of love enfold you
    like a blanket in the night.
And the arms of faith, uphold you
    until the sky is bright.
May life's storm clouds quickly vanish
    as rainbows come your way...
May now walk in sunshine
    with blue skies everyday

—*Toni J. Brown*

Unspoken

Handicapped by words
The mind — four-walled
Is ever seeking an escape
To once convey
The soul's deep yearnings
And say beyond itself
The thought formed
In the caverns of the heart
That language cannot say.
Mind to mind we grope,
Soul to soul, the silence
Knows what words
Can never say....

—*Shirley Lee*

Sunny Morning

he morning enters
ith clashing brass,
nd trumpets echoing
hrough the glass.

e marches over
arth and boulder,
oisting the sunshine
n his shoulder.

ll dressed in gold
nd brilliant green
ith dark brown boots
f earthen sheen.

ith sky-blue eyes
hat envision the best
nd shiny orange medals
cross his broad chest.

e whistles through the dawning
cattering dewdrops where he blew
nd the crowning touch of glory
the world that's born anew.

—*Joanne A. Wright*

nticipation

ones of fire crest the peak
With feet in mirror lake.
quatorial wind fluffs the cheek
Of maiden now awake.

man takes flight on bitter bird
With life and light behind.
ity lights and moon recede
With the captor of his mind.

lan and girl love in flying word
Before the final moment sweet
Then witnessed words ordained by Lord
Flee lips and then the eyes repeat.

—*LeRoy J. Binder*

he Heartbreak

ou swept me off my feet
ith flowers so sweet
e comfort each other
s if you were my lover
ow you've gone away
hen later you would say
love you my beloved
ut I would have moved
o a new home all alone

—*Katherine Bolin, Age 14*

ly Memories

s I sit by his chair
ith his hand in mine
ond memories stir in my heart.
e naps as we sit there
hile I remember the happy days
our marriage of forty years.
he years passed by so swiftly
ull of joy and busy bliss.
he day could be stormy or happy
ut each one ended with a kiss.
efore I leave to go home alone
give him a loving hug
hich may help to atone
or the guilt in my heart
hat I can't take him home with me.

—*Frances E. Tolson*

Lifeboat

Small flimsy raft
Set adrift, afloat
In a swirling storm
Committing self-sacrifice
I alone survive
Hopeless needs lost
A thirsty drink,
Swallow, swallowed
By the waves
Overcome and overwhelmed
Vanish into the endless sea

—*Katherine Oxton*

The Stolen Child

I started this day young
With hope and innocence
But you came
And took my innocence away
Tore from my very soul
All hope of happiness
With your rough hands
You stifled my cries
With the hardness of your body
Claimed all my sunny days
For your pleasure laid claim
To my most secret places
To make yourself a man
You stole a child

—*Jacqueline Cartledge*

Hurt and Sorrow

A child of six treated
with hurt and sorrow.
Those sister of God so holy and pure
always mistreating me rough and blue.
If someone or a priest could
of help me through,
But no one knew I could
only pray to God to see me through.
Even now I'm grown I still can
see those sister of God
Their ghost acting so holy and pure.

—*Carolyn Spoto*

Abortion...

My stomach will soon be swollen
with life so simple and true.
I never thought I'd hear those
words come from you!
I thought you would understand,
and feel the way I do.
I guess I was a fool to believe
those words you swore were true!
How could you ask these three
words from me?
I believe in life not abortion
do you see?
I will have and love this baby
with all of my heart!
I guess we never had love from
the start!
I thought that we knew each
other well.
But now I think you can go to
Hell!

—*Dustie Petrouske*

Only to Love You

Life played its hand each day
With pain and joy along the way,
When we touch our souls Collide
Keeping tender love alive.

Only to love you it's true
I'd walk a live wire with you.
Only to love you each day
My heart lovingly prays.

Given a chance to live free
Would bring happiness to me.
One moment at a time
Will give love God's design.

We'll grow together as one
Playing in summer sun.
Along the beach we'll stroll
Making total love our goal.

—*Emy Star*

"No Snow On Christmas"

'Twas a day in December
With rain and no snow,
But the spirit of Christmas
Was there all-aglow.

The shops were crowded
With people on a spree,
With plastic and greenbacks
To put under the tree.

The snow didn't come
But there was bustling and skelter
With the tree going up
And the Babe in his shelter.

The lights went on
And the trimmings did too,
And everything was set
For Santa and his crew.

Santa came and went
And what do you know?
He forgot to leave us
A blanket of snow.

—*Pacita Johnson*

The 25th of December

On this solemn day of praise,
With snow-capped hills and
    snow white days,
We celebrate the date of birth,
Of Him who created Heaven and earth.

Children waken on the morn,
On which the dear Christ
    Child was born,
To find such gifts beneath the tree,
That fill their hearts so full of glee.

The old folk gather, sing, and pray,
That their children will live their day,
And to God they give the praise,
For their health and happy days.

On this Christmas of '42
With war we hope we'll soon
    be through
Men are fighting so we might save,
This Christmas day to sing
    His praise.

—*Kenneth J. Grout*

The World Today

Towers of steel
  with sections of glass
Blocking the sun
  and destroying the grass

Cages of metal
  with wheels made of rubber
Spewing toxins galore,
  making us all sometimes shudder

Birds with no feathers
  with fire to fly faster
Never singing a song
  sometimes causing a disaster

We separate ourselves
  with walls with no substance
Made of anger and hatred
  and words that can hurt us

We chose to live here
  amongst all the clatter
With faceless expressions
  like it all doesn't matter

We've forgotten what we were taught
  we forgot one another
"What happened to heaven on earth
  and everyone is my brother"

—*Stephen Hare*

I Thought of You

I thought of you Christmas Morning
with the fireplace a-glow,
Yule logs and wreaths made of holly
and the rooftops white with snow.
I thought of you Christmas morning
and the good times that we knew;
Sleigh rides and parties so jolly
and the carols I sang with you.
"Jingle Bells," "12 days of Christmas;"
"Rudolph," with his nose so bright;
"Adeste Fideles," "White Christmas;"
"Joy to the World," "Silent Night."
Mem'ries of you keep returning
as I gaze upon the tree.
I thought of you Christmas morning
and I hope you thought of me.

—*Buddy Overn*

The Game

He jumps with grace,
With the look on his face,
Knowing they're going to win,
They pass to the right,
Pass to the left,
Pass down the court,
Then you see the look in his eyes,
As they grow really wide,
As he shoots and scores again,
The day is not over,
Even though his career is,
For Magic still lives.

—*Brooke Rebber*

The Coast of Maine

I felt home on the coast of Maine,
with the smell of spray
and the feel of rain.
Nestled in her rocky shore
are tales of men in ancient lore
of ships,
of fish,
and lives folks struggled with.
Yes, life was hard and conquered most.
Many so, have left her coast.

The city's pulse feeds me now,
though din and rush have furrowed brow.
I'm full, but wish
of ships,
of fish,
a place my soul can harbor with.
The scent of spray,
the taste of rain,
a man could never be the same
if he's loved the coast of Maine.

—*Patrick C. Fournier*

"A Woman Tanning"

'Don't you realize?'
With wine on her breath,
With sweat under her breasts,
'We were all former Gods,
Marked by tidy oracles
and ached by submerged
Serfdom - so,
We hollowed out this trapdoor
- Our lordly abandonment
Snakes many eyes until
Our rushes entwine onto
The rays -
And this brahmanic ritual?
My mourning bands always
Need mending and only
Sweated knowledge truly
Holds on.'

—*W. Matyjewicz*

To Both of You,

On Your Wedding Day

On one cold and windy day,
  with winter looking on;
All the family gather round,
  the wedding was upon.

A candlelight wedding, with
  flowers everywhere;
A beautiful song was sung, which
  ended with a prayer.

The bride, in shining satin,
  and the groom in stunning gray;
Said their "I do's", at the church,
  then went their married way.

Marriage is the bond, that
  two people share;
Love and keep each other always,
  will show how much you care.

"Always" be happy, with the
  one you love;
For both of you together,
  were "blessed from high above"!

—*Mary A. Conner*

Blessed Sleep

No sweet contentment
Within my chamber.
Where the divine peace?
No, never the gentle stillness
of a home at sleep.
Only the whispering, gnawing
of wasted years.

No lovely strain, no
ruby wine can calm
my impassioned mind.
Past regrets. The barren now.
No dreams of tomorrow.
Come blessed sleep.

—*Fay Franklin*

"Images"

Adrift at sea...
Within the last lifeboat,
torturous moans from the blistering
red humans fill the air.

Parched throats, salt crusted eyelids,
nostrils filled with the stench of
human feces makes it difficult for
the humans to ponder rescue.

Will sunset bring a cool misty
blanket to ease their pain.

As styx waits quietly in the wings?

—*Maureen Everett*

Time

Time was not meant
To be solely of mine
Rather to be spent
Preciously but deliberately sound.

How can one say
It's my time I spend.
Even without our lives
Time would survive alone.

How carelessly we putter
To aforge no path.
When survival of life
Falters in due time.

Complacency of a chartered course
Begins in the fog.
Continuance without direction
Ends in the dark.

Yet alone I ponder
Where am I going.
Should I be wasteful
Or consider the time.

—*Larry H. Bange*

Untitled

Love is such a beautiful thing
  When you have it you want to sing
and dance and play.
  Not just once, but every day

I know the feeling that love will bring
  I have it now and want to sing
and dance and play
  Not just once but every day.

—*Richard L. Marlow*

...ower On the Outside,
...rpent Within

...n, Washington; Oh, Washington
...ithin you live men of worth,
...om the day of your foundation
...u've been a blessing to the earth!

...n, Washington; Oh, Washington
...ith thy words my heart is won.
...ll me all you will do for me
...s you bask shining in the sun.

...will show you richness
...my world of stately art.
...st put your trust in me,
...et us never separate or part.

...h, Washington; Oh, Washington
...thee I will abide;
...ive you my tax dowry
...ith felicity and pride.

...nd I will spend accordingly
...our taxes you have given.
...pon this Earth I promise you,
...ashington shall be as Heaven.

—*Glenn F. Girdham*

...omeless

...o be homeless is to be ice cream
...ithout a cone,
...king without a throne
...ship without a port
...drift endlessly.
...o see the things that
...hey go through each day,
...akes me sad they have
...o live that way.
...o see a child at my feet,
...akes me wish he wasn't on the street.

—*Danielle Hubbling*

Common Memory

...Childhood was once
...ithout cause, bringing
...emories even Santa
...laus.
...But now's the time
... live each day well, and
...eep secrets that one must
...ot tell.
... For someday the words
...e've said will be repeated,
...nd one will find it's a
...isease that will soon
... treated.

—*Christina Walters*

...ruits of the Spirit

...he oranges of life are glistening;
...pon one which oozes sweetness.
...s the seed of inspiration is implanted,
... the caverns of one's mind.
...lope you enjoy the visions before you,
...nd allow the seed to sprout.
...o travel to the dimension,
...here understanding will come about.

—*Barbara Jo Hovey*

The Empty Chair

She sits and stares at the empty chair,
Wondering why - nobody is there!

Waiting for someone to return again,
So things can be as they were when,

The chair was full of fun, for her,
When her master combed her tangled fur.

But he is gone, and won't return,
The empty chair - her only concern!

So she sits, and stares each day,
Wondering why - he went away.

Just a sad-eyed - furry friend -
Whose love does not have an end!

—*Adeline Fleischer*

It's So Cold and Dark Inside!

It's so cold and dark inside!
Won't anyone help?
I feel so alone.
I wish someone could
Explain what is happening.
I hope that I will understand.

It's so cold and dark inside!
At times I wonder why I was
Brought into this God awful world?
I ask at times "Was I a mistake
Or was I meant to be?"

It's so cold and dark inside!
I have had so many losses in my life
That it seems so cold and dark inside.
I hope and pray that one day
Someone or something will turn on
That light inside and it will
Become warm again, inside my lonely heart.
I feel so cold and dark inside!

—*Amanda Yates*

Land of the Free?

Eyes, drinking in the beauty of a
world, a nation's misery.
Ears, with screams so loud,
lost laughter can't be heard.
Hearts, so filled with disgust,
compassion, love, can't be felt.
Understanding, a word, no more
can be understood.
Religion, no more man's own
personal choice.
Freedom, no longer a luxury,
regardless of race!
America, home for the choicest
and best;
Land, stolen from the ones
to whom it was blessed!
Memories, of a life in the past,
before reservations were home.
Futures, no hope for things better,
longing, mourning hearts remain.

—*E. Renae Boyd*

Fly Away With Me?

If both of us had wings,
    Would you fly away with me?
We could soar the open sky
    And fly out across the sea.

Side by side we could fly
    And land wherever we want....
Stay as long as we wish;
    Then, off on another jaunt.

We'd visit worlds unknown....
    Come home when we are through
And see all the family
    To relate our travels to.

We could build our nest
    Way up on the mountain top,
Out on the wide open plain,
    Or anywhere we might stop.

Make friends in the city
    And in the country wide;
If the two of us had wings
    And flew away side by side!

—*James Max Davis*

Winters Hall

White the sun,
Write the cold,
Old blood doth slowly
Creep and crawl.
Stall the rain,
Hold the snow,
Form not ye icicles
To my wall.

A new day, a blue day,
No need to be bereaved, or cry -
But a tear still seems
To make its way,
No matter how I opposing try,
No matter how azure the sky -
Or how the wind doth sigh.

Bless now the kiss, of ice cold lips,
Frozen blank with natures pall.
Catch your breath,
As best ye can-and be ye still
In winters hall.

—*Norman Coburn*

Trust

When a problem comes
You need help on the way,
It's not hard to find
The right words to say.

It's easy to pray
"Lord, hear my prayer,"
But, oh it's so hard
To leave it there.

We take it to Him,
Ask for help for today,
Then pick it back up
As we go on our way.

Lord, help me to learn
As on you I call,
To leave it all there,
You don't need my help at all.

—*Vivian F. Young*

A Christmas Poem

Fireplace so cozy,
Ye, Papa nods us to bed
Up the stairs all children
Await Santa, reindeer and sled.

Mom tucks us in
On Christmas eve night
All covered, snuggled up
Out goes house light

Cookies and cup o' tea
Down stairs on the table lay
Wind whistles through trees
Dreams of bells on a sleigh

O'er a blanket o' snow
Children smile in dreams
Joy, peace in this home
With light of moon beams

Sometimes through night
Goodness will come
Santa, his laughter will be here
Hence Christmas Day, love in our home

—*Teri Berta*

Anniversary

So it's your anniversary
Years of married bliss
Every time you look at each
Other, you still act like
It's your very first kiss.

You have seen hard times
And good times and lived
Through them all.
So your love grows stronger
Cause you're always on
The ball.

So in your book of love
You fill another page
I just hope that you're around
When I get to be your age.

—*Russell Wilson*

A Duckling's Pledge of Love

I think you're absolutely "ducky",
    Yes, indeed I do!
If you will be my valentine,
    I'll pledge my love to you!

I'll strut my stuff in the barnyard
    The minute you say you care;
But, I will simply "quack up",
    If you leave me in despair!!

—*Gloria Anna Ringle*

The Last Request

    The brave young man
    with pride in his land
fell down in the blinding burst.
    He whispered to them
    as they leaned over him,
    "I loved my country first!"

    "Tell all that you see
    that men should be free,
for this is my last uttered sound,"
    he whispered to them
    as the life from within
ran out on the cold, hard ground.

—*Jody Darlene Brow*

This Day

The day began as it did
yesterday
and the day before.
A summer day full of promise
and beauty.
I am warmed by the sun;
soothed by the song of the birds
and the gentle whisper of the wind.

The shrillness of the telephone
intrudes upon this lovely moment.

And then the day is not as it was
yesterday
or the day before.
The beauty and promise of summer
are gone.
The sun no longer warms me
And the birds and the wind together
weep in sorrow
that this day my friend has died.

—*Pat Gualdoni*

Sunset

I would like to share with
you, a Lake Michigan sunset
In November, something truly
to be remembered.

It was an Indian Summer day
That lingers in your mind.
As you rounded the curve
You found orange, blue and gold.

It spoke to you so bold.
It bathed everything in it's light.
Your eyes cannot believe the
Magnificence of that sight.

It gave you such a start
That went straight to your heart.
You wanted to weep, and
Always keep that vision alive.

Your spirit knew the gift that was given,
And on a bleak and gloomy November day.
You recall that wondrous, glorious sunset.
Never growing tired, of the awe, that it
inspired.

—*I. B. Polerecky*

Objectifying

Blue cheese, oh blue cheese
You are as blue as the
macerated tripe of a blue
whale plagued by halitosis
you are ever so many things
at whose approach my
nasal lining shrivels
hastily into a wrinkled blue powder
like the sand at the
bottom of an artificial
lake where blue
puppies liked to swim
until they found it
was just a big paint leak
or the cerulean saliva
of a girl who gagged
over some dressing on
a pile of lettuce that
was sort of green.
Go figure.

—*Marina Vishmidt*

Come Spring Come!

Come spring come!
You are so long in coming
Do not hesitate, come forth
We are lost without you
Let spring be born again.

Come spring come!
You are so long in coming
Fields do not smell of the dew
There is no lawn of green
Where over head the moon light beams

Come spring come!
Bring forth your lovely charms
Let us be thankful for thee
That we may hold in our palm
A flower sent from your arm
Come spring come!
You have been so long in coming!

—*Margaret Bavoso*

Thank You, Lord

Thank you, Lord,
for the birds that sing,
for the church bells that ring,
for rivers that flow,
and the sun that glows,
Thank You for Everything.

Thank you, Lord,
for the miracle of seeds growing,
for Your love overflowing,
for the rainbow in the sky,
for mom with her homemade apple pie,
Thank You for Everything.

Thank you, Lord,
for trials that come my way,
I know you are there throughout my day,
for the rain that falls,
and for the baby that crawls.
Thank You Lord for Everything!

—*Linda Rohland Day*

Flag

You, magnificent stripes of red
You are the fighting men who said
"For freedom is why we're fighting,"
But the price you paid was dying
To keep this country strong standing

Oh! You innocent stripes of white
You are the young who learn with might
You grow with knowledge and wisdom
To give us honor and freedom
To give us a better sounding.

Oh! You glittering stars of gold
You're the ones standing oh so bold
You give this country significance
For it holds great magnificence
to honor this country's springing.

—*Steven L. Knox*

My Dad

My Dad was gentle,
But sometimes tough;
He would use his leather strap
When he'd had enough.
It didn't matter if Dad
Was angry or sad:
He would always have time
To spend with his kids
He was a character,
This Dad of mine.
Pulling pranks on family and friends
All of the time.
But time has gone by
And Daddy is gone
To be with God
In His mansion above.
Someday I'll see him,
That Dad of mine;
Where God's love shines on him
All of the time!

—*Kay Thompson*

ty Poet

ce addiction sets in
u can't stop
u become a serial killer
tacking the keyboard at will
ange creature live inside
ur head
ey show you no mercy
ve no quarter
rce your fingers
do their will
e city is your slaughter house
ke a wife it accommodates
ur moods
esn't seem to mind your
ving her a bad name
u walk her streets
hungry vampire
pping up your own blood
nights when word
ansfusions are not enough

—*A. D. Winans*

'ading"

ade, fade away in the distance
u come, you try to catch me
isappear to the other side
beautiful
ere's fresh air
an breath
ere's no disease
e here is brilliant, to some degree
u should come and see
ly if you were like me
le to fade away
t you're not
rt to help out
d soon you'll be
fade back in and wait for you
wait until your time comes
help you see, it's your time
me with me
we fade away
e earth begins to grow beautiful like it
ed to be.

—*Kristin Beckman*

"Life"

"Life", how vain, how futile thou art;
"You" give us the Moon,
Then take away the Stars;
"You" show us the right,
Then give us the wrong;
What use to struggle,
When all will be gone;
"Your" Brother lies waiting,
In vain knows "He" not;
For sooner or later,
"Time", stops everyone's "clock!"

—*Daniel Jay*

That Something Special

You got that something special.
You have a sense of style.
An Adonis who melts my heart,
simply with a glance of your smile.
You just have a certain flare,
pardon me if I happen to stare.
No one if they dare can ever compare
with your gorgeous silver hair,
and dazzling eyes of sapphire blue.
Are a few of the many things that,
make you so very irresistible.
You're just so genuine fair and
kind having a friend like you
is a gem of the rarest kind.
You've been good to me from the start.
I'll always keep my valentine memories of
you forever next to my heart.
Summing it up with one last rhyme.
I think you're sweet, I think you're fine.
Thank you for being my valentine.

—*Mary L. Strickhouser*

Note to a Husband

Dear man of mine,
You know I see,
That you are working hard for me
Spending all your time away,
Sixteen hours or more a day.
It seems to you that we are bound
Digging deeper in the ground,
But pretty soon all will right.
Our dreams coming into sight.
So smile though I know your tired,
With this I hope you are inspired.
Love me.

—*Davina M. Purnell*

Untitled

An indefinite feeling.
You know the one I mean.
The one we see in the wake of a new day,
The one we know will always stay.
Well, here we are now,
let us celebrate the rise of
the new tide.
Which will bring in the new lovers,
bring in the new beliefs,
bring in the new deaths.
And it shall wash away the old.
This is our feeling of hope,
Meant only to be let down.

—*Daniel Hall*

I Fall In Love

The best and most feeling is
you love and have a sweet kiss...
I can talk loudly about this.
Because my love - the baby is.
He babbles, dances, runs and springs
And what he listens to - he sings.
His golden, silky wavy hair
Is shining like a joyful fire
And when he smiles - all people laugh
Much gladness adds the kid to life.
I loudly talk and that's not shame
"The best is Boston! Baby Sam!"
But then I thought: "Why only Sam?
All kids are wonder! I love them!"

—*Nokhm Azriyel*

Untitled

God
You made us short and tall
Made us think before a fall
Sent us far and sent us wide
Made us feel happy inside
Made us silly and made us wise
Kept us considerably down to size
God
You made us ups and gave us downs
Gave us remedies for frowns
Caused us to stop and think
Pulling up short before the brink
Gave us tools to build a fence
And how to use it with good sense
God You could be, if You choose, aloof
And remain far, far above our roof
But we know You love us still
And are assured You always will
Thank you for so much free rein
We hope, we do, Your approval gain

—*William Morse*

Nothing But Black

The world goes black,
you no longer feel your pain.
The tears you cried
are never to come back again.
Your fear and suffering
are done and gone.
Your soul is set free
and your life is gone.
All you were doing was
lying in bed.
All you did
was wish you were dead.
All those pathetic
thoughts in your head.
All your hate
and longing to be dead.
You pulled it back
and now you are gone.
You played life as a game, now you can
never come back.
How does it feel to see nothing but black?

—*Celina Victoria Wike*

Thank You God, For My Little Dog

My "Ocho" was a gift from you-
   You sent the best You had.
He taught me all You sent him to-
   He loved me, - good or bad.

He possessed a cosmic knowledge
   of what He was about;
He knew His job and destiny-
   And lived it, without doubt.

He was a perfect symbol
   of loyalty and right-
He did, what 'ere He had to do-
   His light - was shining bright.

He took His orders from within,
   the way we all should do.
He never questioned one command-
   He simply followed through...

         Amen.
      —*Lavaughn Ogren*

Spider Magic

Architect of the impossible
you spin a silver thread between
two pillars of my porch:
a veritable Verezzano Bridge, unseen,
suspended in sun.

I find more webs strung
between the hemlock and the vine,
rooted upon the clothes line:
carefully crafted circles
scarce begun.

Unsuspecting, I blunder through,
then brush away the sticky thread
from face and hair and head:
your masterwork
undone.

You weave webs, I dream dreams,
both shatter beyond recall:
your webs, my dreams
together fall
unsung.

      —*Charles P. Edwards*

Those Three Special Words

The music softly playing
You whisper in my ear
But I hesitate to say
Those three words you long to hear
My feelings for you are so unsure
Though we've known each other for years
If I could you know I would
Take away your fears
I've been there for you
And you've been there for me
Our relationship has always had
Trust respect and honesty
You hold me in your arms
As we sway across the floor
I now know how I feel
As you kiss me once more
Those three words you long to hear
I now know I can say
You no longer have to fear
Because I love you in every way

      —*Amie Proctor*

Kingdoms Come from Your Eyes

Kingdoms come from
   your eyes, and I can find
   your lips.

After your arms I was loose
   under the darkness, but you come
   into my life
   and I start to be alive.

Running the winds
   and brought me your body,
      each curve line
   made me crazy.

East dust wind, brought me,
   your hair blonde, and soft

and I took, between my fingers,
   to start to love you.

Nothing can pick up
   this feeling of my heart,
   because I can say everywhere
   I love you.
      —*Chuck Gasso*

They Are...

They are...
   lost
   lonely
   cold
   wet
   afraid.
Huddled somewhere
   dark
   damp.
They are...
   penniless
   willing to
      do
   anything.
They are...
   homeless
      —*Kris Bunch*

Untitled

When your dreams seem all behind you,
   Your memories all afar,
   Just hold this tiny castle
   I've done it lots myself.
You'll feel the warmth inside it
   From every grain of sand,
   For directly in the middle
   I've molded all our plans.
   Be they only for a moment,
   Be they for a long-long time,
   True friendship lasts forever,
   And so this fortress stands...

      —*Margaret Doty Edwards*

You Were There Again

Your the light of my life
Your the sweetness in my sorrow
You keep all of passions promises
As if there were no tomorrow

Your the rose in my winter
Your the voice in my heart
Come love me a stranger
And will never be apart

To love again
The remembrance of a burning desire
You a perfect stranger
Have made my standards higher

The summers end
The crossings begin
Once in this lifetime
You were there again
      —*Nicole K. Best*

Heart's Desire

Sacred stars up in the sky,
Won't you tell me why, oh why;
All the things I want so much,
Must remain outside my touch?

If only I could have but one,
My most sought treasure beneath the sun
It truly would be all I need,
My desire, 'tis like a weed.

My heart can handle nothing less,
Oh how did I get in this mess?
Alas, I fear 'tis not to be,
This one thing denied to me.

So on I wander, not a clue,
What it is I'm meant to do;
On and on the time goes by,
Yet not one tear falls from my eyes.

Endlessly I hope in vain,
That somehow soon, this thing I'll gain;
Although it seems this will not be,
Only time will tell, so we shall see.
      —*Kevin Loeffler*

Over the Rainbow

Somewhere over the rainbow
yours and my dream await.
No matter what it is it awaits.
Traveling up the rainbow to get
there you can see people and
houses everywhere.

All you can do is sit,
wondering when you will get to the top.
Knowing if you forget your dream, it
vanishes into the air.

New people sitting all around you.
One even looks scared.
Crying you hear from behind you, but
not turning in fear of your dream.
Finally, at the top.
Now you and I can enjoy our dreams
till day comes once again.

      —*Shae Schoenherr*

The Farmer and His Wife

A farmer is a special man,
Who is well known for his tan.
Always willing to help his friends,
And is committed to the cattle he tends.
He is King over his lands,
And is used to working with his hands.
Even when the times get rough,
I've never heard him say "enough's, enough."
He just buckles down and does the deed,
With whatever tools he may need.
But without his wife he wouldn't get far,
She is needed to make his life par.
She does more than cook, clean and sew,
She raises his spirits when he feels low.
Together, they run the farm as a team,
Like a well-oiled John Deere machine.
To their two daughters and their son,
They are regarded as number one.
To the best mom and dad in life,
To the farmer and his wife.

—*Colleen Baedke*

War

What does one boy do,
When a friend is so obviously no longer a friend.

What does one boy do,
When there is no more money left to lend.

What does one boy do,
As a man with no more love left to spend.

What does one man do,
When the world is so obviously coming to an end.

What does one girl do,
When there are no more young boys left to send.

What does one woman do,
With a broken heart that will never mend.

what does one death do,
When there are so many more deaths
Left to comprehend.

—*Fi Livings*

The Frolic

The bed will wait,
as I lay empty on the white sands.

As the cool free air on the waters edge
flees slowly from the banks of my heart.

Flowing through my toes,
and crossing over.

The hills are not too high anymore...
as the top is finally in view.

Windstorm in the vast sunlight, then
parading joyously, as the frolic is in place.

—*J. Melodie Zito Balcom*

Title Unknown

In a time no one remembers,
At a place where time's forgot,
The reign of innocence rules over all —
the childlike to ensure —
For not a memory forgotten,
or a story left untold,
this place we call childhood,
and is magical no more.

—*Kelley Smith*

Goodbye My Friend

My gaze is fixed upon the setting sun amid thoughts of wonder.
The reflections and hues emitting from a few puffy clouds,
Are enhanced by the sound of the rippling trees o'er yonder.

What will you see dear friend, as you shed your light anew,
Upon a part of the world hopefully rested.
I will certainly miss you, as I bid you adieu.

Do the people live like us where you're going, dear friend?
Do they bid you goodbye, and welcome you in the morning?
If not, I have a message to send:

Tell them to be like me and take time to think enjoy the stillness.
For we don't only age during the day.
Help us to appreciate life and repulse illness.

I will face the other way sometime later and watch for you.
I hope you will not be lonely without me.
I know that you have others to warm too.

—*Paul Charles*

Recipe for Myself

Take a large dose of compassion
Mix with plenty of self-realization.
Stir in a drop of understanding
and roll in humour.
Handle carefully, or shape will become twisted.
Leave to grow for years and years,
making sure you look inside regularly.
Cook gently, or the outside will become hard,
even when the centre is barely done.
Present confidently
and with love.

—*Dandy A. Pyper*

The Courage

The winning hearts to make us free
No telling why the war was to be.
The soldiers crowding left and right,
Waiting for a daily fight.

Some knew there would be death this day,
But none of the soldiers shied away.
With guns all ready to fire,
Burning in hearts with strong desire,
To make our country free,
They are so generous to you and me.

—*Crystal Lee Miller*

Who Am I?

I am me, myself, an individual, different from everyone else
I am full of emotions
Sometimes I think I am the happiest person on earth
But sometimes I am so sad I feel like going to sleep forever
I want to explore the world and discover the future
Yet I am also afraid of the new things in life
And I am afraid the world will gobble me up
I feel lucky that I was brought into the world
But then again it might've been easier if I didn't exist
I bring happiness to my parents
However I also bring them trouble
I want to fulfill all my dreams
But sometimes I think I am too ambitious
And sometimes I feel hopeless
And I know I won't be able to accomplish anything
I don't think I really know myself
I guess I am just a jumble of feelings, fantasies, actions,
and everything that I am.

—*Wendy Hung*

Irish Blues

A man goes shopping, window hopping, on his wife's birthday.
A bomb is triggered, blasting figures. His life is blown away!
Now his wife looks at her kids and wonders what to say.
How does she tell them daddy's dead? Killed by the IRA.

Recompense, retaliate. Stoke the fire of rage and hate?
Anger people who don't choose, to be a part of Irish blues.

A Derry wife, steps out of church, around her bullets spray.
She barely felt the crossfire that blew her life away!
Now a dad looks at his girl, in sorrow and in pain.
How does he tell his little pearl, mum won't be home again?

Recompense, retaliate. Stoke the fire of rage and hate?
How on earth do you diffuse, the color cause of Irish blues?
Green white and gold, red white and blue, and not forgetting
Orange too.

A man is sleeping, men are creeping, up his dark stairway.
With deep desire, bullets fire. His life is blown away!
Now his wife looks at her kids and wonders what to say.
How does she tell them daddy's dead? Killed by the USA.

Try to mingle, integrate. Douse the fire of rage and hate?
Understand each other's views. Put an end to Irish Blues?

—*Graham Morgan*

Long Ago

Long ago in Bethlehem
A child to us came,
Born of the Virgin Mary
And Jesus was his name.
Lying in a manger on a dark and stormy night,
The shepherds in the field saw an extremely
wonderful sight.

Angels appeared to them
Saying God has sent great love,
He sent his only beloved son
down from above.
They travelled to the manger to prove Christ was born,
And lying in the manger was the baby all forlorn.

Some wise men too had heard the news
And travelled from afar,
They found the baby in swaddling clothes
by following a star.
So when Christmas is mentioned don't only think of a tree,
Remember God sent his only Son for you and for me.

—*Allisha D. Smith*

Forsaken and Alone

It is raining heavily outside
A cold, wintry rain matching the chill in my soul
I have been forsaken by my love
Who no longer loves me
Now I am alone
Cast adrift on an endless sea of loneliness.

You were everything to me
I loved you with all my heart and soul
But now you are gone from my life
Leaving that heart sundered
Shattered into tiny, brittle shards
Pieces that will never fit together again.

You were all and everything to me
Without you I have nothing
Nothing save dust and ashes
Alone, I sink into bleak despair
An eternal midnight of the soul
I am forsaken and alone.

—*Steve Nottingham*

His Eternal Triangle

He,
A cute
Young boy,
Has two girls
Following him:
A blonde-haired one
And a brown-haired one.

The blonde often grins:
"I really want to eat you."
When she kisses his face hard.

The brown always likes to shout:
"My son, my son. You'll be my son."
While she hugs him for emotional fun.

He thrills not because he is afraid of
Being eaten but because he has another date.
His heart throbs not because he feels great
But because he fears he has to be a son's father.

God sends cupid to help him tackle his love complex —
And cupid advises: "Why don't you pick the one you love?"
He replies: "The two fleshes growing on my rib feel equally hot."

—*Yue Ming Chen*

Looking Back

Oh! I wish I was 18 again!
A familiar phrase but think for a moment....
Would you want to live those years again,
Watching someone you love waste away in pain?

Sure there were happy times, moments of bliss,
Recalling who shared that first sweet kiss.
Sad memories too of the boy next door,
Who never returned from the Second World War.
The tears of frustration for a handicapped son.
The smiles of joy for a new grandson.

The years of struggle, doing your best for the ones you love.
Scrimping and saving to get ahead.
Going without till the last child was fed.
Cleared the mortgage! Oh! Happy day!
Don't count the grey hairs, they're here to stay.

Would you really want to be 18 again
    and go through all that once more?
Memories are precious and a gift of God.
    we must not wish for more.

—*Joan W. Gagnon*

Poverty

Right now on a train in a box car
A family huddles together
Just to keep warm
They ride the rails
Not knowing
Where they'll wake up next
The two youngest have never known a home
Their meals may be our leftovers
At time they do not eat for days
But to them it doesn't seem to matter
It seems to be a part of their life
I guess it has become the norm
The baby is coughing
They can only hope he gets well
Someday they say
Their life will improve
Till then
They continue to ride the rails and hope
Tomorrow will bring them happiness.

—*Julie-Dawn Lemke*

Rose

hat is a rose, a creation of delight,
flower you fall in love at first sight.
; scent gives you pleasure, a perfume
u learn to treasure.
rose so gracious in its beauty.
he leaves are soft as satin.
painters phantasy, a musicians rhapsody;
poets gift to dreams of everlasting love.
his is a rose, the flower of delight,
harmony of colour, a symphony in its might.

—*Margaret Werner*

elease Me

As the sadness comes my tears flow free,
A little girl sits under an apple tree.
Forever alone and always crying
'Till she said goodbye and started dying.
I didn't know, she wasn't really dead,
I had no body; just one gigantic head!
hen one night she came to me with magic in her eyes,
Playing with the moonbeam brightening up the skies.
Smiling sadly she touched me and said,
You sure look funny - just one big head.
So remember this, my darling little child
Our journey together is over for a while.
When things get rough with grave concerns
will collect the knowledge you've no time to learn,
Inside your head is the best escape
My magic will give you that break.
As the years go by, the magic I gave you this way
Will be our connection to release me some day.
Although we will be travelling together side by side,
We will not meet again 'till you reach the age I died.

—*Lynn Tyers*

The Final Frontier

Out in the inky darkness of space, floats a planet
a lonely planet
with a tear falling, from an unseen eye!
A quiet eerie serenity enfolds the remains of a lost race.
I float, through the eyes of my subconscious,
and wander, through the strangeness of space
death all around me!
Giant metal robots, wander through the Universe,
Colliding with bursts of light, that shatter the darkness!
Oh! Man, that they call "Human!"
How could you breed such destruction?
And leave a legacy, of hatred, and greed
for eyes, that see not, and ears, that hear no more!
Slowly, ever so slowly, I sink into the whirlpool of
blackness,
where "nothingness" is my friend
in the junkyard of "Human Modernism,"
Where there is no pain, no laughter,
Only silence!

—*Jamie*

Untitled

Surreal spheres;
Your deep pools,
Light as air.
There ethereal haze
Of celestial hues,
silver and blue,
Piercing my soul,
Yet open doors to...
In stolen moments
I swim there.

—*William Charles Vallette*

The Magical Symbol of the Unicorn

The magical symbol of the Unicorn,
a magnificent sight of true devotion.
The expressions of love, friendship and pride.
I never had many friends but then a true friendship was born
in the name of April. I was overwhelmed with emotion.
She was something really special that I cried.

The thought of a new found friend, a Unicorn came over me.
She's the closest friend I've ever known.
I miss her but I still keep in touch.
She's great fun, she's a joy to be with.
I miss her company. Since I met her, our friendship has really
grown. She was my tutor on a course.
Looking back the memories hurt so much.
She's not just any old joy. She's April Joy Jones.
That's her name. What good times we had together.
Helping each other, she brought me out.
I was nervous and shy as I ever was.
I made new friends and she was the best of all.
Looking back on it tears flow as things will never be the same.
The magic of the Unicorn. That's what friends like April are
about. Someone to talk to, share with, confide in.
She's been kind to me. Without her I'm lost.
The Unicorn over me, feelings flow
As April's my dear friend I love. It's beautiful.

—*Edward G. Scullion*

A Life to a Life

What is it that binds a life to a life,
A man to a woman, a husband to a wife.
As in this world he must abide,
He wants an angel by his side.
And when he thinks he's a lonely man,
Along she comes and takes his hand.
He wakes each day and finds her there,
He knows she's someone who always cares.
He makes mistakes but she gives him time,
And through them all, she always shines.
She helps him through and helps him see,
Just who it is that he will be.
He loves her deeply and this he knows,
His love for her will always grow.
The lesson here they know is just,
The lesson here is love and trust.
Remember what binds a life to a life,
It's trust and love, life after life.

—*Terrance Lee Conrad*

October Parting

Dusk deepens
A night hawk lights on a dead cottonwood, waiting
While a barn owl staggers on a bend bough and blinks
At a chipmunk who takes cover in time.
An opal moon surfaces the hills, spilling its radiance
On the water below,
And up from the lake comes the haunting cry of the loon.
A "kokanee" jumps, its pink spawning body
Silvered once again in the moonlight.
A wind stirs in the pines and the cones drops one by one
On a bed of dry leaves blown from the poplars,
And on a damp log a frog begins his night song.
Dew forms on the reed grass by the wharf
And suddenly it's cold, and it is time to go,
Winter is coming.

—*P. M. Gray*

Met An Old Soul

He squatted perched against the curb
a poor man a tramp.
The lunch groups, gossip hounds mingled
so my bench gave room.

My body, jolts with a caution
senses scream alert.
The air dulls, sick decay falls close
but I speak controlled.

His clothes, rags heavily hung on bones
that tales weaved advise.
Beacon lit, he controls masters
a prododist a sage.

My heart, thaws in awe of his prose
those first fears abated.
Now the mood spell-bound, is enthrall
as I'm his student.

Soul-mates, while nature sung in us
with lessons absorbed.
An old man an auger, a guide
anoints me to see.

—*S. Grant*

"Black"

Black
A shade or color taken for granted
Brought down with little time to be saved,
A color judged a shade dark;
Too dark for white mens' eyes.
A culture rich with originality.
People on fire with pride,
A color so wrongly categorized
Leaving our world without peace!

Black
Hungry people starving for love
To love as one, to unite as equals
A color stripped bare of respect
A shade torn in half
For the difference in skin is our world's enemy!

Black, What does it really mean?
When love is felt, it's felt from the heart,
A heart is not masked with color,
Two races like night and day
Not willing to create the sunset of peace!

—*Andrea Marthinsen*

Kuatshua

Kuatshua, I muse. What does it mean?
A strip of sand where whitened sea shells gleam?
Or steady swish of waves upon the shore?
Or blue sky where the sea gulls skim and soar?

Is it the land where trees and shrubs grow free
That lies between the inlet and the sea?
Or where, caught in the driftwood, rocks and sand
I find glass bubbles from a far-off land?

Perhaps that looped tree trunk was, long ago,
A snare to catch a rabbit in the snow.
Or, maybe, some great native god forgot
And left his wooden bracelet on this spot.

Named by the people of an ancient race,
Long, long before I ever saw this place.
What does it mean? What does it mean to me,
This glorious bit of earth and sky and sea?

—*Agnes Fisher*

Masquerade

A crystal mirror, a shattered image,
A thousand eyes stare out from me.
Different names and different faces,
Different voices and different lives
But all belong to me.
A single sliver, a tiny shard, A voice within the wind.
A single face within a thousand, a single voice that cries.
One wave within an ocean, that is what I see,
Find the true image within the maze, find it, find me,
For I no longer know who I see.
I diminish with each passing day,
As more cracks within the crystal appear.
Live them, feel them, know them, be them.
They are me and I am them but I am lost within.
Which image is reality? Which is illusion? Them or me?
Who is the face behind the masquerade mask?
Is it Leah? Is it Alana or Ariadne or is it me?

—*Julie Lynne Rickett*

To Mothers

Today I received a tribute,
A token of joy and pride,
A moment of love and affection,
In our times endless flowing tide.

For a beautiful bouquet was chosen,
By six little hands with care,
It looked, for the world, like dandelions and grass,
But the love and affection were there.

I wondered — just how many mothers,
Throughout the course of time,
Have received a bouquet — as I have,
A "Thanks" from an age in its prime.

And I pray to God to keep with them,
The beautiful innocence of youth,
And to instill in their souls forever,
That love and nature are truth!

—*Arlene Bartley*

Dreaming

I dream of long sandy beaches.
A trite sort of illusion
Held dear by the bored,
The mentally unemployed;
The over-worked, in moments of stress.

Which of the above is me?
Are the others right or wrong,
Or are they merely different.

And why beaches with long waving seaweed hair?
Why not fields or forest or views
Or any of those freedom nature places
That whisper to the soul in torment,
Or to the individually bored and socially acceptable
Little people in little spheres.

Everyone has the right to watch the grass grow.
Yet the thought is too shattering;
Louder than incessant traffic,
Office gossip and city speed.
Silence can be frightening and time
A horrific voice to be filled, somehow...anyhow...dreaming.

—*Sarah Mahon*

reaming About You

metimes, I sit down and just dream about: You and I. Dream
out how our love is so strong, that it's permitting us to float
the sky. And from the joy our love grants us to have, we kiss
ch other as we fly. In a sensuous manner love will never see
ain; in all historical events visible to the eye. I dream how the
sses we give each other, produce countless molecules in the air.
olecules formed by the fusion of harmony within our hearts, and a
e we so want to share. Molecules when inhaled by all living
eatures, cause them to sing and dance. And as the many inhale
r mysterious atoms, so do the lives around us change to love and
nance. It's in this atmosphere within which we fly, that we are
lighted to have the gross company of birds. Each species unique in
ir flamboyant colours, sweetly whistling one song in these
rds... Oh fly with me, you beautiful couple, come fly with me
d soar the sky this way: We'll be your guide as you go wandering,
t let's fly and enjoy this happy day". It must be a dream for
it seems! Such is the expression of thoughts, from the many who
tch us miraculously pass above their heads. Some who are too
ocked by our informal surprise, can't help but to stand
tionlessly; Like living deads. Others who from fear and disbelief,
n for shelter through any unlocked door. But the majority, hail
us in amazing joy and cheer us until we could faintly hear their encore.

—*Stanton Roberts*

ainbow

e fall was over. On the endless road
ross the fields he was alone, a vagrant,
young, so tired, his entangled hair
as touched with grey. His aching heart was where
s violin was, and nothing in that face
ould tell the story of his life, and never
ould anybody know there'd been a child,
muffled up and waiting for a wild
d rainy night to pass and for a rainbow
wake him up at dawn.. Since then he'd changed
had been changed - now he felt out of breath,
biting wind was like a wind of death
r him, he wasn't afraid, nor was he going
fight his fate. He couldn't only let
at childish dream be wrecked, and so he took his violin...

e fall was over and the ground was dry.
little boy was standing by the window,
muffled up and thought it was a dream,
howling wind, so cruel, and a shy
d shining rainbow high in the sky.

—*Natalia Khrutsheva*

eld of Green

ere lies somewhere a field of green
calling to my soul.
me see what I can offer you
you can be so bold.

y soil can nourish seeds which grow
give you food to eat.
y grass can comfort feet which blister
om the summer heat.

y flowers are a spectrum
colors you must see.
itting such aroma
hich summons forth the bee.

y trees can give you shade or fruit
satisfy a hunger.
I'll provide a grave
til the roll is called up yonder.

—*James D. Hodges*

Spilled Ink

Twisted, tormented and filled with rage
Alcoholic nightmares unfold on page
Quiet voices only I can perceive
My soul is trapped I cannot leave

My pen like a dagger I carve the verse
Writing to escape from this evil curse
Loves won, and loves lost, loves yet to be gotten
The bitter sweet thoughts of families forgotten

The pen can heal my pain no longer
I pray for hope and pray to be stronger
My soul cries out I must be free
Then this time the bell, it tolls for me.

—*Jo-anne Dadey*

Life

I sit in a room
All alone
There's no one to talk
Everyone is gone
The light is slowly dimming
As the petals of life slowly fall
I can feel no movement of my body
Everything is still
I can no longer hear the music
I cannot see the precious light
I can only sense the presence
Of the shadowless figure which guides me
Through life
I cannot see it, it's just
A thought that will always be there
All I know is the darkness and silence
That I live with.

—*Apollo Catevatis*

Alone

All alone, cleaning my room,
All alone with a dust pan and a broom.
I only wished that today was the day
I could kick off my boots and fly away.
But I'm sitting, cleaning my sock drawer,
"Stop!, Stop!" I can't take it anymore!
Maybe I could live on a boat,
And write Prince Charming a long, love note.
Or think of a volleyball game I won,
Or be an athlete who could really run!
Now I have to clean this mess,
If you think this is fun, take another guess.
I can't even talk to my friends on the phone,
All I can do is watch my dog chew on a bone.
I can't believe I can't play with a friend
And keep on going 'till the very, very end.
Now that all of my work is done,
I think back...that was kind of fun!

—*Sherilyn Chorney*

Little Girl

I know a little girl
Who has just turned five
So off to school she'll go
With a yearning so alive
To miss her when she goes
To smile at her sadly
But I know she'll come back home
For I'm the little girl's daddy.

—*R. Richmond*

Tempest of Love

Wind tosses my desires; that lonely walk
alone; in my passionate rain; languishing in
romantic shivers of love.

Rain drops, so softly sad; drenching my
asundered heart in that yearning for, you,
CATS. And you care nought.

Cats, now that you've bewitched me, I'm lost
in the serenade of your lambent eyes;
in this wild night. And I'm imperfect for you.

Your euphony, eternally soothing the
tempest of my afflictions. O Seraph! I need your ways;
the FLAMBEAU of INTEGRITY glowing perpetually.
Why did we meet? Tell me how to lose you.

That beguiling smile; so ethereal; captivating
my self; till my eyes freshly pearl.
O BIJOU! Hurt me no more.

CATS, I'm standing cold outside your
soul. I'm so lost in your hearts intricate
labyrinth. Where have I come?
Where are you?

—*Hassan Mian*

Disturbance

Amidst the disturbing cry I wake from my Ignorance.
Along our highways of disturbance they make us Ignore
the criminals of domesticity who live with us.

No reason to stop, they flail at their "property" and sing.
Their song is of the security within our society
to hide them from what they do which no one sees or admits.

Amidst the bruises on flesh we learn to see accidents.
Along our freeways of tolerance we spurn their closed eyes
but we do the same and do not feel guilty, but we should.

No obstacles for them and many in our way, we stop.
Their actions are known but something halts our accusations,
or finding the guilty, guilty of their harsh disturbance.

—*Rhonda M. Miller*

The Lone Little Pine

All alone and forlorn it does stand
Among the mighty poplars grand.
It rests its weary boughs below
The triumphant limbs the oaks bestow.

Tall as the sturdy maples' knees.
The sun's warming rays it never sees.
The lone little pine whispers its tale
Of struggle and woe in the darkened vale.

No one to coax it on its way.
No one who cares enough to say,
"Take courage, draw strength and might,
Someday you'll be victorious. You'll win the fight!"

"Life will be yours little pine.
Sovereignty and headship will be thine.
Mightier than the rest you'll be.
Take courage, little pine, just wait and see."

—*Donna Anderson*

My Summer Garden

The nursery garden had become
an endless green ocean,
splattered with dots of pink,
aqua, yellow and crimson flowers,
that poked their heads out of
the warm earth,
to stare up at the pure blue sky.
Lemony rays of sun shone down
on my little plant family,
with my little chubby shrubs like guards,
standing proudly,
their green chests stuck out
as they protected the children
who opened their petals like tiny hands
to welcome you in.

—*Patti Kennedy*

Untitled

Come, come you eternal love come with bold
and ambition forward a peevish, my mind hath
been come as big as one of yours, my heart
as great as my reason happy ever-more to
bandy words for words and frown for frown.
But now I see our lances are but straws,
our strength as weak, our weakness past compare
then vail your stomachs, for it is no for a fools
and do now place your hands below your husbands
foot, and I expressly am forbid to touch it.
For it engender choler, planteth anger and
better both of us did-fast for how I firmly
am resolved you know that is not to bestow my
youngest beauty daughter because I know you
sing well and love well, I know you very
well and love well, I known you very
well performance her bright future as you singing
very and love you very well too.
But that soft conditions and our hearts should
well be agreed with our external parts.

—*Mike Oshun*

Little Teddy Chatter

Oh! Little Teddy Chatter was a very curious boy
And finding out about things seemed to be his greatest joy.
There wasn't much a doing that Teddy Boy did miss, He was
always saying, "What's that for?" and "Tell me, what is this?"
And when it came to Christmas time, this curious little child
Asked so many, many questions, he almost drove folk wild.

"How old is Santa? Where's he live and has he got a wife?
How does he know if he should bring a boy a doll or knife?
How does he look? And is he Swede, American or Dutch?
Where does he get his presents? And how can he get so much?
When Santa drives on housetops, how does he get so high?
Does he just go long a driving his reindeer through the sky?
How can he come squeezing, down a narrow chimney flue?
Then when the fire's roaring hot, then what does Santa do?"

Until at last on Christmas Eve, this curious little Ted
Asked so many, many questions and would not go to bed.
So he resolved to watch and see St. Nicholas coming down. And
then find out what he did and when he left how he got up again,
He waited 'till he heard a sound, then down the chimney-flue
A "woo, woo, woo" like someone trying to squeeze through.
All eagerly he knelt and peered expecting to grow wise,
But alas just one thing happened, he got soot in his eyes.

—*W. F. Maxted*

oenix

ke Phoenix I have burnt myself to ashes
d from the ashes
ide myself anew.
y prideful plumage torn to shreds,
sung the all-embracing aria.

w like a pariah must start again
wend inroads through wastelands of the self
til I reach the silent well.
headstrong child, who failed to pass
r kindergarten class.

y only retinue - hot whirling desert sand.
e staff - my maker's outstretched hand.
　　　　—Urve Karuks

oodbye But Not Forever

hen the time has come upon me
d I must say goodbye
ill put my trust in Jesus
ho will be with me when I cry

though life will never be the same
hold on to the hope we will meet again
hen Jesus calls me to come home
join you there as he reigns from the throne.

ill cherish the moments that we've shared
d will remember always the ways you cared
though my world has torn apart
rever you'll remain in my heart.

ough the battle is long
d there are obstacles ahead
now one day we will be together
my great saviour said.
　　　　—Jennifer Watts

Happens in Wartime or Just One of Those Things

ey were both young and in uniform,
d in spite of wars alarms
e day they met and fell in love
o each others arms.

ey made no plans for the future,
e future seemed so far away,
they laughed and loved and were happy
ey only lived for the day

/e're here we're in love and together
want nothing more so they said
fter all there's a war on
morrow we might all be dead"

vitably they were posted
units far, far apart
e each said I'll never forget you
love you for ever Sweetheart!

en one day the war was all over
me an end to the fighting and strife
e eventually married another
d he went back home, to his wife.
　　　　—D. M. Nicholson

ening Breeze

ur eyes are as blue as turquoise
ur hair blows against the windy
mmer night, your body glistens
inst the reflection of the moon,
tasy is filled in your heart as
expression on your luscious soft
ile makes the night more beautiful;
ant to spend an eternity with you...
　　　　—Tim McMorrow

Untitled

You put on the radio to get you going
And it has kept you going all these years.
That is because you are a free spirit.
Even when you type you rock and rive, your light, in flight
The rhythm in your fingers do the big boy's letters
Does he know that you rock on the company's time
It's cause you are a well trained secretary - and you know how
to get away with it
You tuck your mother in - the rhythm a little more subtle -a
quiet rhythm but it's still there and you still care
Take your time brush your teeth, put the radio on, make your
hair nice and escape into your past when your were young and
free just like the music we all live in a yellow submarine
some days - rise up and be brave
you are not a slave, raise your arms up to the one who watches
You always - join your arms with him, He wears a crown not a frown
And He never never... ever stop rocking. He rocks the
universe and He will lead you on a dance where ever you may
be and you will dance, dance...where ever you may be
"Cause you can't resist the music.
　　　　—Martin L. Burns

Communion With Nature

I have washed my feet with morning dew
And knelt before the eastern sky,
In wonder lost, and struck with awe
By saffron, red, and green
That play upon the cliffs and vales unknown
And magic lands unseen.

I have bathed my eyes
In seas incarnadine;
I have dipped my soul
In fiery oceans of the west,
When twilight fades and Man and Nature meet
In hushed eternity.

I have sat dumb in growing darkness
And listened to her voice;
I have felt peace descend upon my soul
From her perfumed bowers.
　　　　—Pritam Singh

Smoky Faces

　I saw hope last night, saw it shining through the smoky
Bingo Hall.
　　And like a sermon hope raced from the Bingo callers mouth,
　　　　　to microphone,
　　　And it spilled from tinny sounding speakers
　　　　　to the ears of the downtrodden.
　"B 6" the caller crooned to desperate ears, "Under the B...6."
　　Big women in Muumuus with cigarettes
　　　　dangling from their mouths,
　　　And angry old men in sweaty ball caps
　　　　dabbed their bingo cards.

　They mumbled their mantras to their lucky charms and Gods.
　"Pick me" I saw them thinking, "I hope they pick my number."

　I saw hope last night, saw it shining on the faces in the Bingo
　　　　Hall and I heard it too.
　　　I heard it come from the toothless mouth
　　　　of the man in the John Deere cap.
　　　　"Bingo" he said, and on his face
　　　　　was rapture. On his face was
　　　　　　hope.
　　　　—Clint Andersen

Ode To The Horse

Have you always had a long face?
   And mane instead of hair
Your nose is hooked, your legs are crooked.
   But, do you really care?
We seem to call you silly names
   Like roan, buckskin, piebald
Your not like us you never fuss,
   But seem to like them all.
Tho' horse I've never seen you smile,
   You just eat your oats and hay.
A sugar lump a pat on the rump,
   And I've really made your day.
You seem to be quite clever horse
   Yet when asked, "Would you like hay?"
I would guess, what you mean is "yes",
   But you answer with a "neigh,"
I know your just an animal
   And you do the best you can.
So do not fret, if I was to bet
   It would be on you, not man.

   —Madge Gummow

Happy Mother's Day

When I think of you, Mom, my heart fills with love,
And on this Special Mother's Day, you're all I think of.
I love you so much words cannot say,
I think of you always, each and everyday.
I remember the times when you made me mad,
I'd say such mean things, and now I feel bad
You have loved me always, all through the years,
Through my triumphs, failures, laughters and tears.
We've been through so much, the old and the new,
I wouldn't be where I am, if it weren't for you.
Now I am older, starting my own life,
Soon to be a bride, a wonderful man's wife.
But through my years with him, you'll always be there,
To love me, to hold me, to talk to me, to care.
I want you to be proud of me, I want to do things right
I promise I will do it all, try as I might.
You taught me to be honest proud and strong
With you behind me, Mom, I could never go wrong
So even though I'm not with you, think of me today
Cause in your hands, my heart and love, will forever stay.

   —Lisa Sinclair

The Summer of 1993

   I see a little river that seems so harmless
and safe.
   I see it right before my eyes, it's the opposite
of a waif.

   It turned into where we had fun all summer, to
something that had taken two lives away from us.
   I can still hear their voices in my mind, saying
don't worry, don't make a fuss.

   Everybody loved them, they were the spirits of
the town.
   Now you look at everybody their spirits are all
down.

   It's hard to move on, it's impossible to do.
   You can't forgive and forget, your heart is broken in
two.

   Life just isn't fair, it doesn't make sense.
   Look at what we have to suffer from, look at
the consequence.

   —Joanne Blouin

Waiting

It's late Saturday night,
And she's waiting for him.
I can hear the bed moaning,
As she turns from side to side.
Waiting for his arrival.
She walks down the stairs,
And pulls back the curtain,
To see if he is coming:
But he's not.

He will stay out until the last bottle is empty,
While trying to gyrate his body,
As the younger people do.

I stare at the pieces of metals beside me.
The ones I have to hide on nights like these.
But shouldn't someone hide them from me as well?
Who is he, to hurt her like this?
So, now we both go on -
Waiting.

   —Jennifer Grant

Ode To A Passing Sailor

He stood above; tall, still and proud,
And shouted the command,
And every one that stood below
Stood proud beneath the man.
Through days of wild, and wind-tossed waves,
And nights of stars, and sleepy song,
Each sought, in his or her own way,
To mend the nets, and mend the wrongs.
And when water welcomed him for final rest,
To claim him for her own,
Though each stood silently, side-by-side,
In each sad heart, was home.

   —Dawn Nevills

Life and Death

It's just not fair, how someone so young would die
and the only sound is sadness and the helpless cry
By the one's who care about the dying young
And the only sight is the clouded sun.
No brightness in every hurtful heart
When the tragic day sets everyone apart.
It made me think, I should care about everything
Before they're all gone and there are no birds to sing
No rivers running through the grassy meadows,
Or little boys and girls playing with their shadows.
Taking life for granted just isn't right
If only life were true, no one would fight.
If only everything was happy, and nothing was sad
When nothing would die, or nothing would be bad.
Everything should be loved and admired
Before its life deadline has expired.

   —Tammy Pruden

Line To My Son

The earth in bondage holds the tree
And for her service gathers subsidy
Which the humble tree doth duly pay
With leaves she strews in dismal disarray.

But the sky from its azure dome doth freely pour
Life-leasing light, life-saving heat,
And rending itself with a thunderous roar
Showers reviving rain on all life beneath.

Despite my need to cling to you,
Like the bountiful sky let me be,
And remember that all I gave to you
Was given out of love-gratuitously.

   —Bertha Fernandes

...e Dark Unknown

...y do i long these urges twist and pull
...d their razor sharp teeth devour my spirit
...p don't pull make it quick and kiss
...etter in the morning when my mind is
...mb from the pain that i suffer when
...rkness descends enveloping me in an
...ereal sea of dense emotion with the
...eat of sudden attacks from the unknown
...pths that we keep unknown from our weak
...nds because we lust
...ust for the dark unknown to lay it's
...ck kiss upon my face and take me away
...an insidious world where my desires
...n rampant and i unite with my demon love
   —Rubina Ramji

...e Mirror

...ere's a face behind the glass that's calling out my name
...d there's a tiger in my soul that she's trying to tame.
...on't recognize the smile, or the tear that's in her eye,
...r strange expression wanders her eye's toward the sky.
...at mystery girl knows that there's a paradise to be found
...t me I'm still searching for that is where I'm bound.
...at face keeps believing, but I still hide with doubt
...d I feel that she's the only one that can let the tiger out.
...ho is that girl who answers? Whispering all night long
...e silent, echoing lullaby, she sings my inner song.
...t now the truth has come at last, that girl in there is me.
...d my dreams captured forever, that's where I want to be.
   —Toni P. Bowden

...eauty

...you must think,
...d think you must,
...ink: Goodness, truth, and beauty.

...d in your life,
...seek you will and seek you must,
...ek: Goodness, truth and beauty.

...t only this but more — for all are one —
...d the one is beauty:
...deeds, thoughts and words.

...we're not living for high ideals, then what?
...e we to lie as scum, conceited in self-centeredness?
...love, no art, no music!

...short, no beauty. Not that you cry!
...en take the challenge,
...d find: Your happiness.
   —Julia Dawson

...tience

...t and stare at the bars that surround me
...pears to be no escape
...affic heavy, the pace so fast
...the while I move slow
...stined for where I know not
...certainty fills the air
...ntent to some extend, for peace I have found
...e tide has not come in as yet,
...gh waters yet to calm
...ne passes quickly
...e full of laughter, tears,
...rs
...eams appear untouchable
...at lies beyond I know,
...th perseverance, I can conquer
...r what I want to be
...ll be in the end
   —JoAnne Dacre

"The Way Of Life"

Sunrise, and nature's call
  And wild craze for - the minds,
The fire for - wants, and dash for - hopes,
  For flowers - the mighty winds.

  Fear and fret for the ailing heart
   And blow for empty vaunt.
  And lament for the lost one,
   For living - the woes to haunt.

The fights and wars for lands futile,
  And party strife in row,
To think of foreign strand I fail,
  One land is sky below.

  Sunset, and the drowsy waves,
   And moaning of the sea,
  Then wink of one immortal sleep,
   And farewell world to thee!
   —S. K. Joshi

Frustration

Suddenly the world whirls out of control
And you realize you're all alone.
Yesterday your life was full of smiles and laughs,
Today you stand lonely, left behind and tomorrow
who knows...
Once your heart beat to a joyous rhythm,
Now it only plays the drum roll of fate.
There's an old life behind and a new life before you and
You're standing in between, trying to decide to take a
step forward or back.
Frustrated with the weight of such a decision,
Frustrated to see what is the will of the hand of fate,
Frustrated because you know you can't delay
Frustrated that you might go the wrong way.
Then all frustration dissolves away
And you close your eyes and pray
That you picked the right way.
   —Katalin Erdodi

Raven's Tears

Is it safe to be in life,
as a person in their lives,
scattered in their memories -
loved and missed, withdrawn from it....?

Hidden underneath the mask of death -
is feared and desired life at its best.
My love, I shall say, for whom I lived,
is gone to a past - and in the future,
which they will never share, will be greatly missed.

So violent out there,
their wanting memories,
for it is all they've got of me,
for it is all, they shall ever see.

They feared our time, wanted his, wanted mine!
In rage I fight, I bleed, I cry, since all I've left to hear
for them, carried on wings - in howling northern winds -
is sad and simple one last - good bye-
   —Sonja E. Posod

Trees Our Brothers

Trees, mute and calm, our brothers
as ancient as we are
their fruits and leaves have fed us
since we first arrived

They have warmed us with their flesh
in cruel cold
Protected us from ardent rays
of the sun at its fiercest

Playing with the wind
as living marionettes of twigs and leaves
trees our brothers with their somber mass
parade on the horizon
covered with fog or snow or ice or simply the sun
like the nobles of days gone by
wearing jabots of lace and wigs powdered white

You save us from self-destruction
by fighting the greenhouse effect
and containing environmental pollution
of which we are the compulsive authors
who would kill even you if they could

—*Pierre Meunier*

"A Day in the Life of Beirut."

Squish..hh crash, went the bombs
as it whistle and cries.
Rid-dd-le-le went the bullets as it
roars and flies.

Bombs crashes in the buildings
which rumbles and shakes
cries of fears and prayers as it scatters
over the place.

It's a land divided, east and west
Christians, muslims they all have zest.
Pray together, stay together and become one nation.
Fighting each other, can't help situation.

No kids in the streets, afraid to be beat
as men in green looking quite mean,
roams idly by, don't ask me why?
Guns swung across shoulders, bullets lined their
waist, its a duty to perform and its no disgrace.

Night has fallen, soon a new days dawning
when will this end?
Oh! Please let's be friends.

—*E. Plunkett*

Goodbye

In the beginning there was love
As light and graceful as a dove
But now that dove has flown away
And I know you'll no longer stay

The memories will last forever
Of the time we had together
And though our love could never be
When I close my eyes it's you I see

I hope in time I'll love again
And that my heart will feel the same
And you'll be happy where you are
Though from my thoughts you won't be far.

—*S. Box*

This Shaky Instant

There is at this shaky instant
as many individual human faces
as there has been independent species,
Ours is not so pretty nor noble
to build false hierarchy
placing God wearing our face as pinnacle
while we hold Nature's faceted kingdom
with leashes and bars and chains;
Proliferate us have flipped the pyramid,
forgetting virtue make false attempt
at morality, and, swimming in ethic's mire,
giving God no due's our greatest crime;
Again, always He wearing our face we call
to save us while we sacrifice our chosen
by territories and ethnics and operations,
while weapons beget weapons in nervous
spiralling and terrified imagination hides
behind National Security blankets.

—*T. Alan Schack*

Remembering Locket Love

The prince of poems casted that day a cheerless spirit
As the travelling bard sang words he would never forget.
'Outstanding and gracious locket love, your picture is not
enough. Answer my question; beloved one. What have I done?
What have I done! He drifted into memory's past to embrace her
A splendid woman of grace and beauty every noble would honor
Always dressed in radiant fashion with movements of an angel
The eloquent sound of her voice was incomparable.
Every Lady and gentleman remembered her smile being renown
Neither her wisdom and brightness would ever be cast down

The first time they met was on a pathway of happiness
The warmth of friendship endured to charitable abundance.
It was not for the sake of love but for adequate admiration.
Fate had portrayed two different vogues for the both of them.
Spectre of time made them part and exchange a prize treasure.
Settled and though older she was like that of wine, a pleasure.
The price of poems offered a golden-feathered pen and
illustrious art.
Like a peaceful river the moment touched her humble heart.
The iridescent vogue Nancy gave him a sparkling self-portrait pendant
It was this locket love now that the prince of poems held extravagant.

—*Victor W. Oliveira*

A Cry in the Distant—A Bosnian Warfare

Hear the cries in the distant,
As they forever returneth,
From the corruption, destruction,
Fires of hell, forever burneth.

Hear the cries in the distant,
From shattered lives, innocent eyes,
In a place so subversive,
From a conflict despised.

Hear the cries in the distant,
When there's no one to gain,
And the bloodshed surrounding,
From the torture, the pain.

Hear the cries in the distant,
Reaching out for a prayer,
With no hope of peace,
When all's in despair.

Hear the cries in the distant,
Every echo so near,
From the death and torment,
And when man sheds a tear.

—*MaryAnn Gaston*

emembrance

he mother's eyes they filled with tears,
 they said good-bye.
oping their husbands and sons returned,
d not get wounded or die.

s they gathered and on their way,
ere was no way to yield.
r they had to fight for those back home,
on the battlefield.

 their coats of navy blue,
d hearts so full of pain.
ey knew they could not stop the battle,
d they would fight tomorrow again.

ntil the eleventh day of November,
hen it finally ended.
r our country they all stood,
d for us they defended.

　　　—*Tammy Greencorn*

eaving Home

he homesick pain does all my soul infest,
s time creeps up and seems to draw so near.
y final day of home's sweet pampered best
rives with my anticipated fear.
he day I wave my last goodbye comes due:
 crashes down like Zeus's lightning bolt,
nd deep inside the thunder rumbles through
y aching heart. Compare me to a colt
at's weaned from it's Mother's care and now must face
he world's responsibilities; so too
ust I accept dear Liberty's embrace
nd recognize this independent cue.
 And yet, I am prepared to walk alone
 Despite these pangs of sorrow to which I'm prone.

　　　—*Tiffany Ann Knight*

reaming

ove floats on, through the air
 time ticks at a desired pace.
here is no more fighting or
ckless bombing plaguing this place.
r the clouds are gone,
d the stars are here, in full force,
d dressed to be wished upon.
he ponds are blue, and the red has leaked away.
he eclipse is over and the sun is out.
he children chuckle and walk in love,
ther than marching in hate.
nimals are fruitful and greens are present,
 longer in immediate danger.
od has answered the prayers of his lambs,
d cast hell from the earth.
he Lord has finally taken us
 into his arms, where we are protected.
a, ya right!
m only dreaming.

　　　—*Steve Frank Collins*

urvival

is eyes were of blood red and fury.
aiting to conquer the torment of destruction.
iery breath of a dragon from the pit.
rength of a cyclops from the forest of fear.
he cunning of a wolf from the wild.
peed of a panther cutting through the bladed wind.
e is the victor in this blood battle of darkness.
ow eyes of blood red and fury have become
iercing blue for Survival.

　　　—*Damian C. Pannell*

Remember...

The wind is howling, the sky is dark,
As we stand in silence around the grave
Of the young soldier who was so brave.

Only 18 and off to war.
Not even knowing what was in store.
The bloodshed, the fear, the tears that ran.
It didn't take long to become a man.

He fought hard for freedom, but all in vain,
As one fatal night, he was shot in the rain.
So we gather around to honour this lad,
And remember the youth that he never had.

As we lay down the poppies, so brilliant and red,
Remember, we came to honour the dead.
　　　—*Jeffrey P. Roberge*

Abundant Love

Being a mother at times makes the heart bleed,
as we strive to fulfill with balanced love
each child's need.
We forget how a younger person deciphers our
response of help and advice;
but also yearn for their respect and some
show of love would be nice.
We remember them as little babes we held
so preciously in our arms,
still feeling the need to keep them safe from
the world full of harm.
Forgive us for loving so much, it is hard
to forget ones to whom we gave birth,
for once a mother always a mother
until we pass from this earth.
　　　—*Lillian Sherrer*

Next to Infinity

Happy death, a one night stand.
At first i felt nothing: Then the rush.
i didn't realize the rush was pain, although i've felt it all
along. Vow, what is this place?
Flying: Now walking.
Want to go over there but it looks too far.
Mind power got me there.
On the outside the shock.
i'm pulled back and that place i'm attracted to is far now.
On the outside; the shock!
i'm pulled back further.
What's happening?
i like this place.
It has its own peaceful, eerie, mysterious ways.
Same as the outside in the latter ways.
But here it has peace.
The shock.
They're trying to wake me up.
It only lasted this long but next time will be forever.
i'll wake and tell the story.
　　　—*Fjona Thorson*

Innocence

Beware of a person who appears to have never made a mistake.
The laws of percentages usually indicate a different rate.
Only one man alone achieved that impossible feat.
They rewarded him by turning his body into chopped meat.
My friend, just stay in there and do your very best.
I'm sure you will be rewarded by being blessed.
Not for defeating the traits that were born to you.
But for possessing the innocence of not knowing false from true.
　　　—*A. Derosie*

Untitled

He approached me on a horse
At sunset, he charmed me to a world unknown
We embraced until dawn
I will never forget his fingers locking with mine.

He spoke a passionate promise
He immediately had me for life
We impelled closer
I will never forget how softly his lips touched mine.

He nestled his hand on my flesh
A shiver overcame me
He gently lowered me down on a cloud
I will never forget how calmly he whispered.

He positioned himself upon my body
My stomach aroused with pain
His touch settled my emotion
I will never forget the sensation.

He comforted me in a dream
A warmness fulfilled my heart
I then knew what love was
I will never forget.

—*Amanda Feltus*

At The Sheba Hospital

In beds of living tombstones, yelling with pains, in crippled
barracks falling apart, intermingling into one big pain. With
the crying voices is the voice of a patient in barrack No.
13. This is the voice of approaching death, penetrating deeply
into the veins and whispering perpetually into the sufferer's
ears. At the Sheba Hospital, spasmatic pains accumulate in the
cup of lost time with bitter anxiety and merge with illusions
in the twilight of love. Burst of new life is also inherited
with pains of another human being. Flower beds on the lawn
between the barracks are blooming with colored blossoms, and in
the beds of the terminally ill, the lives are slowly wilting
like the flowers in the vases of hope. Like the colors of the
flowers which fade away: First the red, next to it the blue in
cloudy sadness, and then the cheering, as if eternally, two
faced green, poisonous and prickly, turning into an ugly
yellow, bringing our dreams into sadness. Our eyes are
dimming gazing into squares between detaining barracks, and on
the walls are glowing queries asking where does the pain lead.
Soon the universe will be covered in cloudy grim fall.
As man has no choice of love, no choice of his life, no choice.
But some granules of hope in his hand.

—*Abraham Ben-Aviv*

Killing Time

He stomps on the alarm clock,
Bashes the grandfather with one of his baseball bats,
Smashes his watch with a hammer,
And sets fire to the cuckoo with a flaming match.
Time won't be making him rot anymore;
Time won't be passing him by.
He's seeing to it that time stands still
By making every symbol of time die.
He rips up all the calendars
And shoots the hourglass with a gun.
He thinks the job is finished
And then he remembers the sun ...

And his face ...

—*Chris Donovan*

For Bredell

My daughter's such a sweet, sweet girl.

I'll love her till the end.
Because sometimes she proves to be,
Her father's only friend.
She listens deep, and gives advice,
That's always good I'm sure.
Just like the kind I often find,
Myself giving to her.
Our friendship is as warm and tight,
As the hand within the glove,
Because one of us is always there,
When the other one needs love.

—*Dale Mach*

New Moon

Going somewhere, don't care
Been there, never the same
Catch a fox, kill a deer
Life stinks haven't you heard.
Toxic wastes up for sale
Buyers gong to hell
Why put down the government
No harm was there, catch a fox
Kill deer, save your soul 'til next year.
Tell once and only fears.
Slip away from it all
Give a chance to have a ball.
Got it now, take control
Have the wind meet them all.
Say hello been here before,
Stay awhile build a wall
What a joke, been told before
That fears control, it'll make you
Catch a fox, kill a deer
Betters stay clear away from fears.

—*Heather McConnachie*

A Caribbean Sunrise

The sun takes a peek to survey the small island,
Before it rises in splendor.
Slowly it rises, its rays touching the natives' homes,
Palms, coconut trees all along the 365 beaches.

As dew slowly falls from a Hibiscus petal,
The sun catches it and turns it into a diamond.
As it hits the ground it turns back to dew,
And breaks on the cold, damp ground.

The rays of the sun goes through the natives' windows,
Waking children for school,
And adults for work
Telling them to wake up, its morning.

The sun introduces another glorious day,
And says goodbye to the night
A day of sun and beaches has begun,
With the rising of the sun.

—*Kimolisa Mings*

"In Memory of My Dad"

It's been a year since you've been gone,
So many things were left undone,
So many things were left unsaid,
As we sat beside you bed.
But, still I think you'll always know,
Just how much we loved you so.
Now I hope you're out of pain,
May God take care of you
'Til we meet again.

—*Ruth Wilson*

Place In The Sun

uthorities do the right things,
eside themselves, in their chairs.

oldiers, the honorary thing,
mongst themselves, in the fields.

oes the sun ever get in their eyes?
o introduce me to the sun,
he peoples' sun,
hining on the different flags,
he people's flags
nder the peoples' sun,
nd the sun's people fighting in it's shining.

—*Chris Freund*

1y Sister, My Best Friend

/e've grown together from our childhood years as companions; as
est friends; as sisters. These tears that fills my eyes,

gnifies that the time has come to separate. If I could turn
ack the times I've brought sorrow to your mind I'd replace it

ith love and overfill it with happiness. I'll pray to the
an above to look over you while you're gone; I'll have a

ountdown until you come back home. It's so hard to believe
ow these years have gone by; yet so easy to understand why our

earts haven't strayed. We've shared some good times, we've
uffered some bad times; The good times are to keep in our

emory - the bad times are to forget; good times are to look
rward to, that only I will share with you. Every moment that
breath, I keep praying you won't leave. I don't want us to
row up - but that's the only place we're going. I couldn't be

ore lucky, it's with you, and we are together. We've kept no
ecrets, we're told no lies, and when it came right down to it,
e've always been by each other's side. You've always looked
ut for me; I've always looked up to you; You're my sister - my
est friend.

—*Joni Zagrodney*

roken Vows

stand on the other side of the gate,
eyond the ivy-covered wall. I see you through the cracks
aughing in her face.

see your arm draped carelessly against the tree
/ith the flower between you fingers.
see your dark, wavy hair;
our long lean face and laughing eyes

aughing, always laughing
1 that tempting way.
our dark smoldering eyes twinkle with laughter.
nce I thought there was love in them.

ow I look away from you;
1y heart is filled with agony, pain.
ler orange curls dangling at her temples
nd that sensuous way she smiles at you.

hear you talk to her in that amused way,
he reaches up for the flower and you touch her face.
ou touch her face! I feel it on my own face now;
hat burning feeling fills my breast.

he times you touched my face; brought my lips close to yours!
h, she has pulled away. No stolen kisses today for you.
ver her shoulder she smiles as she trips away.
ou look on and smile with laughter.

hen the gate is open I am startled; I turn and...
ou look up and smile as one who smiles at a stranger.
ou turn and walk away.

—*Renee Schorno*

MacMillan's Pub

There's a place up along the Western Highway,
'Bout four miles from Ararat,
Where the beer stays chilled any time of day,
And you'll always find a welcome mat.

The publican there hails from Edenhope,
'John MacMillan' it says on the bar,
If you know him he's a good enough bloke,
And his pub's the finest by far.

There's a core of regular customers,
Old blokes swapping yarns by the dozen,
One of them's called Bill Sanders-
He use to break horses at Maldon.

Then one day this young chap walks in,
With a mongrel that's painful to see,
And he proclaims, real loud, as he orders a gin,
"He only takes orders from me."

Now Bill says "I'll bet he does what I tell him",
As he drags the mutt to the fireplace,
And with a casual glance he throws him straight in - and says,
"C'mon boy, git outta there!"

—*Victor Ng*

The Miracle of Life

A tiny human being grows inside you
Budding slowly like a beautiful flower
Every kind of emotion crashes over you
Patiently you wait for your flower to bloom,
for that's when its most beautiful
For such a miracle there must be love,
Love, like you've never loved before
That very special flower needs to be nurtured
To be loved enough to grow at its own pace
To be, what it wants to be
We struggle never to let our flower down,
even though someday we may
We have to give our flower enough space to grow,
which may be quite a challenge on our behalf
Wouldn't you rather love and nurture it just
enough not to have it wilt away,
Then to love and nurture it too much and lose it forever?
The miracle of life is a beautiful thing.

—*Jill J. Pasap*

Love Divine

Writing poetry is no talent of mine;
But being so inspired by the Lord,
Like Milton, I invoke the power of God,
All that in me is dark to illumine.

But all in me is only darkness, I say.
Grumble not thus, comes inner voice kind,
With entry of God's thought in mind,
What darkness there can ever stay?

Give to men and women this message fraternal,
Look within, your real self is Divine.
Give up all thought of thine and mine,
For in all is One, Divine and Eternal.

In all creatures and nature you'll see God,
Then you'll love nature and man alike,
Bidding adieu to all hatred and dislike,
For even the void is not of God devoid.

This is the greatest wisdom in life to discern,
There's nothing besides and nothing more to learn.

—*J. A. Jhirad*

"Holding on to You"

Years have gone by since we've been apart,
But I wish it was still all the same,
When you looked in my eyes as we lay down in bed,
By the light of a candle's flame.

Things have all changed now as time has gone by
But we still talk and keep in touch.
There's something about you I just can't forget,
I've never missed anyone so much.

When we're face to face, my heart skips a beat,
And I'm not sure just what I should say.
I wonder sometimes, if you feel that way too,
...always longing for yesterday.

Deep in my heart, I wish every day,
That we could give it just one more try,
But somehow I knew our chances were gone
The day that we said goodbye.

Like the strings on a puppet, you tug at my heart,
Without even knowing you do.
But someday I hope that I'll have the strength
To cut the strings holding on to you.

—*Jo-Anne Dejonckheere*

For Empty P.

A man may love a woman
But is the circle of love truly valid
Or is it just a fleeting
Gift that we feel for a moment in time
Like a note of clear music
  in the
Infinite Silence
  of
Religious Passion.

—*H. Hall*

Deep In My Heart

I thought I could live without love
But now I think I should have looked above
I kept the souvenir deep in my heart
Since the day we fell apart.

I don't love him anymore
But I miss the love he gave me.
It feels like I want it more
Because it has left me.

It was so precious
What we had together,
But I shouldn't even bother
Thinking about us.

I have the souvenir deep in my heart
Since the day we fell apart.
I shall now move on
Or eternally stay a swan.

—*Cathy Maltais*

Foreword

Men speak to the Gods in words from
The heart, sincere words that rise
With intense feeling. Such words reflect
The truth of life's profound concerns.
They are words washed in lakes and rivers,
Purified in fire,
Entrusted to the winds and delivered to the earth.
The philosophical thinking of the Mayas
Unlocks life's mystery in songs and legends.

—*Roberto H. Romano*

Falling Petals

I said "Please write or give me a call;"
But she didn't,
Women are like that I guess,
How I love this woman,
But somehow we just drifted apart,
Life's like that I suppose...
One day of sun, followed by weeks of rain;

Crying in your heart.

The falling petals of our flower of love,
Slow orange and wine sunset
Of the summer sun.

—*Graeme Cameron Shaw*

Oh Canada!

We live, up here in the 'Great White North'
But we cross the boarder back and forth.
Shopping is cheaper down in the south
That's why there is a frown across my mouth.

Our great country so beautiful and vast
But our resources are declining fast.
So we have to find a way to make it stop
Before our resources finally drop!

We Canadians are known for saying 'Eh'
But in fact we don't use it everyday.
We talk like you American guys
Take a look we are the same in and outside

So next time you are wandering up this way,
Make sure you stop in and enjoy your stay.
We are really as friendly as can be
Just stay awhile and you will see

—*Dawn New*

Song Of The Mountain

My foot in the ocean, my head in sky,
By gentle clouds caressed am I,
As I blanket the sun, sinking to rest,
While brushing with crimson the halls
Of the West;
I am lulled by the stream that gaily goes,
Prancing and dancing as downward she flows
To meet the ocean; and as if to tease,
I am playfully kissed by a fresh sea breeze.
Stars wink at me as they silently creep
Into the sky, when earth is asleep;
And the moon paints my silhouette on the
Canvas of night,
With masterful strokes of her lingering
Light;
I reign o'er the earth and blest am I,
With my foot in the ocean, my head in the sky.

—*Selina Pimblett*

My Love

The searing heat of a thousand suns
Burns like the love in my heart for you.
The smell of dew on a sleeping fall morn
Awakens and stirs my passions for you.
The soft billowing clouds hugging the open sky
Comfort my unyielding commitment to you.
The pale moon rising upon a summers eye
Generates my ardent devotion to you.
The flower that lay bare for the bee to suckle
Bestows from me my being to you.
The majestic eagle soaring with undaunted ease
Unveils the eloquent blending of my soul with yours,

—*Leanne Mulhall*

African Marriage Revolution

that yester custom-reinforced traditional marriage
by mutual conferences between potential groom's and bride's
families. Ululating in resonance
pronouncing bride and groom as wife and husband
with or without consent of both potentials
simmered more often than not
prosperity, posterity and longevity graced the couple
bride price was not the in-law motive
but rather the groom's pride was their price tag

Today, family conferences have been couped
by the custom-defying unstable youths
glued together only by cash power
devoid of any genuine mutual love
make marriages bloom and doom at the same occasion

Couped parents in revenge demand inflated bride prices
assorted livestock, clothing, mechanical wealth and four-digit
cash, Oh poor young and subsequent generations
Will government fix a bride-price tag
or will someone abolish bride-price
or ban marriage altogether.
        —W. E. Nkhwanana

Splendor of Summer

A thousand white doves I saw this morning sitting in the grass
by the river... I asked myself where they come from what are
they where they fly. I felt the splendor of summer and the
warmth in the daybreak. Everything cooked golden, faded
through the hot wind... The girl came up to them. She had long
golden hair, and she bore the sun-breath in her hands. The doves
flew on her hands imbibing the warmth and the spring of a dream
she narrated the stories, I couldn't hear well... and they
listened to her, and they followed every step of her. She was
so beautiful... then in a minute she disappeared, surrendered
herself in the warmth of the sun in the endlessness of gold and
splendor... a thousand white doves wided their wings and took
the course of the sky... I remained there sitting in the grass
by the river. I heard how it runs, taking the splendor of
summer and warmth in the daybreak. There was no more gold...
remained just grayish of bottom. Everything changed,
became black, silently. I couldn't bore that, so I stood up
and looked away for the new splendor of summer, a thousand
white doves by the river in the daybreak.
        —Danny Bankovic

You Shine

For every heartbreak that you endure, for all of life's
challenges no matter how small and obscure; there is something
comforting you will find and that is the strength and courage
to see that only through struggle can you shine. When it seems
hopeless and you want to give in; give yourself the credit to
reach that power that comes from within. The roads you took got
you to here and now; the years and tears of lessons that you
must make work for you somehow. Never resent the little falls
you must take; your character and your heart grow from the
repair as they've learned from the break. In everything there's
always some good; don't think, "what if I had..." take a deep
breath and say, "what if I could..." There will always be
storms; you must be strong. Tears are like the rain, necessary in
life but never for long. Put the rocks of the past far behind;
hold close the gems of the future and smile, because like them,
you shine.
        —Candice V. Sheldon

"Christmas Time"

It's Christmas time, and most are smiling,
Children in angel wings look so beguiling.
Stores are piled high with shoppers and gifts,
They're trying to find the wishes on lists
Clutched in their hands as they scurry along,
Rushing to beat the maddening throng.

But, down in the Ghetto, there's a different scene
There's no laughing children, and faces are mean,
As they scurry from trash can to alley looking for a bed.
Just for one night to lay down their heads
They rush to the stores, it's just to keep warm
For them, there will be no Happy Christmas Morn!

It's Christmas time; but where's the spirit?
Is there anyone out there who can hear it?
We must start to listen, about the other choices
We must start to hear the needs of the voices.
The time is now, to be generous and give
That all God's children have a place to live.
        —V. Arlene Bourne

Wasp

Wasp makes me tingle with fear
clad in mustard and black, furry black;
as he buzzes, hovers around my vicinity.
He has the power to kill if eaten,
to hurt painfully if not.
Suspended in dizzy air,
motor rasping away
with dexterous dodge-ability.
But landing in my hair is close enough
brave knight,
I can kill too.

Intestines squashed out,
limbs and tail still wriggling
I watch my morning adversary
and write this elegy.
I didn't want to hurt you,
at pains I set you free
but back you came into
my warm nest,
disturbing my work intensely.
        —M. J. Timms

Untitled

This sleazy guy here
claims that he's in love with me
which is hard to believe
coming from his mouth
he makes me feel like a piece of meat
ready to be bitten into
and he thinks that I like it.
He showers me with gifts
which are probably stolen
and fills my house with red coloured roses.

His obsession must stop
it's driving me mad!
I protest I'm not worth it
but he says he's got it bad.

That's it I give up, I can't take this any longer!
I'll just close my eyes, and pretend that's it's over.

Three months later, he finally gets me
Well, what could I have done?
I was intrigued by his beauty...
Yeah right — It was his money.
        —Voula Tsiakos

Six Cavaliers...

Six cavaliers,
Clinging to their saddles,
Sheltered by their black leather breeches,
Their horses whinnying and dripping with rain,
While their silver spurs were shining
At the flash of striking lightening.

This infernal roundabout frantically
Galloped around the shaky bell-tower
Of a decrepit old church.
The oldish mechanism had broken down.

Petrified, from my bed,
I was observing this wild steeple-chase,
Already foretelling the worst.
Suddenly, this raging thunder-storm,
Unexpectedly, quieted down,
Becoming reasonable again.

Coming out, a timid and fugitive star,
Chancing a quivering glance.
Reassuringly, a luminous moon
Came into sight. With a sigh of relief,
I then, opened wide, my window.

—*Lorraine Hains*

Peace

The sun is setting. The radiant
colors stream across the sky, and
touch the earth's surface.
The soldier's grave stones are
silhouetted against the pink-streaked sky.
A soft breeze just barely stirs the
grass and leaves on the trees.
The flowers on the hill bob their
heads in sorrow.
The sky grows darker, deeper, and
richer. The land turns blue, the stones
turn black against the horizon
Everything turns black.
The earth is peaceful-no more war.

—*Sherry Kindlein*

Untitled

A word of peace
Concentrated on such a small place,
Where sanctuary ceases,
And anger rules a country.

Questions asked by so many
from men across the land,
where the people unlike you and I,
have only dreams of a world of peace.

Yet with all the hatred of today
and deaths that tomorrow may bring,
we must all join together,
uniting the hopes and wishes of each other,
as a world,
as a nation,
as one.

January 14, 1991
—*Rick W. Fodor*

Tears!

I couldn't hear the wind that blew, or feel the rain that fell,
Couldn't see the sunshine through my pain,
Then I saw that little bird, upon my window sill,
And now I know the sun will shine again.
"Cheer-up" he said, his breast was red, his manner bright and gay,
I have a nest to tend, my weepy friend, I must be on my way,
And saying thus, without a fuss, he hopped down to my lawn,
He grabbed a worm, although it squirmed in a moment he was gone.
Although he's gone, I hear his song, and life is not the same,
For from that day, I'm glad to say, I see rainbows in my rain.

—*Donald Wm. Dolson*

As Your Face You Shave It

I know you read it I know you said it you know who gets the
credit. His compass on the trith an hour ago he left St.
Moriah his trusty bark landed on Mt. Ararat Southern
Saskatchewan then his mind not long gone. He decided to write
"The Decalogue" on a majestic monologue he talked to a moose
saw an arctic wolf joined are chorus this claw hit an icy
play toodle so to moose saw decalogue written in crayon? Sacred
blue was his favorite color weather dreary, weary even duller
rainbow sky ever nigh hope for a world for a world of hope and
love, by and by!

As your face you shave it. Even when knowing so many crave it.
Wintry blast over, facing the mast even you brave it.
Money, do you ever save it? As your face you shave it
Height, sleight of hand, you chant of David wave it.

—*Dorothy Hamilton*

Sarajevo

"Is there anybody there?",
cried a voice in despair, but it fell on ears of stone.
The silent cry of ravaged faces, desperate,
anguished, all alone.

War bombs rain on desperate people
dripping shells and bombs that kill,
crescendo, tempo rising, shrilling,
screaming pain, then quiet and still.

Humanity watches from the sidelines
heaving a collective sigh,
clucking at the ravaged faces doing nothing standing by.

Each lamenting at the sorrow on the faces
of woman and child,
change the channel 'till tomorrow
outraged, blase, primitive, wild, are the
sentiments locked in the hearts
of every you and me,
there but for the grace of God,
go you, go they, go we.

—*Sandra Pinto*

Love

Love is true,
True indeed.
You plant it like a new flower seed.
You plant it, care for it, and handle it with care,
and maybe someday it'll still be there.
If you have not found it,
than this is my wish for you,
when you find love you'll share the reality too.

No matter how far you have to go,
there's always love for everyone.
So don't get down or feeling blue;
One of those days, love with find you.

—*Tammy Regular*

'rough the Eyes of Love

look across the room and see you there,
ashing and handsome, with just a touch of arrogance;
he kind of man every woman dreams of.
/hy then are you standing alone?
look around the room and see,
he quick glances and longing looks directed your way.
ou're a man who inspires others.
/hile never really noticing,
he impact you have on their lives.
s you notice my observation of you,
ou smile and look deeply into my eyes,
nd I can feel the power you hold.
remember back all those years ago,
/hen you came to my side as you are now.
am still proud to call you my husband,
he love of my life.

—Trudy Anne Dodd

)ear Teresa

was a tight fist when I met you,
)ays and days ago,
/hen our lives were made of something else
nd even then
till something else from everyone else;
nd you, the first to know,
)r almost know,
eached under my fingers
nd unclenched my grip
' even for just a day.
1 honour of you and in gratitude,
1y fist is now unbent,
low unclosed,
low unknuckled
nd I hold my hand open and up
nd extend it to you,
oftly,
o that we may walk hand in hand
long the way
)own this dusty path newly travelled.

—Kevin J. Sudot

'o Be With You

Sometimes I get so lost
ays pass and this emptiness
fills my heart
when I run
which ever way I go
come back to the place you are
I reach out from the inside
just to feel your tender touch
but this moment keeps slipping away
look to the time with you to keep me
Awake and alive

—Cherie Erica Hackel

Vhat's The Use

/hat's the use in living if your going to die.
/hat's the sense in friendship if you have to say goodbye.
/hy can't life last forever or just a little longer
'ause I love you and you love I suppose it just
asn't meant to be.
/hy does life hurt so much, it confuses me when I
:el your touch.
/hat's the use in loving if your only going to cry.
/hat's the sense in caring if you don't know why.
/hy can't love last forever or just a little longer
'ause I loved you and you loved me.....
suppose it wasn't meant to be.

—Carrianne Byers

Masters of Music

The fairies' sad music,
Dazzling to hear,
Wafts on the breeze to my listening ear.
It rustles like leaves on a windy day,
It splashes like brooks as they sweep on their way.
It shines precious like diamonds,
It glitters pure as gold,
For the fairies sweet music shall never grow old.

The harmonious notes drift over the sea,
Rising and falling, they're calling to me.
Regardless of what anybody might say,
I follow the music that leads to the bay.
There by the moonlight, I glimpse a radiant sight,
A large host of fairies are gathered by night.

Singing and dancing the hours away,
Their enchanting colours blend, from crimson to grey.
Slowly as rays begin streaking the sky,
The fairies hastily wave a good-bye.

Now, their dances with music linger still in my mind,
And perhaps someday soon, the fairies again shall I find.

—Hazel P. Penner

The Ballad Of The Last Rites Kit

Once when with crime, Before its prime,
Death cheated time, And opted
To kill her child, A she ape wild,
A kitten mild Adopted.

But though she sought Its paw and thought
That she had caught A kitten,
This ape whose squeeze Ignored its pleas
Could only seize
A mitten.

And since in fact, They shared a pact,
That made puss act Like fool's gold,
She used to mourn; Yet this forlorn
Love child was born Changeling souled.

This ape saw fit To be a kit,
That made puss flit To glory,
Where apes condemn
No longer them
Of requiem
This story.

—Jeremy Whicher

African Children

O, African children
Do we really have to suffer?
Were we created to suffer,?
Is it Gods making?
Or ours
If its God's making
Why should it be so?
If it's ours
Why sit for it to be so?
What are we doing to come out of it?
We can only come out if we know the cause
But to me, it seems
The cause has still not been found
Do we have to continue suffering
Because the cause has not been found?
What at all should we do
African children.

—Edward Bartels Sackey

Snow

Snow tiny little white stars
Each one with its own destiny
Some to become snowmen or
Snowballs and some to stay untouched.
Lakes turning into great glass windows
Almost unbreakable and then it all
Disappears within the mists of summer
Bringing back the once forgotten
Forests and fields of God's breathtaking painting of nature.

> —*Philip Monaghan*

The Bomber's Song by Moonlight

"Bombs away Skipper, and I think we're still alive,
Don't stick around until the bats of hell come
Just ease the stick forward to a roartin' snortin' dive
and let's push off to somewhere where we're welcome".

Chorus oh! We've knocked the rubber truncheon from the 'nazi'
bullie's hand, and we've done our best to even up the score.
So we'll drink in the mess, to goering and to hess, and Bosch's
who are boss no more.

Below there cousin Fritz, if you ain't been blown to bits,
Don't trouble 'bout the rubble round your door;
It isn't so long; is it since we paid you our last visit?
With any luck there'll still be plenty more.

Skipper to mid-upper, if you want to earn your supper.
Don't watch the flares and flashes all around,
P for Peter has just bought it. Spect a'one-o-nine' has caught it,
don't watch it 'til it bursts upon the ground.

"Easy Fox" to base, by God's almighty grace,
Your permission for a landing s'il vous plait fill up the cup that
cheers, and order seven more beers "Easy Fox" will fight
and run, another day.

> —*H. Dale*

Snow

Last night, it snowed big white flakes that came
Down from the big black sky,
Everything was windy and cold as
The freezing north winds blew by.

The next morning the sky was clear,
And snow sparkled in the sunlight.
Icicles hung from everywhere and
the world looked shiny and white.

At night the sun went down to sleep
And the moon came up to see the world below it.
The north winds called hello,
And then it started to snow, bit by bit.

> —*Tara McCarty*

An Ocean Night

Alone I descend the rarely used path,
Down to the ocean below;
I listen to the waves lapping along the shore,
And marvel at how the wind can blow.
I sit along the water's edge,
And let the tide wash over me;
I listen to the wandering gulls,
And gaze outward at the unending sea.
A ship slips by,
Heading into the sunset;
Its sailors head out to their only home,
As their destinies and the ocean's call have met.
Twilight arrives, and the stars twinkle,
While underneath, the sea is frolicking;
I curl up onto a bank and drift asleep,
Not willing til morning to leave my cozy lodging.

> —*Malcolm Gorrill*

Thoughts of an Artist

Ambitious thoughts creative plans go through my head a lot.
Dreams of owning a store or shop with all its valued stock.
It's clear at times; I'm there, it's mine, the scene is all so set.
The paintings hang on pegged-board walls, the oil still barely wet.
Of all the masterpieces done in my mind so many come and gone.
The texture of the canvas felt; my wrist has twitched along.
A tree I've dreamed of painting; I've painted many times.
But have never had the finished piece, it's home still in my mind.
People I don't even know; their wrinkled faces clear.
I've tried to keep that image, but in light they disappear.
Images leave when my eyes aren't shut "where do they hide all day?
I wish they'd last until the dawn; better yet just stay away.
Tormented nights bring frustrating days, some days are not easy to
start.
Peace would mean so much to me; what a price to pay for art.
One out of ten, either paint, pencil or pen so few worthy of praise.
I only somehow wish I could change my creative nights into days.

> —*Roberta Carroll*

"The Hunted"

They walk, silently, softly
Dressed to kill.
Suits of orange, or white.
Their called the hunter,
I am called the hunted.
I am the game they come out to play.

They see me now, standing proud.
A rack upon my head.
The span I hear them say is the most divine.
The points there must be six at least.
My head they say, "will make them proud"
Mounted, to hang upon their wall.

I'm thinking you hunters, Who dare to enter here.
With sticks made to kill.
This is our home, yet you make us flee

Hunter you call me cagey.
Do you think I got this rack, by standing in your sights?
Hunter I think as I flee once more, hunter come on find me now.
For this game of the hunter, this hunted one, has played before.

> —*Chris Francis*

The Lock

As the click of the lock on the door that just shut,
echoes through the air, the feelings of total despair,
desperation, anger, and self degradation come boiling
up in the pit of the stomach.

In a fleeting moment faster than a heartbeat, they rip
through the chest that has become tight with fear.

Racing onward to the mind screaming with a common voice
that defies resistance, of the sacrifice that must be made
to right the wrong, they slam into the brain with the pain
and consternation of a planet crashing into its own sun.

Then, as quickly as they came, the feelings are swept away
with the realization that we are all just human and another
of God's imperfect creatures.... sometimes, even the best
of us lock our keys in the car.

> —*Trevor G. Spalding*

Universal Nature

...s the beautiful, misty dew,
...dges its way off the lonely flower,
...he sun sneaks out from behind the clouds,
...nd shows off its mighty power,
...rying up the long nights rain,
...nd the mornings dew,
...preading long, violet rays of light
...nd bringing nice weather, too!
...s grass grows long and green,
...nd flowers grow wildly forming a shield,
...hey bring pink and purple colours,
...hat define the beautiful field.
...s the sun slowly sinks away,
...ehind a large, fluffy cloud,
...he big, bright moon comes out,
...lowing with beauty, and feeling proud.
...shines its nighttime light,
...pon a world of dreams,
...nd truly wishes, the world was as
...nocent, as it really seems.

—*Kelly LeBrun*

Memories

...emories playfully skitter across my mind
...luding my grasp, taunting - now within reach, now hard to find
...olleying yesteryear's errors, frothy ideas, incidences — some
...wretched, some kind
...emories haunt me, pursue me, surround me, keep me in a bind
...would readily jettison some, others would make a fair trade
...o provide space for the new ones that only yesterday I made
...ut the precious ones I'd cling to - how quickly they blossom and fade
...nd time is the thief of memories - a contender of whom I'm afraid
...have memories of achievements and victories that give me a good dose of pride
...ut, oops! the failure, the scars, the sadness I would like to forever hide.
...here are memories of growing up, self-discovery, things over which I
...laughed or cried.
...ome memories aren't worth mentioning (I thought by now they'd died).
...ut all memories are but components of the person you now see.
...hough I grow up or grow old or change daily - of this you will agree.
...I should rid myself of them and start afresh with the goal of being free.
...would lose myself forever, without hopes of ever regaining "ME".

—*Pauline Samuels*

Untitled

...have seen the shades of green melt into a blue
...have seen the crush of winter and the resurgence of spring
...have been witness to the tear of the moon and the sun smiling at dawn
...have seen the purple violet bent by the breeze
...have seen the rain melt into dew
...have been witness to nature's birth and death and re-birth
...have plucked the wild rose and suckled the savage strawberry
...have seen the storm mount purple heights and heard it groan and climax
...have swam in the durge and was dried in a blanket of leaves
...have heard the song of the sparrow and watched it dive to
...ip along the grass-thick shore
...have seen the daisy drooping
...have seen the lilac but for a little while
...have seen witness to the birth and death of Gods & God-heads
...have sniffed the perfumed morning. I have kissed the clouds
...ve tripped across. I have seen the round earth naked - we
...ere both naked we clutched our pink wreathing flesh tossing
...e fog like bed covers from our fragile bodies

—*Charles S. Ryan*

Raging Wars

Forthcoming desolation
Empties into riverbends of despair
Pools of hate and anarchy
Flowing wars speed on its rapids of
propaganda
Collected by the Westerly winds
To no avail

Will this blood bath calm?

Outstretched arms grasp for sympathy
Wounded souls spread into the somber lake
Scars afloat
A ceremonial graveyard
Our oasis coexistence
Poisoned
Absorbed by the Sun
Redemption for fishers of death

—*S. M. Veale*

My Romance Of 40

Mischievous eyes, brown eyes.
Eyes, laughter and Tears too.

My tender romance of golden hair
Curly hair, Afro hair
Small hands that caress
Bear hugs.

Precocious painters, dresses and laces,
Fruit of our exile
Nostalgic eyes...friendly laughter...tenderness

Beautiful face, afro hair
Dark skin that washes my native nostalgia.

My roots of exile,
Temperament araucanian,
Demand of pride.

—*Teresa Leon de Paredes*

The Dreamer

I feel myself falling.
Falling into the dark world of sleep.
Blackness washes over me.
Like an ocean wave.
I am no longer in control.
Something else has taken over.
Bliss comes over me.
As I fall from cloud to cloud,
Images pass as I float by.
Suddenly, I'm awake,
Terrified.
For reality has intruded the world of fantasy.
As I realize that I need to face,
My insanity for yet,
Another day.

—*Gillian Douglas*

"Hangin... Someone Cares"

When you feel your world is low
There is something that I think you know -
When ever clouds start turning black
There's rain and then the sun comes back!
The loss of a loved one hurts a lot
But the healing comes from what you've got...
A beautiful family that loves you so
And wants you to hang in so they will know
That their man is strong and will be around
When their little worlds come tumbling down.

—*Sherry D. Johannesson*

Canadian Snowflake

Lacy beauty
Falling to the earth

Crystal dream
Unfolding in geometric flight

Ivory key
Singing a white orchid song

Alabaster soldier
Parachuting to the glacial confrontation

Cold kiss
Keeping the dark dirt warm

—*Christine H. Pfeiffer*

China Doll

I lay alone as always
feeling like an over priced China doll
with crack after crack I cry
I feel the tears come from deep inside my heart,
deep inside my soul.
    The loneliness is over baring,
I can't understand it, and I can't change it.
Is there, will there ever be another way of life
Where loneliness can't break through?
    And still I cry
But then I feel you.
Watching me, caring for me.
I feel you reach out,
crying with me, crying for me.
I suddenly feel not so alone
    And then the realization hits.
That we can never be together
I never see you, I only feel your presence
I can't hear you, can't ever feel your touch.
    And finally, your little China doll falls and breaks.

—*Jillian Schleger*

The Mask

Who is hiding behind the mask-
Feelings are hidden under porcelain smiles
Tears fall unfeeling behind laughing eyes,
You are not ugly, only afraid,
Afraid of feeling, afraid of love
Or just afraid of me.
I will not laugh, I will only
Love,
Whatever is hiding under porcelain smiles.

—*Kristine McKenzie*

Dream....

When we were young
Dreaming was easy,
We grew up suddenly
And forgot how to dream.

Stop and look around!
Are you happy?
Maybe, possibly, certainly.
Again, you can start to dream.

Imagine!
If you would have everything you want.
Can you imagine?
Finally, you would have your purple dream
And be larger than life!

—*Gaylle Aubuchon*

A Better Place To Live

A flaming chariot rules the sky
flying up, up, up so — high,
Making the world hot and dry
Like a dried pool in the summer months;
But when all is said and done
The flaming chariot is our sun.

Our world is so hot and dry
Sickened with pollution and toxic waste
If we don't help save the world we'll all die.
What kind of world will we leave behind
A world full of war and death
We are so cruel and unkind
That we are destroying our only planet, Earth.

What kind of world are we leaving our children.
One filled with all kinds of danger.
If we all helped out a little
To recycle, conserve and save
This world of ours would be;
A better place to live.

—*Ian Larocque*

Life, Death...And Life

I know you fear me, brother,
For my power is like no other.
I always lurk, I always loom,
I'm spreading my impending doom.

Stop, death! I know I can resist you friend!
I've learned to look beyond life's end.
I'll die to live in paradise,
Thereby mastering your great vice.

—*Cynthia Murphy*

The Inhuman Condition

The night-time brings with it a sense of fear
for our very lives.
We sit in our homes and listen, trying to hear,
trying to stay alive
just one more night.
For the night is their time;
it is when they rule the world.
They come at night
from their resting places
so that they may feed upon us.
They desire not our flesh,
for it does not excite them.
What they want
is to drink their wine,
a wine we all know
as blood.
For it is that element
that they need to survive,
to satisfy
their inhuman condition.

—*Tim Hayes*

The Farm.

The farm is freedom.
The farm is wide open space, big blue skies, tall green grass.
On the farm is cute kittens, fuzzy yellow chicks, and soft bales of hay to lay on.
You can cuddle big farm dogs.
You can ride tractors and horses.
You can hear birds chirping, roosters crowing, cows mooing, and lambs baaing.
But the best thing about the farm is my Grandparents are always there.

—*Jenelle McDougall*

Undercover

I'll wait in suspense
for the arrival of the mysterious man
but he hides beneath his cover
like no other can
baffling the minds of
all who await his unveiling
Trying to coax him from his hiding
all of them failing
He laughs at their attempts
as he smiles so smug
Annoying those who try
to push, pull, and tug
He sings a song
of a sly creature and a bush
As the song nears its end
he begins to push
On the roof of his dwelling
as he breaks the lock
And out pops the cunning
Jack-in-the-box.

—*Lana Magnan*

Eyes of the Ancient

I have seen the world grow
For the past five hundred years.
I have seen men and beasts go by,
Countless generations of each.
My home was so different when I was young;
I hardly remember it,
For the sun, winds, and rains of change
Have fallen many a tree and moved many mountains.
I stretched my arms toward the sky,
Always reaching for the life giving sun.
I rooted my feet in the soil of my home,
Touching the soul of the Earth.
I have endured the ever changing seasons
With strength and stability matched by none.
And to this day I stand, strong and proud,
Always watching, always feeling,
Though at times not always understanding what goes on.
But I will remain many, many seasons more,
To watch, ever silent,
Until I touch the sky.

—*Sean R. Burkholder*

Love Across the Miles

Love does exist across our land,
From one coast to the other,
Our children move to a different place,
Their adult life to discover,
To greet life as intended,
The family as one,
Flying across the country to a place they still call home.

Love of brother and sister,
Trust of husband and wife,
Friends and family together,
Loving each other for life.
Unhappiness may come between them,
Jealousy or strife,
When sickness or death befalls them,
The love is there for life.

—*Audrey Duncan Major*

Untitled

The taste of your love
from within me breathes
A lustre of light
that floods my soul,
forever bright.
As dark rays gloom
near head, near sight.
Searching for laughter and love to fight.
Somewhere far a voice doth say,
fear not my love
for in my garden
fragrance enfolds the voice
of a love, that burns.
Whom the love is sent.
Unto you it is given
an ear to hear.
The power of His majesty forever near.

—*Michael Graham Tucker*

The Full Moon Rite

A witch, for she might be called;
    gathers her tools to perform the rite.

In the air the incense burn,
    candles flicker throughout the night.
'Tis the fairies, who dance the moon light.

Cauldron and wand, a crystal sphere.
An alter awaits, for the moon draws near.

High in the heavens she invokes the night,
    gods and goddesses left and right.

Isis, Athena, Odin and Thor,
    hear me now for I implore.

In the circle, circle round,
pixies and leprechauns scatter the ground.

Crooning, chanting, dancing along;
the little people sing their song.

Mortal and spirits are as one;
    the ancient rite has been done.

Moon descending in the cool black night;
Oh, it is a beautiful sight.
Pagan pact and celtic rite.

—*Diana Keeler*

The Unseen Unicorn

A little boy was walking lonely by a stream,
He thought he saw a unicorn,
But it was just a dream,
His mother always said to him "keep watch and you will see"
For when I was a little girl, I saw not one but three,
So on he walked a looking,
But nothing to be found,
What's this, what's this, what's this he called,
A footprint on the ground,
So off he followed slowly going round and round,
OH! Unicorn OH! Unicorn! Why can you not be found,

I wish I wish that I could see
You standing by my side,
And if I'm very lucky, perhaps I'll get a ride,
But dreaming's all this boy could do,
Then saw the reflection in his shoe,
For up above, not on the ground
was where this unicorn could be found,
So home he went to tell his mother
And tomorrow I'm of to find another.

—*Raymond Robinson*

Flies

Sordid and slow
greasy and grey
Stale thoughts stain the twilight

In my pale, placid bedroom, there is a closed door
Life lies behind it with a fancy for my soul

I'm lying on my bed staring at the ceiling
staring at the ceiling
staring into nothing
displeased with myself

I can't "just get a grip"
or make the effort to fit in
I can't "get on with it"
when there's nothing to live
or die for

Over by the window
by the faded curtains
flies hum with malicious laziness
They remind of the public toilets
and my own social stench

In my pale, placid bedroom, there is a closed door
Life lies behind it with a fancy for my soul
—*Simon Baker*

Hope

Hope is a tiny blade of grass
    greening sharply the cold, brown soil
    when winter has withered all plants.

Hope is a rose in a garden
    battling fearlessly the dewdrops
    while drizzles quiver in the morn.

Hope is a sweet song in the air
    harking melodiously a poem
    even as strong winds slap the sky.

Hope is a flicker in the dim
    twinkling courageously steady
    when nightmare comes to spark a grim.

Hope is the last beat of the heart
    resisting stubbornly the call
    of the streaks of death drawing close.

Hope is someone who cares for you
    dares to brave the narrow escape
    from death with you locked in his arms.

Hope is forever a promise
    as if there were no ends to meet.
—*Remedios Nalundasan-Abijan*

Untitled

A little more than, a little less than,
happy are we, are we? Strawberries with the
perfume of rose escalate to my mind,
new hopes, new dreams, all shattered it seems,
such a puzzle too trifling to waste. Shadows
lurk at the corners feeding off our mental energy,
what a vicious act! A splurge of creativity has
surged through my body causing me to bring alive
characters of beyond. The tip-toe of light seeps over
the horizon commanding me to flee, there has been
a choice of two, but what can one do? Blue.... Red...
Purple... what are these to you? Warm or cold? Bright
or dull? Heavy or light? Pain radiates outward as
it feeds and eats your vitality, then you breath... a little
more than, a little less than... Black... only because you
wanted me to. Silently in the back of my mind...I beg.
—*Heidi Fokema*

Poetry

Poetry they say is from the heart,
It brings us together or tears us apart.
Emotions are labeled and put into writing,
Some are tragic, some are exciting.
Words and phrases can relate a lot,
Its why people loved and why they fought.
Rhyme and rhythm add a nice touch,
But its the words and their meaning
That say so much.
—*A. G. Morris*

Fred Astaire

Have you seen those tapping feet
That keep the rhythm of each beat
He wears his top hat and his tails
The wind is soaring through his sails
He's tall and slim and full of charm
A leading lady on his arm
If it isn't Ms Rogers or Leslie Caron
Plenty of others would take him on

Born in the year 1899
He grew to be great in his own time
With sister Adele he was the toast of the stage
But then later, as solo, he showed his own grace
His half-spoken singing held a class of its own
His finesse and good humour were a sight to be shown
For two generations he delighted his fans
Hearing his singing and watching his dance
—*Cleo Peries*

The Seasons Of The Bear

Deep in the heart of a bear something stirs.
He feels a gentle warmth, a sense of beginning,
as he is kissed awake.
It is the Springtime of his life.
The heady days of Summer's heat
follow and a sense of belonging,
filled with all the sights and sounds
Teddy will remember through his life.
The years go by, and other interests
take Teddy's place.
He shivers, as he feels the first chill of Autumn,
and puzzles at this stage of his life.
He is packed away-far from the warmth he used to know.
He feels the bitter cold of winter, the undeserved neglect
at the end of his faithful life.
Someone, please tell our bear the spring
follows Winter. One day, he will be kissed again,
and he will feel the gentle warmth
of the second Springtime of his life.
—*Doreen James*

Isabel

I know a scottish lassie, her name is Isabel
Her hair is gold of colour, her eyes are true bluebell

Her brogue is fascinating, though hard to comprehend
She says lots of ochs and ayes, but she's a Bonnie friend

One day while we were talking, she asked my secret dream
"I'd like to be a poet" said I, at which she let out a scream

"Nay, Nay, Ma Wee friend, you sassanachs are such bairns
There is only one poet, and that's robbie burns"

Now Isabel's a fine lass and such good company
We discuss many subjects but on one cannot agree

She's got this fierce scottish pride and she will never see
That her robbie burns has got nothing on me....
—*Joan Gidman*

olitude

he wind has lost it's way
ere in the flatland so misty and grey.
'alking through this mist at this the close of day
olding hands of quiet.

he silence within the trees
adows the aching fears
f one who walks alone
ver pebbles and life's stone.

soft whisper above me lets us know,
hat even in the flatland misty and grey
he wind is gently holding me in it's arms
ntil I walk again, but not alone.
            —*Merle Cormier*

oodbye

he ticking of the clock, the music stopped playing
ere on my pillow I lie here just praying
s you lie there beside me your chest gently heaving
fumble for words to tell you I'm leaving
here's lots of old cliches but nothing sounds right
:an't find words to tell you in the middle of the night
s nothing you've done or anything you've said
ust think I'm fed up with two in a bed
I go right now it won't hurt so much
I only want to kiss you and then start to touch
ust need some time please give me some space
nd let me go now so I don't lose face
m sorry I love you but I'm not coming back
just cannot work with the things that we lack
on't turn on the light I can't see you cry
st go back to sleep I love you Goodbye.
            —*T. Joint*

od's Gifts

y God knows where I am and he cares for me
e's preparing me for Eternity
n not in a place of my own choosing
it in the end I'll be winning, not losing
od is using my weakness to make me strong
) help me build character as I trudge along
metimes I don't talk to God when things go well
it when trouble arises, He's the one I tell
od gives salvation and it is free
) everyone including you and me
od is good and He wants my love and trust
personal relationship with Him is a must
e Creator can do anything as He's in control
ving the reins to Him will help me attain my goal
) add any more would be redundant
od's gifts to me are so abundant
            —*Judy A. Waugh*

bscurity

bscurity, when the hands of time are no longer your friend
ding from pain's passion reaching for the end
reaming, when the past and future seem so far away
)u squander through the unimportance created by today.

fe can be many things, but it's really what we choose
me win, some obtain mediocrity, unfortunately most loose
bscurity, is it friend or foe
fe becomes a prison, being locked away with no place to go

)u blame your own failure on other people's success
hile constantly remind yourself, you've done your very best
)wn inside you know the truth, that is why you hide
parated from life's pleasure you stop asking way
            —*Donald Jollimore*

Ode to My Unborn Grandchild

What can I promise you, this Christmas Day?
HOPE, for a safe arrival on life's pathway.

LOVE, I'm sure, from "Grand-dads and mothers,"
Uncles and aunts and a host of others.

PEACE, we'll help you to attain.
In a troubled world so filled with pain.

True happiness - why, "the Golden Rule!"
For a loving home - tis the only tool.

That's hope and love - now Charity,
Real compassion - that, sets mind's free.

The first Christmas baby - many ways like you,
With concern for others - to manhood grew.

His footprints are yours, to seek and find,
The greatest blessings on the sands of time.
            —*Pearl Jewett*

The Other Side

Our uncle Krug has left us,
How often I heard him say:
"If you knew what was on the other side
You wouldn't want to stay."
And though he was sightless these past few years
And dwelt in the dark alone,
We walk in a greater darkness
Than he had ever known.

For he knew God in a different way
Than either you or I,
He took the time to talk with him
And never questioned "Why?"
Why his sight was taken,
This very gentle man
Only knew that this was part
Of his heavenly Father's plan.

And today as I sit and think of him,
I am sure I can hear him say:
"Now I know what is on the other side,
I am with my God this day."
            —*Sylvia Wallace*

Volunteers

To you we want to express our thanks
How your kindness has blessed us all
Any time we need you there's
No hesitation when we call
Knowing that we cherish your help

You never fail to be
On time for those who will benefit most
Until the day's complete

Volunteers we offer you
Our total admiration
Lots of people smile and heal from your
Unlimited dedication
Never are you selfish
Taking nothing but time to care
Each of us are
Ever grateful for the way you share
Respectfully we say in truth
Stand tall for being you!
            —*Carolyn Hockley*

God's Garden

I am like a leaf floating through the air on a windy day,
I am like a cat soaking up the warmth of the sun,
I am like a cloud floating through the sky,
I am like a butterfly on a warm summer day,
I am like a sunset with its rustic hues,
I am a flower in God's garden.

—*Adrienne N. Rowlinson*

"He'll Do the Same for You"

There was a time I never thought I needed God in my life.
I believed I'd go on never feeling the strife. I never knew
life was like a two-edged knife.

Then came the day life's pain struck home. It cut me like
a sword. I fell to my knees, cried, oh Lord! He heard my
pleas, He carried me through. He'll do the same for you.

Now when I have trouble, grief or pain, I've only to call
out his name. He holds my hand, restores my faith, He's my
friend it's true. He'll do the same for you.

He wants to be your loving friend, He doesn't care where
you've been. Are you down and help can't be found, you don't
know what to do? Reach but your hand, He brought me through,
He'll do the same for you.

—*Carolyn Janowski*

Victoria Lori

There was a time when I held you, but I had to let go
I came home to the windswept plains
The love that was left behind, how could I know?
She was born in your tears of rain

I tried to forget you, but you were
entombed in my heart refusing to ever let go
We were meant to be forever, together, never apart
Why couldn't I let it show?

Refusing to let go, you found me that day
standing, staring out across the plain
We spoke of our love and how never it would betray
I would never leave you again

The life we have made, it is the road we chose
It's the path we'll take together
The curtains of our love, never will they close
Our love shall be forever

—*Darren J. Patras*

Whispering Pines.

I lie here in the dead of night, my window open wide.
I feel the freshness of the air, the peace and calm outside.
Quite suddenly I hear a sound that through the stillness creeps,
The trees are talking gently now while everybody sleeps.
They're speaking very quietly, they whisper through the night.
They tell each other of events just hidden from our sight.
And as we hear when listening to music played so well,
The great crescendo comes from far, I hear the chorus swell.
Their whispering turns to singing now, oh what a happy strain!
And suddenly the wind just drops and all is quiet again.
Now I can see them in my mind as I did yesterday
They're swaying gently to and fro as if they were at play.
At first they just play quietly, their laughter fills the air,
It's just as if they're giggling, as if they have no care.
They're being very noisy now regardless that we sleep.
But now until the morning breaks they will their vigil keep.
And as I lie awake at night the Lord His watch will keep.
And as I listen to the trees, I'll slowly fall asleep.

—*Angela R. Moesman-Mason*

My Buddy, Elvena

I can't recall a single time when you weren't by my side,
I can't recall a time when you weren't there,
I can't recall you missing any opportunity
To show me just how much you really care.

There were so many times the world had treated me unfairly
There were so many times you dried my tears,
You always had the knack of saying just the right thing
To make me stand and face up to my fears.

You were first to offer words of praise and last to criticize,
You were first to call me up to share your joy,
You were first to hear my happy news in the early morning hours
That I'd finally had a precious baby boy.

I can't recall a single word in anger ever spoken,
I have only happy memories of you,
And I promise you a word in trust I never once have broken,
And I know I can believe the same of you.

As in all the years I know that we will be the same tomorrow,
You never chose to be my judge you're my best friend
You've always been my pride and joy through all the smiles
   and sorrow,
And upon my love you always can depend.

—*Brenda M. Vaudry*

Why Me?

It scares me. It really scares me.
I don't ever want to go home because it scares me.
I'm never happy, I'm always sad and depressed
I wish my life would get better.
I miss him so much it hurts,
But people probably don't care at all.
My sister doesn't care.
I probably shouldn't feel this way
but it scares me.
I wish he was here not out there.
Why can't it be someone else?
Oh, how I miss him.
I can't think about anything else.
All I can think about is him, and
being home scares me because of what happened.
I don't want to go home because of it.
But I have to.
My family makes fun of me because of it.
Why me?
Why not you?

—*Anna Froese*

No Peace of Mind

Nothing resolved, so much more found.
I feel unsolved and not very sound.
If what's on the paper just touches mind's surface,
then I've got a problem and surface I must.
This cobweb, this dust, should soon disappear.
Things would be clear if I could just face my fear.
The mind never naps, just raps,
then wraps them in memories
to bring home one day with the pen.
Such as battles once fought, answers once sought.
As to why men of rum, always have some;
verse, I mean, yet they're never seen
on the front of the book, 'Listen and Look'.
I'd cross the ocean to calm my mind,
afraid of drowning, or what I might find
on the bottom, and bottoming out.
Yet! Failure smells like a pack of hounds
surrounding the pitchers and their mounds.
So! Nothing resolved, so much more found.
My pen is down, I am sorrow bound.

—*Carla Schwarz*

Will Walk Again

have crawled, yes I have crawled
have crawled on my hands and knees
nd now, I am on my knees with my arms up in the air,
ide open, reaching up to the sky for my creator
know someday I will walk again!
will walk with all!
nd when I do, you will know that I am here
or you will see me and you will hear me.
will be walking with my Creator.
de by side, we will walk together.
ogether we will grow and learn to live again.
o live again for all of our lost souls
he lost souls of our loved ones
nd the lost souls of the ones that
have gone and left us behind

es, I will walk again.
—*Darlene Young Pine*

Am Eve

is not as though I am ice that must thaw
have never known the windowpane of winter
have never seen icicles hanging from trees
have never seen dusk white in the moonlight.
is not as though I am a thief in the night
ith a bullet to the head, if you want me dead
am but the vulnerable, the woman, the cause.
am the syllables you see, the notes you manipulate,
e oppressed that you choose to downpress
e one you want in the gutter, the one about whom, you stutter
am the vulnerable, the woman, the cause.
ook a rib, relieved you of your ego
ceived you, conceived you, built you and delivered you.
am the butt of the cigarette tongue, the vulnerable, the cause.
hen next you seek my fingertips, my lips,
hen next you seek my skin, my favors to win
hen next you seek me at dusk
hen next you need to bleed your wounds upon me,
hen next you seek to hide your hurt,
hide your fears in my weaker tears
member, I am Eve, the vulnerable, the woman, the cause.
—*Jean L. Goulbourne*

ntitled

ave to tell you many things, my friend
ave to tell you all about it all
ay be you feel the same way, may be - not at all
u see, I hate misunderstanding
t by this friendship's always ending
u are the friend I don't want to be gone
at's why this poem must be done
nean, please, never think of lying
cause this really can make me crying
you betray me
ill certainly be hurt
t I will never show it
en though I can be all in dirt
d when I fall in love one day
n't let me go too far away
d when I leave my house for many years
st promise me to keep in touch
d even if you are the one that doesn't care
u are the friend I ever needed, you are such!
—*Katya Baranova*

Bosnia

A place in which the ceasefire only changing
    of the cartridgebox.
Jesus and Mohammed crying tears of powder
    Plenty of prisoners- Torture -
    Electricshocks
Wailing of the women and the children
    going louder.
    This sorrow eternal repeating its presence
    over and over again, is this mankind insane?
—*Seppo Kauppinen*

Trusting

    This is very important now in our relationship
    I know your trying hard like you say you do
        I just want everything to work out
            somewhere, somehow I know.

    We must not let things like this break us apart
    because you know already I want you in my heart.
        I see now trusting is hard for us to do,
    but sooner or later this will come true, just let trust take
            its time.

    You say you don't know, you say you don't care,
        are you sure that's what you want to say,
        it's in my mind just getting in the way.
            As I said it's gonna take time,
    just remember one and one can make us combine.
—*Belinda Pompey*

An Ode to Sister

In early October, when spring flowers bloom Down Under,
I learned that dreaded cancer had smitten you, my sister.

Flying across parched lands and oceans deep
Reached Serendip, seeing your forlorn self to weep;
Your warmth and radiance shaded in gloom;
Your large eyes sunken and lost their bloom.

The next day, you were taken to the theater,
To learn too soon, that it was no simple matter.

So they rolled you to the wards again.
For three weeks I shared your agony and pain.

Then in the end, in God's ways to mend,
You breathed your last to a painless end.
—*Peter Seneviratna*

Love Will Keep Us Together

Love will keep us together,
I love you today and always forever.
Jesus will keep us together,
Let us hold hands and bind them in, love will keep us together.

Love will keep us together
the Good Lord is with us forever, heaven will bring us together
let's ask for a blessing, and cry for each other.
Love will keep us together.

Love will keep us together, thank you Lord for loving parents.
The Holy Father will keep us together,
Let us love closer together forever.
Love will keep us together.

Love will keep us together,
We are the Lamb of God,
We lost ones will bind together,
Let us be there for each other. Love will keep us together.

Love will keep us together,
the more we cry, the more we need each other.
Let us realize how much God loves us,
Love will keep us together.
—*Krystal J. Peck*

"Vanessa"

I looked into my heart - and saw its darker side
I reached into my soul - and found someone I despised,
I've stared into the sun - looking for love -
for someone until by blindness I was overcome
I've walked thru the gates of heaven and thru the
fires of hell - I've talked with angels and devils
And still have nothing to tell;
I've felt joy elation the highest of nights
I've laughed thru tears of despair
And died a thousand times;
I've had good intention - thrown back in my face
Sincere love and trust - taken as lust and disgraced
I've known religion to be the cause of every war
I looked into my heart and saw its darker side
And realized that I too am just part of the
crime part of the crime
    called mankind...
    —David Moore

What Do I See, What Do I Feel?

When I look out there what do I see?
    I see the sky, I see the sea,
I see the birds, I see the bees,
    I see the flowers, I see the trees.
The sun is shining everywhere.

    And when I close my eyes, what do I see?
I see the sun, I see the stars,
    I see Jupiter, I see Mars,
I see gold and green and a blue, blue sea,
    I feel the peace, that is me, me, me.
The sun is shining everywhere.

    When I look out there what do I feel?
When I close my eyes I feel it still,
    I feel the love from the birds and bees,
I feel the love from the flowers and trees,
    I feel the love from the sky and sea,
I feel the love that is me, me, me.
    Love is shining everywhere.

    —Adelaide F. M. Rhead

Rosebud

Little daughter, in My Word thou hast found me
I see thee like a flower, an open rose in white and pink
And each day I touch your petals, one by one
As each day you enrich the earth around thee
And when your petals fall and die
Your perfume is at its greatest and the seeds are sown
Yes, in thee, I have a chosen vessel
I am Alpha and Omega, and you will always be mine
I see thine ups and downs but I know the end
I see thy heart because My child, I have it
It is mine, I can feel it's love, it's warmth
And even when you fade from Me
I just water thee a little and thou just brightens up
And My strength runs through thy veins
Even to the tip of thy leaf
Yes and right down to the base of thy root
Yes My love flows through thee with joy
That many can surely see
And that same joy stays, even when thy spirit may seem down
Little daughter, is My song not still within thy heart.

    —Jean Revie

A Season For Dying

As I close the door behind me
I shiver in the cold morning air
Walking briskly now I feel warmer
as the first rays of sunshine
glide across my face.

Further along I go my spirits lifting now
How could anyone be sad in the
midst of so much beauty
The mountains bathed in warm sunshine
and the tree's in their best autumn dress.

Yet as I return along the path
my spirits lift again
And I know that like the leaves
in autumn my love has also died.

As I close the door behind me
I shiver yet again
I know I'll be cold for a long long time.

    —C. M. Evans

Love Song

During twelve o'clock Mass in Terenure,
I spied her kneeling in the center aisle;
Her dusky features limned with Eastern lure
Might have been Eve's enchanting Adam's soul.

Father Wren's prayers were for brotherhood
Of Muslim and Serb; embattled Beiruit;
A communion of souls; crossing of blood;
An end to sectarian strife up North.

Carmel! Soul-daughter of Islam and Rome;
Eden-fruit of passion-wed East and West.
Venus at worship. Come kneel with me,
Love is one race, one colour, one Christ.

Time will reunite the tribes of Babel,
Over bread and wine at a round table.

    —Frank O'Carroll

Chris

Raging with anger and fear,
I stand and remember what happened here.
Wondering why the Lord took you away,
when there was still things to do and say.

Trying to search for reasons why,
it couldn't have been someone else to die.
I wish to God that it wasn't true,
and that it really didn't happen to you.

Thinking of memories from all those years,
always manage to bring me tears.
Knowing that, I never got to say,
that I love you in every possible way.

Not only my brother, but my best friend,
you promised that it would never end.
Remembering how you used to say,
that things get better day by day.

I want you to know, I think of you everyday,
and remember what you used to say.
For it is love in the heart that helps the eyes see,
what life was really meant to be.

    —Carrie Ingebrigtson

The Song of Life

Play me a song, sing it so loud
I want to hear it and all is too loud
The sun setting, far beyond a cloud
Can it hear your words so strong and loud

The winds of change blowing far and wide
I don't know in who else, to deeply confide
Fear and tears, such a great part of my life
They hurt so much, it cuts like a knife

What hope do are children have, so small and sweet
No fresh air, no trees, well what about meat
Animals rushed to grow and produce
When you think of it, what is the use

Education they say, shall be the key
But look at us now, what are we
So smart and strong, so is the man
Then why the heck is our world out of hand

Relax, think and we shall solve
Because the key to life is not to dissolve.

—*Patrick Robidoux*

Shhhh!

What I would want to be if I was anything
I wanted to be in the world, it would be a whisper.
I would want to be a whisper because
you could float almost forever.
I would be given and received,
sometimes I would be gentle but other
times people would rather not hear me.
If I were a whisper I would dance and
sing until I reached my destination.
Whispers are used everywhere, at school while reading,
or when you're telling a secret to a friend.
Whispers can go anywhere, through walls,
down vents, and through glass.
I would be soft and encouraging except
when somebody gets on my nerves.
Whispers can do almost anything!
They can dance, sing, float and soar.
What I would like about being a whisper
is that whispers can't get caught in trees,
they can't fall down and hurt themselves.
But the best thing of all, whispers are never left out.

—*Kristi Penner*

A Very Special Christmas

The village was like a mountain all covered in snow,
I wanted to stay forever, I didn't want to go.
The enchantment I've been here forever although I only got back
    today.
We settled in our little cabin and trimmed our Christmas tree.
When we moved away from here my son was only 3.
It's that special feeling we get with everyone.
To be home with all the family especially dad and mom,
He's almost asleep now but then opens up his eyes
I know now what you mean mom about home and family ties,
I never knew he understood he took me by surprise
I thought he was too young to see, I didn't realize,
He opened up his eyes today you should seen them dance,
He filled my heart with love and pride.
I thank God, yes we've got a second chance.

—*Carmelita Decoff*

Untitled

Tick, tock,
I watch the minutes pass by,
And as the hands go 'round the clock
The sun slides down the sky,
The minutes turn into hours,
As the hours turn into days,
But each second that passes by,
Makes a memory that somehow stays,
You keep it somewhere safe inside
In the far back of your mind,
But a word or feeling can spark this thought,
And make it simple to find,
We're constantly travelling into the future,
Which is constantly becoming the past,
So each day should be spent well,
And cherished like it's your last,
Hopefully when that thought is sparked,
And your mind begins to drift,
The memories of past seconds and minutes,
Will give the corners of your mouth a lift.

—*Heidi Steenbergen*

A Long Day

I welcomed my final morning when I awoke,
I witnessed the pink-gilded sun climb;
I embraced the dew-dipped lilacs,
And listened to the swallow a final time.

The grass caressed my sandaled feet,
While the bumblebee danced me a dance;
The poplars whispered the silent song,
Will surroundings attacking my stance.

Then I walked up unto the stone,
With all surroundings personified.
And I walked, then I knelt,
And with death on my mind, I cried.

I cried for her, a final mourning,
Tears stained the bed of fresh-turned earth.
Alone I cried, alone I'd live,
Angered, my soul, so foul with hurt.

But then I saw how life could be,
When the sun arose in might.
Death passed away, for I saw the day,
And again I shall see the night.

—*Dominic Girard*

My Husband-Title

Sometimes I wonder if it's worth all the pain,
I wonder if I lose more than I gain.
I wonder if there really is any hope,
I feel like I'm dangling near the end of my rope.
But then I look and I see you there,
I can see in your eyes how much you care.
I realize I have a wonderful life,
Because you are my husband and I am your wife.
With you by my side I know I can't lose,
If we build together there's nothing we can't do.
You give me the strength to rise above,
You taught me courage, respect and love.
That's why I adore you and we are together,
And I know that our magic will last forever.

—*Tracy Gravelle*

I Am

I am a solitary soul with an odd sense of humour
I wonder where my dreams go when I'm finished with them
I hear the screams of souls burning in the mines of hell
I see the blood running through my vampire mother's veins
I want to eat my chocolate and contemplate my sins
I am a solitary soul with an odd sense of humour

I pretend I'm a mobster who can't be killed
I feel my life screwing death
I touch a live wire and frizzle to a blackened chunk
I worry about my house being abducted by aliens
I cry when doves drop from exhaustion
I am a solitary soul with an odd sense of humour

I understand the meaning of a leaky faucet
I say that because I'm alone doesn't mean I'm lonely
I dream about being invincible and then falling through the cracks
I try to be the person I was in 1998
I hope to have the last chuckle
I am a solitary soul with an odd sense of humour

—*Eshe Mercer-James*

To Hilda

If I were blind, your eager, bounding feet
I'd recognize upon the crowded street,
And sense your presence in my chamber ere
Your welcome reached my all-expectant ear.

If all were dark, or sight removed, my heart
A swift, accelerated beat would start
To code its happy message to my brain —
"God's in His Heaven, she is here again!"

If I were dead, my spirit free would choose
Its brief, bright span of Paradise to lose
That it might hover near and in your sleep,
And through your day, its loving vigil keep.

If I were left and you had gone before,
How eagerly I'd welcome Death's dark shore
Where, hand in hand, again we'd share
Life's destinies upon a brighter shore.

—*Jeanette Gendall*

A Girl Called Dillon

Alive she cried!
In a mist of passion, the moon slowly rose
Into a world where fruits are born living.

Would you be the one to judge beauty on normality?
Normality?
A true myth of inexperience,
You see,
Normality is only a personal perception of normal.
And all the while people still starve and hunger!
Alive she cried!

Dillon wept for the forgotten children,
Knowing as the next page was turned,
she to would forget.

The call of the wind whistled through halls and stairways,
Tonight was for living!
Seize the day.

Dillon awoke and smiled,
Welcoming the sun of a new day..... and with it,
A new challenge!

—*Andrew Mills*

Soulmates

The sun's rays drip from the heavens.
I'm thinking of you!
The birds sing their final song of eve.
You're thinking of me?
I feel your laughter!
You feel my pain?
Without words, without touch!
You are there!
I am here?

But somehow . . . Together
we find a friendship!
A love?
And maybe . . . the true definition
of soulmate.

—*Valerie Ebert*

Last Impression

Torments like thorns upon my head,
I'm trapped like a clown in a circus,
your image will not age, as I,
Know, that tuxedos can't talk about sorrow,
Though idols hang from the thinnest thread.
Don't mind me if I seem dishevelled.

Words of the wealthy and wise are long, but their views, so
narrow, comfort less than a sweater of cashmere,
My mind has been battered and bevelled,
It'll be a companion when the chilling winds disappear,
Or reappear. But you being a mere photograph,
Until the end, my pictorial epitaph.

—*Anthony Sweeney*

The World Below

When a vee of geese passed overhead
In perfect calligraphy,
I felt the tremor of shifting air
Bestowing their wings on me,

With neck outstretched, I led the flock,
And called to the world below.
"Look! Look up!" I called,
"Look at our travelling show."

I led my flock over rivers and lakes,
Over forests and fields of wheat,
Over herds, serene on the grassy hills,
With shackles of earth on their feet.

And then I woke from my reverie,
With wings wrapped around my hoe.
But I'd led the flock that afternoon,
And laughed at the world below.

—*E. V. Lewis*

The Muddle-Headed Wombat

There once was a muddle-headed Wombat
Who lived with a mouse and a Tabby cat.
The mouse's name was Mouse, the cat's Tabby
(his tabby coat was pretty shabby).
And the wombat's name is Wombat, of course,
And sometimes Tabby's voice goes hoarse
And he cries out "I'm a far too delicate cat
to stand another day of a muddle-headed Wombat!"
(Tabby and Mouse are very clever
but Wombat's muddles last them forever!)
Well, anyway they're best friends
and their friendship never ends.

—*Jasmin Islam*

The God Tree"

Walking down a gravel path, beside a mossy bank,
In the Autumn of my life who is here, to thank?
God throws up a smokescreen, dimly, he is here,
Waiting in a vacuum. Should I begin to care?

My tree, dappled with sunlight is warm against my face.
My arms encircle lovingly, this endless fount of grace.

So tangible, so tall and straight, it shelters me, it bears my weight,
Communion of trunk with mind, never angry, ever kind,
Here for more than my life-span, more reliable than man.
Selfish thoughts of I and me, are centered in my sunsplashed tree.

When heavy hearted, sore with strife, I cuddle close my tree of life,
It soothes my hurt and calms my fear, if God exists, he might be near,
He might be listening to me, as I commune through trunk, with tree.

　　　—Lesley K. Atkinson

That First Robin Of Spring

I was walking to school one day
In the beautiful month of May.
Contemplating the demands of my age
When a disturbing sound provoked my rage.
How dare he whistle at me!
I wonder who it could be..
I turned around to see
He was sitting beneath the tree.
A smile instantly graced my face
As my heart began to quickly pace.
He was standing there, waiting…
His eyes met mine
He looked oh so fine.
It was then I knew - without his saying a thing
I would always love that first Robin of spring!

　　　—Elizabeth Anderson

The Firefly

A flitting little light
　　In the darkness of the night
Mapping out the frenzied course
　　Of a secret, spastic flight.

I wonder where he's off to -
　　What's the purpose of his run?
This tiny little firefly
　　Who dances without sun.

He's like a star from heaven
　　But so close - yet out of reach
And he's joined by fellow dancers
　　Cross the fields and streams and beach.

It's amazing how God's creatures
　　Insignificant and small
Like the little firefly
　　Can fascinate us all!

　　　—Sandra Cooper

No Where To Go

I walk through the long and winding road
As I walk on, the road gets narrow
Where do I go my options limit
As I walk on, the road finally ends.
Where do I go I'm standing all alone
I turn to start again
As I walk on, the road disappears
Where do I go I'm unable to move
I realize my journey is over
Where do I go no one will know.

　　　—Brandy Armstrong

Mountains Have Their Own Magic

The two of them all alone
in the deepness of the mountains
with the magic of their love
whisping through the untouched woods

Now the sun's gone down, and the fires lit
the stars are twinkling brighter than ever
and the moon shines on the silhouette
of two people huddled together

The warmth from their hearts
is enough heat to keep them warm for the night
the fire just adds that gentle touch
and the blanket keeps them safe

His strong embrace
her gentle touch
to be shared forever
up in the freeness of the wild

　　　—Lara Doyle

A Poetic Search For Meaning

In the future I would want to cry,
In the past I would want to laugh and party.
Now I imagine sea gulls and seashores.
We deceive ourselves and this I would want to do honestly!

Inside and far from reality inside my mind,
We see our thoughts through our thoughts,
To make us see ourselves easily, is not for the sake of
　　easiness.
When we love our thoughts, actions are poetry.

The thoughts of our thoughts are like ancestors and we do not
　　find their remains.
The fossils are brittle and take up all our energy to find.
It is in these that we find out origins and our truth!
Searching through the days but not at the expense of ourselves.
Ever looking and ever searching in this great quest.
Here the quest of quests is at hand;
Never to come before we leave.

　　　—Peter Singh

"A Question"

This is tearful
in the season
when
hundreds of clear springs are flowing
some thirsty ones
are pleased with their memories of water.

Isn't it funny
at dawn
when
the eternal sun is appearing
those called the apes
are happy with
the light from a glow worm.

　　　—Saeed Vesal

Cities

Cities are beautiful in the night and the days,
Cities are loud and crowded.
They are big and have lot's of buildings,
Cities smell good because of all the restaurants.
And smell bad because of the pollution in the air.
The food tastes great and sometimes not!
You can touch the wind as cars race by,
You can see the cars and factories too.
Cities are for lot's of people.
Towns for only a few!

　　　—Corey Rutledge

A Taste of Freedom

Armed with need, I must escape this suffocating box
In which I am unmercifully tormented, bound and gagged.
My struggle reaches nothingness; there is no box.

Exhilarated by such freedom, I take the shape of tree
That I might lean toward the sun, blossom and fruit in season.
Thus, in fusion of beauty and worth, find peace.

But I am not meant to be tree; I take nightingale shape
For a different view, and flit about, shamelessly flirting with
clouds, exuberantly singing messages of love and happiness.

My nature is not bird; I become light.
At tremendous speed, I erase the darkness
With its limitations and weights upon the soul.

Finally, I return to my beautiful shape as woman,
Unrestrained by roots or wings or speed,
And quietly walk along the embankment
Watching the Canada Goose being gently pulled
Along the river's edge, her mate at her side,
Five round-eyed goslings following, their necks outstretched,
Listening to the whisperings of the universe.
Like the proud Canada Goose, I rejoice in my taste of freedom.

—*Irena Kohut*

Untitled

The only requirement needed to fulfill is
To start by using own free will
yet somehow it's not always possible to start everything or do
without creating barriers and much ado
waiting to be told
and on an idea - sold
and shown
and all examples - known
and explained
that everything is inter-related and self-sustained
after it was created and maintained
and that the creator
expects created potentials to be fully realized
thus lessons are to be repeated
until their learning is completed
and there is no exception
from that goal of perfection
which includes the unruly
small potato yours truly

—*Alex Bryson*

Farewell

I hope the world you've gone to
Is beautiful and serene
With birds, and trees, and butterflies
And clear cool running streams.

With pastures green, and blue blue skies
Sweet music in the air
And a feeling of contentment
That nothing can compare.

My wish for you is happiness
Wherever you may roam
With love, and health, and joy and peace
More than you've ever known.

May you see all of Gods wonders
More precious than before
And may you carry in your heart
My love forever more.

I'll say farewell, but not goodby
We'll meet again sometime
My very very precious son
I love you more than life.

—*D. Jewison*

Marriage

Was it a poet that once said, what is marriage?
Is it a bond of a man and woman?
No, it is much more than that.
Marriage is love,
Marriage is friendship and trust,
It is not something to be taken lightly.
For serious lovers it means
Till death do us part.
But for un-certain love
The bond will never be there.
Divorce is an escape
But an easy on it isn't.
Consequences can be devastating,
People are not stones which feel no pain.
The human emotion is a great one
Which can be damaged very easily.
So if marriage is an option,
Make sure it will be true
For life is eternal
But love is just a flame.

—*Gavin Begg*

Epilogue for a Ruined Cottage

See this heap of rubble?
It is I ....
And where you stand
My feet lie.

Grace and style I had none.
My strength has gone with age ....
And my site marks naught
To be writ on History's page.

But I gave a rustic shelter
To a family's fleeting dance ......
And on this simple service
I rest content with chance.

Just leave me
As you found me ....
Unless you'll stay for evening shade
To watch my colours gently fade.
Then, maybe you'll wait for the dawn light
And its new fingers groping for a sight
Of the tears of a brooding cloud
Compacting my dust into a greening shroud.

—*K. W. Brooks*

And Malibadex Spoke of Love... and Said...

Love, is the bounty of your hearts in freedom
it is the laughter of the rain unto the mirror of thy hand,
it is the tears that thou shed
for the awakening of thy dreams.

Love, is the volley of the wounded shadow
upon the battlefield of ignorance,
the toil of the morning's hope
unto the kisses of the night,
enfolded shores unto the deep ocean.

O Soul of man known by the nakedness!
For in the burning of your garments
the "truth" springs pure and innocent,
by the chisel of the sun, immortal,
in the stone, you yearn of life!

For life is love's unbounded gift
the crystal crown of "risen" Kings.
Let life be "breath" and love a "quest,"
upon the barren land that stands
of knowledge taunt, of love begot,
where, the brotherhood of man may be reborn.

—*Jorgos Skiathas*

682

Dream To Fly

hen the earth touches the sky
makes me feel as though I should cry
hen I'm with you I feel so shy,
it when you touch me, and I touch you,
eel like I could fly.
ere isn't a day that passes by.
I can't be with you, I can't fly.
hen I walk down my favorite path,
Iream of you by my side.
1, how I wish that we would fly
irough the sky, side by side.
nally that beautiful day came true,
o fly in the sky with you.
Ion't have a clue, how that dream
ime true. Maybe it was the way we both cried
hen we say in our minds the earth and sky,
ake the space for two young birds
st to fly free with one another
their sides

—*Debbie J. Scott*

1other

ing a mother isn't the easiest thing to do oh how frustrating
must have been for you. We never really understand from a
other's point of view we think it's all so easy, and we never
ve a clue of all the pain and anxiety that you felt and knew.
metimes the words I love you are very hard to say and it
esn't get much easier with each passing day. A warm bed,
ce clothes and a safe place to play the love is there, but
ou show it in your own way, we can only hope that the words
me out, we can only hope and pray. Things are coming
gether now, and I can understand why there were many lonely
ghts that you would sit and cry. Trying to do what's right
ou think, heaving a big sigh, I hope they understand someday,
n not telling a lie, she hope's it's not too late, she knows
e'll get by. It only takes one child to set your mind
raight you quickly forget the pain you felt, and even the
te. You ponder their future, you look for help from your
ate but your child looks to you, I'm about to suffer that same
te I love you mom, and it's never too late.

—*Dorothy MacKay*

'hat's the Difference It Makes No Sense

ife is unfair and so unreal
really makes no common sense
:ality just slips away
o disappear day by day
nowledge of life locked within
ot knowing where to start or where to begin
houghts of loneliness and despair
owhere to hide and no soul to care
fe seems to be only a reflection
f devious minds full of deception
ightmares become, Oh so real
nly the lonely knows, how one may feel
it all just an illusion
aat one's life is filled with so much
onfusion
here is the freedom from all this fear
:ar of fear, will it ever disappear
ould it all be just a dream
ith the mind
r some spell that was cast and left behind
'hat's the difference it makes no sense.

—*Debbie Schuchard*

Fantasy

There is a large bright ray of light,
It shines all day, then says goodnight.
It warms the earth, and warms the air,
Making it kind, of a heated affair.

It dries up the clouds, and the big wet pools,
It keeps the students, away from the schools.
It makes adults, wish there was no toil,
For such great days, are a pain to spoil.

As you ponder, under the front willow trees,
Wondering, and planning what will be, will be.
Letting your hassles, and your worries roam,
Letting your dreams, and fantasies come on home.

Of places far away, that some day would be nice to visit.
Of clothing, and foods, that would be exquisite.
Of cars, and boats that race with high speed,
Of shifting gears, and taking no heed.

When all of a sudden, a dark cloud hovers,
Blackening the sun, making you run for cover.
Spoiling you fantasies, and desires,
Returning the earth, to puddles, and mire.

—*Verna Ingenhaag*

"The Darkness Of Desire"

It lay in the corner shrouded by shadow, warm, musky, sensual.
It stirred - rising like a phantom of a childhood lost.

A puppet, injected with a human soul.
A nightmare, infused with a borrowed reality.

It appeared, with uncommon strength, vampiric in intent,
    a photo play for a foul and vengeful spirit.
It emerged, fluid with movement, from a psyche bruised,
    battered and bloodied - angry and deceptive in strength.

In horror, I watched as it moved.
In desperation, I sought refuge in some memory of affection,
    a fortress of parental blessing, some repose of prayer.

In shame, I thought to find haven from its hunger.
In defeat, I accepted there was no order to my badly
    dishevelled world.

It stood, a parody of life, its breath stank - decaying fetus,
its telepathic screech sickeningly familiar. It reached out in
feigned love to embrace, to encompass - me. We vanished into
the night, our forms merging with the murky darkness of desire.
We would return before the dawn to seek rest, expiate, atone
and, if possible, exorcise the guilt once again.

—*Tom Rawls*

Stranger

I was walking down that lonely road
it was cold and dark.
Nowhere could I see anything,
When suddenly I arrive at a crossroad
As I stood pondering which way should I go
then a stranger came by,
which way to the city I asked him
without a spoken word and with a smile
He pointed to the left I turn around took one step
in that direction when I turn back to thank him
To my surprise I found out that I was all alone
so I started walking in the direction that he had
pointed to soon I notice up ahead some city lights
and above the city dawn was lifting up,
now I wonder who was that man name
who had show me the way to the city of life.

—*Marcel Lauzon*

Let Us Save the Earth

When the Lord created the Earth
It was a jewel in space, perfect in its new birth.
But earth was made too silent;
So God thought of something with intent.

Ah...something with life...with human emotion,
Someone to manage earth with fervent devotion,
To break the monotony of silence,
Akin to unmarked graves.

So God blew life into a piece of rib and clay
Thus...man was created and earth will have him from day to day.
But...as man multiplied
Earth's beauty is dangerously close to destruction.

Now lay trampled the valleys, sun scorched the hills
Defiled the running waters, muddled the meandering rills
Most forests had gone bald
Pollution taunts and flourish...

Are we to await our doomsday?
...Man should put a stop to this sadistic trend
For there's the saying that goes:
"When nature reacts, it reacts violently."

— *Joyce C. Abano*

Innocence

I stood there amongst the pines, when I heard it.
It was but a whisper
and yet it touched my very soul.
It was the sweetest melody I had ever heard.
It brought chills to my spine
and a tear formed and slid slowly down my cheek.

As I listened more closely, I heard it's words
It told of passages taken and of unknown worlds
of treasures gathered from near and far
of Love found.....
and lost
It's words were pure, and trusting
Filled with love and joy

Yet somehow I knew
that one day it would be destroyed.
Stripped of its beauty and youth
And as though it had penetrated by thoughts
The melody simply ceased
And I,
began to cry

— *Lorraine Farmer*

Remember...

The words that are spoken, are never heard,
It's like flying in the sky, like a blind bird.
The feelings we shared, are never forgot,
Just like the battles, the soldiers fought.
The hug that was given, you can never feel,
Just like the wars, so big and so real.
Remember the faces, that fought for us,
Then you can forgive, the silent cuss.
Remember the eyes that cried and cried,
Remember, those were the eyes that died.
Remember the blood, scattered all around,
The dead bodies of soldiers, the nurses found.
Remember the poppies, so true and so red,
Cause that was the colour the soldiers bled.
Remember the fields, filled with such love,
The cheerful song, of a snow white dove.
Remember the song, that played and played.
If you keep on remembering,
The memory won't fade.

— *Stacey Hauck*

Untitled

I found a windmill on my travels.
It was rundown and worn.
The windows were broken and shattered
'fore their shutters had been torn.

The action of wind upon its vanes
sent a creak throughout the night.
It frightened me to hear such sounds
from that lonely, haunting sight.

Warily, I crept into its vastness
and laid down for a spell
And when I awoke, I was amazed
at the fresh-like flower smell.

Across the bareness, inside the mill
was a bunch of wild flowers.
It brought to life this run down machine
by the help of nature's powers.

I rolled my bed and walked outside
and took a breath of morning air.
I began to walk, but took one last look...
at that windmill left in despair.

— *Mrs. Kathryn Wilson*

The Child Within

When I was little I played all the time
It was so much fun that life of mine.
Now I am grown but the child is not
She's inside somewhere and is somehow caught.

She wants to play and still have fun
While the adult me wants to hide or run.
What will they say if I play with glee?
Will they frown and somehow laugh at me?

What do I want is the question now.
I want the laughter, can I have it somehow?
Can I be the kid and still be me?
Can I be an adult and still be free?

Why yes I can if I only try
To love myself and not ask why.
So let the child within me be
The child I love in the adult me.

— *Llyn Wren-Lisowski*

What Everything Builds Up To

It's the smile on a face, so innocent and young
It's the taste of candy on the tip of your tongue
It's the freedom of birds soaring high in the sky
It's the tears in your eyes when you wave goodbye
It's the tip of a rose, where there is a bee
It's the rainbow over your head that you like to see
It's the stars in the sky in a night so bright
It's the sunshine in the rain providing the light
It's the helpless body being hanged by a rope
It's the wish you desire when you feel there's no hope
It's the kids playing jump-rope in a playground at school
It's the swimmer's joy when he swims in the pool
It's the princess' beauty when she's holding a flower
It's the pride that you've got when you have all the power
It's the passionate feeling as they look into each other's eyes
It's the sacrifice you make when you tell all those lies
It's the laughs you share when you're around your friends
It's the dream in life, you have, that never ends
It's that feeling of feelings like never of
All these and more build up only for love

— *Yasmene Sabkar*

ve Crimes

Surrender to the passion of the moment with all
tranquility and distress, to the pleasures
a touch, to the softness of a kiss, to wake and
d yourself within the walls of wishful bliss, to
fy the power of love, that divine inspiration of
gic becomes profound with charming ability to grow
th time. The heart slowly anticipates the seat of
otions and affections, with mind, soul, and courage,
ur heart suddenly gets broken, your soul gets stolen,
ur minds gets crushed, and your courage has left you
ying the unsociable fool. But as you probably
eady know that's how the cookie crumbles, or in this
se, you've only become another victimized statistic
a social love crime.

—*Johanne Raymond*

ve Unfounded

vas hooked on you, every of your movements,
ur eyes, your laughter;
, how you teased me so!
t I was too undiscerning, and just one question,
u dropped me from your affection.
vas devastated,
I see that you were infuriated.
ried to patch up, I tried to forget,
t you were always so tensed up, you too could not forget.
on't see you nowadays,
d I'm glad it's this way.
on't blame you wholly,
my fault partly.
w, I strive to live my life as best,
d one day, we'll meet afresh.

—*Chow Sok Chui*

y Sheppard Blue

t fluffy sheep drift
ily, dream like,
ross roof top pastures,
pporting the weight
the sky on rounded backs.
d when the eye turns away
scan blue pastures for straying sheep,
d finding none returns to the flock
ly to find that it is only a cloud.
t not just a cloud, it is magic delayed
d will become once again, if not now,
reature of blue pastures.

—*Krista Martin*

gether

e've spent a good part of our lives together
arned a lot about sharing and giving.
e've learned to accept things we don't understand
d felt things that make life worth living.

ch year is counted as it goes by,
d we look back on the past.
ere's no doubt in my mind when I think of it
is marriage was made to last.

let's raise a glass in a toast to us
the love we'll always share.
the sense of security that we have
owing each will always be there.

—*Shannon Cranston*

Erotica

Come rest your head against my breast
Let me run my fingers through your hair
Let me feel the weight of your masculine strength
Against my gentle body
Let me touch and feel the texture of your golden skin
As it sparkles against the moonlit night
Let me look into your eyes and know the gentle caresses
Of your warming heart
Let me touch your lips
As your smile consumes my every being
Let me know and experience the joy of your thumping heart
As it gladdens with excitement
Let me feel your quick and gentle breath
As your passion soars
And your soul cries out
...Erotica!...
Let me feel the oneness of you
As time
Stands still

—*Ann-Marie Kennedy*

The Fledgling

Soar alone my wayward child.
Like an eagle in the sky.
Do all the things you want to now,
for you will settle by and by.

Just now you feel you do not need me,
that you know all you need to know.
I will just wait here and bide my time,
hiding my tears as I watch you go.

Gone are the days when you ran to me,
when things went wrong or no one would play.
Your small arms tight about my neck,
and I could kiss all the hurt away.

If I learn to let go, will it bring you back?
Will you tell me your secrets once more?
I'll be here if you ever need me,
Isn't that what mothers are for?

—*Joyce G. Shinn*

Victory

At first the opacity was tormenting
like bolts of lightning flashing into the
heart of my eyes - leaving me with a blinding sensation

Though, veracity was carving promises into the distance
Adversity was waiting in silence

The variegation was present like a painters brush
it was illuminating the future

As the spark was ignited
the race to the summit began with
such fierce velocity

Adversity was rising behind it's shadow like the sun -
As it rose it rocketed into the skies
plunging poisoned darts into the eyes of victory

Quietly riding upon the shoulders of adversity
faith uplifted the wounded
eyes of victory

Suddenly the summit appeared so small
it was then that I felt the winds
surrounding me on the summit

—*Patrizia Del Zotto*

Two Times the Fun

The world is full of wonderful things,
Like the joy and laughter a little boy brings.
And when there are two, it's twice the fun.
With the running or jumping and playing in the sun.
The smiles on their faces bring life to your day.
And you wish for their happiness in every way.
You care for and love them your whole life through.
And hope you've taught them to be good and true.
But when the day comes, they are all grown up.
You still see the little boy with the training cup.
The one he tried so hard not to tip,
Just to prove he's a big boy with every little sip.
While looking back at the things that they've done,
You'll be remembering, it's not one but two times the fun.

—*Teri-Lynn Olinik*

Vision

The winds of life are flowing
Like the rivers, brooks and streams
Always running, changing
Creating new whirls and lengths

The flows are always constant
And the winds are always high
For sailing on the open seas
Leaves one on open mind

Creative are the spirals which encircle every line
Lengthy are the flowing waters.
Where crystal visions are denied.

Encounters all along the way are
different never alike.
So much is there to choose from
within the realm of life.

—*Karen Riley*

Untitled

Love is the birds and the buzzing bees.
Love is the flowers and the evergreen trees.
Love is the wings of a gentle white dove,
Sent with a message from Heaven above,
Love is the touch of Jesus hand,
Love is a promise throughout the whole land,
Love is the waves of the deepest blue sea,
Love is the friendship between you and me,
Love is what makes the world go around,
Love is the peacefulness, the silence, no sound,
Love is the time in which we both spend,
and so finally Love, is a blessing forever,
It's a special commitment that combines us together.

—*Lianne Pritchard*

Provide Me

When you came into my life, I was torn in half.
My heart sank like a rock in the waters, it was
closed to everyone.
A wall of brick stood around me that you couldn't
even climb.

Our long walks, our fantasy's and our dreams we shared.
There was so much to talk about, so much to give. My
soul was taken, my passion was thrown, every part
of me was weak, when you were around. All I needed was
someone just like you to come into my life and show me
a way. To forget the past and go on again.

But once again it was my mistake, I was wrong and over
reacted and look at me now! Once again I stand by the
edge of the shore looking upon the ocean, looking no where,
"Lost."

—*Lesleyanne Hilts*

Sympathy

This is most marvelous time to -
Love someone dearly with sharp eye;
Incredible moments surrounded me too,
For blessed companion truth at time.

Whole world around us make feel sorry
Small as bee, flying with deadly sting;
How beautiful greetings devoted today,
With immense compromises for helping.

Song has been wind sound in sky,
Rain as shower above from cloud;
Thunder bolt seems familiar daily,
Frightened cover poor smile as glad.

High, why your appearance so late,
Drastic experience some folks had;
Magic might surprise in right time,
Recover old dreams for centuries sad.

Purple heart wishes in years to come
Possible symbol for society pride;
Together united developments do smile,
Sweet congratulations sent be aware.

—*S. West*

Why?

Rainbow, Rainbow, Watch it shine,
Many colours, favorites of mine.
Beautiful rainbow glittering high,
I begin to wonder how and why?
Glitter and sparkles falling from the sky
Lovely clouds surrounding near by.
Pinks, and yellows and even blues,
the sky contains of many colours
Stars, stars, shinning so nice, just like the taste of
Sugar and spice.
The beach, the beach, feel the sand,
Rubbing against my feet, and my hand
This is part of our nice land.
I glare and stair at the beautiful sky
When suddenly I start to cry.
For everyday its seems as though
things loose there beauty
So let's all pitch in, and put a stop
to polluting.

—*Shira Moss*

The Anguish of a Hostage

Such sweet recall, the solace of my fears
Might bring the peace to stem the tide of tears
Might shield me from eyes burning black with rage
And might yet quench the thirst I can't assuage.

I strain no more to glimpse the smoke charred sky
Through windows barred above me where I lie.
But close my eyes against this squalid hell
And journey to a place I knew so well.

Once there I gaze at an azure blue sky
And watch as wisps of feathered cloud float by
Where wild flowers tremble to the melody
Of earth's sweet music, playing wild and free.

Where, with a passion sweet, I long to be
Wrapped in the arms of one who'll comfort me
For I was captured then in joyous chains
Now nought except the love of her remains.

Through eyes now open, I perceive the stare
Of sweat-soaked captors with their matted hair
My fate is in the hands they rub with glee
Dear God I pray you've not forsaken me.

—*Irene Sorsby*

...intings

...eam - like landscapes:
...ody, slightly blurred.
...rds.
...aring and fragile.
...ls:
...ntle curve on a dense background.
...nrise:
...ivers of light in an unrelenting sea of grays.
...iniature mountains,
...adows of trees,
...gged landscapes,
...rce beauty:
...agments of scenes long past.
  —Agnes Borecka

...ace, Walk With God

...rth, is the name of our planet,
...ther Earth, if she is called by her name.
...e are privileged, and honoured to be here,
...ving proof, life is not just a game.

...ny, are the people, unhappy?
...hat, makes the violence, erupt?
...lling each other, is not the solution,
...lk to each other, listen, take stock.

...rely, for all of the children,
...nose lives, are so precious, and dear.
...ey, are the people, that matters,
...t them on this earth, without fear.

...ny, are people, dying of hunger?
...hat, stops the food, getting through?
...ed the starving, the children, they're the future,
...ve them love, hope, and compassion, too.

...t an end, to the cruelty and suffering,
...ite, join hands, be as one.
...t peace, be the answer, for all men,
...lk with God, and let his will, be done.
  —Shirley Thompson

...parting from Home:

...son, what is that?
...ther, it is the sun.
...en she picked up sand under my feet,
...led in a piece of cloth, she handed it to me.
...rs flowed in both eyes.
...e heart, greatest bearer had endured,
...yers were in complete silence.

...xious eyes of compound women,
...rious heads of little children.
...hers engaged in the "Fatiha".
...e grabbed again a handful of sand from the middle of the
...npound. Musa! This one, wash with it on arrival,
...e other one, forget it on the bottom of your box.

...followed me to the vehicle, always murmuring prayers in
...mouth. She handed over my box to me, the vehicle departed,
...last tears dropped on her chest.
...rs on my little sisters face.

...stood rooted, as the vehicle coughed and smoked.
...e vehicle rolled, my eyes on her spread arms,
...if they were meant to say, please; come back.
  —Bala Sk. Saho

Summer Day Dream

I dream it the sand, listening to the sea
My eyelids clos'd, 'cos' I don't want to see
The people round me lying on the beach.
Whom am I dreaming of while eating a peach?

It is such a long dream, never ending,
So light and so shy as in the sky a cloud;
It contains a lot of things and its meaning
Is not clear enough to be spoken aloud.

If you were here, by me, on the beach,
You would feel the same looking at this cloud,
While biting with me a bit of my peach.....
  —Claudette Clerin

Today

Today it is the hardest thing for me to say goodbye.
My heart and soul are heavy, but I'm far too big to cry.
So when I leave this place of poems, and songs I love so dear,
There'll be so many heavy hearts, and many hidden tears.

But going home can be so sweet; and parties they must end.
And you can make it easier, by being one more friend.
I'd like to add you to my list, then bid a fond farewell,
For if you want to steal a kiss, I'm sure no one will tell.

Perhaps this is the only time, that our two paths will cross.
We'll leave it up to God above, for we know He's the boss.
So may He bless you one and all, who helped to make my day.
And when you're feeling down and out, just take some time to pray.

I know there are miles that separate the places we call home.
With Jesus' love down in your heart, you'll never be alone.
For with so many things to do - like write another poem,
Be happy fellow travelers, we'll meet around God's throne.
  —Gordon R. Hall

The Uncountable Steps

Night stops and it is two o'clock
neither moon nor regrets I am alone
I drift and I ask me
if sometimes God must feel like me.
Nobody in the long street not even a voice
neither a breath of illusion on this night
nor the old beggar nor the cats
nor the one that sell her soul only me.
And I continue walking and it is two o'clock
and where where will be God.

I looked for Him twenty years in the shadows
in the open window in the breaking weaves
in the coffins humid of crying
where life and love die.
He didn't come to me where He will be in what moment
in what index in what alm in what measure
long street and I am alone and without direction
and everything stops and it is two o'clock.
  —Miguel A. Llado

Tribute To Mother

She gives a glorious smile.
From a babe, love and comfort did she give.
She has shown good leadership.
She can make one's heart fill with glee.
Through our youth stages understanding and
 patience she has endured.
She stands afar to see her child and makes
 herself someone so proud.
Then she sighs, "thank God for this child."
A mother who says her job is done.
  —Grace Wells

The Memories I've Never Had

I'd like to have the memories, the ones I've never had
Of the things my mom has told me about her beloved dad;
He passed away sometime ago, awhile; before I came
And even though he's not with me I love him all the same;
I see him in my mother's face no matter what she does
I've seen him in some pictures and I've heard how nice he was;
I have so many questions, about him in my head
It's hard to ask someone else and rely on what they said;
I would have loved to meet him but I've never had the chance
I'd love to have my grandpa here to sit and watch me dance;
I've heard he was a gentleman and he was quite well-known
And at least way up in heaven he will never be alone.

—*Dawn Hallworth*

Blue-Eyed Angels

Ever present yet out of reach,
No expectations for the future.
Experience measured not in years,
But in the life you choose to lead.
Wanting to teach you in every way,
To taste of life, to feel passion,
For experiences beyond the physical.
Let your spirit be joined with mine.
Let your mind be free to wander.
Reach out your hand, let me lead you.
A new beginning on a clear horizon,
Where for a time we will be as one.
Then return to the present to live our lives
With memories of blue-eyed angels.

—*Karen Geurtjens*

The Trap

There is no right or wrong
no good no
bad

they
are but control disguised

designed to
push and shove the spirit in
a box whereby shine fades and freedom suffocates

poor spirit   paralyzed
a captive of morality

is puzzled first
cannot believe

then comes rebellion
outrage

followed quick by guilt
remorse
and

in the end it heaves
...a sigh

the hopelessness of chaste capitulation.

—*Christian lakeBryan*

The Poppy Fields

Looking across at this field full of grace
Where sometime ago war battles took place
A soft summer breeze rocks the carpet of red
For each living poppy a soldier lies dead.

Not far away the graves at attention
A thousand young soldiers too many to mention
See how they're sleeping forever in line
Wasted from evil and war in our time.

—*Tracy E. Payne*

Class Poem of 1927

We finished our high school strife
no matter what we do.

We've gained a foot hold in this life
we can paddle our own canoe

We leave high school glad and gay
thinking our rug in span

But when we're on our way we
Find it's just began

Ah yes it's true we've gained a lot of knowledge
but what better can we do than go and enter college

Be four more years of rip ant tuck but what
is that to us

I'm sure there'll be not better luck
so why make a fuss

And when those years are finished
you can take up what you may
for with an education
your work is what you say.

—*Glen Murray*

The Hat

I'll let you wear your favorite hat.
No - not that hat. What are you
trying to do start a war.
I'll let you wear your favorite hat.
It looks good on you
People turn their heads and stare at you.
That's what you wanted
you got what you wanted.
It's the magic in the hat
I've told you about the hat
I know I have and so do you so wear them.
Don't be afraid. You might get
Saved for later than better
Write them a letter and they'll
never write you back.
The magic is in the hat.

—*Garry M. Currey*

In Memory Of...

Yesterday, left my best friend
now and forever, I won't see her
she fought until the end
and no one ever will replace her.

The only thing that keeps me from going sad
is the knowledge of her well being
but, I'm slowly getting mad
because she was young and willing.

For both of us, when my turn will come
it won't be a sad moment
from then on, just like when we were home
everything will seem to be important.

Meanwhile, I do my best to keep on living
it takes a while to get used to
but if I keep on loving
everything by itself will do.

—*Serge Joly*

ear God

ou have left us the difficult task
f finding out if life is worth living...
e are so fragile!
is so easy to pass from life to death,
at it only takes one second!
d yet we worry so much about earthly things,
ke working more, to earn more, to have more!
then leave what we made, to others...
d also, dear God, there is no Shangri-la in this world,
where can we find the perfect place!
we see everywhere is hunger, pain, war, ambition, envy.
though there are some good and beautiful things,
ere is so much evil!
en cannot live together without fighting,
d those that are good and straight are unpopular,
ey do not fit in...
, perfection becomes an illusion not compatible with reality...
d as every thing takes its time to happen,
d time is so important to us,
so happens that time means nothing to Thou!!!
        —*Marianne Antoniadis*

e Hills of Life

y soul and I climbed the hill
love and life together.
e paused one moment, then stood still.
hen life was never better.

t winds and storms approached the top.
ey blew away my feeling.
ey left me empty at the stop
ith not a thought for healing.

y heart feels lonely as it turns.
ck down that steep embankment.
mourns, it prays, it hopes, it yearns.
r a soul, a chance and encouragement.
        —*H. Glukler*

w Many Aprils?

w many Aprils have I left-
f sight, scent, sound, taste, touch-
sense the blossom-petal'd Spring,
o live, to love so much?

w many Summers have you left-
f roses custom'd hue-
contemplate their perfumed zest,
neath skies of azure blue?

w many Autumns have we left-
f beauty's pain to feel-
rain-kiss'd earth's musk-mellow'd tang
gold-russet leaves reveal?

w many Winters has one left-
f frozen twig-hung dew,
n moons that pulse of karmic debt,
o breathe, and act anew?

w many Aprils are there left-
f dawn, noon, twilight, dusk,
, honed by time the ripe-grain'd soul
ill leave the body husk?
        —*Michael Roy A.T.C., D.A.E.*

Soldier Boys

Still to young to face the facts
Of what they're soon to face.
Youthful soldiers marching off to war
To be heroes of other days.

Mother's cry and sisters weep
As they wave these boys good-bye.
They pray the Lord their souls to keep
And hope they do not die.

Courageous hearts burst full with pride.
Others quiver with fear.
Still they all go off to fight
In this God awful war.

Lord protect their naive souls.
Keep them safe from storm.
Keep them in your safety.
Until once more they come home.
        —*Jessica Young*

Strange Thoughts!

Strange thoughts come into mind
Of who I am and where I am going!

!!Thank God I am growing!!

I am scared to death of all the "daring"
And of the different kind of "caring"

I do not want to lose the ones that I
most love.....

Yet with the change in me
Will they still love and see
That through the growing pain
I still remain

"Deeply devoted".
        —*Elisabeth MacDonald*

Dream World

I have a dream world all my own,
Of woodlands green where I used to roam,
Winding paths of mossy green,
A silence perfect and serene
Broken by the sweetest sound ever heard,
The warbling song of a winging bird,
Honeysuckle fragrance fills the air,
Sunlight shining through the trees,
Honeysuckle perfume fills the air,
Bluebells and wildflowers everywhere,
Then the sunset far beyond,
And the sweet goodnight of a robin's song,
Silence once again descends
Like a prayer on all my woodland friends.
        —*Beatrice M. Willmott*

A Light In The Darkness

Even when it's dark, there's always a light.
You may not see it, you may not know about it, but it's there.

It may not be a candle, or the kind of light you are used to.
It may be someone's own light, within themselves.

Light is a symbol of freshness, something new.
Light is a symbol of happiness.

Dark is a symbol of unhappiness.

Within the dark, there is a light.
Within the unhappiness, there is always a light, even if you
can't see it, or don't know about it, just then.
        —*Clare Rose*

Untitled

Such a crazy world it is today
Oh how it has changed along the way
Always accidents, crime and killing
How can the world be so willing
To let it run so far astray
No longer now able to find the way.
Youths could gather at any time
To ride, to skate, to dance, to dine
No evil thoughts or deeds were done
There was nothing but good clean fun.
A good time was so very cheap then
Back in those hard-up old days when
A sleigh ride, a hay ride could bring more joy
Than is ever dreamed of by today's girl or boy.
There is an aching deep down in my heart
For a world in which I had no part.
Oh Lord, my God, what earthly fate
To have the feeling you were born too late
To miss a life you never knew
And wish for the past to look forward to.

      —C. Crozier-Smith

Yvon, a Poet?

Young, ignorant, confident, decades ago.
Old, wise, cultured, experienced? Perhaps.
Rich? Not too much, enough to survive.
Healthy? How can one feel at seventy?

Unsecured, controversial and abused world.
Violence, greed, power, hatred, vengeance.
Vices, robberies, murders and other felonies.
Nature destroyed. Pollution all over the globe.

Unsecured, controversial and abused world.
Where is the beautiful, love and respect?
Where is the human compassion?
The desire to help each other is dead.

Intellect, science, discovery, evolution?
Things we sometimes hardly control.
Faster communications. The media's
Reporting violence, suffering and gains.

Plentiful motives not to think of poetry.
But young at heart and mind, believing,
the best is yet to come for all and me.
Poetry may be the salvation for humanity.

      —Yvon Andre Gaillard

Writing Home

There's something about a freight train
on a rainy night that reminds me of war
   and the movement of troops.

There's something in the glare of the
electric lights
the waiting steel
and heavy mist
   that needs soldiers to
   complete the scene
cold

and writing home

      —Dan D'Alimonte

Weathering the Storm

We sat by the shore,
on a rock, you and I
Just the two of us
and a darkening sky
Oh where are the thunder clouds
and the wind to tear us down
Where is the lightning
to shake beneath us the ground
It's Apocalypse now
gonna rip out our hearts
Love is no more, just a shape on a box
So what are we doing, hands tightly clasped
on a rock, you and I
in a storm.

      —Margaret Ranger

Song of Amalfi

When God looked down
On a small white town
Set at the edge of the sea,
He placed His hand
On the firm brown sand,
And said, "Peace unto thee".
He blew a breeze through the orange trees,
Warm as a summer night.
Where the breaker mocks
At the tumbled rocks, he painted a pattern of white.
He gave her the fun
Of dancing; the sun
For warmth through the balmy day,
But better by far
He hung on a star
The moon, to swing o'er the bay.
At the foot of the hill,
By the murmuring mill,
He wrote the song of the stream.
So Amalfi stands by her dark brown sands,
Like the sight and the sound of a dream.

      —Donald V. Weeks

Falling Bombs

On hearing the first cuckoo of Spring — this day
On first hearing the whistle of falling bombs.
Walking fast to the shelter one evening with a
neighbor and all the paraphernalia.
The others had gone ahead.
I said to Arthur "what is that strange scream"
All he said was "run".

I think the wright brothers should have been shot.
Planes have invaded my privacy and there is nothing
I can do to escape the noise.
Without them Hiroshima could not have occurred
Nor yet Pearl Harbour or Desert Storm.
The London Blitz — the death of both Sonny and Pa
Lockerbie noise and John's suicide.
Tourists benefits few — air sea rescue — holidays.
We could well do without.
The blue ribbonned ships Mauretania-Normandy
were wonderful
Comfortable, a delightful, civilized way to travel.
Nostalgia and a longing for peace.
What do others think????

      —Irene S. Brown

in

tally wounded and in pain, lies my soul silently
1 the thorny arms of, artificial relationships
onfined within the web, of morals and traditions
main, my unfulfilled dreams, aspirations and hope
ifled is my love under the burden of
1st, honour and responsibility
ackled are my desires by values, laws and trends
fetters lie my dreams, subdued are my emotions
igulfed in the mist of, errors and misjudgment
uffer in silence, the miscarriage of destiny
ive in torment with squelched wishes
y emotions are distraught, my enthusiasm is reticent
y youth is undaring, my love is secretive
y coalition is timorous, my speech is uncommunicative
vish to demolish, annihilate, quell, extinguish and quash
e demon of laws that are a cause for
he, torture, agony and anguish
grieved, burdened and in despair, I toil towards my goal
defeat, conquer and enslave
istoms, culture, norms and mores
　　—Sirajuddin Aziz

le Sand Moon

The gentle breeze pushed small waves up
to the soft sand which reflected the
immering moon,
As the gentle breeze increased to a
rsh wind the once small waves rapidly
anged in to huge rolls of water being
ven on to the shore as if death was
ht behind them,
They rushed on to the beach and washed
reflection of the moon off the once
rfect beach,
Then as if the storm had never happened,
things calmed,
There were no small waves rushing on to
peaceful beach,
And once again glowing moon appeared
the soft, silky sand...
　　—Danett Bothe

adows

ve is gentle, hate anger
e innocent, one cruel
ve is like a candle in the dark
ired a vast ocean of obscurity
ve is morning dew, hate night
ve is knowledge, hate ignorance
wers draw a loving glance
1's heat blinds
e kindles the soul and brightens the universe
e brings confusion and destruction
et makes love with nature
nded with ambition, hate destroys it
e is rational
e is serene, one passionate
e lives in the soul, hard to reach
e is earthy, easy to attain
e cures the human heart
e injuries it furiously
s for us to choose which is worthy of achievement
　　—Sandy Narang

Untitled

It starts when we're young.
Our minds are filled and polluted.
With images of long, flowing hair,
A slim figure, a beautiful dress,
Long winking eyelashes, etc.
These are concepts of beauty.
Little girls don't wear
Something other than what will make them pretty.

They don't play with cars.
Instead they practice being a mommy
With little dolls.
They can't be themselves,
But instead they mirror
And recreate images of "beauty" on T.V.
And dream of who they'll marry
He'll be strong and handsome
And save you from the reality of
Who you are without him
　　—Alana Berringer

In God's First Temple

When the light separated from the day -
Out in the woods I went astray.
The shadows, they drifted, then settled about.
My pain, it was lifted - (I near had to shout!)

About the joys and the peace
That entered my mind;
About the longings... then the love
That was not hard to find.

Oh, the glory that I found there
When I did go astray...
A whole new frame of mind there
When I met the brand new day!
　　—Vera Schwedhelm

Abuser

I hit him
　　Over and over and over.
The anger, frustration and hurt
　　Coming out my fists.

The tears fell from his eyes.
　　The respect he once had for me—gone.
A pain came into my heart,
　　I felt guilty and ashamed.

I couldn't hug him,
　　I couldn't move.
I heard myself say once again,
　　"I'm sorry. That's the last time."

I took a long walk that night.
　　I thought of the reasons I had him.
I thought of how innocent he is.
　　I am his example—a molder.

What he learns from me
　　Will go with him in his mind.
I know I have to change,
　　For his sake and mine.
　　—Andrea Carson

The Tempt To Know

Far, far away in a mystical land,
past deep ocean seas, deserts and sand.
Atop a great mountain, lived the Arcane,
he was fabled to know all, true knowledge he'd gained.
This aged man knew answers, for every question asked,
whether it pertained of the future, present or past.
One day a young man, sad and distraught,
came to him and offered one single thought.
"Is there a God?" The young boy asked.
A worthy challenge of his intellect, the man thought last
Many years have gone by decades long dead,
but the Arcane still pondered on that thought in his head.
When the boy returned, many years since that day,
he thought he'd finally hear, what the man had to say.
But when he approached, he found the dead heap,
of the old man, who had died in his sleep
Among the remains, he found a note grimy and grout,
that stated, "Please stand by, I went to find out...."

  —*Samantha Lee*

A Poem for the World

People bloody people fighting in their wars. Killing other
people for really nothing at all. It started long ago with
slings sticks and stones. Now the world can be wiped out with
weapons that can break our bones. Mankind has always thrived
on death and destruction. Pray the wrong people never get
their finger on the button. The world goes on so they say,
hope we all live to see another day. When will mankind learn
when will the people listen. That life is for living not for
killing. The candle of life is burning away did God really
want it to be this way. The world He created is now in our
hands. Yet people still fight Maim and kill just to say "this
is my land". Is mankind on trial will we be judged. Or left to
our own devices will we be crushed. Jesus died for this world a
long time ago. Yet we all hope his spirit is with us
everywhere we go. If only the evils of war could stop and the
good of peace prevail. The world would be a better place to
live. For the sake of all our children we dare not fail.

  —*Bill Rogerson*

Searching

I look up to the sky to find it dark; with lightening bolts
piercing by heart.
I follow the rainbow to find a pot of gold; only to find
disappointment and despair.
I walk along the milky way to find peace and contentment; only
to find a tornado of torment and tears.
I asked God, "Why am I being punished for I am not a bad person?
As yet no answer has been received.
I look upwards to the sky for a sign of hope; a bright star, or a
moon beam so bright.
Only to find a dark sky with lightening bolts breaking my heart!

  —*Judy Pannell*

My Love

 Across the country you live.
Once we met, we laughed, loved and cried
  But yet so long ago.

  Much time has passed
 but, I still remember
you as if it was yesterday.

  We fell in love there
 on the cold hard floor
 but yet, we did not once
  feel cold or alone.

Now we are gone from there and
 we are alone once more.

  —*John A. Carter*

Mother

You taught me how to read and spell,
Plus writing and arithmetic as well.
You played the piano while I stood at your knee,
And showed me the beauty in poetry.
You led me to respect the law,
Our God, my elders, and "maw and paw!"
You taught me ethics on the side,
And aimed my conscience as my guide.
Some of these gifts I can recognize,
In our kids (and theirs in spite off their size).
In these later years, while in your chair you park,
You can know that you have made your mark,
And will have had a hand in years to come
On things that will shape many a life's outcome.
For lots of future generations
In at least two (and who knows how many more) nations.
We are proud as can be of the legacy
That you've grafted to our family tree!

  —*Bill Nichols*

To a Snow-White Robin

Where is your red breast? Where the brown?
 Poor little bird, so young and frail.
In quaint but lovely snow-white gown, yet helpless on that old
 bare rail.
If I was you I'd rather be a common robin in a tree.

Beware! Dear little bird, beware!
 You're genuine. You're not a fake,
But too conspicuous and rare, for Nature's made a bad mistake.
Your gown so bright but snowy-white won't blend with nature out
 of sight.

Your enemies are all around, both here below and in the trees.
The cats and weasels on the ground can see you now with ample
 ease.
Your enemies the hawk and crow can see you now for where you go

Let 'Mother Nature' take her brush,
 and paint you brown like all your kin,
Then you will blend with any bush and probably thus save your
 skin.
Or otherwise, for what it's worth, you'll not live long on
 Mother Earth.

  —*Thomas Singleton*

Remembering Those Who Fought For Us

Here we stand in silence,
Praying for those who cared.
Praying for those who fought for us,
And praying for those who dared.

Remember the men and women
Who fought in the wars,
Let us remember them with a poppy,
And let them rest peacefully beyond our shores.

I would like to take a moment,
Please join me if you will,
To remember all our loved ones,
Who were brave and have been killed.

So I bless everyone of them,
Who put their lives on stake for us.
And I want to give to them:
My thanks, my love, and my trust.

  —*Michael Manaois*

Galaxies

Exploring galaxies is my dream.
Riding through space on the wings of a beam.
Searching out words, hoping for life.
That is my goal, that is my strife.

Spreading peace through boundless stars.
Telling of love, preventing wars.
Making sure we hear our neighbors
On the planets, in the vapors.

Wishfully hoping, hate disappears.
As I'm sailing through the years.
May all universal life unfold.
And new generations peacefully grow old.
—*Hannah Glukler*

The Child of Man

In a market square in Caesar's Rome, clothed only in a tattered
robe, you stand there on the stage, a statue of flesh on
display, on sale. You look out into the heartless crowd of
your masters with sad empty eyes.

In a dark cavern of the earth, the sounds of steel grinding
steel, of small naked feet kicking the dirt beneath, and the
exhausted cries of hard labour echoes into the mine shaft.
From the corridors of the night, a shining, shimmering light
appears from a lantern's light that silhouettes your small
frail form pushing a cart of stone on tiny rails.

You cling to your mother with all your might
Seeking for strength and for comfort like so many times before.
You scream, you shout, at the top of your lungs
and your wailing cries reveals your fear,
the fear of death's cold touch, the fear of Auschwitz,

From history's past to the modern age, you have been sold and
worked to the bone. Now with the present at hand, I will teach
you how to kill, to steal, to rape; pillage and plunder.
Of the many evils I have done,
leaving you in this world without a future is the worst one.
—*Richard T. Lyonhart*

Joy and Pain

A precious gift
Round tiny face, rosy cheeks,
Downy soft hair,
Ten fingers and toes,
What a joy

First steps, first words,
Smiles and giggles,
What a joy,

First day of school, first hockey game,
First date, first kiss,
What a joy,

First cigarette,
Staying out late,
First words to wound us,

No more a joy,
Only unbearable pain.
—*Rita Fabiano*

all - Winter Fashion

ll-winter fashion critique
ints oriental mystique
btle elegance mingle
nnels, satins, serges, tingle
ocks in free-flowing form
tterfly sleeves coolie-warm
pes, scarfs, sweaters, dresses and skirts
necked jumpsuits, trousers with shirts
rments of whisper-weight wool
ggle-buttoned jackets full
de cinch-belts plus money pouch
azing colors for which we vouch
ft slouchy boots enhance the frame
llmark wrap-ups is the game
arn loosely or all together
doors, outdoors, in any weather.
—*Alan R. Golding*

gonizing Situation

ar! Remote cause and immediate are so many they are -
cial, color, religion - the most by far;
ejudicial, inequity and even hatred,
o wonder our planet in turmoil - often been said.

andela and company - dislikes apartheid -
ohamisans - cursing Christians an ugly attitude';
en some Americans - challenges each other,
use of colour - inequity, killing one another.

me Nations loves 'power' - for National aggrandisment -
ntradicting social and customs - and different government;
creasing armed forces - with ambiguous purpose,
r home defence - preparing for 'invasion', I suppose.

valry attitude - hinders progress, and restarts civilization -
ery one cares to 'champion' - agonizing situation-condition;
ligion - should be the 'mother of peace' - cultured and 'divine',
ly then - peace on earth will prevail - good well to all mankind.
—*Antonio E. Najera, Sr.*

alassa

new the sea:
ality floating coyly by, we slept, then woke together,
ch mirroring the other's secret charms.
r days without eternity, she'd quite forgotten how to be demure,
rnally wielding ocean swords against immortal towers of stone
t dared define her.

e preened herself
h devilish pride the day you left; she seemed at peaceful odds
th terraces, and wicker chairs, and warmth.
e asked you to belong, with her, to umbrella pines that brought
s to the sun.
scribing speech in cadences of furrowed song and wanderlust,
shared the wine.

d when you'd gone,
lifted harrowed arms
f to battle with the clouds
f to shroud the prattling shawls
f to ask:
lone?
But why?
—*C.R. Kamarat*

One Heart

She lives in her darkness
Searching
For the truth
She climbs the right ladder
But it seems to be no use
She can't seem to get over those towering walls
That entrap her inside.
One heart doesn't know
Those feelings she hides.

Love eludes her
And has no meaning
Her darkness grows deeper
And stronger and wider
Enveloping her
Squeezing
Leaving no room for one single breath
Letting her die her undying death
One heart just doesn't know.

—*Nicole VanWezel*

Shadows Of The Night

I stand for hours by my window when sleep will not come,
Searching for an answer to things I should have done.

I reach out in the darkness, I'm drowning in despair,
I pray for strength and courage, to find an answer there.

The darkness settles over me like a black velvet robe,
The stars like studded diamonds a beauty to behold.

I see comfort from its beauty as I gaze into the sky,
A special star to guide me and set my pathway by.

It is sad to think of those that fear shadows of the night,
They get no comfort from the stars that shine for us so bright.

For them the nights are ugly, dark shadows everywhere,
Their minds are filled with terror and they find no solace there.

I wish I could give them courage and faith enough to see
The beauty of the heavens, what comfort it would be.

For God in all his wisdom, the nights I'm sure he blessed
The darkness of the heavens to give us time to rest.

So we must not worry so, if we believe in prayer,
Put our faith up in the stars, we will find an answer there.

—*Texas Jewell Yeates*

Fall

Why do we choose to walk with nature?
September, October, November
And do you perceive what it beholds, as I am seeing?
Can you tell just what you are seeing or is it
impossible?

The colors I see are the indulging complexions of
inspiring lives.
Each leaf merely a reflection of a mortal soul.
Time now for them to recede to the earth,
Forming a blanket of fading life.

Our creator has set forth an explanation of nature,
A pathway in which we too shall follow...
So does nature with the use of its inquiring mind.
It prepares them for the lingering, passionless cold
winter months.

Alas, the awakening of the earth in spring brings forth
a distinct golden tree, for every mortal soul to see.
... still do you see what I see?

—*Petrina Moreg Nina Gillard*

What We Wanted To Be...

Wasting my time,
shaping my mind, to live up to the standards,
that they've told me were mine...
There's an infinity out there,
Of lessening time,
and I know I've only one childhood,
just one life;
but now I see
that these things
they are not mine...

—*Tiffany Izsa*

From Life To Life

From life to life we live and we die,
sharing a dirge or a lullaby,
sharing an hour or a whole lifetime,
leaving in old age or in our prime.

We were brothers once, sisters as well,
perhaps even lovers; who can tell.
We were together then for a moment or more.
We'll be together again, of this I am sure.

And after the march when we're laid to rest,
we'll plot our return and do our best
to be lovers again or brothers-in-arms,
or sisters or friends, drinking loves' charms.

—*J. M. Neil*

The Friday Night

He asked her on a friendly date
She thought it would be really great
He took her to dinner and a dance
He bought her a drink, he spilled on her pants
Later he took her back to his place
Only then did she honestly see his face.
A face he changed so suddenly
He frightened her so terribly
He threw her on the floor
He locked and bolted the door
He promised he wouldn't hurt her
He emptied her soul and almost killed her.
She screamed and cried
She fought and tried
It was hopeless
It was useless
It was awful, what he did
Something she will never forget
What turned out a simple date
Was now complex, it was rape!

—*Kelly Keith*

Drums

To the beat of a drum and the blaring of a trumpet.
The battle has always just began and we are marching to
a final sunset. Wars and rumor of wars are Biblical facts
but, why do we fail to react. For the countless young
men who lie in flanders and other memorial fields, do not
lie in peace for the beat of the drum and the sound of
cannon and trumpet is still vivid in their ears for the war
to end all wars was never meant to be. And there is no
restful peace in eternity for if we do not learn to live in
harmony and friendship armageddon is the end. But the earth
will survive. Lest we forget with all the anthology, there
will be no one there to accept our apology

—*G. Apostolatos*

hantom of the Night

barn owl visits our orchard late each night,
e's often their till the break of light.
er shadow glances my window and sometimes gives me a fright,
en I blink my eyes, and watch her hunt by the moon's light.
ysterious and majestic bird of the night,
rge bright eye's and a face so white.
oking like a spectre of the night, bathed in a silvery white light,
e perches upon a bough of our old pear tree,
oking swiftly to the left and then to the right,
a field mouse scampers from pillar to post,
e see's an unsuspecting mole heading towards an old gate post.
uch quicker than the blink of her large bright eyes,
e's back on the bough with a gulp and a sigh.
hile the field mouse managed to escape with his life,
l that is left of the mole is his wondering soul.
er owlet's will flourish now that pray is rich and rife,
she call's out happily into the dark spangled night,
if to say I'm content with my life.
w wonderfully blessed I am this night,
witness that wondrous bird of the night.

—*Mark Pocklington*

e

ll constant nagging ignored,
ill screams of bitter anger
ouded out by loud voices,
ars build in frustration when no
ice is found to turn to.
mehow it always finds its
y around blockades.
re, they are punishing themselves,
t what about their young?
eryone says that they're the victims,
m too, the victim of circumstance I mean.
ould I keep trying to make them
derstand, or will I get pushed aside again?
ar controls me and panic is easy
reach, what did I do wrong?
ill this song of agony ever go away?

—*Charmaine Hartley*

ar Lynne

emories of you return to me each day,
ice you've been gone my mind has gone astray,
ere were so many things I wanted to say,
w my heart is blue my world is grey.
cause you're gone I have lost my way.

d thou behold your child so sweet,
see her now would be a treat,
w could winter have been so cruel,
take away life's finest jewel?

ur picture still hangs from my wall,
eping at night I dream of you all,
ur husband beside you standing so tall,
ur baby too learning to crawl,
d there you are at the end of a hall,
un to you but only to fall
u turn around ignoring my call,
en I'm awake clutching my doll.

r each of you I have shed a tear,
d I will do so year after year,
n't wait to see you again my dear!

—*Jacquelynn Bourgeois*

Why War?

War - shame, grief and pain, never an end, no regain,
Slaughter, strain, lost terrain,
Powerful factions, heaved apart, sundering ruction, satanic art

Blood, filth, horrific slush, poverty, misery, deadly hush,
How can hate achieve so much?
Fiery fury left unchecked, dazzles saviours finally beckoned.

Children crying, lost, alone, helpless, hopeless, severed bone,
Crippled, crawling, awe-struck moan.
Puny pawns of Man's ambition, their sufferings nag our vision.

Haggard women, drained, tormented, helpless now, alone,
frustrated,
Scrawny, useless, ever mistreated,
Why must life's givers suffer so? Forever abused, never let go

Average man, pounded, grovelling, rootless, restless, past
redeeming, hounded, harried, always sickening,
The hope of the world, kept confounded, spirit gone, his all
destroyed.

Beloved country, smashed to dust, innocent victim of rampant
lust, ageless culture allowed to rust.
Why is peace a dirty word? Will Justice ever again be heard?

—*A. M. Rymer*

Stirrings

Stirrings - the first man and first woman were roused from slumber
Stirrings - they were pulled together in rushing currents and
we were increased in number!
Stirrings - the internal switches are turned on and we react
Stirrings - a shove towards Communicable love not something
   abstract
Stirrings - elevating the mind to a Divine manifestation
Stirrings - fulfillment won't brook any hesitation
Stirrings - excavating problems from their root
Stirrings - unruffling the conscience to ask about truth
Stirrings - a reminder of the past that suddenly haunts
Stirrings - the curiosity of tomorrow itself sensuously flaunts
Stirrings - a mere nothingness takes form by 'becoming'
Stirrings - the senses take their cue and start humming
Stirrings - unzipping the ignorance - now realization is bliss!
Stirrings - urging the desire for loved ones you miss
Stirrings - the heart is gloriously beating - no need for alarm
Stirrings - I want to be the Stirring that gently nudges his
Sea of calm!

—*Anita Bennett*

Fingerprints

Little tiny fingerprints,
Smeared across the wall.
Potatoes, peas, and gravy,
Travel down the hall.

"Who did this?" I calmly say,
Opening the door.
"Uh-oh, Mama." Angel smiles,
"I got some on the floor."

Every day there's fingerprints,
Smeared across that wall.
And I thank the Lord to see them there,
Potatoes, peas, and all.

—*Michele Powell-Baron*

Clerihew On A Clique

Around the room on high-backed chairs they sat with nervous
smiles, their works of art clutched under arms or hidden away
in files or folders, briefcase, bags and such, book, poems,
lay there, dead to all but each one's mindful thoughts of just
what might be said.

A joke exchanged to break the ice; a comment on the weather,
Strangers wanting to be friends to share their works together.
Discussing dialects and speech, never lost for words,
Eyeing each other, wondering if their words were for the birds.

Hesitating, anxious, even though they had rehearsed, until,
when asked, the answer came - "Oh, no! Will you be first?"
So, reading from a page of verse the words came true and clear,
The first of many readings, elocution without fear.

They all relaxed, at last they heard each others' works of art,
The words which took such time and thought but came right from
the heart. The meeting closed, they all went home, inspired
and full of cheer, their efforts for the next blank page
renewed and in top gear.

And so, my friends, who read this now, I thank you for your
time, at least I have conveyed to you, my poetry must rhyme!

—*Brenda Chappell*

Health Is Wealth

(Dedicated to Dorothy Porter)
Smoking and drinking is ruining my life.
That may even be the cause of losing a wife.
Health is wealth are you healthy or not?
Gotta stop it all, gotta give it a shot!
I've been alone for so many years,
plenty of smiles left with tears.
If we keep it up no child no wife,
We have control of ruining our lives.
Health is wealth are you healthy or not?
Gotta stop it all, gotta give it a shot,
Girl if you hear me this message is for you
Take a chance at somebody knew.
I feel so good, in my best of shape
I'll now knock at your door, never ever late.
Health is wealth are you healthy or not?
Gotta stop it all, gotta give it shot.
Most of you who are just like me.
Should realize it seriously

—*Bobby Legault*

That Smile

A little child casts me a smile or
So he bothers even try.
Battered he is and worn out to nothing.
He looks up, and I don't understand the words whispered
They're of some strange language I have never heard,
He sings a song of some glorious day,
So sad, so lonely, but so joyful, and he is not heard.
Then he cries a pitiful, little cry, with his sad face,
And his tiny hands reaches out to me,
Burden with young life, that laboured so and was never free.
It touches mine, and I feel warmth on this bitter night,
And still in this night, I feel his long-lost life.
A little child casts me a smile
Or so he bothers even try
And now his battered little soul has been replaced.
He smiles and we all know that he sees none of this world
But accepts and learns to bear his own fate.

—*Gail James*

Looking Back

Another day of life slips by,
    so quickly now it seems.
Slow moving days of other times,
    are gone just like our dreams.
We look into the mirror,
    how time has took its toll
Who is this person looking back?
    Dark eye's peer at her soul.
The once young, healthy girl now gone.
    Dark hair has turned to gray
But memories of her-still linger
    - inside not far away.

She see's herself in her minds eye -
    As she used to be
Walking down that country road and being so carefree.
    That time of youth so quickly past surely only yesterday -
Yet captured in her heart we know to live on and to stay.

—*Rita Fitzgerald*

Oh Youth

Oh youth, sweet child, why did you have to grow,
So silently you left not saying goodbye.
Do you remember days not long ago,
When we would pass the careless hours by.

For we aspired to celebrate our birth,
And reach our seniority, the goal,
In rocking feasts that shook our minds with mirth,
and friends that grew and freely filled our soul.

But now within I'm deaf, an empty rage,
A silent scream which bends these bones grown tall.
That I should strive for youth in youth, not age,
My heart did not this thought to mind recall.

'Tis in the noise of youthful heedlessness,
That peace is lost in aging restlessness.

—*Jo Rodrigues*

The Recruiter's Lament

Now you look like one who can't be had,
So step up here, we'll talk my lad.
Think of every land you've ever heard from,
All yours to see if you follow the drum!

Ahh, follow the drum, with never a care,
Follow the drum, we'll take you there,
And everyday yah drinks your rum!
All for you if you follow the drum.

Ahh, follow the drum, every day's a vacation,
Follow the drum, with your mates at their station,
And you and your mates will all stick like gum!
All for you if you follow the drum.

Ahh, follow the drum, I hope you've decided,
Follow the drum, all meals are provided,
And every pay tis like a king's ransom!
All for you if you follow the drum.

Follow the drum, you've signed in stone,
Follow the drum, there's no going home,
Every wife a widow, every mother glum.
Poor luckless bastard, you follow the drum.

—*Alan James Lemberg*

Tender Love

Our love is like a delicate rose,
So sweet and soft to touch,
But sometimes it's very hard to love you
So very much.
But when we're both together,
It's your friendship I really love,
Intwine with a tender passion,
Together with a warm caring love.
I can't express my feelings
About the way I care for you,
But way deep down inside me,
I know our love is true.
For one day you'll be with me,
In a world of silent dreams,
So only you and I will know
What true love really means.

—*Mandy Jones*

How Do You Look In The Mirror?

Executing sculptures of thoughts
Roles of rationalization irrationalization...
The intent of acting,
No thesis; of actors that can't act
The giant sculpture of stages of neglect
Denial of ones own thoughts.
The subconscious of truth,
Argumentive bluntness to steel,
Not to please...
Take a stand not to be convicted;
The price of entrance into the window,
Understanding...
To free ones actions.
Can only approach justification to justify,
There is no rage
No rage....
Just, Diva's wondering in the night of darkness.
The sculpture melts down into white powder.
Can only be purchased by the spirit to see the spirit.
The soul, the block to end.

—*Rachelle Deforest*

Heroes

Everyone needs a hero,
Someone who's made the grade,
A person who has won the fight
Even though he was afraid.

A hero is a paradigm
Who we can look up to
Whose life serves as a model
Of what we each can do.

We learn a lot from heroes.
We find that they have erred;
They've stumbled and they've fallen,
Yet they won because they dared.

Even with all odds against them,
Our heroes ventured on,
Gaining strength from their commitments
Till all obstacles were gone.

Now choose yourself a hero,
One you can hold in high esteem.
Then follow his example
As you pursue your dream.

—*Wendie Donabie-Dixon*

My Dad

Why does it seem I'm only here to feel the pain.
Sometimes I get so lost I begin to wonder whether I'm insane.
But it pleases me to know
You're right by my side
helping me to grow.

Yes I love you.

I don't know who is right or wrong
But it's good to have someone around who feels secure and
strong. You and I, we don't know each other very well and in
the process we're both going through our own kind of hell.

Yes I love you.

I've been thinking lately you're okay.
I think that's all we both have to say.
It doesn't matter who is good or bad
Lets both of us be happy together instead of sad.

Yes I love you.

—*Doug Burrows*

Is This Now?

Like a wolf, you watch my soul, take me, and we shall live.
Spirit and body amongst the souls of planetary level, seeing
the self-destruction of themselves.
Have love, in thy inner being, for we are there.
Around, in human garbage, this is the plan, for no-one seeks
tranquility, seeks heart!
Have love, in thy inner being, for we are there
Take-up your bodies, as are, and see the light
coming from the east, and setting in the West,
not the gloom, but the needle of colour that treats us together
Have love, in thy inner being, for we are there.
Save the returnables, of forgiveness, making the use of our
sub-nobility, as our spectrum is but a dot, night to be remembered?

—*Gary Allan Utas*

Bothar na bhFál

The whitened face of a boy soldier
stalking the Falls Road of fences
stops at a door.
He goes down on one knee.
In his rifle-sight he sees
a child throw a ball into the air
the way petrol-bombs are hurled.
A dog barks in Irish
on the Falls Road of fences.

A ball bounces towards the soldier.
The whitened face of a child approaches,
stops at the soldier.
He goes down on one knee.
Reaching for the ball, he sees
a rifle and a wave from the soldier
who does not live there
on the Falls Road of fences.
A dog barks in Irish.

—*Frankie Sewell*

My Badminton Racket

As I step on the court it becomes part of me. The court, my
racket, and I, we are three. We battle together through good
and through bad, we win we are happy, we lose we are sad.
Without my racket I'm frozen in time. Like a boat lost at sea
a poet without rhyme. We're an army at battle fighting for
space. But we take our time we set our own pace. We rely on
each other day in and day out. We control our anger and try
not to pout. No matter the opponent a match or a game an
unstoppable team we will always remain.

—*Lisa Robicheau, 16 yrs.*

Flo

Here I am,
standing in the rain,
my face a liquid mask,
awash with tiny rivers.
Yet I feel the grooves on my face,
carved by my trudging tears,
every mile of their passage,
irrespective of the rain.
Suddenly; joy,
sweet-scented on the dampened breeze a thought of you,
a smile dams the flow of my boulder - tears,
an avalanche of happiness overcomes me.
My tears no longer track but flow,
away,
adrift upon the sky - drop rivers,
and now my eyes are dry, no longer drowning.
So do not cry sweet one,
but think of me,
embrace yourself with loving arms
and I will be there too.

—*Darren Knight*

The Cenotaph

It's just a mass of sand and stone,
Standing silent and all alone.
And from a distance all you see,
Our country's flags, fluttering free.
But go up close and read quite slow,
What is written on its base below.
"To those who served in two great wars"
Their memory will always be ours.
This monument declares our pride,
For all those souls who fought and died.
Their sacrifices had to be,
To keep our future children "free."

—*Ronald P. O'Keefe*

Alone

Alone - what does it mean?
State of mind or reality?
being by oneself, with no other people
just you, and your thoughts
together.

Alone - are we ever really alone?
is the world as isolated as it seems now
or do we lead ourselves to this dark gloom?

Alone or lonely which is it?
Is it both?
or is this your chance to regain your strength
by taking stock of you within.

Alone - is it just a sad dream, maybe dejection? Or are you
simply caged by your own bruised pride? Asking all these
questions while sitting all alone hurt, angry, confused, you
suddenly realize you're talking aloud. Someone must be hearing
you up there is it God listening or some poor spirit who passed
on? Or maybe you're the only one hearing you talk you are
talking to yourself: Now you know you're never alone.

—*L. C. Michael Arundel*

Love - A Definition

Love is an unconditional, eternal, gentle, tender contented
state that if nourished, cared for it cherished, begins to grow
and flourish in direct proportion to those conditions. Without
the conditions love will soon wither and die, leaving one
bewildered, angry and consumed with pain. Love is not being
afraid to tell of your love - not being afraid to be told of
love. The sharing of love will be the greatest of all joys and
will cause your life to be fulfilled. Love is a delicate,
fragile wisp, easily shaken, easily shattered, easily lost - be
kind, be patient - share your loves pains and sorrows - allow
your love to express all things without criticism, without
goes in. Love yourself - be charitable to yourself, forgive
yourself, for how can you do unto others if you cannot do unto
yourself? Love is understanding without the need for
explanation - for what is love but giving - never taking, never
expecting, never demanding - Love has no boundaries, no walls,
no fences for love is unconditional of all obstacles - for love
is understanding and eternal.

—*Bob Marchand*

The Young Man

The young man loved the outdoor life. He was handsome and
stood six foot tall his eyes were the colour of the sky on a
beautiful June day. He loved this time of the year,
September,
the start of the shooting season. He loved to walk the green
fields of his native Ireland. It was just dawn and he could
see the mist and dew on the grass. Suddenly, in the quiet, he
looked up at the sky to see a flock of mallard duck flying over
the lough. He thought of the day ahead.

By noon the young man and his friend, both twenty years old,
had fought the cruel waters of the lough but the lough had won.
As it had many times before.

The lough could be calm and beautiful and in a moment fierce
and cruel. They found the young man when his body reached the
shore. When the mother saw her only son he looked as if
sleeping and she found in the curls which reached his shoulders
some wet sea-weed. Her son would never walk the beautiful
green fields of Ireland again.

—*P. Thompson*

The Man with the Harmonica

(Dedicated to that man in that cold and lonely
subway — because a smile was more than a coin.)

There, underground,
and in his pocket not even a pound,
his hands were cold...
Everything he had, had to be sold.
...and again the harmonica is played.
Oh! I wish I could have stayed.
So I slowly realize,
tears wander through my
   cheeks,
And drop on the street.
Then I ask, I ask to myself:
Will he lucky tonight? Will he find a
   a site?
So there I leave him alone,
with his harmonica playing,
I leave him there praying...
and again I ask to myself:
when will we ever meet again?

—*Mercedes Fonseca Sanchez*

oing On

:sterday, the mowers hummed.
nlight danced on petal, leaf and stem.
day I hear the crush of crisp, brown leaves
neath my feet, along the garden lane.
day I felt the wind, and smelled
e promise of a frosty Eve.
morrow... snow may come
d cover up
l that is left of green.

e seasons come, they pass.
ch bathed in nature's beauty of the hour.
rpetual change, part of the master plan
bring creation to
e miracle of spring.

d as with nature, so with life.
ch step apart...
ch stage an innate beauty bears
on we go.
... up to the sublime Spring.
e Paradise of God.

    —Viola M. Johnstone

e Rain

was not what one could call a rain
at falls down into puddles
d taps on your window pane.
was a though the Heavens
d turned a shower on low
d caused the raindrops to sprinkle
pure as the driven snow.

umbrellas were needed
boots to put on
r in this misty downfall
ou just wanted to walk and walk
til the showers were gone!

ke the roses that are kissed by the dew,
is Heavenly rain has a message for you.
ve each day to the fullest
it snow, rain or sunshine
r when you greet each new morning
ere is no greater gift than Thine!

    —Ethel E. Spencer

idnight Traveler

alking at midnight along the only niche of the world
at has been saved; I am not sad
ing the only person on the earth; nor am I alone.

ou accompany me with each step I take.
ou are the night; silent, fresh, calm.
ou are the mist; almost making me float; lifting my spirits.
ou are the stars; winking at me during my journey.
ou are the soil; rich, fertile, returning the warmth of the
sun long gone.
ou are the grass; carpeting, soothing my bare trodding feet.
ou are the gentle breeze; caressing my hair and whispering
he night's secrets.
ou are a murmuring meandering stream; dancing around me
nd singing lullabies.

en to the end of the earth you are there; and somehow
ave the feeling that no matter where I will go, you
ll always be by my side.

    —M. Rachel Babcock

Distance

There's a distance, come between us,
That I don't quite understand. It's like a mountain
crumbling,
And then turning into sand. With that sand I'd like,
To mould into a castle, a place for us alone,
Away from all life's hassles.

There's a storm, that must be conquered,
So that we, can make amends.
Cause I long, to have, you near me,
In my castle in the end. But we must fight the thunder,
And the lightening, in the skies.
Before we reach our kingdom,
In our castle way up high. So if you care to join me,
In a castle made from sands. Let's learn, more of each other,
Try to love and understand.

For a mould, is a creation, only we,
ourselves can build. It takes a lot of learning, and I'm sure
we have the skills. So if you'd like, to be my partner?
Let us start, with grains of sand,
As we build, our dreams together,
For our castle, hand in hand.

    —Helen Perrault

By No Simple Miracle

She is gone and it is by no simple miracle
that I have not simply become mad

I have left notices in shop windows
"Love lost; golden laughter and green eyes,
passionate about poetry, plays the banjo,
is kind to animals and has peculiar eating habits.
Does not belong to me but would like her back.
Caution: Do not spend time with her
she will pull at your heart like a magnet."

At midnight I have crept into streets
and painted arrows on the roads, exchanged road signs for my
own only to find disappointment when the doorbell rings
forgeries in droves, thinking the signs for them

The extremities I would go to would amaze her
like learning to fly without the aid
of mechanics or wings of any kind
so as to look down on where she could walk
I will not face that she is gone
all I have learnt is by no simple miracle
by no ordinary love, no lazy life

    —Andrew Nash

Someday

Even though I'm not your real Dad
That makes me feel sad.
I will always be here for you
No matter what you do
He may try to buy his way into your heart
I won't that will only tear you apart.
Love is not something bought, it's something earned.
Will he be there for you when there is a lesson to be learned?
Remember who was there to pick you up
When you would cry or answer your questions, "why"...?
Even though this poem won't make you love me,
It's just expressing how I feel.
Emotions for you that are real
Not bought in some corner store
And when he comes to take you
It's my heart that gets tore,
It makes me sad that I'm not your real Dad
But you'll always be my little baby
And hopefully someday, maybe you will call me Dad.

    —Christian Pearson

Friend to Lover

He is my friend, I know he is. Yet, why does he stare at me in
that manner? And why do I seem to be melting?
As he continues to stare, so I search my mind for distractions.

He draws himself closer to me, aware that I am numb. As his
lips touch mine, caress mine, I close my eyes and adhere to
their demands. By doing this, I know that we are over-stepping
the boundaries of friendship. What can I do, except pray that
this is as far as we will allow ourselves to go?

My power to resist him is now non-existent - He has carried me
from my world to his own. A world where his wish is my
command, a world where he is already aware of my wish. I have
travelled so far. It is impossible even to imagine the world I
have just abandoned.

As his tongue travels and meets with my valley, I sigh. My sigh is
more than just a sign of relief, it is an indication that I
have resigned from my own world. I have decided to be a part
of his world. Accepted all his terms and conditions.

Explain this, I can not. He was my friend - now he is my
lover. The transition was rapid.... And very much beyond my
control.

—*Thanjiza Danielle Nkowani*

The Joy Within

The two of you bring great pleasure,
    that my heart is sure.

It all took place in the fall,
    when I received that special call.

One look in your eyes is all it took,
    to know I no longer had to look.

I'm filled with joy watching you two grow,
    since that special day summers ago.

Passing my days with you two,
    brings me pleasure I never knew.

When you hang on so tight at night,
    I know our life is going just right.

Crystol with your eyes so bright,
    they even sparkle in the night.

Trevor with your funny ways,
    makes me laugh throughout my days.

You two are a part of me,
    that's the way we'll always be.

The little things you two do,
    touch my heart and please me too.

—*Judy-Ellen Grant*

Untitled

Love is a two way street.
That's all I can think of when our lips meet.
He broke my heart, now he wants to be friends.
It never ends.
I've fallen for him and I've fallen hard.
Our destiny is just not in the cards.
I look into his eyes and everything I want is there.
How can I make him care?
I can't make him love me or force him to try,
I wouldn't want to love a lie.
I wish our paths were different,
Instead of a one way street,
Then my thoughts would be justified,
The next time our lips meet.

—*Lisa M. Carmanico*

Christmas Eve'

Goodnight Mummie..goodnight Dad
That's the best Christmas eve I've ever had
Decorating the tree and stirring the pud'
Dad said did I make it..as if I could
Up the wooden hill to bed
Oh there's one thing I should have said
Down again, I could see they were glad
When I told them both 'Your my best mom and dad'
Pushing me gently through the door
Mum said 'Up those stairs, I'll tell you no more'
I don't think I slept very much though
I remember father Christmas banging his toe
I switched on the light on a face so sad
'You didn't wake me, and I love you dad

—*R. Vandersypen*

Time Unmeasured

A year, a moment, a lifetime, eons....
The blinking of an eye…
Time unmeasured.. existing somewhere else.
Memories like vapors, rise and melt away
Into the space that holds events of yesterday.

Who can follow the exhaled breath?
It rides on the wings of the wind
To join the space where breath goes.
Place that held purpose and meaning
Is now void of substance known and loved
And has moved to be transformed.
To live… beyond space or breath or memory
Beyond the place where time is
Where only love remains.

—*Marcia G. Androsoff*

Dark Day

Never to see the rising splendor of the sun,
The changing tints upon an early morning hill,
Or watch it blazoned by a crimson twilight fire
Before another slow-receding day is still.
Never to see the countryside soft swept by rain
In muted colours restful to the questing eye;
Mist grey and dusky purple, smoky brown and green,
The pearl and opalescent sheen of new-washed sky.

Waft her the scents of summer and of autumn leaves
That she may know the seasons through the changing year.
Give her the cool, caressing touch of each young breeze
That she may feel it ripple lightly through her hair.
Pour softly into each acute and listening ear
Such charms as bear no relevance to dark or light -
The friendly sounds of passing life for her to hear -
To bring her comfort in her everlasting night.

—*Roxane Houston*

The Hungry Soul

To know,
The child I have within is waiting to be Born.
A soul,
It yearns to live, longing to be loved.
When I let this soul come home,
The home,
To which all returning is no sacrifice,
I will be reborn, and, with that rebirth,
Then,
And only then,
I can give birth to my Hungry Soul.

—*Liz Routier*

...e Day

...rth! The radio blasts on!
...e clock hands mercilessly forwards creep...
...e curtain of sleep is rudely torn.
...freshness pervades over shadows deep.

...tside in the frosty air the figures wait,
...patient to resume their daily cycles...
...es seeing without sight,
...ces keen and bright, anticipating the day's struggles.

...e city silhouetted in the soft grey sky,
...ysteriously beckons, then looms up tall -
...the confusion, a mass of feet fly...
...'nine-to-five homes' to give their all.

...e smell of bread and tangy fruit,
...maybe the cozy place down the street -
...e you wearing jeans or a suit?
...ah, the fragrance divine - save me a seat!

...e homeward train rocks to sleep.
...d the day's events gently blur...
...evening calmness, machine-like I creep,
...fore night's numbness obliterates the uproar.

    —Sanghamitra Sen

...e Knife

...e knife was in the desert.
...e desert looked like an orifice in the sky.
...om which any retribute could appear.
...lamed with a noisome face of something innumerable
...say the least.
...e knife was in the noisome face.
...ychedelic to the human eye.
...e eye of an empiric who carries only one small tool.
...at of a rein.
...hich one belonged to a dead horse.
...ho was killed by a knife.
...the desert.

    —Afshan Ahmad

...eep Not the Kings of Gentiles

...orld sees more than enough this century
...e destructions of our fragile planet in the living memory
...ght from the Arctic Circle across the South Hemisphere
...mans and creatures expelled from their places of abode
...l around our fragile earth,
...eir original habitats are increasingly on the exploit
...th senseless mass destructions in our peace time
...eep not the kings of Gentiles
...use you wash your hands and feet out, and
...atch the slaughter of the few virgin forests around
...here are you gonna run when the voice above say, come?
...here are you gonna hide when ask to speak the truth?
...eep not the Kings of Gentiles 'cause you're dead satellites
...ee no truce nor lay down of arms
...ir planet and its people are now under siege
...weep not the kings of Gentiles 'cause you never care
...lam and Eve never saw all this gloom around,
...the Garden of Eden the bible says
...eep not the kings of Gentiles for you're inert
...l cry out, how can we heal the pains?

    —Don Okoko

Halloween

Imagine the scene, a dark cold night,
The glow of the moon shone an eerie light,
An owl softly hooted to his mate as she flew,
Hunting the hedgerow for a nice tasty shrew.
Then a frightening cackle broke the peace of the night,
And a witch on a broomstick flew into sight,
With a wart on her nose and a long pointed hat,
She was joined on her flight by her ugly black cat.
When out of the darkness a shadow did creep,
What else but a ghost - or was it a sheet?
As it floated across the dew soaked ground,
It opened it's mouth, yet made - not a sound.
All of a sudden strange faces appeared,
Some ugly, some gruesome, but all of them weird,
With brightly lit mouths and noses and eyes,
Their brilliant features lit up the skies.
Through my fear I realized, this wasn't a dream,
'Twas the end of October - of course - Halloween.

    —J. A. Browne

Wasting

Thoughts ricochet piercing
the grey matter splattering the inside
of my bloodied skull!

God! How I long for death!
As the frost settles upon my shattered frame.

Homeless and starved to the point of -
nearly eating out of rubbish bins
by the take-aways.

Warm bed! Where are you? My second womb.
"Here darling embraced by four warm walls
in many an upstairs room."

In the early morning nostrils smell
the food from cafes.
I window glance furniture shops
with enchanting beds.
Yet walk this temporary world and dream -
until the paupers grave.

    —Paul Stocks

The Gamekeeper

Crisp frosty mornings, a 'Tally Ho!' horn
The hunt comes a calling from dusk until
dawn. 'Through windswept fields the
Hounds fast and slow. A fox it's heart
Beating with no-where to go.

Closer and closer the huntsmen come, laughing
And jostling enjoying the fun. Into the woods
A pheasant they scare, squawking and soaring
High into the air. Crack! The birds falls, down
Instantly dead, a gamekeeper whistles his
Gun dog has fled.

Riders and horses, panic awry the gleam
On their boots is now in their eyes all
Muddied and tatty raise high the whips
A flurry of words escaping their lips.

A gamekeeper cries 'be gone from his land,
That cub you've been chasing I tended by
hand.' Surly and cross they turned heel
Astray, the fluffy warm bundle stowed safely away!

    —Joanne N. Parris

Little girl, will you ever know
The joy you have brought me, the love
Overwhelming me every time
I look into your eyes.
While I carried you
Many thoughts and emotions took me
To highs and lows I never knew before.
But nothing ever surpassed
My ever-growing, ever-lasting
Love for you; my little girl.
In my soul, with all my heart,
I will always cherish you, my beautiful girl.
The day you were born. I was born, too.
Now I am, and will always be, a mother
So proud of you
And filled with joy and love forever
Little girl.
　　　　—T. Kwissa

Over the Bullrushes

I see the window over there,
The light gently glowing on whom I care,
In the house, over the Bullrushes.

His shadow falls on the pane
In his hands my love is laying,
On he that lives, over the Bullrushes.

One night a tragedy falls,
A fire rages.
I run for him there, over the Bullrushes

The flames rage on, my love is high
Through the house I go, with an anguished cry,
I see him, my love, over the Bullrushes

He lays under debris just past the stair,
I run and drag him out from there
And onto the lawn, over the Bullrushes

He coughs, a faint smile on his face,
He's safe, he knows, in my arms.
I hear the sirens on their way,
"Thank you, my love" I hear him say
My heart soars, over the Bullrushes.
　　　　—W. Suzanne Robitaille

Freedom One

Freedom one had landed.
The men they were freed.
They flew from Algeria.
To West Germany.
They were held in captivity.
Over in Iran.
American citizen's.
And belonged in their land.

As I sat in my living room watching T.V.
I saw freedom one landing.
In West Germany.
As they walked down the ladder,
And onto the land.
President Carter was there
To shake each man's hand.

Set them free, set them free.
Was everyone's plead.
(Dear Lord) above set them free.
　　　　—Elizabeth Piercey

The Old Man

The old man sits to tell his story of the time when life was pain.
The pain is one that only he can understand.
The sorrow began the day he lost the people that he needed so,
The love he felt was one of trust to live a life like that.
To tell the truth would only cause the life he made to leave,
But to tell a lie of what went on would only cause more pain.
What to do, only he knows the truth for love like that will stay,
In your heart, just one more day than what you want it to be.
The one day came when all pain was gone for it to leave was grea
But why it left is one that only the man will know.
　　　　—Darcy Jansen

The Picture

I saw a picture of you yesterday
The picture was of you standing in the rain
Moving round and round making no sound
Talking to voices underground

I saw an image of you in blue
The image was unkind but somehow true
It was making the cries you do when I roam
I then open my eyes to see I'm alone

The pictures I see are always new
The pictures I see are always of you
Wishing I'm in the pictures that you are too
Is a wish that only she can make true

I'm gonna take a ride to City Untold
I'm gonna take a picture of you in the cold
I'm gonna shout out no then you'd say
You're the source of my wrath to innocent prey!
　　　　—G. A. Kellman

Hellions: Servants Of Hell

On a dragonfly's wing,
The screams of Hellions sing,
torture for infinite years,
spilling blood and tears.
The Hellions know the way,
to make your face turn gray,
and pale as that of a ghost,
for they feed on their living host.
Their faces twisted and torn,
from the way they were when born,
their eyes scream of the pain,
of going to Hell and back again,
their mouths sing of the song of death,
before it steals away man's last breath.
For they are the servants of Hell,
and satan himself shall ring the bell.
Writhing, dying,
floating, flying,
fare thee well,
when you enter the realm of Hell.
　　　　—Tim Hayes

Why?

In this life there are some wonderful things.
　　Some things I don't question like
　　　Why the sun rises and sets
　　　　Why is it so beautiful?

　Why do birds fly south for the winter?
　　How do they know winter's coming?

　　Why is God such a beautiful person?
　　Why hasn't anyone ever seen him?

But the one question I would like to know
　　Why does God put us on earth to love
　　　Someone and then take him away.
　　　　—Jeannie Landry

...ptive Song

...ear them.

...ear them:

     the sighs of the jobless;
     the sobs of the barren;
     the chatter of waifs;
     the tear - drops of widows.

...ear them:

...ear them:

     the echo of their groans;
     the thunder of their lament;
     the chorus of their woes;
     the siren of their sorrows:

...eir sun sinks at mid-day
...owning their day in darkness
...d hope suffocates, like a hanged rat, in their souls
...their day dies.
    —*Otuije Onyema*

...titled

...ting alone in this empty room with no-one around but me.
...e sound stillness... one tear falling, falling onto my lap.
...cloud sits in front of my eyes. I can not see, I do not
...nt to see because it will only hurt. The cloud blocks
...ay the world of my hell.
...w I sit and talk to myself, just talk. I
...'t have friends, I don't want friends.
...ey don't need me. I need me!
...w I'm going back in time. I'm 18 again
...pain, pain and agony. Why I did it is partly unanswered.
...dn't want to do it. She put the knife in my hand and
...ined it with her own blood. The blood that put me here
...iind these bars so alone.
...why am I punished? Suffering, I will die here. Why?
...cause of a word so powerful and uncontrollable. A word
...t can turn anyone insane.
    —*Connie Meyers*

...Be Human

...e storms of life rise and fall like waves.
...e waves crash against the rocks creating caves.
...s here, in the deep, where we hide how we feel
...e other side, trying to disguise what is real.

...some, feelings seem meaningless
...r they are thought to be a weakness.
...be human is to feel, to express emotion
...d not to pretend to go through the motion.

...ey say: Doomed is my life, my life must cease
...put my mind at rest, to find that find peace.

...ife so bad that we must snuff out existence?
...! I say, we must fight with persistence!
...deal with our problems and find a solution,
...e humans have always done, rid our minds of the pollution.

...ey say: Redeemed is my life, my life must not cease
...put my mind at rest, to find that final peace.
    —*Dianna Robins*

Despair

The sky grew dark. The mountain roared.
    The world came to an end.
He stood and watched the tossing sea
    And thought how it began.

The lightning flashed and lit the night.
    The sight was to behold!
He felt so feeble, all alone
    And knew he should be bold.

The earth then cracked and opened wide.
    For smoke he could not see.
He closed his eyes and tried to think
    How such a thing could be.

    "Why me O'Lord," he cried aloud.
      "Why should I be the one
    To witness such a drastic sight
    And live when it was done!"

The smoke did clear. He saw the crowd.
    Of him they weren't aware
And only then he realized
    'Twas only his despair.
    —*Roy Victor Murray*

The Rabbit

Blind faith no longer exists,
The world is too harsh to have it.
The cuts and scrapes, all "Battle wounds"
Will heal with the blood from rabbits.
Innocence is slaughtered daily.
So we'll use his flesh for profit.
Your sheets are stained
With blood from pain,
But think of that poor hare.
An offense he would not dare.
While we persist to love and hate
You eat rabbit from my plate.

His fur was white and oh so pure,
Like starlight in the night.
You tore his fur and ripped his life apart.
Well my friend, I've news for you,
That rabbit was my heart.
    —*Shelley Durocher*

Untitled

His hand so gnarled you'd never link
Them with the hands once dimpled pink,
For now with age and endless toil,
Exhausting work with sows and soil,
Though little pigs rush in a band
To be caressed by soil-stained hand,
Few human beings can endure
The sight of something "So impure!"
He wonders "Does God care so much
For aught but silken textured touch?
Could not a thing of purest gold
Be hidden in harsh hessian's fold?

Before attending Church at night
He scrubs and scrubs to put things right
Still wondering "Does God only care
For those with hands which show no wear?"
If this is so what chance have I
Of going to Heaven when I die!"

But God I know will understand
He'll make allowance for those hands.
    —*P. Smith*

Asking for Him

"Is there a beautiful man out in the universe today?" "Is
there a gruff and rough man willing to play life's game?"
"Is there anyone there who thinks the same?" "Can he feel the
joy of living and loving?" Can he honestly say, Yes, he is giving!
"Will he love as a person and not as a fixture?"
"Does his life include a perfect picture?"
"Was he a drunk, hard and scary?" "Is he still?" "Did he steal,
or treat people unkind?" "Did the police make him toe the
line?" Please do not come forward as you are the wrong man who
is blind. "Do you offer protection from life's bumps and
grinds?" "Do you have broad shoulders strong muscles and a good
mind?" "Are you dependable with a little boy's wonder?" "Are
you looking ahead to see what is up yonder?" "Are you willing
to take risks- adventure, as a sense of play?" If you answer
yes to most of the above, with love. Would you like a little
girl at heart to take your hand and be a part?"

—*Eleanor Weber*

Sisters

Sister, you are my friend, and I look up to you,
there isn't a thing in the world that I wouldn't do.
When I was young you were always by my side.
I would come into your room, and there I would hide.

Do you remember all the talks we kept between us?
you still would love me even when I'd fuss.
You taught me about right and let me learn about wrong,
when I was falling I had your shoulder to lean on.

You took me every where, no matter where you went,
and any article of clothing, you always lent.
You were proud of me like I was of you,
for being my sister and seeing me through.

I had some bad times but you were always there,
holding out your arms and showing you care.
That closeness we had seemed to disappear,
and now it has left me with nothing but tears.

—*Billie-Jo Ferguson*

Days of Summer

It's the days of summer
They are all here
The catcher, the pitcher
The guy with the beer.

The field's not the best
They will settle for less
The thud of the ball
An umpires good call

To be part of the team
Who wants to win or at least be satisfied
With a grin.

Here they are
The large and the small,
Here to play just a game of ball

The game they say is just a sport
Yet somehow they play,
Defending the fort.

It won't stop the wars
Famine or hate
But maybe the game will open the gate

—*E. Jane Danielson*

Husbands

Husbands are special without a doubt
They have much to do as Head of the House
They have to fix the car and mow the lawn
And get up at the crack of dawn
My husband sometimes is a nurse
When I make a mess, he doesn't curse
Husbands know just what to say
If you are having a trying day
If the washer breaks, he says, "Don't cry"
I'll have it fixed in a wink of an eye
And if it needs a part, don't frown
I'll make a little trip to town.
Don't nag, as it grates upon one's nerves
Give him the love and respect he deserves
My husband is a "special" one
If he can't do it — it can't be done
A good husband is a treasure indeed
He fulfills his wife's every need.

—*Judy A. Waugh*

Gun Men

The gunmen are taking lives
They killed the husband and leave the wives
They smoked the crack
And killed the cops
And murdered the Babes upon the breast.
They walked into the bank
With a brave and cruel heart
They order the manager to get flat
And then they do their part.
The gunmen sniff the coke
They did it for a joke
And when they are finish
They closed their eyes,
And said. I'm feeling high.
These cold blooded murderer
Sometimes have to be honoured.
For fear of our lives.
But if God was just like man
I know they would all understand.

—*Lavern Arthurs*

Helena's Golden Wing

Crisp autumn leaves put thee in trance.
They rustic ones began to dance.
Thy wind began to softly blow,
thy cheeks of God began to glow.
Thy ring of Angels doth not sing.
Helena lost a tiny wing.
Thee Angels looked throughout the sky
Helena couldn't even fly
Thee God began to search then smile
In Autumns tree there was a pile.
In rustic golden greenish leaves.
There sits a bird and slowly weaves
Underneath her tiny breast,
She builds a loving mothers nest.
Then slowly to her young she'll sing.
Praise to Helena's Golden Wing.

—*Alexia Panagiotou*

octurnal Liaisons

ese balmy nights of mysterious dreaming:
ey sail in and out of my life
ke quiet messengers streaming
wn a vista of dim lights astrife
ildings that have been imposed upon
 shadows casting out repressed memories.
ese dreams lurk incessantly in the dark pond
 an illusion created by stealthy thieves
10 wait surreptitiously in the background.
pidly, they descend upon this unwitting lady,
trapping me to a time bound
r dispersing the fears of my emotional captivity.
ese nights string together messages
ded with imagery hiding in dark
ices where they've existed through the ages.
y unreconciled memories have entrenched a mark
 deep and uncompromising that strangers
n steal into the depths of my confusion
d like magicians release these wild creatures
 that finally I can meet my illusion.

—*Nicola Bird*

The Place Where You Kissed Me

ent today to the place where you kissed me
king I could mayhap find restful peace,
 instead my heart choked a nostalgia
ich had in this poem its sweetest release.

 soul must needs in your chest again dwell...
 why did you make of my tears your game?
u changed overnight, that much I can tell,
1 I changed as well, you not being the same.

 as there alone, by the world unseen...
 vas so like then... only you were missing.
 t then, love, the harbour and the cold sea wind,
 at do they know of kissing?

—*Laura Chalar*

Vill Never Forget You

e been selfish and uncaring,
 king only of the pain.
e been very unforgiving,
 t I won't do it again.

sk for your forgiveness,
 oing you can be my friend.
 member only the happiness,
 will share 'til the very end.

 a very, very sorry, for what I did to you.
 at you wanted was a different story
 n what I wanted from you.

 u've always been my friend, and you always will be.
 ways there to give a helping hand,
 t's what a friend should be.

 u think we're friends now,
 t to me you're more.
 keep it a secret somehow,
 d try to forget how my heart you tore.

 n't know what love is,
 don't know if I love you.
 t I do know this, that I will never forget you.

—*Anita Neufeld*

Me Feelings: (A Dedication)

I see you clearly in my mind,
This vision frightens me,
Your face appears so soft, yet strong,
And seems to haunt me as each day goes on.

Is this new feeling simple infatuation,
Or is infatuation all that simple?
"Can it be love?", I ask myself.
The answer, "No, you've not known him long."

I wonder what you would do if I told you my thoughts;
Would you run and hide? Or would you tell me how you feel
inside?

Each thought is a question, and none has an answer.
(Or is there an answer unseen?)
My thoughts and feelings puzzle me
Why is it you do what you do to me?

—*Liane Bisaillon*

"Birth of my Grandchild."

For seconds I see her -
Thrust from the womb
Naked, bloody; streaked with her mother's agony.
Mouth torn in a soundless scream
Wrinkled grey hands, straining back
to something forever lost.
Ancient eyes; filled with the knowledge
and horror of centuries past and to come.

In minutes I see her
Suckling at the breast
Silken skin diffused with pink.
Tiny hands folded like flowers at dusk.
Eyes like limpid pools of innocence,
gazing in drowsy wonder at her
mother's face.
Child of my child; the last and greatest joy.

—*Mary E. Maloney*

Time

Time is the keeper of our dreams
Time is never ever what it seems
Time is short; time is long
Time will right what is wrong.

Time can change your life, time can ward off strife
Time is master of the season, time gives space to reason.

Time is the endless search for more
Time to get more than before
Time is present, time is past
Time is that which cannot last.

Time is what we cannot hold
Time cannot be bought or sold,
Time is everything to every man
Time is hard to understand.

Time rules in every domain, time is loss and time is gain
Time can never be but now time is always lost somehow.

Time carries you to your goal
Time can ease your very soul
Time, respect it, to succeed
Time, on time, is all you need.

—*James L. Ferguson*

Do You Ever Think Ahead?

Do you ever think ahead
to days to come or even years.
What is around that next corner,
we all seem to wonder and ponder.
But we still never get to know until it is upon us.

Do you ever think ahead
is it going to be good or bad.
Can you, or can't you wait
for fate to take it's mighty bite.

Do you think of love
just who is going to be that mister right,
or do you think of having fortunes
Only to sit alone and count your last coin that same night,
or is it family that you think of,
and promise this time you really will show up.

Or do you sail through life with out the strife,
With no need to think ahead
Even with nothing at all,
but family and friends
Your still the richest of them all.

—*Traci-L Barker*

If I Were a Dog Instead of a Tree

or My Bark is Better

Oh, what joy to be a pup,
to romp and run, on laps jump up.
What fun to race around a park
emitting oft a playful bark.

How comforting to have a home,
a friendly master, tasty bone,
A life at once both free and kept.
Old willow tree, once dead, has wept.

A tree alive grows in the ground,
Relies on wind to make a sound.
It cannot move, but tries its best
by sending branches east and west.

A tree's exposed to black of night,
to snow and hail and thunderlight.
Dependent on no one, it stands
a witness to clasped lovers' hands.

A dog's a dog, a tree's a tree.
One cannot the other be.
However, trees must often wish
that puppy piss did not exist.

—*Jacquelyn Martin*

Yearnings

Moonlight on an Eastern beach beside a crystal sea
The fragrance of magnolias drifting o'er the lea.
Saharan stars, the Southern cross and trade winds in a tree
Whispering a love song to you my dear and me.

Canoeing on the Humber in a quiet cool lagoon.
The saucy wavelets shimmer beneath a harvest moon.
The breeze in the branches hum a soft seductive tune
And the stars in your eyes dim the stars in the skies on a
    balmy night in June.
The locks and glens of Scotland are entrancing — ever new,
Killarney's lakes and fells are known to people of every hue.
Seattle has its beauty spots and so has Timbuktu.
But anyplace would be Paradise if I could be with you.

—*J. H. Leatham*

Crossing The Line

When one crosses over the line,
to the other side for walking,
How can things or life be fine,
when fit is in the talking?
Anger and self-pity seems the win,
of the young, leave alone;
Drawing in the innocence is sin,
for aid to another is the tone;
Love is great, love is cherish,
but it does take work;
Promiscuity, the inner death of perish,
fallacy thinking is the lurk;
Spirituality, the guise nicety is hidden,
discernment is the key;
Once over the father of lies the bid'n,
then justification the ill to be;
Self-will is the aim to please the heed,
if it feels good do it;
Self-righteousness the calling to head,
Have I done my bit?

—*Lawrence M. Kosedy*

The Stranger

He walks along the busy streets
Travelling back and forth from dusk 'til dawn
He never smiles or speaks a word
Where he comes from nobody knows
For he is a stranger
An outsider
An individual people disregard
For he is a new comer
A new comer not welcome!
The laughter can be heard from a passing car
He lowers his head hiding his watery eyes
For another day has come just the same
He begins walking towards his place
It not very much
But all he can afford
A cardboard box
He call his home…

—*Cory S. Visutski*

Footprints

Twice I am stepped on
Twice I brush myself off

Live and learn, I say

As I turn my face skyward,
I see the ominous shadow of yet another shoe…
Its destination… the very core of my heart

You see, my heart is splattered with footprints
Of many shapes and sizes. Some thankfully, are
Fading, while the signature of a few will remain
Forever.

My heart is not as the sand, prints easily washed
Away by the day's waves,
But more like soft clay,
Impressions which are left too long, turn hard and ugly.

I must be treated gentle, for if you look closely,
You will see I am gentle too.

—*Marji Locket*

Garden Full of Weeds

Ten little fingers, ten little toes
Two bright eyes and a cute little nose.
A smile on your lips and peace upon your face
Welcome to the earth my son this wonderful joyous place.

Shot down by a gunman the innocent victim died
Clutching to her loved one, her face quivered as she cried.
Little children wounded by the hand they often feared
Darkness taking over as we shed another tear.

Prejudice and hatred seeping through the divided walls
War, destruction, murder as yet another victim falls.
Homeless people walking the dark, grim streets of crime
Innocent babies screeching as the gun fired one more time.

Sweet dreams dancing through your head
But someday soon you shall all be dead.
Killed by your brothers who hunger for evil deeds
You are like a flower my son in a garden full of weeds.

I will try to protect you from the wicked world outside
Raising all of your goodness, come out now don't you hide.
Always wear a smile and your faith will get you through
Always remember my face dear son for I will always love you.
      —*Tiffany Richardson*

Soldiers

Off to war the soldiers went
Unloaded their guns and set up their tents

They built a base that would not break
The lives of soldiers the enemies would take

They went to war hoping to win
But the war was just starting to begin

There were shrieking cries of soldiers being shot
While some died others still fought

When the war was over the soldiers went home
Their families came to greet them so they were not alone

They won the war but soldiers died
We all were proud that they had tried
      —*Candace Nikic*

Family Matters

Let us understand;
unnecessary denial and painful heartache,
our elders crying and brotherhood at stake,
what should be done?

Let us imagine;
a sense of pride, glory and above all trust,
our elders sharing precious moments with us,
what could we do?

Let us understand:
our people constantly disagreeing,
neglecting love between human beings,
this respect?

Let us imagine;
our children playing, cherishing life,
a special love shared between husband and wife.
We can learn together.

All my relations.
      —*Candy George*

Specula Lucis

I had been standing still
Up there it rain'd that dream, as bright
  As a cool drizzle in the morning
With an abrupt flavour of nearness.

This sudden shiny shower
Turned to new heavens opening down
  Down as if descending:
  Oh, clotted I was no more, but
  Like a boneless old-man's-beard
  Up, clambering up
I did then see, I did learn it
That even a hoarse matin-tune from afar
Our very days' boredom discolours.

They said perhaps I'd faded away—
  That incumbent rock, I sighted
  At the bottom of my further path—
And the vale beyond - a real womb of glitter.

  Down where our lives' circle
  Is tinged with eternalness,
  I had been standing still.
      —*Flavio F. Poli*

Picturesque

A lovely day,
walking along south downs way,
to help endangered species.

Through bridle paths
and horses trotting pass,
nodding their heads in approval.

The views surrounding countryside,
the flow of rolling hills.
It's nice to help wild life when you can.

Fields a little muddy,
and puddles here and there,
the route being sheer magic.
So glad we were there.
      —*Joyce Redman*

Christmastime

Christmastime in the olden days
Was horses pulling wooden sleighs,
Molasses cookies and popcorn balls,
Rough skating ice and great snowfalls.

The country school with its quaint program,
Featured Simon and Bob, Norene and Pam;
All traded gifts and laughed and sang;
There were candy and nuts, and tinsel to hang.

The white-sheeted curtains were strung on a wire
To hide all the kids who sang in the choir.
Then one by one we took our turn
And spoke the lines we'd had to learn.

Our songs and plays and poems were done,
To some it was torture, but to others fun.
And dads and moms and friends galore
Returned each year to hear some more.

But things have changed since the olden days,
The little old schools and the Christmas plays,
Are history forever but continue to chime,
In the rooms of my head each Christmastime.
      —*L. K. Redinger*

Our Promise

It seems like only yesterday,
we took our vows for life.
I remember well those loving words,
as you took me for your wife.

"I promise to be faithful,
and always honest too,
I will respect, trust, and help;
and always care for you."

"I will share my life with you,"
I know you meant every word.
"Forgive as we've been forgiven,"
those are the lines I heard.

"Through best and worst of what's to come,
as long as we both shall live."
You memorized each solemn vow,
what a special gift to give.

All of those things you promised,
and kept your word so true.
It seems like only yesterday,
I repeated those same vows to you.

—*Allyce Jones*

Inside Looking Out

Life is a series of masks. We wear when we want to impress.
We wear masks to make us appear happy, our true feelings we
just can't express. A sad mask for sorry occasions, to show
that we really do care. A mask that shows placid contentment,
when our hearts are feeling despair. A mask will cover up
feelings, just wear one and then you will know. But when
you're alone with your feelings, your true will surely show.
A mask is a form of deception, it allows you to be someone new.
When you can't cope with being the person inside, you can give
others a much different view. Use your mask as a strong piece
of armour, you can build all the walls that you need. When you
look through the shield you've created, your confidence you
won't impede. A mask allows time to make judgements, to reason
and make and walk out from behind. What's the verdict when
people first see you, when they see you as you want to be. Is
surprise in their eyes when you let down your mask? Do they
like the new person they see? You don't need a mask when alone,
because no one will ever see.   The real you that's hiding in
shadows, what you get, what you see isn't me.

—*Patricia Munt*

The Old Brown Bag The Treasure Trove

We were ready to move to our new home
We'd packed all the boxes but there alone
Sat an old brown bag creased, tattered,
dented with many a journey its true
That old brief case that belonged to you
Not something anyone else would save
But to me it was a treasure cave
Out of it's depths had emerged bounties unknown
A fish, loaf of bread, bottle of wine
Beautiful cards and records we shared alone
Lovely aromatic soaps, scented creme for my hands
and now alone and abandoned it stands.
A romantic reminder of our love
When you courted me with its treasure trove
So near to us that old brown bag will always be
It's part of our lives, yes part of you and me
Just glance at its worn seams
And the memory of a light in the window gleams
Never in all my life through
Would I part with it or part with you.

—*Thelma Ione Barry*

A Winner

A winner is a person who pulls his own
weight around without waiting for anyone else to
do it for him.

A person who knows when to say "no" and then
be proud of that decision

An individual who can look in the mirror
and say that he likes what he sees.

Somebody who is always there to lend a helping
hand to others and do it with a smile.

A person who gives his best effort in everything
he attempts and if he doesn't succeed, he is
willing to try over again and again.

But most of all, a person who never gives up
is a winner because quitters never win
and winners never quit.

—*Annette Marina Gauthier*

Little Boy of Love

Little boy of love
Welcome to our world
Welcome to life
Although it is not perfect
Although it can be cruel
All you need are two things
Love and courage
You ask, what is love?
Love is about caring
It is respect and gentleness
You ask, what is courage?
Courage is standing up for what you believe in
Standing up for who you believe in
And admitting to your mistakes and facing them head on
I say only this to you little boy of love
Love will bring you happiness but sometimes pain
But then courage comes along and saves the day
Live by these rules little boy of love
And you shall be the boy who grew into
A very, very special man

—*Annie Gagnon*

Memories

I know it's weird
what I'm feeling now
I never felt this way before
maybe it's just the same as always
just a different beginning
but the same hurting - ending:
Leaving...
And loosing the moments of good times
they always leave you with a memory of them
and a scar in your heart that doesn't heal
and they know you won't forget
it's almost a disease with no cure or vaccine
that unfortunately - spreads so fast
and you try and try...but...
Nothing changes...
it'll stay this way...now and forever...
These awful memories of previous loves,

—*Dima Hussein*

What Mountains Tell

Oh Mountains ye, of rock so old,
What you tell? While stand so bold,
Your view of earth, far and wide,
All many secrets! Do you hide.

Your snow-clad peaks, reach to the sky,
The climber, see he, those clouds go rolling by,
Your crystal stream, bound round and around,
Dance by day, at your command.

What fossil? Hidden far below,
Tell your time, of long ago,
What crevice deep! Within thy face,
Holds what life's historic case.

What minerals rare - within thy seams,
Gold for man - his wildest dreams,
And tunnel his - with pick and drill,
Oh let him fall, to dust your feet,
For when he's gone, you're be there still.

—*M. F. Soper*

Years of Loneliness

Every time my volcano of hate would erupt with anger and rage.
When ever I saw her happily laughing, giving you that
mischievous grin and talking. Seeing you return that
flirtatious smile, tore my heart and made me cry. It seemed from
your memory I was being erased — Whenever I saw you both face
to face. I wanted to reach out and tell you how I felt,
But every time I talked I hid further in my shell.
You seemed like a stranger, so new and untrue,
And I just couldn't open up, no matter how hard I tried to.
Pretext was something she was so good at,
And when I told you, you never believed that.
The things she had said and done were so mortifying,
In my heart I knew, you thought I was lying.
Because of her molestation, in front of my friends I had to bear
humiliation. At that moment I drew conclusion —
That, for us, break up was the only solution.
You then said you would change your colours for me.
But deceptive to your words you proved to be.
It was circumstances that eventually proved and showed
That "all that glitters is certainly not gold!"

—*Nazish Davar*

Addressing Friends

Wonderful, brilliant and lovely to hear,
When one opens up and lets out some cheer.
A means of exchange for one to a peer,
The mysteries unfold for those with an ear.

Flowing like water as clear as glass,
The people are grouped into a class.
With curing and stealth the speaker will rise,
And deliver a speech that opens their eyes.

Through books and texts we hopefully learn,
To salvage those we wish not to burn.
Revealing the facts which have been found.
Lifting the binding that keeps them bound.

Then those who assemble to listen and hear.
Clap their hands and offer the cheer.
Figures delight of speech with a peer,
The genius is present so bend an ear.

—*J. A. Pietsch*

Sorrow

Why did this young man pierce her very life,
When she wanted but one thing; to end her strife.
For she had been done many a time before,
She could not absorb him because of it all.

She wanted a part of him to be of herself,
Yet she knew all too well that it lay on the shelf.
Another man before him had taken her far,
On a trip that will forever leave her a scar.

How can she tell him his life-string links hers,
When he's not aware of the death-driven thirst.
She'll take her life, if it matters but small,
For reality stays even after the fall.

—*Marion J. Urban*

The Package

The year was 92, the truth I'm tellin' you
When skipper John he really locked the door.
He closed the fishery down-and left us with a frown
The like, of course, we never saw before.

The picture was remote with all our boats afloat
We thought 'twas like it was "just up and go"
But Crosbie shook his fist and said "you cannot fish
Now that's a fact and I am sayin' so".

"Take in your gear today-and stow it all away
Haul up your boats and put them in the pound.
'Cause we will pay the price-and matters will be nice
And in a while the package will be down."

'Twas hard to take that rule-but now we're back in school
Its not too bad at all as we can see.
The fishery it has passed-and Christmas here at last
So here's the best to all in 93.

—*Paul Emberley*

The Intangible Nature

There are folks that blame their brother
when they stumble along the way
Others say it's fate because it happened on that day.
The smart blame the unlearned for the slums and dirty lanes
The salesman blame the markets when he doesn't make his gains.
The gambler trusts his dice as they roll across the board
The fisherman often casts his net when he isn't even moored.
We never want to answer for things that might go wrong
We say it isn't our fault cause we are week and they are strong.
If others shirk their duty and throw caution to the wind
It doesn't mean we should imitate and unkindly treat a friend.
Account for all your actions and be honest in our ways
For each his life must mold to stand in his proper place.

—*Jean Hazel Daugherty*

Someone

Won't you be someone special, someone kind
Someone always on my mind
Won't you be someone to love me, someone to care.
Someone with my life, I'd like to share
Won't you be someone forever, someone together.
Someone who will never say never
Won't you be someone in my dreams
Someone to understand my every means
Won't you be someone to hold my hand
and say it's alright.
Someone who will never give in without a fight.
Someone to kiss me, someone to miss me
Someone who will always stay
Someone to love me in every way.

—*Anna Sawicki*

To My Son

How many more days to wake,
When you feel your heart is about to break.
How many more days to feel sadness,
When you know the days should be gladness.
How many more days of no joy,
When in your heart you still are a boy.
How many more days to live when this
thing won't allow you to give.
The answer is before you, go on a search I
implore you, the way is hard, the road is long.
Your allies are music or sing that song.
No doubt we'll find what where searching for.
We will find that key to unlock that door.
So God give me strength, please keep holding
my hand, I know something is to come and
that something is grand.

    —*H. D. Greenwood*

Home

Home! Where father rules and Mother cares,
Where each child fun with others shares.

Home!
Where work is joy and food is near,
Where no one has a cause for fear.

Home!
Where all the clan at night will pray,
Where all return when skies are gray.

Home!
Where friends will come and go in peace,
Where foes will find they have no place.

Home!
Where roots are laid of character,
Where pride in work is sought after.

    —*Anezi Okoro*

The Carton

It lay on the dew-drenched emerald grass,
Where Erica spilt o'er the verdant lea.
A symbol of thoughtlessness-of an uncaring soul
Too steeped in bitterness idyllic beauty to see.

The children came running-cheeks aglowing with sun.
Their pet pounced on the carton, as a prize he had won.
The arsonist watched trembling, evil eyes afraid
Lest the dog betray him-his plans thus waylaid.
Thoughts torturous and turbid, yet tinged with pity
For these happy tots from the polluted city.
Soon their respite from care for them be no more
And man's darkest nature they would know for sure.

He had found his father, hideous in death,
Hanging in the barn, where life-long he'd toiled.
This sacred place was now used for pleasure
By folks who did not deserve this leisure.

That night, the family returned to the city.
He watched his inferno, feeling no pity.
His friends bought him drinks in the pub that night;
But the carton betrayed him-no more would he fight.

    —*Joan E. Clark*

Serenity

On this earth of heaven and hell
Where good and evil have to dwell
And in this world that is so old
We have to make gentle the bold

We rush around all in despair
Without concern without a care
Mankind caught up with his greed
Worries not for those that really need

Through all the ages man has dwelt
The time has come to find content
Let one and all be of same mind
For its themselves they have to find

All those thoughts we think our own
We have to realize what is shown
In every man this conflict has to cease
Before we humans ever find elusive peace

    —*R. Hargreaves*

Sea Gulls

A flock of gulls threads its way yonder,
Where sea and sky are locked in an embrace.

The birds hover,
Now together,
Now asunder.
You stare in wonder.

Wings folded, wings outspread,
Wing never touching wing,
Yet the flock is a oneness.
To whose command do they bow?
Whose orders do they follow?

The sea gulls dance -
White robed ballerinas in motion -
To the predestined beat,
To the sea's eternal music.
Who was the designer?
Whose was the notion?

Questions remain unuttered.
Grains of sand now slipping through your fingers
Keep the secret, in silence, shuttered.

    —*Levi Shalit*

The Rainbow Frog's Country

Walking through the rain forest
Where the rainbow frog's do live
Raindrops sprinkled over the ground
Glisten and sparkle with every sound

Trees that have grown tall and big
Wonder, how much longer they will exist?
Please, please, leave us alone
on this planet that we call home

Listen, as the cool green breeze
whistles softly between the leaves
Perched high up on the leafy canopy
so many birds can be heard, singing

The possums come up to say "hello"
and this is the message they give
Please, please, don't cut down the trees
or we will have nowhere to live

    —*Elizabeth Navratil*

Untitled

Sitting here full of fear, afraid to move.
Who's there? Behind me!
Please, don't touch me!
  Noooooooo.........
Shame, what did I do?
Why me? What do I do now?
Can't tell anyone.
  He might take more from me.
What next?
The memories...
  My mind continually rapes me.
Take the memories.
  I can't live with the fear.
Help me live.
  I want to be happy.
No more fear.
  Joy in my life.
The more I talk,
  The more free.
Please, will you listen to me?

        —*Annette Bonertz*

As A Child...

As a child I would sit and ponder....
Why is he black?
Why am I white?
Why is he wrong?
And I'm always right.
Why do we live
In worlds so apart?
When we all have a dream
And all have a heart.
Why are we treated
In two different ways?
White men as masters.
Black men as slaves.
I am now older and struck by a realization.
Colour matters only to the ignorant.

        —*Tony Garlinge*

Sad

Sad
Why must love be so sad? It's supposed to be a happy thing
A sharing thing, a giving thing...a caring thing.
It's supposed to pick you up; make you feel alive,
Give you hopes and dreams, so many things.
Sad
Why must new love be so sad?
Who are these strangers we meet, who knock us off our feet?
Give us dreams and plans and then just drift away,
Lost in some foggy space never thinking of what could be
Only of that awful place, of a hurt they once faced
Now wishing to repeat, they retreat
Leaving us all alone hungering from something as yet unknown
Sad
Why must love be so sad? I wish I could make it go away.
Get up and walk away...unscarred, unmarred,
Free and easy and unaffected
Sad
Why must love be so sad
Sad

        —*C. Fenton*

It Could Have Been You

People go on marches to save the bloody whale
Why not spend their energy on the old, infirm and frail?
There's poverty, unemployment and fatal disease
And all they can worry about is the fish in the sea.

Think of the man with no job and no home,
He once owned a car and a life of his own
Now he's a loner, his friends have all gone
He sits in despair wonders where he went wrong.

Think of the child who's been sexually abused
Her life has no meaning she feels dirty and used
The joy of the childhood she never had
It was taken away by a man she called dad

All of the money spent fighting a war
To bring death and destruction, what is it for?
Our young men go off to fight for a land
That spits in your face, buries its head in the sand

What of the starving that live on our earth
How could a whale undermine their worth?
Couldn't we try to do better for them
It could have been you, how'd you feel then?

        —*Lynda Halliday*

As You Go

Why ever do we laugh. Why ever do we cry
Why ever do we love to live
Because He says we never die.

Whatever you may do. Whatever you may see
Whatever you decide
Remember He can see.

Whenever you are lonely. Whenever you are down
Whenever you are by yourself
Remember He is around.

Whoever you are with. Whoever you confide
Whoever you may choose
Remember with the Lord you never lose.

Wherever you may roam
Wherever you may call home
Wherever you may go soon
Remember He always has room.

        —*Olive Bryson Hargreaves*

Always Remember

Always remember a friend is someone who:
        will always be there
        when ever you need them
        they care about you
    They want you to stay safe
        They may not be happy
    With some decisions you make
Because they don't want to see you hurt
    A friend will always understand
        They'll comfort you
        They'll help you through
    All the rough times you ever face
        so always remember
    A friend is someone for life
    Someone you can always trust

        —*Holly Pappel*

Will I?

Seems long since passion filled my life,
   Will I ever find a wife?
Will I ever father a child?
   Will I ever stop being wild?
Will I ever be responsible?
   Will I ever be so dull?
Will I ever fulfill my dream?
   Will I ever be supreme?
Will I ever write a book?
   Will I ever have good luck?
Will I ever have plenty of money
   Will I ever tell a joke that's funny?
Will I ever be at ease?
   Will I ever be any of these?

   —*R. Hudson*

Thoughts by the Pond

Clearer than clear are the waters of life's pond
Wind sweep away the memories that are long gone
I am here now through yesterday, therefore I am
I remember all the colors and then the thoughts
They sweep me still because I was and I am still
The one that will always be part of then and part of now
The sun that shine over the crests shore yesterday and will always
Remind me of a time a place a memory a part of me
I am the strength of my destiny
And the holder of all that crest
Over my mind through memories through soul
I remember a time a place and the feelings I hold inside
Because it was then even now, and forever will
Reminds me how I was I am and I will be
Because the pond will not stay dry nor turn to mud
Because I too will never fade will never be without a soul
And when time takes me way far away
On golden pond thoughts will remain.

   —*Andre Paquette*

My Flask

I have filled a flask
with crystal light,
And placed a lid upon it.

Recollections of a time so pure and rare.

Now I save them for a day
When perhaps cold hands of despair
May grip me.
And the corners of my mind travel
inward.

No cobweb thoughts are in my flask,
just those of silk and fleece.

Thought is good, but not all thought.
I have learned to filter the flood.

   —*Carole Bambullis*

The Wildflower

You gave me once upon a moment,
The token of your love so dear,
Such a lovely way to express,
Your sentiments of endearment;

Gently, so softly, in my hand,
You placed it, and you smiled,
A boyish grin that cast a spell,
Cast happiness, high and wild;

Slowly, once more, we kissed,
Warmth and affection glowed,
As I held against my breast,
My love and exuberance... the wildflower.

   —*Corinne Barton*

Fall Fanfare

Forests — ready to rest — celebrate the onset of renewing sleep
with festive garments heralding Winter-white blankets of snow.
A thousand words might plausibly paint the gaudy, glorious
kaleidoscope of Autumn woods,
but, who would believe — sight unseen — such sumptuous pictures
in thousands of shades of reds and oranges and yellows against
greens? Vermilion, crimson and cadmium reds inflame Sumach
shrub clusters... some sporting dark burgundy velvet plumes.
Fiery Maple trees glow scarlet or wine or brilliant tangerine.
Tints of pumpkin pulse against burnt orange.
Lemon or mustard yellows of Poplar, Birch, Ash or Elm
shine through amber tones, ochres or Maple golds. The russet
or ruby of Oak gleams amid vegetation tinged salmon, coral,
cerise or maroon. The bronze of leathery Beech leaves
glimmers. Interspersed... Pines, Cedars or Spruces stalwartly
ignore the colorful conflagration
while other olive, lime or emerald greens melt into myriad Fall
hues aglow in sparkling sunshine or drenched in glistening rain
... stock-still against exultant blue or wind-whirled beneath
sullen skies misty gray with grief.

   —*Tish P. Sass*

Gods of War

They wasted our world
with their testing of bombs.
The ozone layer has a piece of it gone
They say there's nothing we can
do about it now.
Did we really have a vote anyhow?
The news came out and finally
the truth
They gave us another shot of
that radiation juice.
They take no blame feel no shame
its just part of the Gods of war game.
Hope your testing left you in awe
you made sure no one else saw.
So here's a toast to them one and all.
Thanks for giving our future generation
almost no hope at all.

   —*Karen Wright*

Beyond Time

Sting in the ear of the patient
Withered fingers caress the globe
Soulful dreams mark our presence
Silhouette of blackness before a red sky
Sour worries eaten by the soil
A sanctuary of friends
Summer shade scarring the bats tears

Water fills the world's valley
A drink for those in dying thirst
Trees dance in reunion of the wind
Hooves roll along the field, grazing food
Magical lights crack the now black sky
The moon eaten by the darkness of evil
Featherless creatures fly crying in fear
Soon the clouds pull and creatures "awe"
At the reward of a sky that lives beyond a storm
The stars, and the monstrous stare of the moon
Life is passed its fear and pain
This is our earth
And we passed the storm

   —*Darwin Burns*

.S...... Thank You

Good manners in these stressful times
Would mean so very much
If every day would simply get,
The "please" and "thank you" touch.

This truth was brought home by a sign
I chanced to see one day
In a service station entrance
I passed along the way.

The question spelled out on that sign
I pondered many a mile
"Is it true that simple thank-yous
Have now gone out of style"?

I sincerely hope they haven't.
Their loss would be a shame,
Without these little niceties
Life wouldn't be the same.

Good manners when they're put to use
Will often bring a smile
And just this fact alone is proof
They'll always be worthwhile.
—*Christopher M. Vaylon*

Untitled

Mother you stand so tall and strong your whole being is never
wrong. For us you always stoop down low
in the darkness forever more you'll glow.
Mother you nurtured us with an abundance of love
such an impact on our lives you've had
from a baby to an adult you have taught us to love, care
respect and never to expect, your aura with us for evermore.

Mother like you another there will never be
just like the sun, the moon and sea
always unique - you could never be replaced
in our hearts and minds you will always enter in haste.
Mother your face like a warm embrace
your heart always there you never anticipate.
Mother with one touch you can always predict
any sorrow in our hearts quickly to evict.
Mother you've made us realize so sure
that one day when you're no longer here
rest assured your wisdom and love that you have given to us
will carry on forever more - it was not in vain
Mother your presence will always remain.
—*Theodora Pieri*

Untitled

Father, I am thine, belonging to no others;
Yes, my body remains, but my spirit to you.
My whole being not mine, yours; yet mine.
I must sacrifice my self to the cause of God.
Yes, before all, I must keep my body clean to you,
As well as my soul, and intellect be accepted to you.
I was saved from this degenerated world into heaven:
I have been dead to this world; yes, I am dead.
I must realize this very fact: I am dead to this world.
So take heart for any fate, God overhead.
I'll receive anything, for He stands by me
With a help to go beyond the unsurmountable.

I must remember myself; myself a God's love
No, not for my sake, my Lord's sake I work
Take heart! lose no courage for doing for His sake.
Work hard, the necessities come into my hands
Work hard, so our wants become bountiful.
The world is my Father's; if I ask Him, He gives all.
We are but a breath, only a breath,
So while I am alive, I'll keep praising and loving Him.
—*Mineo Moritani*

Sibling Love

Family's always have each other
Yet nothing's better than a brother
He's there to help when you fall
And always answers if you call.

Across the sea I have a brother
Who years ago vowed to love another
And though the distance keeps us apart
I know I'm always in his heart.

His family grew two, three, four
Now with grandchildren to adore
A laughing face with those to share
Does he know how much I care.

I think I've said all there is to say
And though it's in a simple way
Keep these thoughts within your heart
Of which I know I am a part.

Brother you mean so much to me
To my life you hold a key
All the above is very true
Brother Peter I love you.
—*Wendy Claire Swinfen*

A Special Person

When you look into my eyes,
you can see how much I love you.
You're always there when I need you.
Always supporting me
in all
my endeavors.
Standing by me though
the good
and
the bad.
For being my rock that I can lean on.
For correcting me when I'm wrong, for just
being there and for being my friend, not
just my mother,
I love you.
—*Vonna M. Mayo*

Man's-Unkindness to the Environment!!

Sometimes,
You cannot help - but to drift along hopelessly,
Within the winds of change, along the baffles of time.
As I look along this corridor of life.
at all the trouble and strife,
I wonder what goes on in another's mind,
It seems to me to be so - unkind,
as to let - this earth be destroyed by mankind.

If we could only use our time wisely
on this planet,
Instead of just moving hard junk & granite,
Devastating the Indian's forests,
Polluting the rivers and estuary's,
Destroying the atmosphere.
If we could-only let each other know,
How much we treasure it;
We could-stop all the disasters of the future,
and save this wonderful planet we live upon,
and stop abusing it - so we could use-it,
To let everyone know, we don't want to lose it!
—*Peter Haydock*

Freedom, Don't Deceive Me

Why freedom, in whatever way I think, you're really unfair?
You just glanced to almost all in a nation,
And then stared with concern to selected individuals.
The opulent and impecunious, please try to evaluate
With extra care and open eyes.
Ruminate our justice and carefully adjudicate.
Forced detention for penurious man,
Who is blameless and benighted.
And the brigand who has money and the "right connections"
Not to mention immunity, or their "power of position",
Very often they're untrammelled;
Or if not extenuated, very often vindicated!
Freedom, don't deceive me
For you to stay and be with us fairly,
Why not expound what you want us to do?
Maybe if you subsist, there's no serfdom and injustice,
No more unloved, starving homeless people!

    —Concepcion C. Carenan

Stone Mirage

Circuitous by the clusters of jackpine or spruce
You lead through a river stone mirage to the gate
Beyond that bottle garden is the raw sepia site
Opened for the centennial cherry blossom rockery

As petals fluttered at the mansard eave of North
Hall you assess the vantages of a clay bank just
Romped by expansive meditation hall architecture
It overturned hardpan and pruned cherry roots

Inspired island carpenters reconnoitred over
Lofty rafters and ridgepoles in full view of ships
On the canal their booms and masts swaying slowly
Quiet craftsman were mere dots perched on new rooves

Brace for improbable weight heels sink sideways
Shuffle for foot holds as your orders send huge
Stones home to be rocked out of their nests while
Shovel accommodates lithic corners to budge back

Thus you divide the cascade of romped clay
With grey rocks to be splattered by pink petals
And showers the ground water parted latitudinally
Nourishing ground cover down that sunny corridor

    —Michael Corr, Ph.D.

A Shadow From The Past

  Shadow, how mysterious you are.
    You stick to me like molten tar.
  Shadow, you're a terrible friend.
    But hardly ever are you seen.
  Why is it that I feel so strange,
    Whenever you are in my range?
  I feel so hopeless and terribly bad.

You're like a nightmare that I've never had.
  What can I do to stop you from coming.
  Maybe I'll run, and keep on running.
  Oh help me, I'm in desperate need.
    I want someone to rescue me.
  But shadow, now I seem to know!
    You're a memory from long ago.
    A face I've seen in photo books.
The face of my Grandma, her warmhearted looks.

    —Christine Zitscher

Corruption

O you corruption, you hydraheaded monster!
You this cankerworm of a beast
That has eaten deep into the fabric of our national life.
Where do you come from? Where is your abode?
Your home is not here; Go away!
You have done a lot of havoc in this country; Vamoose!
Everywhere your presence can be felt.
Everywhere your devastating hands can be noticed.
My people cherish you very much.
They accord you a place of pride in all works of life.
In Government you are there.
In the Judiciary your presence can be felt.
Politicians are your friends.
Religious leaders accord you a place of honour
Where in this land do you get what you want
Without greasing people's palms?
In public life? In the private sector?
The story is the same all over.
O corruption, may you be damned!
O corruption, may you for ever die!

    —Mac Araromi

The Better Place

I see her face... full of love but heart-heavy..
'You'll never be home again'.
Forgive me Mumma....
I must travel...my insatiable curiosity drives
me on.
Shocked by my father's tears...
A sudden realization of the depth of pain...
We would not see each other again.
He knew.
I should have said how much I loved you both...
Now I'm separated from my children too.
One day in a far-off place...
We'll be together..
No goodbyes ever again....
I'm looking forward.

    —Valerie J. Smetheram

Poem For Paola For Valentines Day 1993

I have caught a memory of you
Your face etched in that half confident
vulnerable expression only you wear
trying to see, your dark eyes
beautiful, always as if in hiding.
And then it is morning - you leaving for work
Earlier, waking beside you
I listen to the chorus of quiet sounds
that form a part of every dawn
there, your touch, calming me the sweet smell of love on your body
I want to kiss your neck, feel your warmth, breathe in time
stay longer in that place where my skin shivers still,
unravelled by you.

Clouds drifting, deeply, sleepily earthwards
I have found you in the dying of autumn
grey golden leaves now dancing, rediscover the spring
All life like rain, must survive the night
in your raging hidden tender heart there is hope in the stars
Oh elegant, funny, furious you in all the songs,
so much longing seeking a way from what made you this day.

    —Ron Roberts

Marcus

Your heart was not easy to find,
but you led me to it --
      Now, I hope you'll always be mine...

You lift my spirits up
      fill me with laughter
      give me dreams to reach for
You are my "happily ever after."

You're a wonderful man
with eyes of emerald green
and hair of honey gold.
I love you more
than you'll ever know.

To be near you
makes me feel so secure.
I want to be with you forever and ever.
In my heart you are the only one --

      With you I've found my permanent home.

      --C.F.C.

The Willow Tree

Longingly I waited for the night to come,
   Stealthily creeping on the heels of dusk.
A strange aroma suddenly filled the twilight mist ...
   It was your sensuous scent, as you stood there
Beneath the dying shadow of the willow tree, searching for me.

Each night you came upon that barren hill to keep my frozen body warm
   With soft and gentle sighs and whisperings,
To tell my ashen heart I was your only love,
   As once before in life when you would fondle
With your happy tears my fevered brow.

Suddenly your heart leaped; before your eager gaze
   You thought you saw my wavering form and sought
To grasp me in your tender arms, as long ago.

Alas, my love, 'twas not my body you beheld;
   Instead you had embraced my soul
With hopeful eyes, a soul that waited every night
   To smell your fragrance and to kiss again
Your lovely face with my most hungry phantom lips. But you are life
   And I am death. You knew I was not there. You left the tree,
The hill and me, and lost yourself in reverie.

      —George N. Pulos

Dragon

Dragon looked out from his lair, and saw the maid with long gold hair,
white skin blue eyes, so very fair....

His claws withdrew, his forked tail quivered, yellow eyes gleamed in his
head like a lizard....
His belly churned and billowed smoke, from jaws wide open, his green
tongue poked....

Outside his cave, his head raised high, he blew smoke writing in the sky...
Then slowly slithered to the maid, who screamed aghast was sore afraid;

When satisfied and full replete went to his lair and fell asleep....
A year passed then from the cave the dragon stirred and came alive...

No maid was waiting for his meal, no jewels, no gold and no King's seal...
All was quiet all was still, so Dragon inched himself downhill...

The Castle stood a solid wall, the drawbridge high the moat was full...
A Knight came charging, dressed in white, his lance reflected last sunlight....

Full tilt he rode towards the beast, until blasted by Dragon's breath furnace....
The Knights blood boiled — his mount collapsed, and Dragon nibbled on the horse...

Then tore the amour off the Knight, and feasted, feasted through the night...
To his cave the Dragon came, then fell asleep to rise again —
Next Year.

      —Shirley Thrush

York University

When I was but a boy, I inquired of my father to know the
secrets of yon large sinister edifice which had for many years
dominated much of my imaginings just as it had the landscape
for countless eons. As we looked on together, the light of the
sun made it glow red hot as though from the endless torments
and agonies of which, I was too soon to learn it. It glowed
and glowed and glowed. Until the clouds seemed black in
contrast, as black as the smoke in battle. Then he raised his
voice toward the black foreboding shape as though what he
asked, he asked of those poor wretched souls who spent their
eternities fasting in fires. He cried: "Can mortal lips utter
what unspeakable suffering goes on behind those crimson walls?
Can such sounds pass through? For surely my lips would scorch
at the first syllable." So I had to wait; but O that I had
waited longer for that building which loomed ominously in the
distance was Steacie! And now that I have joined the ranks of
the demon I live in the constant and deafening din of battle.
The eternities of torment and the painful anguish of sulphurous
fumes. Until my sins are purged and cleansed away and the smoke
of my torment ascendeth up forever and ever.

      —Christopher J. Graham

Change

What can turn a smile into a frown
   And can turn your world upside down?

What can be both good and bad
   And can also turn happy times into sad?

What can make you feel happy through and through
   And can make you turn a moody blue?

What can take away your very best friend
   And will never, ever, ever end?

What seems like an end, but is really a start
   And puts sharp arrows into your heart?

What is good, bad, and strange?
   The answer to these questions can only be change.

      —Lisa Thupvong

True Love is Suicide

When love visits your lonely heart
Your mind seems to abandon you
The feelings of joy and happiness
Control your every thought
You would do anything for that special someone
You are suddenly a slave to your heart and soul
You would risk your life for these feelings
The best feelings you'll ever experience
Suddenly out of the blue, a bomb is dropped
Your love is not shared by that person anymore
This news is devastating
Your mind just doesn't return
You're dying inside and nothing can help
Rational ideas are a hundred miles away
Now with all your heartbreak and sorrow
All you want to do is hide
The pseudo-relationship has taught you
True love is suicide

      —Stephen Dugdale

BIOGRAPHIES

AASMAN, SHEREE
[b.] September 6, 1972, Walkerton, Ont; [p.] John and Susan Aasman; [ed.] Mayfield High School, College Diploma in Art, graduated with highest honours; [occ.] Veterinary Clinic Grooming Small Animals; [memb.] Eramosa Junior Farmer, Brampgton Fair Ambassador Committe, Completed 13 4-H projects; [hon.] Brampton Fair Ambassador 1992-93. My role was to raise public awareness of country life through public speaking; [pers.] Poetry is a way for me to express my emotions on paper. This poem is a tribute to my grandmother. For to know her was to love her for a wonderful person she was; [a.] Terra Cotta, Ontario

AASMAN, SHEREE
[b.] September 6, 1972, Walkerton, Ontario; [p.] John and Susan Aasman; [ed.] Mayfield High School, College Diploma in Art. Graduated with Highest Honours.; [occ.] Veterinary Clinic Grooming Small Animals; [memb.] Eramosa Junior Farmer, Brampton Fair, Ambassador Committee, Completed 13 4-H projects.; [hon.] Brampton Fair Ambassador 1992-93. My role was to raise public awareness of country life through public speaking.; [pers.] Poetry is a way for me to express my emotions on paper. I dedicate thi spoem to Scott, with all my love. Whose inspiration and devotion is unforgettable; [a.] Terra Cotta, Ontario

ABBOTT, CHERYL LYNN
[b.] November 1, 1966, Lynn Vincent, DL Vincent; [ch.] William, Kayleigh, Christopher, Maria Lynn; [occ.] Secretary; [hon.] Girl Scout Gold Award; [pers.] I wish to thank my mother for showing me the beauty of old folk songs, and my father for instilling in me an appreciation for the English language and a love of poetry; [a.] Rose City, MI

ABIJAN, REMEDIOS NALUNDASAN
[Pen.] Ree Cana; [b.] February 20, Philippines; [ch.] Sharon-sydney; Karl and Ma. Goretti; [ed.] M.A. in Education; Post Graduate in Cultural Anthropology; [occ.] Professor, Social Sciences, Mapua Institute of Technology Manila, Phil; School Director, Academe & Casadeig Study Centre Bulacan, Phil; [memb.] Nature and Environment Study (NEST) Club, Philippines, President Founder; [hon.] "Cum Laude" BSEEd, PNU, Manila; "Editor's Choice Award" for outstanding Poetry 1993, Nat'l. Library of Poetry, USA, UP Scholar, Ph.D program; PNU College Scholar, Bachelor's degree program; [oth. writ.] Instructional materials and books for children published in the Philippines; a collection of poems "A Woman In Escape for Peace"; [pers.] My cultural encounter in Botswana made me a poet. I wrote my poems against the backdrop of the African natural and socio-political environment where I experienced mankind's undying Hope for peace racing with time to survive defeat.; [a.] Los Pinas Metro, Manila, Philippines

ABSHURE, STEVEN RAY
[Pen.] Steve Abshure; [b.] April 1, 1964, Little Rock, AK; [p.] Willie & Kathryn Abshure; [m.] Tammy Abshure, April 4, 1986; [ch.] Dusty Ray Abshure, Cody Allan Abshure, Crystal Rose Abshure; [ed.] Cabot High School, Cabot, AR; [occ.] Automobile Mechanic Truman Baker Dodge, Searcy, AK; [memb.] New Horizon Baptist Church; [pers.] This poem was a gift to my wife it was the first poem I wrote to her.; [a.] Austin, AK

ACCARDO, KATHRYN
[Pen.] Katie Accardo; [b.] March 7, 1982, Goshen, NY; [p.] Richard and Susan Accardo; [ed.] Currently in Junior High School; [occ.] Student; [memb.] Girl Scouts. All-County Chorus, school chorus, church choir, piano-private lessons-performs with group, also New York State Music Association, American Red Cross; [hon.] Presidential Academic Fitness Award, New York State Music Assoc award of Excellence, American Red Cross-Amazing Action Award-Basic Aide Training, Drug Awareness Resistance Education Award, Piano-Certificate of Achievement-Distinguished Accomplishment; [memb.] Published poem in school yearbook, school slogan, other writings as school projects to include poems, stories and a book, also composes songs; [a.] Washingtonville, NY

ACKER, SARAH REBECCA
[b.] April 10, 1978, Toronto, Ont; [p.] Michael Acker, Jean Acker; [ed.] Grade 10, Evely All grade school; [pers.] "Unreconciled", my first piece of writing to be published, expresses my feelings of sorrow for having left my Ontario home, despite my love and appreciation for New Foundland; [a.] Roddickton, NFLD

ADAMS, KEVIN R.
[b.] January 24, 1968, Martinsville, IN; [p.] Joseph Adams (deceased), Linda Adams Noel; [ed.] High school graduate and personal studies; [occ.] Warehouse manager, Indianapolis; [oth. writ.] Non-published personal writings; [pers.] I only wish through my writings that I may stop the hatred that is so apparent on our planet; [a.] Mooresville, IN

ADAMS, LOUIS M.
[b.] May 19, 1919, Madison, WI; [p.] Jesse B. Adams and Josephine Perrill Adams; [m.] Lillie Stamey Adams, June 16, 1947; [ch.] Joseph B. Adams (deceased); [ed.] AB Degree, Univ of IL 1941; [occ.] United Methodist Minister; [memb.] National Geographic Society, Smithsonian Assoc, Greenville, SC Symphony Orchestra, Augusta, GA Symphony Orchestra, Anderson, SC Symphony, Laurens, SC Chorale; [oth. writ.] Poetry since 1942; [pers.] I believe strongly in the redemption of man under Christ and in the mission of people to lead others to that redemption. I am pacifistic, philosophical, at the same time, I think that if something is working, there must be something good about it; [a.] Laurens, SC

ADDISON, ROBERT ELLARD
[Pen.] Robert E. Addison; [b.] December 10, 1937, Atlanta, GA; [p.] Robert and Dorothy Addison; [m.] Minnie Montgomery Addison, April 7, 1963; [ch.] Stephanie Denise, Valerie Eileen, Titus Maurice; [ed.] B.T. Washington-Atlanta, Blayton Business, Franklin and Marshall, New Mexico State, Univ of New Mexico State, Univ of New Mexico, Albuq-Technical-Vocational; [occ.] Pastor/Founder - Global Harvest Christian Fellowship Church; [memb.] Juvenile Probation-Parole Volunteer, Big Brothers, National Chaplan Assoc, National Ministers Assoc, Alpha Psi Omega; [hon.] Ford Foundation Scholar, VA Hospital Volunteer Award, Big Brothers Award, Juvenile Justice Award; [oth. writ.] Poem published in Great Poems of Our Time, p.86; [pers.] My philosophy of life is my deliberated effort to make sensible my beliefs, morals, and behavior and to tie them together so that I may have a basis for action when I am confronted by problems; [a.] Albuquerque, NM

ADKINS, RYAN
[Pen.] Renegade; [b.] November 14, 1981, Cleveland, OH; [p.] Linda and Isaac Adkins; [ed.] St Elizabeth Seton School, Toledo, OH in grade 6; [pers.] Like things about space and legos; [a.] Toledo, OH

AGNA, VANESSA ELIZABETH
[b.] January 12, 1978, Hornell, NY; [p.] Forooq P. and Alice L.; [ed.] Martin Luther King Elementary, Deer Path Middle School, Deer Path Junior High, Lake Forest High School; [occ.] Student at Lake Forest High School; [hon.] Citizenship Award, 1st place in Science Fair, Academic Award at Deer Path Junior High; [oth. writ.] One article in M.L.K. school paper; [pers.] I like to practice random spurts of weirdness. Monty Python has greatly influenced me. If people brought out their pain writing, the world would be happier; [a.] Lake Forest, IL

AGUADO, DAVID
[b.] May 15, 1956, Cuba; [p.] Pierre L. Aguado, Bertha Sanchez; [ch.] Gunther Yhander Aguado; [ed.] Inst for Higher Studies in Pedagogy, Cuba; Univ of Toronto (M.A. & M.Ed.); [occ.] English Teacher - St. Elizabeth Catholic High School, Toronto; [memb.] MLA; NCTE; Toronto Semiotic Circle; Wallace Stevens Assoc; [hon.] Toronto Open Fellowship, Univ of Toronto; [hon.] Dean's List, Teacher's College; [oth. writ.] "Enigmatic Poetry?...What the Author Really Wants to Say!", Toronto Scholars Press (in press); [pers.] What a great joy it is to shape my feelings into rhyme!; [a.] Etobicoke, Ontario

AGUIRRE, PEGGY R.
[b.] February 15, 1950, North Dakota; [p.] Irene & Rolland Fandrich; [m.] Mike Aguirre, October 5 1990; [ch.] Kandra Noel, Tawny Nicole, stepdaughters: Amiee Marie, Michele Lynn; [ed.] Lennox High School, Cerritos Jr. College; [occ.] Self employed property appraiser; [memb.] CRA, CREA; [oth. writ.] Poetry Society Publication, Not Years Too Late, Daniel's Poem; [pers.] Poetry comes from the heart not the pen, my greatest influence comes from my wonderful husband and the guidance of my mother & father.; [a.] Anaheim, CA

AHLFORT, KATARINA
[b.] August 17, 1967, Sweden; [ed.] One year of media education at a Swedish college; Bachelor Degree from Metropolitan State College of Denver in Journalism.; [occ.] Freelance reporter, writing on first novel; [memb.] Swedish Publicist Club, Swedish Union of Journalists, International Federation of Journalists, International Association of Business Communicator (IABC); [hon.] The Best of Colorado 1992, Student Award from Society of Professional Journalists, Honorable Mention for News Writing 1993 from Rocky Mountain Collegiate Media Assocation, Vice President's List, 1993 Award from IABC for speech writing.; [oth. writ.] Articles published in several Swedish daily newspapers, articles published in American weekly newspapers.; [pers.] I want to travel roads, sit in cafes' and write ruthless truths.; [a.] Denver, CO

AKERS, BRAD
[b.] June 20, 1975, Potosi, MO; [p.] Delmer Akers and Terry Gross; [ed.] I am a graduate of valley, K 6 High School located in Caledonia, Missouri. I have future plans to attend college; [memb.] Naitona Honors Society, Students for life; [hon.] I have been given two Who's Who Among American High School Students Awards, and All American Scholar Award. [oth. writ.] I have had several poems that were published in local papers such as the focus, a national publication, "The Galileen Witness" (a christian publication) I have written other poems entitled "At The Touch of God's Hands, Don't Give Up On God, and Christians, Get Up and Go"; [pers.] I strive to reflect the goodness of God and the saving power of Jesus Christ my Lord and Saviour. I hope in my writings to lead lost souls to the Lord. I have been greatly influenced by all of my wonderful Christian friends. [a.] Belgrade, MO

ALBERT, CHESTER LEE
[b.] June 11, 1954, Detroit, MI; [p.] John and Viola Johnson; [m.] Patsy A. Giddens, June 1994; [ch.] Gena C. and Wallace E. Giddens; [ed.] H.S. Ged, Northside High School, Warner Robins, GA; [occ.] Laborer; [hon.] DD214 "Honorable" discharge; [oth. writ.] Many, many copies of poetry written down thru

ie years. None ever recognized; [pers.] Write poetry n any subject, particularly love and personal happenings. Wish to write poetry for greeting cards, have reams of writing country music; [a.] Warner Robins, A

LCORN, SAM J. (AL)
Pen.] Al Howell; [b.] February 22, 1922, Saratoga, X; [p.] Gladys Indepence Spell and Wendell Bertram lcorn; [m.] Mary Lou Alcorn, September 8, 1972; h.] Kenneth James Richards, Sam J. Alcorn, Jr., Villiam (Billy) Alcorn; [ed.] Graduate Boling High chool 1940; Boling, TX Prep Allen Military Academy 1941-1943; Bryan, TX Bachelor Science Degree najor - animal husbandry) Agriculture 1950 Texas &M College; attended 1940, summer 1943, and 946 - 1950; College Station, TX; [occ.] Retired US oast Guard Reserve (May 30, 1980) and Aluminum o of America (ALCOA), November 1, 1984; [memb.] Iethodist Church, Fraternal Order of Eagles, Amerin Legion, National Committee to Preserve Social ecurity and Medicare, American Military Society, merican Assoc of Retired Persons (AARP); [hon.] WII Naval Reserve Victory Medal. US Coast uard Meritorious Service Medal. Honorable Dis-arges - Naval Reserve 1946, US Coast Guart eserve 1980. Total Military Service 25+ yrs. Staff riter with Majestic Records and designated writer ff Roberts Publishing Co; [oth. writ.] "Prince harming", "Dixie Anne", "A Man In Mars", "Scamr In My Camper", "Fly-In'To Heaven (On A paceship)", "Be Not A Screaming Eagle (Or A aunting Dashing Hawk)", "The Way To Hell", Songwritin'", "Just A Joke", "Corpus Christi Blues"; ers.] Favorite Poet: Edgar Allen Poe. I'm branching it to write poems based on historical events and dding color. And as Poe at times tend to add an aura mystery or supernatural. Favorite Artists: Jim eeves, T Texas Tyler, Floyd Tillman; [a.] Palacios, TX

LESTRA, MICHAEL
.] March 10, 1953, Bronx, NY; [p.] Rocco & armela Alestra; [m.] Virginia Alestra, July 7, 1987; h.] Kristen Marie, Kyle Michael; [ed.] Patchogue, edford H.S. SUNY at Stony Brook; [occ.] Former igh, School English Teacher; [hon.] Dean's List; th. writ.] Sociological paper in SUNY at Stony rook's library, poem in a local publication.; [pers.] have been influenced by William Wordsworth's eas of inspiration. Whitman and Frost have left a sting impression, greatly enhancing my work. [a.] ings Park, NY

LEXANDER, ALLISON MICHELLE
.] December 19, 1978; [p.] Keith and Jean Alexander; d.] Freshman, Haynesville High, Honor Student; cc.] H.S. Student, serious studen of Dance; s Sr. ompany Member of LA Dance Theatre, LA Dance oundation, First Baptist Church Youth Choir; [hon.] perintendant's Writing Award, Art Award, LA ate Fair, State 4-H Speaking Award. Performed utcracker with Delta; [hon.] Festival Ballet and LA ance Foundaiton. Graduate of Oma's Fashion gency; [oth. writ.] Poems and short stories.; [pers.] xpress myself best artistically through dance, the ritten word, the visual arts or modeling in front of a mera; [a.] Haynesville, LA

LEXANDER, ANITA
.] August 23, 1937, Malta, MT; [p.] Lars and ther Gullickson; [m.] George Alexander, April 16, 72; [ed.] Melta High, Medical Secretary certificate om Northern Montana College, Lutheran bible stitute, Great Falls Commercial College, IBM Key nch Certificate.; [occ.] Housewife, caring for dis-led husband, who is retired from the military.; nemb.] Lutheran Church, VFW and AFSA, Auxil-ry, AARP, Senior Citizens, International Society of ets.; [hon.] Honor roll in high school, scholarship college, Editor's Choice Award from National

Library of Poets; [oth. writ.] A poem, "Save The Earth," published in "The Coming of Dawn", a compilation of the National Library of Poetry.; [pers.] With extra time at home now to watch TV with my disabled husband, when I learn of things that could be helpful to people, or to preserve the beauty of nature and strength of our country. I like to write poems to share these ideas with others.; [a.] Glasgow, MT

ALLEN, ALICE T.
[Pen.] Alice Towsley Allen; [p.] George Everet Goldsmith and Alice Sophia Kunkeli Goldsmith; [m.] Colonel Charles Kissam Allen, January 20, 1973; [ch.] (Step-children) Barbara Blake and Prof Charles K. Allen, III; [ed.] Columbia Univ; [occ.] Writer, autobio just completed; [memb.] Overseas Press Club of America (ASCAP); [hon.] Listed in Who's Who of America; Who's Who of American Women and other prestigious publications; [oth. writ.] For many years columnist, feature and editorial writings too many to enumerate. Over 85 poems. Some of the publications I worked with: Honolulu Advertiser (7 yrs), Chicago, Tribune, NY Herald Tribune. Magazines: Fashion and Travel Medical World News, Rudder, Doctor's Wife; [pers.] As a newspaper woman and magazine editor and publisher, my career was prompted by my addiction to writing since childhood. Poetry though has been a personal outlet and one I cannot withhold from paper.

ALLEN, CINDY
[b.] April 1, 1969, Torrance, CA; [m.] Partner & Inspiration, Kevin McHugh; [ed.] Currently working on Mass Communications degree at Cal State University, Hayward; [occ.] Food Server; [oth. writ.] Articles have appeared in college publications, including Cal State, Hayward's Escape Magazine.; [pers.] Writing is an outlet for me a catharsis of sorts. Through poetry, I am able to voice my fondest dreams and heal my deepest wounds. My only hope is that my words reach out and touch somebody's heart.; [a.] Hayward, CA

ALLENDE, JENNIFER
[b.] June 15, 1980, Bronx, NY; [p.] Samuel and Arlene Allende; [ed.] Public School 41, Michelangelo 144, Monsignor Scanlon High School; [occ.] Community Service Volunteer and babysitter; [memb.] Library, Carvel, United Bronx Parents, ASPCA Guardians; [hon.] Kindergarten through fifth grade citizenships/SPECDA Completion/sixth through eighth grade honors, science fair 1st place, honorable mention; [oth. writ.] I have a book of my own original poems at home; [pers.] I really wasn't into poetry. For school my teacher said I had to right one, so my sister came to mind. Soon came the poem called "sisters". I dedicate this poem to my sister, Erika Allende; [a.] Bronx, NY

ALLIGOOD, MARY M.
[b.] November 26, 1927, Frostproof, FL; [p.] Joel D. Moser, Mary Burleigh Moser; [m.] Jack Dale Alligood, December 27, 1948; [ch.] Jacquelyn Dayle, Jack Daryl & Linda Lou; [ed.] Babson Park Elementary, Lake Wales High School; [occ.] Homemaker, wife, mother and grandmother, gardener; [memb.] Attend Walker Street Church of God, Lake Wales, FL, Charter member of Polk County Historical & Genealogical Assoc. & Frostproof Historical Society, former Brownie, Girl Scout & Cub Scout Asst. Leader in Babson Park, Babson Park PTA Officer.; [hon.] Lake Wales High School Honor Society; [oth. writ.] Poetry published in newspapers, as well as poetry for family & friends. Historical & Genealogical research of Frostproof, Midland and Wlak-in-the-Water areas.; [pers.] My love of poetry comes down through my mother's "Burleigh" line; and I particularly love the King James version of the bible for its poetic nature.

ALLISON, DESTINY
[b.] April 24, 1978, Dexter, MO; [p.] Lance and Donnie Allison; [ed.] Have completed 8 years of school, am currently a freshman; [memb.] Yearbook Chess Club; [hon.] Won second prize in poetry contest in 7th grade; [oth. writ.] Several poems, a few published in school magazines; [pers.] Poetry is an art, and if you can write, then do so, for yourself, not for others; [a.] Davis Junction, IL

ALLISON, JAMES
[b.] October 11, 1954, Mish, ID; [p.] Leon and Lois Allison; [m.] Sandy M. Allison, March 21, 1981; [ed.] Christian Int'l - 1988, Southern Career Inst - Paralegal Studies/Current, (B.A. in Theology - 1988); [occ.] Self employed; [oth. writ.] I have had 2 poems published in a church bulletin. One poem published in "Best Loved Contemporary Poems" 1979, World of Poetry Press. One poem to come out soon in "Poetry - An American Heritage" thru Western Poetry Assoc; [pers.] My poems are journeys as well as reflections. They are my children reflections of my own bewildered soul on this multi-denominational landscape; [a.] Stafford, VA

ALVAREZ, JULIET
[b.] January 6, 1980, Elmhurst Hosp, NY; [p.] Luisa and Roberta Alvarez; [ed.] William Cooper Junior High School I.S. 73; [occ.] Drawing and writting poems; [hon.] Honor Roll and a poem award; [oth. writ.] Several other poems; [pers.] I write the way I feel that's why most of my poems are about love, friedship and hopes; [a.] New York, NY

AMANTIA, SUE
[b.] August 16, 1937, Lebanon, PA; [p.] John Kimmel, Mae Houser; [ed.] Lebanon Catholic High, RN from Hospital School of Nursing, Lancaster, PA. BA in Anthropology from Univ of New Mexico, Albuquerque, NM. M.S. in Biology from St. Joseph College, West Hartford, CT; [occ.] Research Assistant; [memb.] MENSA (high IQ society), Greenpeace, Sierra Club, Lebanon Valley Hiking Club, Lebanon Community Library Great Books Club, Three Mile Island Alert, Survival Through Understanding (a local peace and justice group), Friends of the Union Canal a branch of Lebanon County Historical Society; [hon.] Orthopedics and Gynecology Awards from St. Joseph Hospital School of Nursing, Lancaster, PA; Dean's List, Univ of New Mexico, Albuquerque, NM; [oth. writ.] Poetry and feminist articles for "Women in Hartford" paper. Poetry and historical articles for "The Daily News" of Lebanon, PA; [pers.] I aspire to share with others, through my poetry, the joy and wonder I feel about the universe, from a multi-hued sunset to a many-faceted human personality; [a.] Lebanon, PA

AMATURY, JOY
[b.] February, 9, 1940, San Francisco, CA; [p.] Lavella and George Amatury; [ch.] Jana Lyn and Floyd Patrice; [ed.] El Monte High, B.A., M.A. Governor's State University; [occ.] Casualty Underwriter Explorer Insurance, Burbank, CA; [oth. writ.] Poems and a children's book (as yet unpublished); [pers.] Through my writing I hope to briefly touch someone's soul, bring a smile to their heart or perhaps cause their mind to ponder a thought or two.; [a.] Lakeview Terrace, CA

AMES, ROBERT
[b.] October 31, 1967, Boston, MA; [p.] Robert F. and Rosemarie Ames; [ed.] Weymouth South High, Boston University, Bridgewater State; [occ.] Manager/Head Chef, Standby Diner & Cafe, Martha's Vineyard; [memb.][oth. writ.] Teamsters, Sigma Chi; [hon.] Dean's List, Meritorious Service, USNR; [pers.] It's important to remember the mistakes and successes of the past, private and public. Because ultimately every generation is called to act. Only with the lessons we have learned will we be successful in

passing on to our children a better place to live; [a.] South University, MA

ANDERSON, AMBERLEE
[b.] December 27, 1978, Murray, UT; [p.] Kelly and Virginia Anderson; [ed.] Cresent View Middle School; [occ.] Student; [hon.] Honor Roll, Winner in Visual Art; [pers.] I like to imagine things and write them in poetic form; [a.] Sandy, UT

ANDERSON, AVIS D.
[Pen.] A. Denise; [b.] December 27, 1953, New Orleans, LA; [p.] Richard E., Sr. and Elva A. Smith; [ch.] Albert L., Letitia O. and Juane' Blake; [ed.] San Diego City College (San Diego, CA), Ganesha High School (Pomona, CA), Sawyers Business College (Pomona, CA); [occ.] Operations Control Coordinator and Teledyne Ryan Aeronautical (SD, CA); [memb.] National Authors Registry (Troy, MI), New Creation Church (San Diego, CA); [hon.] 1994 President's Award (National Library Authors Registry and Iliad Press), Editor's Choice Award 1993 (National Library of Poetry), Honorable Mention 1993 (Iliad Literary Awards Program); [oth. writ.] Celebrations, Chp Two and Memories, August 1993 Edition; The Coming of Dawn, Fall 1993; Upcoming Anthologies, Perceptions 19904 Iliad Press; [pers.] A. Denise loves to write with an envision of passion where the person reading the works is stirred to an ecstatic emotion as being a participant. Her writings entail fiction, playwriting, children stories and a how to book with favorites of poetry; [a.] San Diego, CA

ANDERSON, DIANE
[b.] May 13, 1947, Linden, TX; [p.] Lester and Mildred Mc Michael; [m.] James Anderson (deceased), January 18, 1969; [ch.] Cindy, Eddy, Kara, Carl; [ed.] L-K High Schl., Oscar B. Jones Schl. of Nursing; [occ.] Nurse, I work at Oak Manor Nursing Home; [memb.] New Colony Baptist Church; [oth. writ.] I have written about 20 poems, all my poems are about people I have known -- some are relatives -- some are friends; [pers.] I started writing poetry after my husband died August 23, 1993. I think about a certain person and words will come to me. Every word I write about a person in my poems are true. I think this was God's way of keeping my sanity after my husband died; [a.] Linden, TX

ANDERSON, ELIZABETH
[b.] August 5, 1929, London, Ont; [p.] Patti and Rick Anderson; [ed.] Grade 8; [memb.] The Toronto Children's Chorus, Fitness Membeship; [hon.] Public Speaking, Track and Field, Horseback riding medals and ribbons, vocal music awards. Literary Awards; [memb.] Short stories for children; [pers.] Smile alot - it doesn't cost any money, but it's worth more than any amount of money can buy; [a.] Mississauga, Ontario

ANDERSON, JAMES A.
[Pen.] James Anderson Anderson; [b.] November 17, 1950, Belleville, Ontario, Canada; [p.] Dorothy and Garfield; [m.] Lynn Ruigrok; [ch.] Step Daughters: Patricia and Janet; [ed.] BSc. Coop. Honours, Applied Chemistry, Univ. of Waterloo, Waterloo, Ontario, Canada, Class of '75; [occ.] Plant Mnger., Strudex Fibres Ltd., Waterloo; [memb.] Guelph Curling Club, Canadian Textile Assoc., The Silent Partner and somtimes installer in Lynn's "Decorating Den" franchise; [hon.] My health, safety and accident, ed. prog. was noted in an edition of "Occupational Health and Safety Canada", a few bowling trophies and curling prizes, to be accepted by your contest and published.; [oth. writ.] A collection of poetry, in the hope of publishing a book oneday. I began writing this, past year (1993); [pers.] Guelph, Ontario Canada

ANDERSON, JAMES G.
[Pen.] Jim Anderson; [b.] December 2, 1939, Martin,

TN; [p.] G.K. and Nelle Anderson; [m.] Darlene (Cook) Anderson, May 22, 1960; [ch.] Kathleen, Linda, Kelly, Ann; [ed.] Messick H.S., Memphis, TN; A.A.S, Pierce College, Tacoma, WA, B.S. Adult Ed Southern Illinois Univ, Carbondale, IL, M.S. Soviet/East European Studies Univ of Kansas, Lawrence, KS; [occ.] Guest Lecturer, U.S. Army Engineer School, Intelligence Research; [memb.] Gideons Internationsl; [hon.] University Honors, Dean's List, Chairman of Deacons, First Baptist Church; [oth. writ.] Poems, songs, several technical and professional papers; major research projects published for U.S. Army and D.O.D; Seminars on religion/culture/society/politics of Mid-East and former U.S.S.R and E. Eur; [pers.] As I seek to educate through research and teaching, I seek to enlighten, enrich, bring enjoyment, hope and spiritual strength through poems and songs; [a.] Waynesville, MO

ANGEL, DON
[b.] March 9, 1973, Sullivan, IN; [p.] Erma Lynn Angel, Roy Dennis Angel; [ed.] Hutsonville High School, Hutsonville, IL, Lincoln Trail College, Robinson, IL; [memb.] West Union Christian Church; [hon.] President's List - Lincoln Trail College; [a.] West York, IL

ANGEL, ELIZABETH MARIE
[b.] January 10, 1970, Mesa, AZ; [p.] Johnnie D. Mantolete and Judy A. Mantolete; [m.] Kelly L. Angel, March 25, 1991; [ch.] none; [ed.] Central Heights Elementary, Bullion Plaza Elementary, Lee Kornegay Junior High School, Miami High School; [occ.] Student and HOusewife, Reserve Dispatcher; [memb.] Advocate for abused woman and children, guest speaker against drug abus.; [oth. writ.] Article in the Arizona Silver Belt, speaking against military bashing--1990; [pers.] Great art is something that I cherish and I hope that someday I will be compared to Byron, Shelly or Keates because they are the best and what I'd like to be one day.; [a.] Miami, AZ

ANGRIMSON, GINA
[b.] August 24, 1973, Edina, MN; [p.] Ronald and Shirley Angrimson; [Brothers] Craig, Jim, John, Mark, Jeff; [ed.] Kennedy High Lake and Academy; [occ.] Medical Assistant; [memb.] Model for John Cassablanca, Nativity of Mary Catholic Church; [oth. writ.] A couple of poems in schools literary magazines; [pers.] My poems relfect grieving of the loss of a loved one. I feel they can be used as a source of help for people. This poem is dedicated to my grandfather, Dedrick Angrimson and to all of my family and friends who I love so very much; [a.] Bloomington, MN

ANTONIADIS, MARIANNE
[Pen.] Maria; [b.] November 19, 1949, Panama; [p.] Joseph and Sophia Molino; [m.] Ermolaos Antoniadis, January 19, 1975; [ch.] Constantino and Maria Sophia; [ed.] Degree, Doctor in Medicine, Bachelor in Physical Therapy, Mini speciality in Occupational Medicine; [occ.] Chief, Occupational Health Division, of the Panama Canal Commission; [memb.] U.S. Government Agency President, Medical Society of the Panama Canal Area, Member of the Panamanian Association of Translators and Interpreters, Member of Philantropic Society of Greek Ladies (Philoptohos); [hon.] Six Superior or Outstanding Performance Awards, Promoted to Chief, Clinical Services Branch and thisyear to Division Chief.; [oth. writ.] Many papers and conferences on medical issues, a book on the make; [pers.] I once heard that each person has 3 things to contribute in life: To plant a tree, to have a child and to write a book. I definitely want ot leave one or serveral books behind me, because I love to write, especially to share with others my analysis of life and human behavior. Nobody has the right answers, but one still has to try.; [a.] Panama, Republic of Panama

AQUINO, ABIGAIL S.
[Pen.] Abby, Ging; [b.] Aug. 9, 1974, Olongapo City, Philippines; [p.] Abraham O. Aquino, Verna S. Aquino; [ed.] Olongapo City National High, New Era College, Miramar College; [occ.] CNA, Villa Monte Vista Convalescent Hospital; [memb.] Iglesia Ni Cristo; [hon.] Oustanding Graduate of Speech Pioneer; [oth. writ.] Several poems and editorial columns published in our school organ "Ang Buklod" in the philippines.; [pers.] Use our talents wisely, and always praise and give thanks to the almighty. Thanks to Erman for inspiring me. I live for your love.; [a.] Poway, SD, CA

ARIS, OBADIAH
[b.] May 16, 1978, Georgetown, Ontario, Canada; [ed.] Obadiah's grade 13 OAC credits will be completed by June 1994 with 7 OAC credits and close to other high school credits; [occ.] Student, honour student every year, advanced 3 yrs during school; [memb.] Also a member and student of Young Artist Performance Academy at the Royal Conservatory of Music/Toronto/Ontario/Canada and student of concert pianist, James Anagnoson, (1st places for all Kiwanis Festival Competitions); [oth. writ.] The Great Book on Pollution (workbook for Gr 2 students contest, to be judged in June 1994. It has passed the first elimination on Jan 31, 1994; [pers.] Goal concert pianist and composer. Philosophical statement: All our lives, we struggle to achieve a materia greatness. However, in the end, all our numerou accomplishments and worth are nothing when compared to what we have learned from these astounding feats; [a.] Ontario, Canada

ARMENIO, LISA M.
[b.] September 14, 1970, Providence, RI; [p.] Joseph and Laura Escobar; [m.] Vincent A. Armenio, March 20, 1993; [ed.] Dighton -Rehoboth High School Univ of R.I.; [occ.] Student of URI and Medical Assistant; [memb.] East Coast Tae Kwon Do; [hon.] URI Dean's List; [oth. writ.] Personal unpublished poems; [pers.] I have been influenced by the goodness of people and beauty of nature; [a.] Rehoboth, MA

ARMSTRONG, LA JUANNA MARIE
[b.] May 25, 1971, Dallas, TX; [p.] Doris and Matthew Armstrong; [ch.] Ajah Manae Owens, May 27, 1993; [ed.] Graduated from Warner Robins Sr High in Warner Robins Georgia and attended Georgia College in Milledgville, GA. Majoring in Journalism [occ.] House Mother/Homemaker; [oth. writ.] I have many that I've yet to have published; [pers.] I exist to live and not live to exist for life is filled with so many challenges that to merely exist has already given probable cause for being defeated by life's mos adventurous game of chess; [a.] Atlanta, GA

ARNOLD, JEAN D.
[b.] November 1, 1914, Hogansville, GA; [p.] Annie Pearl and High Darden; [m.] Edwin T. Arnold, M.D. December 26, 1937; [ch.] Ellen, Dr. Edwin Arnold III, Richard Frank; [ed.] Hogansville High School La Grange (GA) College, West Georgia College [occ.] Retired (Former high school teacher); [memb.] Delta Kappa Gramma, Troup County Historical Society, Hogansville First United Methodist Church; [a.] Hogansville, GA

ARNOLD, JULIA
[b.] September 1, 1981, Rolla, MO; [p.] Laurie and Jim Arnold, Brother - Jim; [ed.] Seventh grade; [occ.] Student; [memb.] Softball, basketball, track, soccer [pers.] Special thanks to my 6th grade english teacher Miss Kinne and all the cowboys of Nevada; [a.] Winnemucca, NV

ARREOLA, BELINDA
[b.] February 21, 1978, Los Angeles; [p.] Ruben Arreola, Pamela Macias, (Step-father) Eddie Serna

Sister) Michelle Arreola (14), Rebecca Serna (11); ed.] High School Student Sophmore; [occ.] Student; memb.] YMCA c/o counselor; [hon.] Achievement ward for Speech; [oth. writ.] Personal Poetry Colection; [pers.] "There are many roads to choose rom, but only one to follow." My dad is my inspiraion for writing; [a.] Whittier, CA

RTHURS, LAVERN
».] October 20, 1958, Portland; [p.] Miss Dorrel mith; [m.] Robert Craig; [ch.] Racquel, Jerome, ason, Andre; [ed.] Fair Prospect Secondary School, ong Bay PO; [occ.] Housewife; [pers.] Life is a daily ruggle and each day I pray for strength to go one day a time; [a.] 7 Miles PA, Bull Bay, St Andrew

RUNDEL, L. C. MICHAEL
».] April 17, 1971, Ottawa, Ontario, Canada; [p.] .M.G. Arundel, Louise L.K. Arundel; [ed.] St. »seph's Secondary (Cornwall) Carleton Univ (Otwa); [occ.] Writer/Student; [pers.] I strive to emhasize the importance of self reliance in a world that brow beaten with discouragement and failure, articularly for young people; [a.] Morrisburg, ntario, Canada

RVIN, MYRA JO
en.] MJ; [b.] November 18, Balto, MD; [p.] Earl C, rvin and Doris L. Arvin; [ch.] Thomas A. Fraser II nd Tahrim K.M. Magee-Kromah; [ed.] Eastern Sr. igh, Hunter College, Manhattan, NY, Currently CCC; [occ.] Single mother attending BCCC for an A degree in psychology; [memb.] Arena Players, alto, MD, Screen Actors Guild, Beverly Hills, CA, Expressions" Poetry organization at BCCC; [hon.] Iaryland State Scholastic Awards; [memb.] Three npublished works entitled "Inspirations From My en Sei", "A Brick Wall Fell On My Head" and Myra Jo From Baaltimo"; [pers.] I strive to entertain rough music, dance and dramatic expressions of my ritings. All the while with many years of love, pain nd now healing, I bring to the universe my wisdom nd knowledge for survival; [a.] Baltimore, MD

SRADE, ANNETTE
en.] LaDorris; [b.] January 19, 1946, USA; [p.] hnnie and Lillian Williams; [m.] Melaku Asrade, pril 29, 1974; [ed.] Wilson Sr. High; DC Univ, mple Business School; [occ.] Customs Aid; [memb.] lgrim Baptist Church, NAACP, Vice President Sr hoir; [hon.] Walk America for Healthier Babies, resident Family Reunion Committee of SC, Awards work performance; [oth. writ.] Songs, poems; ers.] Always striving for the prize of the high mark he calling of God; [a.] Chas, SC

THERTON, DEBBIE M.
.] April 2, 1965, Waynesboro, PA; [p.] James E. d Shirley M. Green; [m.] Travis W. Atherton, Sr, ay 28, 1983; [ch.] Travis W. Atherton, Jr; [ed.] reencastle Antrim High School; [occ.] James Rivers atcher/Packer; [pers.] This poem was written after e loss of my father, in memory of him; [a.] reencastle, PA

TTINGER, LINDA KAY-BOONE
.] November 29, 1944; [p.] Ora and Hazel Boone; h.] Arthur Jr., Anthony, Adam; [ed.] Bermudian »rings High School; Thompson School of Business d Technology; [occ.] Buyer at SKF USA Inc., anover, PA; [memb.] Friends of the Library; Ameri-n Business Women's Association.; [hon.] National onor Society in H.S., Dean's List in Business :hool; [a.] Hanover, PA

TWAL, VIKRAM
.] March 7, 1972, India; [p.] Surjit Atwal; [ed.] odern High -New Delhi, India. College - H of Stra niv; [occ.] Student; [memb.] AIESEC - Assoc of t'l Students in Science and Economics and Com-

merce; [hon.] Dean's List; [oth. writ.] Unmarked Grave, Ominous, Shadow of Love, Proud Ribbons, One Man's Vision (article), Casanova; [a.] Westbury, NY

AUBUCHON, GAYLLE SYLVIE
[Pen.] Gaylle Aubuchon; [b.] September 2, 1955, Montreal, Canada; [p.] Raymonde Aubuchon; [m.] Divorced; [ch.] Francois, Jonathan Rainville; [ed.] B. Comm (Concordia University), TQM, Programming and Human Resources; [occ.] Consultant (Business) and Writer; [oth. writ.] Success 94 Calendar, Others for 95'; [pers.] "Imagine if we would focus on self-actualization right from the beginning". I am here to help others succeed. My goals are very diversified.; [a.] Beaconsfield, Quebec, Canada

AUSTIN, CARROL LYNNE
[Pen.] Karal; [b.] August 25, 1948, Des Moines, IA; [p.] Maynard and Virginia Hauge; [m.] Larry Bruce Duncan, February 20, 1994; [ch.] Randall, Dave, and Nicholas Hayes; [ed.] Bachelor of Applied Arts and Sciences from Midwestern State Univ - Wichita Falls, TX; [occ.] Guardianship Coordinator for the ARC of Arizona; [memb.] Vocational Special Needs Education Assoc; ARC; Partners Resource Netword; Iowa Legislative Advocates; Artistic Task Force of Wichita County; [hon.] Art Scholarship - 1987. Sale of two oil paintings in the last six months. Artwork represented by Holman Gallery, Scottsdale, AZ; [oth. writ.] Approximately 50 poems, 15 short stories and a romance novel. Newspaper and newsletter articles. Some published, some not; [pers.] I've always believed, and always will, that each of us has a special purpose in life. If we know our purpose we can help others find theirs; [a.] Phoenix, AZ

AUVIL, (R.N.), PATRICIA M.
[Pen.] Pat, [b.] January 18, 1923, Seattle, WA; [p.] Winifred and Leo Dorgan; [m.] Raymond G. Auvil, M.D., July 3, 1946; [ch.] Carole Anne Caylor (RN BS), Arthur Daniel Auvil, MD, L. Com Wm Paul Auvil, who at present flies for Continental Airlines; [ed.] I received my RN from Glendale Adventist Hospital in 1948 after my daughter was born; [occ.] I love to assist teachers in grade school and especially teach young children to ski. Skiing is my greatest sport. I am a member of the Loma Linda School of Medicine Auxiliary; [hon.] My greatest accomplishments are the success of my children who have reached their goals and are successful and contribute to society, I also drew a manikin and put in on felt so that in my "Wings of Health Club" I could teach the children how to keep their bodies healthy. The children, themselves told about each organ of the body and what to do to keep it functioning properly. Although the manikin had to be redrawn so as to be put on transfer, it is produced and sold by: Betty Lukin's Felts. I wrote a book to go along with the manikin. If anyone wanted one of these manikins and books write me; [oth. writ.] When I find a publishing company to publish my first book of poems, I'll finish the other 2 volumes of "Patricia's Poems for 1/2 Pints": "ABC to Being the Best Me", Vol I, Vol II, Vol III; [pers.] My goal is to place in the teacher's hands books of poems that they can use with puppets, as my daughter did in her kindergarten, that will educate the children to become responsible, healthy, good citizens in this fair country of ours. So many children are not being taught at home how to become good citizens and the slack must be filled by the teachers. The earlier they are taught to be principled, the farther they will go in life; Lone Pine, CA

AVELLAR, RYANE M.
[b.] August 15, 1977, Puyallup, WA; [p.] Tom Davis, Valerie Davis; [ed.] Gig Harbor High; [occ.] Student; [memb.] Gig Harbor Concert and Jazz Bands, Gig Harbor Volleyball, Basketball and Track Teams; [hon.] Gold Medal Winner in the ARCO Jesse Owens

games representing the state of Alaska at the national competitions at the Univ of California - Los Angeles; [oth. writ.] Gig Harbor School paper; [pers.] Music is another of my interests and I combine this and my love of writing by composing music and writing lyrics. I express my feelings through words and music; [a.] Gig Harbor, WA

AZELL, EDWARDS
[Pen.] Dino Edwards; [b.] July 5, 1973, Chicago, IL; [p.] Geneva Edwards, Azell Edwards, Sr.; [ed.] Enrico Ferm, Elementary School, Englewood High School, Richard J. Daley College; [occ.] Car washer, best hand car wash, Chicago, IL; [hon.] Award: In H.S. for entrepreneurship education award: in tv and radio two class for public service announcment, 3rd place. Honor roll in Senior Year of High School; [pers.] Personal Note: I thank God for giving me my talent for writing. Also, I would like to thank my parents for believing in me and my gift for writing.; [a.] Chicago, IL

AZIZ, SIRAJUDDIN
[b.] February 10, 1956, Karachi; [p.] Mr. Abdul Rashid, Mrs. Samiun Rashid; [m.] Zeba Aziz; [ch.] Ali Abdul Azis (son); [ed.] Bachelor of Commerce, Univ of Karachi; [occ.] Banker; [memb.] 1. Inst of Bankers, 2. Hong Kong Society of Training and Development; [hon.] 1 Distinction List at Univ for English Language and Advanced Accountancy, 2. Several Prizes in debates and essay writing; [oth. writ.] I am a regular contributor to local english dailies on varied subjects; [pers.] I endeavour to view only positively all human achievements. I attempt to portray in my writings virtues attending mankind; [a.] Karachi, Pakistan

BACHETTI, PIERO
[b.] October 25, 1969, Windsor, Ontario, Canada; [p.] Giovanni and Serafina Bachetti; [ed.] BA (Honours Italian Language and Literature), B.Ed., Univ of Windsor; [occ.] International Languages Educator; [memb.] Multicultural Council of Windsor and Essex County; [hon.] Italian Studies Scholarship, Windsor Italian Professional and Businessmen's Assoc; [pers.] Humanity is the epitome of multiculturalism, and the threshold of divinity"; [a.] Tecumseh, Prov Ontario

BADILLO, DOREEN M.
[Pen.] Dora B.; [b.] October 12, 1946, Sydney, Australia; [p.] Doreen Dunshea; [ch.] Darren Michael and Danena Alexis; [ed.] Oceanside High, Palomar Jr. College; [occ.] Santa Fe Irrigation District Utility Dept (meter reader); [memb.] Oceanside Pop Warner, Oceanside Bobby Sox (Girls softball), Softball Assoc, Youth Activities, Umpire Assoc; [hon.] Coaching awards from Breakfast Optimist, Elks Lodge, Emblem Club, El Camino High School, All Tournament teams (softball), Honorable awards from youth activities in Oceanside; [oth. writ.] Several poems not published and a few short stories; [pers.] I think of my children and others, I think of my friends, relatives and experiences in life itself. I let thought of mind, heart and feeling surround me as I write. I write on site and inspiration of moment in mind; [a.] Oceanside, CA

BAFEKR, KIARASH
[b.] November 25, 1968, Tehran; [p.] Mohammadali, Roohangiz; [ed.] AS, City College of San Francisco. Currently in process in obtaining Bach of Architecture from IIT (Chicago) with a minor in Philosophy; [occ.] Student, part time odd jobs; [memb.] Amnesty International, Green Peace, Children International; [hon.] Dean's list, several scholarships, first place prize winner of annual, statewide student design competition, 1992 (California); [oth. writ.] In Majorem Dej Honorem, Passage Through Time, War, Cycle, To

My Empress, Fire and several other poems and essays; [pers.] Open yourself to the gentle indifference of this world, and you will find the stranger within you; [a.] Chicago, IL

BAHNA, CAROL LEE
[Pen.] Carol Lee Bahna; [b.] June 3, 1944, NY; [p.] (deceased) Frances and John Bahna; [m.] (former) Felder James (divorced), September 9, 1971; [ch.] Tara Bahna-James (who attends yale); [ed.] 1) MA in Eng and Secondary Ed from City Univ, 2) BA in English with a dual minor of psychology and education from City Univ; [occ.] Teacher in New York City - English Teacher; [memb.] I was a member of Alwin Nicholais professional dance class in 1962-1964 and was in his show "Imago". When I was in Seward Park High School, I was a member of Arista, the chorus and the modern dance club; [hon.] I was a finalist in the New York City Spelling Bee when I was in elementary school. I was in sp in junior high and skipped a grade. I attended Seward Park High School. I was on the honor roll and in honors classes in high school. I received an award for athletics; [oth. writ.] My other writings include over 50 poems and over 40 songs. I write both the music and the lyrics. My songs include folk, pop, and show tunes; [pers.] I have performed my songs in Les Mouche, The Cajun, and in Penn Palace in New York City. I play guitar and piano. I studied voice with Adele Burgoff Rothenberg; [a.] New York, NY

BAHR, AGNES K.
[Pen.] Agnes K. Bahr; [b.] April 20, 1907, Fond du Lac, WI; [p.] Gert Bessie Lainy; [m.] Rudy Bahr (deceased-May 27, 1989), May 19, 1928; [ch.] (6) Hob, Dave, Betty, Dick, Nat, Edgar; [ed.] 8th grade; [occ.] Housewife; [a.] Milwaukee, WI

BAICY, SARAH WILLIAMSON
[Pen.] Sarah Williamson; [b.] March 3, 1918, Lumberton, NC; [p.] G. W. Williamson and Dora McCormick Williamson; [m.] Edward Owen Baicy, June 7, 1941; [ch.] Joan, Edward, John, Robert and William; [ed.] AB degree in English and History. I was educated in North Carolina; [occ.] Retired Homemaker; [pers.] This poem was written in honor of my grandfather John Archibald McCormick of Rowland, NC. He lived 1868-1940. I moved to Maryland in 1949.; [a.] Aberdeen, MD

BAIER, KATIE
[b.] February 19, 1901, Dresdon; [m.] 1955 widowed, 1927; [ed.] High School grad, college courses, Trained Practical Nurse, Home Health Aid; [occ.] Retired - also from volunteer Kaiser Hospital 1990; [memb.] 25 years award this year from Tourist Club "The Nature Friends" San Francisco - Mill Valley; [hon.] Golden Poet Award 1987 for "The Car" by World of Poetry contest by Eddie Lou Cole, Poetry Editor, Sacramento, CA; [oth. writ.] Poems appeared here in the "Alten Heim Retiremt" papers. A lot of poems I wrote and still write - keeping for me and my friends; [pers.] When I look around and back on the life's happenings, it delivers a lot of comics, even in some serious problems. So I keep some memories in little poems waiting for bigger; [a.] Oakland, CA

BAILEY, LONNIE DALE
[b.] January 13, 1957, Pineville, W.VA; [p.] Violet Bailey;l [m.] not married; [ed.] Graduate of Glen Rogers High School, 1 year of college, 11 years training in Regular Army.; [occ.] College student at Southern West Virginia Community College.; [memb.] The Planetary Society, Music writers of America, American Atheist.; [hon.] Name to be on microdot by the Planetary Society, on landers, for the Russian Mars 94' Mission, name on the Planetary Society's SETI (Search for Exttraterrestrial Intelligence) radio-telescope plaque permanently, etc.; [oth. writ.] Numerous poems in anthologies, two books, published,

collection of 22 poems published entitled "When Love Passes You By" articles and stories in "The Register-Herald" newspaper, 8 songs released nationally under the Tin Pan Alley, Inc. music label, etc.; [pers.] I try to cpature beauty, truth and cosmic wonders in action, I prefer to color science as the spirit of curiosity, love and intellectual joys as Percy Shelly painted them best and the darker emotions true too life.; [a.] Rock View, W.VA

BAILEY, NICOLE
[b.] December 4, 1981, Westminster, MD; [p.] Denis and Colleen Bailey; [ch.] None, Have 1 sister, Natasha 10 yrs. old; [ed.] I am a 7th grader at Westminster West Middle School.; [memb.] I belong to orchestra playing violin; [oth. writ.] Other unpublished poetry and short stories.; [pers.] I am interested in the saving of our environment and animals and I include them in some of my writing.; [a.] Westminster, MD

BAILEY, SHANNAH RAE
[Pen.] S. R. Bailey; [b.] April 7, 1978, Rockingham, NC; [p.] Patsy A. Bailey and Ronald L. Adrianse, Jr; [ed.] Chatham Central High; [occ.] Student; [memb.] Fellowship of Christian Athletes. Students Against Drunk Driving, Art Club; [oth. writ.] Recognized for excellence in poetry by the Tri-County English Alliance; [pers.] To June Wicker my inspiration. I can never say how much you mean to me. I'll start by dedicating this poem to you, and I hope that someday you'll know how much I care; [a.] Bennett, NC

BAILEY, TRACEY ETHAN
[Pen.] Eric E.J. Ann Bailey; [b.] June 25, 1974, Hawthorne, CA; [p.] Angel W. Bailey, Alvin James Bailey; [ed.] Monrovia High; [pers.] Art is the collaboration of intellect and emotion expressed in a unique and individual style bringing pleasure and awe to a small or large majority. Which we should strive to accomplish; [a.] San Gabriel, CA

BAIRD, JULIA ANNETTE
[b.] August 19, 1974, Lafallette, TN; [p.] Ronald Jerry Baird and Brenda K. Powers Baird; [ed.] Campbell County High graduate; [occ.] Liberal Health Care Mountain View Nursing Home; [oth. writ.] I have written other poems. A few titles are "Love is the Key", "I'm Thankful", and "Changes", Along with some others. I have never attempted to have any published; [pers.] I would like to dedicate this poem to my parents (Jerry and Brenda Baird). They have always encouraged my writing. Also to Clarence Cowan. He inspired my heart to write this poem; [a.] Speedwell, TN

BAKER, CINDY
[b.] March 11, 1978, Spartonburg; [p.] Libby and Niel Baker; [ed.] I'm in my second year of High School. I attend Berea High School.; [memb.] I'm a member of the National Art Society; [oth. writ.] I'm very interested in music, art, and poetry. I feel honored to have one of my poems in your book.; [pers.] "Life will make anyone think seriously about God and death."; [a.] Greenville, SC

BAKER, RHONDA
[b.] September 23, 1980, Morristown, PA; [p.] Dr. and Mrs. Ronald Baker; [ed.] Saint Titus School; [occ.] Student; [memb.] St. Titus CYO; [hon.] Blue Ribbon Recognition 1993 Academy of Notre Dame, Young Writers Conference, CYO 3-D Award 1992; [a.] East Norriton, PA

BAKER, STEPHANIE
[b.] December 17, 1982, Eastoria, OH; [p.] Steve M. and Martha A. Baker; [ed.] Student at St. Patrick School, Troy, OH; [occ.] Student; [memb.] Girl Scouts, YWCA, 4-H, St. Patrick Church, Troy Soccer Club; [hon.] Honor Student (G.P.A. 4.0); [pers.] I enjoy writing poems about animals because they are

so interesting and lively; [a.] Troy, OH

BAKHLE, ARATI
[b.] April 4, 1975, New Delhi; [p.] Jayant Bakhle an Anita Bakhle; [ed.] Second year medical studen [hon.] 1. First prize in an inter-school poetry-writin contest, 2. First prize in a poetry-reading contest, 3 Participation in poetry-reading programs; [oth. writ. Poems have been published in a local newspaper, 2 Poem has been quoted in an indo-Israel magazine [pers.] Dawn arrives after the dark night, and the su rises, radiant and bright so, don't give up hope whatever be your plight, for hope gives us courage fight with all our might; [a.] Bombay Maharashtr (India)

BALCOM, JO-ANNE MELODIE ZITO
[b.] Ottawa, Ontario; [ch.] Austin, Curtis and Jame [ed.] Completed Gr 10, a 150 hr wordprocessin course, Completed Gr 12 English Writin (nightschool), Correspondence Courses were Ac counting I, Grade 11-12 Typing, Military School Logistics, Large Quantity Cooking, Basic Trainin [occ.] Full-time Single-mother; [memb.] St Joh Ambulance; [hon.] Military Awards; [oth. writ.] have a huge selection of poems and songpoems whic I have written and that I am very proud of. Poetr published with The National Library of Poetry are: H Did Not Exist and this upcoming poem called th Frolic. I would love to know someone who would p my songpoems in the charts; [pers.] My mind speak my poetic words and then my pen writes them. I wi always writ as then my words can always be spoke [a.] Beachburg, Ontario, Canada

BALDACCHINO (JR.), GERARD J.
[b.] October 12, 1971, Quirry, MA; [p.] Gerard ar Sheila; [m.] single; [ed.] GED; [occ.] Fiberglass Bo Builder - Northeast Fiberglass, Waldoboro, MI [oth. writ.] Many poems and a few short stories, nor published though; [pers.] I write from personal refle tions, music and my surroundings. People influenc my writtings most of all; [a.] Damariscotta, ME

BALDWIN, ALLAN RAY
[b.] November 2, 1954, Chicago; [p.] Mary & Josep Baldwin; [ch.] Ravin Angelique Baldwin (Daughter [ed.] Currently working on Masters Degree in Psy chology at Chicago State University; [occ.] Da Collection Technician at U.S. Postal Service; [memb American Red Cross First Aid Instructor; [hon Dean's List at the university of IL (Chicago); nume ous postal service appreciation, incencentive an suggestion (monetary) awards; [hon.] First plac award in postal talent competition; [oth. writ.] Aut mation (Post Office Skit & Video used for orientatic and training); approx. 2 dozen other songs (Gospe R&B, Pop) and inspirational poems; [pers.] "You'v got to have a positive mind and keep your head to th sky, because if a bird din't believe in itself he'd nev be able to fly." [a.] Chicago, IL

BALDYGA, NANCY J.
[b.] October 4, 1931, Springfield, MA; [p.] Frank an Apolonia Lachut; [m.] Edward J, June 6, 1953; [ch Debbie, Connie, Barbara, Elaine, Diane; Grandchi dren: Matthew, Gregory, Sarah, Allie, Ryan, Steffi [ed.] Ware High School; [occ.] Retired; [memb.] Mary's Church parish committees; [hon.] Seven awards for artistically crocheted afghans; [oth. writ Numerous unpublished reflections on family an other things that are close to the heart; [pers.] M poems help me express the pleasure and love I enjoy with my husband and daughters and now with the children; [a.] Ware, MA

BALENT, AMY
[b.] December 19, 1968, Ft. Lauderdal, FL; [p Susan and Alvan Balent; [ed.] Pine Crest Schoo Georgetown University; [occ.] Artist; [hon.] Dean

st, various fine art, writing, and athletic awards; ⸱ers.] Words and visual images are my shoes in the ⸱nce with truth, I wear them to live, to better know ⸱e vitality of the human spirit.; [a.] San Francisco, ⸱A

ALL, EVERETT
⸱d.] Graduate UCLA, English major, minors in ⸱ench, music, drama; [oth. writ.] Published short ⸱ory, "A Painting for Isolde" in New World Writing, ⸱ol 2, Modern American Library, wrote and directed ⸱dio documentaries for United Nations Radio in New ⸱ork, Paris, for five years, creative director for own ⸱dvertising agency in California (25 years) wrote ⸱ems (haikus) to accompany his recent one-person ⸱hibit of paintings and sculpture at the Pacific Asia ⸱useum in Pasadena, CA. (Ball is also a pointer, ⸱ulptor and graphic designer with over fifty shows in ⸱SA, Europe and Australia). Current work: Illustrat-⸱g a collection of his poems, writing a novel, poems, ⸱mpleting a series of paintings: "Lifeline, Theme ⸱d Variations" and programming and announcing ⸱assical music on radio station KDB in Santa Barbara, ⸱ night. His late wife was novelist Jane Eklund Ball. ⸱ree Children.

ALLANCE, VIRGINIA O.
⸱en.] Gini Ballance; [b.] September 21, 1927, Mis-⸱uri; [p.] Ethel and Revere Ogden; [m.] Thaxton A. ⸱llance Jr., October 27, 1949; [ch.] Alan Lee ⸱llance and Stephen Henry Ballance; [ed.] Teachers ⸱edential University of California Los Angeles; ⸱cc.] Fine Arts Teacher Monrovia Adult School; ⸱nemb.] Mid Valley Art League Pasadena Lapidary ⸱ociety, Pasadena Auxiliary of Boys Republic, Sierra ⸱adre United Methodist church, California Teachers ⸱nion; [hon.] Numerous Fine Art Awards: Los ⸱ngeles County Fair, Mid Valley Art League, June ⸱ke Artists Guild Art Show (Calif.); [oth. writ.] ⸱ymphony of the Trees" is my first poem ever to be ⸱bmitted; [pers.] This poem was inspired while ⸱mping along the beautiful and scenic Deschutes ⸱ver in central Oregon. The magnificent Ponderosa ⸱nes, the birds, the wind, and the river created the ⸱notion for this poem. The world could find peace ⸱d rest somewhere in nature or within one's own self; ⸱] Arcadia, CA

ALSAMO, PETER P.
⸱.] June 6, 1966, Brooklyn, NY; [m.] Single; [ed.] ⸱S, 1 yr of college, 1 yr paralegal, legal asst school ⸱ertified. US Coast Guard, and life in general; [occ.] ⸱ivate information service agent (background checks); ⸱th. writ.] A compilation, and auto-biographical ⸱n-fiction work titled "The Truth". I am currently ⸱riting a fiction novel titled "Justice". (non-published ⸱t); [pers.] My work titled "The Truth" is one ⸱mpilation of personal notes, observations and philo-⸱phical statements; [a.] Ft Lauderdale, FL

ALVIN, MARY L.
⸱.] February 5, 1918, NYC; [p.] deceased; [m.] ⸱parated, June 30, 1934; [ch.] 1 daughter; [ed.] High ⸱hool; [occ.] Retired; [memb.] Republican Clubs; ⸱h. writ.] Club Newspaper, Employees Newspaper; ⸱rs.] I would like to see peace throughout the world. ⸱ children happy, well fed and well cared for and ⸱ved; [a.] Dix Hills, NY

AMBULLIS, CAROLE S.
⸱] July 11, 1963, Manchester England; [p.] Trevor ⸱d Irene Walker; [m.] Martin, July 11, 1990; [ed.] ⸱A Special, English Literature, Univ of Alberta, ⸱monton; [occ.] Bookshop Clerk; [memb.] Lake ⸱uise Community Assoc; [hon.] Alexander ⸱therford Scholarships for high school achieve-⸱ent; [oth. writ.] Previously published poetry, un-⸱blished poems and children's books; [pers.] My

grandmother often told me - and it is true - procrasti-nation is the thief of time.

BANGE, LARRY H.
[b.] March 24, 1950, Gettysburg, PA; [p.] Donald H. Bange, Ethel M. Bange; [ch.] Rachael Rae; [ch.] RAchael Rae; [occ.] Data Processing; [memb.] Int'l Soc of Poets; [oth. writ.] Several poems in antholo-gies; including "A Break in the Clouds", "Wind in the Night Sky" and "Outstanding Poets of 1994"; [pers.] Writing should be fun and communicative - an expres-sion of oneself from within. Sensitivity to mankind and his needs of existence expresses love at it's core; [a.] Harrisburg, PA

BANKS, HELEN
[b.] July 20, 1914, Pleasant Lake, IN; [p.] John and Malinda (Houlton) Patton; [m.] (deceased) "Lyle", January 27, 1934; [ch.] Roy, Marjorie, Glenn & Loretta; [ed.] Marshall High School Lambsone Busi-ness College and Manicure Cert - Classic Beauty College; [occ.] Retired and disabled (age 79); [memb.] Active member of LDS Church since 1947; [hon.] 1989 Silver 1991, - academy 1992. Golden (Poetry Awards). Lifetime in "Academy" and award 1993 poems in 5 poetry books, oil paintings over 400 since 1982. Senior Center Volunteer Award. Attended Milton Berle's 85th Birthday award by invitation from Steve Allen (the MC) July 4, 1993 at Beverly Hills, CA (150 celebrities attended); [pers.] The greatest love is remembering those before you, during and after. And leaving things you create for posterity to enjoy; [a.] Mesa, AZ

BANKS, JR. RICHARD L.
[b.] August 9th, 1962, Brooklyn, NY; [p.] Richard L. Banks, Sr., Erika Banks; [m.] Eileen B. Banks, July 2nd, 1983; [ch.] Jessica Maryann, Felicia Jean; [ed.] Franklin K. Lane H.S., Community College of the Air Force; [occ.] Security Officer, Vanguard Security Services; [hon.] High School Honor Society, Armed Forces Expeditionary Medal, Air Force Commenda-tion Medal; [pers.] My life has been a painful quest for greater knowledge and truth of those life forces that surround me daily. My writigns reflect this through a higher consciousness from my inner-being.; [a.] Glendale, AZ

BARANOVA, SKATERINA
[Pen.] Catherine Rush; [b.] July 22, 1976, Moscow, Russia; [p.] Tatyana Baranova, Aleksandr Baranov; [ed.] Alternative school "Modern Education" (11 yrs); [occ.] An interpreter in a Joint Venture" Transripok"; [memb.] The American Center (Ameri-can Library); [oth. writ.] Many poems, which have not been published anywhere yet; [pers.] The grand essentials of happiness are: something to do, someone to love and something to hope for (Chalmers). When one does not have a chance to experience these things in his real life, he is carried away to his dreams. I am carried away to my poetry. That is where my love, my dreams and my hopes and faith live; [a.] Moscow, Russia

BARGO, MARY J.
[Pen.] Mary Walters Bargo; [b.] April 27, 1934, Port Royal, PA; [p.] Thurman and Geraldine Walters; [m.] C.L. "Duke" Bargo, [ch.] Three sons - Mark, Bryne, Joel; [ed.] Graduated from Tuscarora Valley High School, Port Royal, PA; [occ.] Housewife; [memb.] Attend Christian and Missionary Alliance Church, Milroy, PA (C&MA) Church; [oth. writ.] Poetry in local news papers - short articles in the Common Ground magazine, McVey Town, PA. Play piano and sing original songs I wrote in local churches; [pers.] Most of my writings are spiritually inspired. The Lord doesn't speak to me in an audiable voice. It is a feeling in the spirit. Words and melodies run through my head like a typewriter, sometimes like an electric type-writer. The Lord gives me one chance at it. If I don't

write it down or put it on tape it is lost; [a.] Reedsville, PA

BARNES, JAMIE LYN
[b.] December 4, 1978, Michigan; [p.] Larry and Janet Barnes; [occ.] Student at Pilot Mtn. Middle School; [memb.] Environmental Club at my school, member of Pilot View United Methodist Church; [oth. writ.] Close to 14 or 15 other poems. I also enjoy writing stories.; [pers.] Just by being around my friends and family has inspired me to write my poems. Even my enemies have inspired me to write. So I guess just being around people helps.; [a.] Pinnacle, NC

BARNES, JR. WILLIAM ARTHUR
[Pen.] R. J. Senrabaw (pronounced sendraybay); [b.] January 25, 1914, Marston, Missour; [p.] William Arthur Barnes and Mary Marguerite Barnes; [m.] Olive Yost Barnes, August 1, 1937; [ch.] Dr. W.A. Barnes III, Bonnie O. Bennett, Garry E. Barnes, Greg D. Barnes; [ed.] Graduated Marston, Missouri High School 1931. Attended Wilson Teachers College, D.C. and Southeastern Univ., Wash. D.C. MBA-MBS; [occ.] Has been retired from the FBI, Wash. D.C. since June, 1972; [memb.] Ancient Free and Accepted Masons, Eastern Star, NRA; [hon.] Marston, MO, High School 1931. Valedictorian; [oth. writ.] An assortment of poems and lyrics numbering about 180 plus, submitted and copyrighted under the title "Over 150 and Some Nifty."; [pers.] I have been influenced by my dear parents. Both were school teachers at one time. I am a registered voter and consider myself a conservative progressive populist. My ancestors in this country from England are Tho-mas Barnes, to Hartford, Conn. 1635, William Marston to Salem, Mass. 1634. Am still tracing my Joseph A. Carmack and Mary O'Kelley (O'Kelly) lineage.

BARNES, KATHLEEN MARGARET
[Pen.] "Barnseybaby"; [b.] September 27, 1918, Stockport, UK, Cheshire; [p.] George Wm. Harrison, Ellen Harrison; [m.] Bernard Barnes (2nd), Novem-ber 29, 1978; [ch.] Adrian George Harrison (son - BA Modern Languages); [ed.] RC Elementary School; Army Education. A level standard. British Army service 16 yrs, Collector of Taxes - 15 yrs; [occ.] Retired government servant; [memb.] Horticultural Clubs, Blind Social Worker, Flower arranger city and guilds pait one hospital shop volunteer, over 60's clubs, Deaf Assoc Secretary, Committee Member of Ex Army Assn, Committee Member of Church, Golden 9 Flower Clubs; [hon.] Advanced level english language and english literature; [oth. writ.] Several poems and short stories submitted but nothing ac-cepted until now. Thank you; [pers.] Religion is not so much the externals but the way one treats ones neighbor especially the afflicted. That is true religion; [a.] Stockport, Cheshire, UK

BARNES, LISA
[Pen.] Madeline Van Cappio; [b.] January 26, 1979, Hamilton, NY; [p.] Gerald and Laura Barnes; [ed.] Waterville Jr., Sr. High School; [memb.] Jr. High Honor Society, Sr. High Student Council, Drama Club; [hon.] Honor Society Certificate, Most Artistic Ability Award, Academic Honor Achievment Award, Presidential Academic Fitness Award, Student of the Month, Perfect Attendance Award and Optimist Club Certificate; [oth. writ.] A novel titled "Breaking The Rules," a movie script titled a family vacation, a song titled Hawaii and various works of poetry.; [pers.] I feel that poetry is a way of expressing emotion what I am writing in a poem, usually reflects what I am feeling. I write to releieve myself; [a.] Oriskany Falls, NY

BARNETT (JR.), JERRY DON
[b.] April 02, 59, Boise ID; [p.] Jerry Don and Shirley Barnett; [m.] Debbie Dudley Barnett, February 6, 1985; [ch.] Shawn Michael, Jerry Don III, Natalie Ann; [ed.] Lindale High, Tyler Jr College, Univ of Texas at Tyler; [occ.] ETTL Engineers and Consultants, Tyler, TX; [memb.] American Chemical Society; [hon.] Tyler Jr College Certificate of Merit in Psychology, Dean's List; [oth. writ.] Haiku poem published in Tyler Jr College Touchstone in Spring 19988; [pers.] Beauty lies within all things. Wisdom dwells deep within the beauty; [a.] Lindale, TX

BARNETT (JR.), REV. CARL H.
[b.] November 23, 1952, Indpls, IN; [p.] Rev. Carl H. and Cleo Barnett; [m.] Barbara Barnett, September 6, 1986; [ch.] Catrina Barnett, Krystal Gray and Steven Keys; [ed.] Shortridge H.S., ITT Tech, William Tyndale College, Admin USAF; [occ.] Transportation Pepsi Co Food Systems; [memb.] Minister, True Rock Missionary Baptist Church; [oth. writ.] Several poems such as The Void and This is the Day Which, have not been published; [pers.] I reflect my insight of God's word through poetry. It is a way to convey God's word in a different light; [a.] Detroit, MI

BARR, LINDA M.
[b.] June 22, 1962, Grants Pass, OR; [p.] Richard and Donald Barr; [ch.] Courtney Janai Capps and one on the way!; [pers.] My writings reflect all of the love and kindness I have been blessed with. It will get my thru any tragedy in my life especially my beautiful children; [a.] Puyallup, WA

BARRETT, FRANCES K.
[b.] July 4, 1911, Beach, ND; [p.] Walter and Rose Stratton; [m.] (1st) Harold R. Davis, September 10, 1934, (2nd) James R. Barrett, October 31, 1959; [ch.] Harland, Raymond, Wallace, Marvin, Karen, Kaye, Lowell; [ed.] O'Briend School, Black River Falls High - Jackson Co, Teachers Normal - Juneau Co, Teacher Normal - Lacrosse State U; [occ.] Retired; [memb.] St. James Catholic Church, Juneau Co Nutrition Council - Juneau Co Advisory Council - Pres. Scenic Vue Ex Homemakers - Disaster Chairman Redcross for Camp Douglas, WI; [oth. writ.] Published in local paper - Homemaker News; [pers.] Poetry is music for the soul. I especially love H.W. Longfellow. Wish I could have known him; [a.] Camp Douglas, WI

BARRY, THELMA IONE
[b.] January 4, 1935, North Star, Alberta, Canada; [p.] deceased; [m.] Kevin Barry, October 6, 1979; [ch.] (1 son) Sheldon; (1 daughter) Beth; [ed.] Graduated gr 12 - 1953, Business Education 1974, on the job training as Library - Assistant; [occ.] Retired; [memb.] Anglican Church - Reform Party of Canada; [hon.] 2nd prize - Sh St Tast of Salt - Creative Writing Course 1972, Edmonton Public Schools continuing education; [oth. writ.] Many unpublished poems and short stories; [pers.] My philosophy of life is start your day with a smile. Be thankful for being so loved and free in our beautiful country. Go the extra mile for a friend. He may need to do the same for you one day; [a.] Bon Accord, Alta

BARTHLOW, CHARLOTTE
[b.] October 1, 1955, W.VA; [p.] Homer and Carol Barthlow; [ed.] Idaho State University, 1985, Biology degree B.S. 1989 Nursing degree BSN; [occ.] RN; [pers.] Most influenced by the writings and philosophy of Ayn Rand, and poetry of Alice Walker; [a.] Boise, ID

BARTON, CATHERINE
[Pen.] Kae Pollitt, Kae Barton; [b.] September 21, 1911; [p.] Eugene J. Reilly, Catherine Moran; [m.] James J. Barton, November 28, 1992; [ch.] Jeanne Russo, William Semmens, Bonnie C. Moran, Geri McGrath; [ed.] Lincoln High School, Jersey City State College; [occ.] Retired - Volunteer; [memb.] American Assoc for Medical Transcription; [hon.] Golden Poet Award; World of Poetry Award of Merit; [oth. writ.] Many poems published in local newspapers, humorour columns published in senior newsletters; [pers.] I try to keep a little humor in everything. I have been greatly influenced by the writings of my parents; currently by the writings of Erma Bombeck; [a.] Rahway, NJ

BARTON, W. AUSTIN
[Pen.] Agustin T; [b.] September 5, 1929, Niag Falls; [p.] Deceased; [memb.] Single; [ed.] Grade 11 - High school; [occ.] Retired; [memb.] Belong to the Friend Club at the Local Library. Also the Senior Club membership; [hon.] Musical adaptation - instrument - keyboard, musical theory; [oth. writ.] Short stories. Poetry and newspaper articles. Submitting my poem 'The Cross' to the NLP; [pers.] My writing is my main interest and past time, whether it be for fun or profit; [a.] Crystal Beach, Ontario

BASH, JEAN CONNERLY
[b.] August 17, 1913, Sedgwick, CO; [p.] Jesse M. Connerly & Kate Ruth Conner; [m.] Dallas W. Bush, July 12, 1942; [ch.] Edward Jesse, Margaret Shirley, Ballas Wayne Bash Jr., [ed.] Sedgwick County High School Opportunity Business school; [occ.] Retired Secretary; [memb.] First Southern Baptist, Baptist Church of Paradise Valley, Zola Levitt Ministries; [hon.] Named Class Poet at Graduation, 1st place in essay contest. Salutortion at Graduation; [oth. writ.] Printed a book of poetry and distributed 100 copies, called "Love is Forever."; [pers.] Mother read poetry to her children all of our childhood. She quoted them and knew all the authors. Father was a musician and storyteller. There was a long line of poets and artists including Hyrum Powers the sculptor; [a.] Phoenix, AZ

BASILE, MICHELE
[b.] April 20, 1977, Pompton Plains, NJ; [p.] Colleen Basile, Mike Basile; [sibs.] Brother Michael; [ed.] Wayne Hills High School; [occ.] Student; [memb.] Wayne General Hospital Volunteer, Smile Club - Charitable and Civic Program, Annunciation and Civic Program, Annunciation Church Youth Group; [hon.] Smile Club Award of Appreciation, Hospital Youth Service; [a.] Wayne, NJ

BATE, EMMA
[b.] March 18, 1978, Toronto, Ontario; [p.] Barbara Bate and Roger Bate; [ed.] Grade 10, The Humberview School; [occ.] Student; [memb.] Albion/Bolton Fitness Centre.; [hon.] Academic Honours since grade seven, student of the month, citzenship; [oth. writ.] Personal poems written for my loved ones.; [pers.] People must lern that the most important aspect to happiness is love, for without love, there is no happiness.; [a.] Bolton, Ontrio

BATES, DARREN
[b.] June 9, 1969, Montreal, PQ; [p.] Douglas and Claire Bates; [ed.] Mount Royal High School, McGill Univ (B.A.); [occ.] Student (M.Div.); [pers.] "Ask, and it shall be given you; seek, and you shall find; knock, and it shall be opened unto you" (Mtt.7,7); [a.] Montreal, PQ

BATES, DAWN WISTERIA
[Pen.] Yeboa; [b.] August 26, Brooklyn, NY; [p.] Edward and Gladys Bates; [m.] none; [ed.] P.S. 52, Shell Bank Jr. High, City-as-School High School, Hunter College Cuny; [occ.] Freelance Writer, Researcher; [hon.] Undergraduate honor received from the African and Puerto Rican Studies, Department of Hunter College.; [oth. writ.] Poems (Lent, Kikuyu Prayer, Black Tamil) published in poder, a women centered publication. Additionally, I have develope with great effort of spirit, three short stories.; [pers] I have been exposed to superlative writers--havi this blessing, I struggle to write with the analytic clarity of James Baldwin and the abundant fluidity Zora Neale Hurston.; [a.] Deer Park Long IS, N

BATES, JENNIFER E.
[b.] Buffalo, NY; [p.] J. David and Mary Eick; [ch] Devon Robert, born 8/28/91; [ed.] The Kansas C Academy of Learning, GED received 6/89, o semester of college (Austin Community Colleg Austin, TX); [occ.] Writer, I am currently working a novel.; [memb.] Columbia House Video club, t human race.; [oth. writ.] Numerous as yet unpu lished poems and stories, poem published in hi schoool newspaper.; [pers.] My writings focus prim rily on human nature. My goal is to promote harmo among people of all kinds, and to increase t awareness of separating the truth from the lie.; [a Overland Park, KS

BAUMAN, MATTHEW WILLIAM
[b.] September 4, 1967, Ithaca, NY; [p.] Susan and William C. Bauman, Jr.; [ed.] University Oklahoma (Norman) graduated 1991, Bachelor Science in Geography, 1985 graduate Laho Americanb School, Lahore, Pakistan; O Paramedic Assistant; [oth. writ.] None yet (pending).; [pers. have found that writing is and always will be, like a art form in general, important for the doing of the not the art's final accomplishment(s).; [a.] Keoke HI

BAYER, KATHLEEN MARY BAULY
[Pen.] Kathleen Bauly Bayer; [b.] Senior Citize Bury St. Edmunds, England; [p.] Dorothy K. a James E. Bauly; [m.] John B. Bayer (retired Lawye [ch.] Three daughters; [ed.] College trained, Childre Nurse. East Anglian Methodist Boarding Schoc [occ.] Former farmer, children's nurse, housewi [memb.] Tinnitus Association, Greenpeace (a worke [hon.] Prizes for handwork; [oth. writ.] 200 unpu lished poems, one book (pers.) unpublished.; [per To promote the wonders of nature all wildlife a helpless creatures, known to me as "My Jade Circl and "Little Bits of Happiness." [a.] Richmond, K

BAYLIS, JANICE
[b.] July 26, 1928, Beloit, WI; [p.] Ralph & De Hinshaw; [ch.] Bradley, Brian and Allen Bayl [occ.] Occidental, Pepperdine and Columbia Pacifi Ph.D. in Psychology; [occ.] Retired reading speci ist; [memb.] Association for the Study of Dream [oth. writ.] Sleep On It! The Practical Side of Dream -De Vorss & Co. book. Dream Dynamics a Decoding--Sun, Man, Moon, Inc. book; vario articles; [pers.] Promoting everyone's use of th dreams is my passion.

BEANE, KIMBERLY D.
[b.] April 17, 1971, Minnt., ND; [p.] Bobby H. Bea & Sherrill R. Beane; [ed.] Scotland High School, El College, NC, B.A. English Purdue University, c rently working on MA Amr. Literature.; [occ.] Teac ing Assistant and grad student, Purdue Universi [memb.] National Council of Teachers of Englis Defenders of Wildlife, North American Wildlife Pa Foundation (Wolf Park), Amnesty International; [ho Alpgha Chi Honors Society, Sigma Tau Delta (E glish) Omicron Delta Kappa (Leadership), Kap Delta Pi (Education), NC Teaching Fellow, 19 Elon English, Scholar Award, Alpha Psi Ome (Theatre), Dean's List; [oth. writ.] Short sstories a poems published in collegiate literary magazin (Colonnades, Pegasus), article in the Alpha C Recorder; [pers.] I am both awed and influenced the intensity of "poetry of witness". The poem print here is from my own working series, Afterward The Were The children, Poems about Second Generati

locaust Survivors.; [a.] Laurinburg, NC

ARDEN, KATHARINE
] February 11, 1969, Springdale, AR; [p.] Dayle
Mary Luper; [ch.] Ariel Dawn Bearden; [ed.]
aduate of Springdale High School; [occ.] Factor
pervisor; [oth. writ.] "The don't understand" pub-
ed with Treasured Poems of America, Fall 1993.;
rs.] My poems reflect the ups and downs of my
n life and the love I feel for my daughter.; [a.]
ringdale, AR

AULIEU, ERICA D.
] November 30, 1977, Augusta; [p.] Joyce A.
ath; [ed.] I attend Gardiner Area High School
ere I am a sophomore; [memb.] I am a member of
Gardiner High School, JV Cheerleading team.;
n.] In 1993, my freshmen year I received a tophy
being the most dedicated cheerleader on the
shmen team. Also in 1993, I was nominated for
o's who among american high school students.;
n. writ.] Published or soon to be in my high school
wspaper "The Eye of the Tiger."; [pers.] My
try reflects my inner feelings about both my family
boyfriend. Both happy and sad moments.; [a.]
rdiner, ME

CKER, PHILLIP HENRY
April 10, 1942; [p.] Henry Becker and Martha
rchfield; [m.] Susan Becker (divorced 1980); [ch.]
e Beth Becker, Matthew Brady Becker; [ed.] MFA
tis Art Inst, grad 1968, Los Angeles City College,
llywood High grad - 1960, Harvard Military
ool; [occ.] Appt and Canvassing Mgr Southern
if Construction Consultants; [hon.] Art Work
ibited Pasadena Art Museum, CA; Long Beach
Museum, CA; Downey Art Museum, CA; [oth.
t.] None published; [pers.] Take observation that
ear not unusual and show how they illuminate the
y mechanisms of our existence; [a.] Los Angeles,

CKHAM, ELIZABETH
n.] Elisha; [b.] January 17, 1977, Ft. Worth, TX;
.] Joshua High School (still in progress); [memb.]
A; [hon.] Published two years in Who's Who
erica's High School Students; [oth. writ.] Poems
ocal newspapers; [pers.] I have found that my best
rk is based on personal experience, and I hope my
will still be worth writing about in the years to
ne.; [a.] Joshua, TX

CKMAN, KRISTIN
July 20, 1975, Brooklyn, NY; [p.] Steven and
borah Beckman; [ed.] Spotswood High; [occ.]
ck Clerk at Meldisco (K-Mart Footwear Dept);
mb.] Vocational Industrial Clubs of America
CA); [hon.] Who's Who Among American High
ool Students, English trophy, two English medals,
medal, Future Homemakers of America letter,
cational Industrial Clubs of America letter, Aca-
ic letter, Home Economics medal, Medallion
ard, etc; [oth. writ.] Captions and other writings
lished in the Spotswood High yearbook; [pers.]
low your heart and dreams and you can do
thing you wish; [a.] Penn Laird, VA

DARD, JENNIFER MAREN BRIANA
March 17, 1979; [p.] Ronanld and Jean Bedard;
] Eigth grade - Moorehead Junior High; [occ.]
dent; [memb.] Fargo - Moorehead Youth
phany, Mid-night strings, Our savior's Lutheran
rch, Liturgical Dance Choir and Joyful Ringers;
n.] Award winning drawing for Moorehead Public
vice, Co-Concert mistress for Fargo - Moorehead
th Symphany; [pers.] Interested in violin, ice
ing, ballet and modern dance, singing and drama.
ms and precious, preciours are dreams. Dreams
from within. Dreams you'll always have. Don't
nyone take your dreams away, because dreams

are forever.; [a.] Moorhead, MN

BEDWELL, MICHAEL
[b.] August 26, 1950, California; [p.] Bill and Betty
Bedwell; [m.] Diana Bedwell, August 29, 1970; [ch.]
Wendy and Brian; [ed.] Graduate of Downey High
School and two years at Cerritos College; [occ.]
Steam Generating Station Supervisor; [hon.] Various
athletic and automobile racing awards; [oth. writ.]
Several poems of which never have been submitted
for publishing; [pers.] My writing is a vehicle to relate
my personal feelings dealing with the current issues in
my life; [a.] Corona, CA

BEEMAN, LOREEN E.
[Pen.] Emmy; [b.] August 20, 1941, Superior, WI;
[p.] Lawrence and Dorothy Schrieffer; [m.] Elmer
Beeman, October 17, 1959; [ed.] Superior Senior
High, Superior Community College, Lakeshore Tech
Collect - LPM, Medical Dental College; [occ.] Thera-
peutic Cook, Rocky Knoll Health Facility, Plymouth
WI; [memb.] Nord - Rare Disease Disorders progres-
sive Supra Nuclear Palsy Assn, AARP, Future Nurses
Assn, Campers of America; [hon.] Mother of the yr
Award, Dean's List, Superior Comm College, Hon-
orable Mention Award Sparrowgrass Poetry; [oth.
writ.] 2 poems published by Voices of America, 1
poem published by World of Poetry; [pers.] In this
day and age of ones hectic pace, writing and reading
poetry is a relaxing and learing fullfulment for me; [a.]
Plymouth, WI

BEEMER, TONY
[b.] June 14, 1973, Kentucky; [p.] Bonnie and Tim
Beemer; [m.] Single; [ed.] Graduate of New Albany
High School Class of 1991, attending Indiana Univ
Southeast; [occ.] Student; [oth. writ.] Poetry; [pers.]
I am honored to be considered for this award; [a.] New
Albany, IN

BEHLING, BRIAN
[b.] April 9, 1975, Madison, WI; [p.] Nick & Linda
Behling; [ed.] High School Equivalency Diploma;
[occ.] Factory Worker; [hon.] Various Music Awards,
State and local; [oth. writ.] Where Eagles Fly, Black
Rain, God Shall Forgive, Sea of Fright, War, Some-
thing you Can't Explain, Wasting Away, Love,
Storm, One Day At A Time, and various untitled
poems.; [pers.] I believe the meaning of a poem,
song, or book (fictional) or any other work of art,
should be left up to the reader's imagination, not
analized or interprd by so called "critics"; [a.]
Oshkosh, WI

BELCHER, TERRENCE
[b.] January 15, 1963, Queens, NY; [p.] Theodore
Belcher, Barbara Belcher; [ch.] Tiffany Rose, Chris-
topher Thomas; [ed.] HS Francis Lewis College,
Suny Old Westbury, LI; [occ.] Banking - Foreign
Exchange Operations; [hon.] Award of Merit, from
the World of Poetry 4/12/90; [oth. writ.] Lord hear
my cries, reflections, pieces of a dream, forever in
love, you'll never know and my precious jewel;
[pers.] True love is rare and hard to come by. But once
found, it's like a bottomless ocean and knows no
depths and bounds; [a.] Bronx, NY

BELKNAP, JEAN
[b.] Huddersfield, Yorshire England; [p.] William &
Allice Ottewell; [m.] Scott Belknap Jr., November
30, 1944; [ch.] Scott II, Bonnie, Cindy; [ed.] Edu-
cated in England, College: Madonna University
Michigan U.S.A.; [occ.] Retired; [memb.] Rockwood
Congregational Church Questers Society. World War
II British War Brides Group Local U.N.I.C.F., orga-
nizer; [oth. writ.] Two poems published in local
paper.; [pers.] I strive to show the essence of real life
experiences. The great determination of human
nature faced with adversity.; [a.] Gibralter, MI

BELL, ALAYNE MICHELE
[b.] October 3, 1978, Phila, PA; [p.] Jacquelyn Bell,
Handa Bell; [ed.] Philadelphia High School for girls;
[occ.] Student; [memb.] National Geographic Soci-
ety, Cross Country Team (Assistant Manager); [hon.]
Citizenship Award, Academic Awards, Art Awards,
Honorable Mention in fast contest; [oth. writ.] A
poem in past anthology, several editorials in junior
high newspaper; [pers.] Life is hard and painful and
people want to hear about it so...write about it; [a.]
Philadelphia, PA

BELL, MICHAEL LEE
[Pen.] Michael Bell; [b.] December 15, 1981, Hinds
Co.; [p.] Junior and Glenda Bell; [m.] none; [ch.]
none; [ed.] 5th grade, Greenlee Elementary School;
[occ.] None, I am still in school; [memb.] Fox 40 Kids
Club; [hon.] Honor Roll B, Average Award, Principal's
List; [oth. writ.] The Moon; [pers.] The death of my
grandparents inspired me to write this poem. Mr. &
Mrs. Theo Griffin.; [a.] McCool, MS

BEN AVIV, ABRAHAM
[b.] February 28, 1912, Berestechko, Urkan; [p.]
Shmuel Abciuk, Suzi Abciuck (died in holocaust);
[m.] Ester Ben Aviv (1917-1984), September 1,
1939; [ch.] Siona (Ben Aviv), Amitai (Ben Aviv);
[ed.] Architect; [occ.] Architect; [memb.] Ex Free
Masonry; Rotary International; [oth. writ.] 1. A Place
in Heaven, 1964, 2. Strive For Shadow, 1968, 3. Still
Swimming, 1983, 4. Granules Of Time, 1987, 5.
Haiku Poems, 1989; [pers.] Life is not rulled by
philosophy. Empiric Life is real philosophy and
poetry is it's legitimate child. 1932 - immigrated to
Palestine (Israel) as a pioneer of the Zionist move-
ment. 1947 - Fought and was wounded in the War of
Independence of Israel. World Traveler - Visited most
interesting spots in the world including the US which
toured three times. The most astonishing place was
Pearl Harbor where I saw the brutal attack of the
Japanese; [a.] Tel-Aviv, Israel

BENJAMIN, VANESSA CAROL
[b.] August 2, 1969, Washington, DC; [p.] Gwendolyn
and Byron Rankin; [ed.] California State Univ
Northridge - BA, Pasadena High School; [memb.]
New Baptist Church; [hon.] Certified Black Family
Specialist. Scholarship from Delta Sigma Theta Inc,
Pasadena Chapter; [oth. writ.] Article for the Sundial
at Cal State Univ Northridge. Short story for Kapu
Sens Literary magazine. Many other unpublished
poems; [pers.] My poems are written upon inspriation
of my personal experiences. Through struggle, pain
and victory; grace and mercy surrounds me so that I
might show others how to survive, be strong seek
higher peace by loving yourself; [a.] Pasadena, CA

BENSON, JOYCE A.
[Pen.] Joyce Benson; [b.] June 3, 1945, Lynwood,
CA; [p.] Berness C. Ferguson, Ann Ferguson; [m.]
Keith L. Benson, March 9, 1968; [ch.] Darrell Ivan,
Dennis Michael; [ed.] Artesia High, LBTD, AV
College; [occ.] Writer working on a children's book;
[memb.] Epilepsy Society, Bowling League, (AFTRA-
TV and Radio Assoc); [hon.] Two honors in 1992 for
the poem "Being a Woman"; [oth. writ.] "Being
Different" newspaper poems; [pers.] To bring aware-
ness to all, about epilepsy. Hoping to produce the
beauty of everyday life. In all I do - not just my
writings. Knowledge lifes greatest gift; [a.] Lancaster,
CA

BERENS, EVA NATALIE SHURE
[b.] April 14, 1979, Hollywood, FL; [p.] Elaine &
Sheldon Berens; [ed.] The Hewitt School, NYC, 9th
grade; [memb.] Community Service Committee,
Drama Club (Both School organizations); [hon.]
Award of first place in Mathematics League for year
of 1993, Delegate to Packer Model Congress 1993,
Winner of Janet Mayer award for all around achieve-

ments (In school 1993).; [oth. writ.] Several poems have been published in school's literary magazines.; [pers.] I believe emotions are the roots of poetic flowering. I am inspired by observations of people's conduct.; [a.] Greenwich, CT

BERG, DONNA
[Pen.] Donna DeLucca Berg; [b.] April 27, 1959, Blakely; [p.] Thomas & Johanna DeLucca; [m.] Paul Berg, September 23, 1989; [ch.] Amando Pearl; [ed.] Completed High School; [occ.] Homemaker, mother, wife; [hon.] National Honor Society, I was a Ballarina and danced in the theater most of my life, until I married and had a child.; [oth. writ.] Birthday, anniversary cards,; [pers.] Poem is dedicated to Marie, she was a loving friend. Hope your happy living with God.

BERG, HARRY V.
[b.] November 26, 1918, Detroit, MI; [p.] Harry and Anna Berg; [m.] Frances E. Bert, October 21, 1942; [ch.] Douglas M. Berg, Gordon M. Berg; [ed.] BA - Univ of Mich at Ann Arbor, MI, MA - Univ of New Mexico at Albuquerque, NY; [occ.] Part-time Planning and Communications Consultant; [memb.] International Transactional Analysis Assoc (ITAA); [hon.] Phi Delta Kappa - Honorary Educational Fraternity; [oth. writ.] Various journals including; Hospitals ASTD, Design, The Creative Art Mag plus an article (reprinted) in the book, Organizational Environment Relationships plus poems in various local newspapers; [pers.] My poems reflect my feelings about a variety of human relationships from serious to humorous - My poetry studies at the Univ of MI became an inspiration that's lasted over 40 year; [a.] Detroit, MI

BERGQUIST, KATHLEEN
[pen.]Kuria; Kaye; Kat; [b.] September 1, 1957, Mesa, AZ; [p.] Bertil R. and Pearl J. Bergquist; [ch.] Tanum K.; [ed.] Lamson Business College; [hon.] Honor Roll Kino Jr High, AAU swimming ribbons and metal, Salesgirl of the year '77 - Mecca Enterprises, Inc; [oth. writ.] Have collection of quite a variety of poetry that I have done over several years as a hobbie; [pers.] I write for and about various people in my life. I have been inspired by spending time with the Lord and song lyrics. Would like to compile my own book of the better ones I have done; [a.] Mesa, AZ

BERKHAHN, PAULA MARIE
[b.] June 11, 1978; [p.] Richard and Alice Berkhahn; [ed.] Central High School; [occ.] Child care; [pers.] I feel that there can be love and peace in the world if everyone just tried to get along with everyone else. I think there is good in every body and great relationships start with friendships that can help in the future; [a.] West Allis, WI

BERRY, CHARLENE
[b.] February 20, 1951, Titusville, PA; [p.] Michael Savitz, Marilyn Savitz; [ch.] Richard Bruce, Angela Rose; [ed.] Youngsville High School, Mercyhurst College; [occ.] Inspector - Associated Spring/Barnes Group - Corry, PA; [pers.] We can be greatly satisfied if only we know, that our lives have helped someone else to grow.

BERRY, GARY EDWARD
[Pen.] Garrison; [b.] December 29, 1959, Millville, NJ; [p.] David Franklin, Joan Virginia; [ch.] Matthew Edward Berry; [ed.] Staunton Military Academy, Staunton, Virginia 1974-1976; [occ.] (Writer-author); [memb.] Camden County Library Assoc/Berlin Scrabble Club Berlin, NJ; [hon.] Certificates of Highest Achievement in: American Military History and Marksmanship; [oth. writ.] Article published in 1982 Vanguard of Mission Teens Rehabilitation center Re: (Relationships). Current Book Pending Publication: The Poet.....Consisting of a compilation of poetry and stories; [pers.] Periodically emerges with

pen in hand. Incisively clear so that you understand Gods gift of rhyme in a time span. Expressed from the heart to unfold his plan. Words offered as food for thought. The melody in which is often sought; [a.] Berlin, NJ

BERTHOLDE, BONNIE J.
[b.] July 21, 1961, Fall River, MA.; [p.] Mr. and Mrs. Jesse Bertholde; [ed.] Graduated Bible College in Baltimore, MD; [a.] Fall River, MA

BERTRAND, MASLYN
[b.] March 30, 1952, Dominica; [p.] LLoyd and Veronica Bertrand; [ch.] Daniel James; [ed.] Elementary and High School. I am taking a course at the Institute of Children Literature. I have obtained a second High School since I have been in this country. [occ.] None. I have not been able to work due to polio; [hon.] High School, First Aid with the Fire and Ambulance Services; [oth. writ.] Some other poems, short stories, a manuscript. After the storm. I have written to publishers about my work, but they do not want to know. The only ones who do, are the publishers who will publish for a fee; [a.] I was born in the Commonwealth of Dominica. When I was a child I had polio, this did not deter me from doing all the things that children do. I went to school became a teacher, but I always wanted to write about the things and people around me; [a.] Jacksonville, FL

BERTUZZI, RICHARD MARK
[Pen.] Mark Bertuzzi, [b.] July 16, 1957, Ft. Worth, TX; [p.] Richard and Thelma Bertuzzi; [m.] Teri Bertuzzi, July 11, 1981; [ch.] Natalie Nicole, Marci, Michelle, Richard Cameron, Trevor Garrett; [ed.] Memorial High School, Stephen F. Austin State Univ, Rhema Bible School; [occ.] Salesman, Mid-American Research Chemical Corp; [memb.] SFASU Alumni Assoc, Rhema Alumni Assoc, Prison Outreach International; [pers.] I concentrate on putting experiences of life from the visual to pen and ink; [a.] Houston, TX

BEST, DEBORAH
[b.] January 25, 1958, Grenada, WI; [p.] Agatha Taylor; [m.] Anthony R. Best, March 6, 1980; [ch.] Chad Peter, Shawn Anthony, and Elon Ronald; [ed.] Grenada SDA Comprehensive School, Mac Donald's College; [occ.] Bank Worker, Chemical Bank, New York; [memb.] The Smithsonian Institute; [hon.] Achievement Award from Little People Nursery School, Brooklyn, NY for Outstanding dedication (1992); First price received for entry in essay competition in Grenada (1977); [oth. writ.] Enrolled in Institution of Children's Literature and also in Long Ridge Writers Group to write stories for children, ages 6-12 yrs and fiction for adults; [pers.] My inspiration comes from my wonderful life with my husband and our three sons. The adventure has just begun and I thank God for this talent; [a.] Brooklyn, NY

BEVERLY, DAVID
[b.] August 31, 1955, Akron, OH; [p.] A.M. and P.M. Beverly; [ed.] Akron University, currently Western International University; [occ.] Training Specialist with AT&T; [memb.] Unity, Lebanon, NJ, National Society Performance Instruction, American Society Training Development Founder, President of Make a Conscious Choice; [hon.] Civic Awards for work with Telephone Pioneers of America; [oth. writ.] Local publishing and creative creating cards; [pers.] My work is very personal, I always aim to challenge my mind and thought. I hope every reader walks away with a new view.; [a.] Morristown, NJ

BEYNON, DEBRA ANN
[b.] August 20, 1957, Scranton, PA; [p.] Skip & Liz Beynon; [m.] Jerry Mitchell, Fiancee; [ch.] Andrew and Timothy Slagan fromn first marriage; [ed.] A.A. Degree in Accounting from Palo Verde College Blythe, CA; [occ.] Personnel clerk, Palo Verde

Community college; [memb.] California School, Employees Association (C.S.E.A.) Presioent 199 [hon.] Accounting and Word Processing from Pa Verde College. Outstanding Volunteer Service, Computer classes at Chuckawalla Valley State Prison [hon.] Advisory Committee, Presidents & Deans L 1989 through 1990; [oth. writ.] Poems and writings English class.; [pers.] My writing relfect past experiences good and bad that are a great influence in th future. The future is our greatest asset.; [a.] Blyth CA

BHANJA, HIMANGSHU
[Pen.] Baitalik; [b.] September 18, 1937, India; [p Lt. K.P. & Mrs. Binapani Bhanja; [m.] Monjusr Bhanja, July 8, 1953; [ch.] Utpal K. Bhanja, M [ed.] BSME (First Class) Training in India & U First in Rolls Royce Oil Engine School (UK) in 195 [occ.] Test Development Specialist 2 (Engineering New Jersey State Dept. of Personnel; [memb.] Mer ber of the American Society of Mechanical Engineer Fellow & Chartered Engineer of the Institution Engineers (India) (ABB: I.E.(I), Member of AAI (USA).; [hon.] In Durgapur, India I was coun member of IE(I), Chairman of the Local Center IE(Chairman of the Local Center IE (I), Founder, Ge eral Secretary of The Sports Association, Found President of Referee's Assocation, President of t Lions' Club, 100% Presidents' Award from Lio International; [oth. writ.] Several, articles, key-nc address, papers and poetry in papers, souvenirs a bulletins on soci/religious/philosophical and en neering topics; [pers.] Believe in the Tenets of Adua Vedantic Philosophy, innate spiritualism of eve human being, merging with the creator is the summ Bonum of all lives. Fond of analytical and compar tive study and writing on "Ancient Wisdom a modern science, history economics and philosoph [a.] NJ, NJ

BIBB, DEBBIE ANN
[Pen.] "Deb"; [b.] July 4, 1951, Jefferson Cnty, K [p.] Ethel C. and James E. Bibb; [m.] divorced, Ap 11, 1970; [ch.] Shannon Lynn - 23, Kristen - 1 Megan - 9; [ed.] Shawnee High School - graduated 69, Working on a BA at Bellarmine College, Lou ville, KY; [occ.] Administrative Asst; [memb.] Ho pitality Committee at Our Lady of Consolation Chur - 1981, Hospitality Committee at St Cecilia's 198 89, Choir Member 1987-1991; [hon.] My poem "I Wings Upon Your Back" gained recognition in 19 in the Catholice Renew Newsletter in Loui, KY. Als my poem "What Did I Do To Deserve This" wa published in the ECHO newsletter. Outstanding Awa from "ECHO" (Exploited Children Help Organiz tion); [oth. writ.] "What Did I Do To Deserve Thi was nationally televised. Poem was read on the air the founder of ECHO, Lucy Callahan; [pers.] I' always believed that I had a tlent for writing but it to my Mother's death and support from terrific friends encourage me to pursue my dream. Loving frien and the love of my mother gave me the courage follow my dream. I hope to someday be as good Helen Steiner Rice. I admire her work; [a.] Louisvill KY

BIBLE, BETTY J.
[Pen.] Bee Bee; [b.] Feb 16, 1954, Gettysburg, P. [p.] Worth H. Bible, Gayetta Bible; [ed.] New Oxfo High School; [occ.] Factory Worker at Hanov Direct, Hanover, PA; [oth. writ.] A poem about catalog "The Safety Zone", published in the Hanov Direct Newsletter. Poems published in the newslet for St. John's United Church of Christ; [pers.] I wr of things and people I meet along life's road remember them by. Like a painter's portrait; [a.] Ne Oxford, PA

GGS, SCOTT
.] March 5, 1976, DE; [p.] Cathy Zimmerman;
d.] I am a senior at Caravel Academy; [hon.] I have
ver sent any of my works to magazines, or for
blication.; [oth. writ.] I have many writings that I
ep personal.; [pers.] I started serious poetry when
was a freshman in high school. I sue the death of
ree family members, two divorces between my
rents, and personal experiences in my poems.; [a.]
ayton, DE

GGS, TARA
.] July 24, 1980, Austin, TX; [p.] Ronnie & vicki
ggs; [ed.] K-8th Lake Travis ISD; [occ.] 8th grade
ident Lake Travis Middle School; [hon.] Academic
chievement, Certificat of Achievement, A/B Honor
oll; [a.] Austin, TX

NDER, NANCY ROSALEE
] June 13, 1934, Wichita, KS; [p.] Ethel Posey
iderson, Wayne Anderson; [m.] separated; [ch.]
nes W. Burbank, Deborah Burbank, Mike Wilson,
rsta Binder; [ed.] Grad Redondo Beach, CA
ghtschool) El Camino College, Torrance, CA.
esently UAA-Creative Writing 260B; [occ.] Re-
ed LVN/LPN and Church Deaconess. Was in
ildren's theatres "Land of Enchantment". Last play
vas in "Fiddler on the Roof" 1987; [oth. writ.] I am
1 unpublished music writer, and poet until now;
ers.] Wish to thank you for publishing my poem,
iking it possible for older people like myself to have
other opportunity at life; [a.] Chugiak, AK

RD, NICOLA
] January 13, 1966, Antigua, West Indies; [p.] Ena
d Keith Gonsalues; [ch.] Jasim Bird; [ed.] College;
cc.] Jewellery designer, dream counsellor; [oth.
it.] Articles on dreams; [pers.] Poetry captures the
pth of our inner world and transalates it into a
iguage, a rythm. It is through this beat that we touch
e voice of our soul; [a.] Toronto, Ontario

RKHOLZ, ANNA
] April 19, 1978, Milwaukee, WI; [p.] Steven,
ary Birkholz; [brother] William; [ed.] High school
phomore; [occ.] student; [memb.] SRO, Freshman
ass Officer, Sophomore Class Officer. Founder of
he Service Club"; [hon.] '94 Essay Winner, Sac-
nento Optimist Club; [oth. writ.] "The Bounderies
Freedom"; [pers.] I believe strongly in the need for
cial justice. My writings and work in soup kitchens
lect this belief; [a.] Sacramento, CA

ZZELL, JINGER
] October 26, 1964, Queens, NY; [p.] Peni Shellman
iother; [occ.] Actress, Screenwriter; [memb.] Black
mmaker Foundation; [oth. writ.] Poetry: The Book;
rs.] Put God, family and friends first; [a.] Atlanta,
A

ACK, H. BLANDENAH
] March 29, 1933, Chicago, IL; [p.] Mr. and Mrs.
ward Hayes; [m.] James R. Black, Jr, December
, 1954; [ch.] James III, Rev Brigitte, Geoffrey and
egory; [ed.] BS Wilberforce U, Wilberforce, O; BS
ntral State U, IIUN); MS Indiana Univ NW;
uSable High, Chicago, IL); [occ.] Retired Educa-
. (Daniel Hale Williams Elementary School);
emb.] (past) Schools Reading Council, Social Stud-
; Council, NIABSE, First AME Church,
ilberforce, Alumni, Alpha Kappa Alpha Sorority;
in.] 32 yrs in Ed, 29 yrs Gary Community School
irp Nominee Heroes in Education (Readers Digest);
i-founder, author and chairperson of PRIDE pro-
im in Gary, IN (13 yrs); IU Dons, State of Indiana,
it, [oth. writ.] Several poems published in local
wspapers. She Dreamed the Dream, Dr. Daniel
e Williams, Dr. Carter G. Woodson, Winnie
indela, Nelson Mandela, Dr. Charles Leander Hill,
iry to Me, America to Me, Marvin Gaye; [pers.]

Children are our greatest resource. All children can
learn. (plaque inscription) "Your love for children
will live forever". I envy Maya Angelou, Toni
Morrison and J. California Cooper; [a.] Gary, IN

BLAESER, COREY
[b.] July 2, 1965, Eau Claire, WI; [p.] Mr. and Mrs.
Dennis and Joann Blaeser; [ed.] North High School;
[oth. writ.] Poetry and essays none published.; [pers.]
As the impetus for my beginning to write two yers ago
was the most devasting experience of my life. My
opinion that darkness should begreeted and explored
not avoided has been bolstered by the publication of
this, my first submission. Being emotionally healty
does not equal constant happiness.; a Eau Clarie, WI

BLAIR, JOSEPHINE COSMA
[b.] January 26, 1942, Puunene, Maui, HI; [p.]
Manuel and Beatrice Cosma; [m.] David D. Blair,
August 6, 1988; [ch.] Michael Kahala, James Buddy
Haleokalena, and Ilima Marcel, Greig; [ed.] Hana
Elem., Lahainaluna High, Maunaolu Jr. College,
BYU Hawaii; [occ.] Remedial Reading Teacher,
Princess Nahi'enaiena Elementary; [memb.] NEA,
HSTA, Holy Innocents Episcopal Church; [oth. writ.]
Newspaper article published in the Hana Newspaper
entitled "Pekelo Does Hana Proud."; [pers.] "Tita's
Lament" is dedicated to my sister Maddie and all the
proponents of the Hana Golf Course. Whatever the
outcome, may the people be granted future employ-
ment and stability; [a.] Lahaina, Maui, HI

BLAKE, NORMA M.
[Pen.] Sara Bellum, Mons Ols; [b.] October 30, 1949,
Philadelphia, PA; [p.] Norman Walter and Grace
Tilton; [m.] Carol Feldman Blake, October 30, 1983;
[ch.] Poul Olof Stein, Sandra Caryn Koppelman; [ed.]
Rio Salado, Phoenix and Lundelska Laroverket,
Uppsala, Sweden; [occ.] Columnist for the Neural
Network, Phoenix; [memb.] Vasa Order of America;
[hon.] Certified Rattle Snake Eater, April 93; [oth.
writ.] "The Shining Path of the Heart" Revised
Revisionist History "Stargard"; [pers.] Lighten up;
[a.] Phoenix, AZ

BLANKS, SURNELLA
[b.] February 9, 1945, Weymouth, NJ; [p.] Charles
and Rosie Sea; [ch.] Heather, Andrea, Robin and
Rebecca; [pers.] Love of our creator, Jehovah God,
love of family, neighbor, and life, are all things that
i feel priviliged to share with the world; [a.] Philadel-
phia, PA

BLEDSOLE, ROBIN
[Pen.] Robin Bledsole; [b.] January 24, 1980; [p.]
Marty and Pamela Bledsole; [ed.] 8th grade, Armstrong
Jr High, Eastover, NC; [a.] Wade, NC

BLOCHINGER, JODI
[b.] September 10, 1960, St Paul; [p.] Rita and Denny
Bauman; [m.] Mark Blochinger, June 20, 1981; [ch.]
Katie Jean; [ed.] Simley High School. Inver Hills, and
continued classes at St. Thomas previously; [occ.]
Medical Secretary; [hon.] Dean's list; [oth. writ.] I
have always loved writing, but have never submitted
anything previously; [pers.] I believe in the good of all
people and that nothing is as important as love and
family; [a.] Inver Grove Heights, MN

BLOUIN, JOANNE
[b.] January 26, 1978, Winnipeg; [p.] Julie and Roger
Blouin; [ed.] Grade 10; [occ.] Waitress; [hon.] Spe-
cial Academic Mention in grade 9 - June '93, Certifi-
cate of Excellence Softball - June '93, Bronze and
Silver Medals in Manitoba Ringette Provincials; [oth.
writ.] Poems that have not yet been published; [pers.]
I would like to dedicate this poem to Brigitte Ayotte;
[a.] St Jean, Manitoba

BLOUNT, JULIE OAS
[b.] February 13, 1964, Wayland, NY; [p.] Donald &
Alma Oas; [m.] David Blount, April 16, 1988; [ch.]
Nathan Samuel; [ed.] Wayland Central School and
Charles G. May Center; [occ.] Administrative Assis-
tant, Catholic Social Services; [pers.] My family is my
inspiration in all my poetry; [a.] Sarasota, FL

BOBRUK, AIMEE
[b.] April 11, 1981, Huntsville, TX; [p.] Toni and
Walter Bobruk; [ed.] (MPJH) Mance Park Jr High
School - 7th grade; [occ.] Student; [memb.] Hunts-
ville Youth Orchestra, Huntsville Children's Choir,
Huntsville Girls Softball Assoc; World Tang Soo Do
Assoc; [hon.] Tang Soo Do Karate, 1st Degree Black
Belt, 1st place Won Talent Show at school playing
violin. All A's honor roll 7 yrs; [oth. writ.] Several
other poems; none published, yet; [pers.] I love sports
and music, but I write mostly about God, love, and the
earth. I hope to become an environmentalist and help
save the earth; [a.] Huntsville, TX

BOER, JUDITH ANNE
[Pen.] Dewi; [b.] August 1, 1952, Chicago; [p.]
Charles and Rita Zullo; [m.] Dennis Williams, Sr,
August 16, 1972; [ch.] Dawn, Michelle, Dennis Jr,
Nicole, Rebecca; [ed.] Antioch Comm High School,
Inst of Children's Literature; [occ.] Office Manager;
[memb.] National Trust of Historic Preservation;
[oth. writ.] Poems - Believe Me, My Love, War;
[pers.] My poem comes from my heart directly to
paper. I try to reflect my feelings about everyday
situations we all experience. I write about the people
in my life, who mean so much to me; [a.] Ashton, IL

BONANDER. ANDREW J.
[b.] June 5, 1984, Turlock, CA; [p.] Richard and Lori
Bonander; [ed.] Attends 4th grade at Central Valley
Christian School, Atwater, CA; [occ.] Student; [pers.]
If you don't try you won't succeed; [a.] Ballico, CA

BONANSINGA, JANE
[b.] October 1965, Cincinnati, OH; [p.] Wm and
Mary Bonansinga; [ed.] Walnut Hills High, Cincin-
nati, OH; [memb.] National Wildlife Federation, Co-
op America, Amnesty International, Freedom Writ-
ers, Columbus Community Kitchen, Inc; [pers.] Lack-
ing a formal education, I enjoy learning through
reading and my love for people, animals, and nature.
Primarily I draw and write as an avenue of communi-
cating to myself. Largely my work reflects my expe-
riences and struggles with mental illness and the
difficult path to healing. I'm grateful for the fortune of
expression; [a.] Columbus, OH

BOND, ANDREA
[Pen.] Morgan; [b.] September 7, 1978, Winter
Haven, FL; [p.] Sandrea Rauscher & Peter Bond;
[ed.] Chicago, Illinois American High Schooling;
[hon.] Scholastic Achievement of Excellence Awards;
[oth. writ.] Two other poems, and several creative
stories published in junior and senior high.; [pers.]
"Everybody's day starts as somebody's dream" my
feeling and emotions inspire my poetry; [a.] Daven-
port, FL

BOND, HOLLY ANN ABBATOY
[Pen.] Malayna Madison; [b.] December 10, 1975,
Buffalo; [p.] Peter Abbatoy, Carmela Abbatoy; [m.]
Scott Bond, December 18, 1993; [ch.] Areil Ann,
Scott Richard, Erin Pete; [pers.] I have been writing
ever since I was five years old. Poems, short stories
and songs; [a.] Buffalo, NY

BONILLA, MANUEL I.
[b.] October 16, 1976, Puerto Rico; [p.] Manuel
Bonilla, Clara Garcia; [ed.] High school graduate in
Oct of 1993. I'll attend Hamshire College (Mass) in
Feb '94; [hon.] Two consecutive years Who's Who
Award; [oth. writ.] Plenty unpublished poetry and

songs. Currently writing a book in spanish; [pers.] Feel the motion of silence, hear the inner-space sound. My dream is to help people toward a better self-acceptance and to state in a special way the unknown nature and feelings perception often misunderstood; [a.] Trujillo Alto, PR

BONITATIS, NICOLE DANNETTE
[Pen.] Den or Denny; [b.] September 7, 1982, Cherryhill, NJ; [p.] Joseph and Jeanette Bonitatis; [ed.] Clara Barton Elementary; [memb.] DeMarco Dance Studio, Queen of Heaven Catholic Church Camden County; [hon.] Scribbler A& B Honor Roll; [oth. writ.] Other poems published in Scribbler at school; [pers.] My writing comes out of my feelings.; [a.] Cherry Hill, NJ

BOOHER, LORI
[b.] October 18, 1977, Ennis Hospital; [p.] Martha and George; [ed.] 10th grade presently; [occ.] student; [memb.] none; [hon.] Softball Awards and Twirling; [oth. writ.] none; [pers.] My philosophy is to try to make the best of your life and not to ever let other people stop you from being who you want to be; [a.] Ennis, TX

BORCHARDT, Ph.D LOVIE LEE MC BRAYER
[b.] March 4, Harolson County, GA; [p.] William Arthur McBrayer, Sr., Dona Vaughan McBrayer; [m.] Raphael David Borchardt, June 9, 1946; [ch.] Donna Borchardt Cox, Millie Borchardt Matthews; [ed.] M. Ed. Univ. of GA (1961), Athens, GA; Ed. S. Univ of GA (1970), PhD (1980), University of SC, BA Shorter College, Rome, GA (1955); [occ.] Professor; [memb.] Alpha Delta Kappa (Past Pres.), Kappa Delta Phi, AAVP (American Assn. Univ. Professors) Rome Pilots International AAUW/American Assn. of University Women; [hon.] Rosenwald Scholar, Deans List Student, Mrs. Georgia Finalist, Georgia State Poetry Society, National Council Teachers of English; "Who's Who in American Education" 89-90, "Who's Who in the South and Wouthwest" 80-81, "The World Who's Who of Women" Fourth Edition, "Community Leaders and Noteworth Americans" 1978, "Biographical Role of Honor" Second Edition, "Personalities of the South" [oth. writ.] Kappan Publications: "Standing Tall" Who Cares Meeting a Challenge "Improving College and University Teaching, "The Successful Student", International Reading Assn. "Reflections", "It is in giving that we Receive" Christian Singles Magazine", [pers.] My inner most feelings find expression through my poetry, and I hope through it to communicate ot others a spirit of encouragement and faith in the goodness of God; [a.] Rome, GA

BORGGAARD, CLARENCE S.
[Pen.] Born on Farm; [b.] November 29, 1899, Worcester; [ed.] 8 yrs grammar school, Marine Corp WWI, Wig Nt School - Law School, passed Mass. Bar; [occ.] Lawyer - Business Man - Jack-of-all-trades, retired (94 years old); [a.] Mass.

BORTHWICK, DAVID JAMES
[b.] December 21, 1963, Ediwburgh; [p.] Eleanor and Shearer; [ed.] South Morningside primary school - Boroughmuir secondary school; [occ.] Graphic Artist/Jazz Musician (guitar-semi pro); [memb.] Musicians Union - Scotland. Blood Transfusion Service - Blood Donor; [oth. writ.] "A Flight of Doves" - short stories. Plus several other short stories and poems; [pers.] It is a great honor to be selected for the semi-finals of this competition. I try to express my inner most feelings in my writing (sometimes it works!); [a.] Edinburgh

BOTHE, DANETT
[b.] March 1, 1979, Canoe, BC; [p.] Judy Bothe and Ken Bothe; [ed.] Shuswap Jr. High School; [occ.] Student grade nine; [hon.] Merit List; [pers.] I was

inspired by S.E. Hinton to right stories and after enjoying poetry I decided to try writing some.; [a.] Canoe, B.C.

BOULEY, COLLEEN
[b.] December 14, 1976, Monticello, MN; [p.] Richard and Kathleen Bouley; [ed.] So far am completing a high school education. I am presently in 11th grade. Taking a homeschooling course for writing through the Inst of Children's Literature; [occ.] Part-time secretarial work at Pennsylvania Financial Group; [memb.] Member of the National Honors Society for three yrs; [hon.] Received an award for being the most talented writer, in tenth grade. Completed five yrs of honors, English course. Was a member of National Honors Society for three yrs; [oth. writ.] Wrote articles for local newspapers concerning surrounding county 4-H Clubs; [pers.] Have written many poems through a combined effort with a classmate, Melissa Foster, who gives me most of my writing ideas; [a.] Tyrone, PA

BOULEY, JR. DAVID F.
[Pen.] (too many to list); [b.] July 18, 1969, Quincy, MA; [p.] Sandy Bouley & David Bouley; [ed.] Quincy High School UMASS Boston (Life); [occ.] Liquor Store Advertising Coordinator, Human Being; [memb.] Quincy Tennis Club, Humanity; [hon.] Scholar athlete at UMASS Boston, Repeat doubles champion, City of Quincy Annual tennis tournament.; [oth. writ.] Daily journal poetry, short stories, record reviews fiction.; [pers.] I would hope that, if anything, my writing reflects myself. I have been influened by everything from Whitman, Kerouac and Leslie Marmon Silko and Chuck D. and Henry Rollins; [a.] Braintree, MA

BOUWKNECHT, LUMMNY
[Pen.] Lummy; [b.] July 31, 1931, The Netherlands; [p.] Gerrit and Baukje Apperloo (Deceased); [m.] First husband, Mel Bouwknecht (Deceased 1953-80), Second husband, David Inskip, December 19, 1987; [ch.] Daughter Maryke Verhagen, Sons: John Richard, Ronald Andy Bouwknecht, Adopted Sons: Marvin Joe, Gerald Marten; [ed.] The Netherlands; [occ.] Retired; [oth. writ.] For my own pleasure; [pers.] Live one day at a time, Love each other and never give up your dreams.; [a.] Abbotsford, B.C., Canada

BOWE, THELMA SUZANNE
[Pen.] Thelma Bowe; [b.] May 15, 1968, Roseburg, OR; [p.] Frederick & Thelma Matlaff; [m.] Charles P. Bowe, April 17, 1992; [ch.] Samantha J. Seward (from a previous marriage); [ed.] Grundy RV High School Chillicothe Area Vocational Techical School; [occ.] CMT, housewife; [hon.] Who's Who Among High School Students, Best greeter at High School open house.; [oth. writ.] Other poems not published.; [pers.] I try to make everyone in my family happy, however I am able to do this! Inspired about poems by Grandmother Marie; [a.] Chula, MO

BOWEN, MARK A.
[b.] August 15, 1969, Saranac Lake, NY; [p.] Arthur Bowen, Sally Weaver; [m.] Halle Berry (No, just kidding!); [ed.] 1 1/2 yrs. college (Forestry); [occ.] U.S. Army; [memb.] MARS, Musicians Against Racism and Sexism, National Wildlife Federation, NRA, Americare; [hon.] U.S. Army Parachutist Badge, Soldier of the Month, Austrian Commando School; [oth. writ.] Many, but no official publishings; [pers.] I try and let nothing but truth flow from my pen. If my poetry brings tears to one's eyes, than I know I'm in business. Greatest influence, Maya Angelou; [a.] Lake Placid, NY

BOWMAN, PAUL
[b.] November 23, 1956; [pers.] Time is an existance, age is a memory, and life is but a thought, so stare back at the flower, as life catches up. Make you a memory,

and hey, it was just a thought.

BOWSER, JR. CHARLES
[Pen.] Arubacar; [b.] Philadelphia; [p.] Charles ar Amelia Bowser; [ch.] Son, Justin L. Bowser; [ed Advance Acting Student at Freedom Theater, Phila received Teacher's Certificate and Diploma for Chri tian Education at Manna Bible Institute, Phila., Ass ciate Degree in Business, Phila.; [occ.] Actor, Write Novelist, Independent Director; [oth. writ.] Cu rently writing a novel and it will be in the bookstor very soon.; [pers.] Charles has been in movies ar acted in theater. He's looking forward to directir and producing his own screen play, in the nea future.; [a.] Philadelphia, PA

BOYD, DAVID P.
[b.] March 24, 1906, Chicago, IL; [p.] James I Boyd and Adele Elizabeth Boyd (nee Adele Elizabe Wandas); [ed.] Bachelor of Science in Journalism The medill School of Journalism, Northwestern Un versity, 1932; [occ.] Former editor of CRDA New the Chicago Retail Druggists' Association, Chicag 1939 to 1943, Army Air Corps, February 1943 I September 1945, reporter for the La Grange (Illinoi Citizen, 1947 to 1952, worked for Illinois Bureau Employment Security from 1965 to 1974, The Illino State Employment Service, reporter for the Blu Island (Illinois) Sun Standard, 1929 to 1930, report for the Chicago City News Bureau, 1930 to 193 [memb.] Church of the Atonement (Episcopal) Ch cago, member of International Society for Gener: Semantics, member of Sigma Delta Chi Professior Journalist Fraternity since 1929; [oth. writ.] Auth of "How to Discover Your Better Self", Vantag Press, 1959, author of "Stories Behind the News short stories, Vantage Press, 1965, author of "Thorea the Rebel Idealist", Americana Magazine, 1937; [a Chicago, IL

BOYD, DWIGHT PHILIP
[Pen.] Phil Boyd; [b.] October 12, 1939, Cin., OI [p.] Dwight & Geneva Boyd; [m.] Lucy Bethel Boyc July 4, 1959; [ch.] Derrick, Randy, Leta Boyd; [ed 12 years graduated from Sycamore High School, 1 Class Chemical Operator; [hon.] I played in a band i a Vic Club in High School; [oth. writ.] Local publ cations I write songs as well as poetly, I am no writing a book; [pers.] I feel that the Lord has inspire me to write and help others in my writing.; [a Loveland, OH

BOYNTON, JACINTA
[Pen.] Jazzy; [b.] March 31, 1971, Indpls, IN; [p Sandra J. Boynton, Joel R. Boynton; [ed.] Noblesvill HS, currently in CLE (Christian Light Education [oth. writ.] Poems published in NHS literary maga zine; [pers.] I strive to make my poems different from other poets by making them relate to feelings an thoughts people fail to express. My goal as I get olde is to show others to accept people for who they are Not to judge them by color, social status, etc. In othe words, amalgamated; [a.] Indianapolis, IN

BOZZANO, MICHAEL
[b.] June 17, 1971, Winston-Salem; [p.] Toni ar Carlo Bozzano; [ed.] Obtained an Associate in Ar degree from Brevard College, then obtained a bach elors in arts from UnCG. My major was english wii a minor in history; [occ.] Legal review specialist fc First Union Mortgage in Wilmington; [hon.] Honc student at Brevard College and at the North Carolin School of the Arts where I studied Italian; [oth. writ Wrote article for Wilmington Star News and poer "The Caller" was published in Treasured Poets c America; [pers.] My heart and feelings guide my pe and I hope the words I create can help entertain thos who choose to read my poetry; [a.] Wilmington, N(

RACE, CORINNE A.
.] August 18, 1920, Wheatland, WY; [p.] Hazel and oward Drew; [m.] Bob Brace, July 10, 1943; [ch.] 1omas Robert Brace and Valerie Lee Brace; [ed.] A. U. of Denver, 1 yr. Social Work, Univ. of enver; [occ.] Retired; [memb.] Shelton United 1ethodist Church, P.E.O. Chapter B. Wash.; [hon.] ollege Scholarship from High School, Dean's List, of Denver, Nat. Drama Society; [oth. writ.] Short ories life history poems; [pers.] My aim in life is to kind to all my fellow man. Most important is my ith, my family, and my friends in that order.; [a.] rapeview, WA

RAGINSKY, CRAIG
en.] John "Jack" Redmond; [b.] May 14, 1967, ew Haven, CT; [p.] Marilyn & Benjamin Braqiusky; 1.] Crisanta Quinoues Braginsky, [m.]ay 5, 1993; h.] none; [ed.] self-educated; [occ.] Composer, /ricist; [memb.] American Society of Composers d Publishers a.k.a. (A.S.C.A.P); [hon.] 1989 New ork Festival of the Arts, "Best New Composer," my ife's acceptance; [oth. writ.] Numerous songs, undtracks, for film and television; [pers.] 1akespeare, God of my art, and I beneath, ever 2mbling; [a.] New Haven, CT

RAIDA, DOLLY
en.] Dolly; [b.] April 17, 1937, San Francisco; [p.] 2 and Louise Dougherty; [m.] Arthur Braida, Au- 1st 25, 1962; [ch.] Two sons, Joe and Eric, three 1ndchildren: Jessica, Zachary & Jeremy; [ed.] Went rough High School at a Catholic High School, 2sentation High School; [occ.] Homemaker and 2pefully a Poet; [memb.] Was a member of The 1iphany Guild and Their Parish Counsel. For one ar I was president of The Guild. I am a member of 2ir church.; [hon.] None so far, I'm just starting cept for your Merit Award Plaque.; [oth. writ.] I've ritten a collection of poems and a poem w/music to turned into a children's book. Hope to get both 1blished this year.; [pers.] I'm a wife, mother and 1andmother who started writing poetry in May of 92. y grandchildren were my inspiration on the first 2em. If God gave me this talent, I want to try and us to help stop the hate and violence by talking to 1dents while their minds are still young.; [a.] San ancisco, CA

RAIDIS, SUSAN
.] August 13, 1970, Seoul, Korea; [p.] Mary Ellen d Raymond Braidas; [m.] Richard I. Wolfson, 2cember 17, 1994; [ch.] Kira and Alia Wolfson; 1.] Haddon Township High School County College Morris; [occ.] Model; [hon.] Editor's Choice ward; [oth. writ.] "Life" published in the Days of 1tures Past; [pers.] I would like to dedicate my ritings to my family, The Wolfsons. Kira and Alia: 2u are the two most beautiful little girls I know. I ve you. Rich, thank you for everything. You are my spriration; [a.] Marlton, NJ

RAMBLETT, ALMA McDOWELL
en.] Alma McDowell Bramblett; [b.] November ', 1944, Henry Co, KY; [p.] William C. McDowell, 2lia Lee Peyton; [m.] Elmer Lee Bramblett, June 8, '67; [ch.] Jody Lee, Jennifer Elizabeth, William son and Michael Joseph Bramblett; [ed.] Graduated 2m Decatur Central High School - Indiana, 3 yrs 1dway College - Midway, KY; [occ.] Homemaker; 1emb.] Orville, Baptist Church, Pleasureville, KY; 2n.] My greatest honor is knowing Jesus Christ as y Savior and Lord; [oth. writ.] Poems and short 2ries, including "Free at Last", written for Persian 1lf Veterans. "Destiny", and "Tribute to Mother", r our family; [pers.] Poetry is God's gift to me...to ve to others; [a.] Pleasureville, KY

BRAMMER, HAZEL COX
[b.] March 14, 1924, Elliott Co; [p.] James E. and Mary Conncox; [m.] James H. Brammer, Jr, January 7, 1991; [ch.] 1 son - former marriage, 2-step daughters - present; [ed.] Masters Degree, Rank I, Morehead St Univ; [occ.] Retired Teacher; [memb.] Rowan Co Retired Teachers Assoc, KY Retired Teachers Assoc, Church of God; [hon.] RC EA Twenty Seven Years of Teaching - Farmers Elementary - Rowan County. I taught 27 yrs same school, same room, same grade; [pers.] I have written poetry since childhood, but never tried to have anything published. I have been inspired by family experiences and a love for expressing appreciation to others. My poetry is spur of the moment material; [a.] Morehead, KY

BRANCATO, VERONICA
[b.] June 27, 1979, Philadelphia, PA; [p.] Peter Brancato, Veronica Cahil-Brancato; [ed.] Holy Spitit High School; [hon.] $100 savings bond for pro-life contest. Spirit award for school; [oth. writ.] Dad, God's Help, A Christmas Nightmare, Good Night and God Bless You, Pop, Pop, Thanksgiving Poem, The Big Game, to name only a few; [pers.] I don't take what you have for granted because you never really know what you have until you lose it; [a.] Veronica Brancato

BRAND, MEGAN
[b.] July 3, 1982, Moorhead, MN; [p.] Brenda and David Brand; [ed.] Atkinson Elementary Barnesville, MN; [memb.] Barnesville Lutheran Brethren Church; [pers.] I like to write, and have written several poems and stories. My favorite author is Laura Ingells Wilder; [a.] Barnesville, MN

BRANT, MARY
[occ.] U.S.F., Tampa, FL, full-time Graduate Student - Counselor Education; [memb.] N.A.F.E., Murho Sigma, A.C.A., F.M.H.C.A., S.M.H.C.A., Florida Adlerian Society; [hon.] Nat'l. Dean's List; Phi Theta Kappa Honor Fraternity, Phi Chi Chapter; N.A.F.E. Appreciation Plaque Award 89; Outstanding Young American 88'; [oth. writ.] My particular poem was inspired by a sculpture that a special friend of mine thought should be captioned "Homage to Sh_t." This same friend has helped me so immensely. I am no longer that self-righteous "Goody-two-shoes," "Little miss Perfect" but, I hope, with the help of God, an authentic human being!; [a.] Tampa, FL

BRANTLEY, ANTHONY
[b.] August 4, 1964, Shelby, NC; [occ.] Construction; [oth. writ.] Several poems published in local newspaper; [pers.] Poetry can reflect a timeless beauty in its thought, form, and intent. I greatly admire the works of William Wordsworth; [a.] Lattimore, NC

BRAUN, MAJORIE
[Pen.] Marjorie Braun; [b.] December 21, 1968, Baltimore; [p.] John Braun Jr and Anita Braddet Braun; [ed.] GED, AA degree in Elm Ed from HCC 1990, Mother graduated RN program same year at HCC. Briefly attended U of M and Towson State; [occ.] Day Care Teacher; [memb.] NAACP, AAA. Was once a member of a non-profit weight loss group; [hon.] Once won 1st prize in county wide writting competition in high school. In 9th grade at the time; [oth. writ.] None have ever been submitted for publishing, but this recognition from the NLP has given me the courage to reveal more of my private thoughts in the future; [pers.] The poem I wrote for this contest was in memory of my uncle who left his body behind to join the moon and stars. I believe that my grandmother must have felt the way I wrote; [a.] Bel Air, MD

BRAZELL, DR. ROBERT E.
[b.] May 17, 1923, Port Huron, MI; [m.] Gene Brazell, November 25, 1950; [ch.] Kevin Brazell, Colleen Pierson, Kathleen Weissert; [ed.] Cornell Un. Midshipman's School, B.S. Mich. State Univ., M.A. Univ. of Michigan, PH.D. Univ. of Michigan; [occ.] Retired Teacher, Coach, Principal, Travel Lecturer, visited 50 states, 74 countries; [hon.] 1989 U. of Mich. Distinguished Alumnus, Mich. Ass'n Secondary School, Outstanding Leadership Award; [oth. writ.] Dinosaurs Had No Floors, Does An Owl Growl?, Why is The Baby Crying? Freddie The Frog Meets Teddy The Toad, My Wife Always Peels My Peaches, You Can Tell The Retirees and Others, too numerous to mention; [pers.] More than 50 original poetry readings before over 26,000 people in U.S., Canada, Hong Kon, Equador, Turkey, Russia, Germany, Virgin Islands. I write rhyming poetry for children, parents and grandparents.; [a.] Dearborn Hgts., MI

BRAZIL, JENNIFER ANNETTE
[b.] September 10, 1980, Bay Roberts; [p.] Doris and Harry Brazil; [ed.] grade 7; [oth. writ.] Several poems, none published; [pers.] I feel that my poems help me express feelings I have which I can not speak out loud; [a.] Bay Roberts

BRAZZIEL, ALTON FELIX
[b.] November 21, 1901, Barnum, TX; [p.] Felix, Annie Brazziel; [m.] Nellie N. Maxey, November 30, 1927; [ch.] Yvonne Parks; [ed.] Education at Barnum Texas, business college at Port Arthur, TX; [occ.] Retired, former accountant; [memb.] Mason; [oth. writ.] Several other poems. Once had a poem set to music by Bing Crosby and Rosemary Clooney. They asked for poems to be sent in and then they would sing them on the air; [pers.] Like books about History. Mr. Brazziel has seen Haley's Comet twice in his lifetime, in 1904 and in 1980.; [a.] Corrigan, TX

BREAKEY-BALDASAN, LINDA
[Pen.] Brandelyn Brooke; [b.] August 19, 1965, Tampa, FL; [m.] Joseph T. Baldasan, Jr, July 30, 1993; [ch.] Stephen Bryant Cox; [a.] Tampa, FL

BREAUX, ROBERT STUART
[b.] October 17, 1949, New Orleans, LA; [p.] Warren and Miriam Breaux; [m.] Connie Hall Breaux, April 19, 1974; [ch.] Joshua Stuart and Desiree' Monique Breaux; [ed.] West Jefferson High, Del Gado Jr College; [occ.] Letter Carrier USPO, Mandeville, LA; [memb.] US Air Force - 1969-73; [oth. writ.] "To See God", published in "Where Dreams Begin"; [pers.] I try to bring people to God through prayer and forgiveness. God's awareness is available to all the people of the earth; [a.] Mandeville, LA

BREEDLOVE, RENEE
[Pen.] Renee Rowley Breedlove; [b.] December 18, 1959, Haxtun, CO; [p.] Rosalie Monteith and Ronald Rowley; [m.] Steven Earl Breedlove; [ch.] Jason, Steven, Michelle; [a.] Foresthill, CA

BREMER, THEODORE W.
[Pen.] Ted W. Bremer (variations); [b.] April 14, 1910, Wilmington, NC; [p.] Henry M. and Elizabeth Ulrich Bremer; [m.] Emma Davis Bremer (DOB March 17, 1919, December 28, 1941; [ch.] Virginia Wiley, 1942, Elizabeth Bruchon 1946, Theodore M. Bremer 1950; [ed.] N.C. Univ. Chapel Hill, Geo. Washington Univ., Georgetown Univ. Foreign Service School, The Air Univ. (USAF), The Atlanta Law School, Degrees; BA, LLB, LLM. Also, service schools: The Army Quartermaster school, the Adjutant General's School, The Air Force Personal Affairs School; [occ.] Retired U.S. Vets. Admin. Executive and military officer (U.S Army, WWII; Air Force Intelligence, Korean Conflict.; [memb.] National Genealogical Society, Lutheran Church, ELCA, The

Heritage Foundaiton, AF & AM (Masonry), The Retired Officers Assn., Reserve Officers Assn., The National Assn. for Uniformed Services, The National Assn. for Retired Federal Employees et al, Phi Sigma Kappa.; [hon.] The Governor's Hospitality Committee (NC) 1937-39, 32nd Degree Scottish Rite Masonry, Professor Emeritus The Air Univ. (USAF); [oth. writ.] Feature articles in newspapers of North and South Carolina, The Eglin Eagle (USAF), the HRRC brochure (USAF), promotional and trade magazines such as Dixie Business, The South Carolina Magazine. The Carolina-Virginia Retailer, and others. Also a number of unpublished poems.; [pers.] As I contemplate life, my admiration grows for the old masters whose works and thoughts have survived the ravages of time and of our preoccupation with "progress" and I wonder how much of today's art, literature, and philosophy will prove so durable, so timeless. Then, an optimist, I manage to summon the faith that, eventually, the roses will bloom on the wall.; [a.] Annandale, VA

BREMMER, ROSE MARY
[Pen.] Cabbage Patch Kid and Jimmy Dean (my fingers); [b.] October 28, 1979, Pt Pleasant, NJ; [p.] Elliott Bremmer, Susan Bremmer; [brother] Anselmo Joseph Bremmer; [ed.] St. Rose Grammar School (K-6), Wall Intermediate (7-8) Wall High School; [occ.] Worked with disabled children (6th & 7th grade); [hon.] Effort Awards 5th and 6th grade (St. Rose) graduated 8th grade; [oth. writ.] Precious, Racism, Life, and Who Am I -- (never got them published); [pers.] I try to understand the qualities and meaning of life through my 14 years of experience, write what you feel, feelings are important; [a.] Wall, NJ

BRENGLE, TAMMY L.
[b.] November 23, 1970, Baltimore, MD; [p.] Patsy Fogus & James Shifflet; [m.] Max Brengle, September 28, 1991; [ch.] Brandon Robert Brengle (deceased); [ed.] Patterson High; [occ.] Secretary at the Maryland State Penitentiary; [pers.] Without the inspiration of the lost of my son Brandon who only lived for 3 days, I would have never been able to explort my true feeling like this to anyone. I give all my thanks to Brandon. This is dedicated to him.; [a.] Baltimore, MD

BRENHAN, FRANCES ANSTETT
[b.] August 29, 1907, Wilkes Barre, PA; [b.] Frank Anstett, Kathryn Shwalbach Anstett; [m.] Thomas J. Brennan, Jr, (deceased 1953), December 15, 1937; [ed.] Wilkes-Barre City Schools, Art Scholarship to Wilkes Univ, Extension Social Studies, Misericord in College, Dallas, PA, Univ of Penna (Philadelphia); O Retired, Mercy Hospital School of Nursing - Wilke-Barre, PA - class of 1928; [memb.] Charter Member, Wyoming Valley Art League, Wilkes-Barre, PA; Charter member - The National Museum of Women in the Arts, Washington, DC; Charter member - National Museum of The American Indian Smithsonian Inst, Washington, DC; [hon.] Grumbacher Award of Merit Art Scholarship to Wilkes Univ, Director of Arts and Crafts, Georgetown Settlement House, Wilkes-Barre, PA; [hon.] 2nd place, 3rd place winner Dallas, TX fair for Indian Skin painting; [oth paintings] 2nd place prize in juried show, Luzerne Cty Crt Hse, Wilkes-Barre, PA sponsored by "Acorn Guild" A Suqehanna River conservation group; [pers.] Over the years have dedicated myself to the service of others seeking wisdom and strength from my divine creator in keeping the Golden Rule; [a.] Bear Creek, PA

BREWER, KENNETH LIONEL
[b.] August 16, 1961, Williamston NC; [p.] Marie Anna Brewer; [m.] Not married; [ed.] High School Graduate one year of college; [occ.] Parking meter service worker; [memb.] No memberships; [hon.] No Honors; [oth. writ.] I have written many many poems,

when I was an adolescence. I have won a poetry contest in 1979, and publist in a newspaper.; [pers.] I'm a person who has suffered greatly, and suffered many hardships and difficulty of life. I have survived my ordeal from the debt of destruction and despair. I have arise, overcome the evil that has be set me from birth. I'm very gifted and taltented; [a.] Far Rockaway, NY

BREWER, NICHOLE
[b.] November 24, 1982, Baltimore; [p.] Gina and Mark Babka; [occ.] 6th grad, elementary school; [oth. writ.] So far I have only written for my school paper; [a.] Perry Hall, MD

BREWSTER, CHARLOTTE GREENE
[b.] August 29, 1944, Thornton, AR; [p.] Willie & Annie Marean Green; [m.] April 11, 1965, Deceased 1986; [ch.] Leroy Brewster, Jr. and Brigina Briehl Brewster; [ed.] B.S. University of Arkansas at Pine Bluff. Beginning 1st Sem of MLA at Southern Meghodist University Dallas, TX Spring 94'; [occ.] Administrative Asst., Ethnic Studies/SMU; [memb.] Hamilton Park United Methodist Church; [oth. writ.] A dozen plus poems (unpublished, except in the church newspaer, "The Word."; [pers.] All of my poems are reflections of personal experiences. They are mostly spiritual, often with a humorous tone. My writing is quite simple.; [a.] Dallas, TX

BRIDGEMAN, MICHELLE RENYEE
[b.] December 31, 1971, Ft Bragg, NC; [p.] George W. F. Bridgeman; [ed.] I'm currently a sophmore at Chancellor High School; [memb.] FHA (Future Homemakers of America); [oth. writ.] I've written 50 poems, 2 have been used for Christmas cards for relatives. Only "Sadness" has been published; [pers.] The credit isn't entirely mine. And to help you understand there has been many a time when I've let my feelings guide my hand; [a.] Medgesville, WV

BRIEL, KIM
[b.] September 13, 1951, Pottstown, PA; [p.] Linwood and Sarah Briel; [ed.] Boyertown Area High School; [hon.] Various Sports Awards; [a.] Macungie, PA

BRITE, KATHERINE ANN
[Pen.] Kathy; [b.] August 13, 1954, Ft Worth, TX; [p.] Darrell and Hazel McBrayer; [m.] Lindsey A. Brite, June 23, 1972; [ch.] Bobby Allen, Jerod Adam, and Rebecca Ann Brite; [ed.] Mansfield High; [occ.] Restaurant; [oth. writ.] Several writings, none published; [pers.] In this fast paced day in time, I always enjoy the scarce, still moments, to collect my thoughts, which inspires me to write about many things; [a.] Alvarado, TX

BRIZZI, JILLANN
[b.] January 8, 1949, NY; [p.] Anthony and Gilda Brizzi; [ed.] Sewanhara High, Upsala College; [occ.] Music Teacher Brizzi Music Studio; [memb.] (N.Y.S.S.M.A.) (MENC) New York State School Music Assoc., (L.I.M.T.A.) Long Island Music Teacher's Association; (PETA) People for the Ethical Treatment of Animals.; [hon.] Columbia University Honorable Mention for Journalism, First Place Virtuoso, L.I. Long Island, Third Place, Virtuoso, NY State, American Accordionists Association.; [oth. writ.] Article for Daily News; [a.] New Hyde Park, NY

BROADDUS, MARY HENKEL
[b.] August 27, 1882, New Market VA; [p.] Solon G. Henkel & Mary Alice Henkel; [m.] Junius M. Broaddus, 1902; [ch.] John P. Bruce B. & Mary June; [ed.] New Market High School, Dunsmore Business College, Harrisonburg, VA; [occ.] Died October 20, 1964 in Harrisonburg, VA; [memb.] First Baptist Church, Parkersburg, W. VA.; [oth. writ.] Several poems published in local newspapers. "The Heart of

an Indian" was written while staying with her son, teacher on the Apache Indian Reservation at Sa Carlos, Ariz., in 1936.; [pers.] She devoted a gre deal of her time in research of her family history an was an able assistant compiler of "The Henk Geneology" published in 1963.

BROCK, SANDI
[b.] January 9, 1946, Rapid City, SD; [p.] Dub ar Eileen Brock; [ch.] Robyn Parish and Gina Parish [ed.] Bachelor's degree at Sam Houston State Uni Univ of Houston - hrs toward master's, St. Nichol Montessori Training Center; [occ.] Child Care L censing; [memb.] Humble Art League, America Montessori Society; [hon.] Best of Show for c painting, dean's list; 2nd place in "bars" in gymna tics; [oth. writ.] Writing a book of poetry reflectir recovery from divorce; [pers.] My ability to wri verse a gift from God and I will treasure it forever; [a Kingwood, TX

BROOKS, BETTY
[b.] May 21, 1925, Baltimore; [p.] Helen Warren ar Burton Wagoner; [m.] Divorced; [ch.] John Edwa Brooks III (Jeb), Michael Paul Brooks; [ed.] RN (3 y Diploma) Church Home and Hospital Baltimor MD, BA Baldwin Wallace College, Berea, Ohi M.Ed., Cleveland State University, Cleve., Ohi [occ.] Semi-Retired Health Educator; [memb Olmstead Unitarian Universalist Fellowship, P. Faculty Member, Cayahoga Community Colleg Cleveland Zoological Society, Board of Trustee Bide-A-Wee Cat Shelter; [hon.] Psychology Hon Society, Psi Chi 79/80, Outstanding Student, B.W College 1980, Magna Cum Laude, B.W. Colleg 1980; [oth. writ.] Articles in Professional Journal American Journal of Infection Control (AJIC) Apri Oct., Dec., 1983; Journal of Continuing Education i Nursing (JCEN) Sept., Oct. 1985; Health Servic Mgr. 3/79, 8/79, 11/79, 10/80, also American Mar agement Assn. Journal, Solutions to Manageri Dilemas; [pers.] Continue to grow. Broaden yo horizons, Sample new experiences. Never sto learning; [a.] Parma, OH

BROOKS, ERNESTINE VERLISTER
[Pen.] E. V. Brooks; [b.] May 27, 1952, Washingtor D.C.; [p.] Rudolph Russell Smith and Margaret I Smith; [m.] Arthur Brooks, Sr., February 18, 198 [ch.] Jessica, Michelle, Allen, stepchildren: Arthu Jr., Clinton, Kelby, LaDrika, Lessa and Timothy; [a Prince Frederick, MD

BROOKS, SHANE ALLEN
[b.] September 26, 1971, Cols, OH; [p.] Jack ar Geneva Brooks; [m.] Paula Brooks; [ch.] Thoma Allen Brooks; [ed.] Diploma from Grove City Hig School; [occ.] Rotery Corp (Associate); [oth. writ.] have quite a number of other poems with all sorts subjects; [pers.] Learn to be unselfish, understandin and kind. Think with your heart and not with you mind; [a.] Grove City, OH

BROUGHTON, DOROTHY C.
[b.] April 8, 1961, Geneva O. Tooson, Jones, Turne [m.] Rev Willie C. Broughton, Jr, December 2 1984; [ch.] LaTouya, Tiffany, Debonair, Cherisl Charmill; [ed.] Pierce College, Antelope Valley Co lege; [occ.] Homemaker, student; [memb.] Ne Heaven Missionary Baptist Church; [pers.] Giv music a chance it can protect you, correct you eve help mend your soul.

BROW, JAYME
[b.] September 20, 1977, Natick; [oth. writ.] In th past 2 1/2 yrs, I have written 27 other poems. In whic all of them have a very sentimental meaning to them

ROWN, BARBARA PATRICK
] April 24, 1915, Los Angeles; [p.] Margaret
ith, Claude Smith; [m.] Rayner Brown, July 23,
40; [ch.] Zachary, Marthella; [ed.] University of
uthern California, B.A., 1936, M.A. 1943, M.A.
sis: Coleridge and His Highgate Disciples; [occ.]
tired Teacher of English (20 years, California);
n.] Phi Beta Kappa, Phi Kappa Phi; [a.] Los
igeles, CA

ROWN, GEORGETTE M. INNES
] March 20, 1918, Wilmington, DE; [p.] George
eyer (Dec) and Flora Sue Saunders Meyer (Dec);
.] Roy Glen Brown, Jr., March 6, 1991; [ed.]
aduate West Phila. High School 1935, Graduate
al Estate Law School 1945, Graduate Fire, Marine
Cas. Ins. 1946, both from Phila Board of Realtor,
ila., PA. Graduate Phila. Income Tax. Institute
55, Villanova College-Appraisal Courses 1965;
c.] Retired Real Estate and Ins. Broker; [memb.]
tional Assoc. of Realtors Greater Phila. Realty
ard, Phila Womens Realy Assoc. & American
siness Womens Assoc., St. Pauls Lutheran Church,
ceived Golden Poet Awards from World of Poetry
85, 87, 88, 91; [hon.] Woman of the Year-Phila.,
omen's Realty Assoc. 1951, Boss of Year, Amer.
s. Womens Ass. 1963. Gustave A Wick Award
. Phila. Realty Board, The Marquis Who's Who in
World 1990 to & including 1994, 500 Personali-
s of The Worldk Service to Real Estate Profession,
mbridge, England-International Woman of the Year
92, 20th Century Award of Achievement, Certifi-
e of World Leadership 1987 and several others too
merous to mention; [oth. writ.] Poems i.e., Heav-
ly Father Why?, Courage, If, What is a Rhythme?,
y, Peace, Ember, Poets, Sharon, Dr. William
rnheim, Tempest in a Tea Pot, Jim, Anniversary of
ur Ring, Dr. Thomas Shutt, Thank you Lord,
flections, "Our Graduation, Carmella, For Andres
d others.; [pers.] The written word is a true expres-
n of what is in one's heart!; [a.] Boca Raton, FL

ROWN, IRENE SYLVIA
] March 7, 1916, Bow, London; [p.] Alfred
illiam and Lily Williams; [m.] Frederick Charles
own, August 13, 1949; [ed.] Carlyle Secondary
elsea, London; [occ.] Housewife and gardening
atic; [memb.] St. Nicholas Church, Royal Society
the Prevention of Cruelty to Animals (fund raiser)
ds. Royal Society for Protection of mentally handi-
ped society; [oth. writ.] Autobiography, One
man's War; [pers.] Surprised and deeply grateful
have survived world war two. Deeply grateful also
America for coming to our aid. We would now be
der the Nazi wheel if they hadn't.

ROWN, JUDY ANN
] December 7, 1949, Hamilton, OH; [ch.] John
Brown; [ed.] Graduated from Phoenix Union High
hool in Phoenix, AZ; [occ.] Volunteer-worker, I
ve donated my life in helping the people in our state
Michigan, and in America; [hon.] 4 Honor Awards,
ditor Choice Awards, Golden Poet 1990, Golden
et 1991; [oth. writ.] I am never alone, Santa's
ming Home, Sunshine Rainbows and Roses,
ddy's Special Little Angel, America A Land of
auty, Walk Hand in Hand, Lord I Want You To
ow Me The Way, My Secret To Good Fortune;
rs.] What greater gift could I ever receive is to help
erica through the words of poetry. Words which
spoken from within the heart; [a.] Engadine, MI

ROWN, KEVIN
en.] Kevin Brown; [b.] December 28, 1969,
rrytown, NY; [p.] Robert Brown, Maureen Brown;
.] Bachelor of Arts in Psychology. Oneonta State;
c.] Mental Health Counselor, Personal Trainer;
h. writ.] Several poems published in School news-
er; [a.] Mohegan Lake, NY

BROWN, SANDRA MIELAK
[Pen.] Sandra Mielak; [b.] December 27, 1966,
Anaheim, CA; [p.] Eugene B. Mielak & Leilani
Mielak; [m.] Jeffrey M. Brown, August 14, 1993;
[ch.] none; [ed.] El Toro High School, College
Saddleback College; [occ.] Bookkeeper; [hon.] Pen-
manship Award, and Honor Roll List numerous
times.; [pers.] I express my feelings and emotions
through my writings. I have a strong desire to write,
which comes naturally.; [a.] Lake Forest, CA

BROWN, VICTORIA LEE
[Pen.] Vicki Brown; [b.] October 7, 1955, Ohio; [ed.]
Wilmington College, Wilm, OH, Chatfield College,
St Martin, OH; [occ.] Whatever I have to do; [memb.]
Songwriter, performer of original musci playing ac-
tively at Canal St Tavern in Dayton, OH and Bluebird
Cafe in Nashville, TN; [hon.] Harris Memoria Fund
Award for poetry - published "Standing by the Road"
in Woodstock campus literary magazine; [oth. writ.]
Published four songs with "Don't act Your Age Music
Published", (BMI) currently working on an album of
original music with independent record co, "Family
Man Records" represented by Eugene Bick; [pers.]
Don't quit your day job. You just have to be at the
right place at the right time when lightening strikes;
[a.] Sabina, OH

BROWNING, SIMON K.
[b.] February 3, 1971, Southhampton, England; [p.]
Keith Browning, Yvonne Browning; [ed.] Insuffi-
cient English Schools of Little Importance or Impact;
[memb.] Amnesty International; [oth. writ.] Only
other submitted poem, published in Britain in poetry
collection (book); [pers.] With my life, I paint a
picture, With each day, I add a colour; [a.]
Southampton, England

BRUKNER, JANET
[b.] May 15, 1975, Chicago, IL; [p.] Chester Brukner,
Carolina Brukner; [ed.] Holy Trinity High School;
College of Office Technology; [occ.] Cashier, Ser-
vice Assist, Stock, Student; [memb.] Police Explorer;
[hon.] Volleyball, Tiger Award (sportsmanship), stu-
dent council, secretarial asst; [oth. writ.] Several
poems not published anywhere; [pers.] I have been
influenced in poetry by my one and only love Alex!
[a.] Chicago, IL

BRUNS, CINDY
[b.] June 29, 1975, Bellaire, TX; [p.] Ellen and David
Bruns; [ed.] Currently attending Kempner High School
as a senior; [occ.] Child Care Worker; [memb.]
T.A.S.K. - Teens Assist Special Kids; [pers.] No one
gets out of life alive so live life until you die. Don't
worry about asking why, those who don't don't even
try, to live life 'til they die; [a.] Sugarland, TX

BRUSATTI, LOUIS T.
[b.] St. Louis, MO on May 18, 1949; [p.] The first son
of Edith and Louis J. Brusatti. After finishing grade
school he went to St. Louis Prep Sem. - South in St
Louis (1963-67). His undergraduate degree in sociol-
ogy was completed with honors at the Univ of MO,
Columbia, MO (1971). After two years of graduate
theological study at Kenrick Sem. in St. Louis he
joined the Congregation of the Mission (Vincentian
Fathers and Brothers) and went to St. Mary's Semi-
nary in Santa Barbara, CA for novitiate. Vows were
taken on September 27, 1974. He finished the M.Div
degree at DeAndreis Sem. in Lemont, IL and while a
deacon began his D.Min work at The Catholic Univ
in Washington, DC. He was ordained a priest on
November 28, 1975 at St Mary's Sem. in Perryville,
MO. Later, he completed a MS in Pastoral Counseling
from Loyola College in Balt., MD (August, 1978) and
a Cert. in Management Studies from the Univ. of
Denver in CO (Spring 1982). He is cert. as a coun-
selor by the National Board of Cert. Counselors
(1985). By the Spring of 1985, Father Brusatti had

been given the task of establishing a new college
formation program for the Congregation of the Mis-
sion in St Louis. The Fall of 1985 saw the opening of
this new program. Until the Fall of 1990, he was dir.
of Saint-Lazare, the college formation program for
the Congregation of the Mission. He accepted the
position of Academic Dean at Kenrick Sem. In
addition, he was the Dir. of Field Ed. at Aquinas Inst
of Theology. In 1990 Father Brusatti became princi-
pal and rector of St Vincent DePaul High School
Seminary in Lemont, IL. From 1991 until the Fall of
1993, Father Brusatti was a faculty member in the
DePaul Univ School of Education and Dir. of Gradu-
ate Programs for the Schl of Ed. Today he is a full time
Assist Prof. in the Dept of Religious Studies at DePaul
Univ. He continues to teach and write while working
toward tenure. [pers.] I want to live a thankful life and
share what I have been given with others; [a.] Chi-
cago, IL

BRYANT, KERRI
[b.] February 21, 1979, Murphysboro, IL; [p.] John
L. Bryant, Jr and Janice Ostrom, Stepmother - Saralee
Bryant, Stepfather - Bob Ostrom; [ed.] High school
freshman; [occ.] Student at Murphysboro High School;
[memb.] Beta Club, 4-H; [hon.] High Honors in
school and many other awards for academic achieve-
ments; [oth. writ.] Unpublished poems short stories.
Some are published in various magazines, etc; [pers.]
My poems reflect different times, moods, and events
of my life. I try my best to write my poems so others
can feel those feelings too, and understand my thoughts;
[a.] Murphysboro, IL

BRYANT, TRUDY
[b.] December 26, 1954, San Antonio, TX; [p.]
Alexander Wolfe, Carrie Wolfe; [m.] Mark Bryant,
July 22, 1988; [ch.] Amber Jene Bassford; [ed.]
Robert E. Lee High, Labette Community Collee -
A.D.; [occ.] Registered Nurse - Homemaker; [memb.]
United Methodist Women; [pers.] Belief in the "one
true God", can give a human being, spiritual eyes in
which to view the world, and make wise decisions;
[a.] Independence, KS

BUBBICO, LIZ
[b.] October, 10, 1983, Stamford, CT; [p.] Laura and
Richard Bubbico; [ed.] Vineyards Elm. School; [occ.]
Student; [memb.] President of 4-H Club and YMCA;
[hon.] 5th grade Honor Roll, 4th grade Honor Roll,
Presidents Physical Awards, Safety Patrol; [a.] Naples,
FL

BUCK, AMY L.
[b.] August 12, 1971, Atchison, KS; [p.] Dr. Harold
P. Buck, Jr and Dorothy Buck; [ed.] Academy of
Mount St. Scholastica; Benedictine College; [occ.]
Publications Writer, Cleveland Chiropractic College,
Kansas City, MO; [hon.] Dean's Honor List; National
Dean's List Member; [oth. writ.] Numerous news and
feature articles published in Benedictine College's
student newspaper; and for Cleveland Chiropractic
College's student, and alumni publications and press
releases; [pers.] My intentions within poetry strive to
portray the human spirit. A symbol of the dedicated
people in my life who are responsible for teaching me
that patience is truly a virtue and that love is the
greatest gift of all. "True Heart" was inspired by
someone very special and a true gift; [a.] Kansas City,
MO

BUCK, VANESSA A.
[b.] April 16, 1978, Albuquerque, N. MX; [p.]
Wallace and Lena Buck; [ed.] New Mexico Military
Institute, Ft. Wingate High School; [oth. writ.] Sev-
eral poems published in "The Maverick" of NMMI.;
[pers.] I write these poems for friends and about their
problems. Sometimes I write them on my personal
experience.; [a.] Shiprock, NM

BUCKBEE, SANDRA K.
[Pen.] Sandra K. Floyd; [b.] November 14, 1951, Emporia, KS; [p.] Doris G. Malhena and Bob Sternadel,; [m.] Samuel Buckbee, June 20, 1992; [ch.] Cheyennek K. Floyd, Charles W. Floyd, II, Roger L. Floyd; [ed.] Graduated Auburn High School, Rockford, IL, Superior Hair Styling School, Olatha, KS; [occ.] Cosmetologist; [pers.] The words of a poem are the innermost feelings of the poet; [a.] Allen, KS

BUCKLAN, PROFESSOR JOHN ERDELL
[b.]October 3, 1916, Bethlehem, PA; [p.] Charles Erdell and Lillian Schmidt; [m.] Paquita DeLeon, June 21, 1947; [ed.] Graduate The Art School Institue, NYC B.S., MA, Professional Diploma, Teachers College, Columbia University, NYC Photo Schools in Germany, New york School of Photography; [occ.] Retired Professor of Art & Design; [memb.] Kappa Delta Pi, Honorary Society in Education, Louise Bogan Poetry Society.; [hon.] 2nd prize for World Search for Design, Hall of Education, NY World's Fair, 1963. Received US Patent for Selective Color Photography whereby 10,000 colors can be produced on colorprint paper or film, Who's Who in Poetry 1990; [oth. writ.] American Anthology 1989 World of Poetry, Great Poes of the Western World, National Library of Poetry, Five Golden Poet Awards. Distinguished Poet of America, Two Editor's Choice Awards, Whispers in the Wind, Tears of Ire, Outstanding Poet of 1994. Paintings in private collections, Five US Patents; [pers.] I have been blessed in being a modern artist, first in my career, then learning to be a designer, teacher, inventor, world traveler, poet. I have taught thousands to create; [a.] New York City, NY

BUCKLER, TERRY WAYNE
[b.] October 11, 1973, Fenton, MI; [p.] Robin Howard, Kevin Buckler; [ed.] Fenton High School; [occ.] Student; [pers.] Drugs turn good men with hope into lost souls of despair; [a.] Fenton, MI

BUCKLEY, JAMES M.
[b.] June 19, 1912, Jamaica Plain, MA; [p.] Arthur & Katherine Buckley; [m.] Marilyn Buckley, September 11, 1976; [ch.] James m. Buckley, Jr., Carolyn Souza, Bradford Reed; [ed.] jBoston College A.B. 1934, M.Ed. Boston College 1950, Graduate Study at Boston University in the 60's; [occ.] Ret. from Schl. Dept. as Dir. of Adult Ed.; violinist and songwriter; [hon.] Award for 30 yrs. of outstanding service in the school department of the New Bedford, Mass.; [oth. writ.] Poems and songwriter, commencement exercises, speeches; [pers.] It's never too late.; [a.] New Bedford, MA

BUENTELL0-GARZO, VERONICA
[Pen.] Gigi; [b.] June 12, 1969, Brownsville, TX; [p.] Manuel M. Buentello & Gertrudis Buentello; [m.] Ruben Garza, October 24, 1992; [pers.] Only one person has been the inspiration in everything I strive for. My mother lost her battle with cancer on May 3, 1993. Her spirit is alive within my now, and it will remain a part of my life forever; [a.] Brownsville, TX

BUNGE, ROSEMARY C.
[Pen.] Rosie; [b.] September 20, 1948, Heidielberg, W. Germany; [p.] Robert & Clara Fricke; [m.] Dieter Bunge, May 4, 1979; [ch.] Andy Wienecke; [ed.] Southern Alberta, Institute of Technology.; [occ.] Purchasing Manager Fairmont Hot Springs Resort; [hon.] Diploma Commercial Cooking at Bursary Technology.; [oth. writ.] This is my first writing.; [pers.] I wrote this poem, to depict the beauty of the area which I live in, and will always cherish this.; [a.] Hot Springs, B.C. Canada

BUNKER, N. MORGAN
[b.] December 24, 1968, Las Vegas, NV; [p.] Richard and Carole Bunker; [m.] Allyson Bunker, December 18, 1992; [ed.] Currently a senior at the Univ of Utah majoring in english; [oth. writ.] previously published in Bouillabaisse; [pers.] I try to paint pictures of the unnoticed subtelties that are forgotten in the busy heaviness of our day; [a.] Salt Lake City, UT

BURGESS, MARJORIE L.
[b.] Nobember 24, 1928, Whitakers, NC; [p.] Benjamin & Laura Harrison; [m.] Divorced; [ch.] Terence D. Dixon, Michael J. Dixon; [ed.] Eastern District H.S. Brooklyn, NY, John Jay college of Criminal Justice, NYC, NY; [occ.] Retired; [memb.] First Baptist Church, AARP, AAUW, RPEA, Missionary Society, Altar Guild; [pers.] Work hard if you want to realize your dream.; [a.] Hackensack, NJ

BURGESS, ROBERT EUGUENE
[b.] January 14, 1954, Trieste, Italy; [p.] Vaugn & Marina Burgess; [ch.] Edmund Cullen Burgess; [ed.] 71st High, College of the Redwoods, Instituto De Allende (Instituto De Allende); [occ.] General Contractor, Whittier, CA; [oth. writ.] Have written several poems and songs. Some have been recorded.; [pers.] There is a time and a place, that floats on a feeling; [a.] Whittier, CA

BURGOON, SEAN
[b.] September 2, 1981, Herkimer, NY; [p.] Janice and Dennis Burgoon; [ed.] Cobblestone Elementary School, 6th grade; [hon.] Honor Roll; [a.] Rocklin, CA

BURGOS, JUAN A.
[Pen.] Tony; [b.] April 19, 1973, Humacau, PR; [p.] Rosa Diaz/ Juan Burgos; [ch.] D'Anthony A. Burgos; [occ.] Not right now; [hon.] Awarded for best poem of love. Also honored for best titled poem; [oth. writ.] Many poems entered in several contests similar to this one. To be more specific - school poetry contest; [pers.] I give all my great thanks to our God for giving me this special talent. As well for my ex-girl friend, Karen Vega, that which the poem was all about her; [a.] Springfield, MA

BURKE, BILLY J.
[b.] March 15, 1954, Hazard, KY; [p.] Bob and Myrtle Burke; [m.] Dora Burke, January 4, 1974; [ch.] Melissa A. Burke; [occ.] Heavy Equipment Operator; [memb.] Minister of the Church of Christ; [pers.] This poem was written in memory of my dear friend Clay Williams Sr who died of cancer; [a.] Baxter, KY

BURNES, JESSICA J.
[Pen.] Jessica Monty; [b.] November 30, 1976, Coranado, CA; [p.] Pamela and Mark Barnes; [oth. writ.] You can survive which is published in Dance on the Horizon; [pers.] Dreams can come true. I wish to thank my family and friends for their support.; [a.] St. Pete, FL

BURNS, ALISHA
[b.] August 16, 1982, Louisville, KY; [p.] Paul and Sandy Burns; [ed.] Scottsburg Elementary School and William H. English Middle; [occ.] Middle school student; [memb.] Odyssey of the Mind Team; Honor Choir, Flag Corp; School Publication Staff; [hon.] President's Physical Fitness and National Physical Fitness Awards; Honor Student, All A - Academic Awards; [oth. writ.] Several other unpublished poems; [a.] Scottsburg, IN

BURNS, CHRISTY JO
[b.] March 6, 1975, Flint, MI; [p.] Cindy and Gary Grierson; [ed.] Davison High School graduate of 1993; [pers.] Life is to be valued, not taken for

granted; [a.] Gaylord, MI

BURR, JENNIFER LYN
[b.] November 11, 1976, Michigan; [p.] John a〉 Debra Burr; [ed.] Redford Union High School; [occ] Student; [memb.] Student Council, AIDS Awarenes Soccer; [hon.] Many awards that most high scho〉 students get, but the one I am most proud of is "mo creative imagination". Received at Redford Union band camp '93; [oth. writ.] Lost in Joseph's eye〉 Days of Future Past; [pers.] I am having a ve〉 difficult time being a teenager. With parents a〉 friends who support me it is suppose to be mu〉 easier, but it's not. I am also trying to realize why lo〉 hurts so much. A boy whom I love gave up on me a〉 I don't know. I just want him to know I will never gi〉 up on him; [a.] Redford, MI

BURTON, DONELLA
[Pen.] Marley Shaw; [b.] June 7, 1973, Beaumon TX; [p.] Helene Rouse and Donald Burton; [ed.] We Brook Sr High; [occ.] Bail Bonds person - Jeffers〉 County; [memb.] 1993 Debutante, 1993 Nech〉 River Princess, Member of Debate Club, and You Guild; [hon.] Winner of essay contest on Babe Zahari〉 "Who's Who" at high school for outstanding achiev〉 ments, and winner of debate on abortion; [oth. writ〉 Several poems, debates, and essays; [pers.] A lot 〉 my writings are inspired by personal triumphs I'〉 had to make throughout my life; [a.] Beaumont, T

BUTCHER, JOHN C. (CRNA)
[b.] March 27, 1942, Urbana, OH; [p.] Katherine I Butcher; [ch.] Katherine Christy Jon and Bryon; [ed〉 RN Miami Valley Hosp, Dayotn OH 1964; Anesth〉 tist Mayo Clinic 1967, Univ of Redlands BA 197〉 MPA Golden Gate Univ 1979; [occ.] Anesthetist f〉 ACA, CA and Samaritan Health Service Springvill〉 AZ; [memb.] AANA, CANA; [hon.] Past Vice Pr〉 CANA; [oth. writ.] Book of poetry; [pers.] I hav〉 spent most of my life trying to wake up from th〉 illusion of physical life where no power can real〉 affect me. And only the God within can set me fre〉 [a.] Apple Valley, CA

BUTLER, JOHN T.
[b.] October 20, 1938; [occ.] Chauffeur for N Teamsters, Local 868; [pers.] No formal education 〉 poetry. It was just a natural talent that I always kne〉 I could do. I like writing about things that affect m〉 emotionally from life to politics to religion; [a Bronx, NY

BYERS, CARRIANNE
[b.] October 15, 1970, Toronto; [p.] Marion an Crane Byers; [ch.] Kylie Marion Carol Byers Blundell; [ed.] Sutton District High; [occ.] Rece〉 tionist for Keswick Medical Center and waitress 〉 Waterfront Bar and Grill; [memb.] VERT - Volunte〉 Emergency Response Team (C.B. Group); [oth. writ I have many other writings but none that have bee published of my own; [pers.] I would like to thank a〉 the people that told me to do something with m〉 poetry. And the people that are in my life th〉 influenced me to write. I love you all. Thank you; [a Keswick, Ontario

BYRNES, MARTIN A.
[b.] February 7, 1973, New Brighton, PA; [p William and Helen Byrnes; [ed.] Beaver Area Hig School, University of Dayton; [occ.] Full-time stu dent; [memb.] University of Dayton English Associ〉 tion; [hon.] Dean's List; [oth. writ.] Previous publi cation in Poetice Voices of America, Fall 199 edition; [pers.] "As for me, I could leave the worl〉 with today in my eyes."--Truman Capote; [a.] Be〉 ver, PA

ACCAVALLA, JOHN
[.] July 21, 1961, LI, NY; [p.] Anthony and Lee
.ccaualla; [ed.] Attended both the Fashion Inst of
.ch and NY Univ; [occ.] Astrologer/herbalist spe-
.lizing in alternative medicine; [memb.] Volunteer
.rk: "Manhattan Ctr for the Living", "God's Love
. Deliver", "Gay and Lesbian Community Cen-
.", "Friends in Deed"; [hon.] Class talker, Class
.ncer, numerous actor awards. Certificates in
.pnotherapy and past life regression. To be healty,
.ppy and very much alive; [oth. writ.] Endless
.lume of poetry. Current compilation entitled "On
.mpany Time" and I'm sure there's more to come;
.rs.] As an HIV positive, gay man living in NY,
., I have turned my liabilities into assets. Always
.nembering that from pain comes birth and that the
.mpassion of God is for all; [a.] New York City, NY

AHOE, ARIANE LYNN
.] December 27, 1977, Waterloo, IA; [p.] Barbara
.d Michael Cahoe; [ed.] East High School; [occ.]
.st High School; [occ.] Waitress/hostess, Friend-
.p Village Retirement Home, Waterloo, IA; [hon.]
.nor Roll; [pers.] I write to touch my personal
.periences and in hope that people who read my
.ce can somehow relate to them. I owe tremendous
.nks to the ones I love and those who've influenced
. writing; [a.] Evansdale, IA 50707

ALHOUN, ALICE JEAN
.] July 6, 1938, Pueblo, CO; [p.] James Calvin
.ddleston & Alberta Louise Cables; [m.] Marlyn
.an Calhoun Sr., January 16, 1957; [ch.] Marlyn
.arty) D. Calhoun, Sr., Michael W. Calhoun,
.arcia J. Beardsley, Mona L. Allen; [ed.] Graduated
.gh School in 1956 at Centennial High School,
.eblo, CO; [occ.] Housewife, Presently raising 2
.andchildren and writing; [oth. writ.] To date I am
.published, but I press on via lyrics and music,
.etry, short stories and a novel within my mind and
.art that result in many sleepless nights.; [pers.] It's
.portant to remember the past, live for each day,
.ish in life's delights and learn from it's horrors, as
.e speeds on. It's my grand privelege to be a
.mber of the human race.; [a.] Melbourne, FL

ALLAHAN, COLLEEN
.n.] CMC; [b.] September 14, 1949, Watertown,
.Y; [p.] Robert Callahan (deceased) Mary & Robert
.aigret; [m.] Gerald H. Heitzman; [ch.] Marc R.
.um; [ed.] Lyme Central High School, Watertown
.hool of Commerce, & Concord Career Institute for
.dical Asst.; [occ.] Claim Examiner, Central United
.e Insurance Company, Houston, TX; [oth. writ.]
.e homes of many friends and family members all
.er the United States. Have also, with my son, Marc
.Baum, copywritten many poems as song lyrics.;
.rs.] Since childhood, I've written poems to declare
.e, express respect, instill hope, provide inspira-
.n, show sympathy, explain fears, give thanks,
.are joy, bring a smile, or to celebrate just about any
.casion. It's the best way I know to communicate
.ong emotions to those around me.; [a.] Houston,

AMERON, HARRY F.
.] December 21, 1917, Camden, NJ: [p.] Charles
.Berta Cameron; [m.] Divorced; [ch.] Bonnie L.
.ardle; [ed.] Moorestown High, Rutgers University;
.c.] Retired; [pers.] I have written many poems
.nular to this; [a.] Las Vegas, NV

AMERON, JERRY
.n.] J. Rome; [b.] May 21, (I forgot), Elyra, OH;
.c.] Counting the money I'd like to have; [memb.]
.ace in the Human Race; [hon.] Being still alive!;
.h. writ.] If I did, I deny it!; [pers.] My short,
.netimes seem satirical and/or humorous (I hope)
.mes are each written without a repeated word. The
.der thus is spaced repetitious "fill-ins". I'm

challanged when given a subject or person to write
about, and hey, yours truly is available; [a.] Sequim,
WA

CAMPBELL, CAREY LYNN
[b.] August 19, 1979, Atwater, CA; [p.] Dawn & Jack
McLennan; [ed.] Staley Jr. High; [memb.] American
Red Cross, City wide-all country music hall. Acting,
art, and dance, talent school.; [hon.] Chorus, Ameri-
can Red Cross Association. Writing Awards Storys.;
[oth. writ.] Writing for my school newspaper. Illus-
trating school handbooks.; [pers.] I usually write
about family or personal experiences, and through
these poems people should realize that even though
I'm young I know how it feels to have problems.; [a.]
Rome, NY

CAMPBELL, ZACHARY SEAN
[Pen.] Zakk; [b.] February 2, 1982, at home; [p.]
Frank Campbell; [m.] Is this a type of bird? Just
starting to like girls, but they are all older; [ch.] None
-- older brothers act like children; [ed.] 6th grade;
[occ.] It is work trying to stay crazy; [memb.] Human
Race, simi youth baseball team called the Phillies;
[hon.] Most improved academically in my class; I am
my Dad's favorite son but he says that about my 2
older brothers also; [oth. writ.] I can't remember, but
I am writing a novel; [pers.] Don't go to jail, just be
awesome; [a.] Simi Valley, CA

CANBY, DICK
[Pen.] dick canby; [b.] September 15, 1943, Dayton,
OH; [p.] Franc & Edward Canby; [m.] Olga Knyazeva
Canby, September 15, 1990; [ed.] Arizona State
University & Northern Arizona Univ. with degrees in
B.S. in Geology & B.A. in Education; [occ.] Profes-
sional Photographer, Tour Director & Guide; [memb.]
Commissioner on Sedona Parks and Recreation Com-
mission; Member of: Cousteau Society, Wilderness
Society, Greater Yellowstone Coalition, National
Parks & Conservation Association, Earth Island Insti-
tute, World vision, World Wildlife fund, Global
Family, Earchwatch; [oth. writ.] Poems published in:
Unity Magazine, Science of Mind Magazine, Arizona
Highways magazine, "Arizona Anthem" of Arizona
Poets, (a hardbound anthology of poems from Ari-
zona poets); [pers.] My dream & desire is to dedicate
myself, my photography and poetry to the expression
of truth...the truth that we humans are all one species
living on a globe with no continents or hemispheres,
no races or ideologies that separate us from the love
that infuses all mankind...that it is this very love of our
brothers & sisters (and all the earth's other creatures)
that will put us together in the realization that only
human beings will ever change things for the
better...and none of this will begin to happen until we
change our attitudes. The media is the message, and
the message is that Love heals all... but we must work
toward that loving peace by starting with our loved
ones and ourselves... to grab a hold of a reverence for
all life.; [a.] Sedona, AZ

CANTON, LIONEL BRENT
[b.] December 19, 1954, Harlem, NY; [p.] Iris and
Clarence Canton; [ed.] Rollins College, Winter Park,
FL; [pers.] You must live beyond your mistakes.
Everyone falls, the true measure of a person is to keep
getting backup; [a.] New York, NY

CAPOGNA, STEPHANIE MARIE
[b.] July 9, 1980, Bayshore, NY; [p.] Loreto and
Anna Marie Capogna; [ed.] Weldon & Howitt Junior
High School, Farmingdale, NY; [occ.] Student;
[memb.] Drama Club, Company Dancer (local dance
school), MDA Volunteer, Studio Art; [hon.] Creative
Writing, Young Author's Conference, Terrific Kid
Award (Farmingdale School), Student Council Rep.
(AA School); [oth. writ.] Enjoys writing for friends
and family members, Bowling for Girls; [pers.]
Poetry expresses how I feel about our society and

relationships. I hope that my poems will bring
happiness and peace to all.; [a.] No. Massapequa, NY

CAPORALETTI, JENNIFER
[b.] May 19, 1961, Akron; [p.] Louis and Judith
Caporaletti; [ed.] St. Vincent St Mary H.S. Akron
Univ; [occ.] Assistant Manager for BP Oil Company;
[memb.] St Marys Catholic Church; [hon.] National
Honor Society; [oth. writ.] Children's Literature
(beginner) location - Conneticut; [pers.] Our live
should be a reflection of the beauty knowledge, and
wisdom of God, our heavenly father; [a.] Cuyahoga
Falls, OH

CAPWELL, ANNETTE M.
[Pen.] Annette; [b.] April 23, 1963, CO; [p.] Marge
Whaltler and Rudy Estrada; [m.] Bob F. Capwell,
August 25, 1984; [ch.] Joseph, James, Christopher;
[ed.] No High School, GED, 18 mos Jr College;
[occ.] Disabled, CFS, PTSD, Depression; [pers.] My
life - a very close family childhood sexual, physical,
mental abuse, alcholic, addict, battered wife, rape
survivor, chronic, illness, suicidal tendencies, worth-
lessness, hopelessness - recovery - healing; [a.] Do-
ver, NH

CARAVELLO, JOSEPHINE
[b.] May 18, 1920, USA; [p.] Joseph and Mary
Cavallaro; [m.] Benjamin, November 19, 1950; [ch.]
Dolores, Gloria, Richard, Vincent T. Joseph, Joann;
[ed.] Manuel Training High School, American Inst of
Banking, Certificate of Recognition, Office Work
Management; [occ.] Retired; Apple Bank for Sav-
ings; [memb.] St. Raphaels Council of Catholic
Women, Living Waters Prayer Group, St. Raphaels -
Volunteer; [hon.] Cabrini Medical Center Service
Award - 1978, Central Savings Bank, Outstanding
Achievement Award - 1973; [pers.] With God all
things are possible. I love America and all it stands for
with its beautiful flag flying forever; [a.] Lehigh
Acres, FL

CARENAN, CONCEPCION C.
[b.] November 8, 1965, Balayan, Batangas Philip-
pines; [p.] Felix and Corazon Carenan; [m.] Single;
[ed.] High School, Balayan College; [occ.] Service
Staff; [hon.] Received two awards, first prize in essay
writing competition and third prize in poster making
competion.; [oth. writ.] Many poems published in TF
International Magazine, many poems published in
ITS Book of Collection of Poems. Essay for the same
magazien and poems for the "New" newsmagazine
for Filipino's; [pers.] My family, G.S.B. "Bubbles"
and the people around the world are the heart and
sould of my poems and my poems are the direct and
indirect songs of mankind.; [a.] San Juan, Balayan,
Batangas, PHilippines

CAREY, MALIKA S.
[Pen.] Mali Starr; [b.] June 15, 1970, Newark, NY;
[p.] Sandra Honore and Oscar Collins; [ch.] Keith
Carey; [ed.] Essex County College, Irvington High
School; [occ.] Student; [memb.] ECCO College news-
paper; [pers.] Never let anyone fool you into believ-
ing the impossible is unachievable. Make your dreams
and goals your reality never letting the words of others
hold you back; [a.] Newark, NJ

CARLSON, JANE E.
[Pen.] JEC; [b.] May 2, 1966, Jackson, MI; [p.] Jerry
Dean and Phyllis Jean Marshall; [m.] Raymond Lee
Carlson, June 29, 1985; [ch.] Rick Dean and Ashley
Brook; [ed.] Edwardsburg High, Cornel Univ,
Rockhurst College; [occ.] Office cashier, Martins
Supermarket, S.B. IN.; [hon.] "On Going Education;
Rock Hurst College", "Total Management; Cornel
Univ" (4) Awards of Merit for poems written for
"World of Poetry"; [oth. writ.] Published poem
"Bonded by Unmistaken Love", World of Poetry
contest; [pers.] Days go by before our eyes - slow

them down...look...see what fills those days...and then..."Remember When". Poetry is in your heart...Learning how to write it down, is the key!; [a.] South Bend, IN

CARNANA, KATHLEEN LYNN
[Pen.] Kat Carnana; [b.] January 3, 1964, Norfolk, VA; [p.] Will and Betty Klein Schmidt; [m.] Joseph A. Carnana, December 4, 1993; [ed.] High School; [occ.] Machine Operator, nail technician; [pers.] This poem is dedicated to all the abused and neglected children in the world. May God keep you and heal you. Love Kat!; [a.] St Charles, IL

CARR, WILLIAM IRA
[Pen.] Bill or William; [b.] December 30, 1954, Quantico, VA; [p.] Ira Carr and Gwen Carr; [m.] Meryle Noelani Carr, June 19, 1993; [ed.] BA English, Univ of Hawaii, attended UC Berkeley, La Jolla High School; [occ.] Self-employed; [oth. writ.] Some Sonnets; [pers.] I am grateful to Mr. McCann and Mr. Carey, Mu High School english teachers, for introducing me to poetry and literature; [a.] Honolulu, HI

CARRILLO, STEPHANIE
[Pen.] Liz; [b.] January 10, 1982, NYC; [p.] Jacqueline and Cecilo Gomez; [ed.] PS 76X - Bronx, NY, MS 135X - Bronx, NY; [occ.] Student in Middle School; [pers.] I have six sisters. My poems was written when I was 11 yrs old. I enjoy writing and hope to go to college one day.

CARROLL, ROBERTA
[b.] 1945, Windsor, Ontario, Canada; [p.] Mr. & Mrs. Fred Niven; [m.] Thomas Carroll; [ch.] Colleen and Alan, grandson-Todd; [ed.] St Rose High, St John's High Amherstburg, Canada; [occ.] Art Gallery Owner; [oth. writ.] Have compiled a book of poetry. Started writing seriously since 1963. (not published); [pers.] Would like to leave a book of poetry which depicts mooods or times in my life. Which by putting my feelings down helped me to see life a little lighter and got my feelings out.

CARROLLL, ERIN M.
[b.] August 28, 1980, Milw, WI; [p.] Susan and Joel; [ed.] Currently in 7th gr at Elmbrook Middle School; [occ.] Student; [memb.] Renegrades select soccer team, IDUC (I don't use club), Drama Club; [a.] Brookfield, WI

CARSON, TIMOTHEUS H.
[p.] (Late) Roberta Nellie Carson of Little Rock, AR; [m.] Lillian B. Carson, December 21, 1957; [ch.] Andrew Bryan Carson; [ed.] BA Butler Univ, Indiannapolis, IN; Theology - English Modern Languages, Indiannapolis, IN; MA Eng, French, German, Purdue Univ in conjunction with Univ of Paris French Indian Univ German; [occ.] Instructor of English Literature French and German, Amundsen H.S., Chicago, IL; [memb.] Chicago Teachers Union, American Teachers of French, American Teachers of German, American Teachers of Spanish, English Teachers Assoc Indiannapolis, Alliance Francoise Indiannapolis; [hon.] National Honor Society, Dean's List, Indiana Univ '63, Honorary Member of Southwest Regional Council YMCA, Student Christian Assoc, Honorary Presentation, 1967, An Hour With Timotheus Cousin, Indiannapolis, by National Poems in Society; [oth. writ.] (Autobiography) Unpublished: Novels: Stay Young Oh My Dreams, book lengthy manuscript TNILFLINT, Poetry with Greek subtitles; The Celebration of the Spirit, War Song of Africa: Cassette Tapes with original music and poetry and song of IFE, book manuscript: Writers of the Harlem Renaissance Suite of the Revolution in A minor, War Drums, cassette, volume II poetry; [pers.] My sister Mrs. Ruth Long always told me when I was growing up in Arkansas that life is a great war that we

must make our wounds our weapons. I, therefore, would add to that my world view: The last great frontier of nature is mankind; we must, therefore, preserve one another; [a.] Chicago, IL

CARTER, FRANCES
[b.] Iowa; [m.] Married; [ch.] Mother of three, grandmother of six; [oth. writ.] I am currently creating a collection of writings on what God has revealed in his word; [pers.] My poems, my songs paint life as I know it. My desire is for them to bring good to others; [a.] Mooers, NY

CARTER, JOHN A.
[Pen.] Cat; [b.] September 11, 1975, Gander, Newfoundland, Canada; [p.] W.C. Carter and Irene Carter; [ed.] Student at St Paul's High School. Through the Air Cadet program, familarization in Basic Training (1989); Junior Leaders (1990); Junior Instructors (1991); Aero-Engines Tech (1992). Scuba diving course through the PADE organization; [occ.] Student; [memb.] 537 Gander Royal Canadian Air Cadets. Instructing Photography; [hon.] Top Photographer (1992); [oth. writ.] A poem published in "Coming of Dawn"; [pers.] In my writing I try to express some of the feelings that I have at that time; [a.] Gander, Newfoundland, Canada

CARTER, PATRICIA N.
[Pen.] Patricia Nolan; [b.] June 21, 1930; [p.] Margaret and Robert Nolan; [m.] Merle B. Carter, January 17, 1979; [ch.] Robert, Randy, Jonathan, David and Daniel; [ed.] Spotsylvania High Virginia and Houston Bus College; [occ.] Retired; [memb.] Church of Christ, National Childrens Cancer Society, AARP, American Federation of Police Hall of Fame. National Parks Conservation and Committee to Preserve Social Security and Sedicare and Radio Advisory Board; [hon.] National Wheelchair Basketball Assn Cert for Fundraising, School Creative Writing Award, Fire and Safety Award; [oth. writ.] "Point of Interest", Saturday Evening Post, Comedic Children's Poetry. Currently writing an autobiography in fiction form. Also specialize in antidotes and short mystery stories; [pers.] My joy in creating is to glorify the "Lord", and as His instrument to inspire, perhaps, just one other soul to do the same; [a.] Rosenberg, TX

CASH, COLLEEN M.
[b.] April 27, 1947, W. Covina, CA; [p.] Bert and Olive Coltharp; [ch.] 2 daughters: Jenny and Kelly; [ed.] 14 yrs (including 2 yrs of college) - then 3 years of intense writing course in fiction writing; [occ.] Psych nurse at state hospital for criminally insane; [memb.] Digit Fund, United Way, World Vision; [oth. writ.] A novel about 3 spinster sisters living together, trying to survive each others others strong personalities. And many, many poems; [pers.] I've been writing since I was 10 yrs old, but only in the last 15 yrs did I take it seriously. I write about emotions I have actually experienced. Many of them I still cry over, but view them as therapeutic--for me and someone else; [a.] Redlands, CA

CASHERO, JOANN
[b.] December 17, 1932, Roseland, KS; [p.] Joseph Cashero, Esther Cashero; [ed.] Columbus High School; [occ.] Housekeeper and I'm studying flower arrangement; [memb.] The International Society of Poets, The Smithsonian Associates; [hon.] 6 awards, 3 plaques; [oth. writ.] Several poems published in small magazines throughout the US; [pers.] I am proud to be a part of poetry; [a.] Belleone, NE

CASSIDY, STEPHANEE
[b.] November 20, 1972, FL; [p.] Joyce Burnett, Ken Cassidy; [ed.] I'm going to Lake Howell High School. And am in the 9th grade; [oth. writ.] Never been published but too many to list; [pers.] I write all my poems from my heart. They are written from true

feelings that I've had or things that I've been throug Enjoy; [a.] Fern Park, FL

CASTANEDA, CLARISSA
[b.] January 13, 1979, Brawley, CA; [p.] Guillern and Cecilia Castaneda; [ed.] Freshman, 9th grad Central Union High School; [occ.] Student; [memb None at this time; [hon.] Science, student of t month, honor roll, calligraphy writing; [oth. writ Yes, but not published; [pers.] My writing express feelings that people might feel as they go through lif [a.] El Centro, CA

CASTILHO, LYDIA
[b.] January 22, 1936, Hong Kong; [p.] Vasco Gama Xavier (deceased), Melina Alvares Xavi (deceased); [m.] Albert Castilho, July 7, 1957 (Hong Kong; [ch.] Larry, Ken, Brian, Janice ar Linda; [ed.] St. Paul's School, Hong Kong Rockwe International, Seal Beach, CA; [occ.] Corporate Staf [memb.] United Macaista Assoc, Los Angeles, C/ Romance Writers Assoc, Orange County Chapte Los Angeles, CA; [hon.] English Literature an Social Studies; [oth. writ.] Several poems publishe in "Chasing Rainbows" and "Impressions" by Qu Books, "Golden Dreams" by Yes Press, "Poems the Century" by Suwannee Poetry, a collection poetry in "This Friendship Place" by L.C. Marketin short stories in various magazines; [pers.] I strive touch the lives of people in some small way k creating a place of beauty, peace and tranquility wi my writing. I have been very much influenced by t early romantic poets of our times; [a.] Torrance, C

CASTILLO, KARLA V.
[b.] March 20, 1974, Managua, Nicaragua; [p Roberto Castillo, Vilma Castillo; [occ.] Studen [memb.] National Forensic League; [pers.] The brea ing sun represents the beginning of a new day. Eac new day we keep walking through the path of ou lives, and hopefully wish to make them better wi each breaking sun. Life is a wonderful gift that shou not be wasted, just like true friends are special gif that should not be taken for granted. Many people wi enrich our lives, but true friends will make them eve more meaningful. I'm grateful for my life and fc having a friend who has not just been there for me, bu a person who has given a new meaning to every ne day for me; [a.] Thousand Oaks, CA

CASTILLO, TOMAS
[Pen.] Tomas; [b.] July 29, 1920, Manila, PI; [p Tomas Castillo, Perpetua De Mata; [m.] Jovita Arayata December 1, 1947; [ch.] Aurora Castillo, Ramo Castillo, Armando Castillo, Luming Cuajunc Florencia Blancafl; [ed.] Primary, Manila, P.I., E ementary, Manila, P.I., High School, San Diego CA, College, Chula Vista, CA; [occ.] U.S. Nav Retired 25 years, 17 yrs. serviced VA Medical Cent Dietetic Food Service Worker, taken care of disable veteran.; [memb.] Fleet Reserve Assoc., Senior Cit zen Assoc, Republican Presidential Task Force, Tar zanian Club, Philippines it. Cost me a fee of $3,00 Life membership since Oct. 1952 until Nov., activ Navy Good Conduct, 7 medals World War II, 1 Medals, VA Medical Center, 3350, La Jolla villag Dr., Three Award! Saving Lives of Patient! (Di abled), Medal of Merit from President Reasan, Med of Merit from Pres. Bush; [oth. writ.] "Have Whee Will Travel", "Water and Rice Will Rise", "Her Today! Gone Tomorrow", "Remember, The Golde Rule", "Then! Your Trouble, Are Over.""The Li You Save Might Be Your Own," "Take Some, Leav Some," "The One You Love! You Hurt The Most, "We Are All Renters, Born Naked! That Is The Nake Truth"; [a.] San Diego, CA

CAVANESS, LaVONDA
[b.] May 23, 1965, Paragould, AR; [p.] Odis and Ka Gilbee; [m.] William Todd Cavaness, June 16, 1984

n.] Nicholas Todd; [ed.] Greenway High School, olmes Junior College; [a.] Rector, AR

ELICO, ANDREA M.
,] May 19, 1973, Westerly, RI; [p.] Richard J. elico, Jr and Marjorie K. Celico; [ed.] Westerly gh School, Keene State College; [occ.] College dent; [hon.] Executive Editor of The Kronicle, The arbook of Keene State College, selected to attend ception for Natalie Babbitt in April 1993; [oth. rit.] This poem also published in Weaving Our ices III writing anthology, March 1994. Sponsored Women's Crisis Services, Keene, NH; [pers.] though circumstances may yield disappointment, e must continue to hope and be optimistic. Another n will always dry the rain; [a.] Westerly, RI

ERNIGLIA, JOSEPHINE
,] August 3, 1922, Brooklyn, NYC; [p.] Antonio d Severina Fiore; [m.] Stephen Cerniglia, June 17, '45; [ch.] JoAnna, Alice, Vincent; [ed.] Abraham ncoln High School, LaSalle Extention Institute; cc.] Retired; [pers.] So Soon Old, Too Late Smart, ou're Out in the Cold, Without Doing Your Part; [a.] een Acres City, FL

HAINEY, MARTHA L.
,] January 13, 1937, Lynn, MA; [p.] Alexander & abel Warden; [m.] Rudluff E. Chainey, Jr., Sep- mber 1, 1956 (Deceased); [ch.] Four, Cynthia L. ale, Michael E., Chainey, Darlene P. Renfrow, Lisa Hardage; [ed.] completed two years of college; cc.] Emplyed by U.S. Customs Service as a legal cretary for the past three years. Job location is at the wntown Dallas Office of Enforcement.; [memb.] SMBA, AARP, Coordinator for the Combined deral Campaign; [hon.] Elected to the Parish coun- at my former church. Very involved with church tivities, covering many years.; [oth. writ.] I have ritten many other poems and am presently working a novel.; [pers.] Lover of the great outdoors, pecially enjoying boating. Having a little talent in painting.; [a.] Desoto, TX

HALAR, LAURA
,] July 26, 1978, Montevideo, Uruguay; [m.] Julio 9) and Adriana (47); [ed.] Currently doing 6th grade aw), Elbio Fernandez High School, Montevideo, uguay; [occ.] Student; [hon.] 1st prize, 1988 ational Writing Contest; 1st Prize, 1991 Elbio rnandez High School Poetry Contest; [pers.] There e some very special people I would like to thank. nong those are my mom and dad, Rak, Nati, ossana, Adriana, Maria, Noel and flo, who always derstood me and encouraged me to keep on writing. d Willy. I love you. I'll always love you, no matter at; [a.] Montevideo, Uruguay

HAMBERS, CAROLYN S.
,] March 1, 1942, Texas; [p.] Van and Nina anuel; [m.] Terry Chambers, November 14, 1964; .] Corey Gregory and Kendra; [ed.] Feitshans gh School; [memb.] St John Baptist Church; [pers.] elieve in my personal salvation and the salvation of e world. But, right now, I'm in a state of wondering t real doubt, just wondering; [a.] Long Beach, CA

HAMBERS, GILLETTE BERTHA
,] June 26, 1915, Jackson, WY; [p.] Berla and mes Chambers; [m.] Wendell C. Gillette, June 6, 34; [ch.] Glen LaVon; [ed.] High School; [occ.] wner and operator of The Quilt House. Have made ore than 500 Quilts.; [memb.] The Church of Jesus rist of Latter Day Saints, Daughters of Utah oneers, Jackson Hole Museum.; [hon.] Have given any book reviews, readings, and actor in many ays; [oth. writ.] Book, Homesteading with The Elk. ort Stories, now I'll take the Diamonds, No More ack Sheep. Other poems and stage readings.; ers.] I strive to write so that both young, and old will

enjoy the contents. I prefer writing true stories. My book Homesteading with the Elk is a true story about the Early Homesteaders of Jackson Hole WY and 23,000 head of Elk eating the hay stacks; [a.] Victor, ID 83455

CHAMBLISS, SARAH JANE GORDON
[Pen.] Sarah G. Chambliss; [b.] November 3, 1937, Port Gibson; [p.] Mr. and Mrs. Anthony M. Gordon; [m.] A.C. Chambliss, December 24, 1959 (divorced); [ch.] Steven & Vanessa Chambliss; [ed.] Master's Degree and beyond; [occ.] Retired Teacher; [memb.] NEA, MEA, NCTE; COM BAAC, Inc. Founder, Advisory Board Member at Claiborne County Vo-Tech Center, Pine Grove Christian Church Choir President (20 yrs.), MS Cultural Crossroad Board Member (9 yrs.), School Newspaper Co-Editor; [hon.] Star Teacher, 1986 Head of English Dept. Quitman County High School, Head of English Dept. Delta Center High (Desota County); [oth. writ.] The Dark Day, The Beauty of America; [pers.] Godliness has no color. God does not force himself upon us; therefore, many of the circumstances of our lives are determined by the choices we make.; [a.] Port Gibson, MS

CHANDLER, VONDA MARIE
[b.] April 20, 1958, Hopewell, VA; [p.] Johnnie W. and Mary W. Base; [m.] Jacob Calvin Chandler Sr, June 6, 1987; [ch.] Christopher Shane Chandler; [ed.] Prince George Sr. High, America Inst of Banking, J. Sergeant Reynolds Community College, Southside, VA, Community College (presently enrolled); [occ.] Substitute Bus Driver - Brunswick County Schools Full-time student; [pers.] I have very strong emotional feelings and I try to express them through my writings so that other people may share them with me. I have always tried to find the best in everything and every-one; [a.] Ebony, VA

CHAPIN, ELIZABETH
[b.] March 4, 1979, Raleigh, NC; [p.] Gil & Mary Ellen Chapin; [ed.] Central Catholic 9th grader; [hon.] In 5th grade I won an Award of Merit for Outstanding Achievement in Language Arts, creative writing.

CHARIS, BARBARA
[b.] February 26, 1934, Pittsburgh, PA; [p.] Robert and Clara Wakefield; [m.] Divorced, 1956; [ch.] Mitchell, Heidi, David Markel and Tarri Markel Kuzmanic; [ed.] Taylor Allderdice HS, Penn State Univ, Columbia Pacific Univ, MS in Nutrition/ Holistic Health Sciences; [occ.] Health Researcher (33 yrs), started: Charis Holistic Center in 1981; [memb.] National Health Federation (lifetime); Book publicists of Southern California (17 yrs); [oth. writ.] Magazine writing: newspaper contributor and avid letter writer. Four manuscripts and 15 song copyrights. I started writing poetry at 7. Produced and wrote "The Health Beat" on American Radio Network in 1989; [pers.] "In my twenties love meant caring for people close to me; parents, children: spouse and friends. As I enter my sixties - love means caring for the creator, our globe, and all creations. I want to share my love by giving freely of the knowledge, which I have obtained from my journey; [a.] North Hollywood, CA

CHARLES (JR), ELSWORTH
[Pen.] C.S. Worth; [b.] April 25, 1973, Boston, MA; [p.] Merle Charles and Elsworth Charles, Sr; [ed.] Joseph P. Taravella High School. Sophomore at Boston Univ; [occ.] Student/Certified Pharmacy Technician; [memb.] Pre-Med Society, Minority Pre-Health Assoc; [hon.] 1st place - short story in District NAACP ACT - SO Competition. 2nd place - Accounting II in District Future Business Leaders of America Competition; [pers.] In my writing, I make a strong effort to adhere to the laws of universal balance. I allow for the positive and negative qualities of my

characters to be expressed and made noticeable to the reader(s); [a.] Boston, MA

CHARLES, PAUL J.
[b.] April 26, 1932, N.B. Canada; [p.] Mother living - Marjory Lengren; [m.] Joan (remarried), February 15, 1992; [ch.] Four grown sons from former marriage; [ed.] Basic country school in Alberta through JH, Ontario Matriculation through military, Officer staff academic upgrading and Pilot training, 29 yrs in Airforce. Retired with Major rank; [occ.] Manager Safety and Training, Briggs Bus Lines; [memb.] McClure United Church, Northern Alberta Computer Users Group, Royal Canadian Legion, R.C.A.F. Alliance; [hon.] Canadian Forces Decoration with clasp; [oth. writ.] Some childrens short stories and one novel of 32,000 words. None published. Contributed to military training manuals. Wrote Standard Operating Procedures for school bus operators; [pers.] As an outdoorsman, I have always been influenced by poets such as Robert Service and Badger Clark. I have never tried to write poetry, but find on the first try, that it's surprisingly relaxing; [a.] Edmonton, Alberta, Canada

CHATHAM-WOODS, ROBERT
[b.] August 16, 1983, Quebec; [p.] Errol, Barbara Chatham; [ed.] Grade 5; [occ.] Student; [memb.] Lakeside Swin Club, Pointe Claire Canoe Club; [hon.] Swim team ribbons, Badge of Merit for Cub Hobby Show, 9 yrs old when poem was written after seeing a film about Somalia and the suffering children. The teacher asked the class to write our thoughts. My poem is the result; [a.] Pointe Claire, Prov, Quebec

CHEAQUI, HELEN M.
[b.] April 21, 1914, Castleton, KS; [p.] Newell E. and Jessie M. Fountain; [m.] William M. Cheaqui, May 21, 1954; [ch.] Jack L. Crozzer and Elizabeth Joan Curth; [ed.] Graduated from Moline High School, Moline, KS; [occ.] Retired; [memb.] The United Methodist Church; [oth. writ.] Books of Poetry for family and friends, birthday poems, poems on different subjects, mostly religious. I draw the pictures and write the poems for my christmas cards. Poem "A Mother's Thoughts" published in The National Library of Poetry, "The Coming of Dawn."; [pers.] I try to refelct my feelings and thoughts and my faith in my poetry. It gives me a feeling of happiness and satisfaction that my poetry is enjoyed by my family and friends; [a.] Findlay, OH

CHEESEMAN, BARBARA JEAN
[b.] July 29, 1929, Junction City, Perry Co, OH; [p.] Eugene O. and Beatrice Rarick; [m.] James Royce Cheeseman, October 15, 1949; [ch.] Sharon, Deborah, Bonnie, Jean, Julie, (1 grand-daughter) Jessica; [ed.] High School graduate - JCJHS. Took a few classes at Bliss Business College - Columbus, OH and audited some classes of the Cinn Bible Seminary Extension School, CO; [occ.] Retired; [memb.] Currently, North Park Church of Christ, previously 43 yrs member of Northeast Church of Christ, Columbus, OH; [hon.] Teaching Certificates awarded for Bible School and V.B.S. work in churches; [oth. writ.] Compiled a history of the Northeast Church of Christ for a Remembrance Book, 1991. We merged with the Minerva Park Church and became the North Park Church of Christ. Letters to the Editor of the Columbus Dispatch and have had receipes published in the paper. This is my first poem; [a.] Before I was married, I did a sampler of the words of Edwin Markham, "All that we send into the lives of others, comes back into our own", and I try to live by that. As for poetry, I'm very much inspired by Love. "God so love . . . ." John 3:16; [a.] Columbus, OH

CHENOSKY, BRENDA M.
[b.] January 26, 1949, Vancouver, BC, Canada; [p.] Mr. & Mrs. E. F. Neifer; [m.] Graham Chenosky (deceased Aug 12, '92), September 11, 1971; [ch.] Tamara (Apr 12, 1974) Larissa (Apr 10, 1978); [ed.] Graduated, 1993 in June at SFU Von, BA (Kinesiology and Psychology); [occ.] Attending Abbotsford College to upgrade for librarian; [a.] Port Moody, British Columbia, Canada

CHIASSON, KENNETH
[b.] August 30, 1965, Lowell, MA; [ed.] B.A. in English, University of Massachusetts, Lowell; [oth. writ.] First published work; [pers.] I would like to dedicate my poem to my wife, Sandy, whose love has given me, more than anything else, my sense of peace and well-being in life.; [a.] Dracut, MA

CHIEM, LOC (KEVIN)
[Pen.] Kevin Chiem; [b.] July 4, 1978, Vietnam; [p.] Phung Chiem, Quang Chiem; [ed.] Freshman at San Gorgonio; [occ.] Student; [memb.] Blockbuster and Music Plus; [hon.] Student of the Year, Student of the Month, Sports Athletic, etc; [pers.] One of my greatest poets is Jim Morrison. We both have a similar taste in music and in poems. Most of these poems relates to some of the dramatic situations in our society, as well as inside a person's heart; [a.] Highland, CA

CHILBERG, LISA M.
[b.] March 21, 1975, David and Nancy Chilberg; [ed.] Graduating in 1994 from Jefferson County Open School, Lakewood, Colorado; [occ.] Student; [memb.] National Writers Club, Friends of Dinosaur Ridge; [hon.] Masonic Officers Assoc, Jr. Achievement Award, Second and First Place for Senior High Writing in 1990-91 and 1991-92 Jefferson County Schools PTA Reflections Contest; [oth. writ.] Written and produced a three act play, completed one novel and writing a second; [pers.] I am a college bound high school graduate who has yet to find a direction in life, but hopes to contribute to the arts and humanities; [a.] Littleton, CO

CHIN, RITH
[b.] December 10, 1977, Cambodia; [p.] Sauann Oun; [ed.] Mason Middle School, Lincoln High School; [occ.] Clay Art Center; [memb.] BMG Compact Disc Club, Boys and Girls Club.

CHOE, MIWHA
[Pen.] Nevets Murts; [b.] June 11, 1961, Pusan, Korea; [p.] Jeewoon Choe, Shinja Kim; [m.] Stephen Strum, May 29, 1961; [ed.] Graduated from Catholic Medical College in Seoul, Korea; [occ.] Registered Nurse; [oth. writ.] Collected poems of a soul in transition.; [pers.] Love is as love does.; [a.] Playa del Rey, CA

CHRISTOFF, ALEX V.
[p.] Vangel and Helen Christoff (dec'd); [m.] Barbara Christoff; [occ.] Wildlife Preservationist; [memb.] North Shaolin School, Martial Arts, Kung Fu, Hand to Hand Combat Instructor, US Army WWII; [oth. writ.] Poems published in several anthologies; [pers.] Man stretches his hand to distant moon, Infinity bound; yet, himself, earth bound, Coveting eternity's silent sound, Builds an unnamed, boundless tomb; [a.] Springwater, NY

CHRISTOFFERSEN, VIRGINIA ROSE
[Pen.] Virginia Rose Fitzgerald; [b.] November 4, 1918, New York City; [p.] Joseph F. Fitzgerald and Irene A. Sebold; [m.] Rolf Eric Christoffersen, October 1, 1944; [ch.] Dr. Gaye Christoffersen, Dr. Rolf E. Christoffersen, Jr., Robin Repp; [ed.] Finished Master's Program at Cal State, LA; [ed.] Hamilton Jr. High, Battin High in Elizabeth, NJ. Upper 1/3 of class 1936. Mt. San Antonio, AA, California State, BA NY

U Copywriting with C.B. Hotchkiss; [occ.] Writer; [memb.] Founder and Director of the "Valley Writers" in Covina, CA, Family RV Club of West Covina Vand Bakke Ski Club; [hon.] My children's success is my highest honor: Rolf Jr. is a bio-chemist, Gaye is a Political Scientist and Fulbright Scholar and Robin teaches Art and Photography, AA Mt San Antonio College, BA in English, California State College; [oth. writ.] Trilogy, Glory of the Geraldines includes Star of Destiny, The Lovers of Nest, Strongbow and the Sons of Princess Nest. (Unpublished-sending out) Many poems published. "The Door" is part of "The Lost Lake" - unpublished; [pers.] "Do it - and you will have the power"; [a.] West Covina, CA

CISNEROS-VALDEZ, ALVINA
[Pen.] Vina; [b.] January 16, 1971, Grand Junction, CO; [p.] Luis and Julia Cisneros; [m.] Alfred Valdez, April 28, 1986; [ch.] Julie Angel, Robert Anthony, Sheralynn Joanette; [occ.] AKC - Toy poodle breeder, fulltime homemaker - wife - and mother; [oth. writ.] This is my first publication. I've written numerous other poems which I hope also to get published in the near future; [pers.] I discovered the poet in me after the tragic loss of our youngest 17 month old baby girl, Sheralynn's accidental drowning death on April 3, 1992. To me poetry is the song within ones inner self and soul. It's expression should be to the fullest; [a.] Liberal, KS

CIZEK, FRED
[b.] Cedar Rapids, IA; [p.] Charles and Elsie Cizek; [m.] Florence (deceased); [ch.] 1 boy Roy (deceased); [ed.] Musician, Big Band Leader, Ballroom Operator, Ballroom Dance Teacher, Ballet, Home Builder and Designer, Traveling Photographer; [occ.] Traveling Photographer; [hon.] Music Director Boston Ballet while on vaudeville, Grand prize photo winner Chicago, Indiana State and Local, Magazine and Book Photos, Judge Miss Indiana America Contest; [pers.] While traveling all over the world including -- Galapagos Island, South America, Antartic, Russia, Israel, Africa, Australia, Java, India, Ireland, etc. I have found a most interesting and a wonderful way of life that I never thought existed; [a.] W. Terre Haute, Indiana

CLARK, JOAN EVELYN
[Pen.] Evelyn Sefton; [b.] August 24, 1924, Liverpool; [p.] Frank and Olive Leeson; [m.] Major Anthony Clark, May 24, 1950 (divorced 1969); [ch.] David, Lucinda, Paul and Joanne; [ed.] "La Sagesse" Convent School Liverpool, state registered nurse and health visitor; [occ.] Retired; [oth. writ.] "The Brooch" - a historical romance, due to be published this summer (1994); [pers.] I started to write when aged 68 - first with fairy stories for my young grandchildren - Christina and Michael - now living in Florida. Now I am just embarking on a second novel. Retirement should give all a second chance!; [a.] Llanrhystud, Wales, United Kingdom

CLARK, KIM
[Pen.] Kim Pennington; [b.] May 2, 1961, Ft Campbell, KY; [p.] Robert Paul Johnston, I, Laura Emilie Werger, Johnston; [m.] R. Kent Clark, September 8, 1993; [ch.] Shalimar Emily, Chanel Renee, Ariane Rachealle; [ed.] Loveland High; [occ.] Transfer driver, housewife; [oth. writ.] "Where do the tears Go" in the Coming of Dawn. Have written 91 poems. Have entered 38 in a contest due to be announced May, 1994, entitled "It's About Life"; [pers.] All of my poetry begins within my heart and soul and are actual pages of my life or the life of another person. Real life feelings; [a.] Wheatridge, CO

CLARK, KIM
[Pen.] Kim Clark; [b.] May 2, 1961, Ft Campbell, KY; [p.] Robert Johnston I, Laura Johnston; [m.] R. Kent Clark, September 8, 1993; [ch.] Shalimar Emily,

Chanel Renee, Ariane Rachealle; [ed.] Lovela High; [occ.] Housewife, mother; [oth. writ.] poems written one published in the 1993 antholog "The Coming of Dawn". Titled "Where Do T Tears Go?" by: Kimbery Pennington; [pers.] Each my poems reflect a page of my life. I also have the g of writing a page of someone else's life with love a accuracy, with an understanding of hearts and soul [a.] Wheatridge, CO

CLARK, LAURA
[b.] July 24, 1966, Brooklyn, NY; [ch.] Lisa Mar [ed.] Brooklyn College; [occ.] Computer Netwo Coordinator.

CLARK, MICHAEL DIANE
[Pen.] Shelly Bean; [b.] June 23, 1980, Radford; [p Donald and Angela Clark; [ed.] Air Base Elementar Aviano Elementary. Shaw Heights Elementary, Hi Hills Middle School, Pulaski Middle; [occ.] Studen [memb.] Crime Monitors; [hon.] Ace of the Wee Academic, Harp Awards, D.A.R.E; [pers.] My la grandfather inspired me in such a poem from t goodness that has within his heart. I hope to contin finding such inspirational subjects. My writing h always been influenced by my personal contac There's always some good in all people; [a.] Pulask VA

CLARK, PAULINE
[b.] July 30, 1925, Alleghany Co; [p.] Mr. & M T I. Craft; [m.] Richard G. Clark, January 7, 194 [ch.] Stephen Thomas Clark; [ed.] Covington Hi, Schl.; Virginia Western Community College [occ Retired; [memb.] Church of Jesus Christ of Latt Day Saints; [oth. writ.] I write short stories, poen and song lyrics; [pers.] Each new year I make commitment not through resolutions, but throu, activities and challenges that will enrich my life a my fellow man. My goal is to write poetry that w inspire and enrich the ones who read it; [a.] Bue Vista, VA

CLARK, STEPHANIE RAE
[b.] March 5, 1982, Saskatoon; [p.] Calvin Clark a dianne Moebis; [ed.] Attending Grade 6 at Bransk school, Saskatoon, Saskatchewan, Canada; [memb Member of the Saskatoon, Goldfins Swim Club; [a Saskatoo, Canada

CLARK, TODD A.
[b.] May 16, 1970, Newport, OR; [p.] Keith a Karen Clark; [m.] Nita Sue Clark, December 1 1992; [ed.] Graduated High School from Burrough High School in 1989; [occ.] Asst Supervisor, Achiev ment House, San Luis Obispo; [oth. writ.] Seven poems also published by National Library of Poetr Also, in progress of 1st book published by loc publishing facility; [pers.] An open heart is the key an open door; [a.] Morro Bay, CA

CLARK, WALTER REGINALD
[Pen.] M.C. Reality Remnant; [b.] June 6, 196 Harlem, NY; [p.] Amm McDonald and Walter V Clark, Jr.; [m.] Single; [ch.] none; [ed.] Graduate from Julia Richman H.S., NY 1985, went to Bron Community College, NY, from 1985-87 overall student average H.S., college; [occ.] Morgan static (postal office) NY; [memb.] Member of the Lon Beach Seventh Day Adventist Church, Thanks to a members, thanks to the McDonald family and m grandmother Ora Lee Scott.; [hon.] Valedictorian JHS 45, Harlem, NY in 9th grade gave class speec 1981. Thank you to my God son Jamal Deion Jam and his mother and employees at Morgan Post. Office, Stewart Family, Rick, and the Marshall Fam ily, Janie Ford, Molly Porter, Baptized in Adventi Church Summer 1991. Member of several chariti organizations. Also Deacon in training at my church [oth. writ.] Honorable Mentions.; [pers.] Also than

all my family and friens and my cousin in Balti-ore, MD. Also thanks to the Jackson Family, regory, Twanisha, Buzz in family. Thank you to all e people on the grand course, Peace to the nningham Family, and my uncle Gregory Clark in altimore, and to my grandmother Anna L. Nelson ho raised me. Thanks to the Miller family, and my mily in Norfolk, VA. Also Thanks to he Clark amily, Harris Family and members of the eobobaptist Church.; [a.] NY, NY

LARKE, LOIS
.] March 30, 1914, Winston Salem, NC; [p.] Archie and Annie P. Johnson; [m.] Joffre F. Clark (Dec.), ay 1, 1942; [ch.] Joffre T. Clark (dec), Marshall A. arke; [ed.] Palmer Memorial Junior College, Sedalia, C, Catholic Univ. America, George Wash. Univ.; cc.] Retired, Federal Gov., First line supervisor rgeon Generals Office; [memb.] International raphoanolysis Society, Advisory Council Savation rmy, Sherman Corp. Pleasant Plains Civic Assoc., ortheastern Presbyterian Church (sang in choir 47 ars.); [hon.] Awards Salvation Army. Many awards r poetry from World of Poetry, over period of major an 10 years from Edie Cole published in 4 books.; th. writ.] "Excerpts from the Journals of Annie ce" (my mother) Vantage, "Shorts and Shorts" antage, "Poetry" Vantage. Published over 10 usical compositions, Sunrise Records. Junc Artist any mediums); [pers.] I love all of God's children. o not trust all of Gods children. I pray for them. Be re brain is loaded before you shoot off at the mouth. ll of us are guilty); [a.] Washington, DC

LARKE, PAMELA SUE
n.] Pam Clarke; [b.] January 13, 1967, Melbourne, c.; [p.] Rev. Neville and Beth Clarke; [m.] not rried; [occ.] Office Manager for Seaview Elec-nic Services; [memb.] Lifetime member of The ternational Society of Poets and a member of their visory board.; [pers.] I am mostly influenced by the rld around me and the people I meet. Writing has en another way of expressing what I see, feel and perience in life.; [a.] Victoria, Australia

LARKSON, ROSA MARIA
.] Rosemary, Rose; [b.] December 15, 1971, cAllen, TX; [p.] Agustin & Beatrice Sanchez; [m.] avid Scott Clarkson, February 14, 1990; [ch.] erek Scott Clarkson, Devon Ray Clarkson, Dustin e Clarkson; [ed.] Georgetown High School; [occ.] ousewife; [oth. writ.] My Broken Heart, Is it Love, d others which I've kept to myself.; [pers.] What I e to write are subjects important to me. Ones which e can never give up on. Those which we can add eetness to; [a.] Georgetown, TX

LEMONS, CAREY L.
.] January 28, 1968, Phoenix, AZ; [p.] Haywood d Ruby Clemons; [ed.] Trade school, community llege; [occ.] Computer Boards maker; [hon.] Draft-g Technician Degree, others; [oth. writ.] Short ries and other poems (hobby only); [pers.] Writing ings out the person you really are and opens the ors to your lonely soul; [a.] Phoenix, AZ

LEMPSON, ALLAN
en.] Allan Stache Clempson; [b.] October 1, 1949, illiwack; [p.] Fred and Martha Clempson; [ch.] vin Clempson - daughter, Coby Clempson - son; d.] Graduated high school 1968 from Saint Lawrence llege, Ste Foy, PQ Canada the school no longer ists but in its heyday it was affiliated to Laval Univ; emb.] During high school I was a member of an gineers militia unit, lo field squadron based in the ande Alley Armories Quebec City. I attained the nk of corporal and usually spent my summers structing recruits at various locations in and around e city for which service I was paid a daily rate my st job; [oth. writ.] Over the last twenty years I have

compiled a complete book of poetry some of it is good, some of it is very good. Some of it is not so good; [pers.] In 1985, I suffered a brain stem anurism from which by some miracle I have recovered from almost completely. Due to this accident, I have to take medication every day probably for the rest of my life; [a.] Chilliwack, BC

CLERIN, CLAUDETTE LAURE
[Pen.] Claudette Aubert; [b.] May 13, 1921, Marseille, France; [p.] Andre and Elizabeth Eycoffon; [m.] Divorced from L. Roland Clerin; [ch.] David, Peter, Andre, Esther and grandchildren; [ed.] Lycee Longchamp in Marseille, studied classical diciplines, Latin, Old Greek, English. Also, diplomas for short-hand typist in French and English and translation; [occ.] Retired; [oth. writ.] Songs unpublished for which I wrote lyrics and words both in French and English; [pers.] I have been greatly influenced by my uncle Philippe Excoffon in Marseille who wrote "Madame de Lavalliere" inverdes (2.000) for which he got the French honor (Prix Jean Aicard). My parents loved poetry and I studied many wonderful poets both in French and English. My mother wrote poetry and a book; [a.] Miami, FL

CLIMOND, BETH M.
[b.] Bathfriland; [p.] deceased; [m.] John L. Climond, December 25, 1960; [ch.] 2 sons - Keith and Griffith; [ed.] Ineagh School; [occ.] Housewife; [oth. writ.] Several poems in book hope to print at later date for the public to read; [pers.] The sheer joy of knowing that these are inspired words and to actually see them in print; [a.] Bathfriland, Ireland

CLOWNEY, YLONDA k.
[Pen.] Kacey; [b.] August 2, 1960, Detroit, MI; [p.] Sharon Crawford, John Clowney; [ed.] Chadsey High School. I am studying to be a freelance writer with the ICS home study program; [memb.] Alpha Phi Omega "Chi Mu"; [oth. writ.] A Mother's Love, a poem I wrote for my mother; [pers.] Poetry is beauty in motion. I have been influenced by one of my favorite poets Maya Angelou. On a personal note: Strive to be and do the best that you can in what ever you do, that is all you can ask for; [a.] Detroit, MI

CLUXTON, RHODA (DOYLE, REED)
[b.] January 23, 1938, Nicholasville, KY; [p.] Mr. & Mrs. Edward Doyle; [m.] Donald W. Cluxton, May 29, 1976; [ch.] Sgt Michael Lee Reed (deceased), Deborah Lynn Hicks and Pamela Jean Hansford; [ed.] Completed Ged 1986, 1 yr typing and computer training, at Community Action and at Southern State Community College, Laurel Oaks, Wilmington, OH; [occ.] Wife, mother, grandmother and great grand-mother; [memb.] Pleasant Grove Church of God, Clarksville, OH; [hon.] Poem published in the "Space Between" The National Library of Poetry - 1993; [pers.] I have always loved poetry and was taught to recite in my earlier childhood days and it has been a inspiration to me all through my life, I hope my writing will inspire other young people to appreciate the love of poetry as I do; [a.] Wilmington, OH

COATES, JANICE GAIL
[Pen.] J. Coates; [b.] March 7, 1956, Dallas, TX; [ch.] two cats, Rastus and Timba; [ed.] Grand Praire High School, B.S. Texas A&M University; [occ.] Environmental Health Specialist, TX Dept. of Health; [memb.] Various professional organizations, Ameri-can Associaton of University Women; [hon.] Phi Kappa Phi, ETA Sigma Gamma; [oth. writ.] Cur-rently working on a collection of poems of and about the sea; [pers.] Music has long been my solace and my inspiration and has finally led me to pursue some of my dreams (i.e. publication). Better late than never!; [a.] Grand Prairie, TX

COBB, JR. JOSEPH WILLIAM
[Pen.] J.W.; [b.] February 1, 1946, Greenwood, MS; [p.] Joseph W. (Sr.) and Mary Ellen Cobb; [m.] Phellis Eileen Cobb, June 26, 1971, separated; [ch.] one son, Charles Michael Cobb; [ed.] Leflore co. High School, (Itta Bena, MS), MS Delta Community College (Moorhead, MS), Delta State U. (Cleveland, MS), U. Southern MS (Hattiesburg, MS); [occ.] Teacher of Special Education in Greenwood (MS) schools; [memb.] Miss. Educational Associaiton, Associaiton of Early Childhood, Christian Writer's Guild, First Baptist Church (Itta Bena, MS), Sunday School teacher and choir member.; [hon.] Phi Mu Alpha Sinfonia (Honorary Music Fraternity). Trea-surer and drill team for Woodmen of the World.; [oth. writ.] Newspaper articles to (Greenwood, MS) Com-monwealth and The (MS) Baptist Record: Open Letter to Leflore County Students. Christian Theme Parks? Various other articles about christian living.; [pers.] "For me to live is Christ.." (Philippians 1:21). For me to write is also Christ. By poetry or by prose, I wish to turn the world's philosophy to Jesus by His words in writing.; [a.] Itta Bena, MS

COBBS, CAROLYN
[Pen.] The Anointed Writer; [b.] October 17, 1957, Galveston, TX; [p.] Floyd & Florence Tottenham; [m.] September 18, 1978, deceased; [ch.] Rowsheka Cobbs; [ed.] LaMarque High School, College of the Mainland; [occ.] Instructional Assistan; [hon.] Per-fect, attendance grades 1-12, I have also received; [hon.] Tropies and awards for track and field events; [oth. writ.] I have written over 80 poems, I also read them at others churches and funerals. They have been received in over 200 or more homes and still grow-ing.; [pers.] God has anointed me to write poems to express His love and concern for his people. I strive to reflect the Glory of my God in every poem that I write.; [a.] Texas City, TX

COFFEE, CAROL DONNA
[Pen.] Carol Hammer; [b.] April 17, 1967, Pourthourn, MI; [p.] Mary and Myrtle Hammer; [m.] Age 26, 1989, Divorced January 8, 1992; [ch.] Gary Keith Hammer, Amanda Jean Coffee, Shelby Lynn Coffee; [ed.] Marion High School, Marion Mich., Pine River High Night School, Tusten Mich.m, Tresher Lake Job Corp., OK, Carpentry Course; [occ.] Single Mother of three with carpentry on the side; [memb.] Sooner classic car club, Lawton, OK 2 1/2 yrs.; [hon.] Several art contest in elemntary and junior high, two art contest submitted in newspaper in Kalkaska Mich. and several track awards in high school but none for poetry.; [oth. writ.] Several poems some like "Life is a Beach", "A Smile", "Angels", "Friends", "To the Man I Love," "Straight From the Heart," "Day Dreamin" and others and the song straight from the heart.; [pers.] My personal goal is to one day combine all my poetry and have my own book of poetry published so that I will be able to leave my one personal legacy so my own children will have a memory of my life and for the rest of the world to remember me to.; [a.] Tick Faw, LA

COHEN, ERIC
[Pen.] Eric a.k.a. Curly; [b.] April 25, 1962, Brook-lyn, NY; [p.] Leon and Hindi; [ed.] BA/Marketing; [occ.] Medical Sales; [pers.] My greatest satisfaction from my writing is the joy and pleasure it brings to others; [a.] Merrick, NY

COLBURN, HOLLY BETH
[b.] December 22, 1977, Hastings, NE; [p.] Marvin & Marjorie Colburn; [ed.] Student at Adams Central Jr., Sr. High School, Class of 96; [memb.] Jr. National Honor Society, National Honor Society; [hon.] Participant in "Women Investigating Science and the Environment" at the University of Nebraska, Lincol, "A" Honor Roll Student; [oth. writ.] A personal notebook of other poems, none published;

[pers.] When my friends aren't around, a pen and a piece of paper become my friend.; [a.] Juniata, NE

COLE, HELEN VICTORIA
[Pen.] Vic; [b.] February 15, 1908, SC; [p.] Levi, Mary Taylor Stephens; [m.] John B. Cole, July 12, 1930; [ch.] Leah Gray, Gloria Butler; [ed.] Armstrong High, Washington DC, Clatlint State College, Orangeberg, SC; [occ.] Elementary School Teacher, Bamberg, SC; [memb.] Mt Carmel ME Church Bamberg, SC, Trinity ME Orangeberg, SC, Macedonia AME, Flushing, NY, Stephens Amezion High Point, NC; [hon.] Loyal Dedication for Faithful Service. In church school and work place. Trips, pictures, and stories. Appreciation certificate for original artwork, poems and a speaker; [pers.] The bible has been my source of information. For it was God that made and created every living thing. My next place of is people and books, etc; [a.] NY, DCS, NC

COLEMAN, CHRISTINA
[Pen.] Baby Girl, Pickles; [b.] January 16, 1979, Baltimore, MD; [p.] Joseph Coleman & Victoria JOnes; [ed.] Parkdale H.S.; [oth. writ.] I wrote many other poems but never published them.; [pers.] I write in times whn my feelings are really strong for/against someone/something.; [a.] Berwyn Hts., MD

COLEMAN, HENRY D.
[b.] September 11, 1940, Wisner, LA; [p.] Leander and Frances Thomas Coleman; [ed.] BA degree in Sp Ed and Elem Ed, Southern Univ, A&M College graduate studies, NLU Monroe, LA, Holy Cross College, Loyola Univ NO LA; [occ.] Teacher/writer/actor; [memb.] Gloryland MT Gillion BL First District Baptist Assn, Southern Regional National You Conf, National Federation for Blind (JFT), Louisiana Take A Stand Against Drugs (SPETO); [hon.] Royal Ambassador Awards, Special Ed Teacher NFP - Drug Free Youth, NYP Drama and Special Olympics; [oth. writ.] More than 30 plays and skits. Several poems and essays and editorials; [pers.] I strive to reflect the reality of our human purpose and the appreciation of universal trues which challenge our determination and enlighten us to greater wisdom and understanding; [pers.] New Orleans, LA

COLEMAN, JOHN
[b.] April 6, 1902, Scotland; [p.] George and Agnes; [m.] Margaret Esther, February 16, 1929; [ch.] George, Margaret, John Jr.; [ed.] High school; [occ.] Retired; [memb.] Hugh Doyle Senior Center - Davis Ave, New Rochelle, NY. Poem published by above, Thanksgiving; [hon.] Book published, Hanpen Collin, name Legacies; [oth. writ.] Would like my poem published, Stand and Star, New Rochelle, NY; [a.] New Rochelle, NY

COLEMAN, NANCY A.
[Pen.] "Nants" Coleman; [b.] January 11, 1948; [p.] George and Jeanne Coleman; [m.] divorced; [ch.] Eric M. Hinkley (22 yrs), Nancy J. Hinkley (18 yrs); [ed.] High School; [oth. writ.] Wrote one poem that was printed in a small local town newspaper; [pers.] I have several more poems I've written, but never sent off to be published. You're is the first contest I've ever entered. I strive for honesty; [a.] Lititz, PA

COLEMAN, PHYLLIS
[b.] March 30, 1931, Columbus, OH; [m.] Robert K. Coleman, September 22, 1951; [ch.] Carolyn, Steve and Brent (deceased) and reason for my poem; [ed.] Columbus Business College; [occ.] Retired 12-17-93 after 33 1/2 yrs as secretary for the State of OH; [memb.] OH Federation of Republican Women, National Federation of Republican Women, Madison County Women's Republican Club; [hon.] Congressional Resolution on yrs of service with the State of OH. Also a resolution from Governor Voinovich of OH commending me for years of state service.

Awards from OH Federation of Republican Women for leadership role in local women's Republican club. Letters of commendation for my photography regarding ex-President Bush and also Governors and Congressmen and local officials; [oth. writ.] I have a collection of poems I hope to have published. All were written about my son, Brent, who died at age 29 (had a seizure in his sleep). I hope to have some of the proceeds to go to the Brent Coleman Memorial Fund to send children to summer camp; [pers.] My 26 poems I wrote for my son helped me get through my grief. I just wrote about everything concerning him. All his interest, etc. Some are long and story type. I have pictures I took of him and each poem is represented within a jpicture. I had a poem published in local newspapers remembering my son on his birthday and his death; [a.] Columbus, OH

COLLINS, PHOEBE W.
[Pen.] P. Collins; [b.] May 7, 1959, Wekh, W.VA; [p.] John C. Webb & Lillie Webb-Nester; [m.] Gary W. Collins, April 12, 1979; [ch.] Crystal Marie and Sarah Jean; [ed.] AAS Office Systems Technology, New River Community College; [occ.] Mother; [hon.] Dean's List; [pers.] I hope to always glorify and honor the Lord in all that I write.; [a.] Radford, VA

COLLINS, STEVE
[b.] July 4, 1975, Toronto, Ontario; [p.] Linda Armstrong, Jack Collins; [ed.] Orangeville Distric Secondary School; [occ.] Musician; [pers.] Emotions are meant to be felt and expressed, not explained; [a.] Orangeville, Ontario, Canada

COMBS, FRANCES
[b.] April 23, 1969, TN; [p.] Clyde and Louise Bolton; [m.] Barry W. Combs, October 5, 1993; [ch.] Nicole, Amanda, Ambarry Combs; [ed.] Majoring in Psychology, Walters State College - Morristown, TN, Powell Valley High School; [pers.] My wish is for all children to live every hour in peace; [a.] Harrogate, TN

CONNORS, RACHEL
[Pen.] Pokey; [b.] September 13, 1982, Upper Darby, PA; [p.] Kevin and Debra Conners; [ed.] 6th grade student, St Joseph Elementary School, Collingdale, PA; [occ.] Student and poet; [memb.] Briarcliffe Athletic Association; [pers.] I hope one day to be a famous poet and writer; [a.] Glenolden, PA

CONRAD, TERRANCE LEE
[b.] August 2, 1947, Lloydminster Sask, Canada; [p.] Loren Conrad and Helen Conrad; [m.] Isobel Conrad, September 23, 1968; [ch.] September 23, 1968; [ch.] Sean Jared, Lee Alan, Colleen Lauren; [ed.] Lloydminster Composite High School, NAIT, SAIT; [occ.] Power Engineer for Univ of Alberta; [oth. writ.] Cowboy Poetry and poems for and about friends and family; [pers.] I believe it is in love and in nothing else, that we find not only the supreme value of life, but also the supreme reality of life, and indeed, of the universe; [a.] Edmonton, Alberta, Canada

COONER, TAMI A.
[b.] October 3, 1982, Norfolk, VA; [p.] Gregory and Elvira Cooner; [m.] single; [ch.] one sister, Julie Dawn Conner; [ed.] Currently in 6th grade; [occ.] School; [hon.] Poetry award, City of VA Beach Poetry Contest; [hon.] Honor Roll Student 1st place poetry contest, city of VA Beach; [oth. writ.] Personal poems and short stories.; [pers.] I work toward saving the Earth and like to write poetry and short stories. I also enjoy art. My mom inspires me and is in my poems constantly.; [a.] VA Beach, VA

COONS, LEIGH ANN
[Pen.] Leigh Coons; [b.] October 6, 1983, Lou. KY; [p.] Greg and Nancy Coons; [ed.] 4th grade Riverside Elementary School, Jeff. Indiana; [occ.] Student in

school; [memb.] YMCA; [hon.] Honor Roll, chee leader Award and Basket Ball Player Award, Hono for not missing school; [pers.] I also like to d gymnastics and like to hang out with my friends.; [a Jeff, IN

COOPER (JR), ROBERT L.
[Pen.] Robert "Buster" Cooper; [b.] November 1(1946, Zwolle, LA; [p.] Anna, Ruby and Esau Gipsor [ch.] Sonnie, Sherry and Chris; [occ.] Disabled Ve [hon.] Golden Poet Award, Award of Merit fc poems; [oth. writ.] "Let Me See Texas", "Moving T Dallas", "Troubles", "Black I am", "444", "Stanc off In Waco", "1619", "Mahummad Ali", "Youn Men", "Dreamin", "You Are Mother", "Old Man and 3 to 4,000 more poems; [pers.] For one to kno others, they must know oneself; [a.] Dallas, TX

COOPER, BILLIE A.
[b.] October 25, 1927, MO; [p.] W.S. and Sara Cooper; [ed.] University of Colorado; [occ.] Retiree Telecommunications Specialist; [memb.] Valley Vie Bible Church, D.A.R.; [hon.] Beta Gamma Sigm [oth. writ.] Poems and other writings in churc publications.; [a.] Phoenix, AZ

CORAYANNIS, CONSTANTIN A.P.
[Pen.] Constant Dean Apollo Karayans; [b.] Octobe 22, 1919, Nafpactos, Greece; [p.] Apostolo: Anastasia; [m.] Future, Oreo Cookie, not yet se [ch.] from previous marriage, one boy, Pa Corayannis; [ed.] Graduate from Plate Academy fe Teachers. College of Baltimore in General Educa tion. AA Degree Morgan State University in Genera Clinical-Therapeutic Nutrition, Human Ecolog Business Degree; [occ.] Teaching; [memb.] Hellen Nutritionists Association. Hellenic Poets Club an Teachers Club.; [hon.] Dean's List Morgan Sta University, Honoree, Trophy and $5,000 in 198: 1983-84 Marayland Senatorial Scholarship; [ot] writ.] Language: Learn Greek in One Week, Lessor Recorded, Teachers and Retaining; Science: How t become elite as a scientist, Deontology 2, How t Avoid Numerous Mistakes, Deontology 1, Biomed cal Terminology, Dietetics for In and Out (Nosokomeion, Logotechny: Lessons of Poetry, L Ronde de Vie (poems and songs), Dialogues, man theatrical plays, scripts and stories. Roots of Word [pers.] Contrary to the destroyers of poetry, thos who always present an abstrusus mental reaction t the matter, my efforts tend to approach the lyric an the realism guiding to didactic and useful; [a.] Ch cago, IL

CORDONNIER, DON E.
[b.] March 21, 1956, Sidney, OH; [p.] Clarenc Cordonnier and Alvina (Bender) Cordonnier; [m Jean (Miller) Cordonnier, September 9, 1989; [ed Russia High School, Edison State College; [memb Big Brother/Big Sister; [hon.] Dean's List; [pers. try to never lose sight of the truth; [a.] Piqua, OH

CORNACCHIA, AUGUST
[Pen.] "Uncle Augie"; [b.] June 20, 1919, Detroi MI; [m.] Irene L. Cornacchia, February 21, 197([ed.] High School; [occ.] Retired Contractor; [memb Many antique auto clubs; [pers.] I have compose many poems, which I call rhyming verses. Most c these were for special occasions, such as birthday: weddings, funerals retirements, or just friendshir They are usually a spur of the moment thing and ar well liked. Some have been included in the antique ca club publications, which we belong to. My Motto "Anything that brings forth happiness and smiles i worth doing" - Uncle Augie.

CORR, MICHAEL WILLIAM
[Pen.] Degrees: B.S., M.A., M.A., Ph.D.; [b. November 14, 1940, Seattle Washington; [p.] M William John and Ms. Cecilia Corr; [m.] Ms. Kinuy

atsuda (b. Okazaki, Japan), November 13, 1980;
h.] Mr. Anders Schwartz (Childs) Corr, born to Dr.
arbara Francis S.C. Corr, M.A., Chin. Lit., Harvard;
1.C., Univ. of Wash.; [ed.] B.S., Antioch College,
athematics, 1963, M.A. Univ. of Washington,
065, M.A., Geography, U. of Wash., 1981, Ph.D.,
niv. of Washington, Medical Photo-geography, 18
ov. 1985. Kyoto Japanese Language School 68,1
' Candidacy in Philosophy required examinations in
hnobiology, cultural geography, and anthropology
Chinese religion, passed in 1983.; [occ.] Part time
ofessor, English Dept. of Linguistics and Culture,
agoya Univ., and Japanese Welfare University at
ihamatown); [memb.] To many to list.; [hon.] To
any to list; [oth. writ.] To many to list; [pers.] My
mily seems to have been influenced by Harvard
ilosophy professor Douglas Steere, whom I only
ard late in my education. His friends interested me
Buddhism resulting in an introduction to the priest-
od of the Rinzai Sect. of Zen Buddhism. It is the
ly liturgy I remember, and I translate from it. It is
y wives' sect. Tho I seek it, I can only find the way
humanism ala Sartre. Questioned by a Mongolian
eoretical physicist, I remembered from the vows of
y first marriage: "God is that which makes it
ssible for us to love one-another." My 2nd mar-
age is simply "holy."; [a.] WA

ORRAL, AGUIRRE GUILLERMO
en.] Guillermo Corral; [b.] February 23, 1936,
exico; [p.] Silvano Corral and Sara Aguirre; [m.]
nsuelo Corral, July 28, 1957; [ch.] (Five) Guillermo,
orma, Hector, Laura and Silvano; [ed.] Junior
ollege and Technician; [occ.] Refrigeration and
pliance and heating; [memb.] Knights of Columbus
h and 3rd degree, PTA Board Member, Small
siness Administration, National Federation of Small
siness, St. Francis Church Chamber of Commerce;
on.] Faithful navigator of 4th degree, soft ball
ampionship trophies, bowling, sales man of the
ar 1964 in pepsi cola, Intertherm Seal Systems
74, Stanford Univ from the Students, PTA Presi-
nt 1971 and The National Assessment Inst 1990;
th. writ.] My Parents the Bible and I, plus commen-
ries, Poems in local newspaper specials; [pers.] We
ust all help preserve our ecology in order to survive;
] Gallup, NM

OSTA, MARIE C.
en.] MC; [b.] 60+, NYC; [p.] Anthony and Mar-
ret Messina; [m.] Divorced; [ch.] Cherie M. Bonnie
, Stacey M; [ed.] High School; [occ.] R.E. Broker,
tired; [memb.] Servants of Jesus and Mary; [oth.
it.] Short stories, poems, letters from the heart;
ers.] My education scholastically is limited, my
ind and mental capacity unlimited. My thoughts
ep, profound from the recess of my heart; [a.] Kings
rk, NY

OTTON, DAISY L.
] September 6, 1936, Shreveport, LA; [p.] Leola
avis and the late Raymond Davis; [m.] Joe W.
otton, March 11, 1962; [ch.] Douglas, Darryll,
ith and Dale Cotton; [ed.] Ventura Jr. High School
entura Jr. College, Cal State University, Northridge;
cc.] Disability Retirement; [memb.] Trinity Baptist
urch, Ventura Hospice; [oth. writ.] Many others,
e book "Death and Dying for Children", not
blished. One essay in school paper in 1977.; [pers.]
riting for me is like giving birth another time…there
yet so much to be delivered. My inspiration Maya
gelou; [a.] Oxnard, CA

OUGHLIN, DANNY
ers.] Life has its darker moments, but then night
rives with its forbidden promises and rings of fire.;
] Peoria, AZ

COVEY, KAREN
[b.] October 6, 1959, Pulaski, VA; [p.] David and
Jean Covey; [ed.] BA Radford University, MFA
Virginia Commonwealth University; [occ.] Professor
of Speech/Drama New River Community College;
[pers.] By embracing the past we realize our future.;
[a.] Pulaski, VA

COVINGTON, BERNARD A.
[b.] November 6, 1947, New York City; [p.] Grace
and Frederick Covington; [m.] Tina Marie Covington;
[ch.] Edith Jacynthia, Connie Kay, Shuana Kaiesha,
Keith Jamaal, Eva Monie; [hon.] Viet Nam Vet;
[pers.] I love to write about the lessons and blessings
of life. To keep what you have you must give it away;
[a.] Redwood City, CA

COX, MARCIA E.
[b.] December 26, 1959, Monterey County; [p.]
Raymond L. & Ina B. Smith of San Antonio, TX; [ch.]
Tara Marie 12, Tala Danielle 8; [ed.] Widefield High
School, Cal. State Univ., Sacramento; [occ.] Gradu-
ate student in the MBA program, International Stud-
ies, Univ. of Colorado, Colorado Springs.; [oth.
writ.] Senior Class Poem, stories for Guideposts,
helped Tara with her writings, one of which may soon
be published as a book called The Magnificent blue
Whale; [pers.] Live life, each and every day to the
fullest, smell the roses, experience the newness after
a rainfall, contemplate the wonders of life even amidst
the storms, gaze upon sleeping children often, be
thankful always, and smile a lot! Have travelled
extensively and lived in many countries, including
Germany, Iceland, Israel Egypt and the Seychelles
Island; [a.] Colorado Springs, CO

COX, MILDRED
[Pen.] Gigi, BX; [b.] February 23, 1968, Bronx, NY;
[p.] Samuel and Migdalia Vazquez; [m.] Desmond
Cox Jr., October 13, 1990; [ch.] Faith, Desiree,
Cheryse, Jaymie; [ed.] Graduated 1986, Jane Addams
Vocational High School; [occ.] A Collator at Newsday
Inc., Melville, NY (Newspaper); [pers.] I love to
make people smile.; [a.] North Babylon, NY

COX, MITCH
[b.] April 26, 1960, NC; [p.] Cornell/Marlene Cox;
[m.] separated; [ch.] Liam Cox (age 10), Jacob Cox
(age 7); [ed.] BA Wake Forest Univ (English), MA
(English) Duke Univ; [occ.] Teacher; [memb.] Na-
tional Council of Teachers of English, North Carolina
English Teacher's Assoc, Phi Delta Kappa; [hon.] Phi
Beta Kappa (Delta Chapter, Wake Forest Univ) -
1982, Hankins Scholarship - Wake Forest Univ -
(1978-1982). Finalist in Tennessee Writer's Alliance
Fiction Competion 1993; [oth. writ.] Articles in
English Journal, Phi Delta Kappan, "Plane View"
(poem) in Coastal Plains Poetry; [a.] Mebane, NC

CRAINE, KERRI
[b.] August 17, 1981, Johnstown, PA; [p.] Ed & Ann
Craine; [ed.] 7th grade student at Penn Cambria
Middle School in Lilly, PA; [a.] Lilly, PA

CRANFORD, RALPH L.
[Pen.] Ralph Locke; [b.] July 17, 1926, Burke Co,
NC; [p.] George D. Cranford and Oaklone Shuffler
Cranford; [m.] Charlotte Travis Cranford; [m.] Char-
lotte Travis Cranford, March 29, 1947; [ch.] Walter,
Michael, Charlene, Lisa; [ed.] High School - Bells
Creek College - Clevenger Business, completed 2 yrs
Business Administration, Business Law and Account-
ing, and other; [occ.] A volunteer Tutor at CVCC,
Hickory, NC. Currently Tutor English Literacy at
The Catawba Valley Community College. Do Meals
on Wheels For Seniors. Also do volunteer work for
them. The Catawba County Social Services office;
[memb.] Mt. Olive Lutheran Church Lutheran
Laymens League, The Bible-a month Club, Songwriters
Club of America. Top 100 Songwriters Club; [hon.]

Golden Poets award, 1989, 1990, 1991 and 1992.
Silver Poets award for other poems the same years.
Hollywood Gold Record, songwriters award. Various
awards and honors for poems entered in other publi-
cations. It has indeed been an honor to have some of
my poems published by The National Library of
Poetry; [oth. writ.] To date I have authored more than
1,000 Poems, 34 of which has been set to music. Have
self-published three poem books. One How-To-
Manual, and I am presently working on several
manuscripts for books. "I Believe in Angels", "The
Covenant of the Triune God" and God's Laws Versus
Man's Laws"; [pers.] (The Lion Has Laid Down With
The Lamb) (Russia and The Free Nations). I believe
that the days spoken of by the Prophet Daniel, By
Jesus Christ, and His Chosen Apostles is fast ap-
proaching and if I can proclaim the word of God
through Poetry, or other writings, to make people
aware of the returning Lord, I will proclaim it when
ever, or wherever the opportunity arrives. I also
believe that the sinfulness we see around us everyday,
and the signs sent from God in the past year or more
(Tornados, floods, earthquakes) is proof; [a.] New-
ton, NC

CRIBBETT, KATHY R.
[b.] March 31, 1962, Gibson City, IL; [p.] Orville and
Marlene Kupferschmid; [m.] Randy Cribbett; [ed.]
High School. I was recently excepted at the "Institute
of Children's Literature", as a student; [occ.] House-
wife and mother; [oth. writ.] I have written other
poems besides, "The Footprints in the Sand", but this
is the first time I have ever shared my poetry with
anyone. So therefore, I have never been published
before; [pers.] I am very honored to have been chosen
to be published in this very wonderful book. I am so
pleased to be able to share one of my poems with
others; [a.] Forrest, IL

CROMWELL, TAWNYA S.
[Pen.] Tawnya S. Cromwell; [b.] July 7, 1971,
Walnut Creek, CA; [p.] Sheila Leonard and George
Dunaway; [m.] Tim A. Cromwell, February 16,
1991; [ed.] Mt. Diablo High, Universal Beauty Acad-
emy, DVC Community College; [occ.] Cromwell's
Welding Co - clerical assistant; [memb.] Inst of
Children's Literature. Long Ridge Writer's Assoc;
[hon.] I am honored by all who appreciate my
writings. National Library of Poetry; [oth. writ.]
Being born only by chance; [pers.] I strive to write the
goodness of mankind in my poems. I love all my
family dearly; [a.] Concord, CA

CROUCH, MELISSA
[b.] August 9, 1979, Eastview; [p.] James and Lynda
Crouch; [ed.] Freshman in High School; [pers.]
Dedicated to Andrew Jay Gallagher; [a.] Eastview,
KY

CROW, ED LITTLE
[Pen.] Ed Little Crow a.k.a. Little Crow; [b.] Novem-
ber 5, 1941, Ft. Thompson, SD; [p.] Belva and Cecil
Crow; [m.] Sherry H. Stephens, November 10, 1982;
[ch.] Lillian, Kenny, Ron, Raylynn; [ed.] AA degree
- Milwaukee Area Technical college Wisconsin; [occ.]
Indian Affairs Culturist; Lecturer; Advisor; [memb.]
Advisory Council for American Indian Culture Cen-
ter; Founder of Native American Action Committee
for Cultural Perservation; Board Member Williamette
Valley Sacred Sites Committee; [oth. writ.] Poems
published in Wanbli Ho Journal Sinte Gleska College,
SD; Go in Beauty Peace Be With You, by Mary
Eberdt; various periodicals; [pers.] My culture is
being erased from the footnotes of history through
assination, a cultivation, and progress. As an inactive
activist my poems are one way of keeping my culture
alive in the minds of the population; [a.] Veneta, OR

CROW, FELICIA DIANE
[Pen.] Flea; [b.] January 14, 1964, Kaufman; [p.] Bob and Wanda Gunnels; [m.] Scott Crow, April 2, 1983, Brandon Scott Crow (age 4yrs); [ed.] High school graduate, some AIB banking courses; [occ.] Student; [hon.] UIL ready writing; [oth. writ.] I've written lots of poems and songs through the years, but I haven't done anything with them; [pers.] I am happiest when I can make a difference in someone and helping them in some way. I have many thoughts and feelings and express them in writing; [a.] Kemp, TX

CROWDER, STEVEN K.
[b.] March 13, 1960, Evansville, IN; [p.] Rev Rex and Margaret Wallace; [ch.] Roman; [ed.] New Palestine High School, New Palestine, IN; [occ.] Maintenance Supervisor, National Park Service; [hon.] Published author, distinguished army veteran with overseas service; [oth. writ.] Lowen; Lowen II; poems published in Philadelphia's Poetry Forum.

CRUM, GRACE
[Pen.] Candy Williams; [p.] Anna Gaines; [ch.] Sharon, James; [ed.] Cambridge Academy, Harding Business College, Mid America Police Academy; [occ.] Police Officer; [memb.] Police Constable Assn; [oth. writ.] I am currently in the process of finding a publisher for my songs and poems; [pers.] My personal goal is to become a singer and songwriter. My songs were inspired by the late Hank Williams, Sr; [a.] Youngstown, OH

CRUZ, LINA ANASTACIA R.
[Pen.] Linda R. Cruz; [b.] Manila, Philippines; [p.] Pablo and Anastacia R. Cruz; [m.] (deceased) Delfin R. Bacho, 1952; [ch.] Joey C. Bacho, Eddie C. Bacho; [ed.] Bachelor's degree in Education, graduated/completed paralegal course, completed secretarial course; [occ.] County personnel, secretary, stenographer; [memb.] Secretary, Gen Gouglas MacArthur Memorial Foundation (Philippines), Board Secretary, Filipino-American Community in LA, Coalition of Filipino World War II Veterans; [hon.] Honor student, Elem and high school, International Poet of Merit Award from ISP, various certificates of appreciation from the American Legion, Veterans Federation of the Philippines, Loyalty and Dedicated Service to Veterans, scholarship granted in high school; [oth. writ.] Several poems published in various local newspapers, like California Examiner, Herald, LA Press, Mabuhay Mirror. Essays and term papers on various subject matters (Abortion, World War II, Capture and Trial of Yaruaslita); [pers.] 1. Do unto others what you would want others do unto you, 2. If there is a will, there's a way, 3. God helps those who help themselves, 4. Give your smile to everyone, but your heart to only one, 5. Enjoy being of service to others, particularly to veterans, 6. Have faith in the creator; [a.] Los Angeles, CA

CRUZ, VICTORIA A.
[b.] September 23, 1979, Laredo, TX; [p.] Mr. and Mrs. Eduardo Cruz, Jr.; [ed.] 8th grade student; [occ.] Full-time student; [hon.] 1. National Jr Honor Society, 2. Honor Roll, 3. Texas A&M Academic, Enhancement Program; [oth. writ.] Other poems at home; [pers.] I like to write about people who have been an inspiration in my life; [a.] Laredo, TX

CULBERTSON, D. JUNE
[b.] March 2, 1966, Eureka, CA; [p.] Elaine Culbertson; [ch.] Trisha Culbertson (age 7), Barbara Culbertson (age 5); [ed.] Del Norte High Crescent, City College of the Redwoods - Crescent City, Humboldt State Univ; [occ.] Student; [memb.] Member Social Work Club and National Assoc of Social Workers; [oth. writ.] Have had other works published in poetry magazines at College of Redwoods Crescent City, CA; [pers.] My life is my notebook. My work comes from the heart. I live life on lifes terms and am never disappointed with what it offers; [a.] Arcata, CA

CULBRETH, ADA B.
[b.] June 3, 1938, Shelby, NC; [p.] John H. Burson Sr. and Ada S. Burson; [m.] Ollie E. Culbreth Jr., October 22, 1960; [ch.] Lisa M. Culbreth, Donna M. Culbreth, Ollie E. Culbreth III Grand-daughter, Ada E.; [ed.] Washington High Sch., Shelby, NC, Jersey City State College, JC, NJ, BA Degree, MA Degree; [occ.] Teacher, public school #22, Jersey City, New Jersey, Public Speaker, Workshop Instructor.; [memb.] JCEA, NJEA, NEA, Educational associations. NAACP, Smithsonian Assoc., Saint Aloysius parent guild.; [hon.] Education consultant, Asst. Dean local Association, served as Director of Christian Education, Salem Baptist Ch. Program Dir. Youth Advisor, Scholarship Com.; [hon.] Deans list college, Honored for outstanding work in the fields of Education, Religion and Community work, Outstanding Woman of Am.; [oth. writ.] Articles, written a book on Teaching career. Have written over seventy-five speeches.; [pers.] My goal in writing poetry is to show the true meaning of life through writing; [a.] Jersey City, NJ

CULVER, RUTH
[b.] February 26, 1939, W. Germany; [p.] Marta Nusshag nee: Jensen Richard Nusshag; [m.] Edward T. Culver, Jr, November 28, 1958; [ch.] Barbara Bewley and Edwina Richards; [ed.] Boppard a/Rhein 2 yrs Home Economics; [occ.] Housewife, part-time interpreter for Municipal Court; [memb.] Previous member of Mid-Atlantic Independent Newsdealers Association; [hon.] Editor's Choice Award 1993, National Library of Poetry; [oth. writ.] Five poems to be published in the summer of 1994 by Sparrowgrass Poetry Forum. Unpublished Children's Christmas story and book of poems; [pers.] I need a dictionary. My imagination, heart, and soul rhyme it in a poem; [a.] Mays Landing, NJ

CUNNINGHAM (Jr), LEO GUINN
[b.] October 25, 1959, Kansas City, MO; [p.] Leo G. and Batty K. Cunningham; [ed.] Raytown Senior High School, Raytown, MO. Bailey Technical School - auto mechanics school - Kansas City, MO; [occ.] Unemployed; [a.] Independence, MO

CURL, MARK
[b.] June 16, 1954, Detroit, MI; [p.] Mack and Joan Curl; [m.] Douglas Hupp, February 5, 1978; [ed.] Melvindale, H.S., Valley College; [occ.] Retired Manager for Pacific Bell; [memb.] Human Rights Campaign Fund, G.L.A.A.D., American Health Foundation of Los Angeles - Hospice Support for People With AIDS; [hon.] Screen acknowledgement for my work on the movie "Hello and Goodbye". Major article done on my life in Michigan's 2nd largest newspaper; [oth. writ.] Several of my poems have been published in Los Angeles and Nashville; [pers.] I am very involved in human rights, especially those of gays and lesbians. And in God's Kingdom, He loves us one and all; [a.] Sherman Oaks, CA

CURREY, GARRY M.
[Pen.] Grey Raven and Sam Boyce; [b.] June 24, 1951, Roblin; [p.] Merle and Louise Currey; [ch.] Pets: Budgies, Cats, Turtle all wildlife "Children of the World"; [ed.] Broadcasting Graduate, Naitonal Inst. of Broadcasting Canadian Coaching Cert.; [occ.] Private Music Teacher; [memb.] My Creation "Guardians of the Earth Dreams & Space" G.E.O.S. I am the Director, Humane Society, Red Cross; [hon.] Gold, Silver and Bronze Medal; [oth. writ.] Many poems and songs that need publising.; [pers.] If I could stop animal cruelty I would. If I can share the knowledge of God and nature I will. I cry for all the pain, mother earth feels. I want to buy up all natural habitat and create sanctuarys.; [a.] Wpg. Manitoba

CWIKLA, MICHAEL
[b.] December 15, 1977, Fall River, MA; [p.] Ke Cwikla, Barbara Page; [ed.] Sophomore at Bisho Connolly High School, Fall River, MA; [occ.] Stu dent; [oth. writ.] My only other published work wa a poem entitled "Lone" - it was published locally [pers.] In my poetry, I try to top into those genuine happy and nostalgic feelings that no one can reall label or put a finger on; [a.] Somerset, MA

CZARNECKI, JEREMY M.
[b.] October 15, 1982, Ft Carson, CO; [p.] Mark an Dawn Czarnecki; [ed.] Currently in 5th grade; [memb Cub Scouts; [a.] Bellevue, IA

D'ALIMONTE, DAN
[b.] September 13, 1953, Windsor; [ed.] Bachelor Education Honours Degree - English and Philosophy [occ.] Supply Teachery General Labourer; [pers.] consider none of my poetry complete unless it end with the reader's "wow". This is what I aim for in m writing; [a.] Amherstburg, Ontario, Canada

DADEY, JO-ANNE I.
[b.] September 24, 1961, Peterborough, Ontario; [p. Cathy Bacon, Joe Carr; [m.] Dwight E. Dadey, Jul 23, 1983; [ch.] Robin Kayla - Ann Dadey; [occ. Housewife and mom; [oth. writ.] Other poetry writ ten, but none published as of yet; [pers.] I have n other published works, but am currently working o a series of children's books. My husband will be doin the ilustrations for them; [a.] Calgary, Alta

DALANGIN, CRYSTAL
[b.] March 11, 1981, Baltimore, MD; [p.] John an Susan Dalangin; [ed.] Lansdowne Elementary an Arbutus Middle School; [hon.] Presidential Aca demic Achievement Award; [pers.] I try with my be efforts to show the love, happiness, and goodness i life, in my poetry; [a.] Baltimore, MD

DALIOUS, HAROLD G.
[b.] December 10, 1963, Bloomsburg, PA; [p.] Pau and Marguerite Dalious; [m.] Barbara S. August 16 1986; [ch.] Alexander Kyle, Samantha Nicole; [ed. Bloomsburg Area High School, Williamsport Are Community College (Penn State School of Techno ogy); [occ.] Restaurant Manager; [memb.] Interna tional Thespian Society, Lincoln Lanes Mixed Couple Bowling League; [oth. writ.] "Without You", pub lished in the National Library of Poetry's The Comin, of Dawn; [a.] Chambersburg, PA 17201

DANIEL, VALERIE
[Pen.] nee: Auffray; [b.] November 24, 1954 Vancouver, B.C.; [p.] Princess Januanade Bourbo and Dr. Jean Paul Auffray; [m.] Michael R. Daniel [ch.] Naomi Lara, Sebastian Thoms, Sterling James [occ.] homemaker; [pers.] Poetry to me is an antedot to an era of black and whites, where in there is littl nor no time for reflection, beauty or praise. I somehow manages to slip through and open a gatewa to a larger understanding of human natue and th world around us, thereby creating a moments t pause, wonder and find a momentary stillness in ou driven lives; [a.] Bethel, VT

DANIELS, KATHLEEN
[Pen.] Kat; [b.] August 18, 1952, New York; [p.] Mr and Mrs. James Amason; [ch.] Michelle, Earl, Antion Jefferson; [ed.] Pasiley High, Winston Salem, NC [occ.] West Alabama Cleaner, Livingston, AL [memb.] New Jones Baptist Church, Emelle, AL [pers.] I just want the world, to see what mess it is in And to let everyone know that with hope and faith anything is possible.

DARGITZ, JANIE K.
[b.] October 27, 1973, Detroit, MI; [p.] John Dargitz Jeanette Riggs; [ch.] Two sisters, one brother; [ed.

Bethany Lutheran, Forest Park Elementary, Kelly Junior High, East Detroit High School; [occ.] Head Teacher for Toddler Class at Wee Care Child Care Inc.; [oth. writ.] A poem titled "thoughts," published a soft cover book titled "All My Tomorrows."; [pers.] I am very thankful for my ability to express myself through my poetry drawings. But mostly for the love and confidence that my family and friends have in me.; [a.] East Pointe, MI

DARR, THERESA
[b.] May 12, 1974, California; [ed.] Univ of WI - Stevens Point; [hon.] Phi Eta Sigma; [oth. writ.] High school newspaper; [pers.] If it travels from the world to my fingertips it will be written; [a.] Stevens Point, WI

DAUGHERTY, JEAN H.
[b.] September 17, 1927, Naicam Sask; [p.] Cheaster and Aagot Carson; [m.]10/1947 and 5/1985 [ch.] Two sons, Harvey and Dennis Wood; [ed.] Equivalent to Grade Twelve; [occ.] Retired; [oth. writ.] Selection of approximately 100 poems on various subjects. Have considered having them published. Radio Station has used some on their program (Quiet Time); [pers.] I endeavor to paint a picture of beauty of Creation, Joy of Animal and Bird Life as well as the love and inclinations of man as we walk lifes road.; [a.] Golden, BC

DAVAR, NAZISH, F.
[Pen.] Naz, Nazoo; [b.] June 11, 1975, Karachi; [p.] Farhad Davar, Dinaz Davar; [ed.] The Mama Parsi Girls High School. Government College of Commerce and Economics; [occ.] Student (second yr of college); [memb.] Zoroastrian Youth Assn (ZYA). Pakistan Parsi Collegiate Assn (PPCA). Zoroastrian Assn of Pakistan (ZAP); [hon.] Won the Shield in the Habib Bank speech competition. Won 2nd prize in Dubash Art Competition 1989, and 3rd prize in 1991, Won 2nd Prize in school play in 1991.; [oth. writ.] I have written several poems but this was the first time I ever took part in a competition or sent any of my poems for publication; [pers.] My poems reflect me - as I am, what I feel, what I think, what I want, they bring me out from my inner most depths; [a.] Karachi, Pakistan

DAVID, DWIGHT
[b.] October 1, 1952, Lafayette, LA; [p.] Francis and Lola David; [m.] Megara Cassin, August 9, 1986; [ch.] Danielle C. David; [ed.] B.F.A. (76) Univ of Southwestern Louisiana, Lafayette, LA, M.F.A. (79) Univ of New Orleans, N.O.L.A; [occ.] Artist-teacher; [memb.] Longchen Nying Thig, Ed Buddhist Society NY - NJ Center, Fed of Catholic Teachers NY, NY; [hon.] 1987-88 NJ State Fellowship; [oth. writ.] "Temporary Culture" magazine, all editions - "Village Voice" NYC,NY; [pers.] "Nothing is weird and everything has a purpose"; [a.] Philmont, NY

DAVIDSON, ALLISON RENEE
[b.] November 8, 1976, Shreveport; [p.] Robert and Linda Davidson; [occ.] Student - North DeSota High School; [memb.] BETA, FBLA (Future Business Leaders of America), FCA (Fellowship of Christian Athletes), Newspaper Staff (The Talon), FTA (Future Teachers of America), Captain of Danceline, National Honors Society; [hon.] 2nd place - 1991 Young Author's Contest, Honor Roll - North DeSoto High School; [oth. writ.] Poems published in local newspaper; several children's books, school newspaper articles and poems; [pers.] I prefer to show variety in my work -using styles and ideas that almost everyone can relate to in some way; [a.] Mansfield, LA

DAVIES, LEIA
[Pen.] Ruby Tuesday; [b.] December 23, 1978, Framingham, MA; [p.] Jan and Christine Davies; [ed.] King Philip High School, Freshman presently;

[pers.] So often, the bad things are enhanced in our lives that we don't realize that life is good. Living life is the best gift you could possibly give to yourself; [a.] Norfolk, MA

DAVIS, BAHIYYIN
[b.] November 4, 1981, Beloit, WI; [p.] Sharon Davis and George Davis; [ch.] No children, horses - Misty and Sadie; [ed.] Spectrum School; [pers.] I love to write, my real love is horses, and that's what I write about. I've had a lot of good story/poem ideas from my horses, Misty and Sadie. I've been riding for 4 yrs; [a.] Rockford, IL

DAVIS, CHAYA
[Pen.] Chaya S. I. Davis; [b.] July 19, 1979, Chicago, IL; [p.] Lucille Brown; [ch.] none; [ed.] Roosevelt Jr. High, Bellwood, IL and Trinity College Preparatory High School, River Forest, IL; [occ.] Student; [memb.] Student Council Senator, The newspaper, Explorer Scouts of America; [hon.] Certified American Red Cross Peer Instructor, made front page of local newspaper; [oth. writ.] Several poems published in school newspaper, poems written in family newsletter.; [pers.] In my writings, I try to get across a point to the people that reads them. The two people who inspired me to start writing poetry were Maya Angelo and Longston Hughes; [a.] Bellwood, IL

DAVIS, DAVID KARL
[b.] February 19, 1957, Folkstone, England; [p.] (deceased) Mother - Margaret Mary Paul; [m.] Susan Davis, July 31, 1976; [ch.] (10 yr old girl) Natasha Nadine Davis; [ed.] Electronics Technician Dip, Royal Navy Trade Training, Radio Operator/Radio Mechanic, (UV) Open Univ of Science Education; [occ.] Medical Imaging Systems (Xray/CT) Service Rep; [memb.] Previous member of Canadian Theosophical Society; [oth. writ.] Approximately twelve other poems; [pers.] To think, feel and then write. Is a way for man to immortalize his light.

DAVIS, EMILIE M.
[m.] Eric Davis; [ed.] Graduate of Colorado State University; [pers.] "Castle of Our Hearts" was written for my husband in celebration of our one year anniversary..his love inspires me.; [a.] Fort Collins, CO

DAVIS, JR. JOHN HENRY
[b.] March 9, 1979, MS; [p.] John Davis Sr. and Jewel Davis; [ed.] Spratley middle school; [occ.] student 8th grade; [hon.] Honor Roll (9 times) Bug Roll (2 times) (bring up grades) Citizen of the Month twice (2 times) Principal's List (4 times), Warm Fuzzy Award, perfect attendance, science fair, Young Author's Award, 8 math awards; [oth. writ.] I wrote two writings for my English class in 8th grade and both of them was chosen to go in our newspaper. The Daily Press.; [a.] Hampton, VA

DAVIS, LESLEYANNE
[Pen.] Lester; [b.] April 24, 1994, Saskatchewon; [p.] Sandra and Halley Hilts; [ed.] Foamlake Campsite High School, U of S Business College; [occ.] Asst F&B supervisor manager; [oth. writ.] Children's books, fiction stories, poems, short stories; [pers.] During life you become something and someone better than you could imagine. See others as who they really are and not what you want them to be; [a.] Banff, Alberta, Canada

DAVIS, NELLIE ESTELL
[b.] December 28, 1902, Oaklahoma Territory; [p.] Ollie and Laura Moore; [m.] Jay D. Davis Sr., June 30, 1920 (Decesed); [ch.] Seven Children, 28 grandchildren, 42 great grandchildren, 19 great great grandchildren; [ed.] Grammar School and the knocks of life; [occ.] Retired; [oth. writ.] Autobiography (unpublished); [pers.] I have always liked to travel,

see nature at its best and let that show in my writings.; [a.] Corning, CA

DAVIS, SUE JENKINS
[b.] February 29, 1944, Londonderry, N. Ireland; [p.] Edith E. Turner and Stanley E. Jenkins; [m.] Divorced; [ed.] Chuhester High School, Los Angeles Piere College: California State Univ Northridge; [occ.] Teaching Assoc/Graduate Student Cal State Univ Northridge; [memb.] NOW; [hon.] Lifetime member Alpha Gamma Sigma, Dean's List; Member Lambda Pi Eta; Gold and Bronze Medal National Forennis contest; Dean Snyder Scholarship; [oth. writ.] Poems published in school magazine; [pers.] I have been influenced by the poetry of Edwin Muir; [a.] Simi Valley, CA

DAVIS, TONYA RENEE
[Pen.] Tonya D.; [b.] May 11, 1976, Halifax, VA; [p.] Mr. Beverly Davis and Mrs. Willie Davis; [ed.] Halifax Co High School; [occ.] Student; [memb.] Health Occupation Students of America; Student Alliance for Minority Advancement; Future Business Leaders of America; Students Against Drunk Driving; President of Youth Department; Member of Pleasant Grove Baptist Church of Nathalie, Leader of Youth Support Group; [hon.] Various awards from Pleasant Grove Baptist Church of Nathalie, VA; [oth. writ.] Personal writing submitted to English teachers; [pers.] This is a talent I have had for many years, as I have gotten older I reflect my feelings and visions through my poems. I hope they can enlight others, as they have me; [a.] Halifax, VA

DAVISON, LIZA
[b.] August 24, 1978, Annapolis, MD; [p.] James L. Davison, Clare L. Davison; [ed.] Annapolis Senior High School - sophmore; [occ.] Student; [memb.] National Audobon Society, National Wildlife Assoc; [pers.] "A clear conscience is more satisfying than the relief of knowing you got away with a good lie" - Liza Davison; [a.] Annapolis, MD

DAWN, GREY D.M.
[b.] December 17, 1970, Aiken, SC; [p.] Pablo Grey & Dorothy Grey; [ed.] Aiken High School, Morris College; [occ.] Kindergarten Teacher; [hon.] Alpha Kappa Alpha Sorority, Inc.; [oth. writ.] Numerous poems yet to be published; [pers.] To deny is to kill, but to give is to build. Education is the way for prosperity today; [a.] Aiken, SC

DAY, KIMBERLY KAY
[b.] August 22, 1956, Madisonville, KY; [p.] Gary Veazey Day & Shirley Catherine Mitchell; [occ.] Administrative Assistant, Chgo, IL; [hon.] Award of Merit Certificate, Honorable mention for Poem "Yesterday," World of Poetry, Sacramento, CA 3/15/88, Certificate, John Robert Powers School, Chicago, IL (1976), Miss Carpentersville Pageant, Carpentersville, IL (1977); [oth. writ.] I have many poems that I would like to have published into a book someday. I have written on several subjects: geneology, marriage, family, life, love and religious material; [pers.] I have been writing poems for over 20 yrs. When I feel inspired and feel the urge to write, the words just flow. I feel that I have any worthwhile and excellent poems that I would like to share with the world. One of my fav. poets is "Helen Steiner Rice" whom I admire for her inspiring poetry; [a.] Munster, IN

DEAN, HARRY J.
[oth. writ.] Several poems published in Weekly News, a self published, wide variety of poems, titled, "New Old Mining Towns We Built."; [pers.] Early North American poets of the past three centuries influence my life and thoughts.; [a.] Hesperia, CA

DECAPRIO, LORRAINE
[b.] April 23, 1954, Passaic, NJ; [p.] Jean Stolarz & Charles Stolarz; [ch.] Danielle Lauren; [ed.] Pope Pius XII High School, Fairleigh Dickinson University; [occ.] Educator, Pierrepont Elementary School, Rutherford, NJ; [memb.] National Multiple Sclerosis Society; [hon.] Phi Omega Epsilon honor society, Dean's List, cum Laude graduate, * Governor's Teacher Recognition Award*; [pers.] My writing reflects the joys and challenges of life; [a.] Totowa, NJ

DeCESANE, CHRISTINA
[b.] October 5, 1979, Tarzana; [p.] James De Cesare/ Russ and Val Tippy; [ed.] Currently a freshman in high school. I am also on the track team; [occ.] Student; [hon.] In honors English and won an award in 8th grade for the best article in the school newspaper; [oth. writ.] In fourth grade I had a poem called "My Two Dads" published in the Daily News newspaper; [pers.] My grandfather has been the inspiration for the talents that I have. He always encouraged me when I got discouraged. He was the greatest man in the world; [a.] Saugus, CA

DECKARD, DORA J. CRISS
[b.] March 13, 1932, Palestine, TX; [p.] Timothy Criss and Dora Criss; [m.] Warren L. Deckard Sr., (dec.); [ch.] Calvin, Ronnie, LaBertha, Warren Jr.; [ed.] Henry High, Houston-Tillotson, T.S.U., Howard University, TAMU (M.Ed. Concentration Geol.); [occ.] Math Teacher, Lamar H.S. Houston, TS; [memb.] H.F.T., N.C.N.W., Providence Baptist Church, B.T.U. Assistant Director Life membership NAACP, Houston Council of Math, Teachers Delta Sigma Theta Sorority.; [hon.] N.S.F. Study Grants in the amount of $30,000 (1960-68), Rank number 1006 among Outstanding Women of Texas. 1988 honored during Black History Month as "Trail Blazer" by Lamar, PTA and Faculty, Woman at TAMU 1967-68; [oth. writ.] At present I am enrolled in a writing course. "Institute of Children Literature." I love Literature, although I am a science major and math minor.; [pers.] To see that every child learns and growss and feels like a human being.; [a.] Houston, TX

DECKER, EDWARD MACKAY
[b.] March 17, 1952, Jamaica, NY; [p.] Edward and Betty Decker; [ed.] Masters of Science in Education; [occ.] Kindergarten Teacher; [memb.] Nassau Assn for the Education of Young Children; [hon.] Departmental honors in masters program at Queens College; [pers.] In my writings, I often attempt to uncover our tenuous relationship with nature and how it mirrors our spiritual understanding. The words of Pablo Neruda, Corca, and my dear friend, Robert Rose have lodged themselves forever deep in my heart's geography; [a.] Farmingdale, NY

DECKER, ROSEMARY
[Pen.] Rose Decker; [b.] June 8, 1934, NY; [m.] james W. Decker, November 11, 1977; [ch.] Valentine (son), Michael (son), Peggy (daughter), Delores (daughter); [ed.] Berlin High School, in Berlin, NY; [occ.] "Retired" because of my emphysema; [oth. writ.] Some poems published in local newspapers. I only started to write poems last year, so far I have 260 written.; [pers.] God Composes every poem I write, He lets me feel the sadness and he lets me feel the laughter, He is the artist. I am only the writer.; [a.] Hillsdale, NY

DEFOREST, RACHELLE
[b.] June 4, 1970, Kamloops, BC Canada; [p.] Martin and Lorna DeForest; [ed.] Douglas College (Vancouver) Politcal Science, Camoson College, General Studies, Intro to literature; [oth. writ.] Black Angel of des fleurs, short story hasn't been published.; [pers.] The canker of indulgence has been

torn from my spirit. The infatuation with trinkits is no longer lustful, the attraction of truth within myself is no comparison to that of wearing a mask, I no longer exercise the need of forgiveness within the body I live.

DEL CASTILLO, INES
[b.] Cuba; [p.] Celestino Garcia-Victoria Ruiz; [ch.] Joseph and Caridad Maria; [ed.] High, Rosalia Abreu, Havana, Cuba Havana Univ. Some literary courses at Hunter College, NY; [occ.] Art crafts, writing; [memb.] Spanish-American Cultural Link. Circulo de Cultura Panamericano; [hon.] 6 awards in high school. International Prize in Poetry for my book Inmanencia de las Cenizas. 1990. First price poetry, five poems, CA 1990. Honorable mention for my poem Circle of Time, 1990. Poetry prize, poem "Leccion en Puerta De Golpe", Kinsborough College, 1979. Have others. [oth. writ.] Book 50 poems: Hierba Azul, 1989. Anthologies: Cuban Poets in NY 1988, Madrid, Spain. Sonets of Cuba, Miami 1992. Los Rostros de la Gloria, Argentina, 1993. Publications in literary magazines: Osiris, Mass Mairena, PR Circulo Pana-Americano, Miami and others as well as newspapers. I have written prose and some short stories; [pers.] Poetry has been a center of ever green strength to my existence. My verses are mine; each one carries the rhythm of my heart; [a.] Forest Hills, NY

DEL ROSSI, MONICA
[b.] June 11, 1974, Landstuhl, Germany; [p.] Michael and Reena Del Rossi; [ed.] Brussels American School, Univ of Maryland, City Colleges of Chicago - (Belgium), Northern Virginia Community College (Dumfries); [oth. writ.] Lyrics to a mini-album on I Scream Records (side project of Deviate - hardcore band from Belgium); [a.] Dumfries, VA

DELA CRUZ, LISA
[Pen.] Vantaysia; [b.] November 9, 1972, Honolulu, HI; [p.] William A.K. Nihi and Marie Nihi; [ed.] Pahoa High School, Kapiolani Community College, International Correspondence School, Business Mgmnt.; [occ.] Professional Hula Dancer; [hon.] Having my poem being published in the National Library of Poetry; [pers.] I have an easier time to to write my feelings on paper rather than saying them directly. I was inspired to write this poem from one special person in my life, E.A.; [a.] Pahoa, HI

DELA ROSA, REGINALD R.
[b.] May 12, 1970, Honolulu, HI; [p.] Cirilo and Leonora Dela Rosa; [hon.] American Legion School Award, Valedictorian - Hawaii Business College; [pers.] For yesterday is already a dream and tomorrow is only a vision; but today, well lived, makes yesterday a dream of happiness, and every tomorrow a vision of hope; [a.] Honolulu, HI

DELGADO, LIZA MARIE
[b.] February 3, 1962, Elpaso; [p.] Olivina & Gary Rogers; [m.] none; [ch.] none; [ed.] High School, Eastwood Elpaso, TX; [occ.] Realestate, working with parents; [hon.] First poem published in Whispers In The Wind, The National Library of Poetry, Durham Collage, Elpaso, TX; [oth. writ.] None; [pers.] I am disabled and enjoy poetry and writing very much. [a.] Elpaso, TX

DELL, IRENE PRATER
[b.] January 10, 1912, Rural Seneca, MO; [p.] Belle Lynn & Melvin Prater; [m.] Wayne J. Bell, October 7, 1933, (deceased), [ch.] none; [ed.] Salutatorian Grad, Pineville, MO High School, 1929-30, Cottey College, Nevada, MO, Grad. Famous Writer's School; [occ.] Retired, own and manage home farm; [memb.] United Methodist Church, MO Farm Bureau, Republican Presidential Task Force, RNC, The Heritage Foundation; [hon.] Golden & Silver Poet College

Scholarship Poetry Award, Tri-State Writers Guild Ozard Creative writers, Inc.; [oth. writ.] One Book "The Dew of Little Things," articles in Joplin Globe Ozarks Mountaineer, Capper's. Commentaries in National Magazines, poems published in six anthologies; [pers.] Honor truth, stetch the mind, enlarge, the heart, nourish the soul, practice gratitude.; [a.] Carl Junction, MO

DELLAS, LORI-TEE-CSUKARDI
[Pen.] Luara Be Thy Name, Loot The Quiet Starr; [b.] November 24, 1962, Bronx, NY; [p.] Zoltan and Elizabeth Csukardi; [m.] George - James - Dellas; [ch.] Laurissa - Nicolette; [ed.] St. Rose of Lima Rockaway Qns and Beach Channel High School, James Madison High, Kings Borough College, Sheepshead Bay, Bklyn, NY; [occ.] Self-employed w L.G.D., Inc, specializing in above ground pools and decks; [memb.] National Pool and Spa Inst, Tauto School PTA, St Mary's Catholic Church; [oth. writ.] As yet to be revealed; [pers.] Inspired by the faith and strength of my own mother. A mother of ten remembering how she would cry for the goodness of then and for them. My husband with artistic talents of his own, long time frinds Tina Jordan also awaiting a publisher. Last but not least Fr. Dunne of St Patrick Cathedral, NY, NY; [a.] Howell, NJ

DELOREY, K. MARIE
[b.] October 5, 1927, Medford, MA; [p.] Leonell & Alice Delorey; [ed.] Medford High School; studied under poetess Agness Carr; [occ.] Retired; [hon.] Medford High School Class Poem (1945); [oth. writ.] Several poems published in local newspapers and magazines; [pers.] I enjoy writing about current happenings. I was greatly influenced by the poetry of the late James J. Metcalfe author of "Portraits"; [a.] Winchester, MA

DELOSRIOS, JUAN
[Pen.] JDLR; [b.] March 6, 1966, Havana; [p.] Juan and Mercedes; [m.] Maria C. Delosrios, July 5, 1991; [ed.] Hialeah High, Miami Dade Community College, Florida Army National Guard Military Academy; [occ.] Police Officer; [memb.] National Guard Officers Assoc of Florida, National Guard Assoc of the United States; [hon.] Phi-Theta Kappa, Dean's List (Miami Dade Community College); [a.] Miramar FL

DELUCA, MARIA MARTINEZ
[Pen.] Maria Martinez; [b.] November 12, 1980, Brooklyn NY; [p.] Kenneth & Margaret Deluca; [ed.] Alden Terrace elementary School, P.S. 26 (NYC) Louis Pasteur Middle School (M.S. 67); [occ.] Student; [hon.] Honor Roll, M.S. 67, Service League M.S. 67., Gold Cup National, Federation of Music Clubs; [oth. writ.] Essay published in The New York Times; [pers.] My hope is that one day there will be less competition and more appreciation of individual talents, especially in the field of the arts.; [a.] Fresh Meadows, NY

DELZ, CHELSEA
[b.] November 11, 1977, San Angelo, TX; [ed.] Sophomore - Cooper High School; [occ.] Student Cooper High School; [memb.] Cooper High School Choir, Future Homemakers of America; [hon.] Executive Board - Cooper FHA, Presidential Academic Fitness Award 1991-1992; [a.] Abilene, TX

DELZOTTO, PATRIZIA
[b.] April 2, 1962, Rome Italy; [p.] Anna and Francesco Esposito; [m.] David Del Zotto; [ch.] Marc, Deanna and Julian; [ed.] York University, Madonna H.S.; [occ.] Homemaker; [memb.] Local Hospital fundraising committee; [hon.] Have recognition from hospital for my efforts. Also I received a merit award for my publication "The Hunger" in the 1993 Wind In The Night Sky.; [oth. writ.] Working on a novel an

her poetry. I will also be freelancing for a large greeting card company for they enjoy my work and will use it for various greeting cards.; [pers.] All words to flow easily into thy ears. Rather than letting them, slip quckly from thy mouth; [a.] Woodbridge, Ontario

EL-CASTILLO, ELLA MARIE
[Pen.] Virginia Casmey; [b.] September 21, 1922, St. Paul, MN; [p.] Dan, Ethel; [m.] Henry R. Del-Castillo, June 2, 1972; [ch.] John, Brenda, Frances, Marcella; [ed.] Elementary School; [occ.] Home-maker; [hon.] Honorable mention from the world of poetry for the poem "The Miracle"; [oth. writ.] Several poems published in local newspaper. Article President Reagan; [pers.] I have always loved poetry and I hope that I give other people enjoyment from my writing; [a.] Ortonville, MN

EMETRICK, MARY RUSSO
.] August 4, 1942, Syracuse, NY; [p.] Theresa & Nicholas Russo; [ch.] Brian, Katrina, Christopher, Gregory; [ed.] B.S. Speech Communication, 1993 magna cum laude, Syracuse University, Syracuse, NY; [occ.] Assistant Director of Publications, Syracuse University; [memb.] National League of American Penwomen, National Women's Studies Association, American Italian Historical Association, New York State Speech Communication Association, Business and Industry Communicators, listed writer Poets and Writers, Inc. (NYC), American Italian Writers Association; [hon.] Honorable mention (2) 1992 and 1993 Allen Ginsberg Poetry Awards, Paterson, NJ; [oth. writ.] Works published in Plainswoman, Lake Effect, Sinister Wisdom, Voices in Italian Americana, bella figura, Word of Mouth short-short writings by women, Footwork: Paterson Literary Review, The Round Taple, and elsewhere.; [pers.] Much of my creative work focuses on my Italian American heritage. My most recent work includes short-short stories cebntered around women's stories encompassg multi-generational themes. Family stories conitnue to influence my writing. As the first in my family receive a college degree, I strive to put our oral tradition into written form.; [a.] Syracuse, NY

ENSON, LOUISE
.] October 21, 1941, Elk City, OK; [p.] m/m Harvey Duke; [m.] Denny F. Denson, November 8, 1975; [ch.] 3 sons - Bob, Mark and Steven; 6 grandchildren; [ed.] Thru 12, some college courses; [occ.] Real Estate Sales since 1976; [memb.] Various Realtor organizations; [hon.] President - Eugene Board of Realtors - 1983; [pers.] Poem was written while riding in car returning to Oregon from Montana after attending funeral of my mother-in-law, Marjorie Denson.

EPAULA, HENRIQUE
[Pen.] El Bruj (Sorsorer); [b.] December 12, 1928, Brazil; [p.] Antonio de Paula and Amalia Salgado de Paula; [m.] Maria Luiza de Castro, May 31, 1958; [ch.] Julio Cesar and Carlos Alberto, Valerie Walters and Celia (In laws); [ed.] First School and Commercial School; [occ.] Construction Laborer In Brazil I was a sales manager for a chain of newspaper FOLHA DE S. PAULO; [memb.] None; [hon.] Hone; [oth. writ.] Articles about sports for the newspaper Noticias Populares in S. Paulo, Brazil. Many other poems not publibhed yet.; [pers.] I like to write about almost everything. In poetry I prefer the tragic and the romantic. I'm writing a book titled GOD, The Outright Lie.; [a.] Newark, NJ

eROSIE, ALBERT J.
.] November 6, 1927, Toronto; [ch.] 4 - Lynn, Debra, Melodie and Michael; [occ.] Retired; [pers.] Born and raises in Cabbagetown, Toronto. Retired owner of a tree removal business, currently living in the suburbs of Ajax; [a.] Ajax, Ontario, Canada

DeROY, TOMACINA MARIE
[Pen.] Carrot Top; [b.] August 8, 1978, Troy, MO; [p.] Jeff and Sharon DeRoy; [ed.] At time 10th grade, Troy Buchanan High School; [occ.] Student; [pers.] I love having a grandmother who loves to read and write as much as I do. This is a very special gift she has passed on to me. I'm very grateful and pleased to dedicate this to my wonderful grandmother, Mary Lou Schuler; [a.] Moscow Mills, MO

DESALO, CRISTINE
[b.] May 13, 1981, Brooklyn, NY; [p.] Jeanette and Sammy DeSalo; [ed.] Visitation Academy of Brooklyn, NY; [hon.] Principals List; [pers.] In my poems I write down whatever I am feeling at the moment.; [a.] Brooklyn, NY

DETMER, MILDRED
[Pen.] Millie; [b.] February 11, 1938, S.L.C. Utah; [p.] Alfred and Harriet Funk; [m.] Andrew Detmer, July 15, 1967; [ch.] Michael B. Korogi, Kim A. Korogi, Stephanie Frank; [ed.] 12th grade, South High School, S.L.C., Utah.; [occ.] Cashier Hostess; [oth. writ.] I have written 63 poems none published; [pers.] I have been greatly influenced bo both of my daughters for they both have written poems with much feeling. You might say I'm a late bloomer.

DEVINCENT, JUNE
[b.] Winsted, Conn.; [p.] Natale and Al Gosselin; [ch.] Five, John, Nancy, Edward, Jeanne, Christine; [ed.] High School American School, Chicago, Sears and Macy's school of decorating, six years, The Yard School of Art; [occ.] Artist; [memb.] Art League of Bonita Springs, Cape Coral Art League, Charlotte County Art League, Art League of Ft. Myers, Ft. Myers Beach Art Assoc., Lehigh Acres, Fine Arts League, Art League of marco Island, Naples Art Asso. Pine Island Art Asso. Sanibel, Captiva Art Leaque; [hon.] Numerous Awards over past 35 yrs. in fine arts and sales. Most recent 93 all Fla. Fiesta of Art, Lehigh, FL, 3rd place watercolor on rice paper.; [oth. writ.] Additional poetry accepted 12/93 - 1/94 to be published summer 94; [pers.] It is satisfying to at last pursue things. That the everyday business of living prevented over the past 40 years.; [a.] Lehigh, FL

DIAMA, BENJAMIN
[Pen.] Ben Diama; [b.] September 23, 1933, Hilo, Hawaii; [p.] Agapito & Catalina Diama; [ed.] Hilo High School, School of the Art Institute of chicago, University of Hawaii School of Art, Music Education; [occ.] Retired Public School Teacher; [memb.] National Education, Association of America, American Society of Composers, Artists and Publishers, New York Academy of Sciences, Hawaii State Teachers Association, Hawaii State Teachers Association, Hawaii Education Association; [hon.] White House, President Bush, Presidential Order of merit, State of Hawaii Foundation of Arts and Culture Requisition Painting Award.; [oth. writ.] Author of copyright registered "The Calendar Clock Theory of the Universe with Faith" (acknowledged by NASA in 1984), Author of copyright "Beautiful Hawaii" cassette of 14 songs, Author of registered copyright musical play, "The American Dream," a story of Hawaii Immigration; [pers.] I was born kind and taught to be good, therefore inspite of the shortcomings of myself and of my environment. I am always gratified with happiness in my compassionate work of discipline to trust God with love and praise as I relate in friendship with people for peace and brotherhood.; [a.] Kailua Kona, Hawaii

DIAZ, MINERVA
[b.] March 3, 1958, Milwaukee; [p.] Angeles and Felix Cordova; [m.] Hilario Diaz, October 10, 1978; [ch.] Chrisalys and Franceska; [ed.] AA in Liberal Arts, and am currently working on my BA in English;

[occ.] Student and mother and wife; [oth. writ.] I have written lots of poetry, and have always been afraid to let anyone read it; [pers.] Just to know that I am a semi-finalist is enough of a prize for me. I haven't won any awards for any of my writing, and right now, I am very proud of myself; [a.] Plantation, FL

DiCIERO, STACI
[b.] June 9, 1976, Syosset, NY; [p.] Nick and Diane DiCiero; [ed.] I attend Farmingdale High School; [memb.] I'm in Farmingdale Key Club; [pers.] If it wasn't for my friend Teresa's persuading, my poem would not be in this book; [a.] Farmingdale, NY

DICK, DEBORAH JEAN
[b.] June 27, 1955, Jerome, ID; [p.] William Evan and Eleanor June Dick; [ed.] HS North Fremont High Ashton ID, Assoc Degree-Ricks College, BS Degree in Elementary Ed Minor Speech, Drama and Cinn Arts with a speciality in Humanities from Brigham Young Univ; [occ.] I teach the 6th grade at Madison Middle School; [memb.] Delta Kappa Gamma, NAFE, Commanders Club for Disabled American Veterans, and was a member of Toastmasters International; [hon.] Many sports and speaking awards. Have received my CTM in Toastmasters International, won 2nd in a Division B speaking contest in 1991. Am currently the Alpha Beta president in Delta Kappa Gamma; [oth. writ.] My 1st book is in the process of being published; [pers.] Sprinkled throughout my writing, one can see the love I have for family and friends as I travel through life enjoying it's variety; [a.] Rexburg, ID

DICKIE, KIP
[Pen.] S. Sullivan Jr.; [b.] August 8, 1959, Los Angeles, CA; [p.] Shirley M. & Charles K. Dickie; [ed.] Life, and Life Only.; [occ.] Bluesman; [memb.] The League of Soul Crusaders, and Humanity; [hon.] None; [oth. writ.] Billy 'n' Billie (screenplay); The League of Soul Crusaders (Novel); Calamity Cat's and Black Cole Kid's Uncomplicated Guide to Western Moveis for the Simple-Minded Cowperson; many more poems; [pers.] Live for the moment and die for the past; [a.] Prescott and Phoenix, AZ

DILLING, JEN
[b.] 1977, Cleveland, OH; [memb.] Student; [memb.] National Honor Society, French Honor Society, Math Honor Society, National Forensic League, United States Hang Gliding Assoc, Mensa; [hon.] Selected as 1994, Virginia Governor's School candidate; National Forensic League Degree of Honor; 1994 NCTE Writing Contest nominee; publication in school literary magazines; [pers.] I want to evoke something in you when you read my poetry; something that will grow at your chest and linger in your mouth. I hope to be your personal version of Ferlinghetti's man beneath the plaster head of Dante. I am eagerly seeking further publication of any works; [a.] Fairfax, VA

DILLON, JESSICA P.
[Pen.] Jessica Dillon; [b.] December 18, 1975, Chewlah; [p.] Kitten and Steven Dillon; [ed.] Junior in High School; [hon.] on Honor Roll of 1993 to 1994; [pers.] All who have an imagination and a will to make things extravegent maybe a great writer.; [a.] Valley, WA

DIMARIA, MICHAEL ANTHONY
[b.] August 16, 1973, Southfield, MI; [p.] Camern DiMaria and Anna Marie Dimaria; [ed.] Brother Rice High School, current student at St. Leo College; [occ.] Student; [oth. writ.] First Publication; [pers.] I hope as I grow as a writer, I will never give in and water down what I really feel, and what I write. I ahve been greatly influenced by the writings of Arthur Rimbaud; [a.] Bloomfield Hills, MI

DIROBERTS, ARCH
[b.] December 19, 1922, NY; [p.] Robert & Lillian; [m.] Estelle May, 17, 1947 (dec.); [ch.] Kim, Duane, Cliff; [ed.] 2 years college, Louisiana State University; [occ.] Retired NYC Police Lt.; [memb.] Superior Officer's Council, Retired Lieutenants Association.; [hon.] Two Battle Stars WWII (European Theatre), Three Distinguished Awards, NYC Police Dept.; [oth. writ.] Over the years a speech written for various congressional candidates and incumbents and State condidates and incumbants. NYC, ran for Congress in 1976 (Arizona, lot not enough money); [pers.] I am a provo American, a history buff, especially Revolutionary War and Thomas Jefferson is my idol.

DISHART, STEPHANIE M.
[b.] Stephanie Mae Dishart; [b.] July 17, 1982, Charleston, W.VA; [p.] Stephen K. and Susan R. Dishart; [ch.] Brother, Justin E and Sister, Melissa B.; [ed.] Forbes and Franklin Elementary School, Ingomar Middle School; [occ.] Student; [memb.] Ingomar United Methodist Church Bells and choir, Western Penn. School of Gymnastics, Twisters Team; [hon.] Principal Honor Awards 1990-93, Gift of time Honoree 1993; [oth. writ.] School newspaper contributor; [pers.] I feel that my family is very important and this has influenced many of my writings.; [a.] Pittsburgh, PA

DIXON, BRYAN L.
[b.] May 10, 1952, Johnstown, PA; [p.] Dale Dixon Sr., and Virginia Dixon; [m.] Sherry L. Dixon, June 25, 1977; [ch.] Trista Leah; [ed.] Central Cambria High School, Ebensburg, PA, didn't graduate, got a G.E.D. In military, U.S. Army; [occ.] Salesman and clerk, Boscou's Lawn and Garden Dept. Johnston, PA; [memb.] A National Guardsman, 76th Engr. BN HHC, Company; [hon.] Honorable Discharge from U.S. Army, merit Awards on Electronics, Military Safe Driving Award 1973; [oth. writ.] I wrote a poem on the life of a soldier many years ago to my parents. But never published it and some love poems to my ex wife.; [pers.] I wrote to reflect to heartaches of my life and to the ones that must try again. I was deeply hurt in a divorce, which made me to start writing what I feel and need in live; [a.] Nantyglo, PA

DOBBINS, HEATHER
[b.] October 14, 1975, Memphis, TN; [p.] Hamlett Dobbins, Jr and Gail Dobbins; [ed.] Craigmont High School; [occ.] Student at the Univ of TN at Knoxville; [memb.] The Poetry Society of Tennessee, The National Flute Society; [hon.] Univ of TN Dean's List; [oth. writ.] Several poems received awards in the Poetry Society of TN contests; [pers.] Poets are easily impressed and disappointed, but we must keep on knowing people and writing about them and our experiences. "Poetry led me by the hand out of madness" - Anne Sexton; [a.] Knoxville, TN

DODD, TRUDY
[b.] March 27, 1972, Ontario, Canada; [p.] Gilbert and Linda Dodd; [ed.] Eastale Secondary School, Notre Dame H.S., University of Guelph, B.A. English); [occ.] Promotions Analyst, The Guelph mercury; [memb.] Univ. of Guelph Alumni; [hon.] Several awards in local dance and piano competitions; [pers.] When I wrote this poem at seventeen I never dreamed that it would be published. I now know that even the most far reaching dreams can come true.; [a.] Ontario, Canada

DODGEN, DIANNE CARTEE
[b.] March 26, 1942, Williston, FL; [p.] John B. Cartee (d) and Lucretia D. Cartee; [m.] Douglas L. Dodgen, September 27, 1986; [ch.] Maria D. Langley, Cynthia A. Dyer, Billie Ann Dominick; [ed.] Augusta Tech and Academy of Richmond County, Both of Augusta, GA; [occ.] Printing Press Operator with Moore Busn Forms and Systems; [memb.]

O.E.S and Lady of the Shrine; [oth. writ.] National Library of Poetry publication "A Break in the Clouds", entitled "In You I AM", 1993 also, "Together We Walk" in Famous Poets anthology, 1994; [pers.] Dedicated to my 3 wonderful daughters; and my 3 precious grandchildren, Christina Dyanne (16), Frazier (5) and Brittney Ann (17mos), whom I love and am very proud. And also to my wonderful husband who has always encouraged and inspired me. Thanks; [a.] Ninety Six, SC

DOE, JAANE
[b.] 1969, NY; [occ.] Child Care Worker/songwriter, poet; [oth. writ.] The Crystal Catalogue (various songs and poems); [pers.] It is not who we are, but how true we are that really matters; yet there are times when who we are rings truer and leaves a more significant mark on the world, than the actual truth of our existence; [a.] Los Angeles, CA

DOLSON, DONALD WILLIAM
[b.] March 28, 1926, King Township, Ontario, Canada; [p.] John A. & Emma D. Dolson, 1st Mary A. (Berti) Dolson-died, May 16, 1965. 2nd Ruth E. (Holloway) Dolson, 1st August 11, 1951. 2nd May 20, 1978; [ch.] Donna Anne Dolson, March 25, 1953. Now teaches physical education, Gail Jane Dolson, May 11, 1957; [ed.] Public school to grade 8 (1940) radio and TV course at RETS graduated 1957. Oil burner servicing, refrigeration and air conditioning and appliance repair at Standard Engineering approx 1960-61. Apprenticed at Auto spray painting and repair 14 yrs 1946-1959; [occ.] Retired. Last 25 yrs at Coinamatic, (Washers & Dryers); [memb.] Ennerdale Baptist Church, Evangelical Fellowship of Canada, Parkdal High-Park Federal Liberal Assn. Council of Canadians. Voice of Canada Committee. Citizens for Public Justice (CPJ). Canadians Allied in Solidarity with Native People; [hon.] Int'l Society of Poets, Liberal of the Year for Volunteerism 1990; [oth. writ.] Fact, Fancy and Philosophy, self published account of conversion, including over 50 poems, inspired by grief, personal experience and knowledge of God's love. (c) 1970. Heartalk, a more cheerful sentimental one 1972 Satire, Sentiment and Humour, (SSH) 1974. Let There Be Love, 12 pages, 1980. In the Shadow of His Cross, 1992. Also in local papers, single parent, Church newsletters; [pers.] I believe we must return to honoring God and His precepts, stop competing our children out through flipping, and leveraging, Plan Them In! A home is our greatest source of jobs, and satisfaction, it should be put in the "essential" category, because it is, Where Our Heart Is! We must recognize native rights as well; [a.] Toronto, Ontario, Canada

DOME, RICHARD M.
[Pen.] Michael; [b.] June 26, 1951, Glendale, CA; [p.] Mildred Mann; [m.] Kaylyn Dome, November 85; [ch.] Krista Dome; [ed.] Ph.D. Clinical Psychology, B.A. Philosophy; [occ.] Philosopher, Psychologist; [memb.] President, Southern Cal Soc. Clinical Hypnosis; [oth. writ.] San Fernando Poetry Journal; [pers.] Alchemical Process, sove et Coagula, "Dissolve and the Become Complete."; [a.] Westlake Village, CA

DONABIE-DIXON, WENDIE
[b.] December 14, 1950, Belleville, Ontario; [p.] Beatrice and Robert Donabie; [m.] Kenneth Donabie-Dixon, December 9, 1978; [ed.] Etobicoke Collegiate, Humber College, York Univ; [occ.] Writer; would like opportunity to write song lyrics; [memb.] Canadian Society of Childen's Authors, illustrators and performers; [hon.] Poetry award - 2nd prize in 1994 Mississauga Library Literary Competition; [oth. writ.] Several poems published in anthologies, newsletters. Book length children's story in verse currently seeking publication. Also book length collection of poems ready for publication; [pers.] I write poetry to

express our common humanity, using rhyme to reac those who simply want the message, and free verse t connect with those more moved by imagery; [a Mississauga, Ont

DONAHUE, GUY O'HARRA
[Pen.] Guy and Lorraine's Country; [b.] 1953, Sa Fransisco; [p.] Matred & Jack; [ch.] Jessica Ru Donahue (my pride and joy); [ed.] Woodside High Santa Clara University, Petetioning for P.H.D. as certified family, corporate mediator; [occ.] Songwrite (Recorded) Student; [memb.] N.A.U.I., United Brot erhood of Carpenters, Faith Episcopal Church B.M.I [oth. writ.] Many Lyric's, songs recorded last one t date being performed by the artist LuLu Romar many "writing's" still untryed! working on a nove ace's country; [pers.] I strive to live with the influenc of Gods grace for the past, Gods will for the future an patience in the day; [a.] Shingle Springs, CA

DONNER, MARCI LOUISE
[b.] December 11, 1972, Sacramento, CA; [p.] Edi Degener, Robert Donner; [ed.] I'm currently study ing at the University of Nebraska for a B.A. Englis is my major; [occ.] Student; [memb.] I'm a curren member of the Cornhusker Marching Band; [oth writ.] I'm currently working on getting published. I my spare time I write poetry and short stories.; [pers Only memories does time leave as hours, days minutes pass. Only these can we rely on because the can't be stolen or killed. Live each memory for tim is short but memories are yours forever; [a.] Lincoln NE

DORMAN, LITA TRENT
[b.] October 29; W.VA; [p.] Kyle & Virginia Mounts [m.] Wallace D. Dorman; [ch.] Richard J. Tren Joann M. "Nan" Trent; [oth. writ.] A novel (histori cal), short stories, essay, & poems.; [pers.] I realize early in life that I am able to express myself throug my writings, especially poetry. I love the romantics [a.] San Diego, CA

DOSS, JENNIFER
[Pen.] Jenn Doss; [b.] January 23, 1978, Nashua; [p. Clara and Sonny Doss; [ed.] Londonberry High [occ.] Private Music Teacher, part-time; [memb. Student council, Music Dept. Council, Friends o Music Council, Showstoppers Accordian Band, Lea Singer in band Renaissance, Class of 96 Representa tives.; [hon.] Many awards and trophies for accordian keyboard, and singing competitions, academic hono roll; [oth. writ.] Articles for Jr. High Newspaper song lyrics for band.; [pers.] I am thankful for th encouragement of my family and my Aunt Sandy i TX; [a.] Londonberry, NH

DOTTIN, SHARI
[Pen.] Chaaka, Katanga; [b.] March 19, Trinidad WI; [m.] Tena, December 24, 1990; [ch.] Omaari Biko, Fe; [ed.] Bishop Anstey High School Trinidad WI, School of Visual Arts NYC, New School fo Social Research NYC; [occ.] Musician, Artist; [memb. ASCAP, American Society of Naturopathy; [hon. Gold Medal - Trinity School of Music; [oth. writ. Poems and articles published in various magazine and publications; [pers.] I want to convey the beaut of the unseen in the universe to those who do no believe that the world in which we live is truly paradise and is filled with many mysteries.

DOUGLAS, PHYLLIS
[b.] December 19, 1943, Cleveland, OH; [p.] Betty R. Nolan Douglas, (the late) Lionel E. Douglas; [m. (happily divorced); [ch.] Two grandchildren; [ed. Completed H.S. Some college classes. All of life is continuing education; [memb.] Eagles Auxillary 456 Collector of WAMPUM Pocahontas Wenola 51 [hon.] It's an honor, indeed to have the first tw poems I've ever submitted; to be chosen for publica

n; "Meet the Tiger" and "Valley of Dreams"; [oth. rit.] "Valley of Dreams" to be published in "Trea-red Poems of America" by Sparrowgrass Poetry rum, Inc. due Aug 91; [pers.] Loveto Read, dabble oil paint on canvas, love all animals, enjoy most usic, and history; [a.] Martins Ferry, OH

OUGLASS, W.C.
ers.] Anyone can write a poem and those who do em to be very good writers or very bad. To be good it is to be trapped between heaven and hell because etry is a compulsion. I write whether I want to or t. Poets are the most sensitive, Egotistical and ensitive of all writers. Of all the talents I ever had etry is the most frustrating and painful. The public es'nt read it, few people can make a living at it, and t it is savagely criticized by other peots and is often len from the author by those who wish to be known poets. The only satisfaction I've ever gotten from etry is in public recitals of my works. No one will member my words but they will always remember e feeling of the moment. Poetry is the she box of literary world, this is why an obscure janitor can htfully regard himself as one of the finest war poets live in this part of the century. No one will ever low so who can say otherwise.

OULTON, YVONNE
en.] Eve Margaret; [b.] April 6, 1950, Puerto Rico; .] Esther Wagner; [m.] Fabian Doulton, August 12, 93; [ch.] Joseph and David; [ed.] Jericho High hool, NY; [occ.] Musician, Singer, Guitarist; emb.] Writer's Club; [hon.] Musical; [oth. writ.] any others, music, lyrics and poetry of which I entually intend to publish; [pers.] I am but a journer in this particular walk of life. May I touch d be touched by love and may all my endeavors be utiful, for I may not pass this way again...; [a.] cksville, NY

OYLE, FRANCES M.
.] February 5, 1896, OH; [p.] Emma Evert and mes Seaman; [m.] Joseph Francis Doyle, July 27, 16; [ch.] Bavara, Beverly, James T (Ted), Louis , John Edward (died at 1 Mo.), Richard, Myron and arion (Twins), Twila, and Mary E.; [occ.] House-fe and Mother; [memb.] Methodist Church, Essex io; [oth. writ.] Pending; [pers.] Mother of 10, ent her entire life caring for her husband and ildren. The greatest part of her life, they resided at ses, Ohio and/ore Evening Shad, Ark. In 1948, om and Dad, plus the five youngest Children nsplanted to Ark., but for short periods would turn to Ohio to be with the rest of the family and ends.; [a.] North Babylon, NY

RAKE, HELEN S.
en.] Helen Sue Stroman Drake; [b.] March 8, 1922, alde, TX; [p.] William Stroman, Anne Menke roman; [m.] Harrell M. Drake, February 6, 1943; i.] Lynda Ann, Elaine Dianne, Elizabeth Nan, tricia Sue; [ed.] Eagle Pass High School, Texas atheran College; [occ.] Homemaker; [memb.] Faith atheran Church; [pers.] My poetry reflects my deep elings about nature, friendships and my personal th in God; [a.] Seguin, TX

RANE, JOLENE
.] July 2, 1961; [p.] Jack and Nelda Payne; [m.] ndy Darrell Drane; [m.] July 22, 1977; [ch.] Jason, aad and Stephanie Drane; [ed.] Breckinridge County gh and 1 yr at Elizabethtown, KY Community ollege; [occ.] Waitress at "Donna's Diner" in ardinsburg, KY; [pers.] Everyone needs a way to press themselves and the best way I can do that is rough poetry; [a.] Leitchfield, KY

RAPER, BARBARA
.] September 21, 1925, Buffalo, NY; [m.] William Draper, May 6, 1974, Died 1977; [occ.] Retired,

Railroad Secretary-Clerk; [pers.] I am neither writer nor poet, but on one dreary day was inspired to write "Roommate," I hope it may bring the same comfort to others.; [a.] Angola, NY

DRYDEN, HEATHER
[b.] August 19, 1977, Lawrenceburg, IN; [p.] John and Sherry Dryden; [ch.] none; [ed.] Loretto High School, Leoma Elementary School; [occ.] Student; [memb.] Tennis team, FCA, French Club, Spanish Club, Journalism staff; [oth. writ.] Several poems written for school and on my own time.; [pers.] I had the inspiration for this poem of my grandfather whom I lvoed alot, even though he is gone, he's still here in my poem.; [a.] Leoma, TN

DUDASH, SHEILA K.
[b.] December 22, 1967, Syracuse, KY; [p.] Richard and Mauraide Dubash; [ed.] BA in Spanish and minor in education, LeMoyne College, Syracuse, NY. Presently doing graduate work at Suny @ Oswego; [occ.] Spanish translator for Onondaga - Cortland - Madison Boces; [memb.] Syracuse Up Downtowners, Volunteer for numerous charities in Syracuse area; [pers.] I have just finished writing my first book of poetry entitled "Imagined Reality". I hope to have it published by fall of '94; [a.] Liverpool, NY

DUENOW, MARK S.
[Pen.] Dina Marks; [b.] July 7, 1949, Forest City; [p.] Merlyn & LuAnn Duenow; [m.] Cynthia Lynn Duenow, August 1, 1981; [ed.] LeRoy, HS Leroy MN, Troy State University; [occ.] Police Officer; [memb.] Minn. Police and Peace Officers Assoc., National Guard Assoc., Multiple Sclersosis Society; [hon.] Master Army Aviator Bronze Star, 13 Air Medals Vietnam Veteran. Many Army Awards and Decorations; [oth. writ.] Several unpublished poems; [pers.] The many faces of life always are notable; [a.] River Falls, WI

DUGAN, HENRY
[b.] October 28, 1922, Philadelphia, PA; [p.] Anna & Joseph Dugan; [ed.] High School Graduate 1941; [occ.] Writer; [hon.] Republican Legion of Merit Medal, FBI Medals, Police Medals; [oth. writ.] Books and short stories; [pers.] Love what you do. Keep writing until you succeed. It can be done.; [a.] Philadelphia, PA

DUGDALE, STEPHEN
[b.] December 23, 1976, Almonte; [p.] Steve, Darlene Dugdale; [ed.] Carleton Place High School, Grade 12; [occ.] Student; [memb.] I've been playing baseball for 7 yrs; [pers.] Can you please dedicate my poem to my good friend Lisa Harris of Brockville, Ontario if possible; [a.] Carleton Place, Ontario

DUMONT, JAMES A.
[Pen.] James Penant; [b.] September 16, 1964, Medicine Hat, Alta; [p.] Garry and Leona Dumont; [m.] Lorraine Dale Dumont, October 20, 1984; [ch.] Ashley, Alex, Amanda; [ed.] Graduated ED Feehan High School; [occ.] Farm Laborer; [memb.] Undiscovered Province Science Fiction Fan Club; [hon.] Robert P. Connelly Award of Merit, City of Saskatoon Citation for Laudable Conduct; [pers.] This may have been said before but, I write what I feel and feel what I write; [a.] Borden Sask, Canada

DUNAGAN, MICHELE
[Pen.] Michele Dunagan; [b.] July 22, 1976, Somerset, KY; [p.] Ronald and Charlotte Dunagan; [ed.] Will graduate from Southwestern High School in Somerset, KY in June 1994; [oth. writ.] I have 2 poems, "Untitled", and "Mysteries" that are going to be in an anthology from Sparrowgrass Poetry forum in April 1994; [a.] Bronston, KY

DUNBAR, CHRISTOPHER KAY
[b.] February 7, 1965, Fontana, CA; [p.] Marlen and Lois Dunbar; [ed.] Currently attending Northern Arizona University in Flagstaff; [occ.] Full-time student studying elementary education; [pers.] This poem is dedicated to my grandfather Charlie Wardlow, who, along with my grandmother - Margaret Wardlow have given me more beautiful memories than I can count; [a.] Flagstaff, AZ

DUNCAN, KATHY G.
(Sullivan, Mary Jane, Co-Auth)
[b.] January 22, 1964, Heber Springs, AR; [p.] Nellie Watkins, Rev Leroy Thomas; [ch.] Dustian Davis - son, Timothy P. Carroll - son; [ed.] 12th; [occ.] none; [oth. writ.] Have books full of various writings and poetry. My friend and I wrote "My Dream" others stated that we should enter it into this contest. We never dreamed it would actually be excepted; [pers.] Never say never until you've tried nor the good things you do in life be denied.

DUNELLO, CHELSIE
[b.] May 19, 1974, Great Falls, MT; [p.] Midge and Weber; [ed.] School of Aero Space Medicine, Brooks, AFB, TX; [occ.] Aeromedical Technician; [memb.] Yokota players (drama); [hon.] Editor's Choice Award (National Library of Poetry); [oth. writ.] The Coming of Dawn (poem) National Library of Poetry. A Question of Balance (poem) National Library of Poetry; [pers.] I'd like to dedicate this poem and future poems to two very important people in my life. Terry L. Collins - who has had a great influence on my recent work - and Mark Hernandez. Friendship is forever; [a.] Yokota AFB, Japan

DUNLAP, HELEN ELIZABETH
[Pen.] Helen Brown Dunlap; [b.] August 23, 1937, Wellston, OH; [p.] Rev. C. Albert Brown and Margie Brown; [m.] Jerry David Dunlap, June 16, 1985; [ch.] Timothy A. Voght, M. Renee Voght and Kayse E. Hembree; [ed.] Jeffersonville High School, Jeffersonville, IN, IBM, Data Processing; [occ.] Domestic Engineer; [memb.] Calvary Baptist Church, Richmond, IN; [oth. writ.] Several poems published in our church paper "The Voice of Calvary". Also published in our church paper, was the tribute I wrote especially for my dad "A Tribute to Reverend C.A. Brown for his 60 yrs in the ministry"; [pers.] I give the glory to God for the talent he has given me. If you have a talent no matter how big or how small, use it to the best of your ability. To me, it is better to sing a little off key than not to sing at all; [a.] Richmond, IN

DUNN, FRANCES
[b.] February 23, 1941, Alabama; [p.] Bettie and T.J. Graham; [ch.] (Daughter) Carolyn Cutis; [ed.] Still in school; [occ.] Housekeeper; [pers.] I always try to do the best I can in what ever I do. I want my poem to make people happy. I would like to continue writing poems; [a.] Great Neck, NY

DUNNING, ASHLEY
[b.] November 11, 1981, Geneva, NY; [p.] Jim and Jan Dunning; [ed.] 6th grade; Penn Yan Middle School, Liberty St, Penn Yan, NY; [occ.] School; [memb.] C.Y.O. Basketball (girls), Yates County Girls Slow Pitch, Yates County Soccer, Middle School Ski Club, Methodist Church, Yates County 4-H; [hon.] (Highest) Superior Honor Roll; [oth. writ.] Other poems; [pers.] "I enjoy writing poetry about nature and making people feel happy!"; [a.] Dresden, NY

DuPONA, MARCUS
[b.] July 9, 1982, Danbury, CT; [p.] Karen DuPona, Thomas DuPona; [ed.] Home schooled; [occ.] student; [memb.] New Fairfield Historical Society; [hon.] Selected five times to attend prestigious science program for gifted students at Sacred Heart Univ; [hon.]

Won third place in a regional creative writing contest; [oth. writ.] Essay published in "Understanding Our Gifted"; [pers.] I believe that any child who excels at reading can accomplish anything!; [a.] New Fairfield, CT

DUQUESNE, DEANNA
[b.] May 6, 1976, St. Louis, MO; [p.] Linda Duquesne, Gilbert Duquesne; [ed.] Northwest High School graduation, May 1994; [occ.] Sales Assoc at Toys R Us; [memb.] DECA (Distributive Education Clubs of America), Pen and Palette, Northwest Waters, D.A.R.E. (To keep kids off drugs), TRENDS (Turning Recreational Excitement in New Directions); [oth. writ.] Many poems published in school newspapers and a few in the new magazine coming out Young Author's magazine; [pers.] I believe in my talent because I write of what I feel, my writing is from deep within my soul. I believe if everyone examined themselves, world peace would seem an easy task to accomplish thank you for this opportunity; [a.] High Ridge, MO

DUROCHER, SHELLEY
[b.] June 29, 1971j, Windsor; [p.] Pat and Ann Durocher; [occ.] Bank of Nova Scotia, Teller; [pers.] I'm eclectic in my tastes and as a result my writings are ruled by emotion.; [a.] Harrow, ON, Canada

DURRETT, CATHY
[b.] February 13, 1958, Seattle; [p.] Fred and Onibe Carpenter; [ch.] Kenny Durrett and Jason Durrett; [ed.] Eureka Adult - HROP Medical Asst; [occ.] Cashier; [memb.] A member of the Women of the Moose; [pers.] I would just like to thank all the people who encouraged me to keep writing, and I do want to encourage other people to do the same; [a.] Lacey, WA

DUSOVIC, DYAN LIN SCHNELL
[b.] May 31, 1970, Bx. NY; [p.] Robert & Linda Boyle; [m.] Alex Dusovic, September 25, 1993; [ed.] Christopher Columbus, HS; [hon.] Awards in writing and creative arts, NYPD Award for Drug Enforcement Literature.; [pers.] I wish my poem could reflect on those who think about commiting suicide. No matter how bad things get, it will get better and life is your future.; [a.] Temple Terrace, FL

DuVAL, NEDRA
[b.] October 15, 1927, Philadelphia, PA; [p.] Alma and Albert Jenkins; [m.] June 53, (deceased); [ch.] Nedra Jean Shands; [ed.] West Phila High. J Martin school of nursing, schlor dance: Andre Drew and Apex School of Cosmotology; [occ.] Retired now but a volunteer worker at Christ Church Hospital. Ex-singer, dancer Model so also MC Fashion Shows, Teac or any church related or fund raising events. Many, many church awards. I dance award given united nation (have pictures, etc) with partner at a luncheon there 1956. [oth. writ.] "A dance interpretation". I play and sing hymns and old folks songs also on my Hawsaiian Steel guitar at various functions when asked. Have written many poems. Just got nerve enough to attempt to send out, thanks to you!; [pers.] Laughter is medicine, Live love laugh; [a.] Philadelphia, PA

DUVALL, DAN
[Pen.] Dooovall; [b.] January 2, 1971, OH; [p.] David and Diane Duvall; [ed.] Westlake High School, Baldwin-Wallace College; [occ.] Videotape Editor; [memb.] B-W College's Satorl; Greenpeace; The Cleveland Freenet Llama Lovers Society; [oth. writ.] Various unsold television spec scripts and screenplays; one TV public service announcement produced in Cleveland; [pers.] Human beings are inherently creative: Why else would we doodle and tap out melodies when our minds wonder?; [a.] Berea, OH

DWYER, DEBBIE
[b.] December 2, 1970, Tachikawa, Japan; [p.] Paul and Kazuyo Dwyer; [m.] Single; [occ.] CNA, Bethesda at Evanswood, Kingston, MA; [hon.] Dean's List; [oth. writ.] Endless poems and songs; [pers.] Knowledge is power, knowledge is safety, knowledge is happiness.; [a.] Kingston, MA

DYBMAN, NICK N.
[b.] December 23, 1945, China; [p.] Gregory & Alla; [m.] Dora; [ed.] B.A., Queens College, Flushing, NY, Sobelsohn School, Manhattan, NY; [occ.] Songwriter; [hon.] Phi beta Kappa, Magna Cum Laude, Kappa Delta Pi, 1990 & 1991 Golden Poet, World Poetry Society; [oth. writ.] Freedom Is Upstoppable, A Universal Theory of Relativity, Your Not The Only One, Umpire Empire, Sacred Sharon, Hard In Tennessee, Sweet Recovery, Israel Tour, Just Summer Notes; [pers.] Everyone needs to relax more.; [a.] Forest Hills, NY

DYMOND, LORI
[b.] September 14, 1974, Liberty, NY; [p.] Roy and Myrtle Dymnond Sr.; [ch.] none; [ed.] Tri-Valley School, Grahamsville, NY K-12; [occ.] Cashier, Peters Market; [memb.] In High School, Dead Poets Society, National Honors Society, Chorus; [hon.] Honorable Mention In World Of Poetry Contest for the poem "The Rose"; [oth. writ.] Poem in high school yearbook entitled "If There's a God In Heaven"; [pers.] All poets have inspirtions, mine are my mother, father and my wonderful fiance, Chip Smith. I love and thank them all.; [a.] Grahamsville, NY

EATON, BETTY MAE
[Pen.] July 8, 1935, Indpls, IN; [p.] John W. & Dorothy L. Fishback; [m.] Charles H. Eaton, November 19, 1977; [ch.] Cynthia Ann Smith, Mark Allen Smith, Penny Jo Shumaker; [ed.] Tech. High School thru the Jjr. year in Indpls. Ind.; [occ.] Cashier and clerk at Roselyn Bakiers of Ind.; [memb.] Order of Eastern Star (Beechgrove Chapter #465) of Ind. for 29 years.; [hon.] A poem put into a capsule to be opened in 100 years (Oct. 1, 2091) pegasus Time Capsule, World of poetry's 1992, Edition of Who's Who In Poetry, Golden Poet 1990-91; [oth. writ.] The Time Is Now, Your Family Tree, Moma's Hands, Colors, Chase Away the Blues, I Am A Poet; [pers.] I write from real lfie, to make a point and to make others feel they count and are important to me. Life it self is a poem. You only have to look at it through my eyes.; [a.] Indianapolis, IN

EATON, ERROL J.
[b.] July 10, 1968, Huntington, NY; [p.] Edward and Evelyn Eaton; [m.] Tia L. Eaton, September 11, 1992; [ed.] Graduate of Huntington High School, Huntington Station, NY, Basic Military Training Lackland AFB, TX, Aircraft Technical School, Shaw AFB, SC; [occ.] F-16 Aircraft Maintenance Specialist (Crew Chief); [hon.] Air Force Good Conduct Medal, National Defense Service Medal, South West Asia Campaign Medal with Device, Humanitarian Service Medal, Outstanding Unit Award; [pers.] No matter who we are, we should not forget where we came from, or who we could be; [a.] Edwards AFB, CA

EAYRS, ANTHONY CURTIS
[Pen.] Anthony C. Eayrs; [b.] January 6, 1962, Seattle, WA; [p.] Willis E. Eayrs, Miyo Eayrs; [m.] Mary-Jane D. Eayrs, August 21, 1993; [ed.] Queen Anne High School, Seattle, WA, Univ of Washington, Seattle, WA; [occ.] Payroll Accountant, Bartell Drug Company; [memb.] Secretary for the Board of Directors of the Pacific Credit Union, KCTS - TV Fundraiser; [hon.] Phi Theta Kappa, UW High Scholarship List - 2 quarters, Private Pilot's License, Airframe and Powerplant Mechanics License; [oth. writ.] As a true amateur poet, this is the first poem I have ever written that has been published; [pers.] I wrote "A Love For All Time" for my wedding o August 21, 1993 to my lovely wife, Mary-Jane. believe the main goal in life is to love and to learn, an to not be afraid to fail; [a.] Seattle, WA

EBBS, ALBERT
[Pen.] Albert; [b.] November 5, 1954, Louisvill KY; [p.] Warren Henderson Ebbs and Mrs. Judel M. Shaw; [ed.] 3 yrs of college and UCLA, San Monica College and Galveston College; [occ.] Vide producer/owner of Attorney's Media Specialist Houston, TX; [pers.] Let us pray that we reflect God will and blessings throughout our lives - making lov and it's expression, the "Art of Life"; [a.] Houston TX

EBERT, VALIERIE A.
[b.] May 26, 1968, Humboldt, Saskatchewan, Canada [m.] Blair Ebert, August 15, 1992; [ch.] Expectin first child; [ed.] Graduated Annaheim high, Anaheim Saskatchewan, Canada; [pers.] 'One is never entirel what others preceive them to be!' My husband and m child are who inspire me; [a.] Morinville, Alberta Canada

ECHOLS, BONITA
[b.] May 4, 1956, Chicago, IL; [p.] James an Dorothy Echols; [m.] single parent; [m.] DNA; [ed.] Lind Bloom High; Kennedy King Junior College [occ.] Accounting Clerk; [memb.] True Family Salomon Church; 81st and Green Block Club; OE Fraternity; [hon.] Marshall Fields Finest (Employe Excellence Award) 1984; [oth. writ.] Godspel songs and children books presently unpublished; [pers.] W are the creators of our destiny and the captains of ou souls; [a.] Chicago, IL

ECKEL, PATRICIA A. (PAT)
[b.] August 28, 1929, Cols, OH; [p.] Wm an Elleanora Oswalk; [m.] Charles H. Eckel, June 4 1949; [ch.] Twelve, 8 sons and 4 daughters; [ed.] S Mary's High School, Columbus, OH; [occ.] J Penney Co - 20 yrs; [memb.] St Ladislas Church Columbus, OH; [hon.] The love and smiles of m family; [oth. writ.] Many poems pertaining to famil and friendship; [pers.] I firmly believe that faith i God and a loving family work together to make a goo and happy life for all concerned. Also, a sense o humor is a helpful ingredient for a healthy, happy life [a.] Columbus, OH

ECKHARDT, EILEEN
[b.] May 3, 1964, Pelham, NY; [p.] Carolyn & Rud Eckhardt; [m.] John M. Pittarese, May 15, 1992 [ch.] none; [ed.] Mineeola High School, Nationa Honor Society, Top 10 Percent of Class 82: Nassa Community College A.S. BIO-Cum Laude: Cur rently finishing bachelors degree in Business Manage ment at Empire State College; [oth. writ.] I have othe poems in my journal but this is my first published one [pers.] Usually an event I am participating in or a person I have met or know for sometime gives me a idea for a poem. I try to express this particular feelin of the time in my poem.; [a.] Lindenhurst, NY

EDMONDSON, PATRICIA A.
[b.] January 15, 1958, Brunswick, Georgia; [p. Lonnie and Evelyn Newbern; [m.] Ronald D Edmondson, November 19, 1982; [ch.] Shanna an Rebecca Edmondson; [ed.] Currently enrolled full time college student seeking AA, BA in education Will teach elementary; [occ.] Personal Asst to Chai of Basic Education, Grays Harbor College. Also a tutor; [pers.] Thanks to Mrs. Singletary, my seventh grade teacher for encouraging me to write poetry, m God, family, friends, and the beautiful, inspirationa Northwest Territory; [a.] Elma, WA

DWARDS, DANIEL J.
.] January 10, 1972, Racine, WI; [p.] David and onstance Edwards; [ed.] Washington Park High chool, UW, Stevens Point (currently); [occ.] Stuent (UWSP), Custodian (Crest International); [hon.] ean's List (Every now and then); [oth. writ.] This as my first writing, period; [pers.] Always write for ourself and no one else. Stick with your own ideals, ey are what you know best. Recommended readingomics. (There's a lot there people miss!); [a.] evens Point, WI

DWARDS-RANDOLPH, JACQUELYN
.] July 26, 1934, Hbg, PA; [p.] Frank Qantigua & illie Mae Abrahms; [m.] Stanley J. Edwards, Auust 16, 1993; [ch.] George, Dayne & Jocelyn aylor; [ed.] Swatara Township High School, Hbg, ltn, Hghspr, Technical School, Sociology I at HACC lbg. Area Comm. College) Computer Operation at nn State; [occ.] L.P.N. (Retired); [memb.] Post 15 V.F.W. Auxiliary Post 420 American Legion uxiliary, St. Stephen's Episcopal Cathedral; [pers.] came from a poor family, but I feel success and eatness can definitely come from any level if you set our heart and mind to it.; [a.] New Cumberland, PA

GERTON, CAROLYN R.
en.] Carolyn Rae; [b.] October 19, 1966, Lowell, A; [p.] Leslie Atwood, James Edgerton; [m.] Single; h.] Silvanus W. Egerton (my awesome son); [ed.] ashua High continuing education as Mech Tech ngineer major; [occ.] Homemaker and student; [oth. rit.] Not published; [pers.] I hope to touch your heart d capture every beat. I'm greatly influenced by life d I have an incredible respect for the master ngineer. God Bless; [a.] Canaan, ME

HNES, TAMMY
.] January 7, 1963, Mobridge, SD; [p.] Henry and velyn Quenzer; [m.] Kyle Todd Ehnes, June 27, 81; [ch.] Tyler Todd; Karissa LaRee; Austin Jay; d.] Lead High School 12 yrs; [occ.] Domestic ngineer; [memb.] The only membership I have is to e. To try everyday to be the best I can be, loving, lpful, cheerful, honest - just be me!; [hon.] Knowg I have a gift to write and sharing it with others, is hat I consider an honor. I have not yet received any vards but if my writings may touch the souls of hers to see the light so to speak that to me would be much better award of giving to someone than for me actually receive any material rewards, or awards; th. writ.] Poems published in our local newspaper. ne I'm especially proud of is "Through A Mother's yes" published in the Circuit Newsletter - South Dak rent Connection, Sioux Falls,SD; [pers.] My greatt inspiration is music, people and life itself. Life is dance; Without music there is no dance and without nce there is no life. God gave us His grace and a life dance; [a.] Lead, SD

LISSA, ROSEMARIE CALUORI
en.] Angel Pumpkin Caluori; [b.] October 2, 1939, rooklyn, NY; [p.] Rose and Edward Caluori, Sr; [m.] Charles Elissa, Ocotober 4, 1964, divorced December 1968); [ch.] One daughter - Nyla Elissa erez; one grandson - Xavier Charles Perez; [ed.] neonta Univ BS in Ed 1961, 1988 Libi - Long Island usiness Inst, 1978 -Univ of Utah - Utah Teacher ertification, 1983 - Writer's Digest Homestudying Vriting Non-Fiction"; [occ.] Freelance writer, subtute teacher; [memb.] Hands: Handicapped Adults ew Directions in Suffolk, Patchogue Historical ociety (Republican Club) NW Babylon; [hon.] Hons in Business, National Honor Society - HS, Winner Essay Contests, Honorable Mention in songwriting ntests (2) winner of several dance trophies in 1962-; [oth. writ.] Published previously in 3 poetry thologies New Voices 1986, "The Challenger ew", The NY Poetry Society - "Rebuttal" Quill

books: Down Peaceful Paths: "Color Your Rainbow, Pink"; [pers.] I study experience, and learn the hard way while keeping a flexible attitude; [a.] Medford, Long Island, NY

ELLEN, DEBORAH
[b.] 1950; [m.] 1977; [ch.] 3 boys, aged 11, 9, and 5 years.; [ed.] M.D., Psychiatrist, Psychoanalyst, M.A. English Literature; [occ.] Psychiatrist, Psychoanalyst; [oth. writ.] Poem entitled "The Greek Woman and the American Woman.", Published in Treasured Poems of America, Sparrowgrass Poetry Forum, winter 1992. Psychoanalytic article on "Creativity" writing in progress.; [pers.] Make sure that a creative endeavor does not become a destructive endeavor with the poem providing merely a license to indulge in anger.; [a.] Montreal, Province Quebec, Canada

ELLER, CONNIE
[b.] 1960, Brooklyn, NY; [p.] Joseph and Esme Gooding; [m.] Douglas L. Eller, 1987; [ch.] Allyn, Jamica, Epiphany; [ed.] St. Louis Community College at Forest Park, Graduated 1989. Graduate of the High School of Art and Design, New York City 1978.; [occ.] Social work with homeless families, Community Volunteer; [memb.] National Right To Life Committee, Board Member Missouri Right to Life, Eastern Region, The Salvation Army, Euclid Corps, Senior Soldier, Hyde Park (St. Louis, MO) Safety Committee, Co-Coordinator, Missouri, Illinois Life Caravan, Member, Belleville (Illinois) Area Right To Life, Founding member, salvationists for life.; [oth. writ.] Letters published in local newspaper, articles for local newspaper; [pers.] Writing comes from pain and joy, necessity and leisure, youth and maturity. God, through Jesus Christ, is my inspiration and survival.; [a.] St. Louis, MI

ELLINGSON, WILMA A. K.
[Pen.] W.A.K.E.; [b.] April 23, 1922, Linton, ND; [p.] Wilhelm and Magdelena Klaudt; [m.] Orlando V. Ellingson, November 30, 1940; [ch.] Lowell, Mark, Douglas and Robin; [ed.] Eleventh grade; [occ.] Domestic Engineer, retired; [memb.] North Dakota Head Injury Assoc. National H. I. Assn, Life Member Disabled American Veterans Unit, National Planned Parenthood Assn; [hon.] I have received various awards and certificates for volunteer work during the past 12 yrs; [oth. writ.] One other poem was published in the North Dakota Mental Health Publication. Also, am marketing another poem I have written; [pers.] All my writings are based on my personal life experiences; [a.] Bismarck, ND

ELLIS, JAMES H.
[b.] June 11, 1951, Fayette, MS; [m.] Constance Baker Ellis, May 18, 1991; [ch.] Preston D. Ellis, Tyler A. Ellis, Candace A. White; [ed.] Lanier High School, Jackson, MS, Forsyth Technical Community College, Winston-Salem, NC; [occ.] Retired United States air Force, full-time Student; [memb.] American Legion, Disabled American Veterans; [hon.] Recipient of Vietnam Service Medal, Honorable discharged from United States Air Force 1990; [oth. writ.] Two poems published in Tech IX TX - an annual college publication; [pers.] I regarded myself as a closet poet unaware that my poetry spoke for anyone other than myself. My inspiration is life. I write to ease its strife with words of peace to keep in sight. I have been influenced by Harlem Renaissance writers and the early romantic poets; [a.] Winston-Salem, NC

ELMBLAD, HARRIET
[b.] August 28, 1912, Minneapolis, MN; [p.] Willis & Elva (Newton) Wilson; [m.] Donald Robert Elmblad, August 1, 1936; [ed.] High School; [occ.] Retired from Secretary to Supt. of Minnetonka Public Schools 1957 to 1972, before marriage 6 1/2 yrs. Northern States Power Co., Billing & Credit Dept.; [memb.]

Order of Eastern Star; [hon.] Salutatorian of Class of 1929, Excelsior High School (MN) Probably non an honor but a great surprise. Two poems were read on radio, "Kitchen Prayers" and "Thanksgiving" were read in church. My permission was not requested. They were just "chosen." My permission was requested for use in "Decision" Magazine, also for use on radio. I would like to add that at the request of a grandson I have books which I paid for the publication in order to have one for each member of our family of 32 (soon to be 35). My grandson did all the "leg work" and they turned out to be beautiful books. Their title is "In Pictures of Silence." It is 308 pages, hardbound.; [oth. writ.] Close to 50 poems published by Ideals Magazine. Card verses by "Joya Creations" used by Joyce Goad of Tampa, FL; [pers.] I feel that my joy in poetry was a gift inherited from my paternal grandfather who write a little unpublished poetry, and cultivated by my father who talked in "rhyme"; [a.] Minnetonka, MN

ELMORE, ROBERT
[b.] April 26, 1973, Baytown, TX; [p.] Annie Elmore & David Elmore, Sr.; [ed.] Ross S. Sterling High School, Duke University (Junior); [occ.] Student; [memb.] Alpha Phi Omega, Habitat for Humanity, Mt. Rose, Missionary Baptist Church, Black Student Association; [oth. writ.] Several unpublished writings; [pers.] Life is really large, but it's the little things that count. I live each day to the fullest and strive to be good to myself and others.; [a.] Baytown, TX

EMBERLEY, PAUL
[b.] Aug 30, 1917, Bay De Verde, New Foundland; [p.] Williams Jas and Jane Ann Emberley; [m.] Lydia Jacobs, April 27, 1943; [ed.] High school at Bay De Verde. No Univ exp or training; [occ.] Retired postmaster and CNT agent here 40 yrs; [pers.] I have written personally, some of the happenings assoc with my life long activities and my personal accomplishments in public life. [a.] Ba de Verde, Newfoundland

EMIG, BERNADINE C.
[b.] November 18, 1916, Aviston, IL; [m.] Oliver Emig, October 29, 1940, Deceased; [ch.] Three; [occ.] Housewife; [a.] Trenton, IL

ENGLISH, ROBERT G.
[b.] August 12, 1945, Portland, OR; [p.] Mr. and Mrs. Samuel English; [ed.] High school graduate 2 yrs college; [occ.] Author poet photographer; [memb.] Art is - Paris, France, Int'l Society of Poetry, Outstanding Achievement in Poetry - 1993 by ISP; [hon.] Golden Poet 1991-1992, Editor's Choice Award - 1993 (two), Lifetime Member of Int'l Society of Poetry; [oth. writ.] Two short poetry stories selected to be published in Ten Top short stories of 1994. Only yours Susanna My Rose and Poetical Jest my Gestful World will be published by Artis in Paris, France; [pers.] Spring forth a more prolific poetical endeavor throughout the world; [a.] Albuquerque, NM

ERDODI, KATALIN
[b.] August 15, 1980, Debrocen, Hungary; [p.] Ference Erdodi, Katalin Kover; [ed.] Istvan Hatvani Elementary School and Junior High; [occ.] Student; [hon.] Shankar's International Children's Competition Silver Medal; [oth. writ.] Short story published in Shankar's Children's Art Number, a poem published in the local newspaper.; [a.] Debrecen, Hungary

ERICA, STOELTING
[b.] April 13, 1978, Olney, IL; [p.] Stan & Neala Stoelting; [ed.] Presently a sophomore in high school; [memb.] Pep Club, Spanish Club, Student Council; [hon.] Regional winner in county, speech contest, First Student of the Month in Lawrence County, UDA Dance All-Star; [oth. writ.] Several poems given to personal friends and family.; [pers.] I like to be differnt and have unique views on everyday life.; [a.]

Bridgeport, IL

ESAKU, KONDO
[b.] July 25, 1924, Mishima, Japan; [p.] Goro Kondo, Sata Kondo; [m.] Iku Kondo, April 1, 1955; [ch.] Kayoko Opalacz, Satoshi Kondo; [ed.] Yokohama National University, Nihon University, Japan, Carnegie Mellon University; [occ.] Consultant Architect; [memb.] American Institute of Architects, Japanese American Citizens League, Michigan Mushroom Hunters' Club; [hon.] Andrew Mellon Memorial fellowship in Urban Design; [oth. writ.] Essays for 1993 and 1994 New Years Editions of Nichi Bei times; [pers.] A genius Japanese poet "Takuboku Ishikawa" died at age of 27 after leaving various sad poetry in fighting against poverty, consumption and bias. At age of 69, I realize keenly his human fate and pathos on myself too.; [a.] Bloomfield Hills, MI

ESCALON, LISA D.
[b.] September 10, 1976, Amarillo, TX; [p.] John and Robble Escalon; [ed.] (11th grade) Dumas High School; [occ.] Occational baby sitting student at Dumas High School; [memb.] Member of the "Yes" ensemble at BBC (Youth Exahalting the Savior). I am a member of the Dumas Demon High School band, I play the trumpet. I am a leader in an Awana group at church (BBC); [oth. writ.] My poem was published in our school newspaper, the Demon Tale; [pers.] I wrote this poem to help me cope with the death of my two friends. They were both dear friends that I will miss always; [a.] Dumas, TX

ESPERSER, NICOLE
[b.] July 24, 1981; [p.] John and Faye; [ed.] Akron Central School; [occ.] Student; [hon.] Two second place trophies, and ribbons; [oth. writ.] Other poems written for school news; [pers.] I work hard on these poems, it takes alot of thinking. I get most of my ideas from my back yard. I have been greatly influenced by romance; [a.] Akron, NY

ESPOSITO, DONNA MARIE
[Pen.] D. Esposito; [b.] June 1, 1965, Vineland, NJ; [p.] Andrew and Klara Esposito; [ch.] (two) 1 boy who is 2 yrs and 1 girl 4 mos; [ed.] Vineland High School graduate; [occ.] Homemaker; [oth. writ.] Too many to list; [pers.] Although I majored 4 yrs in High School as an Art Major, writing is my choice. My inspiration stems from my childhood. I love nature. I love all animals, they are the "real" people. I just love to express. My hand can't keep us with thoughts I think to put on paper; [a.] Vineland, NJ

ESQUIBEL, PHILLIP E.
[b.] October 2, 1947, New Mexico; [p.] Ralph and Antonia Esquibel; [ed.] El Camino Jr College AA degree 1965-1968; [occ.] Retired; [memb.] World of Poetry; [oth. writ.] World Treasury of Great Poems, vol II, World Treasury of Golden Poems, Who's Who in Poetry, vol III - all by John Campbell, editor and publisher; [pers.] My life is like a giant tree. Its trunk reaching high into the open air. Trying to find something to cling to, always reaching, but very still...Holding onto its very existence, its roots. Phillip C. Esquibel; [pers.] Dearly beloved Jesus...Please restore my spirit with faith in you, to give my mind and body new hope and fill my heart with love and kindness. Please cleanse my soul of all sins, now and forever...Amen; [a.] Torrance, CA

EVANS (MAL), MALKANTHI
[b.] October 23, 1949, Sri Lanka; [p.] Walter Perera, Freeda Perera; [m.] Franklin Evans, August 21, 1982; [ch.] Christopher Evans; [ed.] DVM Univ of Sri Lanka, MSC, Ph.D Univ of Gaelph Ontario, Canada; [occ.] Faculty - Ridgetown Agricultural College, Ontario, Canada; [oth. writ.] Several poems published in the Jewels for Jesus newsletter, scientific papers published in American and Canadian Journals;

[pers.] My poems are based on experience and my personal reflection. I enjoy my son Christopher and I hope my poetry reflects this. I am greatly influenced by the writings of Luci Shaw; [a.] Melbourne, Ontario, Canada

EVANS, CAROL MAYO
[b.] January 13, 1954, Wales; [p.] Lilian and Cecil Evans; [ch.] 1 daughter age 6 1/2 yrs named Philippa; [ed.] Completed high school; [occ.] Part-time waitress and bar person; [memb.] Anglican Church of Wales; [hon.] none; [oth. writ.] Have written several poems and a short story none published so far; [pers.] Have worked at many varied occupations and lived in Canada for four yrs from 1977-81; [a.] Abergynolwyn, Gloynedd, Wales, UK

EVANS, CASEY COSMO
[b.] July 22, 1969, California; [p.] Cheryl Ruth Evans and Steven Charles Evans; [m.] Kristi R. Evans, August 17, 1988; [ch.] Acacia Mar Evans (February 26, 1991); [ed.] The School of Hard Knocks; [occ.] Starving author, song writer, poet. Making ends meet in menial ways [oth. writ.] An unpublished novel and scores of unpublished poems and songs; [pers.] Writing has always been a release for me. My emotions rule my poetry and creative writings. This poem, written in haste, reflects an anger-written in a serene state of mind about self proclaimed know it alls, and how the world would be a better place without them; [a.] Corona, CA

EVANS, NIA
[b.] February 13, 1975, Des Moines, IA; [p.] Connie O. Evans; [ed.] Dowling High School; [occ.] Student; [memb.] Rainbow Coalition, NAACP youth member, and Iowa Buxton Heritage Club; [hon.] 4 years at the Young Drake Writers Conference; [oth. writ.] A variety of short stories and poems published in other anthologies.; [pers.] I like writing. It gives me pleasure to know I accomplished something worthwhile. Watching and listening to the world draws me to write it on paper and then the words themselves come alive and tell a story all on its own.; [a.] Des Moines, IA

EVERLY, KATHERINE M.
[Pen.] Katherine Worth-Everly; [b.] June 19, 1912, Geneva, IL; [p.] John and Sarah Worth; [m.] Raymond H. Everly, February 12, 1943 (Dec.); [ch.] Mary and Stephen (adopted); [ed.] High School, 3 years Nursing and P.G. Pediatrics; [occ.] Retired; [memb.] St. Mary Cathedral Guild, AARP, Cap. Chap. 3146, Wyoth County Historical Soc., R.S.V.P. (one to one tutor), Army Nurse Corps WWII, Catholic Nurses Assoc. (Cheyene), United Medical Center Auxillary; [hon.] AARP Special Citation, for 1990, for "Outstanding Service to the Community", featured in an article in Cheyenne Paper.; [oth. writ.] Sen. Class History for H.S. Yearbook 1930, Article in Modern Maturity, Poem in home town paper 1930, article in Sat. Eve Post.; [pers.] I believe each of us should contribute whatever we can to our community; [a.] Cheyenne, WY

EVERS, GENE
[Pen.] Gene Alexander
[b.] March 26, 1951, Manhattan; [p.] Lee Evers; [ed.] 1) Pearl River HS, 2) Stony Brook College 3) Made Nursing School of Nassau CC; [occ.] Script writer; [hon.] Made Dean's List in Jr High School (Hicksville Jr High School 1964, 1963); [oth. writ.] Assorted poems and a movie script, poem in the chiropractic journal; [pers.] I believe you can reach the truth through the heart and the mind and a soaring spirit. Influenced by Melville and the philosophy of Nietake; [a.] Bethpage, NY

FAISAL, JEHAN
[b.] November 17, 1976, Ames, IA; [p.] Dr. Caroline and Abdulla Faisal; [ed.] Will graduate from Ames High School in May 94; [occ.] Student; [oth. writ.] Several poems published in Des Moines National Poetry Festival; [pers.] I have been influenced by both my Saudi and my American heritage.; [a.] Ames, Iowa

FAKANKUN, D'ARIA
[Pen.] D'aria; [b.] March 21, 1952, VA Bch, VA; [p.] Daria and James Herron; [ch.] Olusegun, Jr, Jame Manigo, Jr (departed this earth January 22, 1994) [memb.] Federal Woman's Program Norfolk Nava Shipyard, Portsmouth, VA, Laubach Reading an Literacy Program; [hon.] Specialized Act Awar from Norfolk Naval Shipyard, 92, Special Act Awar from Norfolk Naval Shipyard, 93; [oth. writ.] Grea American Poetry Anthology, poem published titled No Day Shall Come, thru World of Poetry and spok poetry over radio station WDAS, Phila, PA 1985 fo Senior Citizen Program (have tape), Federal Woman' Program, poem presented in their newsletter; [pers. I love this verse by (Unknown author), Title: The Poe and His Songs, Last Verse: For voices pursue him/he by day, and haunt him/her by night, and he/she listen and needs must obey when the angel says "write" [a.] Norfolk, VA

FALLON, DANIEL JOSEPH
[b.] December 9, 1957, San Francisco; [p.] Williar and Barbara Fallon; [ch.] Riley William Fallon; [ed. Fountain Valle High School, Bachelor of Scienc Degree in Physical Education - Cal State Univ a Fullerton; [occ.] Superior Court Courtroom Clerk [pers.] I am just one of who knows how many poe out there just trying to find himself. We all have th capability to write poetry. All it takes is to live life Each of us will interpret what he sees and feel differently, based on our personalities, our values our hopes and our dreams. What is a poet? To me poet is a man or woman who has experienced passio and emotion in their life and is able to express thos feelings in writing; [a.] Corona, CA

FALLON, TONY
[b.] May 1, 1944, Athlone, Ireland; [p.] Maimi (Living) Bernard (Deceased); [m.] Mary B. Quinn January 31, 1970; [ch.] Brian, Anthony Christopher [ed.] Rahara Ireland Grammar C.B.S. Roscommon Ireland 2 yrs. High, no college.; [occ.] Real Estatg Sales, Disc Jockey; [memb.] Long Island Board o Realtors Ancient Order of Hubernians St. Brendan Association; [hon.] Roscommon Man of the Year in America 1985. Best Ethnic Radio Show Produce 1982-3-4-5. Many many citations from State, City and Federal Officials for Charitable Work an Fundraising; [oth. writ.] Thousands of poems, songs jokes, articles and short stories in Ireland and Americ Newspapers. Numerous copyrights for songs poem and artwork. Also wrote all material for my own radi shows for 15 yrs.; [pers.] Nobody should allow the lack of education to hinder their progress. Boredon will kill more spirits than hard work ever killed. If yo don't read how can you dream.; [a.] Long Beach, NY

FARELLO, FRANK S.
[b.] September 8, 1949, New York City; [p.] Fran and Rose Farello; [m.] Patricia, September 1, 1974 [ch.] Frank, Evamarie, Sean; [ed.] Bishop Loughli High School, New York City Community College Brooklyn College; [occ.] Airline Rep; [memb.] Virg Society; (IFPC) Inst for Philosophical Change; Base ment Brains; Musicians Anonymous; Art and Artists Inc; [hon.] Long Island Slap-on-the-Back Award (1s place); The Humanitarian Handshake House Troph (3rd place); [oth. writ.] Many poems published i local newspapers; short stories, movie reviews, fic tion and non-fiction published as the literary consult ant for the Long Island Dispatch; [pers.] I strive t

educe prejudice by promoting universal brotherhood; [a.] Howard Beach, NY

ARESE, THOMAS V.
[Pen.] T. Bisogno Farese; [b.] June 25, 1933, Newark, NJ; [p.] Thomas and Rose Farese; [ed.] Julliard School of Music, Wolfgang Goethe Inst: Frankfort, /Main W. Germany, Rutgers Univ (BA), Newark, NJ; [occ.] Language Scientist; [memb.] Full member: American Cryonics Society; [hon.] Governor (Board of Director) for: American Cryonics Society - Cupertino, CA; Past (East Bay Chapter): Society for Technical Communications; [oth. writ.] Logo aediatrics, bio-molecular linguistics, Ideotaxy, syncotronic Ideometry, Tableaus and other pictures: forthcoming (Vantage Press), One unguarded moment: writing in progress withholding publication; [pers.] It shall ot be through the use of arms that we command our rightful place, no by submission to a cultist's voice leading us on to the Valley of Death, but by subscribing to benevolent ideas that portend of an reluctable adventure to know the world first hand, without impediments of time and evolution; [a.] Pinole, CA

ARINA, OTIO, TONY
[Pen.] O. T. Farina; [b.] May 18, 1915, Brooklyn, NY; [p.] Deceased; [m.] Maria, November 29, 1952; [ch.] None; [ed.] Junior H.S., Attended Infantry School at Fort Benning, GA; [occ.] Retired; [memb.] OAV Blessed Sacrament Ch.; [hon.] Two published poems, Senior Arizona, Richardson Chamber of Commerce, TX, Gwenty W.W.II, Medals and Citations; [oth. writ.] 400 Copywrighted verses, unpublished, narrations, and lyrics; [pers.] I write for mood, atmosphere and pleasure for others to enjoy. Through range of topics; [a.] Scottsdale, AZ

ARRELL, AMY R.
[Pen.] Armsmere Ravenglass; [b.] April 28, 1959, Los Angels, CA; [p.] Jody Farrell, Edward Farrell; [m.] Marjorie Andreco; [m.] October 11, 1986; [ch.] Daniel Roric Andreco; [ed.] Tamalpais High Mill Valley, CA; Porterville Horse Shoeing School, Porterville, CA; [occ.] Construction Laborer, Farmer; [memb.] People for the Ethical Treatment of Animals, Momazons, Greenpeace, The Tournament Company (a medieval re-enactment group); [oth. writ.] Fantasy novel: For the love of a Queen, several historical short stories, many poems, articles for The Sequoia Sentinel; [pers.] As a lesbian writer and an avid historian, I feel it is through literature (the creating of it and the reading of it) that we may refine sex roles and social structure, thereby realizing more equal society; [a.] Three Rivers, CA

ARRELL, CHARLOTTE R.
[b.] June 7, 1968, Bronx, NY; [p.] Diane Shrum/William D. Farrell; [ed.] Graduated from Immaculata High School in 1987. Completed and graduated 1-yr information systems program at Katherine Gibbs in 1990; [occ.] Secretary; [memb.] Malce monthly donations to the North Shore Animal League; [hon.] Made the honor roll for the first, (and last time), in the 8th grade!, Several academic awards throughout academic career. I've written several poems, starting in my sophomore year in high school. (My English teacher made us keep a journal everyday and that started me to writing poetry); [pers.] Believe in yourself, perservere, trust your instincts, and no matter how difficult your dreams may seem, keep going! Never give up!; [a.] Bronx, NY

ASULO, VENKA
[Pen.] Venka Dyro; [b.] June 4, 1964, Brooklyn, NY; [p.] William & Evelyn Dyro; [m.] Edmund J. Fasulo, May 7, 1993; [occ.] Travel Consultant, C.A. Hanssen & Bros. Inc.; [memb.] Mid-Atlantic Rosemailing Society; [oth. writ.] Greeting Cards, Short Stories, poems; [pers.] Special thanks to my father, for never

giving up.; [a.] Brooklyn, NY

FAULKNER, DONALD
[Pen.] Don; [b.] January 2, 1931, Nashville, GA; [m.] Cauley & Marie Faulkner (both deceased); [m.] Maxylene Adams (maiden name), July 2, 1954; [ch.] Donald Faulkner, Jr; [ed.] Four years college, Temple College, TN, B.A. Degree in Bible and Religion; [occ.] Minister, Lakeland Drive-In Church over 15 yrs.; [memb.] National Literary Society, American Assoction of Ordained Ministers, American Institute of Professionals, National Society of Tax Professionals, Southern Baptist Minister, Temple University Varsity Club; [hon.] Literary Guild of America 1956, National Foundation for Freedom 1959, Academy of Sciences 1981, National Freedom Foundation 1992; [oth. writ.] Various short stories, hundreds of Homitetic works, preparations of weekly sermons; [pers.] I was ordained as a Southern Baptist Minister in July 1954...I have travelled as a Southern Baptist Missionary to Puerto Rico from 1955 to 1958. I have always enjoyed reading religious materials and I have over 1,000 books in my personal library.

FAWLEY, MYRA
[b.] September 24, 1960, Howell, MI; [p.] McClellan & Payline Stampter; [m.] John Ray Fawley, February 13, 1982; [ch.] Johnny, Adam, Kevin; [ed.] Knox Senior High Ancilla College; [occ.] Activities Director; [oth. writ.] Several poems for newsletter each month. Have never had any published before.; [pers.] All of my poems I write from my heart, parents and family are my inspirations as well as the people I work with.; [a.] Knox, IN

FEARN, RODERICK MURRAY
[Pen.] Nil; [b.] January 5, 1931, Iroquois Falls, Ont; [p.] Albert Sidney Fearn, Janet Crombie Robertson; [m.] Hazel Lorne Winningham, November 8, 1969; [ch.] Glenn W. Fearn, Roy W. Gauvreau, Pierre Richard Fearn; [ed.] Grade 12 and two yrs SAIT in Calgary, Alberta; [occ.] Retired; [oth. writ.] Seventy assorted poems by RM Fearn covering; Religious Matters Topography People, places economics, Patriotism compiled and bound by myself; [pers.] My intent to write poetry is to raise the standards of my fellow citizenry in my country. My thoughts are akin to Robert the English poet who is a relative; [a.] Lardston, Ab, Canada

FEDELE, THOMAS
[pers.] To my son, Kenan; You are my inspiration and you make me proud...I love you.

FEDEWICK, EMILY
[b.] Winnipeg; [m.] Single; [ed.] West Kildonan Collegiate, St. James Collegiate University of Winnipeg; [occ.] Secretary; [memb.] Volunteer at the United Nations branch in Winnipeg. Also, volunteer at Dalnavert Museum, a Former Home of 1st Prime Minister's son built in 1895.; [hon.] Won a 3rd prize for an essay I wrote in grade 8 out of all the children in Manitoba, won an award in Grade XII for the highest mark in history; [oth. writ.] Wrote a christmas story in December 93, for a local paper.; [pers.] I want to do things that will make a difference for people and ultimately help them.; [a.] Winnipeg, Manitoba, Canada

FEGER, TAUSHA
[b.] October 12, 1981, Somerset, KY; [p.] David Feger and Cathy Feger-Miller; [ed.] Currently 6th grade student at Southern Middle School, Somerset, KY; [occ.] Student; [memb.] Jr Beta Club, Washington Club, Photography Club, Cadet Girl Scout; [hon.] 1st place local level - 1993 Reflections Literary Contest; [pers.] The biggest part of writing is reading. My 2nd grade teacher, Paula Adams, helped me recognize my talent for writing and love of reading. She was my greatest influence, and still is; [a.]

Somerset, KY

FEIBUSCH, IDA
[b.] April 16, 1925, NYC; [p.] Sadie and Louis Kaplan (deceased); [m.] Rubin (deceased), December 1, 1940; [occ.] Stuart; [ed.] High School grad, Julia-Richman, 1 yr NY City College; [occ.] Housewife; [pers.] It matters not how old you are. It matters only how you think. Go along with the times. They change just like we do; [a.] New York, NY

FEIGELSON, SUSAN B.
[b.] May 12, 1963, Brooklyn, NY; [p.] Theodore Feigelson, Beatrice Feigelson; [ed.] Brooklyn College, Brooklyn, NY, BA History; [pers.] I dedicate my poetry to the memory of my father, Theodore Jerold Feigelson, who was, and will always be, my greatest inspiration; [a.] Brooklyn, NY

FELD, NEAL
[b.] May 9, 1976, Brooklyn, NY; [p.] Stanley Feld, Ph.D., Haya Feld; [ed.] Senior at Hewlett High School, Hewlett, NY; [occ.] Student; [oth. writ.] Works in four genres: 30 short stories, 2 short novels, 1 short play, numerous poems.

FELIX, JULIE
[b.] April 28, 1978, Seoul, S. Korea; [p.] James Felix, Yon Ahn-Felix; [ed.] Columbiana High School; [occ.] High school student; [memb.] SADD, Big Brother/Big Sister Program; [hon.] Presidential Academic Fitness Award; [pers.] My parents gave me love, my teachers gave me knowledge, God gave me faith, but my grandmother taught me how to go after my dreams. To her I owe all of my successes; [a.] Columbiana, OH

FELMET, MOLLY
[b.] January 25, 1976, NC; [p.] Holt and Diane Felmet; [pers.] I dedicate "The Kiss" with all my love to Thomas Holmes who has shown me more love and support than I could ever repay in just one lifetime.; [a.] Bunnlevel, NC

FELTMAN, MARVEL L.
[Pen.] Margo Lane; [b.] March 21, 1924, Onsted, MI; [p.] Irving R. Preston (Poet); [m.] Ida Louise Smith Preston (Poet), March 23, 1968; [ch.] By former marriage, Laura Lee, Douglas, Priscilla; [ed.] 9th grade; [occ.] Retired but owned a Adult Foster Care Hm for 30 yrs; [memb.] Church of Christ, Edun, OH, AARP Retired Citizens, National Rifle Assoc, National Law Enforcement Memorial Fund, US Navy Memorial Plant Owner; [hon.] Having a poem published in The Coming of Dawn, winning second prize for singing Danny Boy when in the 8th grade; [oth. writ.] Have written a book about Adult Foster Care, not published. Poem published in Western Kennel World Calif, about a German Shepherd dog I owned; [pers.] I like to sew. Make quilts. Can't type very well. Had 1/2 sem of typing. Worked hard all my life taking care of people in my foster care home. Enjoy doing for the poor - that where bad times come from; [a.] Edon, OH

FERGUSON, BILLIE-JO (CHILES)
[b.] May 11, 1974, Nelson, BC; [p.] Gordon Chiles and Linda Wiebe; Stepfather - Ivan Wiebe; [m.] Brad Ferguson, July 3, 1993; [ed.] WR Myers, Lethbridge Collegiate Institute, Taber, AB; [hon.] Editors Choice award from The National Library of Poetry contest 1993; Honor Roll; [oth. writ.] "Drinking and Driving," which appeared on T.V. talk show; "The Altar," published in The Coming of Dawn.; [pers.] Ambition, determination, and drive are the keys to success. This poem was written for my sister Kari, and is dedication to all of my sisters.; [a.] Taber, AB Canada

FERNHOLM, RITA
[b.] December 5, Stockholm; [p.] Lars Fernholm and Karin Lundgren Fernholm; [occ.] Student; [pers.] I am from Sweden and Swedish is my native language, but after studying at Knox College in Illinois I write in both English and Swedish.; [a.] Osterskar, Sweden

FERNICOLA, JOSEPH
[Pen.] none; [b.] April 28, 1951, NJ; [p.] Deceased; [ch.] Melissa Dawne, Melynda Jo; [ed.] 2 yrs. college. Major Cultural Anthropology; [occ.] Retired (medically); [memb.] none; [hon.] Dean's List throughout college; [pers.] numerous awards for USMC action while in Vietnam; [oth. writ.] Currently working on a novel, title "Just Family"; [pers.] There really is a Santa Claus, Toto. Don't ask, it's not what you think!.; [a.] Ft. Myers, FL

FIELDER, RICHARD WAYNE
[Pen.] Rickki Wade; [b.] April 19, 1952, Wytheville, VA; [p.] Wade and Katherine Fielder; [m.] Pamela Widener Fielder, September 12, 1975; [ch.] I have no children. (which is a story in its own right); [ed.] Rural Retreat High School, 1970, Wytheville Community College, A.S., 1972, Virginia Tech (VPI & SU), B.S. ACCT. 1974, Presently enrolled in M.S. Taxation program of William Howard Taft University; [occ.] I am a Certified Public Accountant and a Certified Management Accountant with my own accounting, tax and consulting practice.; [memb.] American Institute of CPA's, VSCPA Scholarship Committee, Highlands Chapter, VSCPA, Institute of Management Accountants, American Society of Accountants President, Wythe-Bland Chapter of the Virginia Tech Alumni Association, 1993-94, The Rural Retreat United Methodist Church, where I teach Sunday School, other capacities.; [hon.] Dean's List, Honor Roll, 4th in HS class, voted Most Studious, Magna Cum Laude, WCC-1972, Beta Alpha Psi and Beta Gamma Sigma honorary fraternities, Mechanical Drawing Award in High School, Most Improved, The Deal Carnegie Course 1980; [oth. writ.] "Our Zenity" a poem written in 1968, Senior "Skip-Day" skit in 1970 which was a take-off of the "Hee-Haw" telivision show.; [pers.] I have battled major depression illness all of my life. For years I knew not what was going on. Now that I know most of the hidden skeletons of that history, I feel deprived of an opportunity to know and love my grandparents. From deprivation, not abundance, springs forth the waters of expression, flowing as though let go by a failed dam. Hearts and minds flooded with emotion, both good and bad, produce words twisted into artful phases not unlike the soulds from which they come.; [a.] Wytheville, VA

FIGLIOMENI, FRANK
[b.] November 5, 1966, Albany, NY; [p.] Rocco & Carmela; [m.] Dan,a Fiance', April 95; [ed.] One year State University Albany, NY 1991, Christian Brothers Academy 1985; [occ.] Chef, Owner Figliomeni's Rest Inc.; [hon.] Semi Finalist Minors Cook 1988, Finalist 1993 Rich's Dessert Contest, Honorable Mention, Pork Contest Cook Off 1993; [oth. writ.] none, that are published; [pers.] I only know of two worlds the physical world that we all see and touch and the world in our minds; [a.] Albany, NY

FILIAR, THOMAS
[b.] October 26, 1951, Auburn, NY; [p.] Bohdan and Mary Filiak; [ed.] Univ of Notre Dame, South Bend, IN, Rush Univ, Chicago, IL; [occ.] Medical Technologist; [memb.] American Society of Clinical Pathologists (ASCP); [hon.] Dean's List, Rush Assoc Scholarship, Member, Univ Research Committee; [oth. writ.] Several poems published in literary journals and publications. Working on a collection of poems entitled "Western Rhyme"; [pers.] Poetry is the language of the soul; [a.] Auburn, NY

FILOSA, DEVON
[Pen.] Devon Filosa; [b.] November 2, 1980, Brooklyn; [p.] Deborah and Albert; [ed.] Our Lady of Angels and McKinley Junior High School; [occ.] Student; [hon.] Service Awards (3). Good Conduct and Effort (2); [a.] Brooklyn, NY

FINA, TINA
[b.] February 17, 1961, Houston, TX; [p.] Bill and Racine Watson; [ch.] two daughters, Kristina and Amanda ages 12 & 11; [ed.] Mineral Wells High School, Weatherford College LVN School, Jones Real Estate School, Insurance Agent School, Licensed in each one.; [occ.] Insurance Agent and writing poetry and writing a book; [memb.] International Society of Poets, Holiday hills Country Club; [hon.] Four poems published in National Library of Poetry Anthologies. "Troubled Heart" in On a Threshold of a Dream", "My Dear Friend" in The Coming of Dawn, "Friendship of the Heart" in The Space Between, "One of a Kind" in the Desert sun; [hon.] Editor's Choice Award from International Society of Poets, Lifetime Membership of International Society of Poets; [oth. writ.] Dreaming, My True Blessings, Shall We Dance, Beauty, Put Aside, What Shall Happen, Our Games, Return, My Love, The Art of Poetry, Innocent Man, Bobby, The Cliffs Adventure Oh, Dear Lord.; [pers.] I really enjoy writing poetry. I believe our life experiences help us journey through to become better people and I know the Lord helps us every day. I feel that I have truly been blessed and given a gift to write. I am very thankful; [a.] Mineral Wells, TX

FINDLEY, LELA E.
[b.] December 11, 1913, Nebraska; [p.] JV and Mable Pursel; [m.] divorced, July 18, 1937; [ch.] Darla (deceased), Dorothy, Cathy; [ed.] B.Ed - MA, Psychologist license, Counseling license, Administrative Credential; [occ.] Retired; [memb.] NRTA, CRTA, AARP, 60+ of Calf State at Bakersfield; Trinity Methodist Church, Amaranth, White Shrine, Eastern Star, Alpha Delta Kappa; [hon.] National Defense Act recipient 1967-1968. PTA Life Membership. Women's Society Methodist Church, I have been a Lay Preacher in my church; [oth. writ.] "Three Faiths", "My Education", "An Artist's Hand"; [pers.] My poetry uses God and his blessings as a basis for thought; [a.] Bakersfield, CA

FINKE, MARGARET M.
[Pen.] Peggy Finks; [b.] May 28, 1912, TX; [p.] George & Harriet Porter; [m.] Walter Finke, November 30, 1933; [ch.] Two daughters; [ed.] Two years college; [occ.] Retired; [oth. writ.] Wrote many, never submitted any.; [pers.] I'm now in the eightys, I have five grandchildren and three great-grandchildren and hope I've measured up in some small way to the grandmothers my children had.; [a.] Huntington Beach, CA

FINNEY, SCOTT W.
[Pen.] Will; [b.] February 22, 1970, Logansport, IN; [p.] Tom and Paula Finney; [occ.] Computer Sales & Service, Photography and Writing; [memb.] International Freeland Photographers Organization; [oth. writ.] Publication on State Park in Tennessee (Old Stone Fort); [pers.] My love of writing, and a want to make others happy, has caused the writing of poems so that all reading them may know of the expressions sometimes suppressed because of the stress of daily life. I hope that is some small way I can give someone a happier day; [a.] Manchester, TN

FISH, ROBERT
[b.] January 20, 1954, Ashtabula, OH; [p.] Delores Fish, Guy Fish; [m.] Janet Fish, April 16, 1977; [ch.] Kylan Robert; [ed.] St John High, Univ of Phoenix; [occ.] Principal in the Sage Tax Group; [pers.] I write from the heart with an emphasis on personal relation-

ships; [a.] Gilbert, AZ

FISHER, AGNES
[Pen.] Senga-On-Sculpture; [b.] March 21, 1909 Dundee, Scotland; [p.] John and Agnes McJannes [m.] Leonard, December 18, 1935; [ch.] Lenor Agnes, Robert John, Elizabeth Anne, Gordon Duncan [ed.] Davidson High (Davidson, Sask), North Islan College (B.C. Canada); [occ.] Retired; [memb.] Community Arts Council, North Island Clay Club, Happ Wanderers Club, Campbell River O.A.P. Assn. [hon.] First for sculpture injured show at Madron College, Nanimo, B.C., First for painting at Jurie Show at Prince Rupert B.C.; [oth. writ.] Poems i local papers articles regarding our rain forest. Th Coming Of Dawn.; [pers.] I live in the rain forest b the sea and I care very much about our environmen The sea and the tall trees have inspired me.; [a.] B.C. Canada

FISHER, CELESTE
[b.] February 28, 1983; [a.] Naperville, IL

FITZPATRICK, MAUREEN
[Pen.] Bella Kaplan; [b.] February 20, 1945 Westmount (Montreal) Quebec, Canada; [p.] Stanley Jane Wood; [m.] Victor Fitzpatrick, May 2, 1964 [ch.] Deborah, Susan, Wendy; [ed.] McGill Uni Psychology Major, English Minor; currently workin toward Ph.D in 20th century American and Canadia literature; [occ.] Traveling, discovering constan wonders and dilemmas of the planet earth. Freelanc writing; [oth. writ.] 20th Century American an Canadian Literatue; and to which I a now currentl working on in a continuum towards a Ph.D in 20t Century American and Canadian Literature (20th) [a.] Gloucester (Ottawa Suburb), Canada

FIX, JOHN
[b.] January 26, 1968, San Diego, CA; [p.] Larry an Sandra Fix; [m.] Susan Scrivens Fix; [ed.] Easle High School; [occ.] Intelligence Analyst and Arabi Linguist, US Army; [pers.] Life is like a puzzle. W are all pieces to that puzzle. Once we find our nich in life, we then make a greater contribution to th bigger picture. And before we know it, the puzzle i complete; [a.] Ft Meade, MD

FLANAGAN, DENNIS
[Pen.] Joshua; [b.] December 3, 1972, St Petersburg FL; [ed.] Dixie Hollins High School; [occ.] Unite States Marine Corps; [oth. writ.] Just poetry in various books and magazines; [pers.] Philosophy: feel that the world can do better, so threw writing hope to make that happen.

FLEISCHMANN, MARTHA JO
[b.] December 30, 1955, Detroit; [p.] Leah & Charle Snider, Yosef Fleischmann, April 25, 1982; [ch.] Michael Jacob, Jonathan Aaron, Manuel Abraham [ed.] BBA, Finance (Univ. of MI); [occ.] Home maker; [hon.] National Honor Society, Phi Bet Kappa, 1st Place Women's Original Oratory (State o MI), Branstrom Scholar and Angell Scholar (Univ. o MI); [pers.] Poetry is the best of civilization distille into words.; [a.] Bloomfield Hills, MI

FLEISHMAN, DEBRA JANINE
[b.] December 20, 1968, Los Angeles, CA; [p.] Gary Mitock (7/28/43) and Ronnye Mitock (1/15/45); [m. Jeff Fleishman, February 14, 1992; [ed.] Calabasa High School; [occ.] Receptionist, Desert Vision Palm Springs, CA; [oth. writ.] An additional poen published in "The Coming of Dawn.; [pers.] I an greatly inspired to wirte poetry, due to my husban Jeff, whom I love dearly and will cherish always.; [a. Palm Desert, CA

LEMING, NICOLE
.] August 1, 1979, Staten Island, NY; [p.] Vincent
d Maria Fleming; [ed.] Toms River High School
orth; [occ.] Student; [memb.] Student Council;
am Program; [hon.] Gifted and Talented Program;
ertificate of Merit Board of Education; [oth. writ.]
ublication in the 1993 Anthology of Poetry by
oung Americans; Publications in school newspaper
d magazines; [pers.] Look deeply; care greatly; [a.]
oms River, NJ

LETCHER, KAREN L.
.] September 18, 1956, CA; [p.] George & Marie
kler; [m.] James M. Fletcher Jr., October 27, 1984;
h.] James M. Fletcher III, Jeremy George Thomas
etcher; [ed.] 12 yrs., Camarillo High School; [occ.]
SAF; [memb.] Veterans at Foreign Wars; [oth.
rit.] Lots

LEURY, HELEN C.
.] January 4, 1928, Mineville, NY; [p.] Clyde E.
d Sylvia A. Smith; [m.] Edgar J. Fleury, November
, 1947; [ch.] Sharon M. Keech, David J. Fleury,
mes M. Fleury, (2 grandsons: Joshua M. Keech,
achary A. Keech; [ed.] Graduated (12) years
ineville High School class of 1946, Mineville, NY;
cc.] Housewife (widow); [oth. writ.] Short stories
d poems. 1 poem published in Sparrowgrass Books,
poem published in Quill Books; [pers.] I praise God
r giving me the gift to write, and hope through my
ritings, a window will open for all who read, to share
d enjoy; [a.] Hudson Falls, NY

LORDELIZ, HELEN LENORE
en.] Lenne (Lenore); [b.] July 3, 1920, Athens,
H; [p.] William Edward and Mary Buchanan; [m.]
rlino A. Flordeliz, August 15, 1982; [ch.] 2 sons, 4
ughters, 1 son and 1 twin daughter deceased; [ed.]
yrs, 2 yrs; [occ.] Retired Certified Dietary Service
pv; [memb.] Yes; [hon.] Golden Poet Award 1988
World of Poetry (True Love) under 1980 - my
evious name Lenore Martello; [oth. writ.] Two
blished under Sec Golden Poet Award, 1st one 2nd
em; (A Time to be Free) Quill Books (1982),
idnight Lady pg 30 under former name (L. Martello);
rs.] Since I was in the 3rd grade I started to read and
ve poetry. My first in the glooming and Campells
up dilty I cut them out and made a scrap book from
em. I have many I have not offixed as yet. I want to
nor my lovely teacher Dorothy G. Sweeny for all
r inspiration who lives here; [a.] Brieliant, OH

LORES, MARJORIE ELAINE SUMMERS
.] June 12, 1922, Worcester, MA, USA; [p.] Henry
d Hazel Tracy Gokey; [m.] 1) William Summers
44-1972, Macavio Flores 1979-1994; [ch.] Michele
ccitiello, Steven Summers, Susan Kinkade, Wil-
m Summers (Jr); [ed.] Central High School -
perior Honor Roll; Texas Christian Univ - 2 yrs;
range Memorial Hospital, Montclair State Univ -
ursing School; [occ.] Retired 1993, professional
rse; [memb.] American Chemical Society, Na-
nal Honor Society, Waipahu Jackrabbito Sports
ssn; [hon.] Won 2 National Honor Society College
holarships; [oth. writ.] Collection of Poetry - pre-
ring manuscripts now for publication. Several short
ticles for nurses journal. Few articles on psychic
search. Several childrens stories not yet published;
rs.] Every human emotion and experience is re-
cted in all of any poetry, giving insight into the
use, the effects and cures of a multitude of human
oblems; [a.] Waipahu, HI

LOWERS, J.C.
en.] Bouquet Kid; [b.] November 16, 1948, Broken
w, OK; [p.] Edward Lloyd (dec.) & Tilda Sevenia;
.] X-Ethel Jane Sanders, September 4, 1969; [ch.]
vin Lane, Lloyd Dale (dec), Jason Charles, Mel-
a Dawn, Jeffrey Gregory; [ed.] 1st thru 8th Holly
eek Elm., Idabel Gray High 9th thru 12th.; [occ.]

Supervisor at Pilgrim's Pride Poultry Processing
Plant in Dequeen, Arkansas; [hon.] Eddie Lou Cole's
World of Poetry Honorable Mention in: 1991 3 times,
1990 2 times, 1989-1985 & 1984 1 time Golden Poet
Award in 1991, 1990, 1986, 1985 Silver Poet Award
in 1989 Several poems published in books by Eddie
Lou Cole; [oth. writ.] Song lyrics with music by
Country Creations, Inc. 5 in 1982 and Nashville,
Tennessee, 4 in 1984. Library of Congress Copyright
Office (words only) 3 in 1992 song lyrics; [pers.]
Poems I write is a Gift from God. Some people think
things done or said is by self alone. Without god no
one nor anything would exist. Wake up world facts
are: there was a maker, there will be a taker, the
hereafter is one's choice, either heaven or hell, the
choice only self can make I'm no saint nor preacher
and still have a long way to go. With God's help I hope
for the hereafter (Heaven) one day.; [a.] Broken Bow,
OK

FLOYD, CHRISTOPHER D.
[Pen.] C.D. Floyd; [b.] May 27, 1956, Topeka, KS;
[p.] Donovan and Ruth Margaret Floyd; [ed.]
Tehachapi High, Glendale Community College; [occ.]
Market Research, Winona Market Research Bureau;
[memb.] Society for Creative Anachronism, Arizona
Writers Critique Group; [oth. writ.] First time pub-
lished since college and high school, although I have
several short stories submitted at this time. My first
novel is complete and in it's final draft.; [pers.] I love
God, my parents, the Beatles, Medieval history,
basketball, pepsi and chocolate, in that order. I am
also quite fond of the letter "o"; [a.] Phoenix, AZ

FLOYD, LIZ ROBINSON
[Pen.] Bobbi Simmons; [b.] May 5, 1949, Tuskegee,
AL; [p.] Jerry Robinson, Annie L. Robinson; [m.]
Lodolphus Floyd, July 23, 1988; [ch.] Monica,
Chancey, Michelle, Seporna; [ed.] Tuskegee Inst,
High Alex City State Jr College, Southern Vocational
College, AUM; [occ.] Equipment Technician, VAMC,
Tuskegee, AL; [memb.] American Legion Post 150,
Eastern Star Rosebud Chapter 281; [hon.] Superior
and Outstanding Performance Awards; [pers.] I feel
that poetry is a feeling of the inner soul. One that no
one can see except on paper, and to be able to do this
help to give others joy and consolation; [a.] Auburn,
AL

FLYNN, STEPHEN T.
[b.] August 18, 1951, Bloomington, IL; [p.] Richard
J. and E.L. Flynn; [ed.] Illinois State Univ., and the
Nashville Institute; [occ.] Executive Acct. Specialist
for WMX Technology's; [oth. writ.] Author of "Apples
of Apathy" currently awaiting publication instruciton
manuals on Theory and Practical uses of electronics,
business practice and ethics in the market place both
awaiting publication.; [pers.] My poems are a colleciton
of works written during a love affair with life and a
very special red head. My belief in God and Zen
Buddist teachings hav helped channel both beyond my
poems. I believe in the pursuit of love and the
knowledge that art, love and God are but one.; [a.]
Bloomington, IL

FLYNN, TAMMY L. (KING)
[Pen.] "T."; [b.] October 10, 1965, Janesville, WI;
[p.] Rev. Garfield King and Mrs. Diana Baker; [ch.]
(1 daughter 11 yrs old) "Stasha Lynn" [ed.] Completed
GED 3/93. Currently going to college for
Business Administration; [occ.] Administration As-
sistant for Pollution Cleanup Co, Tpa, FL; [memb.]
Local PTA; [oth. writ.] Several other poems and
personals; [pers.] A "special" thanks to someone very
special whom without, college and publication would
still be only a dream. To you David, with all my heart;
[a.] Tampa, FL

FOERSTER, GARY C.
[b.] April 28, 1947, Bronx, NY; [p.] Violet Jenner
and Herman Foerster; [m.] Valerie Ann Foerster,
April 27, 1969; [ch.] Jennifer, Sharon; [ed.] B.S.
Degree, New York Inst. in Behavior Science and
Criminal Justice; [occ.] Police Sergeant Suffolk County
Police Dept.; [memb.] Superior Officers Assoc.,
Fraternal Order of Police, Drug Recognition Expert.;
[hon.] Internship to the United States Dept. of Trans-
portation in Washington, D.C. 1994-1995; [oth.
writ.] None published; [pers.] Poem written in honor
of my wife Valerie on 11/7/87; [a.] E. Setauket, NY

FOGLE, DON G.
[b.] January 14, 1952, Virginia; [p.] Cecil Donald &
Rose Marie; [m.] Gina, I Love You; [ch.] Susanna,
Evan, Keith, Daisy; [ed.] Graduate of the Greatest
School of Peopleology, The Planet Earth; [occ.]
Resident Artist, Juggler, Clown; [memb.] Lincoln
County 4H; [hon.] Former World Master Freestyle
and self taught Flight Frisbee Champion, privileged to
be a Father; [oth. writ.] Circus Arts curriculum and
advancement program guides. Co-Author, The Fox-
tail Book, Klutz Press California.; [pers.] I believe if
you play games for the reasons you started to in the
first place, i.e. to have fun, you win every time you
play! The most fun wins!; [a.] Toledo, OR

FOLSOM, ELIZABETH
[Pen.] Elizabeth Ellingwood Folsom; [b.] April 15,
1934, Austin, MN; [p.] W.A. Ellingwood Dorothy
Ellingwood; [m.] Franklin H. Folsom, July 1, 1978;
[ch.] Christine, Connie, Colleen, Crystal, Charles,
Berni and Sheila; [ed.] 12 grade; [occ.] Sweeper at
Blackduck School; [hon.] Privilage of having 19
grandchildren; [oth. writ.] I have my collection of
poems but have never entered them in anything
before.; [pers.] Poetry is like a window into ones life
with just enough curtain to keep from revealing all for
the world to see.; [a.] Pennington, MN

FONG, ORLENA WAVERLY
[b.] March 10, 1977, Stanford, CA; [p.] Peggy and
Godfrey Fong; [ed.] Currently a junior at Castilleja
High School; [pers.] "To love and to be loved is to feel
the sun from both sides.; [a.] Los Altos Hills, CA

FONSAH, ESENDUGUE GREG
[b.] September 15, 1958, Tiko, Cameroon, West
Africa; [p.] Joseph B. Fonsah & Mashiana Ebongkie
Fonsah; [m.] Kai Lan Liu Fonsah, June 9, 1984; [ch.]
Derrick Bebongho Fonsah; [ed.] Ph.D. Ag-Econs,
Univ. of Nigeria, Nsukka Msc. Ag-Econs, Univ. of
Kentucky, USA, MBA, Morehead State Uni., BSC
Berea College, Kentucky.; [occ.] Agricultural Econo-
mist and Superintendent, Delmonte Cameroon;
[memb.] Association of MBA Executives 1984;
ACORBAT Association for Cooperation in Banana
Research in the Caribbean and Tropical America
1991-Present; [hon.] Gold Medalist (soccer) The
Blue-Grass State Games, 1987; Certificate of Merit
(Chief Instructor of Kung Fu Martial Art); Labor
Program Award, Berea College 1983; [hon.] Bubors,
Nyerere Athletic Award, Berea College, Athletic
Awa4rd, etc.; [oth. writ.] FONSAH, E.G. and SAND
Chidebelu (1994) Economics of Banana Production
and Marketing in the Tropics, Minerva Press, Lon-
don; [pers.] Hardwork, endurance and perseverance
are the key to success. I get my inspiration from the
poem "Le Laboureur et ses enfants" by La Fontaine
(1621-1695).

FORD, NATALIE PAULINE
[b.] May 9, 1978, El Cajon; [p.] Debbie & Russ Ford;
[ed.] Still in High School, 9th grade; [occ.] Student;
[oth. writ.] Wrote an article on Racism in D.C. Health
Middle level literature book.; [pers.] I dedicate this
poem to all the men and women that almost or did give
their life for the honor of our country.; [a.] Ontario,
CA

FOREMAN, JAMES HAZLETT
[b.] May 2, 1977, Wheeling, WV; [p.] R. Noel Foreman, Anne H. Foreman; [ed.] Linsley School; [occ.] High school student; [memb.] Model UN; History Club; Yearbook Staff; German Club; [oth. writ.] Science Fiction, Historical Fiction, Poetry. Two stories in the Linsly Review; 1992, 1994; [pers.] I write with the idea in mind that people are nothing more than a summation of instinct, knowledge, undying nobility and a heavy smattering of pretentiousness. Some just hide it better than others; [a.] Wheeling, WV

FORSBERG, KYNDRA
[b.] May 10, 1982, Baxter Springs, KS; [p.] Kenneth and Tracy Forsberg; [ed.] McPherson Middle School, McPherson, KS (6th grade); [occ.] Student; [memb.] Harmony Christian Church, McPherson, KS; McPherson YMCA; [hon.] 2nd place - McPherson Middle School, PTA Essay Contest, "An Outstanding Kansas Citizen" - 1993; McPherson Middle School Student of the Week, "Outstanding Achievement" Award - 1993; [pers.] I was ten years old when I wrote this poem for my mother on Mother's Day. The day before my 11th birthday. I enjoy basketball, reading and writing stories and poems; [a.] McPherson, KS

FORSTER, JILL
[b.] October 10, 1954, Sidney; [ed.] B.A. (Hons), Diploma of Educat, PhD; [occ.] Lecturer/Educator; [memb.] Australian Assoc for the Education of Gifted and Talented Children (AAEGT); NSW Inst for Educational Research; NSW Gifted and Talented Assoc; Australian Assoc for Research in Educa (AARE); World Council for Gifted Talented Children, Inc; [hon.] First class honours; Research Awards; PhD in Education; [oth. writ.] Journal articles and editing in education; [pers.] The silence between the waves is one of my sources of inspiration -- similarly, the "Space Between" which perhaps, as T.S. Eliot perceived it, was "half-heard, in the stillness Between two waves of the sea"; [a.] Sidney, Australia

FORTINO, CHRISTINE
[b.] December 20, 1971, Philadelphia, PA; [p.] Albert and Frances Fortino; [ed.] St Maria Goretti HS, St Joseph's Univ; [occ.] Legal Asst/graduate student; [memb.] Cap and Bells Dramatic Arts Society, World Wildlife Fund, Humane Society of the United States, People for the Ethical Treatment of Animals, National Wildlife Fed; [hon.] Who's Who Among American High School Students, 1988-1989; [pers.] Eddie, thank you for being my biggest inspiration. I love you; [a.] Philadelphia, PA

FORTNER, DIANA MAE
[b.] June 3, 1951, Columbus, OH; [p.] Lawrence & Lena Kuhn; [m.] William Earl Fortner, May 25, 1979; [ch.] Rachel Diana, Donald Lee, David Paul; [ed.] Silver Creek Senior High; [occ.] Housekeeper; [memb.] Do volunteer work for American Heart Assoc. and The Kidney Foundation and March of Dimes; [oth. writ.] Other Poems, non published. "Daddy Dear Daddy" "My Little Man"; [pers.] My husband inspired this poem. It seems the people close and dear to me always inspire me to write. I would like to dedicate this to my husband and children; [a.] Sellersburg, IN

FOTAKIS, MARIA
[b.] August 25, 1978, Voorhees, NJ; [p.] George Fotakis, Heidi Milazzo, Bill Milazzo; [ed.] Delsea High School; [occ.] 9th grade student; [pers.] This poem is to my favorite people that inspired me the most: Angelo Rambone and George Fotakis; [a.] Franklinville, NJ

FOWLER, OLIVER E.
[b.] June 23, 1920, IA; [m.] Lillian; [ed.] Univ of Southwest Louisiana 1937-41; [occ.] USAF Ret;

[memb.] Several Civic and Charitable Organizations; [hon.] USAF Air Medal and Commendation Ribbon plus other military awards; [oth. writ.] Song "Five Worms and a Fishin' Pole" - song, "Desert Rat" novel - "Brothers to the Wind" - unpublished - "Legacy of Place' Perdu", "Bride of the Sun-dog"; [a.] Niceville, FL

FOX, MARY BLANCHE
[b.] September 8, 1932, Livingston, TN; [p.] Ruth Mai and Richard Duke; [m.] J. W. Fox, Jr., May 5, 1954, Kimberly Ann Fox, Sisty; [ed.] High School 1951 at Livingston Academy; [occ.] Clerk Typist, Marshall Co., Dept. of Human Resources, Guntersville, AL; [oth. writ.] Published in the National Library of Poetry. I write poems for all occasions in the lives of my friends, happy or sad. Published in hometown newspaper.; [a.] Boaz, AL

FOYS, JOHN
[b.] February 8, 1966, Chicago; [p.] Franfk and Ruth Foys; [ed.] Loyola University of Chicago; [pers.] I seek to express universal human feelings by searching within myself and by observing others.; [a.] Westmont, IL

FRANGOIS, STANLE
[Pen.] Frangois; [b.] January 25, 1973, Haiti; [p.] Eletha Dorsous, Marcel Gowite; [ed.] Ghelsea Vocational H.S., New York Technical College; [occ.] College student employ at "Data Movers"; [memb.] Civil Air Patrol, General Nutritions Center, Chiti's Kick Boxing Club of New York; [hon.] National Honor Society, New York City Chonslu role of Honor sword "Poetry", Cadet of the Year J.R.O.T.C.; [oth. writ.] Several poems published in High School newspapers and year book. The Roses, The Kiss, Blood of a Hero.; [pers.] I try to be the best on everything or anything I do. I thank my Mom and Dad for every successful achievement of my life. Especially my Dad whom never live to see these days of my life.; [a.] Brooklyn, NY

FRANKLIN, ALICIA D.
[b.] March 1, 1968, Chicago, IL; [p.] Grover Franklin & Hazel Franklin; [ed.] Whitney M. Young Magnet H.S., Howard University, B.S. Microbiology 1990, Howard University College of Dentistry; [occ.] Sophomore Dental Student; [memb.] Sigma Gamma Rho Sorority, Inc., American Student Dental Association; [hon.] ETA Sigma Pi (Nat'l Honorary Society of Greek and Latin), Dean's List; [oth. writ.] Other Poems: "Ridin High," " rapped," "Home," "Message to Our Black Youth," Short Story: Final Thoughts; [pers.] Always be true to yourself. Always strive for excellence. Through God all things are possible.; [a.] Chicago, IL

FRANKLIN, MARY ANN (Ed.D)
[b.] February 24, 1921, Boston, MA; [p.] Arthur E. Wheeler and Madeline H. Wheeler Brooks; [m.] Carl M. Franklin, November 29, 1952; [ch.] Evangeline R. H. Franklin-Nash, MD.; [ed.] Howard High School 38, diploma, U of New Hampshire, B.S. 42, U of Buffalo, M.Ed, 48, Harvard Univ, AYI 58-59, Princeton U., S64, Univ of MD, College Park, Ed. D. 82; [occ.] Consultant, H.Ed., Admin. and Mgmt; [memb.] Amer Management Assoc, LA Counseling Assoc, National Conference of Christian and Jews, Admin. Mgmt., Natnl. Assoc for the Advanced... Advancement of Colored People, Urban League, Assoc. for Continuing Higher Ed., former Pres. MD Assoc, H.Ed., S.U.N.O. Faculty Council; [hon.] Natnl. Sc. Foundation Fellowship, Carnegie Ford Fellowship, Phi Sigma Honorary Biological Society, Pi Lambda Theta, Honorary Soc. for Women in Ed.; [oth. writ.] The How and Why of Testing at Elizabeth City State College, 1962, Report on Princeton Univ. Program for Physics Teachers in HBCU's 1964, Learning Summer Camp Code, National Library of

Poetry, 1992, Editor "Academic Affairs Newsletter Morgan State Univ 1980-82, Report on Pre-Colleg Booster Study Prog., Vol. I, II, III; [pers.] I try to liv and to teach to exemplofy principles, values an morals that are based in Judeo Christian teachings t help others solve problems to life situations. Continu to learn reaching for improvements; [a.] New Or leans, LA

FRANKS, CYNTHIA M.
[b.] October 8, 1964, Big Rapids, MI; [p.] Raymon and Barbara Franks; [ed.] Central Michigan Univ NY Univ BA in journalism and sociology); [occ Newswire Editor; [hon.] Merit Scholarship; [oth writ.] Feature length articles, news, reviews, prose poetry and short story book. Published in Michigar New York and California; [pers.] This poem wa written for my grandmother, Genevieve I. Suttor who has recently developed Alzheimer's Disease an currently resides in a Michigan nursing home; [a.] Sa Francisco, CA

FRASER, LORNA A.
[b.] September 19, 1951, St Elizabeth, Jamaica Ralph and Hilda Fraser (deceased); [ed.] St Andrev High School, Univ of the West Indies, BA MA Dip E (to be finalized); [occ.] English teacher, St Hugh' High School (on study leave); [oth. writ.] Unpul lished thesis "Literature Self and Society: the Onto logical Dilemma" in the UWI library, 1993; sever poems published in a local newspaper, "The Sunda Gleamer"; [pers.] I have been writing poetry sinc school days. I try to show the universality of exper ence and man's link to nature as evidenced in th poetry of Wordsworth and Dylan Thomas; [a. Kingston, Jamaica, WI

FRATTO, LOUIS FRANK
[b.] Chicago, IL; [p.] Carmen and Esther; [m Barbara, May 29, 1992; [ed.] 8 yrs grammar, 4 yı high school; [occ.] Truck Driver; [memb.] Broadca Music, Inc (BMI), Nashville Songwriters Assoc; [oth writ.] Poem of my Youth, Possessed, Popcorn an Me, The Girl I Threw Away, (Chocolate Covered (Cherry Pie), Stage Name = Lou Capri; [pers.] I ar a singer-songwriter. I had a few of my songs, playe on the radio; [a.] Cicero, IL

FRAZIER, DENISE LYNNE DUNN
[b.] October 29, 1965, Ottawa, IL; [p.] Raymond G Schink; [p.] Lynne Riordan Schlink; Late Dennis R Dunn; [m.] Kip L. Frazier, August 29, 1992; [ch Colton James; [ed.] Ottawa Twp High School, South ern IL Univ; [occ.] Quality Control and B&B Ele tronics - Ottawa; [memb.] St Patricks Catholic Church American Legion Aux; [hon.] 1st place short story Ruth Rettenborg Writing Award - 1984, OHS Cr ative Writing Contest; [oth. writ.] Have written sho stories, poems for fun. Never have submitted befor this; [a.] Ottawa, IL

FREEMAN, MARILY RENEE
[b.] December 30, 1961, Kansas City, MO; [p James and Charlene Freeman; [ch.] Carl Anthony [ed.] Southeast High, Penn Valley College; [occ Human Services; [memb.] Nation of Islam; [hon Black History Award, Drama Awards and Honors Track and Field, Religious Awards; [oth. writ Published in Kansas City Papers (articles); [pers.] want to feel the higher being, reflect the creator in m writings. I am greatly influenced by the love I have fc my son, Carl Anthony. He is my inspiration in life [a.] Chicago, IL

FRIESEN, MARY
[b.] February 11, 1951, B.C., Canada; [p.] Dave an Tina Fehr; [m.] Wayne Friesen; [ch.] Dean, Shan Darin; [occ.] Homemaker; [oth. writ.] First poe submitted for publication; [pers.] I have writte

umerous poems for family and friends for special ccasions. Am currently working on a book of poems r children. (for publication); [a.] Kamloops, BC, anada

RY, MARY A.
.] February 4, 1913, Ashland, KS; [p.] H.B. and ssie Fry; [pers.] Together, my grandmother and I ave seen over 152 years of life roll by. She was born 1841. I was born in 1913 on a farm in Kansas and randma next door or in my home for 15 years of my e, until her death in 1928. When I was 80 years old ecided to write family stories. My dirty thirties dust orm story opened with this black roller poem.; [a.] shland, KS

UJIWARA, WARREN TADASHI
.] May 5, 1914, Waikapu, Maui, Hawaii; [p.] iichiro Fujiwara and Mitsue Goshi Fujiwara; [m.] ssie Haruko Nakamura Fujiwara, July 12, 1942; h.] Lloyd, Gary, Eric, Mrs. Steven (Sharon) ramham, Mrs. Neal (Nora) Nakamura, Mrs. Donald Flora) Isozaki; [ed.] 6th grade, Honokohua Public chool; Honokohua, Maui, Hawaii; [occ.] Retired ith disability 1952 Sr. Engineer Equipment Me-anic; [oth. writ.] 32 other unpublished imaginative d humorous, stanzas, epic, idyll, ode, and lyric etries; [pers.] Self-educated amateur hobby in writ-g and composing poems or lyrics; [a.] Honolulu, awaii

ULLER, NEVADA LYNN
.] June 11, 1954, Puritan Mines, WV; [p.] Mattie ates and Bernard Yates; [m.] Glenn Fuller, Novem-r 1, 1991; [ch.] April Lynn, Mitchell Glenn, Carol e; [ed.] Norwich Free Academy; [occ.] Home-aker; [oth. writ.] Poems and short stories; [pers.] any are blessed with a heart and mind full of oughts and emotions but few are blessed with the ility to express them; [a.] Norwich, CT

ULLER, OMAR JAMELL
en.] Omar J. Fuller; [b.] April 5, 1983, Det, MI; .] James Fuller, Sharon L. Fuller; [ed.] Fifth grader Marcus Garvey Academy in Detroit; [occ.] Student; emb.] Lemay Church of Christ Youth Committee, e NAACP; [hon.] Young Authors winner of 4th yr a row, 1 time Science Fair Winner, The Mighty Pen inner and other scholastic awards; [oth. writ.] everal short stories printed in the schools Area F. uthors Books; [pers.] I'd like to thank my family and achers for encouraging me to write and special anks to Aunt Barbara and Uncle Earl and my ranny, who I love so dear!; [a.] Detroit, MI

URCHES, MELISSA
.] September 25, 1971, Nashville, TN; [p.] Donna d Keith Thompson; [ed.] La Vergne High, Jefferson ommunity College, Franklin University; [occ.] cords clerk and waitress; [pers.] My dream is ginning to come true.; [a.] Columbus, OH

URMAN, ALEX
.] October 5, 1975; [pers.] I dedicate my poem as ll as my life to my Sarah.; [a.] Northridge, CA

USCO, DIANE M.
.] Paul S. Fusco; [ch.] 1 child, Paul L. Fusco, who as killed in a car accident on December 3, 1988. I rite poetry in his memory; [occ.] Index Clerk in the vingston County Clerk's Office; [oth. writ.] "Re-ember Me" in memory of my son, Paul L. Fusco, blished in the Coming of Dawn in 1993; [pers.] In ving memory of my son, Paul L. Fusco; [a.] vonia, NY

UNDY, TANYA
.] November 12, 1975, Ft Knox, KY; [p.] Lucius d Gloria Gundy; [ed.] Redan High School, Stone ountain Georgia; [occ.] Student at Redan High

School (Senior); [memb.] Students for Black Culture, Literary Magazine; [pers.] Originality is hard to come by, but don't be fake, don't loose ground; [a.] Stone Mountain, GA

GABRIEL, FREDDY
[b.] August 2, 1966, OH; [p.] Agnes Gabriel; [ed.] Death; [occ.] Caaotic Structure Entertainment; [memb.] Ultra sports; [hon.] Life; [oth. writ.] Sex verses, collection of poems and writing; [pers.] Communication is a must for positive friction; [a.] Tempe, AZ

GAGNON, ANNIE
[b.] June 11, 1975, Grand Falls, NB, Canada; [p.] Jacinthe and Ivan Gagnon; [hon.] 2 most valuable player awards in basketball, also a second place medallion in basketball finals, and an athlete of the year award chosen on the basis of sports and academics; [oth. writ.] A score of other poetry writings; [pers.] What comes of my work, comes of my heart; [a.] Buckingham, Quebec, Canada

GAILLARD, YVON ANDRE
[Pen.] John Yag; [b.] October 18, 1923, Sion, Switzerland; [p.] Edouard E. Blanche Gaillard; [m.] 2nd m. Jovita Maria, October 18, 1985; [ch.] Yvon Andre De Chambery Gaillard; [ed.] Catholic College, Brid Switzerland/Arch. Designe at Kunstgewerbeschule Zurich, Switzerland, BA Univ Getulio Vargas, Sao Paulo Brazil; [occ.] Consultor Empresarial Conf, Mainly, researches on human behaviour in business; [memb.] Conselho Federal de Administracao, Ex Alumni Fundacao Getulio Vargas, Sao Paulo, New York Academy of Science; [oth. writ.] In preparation "Can Man Survive" to be published in the US; [pers.] All we aim at is wealth. Through that we spoil our health. We destroy the richness of mind. We age very fast. If you intend to stay young for a long time. Take good care of the treasure present in your mind; [a.] Sao Paulo - Brazil 02/02/94, Yvon Andre Gaillard; [a.] SP, Brazil

GAKIS, ANNA R.
[Pen.] Anna Gakis; [b.] January 1, 1950; [p.] Rose and Peter Karayeanes; [m.] Mr. Lambros Gakis, december 6, 1979; [ch.] Vayia Gakis, age 13 and Rosanna Gakis, age 8; [ed.] High School; [occ.] Housewife; [memb.] International Poetry; [hon.] Merit Awards, Editor's Choice Award; [oth. writ.] I just recently started writing lyrics; [pers.] I would very much like to dedicate "Mother's Expectation" to my mother in law Vayia Gakis and in memory of my mother who passed away, April 1993, Rose Karayeanes, born 1926, died 1993

GALDAMEZ, EMMA
[b.] August 20, 1978, El Salvador; [p.] Ricardo Galdamez, MD, Elsa Galdamez; Sisters: Ana Galdamez, Martha Galdamez; [ed.] PS 120 Q, Rachel Carson IS 237 Q, St Agnes Academic; [occ.] Student; [memb.] Volunteer at The NV Hospital Medical Center of Queens; [pers.] I want to show my gratitude to my parents and Kenny Ortiz for their encouragement and influence. I will strive to write more as I grow older with God's help; [a.] Flushing, NY

GALIANO, ANTHONY JOSEPH
[b.] October 21, 1959, Beth Israel Hospital Passaic, NJ; [p.] Anthony and Lucy Galiano; [ed.] Hill Top Elementary, Thomas Jefferson Middle Lodi High School, Don Bosco Prep High school, Bergen Tech Vocational School, Adult Training School; [occ.] I work in Machine Trade; [memb.] Postal Commemorative Stamp Society; [oth. writ.] Book reports, Thesis on Islamic Religion in Don Basco Prep High School. I got an A+ 100%; [pers.] If man is to save the earth. He must first save himself; [a.] Lodi, NJ

GALINDO, MICHELLE
[Pen.] Michelle Mantooth; [b.] May 15, 1962, Las Vegas, NV; [ch.] Tina 17, Kesha 12, Rustin 5; [ed.] Major in Art, Minor in English; [occ.] Freelance Artist; [oth. writ.] Writing a novel not yet published; [pers.] The emotional expression in writing is similiar to that of my painting; [a.] Austin, TX

GAMEZ, ANGIE
[Pen.] NG Gamez; [b.] March 14, 1952, Edinburg, TX; [p.] Alberto Gamez; [ch.] John W. Morgan, Jr.; [ed.] MPA University of New Mexico; MAM (Emory-Riddle Aeronautical University); [occ.] Senior Planner, Dallas Area Rapid Transit; [hon.] 1971-1972 I.S.U. Homecoming Queen's Court, 1971-1972 I.S.U. Vo-Tech Student Body Secretary, 1983 Congressional Hispanic Caucus Fellow; [oth. writ.] Unpublished Poet (short story), Live or Die (poem), Pageant Creed (poem); [a.] Dallas, TX

GANDHI, NEIL
[b.] March 10, 1981, Parma, OH; [p.] Ashok and Venu Gandhi; [ed.] Holy Family Elementary, Colony Meadows Elementary; First Colony Middle School; [occ.] Student; [memb.] Fort Bend Republican Party; Academics Clubs; First Colony Band (Trumpet); [hon.] 1989-92 Summer Super Reader Award; Invited to read for local library; [pers.] Reading is the key to erudition, and writing is the absolute best way to express yourself. The pen is always mightier than the sword. I also pursue the mankind and goodness in my word; [a.] Sugar Land, TX 77479

GANIO, PETER
[Pen.] M.T. Hart; [b.] July 16, 1975, Vineland, NJ; [p.] Pete and Jeanette Ganio; [ed.] Vineland High School, Currently in first year at Rutgers College of Pharmacy; [occ.] Student, [memb.] Alpha Zeta Omega; [hon.] Honor graduate at Vineland High School, State Champion Swimmer, All-Conference Cross Country Runner, various scholastic awards; [oth. writ.] 1st publication; [a.] Vineland, NJ

GANN, SUE
[b.] September 22, 1952, Tupelo, MI; [p.] Hollis and Wahala Underwood; [m.] Larry E. Gann, March 2, 1973; [ch.] Ramona Sue and Miranda Leigh Gann; [ed.] Itawamba Agriculture High School and Secretarial Training School; [occ.] Housewife; [memb.] Ozark Baptist Church; [oth. writ.] Poems wrote for friends and for church bulletins; [pers.] I strive to reflect the love Jesus has for mankind. He is my inspiration in my writing; [a.] Marietta, MS

GARCIA, ROBERTO
[b.] June 18, 1958, MX; [p.] Roberto and Helena Garcia; [m.] Sylvia Ibarra, November 29, 1980; [ch.] Sylvia, Roberto Jr., and Alberto; [ed.] San Diego High; [oth. writ.] Over 500 poems, several short stories a few fablas, and a novel "Fall of Rebel", all unpublished.; [pers.] This poem is in the memory of my friend Ernesto Mendez Meza; [a.] Lemon Grove, CA

GARDINER, GEORGE H.
[Pen.] G. G. Gilchrist; [b.] May 19, 1926, Brooklyn, NY (Eldest of six children); [p.] Geo H. Gardiner (nee: Daniel P. O'Leary), Viola Catherine (nee: Nolan-Smith; [m.] Barbara Joyce (nee: Chelplak-Perina), Ed.D (Dec 27, 1952: three children, seven grandchildren; [ed.] Divine Word Seminaries; St John's Univ of NY; Teacher's College (BA English, '51), graduate school of arts and sciences; graduate school of education, (MS in Ed, Psychological Counseling, '63); [occ.] 1950-91 Dept of Ed, Diocese of Brooklyn - Queen, NY: teacher (Latin; English); counselor; director of guidance, Asst Principal; 1974-91: Regional Coordinator, Program for the Development of Human Potential; [memb.] APGA, Catholic Classical Society, A Co-founder, first President of

Genesian Guild; Editor of College Newspaper, Yearbook; Editor of College Newspaper, yearbook; Editor of SJU Alumni Magazine; [pers.] "In-principio" erat Verbum..." (John I, 1-14); [a.] NYC, NY

GARITE, STEPHANIE
[b.] February 5, 1942, Brooklyn, NY; [p.] Placido Carbonaro, Jeanette Carbonaro; [m.] Carl Garite, June 27., 1964; [ch.] Peri, Janine, and Danielle; [ed.] Seton Hall High School, Suffolk County Community College; [occ.] Principal Clerk, Suffolk County Government, Hauppauge, NY; [memb.] St. Joseph's RC Church, Lake Ronkonkoma, NY, Employee Assistant Program Committee Member, Sexual Harassment Officer for D.P. Unit; [hon.] Honor Society Pi Alpha Sigma, Presidential Recognition Award for Community Service; [oth. writ.] Another Garden (poem) and Article in McCall's Magazine; [pers.] My poems and writings express the daily happenings of birth and old age and are inspired by family and friends and by the independence I have always been allowed to pursue. I wish my children that same kind of independence and the opportunity to do and become whatever they desire.; [a.] Lake Grove, NY

GARLAND, JENNIFER
[Pen.] Jennie Garland; [b.] December 25, 1973, California; [p.] Glynn E. Garland and Virginia Garland; [ed.] Orland High School, Irvine Valley College; [occ.] Student; [pers.] I hope to write in such a way that people may come to know God's love and grace. I admire God's goodness and I hope that I am able to refelct His goodness in my poetry; [a.] Irvine, CA

GARMAN, HEATHER DAWN
[Pen.] Keona Jane; [b.] November 19, 1972, Lock Haven, PA; [p.] Mr. and Mrs William Garman; [ed.] 1991 graduate of Bucktail Area High School; [occ.] Babysitter, homemaker; [memb.] Was in the FHA for 5 yrs during high school; [a.] North Bend, PA

GARNER, SARAH GERTRUDE
[b.] January 28, 1899, Strasburg, VA; [p.] Angus and Emma Stickley; [m.] George W. Garner, August 12, 1925; [ch.] Wiley Newell Garner, Marshall Stickley Garner; [ed.] BA in music from Mary Baldwin College specializing in piano and organ; [occ.] Retired high school english and history teacher (as well as piano teacher); [memb.] Sheva Church of Christ; [pers.] The grand-daughter of Major John Henry Newell, Sarah has many fond memories of playing at "Belle Grove" Plantation and attending the house parties there; [a.] Gretna, VA

GARRO, BARBARA
[b.] Camden, NJ, February 3, 1943 d. Dominic and Mildred Barbara (Homiak) "BS State Univ of NY 1993, G. [m.] James Edward Stephano, Nov 28, 1964 (div. 1975); [ch.] Victoria Lynne, Karen Maria, CPCU; [occ.] Syndicated business columnist, writer, speaker, "Writer / Producer / Star Performer of syndicated Public Television Show, Mother Goose and Gander", storyteller, poet; lic property/casuality cons NY 1987-1992 Sales, free-lance writer, 1978-; pres Electric Envisions, Inc., 1989-; pres Garro Enterprises, Clifton Park, NY 1989-, Eclectic Envisions, Saratoga Springs, NY, 1989-. Columnist (newspaper column) Corp Talk. 1986 -. Ins. Tips, 1990-. "Communication Lines, 1993" Adv. bd. UpperMerion CATV, King of Prussia, PA, 1987. [mem.] Member Nat Speakers Assn 1986-1992 (bd dirs Albany chpt. 1987-89, CFCU, Nat Assn for Preservation and Perpetuation of Storytelling, "Puppeteers of America", "Society of Children's Book Writers", "International Women's Writing Guild", "American Association of University Women", Hudson Vallen Writers Guild, Saratoga Poets Soc. (co-chair), Toastmasters International Republican. Roman Catholic. Avocations: Outdoors painting, antique collecting and restoring,

humanities, chess, theater. [a.] Saratoga Springs, NY

GARVEY, ELIZABETH
[b.] November 6, 1965, West Islip, NY;l [p.] James Garvey & Mary Garvey; [ed.] West Babylon High School, Siena College; [occ.] Assistant Controller, Reid & Priest, New York, NY; [a.] Valley Stream, NY

GARZA, JAIME J.
[b.] May 1, 1951, Laredo, TX; [p.] Raul R. and Oralia R. Garza; [m.] Delfina Hinojasa Garza, December 14, 1974; [ch.] Omar Javier, Robert Eric; [ed.] Hebbronville High, Texas A&I University; [occ.] Operator, Chemical Industries.; [pers.] As the father of two boys I strive to bring out in them the best they can be. They are a beacon of hope to our future.; [a.] Kingsville, TX

GARZA, SHANNON STACIE
[b.] May 15, 1983, Napoleon; [p.] George J. and Victoria J. Garza; [ed.] 5th grade; [pers.] I want to thank my teacher Kathy Tedrow, for helping me believe in my self, and she believed in me; [a.] Napoleon, OH

GASPAR, GENE A.
[b.] August 26, 1953, New Bedford, MA; [p.] Arthur Gaspar, Barbara Gaspar; [ed.] Old Rochester Regional High School, BS psychology SMU and Rhode Island College; [memb.] Reservation Golf Club; [hon.] Honor Society, Dean's List; [pers.] Divorces and marriages are like death and taxes; [a.] Providence, RI

GASTON, MARY aNN
[b.] June 8, 1965, Simcoe, Ontario; [p.] Bill and German Godlouski; [m.] Kevin Gaston, July 14, 1984; [ch.] Jessica, Justine, Stephanie, Kayla; [ed.] Simcoe Composite; [occ.] Artist; [hon.] ICS Art Certificate; [oth. writ.] Several Children's poems hoping for publication; [pers.] Poetry is but an art; you need an open mind; a willingness to observe, express and strengthen to create a finished piece; [a.] Delhi, Ontario, Canada

GAU, MICHELLE
[b.] March 20, 1982, Tacoma, WA; [p.] Eileen and Mike Gau; [ed.] Elementary School; [occ.] Elementary School; [occ.] 6th grade student; [hon.] A-B honor roll; [oth. writ.] 1 poem published in Anthology of Young Poets; [pers.] I like to write short stories and poems. In my spare time I like to read books; [a.] Moyie Springs, ID

GAUSE, RUSSELL
[Pen.] Fela Hanif (Fay-lah, Hah-neef); [b.] May 4, 1949; Chadbourn, NC; [p.] Garfield Gause, Alice Gause; [m.] Single; [ch.] Tinika, Yasheree and Jamaine Gause; [ed.] Westside High, Chadbourn, NC, Schenectady Community College; [occ.] Dietetic Technician Samuel Stratton, VA Med Center, Albany, NY; [memb.] African American Relations Committee; [hon.] Several Highly Performance Awards in Clinical Nutrition; [oth. writ.] Several poems published; [pers.] As an African American, I'm obligated to write about the harsh realities of western culture and its affect on my people. I've been greatly influenced by the Harlem Renaissance; [a.] Albany, NY

GAUTHIER, JOANNE
[b.] June 24, 1979, Virden, Manitoba, Canada; [p.] Bay Gauthier, Huguette Gauthier; [pers.] Our wildest dreams and fantasies can become reality with the use of a pencil. I think more people should believe in heroes...; [a.] Regina, Saskatchewan, Canada

GAY, CHARLOTTE A.
[Pen.] Charlotte Womack Gay; [b.] June 28, 196? Hamilton, CO; [p.] Larry A. & Lorene Womack; [m Rickey Gay, July 12, 1986; [ch.] Christy Lorer Coulter & Teresa Lynn Coulter; [ed.] Soddy-Dais High, Sequoyah Tech., McKenzie Business Colleg Chattanooga State Community College; [occ.] Ac ministrative Assistant, Leitner, Warner, Moffitt La Firm; [hon.] Honor Graduate in Business, Academ Achievement Business Mgmt., Deans List, 4.0 GPA [oth. writ.] Several unpublished poems; [pers.] Th poem as well as many of my poems, are dedicated & inspired by my two wonderful daughters, Chris & Teresa Coulter. And also my Mother & Fathe who raised me "right": You can achieve if only yc believe.; [a.] Chattanooga, TN

GEDDES, SUE
[b.] August 27, 1953, Los Angeles, CA; [m.] To Geddes; [ch.] Emma (13), Whitney (10); [ed.] BA ar Masters Degree from Univ of LaVerne - LaVern CA, French and English major, French Degree fro Strasburg Univ, France; [occ.] Third grade teache (also credentialed to teach high school French ar English); [memb.] St Luke Lutheran Church, Sunda School Staff; [hon.] Univ graduation with academ honors; delivered and wrote invocation for universi graduation; [oth. writ.] Poetry for school site ar district publication - Alta Loma School Distric poetry for church functions; poem for high schoc graduating class invitation; [pers.] Living in Franc for a year (at age 19) inspired much of my earlie writing (the poem in this anthology included). M writing today is reflective of my two beautiful daugl ters; [a.] LaVerne, CA

GEISTER, JESSICA
[Pen.] Marisela (Mah-dd-e-say-lah); [b.] Decembe 15, 1979, Portland; [p.] Gary Geister and Darily Geister; [ed.] I get a 4.0 or Honor Roll on every repo card and plan on taking extra classes in high schoo [occ.] Child care and school; [memb.] I am a membe of Milwaukee Presbyterian Church in Milwaukee. am a Christian; [hon.] I have been in many tale shows and have earned trophies. I have gotten on th honor roll, citizenship, and 4.0; [oth. writ.] Poem songs, short stories - just for fun, for my ow enjoyment. I have written a song called "Prejudice" Many others "Lollypop", "Open Up", "In"; [pers I am planning to become a doctor in the future so I' taking math and science classes. I love to write poen for my friends and family; [a.] Milwaukee, OR

GEMZA, MISTY
[b.] July 28, 1978, Ft Smith, AR; [p.] Diane ar Andrew Gemza; [ed.] Astronaut High School; [occ Student; [memb.] SADD (Vice-President 91-92 [hon.] Honor's Role, 91-92 Journaler's Award; [otl writ.] Poems published in a school collection; [pers I've found that when our words can't be spoken, w write them down and call them poetry; [a.] Mims, F

GENTILE, ANTHONY
[b.] May 13, 1938, NYC; [p.] Victor and Emr Gentile; [m.] Barbara Vaccaro Gentile, July 26, 195 [ch.] Gina, Kathy, Barbara, Ann, Dean Anthony [ed.] Theodore Roosevelt High; [occ.] Plumbir Contractor, self-employed master plumber in ar around the city of New York; [oth. writ.] Sever poems about God, love, wife, children, life, ar death; [pers.] I strive to reflect my feelings about lif love, God and mankind in all my writings.

GEORGE, SHAWN MICHAEL
[Pen.] Crazy Eddy; [b.] May 7, 1971, Hammond, IN [p.] Danny George; [ed.] Highland High, 2 year Purdue Calumet University; [occ.] Irrigation Specia ist; [memb.] Wally's Dog House, Donatello's Soci Club; [hon.] Vi Sikka Hema, All-Pettit 92; [pers.] TI time we spend collecting memories shall be o

eatest trophy.; [a.] Highland, IN

ERHAUSER (JR), STEPHEN LEE
] May 8, 1971, Spokane, WA; [p.] Steve and nette; [m.] Lori Gerhauser, February 29, 1992; .] Loren and Gerhauser (19 mo); [ed.] Selah High hool, Selah, WA; [occ.] US Coast Guard; [oth. it.] Several unpublished poems; [pers.] I write what uely feel at the time of writing. Sometimes it's the ly way to find myself. Thanks deeply to my mother o inspired me to write and go public; [a.] Alameda,

ERMANY, DAVID E.
en.] Wilhelm Flohr; [b.] September 27, 1958, xas; [p.] John Germany, Erma Germany; [ed.] CP from Southern Nazarene Univ; [occ.] Psy-ologist; [memb.] APA/American Psychological soc; [hon.] President's Honor Roll, Cum Laude; h. writ.] Privately published book "Poems of the art and Soul"; [pers.] To reach for the spiritual otion deep within use through poetry; [a.] Okla-na City, OK

EST, JACQUELINE
] October 22, 1980, New York; [p.] Nina and bert Gest, Sister: Suzanne; [occ.] Student at John Kennedy Middle School, 8th grade; [memb.] tional Junior Honor Society; [pers.] This poem was tten in memory of my special friend, Sarah M.; [a.] rt Jefferson Sta, NY

ETTLER, ANNE S.
en.] Annie; [b.] March 19, 1962, Wash., D.C.; [p.] ceased; [ch.] none; [ed.] Legal Secretary certifi-e. AA in Pre-Business, 25 years an accomplished nist; [occ.] Kitchen Assistant; [memb.] Humane ciety of the United States. U.S. Swim and Fitness.; n.] Honor roll and Dean's List. Editor's Choice ard in Poetry; [oth. writ.] Articles in leading vspapers, poem in newsletter prior poems with t'l Library of Poetry. Also two poems in The ric; [pers.] Why is it we usually band together and p each other best, just when a crisis happens. We d this all the time; [a.] St. Paul, MN

HAZAL, AMANI
] February 10, 1956, Egypt; [p.] Mr. and Mrs. M. ongui; [m.] Mr. Alain Paul Ghuzal, Oct 8, 1977, .] Adam Paul Ghazal; [ed.] Business Administra- (in Toronto), Art History and Oil Painting classes Harper College in Chicago, IL; [occ.] Freelance ter and mother to my son Adam; [oth. writ.] lished article about "The Healing Power of Love" Magazine called Rainbow Bridge which is headed well known writer "Lynn Andrews"; [pers.] I truly eve that in order for us to heal mother earth, we st collectively and consciously release energy ich is not destructive, so we can learn to heal and ive in harmony with ourselves and ultimately on great planet called Mother Earth; [a.] Hoffman ates, IL

IAMBARRESE, BARBARA LYNN
n.] Barbara Giambarrese; [b.] March 21, 1949, erson, NJ; [p.] Edward Stuhr and Matilda Stuhr;] Salvatore Giambarrese, July 22, 1972; [ch.] hleen Cory, Christopher Joseph; [ed.] Midland k High School; Attended Milliken Univ; [occ.] nin Asst; [memb.] United Methodist Church Mid-d Park Magic Scholarship Fund; [pers.] I enjoy ting about my own experiences from my heart, that ink other people can relate to; [a.] Midland Park,

IBBONS, BART M.
n.] "ADG-JGB"; [b.] December 24, 1961, Chi-o, IL; [p.] Bonita and Kenneth Gibbons; [m.] onica M. Gibbons, April 3, 1993; [ch.] Andrrew e Gibbons and Chelsea Lynn Gibbons; [oth. writ.]

When We See, We Cry, Iraq, You Break, With Your Life, Echo's & Years, Will Art?, Warning Wise, Lost Letters, Soldiers Denial, Day Like Tommaro; [pers.] I began writing and continue to write to achieve eternal peace through poetic documentation of my life. To include events that have occured within my time and many thoughts that've entered my mind. [a.] Corona, CA

GIBBS, HEATHER A.
[b.] July 2, 1980, Burlington, VT; [p.] Thomas M. Gibbs, Mary Patricia C. Gibbs; [ed.] Waterbury Elementary, Harwood Union Jr High; [occ.] Babysitting, ski lodge; [memb.] Ducks unlimited, Waterbury - Stowe fish and game; [hon.] Grades 1-6 Presidential award honors through junior high; [pers.] I try to express my feeling through my poems, and also the hearts of those teens in the world that are sometimes not understood; [a.] Waterbury Ctr, VT

GIBBS, JENNIFER LYNN
[Pen.] Jennifer Soll; [b.] March 1, 1978, Mather AFB, Sacramento, CA; [p.] Katherine Soll and Larry Burge; [ed.] Still in High School. I graduate in 1996; [oth. writ.] I do have other writings, but they aren't published; [pers.] I mostly write on how I feel or about life and nature. And have been influenced by many other poets; [a.] Silver Creek, NE

GIBSON, AMBER M.
[b.] November 18, 1979, Duncan, OK; [p.] Darla Beeson and Daniel Gibson; [memb.] At the time attending Highland West Junior High. Honor Roll, Honor Society; [oth. writ.] Just poems and stories in which I love to write but have never won anything before; [pers.] I like to write poems because it give me a chance to write my feelings. My best friend Amanda encouraged me to enter the contest so she helped me alot; [a.] Moore, OK

GIBSON, LAURA
[b.] April 10, 1977, Hershey, PA; [p.] Frances Gibson, Robert Gibson; [pers.] My dreams were so far away until you came into my life. Kristy, you showed me what a friend is. When I needed somebody you were there. You inspired me to write and gave me the courage to live. I thank you for that. You are so very special. Just remember I will always love you; [a.] Annville, PA

GILBERT, PATRICIA
[b.] April 8, 1937, Winston-Salem, NC; [p.] D.E. Jones and Estelle Jones; [m.] widowed; [ch.] Russell E. Gilbert, Richard Jay Gilbert; [ed.] High School; [occ.] Self-employed, semi-retired; [hon.] Silver Certificate for "What My Mother Means To Me"; [oth. writ.] "Me", "Friendship", "Did I?"; [pers.] I write from the heart about the thoughts of how I feel about life and the important people in my life such as family and friends. Poetry is therapy for me; [a.] Richmond, VA

GILBY, KELLY
[b.] August 25, 1980, Bethlehem, PA; [p.] Susan and Lee Gilby; [ed.] Wayne Highland Middle School; [occ.] Student; [oth. writ.] I have had my poem published in Highlights for children and local newspapers; [pers.] My favorite poet is Edgar Allen Poe; [a.] Honesdale, PA

GILES, ANDREA NICOLE
[b.] August 15, 1974, Melrose Park, IL; [p.] Morton West High School, Berwyn, IL; [oth. writ.] Many other poems and lyric songs not yet published; [pers.] My words are inspired by truth, nature an death, misted violet and cerulean making up the intensity of a raw energy life.; [a.] Hedgesville, W.VA.

GILKEY, OLA
[b.] November 12, 1960, San Fernando, CA; [p.] Henry and Iola Gilkey; [ed.] San Fernando High School, California St Univ Northridge; [occ.] Parale-gal; [memb.] West Angeles Church of God in Christ; Los Angeles Paralegal Assoc; [hon.] Distinguished Service Award, US Olympic Festival (volunteer); [pers.] I am a sentimental romantic with an appetite for self-discovery. I am young at heart with a craving for the unexplored, God's natural wonders and a desire to share through writing; [a.] Harbor City, CA

GILLARD, PETRINA
[Pen.] Morag Nina; [b.] April 18, 1977, Raddickton; [p.] Frank Gillard, Annie Gillard; [ed.] Evely Integraded, Roddickton, Newfoundland; High school student; [occ.] Part time sales clerk; part time working in an arcade; [hon.] Music award (piano) from the Kiwanis Festival, Grand Falls, NFLD, (1988); [oth. writ.] Writings and poems pub listed in local newspa-pers, articles in the Northern Pen; [pers.] God Bless all; it is my wish, to see lasting peace for all men who live well, and attain such desirement. I live to relect these wishes; I am in love with writings from the Victorian age, especially Charles Dickens!; [a.] Roddickton, NFLD

GILLESPIE, LEONARD X.
[b.] July 9, 1950, Danville, VA; [p.] Leonard and Savannah Gillespie; [ed.] BS, Haverford College, Haverford, PA; JD, New York Univ School of Law, NY, NY; [occ.] Attorney; [memb.] New York Trial Lawyers Assoc Education Committee, Congressuan Edouphus Towns; [oth. writ.] Several unpublished poems as well as a play in progress; [pers.] I feel that poetry and all forms of art is an experience alive on all levels of our consciousness. I always marvel at the sense of the eternal that is part of a good poem; [a.] Brooklyn, NY

GILLIS, JENNIFER A.
[b.] February 1, 1974, Marquette, MI; [p.] Jeff and Linda Gillis; [ed.] Bay Port High School; [occ.] Photographer; [hon.] Several music awards, high honor roll in high school; [oth. writ.] Several short stories, essays; [pers.] I write poetry mainly as a form of self-expression. I can better express my feelings in my poems. It is a great form of Therapy! I greatly admire the poetry of Emily Dickenson; [a.] Green Bay, WI

GILMORE, ANTOINETTE GONZALES
[Pen.] Toni; [b.] November 7, 1953, Trinidad; [p.] Tony & Louise Gonzales; [p.] John T. Gilmore, June 13, 1982; [ch.] none raised duschunds; [ed.] Minot in psychology, education AAS Journalism; [occ.] House-wife; [memb.] Member of World Wide Church of God, 4 years the former secretary of the Colorado Association of Public Employees.; [hon.] Dean's List, Phi Beta Kappa, French Award, Spanish Award Capt. ROTC, Who's Who In Poetry 1978; [oth. writ.] Poem in American Collegiate Poets 1975, Juvenile Poems Book, 1 poem 1979, collection of poems by Iowa Colo. & Michigan Society of Poets, 1 poem 1976.; [pers.] No matter what our race, our back-ground, our circumstance, we owe it to ourselves and to future generations to live for one another in the dignity and in the image of God who created us.; [a.] Trinidad, Colo.

GIORDANO, MELINDA ANNE
[Pen.] Linda Giordano; [b.] March 20, 1980, Whittier Hosp.; [p.] Mike and Liz Giordano; [ed.] Huntington Middle School; [occ.] Student and Barbizon Model-ing School Student.; [memb.] A.S.B. Assistant Stu-dent body (almost over); [hon.] Scholastic Awards, Citizenship Awards, and National Philanthropy Award. Also sports awards.; [a.] San Marino, CA

GIRDHAM, GLENN F.
[b.] July 9, 1944, Wausoon, OH; [p.] Glenwood Girdham, Belva Paxson Girdham; [m.] Divorced, but friends, May 17, 1970; [ch.] Matthew John, Joline Angela; [ed.] Morenci High school, U.S. Military Intelligence School; [occ.] Writer, businessman, investor, Morenci, MI; [oth. writ.] Several unpublished poems, 120+ short stories usually 2 typed pages in length. All are presently unpublished, written within a one-year time limit; [pers.] I write story material with a twist at the end. I try to make each interesting. I am open to all subjects but attempt to keep content suitable for my family. I believe in original, creative reality in searching my mind to write its' thoughts; [a.] Morenci, MI

GITTENS, KAREN
[b.] August 10, 1976, Trinidad, WI; [p.] Carol & David Gittens; [ed.] High School; [occ.] Student; [oth. writ.] None; [a.] Anaheim, CA

GLAPIE, JOHNETTA
[Pen.] Netta; [b.] June 22, 1977, Washington, DC; [p.] Beverly Mayes, John Glaspie; [ed.] Laurel High School; [memb.] Student Government Assoc; [hon.] Biology and Science Awards; [oth. writ.] I haven't had any of my poems published. I do have other writings that I haven't shown anyone; [pers.] I feel that poetry is a perfect way to express your feelings and everyone should try it. I have been influenced through and by experiences in my life; [a.] Landover, MD

GLENN, JEAN W.
[Pen.] Danielle Angeleque; [b.] January 1, 1951, Phila, PA; [p.] Euguene and Alice Wilkerson; [m.] James A. Glenn, July 15, 1989; [ch.] Stacy, Nate, Jean R. & Khalil; [ed.] South Phila High School, National School of Science and Tech.; [occ.] Data Entry Board of Trustee Univ. of PA.; [hon.] Dean's List at National School of Science and Tech.; [pers.] I strive to give inspiration to others in my writing.

GLENN-TATE, CAROLYN
[b.] August 14, 1950, Winston-Salem, NC; [p.] Mr & Mrs Willie M. Glenn, Sr; [m.] Richard Lee Tate; [ch.] (2 daughters) England and Moya Tate; [ed.] Friendship Jr College - Rock Hill, SC, Salem College - Winston-Salem, NC; [oth. writ.] Several poems published during my college years and one novel under pen name; [pers.] The beginning of life follows us through the ending of life, and there is no escaping our roots even if they lie dormant; [a.] Muncie, IN

GLINSKI, FRANK ZDZISLAW
[b.] 1928 in Wyrzysk, Poland; [ed.] in Poland, Germany and USA (Rutgers Univ in Newark, NJ; [m.] 1950 to former Eugenia Pilc; [ch.] Lech b. 1953 and Evon b. 1959; [occ.] emigrated to USA in 1965 - worked in management of Simmons Co. in Elizabeth, NJ for 25 yrs.; [oth. writ.] His writing in Polish, German and English - has appeared in Europe; newspapers and cultural magazines - "History of textile industry in Lower Silesia" 3v 63 "15 yrs biography" Wroclaw - Poland, "Memoir" SGH Warsaw - Poland; poems and writings appeared in USA: "The Coming of Dawn" - (Editor's Choice Award), National Library of Poetry, "Contemp. Poets of America and Britain" - Durrance Publ. Comp., "Famos Poets Antology" - Famos Poets Soc Hollywood, CA, "Poetry: An American Heritage" Western Poetry Ass Colorado Spr, "A Touch of Poetry" Poetry Int'l - Alachua, FL, "Poetic Voices of America" - Sparrowgrass Poetry Forum, Sisterville, WV, "American Poetry Annual 1993" - The Amherst Society, Baltimore, MD, "Once Upon A Song" - Yes Press - Waynesboro, TN, "Poems of Our Times" - Suwannee Poetry - Suwannee, FL, "The Sound of Poetry" (cass tape); [hon.] The National Library of Poetry, "Memories" - (honorable mention) Iliad Press -Troy, MI,

"Inspiration In Ink" - (Accomplishment of Merit), Creative Arts and Science Enterprises - Painted Post, NY, The American Poetry Society - (Book of Selected Poems) - Midland, TX, "Special Poets Series" - Yes Press -Waynesboro, TN, "Visions" - Contemporary Poets Series - selection of poems, "American Poet's Forum", "Bedpost", "Biographies", "Starburst", "West Orange Chronicle", "Gwiazda Polarna", "1994 President's Award For Literary Excellence", "Perceptions", "The Space Between", "Chasing Rainbows and Ribbons"; [memb.] Int'l Soc of Poets, Int'l Society of Authors and Artists, The American Poetry Society, The National Authors Registry; [pers.] I am greatly influenced by the romantic poets and enjoying - retirement - golf - poetry, not always in this order....

GLUKLER, HANNELORE M.
[Pen.] Hannah; [b.] March 17, 1941, Germany; [p.] Wilhelm and Louise Bachmayer; [m.] Emile U. Glukler, May 29, 1993 (2x widowed); [ch.] Bianca, Denise, Garrett, Michael, Mark, Trent; [ed.] Gv 12 and College Business Major; [occ.] Retired business woman [memb.] Various business memberships; [hon.] Various business honors and awards; [oth. writ.] Published newsletter "The Mudslinger"; [pers.] Words may either be used for love or wars. It's up to us to use them wisely; [a.] Mission, BC, Canada

GOERING, ART
[b.] December 10, Kansas; [p.] John C. Goering; [m.] Adina Wedell Goering, October 12, 1899; [ch.] Lydia, Phily J., Edwin J., Benjamin J. Berth, A. John W, Arthur J. Lorene, Lilie E., Martin H. and Evelyn Goering, Ellen E., Harold W. Schrag; [ed.] Varries from 8th grade on to high school, college; [occ.] History major with 16 yrs as principal; [memb.] Of and participating in county political organization, H. Newton, KS; [hon.] A suit for acquiring assigned quota in selling corn and other related farm seeds. Also a certificate for having attended the 8th grade without being neither absent or tardy; [oth. writ.] Inteligence is like a river - the deeper it flows less noise it makes. There is no way to peace, Peace is the Way; [pers.] We were all born in rural home to bible reading christian parents who always sought to bring their children up in the nuture and admonition of the Lord. And on confession of faith in Christ as Savior and remained member of churches to which we belong.

GOERING, ELIZABETH
[b.] May 26, 1975, Detroit, MI; [p.] Karl Goering, Marilynn Goering; [ed.] Greenhills School, Ann Arbor, MI Shenendehowa High, Clifton Park, NY; [occ.] Student at Eckerd College, St Petersburg, FL; [memb.] Amnesty International; [oth. writ.] Several poems published in Greenhills School annual book featuring student artists; [pers.] I write from my soul and hope that others are able to distinguish their own personal message through my writings; [a.] Northville, MI

GOFF, MICHAEL
[Pen.] Now and then; [b.] August 10, 1948, New Orleans; [p.] Irving and Sophie; [m.] Looking, dispite govt interference; [occ.] Photographic artist; [hon.] Misc photo prize, nothing recent; [oth. writ.] Nothing for public published distribution: 1993 supreme court case; [pers.] Whether "booger" is Gematria for "blunderbuss"; Who really knows what goes, where it comes from? To Clown, something on made-face is all possible wrong. "Green TV, go off..."; TV Timers are the leading cause of house fires. "Secretive Policy..."; Key phrase in 176 US 167 (supreme court). "All We Can Be..."; Recruiting slogan. "Lint...Mint"; Fibers in cash, a pseudo non-vulgarization? Me? I'm persecuted under my name (no lie). Rarely use it: Hemingway, for whom the bell tolls, Gunvivers) on and on. This poem is a risk (serious threat of arbitrary domestic torture). But I'm looking for a fearless female friend. Have a nice day, serious

govt believers and all! I've never been left alone by govt long enough to commit a crime, even a marria by govt standards!; [a.] Vermontville, NY

GOLD, MARK
[b.] July 11, 1962, Bronx, NY; [oth. writ.] Sh stories: "Casual Death", "Passing Through", "So Still Breathe in Restless Sleep." Collection of poe entitled "Poetry for the Sucidal Yet Optimistic."; [Smithtown, NY

GOLLINGS, ADDIE
[b.] October 26, 1921, Big Falls, MN; [p.] Robert Hilda Leak; [m.] George; [ch.] Sandra, Ter Deborah, grandchildren: Jon, Chaunte, Jennif Benjamin, great grandchildren: Ryan, Taylor, Tes Brandon; [ed.] High School, Welcome Wagon, Tra ing, took some speciality classes; [occ.] Retire [memb.] Grange, Senior Citizens; [oth. writ.] No ing published, just written for my own enjoyme [pers.] A homemaker most of my life-worked a welcome wagon hostess in late 50's and early 60 Owned and operated a fabric shop, taught sewing a knitting for 7 yrs., retired from apt. management seniors.; [a.] Snohomish, WN

GOMES, J. ANTHONY
[Pen.] Tony Gomes; [b.] February 29, 1944, Bomb [p.] Agostinho Gomes, Olimpia Souza; [m.] Mar Flores (deceased), January 10, 1970; [ch.] Tar Raquel Gomes; [ed.] Doctor of Medicine (M [occ.] MD Professor of Medicine, Mount Sinai Sch of Medicine; [memb.] New York Academy of S ences, North American Society of Pacing and Fsecti physiology, poets house, member at large: Inst Mene Braganza; [hon.] Listed in Best Doctors in Ameri Listed in Int'l Biographies - London, England, M Award, Fellow - American College of Cardiolog Fellow - American Heart Assoc; [oth. writ.] Seve poems published in magazines; published more th 100 original articles in major medical journals p lished text book on Electro cardiography (Khuw Acad Publishers); [pers.] I try to reflect the changi seasons of life. The plight of the book, nature and environment in my writings always with a streak optimism; [a.] NY, NY

GOMES, STACEY L.
[b.] June 5, 1976, West Warwick; [p.] Debra Gomes and Gordon L. Gomes, Sr. (deceased); [r engaged to Joseph J. Foertsch, 1995; [ed.] W Warwick High School; [occ.] Crew Train McDonalds; [oth. writ.] A few poems a cou essays; [pers.] What one experiences, and how th react makes each the unique person they are...And. something is calling you, don't keep hitting "snooze button". One day it may not call to y anymore; [a.] West Warwick, RI

GOMEZ, SABINO
[b.] February 25, 1947, ElPaso, TX; [p.] Sab Gomez and Petra Gomez; [ed.] Austin High Scho [occ.] Electrical Buyer Wells Gardner Electrical Cor [pers.] Through Genetic Engineering we will be a to explore space, but first we must learn to live, a family, here on earth.; [a.] Chicago, IL

GONZALEZ, BRENDA MORALES
[b.] June 21, 1977, Puerto Rico; [p.] Janette Gonza and Efrain Morales; [ed.] Union High School; [oc Student; [memb.] First Baptist Church of Uni Youth Group - President, Young Artists Worksh Theatre of Union; [hon.] Honors for playwriti medals; [oth. writ.] Small plays which have be performed at Union High School, poems and sh stories; [pers.] Life is a big puzzle and through writings I see the pieces come together; [a.] Union,

ONZALEZ, LISA
] February 19, 1979, Brownsville, TX; [p.]
mando Gonzalez, Aguedo Gonzalez; [ed.] Lopez
gh School, ninth grade; [occ.] High school student;
emb.] National Junior Honor Society (Perkins
ddle School); [hon.] Most Valuable Player (6th);
 5% (7&8th), Outstanding Band Service (7th), and
st outstanding student in English; [pers.] I write my
etry to get out of the hatred and racism in the world,
t is why I don't understand how a person could
ve hatred or be a racist against a precious life; [a.]
ownsville, TX

ONZALEZ, MARTI
] February 26, 1954; [p.] Atanacio and Eleuteria
rnandez; [ch.] Val, Jeremy, Dena, Sean Gonzalez;
.] Lubbock High; [occ.] Learn, Inc, Secretary for
ent Search Program; [pers.] Writing is the most
filling way for me to express my innermost thoughts
feelings. I am inspired and motivated by knowing
t others can relate to my writing; [a.] Lubbock, TX

ONZALEZ, THERESA
] November 29, 1962, San Jose, CA; [p.] Enrique
 Clara Estrada; [m.] Jose Gonzalez, March 28,
37; [ch.] Jose II, Eric, Michaelangelo and Daniel
nzalez; [ed.] Lodi High School, MIT Business
llege, San Joaquin Delta College; [occ.] House-
e; [hon.] Principals Honor Roll; [oth. writ.] Per-
al poems I keep in my personal collection; [pers.]
 poems I write are straight from the heart, and not
tten for financial gain, just my own personal
perience; [a.] Hollister, CA

OODWIN, BONNIE MCLEAN
] April 9, 1950, Masury, OH; [p.] John and
elma McLean; [memb.] Gary Goodwin, June 30,
73; [ch.] John Gary Goodwin and Gary Goodwin;
.] Hubbard High School, Ohio Columbus Business
iversity, OH; [occ.] Personnel, Ohio Bureau of
ployment Services, Lima, OH; [memb.] PTA;
n.] Spelling Bee, Runner Up; [oth. writ.] Calendar
ies, What I Wish For You (both poems) pub-
ed.; [a.] Wapakoneta, OH

ORDON, DONNA P.
n.] Pasty Gordon, [b.] May 9, 1958, Grand Forks,
; [m.] Oscar Gordon, January 9, 1978; [ch.]
ce and Sarah; [ed.] Northeastern State Univ -
lequah, OK, BS in Special Education; [occ.] L.D.
her at Glenpool Middle School in Oklahoma;
mb.] Oklahoma Caged Bird Society; [hon.] Magna
 Laude; Educational Honor Society; Kappa Delta;
 Theta Kappa; Dean and President Honor Roll;
rs.] I teach my students to write and touch their
otions so they will learn to reach out and touch the
rld. Look out world! They're are some beautiful
ple coming out to help make you better; [a.] Tulsa,

ORRILL, MALCOLM
as born the youngest of six children on March 7,
7. I graduated from Westile Composite High
ool in 1985 but, I hate to admit, I did not like
try until I attended the Univ of Prince Edward
nd from 1985-1989 (I received a BA degree with
ajor in history). During my last two years at UPEI
gularly contributed short stories and poems to
 Gem (the student newspaper). Currently I am
rking at the Atlantic "Wind Test Site in North
e, PEI. When this job ends at the end of March,
pe to find employment pertaining to computers. I
e written two novels but so far no one has offered
en crazy enough?) to publish either of them.
wever, I am hopeful that I can get my first
ection of poems, Idle Thoughts, published some-
 this year. When writing poetry, I try to create
ple and situations that people can easily relate to.
 to entertain people while also making them think.
ew up on a farm and I believe that influences many

of my poems. I am a large fan of Lucy Maud
Montgomery and Ernest Hemingway. I am also a
huge Star Trek fan. I love country music-some of my
favorite acts are Patricia Conroy, Pairie Oyster, Suzy
Bogguss and Dan Seals; [a.] Prince Edward Island,
Canada

GOYETTE, CAROLYN M.
[b.] October 28, 1937, Ecorse, MI; [p.] Emma Fesko
and Joseph Goyette; [m.] David I. Katz, September
24, 1978; [ch.] none; [ed.] Doctoral candidate in
multicultural education, studied sculpture for seven
years with Fereug Varga; [occ.] Teacher, Wayne
State University, part-time; [memb.] Sculptors Guild
of Michigan; [hon.] Scarab Club, Detroit, sculpting
award, Women's Caucus for the Arts, sculpting
award; [hon.] Travelled to former U.S.S.R in first
major education exchange, 1989; [oth. writ.] short
stories, collection of poems when I get to 100, I'll
publish; [pers.] As a small child my father built me a
sandbox. He taught me to play. The sand has
changed, but the lesson didn't; [a.] Clarkston, MI

GRANT, BARBARA B.
[Pen.] Barby Gee; [b.] July 25, 1931, Greenville, SC;
[p.] Alvin and Louvenia Anderson; [m.] Chester E.
Grant; [ch.] Kay, Donna and Anna; [occ.] Retired
Driver Education Teacher; [memb.] National Safety
Council, Texas Safety Assoc; [hon.] Lifetime Mem-
bership in professional Organization, Texas Driver
and Traffic Safety Education Assoc, Outstanding
achievement award for work on State organization
magazine both local and state; [pers.] To me poetry
must rhyme while telling a story. My favorite poems
are Trees and In Flanders Field. Poetry must flow like
pouring water from a glass; [oth. writ.] Several
newspaper articles.

GRANT, NICHOL
[Pen.] Nickie Gee; [b.] January 21, 1976, Barbados;
[p.] John Grant, Isha Grant; [ed.] Berrien High
School, International Correspondence Schools; [occ.]
Student; [a.] Madison, AL

GRANT, SHIRLEY B.
[b.] March 3, 1950, Toronto, Ontario; [m.] Albert E.
Grant, August 6, 1966; [ch.] Krista Lynne; [memb.]
A.R.E. Assoc., Dynamic Life Systems, Inc., Nuage
Esoteric Wisdom, Enhancing Self Development
(N.E.W.E.S.) Inc.; [hon.] Docete Award, R.C.
ARchdiocese, Hfx. N.S.; [oth. writ.] Short stories,
(nonfiction/fiction) novels, essays, (mainstream and
lieterary) [pers.] A student of E. Poe., S. Fitzgerald
and A. alker, C. Pinkola Estes, I'm drawn to the
"vivid and continuous dream," (J. Gardner), a guest
to fulfill the soul's expressions, voiced within the
literary landscape of options.; [a.] Armdale, Canada

GRAY, FIONA
[Pen.] Fiona McKenzie; [b.] Coleraine N. Ireland;
[p.] Harold and Clarie Wray; [m.] Duncan; [ch.]
Stuart, Kristin, Lisa; [ed.] Queen's University, Belfast,
N. Ireland; [occ.] French Immerson, Teacher, Ladner,
B.C.; [pers.] I am constantly seeking to express
verbally, the visual metaphors my experiences con-
jure up in my mind, bringing order and sometimes
closure to them.; [a.] Delta, BC Canada

GRAY, LYLE
[b.] April 22, 1919, Richland County, WI; [p.]
Melvin and Ida Gray; [m.] Marie Anderson Gray,
November 6, 1940, deceased; [ch.] one Diana L.
Gray, Masters Degree in English. Taught 26 yrs in
High School. Deceased at age 51; [ed.] Graduated
from 8th grade. Went to MATC to work on GED at
age 72. Hve made through three subjects. This is
where I started writing poems.; [occ.] Retired; [oth.
writ.] I have written around 18 poems in the last two
years. Most of my poems are religious.; [pers.] God
is our author and maker and our helper in every

occasion.; [a.] Fort Atkinson, WI

GREEN, ELDRED IBIBIEM
[b.] May 16, 1957; [p.] Titus and Adeline Green; [m.]
Constance Douye Green, October 7, 1989; [ed.]
Baptist High School, Port Harcourt; Univ of Port
Harcourt, Port Harcourt; Univ of Ibadan,Ibadan; All
in Nigeria; [occ.] Literature lecturer, Univ of Bangui,
Bangui, Central Af Rep; [memb.] Rivers Reader's
Committee, Port Harcourt; Nigerian Inst of Public
Relations, Port Harcourt; Executive Committee of the
Ibani Christian Fellowship; [hon.] Dean's List, School
of Humanities, Univ of Pharcourt (1977-81); Federal
Merit Award Scholar (1978-81); Prize for best gradu-
ating studt, Literature, Univ of P. Harcourt (1981);
Univ of P. Harcourt Scholar at the Univ of Ibadan
(1982-83); [oth. writ.] Poems in Literary Journals,
Literary Criticism in Academic Journals, several
articles published in the Nigerian Tide newspaper, P.
Harcourt; [pers.] I believe in God, I am an optimist
and love experimenting with ideas and forms; [a.]
Lagos, Nigeria

GREENBERG, LINDA
[b.] May 3, 1978, Los Angeles, CA; [p.] William
Greenberg, Ana Guardado; [ed.] I am enrolled at
Santa Monica High School, and am in my sophomore
year; [oth. writ.] I am currently working on a science-
fiction fantasy novel for children and pre-teens;
[pers.] I do not rebel against conventionality, nor do
I foster it. Poetry is an art which demands neither,
accepts both, and asks only for root emotions and
convictions; [a.] Santa Monica, CA

GREENE, HILL
[b.] 1925, California; [m.] Ann Greene; [ed.] Pomona
College (BA); [occ.] Art Collector/Poet and Retired
Journalist; [pers.] Favorite poets: Browning, Masefield,
Frost, Millay.

GREIGER, MELISSA MARIA
[Pen.] Nick: Dee-Da; [b.] October 5, 1983, Surrey,
B.C; [p.] Mona and Ritchie Geiger; [ed.] Attending
Horse Lake Elementary School 100 Mile House B.C.
Canada, previously from Bear Creek Elem. in Sur-
vey, B.C. Home of Carol Dixon the best school
student secretary; [oth. writ.] Not sent in, I am
something all round and orange, and my name is
Jacky George, I have two eyes just like you, and my
best friend says Boo!! What am I???; [pers.] Thanks
to my Grandma for making this possible. All of my
love Melissa; [a.] BC, Canada

GRESS, EBERHARD W.
[b.] July 31, 1927, Stuttgart; [p.] Dr. Richard and
Helene Gress; [m.] Eva B. Gress, August 12, 1969;
[ch.] Dirk Wilhelm, Michael Frederick Gress; [ed.]
Friedrichs Gymnasium (Humanitas) Kassel - Ger-
many. Academy for performing Arts, Kassel and
Frankfurt; [occ.] Actively retired; [memb.] German-
American Heritage Society. Lifetime Hon Board
member Int's Society of Poets; [hon.] Volunteer
teacher of the year. Age of Enlightenment Award.
Golden Poet Award. German-American Friendship
Award. Cross of Merit; [oth. writ.] Poems and
Columns published in German and American Journals
and Newspapers. Opera Libretto "From Hate to
Hope"; [pers.] Recording mankinds struggle in its
tragic and humorous happenings. Open peoples eyes
to the ever trying manipulators; [a.] Sarasota, FL

GREY, TOYRE
My family and friends call me Toy for short. I'm a
11th grader at Pontiac Northern High School. I was
born in Detroit, MI. I'm 56 and have 2 sisters and 2
brothers named Ta'Litha, Destiny Darmaris, Christo-
pher Grey. I loved to Rollerskate and go shopping and
do hair. I just want to give special thanks to Ms.
Jacklique Ross, Mrs. Melissa Hardenburgh and Ms.
Ivy Chism and a very special person which is my

mother that encourage me to keep trying and to never give up on all my hopes and dreams, Ms. Terre Williams. I dedicate this poem to Bennie Hodges and to tell my best friend she can do it to (Masturella Ford) and the late Ramona Smith.

GRIEWAHN, JENNIFER
[b.] January 21, 1979, Adrian, MI; [p.] Gary and Nancy; [ed.] Currently a freshman at Adrian High School; [occ.] Student; [memb.] Adrian High varsity swim team, AHS German Club, St John's Senior Youth Group; [hon.] Varsity letter for swimming, Presidental Academic Fitness Award, Michigan State Board of Education Certificate of Recognition for Essential Skills Reading Test; [oth. writ.] None published; [pers.] Be yourself; stand up for what you believe in; [a.] Adrian, MI

GRIFFIN, BARBARA
[b.] Oyster Bay, NY; [p.] Rose and Arthur Brown; [m.] John Griffin, November 27, 1949; [ch.] jay, Laurel, Jon, Scott, Melissa; [ed.] Oyster Bay High School; [occ.] Retired; [oth. writ.] Western "Ride The Lonely Country" published in 1975. Poems in other books. A vision, a verse, poetry press 1978, Important American Poets and Songwriters of 1948 and 1949.; [pers.] I would like to dedicate this poem to Jon who left us in 1993, a fine police officer a beloved son.; [a.] Islip, NY

GRIFFIN, GYNETH
[b.] July 8, 1921, Richland County, WI.; [p.] Ernest & Ethel Panfrey Gray; [m.] Armo Griffin, June 10, 1989; [ch.] one son by previous marriage, five step-children. All married.; [ed.] Three years of college; [occ.] Retired fram wife.; [memb.] Free Methodist Church; [oth. writ.] I have several poems I have written since high school days.; [pers.] One poem is about my son's car. "That's Where My Money Goes," another is a humorous account of my many surgeries. One poem, written in high school, "I Hear The Distant Thunder Rumblin In The Hills.; [a.] Richland Center, WI

GRIFFIN, JUDD
[b.] February 23, 1929, Milwaukee, WI; [p.] Lila Ruth and John Walter; [m.] Annette Eileen and Karen Marie; [ch.] Colleen Marie, Mark Judd, Linda Ann, Cathleen Ruth and Tina Lee; [ed.] Milwaukee State Teachers College; [occ.] Furniture Mover; [memb.] Marine Corp League VFW Post 388; [oth. writ.] Unpublished sardonic stories told in rhyme; [pers.] Try not to create phantom barriers when contemplating future endeavors; [a.] Milwaukee, WI

GRIFFITH, YULU
[b.] January 24, 1972, Kingstown, St. Vincent; [p.] Edward and Patricia Griffith; [ed.] Petersville School, St. Vincent Girls' High School; [occ.] Library Assistant at National Archives, St. Vincent; [memb.] Friends of the Library Comm, Museums Assoc of the Caribbean; [hon.] Student of the Year (GHS) 1987, Headgirl (GHS) 1988, 1st prize (behavioral science), National Schools Science Fair (1989); [pers.] I believe that young people should empower themselves by becoming more aware and by exploring avenues of self expression. I want to demonstrate this. I must express myself; [a.] Kingstown, St. Vincent of the Grenadines

GRILLO, CAROL G.
[Pen.] C. G. Girllo; [b.] March 21, 1939, Salem, MA; [p.] Early years raised in an orphanage; [ch.] Daughters, Christine C. & Karen G. Grillo; [ed.] High School, Computer Courses, Metropolitan Museum of Fine Arts, Mail Order Classes, Courses Ciompleted, Still Life Art Classes, REal Estate Courses, Journalism Courses; [occ.] Methuen Zoning Board of Appeals Secretary.; [memb.] Massachusetts Real Estate Association, Volunteer in several charities. Notary

Public. Secretary, Methuen Little League.; [hon.] Dean's List, Honor Roll while in orphanage school of public school system.; [oth. writ.] Unpublished: poems, childrens story, other incomplete works.; [pers.] My intent is to put into words, what people see and feel, and hopefully understand that we all go through the same life feeling the same things. We all must have compassion, for the sake of all humanity. Our dreams can be our achievements.; [a.] Methuen, MA

GRIMBERG, IRENE
[b.] June 27, 1930, Poland; [p.] Wilhelm and Stella Rippel; [m.] divorced; [ch.] Sandra Grimberg; [ed.] BA Sociology (New School for Social Research), Art History studied (Italy, Univ of Pevugia); [occ.] Freelance Writer; [memb.] Mothers Against Drunk Driving, Friends of NY Public Library, Peta, IFAW, Doris Day Animal League, The National Humane Education Society; [hon.] Golden Poet Award; [oth. writ.] Poem in an anthology "Sarah's daughters sing". An article on the subject of art and a poem in "Voice of the Woman Survivor" in New York Central Public Library Jewish section, and Golden Poetry Club Anthology a poem; [pers.] I believe that most important is the charity to all living creatures both people and animals. All those who share this earth with us are entitled to our assistance. We have no right to harm them or cause them pain; [a.] New York, NY

GRIMES, HELEN
[b.] April 15, 1965, Glens Falls Hosp.; [p.] Antoinette C. Haley; [m.] Archie M. Grimes, August 19, 1988; [ch.] Daniel James, robin Lynn, Danielle Grimes; [ed.] Fort Edward High School; [occ.] Full time mother; [hon.] North American Correspondence School, Diploma, Wildlife Forestry Conservation.; [pers.] I have been greatly influenced by my Daughter: Danielle Elizabeth Grimes who was born 5/17/89 with a birth defect. The poem was written about Danielle, from the heart.; [a.] Lake George, NY

GRIMES, KAY F.
[Pen.] Francois Carter, KC Grimes - Brown; [b.] April 24, Decatur, IL; [p.] Bernice and Cleveland Vernon Grimes; [ch.] Nastajjea' Aurjeon, Shaunessy Carterell Grimes (siblings, Trey and Craig Grimes); [ed.] Enterprise, Roosevelt MacArthur High School, to study law at Lasalle University; [occ.] Copywriter; [memb.] American Animal League, CAA, The Children's Institute of Literature; [hon.] "Dean's List," "Award of Achievements," "Scholarship to the International School of Astrology," "National Honor Society."; [oth. writ.] "Time," "The Prince's Magic Marbles," "Nothing Sacred- autobiography" "A Monster's Tale"; [pers.] I agree with Victor Hugo, Master of poetry and romance. "Take a moments rest? Impossible!" he used to say "A little work bores me, but much work is a pleasure."; [a.] Decatur, IL

GRINDSTAFF, TERESA
[b.] October 19, 1960, Maryville, TN; [p.] Henry (deceased) and Ellen Poplin; [m.] Richard Grindstaff, September 22, 1981; [ch.] Cedrick Cole Grindstaff, Hannah Elizabeth Grindstaff; [ed.] Everett and Heritage; [occ.] Financial Advisor/Assistant to Customers of Local Customers of Local Home Builder; [memb.] Promotional Chairman of the Maryville Christian School and President of Women's Missionary Union at Six Mile Missionary Baptist Church; [hon.] None yet but I hope my writing will someday gain great recognition; [oth. writ.] From school newspapers to other local publications; [pers.] I have been writing poetry, songs, and short stories since I was a child. My dad was my greatest inspiration at that time. It seems to be a gift to write and is surely a blessing; [a.] Maryville, TN

GROGAN, ERIKA
[b.] January 7, 1983, Toronto, Ontario; [p.] Bruna and John Grogan; [ed.] Grade Six and Grade Six

gifted programme; [occ.] Student; [memb.] Nation Geographic Society (Junior) and Always Frien Forever Club - by: Scholastics; [hon.] Gold and Silv in Science Fair Superitendancy; [oth. writ.] Seco Place for Public Speaking Contest, representing M Gracie's Grade 6 class topic - genetrics; [pers.] Th has proven to me to never give up writing even i think I'm not good enough; [a.] Toronto, Ontari Canada

GROSE, ALLAHALINE
[Pen.] Gal; [b.] February 6, 1930, Longacre, W.V. [p.] Bert & Katherine Pritt; [m.] Robert D. Gros January 10, 1949; [ch.] Barbara, Linda, Brend Robert Jr., Roxane, Eric; [ed.] 8th Grade; [occ Housewife, retired; [oth. writ.] Just write poems like to set down and write my thoughts, of thing remember of growing up. It's great memories of t past.; [pers.] The National Library of Poetry sent a letter of expertise. I never expected anything ln these. I give thanks to God, up above, to someone li you, with this kind of love.; [a.] Tampa, FL

GROVE, LEAH M.
[Pen.] Le Le; [b.] January 31, 1979, California; [Jois Smyth and Steven Grove; [ed.] Tempe Hig [occ.] Student; [hon.] Silver award for academics the 7th grade; [oth. writ.] None that have be published; [pers.] Be you and not me; [a.] Tempe, A

GRUBER, MARY JANE
[b.] September 23, 1924, St. Paul, MN; [p.] Hube and Mary Casper; [m.] Frank E. Gruber, Septemb 12, 1944; [ch.] Richard, Jeanne-Marie, Tricia, Gre Deanna, Anita, Cathy, Frank; [ed.] Monroe H.S., Paul Vocational for Activity Director; [occ.] Acti ties in Baldwin Care Center; [memb.] St. Mary Church, Hammond, WI, American Legion Auxilia [hon.] Certificate of Merit for Quality Service in Ca Center; [oth. writ.] Autobiography (Book) "I Did Stop To Smell the Roses" published 1990.; [per The frequent waste of the precious gifts, food a water, has always been a concern to me. T motivated me to write the poem.; [a.] Baldw Wisconsin.

GRUHN, KENNETH
[b.] October 9, 1923, Chicago; [p.] Deceased; [n Hazel, November 23, 1979; [ch.] None personally step daughter: Sandra Atwood; [ed.] Chicago's M sical College and other occupational learnings; [oc Retired; [oth. writ.] Analytical and interpretati Endeavors as an essayist and other poetic worl [pers.] With the plethora of life's unexpected stres and tribulations, if one can reach any stimulus w improvement, by the increased efforts to survive, subsequent conversion from improvement to achiev ment will surely prove one has been blessed.; [Chicago, IL

GRUMBINE, MEGAN
[b.] March 8, 1980, Baltimore, MD; [p.] Karen a Loren Grumbine; [ed.] Attending Severn River Jun High School as an eighth grader; [occ.] stude [pers.] If words were just for practical use, the would be no poets on earth; [a.] Annapolis, MD

GUARINO, KEVIN S.
[b.] April 13, 1968, Easton; [p.] Louis and Jud Guarino; [ch.] Godson and Nephew: Michael Lo Souza; [ed.] Oliver Ames High School, Dean Jun College, Bridgewater State College; [occ.] Self-e ployed carpenter; [memb.] Boy Scouts of Americ Asst Scoutmaster, Asst Camp Director and Explo Advisor; [hon.] Eagle Scout; [pers.] Each day I ar new person, thanks to poetry and literature, brou to me by close friends and excellent teachers. Spec thanks to John Bohane and Jeff Hammond, "T Librarians"; [a.] N. Easton, MA

JERNSEY, JOSEPH D.
] April 4, 1977, Bay City, MI; [p.] John & .rgaret Guernsey; [ed.] Currently attending U of D uit High, Detroit, MI; [occ.] Student; [oth. writ.] poem published in a school literary magazine.; rs.] Through my writing, I attempt to discover uty in places few people would expect to find it.; Royal Oak, MI

JMINSKI, PAUL
n.] SamSon; [b.] July 15, 1954, Buffalo, NY; [p.] xander & Gertrude; [ch.] Paul, Catherine and .gy; [ed.] Graduate of Buffalo State College in w York; [occ.] American Red Cross Caseworker; .mb.] Bread of Life Christian Church, Buffalo, w York, Total Christian Television, Prayer Part- ; [hon.] West Sencea West Honor Society; [oth. t.] Lost & Found, Why witness, credit goes to the ly Spirit and I thank God that I can be used as a sel; [pers.] I believe Jesus is coming soon and he d "yue must be born again" -- John 3:7 I Love us!; [a.] Buffalo, NY

JMMOW, MADGE
May 7, 1923, Leo, AB; [p.] Amelia and Frank ver; [m.] Malcolm Gummow, June 27, 1946; .] Dale, Gary, Dennis, Marlene, Heather; [occ.] ired; [memb.] Royal Canadian Legion, Senior .iety, Wayside Chapel; [hon.] Award for Teaching .racy Classes; [oth. writ.] Poems published in local .er and Western Producer, Regina.

JNN, CHRISTOPHER
April 18, 1959, Lanett, AL; [p.] James and Ruth .nn; [m.] Julie Gunn, March 15, 1992; [ch.] Carley .nn, Drew Gunn, B.J. Finney, Andria Finney; [ed.] .ett High School, Community College of the Air .ce, LeTourneau University; [occ.] Systems Engi- .r; [a.] Greenville, TX

NTER, DANNY W.
January 21, 1970, Kansas City; [p.] Earl W. .ter, Vernetta R. Lungstrum; [ed.] Turner High .ool; [occ.] Distribution Clerk - Fleming Foods; .rs.] While it's easy to speak or write what's in your .rt, many are afraid or unable. The heart never lies I thank the Lord that I am afraid to listen to mine; Independence, MO

AGEN, DONOVAN
November 21, 1969, Copenhagen; [p.] Ronelle .nham; Mark Haagensen; [ed.] Matric Senior Cer- .ate; [memb.] Old Dalian Union; [oth. writ.] .ered a poem for previous publication, "Whispers .he Wind"; [a.] Johannesburg (South Africa)

AKINSON, NATHANIE
August 30, 1971, Rapid City, SD; [p.] Richard Gayla Haakinson; [ed.] Rocky Mountain High .ool, Front Range Community College, University Colordo; [occ.] Lazy Worthless Songwriter, Poet, .hor Deadbeat; [hon.] National Merit Scholar, .o's Who of American High School Students, Best .ion Award from Chrysalis, the Front Range .nmunity College literary magazine.; [oth. writ.] .try, Fiction and essays published in Chrysalis, .ing & Fall 93, poetry in some underground pub- .tions.; [pers.] Poetry is a game, an artifice, style .ore substance is my artistic motto. My poetry is .ely influenced by songwriters such as Bob Dylan, .n Prine, Tom Waits and Lou Reed.; [a.] Ft. .ins, CO

AN, SHERYL A.
October 24, 1959, Anaheim, CA; [p.] Vernon Shirley Adelmund; [m.] James Kinney, signifi- .t other; [ch.] Willy and Stacy Haan; [ed.] Ellsworth .nmunity College; [occ.] Medication Manager at .adows group home; [memb.] American Quarter .se Assn, Iowa Horse Protection League, VietNam

Veterans Wives Support Group; [hon.] Academic Honors Graduate, Deans List; [oth. writ.] Opinion page articles leading to investigative reports; [pers.] I find writing to be a great release, more relaxing than therapy, more emotional than music, more insightful than the human eye; [a.] Aplington, IA

HADAD, ALVIN NATHAN
[b.] Boston, MA, June 13, 1943; [p.] Norma Tobias and Morris Hadad; [pers.] After long neglecting the urge to write, at age 50, I've begun to publish and coming together with this bit of creativity in me has been like finding a new life.; [a.] Newburgh, NY

HAGER, AMANDA
[b.] June 16, 1980, Tacoma, WA; [p.] David D. Hager and Alisa M. Hager; [ed.] K-8th grade (K:Ulm American School - Ulm Germany 1st - 2nd grd - Amanda Arnold School - Kansas 3rd-5th Cascade Elementary - Washington 6th-8th Cedarcrest Middle School, WA; [occ.] Student/unpublished writer; [oth. writ.] High Seas Voyager (not yet published); [pers.] Though I am only thirteen, I have high hopes for becoming a professional novel writer soon. My favor- ite music group would have to me The Moody Blues, it helps me relax and think. In my opinion, having my poem published in this book is a big step in the right direction; [a.] Marysville, WA

HAGERTY, DAWN M.
[b.] May 4, 1924, Chicago, IL; [p.] Carmen and Anna Zarlinga; [m.] Gerald W. Hagerty, September 10, 1972; [ch.] Lt Commander Val Jon Jensen (Chaplain - US Navy); [ed.] Trinity High School (River Forest Illinois); Univ of Chicago; and dancing training from 3 years old - until becoming a professional; [occ.] Wife of an ordained minister; [memb.] National Honor Society; International Federation for Animal Welfare; National Committee to Preserve Social Se- curity and Medicare; Humane Society of the United States; [hon.] National Honor Society; Volunteer work at Kenmore-Mercy Hospital in Kenmore; Chari- table works for Village Independent Church in Williamsville, NY; [oth. writ.] Newspaper articles; autobiography entitled "A Dancer's Crooked Path to the Lord," (under the pen name Crystal Bart); [pers.] I hope to show the interest God has in those who follow Him and how He can lead us if we lean on Him, The Great Creator; [a.] Williamsville, NY

HAGGERTY, MARK
[b.] August 8, 1948, Prov., RI; [p.] Donald M. and Jane C. Haggerty; [ed.] Associate in Arts, Commu- nity College of R.I. 1970, Shindler Fellow, Fuller Museum of Art, Brockton, MA 1985 B.F.A., Art Institute of Boston 1990, Graduate Level, Human Development Course, Eastern Nazarene College 1992; [occ.] Poet, Illustrator; [memb.] Life Member, Inter- national Society of Poets, Secular Franciscan Order, Holy Name Society, Assoc., Mem., Legion of Mary, Boston Athenum, Associate Member, Guild of Bos- ton Artists, Air Force Sergeants Associaiton; [hon.] Dean's List, Community Col. of RI 1969, Shindler Fellow, Fuller Museum of Art, Brockton, 1985, Highest Honors Graduate. Art Institute of Boston, 1990, 1st Prize " No Greater Love Day", Poetry Contest, Brockton, VA Hosp., poem "Lovin' Breezes included in "Sound of Poetry" tape (NLP, Editor's Favorite Poets), poem "The Summer Shapes" awarded same honor, poem "Spring is Just Four Days Away", included in Nat'l Library's "Outstanding Poets 1994, selection of poems "An Open Door to Seasons Four" included in NLP tape series "Visions"; [oth. writ.] Numerous poems on love, spirituality, nature, tran- quility, to be compiled into collections and submitted to publishers children book "Slippy Sloth' recently released by vantage press, NY, A second children's book has been prepared; [pers.] What one sees, feels and hears in varied situations and in relation to varied subjects can unexpectedly lead the individual to

inspired verse.; [a.] Brockton, MA

HAGLUND, PAULA J.
[b.] August 10, 1977, Beaver, UT; [p.] Mary Haglund and Roger Haglund; [hon.] 3rd place literature, reflections contest; [oth. writ.] 3 poems published by Sparrowgrass Poetry, Forum, Inc; [pers.] Fate cannot change what destiny has predetermined; [a.] Kanosh, UT

HAGUE, JR. HENRY H.
[b.] August 14, 1952, Houston, TX; [p.] Henry & Norma Hague; [ed.] B.B.A. Marketing, University of Houston; [occ.] Purchasing Agent Continental Air- lines; [memb.] Second Baptist Church; [oth. writ.] Personal Book of poems titled "Not Just Today, But Always." (not published); [pers.] I write from my heart and believe that the purest love is that of God's love for mankind.; [a.] Houston, TX

HAHN, DAVID MICHAEL
[Pen.] None yet!; [b.] November 14, 1976, Utica, NY; [p.] Lynne Boutet, Jack Hahn; [m.] (Girlfriend) Shelley Scott; [ch.] Maranda Nicole Hahn; [ed.] Senior in high school; Brookside High School, Brooks Lane Chadwick, NY; [occ.] Full-time student; [oth. writ.] Other poems, but none have been published; [pers.] Don't ever get so wrapped in your own beauty that you can't recognize the beauty of others; [a.] New Hartford, NY

HAHN, SARA
[b.] January 27, 1983, Hollywood, CA; [p.] Joel Hahn & Linda Hahn; [ed.] Currently a student at Washington Elementary School, in the fifth grade; [memb.] Washington Elementary School Student Council, Gifted and Talented Education (GATE); [hon.] Washington Elementary Creative Writing Awards, grades 1 through 4, Elected Student Council; [hon.] Recording Secretary, 1993; [oth. writ.] Pub- lished in American Heart Association Newsletter, Whiz Kids Digest, The Washington Bell Newsletter; [pers.] I enjoy writing to express my emotions. I hope to be a journalist and author when I grow up.; [a.] San Gabriel, CA

HALE, SHANNA
[b.] March 2, 1976, Heidleburg, West Germany; [p.] Thomas, Carolyn Hale; [ed.] Boswell High School; [occ.] Fast Food, Golden Fried Chicken; [memb.] Thespians, Saginaw Church of Christ Youth Group; [hon.] National Honor Society, Optomist Club Award; [oth. writ.] Several poems in Treasured Poems of America several short stories yet unpublished; [pers.] I am mankind's tonge. I write what he cannot or will not say; therefore, I am the world; [a.] Saginaw, TX

HALL, DANIEL EDWARD
[b.] Houston, TX; [m.] Girlfriend for two years, Natalie Pierre; [oth. writ.] I enjoy writing short stories, scripts, and plays as well as writing poetry.; [pers.] I've been greatly influenced by Friedrich Nietzsfche and I'd like to say that if only one person reads and enjoys my writings then it is all worthwhile.; [a.] Las Vegas, NV

HALL, HEIDI M.
[b.] July 4, 1972, Nova Scotia, Canada; [p.] Ellen M. Hall; [ed.] Completed grade 12 high school education - graduated 1991; [occ.] Military Reserves of Canada 84 Indep Fd Bty Yarmouth; [hon.] Class of '77 Creative Writing Award - Best All-Around Creative Writing; [oth. writ.] Several unpublished poems and short stories; [pers.] I reflect my romantic discontent with the world around me in my writings. I have been greatly influenced by Edgar Allan Poe and Jrr Tolkein, among others; [a.] Yarmouth County, Nova Scotia, Canada

HALL, WENDY R.
[b.] August 19, 1958, Benton Harbor, MI; [p.] Harold and Dorothy Blankenship; [m.] Walter E. Hall, January 1, 1984; [ch.] David Lee and Kevin Edward; [ed.] Eau Claire High Graduate; [oth. writ.] Several poems published in our local newspapers; [pers.] I truely enjoy writing poetry, and if I've touched one heart through my writing, then I've accomplished what I set out to do. Loving what I do, and making people happy too; [a.] Greenwood, AR

HALLFORD, JAEMS W.
[Pen.] Wayman Hallford

HALLIDAY, LYNDA
[b.] March 6, 1967, Luton, England; [p.] Ann Jeffs; Partner: Jon Fuller; [ed.] Queensbury High School, Dunstable College; [occ.] Social Worker; [oth. writ.] Numerous, Unpublished; [pers.] My writings come from personal observations which in some way may relate to others experiences, although ultimately the words are a release for my own emotions; [a.] Luton, Bedfordshire, England

HALSTED, JAMES P.
[Pen.] J.P.H.; [b.] October 9, 1965, Camden, NJ; [p.] Francis & Mary Holsted; [m.] Charleen, September 14, 1991; [ch.] none; [oth. writ.] None published but pages of others as good as the one presented in this anthology; [pers.] Words written on paper are taken from my heart hoping people understand where I'm coming from, but realizing every person has there own thoughts toward life.; [a.] Maple Shade, NJ

HAMILTON, ANGELA
[Pen.] Angelica LaShore; [b.] August 7, 1996, Milwaukee, WI; [p.] Augustine Hamilton, Worley Hamilton; [ed.] High School Student; [memb.] Young Educator's Society; [pers.] I would like to thank my parents for the wonderful up bringing and for teaching me how to enjoy life and all it has to offer. I would like to thank Shanta Hamilton and Joe Bradford for being great friends; [a.] Milwaukee, WI

HAMILTON, BRENDA
[b.] September 11, 1955, Saginaw, MI; [p.] Beverly Meeker, Wayne Borden; [m.] Richard Hamilton, June 3, 1989; [ch.] Jennifer Johnson, Tara Battles, Jenny Hamilton; [ed.] Davison High School Grad., Rhema Correspondence Bible School Grad., three certificates from Christ thru the nations.; [occ.] Caregiver, homemaker, care for my 91 yr. old mother in law; [memb.] Beaver Lake Community Church AARjP; [oth. writ.] I have written over 60 poems. None have been published yet but I plan to in the future.; [pers.] I strive to reflect my lvoe for the Lord in my poems. I am totally inspired by Him when I write. I love the lord with all my heart and I want to share that love with othrs.; [a.] Alpena, MI

HAMLAR, PORTIA Y.T.
[Pen.] Treena Holm; [b.] Montgomery, AL; [p.] H. Council Trenholm, Sr, Portia Lee Trenholm; [ed.] BA - Alabama State Univ; MA - Michigan State Univ; JD - Univ of Detroit; [occ.] Attorney; Technology Center Coor; Creative Writing Instructor; [memb.] State Bar of Michigan Environmental Law Section; State Bar of Illinois; [hon.] Alpha Kappa Mu; Mu Phi Epsilon; Kappa Beta Pi; Univ of Detroit Law Review; Who's Who of American Woman (1978); The World's Who's Who of Women (1978); [oth. writ.] Two law review articles; book on occupational safety and health law; Ed, Michigan Environmental Law Case Digest; numerous educational and cultural grant applications; [pers.] My non-legal nonfiction writings reflect my personal experiences and observations on human relationships and contemporary life.

HAMMEL, LESTER L.
[b.] August 15, 1960, Keokuk, IA; [p.] Lester and Patricia Hammel, January 21, 1994; [ch.] Chela Carlisly; [ed.] Keokuk Senior High School; [occ.] Langen Bach Wood Products - Maintenance; [oth. writ.] Romantic poem contest winner - Carribean Satellite Network; [a.] Montrose, IA

HAMMERBECK, GEORGE EDWARD
[b.] April 5, 1971, Louisville, KY; [ed.] Boston University, BA Political Science from University of Louisville; [occ.] Receptionist; [memb.] Golden Key National Honors Society, American Civil Liberties Union; [oth. writ.] Poems published in Chance and Rant magazines; [pers.] My poems are snapshots. I write them largely for that reason. I guess the things I oppose are work, television, and expensive drink prices at bars. I avoid wearing watches. I like ska music.

HAN, NELLA J.
[Pen.] Nella J. Han; [b.] October 12, 1938, Allison Park, Allegheny County, PA; [p.] Guido Chini, Diana Chini; [m.] Chaesoo Han, January 28, 1986; [ch.] (4) Donald A. Lutz, Denise A. Klimkowicz, Diana J. Lutz, Debra L. Lutz; [ed.] Graduated Springdale High School; [occ.] Homemaker; [hon.] Played a stage role in the performance "Bodhistava" (on the path to meet Buddha) at the "Mandala" theater, Los Angeles, CA on November 27, 1993; [pers.] The world is an open book and my inspiration comes from a higher source - our creator. I find peace by putting the deep feelings stirring within me into writing with the hope of enriching the lives of others; [a.] Los Angeles, CA

HAND, MARK
[b.] November 7, 1950, Phoenix, AZ; [p.] Raymond & Robbie Hand, April 23, 1988; [ch.] Adam Mark, Travis Joseph; [ed.] Saguaro High School, Sheet Metal Mechanic School, U.S. Navy; [occ.] Aerospace Welder, Allied Signal Aerospace, Phx., AZ; [memb.] National Rifle Association, Allied Signal "Go" Club (Charity); [hon.] My greatest honor and award is my family and the satisfaction I get when someone appreciates my writings; [oth. writ.] Until this time, all of my writings have gone to loved ones as gifts. Those and others in my file hopefully someday will be published.; [pers.] Most of my writings are influenced by the realities of life, or deep down emotions that cannot be expressed verbally, but only with a pen; [a.] Maricopa, AZ

HANLEY, JENNIFER ASHLEY
[b.] August 14, 1980, Burbank; [p.] Jeff & Sheri Hanley; [occ.] Student at John Muir Middle School; [a.] Burbank, CA

HANLON, SHARON A.
[b.] July 23, 1949, Waterbury, CT; [p.] William D. and Helen G. Pettit; [m.] David C. Hanlon, Sr, August 22, 1980; [ch.] Sheri Lynn, Vicki Lee, Bobbi Jean, Granddaughter: Tailor Evelyn; [ed.] 1 yr H.S.; [occ.] Notary Public, housewife; [hon.] Poetry awards from contests; [oth. writ.] Several other poems, one of which was published; [pers.] This poem was written specifically for my mother, Helen G. Pettit who died July 13, 1993. "Love Ya"; [a.] Waterbury, CT

HANNAN, BEVERLY CARROLL
[Pen.] Beverly C. Hannan; [b.] December 25, 1925, Yakima, WA; [p.] WM Rathbun and Alfrida Rathbun; [m.] Robert Donahue Hannan, July 26, 1946; [ch.] (4) one son and 3 daughters, Mark, Mary, Julie and Amy; [ed.] Assoc of Art in primary teaching; [occ.] Retired meat wrapper for 23 yrs; [memb.] Am Heart Assn, Volunteer for Los Robles Hospital in Nursery; [hon.] Our son is a reg. nurse, Mary a teacher of special ed for children, Julie is a veteranarian here in

Cal and Amy a dental assistant in Washington Sta Its' an honor just being a mother to these four; [o writ.] Childrens stories for my nine grand-childr Some poetry published in paper for our firemen Simi Valley; [a.] Simi Valley, CA

HANSEN, TARAHL
[b.] April 21, 1982, Rochester; [p.] Dale and Lau [ed.] Kendall Elementary, currently in grade 6; [ho Selected to participate in New York State Music As Flute Soloist/Duet, Citizen Award from Senator J B. Daily; [oth. writ.] Numerous poems and sh stories unpublished; [pers.] To be yourself, not so one you aren't; [a.] Kendall, NY

HANSON, JUDITY R.
[b.] March 12, 1940, Greeley, CO; [p.] Selmer Rein & Gladys L. Holick; [m.] March 10, 19 Divorced; [ch.] Four children of previous marri (father deceased); [ed.] 12 yrs., graduated; [o Retired; [pers.] I live each day to the fullest always live for what tomorrow brings. And to sh my love and happiness with those I care so mu about!; [a.] Mesa, AZ

HANTMAN, BARBARA
[b.] July 3, 1954, Brooklyn, NY; [p.] Abrah Hantman, Sarah Hantman; [ed.] Bayside High, Que College, CUNY and Teacher's College, Colum University; [occ.] English teacher, NYC pul schools; [memb.] Fresh Meadows Poets and Soci for Humanistic Judasim; [hon.] Phi Beta Kappa; [o writ.] "The Vintners These Days" appeared in "Wl pers in the Wind" and was recorded on the accom nying tape, "The Sound of Poetry," by Ira Westre for The National Library of Poetry. Verse will app in a forthcoming issue of "Freshet" sponsored Fresh Meadows Poets.; [pers.] My muse was freed a poetry writing class at NYU's School of Continu Education. In exploring the human condition and own ethnicity by way of verse, I often come to a d sense of wistfulness; [a.] Whitestone, NY

HARCLERODE, STACY
[b.] May 2, 1968, Harrisburg, PA; [p.] James a Cherie Harclerode; [m.] Fiance Michael D. Car [ed.] Middleburg Joint High School; [occ.] Weld Pipecutter, part-time Inventor; [oth. writ.] Seve poems and plays that were used in my High Sch Drama Club. I am currently working on my novel a afterwards plan to write my biography.; [pers. personaly feel society has strayed fromj the age old of story telling. We have forgotten the pleasure reading the written word and the feeling one can co away with by reading someones personal trials a relaizing we are all connected by life experience [a.] McVeytown, PA

HARDWICK, NAN-MARIE
[b.] July 18, 1937, Winnipeg, Manitoba, Can.; [Nestor and Marie Orlesky; [m.] Ronald Ge Hardwick, April 19, 1958; [ch.] Shane, Kelly, Dan and Jean; [ed.] University of Winnipeg and Univ sity of Lethbridge; [occ.] Working on small book poetry and ideas; [memb.] Illness does not pen membership my interests are: family, nature, philo phy, poetry, history and people.; [hon.] Hon courses in Human Nature and Ethics (Philosoph [oth. writ.] As stated earlier, won poetry contest 19 by Canadian Authors Assoc. for poem "Ni Therapy"; [pers.] I love the earth and all her creatu and morn the treatment of our first mother. I dee believe in a power greater than all we perceive.; [Winnipeg, Manitoba, Canada

HARGREAVES, OLIVE
[Pen.] Olive Bayson Hargreaves; [b.] September 1957, Saskatchewan; [p.] Murray and Vivien Brys [m.] Roy Hargreaves, September 6, 1975; [c Brandon, Julie, Brock; [ed.] Young McClellan Hi

c.] Full time wife, mother, nursing home, gov't ...ployee; [pers.] Most of my poems or writings are ...pired by a certain person or sitation. They show ...pport and encouragement. I am greatly influenced ... my faith in God and His word.; [a.] Watrous, Prqu. ...sk.

ARKINS, NANCY
...] December 5, 1935, Memphis, TN; [p.] Dr. and ...rs. Malcolm Prewitt; [m.] James Harkins, February ...959; [ch.] Jon, Karen, Paul and Chris, Jon ...alcolm, Karen Elizabeth, Paul Matthew, Christo- ...er Lee; [ed.] Graduated from high school and went ...ss than a yr. to art college.; [occ.] Homemaker or ...omestic Engineer"; [hon.] I've won several trips, ...cause of winning coloring contests, one of them put ...y family in a Penthouse in Canada. The latest ...ntest I won was a couple of yrs. ago.; [oth. writ.] ...his is the only poem I have ever written.; [pers.] I ...ould admire the beauty of Mt. Rainier each time we ...ould travel around Seattle, we were stationed there ...e last thre yrs. of my husband's 24 years in the ...nited States Marine Corps. I served 3 yrs. in the Air ...orce in the Supply Field; [a.] Chandler, AZ

ARPER, DENIS
..] February 19, 1971, CA; [p.] Lief & Laura Ayen; ...m.] Michael Harper, March 26, 1993; [ch.] Anastasia, ...arper; [ed.] Currently attending Mesa Community ...ollege to transfer to ASU and receive a degree in ...nglish Education; [occ.] Student; [pers.] If the world ...as upside down, I'd be tall.; [a.] Mesa, AZ

ARRINGTON, MOLLY
...b.] September 16, 1978, Brentwood, TN; [p.] Michael ...nd Madeline; [ed.] 9th grader at Humble High ...chool; [memb.] National Charity League and Key ...lub; [hon.] All A honor roll during middle school. ... A & B honor roll as of yet in high school; [oth. writ.] ...everal poems; [pers.] Don't take anything for granted, ...f you have a special gift, use it to further your life; [a.] ...umble, TX

HARRIS, GWENDOLYN D.
...b.] May 3, Coahoma, MS; [p.] Henry and Alva ...arris; [ed.] Tougaloo College, Georgia Inst of ...echnology, Vanderbilt Univ; [occ.] Law Student; ...a.] Huntsville, AL

HARRIS, RACHEL ANN
[Pen.] Rock; [b.] March 28, 1963; [p.] God Raised Me; [ed.] Muncie Christian High School; [occ.] Gymnastics is my spiritual calling; [hon.] Was 4th place in my freshman class and 4th place in the building champion in the spelling B contest at Northwest Jr High School; [oth. writ.] Wrote for the Reflection Newsletter at the Johnson County Residential Care Facility. And have written other numerour poems and songs; [pers.] All my writings are inspired by the Holy Spirit which is the reflection of my personal relationship with God.; [a.] Kansas City, KS

HARRIS, RAJEAN
[Pen.] Rajean Harris; [b.] June 3, 1972, OR; [p.] Glenda Cave, Hardy Cave; [ch.] Rayana Thanh Nguyen; [ed.] St. Helens High School, Tongue Point Job Corps; [occ.] Motherhood; [hon.] Motherhood; [pers.] The beauty of earth are in our thoughts. Let there be peace in our minds and be good to one another. God bless; [a.] Evans, WA

HARRIS, SHANNON DEE
[b.] July 24, 1970, Yuba City, CA; [p.] Franklin P. Harris and Judy Brooks; [ch.] Torrey Michael and Taylor Jenae; [ed.] Lindhurst High school, Yuba Community College; [occ.] Homemaker, Nail Technician; [hon.] FFA Leadership, Public Speaking; [oth. writ.] Various poems of many topics/never submitted for publishing; [pers.] You do not have to be a Harvard Graduate to pick up a pen and place your

thoughts on paper. Find your inspiration, and follow it; [a.] Yuba City, CA

HARRISON, PAMELA
[b.] March 26, 1942, Lymington, Southampton, England (UK); [p.] Phyllis Mary Harrison, Private Edward Harrison (Middx Regr) 1st btn; [ed.] The Gordon General School (secondary modern England, (UK); [occ.] Part time Draughts Woman Tracer with: Imperial College, London (UK) (Soul Mechanics); [memb.] The Royal British Legion (Associated Member); Honorary Member of the Middlesex Regiment (DCO); [hon.] Published in "Poppy Fields" for: Poetry Now War Anthology (1992); Editor's Choice Award contest in "Where Dreams Begin". The National Library of Poetry (1993); [pers.] Looking forward in the near future to continue with my poems and to share my inner thoughts with other poets; [a.] Chelsea, London, UK

HART, JULIE
[b.] September 26, 1952, Toppenish, WA; [p.] Maizie Abercrombie, Arnold Abercrombie; [m.] divorced, June 3, 1973; [ch.] Rebecca, Sarah; [ed.] Goldendale High School, Yakima Valley Community College; [occ.] Newspaper reporter/photographer; [memb.] Soroptimist International Lower Valley Crisis and Support Services; Valley Musical Company; [hon.] Washington Newspaper Publisher's Assoc writing and Alsign Awards. Awards of Appreciation from Sunnyside School District; [oth. writ.] Several poems published in college literary magazines and newspapers; [pers.] My aim is to derive honesty of feelings which uncovering humanity of self; [a.] Sunnyville, WA

HARTMANN, MICHAEL
[Pen.] Michael D. Hartmann; [b.] April 9, 1983, Manhasset; [p.] Linda and Thomas; [ed.] Grades 1-3; [oth. writ.] "A Light of Black," "The White Leaf," "The Chosen Christmas," "The Upsurd," "The Way of Love,""Her Eyes."; [pers.] I write to express myself and I am involved in other arts as well such as dance; [a.] Dix Hills, NY

HARTSHORNE, HARRY E.
[b.] February 2, 1926, Detroit; [p.] Harry & Florence (nee McArdle); [m.] Dorothy M. (nee Lentes), March 31, 1951; [ch.] Sandra, Bryn, Kevin and Neal; [ed.] S.W. Essex Tech. Coll., London Eng.; [occ.] Retired; [memb.] Elks, V.V.W., A.A.R.P., W.W.II 94th Inf. Div. Association; [oth. writ.] One unpublished short story "Nicholas' Guardian Angel"; [pers.] Arm Chair Crusader Against Injustice; [a.] Northvile, MI

HARVEY, JAMES L.
[Pen.] Jay Harvey; [b.] May 6, 1918, Chattanooga, TN; [p.] John & Zelphia Harvey (Deceased); [m.] Elmae Allen Harvey, October 3, 1945 (Deceased October 25, 1989; [ch.] James R. Mary Deborah and Zelphia Jeanette; [ed.] 8th Grade; [occ.] Retired; [memb.] Meth. Church, Masonic Lodge american Legion and DAV; [memb.] 19 Other Poems. Some have been put to music. I am now working on my autobiography; [pers.] I am 75 years old and I wrote my first when I was 73 years and 8 months old. I had music put to it. There is a personal story behind every one of my poems. When I was younger I like to walk in the woods and listen to nature. Thinking about my walks in the woods inspired me to write "Hear The Master Talk."; [a.] West Liberty, KY;

HARVEY, ROBERT
[b.]j August 21, 1964, Nash Creek, NB; [p.] Murray and Emaline Harvey; [ed.] Bachelor of Business Adm. College Militaire royal, St. Jean, Que; [occ.] Logistics Officer, Canadian Forces,; [memb.] Aitken Alumni, Lambda Ottawa, Anciens de CMR; [hon.] Numerous sporting awards in amateur hockey and

cross-country running. Third in New Brunswick Public Speaking 1979; [oth. writ.] Poems published in local newspaper. Articles in the UNB Mushroom, CMR Rempart, and RMC student paper.; [pers.] Life is only what we make of it. A fly is only interested in a spider once he has spun his web. Life is only exciting if we live it to the fullest with happiness and love.; [a.] St. Jean, Quebec

HARVEY, SHEILA G.
[b.] March 25, 1957, Galveston, TX; [p.] Dave and Irene Branstetter; [m.] Terry J. Harvey, July 28, 1985; [ch.] Danna Lynnette Rogers, Teri-Jo Harvey; [occ.] D.A. Operator Southwestern Bell 14 yrs.; [memb.] Five Star Music Masters; [oth. writ.] Songs and poems, short stories, children's books; [pers.] Writing poetry has been a passion since Jr. High School. I was greatly influenced by my 2nd jgrade teacher, who was also my 7th grade English teacher.; [a.] Santa Fe, TX

HASS, CAMI
[b.] March 25, 1980, Ft Benning, GA; [p.] Bob and Dorothy DeMaio; [ed.] 8th grade, start high school next year; [occ.] student; Organizations: Worked with City of Casa Grande, Camp Pee Wee, Teen Council; [hon.] Soccer, honor roll, principals list, wrote book in 6th grade got award; [pers.] I feel very strongly about that do or might harm somebody. I take all of that sadness and I put it into words; [a.] Casa Grande, AZ

HASSELL, TODD EMMITT
[b.] April 10, 1965, Rockville Center (NY); [p.] Pauline and Edwin Hassell; [pers.] I dedicate this poem to my dear mother, Pauline Malone Hassell; professional writer, counselor, astrologer, and most of all wholesome loving mother of ten children. She has given me the purpose through love and caring to create, to share, to have compassion and love.

HAUSCHILDT, CHRISTINE
[b.] April 4, 1969, St Louis, MO; [p.] Roger Hauschildt, Carol Kennedy; [ed.] Pursuing a BA of English at McPherson College; [occ.] Student; [oth. writ.] Several short fiction stories pending publication, editorial writer for college newspaper; [pers.] I am influenced by contemporary writers of the US. Through writing, I have overcome many obstacles; [a.] McPherson, KS

HAVA-ROBBINS, NADEZDA
[b.] November 9, 1952, Prague, Czechoslovakia; [p.] Maria and Milos Hava, MD, Ph.D; [m.] Peter S. Robbins, MD, November 16, 1985; [ch.] David Alexander Robbins; [ed.] Performing Arts, Ballet, BA Philosophy; Psychology - U of Kansas at Lawrence, MA Counseling; Guidance U of Missouri at KC; [occ.] Medical Office Manager; [hon.] First prize - French Poetry Contest - Academic Fair, KCMO 1971, "Life Saver Award" - American Cancer Society; [oth. writ.] Collection of poems, and adaptations of Czech Fairytales for English - unpublished; [pers.] To be able to freely translate emotions, feelings, and thoughts with spontaneous harmony into a creative expression of any kind is to become alive!; And to be alive is to make dreams come true; [a.] Honolulu, HI

HAWKINS, AMY
[b.] January 2, 1979, Hagerstown, MD; [p.] Anna Kreps, Lew Kreps; [ed.] Williamsport High School, Williamsport, MD; [occ.] Student; [memb.] Cheerleading; [hon.] Modeling; [oth. writ.] Poem published in newspaper (special selection from eighth grade teacher); [pers.] When writing my heart is more powerful than my pen. I have been greatly influenced by Mrs. Kathy Hose; [a.] Williamsport, MD

HAWKINS, SHAYLA
[b.] September 10, 1976, Detroit, MI; [p.] Shirley Hawkins, Edward Hawkins; [ed.] Renaissance High School; [occ.] High school student; [memb.] Future Writer's Club, Drama Club, Foreign Language Club, Public Announcements Staff; [hon.] Honor Roll, National Honor Society, Who's Who Among American High School Students; [oth. writ.] Several poems published in high school newspaper The Stentor; [pers.] "What you are is God's gift to you; what you become is your gift to God"; [a.] Detroit, MI

HAYDEN, PAT
[b.] Connecticut; [ch.] (four children) Raymond, Ann, Larry, Kate; [ed.] BS in English Literature from Central Conn State Univ, MA, Trinity College English Literature, post grad work at Wesbyan in writing workshops; [occ.] Teacher of English at Rocky Hill High School; [memb.] St Elizabeth Seton Church; [oth. writ.] Poems published in local paper on the history of our town; [pers.] I have been influenced by many of the Irish writers and poets from Yeats to Healy. I also respond to some of the starkness of modern poets such as Mary Oliver; [a.] Rock Hill, CT

HAYDOCK, PETER
[Pen.] (Lord) Peter Haydock; [b.] September 9, 1969, (Chatham) Kent; [p.] Prof Lawrence & Mrs. Pauline (Anne) Haydock; [ed.] 1) Fernwood School, Wollaton, Nottingham, UK, 2) Bronxtowe College, 3) Nottingham Trent Univ, Nottingham England, UK; [occ.] Student photographer/new-age poet and musician; [memb.] 1) The Poetry Society of London, 2) The New Mechanics Institute Poetry Society/Nottm, 3) Amateur Royal Society of Photography, 4) Beeston Camera Club, 5) Stapleford Creative Writing Group, Nottm/Uk; [hon.] BTEC National Certificate in Electronics GCE/CSE: English Language, Mathematics, Geography, Chemistry, Technology (industrial); [oth. writ.] An extensive collection of poetry, which is continously being updated and added to for publication as one or more complete books of my work; [pers.] "In all my writing, photography and art work. I try to direct attention to the preservation of the environment, to make people think about their relationships to others and the universe.; [a.] Nottingham (England), UK

HAYES, CARA
[b.] February 9, 1978, Cullman, Alabama; [p.] Barbara and Sam Hayes; [ed.] Los Angeles Baptist High School; [occ.] Student; [memb.] Panorama Baptist Church Youth Board, Los Angeles Baptist High School Drill Team; [hon.] Los Angeles Baptist School 4.0 Award and Drill Team Coach's Award; [oth. writ.] Poem in the Los Angeles Baptist Literary magazine; [pers.] I hope that God and His influence in my life can be seen through my writing; [a.] Mission Hills, CA

HAYMAN, CHARISE
[b.] April 14, 1975, Detroit, MI; [p.] George Hayman, Valerie Hayman; [ch.] Kristen Avonne Hayman; [ed.] Moorestown Friends School, Rutgers Univ (I am presently a freshman); [hon.] Annual Delta Teens Writing Award; [oth. writ.] Poems published in high school literary magazine; [a.] Willingboro, NJ

HAYNES, CYNTHIA
[Pen.] Cindy Haynes; [b.] February 27, 1976, Ft. Campbello, KY; [p.] Rita & Richard Haynes; [ed.] High School Senior; [occ.] Student; [hon.] Attended South Carolina Governor's School for The Arts in the area of Creative Writing; [oth. writ.] Several poems and one short story published in Literary Magazine; [a.] HQ EUCOM, Unit 30400 Box 1113, APO AE Germany

HEALEY, FELIX, M.
[b.] October 3, 1947, St Agnes Hospital Baltimore, MD; [m.] Catherine A. Healey, September 13, 1970; [ch.] Chyrel and Brandi, Sherry and Brandi; [ed.] Two years of college, commercial art, aircraft mechanic and minister of the Word of God; [occ.] Letter Carrier, US Postal Service; [memb.] Part-time minister and artist, along with my love of writing poetry; [oth. writ.] The Plastic Society World of Poetry (California), Measure Me, Took honors in 1991, Dad and me same year; [pers.] Poetry is the expression of the inner self, the deep thinking of the mine, mixed with the heart felt, process of the emotional threaded with life, tales twined thru out; [a.] North Port, FL

HEBRANK, WILLIAM
[b.] August 28, 1959, Weisbaden, Germany; [p.] Ferdinand and Magdalena Hebrank; [ch.] William Brandon, Nicole Marie, Thomas Ford; [ed.] Platte Canyon High, Colorado School of Mines, Metropolitan State College; [occ.] Owner/President "Impressions" advertising artist; [pers.] If we could get the children to recite my writing...If only on thanksgiving...then maybe it could change a few lines. It may not be much, but it would be a much needed start; [a.] Denver, CO

HEDAYATI, JEANETTE
[b.] Washington, DC; [ed.] BA degree in history; [occ.] Hearing Instrument Specialist, Writer; [memb.] Baha'I Faith, Lions Club; [hon.] From Lions Clubs International; [oth. writ.] Loving Trees, Horizons, Research papers on Baha'i Writings; [pers.] My writings are influenced by the teachings of Baha'u'llah, for He said, "The utterance of God is a lamp, whose light is these words: Ye are the fruits of one tree, and the leaves of one branch. Deal ye one with another with the utmost love and harmony, with friendliness and fellowship"; [a.] Graham, TX

HEDEEN, MELISSA A.
[Pen.] Presley Ann; [b.] August 7, 1977, Norwalk, OH; [p.] Judy Eckstein, Eric Hedeen; [m.] not married; [ch.] none; [ed.] Willard High School, I'm now in the 11th grade.; [occ.] Student; [memb.] Plymouth American Legion, Auxiliary. Young Author's Club, American Heart Association; [oth. writ.] Nothing that has been published, but a lot of individual poems that I keep to myself.; [pers.] Poetry is an artform, of ones individual acceptance of this world and to this world. You either learn to hate it, but accept it or to love it and buildd it, as I did. Poetry is Reality; [a.] Willard, OH

HEGEDUS, EVELYN
[b.] February 19, 1922, Warsaw, IL; [p.] Elma and John Herren; [m.] Deceased; [ch.] Seven children, John Warning, Roger Warning, Pat Byers, Jo Silvestri, Sandra Hewitt, Betty Houston, Theresa Fowler; [ed.] I made it through the 8th grade, 1 of 14 children including twin sisters, twin brothers and I am one of a set of triplets; [occ.] Retired; [oth. writ.] I've only wrote poetry since I was age 13; [pers.] I grew up on a farm in the mid west Illinois and Missouri. All my poems are from the Heart, all true experiences. I've written over one-hundred; [a.] St. Petersburg, FL

HEIMANN, VERDA M.
[Pen.] Verdi; [b.] May 17, 1917, Baird, TX; [p.] John Q. & Sarah Morrison; [m.] Louis Heimann, Jr., June 3, 1950; [ch.] Sharon 42, Cathy 40, Louis III 38, 7 grandchildren; [ed.] High School, Nursing School, some college; [occ.] Retired 1987; [memb.] Zion Lutheran Church, Ex-member American Nurses Assn., Texas Public Employees Assn., Kerr Co., Wood Carvers, Texas Wood Carvers Assn.; [hon.] Gold Medal at age of 12 for highest grade average in art, Medal in U.I.L. for essay, Salutatorian of High School graduation class; [oth. writ.] Informative articles for local newspaper to explain progress of

resocialization project which I supervised, have h one poem published; [pers.] Love to write poetr words that rhyme come asy for me sometimes I wal up with a poem running through my head, all I hav to do is get up and write it down.; [a.] Kerrville, T

HEINTSCHEL, MICHAEL
[b.] January 10, 1978, Abilene, TX; [p.] Raymor and Belinda Heintschel; [ed.] Currently sophmore Ross S. Sterling High School of Baytown; [occ Student; [hon.] Letterman in football; [a.] Baytow TX

HEMPE, KEVIN
[b.] May 5, 1966, California; [p.] David Hemp a and Becky Hemp; [m.] Yolanda Hempe; [m.] Ju 29, 1992; [ch.] Carlos, Garrett and Cassandra; [ed BA in Visual Communications; [occ.] United Stat Marine; [memb.] USM (Univ of science, music a culture); [oth. writ.] Just poems to my wife; [pers Please read from the Bible: Romans 3:23, 3:10; Isai 64:6; Romans 6:23; John 3:16-21; Romans 5:6- John 3:3, 14:6; Revelations 3:20; I John I:9 Roma 10:13, 10:9,10; I John 5:13; II Corinthians 5:17; a 1 John 2:4; [a.] 29 Palms, CA

HENDEL, CHRISTINE
[b.] September 23, 1976, Eugene, OR; [p.] Rudi a Catherine Hendel; [ed.] Summit High School, w attend college fall '94; [occ.] Student; [memb.] Sur mit Symphony Orchestra; [oth. writ.] Assorted p ems, essays, and short stories; [pers.] My art; scul ture, painting, violin and literature alike, is merely mirror of my own heart and soul. Just as simple a just as pure; [a.] Summit, NJ

HENK, LYNN E.
[b.] March 25, 1945, Evanston, IL; [p.] Walter H. Anne L. Seidel; [m.] Charles W. Henk, March 1 1970; [ch.] none; [ed.] Evanston Township Hig School, Evanston Business College; [occ.] part-tin secretary for lawyer in Berwyn, Illinois; [memb Business and Professional Women's Club of Evansto [hon.] Paul Harris Fellow from the Rotary Foundati of Rotary International (worked for Rotary Intern tional for 26 years, then retired); [oth. writ.] Poe "Love in America", printed in "U.S. in Clover 76 Poem "A Holy Wish" printed in "Our 20th Centur Gretest Poems." Poem "It's In The Stars" printed "The Coming of Dawn."; [pers.] The poems that write come out of feelings that I have of the thing experience and see. Love and beauty is all around u and I like to write about those feelings.; [a.] Cicer IL

HENRIE, PAMELA A.
[Pen.] Pammie; [b.] May 6, 1968, Arlington Height IL; [p.] Camiel and Christine Van Dorne; [m.] Cor Henrie, October 31, 1992; [ch.] Lacey Ann Henr (age 4); [ed.] Graduated from Crystal Lake Sou High School, Crystal Lake, IL - college - Robe Morris College, Carthage, IL; Study legal and adm istrative; [occ.] Housewife; [memb.] Belonged to t ski club in 7th and 8th grade. Was a girl scout until n junior year; [hon.] Perfect attendance in certain s mesters in high school; [oth. writ.] I have writte many poems from the time I was 12 until today to m father, husband, friends and working on one to m daughter; [pers.] I was born and raised in Illino living most of my life in a small town called Lake-I The-Hills, I had gotten married and moved to th small town Carthage where I attended college provide a more relaxing, secure and safe environme for my family. I love making all people feel importa and appreciated with true feelings I put into poem [a.] Carthage, IL

HENRY, HELEN
[Pen.] Helen Moore Henry; [b.] May 16, 1922, Batt Creek, NE; [p.] Paul Moore and Barbara (Souvignie

oore; [m.] Aaron S. Henry, Jr (deceased), Decemer 26, 1944; [ed.] Wayne State College BAE plus 22 ours of graduate study - A average. Univ of Lincoln, e; [occ.] Retired Elem. Teacher and Community ol. Worker - no salary for volunteer work; [memb.] t'l Society of Authors and Artists, Member of ational Author's Registry, Kappa Delta Pi (1967), E State Historical Society; Secretary of Madison Co istorical Society, Treasurer of Madison Woman's lub; American Assoc, Smithsonian Inst, NEAR, SEAR, St Leonards Catholic Church and Guild, merican Legion Aux, AARP, Church Parish Coun- l Member 2 yrs, Jail Ministry - 2 yrs; [hon.] NSEA ert of Special Recognition May 1987 NSHS Certifi- te of Appreciation Oct 6, 1989, Won 1st place in ate Contest 1983 for History of American Legion ux. Won 2nd place in another State Contest for istory of Amer Legion Aux 1984. Honor graduate om college - certificate from high school academy of nor; graduated Cum Laude at Wayne State Madi- n High School Academy of Honor by students at tirement; [oth. writ.] Have had many publications in agazines and newspapers. Poetry: "Beauty", "In- ght of the Ode to Senior Citizens, Reunion-Class e'll Never See Tomorrow. One short story: (unpub- hed) How the 3 Bears Saved. One 577 page Family istory. All poetry accepted for publication one short ory accepted; [pers.] "Let me live in a house by the de of a road and be a friend to America and ankind"; [a.] Madison, NE

ENRY, STEVEN WAYNE
en.] Captain; [b.] November 6, 1962, Phoenix, Z; [p.] Roberta & Lee Henry; [m.] Michelle mmons-Henry, August 3, 1992; [ed.] South Moun- n H.S. Grad., Attended ASU; [occ.] Budding ntrepreneur; [memb.] M.U.S.A.C. (Musically Unit- g Successfully Aiding Children); [hon.] Recogni- n of poetry by one of the most distinguished rican-American poets of Arizona. ASU/Honorable ention, Voices of Africa, Honorable mention for tstanding poetry writing.; [oth. writ.] Stainglass ue, Flaming Heart, Rhythm of Unforgotten Time, a Maiden, Changes Turn, Souls Freedom Flight d Emerald Sea Amber Sunl; [pers.] Living for most ople is Hell, it's the inkling of a brain cell derived om a fearful heart. Heaven is to hard to ask for and simple for the giving, simple and true; [a.] Phoenix, Z

ERMANN, NANCY
.] April 25, 1968, Staten Island, NY; [p.] Mr. and rs. Charles F. Hermann, III; [ed.] Curtis High hool, Sophmore at Wagner College studying soci- gy; [occ.] Certified Nursing Asst at Eger Health re Center; [memb.] Member with the Assoc: Na- nal Dart League; [oth. writ.] Poems on leisure time t published; [pers.] I am inspired by Alexander pe. I write during my leisure time to relax. I would pe to help someone relate to what I write. I strive for e enjoyment that of myself and others reading it; [a.] aten Island, NY

ERMES, ANN
.] Janury 13, 1963, Surrey, B.C. Canada; [p.] Mr. d Mrs. henry Kuipers; [m.] Ray Hermes, April 2, 94; [ed.] High School Graduate (Grade 12) Oph- almic Assistant Diploma; [occ.] Housewife; [oth. it.] unpublished poems and songs; [pers.] When I ked Jesus into my life is when I started writing my elings on paper which just flowered into poetry and/ song; [a.] Lynnwood, WA

ERNANDEZ, BARBRA K.
.] December 29, 1943, Tillamook, Oregon; [p.] over & Dorothy Coe; [m.] Ruben Hernandez, Sr., gust 16, 1963; [ch.] Denise Alexander, Lynette ernandez, Ruben, Hernandez Jr., Stephanie adshaw; [hon.] Being a wife, parent and grandpar- t; [pers.] Life should be embraced and cherished for

it is "all" that we have.; [a.] Stockton, CA

HERNANDEZ, KILEY JOSEPH
[b.] November 26, 1977, Wichita, KS; [p.] Rhonda M. Hurst; [ed.] Brooks Middle Magnet, Wichita Heights High School; [occ.] Student; [memb.] Feed- ing Our Children Under Starvation (FOCUS); [hon.] Achievement Award: Interviewing skills in business; [oth. writ.] The Door, The Beating Heart, The Gray Ghost; [pers.] No matter how hard you try, you will fail at some point. I guess life was meant to fail, in order to succeed. That's the true meaning of knowing everything. Being able to except failure and challenge it; [a.] Wichita, KS

HERRBACH, JEANETTE L.
[b.] July 16, 1951, Erie, PA; [p.] Carl and Nancy Egolf; [m.] Allan M. Herrbach, September 22, 1984; [ch.] Theresa L. Cross; [ed.] Essex Jct High, Champlain College; [occ.] Owner of home-based business for custom leather products; [memb.] American Horse Shows Assoc, American Morgan Horse Assoc, NM Morgan Horse Club, Roadrunner Leather Artisans Guild; [hon.] Runner-up, Vermont Federation State Music Scholarship; 1st and 2nd place award in American Morgan Horse Assn Art Contest; [pers.] I believe my appreciation of art and music has enabled me to expand my creativity through my leather art and poetry; [a.] Bosque Farms, NM

HERRERA, ERNEST A.
[b.] May 16, 1970, Denver; [p.] Joseph & Elhira Herrar; [m.] none; [ch.] none; [ed.] Junior Chamber of Commerce. Special Projects Committee Assistant; [memb.] Foreign Language Club, Club Morales; [hon.] 1986 - 2nd Place State Football 2nd, 1987, 3rd Place State Wrestling 112 lbs., 2nd, 5th place state powerlifting 1988 130 lbs.; [oth. writ.] none; [pers.] True success is found within.; [a.] Pueblo, CO

HERZ, DONNA
[b.] February 3, 1950, Philadelphia, PA; [p.] Donald Brown, Ellen Halberstadt; [m.] Norman Herz, June 11, 1977; [ch.] Matthew Adam, Robin Elizabeth; [ed.] Wissahickon High, Bennett College; [occ.] Homemaker, education activist; [oth. writ.] Several articles published in a local arts magazine, articles for a company newsletter; [pers.] I think of writing poetry as painting with words, the paper is my canvas, the words my palette; [a.] Denver, CO

HESS, KIM
[b.] February 17, 1980, St. Henry, OH; [ch.] None, 2 Brothers and 1 Sister, Kelly, Brad, Brent; [ed.] 8th Grade, St. Henry Consolidated Local Schools; [occ.] Student; [memb.] Brownies, Youth Group, Middle School Volleyball, Basketball, and Cheerleader, Stu- dents Teaching About Resistance (STAR), Power of the Pen; [hon.] Honor Roll; [pers.] Don't let anyone steal your dream! If you can dream it, it will happen. If you really work toward something, believe in yourself and it will heppen in one way or another; [a.] St. Henry, OH

HICKLIN, JAMES K.
[b.] November 21, 1962, Los Angeles; [p.] Myra J. Boling and James R. Hicklin; [occ.] Cashier, Califor- nia Commerce Club, Commerce, CA; [oth. writ.] Dedications in local newspapers; [pers.] Poetry should touch the soul, and inspire the mind to reach ever higher for the infinite desires of the heart.; [a.] Bell Gardens, CA

HIGHAM, MARILYN
[Pen.] Sybil Brown; [b.] Conn.; [p.] Dorothea and James Brown; [ch.] Marilyn Sybil and Marvin Irwin and Phyllis Linda; [ed.] Educated in Conn. in Early Childhood Education; [memb.] National Geographic; [oth. writ.] Small, local publication; [pers.] I have been influenced by major british writers in writing

style and thought, wondering through ancient history around the globe, led by nursery ballads and children's favored classroom tales.; [a.] Seymour, CT

HILDEN, ALTON
[b.] February 1, 1907, Minnesota; [p.] Deceased; [m.] Helen Jane H.; [ch.] None; [ed.] B. of Science 1929, U. of M. of Arts 1935. Minnesota H.S. teacher, Coach, Principal, Immigrant Inspection, Naval Officer 28 years.; [occ.] Retired USN, CDR.; [memb.] A.F.A. Masons, B.P.E. Elks., American Legion, Military Order of World Wars.

HILL, RANDI
[b.] January 6, Norway; [p.] Anne Beth and Ay Januila; [m.] Divorced; [ch.] none; [occ.] P.R. Div./ Assist. GNP Crescendo Records; [oth. writ.] In progress: 3 poetry books with photos, children's book and greeting cards; [pers.] Love conquers all!; [a.] Hollywood, CA

HILLERT, JESSICA R.
[Pen.] Jessie; [b.] May 29, 1984, Alpena; [p.] David and Debra; [ed.] 4th grader--Ella White Elementary; [occ.] Student; [memb.] Community Childrens Con- cert Choir. 4-D 2nd Street Dance Company; [oth. writ.] This is my "real" first. I love poetry!; [pers.] I had to write a paper for school. It had to have something to do with a reflection. The refrigerator handle cut off my nose. Thus my poem; [a.] Alpena, MI

HINSDALE, ALENE JOHNSON
[b.] April 19, 1913; [p.] JD - Alice Johnson (de- ceased); [m.] deceased, 1921, June 21, 1941; [ch.] Z. Carl A., Mary Elizabeth; [ed.] 5 grade; [occ.] House- wife; [memb.] YMCA St Delight Church; [hon.] Trophys, bowling; [oth. writ.] I write a lot; [pers.] I have Elvis Presley Collection records - Xmas carols. RJ Reynolds for (Forsyth Legritts); [a.] Winston- Salem, NC

HIROZAWA, SHUREI
[b.] May 12, 1919, Eleele, HI; [p.] Masaichi and Sada Hirozawa; [m.] Betty F. Hirozawa, October 5, 1957; [ch.] Gail Reiko, Joan Emiko, Robert Kenji; [ed.] Waimea High, Hamline Univ, Univ of IA (BA); [occ.] Retired; [memb.] Society of Professional Jour- nalists, Hawaii Chapter; Hawaii Economic Assoc; [hon.] Distinguished Service Award, Society of Pro- fessional Journalists, Hawaii Chapter; [oth. writ.] Honolulu Star-Bulletin, reporter and business editor; First Hawaiian Bank, economic reports. Poem pub- lished in the Hawaii Review, Univ of Hawaii, 1993; [a.] Honolulu, HI

HIZER, GLORIA E.
[b.] July 30, 1936, Drafter, Michigan; [p.] Vilho and elma Huhtala; [m.] Eugene R., February 7, 1990; [ch.] Donald W., Michael J., and Kathy Quigley and Teri A. Marchetti, [ed.] Superior High; [occ.] Retired was office manager of local utility company business office; [occ.] Couple poems published in local news- papers. I have a portfolio of over 200 poems and some short articles on personal issues. All my poetry began after August 12, 1991; [pers.] I am a strong believer in the brotherhood of man and writings reflect my study of man and his problems, sometimes in a serious vein, other times in humor.; [a.] Kincheloe, MI

HLABSE, STEVEN RICHARD
[Pen.] Steven Richard Anthony; [b.] August 16, 1950, Cleveland, OH; [p.] Richard & Antoinette hlabse; [m.] Divorced; [ch.] Steven Brandon, Geoffrey Anton, Jason Richard, Justin Michael; [ed.] H.S. Diploma, Auburn Career Center (Auto Mechanics); [occ.] La- borer for the City of Wickliffe Service Dept.; [memb.] Wickliffe H.S., Marching Band Boosters, Wickliffe H.S. Forum; [hon.] Life itself is an honor and an award; [oth. writ.] This is my first entry as a poem.

I've written several editorial comments of the years in a local newspaper.; [pers.] All things will work according to the great plan of the creator. When we try to alter the plan in any way, we just mess up the honor & award.; [a.] Willoughby, OH

HOCKLEY, CAROLYN
[b.] November 10, 1966, Halifax, Nova Scotia; [p.] Fred and Louise Hockley; [ed.] Bachelor of Arts Degree, Acadia Univ, Nova Scotia Public Relations Certificate, Humber College, Ontario; [occ.] Public Relations Asst, West Park Hospital, Toronto, Ontario; [pers.] Each word I pen I dedicate to my grandmother. May she be at peace, Mrs. Winnifred Hockley; [a.] Toronto, Ontario, Canada

HOFFBERG, REBECCA
[b.] March 14, 1981, Washington, DC; [p.] Howard & Esther Hoffberg; [ch.] Siblings, Danielle, Adam, Sra, Harris Hoffberg; [ed.] Deer Park Middle School Cedarmere Elementary School, JCC Nursery School; [occ.] Student 7th grader; [memb.] Kadima, Teen Connections, student council, peer mediator, history club, drama club, honors band, former girl scout; [hon.] Honor Roll in religious and public school, academic excellence award (for straight A's) lead in school play (Anne Frank), Red Cross, Babysitting Card, Perfect Attendance Award, Karen Sach's Dance Acad., Tennis Intramural Champ; [oth. writ.] Enjoy writing short stories, poems, monologies and plays.; [pers.] If I'm not for myself, who will be for me? If I'm only for myself, what good am I?; [a.] Reisterstown, MD

HOFFER, AARON
[b.] July 6, 1946, Springfield, OH; [p.] Mary Mounts; [occ.] Oakland Community College, Wayne State Univ; [oth. writ.] Personal unpublished pieces; [pers.] I strive to manipulate the written language in order to express ideas, ideals, and concept of a higher self. In doing so, it is my hope that a higher plateau of understanding is reached; [a.] Detroit, MI

HOFFMANN, PEGGY G.
[Pen.] Peggy G. Hoffmann; [b.] August 8, 1924, Muskegon, MI; [p.] Bernice and Tom Andersen; [m.] William D. Hoffman, August 7, 1975; [ch.] Jan, Daniel and Susan; [ed.] Michigan National Music Camp, Glendale Community College, CA; [occ.] Homemaker; [memb.] Church of Lighted Window, Council of British Societies, Glendale Woman's Club; [hon.] Golden Poet 1991 by World of Poetry, Editor's Choice Award by the National Library of Poetry; [oth. writ.] Various short stories published by Glendale Community College; [pers.] To enhance beauty for the reader's delight; [a.] La Crescenta, CA

HOGAN, KENNETH B.
[b.] April 5, 1965, Rockaway Beach, NY; [ed.] Xaverian High School, Brooklyn, NY, American College of Pre Hospital Medicine, N.O. LA with A.S. in EMS Management; [occ.] NYC Firefighter, Instructor, Training Academy; [memb.] American Red Cross, American Heart Association, United States Lifesaving Association; [oth. writ.] One book "The Old Firehouse" published in 1993. Several short stories and articles have appeared in fire service magazines.; [pers.] Influenced greatly by 19th century American poets and short story writers. The author, a former lifeguard of 11 years, continues to reflect His love of the ocean and beach in his writings.; [a.] Breezy Point, NY

HOGUE, JENNIFER MARIE
[b.] September 21, 1982, Ravenna, OH; [p.] James Hogue (Jr), Brenda Hogue; [ed.] Brown Middle School, Ravenna, OH; [occ.] Student; [memb.] Student Council; [pers.] Jennifer is a 6th grade student at Brown Middle School. She is 11 yrs old. And enjoys computers, keyboard, music, and loves writing po-

ems and short stories. She has one brother Jim Hogue who is 16; [a.] Ravenna, OH

HOLLEY, ALISA
[b.] January 22, 1980, Detroit, MI; [p.] Desiree and John Holley; [ed.] Saint Juliana, Detroit, MI; [hon.] National Junior Honor Society, Ronald E. McNaire Chapter President; [a.] Detroit, MI

HOLM, KATIE
[b.] August 9, 1979, Chicago, IL; [p.] Lloyd D. Holm, Jan L. Williams; [ed.] High school freshman; [occ.] Student; [hon.] Science Merit Award grade 9, Math grade 7, English grade 7, Social Studies grade 7, Spelling Bee grade 6 and 8; [pers.] The poetry that I write comes from my innermost feelings. Many of my friends and family encourage me to write my feelings down. This is my way of escape; [a.] Hanover, IN

HOLMES, ROSIE LEE
[Pen.] Rosie Holmes; [b.] April 4, 1918, Mt. Rose AR; [p.] William and Sarah Brown; [m.] James H. Holmes, Sr, November 28, 1936; [ch.] Dr. James Holmes, Delores Standifer, Carolyn Slade; [ed.] Completed the 8th grade in Mt. Rose Arkansas; [occ.] Foster grandparent; [memb.] Deaconess Fresno Westside SDA Church; [oth. writ.] 1978 poem published in "A Different Drummer", poem published in "New Voices in American Poetry 1980", "Life at Best": Booklet published with a true life story and twenty original poems written by Rosie Lee Holmes - 1993; [pers.] I am deeply moved by others when they express their appreciation for the poems that I have written. And by the Grace of God, I wish to continue with this God - given talent; [a.] Fresno, CA

HOLMSEN, ALEXANDER
[b.] September 21, 1931, Southampton, NY; [p.] Nicholas and Ellen Holmsen; [m.] Elizabeth Blanco-Fombona, March 31, 1959; [ch.] Alexander T. Jr, Stephen Bigelow; [ed.] St. Paul's School (Concord, NH), University of Virginia, Middlebury College; [occ.] Journalist; [oth. writ.] From: "On The Nature of the Universe", "One-Way Street," a novel of Wall Street, Meredita Press, 1967, poem: "L.A. Lament, 1992" Los Angeles Times Book Review, Sunday May 24, 1992; [pers.] And yet, if a man would guide his live by true philosophy, he will find ample riches in a modes livelihood enjoyed with a tranquil mind. "Lucretius 3rd Century B.C.; [a.] Monrovia, CA

HOLT, GLADYS LAVERNE
[Pen.] LaVerne Holt; [b.] September 21, 1941, Lou., KY; [p.] Wm. M. Hill & Geneva L. Walls; [m.] William L. Holt, February 25, 1960; [ch.] Mary Renee & Loyed Jr.; [ed.] Jefferson County Education Center; [memb.] Free Gospel Missions, Inc., Ladies Aux. V.F.W.; [oth. writ.] Several poems published in local papers. Music and words in my religious affiliation; [pers.] I am inspired by people. Their laughter, tears, joy and sadness. I hope to reflect these emotions in my writing.; [a.] Sellersburg, IN

HOLTZ, LYNN MARIE
[b.] December 28, 1959, Toronto, Ont.; [p.] John & Evelyn Gibson; [m.] Gerry James Holtz, July 3, 1993; [ch.] Lyndsy Ann, Robert John (twins); [ed.] Westwood Secondary High; [occ.] Artist; [oth. writ.] Several short stories an published in various media.; [pers.] All we have to do is open our eyes, our minds will quickly follow to uncover a multitude of wonders.; [a.] Peterborough, Ontario Canada

HONSON, MARION
[b.] November 26, 1924, Alabama; [p.] Mary and Frank Little; [m.] Stanly Honson (deceased), February 13, 1969; [ch.] one stepson; [ed.] 8th grade at Rosenwall Elementary School, Alabama; [occ.] Retired; [memb.] Andrew Jackson Senior Ctr, Emaculate

Conception Church; [oth. writ.] Mrs. Hinson started writing during the summer of 1993 at the Andrew Jackson Senior Center in the one day per week poetry classes; [pers.] Ms. Honson was inspired to write this poem after thinking about the injustice she had experienced living in a multicultural community in the Bronx, NY.

HOOPER, MICHAEL
[b.] November 10, 1976, San Jose, CA; [p.] Frank Hooper/Carolyn Hooper; [ed.] Currently a high school senior at Bellarmine College Preparatory. In the process of applying to a four year university; [occ.] Full-time student; [memb.] The Bellarmine League of Poets and Literary Society/Surfrides Foundation; [hon.] Dean's List/Honor Society/Saratoga Optimist Club Citizenship Award; [oth. writ.] Recently published in The Coming of Dawn by the National Library of Poetry; [pers.] To act on each moment as if it were my last and savor each breath I take. This is how I live my life and what I try to portray in all of my writing; [a.] San Jose, CA

HOOPES, HELEN M.
(Deceased) [b.] September 7, 1915, Salem, OH; [p.] Mr. and Mrs. Eugene Charlton; [m.] James H. Hoopes, April 26, 1934; [ch.] Carolyn Harrington and Ruth Wagmiller; [ed.] 12 yrs public school; [hon.] Margie Hiscox; [pers.] Mom enjoyed writing, poems and I found this poem in one of her cook books and decided to enter the contest. She would be proud if she knew; Submitted by Ruth Wagmiller - Daughter

HOPKE, NICOLE
[Pen.] Nic; [b.] April 21, 1979, Westaskiwin, AB; [p.] Audrey; [ed.] Grade 8, Clear Vista School in Westaskiwin, Alberta, Canada; [occ.] Student; [hon.] 3rd place in the 93 country track meet, 6th place finish in the 93 cross country run.; [oth. writ.] Several poems yet unpublished.; [pers.] Good things happen to those who wait. People have different talents, trust yourself that things will work out.; [a.] Wetaskiwin, Alberta, Canada

HORGER, SARAH KIRSTIN
[b.] January 8, 1975, Rochester; [p.] Steven Horger, Joanie Horger; Sibling: brother - Ethan Horger; [ed.] Lake Orion High School, Class of '93, Oakland Community College; [memb.] American Moo Du Kwan Assoc (martial arts), Karate Inst of America; [hon.] Blackbelt, martial arts instruction certification; [oth. writ.] Several unpublished short stories, children's stories, and poetry; [pers.] "Truth does not change although your perception of it may vary or alter drastically." John and Lyn St. Clair Thomas, Eyes of the Bolder; [a.] Lake Orion, MI

HOROSZEWSKI, JOHN
[b.] June 30, 1956, Glen Cove, NY; [p.] John & Genevieve; [m.] Cheryl Ann, May 23, 1981; [ch.] Danielle Francis, Devin John; [ed.] Sayville High School, Suffolk Community College; [occ.] Program Material Coordinator, Grumman Aerospace; [hon.] PH Alpha Sigma (Dean's List), Graduated with Distinction; [oth. writ.] "The Portrait" was my first submittal. Other poems I have completed include "The Tree". "Daybreak", "Veil of Slumber." [pers.] I strive to have my writings reveal my inner self. I vent my frustrations and anger in many, but also express my love and joy in others.; [a.] Islip, NY

HOROWITZ, SHERRY
[b.] Oceanside, NY; [p.] Daniel and Rita Leonardi; [ch.] Robert Michael and Jonathan Julian; [ed.] Uniondale High School, Kree International, My Real Estate School; [occ.] Real Estate, Sales consultant Northmassapequa, NY; [oth. writ.] Several poems unpublished to date.; [pers.] I believe distance is measured in the desire to get there. Distance being special or emotional.; [a.] Farmingdale, NY

HOSKINS, JoANN (T)
[b.] October 28, 1939, O'Donald, TX; [p.] Mr. and Mrs. J. F. Tidwell; [m.] Jack L. Hoskins, April 24, 1970; [ch.] (one daughter) Lisa M. Hoskins; [ed.] Hobbs, NM; [occ.] Housewife; [pers.] I want to dedicate this poem in memory of my parents, JF and Jewel Tidwell and (bro) Jessie and (sister) Frances; [a.] El Paso, TX

HOUSE, DENNIS K.
[b.] May 27, 1955, W. Memphis, AK; [p.] Lawrence House, Dorothy Elliott; [ed.] Brown County High, IN, advanced electronic training, U.S. Navy 25 yrs. of musical study; [occ.] National Sales Rep, specializing in environmentally safe alternatives; [hon.] 11th Naval District talent, contest runner up 76' honorable discharge U.S., Navy, 79, Formal Recital, (Balboa Park Recital Hall) SD, CA 87, (Original Compositions), Golden Poet Award 91, (World of Poetry Press); [oth. writ.] One poem and one musical composition performance piece published, many unpublished poetic as well as musical compositions.; [pers.] The great spirit leads me, I do but follow.; [a.] Phoenix, AZ

HOUSE, RHONDA L.
[b.] June 11, 1975, Evansville, IN; [p.] Charmain and Michael House; [ed.] San Diego High School; [occ.] Student; [memb.] FBLA (Future Business Leaders of America); [hon.] Writing Celebration, Honor Roll, Perfect Attendance, Presidential Fitness Award, and Editor of Poetry section in school newspaper; [oth. writ.] Many poems, horoscope section, and a few stories published in high school newspaper. (The Russ); [pers.] I try to express the pressures and frustrations of my age group in today's society; [a.] Evansville, IN

HOVEY, BARBARA J.
[b.] February 10, 1957, Milwaukee; [p.] Clem and Irene Sharafinski; [m.] Charles F. Hovey, Jr; [occ.] Student; [hon.] President's List; [oth. writ.] September 19, 1992 I wrote 350 poems in two days and have continued since; [pers.] I see no color or status just people free or still in bondage within; [a.] Davenport, IA

HOWARD, KATHLEEN M.
[Pen.] Kathleen, Kathy Katherine, Kathryn; [b.] August 25, 1968, Mentun; [p.] Peter and Judy Broderick; [m.] Ken Howard, May 6, 1990; [ch.] Miranda Rose (3-3-91); [ed.] Northeast Voc "87", Health care; [occ.] Poet - housewife; [memb.] VICA; [hon.] Editor's Choice Award 1993, The National Library of Poetry. Couple of poems have been published in books; [oth. writ.] Rose of life, many others; [pers.] I'm grateful I have the talent to share with the ones who influenced me to strive to be my own self in my poetry. I love you all who inspired me to write - Grammy Groleau died of cancer, Nov 20, 1993; [a.] Malden, MA

HOWARD, M. RUTH
[Pen.] Sam - Kitten; [b.] November 4, 1910, Maryville, TN; [p.] George and Laura Belle Stinnett; [m.] Richard L. Howard, February 14, 1976; [ch.] James Taft Watts, Thomas Elbert Watts, Charles Howard Watts; [ed.] 7 yrs grade GED Diploma - 1964, Teacher - who inspired me to become a nurse and to write poetry, Miss Mary Jane Goddard; [occ.] Am non-retire nurse; [memb.] Eastern Star; [memb.] Bowling League - Ventura County am a 'volunteer' anyone who needs me I am there to help; [hon.] I wrote my first poem at age 13 - and have been jotting down my thoughts ever since. Several Merit Awards 2 plaques and my poems - poet of year; [oth. writ.] Couple short stories (unprinted). Have collection of original poems approx 300. Wish I could get them printed in book; [pers.] " To be a friend to one and all give my aid wherever I can. To live a good life, enjoy and keep going". Motto - "Love, and trust the Lord, because He is my Salvation"; [a.] Port Hueneme, CA

HOWE, LOWELL
[Pen.] Stone Buffalo; [b.] November 20, 1958, Los Angeles; [p.] Jay & Rose Howard; [m.] Brenda Howe, April 8, 1978; [ed.] Jordan High, Long Beach, City Streets, Corporate America; [hon.] Multi "Golden Poet" award winner, two time "Silver Poet," but truly honored by the love of a good woman, Thanks Babe! Special Thanks, Uncle Don, Grandma, Jay, Mom, and Grandma Alice...You're all part of everything I think, say and do!; [pers.] "Look past the height and the breadth, to the heaven..to find depth, once thought inaccessible!"; [a.] Desert Hot Springs, CA

HUDSON, DINORAH
[Pen.] Dina; [b.] November 12, 1976, NY; [p.] John Hudson, Roselina Calderon; [ed.] Academy of Mt. St. Ursula (High School); [occ.] Student; [pers.] As sure as your life will end, time, in it's haste will have rolled by. Will it find you an unhappy failure or pleased with a dream you did not let die.

HUDSON, ROBERT JAMES
[b.] june 26, 1966, New Millerdam; [p.] James Hudson, Edith Hudson; [ed.] Kettlethorpe High, The Univ of Life; [occ.] unemployed; [memb.] Trogite Warriors; [hon.] Life and Love; [oth. writ.] Over a hundred screaming for print; [pers.] … Can I really see me is it how I should do will I see the whole truth or what I want to be true. Taken from soul search; [a.] Wakefield, Yorkshire

HUGHES, A.B.
[Pen.] Albert Hughes; [b.] November 23, 1929, Nottingham; [p.] Albert and Sara Harriet Hughes; [m.] Kathleen Hughes, March 24, 1956; [ch.] Michael and Pamela; [ed.] Cavendish Secondary Modern; [occ.] Retired because of ill health; [memb.] Nottingham Writers Club; [hon.] Writer of the Month, "Evening Post"; [oth. writ.] "Nelly" the story of a boat, "Sara", "Maggie" the story of a duck, "The Bombj", "The Key", "G A Custer's Men", poems in "Poems of the Midlands", "Living in the 70's and 80's and "Tears of Fire" and "My First Book of Poetry"; [pers.] The aim of my writing is to give people the maximum of enjoyment, be they young or old, rich or poor; [a.] Radcliffe-on-Trent, Nottingham, England

HULT, HELENA C. (MRS. JOHN L.)
[Pen.] Helena Hult; [b.] June 13, 1916, Id Falls, ID, USA; [p.] Rev and Mrs. Luther I. Cornay; [m.] John L. Hult, Ph.D (Nuclear Physics), March 27, 1943; [ch.] John Tod Hult, Holly Jean Hult Stearns (Mrs. Michael Stearns); [ed.] Dipl., Michigan City, IN, BA Immaculate Heart College, CA, Advanced Studies: Univ. of Calif, LA, CA; [occ.] Retired, writing, studying poetry writ. and narrative writ., CA Lutheran Univ., Thousand Oaks; [memb.] Ascension Lutheran Church, Thousand Oaks, CA; IAVE (Int'l Assoc for Vol. Effort); [hon.] 1958 - LA Cnty Med. Assoc. Bay Dist. second annual outstanding achievement award in mental health; 1964 CA State PTA hon. life memb.; 1978 - Santa Monica Woman of the Year; 1979 "Cover Girl" - Independent Journal Nwspaper supplement; 1981, Protestant Humanitarian Award of Nat. Conf. of Christians and Jews, Santa Monica, CA; 1982 first annual Helen Wallace Humanitarian Award of Santa Monica-Westside Comm. Serv. Cncl.; 1982 - Dir. Emeritus, Lifetime Board Memb., Wise; 1984 - Reg. in World Who's Who of Women, Cambridge, Eng.; 1984 Outstanding Leadership and Community Serv. Award of Wise Century Plaza Hotel; 1987 - Elected to: Who's Who in California 1988 and 1990; 1989 - w/husband - Commendation for Outstanding Contributions to the Intnl. Assoc for Vol. Effort (IAVE), Israel, as founding members/officer; 1989 - Golden Poet Award, World of Poetry, DC, Washington-Hilton Hotel, Sept 1-3 Poets from 30 countries; [oth. writ.] Former news reporter, Nixon newspapers, Indiana: By-line Weekly feature, special assignments with theater, orchestras, etc. and social events; [pers.] Affirming those we live and work with whom we work and live, encouraging the best in them, is important to accomplishment of mutual beneficial goals, and in fulfillment of gifted promise; [a.] Thousand Oaks, CA

HULTIN, LORIE
[b.] April 1, 1961, Breckenridge, MN; [p.] Richard Denzel and (the late) Sharon Denzel; [m.] John Hultin, June 30, 1990; [ch.] Tyler Michael, Tanner John; [ed.] Fergus Falls Sr High Fergus Falls Community College, Alexandria Vo-Tech; [occ.] Licensed Daycare Provider; [oth. writ.] Several poems I've written for myself and others; [pers.] I write my poems to release my inner feelings and emotions. I hope they will touch the hearts of many; [a.] Fergus Falls, MN

HUNSICKER, BETH MEGHAN
[b.] October 29, 1978, Dover, NJ; [p.] William and Carol Hunsicker; [ed.] Mt View Elementary, Fleetwood Middle School, one year in Fleetwood High School; [occ.] Waitress in an Italian restaurant; [memb.] Band front and the Fleetwood Pep Club; [hon.] Honor Roll, High Honors Student of the month, Basketball manager, and the Presidental Academic Fitness Award signed by the President of the United States; [oth. writ.] "Love" published in a local newspaper and four other poems titled: "All I Want", "The One", "But Feelings Always Change", "The Best Part of My Life"; [pers.] My writings influence my inner most feelings about the special people in my life; [a.] Blandon, PA

HUNT, ALLEN
[b.] July 27, 1944, South Haven, MI; [ch.] Jill Annette and Bridget Suzanne; [oth. writ.] Writing has been a lifelong hobby. I've written for my own satisfaction, and for the entertainment of others. Nothing published to date; [pers.] It's always so hard to accept the death of a loved one. It's extremely difficult when it's a son or a daughter in their youth, with a whole lifetime ahead of them.; [a.] South Haven, MI

HUNT, CLAUDETTE
[b.] December 20, 1969, Clinton, IN; [p.] Penny and Gaylord Shull; [ch.] 3 David, Anna Marie and Paul; [ed.] High school; Turkey Run High School, GED; [occ.] Homemaker; [hon.] 3 medals in high school choir contests; [oth. writ.] Several personal poems. No others published; [pers.] My poem was written, because of a miscarage in 1989, it took two years to find the words. I dedicate this poem to Richard Mason Hunt my unborn son; [a.] Rockville, IN

HUNTER, ROSE MARY
[b.] March 30, 1965, Marinette, WI; [p.] Beatrice Kent William Kent; [m.] Donald R. Dettman, October 26, 1991; [ed.] Mariette High School, Inst of Childrens Writting School; [occ.] Housewife, poet childrens writter; [memb.] The National Library of poetry. Humane Society. Quill Books. International Society of Poets; [hon.] Golden Poet 1991, Editors Choice Award 1993, Award of Merits; [oth. writ.] What makes a best friend? (poem) Giving Thanks (poem) The Heart of Gold (poem) Happy Graduation (poem) My Best Friend (Poem) Christ's Spirit (Poem) All published in poets books; [pers.] My goal is to one day get a childrens book published. I'm thankful for the many gifts Heavenly Father has given me; [a.] Marinette, WI

HURST, WINNIE
[b.] January 8, 1933, Johnson Co; [p.] both dead; [m.] divorced; [ch.] 7; [ed.] 8th grade; [memb.] No membership at the time; [pers.] Well, I just thought about doing this so I decided to try it so I did. I just thought it up in my mind; [a.] Harrison, GA

HUSSEIN, ADIMA
[b.] December 14, 1980, Dubai; [p.] Toufiq and Salma Hussein; [m.] I'm still available; [ed.] I study at Almawaker School in Dubai, Garhood; [occ.] I'm still a student; [memb.] Dedicated to school and studies. I'm in the computer club in our school.; [hon.] Two merit awards from schl., and an enormous amount of appreciation cards from schl. for my great efforts (about 27 of them in the past 2 yrs); [oth. writ.] I write love poems, and poems about the racist attacks, short stories, I'm half way through my biography songs. I'm very good in writing essays at school, I usually get 90's; [pers.] I may have the talent but I owe it all to Miss Nickolette, my eng. teacher, because she's the one who encouraged me to go one with my writings. And, thanks for wanting to publish my poems. It made me really happy; [a.] Dubai, Uae

HUTSKAL, KATHLEEN
[b.] April 12, Bonnyville; [m.] George Hutskal, 1944; [ch.] 3; [ed.] No high school; [occ.] Farmers wife; [oth. writ.] I write song poems; [pers.] I did not have the chance to do the things I would have liked to do. But I've always wanted to write. Me and spouse work for a living. There's, nothing much I could write about myself; [a.] Alberta, Canada

HUXFORD, COLETTE L.
[b.] May 17, 1972, Inglewood, CA; [p.] Bonnie and the late Max Huford; [ed.] Shenandoah High School, Purdue Univ - Creative Writing and English Education; [occ.] Student; [memb.] Purdue Writing Lab Tutor, Group Bible Studies, Campus Baptist Fellowship, East Lynn Christian Church; [hon.] Phi Beta Kappa, Phi Kappa Phi, Kappa Delta Pi, Dean's List, Kappa Kappa Kappa State Scholarship Winner, Golden Key National Honor Society; [oth. writ.] Poem in Potpourri; [pers.] I thank my Lord for giving me the gift of writing, so that I may bring glory to Him; [a.] Middletown, IN

HYMAN, NORMAN S.
[b.] Ithaca, NY; [m.] Ralph A. Hyman; [ch.] Son & Family; [ed.] B.A. Univ. of Rochester; [pers.] I believe that nature is the poetry of the world.

ILOG, THERESA BRIZUELA
[b.] June 17, 1970, Manila, Phil; [p.] Pedro and Teresita Ilog; [ed.] Davis High School, Modesto Junior College; [occ.] School Instructor, part-time sales; [memb.] Free Methodist Church; [hon.] Miss Stanislaus "Congeniality" Award 1993, "Young Miss of America" 1st runner up. "Jr Miss" finalist. "Dunlaps" spirit Award; [oth. writ.] Won Best Essay Contest in 1992 "Young Miss of America" pageant, held in Los Angeles, California; [pers.] If I was to give up hope, what would be the point in living?; [a.] Modesto, CA

INMAN, MELISSA LYNN
[b.] October 28, 1980; Orange, CA; [p.] Dana Inman and Jeanette C. Inman; [ed.] Current Status: 8th grader at Saint John the Baptist School; [memb.] Sacred Heart of Jesus Retreat Center Teen Club; [pers.] I write to express my feelings. Apparently my feelings mean a lot to many who read my poems; [a.] Santa Ana, CA

IRISH, ROSEMARY
[b.] April 8, 1962, Manchester, NH; [p.] Paul F. and Margaret T. (O'Leary) Murphy, Sr; [m.] Shawn William Irish, September 29, 1989; [ed.] Manchester Memorial High; [occ.] Housewife; [memb.] League of American Wheelmen; [hon.] Certificate of Appreciation from US Navy, Editor's Choice Award from the National Library of Poetry; [oth. writ.] Poetry published in The Coming of Dawn and In The Desert Sun. Also a notebook full of unpublished work; [pers.] Many thanks to my loving husband Shawn for all his support both silent and spoken. I'll love you always; [a.] Aiea, HI

IRVING, DANIEL PAUL
[b.] July 10, 1972, Ft Dix, NJ; [p.] Brian and Lisa Irving; [ed.] Seventy First Sr High, Univ of North Carolina at Greensboro; [occ.] Student, ROTC Cadet; [hon.] Honor graduate ROTC Advanced Camp; [oth. writ.] Several poems none currently published; [pers.] Never give up; [a.] Fayetteville, NC

ISLAM, JASMIN
[b.] March 14, 1984, Subiaco, Western Australia; [p.] Aziz and Akhtar Islam; [ed.] Upper Primary (grade 5); [occ.] Student; [hon.] Earth Worm Environmental Award for schools state champion and national finalist; [oth. writ.] Several poems published in school magazine; [pers.] Poems are works of art drawn with words; [a.] Rossmoyne, W. Australia

IVY, RICHARD
[b.] April 22, 1970, Dallas, TX; [p.] Richard Ivy, Sr. and Janis Skinner; [ed.] Mt. Ararat High Schl., Penobscot Job Corp.; [memb.] Alamo City Baptist Church, Flat Earth Artists; [oth. writ.] Will appear Flat Earch Artists, Ear to the Ground II poetry camp.; [pers.] These troubles and sufferings of ours are after all quite small and won't last very long, yet this short time of distress will result in God's richest blessings upon us forever and ever. 2 Corinth, 4:17.; [a.] San Antonio, TX.

JACKIEWICZ, JOSEPH S.
[b.] March 3, 1931, Jersey City, NJ; [p.] Stephen and Regina Jackiewicz; [m.] (1st) Frances Oldinsky (deceased), June 26, 1954; (2nd) Aleksandra Szymura, July 2, 1977; [ch.] Joseph Jr., Anne Frances, Damian Joseph, Adam Joseph; [ed.] Ferris High School, Jersey City, NJ; St Peter's College; [occ.] Retired; [memb.] Knights of Columbus, The Rev Thomas F. Canty Council #3197, Hillside, NJ, RSVP (Retired Seniors Volunteer Program) NJ, Senior Citizens Hillside, NJ; [hon.] 40 yrs Certificate, Knights of Columbus; [pers.] As a senior citizen to reach out to everyone with written words spoke, by me in loniness, but shouted out in printed text; [a.] Hillside, NJ

JACKSON, ALLISON RENAE
[Pen.] Alli, A.J.; [b.] February 20, 1980, California; [p.] Melinda and David; [ed.] Oscoda Elem School - Oscoda, MI, Cedar Lake elem - Oscoda, MI, Brewbaker Elem, Montgomery, AL, Ramstein Elem, Kaiserslauturn Germany, Tunner Jr High, Frankfurt, Germany, St Bede Catholic School, Montgomery, AL; [pers.] I have been influenced by my brother, my parents and great poets such as William Shakespear and Edgar Allen Poe.; [a.] Montgomery, AL

JACKSON, AMANDA
[b.] February 20, 1979, Goldsboro, NC; [p.] Sam and Paulette Jackson; [ed.] I am a freshman at Goldsboro High School class of '97. I hope to go to East Carolina Univ in Greenville, NC upon my graduation to be a journalist or primary school teacher; [hon.] I was awarded 2 certificates of recognition for creative writing and for the same poem in the Wayne Collection. I also received an academic award for poetry in 4th grade; [oth. writ.] I wrote a story in the 7th grade and received a grade of 95. I was told it would make a great soap opera; [pers.] My inspiration is my parents, grandparents, my boyfriend: Tommie Heath, and my best friend: Amanda Grant. One special person is Mrs Susan Stone-Hawkins who helped me. To learn how good a writer I am and she also helped get my poem printed the first time in the Wayne Collection. My mom also helped me realize I could do more than run my mouth and chase boys. My boyfriend and best friend have gave me so much love and said lots of things that inspire me. For the teenagers who may read this, please remember: "Do not let your mouth or bad actions overrule your success. I want the people mentioned above to know I love them and will cherish them forever; [a.] Goldsboro, NC

JACKSON, BENJAMIN
[Pen.] "Action Jackson"; [b.] April 5, 1967, Ashburn, GA; [p.] John and Leola Jackson; [m.] Janet Annette (Thomas) Jackson, January 26, 1991; [ed.] High School (Turner County High) graduation: May 1986; [occ.] U.S. Navy Second Class Petty Officer; [hon.] Navy Good Conduct Medal; Navy Commendation Medal; [pers.] Always believe within yourself and know you can achieve the highest goal "you" set to accomplish. "Stay away from drugs"; [a.] Ashburn, GA

JACKSON, JENELLE-MARQUERITE
[Pen.] Kitty Jackson; [b.] June 11, 1968, Chicago, IL; [p.] Shielah Jackson; [ed.] Life (Wink!); [occ.] Military Policewoman, stand-up comedienne, freelance writer; [oth. writ.] Poetry, children stories short stories; [pers.] All my life I've always pursued that small patch of sunshine just out of the rains reach, yet it never stay in one place for long, life for me is the pursuit of a permanent patch of sunshine; [a.] Kunsan, AB, Korea

JACKSON, ROSEMARIE
[b.] March 11, 1930; Walkerville, Ontario, Canada; [p.] Harper Brown, Agnes Brown; [ch.] Earl Stanley, Steven Anthony, Marzs Louise, Reuben, Jr, Michael Timothy, Annette Denise, karyn Elizabeth; [ed.] Ypsilanti High, Highland Park Community College; [occ.] Latch Key Aide, Herlong Cathedral School; [hon.] Dean's List, Certificate of Achievement, Certificates of Honor, Diploma in The Writing for Magazines Course from the Inst of Children's Literature; [pers.] It is my hope and prayer that my poems will bring consolation, enjoyment and spiritual peace to people everywhere. I have been writing poetry since high school; [a.] Detroit, MI

JACKSON, TIFFANY C.
[b.] February 21, 1982, Virginia; [p.] Sherry Lee Jackson and Wendell Edgar Parker; [ed.] Olive Elementary, Empresa Elementary, Roosevelt Middle School; [occ.] Student; [memb.] ASB President of the 6th grade student body. Young Ambassador; [pers.] I dedicate this to my mother, father and family. I'd like to thank my teachers and friends. I appreciate your support; [a.] Oceanside, CA

JACOBS, ROBERT
[Pen.] Seth Jacobs; [b.] June 29, 1971; [ed.] San Diego State University, English Major, Buena High School, Ventura; [memb.] Sigma Phi Epsilon Fraternity, California Delta; [pers.] Sometimes the simple things in life get you through life.; [a.] San Diego, CA

JAKSTAS, REGINA
[b.] April 23, 1953, Newark, NJ; [p.] Regina E. Jakstas (deceased 1979), Stasys Jakstas (deceased) 1979; [m.] single; [ed.] North Salem High School, North Salem, NY - Diploma, School of Visual Arts, New York, NY - 1 yr (fall 71, spring 72). The Cooper Union School of Art (Fine Arts) 3yr - 1 Cooper Square, NY (fall 72-spring 75); [occ.] United States Navy - since 1980, Petty Officer First Class, Boatswain's Mate, Weapons Quality Assurance Inspector, Weight Test, Supervisor, Security Watchstander, Training; [memb.] Member of Columbia Video Club; own over 50 Horror Videos and am still collecting them; Member Bose Music and Video Club, Rock and Roll and Classical taste. Am a

vegetarian since 1965. Health food enthusiast, and physical fitness. Lithuanian ancestry - aunt and uncle close by 'Svoinickas'; [hon.] 3 Navy Good Conduct Awards, 3 Battle `E's', National Defense Medal, Southwest Asia Service Medal, Rifle Marksman, Meritorious Unit Commendation. Four Sea Service Awards; [oth. writ.] Nothing published, also like to draw whenever possible. Earlier poems from school; [pers.] Like horror stories, modern and classical. When I was in grade school liked to read Edgar Alan Poe and HG Welles. Still admire their stories. Favorite poet is William Butler Yeats. I would want my writing and poetry to be entertaining, intricate indetail and `lofty.' A place to let the imagination live, that does not relate to the usual physical world; [a.] Norfolk, VA

JAMES, DANDREA V.
[Pen.] "Brown Girl"; [b.] September 1, 1961, New York, NY; [ed.] BS Behavioral Sciences; Mercy College - Dobbs Ferry, NY, Foreign Language: French, Japanese; [memb.] Canaan Baptist Church of Christ, New York, NY; [hon.] Marion Ohara Award for Creative Writing; James Hackett Medal For Public Speaking and Oral Interpretation; [pers.] What little we each do to promote love, peace, and harmony, will do a lot for the world. Love is uplifting, compassion is comfort-impart them on mankind; [a.] New York, NY

JAMES, ESHE MERCER
[b.] September 11, 1980, Toronto, Ontario; [p.] Dr. Errol James, Erica Mercer; [ed.] Currently in a Gr 8 gifted program; [occ.] Student at Deer Park Public School, Toronto, Ontario, Canada; [hon.] Gr 7 Honor Roll, Grade 8 Honor Roll; [a.] Toronto, Ontario

JANCSY, PAUL
[b.] July 15, 1979, Melrose, MA; [p.] Debby Cogan, Paul Janesy; [ed.] I am in 8th grade; [occ.] Student; [memb.] Civil Air Patrol, Saratoga Public Library, Schennectady; [hon.] Cadet Airman for C.A.P. 1st in my social studies class in National Georgraphy Bee, Honor Roll, Saratogo Springs Junior High School; [oth. writ.] none published; [pers.] I strive to stress the idea of a free world where there is no predudice and we can all live in harmony.; [a.] Saratoga Springs, NY

JANOWSKI, CAROLYN
[Pen.] CJ; [b.] January 1, 1935, Noerdeen, WA; [p.] Carl and Dolly Carrigan; [m.] (the late) Henry Janowski, March 25, 1955; [ch.] Edward, Debbie, Michael, Sheryl, Steven, Hank, Frank; [ed.] Sr high school grad Elma High School, Elma, WA; [occ.] Retired Motel Hotel housekeeper; [memb.] The "100" Club (poetry, song lyric club) Quincy, MA; [hon.] An honorable mention award in a Nashville contest. Certificate of Merit and Song of the month from Talent and Associated Cos, Quincy, MA. Editor's Choice Award from the National Library of Poetry; [oth. writ.] I have had several of my song lyrics recorded by recording artist; [pers.] I like to write words of praise and helpful words; [a.] Abbotsford, BC, Canada

JANSEN, DARCY LEIGH
[b.] May 5, 1977, Edmonton, Alberta; [p.] Dirk and Val; [ed.] G 1-6 James Mowat; Gr 7-9 Fort J-Saskatchewan Junior High; Gr 10-11 Fort Sr High; [memb.] Fort Saskatchewan Community Band, 2 yrs play trumpet, Navy League Cadet for 3 yrs; [hon.] Has numerous awards in the athletic field; [pers.] Darcy works very hard at everything she does. She is a very sensitive girl and uses her time well. She's very active in school and do exceptionally well at everything she does. And above all is a very lovely daughter and sister. She has 2 sisters, twins - Demi and Dale aged 15 and 2 brothers Dick age 28 and Danay 27. We are very proud to have Darcy as our daughter and we hope this will be a nice surprize for her. Hope she

continue to write; [a.] Fort Saskatchewan, Alberta, Canada

JANUSZ, ANNA
[b.] July 18, 1952, Warsaw, Poland; [p.] Maria and Wladyslaw Janusz; [m.] Divorced; [ed.] Atkinson College, York Univ Toronto, Humber College Toronto; [occ.] Computer Consultant; [oth. writ.] No previous publications; [pers.] Life, its sorrows and happiness are my inspiration; [a.] Toronto, Ontario

JARRETT, CECILE A.
[b.] March 16, 1966, Jamaica, West Indies; [p.] Janette and Dacosta Biggs; [m.] Howard A. G. Jarrett, February 3, 1990; [ch.] Tiffany and Steffan; [ed.] Ardenne High - Jamaica WI, Queensborough Community College - NY; [occ.] Travel Consultant; [oth. writ.] I possess several poems and short stories which I hope to publish in the near future; [pers.] I am concerned about the injustice I see. My writings reflect how I feel, and my hope for change; [a.] Norcross, GA

JEANETTE, ANITA
[b.] May 28, 1975, Santa Barbara, CA; [p.] Carol Barkowsky; [ch.] Joshua Troy Jeanette; [ed.] 10th grade, 1 yr. adult school; [occ.] Poet and novelist avon representative; [memb.] KSF (Klingon Strike Force) Fan Club & A.W.P. (American Writer's Program); [oth. writ.] Over 30 poems published in various anthologies all over the country; [pers.] All poets need their pain.; [a.] La Mesa, CA

JEFFERIES, AMBER
[b.] July 29, 1978, Gastomia; [p.] Tom & Vicki Jefferies; [ed.] 9th grade at Grier Jr. High in Gastonia, NC at the present time; [occ.] Student 9th grade; [memb.] Christ United Methodist Church, Jr. Civitan, S.E.A.C, Pep Club, Student Council Representative; [hon.] Homecoming Princess for Cheerleading Ribbons for other poems, Cheer leader, co-captain; [oth. writ.] Remembering When, Friends, The Feel, Love, Awaking, The Old Man; [pers.] I enjoy writing poems on happy and sad things. My past english teachers, Mrs. Pearl Patrick and Mrs. Linda Peters influenced me into writing poems. I send a special thanks to them.; [a.] Gastonia, NC

JELIS, SUSAN
[Pen.] S.L. Jelis; [b.] February 10, 1969, Poughkeepsie, NY; [p.] Carolyn Weeks-George and John A. George; [m.] Gary Jelis, May 9, 1989; [ch.] Harley Kenneth Jelis; [ed.] Life; [occ.] Currently working on a series of children's books; [memb.] National Trust for Historic Preservation; [pers.] Be yourself at all cost. The peace and happiness you will feel inside is worth much more than the nonsense others might say about you.; [a.] Pleasant Valley, NY

JENKINS, JOHN
[b.] January 24, 1955, Georgia; [p.] Junior & Louvenia Jenkins; [m.] Leontyne R. Jenkins, December 31, 1977; [ch.] Mercedes, Leontyne & John Jr.; [ed.] A.S., Ventura, CA, B.S., California State University, Northridge, CA; [occ.] Technical Support; [hon.] Silver Poet 1986; [pers.] Love The Lord

JENKINS, LORNA
[b.] January 23, 1063, Nothingham, England; [p.] Alamo, Alvin Jenkins; [ch.] Crystal, Gary Jenkins; [ed.] Grade 12; [memb.] Dominos Club; [hon.] Holder of B2 license, holder of 2 Safe Driving Award; [oth. writ.] Have other poems, wrote 4 songs.

JENKIS, GARY
[b.] August 28, 1944, Caraway, AR; [p.] Joy Jenkins; [m.] Betty Jenkins, April 10, 1976; [ch.] Charlette, Daniel, Diana, Kevin, Spring & Jennifer; [ed.] Self Educated, G.E.D.; [occ.] Welder; [memb.] Calvary Baptist Church; [oth. writ.] Children's poems &

stories; [pers.] I feel my writing is a gift from God, I wish to share it with other people as a witness.; [a.] Carpentersville, IL

JERPE, ANDREW
[b.] April 9, 1946, Pittsburg; [p.] James A. Jerpe, Grace McLain; [m.] Single; [ed.] Dekalb College/ Atlanta GA, Graduated in 1993 with a degree in Engineering.; [occ.] Technical Instructor, Marketing Spokesperson, LXE, Inc. Atlanta, GA; [pers.]The remarkable thing about poetry (in addition to its ability to evoke a powerful catharsis) is its great flexability: it can be narrative or dramatic, didactic or just plain fun.; [a.] Atlanta, GA

JESS, JOYCE ANN
[b.] Born and reared on Chicago's NW side. She now resides in the SW of USA and plans to finish her higher education. She says "be good to yourself and others too".

JESSICA, CUCKLER
[b.] August 14, 1976, Freeport, IL; [p.] Tammy Cuckler, Unknown; [ed.] Mt. Carroll High School; [occ.] Student (Senior) Mt. Carroll High School; [memb.] Students Against Drunk Driving (S.A.D.D.), Mt. Carroll High School yearbook staff; [oth. writ.] Articles for Waukarusa (Mt. Carroll High School Yearbook); [pers.] I find poetry and songwriting an effective release for overwhelming thoughts and feelings. People would probably be much happier if they'd just pick up a pen and write it all down.; [a.] Mt. Carroll, IL

JEWETT, PEARL (BROWN)
[pers.] Dedicated to my grand-daughter Shelly-Marie Norton, (born Hamilton, Ont); [a.] Stoney Creek, Ontario, Canada

JHIRAD, J.A. (Jacob Aaron Jhirad)
[b.] October 2, 1927, Jabalpur-india; [p.] (late) Dr. A.E. Jhirad and (late) Mary Jhirad; [m.] Mrs. Abigael J. Jhirad 1964; [ch.] 3 sons and 1 daughter (Ronen, Joel, Leon and Leena); [ed.] MA (English Literature) and LL 13; [occ.] Pensioner; [hon.] (1) Passed with honours and topped the list of successful candidates of Hindi Pragyaz Praveen Examinations, (2) First prize in central railway Hindi Essay Competition, (3) First Prize in Inter-Railway Essay (Hindi) Competition at Railway Board Level in New-Delhi; [oth. writ.] Wrote a book entitled "God, Man and Religion"; [pers.] Influenced by Indian philosophy particularly by Maharshy Ramanna. Consider man's real self to be divine and eternal. See God in every person and everything. Consider all acts to be done by God Himself; [a.] Rehovot, Israel

JOAN, GIDMAN
[b.] September 7, 1939, Liverpool, England; [m.] Alf Gidman, December 22, 1962; [ch.] Pamela and Stephen; [ed.] Attended Liverpool Girls College, England; [pers.] I love to laugh, laughter is tonic for the soul. I am lucky to have a family that provides me with lots of chuckles and many guffaws; [a.] Ayr, On., Canada

JOHNSON, ALFRED (JR.)
[b.] September 7, 1956, Kemptville Novia, Scotia; [p.] Alfred Johnson Sr, Elsie Johnson; [m.] Laura Johnson, April 3, 1992; [ch.] Anna Marie, Brandy Lee Mae, Alfred Cody, Eleanor Caroline Jean; [ed.] Moria Secondary; [occ.] Machine Operator; [oth. writ.] Write poems for family and friends, but have never sent any in before for publication; [pers.] My poetry is written on a personal level, they are usually of personal interest to whom I am writing them for; [a.] Cherry Valley, Ontario, Canada

JOHNSON, ANTHONY
[Pen.] A. Christian, November 5, 1968; [ed.] Assoc of Arts Degree; [occ.] Manager - Sherwin Williams; [oth. writ.] Over 30 poems in my own collection; [pers.] I try to appreciate the depth and substance of what life has to give, rather than the style and imagery; [a.] Houston, TX

JOHNSON, HEATHER
[b.] January 13, 1979, Ansonia, CT; [p.] Deborah Johnson, Philip Johnson; [ed.] Prendergast Elementary, Ansonia High School; [occ.] Student; [memb.] Ski Club; [hon.] Cheerleading awards, student of the month; [oth. writ.] Several poems in my private poem folder at home; [pers.] I was inspired by my best friend, Heather Martineau, who taught me there's a brighter side to everything; [a.] Ansonia, CT

JOHNSON, JOY
[b.] May 23, 1978, New York; [p.] Enid Johnson; [ed.] High School, St. Michael's Academy in Manhattan currently, 10th grade; [occ.] Student; [pers.] I'm grateful to God. This just proves that anyone can do whatever they set their mind to. Oh, and thanks, Mom!; [a.] Bronx, NY

JOHNSON, KELLY
[b.] November 29, 1976, Kingster, PA; [p.] Don and Jackie Johnson; [ed.] Presently enrolled student, 11th grade, Bishop O'Reilly H.S., Kingston, PA; [occ.] Teachers Aide; [pers.] I write and you read. If you can relate all the more meaningful my writing is; [a.] Kingston, PA

JOHNSON, LOUISE
[b.] August 7, 1922, Smithfield, NC; [p.] Zoe L. Coats & Effie Flowers Coats; [m.] Lawrence A. Johnson, February 14, 1943; [ch.] Lawrence Jr., Michael Leon; [ed.] High School, Community College, creative writing courses; [occ.] Retired, volunteer work with children; [memb.] Hillcrest Baptist Church; [hon.] First place in poetry contest on local radio; [oth. writ.] Several poems and short articles in local newspapers. Short stories and children's books; [pers.] I will not have lived my life in vain if I can make a difference in the lives of the children I help; [a.] Bryan, TX

JOHNSON, MARY
[b.] December 19, 1957; [p.] Glen and Josephine Aschauer; [m.] Clay Johnson, June 21, 1980; [ch.] Lacey Lanae 12, Kelli JoAnn 10; [ed.] High School Grad, Union Grove High School; [occ.] Factory; [oth. writ.] A collection of poems from elementary through high school; [pers.] To be the necest mother I can be. Be honest, and compassionate to my husband and most of all to God.; [a.] Union Grove, WI

JOHNSON, SUSAN
[Pen.] Susan Marie; [b.] October 16, 1976, Allentown, PA; [p.] William and Sara Johnson; [ed.] Cocalico High, Denver, PA; [occ.] Student (12th grade); [memb.] St. Albans Episcopal Church Choir; VICA (Vocational Industrial Clubs of America); [hon.] National Honor Society; [oth. writ.] Other poems and short stories in my freetime; [pers.] I want to give inspiration and hope to those who read my writing. I want people to know dreams really can come true!; [a.] Reinholds, PA

JOHNSON, TIFFANY
[b.] May 25, 1993; [p.] Tonnee and James Johnson; [ed.] I am currently in 8th grade at Hughes Middle School in Burleson; [occ.] Student; [memb.] I'm a member of the National Junior Honor Society; [hon.] I have received trophies for my athletic abilities; [oth. writ.] Collection of unpublished poetry since 1991; [a.] Burleson, TX

JOHNSON, TORINO
[b.] April 15, 1974, St Louis, MO; [p.] Loraine Johnson; [ed.] Beaumont High School, Univ of Missouri - Rola; [occ.] Student-- Junior at the Univ of Missouri-Rolla; [memb.] Mathematics Assoc of America, Assoc of Black Students (UMR), Incubator Scientist Soc.; [hon.] Hon. Mention - NAACP, Afro-Cultural, Technological, and Scientific Olympics, several science competition awards and numerous scholarships; [oth. writ.] Several poems were written in leisure time, including "So Often", "Exceptional", and "Within You...For You"; [pers.] I want to be successful, a successful black man. I watched others fail before me, and I vowed not to fail at anything. I want to prove that there are talented black people in the world. My writing is not just for me, it's for everyone to enjoy; [a.] St. Louis, MO

JOHNSON, VINCENT L.
I write according to how each poem relates to the times, personal experience or mood of thinking. I possess many poems and am seeking a publisher. I am positive upon review of my work, someone will recognize its value in a way that's equally beneficial. The quality of my poems are very like the one chosen for publication; would you or someone you know be interested in sponsoring me as a poet?; [a.] Chicago, IL

JOHNSTON, SARAH
[b.] June 1, 1977, Victoria, B.C.; [p.] John and Dianne Johnston; [ed.] Senior Secondary High School, Grade 11; [hon.] Royal Canadian Legion, Remembrance day literary contest 1993. Expressions, A compilation of feelings, publication of poems 1993; [pers.] Involved in soccer and baseball; [a.] Sooke, B.C., Canada

JOHNSTONE, VIOLA
[p.] Johnstone, Gilmore and Margaret; [ed.] Acadia University 45', Wolfville, N.S. (BSC in HEa); [occ.] Retired; [memb.] Elder, Presbyterian Church, Clan Donald, Member Sr., Adult Friendship Group (Numerous Charities and Assoc.); [hon.] Trivial; [oth. writ.] six, 3 act plays ((farce produced) for senior ladies, Silver Notes (devotional poems) The friend (devotional poems) many poems and short clips through the years, mainly religious; [pers.] I write of what I see around me, coloured by what I feel within.; [a.] Thorburn, Nova Scotia, Canada

JOINT, TRACIE ELAINE
[b.] April 27, 1968, London; [p.] Marjorie and Ernest Adshead; [m.] Duncan Edward Joint, May 21, 1988; [ch.] Marcus and Leslie Joint; [ed.] White Rock Primary Paignton Community College; [occ.] Catering Assistant; [oth. writ.] Many poems and a series of educational childrens poetry books with a central character. Many stories about the character yet to find a willing published; [pers.] I hope to see my books, which I believe incorporate both a fun and educational aspect. In print and on the bookshop shelves for the people who will most appreciate them, children!

JOLLIFF, PAULA
[b.] August 8, 1958, Miami; [p.] Paul Prescott, Ruth Prescott; [m.] Dave Jolliff, October 5, 1991; [ed.] Belton-Honea Path High Schl., Forrest College, Tri-Cnty. Tech. College; [occ.] Housewife, budding writer; [memb.] Forest Hill Baptist Church; [hon.] Golden Poet 1990, Golden Poet 1991; Award of Merit - 1990 for poem "Spring"; Award of Merit - 1990 for poem "Jesus"; Editor's Choice Award 1993 from National Library of Poetry; [oth. writ.] Several poems pub. in other anthologies including the poem "Life" in the anthology Whispers in the Wind.; [pers.] I try to write about what God has done for me and the wonderss He has created. I have been influenced greatly by nature; [a.] Honea Path, SC

JONES (JR.), NATHURLON
[b.] November 12, 1949, Rocky Mount, NC; [p.] Nathaurlon, Sr and Vera Jones; [m.] Vanessa S.T. Jones (deceased (April 4, 1977); [ch.] Nathaurlon Jones, III; Kashif N. Jones; [ed.] Graduate of Booker T. Washington High Schl., undergrad at Borough of Manhattan Comm. College; [occ.] Ret. Veteran, disabled; [memb.] Voodoo Religion - and the African American Comm. - Vietnam Veterans of America; [hon.] VA Ed. Awards and Incarceration by Injustice Award, Parenthood; [oth. writ.] Unpublished poems and poems destroyed by my fury 2 volumes...; [pers.] I have helped many people to succeed in this life time around and in my hour of need only the spirit helped me, so I could continue to help other people and myself...; [a.] Attica, NY

JONES, ALLYCE
[b.] April 8, 1960, Provost, Alberta; [p.] Clarence and Stella Hoff; [m.] Grant Jones, August 2, 1980; [ch.] Tanya, Yvonne, Dylan; [ed.] Metiskow School (gr 1-8), Hughenden Public School (9-12), Alberta Vocational Centre, Edmonton, Alberta; [occ.] Licensed Practical Nurse at Provost Municipal Health Care Centre; [hon.] Won a valentines contest and was printed in Provost News (local paper); [oth. writ.] I have other poems I've written for my families history book or as a hoby. I have written personal poems for gifts; [pers.] I write from the heart. I am influenced by the love for my husband and children; encouraged by family and friends; [a.] Czar, Alberta, Canada

JONES, BETTY JEWELL
[b.] August 13, 1939, Vanndale, AK; [p.] Gladys and Levin Jones; [pers.] Dedicated to my Aunt Laura for her support.

JONES, BRENDA
[b.] November 15, 1974; [p.] Walter & Barbara Jones; [ed.] Truman High, attending Salem-Teikyo University; [memb.] Baptist Campus Ministry; [oth. writ.] Never published before.l; [pers.] My pain influence came from my dear friends who's support kept my writing.; [a.] Salem, WV

JONES, CHRISTINE McDONAGH
[Pen.] Xena; [b.] July 24, 1969, Aurora, IL; [p.] Irene & Roy McDonagh; [ed.] Project Individual Education (P.I.E.); [occ.] Actress; [oth. writ.] Several unpublished poems and short stories; [pers.] Try your best at everything you do, this way, even if you don't publicly succeed, you'll always be personally successful.; [a.] Justice, IL

JONES, FRIEDA
[Pen.] Rhedd Jones; [b.] October 18, 1961, Virginia; [ed.] High School graduate (1980), Bronx Comm College (1yr), NY School Food and Hotel Mgmt; [occ.] Deli Clerk, NYC; [oth. writ.] Currently working on a biography; [pers.] I have always believed that a person should utilize whatever knowledge he/she has acquired. Never believe that your limits are in sight; [a.] Bronx, NY

JONES, JUDY A. SWAIN
[Pen.] Honey Saunders; [b.] November 16, 1965, Miami, FL; [p.] Rev and Mrs Albert Swain, Sr; [ch.] Dominique and Brittany Jones (2 girls ages 5 & 3 yrs); [ed.] Miami Northwestern Senior High - Atlanta, GA; Spelman College - BA English; Nova Univ. (currently in grad. prog.); [occ.] English teacher (6th grade), St. Monica Catholic Schl.; [memb.] Friendship Baptist Church - Miami, FL Mass Choir; NAACP Miami, FL; Spelman Alumnae Chapter; [hon.] Peer Teacher Prof. Orientation Prog. (POP); GA Governors Internship 1987; Innercity Scholarship Recipient - Miami, FL 1983-87; [oth. writ.] Focus Magazine 1983-87 (Spelman College's Literary Magazine) Poetry Only; Teletalk Newsletter (editor) Avanti Press Miami, FL; [pers.] "I can do all things through

Christ." My goal is to reach the hearts of my readers and tell their story, be their voice." [a.] Miami, FL

JONES, MANDY
[b.] August 19, 1969; Knottingley, West Yorkshire; [p.] George Morfet, Brenda Morfet; [m.] Tim Jones, June 4, 1993; [ed.] Knottingley High School; [occ.] Clothing presser; [hon.] This the first time I've let the public see this. So I really hope I do very well. [oth. writ.] I've written a few poems, but no one has really seen them; [pers.] I love writing poems. It's good for relaxing; [a.] West Yorkshire, England

JONES, THEOLA
[b.] February 2, 1929, Hot Springs, AR; [m.] Aaron Jones, Jr; [ch.] Aaron, Rita, Dennis; [ed.] BS Degree Gerontology, Minor: Journalism - Public Relations Madonna Univ. - Livonia, MI; [occ.] Retired; [memb.] Delta Sigma Theta - inkster Alumnae Chapter, Kappa Gamma R, Sigma Phi Omega, Top Ladies of Distinction, Inkster Goodfellows, Aging Commission - City of Inkster, Smith Chapel AME Church; [hon.] 150 Lady Award - State of MI, 1990 Winner - Collegiate Poetry Contest; [oth. writ.] (former) Ledger Star - Special Writer; [pers.] Think positive - Act positive - have faith - love God; [a.] Inkster, MI

JORDAN, CLARA EDITH
[Pen.] Jody Jordan; [b.] June 2, 1903, Barnard, Missouri; [p.] Joe and Belle Holaday; [m.] A. Dale, December 24, 1927; [ch.] (2) Joe Neal Jordan, Adala B. Jordan Muhlenbruck; [hon.] Blue and Purple Ribbons in Creative Writing; [oth. writ.] Short stories, various styles of poetry; [a.] Sheridan, WY

JORDANIDES, AMY
[b.] May 10, 1971, Derby, CT; [p.] Richard & Ruth Chandler; [m.] Stephen Jordanides, May 29, 1993; [ed.] New Covenant School, Teikyo Post University; [occ.] Admissions recruiter, Teikyo Post University; [memb.] Intercessors for Haiti; [hon.] Presidental Scholarship Award and Dean's List, Teikyo Post University; [a.] Ansonia, CT

JUDKINS, LEMMA
[Pen.] Ammel; [b.] March 14, 1945, Alabama; [p.] Joseph and Della Wyckoff; [m.] Widow; [ch.] Kenya, Terrance and Tyrone; [ed.] Zana High School, Daviston Alabama; [occ.] Textile Worker; [memb.] Saleeta Baptist Church Matrons; [oth. writ.] Poems and short stories just as a hobby; [pers.] My writing to me is a way of being my self. And the true devotion of my life to Jesus Christ and my family, with the hope of reaching some one else; [a.] Rockford, AL

JUGILON, GAYLE
[b.] September 3, 1967, Parma, OH; [p.] Eleanore & Alex Juguilon; [ed.] North Royalton High, Kent State University, Widener University School of Law.; [occ.] 3rd year law student; [memb.] American Bar Association.; [pers.] I amn motivated by the quest for knowledge and the desire to never stop learning.

JUGUILON, BRIAN
[Pen.] B. Rawlins Easton; [b.] January 7, 1970, Parma, OH; [ed.] Univ of Akron; [occ.] Student; [pers.] I am intrigued with nature and the heavens as well as with human consciousness, and I try to incorporate these into my writings; [a.] North Royalton, OH

JUVE, LORRIE
[b.] December 31, 1963, GA; [p.] Ordean & Lucy Juve; [ch.] Joshua Bonifaz; [ed.] Neptune High, Long Branch Vocational for Cosmetology; [occ.] Cosmetologist; [memb.] National Riffal Assoc. American National Society for Wild Life.; [oth. writ.] Several poems not yet published.; [pers.] My poetry is a reflection of my sould which has been set free by one man. To Joseph Dawson Evans, Thanks for all the love and inspiration.; [a.] Neptune, NJ

KABE, AINO KOHALOO
[b.] April 14, 1914, Estonia; [p.] Elvine & August; [m.] Herman Robert Kabe, 8/1/42; [ch.] Lenne, Elo Riuit, Alvan Mehis Kabe; [ed.] Art University of Tallinn 1943, Santa Monica City College 1970, Ed. Taska atelijce (masters) 1936, UCLA appreciation of Art.; [occ.] Retired, poetry, artist, homemaker; [memb.] ENUS (University Women's Sorority) Hon. Charter Memb., Internatnl. Assoc. of Poets, A.G.B. Hon. Soc. (AA Dean's List) Estonian Seniors Club, Lutheran Church leadership, Choir memb.; [hon.] Sev. first prizes for Art. Lifetime Charter memb. in Internatnl. Assoc. of Poets. Sev. Hon. Mention and Semi-final prizes for my poetry Golden Poet Award 1991, 1992.; [oth. writ.] Poetry book "Tuulemaa-Motteruni 1987, and Ule Kavguste 1992 (printed in free Estonia). 7 novels ready for printing and 50 pomes in english...which have printed in Anthologies (12) 24 poems on tape "Visions", 4 on Sound of Poetry.; [pers.] My dream is to have my poems in english published. The manuscript is ready and waiting to be published. Poetry is my key to unlock minds mysteries. Things happening around me..ask for attention!; [a.] Santa Monica, CA

KACHEL, ELAINE
[b.] September 20, 1918, Pagosa Spgs, CO; [p.] Dr. Bert Ellsworth and Anna Elsworth; [m.] Roy C. Kachel, 9/2/1938; [ch.] Karen Kachel, Kathleen Kachel Hauff; [ed.] High Schl. and 2 yrs Univ of Washington; [occ.] Homemaker; [memb.] Smohomish Co Historical Soc., WA; Marysville, WA Historical Soc.; Stilaguamish Senior Cntr; [hon.] Hon. Soc. in both high schl. and univ; [oth. writ.] Poem pub. in local newspapers. Book of poetry, "Homespun", in 1982 - self-published; [pers.] I enjoy writing poems about our extensive travels; family; local history and friends; [a.] Marysville, WA

KADNER, WENDY
[Pen.] Wendy S. Wendy Sux; [b.] February 24, 1961, Osage, IN; [p.] Edward and Marcia Mullen; [m.] Russell R. Decker, my best friend of 10 yrs; [ch.] Justin Kadner, Erin Kadner, Joshua Deaker and Trevor Decker; [ed.] 1979 Grad. from Osage Community High Schl.; [occ.] House mouse, poet, mother, artist; [hon.] Editor's Choice Award for poem, Best Friends, entered last year 1993. "A Break in the Clouds"; Upcoming Famous Poets Society is publishing "Only Six Months to Go"; [oth. writ.] In Anthology 1993, "A Break in the Clouds", I have poem "Best Friends" dedicated to Becky Wydent; [pers.] Even though my son is somewhere in this world. Should something ever happen to me. I want him to read this and know "I've always loved him"; [a.] Floyd, IN

KAISERSHOT, KAREN
[b.] December 4, 1956, Parkers Prairie, MN; [m.] Marvin Kaisershot; [ch.] Katy May, Morgan Erin; [occ.] Cryptologic Tech. United States Navy; [pers.] I write to keep in touch with a given inner strength and stability. Too often situations, surroundings and society are wrongly accused for the traits we find displeasing in ourselves and others. It is humanly preferable to blame the external elements than to look within ourselves for change; [a.] Westerly, RI

KAMINSKI, AMANDA
[b.] July 8, 1979; [p.] Ruth and Ken Kaminski; [ed.] Will soon be a sophomore in high school; [memb.] Memb. of the school yearbook; [oth. writ.] Memb. of yearbook staff, on the schl. paper in eighth grade, and on schl. paper in fifth and sixth grade.; [pers.] Even though people say I'm a good writer, I, myself, will never believe that. I just can't be convinced.; [a.] Glenwood, IL

KANE, ALLAN S.
[b.] August 1, 1965, Philadelphia, PA; [m.] Michele;

[ch.] Lynn Marie and Amber; [ed.] Wm Penn Charter School, Stockton State College, St. Joseph's Univ; [occ.] Police Officer, Galloway Twp, NJ; [pers.] When did violence become a basic human need?; [a.] Smithville, NJ

KANETAKE, IRENE Y.
[b.] Hawaii; [p.] Shizu & Shitatsu Miyagi; [m.] Choki Kanetake, 12/28/1941; [ch.] Stanley & Wesley Kanetake; [ed.] McKinley High, still attending, University of Hawaii, Sen. Program; [occ.] Realtor; [memb.] Choon Shisha Poem Club, Thursday Luncheon Club; [pers.] In writing poetry, I've come to know another dimension of myself. I am indebted to Professor Rob Wilson, who is also a published poet, and who encouraged me to keep writing poetry.; [a.] Honolulu, HI

KAPHING, JOHN C.
[b.] November 12, 1960, St. Paul, MN; [p.] Gerald E. Kaphing and the late Barbara H. Kaphing; [ed.] Janesville, WI, Craig High, Grad. of Univ. of Wisconsin, Madison; [occ.] President, FSSI, Inc., Tulson, AZ; [memb.] Delta Upsilon Fraternity, NRA, National Geographic Soc.; [hon.] U.S. Army, "Jungle Expert", ACM Award; [oth. writ.] In Progress; [pers.] Reality is as you perceive it life is all around you...live it. I have been greatly influenced and thankfully, so by my mother and father; [a.] Phoenix, AZ

KAPSON, FLORENCE
[Pen.] Flo K.; [b.] June 26, 1934, Brooklyn, NY; [p.] Robert & Ethel Hynes; [m.] Kenneth Kapson, 9/2 1961; [ch.] Kenneth John Kapson; [ed.] St. John's Grammar Schl., All Saints High Schl., Studies & Cert. in the Field of Alcoholism.; [oth. writ.] Personal and Spiritual, Diaries. Gift poems for family and friends.; [pers.] "My feelings and thoughts expressed in my poems relate "to others," "words"--that fill my head, spring from my heart, speaking soul to soul."; [a.] Freeport, NY

KARPER, ANNABELLE H.
[b.] June 14, 1976, Westport, CT; [p.] Diane Karper & Stephen Karper; [ed.] Fay Schl., Westminster Schl; [hon.] Fourth Place in a poetry contest in North Hampton, MA; [pers.] I am inspired by the beauty of light and my love for my friends; [a.] Nantucket, MA

KARUKS, URVE
[b.] January 18, 1936, Tallinn, Estonia; [p.] Voldemar and Elvine Aasoja; [m.] Ergo Karuks, 8/9/1956; [ch.] Alar (son), Linda (daughter); [ed.] Jarvis Collegiate Inst, Toronto, 1955; grade 13 grad.; Univ of Toronto, 1966, BA Sociology and Eng. Lit; [memb.] Internatnl. PEN; [hon.] 1969 Poetry Award - "Canadian-Estonian Lit. Award Committee"; 1979 1st Prize in Poetry from the "Estonian Art Centre Cultural Fund"; Published three books of poetry: SAVI (Clay), Toronto, 1968; Kodakondur (Hunter of the Homestead), Publ. "Mana", Toronto, 1976; Laotusse Lendama Laukast (Soar from the Swamp to the Stars), Publ. "Eesti Raamat", Tallinn, Estonia, 1992; All three are written in the Estonian language. Also published poems in lit. mags.; [pers.] I came to this earth with a mission to learn how to become Human and then find my way back to God; [a.] Toronto, Ontario, Canada

KASTIN, KATHERINE CRAWFORD
[b.] February 1, 1982, Mass.; [p.] Dan Crawford, Stephanie Crawford, Matthew Kashin; [ed.] The Village Schl. and City of London Schls. for girls; [occ.] Student and prof. actress; [oth. writ.] Currently working on a collection of humorous cat poems, have written many other poems and illustrated stories; [pers.] I only write when feeling inspired and although I do not write only about animals. My great love of animals has produced the passion for many of my poems; [a.] London, England

KAUCHER, LINDA L.
[Pen.] Lindsay Mary Rogers; [b.] May 16, 1947, New York; [p.] Evelyn and William Kaufmann; [m.] Roger Kaucher, October 30, 1971; [ed.] High school graduate; [occ.] Office worker; [memb.] National Author's Registry; [oth. writ.] Two poems published in other anthologies, a full-length feature screenplay entitled "cold sweat", treatments for future scripts; [pers.] My goal is to have my scripts produced into movies. I also hope more of my poems will be an inspiration to many; [a.] Edison, NJ

KAUFMANN, GARY A.
[b.] March 29, 1948, Casper, WY; [p.] Wayne and Thelma (Hart) Kaufmann; [m.] Never married; [ed.] 17 1/2 yrs. of total schooling, mostly in computers, accoutning, and business in higher education.; [occ.] Disabled American Veteran and Social Security Disabled; [memb.] DAV, NRA, Nature Conservancy, Anglers United, North American Fishing Club and Hungint Club; [hon.] Purple Heart, Four Semesters on Dean's List at Yavapai College, Five yrs. Veterans Adminsitration Service Award. Citation for Constributions from Chpt. 10 DAV, I feel honored because of God, my parents and my sister; [oth. writ.] Four line poems for each mont, spirit letters to vietman casualiteis, sayings, 12 poems on vietnam, 19 poems on faith, family, christmas, lonesomeness, etc., 4 personal experience storeis, 6 literature critiques.; [pers.] Poetry comes from personal experience, which puts me in a quandary. When I dwell on some past events, I write a tradgety type poetry and when I dwell elsewhere, I write uplifting poetry.; [a.] Prescott, AZ

KAVANAH, DENISE
[b.] April 1, 1964, Cornwall, NY; [p.] Teresa Kavanah and Thomas J. Kavanah (deceased); [ed.] B.A. in Psychology, Marist College, Poughkeepsie, NY; [occ.] Human Services Field, Residential School for Children with Emotional Disturbances; [hon.] Receiver of Excellency in Psychology in 1986.   Dean's list throughout 4 years of college; [oth. writ.] I have written many poems reflecting my personal experiences but at this time have not attempted to publish any of them.; [pers.] I believe that every person has the ability to overcome difficulties in their life. although we may never arrive at our destination there are always other's to help us on our journey; [a.] Stantsburg, NY

KAY, DEBORAH
[Pen.] Debo; [b.] October 23, 1980, Shreveport, LA; [p.] Manuel and Hilda Kay; [ed.] Elementary/Middle School; Plain Dealing Academy Herndon Magnet; [occ.] 8th grader at Herndon Magnet Middle School; [memb.] 4-H; [hon.] Elected on May 18, 1990 for membership in the National Junior Beta Club; [oth. writ.] Song (just 1), 4 more poems; [pers.] I hope to become a lawyer or a writer in the future; [a.] Hosston, LA

KEELER, DIANA
[b.] January 12, 1967, Brockville, Ontario Canada; [p.] Shirley Flegg, Wesley Steele; [m.] Troy Keeler, May 22, 1990; [ch.] Amanda Rose Ann Keller, Megan Emerald Rose Keeler; [ed.] Seaway District High, Iroquois, Ont.; [occ.] Potential writer and domestic engineer (housewife); [hon.] Kinsmen Club Award; [oth. writ.] Many short stories, prose poems, unpublished as yet.; [pers.] Dream your passion, and fly like the eagle.; [a.] Ontario, Canada

KEELS, DON JR.
[b.] January 6, 1976, Gallipolis; [p.] Don & Brenda Keels; [ed.] Senior at Jackson High School; [hon.] Honor Roll and Merit Scholar.   Recipient of Applachian Peace Award.   Published Twice in Who's Who Among American High School Students; [pers.] If a

person listens carefully to their hearts, they can achieve anything in this world.   Let no one tell you different.

KELCH, RUSSELL L.
[Pen.] Russell Kelly; [b.] September 17, 1913, Kansas; [p.] Harry and Alma Kelob (both deceased); [m.] Clara Louise Kelob (deceased 1993), November 2, 1941; [ch.] Russell L. Kelch II (deceased), Rebecca Louise Kelch (born 1946); [ed.] High School 1930 GCS Ft Sill Class '38 1942, C&GS Assoc Course 1960; [occ.] Retired 1979, Tech writer aircraft, Army 34 years; [memb.] Retired Officer Assn, Nat Rifle Assn, Battle of Normandy Foundation; [hon.] Campagne Stars 5 Battles, ETO Normandy N Franc Rhineland, Ardennes Central Europe, Editor's Choice Award 1993, Bird Feeders in Winter, published in Coming of Dawn; [oth. writ.] Two poems to be published, Space Between and Dance on the Horizon. Have a book in Progress called Horse Hide Gloves and Red Bananas about 1931 to 1940 years; [pers.] I have always been an admirer of Rudyard Kipling, especially Tommy and Fuzzy Wuzzy; [a.] Derby, Kansas

KELHAMI, CHAD
[Pen.] Tchad Martin Vardaman; [b.] June 4, 1975, Kendallville, IN; [p.] George & Loraine Kelham; [ed.] Garrett High School; [oth. writ.] Two poems published in the Garrett Clipper, a local newspaper; [oth. writ.] In my writing, I am saying something I can't usually say outloud, but I always make a positive statement happen, for others to understand.; [a.] Avilla, IN

KELLY, CLAUDE E.
[Pen.] E.C.; [b.] February 18, 1922, Det.; [m.] Louise M. Kelly, January 26, 1944; [ch.] Lynn, Craig, Duane; [ed.] 5 1/2 years college.; [occ.] Retired; [oth. writ.] Non-Commercial; [a.] Park Ridge, IL

KELLY, DEAMUS
[Pen.] Gloves; [b.] August 5, 1933, Castlebar W. Mayo Ireland; [p.] Thomas Kelly (RIP) & Eileen Keane (RIP); [m.] Eileen Reynolds 1976-1986 (RIP); [ch.] none; [ed.] BA, Hons. Philosophy, Unviersity College, Dublin, Qualified Theologian; [occ.] Security Officer; [memb.] Associate Holy Ghost, Gathers, Kiammage Manor, Dublin; [hon.] Poem, included in The Space Between; [oth. writ.] The Mystery of Women, (Evening Press Dublin, short poem); [pers.] The world, cold comfort, women, warm comfort; [a.] Dublin, Ireland

KELLY, DON
[b.] February 15, 1935, Ireland; [p.] Michael and Elizabeth; [m.] Patricia, May 16, 1964; [ch.] Sheila, Colleen, Sean and Tara; [ed.] High School, 2 yrs. College (Suffolk Community College); [occ.] Head Custodian, Sewanhaka High School; [memb.] Knights of Columbus, American Chess Federation, Extraordinary Minister, Pioneer Assistance Assoc., Gaelic Athletic Assoc.; [hon.] College Graduate, Summa Cum Laude, Soldier of the year, Fort Dix, NJ., Gaelic Athletic Champion; [oth. writ.] Short stories, book of poetry; [pers.] We are judged not merely by the goals preached, but by adhearing to the basic rules of decency.; [a.] Oyster Bay, NY

KELLY, KELLY
[b.] April 8, 1972, Alexandria, LA; [p.] Leonard and Parlee Kelly; [ed.] Graduated from Lak Highlands HS in Dallas, Degree in grant writing and consulting for non-profit organizations; [occ.] Product distribution center organizer; [memb.] Love Outreach Evangelistic Penticostal Church Board of Directors, Youth Ministes, Youth Evangelist; [hon.] English Literature recitation. Outstanding biblicol writings by subject

matter; [oth. writ.] Other poems and biblical writings inspired by the Holy Ghost; [pers.] The best writer is one who can feel what he writes and effectively channel those feelings into a positive point for living [a.] Dallas, TX

KELLY, TERRY
[b.] November 3, 1961, Los Angeles, CA; [p.] Judy and Joe Kelly; [m.] Chris (Newbury), December 21, 1991; [ed.] BA, San Francisco State Univ; AA, City College San Francisco; graduated Wm Niff High, LA Mirada, CA; [occ.] Television Writer; [pers.] "Give me a fat, meaty rabbit and I'll give you dinner".

KELM, LOUISE MABEL
[Pen.] Lou Kelm; [b.] August 14, 1921, Lockport, IL; [p.] Steve and Marie Pesavento; [m.] Leo Joseph Kelm, February 14, 1942; [ch.] Joseph (Dec.) Larry, Louis Kelm; [ed.] Sacred Heart 8th grade, Lockport High School, given a college grant, but due to finances of parents, went to work; [occ.] Homemaker, Volunteer; [memb.] V.F.W. Auxilary American Legion Aux. Altar & Rosary Society; [hon.] Citation for Poppy Displays, volunteer work at hospital, poems written for outgoing commanders at Post Home; [oth. writ.] Many poems mostly concerning our men who served in the war.; [pers.] I can express my feelings in poetry especially about the beauty of God's world; [a.] Lockport, IL

KELSEY, LEIGH ANNE
[b.] May 10, 1979, Tacoma, WA; [p.] Gray and John Kelsey; [ed.] 9th grade, Thomas Edison High School; [occ.] Student; [memb.] Edison H.S. Marching, and Jazz Band, Edison H.S. Ecology Club; [hon.] Selected for Gifted & Talented (GT) English in 8th and 9th grade; [pers.] Wrigint poetry says so much of you. People can know who you are just be reading one of your poems.; [a.] Alexandria, VA

KENDRICK, AJIKE KORENTHA
[b.] June 20, 1968, NY, NY; [p.] Francina Y. Kendrick, John Organ; Partner: Dawn Morrison; [ed.] Clara Barton HS, Shaw Univ, 1993; [hon.] Cum Laude, Dean's List; [pers.] I have been greatly influenced by Ntozake Shange. I seek to express the beauty of my reality as I relate to the world we live in; [a.] Brooklyn, NY

KENNEDY, ANN MARIE
[b.] January 23, 1956; [ch.] Deanna E. Ceclia; [ed.] Seneca College of Applied Arts and Technology, Mohawk College of Applied Arts and Technology. Toronto School of Arts.; [occ.] Program Coordinator, Artist.; [oth. writ.] Just completed my first book of poems and presently in search of a publisher.; [pers.] My greatest influence has been that of my own Journey. A journey that has led to the quest and the discoveries. New awareness, renewed consciousness and a better understanding of self; [a.] Toronto, Ontario

KENNEDY, JIM
[b.] January 6, 1929, Zachary, LA; [p.] Deceased; [m.] divorced, October 24, 1952; [ch.] Kim, Tonnel, Andy, Micah, Jude; [ed.] Finished 9th grade; [oth. writ.] About 15 short stories. Between 80 and 100 poems.

KENNEDY, PATTI BARRON
[Pen.] P. Kennedy; [b.] September 22, 1966, St Johns NF; [p.] Sarah, William Barron; [m.] Don Kennedy; [m.] June 16, 1990; [ch.] William Jonathan, Donald Brett; [ed.] Whitbourne High, Placentia Vocational College; [occ.] Secretary St Alphonsus RC Parish; [memb.] 2nd Lieutenant/Administration Officer 2584, Whitbourne Army Cadets Volunteer for CNIB, Coordinator: 1993 World Day of Prayer (Whitbourne); [hon.] Graduated Gr 12 with distinction Whitbourne

gh; [oth. writ.] History of 2584 Whitbourne Army
det Corps, published by RCAC Historical Society
part of the history of the Cadet movement in NFLD
Labrador; [a.] Whitbourne, NF

ERBS, MANDY
] May 22, 1974, Chicago, IL; [p.] Margaret and
onald Kerbs, Sr; [ed.] Charles J. Sahs Elementary
hool, Reavis High School; [memb.] Alabama Fan
ub, Billy Ray Cyrus Fan Club; [hon.] Leadership
ard in 1993, Perfect Attendance Award in 1990;
h. writ.] Several other poems and a couple of short
ries; [pers.] I write my feelings in my poems. If you
d my poems you will know how much pain and hurt
elt and still feel about everything; [a.] Chicago, IL

ERCHEVAL, RUTH ANNA JORENE
en.] RJK; [b.] June 12, 1976, Torrance, CA; [p.]
l and Terri Kercheval; [ed.] Pre-school and Kinder-
rten - Torrance, CA. Kindergarten through 8th
ade - Sullivan, IL High School, Myrtle, MO; [occ.]
ident at Couch High (Senior); [memb.] Library
ub, Peer Helper; [hon.] I have won two ribbons for
intings. My first published poem is my best one yet;
h. writ.] I have written numerous poems. Like
ears", "Am I Alone", "Do You Feel The Same" to
me a few. I have several more written. I also plan
continue writing; [pers.] This poem is dedicated to
sister. To me "Death is the ultimate adventure".
u always will have an idea of what will happen
eryday of your life. Yet, death is still filled w/
ystery; [a.] Myrtle, MO

ERMON, ELIZABETH F.
] January 3, 1980, Asheboro, NC; [p.] Todd
rmon, Mary Weathrspoon; [ed.] Annie H. Snipes
ementary, and attending D.C. Virgo Middle School;
cc.] Student; [memb.] Wesley Memorial United
ethodist Church, Drama Club, Fifth Ave Methodist
YF; [hon.] Second Year Spelling Bee Class Cham-
on, Presidential Academic Fitness Award, Duke
niv TIP Program, Arts displayed; [oth. writ.] Nu-
erous other writings; [pers.] No matter how much
ne I spend writing, it's the time I don't that pesters
 heart and mind; [a.] Wilmington, NC

ERN, DEENA MARIE
] July 22, 1967, Newhyde Park, NY; [p.] Neil
rn, Rita Lazada; [ch.] Ashley Michele (Age 3);
l.] H.S. of Art & Design, NY; [occ.] Self Em-
oyed; [oth. writ.] I have written poetry since I am 11
ars old, this is the first time any of my poetry has
en published.; [pers.] I believe that letting go of
otions onto paper can make for beautiful poetry.
 of my poems have been written according to my
pes, dreams and fears.; [a.] Mineola, NY

ERPCHAR, SALLY
] June 26, 1961, Houston, TX; [m.] Christian
rpchar; [ch.] Daniel, David, and Katherine; [ed.]
 Literature, Univ of Houston-Clear Lake; [occ.]
ident; [memb.] Sigma Delta Tau, Phi Theta Kappa,
i Alpha Theta, NOW, MENSA; [oth. writ.] "Jet-
s" published in the UHCL Bayousphere, 1992;
] Carpe Diem for we are dying; [a.] League
ty, TX

ERR, KLEON HARDING
rmer State Senator, educator; [b.] Plain City, UT,
or 26, 1911; s. William A. and Rosemond (Harding)
; m. Katherine Abbott, Mar 15, 1941; [ch.]
thleen, William A., Rebecca Rae. AS, Weber
ll., 1936; BA, George Washington U., 1939; MS,
ah State U., Logan, 1946. Tchr., Bear River High
h., Trenton, Utah, 1940-56, prin. jr. high sch.,
56-60, prin. Bear River High Sch., 1960-71; city
stice Tremonton, 1941-46; sec. to Senator Arthur
Watkins, 1947. Mayor, Tremonton City, 1948-53;
em. Utah Local Govt. Survey Commn., 1954-55;
em. Utah Ho. of Reps., 1953-64, chmn. appropria-

tion com., 1959-, majority leader, 1963; mem. Utah
Legis. Council. Author: (poetry) Open My Eyes,
1983, We Remember, 1983, Trouble in the Amen
Corner, 1985, Past Imperfect, 1988, A Helping
Hand, 1990, Sound of Silence, 1991, Power Behind
the Throne, 1992, Unreachable Goal?, 1993; (his-
tory) Those Who Served Box Elder County, 1984,
Those Who Served Tremonton City, 1985, Diamond
in the Rough, 1987, Facts of Life, 1987, Gettin' and
Givin', 1989. Dist. dir. vocat. edn. Box Elder Sch.
Dist. Recipient Alpha Delta Kappa award for out-
standing contbn. to edn., 1982, award for outstanding
contbrs. to edn. and govt. Theta Chpt. Alpha Beta
Kappa, 1982, Excellence Achieved in Promotion of
Tourism award, Allied Category award Utah Travel
Counc., 1988, Merit award, 1993, Andy Rhytting
Community Svc. award, 1991; named Tourism Am-
bassador of Month, 1986. Mem. NEA, Utah, Box
Elder edn. assns., Nat., Utah secondary schs. prins.
assns., Bear River Valley. C. of C. (sec., mgr. 1955-
58), Lions Kiwanis, Phi Delta Kappa. Mem. Ch. of
Jesus Christ of Latter-day Saints. [a.] Tremonton, UT

KESO, SARAH KRISTEN
[Pen.] Brooke S. Fields; [b.] December 14, 1977,
Sharon, PA; [p.] Barbara and Ronald Keso; [ed.]
Sophomore at Brookfield High School, Brookfield,
OH; [occ.] Student; [memb.] Volleyball, Track,
Basketball, Tennis, Student Council, Octagon Club,
Sophomore Class President, English Festival; [hon.]
8th Grade Student Athlete of the Year; [a.] Brookfield,
OH

KEYS, ADDIE
[Pen.] Mme Niruma; For more than 20 years, the
process of forging the classics, vocal, dance and
dramatic training, with native and articulate talent,
has developed in each turn of the process, a product
unique in its own emergence. NiRuma, the classically
trained vocalist, dancer and dramatist emerges as the
highly skilled and trained artist, a tribute to those years
spent in forging and molding her talents. NiRuma, the
vocalist, lyricist, dancer and dramatist who conveys
the freedom message of spirit, mysticism, and mo-
tion, emerges as the end-product of this process, ever
accomplishing, growing, sharing, teaching, contrib-
uting. Produced and directed a dramatic presentation
for the Southern Society of Anatomists Convention,
Nashville, TN.

KILDAY, BILLIE
[b.] November 18, 1933, Baguio, PI; [p.] William H.
Reese, Susana S. Reese; [m.] Bernard L. Kilday, Jr;
[ch.] John, Kathryn, Jim, Granddaughter Kim; [pers.]
I like to celebrate and honor the preciousness, good-
ness, and intelligence of our children. My inspiration
comes from my Granddaughter Kim Kilday, now 3
years old, who lives in Gresham, OR; [a.] Lake Forest
and Dana Point, CA

KING, DAVID P.
[b.] January 26, 1954, Bakersfield, CA; [p.] Betty C.
& Argil King Sr.; [m.] Marcia Bucchianeri King, June
29, 1986; [ch.] none; [ed.] South High, Pasadena,
CA, City College; [occ.] Custodial Leadman for
Ambassador College; [memb.] American Red Cross,
World Wide Church of God, Usher Coordinator,
Outreach for Elderly Seniors, Homeless Shelters.;
[hon.] First & Second place ribbons in high school for
Best Poetry, Japanese Haiku's, standard poetry; [oth.
writ.] Hudnred's of poems, different styles, several
song poems, Ballads, country rock, religous.; [pers.]
I strive to serve the world through my writings. As
long as there is ink, there will be paper. As long as
there is time, there will be verse. As long as there are
oceans, there are breakers. As long as there is
thought, writers will emerge.; [a.] Los Angeles, CA

KING, ESTHER
[b.] November 30, 1933, Chicago, IL; [p.] Simon &
Mae Handzik; [m.] Russell King, August 10, 1973;
[ch.] God Children: Nancy Kent, James Augustine;
[ed.] Laurdes High; [occ.] Homemaker; [pers.] I wish
to share with others any God given talents I may
possess as homage and gratitute to my source.; [a.]
Orland Park, IL

KING, JERRY
[Pen.] Glenn Scott; [b.] March 16, 1967, KI Sawyer,
MI; [p.] Jim & Joyce King; [ed.] Red River High,
North Central bible College (B.A.), Gordon-Conwell
Theological Seminary (current, MA in Theology);
[occ.] Student, Gordon-Conwell Theological Semi-
nary; [memb.] None current; [hon.] Who's Who High
School, Who's Who, Colleges and Universities, Eagle
Scout, Nat. Honor Society, Silver and Gold Honor
Society (College), Summa Cum Laude, 2nd Regional
in German; [oth. writ.] None published; [pers.] The
human heart is the bastion of writing resource.; [a.]
Grand Forks, ND

KING, KALISKA
[Pen.] Kaliska King; [b.] February 22, 1978, Salem,
OR; [p.] Gale Williams and Rocky King; [occ.]
Student; [memb.] YMCA Leadership Club, Future
Business Leaders of America, and 4-H Horses and
dogs; [hon.] Lot's of horse back riding awards;
[pers.] I owe a lot of my poetry to my grandmother
Betty Elizabeth Keays Williams, to me the greatest
poet around; [a.] Salem, OR

KING, MAX
[b.] November 15, Edison, GA; [p.] David Fillmore
and Julia; [ch.] David, Carol, DuVal, Julie, Johnson,
Enrico, William, Lorenzo, Steven, Hosteen; [ed.]
Jordan High School, Columbus, GA, Utah Tech
College, SLC, UT; [occ.] "Tired"; [memb.]
Songwriters, Arts, Poetry, National Sheriff's Assoc
Retired. Seafares Int'l Union, VA-50 Army, Navy
43, US Merchant Seamen 54; [hon.] Korean Service
Bar and Medal awarded for service under combat
conditions, 1950 to September 30, 1953; [oth. writ.]
Childrens songs and books ("Winnie", "The Frog")
and published; [pers.] Nutrition for longevity and the
soul. The best known ingredient, love; [a.] Kingman,
AZ

KING, NICOLE
[b.] September 23, 1979, Valencia, CA; [p.] Fred and
Penny King; [ed.] Vineyard Christian School; [occ.]
Student; [hon.] Citizenship, 1st Place Basketball,
Student of the Month; [pers.] Never give up, follow
your hopes and dreams, expressing myself in poetry
is fun; [a.] Quartz Hill, CA

KIRK, DONNA L.
[b.] May 30, 1959, Reading Hospital; [p.] Joan E.
Kirk, Edward P. Kirk (Deceased); [ed.] Graduate,
Twin Valley High School; [occ.] Bank Teller, Bank
of PA, Honey Brook, PA; [oth. writ.] Poetic Voices
of America 1990, 91, 92, National Library of Poetry,
Where Dreams Begin, Whispers in the Wind, Our
World's Most Treasured Poems, Selected Works of
Our World's Best Poets; [pers.] This poem is dedi-
cated to the memory of Connor Clapton, son of Blues
Guitarist Eric Clapton; [a.] Geigertown, PA

KIRKSEY, LYNETTE
[b.] November 16, 1947, Phoenix, AZ; [m.] Married;
[ch.] one child; [ed.] Phoenix Union High, Phoenix
College, Arizona State University; [occ.] Elementary
School Teacher in the Roosevelt School District;
[memb.] N.E.A.; [hon.] Personal poetry reading at
the South Mountain Baptist Churches, Mothers and
Daughters Tea.; [oth. writ.] Collection of personal
poems; [pers.] Mrs. Brown and Ms. Stewart, Thank
you for making poetry a vital part of my life which
began in your English classes.; [a.] Phoenix, AZ

KLASSEN, HELEN
[b.] July 13, 1975, Tillsonburg; [p.] Bernard & Maria Klassen; [ed.] Graduated from East Elgin Secondary School; [occ.] Babysitter; [hon.] Grade 9 Math Award; [oth. writ.] Never wrote anything before. Breaking up with my boyfriend inspired me to write this poewm.; [pers.] In my spare time I like to listen to music, but I have the most fun when I'm with with my friends.; [a.] Vienna, Ontario

KLEIN, JOY G.
[Pen.] Joy G. Klein; [b.] December 19, 1931, Brooklyn, NY; [p.] Solomon J. Schwartz, DDS, Eleanor Schwartz; [m.] Divorced; [ch.] (1 son) Robert Allan Klein, (NMT Certified Message Thereapist) DOB: March 9, 1956; (2 grandchildren) David (10) and Marcie Klein (8); [ed.] Syracuse Univ., NY Univ. Schl. of Ed. BS Degree, NYS Cert. Ed. Dept.; Teacher Regular NYC Day Elem. also NYC and NYS Nursery Prek and Kg; Equivalent Masters Degree of in service courses; [occ.] Ret. as of March 1, 1990; I taught 30 yrs in NYC public schools and I enjoyed my profession, working with children, other colleagues, parents and administrators. I am now, again, writing poetry. I was also Teacher-Director of NYC private Nursery (NYS Certified)-Kg Schl. in Brooklyn, NY, previous to my NYC teaching career in pub. schls.; [memb.] Regular member congregant - Temple Congregation Children of Israel in Athens, GA, and Sisterhood. I appreciate the services and skillful presentation of the Adult Ed. Courses given by Rabbi Ronald Gerson; [hon.] Many certificates of appreciation awarded to me by officials re: Ed., also parents, also by UFT Pres. Sandra Feldman, on my retireent March 1, 1990. I was music coordinator at my pub. schl., too, and played piano led the Glee Club and Chorus. I also choreographed some mini-field day dance and aerobic events.; [pers.] May I continue to add, as a new resident, and a permanent resident to Athens, Georgia, I appreciate fine and nice friends; Jeff, also my sincere, friend, here, Michael, who is my Temple friend - and along with Rabbi Gerson, make me feel very comfortable and welcome. I sincerely wish we all, with my family in Athens, Georgia, enjoy each day with health, happiness, and prosperity, and peace!; [a.] Athens, GA

KLUESNER, SUSAN M.
[b.] December 24, 1958, Elgin, IL; [p.] Chris Stewart/ Norman Gilbert; [m.] Scott W. Kluesner, November 10, 1979; [ch.] My 3 dogs, JD, Misty, Jammer; [ed.] GED; [occ.] Bindery for Alphagraphics Telemarketing for Market Link; [memb.] On board of directors for "Help the Animals" a non-profit organization dedicated to pets. We help pay for veterinary bills, food, and finding them homes; [hon.] To have my poem published; [oth. writ.] I write poetry a lot but this is my first published poem; [pers.] I thank the Lord for being able to write. Life is so short and every moment should count. Is your cup half full or half empty?; [a.] Des Moines, IA

KMIEC, JAMIE ELAINE
[b.] June 28, 1977; [b.] Houston, TX; [p.] James and Jefferie Kmiec; [ed.] Inez Carroll Elementary; TS Grantham Middle School; currently a junior at Aldine Senior High School; [memb.] National Honor Society, Photography Club, Ecology Club - President, Junior Achievement - Vice President, History Bowl, Boys Varsity Soccer -Team Manager; [hon.] Who's Who Among America's High School Student's; various academic, theatrical and artistic awards; an invitation to the 10th Annual Washington Journal Conference; Texas Media Art Awards 3rd place photography recipient; [oth. writ.] "The Betrayer"; Hundreds of unpublished poems and essays; [pers.] Believe in something;; This poem is for Bob and for Christopher who helped me find my voice; [a.] Houston, TX 77037

KNESEK-KUBELKA, MARGARET
[a.] Richmond, TX

KNIESPECK, MICHAEL J.
[Pen.] J. Michael Benczyk; [b.] October 19, 1973, Detroit; [p.] Michael and susan; [ed.] Currently studying mental health and psychology; [occ.] student (full-time); [oth. writ.] Occasional article for local senior citizen newspaper; [pers.] My writings always reflect issues involved in human service and welfare.; [a.] Rochester Hills, MI

KNIFFEN, RICHARD C.
[Pen.] C-NA; [b.] December 26, 1960, Lansing, MI; [p.] Richard W. Kniffen and Gloria J. Duffey; [m.] April 22, 1983; [ch.] Chad, Nick and Alyssa; [ed.] Lansing Everett High, Lansing Com Collete; [occ.] Assembly (Auto) Saturn; [hon.] Phi Theta Kappa; [oth. writ.] Editorials and Business Reports; [pers.] The happiest moments of my life have been the few which I have passed at home in the bosom of my family - Thomas Jefferson; [a.] Spring Hill, TN

KNIGHT, TIFFANY ANN
[b.] January 16, 1974, Lethbridge, AB; [p.] Lennis and Diana Knight; [ed.] Grade 1-5 St Joseph's School Coaldale; grade 6-12 National Ballet School, Toronto, Ontario; graduate year - Intensive Dance Training, NBS (as above); [occ.] Apprenticeship with The National Ballet of Canada; [hon.] Peter Dwyer Scholarship, Willington Award, Norcen Award Mona Lubin Scholarship all at NBS; [pers.] "Just do it!" Nike; [a.] Coaldale, Alberta

KNIGHT, VERA J.
[b.] October 9, 1931, McKeesport, PA; [p.] John and Bessie Thomas; [m.] Jack R. Knight, September 18, 1953; [ch.] Lee R. Knight, Laura E. Knight; [ed.] High school graduate; [occ.] Homemaker; [memb.] Norman Vincent Peale - Positive Thinking Club - Peale Center for Christian Living, First Presbyterian Church of Santa Monica; [hon.] PTA President and PTA Honor Award; [pers.] I have been greatly influenced by my wonderful parents, my brothers and sisters, and my church and the beautiful people of McKeesport, PA; [a.] Santa Monica, CA

KNOX, DOROTHY B.
[Pen.] Dorothy Brent; [b.] March 10, 1940, Jayess, MS; [p.] Robert & Juanita Brent; [m.] Stanley R. Knox, October 23, 1960; [ch.] none; [ed.] B.S., Wayne State, IL, Detroit, MI, FBI National Academy Graduate, 1979; [occ.] Deputy Chief, Detroit Police Dept.; [memb.] Women Police of Michigan, Michigan Association of Chiefs of Police, International Assn. of Chiefs of Police, Crime Prevention Assn. of Michigan; [hon.] Payne-Pullman Door Openers Award, 1993; [oth. writ.] Article in FBI Bulletin April 1980 ("A Procedural Model for Processing Citizens Complaints"); [pers.] Poetry is muchic for the soul.; [a.] Detroit, MI

KOBAYASHI, GEORGE, JOJI
[b.] January 27, 1952, Santa Monica, CA; [p.] Osamo & Tomiko Kobayashi; [m.] Single; [ed.] Gardena High School, A.A. Degre in Liberal Arts, L.A. Herbor College; [occ.] Unemployed, disabled; [hon.] Goodwill Client of the Month, Reception Line (Torrance Marriott) met original Mr. Marriott in person; [oth. writ.] Poems published in "The Coming of Dawn"; [pers.] I believe in the Bible; [a.] Gardena, CA

KOCH, EVELYN
[b.] 1904, Brillion; [p.] Min & Chris Tschantz; [m.] Ralpk Koch, May 15, 1926; [ch.] Jacquely Ann; [ed.] High School, Brillion OshKosh Normal; [occ.] Retired, 90 years-age; [memb.] United Methodist Church, Retired Choir AARP Member, Writers Club; [hon.] Declamation Going of the White Swan, World Poe■ Award, Gold & Silver Award, Honorable Mentio■ [oth. writ.] "The Burning Ship", "Farm Life 70 Yea■ Ago", "My Treasure Chest" (a book of my poem■ [pers.] The University at Madison has "Yarns Yesteryears," contest every year. Also won a che■ My aim in life is to make someone laugh or sm■ everyday.; [a.] West Bend, WI

KOEHLER, MARTHA PETERSON
[b.] December 27, 1904, Tidaholm, Sweden; [p■ John & Helna Peterson; [m.] Edward Fenton Koehle■ December 4, 1943; [ch.] none; [ed.] Evanston Coll■ giate Institue (now Kendall College), Northweste■ Univ.; [occ.] Retired; [memb.] Wesley United Me■ odist Church, Edison, NJ, Northwestern Alum■ Assoc., Hill and Valley (UT) Church, Women Unite■ AARP; [hon.] Scholarship to Northwestern, 70 ye■ membership certificate-Wesley Church; [hon.] Wo■ cited on Channel 13 news; [oth. writ.] Ralph Wal■ Emerson and Other Poems. A play based on life■ Handel. (Produced.) A few poems and articles■ magazines. Published in Anthology of New Jers■ Poets; [pers.] Burial of Sir Winston, brought lette■ from Queen Elizabeth, Mrs. Churchill. Have tried■ lift the human spirits and to eliminate injustice of ■ times; [a.] Neptune, NJ

KOENIG, REBECCA
[b.] September 30, 1981, Saskatoon, Canada; [p■ Norma and Bob Koenig; [ed.] 7th grade at Dougl■ McArthur Junior High, Jonesboro, AR; [occ.] St■ dent; [memb.] Jonesboro Swim Team; [hon.] 4 ■ GPA; [pers.] I love writing poetry because I li■ thinking of the words to write, and making the poe■ come alive. I can tell my feelings bout things, alm■ like drawing a picture; [a.] Jonesboro, AR

KOHN, KIMBERLY ANN
[b.] November 15, 1974, Springville, NY; [p.] Lorai■ and Calvin Kohn; [m.] not married; [ch.] no childre■ [ed.] Currently attending Fredonia State University■ an Elementary Education Major with a concentrati■ in English and minor in Psychology; [occ.] Studer■ [hon.] Dean's List; [oth. writ.] Several poems whi■ were published in local newspaper; [pers.] Poetry■ Artwork. Read it and write it with true feeling.; [a■ North Collins, NY

KOSSOW, SUELLEN E.
[b.] July 23, 1953, Milwaukee, WI;l [p.] John ■ Kossow and Patricia Mulvaney Kossow; [m.] non■ [ch.] none; [ed.] B.S. Barry University, M.B.A■ Univ. of Miami; [occ.] President, Owner, Gabri■ Kossow and Morgan Inc. (GKM) Advertising, Ma■ keting P. Reladbus Conssultants; [memb.] Adverti■ ing Federation of America, Broward Chamber ■ Commerce; [hon.] Who's Who of American Wome■ [oth. writ.] Vearious poems and articles published ■ published in newspapers and literary magazine■ Addy Winner; [pers.] My poems are the expression ■ my passion for life.; [a.] Miami Springs, FL

KOSTIC, OLGA
[b.] June 1, 1978, Toronto, ON; [p.] Bata V. Kosti■ Gordana Kostic; [ed.] Silverthorn Collegiate Ins■ [occ.] Student; [pers.] My favorite type of poetry ■ the kind in which I can recognize my own though■ and emotins. It is very gratifying to see other peop■ being able to identify with the feelings expressed ■ my poems; [a.] Toronto, Ont

KOTLINSKI, MICHAEL A.
[Pen.] Michael A. Kotlinski; [b.] November 2, 195■ Chicago, IL; [p.] Eugene B. Kotlinski, Lottie ■ Kozoil; [ed.] Glenbrook North High School, Lak■ County College - A few construction courses; [occ■ Mailman, Northbrook, IL; [oth. writ.] The Nation■ Library of Poetry - The Spirit Star, Unspoken Lov■ Enlightenment; [pers.] Wishing one day to attain th■

sdom of thought to understand the wonders of istence and its infinity; [a.] Gurnee, IL

OVILIC, MARYANN
.] March 22, 1956, Chicago, IL; [p.] Petar (Bajica) id Ivana Martinovich; [m.] Nikola Kovilic; Novem- r 23, 1974; [ch.] Radovan (Rodney), Danilo (Donny); d.] Nazerath Academy, Elmhurst College, Bach- or of Science in Business Administration; [occ.] orporate Officer; [memb.] American Small Busi- ess Assoc, National Women in Construction JAWIC); [hon.] Deans List; [pers.] Gods grace and fes journey are my inspiration for creative expres- on; [a.] Chicago, IL

OWALCZYK, ARTHUR
Pen.] Przemek Kowalczyk; [b.] June 12, 1960, rakow, Poland; [p.] Ryszard, Regina Kowalczyk; m.] Jolanta; [ch.] Przemystaw; [memb.] Polski siazek Wedkarski, Stowarzyszenie Wolnej Mysli, wiatowy Front Na Rzecz Odbudouy Czlowieka; oth. writ.] Booklet of Poetry called "The Big For- st"; [pers.] Most people are lost in life. They forget hat there is much more to do and to think about than money and comfort. I'll try to wake them up; [a.] Iillsboro, OR

OWALCZYK, DOMINIC
b.] September 28, 1975, Chicago, IL; [p.] Joseph and Krystyna Kowalczyk; Sisters: Claudia, Lisa, and Monica; [ed.] John Hersey High School, Emilii Platter Polish School, IL State Univ; [occ.] Full-time student at Illinois State Univ; [memb.] NASTAR Ski Racing; [oth. writ.] Poems to be published in two languages and songs; [pers.] I try to live life as it is, through my eyes and no one else's; [a.] Normal, IL

KOZLOWSKI, FLORENCE
[b.] Chicago, IL; [ch.] Mother of three, grandmother of three; [ed.] Attended Oakton College and North- western University (Evanston Campus); [occ.] New (hopeful) writer I am a freelance painter and sculptor.; [memb.] American Society of Artists, Member of Ioto Sigma Epsiton Sorority of Northwestern Univ. Evanston Campus; [oth. writ.] Not published, autobi- ography, fiction, essays, short stories. Novel in progress.; [pers.] Yesterday is gone, tomorrow is not yet born. So all we have is now. "Use it."; [a.] Chicago, IL

KRAGTHORPE, ILA JEAN
[b.] October 17, 1931, Mpls, MN; [p.] Ruth Schimmel Warrington; [m.] Ronald E. Kragthorpe, December 30, 1950; [ch.] Kristin Maria, Kimberly Ann, William David; [ed.] BA - Calif Lutheran Univ 1979; MA Cal State Univ Northridge; ESL Certif, Univ Calif Santa Barbara; [occ.] English/ESL Instructor: Moorpark College, Moorpark, CA; [memb.] Victim Offender Reconciliation Program, VA County, CA; Holy Trin- ity Lutheran Church; Telecare Ministry; Memorial Committee; [hon.] Scholastic Honor Society; Who's Who/Amer Univ Dean's Award: Cal Lutheran; Phi Kappa Phi, Judge Julian Beck Award: CSUN; [oth. writ.] "Homecoming"; "A Matter of the Heart": LCA, Phila, PA "Sharing A Heritage" Learning With, LCA, Phila, PA; Selected Poetry: Pegasus, Morning Glory; [pers.] Grace, and therefore hope, are possible in all things. But we must seek the out in ourselves and in one another; [a.] Thousand Oaks, CA

KRAH, BETTY
[Pen.] Elizabeth Poetkau Krahn; [b.] June 18, 1944, Winkler; [p.] Both Deceased; [m.] Jim Krahn, July 14, 1973; [ch.] Two Girls, Lavonne Lynn aged 19 and Julia Kaye aged 15; [ed.] Teaching certificate from Man. Teachers' Colelge. Bach. of Sc. in Educ. from Bethel College, Bach. of Christian Educ. from Can. Mennonite Bible College.; [occ.] Homemaking; [memb.] I serve on the board of the Mennonite

Collegiate Institute; [oth. writ.] I publish a poem in our church newspaper every month. I have published a number of poems in the Collegiates alumni newslet- ter.; [pers.] I aspire to glorify and praise God and his beautiful creations in my writing.; [a.] Winkler Manitoba, Canada

KRALIK, RICHARD PAUL
[Pen.] Richard Paul; [b.] August 29, 1964, Hoboken, NJ; [p.] Richard Kralik & Laurena Phegn; [m.] Someday…; [ed.] Bergenfield High, Bergen Commu- nity College; [pers.] Creations motivated by love are best, for reader and writer. That which makes us think, feel…these things live with us long after we put down…They make us better, for having read them.; [a.] Bergenfield, NJ

KRANNING, DORA SILVA
[b.] March 2, 1946, Zurich; [p.] Walter and Anna Kranning; [m.] Divorced; [ed.] European education, Switzerland Regal Ballet School, London; [occ.] Ballet teacher, Glendale College, Lyricist, Shiva Diva Music; [memb.] Women in Theatre, LA; [oth. writ.] Several lyrics to pop songs, Shiva, Dive Mag. Article, Noho Magazine; [pers.] Poetry like all the other art forms touches the inner truth of mankind.; [a.] Burbank, CA

KRANTZ, NORMA J.
[Pen.] Norma Coursey Krantz; [b.] May 19, 1927, Atlanta, GA; [m.] December 8, 1945; [ch.] Four children; [pers.] This poem is taken from my unpub- lished book Only In The Silence. My writings have come from my personal spiritual growth. It has been my privilege for over twenty years to be the spiritual parent to all of the men and women that God has placed in my path. I feel I have been called to encourage and uplift His children, for I know He loves us all just as we are and where we are. I know He wants to be for everyone the Friend and Counselor He is to me.; [a.] Erie, PA

KREHBIEL, JANE-ALEXANDRA
[Pen.] Jane Ross Rogers (as recording artist); [b.] August 14, 1959, San Rafael, CA; [p.] Lawrence Kelsey, Lilian Kelsey; [m.] David Krehbiel; [ch.] Stephanie, Adam and Matthew; [ed.] RN degree, studying also for environmental science degree; [occ.] RN, writer; [oth. writ.] Numerous published articles on nursing, parenting, asthma proofing, time man- agement and homeschooling. A frequent contributor to Pediatric Connection Magazine; [pers.] I strive to enjoy and understand all the things in which I am interested and also to set this example for my children; [a.] Chesterfield, VA

KRISEL, DARLENE
[b.] May 8, 1957, Detroit, MI; [p.] Dorothy Jean Fluker; [m.] John Boyd Krisel, Jr, May 9, 1981; [ch.] John Boyd III, Julia Brianne; [ed.] Redford High School, Univ of Detroit, Wayne State Univ, Cam- bridge Business School; [occ.] Temporary Adminis- trative Assistant for WDIV Channel 4; [hon.] Kappa Kitten Cum Laude graduate from Cambridge Busi- ness School; Shorthand Award pin; [oth. writ.] Poem published in the Michigan Chronicle; [pers.] My writing reflects my moods and my outlook on life. I put my feelings into my writing. I have been influ- enced by the poems of Maya Angelou. I someday hope to be as wonderful as she is; [a.] Oak Park, MI

KROCK, WILLIAM A.
[b.] March 13, 1943, Chicago, IL; [p.] William, Florence; [ch.] Anthony, Katherine, Kristina; [ed.] Lakeview H.S., Roosevelt University, University of Hawaii; [occ.] Sales, Writing Business Name: Dreamaker; [memb.] President, Parents without part- ners, local chapter #150; [oth. writ.] Never been published, although I have a wealth of poems and stories I'm currently Cataloging.; [pers.] This poem

is dedicated to the loving memories gifted to me by Mele. May she never stop giving.; [a.] Honolulu, HI

KROLICK, JAMIE KYLE
[Pen.] Jamie Kyle; [b.] November 26, 1963, Long Beach, NY; [p.] Stanley & Barbara Krolick; [m.] Eugene F. McGillian, June 5, 1994; [ch.] none; [ed.] SUNY at Ston Brook; [occ.] Writer, Editor, Children's Television Workshop; [oth. writ.] Several children's books, plays, short stories, and essays in children's publications (published by Children's Television Workshop); [pers.] Writing is my favorite vice and my true love.; [a.] Bayside, NY

KROMER, DELLA HARRISON
[b.] April 10, 1925, Waite Water, KS; [p.] Mabel Miller, Ray Harrison; [m.] Kermit Kromer, June 17, 1945; [ch.] Nova Joelene Alderfer and Lreda Dianne Horutz; [ed.] High School, Newton Kansas and Valley Center Kansas, Wilton Cake Decorating School, Potstown, PA; [occ.] Retired; [memb.] Ladies Auxilary, Polk Township Fire Co., volunteer; [hon.] Many hand crafted articles, Westend Fair, Gilbert, PA, Wedding Cakes, Potstown, PA, Special Ocasion cakes, Potstown, PA; [oth. writ.] Big Sister, to Nona, to Loreda, Off Where Has The Time Gone? to virgina, Autumn, Lee, all published in National Library of Poetry Books; [pers.] I enjoy writing poetry mostly about our family because next to God, family is the most important thing in the world to me. I also have been tracing our family history for 18 years. I love finding out about our ancestors.; [a.] Kunkletown, Pa

KRUPCHECK III, JOHN I
[b.] June 17, 1967, Boston, MA; [p.] John & Patricia Krupcheck; [m.] Engaged to Sheila Treanor; [ed.] Christopher Columbus H.S., Bunker Hill College; [occ.] Computer Operator; [oth. writ.] Several poems published in school literary magazine. One poem published in an anthology to be out spring 94'.; [pers.] I've learned over the years to write from my heart and soul. Heart and soul is what touches people.; [a.] Charlestown, MA

KRZYZANIAK, CRYSTAL LYNN
[b.] March 30, 1980, Wayne, MI; [p.] Gregory and Michelle Cooper; [ed.] Student at John Marshall Junior High School; [hon.] Student of the Month November/December 93. Honor Roll student; [pers.] This poem is dedicated to my grandfather who died March 19, 1992, and also to my grandmother, who he loved so much; [a.] Inkster, MI

KUBIAK, TERRI JEANNETTE
[Pen.] T. J. Kubiak; [b.] June 1, 1974, Indiana; [p.] Sherry Kubiak; [ed.] Fort Zum Walt North High, St. Charles Community College; [occ.] Part-time Stu- dent; [pers.] My writings show the deep emotions about how troubled I can be about certain subjects. They do not emphasize enough on how troubled one can be and still my writings touch me. I mainly keep my writings to myself, and still I write in silence; [a.] O'Fallon, MO

KUBOSH, FELIX MICHAEL
[Pen.] Mike Kubosh; [b.] February 27, 1951, New Gulf, TX; [p.] Felix Kubosh, Francis Kubosh; [ch.] Shelley Gibson, Scott Kubosh, Chris Kubosh; [ed.] South Park High School, International Bible Inst and Seminary, Orlando, FL, Masters of Theology; [occ.] Writer, lecturer; [memb.] Lion's Club International FCF - Frontiersmen Camping Fraternity, National Republican Party, Boy Scouts of America; [hon.] Magnum Cum Laude graduate, Honors College Gradu- ate Balford Award of Excellence in writing, South Park High School Magnum Cum Laude Grad; [oth. writ.] Books: Crime Awareness Tips, The Best of Mike Funny and Serious, Lonliness the Test of Leadership; [pers.] I fell in love with life and every- thing changed. Now I know what happens really is

and I share it everyday with those about me; [a.] Pledger, TX

KUHN, JULIA KAREN
[Pen.] Julie K. Kuhn; [b.] September 26, 1958; [p.] Bert Friesen, Hilda Friesen; [m.] Douglas Kuhn, February 06, 1982; [ch.] William Corey Joseph Kuhn, Carrie Rae Kuhn; [occ.] Family Child Care Provider, Mother, and Farm Wife; [memb.] Manitoba Child Care Assoc. Family Day Day Care Association of Manitoba, Canadian Children's Book Centre; [oth. writ.] Articles for the Manitoba Child Care Assoc and Family Day Care Assoc, Newsletter; [pers.] I try to write from the heart; [a.] Woodside, Manitoba

KURIMSKI, LYNN D.
[Pen.] Lynn Duggan; [b.] September 3, 1973, Toronto; [p.] Gertrud Koche Ray Duggan; [ch.] Christopher Kurimski 3 1/2, Amber Laury 3 weeks; [ed.] Last grade completed 8; [occ.] Housemother; [pers.] My poem was written from my heart, it belongs to Amber's father James Laury, Who I loved, lost and now am loving once again.; [a.] Ottawa, Ontario

KUZMA, ANNIE
[Pen.] Annie McLeod Kuzma; [p.] Scotland; [p.] John and Margaret McLeod; [m.] Husband deceased; [ed.] Finished higher grade; [pers.] I had a small book of poetry published, which could not have been accomplished except for a dear friend, Lucy. Who encouraged me to push ahead; [a.] Tinley Park, IL

KWISSA, TRACY
[Pen.] T.A. Kwissa; [b.] July 8, 1918, Ottawa, Ont; [p.] Richard and Judy Kwissa; [p.] Richard and Judy Kwissa; [ch.] Emily Rose Kwissa (1 yr old); [ed.] Certificate of Legal Assistant completed at Algonquin college, April 1994; [memb.] Humane Society, World Wildlife Federation, President (1989-1990) and member of Ontario Students Against Impaired Driving (OSAID) Literacy For The World Member (1990); [hon.] Public Speaking, Contestant in Miss Carleton Place Pageant 1990. Head writer and Editor of Paw Print (High School Newspaper) President of OSAID; [oth. writ.] I have written many, many poems and three children's books, but none have been published articles published in Carleton Place H.S. Newspaper (Paw Print); [pers.] All I want out of life is to be happy. My poems help me to reflect on my life. Through my writing I hope to keep my perspective and always remember that only I can ensure my own happiness; [a.] Carleton Place, Ontario, Canada

LA'AU, LESLEY N.
[b.] February 11, 1980, Hilo, HI; [p.] Jack E. & Lilson La'au; [ed.] Student, Waimea Elementary & Intermediate School; [memb.] Three years Nippon Kokusai Karate Cntr. Academic & Scholastic Honor Roll, Student Council Committee; [hon.] Scholastic & Academic Editors' Choice for "Save Our Planet" poem in Whisper in the Wind Book.; [oth. writ.] Save Our Planet, Shadows of Darkness, Shadows of the Forest, numerous others submitted to National Library.; [pers.] Writing comes naturally to me, just like people writing letters, I put words on paper and they become poetry; [a.] Kamuela, HI

LACY, DAVID A.
[b.] May 18, 1968, Norristown, PA; [p.] Barbara and Joe Stevens and Donald Lacy; [ed.] Norristown High, Armory School of Arts; [occ.] Operations manager, Browns Furn and Design, Independent Artist; [pers.] Personal inspiration come from my fiancee; Allison, without her poetry would be useless to me...; [a.] Lake Worth, FL

LACY-WILLIAMS, SHERYL D.
[Pen.] Denice Givens; [b.] June 24, 1957, Little Rock, AR; [p.] Mary Givens and Willie Givens; [m.] George E. Williams, October 12, 1991; [ch.] Kim-berly Crishoe and Shabre Tonei Lacy; [ed.] Tillar High School and Univ of Arkansas at Little Rock; [occ.] Secretary/Substitute teacher, Prince George's County Schools; [memb.] Phi Beta Lambda, Marlton PTA and Full Gospel AME Zion, [oth. writ.] Other poems and short stories not published just shared with close friends; [pers.] I write to express my personal experiences and my love for God and his blessings; [a.] Upper Marlboro, MD

LAGIRS, PETER
[b.] 20th Century, Earth; [p.] Father & Mother; [m.] Absolute being, Incidental; [ch.] Absolute Creations; [ed.] The procss of Living; [occ.] Living in Languages and other; [memb.] Human Race; [hon.] Chosen for love.; [oth. writ.] Guest Editorialist for local newspaper, one poem previously published, many written; [pers.] Poetry is the connection between truth and infinity.; [a.] Napernur, IL

LAIRSON, TINA MARIE
[Pen.] Tina Lairson; [b.] July 2, 1965, General Hos,; [p.] Raymond and Ernestine Lairson; [m.] Ronnie Williams, February 14, 1993; [ch.] Gustavo Robio, Anthony Velez, Shureue Trevino; [ed.] Myler St Elem, LaPuente High School; [occ.] Street Maiuance Worker; [oth. writ.] I have other poems I've written, but none of them have been published.

LAKE, VANESSA
[b.] August 13, 1971, Knoxville, TN; [p.] Paul Johnson, Donna Johnson; [ch.] Jazmon Aurora; [ed.] Holston High, Rice College; [pers.] My inspiration came from my having to choose between the birth of my child or saving my marriage.

LALAGA, ANNA
[b.] Salamis ; [p.] Pamagiotis and Chatherine Papassotiriou; [m.] George; [ch.] A daughter, Mika (she is a lawyer); [ed.] Music, painting, accountancy; [memb.] Civilized Centre of my municipality. Soloist in our (church) choir. International Society of Greek Writers; [hon.] I have got some; [oth. writ.] I write poems. I also keep the main articles in our local newspaper and in several literary magazines; [pers.] Contributing to the civilized development in my town; [a.] Salamis, Greece

LALOR, ELIZABETH
[b.] July 21, 1929, Brooklyn, NY; [p.] Herman and Adelheid Poelker; [m.] Richard Lalor, April 11, 1971 (dec. 4/12/93); [ch.] Bruce, Robert; [ed.] M.S. Fordham Univ.; [occ.] Retired Math Teacher, Adm. Freeport Public Schools, nY; [hon.] #M Impact Teacher, 1967; [oth. writ.] Mathematics: Back to Basis (Mathematical Alternatives, Inc. NY 1978); [pers.] An avid reader, I am deeply influenced by current cosmic awareness and spiritual reawakening. Each of us can be a power for good in the age of the spirit.; [a.] Jupiter, FL

LANDGREBE, DANIEL M.
[b.] October 22, 1977, Somers, NY; [p.] Deborah and Donald Landgrebe; [ch.] 1 Brother, 1 Sister; [ed.] High school sophomore, John Jay HS, Cross River, NY; [occ.] High school student; [memb.] Boy scouts, Royal Rangers; [hon.] Honor student; [oth. writ.] Poems and short stories; [a.] Yorktown Hgts, NY

LANDPHERE, DEB
[b.] July 14, 1954; [ch.] Jennifer and Katie; [ed.] Moorhead State Univ, Moorhead, MN; [a.] Fargo, ND

LANGHAM, NORMA
[Pen.] Noel; [p.] Alfred S. and Mary Edith Langham; [ed.] Ohio State Uiv, BSC, Pasadena Playhouse, BTA, Stanford Univ, MA; [occ.] Professor Emeritus Theatre, California Univ of PA, Playwrite, composer, poet, inventor, play producer, public speaker; [memb.] Dramatist League; Mensa; Internation Platform Assoc; Amer Assoc Univ Women; DA* Presbyterian Church (Elder) Calif PA Communi and Church Choirs; [hon.] Alpha Psi Omega; Om cron, Nu; AAUW Calif PA, Outstanding Woma* Freedom Foundations award for play, DAR Nat'l ar PA awards for historic plays, Calif Univ of P. Alumni Award for Service, PA Bicentennial Commi sion Award, Calif Univ of PA distinguished facul* award; 1993 International Platform Assoc Poetr Award. Who's Who in the East; In the World; I Education; and of American Women; [oth. writ. Numerous play, produced; poetry published; musi performed; text "Public Speaking: Science of the Ar play published "Magic in the Sky"; [pers.] I work i* service to God and thus my pen name, Noel, take* from the initials of my name; [a.] California, PA

LANKENAU, ANITA
[Pen.] Mary Anita Byrne; [b.] May 4, 1919, Cincinnati, OH; [p.] Thomas J. and Anna Byrne; [m.* Richard F. Lankenau, July 24, 1939; [ch.] Five; [ed. Notre Dame Academy Graduate 2 yrs college, Home courses pertaining to writing; [hon.] Golden Poe* Award; [oth. writ.] Obstinate Embryo, an autobiography; [pers.] All things work together for good for him who trusts in God; [a.] Dayton, OH

LAPOLT, EDA
[b.] March 11, 1956, Monticello; [p.] Norman and Mary Pittuluga; [m.] Howard LaPolt, September 4, 1982; [ed.] Monticello High School, Orange Co. Community College; [occ.] Purchasing/Inventory Control; [hon.] Editor's Choice Award, The National Library of Poetry; [oth. writ.] "An Angel Named Hovt"; [pers.] To Mom & Vivian, your love is my inspiration. To David Fulkenmeyer and to Juliet, two special friends who have helped me get this far.

LATTERELL, DATHAN
[Pen.] Goob; [b.] January 6, 1975, Bemidii, MN; [p.] Daryl Latterell, Sally Latterell; [ed.] Kelliher High, Hennepin Technical College, St Cloud State Univ; [occ.] Student; [memb.] YMCA; [hon.] Who's Who Among American High School Students. "A" Honor Roll; [pers.] I think the late Cliff Burton stated it best, "To Live Is To Die." My quote is not as great, but..., "If life is the beginning to some, why is it the end to others"; [a.] St Cloud, MN

LAUENBORG, MARGARET
[b.] July 4, 1956, Sweden; Date of Engagement: March 16, 1994; [ed.] High School, although I plan to return and get my degree in writing and english; [occ.] Secretary for a dozen years; [pers.] I have been gifted with the ability to write for others and with the capacity to be a conduit of love. It is a pleasure to accept this responsibility; [a.] San Jose, CA

LAUZON, MARCEL
[Pen.] Denis Roson; [b.] February 1937, Hull, PQ; [p.] Alred Lauzon/Victoria Corneau; [m.] Therese Dupuis, July 13, 1963; [ch.] 3; [ed.] High school; [occ.] Registered Nursing Asst, Ontario.

LAWRYNIW, KELLY
[b.] August 11, 1979, Timmins, Canada; [p.] Orest Lawryniw; [ed.] Up to grade eight, now in grade 9; [occ.] Student; [hon.] Honor roll, gr 8; [oth. writ.] Poems published in local newspaper; [pers.] "I believe that all authors must have a great amount of patience in order to create such interesting works of art"; [a.] Timmins, Ont, Canada

LAZAN, TRISHA
[b.] April 1, 1968, Erie, PA; [p.] Jim and Penny Henderson; [m.] Ronald Lazon, March 7, 1992; [ed.] Northwestern High; Albion, PA - graduated 1986; [occ.] Dental receptionist O'Leary Dental Group; Girard, PA; [a.] East Springfield, PA

LAZARUS, ARTHUR
[b.] March 10, 1926, Wheeling, WV; [p.] Fannie Lazarus and Nathan Lazarus; [m.] June Lazarus, June 12, 1949; [ch.] Mark Alan Lazarus, Robyn Sue Lazarus; [ed.] B.S., Roosevelt Univ; [occ.] Direct Mail Sales Promotion Salesman; [memb.] American Legion, Couples Club; [hon.] Two Golden Poet's Awards. Military: Bronze Star Medal, Purple Heart Medal, Combat Infantry Badge, Distinguished Unit Badge, and five other various service awards; [oth. writ.] "Camelot", published in great poems of the Western World, Volume II; [pers.] Word's crafted to perfection can express those thoughts I would be too embarrassed to put into words; [a.] Glenview, IL

LAZORE, NOAH A.
[b.] July 22, 1959, Cornwall, Ontario; [p.] John and Louise Lazore; Fiancee: Sofie "Dell" Publico; [ed.] Osbourn High, Ulster County Community College, Suny at New Paltz; [occ.] Counselor; [memb.] Mystic Warrior Society for the Mohawk Nation at Akwesasne; [hon.] Graduated with distinction twice at UCCC and once Suny At New Paltz; Certificate of Academic Achievement for Scholastic Excellence and Extraordinary dedication to self-improvement; scholarship awards by the Native American Indian Education Unit and the Akwesasne Mohawk Board of Education; [oth. writ.] Articles for the Indian Times newspaper; [pers.] I owe everything to my beautiful and wonderful parents. Especially my father who has been my greatest inspiration in my strive for excellence and self-improvement and everyone in my family who have been loyal; [a.] Akwesasne, NY

LEAL, CARMEN
[b.] October 9, 1954, Houston; [p.] Mr. and Mrs. Andrew H. Garcia; [m.] Raul Leal, April 21, 1979; [ch.] Gracy Leal, 14 yrs; [ed.] Douglas Mac Arthur High, Sam Houston State University, Huntsville, TX, Received my B.A.T. 4 yr. degree.; [occ.] Elementary Teacher 11 yrs. as Bilingual Elem. Teacher; [memb.] National Association for Bilingual Education, P.T.A. Parents Teacher's Association; [hon.] 5 yr. Teaching Pin and 10 yr. Teaching Pin from Aldine Independent School District; [oth. writ.] "Sin Ti" (Without You), "Just Like Her," "Mother, If I Could," "The Time Has Come", "Mi Madrecita" (My Mom); [pers.] Listen and trust your heart for it has a lot to say. [a.] Houston, TX

LEAR, JONATHAN D.
[b.] May 12, 1973, Tokyo, Japan; [p.] Mr. and Mrs. Michael D. Lear; [occ.] United States Air Force Stationed at MacDill AFB, FL; [oth. writ.] I have a small compilation of poems titled "Poetry Four the Mind"; [pers.] I have greatly been influenced by the recent out break of coffee houses around the nation. My inspiration is an author known as Max Blagg.; [a.] MacDill AFB, FL

LeBLANC, BERNADETTE
[Pen.] Bernadette; [b.] River Rouge, MI; [ch.] Ten; [ed.] Our Lady of Lourdes High, Henry Ford Community College, Wayne County Community College, Wayne County Community College, Wayne State Univ; [occ.] Retired, Secretary/Office Manager; [memb.] Detroit Inst of Arts, Volunteer Committee, 14 years, recently joined Speakers Bureau, Detroit Inst of Arts, includes original poetry in presentations. Member Writer's Group, Hidden Pond Manor; [hon.] Editor's Choice Award, National Library of Poetry, two poems published in Cat Tales Newsletter; [oth. writ.] Work in progress a book length collection of poetry; [a.] Ypsilanti, MI

LeBRUN, KELLY
[b.] March 30, 1980, Shawville; [p.] Don and Elizabeth LeBrun; [ed.] High School, grade 8; [occ.] Student; [oth. writ.] "Decisions" year book. "Finally my Destiny" Pontiac Journal. (newspaper) "Deadly

Silence" creative writing book (high school); [a.] Shawville, Quebec, Canada

LeCORCHICK, NELDA
[Pen.] Nelda LeCorchick; [b.] September 30, 1925, Merna, NE; [p.] Jennie and Murray Bailey; [m.] Edwin, September 10, 1946; [ch.] Charles Joseph, Jenny Lou; [ed.] K-12, 1 yr college; [occ.] Housewife; [memb.] Optimist Club Colo Retired Teachers Organization; [hon.] Valedictorian High School, certificate for my work with cancer fund. (Section Chairman); [oth. writ.] Book of my life - "My Little House on the Prairie". Short story - God's Littlest Christmas Angel; [pers.] I was the sixth child in a family of eight. My mother died when I was 12. I had the best and braviest daddy in the whole world; [a.] Aurora, CO

LEDBETTER, CRYSTAL
[b.] September 21, 1978, Amarillo, TX; [p.] Elaine Hill and J.D. Ledbetter; [ed.] Elementary -- 9th grade; so far; [occ.] High school student; [hon.] I've received over forty (40) awards from school for my grades, including the "American Legion School Award"; [oth. writ.] Several other poems, but none published; [pers.] My poems come from my heart and mind. I hope to go far with my poetry; [a.] Amarillo, TX

LEE, ALYSSA YOUA
[b.] April 6, 1973, Laos; [p.] Wangtoua and Phoua Lee; [ed.] Garinger high, Univ of North Carolina at Chapel Hill; [occ.] Student, Univ of NC at Chapel Hill; [memb.] Emerging Leaders of America, Womentoring Program, Asian Students Assoc, Carolina Fever, The International Society of Poetry, ISP Advisory Panel; [hon.] Induction to and lifetime member of the International Society of Poetry, Editor's Choice Award for poem "Just Another Stranger"; [oth. writ.] Several poems published in local newspapers, poem published in poetry anthology Where Dreams Begin; [pers.] I believe each day brings a chance to do better so no matter what happens, the sun will rise tomorrow; [a.] Chapel Hill, NC

LEE, MICHAEL A.
[Pen.] Jacque Fortier; [b.] January 31, 1972, San Bernarding, CA; [p.] Larry, Susan Lee; [m.] Single; [ed.] Cajon High, Cal-State University San Bernardino; [occ.] Full-Time Student; [memb.] Postal Commemorative Society, BMG, Pittsburgh, Poetry Series; [oth. writ.] Few poems published in local newspapers and three books of unpublished, unseen material of my own works; [pers.] The free moments of thought and imagination which are given to all are oh so simple. But those who know the precious value of such tools, hold fast the sendamentality of thought, and know its true infinite worth.; [a.] San Bernardino, CA

LEE, NANCY
[b.] November 11, 1951, Manitoba; [p.] Norah Lee (My inspiration) divorced; [ch.] Lorne, Derek, Wayde (whom I love dearly); [ed.] Fenelon Falls Secondary School; [occ.] Health Care Aide; [oth. writ.] Writing for birthday's, weddings, showers, etc; [pers.] I believe one should be who they are, for what they are, not what society wants them to be. I would like to thank my mother for standing by me; [a.] Ontario, Canada

LEE, SAMANTHA
[b.] April 7, 1979; [p.] John and Vicki Lee; Siblings: Joyce and Stephen Lee; [ed.] KRTCS, St Thomas Aquinas (Top student); [pers.] Interest/hobbies - horseback riding, swimming, shopping, helping others, stocks/betting on games, etc. Thank you's - I would like to thank you all my friends and family for all their influence and help. Especially, my parents and the National Library of Poetry for this golden

opportunity for this publication to be possible. Thank-you.

LEFEBVRE, MARY ANN
[b.] June 29, 1954, Methuen, MA; [p.] Stephen and Josephine Catalano; [m.] James Lefebvre, June 30, 1974; [ch.] Christopher, Charise, David, Stephen Lefebvre; [ed.] Tenney High School, Methuen MA, LaBarron Hairdressing Academy, New Life Bible Inst; [occ.] Mother, home school teacher, and wife, poet; [memb.] New Life Christian Assembly, Haverhill, MA - Church; [hon.] Graduated with high honors; [pers.] I pray that my poems would be inspired by God, and that he would touch many hearts and bring many people to a saving knowledge of Jesus Christ as they read them; [a.] Methuen, MA

LEFKOWITZ, AARON MARC
[Pen.] Aaron Lefkowitz, Aaron Marc; [b.] October 13, 1971, NY; [p.] Barbara & Elliot J. Lefkowitz; [ed.] Scarsdale High School, University of Wisconsin, BS, Marketing, Management; [occ.] Management; [memb.] Alpa Epsilon Pi Fraternity; [oth. writ.] I have written over 250 poems. Numerous works are in progress, including a novel and a story for children written in verse.; [pers.] I have only been writing for a year and would someday like to see my poetry used as song lyrics.; [a.] Scarsdale, NY

LEFTWICH, SAMUEL
[b.] August 14, 1948, Dallas, TX; [p.] James & Amy Leftwich; [ed.] Southern Methodist University; [memb.] Grace Caathedral, San Francisco; [oth. writ.] Various poems written to celebrate special events, to honor special people. A lengthly work in progress about Sante Fe.; [pers.] In this "Age of Fracture" I write of the rich threads which bind us into the fabric of community and fellowship and which give us cause for celebration and renewal; [a.] San Francisco, CA

LEIDBERG, MICHAEL
[b.] September 9, 1971, Chelmsford, MA; [p.] David A.; Della E.; [ed.] U-Mass Lowell, Major: Criminal Law, Minor: Political Science, GPA: 3.5; BA degree in May '94; [occ.] Legal Intern; [hon.] Dean's List; [pers.] I enjoy poetry as a form of romantic expressionism. To me there is nothing better than a carefully crafted poem to express one's feelings, thoughts and desires; [a.] Westford, MA

LEITERMAN, ROSE
[ed.] BA - Pre-Medical - Brooklyn College, New York City; MA - Education of Exceptional Children, Brooklyn College; MA - Guidance, Counceling, Administration and Supervision, Hofstra Univ, Long Island, NY; Sixty (60) credits of University level in Education, Teaching of Reading, Arts and Crafts, Leadership; [memb.] Member of Code Enforcement Board - 3 years; From 1985 to 1990 - 5 years President of Environ Condo II Assoc; Elected 1987 as a member Democratic Executive Committee; Active incessantly in the affairs of City of Lauderhill attending Council Meetings, Speaking at Public Communications, etc; For the past two years, I have been a member of the Recycling Committee for Lauderhill, etc, etc., etc; [oth. writ.] Wrote and published 2 books of poetry; [a.] Lauderhill, FL

LEMKE, JULIE DAWN
[b.] December 1, 1973, Drayton Valley, AB, Canada; [p.] Lawrence and Donna Lemke; [ed.] High school graduate, Frank Maddock High School, Drayton Valley, Alberta, Canada; [memb.] Guider with girl guides of Canada for 2 1/2 yrs; [pers.] Thank you to English teachers Mrs. Jan Atkins (grade 11), Mr. George Matheson (grade 12) for giving me my appreciation of poetry; [a.] Drayton Valley, Alberta, Canada

LENNARD, NIKASHA SCOTT
[b.] July 30, 1976, Mobile, AL; [p.] Joycelyn and Terry Lennard; [ed.] 12 grader at Booker T. Washington High School; [occ.] Student; [memb.] Future Business Leaders of America, Future Farmers of America, Cooperative Education Program and Literary Art Guild.; [hon.] Miss Future Farmers of America; [a.] Tuskegee, AL

LENZMEIER, LOUIS
[b.] August 9, 1974, St. Cloud, MN; [p.] Mickey and Carol Lenzmeier; [ed.] Kimball Area High school, currently attending St. Cloud State University. I am an English major.; [occ.] A part-time Assistant Residental Counselor at the Mother Theresa HOme in Cold Spring, MN; [hon.] Won the Xerox Award for Excellence in Fine Arts and Humanities; [a.] Kimball, MN

LEO, ROSA
[b.] July 7, 1970; [p.] Toronto; [p.] Mr. Antimo Leo, Mrs. Santino Leo; [ed.] Bishop Marrocco, Thomas Merton CSS; [occ.] Receptionist - Univ of Toronto; [hon.] BMTM Honour Society; [oth. writ.] Moon Lit Waltz published in "Tears of Fire"; [pers.] Here's to the good friends who have brought much more than laugh lines to my life. (Liz, Guida, Glenda, Rosa, Grace, Cathy, Steve, Isabel, Mary, Jo, Jesse); [a.] Toronto, Ontario, Canada

LEON, TERESA
[b.] March 4, 1940, Valparaiso; [p.] Irma Latoja and Osvaldo Leon; [m.] Juan Gustavo Paredes, December 29, 1955; [ch.] (7) Juan G., Ana, Rosalinda, Irma, Ivan osvaldo, and Sofia. 10 grandchildren: Alex, Daniela J.J., Vanessa, Jordan, Sebastian, Delfina, Catherine Simon and Leonardo; [ed.] Finished primary school in Chile, South America. In Canada took a college english course; [occ.] Housewife; [oth. writ.] Published a poetry book named "Poesia Errante" in May 1993. Presently working in children's stories; [pers.] My inspiration, the sweetness of many of my poems are dedicated to my grandchildren. Passing on the family history and the culture from which we come from; [a.] Toronto, Ontario, Canada

LEONARD, STEVEN
[b.] March 26, 1950, San Rafael, CA; [p.] Mr and Mrs Arnold Leonard; [m.] Ariane Leonard, July 10, 1976; [ch.] Joel (14 1/2), Gabriel (13); [ed.] Nevada Union High, College of the Redwoods, UC Davis; [occ.] Graphics Artist; [memb.] Shaarei Hashamayim Congregation; [oth. writ.] Poems and songs unpublished; [pers.] I believe creativity is the nature of the creator, whose image we bear and whose spirit yearns expression. I love to write and draw, and I hope others can enjoy my work; [a.] N. Massapequa, NY

LESNIEWSKI, KARI ANN
[Pen.] Kari Ann; [b.] December 22, 1980, Woodland, CA; [p.] Joseph Lesniewski, Linda Irvine and Jerrel Irvine; [ed.] Willow Spring Elementary (K-4), Gibson Elementary (5-6th); [occ.] 7th grade student at Douglas Jr High in Woodland, CA; [memb.] LDS Church, president of Beehive Class; [hon.] Several 100% Attendance Awards for school, 1st place and 3rd place trophies for girls Powder Puff Baseball; My poem "A Nice Lady" was written about Bonnie Carr, a yard duty attendant at Gibson Elementary who is kind, caring, and easy to talk too; [a.] Woodland, CA

LESNIEWSKI, KEVIN D.
[b.] June 20, 1954, Chicago, IL; [p.] Dominic and Dorothy; [m.] Sandra Lynn; [ch.] John Kevin, Sarah Katherine; [occ.] Analyst; [memb.] United Way; [hon.] Dean's List Elgin Community College; [pers.] I write about life as if appears to me to be; [a.] Lake In The Hills, IL

LESTER, MARSHA C.
[Pen.] Marsha "Christoffel" Lester; [b.] March 2, 1948, Indpls., IN; [p.] Edward F. and Gladys M. Boswell; [m.] Gregory A. Lester, September 6, 1992; [ch.] Tiffiny N. Thompson; [memb.] Memorial Area Newcomers Club, "I'm editor of the newsletter"; [hon.] Toastmasters several awards for speaches.; [oth. writ.] "Watch for Daddy" Novel seeking publication; [pers.] "I wonder, do I feel, so that I may wirte, or do I write, because I feel? My pen is always guided by emotions, and emotion is always somehow freed by the pen.; [a.] Houston, TX

LEWIS, ELIZABETH M.
[Pen.] Betty Lewis. [b.] Kansas City, MO.; I moved to Baltimore where I attended Johns Hopkins Univ. I received my degree of BS there. I taught school in the public schools of Baltimore for thirty years, and have enjoyed writing poetry all of my life. I have published poems in various school and square dance magazines. I was an avid square dancer. Now I am retired to writing poetry, playing bridge, oil painting, and gardening; [a.] Baltimore, MD

LEWIS, EVELYN
[Pen.] Evelyn Vanderberg; [b.] 1927, Edmonton, Alberta; [p.] Hazel and Richard Vanderberg; [ch.] One daughter, Jody, and four grandsons, Stacy, Troy, James and Trevor; [ed.] High school and one creative writing course; [occ.] Retired; [oth. writ.] Have had poetry accepted in small publications in the US and Canada and have published four books of poetry, one of them Limerick; [pers.] I find that a word, a phrase, a joke, a political statement, an emotion are all food for poetry. I mustn't forget the Rocky Mountains. Each peak and valley hides a poem, as well; [a.] Spruce View, Alberta, Canada

LEWIS, JOY
[Pen.] Julie Lewis; [b.] July 12, 1946, Santa Monica; [p.] Joyce White and Robert Lewis; [ed.] MFA Degree - UCLA - Dept of Theatre Arts with specialization in screenwriting; [occ.] Artist and writer; [memb.] Writer's Group of Los Angeles, SAG, AFTRA; [hon.] MFA UCLA; [oth. writ.] Screenplays, plays, and poems performed my own work on Century Cable TV in LA; [pers.] I want to express and explore my deepest feelings and communicate with others. I feel poetry is a way to go beyond everyday reality; [a.] W. LA, CA

LEWIS, MARJORIE WINCHELL
[Pen.] Marjorie W. Lewis; [b.] September 29, 1913, Phila, PA; [p.] Elsie Stearly Winchell & Samuel Dickson Winchell; [m.] Don E. Lewis, May 23, 1942; [ch.] Son, Dickson W. Lewis and three grandchildren, Christopher, Jeffrey and Paige.; [ed.] Upper Darby High School, 1930 and Palmer Business Colege 1932. Graduated as Salutatorian of Class, from Palmer.; [occ.] Retired, was former Journalist and feature writer and reporter for former Upper Darby News and Phila Bulletin; [memb.] Life-time member International Society of Poets and Member of Advisory Board. Former President of Phila. Professional Writers' Club, Active Red Cross Instructor, and former President of Upper Darby Junior Women's Republican Club, Den Mother and Sunday School teacher, Town Watch and other community activities.; [hon.] Awards of Merit for Poetry and Semifinalist at ISP Symposium in Washington, DC 1993; [oth. writ.] Features stories and even many obituaries, resulting in my poem "Death Is My By-Line" which became my first published poem with former World of Poetry in 1991 for which I received an Award of Merit.; [pers.] I urge all aspiring poets, young and old to Go For It, when one door closes, another opens. Dreams do come full circle; [a.] Havertown, PA

LEWIS, STEVEN P.
[b.] June 8, 1970, Cleveland, OH; [p.] Reese and Stella Lewis; [m.] none; [ed.] Garfield Heights High, Cleveland State University; [occ.] Correspondent, Sun Newspapers; [hon.] Dean's List; [oth. writ.] Several unpublished works of poetry, several published news articles in loca newspapers; [pers.] Poetry is written from the heart based on one's past experiences. It is the freest form of expression. There should be no rules to poetry; [a.] Garfield Heights, OH

LEWIS, SYLVIA
[b.] April 11, 1953, Sumter, SC; [p.] Lottie Lee Smith; [m.] William R. Lewis, August 16, 1985; [ch.] (3) Gavin Kyle - 22, Renee Lynn - 20, Randy Allen - 14; [ed.] High School. Reared in Baltimore, MD. Completed high school in S.C.; [occ.] Writer, songwriter. I have recently had a song published; [oth. writ.] I have several songs also poems, essays, and I am currently writing a mystery novel. Also I have had recipes published in a cookbook for charity purposes; [pers.] My writing reflects a persons positive perspective outlook to life. Inspiration is due to Edgar Allen Poe; [a.] Dillon, SC

LEWIS, WILLENE LOUISE VEAZEY
[b.] November 22, 1918, Wilmington, DE; [p.] William M., Florence, Anna Veazey; [m.] Russell Lewis, November 22, 1957; [ch.] Pamela Sharon L. Hedrick; [ed.] Certification in Fashion Illustration and Bachelor of Fine Arts in Education; Former Philadelphia Museum School of Art, PA; Hugh Breckenridge Summer School of Art, Gloucester, MA; Eliot O'Hara Water Color School, Goose Rocks Beach me; [occ.] Retired, but do freelance art; [memb.] NARFE (National Assoc of Retired Federal Employees); First Presbyterian Church in Winchester, VA; Life Member of Rehoboth Art League, Rehoboth Beach, DE since its inception (mid 1930's); [hon.] In art: 1st and 2nd prize for posters when sliced bread was introduced, 1930; Safety Poster contest in mid-1930's -both in Wilmington, DE; As a technical illustrator, "First in Illustrations in Society of Federal Artists and Designers in mid 1960's (1964) (Naval Ordinance laboratory); [oth. writ.] Feature story articles for inhouse organ at old naval ordnance laboratory, White Oak, Silver Spring, MD; Several "Letters to the Editor" published in "The Winchester Star"; [pers.] Committed to maintaining a high standard of quality, and an eternal student in my quest for truth, I believe in the essential goodness of man; [a.] Winchester, VA

LIBBY, BRIGITTE B.
[b.] April 24, 1982, Boston; [p.] Beryl Benacerraf and Peter Libby; [ed.] Currenly in 6th grade; [occ.] student at the Winsor School; [oth. writ.] many poems and short stories; [pers.] I am an 11 year old who loves nature and aspires to be a writer.; [a.] Boston, MA

LIEBLING, LESLIE ILENE
[b.] April 15, 1974, Nassau County; [p.] Richard and Brenda Liebling; [ed.] Sophomore at Suny Genesco High School, 1988-1992, John F. Kennedy H.S.; [occ.] Student; [hon.] Long Island Teen Talent winner 1991 Piano; Spanish Honor Society; English Award - POB JFK High School; Humanities and Social Services Award from Xerox Corporation; Dean's List of Suny Genesco; [oth. writ.] Several poems published in high school journal; [a.] Plainview, NY

LIMANDRI, EMANUELA
[b.] May 28, 1970, Queens, NY; [pers.] Self-worth is the most important lesson an individual can learn. I would like to thank all of my friends, Michael Moorcock, M. Mascitti, and most importantly, my mother, Francesca Calabro.; [a.] Long Island City, NY

LINCOLN, VERNUS JOHNSON
Pen.] Vernus Christine Lincoln; [b.] Idaho; [ch.]
Dianja Lincoln Andrus, Lawrence Dale Lincoln;
ed.] High School Graduate with extensive post gradu-
ate studies, musical training; [hon.] Honorary Life
Membership in the National Congress of Parent-
Teachers Assoc. for service in the field of child
welfare.; [oth. writ.] Lyrics for several successfull
published songs.; [pers.] Have authored two books of
poetry; [a.] Torrance, CA

LINDSEY, SHARON E.
[b.] March 19, 1958, Turlock, CA; [p.] Bill and Helen
Daniel; [m.] Kenneth J. Lindsey, November 22,
1986; [ch.] Caroline and Steven Corbin, Kevin Lindsey;
[ed.] Turlock High 1976 grad, Modesto Jr College
grad 1984 in Dental Assisting; [occ.] US Postal
Service letter carrier; [memb.] VFW Ladies Aux No.
5059, National Assoc of Letter Carriers Union Local
213; [hon.] Graduated with honors MJC; [pers.]
Good things can be found even in the worst of life's
situations, it just depends on one's attitude toward life;
[a.] Turlock, CA

LINGARD, JO-ANNE C.
[Pen.] Lady J.; [b.] Port Hope, Ontario; [ch.] Shane
Matthew, Christopher Thomas; [ed.] AB Recreation
Administration Diploma, Working on Diploma in
Travel and Tourism; [occ.] Play School Coordinator;
[oth. writ.] Poem published in Toronto newspaper;
[pers.] Travel, education, and the courage to follow
your dreams; However long it takes; Makes the
experiences along the way worth while. I write from
the heart of experience; [a.] Castor, AB, Canada

LINGER, ROSETTA
[Pen.] Rosetta H. Linger; [b.] April 21, 1959,
Buckhannon; [p.] Wesley J. and Dessie L. Tenney;
[m.] Gary N. Linger, June 2, 1975; [ch.] Wendy
Dawn Linger, Sammie Neil Linger, Misty Rose
Linger, Stormy Allen Linger; [ed.] Finished 10th
grade; [occ.] Housewife - writer - poet; [memb.]
International Society of Poets, North American Fish-
ing Club; [hon.] Editor's Choice Award, The Na-
tional Library of Poetry for The Flame of Eternal
Love; [oth. writ.] The Flame of Eternal Love, Look-
ing at the World Through the Eyes of a Child; [pers.]
Just a rag muffin is my story of Cinderella of the 90's.
This is for my daughters Wendy and Misty; [a.]
Buckhannon, WV

LING-KWAN, LOUISE LUK
[Pen.] Green Apple; [b.] Hong Kong; [p.] Mr. Luk
Kai-Sang (deceased), Madam Kan Lau-Kiu; [m.] Mr.
Tony Chan; [ch.] (1 girl 2 1/2 yrs old) Chan Tak-Yin;
[ed.] Graduate from the Faculty of Arts, the Univ of
Hong Kong with BA (Hons) Degree in 1985, Major
in English studies and minor in English and European
History; [occ.] Exhibition Co-ordinator Hong Kong
Productivity History; [memb.] Lady Ho Tung Gradu-
ates' Assoc (Univ of Hong Kong); [hon.] For thought.
And hope you as my readers will enjoy reading my
writing and welcome to hear your comments, BA
(hons) 1985; [oth. writ.] Writings of poetry, prose and
short stories in Univ days; [pers.] I am a Chinese born
in Hong Kong. With an Asian background in Hong
Kong in which the East meets West, there are plenty
of interesting topics and food for writing. Writing is
one of my greatest life aspirations and I hope to share
my joy of writings to other people worldwide and
across national boundaries. As the 1997 question is
getting more close to Hong Kong, I believe I have
more food.

LIPINSKY, JASON
[b.] October 6, 1975, Montreal, Canada; [p.] Richard
and Elaine Lipinsky; [occ.] Student; [oth. writ.] This
is the first writing I have submitted to a contest or
publisher.; [pers.] Each poem I write is a pice of
myself. If you understand my poetry, you know me

better than even I do. I thank Greg Gaffin for being
an inspiration.; [a.] Algonquin, IL

LIPSON, MICHAEL
[b.] December 10, 1978, Royal Oak, MI; [p.] Lawrence
Lipson and Doreen Berg; [m.] Music, 1989; [ch.]
Twins: A Flat and G Sharp, Fermata on F; [ed.]
Farmington Harrison High School; [occ.] High school
student; I applied at a Dunkin' Donuts where I'd be
serving…um, doughnuts!!!!!; [memb.] SADD, Jun-
ior Achievement, Marching Band, Jazz Band,
Synmphony Band, etc, Student Council, anything
else to keep me occupied: I play tenor sax/bass
clarinet, soprano/contrabass clarinet; [hon.] Part of
1993 Flight III state champion marching band, presi-
dent of my Junior Achievement company (SLAMM
Ent) vice-president of Freshman Board, student Round
Table treasurer of SADD, 1st place in county spelling
bee…the list goes on and on…; [oth. writ.] Movie
Critiques for local newspapers, articles for school
newspaper, poems/stories for school anthologies;
[pers.] "Writing is a freedom - freedom from one's
cares, one's worries. Words can take you to a magical
world. I've been there and I've wrote about it…"; [a.]
Farmington Hills, MI

LISTER, JESSICA ANN
[b.] December 12, 1976, Baltimore, MD; [p.] Charles
Francis Lister, Barbara Ann Lister; [ed.] North Carroll
High, incoming college freshman (fall of 94-95) at
Carroll Community College; [occ.] Aspiring to be a
writer/child psychologist; [memb.] American Legion
Auxiliary; [oth. writ.] Several other poems, short
stories and continuous work on my first book; [pers.]
I strive to achieve recognition through my writings as
well as personal success; mom, dad, thanks for always
being supportive of me; [a.] Manchester, MD

LITTLE, JAMES G.
[b.] November 10, 1965, Mt. Kisco, NY; [p.] Darrel
J. Little and Frnces Little; [ed.] S.U.N.Y. Potsdam,
PACE University, Santa Monica College, UCLA
Extension; [occ.] Concierge, Peninsula Hotel Beverly
Hills; [memb.] Los Angeles Comcierge Association,
National Notary Association; [pers.] My writing tries
to reflect the feelings of confusion and uncertainty
faced by a generation that grew up in a world of weak
morality. Ruled by the political turmil and fashion
fads of the seventies, the treat of nuclear war and
financial greed of the eighties, and the increasing
social problems and fear of intimacy spurred by the
A.I.D.S. crisis of the nineties, I write for my peers,
the generation of over achievers without a cause.; [a.]
Santa Monica, CA

LITTLEJOHN, JAMES E.
[b.] June 28, 1980, Pasadena, CA; [p.] Donna &
Robert Littlejohn; [ed.] I am in the 8th grade at Our
Lady of the Assumption School in claremont deciding
were to go to high school; [occ.] Student; [memb.] I
am interested in the stock market and buy ans sell
stock occasion. I am an avid comid book collector and
trader. I was a member of the championship footbal
team of my school. I enjoy sports very much. I would
like to become a scientist.; [hon.] I have been awarded
an "Americanism in Action" award and many aca-
demic honors but this is my first award of this
magnitude; [oth. writ.] I've written many things like
poems and short stories but this is the first I have had
submitted.; [pers.] I enjoy writing, especially poetry.
I get inspired by beautiful places, or important people.
I'd like to thank my grandpa for inspiring me and my
grandma for submitting this poem.; [a.] Claremont,
CA

LOGAN, KATHERINE
[Pen.] Kat; [b.] January 14, 1967, San Diego, CA;
[p.] Margie Best, Larry Logan; [ed.] High School;
[occ.] Car painters helper; [oth. writ.] My personal
book of poems; [pers.] Instead of trying to impress

others, try impressing yourself; [a.] Havelock, NC

LOJAS, FRANCISZEK
[Pen.] Kosla; [b.] October 30, 1946, Poronin, Po-
land; [p.] Franciszek Ludwina; [m.] Kazimiera Lapa,
July 11, 1971; [ch.] Dariusz, Franciszek; [ed.] 7 -
grades, Gramma School - Poland; [occ.] Wood Carver;
[memb.] Polish Highlanders Aliance in America and
in Poland, Stowarzysz Enie Tworcow Ludowych W
Lublinie - Poland; [hon.] 10 Diplomas for Best Poems
in different contests, 24 awards for participating in
contests in a few countries; [oth. writ.] Three short
poem books. Various poems were published in 20
newspapers all over the world; [pers.] I love people
everywhere and I love peace and this reflects in my
work; [a.] Chicago, IL

LOMBARDO, ALEXANDRA WIEST
[Pen.] Talia Negra; [b.] Brooklyn, NY; [p.] John
Wiest and Ligia Evanchik Wiest; [ch.] Twins, Krista
Danielle & Stefanie Nicole; [ed.] William Cullen
Bryant H.S., Long Island University (Brooklyn Cam-
pus); [occ.] Elementary School Educator; [memb.]
Association for Supervision and Curriculum Devel-
opment (ASCD), The Living Bank; [hon.] Horace
Greeley Hall of Fame Award, Ollie B. Ritchie Award;
[oth. writ.] I have also written the following poems,
but as of 1/94 none have been published (4 are
pending publication), Searching, Your Eyes, The
Sea, A Rebirth, As The Sunsets, Fear, The Might
One, Night, Spring, A Love; [pers.] Poetry written
from the heart, captures the soul.; [a.] Elwood, NY

LONG, KEANNA KAVEHI
[b.] June 16, 1978, Salt Lake City, UT; [p.] Judith
Long Settel and Mark Settell; [ed.] Completing 9th
grade at present - music student with concentration on
languages and other cultures; [occ.] Student/Ridge
Top Junior High School, Silverdale, WA; [memb.]
Church Youth Group wich concentrates on service
and self improvement; [hon.] Reflections Cert Pro-
gram, 1990, drawing award; [oth. writ.] Unpublished
novel nd numerous poems; [pers.] I believe in giving
assistance to the under priviledged and offering proper
education; [a.] Silverdale, WA

LONG, MONIQUE MARIE
[b.] February 12, 1962, Los Angeles; [p.] [pers.] icholas
& Anna Long; [ch.] Brother: Darius Long; [ed.] B.S.
Degree: Woodbury University Major, Fashion De-
sign, Minor, Business AA Degree, Mt. San Antonio
college; [occ.] Designer, Motion Picture Costumer,
Stylist; [memb.] IATSE #705, Nabet #57; [hon.]
Dean's List, Alpha Gamma Sigma; [pers.] Dream a
thousand dreams and never let them go, live a life of
Zen, of what is good and bad? Look at the world
through rose colored glasses, for only then will you
see..beyond..to the true beauty of life!; [a.] South
Pasadena, CA

LONG, TOMMY W.
[b.] July 22, 1957, Hollandale, MS; [p.] Mrs. Jamie
R. Long and the Late E. L. Long; [m.] Divorced;
[ed.] Graduate of Greenville Christian School,
Greenville, MS 1975.; [occ.] Sales Representative
Lance Inc. Charlotte, NC; [memb.] Pleasant Hill
Baptist Church, Tyler TX, Adult choir, Pleasant Hill
Baptist Church; [oth. writ.] I have written several
tribute poems in memory of my father, and in honor
of the birth of my nephew; [pers.] I wish that the
emotion I feel in each poem will be felt by each person
that reads them. I love poems and stories that are
tributes to someone who has touched other peoples
lives.; [a.] Whitehouse, TX

LONGOSKY, KATHERINE A.
[Pen.] Katy Longosky; [b.] August 9, 1984, Durham,
NC; [p.] Carl and Susan Longosky; [ed.] Derrick City
Elementary School; [occ.] Student (4th grade) at
Derrick City Elem School; [memb.] Girl Scouts of

America, Friendship Connection, St Francis of Assisi Church Choir, Derrick City Chorus and Show Choir, Peggy Johnson's jaz (dance) class; [hon.] Editor's Choice Award from National Library of Poetry: for poem "Into the Past", Bradford Creatie and Performing Arts 1993-94 winner for literature for elementary level (grades 4-6), High Honor Roll; [oth. writ.] Poem "Into the Past" published in "The Coming of Dawn", several poems, short stories, and a play which won the 1993-94 BCPAC Award for literature for elementary students; [pers.] I love to express my thoughts and feelings in poetry and I enjoy the reactions of my family and friends to my work. I'd like to dedicate my poem to the teachers at Derrick City school and to the National Wildlife Federation; [a.] Bradford, PA

LORD, STACY
[b.] April 11, 1980, Women and Infants; [p.] Donna and Steve Lord; [ed.] St Mary Academy, Bay View Academy; [occ.] Attending school; [memb.] Kenbrin Swim and Tennis Club; [hon.] Grades K-6, 2nd honors, grades 7 & 8 2nd grant science fair; [pers.] This is a tribute to my father who was killed in a bad automobile accident: I love you dad, 1994; [a.] Riverside, RI

LORETTO, CHRISTY
[b.] March 18, 1977, Upland, PA; [p.] Susan, Samuel Loretto; [ed.] Chichester High; [occ.] Part-time Kmart; [pers.] I'd like to thank my family and my creative writing teacher, Mrs. Cop, for all their support; [a.] Marcus Hook, PA

LOVING, COLLIER M.
[b.] July 7, 1924, Chicago, IL; [p.] Hugh and Ruth Loving; [m.] Kathleen R. Loving, March 2, 1981; [ch.] 7 of two marriages; [ed.] BS Retailing and Merchandising Washington Univ, St Louis, MO (1949); [occ.] Retired; [memb.] Lifetime Honorary Member, Sporting Goods Agents Assoc; Board of Directors, Hayward Golf and Tennis Club, Hayward, WI; [hon.] Bronze Star 1945. Member Eta Mu Pi, National Honorary Retailing Society. Hall of Fame, Sporting Goods Agents Assoc. 1989; [oth. writ.] Articles in newspapers Minn, Arizona, Wis. Also Sporting Goods "Dealer"; [pers.] "Retain your friends through the written word. Let your enemies settle quietly into the dust of time. Leave your mark with words...deeds are soon forgotten. Write from your heart; not your checkbook. Write the truth and have the guts to stand by your words. Respect history; [a.] Stone Lake, WI

LOWERY, HELEN LaVERNE
[Pen.] Helen Lowery; [b.] March 1, 1939, Freeport, TX; [p.] J. H. Ray, Oleta Hatchcock Ray; [m.] David L. Lowery; [m.] June 14, 1957; [ch.] LaDonna, Lisa, Jarrod, Michael; [ed.] Brazosport High, Class of 1957; [occ.] Office Work for land developer; [memb.] Friendship Baptist Church; [oth. writ.] This is the first time I have submitted any of my work; [pers.] There is a lot of thought in what I write about. I hope it gives the reader pleasure and thoughts that stay with them; [a.] Lake Jackson, TX

LOWERY, HELEN LAVERNE
[Pen.] Helen Lowery; [b.] March 1, 1939, Freeport, TX; [p.] J. H. Ray, Oleta Hathcock Ray; [m.] David L. Lowery, June 14, 1957; [ch.] LaDonna, Lisa, Jarrod, Michael; [ed.] High School Graduate, class of 1957, Brazosport High School; [occ.] Office work for Land Developing Company; [memb.] Friendship Baptist Church; [oth. writ.] This is the first time I have submitted any of my work.; [pers.] There is a lot of thought in what I write about. I hope it gives the reader pleasure and something to think about.; [a.] Lake Jackson, TX

LOWERY, JENNIFER
[b.] November 26, 1975, Berwick; [p.] Mr. & Mrs. Dennis Lowery; [ed.] I'm a senior at Berwick Area Senior High School. Plan to attend college upon graduation.; [memb.] FBLA, Cheerleading, Chorus, Yearbook, Keyette Club; [a.] Berwick, PA

LOWTHER, BRIAN SCOTT
[Pen.] (1) T-Bear; [b.] October 13, 1973, Omaha, NE; [p.] Eugene E. and Linda K. Lowther; [ed.] Daniel J. Gross High School, Wayne State College; [occ.] (1) WSC Student studying to become an Elementary Music Teacher. (2) Bakery Sales Representative, Baker's Supermarkets, Omaha, NE; [oth. writ.] Over 50 love poems written; [pers.] Thanks to all my teddy bears friends and family, especially: Lori, Mom, Dad, Rachael, Kristin, Bobby, Grandma and Grandpa, Mary Ann, Carol, Kenny, Terri and Danny's Family, Sheri and Dale, Patty and Jessica, Gary and Evie, Mark, Mike and Kris's Family, Deb and Mike, Chad M., April, Mary Jo, Shawn, John, Shaste, Chad F., Garret, S. Frans's Family, M. McGee's Family, Jim, Edith, Kenny Brian, Philip, and Julie Macklin, for continuing to illustrate an Image of Inspiration for me to follow always. All my poems come straight from the bottom of my teddy bear heart and soul; [a.] Omaha, NE

LUCIO, JUANA
[b.] March 23, 1977, Normal, IL; [p.] Lila Lucio; [m.] Single; [ed.] Junior in Olympia High Scool at the time the poem was written; [occ.] Student; [memb.] St. Joseph Hospital Volunteer Service; [oth. writ.] Several other poems, but none were ever published; [pers.] I write my poems from my own life. I wrote what I would think, what I would feel if I was ever in love with the right man.; [a.] Minier, IL

LUCY, LILEBEL
[Pen.] Lilibel Pazoureck Lucy; [b.] Yukon, OK; [p.] Mr. and Mrs. Frank J. Pazoureck; [m.] Otto Lucy (deceased); [ch.] Robert F. Lucy; [ed.] AA - MA, Central State Univ, Univ of OK; [occ.] Retired Teacher of Okla City Public Schools; [memb.] Am Heart Assoc and Cancer Society. Honorary Teacher's Sorority Kappa Kappadota American Assoc of Univ Women; [hon.] Honorary Woman of the South. Crown Heights Christian Church, Life Member - Poetry Society of Oklahoma; Sponsor - Sonnet Award of PSO (Judge of Contests); [oth. writ.] Poetry published in Oklahoma and other states. Thirteen fifteen minute radio dramas used in English Depts of Okla City Schools Poetry Award of North American Poetry Assoc; [pers.] Life is a marvelous revolution, sometimes sad but never boring. Travel around the world, etc; [a.] Oklahoma City, OK

LUKIN, BONNIE JEAN
[b.] July 20, 1942, Vallejo, CA; [p.] Francisco and Flora Pedrasa; [m.] Mario Lukin; [ch.] Jill Lynette Negrin and Joy Annette Negrin; [ed.] Santa Cruz High School, Santa Cruz County, CA; [occ.] Writer/photographer; [memb.] Santa Cruz Camera Club, Santa Cruz, CA; Watsonville Camera Club, Watsonville, CA; [hon.] Achievements: Dance instructor 25 yrs. Owned and operated the Santa Cruz Academy of Dance and Music which encompassed drama. Initiated and formed the Santa Cruz Ballet Company and it's non-profit static. Co-ordinated and presented dance productions utilizing and combining Cabrillo College music instructors, professionals, and students. Made dance instruction available for under privileged children and minority groups. Introduced dance as a therapy for emotionally disturbed and physically handicapped children; [oth. writ.] Author of "Survivals Cry For Change"; [pers.] Life Is Change invented by human beings, creating a chain reaction. Yet human nature resists change. Some fear the unknown, some are ignorant, and Greed repeats the wars of life's tragedies; [a.] Watsonville, CA

LUM, GRETCHEN YATES
[b.] June 10, 1945, Honolulu, Hawaii; [p.] Francis C Annabelle Yates; [m.] Divorced; [ch.] Jadine A Lum; [ed.] Calif College of Arts and Crafts, BF. degree; [occ.] Graphic Artist/Fine Artist and Busines Woman; [memb.] Council for the Arts for the Aldric Museum of Contemporary Art; [hon.] Merit Awar 1989, Golden Award 1990 from World of Poetry published poetry in 2 anthologies - Golden Poems o Western World and World Treasury of Golden Po ems; [oth. writ.] Completed studies in India and wrot a illustrated poetry from that year and one-half (nov recording this poetry); [pers.] Discovery is at the roo of all my poetry as is inner contemplation and sel realization; [a.] Presently returning to India

LUNA, LORETTA A.
[Pen.] Karen's Addict; [b.] May 5, 1963, Ventura CA; [p.] Jose, Luna, Jennie Luna; [ed.] Rio Mesa High grad '81, Camarillo Adult Ed, June 14, 1985. Certified Nurse Asst, Simi Valley Adult Ed, June 30, 1992; Medical Asst Cert License; [occ.] Private Nurse; [memb.] Member of the Candelaria American Indian Council; [pers.] I believe that poetry is a beautiful method by which an individual can express their deepest emotions and creativity that enters their most inner experiences and thoughts; [a.] Oxnard, CA

LUND, SHARON
[Pen.] Sharon Apgar Lund; [b.] January 8, 1941, Kalispell, MT; [p.] Harvey and Dorothy Apgar; [m.] Dale K. Lund, March 9, 1960; [ch.] Michelle Kay Bydalek, Lisa Rena Lund.

LUNSFORD, DAVID
[b.] February 21, 1972, Fort Lauderdale, FL; [p.] Larry & Barbara Lunsford; [ed.] Northeast High School; [occ.] Active Duty U.S. Navy; [memb.] Surfrider Foundation; [pers.] I believe that this earth is our last hope. I feel that we ar killing, ourselves by kinng her. I hope everyone will open their eyes to truth; [a.] Fort Lauderdale, FL

LUSTGARTEN, CAROL L.
[b.] March 20, 1956, Oceanside, NY; [p.] David and Rhea Lutgarten; [ed.] BSW, Buffalo State, MSW, Stony Brook, NY; [occ.] Social Worker (day job), writer and artist; [memb.] Charter member of the United States Holocaust Memorial Museum, member of Full Moon, improv group, Boston; [hon.] Have written and self-published 5 poetry books, co-wrote another with my business partner. I am part of the Wild Pens, Spontaneous writing on demand, appearing at Street Fairs and a bookstore once a month in Boston. [oth. writ.] Currently writing another book. I've written a few skits which were performed at an improv/sketch comedy benefit for the homeless.; [pers.] Writers are the artists of the world; [a.] Boston, MA

LUTHER, GRETCHEN AMANDA
[Pen.] G. A. Luther; [b.] January 1, 1977, Floyd Co, IN; [p.] Lynn Luther, Alan Luther; [ed.] South Central High, Oak Forest High; [memb.] Art, dance, drama, Student Council, yearbook, Spanish Clubs; [hon.] Sports, art, drama; [oth. writ.] Several poems and short stories; [pers.] Do or write what you feel, by that you can't go wrong. Know who your true friends are and don't waste your life; [a.] Crestwood, IL

LUX, JANET
[b.] May 13, 1953; [m.] yes; [ed.] George Washington High School, Arapahoc Community College; [occ.] Secretary/Graphic Designer; [oth. writ.] Published articles in company newsletters, magazine - "Wolf Hybrid Times," semi-finalist in nationwide photography contest, winner in national organization logo contest; unpublished collection of children's short stories; [pers.] The poem submitted for this

ontest was written by myself when I was 16 yrs old. have always liked this one and find it interesting that 25 year old poem still reflects my feelings now and lso the feelings of others as well; [a.] Englewood, CO

.YONHART, RICHARD THOMAS
b.] February 10, 1969, Saigon, VN; [ed.] Newspa-er Inst of America; H&R Block income tax course, lberta College, St Joseph Composite High School; occ.] Hotel casual worker and student of the NIA; memb.] The Sir Winston Churchill Squadron - Air adets, SJCH Football Volleyball and Basketball eams. Speech and Debate Club, Weight training lub; [oth. writ.] Lost Love (short story); When the ion Roars, Stryker's War, The Evil Within (unfin-shed novels); Love Offerings (poem). All unpub-ished. There are others but too many to mention; pers.] "I see story telling, be it fiction or non-fiction, s a doorway into another world, where the author or speaker, is your tour guide; provides the readers a hance to explore different realms of existence or other places."; [a.] Edmonton, Alberta, Canada

LYONS, GRETCHEN
b.] May 17, 1960, Decatur, IL; [p.] Tom and Linda Strahl; [m.] Joseph Lyons, July 9, 1988; [ch.] Jordan Elizabeth, Justin Thomas; [ed.] Jefferson HS, Lafayette Indiana; Purdue Univ BA, 1982, W. Lafayette, IN; occ.] Elementary/special education teacher; [hon.] Graduated with distinction from Purdue Univ; [pers.] I have always used poetry as a way to express my moods and feelings. I've been influenced by my loving, caring family; [a.] Tampa, FL

LYONS, VERNA R.
[b.] July 4, 1921, IA; [p.] J.D. and Lillian; [m.] Doretha M., June 15, 1947; [ch.] Richard A. and Jolee; [ed.] Strawberry Pt. High School, several correspondence courses; [occ.] Retired; [memb.] American Legion, Strawberry Point Lions, Masonic Lodge, Elkahr Shrine; [hon.] Three Term Mayor of Strawberry Point, IA; [oth. writ.] Several poems published in local newspapers; [pers.] I enjoy writing poetry for the benefit of others to enjoy. To me poems should have a story to tell as well as a rhythm when they are read.; [a.] Strawberry Point, IA

MACALUSO, PETE
[b.] December 17, 1967, Brookhaven, NY; [p.] Anthony and Karen Macaluso; [ed.] BSBA Appala-chian State Univ, Boone, NC. Westhampton Beach HS, Westhampton Beach, NY; [occ.] Junk bond traders asst, Merrill Lynch, NYC; [memb.] New York Sportfishing Federation, Cooperative Shark Tagging Program Volunteer, Greenpeace, American Littoral Society; [hon.] Outstanding Leadership Award - ASU Club Football 1990, Outstanding Contribution Award - ASU Club Football 1989, 1990, Letter of Commendation from ASU Dept of Recreation, 1991, 1993. Editor's Choice Award by National Library of Poetry; [oth. writ.] Poems "Los Angeles" published in Coming of Dawn, "Augustina" published in Dust-ing Off Dreams; [pers.] I am influenced by life around me from daily reflection, CNN, Newsweek, MTV, adolescence and moodswings to such greats as Henry Miller, Voltaire, Blake, Jim Morrison, Kerouac, Dr. Hunter S. Thompson, Dorothy Parker, Cousteau, Rimband and Carl Sagan. My writing encompasses travel, adventure and the grace and disgrace of the human condition; [a.] East Moriches, NY

MACANGO, LORI
[b.] August 21, 1978, Glen Cove, NY; [p.] Sue and Dennis MaCanyo; [ed.] Saint Anthony's High School; [occ.] Student; [pers.] Time spent in ignorance is time wasted.; [a.] Seaford, NY

MACDONALD, ELIZABETH
[b.] February 17, 1934, Djakarta, Indonesia; [p.] Dr. and Mrs. Hugo Corrie; [m.] Hugh MacDonald, May

4, 1990; [ch.] Previous marriage, Johanna Arianne, Audrey, Steven, Maarten; [ed.] High School Hol-land; [occ.] Retired Shopkeeper; [pers.] This poem was written at a period in my life. When I recommitted my life to God. As a reborn Christian my whole life style changed and with it came a freedom I never had known before.; [a.] Tatea Labe, B.C.

MACKENZIE, NANCY
[b.] July 14, 1953, Brooklyn, NY; [p.] Henry F. and Clare M. Gioranelli; [m.] Robert L. Mackenzie, November 27, 1982; [ch.] (son) Brian Thomas Lauch (previous marriage); [ed.] New York Inst of Technol-ogy, BS in Accounting; [occ.] Vice President and Director of Internal Audit for Roslyn Savings Bank; [memb.] The Inst of Internal Auditors; [hon.] Dean's List, graduated Magna Cum Laude; [oth. writ.] As editor in chief of my high school newspaper, I initiated and contributed to a literary supplement called "Sweet Dreams and Flying Machines"; [pers.] This, my first published work, is dedicated to my father, who taught me to respect the written word, and to my mother, who cherished her daughte's poems; [a.] East Norwich, NY

MACNEIL, CHERYL
[b.] June 1, 1947, Schenectady, NY; [p.] George & Myrtle Ives; [m.] Randall MacNeil, July 8, 1967; [ch.] Wndy MacNeil Carpenter, Eric Todd MacNeil; [ed.] Shenendehawa Centra School, Schenectady County Community College, SUNY Empire State College; [occ.] Public Relations Consultant; [memb.] Soroptimist International of Schenectady, NAFE Na-tional Association of Female Executives, Scotia United Methodist Church, Memorial Chairperson; [hon.] Who's Who American Junior Colleges, Scotia-Glenville, PTA Founders Life membership; [oth. writ.] Article published in, In Accord Magazine.; [pers.] Writing, for me is painting Life's moments with words; [a.] Scotia, NY

MacPHERSON, CATHERINE
[Pen.] Cathy MacPherson; [b.] September 14, 1978, NC; [p.] Bea and Ray MacPherson; [ed.] Kyrene Jr High, Marcos de Niza High School; [occ.] Student at Marcos de Niza; [oth. writ.] Not published yet; [pers.] I have been influenced by great poets, music, famouns bands, and my late mother. I believe you can accomplish anything if you just believe and keep the faith; [a.] Temple, AZ

MAGIS, BARBARA A.
[b.] October 8, 1952, Chicago, IL; [p.] Norbert and Evelyn Leparski; [m.] Michael K. Magis, June 22, 1974; [ch.] Matthew Norbert, David Michael, Kelly Lauren; [ed.] St Augustine HS, Chicago, IL; Lewis Univ, Lockport, IL; [occ.] Tech Support Supv, AT&T Comm, Domestic and Int'l Swt; [oth. writ.] The Perfect Picture, Life's Legacy - published in local newspaper; [pers.] If we are all shared our talents, how rich the world would be! A life in perfect balance, built on the word "we", instead of "me"; [a.] Lisle, IL

MAGIT, TAI OPIA
[Pen.] Kalgana; [b.] October 20, 1978, Chicago, IL; [p.] Anne Frank Magit, Paul B. Magit; [ed.] Interna-tional Boarding School in UK (graduating summer '94), Name of Sch Ko-Hsuan; [occ.] Student.

MAGNAN, LANA CARRIE
[b.] November 23, 1979, Edmonton, Alberta, Canada; [p.] Henri and Caroline Magnan; [ed.] Junior high graduate 1994 (grade nine - Alberta, Canada); [occ.] Grade school student (currently - grade nine); [memb.] Calmar Junior Curling Club, Attend Leduc School of Music of Piano, St Margaret - Mary Catholic Parish (lector); [hon.] Grade 4 thru 8 honor role. Honor Role - 90% + average; [oth. writ.] Winning rememberance Day poems in regional contests, various poems, short

stories, and essays; [pers.] I write because I find it the most expressive way to convey my thoughts and feelings; [a.] Calmar, Alberta, Canada

MAGNO, GIL
[b.] Madeira Island; [ed.] West High School, RI, Boston Conservatory of Music, Bachelor of Arts; [occ.] Educational Consultant in English ASL, Music and Personal Magnetism; [memb.] The Charles J. Givens Organization, Rosicrucian Order, AMORC; [oth. writ.] Short stories and poems in local papers, book "How to Attract Your Love-Life-Partner." Currently working on book, "Confidence, Self-Ex-pression and Personal Magnetism." Reviser and expander of the words of Webster Edgerly on Per-sonal Magnetism under the new title "The Person Magetism Home Study Course on All Human Pow-ers." [pers.] Life is a school. The arts are some of its books. Study them well through observation and action. Follow no one. Your existence needs no apology when you are just with your creations; [a.] Miami Beach, FL

MAITRA, SOMA
[b.] October 24, 1978, Caleutta, India; [p.] Subio and Sante Maitra; [ed.] Student at Ward Melville High School, NY; [occ.] Full time student at Ward Melville High School. Children's editor of Sangbadik Inc., Westbury, NY; [memb.] National Junior Honor So-ciety, student government; [hon.] High school honors student, Living authors Award; [oth. writ.] Several poems and articles published in Sangbadik and Kalei-doscope; [a.] Stony Brook, NY

MALONEY, MARY
[b.] August 13, 1942, Sweet Bay; [p.] Matthew and Theresa Nolan; [m.] William, April 19, 1955; [ch.] 4 sons - Joseph, Kenneth, Neal and Darryl; [ed.] High School Grad. Teacher's Certificate - taught elemen-tary school for 3 yrs; [occ.] Housewife; [a.] New-foundland, Canada

MALOTT, CHRIS
[Pen.] Christopher Malott; [b.] November 8, 1971, Ft. Wayne, IN; [p.] James and Sandra Malott; [ed.] Northside High School; w Written many other poems yet published.; [pers.] We all live in this world we try to live the best we can, we try to take care of everyone so we can live in pure harmony. Influenced by Jim Morrison who's poetry reflected a time of change.; [a.] Ft. Wayne, IN

MALTAIS, CATHY
[Pen.] Crag; [b.] February 21, 1978, Montreal; [p.] Nancy Proulx, Gaston Maltais; [ed.] Bernard Corbin (elementary). Nicolas - Gatineau (secondary). I am now in secondary 4; [occ.] student; [memb.] Student newspaper and school radio; [hon.] First prize for a poem at school; [oth. writ.] Other poem published in "Whispers in the Wind" and several in school news-papers. I write a lot in French and in English; [pers.] I believe that by dreaming you make life better. I love to write about things I feel or see around me; [a.] Gatineau, Quebec, Canada

MANAOIS, MICHAEL ANGELO
[Pen.] Mike; [b.] November 14, 1979, Toronto, Ontario; [p.] Constancio and Linda Manaois; [ed.] St. Michael's College (first year high school); [hon.] Public speaking finalist, Math-Science Fair Finalist, The Royal Canadian Legion Literary Contest District Level; Finalist for poem Validictorian for Elementary Schooling; [oth. writ.] Children's story - published in New York City; [pers.] I strive to express my inner-most feelings towards my poetry. I focus mainly on love, grief, and friendship which all influence me to write; [a.] Mississauga, Ontario, Canada

MANKINS, TARA
[b.] March 23, 1978, Santa Monica, CA; [p.] Walter

and Janet Mankins; [ed.] Righetti High School; [occ.] Student at Righetti High School in Santa Maria, CA; [memb.] Campus Clubs: JSA, Youth to Youth, weight lifting club, class president; [hon.] School: Dean's List, high honor roll, honor roll, HOBY Leadership Seminar, Who's Who Among American High School students, Community: DARE role model; [pers.] I enjoy writing with symbolism, multiple meanings, and an air of mystery; [a.] Santa Maria, CA

MANNING, EDWARD W.
[Pen.] Vagabond Ed; [b.] October 11, 1923, Orduny, CO; [m.] Barbara, February 14, 1945; [ch.] one; [ed.] Cal State; [occ.] Retired - work with LVA as a tutor; [memb.] many; [hon.] few; [oth. writ.] Musings of a Vagabond - book, made in Montana - book, "On the Hillside" short story, "The Cone Sailor", Navy Memorial - DC; [pers.] I just try to write what can be understood; [a.] Wildhorse Plains, MT

MANNING, LENA
[b.] August 1, 1977, Lethbridge, AB, Canada; [p.] Fred and Pat Manning; [ed.] Lamont Jr/Sr High School Lamont AB Canada; [occ.] Student; [hon.] Two remembrance Day Essay Contest Cert from The Royal Canadian Legion (Alberta - NWT Command). 1. First prize Legion Branch Level, 2. Second place Senior Essay Zone Level; [a.] Chipmen, AB, Canada

MARAFFAH, SHAHRZAD
[Pen.] Shari Maraffah; [b.] January 27, 1958, Persia; [p.] Saeed and Ghodsieh Moraffah; [ed.] Graduate of school of dental hygiene; [occ.] Exporter of family iventions of new designed products; [memb.] National Assembly of Bahai faith (Bahai world center Haifa Israel); [hon.] Name appears as a lyrics writer for song (Heart beat) on low rider sound track (album/tape/CD). Can be found in record stores. Song was produced wrote and programmed by brother (Brian Wayy). He is signed by MCA record company; [oth. writ.] Various poems for a well known card company. Lyrics for record company; [pers.] Every poet has a heart of gold, and every time they want to share, they melt the gold from their heart, and let it flow to their fingers and onto the paper; [a.] LA Mirada, CA

MARCANO, SHARNTA
[b.] September 16, 1978, Reading, PA; [p.] Selwyn, Germaine Marcano; [ed.] Attending Holy Name High School of Rdg. DA; [occ.] Student; [oth. writ.] I have several other poems but none of them ever published.; [pers.] I love to write it is one gift that have and I know I am good at. It helps me express myself.; [a.] Reading, PA

MARK, NEWPHER JR.
[b.] November 8, 1969, Bethesda, MD; [p.] Mark Newpher & Sally Newpher; [occ.] Student of Watch-making; [a.] Potomac, MD

MARLOW, SUSAN A.
[b.] January 12, 1960, Long Beach, CA; [p.] Maryin Bullock, Jeanette Bullock; [m.] John Marlow, March 5, 1988; [ch.] Ryan Grant, Jeffrey Austin; [ed.] Westminster High, Orange Coast College, Compter Cert Prog CSULB, College of the Canyons; [occ.] Full-time mother an part-time merchandiser, gifts in the attic, Lancaster, CA; [oth. writ.] Several I am seeking to have published; [pers.] I enjoy writing poetry about places I've traveled because as I read them back, it allows me to return to those places once again in my minds eye; [a.] Palmdale, CA

MARQUIS, ANTHONY J.
[b.] July 4, 1935, Peabody; [p.] Alice, Philip Marquis; [ch.] (1) Jill-Ann; [ed.] Lowell Univ, Northern Essex; [occ.] Writer, landscaper, Psudo-agent for writers; [oth. writ.] "Garden Tips", How to Home Gardening. Crossword puzzles, Ezy-tuff. And a Land-scaping course w/Q&A; [pers.] Always looking for

alternative ways of doing things. Never taking things for granted and blessing every day of my learning life; [a.] Lawrence, MA

MARS, ELLA SHAUNA
[b.] San Saba, TX; [p.] Father: Full Comanche Mother Iris; [ed.] Usual and Business school with P.G. work as legal secretary, earned certificates, 5 yrs. commercial art, journalism, 3 yrs. teacher training course in bible studies, various writing courses, music studies; [memb.] Church of Christ, all other memberships, studies and schedules have been canceled, overload has about destroyed my sense of freedom.; [oth. writ.] Newspapers in Texas and Okla. (straight news, human interest, features, columns), Column in Woman's Magazine, Articles in Magazine, Articles in Magazines, Christian Publications, Six books, four of them are books for Indian children, 6, poem in two collections and a magazine.; [pers.] To know freedom I must love, respect and reverence God and live within his law, I study his word that I may understand and grow spiritually. To enhance this freedom I must know, appreciate and respect the laws of nature. To use the laws I study the wisdom of the old Neuma this I may absorb the beauty and rejuvenating power of nature.; [a.] Scurry, TX

MARSH, NOEL G.
[b.] April 6, 1974, Tucson, AZ; [p.] Margaret Marsh; [m.] Single; [ed.] Attending Mesa Comm. College. Graduated from Dobson High School, Mesa Arizona; [occ.] Student; [memb.] Vice Chair of the District 6 of Arizona Demacratic Party; [oth. writ.] Several poems published in High School literary Arts Magazine.; [pers.] In my writing I try to reflect all of what happens in life, some of the good and some of the bad. If I can make someone see that there is someone else feeling the same way, then I have done my job as a writer.; [a.] Chandler, AZ

MARSHALL, JEFFREY ERIC
[b.] May 28, 1964, Newburyport, MA; [p.] Joseph and Pauline Marshall; [ed.] Sanborn Regional High; [Oth. writ.] This is my first published writing.;[pers.] This poem was chosen by my father to send in out of all my poems three months before he passed away. I dedicate this poem to the greatest man I've ever known, my father.; [a.] E. Kingston, NH

MARSHALL, STEVE
[b.] July 27, 1970, Brooklyn, NY; [p.] George & Anita Marshall; [ed.] Graduated Wallington High School, June 1988; [occ.] Market Research; [memb.] none; [hon.] Graduate of Long Ridgewriter's Group; [oth. writ.] "Rituals of Terror" an anthology of contemporary modern day horror that includes 8 short stories.; [pers.] "Writing is not hard, it is life that is difficult. If you're not writing for yourself, you're in the wrong business.; [a.] Stamford, CT

MARTELL JR., JOE
[b.] May 7, 1952, El Paso, TX; [p.] Jose & Amparo Martell; [ch.] Adam Joseph, Jason Andrew, Joseph Andrew; [ed.] Yslera High School, Computer Learning Center; [occ.] Computer Operator; [pers.] I feel that everyone should try to express their feelings in a poem whether it rhymes or not. All it takes is a little inspiration. Inspiration I get from my beautiful "Jasmine."; [a.] El Paso, TX

MARTIN, ALTA MARIE SHANNON
[b.] April 28, 1907, Clinton County; [p.] Hugh Elbert & Mary Ann Shannon; [m.] Hugh C. Martin (deceased), June 5, 1927; [ch.] Two girsl, Margaret Frost & Madellyn Everett; [ed.] Rural Schools and high school, belonged to a Dramatic Club, Debate team, Music Club, Basketball team. Started writing poetry for birthdays and weddings. My mother wrote poetry for her own pleasure; [occ.] Clerk in Dad's grocery store, later in a dry goods store. Was Deputy

County Collector 13 years, Medical Clinic Receptio-ist 17 years.; [memb.]w I have belonged to th Business & Professional Club, Chairman of the Clint County Democratic Club Treasurer of our sunda School class, belong to 2 Bowling Clubs, and Pres dent of a local Women's Club.; [hon.] I won man award in John Campbells Poetry Club in Sacrament CA, 2 plaques, one Cassette tape of one of my poem a cash award, naming an addition in Plattsburg, an cash award for a essay for a lumber company. Fou grandchildren, Seven great grandchildren two ste great grandchildren; [oth. writ.] In O.A.T.S. Maga zine, young at Heart Magazine, have had two poer books published locally.; [pers.] I've been writing fo 40 years. I am a volunteer at the Senior Citizen Clu in Plattsburg, MO. I've Vice President of the Orga nization, Activity Leader and Cashier. I have lived i many towns near by, due to the depression years; [a. Plattsburg, MO

MARTIN, DORIS L.
[Pen.] Dee J. Mark; [b.] May 29, 1966, New Castle PA; [p.] Vella Jones, Wally Jones; [m.] Rick E Martin, December 7, 1990; [ch.] Misty (10), Robyr (8), Joey (7), Jessica (3), (adpt) Suzanne (18); [ed.] Currently attending GED classes at lower Columbia College. Plans to further education; [occ.] House-wife, mother, student; [hon.] up and coming employee from Melaleuca, Inc, Nov 1991; [oth. writ.] Other poems; [pers.] To ensure the happiness of those around you; first make sure that you have the capabili-ties to make yourself happy; [a.] Kelso, WA

MARTIN, ESTELLE SMITH
[b.] February 19, 1919, Livington Parish; [p.] Bryan & Thelma Smith; [m.] Deceased; [ch.] Three; [ed.] Finished High School; [occ.] Retired; [oth. writ.] Yes; [pers.] I like writing gospel songs and poems; [a.] Springfield, LA

MARTIN, MARGARET C.
[b.] July 27, 1933, Hickory Grove, SC; [p.] James Wylie, Mary Wylie; [m.] Arthur Martin, March 6, 1955; [ch.] Bonita Louann, Regina Sue, Matilda Kaye; [ed.] Blacksburg High; [occ.] Housewife; [hon.] The National Library of Poetry Editor's Choice Award 1993 for "I Love You My Dear"; [oth. writ.] Poem, "I Love You My Dear", published by The National Library of Poetry in "The Coming of Dawn". Has written three children's books waiting publica-tion; [pers.] God and my family come first in my life. The love is ever lasting. If your heart's full of love, there's no room for hatred; [a.] Blacksburg, SC

MARTIN, SABRINA
[b.] November 4, 1967, Castle, Germany; [p.] Ann Martin & Louis Eulenfeld; [m.] Dennis J. Martin, February 14, 1986; [ch.] Kris Lee Martin and Michael Scott Martin; [ed.] Richard King High; [occ.] House-wife, Mother; [memb.] Blood Donor; [hon.] Naval Junior Reserves Officers Training Corps, the birth of both of my two sons; [oth. writ.] none; [pers.] I am very fascinated by the unknown. Writing helps me release my inner most personal thoughts.; [a.] San Bernardino, CA

MARTINEZ, ANTONIA
[b.] July 23, 1942, Puerto Rico; [m.] Joseph Cartelli; [ch.] George, Raymond, Nadine; [ed.] Julia Rich-mond H.S., Nursing; [oth. writ.] Poems published in various periodicals; [pers.] There is nothing like a loving family. I thank my brother Angel Luis for his love and encouragement; [a.] New York, NY

MARTINEZ, SUSAN R.
[b.] Wilton, ME; [p.] W.F. Kenney, Jr; [pers.] Dedicated to RAI; [a.] Fort Bragg, NC

MARTINOES, MARYE C.
[Pen.] Marye Martinoes; [b.] December 4, 1952,

nnsylvania; [p.] Mary McAfee, Peter Martinoes; ...] Three children, Catherine, Mari, Peter; [ed.] S. graduate, New york, Triple Cities Beauty School, ...duate 5th Ave. School of Modeling, NYC; [occ.] ...nager of an Engine Rebuilding Co., Phoeniz, AZ; ...emb.] St. Francis Xavier church, Arizona Puma ...ack Club, past member.; [hon.] 1st Runner up Miss ...enage America at age 17. Palisades PK, NJ, Miss ...w York; [oth. writ.] Whispering Winds, I Remem-...r The Day, Can I Have a Loan (these are just a few ...my writings); [pers.] Everything, I have written, I ...ve to Catherine Skelly, a 10th grade English teacher ...th a lot of patience. Have several poems written to ...blish for a poetry book; [a.] Phoenix, AZ

ARTORI, MERRI
...] November 6, 1950, Evanston, Ill; [p.] Peter J. ...d Joan Martor; [m.] Mervyn Stein M.D., August 5, ...79; [ch.] Stephen R. Stein; [ed.] University of San ...rancisco 1973, B.S.N., University of California at ...n Francisco, 1977, Graduate Program Nurse Prac-...tioner in Medicine; [occ.] Nurse Practitioner, Pri-...te Practice, Marin County, CA; [memb.] American ...urses Association, American Academy of Nurse ...ractitioners, California Nurse Association; [hon.] ...cademic honors in college (Dean's List, Presidents ...ist). Academic honors in graduate school; [oth. ...rit.] I have written and lectured on heath care reform ...n the US; [pers.] I have written several poems since ...e age of 12. Short satrical pieces and poems that ...apture human emotion are my best works. Ralph ...Valdo Emerson, Robert Frost and Sara Teasdale are ...ny favorite writers for grace and style; [a.] Novato, ...A

MASON, DANA J.
...] August 1, 1964; [p.] Sandra J. and David E. ...Mason; [ed.] Crowley High, Univ of North TX; ...occ.] Night Dispatcher, City of Wichita Falls; [memb.] ...Agape Church; [oth. writ.] Several other poems ...vritten through the inspiration of the Holy Spitit; ...pers.] God loves you so much that He sent His only ...son to die on the cross alone so that you can live with ...Him someday in His Perfect Kingdom. Just open your ...heart to Jesus and accept Him as your savour and ...Live!; [a.] Wichita Falls, TX

MASON, DARRIN
...b.] July 22, 1969, San Francisco, CA; [p.] Claude Mason, Norma Mason; [ed.] Currently in second year of college for computer programming at National College, Sioux Falls, SD; [occ.] Electronics Assembler at Raven Industries, Sioux Falls, SD; [hon.] Dean's List; [oth. writ.] Many unpublished poems of various themes; [a.] Sious Falls, SD

MASON, KIMLA DENISE
[b.] April 9, 1975, Hollandale; [p.] Mr. and Mrs. Pearl Mason Jr; [ed.] Greenville High School; [occ.] Senior; [oth. writ.] A poem I made up while I was sitting down thinking about this boy that I was in love with and still is, the name is when I think; [pers.] Reality, romance, and creative imagination is what helped me engage in my new hidden talent that have suddenly come to light after my thinking about my sunshine at night; [a.] Greenville, MS

MASSEY, RILDA
[Pen.] Jan Massey; [b.] February 8, 1969, Groesbeck, TX; [p.] Barry and Delta Sterling; [m.] Edward Massey, August 18, 1986; [ch.] Amanda Massey 7 yrs. and Avis Massey 4 yrs.; [ed.] G.E.D. Mexia, High; [occ.] Store Clerk; [hon.] Damanique...Always on our minds) This poem is an honor to have published.; [oth. writ.] I have written many other poems, in which in the future I wish to have published Title "A Prayer For Daddy"; [pers.] Feelings are a wonderful thing. Because my feelings are what influence me and my writing.; [a.] Mexia, TX

MASSEY, TOM L.
[b.] April 8, 1966, Dbn Hgts, MI; [p.] Robert Massey, Sandra Massey; [ed.] Crestwood HS. Attended Henry Ford Junior College; [occ.] Sales; [oth. writ.] Many other poems, non-published. "like no other place I know". "who's the one who loves us still"; [pers.] Tomorrows may never come, share love and tenderness from your heart, before you can only say. I wished I had; [a.] Dbn Hgts, MI

MASSINELLO, STEPHEN ROBERT
[Pen.] S. Robert Massinello; [b.] December 17, 1973, Portchester, NY; [p.] Steve and Gerry Massinello; [ed.] RYE High School Graduate, 1 semester, Iona College, 1 semester WCC, now attending Mercy College; [occ.] Pitney Bowes Mailroom; [pers.] Listen to your heart, and follow your dreams. Find your boundaries and break them. But stay true to yourself. Inspiration is the key to success.; [a.] Rye, NY

MASTROPASQUA, ELISA
[Pen.] Elisa Munao; [b.] May 15, 1961, Argentina; [ed.] English Specialist, Univ of Toronto, MA in English, Univ of Toronto; [occ.] Spanish Tutor; [hon.] 2nd prize in the 1993 National Library of Poetry contest, honorable mention in the Humanitas Int'l Poetry Contest (1993); [pers.] Life, as Virginia Woolf pointed out, is "an endless interrogation". My poems are variations on that infinite questioning; [a.] Toronto, Ontario

MATEJIC, GEORGE WAYNE
[b.] August 8, 1940, Sault Ste Marie, Ontario, Canada; [p.] Matthew and Kathleen Matejic; [m.] Maralyn Matejic, July 31, 1971; [ch.] Nil; [ed.] high school, working experience - road of lumps and bumps; [occ.] Planning and Development Recreational Lands - 850,000 acres; [memb.] Elks Lodge - 341; [hon.] City Sault Ste Marie Conservation Award; [oth. writ.] Teachers Reference Book - Holt Rienhart-Winston, Ontario Outdoors Northern Sportsman; [pers.] I strive to learn from my mistakes, and to live each moment of each day and treat others as I myself would want to be treated; [a.] Sault Ste Marie, Ontario, Canada

MATITS, LORI
[b.] September 10, 1994, Paterson, NJ; [p.] Rita and Robert Matits; [ed.] Manchester Regional H.S., Penn State University; [occ.] Marketing Representative, U.S. Healthcare; [memb.] American Heart Association, American College of Sports Medicine; [hon.] High School, Student Council President, Girls, Athletic Association President, Homecome Queen, National Honor Society, College, Dean's List; [pers.] My inspiration for writing poetry always comes from my heart, for this is my way of conveying my emotions and feelings for others.; [a.] Totowa, NJ

MATTHEWS, BONNIE MARIE
[b.] July 18, 1977, Clarksville, TN; [p.] buddy and Faye Matthews; [ed.] Currently a student at Russellville High School; [occ.] Student; [memb.] National Honor Society, National Forensic League; [hon.] Regional Science Awards in Zoology and Environmental Science, Various Speech Awards; [pers.] Poetry is the outlet I employ to express my innermost feelings. Great women poets with the same mindset, like plath and sexton, are my strongest influences; [a.] Russellville, KY

MATTHEWS, RHONDA L.
[Pen.] Rhonda; [b.] July 8, 1954, Chicago, IL; [p.] Thomas Carlyle Fleming, Louise Fleming; [m.] Vernon Matthews, October 12, 1973; [ch.] Carlita, Jodi, Tiree; [ed.] George Washington High School, Carver, North Park College, William L. Dawson Skill Center; [pers.] LIfe in the nineties is full of distractions some negative, some positive, and some unavoidable. But if a person is striving for something positive in life, most quests can be accomplished

through inner strength; [a.] Evanston, IL

MATTINGLY, CHRISTA MICHELE
[b.] November 2, 1982; [p.] Richard Mattingly & Sharon Sitzer; [ed.] Kitty Stone Elem. 5th; [occ.] Student at Kitty Stone Elementary; [oth. writ.] (None published) The Earth (poem), The Story of Black Renegade and The Apple Orchard; [pers.] I have not accomplished many things, but I feel like this will be a start, éven though I am only 11 years old. I like poetry.; [a.] Jacksonville, AL

MATTLI, ARTHUR
[b.] April 13, 1963, Lucerne (Switzerland); [occ.] International Lawyer; [pers.] In poetry, the art of disputes is often unappreciated. Disputes, however, are inherent culture of mankind. And we should remember that the space between the protagonist of a dispute is not always a filling of hate and distinction, but often affection and love. Disputes in poetry open a new perception of human behavior; [a.] Brooklyn, NY

MAUGERE, DENNIS
[b.] Newark, NJ; [p.] William and Virginia Maugere; [m.] Joanne Cella Maugere; [ch.] Lisa Marie, Anthony Paul, Lauren Michelle; [ed.] BA, History, Univ of FL; MAT, American History 19th Century: Slavery, Civil War Reconstruction, Minors: Political Science, Social Foundations of Education, Univ of FL; [occ.] Educator, secondary and post-secondary levels, Cooper City High School and Broward Community College, Broward County, FL; [memb.] American Historical Assoc; Phi Alpha Theta, International Honor Society in History; Who's Who Among America's Teachers; U.S. Citizen Ambassador Selectee (History Education Delegation to Russia and Latvia); Member, Editorial Advisory Board, Western Civilization: A Brief History, Robin Winks, Yale Univ; Honoree, "Outstanding Past Service", Chairman of the Broward County Advisory Board for the Disabled; three Presidential invitations to attend the Annual Meeting of the President's Committee on Employment of the Handicapped, Washington, DC; Guest of Honor, "Laramore Radar Poetry Group", Miami, FL, reading of "Time/Being"; [a.] Hollywood, FL

MAUNEY, JESSICA
[b.] August 11, 1980, Hickory, NC; [p.] William & Amy Mouney; [ch.] Grandparents: Annie J. Black, Carol and Ted Mauney, Ned and Janice Bolick; [ed.] Crystal River Middle School; [occ.] Student and aspiring journalist; [hon.] Academic Achievement Award 92' 93'; [pers.] My poem was inspired by a friend in need. I would like to thank her for her encouragement and love; a Crystal River, FL

MAURER, FRANK H.
[b.] April 29, 1950, Erding, W. Germany, Nee: Helmut Maurer; [p.] Lilli and Helmut Maurer; [m.] Sherrie Maurer, July 12, 1975; [ch.] Eric, Ryan and Alex; [ed.] BS Community Health Management, Univ of Cincinnati: MBA - Southern IL Univ, Edwardsville; [occ.] Consultant, Trainer, Speaker on Mental Health Issues; [memb.] Various Arizona Boards and Committees related to the statewide Behavioral Health Care Delivery System; [oth. writ.] Numerous poems describing first hand experiences with mental illness. Advocacy articles in newsletters, newspapers. Professional articles on psychiatric rehabilitation; [pers.] Sursum Ad Summum (Rise to the Highest) you can "rise to the highest" at any station in life!; [a.] Phoenix, AZ

MAYO, VONNA M.
[b.] September 20, 1973, Kahnawake; [p.] Constance Foote Mayo; [ed.] Kahnawake Survival School, High School diploma class of 92; [oth. writ.] Words, by Vonna M. Mayo, privately published in 1993, con-

taining 14 poems. All written by Vonna M. Mayo.

MAYS, CHARLES LAMAR
[Pen.] Lamar; [b.] September 16, 1937, Marks, MS; [p.] Charlie & Lottie Mays, April 16, 1956; [ch.] Charles Jr. Annett, Walter, Chris; [ed.] Marks - Ft. Myers High, Capt. City Buss. College; [occ.] Self-Employed, M&M Research & Development; [memb.] Oak Grove Church of God, Mason, Moose Lodge; [hon.] Silver Poets Award 1990; [oth. writ.] Poems published in Newspapers; [pers.] Time is held in the pen of poetry; [a.] Lehigh Acres, FL

McCALLUM, BRIDGET
[b.] August 27, 1968, Kamloops, BC; [ch.] Kayla Elizabeth, Kyra Majory; [ed.] Clearwater secondary; [occ.] Domestic Engineer; [pers.] I try to paint more than pictures with my words. I try to paint emotions so others may understand them; [a.] Clearwater, BC

McCARNEY, R. JEAN
[b.] June 25, 1977, Norfolk, VA; [p.] Sandee Lund; [ed.] Anita High School; [occ.] Student; [memb.] Speech/debate team swing choir, cheerleading, vollyball, track, yearbook, newspaper, honor role; [hon.] President of Class, Editor Yearbook, Editor of newspaper, HOBY; [oth. writ.] Several editorials in local newspaper; [pers.] Writing gives me the ability to express myself in a way people can relate to. I try to make difficult subjects easier to talk about; [a.] Anita, IA

McCARTHY, PHILIP JOSEPH
[b.] August 21, 1967, Weymouth, MA; [ed.] Various High Schools, graduated from BCC Fall River, MA, Northeast Broadcasting School Boston, MA; [oth. writ.] Several other poems as well as songs, which the author currently performs with his bandmates in Strange Brew; [pers.] The poem of mine found in this book, is hereby dedicated to all those other Night Owls out there. You ae not alone. Until we meet again, I leave you with these words. "Spend Our Time Chasing Dreams and Diversions, and Tending to our Wounded Vanities...If the Rapture Were to Come Tomorrow, we'd all be forced to plead Insanity". (From "Petty Jealously" copyright 1992, 1993 by the author); [a.] North Easton, MA

McCARTY, COLLEEN M.
[Pen.] Colleen Marie; [b.] May 11, 1969, Port Jefferson, LI; [p.] James B. McCarty, Jr, Arlene M. McCarthy; [ed.] Sachem High School, Long Island, Suffolk County Community College, Selden, Long Island; [occ.] Supermarket/retail, Wolbrook, Long island; [oth. writ.] A collection of poems written over the years, but to date, I have elected to keep personal; [pers.] Through my writing, I strive to express my true feelings, the ones hidden deep within my heart and soul. As a result, of my father's death on July 19, 1993, the poem submitted is in his memory; [a.] Lake Ronkonkoma, NY

McCARTY, TARA ALLISON
[b.] February 23, 1981, Montreal; [p.] Susan and Donald McCarty; [ed.] St. Paul Elementary School, Beaconsfield, Queen of Angels Academy, Forval; [occ.] Student at Queen of Angels; [memb.] YMCA Ski Club, Girl Guides of Canada, Q.A.A. Drama Club.; [pers.] Thanks to Mrs. Gail Monaghan of St. Paul Elementary School, Beafconsfield, who inspired me to write this poem.; [a.] Kirkland, Mont. Quebec

McCAULEY, HEATHER
[b.] October 27, 1977; [p.] Michele McCauley and Paul McCauley; [a.] Dunmore, PA

McCLYMENT, AUDREY
[b.] April 4, 1978, Easton, MD; [p.] Frank-Maxine McClyment; [ed.] Up to 10th grade in Colonel Richardson High School; [memb.] Columbia Music Membership; [hon.] Student of the month, honor and merit role in school; [oth. writ.] Poems for english class and friends; [a.] Preston, MD

McCONNACHIE, HEATHER
[b.] February 27, 1971, Vancouver, BC; [m.] David Todd McConnell; [ch.] Candice Victoria McConnell; [ed.] Alpha Secondary School, Trinity College, grade 6 drama with merit - 1988, Toronto Univ grade 6, speech arts, first class honors '84; [memb.] Performing Arts Festival 1983-1993, '83 Junior Speech Representative, '88 Intermediate Honor Performance and Representative; [hon.] CDMF Speech Arts Bursary's 1983, 1984, 1988; [a.] Surrey, BC, Canada

McCOY, PATRICIA J.
[b.] January 13, 1929, Peoria, IL; [p.] John & Mable Edenburn; [m.] Neil B. McCoy, June 30, 1990; [ch.] Two, Deborah Kay Goeke, Joyce Lynn Gallion; [ed.] High School, manual High School, Peoria, IL, College Level Secretarial Courses; [occ.] Retired, Personnel Officer, Marcus Daly Hospita, Hamilton, Mt., Present, Music Director, First Baptist Church, Hamilton, Montana; [memb.] American Business Women's Assoc. (20 year member). Marcus Daly Hospital Auxiliary (Volunteer Gift Shop); [hon.] Literary Award & Sir Galahad Award for prose in High School; [oth. writ.] This is my first attempt at poetry other than short poems for birthdays & anniversaries; [pers.] In each writing I wish to reflect my God-given love of mankind as well as to reach the hearts of individuals to aid them in improving their relationship with others.; [a.] Hamilton, Montana

McCREA, TREY
[b.] November 21, 1977, Houston, TX; [p.] Llew and Diane McCrea; [ed.] 1993-4 Sophomore Belton High School, Belton, TX; [occ.] High School Student; [memb.] Belton High School Varsity Choir, Teen Involvement; [hon.] Recipient of Presidential Academic Fitness Award 1989 & 1992, DAR Citizenship Award 1991, Outstanding Student Advanced Physical Science 1993, Outstanding Student Advanced Geometry, Top 5% of class academic awards 1992 & 1993; [oth. writ.] The Coming of Dawn "Jets"; [a.] Belton, TX

McCUE, DANIEL J.
[b.] September 23, 1970, Philadelphia [p.] Joseph McCue, Patricia McCue; [ed.] Clearview High School, Univ of PA - BA Tulane Univ - Graduate School; [occ.] Graduate Student in Anthropology; [a.] Mantun, NJ

McCULLOUGH, JON
[Pen.] J.D.M.; [b.] December 20, 1968, Newport Beach, CA; [p.] Maroe Neely, Robyn mcCullough; [ed.] Junior at Southwestern Assemblies of God College.; [occ.] Student; [hon.] Other poems published. Athletic honors etc.; [oth. writ.] Short stories, songs, and many other poems (60), I am seeking to publish all my poems for the first time.; [pers.] Whatever talent I have been given, I give all the glory to Jesus Christ the son of god, who rose from the dead to save my soul. I always try to show his love in my writing.; [a.] Waxahachie, TX

McDOUGALL, JENELLE LYNN
[b.] May 5, 1985, Calgary; [p.] David and Cheryl McDougall; [ed.] Grade Three; [hon.] Has always been an honor student in elementary school; [pers.] Jenelle is a figure skater with six gold medals. She loves to spend time in the country. Her poem was written to her grandmother for her birthday.; [a.] Calgary, Canada

McDOWELL, MELINDA ANNE
[b.] April 11, 1974, St. Petersburg, FL; [m.] Fiance Margie Hildebrand and Dr. Ronald McDowell; David Lee Sutton, July 13, 1994; [ch.] Pinellas County Center for the Arjts; [memb.] United State Pony Club, MMM Ranch.; [hon.] Dean's list for yrs., Colorado Outward Bound School graduate National Piano Playing Auditions Certificate; [oth. writ.] Several poems and songs; [pers.] Life for me is like a beautiful mountain, it may be rocky at times, but I will not quit climbing until I reach the top; [a.] Steamboat Springs, CO

McDUFFIE, ANNIE LAURA
[b.] January 17, 1936, AL; [m.] Ralph McDuffie, August 28, 1960; [ch.] Shirley, Shelby, Patrice, Ralph II, and Keith; [ed.] Inglewood High Adult Education. MA English Literature Calif St Univ Comm College Teaching Cert; [occ.] Rehabilitatio Spec Willing Workers, Los Angeles, CA; [memb.] Second Mt Nebo Board of Educ; [hon.] Dean's List Summa Cum Laude; [oth. writ.] Registered with Library Cong. Articles published in LA Times, Wave, Whole Life and Times; [pers.] I endeavor to depict God as the source of my inspiration in my writings; secondly, I was greatly influenced by the works of the metaphysical poets; [a.] Inglewood, CA

McELMURRAY, ERIC LEE
[Pen.] Eric Lee MacGiolla Mhuire; [b.] January 15, 1993, Wilmington, NC; [p.] Eli and Emma McElmurray; [ed.] Bay City High School; [occ.] United States Navy Cryptologic Technician Maintenance; [pers.] I express my true feelings about life through all my poetry. I would like to dedicate my poems to my true love, Cassandra. My favorite poet is Edgar Allen Poe.; [a.] Bay City, TX

McGARY, BRYNDA
[b.] December 19, 1973, Phoenix, AZ; [p.] Jerry McGary, Annette Burt; [ch.] Eukyshia Shannette; [ed.] West High School, Waterloo Hawkeye Community College, Univ of Northern Iowa; [occ.] Student; [oth. writ.] Many poems not yet published; [pers.] My writings reflect love and emotions. I greatly admire all poets; [a.] Waterloo, IA

McGHEE, CEDRIC L.
[b.] May 30, 1972, San Antonio, TX; [p.] Lena N. McGhee, Curtis L. McGhee; [m.] Someday hopefully; [ch.] none; [ed.] Dayton, OH, Colonel White H.S., currently attending the Ohio State University for an engineering degree; [memb.] National Society of Black Engineers (NSBE) BUEC, Ohio State Chapter; [hon.] BUEC member of the year 1993 and oratorical contest winner; [oth. writ.] Some poems about to be published from Sparrowgrass Forum, Iliad Poetry, Arcadia Poetry, the Amherst Society and National Library of Poetry. In My Dreams, Sweet Dreams, Riding Blood Thirsty, Delicious; [pers.] I write based on personal feelings. I'm not a writer of set structures such as jambic pentameter. My personal feelings are part of being a man. I strive to be the best man that I can be, and it shows in my poetry; [a.] Columbus, OH

McGINNISS, KENNETH J.
[ch.] Susan, Michael, Stephen, Paul, Nancy, Kerry, Kelly; [ed.] St. John's University, B.A., MS-ED, MA, Pol. Sci.; [occ.] Actor, Director, Broad Hollow Theaters of Long Islandy; [memb.] Executive Board, New York State Social Studies Supervisors Association; [pers.] "I love you all the trees" was something my mother always said. I dedicate this poem to her, my children and to Nina; [a.] E. Setauket, NY

McGLOIN, SOPHIE
[b.] February 12, 1922, Newark, NJ; [p.] Alexandra and Ignatzy Krasucki; [m.] Eddie McGloin, May 24, 1944; [ed.] BS in education; Major - history; Minor - english; Wayne St U, Det MI; [occ.] Retired teacher of history - Central HS, Det; [memb.] Detroit Federation - American Federation of Teachers; Wayne St

lumni; MI Democratic Party; [hon.] I consider it a great honor to have served as a Vice President (longest serving in the history of the union) of the Detroit Federation of Teachers; [oth. writ.] Served as Editorial Bd Member of DFT Detroit Teacher, as well as writer. Poems published in Det Teacher. Written articles for Detroit Labor News; [pers.] Am heavily influenced by my observation of nature, animals, birds. The mystery of life and death often influence my melancholy writings. I still correspond with friends; [a.] Detroit, MI

McGOWAN, DEBRA LEE
[b.] July 26, 1960, Nacogdoches, TX; [ch.] Ja'Coby Robert McGowan; [occ.] Owner, McGowan Transcription Services, Houston; [oth. writ.] Numerous publications over a fifteen year period; [pers.] To write poetry is to dream aloud. To share poetry is to share that dream; [a.] Houston, TX

McGUCKIN, GLENN M.
[b.] June 23, 1906, Pittsville, MO; [p.] George and Pearl McGuckin; [m.] Ruth Brookhart (died 9 1/2 yrs ago of cancer), February 16, 1956; [ch.] none; we were 49 and 48 yrs at marriage; [ed.] BS in Physics, U of IL; one summer grad physics, U of OK; [occ.] retired; [memb.] Formerly: American Assoc of Petroleum Geologists; and American Geophysical Society; [hon.] High school valedictorian; [oth. writ.] 4 - volume autobiography, 2 page study of certain biblical prophecies produced "The Future of Israel" in 1968; [pers.] I try to treat everyone as I would be treated (Jesus teaching). For 30 yrs my wife and I have heavily supported the Wycliffe Bible Translators, 6,000 trained linguists working, just now, in 1,000 never-written languages; ultimate goal; translation of the New Testament into each language and the people taught to read and write; [a.] Norman, OK

McGUINNES (H.), BEVERLY
[b.] February 28, 1923, Albion, ME; [p.] Ruth and Clarence Hussey (dec); [m.] John F, September 19, 1952; [ch.] 3 (one deceased - Pearl), Ruth Allen, Mearlene Lombardi; [ed.] High school; [occ.] Retired housewife; [memb.] American Legion VFW; [hon.] Awards in Clubs for Volunteer Work (Awards in Bowling); [oth. writ.] A Book - not published. Many, many poems; [pers.] I had one poem published several years ago, but have kept things on a low keel since my daughter passed away last September 1993; [a.] Skoshegan, ME

McGUIRE, MICKY W.
[b.] February 12, 1960, Colorado Springs; [p.] Mr. & Mrs. Gerald McGuire; [ed.] Mountainview High Master Course Microcomputer Repair; [occ.] Technical Systems Analyst - Sonoma Valley Hospital; [memb.] American Sailing Association, Scuba Schools International; [hon.] Crown bearer for Gov. Love, CO 1965, Most Valuable Player, Mountain View High School football 1978; [hon.] Employee of the Quarter Summer 1993, Sonoma Valley Hospital; [oth. writ.] Personal poems written of experiences, and for family and friends; [pers.] I am that I am. Every person is a door, an opportunity to learn of lifes experiences.; [a.] Sonoma, CA

McINERNEY, COLLEEN
[b.] January 6, 1951, Midland, Ontario; [p.] Cecile and Daniel McInerney; [m.] Irwin Brathwaite, October 22, 1988; [ch.] Shawn Wayne 13 yrs., Caitlin Rae 5 yrs.; [ed.] Early Childhood Bachelor of Education Degree McGill University Montreal; [occ.] Yoga, Meditation Teacher; [memb.] Board of Director for Housing Cooperative, on Board for Milton Park Recreation Assoc., Board Member at Stratheam Arts and Intercultural Center, Member of Spiritual Science Fellowship.; [hon.] No honors or awards but I am reverened of the Universal Life Church; [oth. writ.] Many children's stories, and some short stories, none of which have been published.; [pers.] I believe the time has come for all men/women and children to raise up their hearts and join hands in the knowledge that we are all truly brothers and sisters.; [a.] Montreal Quebec, Canada

McINTOSH, JUANITA
[b.] December 20, 1932, KY; [p.] Ford and Ida (Morris) Spurlock; [m.] William J. McIntosh; [ch.] Larry, Venita, Jerry, Darlene, grandchildren: Nicolas, Emma, Brandon and Travis, son-in-law: Domingo, daughter-in-law Shirley.; [occ.] Homemaker; [oth. writ.] Several poems, I have always loved poetry.; [pers.] I love the outdoors and raising flowers, I love feeding the birds, in winter and the little hummingbirds in the summer. Some of my hobbies are, collecting, post cards and owls.; [a.] Buckhorn, KY

McINTYRE, MARY
[b.] May 27, 1950, CA; [ch.] One; [oth. writ.] Published in numerous poetry publications.; [pers.] Mary McIntrye is a Navajo Indian orphan who came into this world a premature epileptic baby addicted to heroine and alcohol. She spent her childhood in a foster home and many of her adolescent years in institution's for treatment of mental illness and alcoholism. She lived the majority of her adult life in poverty as a disabled person. Today, with 14 years of sobriety, Mary is a drug and alcoholism counselor in an Indian Recovery home. She shares with others her spiritual life and brings joy and hope to all who know the adversity that she has overcome. Mary's poetry are the songs of her Indian spirit that reflect her understanding of the condition of the human heart and her love. Signed, One of the many who know and love her.

McKELVEY, LAWRENCE P.
[Pen.] jGenoa; [b.] March 26, 1934, Monroe, MI; [p.] Paul and Florence McKelvey; [m.] Divorced; [ch.] Karen, Dana, Holly; [ed.] College Graduate, Central Michigan University; [occ.] Business Owner, Insurance Claims; [oth. writ.] Various poems and short stories; [pers.] Thoughts and feelings are derived through spiritual influence; [a.] Royal Oak, MI

McKENZIE, KRISTINE
[Pen.] Kristine, McKenzie; [b.] August 25, 1973, Toronto; [p.] Donald and Kathleen Wood; [ed.] OAC (Ontario Academic Credit) and high school diploma. Currently, St. Lawrence College; registered nursing program; [occ.] Student; [memb.] Royal Life Saving Society of Canada and Red Cross Society; [oth. writ.] Several poems published in high school anthology "Constellation". Student editor of Constellation during high school senior year; [pers.] I'd like to thank my high school english and creative writing teachers for helping me to bring my thoughts and my creativity from my mind to the paper; [a.] Brockville, Ontario, Canada

McKESSON, AMANDA LYNN
[b.] June 26, 1980, Plymouth, IN; [p.] Jon D. McKesson and Lynne E. Erickson; [ed.] Lincoln Junior High School, Ploymouth IN; [occ.] Student; [memb.] Band, Cheerleading, U.S. Tennis Assoc.; [hon.] Regional Band Selection, Jr. High Language Arts Award, Lincoln List; [oth. writ.] Several poems and essays; [pers.] Individual rights for all including young women; [a.] Plymouth, IN

McKINNEY, DIANE
[b.] May 12, 1979, El Centro, CA; [p.] Cheryl and Rick McKinney; [ed.] I am going to Atascadero High School where I am in the 9th grade; [memb.] I am a member of Atascadero Creekside lanes. I am very active in bowling; [hon.] I have been student of the month this year; [oth. writ.] I have done research papers that I have gotten A's on; [pers.] I would like to thank Mr. Kirk Smith, one of my English teacher's from 8th grade. He has always helped me with my writings; [a.] Atascadero, CA

McKNIGHT, ALEXANDER W.
[b.] June 14, 1929, Oakland, CA; [p.] Duncan & Christina McKnight; [m.] Ayame McKnight, August 14, 1963 Tokyo, Japan; [ch.] none (Although our cat is "family"); [ed.] Victoria High School (Edmonton, Alberta, Canada); [occ.] Retired Ship's Purser (U.S. Navy Military Sealift Command, Pacific); [memb.] U.S. Naval Institute (Associate), National Assoc. of Retired Federal Employees, Kyushu Military Retiree Association; [oth. writ.] Poem "Remembering Diz" published in Cadence Magazine, April 1993; [pers.] To live one day at a time.; [a.] Sasebo City, Nagasaki-Ken, Japan

McLEOD, ROGERS PATRICK
[Pen.] Pat McLeod; [b.] January 28, 1937, Augusta, TX; [p.] Leonard and Emma McLeod; [m.] Jean Collins McLeod, November 26, 1959; [ch.] Patsy Jean, David patrick, Molly Annelle, Emily Anne; [ed.] Boling High School, Wharton County Junior College, Sam Houston State University; [occ.] Retired History Teacher; [memb.] Association of Texas Professional Ediucators; [hon.] National Phi Theta Kappa, Best Poetry Award 1957; [pers.] My inner feelings are released through my poetry. I have learned to write down my poetry whenever it occurs, day or night.; [a.] Bay City, TX

McMAHAN, IVY
[b.] September 15, 1980, Scotts, ZA; [p.] Connie & Jesse McMahan; [ed.] Seventh grade student at Desert Shadows Middle School; [oth. writ.] I enjoy writing poems often, for fun.; [pers.] I like to play a variety of sports for fun and other activities. I love drawing, in my spare time I play basketball with the neighbors, or play the piano.; [a.] Scottsdale, AZ

McMORRIS (II), JAMES O.
[Pen.] Mac-Mo, The Mac; [b.] October 15, 1973, Washington, DC; [p.] James and Jacqueline McMorris; [ed.] Cheyney Univ of Pennsylvania - 2nd semester junior; [occ.] Author, student; [memb.] Alpha Phi Alpha Fraternity, Inc, Cheyney Record Newspaper, Cheyney Videography Club, etc; [hon.] Homecoming King (1993), Funniest Individual Award (spring 1993), National Dean's List, Honor Roll for 3 yrs straight, All American Scholar; [oth. writ.] The Black Youth Mentality (not yet published), other short poems (not yet published); [pers.] Knowledge is power. In today's cruel society, power seems to be extinct for many of the lower and middle class citizens. We need knowledge to bring into the forefront. We do not need dictatorship in this country. Therefore, power must be shared equally; [a.] Washington, DC

McNAMEE, ARTHUR
[b.] January 26, 1960, Amburg, Germany; [p.] Patrick and Catherine McNamee; [m.] Jean D. McNamee, April 19, 1985; [ch.] John P. McNamee; [ed.] Adelphi University; [occ.] Claim Adjuster; [oth. writ.] "Sand Castles" Our Twentieth Century's Greatest Poems. Several poems published in newspapers, and periodicals. An article published in Malvelne/Lynbrook Community Times; [a.] F. Massa pegua, NY

McNUTT, IDA JEAN
[Pen.] Jean McNutt; [b.] May 20, 1925, Muskegon, MI; [p.] Don J. & Beatrice (Covell) Irwin; [m.] Harvey McNutt, March 24, 1952; [ch.] Von, Roger, Barry, Douglas & Elaina; [occ.] Retired from 10 yrs. of Community Social Worker; [memb.] American Legion Auxiliary; [hon.] A book of Poems "Poems to Ponder" (Unpublished); [pers.] I feel that home and family are the worlds largest asset. Most of my writings are actual experiences in that area. I am truly satisfied when a reader tells me they know how I feel

and they have been there.; [a.] Saranac, MI

McPHERSON, HEIDI
[Pen.] Mickey or Little Baby; [b.] April 19, 1979, Chester, CA; [ed.] Started going to Galt High and planning on attending college; [oth. writ.] I write for myself none of the others have been published, maybe they will be someday; [pers.] If you believe anything can happen; [a.] Galt, CA

McQUADE, LYNNE
[b.] October 23, 1959, Bayshore, NY; [p.] Rober and Marie Davenport; [m.] William McQuade, September 9, 1979; [ch.] Kelly Lynne, Tracy Laura; [ed.] Smithtown High School, Wilfred Beauty School; [occ.] Housewife and mother; [memb.] Women's International Bowling Congress. School PTA; [oth. writ.] Several poems, none of which have yet been submitted; [pers.] My writings come straight from the heart and are mainly based around my husband and family; [a.] Nesconset, NY

McRAE, ELIZABETH
[b.] November 7, 1959, Louisville, KY; [p.] Jesse & Rosa Farley; [m.] Clinton McRae, Jr., August 2, 1985; [ch.] Theodore, Jessica & Jackie; [ed.] Mountain View High; [occ.] Mother/Homemaker; [oth. writ.] Collection of poems & songs; [pers.] Every good and perfect gift comes from the Father and it is to Him. I give glory.; [a.] Bremerton, WA

McZEAL, WANDA J.
[b.] January 9, 1957, LaPorte, TX; [p.] Grace Rosette Sims, Morris Manuel, Sr.; [ch.] Lathanias McZeal and Winston McZeal; [ed.] Welsh High School, McNeese State University, Texas Southern University, Jeff-Davis Vo-Tech School; [occ.] Secretary 2; [memb.] LA State Youth Conference Committee Member; [hon.] LA State Youth Conference committee Plaque, Dean's List, J.D. Sheriff Recognition Program.; [oth. writ.] Wrote a book cannot find a publisher.; [pers.] I want the poetry I write to be read all. It has meaning, concerns reality.; [a.] Crowley, LA

MEADE, FRANCES E.
[Pen.] Efram Malik; [b.] February 25, 1938, Philadelphia, PA; [p.] Russell and Lucille Meade; [ed.] 1. St Joseph's School of Nursing (Phila, PA); 2. St Louis Univ (St Louis, MO); [occ.] Registered Nurse Dept of Health - St Louis County.

MEADE, TIMOTHY M.
[Pen.] T. Matthew Meade; [b.] April 2, 1967, Cleveland, OH; [p.] Ercel Meade, Gloria Meade; [ed.] Berean College, Wooster Business College, Leone Tech; [hon.] Dean's List, Honor Roll; [pers.] "Perfection may not be attainable in a lifetime, but it is none te less to be striven for"; [a.] Chippewa Lake, OH

MEANS, ELIZABETH SUZETTE
[b.] September 17, 1949, Vernon, TX; [p.] Alton Abston; [m.] Helen Abston, January 18, 1992 (Divorced); [ch.] 3 stepchildren; [ed.] Bachelor of Science in Education, Minor: Math from Midwestern State University in May 1971; [occ.] Secretary; [hon.] Valedictorian of 8th Grade, Thalia, TX; [oth. writ.] Other poems not published; [pers.] My poetic ability is a God, given talent and I wish to give him the credit for my accomplishments while here on earch; [a.] Floydada, TX

MEDINA MOTTA, FRANCISCO JAVIER
[b.] February 22, 1936, Izabal, Guatemala; [p.] Jos'e Medina, (A civil servant who loved literature and poetry.), and Virginia Motta, (A housewife converted to business woman when her husband stopped work becuase of illness and their three children were little people.); [pers.] Bertha, the elder sister died very young in 1961; Jos'e, his broter, works as Editor of an agricultural magazine in the United States. Under

his father's influence, Francisco began writing from childhood. At 13 he was director of the mural newspaper in the elementary school. Afterwards, in 1955, he worked as an official journalist in Nicaragua. He has written a novel, short stories, essays and poetry; studied theology in a Guatemalan University and is father of two daughters and four sons.; [a.] Guatemala, Centro America

MEDLEY, RUTH
[b.] october 11, 1913, KY; [p.] William & Monino Wathen; [m.] Arville Medley (dec.), March 29, 1932; [ch.] Carl, David, Medley, Martha, Fenton, Mildred Pedly, Dalore Sawder (dec.); [ed.] Two years high school; [occ.] Retired; [memb.] St. Mary's Magaline Church (Catholic); [oth. writ.] Sonny and Me, published in local newspaper, only thirty nine published in local newspapers.; [pers.] I widow since 1949, owned and operated a market of General Store food, clothing, hardware and animal feed for twenty eight years.; [a.] Sorgho, KY

MEGYERI, LOU C.
[b.] Lockport, NY; [p.] Norma Johnson, Jerry Nugent; [m.] Joseph Megyeri; [occ.] President, Literary Creations, Green Mountain, CO; [oth. writ.] Last Call Drive - humorous suspense. The Camper With Wings - children's book. Case Games - humorous suspense thriller; [pers.] "Writing to me is an uncontrollable passion, the best means of self entertainment I have ever experienced."

MEINE, SHAWN J.
[b.] September 30, 1975, Phoenix, AZ; [p.] Karen B. Meine & James D. Meine; [m.] unmarried; [ed.] Plan to attend ASU with a degree in Electrical Engineering; [occ.] Student; [oth. writ.] I have completed my first book of poems, which I would like to have published.; [pers.] "The better God told a tale about himself, yet I wreak without ignorance, and you are but a blip in evolution."; [a.] Phoenix, AZ

MEJIA, MARIA
[b.] August 8, 1979, Glendale, CA; [p.] Mario & Erlinda Mejia; [ed.] St. Thomas More, currently attending Immaculate Heart High School; [hon.] Received an award for excellence in creative writing; [oth. writ.] Several published poems and short stories; [pers.] Enjoy what life has to offer because you may never have a chance to do it all again.; [a.] Alhambra, CA

MELCHIORRE, CHARLES
[Pen.] Charles Thomas Payne; [b.] June 16, 1957, West Chester, PA; [ed.] Oakland Community College, Assoc Business; [occ.] Poet/GM/Pontiac; [pers.] Simplicity is the highest form of complexity; [a.] Clarkston, MI

MELTON, REX
[Pen.] Rex Farris Melton; [b.] September 5, 1966, Greensburg, KY; [p.] Farris Melton, Brenda Cox; [m.] Kimberly Joe, January, 1990; [ch.] Nikki Dartaniel, Matthew Kalup, Ashely Brook; [ed.] Cambellsville High, Lees College, Morehead State University; [occ.] Teacher's Aid, Free-Lance Writer; [memb.] Roman Catholic Church; [hon.] Magna Cum Laude, Dean's List; [oth. writ.] Prose, Her love--My love, various poems; [pers.] This poem herein is dedicated, to my home State of Kentucky and her brave ancestry.; [a.] Campbellsville, KY

MENCHES, PATRICIA
[b.] November 3, 1975, Phoenix, AZ; [p.] Katherine and John Gearig; [m.] Engaged to Mike Noto, April 8, 1995; [ed.] Graduated high school and plan to go to community college; [occ.] Cashier at local store; [oth. writ.] Have written several poems but none published yet; [pers.] I would like to dedicate this poem to my mother, who knew nothing about my

writings and also to my grandfather who pushed ℝ to continue writing; [a.] Sunrise, IL

MENDOZA, JR. A.
[b.] November 7, 1963, St. Bernard Parish, LA; [ⱷ Anthony & Linda Mendoza; [ch.] I have no childre but the most adorable God daughter Bethiney Ly Mendoza. She is the child of my twin brother Jose Mendoza; [ed.] I am a product of St. Bernard Parish fine public schools; [hon.] The only honor as of nov is having my second poem published by ya'll. I thank ya'll for the notice, and the helping hand.; [ot writ.] I only have one published poem "Nativity that's in "The Coming of Dawn" I have many mo unpublished poems, and much more waiting for li through me.; [pers.] My abstract look at life shou appear in my poetry, my poems are fragments of n life. "The need is a must, through the pen of my life." [a.] Arabi, LO

MENELEY, SUSAN
[Pen.] Lily Gaines; [b.] March 25, 1943, Geneva, Il [p.] Frederick and Lucille Wachter; [ch.] Mega Meneley; [occ.] Writer/Fine Artist; [memb.] Interna tional Womans Writers Guild New York; [hon National Honor Society; [oth. writ.] Poetry, fictio children's books (emphasis on self esteem and unlim ited possibility); [pers.] Excellent woman is a selec tion from an anthology; of poetry entitled, Quietus dedicated as a tribute to the poet's deceased mother first, presented at her memorial; [a.] Chicago, IL

MENZZASALMA, ROSSI
[Pen.] Rossi Menzza; [b.] January 10, 1926, Brook lyn, NY; [p.] Joseph and Natalie Menzzasalma; [m. deceased, November 22, 1952; [ch.] Joel Menzzasalm (1-6-54); [ed.] Bloomingburg High, Sullivan County NY; Farmingdale Agricultural College, Long Island NY; [occ.] Retired construction supervisor; [memb. Bricklayers Local 41, Long Island City, NY; [hon. Medals from WWII include The Victory, Rome Arnc Campaign, and the Good Conduct Medals; [oth. writ.] Several unpublished poems, and currently, I am working on my autobiography; [pers.] The poet, Thomas E. Kennedy, who was a friend and neighbor, published Doors To A Hidden World, through Van tage Press in 1963. It was that book of poetry that inspired me to write. History will repeat, only in a different way. The rulers will be ruled. The bottom fence rail will be on top; [a.] Old Bethpage, NY

MEREDITH, MARTA
[Pen.] Marta Vaughn; [b.] December 27, 1952, Milw, WI; [p.] Otis F. Swinger, II and Vaun Swiger; [m.] George Meredith, April 21, 1978; [ch.] Bryant Meredity (August 12, 1976); [ed.] Shorewood HS, MATC, Ricks College; [occ.] Unemployed; [hon.] 1st, 2nd, and 3rd place in state solo and ensemble competition; Competitor in National Piano Guild Auditions. Scholarship to UW Madison Summer Music Clinic - Outstanding Performance Award; [oth. writ.] Many poems, prose and philosophical works not published thus far; [pers.] As I meditate the words flow thru me. Like I'm a conduit from another source; [a.] MIlwaukee, WI

MERRELL, RICKY
[Pen.] Rick; [b.] October 11, 1968, St. Jones Hosp Canton, GA; [p.] Burt Merrell and Kathleen Pendley; [ed.] Graduated from Pickens High School in 1988; [occ.] Working at Cryogenic Services, Inc; [oth. writ.] I have other poems, but they have never been published; [pers.] Poetry is a hobby for me. I enjoy it a lot. The art of writing poetry is the artist in itself. But I never expected my poem to be selected or published, but I'm excited about it; [a.] Jasper, GA

MERTZ, JUDITH
[b.] February 20, 1941, Allentown, PA; [p.] John F. and Pearl M. Ohmacht; [m.] deceased; [ch.] 4 boys,

girls and 17 grandchildren; [ed.] Graduated by way GED in 1977 - 20 yrs after quitting HS to help my ....mily financially; [occ.] Retired Trinity Lutheran ....emorial Church of Catasauqua; [hon.] I have ...hieved 5 "Mother of the Year" awards; [oth. writ.] ....ad a book made up containing 53 pages of poetry. .is however very personal as to the fact that the poetry ....lates to my true life. Thus books are given to family ....d friends only titled "A Life Time of Memories"; ...ers.] I think you are wonderful for publishing poems ...om people of all walks of life. Thank you; [a.] ...atasauqua, PA

...ESTAZ, STACY
...en.] Jasmine Rasha; [b.] January 10, 1977, West ....orvina; [p.] Darlene Saunders and Davis Mestaz; ...d.] Giano Intermediate El Rancho High School; ...ers.] I want to emphasize the emotions of life. I was ...spired by my lovely and supportive seventh grde ...nglish teacher Mrs. Snyder; [a.] Pico Rivera, Corvina

...IEYER, CATHERINE
...b.] July 19, 1979, Monticello, IN; [p.] Dave and Jean ....eyer; [ed.] Currently attending Mattoon High School ...n Mattoon, Illinois; [oth. writ.] Many poems and ...nfinished novels; [pers.] Never under -estimate ....ourself, work with your personal situations and ...lways believe in yourself and your work.; [a.] ....attoon, IL

...IEYERS, CONNIE
...b.] March 27, 1978, CA; [p.] Marina Meyers; [ed.] ....oorpark High School, Oxnard High School; [occ.] ...igh School Sophomore; [oth. writ.] none published; ....pers.] Don't let life's insanities pull you under. Time .s at the essence and the future is arranged by fate; [a.] ....xnard, CA

MIANI, ANN MARIE R.
.b.] October 16, 1980, New Haven, CT; [p.] Mr. and ....rs. Joseph P. Miani; [ed.] Bradley Elem School, ...erby Intermediate School, Derby High School; ....occ.] Student; [memb.] Cheerleading, Dancing, Spanish Club, Drama Club; [hon.] DARE Award, Honors in School, Science Awards; [oth. writ.] Several poems and short stories published in my school newspaper the Pow-Wow; [pers.] I am very honored to have my poem published in "The Space Between". I hope it inspires young poets to write what they feel, instead of what teachers want them to write; [a.] Derby, CT

MICHAEL, MARY A.
[b.] November 24, 1921, Huntington, W.VA; [p.] Claude and Garnett Lakin; [m.] James Michael, June 20, 1941 (died 1991); [ch.] Two, Greg Michael, Teacher, Carol M. Masterson, Business Owner; [ed.] High School Grad., Fort Gay, W.Va.; [occ.] Retired from family owned business.; [memb.] O.E.S Order of Eastern Star, So. Point Christian Church Chair; [hon.] Personal Prizes; [oth. writ.] Short stories; [pers.] I love to read and write and just be a friendly happy person. Have lots of friends and love my children & grandchildren; [a.] South Point, OH

MICHELE, CHOW
[Pen.] M. Chow; [b.] January 2, 1963, Singapore; [p.] Gordon and Mary Chow; [m.] (looking for one); [ed.] General Cambridge Exam, Marymount Convent School; [occ.] Legal Secretary; [memb.] YMCA; [memb.] Silver Award for 1st place in Singapore in stenography - 1988; [oth. writ.] Not yet. Just started; [pers.] I like to note about people and life; thoughts, actions, pleasures, the human race and its complexities and diversity, all about life; [a.] Singapore

MICHELS, TREVOR
[b.] September 8, 1972, Louisville, KY; [p.] Roger and Pat Michels; [ed.] Graduated 1991 from Crawford County HS; (now) Junior at Univ of Evansville; Major: Math and Secondary Education; Minor: En-

glish; [memb.] IHSAA Official in Basketball, U of E Cross-Country Team; [hon.] Courier Journal Award of Excellence - 4 yrs. Who's Who - 4 yrs All State Cross-Country Team - 3 yrs; [oth. writ.] The Race - published in Whispers in the Wind; [pers.] Always be the best you can be; [a.] Marengo, IN

MICIOTTA, JR. DOMINICK T.
[b.] June 3, 1969, Brooklyn, NY; [p.] Alice and The Late Dominick Miciotta; [ed.] Dillard School of the Performing Arts, Franklin Pierce College, B.A., Theatre Arts; [occ.] Customer Service Rep., Florida Fillers, Inc.; [memb.] Memorial Sloan-Kettering Cancer Research Center, NY; [oth. writ.] Through poetry is his first love, Mr. Miciotta enjoys writing lyrics, plays and short stories. "On a Peaceful Night" is his first published work.; [pers.] Sylvia Plath once wrote, "I write because there is a vice in me which will not be still." I hope to encourage everyone to hear th epece which can exist in the hearts of humankind.; [a.] Carol Springs, FL

MIKES, DORAE ANN
[b.] September 6, 1975, Sequin, TX; [p.] Gene and Terri Mikes; [ed.] Joe F. Saegert Middle School, Sequin High school; [occ.] Student; [memb.] Matador Band; [pers.] A lot of love and support from my family and friends, and teachers has been the greatest influence upon my writing. I find that when I write, I try to answer the same questions others may be asking themselves; [a.] Sequin, TX

MILLARD, CHARLES A.
[b.] September 7, 1934, IL; [p.] deceased; [m.] Darlene, February 12, 1966; [ch.] A boy, George 25, a girl Michele 27.; [ed.] Sr., H.S. subjects being studied now are Physics, Philosophy and Psychology. Doing it myself.; [occ.] SSI retirement, I have chronic progressive M.S., had for the last 35 years; [memb.] A.N.A., C.N.A., A.I.N.A., un related; [hon.] None, its only been the last 6 months that I have let other than close friends, "see" the inside; [oth. writ.] "Cobwebs of time", "Winter of", "Always", "Life", "The Darkness", "Hallowe'en"; [pers.] I find writing, painting, playing music etc., etc., an "altered State of consciousness" and the need to express our feelings in so doing, I "Paint" what I "Hear", and "Write" what I "see". Now, that I am almost 60, I would like to live long enough to really learn to "paint" and "write".; [a.] Chicago, IL

MILLER, CRYSTAL LEE
[Pen.] Crystal Miller; [b.] April 7, 1982, Saskatoon, Saskatchewan, Canada; [p.] Merrilyn Miller; [occ.] Student; [memb.] Manitoba Figure Skating Assoc, Neepawa Gymnastics Club, Avid Swimmer (one more level to complete before she can begin the lifesaving course in swimming). Taking fourth year of piano; [hon.] Received divisional book award in grade 3 for language arts skills. Crystal has been involved in several dramas and musicals through school and church, including a musical, "Get on Board" in which she was the narrator of seventeen pages of script while only in grade 3; [oth. writ.] None published. Has written anumber of children's books. Attended a young author's conference with Paulette Bourgeois (Franklin Children's Book series author) in grade 2 for writing a children's book titled "The Kitten and The Seamonster". [pers.] Crystal wrote The Courage in grade 5 for Remembrance Day. She has taken a keen interest in World War II as her grandpa Miller is a veteran and his brother was a soldier who lost his life in that war; [a.] Minnedosa, Manitoba, Canada

MILLER, GRACE M.
[b.] August 19, 1952, Brooklyn, NY; [p.] Anthony & Lena Dispigno; [m.] David F. Miller, June 30, 1974; [ch.] David Anthony, Mark Francis, Diana Leigh, Jeremy Matthew; [ed.] Lynbrook High School stud-

ied Theology; [occ.] Homemaker Caring for other children; [memb.] Religious Instructor PTA member, class mother; [oth. writ.] Many poems written; [pers.] I believe that dreams never die.; [a.] Lynbrook, NY

MILLER, JAMIE
[b.] April 10, 1978, Indiana; [p.] Betty and James Miller; [ed.] Attending Buffalo Senior High; [occ.] Student; [oth. writ.] I was published in the "Large Sky Reaches Down"; [pers.] Paper is the only way for me to get my true feelings out. Poetry has helped me through some bad times; [a.] Buffalo, MN

MILLER, JANAY
[b.] September 1, 1977, Spfld, OR; [p.] Bradley S. Miller, Geri L. Miller-Hyland; [ed.] Currently a junior at Thurston High School; [memb.] Young Life, Financial Director of Thurston High; [pers.] Forbidden Love is written for all hearts who have been so badly broken that they are unable to express their true feelings. I dedicate this poem to Brian, who is the only "Apple" for my eyes, and who I will always want, need, and love; [a.] Springfield, OR

MILLER, MARY C.
[b.] May 8, 1919, Iron Mtn, MI; [p.] Vincenzo Gregori and Rachael; [m.] Jerome M. Miller, June 25, 1938; [ch.] 2 daughters - Barbara J. Kramer, Kathleen M. Yaggie; [ed.] High school - 1937, Nath Honor - Cum Laude (grad) junior yr; could not attend college because of financial problem at that time 1937; [occ.] Watercolor Artist Retired Floral Designer and Business Owner; [memb.] Pine Grove C. Club - Chippewa Club. Iron Mtn Kingsford Women's Club, Tuesday Literary Club (charter member) and founder SS Mary's and Joseph Catholic Diocese Northwoods Art League and Scholarship Committee, Adult Education Organization and Teacher; [hon.] 2nd award in Int'l National Art in 1988 - Won many local and state awards for my painting in Oils and Water Color of the Impressionistic School; Honored by St of MI for Watercolor by Gov. Blanchard; [oth. writ.] Many poems unrecorded, but enjoyed by my family and friends. Several in my possession have never been submitted prior to this. But english teachers recommended that I continue to write tho college was not possible; [pers.] Impressions of Days Gone By and Flowers and Nature have been my inspiration. Have been greatly influenced by mood and impressionistic writers especially poets. Written poetry every year for 35 years; [a.] Iron Mtn, MI

MILLER, MICHAEL T.
[b.] June 22, 1965, Minneapolis, MN; [p.] Paul & Judy Miller; [ed.] North Central High School, Indianapolis, Indiana University; [occ.] Certified Public Accountant, Neuwisser, Flygare and Szarzyaski; [memb.] AICPA, MNCPA; [hon.] Two-time winner of poetry contest sponsored by Indiana chapter of the National Society of Arts and letters, 1981 & 1982; [oth. writ.] Poetry published in annual high school anthology, "Etchings in Thought", 1981-83. Wrote numerous articles for high school newspaper, "The Northern Lights."; [pers.] Love is important, complex, and at times, elusive. I try to use the structure and texture of poetry to grasp the essence of love without having it. Other times, I write to dispel the darkness of my thoughts.; [a.] Minneapolis, MN

MILLER, MICHAELA C.
[b.] September 27, 1957, Germany; [p.] Sam and Nance Webb; [ch.] Robert James Miller; [occ.] Watercolor Artist (published) and freelance writer; [memb.] Hawaii Watercolor Society Copely Society of Boston, American League of Pen Women; [hon.] Numerous awards for watercolors in varied juried shows; [pers.] I believe strongly in nobility - nothing lovely is truly beautiful without it. I seek this elusive quality in my paintings as well as the written word, with the humble awareness that this comes only from

a character tireless in its own personal quest; [a.] Honolulu, HI

MILLER, ROBERT
[b.] February 7, 1977, Loving, Covina, CA; [p.] Robert & Karen Miller; [ed.] Currently a Junior at Rubidoux High School; [hon.] Academic Achievement Awards; [pers.] I don't worry what others think or say about me. My writing usually reflects how I feel at that time or it reflects things that are around me.; [a.] Riverside, CA

MILLER, RUTH
[b.] January 21, 1950, Brevard; [p.] Arthur and Dollie Riddle; [m.] Clifton Miller, December 2, 1969; [ch.] Alice Wayne and Joseph Miller; [pers.] I love expressing my heart felt thoughts in poetry. The poem "When I Used to Tie Your Shoes" was written for my daughter, Alice Miller; [a.] Rosman, NC

MILLER, TAMMILA (WEAKLEY)
[Pen.] Tammila M. Miller; [b.] January 19, 1969, Lutesville, MO; [p.] E. Glen Weakley, Joyce (Jordan) Weakley; [m.] Lee A. Miller, May 20, 1989; [ch.] Deborah Nicole (born July 29, 1990 in Germany), Brother: Delbert Weakley; [ed.] 1988 Graduate of Woodland R-4 High School, CNA training at Bond's Nursing Care Center, 1 year at Univ of Missouri; [memb.] Compassionate Friends and Mid-Tex Chapter, MADD; [hon.] VFW Literary Award - 1987; [oth. writ.] I've sent in other poems to "Compassionate - Friends" Chapters for those who've also suffered from Bereavement; [pers.] The life of a child born through love is the most precious gift in life; [a.] Grassy, MO

MILLIARD, LARONDA
[b.] May 15, 1978, Houston, TX; [pers.] Self Influenced; [a.] Sugarland, TX

MILLS, JON K.
[b.] November 3, 1964, Springfield, IL; [p.] Richard and Rachel Mills; [ed.] Doctor of Psychology degree; [occ.] Asst Prof of Psychology; [memb.] Amer Psych Assoc and American Philosophical Assoc; [hon.] Numerous Awards, scholarships and fellowships. Outstanding Doctoral Graduate of the Year Award, 1992; [oth. writ.] Numerous articles published in professional journals; [pers.] Destiny is never predetermined. It can only be and is necessarily determined; [a.] Romeoville, IL

MILLS, WILLIE HAYES
[Pen.] Willie Mills; [b.] February 9, 1938, AL; [p.] Elizabeth Jones; [ch.] Cynthia Mills, Angela Mills; [ed.] 10 grade, Pickens County High; [oth. writ.] Songwriter "Remember Me Darling"; [pers.] Yes, I have something to say, I have been writing poetry for 15 years, and I haven't got no place with my work yet; [a.] Ethelsville, AL

MILOSZ, GRACE
[Pen.] Grace Vincent; [b.] November 9, 1957, Calgary, Canada; [p.] Leon Milosz, Genowefa Milosz; [m.] Dan Vincent, July 17, 1994; [ed.] Bishop Carroll HS, Southern Alberta Inst of Tech; [occ.] Chemical Technologist; [hon.] Graduated with honors, CH.T., Imperial Oil Award, IODE Bursary; [a.] Fullerton, CA

MINES, ROSETTE
[b.] April 1, 1929, Brooklyn, NY; [p.] Samuel Esther; [ed.] Graduate from Erosnus Hall High School also studied at Brooklyn College; [occ.] Own Bus Cust Service Printers; [memb.] Artist League of Brooklyn Honorable Mentions; [oth. writ.] Poetic Eloquence, Feelings Magazine and National Library of Poetry creating through writing or painting is my love; [pers.] Feelings life's air being close and in touch by painting or writing can make me alive warm and thoughtfull; [a.] Brooklyn, NY

MINGS, KIMDLISA
[b.] February 13, 1980, Antigua; [p.] Stanford and Janet Mings; [ed.] Grade 8, high school (Antigua Girl's High School); [occ.] Student; [oth. writ.] Several poems (not published); [pers.] "Without a poem now and then, life is like a blank page"; [a.] Antigua, WI

MINNINGER, DANIEL R.
[Pen.] Ross Daniels; [b.] August 11, 1964, Pottstown, PA; [p.] Hazel and William Minninger; [ed.] Graduated Boyertown Area Senior High School (Pennsylvania) some college courses, plus numerous course in the Air Force; [occ.] Staff Sargeant, US Air Force; [memb.] Hemlock Society; [hon.] US Air Force Commendation Medal, US Air Force Achievement Medal (twice); [oth. writ.] Numerous unpublished poems; [pers.] Live all your dreams to the fullest, for we never know when or where our roads will come to an end.

MIR, NESTOR
[b.] September 8, 1932, Cuba; [m.] Emilia, May 30, 1953; [ch.] Oscar, Ari and Robert; [ed.] Accounting; [pers.] I have written many poems most of them in spanish, which I do for my own enjoyment, I have never published any. I have been too busy helping my children and now grandchildren.

MIRKOVIC, WALTER
[b.] August 3, 1970, Jersey City, NJ; [ed.] Brick Memorial High, Devry Technical Institute; [hon.] Dean's List; [pers.] I love writing, it may sound strange, but my poetry seems to flow out on to paper from nowhere. It's a gift from God.; [a.] Brick, NJ

MISEWICH, GEORGE
[Pen.] Luke; [b.] January 17, 1930, Richmond, BC, Canada; [p.] George and Eustace Misewich; [m.] Lilian Agnes, Belford (Feb 10, 1935), December 17, 1954; [ch.] (4) Bradley, Bruce, Shelley and Todd; [ed.] Grade 12, high school graduation, John Oliver High - June 1949, Vancouver, BC, Canada; [occ.] Retired; [oth. writ.] Newspaper articles; [pers.] "To each his own. Imaginative. Responsive"; [a.] Abbotsford, BC, Canada

MITCHELL, DANA LEE
[Pen.] Dana Mitchell/Dana L. Mitchell; [b.] October 13, 1980, Charlottesville, VA; [p.] Douglas and Laura Mitchell; Family: Twin Sister - Shana, Brother - Jacob; [ed.] 8th grader at Johnson Williams Middle School. Currently studying latin and algebra; [occ.] Student future marine biologist; [memb.] Virginia St Appaloosa Assoc Freestate Appaloosa Assoc - Student Council Admin, Chess Club Cooking Club; [hon.] 1990 Lord Fairfax Community College Soil and Water District Award Winner, Presidential Academic Award, Merit Finalist 1992 Virginia Future Miss Achievement and Awards; [oth. writ.] (LFCC) "Don't Pollute", (Zenith) "The Breeze"; [pers.] I am greatly encouraged by my family and believe that everyone should try writing at least once!; [a.] Berryville, VA

MOHANDIE, KRIS
[Pen.] Jimi Waterman; [b.] July 5, 1963, Inglewood, CA; [p.] Linda Senechal, Lee Mohandie; [ed.] Ph.D. Clinical Psychology, California School of Professional Psychology Los Angels, BA Bachelor Science Cal Poly Romona; [occ.] Police Psychologist, LAPD; [pers.] I write about what I feel and what moves through me.; [a.] Pasadena, CA

MONTEIRO, KELLY L.
[b.] September 9, 1975, New Bedford, MA; [p.] Renee Savoie & Kenneth Monteiro; [ed.] Fairhaven High School, Emmanuel College; [occ.] Student; [hon.] Dean's List, Dave Cowen's Award Nominee, Presidential Academic Award, Getting a poem published; [oth. writ.] Poems and stories and song lyrics

but not yet published; [pers.] Writing is a way for m to deal with the many feelings, emotions, and though I sometimes have--I find it an easier way to expre myself rather than speaking. Actions may spea louder than words, but words are more powerful tha people seem to relize; [a.] New Bedford, MA

MONTERO-ELBAO, VICTORIA LOKELANI
[Pen.] Lani Elbao; [b.] June 30, 1981, Temple, TX [p.] Jose E. Elbao and Lorraine M. Elbao; [ed Fairway Middle School; [occ.] Student; [memb.] Joseph Choir.

MONTGOMERY, JAMES H.
[Pen.] J. Herbert Montgomery; [b.] January 31 1945, Frankfort, KY; [p.] Mary and Edmond; [ch.] 3 [ed.] Northeastern High School, Det MI; MI St Univ E. Lansing (2 yrs); [occ.] Deputy Sheriff; [pers.] W are not physical bodies leaving spiritual experiences we are spiritual beings having human experiences [a.] Detroit, MI

MONTGOMERY, TRESA
[b.] December 15, 1977; [p.] Barb Bailey Montgom ery and Henry Heichert; Sisters: Tammy, Penny, Cory, Barbie; Niece: Alicia; [ed.] In grade 11 a Robert Usher High School, Regina, Sask, Canada; [occ.] Student.

MONTOUR, SUSAN
[b.] March 20, 1957, Balto; [p.] Mr. and Mrs. Roland Reiser, Sr; [m.] George Montour, Jr, November 15, 1986; [ch.] Chris 5, Eric 2; [ed.] High School class 75, Mergenthalau Voc Tech High School; [occ.] Homemaker/part-time insurance agent; [pers.] I have been writing poems for a long time. This is my first publication. I enjoy expressing myself through poetry. I write for enjoyment. My oldest son loves to read what I write. He is my biggest fan; [a.] Hollywood, MD

MOON, MICHAEL SHAWN
[b.] September 23, 1973, Lewisburg, PA; [p.] Eric B. & Carol Moon; [ed.] High School Graduate but am seriously considering going to college for art, went to high school at Shikellamy High; [occ.] Unemployed; [memb.] Member of Alcoholics Anonymous, Member of National Art Honor Society; [hon.] Several certificates and honorable mentions for my artwork in high school; [oth. writ.] "MY Life" was the first poem I ever wrote.; [pers.] I'm involved with a variety of arts. I enjoy writing poetry, drawing and sketching, pen and ink and playing my drumset. I find my most successful pieces of art being most successful when they come from the heart. That is were "my life" came from.; [a.] Northumberland, PA

MOORE, DARGAM FISHBURNE
[Pen.] Dargam F. Moore; [b.] April 14, 1940, Walterboro, SC; [p.] Mr. and Mrs. L. G. Fishburne; [m.] divorced; [ch.] Four; [ed.] St Mary's Jr College, Raleigh, NC, USC - Cola JC; [occ.] Retired - Probation Counselor for 12 yrs; [memb.] Colonial Dames Nature Conservancy of SC, SC Preservation Society, Junior League of Cola, SC; [oth. writ.] Other poems - freelance; [a.] Walterboro, SC

MOORE, DAVID
[b.] February 15, 1968, Sydney, Australia; [ed.] Liverpool Tech College; [occ.] Shop Assistant; [oth. writ.] Many songs and poems -- none of which have been recorded or published - mainly because I don't usually let anyone hear them!; [pers.] Wounds of the flesh - in time will heal - but the wounded heart - you forever feel; [a.] Hemel Hempstead, Herts, UK

MOORE, DEREK W.
[b.] July 21, 1972, Lakeview, MI; [p.] Mary Elna Dauchy; [ed.] Washtenaw Community College 1/93 to present, Grand Rapids Community College 9/90-4/

..., Cedar Springs High School, Diploma 6/90; [occ.] ...udent, prep cook and assistant manager; [memb.] ...ational Eagle Scout Assoc., American Culinary ...dertion, Green Peace, Howard City Conservation ...lub; [hon.] Eagle Scout, Boy Scouts of America, ...est Michigan Shores Council, Troop 222 3/14/90, ...edar Springs High School Excellence and Award in ...gricultural Education 1990. Michigan and National ...ood Service, Sanitation Certification, many others in ...oy Scouts of America and F.F.A.; [oth. writ.] An ...rticle written for international magazine, published ...n The Perspectives network, winter 1994, Vol IV ...ssue. Other poetry and writings about my life ...xperiences and feelings.; [pers.] I understand human ...eeds and the need for human companship. I, as well ...s others, can see this as I write about my life ...xperiences. It is in this that I strive to make it better ...or the generations that take our place. My eternal ...ish is that no person endure the enevitible evil ...ardships of life and that I've gone through that ...iolence will cease, that we enduce and live life for ...oday as well as tomorrow and the people of all races ...eligions, and sex live in peace and harmony.; [a.] ...nn Arbor, MI

MOORE, EVE
[b.] June 6, 1919, Wilmington, CA; [p.] Ellawen & Francis Fein; [m.] Fred Moore, February 19, 1938; [ch.] Terry Moore, Greg Moore; [ed.] Bakersfield Grammer and High School, Costa Mesa Jr. College; [occ.] Retired Secretary, Retired Portrait Artist; [memb.] Delta Theta Tau Sorority, Church of Religious Science, Bakersfield Art Assoc., Bakersfield Business & Professional Women's Club, Bakersfield Community Theater; [hon.] Foremost Portrait Artist of Kern Co., Cal. (Bakersfield Newspaper Quote) 1992 Who's Who In Poetry, Etc. Popular, etc. Popular vote a 1948 Kern Co. Fair for Portrait in OR, three times more votes than any other, standing ovation at community theatre (Lettie in "Uncle Harry") does this count.; [oth. writ.] A book of poetry, "Grant Me Voice" (How I would love to see it published, I haven't known how to go about that. It would be well recieved by the public considering many comments. (148 poems to date); [pers.] If my thought is truly worthy and if all souls are nurtured by worthy thoughts, and if I, in regal splendor, hide my meaning in esoteric phrases and the sound and rhythm is all that's heard by those who read then I have failed and should lay down my pen and start a new; [a.] Minneapolis, MI

MOORE, JEWEL LYNN
[Pen.] Julie; [b.] October 28, 1977, Elmendorf AFB, AK; [p.] Lonnie and Debra Moore, Jr; [ed.] Sophomore at Freedom High School, Morganton, No Car; [hon.] Received a letter from a congressman in Sacramento, CA when she was in the 5th grade for a letter written to request funds for her school; [pers.] Writing poetry is a way of expressing my feelings when I am frustrated; [a.] Morganton, NC

MOORE, MIESHA DAWN
[b.] October 11, 1981, Muskogee, OK; [p.] Ricky and Sheila Moore; [ed.] 6th Grade; [occ.] Student; [memb.] Grace Episcopal Church member, Gifted Student Program at Oktaha Elementary, Oktaha Elementary Band. Grace Episcopal Youth Group.; [hon.] "World Peace" and "Year 2050" poster winner for Delta Kappa Gamma. Honor Roll student 1st chair flutist, member of the gifted student program at Oktaha Elementary; [pers.] "Whatever you do keep trying"; [a.] Oktaha, OK

MOORE, OPHELIA
[b.] August 17, 1941, Dillon, SC; [p.] Nora Steele and Clyde Steele; [m.] Robert Moore, July 26, 1958; [ch.] Violet M. Glenn, Orneze Moore, Adrienne Turner; [ed.] William Howard Taft H.S.; [occ.] Homemaker (Interior Decorator); [memb.] Graham

Temple (Church of God and Christ); [hon.] none; [oth. writ.] none; [pers.] I write poetry from experiences and from feelings I hold within. I write poetry because I'm working toward the feeling of accomplishment.; [a.] Laurinburg, NC

MOORING, JUNE P.
[b.] December 13, 1945, Seven Springs, NC; [p.] Roy and Rabia Price; [ch.] Alicia Dawn Mooring, William Lee Mooring, Jr; [ed.] Ongoing Management Training by Coldwell Banker-Broker/Management Consultant; [occ.] Asst Vice President and Managing Broker, Abbitt Realty, Newport News, VA; [memb.] Virginia Assn of Realtors, Virginia Peninsula Assn of Realtors; [hon.] Distinguished Visitor Award - Seymour Johnson AFB. Awarded by the Base Commander for outstanding community service. Cert of Appreciation - NC Special Olympics; [pers.] My writings are dedicated to my loving family, whose inspiration has given me the richest of blessings. I love you mother, daddy, Bobbie, LaRue, Dawn and Lee; [a.] Newport News, VA

MORA, MADELINE
[b.] October 24, 1972, Brooklyn, NY; [p.] Louis & Loretta Mora; [m.] To Be..Matthew E. Hichks, May 26, 1995; [ed.] Bishop Kearney H.S., Monmouth College; [hon.] English Alumni Scholarship; [oth. writ.] Production of one-act play- "Sanitation Symphony", Publication of poems in a compilation entitled "The Eagle Spirit"; [pers.] I write because it is in me to do so, to not write would be a rejection of self.; [a.] Middletown, NJ

MOREY, FRANCINE
[Pen.] Francine Pollack; [b.] April 20, 1932, Jamaica; [p.] Eric and Linden Pollack; [m.] Eric Morey, April 20, 1974; [ch.] Geraldine, Elaina, Anthony, Manuel, Naomi, Wayne, Linden, Chris; [ed.] St John's Primary, St Hildas, Miss Trap's Private, PCC; [occ.] Retired; [memb.] AARP, Legion of Presidential Task Force; [hon.] Awards from President Regan and President Bush; [oth. writ.] Poems, song writing; [pers.] Be happy with what you have, if one can do better, do better. I believe happiness is a state of mind; [a.] Pasadena, CA

MORFORD, RHONDA S.
[b.] May 21, 1975, Kansas City, MO; [p.] Ronald and Wanda Morford; [ed.] Grandview High School, currently enrolled as a Freshman at Missouri Western State College; [a.] Grandview, MO

MORGAN, AUGUSTES
[Pen.] Guss Morgan; [b.] January 5, 1926, McMinn, TN; [p.] Frank Houston, Laura Houston; [m.] Arlee Morgan; May 18, 1920, October 14, 1944; [ch.] Larry Frank, Gaynell; [ed.] Finish 10th grade. Got my GED 1982; [occ.] Volunteer at Charleston Senior Center; [memb.] Bellefounte Baptist Church, Empty Stocking Fund (For foster children Christmas) Senior Center; [hon.] Humanitarian Award, Tennessee Foster Parent of Year in 1991, Certificate of Achievement of Good Citizenship from Sheriff Dan Gilley; [oth. writ.] Wrote other poem not published; [pers.] Love to help other, Foster Parent for 17 yrs raised six of my Foster Children they still call us Mom and Dad. Their children call us Grandmama and Granddaddy; [a.] Charleston, TN

MORGAN, THERESA A.
[b.] July 4, 1971, Milwaukee, WI; [p.] William E. Morgan Jr., & Maxine Morgan; [ed.] John Marshall High, Marquette University; [pers.] Inspiration and Spontanity are the keys to my creativity; [a.] Milwaukee, WI

MORIN, NICOLE
A senior at Van Buren High School. She was given eight awards on Academic Awards night. She has

been secretary of her class for four years and was active in the following activities: all drama, (taking best actress 1993), baseball, soccer, gifted and talented, church activities volunteer, catalogued books at the library in her spare time, karate, band, cheerleading, pre-naval training and very active in Project Grad. She took first place regionals and third place in the state finals in accounting in her junior year, Senior year, Presidential Academic Fitness Award for outstanding academic achievement, high honors three out of three quarters and Husson College Business woman of the year, Regionals (Beam contest - first place, Administrative Office procedures and second place Accounting II: first place, Administrative Office Procedures, first place, Accounting II, and first place, Business Computor Applications - Van Buren District. Upon graduation, Morin will leave for the US Navy. She has been selected for officer training and will do her basic in Orlando, FL. She is the grand-daughter of Guy and Jane Morin of Hamlin. She left for the Navy July 1, 1994 and graduated basic in Aug. She was then sent to the San Diego Naval Base and was enrolled into the BOOST Officer's Training Program. She has been awarded 2 commendations for working with underprivileged children on her off time. She will graduate June 3 and after a 20 day leave she will be sent to AZ St Univ. She will then be required to serve 4 yrs of college naval program. Upon completion, she will be reactivated, Full Officer status.

MORITANI, MINEO
[b.] October 21, 1944, Kasawa, Japan; [p.] Kataro, Asae Moritani; [m.] Keiko Moritani, March 15, 1974; [ch.] Mirei, Monica, Hosana, Shigeoki, Shinki; [ed.] Tokyo Univ of Education, D.LiH DEJ (Lafayette Univ) Ph.D (Open Int'l Univ); [occ.] Asst Prof Bukkyo Univ; [memb.] PEN Int'l; [hon.] Cultural Doctorate (world univ) Madhusudan Academy Prize (Indian, Calcutta), LHD, World Univ of America; [oth. writ.] Theoretical Study of John Multon, vol 3; [pers.] I serve the Lord, to manifest His Glory; [a.] Kobe, Japan

MORRIS, JENNIFER
[b.] July 7, 1975, Dayton, OH; [p.] Patrick Morris and Suzanne Pennypacker; [ed.] Hellgate High School, Cornell College; [occ.] Student; [memb.] Womyn 4 Womyn; [hon.] Academic Honors throughout high school; [oth. writ.] Poems and short stories published in school anthology and local paper.; [pers.] I need to write to release my inner feelings. Without writing I wouldn't have the will to survive.; [a.] Mt. Vernon, IA

MORRIS, MARK
[b.] February 15, 1970, Pasadena, CA; [p.] Drew Morris & Connie Morris; [ed.] San Marino High School, Baylor University; [memb.] Kappa Sigma Fraternity Golden Key National Honor Society; [a.] San Marino, CA

MORRIS, RASHIAH
[b.] October 23, 1971, Harley, NY; [p.] Sarah and William Morris; [ed.] Suny (State Univ of NY) at Albany; [memb.] NAACP, Black Women's Coalition, Albany State Univ Black Alliance and the All African People Revolutionary Party; [hon.] Who's Who Among American High School Students, Mount Vernon High School Scholarship Award; [oth. writ.] I express what I'm feeling in my writing; [pers.] Writing is my favorite past time which I have enjoyed for many years; [a.] Mount Vernon, NY

MORRISON, ARTHUR R.
[b.] April 4, 1931, Bayonne, New Jersey; [p.] John S. and Mable M.; [m.] Majorie L., October 2, 1976; [ch.] Sharon, Patricia, Arthur, Leonard, Brian, David; [ed.] Patterson Jr., High, Balto. MD, Paterson High, Baltimore, MD, Baltimore city College (LUTC), CLUE, City College of Baltimore, MD; [occ.] Re-

tired (Security Field); [memb.] Grand Lodge A.F. & A.M. Mason's 30 years, Maryland Song Writer's Assoc., Nashville, TN, Top Records AM41086 (5 poems put to music); [hon.] Editors Choice Award, When A Writer Dies, National Library of Poetry 1989, Star Search Award, Out Of My Mind by Wayne Presley, 1992; [oth. writ.] Disabled American Veteran's Mag. Biography John S. Morrison WWI and WWII Born, 1898, Circulation 35,000. Paradise Valley News Paper, 1993" Mayor Johnson recall" circulation 50,000, 28 other poems published; [pers.] I write as I have lived it. Sometimes happy. Sometimes sad. A lesson learned or a lesson earned. Along lifes way. With out my wife Marjorie inspiration and love..my writing would not be possible. I have presently finished my fifth book in a series of westerns I am writing. I am now starting a series of Mystery Detective pocket books.; [a.] Phoeniz, AZ

MORROW, VIVIAN GRAY
[b.] December 18, 1913, Sapulpa, OK; [p.] Elam and Nora Gray (dec); [m.] (dec) Glenn O. Morrow, April 11, 1939; [ch.] 2 - Pamela Foley, Mark Morrow; [ed.] High school graduate, creative writing course (Olympic College); [occ.] Retired (former telephone supervisor); [memb.] Lincoln Bible Church Bremerton, WA; [hon.] Class poet in high school. A poem published in the Univ of Wash Hosp (TCU) newsletter. I have written one song (words and music) been copyrighted; [oth. writ.] Prose and poetry. I have had one poem published in "Decision" magazine. I have had others published in local publications. A number of letters to editors published; [pers.] I have a deep personal faith in God, and desire to honor him in my writings. Also, to minister to others and encourage them in all that I write; [a.] Bremerton, WA

MOSHIER, LOUISE C.
[b.] December 2, 1915, Little Falls, NY; [p.] Ferdinand and Mary Moshier; [ed.] St. Mary's HS Little Falls, NY; College: Immaculata, PA received BS degree 1950: Columbia, U, NY; Internship at Presb Hosp 1 yr Dietitian; [occ.] Surgical nurse and dietitian, currently retired; [memb.] ADA; [oth. writ.] Several poems published in several poem books and newspaper. Several recipes published in Syracuse Newspaper.

MOSS, JETTIE M.
[b.] January 1, 1927, AR; [p.] Mary and Tilton Richrdson; [m.] Edward Moss, (dec.), September 3, 1955; [ch.] Anita, Linda, Edwina, Joyce, Edward Jr., Lisa, Rickly; [ed.] Elyria High School, Elyria, Ohio; [oth. writ.] I have written other poems and I have assembled many in my own book.; [pers.] In my poems, I try to write of the realities of life and bring joy to others.; [a.] Chicago, IL

MOYER, CAROL
[b.] June 23, 1939, Pittsburgh; [p.] Marie and Carl Thoma; [m.] John L. Moyer, December 18, 1981; [ed.] BS in English, Carnegie Mellon Univ, graduate work in English and Library Science, Univ of Pittsburgh; [occ.] Rehabilitation Counselor/mentally ill; [hon.] Quill and Scroll Award; [oth. writ.] Amateur writing only, to include satirical travelogues, greeting cards; [pers.] I try to capture the tragi -comic aspects of life; [a.] Pittsburgh, PA

MUDGETT, SEAN P.
[Pen.] Luratic Prince; [b.] January 12, 1972, Earth; [p.] One of 'em's dead, Diane K.; [m.] Would be dead if I could find her; [m.] Never happened; [ch.] None that I know of; [ed.] I ain't got none. Ha, Ha; [occ.] Bum; [memb.] Unfortunately, the human race; [oth. writ.] Some poems, short stories and a song here and there; [pers.] Fich Di, du miserabler whorenson! It's German, you figure it out; [a.] Fish Kill, NY

MUELLER, MARY ROSE
[b.] March 16, 1953, St. Paul, MN; [p.] John and Mildred Sonstegard; [ch.] Dustin John Mueller; [ed.] BS English/Education/Speech/Theatre (Minor), St. Cloud State Univ, MN; AA Golden Valley Luth Jr College, Golden Valley, MN; [occ.] Technical Publications Editor; Public Affairs Specialist; [memb.] Smithsonian Inst; Leadership Killeen, Killeen, TX; [hon.] Member of Leadership - Killeen, TX; Mayor's Award for Excellence, Temple, TX; Commander's Coin, Test and Experimentation Command; Fort Hood, TX; Phi Kappa Phi Honor Society; [oth. writ.] Numerous articles in Fort Hood Sentinel (newspaper), Fort Hood, TX; articles in Aviation Digest; [pers.] Realizing that the continuum of life is heavily weighted by the integrity of the living, I strive to achieve my ideal weight; [a.] Killeen, TX

MUHAMMAD, MARYAM E.
[b.] April 18, 1936, Detroit, MI; [p.] Eddie Dew and Catherine Roland; [m.] Divorcee; [ch.] Ricardo Ware, Mary K. Muhammad, Sameerah, Wahad, Rahaman and Rahim Muhammad; [ed.] Microcomputer Training - Wayne Community College. MSC Skill Training. Lic Beauty Operator; [occ.] Retired Disabled worker (State of MI - DSS); [memb.] Sera - DAC for retired State of MI employees. Public and private shcool parents organizations; [hon.] Outstanding service Western High School, Humanitarian - MYC, Chicago, IL. Humanitarian Huron Valley Woman Facility. Community Service Neighbor Watch-City of Detroit Outstanding Service (sis. Clara Muhammads School; [oth. writ.] Reflect Upon the Whirl of Emotions (book of 40 poems). Bible Commentary for Reference A Muslim is Humble; [pers.] "Our destiny depends on how we live"; [a.] Detroit, MI

MULLER, PATRICIA MCGILL
[b.] October 13, 1946, Philadelphia, PA; [p.] Jeanne & Bill McGill; [m.] William Harry Muller, September 18, 1976; [ch.] Rebecca Anne, Mark William, Matthew Thomas; [ed.] St. Francis School of Nursing, University of Virginia and St. Joseph's College; [a.] Ashburn, VA

MUNSON, DANNICE
[b.] October 19, 1935, International Falls, MN; [ch.] Holly Munson-Wermiel, Susan Munson Lonsinger and Mark Munson; [ed.] Bachelor Science degree in journalism. Arizona State Univ, Walter Cronkite School Journalism 1976; Assoc degree, Scottsdale Community College 1973, Scottsdale, AZ; [occ.] PT receptionist, Lincoln Learning Center, John C. Lincoln Hospital, Phoenix, AZ and also Manpower at Phoenix Civic Center, Phx, AZ, includes Symphony Hall; PT Manpower temporary service. Through Manpower, I have worked part-time for more than three years at Phx Symphony Hall as an usher and also at Phx Civic Center; [hon.] (1973) Phi Thela Kappa, Scottsdale Community College, Scottsdale, AZ; [oth. writ.] While attending AZ State Univ 1973-76, wrote for the State Press, the Univ newspaper; [pers.] Through prayer each day give honor to our God and thank our Father for the new blessings still coming into my life. Also, I continue to strive to make use of my artistic abilities; [a.] Phoenix, AZ

MURDOCK, ARAMATHEA EVE
[b.] October 14, 1978, Denver, CO; [memb.] Amnesty Int'l; [hon.] Daughters of the American Revolution essay contest; [pers.] Special thanks to everyone who has kept me alive; Thank you God; [a.] Bath, ME

MURRAY, MACHEL BALLARD
[b.] July 19, 1959, Newport, RI; [p.] Richard Ballard, Ron & Virginia Anderson; [ed.] Riverdale High School, Graduated 1977; [occ.] Automotive Parts Counter Person, Lohse Automotive; [oth. writ.] Have recently written several poems. None have been published.; [a.] Rapids City, IL

MURRAY, TIMOTHY IRWIN
[Pen.] T.I.M. "T.C." Skull; [b.] January 13, 1967, LaPorte, IN; [p.] Dan Murray and Donna J. Stotle R. Murray, Jones; [ed.] LaPorte High School; [occ.] Babysitter and Housekeeper; [oth. writ.] unpublished; [pers.] I write poems and books all the time yet show them to very few. All who see them love them but still I kept them hide. This poem proves any thing i possible. So take a chance and send one off; [a.] Fish Lake, IN

MUSCIANESE, LAUREN CHRISTINA
[Pen.] Daisy, Ivy, Beb, Shyanne/Shy, Sky; [b.] June 23, 1979 (cancer), Newport News, VA (Hampton); [p.] Peter M. Muscianese and Agnes A.P. Muscianese; [ed.] Secur Notre Dame in Belgium Prek - 2nd grade Bronxville School from 3rd presend 9th grade; [memb.] 2 youth groups, the GA council at school. A concert choir as well as a madrigal and women's enssemble; [oth. writ.] "Off To War", poem published in "Whispers in the Wind". A book of poetry and several poems about my life; [pers.] "True friends are like Ivy and the wall. Both stand togethre and together they fall". "The dependable Daisy is a good friend in all weather". I have always compared life to a painting, plain and simple yet unexplainable. I will never stop writing it is my love although it is my dream to someday become an actress which is my passion; [a.] Bronxville, NY

MUSMACHY, FRANCES
[Pen.] Musch; [b.] November 13, 1922, Brooklyn; [p.] deceased; [m.] deceased, July 19, 1942; [ch.] (3) 2-boys, 1-girl; [ed.] 8 grade; [occ.] Retired.

MUSSINGTON, RENA
[b.] February 5, 1972, Manhattan, NY; [p.] Jean Christopher; [ed.] James Monroe High School, Bronx State Univ College at Fredonia, Fredonia, NY; [occ.] Student; [memb.] Black Student Union, Junior Class Representative; [pers.] I feel the best works of art are those that express how an author views the world. I have been greatly influenced by three African-American poets, i.e., Gwendolyn Brooks, Nikki Giovanni, and Langston Hughes; [a.] Fredonia, NY

NA, VICTOR
[b.] September 24, 1977, Malaysia; [p.] Chee Min Na, Martha Chang; [ed.] Currently studying at Carey Baptist Grammar School, Melbourne, Victoria Austrial; [occ.] Student; [memb.] none; [pers.] My favorite works are the Shakespearen Sonnets and the Australian Ballads of "Banjo" Paterson and Henry Lawson.; [a.] Melbourne, Aust., Victoria

NAJERA, SR. ANTONIO E.
[Pen.] Tony, Toning; [b.] May 10, 1915, Agno, Panga, Sinan, Philippines; [p.] Mariano Norico Najera; [m.] Natalia Espanol Najera; [ch.] Children 9 (5 boys & 5 girls); [ed.] Stationary Engineering Chemical Engineering (Under-grad.); [occ.] Retired; [memb.] American Legion, Post 2, Canada Chapter, Phillippine - Canadian Senior's Club; [hon.] As USAFFE Veteran (United Armed Forces In The Far East), States Army in the Far East, received three medals and five ribbons.; [oth. writ.] As to poetry contest, harvested over 23 Merits of Awards and five (5) yearly golden poet of awards, consicutively, 1985, 1986, 1987, 1988, and 1989 at Sacramento, Poetrygram Contes.; [pers.] With the case of the Marcoses, the most abused couple, The Media had gone too far, too long. Freedom of the Press, defeated its purpose. Hence avoid Politics, its a Dirty Business.; [a.] Toronto, Ontario Canada

NANCE, ANETTE K.
[b.] Alona; [b.] June 5, 1955, Stipshausen, Germany; [p.] Karl Faller, Annelisese; [m.] Leon B. Nance, July 2, 1981; [ed.] IDAR-Oberstein-High School; University of Tuebingen; University of Frankfurt; Monterey

eninsula College; [occ.] English School Teacher, Private); [oth. writ.] Personal poems waiting to be published and short stories for children learning to read english; [pers.] My writings reflect the primary essence of creation and inner emotions materializing themselves in progressive development as self-fulfilling prophecies in the secondary outer world.

ASON, TRACY
[Pen.] Tracy Lynn Nason; [b.] October 24, 1979, Portland; [p.] Ralph Mason, Jr. and Susan Mason.; [ed.] 8th grader at Saco Middle School; [memb.] Yearbook staff; [hon.] Honor Roll; [oth. writ.] Poems that only friends and family have read. Nothing else published.; [pers.] You never miss what you have until it's gone; [a.] Saco, ME

ATER, RAFAEL HONG
[b.] January 15, 1976, Seoul, Korea; [p.] Raymond Ater; [ed.] Maynard Evans High School, Junior Class; [occ.] Assistant Server at China Coast Restaurant; [memb.] Evans Career Path Program; [hon.] Outstanding Service in Red Cross Teen Corps.; [oth. writ.] Other poems not published; [pers.] Poem's are more than words on paper. Poetry reflects the feelings of your heart.; [a.] Orlando, FL

AUMANN, JOHN E.
[b.] August 18, 1963, Long Island; [p.] Catherine and Edward Naumann; [ed.] Primarily self-educated; [occ.] Art and Antique restorer, Historical Consultant, Artist; [oth. writ.] Unpublished poetry and philosophy, letters of love, frienship, and commentary. Ghostwriter; [pers.] After you have done and said what eases others, be sure to say and do what pleases you.; [a.] Hempstead, IL

AVRATIL, ELIZABETH
[b.] July 3, 1952, Brisbane; [p.] Elmer and Isabel (Mitchell) Navratil; [ed.] High School Certificate; studied playwrighting at QUT Kelvin Grove, Queensland; [occ.] Actress, Comedian, Playwright, Poet; [memb.] Queensland Writers' Centre, Access Arts Inc., Queensland Community Arts Network, Rock'n'Roll Circus, Grin and tonic Theatre Troups; [oth. writ.] I have had a few articles published in magazines. I write my own material for my stand-up comedy routines. I co-wrote the play "Glimpses in the Dark" which was produced in 1992. Another play I wrote, "The Lives of Sara" is currently being workshoped by the the Queensland Performing Arts Trust with the possibility of it being produced in 1995. My poem "Standing Feet" was published in "The Coming of Dawn"; [pers.] I only started writing three years ago as a way of creating more work for myself. I get a great deal of enjoyment from my writings especially when I hear the audiences, laughing during my comedy routines.; [a.] Brisbane, Quensland, Australia

ODULE, ERASMUS CHINEMELU
[b.] June 15, 1967, Port Harcourt; [p.] Christopher Odulue, Rita Ndulue; [ed.] B.A., Hons. Archaeology, M.A. Mass Communicaiton, University of Niceria Usukka; [occ.] Just rounded up my Masters Degree Programme, will shortly attend interview for employment.; [hon.] Director's Certificate of commendaiton for Meritorious Service, Katsina State, National Youth Service Corps., 1991; [oth. writ.] numerous articles and poems published in both national and local dailies in Nigeria including Musings of A Patriot (Eighty Three poems for National Coniousness) yet to be published.; [pers.] I sensitise the numb feelings of my society to the agonising and despicable plight of the down-trodden hoipolloi in my country. I believe in justice, fairplay and respect for human rights.; [a.] Aba, Abia

EAGU, JOHN
[Pen.] August 28, 1921, Garret, IN; [p.] John and Victoria Neagu; [m.] Katherine L. Neagu, September 14, 1946; [ch.] Doreen L. Mudrich, John Raymond Neagu; [ed.] Garrett High School, Indiana Extension University; [occ.] Retired from real estate brokerage business.; [memb.] Various veterans organizations.; [hon.] Was part of 49 editors invited to the White House for briefing on vietnam war by President L. B. Johnson; [oth. writ.] Many short stories, essays, and poems.; [pers.] Always try to convey a gentle message; [a.] Mendon, MI

NEIDLINGER, JR. PUAL E.
[b.] June 23, 1938, San Francisco; [p.] Paul Sr., Lillian Brown (dec.); [ch.] Paul III, Christian M., Jeffery Shane, and Jennifer E.; [ed.] Hight School, Bible Correspondence courses, Assy. of God, Calif.; [memb.] Full Gospel Business Mans Fellowship International; [hon.] Good Conduct Medal twice, Air Force Outstanding Unit Citation Award, 1958 France, Outstanding Cated of year, 1955; [oth. writ.] Plays, unpublished, The Day Mr. Lord Made The Right Choice, Coversation of Susan, The Fall of Johnnie Pillars, an the charted course of Samuel J. Book, novels, a seven set series, entitled The Continues Story Of The Two Witnessess, Changing World Power, The Easy Days, God New Fight, The Works Finished..; [a.] Navato, CA

NELSON, BESSIE
[Pen.] Justina Shackerfoot; [b.] September 8, 1958, Headland, AL; [p.] Perry Walker Sr., and Hilda Walker; [m.] June 8, 1968, Willie Nelson Sr., (October 15, 1950); [ch.] Willie Junior, Kirby Demond; [ed.] Carter Parramore, Middleton High, Washington College; [occ.] Religious Head Clerk, Metropolitan Ministry, Tampa, FL; [hon.] Spelling Honoree, Modeling Trainee; [pers.] I strive to reach each and every heart through my writings. I was influenced enarly in my life by people. People's are Pearls and Gems.; [a.] Temple Terrace, FL

NELSON, BRANDI
[Pen.] Brandi Lynn Nelson; [b.] May 4, 1976, Kingman, ZA; [p.] Jim and Carolyn Nelson; [ed.] Valentine Elementary School (K-8) (9-12); [memb.] Rodeo Club, FFA; [hon.] Who's Who In American Schools.; [oth. writ.] I have written numerous other poems and short stories.; [pers.] I love to write. I use writing as an outlet for my inner feelings. I feel that everyone should.; [a.] Peach Springs, AZ

NELSON, COSNTANCE A.
[b.] November 22, 1957, Gaylord, MI; [p.] Charles E. Margaret R. Richards; [m.] Michael J. Nelson, September 18, 1992; [ch.] Leeann M. Hunt, Kern T. Hunt, John M. Nelson, Sara J. Nelson; [ed.] St. Mary's Cathedra High School, Gaylord, MI; [occ.] Restaurant Manager; [memb.] M.A.D.D.; [hon.] National Honors Society High School Graduate; [pers.] I enjoy writing little poems and jingles to make others laugh and smile.; [a.] Gaylord, MI

NELSON, QUETTA MARIE
[Pen.] Maria Jones; [b.] May 24, 1944, Stuttgard, AK; [p.] Ralph Johnston & Edith Johnston; [m.] Walter Pierce Nelson, October 19, 1962; [ch.] Robin age 30, Randall age 27; [ed.] Cushman Elementary, Cushman Jr. High, Cushman Sr. High; [occ.] Assembly Line Factory, Worker White Rodgers Co. Batesville, Ark.; [oth. writ.] Other poems written in precious loving memory of friends and relatives who have passed on published in Batesville Daily Guard our local newspaper; [pers.] Time is fleeting and life is precious so I believe that by being kind and considerate of other people is one of life's greatest achievements; [a.] Batesville, AK

NELSON, ROSS
[Pen.] Rossi Nelson; [b.] April 28, 1944, El Paso, TX; [p.] Rowena S. Nelson, dad deceased; [ch.] Wes, 27 (son), Tony 24 (son); [ed.] Venice High, L.A. Calif. Assoc. of degree in Theology: Indiana Cosmetology License North Carolina, (Landmark Education Professional S.B. Calif; [occ.] Freelance Artist, Office Manager; [memb.] Maui Scuba Divers Assoc.; [hon.] American School Girl Award, Leadership Training Certificate, Hair and Costume Design Trophy 1st Place, Art Pastel Awards, Rodeo School Certificates; [oth. writ.] The Twig Times, Book of Poetry in progress, title "True to Life"; [pers.] Every person is special a unique individual standing in possiblity and power causing a world transformed now and for generations to come.; [a.] Santa Barbara, CA

NELSON, SCOTT PAUL
[b.] April 11, 1975, Lowell, MA; [p.] Clarence and Donna Nelson; [ed.] Oxbow High, VT; [occ.] Computer Systems Operator in the Air Force; [oth. writ.] In Progress; [pers.] The most lonely place in the world is the human heart when love is absent.; [a.] Ft. Myer, VA

NEUSCH, ELISABETH A.
[b.] November 14, 1978, Amarillo, TX; [p.] Edwin and Patricia Neusch; [ed.] San Houston Middle School, Tascosa High School; [occ.] Student; [memb.] Tascosa High Student Council, Kiwanis Club International, Bell Avenue Church of Christ, Tascosa High Advanced Orchestra, UNI drug prevention team; [hon.] Superintendant's Scholars List; Junior National Honor Society; National School Orchestra Award; [oth. writ.] Several poems written for personal enjoyment and not yet published in any form.; [pers.] The creation of poetry, like music, should come from the heart. I write with my heart and try to touch my poems with realism and truth.; [a.] Amarillo, TX

NEW, DAWN
[b.] September 25, 1976, Barrie, Ontario Canada; [p.] Richard and Karen New; [ed.] Barrie North Collegiate; [pers.] Life is a bowl of cherries, just watch out for the pits.; [a.] Barrie, Ontario

NEWCOMB, MARC GARLAN
[b.] January 20, 1972, Erie, PA; [p.] Garlan & Vicki Newcomb; [ed.] 1990 Graduate of Bethel Christian Academy. I have been accepted to the IUP Culinary Institue and will attend in the fall of 1994; [occ.] Fish Department Manager at local Pet Store, Musician.; [memb.] Glenwood Branch YMCA, National Rifle Association, Tommy Bolin Lives Club; [hon.] Dedicated to Service Award from Brown Bros. Loblaws, July 1991, Certificate of Versitility B.b. Loblaws, Dec. 1991, Best Actor inb a minor Role, "On Holy Ground" 1988 Bethel Christian Academy, Most Improved Actor "David" 1989 Bethel Christian Academy, Top Rock Guitarist Erie, PA 1993, Most Versatile Musician 1993;l [oth. writ.] "Crystal Eyes" (Amini Rock Opera), "Adia Nada", "Forever," "Special Place," "The Rose of Thorn," "I.B.U.B. We Be." "I will, to will, they will," "Salvation Epitaph", "Hope", "Dark Bell," "Shower Me The Blue Light" "Passages between the realms of Death," "The Devil's Best Friend," "The Lillies."; [pers.] "Artists throughout time have been known to be a bit eccentric. To weighout the balance between creativity and madness is where, in my opinion, artistic giants exist. In short, oddness is how the world perceives Genius."; [a.] Erie, PA

NEWMAN, ANNA
[b.] March 3, 1964, Parma City, FL; [p.] Roy and Catherine Newman; [ed.] High School, AMC, Amdor County; [occ.] Food server at Satter Creek, Back Roads Coffe House; [memb.] Gold Country People, First Area Counsel People First California; [hon.] Ten awards, special olympics, three church awards, spelling bee, bicycle sale; [oth. writ.] Story for AME preacher board.; [pers.] I write for myself and not at

people who want it.; [a.] Jackson, CA

NEWMAN, BENEDICT JOSEPH
[Pen.] Benny Newmn; [b.] February 25, 1952, Boyds Cove; [p.] Joseph and Bernadette Newman; [m.] Nora D. Donahue, Common Law January 1, 1980; [ch.] Sonya Bernadette Donahue, Matthew Benedict Newman; [ed.] Grade 12, 1st year Memorial University of NFLD; [occ.] Laborer; [memb.] Recreation Comm. Boyd's Cove; [hon.] Nil; [oth. writ.] I am an affiliate with Pro Can, Don Mills Ontario, where I have several song's copyrighted. A couple of more poems also.; [pers.] I like to live live one day at a time. I find plans are the seed of disappointment, so I just prepare for tomorrow, rather than plan. My philosophy is: necessity is the mother of invention, imagination is the father.; [a.] Boyd's Cove, NFLD.

NEWTON, PEGGY JO.
[Pen.] Peg's Prattle; [b.] October 9, 1933, Pine Bluff, AR; [p.] Cecil Owen and Helen jacks Owen; [m.] Freddie Newton, June 28, 1952 (Deceased 11/15/81); [ch.] Fredrica, Dannile, Gina, Amanda, and Marci; [ed.] High School; [occ.] Owner, Bar & Grill, Freddie's Bar-B-Q; [memb.] St. Alban's Episcopal Ch. Amer. Legion, VFW.; [hon.] "Little Things" published Nat'l Lib. 1992; [oth. writ.] Letters to editorials school paper.; [pers.] Writing is an emotional release from deep within the soul, a pouring out of the suppressed feelings in the hope that it will help someone else.; [a.] Stuttgart, AR

NG, STACY
[b.] August 10, 1978, Children Hospital; [p.] Irene Ng, Alfred Cheng; [ed.] Serramonte High, Ben Franklin Junior High School; [pers.] I want to spread my feeling to the winter.; [a.] Daly City, CA

NIBERT, HEATHER RENEE'
[b.] November 18, 1978, Point Pleasant, W.VA; [p.] Barbara and Ricky Nibert; [ed.] Sunny Side Elementary, Hannan High School, Giggleworks Clown Training; [occ.] Attend School; [memb.] Go Getters, 4-H Club, "Love Troop" clown group band.; [oth. writ.] "Untitled", "To the One I Love," "A Search For Words," "Would He", "Lost So Much, Gained So Much Too."; [pers.] I believe a poem is a way of wording your dreams. I always say "A dream is shread of hope, lingering in your mind. Hold on to your dreams and truth in them you'll find."; [a.] Apple Grove, W.VA

NICHOLS, TIMOTHY ALAN
[b.] August 2, 1970, Warren, MI; [p.] Bill Nichols & Ruth Nichols; [ed.] Abilene Christian University; [occ.] Graduate Student, MBA Program at Memphis State U.; [oth. writ.] Collection of poems written through the years.; [pers.] As I look up into the evening sky, I see a burning desire flowing from each individual cloud longing for a soul to devour its mastery of devine inspiration.; [a.] Memphis, TN

NIELSEN, LONE GOUL
[b.] December 17, 1971, Slagelse, Denmark; [p.] Hanne & Svend Aage Nielsen; [ed.] Hairdresser; [occ.] Au Pair; [memb.] The Danish Scout Organization (DDS); [oth. writ.] Several poems and some fairytales/stories still unpublished.; [pers.] I'm inspired by the hardness of life, that turns those special moments into beauty. It is about feelings that could belong to anybody.; [a.] Shaker Heights, OH

NIERMAN, MAJORITY
[b.] August 15, 1936, Fairplay, CO; [p.] Warren H. yarroll; [m.] Leon K. Nierman, March 18, 1956; [ch.] Sharon, Darlene, Steve and grandchildren: Amy, Kelly, Terri, Emily and Erica; [ed.] Prov High School, North Harris County College, LaSalle Univ.; [occ.] Student and writer; [memb.] Resurrection Lutheran Church; [hon.] President of Thespians,

First Place State Debate, Student Council for four years. Past President of Management Company for Physicians. Who's Who of American Women, 1985-86 Edition; [oth. writ.] Several short stories; [pers.] Don't dwell on the bad things, look for the good, have faith and never give up your dream.; [a.] Houston, TX

NIVEN, VICTORIA
[b.] January 24, 1969, Annapolis, MD; [p.] Henry and Wanda Niven; [ed.] M.A. University of Baltimore, B.A. Goucher College; [occ.] Graphic Designer; [memb.] The National Museum of Women in the Arts; [oth. writ.] Coelacanth, a group of women writers once believed to have been extinct.l; [pers.] The problem isn't that love ends, it's that it never ends. Nietzsche. This is why I write.; [a.] Baltimore, MD

NIX, CHRISTOPHER STEVEN
[Pen.] Chris Nix; [b.] March 9, 1976, Jackson, Tn; [p.] John A. and Jean D. Nix; [ed.] Cherry Creek High School, Englewood, CO; [occ.] Student; [pers.] It is indeed an honor to both myself and my family to have my first publication. I hope this will inspire others as it does me.; [a.] Englewood, CO

NIXON, DEWEY
[b.] October 17, 1942, Flint, MI; [p.] William and Dora Nixon; [m.] Catherine Viau Nixon, September 27, 1969; [ch.] Christina Nixon Collins, Regina and Melissa Nixon; [ed.] Grad. Flint Northern High 1961, Attended Flint J.C. 1962, Army Med. Corps Europe 1965-1966, Attended Det. Coll. of Business 1974-76. Also graduated Electronic Computer Programming Institute 1971; [occ.] 31 1/2 years at G.M. C.P.C. Flint V8 Eng.; [memb.] Amuets, AARP Past Member Westwood Hts. Lions Club; [hon.] Several Bowling and Drag Racing Trophies; [oth. writ.] Song copywritten not published "Thief with the Light" have other songs or poems none published.; [pers.] Jack of all trades master of none. Graduated from school of hard knocks also, toured U.S. and Europe; [a.] Flint, MI

NKHWANANA, WAFF ELLIOT
[Pen.] Waff; [b.] January 1, 1963, Mosojane, Botswana; [p.] Shyte Nkhwanana and Tjibuya Nkhwanana; [m.] Wananai Nkhwanana, May 18, 1993; [ch.] Michael Stuart and Chiang Cheng; [ed.] P.S. L.E.C (Zwenshambe) J.C. & COSC (Selebi Phikwe), Prsc and Dip. Sec. Educ. (U.B.), B.Ed. Sci. Ed. (pursuing at UB0; [occ.] Student (UB); [oth. writ.] Several poems published in local newspapers (Botswana and overseas (USA) journals, eg The Kalahari Review. I have a manuscript of 70 original wide-theme poems for volume publication.; [pers.] Let not our aspirations and appreciations depreciate and deteriorate.; [a.] Let not our aspirtions and appreciations depreciate and deteriorate; [a.] Gaborone, Botswana

NOBLE, NICK
[occ.] Unemployed; [hon.] Two awards as Outstanding Service as Library Assistant in Jr. High School one award as Learning Lab Assistant in Jr. High School. On the Honor Roll in Jr. High School. Did work as a VA Hospital Volunteer; [oth. writ.] I wrote a lot of poetry that is unpublished as well as philosophical, that are unpublished.; [pers.] I have been influenced by a lot of things around me but my poems come from me deep inside myself. I hope I can some day write more and I hope its published so others may read it and learn, more things, better for themselves and others.; [a.] Largo, FL

NOLL, JEWEL E.
[b.] April 12, 1983, Waukesha, SI; [p.] Thomas & Beverly Noll; [ch.] Brother, Dustin Noll; [ed.] 5th grde student, Waukesha School Dist. Hillcrest School; [occ.] Student; [memb.] Young authors conference,

school district of Waukesha; [hon.] "Celebrate th Writer" young authors conference 1993. "Hom work that unforgettable word"; Honorable Mentio "Why I think my Mom would make a good Pres dent", Waukesha Freeman Newspaper; [pers.] Spel ing and punctuation doesn't matter until the fin draft.; [a.] Saukesha, WI

NONNEMACHER, MARTIN ALLEN
[Pen.] Marty or Man; [b.] February 20, 1959, Reseda CA; [p.] Carl K. Nonnemacher, Jennifer Wilson; [m Dianna "Rupe" May 8, 1987 and Crystal "Stoner' May 20, 1980; [ch.] Tristan James (5 yrs) son, 4/13 88, Danielle Marie (12 yrs.) daughter, 12/20/8 [ed.] Chatsworth High, GED, Pierce Jr. College, CA Northland Pioneer AZ, Santa Fe Community NM SCI Southern Careert Institute, FL; [occ.] Disabled Paralegal, Part-time Writer/Poet; [memb.] Worl wide Church of God, Professional Career Develop ment Institute, School of Paralegal Studies, Interna tional Correspondence (Russian), The National L brary of Poetry, National Geographic, America Family Publishers, Newsweek; [hon.] SCI, Top 5 Aptitude, N.R.M. (Natural Resources Management Chemical Control Lic. #N553192778, G.E.D., En glish Comp., Substance Abuse, Santa Fe Comm NM, Psychology, Gourmet Cooking, Domestic Hom making; [oth. writ.] Political letter(s) of Civil Right Cases, Congressional News, WAD.C.., Tribun (albu.NM) Civil Rights 1983, Reader's Digest (Rapi Release/Prison, Civil Rights Letter(s) Public Com plaints, L.A. Times, Local Papers, CA, NM, OF AZ, WA, WAD.C.; [pers.] Do not neglect to sho hospitatlity to strangers, for by this some have ente tained angels without knowing. This I pray, that you love may around still more and more in real know edge and all discernment. Praise God; [a.] Tacoma WA

NORLING, SAMUEL A.
[b.] July 3, 1956, Youngstown, Ohio; [p.] Willia and Georgia Norling; [ed.] Springfield Local H.S. B degree in Mechanical Eng., Youngstown State Un versity; [occ.] Project Engineer Packard Electric Div of G.M.; [memb.] American Society of Mechanica Engineers, Society of Automotive Engineers, Ne Middletown Free Methodist Church; [hon.] Tau Bet Pi, two US Patents; [oth. writ.] Several poems non published; [pers.] In pursuit of the stars, as a colleg freshman, I encountered the rock of ages. My life an writings have not since been the same.; [a.] Ne Middletown, OH

NORMAN, KRYSTAL
[b.] April 30, 1982, Patchogue; [p.] Katherin Norman; [ed.] Challenge Program (Gifted & Talente Program) Saxton Middle School; [occ.] 6th grad student; [memb.] Honor Society, Honor Roll, Meri List; [hon.] N.Y.S.S.M.A., Solo & Duet Award Renaissance Program; [oth. writ.] Poems: The Sun The Human Race, Poetic Phrases, Why can't I fly Shoofly to Razzamatazz. Short stories: The Class room; [pers.] Intrigue, suspense, and a twist of th plot. That is what my writing is all about.; [a.] Patchague, NY

NORSTRAND, IRIS FLETCHER
[b.] November 21, 1915, Brooklyn, NY; [p.] Viole Marie Anderson & Matthew Emerson Fletcher; [m. Dr. Severin Anton Norstrand, May 20, 1941; [ch. Virginia Helene Villano, Thomas Fletcher Norstrand Dr. Lucille Norstrand; [ed.] Bay Ridge High Schl. Brooklyn College, Long Island College of Medicine MA and Ph.D. in biochemistry., M.D.; [occ.] Physi cian (Neurologist and Psychiatrist), Brooklyn, VA Medical Center, Clinical Prof. of Neurology, SUNY Health Science Cntr. at Bklyn.; [memb.] Assoc. o Univ. Professors of Neurology, Fellow of the Amer can Psychiatric Assoc. and Fellow of the America Academy of Neurology, Memb. of the Intnatl. Asso

f Neurochemistry, Board of Directors, American Medical EEG Assoc.; Memb.of the American Assoc. f Geriatric Psychiatry.; [hon.] Pres. of the Natl. ssoc. of VA Physicians (1989-1991), Pres. of the American med. EEG Assoc. (1987), First woman res. of the Brooklyn Neurological Assoc.; [hon.] 994 Special Achievement Award from the Alumni ssoc., City Univ. (Biochemistry); [oth. writ.] 47 medical papers. 2 musical compositions.; [pers.] The asic philosophy of Brooklyn College, my alma mater pplies to my life, i.e. "Nihil sine magno labore".;

NOWICKI, JESSICA KELLER
b.] April 17, 1974, Milwaukee, Wi; [p.] James and Van Nowicki; [ed.] Marquette University freshman year, Concordia University, presently UW, LaCrosse, Junior Year (next year); [occ.] Student, backpacker, naturalist, artist, aries; [memb.] Student of N.O.L.S. National Outdoor Leadership School) Go on back-packing trips for up to 30 days at a time; [hon.] Writer of the month of April is H.S.; [oth. writ.] none published, I generally write for my own health, I sent this poem in on a whim, glad I did; [pers.] I find that expressing my thoughts and feelings through poetry can be therapeutic. I tend to write for myself with no format. When it's raw, the emotions show whether it's gramatically correct or not.; [a.] Cedarburg, WI

NOWOCIN, WILDA ANN
[Pen.] Willie; [p.] Vera Johnson; [m.] Divorced; [ch.] Tina, Tony, Eddie, P.J. and Chris; [ed.] High School Diploma; [pers.] I am 51 years of age. I have five grown children. I am enjoying being able to write some of my feelings and thoughts in poems. I hope that someone can have some enjoyment from them.; [a.] Aiken, SC

OBAOB, SOCORRO F.
[Pen.] Cora; [b.] December 21, 1911, Mambusao, Capiz, Phillippines; [p.] All Deceased; [m.] De-ceased, january 7, 1938; [ch.] Rosemary Romero Mittenthal MSN, Myrna Obaob Aguila RN, BSN, Miguel O. Fernandez, Med. Tech.; [ed.] M.A. Arellano University Phillippines; [occ.] Retired Spe-cial Educ. Teacher, Phillippines 1930-1975,; [memb.] Chicago Organizaitons: Fil-Am Catholic Guild, Chi-cago Senior Citizen's Club, Founder and First Present Fil-Am Grand Pa-Rents Association of Chicago (FA6PAC) 1988-1990; [hon.] Constant Winner in Elem. District Academic Contest, 1918-24, Valedic-torian in grade VII, 1925, District Contest Presenta-tion Award 1959, First Prize Winner in both Headress and Costume.; [oth. writ.] Articles published in local newspapers such as grandparents plea for fairness and justice, salutation songs, etc., Viatimes, Chicago, Illinois; [pers.] I portray in my writings my past experiences especially those hard times to encourage readers not to give up bot to struggle hard and survive. My motto is, if there is sacrifice, there is success.; [a.] Chicago, IL

O'BRIEN, MICHELLE LYNN
[b.] June 3, 1967, Wash., D.C.; [p.] John & Linda O'Brien; [ed.] B.A. Social Science from Gardner Webb College, Cum Laude; [a.] Sterling, VA

O'CONNOR, ANGIE
[b.] July 18, 1974; San Diego; [p.] Melinda E. Arnold, Thomas O' Connor; [m.] Boyfriend, Bran-don Cyrus Peery; [ch.] none; [ed.] Attending Seattle Central Community College. High Schools, Charles Wright Academy and Decatur High School; [occ.] College Student; [memb.] None; [pers.] I'd like to thank my parents and Brandon for all the love and support they're given me. Also, my 10th grade English Teacher Mrs. Pughe for turning me on to poetry; [a.] Seattle, WA

O'GORMAN, JR. JERRY
[b.] November 13, 1979, Salt Lake City, Utah; [p.] Jerry and Linda O'Gorman; [ed.] Currently in Mont-gomery Blair High School (9th grade); [occ.] student; [memb.] United States Tennis Associaiton (USTA); [pers.] "Seven And One" is dedicated to the Charles Town Jr. High 1993 Varsity Football Team. The most dedicated team in West Virginia.; [a.] Silver Spring, MD

O'NEILL, RHONDA R.
[Pen.] Autumn O'Neil; [b.] April 30, 1971, Elgin, IL; [p.] John & Renee' O'Neill; [ed.] Schaumburg High School USMC Aviation Operations Specialist School, School of Wicca; [occ.] United States Marine Avia-tion Operations Specialist; [memb.] World Wildlife Federation, National Audwoon Society; [oth. writ.] One poem published in local literary magazine.; [pers.] My goal as a writer is to bring out the truth through words.; [a.] Schaumberg, IL

O'RIORDEN, LAURA
[b.] December 23, 1968, Sarasota, FL; [p.] John J. O'Riorden, Margie Copes; [ed.] Cardinal Mooney High, University of Florida, University of South Florida, College of Medicine; [occ.] Student, Tampa Florida; [memb.] Phi Beta Kappa, Phi Kappa Phi, Alpha Epsilon Delta, American Family Physician.; [hon.] Dean's List, President's Honor Roll, Golden Key, National Honor Society, Outward Bound Alum-nus; [oth. writ.] Article published in premedical journal, poems in school literary magazine and in other poetry collection.; [pers.] The more often I write, the more inspiration in sparked inside my heart. Life is a work of art, you make what you want out of its illusions.; [a.] Tampa, FL

O'ROURKE, CORINNE
[b.] January 20, 1981, S. Nassau Hosp., NY; [p.] Mary Ann and Kevin O'Rourke; [ed.] Attends Woodmere Middle School; [occ.] Babysitter; [hon.] Won the Gerald Glazer Award of Excellence, Honor Roll two years in a row.; [oth. writ.] Two poems in the school newspaper; [pers.] I'd like to thank my sixth grade English teacher Ms. Packer for influencing me to enter my poems.; [a.] Hewlett, NY

OKOKO, DON
[b.] December 1, 1954, Nigeria; [p.] Chief Okoko and Jenny; [m.] Ini Don Okoko (Mrs.), October 15, 1988; [ch.] Master Atanganam Okoko, Miss Jennifer D. Okoko; [ed.] Ibadan Polytech, Nig. CBS, London, England, Wili London England, Hunnberside, C.H. Educ. Hull; [occ.] Author; [memb.] MILDM, FCI, Minstia, MlnstAM; [hon.] MBA PGD, ADV.DIP; [oth. writ.] Mother and Child, African Skies, Wailing Bats, the Harmattan Vengeance, The King's Con-quest and several other poems; [pers.] My artistry always strives to focus on the love of nature and the welfare of mankind.

OLIVEIRA, VICTOR W.
[b.] March 23, 1966, Woodstock; [p.] Edunio Oliveira (deceased) and Inez Cabral Oliveira; [ed.] High School Diploma, currently writing course with N.I.A.; [occ.] Janitorial; [memb.] Oxford County Right to Life, Knights of Columbus, League of the Immaculate Heart of Mary; [hon.] Two Editorial Choice Awards from the National Library of Poetry. Invited three times to the International Society of Poets Symposium in Washington, D.C.; [oth. writ.] A lyric put in a showcase album by Mascho Record Company. Fea-turing my title "Lovewaves" 89, Four other poems in the National Library of Poetry and have written letters to the editors in my hometown; [pers.] In these troubling times for oneself to stay loyal to God, Ciountry and neighbor we need to pray more and provide charity to all. Here is a prayer of self-dedication to Jesus Christ who is being mocked by the New Age Movement. Lord Jesus Christ take all my

freedom, my memory, my understanding, and my will. All that I have and cherish, you have given me. I surrender it all to be guided by your will. Your grace and your love are wealth enough for me. Give me these, Lord Jesus, and I ask for nothing more; [a.] Woodstock, Ontario

OLLIVIER, DONNA L.
[b.] September 16, 1946, Nova Scotia, Canada; [p.] Harry & Marie Haynes; [m.] Alan Sr., February 23, 1962; [ch.] Three boys, Allan Jr., Larry, Brian; [ed.] High School; [occ.] Housewife & Mother; [memb.] Titanic Historical Society; [hon.] Hobbies: Knitting, reading, collection (coins, spoons, daltons; [oth. writ.] other poems; [pers.] "Not to live for tomorrow because you will miss today.; [a.] Timminus, Ontario, Canada

OLMSTEAD, NED
[b.] January 24, 1936, Chicago, IL; [p.] Gordon Olmstead and Ruth Krepas; [m.] Mary Faye Olmstead, December 17, 1966; [ch.] Vanessa Ruth, Shawn Cameron; [ed.] Waukegan Twp. H.S., Ringling School of Art, Sarasota, FL; [occ.] Structural Eng. Tech., Navy; [memb.] Toastmasters Int. Backporch Story-tellers; [oth. writ.] Articles in Toastmaster Magazine; [pers.] I write my own stories and poems to uplift the soul and bring a smile to one's life! I get my inspiration from the Bible; [a.] Summerville, SC

OLSON, ALICIA
[Pen.] Lana Winstead; [b.] January 14, 1977, Man-hattan, NY; [p.] Daphne and Chuck Olson; [m.] Not married; [ed.] Brewster High School; [occ.] Admin-istrative Assistant; [oth. writ.] Currently in the middle of a book. Many other unpublished poems.; [pers.] Writing to me is a way solely to express yourself. If you have strong feeling about something write them down. Who knows what might come of it.; [a.] Brewster, NY

ORARA, JUAN D.
[Pen.] Johnny; [b.] June 24, 1904, Bolinao, Pangasinan, Philippines; [p.] Baldomero Orara and Pascuala Natino (both dec.); [m.] Maria de Gusman, July 4, 1928; [ch.] Juan, Jr., Emmanuel, Salvador, Lourdes, Daniel, Victory, Rachel; [ed.] Bachelor of Science in Education; [occ.] Teaching English as Second Language (to Latinos), Teaching Spanish (to Americans); Teaching Philipino to American, both Filipinos; [memb.] American Legion, Post 287, as Chaplain, Disabled American Veterans, Ch. 17 as Chaplain, Ex-Prisoners of WW2, L.B. as Chaplain, Film. Am. Vets. of WW2, Sta. Fe, L.B. as Chaplain, Missionary of the Church of Fullfillment; [hon.] Model employee of National Asian Pacific Center on Aging (Los Angeles, CA), Philanthropy medal (Vol-unteer Team, L.B.), Certificate of hon. mention (from World of Poetry); [oth. writ.] My Supreme Quest, Immortality, Looking Back, The Millennium, My Wife, and many lost writings.; [pers.] Make the most our of the least and the best out of the worst. (orginal learned through experience); [a.] Wilmington, CA

ORISON, KAREN D.
[b.] July 18, 1942, Everett, WA; [p.] Don & Erma Welch; [m.] Widow of Stan Orison, August 30, 1963; [ch.] Two sons, Douglas Dwain and Steven Lawrence; [pers.] The poem entered came from my questions to a higher being during the many sleepless nights following the death of my youngest son, Steven; [a.] Sun Lakes, AZ

ORLOWSKI, BONNIE F.
[b.] January 1, 1956, IL; [p.] Steven A. & Josephine S. Orlowski; [ch.] Amy C. Yurek, Annie F. Yurek, April M. Yurek; [occ.] Waitress; [pers.] Currently, I am working as a waitress, and I am returning to college this year to pursue my interest in the legal field. I do plan on continuing my writing also.; [a.]

Van Nuys, CA

OSTWIND, HOWARD
[b.] October 12, 1938, Bronx, NY; [p.] Samuel and Adele; [m.] Marcia Edelman Ostwind; [ch.] Kara, David, grandaughter: Shaina Erin; [ed.] Masters Gegree from Brooklyn College, City University of NY; [occ.] Psychotherapist; [memb.] American Assoc. of Counseling and Development. West Side Artists Assoc.; [oth. writ.] A number of poems published in various poetry and literary magazines. A number of newspaper articles dealing with the plight of visual artists in America.; [pers.] I am very concerned about the extent of social neglect inflicted on the powerless of our society. My poetry often reflects this concern.; [a.] New York, NY

OVERTON, CORTEZ
[b.] September 27, 1948, Chicago; [p.] Mary, Josh Overton; [ch.] Felicia & Kimberly; [ed.] St. Joachim School, Chicago Vocational School, Molor College; [occ.] Hospital Technician Song Writer; [oth. writ.] Over one hundred songs and poems to date, one short story one play near completion.; [pers.] He is the word, read him He is the song, listen to His music, let all of us make balance and love, so all may live in peace.; [a.] Chicago, IL

OWEN, LARRY PAUL
[Pen.] Larry Paul Owen, Little Red Rhymer; [b.] September 22, 1947, Tulsa, OK; [p.] Tedd and Lois Owen; [m.] Kim, July 24, 1971; [ch.] Daughters, Nicole and Jamie; [ed.] George Washington High School in San Francisco, Bethany Bible Colege (2 yrs.) in Santa Cruz, CA; [occ.] Associate Pastor at the Harbor Church in Lomita, CA; [oth. writ.] Many poems used for Church work and special occasions.; [pers.] The Lord Jesus Christ is my greatest inspiration, the source of my desire to be creative. and the greatest joy of all fulfillment.; [a.] Lomita, CA

OWENSBY, RAYMOND L.
[Pen.] Raymond L. Owensby; [b.] January 29, 1970, Cincinnati, OH; [p.] Raymond A. & Chinesha Owensby; [m.] Jacqueline Johnson, December 23, 1989; [ch.] Raymond L. Owensby, Jr.; [ed.] High School, Some College; [occ.] Government Employee; [oth. writ.] This is my first poem I've ever submitted.; [pers.] In my writings, I try to show people that God is the creator of all, and through his likeness, we can love one another.; [a.] Ramstein, Germany

PACE, MATHEW JESS
[Pen.] Mathew J. Pace; [b.] April 11, 1980, Phoenix, AZ; [p.] Yvette Lass, Tim Lass, Dan Pace; [ed.] Garden Lakes Elementary School, 8th grade; [occ.] Student; [memb.] US Practical Shooting Assoc/IPSC; [hon.] Principals list; [pers.] Write what you feel no matter what others say; [a.] Phoenix, Az

PAGAN, JAYSON
[Pen.] Always "I"; [b.] January 13, 1978, Barnes Hosp.; [p.] Sandra & Jim Pagan; [m.] Time will tell- I think, to early to know; [ch.] I will have two; [ed.] Marine Gradeschool and Triad High School, grade 10, I love Spanish; [occ.] Friend to everyone; [memb.] Yearbook Staff, Camera Club, Track, Art Club, Spanish Club; [hon.] Art Awards, Two First Place and Two Second Place, Exchange Student to Spain in "94"; [oth. writ.] I have written several poems, and have been influenced by many different people, but most, my friends; [pers.] Good can be found in all of my poems, though some may make ya' cry, friends enemies, loves and cries, some may live and some may die; [a.] Marine, IL

PALANCA, RAMON G.
[b.] June 23, 1928, Manila; [p.] Rosa & Carlos Palanca Sr.; [m.] Janice Yvonne Palanca, June 5, 1968; [ch.] Ramon Palanca Jr.; [ed.] 1949 High School, Ateneo deManila, 1953 College, San Beda, Bachelor of Com. Science; [occ.] Retired; [memb.] Manila Polo Club, Manila Yatch Club, Wack Wack Golf and Country Club; [oth. writ.] Other poems and essays; [pers.] To love is to give until it hurts; [a.] Los Vegas, NV

PALOMA, JOSEPH A.
[Pen.] J. Anthony; [b.] March 29, 1969, Chicago; [p.] Mr. and Mrs. Blas J. Paloma; [m.] Mrs. Christine M. Paloma, May 15, 1993; [ch.] First child due June 9, 1994; [ed.] Pursueing a degree in mathematics; [occ.] Employed by Chicago Board of Trade; [hon.] Who's Who Among American High school Students (2 yrs), US Achievement Academy (1987); [pers.] Live each day as if it were a new beginning; [a.] Hammond, IN

PAPIN, LINDA
[b.] May 23, 1952, Wichita, KS; [p.] Floyd & Melva Papin; [m.] Divorced; [ch.] one, Nicholas, age 11; [ed.] Columbine Elementary, Cole Jr. High, Manual High, Western State College; [occ.] Office Manager, Executive Career Consultants; [oth. writ.] Whispering Dreams, published in the Denver Safe House newspaper; [pers.] I try to write what my heart feels. Directness and honesty are two components I try to put in all of my writings. I believe if you trust in your heart you won't be discouraged.; [a.] Denver, CO

PAPPAS-BROOKS, ARETHA
[b.] August 13, 1944, LA, California; [p.] Ruth and Millwea Brooks; [ch.] Three Children, Darrell, Byron and Kellyn; [ed.] Currently attending local school at Antelope Valley College. I attended Manual Arts High School; [occ.] I am a retired administrative Assistant.; [memb.] Delores Missions, Antelope Valley Christian Center.; [hon.] I have received both the "Gold" and "Silver" Poet awards from World of Poetry; [oth. writ.] I have several unpublished poems.; [pers.] I have been moved and influenced by the contemporary poets. I am interested in addressing todays issues and how we can make a differencel; [a.] Quartz Hill, CA

PAQUETTE, ANDRE
[Pen.] Nick Damaru; [b.] August 3, 1956, Val Dor, Quebec; [p.] Gisele Audet, Armand Paquette; [m.] Lise Beauvals; [ch.] Amy-Lee, Daniel, Ann-Marie; [occ.] Aircraft maintenance engineer; [memb.] Federation Des Astronomes Amateurs Du Quebec; [pers.] I am in a personal quest to understand man's place in the universe. My perception of our being and uniqueness is reflected through my writings. I long to understand why and what we are; [a.] St Anne Des Lac, Quebec, Canada

PAQUIN, JEAN LOUISE
[Pen.] Lucy Pepper; [b.] January 12, 1971; [p.] John Paquin, Jude Paquin; [ed.] Braintree High School, Massachusetts College of Arts; [occ.] Nurses Aid/ Florist Artists Model; [hon.] BFA in painting; [oth. writ.] Selected poems published in repartee literary forum. Self published book of poetry, entitled I, II, III; [pers.] Everything connects -- the ground to the body to the brain to our surroundings to interactions with other individuals and their thoughts, I must write about these relationships; [a.] Brighton, MA

PARKER, ANGELA
[Pen.] Angie Parker; [b.] June 7, 1976, Lansing, MI; [p.] Philip Parker, Doris Nixon; [ed.] Everett High, Lansing Community College; [occ.] Courtesy Clerk, Kroger Grocery Store; [hon.] Outstanding Writer Award, Outstanding Editor in High School; [oth. writ.] Several poems and articles in H.S. newspaper, "Off the Wall". Poems and drawings published in Ele's Place newsletter; [pers.] If you believe in yourself you can do anything. Don't let other people get in your way and bring you down; [a.] Lansing, M

PARKER, CRYSTAL DAWN
[b.] April 21, 1975, Wynne, AR; [p.] Randy Barbara Parker; [ed.] Student at Wynne High School; [oth. writ.] Poem published in school flight.; [pers] When critisism falls upon you hold your head high a I have done, because no one can take away you dreams and goals within; [a.] Wynne, AR

PARKER, JOAN S.
[p.] John and Grace Smith; [m.] Charles M. Parke [ch.] Kim Litscher, Kevin Arnold; [ed.] High Schoo Culpeper Co; [occ.] Proof operator, Second Nationa Bank; [pers.] Expression just seems to flow an cleanse the soul through writing. I would love to writ books for children; [a.] Culpeper, VA

PARKER, PERCY G.
[Pen.] F. Parker Wellington; [b.] December 11 1959, Atlanta, GA; [p.] Francis Lorraine (Greene) Wellington L. Parker; [ch.] Jonathan Gregory Parker Justin Wellington Parker; [ed.] Southwest High Schoo (Atlanta); Howard Univ; [occ.] US Army Aviator [pers.] If you enjoy this snapshot of my work be on the look out for my up coming book "A Sortrd, Sordic Life". Not yet published; [a.] Orlando, FL

PARRELLA, MICHAEL A.
[Pen.] Michael Parr; [b.] October 17, 1945, Brooklyn, NY; [p.] Matilda and Charlie Parrella; [m.] Debora M. Kurtz-Parrella, August 27, 1983; [ch.] none; [ed.] Woodrow Willson High, Queens Borough College, NY; [occ.] Building Tech II, Plumber; [memb.] N.R.A., BASS; [hon.] Gold 1958 880 yd. Dash in Lincoln Hall NY, Silver, Diving Blue Ribbon 100 yd dash 1959.; [pers.] Sometimes I sit back and close my eye's, and see a young boy. I even hear his crus. He is laying under a car out from the rain. he dreams of tomorrow not todays pain. I think you already know the boy's name; [a.] Centereach, NY

PATRICK, GINA RENEE
[b.] May 9, 1977, Fayett Co, KY; [p.] Perry and Cleda Patrick; [ed.] 11th grade Menifee County High School; [occ.] Student; [memb.] Church, Clay City Holliness; [pers.] I only hope to rach the hearts of others through my writings, and for people to know that everyone has good qualities if they just look; [a.] Frenchburg, KY

PATTERSON, ROBERT O.
[b.] March 18, 1943, New London, CT; [p.] Robert & Pauline Patterson; [ch.] Jason, Brianna Marie; [ed.] Lockport Central High, Lockport, IL, Glassboro State College, Glassboro, NJ; [occ.] Program Driector, WLYH-TV Gateway Communications, Inc. Lebanon, PA; [memb.] NATPE Interntional, Kiwanis, American Legion; [hon.] Magna Cum Laude, Who's Who In American Business, Glassboro State College Distinguished Alumnus, Television; [pers.] Thanks Mom & Dad; [a.] Manheim, PA

PATTON, BERTHA P.
[b.] August 10, 1919, Georgia; [p.] Mary and John Pogers; [m.] Roy Patton, June 1957; [ch.] Curtis and Doris; [ed.] Law tric o college case Western Resplup Wilkins Beauty School of Cosmetology; [occ.] Poetess on WABQ radio station; [memb.] Member of the Helen S. Brown Senior Chosen Queen of the Center along with Mr. Voe Spates as King, member of Parkwood CME Church; [hon.] Attended eight annual conventions, received 7 certificates of Editor's Choice Award, merit in plastic, honored in Black Women - Pen an Image Program; [oth. writ.] Several books published the most noteable, My Inspirational Breakthrough, presented Harriet Tubman Hall of Fame Award - Golden Poet trophy and inducted into the prestigious Homer Honor Society of International Poet; [pers.] Look up, look out, look within and with

...ut a doubt you will find what life is all about; [a.] ...vehio, OH

ATTON, EDWARD LEE
[Pen.] Lee Edwards; [b.] August 27, 1936, Bedford, ...N; [p.] Earl and Dolores Patton; [m.] Beverly (Grego) ...atton, December 23, 1958; [ch.] Anthonly Lee, Lori ...ean, Lisa Ann (Soloman) Patton; [ed.] Mitchell High ...chool; [occ.] Chrysler Transmission (machine operator); [oth. writ.] This is the only composition I have ...ver submitted for publication; [pers.] I tend to write ...oetry from a personal standpoint and novel from a ...ictional view point; [a.] Kokomo, IN

PAZ, ANGELA NATALIA
...b.] March 18, 1975, Bethlehem, PA; [p.] Juan & ...ylvia Paz; [ed.] Saucon Valley High School, Moravian ...College; [occ.] Waitress, Student; [pers.] My poetry ...s my emotion captured at its most felt moment.; [a.] Bethlehem, PA

PEABODY, GEORGE W.
...b.] October 23, 1918, Paso Robles, CA; [p.] Blanche Wilkes and George T. Peabody; [m.] Patricia C. Peabody. Nee: Davies, June 13, 1942; [ch.] Gregory D., George G., Laurence D., and Geoffrey D.; [ed.] Assoc of Arts Degree at Pasadena Jr College, LA Co, CA; Foundry Practice at Antioch College, Yellow Springs, OH; [occ.] Retired Aircraft Industrial Engineer; [memb.] Historian, El Dorado Co Committee on the Bicentennial of the US Constitution. Honorary Member, Heritage Assoc of El Dorado County, CA. Boy Scouts and 4H Club project leader at large; [hon.] Outstanding Scouter Award; Distinguished Citizen Award. Military Service: USMC WWII, battle for Iwo Jima, Purple Heart Award; [oth. writ.] Four local history books published, a human relations and a book of poetry published, many newspaper articles printed; [pers.] Give a smile and get a smile. Give a hug and get a hug. Love, and be loved; [a.] Placerville, CA

PEARLMAN, EDWARD L.
[Pen.] Louis; [b.] April 11; [m.] Celia M. Pearlman, January 15, 1929; [ch.] Bobby, Sandra, Freddie Pearlman; [occ.] Retired

PEARSON, CHRISTIAN
[b.] April 3, 1974, Oshawa, Ont; [p.] Christine and Bob Pearson; [ed.] Grade twelve; [occ.] Detailer at Ziebart Tidy Car; [oth. writ.] I enjoy writing children's stories. I am previously enrolled in a correspondence college. The Inst of Children's Literature; [pers.] I write to express how I feel; [a.] Oshawa, Ontario

PEARSON, VERNA MARIE
[b.] October 1921, Oklahoma; [p.] Ike & Mary Wasda; [m.] William Pearson, 24 years ago; [ch.] none; [ed.] High School, Oklahoma; [occ.] L.V.N. Nurse; [memb.] SCAAN; [hon.] My Pastor has it, I sold some corys to cripled children; [oth. writ.] My husband wrote the book called "Tunnel"; [pers.] I carry a cross in my pocket A.I.; [a.] Long Beach, CA

PEARSON, WENDY LUELLA
[b.] August 3, 1980, Terre Haute; [p.] Jerry and Mary; [ed.] Currently 8th grade, 7th grade at time of writing.; [memb.] YWCE, YMCA, Creative Writing Club, Indianapolis Soap Box Derby, People to People Student Ambassador Program, 8th grade basketball team.; [hon.] Honor Roll, Baseball All-stars, Physical Fitness Award, Gymnastic and Track and Field Award, 1992 Second Place National Soap Box.; [hon.] Derby Champion, 1993 Third Place International Soap Box Derby; [oth. writ.] "Thanksgiving in North Carolina," many other poems, "The Cheetah Family."; [pers.] Do not wait for life to happen, make it happen. Be creative and aggressive with everything you do. Set goals in life and work to achieve them. Never give up on dreams.; [a.] Kokomo, IN

PEDERSON, THEODORE DAVID
[b.] October 10, 1932, Forsyth, MT; [p.] Pastor Tobias & Gertrude Pederson; [ed.] Trinity Lutehran Gr., Sterling Cdo., St. Paul's College, Concordia, MO, Northwestern College, Watertown, Wis., Bethany Lutheran Seminary, Mankato, MN; [occ.] Christian work, piano teacher, care for aged father; [oth. writ.] Articles relating to Christian teaching and biographies. I have been much influenced by Christian hymns and early American poetry.; [pers.] What is a person profited if he gain the world, and lose his soul? John 17,3 tells us that the only real God is the God who sent Jesus Christ into the world, and to know this God is to have everlasting life. John 3,36.; [a.] Sioux City, IA

PEITSCH, KRISTI LYNN
[b.] March 20, 1982, Saginaw, MI; [p.] Dorayneand Julium Peitsch; [ed.] I'm a sixth grader at Handy Intermediate in Bay City, MI; [occ.] Student; [memb.] Bits 'n' Pieces 4-H club, Critters 'n' Kids 4-H; [hon.] Presidential Academic Award, 1st place be an author; [oth. writ.] Be An Author Book published in Library, a poem published in local newspaper; [a.] Essexville, MI

PEMBERTON, BRANDI
[b.] August 1, 1979, Lawrence CO; [p.] Diane and Lindsey; [ed.] Freshman academic classes at Rock Hill High School; [occ.] Student; [oth. writ.] Poems written for personal and family enjoyment; [pers.] "You can do anything you want to do if you set your mind to it"; [a.] Ironton, OH

PEMBERTON, DALE
[b.] April 18, 1932, Big Flat, AZ; [p.] C.W. and M.E. Pemberton; [m.] Maxine Treat, April 8, 1961; [ch.] Kenneth; [ed.] BA Journalism, HS Sunyside, WA, Wichita Univ; [occ.] Retired Farmer; [oth. writ.] Several poems published in local papers; [pers.] I always play the hand I'm dealt; [a.] Big Flat, AR

PENA, REBECCA GONZALES
[b.] July 11, 1964, Hart Michigan; [p.] Cmilo Juan Gonzales and Maria De Anda Gonzales; [m.] Reynaldo Pena, July 17, 1983; [ch.] Raquel Ann and Reynaldo Jr.; [ed.] Present, Sophmore in Houston Community College, Mission High School; [occ.] Landscraper; [memb.] World Vision Sponsor, Parent Teacher Organizaton fundraiser, United Way Volunteer; [hon.] State Best Comedy Actress Trophy (High School) Catholic War Veterans Sweethear 1st, Pre-Law Sweetheart, Pan American Club Sweethart, Rio Grande, Valley Princess 1981, 2 science all "A" trophies, love and praise from my husband and children; [oth. writ.] 210 unpublished songs an dpoems in /English and Spanish my life has been a bit hectic to publish them, but my day will come; [pers.] i come from a migant field working family of eleven children. I was the eleventh child. I was taught to work hard and to educate myself in every aspect of life. My philosophy "With God, My life thrives on my sprit's everlasting strength; [a.] Missouri City, TX

PENNY, DENISE MCVAY
[b.] May 31, 1968, Corbin, KY; [p.] Virgil and Brenda mcVay; [m.] Rick Penny, February 20, 1988; [ch.] Candice Raschelle; [ed.] Laurel County High, vogue Modeling School; [occ.] Housewife/Mother; [memb.] Hopewell Baptist Church, Save The Whales, top Records Songwriters Assoc.; [hon.] Honors in writing, Golden Globe Award, two Awards of Merit, Silver Poet Award; [oth. writ.] Songs for recording poem published in "Whispers In The Wind," several for public readings, hudnreds of other poems, several short stories.; [pers.] I deeply feel that everything I write is a gift from God, and is inspired by all the people that touch my life."; [a.] Independence, KY

PEPPER, PENNEY
[Pen.] Penney Phyllaine Pepper; [b.] February 27, 1970, Rochester, NY; [p.] Frank & Madelaina Pepper; [ed.] Benicia High School, Diablo Valley College, Regional Occupational Program (R.O.P.) Martinez Adult School; [occ.] Student; [hon.] Channel 7 (KGS San Francisco) 1980; [oth. writ.] 1991-1992 short story for children's literature; [pers.] I've been greatly influenced by writing from personal experiences of my life. Also by my dreams, my aspirations, my ideas, my questions. I write in the hope that somehow it will help someone else; [a.] Pacheco, CA

PEREIRA, LINDA TSETSI
[Pen.] Lin; [b.] Boston; [p.] Dede and Michael Tsetsi; Mark Pereira; [ch.] Kraig, Brandon and Elisha; [ed.] Tiverton Jr. Sr. High, Fisher Jr College, Mass College of Pharmacy; [oth. writ.] Poem published in high school newspaper (fragments). Accepted to Inst of Children's Literature in Connecticut. Accepted to National Writer's Inst; [pers.] This poem is dedicated to my mother and father - Who always encouraged and supported my writing; [a.] Charlestown, NH

PEREZ, ANISA
[b.] March 18, 1971, Houston, TX; [p.] Vicente and Connie Perez; [ed.] BA in English, Univ of St Thomas; Houston, TX; [occ.] Temp work in London, England. Going back to grad school; [memb.] BUNAC (British Univ North American Club); [hon.] Phi Theta Kappa, Dean's List, Honored graduating english student for editing The Sampler (campus literary magazine); [oth. writ.] Published in: Pagan America: an anthology of New American Poetry, Concho River Review, and local literary magazines on college campuses; [pers.] Writing has been my source of growth. I love to write (Journals, letters, poetry, etc). I have a passion for it! I'm tired of playing battle of the sexes w/men, so I write all forms of poetry based on conflicts w/in society dealing w/men and women. It's a release to it all; [a.] (perm) Houston, TX, (temp) London, England

PEREZ, WILLIAM
[Pen.] Will; [b.] February 4, 1966, CA; [p.] Cruz and Ysalia Perez; [ed.] Notre Dame HS, UCLA; [occ.] Student; [oth. writ.] Novelty - (Living with a compound, no one knows, not the thought, etc.) From A Sole to Soul. For Too Many Moments. Hidden. Honesty; [pers.] The ability to evoke feelings through words is a powerful gift. I can only hope that with this gift I have, in some way, touched the reader darkness through a shade of grey is sometimes quite beautiful; [a.] Panorama, CA

PERKINS, MARIAN LaVERNE
[b.] December 9, 1956, Atlanta, GA; [p.] Rev Franklin E. Perkins, Jr and the late Mrs. Margaret R. Perkins; [ed.] Southwest High School; BA/Psychology -- Davidson College, NC; [memb.] The True Light Baptist Church; Hobbies: Reading, singing; inspirational Music: writing; teaching; [hon.] Elementary and high school valedictorian; Who's Who Among American High School Students; Nat'l Honor Society NSFNSS Finalist; [oth. writ.] No other published works; [pers.] I no longer measure myself using the standards of this world. I regard every day that I am able to get up a triumph. I know that God's grace is amazing. And attempt to convey His love in my writings; [a.] Atlanta, GA

PEROO, JOANNE
[Pen.] Pony; [b.] April 30, 1973, Guyana; [p.] Shantie and Fredrick Peroo; [ed.] John Bowne High School, College of insurance - CPCU, Major: Insurance Specialist. Title: Chartered Property Casualty; [occ.] Underwriter Claims Examiner, Claims negotiator; [memb.] YMCA, CPCU Candidate, Variety

Volleyball player, Lincoln Douglas Debate; [hon.] Volleyball award, Awards and Achievement in Math, Honor Writing, English and Science, John Bown High School's Dean List; [oth. writ.] None - this is my first; [pers.] I try to make a difference in society today, I try to be different and I have try to be likeable, but I sometimes fail. The only thing I believe is without any effort there cannot be any luck; [a.] Hollis, NY

PERRICELLI, TONY
[b.] March 24, 1975, Columbia, SC; [p.] Bill and Kay Perricelli; [ed.] Ben Lippen High School - Columbia, SC; Winthrop Univ (currently a student); [occ.] Student; [memb.] Baptist Student Union, Reformed Univ Fellowship; [hon.] Salutatorian, Ben Lippen 1993; Assoc of Christian Schools, Int Distinguished Student, Trustee's Scholar - Winthrop; [pers.] My desire is to use the talent God has given me in order to glorify His name. God loves us so much and I want to give Him the praise He deserves. He is my inspiration and my salvation. He is the reason for all of my success; [a.] Rock Hill, SC

PERSINGER, C. SUSAN
[b.] July 22, 1956, Covington, VA; [p.] Adopted by: Lee H. and Elizabeth B. Persinger; [ed.] St. Andrews Presbyterian College, University of North Carolina at Greensboro.; [occ.] Public School Elementary Music Teacher; [memb.] Orange County Association of Educators, North Carolina Association of Educators; [hon.] Teacher of the Year, Central Elementary School (92-93), Author of Awarded Governor's Award; [pers.] It is my deepest hope that through truth in expression, multicultural issues will soon transform into understanding, compassion and affirmation. My external gratitude and love to my caretaker as a child and ever present influence in my life, Yvonne Young.; [a.] Carrboro, NC

PETERS, ALFREDA M.
[Pen.] Anna Dixie; [b.] March 24, 1939, Halifax, NS, Canada; [p.] Mr. Ross Dixon, Mrs. Amy Dixon; [m.] Mr. Charles E. Peters, July 29, 1966; [ch.] Natalie Jewel, Catherine Elaine, Ramon Scott, Ross Edward, Max Hebert; [ed.] St Steven's elementary (Can), National College (Can) San Jacinto College (TX) Laurel School - (Phoenix, AZ); [ed.] Private Duty Nurse; [memb.] Notre Dame RC, Church Hou, TX; [hon.] Received a diploma from Quebec school of practical nursing, Laural School - Diploma for Dentist Assistant; [oth. writ.] My recipe got published in a cookbook called Who's Cooking What In America, edited by Phyllis Hanes. My recipe called "Blue Berry Dove". I write other poems and stories for a passtime and only for self use; [pers.] I always dreamed of becoming a writer or poet someday. My mother used to read poems and children stories to me at a very young age. My favorite poem was "Hiawaita"; [a.] Houston, TX

PETERSEN, KkARI
[Pen.] Kari Aljker; [b.] April 24, 1971; [p.] Lin Petersen; [m.] Giovanni D'Ottavio, May 21, 1994; [ch.] Jenna Christian D'Ottavio; [ed.] Univ of South Dakota attending my fifth year there MCOM major. Advertising emphasis. Spanish, English and communication disorders and (Minors); [occ.] Student; [memb.] PRSSA (Public Relations Student Society of America); [pers.] I try to be creative while reflecting reality in our everyday lives; [a.] Sergeant Bluff, IA

PETERSON, JANICE
[b.] December 20, 1940, Wynne, AK; [p.] Deward & Elsie Jones; [m.] Frank Peterson, March 29, 1959; [ch.] Susan Hare, grandchildren: Douglas, Jared, Stephanie Hare; [ed.] Vanndale High, Vanndale, AK, Motorola University, Mesa, AZ; [occ.] Inventory Control Clerk, Motorola Inc. Mesa, AZ; [memb.] Southern Baptist Church; [hon.] Six Sigma (3 years); [oth. writ.] Several poems for company paper. Sev-

eral for church, many un-circulated.; [pers.] I am a very personal person, I love to express myself by writing poems. Especially about nature, and all the beautiful things that god has given us.; [a.] Apache Jct., AZ

PETRACO, NICHOLAS
[b.] October 16, 1947, Queens, NY; [p.] Dominick Sr and Ignazia; [m.] Mary Elizabeth Koslap, June 21, 1970; [ch.] Nicholas and John; [ed.] BS Chemistry, MS Forensic Sciences. Both John Jay College of Criminal Justice, CUNY; [occ.] Criminalist, retireed New York City Police Detective; [memb.] Fellow New York Microscopic Society, Fellow American Academy of Forensic Science, Diplomat American Board of Criminalistics; [hon.] 1979 Dean Hawley Award, John Jay College, 1987 National Law Enforcement Award Recipient; [oth. writ.] Mystery Short Stories, Many Technical Publications; [pers.] I seek the truth; [a.] Long Island, NY

PETTY, LOUIS J.
[Pen.] Lou Petty; [b.] March 19, 1919, Port Chester; [p.] Deceased; [m.] April 1946, Deceased; [ch.] Eight: Tom, Gary, Daniel, Kathy, Michelle, Linda, Elanor, Louis Jr.; [ed.] High School; [occ.] Retired; [memb.] Veteran's Foreign Wars, Knights of Columus, Stamp Club, Holy Name Society (president); [oth. writ.] Sixty-three poems, children's short stories, most published in local weekly newspaper, started writing while in service WWI, ETO; [a.] Port Chester, NY

PEZZI, MARIO MICHAEL
[Pen.] Mario Pezzi; [b.] February 9, 1929, Stamford, CT; [p.] Salvatore and Caroline Pezzi; [occ.] Retired; [oth. writ.] "An Indian Told Me So," published at The University of Connecticut, Vertuoso of the Fiddle, and "A Marvellous Creation" (both not published as of yet).; [pers.] My poetry portrays my experiences and inner thoughts. I rely on my imagination to carry me on further and further.

PFEIFFER, CHRISTINE HERLEMAN
[b.] March 6, 1953, Evanston, IL; [p.] William and Terry Herleman; [m.] Michael Pfeiffer, January 31, 1976; [ch.] Cynthia and Michael; [ed.] Univ of Illinois; [occ.] Writer and homemaker; [oth. writ.] Various editorials, essays and poems; [pers.] I moved to Canada with my family in February, 1991. My inspiration is the beauty of the Canadian earth, the beauty of the Canadian sky and the beauty of the Canadian people; [a.] Calgary, Alberta, Canada

PHILLIPS, MARK PETER
[b.] January 3, 1956, Pittsfield, MA; [p.] James R. Phillips, Jr, Ruth Eleanor Davidson Phillips; [m.] Nancy A. Phillips, March 23, 1991; [ch.] Shannon Claire Phillips, Emily Rachel Phillips; [ed.] Glenrock Jr/Sr High School, grad 1974, USN - 1974-75, NH College - some courses; [occ.] Disabled restaurant chef/mgr. I am a "Mr. Mom"; [memb.] DAV Commanders Club; WWF, NPCA, The Smithsonian Assoc, Reader's Digest; [oth. writ.] 2 poems published in local newspaper (Manassas, VA), Friday, July 13, 198 ; Collection of Poems - waiting for publisher; [pers.] Fiercely patriotic "For God and Country"; Most of my poetry is of a romantic nature. I am romantic, a sentimentalist and I strive to give all I can to help my fellow humans and believe in the Native American Ways; [a.] Port Charlotte, FL

PHILLIPS, PEARL LIGON
[Pen.] I was Polly to my father, for myself "Precious Gem" just for fun; [b.] May 19, Tuskegee, AL; [p.] John Ligon Jr. and Leola Torrence Ligon; [m.] Ex Spous, L.A. Phillips, June 9, 1974; [ch.] One Son Daryl Jiligon; [ed.] Finished High School at Tuskegee Institue 2 yrs. at Bama State Teachers College. Attended NASS Community College in Garden City,

NY; [occ.] Translator Adminstrator for NYNEX Gargen City, NY; [oth. writ.] 1st poem titled "Awaing My Love" published. 2nd "I Can See God Everything." published copy with the Library Congress.; [pers.] I enjoy writing poetry in my spa time. I have a true fascination concerning the thing of God. I am greatly influenced to write when I s things of nature that no man could ever do.; [a.] Lor Beach, NY

PICA, JAMES
[b.] February 15, 1975, Bronx, NY; [p.] Linda Pi Barbal and Ted Barbal; [ed.] St. John's Prep Hig School. Now attending Hunter College; [hon.] Hig School, second honors freshman, sophomore, senio years.; [oth. writ.] Variety of love poems, free verse and rhyming poems. Another love poem is publishe in the Arcadia Press Anthology.; [pers.] I owe all m' inspirations to my girlfriend Agnes whom I dedicat all of my poetry to.; [a.] Astoria, NY

PICARELLO, ANDREA'
[Pen.] Poe Tyler, Alexandria Poe; [b.] March 24 1979, Long Island, NY; [p.] Joe & Rose Picarello [ed.] Hylton Senior High; [memb.] PWSI Soccer Ecology Club, Impowered Bulldogs.; [hon.] Two pages of poems in the school magazine.; [oth. writ.] 26 other poems I've written for school papers, friends, or just for me.; [pers.] I feel poetry should come from your soul, and reflect your inner and truest feelings. I have been greatly influenced by the poet Edgar Allen Poe.; [a.] Dale City, VA

PICKETT, FRANCES REED
[Pen.] Frances Reed; [b.] Clarksdale, MS; [ch.] Ryan Michael and Schuyler Douglas; [ed.] Bachelor of Science degree from Univ of South Alabama in Mobile Alabama; [occ.] Social worker; [memb.] Charter member of the Univ of South Alabama Sociology Club. Member of the Baldwin County Jobs Advisory Council (Alabama); [pers.] My writing reflects my feelings, views on life, childhood memories and experiences as an adult; [a.] Montrose, AL

PICKNELL, DIANA M.
[b.] February 23, 1955, Seattle, WA; [p.] Clyde and Jean Ries; [ed.] South Kitsap High School, Port Orchard, WA (1973), Lutheran Bible Inst, Seattle, WA (1977); [occ.] Legal Technician; [memb.] National Audubon Society; [hon.] MSPB Chairman's Award for Excellence (1992); [a.] Seattle, WA

PIERI, THEODORA
[b.] February 15, 1957, London, England; [p.] Michael and Sotira Haji Petrov (both from Greek cypriots); [ch.] Andrea (15), George (12); [ed.] Acland Burghley Secondary School, Marjery Hurst Secretarial College. (Currently studying creative writing and poetry appreciation -- evening classes); [occ.] Secretary; [oth. writ.] 3 poems being published in an anthology called 1Lunatics Lovers and Poets' in bookstores May. Entered Bard of the year contest last year, came 76 in top 200; [pers.] Writing poetry is an emotional release. An exposure of feelings and thoughts.

PIERRE, MEUNIER
[b.] July 10, 1926, Grand France; [p.] Andre Meunier, Jeanne Meunier; [memb.] Chairman Alliance Francaise Maiduguri (French Culture Centre); Nigerian Conservation Fund; Club Des Poetes, Paris France; [oth. writ.] 90 children stories, 20 short stories, 15 theatre plays for adults, 10 theatre plays for children, 1 autobiographical novel (in french); [pers.] I have been greatly influenced by my 45 years in Nigeria. Born French, naturalized to become a Nigerian citizen. All my writings are available both in French and English except the novel; [a.] Maiduguri, Nigeria

PILLSBURY, CRAIG ANTHONY
[b.] November 2, 1956, New York; [p.] Mr. & Mrs.

Elwin L. Pillsbury, Sr; [ed.] GED, graduate of J. Sargeant Reynolds Comm College Certificate in Respiratory Therapy 1983-1985; [occ.] Retired Disabled Respiratory Therapy Technician; [memb.] JSRCC Alumni, American Kidney Foundation, American Assoc of Respiratory Care and VA Assoc of Respiratory Care 1985-1987; [oth. writ.] Several poems unpublished; [pers.] The extent and ability of what one can do goes beyond what can be imagined or dreamed for all things are possible if you just believe; [a.] Chester, VA

PINE, DARLENE YOUNG
[b.] November 10, 1960, Cardston, Alt; [p.] Kathleen and Raymond Young Pine; [ch.] Denise, Kesler, Violet; [ed.] grade 8; [occ.] homemaker; [memb.] Medicine Hate Rock Club, Women's Healing Circle; [pers.] The Creator sent me a vision of this poem. When I was struggling to recover from all types of abuse (alcoholism, wife and sexual abuse, etc). This poem was given to me so I could be lead back to the Creator. he is the only one who is able to help through out all my difficulties; [a.] Medicine Hat, Alberta, Canada

PINO, RICK
[b.] April 7, 1975, Syosset, NY; [ed.] West Deptford High School, Westville, NJ; [occ.] Secondary Education/History Student at Seton Hall Univ; [memb.] De Molay, Seton Hall Forensics Team, Seton Hall 's Literary Magazine, "Renaissance"; [pers.] I would probably like to thank my family, God and my sixth grade English teacher, Mrs. Jean Cervone, whose teachings inspired me to enhance my creative writing abilities; [a.] Mantua, NJ

PINTO, SANDRA
[b.] June 30, 1946, Rhodesia; [p.] George and Rose Davis; [m.] Leander Pinto, December 21, 1968; [ch.] Michelle; [ed.] Morgan High Hillside Teacher's Training college, Bulawayo Rhodesia; [occ.] School Teacher; [oth. writ.] I am in the process of writing a book on a group of people I call the "silent majority"; [pers.] I believe intrinsically in th epower of the spoken and written word. We have all, at our disposal, the means to build bridges, and break down walls. The power of the pen is mightier; [a.] Switzerland

PISANKO, CAROL ANN
[b.] November 4, 1952, Chicago, IL; [p.] Edward Jamroz - Dolores Jamroz; [m.] Richard M. Pisamko, January 16, 1970; [ch.] Michael (14), Matthew (10); [ed.] Holy Name Cathedral High School, College of Dupage; [occ.] Floral Designe; [oth. writ.] These have not been submitted yet. Gold, Gold, Gold; Wolf; Mother; [pers.] Depth and sensitivity are reflected in my writing. I am greatly influenced by my surroundings. Look and listen to the world around you; [a.] Darien, IL

PITTENGER, TIMOTHY J.
[Pen.] T. J. Pittenger; [b.] July 17, 1952, Flint, MI; [p.] Dallas and betty Pittenger; [m.] Divorced; [ch.] Valerie Lynn; [ed.] Lakeville H.S., Otisville, MI; [occ.] Road Con; [memb.] Michigan United Conservation Club, National Geographic Society; [oth. writ.] Many other poem's about nature, wildlife a personal character's and philosophy. but never tried to publish my work before.; [pers.] I write mostly about what I see and feel around me. I think too many people, go through life without stopping and feeling this beautiful place we call earth!; [a.] Curtis, MI

PITTMAN, JESSICA K.
[b.] January 22, 1979, Oak Ridge; [p.] Steve and Sandy Poling/Eddie and Judy Pittman; [ed.] Clinton High School; [occ.] Student; [memb.] Cheerleading, FED-UP (Fighting Environmental Destruction for Universal Presentation), Youth For Christ, National

Honors Society, All American (Cheerleading); [hon.] All American-National Cheerleading Association; US Achievement Academy: All American Scholar and National Honor Roll Scholar; [oth. writ.] I have many poems, but I haven't named them yet; [pers.] I believe that through Christ all things are made great. Believe God will stand by you and provide for you, and He will. Follow His word, and you will have eternal life; [a.] Clinton, TN

PITTMAN, TODD
[b.] March 10, 1965, Springdale; [p.] William Pittman, Leona Pittman; [ed.] I attended SOP's Arm Central High, but only completed grade 10; [oth. writ.] I have other writings, but they have not been published in any kind of association; [pers.] I like writing poems. It gives me some sort of mental outlet. I write the way I feel. If I'm sad, I write something sad or if I'm angry I write something angry, etc; [a.] Canada

PLOURDE, PATRICIA
[b.] January 15, 1959, Goldsboro, NC; [p.] Bill & Betty Howell; [m.] Johnny Joseph Plourde, August 7; [ch.] Jessica Leigh, Stacey Marie; [ed.] Rosewood High; [occ.] Nail technician; [pers.] My poems are written for when I am searching for when I am reaching and especially for when I am remembering.; [a.] Goldsboro, NC

PLUGGE, CHRISTINA
[b.] June 25, 1980; [p.] Beverly Plugge and Walter Viles; [ed.] 8th grade; [occ.] school student; [hon.] Honor student; [a.] Pittsfield, ME

PLUHOWKSI, JULIA
[b.] December 25, 1981, White Plains, NY; [p.] Drucilla Minte, John Pluhowski; [ed.] Upper Nyack Elementary, currently attending Nyack Middle School; [memb.] Girl Scouts of America; [hon.] Numerous awards for academic and artistic excellence, including high honor roll and dance scholarships; [oth. writ.] Several unpublished stories and poems; [a.] Nyack, NY

PLUMMER, ELIZABETH
[Pen.] E. Plummer; [b.] October 18, 1919, Marion Co, IN; [p.] Mr. and Mrs. John L. Kleyn; [m.] Raymond L. Plummer, May 18, 1942; [ch.] 4 children - 9 grandchildren; [ed.] High school graduate studied "Riley's" poems; [occ.] Retired, farm background; [hon.] Short article in Parade magazine. Have placed in Riley Day Festival - poets on Podium - 1st - 1993, 3rd - 1992; [oth. writ.] Tribute to the working man - (honorable mention) - 1992 - World of Poetry. Was invited to read poem in Sacramento, CA 1991; [pers.] I like to write about happenings, events, friends, ask me to write poems for certain occasions. Like poems with spiritual meanings; [a.] Greenfield, IN

PLUNKETT
[Pen.] Eukene Veronica; [b.] August 19, 1965, St Catherine, Jamaica; [p.] Ronald Plunkett, Gloria Plunkett; [ed.] Excelsior Community College, St Mary's College, St Mary's All Age School, St Mary's Basic School; [occ.] Student; [pers.] I try to understand the nature of people in my writings and tries to include a touch of my own everyday experiences; [a.] Kingston 12, JWI

POCKLINGTON, MARK ANTHONY
[b.] December 7, 1960, Worksop Notts U.K.; [m.] Emma Francesca Pocklington and Michael James Pocklington; [ed.] Henry Hartland Comprehensive; [pers.] "Poetry," is a benison from Bod. It furnishes our sould with benignity. And allows us to dwell on the beauty of mankind.

POGOREL, BERNARD
[b.] December 5th, 1916, Brooklyn; [m.] Bernice;

[ch.] Barry, Reba, Esther; [occ.] Physician, MD; [hon.] WWII awards -- 5 Campaign Ribbons, 1 Silver Star, 2 Bronze Stars, 1 Purple Heart; [oth. writ.] 2 short stories and several poems. A dozen medical articles; [pers.] Influenced by my experiences as a physician and as a contest medical officer in WWII; [a.] Los Angeles, CA

POLING, DONALD R.
[b.] November 6, 1972, Connersville, IN; [p.] Patricia Cooper and Donald Poling, Sr; [ed.] St Michael's Catholic School (1-8); Brookville High School (9-10); American Sr High (11-12); Art Instructional School (2 yrs); Life 21 (yrs); [occ.] Warehouse employees and Driver for Horizon Farms, Miami, FL; [memb.] Smithsonian National Assoc; The Human Race; The Planetary Society; National Geographic; Comic Collectors of America; American Museum of Natural History; National Preservation for Hardcore Lifestyles; [hon.] 2 Blue Ribbon Awards for Artistic Excellence; Editor's Choice Award from "Whispers In The Wind" from National Library of Poetry for Poem entitled "Words of Affection"; [oth. writ.] "Words of Affection" in Whispers in the Wind (Nat'l Library of Poetry); "War" in Contemporary Poets of America and Gr Britain (Dorrance Publishing); "Waiting" in The Space Between (Nat'l Library of Poetry); [pers.] If you wiped away the righteous indignation stemming from organized religion and recial tension from over abundant racial pride and ignorance of other races, there would be no conflices in society; there is only one race, the human race!; [a.] Miami, FL

POLLOCK, DAWN M.
[b.] October 8, 1966, Guelph, Ontario; [p.] Clarke and Helen Pollock; [ed.] Honours B.A. Univ. of Guelph, D.SW diploma, Georgian College Onillia; [occ.] Residential Counsellor; [oth. writ.] Several other poems and writings all of which are unpublished; [pers.] Above all I dedicate this poem to Joan Morgan who will always remain a source of inspiration and coruage for me, and to Cheryl who realizes that Charlie isn't so lonesome when he's around the both of us. Friends forever.; [a.] Toronto, Ontario Canada

POLLOCK, GLENN ANDREW
[b.] January 13, 1972, [occ.] Electrician; [pers.] Not for the faint hearted, nor one who claims to hold the secret of everything and all that is unknown; [a.] Northern Ireland

PONUSHIS, ALEXA DYAN
[b.] March 4, 1982, Ft Myers, FL; [p.] Karen and Jerry Krieger and Dieno Ponushis; Siblings: Athena (14 yrs), Joseph (2yrs); [ed.] Presently 6th grade - middle school, Good Shepherd Lutheran; [occ.] student; [memb.] Particpate in basketball/volley ball/soccer; [hon.] 'A' Honor Roll grades 1-6, 1991 1st place spelling bee, science fair's 1st and 3rd places; [oth. writ.] Several poems/songs/short stories (none published - none submitted for publication); [a.] Fort Myers, FL

POOLE, ANNIE MAE KEELING
[Pen.] A. Keeling Poole; [b.] November 24, 1911, Keysville, VA; [p.] Gabrielle King & Frederick Keeling; [m.] Cecil R. Poole (deceased) April 7, 1934; [ch.] Gabrielle Judith P. Ryon, Rebecca P. Jones; [ed.] High School, and Harvard Classics Avid Reader & Thinker; [occ.] Writing; [memb.] Smithsonian, Heritage Foundation, Peakland Baptist Church; [hon.] My work with little children was appreciated by my church, and honored by the children; [oth. writ.] I wrote many songs in earlier years but never had anything published.; [pers.] I am forever awed by the beauty and wonder of nature, and science use of it, often 'just because it's there'.; [a.] Lynchburg, VA

POPE, JR. JOHN J.
[Pen.] John J. Pope; [b.] June 4, 1967, Patuxent river, MO; [m.] Lisa M. Pope, August 15, 1992; [ed.] B.A. North Park College, M.S. Economics, Indiana State University; [occ.] Stockbroker; [memb.] American Institute for Economic Research, National Association of Business Economists, Amnerican Num-smatics Association; [hon.] In Sbsentia Fellow, The American Institue for Economic Research; [a.] Bloomington, MN

POPE, MAJELLA COURTNEY NIPPERT
[b.] April 17,k 1979, San Leandro, CA; [p.] Ronald & Elizabeth Pope; [ed.] Cleveland Elementary Stockton, Woodlake Elem. San Antonio, TX, Kelley Elementary Riatto, CA, Frisbie Middle Schl. Rialto, CA, Rialto High Schl. Rialto, CA, CA State San Bernardino; [occ.] Student Freshman 5.0 GPA; [memb.] Black Future Leaders; [hon.] 1st Place Black History 1993, 1st Place Red Ribbon, Writing Contest 1992, 1st Place Spelling Bee 1991 and many academic awards from my schools; [oth. writ.] Helped produce Frisbie Middle School newsletter; [pers.] One day I hope to become a Supreme Court Justice; [a.] San Bernardino, CA

PORZIO, BETHANY
[b.] March 5, 1977, Bay Shore; [p.] Donna & Robert Porzio; [ed.] High School Student; [hon.] Psychology Club; [oth. writ.] Poems for friends; [pers.] I write about my own personal feelings. I have a positive attitude towards life and I love poetry; [a.] Hauppauge, NY

POSMA, MICHELLE LYNN
[b.] August 31, 1970, Charlevoix, MI; [p.] Thomas Posma, Karen Posma (Walhalla, MI); [ed.] Mason County Central High School, Scottville, MI; [occ.] Working on my degree in the medical field; [hon.] 1993 "Editor's Choice Award" by The National Library of Poetry; [oth. writ.] First poem published in the anthology "The Coming of Dawn" in 1993. I'm currently working on having a play produced, that I wrote based on youth drug abuse and the dangers of using drugs; [pers.] I've been writing poetry and short stories for 11 yrs. I will continue enhancing the silent depth of emotions through poetry; [a.] Harbor Springs, MI

POSOD, SONJA G.
[b.] December 26, 1961, Austria; [oth. writ.] Book of Poetry booktitle, "Aimless" printed and distributed by author.; [a.] Cookstown, Ontario

POSTINS, TERRY CADIEUX
[b.] November 25, 1948, Detroit; [p.] Clarence and Fay Cadieux; [ch.] Matthew and Joshua; [ed.] Central Michigan Univ; [occ.] Research Director - FOX 51; [memb.] Great Texas Balloon Race Board; [hon.] Writing awards - IABC/Detroit, and Southeastern Michigan Public Relations Assn, Addy Award - East Texas Ad Federation; [oth. writ.] Article, Michigan Hospitals magazine, recruitment film for Paris Jr College jewelry school, 30 commercials for psychiatric hospital, other poems as yet unpublished; [pers.] "Living" was written as a tribute to a member of the Great Texas Balloon Race Board upon his death. It is also a statement as to how I try to live my life. My poems are just one candle in the dark to remind others of the gentle moments that enhance our humanity and spirit; [a.] Longview, TX

POTTER, JERRY L.
[Pen.] Jay Louis; [b.] July 10, 1936, Detroit; [p.] William and Ross Harris Potter; [m.] Sheila E., September 11, 1971; [ch.] 3-from prev marriage, Teresa, Daryl (deceased), Jeffrey; [ed.] Cass Technical HS - GED; [occ.] Meat Packing Driver; [memb.] Am currently serving as an elder in the Murray Hill Congregation of Jehovah's Witnesses, in Detroit, MI;

[oth. writ.] Only personal poems written for some of our friends for special occasions such as: 50th wedding anniversary; for workmates at prev job with loss of my son in 1984; and for friends inour prev congregations. We served in as an elder upon leaving them; [pers.] From my early years in elementary school. I have had a desire to sing and write songs which I was able to do after organizaing and particpating in several male singing groups, singing songs ranging from rhythm and blues to barbershop music. I have recordings of some of these accomplishments; [a.] Detroit, MI

POUNDERS, BETTY P.
[Pen.] Betty or Bet Pounders; [b.] January 30, 1934, London, England; [p.] Doris and Albert Ackland; [m.] Archie L. Pounders, July 27, 1955; [ch.] JoAnne 37, Lee 36, Christopher 29; [ed.] English Grammar, went to work at fourteen years old to support mother; [occ.] housewife; [memb.] Transatlantic Brides & Parents Assoc., Air Force Sergs. Assoc. Aux.; [hon.] When my son's played sports for "Boys Club's of America, I formed the Mothers Club" to make money for uniforms etc.; [oth. writ.] Poems about motorcycle road racing, Lee was quite famous for two years and eight months. Also my daughter J. Anne became an R.N., wrote "In Honor Of The Nursing Class of 1991, Germanna Community College Grove, Locust, VA.; [pers.] I didn't have much of a life growing up in World War two. Had a terrific mother, the greatest day, I met my husband came to the states, had three superkids. Have alway's been happy with my life; [a.] Orlando, FL

POWELL, ALICE M.
[b.] August 29, 1914, Teanaway, Washington; [p.] John & Anna Lindbert; [ch.] Thomas A. Powell and Dirk Wm. Powell; [ed.] High School, Business College; [occ.] Retired Secretary; [memb.] Columbia Club, Swedish Club, Nordic Scandinavian Historical Museum, American Legion, Eagles Clug, Puget Power, Former member World Affairs Council, Foundation for International Understanding of Students; [hon.] Volunteer Work, Cooperative Extension Service of Washington, Washington State University, R.S.V.P., Senior Literacy Tutor, Senior Services of Washington; [hon.] SKAC, Volunteer Secretary, Training for handicapped.; [oth. writ.] Have written the family history (The Lindberg Saga) and other writings but never submitted them or had them published.; [pers.] I wrote the poem as a tribute to my husband Bill. He passed away in 1953 suddenly of a heart attack, married April 6, 1946.; [a.] Kent, WA

POWELL, BARON MICHELE
[b.] March 20, 1966, Vancouver, BC; [p.] Gerald Powell, Geraldine Powell; [m.] Kent Baron, September 8, 1990; [ch.] Nicholas Randall, Amanda Tere; [ed.] Graduate, Seaquam Secondary 1984; [occ.] Mother of two and aspiring author; [hon.] Honorable mention in school dist #36 - Discover The Writer Within" contest - 1993; [oth. writ.] Poem: Friends published in "Canadian Living Magazine" 1979, International Year of the Child Contest; [pers.] Look to the children for courage, for anything is possible in their eyes; [a.] Surrey, BC, Canada

POWELL, WILSON, M.
[Pen.] Wilson Powell; [b.] June 24, 1932, Cambridge, MS; [p.] Wilson M., Fredrika R.; [m.] Joan A., November 29, 1958; [ch.] 3 boy - 1 girl; [ed.] undergraduate, U of Cal - Berkeley, U of Com - Stours; [occ.] Hazardous Materials Management Consultant; [memb.] Institute Hazardous Materials Management, MO Coalition for Environment, Air and Waste Management Coalition, YMCA Writer's Voice; [oth. writ.] "Eyes of Korea" poem soon to be published by Center for Study of Korean Conflict in "The Hermit Kingdom Poems of the Korean War". My own newsletter "The Hazardous Material Ari-

zona"; [pers.] While having written poetry sporadically over the years, I am now quite seriously usin poetry to uncover and illuminate my own true rela tionship with God and Creation; [a.] Ballurin, MO

POWERS, SHANNON
[b.] September 10, 1977, Beaumont, TX; [p.] Pam and Pike Powers; [ed.] Currently a sophmore in high school, will graduate in 1996; [occ.] Student at S Stephen's Episcopal School; [memb.] Spanish Club, Martin Luther King Scholarship Fund Committee; [hon.] Duke Talent Search, National Junior Honor Society; [pers.] As I write I will try to get to the hear of the issue at hand but I must point out that these are the ways I see things and that is all. I have been inspired by everyone I have ever met or seen; [a.] Austin, TX

PRATUCH, WILLIAM
[b.] November 14, 1923, New York City; [p.] William and Louise Pratuch (deceased); [m.] Marian Pratuch, July 13, 1946; [ch.] (Two) William Pratuch III and Philip Pratuch (Two) grandchildren - Danial and Anthony Pratuch; [ed.] JHS 73 Queens NY, Newtown HS, LI, NY, US Navy Fire Control School Newport, RI, US Navy Advanced Fire Control School Anacostia, Wash, DC, Central Radio/Television School, Kansas City, MO; [occ.] Retired; [hon.] Three Battle Stars, World War II, serving on USS Baldwin DD 624; [oth. writ.] Except for a diary (unpublished), kept during time in Navy during WWII; [pers.] I have been inspired by Indian Culture since moving to Arizona. I wrote this poem for a friend's daughter's wedding; [a.] Sun Lakes, AZ

PREBEG, MELISSA
[Pen.] Lizard; [b.] October 16, 1976, Tomahawk, Wi; [p.] Sandra and Joseph Prebeg; [ch.] Dog, cats, rabbit, rat; [ed.] Presently a Junior in high school; [occ.] High School, Pizza Hut Cook; [memb.] 4-H (so far nine years), school orchestra; [hon.] Won a poetry contest in third grade; [oth. writ.] Reality sleep, and numerous untitled pieces, none of which have been published; [pers.] Write solely to please yourself, no one cares about your writing as much as you.; [a.] Sun Prairie, WI

PRESTON, DEBBIE
[b.] July 25, 1956, Hartford, CT; [ch.] Salvatore, Tina, Kim, Heather, Robert; [ed.] Conard High School, Greater Hartford Community College; [occ.] Special Education Transit Driver; [pers.] I have been influenced by my new love Mac, who has helped me to believe in myself once again; [a.] Hartford, CT

PRICE, THOMAS H.
[b.] May 31, 1916, Oak Park, IL; [p.] Elmer Price, Sylvia Price; [m.] Roberta M. Price, September 4, 1943; Claudine S. Stine-Price, August 25, 1991; [ch.] David Thomas, John Holton, Martha Jane, Paul Robert, Rachel Marie; [ed.] BA (philosophy) Central College (IA) M. Div, Los Angeles Baptist Theological Seminary; [occ.] Retired; [memb.] American Philarelic Society; 775th Tanker Assn (WWII); [hon.] Professor Emeritus, The Master's College (Newhall, CA); [pers.] I must say, in my own way, what I must say, to my own day; [a.] Newhall, CA

PRIMAVERA, ROBERT E.
[b.] June 3, 1934, Philadelphia, PA; [p.] Alexander and Henrietta Primavera; [m.] Dorothy E. Primavera, August 27, 1966; [ch.] Michael, Stephen, Cynthia; [ed.] BS Univ of MD; [occ.] Retired Westinghouse Engineering Publications Supervisor; [memb.] Society of Logistics Engineers; Writers Digest Book Club; [hon.] Dean's List U of M; Outstanding Contributing Award - Society of Logistics Engrs (sole); General Excellence - Veterans of Foreign Wars; [oth. writ.] Dozens of Technical Manuals and Documents for both defense and commercial industries; [pers.] Writ-

en by another, but excellent advice. Give to the world the best that you have and the best will come back to you; [a.] Berlin, MD

PRINCE, ERIK ALEXANDER
[b.] November 29, 1967, Silver Spring, MD; [p.] Leslie and Brenda Prince; [ed.] Stafford High, Virginia Commonwealth University; [occ.] Aircrew member, USAF; [oth. writ.] "Alone" published in Coming of Dawn Anthology; [a.] Plattsburgh AFB, NY

PRINCE, WAYNE
[b.] May 21, 1955, Winchester, TN; [p.] Ruth Bevels, Bobby Bevels; [ed.] Madison High School, Volunteer State Community College, Middle Tennessee State Univ; [occ.] Nightclub management; [memb.] American Orchid Society, Greenpeace; [hon.] Graduated cum laude; [pers.] Writing in my case is a form of therapy, a cleansing of the soul; [a.] Madison, TN

PRINSEN, SALLY
[b.] Sheboygan, WI; [p.] William and Kate Schulte; [m.] Arthur H. Bagemehl (deceased), 1935; [m.] Walter J. Prinsen; [ed.] Sheboygan school system; [occ.] Beautician. Currently a housewife and floral designer; [memb.] St Pauls United Church of Christ, Lakeland College Womans Auxiliary, Sheboygan County Historical Soc; [hon.] Poems of mine were published in the Sheboygan Press a long time ago; [oth. writ.] In 1990, I saw an add about a contest by the World of Poetry so I sent a check and poems. I learned from the National Library of Poetry that World of Poetry was bankrupt, so they offered to publish my poems; [pers.] So now I have this wonderfully handsome book containing my poems and enjoy it. I read good books, biographies of famous people, use maps, and enjoy history; [a.] Sheboygan, WI

PRITCHARD, CAROL
[b.] December 17, 1950, S. Ockendon; [p.] Eric & Phllis Perry; [m.] Separated; [ch.] David and Erica; [occ.] Single Parent not working.; [a.] South Ockendon Essex, England

PRITCHARD, LIANNE
[Pen.] Liandra; [b.] January 22, 1974, Neath; [p.] Mal Pritchard, Margaret Vaughan, Stepfather: David Thomas Vaughan; [ed.] Lllangating comprehensive school, Cadoxton, Neath; [occ.] Factory worker Lucas Sei Wiring Systems; [oth. writ.] Only one poem ever published which was in the local church magazine. My work reflects a lot on religion as I feel it plays a big part in my life; [pers.] I would like to take the opportunity to thank all those who have given me strength and encouragement to accomplish the best things in my life. Especially my mother and stepfather and fiancee, Antonio Vazquez Romero. Who brings out the best in me. But the most gratitude goes out to my father who sadly passed away. I feel it was him who made me what I am today; [a.] Neath W. Glam, S. Wales, UK

PROUD, ERIC MATTHEW
[Pen.] Puppy; [b.] September 27, 1968, Chicago; [p.] Theodore and Camille; [ed.] Hoffman Estates High School, Millikin Univ; [occ.] Systems Engineering; [memb.] Alpha Tau Omega Social Fraternity, Omicron Delta Kappa, Inst of Industrial Engineering; [hon.] OMICRON Delta Kappa Leadership Fraternity; [pers.] Life is worth living, people are worth loving, and only God is Truth; [a.] Royal Oak, MI

PRUITT, NINA S.
[Pen.] Nina's; [b.] October 17, 1916, NC; [p.] Gordon and Dara Hendrix; [m.] Clarence Pruitt, November 13, 1939; [ch.] Robert Lee Pruitt; [ed.] 7th Grade; [occ.] Housewife; [memb.] None, except Christian in Baptist Church, Baptist View Church, Forest Hill, MD; [hon.] Small Gift's, Flowers, Dinner's

out in Restaurants; Local Radio Station "Mother's Day Poem's"; [oth. writ.] Just a peom for a sister or friend; [pers.] Just a note to family or friends; [a.] Forest Hill, MD

PUHIERA, JULIETT
[Pen.] Mickey; [b.] October 16, 1978, Nicaragua; [p.] Julio Puhiera, Dina Puhiera; [ed.] Cardinal Dougherty High School; [memb.] Community Service Corp, Prime; [hon.] Honor Roll, Perfect Attendance; [pers.] In my writing, I like to express my emotions, imagination, and my childhood fantasies. I am influenced by the atmosphere I live in and the people around me; [a.] Philadelphia, PA

PULOS, GEORGE N.
[Pen.] Yoryis; [b.] June 1, 1922, Elmira, NY; [p.] Nicholas & Stella Pulos; [m.] Rita K. Pulos; [ed.] Graduate of Seminary, AB Univ. of MD, completed graduate work, forms in govt. adm.; [occ.] retired, former govt. employee; [oth. writ.] Have written numerous poems. Have not tried to publish any. I paint oils under the name of Yoryis and compose classical music.; [pers.] I strive to define mankind as I see him (her). I do not like what I see! I hope my poetry will influence the behavior of some of humanity.; [a.] Salt Lake City, Utah

PUTNAM, SHANNA
[b.] August 3, 1980, KC, MO; [p.] Georgia Barnes, Martin Putnam; [ed.] 8th grader at Yeokum Middle School; [memb.] National Junior Honor Society (NJHS); [hon.] Nominee for Student of the Month, NJHS; [a.] Belton, MO

PYPER, DANDY
[b.] December 14, 1957, London, England; [ch.] Two; [occ.] Part-time: Librarian and teacher of english conversation, full-time mother; [memb.] Open poetry conventicle Wandsworth, London; [oth. writ.] Poem published in poetry now 1994 anthology. Several articles published in magazines; [pers.] Behind the face we each show the world, mankind shares many of the same vulnerabilities I would like this to be reflected in my poetry; [a.] London, England

QUALLEY, APRIL
[b.] August 10, 1972, Kimball, NE; [p.] Roxanne and Steve Qualley; [ed.] Currently attending Shoreline Community College; [hon.] Honorable Mention for oil painting entered in local art exhibit; [pers.] The key to understanding the beauty in each of us lies within the power of nature.; [a.] Seattle, WA

QUESTELL, EDWARD MENDEZ
[b.] March 8, 1939, NY; [p.] Edward Questell, Teresa; [m.] Mary R. Questell, March 16, 1965; [ch.] Deserie L. Questell, Vanessa S. Questell, Brandon Questell; [ed.] Chelsea High School; [occ.] New York Hospital, PSA; [memb.] St Francis Chantal Church; [oth. writ.] He is the All Mighty, He Calls Himself Cupid, The Ocean, I'm carrying Mine Cross, You Can't Erase Me, Morning Promises, Majic of Your Love, Always Remember You, I Will Cry A Tear For You.; [pers.] "Every perfect love (n) gift is from God above. God gave me the inspiration to write this poem". "The Space Between" the Heavenly Father (n) I is His son Jesus Christ; [a.] New York, NY

QUINN, JUDY WEBB
[b.] January 11, 1949, Gilmer, TX; [p.] H.G. & Louise Webb; [m.] Boyfriend, Sonny Moss; [ch.] Tony, Julia, Rex, Grandchildren: Jennifer & Elizabeth Wetzel; [ed.] Quitman High School (home of Sissy Spacek); [occ.] Grandy's in Sulphur Springs, TX; [hon.] Recognized at two churches for the plays I wrote in which was put on by the local youth dept.; [oth. writ.] Have had one poem published in local

newspaper. I've written many unpublished songs and plays.; [pers.] I enjoy writing so much. I believe God gave me my writing talent. I express my ideas, thoughts and love best in poems, songs and plays. I'd love to share my talents with others to enjoy.; [a.] Como, TX

RABB, LEONARD
[Pen.] Bismi R.; [b.] February 1, 1956, Brooklyn; [p.] Alexander and Salliemae Rabb; [ch.] Dareema, Jameek, Quanisha, Bismillah, Asiatic; [ed.] H.S. Graduate; [occ.] Struggling Poet; [pers.] I strive for growth and personal identification, it is my desire for others to reach their pinnacle through my writing. I have been greatly influenced by the Late Langston Huges; [a.] Brooklyn, NY

RACKLEY, ANNE C.
[b.] August 5, 1978, Falls Church, VA; [p.] Sanford and Gail Rackley; [ed.] Currently a 9th grade student at Pine Forest Jr. High, Fay, NC, graduate of Roland's International School of Modelling, Ray, NC; [occ.] Student; [memb.] St. Elizabeth Ann Seton Catholic Church, Fay, NC; [hon.] Won title "Queen, Young Miss American Youth Future Star" 1988; [oth. writ.] 1992 self-published book of poetry entitled "Sweet and Sour Stories", Poem 1993, entitled "Jesus" published in book Dearly Beloved..Dearly Bought of American Arts Association.; [pers.] I write what I feel in my heart and soul at a particular moment.; [a.] Fayetteville, NC

RAM, BISSOONDAT
[Pen.] Japs'; [b.] February 15, 1951, Guyana, S.A.; [p.] Lakhan Ram & Budhni Ram; [m.] Liladti Ram, June 24, 1970; [ch.] Ganesh D. Ram, Noresh D. Ram, Vishnu D. Ram, Malinie D. Ram; [ed.] Cornelia IDA School, Guyana S.A., Wood Working Centre Hague, Guyana, S.A.; [occ.] Construction Manager, A.C.T.; [memb.] Swarsattie Cultural Group, Minnesota Hindu, Dharmic Sabha (MHDS) Vice President; [hon.] Residential Building Contractor, Chicago; [oth. writ.] Songwriter for 15 songs which 5 are currently in production on commercial recording Tin Pan Ally Inc.; [pers.] I want to write about human actions on this earth, and solutions to help solve them, my writing must go out to the world for all nations; [a.] Minneapolis, MN

RAMEY, EARLEEN LAVONNE
[Pen.] Von; [m.] Joe E. Ramey; [occ.] Brown & Root, Inc., construction worker; [oth. writ.] "By My Windo," "Can he Service the Sand of Time", plus many more, I hope to share one day so others will enjoy them as much as I do.; [pers.] My inspiration comes from within, within all of us we share the same feelings, which only in time and Gods help, my soul then opens to write.; [a.] Channelview, TX

RAMMELL, ELISE
[b.] February 8, 1963, Newark, OH; [p.] Rube Gayheart and Vivian Gayheart; [m.] S. Kelly Rammell, June 28, 1986; [ch.] Angela Hope, nicholas Jay, Michele Fae; [ed.] Utica High, International Correspondence Schools, School of Child Day Care Management, have attended Central Ohio Technical College's R.N. program.; [occ.] Homemaker, Child Care Provider; [pers.] I would like to do what I can to help my fellow mankind in my lifetimne. Also, I just hope that people will enjoy my poetry.; [a.] Utica, OH

RAMMELL, S. KELLY
[b.] January 4, 1964, Columbus, OH; [p.] Michael S. and Marcella E. Rammel; [m.] Elise F. Rammel, June 28, 1986; [ch.] Angel Hope, Nicolas Jay and Michele Fae; [ed.] Utica High School, Columbus Technical Institute, Licking County, JVS Adult Resource Center; [occ.] Office Assistant State of Ohio, Rehabilitition Services Comm.; [memb.] Choir Director, Deacon, CMF President, St. Louisville Christian Church (Dis-

ciples of Christ); [oth. writ.] Several poems in local newspapers, newsletter. I participate in local poetry readings.; [pers.] My writing is influenced by the wonders of nature. I enjoy writing vivid descriptive verse of what man may tend to overlook in this modern world. Free verse is the medium in which I create.; [a.] Utica, OH

RAMSDELL, ANDY
[b.] December 1, 1977, Down East Community Hospital; [p.] Howard & Terry Ramsdell; [ed.] Bay Ridge Elementary, currently attending Washington Academy High School; [occ.] None Yet; [hon.] SAD #77, High Honors, and Honors SAD #77, Softball and Volleyball Awards; [oth. writ.] I have written several poems, sent some to magazines such as Seventeen, Teen; [pers.] My poetry is based on my feeling, or emotions. I feel a sense of peace when I right my poetry, and I hope others will feel the same when they read it; [a.] East Machias, MA

RANDALL, EVITTS
[b.] November 11, 1961, Joliet, IL; [p.] Howard R. Evitts, Mary L. Evitts; [ed.] Vienna High; [oth. writ.] Yes; [pers.] A special thanks to Pete Townshend for his songs and showing me the power of words.; [a.] Simpson, IL

RANDALL, JOAN
[b.] November 9, 1933, Elgin, IL; [ch.] Richard Ralph, Cynthia Louise, Catherine Sue, Margaret Ann, Patricia Lynn, Robert William; [ed.] St. Scholastica High School; [occ.] Supervisor, Enco Manufacturing co.; [hon.] Scholastic Art Award, Gold Medal for Illinois Speed Roller Skating; [pers.] I want to make a positive difference to all who read my poems, and identify with them.; [a.] Stickney, IL

RANGER, MARGARET
[b.] February 14, 1968, Epsom, England; [occ.] Medical Office Asst; [oth. writ.] A poem published in a book for the Powell River School District, currently working on a fiction novel; [pers.] I've always believed in the freedom of speech and the choice to listen; [a.] Powell River, BC, Canada

RANUCCI, PATRICIA JOYCE
[b.] May 1, 1940, Bpt. Ct.; [p.] John & Dorothy Nicolazzo; [m.] Frank V. Ranucci; [ch.] Gina and Frank Jr.; [oth. writ.] Several articles in local newspaper.; [pers.] My father was a writer and inventor. He wrote many articles in local newspapers in Conn. and Calif. He also wrote a book which was published.; [a.] Bpt. Ct.

RASO, MARY M.
[Pen.] Jeanne; [b.] July 29, 1938, Brooklyn, NY; [p.] Dennis & Mabel Peitas; [ch.] Lisa Ann, Peter and Michael; [ed.] Richmond Hill H.S.; [occ.] Medical Coordinator; [oth. writ.] "The Groom", "Chosen Daughter", "Peter", "A Friend, A Sister", "To An Ex-Husband", "Michael", "Laura Nicole", "Happy 30th Birthday", "My Special Agenl" "Ken (my son)" "Sister"; [pers.] My writing has been influenced by the strength and deep love of my children along with the love of life.; [a.] No. Valley Stream, NY

RAWLS, BOBBY THOMAS
[Pen.] Tom Rawls; [b.] January 28, 1957, Lakeland, FL; [p.] Bob and Betty Rawls; [m.] Denise, March 6, 1982; [ch.] Joel, Rebekah and Daniel; [ed.] Miami High School, Gold Coast Qld. Australia, Common Wealth Bible College, Katoonba College, NSW,; [occ.] Missionary Serving the Lord in Thailand; [memb.] Australian Writers Guild, Fellowship of Australian Writers, Australian Society of Authors; [oth. writ.] Poem and short story in graduation high school magazine, editorial staff and contributor to grad. mag. from Theological College (CBC) to frequent contributor to magazines "Australian Evangel

and Missions Update; [pers.] To celebrate individuality and the eccentricities of life. To be real and make sure I enjoy being me.; [a.] Bangkok, Thailand

RAY, TRACY
[b.] July 16, 1974, Laurel, MS; [p.] Mark and Glenda Ray/Kathy and Scott Sherman; [ed.] Graduated West Jones High School, now attending Jones Jr. College; [occ.] Arobic Instructor/student; [hon.] Dean's List at school, Who's Who Among America's High School Students, Sociology Award, Most Outstanding and Team Captain Award; [a.] Laurel, MS

RAYMOND, HAZEL L.
[Pen.] Hazel Louise Kvin/Aug; [b.] January 3, 1910, Legrand, IA; [p.] Jacob and Minnie Kvinlaug; [m.] Maxwell Raymond, September 23, 1958; [ch.] Sharon Ann, Ronald David; [ed.] Graduated Gilman High School, Graduated Grinnell Community Hospital and University of IA, Nursing Training School; [occ.] Retired; [memb.] United Church of Christ Americn Legion Auxiliary American Red Cross, State Nurses Associaiton IA, Federated Women's Club; [hon.] Nursing Awards, American Legion Aux. Award, Voluntary work awards; [oth. writ.] Have written many poems and memorials but none for publications.; [pers.] I try to show the faith and love of Jesus Christ in my writings and in my everyday life.

READ, ROBBIE
[b.] July 20, 1948, Olney, TX; [p.] Richard J. and Billie Taylor; [m.] Dwight L. Read, November 23, 1972; [ch.] son, Kelley Keith Read married to Trady Read; [occ.] Artist/Jewelry Maker; [memb.] Southwestern Watercolor Society, San Antonio Watercolor Group, Waterloo Watercolor Group of Austin, TX; [hon.] Many art awards including Best of Show, Judges Choice and Peoples Choice nominated to the North Texas, Women's Hall of Fame in 1988 for artistic endeavors; [oth. writ.] Wrote weekly newspaper column for the Graham Leader for a number of years.; [pers.] I've always been invoved in the creative process, but have only resently began writing poetry. Like my paintings, what I write has to reflect my own experiences and feelings. It must have content of the soul.; [a.] Graham, TX

REAGAN, CHEVETTE
[b.] October 11, 1969, Phoenix, AZ; [p.] Donna Ealin and Willie Ray Reagan; [ed.] South Mountain H.S., Northern University, Arizona; [occ.] Personnel Director, Super Technologies; [memb.] NAACP, Black Women's Task Force, American Heart Assoc.; [hon.] National Honor Roll, Who's Who, Employee of the MOnth 5/92; [pers.] I express myself through my writings whether good or bad. I have always stressed to myself that I am as good as I allow myself to be.; [a.] Phoenix, AZ

REDFERN, ALSON ROSCOE
[b.] April 25, 1935, Crossplains, TN; [p.] David and Doug Redfern; [m.] Elda, 1956, Divorced 1960; [ch.] Paul, David, Eva; [ed.] Two years, junior college, music and art, creative waiting; [occ.] songwriter; [oth. writ.] 60 songs unpublished, 7 poems unpublished.; [pers.] The free world nations are the keeper of the keys. They should use those keys to unlock the doors of freedom and respect for all individual rights "At All Cost."; [a.] K. City, MO

REDONDO, LORRAINE
[b.] March 13, 1951, Los Angeles, CA; [p.] Alfred & Anita Rubio; [ch.] Nicholas; [ed.] El Rancho High School; [occ.] Executive Secretary; [oth. writ.] Several poems submitted for publication. This will be my first publication.; [pers.] I'm a simple person desiring to capture human sentiment in a complicated world.

REED, A. HOWARD
[Pen.] Howard Reed; [b.] May 26, 1940, Great Fall MT; [p.] Albert & Phyllis Reed; [m.] Margot Chene Reed, April 22, 1989; [ch.] Andrew Howard, Chris topher Clyde; [ed.] herbert Hoover High School California State Polytechnic University, B.S. Archi tectural Engineering; [occ.] Architect; [memb.] Vari ous Professional Organizations; [hon.] Scarab, Dean' List, Photography & Graphis Contest Winner; [oth writ.] Several hundred unpublished poems and shor stories. Self published philosophical essays for : metaphysical news letter and architectural criticism op-ed pieces for local newspapers.; [pers.] My influ ences include Lewis Mumford, Ayn Rand, Victo Hugo & Goethe and the rythm & structure of Jazz and Blues. I write about emotions and humanness and the beauty of our world and our stewardship there of; [a.] Flagstaff, AZ

REED, DENNIS WILLIAM
[b.] September 26, 1937, NY; [p.] Smith and Meryl Reed; [m.] Judity E. Reed, June 16, 1968; [ch.] Karen and Michael Reed; [ed.] Four years college; [occ.] Manager, Securities Industry; [memb.] none; [hon.] none; [oth. writ.] none; [pers.] I have always loved the poetic form for its power, economy and textures. In certain poems, word such as cathedral and exulttion, never fail to dazzle me.; [a.] New York, NY

REED, JOHN E.
[Pen.] John Reed; [b.] January 12, 1915, Rockfield, IN; [p.] Edmund Reed & Margaret Reed; [m.] B. Elizabeth Reed, July 6, 1935; [ch.] Elizabeth Ann, Charlotte; [ed.] Redford High, Tulsa University, University of Houston, Famous Writers School Correspondence; [occ.] Retired; [memb.] Life Enrichment of Houston, AARP, English First, Shell Alumni Assoc.; [hon.] Past President, New Orleans Personnel Assoc., Marian High School PTO, Shell Alumni Assoc., Board Member, Life Enrichment of Houston; [oth. writ.] Columnist Clarion (local newspaper) contributor editor Shell House Organs, contributor, local newspaper editorial columns; [pers.] Now that I have time I hope to be successful in writing poetry as a newspaper columnist of off-beat subjects.; [a.] Houston, TX

REES, VALERIE
[b.] August 15, 1945, London; [m.] August 14, 1965, Divorced 1991; [occ.] Secretary in a busy dental surgery.; [memb.] United Reformed Church, Ingatestone; [oth. writ.] 20 plus poems published in my church monthly magazine. Some poems written for a particular service with a theme.; [pers.] "Personal Reflections" was the first of many poems I have written that describe an experience I have had or my thoughts and personal feelings. I hope that my work will be a witness to God; [a.] Ingatestone, Essex England

REESE, JEANETTE
[Pen.] Jeanae Little One; [b.] October 10, 1969, Ann Arbor, MI; [p.] Spirit Mother Nancy; [ch.] none; [ed.] Fourteen and a half years of schooling with 3.8 and 4.0 grades at Washtenau Community college.; [occ.] Writer and Artist; [memb.] American Kidney Assoc., Health Occupations Students of America, Girl Scouts of America, German Exchange Program, Ann Arbor Art Associations, Manchester Drama Club, Washtenaw Parks and Recreation; [hon.] Merit award from Kidney Foundation, 1st place in regional competition for HOSA, Achievement award for Health OCC., Dean's List, Ann Arbor Deaf Club, Heydlauf Scholarship, Art Honors; [oth. writ.] Poetry and prose published in local presses; [pers.] Most of my writing is influenced by my mental and spiritual aspects of myself. My greatest teachers are the ones who have believed in me and helped me materialize into someone I started knowing; [a.] Tecumseh, MI

REEVES, ARRIANNA LEIGH
b.] December 10, 1975, Greenville, NC; [p.] Delores
ean Reeves; [ed.] High School Senior, JH Rose High
chool; [occ.] Student, JH Rose High School; [memb.]
Member of the Minority Affairs Club at JH Rose High
chool. Member of the "Rampant Battalion" drill
eam Army JROTC; [hon.] Veteran of Foreign Wars
Ribbon, Certificate of Appreciation from the State
Employees Assoc of North Carolina; [pers.] I have
always loved poetry. Being able to express your
intermost thoughts and feelings on paper is the great-
est gift I possess, and for this I thank God, and my
mother, Delores. Always write what you feel; [a.]
Greenville, NC

REEVES, PATRICIA-WADDELL
[b.] Phila, PA; [p.] Nancy & Cornelius Waddell; [m.]
Nathaneil Reeves, Jr, July 16, 1983; [ch.] Kyanna
Nyel Reeves; [ed.] Overbrook High School, Cheyney
University B.S., Antioch University M.Ed; [occ.]
Special Education Teacher, Phila. School District;
[memb.] black Woman's Educaitonal Alliance, Ameri-
can Federation of Teachers, PA Area Science Teach-
ers Association, Winslow Township school District
Advisory Committee, Winslow Township, Withdrawl
Advisroy Committee; [hon.] Certificate of recogni-
tion for Mastery Learning Program; [oth. writ.]
Article for Renaissance Magazine; [pers.] I believe
that the true essence of life comes not from how long
you live, but how well you live. A tribute to my
brothers; [a.] Sicklerville, NJ

REINBEAU, RONALD
[b.] June 7, 1947, Newark; [p.] Bill & Ruth Reinbeau;
[m.] Eva Lee Reinbeau, August 21, 1987; [ch.]
Michelle Reinbeau, Patricia Reinbeau; [ed.] Shadyside
High; [occ.] Glassmaker, Holophane Co.; [memb.]
A.F.G.W.U.; [oth. writ.] Poems published in news-
papers; [a.] Newark, OH

REIS, DEBORA VESTAL
[Pen.] Sarah Elizabeth Marlow; [b.] March 18, 1953,
Dallas, TX; [p.] Calvin and Louise Vestal; [m.]
Michael Reis; [ch.] Christopher & Randon

REISCH, LAURIE C.
[Pen.] Corinne Alexander; [b.] May 6, 1957, Berlin,
NH; [p.] Alexander and Irene D.W. Misnil; [m.]
Russell M. Reisch, June 18, 1979; [ch.] Brandon
Russell and Shayne Alexander; [ed.] Behavior Sci-
ence. I am at age 36, now attending college and
deriving a great deal of pleasure from freelance
writing.; [occ.] Presently a student and homemaker
who writes as a hobby.; [memb.] Phi Beta Kappa;
[hon.] Editor's Choice Award for Day of Contempla-
tion, Certificate of Merit for As Little Children and
Golden Poet awarded piece on cassette, completing a
poem I love is my favorite award; [oth. writ.] As Little
Children is published in Who's Who in Poety Today,
Our World's Favorite Poetry, Day of Contemplation
is in Whispering Winds. Much unpublished poetry
and presently (2 books) manuscripting 2 books. Quill
also has published my work.; [pers.] Visual and
guided imagery in creative writing is my way of being
able to paint a picture. Peotry is an artform and is my
painting. This is why National Library of Poetry so
pleases me by showcasing individual poems of mine.
I value each poem. They are me and mine, a soul on
print as are all other poets.

REISEN, REANA
[b.] July 29, 1983, Milton; [ch.] Siblings: Johnathan
age 8, and Jessica age 5; [ed.] Reana is currently in the
5th grade at Berryhill Elem. Reana plans to be a
Veterinarian; [hon.] Reana has a collection of Terrific
Kid Awards; [oth. writ.] Reana loves to write but this
is her first published writing.; [pers.] I wish everyone
would realize the importance of saving the rainforest
and protecting the environment and do something
about it.; [a.] Milton, FL

RENIC, VIRSEY
[b.] June 24, 1913, Marietta; [p.] John and Hemons
Richey; [m.] Rayford Renick, June 16, 1936; [ch.]
Rayford Jr., Rilda Hicks and Sandra Hall; [ed.] B.S.
from Oklahoma A&M and a masters friom South
Eastern College at Durant, OK; [occ.] Retired from
teaching 21 years; [memb.] Retired Teacher's AARP,
RSVP, OK, Coalition of Aging, Aromre Art Guild,
Homemakers Club, Marietta Church of Christ; [hon.]
Represents the Aging in Washington, DC. Won 20
awards in art in Okla., Texas and L.A.; [oth. writ.]
My life history, I keep a diary; [pers.] I stay busy!
"An idol brain is the devils workshop. My husband
died 1991 with a heart attack; [a.] Marietta, OK

REULE, JEAN
[b.] October 9, 1931, Scotland; [p.] James and Jean
Green; [m.] William, October 4, 1950 (Deceased 12/
31/93); [ch.] James William, William Arthur, Eric
Nicholas; [ed.] Hyndland Secondary High School,
Scotland Music R.S.A. of M.; [occ.] Self-employed,
printing and typesetting.; [memb.] Fislers of Men,
Hi-way Church (band master); [hon.] Pin for serving
as a volunteer in the Hamilton Detention Centre for 5
years, Certificate from 100 Hunley St. for Counsel-
ling 5 years.; [oth. writ.] I have hundreds and
hundreds of poems. Alos 14 booklets, Tracts (The
Tracts are published and given out free in many
countries); [pers.] When I have a quiet time, just for
a few moments, I can usually write a poem.; [a.]
Englehard, Ontario

REYNOLDS, DAVID
[b.] December 11, 1975, Washington, DC; [p.]
Charles & Susan Reynolds; [ed.] Leonardtown High
School; [occ.] Student at Campbell Univ.; [pers.] I try
to bring out the beauty in everything through my
poetry. I also try to expose some of the rights and
wrongs that our society does. I was influenced by Jack
Kerouac and Victor Cruz and E.E. Cummings.; [a.]
Hollywood, MD

REYNOLDS, JOHANNA
[Pen.] Johanna; [b.] May 25, 1935, Almelo, the
Netherlands; [ch.] Roan, Eva, Leah Reynolds; [ed.]
B.A. major Psych. M.S. in Education, Major in
Guidance and Counseling, Youngstown, OH, R.N.
Netherlands, CA RN since 1987; [occ.] RN Psych.
White Memorial Med Center.; [pers.] Trying to make
sense of it all.; [a.] LA, CA

RICE, ARTHURINE B.
[b.] March 31, 1952, Nyack, NY; [p.] Carolyn N. B.
Serveance; [ch.] Hasan Jamal and Sabriya Rice; [ed.]
Washington Technical Inst., Associate of Arts,
Benedict College, Bachelors of Social Works, Webster
University, Master of Arts; [occ.] Licensed Social
Worker with the State of South Carolina; [memb.]
Second Nazareth Baptist Church, Columbia High
School Band Booster Club and National Eastern Stars;
[hon.] Certificate of Service Award from the State of
South Carolina for more than ten (10) years of service;
[oth. writ.] This Perfect Place, A Lovely Season, Our
Missing Star, Moonlit Love, A Complete Ecstasy, A
Tender Touch, The Child Who Blamed, Blames No
More. These are unpublished works; [pers.] Life is
a piece of paer, write something.; [a.] Columbia, SC

RICHARDS, AMBER JOY
[Pen.] Amber Richards; [b.] February 25, 1981,
Harbor City, CA; [p.] Vicki & Roger Hammitt; [ch.]
Siblings, Krystle Ann, Stephanie Ann, Megan Elaine,
Aaron Dean, Brandon Scott; [ed.] Crestwood El-
ementary, San Pedro, CA, currently attending Dodson
Jr. High School, 7th grade; [occ.] Student; [memb.]
Dodson Jr. High Drama Club, Los Angeles Public
Library; [hon.] 1992 First place Crestwood Elem.
Spelling Bee (fifth grade) 1992 First Place San Pedro
Complex Spelling Bee, 1993 First Place, Crestwood
Elem. Spelling Bee 6th grade, 1993 First Place San

Pedro Complex Spelling Bee; [oth. writ.] I have
written many poems, but this is the first I've ever
submitted.; [pers.] I enjoy reading and writing in my
sparetime. My influences depend on my mood.; [a.]
San Pedro, CA

RICHARDS, SCOTT VINCENT
[b.] November 18, 1935, Kansas City, KS; [p.] Orvie
L. Staats, Lena B. Staats; [ed.] Northeast High
School, Kansas City, Missouri; [occ.] Unemployed;
[memb.] International Guild of Occult Sciences Re-
search Society; [hon.] Several Certificates of Merit
and Golden Poet Awards; [oth. writ.] Several poems
published by local newspaper, as well as several
poems published by World of Poetry, American
Poetry Association, The National Library of Poetry,
Literary Focus and Quill Books; [pers.] My poetry
comes from my own life, and I try to show through it
lessons of life; and people we've loved never really
die, for their love and memories live on in our hearts
always.; [a.] Beaver Dam, KY

RICHARDSON, ALYSON
[b.] March 27, 1980, Greensboro; [p.] Peggy & Dean
Richardson; [ed.] Currently in 8th grade; [occ.]
Student; [memb.] Save the earch club at school;
[hon.] Student council, honor roll, ecological essay
contest won savings band, tested by Duke University
TIP testing.; [oth. writ.] Other short stories and poems
but, none have been published before now; [pers.] Let
your heart not be troubled: ye believe in God believe
also in me (John 14:1) The power of God revived me
from the heart-ache and helped me discover a talent.
He can do the same for you.; [a.] McLeansville, NC

RICHMOND, ROBYN
[p.] Ron & Karen Richmond; [ch.] Bonna Robyn,
Keith Richmond; [ed.] I am attending Wylie Senior
High School; [memb.] Disipleship classes at my local
church.; [hon.] First Place U.I.L., Sprint Literary
meet, District 10AAA, 1991; [oth. writ.] My love
lifts; high, U.S. Straight Ahead.; [pers.] I never
neglect myself of doing wrong, I just try to set myself
with goodness of life and poetry that revolves around
my future.; [a.] Wylie, TX

RICKS, JOSEPH
[b.] May 3, 1975, Wilson, NC; [p.] David & Shirley
Ricks; [ed.] East Duplin High School, Barton Col-
lege; [occ.] Student; [memb.] Alpha Omega, Sandy
Plain FWB Church; [hon.] National English Merit
Award; [pers.] In God I trust, for without him I would
not be able to write.; [a.] Pink Hill, NC

RIDDLE, RUSSELL J.
[Pen.] R. J. Ridl; [b.] September 23, 1958, Greensburg,
PA; [p.] Bob & Audrie; [ed.] B.S. Chemical Engi-
neering, Penn State, 1980; [pers.] The most important
thing in life is acceptance of others. The most difficult
thing in life is to admit shortcomings, make ammends
and follow a new path. The most beautiful thing in life
is being in love; [a.] Waverly, OH

RIDDLEBERGER, JR. WILLIAM
[Pen.] Bill; [b.] November 19, 1933, Covington, VA;
[p.] Lillie and Harold Riddleberger; [m.] 1st, Carol S.
Riddleberger, December 22, 1956 (5 children); 2nd-
L. Faye Riddleberger, December 17, 1989; [ch.]
Richard Harold, Rhonda Carol, David Wayne, Dana
Yvonne, William Barrett; [ed.] Covington Sr. High
School, Engineering (Mechanical) Bluefield Coll.
VA., A.A. American Rauer College, Sacramento,
Colifornia, B.S. Charleston Southern University,
Charleston, South Carolina, B.S. Charleston South
Carolina; USAF Vet. Officer Flight Training, South
Carolina Graduate of SC Law Enforcement Training
Academy. Also licensed Firearms Inst.; [occ.] Presi-
dent and owner of respond enterprise inc. for 20
years, a private law enforcement agency; [memb.]

SCLEOA, South Carolina Law Enforcement Officers Assoc., Summerville Baptist Church Deacon; [hon.] Previously listed in Personalities of the South. Appointed to US Senate Advisory Sub Committee for the safe use of Lasers in industry, major and minor in business and economics at receipt of B.S. Degree received highest honors.; [oth. writ.] Several poems in busienss and technical journals. Also poems in local and state news and sports papers. [pers.] "What I do today is important because I am paying a day of my life for it. What I accomplish must be worthwhile because the price is high.; [a.] Summerville, SC

RIEPE, CHARLOTTE
[Pen.] Carmen; [b.] May 31, 1915, Lisco, NE; [p.] deceased; [m.] deceased; [ed.] High school, Loveland, CO, Denver University night classes, 2 years. Eleven years musical training, violin, organ, theory.; [occ.] Retired from 30 years, do volunteer research and proof reading for author Mary A. DeVries.; [memb.] Currently, International Society of Poets, Formerly, National Writers Club, Denver Arizona State Poetry Society, and Yavapai Symphony Assn., Arizona.; [hon.] First prize (poetry) National Writers Club, Denver 1966. Poems published in several poetry magazines. Poems published in six anthologies; [oth. writ.] Composed a song "Firs Love" published and recorded by M.S.R. Records Co., Hollywood, CA 1974; [pers.] I like poetry with uplifting themes of courage, morals and hoe and the victory of right over wrong.; [a.] Sedona, AZ

RIETTA, MARY LOUISE
[b.] January 21, 1967; [p.] Robert Gomez Sr., and Sarah Gomez; [m.] Phil James Rietta, June 3, 1985; [ch.] Christina Marie 1986, Andrew James 1988, Sarah Catherine 1990; [occ.] Housewife and Student Writer (Institute of Children Literature); [oth. writ.] Many poems and short stories never published.; [pers.] I believe that what you feel in your heart should be said!; [a.] Azusa, CA

RIGGIN, CHARLES
[b.] February 6, 1927, Okla.; [p.] Jerry and Mary Riggin (dec); [m.] Patsy Ruth Riggin (dec.), July 26, 1948; [ch.] Nine, all grown and married: Charles, Jerrell, Patsy, Susan, Harvey, Mary, Anna, Genevive, Maureen; [occ.] Retired Plumber; [oth. writ.] The Golden Sea, My Friend, The Iran Hostage Rescue, Young Warriors, The Little Irish Lad, Shawnee By the River, The Bucking Machine; [pers.] I have never had any of these published in any kind of publication. I felt they did not measure up to other writer's.; [a.] Shawnee, OK

RIMNEY, KEVIN
[b.] May 30, 1978, Stony Plain, Alberta; [p.] Fred Rimney, Linda Rimney; [ed.] Currently in Grade 10 at Stony Memorial Composit High; [oth. writ.] Several other poems and short stories; Influences: J.R.R. Tolkien, Dave Mustaine, Metallica, Tim Burton; [pers.] Most of my work has a dark edge to it, this expresses the dark side of mankind, his actions and emotions; [a.] Alberta, Canada

RING, ABRAM
[b.] August 13, 1978, Front Royal, VA; [p.] Larry & Brenda Ring; [ed.] Warren Couty High School (so far); [pers.] I believe that this county has a lot of problems. I also believe that this country could be a better place if the government and other authority figures would listen to the public, especially the younger generation, a whole lot better. Not many people take us seriously because of what we look like, believe in, and our age. It makes me sick.; [a.] Front Royal, VA

RISE, NISSA VIANE
[b.] October 22, 1978, Sunnyside, WA; [p.] Ina Rise and John Rise; [ed.] Freshman in High School; [occ.]

Student; [oth. writ.] "Why Do We Laugh" published in local newspaper.; [pers.] I enjoy writing poetry because I love to express my feelings and I like seeing people's reactions before and after reading my poem or poems.

RIVERA, EDWIN
[b.] November 14, 1968, NYC; [p.] Maria Rivera, Sotero Rivero Sr.; [ed.] Western CT State, University Criminal Law Major.; [occ.] Body Guard, Student Writer; [memb.] Golds Gym Member; [hon.] Art Award High School, Drawing Art, Spanish; [oth. writ.] Souss for Rainbow Records, L.A. California Hollywood.; [pers.] A Dream is just a Dream to all, but to your mind it's a reality. The gift of life is salvation, Jesus Christ. Thank You.; [a.] Danbury, CT

RIVERA, MATHAIS
[Pen.] Collaw; [b.] May 14, 1975, NY; [m.] Yulitza J. Rivera, year 2003; [ed.] Cardinal Spellman H.S. University at Buffalo; [oth. writ.] Many; [pers.] With you reading this, I start my time with my name. How long before I reach the shadows of the end? A journey, not, for me, but for all who die because they were born?

ROBERSON, TERRY LYNN
[Pen.] Trent; [b.] June 16, 1957, Decature, IL; [p.] Will H. and Hazel; [ch.] Foster: Maurice Stanley, Pierce Bradford, Andre Morgan, Steve Morgan, Anthony Phillips; [ed.] High School Graduate of MacArthur High; [occ.] Cashier, Cook, Millikin University; [oth. writ.] Presently working on book to be publish soon "Soul Survivor" a handbook and guide for ministering to youth involved in drugs, gangs and peer pressure.; [pers.] I strive very hard to bring God in his fullness to the world through my writing and showing love, understanding and appreciation to mankind.; [a.] Decatur, IL

ROBERTS, ALICE M.
[Pen.] Freckles; [b.] October 17, 1952, Danville, VA; [p.] James and Amanda McCullor; [m.] Robert T. Roberts, March 7, 1981; [ch.] Juanita Denise, Melanie Danielle; [ed.] Bartlett Yancey Senior High School, Piedmont Tech., Danville Community College; [occ.] (CNA) Certify Nursing Assistant, Danville Regional Medical Center, Danville, VA; [memb.] Volunteer for Danville Regional Medical Center, Poetry Reading by Danville Parks and Recreation Department; [hon.] Graduate Summa Cum Laude for CNA, Volunteer Department, 15 years of service to the Memorial Hospital of Danville, VA; [oth. writ.] I write poems for friends, publish one "Whisper in the Wind", Publish once "The Space Between."; [pers.] I write from my feelings and from all the interested people I meet in my day to day life.; [a.] Danville, VA

ROBERTS, TERRANCE, JR.
[Pen.] Terry; [b.] August 13, 1953, Lansingmi; [p.] Geraldine and Terrance Sr.; [ed.] Some College; [hon.] Honor Roll; [oth. writ.] Short short stories; [pers.] Take life in stride. Retain your pride.; [a.] Tampa, FL

ROBERTSON, NANCY
[b.] February 18, 1953, Atlanta, GA; [p.] John & Hazel Ingram; [m.] Phil Robertson; [ch.] Beth Lambert, Tommy Vaughan, Lee Vaughan, Andy Vaughan, Phil Robert Jr.,; [occ.] Cooks helper at Central Ark. Hosp.; [a.] Sercy, AK

ROBINSON, BYRON
[b.] January 27, 1963, Miami, FL; [p.] Dewey and Helen Robinson; [ed.] School of Hard Knox; [occ.] Entrepreneur Distributor for Interior Design Nutritionals; [hon.] Brown Belt Karate College, Blue Ribbon in Art Show, WWI Merchandisers Award; [oth. writ.] Judgement Day, Beware, Time changed, Prices, The Game, It's To Late, The Sun, The

Philosopher, Out Loud, A Wise Man, Hell, Fellings Shattered Past, Songs: A shot at the light, dame [pers.] Life as we know it can end at anytime. But i we accept the lord as our savior we will live forever In God all things are possible if you believe.; [a. Miami, FL

ROBINSON, MIRIAM KNOX
[b.] July 19, 1938, Atlanta, GA; [p.] Lessie Knox and Nazareth Knox, Sr. (deceased 11/93); [m.] Divorced; [ch.] Monica, Janis and Kimberly, Grandsons: Brandon, Bradley and Zachariah; [ed.] L. J. Price High, Morris Brown College; [occ.] Unemployed (state employee) free lance writer; [memb.] First Mt. Selah Baptist Church, International Society of Authors & Artists, Atlanta Lawn Tennis Association (ALTA), Executive Board member of Coalition for Equality of African American State Employees (CEASE); [hon.] Singles and doubles awards in various local Tennis Tournaments, Certificate of Merit by American Press; [oth. writ.] Tennis Column in The Atlanta News Weekly 1991 to present, four poems for publication in an anthology of poems.; [pers.] I like to make my writings simply for the enjoyment of meaningful messages; [a.] Decatur, GA

ROBINSON, NATHANIEL
[Pen.] Amante; [b.] February 10, 1954, Beaufort, SC; [p.] Nathan & Estella Robinson; [m.] Sandra Kay Britt-Robinson, March 5, 1993; [ch.] Nathaniel Robinson, Jr.; [ed.] B.S. (Biology) Voorhees College, M.S. (Biology) Atlanta University; [occ.] USAF Staff Officer; Part-time Financier; [memb.] Alpha Phi Alpha; Alpha Phi Omega, Lifetime Honor Society and AF Association Member, Prince Hall F&AM; [hon.] Outstanding Young Men of America, Who's Who Among Students in American Colleges & Universities, Summa Cum Laude and Valedictorian (College).; [oth. writ.] Several poems published in high school and college newspapers, one narrative and 40+ unpublished poems.; [pers.] Writing a work is so much like taking a journey... it may be hard gathering the thoughts; however, the serene process and soothing result make it all continually worthwhile.; [a.] Chesapeake, VA

ROBITAILLE, W. SUZANNE
[b.] October 15, 1980, Toronto, Ontario; [p.] William Robitaille, Wendy Robitaille; [ed.] Grade 8, Penson Public School, Grovedale Alberta; [occ.] Student; [hon.] Academic Awards for grade 5 & 6.

ROCKINGHAM JR., RUFUS
[b.] May 28, 1949, Phila., PA; [p.] rufus Sr., & Willie Pearl; [m.] Alma, January 8, 1986; [ch.] Renee Helen; [ed.] Graduate of Thomas A. Edison High School in Philadelphia, PA, one year of college at Burhington Community College in NJ; [occ.] Driver, Photographer; [memb.] none; [hon.] I have received several awards for my work and an award of Honorable Mention for my recent works with other publishers.; [oth. writ.] Other poems published with World of Poetry, Quill Books, American Poetry Anthology of 1983.; [pers.] Poetry has seemed to have a way of taking care of itself for centuries, in it's own class I look forward to continuing my writing and perhaps one day, I will be nominated for the big one.; [a.] Pemberton, NJ

ROCKLIFFE, HAROLD J.
[Pen.] Halj; [b.] November 29, 1927, Pittsburgh, PA; [m.] Cynthia B. Rockliffe, February 11, 1978; [ch.] Keith, Chris, Jamerson, Karen, Ruth and Beth; [ed.] South Hills High, Pittsburgh, PA; Univ. of Kentucky and Univ. of Arizona; [occ.] Retired, Mgr./Supervisor Appraisal Section, AZ Dept. of Transportation; [memb.] National Assn. of Real Estate Appraisers. Owner, Rockliffe Appraisals Erc.; [oth. writ.] none, except for my own amusement.; [pers.] I like to write for the challenge of saying something, sometimes

worth while, in a few words and in everyday language. Of course, some of the things I write and say have duel meanings.; [a.] Youngtown, AZ

RODGERS, ALSACE
[Pen.] Baseemah Abdullah; [b.] November 10, 1928, Chigo, Il.; [p.] Halbert & Mattie Landers; [ch.] Eric, Lyra, Herbert, Otto, Charles Twins--Denise & Dennis, David & Daniel; [ed.] Du Sable High, Kennedy King College, Loop College, Asst. Teacher (9 yrs.), Univ. of Islam, American Floral Art School; [hon.] Mothers Day Poem won a prize in Chgo. Sun Times; [oth. writ.] Severl greeting cards poems. Personal book of poems.; [pers.] Helping to guide youths and others toward education. To help them see what can be accomplished thru education, the wonders of the world with its beauty in many forms. Poetry helps to express that.; [a.] Chicago, IL

RODGERS, WILL
[b.] March 11, 1964, Detroit; [p.] Rosalyn G. and billy Rodgers; [ed.] Courtis Elementary, German Township Junior High, German Township Senior High, Bachelors Degree in Journalism and English from California University of Pennsylvania; [occ.] Communications Coordinator; [memb.] Phi Beta Sigma Fraternity Inc. Sigma Tau Delta, Pi Gamma Mu, African Americans Uniting for Life, United Methodist Church; [oth. writ.] Screen adaptations of James Baldwin's "Sonny's Blues", "When The Night Falls," "My Family and Christmas," short story.; [pers.] Love is the common denominator of life. Nothing can exist without it nothing matters without it it.; [a.] St. Petersburg, FL

RODREIQUEZ, JOE
[Pen.] J.R.; [b.] August 18, 1972, Taft, TX; [p.] Jesus Rodriquez, Sylvia Rodriquez; [m.] Esmeralda G. Rodriquez; [ed.] Mary Carroll High School; [hon.] Football Scholarship, Art Institute of Houston; [pers.] I have been deeply influenced by the different powers of love. Dedicated to myself.; [a.] Corpus Christi, TX

RODRIGUES, JOAO
[b.] March 8, 1955, Cape Town, South Africa; [p.] Joao and Natividale Rodrigues; [ed.] Licentiate in Theology at Urbaniana University Rome, Italy (1980); [occ.] Missionary priest serving in Witbank Diocese of South Africa; [oth. writ.] Mostly lyrical writings used in musical compositions, also spiritual reflections published in a Cape Town Yoga Magazine.; [pers.] Poetry, the written form of the vocal mystery, speaks for those who listen to lye, and, when all else faisl, it alone succeeds in opening the doors of long closed hearts.; [a.] Plumstead, Cape, South Africa

ROE, JENNIFER LEE
[b.] November 25, 1980, Easton, MD; [p.] Jeanne Marie and Robert Lee Roe Jr.; [m.] Single; [ed.] Colonel Richardson, Middle School Completed 7th grade, Honors English Classes, Honor Roll 8 years; [memb.] Little League Softball 4 years, Band Front 2 years, 4-H Club, 1 year, Basketball Intermerials 2 years, Cheerleading 3 years, Teen Directions, 1 year, Teen Group Easton Nazarene Church; [hon.] Citizenship award, Honor Roll awards (7), Softball trophies (4), Merit Roll award (2), 1st place 2 mile track, 2nd place softball thro, 1st place 100 yd relay; [pers.] I work hard to achieve my goals.; [a.] Preston, MD

ROGERS, JANESE MARIE
[b.] January 7, 1977, Cumberland County; [p.] Roy and Rachel Rogers; [m.] not married; [ed.] South Cumberland Elementary and Cumberland County High School currently in the eleventh grade; [memb.] Vandever Baptist church; [oth. writ.] This was my first.; [pers.] My goal is to remind people of the beauties that go unnoticed. Through the words that I might say, I hope to inspire others like me.; [a.] Crossville, TN

ROGERS, JR. JOHNNY
[b.] May 19, 1946, Florence, SC; [p.] Johnny rogers Sr. and Katie Elizabeth Price Rogers; [m.] Divorced; [ch.] none; [ed.] A.A. Business Administration 1971, Brevard Community College, Cocoa, FL, B.S. Business Administration 1978, Francis Marion College, Florence, SC; [occ.] Registered Respiratory Therapist, Duke University Medical Center, Durham, NC; [memb.] Active member: American Assoc. for Respiratory Care and the National Board for Respiratory Care. Charter Lifetime Member. The International Society of Poets.; [hon.] World of Poetry, Golden Poet 1990, 91, 92. Five Honorable Mentions, 1990, 1991. The International Society of Poets: Poet of Merit, 1992, 1993. Two Editor's Choice Awards, 1993; [oth. writ.] World of poetry Press, 13 poems, World of Poetry Anthology 1991, 13 Poems Selected Works of Our World's Best Poets 1992, 1 Poem, Poems That Will Live Forever 1992. Duke University Medical Center, one poem, Chapbook, They Wrote Us A Poem 1993, The National Library of Poetry, 13 poems, Our World's Favorite Poems and Who's Who In Poetry, 1993, 1 poem, Whispers In the Wind, 1993, 1 Poem, Outstanding Poets of 1994, currently being published.; [pers.] I strive to reflect humanity, nature, and I write lyrics for song poems on a wide variety of subjects.; [a.] Durham, NC

ROGERS, SR., LEON
[Pen.] Le Rog; [b.] March 29, 1946, Chicago, IL; [p.] James W. & Laura E. Rogers; [m.] Elizabeth Ann Rogers; [ch.] John, Sarah, Bridgette, Lisa, Leon II, Trelisa and Laura; [ed.] Long Beach City College, A.A., Roosevelt Univ., B.S.B.A., De Paul Univ. 2 yrs Graduate Study Taxation. Currently grad. student in English, Chicago State Univ.; [occ.] Disability Retirement; [memb.] Beta Gamma Sigma, Disabled American Veterans, American Legion; [hon.] Beta Gamma Sigma, Dean's List, Outstanding Manager 1985 State of California; [oth. writ.] Several poems, short stories, and essays.; [pers.] One must put oneself first, so that one can put others before self.; [a.] South Holland, IL

ROGERS, THOMAS E.
[b.] November 24, 1970, Nashville, TN; [p.] Buck and Virginia Rogers; [m.] Tracey, May 16, 1992; [ed.] Battle Ground Academy, Belmont University, Middle Tennessee State University; [occ.] Student; [memb.] Sigma Tau Delta, Gamma Beta Phi; [oth. writ.] Small collection of poems and short stories that have yet to be published.; [pers.] To me, Poetry is like a hidden appendage. Without warning, it touches you, shakes you, then lets you go, hopefully better off.; [a.] Antioch, TN

ROGERSON, BILL
[b.] July 5, 1953, Liverpool; [p.] Bill and Ida Rogerson; [m.] Single; [ed.] High School Education Litherland High School, for boys in the city of Liverpool England.; [occ.] Former Driver, recently medically retired; [oth. writ.] This is the first time I have ever sent anything to be published that has been accepted.; [pers.] I tend to write poetry with meaning and hope to share my thoughts with other people, I also write poetry with the intension of helping people, think about things they may not have thought about before.; [a.] Liverpool, England

ROGOVEIN, REISA M.
[b.] March 1, 1951, Montreal, Canada; [p.] Harry and Ada Rogovein; [ed.] Bachelor's Degree from University of Miami, Master's Degree from Houston Baptist University; [occ.] English Instructor at Houston Community College; [memb.] Texas Junior College, Teacher's Association; [hon.] Favorite Instructor (Spring 93'), Instructor most likely to help her students (spring 93'); [oth. writ.] Poetry published in "Southwestern Studies" and in "Teaching English in

The Community College"; [pers.] The struggle for survival is the impetus behind my work. Although I may not survive, perhaps my poetry will.; [a.] Houston, TX

ROHLOFF, JANE M.
[b.] May 10, 1965, Slayton, MN; [p.] Gary and Karen Onken; [m.] Terry L. Rohloff, September 1, 1984; [ch.] Zachary Gerald, Nichole Marie; [ed.] Slayton High School (Slayton, MN), Granite Falls AVTI (Granite Falls, MN); [occ.] Stay-at-home mom; [oth. writ.] none published; [pers.] I believe hard work, honesty, and dedication are qualities which are possessed by every good person. My poetry comes from my heart and has been inspired by people with those qualities.; [a.] Hadley, MN

ROHRER, EIKA
[b.] March 7, 1968; [p.] Willis L. and Bodil Rohrer; [ed.] Natrona County High, Associated Schools, Inc., Eastern Wyoming College; [occ.] Student, veterinary technology and veterinary medicine; [memb.] North American Veterinary Technician Association.; [hon.] Phi Theta Kappa, President's Honor Roll; [oth. writ.] Article for the Eastern Community; [pers.] Every nuance is important to the content of the poem. Each poem can be read superficially or with deep thought and emotion.; [a.] Casper, WY

ROLSON, JUNE RITA
[Pen.] Andreana Seaton; [b.] April 9, 1939, Toronto, Ont; [p.] Robt F.G. Atkins and Mary Margaret (Ruthledge) Atkins; [m.] Donald Joseph Rolson, August 18, 1970 (Kamloops, BC); [ed.] Parkdale Collegiate, Cariboo College; [occ.] Homemaker/writer and Tutor; [memb.] Canadian Diabetic Assoc, Volunteer Firefighter and Radio Operator, Local Charities BC Federation of Writer's; [hon.] Editor's Choice Award; [oth. writ.] Articles written in local newspaper, 6 completed manuscripts children's adventure stories; [pers.] My best inspiration for all of my writings comes from the love in my heart for family and friends, from things that surroung our daily life itself. I believe in the past, I believe in the future, but most of all I believe we should face both of them with a smile; [a.] Forest Grove, NC

ROMAN, ALEX
[b.] March 6, 1974, S.F., CA; [ed.] Carlmont High School, American Conservatory Theater, SF, CA; [occ.] Actor; [hon.] Director's Merit Scholarship 1991; [pers.] In poetry, I can express the many emotions and feelings that go through me as an actor.; [a.] Costa Mesa, CA

ROMANO, ROBERTO
[Pen.] Leociro; [b.] August 3, 1923, Mexico, D.F.; [p.] Francisco, Luz maria; [m.] Magali, October 17, 1964; [ch.] Rocco 26 yrs, Ali 24, Ric 22; [ed.] Brooklyn College, Brooklyn NY; [occ.] Hotelier, Hotel Industry Teacher; [memb.] Assc. Mex. Hoteles; y Motels, A.C., Palenoue, Chiapas and Mexico, D.F., Senior High School College, Palenque, Chiapas Mexico; [hon.] The Best of Mexico Writers Contest, Tourism Office, Guadalajara, Ja. Mexico;, Writig, Palenque Maya Culture; [oth. writ.] Paradise, Listen to me son, Religion the refuge of the actual spiritual crisis; [pers.] I am inspired in the Socrates symbol "know better yourselve" (Gnothi-seauton-Noscette ipsum), he found in the Apollo temple pediment in Delphi, has been my inspiration to improve myself and others close to me.; [a.] Palemque, Chiapas, Mexico

ROMANO, ROBERTO
[Pen.] Leociro; [b.] August 3, 1923, Mexico, D.F.; [p.] Francisco, Luz Maria; [m.] Magali, October 17, 1964; [ch.] Rocco (26 yrs), Ali (24 yrs), Ric (22 yrs); [ed.] Brooklyn College, Brooklyn, NY; [occ.] Hotelier, Hotel Industry Teacher; [memb.] Assoc Mex

Hoteles y Moteles, AC, Palenoue, Chiapas and Mexico, DF, Senior High School, College, Palenque, Chiapas, Mexico; [hon.] The Best of Mexico Writers Contest, Tourism Office, Guadalajara, Jal, Mexico, Writing, Palenquue Mays Culture, Paradise; [oth. writ.] Listen to me son. Religion the refust of the actual spiritual crisis; [pers.] I am inspired in the Socrates symbol "Know better yourselve", "Bnothi-seauton -

ROMANO, TARA
[b.] September 17, 1979, North Bergen; [p.] Susan Romano, George Romano; [ed.] Still in High School 9th grade.; [pers.] My writings are based on my own experiences and beliefs. I hope my poetry helps to give people a sense of warmth and creativity that they can share.; [a.] Glenwood, NJ

ROMEO, MICHELE
[b.] April 3, 1959, Flushing, NY; [p.] Vincent and Rosalie Romeo (dec.); [ed.] Smithtown High School East, St. James, NY, Suffolk County Community College, Seiden, NY, State University of New York at Stony Brook, B.A. Sociology; [occ.] Counselor; [memb.] American Cancer Society, American Cichild Association, International Wildlife Federation, Cousteau Society, Dean's List 1979; [oth. writ.] Other poems published in local Stonybrook publications.; [pers.] I am committed to nature, preserving the beuty and all of the creatures we must share this wonderful planet with. They have much to teach us.; [a.] Medford, NY

ROMERO, ALBA IRIS
[b.] October 21, 1956, Dominican Rep.; [p.] Sergio and Regina Lopez; [m.] Bienvenido Romero, May 26, 1977; [ch.] Marisol Romero and Cristina Victoria Romero; [ed.] Roberto Clemente H.S., Chi. Il, 1975, University of Illinois Circle Campus 1976, Lk. Michigan Community College, Benton Harbor, Michigan; [occ.] Computer Graphics, Writer; [oth. writ.] Rise and Fall of a dictator Rafael Leonidas Trujillo 1988, Divorce, poem 1993, Marisol, poem 1994; [pers.] I find myself drawn to write about those issues that are important to me personally. Poetry, descrimination, drug abuse, violence, love and hate, and the state of the world we live in today.; [a.] Orlando, FL

ROSCOE, NICOLE CHRISTIE
[b.] May 2, 1983, Pequannock, NJ; [p.] Mark Roscoe & Cheryl Roscoe; [ch.] Sisters: Danielle Lyn, Tiffany Ann, Brittany Ann; [ed.] Aaron Decker school and currently in fifth grade at Richard Butler school; [memb.] Church choir, school band member (flute), gymnastics and Aim program (Ability, Interest, Motivation).; [hon.] Honor roll student in 5th grade, received Presidential Achievement Award, also awards in Math, Reading, Writing and Spelling.; [oth. writ.] Several poems still to be noticed.; [pers.] I would like to especially thank Mrs. Connie Petner my second grade AIM teacher who encouraged me to read and write poetry. My other teachers, Mrs. Hanish (AIM), Mrs. Egan (Homeroom), Mrs. Struble (AIM), Mrs. Struble (reading lab) and my cousin Michele Basile who told me to enter my poem.; [a.] Butler, NJ

ROSE, JENNIFER ANN
[Pen.] Jennifer Wagner; [b.] December 21, 1971, Milwaukee, Wis.; [p.] Max and Sandra Wagner; [m.] Christopher S. Rose, May 15, 1992, USMC; [ch.] Aaron Weil (dob 1/27/91, Marina Rose (dob 2/12/93); [ed.] 10th grade (process of H.S. Diploma); [occ.] none due to medical problems; [memb.] American Red Cross Volunteer Instructor of CPR & 1st Aid, Volunteer for "Helping Children of the Streets" (HCOS); [hon.] Chess Champion in grade school, Honor Roll in grade school, and now this (a dream coming true); [oth. writ.] Many poems from growing up alone, in a harsh world filled with only a pen and

pad in hand. Subjects of them vary from one extreme to another.; [pers.] I've grown up on my own from the streets and have been through many good and bad experiences. I was never given the chance to show myself, except through my poetry that comes from my heart. I hope that the people who read my poem may be able to someway help me get the chance to show everyone the rest of my experiences, lessons, and self-shown knowledge; [a.] Mobile Alabama

ROSE, JERRY
[Pen.] Baby "A"; [b.] January 19, 1953, Orlando, FL; [p.] Mollie Mae Richardson; [m.] Stella Marie Rose, March 24, 1978; [ch.] Monika Marie, Jerry Jr., Samaria and Salena; [ed.] North Dorchester High School, Hurlock, MD, Craven Community College, New Bern, North Carolina; [occ.] Machine Mechanic Crowal Cork & Seal, Winchester, VA; [oth. writ.] Several Poems and song's in my personal notebook; [pers.] I write to give Reader's a closer Insight of the Real World and what would happen if love was the quick temper to replace violence. I love the old and new writings of poets; [a.] Winchester, VA

ROSE, MARY C.
[b.] November 13, 1926, Wildwood, NJ; [p.] Alda Baldwin and Wm. A. Baldwin Sr.; [m.] Alfred G. Rose, August 18, 1946; [ch.] William George, james Allen, sue Ann (Mary C.) Cathy; [ed.] I am a high school graduate from Cape May, NJ. I also attended the vocational school in Cape May Court House, NJ; [occ.] Retired; [memb.] Green Creek Fire Co. Auxiliary. I taught ceramics for the vocational school and owned my own studio.; [hon.] Volunteer Community Services and Clown Entertainment (Noting off Color); [oth. writ.] "Perhaps" published by The National Library of Poetry in "Time Coming of Dawn." One song published and several poems accepted and published in Poetry Journals.; [pers.] I write collective anthologies of inspirational, and spiritual reflections. I also write of "The Clown", that we ach portray.; [a.] Del Haven, NJ

ROSEN, MELVILLE G.
[b.] September 20, 1923, Brooklyn, NY; [occ.] Retired, Chairman Emeritus and Professor, SUNY Stony Brook, NY; [a.] Deer Park, NY

ROSENFELD, NORMA
[b.] August 14, 1922, Detroit, MI; [p.] Gertrude and Morris Shapiro; [m.] J. Jack Rosenfeld, February 20, 1954; [ch.] Mimi B. Rosenfeld and Wendy Ann Rosenfeld; [ed.] Wayne State University; [occ.] Writing Poetry and Fiction; [hon.] Wayne State Scholarship; [oth. writ.] Decades of advertising copywriting which taught me to use a minimum of words to create a maximum of emotions and desires.; [pers.] I have tried to lvie my own version of a full life and, any mistakes will be my failings, the good parts will be my accomplishments.; [a.] Ventura, CA

ROSENICK, BOB
[b.] April 3, 1972, Dearborn, MI; [p.] Rosemary Rosenick/Bruce Ellis; [ed.] Roosevelt High School, Wyandotte, MI; [occ.] Restaurant Cook Singer/Songwriter; [memb.] Lead Vocals for Paranormal Spectrum; [oth. writ.] Wish, Join in the Blood Feast, Purple Lady Satisfaction, Emotion, Knowing You, My Nessie, Factions, Such is Life, among countless others; [pers.] Fear is the most dark and sinister of all Human emotions, it alone can render it's victim in a complete state of mental paralysis which cannot be broken until the victims darkest fears are overcome; [a.] Ecorse, MI

ROSS, MICHAEL T.
[b.] January 13, 1974, Elko, Nevada; [p.] Thomas Bacon, Andrea Sue; [ed.] Gilford High, New Hampshire, Paradise Valley High, Arizona; [occ.] Assistant Manager for McDonald's Corporation; [hon.] Presi-

dential Academic Fitness Award, Tandy Technology Award for Academic Achievement in top two percent Paradise Valley, McDonald's Corporation Top Rank in Basic Operations course; [oth. writ.] Personal library of short stories and peotic works, unpublished.; [pers.] The sands of life are eternally existent but their arrangement in the hourglass is entirely up to you.; [a.] Phoenix, AZ

ROSS, RUTH CONNOR
[b.] February 23, 1924, Kannarous, NC; [p.] Rev. & Mrs. O.W. Connor; [m.] Artis Ross, deceased; [ch.] Kerry, Tamera, Reuben, Delores; [ed.] B.S. Behavior Science, Masters of Education, Westminster College of Salt Lake City (both degrees); [occ.] Retired Counselfor, S.L. Community College; [memb.] Calvary Baptist Church, Life Member NAACP, Heroines of Jericho, Msonic Auxilliary; [hon.] Commendations from the Governor of the State, former Government Calvin Ramton, the former Mayor of the city J. Bracken Lee. Together we care award from channel 2, Oct. 1980; [oth. writ.] Poetry, prose, short plays. I am in the process of arranging a book of poetry and prose.; [pers.] One should strive to better the community, city and the state in which one lives. Always being mindful that one should add to rather than detract from the quality of life of its' citizentry.; [a.] Salt Lake City, Utah

ROSS, STEPHEN
[Pen.] Hammerd Wolfduty; [b.] May 17, 1953, Fort Worth; [p.] Walter Sabina Ross; [ch.] Stephen Jr., Jennifer, and Joshua; [ed.] 2 years college; [occ.] Telephony, Meridian/Northern Telecom; [hon.] IPMS Model Car Contest, approx. 50 trophies, master model builder; [oth. writ.] poems, poems, poems, contemporary poems for everone's enjoyment, everyone relates.; [pers.] Self-esteem is what you give yourself for being good.; [a.] Cortland, NY

ROSSEAU, TAMARA
[b.] March 24, 1977, Long Island, NY; [p.] Mews Rousseau and Maryse Rousseau; [ed.] St Brigid's Elementary School, Sacred Heart Academy High School; [occ.] Student; [memb.] Defenders Club, Service Club, French Club; [hon.] Who's Who Among American Highschool Students, Nominee for Student Ambassador Programs; [oth. writ.] First piece submitted; [a.] Westbury, NY

ROSSMAN, GEORGE W.
[b.] August 17, 1952, Ottawa, Ont.l; [ed.] Ph.D., M.Sc., Hons. B.A.; [occ.] Mathematics Professor; [memb.] The Society of Rheology, SIAM Section on CFD (Computational Fluid Dynamics); [hon.] Summer Fellowship, Central Michigan University, 1993-94; [oth. writ.] eight applied math publicaitons; [pers.] I try to write a modern art.; [a.] Mt. Pleasant, MI

ROSSOK, JESSICA
[b.] July 29, 1980, Greencastle, TN; [p.] Ron Rossok and Tootie Rossok; [ed.] Van Buren Elementary, North Clay Jr. High; [memb.] Girl Scouts of America, 4-H, North Clay Choir; [hon.] I received numerous Art Awards in Grade School; [oth. writ.] I have written many other poems, but none have been published.; [pers.] I am a 13 year old girl who usually just writes about the feelings I have and the moral feelings of a teenager. This specific poem is about a very special guy I knew.; [a.] Carbon, IN

ROUTIER, ELIZABETH
[b.] June 6, 1951, Jersey Channel, Island; [occ.] Freelance Holistic Caterer; [memb.] Amnesty International, MANA, Musicians Against Nuclear Arms; [oth. writ.] "Little People" Alternative cookbood for new age parents and children "song cycle" classical orientation.; [pers.] That which doesn't kill us makes us stronger.; [a.] London England

OWAN, JANET P.
.] January 8, 1934, Honolulu, HI; [p.] Henry O.
faender and Ann McLelland Pfaender; [m.] Alan H.
owan, August 8, 1953; [ch.] William Bill H. Rowan
nd Linda Jean Rowan; [ed.] Punahou School 1952,
reson State University 1952-1953, Univ. of Hawaii
953, one semester; [occ.] Retired outdoor education
oordinator for 6th graders; [memb.] American Phila-
lic Society, Friends of American Assoc. University
f Women, Elected member Manou Neighborhood
oard 1993-94, American Fox Terrier Club, Malama
) Manoa Service Social Club, Hawaii Maritime
enter, Hawaiian Kennel Club; [oth. writ.] Articles
nd newsletters for Hawaiian Kennel Club. Unpub-
shed essays.; [pers.] Teaching young people in the
ut-of-doors over the years has broadened my own
waremess of the riches abounding in our natural
vorld. Poetry is a way to capture the swift, single
econd of an owl's flight.; [a.] Honolulu, HI

ROWLAND, CHRISTOPHER LEE
[Pen.] Christopher, Lee, Chris; [b.] July 15, 1966,
Apple Valley, Calif; [p.] Patricia Ann and Ivan O.
Rowland; [ed.] Apple Valley High School, Victory
Valley College (AA), The Otis Art Institute (BFA);
[occ.] Photographer; [oth. writ.] Many stories and
poems and essays (currently organizing for a book);
[pers.] It's all in how you look at it.; [a.] Los Angeles,
CA

ROWLINSON, ADRIENNE
[b.] October 4, 1980, Ontario, Canada; [p.] David
and Janice Rowlinson; [ch.] Brother, Davey
Rowlinson; [ed.] R.M. Moore Public School; [occ.]
Student; [pers.] If you think you can, you can, go after
your dreams.

ROY, LIA ALICIA
[b.] October 6, 1970, Nova Scotia Canada; [p.] Edie
and Gordon Ray; [ed.] Currently enrolled in the
English Honours Program at the University of Victoria
and have been accepted in the M.A. program at
Queen's University for 1994/95; [occ.] Student; [oth.
writ.] I have written several other poems, short stories
about the experience of depression and a modern
adaptation of the greek tragedy Antigone which reaks
with the distorted perceptions of a manic depressive
individual.; [pers.] I am a manic depressive poet
concerned with the experience of manic depressive
illness. I have been strongly influenced by Virgina
Woolf and Sylvia Pluth. My personal philosophy is
off yourself or die.; [a.] Victoria, B.C. Canada

ROY, MICHAEL
[b.] April 20, 1928, London England; [ed.] Upton
Grammar, Berkshire, Newland Park College, Bucks,
Hornsey College of Art, London, UK; [occ.] Profes-
sional Artist; [hon.] Art Teachers Certificate, Read-
ing University, Diploma in Art Education, London
University; [oth. writ.] "The Art Lark", 1992, poem
"Radiations" in Poetry Now 1994; [pers.] "Art (po-
etry) is born of image and reality, a stream 'twixt
memory and dream."; [a.] Southampton, England

RUBIO, JENELLE C.
[Pen.] Emma Forrester; [b.] March 8, 1977,
Smithtown; [p.] Patricia Rubio and Edward Rubio;
[ed.] Longwood H.S.; [occ.] High School Student;
[hon.] Longwood H.S. Honor Roll, Nat'l Jr. Honor
Society, Science Award, Foreign Language Award,
Social Studies Award, NY State Legislative Commis-
sion on Water Resoruces by Senator Trunzo, 2nd
place poetry award from school district.; [pers.] My
writings are to express my inner thoughts and to have
my readers explore various points of views of life.
Writing is the declaration of feelings.; [a.] Ridge, NY

RUGNETTA, ANDREA
[b.] March 28, 1975, L.I.; [p.] Pam and James
Rugnetta; [ed.] John Lewis Childs School Floral Park
Memorial High School, Nassau Community College

(presently); [memb.] Honors program at N.C.C.;
[hon.] Bronze Medal for honors (high school) $1,000
scholarship from Women's Federation, many finan-
cial awards at N.C.C.; [pers.] "Children are the
seedlings of life growing in a world of flowers, help
their future be their sunlight."; [a.] Floral Park, NY

RUMSEY, AUTUMN J.
[Pen.] Autumn Joy; [b.] November 18, 1978,
Wellsboro, PA; [p.] Dennis F. Rumsey, Kathy A.
Rumsey; [ed.] Freshman in High School (Williamson
Jr., Sr. High): [occ.] Student; [memb.] none; [oth.
writ.] Poems written, "Tears," "Woman and Child",
"Dancing by the Ocean," "Forever," etc.; [pers.] The
number of years you've been writing doesn't matter
as much, as the number of heart-beats you put in to the
poem. It's not age, its ability; [a.] Lawrenceville, PA

RUNION, MELISSA M.
[b.] August 25, 1979, Medina, OH; [p.] Ronald &
Jean Runion; [ed.] Currently freshman at Keyston
High School; [occ.] Full time student; [memb.] 4-H,
FHA; [oth. writ.] Wrote for the "Pass it On" page in
the Chronicle-Telegram.; [pers.] I like to write be-
cause I can get my feelings out and I don't have to
worry what other people think.; [a.] Wellington, OH

RUNYON, THEODORE H.
[Pen.] Ted; [b.] November 8, 1919, Newark, NJ; [p.]
T.W.S. Runyon, Martha C. Radke Runyon; [m.]
Mildred C. (Kyle) Carol Runyon, May 10, 1946;
[ch.] Susan, Ted, Bill, Dan; [ed.] Brown Mil. Acad.
H.S. Univ. of Calif. Berkley C, Engr. Mech. Geo
Wash. U. Forn. Affrs. Dean's List, So. Western Coll.
AS Real Estate, Cmd & Gen Staff, Air Cmd & Gen
Staff NATO DefColl.; [occ.] 32 years Navy, Army,
AF Ret. Colonel AF, Instr. R.E. So. Western Coll.
R.E. Broker Prudential Cal. Realty; [memb.] U.S.
Navy Lg., The Ret. Off. Assoc., Luthern Church
Council, Past Pres. of each, R.E. Cert. Inst. Ca.Ed.
Asoc. Coronado Assoc. of RE Calif. Education
Assoc.; [hon.] Comd. Pilot, Master Missileman,
Legion Of Merit, DEC, Air Medal, Purple Hear,
POW medal, Campaign Medals, American and ETO
Alpha Sigma Lambda; [oth. writ.] Honor Thesis
"Military in Space, What Should Be Done" The
National War College, Wash. D.C. 1963. Top Secret
Study on Middle East, India, Pakistan, participant.
Real Estate Column local newspaper. Numerous
poems, for Church Poets Corner; [pers.] I believe that
Poetry like beautiful Music brings Joy to the Heart and
Peace to the Mind "Now Good Shepherd hear the
Prayer of your sheep here and everywhere from my
poem "Your Sheep are Calling"; [a.] Coronado, CA

RUSHWORTH, LAYNE
[b.] may 13, 1978, SLC; [p.] Harold and Coleen;
[ed.] I am a sophomore at West High School; [occ.]
Student; [hon.] Hope of America, Honors Roll;
[pers.] I base my poetry on love. I use the people in
my life that I love with all my heart as inspiration.; [a.]
Salt Lake City, Utah

RUSSELL, MARK E.
[Pen.] The Pentecostal Poet; [b.] November 7, 1969,
Chicago; [p.] Willie & Blanche Russell; [m.] Nina M.
Russell, July 22, 1990; [ch.] Marquis and Willie III (2
sons); [ed.] College in Process; [occ.] Protective
Service Officer (PSO) Motorola; [memb.] Brother-
hood at Gethsemane Apostolic, Pentecostal Church;
[hon.] Served 4 years in United States Marine Corp.;
[oth. writ.] Many Christians, uplifting and love poems
written, never had anything published, but shall
keepwriting. Mostly write Christian type, inspiring
poems. Also writing Gospel songs.; [pers.] I liken all
my accomplishments as being blessings from the
Lord.; [a.] Mesa, AZ

RUSSELL, SHANTON
[b.] July 30, 1973, Chicago; [p.] Sherry Townsend,

Manuel Russell; [ed.] Seen Metropolitan Academy of
Liberal Arts and Technology, Northern Illinois Uni-
versity; [occ.] Clerk, Chicago Board of Trade; [memb.]
National Residence Hall Associaiton at Northern
Illinois University, Nation of Islam; [hon.] Winner of
1991 Toyota U.S.A. Foundation & Pegasus Players,
young Playwrights Festival; [oth. writ.] Award win-
ning play "Black Ink on Black Paper," Composition
published in a textbook entitled "Reflections of the
American Dream"; [pers.] The individual who has the
proper education, discipline and the true knowledge
of self will accomplish great things.; [a.] Chicago, IL

RUSSELL, YVONNE MARY
[b.] July 2, 1935, England; [p.] Albert and Frances
Rose Mackey (both dec.); [m.] Donald Roland Russell,
August 30, 1958; [ch.] Amanda Jill; [ed.] Pitmans
College Wimbledon; [occ.] Reporter for Spirit; [oth.
writ.] not yet published, 60 books dedicated by my
spirit communicator over a period of 10 years (1984-
94) including lectures on clairaudience, clairvoyance
and c/sentients. The Out of Body Experience. Book
of Love in Rhyme, Titles include The New Book of
Life, The Science of Life, Knowledge of The Spirit,
etc.; [pers.] The Templars of Life who dictate the
words for the books I mention are desirous of having
their works published in America.; [a.] Sevenoaks,
Kent England

RYAN, CHARLES SCOTT
[Pen.] Charles S. Ryan; [b.] April 16, 1970, NY; [p.]
Jeffrey Howard Ryan and Martha C. Ryan; [m.] Carol
Ann Ryan, June 17, 1989; [ed.] Golden Secondary
School, Dalhousie University; [oth. writ.] Several
poems published in Drift a Toronto based Magazine;
[pers.] Through my poetry I wish to unify the mental,
physical and spiritual aspects of my experiences; [a.]
Golden, British Columbia

RYAN, ELSIE M.
[b.] February 19, 1931, St. Elizabeth, Jamaica, WI;
[p.] Charles and Rose Williams; [m.] Maj. (Ret'd)
Matthew J. Ryan; [ch.] Mrs. Pauline Lawrence,
Donald & Clay Washington; [ed.] Red Bank High, St.
Thomas, Moore Business College, Westminster Busi-
ness College; [occ.] Admin. Assistant; [memb.] So-
ciety of Military Widows, Nat'l. Assoc. for Uni-
formed Svcs, Nat'l Assoc. of Female Executives,
Nat'l. Library of Poetry, Int'l Society of Poets Advi-
sory Committee; [hon.] 1991 & 1992 World of Poetry
golden Poets Award, 1993 Nat'l Library of Poetry
Editors' Choice Award, 1993 Int'l Poet of Merit
Award; [oth. writ.] Love's Journey (soon to be
marketed); [pers.] My poems are inspired by me
religious belief, my family, various people and places
encountered. Hobbies include meeting people, travel,
dancing, theater and the arts.; [a.] Bayside, NY

RYAN, MARY A. FRENCH
[b.] July 14, 1924, Boston, MA; [p.] George and
Evangeline French; [m.] Ray E. Ryan, August 1,
1946; [ch.] one foster daughter, Shirley I. Nutting;
[ed.] Continuous, 1942 Tabor Academy, Marion,
MA, 1989 Pierce College, Tacoma, WA, AAS, 1991
The Evergreen State College, Ohy, WA, BA; [occ.]
Writing Instructor and part-time editing consultant,
Director, Writers' Center Pierce College; [memb.]
Phi Theta Kappa Alumni, Chapter EG, P.E.O. Olym-
pia, WA, Nisqually Poet's Assn. Olympia, WA, Adah
Chapter OE.S. Magna, Utah; [hon.] Varied, Honor-
able Mention, Washington State Poets Assoc., 1989;
[oth. writ.] Vignettes from the Duck Pond In, Love
and other faibles, Christmas Letters from the Duck
Pond Inn; [pers.] I believe knowledge is to be shared
with others, agape love exists today, and spirits
departed still speak if we listen; [a.] Olympia, WA

SABATINO, JR. ALEXANDER
[b.] August 9, 1951, NY; [p.] Mary Fasano & Alexander Sabatino Sr.; [ed.] M.A. Teacher's College, Columbia U.; [occ.] Math Teacher, Seward Park H.S., NYC, NYC Tech College, CUNY; [memb.] Scholars Circle, UFT; [hon.] Empire State Fellowship, National Endowment For The Humanities; [oth. writ.] Poems published in school newsletter, Articles for Errorgram; [a.] Mt. Vernon, NY

SABATKA, KATHLEEN PANNUNZIO
[Pen.] Katarina Elizabeth Ashley; [b.] January 12, 1964, Youngstown, OH; [p.] Edward and Linda Medellin; [ch.] Duane John, Ryan Joseph, Jocelyn Elizabeth, Jessica Kathleen Ashley; [ed.] Austintown Fitch High School, Youngstown State Univ; [occ.] Homemaker (mother); [memb.] Andover Church of Christ; [hon.] Youngstown State Univ, Dean's List; [oth. writ.] I've wrote many other poems for my children and also other pieces pertaining to life and love. I can proudly say, this is the first piece of poetry I've had published. I would like to dedicate it to my children with love; [pers.] I have been greatly inspired over the years by the intense love I feel for my children and the love they have returned to me. I feel the Lord has blessed me with a great gift and in return for this gift I feel I need to share it with others. I only hope through my words I may bring happiness into someone elses life; [a.] Andover, OH

SAGE, LILLIAN B.
[Pen.] Lillian Belle Sage; [b.] 1899, Genese, NY; [p.] deceased; [m.] deceased, June 2, 1921; [ed.] 8th grade; [hon.] For Canandaqua Statue of Gesture for court house and police station, Chamber of Commerce. Several merits, no cash. Honor rolls, etc; [oth. writ.] A few excepted in small paper. Several on file for I deals; [pers.] I will decide on book later. Feel sure of at least one; [a.] Canandaqua, NY

SALAMON, NICOLE M.
[b.] May 2, 1977, Canton, OH; [ed.] 10th grade, St Thomas Aquinas High School, Our Lady of Peace grade school; [occ.] Student; [memb.] Spanish Club and Hospice; [hon.] Softball and volleyball awards, cheerleading; [pers.] My poetry is inspired by everyday life; [a.] Canton, OH

SALGADO-CASTILLO, ANA
[b.] June 25, 1961, Ecuador; [p.] Luz & Ancelmo Castillo; [m.] Gumaro Salgado, June 14, 1990; [ed.] Dawson Skill Institute; [occ.] Trainer/Supervisor for Soc. Serv. Agency; [hon.] Recipient of the 1987 Latino Scholarship Award, Honorable Mention in the Black History Essay Contest in 1981; [oth. writ.] My own personal writings; [pers.] My writing is influenced by the feelings other people have in their lives. I just close my eyes and imagine…!; [a.] Chicago, IL

SALIH, DONNA NIELSEN
[b.] April 22, 1939, Libby Montana; [p.] Don L. Nielsen, Valden E. Nielsen; [m.] January 3, 1976, Mohamed A. Salin - deceased; [ch.] Donald Nels; [ed.] Clinical Social Worker; [occ.] Artist - Painter, Poet; [pers.] Born a diabetic, disabled because of my work on the Pine Ridge Reservation in South Dakota. Caught T.B. and hepatitis B. Now living on Social Security disability. Hoping to make a income from my painting and poetry; [pers.] Life should be about excellence.

SAMUELS, PAULINE YOLANDA
[b.] June 30, 1962, Delize; [p.] Philip & Dotsie Samuels; [ed.] Belmopan Comprehensive School, Belize Technical College; [occ.] Administrative Assistant, Public Relations Dept. Belize Social Security; [oth. writ.] Editorial Column for Social Security News, Several poems yet unpublished.; [pers.] These poems were not written for the sake of poetry, even though there may be beauty in that. These poems,

originally, were not written to be shared or viewed by others for their criticism nor their enjoyment. (I offer no apology for that.) These poems are expressions, torn from the heart, of real, vivid and poignant experiences. They were written during struggles, in the midst of tears, of joy, all in a striving to understand God, Self and Life! In reading them, if some soul can relate to these struggles, can be encouraged in the knowledge that we all experience the same things, can be challenged to carry on the ques' to discover and achieve all God meant for him/her…then, to God be the glory!

SANCHEZ, TONY P.
[b.] March 9, 1929, Phoenix, AZ; [p.] Antonio and Ramona Sanchez; [m.] Alice D. Sanchez, June 20, 1954; [ch.] (6) Tony Jr, Arthur, Rebecca, Yolanda, Lydia and Andrea; [ed.] 3 yrs high school, Wilson - PUHS; [occ.] Self employed welder; [memb.] American Legion post 41; [hon.] In Army - CIB - Parachute Wings - Purple Heart; [oth. writ.] Dozens of songs w/ words and music; [pers.] Young or old -- go for it, success.

SANDBERG, TODD L.
[b.] August 19, 1971, Lincoln, NE; [p.] Oscar and Judy Sandberg; [ed.] Lincoln High, Doane College; [occ.] Full-time Student; [memb.] Doane Owl School Newspaper KDNE 91.9FM (School radio) Doane College Varsity Baseball; [hon.] Golden Leaf Awards; Nebraska Collegiate Press Assoc '92-'93. 1st place best sports tory. Honorable Mention - Best Sports Feature Doane College: Marianne Clarke Writing Award; [oth. writ.] Doane Owl - Sports Column "Behind Home Plate"; [pers.] I enjoy writing because it's the best way I know to share my ideas: My own quote "Once you've lock the door to your imagination, better not forget the combination; [a.] Crete, NE

SANDER, JAMES W.
[b.] February 6, 1957, Wilkie, Sask; [p.] Jerry and Theresa Sander; [m.] Joanne I. Sander; [ch.] Adam, Andrea, Mathew Jonah; [ed.] Bachelor of Education: Univ of Saskatchewan; High School - McLurg High, Wilkie, Sask; [occ.] English, Social Studies, and Christian Ethics Teacher; [memb.] Lions International; Parkland Teachers Assoc Executive, Saskatchewan Wildlife Federation; [hon.] General Proficiency Graduation Award; [oth. writ.] Short story - "Suspicion" done on CBC Radio; Short story - "Pick Those Rocks", published in Western People Magazine; [a.] Debden, Sask

SANDERS, LEAH A.
[Pen.] Leah Whitney, Sand and Lyman, Rhyminsimon (children's literature); [b.] April 29, 1936, K.C. MO; [m.] deceased; [ch.] Five; [ed.] Central H.S., KC MO, Wentworth (Jr. College) Lexington, MO, Missouri U. at KC (UMKC); [occ.] Retired; [memb.] Women Leader's Roundtable, MS Society, Sierra Club, ASPCA; [pers.] I write social comment and about the human condition, all sentient beings and the earth, word we share. Gretly influenced by Whitman, Walker, Rich; [a.] Kansas City, MO

SANTIAGO, THOM
[b.] August 21, 1948, HI; [p.] Thomas Santiago & Adeline Smith; [ed.] Bachelor of Arts in Drama from San Francisco State University; [occ.] Claims representative with the Social Security Adminstration; [oth. writ.] Film music critic for "Soundtrack Collectors Quarterly" 1982-1985 published out of Belgium. Have also writen video reviews for Tower Records In-house Magazine; [a.] North Hollywood, CA

SARGENT, HAROLD ROSS
[b.] March 10, 1926, PA; [p.] Everett and Opal Sargent; [m.] Mary Conner, June 4; [ch.] Daniel, David, Harold, Karen; [ed.] Edinboro Univ - BS, Pitt - MS, Penn State - DED; [occ.] Broker; [a.] Hermit-

age, PA

SARNELLI (JR.), THOMAS J.
[b.] November 6, 1956, Brooklyn, NY; [p.] Thom and Eva Sarnelli; [m.] Jill Frances Sarnelli, June 1 1982; [ch.] Maria Theresa, Courtney Leigh, Sea Thomas; [ed.] High School grad; certified paralega [oth. writ.] 3 volumes of poetry (app 80 poems) yet be published. 2 short mysteries (yet to be published My imagination, others inspiration along with modicum of procrastination and determination; er hance ones ability to pen a verse or story; [a. Baldwin, NY

SATYENDRA, PEERTHOM
[b.] March 27, 1976, Mauritius; [p.] Dr. Satteeanun & Dulary Peerthum; [ed.] Xavier High School, St Stephens Grammar School; [occ.] Student; [memb. School Newspaper, Yearbook, Literary Magazine Political Affairs Club, French Club, National Hono Society, Junior Reserve Officer Training Cadets [hon.] JROTC Academic Achievement Award, Firs Honors, Participant at States Finals for Student Congress, School Finalist in National Geographic Contest, Recipient of Senior Army Instructor's Commendation Award; [oth. writ.] Stories and Poems published in school literary magazine "Lexicon" writings published in school newspaper in "Xavier Review"; [pers.] I write for the greater good of all men, I express myself best through my writings and try to get my message across to my fellow man.; [a.] New York, NY

SAUDER, DIANNA
[b.] November 10, 1974, Fort McMurray, Alberta; [p.] Clive Desmond and Denise Robins; [m.] John Anthony Sauder, December 18, 1993; [ch.] Rachel Kimberley Sauder; [ed.] Fort McMurray Composit High School; [occ.] Homemaker; [hon.] Received a plaque for outstanding achievement in a newly introduced Cree language class in high school; [oth. writ.] Submitted 1 poem to the Sparrow Grass Poetry Forum in W.V., which was approved for publication in their poetry anthology; [pers.] My poems reflect real life situations as I see them, and my poems are usually created from one inspiring sentence that comes to me in the spur of the moment; [a.] Fort McMurray, Canada

SAUNDERS, ASHLEY
[b.] Mar 16, 1945, Bimini, Bahamas; [p.] Milton Saunders, Alicia Saunders; [ed.] Miami - Dade Community College, Univ of Wisconsin - Madison, Harvard Univ; [occ.] Agricultural Science Teacher, Bimini All-Age School, Bimini Bahamas; [memb.] Wisconsin Alumni Ass, Bahamas Writers Ass; [hon.] 1. Certificate of Honor (Bahamas Government); 2. Certificate of Honor (Bahamas National Art Festival); [oth. writ.] Have written four (4) books of poetry: "Voyage into the Sunset" (1976), "The Sun Makes It Red" (1977), "The Night of the Lionhead" (1979), "Searching for Atlantis" (1980). Also written two history of Bimini books; [pers.] I strive for sensitivity, expansion, and universality in my writing. I have been greatly influenced by Ernest Hemingway; [a.] Miami, FL

SAVAG, RENEE D.
[Pen.] Renee DiMaria Savag; [b.] October 11, 1955, Steubenville, OH; [p.] Martha DiMaria - Gene DiMaria; [ch.] Thom (14); [ed.] Catholic Central HS, Steub, OH, CGS Beauty Academy, Steub, OH, Pima Community College, Tucson, AZ; [occ.] Controller, Allied Precious Metals; [memb.] Former Ayso Board Member, St Matthews Episcopal Church; [oth. writ.] Currently preparing many songs for copyright and seeking publication (country songs); [pers.] My writing comes from deep within my heart and I strive to touch the heart of the reader with each word that I write; [a.] Tucson, AZ

SAVAGE, HOLLY L.
[b.] December 17, 1976; [p.] James and Trudy Savage; [ed.] Currently a Junior at Lafayette Sr. High School; [occ.] Student; [memb.] Sweet Adelines International, Lafayette High school Choir and High School orchestra; [hon.] Piano Awards, Choir Awards; [pers.] To each is own strive to be the best put your mind and soul always to the test and stive to be the best; a Ellisville, MO

SAWICKI, ANNA E.
[b.] June 4, 1967, Elliot Lake, Ontario; [p.] Horst and Alice Sawicki; [ch.] Sahara Tina Sawicki; [ed.] Northern College in Kirkland Lake, Ontario; [occ.] Social Worker and Artist; [memb.] Volunterr for Children's Aid Society and Monteith Correctional Complex; [pers.] Any poems I've ever wrote, has come from my deepest inner emotions and the emotions of others around me. I find it to be a great therapy (healing); [a.] Kirkland Lake, Ontario, Canada

SAWYER, DEBRA
[Pen.] Debbi Eastman; [b.] January 22, 1978, Bristol, CT; [p.] Dale and John; [ed.] Lyndon Institute South Side School, Memorial Boulevard; [occ.] Student; [oth. writ.] Enter school contest with stories and poems; [pers.] I express my own feelings and to tell about my friends how I see it.; [a.] Lyndonville, VT

SAWYER, JERI
[b.] August 7, 1933, Pontiac, MI; [p.] Floyd and Edna Lovett; [m.] John Sawyer, November 7, 1953; [ch.] 2 daughters - Robin, Teri; [ed.] BS Elem Education Oakland Univ, Rochester, MI; [occ.] Retired from teaching; [memb.] AAUW, Michigan Women's Commission - Essay Judge - Volunteer; [hon.] Graduated Summa Cum Laude from Oakland Univ, 1975; [oth. writ.] This is the first time I have submitted any of my work for publication; [pers.] My writing (essays, poetry, short stories) allows me to express my innermost thoughts in a way I would not do orally; [a.] Clarkston, MI

SAWYER, KARIN MARIA
[b.] August 3, 1981, Tacoma, WA; [p.] Lawanza Sawyer and Edward Sawyer; [ed.] 7th grade at Stewart Middle School; [occ.] student (STRIVE) Strive youth program; [memb.] ASB - Associative Student Body. Representative member of STRIVE. Yuth Choir at Stewart Middle School; [a.] Tacoma, WA

SAXNER, DAVID
[b.] February 17, 1948, Chicago; [p.] Minette and Philip; [m.] Rikke Vognsen; [ch.] Medea Grillos, Sakner; [occ.] Self-Employed; [hon.] Placed second in national contest sponsored by PEN (Poets, Essayists and Novelists) in 1974.; [oth. writ.] Published in PEN, Bitterrot and several other poetry magazines and newspapers in the US and France. This is the first poem I've submitted for publication in 20 years.; [pers.] Influenced by the Bay Area Beat Poets, writers from the Harlem renaissance and political poets from the 60's and 70's. Poetry in its implest form is a powerful tool for communication, especially for the traditional non-reader.; [a.] Chicago, IL

SAYRE, ELIZABETH JANE
[b.] November 21, 1920, Wpokane, WA; [m.] September 26, 1942 (divorced 9/67; [ch.] Richard Layton, Attorney, Spokane, WA, 1953, Robert Charles 1957-1984.; [ed.] St. Nicholas School (now Lakeside School) Seattle, WA, Stanford University, 1938-42 (B.A. History), University of Wash. 1971 (M. Ed.,) (L. Arts, Lit), Seattle Pacific U., Seattle, 1975, 1975 (Ed. Adminstration Principalship); [occ.] Retired. Live on Lake Washington Waterfront in Covenant Shores retirement complex; [memb.] Haiku Society of America, Washington Poets Association, Northwest Haiku Society, Mercer Island Visual Arts League.;

[hon.] Chemistry Cup, H.S. Senior Year, Phi Alpha Theta (History, U. of Wash. 1972); [oth. writ.] Published Educational Research (Special Education, short story, poems, Haikus.; [pers.] Continued exploration of new discoveries in science, Technology, and nature; plus new appreciation of the Arts have made my retirement a delight. My hope is for some return to peace and balance so life can iniversally become a fulfilling experience rather than a constant struggle for survival.; [a.] Mercer Island, WA

SCALLORN, ANN DENICE
[Pen.] Ann Scallorn; [b.] February 4, 1975, Dallas, TX; [p.] Charles and Carol Scallorn; [ed.] Greater Atlanta Christian School, (freshman) Reinhardt College; [pers.] Psalm 23, Isaiah 40.31; [a.] Atlanta, GA

SCHACHT, NANCY
[Pen.] Low Louie; [b.] June 2, 1952, Green Bay; [p.] Mr. & Mrs. Wesley Schacht; [m.] Bob Medici, March 12, 1994; [ed.] High School, A.A.S. Forestry, Flathead Valley Comm. College, Kalispell Mont.; [occ.] Nurse assistant parttime retired in 1990.; [hon.] National Honor Society, Safety Award; [pers.] I try to reflect a dream of the future when all people can live, worship and be happy in peace.; [a.] Green Bay, WI

SCHACK, T. ALAN
[b.] April 14, 1969, Denver; [ed.] Colorado State Univ; [occ.] Freelance Writer; [pers.] One line of truth. In writing painting, music, whatever - all I'm after is one line of truth; [a.] Amsterdam, Netherlands

SCHALLOCK, GINA M.
[b.] April 22, 1974, La Crosse, WI; [p.] Glen V. and Donna K. Schallock; [ed.] West Salem High school, USAF Basic Training, USAF Security Police Tech Training, US Army Air Base Ground Defense; [occ.] US Air Force Security Police Person; [oth. writ.] Several poems and short stories, not yet published; [pers.] In most of my writing I reflect emotions dealt with through hardships endured; [a.] Grand Forks AFB, ND

SCHAMEHORN, MARTHA
[b.] September 18, 1973, Timmins, Ontario; [p.] Laura and Paul Kinnamen; [ch.] Kimberly Anne and Cody Paul; [occ.] Currently finishing my high school and nurses aid at home; [pers.] I was influenced by my boyfriend who I wrote this poem for his 28th b-day. I would like to thank you, Andy Lupton; [a.] Port Sydney, Ontario, Canada

SCHEFFLER, DAVID DUANE
[Pen.] Sir Ramsey Ranon; [b.] August 23, 1980; [p.] Randy and Carol Scheffler; [ed.] 8th grade currently - 13 yrs of age; [oth. writ.] An article in the Ellington weekly newspaper on Magic Johnson's second retirement from basketball. No other published works. Beside this poems of course; [pers.] I am a faithful and devoted member of the Worldwide Church of God and urge everyone reading this to strive for oneness with and closeness to God, whatever and whoever you believe him to be; [a.] Cape Girardeau, MO

SCHEIBELHUT, JOHN
[b.] March 28, 1965, Pottsville, PA; [p.] Jim and Shirley Scheibelhut; [occ.] Police Officer; [hon.] Served in the United States Air Force in Europe from 1985 thru 1988.; [pers.] This poem was written in the fall of 1993 for a girl that I cared a great deal for and still do. I dedicate this to Tracy, thank you for this inspiration.

SCHIEBER, ED
[b.] December 1, 1963, Earth; [memb.] Member of humanity; [oth. writ.] Miscellaneous; [pers.] The destitute, downtrodden denizens of skid row in downtown Los Angeles, have shown me the way to on high. God bless my teachers.

SCHMIDT, MARY L.
[Pen.] WindRider; [b.] October 9, 1945, Chicago; [p.] Wm Miller, Velma Honey; [m.] divorced; [ch.] William, David, Anna; [ed.] MA Webster Univ 1989, Media Communications; [memb.] Not so Dulcimer Club; Gateway Storytellers; [hon.] Phi Thetta Kappa; Role Model, Women's Re-entry Program; Journalism Foundation of St Louis choloarships 198., 1987, 1988; DWAA Journalism award 1970; Journalism awards, SLCC, Meramec, 1985, 1986; [oth. writ.] Feature articles for local, national and international publications; 1989 poetry and 1984 short story, currents literary magazine; American Anthology of High School Poetry 1962, 1963; [pers.] I strive to achieve true Bardic tradition in my songs, stories and poetry, presenting life's passages and lessons in a manner that makes them pleasant to remember; [a.] St Louis, MO

SCHMNIDT, AIMEE ELIZABETH
[b.] July 21, 1978, Long Island; [p.] Josef and Mary Lou Schmidt; [ed.] Taconic Hills High School, Upstate New York; [occ.] Student; [oth. writ.] "Man In The Moon", "She Walks," "Our World," "Racial Discrimance" "Stoned Again."; [pers.] "Live every moment, love everyday. Because before you know it, your precious time have slipped away." Thank you to my supporting family, friends and especially Andrea and Sean. I love you all.; [a.] Ancram, NY

SCHNURR, JOHN W.
[b.] October 5, 1929, Kenosha, WI; [p.] Marlin Schnurr, Charlotte Schnurr; [m.] Phyllis Shaffer, June 28, 1953; [ch.] Jane, Rebecca, John, Neil; [ed.] Wilmot High, Univ of WI, Madison; [occ.] Businessman; [hon.] High honors, Univ of WI 1949, 1951, Phi Eta Sigma, Alpha Zeta; [oth. writ.] Novel, "The Silver Ribbon" (unpub), Epic poem, "Only Two Miles To Go"; [a.] Wilmot, WI

SCHREIBER, LISA
[b.] November 6, 1980, Fredericksburg, VA; [p.] Ken and Roberta Schreiber; [ed.] Enters Stafford Senior High School September 8, 1994; [occ.] Student; [memb.] Student Council Association, National Junior Honor Society, Year book sta 88; [a.] Falmouth, VA

SCHROEDER-RADCLIFFE, ELEANOR
[b.] April 23, 1914, Detroit, MI; [p.] Walter and Clara Schroeder; [m.] Carlyle Fogene Radcliffe, April 29, 1939; [ch.] Carolyn, Barbara Ann, Robert; [ed.] East Comm High; Del Mar Beauty School; Associate Degree in Humanity; [occ.] Retired; [memb.] Trinity Luth Church, Upper Pen of Mich Home Nursing, Retired Senior Volunteer Prog, National Audobon Society, Oil and Water Color Art School; [hon.] Who's Who in US Writers, Editors and Poets, Distinguished Leadership Award. Several Award of Merit, Silver Poet Awards - World of Poetry; [oth. writ.] Great Poems of Today, Great American Poetry Anthology. Poems published in home paper. Poems for church letter. Local newsletters; [pers.] I want to show love for people. With the romantic love of nature, and the love of God for man. Strive to show it in my poetry; [a.] Marquette, MI

SCHURLE, DONNA
[b.] January 8, 1956, Junction City, Kansas; [p.] Melvin & Reta Bixay; [m.] Dewayne Schurle, May 26, 1972; [ch.] Michael & Brandy Schurle; [ed.] Riley County High School Currently enrolled in ICS School of Journalism and the Long Ridge Writers Group; [occ.] Jr. High School Secretary, Blue Valley Middle School, Randolph, KS; [memb.] ABWA, MADD; [oth. writ.] Short story published in Farm Wife Magazine, 1976; Several poems were published in High School Yearbook, 1974; [pers.] All of my writing reflects the emotions and feelings of family

and friends. These are the important things in life. Without them I would be nothing.; [a.] Manhattan, KS

SCHUTT, CHRIS A.
[Pen.] T. N. Grani; [b.] June 24, 1948, Jefferson City, TN; [p.] L.W. and Virena Jennings; [ch.] Christy and Eric (2); [ed.] H.S. graduate w/60 hrs college; [occ.] Secretary; [memb.] Time is a continuum through which all human spirits must pass. But how far are truly fortunate enough to pass through it possessing the sublime, heartfelt knowledge of true romance; [pers.] That feeling deep in your soul that only one person in the universe can bring forth which makes this passing for these few alone so much more than just mere existence.

SCHUTT, JACLYN
[b.] March 30, 1978, Madera, CA; [p.] Penny Schutt; [ed.] Currently in 8th grade; [occ.] Student at Tenaya Elementary; [oth. writ.] Poetry of different things like love poems, animal poems. Also short stories or funny stories; [pers.] I enjoy poetry. It's a way for me to let my feelings be known.; [a.] Greveland, CA

SCHWARZ, AMY E.
[m.] Alan D. Schwarz, December 20, 1986; [ch.] Nicole and Elizabeth; [oth. writ.] First poem ever to have published. Has compiled many other writings on a personal notebook for release in the near future; [a.] Milton, WI

SCHWEDHELM, VERA
[Pen.] Rusti Schwedhelm; [b.] August 27, 1957, New Glasgow, Nova Scotia; [p.] Iris and Arthur Busby; [ch.] 2 - Katie (16), Erich (6); [ed.] 12; [occ.] Homemaker and writer; [hon.] Acting trophy, early essay contest winner, 3 wrist wrestling trophies; [oth. writ.] Poetry, short stories. Newspaper articles; [pers.] Reach for a star, and when you grab it, hold on tightly!; [a.] Hagar, Ont

SCHWEITZER, CATHERINE
[b.] April 26, 1977, Maryville, MO; [p.] Harold Wayne and Diana Schweitzer; [ed.] Graduate from Kickapoo high school in 1995. Plan to attend Cottey College in Nevada, MO; [occ.] Work on temporary Production for Springfield Workshops, Inc; [memb.] For school I am a member of Friends, Drama Club, Secretary of Thespians, and President of Ambassadors Club. I am on the West Missouri Espiscopal Diocese Youth Board; [pers.] Poetry comes from the heart. It sometimes can only be understood by the one who wrote it; [a.] Springfield, MO

SCOTT, APRIL DENISE
[Pen.] "Bell"; [b.] March 23, 1965; [p.] Marilyn and Willie Pace; [m.] Jeremiah Scott, September 12, 1993; [ch.] Rockea, Christopher, Aundrea, Kenneth Jr; [ed.] Wayne High School, IVT College, CAM, CAHM; [occ.] Elderly Housing Manager for Goodwin Plaza, Indpls, IN; [memb.] A member of Light of the World Christian Church; [pers.] Life is wonderful. Taking it one day at a time, knowing that tomorrow is not promised. To God be the Glory; [a.] Indianapolis, IN

SCOTT, BRYAN
[b.] May 14, 1967, Milford, CT; [p.] Cynthia and James Simpson; [ed.] BA in Journalism, Colorado State Univ; [occ.] Social Critic; [memb.] Craven Consumers of Cuban Cigars Society (founding member); [hon.] Contributed opening segment to AP-award winning documentary, 'Silent Epidemic'; [oth. writ.] Novels: My Head is a Race Car, The City Trembles. Screenplays: Fifteen in the Sun, The Wild and the Brave; [pers.] I shall devour my detractors, convert my doubters, and stand laughing in the end; [a.] Boulder, CO

SCOTT, DEBBIE J.
[Pen.] Debbie Scott; [b.] April 18, 1964, Calgary.

SCOTT, GWENDOLYN BLANCHARD
[b.] September 4, 1955, Compton, CA; [p.] Blanchard and Genevia Smith; [m.] Louis Edward Scott, Jr, November 9, 1986; [ch.] Ebony Danielle Massie; [ed.] Centennial High, Univ of CA, Santa Barbara, Southwestern Univ, School of Law; [occ.] Educator; [pers.] Education opens the windows of the world which lets light shine into our lives; [a.] Hesperia, CA

SCOTTO, GERALDINE L.
[b.] Brooklyn, NY; [p.] Rudolph & Filomena Polizzi; [m.] Philip Scotto, September 30, 1967; [ch.] One daughter, Danielle; [ed.] B.A. Brooklyn College, MA Brooklyn College; [occ.] Teacher of English; [hon.] Impact II Grant, 1992, Teacher of Excellence Award, New York State Council of Teachers of English, 1993, Nominated for Reliance Award, District 18, NY 1993; [oth. writ.] Articles published in The Experienced Teacher's Handbook, 1992 and Voices and visions, 1992 Poem "The Canterberry Tales Completed" published in riverrun, 1985.; [pers.] My dad gave to me the greatest gift of all, the gift of laughter. I hope that I can pass that on to others.; [a.] Brooklyn, NY

SCRUGGS, BESSIE M.
[b.] April 7, 1949, MS; [p.] Lucy & Willie Scruggs; [ch.] One; [ed.] High School, some college courses; [occ.] Asst. Cook, certified meditation tech.; [memb.] canaan Gailee Baptist; [hon.] Holds certificate from New World Bible Insitute, some from church organizations; [oth. writ.] Some writing I do myself and read on church programs, nothing published.; [pers.] In my writings I try to keep the focus on Jesus, and to let him use me through my writings and sayings to entice other people; [a.] Madison, IL

SEAVER, ELIZABETH
[b.] January 21, 1914, Malone, NY; [p.] Nap and Harriet Pelkey; [m.] George Seaver, May 31, 1948 (2nd marriage); [ch.] Joan Harrigan, Nancy Miller, Richard Seaver; [ed.] St Joseph High; [occ.] Retired; [oth. writ.] Family poems; [pers.] 80 years old. Stroke in 1980. Has done poems for family for years. Is a bed patient; [a.] Malone, NY

SEEGERT, JENNIFER K.
[b.] November 22, 1970, Monroe, MI; [p.] Kenneth and Janet Seegert; [ch.] (1) Sarah Kay Seegert (22 mos); [ed.] Summerfield High School, Monroe Community College; [occ.] Secretary, Seegert and Seegert, Inc, Petersburg, MI; [memb.] United Methodist Church; [pers.] I hope to create an emotional response in my writing, and I use my life as my canvas; [a.] Riga, MI

SEEWALD, MICHELLE
[b.] October 1, 1980, Denver, CO; [a.] Sam Seewald, Karen Seewald; [ed.] BMH Preschool, Virginia Court Elementary, Mission Viejo Elementary, Laredo Middle School; [occ.] Student; [memb.] Spartan basketball, Spartan softball, Laredo basketball, Millers Dance Studio, Virginia Court Student Council, Laredo Student Council; [hon.] 4.0 honor roll, Trophys for basketball and softball, certificate for modeling; [oth. writ.] A Sister, So Beautiful, Love, California, Chicago, New York, Death; [pers.] I enjoy writing about my feelings and the life around me. I have been greatly influenced and encouraged by my grandmother, and my great-grandfather; [a.] Aurora, CO

SEIDEL, JAQUELINE K.
[Pen.] Jackie Seidel; [b.] February 3, 1979, Sellersville; [p.] Tom and Tesha Seidel, Debbie Albright; Siblings: Carissa - 13, Ilona - 7, and T.J. (2); [ed.] Pennridge Central Jr High School; [occ.] Student; [oth. writ.] I enjoy writing poems as a hobby; [pers.]

My writings are an expressing of my true inne feelings. A special thanks to my father; [a.] Sellersville PA

SELF, WILLIAM ERIC
[Pen.] May 14, 1946, Falls City, NE; [p.] Nolan and Wilma P. Self; [m.] Judith Ann Self, June 2, 1969, [ch.] (3) Janayhe, Joseph, Zachary; [ed.] Junctior City High School, Denver Community College, Kansas State Univ at Manhattan, KS; [occ.] Writer, Teacher, Real Estate Appraiser, Kauai, HI; [memb.] Kauai Viet Nam Veteran's Assoc, Member International Tae Kwon Do Assoc. 9th and 10th Cavalry Assoc, (US Horse Cavalry); [hon.] Husband, father, man, poet; [oth. writ.] Numerous poems. (2) short novels. A single act play. Newspaper articles; [pers.] We all stand between a pebble and a mountain, between doubt and potential, while in search of ourselves. Yet void of adversity, what would freedom be?; [a.] Koloa, HI

SELLERS, WALLACE W.
[b.] January 24, 1971, Wilmington, NC; [p.] William Wallace & Claudia Orrell Sellers; [m.] Gwen Gallagher Sellers, January 30, 1946; [ch.] None; [ed.] B.S., College of William and Mary; M.S., Vanderbilt Univ.; [occ.] Retired scientist and marketing executive; [memb.] Elder Presbyterian Church (U.S.A.); member of Southampton Hospital Volunteer Auxiliary: former member of American Electroplaters Society, Electrochemical Society, Society of Automotive Engineers, Nat'l. Assoc. Corrosion Engineers, New York academy of Science, Fellow, American Institute of Chemists; [hon.] Phi Beta Kappa, Theta Chi Delta, Sigma Chi Sigma, recipient of two gold medals, one silver medal and George Hagaboom award for technical papers, invitational lecturer in Australia, Japan and other foreign countries, formerly listed in American Men of Science and Who's Who in the East.; [oth. writ.] Technical papers and poem in Poems of Praise (Anderie Poetry Press); [pers.] Believing that God needs us as much as we need Him, I am persuaded that our chief purpose in life is to serve as His instruments of love and good. For He can do no more for us than He can do through us.; [a.] Water Mill, NY

SELLMYER, CHALLE
[b.] February 12, 1986, Dallas, TX; [p.] John and Paula Sellmyer; [ed.] 2nd grader at Austin Elementary in Mesquite, TX; [occ.] Elementary student; [memb.] Church choir at Wilshire Baptist, school reading club, Girls Auxillary for Missions, Brownies; [hon.] Straight A Honor Roll every six weeks. Principal's Award (Best all-around student in your entire grade) for the 1st grade; [pers.] My wish for our world is for it to get peaceful. The news is always bad and I wish it could be about good things that happen instead. I also wish people would stop killing endangered animals; [a.] Mesquite

SENEVIRATNA, PETER
[b.] December 30, 1927, Sri Lanka, Colombo; [p.] Miguel and Elizabeth (both deceased); [m.] Saku Seneviratna, February 15, 1974; [ch.] Manel, Chitra (daughters), Rohan and Gamini (Sons); [ed.] In Sri Lanka (primary and secondary) India, the UK and USA. (Unif of Professional Ph.D (Univ of London, Fellow of the Royal College of Veterinary Surgeons (England); Retired Academic - was professor of Veterinary Science - Univ of Ceylon (1966-1973); [memb.] 1. Royal College of Veterinary Surgeons England, 2. Australian Veterinary, 3. Australian Society of Parasitology; [hon.] Colombo Plan Scholar (1955-58) in England, Post Doctoral Fulbright Scholar at David Campus of Univ of California (1963-64); [oth. writ.] Book - Diseases of Poultry in the U.K. Over 65 research publications on veterinary science and parasitology; [pers.] This the the first poem I have written. Poetry is the best way to experience one's

motions and ideas, particularly in retirement -- short and science; [a.] Canberra, Australia

EWELL, FRANKIE
b.] April 8, 1968, Nottingham, England; [p.] Sean Sewell, Geralding Mallon; [ed.] St Mary's Christian Brother's Grammar School, Glen Rd Belfast II. The Univ of Belfast, Univ Road, Belfast Rt 7 Inn, Ireland; occ.] Freelance Journalist; [memb.] Member of staff of "The Honest Ulsterman" literary journal; [hon.] Blayney Exhibition 1990/91; Esther Ballantine Prize for English (February 1993); Foundation Award February 1993). Prize for best short story during Belfast Festival 1989. Greenan Lodge Medal (for history - 1984); [oth. writ.] Irish language editor of and contributor to "Brangle" an anthology of new writing from Univ of Belfast, 1993. Supervisor of Irish language section of "Honest Ulsterman". Contributor of articles to "Fortnight" magazine; [pers.] "Bothar na LL Fal" is Irish for the Falls Rd. It means literally "road of fenses", although "fal" originally meant "the space between fenses" usually a field. The poem highlights the distance or space between human beings caused by history, politics, imperialism; [a.] Belfast, Ireland

SHABAZZ, BILAL
[Pen.] Roscoe Edwards; [b.] March 2, 1948, NYC; [m.] Divorced; [ch.] Roscoe K. Edwards, Adrienne D. Edwards, Monique Edwards; [ed.] College of New Rochelle - BA; [occ.] Bus Operator; [hon.] 2nd pl award for "Prose on Life", a poem. Certificate of Merit for "Two Days in South Africa", both written under the name Roscoe Edwards; [oth. writ.] Various poems and short stories. A novella, "Tragic Magic"; [pers.] Be true to God, yourself, and your loved ones; [a.] Bronx, NY

SHACHTER, JOHN A.
[b.] June 29, 1963, Berwyn, IL; [p.] Marvin and Diana Shachter; [m.] Laura L. Shachter; [m.] May 27, 1989; [ch.] Ashley Nicole Shachter, Melissa Allison Shachte; [ed.] Rolling Meadows HS, Chicago Citywide, Morton College, Roosevelt Univ; [occ.] Amway Distributor; [memb.] Phi Theta Kappa, National Honor Society; [oth. writ.] Placid Anxiety; Frayed Wire; Fraid Not; Teddy Bear; Broken Heart; Kathy (8/6); [pers.] We are students of those who went before, and teachers to those who follow. So learn well the lessons of the day for a promising tomorrow; [a.] North Riverside, IL

SHAH, DEMETRIA EVE
[Pen.] Dee or Dee Dee; [b.] December 16, 1953, Scranton, PA; [p.] Joseph Sembrat, Olga Sembrat; [m.] Siddharth K. Shah, February 3, 1973; [ch.] Aaron T. Shah; [ed.] Marywood Seminary, 1 yr - Lackawanna Jr College; [occ.] Babysitter; [oth. writ.] 1 short story published in local newspaper "The Suncoast News"; [pers.] My dear grandmother has inspired me to write "When Death Comes Calling" (she passed away in '83). I am a simple writer and a wholehearted writer; [a.] Palm Harbor, FL

SHANHOLTZER, CYNTHIA (KISH)
[b.] May 19, 1964, Laurel, MD; [p.] Kathryn Snapp and Alfred Shanholtzer; [m.] Donald Kish, August 26, 1988; [occ.] Area Mgr, Retail Germany; [hon.] Various Awards in Art; [pers.] I hope to see a growing awareness for the environment. Only mankind can make the difference.

SHARITZ, JOSEPHINE M.
[b.] June 29, 1912, Atlanta, GA; [p.] Deceased; [m.] Deceased, World War II, 1st Lt. Thorold J. Sharitz, December 28, 1932; [ch.] Lst. Lt. Charles J. Sharitz (Dec.), Mrs. Clyde Ray Ward, lives in Huntsville, AL, works for NASA and Army of Defense (Space) Librarian; [ed.] Fla. State University, Tallahesse, FL, University of Miami, Barry University, Skidmore

Univ., History of Chinese Art, (taken course); [occ.] Artist, Write poetry, short stories; [memb.] Larramore Rader Poetry Group, Miami, Fla. Professional Membership in teaching art in schools in Miami, Fl.; [hon.] Anthology of love poems "Remember Me", Fla. State Literary Magazine 2 Cinquins. People ask me to read my poetry. They like my paintings. Talaria, Literary Magazine at Florida State University at Tallashessee, FL,. Three poems honored in Magazines. "Remember Me," published in World Anthology of Love Poems, 1983 Miami, FL, other poems not listed.; [pers.] I love nature and I am inspired by nature both in my poetry and painting. Poems sing to me in my mind., and I have to write them down. They sky, trees, birds and my love of people inspire me to write.; [a.] Atlanga, GA

SHARPE, JESSICA, MARIA
[Pen.] Chastity; [b.] February 1, 1980, Charlotte, NC; [p.] Joe & Jill Sharpe; [ed.] Currently in 8th grade, plan to finish high school, then go to Duke University in Chapel Hill, North Cardina; [memb.] I am a member of the Drama Club at my church, the marching & concert bands at my school, and also the rifle division of the Colour Guard; [hon.] My first poem ever written was published in the Anthology of Poetry by Young Americans (1991 edition), awarded "Best Hustler" by teammates in my 2nd year of basketball; [oth. writ.] "Without You," "Wonderings," "Without the Pain" (poems), "The Tin box," "Perhaps Dreaming" (short stories); [pers.] I've played volleyball for 2 years and am in my 4th year of playing basketball. I know the depths of depression and the heights of happiness. Whatever happens, just hond on, and pray.; [a.] Bartlett, TN

SHARPS, CLARISSE YVONNE GOETHE
[Pen.] C. Goethe Sharpes; [b.] June 28, 1953, Los Angels, CA; [p.] Otto Wayne Goethe and Doris Juanity Goethe; [occ.] Legal Technician; [a.] Heidelberg, Germany, Baden Wuerttemberg

SHARROW, TRACY-LYNN
[b.] July 3, 1982, Cornwall, Ontario; [p.] Wanda and Ken Sharrow; [ed.] Akwesasne Mohawk School, Cornwall Island, Akwesasne, Cornwall, Ontario; [occ.] School Student, grade 6; [pers.] I am very happy you picked my poem to be printed.

SHAULIS, HELEN EILEEN
[b.] July 25, 1968, Penn; [p.] Darlene Wachowiak; [m.] Rick E. Shaulis; [ch.] Cody Lee, Kelsey Lea, Cameron Lee; [occ.] Sales; [oth. writ.] Articles published in local newspapers. Unfinished historical novel; [pers.] My words art to those great people whom once roamed these lands with the freedom and inner peace only they could understand thru their unselfish respect for life. And to my 3 wonderful children. Always look to the sky!; [a.] Seagertown, PA

SHAW, BARBARA JEAN
[Pen.] Barbara Shaw; [b.] August 28, 1963, New York; [p.] Peter and Linda Shaw; [ed.] Fashion Inst of Tech - NYC; [occ.] Exclusive agent for Xavier danard (footwear) USA and Canada; [memb.] While in college I was a member of DECA. I won a New York State competition in fashion buying and pricing; [hon.] Made the honor roll while attend FIT; [oth. writ.] Started writing a novel in Paris called "A Moment in Time", by Barbara Shaw; [pers.] The impact of writing a poem comes from an emotional experience that exist within oneself. Being able to express one's most inner self is a gift that only creative people can see; [a.] New York, NY

SHAW, DAWN ELIZABETH TORPIN
[b.] July 12, 1969, Edmonton, Alberta; [m.] Charles Glen Shaw, March 10, 1989; [ch.] Ruby Jean, Owen Lee; [ed.] South Delta Senior Secondary High School,

BC, Canada; [occ.] Currently enrolled full-time at Spokane Community College; [hon.] Vice-President Honor Roll (3.0-3.4) GPA 3 quarters in SCC; [pers.] Poetry is my way of expressing my feelings; [a.] Airway Heights, WA

SHELDON, CANDICE V.
[b.] February 14, 1965, Toronto; [ed.] York Univ - Toronto, graduated with backelor of fine arts in film; [occ.] Sales asst; [hon.] Dean's Honor Roll; [oth. writ.] Short articles in magazines. Articles in Univ newspaper; [pers.] I have tried so hard to make a career out of writing and often got disappointed. I have learned though that there's personal worth and fulfillment in just writing at all; [a.] Toronto, Ontario, Canada

SHELTON, DAYLENE
[b.] January 29, 1976, Idabel, OK; [p.] Roger and Mary Lou Shelton; [ed.] Haworth High, Haworth, OK; [memb.] High school student council, National and Oklahoma High Honor Societies, member of the high school Academic Team. Haworth Stars (drug free club); [hon.] Academic awards in Algebra I and II, Geometry, English I, II and II, World History, American History, Biology, Physical Science and Valedictorian of my 9th and 12th grade classes; [a.] Haworth, OK

SHERRER, LILLIAN
[b.] May 2, 1934, Highwater, Quebeck; [m.] July 15, 1953; [ch.] Six children and seven grandchildren; [ed.] high school [occ.] Convenience Store owner and semi-retired farmer's wife; [oth. writ.] Self-published (locally) a book of short stories and poems - number two on the way. Several poems and one short story published in local papers; [pers.] Interested in a market for writings of rural life - when I was a child - story form; [a.] Mansonville, Quebec, Canada

SHERWIN, SAMUEL ERIC
[Pen.] Sam Sherwin; [b.] December 12, 1974, Cleveland, OH; [p.] Jeff and Mary Jo Sherwin; [ed.] Charles F. Brush High School grad, freshman - OH Stat Univ; [occ.] Student; [memb.] US Chess Federation; [hon.] Member of several indoor soccer championship teams. 1988 Parma Class Open Champion Class D; [pers.] "You're Playing With Stars" is dedicated to Ann and Gwen; [a.] Columbus, OH

SHIELDS, FSC. BROTHER ALFRED
[Pen.] Brother Larry Shields, FSC; [b.] June 14, 1913, Symerton, IL; [p.] Hugh and Ellen Shields; [ed.] Grade school one room school house, High School, DeLaSalle in Joliet, IL, College, Manhattan U., De Paul U. of Chicago St., Mary's College of Winona, MI University of Santo Tomas, PI; [occ.] Fund Raising for the Christian Brothers, helping the needy, writing poetry; [memb.] Biology Teachers Associaiton of the P.I., Splunkers Association, Red Cross; [hon.] Editor of Biology Journal, Full U. Professor, U. Board member, Gold Medal from World of Poetry, Cal.; [oth. writ.] Articles for a Religion Book Editorials for a Biology Journal, poetry for friends for Red Cross work; [pers.] Live one day at a time, do things for others, keep in touch with God, be happy when friends and students are honored, be generous with free time.; [a.] Westchester, IL

SHINN, JOYCE G.
[b.] 1928, London, England; [m.] John D. Shinn; [ch.] Pauline Joy; [ed.] Plaistow Grammar School; [occ.] Retied; [memb.] Mensa, DDA committee (local); [oth. writ.] Several poems published in "first time", one in "Poppy Fields". Article in "Yours", article in A.R.C, first short novel being publishes; [pers.] I feel that poetry writing is a purely personal thing driven by emotion, sometimes love, or sadness and very often ager at man's inhumanity to man; [a.] Benfleet, Essex, UK

SHIPPAN, CHARLES ANTHONY
[b.] July 10, 1963, Chichester, England; [p.] Pamela Anne Tressillian and Mike Shippan; [ed.] American Univ, BA Fl Inst of Technology, MBA, Widener School of Law, JD; [occ.] Law Clerk, Wilson, Elser Moskowitz, Edelman of Dicker; [memb.] Who's Who Worldwide; [pers.] Each generation belongs to its communicators; [a.] Wilmington, DE

SHIRLEY, BECKY
[b.] March 21, 1979, Panama City, FL; [p.] Burl and Lois Shirley; [occ.] High school student.

SHOLTIS, CHRISTOPHER AARON
[b.] October 7, 1974, Fairfax, VA; [p.] Charlynn and Steven Sholtis; [ed.] Central Dauplin East High School; [occ.] Porter for Penn National Race Track; [memb.] Surfrider Foundation and some Union I think.; [hon.] Nothing important.; [oth. writ.] Various local publishings, currently working on a compilation of works.; [pers.] Tell me what I am, I'll tell you what I will be, You told me nothing. I told you everthing.; [a.] Harrisburg, PA

SHOTWELL, MACHUT J.A.
[b.] May 25, 1975, Jorhat (Assam, India); [p.] Rev. Tuisem Shishad, Margaret Shishak; [ed.] Woodstock Christian International School (Mussoorie, India), Calvin College - 1st yr - (Grand Rapids, MI); [occ.] Student; [hon.] Dean's List; [oth. writ.] No other work of mine has been published yet. Chief Editor of high school yearbook, contributed to its text.; [pers.] The profoundest influence on my life, and thus my writing, has been Jesus Christ. i strive to reflect His call to social action in my work; [a.] Grand Rapids, MI

SHOTWELL, STACEY ANN
[Pen.] Saknas or Kalei; [b.] August 8, 1976, Walnut Creek, CA; [p.] Craig and Yvonne Shotwell; [ed.] I am currently enrolled at Monte Vista High School as a senior; [occ.] Student; [memb.] I am a member of the National Honors Society, the California's Scholars Federation, and Interact. (Those are all clubs at my high school); [hon.] Six semesters on the principal' honor role, various trophies for softball, 1993 Business and Education First Place Roundtable Award in Film/Video, and semifinalist in poetry contest by Sparrowgrass; [oth. writ.] One poem published in my school's newspaper and one poem published in Poetic Voices of America; [pers.] I wish to express that poetry is the connection to the thoughts beyond the daily drum of life. It is the instrument for the poundings of the spirit. In my writings I only hope to inspire the same enlightenment; [a.] Danville, CA

SHUFFLER, SGT. IRVING L.
[b.] October 10, 1916, Frederick, MD; [p.] Irving L. Sr. & Mary Catherine; [m.] Three, Jane McSherrie, Margie Ilene Morris, Mann Kepolinger, April 2, 1940, May 3, 1943, Nov. 20, 1945; [ch.] Three sons, Douglas, Karl Juan, Thomas Michael; [ed.] Frederick, MD High School; [occ.] Retired CTC Opr. Chessie System Lurgan Tower; [memb.] BRAC 2nd Air Div. USAF 8th AF Founder Asst. to American Museum, Oxford, Eng.; [hon.] Honored by Sir Winston Churchill in 1944, for poem "Prayer for Victory." 9 Stars, 2 Pres. Citation, Ofc. Air Medal, Purple Heart, served in USA AF Overseas Dec. 15, 1942 to May 8, 1945; [oth. writ.] "No Other Girl in World" (song) Dedicated to Janice Louise Brown of Blackburg, VA, (song) "Remember The Girl Back Home" I'll Be Back When It's Over, Over There. It's Great To Be In The Army.; [pers.] I believe as the nation sings and dances its morals. Lets get back to safe and sane poetry and music; [a.] Chambusburg, PA

SHULTS, ANY RENEE DUMAS
[b.] August 12, 1972, Rensselaer, Indiana; [p.] Louis & Janet Dumas; [m.] Eric Russell Shults, July 13, 1991; [ch.] Karrington Michelle Shults; [ed.] Kankakee Valley High School, International Correspondence Schools; [occ.] Executive Secretary, JCM Enterprises, Ltd., Williamsville, NY; s Who's Who Among American High School Students, International business Women of America, Brushwood United Methodist Church, Business Professionals of America; [hon.] Who's Who Among American High School Students, Business Professionals of America National Winner; [oth. writ.] Several poems and short stories to hopefully be published one day; [pers.] This poem is dedicated to my first love and inspiration, Timothy Robert Steinke; [a.] Rensselear, IN

SICA, BROOK
[b.] July 18, 1980, NY; [p.] Diane Sica; [ed.] Hillsborough Middle School as of now 7th grade; [occ.] Student; [memb.] Girl Scouts, Faith Lutheran Church, Ballet dancing, Cheerleading, Softball; [hon.] 4th place in National Colgate Award, 2nd place for 100 points of life for girl scouts.

SIDBURY, KAREN E.
[Pen.] Let's see how famous I become; [b.] June 4, 1965, Charleston, SC; [p.] Furman and Josephine Sidbury; [ed.] Lackey High School; [occ.] Patient Accounts Representative for Drs Wener, Boyle and Assoc, PA; [memb.] The Official Star Tred Fan Club. Formerly of The National Society of Honored Thespians; [oth. writ.] Several poems and a few prose pieces. Previously published work in my high school literary magazine; [pers.] For me writing is a personal exorcism of negative emotions. It's a way purifying your soul without being judged by those not understanding; [a.] Indian Head, MD

SIGWALT, SHIRELY
[b.] May 13, 1963, Hinsdale, IL; [ch.] Kenneth Warren; [ed.] Downers Grove, South High School; [occ.] Eagle Foods Union Local 1540; [oth. writ.] I have written several poems in the past but never submitted any of them to anyone.; [pers.] The poetry I write comes from the heart and reflects my own personal experiences.; [a.] Downers Grove, IL

SILBERT, BETH ANN
[b.] March 22, 1978, Morristown, NJ; [p.] Andrew & Sue Silbert; [ed.] Sophomore at Parsippany High School; [hon.] Who's Who in American High School Students for History Acting credits: Beggar Woman (a lead) in Stephen Sondheim's "Sweeney Todd" at French Woods Festival of Performing Arts, Montclair Operetta Club - "Pirates of Penzance"; [oth. writ.] Several poems only one of which, "Solitude" has been published in "The Totem" the Parsippany High School literary magazine; [a.] Lake Hiawatha, NJ

SILVA, MIRNA M.
[b.] February 5, 1965, Mexico; [p.] Isaias & Manuela Silva; [ed.] Galena Park Sr. High, HCC and University of Houston; [occ.] Investment Banking; [memb.] Tejas Auxiliary of Assistance League of Houston, Alvin Art League and Worldwide Church of God; [hon.] Dean's List, Poetry in Motion Award from my place of employment (MGSI); [oth. writ.] Having a collection of poetry that I have not submitted to anyone. This poem is the first I entered in a contest.; [pers.] Im my writing I let my heart speak. It takes over and searches the deepest of thoughts that man ponders. The Psalms of the bible have greatly influenced my poetry.; [a.] Houston, TX

SIMMERS, CHRISTOPHER
[b.] July 30, 1984, California; [p.] John and Margie Simmers; [occ.] Student in 4th grade

SIMON, GERADESSIEL
[b.] May 21, 1952, Chicago; [p.] Abraham and Sarah; [m.] "Awaiting her time"; [ed.] Catholic grammer, vocational trade, business - tailoring, Chicato City Colleges, Word of God Theological; [occ.] Office of Prophet in ministry of the Gospel of Jesu Christ...;[memb.] Hebrew - Ethiopian Communit Asso, American Indian Center as Blackfeet Natio member; Gershomite - Levites Inter. Wealth Merchantment of Heaven's Kingdom; Pioneers: Prophets, Psalmists, oets; [hon.] Living the Word of Go Award (National), Vessell of Honor Award (1979) For Creative Television Works (1988), Original Ancient Arts HARP (1988), Righteous Judgmen Honor (1993), The Endurance Award; [oth. writ. Book of Bbooks, Just Living by Faith, The Ancien and Artistic Prophets - Today: Holy Saints Do Stil Live! Proverbs, Psalsm, Parables - now. [pers.] A: my stated name or as my name states: my assignmen here is to inspire, restore, encourage life, happiness, and contentment based upon The Book of Life - The Word of God; [a.] Gary, IN

SIMON, TAMEKA
[Pen.] Me - me; [b.] April 3, 1980, Ft Worth, TX; [p.] Clifton and Linda Simon; Sisters and Brothers: Clifton Simon, Jr, Frank Simon, Latasha Simon, Shandra Simon; [ed.] Forest Hill Elem Forest Oak Middle School, Glen Crest Middle School, Ft Worth, TX; [occ.] Modeling Ind Dallas; [memb.] Junior Honors Society. Asst Secretary for Humble Chapel Church, Spriti Team, SELF Club; [oth. writ.] Several poems that I write to keep for my self; [pers.] I enjoy writing because I can express my feelings through writing; [a.] Ft Worth, TX

SIMPSON, CRYSTAL TEVA
[Pen.] Crystal; [b.] May 16, 1982, Columbus, GA; [p.] Dexter and Janice Simpson; [ed.] I am in the 6th grade at Sanford Middle School in Lee County, AL; [memb.] I am a member of the 6th grade band. Have been an A & B student for several years now. Held office in 5th grade student council; [hon.] Receive student of the week on 3 occasions. A member of the Greater Peace Baptist Church where I am a member of the Junior Choir, and the Secretary of the Ushers; [oth. writ.] first writing; [pers.] I think that through pray and determination there is no limit to my accomplishments. My favorite color is purple. My favorite animal (although mythical) is the Unicorn!; [a.] Salem, AL

SIMPSON, KATHLEEN O'HARA
[b.] April 14, 1946, Balto, MD; [p.] James and Neva O'hara; [m.] William J. Simpson, April 6, 1973; [ch.] Brady William and Casey Veronica; [ed.] Dundalk Community College (AA); Berean Bible Inst; People's Law School; Dundalk Night School; Berlitz Language Center; [occ.] AT&T Federal Admin Asso; [memb.] Bethel Assembly of God, Littletown, PA; AT&T Defense Communications Newsletter editor; [hon.] Honors graduate; Dean's List; charter member Dundalk Thespians; [oth. writ.] Several poems published in local newspapers; [pers.] My poetry is a reflection of my highest emotions, my deepest grief and my widest love; [a.] Westminster, MD

SINGSHEIM, JESSICA LYNN
[Pen.] Jessica L. Singsheim; [b.] October 31, 1980, Milw, WI; [p.] Robert and Cindy Singsheim; [ed.] General education in 7th grade; [occ.] School; [memb.] Model's Club; [hon.] My poetry awards. (2 certificates and $10), 2nd place ribbon for running DARE certificate; [oth. writ.] Poetry (all poems); [pers.] I want the world to be a better place for us in the future; [a.] Sussex, WI

SKALTSAS, KORI
[b.] August 21, 1979, Valparaiso, IN; [p.] Chris Skaltsas, Jane Hayes; [ed.] Eastlake High School, want to go to University of Florida to become a Veternarian; [memb.] Marine Biology Club at school; [hon.] Honor Roll Certificate; [oth. writ.] One poem published in a newspaper called Alligator Express.; [pers.] I really put effort into my poems and I'm really

outgoing and a hard worker. I enjoy reading poetry books, also. And I wanted to say I really love my Dad and my Mom for helping me. If I happen to win the grand prize, I will put it in my savings account.; [a.] Palm Harbor, FL

SKAVINSKI, SARAH ELIZABETH
[Pen.] Sadie Beth Skavar; [b.] April 25, 1976, Greensburg, PA; [p.] Greg and Connie Skavinski; [ed.] Oakton High - senior; [oth. writ.] Personal poems, several poems published in shcool paper; [pers.] I believe poetry should come from deep inside your heart and soul. Always, LAF; [a.] Herndon, VA

SKERKAVICH, LISA
[Pen.] Frankie; [b.] February 9, 1979, Youngstown, OH; [p.] Raymond Skerkavich, Patricia Bokanovich; [m.] none; [ch.] none; [ed.] Holy Name School, St. Brendan's School, Canfield Middle School, Canfield High School; [memb.] Key Club, Y-teens; [hon.] 2nd place regional History Day, 1st place bowling league; [oth. writ.] I write a lot of poems in my spare time.; [pers.] I like to write whenever I have a lot on my mind. I like to stress my feelings in my poems.; [a.] Canfield, OH

SLACK, KEVIN
[Pen.] Kevin J. Sudot; [b.] November 5, 1969, Hagersville, Ontario; [p.] Wilbert Slack, Donna Slack; [ed.] Hagersville Secondary School, Hagersville; Univ of Western Ontario, London, Ontario; [occ.] X-tra! Toronto's Gay and Lesbian Bi-weekly, Freelance Artist; [hon.] Bachelor of Arts, English and Visual Arts, Univ of Western Ontario, Dean's List; Faculty Entrance Scholarship, UNO; [oth. writ.] Several poems published in the symposium, A Student Arts Magazine, UNO; Poetry readings at the now defunct Juice for Life, Toronto; [pers.] People are far too concerned about differences; the world seems to be fragmenting into so many special interest groups they will eventually exclude everyone. I write not to mark my differences but in order to explore a common space; [a.] Toronto, Ontario

SLEGER, KIM
[b.] August 22, 1974, Sturgeon Bay, WI; [p.] Donald Sleger, Dyan Sleger; [ed.] Menominee High School, Menominee, MI; [memb.] Former member of Business Professionals of America; [hon.] Business Professionals of America - national competition winner, awards in legal applications and administrative specialist; [oth. writ.] Other poetry published in high school year book; [pers.] "Success is an attitude"; [a.] Sturgeon Bay, WI

SLIGHT, CAROLYN S.
[b.] November 26, 1949, Norfolk County; [p.] Isiah and Iola B. Slayton; [m.] divorced; [ch.] Percy Theran Slight; [ed.] G in Carver High School, Chesapeake, VA Norfolk State College; [occ.] Crane Operator Supervisor; [memb.] Federal Management Assn, Cathedral of Faith Church of God In Christ, Santuary Choir, Women Chorus; My writings are to uplift the spirits of mankind with grace and dignity. And to show the glory of God almighty; [a.] Chesapeake, VA

SMALLWOOD, KATHY
[b.] August 31, 1956, Ozark, AL; [p.] Sanders Swan, Effie Swan; [m.] Carmen Smallwood, July 28, 1986; [ch.] Samuel Jerome Wesley, Adam Troy Vincent; [ed.] Thomas Jefferson High, Central TX College; [occ.] Staff Sergeant US Army; [occ.] The 700 Club; [hon.] 4 Army Commendations, 2 Army Achievement Awards; [oth. writ.] Several unpublished writings; [pers.] In my writing, I try to reflect my love for God, my family and this country, because without these, there would be no inspiration; [a.] Radcliff, KY

SMELSER, KATHLEEN
[b.] August 12, 1968, Phila, PA; [p.] Ruth Smelser, Doyle Smelser; [ch.] Sean D. Jones; [memb.] North Shore Animal League; [pers.] Dedicated to Ruth McCallum, Sean Jones, Barbara Smelser and our Lord; [a.] Phila, PA

SMETHERAM, VALERIE
[b.] July 8, 1936, Selbourne, U.K.; [p.] William and Daisy Gates; [m.] Richard L. Smetheram, February 22, 1976; [ch.] Graham 26, Peter 22; [ed.] Very limited formal education due to lack of opportunity. However I have tried to rectify this by wide reading and an interest in many subjects. Throughout my life I have had a great love for literature.; [occ.] Pastoral Assistant; [memb.] Writers Groups, Seniors Assoc., Womens Club; [oth. writ.] Numerous articles short stories and poetry, some of which have been published (mostly poetry). Although I recall writing little stories in primary school I did not really start writing seriously until about 4 years ago.; [pers.] I would like to make a truly positive contribution in this world particularly in the area of promoting goodwill betwen people of all races. I am passionately iterested in the study of cultures other than my own.; [a.] Brisbane, Australia

SMETTERS, CASEY
[b.] December 5, 1981, Wooddale; [p.] Sharon Smetters; [ed.] 6th grade; [pers.] I've been inspired to write poetry from my grandfather Carl F. Stratton who is a member of the international poet society.; [a.] Bohingbrook, FL

SMITH, BECCI
[b.] June 3, 1973, Williamsport, PA; [ed.] Montoursville High School, Currently enrolled at Bloomsburg University; [a.] Trout Run, PA

SMITH, BEVERLY A.
[Pen.] Alice Faye; [b.] November 2, 1945, Athens, GA; [p.] Charlie Annie Lee Hawkins; [m.] Bruce Smith, May 17, 1966 (Divorced July 28, 1990); [ch.] Wendy, Bruce & Alicia; [ed.] B.S. Special Ed., Wayne State, Master Education Psy.; [occ.] Sp. Ed Teacher Cody H.S., in Detroit, part-time Real Estate Agent; [hon.] An Honoree for Horace Mann Society 1976, Honored as a Michigan 150, First Lady Award Nominee in Observance of Mich. Sesquicennial; [oth. writ.] Many poems based on reflections of love, life and obsession from a woman's viewpoint that are waiting for a publisher.; [pers.] I've always reached out to help others and have been very sensitive to others need. The poems are inspirational to all who read.; [a.] Detroit, MI

SMITH, BILLIE SUE
[b.] July 3, 1940, Coushatta, LA; [ed.] Highland High School, Alburgue, New Mexico. I am attending Harrisburg Area Community College, Lebanon Campus in PA part-time.; [occ.] I am a teachers assistant with Lancaster lebanan IU 13 for over 20 years.; [hon.] Dean's List; [oth. writ.] "All Hallows Eve" a short piece of fiction and poems titled "Midnight" and "Time" published in The Grand Illusion, Thoughts III" by the Harrisburg Area community college, Labanon Campus, 1993; [pers.] i am a southern born woman that enjoys writing. It's my family that gives meaning to my life and purpose to my days. Writing is as much a part of my life as breathing, without it I could not exist.; [a.] Lebanon, PA

SMITH, CHRISTIE LESLIE
[b.] October 29, 1971, Harlan, KY; [p.] Charles and Oneda Spurlock; [m.] Michael Wayne Smith, January 2, 1993; [ch.] Pregnant with first child; [ed.] James A. Cawood High, Harland, KY; [occ.] Housewife and mother to be; [oth. writ.] I have a collection of poems that I have written through my life, that have not been released to anyone.; [pers.] I write my poems from my own personal experiences hoping that someone can feel the emotions from my writings as I feel in reality.; [a.] Harland, KY

SMITH, DONNA KAY
[Pen.] Donna Postlethwaite-Smith; [b.] March 21, 1957, Cameron; [p.] Robert R. Postlethwaite; [m.] Edith Chaplin-Postlethwaite, December 14, 1984; [ch.] Joshua Lee, Jacqueline Marie, Rebekah Dawn; [ed.] Cameron High School, Waynesburgh College, Canada College; [occ.] Mother/Wife; [memb.] P.T.A., Suzuki Violin Assoc.; [hon.] Who's Who Among American High School Students; [hon.] Dean's List, Canada College; [pers.] Some people cannot read poetry and enjoy themselves until they grow and understand what is said in the words.; [a.] Cameron, WV

SMITH, DONNAMARIA
[Pen.] Donna M. Smith; [b.] July 17, 1976, Philadelphia; [p.] Elizabeth Smith-Mills; [ed.] Olney High School, ACT School - Nursing Asst., Business Technical Ins - Data Entry, PSD - Sign Language Part I; [occ.] Volunteer at Free Library of Philadelphia; [hon.] Business Technical Ins, High Honors Dean's List and Special Achievement Award, Leadership Award in Jr High School, High Honors at ACT School of Nursing Asst; [oth. writ.] A poem published with the Famous Poet Society; [pers.] I tell my philosophy on some concerning knowledge. Because, I speak with inspiration that is well meant; [a.] Philadelphia, PA

SMITH, ERIN MARIE
[b.] November 3, 1979, Erie, PA; [p.] David and Marily; [ed.] Preschool and K-8; [occ.] Student; [memb.] YMCA Westwood, Racquet Club, St Peter's Tennis Team (#1 doubles); [hon.] #1 Doubles Tennis, City of Erie Parochial Tournament, 1st or 2nd honors - all 8 yrs of school, food bank poster, contest (2nd place); [oth. writ.] Dedication page for grade school yearbook, creative writing in school, collection of poetry - ongoing, biography of grandmother, autobiography, multiple term papers for school; [pers.] "Someday I hope to publish my own book of poetry". I write because it gives me pleasure and it makes me proud of myself"; [a.] Erie, PA

SMITH, HOLLI
[b.] December 27, 1976, San Diego, CA; [p.] Natalie Kaspar; [ed.] Chambersburg area Senior High; [occ.] Waitress at 5 Point Diner; [hon.] Got a certificate in english for liking to write so much; [oth. writ.] Teacher's that read my poems liked them alot.; [pers.] I thought about writing poems, when I learned more about life, and the things around me, the outdoors was a great affect too.; [a.] Chambersburg, PA

SMITH, HOLLY NOELLE
[b.] December 3, 1978, Hagerstown, MD; [p.] Paul and Vicky Smith; [ed.] Currently a student at Clear Spring High School and taking correspondence course with the Inst of Children's Literature; [hon.] Numerous High Academic Achievement Awards including honors from the US Achievement Academic, several Presidential Academic Fitness Awards and an all American Scholar Award; [pers.] "From childhood's hour I have not been as others were -- I have not seen as others saw" -- Alone, Edgar Allan Poe; [a.] Clear Spring, MD

SMITH, JAMIE
[Pen.] J.C. Smith; [b.] October 19, 1976, Jacksonville, FL; [p.] Greg and Renee Smith; [ed.] Martin High School, Arlington, TX, Young Jr., High, Arlington, TX, Yucca Elementary, Palmdale, CA; [occ.] Student, part-time job at a move theatre, Arlington, TX; [memb.] none; [hon.] none; [oth. writ.] first poem ever published; [pers.] Poetry is my way of escape, taking me to my dreams; [a.] Arlington, TX

SMITH, JAYNE ROSEANNE
[Pen.] Jayni Rose, Angel Khomadia; [b.] May 30th; [pers.] Just to ad, that my writings come from many fields of pain; personal, imaginable, and so forth. My veneration to man is inspired deeply by music. I am very much so, a sacred poet.

SMITH, JOANNE
[b.] September 22, 1968, Clitheroe; [p.] Geoffrey Smith/Christine Horrocks; [ed.] St Augustine's RC High, St Mary's 6th Form College, Blackburn College, Accrington College; [occ.] Unemployed Secretary/VDU Operator; [memb.] Stefanie Power's Official Fan Club, Clitheroe Singers (Community Choir); [oth. writ.] Short story published in Anthology "New Fiction-Shorts from Lancashire", and poem published in anthology "As Seen on TV-Your Favorites" (Both in England); [pers.] My poem included in this anthology is dedicated to TV stars Robert Wager and Stefanie Powers, whose close and loving friendship inspired it; [a.] Clitheroe, Lancashire, England

SMITH, KELLI L.
[b.] April 23, 1972, Lynn, MA; [p.] Janet Melanson; [m.] Jody B. Smith, January 23, 1993; [ch.] Farren A. Smith; [ed.] Brockton High School; [hon.] 1990 Brockton High Poetry Contest, 2nd Place Award for "Child In Me"; [oth. writ.] Several poems I have written but have not submitted them. 2nd place in 1990 at Brockton High Poetryu Contes, "Child iin Me"; [pers.] My poems come from the heart, on how I feel or what I see around me. I love to write an was influenced by some "special people" in my life.; [a.] Salem, MA

SMITH, LEAH
[b.] November 17, 1973, Miami, FL; [p.] James S. Smith, Terry A. Smith; [ed.] George Washington High, Radford Univ, Danville Community College; [occ.] Student; [hon.] Dean's List, Honor graduate; [oth. writ.] Published poems in high schl. literary mag. and Radord's The Gaelic; [pers.] I hope that others are affected some how by my words. Favorite poets are Sylvia Plath and Stevie Smith; [a.] Danville, VA

SMITH, LILLIAN
[b.] February 27, 1911, Arkansas; [p.] Marcella and Jackson Bell; [m.] Clois Smith, December 7, 1933; [ch.] Patsy Smith Roman, grandchildren: Sandra Roman and Thomas Roman, great grandchildren: Thomas Ronald Roman; [ed.] College; Central State Teachers, Edmond, OK; [occ.] Cancer Survivo, retired; [hon.] Gold Medal - Scholastic Achievement - high school 1928-29 Marlow OK; [oth. writ.] Poems - Rod McKuen influencial; [pers.] Thomas Ronald Roman - great grandson to whem this poem is dedicated; [a.] Alhambra, CA

SMITH, LISA MARIE
[b.] (13 yrs old) January 11, 1981, Lou, KY; [p.] Gary D. Smith, Jennifer Rankin; Sister: Michelle Lynn Smith; [ed.] 7th grade middle school, River Valley, Jeffersonville, IN; [hon.] Honor roll all through elementary and middle school.

SMITH, SARALYN V.
[b.] January 25, 1974, Covington, LA; [p.] Russell A. and Vayon G. Smith; [m.] not married; [ed.] Summit Valley Christian School, Yellowstone Baptist College, and North Greenville College.; [occ.] Montana Silversmith, Billings, MT; [memb.] Yellowstone Baptist College Ministry Team, Park City Baptist Church; [hon.] Honor student at North Greenville College in Tigerville, SC. This is my first publication, as well as my only entry so far.; [oth. writ.] I have written hundreds of poems but I have never sent any of them to be published or copyrighted.; [pers.] I believe in Jesus Christ my Lord and Saviour and I believe the Holy Bible is truth. Therefore, I pattern my life and

writings after Matthew 6:21 "For where your treasure is, there your heart will be also." (NIV); [a.] Whitehall, MT

SMITH, TED
[Pen.] B.T. Goldsmith; [b.] June 28, 1928, Asheville, NC; [p.] Deceased; [m.] Mae W. Smith; [m.] June 4, 1951; [ch.] Dan (39), Rick (36), Dianne (34), Who's Who, etc; [ed.] AB Berea College, MED Emory Univ, ED.S and Ed.D - Univ GA and U AL; [occ.] Info Tech at Amer Secur Ins Gp; [memb.] Natnl Ed Assoc, Gr Ed Assoc, PAGE, DeKalb Civitan Club; [hon.] Trophies and Letter in Basketball, Gymnastics, Swimming, Golf. Awards in the Civic Club as President, Prog Chmn, Safety Chmn, Jr Club Sponsorships, Athletic honors, trophies; [oth. writ.] 3 manuscripts to become books: (A) The Principal of the Thing (about the principalship) (B) Quest of Mind; Crest of Spirit: An Anotomy of Faith and Joy, (C) Just Between Plain Folk; [pers.] Most of my studies and writing since the Masters Prog have been in the "Values" area; [a.] Lithonia, GA

SMITH, THADDAEUS
[b.] May 24, 1975, Houston, TX; [p.] Rev and Mrs Carolyn Hubbard; [ed.] 11 yrs public education Keaney Elem, Northwood Middle School, Mary Brantly Smiley High School, 1 yr private Varnett Academy; [occ.] Navy enlisted personnel; [hon.] Drama (middle school), 7 superior,, 5 excellent ribbons, 2nd place Vocal Performance Trophy, 4th Honor English Award. NAACP participant 10% in Naval Company (boot camp) in Great Lakes; [oth. writ.] (songs) All I Know Is You Lady, Cold and Lonely Nights, Smooth Sailing; [pers.] If God allows, I'll do the best I can while I can because this life is short and I'm a pilgrim trying to find my way home; [a.] Houston, TX

SMITH, THOMAS G.
[Pen.] Tom Smith; [b.] April 9, 1930, Phoenix, AZ; [p.] Samuel J. Smith, Nora Lucile Smith; [m.] Jimmie Jean Watson (Smith), January 11, 1956; [ch.] Launi Jean, Stacy Lynn, Kelly Rene, Becky Denise; [ed.] B.S. Nautical Science, U.S. Merchant Marine Academy, Diploma, Engineering Science, U.S. Naval Post Graduate School, B.A. and M.A., Secondary Education, Arizona State University; [occ.] Retired 20 year Navy Pilot, 16 years H.S. Teacher, science math; [memb.] The Retired Officer's Association, Tailhook Association, Naval Aviation Museum Foundation, VFW; [hon.] Numerous military awards and decorations; [oth. writ.] Lt. Lee K. Fawcett, USN (Novel), Air Arizona (Novel), *Milk Run (short story), Not His War (short story), Ghost of Roger's Hall (short story), Ghost of Roger's Hall (short story), The fea (poem), These are Poems (volume of poetry), Published with agent at present time.; [a.] Phoeniz, AZ

SMITHHART, DIANNA
[b.] August 18, 1955, Ottumwa, IA; [p.] Robert & Patricia Marts; [m.] Scott Smithhard, February 2, 1974; [ch.] Dawn Louise, Jacob Scott; [ed.] Cardinal Community High School, Kirkwood Community College; [occ.] Medical Secretary, St. Luke's Hospital, Cedar Rapids, IA; [hon.] Dean's List; [a.] Williamsburg, IA

SNELL, MERRILL W.
[b.] November 12, 1916, Gretna, NE; [p.] Geroge W. and Gertrude C. Snell; [m.] Alma J. Snell, June 1, 1940; [ch.] one daugheter, Carol; [ed.] Elementary, High School, Pacific Coast Banking School Grad. (Univ. Of Washington), various accounting and tax college courses.; [occ.] Retired from banking; [memb.] Fallbrook, CA Masonic Lodge, AL Bahr Shrine Club-San Diego, CA Eastern Star, Fallbrook, CA (Treas), Boots and Slippers Square Dance, Fallbrook, Avacado Pairs Dance Club Fallbrook; [hon.] No literary awards, have only recently written poems.;

[oth. writ.] A poem entitled "Body Supplements and The Price of Temptation" was published in "The California" on 11/30/93. It concerns (discourages use of narcotics and dope by today's youth (Etal); [pers.] In any composition, I try to point out the good, or evil and hope that shedding some light on a subject will eventually contribute to remedy or improvement.; [a.] Temecula, CA

SNOW, SHANNON
[b.] July 4, 1979, Southfield, Michigan; [p.] Lex and Sandra Snow; [ed.] I am now a Freshman at Clarkston High School in Clarkson, Michigan; [memb.] I am a member of ISIA, (Ice Skating Institute of America); [hon.] I won an essay writing contest, and got to be in a Michigan Parade; [a.] Clarkston, MI

SNOWDEN, VIRGINIA
[Pen.] Midnight; [b.] November 23, 1993, Orange Memorial Hospital; [p.] Cathy Bryant; [ed.] 9th grade Clifford J. Scott; [occ.] student; [memb.] Writers Collective Club; [oth. writ.] More poems, plays, short stories and novels, movie scripts (non every sdd); [pers.] Love is life, life is love. So take the time out to love for long life; [a.] East Orange, NJ

SNYDER (JR.), JOHN
[b.] November 21, 1959, Fort Lauderdale, FL; [p.] John Snyder and Sarah Snyder; [ch.] John Snyder, III; [ed.] Behavioral Science Major, Bachelor of Arts, National Univ San Diego, CA; [memb.] Unity North Church, Marietta, GA; National Head Injury Assoc; [hon.] Leadership Award, National Univ, San Diego, CA 1991. US Navy Drug/Alcohol Counselor of the Year; [oth. writ.] Collective Book of poems: "Poetic Awakening"; [pers.] I am ever so grateful to be aware that we are all equal; connected in spirit; [a.] Walesta, GA

SNYDER, CHRISTIE
[Pen.] Dreamulea; [b.] December 13, 1974, Warren, PA; [p.] James Snyder, Cheryl Hegerty; [ed.] West Allegheny High School; [oth. writ.] Poems published in other anthologies and short story published in national magazine; [pers.] Seek, within yourself, the harmonic balance of nature and spirit; [a.] Portersville, PA

SO, GERALD
[Pen.] Just So; [b.] October 5, 1974, Philippines; [p.] Henry B. So and Flora Te So; [ed.] St. Mary's High School, Hofstra University; [occ.] Student; [hon.] Four - Year High School Award for Excellence in English, Hofstra University Dean's List; [oth. writ.] Several unpublished poems and short stories; [pers.] Ever day I try to find myself and to be who I am.; [a.] Old Westbury, NY

SOMBRA, GLAUCIO
[Pen.] Henrick Sombra; [b.] August 4, 1962, Fort Meza; [p.] Antonio Sombra, Odalea Sombra; [m.] Marta Sombra, October 15, 1993; [ch.] Elisa Sombra; [ed.] Until the fifth year of faculty of medicine; [occ.] Writer; [oth. writ.] "Cranium", "The Curse of the Moth" not yet published. Note: All the above mentioned are science fiction books, and mystery books; [pers.] "Only some are uncommon, but only one is the king, in love and everything"; [a.] Fortaleza, Brazil

SOMMERFELD, MANDY L.
[b.] November 12, 1975, Columbia, MO; [p.] Dennis M. and Connie L. Holder; [ed.] Maple Grove Elem, Cedar Hill Middle, and Moberly Senior High; [occ.] Student; [memb.] DECA, VICA, POSSE, Drama Club, FHA, and PETA; [hon.] Perfect attendance awards, one short story award; [oth. writ.] Several unpublished short stories and poems; [pers.] I feel my poetry reflects what I am feeling inside on things that are taking place in my life. My parents and friends have given me inspiration to do my best work; [a.]

ittmer, MO

SONGER, SHELLY C.
.] April 7, 1951, Illinois; [m.] divorced; [ch.] almon Anthony Songer, Brooke Allyn Songer; [ed.] Gateway Community College; Community College f Southern Nevada; [occ.] Senior Zoning Specialist Clark Co; [hon.] Leadership Forum of Clark County; oth. writ.] Various poetic works. Also Photographic shows; [pers.] I want to make people think, feel, and look into themselves. I want people to understand their prejudices rather right or wrong and to be themselves; [a.] Las Vegas, NV

SONNIER (JR), JEAN A.
Pen.] Jeannie or Jas; [b.] March 8, 1976, LA, CA; p.] Wilbert Sonnier, Jean Sonnier; [ed.] St Bernard high school in Playa del Rey, CA; [hon.] One of my poems was submitted and published in my high school's literary arts magazine; [pers.] I have written several poems and plan to enter them in more contest; [pers.] When I write poems it's not my imagination written on paper, it is what I have experienced. Hopefully, I'll start writing of happier things; [a.] Inglewood, CA

SOPER, MICHAEL S.
[b.] June 7, 1926, London, Exmid Chiswick; [p.] both deceased; [m.] Eileen Soper, January 20, 1951; [ch.] Two sons married, daughter single; [ed.] College education plus agriculture college for NDA; [occ.] Retired; [oth. writ.] Writings of about 250 poems. 5 children's books ages 4-16 yrs not published. 3 ballads song writing, one musical show plus 4 others for church; [pers.] Father head master and Vicar. Lifetime gardener. Two poems written. Dedication to the below previous head gardner for Sir Henry Moore (sculptor). Work read in local shcools I admire works of Lord Tennyson and all childrens books of poems; [a.] Much Hadham Herts, England

SORRENTINO, SARAH
[Pen.] Daisy; [b.] April 29, 1980, IL; [p.] Paul and Mary Sorrentino; [oth. writ.] I have written many poems, none published; [pers.] In my poems I show my love for my family, friends and home; [a.] Naperville, IL

SOTIS, ANDREA
[b.] January 10, 1978, Los Angeles; [p.] Tomaline Guerrero and Cliff Sotis; [ed.] Mary Star of the Sea H.S.; [occ.] Student, Jr; [hon.] CFS, NHS; [oth. writ.] "My Best Friend" in National Library of Poetry's, "Whispers in the Wind"; [a.] Wilimington, CA

SOWELL, APRIL MARI
[b.] April 8, 1980, Murray, KY; [p.] Mark Duane and Rita Faye Sowell; Sister: Angela Faye Sowell, Brother - Joshua Brent Sowell; [ed.] 8th grade - Springville School; [occ.] 8th grade; [memb.] National Junior Beta Club - Drug Free Club; [hon.] 1st place Academic Fair Language Arts Division, 2nd place Academic Fair Language Arts Division; [oth. writ.] Many unpublished poems - few short stories; [pers.] I want to make my family and me proud; and to show others you don't have to have lots of money to succeed; [a.] Springville, TN

SPALDING, TREVOR GORDON
[b.] October 31, 1961, Calgary, Alberta; [p.] Charles and Marilyn Spalding; [m.] Catherine Spalding; [ch.] Tanner and Miranda; [pers.] Lord if I have but one life to live, let it be filled with the love and laughter of family and friends; [a.] Calgary, Alberta

SPECHLER, DIANA
[b.] June 15, 1979, Boston, MA; [p.] Stuart and Cindy Spechler; [ed.] I am currently a freshman at Newton North High School in Newton, MA; [pers.] "Two roads diverged in a wood, and I -- I took the one less

traveled by, And that has made all the differenct". -- Robert Frost; [a.] Newton, MA

SPECK, PAT
[Pen.] Patsy Calfee Speck; [b.] May 5, 1938, Harlingen, TX; [p.] Buddie Ann Speckj Tucek; [ed.] High School graduate, 1 year college, Pan American, Edingburg, TX, Art History Course, Florence Italy 1985, Art History Course, Paris France, numerous writing courses.; [occ.] Rancher, Artist and Free Lance Writer (Published); [memb.] Texas Folklore Society Cowby Symposium, Speaker and member, member of permanent donor. "South Western Writer's Collection" Southwest Texas, University, San Marcos, TX, Albert B. Alkek Library; [oth. writ.] Collection of Fiction, Short Stories, two volumes of Poetry, one fiction novel work in progress, several essays, non fiction, ranch accounts.; [pers.] Like all of us I am an eternal traveler on the road of purpose and understanding, I am "The Ouest".

SPELMAN, TIMOTHY LEE
[b.] November 28, 1962, Concord, NH; [p.] Howard and Delmae; [ch.] Timothy Jr (Aug 10, 1992); [ed.] High school grad w/2 yrs college business mngt; [occ.] Station mngr Mobil Gas Station; [hon.] Eagle Scout Boy Scouts of America; [oth. writ.] Unpublished Journal of short stories and poem entitled "Through Silent Words"; [pers.] Situations that reflect our past experiences help us to gain knowledge and wisdom in dealing with the future; [a.] Scottsdale, AZ

SPENCER, CAROLYN
[b.] Chandler, Minnesota; [m.] James Spencer; [ch.] Mark and Jay; [ed.] High School, Chandler, MN. State College, Mankato, MN. University of California at Los Angeles, CA; [occ.] Retired from 30 yrs. of teaching; [pers.] My inspiration comes from the Bible. I believe that love is perfect and eternal. I believe in honesty, truth, faith and hope, but if one has love, nothing more is needed. I Corinthians, 13; [a.] Rosemead, CA

SPENCER, ETHEL E.
[b.] April 9, 1939, Holtville, NB; [p.] Fred and Thelma Fowler; [m.] Terrance Spencer, November 15, 1958; [ch.] (2) 29 yrs son - Timothy O'Neil, and 21 yrs daughter - Heidi Taryn Elaine; [ed.] Graduate Upper Miramichi Regional High School, Boistown, NB, Boistown is the Geographical Center of New Brunswick, Canada; [occ.] Secretary; [memb.] United Church Women's Group and Women's Inst Group and Choir Member and belonged to oil painting class as a hobby (first time at this) but class no longer being held; [oth. writ.] First time I have ever submitted a poem. I have composed a poem or verse for co-workers who were retiring, leaving, birthdays, etc, but this is a first for me; [pers.] I am the 7th child in a family of 14, 12 of whom are still living. My father was a guide on the Beautiful Miramichi River, as well as a lumberman, working in the woods for a living. He is the only fishing guide from this area to have had a song made up about him and it is very popular in concerts and on our radio. It is entitled, "Big Fred Fowler the Guidin' Man". It is sung by Mavid O'Donnel, a well-known local country singing artists from our area. My Dad is 84 yrs old and still enjoying life. I could be just relaxing or driving along - maybe see a beautiful blue sky -birds butterflys, deer, and words seem to come to me and I wonder "does anyone else see this beauty" and really take the time to really appreciate it and I put the words to poetry; [a.] Boistown, NB, Canada

SPIESS, ERIN
[b.] December 1, 1981, Wauseon, OH; [p.] Jerry & Vickie Spiess; [occ.] 6th grade student; [memb.] band, basketball, piano playing; [hon.] Honor oll; [oth. writ.] God's Child; [a.] Liberty Center, OH

SPOTO, CAROLYN
[b.] December 10, 1957, Tampa, FL; [ch.] 1 daughter; [ed.] Hillsborough High Tampa FL, graduated 12th grade June 1976; [oth. writ.] In high school english poetry classes, wrote poetry and stories, since I draw, I drew pictures to go with the stories; [pers.] In my poetry writing, I want people to see where I am coming from, what I went through, so maybe, hopefully, I never have to suffer again; [a.] Tampa, FL

STAFFORD, DEBRA
[b.] April 19, 1951, Bremerton, WA; [p.] Mary Ward and Charles Ward; [ch.] Melisa Ward, Shawn Stafford and Nathan Ward; [ed.] High School graduate; [occ.] Janitor for Lamb Grays Harbor Co, Hoquiam, WA; [pers.] My claim to fame are my children. They have excelled far beyond what I accomplished in school. I feel the children are so very important, they are out future. I try to touch lives in a positive way; [a.] Aberdeen, WA

STAKER, JOE J.
[Pen.] The Old Scribbler; [b.] March 29, 1916, Beaver, OK; [m.] Kathryn Staker, January 1, 1939; [ch.] Marlene Kay Staker Mitchell and Thomas Joe Staker; [occ.] Retired; [memb.] york Rite, Masonic Lodge Blue, Chapter, Council & Commandery Methodist; [hon.] World War 2 Veteran Service, Intelligence & Reconnaissance, South West Pacific Theatre; [oth. writ.] Children's Story's, short story's and poetry (poem) Escape route, Editor's Choice Award, National Library of Poetry, The Coming of Dawn.; [pers.] I feel my writing reflects the experiences of the seventy eight year old common man, Who is in step with our World, Regardless of our many mistakes; [a.] Liberal, KS

STAMATIOU, KIKI
[b.] July 4, 1969, Kalamazoo, MI; [p.] Odyssey and Toula Stamatiou; [ed.] Mattawan High School, Diploma conferred 1988, KVCC, Associate of Arts Degree conferred 1990, Western Mich. Univ., Bachelor of Arts Degree conferred 1992.; [occ.] Writer; [memb.] Songwriters Club of America; [hon.] High School Honor Rioll 1986-87, Cert. of Award for Excellence in Ed. from Greek Annunciation Orthodox Church 1987-88 from State of MI. 1988, Dean's list at KVEE 1990, a finalist in Chesterfield Film Company, Playwriting Comp.; [oth. writ.] Poem was made into a music record on Tin Pan Alley Label 1989, lyrics were published in Profiles in Music Award pub.1989 edition.; [pers.] "Hollering doesn't solve problems, talking does; [a.] Kalamazoo, MI

STAMATIS, STEVEN P.
[b.] February 4, 1938, Greece; [p.] Deceased; [m.] Betty Stamatis, November 22, 1964; [ch.] two sons age 24 and 26, Jason and Perrin; [ed.] Attended Holy Cross Seminary, Univ. of Illinois (Urbana): B.A. 63', DePaul University (Chgo.): M.A. 67'; [occ.] managing printing and publishing company; [memb.] Poetry judge, youth committee annual diocesan Midwest Ovatorical and Arts Festival, Orthodox Christian Laity, Mt. Athos Group.; [oth. writ.] Published poems in local and regional religous journals, essay and a short story; [pers.] As I'm growing more aware, I'm no longer saddened by my inability to change things.; [a.] Addison, IL

STANFORD, PEARL L.
[Pen.] Pearls; [b.] September 10, 1925, Pullman, Washington; [p.] Alfie & Lou Cane; [m.] Richard Stanford, December 11, 1977; [ch.] Three living, Three deceased; [ed.] Graduated High School 1944, Pullman, WN; [occ.] Retired; [memb.] United Methodist, DAV, AARP; [hon.] I wrote poems for my High School paper. Read a few over radio in Ho's in Pullman. Got Honorable Mention in some contests lately; [oth. writ.] High Desert Country, Dieters Delimma, Grandmother "EM"; [pers.] I prefer to

write about things ! have experienced, or people I know. About country and weather and old times long ago.; [a.] Payette, ID

STANS, ROSARIA
[Pen.] Sarina Sue Stans; [b.] April 26, 1915, NY, NY; [p.] Mary and John Lociano; [m.] Louis Stans, July 17, 1944; [ch.] Maria Bernadette Hunt, Louis John Stans; [ed.] High School and Business School; [occ.] Retired; [hon.] World of Poetry (Edie Lou Cole); [oth. writ.] To Comfort You, Outcast, My Prayer, In Gratitude, Discretion; [pers.] My seventh grade english teacher told me to continue to write "For", she said, "you have talent and you'll reach your goal" so I did, I kept writing.

STANTON, ROBERTS
[Pen.] Stan; [b.] March 1, 1959, Guyana; [p.] Samuel & Stella Roberts; [m.] Rosamund Hughes-Roberts, May 24, 1986;; [ed.] St. Aloysius Roman Catholic School, Berbice Educational Institute, New Amsterdam Technical Institute; [occ.] Operator, Ford Motor Company, Dagenham, Essex; [oth. writ.] Various poems written for organizaitons and individuals to their request and approved satisfaction. I'm now seeking publicaiton of over 180 unique poems; [pers.] Within each of us, there's an ability to love. If we strive to master the art of loving ourselves and fellow human beings, we'll find the fulfilling magic there is in true love. My writing is to aid such human growth.; [a.] London England

STARK, JOHN LACASELL
[b.] January 31, 1957, LA, CA; [p.] Mary Lacasella and Russell Stark; [m.] Maria Torres Stark, March 94; [ed.] BA Univ of Utah, Salt Lake City, UT; [occ.] Insurance Agent Automobile Club of CA; [oth. writ.] Various poems and writings unpublished; [pers.] I write from the heart. I believe that 'Love' is our quest in life. I hope that the people I meet in life are touched by the love I give in both my walk with God and my writings. This poem is dedicated to my grandparents: Bea and Nick Lacasella and inspired by my wife, Maria; [a.] Malibu, CA

STEENBRGEN, HEIDI
[b.] November 22, 1979, St Cath, Ont, Canada; [p.] John and Lynne Steenberg; Sister - Candis, Brother - James; [ed.] Pope John Paul II Elementary School, St Joseph's High School. Grade 9; [occ.] Honours Student; Interests: Drawing, singing, writing poetry, guitar, reading; [hon.] Wrote poem for grade 8 graduation ceremony, received the grade 8 music award; [pers.] Poetry is, to me, what a diary may be for another. I can express thoughts and emotions without boundaries or recrimination; [a.] Stroud, Ontario, Canada

STEINER, ARIAN L.
[b.] September 28, 1983, Porth Austrailia; [p.] Peter & Arlene; [ed.] 4th grade; [occ.] Student, Markham School, Mt. Lebanon, PA; [hon.] Black Belt, Tang Soo Do Karate, "Shark", Red Cross Swimming; [oth. writ.] Poem "Roses" published in Markham School.; [pers.] The poet who has influenced me the most is Jack Prelutsky.; [a.] Mt. Lebanon, PA

STEIRER, MARY ANN WAGNER
[Pen.] "Bo" (as a nickname) given by "Harry"; [b.] July 30, 1928, East Hampton, MA; [ch.] Ron, Pat, Larry; [ed.] Graduate of the Springfield Tech Inst, Springfield Mass in Nursing State Board Exams in Boston, MA; [occ.] Retired from the Nursing Profession; [memb.] American Nursing Assn; [hon.] Who's Who in Poetry from World of Poetry in 1979 and Poetry Hall of Fame Tampa, FL 1979. Presidential Sports Award from President Bill Clinton for fitness walking and Gov Lawton Chiles cert of completion excercise walking 450 miles - equivalent to the State of FL; [oth. writ.] Have 38 poems published in

various anthologies. Has written in the medical newsletter and local newspaper; [pers.] I get an inspiration to write when I walk because I'm so close to nature then. Also ideas come to me when I play the organ. My poems express a message at times that I have experienced myself. When I see the beauty of nature; brings me close to God. And I see God's fingerprints all around me; [a.] Port Richey, FL

STEPHEN, ABEL JESWILL
[b.] January 10, 1970, Perambur, India; [p.] Albert & Sukumari Stephen; [m.] Penelope Rani Stephen; [ed.] Stuyvesant H.S., Brooklyn College (B.S. Biology); [occ.] Medical Technologist; [pers.] The best book to read is the Bible.; [a.] Brooklyn, NY

STEVENS, NICHOLE
[b.] March 26, 1977, Indpls, IN; [p.] William Stevens & Maria Stevens; [ed.] Lawrence Central High School; [occ.] Actress; [memb.] LC Drama Club, Sound Connection Mixed Showchoir; [hon.] Two 1st place medals in ISMA competition (vocal). 2nd place in Shakespear competition; [oth. writ.] Over 30 examples of poetry and free writing, the beginnings of a novel and a play.; [pers.] I thrive on finding the beauty of life. We should always be free to think and dream and feel. One must dream of the impossible, then accomplish it. I dream of the mideval day, then I bring it to life with my words.; [a.] Indianapolis, IN

STEWARD, DANNY RENAY
[Pen.] TVP; [b.] June 3, 1972, Denmark, SC; [p.] John and Dora Steward; [ed.] Denmark - Olar High. Various Naval Tech Schools; [occ.] Gunner's Mate (missle), US Navy; [memb.] Henry Ford Baptist Church; [hon.] Letter of Appreciation, National Defense; [oth. writ.] None published; [pers.] To see the future you must learn and treasure the past, be true of heart with a strong mind and a will of steel, the world can be conquered; [a.] Denmark, SC

STEWART, BRIAN
[b.] December 27, 1976, Windsor, Ontario; [p.] Larry and Judy Stewart; [ed.] Am currently in Gr 12 at Riverside Secondary; [memb.] Member of the Canadian Chess Federation. Have been in the scouting movement for 9 yrs. Parkview Public School; [hon.] Top Academic Award - Grade School - 1990, Chief Scout Award of Canada High School Honor Roll; [oth. writ.] Worlds within a world, Those who fight the rain, Winter Magic; [pers.] We must tread carefully through the unknown waters of our future, especially when in a society where morality and sensibilty are becoming less and less the norm; [a.] Windsor, Ontario, Canada

STEWART, KEITH R.
[b.] October 11, 1970, Fontana, CA; [p.] Martha N. Stewart, Kenneth R. Stewart; [ed.] I have an A.A. from Chaffey College and I am a Senior at California State Polytechnic University, Pomona, majoring in International Business.; [occ.] I am a part-time supervisor for United Parcel Service; [memb.] Upland City Council, Integrated Waste Advisory Committee; [pers.] I am intrigued by the nation that ideas, especially in the form of books, have the power to transcend timne. This book is a form of obscure immortality.; [a.] Upland, CA

STEWART, WILLIAM WATSON
[b.] May 11, 1970, Athens, GA; [p.] William Caldwell & Caliope Stewart; [ed.] Messiah College; [occ.] Travel entrepreneur student; [pers.] We can fill a universe with all the lost thoughts of a lifetime. Bind those thoughts in manuscript and they can fill the world with emotion.; [a.] Fayetteville, PA

STEWART-ROBERS, VALETTA R.
[Pen.] Su Rae Valett; [b.] April 30, 1962, Peru, IN; [p.] Ira E. Stewart and Rosetta N. Stewart-Cox; [ch.]

Chevas La'Mar and Shamir Kantrell; [ed.] Close HS OKC, OK; Central TX College, Killeen, T. Stroudsburg Allentown School of Cosmetology; [occ Cosmetology Teacher and Beauty Manufacture Representative; [oth. writ.] When Death Comes To Point; I Remember; a few poems published in fir world news of Allentown, PA; [pers.] I believe th what one cannot say by speaking, one must show b doing or express in writing; [a.] Allentown, PA

STIEBER, MICHAEL J.
[b.] June 24, 1959, Buffalo, NY; [p.] Helmut D. an Loni Stieber; [m.] Linda L. Stieber, November 2C 1993; [ch.] John Thomas Ronco; [ed.] Bishop Timo High, Canisius College, Suny at Buffalo; [occ. Budget/Management Analyst City of Orlando; [hon Beta Gamma Sigma National Business Honor Societ Dean's List; [pers.] Although I can't write music, enjoy writing lyrics for country songs. My influence are my own experiences along with those others; [a. Orlando, FL

STINSON, JACQUELINE
[Pen.] Jackie Stinson; [b.] February 24, 1928, Ster ling, IN; [p.] Rose, Czor Hershberger; [m.] Harold E Stinson, July 26, 1946 (47 yrs.); [ch.] son Jeff daughter Mary Jennifer, two grandchildren; [ed. Franklin High and B.S. in Elem. Educ. at Franklin College, Franklin, Indiana; [occ.] Retired, Church Volunteers, Teaching, choir, poetry; [memb.] Presbyterian Church USA, Children's Home Society, The Order of The Eastern Star, AWA, Alpha Delta Zeta Sorority; [hon.] Who's Who in Americ. Colleges and Univ., Alpha, Magna Cume Laude from Franklin College 56', PTS Service Award, In Poetry: 90, 91, 92 Golden Poet, Ruby Poet, 3 Anthologies 1990-1993, 2 HS Queens, Yell Leader 5 yrs.; [oth. writ.] Have over 1050 poems, Desert Storm: In the US Pentaton Count Your Blessings, Only God Knows, O' Giver of Life. Lyrics for church Easter Anthem and a cantata, a Christmas Carol, and Benediction my work has been used in newspapers, "Care Centers" pened for Life Care Centers, Inc. Desert Storm in the U.S. Pentagon; [oth. writ.] My writings are outgrowths of reflection, bible teaching and study! Also do some social and seasonal ones. Since 7 yrs. I was orphaned but God became, my Father and I've longed to lift others and point their eyes upward to the source of all love, hope, joy and peace. Basically want to comfort and help others help selves.

STOCKDILL, JEFFREY J.
[Pen.] Jeskin Dodd; [b.] August 10, 1970, MI; [p.] Ronald & Marlene Stockdill; [ed.] Horizon High School, Arizona State University; [pers.] Don't be afraid to change, lest you become afraid to live.; [a.] Scottsdale, AZ

STOCKS, PAUL
[b.] January 14, 1950, Manchester, US; [p.] Joseph Stocks, Sheila Stocks; [m.] Janet Elizabeth; [ch.] Son - Lanjul Kalan; [memb.] Poetry Now, Peterborough, Cambridgeshire; [hon.] City and guilds of London Inst, Hotel and Catering, Health, Safety and Hygiene; [oth. writ.] Previous works published in five anthology books; [pers.] I breathe life's happenings and truly write the experiences; [a.] Peterborough, Cambridgeshire, UK

STOKNER, NATALIE SUSAN
[b.] July 16, 1971, Montreal, Quebec; [p.] Norma Roberts (mother), Stefan Stokner (father), Kenneth Roberts (step-father); [ed.] Graduated from High School in Quebec in 1988, moved to nOva Scotia, did a year of school and graduated from the certified nursing assistant program in 1993.; [occ.] I am a certified nursing assistant.; [memb.] I am a member of the certified nursing assistant, Association of Nova Scotia.; [hon.] In 1990 I received the Dr. Gordon Thomas award in cretive writing and excellence in

rama Award and also in 1990 I recieved an award for
~rst in Law Class and 1st runner up in Miss Friendship
~ward in the Eastern Nova Scotia Exhibition.; [oth.
rit.] I have a personal scrap book of over 30 other
~oems I have written, including my high school
~raduation poem which was published in my year-
~ook and also a poem written for my nursing instruc-
~rs.; [pers.] I enjoy reading poetry and experiencing
, I like all poetry, but as for myself I don't specifi-
~lly set out to write a poem I just write what comes
~om my heart.; [a.] Halifax, Nova Scotia

~TONE, CHARLENE LEE
~b.] May 7, 1935, Dunkirk, NY; [p.] Clark Lee
~hafer and Velma Matie Shafer; [ch.] Ted Stone, Jr.,
~esse R. Stone, Sheri Bowman; [ed.] Dunkirk High
~chool, Dunkirk, NY and Temple Union High School,
~empe, AZ; [occ.] Care Companion; [pers.] Writing
~s an emotional fulfillment for me. Its the voice of
~nspoken thoughts and feelings abounding in every-
~ay life.; [a.] Prescot, AZ

~TONE, LISA DANIELLE
~b.] October 18, 1976, Morgantown, WV; [p.] Mike
~tone & Thelma Stone; [pers.] In memory of "Scott"
~lease watch over me near and far darling, you are my
~shooting star.; [a.] Morgantown, WV

~TONE, SANDRA WALLRAVEN
~b.] June 17, 1939 Springer, OK; [p.] Homer Elps
Wallrave, Hortense Culpepper Wallraven; [m.] Leo
Aldon Stone (2nd hus), June 21, 1962; [ch.] Lisa
Sherilyn Talley, Roland Aldon Stone, Tony Ray
Willson, Danny Lee Stone; [ed.] Lee Elementary
School - Okla City, Capitol Hill High School - Okla
~City, Amarillo (Texas) College; [occ.] Housewife
and curatorial volunteer - Reno County Museum;
[memb.] Democratic Party Reno County Historical
Society (Kans); [hon.] Golden Poet - 1990, 1991,
1992. Honorable Mention - World of Poetry 4 poems
(5 certificates, one made it twice), Editor's Choice
Award - National Library of Poetry; [oth. writ.]
"Dear Washington, DC", Amarillo Advocate, 1972.
"Through the Past Via Postcards" Reno County
Historical Society "Legacy". Poems in "Poems That
Will Forever", and "Whispers in the Wind". Columns
in newspaper supplement "Neighbors". (The
Hutchinson News). Also make books of poetry, short
stories of novels to give to family and friends; [pers.]
We are all part of the cosmos; our struggles, our
defeats and our victories serve a purpose. Because of
the diversity of life, none of us is exactly like another.
We should respect these differences and take joy in
them; [a.] Hutchinson, KS

STOUGH, RYAN ADLAI
[b.] March 12, 1971, Pasadena, CA; [p.] William and
Scarlett Stough; [ed.] St Clair High School, East
Central College, Univ of Missouri - Rolla (UMR). I
will graduate from UMR in May 1994; [occ.] Student
majoring in mechanical engineering at UMR; [memb.]
Pi Tau Sigma National Honorary Mechanical Engi-
neering Fraternity, American Society of Mechanical
Engineers; [oth. writ.] Previously unpublished; [pers.]
I prefer to write poetry that does not adhere to any
form or style. This allows me to concentrate on the
message or theme of the poem; [a.] Rolla, MO

STRICKHOUSER, MARY L.
[b.] August 8, 1963, Carlisle, PA; [p.] Mr. and Mrs.
Fred E. Strickhouser, Jr.; [ed.] Biglerville High
School, Biglerville, PA; [occ.] Pasteup/Bindery La-
bor at Herff Jone year books; [hon.] Won 1st place in
Adams county Pet-of-the year contest; [pers.] This
poem is dedicated to Tom Altemose, My inspiration
my friend. [a.] Gardner's, PA

STRICKLAND, DEBBIE
[b.] May 15, 1955, GA; [p.] Foster Home; [ch.] Jacob
Lee Strickland, 13 yrs. old; [ed.] High School; [occ.]

Disability; [oth. writ.] Just poems; [pers.] God condems
no one, why should I.; [a.] Maryville, LA

STRICKLAND, TINA M.
[b.] December 10, 1963, Decatur, IL; [p.] Charles
and Bernice Loury; [m.] Clifton Strickland, April 20,
1985; [ch.] Ashley and David; [ed.] AS in Biology;
currently pursuing BA in Psychology at DePaul Univ
Chicago; [occ.] Admin Asst - Kendall College;
[memb.] Carey Tercentenary AME Church; [pers.]
My foundation and beliefs are deeply rooted in God.

STRIDBORG, TRUDI G.
[b.] May 8, 1952, Oakland, CA; [p.] Dolores Friedrich,
Harold Stridborg; [ed.] AAS Hearing Impaired Ser-
vices (interpreting) Spokane Falls Community Col-
lege in Spokane, Washington; [occ.] Interpreter for
the deaf, part-time student; [memb.] Literary Volun-
teers of America, United Way, Friends of the Library,
VISTA (volunteers in service to America); [hon.]
College - President's honor roll, VISTA certificate of
appreciation; [oth. writ.] Many poems published in
local papers and newsletters; [pers.] Something won-
derful is always just around the corner; [a.] Plummer,
ID

STROCK, TAMMY
[b.] August 14, 1968, Cary Hill, PA; [p.] Bill and
Nancy Strock; [m.] John Strock, February 4, 1994;
[ed.] Cedar Cliff High. Will be attending Wilson
College in Fall 1994 for Veterinary Technology;
[hon.] Honorable discharge from US Navy in Nov
1993; [oth. writ.] Working on writing my first fantasy
novel, have written other poems, unpublished; [pers.]
I've loved to write since I was a child. This is my first
published writing and I am very excited. I hope to do
much more; [a.] Chambersburg, PA

STROUD, SONYA LOUISE
[b.] October 24, 1976, Fairfax, VA; [p.] Robert and
Kathleen Stroud; [ed.] Planning to attend OH State
Univ in the Fall of 1994; [occ.] Student; [a.] Sterling,
VA

SUDERS, JOSEPH A.
[Pen.] Josef Anthony; [b.] February 2, 1959, Altoona,
PA; [p.] Richard E. & Clementine T. Suders; [m.]
Young S. Suders, July 2, 1987; [ch.] Crystal L.,
Joseph A. Jr., Michael A., Aaron W., Hana L.
Suders; [ed.] High School Grad.; [occ.] U.S. Army;
[memb.] None; [hon.] None; [oth. writ.] Several
poems and songs written over the past 20 years. Most
were personal writings, some written and presented as
gifts. This is my first attempt at officially entering a
contest or publication.; [pers.] Most of my writings
are from personal experiences with various situations
in my life, (good and bad). I like blending nature and
love together to feel the results of my poetry. My
influence in Robert Frost.

SULLIVAN, MARY L.
[b.] April 11, 1954, Palm Springs; [ed.] BS - Cal Poly
Pomona, Teaching Credential English and LH, Mas-
ters LH at CSULA; [occ.] Special education teacher,
Washington Middle School, CA; [memb.] Pi Lambda
Theta, Alphas Psi Chapter; California Teacher's
Assn; The Council for Exception Children; [hon.]
CSULA grant, Mort Herz Memorial Scholarship,
Marian Wagstaff Scholarship; [oth. writ.] Poems
published in anthologies, Golden Poet Award World
of Poetry.

SUMMERLIN (JR.), CHAPLAIN JAMES C.
[b.] October 3, 1956, Homerville, GA; [p.] James C.
Summerlin Sr and Dr. Nanjo Dube; [m.] Sarah
Copeland Summerlin, January 5, 1991; [ch.] Previ-
ous marriage: Cynthia Ann Summerlin; [ed.] High
school grad; college grade, Seminary grad degrees;
BA Th.B; Appointment as Diplomate Counselor;
Doctor of Divinity; [occ.] Christian Clinical Coun-

selor; Chaplain; [memb.] International Assn of Chris-
tian Clinical Counselors; National Chaplains Assn;
American Evangelistic Assn Suffolk, VA, Ministerial
Assn, International Society of Poets - Life Member
and Advisory Panel Member; [hon.] Certified Lay
Speaker of United Methodist Church. Who's Who i
Poetry (World of Poetry); Golden Poet 89-92-93;
[pers.] Happy to have had poems published in The
Coming of Dawn, Tears of Fire, and The Space
Between; Who's Who in Poetry; [a.] Suffolk, VA

SUMMERS, SUSAN
[Pen.] Shoshannah Presson; [b.] August 8, 1952,
Portsmouth, VA; [m.] Donald Summers; [ch.] Shelly,
Stephanie, Susanna and Joshua; [ed.] Woodrow Wil-
son High, Central Virginia College; [occ.] Litigation
Paralegal, Edmunds and Williams Law Firm,
Lynchburg, VA; [pers.] I strive to reflect the love of
God for mankind in my writing. I have been greatly
influenced by "Him"; [a.] Rustburg VA

SWANSON, BONNIE L.
[b.] January 13, 1960, Des Moines, IA; [m.] Alan V.
Swanson; [ch.] Angela, Andrew; [ed.] High school,
Nebraska, currently taking writing courses in child
development. Have taken bookkeeping classes; [occ.]
Day Care Assistant; [memb.] St. John's Lutheran
Church S.S. teacher, Luther League Leader Board
Member, Prevention Child Abuse; [hon.] Poem pub-
lished "Coming of Dawn" wrote a commercial for
Prevention of Child Abuse.; [oth. writ.] Articles
published in local newspaper, poem published "Com-
ing of the Dawn," writings for Prevention of Child
Abuse (published). I write verses, for cards, local
businesses.; [a.] Madrid, IA

SWANSON, GLEEN A.
[b.] August 1, 1914, Cannon Falls, MI; [p.] Algot W.
& Esther J. Swanson, March 16, 1949; [ch.] Margaret
Doucette, Sharon Crowley, William K. Swanson;
[ed.] BBA University of Minnesota, American Insti-
tute of Banking; [occ.] Retired Small Bus. Adm.
Development Specialist, Previous Lobbyist for Inde-
pendent Bankers Assn.; [memb.] Delta Sigma Pi,
(Prof. Business Fraternity) Masonic Order, Lutheran
Church of the Redeemer, American Scandinavian
Assn., American Legion, Capital Cotillion Club.;
[hon.] Public Contact Awards (1972) Secretary of
Defense Commendation 1972, American Legion
Scholarship and Sportsmanship Award (H.S.); [oth.
writ.] Expression in poetic verse. Tell It To Tallahas-
see (1984).; [pers.] Enjoy reflections on nature and
man's humble efforts to succeed in evil society.; [a.]
Fairfax, VA

SWEARSON, CARL
[b.] July 28, 1951, Rugby, ND; [p.] William and
Agnes Swearson; [m.] Georgianna Dunlap Swearson,
July 1, 1982; [ch.] Ben (10), Helen (7), Joseph (5),
Daniel (4); [ed.] Towner High, North Dakota State
Univ, Unification Theological Seminary; [occ.] Mar-
keting Representative, John Hancock Financial Ser-
vices; [memb.] American Legion, American Free-
dom Coalition, Overland Historical Society, Alpha
Gamma Rho Fraternity, Missouri Family Network,
Pachyderms, Unification Church; [oth. writ.] This is
my first attempt at publishing; [pers.] This poem was
written as a tribut to my mother-in-law, Helen Dunlap,
a wonderful person and a dear friend. I miss her
deeply; [a.] Overland, MO

SWEENEY, LORI ANN
[b.] March 16, 1959, Long Island; [p.] Philip and
Mary Schneider; [m.] Lawrence Sweeney, Jr, July 6,
1992; [ch.] Traci Ann Brooks, Brandon Brooks; [ed.]
Copiague High Plaza Business Inst; [occ.] Writer;
[memb.] Middleburgh Little League; [hon.] Dean's
List 1985, President's List 1984; EMT Training
Volunteer, Training in Care for Servers, Red Cross
CPR Certified; [oth. writ.] Poem published in

Odessey's, also published in Treasured Poems of America; [pers.] Both my children are my inspiration. Without them giving me joy and heartache I wouldn't be able to write with emotion; [a.] Middleburgh, NY

SWIFT, CHAD
[b.] January 12, 1978, Dalton, GA; [p.] Steve Swift and Brenda Glenn; [occ.] Student at Dalton High School; [memb.] Young Life, Environmental Action Club, Junior Achievement, SSS; [pers.] Will you live your dreams or dream away your life?

SWIFT, LIZ
[b.] July 4, 1947, West Ridge, AR; [p.] Clyde and Viola Howard; [m.] Bert Swift; [ch.] Libby, Andy, Danny, grandchildren: Dennis and Gilbert; [ed.] 11 grade; [occ.] Resident manager for national church residences; [memb.] HEB Chamber of Commerce; [hon.] I have received 2 Editor's Choice Award for Goodbye My Love and You Could Have Heard a Pin Drop. 2 of my poems have been chosen to go on a musical cassette tape; [oth. writ.] You Could Have Heard a Pin Drop, Goodbye My Love, Where Would I Be, and Our Mother; [pers.] I would like to dedicate this poem to my husband Bert. I love to write poetry. It helps to relax me. And I want to thank God for giving me this wonderful gift and I would like to thank the National Library of Poetry; [a.] Bedford, TX

SWINEFORD, ELIZABETH
[Pen.] Elizabeth Benner Swineford; [b.] September 1, 1922, Lewistown; [p.] John and Elizabeth (Gruver) Benner; [m.] Roy T. Swineford (deceased 1990), September 21, 1940; [ch.] Eight (5 boys and 3 girls); [oth. writ.] Poem - "A Rose" (Is God's Creation), published in The Coming of Dawn, by the National Library of Poetry; [a.] Lewiston, PA

SZABO, JULIE
[b.] February 13, 1944, Ottawa, Ontario, Canada; [p.] Jules and Annie Banville; [ch.] Frank, Tom, Tammy and Wendy; Grandchildren: Leslie, Mathew and Nicole; [ed.] Basic training for skill development - Algonquin College; [oth. writ.] Booklet of poetry "Prelude to Ballad of a Clown" ISBN 0-9697237-0-9 published in 1993; [pers.] Give your best all the time. Love fully. Don't wait for a miracle. Make your own; [a.] Ottawa, Ontario, Canada

SZUCS, PATRICIA E.
[b.] october 30, 1946, Bridgeport, CT; [p.] Betty & William Nagy Sr. and Charles Szucs; [ch.] Shelly Desmarais; [ed.] BS Education, Southern Connecticut State College; [pers.] Title examiner; [memb.] I listed 3 parents, as my father is deceased and now I have a step-father. I wish for peace.

SZYMANSKI, SCOTTK F.P.
[Pen.] Francis Pete; [b.] January 28, 1972, Toledo; [p.] Robert & Margaret Symanski; [pers.] In order to walk in heaven, you must first step through hell.; [a.] Columbus, OH

TABACHNIKOFF, TANYA
[b.] December 12, 1964, New York; [p.] Robert and Anneke Tabachnikoff; [ed.] Graduated from the Pine View Program in 1982; holds a BA in History from Wellesley College; [occ.] Public Relations Director for Marlboro College, Marlboro, VT; [pers.] It is a great honor to be included in your anthology. Many thanks!; [a.] Brattleboro, VT

TAFOYA, KAREN
[b.] November 13, 1973, Delta, CO; [p.] Robert TaFoya, Barbara McHugh; [ed.] Paonia High School; [occ.] Laundry Aide at Bethesda Nursing Home; [oth. writ.] I write stories; [pers.] My favorite quotation is "Beauty Is A Witch, Against Whose Charms Faith Melteth Into Blood." Shakespear; [a.] Paonia, CO

TALLMAN, EVELYN T.
[b.] November 13, 1922, So Westevlo, NY; [p.] Hazel F. Mabie; [m.] (deceased) Raymond H. Tallman, January 23, 1940; [ch.] Ralph R. Tallman; [ed.] Greenville High School, National Baking School, Diversey, Parkway, Chicago, IL; [occ.] Retired cook and baker; [memb.] Social Service by Albany County Social Security Benefits; [hon.] Awarded by social security benefits; [oth. writ.] World of Poetry, Sacramento, CA

TALMI, GIL
[b.] December 15, 1968, Louisville, KY; [p.] Yoav Talmi & Erella Talmi; [ed.] B.A. Music Composition at UCLA (completing); [occ.] Composer, Music for Film; [memb.] Save the Children; [hon.] National Emmy Nomination, Best Music for News/Documentaries, CBS 1991, "A Year to Remember with Dan Rather," Awards from Israeli Ministry of Cultural Education (play) French Cultural Attache to Israel (play); [oth. writ.] "(P)age Numbers," "Daffodils, Petunis, Plutonium and more," (poetry) book.; [pers.] Life is not about having all the answers, it is about posing the right questions. Isn't it?; [a.] Los Angeles, CA

TASHJIAN, ISAAC
[Pen.] Nane; [b.] November 16, 1966, Beirut, Lebanon; [p.] Marie & Kevork Tashjian; [ed.] Glendale High, Glendale Community College, California State University, Northridge; [occ.] Undergraduate Mathematics Student; [memb.] California Community College Honor Scholarship Society; [hon.] Alpha Gamma Sigma, Dean's List; [pers.] Love Life, abhor hate, and adoring peace establish thy fate; [a.] Sunland, CA

TATEM, JENNIFER (BOWDEN)
[Pen.] Jennifer Bowden; [b.] May 26, 1953, NYE; [p.] Dearie Bowden Clarence Bowden; [m.] deceased, September 29, 1980; [ch.] 5 sons; [ed.] Attended Monroe College for Business 1990-91. Now attending the College of New Rochelle for Social Work; [hon.] A Certificate from Federal Emergency Management Agency for working with them for hurricane Hugo that hit the Virgin Islands; [oth. writ.] Created a commercial during a government election in the Virgin Islands in the early eighties which was aired; [pers.] Life is a gift, and each day I'm given another chance to become a better me; [a.] Bronx, NY

TATUM, MARGARET HAMILTON
[b.] September 10, 1914, Cleveland, TN; [p.] William Hamilton, Sallie Lawson Hamilton; [m.] Claude Britton Tatum, March 13, 1937; [ch.] Larry Tatum, Bernita Tatum Wells; [ed.] Elementary and high schools of Bradley County, TN; attended University of Chattanooga and University of Tennessee; [occ.] Retired owned ladies store for 27 years; [memb.] North Cleveland Baptist Church, Cleveland Womans Club, Cleveland Music Club, Bradley County Historical Society, AARP, Business and Professional Womens Club; [hon.] Placed in Who's Who in Sales and Marketing; song "Let Freedom Ring" approved by TN Gov Lamar Alexander as an official Homecoming '86 song for the state; [oth. writ.] Authored a family history book; have written numerous songs and poems; [pers.] I write about people - to encourage them to make a more useful life. Many of my songs and poems are of a patriotic or religious nature. Love is one of my favorite themes; [a.] Cleveland, TN

TAYLOR, CAROLE ANNE
[b.] May 23, 1964, Oakland; [p.] Larry and Betty Taylor; [ed.] Presentation Academy, Spalding College; [occ.] Krogers Louisville, KY; [memb.] St Francis of Rome Church, Honorary member of Leukemia Society; [hon.] Deans List. Will graduate Magna Cum Laude, Volunteer of the Year (St gudes jux); [oth. writ.] Heart Song, hopefully will get published. This is my 8th published poem; [pers.]

Don't forget the light within the world is dark but only act of goodness can destroy the dark; [a.] Louisville KY

TAYLOR, EARLE F.
[b.] May 24, 1914, Vermont - Deceased March 29 1994; [p.] Ethan and Sue E. Taylor; [m.] Mary E Taylor, June 1939; [ch.] John, Eleanor and Bett Ann; [ed.] B.A. and M.S. in Geology, U. of Iowa two years U. of Illinois, one year U. of Syracuse [occ.] President Taylor and Associates Inc.; [memb.] American Assoc. of Petroleum Geologists; Houston Geological Socity, American Institute Mining and Metellurgical Engineers.; [hon.] Legion of Honor (AIME), member Illinois Chapter Sima Xi; [oth. writ.] Geology and oil fields of Brazil (1952), Oi Development in Eastern S. America (1963), Early Exploration for Hydrocarbon in the N. American Arctic 1990, 50 years in the oil patch 1990.; [a.] Houston, TX

TAYLOR, FRANCEINE M.
[Pen.] Franceine - Michelle; [b.] November 14, 1963; Newark, NJ; [p.] Christine Taylor Hatten, Dennis Taylor; [ch.] Godchild: Taheerah Iman Superior Talbert; [ed.] Univ High Rutgers, the State Univ of New Jersey; [occ.] Certified Computer Data Entry and Typing Instructor, The Academy of Professional Development, Edison, NJ, Purchasing Expediter, Tops Appliance City Corporate Office, Edison, NJ; [pers.] As a writer, I write to express my thoughts, my fears, my happiness and my successes. I hope you, the reader, find peace in my writing. Knowing you have a friend somewhere. Someone who hears your cry, someone who knows your pain and someone who's on your side. Thank you for taking the time out to read my work...Peace; [a.] Piscataway, NJ

TAYLOR, GEORGE W.
[Pen.] Fonzo Merrian; [b.] September 6, 1935, Longview, TX; [p.] Buster & Thelma Taylor; [m.] Eleanor Menou Taylor, April 16, 1960; [ch.] Mark Wayne, Angila Marie, Julia Annette; [ed.] Acadia Baptist Academy, Eunice, Louisiana, Northwestern State College, Natchitoches, Louisiana; [occ.] Computer Services Sales; [hon.] Many sales and achievement awards; [oth. writ.] Many poems over the years, this is my first poem submitted or shared with those other than my spouse.; [pers.] I do not write on a scheduled basis, only when on an emotional high or low.; [a.] Houston, TX

TAYLOR, JEANA
[Pen.] J. Taylor; [b.] June 18, 1959, Chaffee, MO; [m.] David Taylor, June 2, 1990; [ed.] Chaffee High School; [occ.] Writer; [memb.] Coastal Writers Club of Florence Oregon; [hon.] American Legion Speech Award; [oth. writ.] Two children's books, The Forgotten Smile, The Unlikely Hero; [pers.] I am drawn to young adventurous, stories of imagination and nature at this stage of my career, although I plan to persue other styles of writing. Looking around the world I see many stories that deserve to be written; [a.] Mapleton, OR

TAYLOR, JESSIE
[b.] July 4, 1917, Wise Co, TX; [p.] John and Jannie Read; [m.] Clyde Terry Taylor, April 24, 1971; [ch.] Anita, Bobbie, Terry L., Sandra K. and Mike; [ed.] High school, graduate of Business College. Also Life Underwriters - graduate; several correspondence courses; [occ.] Retired from Kentuck Central Life Inso Co; [memb.] While working - American Business Assn Sec Treasury of American Heart Assn; International Society of Poets, also Tarrant County, TX Poetry Society - OES Baptist; [hon.] National Quality Award - several other insurance awards, several poetry merit awards; [pers.] I felt honored to receive the National Quality Award also the Merit Awards for Poetry; [a.] Avdo, TX

TAYLOR, MICHELE
».] August 28, 1978, Baycity, MI; [p.] Adolph, Betty Taylor; [ed.] Richardson Middle School - Oscoda Mich - 8th grade; [oth. writ.] "Walking Along, I Find Myself Lost", in the Bay City Times newspaper; pers.] If God turned out the light, everyone would be the same color; And that would make everything right!

TEAGARDIN, BARBARA LOUISE
b.] June 26, 1955, Denver, CO; [p.] William and Isabelle Brophy; [m.] Ralph D. Teagardin, Jr., August 20, 1988; [ch.] Angela Harper and Timothy Harper; [ed.] Centarus High School, Lewisville, CO; occ.] Homemaker, Owner and Designer of Barb's Craft's; [pers.] Creating things that make people happy is the joy of my life.

TEDESCO, SHARON
b.] June 25, 1963, Kentucky; [p.] Donald Canny, Josephine Canny; [m.] Gerald Tedesco, October 19, 1968; [ed.] Longwood High; [occ.] Purchasing Agent; [oth. writ.] I have a poem published in Poetic Voices of America (spring 1991); [pers.] I wrote this poem in memory of my mother-in-law, Florence Tedesco. A woman I respect and admire greatly, who lost her battle to lung cancer last year, but will stay in our hearts forever; [a.] North Patchogue, NY

TERRY, ROBERT DANIEL
[b.] September 28, 1949, Concord, MA; [p.] Barbara Rose, Thomas D; [ch.] Timothy Michael; [ed.] Weare High School, Weare, NH; [occ.] Surviving within the vertical shadows; [oth. writ.] "Angel In My Pillow", published by "Being" magazine an unpublished collection of poetry titled - "The Woodpile"; [pers.] Poetry is the blood coursing through the veins of the body of literature; [a.] Roan Mountain, TN

TESSENSOHN, LESA
[Pen.] Moriah McCall; [b.] February 24, 1957, Wiltshire, Eng.; [p.] Wm. McCallister, Delores Glasgow; [m.] James Tessensohn, March 1, 1975; [ch.] Mandy, Jeanna, Jessica; [ed.] Deland High, Daytona Beach Community College, Nursing Major; [occ.] Walidation/Calibration Technician; [memb.] Emmaus Lutheran Church; [hon.] Presidential acknowledgement for patriotic poem "keeper of the dream" as well as read on radio. Other poems printed in local newspaper; [oth. writ.] "The Lyric Dawn," "Borealis Bay" published 1993.; [pers.] I strive to create a picture to use words as an artist uses paint. The one great influence in my life has been and is my father. This is for him.; [a.] Deland, FL

TETRO, HAROLD M.
[b.] June 18, 1925, Hartford, CT; [p.] Harold M. and Frances L. Tetro; [m.] Rae Tetro, October 21, 1960; [ch.] Brenda and Sheila; [occ.] Retired; [memb.] VFW and Amer Legion, served in US Army from October 29, 1945 thru Feb 2, 1952 with service in Germany and Korea as Motor Sgt a Squad Leader, attained the rand of SFC; [hon.] Received award for Military Merit while serving in Korea for outstanding dedication to duty under close combat conditions; [oth. writ.] Other poetry such as The Rainbow of Love, Palm Beach, FL, Thanksgiving, The Bells, My Lonely Heart, A Peaceful World, Songs Toylin, The Perkinese and Island of Romance, all unpublished; [pers.] Enjoy writing poetry and songs as a hobby. Writing poetry and songs helps to release the inner tensions and feelings. Allowing a person to live 2 more peaceful life; [a.] Palm Beach Gardens, FL

THACKER, AGNES
[Pen.] AG; [b.] June 23, 1950, Brooklyn, NY; [p.] Vincent and Josephine Trama; [m.] James Thacker, September 24, 1992; [ch.] Rosanne Pepitone, Charles "Ragu" Pepitone (no longer with us, here); [ed.] High school, School of Cosmetology, Specialty License in

Nails and Skin; [occ.] Esthetician/Nail Technician; [oth. writ.] I have written many poems since the death (murder) of my son. I hope to publish them so I may reach someone in need as I was. All my work is dedicated to my beloved son "Ragu" (Charles Pepitone); [pers.] I would like to publish my other poems of inspiration that deal with the deep-seated emotions oe goes through when losing a child. To be able to reach the void that no one seems to understand but one who has been there; [a.] Stuart, FL

THIEL, SPENCER
[b.] February 15, 1979, Merriam, KS; [p.] Gret and Susan Thiel; [ed.] Presently a Freshman in High School; [memb.] Plays soccer and baseball; [hon.] First place in the county for essay on drug abuse. First place for poem written for Poetry Society of TX; [a.] Plano, TX

THOMAS, EMMA WORMLEY
[b.] April 20, 1920, Washington, DC; [p.] Luther and Wilhelmina Wormley (dec); [m.] George W. Thomas (deceased), November 17, 1948; [ch.] Karen T. Boyd, Barry W. Thomas; grandchildren: Jennifer and Christopher Thomas and Michael Boyd; [ed.] Dunbar High (DC); Miner Teachers College (DC) BS; Howard UMA; Catholic U (Adv. Studies, Romance Langs); [occ.] Retired teacher of English (DC) and Montgomery College (MD); [memb.] Woodridge Civic Assoc; Howard U. Alumni Assoc; UDC Alumni; Natl Council Teachers of English; DC Retired Teachers Assoc; American Assoc of Univ Women; NAACP; [hon.] Outstanding Teacher of Year - 1968, 1973 -- Research Club of DC; Listed in: Outstanding Secondary Educators of America, 1974; Outstanding Black Educators of America, 1973; Who's Who in American Education, 1989-90; [oth. writ.] Feature writer of: several articles for the old Washington Star; several articles for The Crisis; "The Burnt-Out Teacher Syndrome," The Washington Post, April 20, 1980; "On Teaching Shakespeare to High School Students," California Assoc Eng Journal, 1981; [pers.] I feel that every man in this vast world, wherever and whoever he may be, is my brother, and what affects him also affects me; [a.] Washington, DC

THOMAS, LONNIE E.
[b.] August 3, 1942, Philadelphia, PA; [p.] Mary Thomas and Lonnie b. Thomas; [m.] Mattie Thomas, December 31, 1963; [ch.] Gary Wayne, Sandra Dean and Joseph Bert; [ed.] Hillside High, Morris County College; [occ.] Security Supervisor; [memb.] Union Baptist Church Gospel Chorus, Senior Choir and Male Chorus; [hon.] Dean's List; [oth. writ.] Poems published in school and the National Library of Poetry; [pers.] I write to reflect my feelings about the world today and the way I think it should be. I am greatly influenced by God's word and his teachings.; [a.] Morristown, NJ

THOMAS, VALERIE M.
[Pen.] Val Larie; [b.] February 20, 1920, Philadelphia, PA; [p.] Deceased; [m.] Warren J. Thomas (Thomas), June 4, 1971; [ed.] St. Joseph's Academy - 1937, Plus two years Post (Commercial), both in Penna; [occ.] Housewife; [memb.] AARP, Sun Coast Hospital, Cosmetology Board of Education (graduated Aug 1980), Gulfport Cosmetology College, FL; [hon.] Diplomas for above.

THOMPSON, CLAUDIA
[b.] February 1, 1958, Urbana, IL; [p.] Frank and Eleanor Thompson, Deceased; [m.] Significant Other: Michael Ditz, 16 1/2 years together; [ed.] BA in History/ Women's Studies from Case Western Reserve University in Cleveland, Ohio; 1980; [occ.] Legal Assistant, Santa Monica, California Office of the city Attorney; [memb.] Amnesty International, Planned Parenthood, National Abortion Rights Action League; [hon.] Phi Beta Kappa, graduated from

college summa cum laude, Mortar Board; [oth. writ.] Currently working on a book of poems regarding my personal experience as an incest survivor.; [pers.] I have a deep commitment to women and women's issues, particulary toward battered women and incest survivors; [a.] Los Angeles, CA

THOMPSON, DAWN MARIE
[b.] November 15, 1976, Waverly; [p.] Charles and Carolyn; [ed.] Greene Elementary K-6, Greene Community High School 7-10, deceased July 4, 1993, car accident; [occ.] Enjoyed working at Whistle Stop Ice Cream Shop and Babysitting; [memb.] High School Band, Chorus, Valleyball, Basketball, Track, Softball, Golf, Little League, Girl Scouts, Teen Betterment; [hon.] Selected High School Princess of her class 9th and 10th grade, lettered, softball, track, chorus, band; [oth. writ.] First for High School Autobiography; [pers.] Dawn liked to make people smile. She showed other kids you could have fun by being a goofy who liked sports. By Carolyn Thompson; [a.] Greene, IO

THOMPSON, ELISABETH S.
[b.] November 29, 1960, Pryor, OK; [p.] Silas T. and Polly Suffridge; [m.] Eddie M. Thompson, July 24, 1979; [ch.] Tyrel Jacob; Whitney Elyse; [ed.] High school - Vinita High School; [occ.] Homemaker, seamstress; [hon.] Who's Who Among American High school Students 1978-1979; [oth. writ.] Numerous other unpublished poems; [pers.] I taker personal control of my life, with God being my master, instead of allowing life to control me and I accept personal responsibility for my life as it is, regardless of anyone else's influence; [a.] Vinita, OK

THOMPSON, SHIRLEY
[Pen.] Cheryl Crozier; [b.] Kelso, Scotland; [p.] Helen and George Linday Crozier; [m.] Alexander J. Thompson, March 30, 1954; [ch.] Lesley Helen, John Alexander Johnson; [ed.] Kelso High, Calmulloch College, Cumberland College; [memb.] International Society of Poets, writers formum and poetry now. Verse, poets and Peterloo Poetry Society. Member of the poetry society of Greatbritian.; [hon.] Honours Award in Music. Editors Choice Award, in North American Poetry Compeetition 1993; [oth. writ.] Poems published in local newspaper. Poems published in anthologies "Second time Single", "Break in the Clouds" and "An Invitation to Poetry" "People Like Us." Also wirte children's books and poetry; [pers.] Poetry is a way of expressing myself, searching and drawing on that reserve of knowledge and words. To be able to share with my fellowman. The pleasure and Joy that poetry can give and to strive for peace, through poetry. [a.] Cumbernauld, Scotland

THOMPSON, SONDRA L.
[b.] August 13, 1968, Panama City, FL; [p.] Karmel and Larry Kent; [m.] Clifford L. Thompson, November 7, 1992; [ed.] AA Degree, BA degree in Education (April 30, 1994); [p.] Prospective teacher; [memb.] Phi Theta Kappa (honors fraternity) 1st Baptist Church of Bagdad; [hon.] Numerous President's and Dean's List Awards (for high academic achievement), Outstanding Academic Achievement Award, graduated w/AA w/highest honors graduated w/BA magna cum laude; [pers.] "No matter how bad things are for me now, someone else is worse off than I". I think of this fact when my days are dark. It helps me to be grateful for all that I do have; [a.] Pace, FL

TISLER, DEBRA
[b.] September 14, 1958, Waynesboro, TN; [p.] Martha and Earl Luna; Mate: Dennis W. Eddy; [ch.] Casey Richard, Christopher David, Yahsha Na'Lyn; [ed.] Currently a student at mid-Michigan Community College (math major); [occ.] Math tutor and college math lab instructor; [memb.] Michigan Tutorial Assoc, Phi Theta Kappa National Honor Frater-

nity; [hon.] Phi Theta Kappa, High Honors List, Academic scholarships; [oth. writ.] Short stories, essays (not published); [pers.] Recognition supplies direction to future achievement; [a.] Beaverton, MI

TITEL, MYRTLE E.
[b.] December 21, 1914, Town of Sherman; [p.] (deceased) Mr and Mrs P. Haag; [m.] (deceased) Henry W. Titel, September 4, 1937; [ch.] 7; [ed.] 8th grade; [occ.] Retired; [memb.] Senior Citizens Sheboygan Historical Soc, Trinity Methodist Church Adell Homemakers, Lyndon Grange #713, Community Players, JMK Arts; [hon.] 2nd Prize Acrylic Painting - State Homemaker. Book from Grange for a written article (Long Ago); [pers.] My first attempt at composing a poem. It is fun. I work on it in my spare time or if I can't sleep at night. Many things about nature can be expressed in rhyme; [a.] Waldo, WI

TODD, VIRGINIA
[Pen.] "Petunia Flowers"; [b.] July 16, 1925, Toledo, OH; [p.] Charles and Thelma Janney; [m.] Forrest McMichael, June 19, 1945 (dec.), Now--C.D. Todd January 15, 1983; [ch.] Donald, David, Karen, grandchildren: Scott, Melanie, Joshua, Kelly, Darren; [ed.] Bachelor Degree in Ed. Master's Degree in Early Childhood.; [occ.] Retired Teacher taught in Ohio, Michigan and Texas; [memb.] Retired Teachers (taught 34 years), Women's Aglow, Flame Fellowship, Assembles of God; [hon.] 112 Ribbons in Painting (oil, watercolor, acrylic), art, painting, Salutorian in High School; [oth. writ.] A Bed of Roses, Oh If, Mighty Rushing Wind, written 24 Christian songs, 4 published so far. A poetry book "Poetry Time from My Heart A Line" containing 32 poems; [pers.] I express the feelings of my heart as I walk the pathway of life here on earth desiring to give GOD the talents He's given me to share with the world. [a.] Gainesville, TX

TOMOKANE, FRANCIA Q.
[Pen.] Franie; [b.] January 17, 1980, Saipan; [p.] Frank Tomokane, Anicia Tomakane; [ed.] Mount Carmel Elementary School, Marianas Baptist Academy; [occ.] Student; [hon.] Writing Comp, Energy Awareness Poster Aw (1st), Music, A - Honor Roll; [oth. writ.] I have wrote many but they were not published. One or two of our local newspapers have just offered to begin publishing my poems once weekly beginning, January 1994; [a.] Saipan, MP

TOOLSIE, RAMPERSAUD
[b.] July 8, 1930, Lancaster Cor Guyana; [p.] Toolsie, Sukhri Toolsie; [m.] Doris, April 22, 1951; [ch.] 3 boys, 2 girls; [ed.] Grade 8-9; [occ.] Retired; [oth. writ.] Musical notes and lyrics "Country and Town", a recording schedule to release April 6, 1994; [pers.] I am trying to promote peace thru straight talk; [a.] Thorold, Ontario, Canada

TORRES, SANTOS J.
[Pen.] Saints; [b.] November 1, 1929, East Chicago, IL; [p.] Aristeo and Telesfora Torres; [m.] Lupe torres, October 20, 1947; [ch.] Sylvia, Lupe, Santos, Jaime, Sam, Mark, Michael, Marsha; [ed.] High School; [occ.] Electric Shop Repairman; [memb.] S.W.A., Union Local #1011, Our Lady of Guadalupe Church; [hon.] Kathrine House Free Throw Contest, Babe Ruth Championship (Coach), Coached Catholic Youth Organization (CYO) Basketball Championships Gr. Sch/High School for Our Lady of Guadolupe Church, Baseball, Basketball, Coaching; [oth. writ.] none; [pers.] I strive to be myself within and hope that people will open up as I have. I feel people shut themselves up and don't really let their feelings out.; [a.] East Chicago, IN

TORUNO, JULIO CASTELLON
[Pen.] Julio Castellon; [b.] April 12, 1960, Leon, Nicaragua; [p.] Jose L. Castellon, Teresa Castellon, T; [m.] Gioconda Martinez C., December 17, 1983;

[ch.] Sandra Castellon, Julio Castellon; [ed.] Bachilor and Accounter; [occ.] Typewriter; [memb.] Baptist Church of Washington; [oth. writ.] Hispanic poem; [pers.] Usually or always God is present in all my poems, and my life; [a.] Washington, DC

TOWNLEY, DIANE L.
[Pen.] Diane Leigh; [b.] August 26, 1943, Detroit; [p.] Nettiec (Gaines) Jones, Brook O. Jones; [m.] Kenneth W. Townley, August 26, 1961; [ch.] Jane Lee, David Troy, Suzanne Elizabeth; [pers.] Inspiration: My mother, and the love my father had for her, demonstrated in poems he chose to read.; [a.] Grosse Il., MI

TOWSEND, L'RON
[Pen.] Phorel; [b.] July 12, 1943, Washington, DC; [p.] L.E. and Ona Mae Towsend; [ed.] Self-educated West Coast Trade BA, Century 21 real estate, Foot reflexology, med course; [occ.] Disabled, formerly sub-contractor; [memb.] Order of Dumalay Shirenner and Brotherhood of MAL; [oth. writ.] Pacha Publications, The Flower Jasmine, 1993; Earth Boy, 1993; Bless It Be The Father - 1993; Daily Payer - 1993; Light Rays - 1993; [pers.] I am what I am, not part of me here and not part of me their. I am somebody, with something to say; [a.] Los Angeles, CA

TRAFTON, ELLEN C.I.
[b.] December 24, 1950, Norwood, MA; [p.] Hazel & Walter Zacofsky; [m.] W. L. Trafton, October 14, 1978; [ch.] William Adams; [ed.] Thomas A. Edison High School (Alexandria, VA), Northern Virginia Community College (Annandale, VA); [occ.] Real Estate Investor, St. Crois, U.S. Virgin Islands; [oth. writ.] Autumn, Winter, Virginia (published: St. Croix Avis; USVI) Not yet published: A Quite Lake, Crucian Skies, St. Croix, We're Not Alone; [pers.] The inpiration for my poetry is based entirely on my own life experience. It is my wish that, through my writing, I can touch the hearts of many people and give them hope, understanding, and peace of mind.; [a.] Rancho Bernardo, CA

TRAMONTIN, AUNE
[b.] September 10, 1913, Minnesota; [m.] July 17, 1950; [ed.] Wrote poems for all who call and ask. Many poems published in our local paper; [occ.] Retired; [memb.] Womens Club, Lady Elks, Golden Agers; [hon.] Proficiency Medal in Nursing; [oth. writ.] Book published "Thoughts in Verse", copyright 1989; All monies went to "Bay Cliff" handicapped children; [pers.] Lived most of my life in Calgary, Alberta, Vancouver, BC. Volunteer work Mondays Americana - Nursing Home Volunteer work Wednesdays St Vincent de Paul - To help the needy; [a.] Iron Mountain, MI

TRAUM, MARY M.
[Pen.] Marie Traum; [b.] July 31, 1974, Cocoa Beach, FL; [p.] Herman & Margaret Trauman; [ed.] Merritt Island High, Brevard Community College; [occ.] Cashier at Wal-Mart, Merritt IS., FL; [memb.] Cape Canaveral Hospital Auxiliary; [hon.] Dean's List; [a.] Merritt Island, FL

TREANOR, JAMIE LYNN
[b.] September 18, 1966; St Catharines, Ontario; Children: Robert Craig Murray, Eric Burton; Occupation: Mother; [memb.] L.A. Br 17 Thorold; [oth. writ.] Currently composing a collection of short stories, poetry, and various literary works; [pers.] I believe that people are people and discrimination or prejudism in any degree is very wrong. In my writing I try to reflect a more favourable world for all mankind; Thank you to Joseph for your continued support; [a.] Fonthill, Ontario, Canada

TRENT, HENRY R.
[b.] January 11, 1916, Marietta, OK; [p.] Asa &

Ethel; [m.] Sally Lancaster, July 15, 1938; [ch.] Elain, Kathy; [ed.] 90 college literture hours, mostl literature all phases of English.; [occ.] Retired; [hon.] Past Official REA Express, Man of Year.; [pers.] have always loved poetry, no submissions for publ cation.; [a.] Weslaco, TX

TRIBBLE, AIYISHA NATYLIE
[Pen.] Ish & Little Tribble; [b.] April 11, 1983 Maryland; [p.] Dr. Israel Tribble Jr. and Velm Tribble; [ed.] 5th grade; [occ.] Student; [memb. Iowa City Public Library and Sweetarts 'n Kids Club [hon.] Poems accepted for publication in local pape young writers column, Iowa City Press-Citizen Apr 11, 1992; [oth. writ.] The Fact, Colors, the Big Race Sadness, Find Me, Hair; [pers.] I write my feeling through my poems. Writing makes me feel happy. [a.] Iowa City, IA

TRIMBLE, CAMISHA SHAUNTA
[b.] February 29, 1972, California; [p.] Vanessa Fluker; [ch.] one child, Keitryce Amisha Williams [ed.] Centennial High School, California State University, Long Beach; [occ.] Student; [memb.] New Haven C.O.G.I.C., Young Women Christian Council; [oth. writ.] Second place winner of an essa contest sponsored by Delta Sigma Theta, South Bay Alumnae Chapter, Several High School Essay, Speach Contest; [pers.] I write because it's the only true way that I can express myself freely and uninterrupted. It's a gift from God that I cherish and am grateful for.; [a.] Compton, CA

TUBE, MELISSA
[Pen.] Missy; [b.] February 2, 1975, MI; [p.] Joyce Webb; [ed.] Student; [a.] Clarkton, MO

TUCKER, MICHAEL GRAHAM
[b.] February 28, 1963, Burnaby, BC; [p.] Herbert Earl Tucker, Margaret June Turner; [m.] Susan Lynn Tucker, February 28, 1987; [ch.] Steven Michael, David James, Angela Rose; [ed.] Centennial High; [pers.] If we had the mercy of love we would have compassion. If we had the love of mercy, we would be free; [a.] Aldergrove, BC, Canada

TUCKER, STEVEN LEE
[b.] January 1, 1966, Fairfax, VA; [p.] Clarence Lee Tucker III, Betty Tucker; [ch.] Steven Lee Tucker Jr.; [ed.] Deer Valley High, Central Arizona College; [occ.] Student; [hon.] Honor's and Dean's List; [oth. writ.] Comprehensive Variety of Unpublished writings, poems, books, short stories and anecodotes; [pers.] I have gained my strength, my courage, my endurance, my determination and my inspiration from three wonderful ladies, my mother, Betty Tucker, my grandmother, Arlyne Parrotta and my first love, Valenia Stutzman. I owe a special mention to Robert M. Schaefer.; [a.] Phoenix, AZ

TULLER, TRESA M.
[b.] February 26, 1969, Fort Wayne, IN; [p.] Carol A. Garvey; [m.] Doyle L. Tulley, October 6, 1991; [ed.] Graduate of Wayne High School in 1989. I am currently a student at the Idea Center where I'm working to become a medical office assistant; [occ.] Homemaker and full time student; [memb.] Beacon Light Chapel of Churubusco Indiana. Former member of the Jesters of Saint Francis College. A drama troop for physically and mentally challenged young people; [hon.] Received recognition from Southside Optomists Club of Fort Wayne in 1981; [oth. writ.] Other works which have been published include: A Soft Goodbye, published in the summer 1993 edition of Treasured Poems of America; [pers.] This poem was written in loving memory of Dan Katt. The person who taught me that being a parent means more than giving a child a name, it means giving them love; [a.] Churubusco; IN

UTTLE, KENNETH WILLIAM
[Pen.] Kenneth W. Tuttle; [b.] March 11, 1908, Mt
[view], AR; [p.] W.E. and Mae Tuttle; [m.] Blanche
[.]. Tuttle, July 19, 1942; [ch.] Dale Edward Tuttle,
[B]renda Ruth Quetano; [ed.] High school; [occ.]
[r]etired Service Station Dealer; [memb.] Veterans of
[F]oreign Wars; [oth. writ.] 10 gospel songs - words
[an]d music, printed by 3 different music companies;
[a.] San Jose, CA

[T]WYMON, DANIELLE M.
[b.] November 17, 1976, Det, MI; [p.] Ronald and
[M]arlene Twymon; [ed.] I will be a graduate of
[H]amtramck High School June of 1994; [occ.] Secre-
[ta]ry for the 31st district court in Hamtramck; [memb.]
[I a]m a member of the Michigan Assoc of Student
[C]ouncil's Leadership Program and Macedonia Bap-
[ti]st Church; [hon.] Michigan Assoc of Student Coun-
[ci]ls from Grand Valley State Univ; Honors in Music;
[H]onors in Science; Honors of Vice President of
[S]tudent Councils of Hamtramck High School; [oth.
w]rit.] Dear God I'm only 15, which was published in
[t]he Wayne State (Univ) school newspaper; [pers.]
[N]ext to my parents Langston Hughes is an inspiration
[a]nd I plan to go to college for journalism. My Motto:
[H]old fast to dreams for if dreams die life is like a
[b]roken wiged bird that cannot fly…; [a.] Hamtramck,
[M]I

[T]YLER, BRAD
[b.] November, 11, 1978, Bradford, TX; [p.] David
[T]yler and Connie Tyler; [ed.] Student at Richland
[H]igh School; [hon.] Was involved in PEAK (Pupils
[E]xcelling in Ability and Knowledge) Project; Re-
[c]eived Presidential Academic Fitness Award; Hon-
[o]red by mid-cities Optimist Club during Youth Ap-
[p]reciation as Outstanding student; [pers.] I truly have
[a] wonderful, loving family, and I cherish each day we
[h]ave together. I feel very blessed and thankful for the
[t]alents and abilities God has given me. I strive daily
[t]o do and be the best that I can; [a.] Ft Worth, TX

ULLERY, MICHELE RENEE
[b.] April 8, 1983, Dayton, OH; [p.] Rod Ullery,
Tammy Ullery; [ed.] Educated at home; [pers.] This
poem was read at my Uncle's funeral service; [a.]
Arcanum, OH

UPADHYAYA, AMEET R.
[b.] January 26, 1977, London, (UK); [p.] Raj and
Gita Upadhyaya; [ed.] Junior year of high school;
[occ.] Student; [memb.] Wyandotte Hospital and
Medical Center Youth Volunteer; [hon.] Academic
Varsity Letter of Achievement, Represented in 1992-
93 Edition of Who's Who among American High
School students; [oth. writ.] Wrote short stories and
articles for school newspapers, honored by school
district for writing an essay on "Why I Plan To Stay
Drug Free"; [pers.] Life is as corrupt as it is splendid;
by identifying and dealing with its corruptions, we can
truly revel in its splendor. I have been inspired by my
parents and brother; [a.] Southgate, MI

URBAN, MARION
[b.] November 12, 1948, Germany; [p.] Lothar and
Jutta Hartl; [m.] Alfred Urban, August 8, 1970; [ch.]
Claudia yvonne Urban; [ed.] Henry Wise Wood Sr.
High, Calgary, AB Post, Secondary Coruses Busi-
ness; [occ.] Self-employed, Business Service and
marketing; [memb.] None at present (no time!);
[hon.] Drama, Creative Writing; [pers.] Poetry evolves
from the soul when one or more of the senses are
aroused.; [a.] Valleyview, Prov. Alberta, Canada

UTAS, GARY A.
[Pen.] Allan Utas; [b.] April 11, 1945, Edmonton,
AB; [p.] John Denmer (D) Vera E. Utas; [ch.] Shauna
Lee, Tyler Adam; [ed.] High school grad SWA;
[occ.] Historian/retired poet, APV; [memb.] Conser-
vancy Nature Canada, Canadian Art Foundation, The

Royal Canadian Geographical Society Ex: showing
Saskatchewan Archieves Board (Regina); [hon.] 1st
Vice President Midnight Twilight Tourist Assoc.
Zone 14, Noble Mention by R. Anderson 12 National
Vice Pres Inst of Management Accounting 4 USA
states, Appreciation Extended for my invitation and
interest in the ecosystem by the Office and Dean Univ
Nebraska - Lincoln; [oth. writ.] (International Agri-
cultural Research), The Little Grave 1968, The Ne-
braskan Migration to Alberta 1900-1913, The Night
I'll Never Forget, The Klondyke Trail Through the
Fragile Kewatin Formation Sandhills; [pers.] Being
born in Edmonton at 2 after WWII. I was raised out
in the Bush in a 3 room log cabin. At 18 left and
travelled into the Northwest Territories. Here I learned
to intermingle with the inuit, dene, native nations and
metis; [a.] Edmonton, Alberta, Canada

VAARWERK (JR.), WILLIAM
[b.] June 14, 1973, Virginia; [p.] Phyllis Mueller;
[ed.] Bennett High, Alfred State College of Tech;
[occ.] Writer; [memb.] American Red Cross; [hon.]
Educational Opportunity Program; [oth. writ.] Many
poems not published. Working on a novel to be
finished by 1995; [pers.] Poetry is the display of
human thought and emotion, my thought and emo-
tion, my thought's are to be heard; [a.] Buffalo, NY

VAJRACHARYA, SUWARN
[Pen.] Lunswan, Neva; [b.] July 3, 1962, Kathmandu;
[p.] Ratnaman, Chandradevi Vajracharya; [ed.] Gradu-
ate school of Intenational Relations, International
Univ of Japan; [occ.] Operations Coordinator Inter-
national Herald Tribune, Tokyo; [memb.] Neva Cul-
tural Foundation, Asian Buddhist Congress; [hon.]
President's Award For High School Graduates; [oth.
writ.] Several poems published in magazines in Sri
Lanka and in Japan. Articles published in "The
Island" and "The Daily News" in Colombo,
"Anandabhumi" in Kathmandu; [pers.] Envoy not
any you will be admired. Hate not any you will be pure
hearted. Desire not any you will sleep well. Enjoy the
peace you will thus hail; [a.] Tokyo, Japan

VALLO, CHARLES J.
[b.] February 2, 1916, Murphysboro, IL; [p.] Mr.
and Mrs. Charles Vallo, Sr; [m.] Lucille M. Vallo,
September 27, 1952; [ed.] High school, college -
Southern IL Univ, Carbondale, IL; [occ.] Grocery
Business twenty years and Political Offices, Tax
Assessor, Twp Supervisor and State of IL Property
Control Inspector. Army veteran 47 months, several
medals; [pers.] I have seen yesterday. I know not
about tomorrow. But I love the joy of today; [a.]
Murphysboro, IL

VanBUSKIRK, JENNIFER
[b.] February 21, 1980, England; [p.] Kelly and
Rebecca VanBuskirk; [ed.] Rudder Middle School,
Current 8th grade student; [occ.] Student; [memb.]
Univ Interscholastic league, Honor Society, Drama
Club, Science Club; [hon.] 1st Place - Leon Valley
Elementary Cultural Arts, 1st Place "Just Say No To
Drugs" essay, 3rd place Univ Interscholastic league
for school district; [oth. writ.] Several poems pub-
lished in school literary book, short stories published
in school newspaper; [pers.] "Be who you are - don't
change yourself to meet others standards"; [a.] San
Antonio, TX

VANDERSYPEN, ROY
[Pen.] Van; [b.] March 27, 1927, London; [p.]
Ludovic Vandersypen, Elizabeth Perry; [m.] Joan
Margeret Vanderspen, August 18, 1951; [ed.] via
scholarships/merits; [occ.] Retired, General Motors
Lts.; [oth. writ.] Two other poems published with
many works unpublished as yet. 1991 Peotry Now,
poem called 'Rush', 1992 Central Voices Poem
"Young Enough", Saginaw Steering Gear Hendon,
Ondon

VANDERVER, BRIAN
[Pen.] Beaner; [b.] September 29, 1975, Bl Island,
IL; [p.] George and Kathleen; [ed.] Shepard High
School, Morraine Valley College; [occ.] Student,
Plastics Worker; [memb.] Bowling Club; [a.] Chi-
cago, IL

VANDERVORT, AMANDA
[b.] April 2, 1979, Mt. Vernon Washington; [p.] Barb
and Les Vandervort; [ed.] Sabino High School; [occ.]
Student; [memb.] Sabino H.S. and AYSO soccer
teams; [oth. writ.] Published in "Anthology of Poetry
by Young Americans") "Clean Up My Room?!";
[pers.] I dedicate my poem to the late Steven Ray
Price, who was always there with a warm smile and
a helping hand. He passed away July 27, 1993, may
he Rest In Peace.; [a.] Tucson, AZ

VARGAS, LUCY
[b.] December 10, 1964, New York City; [p.] (mom)
Placida Duran; [ed.] Rutgers Univ, BA Journalism
and Theatre Arts 1987; [occ.] Actress. I teach ESL
(English as a second language) to pay the bills;
[memb.] Screen Actors Guild; [a.] Hollywood, CA

VAUDRY, BRENDA
[b.] February 19, 1949, Kingston, Ontario, Canada;
[p.] Wilfred and Mary Marshall; [m.] Legally sepa-
rated; [ch.] Son - Timothy Vaudry (born: June 24,
1978); [ed.] Grade Eleven, Business and Academic;
[occ.] Telephone Operator Bell Canada - 26 yrs;
[memb.] Vice President, Operator Services Commu-
nications, Energy, Paper Workers Union of Canada,
Local 31 Kingston, Co-Chair, Safety and Health.
Communications, Energy and Paperworkers Union
of Canada, Local 31, Oper. Serv., Kingston; [oth. writ.]
Much poetry written this is the first attempt for
publication; [pers.] For every thorn in my life there
have been a dozen roses; I dedicate my poetry to the
Loyal Roses in my life; [a.] Kingston, Ontario, Canada

VAYLON, CHRISTOPHER M.
[b.] December 24, 1940, Leeds, England; [p.] Mr.
and Mrs. Leonard Firth-Vaylon; [m.] Starr Joelle
Vaylon, May 14, 1960; [ch.] Myles Vaylon - resident
in Portland, OR; [ed.] Milton High School, Milton,
Ontario, Canada. Largely self-taught due to extensive
reading and life experience; [occ.] Medically - retired
- disabling spinal disease - osteoarthritis; [memb.]
Canadian Arthritis Assoc, Holy Family Hospital So-
ciety, International Order of Foresters; [hon.] Honors
Roll throughout high school. Commendations for
Achievement in English; [oth. writ.] I have written a
great deal of Christian poetry. Additionally, I have
been pleased to write personalized poetry for wed-
dings, birthdays, anniversaries, retirements, bereave-
ments, etc; [pers.] I strive to write in an easy to
understand style about things that affect most every-
one; events, subjects, thoughts, observations, etc. I
attempt to convey a message without being preachy or
opinionated; [a.] Surrey, BC, Canada

VELA, TONY
[b.] January 3, 1969, Dinuba, CA; [p.] Tony Vela,
Lucy Vela; [ed.] Madison High, Westbury High;
[occ.] Sales Clerk For Department Store (Wal-mart);
[pers.] Sometimes when I'm alone something will go
through me so fast, that if I don't have a pen and piece
of paper to quickly write it down, I will forget it. After
reading what I wrote I cannot believe I wrote it. I don't
know where it comes from; [a.] Houston, TX

VELASCO, MELODY MARRERO
[Pen.] Ding; [b.] March 14, 1980, Los Angeles; [p.]
Nover and Bety Velasco; [ed.] An 8th grade student
attending Luther Burbank Middle School in Highland
Park, Los Angeles; [memb.] President of KARE
(Kids Army to Rescue the Environment) Club; BIBAK
Youth Club (a cultural group); [hon.] Graduated from
elementary with honor roll awards, yearbook, and

student of the year. Received 2 recognition certificates for an environmental landscaping project and Academic excellence in school; [oth. writ.] Article published in the Daily News Newspaper, Environment article published in the Igorot Quarterly; [pers.] Life Is A Mystery, Love Is A Crime. Protect the environment because it's all we got. Mother Earth gave us everything we have, we should give something back by protecting it; [a.] Los Angeles, CA

VELAZQUEZ, NORBERT
[b.] September 9, 1971, New York; [p.] Luz Velazquez, Manuel Velazquez; [ed.] Currently in Hunter College; [occ.] Shipping Administrator; [oth. writ.] Other poems can only be found in the hands of old girl friends or some few very good friends.; [pers.] No matter how much it may hurt, never give up searching for your true love. Once you find it noting can compre to the warmth you'll feel inside.; [a.] New York, NY

VENDRICK, MELISSA DAWN
[b.] December 5, 1975, Norfolk, VA; [p.] Baxter and Kathleen Vendrick; [ed.] Ryan Academy of Norfolk, Hollins College; [pers.] Keep exploring your mind, and you'll eventually find what you're looking for; [a.] Norfolk, VA

VERLINDA, ALLEN J.
[Pen.] Josette; [b.] July 15, 1967, Jersey City, NJ; [p.] (Guardian) Larry Franklin and Alma Allen; [ed.] Saint Mary's High School, Jersey City State College.; [occ.] Student special Education Major; [memb.] Council for the Exceptional Children, The Museum of National History, The Smithsonian; [oth. writ.] Written other poetry and children's book, to be published.; [pers.] I strive for your goals and to do from what's in your heart. Always remember God first, and he will make a way for your dreams to come true. Never lose faith.; [a.] Jersey City, NJ

VERMIGLIO, PHIL
[hon.] Macomb County, Michigan Citizen of the Year; [oth. writ.] Personal collection of poetry; [a.] Harrison Township, MI

VERSOCKI (JR.), MICHAEL
[b.] April 16, 1972, Freeport, NY; [p.] Michael Sr., Susan; [ed.] Freeport High School, Nassau Community College - Associates Degree, Suny Westbury - Communications Mgr; [occ.] Student; [memb.] South Nassau Christian Church; [oth. writ.] Various poems and degree lyrics; [pers.] I allow my heart to dictate what it is that I write. For me the best poems come from the heart; [a.] Freeport, NY

VESAL, SAEED
[b.] November 14, 1978, Tehran; [p.] Mahmood Vesal, Raziyeh Rezazadeh; [ed.] High school student, third grade, math branch; [occ.] Student; [memb.] I have been a member of the cultural center for children and young adults and I have direct contacts with some Literary Journals at home; [hon.] I placed first in a poem competition in school. And afterward, I placed first at district and town level; [oth. writ.] One of my poems called "Life" was published by one of the Literary magazines here; [pers.] I am mostly interested in the reality of life and my poems are mainly in this conneuion; [a.] Tehran, Tehran

VICK, DOROTHY A.
[b.] May 11, 1934, MA; [m.] Richard E. Vick, October 9, 1960; [ch.] Steven Vick, Susan Delatorre, two grandsons Jeffrey and Jonathan Delatorre; [occ.] Homemaker; [pers.] Poetry, to me, expresses the joys and sadness of life as well as the beauty of our world.; [a.] Mission Hills, CA

VILLANUEVA, JOSEPH
[b.] December 4, 1976, L.A., CA; [p.] Joseph and Lucy Villanueva; [ed.] 94' Ramey School Graduate. I plan to study science at a Unviersity in Florida; [oth. writ.] Many unpublished poems; [pers.] On separate sheet of paper; [a.] Aguadilla, P.R.

VISHMIDT, MARINA
[Pen.] M. Trilby V.; [b.] May 6, 1976, Kharkov, Ukraine; [p.] Nina Vishmidt; [ed.] Senior in Bronx High School of Science; [occ.] Student; [memb.] Various - NYSINARAL, Justice for Animals, PETA, Friends of Animals, MST 3000 Fan Club; [hon.] Who's Who of American High School Students; [oth. writ.] Staff member of EA, underground feminist journal; edit own magazine; contribute to assorted underground press manifestations; [pers.] "'Roughly, 00000000000000006624'. 'Roughly! It's near to 0000000000000000000000000000000000006624'"- William Gaddis. I am partial to the decorative arts; [a.] Jackson Heights, NY

VISUTSKI, CORY S.
[b.] August 24, 1974, Pembroke; [p.] Marilyn and Edward Visutski; [ed.] High school at Opeongo, 1 yr of electronics at Algonquin College Ottawa currently persuing graphic designs; [occ.] Student; [pers.] Poetry is a combination of thoughts and feelings brought together to perform magic; [a.] Kanata, Ontario

VIXO, LEONA JEN
[Pen.] Leah Jean Vixo; [b.] May 5, 1931, White Earth, North Dakota; P Hjalmer and Rachel Frosted; M Darby P. Vixo, August 21, 1949; [ch.] Lynette Danaye, Darcy Lynn and Danna LaMae; [ed.] Tioga High, South Puget Sound Community College; O Job Service Specialist II; [m.] Faith Assembly of Lacey, W2 Prison Ministries, Sweet Adelines Choral Group; [hon.] 3 Washington State Dept. of Corrections Certificate of Appreciation awards, 2 brainstrom suggestions Certificate of Commendations awards, Certificate of Recognition award for music instruction, appreciation award for more than 24 years of public service rendered for the state of Washington, two year Bible study completion award; [oth. writ.] Several poems published in local newspapers, school papers, Tioga Historical Society, Norman Lutehran Church, copyrights in the National Library of Congress in Washington, D.C.; [pers.] I was greatly influenced by my elementary literary teacher who delivered into the meaning of each poetic authors writings with intent expression, as she recited poetry before the class. I give all glory to God for the gift given me to write poetry.; [a.] Olympia, WA

VOLLE, CHRISTIE
[Pen.] Kristi Volle; [b.] February 4, 1959, NC; [p.] Leslie Edward Volle Sr., Dorothy Neese Volle; [m.] Divorced; [ch.] Michael Russell Nelson, Nicholas Courtland Nelson; [memb.] 1976 Member of the National Society of Published Poets; [oth. writ.] "Halucinated City" and "I'm Alive" 1976 Clover Collection of Poetry.; [pers.] To God be the glory. In the best of times and the worst of times, God will see us through this adventure which is live.; [a.] Climax, NC

VON DIPPE, PATRICIA
[b.] March 3, 1937, South Africa; [ed.] Ph.D. University of Arkansas; [occ.] Biochemical Researcher and Teacher; [pers.] Influences on my poetry arve very wide spread and diffuse. I admire John Donne, Shakespeare, but also James Elroy Flecker and Dylan Thomas; [a.] Manhattan Beach, CA

VOSKOBOYNIKO, ELNA
[b.] November 7, 1977, Odessa, USSR; [p.] Yeugeny and Marina Voskoboynikov; [ed.] Nefesh Academy High School for girls; [hon.] Honor roll; [oth. writ.] Several other poems and stories; [pers.] I think that people should learn more about other nations and their

history. Ignorance results in animosity and in a wor as hostile as ours there's no room for anymore hatre [a.] New York, NY

VYAS, HAMEL
[b.] July 15, 1969; [b.] Ahmedabad, India; [p Vasudev and Minaxi Vyas; Background: Raised Toronto, Canada. Presently studying law in Del ware; [ed.] Majored in political science at York Uni (Toronto, Canada); [pers.] Get up and set you shoulder to the wheel - how long is this life for? As yo have come into this world, leave some mark behind Otherwise, where is the difference between you an the trees and stones? They too come into existence decay and die; [a.] Wilmington, DE

WADE, CAROLYN
[b.] December 8, 1945, Santa Paula, CA; [ch.] Fiv daughters; [ed.] Citrus College, Glendora, CA; [occ. Massage therapist; [hon.] Dean's list, 2nd priz winner, literary contest, Citrus College.; [oth. writ. Short story and several poems published in Litru magazine, a Citrus College publication, as well a several other poems, short stories and essays, as ye unpublished.; [pers.] Even as a young child I wa moved by the power of words to create and express feeling. The ability to make me feel something is wha I value in other writers and the gift I strive to bring t my readers; [a.] Cherry Valley, CA

WAGNER, WENDY
[b.] May 10, 1944; [ed.] B.A. in English, M.A. in English, Certificate of Advanced study in Counseling; [occ.] National Certified Counselor, Consultant on Disbility Rights; [memb.] American Counseling Association, American Group Counseling Assoc., Chi Sigma Iota, Nassau Counselors Assoc., Committee for the Handicapped-chair, Beta Sigma Phi; [hon.] The Assembly of the State of New York Certificate of Merit, Nassau County Citation, Charlotte Newcombe Award; [oth. writ.] Shadows, Ties, You Understand, You and I, I will not Whisper, published poetry, short stories, newspaper articles and column; [a.] Seaford, NY

WALKER, SHERI
[b.] May 28, 1955, Seattle, WA; [p.] Marvin & Evelyn Walker; [ed.] Graduated High School, Renton High, Seattle, WA; [occ.] Unemployed, homemaker; [memb.] Cat lovers of America; [hon.] This is my first poem that I've entered in any contest to make it this far is an honor to say the least.; [pers.] I believe that we should look out for those who can't do it for themselves and that we are responsible for the well being of all living things, two legged and four, no matter how old or young; [a.] Seattle, WA

WALLACE, M. A.
[b.] September 13, 1971, Riverside, CA; [p.] LTC and Mrs. John W. Wallace; [ed.] AFCENT International High School (Brunssum, The Netherlands); U.S. Air Force Academy; [occ.] Sales Associate, Marriott Hotels and Resorts; [memb.] American Academy of the Martial Arts, Friends and Families of POWs/MIAs; [pers.] "It is better to die a pice of broken jade than to live a life of clay." --Bruce Lee. Thanks to Mom, Dad, Toots, Burke, Jen, Kim, Dave, Susan, the Huffss, Chaplain Stendahl, Major Bischoff and Finally The Lord.; [a.] Omaha, NE

WALLACE, MARVIN
[b.] March 8, 1940, Portland, OR; [p.] Wilbur R. and Irene Wallace; [m.] Elsa E. Wallace, September 22, 1970; [ch.] John-Paul R. Wallace, Stephanie P. McClure and Brian R. Wallace; [ed.] 1984, B.A. Social Science Marylhurst College, 1988 MPA Public Admin. Portland State Univ.; [occ.] Businessman, self employed; [oth. writ.] Upward of 40 poems of various subject matter; [pers.] "Honesty is not the best policy...it is the only policy!; [a.] Beavercreek, OR

WALLACE, RON
[Pen.] David England; [b.] September 10, 1954, Stamford, Conn; [ed.] Elkhard High School, Elkhard Indiana; [occ.] Truth is disabled from corporate copywriting job, diagnosed as schizo-affective schizophrenia, perhaps why writing style and themes have different wanted quality. Also, musically, piano, inclined.; [hon.] Vice President of National Honor Society, Presiden of Midwest Award Winning Junior Achievement...etc. Dean's List, U. of North Carolina, Graduate of Kalamazoo College, Michigan; [oth. writ.] B.A. English, Creative Writing 1976, 8 manuscripts to date, plus book of poems, different, writing, creative, looking for boom, literary, experimental lit agent.; [pers.] Looking to graduate from disability with wide publishing success.

WALLENBORN, ANDREA P.
[Pen.] Philippa; [b.] March 29, 1971, Michigan; [p.] Paul and Sibylla - from Germany; [ed.] Studying at Metropolitan State College in Denver, CO. I am getting certified for early childhood education (K-3); [occ.] I am a nanny; [oth. writ.] I have had a few poems and sports stories (articles) in the "Prospector" - community college newspaper. Other than that I have not been published; [pers.] I write so as not to feel alone; [a.] Denver, CO

WALLIS, JANE L.
[b.] November 21, 1917, Brainerd, MN; [p.] Dewitt & Rose Holleman; [m.] Clarence (deceased), May 22, 1937; [ch.] Marjorie Niemann, Carol Hawbaker; [occ.] Ret. School Secty.; [oth. writ.] Poem "Beauty" published in 1993 in "Coming of Dawn."

WALRATH, SHANNA S.
[b.] March 30, 1978, Sterling, IL; [p.] Charles F. and Suzanne F. Walrath; [ed.] Sophomore, Sterling High School; [occ.] Student; [memb.] Wesley United Methodist Church/Sterling; Natural Helpers/Sterling H.S., Sterling High School Volleyball, Basketball and Softball Teams; [hon.] 3 years of awards in young author's program in grade school, an excellent in the Illinois History Competition (8th grade), High Honor Roll; [oth. writ.] Poem published in local paper and read over local radio station, written while in second grade; [a.] Sterling, IL

WALTERS, CHRISTINA
[b.] October 31, 1966, Albuquerque, NM; [p.] Al Weber, Maria Weber; [m.] John Walters, May 10, 1985; [ch.] Julia Nadine, Alicia Marie; [ed.] Manzano High; [occ.] Housewife and mother; [memb.] Member of the Worldwide Organization of Jehovah's Witnesses, National Headache Foundation; [hon.] Musicianship Awards for the Violin, Parent Volunteer Awards; [pers.] Finding happiness comes from within. Reach down into your heart and pull out what's inside; because to live is to feel and feelings can either be used or abused; [a.] Costa Mesa, CA

WALTERS, FRENCHY
[Pen.] Grandma "D"; aka Dorothy Boville; [b.] September 23, 1922, Coleman, WI; [p.] Dave Boville/ Ethel Hutchinson; [m.] Ralph G. Walters, February 12, 1944; [ch.] Jeanne Marie, Suzanne Mary, Jerald Joseph, Michelle Marie, Jeffrey Joseph; [ed.] Coleman High School, Milwaukee Business Institute; [occ.] Entrepeneur - poetry in magnets and plaques; [memb.] 4-H Adult Leader, Legion Auxiliary, Homemakers, Altar Society; [hon.] 4-H Leadership Award; [oth. writ.] Several poems in progress and an autobiography, A Cup Overflowing; [pers.] I write about human experiences, struggles, and triumphs to pass on to my next generations; [a.] Hiwasse, AR

WALTERS, KRISTY
[b.] July 26, 1982, Flint, MI; [p.] Ed Walters and Linda Weeks; [ed.] Currently in 6th grade; [oth. writ.] Two times in the Carman Courrier and one time

in the Wide Awake Club of the Flint Journal.; [pers.] I enjoy spendin gtime with my 6 animals, one sister, Brandy and friends. I'd like to become a writer like my gret great grandfather and be a policewomen; [a.] Corunna, MI

WALTON, NIKKI
[b.] February 11, 1977, Ahoskie, NC; [p.] Clarence & Marion Walton; [ed.] Hertford County High School; [occ.] High School Student; [memb.] Future Business Leaders of America, Oxley Hill Baptist Church Junior Usher Board, First Baptist Winton Youth Choir; [hon.] National English Merit Award, Who's Who Among American High School Students, National Leadership and Service Award; [oth. writ.] My other writings are just things I write when I'm down or happy, but none have ever been published.; [pers.] I just love to write poems about love or relationships. I am influenced greatly by my friends because I let them read my poems and they encourage me.; [a.] Ahoskie, NC

WANDER, JENNIFER
[b.] June 8, 1980, Brooklyn; [p.] Chris and Larry Wander; [ed.] St Francis Elementary, Mount St Mary's High School; [occ.] Student; [a.] Metuchen, NJ

WANDERMAN (JR), RICHARD GORDON
[b.] April 12, 1970, Brooklyn, NY; [p.] Dr. Nancy A. Chase, Dr. Richard G. Wanderman, Sr; [ed.] Memphis Univ School (secondary), Memphis State Univ, Univ of South Alabama (BA), Univ of Warwick, England (MA); [occ.] 1) M.A. Student in Philosophy and Literature. 2) MA Student in French Studies; [memb.] Founder and ex-president of the Univ of South Alabama Philosophical Foundation; Univ of Warwick Film Society; Univ of Warwick American Football Club - Warwick Wolves; [hon.] MSU Honors Certificate; Gamma Beta Phi; Reading at USA for the Department of English - Creative Writing; Dean's List, several times; President's List; [oth. writ.] Several poems published locally, short stories submitted (hopefully!) and a novel entitled Dionysus and the Crucified, presently being submitted for consideration as well. Also, many philosophical papers, one play, and a movie script; [pers.] Credo quia absurdum...hinc illoe lacrimoe; [a.] Memphis, TN

WARD, TIFFANY E.
[b.] October 7, 1980, Boynton Beach, FL; [p.] Judy A. Ward and John A. Ward (deceased 6/19/79); [ed.] 7th grader, Congress Middle School, Boynton Beach, FL; [occ.] Student; [hon.] Honor roll; [pers.] My Dad passed away on June 19, 1993 and his wishes were for him to be cremated and his ashes spread in the ocean because he loved the ocean. I wrote this poem to express how I felt about my Dad being cremated over the ocean. My Dad's ashes may be in the ocean but this soul is in me; [a.] Boynton Beach, FL

WARNER, RUTH
[b.] October 6, 1923, Toledo, OH; [p.] David B. Edwards & Pearl (Beyer) Edwards; [m.] Neal E. Warner, October 27, 1945; [ch.] Craig A. Warner; [ed.] Woodward High School, Statzenburger Secretarial School; [occ.] Housewife (former secretary); [memb.] The International Society of Poets, The International Society of Authors and Artists; [hon.] Golden Globe Award 1991, Golden Globe Trophy 1992, Int. Poet of Merit Award 1993, Four Awards of Merit Certs. from World of Poetry, Honorable Mentions from Sparrowgrass Poetry Forum, Cader Publishing Ltd. and Int. Soc. of Authors and Artists; [pers.] Poetry is the greatest therapy in the world. If an injustice occurs, write about it. It will release anger and also tell the victim and the world that someone cares.; [a.] Northwood, OH

WASHBURN, CHARLES C.
[b.] May 1, 1938, Memphis, TN; [ch.] Lindsey Catherine and Logan Charles; [ed.] Booker T. Washington High, Kentucky State University, Milwaukee Institute of Technology, Syracuse University; [memb.] Directors Guild of America, Writers Guild of America, Pacific Pioneer Broadcasters; [oth. writ.] Poems, song lyrics, motion picture and television scripts, magazine articles; [pers.] Whether morn, noon or night, a good writer must write.; [a.] Woodland Hills, CA

WASHINGTON, AMBERLY J.
[Pen.] A.J.; [b.] February 17, 1982, Dallas, TX; [p.] Valerie Washington and Calvin Neal; [ed.] Student, 6th grade; [occ.] Student; [memb.] 6th grade band, alto sax, church 1st Bapt. Church, Hamilton Park; [hon.] A & B Honor Roll Award of Distinction, Magna cum Laude, Award of Excellence, Handwriting Certificate, young author's extravaganza; [hon.] Ms. Pre-Teen Texas, Ms. Photogenic 1992, speech finalist, Ms. Pre-teen, Texas, National Finalist, Ms Pre-Teen; [pers.] I am a youth who has pride in my present and will always have hope in the future.; [a.] McKinney, TX

WASHINGTON, EDDIE V.
[b.] March 13, 1945, Camden, MI; [p.] Mack and Maggie Washington; [m.] Rosetta, August 29, 1970; [ch.] Michael, Shon and Makeba; [ed.] Tolleston High - Gary, IN Calumet College of Whiting in (student); [occ.] Industrial Worker Burns Harbor IN; [oth. writ.] Fly Butterfly, Ragged Houses, Ugly People, And Me, and many more; [pers.] To be or not to be is not the question; it's the answer; [a.] Gary, IN

WASHINGTON, HOUSTON ANDREW
[b.] April 7, 1980, Nola; [p.] Ernestine M. Washington; [ed.] St. Raymond K-3, St. Philip the Apostle 4-7, Attending Jesuit High School; [memb.] Junior Knights of St. Peter Calver

WATERS, THERES
[Pen.] Terror; [b.] January 18, 1981, LaGrange, IL; [p.] Theresa and Tom; [ed.] Kindergarden thru 7th grade so far; [occ.] Student; [memb.] Teen Magazine, Girl Scout, (former) Brownie and Juniors; [hon.] 6th grade B Honor Roll and 4 quarters, 7th grade B Honor Roll, 1st and 2nd quarters, Vocal music student of the week, 7th grade; [oth. writ.] Songs and other poems, I have'nt named. Also short sotires; [pers.] I just entered for fun, I never imagined I would be publshed or even picked. I've learned anything is possible if you just try.; [a.] Warsaw, MO

WATKINS, VIOLET R.
[b.] March 1, 1934, Independence, VA; [p.] William & Gillie Arnold Watson; [m.] James Ralph Watkins, February 4th, 1950; [ch.] Tammy W. Davis 36, Jamey Todd Watkins 29; [ed.] One Room School, Virginia, Education Continuing, Lettering Degree, Teacher of Art and Calligraphy; [occ.] Owner and Manager of Watkins Enterprises Services; [memb.] Davidson County Writers Guild--Arts Council Charter Memb., Calvary Church; [hon.] Award for "Snow Fall at Dusk" - unpublished; [oth. writ.] Many writings in magazines, poem written for President Nixon, "What It Means To Be An American", Working on a book, Title Country Lanes, Poetry, three poems accepted by Ideals Pub.; [pers.] To let each one of my writings paint a picture of its own.; [a.] Lexington, NC

WATSON, JOYCE E.
[b.] January 1, 1955, Bryan, TX; [p.] Calvin and Reta Heptinstall; [m.] Gordon R. Watson - US Army, August 20, 1985; [ch.] Christopher and Jonathan (twins age 4); [ed.] Graduated at West Jones High School - Laurel, MS; Finished 1 yr at SE Baptist College; Jones Jr College; [occ.] Housewife; [oth.

writ.] Poems printd in book form but not published. Prayers and Thoughts in the process of finishing this book handwritten and not published; [pers.] I have a purpose for each poem I write and can personal relate to some things that I have experienced in life or have been a part of my life at some time. Little children learn to pray is special, because children are so sweet and innocent in the way they pray. My own children pray for everyone and everything you can imagine; [a.] Lawton, OK

WATTENBARGER, CORY
[Pen.] Cory W.; [b.] April 16, 1964, Pomona, CA; [p.] Bud and Jean Wattenbarger; [ed.] Redland's High School; [occ.] Construction - Worker; Several poems unpublished; [pers.] My inspirations, come from real life situations. Seens through the eye's of a blue collar man; [a.] Hesperia, CA

WATTS, LORI MARGARET
[Pen.] Noni (9); [b.] December 13, 1970, Bridgeport; [p.] Herman Thomas Watts and Margaret D. Watts; [ed.] Central Magnet Component, Housatonia Comm. Coll. and Institute of Children's Literature; [occ.] Cleaning Service; [hon.] Editor's Choice Award; [oth. writ.] "Life" poem which appears in "The Coming of Dawn and many other poems and short stories that haven't been published.; [pers.] Writing about your life and experiences are the best pieces of poetry anyone can create. Poem meant for a dear person SCR; [a.] Bridgeport, CT

WATTS, MARSHA SUAANNE
[Pen.] "Morning Glory"; [b.] MNarch 24, 1948, Somerset, PA; [p.] Paul E. and Marian K. Lowry; [m.] Mr. John Robert Watts, September 15, 1990; [ed.] Somerset Area High Schools, Kent State University, Kent, Ohio, Indiana Univrsity of PA, Indiana, PA., Northern Michigan University, Marquette, MI; [occ.] Homemaker, Certified Home Economist, Registered Dietitian.; [memb.] The American Dietetic Associaiton, Chicago, The American Home Economics Assoc., Sorority, Beta Sigma Phi, Disabled American Veterans, Life Member, St. John's Lutheran Church; [hon.] Women in Military Service for America, High School and College, Honor Rolls, Home Economics, Sorority, Kappa Omicron Phi; [oth. writ.] Several other poems.; [pers.] I believe in the accomplishments of self-achievements in order to strive for the non-violence and survival of man's environment.; [a.] Tampa, FL

WATTS, SCOTT A.
[Pen.] S.A. Watts; [b.] April 10, 1972, So. Chas., W.V.; [p.] Harold F. Watts, Lois J. Watts; [ed.] St. Albans High, St. Albans, WV; [occ.] Security Police, U.S.A.F.; [pers.] Looking deep within the words and within yourself could have so much meaning. My advise to anyone is to never stop exploring, feel free with the world and everything in it!; [a.] Waimanalo, HI

WAXMAN, TERI
[b.] December 25, 1957, Little Rock, AR; [ch.] Daniel Benjamin & Dillon Beck; [ed.] UM, St. Louis; [occ.] CPA; [pers.] This is a poem that I wrote to thank my sister for an anniversary gift she gave to me. My mom (a seamstress) had started a satin pillow cases as a wedding fit for me before she was diagnosed with cancer. She never got around to finishing the cases before she died. My sister found them when whe was going through my mom's thing and had a good friend (Emily) finish them so that she could give them to me for my wedding anniversary. When I opened the package and saw the gift that had long since been forgotte, I was deeply moved and inspired to write this poem.; [a.] St. Louis, MO

WEAR, FRANK
[b.] March 7, 1964; [m.] Jeanne-Marie Tyte; [ed.]

B.S. Mechanicl Engineering at Georgia Tech.; [occ.] Engineer; [memb.] International Associaiton of Scientologist, Church of Scientology of Georgia; [hon.] Graduated with Honors (GA Tech); [pers.] Thanks to Steve Cole, Mrs. Carey and both of my parents. Thanks mostly to L. Ron Hubbard; [a.] Hendersonville, NC

WEBB, DEBBIE ROSE
[b.] October 18, 1970, Nain; [p.] Henry and Andrea Webb; [ed.] Jens Haven Memorial School and Labrador College; [occ.] Cashier at Jenkins take-out, Nain; [memb.] Canadian Rangers Labrader Inuit Assoc; [oth. writ.] I've written many poems but they were never recognized until now. (I was too shy to send them out to any one.); [pers.] I pour my feelings out in my poems. I put in to them exactly how I feel, it is my way of expressing myself and I love writing them; [a.] Nain, Labrador, Canada

WEBSTER, FREDERICK
[b.] November 25, 1939, Sheffield, England; [p.] Horace & Ada Webster; [m.] Sybil, October 1967; [ch.] William, Kate; [ed.] Crookesmoor Boy's School, Sheffield England, then privately; [occ.] Writer; [hon.] First Prize with Distinction, Warfedale Literary Festival, England for Poetry; [oth. writ.] Poetry published in various anthologies in England. "Simpleton On The Path" a collection of poems published in 1992 by Hedgehog Press, England.; [pers.] We are constantly subjected to relentles sand indiscriminate information artlessly purveyed. Peotry enables us, for a while at least, to dwell upon a single thought and rejoice in the glorious use of language.; [a.] Granada, Spain

WEBSTER, KATHERINE LOUISE
[b.] July 24, 1954, IN; [p.] James H. and Ellen Lewis; [m.] Scot ray Webster, August 29, 1991; [ch.] Kimberly Ann Shealy & Douglas James Wandoff; [ed.] 10th grade Bowling Green High, Bowling Green, KY; [occ.] Homemaker; [pers.] I hoped to rekindle the true meaning of the holiday spirit in children and adults alike. I have always had a special feeling for the holiday seasons.; [a.] Morgantown, KY

WEBSTER, RONALD EDWARD
[Pen.] Don-Ron Webster; [b.] March 2, 1958, Chicago, IL; [p.] Jesse and Dorothy Webster; [m.] Lillian Ruth Webster, August 29, 1992; [ch.] Antrdua Roneca Webster, Ronald Webster II; [ed.] Didn't finish high school, but got G.E.D, went on to Army, then college (ASU) from there to trade school, Trenholm Tech, I am there currently.; [occ.] Trailor, Writer of poetry and songs; [memb.] International Society of poets, nominated 13 August 1993. U.S. Army 9 yers and 6 months Airforce national Guard 3 yrs, Rank of SSG, Staff Sgt.; [hon.] Poet of the year ISP, Montgomery (POTY) and local publications; [oth. writ.] Song's mostly, music currently working on writing a book, I won't give away the title but it's, I think, good.; [pers.] I accepted Jusus as my personal savior. I am no longer in control of my destiny, he'll lead the way now, trusting and believing in that, I know I'll have much increase and success, thanks; [a.] Montgomery, AL

WECKESSER, LORI MICHELE
[b.] August 15, 1975, Middletown, CT; [ed.] Coginchaug High, The University of Conecticut; [occ.] Student; [memb.] Greenpeace, Humane Society; [oth. writ.] Poems published in "Dusting Off Dreams" and "Quest of a Dream"; [pers.] Let me tell you what I've seen, the places I've been, the forests of deep forest green and also the cave people, who made their home for me.; [a.] Middlefield, CT

WEIBLE, MELISSA
[Pen.] Mel; [b.] April 7, 1978, St. Louis; [p.] Jim and

Linda Weible; [ed.] Sophomore at Ursuline Academ (high school); [occ.] Student and working on an actin career.; [memb.] Missouri Thespians, Bonhomm Presbyterian Church, Spanish Club, Drama Club Varsity Speech Team; [hon.] First Place on Varsit Speech Team, reading poetry, Student of the Month 1st place in non stop Spanish conservation at a Foreig Language bowl; [oth. writ.] I write poems, articles prose and episodes to t.v. shows which I hope to se produced in the future.; [pers.] Through my acting, have found another way to communicate my thought and ideas and I express them through my writings. believe that words sometimes speak louder than actions.; [a.] Chesterfield, MO

WEINSTEIN, LEA MONICA
[b.] December 2, 1976, Bronx, NY; [p.] Robert & Ellena Weinstein; [ed.] Lakeland High School; [occ.] Student, Paralegal Assistant; [oth. writ.] Several poems including "A Darkness Grows" "In a Field of Emotion" and "Florida", published in Lakeland H.S. Newspaper, and two novels.; [pers.] Poetry is a tool that I use to process what I see in the world around me. The poems that I write are my voice to express how I feel inside.; [a.] Yorktown Heights, NY

WEISS, DANNY L.
[b.] May 26, 1948, Eureka, CA; [p.] Helen M. Weiss; [ch.] Daughter, 19 yrs. old, Zephera A. Weiss; [ed.] San Lorenzo Valley High School, Felton, CA; Cabrillo College A.A. Degree; Computer Technology, Networking; [occ.] Computer Tech, Property Management; [memb.] Reservation Order, AMORC, Ancient Mystical Order of the Ross Cross); [oth. writ.] Publish quarterly, newsletter called ISCE, " about ancient legends that relate to UFO's, membership conducting expedition to North Pole, Reenactment of Admiral Richard E. Surd. Book: Nordie Connection; [pers.] Paradise is a world within us and the world where the human race resides. It is the latter that I am deeply concerned with.; [a.] Felton, CA

WELBORN, YVONNE M.
[Pen.] Yvonne Dufak, Hogue Welborn; [b.] January 19, 1950, MI; [p.] Step father raised me, Louis & Josephine Dufek, Jack Hague Real Dad died; [ch.] Jesse Welborn, James Welborn, II; [ed.] Belleville High School; [occ.] Grocery Associate; [oth. writ.] A poem of my Father published in the Ypsilanti Press in 1977. I have written many poems since 1977.; [pers.] I have written several short stories, none been published, I like writing and some day like to be a journalist.; [a.] Ypsilanti, MI

WELBORNE, ROBBIE MATONKA
[Pen.] Toka; [b.] February 8, 1969, Washington, DC; [p.] Robert & Mamie Welborne; [ed.] Bachelor of Science Degree in Psychology from Towson State University. Pursuing a Master's Degree in Human Resource Development from Towson State University; [occ.] Full-time graduate student at Towson State University, Towson, MD; [memb.] Alpha Kappa Alpha Sorority, Inc.; Multicultural Committee; African American Acting Troope; [hon.] 4.0 G.P.A., Delegate Scholarship, Graduate Assistant; [oth. writ.] Also published in Towson State University's "Grub Street."; [pers.] Writing has given me a whole new way of looking at the world and expressing the feelings that most of us experience everyday.

WELCH, KELLI RIAN
[b.] October 31, 1977; [p.] Lantz and Sara Evans; [ed.] 11th grade at Hampshire High School; [hon.] I usually am on the 3.5 honor roll or higher; [oth. writ.] poems published in the school newspaper when I was in Junior High. But I have a lot of poems that I think are good that I hope to publish someday.; [pers.] My poems are mostly about my life and what I feel. I usually have to write when I'm going through something in life. So sometimes I don't write for weeks at

time.; [a.] Springfield, WV

WELLS, AL
.] April 3, 1924, Portland, OR; [p.] Nephew of Mary Caroline Davies, poet and author.; [m.] Joyce , June 2, 1951; [ch.] Judy, Nancy, David, anny, Bonnie, Karen, Becky; [ed.] 1 yr. college, WWII Veteran (France & Germany); [memb.] Masonic Lodge, Past Master; [hon.] Grand Prize in Upstart Crow Bookstores, CA, Poetry Contes, 1987; oth. writ.] The Transcordian Connection, Rhymes of Renewal, many thological booklets and essays.; [pers.] Also wrote this poem shortly before his death on November 29, 1993. If reflects his confidence in God's love for us and his own respect for the wonderful peace and life that continues on after death.; [a.] Welches, OR

WELLS, GRACE VILMA
Pen.] Wells, Grace; [b.] March 1, 1979, Bahamas; p.] James and Mary Wells; [ch.] Shaqonya Elizabeth Wells; [ed.] James A. Pinder, Kingsway Academy, Industrial Training Center; [occ.] Pre-school teacher, Wells Private Tutoring; [oth. writ.] Book publish by The Nassau Guardian; [pers.] I begin to write poetry because I wanted to create an imaginative world for my readers to feel love and enjoyment; [a.] Nassau, NP, Bahamas

WELLS, TENDA H.
[Pen.] TLC; [b.] May 16, 1980, NY; [p.] Curtis & Mildred Hall; [ed.] 7th Grade PS #15, Jersey City; [occ.] Student; [memb.] Bethel Baptist Church, Sing In the Choir; [hon.] In Writing poems in class.; [pers.] Being honest is the best medicine you can take.; [pers.] Jersey, NJ

WENDT, FAYE
[b.] November 30, 1925, Pleasanton, NC; [p.] John and Anna Geisler; [m.] Donald Wendt, June 16, 1945; [ch.] Richard Dean; [ed.] Graduate of UNK, Kearny, NC Bachelor of Science, plus gradugate hours; [occ.] Retired Teacher; [memb.] M.S.E.A., N.E.A., Buffalo Co. Retired Teachers, St. Gabriel's Catholic Church; [oth. writ.] Have had several short poems published; [pers.] Our future lies in the hands of the children we are educating today.

WENNER, WALLIS
[Pen.] Pipestem; [b.] November 9, 1919, Yakina, WA; [p.] Forence Williams and C. Stanley Wenner; [m.] Barbara Carpenter, November 13, 1942; [ch.] Lisa and Thorne; [ed.] Polytechnic High School S.F. and Calif. School of Fine Arts in San Mateo, Jr. Colelge USAFF Seoul Korea; [occ.] Retired, doing illustrations for Marin Audubon Society "LOG" and Sierra Club, Marin, CA; [memb.] Nat'l. Society of Art Directors, AFAO Club, Audubon Society of Marin CO.; [hon.] Point of Sale display for Blitz Weinhard, SFAD Club, 2nd prize for poem in Pacific Coast Poetry Contest, Sacramento, CA; [oth. writ.] "Banana Slugs Ain't Got Savoir Faire" Indiana Slugs Have Feelings Too!"; [pers.] Sonnets, Satyrigal, Erotic, Political are Best Way to express my shortcomings, feelings and outlook such as it is.; [a.] Mill Valley, CA

WESLEY, SHERRI RENE
[b.] May 30, 1965, Chicago; [p.] Leonard & Ann White; [m.] John Wesley Jr., June 4, 1988; [ch.] John Wesley III; [ed.] G.H. Corlis High School Olive Harvey College; [p.] Productive Asst. United Parcel Servcie; [memb.] Burnside Church Big Sisters Christian Warriors Choir Click for Christ Ensemble; [hon.] Employee of the Month for two consecutive month's; [oth. writ.] Black Child, His Eye Is On The Sparrow, Making The Right Choice, Adam, This Is Reality, Burnside In Review; [pers.] To God be the glory for all that he has done. Without him in my life I couldn't do anything.; [a.] Chicago, IL

WEST, DIIYL WILL
[Pen.] Dick Princewill; [b.] January 17, 1964, Aba, Abia State; [p.] Late Godfrey W.T. William Dodoiyi and Patience N. William West; [ed.] Yaba College of Technology Yaba, Lagos Nigeria; [occ.] Secretary, Computer Executive; [memb.] Association of West African young Writers; [oth. writ.] Several poems and feature articles published in Nigerian newspapers and magazines including "National Concord" and "Family Magazine.; [pers.] "My life is a living testimony." I believe that living or survival is not enough, living satisfied and making others happy is what life should be all about.; [pers.] Lagos, Nigeria

WEST, RICHARD R.
[Pen.] Ricky; [b.] November 4, 1955, Manhattan; [p.] Richard M. and Catherine M West; [m.] Joan M. West, September 5, 1980; [ch.] Many, my poems and music are my children; [ed.] St Amenics Grade Sch, Rice HS, Pioneer Computer Systems (SF, CA), NY School of Music Manhattan School of usic; [occ.] Poet/Composer AV Technician CLK Receptionist Office Support; [memb.] Active participant in several (musical) venues outrage, sound rythym gtr voice assembly, drums Lt Commander Rythym Gtr Voice, WNYC Jaz Sax Bass and Trumpets; [hon.] Two certificates of completion for computer studies in Dos and cotus programs, data base III; [ed.] Among numerous poems and compositions most noted are, writings for sound assembly, Lt Commander Delux and Chasing The Leopard; [pers.] (1) Confidence is an act of faith. Be yourself and someday your mentors with. Be your admirers. Wipe the slate clean. Every nite to make room for the lessons of the day; [a.] New York, NY

WEST, SID
[Pen.] Mrs. M. Ethel, Priestly; [b.] October 3, 1923, Latvia; [ed.] British Marine Navigation and Engineering School in Fleusburg; [occ.] Pens; [memb.] The Poetry Socity in London, England; [oth. writ.] I have brand new books. Two months go produced, seek publishers. Dall, "Leaf" 750 pp, as sample book; [pers.] Much surprised about this, mean your past. My mind crossed to wealth, Great America, please help. Have much to offer and valued manuscripts. Could you establish since contest, viw future luck. I keep you in my memory - please write!; [a.] Bedford Beds, England

WHEATLEY, HAROLD R.
[Pen.] Hal Wheatley; [b.] August 17, 1931, Tennessee; [p.] Luther and Allie Wheatley; [m.] Betty J. Wheatley, September 26, 1954; [ch.] Mark (Dec.), Laura and Jennifer; [ed.] MA, English, General, Secretary Teaching Credential; [occ.] Real Estate Broker; [memb.] NEA, National Education Association, San Fernando Valley Association of Realtors (SEVAR), California Association of Realtors (CAR), National Association Realtors (NAR); [hon.] Stanford University Award Teacher with Most Influence upon an Honors Graduate; [oth. writ.] Poetry and Song Lyrics; [pers.] Like Crevices in concrete, the cracks in orthodoxy provide the soil from which sprout the green ideas of renewal. Or, as the philosopher said, "Out of the Mud Grows the Lotus."; [a.] Valencia, CA

WHEELER, ALISHA PATRICE
[b.] September 26, 1979, VA; [p.] David and Kathi Whitmore; [ed.] 9th grader; [oth. writ.] Writers short stories and poetry.; [pers.] Enjoys writing about her feelings and emotions. Uses her writing as an outlet and to speak on various issues.; [a.] Burke, VA

WHICHER, JEREMY
[b.] September 12, 1936, in Somerset, England, and I arrived in Canada on August 11, 1953.; [pers.] My philosophical statement, which has no psychiatric significance, is that 'Our choices must be determined for us unless their causes are also choices and so on

back and infinitum, which is impossible; [a.] Victoria, BC, Canada

WHITE, DARWIN D. JONATHAN
[Pen.] D. Jonathan White; [b.] November 17, 1942; [ch.] Shannan, Grandchildren: Robert, Ariel, Dara; [ed.] B.S.M.E.; [p.] Self-employed; [oth. writ.] Blossoms from the vine for my children's children (unpublished)

WHITE, DAVID C.
[Pen.] D.C. White; [b.] March 12, 1970; [p.] Don & Margara White; [ed.] Hilmar High School; [occ.] Job coach for devdelopmentally challenged at "Community Intigrated Work Program; [hon.] Excellence in Arts & Literature, Fresno State University, CA; [oth. writ.] Several lyrics written for Starlite Records, Jacksonville, Florida; [pers.] When you take away the fear, the pain becomes treatable; [a.] Modest, CA

WHITE, JASMINE L.
[b.] November 23, 1969, Jamaica; [p.] Thomas and Bromelda White; [ch.] Sanoya White; [ed.] Dunoon Tech. High School, JA. WI; [occ.] Restaurant Manager.; [pers.] We are our brothers keeper. Live up to the creator in us.; [a.] Brooklyn, NY

WHITE, JESSICA GAIL
[Pen.] Jessie; [b.] April 15, 1981, Charleston, W.VA; [p.] Norman and Patricia White; [hon.] I was one of 13 winners for a state wide contest "Write for Fright"; [oth. writ.] Roses, Make No Bones About It, The Sacred Key, Sky Pictures, Time and Believe It.; [pers.] I am very thankful to my mother and English teacher Miss Babbey. They were very helpful too me and still are. They are the one's who persuaded me to enter this contest. I'm very thankful to you. God Bless.; [a.] Charleston, W.VA

WHITE, MICHELLE
[b.] January 26, 1979, Long Beach; [ed.] Artesia High School; [oth. writ.] I write personal poetry daily on the events and thoughts that take place that day. I keep a book of poetry with these poems in it.; [pers.] Poetry, music and drawings inspire me in my own work. I highly look up to and respect any poet, musician, or artist who can express themselves without being fearful of wht others might think of them.; [a.] Lakewood, CA

WHITE, NORMAN
[Pen.] Norm White; [b.] March 2, 1927, Easton, PA; [p.] Garrison & Jenny White; [m.] Winnie White, June 28, 1986; [ch.] Noel, Ware, Kevin and Mary my step daughter; [ed.] I earned a bachelor of Laws Degree in 1972 from LaSalle Extension University, Chicago, IL; [occ.] Retired, 1989; [memb.] Life Membership Charter, Membership in The Lasalle Alumni Club in Honor of the Universitys 60th Anniversary.; [hon.] The 33rd and last degree of ancient and accepted Scottish rite of fee masonary was conferded on Norman White August 4, 1984; [oth. writ.] I have a uncompleted book that I hope to finish. I also hope to start a book of quotes that I will write myself.; [pers.] I would like to share with who ever reads from Helen Steiner. Race these words, don't give me the praise or would by acclaim for the words that you read are not mine..I borrowed them all to share with you from our havenly father above.; [a.] Ralway, NY

WHITE, PETER J.
[b.] July 24, 1970, Warsaw, NY; [m.] April L. White, June 25, 1994; [ed.] Dansville C.H.S., U.S. Army, Pima Community College; [occ.] Assistant Chef, Japanese restaurant, Tracy, C.A.; [oth. writ.] Two books of poetry currently unpublished, also a book of short stories in the works; [pers.] We are all fools on this great green galleon, revolving ourselves into oblivion.; [a.] Tracy, CA

WHITEHOUSE, LISA
[b.] April 25, 1971, Maine; [ch.] JJ; [oth. writ.] Pretend; Eternal Love, Passing On; [a.] Gardiner, ME

WHITESIDE, KELLIE
[b.] March 17, 1966, Brampton; [p.] James and Hendrika Hope; [m.] Jefferey A. Whiteside, October 8, 1988; [occ.] Cartoonist; [memb.] American Quarter Horse Assoc Evangelical Missionary Church of Canada; [oth. writ.] Published work as a cartoonist with comic strip "Remorse The Horse"; [pers.] Ten little two letter words: if it is to be, it is up to me. (My actions are responsible for my destiny); [a.] Wyevale, Ontario, Canada

WICKHAM, JACKSON B.
[Pen.] Jay Wickham; [b.] September 4, 1972, Clarksville, TN; [p.] Mr. & Mrs. Jack M. Wickham; [ed.] Austin Peay State University, 2 yrs. Clarksville, TN; [occ.] Actor; [memb.] South Eastern Theatre Conference, Florida Professional Theatre Association; [hon.] Alpha Psi Omega; [oth. writ.] An essay on the works of Flannery O' Connor, published in a guide to writing research papers.; [pers.] I've no truly profound statement to make, so I'll give up an axiom; In all you do, in all you create, in all you write, in all you act, in all you are, get to the point. I really have nothing else to say.; [a.] Clarksville, TN

WIEMER, F. EVELYN
[b.] July 18, 1927, Edina, MO; [p.] Pauline Witte & John Witte; [m.] David Louis Wiemer, September 17, 1950, Divorced February 4, 1986; [ch.] David Alan, Douglas Jon, Diana Lynn and Daniel Jay; [ed.] High School (Edina, MO) some college classes (Iowa State College, Ames, Iowa); [occ.] Homemaker, Professional Volunteer; [memb.] St. Mark Luth. Church., Sun School Teacher 40 yrs., plus circle leader; [hon.] Valadeictorian, nominated to State Board of Lut. Church Women; [oth. writ.] In small newspapers and local magazines; [pers.] Since we travel through this life only once, it behooves us to make our trip meaningful and worthwhile.; [a.] Rockford, IL

WIGGINS, EILEEN
[b.] May 18, 1944, Somerset, PA; [p.] Arthur and Mabel Seese; [m.] Dell Robert Wiggins, September 30, 1961; [ch.] Tim Wiggins, Carla Lowery; [ed.] Graduated Adult Classes, Buchanan High School, Buchanan, MI 1975; [occ.] Homemaker; [memb.] Suburban Gardens Church of Christ; [hon.] After seeing singer songwriter Conway Twitty in concert I sent him a poem I had written about him and he sent me a thank you, with an 8x10 autographed picture; [pers.] I only write about things I know about personally or feel very strongly about. I strongly believe any special talent is a gift from God and should not be wasted.; [a.] Buchanan, MI

WILHITE, DALE A.
[b.] February 7, 1960, Aurora, CO; [p.] Lowey, Shirley Wilhite; [m.] Single; [ed.] Graduated from poet, St. Joe High, Associate Degree in Sacred Literature, Dothan Alrdama, 1987-1985; [occ.] King Kam Hotel; [hon.] Magna Cum Laude, June 9, 1988; [oth. writ.] The biblical Book of Knowledge, self-publication 48 pages. Also editor of "The Fundamentalist News Letter.; [pers.] The Biblical Book of knowledge.

WILK, HEATHER ELLYN
[b.] May 15, 1978, Chicago; [p.] Michael & Faith Wilk; [ed.] John C. Dore Elementary, Presently a sophomre at John F. Kennedy High School; [occ.] Student; [memb.] Student Leadership, Volleyball, Student Council, Key Club; [hon.] Spirit of Achievement Award, Math Counts Award, American Legion Award, Presidential Academic fitness Award, All American Eagles Congressional Award.; [oth. writ.]

Other poems published in school newspaper.; [a.] Chicago, IL

WILKENING, KAREN L.
[Pen.] The Rolodex Madam; [b.] Sagittarius, NYC; [occ.] Motivator, Author, Speaker, former Real Estate, Systems Analysis, Corporate Manager, Madam of Exclusive Call Girl Service, Fugitive and Prison Inmate; [hon.] There have been over 300 articles written about my case and myself. I've been interviewed on National Shows such as Maury Povich, Jenny Jones, Morton Downey Jr., Jane Whitney, Canada's Shirley Show, CNN, Inside Edition and Hard Copy.; [oth. writ.] I wrote "Cat Zen" in appreciation of the yard cats in prison. Currently writing my autobiography.; [pers.] My motto is "Love is Power."; [a.] San Diego, CA

WILKINS, EMANUEL RENO
[b.] August 2, 1944, Savannah, GA; [p.] Annie & Joseph Wilkins: [ed.] Sol C. Johnson High School, Diploma Claflin Univ. B.S. Pre-Med, New York School of Announcing and Speech, Diploma, Post Grad, NYU Columbia, S.U.N.Y., Hunter Brooksdale; [occ.] Psychiatric, Social Worker City of New York, Disc Jockey; [memb.] SSEU Local 371, Phi Beta Sigma, Frat Usher Alpha Kappa Mu, Honor Society, Life Time Member Flonk Callen Boys Club of America; [hon.] Spanish Award, Football, Basketball, Track and Physics Award, voted best Disc Jockey class of 1975, Usher Alpha Kappa Mu Honor Society, Honor Roll and Dean's List; [oth. writ.] "Faith," Destructive Aids," "The Beauty of Nature," "Follow Your Dreams," "Devastation at Grand Central Station," "Math Concaptions," "Personal Angels," "Demons."; [pers.] Always help someone less fortunate than you, but at any and all times reach for stars because heaven await the righteous; [a.] New York, NY

WILLIAMS, ALICE HEARD
[b.] June 8, 1928, Hope, Ark.; [p.] Joseph Richard & Daisy Huffman Heard; [m.] James G. Williams, June 8, 1949; [ch.] Daisy Heard Williams Warnalis and Holly Heard Williams; [ed.] DFA University of London (England) BA Oklahoma State University; [occ.] Lecturer, Art and Architectural Appreciation; [memb.] The English-Speaking Union; The Oxford Society; The National League of American Pen Women; Kappa Delta Sorority; The Lygon Family and Kinsmen Association, St. Barnabas Episcopal Church, Lynchburg, VA; [occ.] Past President, National League American Pen Women, Boca Raton FL Branch. Poetry chosen for South Carolina Anthology of Poetry; third place poetry winner in Clearwater, FL national poetry contest; [pers.] Strong family associations and experiences in life which moved me most have instigated most of my poetry--friendships with grand children, travels, living abroad, my garden--all providing inspiration for poetry.; [a.] Lynchburg, VA

WILLIAMS, ARTENA MAE SHERMAN
[Pen.] Little Teanie, Teanie and Tina; [b.] March 27, 1940, Kansas City, KS; [p.] Leon Sherman, and Artena M. Sheppard; [ch.] Clarence Smith Jr., Sheilah Renee Smith and Jackie JoAnn Williams; [ed.] Summer High, Sanders School of Beauty Culture, Kans. City. Ks., Jr. College; [occ.] Para-Legal Student at KCKCJC, Single Head of Household.; [memb.] Allen Chapel A.M.E. Church Ks. Cty., Ks. and Summer High Alumni, Class of 1958; [hon.] Cosmetology State Styling Awards and Local Styling Awards. Effective Leadership Skills Seminar and Principles of Management Seminar, Trans World Arilines, Biblical Literature Black History, Donnelly College KCK Certificate of Achievement, Dept. of SRS, Kans.; [oth. writ.] As Attorney Pro Se, In Forma Pauperis, copyright pending "No Say", no oral argument. Poem submitted to National Library of Poetry, will be printed in "The Space Between" (Spring 1994).

Copyrighted unpublished book of poetry, "Lor Lord Here I Am Again".; [pers.] "Reality can only l achieved, in dreams of fairness, when all concer think alike, not separetly, about the same thoughts, f same reasons, ex: Fairness. I have given appreciatio greatly influence by all Great Men and Women fro the past and present.; [a.] Kansas City, KS

WILLIAMS (JR), CLIFFTON O.
[b.] January 21, 1966, Richmond; [p.] Mary an Clifton, Sr; Step-father: William Green; [ed.] Joh Marshall High School, 1 yr Virginia State; [occ.] A C Mechanic; [hon.] Football 1st team all state 1st tear all district 1985 all star game Touch Down Club; [oth writ.] Mom's Cooking Soup, My Role Model's Gon Away, Before a Color a Child of God, Value Educa tion, She's Gone But Not Forgotten; [pers.] Take tim to lern your history as well as other, to down a ma is not to know his or her history. In God I trust; [a. Richmond, VA

WILLIAMS, MARI
[b.] January 26, 1946, D.C.; [p.] Dec.; [p.] Dec. [ch.] Yolantte, Sheree and Nicole Baker; [ed.] B.A D.C. Teachers College, 1971 M.ED University o MD, Pralegal Certificate, University of MD; [occ. Foster Care Advocate, Council of Governments; [memb.] Nat.l Council of Teachers of Eng., Retired Senior Vol. Board, AHDP, Adult Health Develop ment Program (Univ. of MD) Board Member, AAWG African American Writer's Guld, Women's Museum, AKA Sorority, Emeritus Teacher Program, U.S. Servas International Host Program; [hon.] Outstand ing Merit, RSVP, Council of Governments, Emeritus Teacher Foundation, Outstanding Service, Youth for Understanding, Golden Poet Award, 1987; [oth. writ.] Publication of Book of Poetry "Waiting for a Dream" "Araremix", Poem on video called "Miracle on Saturday Morning" "Servas at Home" Servas Newsletter; [pers.] I believe true happiness arises from the equipment of oneself, hence the beauty of the universe is unfolded each day to revelation of truth in potential.; [a.] Washington, DC

WILLIAMS, MARTHA G.
[b.] June 11, 1932, Coatesville, PA; [m.] James J. Williams, June 12, 1954; [ch.] Winifred McGee, Wanda Shank; [ed.] Coatesville High School, Westchester University, B.S. Graduate work at Westchester and Millersville Universities; [occ.] Retired Math Teacher; [memb.] PSEA, NEA, Smithsonian, Penningtonville Presbyterian Church, International Wizard of OZ Club; [hon.] Scholarships from Scott High School and Estchester University; [oth. writ.] "Christmas" in Voices of America, "A Pleasant Trip" in On the Threshold of a Dream, "A Friend" in Treasured Poems of America, "My Grandson" in Treasured Poems of America (Winter); [pers.] To believe in yourself is important. Also to be willing to give of yourself to others in kindness and love; [a.] Atglen RD1, PA

WILLIAMS, RODNEY CORTEZ
[b.] March 5, 1967, Loraine, TX; [p.] Sylvester J. Williams and Ruby Williams; [m.] Fiancee, Tami M. Franklin; [ch.] Bianna Cherise; [ed.] Copperas Cove High, Universal Technical Institute; [occ.] Technician, Certified Cove Ford Dealership; [pers.] I dedicate this poem to my best friend, my future wife, and better half, Tami M. Franklin. It was through her overwhelming love tht this poem was written. And it is through her heart that I have come to deeply love the woman she has become. I love you punkin.; [a.] Garland, TX

WILLIAMSON, DAWN
[Pen.] Jade Kavik, Katrina Bousch; [b.] February 5, 1981, Winston-Salem; [p.] Ben and Melanie Williamson; [ed.] Pinebrook Elem, North David Junior High; [hon.] A Honor Roll, President Physical

tness Award; [oth. writ.] Poems; Why did you have go? and Autumn Illustrated book; Sally's Surprise; ers.] I like to write poems that draw a picture in a ·rson's mind when they read it; [a.] Mocksville, NC

/ILLIS, JO DEE
·.] March 19, 1974, Springfield, MO; [p.] Saundra ·ngenthron and Joe Willis; [ed.] Currently attending ·outhwest MO State Univ; [oth. writ.] Several po- ·ns, short stories and plays all not published due to ·e fact that I've never sent any in before this; [pers.] ·Vriting is something to have fun with, something to · free with, an own personal truth; [a.] Ozark, MO

·VILSON, DAVID M.
·b.] October 22, 1946, Tacoma, WA; [m.] Divorced; ·ch.] Angela Lynn & Erika Lynn; [ed.] High School; ·occ.] Weightmaster and Free-Lance Photographer; ·hon.] Photographer of the Year (Black & White) ·1991 and 1992 "Western Photographer Magazine."; ·oth. writ.] "Far Away" and "Pinkville" (not pub- ·ished) numerous photos (including 4 covers) in ·Western Photographer Magazine. Also a few articles ·s some magazine.; [pers.] "I dieciate my poem (When ·Will There Be An End To War) to all of the worlds ·victims of war."; [a.] Bellflower, CA

WILSON, JEN
[Pen.] Pheobe Marks, Elizabeth Tara; [b.] July 1, 1978, Grand Praire, TX; [p.] Dr. and Mrs. Robert S. Wilson; [ed.] Currently enrolled in All Saints Episco- pal Upper School, Fort Worth, TX; [occ.] Student- 9th grade; [memb.] A member of the Grand Lake Yacht Club, Grand Lake, CO, member of the Ft. Worth Academy Yearbook Staff, Journalism Club & Assistant Editor of the F.W.A. Literary Magazine.; [hon.] School Sportsmanship Award at Ft. Wroth Academy, Outstanding Achievements in the Theatri- cal Ability Award; [hon.] Graduated from Fort Worth Academy Middle School with High Honors; [oth. writ.] Several poems published in school magazines; [pers.] I was put on this earth to live out loud, and I achieve this through my poetry; [a.] Granbury, TX

WILSON, JESSICA
[b.] June 22, 1978, Jeannette, PA; [p.] Thomas and Gloria Wilson; [ed.] Norvelt Elementary, Mt. Pleas- ant High School; [occ.] High School Student; [memb.] Girl Scouts, Frick Hospital Explorers, Mt. Pleasant Stage Crew, Mt. Pleasant S.A.D.D.; [hon.] Who's Who Among American High School Students, High School Honor Roll; [pers.] My writings express my feelings and I am often influenced by my good freinds and their problem.; [a.] Greensburg, PA

WILSON, KATHRYN R.
[Pen.] Kaspar #3; [b.] March 4, 1969, Westlock, Alberta; [p.] Mary Bucholtz; [m.] Kevin Wilson, August 4, 1990; [ch.] Timothy James, Chad Robert, Suzanne Amber (Bucholtz/Wilson); [ed.] I have com- pleted my grade twelve level of high school; [occ.] I am currently a house wife and enjoy watching my children grow; [memb.] I am a member of the doubleday book club and also a member of the literary guild and atlas editions; [hon.] I was awarded the 'Best Mother' award by my children last Easter!; [oth. writ.] I have written numerous poems and one short story; [pers.] Poetry is an expression of one's inner feelings and emotions. I express most all my feelings on paper with the help of a guiding pen. I find it to be my soul's way of staying in touch with reality!; [a.] Hinton, Alberta, Canada

WILSON, MARVIN P.
[b.] October 7, 1957, Wilmington, Nc; [p.] Marvia a Guinevere Wilson; [ed.] B.A., Economics, Business Management, N.C. State Univ., M.S., Systems Man- agement, Univ. of Southern California, A.A.S. Fi- nancial Management, Community College of the Air Force.; [occ.] Budget Analyst, Defense Printing Ser-

vice; [memb.] American Society of Militry Comptrol- lers; [hon.] U.S. Air Force, Meritorius Service Medal, Commendation Medal, Achievement Medal; [oth. writ.] Poem "Nature Held Captive."

WILSON, THERESA VICTORIA
[Pen.] Tessie; [b.] September 18, 1947, Wash. D.C.; [p.] Mary Lynn Wilson (Dec.) and Thomas L. Wil- son; [m.] Single; [pers.] The poems I write are heartfelt expressions from my personal experiences. "All gifts are from God, and with God all things are possible."; [a.] Temple Hills, MD]

WINIK, PATRICIA
[Pen.] Paw; [b.] September 20, 1944, Macon Geor- gia; [p.] Melvin & Helen Perdue; [m.] Joseph Wil- liam, September 22, 1962; [ch.] Leslie Rene, Suzanne Marie; [ed.] Lake Worth High, Lake Worth, FL, Penn State U. Correspondence Course; [occ.] Secre- tary/Bookkeeper; [memb.] Past member of our vol- unteer fire & ambulance co. Ambuland Corp. mem- ber trained in advanced first aid and C.P.R.; [hon.] First Woman President of a Volunteer Fire Co. in my county.; [oth. writ.] I was a weekly newspaper correspondent for four years.; [pers.] My love for my family has been a great inspiration for my poetry.; [a.] Lakewood, PA

WIPPEL, STEPHEN ALEX
[b.] May 30, 1949, Huntington, W.VA; [p.] Richard and Rosalie Wippel; [m.] Sonya Christina Wippel, December 31, 1986; [ch.] Brianna, Stacey, Ryan and Pamela; [ed.] B.A. Physics, 1971, Florida Atlantic University, Boca Raton, FL, B.S. Geology 1974.; [occ.] Geophysicist, Sameran Oil Corp., Geology teacher, North Harris College; [memb.] American Associate Petroleum Geologists, AAPG, Adjunct In- struct, North Harris College, Houston, TX; [hon.] Who's Who in Southwest, P.C. World, May 1987, Interview on the Future of Computing; [oth. writ.] Several papers on geology. Mostly published poems and essays.; [pers.] My poems, two essays, reflect the metaphisical side of life. I like to investigate the interweaving of nature and self. Influenced greatly by the transdentalists.; [a.] Houston, TX

WISE, PAULA SHANAYE
[b.] October 16, 1979, Hammond, Ind.; [p.] Paul and Genevieve Wise; [ed.] 8th Grader at Kennedy King Middle School; [occ.] Full Time Student; [hon.] Consistent Academic Honor Student; [oth. writ.] Several Young Children Stories. Several poems that I'm currently gathering into a collection hopefully for publishing; [pers.] "Rise" is a poem that reflects my outlook on life. It's sentiments are more profound, since being diagnosed with Cancer. Though 14 years old, I hope to continue to have my other works published, read and appreciated.; [a.] Gary, IN

WISE, RYAN
[b.] July 17, 1978, Jacksonville, FL; [p.] Diane & Evan Wise; [occ.] Currently a sophomore at Naperville North High School, Naperville, IL; [hon.] D.A.R. Essay award, 2nd place, 1992; [a.] Naperville, IL

WISSNER, ILSE ERNA
[Pen.] Ilse Wissner; [b.] August 10, 1925, Lyck, E. Pr., Germany; [p.] Friedrich and marie, Trentowski, Germany (dec.); [m.] Earl W. Wissner (dec. 1961); [m.] Dec. 23, 1950; [ch.] William Earl, Robert Otto; [ed.] H.S. Friedland, E. Pr., Germany Coll. of Ed. Wurzburg, Germany, Madonna University Livonia, Michigan, Wayne State University Detroit, Mich; [occ.] Retired teacher of elem. and second. education; [memb.] Amer. Assoc. of Retired Persons (AARP), Mich. Assoc. of Retired School Personnel (MARSP); [hon.] Member of Lambda Iota Tau, International Literature Honor Society; [oth. writ.] Short Stories, Children stories, poems, non published; [pers.] I immigrated from Germany to the United States in Jan.

1950. My poems are inspired by personal experi- ences, feelings and reflections. I try to share my thoughts in themes that, hopefully, will touch the interest and appreciation of many traders.; [a.] Livo- nia, MI

WOLFE, DICK EDWARD
[Pen.] Dick Haute; [b.] February 20, 1910, Evans- ville, IN; [p.] Emma M. & Walter G. Wolfe; [m.] Katharine L. Wolfe, 1930; [ch.] Dorothy Louise Schorken; [ed.] High School, [occ.] Poet Laureate of San Pedro; [hon.] Senior Historian of San Pedro CA; [pers.] May 12, 1978 I was appointed Poet Laureate of San Pedro by the Los Angeles City Council by a resolution. Introduced by John S. Gibson, President Emneritus of the council.; [a.] Los Angeles, CA

WOLTERS, JENNIFER
[b.] July 17, 1977, Milwaukee; [p.] Fred and Char- lotte Wolters; [ed.] Whitefish Bay High School; [occ.] A High School Junior at Whitefish Bay High School; [hon.] Presidential Academic Fitness Award..(Drama Club) Best New Actress Award.. National AATG German Test Award; [oth. writ.] Short story pub- lished in anthology "The Ugly Caterpillar. Publishings in school literary mazaginzes throughout school ca- reer.; [pers.] Poetry and musica are like the finest perfumes of culture, lingering softly on the air, they hold the powers to make us recall memories buried deep in the corners of our souls, adding spice to something otherwise common.; [a.] Whitefish Bay, WI

WONG, MINKAI EDMOND
[Pen.] November 14, 1947, Shanghai, China; [p.] Pui Wo W. & Kam Chu Wong; [m.] Alice Wai Yee Lee, October 12, 1974; [ch.] Vinyse Kaye Wong; [ed.] Raimondi College, Hong Kong, Concordia Univer- sity, Montreal; [occ.] Chartered Accountant special- ized in business planning and consultation.; [memb.] Institute of Chartered Accountants of Ontario; Inter- national Society of Certified Public Accountants; Academy of Professional Consultants and Advisors, Institute of Management, U.K.; Toronto Canadian Chinese Artists Centre.; [pers.] I would endeavor to explore, understand, and write more about "the truths" in life, particularly the controversial aspects of them.; [a.] Metropolitan Toronto, Ontario

WOOD, JESSICA INEZ
[b.] May 3, 1977, Aiken; [p.] Billy and Inez Wood; [memb.] Beta Club, Math League, Student Council, Church Youth Council, FCA, FBLA; [hon.] Hugh O'Brian Leadership Award, Gateway Program 1993, Art Awards, Presidential Academic Fitness Award, Honor Roll, "Miss Junior" Beauty Pageant; w Several of my works have appeared in school and community papers; [pers.] Frost, Longfellow and Whitman have encouraged me to unveil benevolence and to reach the hearts of those who thrive off of the aesthetic beauty of live and nature; [a.] Batesburg, SC

WOOD, LAURIE A.
[b.] February 13, 1960, Yonkers; [p.] Frank Cesario and Patricia DeNitto; [ch.] Robert Wood 8, Alicia Wood 7, Scot Kielbasa 12; [ed.] Dutchess Commu- nity College, Liscensed Emergency Medical Technicain; [occ.] Developmental Aide for Develop- mentally Disabled Adults; [memb.] Member of Wassaic, Volunteer Fire House, Firefighter, EMT; [pers.] My writing reflects feelings of not forgetting what's important in life, and being able to enjoy it.; [a.] Wassaic, NY

WOOD, LORILEE J.
[Pen.] Lee Wood; [b.] September 9, 1941, Raymond, WA; [p.] Archie E. & Ellen M. Loop; [m.] Frank W. Wood, September 22, 1972,; [ch.] Lori, Archie, Birdie, Margi and Renee' step-Charmaine, Bill & Toby; [ed.] graduated from Flowing Wells high in Tucson, AZ, 52 years of being a student of life.; [occ.]

Mother of 8, grandmother of 12, wife, artist, job coordinator for co-owned business with husband Frank; [memb.] none; [hon.] Editors Award in "Wind In The Night Sky", for "The Deception of Reality." Published by the National Library of Poetry in 1993. They also published "The Bitterest of All Medicines" in Outstanding poets of 1994.; [oth. writ.] Several unpublished poems and philosophical sayings, about friends and family. Also a family cookbook, unpublished.; [pers.] My poetry has been a release, therapy if you like, for when life gets a little brutal and hard to live with. I also have been noted to have a sharp pen in letters to the editor of the local papers, when intolerance of people makes me angry.; [a.] Mortesano, WA

WOODFORD, JORDAN
[b.] January 20, 1979, Washington, D.C; [p.] Dr. Carrol and Reyan Woodford; [ed.] Currently attending Glenelg country School 9th grade Glenelg, MD; [occ.] 9th gr. student at Glenela Country School; [memb.] Jack and Jill of America, Inc., St. John United; [hon.] Winner Barlow PUblic Speaking Contest 1992, Winner Barlow Public Speaking contes, 1993, G.C.S. English Prize 1993, French Award 1993, Glenelg County School Faculty Prize 1993, Second Scholar Prize 1993; [oth. writ.] Poetry and short stories published in the Columbia Flier (local newspapers) and school literary magazine.; [a.] Ellicott City, MD

WOODRING, DAWN ALICIA
[Pen.] Ashley Thomas; [b.] January 11, 1970, Chigo. IL; [p.] Paul Raymond Woodring and Lauretta Woodring; [ed.] Academy of Our Lady High School. Robert Morris Business College; [occ.] Home Health Aide for the elderly or disabled; [oth. writ.] Currently working on a collection of poems in hopes of future publications.; [pers.] The orgin of my inspiration comes from a priceless gem from up above. It allows me to write not only from my life's own experience but to write about the lives of others through my eyes.; [a.] Chgo., IL

WOODROFFE, TYISHA JOY
[b.] August 17, 1979; [p.] Thomas and Henrietta Woodroffe; [ed.] Villa Maria Academy grade school and Jr. high school at St. Catharine Academy; [hon.] 1st Honors at St. Catharines, half scholarship for freshman year of high school; [pers.] I try to reflect real life in my writing from a team perspective.; [a.] Bronx, NY

WOODS, JANIE
[b.] March 8, 1956, TN; [p.] H.P. & Geneva Fitzhugh; [m.] Divorced; [ch.] Tanya A. Wood and Richard L. Woods; [ed.] 12th grade graduate; [occ.] Disabled; [oth. writ.] Many.

WORRELL, ANTHONY L.
[b.] July 25, 1965, Barbados; [p.] Esther & Joseph Warrell; [ed.] University of The West Indies, Cave Hill Campus, B.A. English, Lit. Linguistics, Sociology; [occ.] Student and Inventory Clerk; [oth. writ.] Essays, "Letters to the Editor" in the Nation in Barbados Biography, feature article in Caribbean Week.; [pers.] To me they ask why I be so distraught has not life, time to mankid taught that change and change we all must suffer. That nothing be on earth forever? Each day I embrace the permanencle of change more firmly, to Reina; [a.] Brookly, NY

WOYTOWICH, VICTOR J.
[Pen.] Kyle Christopher; [b.] August 14, 1961, NY; [p.] Andrew & Gloria; [ed.] Lincoln High, Mercy College, A.S., Pace University, B.S.; [occ.] Data Management, Loral Electronic Systems; [memb.] St. Ann's Catholic Church and Choir, Loral Forum; [hon.] Kappa Mu Epsilon, Math Honors Society; [oth. writ.] Several Poems published. Numerous

short stories, poems and collections completed.; [pers.] Love, sex, life loneliness, solitude, death. I write about what causes us to suffer and grow, or struggle and quit; [a.] Yonkers, NY

WRIGHT, CHRISTINE A.
[b.] November 9, 1951, CA; [ed.] College Grad. nursing Pepperdine University classes in Trust/Banking; [occ.] Writer, Personal Consultant/Professional Growth Consultant. Previously an AVP in Banking and a nurse. One of my dreams is to write lyrics for current artists (songs). The most important part of what I write is that it somehow touches someone; [hon.] Conducted extensive growth workshops in the U.S. and New Zealand.; [oth. writ.] Give me 1 or 2 words and I will write about it in a free flowing format.; [pers.] When all else fails I've always got my pen. business: All Wright Productions, Always is never as long as you think it is. I write poetry, prose stories.; [a.] Boise, ID

WRIGHT, COREAN
[Pen.] Pudden; [b.] October 10, Caroline County; [p.] Louise Boone Wright and Beacon Willie Wright, Sr.; [ch.] Towana Ann, Lisa Denise, Deborah Jean, Constance, J. Wayne and Jonathan; [ed.] Union High School, Bowling Green, VA. "Credits, Germana College in Meditation, "Parents and Adolesence Conflicts"; [occ.] "Dual Homemaker" and Community Activist; [memb.] J.C. "Penney" Golden Rule Award "Medallion", Mentah Health Assoc. and Bethany Christian Services of Fredericksburg, VA; [hon.] J. C. Penney, "Golden Rule" award.; [oth. writ.] A Special Star "The Stars", "The Ocean", "My Dreamboat", "Our Love," "Dear God", "God Forgive" when I judge harsly and many, many others. Member & Ebenezer Baptist Church; [pers.] I am blessed to have been reared in christian home, by both parents, 1 sister Elizabeth, 4 brothers Jessee, Robert Willie, Jr. and Lear's, Always been involved in Community Services and loved people. My writings is a love for "life" the creation; [a.] Caroline County, VA

WRIGHT, TALIA
[Pen.] Jaclyn Wright; [b.] January 12, 1981, Oak Ridge, TN; [p.] James and Theresa Wright; [ed.] Kingston Elementary. I am in Cherokee Middle School at this time; [hon.] Beta Club; [oth. writ.] No titled publication in "Anthology of Poetry by Young Americans"; [a.] Kingston, TN

WRIGHT, THOMAS
[b.] June 27, 1959, Dallas, TX; [p.] Willie T. Wright and Carolyn Sue Wright; [m.] Carolyn Marie, June 15, 1991; [ed.] 6th grade, self-taught high school dropout; [occ.] Eligibility Specialist, Texas Department of Human Services; [oth. writ.] Dozens of unpublished lyrics that "pursue the signs of the times," self-published, "The Art of Getting a Job." Currently writing serious work entitled "Society's Child."; [pers.] "Thoughts never die. Meredly go 'round and 'round, like the water runs through the river, up into the sky, and back again, thoughts never die.; [a.] Garland, TX

WYKOFF, ANGELA
[b.] November, 1, 1979, Grand Prairie, TX; Rick Wykoff, Donna Wykoff; [ed.] Newberry High School; [memb.] Marching band, jazz band, indoor guard, symphonic band; [hon.] Most improved middel school band member, academic honor roll, pride medal, most outstanding middle school band member. Superior solos and ensembles/all county honor band; [oth. writ.] Greed, Rain, Worries, The Sea, The Seasons, A Mystery, Sunny Days, Snow, Daydreams, Song of a Bird, The White Dove, A Magical Mystery Tour, Colorful Rainbows, Unicorns, A Star; [pers.] When I write my poems, I think of different things, usually, it's the way I feel inside. I even write about places I

wish I could bring to life. The poem "Chris" dedicated to my loving, deceased cat; [a.] Newberr FL

WYSOCKI, CATHY
[b.] February 12, 1955, Gary, IN; [p.] Julia , Michael Wysocki; [m.] Wayne Hopkins; [ch.] Do, "Lucky"; [ed.] Immaculate Heart College, LA., C San Francisco State Univ., B.A. Painting.; [occ Visual artist and writer.; [oth. writ.] "Divinia" illu trated book exhibited at Boston Public Library an favorably reviewed in Boston Globe (9-12-91); [pers Birth, death, transformation, humor, they all figur prominently in my written and visual work, as they d in the fleshy world; [a.] Merrimac, MA

YAGERIC, BARBARA A.
[b.] April 2, 1937, Cleveland, OH; [p.] Olga M. an Joseph S. Yageric; [ed.] Mt St Mary Academy (HS) Univ of VA at Alexandria, VA; Suny Buffalo a Amherst, Amherst, NY; [occ.] Freelance Writer Public Relations/Advertising Promotion; [memb.] M St Mary Alumnae Board; Amherst Museum; Daeme College Assoc Board and Zonta Club of Amherst, [hon.] Honor Roll; Volunteer of Year-Amherst Museum; Editors Choice-NLP; [oth. writ.] Many poem - some have won a Blue Ribbon at the Country Fair-Amherst Museum; play for State Convention; short story; articles and two children's stories; [pers.] Some of my poetry is a tribute to my wonderful parents who were a tremendous effect on my life; to nature and life which are beautiful. My short stories and articles deal with reality; [a.] Williamsville, NY

YAHN, STEPHANIE J.
[b.] April 30, 1975, Washington C.H., Ohio; [p.] Deborah Bongiovanni and Jim Yahn; [m.] Engaged to Michael Badini; [ed.] Comsewogue H.S., Stony Brook College; [occ.] Accounts Receivable/Customer Service; [memb.] American Diabetes Association; [hon.] National Honor Society; [pers.] Life is my motivation for writing and writing is my motivation for life.; [a.] Port Jefferson Station, NY

YAMAMOTO, MARI
[b.] February 28, 1977; [p.] James and Karen Yamamoto; [ed.] Kapaa Elementary School, Kapaa High and Intermediate School; [occ.] High School student, Piano student teacher; [memb.] Kapaa High Show Choir, Key Club, Japanese Club, Tennis Team; [hon.] Chorus VP-'92, Class President - '93, Kupura Writing Contest Winner, Honor Roll, Tennis Team Captain; [oth. writ.] Poems published in student booklets; [a.] Kapaa, HI

YAMAMOTO, SANDII
[b.] August 3, 1953, Redwood City, CA; [p.] George and Louise Yamamoto; [ch.] Heather and J.J. Omoto; [ed.] Palo Alto High, Palo Alto, CA; Foothill Jr College, Mt View, CA; [occ.] Medical Asst/Receptionist, Benjamin Richards, MD, FACS, PC, Monterey, CA; [oth. writ.] Published a Poem in the Amherst Society Book; [pers.] I enjoy writing poetry, I have been encouraged by my family and friends, they are the one's I love and for my success; [a.] Monterey, CA

YANCHYSHYN, MADELYN
[m.] Married to a lieutenant who appeared on "Top Cops."; [ch.] Mother of 4, grandmother of 6; [hon.] Golden Poet Award 1986; [oth. writ.] "The Smallest Light" published in Treasured Poems of American Book.; [pers.] My inspiration is God, and through life's experiences in which He's guided me and taught me that nothing is happenstance. All is for a divine plan and purpose to them that love God.

YANG, C.W.
[b.] October 2, 1924, Taiwan; [p.] C.M. Yang, J. Chem; [m.] Shueim Yang, January 27, 1944; [ch.]

ınyu Yang, Tanyu Yang; [ed.] National Taiwan ıniv, Michigan State Univ, California State Poly-chnic Univ; [occ.] Retired; [memb.] Taiwanese ıssoc; [hon.] Letter of Appreciation, U.S. Army; ıth. writ.] Farm Machinery and Implement; [a.] ıverland Park, KS

ATES, WILLIAM
ı́en.] Zeka or Greasy Bear; [b.] September 30, 1945, ı́ake Co; [ed.] I have 14 years of education; [occ.] ı̇alesman, General Labor; Hospital Works; [oth. ı̇rit.] I have been writting for some years; [pers.] ı́hat's my original work. I am the sole copyright ı̇wner; [a.] Raleigh, NC

EATES, TEXAS JEWELL
ı́Pen.] Texas; [b.] March 15, 1917, TX; [p.] Van and ı̇sabell Reeder; [m.] John Yeates, August 10, 1940; ı̇ch.] Twins - (Delnor - Elnor), Judy, Loree and ı̇obert; [ed.] Grade nine, one room country school. ı̇asic sales, advanced sales, product knowledge, ı̇emonstration course; [occ.] Sales until retired 1989; ı́hon.] Honorary Award on a poem I submitted and on ı̇everal short true stories. Won several prizes in local ı̇apers for poems and stories; [oth. writ.] "Echoes of ı̇he Past", "My Fathers Dream", "My Best Friend", ı̇Adventures from the Northlands", "Most Exciting ı̇Experience"; [pers.] I like to write of the early days ı̇when we left Texas 1920 to live on a homestead in ı̇Northern Alberta. I write simple poems for children ı̇to understand and grown ups to appreciate; [a.] Edmonton, Alberta, Canada

YORK, PATRICIA J.
[Pen.] Pattie York; [b.] July 11, 1931, Dallas, TX; [p.] Vernon Anderson, Margie Anderson; [m.] Bill York, November 4, 1949; [ch.] William Randy, Michael Glenn; grandchildren - Clay, Cory, Blake; [ed.] North Dallas High; [occ.] Home Maker; [memb.] Casa View Baptist Church, Hardy Listener's Book Review Club, Garland Christian Women's Club, Poetry Society of TX; [hon.] I am honored to have been chose to be a speaker for Stonecroft Ministries. I speak to Christian Business and Professional Women and Christian Women's Clubs throughout Texas; [oth. writ.] "A Time of Thanks", "Texas", "Easter Celebration", "Freedom". "Why", "Heart of Love", "My Treasure Chest of Memories", "Seasons of My Life", "Time", "The Priorities of Christmas", "Too Late", "Waiting For You", "Sharing", "Wise Love"; [pers.] I thank God for giving me the gift of poetry. I strive to write uplifting poems that reflect the beauty in the world. Poetry, like music, can touch the heart and soul when nothing else can; [a.] Dallas, TX

YORKE, RICHARD A. ALEXANDER COTTAM
[Pen.] Raacy; [b.] October 26, 1956; [p.] Halifax, Nova Scotia, Canada; [p.] (Biological) Alan and Maxine; (Adoptive) Robie and Muriel; [m.] Di-vorced; [ch.] Richard Alexander Adrian (Riki), Judith Elizabeth (Jodi), Roderick Vernon (Rodi); [ed.] Grade XI; [occ.] Free Lancer; [memb.] Royal Canadian Legion, Branch 106, Debert, NS; [oth. writ.] "A Ray of Hope", Chapel; Recordings, Boston, MA, US (spiritual song); [pers.] We are all as one with Mother Earth. I try in my everyday life, as well as in my work, to perceive the goodness in all. Positive thinking, on a universal level, is necessary for the rehabilitation of Mother Earth and her inhabitions; [a.] Debert, Nova Scotia, Canada

YOST, RUTH M.
[b.] April 25, 1932, Reading, PA; [p.] Katherine Tietz, Herman Heidenreich; [m.] George E. Yost, June 30, 1951 (divorced); [ch.] Clifford, Cynthia, Timothy; 8 grandchildren, 1 great-grandchildren; [ed.] Graduated Pottstown High School class of 1950; [occ.] Retired doing volunteer work; [oth. writ.] Articles in local newsletters; [pers.] I have faith that God will help me through difficult times and that

everything in life is a learning experience. I try to do my best and help others. I am a survivor.

YOUNG, TAMMY
[b.] August 16, 1970, Herrin, IL; [p.] Ritchie Tutkus, Paula Tutkus; [m.] Brett Young, November 21, 1987; [ch.] Kelsey DeAnne Young, James Mitchell Young; [ed.] Herrin High School, John A. Logan College; [occ.] Student; [pers.] I write to work through feel-ings, and problems in my life. I never thought of my writings as poetry, it was my way of expressing what I feel inside my heart and mind; [a.] Herrin, IL

YOUNG, TONY D.
[b.] January 9, 1949, Detroit, MI; [p.] Robert, Evelyn Young; [m.] Carolyn D. Young, May 24, 1983; [ch.] Dawn, Kenyata, Tony Jr.; [ed.] High School Grad, Eastern High 1967, Detroit Mich.; [occ.] Laborer, Chrysler Corp., Eldon Axle; [memb.] U.A.W., Lo-cal 961; [hon.] Vietnam Service Award.; [oth. writ.] unpublished shorts, shorts, "The Fly", "The Man In Apartment 2-5", "The Flagpole", "Waiting For the Boogy Man", "Shocked," "A Hole In The Wall."; [pers.] Pursue your dreams; [a.] Detroit, MI

YOUNG, VIVIAN F.
[b.] April 9, 1919, Eligin, OH; [p.] Elva & Charles Coffman; [m.] Rev. Delmar J. Young, Sr., June 4, 1939; [ch.] Delmar Jay, Jr, Marilyn Kay, Mary Alice and John Edward; [ed.] Graduation High School, Manila, Ind.; [occ.] Home-maker; [memb.] We took Dorothy Rose into our home in 1964 as another "daughter." We are now retired.; [oth. writ.] My children put together a group of my poems for a Mothers Day Gift; [pers.] I feel that any talent I have comes from God, and I am happy if someone can get some help and enjoyment from them. Many of my poems were inspired by my husband's sermons.; [a.] Deshler, OH

YRUEGAS, MARY ELIZABETH
[Pen.] Mary Cantu; [b.] July 10, 1949, Kingsville, TX; [p.] Marcelino B. & Concepcion V. Cantu; [m.] Nestor Yruegas Jr., August 6, 1965; [ch.] Deborah Jean, Nestor Phillip, Ann Marie, Twins--Daniel Duane, Deanna Denise; [ed.] Sudan High School, Sudan, TX; [occ.] Housewife; [memb.] Girl Scouts 1972, Dearborn, MI, PTA Member 1990, Fund Raising; [pers.] Have been writing poems since Jr. High, but never felt I had talent good enough for publishing til now. Thank you, National Library; [a.] Falfurrias, TX

YURGEL, CHRISTINE
[b.] November 1, 1978, Edison, NJ; [p.] Frances and Robert Yurgel; [ed.] Attending South Plainfield High School 9th grade; [pers.] I write poetry because I write my feelings, it makes me feel better. I think everyone should love not hate; [a.] So Plfd, NJ

ZADEH, SANDRA MARIE
[b.] October 21, 1975, MA; [p.] Glenn and Anita Zadeh; [ed.] Temple Christian Academy; [occ.] J.C. Penny; [hon.] Salutitorian, Who's Who In America; [pers.] To me, poetry is a way of communication. It helps you let others know how you are feeling. Poetry also helps to lower stress you may have locked up inside; [a.] Randolph, MA

ZAFER, (STEVEN)
[b.] August 18, 1972, Perth, Australia; [p.] Nicolas and Irene Zafer; [ed.] 1. Trinity College, Perth (secondary education); 2. Curtin Univ, Perth (Ter-tiary education); [occ.] Student in 3rd and final year of bachelor of pharmacy degree; [hon.] Senior Prefect Trinity College 1989, Captain of 1st XI Cricket Team 1989, Member of 1st XVIII Football Team 1989; [pers.] I believe that much of what we perceive as reality, is, in all reality, a convex binding of dream and fantasy; [a.] Perth, Western Australia

ZAMORA, JUAN CARLOS
[b.] February 28, 1960, Cuba; [m.] Only one girl in faraway; [ed.] Self taught, old relationship with Pascal, Aristotle, Hegel and Saint Thomas; [occ.] Working factory, Aristocrat and Legionary; [memb.] Catholic Church; [hon.] In my country some premium of poetry, some dreams, and some prison; [oth. writ.] A book "He won't be able to come back now" poems in review.; [pers.] The deep longing of any poet is being able to keep silent, being silent profoundly and lovely before the being.; [a.] Wonder Lake, IL

ZERDEN, CRISSY LEE
[b.] January 30, 1979, NJ; [p.] Rosemary and Joseph Zerden; [occ.] I attend Jim Thorpe High School; [pers.] I write poetry to express the way I feel about things. I hope those who read my poems can relate to them and that they might help them through troubled times; [a.] Albrightsville, PA

ZEZULINSKI, DONALD
[b.] September 28, 1965, Oceanside, NY; [p.] Henry and Margaret Zezulinski; [memb.] Clear Mountain Zen Center, Oxfam, Amnesty International, World Wildlife Fund, National Parks and Conservation Ass, and The Mountain Ascending Men's Alliance; [oth. writ.] In the process of writing several novels, and designer and self-published book of chants for the Clear Mountain Zen Center; [pers.] To creatively manifest and express that nature which is realized in me, "Shu Jo Mu Hen Sei Gan Do"; [a.] Island Park, NY

ZIAEI, SHADI
[b.] march 5, 1969, Iran; [p.] Nasrin and Reza; [pers.] A trace of light remains, distant...but genuine, Dim...but intense, which keeps me going even in the darkest nights when I can't write; [a.] Pleasant Hill, CA;

ZIECNE, WILLIAM LOUIS
[Pen.] Z-man or WLZ; [b.] September 18, 1951, Aurora, IL; [p.] Verna, Louise and Edward William; [m.] Subin, October 12, 1973; [ch.] (daughter) Mameaw, (grandsons) Mitchell and Joey; (grand-daughter) Renee; [ed.] High school grad. Some college 20 years with the US Air Force, Noncommis-sioned Leadership School; [occ.] Warehouse Worker with interstate Batteries of Hawaii; [memb.] Non Commission Officer Association, Air Force Ser-geants Assoc, Vista Video of Wahiawa, Blockbuster Video, Hickam AFB NCO Club, Hawaii Public Library and Hickam AFB Library; [hon.] Vietnam Service Medal, Republic of Vietnam Campaign Medal, Air Force Commendation Medal, Air Force Out-standing Unit Award, Air Force Good Conduct Medal, and the best storyteller at a boy scout meeting; [oth. writ.] Some. But, not published at this time; [pers.] If I can touch, excite or motivate, another persons mind into believing themselves a someone that can make a difference. Then, I am thankful for the opportunity; [a.] Wahiawa, Hawaii

ZIELKE, SYLVIA
[Pen.] Syl; [b.] September 3, 1944, Joliet, IL; [p.] Edward and Mary Ziesemer; [ch.] My son is the Olympic Coach for Bahrain. Donovan (Chip) Zielke, Dawn Michaele (Zielke) Harn, grandchild Michael Harn; [ed.] Lockport Twp High School, MacCormick Junior College, Joliet Junior College (Past President of) DeBoer Oil Corp, (Past President of) DB Deli; [occ.] Fund Development and Big Brothers/Sisters and Trinity Ser. Inc, Founding Board Member for the Greater Chapter of the United States UNIFEM Divi-sion. Past Area Director of Zonta. Past Founder of the Will Cook Zonta. Past VP of the Joliet Zonta, NSFRE, PPA, Grundy County Task Force Grundy County Chamber; [hon.] One of 100 women chosen from 35,000 women from around the world for the "Century Club" for Achievement. Honored for my

photography works as a copywriter artist in the local area. Audience with the Grand Duke of Luxembourg. Presented Him with a copywriter photo. Currently on Display in Palace; [oth. writ.] Short Pose/stories/ poems. Photo's in area papers; [pers.] I believe in life. I almost lost mine in a head-on auto accident. I try to reflect upon the awakening process as I traveled back to the world as I saw it then and now. I lost love and found it again to rejoice in the beauty of the world around me. By writing of this experience, I hope to help others see hope when there is none present in their lives as they read my creations from the heart; [a.] Morris, IL

ZILLMER, RONNIE ALLEN
[Pen.] Ron Zillmer; [b.] November 1, 1957, Wiesbaden, W. Germany; [p.] Gertrude Paul Becker, Denny Roy Zillmer; [m.] Karen Sue Zillmer, August 9, 1987; [ch.] Collin Allan, Brandon Alexl; [ed.] High School, Otherwise self educated; [occ.] Dock worker; [hon.] "Winter Remains" Editor's Choice Award, 1993 National Library of Poetry "Coming of Dawn"; [oth. writ.] Short story collection entitled "Disenchanting Tales of the Maladjusted Among Us" (manuscript of same soon to be completed).; [pers.] It is who you are, How you are, when you are: Yours but for the doing.; [a.] Fergus Falls, MN

ZIMMERMAN, MALIA M.
[b.] September 6, 1968, Honolulu, HI; [p.] Dennis and Suzanne McLaughlin; [m.] tom Zimmerman, August 15, 1992; [ch.] none; [ed.] Maryknoll High School, HI, Chaminade University of Hawaii, BA in Communications, Minors in Business and Drama; [occ.] Marketing, Fund Raising; [pers.] Be strong. Be smart. Be Passionate. Be true to yourself. Make the world a better place.; [a.] Honolulu, HI

ZITSCHER, CHRISTINE
[b.] January 3, 1980, Vancouver; [p.] Gisela and Axel Zitscher; [ed.] Attending SDSS, grade 8; [occ.] Student; [hon.] School honor role; [oth. writ.] Rainbow of Love, etc. (other poems and short stories); [a.] Vancouver, BC

INDEX

Dockery-Wilson, Constance Ruth 362
Dockstader Sr., Harvey Joseph 193
Dodd, Trudy Anne 669
Dodgen, Dianne C. 571
Doe, Jaane 458
Doeurk, Vanny 623
Doherty, B. 426
Dolson, Donald Wm. 668
Dombrowski, Dina 259
Dome, Richard Michael 79
Donabie-Dixon, Wendie 697
Donahue, Guy 40
Donaldson, Leslie 294
Donner, Marci Louise 281
Donovan, Chris 664
Doombadfe, Amebi 132
Doombadze, Amelie 136
Dorado, Daniel 467
Dorneker, Meredith 365
Doroscan, Maggie 624
Dorste, Rosalie 432
Dorworth, Alice 171
Dostal, Jeffrey 469
Dottin, Shari 175
Dotts, Anita 487
Doub, Misty 382
Dougherty, Ellen 287
Dougherty, Marcella R. 33
Doughty, Cristy 414
Doughty, Linda J. 611
Doughty, Naomi L. 436
Douglas, Gillian 671
Douglas, Phyllis 17
Douglas, William C. 514
Douglas-Robledo, Vicki 520
Dowd, Dolly M. 61
Dowdy, Will-O May F. 5
Dowell, Chris R. 588
Downey, Laurie Jean 417
Doyle, Frances M. 240
Doyle, Frances M. 578
Doyle, Lara 681
Drake, Edward A. 439
Drake, Helen Sue Stroman 84
Drane, Jolene 246
Draper, Barbara 151
Draper, Janet 620
Dreffs, Neil 18
Drennan, Marilyn 474
Drongoski, Patricia 65
Drought, Rodney 379
Dryden, Heather 293
Du Val, Nedra 66
DuBray, Patrick R. 119
DuPona, Marcus 105
Dubina, Anne 460
Dubovik, Nova 310
Duck, Teresa 288
Dudash, Sheila K. 389
Dudley, Carrie 544
Dufek-Hogue Welborn, Yvonne 54
Duffy, Alaina E. 616
Duffy, Gail 597
Dugaw, Dakin 127
Dugdale, Stephen 715
Dugen, Henry J. 355
Duhon, Amanda 82
Duitsman, Joyce L. 168
Dumond, Scott 516
Dumont, Lorraine 484
Dunagan, Michele Marie 468
Dunbar, Christopher Kay 394
Duncan, Bryan H. 384
Duncan, Linda 506
Duncan, Stephanie 21
Duncan. Kathy & Sullivan, Mary J. 336
Dunlap, Gina E. 423
Dunlap, Helen Brown 47
Dunn, Frances 263
Dunn, Michael P. 133

Dunn, Shirley 433
Dunning, Ashley 463
Dupaquier, Dorienne 565
Dupas, Lorraine 589
Duquesne, Deanna 349
Durene, Chantel 195
Durham, Mary 360
Durocher, Shelley 703
Durrett, Cathy 343
Durrin, Gina 178
Durront, Shauna 485
Dusovic, Dyan 426
Duvall, Dan S. 460
Duvall, Heather 366
Duynhouwer, Melissa 84
Duzyk, Sonya 140
Dvorak-Meyer, Evelyn 88
Dwyer, Debbi 323
Dwyer, Susanne 179
Dybman, Nick N. 614
Dyer, Barbara 487
Dyer, Mack and Brenton, Nick 299
Dyer, Wenda 205
Dyke, Carmelita 123
Dykhuizen, Dorothy 642
Dykins, Vi 26
Dymond, Lori 400
Dyro, Venka 592
Dziepak, Damien 195
Eakins, Cindy 477
Earley, 203
East, Victoria 612
Eastmond, Rita 104
Eaton, Betty M. 123
Eaton, Errol 337
Eayrs, Anthony C. 421
Ebbs, Albert 351
Eben, Shannon 176
Eberhardt, Vera Heide 368
Ebert, Valerie 680
Echols, Bonita 582
Eckel, Patricia 619
Eckerle, Philip A. 44
Eckert, Charnelle 346
Eckhardt, Eileen 98
Ecklund, Rae Anna 99
Edelman, Lynn 312
Eden, Robin 254
Edens, Jamie 303
Edmonds, Ronald V. 4
Edmondson, Patricia 195
Edwards, A. Mahlon 629
Edwards, Azell 218
Edwards, Charles P. 652
Edwards, Margaret Doty 652
Edwards, Rita 295
Ehlers, Melvin T. 435
Ehnes, Tammy 94
Eichelbaum, Pat 129
Eiland, Frances Parton 219
Einhorn, May Stern 626
Eisenshtat, Marc 233
Elam, Greg 143
Elam, Molly 8
Elbao, Lani 352
Elek, J. M. 306
Elipani, Nikki 372
Elkins, Holly 350
Ellen, Deborah 479
Ellenburg-Stevens, April 422
Eller, Constance 99
Eller, Leanne 98
Ellingson, Wilma A. K. 47
Elliott, C. S. 29
Elliott, June Allegra 86
Ellis, James H. 336
Ellis, Stephanie 507
Ellison, Catherine S. 219
Ellison, Donna L. 87
Ellner, Fanne 393

Elmblad, Harried 582
Elpiner, Margaret 181
Emberley, Paul 709
Emerson, Geoffrey Charles 370
Emig, Bernadine C. 371
Emma, Elizabeth 436
Emmerson, Henry O. 594
Emmerson, Theresa 484
Engelhardt, Charles 625
English, Robert G. 543
Engstrom, Kristen 452
Engstrom, Kristen 634
Eno, Thomas Edison Takeru 196
Enos, Hilma 558
Enright, Sean D. 521
Enriquez, Carlos 39
Ensley-Walton, Barbara 267
Epker, Alison 51
Epperson, Kenneth H. 422
Erdell, John 64
Erdman, Amanda 374
Erdodi, Katalin 661
Erinkitola, Jai 265
Esau, Brenda 96
Escalon, Lisa 19
Esch, Dana 266
Esch, Stephen 409
Eschbach, Michele 633
Escudero, Rosalina 151
Esmond, Sarah 215
Esposito, Dana 81
Esposito, Viola Cedol 167
Esquibel, Phillip E. 428
Essig, Richard 116
Estes, Martha 464
Estevens, Michael 13
Etterlee, Chris 86
Evans, Bethel Nunley 139
Evans, Brian 543
Evans, Casey 635
Evans, E. M. 678
Evans, Lee 50
Evans, Mal 484
Evans, Nia M. 319
Evans, Patricia 263
Evans, Riley 618
Evans, Tamara Lenore 101
Everett, Marie 80
Everett, Maureen 648
Evers, Gene 365
Evitts, Randall R. 23
Evoy, Sue 411
Ewald, Abbey 365
Faber, Sally 527
Fabiano, Rita 693
Fairfield, Austin R. 451
Faisal, Jehan A. 337
Fakankun, D'Aria 50
Fales, Alice 124
Fallon, Dan 556
Fallon, Tony 28
Fanning, Frances 262
Farbstein, Peter 644
Farello, Frank S. 354
Farese, Thomas V. 100
Faria, Sandy 247
Farina, O.T. 178
Farley, Edward 576
Farmer, Linda L. 503
Farmer, Lorraine 684
Farr, Betty J. 46
Farrare, Allynn G. 358
Farrell, A.R. 562
Farrell, Charlotte R. 266
Farrell, Kathy 72
Farrior, Evan B. 217
Fass, Amy 527
Faulkner, Donald 89
Fawley, Myra 329
FeBuary, Charles S. 276

Fearn, Roderick Murray 462
Fedele, Thomas Kenan 46
Fedewick, Emily 388
Feger, Tausha 105
Feibusch, Ida 581
Feigelson, Susan B. 496
Feld, Neal 27
Felix, Julie 593
Felmet, Molly 443
Felter, Dave 633
Feltman, Marvel L. 442
Feltus, Amanda 664
Fengler, Emily 353
Fenn, Joe 539
Fenton, C. 711
Fenton, Joanne I. 242
Feralio, Flo 90
Ferguson, Billie-Jo 704
Ferguson, James L. 705
Ferguson, Laura C.K. 605
Fermin, Arlene 399
Fernandes, Bertha 660
Fernholm, Rita 276
Fernicola, Joseph 370
Ferrante, Stephanie Dawn 448
Ferreira, Kimberly 79
Ferrell, Frank E. 131
Ferris, Phyllis M. 373
Fiedler, Tom 160
Field, Mary 57
Fielder, Richard W. 576
Fields, Donna 164
Fields, Jenni 454
Figliomeni, Frank 306
File, Evelyn 431
Filiak, Thomas 631
Fillinger, Cherise 402
Filosa, Devon C. 358
Fina, Tina 138
Finale, Humberto 219
Fink, Daniel 589
Fink, Dudley D. 472
Finke, Peggy 383
Finnegan, Francis X. 625
Finnegan, Jenny 188
Finney, Scott W. 519
Fischer, Gwen 626
Fischer, Marylin 71
Fischer, Myron R. 342
Fischer, Phelicia 35
Fischer, Ruth M. 459
Fish, Amanda 210
Fish, Robert A. 274
Fisher, Agnes 656
Fisher, Celeste 251
Fitch, Dee 179
Fithian, Stacey 270
Fitzgerald, Rita 696
Fitzpatrick, Maureen 406
Fix, John P. 367
Fladmo, Lee 38
Flanagan, Dennis R. 193
Flanery, Michelle 286
Flannery, Norma L. 218
Flaster, Jeff 309
Fleischer, Adeline 649
Fleischmann, Martha Jo 397
Fleishman, Debra J. 143
Fleishman, Debra J. 50
Fleming, Jeffrey 371
Fleming, Nicole 424
Flemming, Dakar 114
Flenner, Keli 533
Flesher, Theresa 520
Fletcher, Karen L. 79
Fleury, Helen C. 137
Fleury, Junior 308
Flo, Joan C. 599
Flordeliz, Helen Lenore 212
Flores, Marjorie Elaine 92

Green, Pats 157
Greenberg, Linda 507
Greencorn, Tammy 663
Greene, Hill 91
Greene, Jay 289
Greene, Mark 75
Greene, Patricia A. 197
Greenway, Charles N. 311
Greenwood, Bertha Woods 147
Greenwood, H. D. 710
Greer, Tracy 626
Gregg, Leslee 132
Gregory Jr., John P. 599
Grew, Desirae 467
Grey II, Joseph E. 440
Grey, Dawn 325
Grey, Toy 523
Gribble, Monica L. 26
Griewahn, Jennifer 445
Griffin, Barbara 401
Griffin, Eunice Pegram 86
Griffin, Gyneth 97
Griffin, Judd 349
Griffith, Barbara G. 615
Griffith, Yulu 477
Grillo, Carol G. 128
Grimberg, Irene 384
Grimes, Helen 176
Grimes, Ralph E. 94
Grimes, Ronald 184
Grimes-Brown, KC 35
Grindstaff, Teresa 525
Griswold, Catherine 349
Grogan, Erika 476
Grohovsky, Laura J. 600
Grose, Allahaline 249
Grossfield, Harriet 439
Grossman, George 528
Grossman, Seth 77
Grout, Kenneth J. 647
Grove, Leah M. 380
Grubbs, Kyle 621
Gruber, Mary Jane 244
Gruhn, Kenneth P. 221
Grumbine, Megan 94
Grushoff, Kenna Morris 444
Gryziec, Heather 415
Gualdoni, Pat 650
Guarino, Kevin S. 416
Guernsey, Joe 76
Guerra, Dorothy 17
Guerrero, Ruthy M. 142
Guidmore, C. Virginia 125
Gulla, Stephen P. 4
Guminski, Paul 12
Gummow, Madge 660
Gundy, Tanya 196
Gunn, Christopher 633
Gunter, Danny W. 599
Gurecki, Ellesha L. 609
Gursky, Adolph F. 425
Gustafson, Aaron 645
Gustafson, Bill 190
Gutierrez, Tamara 559
Guy, Dennis 233
Guy, Marie Murray 17
Guyewski, Dorothy 532
Guzman, Larry 375
Guzman, Raymond 297
Guzzetti, Christine 257
Haagensen, D. 477
Haakinson, Nathaniel 574
Haan, Sheryl A. 513
Haas, Karen Marie 331
Haben, Amy 23
Hackel, Cherie Erica 669
Hacker, Aubri 370
Hackett, Bret 528
Hackett, Paul 498
Hadad, Alvin 463

Haedike-Byrd, Sandra 195
Haen, Patricia 610
Hagen, Sarah 299
Hager, Amanda 345
Hagerty, Dawn M. 209
Haggerty, Mark W. 642
Hagglund, Martin 620
Hagin, Agnes M. 352
Haglund, Paula 605
Hague Jr., Henry H. 591
Hahn, Angela 471
Hahn, David 434
Hahn, Sara 490
Haines, Sarah F. 102
Haines, SunShine 55
Hains, Lorraine 668
Hale, Jennifer 389
Hale, Shanna 394
Haley, James Edgar 210
Haley, James Edgar 548
Haley, Shannon 385
Halicky, Dj 384
Halko, Melissa 404
Hall, Belinda 92
Hall, Colleen 290
Hall, Daniel 651
Hall, Erin 641
Hall, Gordon R. 687
Hall, H. 666
Hall, Tamra 414
Hall, Wendy 256
Hallford, Wayman 443
Halliday, Lynda 711
Hallman, Mara Kathleen 475
Hallmark, Jerry 413
Hallworth, Dawn 688
Halsted, J. P. 45
Halsted, J.P. 262
Halterman, Jessika 608
Hamblin, Cathy J. 91
Hamblin, Joe Alan 327
Hambling, Christine 474
Hamilton, Andrew 212
Hamilton, Brenda 216
Hamilton, Dorothy 668
Hamilton, Lindsay 197
Hamlar, Portia 375
Hammel, Lester L. 546
Hammerbeck, George Edward 324
Hammock, Chad 12
Hammood, Kristen 603
Hampton, Susan 156
Han, Nella J. 61
Hanacek, Andrew J. 260
Hanami, Dan 536
Hanash, Rami S. 83
Hancock, Erin 233
Hancock, Melody 444
Hand, Amy 538
Hande, Stefanie 617
Handlewich, Erica 527
Hanelt, Sabrina 310
Hanes, Lynna 570
Haney, Thomas 515
Hanks, Alexandrea 266
Hanley, Eugene W. 642
Hanley, Jennifer 390
Hanlon, Sharon A. 86
Hannan, Beverly C. 355
Hanneman, Loretta 372
Hannon, Terri 141
Hansell, Lola 98
Hansell, Lola I. 619
Hansen, Erik 611
Hansen, Merle C. 133
Hansen, Michelle 263
Hansen, Tarah 525
Hansen-Daigneau, Margaret F. 87
Hanson, Delores D. 3
Hanson, Judy R. 605

Hanstedt, Constance 418
Hantman, Barbara 55
Harbor, Ronda 363
Harclerode, Stacy 15
Hardiman, Dianne E. Smith 169
Hardin, Theresa 257
Harding, Daniel J. 72
Hardwick, Nan-Marie 508
Hardy, Cheryl Dawn 473
Hardy, Julia Irene 248
Hare, Stephen 648
Hargett, Tony R. 379
Hargreaves, Heather 153
Hargreaves, Olive Bryson 711
Hargreaves, R. 710
Hargrove, Patricia D. 72
Harkins, Nancy 101
Harmon, Ellie 315
Harper, Denise 275
Harrell, Kim 17
Harrington, David S. 303
Harrington, Molly Ann 575
Harris, Cheryl Audrey 220
Harris, Helen A. 186
Harris, Jeannetta 332
Harris, Leslie 334
Harris, Rachel Ann 410
Harris, Rajean 103
Harris, Shannon Dee 501
Harris, Tracy 62
Harris, W.T. 124
Harrison, Berta Louise 264
Harrison, Brian 232
Harrison, Carmen R. 264
Harrison, Dolsonee 418
Harrison, Linda A. 139
Harrison, Paige 276
Harrison, Pamela 481
Harry, Bea 66
Hart, Carolyn D. 201
Hart, Dennisha 621
Hart, Kim 40
Harth, Briana 432
Hartley, Charmaine 695
Hartlieb, Emily 385
Hartman, Viola 637
Hartmann, Michael D. 287
Hartshorne, Harry E. 280
Hartzell, Ruth 328
Hartzler, Thomas J. 240
Harvey, Bob 483
Harvey, Jay 387
Harvey, Robert 455
Harvey, Sheila 103
Hass, Cami 241
Hassell, Todd E. 88
Hastings, Barry 445
Hastings, Patsy 210
Hauck, Stacey 684
Hauenstein, Wendell E. 11
Haug, Elizabeth 514
Hauschildt, Christine 469
Hava-Robbins, Nadia 646
Havlik, Katrin 112
Hawkins, Dan E. 413
Hawkins, Kristin 170
Hawkins, Shayla 66
Hawkins, Vance 74
Hawks, Jonathan Lee 638
Haws, Ralph Leon 74
Hayden, Pat 361
Haydock, Peter 713
Hayes, Cara 433
Hayes, Tim 672
Hayes, Tim 702
Haygood, Ty 156
Haynie, Amoya Ray 302
Hazel, Todd 623
Healey, Felix M. 56
Heap, Harbon B. 268

Heard, Randall A. 465
Heard, Rhonda Kay 121
Hearn, Adrienne 402
Heatley, Nicole 525
Hebrank, William C. 563
Hedayati, Jeanette 168
Hedding, Margaret L. 129
Hedeen, Melissa A. 295
Hedrick, Kenneth 627
Hedrick, Richard Lee 607
Heffington, Mark 1, 54
Hegedus, Evelyn 288
Heger, Lori 574
Heidrick, Doug 595
Heimann, Verda 505
Heimerl, Carla 205
Heinekamp, Lucille H. 163
Heins, Lesley Ann 7
Heintschel, Michael 157
Heiser, Maria 21
Heitkamp, Marie 237
Heller, Melissa 597
Hemingway, Everlena 262
Hemmen, K. 41
Hempe, Kevin 161
Hemsworth, Patricia 639
Hendel, Christine 302
Henderson, Laurice H. 207
Hendler, Lee M. 28
Hendricks, Lori 228
Henk, Lynn E. 630
Henrie, Pamela A. 458
Henry, Heather 153
Henry, Helen Moore 41
Henry, Helen Moore 94
Henry, Steven W. 254
Henson, Beverly 628
Henson, Chris 424
Henson, Maggie 453
Henson, Ronald Homer 613
Herbert, Rebecca 637
Hermann, Nancy 624
Hermes, Ann 615
Hernandez, Barbra K. 250
Hernandez, Barbara L. 338
Hernandez, Kiley 174
Hernandez, Valentina 249
Hernandez, Victor 550
Herndon, Kathleen E. 605
Herrbach, Jeanette Lynn 366
Herz, Donna 303
Herzing, Kelly B. 607
Herzinger, Shana 99
Herzog, Deborah 254
Herzog, Phyllis 196
Hess, Alison 331
Hess, Dana 71
Hess, Lillian Lane 472
Hester Jr., Purnell Wade 370
Hetrick, Sandra 449
Heuman, Herbert N. 400
Hewitt, Jim 405
Hiatt, James 192
Hickey, Trudy 483
Hicklin, James K. 568
Hicks, Bernard 380
Hicks, Elsie L. 589
Higgins, James J. 342
Higham, Marilyn S. Brown 443
Higley, Tammi 501
Hilden, Alton H. 98
Hill, Annette Main 591
Hill, Mike 32
Hill, Randi 357
Hill, Ruth S. 640
Hill, Sarah 107
Hill, Steve J. 411
Hillebrand, Elvera 206
Hillert, Jessica R. 586
Hilts, Carl 325

Sheldon, Candice V. 667
Shelton, Dave 107
Shelton, Daylene 294
Shepard, John W. 529
Shepherd, Natalie 35
Sher, Dana 104
Sherer, Jay 364
Sherman, Virginia Lynn 23
Sherrer, Lillian 663
Sherwin, Sam 211
Sherwood, Richard 452
Shield, Richard 354
Shields, FSC, Larry 598
Shields, Lorin 109
Shimizu, Risa 415
Shimp, Mary Lucy 349
Shimp, Mary Lucy 610
Shinn, Joyce G. 685
Shippam, Charles Anthony 267
Shirley, Rebecca 392
Shishak, Machut 272
Shivener, Angie 262
Shockley, Monte R. 114
Sholtis, Christopher Aaron 595
Short, Dawn E. 550
Short, Tarah 481
Shortfellow, A 613
Shortt, Carolyn F. 267
Shotwell, Stacey Ann Kalei 510
Shrieve, Jessica 371
Shuffler Jr., Irving L. 417
Shults, Amy Renee (Dumas) 578
Shuman, Marjorie Murphy 12
Shutey, Maggie 624
Sica, Brook 470
Sidmore, Bonita 390
Siebert, Heather 427
Sigler, David 147
Sigwalt, Shirley 405
Silbert, Beth 227
Silkiss, Dana 74
Silva, Lanette Y. 250
Silva, Mirna. M. 538
Simmers, Christopher 346
Simmons, Nina 10
Simmons, Nina 280
Simon, GeraDessiel 330
Simon, Tameka 208
Simone, Anthony 330
Simpson, Antony W. 69
Simpson, Darlene 271
Simpson, Isla 545
Simpson, Kathleen O'Hara 456
Sims, Anthony 534
Sims, Brandy G. 257
Sims, Mary 613
Sims, Miriam S. 626
Sinclair, Lisa 660
Sinex, Kayla 170
Singh, Peter 681
Singh, Pritam 659
Singleton, Thomas 692
Singsheim, Jessica 399
Sjolin, Heather 558
Skaltsas, Kori 390
Skarnes, Madelyn K. 125
Skavinski, Sarah Elizabeth 255
Skerdavich, Lisa 423
Skiathas, Jorgos 682
Skoler, Ellie 297
Skousen, Shirley Marshall 118
Skyrm, Paul 217
Slansky, Lisa G. 419
Slaton, Jessie 411
Sleger, Kim 399
Slight, Carolyn Slayton 341
Slovak, J.P. 81
Small, Shannon 521
Smallwood, Jane 97
Smallwood, Kathy C. 149

Smally, Rachel 453
Smelser, Kathleen 7
Smetheram, Valerie J. 714
Smetters, Casey 420
Smiley, Phyllis 441
Smith, Allisha D. 654
Smith, Becci 453
Smith, Benny G. 456
Smith, Beverly 449
Smith, Billie Sue 112
Smith, Carla M. 89
Smith, Carmen J. 464
Smith, Charisa A. 448
Smith, Christie Leslie 375
Smith, Dana M. 415
Smith, David D. 56
Smith, Dawn 120
Smith, Dena Rae 290
Smith, Donna Kay 310
Smith, Donnamaria 162
Smith, Douglas R. 230
Smith, Erin M. 313
Smith, Ethel L. 183
Smith, Frances Taylor 44
Smith, Harold C. 246
Smith, Holli 153
Smith, Holly 609
Smith, Holly 97
Smith, Jackie 470
Smith, Jamal 268
Smith, Jo-Anne 593
Smith, Joanne 474
Smith, Joseph T. 106
Smith, Kelley 653
Smith, Kelli 274
Smith, Kristin 91
Smith, Leah L. 363
Smith, Lillian I. 121
Smith, Lisa M. 274
Smith, Lisa Marie 48
Smith, Lynne 489
Smith, Maggie 373
Smith, Mary Lou 162
Smith, Meredith E. 67
Smith, Nicole 277
Smith, Ozella 59
Smith, P. 703
Smith, Peggy L. 100
Smith, Rebecca 355
Smith, Roger L. 275
Smith, Sandra 484
Smith, Saralyn V. 31
Smith, Stacey 476
Smith, Ted 511
Smith, Terry 506
Smith, Thaddeus 500
Smith, Thomas G. 207
Smith, Tiffany 296
Smith, Tony Andre' 507
Smith, Winifred 524
Smithhart, Dianna 299
Smits, Addie 364
Smylie, Glenn 101
Snape, Margie 34
Sneed, Shanna 521
Snell, Kim R. 237
Snell, Merrill W. 542
Snodgrass, Jeanette 148
Snow, Shannon 518
Snowden, Virginia 587
Snyder, Bertha 42
Snyder, Billie 256
Snyder, Christie 394
Snyder, Darla 102
Snyder, John 439
So, Just 262
Soerheide, Thelma 247
Sokal, Amy 620
Sokol, Andrea Joanne 373
Solomon, Mandy 31

Sombra, Glaucio 485
Somerville, Stacy 352
Sommer, Jennifer 91
Sommerfeld, Mandi 318
Sonessa, Josephine E. 44
Songer, Shelly 498
Sonnier, Jean A. 282
Soper, M. F. 709
Sorensen, Lisle 3
Sorensen, Mark 301
Sorrentino, Sarah 525
Sorsby, Irene 686
Sotis, Andrea 246
Southern, Angela 621
Sowell, April 321
Spadafora, Melita 152
Spalding, Trevor G. 670
Spangler II, William D. 232
Spanier, Stuart L. 509
Spano, Charles F. 83
Spardy, Jennifer 205
Sparkman, Kenneth Lloyd 480
Sparks, Dawn 198
Spataro, Ron 368
Spaulding, Midge 121
Spaulding, Sanford 491
Spechler, Diana 71
Speck, Pat 373
Spelman, Tim L. 65
Spence, Lily 474
Spencer, Alice T. 228
Spencer, Carolyn 105
Spencer, Ethel E. 699
Spencer, Mary Lou 620
Spencer, Rachel 626
Spiess, Erin Renee 642
Spillman, Robert L. 392
Spitzig, Heidi 85
Spivak, Wanita 266
Spivey, Edwin P. 201
Spivey, Edwin P. 625
Spoto, Carolyn 647
Spreen, Esther Tombaugh 94
Spyra, Carrie 432
Squeglia, Cindy 49
Squires, S. 638
St. Clair, Jerry G. 200
Stafford, Debra L. 637
Stafford, Jerry L. 216
Stagnolia, James 312
Stahl, Yvonne A. 517
Staiano, Lynnmarie 304
Staker, Joe J. 187
Stallings, Dorothy 376
Stamatiou, Kiki 81
Stamatis, Steven P. 632
Standley, Reed L. 353
Stanford, Pearl 16
Stanley, Amy 36
Stanley, Christine 121
Stanley, Levater B. 625
Stans, Sarina Sue 524
Stansbury, Brandye 154
Stanton, Amy Ann 185
Stanton, Maralyn 438
Stapleton Jr., Luther Darnell 282
Star, Emy 647
Starcher, Jill 33
Stark, John Lacasella 225
Stark, Regina M. 607
Starr, Sarah 606
Starr, Suzanne Jean 518
Stasierowski, Gary 585
Stauba, Melanie-Lynn 509
Steele, Runell 9
Steenbergen, Heidi 679
Stefani, Chas Q. 280
Steiner, Arian 312
Steiner, M. E. 42
Steiner, M. Elisabeth 556

Steinka, Eva E. 189
Steinwand, Fred 479
Steirer, Mary Ann Wagner 11
Stenzler, Steven 496
Stevens, Nichole 223
Steward, Danny R. 533
Stewart, Avis R. 101
Stewart, Brittany 580
Stewart, Cynthia 27
Stewart, Donese J. 275
Stewart, Kate 636
Stewart, Keith R. 296
Stewart, Lillian 69
Stewart, Patti Clifford 52
Stewart, Trudy 154
Stewart, William 408
Stewart-Tornai, Nancy 616
Stieber, Michael J. 322
Stigger, Regina 163
Stillwell, Helen Jean 371
Stimson, Heidi Buker 113
Stinson, Jackie 584
Stivers, Teena 109
Stobbe, C. W. 19
Stockdale, Patsy 28
Stockdill, Jeffrey J. 30
Stocker, Shana 495
Stocks, Paul 701
Stoecklein, Edward 166
Stoelting, Erica 19
Stojansul, Joe 143
Stokes, Carolyn Ashe 65
Stokes, Grace 218
Stokes, Kim 139
Stokner, Natalie 491
Stone, Charlene Lee 329
Stone, Judy L. 617
Stone, Sandra Wallraven 493
Stone, Walter V. 98
Story, Kay T. 180
Stough, Ryan A. 533
Stout, Orvil 190
Stover, Christi 309
Stowe, Angie N. 285
Stratton, Kimberly L. 350
Strausbaugh, Ted R. 512
Strausser, Anne E. 557
Strickland, Debbie 181
Strickland, Eva 354
Strickland, Marj 645
Strickland, Tina M. 366
Stridborg, Trudi G. 216
Strikhouser, Mary L. 651
Strittmatter, Carey 311
Strock, Tammy L. 521
Stroda, Traci 607
Stroh, Albert 23
Strohm, Tony 496
Stroud, Sonya 512
Strum, Stephen B. 212
Strunk, Mary Lou 391
Stuart, Phyllis Neely 335
Stumpf, Martha 584
Stumphf, Fay E. 158
Sturgeon, Annette 482
Sturm, Amy 277
Sturtevant, Renae J. 406
Stutzman, Becca 38
Stuurman, Sherry 152
Stypula, Susan L. 494
Subra, John E. 12
Suders, Joseph A. 278
Sudot, Kevin J. 669
Suldon, Annissia D. 147
Sullivan, David A. 304
Sullivan, Edward F. 224
Sullivan, Ginamarie 118
Sullivan, James F. 168
Sullivan, Joan P. 177
Sullivan, Katie 350